Canadian Income Tax Law

3rd Edition

David G. Duff   Benjamin Alarie
Kim Brooks   Lisa Philipps

LexisNexis

Canadian Income Tax Law, 3rd Edition
© LexisNexis Canada Inc. 2009
July 2009

Members of the LexisNexis Group worldwide

Canada	LexisNexis Canada Inc, 123 Commerce Valley Dr. E. Suite 700, MARKHAM, Ontario
Australia	Butterworths, a Division of Reed International Books Australia Pty Ltd, CHATSWOOD, New South Wales
Austria	ARD Betriebsdienst and Verlag Orac, VIENNA
Czech Republic	Orac, sro, PRAGUE
France	Éditions du Juris-Classeur SA, PARIS
Hong Kong	Butterworths Asia (Hong Kong), HONG KONG
Hungary	Hvg Orac, BUDAPEST
India	Butterworths India, NEW DELHI
Ireland	Butterworths (Ireland) Ltd, DUBLIN
Italy	Giuffré, MILAN
Malaysia	Malayan Law Journal Sdn Bhd, KUALA LUMPUR
New Zealand	Butterworths of New Zealand, WELLINGTON
Poland	Wydawnictwa Prawnicze PWN, WARSAW
Singapore	Butterworths Asia, SINGAPORE
South Africa	Butterworth Publishers (Pty) Ltd, DURBAN
Switzerland	Stämpfli Verlag AG, BERNE
United Kingdom	Butterworths Tolley, a Division of Reed Elsevier (UK), LONDON, WC2A
USA	LexisNexis, DAYTON, Ohio

Library and Archives Canada Cataloguing in Publication

Canadian income tax law / David Duff ... [et al.]. — 3rd ed.

First ed. Written by David G. Duff.
Includes index.
ISBN 978-0-433-46056-5

1. Income Tax — Law and legislation — Canada — Textbooks. 2. Income tax — Law and legislation — Canada — Cases. I. Duff, David, 1959- II. Duff, David, 1959- . Canadian income tax law.

KE5759.C34 2006   343.7105'2   C2006-904517-8
KF6370.ZA2C34 2006

Printed and bound in Canada.

Preface to First Edition

This book began in the summer of 1997 after my first year of teaching Canadian income tax law at the University of Toronto Faculty of Law. Although the book was developed primarily for use in a basic course on Canadian income tax law, I hope that it will be of value not only to students and tax teachers, but also to tax lawyers and accountants, tax administrators, judges, policy makers, and anyone else interested in learning about Canadian income tax law.

In writing the book, my aim has been to make the study of Canadian income tax law both interesting and accessible, without avoiding any of the technical detail that is necessarily involved in this field of law. By combining the features of a textbook and a casebook and devoting attention both to the text of the *Income Tax Act* and to cases in which the Act has been interpreted and applied, the book is intended to provide a basis for a critical understanding of the law and policy of Canadian income taxation.

Not surprisingly, the development of this book has benefited from the support and encouragement of many people. Through the Cecil A. Wright Foundation, the University of Toronto provided financial support to hire summer research assistants who worked on various aspects of the book. Colleagues, particularly Neil Brooks and Lisa Philipps at Osgoode Hall Law School, provided crucial encouragement to sustain me through what at times seemed like a never-ending project, as did my partner, Mary Liston, who endured my ups and downs with her characteristic equanimity. Student research assistants Ben Barnes, Chris Bystrom, Angus Grant, Sky Jondahl, Glen Loutzenhiser, Elizabeth Moore, Aaron Palmer, Simon Proulx, and John Toffoletto provided invaluable help gathering materials and researching specific topics. Jim Lyons devoted particular care and countless hours to the task of editing the document. Paul Emond merits special thanks for his decision to publish the book and for his patience awaiting its completion, as does the Canadian Tax Foundation for agreeing to co-publish the book and to reproduce it in the form of a CD-ROM. Finally, and above all, I am indebted to the students in my tax classes, whose insights and critical engagement with earlier versions of the book have had a decisive impact on its final form.

David G. Duff
June 2002

Preface to Second Edition

Law, as a student in a course taught by my partner Mary Liston wrote on a final exam, is "a moving target in a living tree". The metaphor is particularly apt for Canadian income tax law, which continues to change as taxpayers plan their affairs, Parliament amends the *Income Tax Act*, and courts interpret its provisions. As a snapshot of this moving target, a book like this must be frequently revised in order retain its validity and relevance.

The first edition of this book was published in 2003 and was current for statutory provisions and judicial decisions up to the summer of 2002. Since then, legislative and judicial activity has generated numerous changes that have rendered parts of the book outdated and inaccurate. In addition to regular changes to rates and credit amounts, statutory amendments have affected the taxation of options to acquire securities, the taxation of non-competition payments, and the deductibility of fines and penalties. Judicial decisions have affected numerous aspects of Canadian income tax law, perhaps none more so than the Supreme Court of Canada's first decisions on the general anti-avoidance rule, released in the fall of 2005. The current edition of Canadian Income Tax Law incorporates all significant statutory and judicial developments up to the summer of 2006.

In addition to these changes to the substance of the book, the second edition reflects two important changes in the process of its production. First, in putting together the second edition, I am extremely pleased to have been joined by my colleagues Benjamin Alarie at the University of Toronto Faculty of Law, Kim Brooks at the University of British Columbia Faculty of Law, and Lisa Philipps at Osgoode Hall Law School of York University. Over time, the book should benefit greatly from this broader input and the insights that each of us gains from using the book in our tax classes. Second, I am also pleased that LexisNexis has agreed to publish and promote the second edition. With its support, I hope that the book will reach a broad audience, including tax lawyers and accountants, tax administrators, judges and policy-makers, as well as tax students and tax teachers.

One final note: the first edition of this book was dedicated to my mother Jean (1927-2000) who, I noted, "taught me that attention to detail in any pursuit is always a virtue." I hope that this attention to detail is as apparent in this second edition as it was in the first, and that it contributes to the book's aim to encourage not only an interest in Canadian income tax law, but also an informed understanding of this area of law.

David G. Duff
September 2006

Preface to Third Edition

It is a great pleasure to write a preface to the third edition of this book which, since its introduction only a few years ago, has managed to establish a strong presence in tax law courses taught throughout Canada. From the outset, this book has sought to take tax law seriously – to provide readers with the necessary material to develop a solid grasp of the basic structure of the Canadian *Income Tax Act* and a critical understanding of the leading judicial decisions through which this statute is interpreted and applied. As a book that takes tax law seriously, regular revisions are inevitable.

This edition continues a process of substantive revision that began with the second edition, facilitated at that time by the addition of co-authors Benjamin Alarie, Kim Brooks and Lisa Philipps. In addition to revisions designed to reflect statutory and judicial developments, this process also involves revisions based on our continuing experience with the book as a vehicle for teaching Canadian income tax law. Changes to reflect legal developments include new excerpts from important Supreme Court of Canada decisions in *Tsiaprailis v. Canada*, [2005] S.C.J. No. 9, [2005] 2 C.T.C. 1, 2005 D.T.C. 5119 (S.C.C.) [Chapter 4] and *Lipson v. Canada*, [2009] S.C.J. No. 1, [2009] 1 C.T.C. 314, 2009 D.T.C. 5015 (S.C.C.) [Chapter 8]. Changes to improve the book for teaching purposes include new sections on principles for evaluating tax provisions [Chapter 1], the tax treatment of relocation assistance [Chapter 4], and tax-deferred and other special income arrangements [Chapter 7], as well as more suitable case excerpts to illustrate the concept of a personal services business [Chapter 4] and the reasonableness limitation in section 67 [Chapter 8]. Finally, revisions have generally reduced the number of notes and questions following case excerpts and added numerical examples from time to time to illustrate the operation of specific rules. The third edition of Canadian Income Tax Law incorporates all significant statutory and judicial developments up to the summer of 2009.

In addition to these changes, the three years since the last edition of the book have also brought major changes in the professional lives of two of the authors. In July 2007, Kim Brooks moved from the Faculty of Law at the University of British Columbia in Vancouver to the Faculty of Law at McGill University in Montreal, where she was appointed the H. Heward Stikeman Chair in the Law of Taxation. In July 2009, after visiting for the 2008-2009 academic year, I moved from the Faculty of Law at the University of Toronto to the Faculty of Law at the University of British Columbia.

Finally, on behalf of myself and my co-authors, I would like to express our thanks to LexisNexis for continuing to publish and promote this book. With its support, I hope that Canadian Income Tax Law will continue to provide a solid basis for law students and other interested readers to learn and reflect upon this important area of law.

David G. Duff
Vancouver, B.C.
June 2009

About the Authors

David G. Duff joined the Faculty of Law at the University of British Columbia as a visiting professor during the 2008-2009 academic year and a full professor in July 2009. Before moving to U.B.C., he taught tax law at the University of Toronto Faculty of Law from 1996 to 2008. Professor Duff has published widely in the areas of tax law and policy and was the sole author of the first edition of *Canadian Income Tax Law*. He is a member of the Board of Governors of the Canadian Tax Foundation, a member of the Law Society of Upper Canada and the International Fiscal Association, an Adjunct Research Fellow in Business Law and Economics at the Faculty of Business and Economics at Monash University, and an International Research Fellow at the Oxford University Centre for Business Taxation. Prior to his academic career, he was a tax associate at the Toronto office of Stikeman Elliott LLP.

Benjamin Alarie is a professor at the Faculty of Law at the University of Toronto. After completing graduate work in law at Yale Law School, he clerked for Madam Justice Arbour of the Supreme Court of Canada and was called to the Bar of Ontario. Professor Alarie researches and teaches principally in taxation law, and also has research interests in contracts and judicial decision-making. Professor Alarie's research has appeared in numerous edited volumes and leading Canadian and international journals. Professor Alarie is Vice-President and President-Elect of the Canadian Law and Economics Association, an Adjunct Research Fellow in Business Law and Economics at the Faculty of Business and Economics at Monash University, a member of the Canadian Tax Foundation, a member of the International Fiscal Association, an invited full member of the Academia Tributária das Americas, and the organizer of the James Hausman Tax Law and Policy Workshop. Professor Alarie was awarded the 2009 Alan Mewett QC Prize for excellence in teaching by the class of 2009 at the Faculty of Law of the University of Toronto.

Kim Brooks was appointed the H. Heward Stikeman Chair in the Law of Taxation at the Faculty of Law at McGill University in July 2004. Prior to joining the Faculty of Law at McGill, she taught at the faculties of law at the University of British Columbia from 2004 to 2007 and Queen's University from 2001 to 2004. Her primary research interests lie in the areas of corporate and international tax law and policy, and she is currently working on a SSHRC-funded project on tax treaties and their effects on revenue allocation between high- and low-income countries. Professor Brooks is a member of the Canadian Tax Foundation, the International Fiscal Association, and the National Tax Association, is Chair of the Women's Legal Education and Action Fund (LEAF), the managing editor of the Canadian Journal of Women and the Law, and Past President of the

Canadian Association of Law Teachers. Prior to her academic career, she practiced as a tax lawyer with Stikeman Elliot LLP in their Toronto and London (U.K.) offices.

Lisa Philipps was appointed to the faculty of Osgoode Hall Law School of York University in 1996. She teaches courses in personal income tax, taxation of trusts and estates, and tax lawyering, and is currently serving as Associate Dean (Research, Graduate Studies and Institutional Relations). Before joining the faculty at Osgoode she taught in the law faculties at the University of Victoria and the University of British Columbia. Professor Philipps has written a broad range of articles and book chapters on topics related to taxation law, fiscal policy, and feminist legal theory. She is a member of the Canadian Tax Foundation and treasurer of the Canadian Journal of Women and the Law. Prior to her academic career she was a tax associate at Blake, Cassels & Graydon LLP in Toronto.

Table of Contents

Detailed Table of Contents

Table of Cases

A page number in boldface type indicates that the text of the case or a portion thereof is reproduced. A page number in lightface indicates that the case is merely quoted briefly or discussed. Cases mentioned within excerpts and footnotes are not listed.

A

B

C

D

E

F

G

H

I

J

K

L

M

N

O

P

P

Q

R

S

T

U

V

W

Y

Z

PART ONE

Introduction

The *Income Tax Act*, R.S.C. 1985, c. 1 (5th Supp.), as amended (herein referred to as "the Act") is a daunting document. At the time of writing, the most recent CCH version of the Act, 86th ed. (2008), including historical references and various annotations, runs for 2,039 pages. Including regulations and other related statutes and treaties, the published text exceeds 2,900 pages. The Act itself consists of 40 "parts", numerous "divisions", various "subdivisions", and a multitude of sections, subsections, paragraphs, subparagraphs, clauses, subclauses, and even a few sub-subclauses!

At first, this length and complexity suggest incoherence. Indeed, with the constant amendments to the Act since its predecessor was introduced in 1917, it might be argued that the Act lacks any coherent structure or purpose and comprises nothing more than a series of relatively arbitrary rules adopted in response to unforeseen circumstances and prevailing political sentiments. There is, no doubt, some truth to this picture. One would be hard pressed to describe the evolution of the Act and the process of statutory amendment as the direct and logical unfolding of a single all-embracing idea! Nonetheless, as a product of human reason, it is also arguable that the *Income Tax Act*, like much of the common law, contains a form of "immanent" rationality — a structure and purpose embodied in the various provisions of the text that gives it a coherent meaning accessible to the determined interpreter. It is this understanding of the structure and purpose of the *Income Tax Act* that this book is intended to encourage.

To achieve this understanding, however, one cannot simply read the provisions of the Act from page 1 to page 2,039, section 1 to 262. The text of the Act is important, indeed crucial, but the text alone — especially if one refers only to the most recent version of the Act — is grossly incomplete. First, the text itself is the product of its history and takes its meaning from this history as well as its current language. Second, the text, like all law, has meaning only insofar as it is applied to concrete facts; consequently, the text derives its meaning as much from the cases in which it is applied as from the otherwise lifeless words in which it is framed. Indeed, to the extent that statutory amendments reflect a legislative response to judicial decisions, the very words of the Act are themselves a product of an ongoing conversation between the text and the facts. Finally, the text takes its meaning from its irreducible purpose —

to levy an income tax. To the extent that an income tax necessarily has a particular form, the Act itself must embody this form in its various provisions.

Chapters 1 to 3 are intended to establish the necessary foundations on which an understanding of the *Income Tax Act* may be based. Chapter 1 contains an introduction to the Canadian income tax, reviewing its history and basic structure as embodied in the provisions of the Act. Chapter 2 is devoted to statutory interpretation, reviewing the various factors that courts may consider in order to determine the meaning of a statutory provision; alternative doctrines that Canadian courts have employed in order to interpret the *Income Tax Act*; and specific sources to which Canadian courts refer for this purpose. Chapter 3 examines judicial and statutory approaches to tax avoidance that play a central role in the application of the Act to specific facts.

CHAPTER ONE

Introduction to the Income Tax

I. INTRODUCTION

To understand the *Income Tax Act*, it is helpful to begin by considering the role and history of the income tax in Canada and the basic structure of the tax that this statute is designed to collect. This chapter provides an introduction to the Canadian income tax by reviewing its role and history as well as its basic structure.

II. ROLE AND HISTORY OF THE INCOME TAX

Although taxes, tithes, or tributes of one form or another have been collected in most societies throughout the course of human civilization, broad-based income taxes like the federal income tax are a relatively recent development, associated with the formation of modern nation states, the emergence of modern market economies, and the increased social and economic role of modern governments. In order to appreciate the role and history of the income tax in Canada, it is useful to begin by reviewing the economic purposes of modern governments and the various methods by which governments can obtain revenues to finance these purposes.

A. Economic Purposes of Modern Government

Within a modern market economy, in which voluntary exchanges play a central role in the allocation and distribution of economic resources, at least four economic purposes may be attributed to the public sector.[1]

First, since private markets do not automatically ensure the most efficient allocation of economic resources, modern governments have an important role to play to address so-called market failures. For example, to the extent that certain goods or services (for example, national defence or research and development) provide benefits that cannot be easily restricted to those willing to pay for the relevant good or service, economic theory suggests that private

---

[1] For a useful introduction to these "fiscal functions," see Richard A. Musgrave, Peggy B. Musgrave & Richard M. Bird, *Public Finance in Theory and Practice*, 1st Cdn. ed. (Toronto: McGraw-Hill Ryerson, 1987).

markets will undersupply the good or service, since "free riders" can benefit from its provision without contributing to its cost. Alternatively, where the production or consumption of a good or service has a negative effect on third parties (for example, pollution), economic theory suggests that private markets will oversupply the good or service to the extent that these external costs are not taken into account by the parties to the transaction. Other market failures occur in the case of "natural monopolies" where the most efficient method of delivering a good or service (for example, certain kinds of transportation and communication) precludes the advantages of market competition. In the case of the first kind of market failure, the public sector is able to eliminate the free-rider problem by providing these "public goods and services" itself (for example, national defence) or subsidizing their provision by private parties (for example, research and development) and allocating the associated costs through compulsory taxes. Similarly, other kinds of market failures may justify governmental responses in the form of public regulation or corrective taxes (for example, for the protection of the environment), or direct public provision of goods and services (for example, transportation and communication).[2] Among economists, the role of modern governments in addressing these market failures is described as the "allocation function".

Second, notwithstanding a generalized preference for individual choice and voluntary exchange, collective values and paternalistic considerations may justify a public role in the allocation of certain categories of goods and services irrespective of efficiency concerns. Public education, for example, serves both a collective purpose in bringing children of different backgrounds together and a paternalistic aim in providing children opportunities for meaningful choices as adults. Likewise, public health care reflects a paternalistic concern about the need for health insurance and a collective judgment that medical services should be allocated on the basis of need, not market demand. Similarly, mandatory public pension plans are based on a paternalistic concern about the welfare of those who do not provide for their own retirement. Although a public role in the provision of these "merit goods" is less readily accepted in traditional economic theories of the public sector,[3] the collective and paternalistic considerations that underlie public provision of these goods and services are no less significant as a determinant of public policy and constitute a separate justification for the "allocation function" of modern governments.

Third, since the distribution of economic resources in a market economy depends on prior "factor endowments" (earning abilities and wealth) and fluctuations in supply and demand, each of which may be considered at least somewhat arbitrary, it is generally accepted that modern governments have an important role to play in moderating the distributive outcomes of the market

---

[2]   On the role of taxation for these regulatory purposes, see Satya Poddar, "Taxation and Regulation" in Richard M. Bird & Jack M. Mintz, eds., *Taxation to 2000 and Beyond*, Canadian Tax Paper No. 93 (Toronto: Canadian Tax Foundation, 1992).

[3]   See, for example, the discussion of "merit goods" in Musgrave, Musgrave & Bird, *Public Finance in Theory and Practice*, 1st Cdn. ed. (Toronto: McGraw-Hill Ryerson, 1987) at 70-73.

economy by redistributing economic resources from those favoured by the market economy to those who are less advantaged.[4] Although this redistribution may be achieved through transfer programs aimed at economically disadvantaged individuals or groups, this "distribution function" may also be pursued through the imposition of a heavier tax burden on those who are economically more fortunate.

Finally, since market economies are prone to business cycles in which aggregate demand exceeds aggregate supply (leading to inflation) or aggregate supply exceeds aggregate demand (leading to unemployment and low growth), modern governments generally employ fiscal and monetary policies in the pursuit of relative price stability, full employment, and economic growth. Through fiscal policy, for example, governments can reduce aggregate demand and inflation by raising taxes, reducing spending on privately provided goods and services, or running a budgetary surplus, or increase aggregate demand and reduce unemployment by reducing taxes, increasing spending on privately supplied goods and services, or borrowing money and running a deficit.[5] To the extent that revenues collected from certain kinds of taxes (for example, income and consumption taxes) tend to correspond to changes in economic conditions, increasing as economic activity increases and decreasing as economic activity decreases, these taxes function as "automatic stabilizers" in the pursuit of this "stabilization function".

Moving from theory to practice, a review of federal budgetary expenditures and consolidated budgetary expenditures of provincial and municipal governments demonstrates the extent to which these governments pursue the allocation and distribution functions outlined above.[6] According to figures for the 2006-07 fiscal year (see Table 1), the federal government devotes more than 40 per cent of budgetary expenditures on transfers to persons and governments, with additional expenditures devoted to Indian affairs and northern development. Together, these transfers and direct spending programs reflect a substantial role for the federal government in the redistribution of economic resources to economically disadvantaged individuals and groups.[7] Other federal expenditures fit neatly into the categories of public goods and services (for example, national defence) or natural monopolies (Crown corporations).

---

[4] For a compelling philosophical account for this kind of redistribution, see John Rawls, *A Theory of Justice* (Cambridge, MA: Harvard University Press, 1971). See also Ronald Dworkin, *Sovereign Virtue: The Theory and Practice of Equality* (Massachusetts: Harvard University Press, 2000) at Chapter 2.

[5] Although less common, fiscal policy can also focus on the "supply side" of the equation, increasing aggregate supply by lowering taxes on labour and capital, subsidizing investment, or increasing spending on public infrastructure.

[6] While changes in government budgets from year to year could be used to illustrate the use of fiscal policy in pursuit of the stabilization function, this role is difficult to discern from annual budgets taken in isolation.

[7] As indicated earlier, this distribution function is also pursued through the collection of federal taxes, especially the income tax.

Table 1: Federal Budgetary Expenditures, 2006-2007

Expenditure Category	Billions of dollars	Percentage of total expenditures
Transfers to persons		
Elderly benefits	30.3	13.6
Employment Insurance	14.1	6.3
Children's benefits	11.2	5.0
Total	55.6	25.0
Transfers to governments		
Support for health and other programs	28.6	12.9
Canada's cities and communities	0.6	0.3
Clean Air and Climate Change Trust Fund	1.5	0.7
Patient Wait Times Guarantee Trust	0.6	0.3
Early learning and child care	0.7	0.3
Fiscal arrangements and other transfers	13.1	5.9
Transition Trust	0.6	0.3
Alternative payments for standing programs	-3.2	-1.4
Total	42.5	19.1
Total transfers to persons and governments	98.1	44.1
Subsidies and other transfers		
Agriculture and agri-food	3.1	1.4
Foreign affairs and international trade	4.0	1.8
Health Canada	2.5	1.1
Human resources development	1.9	0.9
Indian affairs and northern development	5.2	2.3
Industry/regional agencies/granting councils	3.2	1.4
Other	6.9	3.1
Total	26.8	12.1

Expenditure Category	Billions of dollars	Percentage of total expenditures
Other program expenses		
Crown corporations	7.2	3.2
Defence	15.7	7.1
All other departments and agencies	40.4	18.2
Total other program expenses	63.3	28.5
Net program expenses	188.3	84.7
Public debt charges	33.9	15.3
Net expenses	222.2	100.0

Source: Canada, Department of Finance, Annual Financial Report of the Government of Canada Fiscal Year 2006-2007, available online at <http://www.fin.gc.ca/afr/2007/AFR2007_1e.html# TotalExpenses>. Note: Numbers may not add up due to rounding.

While provincial and municipal government expenditures reflect a similar emphasis on the allocation and distribution of economic resources (Table 2), constitutional responsibilities and practical constraints have caused these levels of government to place a greater emphasis on the allocation function than on the distribution function, devoting over 50 per cent of consolidated expenditures to the provision of merit goods in the areas of health, education and housing, and another 21.6 per cent of consolidated expenditures to the delivery of various public goods and services (transportation and communications, protection of persons and property, resource conservation and industrial development, the environment, and recreation and culture). Given their constitutional jurisdiction over property and civil rights,[8] provincial governments and the municipalities they oversee have primary responsibility for the delivery of major spending programs in the areas of health, education, and public infrastructure. As a practical matter, moreover, provincial and municipal governments are more limited in their ability to redistribute economic resources than the federal government, which can impose taxes on a nationwide level and redistribute resources among different regions. As a result, while provincial and municipal governments devote 15.2 per cent of consolidated expenditures to redistribution in the form of social services, these programs are heavily supported by transfers from the federal government.

---

[8] See s. 92(13) of the *Constitution Act, 1867*.

Table 2: Consolidated Provincial and Municipal Budgetary Expenditures, 2007

Expenditure Category	Billions of dollars	Percentage of total expenditures
Health	102.3	27.6
Education	83.9	22.7
Social services	56.3	15.2
Transportation and communications	24.0	6.5
Protection of persons and property	20.5	5.5
Resource conservation and industrial development	12.7	3.4
General services	11.6	3.1
Environment	12.6	3.4
Recreation and culture	10.5	2.8
Housing	4.0	1.1
Regional planning and development	2.2	0.6
Labour, employment and immigration	1.0	0.3
Research establishments	0.7	0.2
Other	0.9	0.2
Debt charges	26.5	7.2
Total expenditure	**370.3**	100.0

Source: Statistics Canada, as reproduced in Karin Treff and David B. Perry, *Finances of the Nation 2007* (Toronto: Canadian Tax Foundation, 2008), Table A.3 at A:5.
Note: Numbers may not add up due to rounding.

B. Sources of Revenue

Having reviewed the economic purposes of modern governments and the various transfer and spending programs pursued by different levels of government in Canada, it is immediately apparent that these governments require substantial annual revenues to finance their cost. Although taxes are the main method by which modern governments obtain the necessary revenues to pursue the economic purposes outlined earlier, they are neither the only way to pursue these purposes nor always the best way.

Although a review of federal budgetary revenues and consolidated budgetary revenues of provincial and municipal governments suggests that Canadian governments obtain some revenues from investment income and the sale of goods and services (Tables 3 and 4), the most prominent alternatives to taxation as a source of public finance involve borrowing and printing money.[9] By 2005, for example, cumulative federal, provincial, and municipal debt approached $800 billion ($791.2 billion exactly).[10] Alternatively, national governments, which maintain a monopoly over the creation of domestic currency, might opt to finance government expenditures through "seignorage" by printing money.

As a means of financing investments in public assets yielding economic returns over a number of years, or as a component of government fiscal policy to stimulate economic activity during economic downturns, borrowing money may represent a better source of public finance than taxation. Likewise, where increases in the money supply are necessary to keep pace with increases in national output or to stabilize the economy by stimulating aggregate demand, taxation is no substitute for printing money. Nonetheless, while each of these alternative methods of financing government is likely to be administratively less costly than the collection of taxes, there are several reasons why reliance on these alternatives is generally less desirable than taxation.

With respect to borrowing money, one need only examine the substantial share of government expenditures devoted to public debt charges (Tables 1 and 2) to appreciate the extent to which interest expenses on borrowed funds can consume scarce resources that might otherwise be used to pursue important allocative and distributive objectives. In addition, to the extent that government borrowing increases interest rates by increasing the demand for borrowed funds, this form of public finance may "crowd out" private investment and impede economic growth. Finally, by shifting the cost of government expenditures to future generations, government borrowing can be an inequitable method of public finance.

Likewise, printing money can be both economically disruptive and distributively inequitable as a source of government revenue. To the extent that increases in the money supply exceed increases in national output, printing money produces inflationary pressures, the most extreme examples of which are periods of "hyperinflation" in which domestic currencies become essentially worthless. Where printing money causes inflation, moreover, this method of raising revenue is arbitrary and unfair, favouring debtors over creditors (since the former are able to repay debts with devalued currency) and imposing a particularly heavy burden on those with fixed incomes such as pensioners.

---

[9] For an excellent discussion of alternatives to taxation as a source of government revenue, see Canada, *Report of the Royal Commission on Taxation*, 6 vols. (Ottawa: Queen's Printer, 1966), Vol. 2 at 1-5.

[10] Karin Treff and David B. Perry, *Finances of the Nation 2007* (Toronto: Canadian Tax Foundation, 2007), 15:2.

   As a result, while it may be economically and distributively appropriate for governments to borrow and print money in certain circumstances, taxation is generally viewed as a preferable method of financing government. Although taxes can produce economic distortions and necessitate collection costs for governments and compliance costs for taxpayers, these adverse impacts are generally less than those associated with borrowing or printing money. Indeed, one of the main objectives in the choice among different taxes and the design of particular taxes is to minimize the attendant costs of economic distortions and tax collection. Moreover, unlike borrowing or printing money, taxation permits the cost of government expenditures to be allocated in a manner that is based on generally accepted notions of fairness.

C. Taxation and the Income Tax

A "tax", as an ordinary dictionary definition explains, is "a contribution to government revenue *compulsorily* levied on individuals, property, or businesses".[11] Although this definition excludes some sources of government revenue from the category of taxation, a look at federal budgetary revenues and consolidated budgetary revenues of provincial and municipal governments (Tables 3 and 4) demonstrates that these revenues are derived mostly from taxation.[12] In addition, as the figures indicate, these governments collect a variety of taxes, including personal and corporate income taxes, various kinds of sales or consumption taxes, assorted payroll taxes, social insurance levies, and property taxes. Other developed countries also depend on a mix of taxes, comprising individual and corporate income taxes, various kinds of consumption taxes, payroll taxes, and property taxes.[13]

---

[11] *The Canadian Oxford Dictionary*, 2d ed. (emphasis added).

[12] This is particularly true at the federal level, where over 84 per cent of budgetary revenues for the 2006-07 fiscal years were derived from taxes. While taxes remain the primary source of revenue at the provincial and municipal levels, these governments derive a much larger share of total budgetary revenues from the sale of goods and services, investment income, and cash transfers from other levels of government.

[13] For a useful comparison of taxes levied in different developed countries, see David B. Perry, "International Tax Comparisons" Fiscal Figures feature (1997) Vol. 45 No. 5 Can. Tax J. 1180. As a general rule, other developed countries rely less on personal income taxes than Canadian governments and more on social security contributions in the form of payroll taxes. See also OECD, *Revenue Statistics, 1965-2006* (OECD, 2007), Tables 10-19.

Table 3: Federal Budgetary Revenues, 2006-2007

Revenue Source	Billions of dollars	Percentage of total tax revenues	Percentage of total revenues
Income tax			
Personal income tax	110.5	55.7	46.8
Corporate income tax	37.7	19.0	16.0
Other	4.9	2.5	2.1
Total income tax	153.1	77.2	64.9
Other taxes and duties			
Goods and services tax	31.3	15.8	13.3
Customs import duties	3.7	1.9	1.6
Energy taxes	5.1	2.6	2.2
Air travellers security charge	0.4	0.2	0.2
Other excise taxes and duties	4.8	2.4	2.0
Total	45.3	22.8	19.2
Total tax revenue	**198.4**	100.0	84.1
Employment insurance premium revenue	16.8	-	7.1
Other revenue	20.8	-	8.8
Total budgetary revenues	**236.0**		100.0

Source: Canada, Department of Finance, Annual Financial Report of the Government of Canada 2006-2007, available online at <http://www.fin.gc.ca/afr/2007/AFR2007_1e.html#Budgetary >.
Note: Numbers may not add up due to rounding.

Table 4: Consolidated Provincial and Municipal Budgetary Revenues, 2007

Revenue Source	Billions of dollars	Percentage of non-property tax revenues	Percentage of total revenues
Income tax			
Personal income tax	70.5	46.4	21.9
Corporate income tax	19.9	13.1	6.2
Other	0.7	0.5	0.2
Total income tax	91.1	60.0	28.3
Consumption taxes			
General sales taxes	35.3	23.2	11.0
Gasoline and motive fuel	8.0	5.3	2.5
Alcoholic beverages and tobacco	4.9	3.2	1.5
Other	12.5	8.2	3.9
Total consumption taxes	60.8	40.0	18.9
Total non-property taxes	**151.9**	100.0	47.2
Property and related taxes	51.4		16.0
Health and drug insurance premiums	3.3		1.0
Contributions to social security plans	12.1		3.8
Miscellaneous taxes	18.4		5.7
Sales of goods and services	41.8		13.0
Investment income	37.2		11.6
Other revenue	5.5		1.7
Total budgetary revenues	**321.7**		100.0

Source: Statistics Canada, as reproduced in Karin Treff and David B. Perry, *Finances of the Nation 2007* (Toronto: Canadian Tax Foundation, 2008), Table A.1 at A:2. Note: Numbers may not add up due to rounding.

While the declared purpose of the new tax was to raise revenues to finance the war effort, the tax was deliberately designed to raise these revenues only from more affluent Canadians who it was felt could bear a greater share of the financial burden. Under the original provisions of the *Income War Tax Act*, therefore, individuals paid no tax until their incomes exceeded $1,500, while married taxpayers paid no tax until their incomes exceeded $3,000.[20] Above these amounts, tax was levied at progressive rates, ranging from 4 per cent on amounts up to $6,000 to 29 per cent on income exceeding $100,000.[21] Although dollar amounts and percentage figures have changed frequently over the years, basic exemptions and progressive rates have remained constant features of the federal income tax. For the 2008 taxation year, for example, the Act exempts the first $9,600 of each individual's income (increased to $19,200 for an individual supporting a spouse or common law partner or related dependant who earns no more than $751[22]), and applies at rates of 15 per cent on amounts up to $37,885, 22 per cent on amounts from $36,379 to $75,769, 26 per cent on amounts from $75,770 to $123,184, and 29 per cent on amounts exceeding $123,184.[23]

Given the exemption of what were at the time substantial dollar amounts, it is not surprising that the original income tax accounted for a small percentage of federal tax revenues and applied only to a limited number of relatively affluent Canadians. In 1926, for example, the personal income tax raised only 5.1 per cent of federal tax revenues, the vast majority of which continued to be derived from customs duties and excise taxes.[24] Fewer than 200,000 Canadians paid income tax in 1934, a much smaller proportion of the population than the more than 15.5 million Canadians who pay income tax today.[25]

As revenue needs motivated the introduction of the federal income tax in 1917, so also did revenue needs prompt the introduction of provincial income taxes in the 1920s and 1930s and the transformation of these taxes into broad-

---

[20] See para. 4(1)(a) of the *Income War Tax Act*, S.C. 1917, c. 28. The higher exemption for married taxpayers created an anomaly where both spouses earned income, resulting in a combined exemption for a married couple of up to $6,000. This anomaly was addressed by subsequent amendments requiring the exemption to be split between the spouses.

[21] See subs. 4(1) of the *Income War Tax Act*.

[22] For subsequent taxation years, these exempt amounts are indexed for inflation on an annual basis under s. 117.1. In addition to these annual increases, subsections 118(3.1) to (3.3) provide for additional increases to reach a basic personal amount of no less than $10,100 in 2009 (increased to no less than $18,500 for an individual supporting a spouse or common law partner earning no more than $850).

[23] See subs. 117(2) of the Act. Each of the "rate brackets" defined by subs. 117(2) is indexed for inflation on an annual basis under s. 117.1. As explained later in this chapter, provincial income tax must be added to these rates in order to determine the full rates of tax payable by individuals at different levels of income.

[24] See Richard A. Musgrave, Peggy B. Musgrave & Richard M. Bird, *Public Finance in Theory and Practice*, 1st Cdn. ed. (Toronto: McGraw Hill Rycrson, 1987) at 298.

[25] See Karin Treff and David B. Perry, *Finances of the Nation 2007* (Toronto: Canadian Tax Foundation, 2007) at 3:2.

based "mass taxes" in the post-war period. Faced with mounting expenditures on public infrastructure to support economic development and on social relief with the onset of the Great Depression, most provinces had enacted their own income taxes by the end of the 1930s. Even in 1939, however, personal income taxes supplied a small proportion of tax revenues for both levels of government, accounting for 9.9 per cent of federal tax revenues and 5.9 per cent of provincial tax revenues in that year.[26]

The Second World War and the growth of the welfare state in the post-war period completed the transformation of the income tax into the mass tax that it is today. During the war, provincial governments agreed to abandon their income taxes in exchange for cash grants from the federal government, which levied the only Canadian income tax from 1941 to 1947.[27] Also during the war the federal government broadened the reach of the income tax by reducing personal exemptions and increasing rates, providing targeted relief, however, in the form of specific deductions for taxpayers with extraordinary medical expenses or disabilities. Under amendments enacted in 1942, personal exemptions fell to $660 for single persons and $1,200 for married persons supporting a spouse, above which taxpayers were subject to a "normal tax" of 7 per cent and "graduated tax" ranging from 30 to 85 per cent.[28] By 1945, the personal income tax accounted for almost one-third of federal tax revenues, with corporate income taxes representing a further 26.8 per cent.[29] From 1938 to 1945, the number of Canadians paying tax increased from fewer than 300,000 to more than 2.2 million.[30]

Shortly after the war, the federal government persuaded most provinces to refrain from re-enacting their own income taxes in exchange for continued cash payments under so-called tax-rental agreements established in 1947.[31] Although these agreements were terminated in 1962 when participating provinces decided

---

[26] See Richard A. Musgrave, Peggy B. Musgrave & Richard M. Bird, *Public Finance in Theory and Practice*, 1st Cdn. ed. (Toronto: McGraw-Hill Ryerson, 1987) at 298.

[27] For a detailed history of these agreements and the process leading to their negotiation, see Ernest H. Smith, *Federal-Provincial Tax Sharing and Centralized Tax Collection in Canada*, Special Studies in Taxation and Public Finance No. 1 (Toronto: Canadian Tax Foundation, 1998) at Chapter 3.

[28] Gwyneth McGregor, *Personal Exemptions and Deductions Under the Income Tax, with Special Reference to Canada, the U.S. and the U.K.*, Canadian Tax Paper No. 31 (Toronto: Canadian Tax Foundation, 1962) at 44.

[29] Calculated from figures presented in David B. Perry, "Fiscal Figures: The Evolution of Tax Collections Over the Past Half Century" (1995) Vol. 43 No. 5 Can. Tax J. 1077.

[30] See Karin Treff and David B. Perry, *Finances of the Nation* 2005 (Toronto: Canadian Tax Foundation, 2005) at 3:2.

[31] See Ernest H. Smith, *Federal-Provincial Tax Sharing and Centralized Tax Collection in Canada*, Special Studies in Taxation and Public Finance No. 1 (Toronto: Canadian Tax Foundation, 1998) at Chapter 4. Although Ontario and Quebec refused to enter into these agreements in 1947, Ontario accepted the arrangement on its renewal in 1952. See *ibid.*, Chapter 5.

to introduce their own income taxes,[32] the federal government has continued to collect most provincial income taxes under "tax-collection agreements" according to which the federal government has agreed to administer the collection of provincial income taxes at little or no charge provided that these taxes retain most of the same structural features as the federal income tax.[33] As a result of these agreements, to which most provinces have subscribed,[34] the federal income tax constitutes the basis of most provincial income taxes.

Also, shortly after the Second World War, the federal government took steps to make the income tax a permanent source of revenue, repealing the *Income*

---

[32] In order to allow provinces to introduce their own income taxes without increasing combined federal and provincial income taxes, the federal government introduced a credit against federal income tax otherwise payable, effectively lowering the federal tax rates applicable to income subject to provincial income tax. See subs. 33(1) of the 1952 Act, which allowed a credit of 10 per cent for 1957, 13 per cent from 1958 to 1961, 16 per cent for 1962, 17 per cent for 1963, 18 per cent for 1964, 21 per cent for 1965, 24 per cent for 1966, and 28 per cent from 1967 to 1971. This credit was repealed in 1972, when the federal government opted to achieve the same result more directly by lowering general rates and introducing an additional tax on income not earned in a province under subs. 120(1) of the Act. In subsequent years, the federal government has conferred more "tax room" on provincial governments by lowering federal income tax rates in 1977, 1982 and again in 1988. Not surprisingly, during these years, provincial income tax rates increased substantially, rising from a range of 30.5 to 42.5 per cent of basic federal tax for provinces participating in the tax-collection agreements in 1972 to a range of 44 to 62 per cent of basic tax for provinces and territories participating in the tax-collection agreements in 1990, excluding provincial surtaxes. See David B. Perry, *Financing the Canadian Federation, 1867 to 1995: Setting the Stage for Change*, Canadian Tax Paper No. 102 (Toronto: Canadian Tax Foundation, 1997), Tables 6.1 and 7.3.

[33] For a detailed discussion of these agreements and the process leading to their negotiation, see Ernest H. Smith, *Federal-Provincial Tax Sharing and Centralized Tax Collection in Canada*, Special Studies in Taxation and Public Finance No. 1 (Toronto: Canadian Tax Foundation, 1998) at Chapters 9-12. Until 1998, these agreements generally required provincial governments to levy their income taxes as a fixed percentage of basic federal tax payable, the effect of which was to cause participating provinces to "piggyback" on the federal rate structure and federal non-refundable credits, as well as accept the federal definition of taxable income, the annual accounting period, and the individual tax unit. Under a new set of guidelines adopted in 1998, provincial income taxes may be based on the federal definition of taxable income, permitting provinces much greater flexibility to establish their own rate structures and their own credits. See Canada, Department of Finance and Canada Customs and Revenue Agency, *Federal Administration of Provincial Taxes: New Directions* (January 2000). For useful discussions of the causes of and policy issues surrounding these changes, see Munir A. Sheikh and Michel Carreau, "A Federal Perspective on the Role and Operation of the Tax Collection Agreements" (1999) Vol. 47 No. 4 Can. Tax J. 845; Thomas J. Courchene, "National Versus Regional Concerns: A Provincial Perspective on the Role and Operation of the Tax Collection Agreements" (1999) Vol. 47 No. 4 Can. Tax J. 861; and Alan Macnaughton, "Compliance and Administration Issues Under the Tax Collection Agreements" (1999) Vol. 47 No. 5 Can. Tax J. 890.

[34] All provinces but Quebec have entered into agreements with the federal government for the collection of personal income taxes and two provinces (Alberta and Quebec) have opted to collect their own corporate income taxes.

War Tax Act and enacting a successor *Income Tax Act*, S.C. 1948, c. 52, which among other things eliminated much of the administrative discretion that had existed under the previous statute. Subsequent amendments were consolidated in a revised *Income Tax Act* adopted in 1952. Under this statute, personal exemptions were set at $1,000 for a single person and $2,000 for a married person supporting a spouse.[35] Above these thresholds, progressive rates ranged from 16 per cent on the first $1,000 of taxable income to 80 per cent on amounts exceeding $400,000.[36] Despite regular revisions to the 1952 Act, these exemptions and rates remained largely unchanged throughout the 1950s and 1960s, producing substantial increases in federal revenues as income levels increased during the post-war period and inflation reduced the real value of the personal exemptions and lower rate brackets. By 1970, the personal income tax had become the largest single source of federal tax revenue, accounting for 44.3 per cent of aggregate federal tax revenues.[37] In that year, over 7.6 million Canadians paid income tax.[38]

As the income tax assumed increasing importance in the federal revenue system, the federal government concluded that the tax merited a more thorough review than that permitted by piecemeal amendments, and appointed a Royal Commission on Taxation (*i.e.*, the Carter Commission) in 1962, chaired by a Toronto accountant named Kenneth Carter. When the Carter Commission released its six-volume report in 1966,[39] it was widely hailed as one of the most sophisticated evaluations of the income tax of any country ever produced.[40] While the federal government's response to the report was slow in coming,[41] the report's recommendations played a significant role in a revised *Income Tax Act*

---

[35] See paras. 26(1)(b) and (a) of the *Income Tax Act*, R.S.C. 1952, c. 148. Additional exemptions, the dollar amounts of which were increased in 1957 and 1962, applied for specific relatives dependent on the taxpayer for support. See paras. 26(1)(c) and (d), para. 26(1)(ba) (enacted in 1955) and paras. 26(1)(ca) and (da) (enacted in 1965).

[36] See subs. 32(1) of the 1952 Act, as it applied to taxation years prior to 1955. In addition to these basic rates, subs. 32(3) imposed a separate 4 per cent tax on investment income from sources outside Canada, making the combined top marginal rate on income from these sources 84 per cent during this period.

[37] See Richard A. Musgrave, Peggy B. Musgrave & Richard M. Bird, *Public Finance in Theory and Practice*, 1st Cdn. ed. (Toronto: McGraw-Hill Ryerson, 1987) at 298.

[38] See Karin Treff and David B. Perry, *Finances of the Nation 2005* (Toronto: Canadian Tax Foundation, 2005) at 3:2.

[39] *Report of the Royal Commission on Taxation*, 6 vols. (Ottawa: Queen's Printer, 1966).

[40] For contemporary reviews of the Carter Commission report, see Meyer Bucovetsky & Richard M. Bird, "Tax Reform in Canada — A Progress Report" (1972) 25 National Tax Journal 15. For a retrospective review 20 years after its release, see W. Neil Brooks, ed., *The Quest for Tax Reform: The Royal Commission on Taxation Twenty Years Later* (Toronto: Carswell, 1988).

[41] In 1969, then Minister of Finance Edgar Benson released a government white paper setting out the government's proposed amendments to the *Income Tax Act*: Hon. E.J. Benson, *Proposals for Tax Reform* (Ottawa: Queen's Printer, 1969). These proposals were reviewed by standing committees of both houses of Parliament before the government released its final proposals in June 1971.

introduced in 1972 (S.C. 1970-71-72, c. 63, section 1). Although subject to a multitude of amendments over the last three decades, this statute remains in force to this day.

Among the many revisions resulting from the report of the Carter Commission, the most significant involved measures to expand the scope of the tax by increasing the categories of income subject to tax;[42] the introduction of new deductions for moving expenses, child-care expenses, and students in full-time attendance in post-secondary education;[43] increases in the personal exemptions to $1,500 for single taxpayers and $2,850 for married taxpayers; a reduction in the number of rate brackets from 17 to 13; and significant reductions both in the top federal rate, which fell from 80 per cent to 47 per cent, and in the income level above which this rate applied, which fell from taxable income exceeding $400,000 to taxable income exceeding $60,000.[44] Subsequent amendments reduced the top federal rate still further to 43 per cent in 1977, 34 per cent in 1982, and 29 per cent in 1988, and reduced the number of rate brackets to 10 in 1982 and 3 in 1988.[45] For 2001 and subsequent taxation years, the federal government introduced a fourth rate bracket, increasing the income level to which the top rate of 29 per cent applies from approximately $60,000 to $100,000. For the 2008 taxation year, this top rate bracket starts at $123,184.

Other significant structural amendments to the federal income tax since 1972 include: (1) the indexation of personal exemptions and rate brackets for inflation in 1974, the partial de-indexation of these amounts in 1986, and a return to full indexation in the year 2000;[46] (2) the conversion of personal exemptions and provisions for other amounts (for example, charitable contributions, medical expenses, tuition fees, and education amounts) from deductions to credits in 1988;[47] (3) the increased use of the *Income Tax Act* as an instrument of federal economic and social policy through the enactment of numerous tax credits to encourage specific kinds of investments;[48] and (4) the introduction of refundable

---

[42] These measures are examined later in this chapter in the discussion of the tax base.

[43] See s. 62 (moving expenses) and 63 (child-care expenses), and the deduction in former paras. 110(1)(g) and (h) (education amount). Sections 62 and 63 are examined in Chapter 7. The last of these deductions, which used to apply in computing the taxable income of the student or supporting individual, was converted to a credit in 1988. See s. 118.6.

[44] See subs. 117(2) of the Act as it applied from 1972 to 1976.

[45] See subs. 117(2) of the Act as it applied from 1972 to 2000.

[46] See s. 117.1, added by S.C. 1973-74, c. 30, s. 15. From 1986 to 2000, these amounts were indexed only to the extent that the annual inflation rate exceeded 3 per cent. For a critical commentary on the effects of the resulting "bracket creep," see Finn Poschmann, *Inflated Taxes, Deflated Paycheques* (Toronto: C.D. Howe Institute, 1998).

[47] The distinction between deductions and credits and the rationale for this amendment are explained later in this chapter.

[48] See s. 125.1 (corporate manufacturing and processing profits credit introduced in 1973), subs. 127(5)-(11) (investment tax credit introduced in 1975), s. 127.1 (refundable investment tax credit introduced in 1982), s. 127.2 (share-purchase tax credit introduced in 1982), s. 127.3 (scientific research and experimental development tax credit introduced in 1982), s. 127.4

tax credits designed to provide direct transfer payments to low-income Canadians through the administrative mechanism of the *Income Tax Act*.[49]

III. BASIC STRUCTURE OF THE INCOME TAX

An income tax consists of at least four basic elements: a "tax unit", which is subject to the tax; a "tax base", on which the tax is assessed; an "accounting period," over which period of time income is computed; and a structure of "tax rates", which are applied to determine the amount of tax payable. In Canada, as in many other countries, the income tax also includes "tax credits," which operate to reduce tax otherwise payable or to provide direct payments in the form of tax refunds.

Three of these elements can be identified in the basic charging provision of the income tax in subsection 2(1) of the *Income Tax Act*, which states:

> An income tax shall be paid, as required by this Act, on the taxable income for each taxation year of every person resident in Canada at any time in the year.

The fourth element appears in subsection 117(2), subject to subsection 117(3), which defines the basic amount of tax payable by individuals after 2006 as:

(a) 15% of the amount taxable, if the amount taxable is equal to or less than … $36,378;

(b) if the amount taxable is greater than … $36,378 and is equal to or less than … $72,756, the amount determined in respect of the taxation year under paragraph (a) plus 22% of the amount by which the amount taxable exceeds … $36,378 …;

(c) if the amount taxable is greater than … $72,756, but is equal to or less than … $118,825, the total of the amounts determined in respect of the taxation year under paragraphs (a) and (b) plus 26% of the amount by which the amount taxable exceeds … $72,756; and

(d) if the amount taxable is greater than … $118,825, the total of the amounts determined in respect of the taxation year under paragraphs (a), (b) and (c) plus 29% of the amount by which the amount taxable exceeds … $118,825.

For taxation years after 2006, these "rate brackets" are indexed for inflation on an annual basis under section 117.1 of the Act.

Section 122 defines the tax generally payable by an *inter vivos* trust as 29 per cent of its amount taxable, and subsection 123(1) defines the basic amount of tax payable by corporations as "38% of its amount taxable for the year".[50] For our

---

(labour-sponsored funds tax credit introduced in 1985), s. 125.4 (Canadian film or video production tax credit introduced in 1995), and s. 125.5 (film or video production services tax credit introduced in 1997).

[49] See s. 122.5 (GST credit introduced in 1989), s. 122.6 (child tax benefit introduced in 1993), and s. 122.51 (refundable medical expense supplement introduced in 1997).

[50] For corporate income earned in any Canadian province, this rate is effectively reduced to 28 per cent by subs. 124(1), which reduces federal corporate income tax payable in order to allow provinces to levy corporate income tax. Corporate tax rates are subject to further reductions

purposes, there is no need to examine the rates of tax applicable to *inter vivos* trusts and corporations.[51]

According to these provisions, therefore, income tax is imposed on "every person resident in Canada at any time in the year," based on the "taxable income" of these persons, measured over a period of "each taxation year", and computed at graduated or "progressive" rates of 15 per cent, 22 per cent, 26 per cent, and 29 per cent for individuals and at single or "flat" rates of 29 per cent for *inter vivos* trusts and 38 per cent (subject to various adjustments) for corporations. Without venturing any further into the body of the *Income Tax Act*, therefore, these provisions provide a preliminary description of the tax unit ("every person resident in Canada at any time in the year"); the tax base ("taxable income"); the basic accounting period ("each taxation year"); and the tax rates applicable to individuals (15 per cent, 22 per cent, 26 per cent, and 29 per cent), *inter vivos* trusts (29 per cent), and corporations (38 per cent).

While the rates of tax applicable to individuals are relatively straightforward, the same cannot be said of any of the other elements comprising the basic structure of the Canadian income tax. Indeed, the bulk of this book (Chapters 4 to 8) is devoted to a detailed examination of the various statutory and judicial rules defining the tax base for the Canadian income tax. As a foundation for this detailed inquiry, the following sections of this chapter provide an introduction to the basic structure of the Canadian income tax, considering the concepts and statutory definitions of the tax unit, the tax base, the accounting period, tax rates, and refundable and non-refundable credits.

A. Tax Unit

The unit or units of an income tax may be defined as the person or persons to whom the tax applies. According to subsection 2(1) of the *Income Tax Act*, the basic unit of the tax imposed under Part I of the Act is "every person resident in Canada at any time in the year".[52] In order to understand the specific tax unit or

---

under a schedule of phased rate reductions under s. 123.4 of the Act, and under separate provisions applicable to manufacturing and processing profits and the "active business income" of "Canadian-controlled private corporations."

51 While the rate for *inter vivos* trusts is relatively straightforward and is intended to prevent income splitting by taxing trust income at the top marginal rate, the rate applicable to corporations is subject to a number of adjustments based on the kind of corporation and the category of income subject to tax. These provisions are best examined in courses on the taxation of trusts and estates, and the taxation of corporations and their shareholders.

52 Although the Act also applies to non-resident persons in certain circumstances, there is no need for us to examine these provisions in detail. See subs. 2(3), which levies a tax on non-residents who were "employed in Canada, ... carried on business in Canada, or ... disposed of a taxable Canadian property, at any time in the year or a previous year," based on the non-resident's "taxable income earned in Canada" during the year (as defined by the rules in Division D of Part I of the Act, comprising ss. 115, 115.1, 115.2, and 116). See also Part XIII of the Act, which imposes "withholding taxes" on interest, dividends, rental payments, and royalties paid by

units to which the Canadian income tax applies, therefore, it is necessary to determine both the meaning of a "person" for the purposes of the *Income Tax Act*, and the criteria whereby such persons may be held to be resident in Canada at any time in the year. The following discussion examines each of these aspects of the tax unit for the Canadian income tax.

1. Persons

According to subsection 248(1) of the Act, the word "person" or "any word or expression descriptive of a person" is defined to include "any corporation, and any entity exempt, because of subsection 149(1) from tax under Part I on all or part of the entity's taxable income and the heirs, executors, liquidators of a succession, administrators, or other legal representatives of such a person, according to the law of that part of Canada to which the context extends". Because this definition merely expands on the ordinary meaning of the word "person", without defining this ordinary meaning, it is useful to consider dictionary definitions, which define a "person" as "an individual human being".[53] Since subsection 248(1) defines an "individual" as "a person other than a corporation," it follows that the *Income Tax Act* applies to individuals and the other persons included under the extended definition of "person" in subsection 248(1) of the Act — provided that they are resident in Canada at any time in the relevant taxation year.

For our purposes, there is no need to examine the taxation of corporations or estates,[54] nor the special rules applicable to tax-exempt entities.[55] Since the income tax imposed under Part I of the Act applies to "every person", however, it is worth noting that most of the statutory provisions governing the computation of a person's taxable income for a taxation year apply to these persons as well as individuals. Of greater relevance for our purposes, however, is the choice between the individual and other units (for example, spouses or families) for personal income taxation, the implications of individual taxation under an income tax levied at progressive rates, and the recognition of broader

---

Canadian residents to non-residents. These provisions are best examined in a course on international taxation.

[53] See, for example, *The Canadian Oxford Dictionary*, 2d ed. and *The Concise Oxford English Dictionary*, 11th ed.

[54] See subdivisions h and k of Division B and subdivision b of Division E of Part 1 of the Act. These provisions and the tax topics are best examined in courses on the taxation of corporations and the taxation of trusts and estates.

[55] Among the persons exempt from income tax by virtue of subs. 149(1) are employees of other countries (paras. 149(1)(a) and (b)), municipalities and municipal and provincial corporations (paras. 149(1)(c) and (d)), agricultural organizations, boards of trade, and chambers of commerce (para. 149(1)(e)), labour unions (para. 149(1)(k)), charitable or non-profit organizations (paras. 149(1)(f), (i), (j), and (l)), and various kinds of deferred income plans (paras. 149(1)(o), (o.1), (o.2), (o.4), (r), (s), and (u)).

family relationships in several provisions of the *Income Tax Act* notwithstanding its use of the individual as the basic unit of personal income taxation.

a. Choice of Unit

While the individual may seem like the most obvious choice as the basic unit for the personal income tax, this unit is neither universally employed in the income taxes of other developed countries nor universally approved by those evaluating the design of the income tax. In the United States, for example, income tax applies to the aggregate income of married couples, whose combined income is taxed at different rates from those applied to single or unmarried individuals.[56] France, on the other hand, combines the incomes of married couples and dependent children under a "quotient" system whereby progressive rates are applied to separate parts of the aggregate familial income based on the number of individuals in the family, with each adult counting as one part, each child counting as half a part, and an additional half part for couples with three or more children.[57] Although Canada has maintained the individual as the basic unit of income taxation since the *Income War Tax Act* was enacted in 1917, commentators have often favoured broader spousal or familial units. In 1966, for example, the Carter Commission recommended the adoption of a family unit "consisting of husband, wife and dependant children, if any".[58] In the late 1990s, when the federal government conducted a review of family taxation in Canada, both the then Reform/Alliance Party of Canada and the then Progressive Conservative Party of Canada favoured a spousal or family unit for the income tax.[59]

Contrasting views on the preferred unit of tax for a personal income tax turn on differing perspectives on the purpose of an income tax, alternative conceptions of the family and spousal relationships, and opposing judgments regarding the social and economic consequences of different tax units.[60] While arguments for an individual tax unit generally favour a concept of distributive justice according to which the income tax is based on the economic power that persons derive from their entitlement to and effective control over income (the

---

[56] For an excellent analysis of the US system of "joint returns," see Lawrence Zelenak, "Marriage and the Income Tax" (1994) 67 S. Cal. L. Rev. 339.

[57] For a description of the French quotient system, see Louise Dulude, "Taxation of the Spouses: A Comparison of Canadian, American, British, French and Swedish Law" (1985) 23 Osgoode Hall L.J. 67 at 71-73.

[58] *Report of the Royal Commission on Taxation*, 6 vols. (Ottawa: Queen's Printer, 1966) Vol. 3 at 122.

[59] See, for example, the statement of Eric Lowther, Reform/Alliance MP for Calgary Centre, House of Commons, *Debates*, February 2, 1999.

[60] For a more lengthy treatment of these issues, see David G. Duff, "Tax Policy and the Family: A North American Perspective" in *Proceedings of the Fifteenth Annual Conference of the Foundation for Fiscal Studies* (Dublin: Foundation for Fiscal Studies, 2000).

"control principle"),[61] for example, arguments for a spousal or familial unit typically support an allocation of tax burdens according to the economic benefits that persons derive from income received by themselves or others, rather than legal entitlement to or effective control over this income (the "benefit principle").[62] Since legal scholars tend to emphasize rights and responsibilities, while economists focus on welfare, it is perhaps not surprising that the former are more inclined to favour an individual tax unit while the latter are more apt to support a spousal or familial unit.

With respect to conceptions of the family, advocates of a spousal or familial unit tend to regard these groupings as the collective owners and shared beneficiaries of the income received by individual members.[63] On this basis, regardless of the conception of distributive justice on which the income tax is based, the tax should be applied to the aggregate income of these units rather than the income of each individual. Where the tax is based on the benefits provided by this income, however, economies from living together suggest that couples should be taxed more heavily than two single individuals with half the combined income of the couple, and that a similar principle should apply to the aggregate income of familial units of different sizes.[64] Indeed, this result is achieved in the United States, which applies a different rate schedule to married couples and unmarried individuals. In contrast, those favouring an individual tax unit emphasize both the individual nature of each recipient's entitlement to and effective control over his or her income and the differential benefits enjoyed by each spouse or familial member based on this legal entitlement, reasoning that an individual unit is preferred under either the control or the benefit principle.[65] Moreover, to the extent that the income tax is based on the benefits derived from income, advocates of an individual unit suggest that the diversity of groupings

---

[61] See, for example, Neil Brooks, "The Irrelevance of Conjugal Relationships in Assessing Tax Liability" in John G. Head & Richard Krever, eds., *Tax Units and the Tax Rate Scale* (Melbourne: Australian Tax Research Foundation, 1996), 35. See also Lawrence Zelenak, "Marriage and the Income Tax" (1994) 67 S. Cal. L. Rev. 339 at 354-58.

[62] See, for example, Michael J. McIntyre & Oliver Oldman, "Taxation of the Family in a Comprehensive and Simplified Income Tax" (1977) 90 Harv. L. Rev. 1573.

[63] See, for example, the *Report of the Royal Commission on Taxation*, 6 vols. (Ottawa: Queen's Printer, 1966) Vol. 3 at 123, characterizing the family as "the basic economic unit of society." See also Michael J. McIntyre & Oliver Oldman, *ibid.*, who argue that the benefits derived from income received by married persons are shared equally by the couple.

[64] See the *Report of the Royal Commission on Taxation*, 6 vols. (Ottawa: Queen's Printer, 1966) Vol. 3 at 117 explaining that "while two cannot live as cheaply as one, economies are possible when two people share bed and board." and concluding as a result that "the tax payable by a married couple should be greater than the sum of the income taxes payable by two single individuals, each of whom has one half the income of the couple."

[65] See, for example, Neil Brooks, "The Irrelevance of Conjugal Relationships in Assessing Tax Liability" in John G. Head & Richard Krever, eds., *Tax Units and the Tax Rate Scale* (Melbourne: Australian Tax Research Foundation, 1996), and Lawrence Zelenak, "Marriage and the Income Tax" (1994) 67 S. Cal. L. Rev. 339 at 348-58.

within which economic resources are shared to a greater or lesser extent (for example, unmarried couples, same-sex couples, extended families, and other persons sharing accommodation) and the impact on personal autonomy necessary to monitor these diverse relationships make it difficult to properly define and unacceptable to effectively administer any tax unit other than the individual.

Regarding the consequences of different tax units, advocates of an individual tax unit have advanced two further objections to a spousal or familial unit in a tax system with graduated or progressive rates: first, that it violates tax neutrality by either encouraging or discouraging the existence of the relevant unit;[66] second, that it discourages participation in the paid labour force by so-called secondary earners (primarily women) by "stacking" their income on top of that already received by the primary earner.[67] Although there is little empirical evidence that tax penalties on dual-income-earning married couples in the United States have had a significant impact on the marriage rate,[68] a growing body of literature suggests that the tax disincentives for "secondary earners" in the United States may be substantial.[69] Indeed, the US Congressional Budget Office estimates that the effect of the rate structure alone causes lower-income

---

[66] In the United States, where a separate rate schedule applies to married couples, the relationship between these rates and those applicable to unmarried individuals creates a "marriage penalty" for couples with relatively equal incomes and a "marriage bonus" for couples with significant disparities in incomes, creating a tax incentive for single-income-earning couples to marry and a tax disincentive for dual-income-earning couples to marry. As female labour force participation has increased over the last 30 years, the number of couples facing a marriage penalty has increased, while the number experiencing a marriage bonus has decreased, prompting increasing political attention in the United States. See, for example, Congress of the United States, *For Better or For Worse: Marriage and the Federal Income Tax* (Washington, DC: Congressional Budget Office, 1997).

[67] For criticisms of the US tax system on this basis, see Boris Bittker, "Federal Income Taxation and the Family" (1975) 27 Stan. L. Rev 1389 at 1431-42; Pamela B. Gann, "Abandoning Marital Status as a Factor in Allocating Income Tax Burdens" (1980) 59 Tex. L. Rev 1 at 39-46; Laura Ann Davis, Note, "A Feminist Justification for the Adoption of an Individual Filing System" (1988) 62 S. Cal. L. Rev 197 at 210-19; and Edward J. McCaffery, "Taxation and the Family: A Fresh Look at Behavioral Gender Bias in the Code" (1993) 40 UCLA L. Rev. 983 at 1037-53.

[68] For a brief review of this literature, see Gann, *ibid.*, at 12-14. See also David L. Sjoquist & Mary Beth Walker, "The Marriage Tax and the Rate and Timing of Marriage" (1995) 48 National Tax Journal 547, who conclude that marriage tax penalties have had no significant impact on the decision to marry, but may encourage couples to delay marriages for a few months in order to avoid paying higher taxes for a single year.

[69] See Edward J. McCaffery, *Taxing Women* (Chicago: University of Chicago Press, 1997) at 10-12. For this reason, the US Congress introduced a special "earned income deduction" in 1981, allowing dual-income-earning couples to deduct 10 per cent of the lower-income spouse's income up to $30,000. With the flattening of the US rate scale in the mid-1980s, however, the deduction was repealed in 1987. See Pamela Gann, "The Earned Income Deduction: Congress's 1981 Response to the 'Marriage Penalty Tax'" (1983) 68 Cornell L. Rev. 468.

spouses to work between 4 and 7 per cent less than they would if they could file individual returns.[70] Notwithstanding these concerns, advocates of a spousal or familial unit tend to regard any behavioural responses as either minimal or socially desirable,[71] and in any event outweighed by the view that equal-income couples (or families) should bear equal tax burdens.[72]

While the purpose of this discussion is not to advocate a preferred tax unit for the personal income tax, but to examine the various reasons underlying the choice of one unit or another, it is relevant to note that most developed countries have moved in the direction of individual taxation,[73] and most academic commentators in Canada, the United States, and other jurisdictions favour this choice of tax unit.[74] For its part, moreover, the Supreme Court of Canada has affirmed the entitlement or control principle underlying the choice of the individual unit, rejecting a taxpayer's argument that income received under Quebec's community of property regime should be split equally with his wife for tax purposes on the grounds that the *Income Tax Act* "imposes the income tax on the person and not the property" and that "only the person who has the absolute enjoyment of the income is liable to pay tax without any regard whatsoever to any restraint that there might be on his right to free disposition of the income".[75] Notwithstanding the arguments of the Carter Commission and others advocating a spousal or familial unit, it is unlikely that the individual will be replaced as the basic unit of the personal income tax in Canada at any time in the foreseeable future.

---

[70] Congress of the United States, *For Better or For Worse: Marriage and the Federal Tax* (Washington, DC: Congressional Budget Office, 1997) at 12.

[71] To the extent that a spousal or familial unit produces a tax bonus for single-earner couples, it is not surprising that these units are more likely to be favoured by those more sympathetic to "traditional" families with a stay-at-home parent. Most feminists, on the other hand, are generally opposed to tax units other than the individual. See, for example, Louise Dulude, "Joint Taxation of Spouses — A Feminist View" (1979) 1 Canadian Taxation 8; Kathleen Lahey, "The Tax Unit in Income Tax Theory" in E. Diane Pask, Kathleen E. Mahoney, and Catherine A. Brown, eds., *Women, the Law and the Economy* (Toronto: Butterworths, 1985); and Maureen Maloney, "What Is the Appropriate Tax Unit for the 1990s and Beyond?" in Allan M. Maslove, ed., *Issues in the Taxation of Individuals* (Toronto: University of Toronto Press, 1994), 116.

[72] See, for example, Michael J. McIntyre and Oliver Oldman, "Taxation of the Family in a Comprehensive and Simplified Income Tax" (1977) 90 Harv. L. Rev. 1573.

[73] For a discussion of reforms in the United Kingdom, which adopted individual-unit taxation in 1990, see Andrew Dilnot, Paul Johnson & Graham Stark, "Savings, Independent Taxation and the 1990 Budget" (1990) 11 Fiscal Studies 27.

[74] See the authorities cited in Neil Brooks, "The Irrelevance of Conjugal Relationships in Assessing Tax Liability" in John G. Head & Richard Krever, eds., *Tax Units and the Tax Rate Scale* (Melbourne: Australian Tax Research Foundation, 1996) at 37-39.

[75] *Sura v. M.N.R.* (1961), 32 D.L.R. (2d) 282, at 284 (S.C.C.), *per* Taschereau J, citing *McLeod v. Minister of Customs and Excise*, [1926] S.C.J. No. 25, [1917-27] C.T.C. 290 at 296 (S.C.C.).

b. Implications of Individual Taxation Under Progressive Rates

Aside from the factors considered thus far, the choice of the individual as the basic unit for the personal income tax has two important implications where tax is levied at progressive rates. First, since these progressive rates apply to the separate incomes of individual taxpayers rather than the combined incomes of spousal or familial units, couples or families with the same total income can face different tax burdens depending on the share of this aggregate amount received by each individual. Second, since the aggregate tax on couples or families in which each member receives a share of the total income is less than the tax on couples or families in which the same aggregate income is received by a single member, the combination of progressive rates and an individual unit creates a strong incentive for taxpayers to split their incomes with an otherwise low-income spouse or child.

Each of these implications is illustrated in Table 5, which compares the aggregate federal income tax (before credits) payable in 2008 by a family in which the total income of the family is received by one member alone, equally by two members (for example, two spouses or common law partners), and equally by four members (for example, two spouses or common law partners and two children). As a result of progressivity, a family in which an aggregate income of $140,000 is received by one member will pay almost $5,800 more in basic federal tax than a family in which this aggregate income is shared between two members of the family, and over $10,300 more in basic federal tax than a family in which this income is divided equally among four family members.

Table 5: Basic Federal Tax (Before Credits) on Families with $140,000 Total Income, 2008

Family type	Taxable income of each family member	Tax on each family member	Aggregate tax on family
Single-earner family			
Spouse 1	$140,000	$26,345 + 29% of income over $123,184 (=$31,221.64)	$31,221.64
Spouse 2 and children	—	—	
Dual-earner family			
Spouse 1	$ 70,000	$5,683 + 22% of income over $37,885 (=$12,748.30)	$25,496.60
Spouse 2	$ 70,000	$5,683 + 22% of income over $37,885 (=$12,748.30)	

Family type	Taxable income of each family member	Tax on each family member	Aggregate tax on family
Children	—	—	
Multiple-earner family			
Spouse 1	$ 35,000	15% of income up to $37,885 (= $5,250.00)	$21,000.00
Spouse 2	$ 35,000	15% of income up to $37,885 (= $5,250.00)	
Child 1	$ 35,000	15% of income up to $37,885 (= $5,250.00)	
Child 2	$ 35,000	15% of income up to $37,885 (= $5,250.00)	

For some commentators, the difference in tax payable by a single- and dual-earner couple is defended on the grounds that the single-earner couple generally derives additional "imputed income" from the otherwise untaxed services provided by a stay-at-home spouse (for example, child care, meal preparation, and house cleaning).[76] This additional burden, however, is not only unrelated to any measure of this imputed income but does not depend on the actual provision of such untaxed services (which might be provided by a nanny or housekeeper paid out of income that has been subject to tax). Nor does this argument explain the differential treatment between dual- and multiple-earner families illustrated in Table 5. Moreover, since the income tax does not generally apply to imputed income, it is arguably unfair to single out this form of imputed income for special treatment.[77]

As a result, where couples or families with the same combined money incomes face different aggregate tax burdens, this result is best understood not as a deliberate policy to achieve equity among spouses or families with similar incomes more broadly defined (that is, including in addition to money incomes the imputed income from domestic services), but as a necessary implication of individual taxation under an income tax levied at progressive rates. Under a progressive income tax with an individual tax unit, in other words, equity

---

[76] See, for example, Peter W. Hogg, Joanne E. Magee & Jinyan Li, *Principles of Canadian Income Tax Law*, 6th ed. (Toronto: Carswell, 2007) at 420, explaining that "[t]he present higher tax on the one-job family could be defended as an indirect recognition of that family's higher imputed income from unpaid household services." See also Robin W. Broadway and Harry M. Kitchen, *Canadian Tax Policy*, 3d ed., Canadian Tax Paper No. 103 (Toronto: Canadian Tax Foundation, 1999) at 171-73.

[77] See the *Report of the Royal Commission on Taxation*, 6 vols. (Ottawa: Queen's Printer, 1966) Vol. 3 at 118. For more general arguments against the inclusion of any form of imputed income in the income tax, see Thomas Chancellor, "Imputed Income and the Ideal Income Tax" (1988) 67 Or. L. Review 561.

demands equal taxation of equal-income *individuals*, not equal taxation of equal-income couples or families.

Notwithstanding this policy choice, however, the Canadian tax system has also sought to maintain the progressivity of the income tax by opposing deliberate efforts to split income with a lower-income spouse or child where the income is not actually earned by the spouse or child. Subsection 56(2), for example, codifies a doctrine of indirect or constructive receipt according to which an amount that would be included in a taxpayer's income if received by the taxpayer is taxable to the taxpayer if it is diverted to another person for the taxpayer's benefit or the benefit of that other person.[78] Specific "attribution rules" go further, deeming income from property that is transferred to a spouse or common-law partner or to a related minor to have been received by the taxpayer from whom the property is transferred and not by the spouse, common-law partner, or related minor to whom the income is actually transferred.[79] For this and other purposes in the Act, subsection 248(1) defines a "common-law partner" at any time as "a person who cohabits at that time in a conjugal relationship with the taxpayer," provided that the period of cohabitation has been "for a continuous period of at least one year"[80] or the taxpayer and the common-law partner are the parents of a child.[81] Related minors include children and other descendants (grandchildren, great-grandchildren, etc.), nieces and nephews, and siblings, provided that they are under 18 years of age.[82]

---

[78] This rule, which was originally enacted as subs. 16(1) of the 1948 Act, is briefly considered in Chapter 4. For an analysis of this provision in the context of a Supreme Court of Canada decision involving income splitting through corporate share capital structures authorizing the payment of discretionary dividends on classes of shares typically held by lower-income spouses and children, see David G. Duff, "Neuman and Beyond: Income Splitting, Tax Avoidance, and Statutory Interpretation in the Supreme Court of Canada" (1999) 32 Can. Bus. L.J. 345.

[79] See subs. 74.1(1) and (2) of the Act, which deem any income or loss from property transferred or loaned to a spouse, common-law partner, or minor child or property substituted therefore to be that of the transferor or lender and not that of the recipient. See also para. 248(5)(a), which deems property substituted for substituted property to be substituted property; the attribution rule for capital gains and losses on property transferred or loaned to a spouse or common-law partner in s. 74.2; and s. 75.1, which applies to certain transfers of farm property to a minor child. These rules are examined in Chapter 8.

[80] See para. (a) of the definition of "common-law partner" in subs. 248(1) of the Act. Where the taxpayer ceases to cohabit with a common-law partner, the definition deems the persons to be cohabiting in a conjugal relationship "unless they were not cohabiting at the particular time for a period of at least 90 days ... because of a breakdown of their conjugal relationship."

[81] See para. (a) of the definition of "common-law partner" in subs. 248(1) of the Act. For this purpose, the meaning of the words "child" and "parent" are to be read without reference to specific elements of the extended definitions of these terms in s. 252.

[82] See the attribution rule in subs. 74.1(2) of the Act, which refers to "a person ... under 18 years of age" who does not deal with the taxpayer "at arm's length" or is the niece or nephew of the taxpayer. Non-arm's-length dealings are defined in subs. 251(1), which deems "related persons" not to deal with each other at arm's length. According to para. 251(2)(a), "individuals connected by blood relationship, marriage or common-law partnership or adoption" are "related" for the

Other rules apply where taxpayers attempt to split income with persons with whom they do not "deal at arm's length" by transferring rights to income,[83] making interest-free or low-interest loans,[84] or selling property for more or less than its fair market value.[85] For this and other purposes in the Act, subsection 251(1) stipulates that:

(a) related persons shall be deemed not to deal with each other at arm's length;

(b) a taxpayer and a personal trust (other than a trust described in any of paragraphs (a) to (e.1) of the definition "trust" in subsection 108(1)) are deemed not to deal with each other at arm's length if the taxpayer, or any person not dealing at arm's length with the taxpayer, would be beneficially interested in the trust if subsection 248(25) were read without reference to subclauses 248(25)(b)(iii)(A)(II) to (IV); and

(c) where paragraph (b) does not apply, it is a question of fact whether persons not related to each other are at a particular time dealing with each other at arm's length.

In turn, paragraph 251(2)(a) states that "individuals connected by blood relationship, marriage or common-law partnership or adoption" are "related" for the purposes of the Act, while subsection 251(6) provides that persons are connected by:

(a) blood relationship if one is the child or other descendant of the other or one is the brother or sister of the other;

(b) marriage if one is married to the other or to a person who is connected by blood relationship to the other;

(b.1) common-law partnership if one is in a common-law partnership with the other or with a person who is connected by blood relationship with the other; and

---

purposes of the Act. According to para. 251(6)(a), persons are connected by blood relationship if one is the child or other descendant of the other or one is the brother or sister of the other. The words "child," "brother," and "sister" are further defined in s. 252.

[83] See subs. 56(4), which requires taxpayers who transfer or assign "the right to an amount ... that would, if the right had not been so transferred or assigned, be included in computing the taxpayer's income" to include the amount in computing their income "unless the income is from property and the taxpayer has also transferred or assigned the property." This provision is considered in Chapter 4.

[84] See subs. 56(4.1)-(4.3), which attribute to the creditor income from the loaned property, property that the loan or indebtedness enabled or assisted the recipient to acquire, or property substituted for this property where "it can reasonably be considered that one of the main reasons for making the loan or incurring the indebtedness was to reduce or avoid tax" by causing the income to be received by the debtor (para. 56(4.1)(b)). These provisions are discussed in Chapter 8.

[85] See para. 69(1)(a), which deems taxpayers who have acquired anything from a person with whom they do not deal at arm's length at an amount in excess of its fair market value to have acquired it at that fair market value; and para. 69(1)(b), which deems taxpayers who have disposed of anything to a person with whom they do not deal at arm's length for no proceeds or for proceeds less than fair market value to have disposed of it for proceeds equal to that fair market value. These provisions are examined in Chapter 8.

(c) adoption if one has been adopted, either legally or in fact, as the child of the other or as a child of a person who is so connected by blood relationship (otherwise than as a brother or sister) to the other.

The effect of these provisions, for the purposes of which one should also consult the extended meanings of child, spouse, and other family relationships in section 252, is to limit opportunities for income-splitting among a much larger group of family members than those subject to the attribution rules described earlier.

In addition to these rules, section 120.4 imposes a special "income-splitting tax" on certain types of income received by individuals under the age of 18.[86] This provision, which was introduced in the 1999 federal budget in response to judicial decisions permitting the splitting of income through private corporations and trusts,[87] eliminates any advantages from these income-splitting techniques by taxing passive income from these sources at the top federal rate of 29 per cent rather than the normal graduated rates applicable to other kinds of income.[88] A similar response to income splitting explains a special rule in subsection 122(1) of the Act, according to which *inter vivos* trusts are also taxable at the top federal rate of 29 per cent.

While many of these rules are consistent with the entitlement or control principle underlying the choice of the individual tax unit (since the taxpayer has either initial entitlement to or effective control over the income subject to tax), others, such as the attribution rules for property transferred from one spouse to another, are less easily understood. Since the transferee spouse is legally entitled to the income or capital gain derived from the transferred property, the choice of an individual tax unit suggests that these amounts should be taxed in the hands of the transferee, unless it is assumed that the transferor spouse retains effective control over the amounts received by the transferee.

While prevailing gender relationships may have supported this assumption when the first attribution rule was enacted in 1917,[89] it is less plausible today.

---

[86] See the definitions of "split income" and "specified individual" in subs. 120.4(1) of the Act.

[87] See Canada, Department of Finance, The Budget Plan 1999, February 16, 1999, annex 7, at 193-94 and 238-39. The key cases in this respect are *Neuman v. M.N.R.*, [1998] S.C.J. No. 37, [1998] 3 C.T.C. 117, 98 D.T.C. 6297 (S.C.C.); and *R. v. Ferrel*, [1999] F.C.J. No. 102, [1999] 2 C.T.C. 101, 99 D.T.C. 5111 (F.C.A.). The *Neuman* case and the proposed amendments are discussed in David G. Duff, "Neuman and Beyond: Income Splitting, Tax Avoidance, and Statutory Interpretation in the Supreme Court of Canada" (1999) 32 Can. Bus. L.J. 345. See also Maureen Donnelly, Joanne Magee, and Allister Young, "Income Splitting and the New Kiddie Tax: Major Changes for Minor Children" (2000) Vol. 48 No. 4 Can. Tax J. 979.

[88] See subs. 120.4(2) of the Act.

[89] See subs. 4(4) of the *Income War Tax Act*, according to which:

[a] person who, after the first day of August 1917, has reduced his income by the transfer or assignment of any real or personal, movable or immovable property, to such person's wife or husband, as the case may be, or to any member of the family of such person, shall, nevertheless, be liable to be taxed as if such transfer or assignment had not been made, unless the Minister is satisfied that such transfer or assignment was not made for the purpose of evading the taxes imposed under this Act or any part thereof.

Indeed, to the extent that men earn higher incomes and accumulate more wealth than women, repeal of the spousal attribution rules might be welcomed for the additional reason that it would encourage transfers of property from high-income spouses (who tend to be men) to lower-income spouses (who tend to be women).[90] Although this reform would benefit only middle- and high-income families with property that could be transferred from one spouse to another, it would, as Professor Brooks explains, promote "a more equitable distribution of wealth" between spouses and recognize "the autonomy of women for tax purposes".[91] Other reforms might permit a limited form of income splitting among less affluent couples by allowing income-earning spouses to deduct payments to caregiving spouses under the child-care expense deduction in section 63 of the Act.[92]

c. Recognition of Family Relationships

As provisions like the attribution rules illustrate, the *Income Tax Act* takes family relationships into account for a variety of specific purposes, notwithstanding that it uses the individual as the basic unit of personal income taxation. In addition to the attribution rules and rules dealing with non-arm's-length transactions, the Act contains several provisions in which family relationships are taken into account in determining the amount of tax payable by individuals.

Among these provisions, the most obvious are the personal credits in subsection 118(1), which exempt a basic amount of income from tax by providing a credit against federal income tax otherwise payable. While the basic personal amount is set at $9,600 for 2008,[93] this exemption is increased by up to $9,600 for taxpayers supporting a cohabiting spouse or common-law partner or related dependant who earns no more than $759.[94] Additional credits are available for each disabled dependant over age 17,[95] and for taxpayers who share

---

[90] For a similar argument to this effect, see Peter W. Hogg, Joanne E. Magee & Jinyan Li, *Principles of Canadian Income Tax Law*, 6th ed. (Toronto: Carswell, 2007) at 423.

[91] Neil Brooks, "The Irrelevance of Conjugal Relationships in Assessing Tax Liability" in John G. Head & Richard Krever, eds., *Tax Units and the Tax Rate Scale* (Melbourne: Australian Tax Research Foundation, 1996) at 74.

[92] As currently drafted, this deduction must be claimed by the lower-income spouse and is available only for child care provided by someone other than a parent or minor child. For a proposal to this effect, see David G. Duff, "Tax Policy and the Family: A North American Perspective" in *Proceedings of the Fifteenth Annual Conference of the Foundation for Fiscal Studies* (Dublin: Foundation for Fiscal Studies, 2000) at 73-74.

[93] See para. 118(1)B(c) of the Act, as indexed by s. 117.1.

[94] See paras. 118(1)B(a) and (b) of the Act, as indexed by s. 117.1.

[95] See para. 118(1)B(d) of the Act. For this purpose, subs. 118(6) defines a dependant as "a person who at any time in the year is dependent on the individual for support and is (a) the child or grandchild of the individual or of the individual's spouse or common-law partner; or (b) the

accommodation with aged or disabled relatives over age 17.[96] Before 1993, the Act also allowed a credit for each dependent child.[97]

Most recently, as announced as part of its *Tax Fairness Plan* in October 2006, the Conservative government provided additional recognition for family relationships through its introduction of pension income splitting for Canadian residents.[98] Effective beginning in the 2007 taxation year, the *Income Tax Act* enables an individual to allocate up to one-half of his or her eligible pension income to his or her spouse or common-law partner. The transferee must include the allocated amount in her income, and the transferor deducts the allocated amount from his income. The result is that seniors are able to split at least some of their pension income. The provision does not require that any of the pension income actually be transferred to the lower-income spouse.

Other provisions recognizing the interdependence of family relationships include the medical expense credit in section 118.2, which allows taxpayers to claim medical expenses in respect of services provided to the taxpayer, the taxpayer's spouse, or a dependant;[99] the disability credit in section 118.3, which may be claimed by an individual in respect of whom the disabled person is a dependant;[100] rules allowing taxpayers to transfer certain unused tax credits to a spouse, or common-law partner, parent, or grandparent;[101] "rollover rules" deferring otherwise applicable taxes on transfers of property between spouses or common-law partners and on transfers of farm property from a parent to a child;[102] and refundable tax credits (transfer payments delivered through the *Income Tax Act*), the amount of which depends on the aggregate income of the taxpayer and his or her cohabiting spouse or common-law partner.[103]

---

parent, grandparent, brother, sister, uncle, aunt, niece or nephew, if resident in Canada at any time in the year, of the individual or the individual's spouse or common-law partner."

[96] See para. 118(1)B(c.1) of the Act.

[97] See former subpara. 118(1)B(d)(i). This credit was repealed with the introduction in 1993 of the refundable child tax benefit in ss. 122.6 to 122.64 of the Act.

[98] See s. 60.03 of the Act.

[99] See the definition of allowable medical expenses in subs. 118.2(2) of the Act. For the purpose of this provision, a dependant is given the same meaning as in subs. 118(6). Similarly, as an administrative practice, the Canada Revenue Agency allows a taxpayer to claim a credit for charitable contributions made by the taxpayer, the taxpayer's spouse, or a dependant, notwithstanding the statutory requirement in subs. 118.1(1) that the credit must be claimed by the individual who makes the gift.

[100] See subs. 118.3(2) of the Act.

[101] See s. 118.8 of the Act (transfer of unused age, pension, disability, tuition, and education tax credits to a spouse), and s. 118.9 (transfer of tuition and education credits to a parent or grandparent).

[102] See subs. 73(1) and 70(6) of the Act *(inter vivos* and testamentary transfers to spouses or spousal trusts), and subs. 73(3) and (4) and 70(9) to (9.2) *(inter vivos* and testamentary transfers of farm property to children). These provisions are discussed in Chapter 6.

[103] See s. 122.5 of the Act (GST credit), ss. 122.6 to 122.64 (Canada child tax benefit), and s. 122.51 (refundable medical expense supplement).

While an assessment of the rollover rules is best left to the detailed examination of these provisions in Chapter 6 of this book, it is useful to consider the arguments for and against the other rules in the light of related arguments over the choice of the tax unit. Although the control principle underlying the choice of the individual tax unit might suggest the irrelevance of any family relationships to the computation of an individual's tax liability, the existence of legal and ethical support obligations arguably reduces the individual's effective control over the income to which he or she is legally entitled. On this basis, exemptions for the basic costs of supporting economically dependent spouses, children, and other relatives, and additional relief for extraordinary costs related to medical care or disability, might be justified on the grounds that these costs reduce the taxpayer's ability to pay. Indeed, this argument is frequently invoked to advocate restoration of the basic exemption for dependent children, which was repealed in 1993.[104] On the other hand, where these support obligations are viewed as personal choices (for example, to support a stay-at-home spouse, to have children, or to care for an aged or disabled relative), it is arguable that their associated costs should be regarded as discretionary expenses resulting from the taxpayer's effective control over the income from which these expenses are made.[105]

As for transfer payments such as the child tax benefit delivered through the *Income Tax Act* in the form of refundable credits, the aggregation of spousal incomes indicates the choice of a spousal tax unit in contrast to the individual tax unit used elsewhere in the Act. For some observers, this dual approach is difficult to justify and points toward replacement of the individual unit with a spousal or family unit. According to Hogg, Magee, and Li, for example:

> [It] is not easy to see why we should pool the shared consumption of poor families because that will reduce their entitlement to income support, but we should not pool the shared consumption of more affluent families because that would increase their liability to pay tax.
>
> Moreover, it is arguable that income support and income tax should as a matter of policy be treated as two sides of the same coin. The refundable credits provide a limited model for a negative income tax, under which any taxfiler reporting income below a stipulated "poverty line" would receive a payment from the government. ... If a negative income tax were implemented, the poverty line would probably be defined by reference to family income rather than individual income. But if family income becomes the basis for entitlement to tax

---

[104] See, for example, Kenneth J. Boessenkool & James B. Davies, "Giving Mom and Dad a Break: Returning Fairness to Families in Canada's Tax and Transfer System" Commentary 117 (Toronto: C.D. Howe Institute, November 1998).

[105] See, for example, Neil Brooks, "The Irrelevance of Conjugal Relationships in Assessing Tax Liability" in John G. Head & Richard Krever, eds., *Tax Units and the Tax Rate Scale* (Melbourne: Australian Tax Research Foundation, 1996) at 73, who argues that "as a matter of tax justice, there is no reason why someone who voluntarily undertakes to support a spouse at home should be considered to have a reduced ability to pay." For a similar argument with respect to children, see Henry C. Simons, *Personal Income Taxation, the Definition of Income as a Problem of Fiscal Policy* (Chicago: University of Chicago Press, 1938) at 140.

"refunds" to the poor, it is going to be very difficult to explain why it should not also be the basis for tax liability for everyone else.[106]

Since the basic purposes of a negative income tax (to ameliorate poverty and improve human welfare) differ from those of the positive income tax (to moderate inequalities in the pre-tax distribution of income and raise revenues in an equitable manner), however, it is arguable that the appropriate units for these different policy goals might differ. As Professor Brooks explains:

> there is no normative inconsistency in basing the tax system on individuals but transfer payments, whether delivered through the tax system or not, on the aggregation of family income. Transfer payments in order to relieve poverty should quite sensibly be based upon some function of consumption instead of control of income. Thus, although a control-based tax system should keep spousal income separate, a consumption-based anti-poverty program should combine spousal income.[107]

2. Residence in Canada

Although the Canadian income tax applies to non-residents under specified circumstances,[108] the main jurisdictional basis on which Canadian income tax is imposed is Canadian residence. As a general rule, Canadian residents are subject to tax on their worldwide income, though the *Income Tax Act* permits a non-refundable credit for income taxes paid to foreign governments and income from some foreign sources is exempt from Canadian income tax under bilateral tax treaties.[109] The choice of Canadian residence as a criterion for Canadian income taxation reflects a policy conclusion shared by many countries that residence in

---

[106] Peter W. Hogg, Joanne E. Magee & Jinyan Li, *Principles of Canadian Income Tax Law*, 6th ed. (Toronto: Carswell, 2007) at 422.

[107] Neil Brooks, "The Irrelevance of Conjugal Relationships in Assessing Tax Liability" in John G. Head & Richard Krever, eds., *Tax Units and the Tax Rate Scale* (Melbourne: Australian Tax Research Foundation, 1996) at 78.

[108] Although the Act also applies to non-resident persons in certain circumstances, there is no need for us to examine these provisions in detail. See subs. 2(3), which levies a tax on non-residents who were "employed in Canada, ... carried on business in Canada, or ... disposed of a taxable Canadian property, at any time in the year or a previous year," based on the non-resident's "taxable income earned in Canada" during the year (as defined by the rules in Division D of Part I of the Act, comprising ss. 115, 115.1, 115.2, and 116). See also Part XIII of the Act, which imposes "withholding taxes" on interest, dividends, rental payments, and royalties paid by Canadian residents to non-residents. These provisions are best examined in a course on international taxation.

[109] See s. 126 of the Act (foreign tax credit) and any of the many bilateral tax treaties that the government of Canada has signed. Where a taxpayer is resident in Canada throughout part of a taxation year and non-resident throughout another part of the year, s. 114 provides relief from tax on worldwide income during the period of non-residence, including in the taxpayer's income for this period only the taxpayer's "taxable income earned in Canada" as defined in s. 115. These provisions and Canada's bilateral tax treaties are best examined in a course on international taxation.

a jurisdiction provides both a practicable and normati███ ████
the imposition and collection of a tax on income.[110]

Like the word "person," which is subject only to ████
subsection 248(1) of the Act, the concept of Canadian ██
the *Income Tax Act*, except for specific rules in sect██
meaning of residence otherwise defined or deem tax██
Canada under certain circumstances. As an initial mat██ ████
courts have held that the concept of residence "shou██
ascribed ... by common usage".[111]

For individuals, the Supreme Court of Canada (in ██
example) has referred to dictionary definitions of the
"[t]o dwell permanently or for a considerable time, to ha██
abode, to live, in or at a particular place",[112] to con██
"chiefly a matter of the degree to which a person in min██
maintains or centralizes his ordinary mode of living with
relations, interests and conveniences at or in the place in ██
to Rand J (at para. 4):

> [t]he gradation of degrees of time, object, intention, continu██
> circumstances shows, I think, that in common parlance "residing" i██
> elements, all of which must be satisfied in each instance. It is quite██
> precise and inclusive definition. It is highly flexible, and its many
> not only in the contexts of different matters, but also in different as██
> In one case it is satisfied by certain elements, in another by others, so██

---

[110] For useful discussions of the different jurisdictional bases on w██
applied, see Douglas J. Sherbaniuk, Henry E. Hutcheon & Pearley R██
Tax — Residence, Domicile or Citizenship?" in *Report of Proceedi██*
Conference, 1963 Conference Report (Toronto: Canadian Tax Foun██
C. Bale, "The Basis of Taxation," in Brian Hansen, Vern Krishn██
Canadian Taxation (Toronto: DeBoo, 1981), 21 at 24-30; and Peter ██
& Jinyan Li, *Principles of Canadian Income Tax Law*, 6th ed. (Toro██
66. While citizenship establishes a "bright-line" test for taxation,
overbroad and under inclusive — including non-resident citizens ██
taxing jurisdiction may be minimal or non-existent and excludin██
residents. Domicile, on the other hand, which turns on residence wi██
permanently, is arguably too subjective a test, which may exclude██
facilitate the avoidance of tax. As a general rule, countries tax resi██
incomes and non-residents on all income having its source in the coun██
income taxes paid to other countries. For a useful discussion of t██
principles of taxation, see Donald J.S. Brean, "Here or There? The██
Principles of International Taxation" in Richard M. Bird & Jack M.
2000 and Beyond, Canadian Tax Paper No. 93 (Toronto: Canadian Tax

[111] *Thomson v. M.N.R.*, [1946] S.C.J. No. 5, [1946] C.T.C. 51, 2 D.T.C. 81 ██
See also *Beament v. M.N.R.*, [1952] S.C.J. No. 38, [1952] C.T.C. 327,
and Rand J's opinion in *Thomson*, which refers to "common parlance".

[112] *Shorter Oxford English Dictionary*, cited in *Thomson, ibid.*

[113] *Thomson, ibid., per* Rand J.

"refunds" to the poor, it is going to be very difficult to explain why it should not also be the basis for tax liability for everyone else.[106]

Since the basic purposes of a negative income tax (to ameliorate poverty and improve human welfare) differ from those of the positive income tax (to moderate inequalities in the pre-tax distribution of income and raise revenues in an equitable manner), however, it is arguable that the appropriate units for these different policy goals might differ. As Professor Brooks explains:

> there is no normative inconsistency in basing the tax system on individuals but transfer payments, whether delivered through the tax system or not, on the aggregation of family income. Transfer payments in order to relieve poverty should quite sensibly be based upon some function of consumption instead of control of income. Thus, although a control-based tax system should keep spousal income separate, a consumption-based anti-poverty program should combine spousal income.[107]

2. Residence in Canada

Although the Canadian income tax applies to non-residents under specified circumstances,[108] the main jurisdictional basis on which Canadian income tax is imposed is Canadian residence. As a general rule, Canadian residents are subject to tax on their worldwide income, though the *Income Tax Act* permits a non-refundable credit for income taxes paid to foreign governments and income from some foreign sources is exempt from Canadian income tax under bilateral tax treaties.[109] The choice of Canadian residence as a criterion for Canadian income taxation reflects a policy conclusion shared by many countries that residence in

---

[106] Peter W. Hogg, Joanne E. Magee & Jinyan Li, *Principles of Canadian Income Tax Law*, 6th ed. (Toronto: Carswell, 2007) at 422.

[107] Neil Brooks, "The Irrelevance of Conjugal Relationships in Assessing Tax Liability" in John G. Head & Richard Krever, eds., *Tax Units and the Tax Rate Scale* (Melbourne: Australian Tax Research Foundation, 1996) at 78.

[108] Although the Act also applies to non-resident persons in certain circumstances, there is no need for us to examine these provisions in detail. See subs. 2(3), which levies a tax on non-residents who were "employed in Canada, ... carried on business in Canada, or ... disposed of a taxable Canadian property, at any time in the year or a previous year," based on the non-resident's "taxable income earned in Canada" during the year (as defined by the rules in Division D of Part I of the Act, comprising ss. 115, 115.1, 115.2, and 116). See also Part XIII of the Act, which imposes "withholding taxes" on interest, dividends, rental payments, and royalties paid by Canadian residents to non-residents. These provisions are best examined in a course on international taxation.

[109] See s. 126 of the Act (foreign tax credit) and any of the many bilateral tax treaties that the government of Canada has signed. Where a taxpayer is resident in Canada throughout part of a taxation year and non-resident throughout another part of the year, s. 114 provides relief from tax on worldwide income during the period of non-residence, including in the taxpayer's income for this period only the taxpayer's "taxable income earned in Canada" as defined in s. 115. These provisions and Canada's bilateral tax treaties are best examined in a course on international taxation.

a jurisdiction provides both a practicable and normatively justifiable basis for the imposition and collection of a tax on income.[110]

Like the word "person," which is subject only to an extended definition in subsection 248(1) of the Act, the concept of Canadian residence is undefined in the *Income Tax Act*, except for specific rules in section 250 that extend the meaning of residence otherwise defined or deem taxpayers to be resident in Canada under certain circumstances. As an initial matter, therefore, Canadian courts have held that the concept of residence "should receive the meaning ascribed ... by common usage".[111]

For individuals, the Supreme Court of Canada (in *Thomson v. M.N.R.*, for example) has referred to dictionary definitions of the word "reside" as being "[t]o dwell permanently or for a considerable time, to have one's settled or usual abode, to live, in or at a particular place",[112] to conclude that residence is "chiefly a matter of the degree to which a person in mind and fact settles into or maintains or centralizes his ordinary mode of living with its accessories in social relations, interests and conveniences at or in the place in question".[113] According to Rand J (at para. 4):

> [t]he gradation of degrees of time, object, intention, continuity and other relevant circumstances shows, I think, that in common parlance "residing" is not a term of invariable elements, all of which must be satisfied in each instance. It is quite impossible to give it a precise and inclusive definition. It is highly flexible, and its many shades of meaning vary not only in the contexts of different matters, but also in different aspects of the same matter. In one case it is satisfied by certain elements, in another by others, some common, some new.

---

[110] For useful discussions of the different jurisdictional bases on which income tax might be applied, see Douglas J. Sherbaniuk, Henry E. Hutcheon & Pearley R. Brissenden, "Liability for Tax — Residence, Domicile or Citizenship?" in *Report of Proceedings of the Seventeenth Tax Conference*, 1963 Conference Report (Toronto: Canadian Tax Foundation, 1964), 315; Gordon C. Bale, "The Basis of Taxation," in Brian Hansen, Vern Krishna & James Rendall, eds., *Canadian Taxation* (Toronto: DeBoo, 1981), 21 at 24-30; and Peter W. Hogg, Joanne E. Magee & Jinyan Li, *Principles of Canadian Income Tax Law*, 6th ed. (Toronto: Carswell, 2007) at 65-66. While citizenship establishes a "bright-line" test for taxation, it is generally viewed as overbroad and under inclusive — including non-resident citizens whose connection with the taxing jurisdiction may be minimal or non-existent and excluding non-citizen permanent residents. Domicile, on the other hand, which turns on residence with an intention to remain permanently, is arguably too subjective a test, which may exclude long-time residents and facilitate the avoidance of tax. As a general rule, countries tax residents on their worldwide incomes and non-residents on all income having its source in the country, providing a credit for income taxes paid to other countries. For a useful discussion of the residence and source principles of taxation, see Donald J.S. Brean, "Here or There? The Source and Residence Principles of International Taxation" in Richard M. Bird & Jack M. Mintz, eds., *Taxation to 2000 and Beyond*, Canadian Tax Paper No. 93 (Toronto: Canadian Tax Foundation, 1992).

[111] *Thomson v. M.N.R.*, [1946] S.C.J. No. 5, [1946] C.T.C. 51, 2 D.T.C. 812 (S.C.C.), *per* Kerwin J. See also *Beament v. M.N.R.*, [1952] S.C.J. No. 38, [1952] C.T.C. 327, 52 D.T.C. 1183 (S.C.C.) and Rand J's opinion in *Thomson*, which refers to "common parlance".

[112] *Shorter Oxford English Dictionary*, cited in *Thomson*, *ibid.*

[113] *Thomson*, *ibid.*, *per* Rand J.

On this basis, where the residence of an individual is at issue, Canadian courts and revenue authorities are required to engage in a detailed inquiry into the taxpayer's ordinary mode of living in order to determine whether the taxpayer is resident in Canada. Although the nature of this factual determination makes it difficult to formulate general principles, cases have established at least some guidelines that courts, commentators, and the Canadian revenue authorities have identified.[114] According to these sources:

1. For the purposes of income tax legislation, it must be assumed that every person has at all times a residence.[115]

2. A person may be resident in more than one country at the same time.[116]

3. Residence is primarily a question of fact.[117]

4. While a taxpayer's intentions to reside in a particular jurisdiction may be relevant to the determination of residence,[118] these intentions are not determinative,[119] but "must always be viewed objectively against all the surrounding facts".[120] In this respect, the concept of "residence" must be distinguished from that of "domicile," which turns largely on the individual's intentions.[121]

---

[114] For useful reviews of these guidelines, see Brian G. Hansen, "Individual Residence," in *Report of Proceedings of the Twenty-Ninth Tax Conference*, 1977 Conference Report (Toronto: Canadian Tax Foundation, 1978), 682; Gordon C. Bale, "The Basis of Taxation," in Brian Hansen, Vern Krishna & James Rendall, eds., *Canadian Taxation* (Toronto: DeBoo, 1981) at 30-42; and Edwin C. Kroft, "Jurisdiction To Tax: An Update" in *Tax Planning for Canada-US and International Transactions*, 1983 Corporate Management Tax Conference (Toronto: Canadian Tax Foundation, 1994) at 1:6-20. See also *Lee v. M.N.R.*, [1990] 1 C.T.C. 2082 (T.C.C.); (1989) 90 D.T.C. 1014 (T.C.C.); and *Interpretation Bulletin* IT-221R3, "Determination of an Individual's Residence Status" December 21, 2001.

[115] *Thomson v. M.N.R.*, [1946] S.C.J. No. 5, [1946] C.T.C. 51, 2 D.T.C. 812 (S.C.C.), *per* Kerwin J. See also *Beament v. M.N.R.*, [1952] S.C.J. No. 38, [1952] C.T.C. 327, 52 D.T.C. 1183 (S.C.C.) and Rand J's opinion in *Thomson*, which refers to "common parlance".

[116] *Ibid.* This statement is now subject to the provisions of bilateral tax treaties, which generally deem individuals to be a resident of one of the contracting states. See, for example, art. IV(2) of the Canada-US tax convention.

[117] *Thomson v. M.N.R.*, [1946] S.C.J. No. 5, [1946] C.T.C. 51, 2 D.T.C. 812 (S.C.C.), *per* Kerwin J. See also *Beament v. M.N.R.*, [1952] S.C.J. No. 38, [1952] C.T.C. 327, 52 D.T.C. 1183 (S.C.C.) and Rand J's opinion in *Thomson*, which refers to "common parlance". See also *R. v. Reeder*, [1975] C.T.C. 256, 75 D.T.C. 5160 (F.C.T.D.). For a critical analysis of this characterization, describing the question as one of mixed fact and law, see Gordon C. Bale, "The Basis of Taxation," in Brian Hansen, Vern Krishna & James Rendall, eds., *Canadian Taxation* (Toronto: DeBoo, 1981) at 31-32.

[118] *Thomson v. M.N.R.*, [1946] S.C.J. No. 5, [1946] C.T.C. 51, 2 D.T.C. 812 (S.C.C.), *per* Kerwin J. See also *Beament v. M.N.R.*, [1952] S.C.J. No. 38, [1952] C.T.C. 327, 52 D.T.C. 1183 (S.C.C.) and Rand J's opinion in *Thomson*, which refers to "common parlance".

[119] *Beament v. M.N.R.*, [1952] S.C.J. No. 38, [1952] C.T.C. 327, 52 D.T.C. 1183 (S.C.C.).

[120] *Erikson v. Canada*, [1975] C.T.C. 624, 75 D.T.C. 5429 (F.C.T.D.).

[121] *Lee v. M.N.R.*, [1990] 1 C.T.C. 2082, (1989) 90 D.T.C. 1014 (T.C.C.).

5.   Residence generally involves either the taxpayer's physical presence in the jurisdiction or the ownership of or right to occupy a building in the jurisdiction.[122] Where a taxpayer is not physically present in the jurisdiction, residence may turn on social or economic ties including the residence of family members,[123] memberships in religious organizations, clubs, unions or professional organizations,[124] ownership of property,[125] and bank accounts.[126] According to the Canada Revenue Agency (CRA, formerly the Canada Customs and Revenue Agency and prior to that Revenue Canada), the "most significant residential ties" of an individual are "the individual's (a) dwelling place (or places), (b) spouse or common-law partner, and (c) dependants".[127] In addition, the CRA explains (in IT-221R3, paragraph 8), the following "secondary residential ties" may also be taken into account "in determining the residence status of an individual while outside Canada":

(a)   personal property in Canada (such as furniture, clothing, automobiles and recreational vehicles),

(b)   social ties with Canada (such as memberships in Canadian recreational and religious organizations),

---

[122]   *Beament, ibid.* See also Gordon C. Bale, "The Basis of Taxation," in Brian Hansen, Vern Krishna & James Rendall, eds., *Canadian Taxation* (Toronto: DeBoo, 1981) at 38-39. As explained below, subs. 250(3) expands on this meaning by extending the statutory meaning of residence to include persons "ordinarily resident in Canada."

[123]   See, for example, *Russell v. M.N.R.*, [1949] C.T.C. 13, 49 D.T.C. 536 (Ex. Ct.), where the taxpayer's wife and children resided in Canada while he worked overseas for three years. For a contrary result, see *Schujahn v. M.N.R.*, [1962] C.T.C. 364, 62 D.T.C. 1225 (Ex. Ct.), in which the taxpayer, a US citizen who lived in Toronto from 1954 until August 2, 1957, when he was recalled to his employer's head office in the United States, was held to have given up Canadian residence on August 2, 1957, even though his family remained in Canada until the family home was sold in February 1958. As a general rule, this consideration does not apply where the taxpayer is separated or divorced. See, for example, *Erikson v. Canada*, [1975] C.T.C. 624, 75 D.T.C. 5429 (F.C.T.D.); *Griffiths v. Canada*, [1978] C.T.C. 372, 78 D.T.C. 6268 (F.C.T.D.); and *York v. M.N.R.*, [1980] C.T.C. 2845, 80 D.T.C. 1749 (T.R.B.).

[124]   *Lee v. M.N.R.*, [1990] 1 C.T.C. 2082, 90 D.T.C. 1014 (T.C.C.). See also Brian G. Hansen, "Individual Residence," in *Report of Proceedings of the Twenty-Ninth Tax Conference*, 1977 Conference Report (Toronto: Canadian Tax Foundation, 1978), 694.

[125]   See, for example, *Thomson v. M.N.R.*, [1946] S.C.J. No. 5, [1946] C.T.C. 51, 2 D.T.C. 812 (S.C.C.), where the taxpayer, a Canadian citizen and former resident, acquired a home in New Brunswick where he spent most summers. Where a taxpayer who has not previously resided in Canada acquires property in Canada, this alone does not establish Canadian residence. See, for example, *Meldrum v. M.N.R.* (1950), 2 Tax ABC 63, 50 D.T.C 232.

[126]   See, for example, *Glow v. M.N.R.*, [1992] F.C.J. No. 726, [1992] 2 C.T.C. 245, 92 D.T.C. 6467 (F.C.T.D.), in which the taxpayer, who worked in Nigeria in 1976 and 1977, was determined to have retained his Canadian residence on the basis, *inter alia*, that he maintained a Canadian bank account and his Canadian registered retirement savings plans.

[127]   1T-221R3, para. 5.

(c)   economic ties with Canada (such as employment with a Canadian employer and active involvement in a Canadian business, and Canadian bank accounts, retirement savings plans, credit cards, and securities accounts),

(d)   landed immigrant status or appropriate work permits in Canada,

(e)   hospitalization and medical insurance coverage from a province or territory of Canada,

(f)   a driver's license from a province or territory of Canada,

(g)   a vehicle registered in a province or territory of Canada,

(h)   a seasonal dwelling place in Canada or a leased dwelling place...,

(i)   a Canadian passport, and

(j)   memberships in Canadian unions or professional organizations.

Although "of limited importance except when taken together with other residential ties", the CRA also mentions "the retention of a Canadian mailing address, post office box, or safety deposit box, personal stationery (including business cards) showing a Canadian address, telephone listings in Canada, and local (Canadian) newspaper and magazine subscriptions" (IT-221R3, paragraph 9).

6.   Where a taxpayer has resided in Canada for a lengthy period of time, clear and "virtually irreversible" measures are required to terminate this residency.[128] In these circumstances, evidence of social and economic connections may play an important role. Where a taxpayer claims to be a resident in another jurisdiction, but does not pay income tax or file tax returns in this jurisdiction, this may also suggest that the taxpayer has retained Canadian residence.[129]

For corporations, Canadian courts have generally referred to the House of Lords decision in *De Beers Consolidated Mines Limited v. Howe*, [1906] A.C. 455 at 458, in which Lord Loreburn LC held that:

a company resides for the purposes of income tax where its real business is carried on. ... I regard that as the true rule, and the real business is carried on where central management and control actually abides.

Although English courts have employed a *de facto* control test to determine corporate residence, looking beyond *de jure* control by the board of directors

---

[128]   *Erickson v. M.N.R.*, [1980] C.T.C. 2117, 80 D.T.C. 1118 (T.R.B.). See also *Thomson v. M.N.R.*, [1946] S.C.J. No. 5, [1946] C.T.C. 51, 2 D.T.C. 812 (S.C.C.); Brian G. Hansen, "Individual Residence," in *Report of Proceedings of the Twenty-Ninth Tax Conference* 1977 Conference Report (Toronto: Canadian Tax Foundation, 1978) at 695; Gordon C. Bale, "The Basis of Taxation," in Brian Hansen, Vern Krishna & James Rendall, eds., *Canadian Taxation* (Toronto: DeBoo, 1981) at 40-41.1.

[129]   See, for example, *Thomson v. M.N.R.*, [1946] S.C.J. No. 5, [1946] C.T.C. 51, 2 D.T.C. 812 (S.C.C.). See also *Morton v. M.N.R.*, [1976] C.T.C. 2463, 76 D.T.C. 1275 (T.R.B.).

where effective control is exercised by a corporation's majority shareholder,[130] Canadian courts have generally held that "central management and control" abides in the jurisdiction in which a majority of the board of directors resides and meets.[131] Likewise, in *Dill v. Canada*, [1978] C.T.C. 539, 78 D.T.C. 6376 (F.C.T.D.), Gibson J held that a trust resides in the jurisdiction in which a majority of the trustees reside.[132]

In addition to these judicial principles, the Act also contains specific rules extending the ordinary meaning of residence and deeming individuals and corporations to be resident in Canada under specific circumstances. According to subsection 250(3), "a reference to a person resident in Canada includes a person who was at the relevant time ordinarily resident in Canada". Although early cases regarded this language as "superfluous" on the grounds that the ordinary meaning of residence implies a degree of permanence or continuity,[133] more recent decisions have relied on this provision to conclude that taxpayers who neither lived in Canada nor maintained a Canadian dwelling during one or more years were nonetheless "ordinarily resident" in Canada over a longer period of time.[134] As Taschereau J (dissenting) suggested in *Thomson v. M.N.R.* (at para. 34):

> [t]he context ... indicates that the words "ordinarily resident" are broader than the word "residing," and that the former were used to cover a field that the latter did not occupy. The aim of Parliament was to tax, not only the residents of Canada, those who have here their permanent home, their settled abode, but also, those who live here most of the time, even if they are absent on temporary occasions. The first group comes under the classification of "residents," and the second under that of "ordinarily residents."

According to paragraph 250(1)(a), a person is deemed to have been resident in Canada throughout a taxation year if the person "sojourned in Canada in the

---

[130] *Unit Construction Co. v. Bullock*, [1960] A.C. 351 (H.L.).

[131] See, for example, *Sifneos v. M.N.R.*, [1968] Tax ABC 652, 68 D.T.C. 522 (tax A.B.C.); *Zehnder and Co. v. M.N.R.*, [1970] C.T.C. 85, 70 D.T.C. 6064 (Ex. Ct.); and *Bedford Overseas Freighters v. M.N.R.*, [1970] C.T.C. 69, 70 D.T.C. 6072 (Ex. Ct.). For useful discussions of corporate residence, see Robert Couzin, *Corporate Residence and International Taxation* (Amsterdam: International Bureau of Fiscal Documentation, 2002); O.A. Pyrcz, "The Basis of Canadian Corporate Taxation: Residence" (1973), 21 Can. Tax J. 374; and Gordon C. Bale, "The Basis of Taxation," in Brian Hansen, Vern Krishna & James Rendall, eds., *Canadian Taxation* (Toronto: DeBoo, 1981) at 44-49.

[132] See also *Interpretation Bulletin* IT-447, "Residence of a Trust or Estate," May 30, 1980.

[133] *Thomson v. M.N.R.*, [1946] S.C.J. No. 5, [1946] C.T.C. 51, 2 D.T.C. 812 (S.C.C.), *per* Rand J. See also *Beament v. M.N.R.*, [1952] S.C.J. No. 38, [1952] C.T.C. 327, 52 D.T.C. 1183 (S.C.C.) and Rand J's opinion in *Thomson*, which refers to "common parlance".

[134] See, for example, *Smith v. M.N.R.*, [1973] C.T.C. 2097, 73 D.T.C. 85 (T.R.B.); *R. v. Reeder*, [1975] C.T.C. 256, 75 D.T.C. 5160 (F.C.T.D.); *Eastwood v. M.N.R.*, [1975] C.T.C. 2156, 75 D.T.C. 126 (T.R.B.); *Canada v. Sherwood*, [1978] C.T.C. 713, 78 D.T.C. 6470 (F.C.T.D.); *Rajotte v. M.N.R.*, [1979] C.T.C. 2555, 79 D.T.C. 436 (T.R.B.); *Saunders v. M.N.R.*, [1980] C.T.C. 2436, 80 D.T.C. 1392 (T.R.B.); and *Roy v. M.N.R.*, [1983] C.T.C. 2644, 83 D.T.C. 576 (T.R.B.).

year for a period of, or periods the total of which is, 183 days or more." In *Thomson*, the Supreme Court of Canada referred to dictionary definitions of the word "sojourn" as "to make temporary stay in a place; to remain or reside for a time" to conclude (at para. 55) that this language applies to "presence in Canada where the nature of the stay is either outside the range of residence or what is commonly understood as temporary residence or residence for a temporary purpose". In one of the few cases in which this provision has been considered, two Americans who lived in Michigan but worked in Canada more than 183 days a year were held not to have sojourned in Canada.[135] According to the court:

> [i]n *The Shorter Oxford English Dictionary* the meaning of "sojourn" is given as "to make a temporary stay in a place; to remain or reside for a time." In perusing numerous cases decided by the Canadian and British courts, it is obvious that coming from one country to work for the day at a place of business in another country and thereafter returning to one's permanent residence in the evening is not tantamount to making a temporary stay in the sense of establishing even a temporary residence in the county where the business enterprise is situate.

As a result, while a person who "sojourns" in Canada lacks the permanence to be considered "resident" or "ordinarily resident", the person must have a more settled connection than daily visits to work.

Like paragraph 250(1)(a), paragraphs 250(1)(b) to (g) also deem individuals to be resident in Canada throughout the year, but apply to specific categories of taxpayers who were members of the Canadian Forces, foreign diplomats, foreign aid workers, overseas teachers with the Canadian Forces, children of these persons, or exempt from tax in another country under a tax treaty with that country on account of their relationship with a Canadian resident. Finally, subsection 250(4) deems corporations to have been resident in Canada throughout a taxation year if they were incorporated in Canada after April 26, 1965 or were incorporated in Canada prior to April 27, 1965 and at any time thereafter were resident in Canada or carried on business in Canada. For companies incorporated in Canada after April 26, 1965, this rule effectively displaces the "central management and control" requirement with a test of corporate citizenship based on jurisdiction of incorporation.[136] For companies incorporated before April 26, 1965, central management and control may play a continuing role. For our purposes, however, there is no need to examine this deeming provision in detail.[137]

---

[135] *R. & L. Food Distributors Limited v. M.N.R.*, [1977] C.T.C. 2579, 77 D.T.C. 411 (T.R.B.).

[136] Where a corporation that is incorporated in Canada is granted articles of continuance in another jurisdiction, subs. 250(5.1) deems the corporation to have been incorporated in the other jurisdiction from the time of continuation.

[137] For cases on the requirement that a corporation have "carried on business in Canada," see *Tara Exploration and Development Co. Ltd. v. M.N.R.*, [1970] C.T.C. 557, 70 D.T.C. 6370 (Ex. Ct.); *Cutlers Guild Limited v. Canada*, [1981] F.C.J. No. 215, [1981] C.T.C. 115, 81 D.T.C. 5093 (F.C.T.D.); *Gurd's Products Co. Ltd. and Grantison Holdings Inc. v. Canada* [1981] C.T.C.

B. Tax Base

The tax base for an income tax may be defined as the amount to which the rate or rates of tax is applied to determine the amount of tax payable. More specifically, the tax base includes the rules related to the measurement of income, whether exemptions, deductions, or inclusions. Simply put, inclusions are amounts that are added in computing a taxpayer's income, while deductions are subtracted from these amounts and exemptions are excluded altogether. The definition of the income tax base is one of the key issues in tax policy and the rationale for most of the rules found in Part I of the *Income Tax Act*.[138]

As indicated earlier, subsection 2(1) of the Act defines the tax base for the purposes of the Canadian income tax as the taxpayer's "taxable income" for each taxation year. In turn, subsection 2(2) defines the taxable income of a taxpayer for a taxation year as "the taxpayer's income for the year plus the additions and minus the deductions permitted by Division C". Section 3, moreover, defines a taxpayer's income for a taxation year by means of a verbal formula that adds the amounts specified in paragraphs (a) and (b) and subtracts the amounts specified in paragraphs (c) and (d).[139] The following discussion examines these and other provisions in more detail, providing a general overview of the inclusions, deductions, and exemptions that comprise the computation of a taxpayer's taxable income for the purposes of the Canadian income tax.

195, 81 D.T.C. 5153 (F.C.T.D.), rev'd. [1985] 2 C.T.C. 85, 85 D.T.C. 5314 (F.C.A.); and *G.L.S. Leasco Inc.,. v. M.N.R.*, [1986] T.C.J. No. 403, [1986] 2 C.T.C. 2034, 86 D.T.C. 1484 (T.C.C.). These cases, and the test for corporate residence more generally, are best examined in courses on corporate income taxation or international taxation.

[138] For an excellent debate on the policy choices that enter into the definition of the income tax base, see Boris I. Bittker, "A 'Comprehensive Tax Base' as a Goal of Income Tax Reform" (1966-67) 80 Harv. L. Rev 925; Richard A. Musgrave, "In Defense of an Income Concept" (1967) 81 Harv. L. Rev 44; Jonathan Pechman, "Comprehensive Income Taxation: A Comment" (1967) 81 Harv. L. Rev 63; Charles Galvin, "More on Boris Bittker and the Comprehensive Tax Base: The Practicalities of Tax Reform and the ABA's CSTR" (1968), 81 Harv. L. Rev 1016; and Boris I. Bittker, "Comprehensive Income Taxation: A Response" (1968), 81 Harv. L. Rev 1032. For a more recent discussion, see Victor Thuronyi, "The Concept of Income" (1990) 46 Tax L. Rev. 45.

[139] Because paras (c) and (d) use the words "the amount, if any" by which specified amounts exceed other amounts, a taxpayer's income for a taxation year cannot be negative. Where taxpayers incur losses that exceed their income from other sources, however, these losses may be deducted under s. 111 in computing the taxpayer's "taxable income" in certain other taxation years. According to para. (e), where a positive amount is determined under para. (d), the amount so determined is the taxpayer's income for the year. Where the amount determined under para. (d) is zero, para. (f) deems the taxpayer "to have income for the year in an amount equal to zero." Paragraph (f) ensures that a taxpayer with zero income will be regarded as the lower-income spouse for the purpose of the child care expense deduction.

1. Inclusions

According to section 3 of the Act, the income of a taxpayer for a taxation year is determined first by adding the amounts referred to in paragraph (a) and the amount specified in paragraph (b). As a result, although the Act contains numerous rules specifying amounts that must be included in computing a taxpayer's income for a taxation year,[140] these two paragraphs describe these inclusions at the most general level.

Paragraph 3(a) requires taxpayers to include "the total of all amounts each of which is the taxpayer's income for the year (other than a taxable capital gain from the disposition of a property) from a source inside or outside Canada, including, without restricting the generality of the foregoing, the taxpayer's income for the year from each office, employment, business and property". The rules governing the computation of a taxpayer's income or loss from an office or employment are found in sections 5 to 8, which together constitute subdivision a of Division B of Part I of the Act.[141] Subdivision b of Division B of Part I, comprising sections 9 to 37 of the Act, contains rules governing a taxpayer's income or loss from a business or property.[142] Subdivision d of Division B of Part I (sections 56 to 59.1) specifies various other amounts that must be included in a taxpayer's income.[143]

Paragraph 3(b) requires taxpayers to include the amount by which the total of the taxpayer's "taxable capital gains for the year from dispositions of property other than listed personal property" and the taxpayer's "net gain for the year from dispositions of listed personal property" exceeds the amount by which the taxpayer's "allowable capital losses for the year from dispositions of property other than listed personal property" exceeds the taxpayer's "allowable business investment losses".[144] The rules defining these amounts are found in subdivision c of Division B of Part I, comprising sections 38 to 55 of the Act.[145] For present purposes, the amount determined under paragraph 3(b) may be described as the taxpayer's net taxable capital gain for the year.[146] In general, section 38 of the

---

[140] These rules are examined in Chapters 4 to 7.

[141] See Chapter 4.

[142] See Chapter 5.

[143] See Chapter 7.

[144] For the purposes of this chapter, there is no need to examine these terms in detail. In general, however, gains or losses from the disposition of property that are not taken into account in computing a taxpayer's income or loss from a business are characterized as capital gains or capital losses; the taxable and allowable portion of these gains and losses is generally one-half under s. 38 of the Act; listed personal property is a separate category of property the gains and losses from which are subject to a separate set of rules and offset against each other under s. 41; and business investment losses are a separate category of capital losses resulting from the disposition of shares or debt of a small business corporation. See Chapter 6.

[145] See Chapter 6.

[146] This term is used in Vern Krishna, *The Fundamentals of Canadian Income Tax*, 9th ed. (Toronto: Carswell, 2006) at 442.

Act defines the "taxable" portion of a capital gain and the "allowable" portion of a capital loss as one-half of the gain or loss otherwise determined.[147]

In summary, then, paragraphs 3(a) and (b) require taxpayers to include their income from all sources (including each office, employment, business, and property), as well as net taxable capital gains from the disposition of property. The following discussion provides a general introduction to these concepts, considering the characteristics of "income" according to its ordinary meaning, the source concept of income on which paragraph 3(a) is based, alternative conceptions of income that influenced the Canadian Royal Commission on Taxation (the Carter Commission), and the federal government's response to the Commission's report in 1972.

a. Income

Although paragraph 3(a) requires taxpayers to include their "income for the year (other than a taxable capital gain from the disposition of a property) from a source inside or outside Canada", neither this provision nor any other in the Act defines the word "income". Consequently, as the Supreme Court of Canada emphasized in *Curran v. M.N.R.*, [1959] S.C.J. No. 66, [1959] C.T.C. 416, 59 D.T.C. 1247 (S.C.C.) (at para. 6), the word "must receive its ordinary meaning bearing in mind ... the ordinary concepts and usages of mankind".[148]

According to *The Concise Oxford English Dictionary*, 11th ed., "income" is defined as the "money received, especially on a regular basis, for work or through investments". The word "capital", on the other hand, is defined as "wealth owned by a person or organization or invested, lent, or borrowed, while "consumption" is defined as the "the action or process of consuming". On this basis, therefore, one might distinguish an income tax that applies to the *flow* of a taxpayer's "receipts" *over a specific period of time* (typically a year), from a *capital or wealth tax* that applies to the *stock* of capital or wealth held by a taxpayer *at a particular point in time* and a *consumption or expenditure tax* that applies to a particular *use* of the taxpayer's income or capital *to purchase goods and services*.[149] As well, it would seem, one might distinguish income from

---

[147] This inclusion rate has varied since the Canadian income tax first recognized capital gains and losses in 1972, increasing from one-half during the taxation year 1972 to 1987 to two-thirds in 1988 and 1989 and three-quarters from 1990 to February 28, 2000 when the federal government reduced the inclusion rate to two-thirds. As of October 18, 2000, this fraction was further reduced to one-half.

[148] See also *Wood v. M.N.R.*, [1969] S.C.J. No. 1, [1969] C.T.C. 57, 69 D.T.C. 5073 (S.C.C.): "Income is to be understood in its plain ordinary sense and given its natural meaning."

[149] Although the federal government and several provinces impose corporate capital taxes, and provincial and municipal governments levy real property taxes, Canada does not have a broad-based capital or wealth tax like the "annual net wealth taxes" imposed in several European countries. In contrast, the federal government and all provinces but Alberta levy broad-based consumption or expenditure taxes in the form of value-added or retail sales taxes, and most of these governments impose so-called excise taxes on the consumption of specific goods (for

other receipts such as gifts and inheritances on the basis that the former are *periodical* receipts "appearing or occurring at intervals",[150] while the latter are generally irregular or non-recurring.

Although Canadian courts do not appear to have found it necessary to distinguish between income and consumption for the purpose of applying the income tax, several cases have emphasized the distinction between income and capital. In *Shaw v. M.N.R.*, [1938-39] C.T.C. 346 (S.C.C.), for example, where the taxpayer received monthly payments of $700 under a contract of life insurance for which her late husband had paid cumulative premiums exceeding $37,000, the court held that the monthly payments were on account of capital, not income within the meaning of section 3 of the *Income War Tax Act, 1917*, S.C. 1917, c. 28, which included among other amounts the taxpayer's "annual net profit or gain or gratuity" from various sources, "the income from but not the value of property acquired by gift, bequest, devise or descent", and "the income from but not the proceeds of life insurance policies paid upon the death of the person insured". Rejecting the Minister's argument that the full amount of each payment was income to the taxpayer, Duff CJC concluded (at para. 9) that:

[t]he legislature, it seems to me, is at pains to emphasize the distinction between income and the source of income. The income derived from the capital source is income for the purposes of the Act. The source is not income for the purposes of the Act.

example, alcohol, tobacco, and gasoline). While taxes on consumption or expenditure are typically levied in the form of sales or excise taxes imposed at the point of sale, such taxes might also be based on a taxpayer's consumption over a period of time (for example, a year) by allowing taxpayers to deduct all savings from income otherwise taxable under an income tax. Indeed, to the extent that specific features of the existing income tax reduce or eliminate tax on certain kinds of savings (for example, retirement savings), it is often argued that the existing "income tax" is actually a hybrid income-consumption tax. On the taxation of capital or wealth, see Organisation for Economic Co-operation and Development, *Taxation of Net Wealth, Capital Transfers and Capital Gains of Individuals* (Paris: OECD, 1988); James Cutt, "A Net Wealth Tax for Canada?" (1969) 17 Can. Tax J. 298; Alex C. Michalos, "The Case for a Progressive Annual Net Wealth Tax" (1988) 2:2 *Public Affairs Quarterly* 105; and Robert D. Brown, "A Primer on the Implementation of Wealth Taxes" (1991) 17 Can. Pub. Pol'y 335. On the taxation of consumption in the form of sales and excise taxes, see Satya Poddar and Morley English, "Fifty Years of Commodity Taxation: Key Events and Lessons for the Future" (1995) 43 Can. Tax J. 1096; and Sijbren Cnossen, "VAT and RST: A Comparison" (1987) 35 Can. Tax J. 559. On the theory of a hybrid income-consumption tax, see Henry J. Aaron, Harvey Galper & Joseph A. Pechman, eds., *Uneasy Compromise: Problems of a Hybrid Income-Consumption Tax* (Washington, DC: Brookings Institution, 1988); and Edward McCaffery, "Tax Policy Under a Hybrid Income-Consumption Tax" (1992) 70 Tex. L. Rev. 1145. On the relative merits of income and consumption taxation, see William D. Andrews, "A Consumption-Type or Cash Flow Personal Income Tax" (1974) 87 Harv. L. Rev. 1113; Alan Gunn, "The Case for an Income Tax" (1979) 46 U. Chicago L. Rev. 370; Alvin Warren, "Would a Consumption Tax Be Fairer Than an Income Tax?" (1980) 89 Yale L.J. 1081; and Charles R. O'Kelley, "Rawls, Justice, and the Income Tax" (1981) 6 Ga. L. Rev. 1.

[150] See the definition of periodic in *The Concise Oxford English Dictionary*, 11th ed.

Likewise, in *Wilder v. M.N.R.*, [1951] S.C.J. No. 36, [1951] C.T.C. 304 (S.C.C.), where the taxpayer sold his real estate business for a life annuity providing monthly payments of $1,000, the court accepted the taxpayer's argument that the monthly payments were "repayments of capital", not income within the meaning of section 3 of the *Income War Tax Act*. According to Rinfret CJC: "The whole economy of Section 3 — and for that matter all of the *Income War Tax Act* — is that it taxes income and not capital." Although annuity payments are now subject to tax under paragraph 56(1)(d) of the *Income Tax Act*, the basic principle of these decisions, that the income tax applies to income not capital, is expressed in paragraph 60(a), which allows a deduction for the "*capital element of each annuity payment included by virtue of paragraph 56(1)(d)*" (emphasis added).[151]

As well, a number of cases have distinguished between taxable income and non-taxable prizes or gifts on the basis that the latter receipts are irregular, non-recurring, or unexpected.[152] On the other hand, Canadian courts have also characterized isolated or non-recurring payments as "annual profits or gains" under the *Income War Tax Act* where these amounts were derived from a "source of income" within the meaning of that Act.[153] As Thorson P observed in *Consolidated Textiles Ltd. v. M.N.R.*, [1947] C.T.C. 63, 3 D.T.C. 958 (Ex. Ct.) (at para. 8):

> the word "annual" as applied to profit or gain or gratuity does not mean that the profit or gain or gratuity must necessarily be of a recurring nature from year to year, but rather that it is the profit or gain or gratuity of or in or during the year in respect of which the assessment is

---

[151] Paragraphs 56(1)(d) and 60(a) are considered in Chapter 7.

[152] See, for example, *Rother v. M.N.R.* (1955), 12 Tax ABC 379, 55 D.T.C. 227 (Tax A.B.C.); *Abraham v. M.N.R.* (1960), 24 Tax ABC 133 (Tax A.B.C.); *Federal Farms Limited v. M.N.R.*, [1959] C.T.C. 98, 59 D.T.C. 1050 (Ex. Ct.); and *Phaneuf Estate v. Canada*, [1977] A.C.F. no. 261, [1978] C.T.C. 21, 78 D.T.C. 6001 (F.C.T.D.). See also *Bellingham v. Canada*, [1995] F.C.J. No. 1602, [1996] 1 C.T.C. 187, [1995] 96 D.T.C. 6075 (F.C.A.), which refers (at para. 35) to a more "problematic" category of "windfall gains." The decisions in *Abraham* and *Federal Farms* are reproduced and *Rother* and *Bellingham* are discussed in Chapter 5. *Phaneuf Estate* is discussed in Chapter 4.

[153] See, for example, *Atlantic Sugar Refineries v. M.N.R.*, [1949] S.C.J. No. 38, [1949] C.T.C. 196 (S.C.C.) (holding that isolated profits from transactions in raw sugar futures were income from the taxpayer's regular business activities of buying, refining, and selling raw sugar); *McDonough v. M.N.R.*, [1949] Ex. C.J. No. 14, [1949] C.T.C. 213 (Ex. Ct.) (holding that isolated profits from the acquisition and resale of shares in a mining company in the organization and promotion of which the taxpayer played a central role were income from a mine promotion business carried on by the taxpayer); and *Goldman v. M.N.R.*, [1953] S.C.J. No. 7, [1953] C.T.C. 95, 53 D.T.C. 1096 (S.C.C.) (holding that an unexpected, non-recurring, and gratuitous commission received by the taxpayer for serving as the chair of a committee of shareholders overseeing the reorganization of a company then in receivership was taxable "remuneration" within the meaning of the *Income War Tax Act*). *Goldman* is reproduced in Chapter 4.

made. The word may thus include an item of income that may occur only once: *vide Ryall v. Hoare* [1923] 2 K.B. 447 at p. 455; *Martin v. Lowry* [1926] 1 K.B. 550.[154]

More recent cases including irregular and non-recurring receipts in computing taxpayers' net incomes suggest that the same principles apply to the *Income Tax Act.*[155]

b. Source Concept of Income

According to paragraph 3(a), taxpayers need not include all "income", however defined, but only "income ... (other than a taxable capital gain from the disposition of a property) from a source". Although this provision identifies four specific sources the income from which taxpayers must include (each office, employment, business, and property), the words "without restricting the generality of the foregoing" suggest that these specified sources are not exhaustive. Subdivision d, for example, contains several other sources of income that must be included in computing a taxpayer's income for a taxation year. Beyond these specific provisions, the Supreme Court of Canada has held that the language of paragraph 3(a) also contemplates income from sources that are not specified in the Act.[156]

While courts and commentators have occasionally considered taxable capital gains as an additional source of income,[157] this type of income is best understood as income from the disposition of property that may itself constitute a source of income, rather than income from a source itself. Indeed, the language of paragraph 3(a), which separates the words "income for the year" and "from a source" by the parenthetical words "other than a taxable capital gain from the

---

[154] In *Ryall v. Hoare; Ryall v. Honeywill*, [1923] 2 K.B. 447, the taxpayers argued that isolated commissions received for personally guaranteeing a bank overdraft of a company were not "annual profits or gains" within the meaning of Case VI of Schedule D of the UK *Income Tax Act*. Rowlatt J upheld the assessment on the basis (at 455) that the word "annual" meant "calculated in any one year." In *Martin v. Lowry*, [1926] 1 K.B. 550, profits from an isolated purchase and sale of a vast quantity of linen were characterized as annual profits belonging to the year of assessment and therefore taxable under case VI of schedule D of the UK *Income Tax Act*. See also *Morrison v. M.N.R.*, [1917-27] C.T.C. 343 (Ex. Ct), where Audette J concluded (at para. 22) that the word "annual" in s. 3 of the *Income War Tax Act* "is used to mean all profits during the year."

[155] The cases are far too numerous to cite here. See Chapters 4 to 7.

[156] *Schwartz v. Canada*, [1996] S.C.J. No. 15, [1996] 1 C.T.C. 303, 96 D.T.C. 6103 (S.C.C.). See also *Bellingham v. Canada*, [1995] F.C.J. No. 1602, [1996] 1 C.T.C. 187, [1995] 96 D.T.C. 6075 (F.C.A.).

[157] See, for example, *Schwartz, ibid.*, where the Supreme Court referred to "capital gains" as one of "the five principal sources from which income can be generated: office, employment, business, property and capital gains"; and Vern Krishna, *The Fundamentals of Canadian Income Tax*, 9th ed. (Toronto: Carswell, 2006) at 138, who describes "capital gains" as one of the "named sources" of income.

disposition of property", might be read to suggest (if somewhat awkwardly) that this category of income is not "from a source".

The origin of the source concept of income is rooted in the economic thought of classical political economists like Adam Smith, who defined income in terms of three productive sources: wages of labour, profits or interest of capital, and rent of land.[158] According to Adam Smith:

> [w]hoever derives his revenue from a fund which is his own, must draw it either from his labour, from his stock, or from his land. The revenue derived from labour is called wages. That derived from stock, by the person who manages or employs it, is called profit. That derived from it by the person who does not employ it himself, but lends it to another, is called the interest or the use of money. It is the compensation which the borrower pays to the lender, for the profit which he has an opportunity of making by the use of the money ... . The revenue which proceeds altogether from land, is called rent, and belongs to the landlord. ... All taxes, and all the revenue which is founded upon them ... are ultimately derived from some one or other of those three original sources of revenue, and are paid either immediately or mediately from the wages of labour, the profits of stock, or the rent of land.[159]

In this passage, it is not difficult to discern the four specific sources of income identified in paragraph 3(a) of the Act: office and employment, from which "the wages of labour" are derived; business, from which "the profits of stock" are derived; and property, from which "the interest or use of money" and "the rent of land" are derived.

In the United Kingdom, the source concept of income was adopted in the income tax introduced by Lord Addington in 1803, which classified different sources of income into specific "schedules" with tax levied on income as defined by each schedule.[160] Though modified, these schedules remain the basis of income taxation in Great Britain. As a result, if an item of revenue does not fall within one of these schedules, it is not taxable.

In addition, on the assumption that "income" must be derived from a productive source, English courts traditionally excluded two kinds of receipts from the "annual profits or gains" subject to tax under Case VI of Schedule D:

---

[158] See Adam Smith, *An Inquiry into the Nature and Causes of the Wealth of Nations* (Chicago: University of Chicago Press, 1976).

[159] *Ibid.*, at 59 (Book I, Chapter VI).

[160] 1803 (UK), 43 Geo. III, c. 122. The original version of the UK Act contained five such "schedules" (A to E), of which Schedule D was subdivided into six "cases." Schedule A, "The Landlord's Tax," was levied on the annual value of land. Schedule B, "The Farmer's Tax," applied to the occupation of farming. Schedule C applied to income payable out of any public revenue. Schedule D taxed income from "any kind of property," of which Case I applied to income from trades and manufactures, Case II dealt with income from professions and employments, Case III covered profits of uncertain annual value (for example, from mines or canals), Case IV taxed interest from securities abroad, Case V applied to income from professions abroad, and Case VI imposed tax on annual profits not charged under any other case or schedule. Finally, Schedule E imposed a tax on pensions, annuities, and the "emoluments" of any public office or employment.

gains from the sale of property held by the taxpayer as a source of income,[161] and gifts and other amounts received by the taxpayer without organized effort or consideration.[162] As Rowlatt J explained in *Ryall v. Hoare; Ryall v. Honeywill*, [1923] 2 K.B. 447 at 454 (K.B.):

> [f]irst, anything in the nature of capital accretion is excluded as being outside the scope and meaning of these Acts confirmed by the usage of a century. For this reason, a casual profit made on an isolated purchase and sale, unless merged with similar transactions in the carrying on of a trade or business is not liable to tax. "Profits or gains" in Case 6 refer to the interest or fruit as opposed to the principal or root of the tree. The second class of cases to be excluded consists of gifts and receipts whether the emolument is from a gift *inter vivos* or by will or from finding an article of value or from winning a bet. All these cases must be ruled out because they are not profits or gains at all.

While the former receipts were characterized as non-taxable capital gains from the realization of an investment, the latter were characterized as non-taxable gains from the transfer of property rather than the creation of new wealth.[163]

In Canada, the source concept was adopted in subsection 3(1) of the *Income War Tax Act*, which defined "income" as:

> the annual net profit or gain or gratuity ... received by a person from any office or employment, or from any profession or calling or from any trade, manufacture or business ... the interest, dividends or profits ... received from money ... or from stocks, or from any other investment, ... and also the annual profit or gain from any other source.

This concept was retained in section 3 of the 1948 and 1952 *Income Tax Act*, which defined the income of a taxpayer for a taxation year as the taxpayer's "income for the year from all sources" including "without restricting the generality of the foregoing" the taxpayer's "income for the year from all (a) businesses, (b) property, and (c) offices and employments". These four sources of income are now identified in paragraph 3(a), which replaced section 3 in 1972, at which time paragraph 3(b) and subdivisions c and d were enacted,

---

[161] See, for example, *Californian Copper Syndicate Ltd. v. Harris* (1904), 5 Tax Cas 159 at 165 (Ct. of Ex. (Scot.)), where Lord Justice Clerk stated that:
> [i]t is quite a well settled principle in dealing with questions of assessment of Income Tax, that where the owner of an ordinary investment chooses to realize it, and obtains a greater price for it than he originally acquired it at, the enhanced price is not profit in the sense of Schedule D of the *Income Tax Act* of 1842 assessable to Income Tax.

[162] See, for example, *Graham v. Green (Inspector of Taxes)* (1925), 9 Tax Cas 309 at 311 (K.B.), where gains from betting on horses "on such a large and sustained scale ... that [the taxpayer] made an income out of it" were held not to be "profits or gains" within the meaning of Case VI of Schedule D of the UK Act.

[163] See the discussion of these cases in *Bellingham v. Canada*, [1995] F.C.J. No. 1602, [1996] 1 C.T.C. 187, [1995] 96 D.T.C. 6075 (F.C.A.). Although transfers of wealth have not been subject to income tax in the United Kingdom, they have traditionally been taxed under separate estate and gift taxes and are currently subject to tax under a combined capital transfer tax. Most developed countries, with the exceptions of Canada, Australia, and New Zealand, levy separate taxes on the transfer of wealth. See Ontario Fair Tax Commission, *Fair Taxation in a Changing World* (Toronto: University of Toronto Press, 1993) at 360-93.

requiring taxpayers to include taxable capital gains and various "other sources of income" in computing their income for the year.

As in the United Kingdom, the source concept of income on which the Canadian income tax is based requires that a taxpayer's income or loss from each source (including sources of the same kind) be computed separately and only subsequently aggregated under section 3 to determine the taxpayer's net income from all sources. As paragraph 4(1)(a) explains, for the purposes of the Act:

> a taxpayer's income or loss for a taxation year from an office, employment, business, property or other source ... is the taxpayer's income or loss, as the case may be, computed in accordance with this Act on the assumption that the taxpayer had during the taxation year no income or loss except from that source ... , and was allowed no deductions in computing the taxpayer's income for the taxation year except such deductions as may reasonably be regarded as wholly applicable to that source ... , and except such part of any other deductions as may reasonably be regarded as applicable thereto.

In certain circumstances, the Act prevents taxpayers from deducting losses from one source or from all sources of one kind against income from other sources.[164]

Notwithstanding this similarity between the Canadian income tax and its English counterpart, the Canadian version of the source concept differs from that of the United Kingdom by referring to income from all sources, out of which "without restricting the generality of the foregoing" the four traditional sources ("each office, employment, business, and property") are specifically identified. Consequently, as the Federal Court of Appeal observed in *Bellingham v. Canada*, [1995] F.C.J. No. 1602, [1996] 1 C.T.C. 187, [1995] 96 D.T.C. 6075 (F.C.A.) (at para. 28):

> [p]aragraph 3(a) makes it clear that the named sources are not exhaustive and, thus, income can arise from other unidentified sources. In summary, Parliament has chosen to define income by reference to a restrictive doctrine while recasting it in such a manner as to achieve broader ends.

A majority of the Supreme Court of Canada reached a similar conclusion in *Schwartz v. Canada*, [1996] S.C.J. No. 15, [1996] 1 C.T.C. 303, 96 D.T.C. 6103 (S.C.C.) (at para. 50), affirming that "income from *all* sources, enumerated or not, expressly provided for in subdivision d or not" are "taxable under the Act".

Despite this general language, however, Canadian courts have, with a few notable exceptions,[165] tended to follow UK practice by limiting the sources of

---

[164] See, for example, s. 31, which limits the extent to which certain farm losses may be deducted against income from other sources, and subs. 18(12), which prohibits the deduction of losses resulting from expenses related to a home office in computing a taxpayer's income from other sources. These provisions are considered in Chapter 5. A similar result is achieved for allowable capital losses by para. 3(b), which generally can be deducted only against taxable capital gains. See the discussion of deductions later in this chapter.

[165] The leading cases are *Curran v. M.N.R.*, [1959] S.C.J. No. 66, [1959] C.T.C. 416, 59 D.T.C. 1247 (S.C.C.), which is reproduced in Chapter 4 and *Schwartz v. Canada*, [1996] S.C.J. No. 15, [1996] 1 C.T.C. 303, 96 D.T.C. 6103 (S.C.C.), which is reproduced in Chapter 7. See also the

taxable receipts to those specifically identified in the Act.[166] For this reason, the Act has been subject to numerous amendments designed to include amounts otherwise excluded in computing a taxpayer's income from a particular source or from all sources as a whole.[167] Likewise, adopting the English view that income must be derived from a productive source, Canadian courts traditionally excluded capital gains, gifts, and other fortuitous receipts from the scope of the income tax.[168] It was to reverse this result in part that subdivisions c and d were enacted in 1972.

c. US Approach

The United States enacted an income tax in 1913, only a few years before the *Income War Tax Act* was introduced in Canada. According to paragraph 2(a) of a revised version of this statute enacted in 1916, the "net income of a taxable person" was defined to include:

> gains, profits, and income derived from salaries, wages, or compensation for personal service ... of whatever kind and in whatever form paid, or from professions, vocations, trades, businesses, commerce, or sales, or dealings in property, whether real or personal, growing out of the ownership or use of or interest in such property; also from interest, rent, dividends, securities, or the transaction of any business carried on for gain or profit, or gains or profits and income derived from any source whatever.

Exchequer Court decision in *Wood v. M.N.R.*, [1967] C.T.C. 66, 67 D.T.C. 5045 (Ex. Ct.), which was reversed by the Supreme Court of Canada, [1969] S.C.J. No. 1, [1969] C.T.C. 57, 69 D.T.C. 5073 (S.C.C.); and the Federal Court of Appeal decision in *Canada v. Fries*, [1989] F.C.J. No. 407, [1989] 1 C.T.C. 471, 89 D.T.C. 5240 (F.C.A.), which was also reversed by the Supreme Court of Canada, [1990] S.C.J. No. 109, [1990] 2 C.T.C. 439, 90 D.T.C. 6662 (S.C.C.). The Supreme Court of Canada decision in *Wood* is reproduced in Chapter 6. The Federal Court of Appeal and Supreme Court of Canada decisions in *Fries* are reproduced in Chapter 4.

[166] Although too numerous to cite here, these cases are considered in Chapters 4 to 7. The most recent example of this tendency is the minority decision in *Schwartz, ibid.*, which is reproduced in Chapter 7.

[167] See, for example, para. 12(1)(g), which includes in computing a taxpayer's income from a business or property "any amount received by the taxpayer in the year that was dependent on the use of or production from property"; para. 12(1)(x), which includes in computing a taxpayer's income from a business or property certain payments made as inducements, refunds, reimbursements, contributions, allowances, or assistance; para. 56(1)(n) and (o), which include in a taxpayer's net income from all sources scholarships, fellowships, bursaries, prizes, and research grants; and subpara. 56(1)(a)(ii), which includes in a taxpayer's net income from all sources "retiring allowances" as defined in subs. 248(1). Paragraphs 12(1)(g) and (x) are examined in Chapter 5. Paragraphs 56(1)(n) and (o) and subpara. 56(1)(a)(ii) are examined in Chapter 7.

[168] These cases are also too numerous to cite here, but are considered in Chapters 4 to 7. See also the discussion of these cases in *Bellingham v. Canada*, [1995] F.C.J. No. 1602, [1996] 1 C.T.C. 187, [1995] 96 D.T.C. 6075 (F.C.A.), and *Schwartz v. Canada*, [1996] S.C.J. No. 15, [1996] 1 C.T.C. 303, 96 D.T.C. 6103 (S.C.C.).

Although the US legislation has been amended frequently over the last 80 years, it still contains a general provision including in "gross income" all "gains or profits and income derived from any source whatever".

Despite the reference to income "derived from any source", the specific categories of income identified in this provision arguably suggest a different concept of source than that developed in the United Kingdom and Canada, defined not only in terms of productivity but also according to the various forms in which income may be received, for example, "income derived from salaries, wages, or compensation for personal service" and income "from interest, rent, [or] dividends". In addition, the specific inclusion of "gains, profits, and income" is potentially much broader than the Canadian inclusion of a taxpayer's "income" from each source.

In any event, on the basis of this statutory language, US courts have held that the US income tax applies to capital gains,[169] gifts and inheritances,[170] and other fortuitous receipts such as punitive damages.[171] In *Commissioner v. Glenshaw Glass Co.*, 348 US 426 (1955), in which the US Supreme Court held that an amount paid in settlement of a claim for exemplary damages under federal antitrust laws was income for the purposes of the US statute, Chief Justice Warren stated of the provision quoted above (at 429-30) that:

> Congress applied no limitations as to the source of taxable receipts, nor restrictive labels as to their nature. And the Court has given a liberal construction to this broad phraseology in recognition of the intention of Congress to tax all gains except those specifically exempted.

Citing several other decisions of the US Supreme Court, he then explained (at 430) that:

> [s]uch decisions demonstrate that we cannot but ascribe content to the catchall provision ... "gains or profits and income derived from any source whatever." The importance of that phrase has been too frequently recognized since its first appearance in the Revenue Act of 1913 to say that it adds nothing to the meaning of "gross income."

---

[169] *Eisner v. Macomber*, 252 US 189 (1920). Although the court held that the US *Revenue Act* of 1916 applied to capital gains, the decision also held that the concept of income suggested by the 16th amendment to the US Constitution and employed in the Act did not apply to increases in the value of property (accrued gains) that had not been converted into cash (realized) through the sale or other disposition of the properly. Thus, the US Act applied to realized but not accrued capital gains.

[170] *Irwin v. Gavit*, 268 US 161 (1925). By statute, the US legislation, like s. 3 of the *Income War Tax Act*, included "the income from but not the value of property acquired by gift, bequest, devise or descent." This explicit exemption, in recognition of the separate taxation of gifts and bequests under a combined gift and estate tax, is currently found in s. 102 of the *Internal Revenue Code*. In *Gavit*, where the taxpayer received a bequest of an income interest in a trust that could last no longer than 15 years, the US Supreme Court held that the income, which was paid quarterly, did not come within the statutory exemption for "property acquired by gift, bequest, devise or descend."

[171] *Commissioner v. Glenshaw Glass Co.*, 348 US 425 (1955).

Finally, referring specifically to the amount paid in settlement of the claim for exemplary damages, Chief Justice Warren concluded (at 431):

> Here we have instances of undeniable accessions to wealth, clearly realized, and over which the taxpayers have complete dominion. The mere fact that the payments were extracted from the wrongdoers as punishment for unlawful conduct cannot detract from their character as taxable income to the recipients.

d. Haig-Simons Definition

In the context of the US income tax, US economists Robert Murray Haig and Henry C. Simons developed an alternative concept of income strikingly at odds with the source concept on which interpretation of the Canadian legislation has traditionally been based.[172] According to Simons, while the concept that income must be derived from a productive source may be true as a matter of economic theory and national income accounting, there is no obvious reason why this concept should be employed in order to determine the appropriate base of a tax designed to allocate the cost of government expenditures among members of the community in a fair and equitable manner. Thus, he explained, the view that "personal income is merely a share in the total income of society" and the idea that "income taxes must bear — presumably by definition! — only on the net social income as it accrues to individuals" must be disregarded as "irrelevant" to the real issue of defining an appropriate tax base.[173]

Finally, suggesting that personal income "connotes, broadly, the exercise of control over the use of society's scarce resources", Simons suggested that:

> [p]ersonal income may be defined as the algebraic sum of (1) the market value of rights exercised in consumption and (2) the change in the value of the store of property rights between the beginning and end of the period in question.[174]

Similarly, Haig had proposed as an "economic" definition of "income": "the money value of the net accretion to one's economic power between two points of time".[175]

Among the many implications of this definition of the tax base, it would include in income all gifts and other fortuitous receipts as well as capital gains.[176] In principle, moreover, this definition would include in income not only

---

[172] See R.M. Haig, "The Concept of Income — Economic and Legal Aspects" in R.M. Haig, ed., *The Federal Income Tax* (New York: Columbia University Press, 1920) at 27; and Henry C. Simons, *Personal Income Taxation, the Definition of Income as a Problem of Fiscal Policy* (Chicago: University of Chicago Press, 1938).

[173] Simons, *ibid.*, at 47-48.

[174] *Ibid.*, at 49 and 50.

[175] R.M. Haig, "The Concept of Income — Economic and Legal Aspects" in R.M. Haig, ed., *The Federal Income Tax* (New York: Columbia University Press, 1920) at 59.

[176] See Henry C. Simons, *Personal Income Taxation, the Definition of Income as a Problem of Fiscal Policy* (Chicago: University of Chicago Press, 1938), Chapters VI ("Gratuitous Receipts") and VII ("Capital Gains"). Another important implication, which is not discussed

capital gains that are "realized" when property is sold, but "accrued" capital gains on property that has increased in value over the course of a taxation year, even if the property is not sold during the taxation year.[177] For administrative reasons, however, Simons accepted "the realization criterion" as "a practical necessity".[178]

e. Carter Commission

For the Canadian Royal Commission on Taxation (the Carter Commission), appointed by the Diefenbaker government in September 1962, the concept of income proposed by Henry Simons and Robert Haig was an attractive alternative to the source concept on the basis of which the Canadian income tax had not been applied to capital gains, gifts and inheritances, and other fortuitous receipts. Referring to US data from 1963 that showed that capital gains accounted for only 4 per cent of all reported income, but 48 per cent of income for taxpayers earning between $100,000 and $200,000 and 128 per cent of income for taxpayers earning more than $200,000,[179] the Carter Commission regarded the adoption of a more comprehensive definition of income along the lines proposed by Haig and Simons as necessary both to the equity and the efficiency of the Canadian tax system.[180] According to the commission:

---

here, is the taxation of "imputed income" from services and property. See *ibid.*, Chapter V ("Income in Kind"). For a useful discussion of "imputed income" in the context of the comprehensive tax base, see Peter W. Hogg, Joanne E. Magee & Jinyan Li, *Principles of Canadian Income Tax Law*, 6th ed. (Toronto: Carswell, 2007) at 105-108. For a more extensive discussion that is highly critical of the taxation of imputed income, see Thomas Chancellor, "Imputed Income and the Ideal Income Tax" (1988) 67 Or. L. Rev. 561.

[177] In this sense, Simons' definition of "personal income" went beyond the decision of the US Supreme Court in *Eisner v. Macomber*, 252 US 189 (1920).

[178] Henry C. Simons, *Personal Income Taxation, the Definition of Income as a Problem of Fiscal Policy* (Chicago: University of Chicago Press, 1938) at 153. Traditionally, the administrative concerns with accrual taxation of capital gains have been twofold: (1) that it would require annual valuation of property that has not been sold in a transaction resulting in a market value on which tax may be based; and (2) that it would impose a cash obligation on taxpayers at a time when they may not have the cash to discharge the tax liability (because the property that has increased in value has not been sold). In recent years, a number of proposals have been put forward for the accrual taxation of capital gains. See, for example, Pamela Gann, "Neutral Taxation of Capital Income: An Achievable Goal" (1985) 48 Law & Contemp. Probs. 78; David J. Shakow, "Taxation Without Realization: A Proposal for Accrual Taxation" (1986) 134 U. Pa. L. Rev. 1111; and Mary Louise Fellows, "A Comprehensive Attack on Tax Deferral" (1990) 88 Mich. L. Rev. 722.

[179] *Report of the Royal Commission on Taxation*, 6 vols. (Ottawa: Queen's Printer, 1966), Vol. 3 at 332.

[180] By broadening the tax base, the commission proposed that the top marginal tax rate could be reduced from 80 per cent, as it was at the time, to 50 per cent, thereby reducing tax-induced distortions and lessening incentives to avoid or evade tax.

We are completely persuaded that taxes should be allocated according to the changes in the economic power of individuals and families. If a man obtains increased command over goods and services for his personal satisfaction we do not believe it matters, from the point of view of taxation, whether he earned it through working, gained it through operating a business, received it because he held property, made it by selling property or was given it by a relative. Nor do we believe it matters whether the increased command over goods and services was in cash or in kind. Nor do we believe it matters whether the increase in economic power was expected or unexpected, whether it was a unique or recurrent event, whether the man suffered to get the increase in economic power or it fell in his lap without effort.

All of these considerations should be ignored either because they are impossible to determine objectively in practice or because they are irrelevant in principle, or both. By adopting a base that measures changes in the power, whether exercised or not, to consume goods and services we obtain certainty, consistency and equity.[181]

Reporting in December 1966, the Carter Commission proposed as the concept of income by which the Canadian *Income Tax Act* should be informed, a "comprehensive tax base" defined as "the sum of the market value of goods and services consumed or given away in the taxation year by the tax unit, plus the annual change in the market value of the assets held by the unit".[182] On this basis, but taking into account a number of administrative challenges to the implementation of a pure comprehensive tax base, the report recommended among other things that capital gains be fully taxable when realized,[183] that gifts and inheritances be included in a taxpayer's income,[184] and that other kinds of windfall gains be similarly subject to income tax.[185] Although the Carter Commission concluded that the administrative challenges to taxing accrued capital gains were insurmountable, it recommended that property be subject to a "deemed disposition", which would trigger tax on death, on the making of a gift, and on giving up Canadian residence.[186]

Although receptive to many of the report's recommendations, the Trudeau government, which had been elected in 1968, rejected the Carter Commission's idea of the comprehensive tax base.[187] Nonetheless, after considerable consultation and the release of a government white paper, the government introduced legislation in 1971 that included half of all realized capital gains in each taxpayer's income for a taxation year, with half of all realized capital losses allowed as a deduction against taxable capital gains. Consistent with the Carter Commission's recommendation, the legislation also proposed that property be

---

[181] *Report of the Royal Commission on Taxation*, 6 vols. (Ottawa: Queen's Printer, 1966), Vol. 1 at 9-10.

[182] *Ibid.*, Vol. 3 at 39.

[183] *Ibid.*, Vol. 1 at 13-15. See also Vol. 3, Chapter 15.

[184] *Ibid.*, Vol. 1 at 16-17 and 19. See also Vol. 3, Chapter 17. In conjunction with this recommendation, the commission also recommended the repeal of the existing federal gift and estate taxes. See Vol. 1 at 19.

[185] *Ibid.*, Vol. 1 at 16. See also Vol. 3 at 526-27.

[186] *Ibid.*, Vol. 3 at 368-80.

[187] Hon. E.J. Benson, *Proposals for Tax Reform* (Ottawa: Queen's Printer, 1969) at 36, para. 3.3.

subject to a deemed disposition to trigger accrued gains on death, on the making of a gift, and on giving up Canadian residence.

These proposals were enacted into law effective January 1, 1972, with the enactment of paragraph 3(b) and subdivision c of Division B of Part I of the Act, the introduction of detailed transitional rules to exempt capital gains that had accrued prior to this date,[188] and the enactment of special rules deeming property to be disposed of when transferred by gift or at death and when a taxpayer ceases to be a resident of Canada.[189] While the "inclusion rate" for capital gains and capital losses was increased from one-half to two-thirds for 1988 and 1989 and to three-quarters in 1990, subsequent reductions in this fraction to two-thirds on February 28, 2000 and one-half as of October 18, 2000 have restored the original "tax preference" for this category of income.[190]

With respect to gifts and inheritances, the government did not accept the Commission's recommendation that these amounts be included in the statutory definition of "income". On the contrary, implementing one part of the Carter Commission's report recommendation on the taxation of gifts and inheritances, the federal government repealed its gift and estate taxes effective January 1, 1972, abandoning the taxation of wealth transfers to the provinces, three of which (British Columbia, Ontario, and Quebec) levied their own gift and succession duties at the time.[191]

The rationale offered by the government for this decision, which was neither recommended in the white paper nor widely discussed at the time, was that the introduction of a deemed disposition on transfers of property by gift or at death required a reduction in the combined rate of federal and provincial taxation on the transfer of wealth.[192] Since the federal government remitted 75 per cent of its gift and estate tax revenues to provinces that did not collect their own gift and

---

[188] These are found in the Income Tax Application Rules, 1971 (ITARs). This book does not examine the transitional rules associated with the introduction of capital gains tax in 1972.

[189] These rules, which were enacted in 1972, are now contained in subs. 70(5), 69(1), and 128.1(4) of the Act. In order to prevent the extended deferral of capital gains that would otherwise be possible for property held by a trust, subs. 104(4) deems trust property to be disposed of every 21 years.

[190] Despite the inclusion of capital gains as income in the United States, capital gains have received preferential treatment under specific statutory provisions during most years since the current statute was first enacted in 1913. When the Carter Commission reported in 1966, only half of "long-term" capital gains were taxable in the United States, which explains why the Canadian government subsequently settled on this "inclusion rate" for "taxable" capital gains. Although the United States taxed capital gains at the same rate as ordinary income in the late 1980s and early 1990s, subsequent amendments in the mid-1990s restored a tax preference for this category of income. Perhaps not surprisingly, therefore, movements in the Canadian inclusion rate for capital gains have tended to follow developments in the United States.

[191] On the repeal of these taxes in Canada, see Richard Bird, "Canada's Vanishing Death Taxes" (1978) 16 Osgoode Hall L.J. 133; David G. Duff, "The Abolition of Wealth Transfer Taxes in Canada" in John Tiley ed., *Studies in the History of Tax Law, Volume II*, (Oxford: Hart Publishing 2006), Chapter 12.

[192] See George E. Carter, "Federal Abandonment of the Estate Tax: The Intergovernmental Fiscal Dimension" (1973) 21 Can. Tax J. 232.

succession duties and provided a credit against federal tax for provinces that did levy their own provincial duties, the government reasoned that an appropriate reduction in the combined federal-provincial rate could be achieved by withdrawing from the field and leaving it up to provincial governments to levy their own wealth transfer taxes. As a transitional measure, however, the federal government offered to collect provincial wealth transfer taxes on a province's behalf for a limited number of years.

In response to these developments, of those provinces that did not levy their own gift and succession duties at the time, all but Alberta enacted provincial wealth transfer taxes to become effective January 1, 1972. Fearing that affluent residents might relocate to Alberta, however, some provinces never implemented these taxes and most were repealed shortly after their enactment. Ontario repealed its gift and succession duties in 1978, and Quebec, the last Canadian province to levy a separate tax on the transfer of wealth, repealed its gift and succession duty in 1985. As a result, Canada is one of only a few developed countries in which intergenerational transfers of wealth are generally free of tax.[193]

With respect to other fortuitous receipts such as prizes, lottery proceeds, and gambling winnings, the government neither accepted nor explicitly rejected the Carter Commission's proposal that these amounts be included in a taxpayer's income for a taxation year. Nonetheless, new paragraph 56(1)(n), enacted effective for 1972 and subsequent taxation years, stipulated that amounts received by a taxpayer "on account of ... a prize for achievement in a field of endeavour ordinarily carried on by the taxpayer" should be included in a taxpayer's income.[194] Whether other kinds of unexpected and non-recurring receipts are contemplated by the word "income" in the Canadian *Income Tax Act* continues to be subject to interpretation by the courts.[195]

---

[193] See, for example, Organisation for Economic Co-operation and Development, *Taxation of Net Wealth, Capital Transfers and Capital Gains of Individuals* (Paris: OECD, 1988). The statement in the text is, of course, subject to the deemed disposition provisions, which apply only to accrued gains in the value of property transferred, not the aggregate value of property transferred. In addition, several provinces impose low-rate "probate fees" based on the value of estates subject to probate on death. For arguments for the re-enactment of a wealth transfer tax in Canada, see Maureen Maloney, "Distributive Justice: That Is the Wealth Tax Issue" (1988) 20 Ottawa L. R. 601; and David G. Duff, "Taxing Inherited Wealth: A Philosophical Argument" (1993) 6 Can. J.L.& Jur. 3. See also the recommendation of the Ontario Fair Tax Commission that the federal government should re-enact a wealth transfer tax: *Fair Taxation in a Changing World* (Toronto: University of Toronto Press 1993) at Chapter 19. For opposing views, see David Ward, "The Case Against Capital Taxes" (1980) 2 Can. Tax'n: J. Tax Pol'y 31; and W.E. Crawford, "Provincial Wealth Taxes? The Numbers Just Don't Justify Them," Personal Tax Planning feature (1993) 41 Can. Tax J. 150. See also Roger S. Smith, *Personal Wealth Taxation: Canadian Tax Policy in a Historical and International Setting*, Canadian Tax Paper No. 97 (Toronto: Canadian Tax Foundation, 1993).

[194] Paragraph 56(1)(n) is examined in Chapter 7.

[195] See, for example, *Schwartz v. Canada*, [1996] S.C.J. No. 15, [1996] 1 C.T.C. 303, 96 D.T.C. 6103 (S.C.C.) and *Bellingham v. Canada*, [1995] F.C.J. No. 1602, [1996] 1 C.T.C. 187, [1995] 96 D.T.C. 6075 (F.C.A.).

Among its other implications, the Carter Commission's comprehensive tax base would also include in income various kinds of government transfer payments (for example, unemployment insurance and worker's compensation) that were not subject to tax when the Commission reported in December 1966. Thus, among its many other recommendations, the Commission also proposed that these government transfer payments be fully included in a taxpayer's income for a taxation year.[196]

For the most part, this recommendation was accepted by the government, which amended the Act by including in new subdivision d of Division B of Part I of the Act ("Other Sources of Income") unemployment insurance benefits and other payments in recognition of employment dislocation;[197] scholarships, fellowships and bursaries;[198] and research grants.[199] Other amounts included in computing a taxpayer's income under subdivision d had been included under various provisions of the 1952 Act.[200]

2. Deductions

As with inclusions, the *Income Tax Act* contains numerous rules specifying amounts that may be deducted in computing a taxpayer's income for a taxation year.[201] Some of these rules apply to the computation of a taxpayer's income or loss from a specific source or to the computation of capital gains or losses, allowing the deduction of various costs that must be incurred in order to produce this income.[202] Other deductions are contained in subdivision e of Division B of

---

[196] *Report of the Royal Commission on Taxation*, 6 Vols. (Ottawa: Queen's Printer, 1966), Vol. 3 at 17. See also Chapter 18 of the report.

[197] See subparas. 56(1)(a)(iv), (v), and (vi) of the Act and regulation 5502. These provisions are examined in Chapter 7.

[198] See para. 56(1)(n) of the Act. More recently, the *Income Tax Act* has been amended to exempt scholarships, fellowships, and bursaries where the recipient is enrolled in an educational program for which the education credit may be deducted under subs. 118.6(2) of the Act. See para. 56(3)(a) of the Act. These provisions are examined in Chapter 7.

[199] See para. 56(1)(o) of the Act. This provision is examined in Chapter 7.

[200] See, for example, subparas. 56(1)(a)(i), (ii), and (iii) (superannuation or pension benefits, retiring allowances, and death benefits), which replaced subparas. 6(1)(a)(iv), (v), and (vi) of the 1952 Act, and para. 56(1)(b) (support), which replaced para. 6(1)(b) of the 1952 Act.

[201] These rules are examined in Chapters 4 to 7.

[202] In computing a taxpayer's capital gain or loss from the disposition of a property, for example, taxpayers may deduct from the proceeds received both the cost of the property to the taxpayer and the cost of outlays or expenses made or incurred by the taxpayer for the purpose of making the disposition. Similarly, subs. 9(1) defines a taxpayer's income from a business or property as the taxpayer's "profit" from that source — a concept that implicitly authorizes the deduction of ordinary expenses that must be incurred in order to obtain this income. Although allowable deductions in computing a taxpayer's income from an office or employment are much more limited, s. 8 allows taxpayers to deduct various amounts as specified in computing any income from these sources. In addition to these specific deductions, former para. 8(1)(a) permitted employees to deduct a standard amount equal to the lesser of $500 and 20 per cent of income

Part I of the Act, comprising sections 60 to 66.8,[203] and are referred to in paragraph 3(c), which permits the deduction of these subdivision e deductions except to the extent that they have been "taken into account" in determining the total referred to in paragraph 3(a) by their deduction in computing the taxpayer's income from one or more of these sources.[204] Yet other rules permit the deduction of losses, which may be deducted against all other income under paragraph 3(d) in the case of losses from an office, employment, business, or property as well as allowable business investment losses, but are restricted under paragraph 3(b) for other allowable capital losses from dispositions of property other than listed personal property to the total of the taxpayer's taxable capital gains for the year from dispositions of property and the taxpayer's taxable net gain for the year from dispositions of listed personal property.[205]

In addition to these deductions, Division C of Part I of the Act, which comprises sections 109 to 114.2, allows taxpayers to deduct other amounts in computing their taxable income. For our purposes, the key provisions in this division are paragraph 110(1)(d) (providing a deduction for certain kinds of employee stock options), paragraph 110(1)(f) (allowing taxpayers to deduct, among other things, social assistance payments and workers' compensation), paragraph 110(1)(h) (permitting taxpayers to deduct specific amounts included in their income in respect of a home relocation loan), section 110.1 (allowing corporations to deduct the value of certain kinds of gifts), section 110.6 (allowing individuals to deduct a cumulative lifetime amount with respect to capital gains arising on the disposition of certain kinds of property), section 110.7 (providing a special deduction for persons resident in northern parts of Canada), and section 111 (allowing individual and corporate taxpayers to deduct

---

from all offices and employments plus taxable training allowances and research grants. This "employment expense deduction" was repealed effective for 1988 and subsequent taxation years.

[203] These deductions are examined in Chapter 7.

[204] The relationship between the deduction of amounts under subdivision e and the deduction of the same amount in computing a taxpayer's income from a source is considered in *Symes v. Canada*, [1993] S.C.J. No. 131, [1994] 1 C.T.C. 40, (1993) 94 D.T.C. 6001 (S.C.C.). See also para. 248(28)(a) (formerly subs. 4(4)), according to which, "[u]nless a contrary intention is evident, no provision of this Act shall be read or construed ... to ... permit the deduction ... in computing a taxpayer's income ... for a taxation year ... of any amount to the extent that the amount has already been ... deducted ... in computing such income ... for the year." Unlike para. 248(28)(a), which provides only that an amount shall not be deducted twice, para. 3(c) stipulates that an amount which may be deductible under subdivision e or in computing a taxpayer's income from a source shall be deducted in computing the taxpayer's income from the source.

[205] In general, gains or losses from the disposition of property that are not taken into account in computing a taxpayer's income or loss from a business are characterized as capital gains or capital losses; the taxable and allowable portion of these gains and losses is generally one-half under s. 38 of the Act; and listed personal property is a separate category of property the gains and losses from which are subject to a separate set of rules and offset against each other under s. 41. For the purposes of this chapter, the key point is that deductions for allowable capital losses are generally restricted to the amount of the taxpayer's taxable capital gains for the year.

losses from certain other taxation years that may be "carried over" to the taxation year for which taxable income is computed).

Although much tax policy analysis regarding the definition of the "income tax base" has tended to concentrate on the subject of inclusions,[206] the question of deductions is also important and often considered.[207] For most commentators, a deduction for costs that must be incurred by a taxpayer in order to obtain income of different kinds is necessary on grounds of equity and efficiency, since a tax on gross receipts rather than net gains would exaggerate the economic resources available to those who must incur larger costs in order to obtain these receipts and discourage these activities by lowering their after-tax rate of return more than the reduction for lower-cost enterprises.[208] Likewise, a deduction for losses incurred in the pursuit of an income-earning activity may be justified on equity and efficiency grounds, since the failure to recognize such losses would exaggerate the taxable capacity of those who have incurred these losses and discourage more risky enterprises.[209] Other commentators support further deductions to exempt a basic amount of income necessary to provide for living expenses and to recognize differences in taxpayers' relative abilities to pay arising from legal responsibilities to support family members and involuntary expenses associated with a mental or physical disability or uninsured health care costs.[210] Yet other deductions function as incentives or "tax expendi-

---

[206] Henry C. Simons, *Personal Income Taxation, the Definition of Income as a Problem of Fiscal Policy* (Chicago: University of Chicago Press, 1938), 140.

[207] See, for example, Robin W. Boadway and Harry M. Kitchen, *Canadian Tax Policy*, 3d ed., Canadian Tax Paper No. 103 (Toronto: Canadian Tax Foundation, 1999) at 116-25. For an excellent discussion of the policy considerations regarding the deduction of expenses under a personal income tax, see Tim Edgar, "The Concept of Taxable Consumption and the Deductibility of Expenses Under an Ideal Personal Income Tax Base" in *Tax Conversations: A Guide to Key Issues in the Tax Reform Debate, Essays in Honour of John G. Head*, Richard Krever, ed., (London: Kluwer Law International, 1997) at 293-363.

[208] See, for example, Richard Goode, *The Individual Income Tax*, rev. ed. (Washington: The Brookings Institution, 1976), 75; and Wayne R. Thirsk, "Giving Credit Where Credit Is Due: The Choice Between Credits and Deductions Under the Individual Income Tax in Canada" (1980) 28 Can. Tax J. 32 at 33.

[209] Indeed, to the extent that the income tax limits the deduction of losses in a taxation year to other income in that taxation year, and limits the deduction of most allowable capital losses to the total of the taxpayer's taxable capital gains and net gains for the year, providing only limited opportunities for the "carryover" of losses to other taxation years under s. 111, it is often argued that the current rules discourage risky activities by limiting the recognition of losses. See, for example, Jack M. Mintz, "Economic Implications of Non-Refundability of Tax Losses," in *Policy Options for the Treatment of Tax Losses* (Toronto: Clarkson Gordon Foundation, 1991), 4:1-43.

[210] See, for example, A. Pierre Cloutier and Bernard Fortin, "Converting Exemptions and Deductions into Credits: An Economic Assessment" in Jack M. Mintz and John Whalley, eds. *The Economic Impacts of Tax Reform*, Canadian Tax Paper No. 84 (Toronto: Canadian Tax Foundation, 1989), 45 at 54-62; and David G. Duff, "Disability and the Income Tax" (2000) 45 McGill L.J. 797.

tures"[211] designed to encourage specific kinds of behaviour, such as saving for retirement,[212] the growth of a small business,[213] or contributions to charitable organizations.[214]

Since a deduction reduces the tax payable by a high-income taxpayer under a progressive income tax by an amount that is greater than the reduction for low-income taxpayers, deductions are generally viewed as an inequitable way to pursue any policy goal other than the accurate measurement of income.[215] Where charitable contributions are encouraged by means of a deduction, for example, taxpayers who are subject to a 40 per cent marginal rate of tax obtain a reduction of 40 cents on each dollar contributed, while those subject to a 20 per cent marginal rate of tax obtain a reduction of only 20 cents on each dollar contributed. Since an "accurate measurement of income" depends on one's concept of the income tax base, however, a proper assessment of any deduction from a tax policy perspective requires both an evaluation of the purpose of the deduction and a judgment regarding the appropriate income tax base.

While deductions for many costs that are incurred to obtain different kinds of income are relatively uncontroversial, expenses having an identifiable personal aspect are much more difficult to characterize.[216] On the one hand, tuition fees for post-secondary education, which were deductible before 1988 under former paragraphs 60(e) to (g) of the Act, are now recognized in section 118.5, which provides a non-refundable credit against basic federal tax payable computed at the lowest marginal rate (15 per cent for 2008). Likewise, employment insurance (EI) premiums and Canada/Quebec Pension Plan (CPP/QPP) contributions, which were deductible in computing a taxpayer's income from an office or employment under former paragraphs 8(1)(k) and (1) of the Act, are now subject to a non-refundable credit against basic federal tax payable under section 118.7. On the other hand, sections 62 and 63, which were enacted in 1972, permit the deduction of certain moving expenses and child-care expenses,

---

[211] This term was popularized by Stanley Surrey, who distinguished between deductions that are essential to the definition of the "normative" income tax base and those that function as a form of government spending designed to encourage specific kinds of behaviour. See, for example, Stanley S. Surrey, "Tax Incentives as a Device for Implementing Government Policy: A Comparison with Direct Expenditures" (1970) 83 Harv. L. Rev 705; and Stanley S. Surrey and Paul R. McDaniel, *Tax Expenditures* (Cambridge, MA: Harvard University Press, 1985).

[212] See, for example, the deduction of contributions to a registered retirement pension plan under para. 60(i) and subs. 146(5) of the Act.

[213] See, for example, the cumulative lifetime deduction in subs. 110.6(2.1) for up to $500,000 of capital gains from the disposition of shares of a "qualified small business corporation."

[214] See the deduction for certain gifts by corporations in s. 110.1 of the Act.

[215] Peter W. Hogg, Joanne E. Magee & Jinyan Li, *Principles of Canadian Income Tax Law*, 6th ed. (Toronto: Carswell, 2007) at 470-71.

[216] For a useful analysis of many of these issues, see Daniel I. Halperin, "Business Deductions for Personal Living Expenses: A Uniform Approach to an Unsolved Problem" (1974) 122 U. Pa. L. Rev. 859.

which courts had previously regarded as personal and non-deductible.[217] Although the treatment of tuition and moving expenses has not been subject to much analysis in Canada,[218] commentators have often criticized the child-care expense deduction as an inequitable subsidy that favours high-income taxpayers over low-income taxpayers.[219] Others, however, defend a deduction for these expenses (at least up to a basic amount necessary to obtain child-care services of a reasonable quality) on equity and efficiency grounds, as a legitimate cost of earning income and a necessary measure to eliminate a disincentive to participation in the paid labour force by "secondary earners" (typically women) resulting from the non-taxation of self-performed child care.[220] Much the same arguments could also be made for and against deductions for tuition fees, payroll taxes, and moving expenses.

In addition to these provisions, others limit or prohibit the deduction of certain costs of obtaining income where these expenses are judged to confer a personal benefit. Although the most prominent of these provisions is section 67.1, which limits deductions for meals and entertainment to 50 per cent of the amount otherwise allowed,[221] other provisions limit deductions for home offices and passenger vehicles,[222] and prohibit the deduction of club fees and expenses

---

[217] See, for example, *Karp v. M.N.R.*, [1968] Tax ABC 1018, 68 D.T.C. 742 (Tax A.B.C.) (disallowing the deduction of moving expenses in computing a taxpayer's income from a business); and *No. 68 v. M.N.R.* (1952), 7 Tax ABC 110, 52 D.T.C. 333 (Tax A.B.C.) (disallowing the deduction of child-care expenses in computing the taxpayer's income from an optometry business). Sections 62 and 63 are examined in Chapter 7.

[218] In contrast, a substantial body of US scholarship has examined the appropriate tax treatment of tuition fees and other costs of higher education. See, for example, John K. McNulty, "Tax Policy and Tuition Credit Legislation: Federal Income Tax Allowances for Personal Costs of Higher Education" (1973) 61 Cal. L. Rev. 1; Clifford Gross, "Tax Treatment of Education Expenses: Perspectives from Normative Theory" (1988) 55 U. Chicago L. Rev. 916; Loretta Collins Argrett, "Tax Treatment of Higher Education Expenditures: An Unfair Investment Disincentive" (1990) 41 Syracuse L. Rev. 621; David S. Davenport, "Education and Human Capital: Pursuing an Ideal Income Tax and a Sensible Tax Policy" (1992) 42 Case W. Res. L. Rev. 793; Hamish P.M. Hume, "The Business of Learning: When and How the Cost of Education Should Be Recognized" (1995) 81 Va. L. Rev. 887; and Cynthia E. Garabedian, "Note. Tax Breaks for Higher Education: Tax Policy or Tax Pandering?" (1998) 18 Va. Tax Rev. 217.

[219] See, for example, Ontario Fair Tax Commission, *Working Group Report: Women and Taxation* (Toronto: Fair Tax Commission, 1992); and Claire Young, "Child Care: A Taxing Issue?" (1994) 39 McGill L.J. 539.

[220] See, for example, Mary L. Heen, "Welfare Reform, Child Care Costs and Taxes: Delivering Increased Work-Related Child Care Benefits to Low-Income Families" (1995) 13 Yale L. & Pol'y Rev. 173 at 207-9; and Edward J. McCaffery, "Taxation and the Family: A Fresh Look at Behavioral Gender Bias in the Code" (1993) 40 UCLA L. Rev. 983 at 106-20.

[221] This provision is examined in Chapter 8.

[222] See subs. 8(13) and 18(12) of the Act (home offices), and para. 13(7)(g) and ss. 67.2 to 67.4 (passenger vehicles). These provisions are discussed or examined in Chapters 4 and 5.

related to the maintenance of recreational facilities.[223] Yet other provisions play an explicit regulatory role by prohibiting the deduction of advertising in non-Canadian newspapers directed primarily at a Canadian market (section 19), or the deduction of bribes constituting an offence under section 3 of the *Corruption of Foreign Public Officials Act* or under various provisions of the *Criminal Code* (section 67.5).

With respect to other provisions exempting a basic amount for personal living expenses and recognizing differences in taxpayers' relative abilities to pay, debates turn less on the purpose of the provision at issue than the concept of the income tax base against which it is judged. Where deductions for family obligations, personal living expenses, and other involuntary expenses are considered necessary to exempt basic living costs and to properly compare the taxable capacities of differently situated taxpayers, the purpose of these deductions can be characterized as an "accurate measurement of income". Where these expenses are regarded as essentially discretionary or otherwise irrelevant to the definition of an appropriate income tax base, their deduction is logically characterized as an inequitable subsidy favouring high-income taxpayers over low-income taxpayers.

Although many commentators have criticized deductions for basic living costs and other personal expenses on the grounds that these constitute an inequitable subsidy worth more to high-income taxpayers than low-income taxpayers,[224] these critics appear to have devoted less attention to a normative justification for an income tax that applies to each taxpayer's aggregate net income notwithstanding necessary living expenses and differences in personal circumstances. In contrast, commentators supporting deductions for these kinds of expenses favour a concept of the appropriate income tax base that exempts a limited amount of income necessary to cover basic living expenses and adjusts the computation of each taxpayer's taxable income in order to obtain a more precise measurement of taxpayers' relative abilities to pay.[225]

---

[223] See para. 18(1)(l) of the Act, which is examined in Chapter 5.

[224] For a prominent statement of this view, see Canada, *The Hidden Welfare System: A Report by the National Council of Welfare on the Personal Income Tax System in Canada* (Ottawa: National Council on Welfare, 1976); and Canada, *The Hidden Welfare System Revisited: A Report by the National Council of Welfare on the Growth in Tax Expenditures* (Ottawa: National Council on Welfare, 1979). See also Thomas F. Pogue, "Deductions Versus Credits: A Comment" (1974) 27 National Tax Journal 659; and Neil Brooks, "The Irrelevance of Conjugal Relationships in Assessing Tax Liability" in John G. Head & Richard Krever, eds., *Tax Units and the Tax Rate Scale* (Melbourne: Australian Tax Research Foundation, 1996).

[225] See, for example, Quebec, Ministère des Finances, *While Paper on the Personal Tax and Transfer Systems (Introductory Paper)* (Quebec: le Ministère, 1984); Adil Sayeed, "Choosing Between Tax Credits and Exemptions for Dependent Children" (1985) 33 Can. Tax J. 975; and A. Pierre Cloutier and Bernard Fortin, "Converting Exemptions and Deductions into Credits: An Economic Assessment" in Jack M. Mintz and John Whalley, eds. *The Economic Impacts of Tax Reform*, Canadian Tax Paper No. 84 (Toronto: Canadian Tax Foundation, 1989) at 55.

Whatever the arguments for and against alternative conceptions of the appropriate income tax base, the federal government appears to have accepted the argument that these deductions constitute inequitable subsidies. In 1988, it repealed a number of provisions permitting the deduction of personal amounts in computing an individual's taxable income,[226] converting these deductions into non-refundable credits computed at the lowest marginal rate.[227] Although the 1987 white paper in which these amendments were announced declared that they would enhance the equity of the income tax by providing "the same reduction of tax to all taxpayers, regardless of their level of income",[228] the document said nothing about the concept of the income tax base on which this view of tax equity relied. As a result, as two critics have explained:

> [t]his argument is not totally convincing, since it assumes what is to be proved — namely that assessed gross income is the equitable tax base. One can argue with equal plausibility that gross income net of certain exemptions and deductions yields a better approximation of "true" income than does gross income alone. According to the latter view, exemptions and deductions are not "upside-down" subsidies but rather adjustments in gross income made in order to refine the tax base. Thus certain exemptions and deductions may be regarded as surrogates for the minimum costs required to cover the basic necessities of life. Given this conclusion, these essential costs should be removed, along with the costs of earning income, from total income in arriving at taxable income.[229]

More sceptically, these critics have suggested that the conversion of what were deductions in computing taxable income into non-refundable credits against basic federal tax payable may have been "a disguised way of moving the marginal rate schedule upward" in order to offset reductions in the "official" tax rates that accompanied the 1988 reforms.[230] As Table 6 demonstrates, where taxpayers are subject to progressive rates of 17 per cent on taxable income up to $27,500, 26 per cent on taxable income between $27,500 and $55,000, and 29 per cent on taxable income exceeding $55,000 (the rate structure introduced in 1988), the conversion of a $6,000 deduction to a $6,000 non-refundable credit computed at the lowest marginal rate (the amount of the "single status" credit

---

[226] See former s. 109, permitting a deduction for basic living expenses as well as the cost of supporting a cohabiting spouse and dependant children; former para. 110(1)(c), allowing a deduction for uninsured medical expenses; and former paras. 110(1)(c), (e.1), and (e.2), providing for mental or physical impairment.

[227] See s. 118 of the Act (personal tax credits), s. 118.2 (medical expenses tax credit), and ss. 118.3 and 118.4 (disability tax credit). A notable exception to this pattern is the deduction in s. 110.7, which accounts for higher living costs in northern Canada by allowing northern residents to claim a deduction in computing taxable income. Enacted in 1987, this deduction was not converted to a non-refundable credit in 1988.

[228] Department of Finance, *Tax Reform 1987: Income Tax Reform* (Ottawa: Department of Finance, June 18, 1987).

[229] A. Pierre Cloutier and Bernard Fortin, "Converting Exemptions and Deductions into Credits: An Economic Assessment" in Jack M. Mintz and John Whalley, eds. *The Economic Impacts of Tax Reform*, Canadian Tax Paper No. 84 (Toronto: Canadian Tax Foundation, 1989) at 71-72.

[230] *Ibid.*, at 72-73.

introduced in 1988) produces a hidden reduction in the income brackets to which the rates apply by the amount of the deduction/credit.

Table 6: Conversion of Deductions to Non-Refundable Credits

Taxable income	Statutory rates	Income ranges to which rates apply	
		With $6,000 deduction	*With $6,000 credit*
$0-$27,500	17%	$ 6,000-$33,500	$ 6,000-$27,500
$27,500-$55,000	26%	$33,500-$61,000	$27,500-$55,000
Over $55,000	29%	Over $61,000	Over $55,000

While the conversion of a deduction that is available to all taxpayers into such a non-refundable credit affects all taxpayers and does not shift the tax burden among different taxpayers, the conversion of a deduction that is available only to some taxpayers (for example, for medical expenses or the costs of supporting a dependent child) affects only their taxes, thereby increasing the relative burden of taxpayers who find themselves in these circumstances as compared with other taxpayers. Perhaps not surprisingly, therefore, commentators continue to debate the merits of the conversion of many of these deductions to non-refundable credits in 1988.[231]

In contrast to these continuing debates over the merits of deductions versus credits for personal expenses, deductions are generally regarded as an inequitable way to pursue policy goals other than the accurate measurement of income.[232] Notwithstanding this concern, however, the Canadian income tax continues to permit deductions to encourage specific kinds of behaviour such as saving for retirement and the growth of small businesses.[233] Although deductions for retirement savings, which are eventually taxed when received as benefits out of the retirement fund, may be justified as an exception to the annual accounting period generally used to compute taxable income and

---

[231] See, for example, Kenneth J. Boessenkool & James B. Davies, "Giving Mom and Dad a Break: Returning Fairness to Families in Canada's Tax and Transfer System" Commentary 117 (Toronto: C.D. Howe Institute, November 1998); and David G. Duff, "Disability and the Income Tax" (2000) 45 McGill L.J. 797.

[232] See Stanley S. Surrey and Paul R. McDaniel, *Tax Expenditures* (Cambridge, MA: Harvard University Press, 1985).

[233] See, for example, the deduction of contributions to a registered retirement pension plan under para. 60(i) and subs. 146(5) of the Act, and the cumulative lifetime deduction in subs. 110.6(2.1) for up to $500,000 of capital gains from the disposition of shares of a "qualified small business corporation."

therefore a means for measuring income over a longer period of time,[234] the deduction in subsection 110.6(2.1) for up to $750,000 of capital gains realized during an individual's lifetime on the disposition of shares of a qualified small business corporation is deliberately designed to encourage the growth of these kinds of enterprises. To the extent that this deduction is worth more to high-income taxpayers than it is to low-income taxpayers, therefore, it is justifiably criticized as an "upside-down" subsidy.[235]

In addition to these provisions, former paragraphs 110(1)(a) and (b) of the Act used to permit a deduction for charitable contributions and gifts to the Crown in computing an individual's taxable income. Concluding that this kind of tax incentive favoured charitable giving by high-income taxpayers, the federal government repealed these deductions in 1988, introducing in their place a non-refundable credit for these kinds of gifts in section 118.1 of the Act. Unlike other non-refundable credits, which are computed at the lowest marginal rate (15 per cent for 2008), the credit for these gifts is computed at the lowest marginal rate for the first $200 claimed in the year, and 29 per cent for annual contributions exceeding $200.[236] Although this "two-tier" credit appears to be more equitable than a deduction, empirical analysis suggests that the distributional impact of the credit differs little from a deduction, since low-income claimants are less likely to exceed the $200 threshold, while average contributions by high-income claimants greatly exceed this amount.[237]

3. Exemptions

Although deductions and exemptions both reduce the amount of a taxpayer's taxable income, the former operate by way of subtractions from income otherwise determined, while the latter are excluded at the outset. Conventionally, however, the word "exemption" is often applied to deductions and credits as well as exclusions, where the effect of these provisions is to

---

[234] See, for example, Neil Bruce, "Ability to Pay and Comprehensive Income Taxation: Annual or Lifetime Basis?" in W. Neil Brooks, ed., *The Quest for Tax Reform: The Royal Commission on Taxation Twenty Years Later* (Toronto: Carswell, 1988) at 157. In a related argument, deductions for retirement savings are also supported on the basis that the "income tax" is better viewed as a "hybrid" income-consumption tax. See, for example, Edward McCaffery, "Tax Policy Under a Hybrid Income-Consumption Tax" (1992) 70 Tex. L. Rev. 1145. For a critical evaluation of these provisions as tax expenditures, see Barbara Austin, "Policies, Preferences, and Perversions in the Tax-Assisted Retirement Savings System" (1996) 41 McGill L. J. 571.

[235] For a critical analysis of this provision, see Jack Mintz & Stephen R. Richardson, eds., "Symposium: The Canadian Experience of the Lifetime Capital Gains Exemption" (1995) 21 Can. Pub. Pol'y S1-S241.

[236] See the formula in subs. 118.1(3) of the Act.

[237] See David G. Duff, "Charitable Contributions and the Personal Income Tax: Evaluating the Canadian Credit," in Jim Phillips, Bruce Chapman & David Stevens, eds., *Between State and Market: Essays on Charities Law and Policy in Canada* (Montreal and Kingston: Queen's University Press, 2001) 407 at 419.

exclude certain kinds or amounts of income from tax. On this broad definition, the *Income Tax Act* contains many exemptions, though these are much less numerous than the various inclusions and deductions discussed earlier.

As with the many deductions contained in the Act, some of these exemptions apply to the computation of a taxpayer's income or loss from a specific source or to the computation of a taxpayer's taxable capital gains. Subsection 6(16) of the Act, for example, exempts various disability-related employment benefits, while subsection 6(6) exempts reasonable allowances for board and lodging at and transportation to and from a special or remote work site, and subsection 6(20) exempts the first $15,000 and half of any amount exceeding this threshold that is paid to the taxpayer in respect of an "eligible housing loss".[238] Similarly, subparagraph 39(1)(a)(i.1) of the Act exempts all capital gains on gifts of certain cultural property to designated institutions, while paragraph 40(2)(b) exempts gains on the disposition of a taxpayer's "principal residence" and subsection 39(2) exempts the first $200 of an individual's capital gains for a taxation year from the disposition of foreign currencies.[239] More generally, paragraph 38(a) exempts one-half of all capital gains by defining the "taxable" portion of a taxpayer's capital gain for a taxation year from the disposition of any property as "½ of the taxpayer's capital gain for the year from the disposition of the property," while paragraphs 38(a.1) and (a.2) exempt capital gains on specified gifts of publicly traded shares and ecological properties by stipulating that the taxpayer's capital gain for the year from these kinds of dispositions is "equal to zero".[240]

Other exemptions take the form of deductions in computing a taxpayer's taxable income, or non-refundable credits in computing the taxpayer's tax payable. Paragraph 110(1)(d) of the Act, for example, exempts half the amount otherwise included as a taxable benefit under section 7 in respect of certain employee stock options, equating the taxation of these employment benefits to the taxation of capital gains, while paragraph 110(1)(j) exempts any deemed interest on the first $25,000 of a "home relocation loan" that would otherwise be included in respect of an interest-free or low-interest loan provided by the taxpayer's employer under section 80.4.[241] Similarly, section 110.6 exempts the first $750,000 of all capital gains realized during an individual's lifetime on the disposition of "qualified farm property" or the shares of a "qualified small business corporation",[242] while paragraph 110(1)(f) effectively exempts all

---

[238] These provisions are discussed in Chapter 4.

[239] These provisions are examined or discussed in Chapter 6.

[240] These provisions are discussed in Chapter 6.

[241] These provisions are discussed in Chapter 4.

[242] See subs. 110.6(2) and (2.1) of the Act. This deduction was enacted effective for 1985 and subsequent taxation years, though the amount of the deduction was phased in between 1985 and 1990. For taxation years prior to 1996, this deduction also applied to the first $100,000 of a taxpayer's lifetime capital gains realized from the disposition of most other kinds of property. See subs. 110.6(3). This general deduction was repealed in 1995.

social assistance and workers' compensation payments by permitting taxpayers to deduct "any social assistance payment made on the basis of a means, needs or income test" that is otherwise included in computing the taxpayer's income for the year, and "any amount that is ... compensation received under an employees' or workers' compensation law of Canada or a province in respect of an injury, disability or death" that is otherwise included in computing the taxpayer's income for the year under paragraph 56(1)(v).[243] In addition to these deductions, the non-refundable credits in section 118 of the Act are often characterized as "personal exemptions" because they operate to exempt a basic amount of income from tax.

More particularly, the Act lists a number of explicit exemptions that are specifically excluded in computing a taxpayer's income for a taxation year under section 81, which constitutes subdivision g of Division B of Part I of the Act. Some of these exemptions relate to various kinds of expense allowances: for members of a provincial legislature, for certain officers of municipalities, municipal boards, or school boards, and for certain kinds of travel expenses (subsections 81(2), (3), and (3.1), respectively). Others relate to payments made under specific government programs, for example, pensions related to wartime service (paragraphs 81(1)(d) and (e)), payments in respect of death or injury sustained in the Halifax explosion of 1917 (paragraph 81(1)(f)), and compensation paid by the Federal Republic of Germany to victims of Nazi persecution (paragraph 81(1)(g)). Paragraphs 81(1)(g.1) and (g.2) exempt income and capital gains from the disposition of property acquired as damages in respect of physical or mental injury for taxation years in which the injured person was 21 years of age or younger.[244] Finally, paragraph 81(1)(a) exempts amounts that are "declared to be exempt from income tax by any other enactment of Parliament."[245] Together with section 87 of the *Indian Act*, R.S.C. 1985, c. I-5,[246] this provision has been relied on to exempt the income of an

---

[243] These provisions are discussed in Chapter 7.

[244] See also subs. 81(5), which permits the injured person described in para. 81(1)(g.1) to "step up" the cost base of capital property acquired as damages in respect of physical or mental injury upon attaining the age of 21. On this basis, capital gains that have accrued during taxation years when the injured person was less than 21 years of age are not subject to tax once that person reaches the age of 21.

[245] This provision goes on to exclude from the scope of this exemption "an amount received or receivable by an individual that is exempt by virtue of a provision contained in a tax convention or agreement with another country that has the force of law in Canada." While these payments are included in computing net income, they are deductible in computing taxable income under subpara. 110(1)(f)(i) of the Act. While this deduction offsets the inclusion for the purposes of computing tax payable under subs. 117(2), the inclusion of these amounts in net income may affect the amount of tax credits that may be claimed under s. 118.1 of the Act (credit for charitable gifts) or s. 118.2 (medical expenses tax credit).

[246] According to s. 87(1)(b) of this statute: "Notwithstanding any other Act of Parliament or any Act of the legislature of a province ... the following property is exempt from taxation, namely, ... the personal property of an Indian or a band situated on a reserve." According to s. 87(2): "No

"Indian" or "band" (within the meaning of the *Indian Act)* where the income is connected in a meaningful sense to a reserve.[247]

As with the many deductions considered earlier, these exemptions fulfill a number of different policy goals. In some cases, the exemption concerns a benefit or allowance that may confer little in the way of any material advantage and merely offsets costs that the taxpayer might otherwise be required to incur in order to fulfill the duties of an office or employment or to obtain income from another source.[248] In other cases, such as the non-refundable tax credits in section 118, exemptions account for differences in personal circumstances. Yet other exemptions provide selective relief to taxpayers receiving specific kinds of income such as social assistance and compensation for workplace and other injuries. Finally, paragraph 81(1)(a) and the *Indian Act* arguably recognize the jurisdictional autonomy of Canada's First Nations, while other exemptions create incentives for specific kinds of behaviour, like home ownership,[249] employee stock ownership,[250] investments in capital property,[251] and contributions of certain kinds of property to designated organizations.[252]

Except for the jurisdictional considerations applicable to the aboriginal tax exemption, the tax policy considerations relevant to these different exemptions are generally similar to those for deductions in computing a taxpayer's income or taxable income. Where exemptions are designed to provide an accurate measurement of each taxpayer's income by excluding amounts that confer little or no material advantage, they would appear to be relatively uncontroversial. Conversely, where exemptions are designed to refine this measure by accounting for personal circumstances, the appropriate form of the exemption (exclusion, deduction, or credit) remains a matter of considerable debate. Finally, where exemptions relieve taxpayers receiving specific kinds of income or function as tax incentives by excluding specific amounts from income, they

---

Indian or band is subject to taxation in respect of the ownership, occupation, possession or use of any property mentioned in para. (1)(a) or (b) or is otherwise subject to taxation in respect of any such property."

[247] See *R. v. Nowegijick*, [1983] S.C.J. No. 5, [1983] C.T.C. 20, 83 D.T.C. 5041 (S.C.C.); and *Williams v. M.N.R.*, [1992] S.C.J. No. 36, [1992] 1 C.T.C. 225, 92 D.T.C. 6320 (S.C.C.).

[248] Examples might be the exemption for reasonable allowances for board and lodging at and transportation to and from a special or remote work site in subs. 6(6) of the Act; the exemption for disability-related employment benefits in subs. 6(16); the limited exemption in respect of an "eligible housing loss" in subs. 6(20): the deduction for deemed interest in respect of a home relocation loan in para. 110(1)(j); and the exempt allowances in subs. 81(2), (3), and (3.1).

[249] See para. 40(2)(b) of the Act (principal residence exemption).

[250] See para. 110(1)(d) of the Act (deduction for employee stock options).

[251] See ss. 38 (exemption for half of all capital gains) and 110.6 (lifetime capital gains deduction for dispositions of qualifying farm property and shares of a qualified small business corporation).

[252] See paras. 38(a.1) and (a.2) of the Act (three-quarters exemption on capital gains arising from gifts of publicly traded shares and ecological property) and subpara. 39(1)(a)(i.1) (full exemption on capital gains arising from gifts of cultural property).

are subject to the same equity concerns regarding the use of deductions for these purposes — that they favour high-income taxpayers over low-income taxpayers by conferring greater tax savings on the former than the latter. Although an exemption for social assistance payments might be justified as part of a combined "tax and transfer" system in which it would be irrational for governments to transfer and simultaneously tax payments that are "made on the basis of a means, needs or income test",[253] the same cannot be said of workers' compensation and other kinds of injury compensation that may be received by high-income taxpayers as well as low-income taxpayers. Indeed, where these kinds of compensation are not subject to tax, those who would otherwise be required to pay sufficient compensation to cover applicable taxes receive an implicit subsidy equal to the amount of the forgone tax revenue.

C. Accounting Period

According to subsection 2(1) of the Act, an income tax shall be paid on "the taxable income *for each taxation year* of every person resident in Canada at any time of the year" (emphasis added). Likewise, subsection 2(2) defines the "taxable income of a taxpayer *for a taxation year*" as "the taxpayer's income *for the year* plus the additions and minus the deductions permitted by Division C", while section 3 defines the "income of a taxpayer *for a taxation year*" by reference to various amounts determined "*for the year*" (emphasis added). As explained earlier, these provisions define the basic accounting period of the income tax as a "taxation year." The following discussion considers the meaning of this term, the implications of this annual accounting period for computing a taxpayer's income, and various other accounting periods that the *Income Tax Act* uses for specific purposes.

1. Taxation Year

The term "taxation year" is defined in subsection 249(1) of the Act, which stipulates for the purposes of the Act that a "taxation year" is a "fiscal period" in the case of a corporation and a "calendar year" in the case of an individual. In addition, subject to sections 34.1 and 34.2 (with which we need not concern ourselves here),[254] subsection 11(1) states that "where an individual is a proprietor of a business, the individual's income from the business for a taxation year is deemed to be the individual's income from the business for the fiscal periods of the business that end in the year." Thus, while the basic accounting

---

[253] See the language of para. 56(1)(u) of the Act, which applies to social assistance payments "made on the basis of a means, needs or income test."

[254] Section 34.1 contains a complicated set of rules applicable to an individual who elects under subs. 249.1(4) to maintain a fiscal period that does not coincide with a calendar year. Section 34.2 is a transitional rule related to the introduction of s. 249.1, which came into effect in 1995.

period for an individual is a "calendar year," the basic accounting period for a corporation and a business is a "fiscal period".

Although the *Income Tax Act* does not define the term "calendar year", paragraph 37(1)(a) of the federal *Interpretation Act*, R.S.C. 1985, c. I-21, as amended, defines a "calendar year" as "a period of twelve consecutive months commencing on January 1". The term "fiscal period" is subject to a detailed statutory definition in section 249.1. This provision, which came into effect in 1995, replaced the former definition in subsection 248(1) of the Act, according to which a fiscal period was defined as:

> the period for which the accounts of the business of the taxpayer have been ordinarily made up and accepted for purposes of assessment under this Act and, in the absence of an established practice, the fiscal period is that adopted by the taxpayer, but no fiscal period may exceed
>
> (a)   in the case of a corporation, 53 weeks, and
>
> (b)   in the case of any other taxpayer, 12 months,
>
> and no change in a usual and accepted fiscal period may be made for the purposes of this Act without the concurrence of the Minister.

Thus, the former rule allowed corporations and individuals with business income to select their own accounting period, subject to the requirements that this period be consistent from one year to the next (subject to change with the concurrence of the Minister) and that it not exceed 53 weeks in the case of a corporation or 12 months in the case of any other taxpayer. The different period for corporations was intended to provide a degree of flexibility for corporate taxpayers to select a convenient year-end (for example, the fourth Friday in March) without having to adjust this day to conform to the requirements of the calendar.

Since corporations are required to remit tax on a monthly basis, the ability of a corporation to select a fiscal period that does not coincide with a calendar year is generally of little consequence. In the case of an individual taxpayer, however, the ability to select an "off-calendar" fiscal period for the purpose of subsection 11(1) used to permit a taxpayer with income from a business to postpone tax on that income by selecting a fiscal period for that business ending in the following calendar year. By selecting January 31 as the year end of the business, for example, the income of the business from February 1 to December 31 would, under subsection 11(1), not be included in the taxpayer's income until the following calendar year.

Effective for 1995 and subsequent taxation years, the ability of a taxpayer to defer income from a business in this way was ended by the enactment of section 249.1 of the Act, which adds to the restrictions on the choice of a fiscal period in the former definition the further requirement in paragraph 249.1(1)(b) that in the case of most individuals and partnerships no fiscal period may end after the end of the calendar year in which the period began.[255] Paragraphs 249.1(1)(a) and (c) reproduce the limitations in the former definition of the term "fiscal period", while subsection 249.1(7) reproduces the prohibition against any change in a fiscal period without the concurrence of the Minister.

Where a taxation year is referred to by reference to a calendar year, subsection 249(1) of the Act also stipulates that "the reference is to the taxation year or years coinciding with, or ending in, that year". Similarly, subsection 11(2) stipulates that where an individual's income for a taxation year includes income from a business the fiscal period of which does not coincide with the calendar year, references to the words taxation year or year indicate the fiscal period of the business ending in the year. As a result, for a corporation or a business with an "off-calendar" fiscal period, the 2008 taxation year refers to one or more fiscal periods ending between January 1 and December 31, 2008. In the case of an individual, the 2008 taxation year refers to the period from January 1 to December 31, 2008.

2. Implications

Although it is customary to think of accounting in terms of annual periods, there is no necessary reason why this period as opposed to any other should have been selected as the basis for computing a taxpayer's income. Nonetheless, originating in the experience of an annual harvest, annual accounting has a long history in western culture and appears to provide a convenient and administratively manageable period over which to measure a taxpayer's ability to pay tax.

Regardless of the rationale for this basic accounting period, it has three important implications for the operation of the income tax. First, if tax is to be based on each taxpayer's income for each taxation year, returns must be filed and tax paid on an annual basis.[256] Second, as the amendments to the definition of the term "fiscal period" suggest, the division of what is often a continuous flow of income into discrete yearly periods creates incentives for taxpayers to postpone the payment of tax by attempting to delay the recognition of income to subsequent taxation years or accelerating the recognition of deductions or credits to the current taxation year.[257] Not surprisingly, therefore, the *Income Tax Act* contains numerous timing rules governing the accounting period in which amounts must be included or may be deducted in computing a taxpayer's

---

[255] Under certain circumstances, taxpayers to whom para. 249.1(1)(b) would otherwise apply may elect to retain an "off-calendar fiscal period" under subs. 249.1(4), in which case they are subject to the special rule in s. 34.1. This book does not examine the election, nor the rules in s. 34.1.

[256] See Peter W. Hogg, Joanne E. Magee & Jinyan Li, *Principles of Canadian Income Tax Law*, 6th ed. (Toronto: Thomson Carswell, 2007) at 555-58 ("Filing of Tax Returns" and "Payment of Tax").

[257] See *ibid.*, at 28-30 ("Tax Value of Money" and "Tax Deferral").

income for a taxation year.[258] Third, where income is subject to tax at graduated rates, as in Canada, an annual accounting period may cause relative hardship to taxpayers whose income fluctuates and "bunches" in single years compared with a taxpayer whose income is more consistent from year to year.[259]

3. Other Accounting Periods

Despite the annual accounting period that serves as the basic period for computing a taxpayer's income, the *Income Tax Act* has often allowed and continues to permit certain other accounting periods for specific purposes. Former section 119, for example, allowed individuals whose "chief source of income has been farming or fishing for a taxation year ... and the 4 immediately preceding years for which the individual has filed returns" to compute their tax payable by "block averaging" their taxable income over a five-year period. (Former section 119 was repealed and replaced with a different rule by S.C. 2001, c. 17, section 102(1), applicable to 1995 and subsequent taxation years.) Before 1988, the Act permitted individual taxpayers to engage in a limited form of "forward averaging" by which they could, under specific circumstances, postpone recognition of certain amounts by acquiring an "income-averaging annuity contract".[260] A different kind of forward averaging is still possible under various retirement savings provisions of the Act, which permit taxpayers to deduct specific amounts contributed to registered savings plans, which are subject to tax only upon withdrawal.[261] Although often characterized as tax expenditures,[262] these provisions also create a longer lifetime accounting period for income that is saved for retirement.

In addition to these provisions, section 111 of the Act establishes yet another kind of accounting period by allowing taxpayers to "carry over" unutilized losses from other taxation years to be deducted in computing a taxpayer's taxable income. For this purpose, as in section 3, the Act distinguishes between unutilized allowable capital losses, which are generally deductible only against net taxable capital gains in the taxation year to which the loss is carried over, and other unutilized losses that are fully deductible in computing the taxpayer's taxable income for the taxation year to which the loss is carried over. Under

---

[258] See the brief discussion of various timing rules in Chapter 3, and the more lengthy examinations of timing issues in Chapters 4 and 5. See also the section on recognition and non-recognition rules in Chapter 6.

[259] See Peter W. Hogg, Joanne E. Magee & Jinyan Li, *Principles of Canadian Income Tax Law*, 6th ed. (Toronto: Thomson Carswell, 2007) at 20 ("Income Fluctuation").

[260] See former s. 110.4 of the Act, current ss. 61 and 61.1, and current paras. 56(1)(e) and (f). For a brief discussion of income averaging, see Hogg, Magee, and Li, *ibid.*, at 20.

[261] For a useful overview of these provisions, see Hogg, Magee, and Li, *ibid.*, at 376-89 ("Tax-Assisted Private Pension Plans"). These provisions are discussed in Chapter 7.

[262] See, for example, Barbara Austin, "Policies, Preferences, and Perversions in the Tax-Assisted Retirement Savings System" (1996) 41 McGill L. J. 571.

subsection 111(8), the former losses are defined as "net capital losses" while the latter are defined as "non-capital losses".[263]

According to paragraph 111(1)(a) of the Act, for the purpose of computing a taxpayer's taxable income for a taxation year, the taxpayer may deduct "such portion as the taxpayer may claim" of the taxpayer's "non-capital losses" for "the 20 taxation years immediately preceding and the 3 taxation years immediately following the year". In other words, a non-capital loss may be carried forward for 20 taxation years or back for 3 taxation years — establishing a 24-year accounting period. Under paragraph 111(1)(b), a taxpayer may deduct net capital losses from any taxation year preceding the taxation year and from the 3 taxation years immediately following the taxation year. As a result, net capital losses may be carried back for 3 taxation years and carried forward indefinitely.[264]

The preamble to subsection 111(1) states that for the purpose of computing a taxpayer's taxable income for a taxation year, "such portion as the taxpayer may claim" may be deducted. As a result, subject to certain restrictions expressed in other provisions of section 111, taxpayers are free to allocate these losses to taxation years for which they obtain the greatest tax benefit. The key restrictions are contained in subsections 111(3) and (1.1). Paragraph 111(3)(b) sets out an ordering rule whereby taxpayers must deduct losses from earlier taxation years before deducting losses from any particular taxation year. Paragraph 111(3)(a) provides that taxpayers can deduct losses from other taxation years only to the extent that they have not already been deducted in previous taxation years. In general, subsection 111(1.1) permits net capital losses to be deducted only against net taxable capital gains for a taxation year as determined under paragraph 3(b). Subsection 111(2), however, allows taxpayers to deduct net capital losses against income from all sources in the year of death or the immediately preceding taxation year.

Thus, while non-capital losses can be deducted against income from all sources, this deduction is generally limited to a 24-year period comprising the previous 3 taxation years (a 3-year "carryback") and the following 20 taxation years (a 20-year "carryforward"), except where the non-capital loss is an allowable business investment loss, in which case the loss converts to a net capital loss after 10 years. While net capital losses may be carried forward indefinitely (and carried back 3 taxation years), they are generally deductible only against net taxable capital gains for a taxation year, except in the taxpayer's year of death and the immediately preceding taxation year, in which case they are deductible against income from all sources.

---

[263] Section 111 also allows for the carryover of "farm losses," "restricted farm losses," and "limited partnership losses." For the purposes of this chapter, there is no need to examine these losses in detail.

[264] By virtue of item C in the definition of "net capital loss" in subs. 111(8), allowable business investment losses, which are otherwise included in computing a taxpayer's non-capital loss, are included in the taxpayer's net capital loss after ten years.

D. Tax Rates

The rates of tax for a personal income tax are among the most controversial topics in the design of the tax, affecting in a direct and relatively transparent way the distribution of the tax burden among taxpayers in different income groups. While the choice of the tax unit, tax base, and accounting period concerns the manner in which the tax burden is distributed among similarly situated taxpayers, the selection of rates and rate structures determine the manner in which these burdens are distributed among taxpayers who are differently situated. The former questions are generally described as matters of horizontal equity; the latter concern vertical equity.

In Canada and other developed countries, personal income taxes have traditionally been applied at graduated or progressive rates above basic exemptions excluding minimum amounts of income from tax. Over the last two decades, however, these countries have generally reduced both the number of rates and the gap between the highest and lowest rates. In 1970, for example, the Canadian *Income Tax Act* contained 17 rates ranging from 11 per cent on taxable income up to $1,000 to 80 per cent on taxable income exceeding $400,000.[265] For the 2008 taxation year, the Act contains four statutory rates, ranging from 15 per cent on taxable income up to $37,885 to 29 per cent on taxable income exceeding $123,184.[266]

In recent years, moreover, critics of progressive income taxation have advocated so-called flat taxes under which income would be taxed at a single rate above a basic exemption.[267] Indeed, with changes to the federal-provincial tax collection agreements allowing provinces to levy their income taxes as a percentage of taxable income instead of basic federal tax payable,[268] Alberta

---

[265] See subs. 32(1) of the 1952 Act as it read in 1970.

[266] See subs. 117(2) of the Act. For taxation years after 2001, these rate brackets have been indexed for inflation by s. 117.1.

[267] See for example, Robert E. Hall and Alvin Rabushka, *The Flat Tax*, 2d ed. (Stanford: Hoover Institution Press, 1995); Michael Walker, *On Flat-Rate Tax Proposals* (Vancouver: Fraser Institute, 1983); and Patrick Basham and Jason Clemens, *Flat Tax: Principles and Issues* (Vancouver: Fraser Institute, 2001). See also the Canadian Alliance party's January 2000 proposal to enact a single rate tax of 17 per cent with increased personal and spousal exemptions of $10,000 and a $3,000 exemption for each dependent child: Canadian Alliance, *Solution 17* (Calgary: Canadian Alliance, January 2000).

[268] For a detailed discussion of these agreements and the process leading to their negotiation, see Ernest H. Smith, *Federal-Provincial Tax Sharing and Centralized Tax Collection in Canada*, Special Studies in Taxation and Public Finance No. 1 (Toronto: Canadian Tax Foundation, 1998) at Chapters 9-12. Until 1998, these agreements generally required provincial governments to levy their income taxes as a fixed percentage of basic federal tax payable, the effect of which was to cause participating provinces to "piggyback" on the federal rate structure and federal non-refundable credits, as well as accept the federal definition of taxable income, the annual accounting period, and the individual tax unit. Under a new set of guidelines adopted in 1998, provincial income taxes may be based on the federal definition of taxable income, permitting provinces much greater flexibility to establish their own rate structures and their own credits.

introduced a single rate income tax in 2001, which applies at a flat rate of 10 per cent above personal exemptions for 2008 of $16,161 for each taxpayer and $16,161 for each spouse or common law partner.[269] In order to evaluate this and other possible reforms to the structure of income tax rates in Canada, it is necessary to consider the arguments for and against progressive personal income taxation, and the manner in which a progressive rate structure may be designed.

While this introductory chapter cannot provide a comprehensive analysis of the arguments for and against progressive income taxation,[270] it is not surprising that differing views on this subject, like those regarding the choice of the tax unit, turn on underlying disagreements over the purposes of the income tax, and the effects of different rate structures on social and economic behaviour. Advocates of progressivity, for example, tend to question the distributive justice of pre-tax incomes, emphasizing the redistributive function of the income tax to moderate inequalities resulting from the operation of the market economy.[271]

See Canada, Department of Finance and Canada Customs and Revenue Agency, *Federal Administration of Provincial Taxes: New Directions* (January 2000). For useful discussions of the causes of and policy issues surrounding these changes, see Munir A. Sheikh and Michel Carreau, "A Federal Perspective on the Role and Operation of the Tax Collection Agreements" (1999) 47 Can. Tax J. 845; Thomas J. Courchene, "National Versus Regional Concerns: A Provincial Perspective on the Role and Operation of the Tax Collection Agreements" (1999) 47 Can. Tax J. 861; and Alan Macnaughton, "Compliance and Administration Issues Under the Tax Collection Agreements" (1999) 47 Can. Tax J. 890.

[269] These amendments were originally announced in the 1999 Alberta budget, which proposed a single rate of 11 per cent and exemptions of $11,620. See Stockwell Day, "A New Tax Plan for Albertans," Budget 99 Fiscal and Business Plan Documents, March 11, 1999. For an excellent analysis of the Alberta proposals, see Melville L. McMillan, "Alberta's Single-Rate Tax: Some Implications and Alternatives" (2000) 48 Can. Tax J. 1019. Although all other provinces have moved to a tax on taxable income for the year 2001, each of these income taxes is levied at graduated rates, which range from a low of 6.2 to 11.16 per cent in Ontario to a high of 17 to 24.5 per cent in Quebec. In addition, some provinces impose surtaxes that increase the effective rates for high-income taxpayers. In Ontario, for example, high-income surtaxes of 20 and 36 per cent increase the effective top marginal rate from 11.16 to 17.41 per cent, which is higher than the top marginal rate in most other provinces.

[270] For an excellent overview of some of the key philosophical issues in the debate, see Donna M. Byrne, "Progressive Taxation Revisited" (1995) 37 Ariz. L. Rev. 739. For other notable treatments, see Walter J. Blum and Harry Kalven Jr., *The Uneasy Case for Progressive Taxation*, Midway Reprint (Chicago: University of Chicago Press, 1978); Joseph Bankman and Thomas Griffith, "Social Welfare and the Rate Structure: A New Look at Progressive Taxation" (1987) 75 Cal. L. Rev. 1905; and Lawrence Zelenak and Kemper Moreland, "Can the Graduated Income Tax Survive Optimal Analysis?" (1999) 53 Tax L. Rev. 51. For an excellent review of the many flat-tax proposals in Canada and the United States, see Neil Brooks, "Flattening the Claims of Flat Taxers" (1998) 21 Dal. L. J. 287.

[271] See, for example, Ronald Dworkin, *Sovereign Virtue: The Theory and Practice of Equality* (Massachusetts: Harvard University Press, 2000), Chapter 2; Charles R. O'Kelley, "Rawls, Justice and the Income Tax" (1981) 16 Ga. L. Rev. 1; and Marjorie E. Kornhauser, "The Rhetoric of the Anti-Progressive Income Tax Movement: A Typical Male Reaction" (1987) 86 Mich. L. Rev. 465.

Other arguments emphasize the greater proportionate ability to pay of high-income taxpayers, for whom a larger proportion of income is available for discretionary use, and the stabilization function of the progressive income tax, which collects proportionately more or less revenue as economic activity increases or decreases.[272] Flat-tax advocates, on the other hand, generally question the redistributive function of the income tax, challenging the implications of this redistribution for prevailing notions of private property,[273] and questioning the fiscal accountability of a tax designed to fall disproportionately on a minority of high-income taxpayers.[274] In addition, critics of progressive taxation tend to argue that graduated rates discourage work effort, risk taking, and savings; encourage tax avoidance and evasion; and increase the complexity of the income tax and its administration.[275]

While disagreements regarding the redistributive role of the income tax reflect philosophical outlooks with respect to which reasonable people may differ, arguments about the social and economic impacts of progressivity are empirical matters for which empirical evidence may be examined. In this respect, most studies are sceptical about the allegedly deleterious effects of progressive income tax rates.[276] While exceptionally high marginal tax rates such as the 80 per cent rate that the Canadian income tax once applied to taxable income exceeding $400,000 might be expected to affect economic behaviour, discouraging productive activities and encouraging unproductive avoidance and evasion, these results are attributable to the percentage rate itself, not the rate structure.

Likewise, while a progressive rate structure may encourage income splitting under an income tax with an individual tax unit, income splitting, which

---

[272] See, for example, *Report of the Royal Commission on Taxation*, 6 vols. (Ottawa: Queen's Printer, 1966), Vol. 3.

[273] See, for example, A. Kenneth Eaton, *Essays in Taxation*, Canadian Tax Paper No. 44 (Toronto: Canadian Tax Foundation, 1966), 27, who argues that progressive taxation is "inconsistent with the concept of private property." See also Walter J. Blum and Harry Kalven Jr., *The Uneasy Case for Progressive Taxation*, Midway Reprint (Chicago: University of Chicago Press, 1978).

[274] See, for example, Ludwig von Mises, *Human Action: A Treatise on Economics* (New Haven, CT: Yale University Press, 1949), 803; and Friedrich Hayek, *The Constitution of Liberty* (Chicago: University of Chicago Press, 1960), 322, who argues that "[i]f a reasonable system of taxation is to be achieved, people must recognize as a principle that the majority which determines what the total amount of taxation should be must also bear it at the maximum rate."

[275] See, for example, Walter J. Blum and Harry Kalven Jr., *The Uneasy Case for Progressive Taxation*, Midway Reprint (Chicago: University of Chicago Press, 1978); A. Kenneth Eaton, *Essays in Taxation*, Canadian Tax Paper No. 44 (Toronto: Canadian Tax Foundation, 1966), 27 at 31–32; Michael Walker, *On Flat-Rate Tax Proposals* (Vancouver: Fraser Institute, 1983) at 38; and Patrick Basham and Jason Clemens, *Flat Tax: Principles and Issues* (Vancouver: Fraser Institute, 2001).

[276] For a useful review of these studies, see Neil Brooks, "Flattening the Claims of Flat Taxers" (1998) 21 Dal. L. J. 287 at 313-69. See also Joseph Bankman and Thomas Griffith, "Social Welfare and the Rate Structure: A New Look at Progressive Taxation" (1987) 75 Cal. L. Rev. 1905.

accounts for a relatively small proportion of tax avoidance, may not be inconsistent with the goals of an individual income tax, and can be addressed by various statutory anti-avoidance rules. (See the discussion under the heading "Tax Unit"). In any event, to the extent that flat taxes include personal exemptions that are not transferable among family members, these taxes can encourage income splitting themselves.[277]

As for the argument that a flat rate will reduce the complexity of the income tax, one can do no better than to cite Professor Brooks's response as follows:

> In spite of the apparent urgency of simplifying the tax system, the proposition that flattening the rates of tax will do so is patent nonsense. None of the difficulties of understanding the Act, the mistakes that professionals make in filing returns, the wrong answers that Revenue Canada [now CRA] agents give in answering taxpayer's questions over the telephone, or headaches involved in filling out a tax return, has to do with applying the tax rates. The section of the Act that sets out the tax rates is one of the most straightforward: it is scarcely a dozen lines. It has not been the subject of any court case or interpretive problems, so far as I am aware. No one has trouble applying the section. Further, once someone's taxable income is calculated on their tax return, a grade three student can calculate the tax owing, no matter how many rates there are. Whether the tax structure has 2 or 87 rates, once taxable income is determined the calculation of tax owing requires only 2 lines on the return.[278]

Since flat taxes with personal exemptions are actually two-rate taxes, with a "zero rate" defined by the personal exemption, this argument suggests that they are no less complex than a progressive income tax with two or more statutory rates.

E. Tax Credits

Unlike deductions, which reduce the amount of income tax payable by a taxpayer by decreasing the taxpayer's income or taxable income, tax credits are subtracted directly from the amount of tax otherwise payable or credited to the taxpayer as a payment of tax, resulting in a reduction of tax otherwise payable or a tax refund where no tax is otherwise owing. Where a credit is subtracted directly from tax otherwise payable, the credit is called a non-refundable credit. Where a credit operates as an overpayment of tax, it is described as refundable.

In computing the amount of tax payable by individuals and corporations, Division E of Part I of the *Income Tax Act* contains numerous tax credits, both non-refundable and refundable. Some of these credits recognize taxes that are paid to another jurisdiction,[279] or assumed to have been paid by a corporation paying taxable dividends.[280] Others apply only to corporate taxpayers,

---

[277] While Alberta's proposed flat tax eliminates incentives for income splitting with spouses by providing a spousal exemption equal to the basic personal exemption, for example, incentives remain to split income with minor children.

[278] Neil Brooks, "Flattening the Claims of Flat Taxers" (1998) 21 Dal. L. J. 287 at 315.

[279] See s. 126 of the Act (foreign tax credit) and subs. 127(1) (logging tax credit).

[280] See s. 121 of the Act.

encouraging specific kinds of enterprises and activities[281] or limiting the combined burden of income and other federal taxes.[282] Yet others apply to all taxpayers, creating incentives for specific kinds of investments,[283] or for making contributions to registered political parties.[284] For the purposes of this chapter, there is no need to consider these credits in detail,[285] except to note the decreasing rate structure of the political contributions credit — a non-refundable credit that, unlike the increasing rates for the charitable contributions credit, is computed at 75 per cent of annual contributions up to $400, 50 per cent for the next $350 contributed in the taxation year, and 33⅓ per cent for the next $525. Consistent with the goals of a democratic society, this credit provides the greatest benefit to small contributions and less support to larger contributions.

In addition to these credits, the Act contains several tax credits that are available only to individuals. Subsection 118(1), for example, contains various "personal credits" that exempt a basic amount of an individual's income from tax by providing non-refundable credits computed at the lowest marginal rate of tax.[286] For disabled individuals, sections 118.3 and 118.4 provide a further non-refundable credit, also computed at the lowest marginal rate, which recognizes additional undocumented living expenses that must be incurred by these taxpayers.[287] A similar rationale explains the age credit in subsection 118(2) of the Act, which is also computed at the lowest marginal rate, though this non-refundable credit is reduced and ultimately eliminated for taxpayers with incomes exceeding $26,941. In addition to these amounts, individuals can claim other non-refundable credits for the first $2,000 of any pension income received in the year,[288] for charitable contributions,[289] for uninsured medical expenses,[290]

---

[281] See s. 124 (provincial abatement), s. 125 (small business deduction), s. 125.1 (deduction for manufacturing and processing profits), s. 125.4 (Canadian film or video production tax credit), and s. 125.5 (film or video production services tax credit).

[282] See ss. 125.2 and 125.3 (credits for capital taxes paid under Parts VI and I.3 of the Act).

[283] See subs. 127(5)-(35) (investment tax credit), s. 127.1 (refundable investment tax credit), and s. 127.4 (labour-sponsored funds tax credit).

[284] See subs. 127(3)-(4.2) of the Act.

[285] Many of these credits are best examined in courses on international taxation or the taxation of corporations and their shareholders.

[286] See the discussion of these credits in the section on recognition of family relationships in this chapter.

[287] For a detailed evaluation of these provisions, see David G. Duff, "Disability and the Income Tax" (2000) 45 McGill L.J. 797 at 823-41.

[288] See subs. 118(3) of the Act.

[289] See s. 118.1 of the Act. For a detailed evaluation of this provision, see David G. Duff, "Charitable Contributions and the Personal Income Tax: Evaluating the Canadian Credit," in Jim Phillips, Bruce Chapman & David Stevens, eds., *Between State and Market: Essays on Charities Law and Policy in Canada* (Montreal and Kingston: Queen's University Press, 2001), 407.

[290] See s. 118.2 of the Act. For a detailed evaluation of this provision, see David G. Duff, "Disability and the Income Tax" (2000) 45 McGill L.J. 797 at 809-23.

for tuition fees and other education expenses,[291] and for EI premiums and CPP/QPP contributions.[292] Although the rate of the charitable contributions credit increases for annual contributions exceeding $200, the other non-refundable credits available to individuals are computed at the lowest marginal rate.

Finally, the Act contains three refundable credits for individuals, which deem individuals to have made a payment or overpayment of tax under certain circumstances. The so-called GST credit in section 122.5, which was enacted when the federal Goods and Services Tax (GST) was introduced in 1990, provides a quarterly payment to low-income taxpayers to offset the impact of the GST. The refundable medical expense supplement in section 122.51, on the other hand, reimburses 25 per cent of uninsured medical expenses incurred by low-income taxpayers, up to a maximum amount of $1,000 per year. Finally, the child tax benefit in sections 122.61 to 122.64 of the Act provides monthly payments to low-income families with dependent children up to an annual amount of approximately $2,800 per child, increased by $2,300 in the case of disabled children.[293] While the refundable medical expense supplement functions as a form of medical insurance for low-income individuals, the GST credit and child tax benefit constitute federal transfer payments delivered through the mechanism of the *Income Tax Act.*

The policy considerations affecting the choice between credits and deductions were discussed earlier in this chapter. While deductions are generally regarded as an appropriate method to obtain an accurate measure of a taxpayer's income, they are widely criticized as an inequitable way to encourage specific kinds of behaviour on the grounds that they benefit high-income taxpayers subject to higher tax rates more than low-income taxpayers subject to lower marginal rates. For this reason, in 1988 the federal government converted most personal exemptions and deductions into non-refundable credits computed at the lowest marginal rate. Although the government did not provide a normative justification for the concept of the income tax base on which its view of tax equity relied, the necessary implication of this policy choice is that these non-refundable credits are properly viewed as tax expenditures that encourage qualifying activities or subsidize eligible taxpayers.

From this perspective, however, while non-refundable credits may be preferable to deductions, they share a basic defect in failing to provide any assistance to persons whose incomes are too low to pay any tax at all. Although a non-refundable tax credit computed at a single rate may have the same value to

---

[291] See s. 118.5 of the Act (tuition credit), s. 118.6 (education amount), s. 118.6(2.1) (textbook credit), s. 118.61 (carry forward of unused tuition and education credits), and s. 118.62 (credit for interest on student loans).

[292] See s. 118.7 of the Act.

[293] For an excellent explanation of the origins and structure of this refundable credit, see Felicity Stairs, "The Canada Child Tax Benefit: Income Support and the Tax System" (1999) 14 J.L. & Soc. Pol'y 123.

high-and low-income taxpayers with tax otherwise payable, it has little or no value to persons whose tax otherwise payable is minimal or non-existent. Not surprisingly, therefore, some commentators favour the conversion of many non-refundable credits into refundable credits that would provide an equal benefit to all persons eligible for the credit, whether or not they are subject to tax.[294]

To the extent that these credits are intended to encourage qualifying activities or subsidize eligible taxpayers, refundability is undoubtedly a more equitable way to provide this assistance.[295] While a non-refundable credit like the foreign tax credit is an appropriate way to recognize income taxes paid to another country without providing any relief in excess of the amount of tax that would otherwise be payable on this income in Canada, incentives and subsidies delivered in the form of non-refundable credits are properly criticized as inequitable kinds of tax expenditures. Where the goal is to achieve an accurate measurement of each taxpayer's income, on the other hand, a non-refundable credit is inferior to a deduction, increasing the effective rates on taxpayers for whom an adjustment in computing income or taxable income is more appropriate. For the most part, therefore, the non-refundable credits contained in Division E of Part I of the Act are an inappropriate hybrid, achieving neither the proper goals of a deduction designed to provide an accurate measurement of each taxpayer's ability to pay, nor an equitable method of encouraging specific activities or subsidizing particular individuals.

IV. EVALUATING INCOME TAX PROVISIONS

The previous section detailed the basic structural elements of any income tax system: each system has to define a unit, base, period, rate, and establish rules governing its administration. These elements comprise what is frequently referred to as the "technical tax system". In evaluating the technical tax system, tax policy analysts generally turn to three criteria: equity, neutrality, and administrability.

The concept of equity has two components: horizontal and vertical equity. Horizontal equity requires that individuals who are similarly situated be treated the same. The difficulty arises in determining when two individuals are similarly situated for tax purposes. The appropriate reference point, given that the income

---

[294] See, for example. Standing Committee on Human Rights and the Status of Disabled Persons, *As True as Taxes: Disability and the Income Tax System*, March 1993, 13-14, recommending the conversion of the non-refundable disability tax credit to a refundable credit. See also David G. Duff, "Charitable Contributions and the Personal Income Tax: Evaluating the Canadian Credit," in Jim Phillips, Bruce Chapman & David Stevens, eds., *Between State and Market: Essays on Charities Law and Policy in Canada* (Montreal and Kingston: Queen's University Press, 2001) at 436, criticizing the non-refundability of the charitable contributions tax credit.

[295] Where this assistance is directed at low-income taxpayers, the amount of the credit can be reduced and eventually eliminated as income increases, as is the case with the refundable GST credit, refundable medical expense supplement, and the refundable child tax credit.

tax is designed to be levied based on taxpayers' incomes, is income. Vertical equity requires that taxpayers with differing incomes be taxed differently. This aspect of the equity criterion draws on the concept of ability to pay. A taxpayer who receives greater income has a greater ability to pay than a taxpayer with lesser income, and therefore the income tax system ought to require the higher-income taxpayer to pay more tax.

A second criterion for judging a good tax system is neutrality. The tax system should not affect people's choices. According to the neutrality criterion, it should be assumed that people make choices that are in their own best interest, and therefore, to the extent possible, their choices should remain after tax what they would be in a world without taxes.

Finally, technical tax systems are regularly evaluated against an administrability criterion. To the extent possible, the tax system should be easy to comply with, the provisions should be difficult to evade, it should be easy for tax administrators to enforce, and so on.

The above evaluative criteria are widely accepted as providing an effective framework for analyzing the technical income tax system; however, tax policy analysts have recognized since at least 1968 that there are a large number of provisions in income tax legislation that have nothing to do with defining the unit, base, period, rate, or administration of the tax based upon the three traditional tax evaluative criteria. In 1967, while working with the United States Treasury Department, Stanley Surrey, a U.S. tax scholar, characterized these provisions as "tax expenditures" since, although they were found in the tax system, they were analogous to government expenditure measures.

The fact that provisions in the tax system can serve as the functional equivalents of direct government spending programs is easy to illustrate. The government might choose, for example, to support and encourage children's physical fitness by agreeing to pick up a percentage of the cost of the fees that parents have to pay to enroll their children in programs involving physical activities. Under a direct spending program, parents who submit their receipts for the fees to the designated government agency would directly receive a cheque for (to illustrate) 25 per cent of the cost (up to some maximum amount). But the government might achieve almost the identical result by providing that parents could claim a tax credit against their tax liability equal to 25 per cent of the eligible fees paid. If a government chooses to deliver the spending program through the tax system, what the government has effectively done is collect the taxes owing by the parent, and then written the parent who has enrolled her child in a physical fitness program a cheque to help offset the costs of that program. These cheques simply cancel each other out, and the government collects less tax from the parent.

Where a provision in the income tax legislation is best understood as a tax expenditure (and the provision may come in the form of a credit, deduction, or exemption), it is usually evaluated using the same criteria we use to evaluate other government spending programs. Tax policy makers first ask what the government objectives are in offering the spending program. They then ask a range of questions related to whether the spending program is effective: is the program target efficient? (*e.g.*, do the intended recipients receive it, and are those who should not receive it excluded from its receipt?); what are the distributional consequences? (*e.g.*, do high- or low-income individuals or families receive more of the benefits? Do some kinds of groups receive greater benefits than other (*i.e.*, women, or disabled individuals, or single individuals) and if so, is that appropriate?); and is the program administrable (*e.g.*, can the government keep track of how much it costs? Is it easy for people who qualify for the spending program to receive it? Does its delivery through the tax system exclude people who should receive it (for low-income people or aboriginal people who may not file tax returns)?).

In the over 40 years since Surrey's articulation of the tax expenditure concept, it has been subject to critique. Scholars have claimed that it is difficult in some cases to distinguish between tax expenditure and technical tax provisions and that the amount spent through tax expenditures is hard to determine, for example. Nevertheless, the conceptual distinction between technical tax provisions and tax expenditures, and the separate articulation of the evaluative criteria that might be used to determine the effectiveness of both the technical tax system and the tax expenditures embedded in income tax legislation have proved enormously helpful in clarifying thinking about the income tax.

CHAPTER TWO

Introduction to Statutory Interpretation

I. INTRODUCTION

As the concept of "income" discussed in Chapter 1 suggests, tax law depends critically on the interpretation of words. In *Commissioner v. Glenshaw Glass Co.*, 348 US 426 (1955), Chief Justice Warren stated that the US Supreme Court had given a "liberal construction" to the "broad phraseology" of the basic charging section of the US income tax Act "in recognition of the intention of Congress to tax all gains except those specifically exempted." In the United Kingdom and Canada, however, the courts generally adopted a much stricter approach to the interpretation of taxing statutes, according to which statutory language was to be construed literally and ambiguities in taxing provisions were to be resolved in the taxpayer's favour.[1] As a result, it followed, the language of the statute was not extended to items not specifically enumerated in the Act.

More recently, however, Canadian courts have broken with this tradition, adopting a more expansive approach to statutory interpretation based less on a literal reading of statutory provisions and more on the objects and intentions pursued through the statutory text. For example, in *Stubart Investments Ltd. v. Canada*, [1984] S.C.J. No. 25, [1984] C.T.C. 294, 84 D.T.C. 6305 (S.C.C.) (at C.T.C. 316), the Supreme Court of Canada affirmed the "modern rule" set out in E.A. Driedger's *Construction of Statutes*, 2d ed. (Toronto: Butterworths, 1983) at 87, according to which "the words of an Act are to be read in their entire context and in their grammatical and ordinary sense harmoniously with the scheme of the Act, the object of the Act, and the intention of Parliament." Since *Stubart* the Supreme Court of Canada has affirmed this approach to statutory interpretation on numerous occasions.[2]

---

[1] Ambiguities in provisions setting out deductions or exemptions, on the other hand, were to be resolved against the taxpayer. Strict construction is examined later in this chapter in Section III.A.

[2] See, *e.g.*, *Antosko v. M.N.R.*, [1994] S.C.J. No. 46 at para. 28, [1994] 2 C.T.C. 25, 94 D.T.C. 6314 (S.C.C.); *Friesen v. Canada*, [1995] S.C.J. No. 71, [1995] 2 C.T.C. 369 at para. 15, 95 D.T.C. 5551 (S.C.C.); *Schwartz v. Canada*, [1996] S.C.J. No. 15, [1996] 1 C.T.C. 303 at para. 74, 96 D.T.C. 6103 (SCC); *65302 British Columbia Ltd. v. Canada*, [1999] S.C.J. No. 69,

This chapter provides an introduction to the interpretation of the *Income Tax Act*, looking at various factors that courts may consider in order to determine the meaning of a statutory provision, key doctrines that Canadian courts have employed in order to interpret the *Income Tax Act*, and specific sources to which Canadian courts refer for this purpose. Section II reviews the different interpretive elements or considerations identified by Driedger and others who have written on the subject of statutory interpretation: the words of the statute, the context in which these words are to be read, the scheme of the Act, statutory purposes, legislative intentions, and the consequences of alternative interpretations.[3] Section III examines the main interpretive doctrines that Canadian courts have employed to interpret the *Income Tax Act*, looking at the strict construction rule that shaped early tax jurisprudence and the so-called modern rule affirmed by the Supreme Court of Canada in *Stubart*.[4] Section IV reviews the specific sources to which Canadian courts refer in order to interpret the *Income Tax Act*.

II. INTERPRETIVE CONSIDERATIONS

In the passage from Driedger's *Construction of Statutes*, five factors are identified as relevant to the interpretation of a statutory provision: the words of the statute, the context in which these words are to be read, the scheme of the statute, the object of the statute, and the intentions of the legislature. In addition to these five factors, courts frequently consider the consequences of alternative interpretations as a further element in the interpretive process. This section reviews each of these considerations and their role in statutory interpretation.

[2000] 1 C.T.C. 57 at para. 50, [1999] 99 D.T.C. 5799 (SCC); *Will-Kare Paving & Contracting Ltd. v. Canada*, [2000] S.C.J. No. 35, [2000] 3 C.T.C. 463 at para. 32, 2000 D.T.C. 6467 (S.C.C.); *Ludmer v. Canada*, [2001] S.C.J. No. 58, [2002] 1 C.T.C. 95 at para. 36, 2001 D.T.C. 5505 (S.C.C.); *Markevich v. Canada*, [2003] S.C.J. No. 8, 2003 D.T.C. 5185 at para. 12 (S.C.C.); and *Canada Trustco Mortgage Co. v. Canada*, [2005] S.C.J. No. 56, [2005] 5 C.T.C. 215, 2005 D.T.C. 5523 (S.C.C.) at para. 10.

3   For more thorough treatments of these interpretive considerations, see Ruth Sullivan, ed., *Driedger on the Construction of Statutes*, 3d ed. (Toronto: LexisNexis Butterworths, 1994); Ruth Sullivan, *Statutory Interpretation* (Concord: Irwin Law, 1997); Pierre-André Côté, *The Interpretation of Legislation in Canada*, 3d ed. (Toronto: Carswell, 2000); and Randal Graham, *Statutory Interpretation: Theory and Practice* (Toronto: Emond Montgomery, 2001).

4   For a more detailed examination of the interpretive doctrines, see David G. Duff, "Interpreting the Income Tax Act — Part 1: Interpretive Doctrines" (1999) Vol. 47 No. 3 Can. Tax J. 464 and David G. Duff, "Interpreting the Income Tax Act — Part 2: Toward a Pragmatic Approach" (1999) Vol. 47 No. 4 Can. Tax J. 741.

A. Words

In order to interpret a statutory text, one must have a text to interpret. As the starting point for statutory interpretation, therefore, it makes sense to look at the words of the statutory text. Indeed, attention to the words of the statute is a basic tenet of statutory interpretation, constraining judicial discretion and reflecting widely held values associated with legislative supremacy and the rule of law. As William Eskridge and Philip Frickey explain:

> Formally, all that is enacted into law is the statutory text, and at the very least legislative supremacy means that an interpreter must be attentive to the text. Functionally, citizens and lawmakers will rely on the apparent meaning of statutory texts. Textual primacy can also be a useful concrete limit on judicial power.[5]

Not surprisingly, therefore, Driedger's "modern rule" begins with the words of the Act.

Words, however, do not speak for themselves — at least not with fixed and certain meanings of universal application. On the contrary, as any dictionary illustrates, words typically have multiple meanings, any one of which is taken on only in the context of particular utterances. To take one obvious example, the word "profit" can mean "bring advantage to" or "be benefited or assisted" when used as a verb, or "advantage, benefit" or "pecuniary gain, excess of returns over outlay" when used as a noun (*Concise Oxford Dictionary*, 7th ed.). In the context of subsection 9(1) of the *Income Tax Act*, which stipulates that "a taxpayer's income ... from a business or property is the taxpayer's profit from that business or property", the grammatical structure of the sentence tells us that the word "profit" is used as a noun, while the provision's role in the context of the income tax favours the definition "pecuniary gain, excess of returns over outlay."

As this example illustrates, the meaning of a particular word cannot be determined in isolation, but depends on the context in which it is employed. As Driedger explains (*Construction of Statutes*, 2d ed. (Toronto: LexisNexis Butterworths, 1983) at 3):

> Words, when read *by themselves* in the abstract can hardly be said to have meanings. A dictionary may give many definitions of a word, but it cannot have a meaning until it is connected with other words or things so as to express an idea.

More generally, as US Judge Learned Hand observed:

---

[5] William Eskridge Jr. & Philip Frickey, "Statutory Interpretation as Practical Reasoning" (1990) 42 Stan. L. Rev. 321, at 354.

> Words are not pebbles in alien juxtaposition; they have only a communal existence; and not only does the meaning of each interpenetrate the other, but all in their aggregate take their purport from the setting in which they are used.[6]

In subsection 9(1), for example, the meaning of the word "profit" depends both on its connection with other words in this statutory provision and on its setting within the income tax as a whole.

B. Context

Recognizing that the meaning of individual words depends on the context in which they are employed, Driedger's "modern rule" emphasizes that the words of a statute are "to be read in their entire context and in their grammatical and ordinary sense" (*Construction of Statutes*, 2d ed. at 87). The grammatical sense of a word depends on the structure of the provision in which the word is found and the rules and conventions of the language in which the statute is written (the syntax of the text). The ordinary meaning of a word depends on the repository of its conventional uses that are collected in dictionary definitions (its semantic characteristics),[7] and the immediate context of the statutory provision in which the word appears.[8] The context of a statutory text has been described in "its broadest sense" as "anything that contributes to a text's meaning, other than the text itself."[9]

In discussing the context in which the words of a statute are to be read, commentators often distinguish between the "internal context" of the statutory text, and its "external context."[10] According to Driedger, the internal context of the statutory text refers to "everything contained within the four corners of the Act",[11] including the words of the statute, the title of the statute, headings,

---

[6]   *National Labor Relations Board v. Federbush Co.*, 121 F.2d 954, at 957 (2d Cir. 1941). For an excellent account of Judge Hand's approach to statutory interpretation, see Archibald Cox, "Judge Learned Hand and the Interpretation of Statutes" (1947) 60 Harv. L. Rev. 370.

[7]   See, for example, Driedger, *Construction of Statutes*, 2d ed. (Toronto: LexisNexis Butterworths, 1983) at 5: "A meaning may be said to be ordinary if it is to be found in the dictionary". See also Sullivan, ed., *Driedger on the Construction of Statutes*, 3d ed. (Toronto: LexisNexis Butterworths, 1994) at 12, suggesting that "a dictionary definition ... fixes the outer limits of ordinary meaning. It offers a more or less complete characterization of the conventional ways in which a word or expression is used by literate and informed persons within a linguistic community. It thus indicates the possible range of meanings that the word or expression is capable of bearing".

[8]   Sullivan, *Driedger on the Construction of Statutes, ibid.*, at 8: "The 'ordinary meaning' of a text is the meaning that is understood by a competent user of language upon reading the words in their immediate context".

[9]   *Ibid.*, at 193.

[10]   See, for example, Driedger, *Construction of Statutes*, 2d ed., (Toronto: LexisNexis Butterworths, 1983) at 107-8; William D. Popkin, "The Collaborative Model of Statutory Interpretation" (1988) 61 S. Cal. L. Rev. 541 at 593; and George H. Taylor, "Structural Textualism" (1995) 75 BU Law Review 321 at 359-83.

[11]   Driedger, *ibid.*, at 107.

preambles, marginal notes, and section numbers.[12] The external context of a statutory text, on the other hand, has been described as "information about the world outside the statute that sheds light on the text's meaning", including "the common understanding of the language that the writer and reader are likely to share, the purposes of the text, and the surrounding background of values in which the text is adopted".[13] While the meaning of a statutory text depends partly on its internal context, it also depends on various external assumptions that the reader necessarily brings to the text regarding the conventional use of a shared language, the purpose and subject matter of the text, and the legal and cultural norms of the society in which the statute is enacted and operates. As a result, while it is conceptually possible to classify the context of a statutory text into internal and external aspects, their influence on the meaning of any particular text is inevitably intertwined.

In addition to this distinction between the internal and external context of a statutory text, commentators also distinguish between the immediate context of a statutory provision and the broader context of the statute as a whole.[14] Beginning with the immediate context of a statutory provision, it is possible to formulate an initial impression of the text's meaning based on the potential meaning of individual words, the grammatical structure of the relevant provision, conventional associations among different words, and assumptions regarding the purpose of the provision and the manner in which it is drafted. As Ruth Sullivan explains, this immediate context is often sufficient to limit vagueness and resolve any ambiguities in the meaning of words considered in isolation:

> For example, the word "fair" can be (1) a noun meaning "a public exhibition" or (2) an adjective meaning "just" or "equitable". In the sentence "The fair has been cancelled", meaning (1) must be intended because meaning (2) would violate the rules of English syntax and it is assumed that the legislature does not make grammatical mistakes. Similarly, the word "entertain" can mean (1) "amuse" or (2) "consider". In the expression "entertain an idea" it must have meaning (2), for given the semantic features of the word "idea", meaning (1) in this context is incoherent. In the sentence "No person shall operate a plane without a licence", the word "plane" could refer to (1) the vehicle or (2) the tool. Meaning (2) is unlikely, however, because it is unconventional to speak of "operating" a carpenter's plane. The word "operating" is associated with machinery driven by fuel or electricity rather than with simple tools. Meaning (2) is also unlikely because it is hard to see what purpose could be served by introducing a licensing requirement for the use of a simple tool; the costs would be significant and there are not apparent benefits. Finally, consider the sentence "No person shall discharge a gun in a public roadway except for the purpose of killing a dangerous animal or a police officer in the pursuit of duty". In this sentence, the words "a police officer" could be understood to follow (1) "except for" or (2) "killing". Possibility (1) is

---

[12] *Ibid.*, at 109-148, "Internal Context".

[13] Popkin, "The Collaborative Model of Statutory Interpretation (1988) 61 S. Cal. Law. Rev. at 593.

[14] See, for example, Sullivan, ed., *Driedger on the Construction of Statutes*, 3d ed. (Toronto: LexisNexis Butterworths, 1994) at 197-213 ("The Immediate Context") and 245-84 ("The Act as a Whole").

clearly intended, however, because possibility (2) is out of the question: no sensible legislature would forbid the shooting of guns subject to an exception that allowed police officers to be shot while performing their duties.[15]

While these examples are relatively straightforward, they illustrate how each reader's understanding of grammar, semantics, and the world more generally are combined — often unconsciously — to derive meaning from a particular text.

When judges interpret statutory provisions, they also rely on these factors to establish the grammatical and ordinary sense of a statutory text in its immediate context — typically without explicit comment and often without awareness. In addition, however, more formal recognition of the role of immediate context on statutory meaning is apparent in two principles or canons of statutory construction to which judges may refer in specific circumstances. According to the "associated words rule" *(noscitur a sociis)*, the meaning of words or phrases that perform a parallel function within a provision and are linked by the conjunctions "and" or "or" are assumed to be influenced by each other.[16] In paragraph 56(1)(n) of the *Income Tax Act*, for example, which includes in computing a taxpayer's income amounts received as a "scholarship, fellowship, or bursary, or a prize for achievement in a field of endeavour ordinarily carried on by the taxpayer", it seems reasonable to give the word prize a broader meaning than "an award for victory in a competition or contest with others" because of its association with the words scholarship, fellowship, and bursary.[17] According to the "limited class rule" *(ejusdem generis)*, the meaning of a general word or phrase following a list of specific words of phrases is assumed to be limited to "the genus of the narrow enumeration that precedes it".[18] In subsection 5(1) of the *Income Tax Act*, for example, which includes in computing a taxpayer's income from an office or employment "the salary, wages and other remuneration, including gratuities" received by the taxpayer, the word "remuneration" is reasonably limited to cash compensation in a form similar to salary, wages, and gratuities (see Chapter 4). Although traditionally regarded as binding rules of legal interpretation, these canons of statutory construction are better understood as guidelines reflecting linguistic conventions that are often but not always employed. Indeed, certain provisions may be

---

[15] *Ibid.*, at 13-14.

[16] *Ibid.*, at 200-2. See also Sullivan, *Statutory Interpretation*, (Concord: Irwin Law, 1997) at 63-65, adding (at 63) that in these circumstances "[t]he interpreter looks for a pattern or a common theme in the words or phrases which may be relied on to resolve ambiguity or fix the scope of the provision".

[17] *Canada v. Savage*, [1983] S.C.J. No. 81, [1983] C.T.C. 393; 83 D.T.C. 5409 (S.C.C.). This case is excerpted later in this book in Chapters 4 and 7.

[18] *National Bank of Greece (Canada) v. Katsikonouris*, [1990] S.C.J. No. 95, 74 D.L.R. (4th) 197 (S.C.C.), per La Forest J, at 203. See the discussion of this canon in Sullivan, *Driedger on the Construction of Statutes*, 3d ed. (Toronto: LexisNexis Butterworths, 1994) at 203-13, emphasizing the need both for an identifiable class to which the specific items set out in the provision belong and for the general word or phrase to be broader than the specific items for the canon to apply; and Sullivan, *Statutory Interpretation*, (Concord: Irwin Law, 1997) at 65-66.

drafted specifically to defeat the application of these interpretive canons: in paragraph 6(1)(a) of the *Income Tax Act*, for example, which includes in computing a taxpayer's income from an office or employment "the value of board, lodging and other benefits of any kind whatever", the words "of any kind whatever" are clearly designed to ensure that the meaning of the words "other benefits" is not confined narrowly to benefits like board and lodging.

While the immediate context of a statutory text is generally sufficient to establish its "grammatical and ordinary sense",[19] any initial impressions arrived at on this basis are properly tested by considering the rest of the Act of which the provision is merely a component.[20] Where a statute contains specific definitions or interpretive guidelines, for example, like those in Part XVII of the *Income Tax Act* or those applicable to specific portions of the Act,[21] these provisions may affect the meaning of a statutory text that one might otherwise reach by reading a provision in isolation. The meaning of a taxpayer's income from a business, for example, is significantly affected by the extended definition of this word in subsection 248(1) to include, among other endeavours, "an adventure or concern in the nature of trade" (see Chapter 5). Likewise, the meaning of a specific word or provision may be influenced by headings, preambles and marginal notes, related provisions, or the structure of the Act as a whole. These factors comprise the statutory scheme, and are examined under this heading.

C. Statutory Scheme

As the grammatical and ordinary meaning of the individual words of a statutory text depends on their connection with other words in the immediate context of the statutory provision in which they appear, so also the meaning of individual provisions depends on their relationship with other provisions and structural features comprising the broader context of the statutory scheme. To the extent that the words of a statute are to be read in their "entire context", therefore,

Driedger's "modern rule" emphasizes that these words should be interpreted "harmoniously with the scheme of the Act".[22]

---

[19] Sullivan, Driedger on the Construction of Statutes, *ibid.*, at 3.

[20] *Ibid.*, at 245-46.

[21] See, for example, s. 54, which contains definitions applicable to subdivision c of Division B of Part I of the Act (taxable capital gains); s. 89, which contains definitions applicable to subdivision h of Division B of Part I of the Act (corporations resident in Canada); s. 108, which contains definitions applicable to subdivision k of Division B of Part I of the Act (trusts and beneficiaries); and ss. 13(21), which contains definitions applicable to the capital cost allowance rules in s. 13 of the *Income Tax Act*.

[22] Driedger, *Construction of Statutes*, 2nd ed., (Toronto: LexisNexis Butterworths, 1983) at 87. See also at 36: "The relation of the various provisions of a statute to each other is also relevant

For Driedger, the statutory scheme is closely connected with the objects or purposes of the statute, which constitute the initial foundation on which the statutory scheme is based. Discussing the manner in which statutes are drafted, he explains:

> A statute begins with an objective that may be called a political or social objective. This objective is but a vision of the ultimate end the desired law is intended to achieve. The means for the attainment of that objective must then be devised; these will be embodied in some social, financial, political, economic, legal or other plan. At this stage a legislative draftsman, who has been made fully conversant with the objective and the means, as well as the law relating thereto, will conceive a legislative scheme, that is to say, a framework or outline of the individual statutory provisions that are required to give effect to the social, economic or other plan. Then he writes the words, taking care to see that everything he writes fits into this scheme, that he has given legislative expression to the plan and that the instrument will attain its object.[23]

As a result, the statutory scheme mediates between the broad social and political goals underlying the statute and the specific provisions through which these objectives are implemented.

Assuming the existence of a logical and coherent statutory scheme, courts have developed several presumptions about the manner in which statutes ought to be interpreted. With respect to the language of a statute, for example, courts generally assume that legislatures do not use words unnecessarily, so that every word has a role and meaning within the statutory scheme.[24] In paragraph 39(4)(a) of the *Income Tax Act*, for example, which prohibits anyone who is "a trader or dealer in securities" from electing capital gains treatment on the disposition of "Canadian securities", this "presumption against tautology" suggests that a "trader in securities" means something other than a "dealer in securities" (see Chapter 6). Likewise, courts assume that legislatures employ a consistent method of expression throughout each statute, such that identical words or phrases are given the same meaning while different words and phrases are given different meanings.[25] On this basis, for example, the Supreme Court of

---

in determining their meaning or scope. This factor is called the 'scheme' or 'framework' of the Act, and a provision should, if possible, be so construed as to fit into that scheme or framework".

[23] *Ibid.*, at 73.

[24] See, for example, Driedger, *Construction of Statutes*, 2d ed., *ibid.*, at 92: "In a well drafted statute there is a coherent scheme and every word in the statute has a place in that scheme. Words should not be put into a statute unless they have a grammatical or substantive function. A reader of statutes, therefore, has the right to assume, at least as a starting point, that every word has meaning and function". See also Sullivan, ed., *Driedger on the Construction of Statutes*, 3d ed. (Toronto: LexisNexis Butterworths, 1994), at 159-63 ("The Presumption Against Tautology"); and Sullivan, *Statutory Interpretation*, (Concord: Irwin Law, 1997) at 67-68 ("Every Word Must Be Given Meaning").

[25] See, for example, Driedger, *Construction of Statutes*, 2d ed., *ibid.*, at 93-94 ("Consistency of Meaning"); Sullivan, ed., *Driedger on the Construction of Statutes, ibid.*, at 163-68 ("The Presumption of Consistent Expression"); and Sullivan, *Statutory Interpretation, ibid.*, at 69-70 ("Same Words, Same Meaning; Different Words, Different Meaning").

Canada ruled that subparagraph 56(1)(a)(ii) of the *Income Tax Act*, which includes in computing a taxpayer's income amounts received as a "retiring allowance", does not include damages for the breach of an employment contract before the taxpayer commences the employment relationship — since the statutory definition of a "retiring allowance" in subsection 248(1) refers to amounts received "in respect of a loss of an office or employment" not the loss of "an intended office or employment" (which language appears in subsection 80.4(1) of the Act).[26]

In addition to these linguistic presumptions, courts also assume that both the provisions and the structure of each statute (for example, the arrangement of sections and subdivisions) are designed to implement a coherent statutory scheme. As Professor Sullivan explains:

> It is presumed that the provisions of legislation are meant to work together, both logically and teleologically, as parts of a functioning whole. The parts are presumed to fit together logically to form a rational, internally consistent framework; and because the framework has a purpose the parts are also presumed to work together dynamically, each contributing something toward accomplishing the intended goal.[27]

For this reason, courts generally presume that statutes contain no internal contradictions or inconsistencies, and interpret statutory provisions to avoid such inconsistencies whenever possible.[28] For example, in *Symes v. Canada*,[29] the Supreme Court of Canada concluded that the taxpayer could not deduct child-care expenses under the general rules governing the deductibility of business expenses in subsections 9(1) and 18(1) in order to avoid any conflict with the more limited statutory deduction for child-care expenses in section 63 of the Act.[30] Where two provisions appear to conflict, moreover, courts apply a principle of implied exception *(generalia specialibus non derogant)* to prefer the more specific provision to the more general. On this basis, for example, the Supreme Court of Canada decision in *Canada v. Savage*,[31] held that a prize that a taxpayer had received in the course of her employment was exempt under paragraph 56(1)(n) of the *Income Tax Act* as it then read, rather than taxable as an employment benefit under paragraph 6(1)(a).[32] Similarly, in *Schwartz v.*

---

[26] *Schwartz v. Canada*, [1996] S.C.J. No. 15, [1996] 1 C.T.C. 303; 96 D.T.C. 6103 (S.C.C.). This case is excerpted in Chapter 7.

[27] Sullivan, ed., *Driedger on the Construction of Statutes*, 3d ed. (Toronto: LexisNexis Butterworths, 1994) at 176.

[28] For a detailed discussion of these interpretive techniques, see *ibid.*, at 176-92.

[29] [1993] S.C.J. No. 131, [1994] 1 C.T.C. 40, (1993) 94 D.T.C. 6001 (S.C.C.).

[30] This case is discussed in Chapter 7. For a critical examination of the decision, see Duff, "Interpreting the Income Tax Act — Part 1: Interpretive Doctrines" (1999) Vol. 47 No. 3 Can. Tax J. 464, at 526-32.

[31] [1983] S.C.J. No. 81, [1983] C.T.C. 393, 83 D.T.C. 5409 (S.C.C.).

[32] This case is excerpted in Chapters 4 (characterization as an employment benefit) and 7 (characterization as a prize). The decision was subsequently reversed by legislative amendment. See Chapter 7.

Canada,[33] the Supreme Court of Canada relied upon this principle to conclude that a damage payment arising from the breach of an employment contract was subject to the specific rule governing "retiring allowances" in subparagraph 56(1)(a)(ii) of the *Income Tax Act* and not taxable under the general rule in paragraph 3(a) requiring taxpayers to include income from all sources. (This case is excerpted in Chapter 7.)

Yet another presumption of statutory interpretation applies both to the language and structure of a statute, imputing meaning to the absence of certain words or the departure from an established pattern. According to the principle of implied exclusion *(expressio unius est exclusio alterius)*, courts may conclude that the legislature intended to exclude something where it has expressly included something else that is similar to the excluded item.[34] In *Schwartz*, for example, the absence of the phrase "loss of an intended office or employment" in the statutory definition of a "retiring allowance" in subsection 248(1) of the *Income Tax Act* led the court to conclude that the legislature had deliberately excluded the damages at issue from the scope of this provision. Likewise in *65302 British Columbia Ltd. v. Canada*,[35] a majority of the Supreme Court of Canada relied on the absence of a statutory rule prohibiting the deduction of fines and penalties like the prohibition in section 67.5 disallowing the deduction of illegal bribes to conclude that the legislature intended to allow taxpayers to deduct fines and penalties arising from the violation of other statutes and regulatory schemes.[36]

While these interpretive principles generally reflect plausible assumptions as to the legislature's likely intentions and expectations, they may also incorporate judicially established norms regarding the manner in which statutes ought to be understood and drafted. Not infrequently, for example, courts insist that if the legislature had intended a particular result, it not only "would have" drafted a statute in a particular way but "should have" drafted the statute in this manner. For example, in *M.N.R. v. MacInnes*,[37] (excerpted later in this chapter), the Exchequer Court concluded that the income attribution rule in subsection 32(2) of the *Income War Tax Act*, which applied to income derived from property

---

[33] [1996] S.C.J. No. 15, [1996] 1 C.T.C. 303, 96 D.T.C. 6103 (S.C.C.).

[34] See, for example, Driedger, *Construction of Statutes*, 2d ed. (Toronto: LexisNexis Butterworths, 1983), at 119-25 ("Expressio Unius Est Exclusio Alterius"); Sullivan, ed., *Driedger on the Construction of Statutes*, 3d ed. (Toronto: LexisNexis Butterworths, 1994) at 168-76 ("Implied Exclusion (Expressio Unius Est Exclusio Alterius)"); and Sullivan, *Statutory Interpretation*, (Concord: Irwin Law, 1997) at 73-75 ("Implied Exclusion (Expressio Unius Est Exclusio Alterius)").

[35] [1999] S.C.J. No. 69, [2000] 1 C.T.C. 57, [1999] 99 D.T.C. 5799 (S.C.C.).

[36] This case is excerpted in Chapter 5. For a critical analysis of this decision, see David G. Duff, "Deductibility of Fines and Penalties Under the Income Tax Act: Public Policy, Statutory Interpretation, and the Scheme of the Act in 65302 BC Ltd" (2001) 34 Can. Bus. L.J. 336.

[37] [1954] C.T.C. 50, 54 D.T.C. 1031 (Ex. Ct.).

transferred from one spouse to another "or from property substituted therefor", did not apply to income from property substituted for substituted property on the grounds that:

> if Parliament had intended that a husband should be liable to tax in respect of income derived not only from property transferred by him to his wife and property substituted therefor but also from property substituted for such substituted property it should have expressed its intention in clear terms.

Whether this sort of interpretive approach is consistent with the principle of legislative supremacy is doubtful.

To the extent that these interpretive principles are designed to discern the legislature's actual intentions and expectations, therefore, commentators suggest that they should be applied cautiously. With respect to the presumption against tautology, for example, Driedger cautions that "[s]tatutes are not perfect; many statutes are not well drafted; and many statutes do contain unnecessary words".[38] In addition, Professor Sullivan observes "[o]ften tautologous words are added *ex abundanti cautela*, out of an abundance of caution, to reduce the possibility of future misunderstanding or mistake".[39] Likewise, the presumption of consistent expression depends on a range of factors, including:

> the proximity of the words to one another, the similarity of their contexts, how often they recur in the legislation, the extent to which they constitute a distinctive pattern of expression, their place in the legislative scheme, whether the legislation appears to have been carefully drafted, and how often it has been amended.[40]

Least reliable, perhaps, is the principle of implied exclusion, the strength of which depends on the likelihood that the legislature would have expressly included the particular item at issue had it not intended to exclude it.[41] As a result, it seems, this canon of statutory construction is employed as often to insist on explicit statutory drafting as it is to discern legislative intent.

---

[38] Driedger, *Construction of Statutes*, 2d ed. (Toronto: LexisNexis Butterworths, 1983) at 92.

[39] Sullivan, ed., *Driedger on the Construction of Statutes*, 3d ed. (Toronto: LexisNexis Butterworths, 1994) at 162.

[40] *Ibid.*, at 166. See also *ibid.*, at 167, explaining that "[o]ne problem with the presumption of consistent expression is that it does not necessarily reflect the realities of legislative drafting. Much legislation is lengthy and complicated; there is not always time for careful editing. Amendments that are made in committee and based on political compromise are often drafted with little regard to the niceties of style. It is not surprising, then, that inadvertent discrepancies occur within a single Act". In addition, Sullivan explains the presumption of consistent expression "conflicts to some extent with the contextual principle in interpretation, which emphasizes that meaning is dependent on context. Identical words may not have identical meanings once they are placed in different contexts and used for different purposes. This is particularly true of general or abstract words".

[41] For a critical evaluation of this presumption, see John Willis, "Statute Interpretation in a Nutshell" (1938) 16 Can. Bar. Rev. 1 at 7-8. See also Karl Llewellyn, "Remarks on the Theory of Appellate Decision and the Rules or Canons About How Statutes Are To Be Construed" (1950) 3 Vand. L. Rev. 395.

D. Statutory Purposes

As Driedger's description of the process of statutory drafting suggests,[42] there is a close relationship between the scheme of a statute and the objects or purposes that this scheme is designed to advance. Since statutes are never enacted for the sake of their details, but only to pursue broader political or social goals,[43] it makes sense to take these objectives into account as part of the context in which the words of an Act are properly understood. Indeed, the Supreme Court of Canada has suggested that:

> it is always necessary in construing a statute, and in dealing with the words you find in it, to consider the object with which the statute was passed, because it enables one to understand the meaning of the words introduced into the enactment.[44]

By interpreting statutory provisions in light of their objectives, moreover, courts contribute to the fulfillment of these political and social goals in a manner consistent with the proper role of an unelected judiciary in a democratic society.[45] For these reasons, Driedger's "modern rule" suggests that the words of a statute should be read "harmoniously with ... the object of the Act" as well as the statutory scheme.

Although it is customary to speak of "the" object or purpose of a statute, as if it were singular, most statutes have several purposes, none of which is pursued to the exclusion of all others.[46] The income tax, for example, is designed not only to raise revenue for government purposes, but also to do so in an equitable manner, and to promote various social and economic policies including the redistribution of economic resources (see Chapter 1). While anti-avoidance rules and provisions requiring taxpayers to include amounts in computing their income reflect revenue-raising and equity objectives, provisions allowing taxpayers to claim deductions or credits reflect equity goals where they are designed to accommodate differences in taxable capacities, and broader public policy goals where they are designed to encourage certain kinds of behaviour (for example, saving or investment). As statutory drafters endeavour to arrange

---

42 Driedger, *Construction of Statutes*, 2d ed. (Toronto: LexisNexis Butterworths, 1983), Section II.B.

43 J.A. Corry, "Administrative Law and the Interpretation of Statutes" (1936) 1 U.T.L.J. 286 at 292: "No enactment is ever passed for the sake of its details; it is passed in an attempt to realize a social purpose. It is what is variously called the aim and object of the enactment, the spirit of the legislation, the mischief and the remedy".

44 *Ref Re Educational System in Island of Montreal*, [1926] S.C.J. No. 6, [1926] S.C.R. 246 at 247 (S.C.C.), *per* Anglin CJC, citing *Reigate Rural District Council v. Sutton Water District Co.* (1908), 99 L.T.R. 168 at 170.

45 See Corry, "Administrative Law and the Interpretation of Statutes" (1936) 1 U.T.L.J. 286 at 289, emphasizing the importance of "intelligent judicial co-operation" in a parliamentary democracy in "the fulfillment of the aims and objects of parliament".

46 Sullivan, ed., Driedger on the Construction of Statutes, 3d ed. (Toronto: LexisNexis Butterworths, 1994) at 47.

different statutory objectives into a coherent statutory scheme, so should courts attempt to interpret statutes in a manner that both recognizes the multiple purposes that they embody and minimizes unnecessary conflicts among potentially competing objectives. Not surprisingly, this task has been characterized as "the most difficult aspect of purposive analysis" and "one of the more discretionary aspects of statutory interpretation".[47]

In order to establish the purposes of a statute or provision, courts may employ two broadly distinguishable approaches.[48] First, where these purposes are explained in the statute itself, or in extra-statutory materials like commission reports, ministerial statements, government publications, or academic texts, courts are apt to refer to these authoritative sources. While preambles and formal purpose statements contained in the body of a statute constitute the most authoritative evidence of statutory purposes, Canadian courts have also affirmed the admissibility of external materials as evidence of these purposes. As Professor Sullivan explains:

> The reports of Law Reform Commissions, Parliamentary Commissions and other similar studies have long been admissible as evidence of the mischief or evil legislation was designed to overcome. More recently, the courts have begun to look to these and other sources as direct evidence of legislative purpose. Statements made about a statute in the legislature, especially by Ministers introducing or defending it, are admissible and may be considered sufficiently reliable to serve as direct or indirect evidence of legislative purpose. Statements issued by government departments or agencies involved in the administration of legislation may also be looked at.[49]

In addition, she notes:

> In numerous cases the courts have adopted explanations of purpose offered by legal scholars in textbooks, monographs or law review articles. The authority of these accounts depends on the quality of the research and the cogency of the analysis and argument presented by the author. This source is routinely relied upon by the Supreme Court of Canada.[50]

Although the *Income Tax Act* contains no preamble, nor many explicit statements regarding the purposes of specific provisions,[51] Canadian courts routinely consult extrinsic materials on the purpose and scope of specific provisions of this statute. In *Symes v. Canada*,[52] for example, a majority of the Supreme Court of Canada (at C.T.C. 65-66) relied on a federal government white paper that preceded the enactment of the child-care expense deduction in section 63 of the *Income Tax Act* to support its conclusion that the taxpayer could not deduct child-care expenses under the general rules governing the

---

[47] *Ibid.*, at 48.

[48] See *ibid.*, at 50-59.

[49] *Ibid.*, at 52 (notes omitted).

[50] *Ibid.*, (notes omitted).

[51] In a few circumstances, the Act stipulates that a provision has been enacted "for greater certainty", suggesting that its purpose is largely interpretive. See, for example, subsections 12(2) and 245(4).

[52] [1993] S.C.J. No. 131, [1994] 1 C.T.C. 40, (1993) 94 D.T.C. 6001 (S.C.C.).

deductibility of business expenses, but was restricted to the more limited deduction in section 63.[53] In other income tax cases, the Federal Court of Appeal has considered statements of statutory purposes made by the Minister of Finance during the release of a federal budget or in explanatory information prepared by the Department of Finance to accompany legislative amendments.[54] Yet other cases have cited academic commentary on the purpose of specific provisions.[55] While the partisan nature of parliamentary debates and budget statements suggests that these materials should be treated with considerable caution,[56] this is less true of academic commentary and Department of Finance explanatory information, which are intended to be impartial.[57] In any event, the Federal Court of Appeal has suggested that the relevance of extrinsic materials is best addressed by ruling on their weight, rather than their admissibility.[58]

---

[53] Citing E.J. Benson, *Proposals for Tax Reform* (Ottawa: Department of Finance, 1969), paras. 2.7 and 2.9 (proposing "on social as well as economic grounds to permit a tax deduction for child care expenses, under carefully controlled terms" to "assist many mothers who work or want to work to provide or supplement the family income, but are discouraged by the cost of having their children cared for"). This case is discussed in Chapter 7.

[54] See *Lor-Wes Contracting v. Canada*, [1985] A.C.F. no 178, [1985] 2 C.T.C. 79, 85 D.T.C. 5310 (F.C.A.), in which MacGuigan JA referred to the budget statement of June 23, 1975 to support his conclusion that the taxpayer, which carried on a contracting business building logging roads for logging companies, was eligible for an investment tax credit under subsection 127(5) on the basis that the property was "used" by the taxpayer "primarily for the purpose of ... logging"; and *Maritime Telephone & Telegraph v. Canada*, [1992] F.C.J. No. 131, [1992] 1 C.T.C. 264, 92 D.T.C. 6191 (F.C.A.), where the court cited Department of Finance explanatory information to support its conclusion that amendments to para. 12(1)(b) did not authorize the taxpayer's use of a "billed" method of accounting for revenues associated with telecommunication services provided in the taxpayer's taxation year.

[55] See, for example, *Lowe v. Canada*, [1996] F.C.J. No. 319, [1996] 2 C.T.C. 33 (F.C.A.), citing Vern Krishna, *The Fundamentals of Canadian Income Tax*, 4th ed. (Scarborough, ON: Carswell, 1993), at 161, in which Professor Krishna explains that the purpose of para. 6(1)(a) of the *Income Tax Act*, which includes "the value of board, lodging and other benefits of any kind whatever" in computing a taxpayer's income from an office or employment "is intended to equalize the tax payable by employees who receive their compensation in cash with the amount payable by those who receive compensation in cash and in kind". This case is excerpted in Chapter 4.

[56] See, for example, *R v. Heywood*, [1994] S.C.J. No. 101, 120 DLR (4th) 348 at 380-81 (S.C.C.), *per* Cory J, noting that "the political nature of parliamentary debates brings into question the reliability of the statements made".

[57] See Stephen W. Bowman, "Interpretation of Tax Legislation: The Evolution of Purposive Analysis" (1995) Vol. 43 No. 5 Can. Tax J. 1167 at 1188, observing that Department of Finance explanatory materials are "intended to inform the public as to the intended meaning and purpose of the legislation", are "official statements" issued by the Department of Finance in the name of the Minister, and are generally "non-partisan, and reflect a considered view rather than a polemic".

[58] *Fibreco Pulp Inc. v. Canada*, [1995] F.C.J. No. 934, [1995] 2 C.T.C. 172, 95 D.T.C. 5412 (F.C.A.), *per* Hugessen JA (at C.T.C. 174).

Where authoritative statements of statutory purposes are absent, courts tend to draw inferences about these purposes from the statute itself, read in the context of the scheme of the Act, the circumstances in which it was enacted, and the way in which it has evolved through successive amendments.[59] For this purpose, Professor Sullivan explains, courts rely on various assumptions or "norms of plausibility" regarding "how the world works, what sorts of things can be known, which effects flow from which causes, which effects are desirable, what makes sense and so on".[60] Although these norms exercise some constraint on judicial inferences of statutory purpose,[61] different background assumptions can produce different inferences.[62] Given a multiplicity of potential purposes, moreover, different inferences are possible even among those sharing the same norms of plausibility. As Professor Sullivan illustrates:

> The purpose of a scheme to license the use of chemical pesticides on residential property ... could be to protect the health of residents or the health of workers or both, to raise revenue for the government, to supervise the consumer contracts made by lawn care companies, to protect certain plant or insect species, and more.[63]

Finally, she observes, courts have "considerable freedom in formulating their descriptions of legislative purpose" — emphasizing a particular provision or the scheme of the Act as a whole, and characterizing statutory purposes at different levels of generality.[64] For all these reasons, courts should be careful not to rely too heavily on inferences of statutory purposes where these inferences are not clearly supported by the words of the statute or the scheme of the Act.

Although Canadian courts are generally cautious in making inferences about the purposes of specific provisions of the *Income Tax Act*, a few notable examples can be mentioned. For example, in *Bronfman Trust v. Canada*,[65] (excerpted in Chapter 5), the Supreme Court of Canada relied on the text of subparagraph 20(1)(c)(i) of the Act alone to conclude that this provision, which permits a deduction for interest on "borrowed money used for the purpose of earning income from a business or property (other than borrowed money used to

---

[59] Sullivan, ed., *Driedger on the Construction of Statutes*, 3d ed. (Toronto: LexisNexis Butterworths, 1994) at 52-59. See also the discussion of "Legislative Evolution", *ibid.*, at 449-59.

[60] *Ibid.*, at 52-53, adding at 53: "The full range of assumptions relied on in drawing even a simple inference is likely to be too diverse to catalogue. For the most part these assumptions are not thought about; they are 'taken for granted' and therefore do not require thought. However, it is the presence of these assumptions that makes it possible to go from the bare words of a text to the reasons for the text with greater or lesser assurance".

[61] *Ibid.*, at 60, explaining that "[n]orms of plausibility resemble the conventions of language in that they are shared by members of a community. The more widely they are shared, the more self-evident they appear to be to those who accept them".

[62] *Ibid.*, observing that "the degree of assent or importance attaching to such norms can vary sharply among persons of groups of persons within society" and adding that "[p]ersons who do not share the same norms are unlikely to draw the same inferences".

[63] *Ibid.*

[64] *Ibid.*

[65] [1987] S.C.J. No. 1, [1987] 1 C.T.C. 117, 87 D.T.C. 5059 (S.C.C.).

acquire property the income from which would be exempt or to acquire a life insurance policy)", was enacted "in order to encourage the accumulation of capital which would produce taxable income" (at C.T.C. 124).[66] On this basis, it concluded, the taxpayer trust, which sought to deduct interest on borrowed money used to finance a distribution of capital to a beneficiary of the trust on the grounds that the funds were used indirectly to preserve income-producing assets, could not deduct the interest paid on the borrowed funds.

Likewise, in *McClurg v. Canada*,[67] a majority of the Supreme Court of Canada relied solely on the text of subsection 56(2), which stipulates that:

> [a] payment or transfer of property made pursuant to the direction of, or with the concurrence of, a taxpayer to some other person for the benefit of the taxpayer or as a benefit that the taxpayer desired to have conferred on the other person ... shall be included in computing the taxpayer's income to the extent that it would be if the payment or transfer had been made to the taxpayer,

to conclude that the provision "is obviously designed to prevent avoidance by the taxpayer, through the direction to a third party, of receipts which he or she would otherwise have obtained" (at C.T.C. 183-84). On this basis, it concluded, since dividends, if not declared and paid, "would not otherwise have been received by the taxpayer" but "would simply have been retained as earnings by the company", the payment of a dividend "cannot legitimately be considered as within the parameters of the legislative intent of s. 56(2)" (at C.T.C. 184).[68]

In *Canada v. Golden*,[69] (discussed in Chapter 8), on the other hand, a majority of the Supreme Court of Canada considered the scheme of the *Income Tax Act* and the evolution of section 68 of the Act to conclude that Parliament had not "intended to abandon the aims" of a similarly worded provision when it repealed this provision and enacted section 68 in 1972.[70] On this basis, it held, section 68, which applied "[w]here an amount can reasonably be regarded as being in part the consideration for the disposition of any property of a taxpayer and as being in part consideration for something else", should be interpreted to apply to a transaction involving the sale of depreciable and non-depreciable property, even though the transaction did not involve something else other than property.

---

[66] *Ibid.*, (C.T.C. at 124). For a brief discussion of this case, see Duff, "Interpreting the Income Tax Act — Part 1: Interpretative Doctrines" (1999) Vol. 47 No. 3 Can. Tax J. at 489-94.

[67] [1990] S.C.J. No. 134, [1991] 1 C.T.C. 169, (1990) 91 D.T.C. 5001 (S.C.C.).

[68] For a critical examination of this decision, see Duff, "Interpreting the Income Tax Act—Part 1: Interpretive Doctrines" (1999) Vol. 47 No. 3 Can. Tax J. at 494-501. See also the discussion of the court's subsequent decision in *Neuman v. Canada*, [1998] S.C.J. No. 37, [1998] 3 C.T.C. 117, 98 D.T.C. 6297 (S.C.C.), *ibid.*, at 501-4 and in David G. Duff, "Neuman and Beyond: Income Splitting, Tax Avoidance, and Statutory Interpretation in the Supreme Court of Canada" (1999) 32 Can. Bus. L. J. 345.

[69] [1986] S.C.J. No. 5, [1986] 1 C.T.C. 274, 86 D.T.C. 6138 (S.C.C.).

[70] *Ibid.*, (C.T.C. at 277). For a brief discussion of this case, see Duff, "Interpreting the Income Tax Act — Part 1", *ibid.*, at 521-25.

E. Legislative Intent

While the purposes of a statute or provision refer to the general objectives pursued through the statutory scheme or individual provision, the concept of legislative intent denotes the specific meaning that the legislature would have given to the provision in the context of a given fact situation.[71] To the extent that the legislature is the primary source of lawmaking in a democratic society, these intentions or expectations have special significance in statutory interpretation, informing the text, scheme, and purposes of the statute, and limiting judicial discretion and power.[72] Indeed courts have long affirmed that "the only rule for the construction of Acts of Parliament is that they should be construed according to the intent of the Parliament which passed the Act".[73] Understandably, therefore, Driedger's "modern rule" for statutory interpretation provides that the words of a statute are to be read "harmoniously with ... the intention of Parliament" as well as the scheme and object of the Act.

As with the purposes of a statute or provision, however, legislative intentions are more easily defined than established. Indeed, to the extent that legislators are unlikely to accord identical meanings to statutory provisions, and may not even be familiar with the details of the legislation they enact, it is often argued that the intent of a legislative body is a legal fiction that is not only unknowable in practice but unachievable in principle.[74] Consequently, Driedger observes, the

---

[71] See, for example, James M. Landis, "A Note on 'Statutory Interpretation'" (1930) 43 Harv. L. Rev. 886 at 888, defining legislative intent as the "immediate concept of meaning" contemplated by the legislature; Cox, "Judge Learned Hand and the Interpretation of Statutes" (1947) 60 Harv. L. Rev. 370 at 471, defining legislative intent in terms of "the specific particularized application which the statute was 'intended' to be given"; and Gerald C. MacCallum, "Legislative Intent" (1966) 75 Yale L. J. 754, distinguishing between the concepts of "purpose" and "intended meaning".

[72] Eskridge and Frickey, "Statutory Interpretation as Practical Reasoning" (1990) 42 Stan. L. Rev. 321 at 356.

[73] *Sussex Peerage Case* (1844), 8 E.R. 1034, 11 Cl. & F. 85 at 144 (H.L.), *per* Lord Chief Justice Tindal.

[74] See, for example, Max Radin, "Statutory Interpretation" (1930) 43 Harv. L. Rev. 863 at 870, concluding that "[a] legislature certainly has no intention whatever in connection with words which some two or three men drafted, which a considerable number rejected, and in regard to which many of the approving majority might have had, and often demonstrably did have, different ideas and beliefs. ... The chances that of several hundred men each will have exactly the same determinate situations in mind as possible reductions of a given determinable, are infinitesimally small". See also Harry Willmer Jones, "Statutory Doubts and Legislative Intention" (1940) 40 Colum. L. Rev. 957 at 968, concluding that "[i]f legislative 'intention' is supposed to signify a construction placed upon statutory language by every individual member of the two enacting houses, it is, obviously, a concept of purely fictitious status"; Willis, "Statute Interpretation in a Nutshell" (1938) 16 Can. Bar. Rev. 1 at 3, explaining that "[t]he expression ['the intent of the Legislature'] does not refer to actual intent — a composite body can hardly have a single intent ..".; and Corry, "Administrative Law and the Interpretation of Statutes" (1936) 1 U.T.L.J. 286 at 290, noting that "[e]ven the majority who vote for complex

only "real" legislative intention is "an agreement by the majority that the words in the bill express what is to be known as the intention of Parliament".[75] For this reason, some have argued, the only "legislative intent" worth considering is that expressed through the words of the statute.[76]

Notwithstanding this theoretical challenge, commentators consider four kinds of legislative intent relevant to the process of statutory interpretation. First, where a legislature has enacted specific rules to govern the interpretation of other statutes, the words of these statutes are properly read in light of these "express declarations" of legislative intent.[77] In Canada, for example, the federal *Interpretation Act*, R.S.C. 1985, c. I-21, contains several such rules. Among these, section 11 stipulates that the word "shall" is "to be construed as imperative" and the word "may" as "permissive". Other rules affect the computation of time periods under other statutes, providing, for example, that "[w]here anything is to be done within a time after, from, of or before a specified day, the time does not include that day" (section 27(5)).[78] Yet other rules contain definitions, for example that the expression "calendar year" means "a period of twelve consecutive months commencing on January 1" (section 37(1)(a)).[79] Other provisions, such as those governing the repeal and amendment of statutory provisions, constitute substantive rules of law, providing, for example, that:

> [t]he amendment of an enactment shall not be deemed to be or to involve a declaration that the law under that enactment was or was considered by Parliament or other body or person by whom the enactment was enacted to have been different from the law as it is under the enactment as amended [section 45(2)].

and that:

> [a] re-enactment, revision, consolidation or amendment of an enactment shall not be deemed to be or to involve an adoption of the construction that has by judicial decision or otherwise been placed on the language used in the enactment or on similar language [section 45(4)].

More recently, the *Interpretation Act* was amended by the enactment of sections 8.1 and 8.2 (added by S.C. 2001, c. 4, section 8, proclaimed in force June 1, 2001). These provisions stipulate:

---

legislation do not have any common intention as to its detailed provisions. Their vote indicates party dragooning rather than approval and appreciation of the measure". For a more recent statement of this position, see Kenneth A. Shepsle, "Congress Is a 'They,' Not an 'It': Legislative Intent as Oxymoron" (1992), 12 Int'l Rev. L. & Econ. 239.

[75] Driedger, *Construction of Statutes*, 2d ed., (Toronto: LexisNexis Butterworths, 1983) at 106.

[76] See, for example, Frank H. Easterbrook, "The Role of Original Intent in Statutory Construction" (1988) 11 Harv. J. L. & Pub. Pol'y 59.

[77] See Driedger, *Construction of Statutes*, 2d ed. (Toronto: LexisNexis Butterworths, 1983) at 241-46 ("Declarations of Intent").

[78] For other rules dealing with the computation of time, see ss. 27(1) to (4) and ss. 26 and 28 to 30.

[79] For other definitions, see ss. 35 to 39.

8.1 Both the common law and the civil law are equally authoritative and recognized sources of the law of property and civil rights in Canada and, unless otherwise provided by law, if in interpreting an enactment it is necessary to refer to a province's rules, principles or concepts forming part of the law of property and civil rights, reference must be made to the rules, principles and concepts in force in the province at the time the enactment is being applied.

8.2 Unless otherwise provided by law, when an enactment contains both civil law and common law terminology, or terminology that has a different meaning in the civil law and the common law, the civil law terminology or meaning is to be adopted in the Province of Quebec and the common law terminology or meaning is to be adopted in the other provinces.

Since the *Interpretation Act* expressly "applies, unless a contrary intention appears, to every enactment, whether enacted before or after the commencement of this Act" (section 3(1)), the *Income Tax Act* must be interpreted harmoniously with these declared legislative intentions.

Second, and more controversially, where those most closely associated with the drafting or sponsoring of a statute or amendment have expressed their views in extrastatutory materials like committee reports, legislative debates, and explanatory information released by government departments responsible for drafting the statute or amendment, it is often argued that these materials should be admitted as evidence of the effective intentions of the legislature as a whole.[80] Although English and Canadian courts traditionally refused to consider information comprising the so-called legislative history of an enactment as direct evidence of legislative intent,[81] US courts have long recognized these

---

[80] See, for example, John M. Kernochan, "Statutory Interpretation: An Outline of Method" (1976-77) 3 Dal. L. J. 331 at 347, concluding that "[i]t is practicable and realistic in relation to purposes and even to details of legislation that the views of those to whom the legislators delegate responsibility should be taken as standing for the views of the legislature". See also Landis, "A Note on 'Statutory Interpretation'" (1930) 43 Harv. L. Rev. 886 at 888-89; Jones, "Statutory Doubts and Legislative Intention" (1940) 40 Colum. L. Rev. 957 at 968-70; and Reed Dickerson, "Statutory Interpretation: A Peek into the Mind and Will of a Legislature" (1975) 50 Ind. L. J. 206 at 210-13.

[81] See Sullivan, ed., *Driedger on the Construction of Statutes*, (Concord: Irwin Law, 1997) at 431-49 ("Legislative History"); and Ruth Sullivan, *Statutory Interpretation* (Concord: Irwin Law, 1997) at 200-7 ("Legislative History"). As Sullivan explains, the main reasons for this exclusionary rule are that these extrastatutory materials are nothing more than the personal opinions of participants in the legislative process and not law, and that the inaccessibility of much of this information makes it difficult and costly to obtain. For an excellent analysis of arguments for and against the "authority value" of legislative history as "evidence of specific legislative intent", see William N. Eskridge Jr., "Legislative History Values" (1990) 66 Chicago-Kent L. Rev. 365 at 369-91. For other discussions of the role of legislative history in statutory interpretation, see D.G. Kilgour, "The Rule Against the Use of Legislative History: 'Canon of Construction or Counsel of Caution'?" (1952) 30 Can. Bar Rev. 769; J.A. Corry, "The Use of Legislative History in the Interpretation of Statutes" (1954) 32 Can. Bar Rev. 624; Reed Dickerson, "Statutory Interpretation: Dipping into Legislative History" (1982-83) 11 Hofstra L. Rev. 1125; Patricia Wald, "Some Observations on the Use of Legislative History in the 1981 Supreme Court Term" (1983) 68 Iowa L. Rev. 195; Kenneth W. Starr, "Observations About the Use of Legislative History" [1987] Duke L. J. 371; Abner K. Mikva,

extrastatutory materials as evidence of specific legislative intent.[82] More recently, English and Canadian courts have begun to admit evidence of legislative history not only to establish the external context for and purpose of a statute or provision,[83] but also as evidence of the legislature's intended meaning.[84] For example, in *Pepper (Inspector of Taxes) v. Hart*,[85] which involved the valuation of a fringe benefit received by several schoolteachers whose children were charged reduced fees to attend the school at which their parents taught, the English House of Lords relied on a statement by the financial secretary in the House of Commons that the benefit in cases of this kind "will be assessed on the cost to the employer, which would be very small indeed in this case",[86] to conclude that the value of the benefit should be determined according to its

---

"A Reply to Judge Starr's Observations" [1987] Duke L. J. 380; Frank H. Easterbrook, "What Does Legislative History Tell Us?" (1990) 66 Chicago-Kent L. Rev. 441; Nicholas S. Zeppos, "Legislative History and the Interpretation of Statutes: Toward a Fact-Finding Model of Statutory Interpretation" (1990) 76 Va. L. Rev. 1295; W. David Slawson, "Legislative History and the Need To Bring Statutory Interpretation Under the Rule of Law" (1992) 44 Stan. L. Rev. 383; Note, "Why Learned Hand Would Never Consult Legislative History Today" (1992) 105 Harv. L. Rev. 1005; Stephen Breyer, "On the Uses of Legislative History in Interpreting Statutes" (1992) 65 S. Cal. L. Rev. 845; Gordon Bale, "Parliamentary Debates and Statutory Interpretation: Switching on the Light or Rummaging in the Ashcans of the Legislative Process" (1995) 74 Can. Bar Rev. 1; and S. Beaulac, "Parliamentary Debates in Statutory Interpretation: A Question of Admissibility or Weight?" (1998) 43 McGill L. J. 287.

[82] See, for example, *Church of the Holy Trinity v. United States*, 143 US 457 (1892), in which the US Supreme Court consulted Senate and House committee reports to help construe an ambiguous statutory term. See also *Boston Sand & Gravel Co. v. United States*, 278 US 41 (1928), in which Justice Holmes relied on legislative history to interpret statutory language that the dissenters found ambiguous; and *United States v. American Trucking Associations*, 310 US 534, at 543-44 (1940), in which the court declared that "[w]hen aid to construction of the meaning of words, as used in the statute, is available, there certainly can be no 'rule of law' which forbids its use, however clear the words may appear on 'superficial examination.'"

[83] See, for example, *R v. Morgentaler*, [1993] S.C.J. No. 95, [1993] 3 S.C.R. 463 at 484 (S.C.C.), per Sopinka J, explaining that "the former exclusionary rule regarding evidence of legislative history has gradually been relaxed... , but until recently the courts have balked at admitting evidence of legislative debates and speeches. ... The main criticism of such evidence has been that it cannot represent the 'intent' of the legislature, an incorporeal body, but that is equally true of other forms of legislative history. Provided that the court remains mindful of the limited reliability and weight of Hansard evidence, it should be admitted as relevant to both the background and purpose of legislation". See also *Lor-Wes Contracting Ltd. v. Canada*, [1985] A.C.F. no. 178, [1985] 2 C.T.C. 79, 85 D.T.C. 5310 at 5314 (F.C.A.), per MacGuigan JA, declaring that "Hansard may be used, like the report of a commission of enquiry, in order to expose and examine the mischief, evil or condition to which the Legislature was directing its attention". On the "purpose value" of legislative history as "evidence of general intent", see Eskridge, "Legislative History Values" (1990) 66 Chicago-Kent L. Rev. 365 at 391-417.

[84] See Sullivan, ed., *Driedger on the Construction of Statutes*, 3d ed. (Toronto: LexisNexis Butterworths, 1994) at 446-49.

[85] [1992] 3 W.L.R. 1032 (H.L.).

[86] HC Debates, 22 June 1976, col. 1095 (UK).

marginal cost (which was nil due to surplus capacity) rather than the average cost of the education provided to all students.[87] According to Lord Browne-Wilkinson (at 1061):

> the exclusionary rule should be relaxed so as to permit reference to Parliamentary material where (a) legislation is ambiguous or obscure, or leads to an absurdity; (b) the material relied upon consists of one or more statements by a Minister or other promoter of the Bill together if necessary with such other Parliamentary material as is necessary to understand such statements and their effect; (c) the statements relied upon are clear.[88]

Although recognizing that extrastatutory evidence of legislative intent may be difficult and costly to obtain, he concluded:

> I do not think that the practical difficulties arising from a limited relaxation of the rule are sufficient to outweigh the basic need for the courts to give effect to the words enacted by Parliament in the sense that they were intended by Parliament to bear. Courts are frequently criticized for their failure to do that. ... The courts should not deny themselves the light which Parliamentary materials may shed on the meaning of words Parliament has used and thereby risk subjecting the individual to a law which Parliament never intended to enact.[89]

Similarly, in *Will-Kare Paving & Contracting Ltd. v. Canada*,[90] (excerpted later in this chapter), Binnie J (dissenting) relied on detailed statements by the Minister of Finance and senior government officials as evidence of "Parliament's intent" to make various tax incentives for property used primarily in the "manufacturing and processing or goods for sale" available to taxpayers who manufacture or process goods that are sold as part of a contract for work and materials.

Third, in the same way that courts draw inferences about statutory purposes from the words of an Act read in the context of the statutory scheme, its external context, and the evolution of the statute or provision through successive amendments, so also may they surmise legislative intentions by considering these factors as well as the purposes of the statute or provision. As US Judge Learned Hand advised in one decision:

> We can best reach the meaning here, as always, by recourse to the underlying purpose, and with that as a guide, by trying to project upon the specific occasion how we think persons, actuated by such a purpose, would have dealt with it, if it had been presented to them at the time.[91]

---

[87] For a useful discussion of the case, see Bale, "Parliamentary Debates and Statutory Interpretation Switching on the light or Rummaging in the Ashcans of Legislative Process" (1995) 74 Can. Bar. Rev. 1 at 13-17. For a similar case in the Canadian context, see *Detchon v. Canada*, [1995] T.C.J. No. 1342, [1996] 1 C.T.C. 2475 (T.C.C.), which is excerpted in Chapter 4.

[88] *Pepper (Inspector of Taxes) v. Hart*, [1992] 3 W.L.R. 1032 at 1061 (H.L.).

[89] *Ibid.*, at 1059.

[90] [2000] S.C.J. No. 35, [2000] 3 C.T.C. 463, 2000 D.T.C. 6467 (S.C.C.).

[91] *Borella v. Borden Co.*, 145 F.2d 63, at 64 (2d Cir. 1944), affd 325 US 679 (1945). For a more recent exposition of this interpretive approach, see Richard A. Posner, *The Problems of*

On the basis of this contextual and purposive analysis, the Supreme Court of Canada has drawn inferences about legislative intentions in several income tax cases.[92] For the same reasons that courts should exercise caution in drawing inferences of statutory purposes where these are not clearly supported by the words of the statute or the scheme of the Act, however, courts should also be careful not to rely too heavily on inferences of legislative intentions where these are not similarly supported by the statutory text, the statutory scheme, or the purposes of the Act. Of particular concern is the inference, adopted in at least one Supreme Court of Canada tax decision (*Schwartz v. Canada*[93]), that legislative inaction in the face of a particular judicial interpretation signifies a deliberate legislative intent to affirm this interpretation. Like the principle of implied exclusion discussed earlier, a presumption that reads meaning into the absence of something that one might otherwise expect is highly unreliable. While legislative inaction might suggest assent to the interpretation, it might also reflect ignorance of its existence, legislative inertia, or opposition to legislative amendment by well-organized interests.[94] Much more reliable is the inference, often confirmed by extrinsic evidence, that an amendment was intended to reverse a particular interpretation adopted in one or more judicial decisions. Not long after the Supreme Court of Canada decision in (*Savage*[95]), for example, paragraph 56(1)(n) was amended (by S.C. 1986, c. 6, section 28(1)) to exclude from the provision "amounts received in the course of business, and amounts received in respect of, in the course of or by virtue of an office or employment". The effect and purpose of this amendment, confirmed in explanatory material released by the Department of Finance, was to reverse the decision in *Savage*.

Finally, just as courts rely on shared linguistic conventions to presume that the legislature intended a particular meaning by the selection and arrangement of specific words, so also do they make presumptions about legislative intentions based on norms and values reflected in the broader legal and political culture.[96]

Jurisprudence (Cambridge: Harvard University Press, 1990) at 273, referring to this method as "imaginative reconstruction".

[92] See, for example, *Canada v. Golden*, [1986] S.C.J. No. 5, [1986] 1 C.T.C. 274, 86 D.T.C. 6138 (S.C.C.) *McClurg v. Canada*, [1990] S.C.J. No. 134, [1991] 1 C.T.C. 169, 91 D.T.C. 5001 (S.C.C.); *Symes v. Canada*, [1993] S.C.J. No. 131, [1994] 1 C.T.C. 40, (1993) 94 D.T.C. 6001 (S.C.C.); *Schwartz v. Canada*, [1996] S.C.J. No. 15, [1996] 1 C.T.C. 303, 96 D.T.C. 6103 (S.C.C.); *65302 British Columbia Ltd. v. Canada*, [1999] S.C.J. No. 69, [2000] 1 C.T.C. 57, (1999) 99 D.T.C. 5799 (S.C.C.).

[93] [1996] S.C.J. No. 15, [1996] 1 C.T.C. 303, 96 D.T.C. 6103 (S.C.C.).

[94] For an excellent analysis of the role of legislative inaction in statutory interpretation, see William N. Eskridge Jr., "Interpreting Legislative Inaction" (1988) 87 Mich. L. Rev. 67.

[95] [1983] S.C.J. No. 81, [1983] C.T.C. 393, 83 D.T.C. 5409 (S.C.C.).

[96] See, for example, Driedger, *Construction of Statutes*, 2d ed. (Toronto: LexisNexis Butterworths, 1983), at 183-221 ("External Sources of Parliamentary Intent"); Sullivan, ed., *Driedger on the Construction of Statutes*, 3d ed. (Toronto: LexisNexis Butterworths, 1994) at 285-96 ("Related Legislation"), 297-316 ("Relationship Between Legislation and the Common Law"), 317-54

Among these presumptions are: (1) that the legislature intends different statutes and regulatory schemes to operate as a coherent whole, so that statutes on the same subject *(in pari materia)* should be construed together as parts of a single system and statutes on different subjects should be interpreted to avoid inconsistencies or contradictions;[97] (2) that, although legislation supersedes the private law, legislatures respect the private law, rely on private law concepts and terms in drafting legislation, and do not intend to interfere with private law rights nor change the private law without clearly and explicitly so doing;[98] (3) that legislation is not intended to have retroactive application unless explicitly so stated;[99] (4) that the legislature intends its enactments to comply with constitutional and international law;[100] and (5) and that the legislature does not intend its enactments to apply beyond its own territory.[101] Like the textual canons of construction discussed earlier, these "substantive canons of construction" reflect both plausible assumptions as to the legislature's likely intentions and expectations, and judicially imposed norms regarding the manner in which statutes ought to be understood. Although these presumptions can be defeated by clear statements to the contrary, they function as quasi-constitutional guidelines to statutory interpretation.[102] For this reason, courts and commentators have emphasized that courts should exercise considerable caution in formulating and applying these presumptions to ensure that they reflect "changing social values" and leave the legislature "the widest possible scope in the performance of its task of adjusting private rights to meet evolving social realities".[103] Otherwise, it would be difficult to justify the use of these presumptions in a democratic society.

("Presumptions of Legislative Intent"), 355-83 ("Strict and Liberal Construction"), and 383-415 ("Special Rules"); and Sullivan, *Statutory Interpretation*, (Concord: Irwin Law, 1997) at 167-98 ("Policy Analysis").

[97] See Sullivan, ed., *Driedger on the Construction of Statutes*, 2d ed (Toronto: LexisNexis Butterworths, 1983) at 285-90 ("Statutes on the Same Subject") and "Statute Book as a Whole").

[98] See *ibid.*, at 297-316 ("Relationship Between Legislation and the Common Law").

[99] See *ibid.*, at 512-25 ("The Retroactive Application of Law").

[100] See *ibid.*, at 322-29 ("Compliance with Constitutional Law") and 330-33 ("Compliance with International Law").

[101] See *ibid.*, at 333-43 ("Territorial Application").

[102] See, for example, William N. Eskridge Jr. and Philip P. Frickey, "Quasi-Constitutional Law: Clear Statement Rules as Constitutional Lawmaking" (1992) 45 Vand. L. Rev. 593.

[103] *NB v. Estabrooks Pontiac Buick Ltd.*, [1982] N.B.J. No. 397, 44 N.B.R. (2d) 201 at 213-14 (N.B.C.A.), *per* La Forest JA (as he then was). For academic commentary to the same effect, see William N. Eskridge Jr., "Public Values in Statutory Interpretation" (1989) 137 U. Pa. L. Rev. 1007 and Cass R. Sunstein, "Interpreting Statutes in the Regulatory State" (1989) 103 Harv. L. Rev. 405.

F. Consequences

In addition to the other interpretive considerations examined in this section, courts often consider the consequences of alternative interpretations in settling on a preferred meaning for a statutory text.[104] Perhaps this is not surprising, since judges who are required to interpret statutory provisions are not engaged in an abstract or academic exercise about its possible meaning, but in a thoroughly practical enterprise regarding its application to a specific set of facts.[105] As a result, where the consequences of a particular interpretation seem absurd, unreasonable, or unjust, it is understandable that courts tend to gravitate toward alternative interpretations that seem more rational, reasonable, and fair. Furthermore, as Cass Sunstein observes:

> Because courts are able to focus upon the concrete and often unforeseeable effects of general statutory provisions, ... they are in a better position [than the legislature] to judge whether a particular provision produces peculiar consequences in a particular setting.[106]

For this reason, he explains, since it is "unrealistic to think that any legislature can or should correct every such problem" a strong presumption against unjust or unreasonable consequences is "entirely legitimate — at least if the injustice or irrationality is palpable and there is no affirmative evidence that the legislature intended the result".[107] Like other presumptions of legislative intent, therefore, consequential analysis is consistent with the legislature's likely intentions and expectations,[108] and substantive norms about the way that statutes ought to be understood and applied. Consequently, it is important that these consequential

---

[104] See Sullivan, ed., *Driedger on the Construction of Statutes*, 3d ed. (Toronto: LexisNexis Butterworths, 1994) at 79-99 ("Avoiding Absurd Consequences") and Sullivan, *Statutory Interpretation*, (Concord: Irwin Law, 1997) at 149-56 ("The Consequential Analysis or Absurdity Rule").

[105] See Sullivan, ed., *Driedger on the Construction of Statutes*, 3d ed. (Toronto: LexisNexis Butterworths, 1994) at 79.

[106] Sunstein, "Interpreting Statutes in the Regulatory State" (1989) 103 Harv. L. Rev. 405 at 482.

[107] *Ibid.*

[108] See, for example, *Waugh v. Pedneault*, [1948] B.C.J. No. 1, [1949] 1 W.W.R. 14 at 15 (B.C.C.A.), *per* O'Halloran J, stating that:

> [t]he Legislature cannot be presumed to act unreasonably or unjustly, for that would be acting against the public interest. The members of the Legislature are elected by the people to protect the public interest, and that means acting fairly and justly in all circumstances. Words used in the enactments of the Legislature must be construed upon that premise. That is the real 'intent' of the Legislature.

See also Aristotle, *Nichomachean Ethics*, trans. Terence Irwin (Indianapolis: Hackett, 1985), book V, paragraph 1137b, suggesting that "whenever the law makes a universal rule, but in this particular case what happens violates the [intended scope of] the universal rule, here the legislator falls short, and has made an error by making an unconditional rule. Then it is correct to rectify the deficiency; this is what the legislator would have said himself if he had been present there, and what he would have prescribed, had he known, in his legislation."

considerations reflect normative standards that are widely shared in the legal and political culture.

Although the Supreme Court of Canada has cautioned in at least one income tax case (*Canada v. Antosko*[109]) that, where the words of a statutory provision are not ambiguous, "a normative assessment of the consequences of the application of a given provision is within the ambit of the legislature, not the courts", consequential considerations may suggest textual ambiguities that are not otherwise apparent. For this reason, Professor Sullivan suggests that consequential considerations are always relevant to statutory interpretation, suggesting that:

> [a]n appropriate interpretation is one that can be justified in terms of (a) its plausibility, that is, its compliance with the legislative text; (b) its efficacy, that is, its promotion of the legislative purpose; and (c) its acceptability, that is, the outcome is reasonable and just.[110]

While the most persuasive interpretations are able to bring these different interpretive considerations into mutual harmony,[111] where these factors remain implacably opposed, legislative supremacy suggests that greater weight be given to textual and purposive considerations than to consequential considerations.[112]

Whatever the appropriate role and weight given to consequential considerations in statutory interpretation, the Supreme Court of Canada has considered the consequences of alternative interpretations in several income tax cases. For example, in *Moldowan v. Canada*,[113] (discussed in Chapter 5), where the court was called upon to interpret former subsection 13(1) (now subsection 31(1)) of the *Income Tax Act*, which limits the loss that a taxpayer may claim from farming businesses where the taxpayer's "chief source of income" for the taxation year is "neither farming nor a combination of farming and some other source of income", the decision rejected a literal reading of the provision on the grounds of irrationality or absurdity. Recognizing that a literal reading of these words could mean that the limitation would either always apply since farming could never be a chief source of income in a taxation year in which it resulted in a loss, or never apply since the arithmetic combination of farm losses and income from another source could constitute a chief source, Dickson J (as he then was) fashioned a more purposive interpretation of the words "chief source of income" and the manner in which a taxpayer may "combine" two or more sources of income as "the only way in which the section can have meaning".[114]

---

[109] [1994] S.C.J. No. 46, [1994] 2 C.T.C. 25, 94 D.T.C. 6314 (S.C.C.).

[110] Sullivan, ed., *Driedger on the Construction of Statutes*, 3d ed. (Toronto: LexisNexis Butterworths, 1994) at 131.

[111] See Duff, "Interpreting the Income Tax Act — Part 2: "Toward a Pragmatic Approach (1999) Vol. 47 No. 4 Can. Tax J. 741 at 793-95.

[112] *Ibid.*, at 795-97.

[113] [1977] S.C.J. No. 55, [1977] C.T.C. 310, 77 D.T.C. 5213 (S.C.C.).

[114] *Ibid.*, at C.T.C. 313.

In *Friesen v. Canada*,[115] where the taxpayer sought to rely on subsection 10(1) as it then read to deduct unrealized losses resulting from decreases in the value of real property held for the purpose of resale, Iacobucci J's dissenting opinion suggested that the consequences of such an interpretation would be unreasonable, requiring taxpayers to engage in difficult and costly annual valuations of all such property, absent any actual sale.[116] Finally, in *Bronfman Trust v. Canada*,[117] where the taxpayer trust sought to deduct interest on borrowed funds used to finance a distribution of capital to a beneficiary of the trust on the grounds that the borrowed money was used indirectly to preserve income-producing assets, the court concluded that "the consequences of the interpretation sought by the trust" would be unfair as between affluent taxpayers with income-earning property and less affluent taxpayers without such assets. According to Dickson CJC:

> In order for the trust to succeed, subparagraph 20(1)(c)(i) would have to be interpreted so that a deduction would be permitted for borrowings by any taxpayer who owned income-producing assets. Such a taxpayer could, on this view, apply the proceeds of a loan to purchase a life-insurance policy, to take a vacation, to buy speculative properties, or to engage in any other non-income-earning or ineligible activity. Nevertheless, the interest would be deductible. A less wealthy taxpayer, with no income-earning assets, would not be able to deduct interest payments on loans used in the identical fashion. Such an interpretation would be unfair as between taxpayers and would make a mockery of the statutory requirement that, for interest payments to be deductible, borrowed money must be used for circumscribed income-producing purposes.[118]

Together with the court's purposive analysis of subparagraph 20(1)(c)(i), this consequential analysis arguably creates a compelling argument against deductibility on the facts of the case.

III. INTERPRETIVE DOCTRINES

In order to interpret the *Income Tax Act*, Canadian courts have favoured different interpretive doctrines that recognize and rank some or all of the interpretive considerations examined in the previous section. As indicated in the introduction to this chapter, Canadian courts traditionally adopted a strict approach according to which statutory language was construed literally and ambiguities in taxing provisions were resolved in the taxpayer's favour. In *Stubart Investments Ltd. v. Canada*,[119] however, the Supreme Court of Canada rejected this doctrine, affirming instead a "modern rule" according to which the words of the *Income Tax Act* are to be read "in their entire context, and in their grammatical and ordinary sense, harmoniously with the scheme of the Act, the

---

[115] [1995] S.C.J. No. 71, [1995] 2 C.T.C. 369, 95 D.T.C. 5551 (S.C.C.).
[116] *Ibid.*, at C.T.C. 405-06.
[117] [1987] S.C.J. No. 1, [1987] 1 C.T.C. 117, 87 D.T.C. 5059 (S.C.C.).
[118] *Ibid.*, at C.T.C. 126.
[119] [1984] S.C.J. No. 25, [1984] C.T.C. 294, 84 D.T.C. 6305 (S.C.C.).

object of the Act, and the intention of Parliament".[120] This section reviews the strict construction rule and so-called modern rule.

A. Strict Construction

For many years, the dominant approach to the interpretation of tax legislation in Canada involved strict construction, according to which statutory language was construed literally, ambiguities in taxing provisions were resolved in favour of the taxpayer, and ambiguities in provisions setting out deductions or exemptions were resolved against the taxpayer.[121] Among judicial expressions of the doctrine that taxing statutes should be strictly construed, the leading statement is undoubtedly that of Lord Cairns in *Partington v. Attorney-General* (1869), LR 4 HL 100 (H.L. (Eng)), who expressed "the principle of all fiscal legislation" as follows (at 122):

> [I]f the person sought to be taxed comes within the letter of the law he must be taxed, however great the hardship may appear to the judicial mind to be. On the other hand, if the Crown, seeking to recover the tax, cannot bring the subject within the letter of the law, the subject is free, however apparently within the spirit of the law the case might otherwise appear to be. In other words, if there be admissible, in any statute, what is called equitable construction, certainly such a construction is not admissible in a taxing statute where you simply adhere to the words of the statute.[122]

A similar view appears in *Cape Brandy Syndicate v. IRC*, [1921] 1 K.B. 64 (K.B.), where Rowlatt J stated (at 71) that:

> in a taxing Act one has to look merely at what is clearly said. There is no room for any intendment. There is no equity about a tax. There is no presumption as to a tax. Nothing is to be read in, nothing is to be implied. One can only look fairly at the language used.[123]

---

[120] *Ibid.*, at C.T.C. 316, citing Driedger, *Construction of Statutes*, 2d ed. (Toronto: LexisNexis Butterworths, 1983).

[121] This discussion of strict construction is based on Duff, "Interpreting the Income Tax Act — Part 1: Interpretive Doctrines" (1999) Vol. 47 No. 3 Can. Tax J. 464 at 469-85. For useful reviews of the doctrine of strict construction, see Gerald D. Sanagan, "The Construction of Taxing Statutes" (1940) 18 Can. Bar Rev. 43; Gwyneth McGregor, "Literal or Liberal? Trends in the Interpretation of Income Tax Law" (1954) 32 Can. Bar Rev. 281; J.T. Thorson, "Canada" (1965) Vol. 50a Cahiers de droit fiscal international: The Interpretation of Tax Laws with Special Reference to Form and Substance (London: International Fiscal Association, 1965), 75; Gwyneth McGregor, "Interpretation of Taxing Statutes: Whither Canada?" (1968) 16 Can. Tax J. 122; Douglas J. Sherbaniuk, "Tax Avoidance — Recent Developments" in *Report of Proceedings of the Twenty-First Tax Conference* (Toronto: Canadian Tax Foundation, 1969) at 430; and Bowman, "Interpretation of Tax Legislation: The Evolution of Purposive Analysis" at 1169-74.

[122] See also *Cox v. Rabbits* (1878), 3 A.C. 473, where Lord Cairns stated that "a taxing Act must be construed strictly; you must find words to impose the tax, and if words are not found which impose the tax, it is not to be imposed".

[123] This passage was affirmed in *Canadian Eagle Oil Co. Ltd. v. The King*, [1946] A.C. 119 at 140 (H.L.), *per* Viscount Simon LC and *Mangin v. IRC*, [1971] A.C. 739 at 746 (H.L.).

Each of these statements was adopted by Canadian courts and, until *Stubart*, affirmed as the primary rule for interpreting tax legislation in Canada.[124] As an initial matter, therefore, strict construction required the courts to adhere to the "letter of the law" reflected in the "words of the statute", notwithstanding the "spirit of the law" (expressed in the scheme of the Act, the object of the Act, or the intention of Parliament), nor the consequences of the court's interpretation, which, according to Lord Cairns, must be disregarded "however great the hardship may appear to the judicial mind to be".

The first presumption, favouring the taxpayer in cases of ambiguous taxing provisions, follows directly from the literal approach outlined in *Partington*. As Lord Cairns stated in *Cox v. Rabbits* (1878), 3 AC 473 at 478, "a taxing Act must be construed strictly; you must find words to impose the tax, and if words are not found which impose the tax, it is not to be imposed". Consequently, as Fitzgibbon LJ explained in *In Re Finance Act, 1894* and *In Re the Estate of Rev George Studdert*, [1900] 2 I.R. 400 at 410, tax statutes are "subject to the rule that no tax can be imposed except by words which are clear, and the benefit of the doubt is the right of the subject". As with the passages from *Partington* and *Cape Brandy Syndicate*, each of these statements was affirmed by Canadian courts.[125]

The second presumption, favouring the taxing authorities in cases of ambiguous benefit provisions, stems from the rule against equitable construction expressed by Lord Cairns in *Partington*, and the further assumption, expressed most clearly in Lord Halsbury's decision in *Tennant v. Smith*, [1892] A.C. 150 at 154, that taxing statutes have no purpose other than the collection of tax:

---

[124] For references to the rule in *Partington, v. Attorney-General* (1869), L.R. 4 H.L. 100 (H.L.) see *Canada v. Crabbs*, [1928-34] C.T.C. 288, 1 D.T.C. 272 (S.C.C.); *Worthington v. Attorney-General Manitoba*, [1936] S.C.J. No. 4, [1935-37] C.T.C. 193 (S.C.C.); *Canada v. Montreal Telegraph Company*, [1945] S.C.J. No. 34, [1945] C.T.C. 287 (S.C.C.); *M.N.R. v. Sheldon's Engineering Ltd.*, [1955] S.C.J. No. 41, [1955] C.T.C. 174, 55 D.T.C. 1110 (S.C.C.); and *Canada v. Malloney's Studio v. Canada*, [1979] S.C.J. No. 52, [1979] C.T.C. 206; 79 D.T.C. 5124 (S.C.C.). For references to the passage from the *Cape Brandy Syndicate* case, [1921] 1 K.B. 64 (K.B.), see *M.N.R. v. Panther Oil & Grease Manufacturing Co.*, [1961] C.T.C. 363, 61 D.T.C. 1222 (Ex. Ct.); *M.N.R. v. Begin*, [1962] C.T.C. 148, 62 D.T.C. 1099 (Ex. Ct.); *Canada v. Harman*, [1978] A.C.F. no. 225 [1979] C.T.C. 12, 79 D.T.C. 5037 (F.C.T.D.), aff'd. [1980] A.C.F. no. 18, [1980] C.T.C. 83, 80 D.T.C. 6052 (F.C.A.); and *Stonehouse v. Quebec (Procurer general)*, [1978] S.C.J. No. 49, [1979] C.T.C. 233 (S.C.C.).

[125] For references to Lord Cairns's statement in *Cox v. Rabbits*, see *Patrick v. M.N.R.*, [1935-37] C.T.C. 58 (Ex. Ct.); *Canada v. Imperial Tobacco Co.*, [1938-39] C.T.C. 283 (Ex. Ct.); *O'Connor v. M.N.R.*, [1943] C.T.C. 255, 2 D.T.C. 637 (Ex. Ct.); *Canada v. British Columbia Electric Railway Co.*, [1945] C.T.C. 162 (Ex. Ct.); and *Rolland Paper Co. v. M.N.R.*, [1960] C.T.C. 158, 60 D.T.C. 1095 (Ex. Ct.). For references to the Fitzgibbon LJ's statement in *In Re Finance Act, 1894* and *In Re the Estate of Rev George Studdert*, see *R v. Crabbs*, [1934] S.C.J. No. 34, [1928-34] C.T.C. 288, 1 D.T.C. 272 (S.C.C.) and *Precision Small Parts Ltd. v. M.N.R.*, [1982] C.T.C. 2799, 82 D.T.C. 1811 (T.R.B.).

in a taxing Act it is impossible, I believe, to assume any intention, any governing purpose in the Act, to do more than take such tax as the statute imposes. In various cases the principle of construction of a taxing Act has been referred to in various forms, but I believe they may be all reduced to this, that inasmuch as you have no right to assume that there is any governing object which a taxing Act is intended to attain other than that which it has expressed by making such and such objects the intended subject of taxation, you must see whether a tax is expressly imposed.

Since the latter assumption implied that "taxation is the rule and exemption the exception", it followed, as Ritchie CJ concluded in *Wylie v. City of Montreal* (1886), 12 S.C.R. 384 at 386, that "the intention to exempt must be expressed in clear unambiguous language ... and therefore ... be strictly construed".

Among the many applications of strict construction to the interpretation of the *Income Tax Act*, one of the most illustrative is *M.N.R. v. MacInnes*, [1954] C.T.C. 50, 54 D.T.C. 1031 (Ex. Ct.) which involved the application of an attribution rule designed to prevent the avoidance of tax through income splitting by deeming income derived from property transferred from one spouse to another "or from property substituted therefor" to be taxable to the transferor as if the transfer had not been made.[126] Although the *Income Tax Act* was amended in 1950 by the introduction of a separate provision stipulating that:

> where a person has disposed of or exchanged a particular property and acquired another property in substitution therefor and subsequently, by one or more further transactions, has effected one or more further substitutions, the property acquired by such transactions shall be deemed to have been substituted for the particular property,[127]

this amendment did not apply to the years at issue in *MacInnes*.

M.N.R. v. MacInnes
[1954] C.T.C. 50; 54 D.T.C. 1031 (Ex. Ct.)

THORSON P: ... There is agreement on the facts. From about 1939 and up to March, 1947 the respondent made gifts of money and bonds to the value of more than $9,000 to his wife Agnes MacInnes. With the money she purchased other bonds. In March, 1947 she sold some $9,000 worth of these bonds and on March 21, 1947, deposited $9,486.36 in her savings account. On April 8, 1947, she handed the respondent her cheque for $9,000 to enable him to buy for her 900 treasury shares of Western Canada Steamships Limited of the nominal or par value of $10 each and the respondent bought the said shares for and on her behalf and also bought shares for and on behalf of other persons ... On August 29, 1947 the respondent sold the said shares for his wife together with the shares which he had bought for other persons to Torcan Limited for $73.125 per share

---

[126] See subs. 32(2) of the *Income War Tax Act*. This provision is the direct predecessor to the current attribution rule in subs. 74.1(1) of the current *Income Tax Act*. The attribution rules are examined in Chapter 8.

[127] See subs. 22(3) of the *1948 Income Tax Act* (as amended). This provision is the direct predecessor to para. 248(5)(a) of the current *Income Tax Act*.

and on the same day purchased for her and the other persons common and preferred shares of Western Canada Steamship Company Limited in her name and in their names respectively and issued his cheque to her for $28,800.00, being the balance of the proceeds of the sale of the 900 shares of Western Canada Steamships Limited. She invested this sum in other securities and in 1948 received income from these securities and from the preferred shares of Western Canada Steamship Company Limited amounting to $2,606.68. In assessing the respondent for 1948 the Minister added this amount to the amount of taxable income reported by him on his return. The respondent objected to the assessment and appealed ... . The appeal turned on whether the facts brought the case within the ambit of Section 32(2) of the *Income War Tax Act*, RSC 1927, c. 97, which provides as follows:

> Where a husband transfers property to his wife, or *vice versa*, the husband or the wife, as the case may be, shall nevertheless be liable to be taxed on the income derived from such property or from property substituted therefor as if such transfer had not been made.

...

The issue in the appeal is a very narrow one, namely, whether the term "property substituted therefor" in Section 32(2) of the Act includes property substituted for substituted property.

...

Section 32(2) of the *Income War Tax Act* is a special provision imposing upon a taxpayer a tax liability under certain specified circumstances which, apart from the section, would not have rested upon him. It is, therefore, essential to valid imposition of liability under the section that it should clearly apply to the facts of the case. It is well established that a tax liability cannot be fastened upon a person unless his case comes within the express terms of the enactment by which it is imposed. It is the letter of the law that governs in a taxing Act. This was laid down by the House of Lords in the leading case of *Partington v. Attorney General* (1869), LR 4 HL 100 at 122 where Lord Cairns made the classic statement:

> If the person sought to be taxed comes within the letter of the law he must be taxed, however great the hardship may appear to the judicial mind to be. On the other hand, if the Crown seeking to recover the tax cannot bring the subject within the letter of the law, the subject is free, however apparently within the spirit of the law the case might otherwise appear to be.

Moreover, the Court has no right to assume that a transaction is within the intention or purpose of a taxing Act if it does not fall within its express terms. There is no intention to tax other than that which its words express. Lord Halsbury LC put this rule clearly in *Tennant v. Smith*, [1892] AC 150 at 154 where he said:

> And when I say "what is tended to be taxed", I mean what is the intention of the Act as expressed in its provisions, because in a taxing Act it is impossible, I believe, to assume any intention, any governing purpose in the Act, to do more than take such tax as the statute imposes. In various cases the principle of construction of a taxing Act has been referred to in various forms but I believe they may all be reduced to this, that inasmuch as you have no

114

right to assume that there is any governing object which a taxing Act is intended to attain other than that which it has expressed by making such and such objects the intended subject for taxation, you must see whether the tax is expressly imposed.

Cases, therefore, under the Taxing Acts always resolve themselves into the question whether or not the words of the Act have reached the alleged subject of taxation.

These are basic principles of income tax law.

Consequently, if Parliament had intended that a husband should be liable to tax in respect of income derived not only from property transferred by him to his wife and property substituted therefor but also from property substituted for such substituted property it should have expressed its intention in clear terms. It could easily have done so. Just as in the case of the proviso to Section 6(1)(n) Parliament expressly stated that the term "previous owner" included a series of owners so it could have declared in Section 32(2) that "property substituted therefor" included property substituted for substituted property regardless of the number of substitutions, as in fact, it did when it enacted Section 22(3) of the *Income Tax Act*, Statutes of Canada 1947-48, c. 52, by Section 6(1) of the Statutes of 1952, c. 29. While this, of course, nullifies the effect of the decision appealed from in respect of assessments for 1952 and subsequent years it has no bearing on the present case which must be dealt with under the law as it stood in 1948 when the assessment appealed from was made.

In my opinion, since Section 32(2) does not expressly extend the liability of the husband to be taxed on the income derived from property transferred by him to his wife or from property substituted therefor to the income derived from property substituted for such substituted property he is not liable under the section. ...

Judgment accordingly.

NOTES AND QUESTIONS

1.   On what basis does the court conclude in *MacInnes* that the income received by Mrs. MacInnes was not subject to the rule in subsection 32(2) of the *Income War Tax Act*?

2.   What, if any, role do the scheme of the Act, the purposes of the Act, and the intentions of Parliament play in the court's decision in *MacInnes*?

3.   What is the "ordinary and grammatical" meaning of subsection 32(2) of the *Income War Tax Act*? Is it inconsistent with the words of the provision to interpret the expression "property substituted therefor" to include property substituted for substituted property *ad infinitum*?

4.   Of what, if any, relevance to the decision in *MacInnes* is the enactment of subsection 22(3) of the 1948 *Income Tax Act* (now paragraph 248(5)(a)) in 1950? What role, if any, should subsequent amendments play in the interpretation of statutes during years before these amendments?

5.   For criticisms of the decision in *MacInnes*, see Gwyneth McGregor,[128] commenting that "it would seem to be perfectly clear that the wording, 'or property substituted therefor,' is sufficiently wide to cover any number of substitutions, and that to require the Act to state explicitly that more than one substitution is included is not only unnecessary but amounts to a refusal to give the existing language its plain meaning"; and Douglas J. Sherbaniuk,[129] arguing that the court should have let the words of the provision "draw nourishment from their purpose" by giving the statutory words "a less restrictive and more reasonable interpretation".

6.   Consider the implications of the strict construction rule for the manner in which the *Income Tax Act* has been drafted. Although subsection 22(3) of the 1948 *Income Tax Act* (now paragraph 248(5)(a)) was enacted before the decision in *MacInnes*, it is a predictable legislative response to an interpretive doctrine requiring that taxpayers must be brought within the letter of the law irrespective of its spirit. Indeed, much of the length and complexity of the *Income Tax Act* is the product of statutory amendments designed, as one commentator has written, to "plug the gaps exposed by restrictive interpretations by the courts".[130] As Professor Sherbaniuk explained: "the stricter the construction of statutory language, the more the need for detailed specific provisions, and the greater the likelihood of creating a hopelessly complex, unmanageable labyrinth".[131]

7.   Consider also the implications of the strict rule of construction for the interpretation of the word "income" in section 3 of the Act. In *Bellingham v. Canada*,[132] Robertson JA, referring to the "narrow construction" given to the source concept of income, suggests that:

> [t]he restrictive interpretation imposed on paragraph 3(a) can be traced, at least in part, to the pre-1984 understanding that ambiguities in the charging sections of taxing statutes — being penal in nature — were to be resolved in favour of the taxpayer.

8.   Although strict construction generally favoured taxpayers by granting them the benefit of the doubt when they were not caught by the literal words of taxing provisions, the assumption that tax statutes have no purpose other than tax collection and the conclusion that consequences must be disregarded "however great the hardship may appear to the judicial mind to be" could also work to

---

[128] McGregor. "Literal or Liberal?" "Trends in the Interpretation of Income Tax Law" (1954) 32 Can. Bar Rev. 281 at 296.

[129] Sherbaniuk, "Tax Avoidance — Recent Developments" in Report of Proceedings at the Twenty-First Tax Conference (Toronto: Canadian Tax Foundation, 1969) at 435.

[130] Bowman, "Interpretation of Tax Legislation: The Evolution of Purposive Analysis" (1995) Vol. 43 No. 5 Can. Tax. J. 1167 at 1184.

[131] Sherbaniuk, "Tax Avoidance — Recent Developments" in Report of Proceedings at the Twenty-First Tax Conference (Toronto: Canadian Tax Foundation, 1969) at 439.

[132] [1995] F.C.J. No. 1602, [1996] 1 C.T.C. 187 at 197 (F.C.A.).

their disadvantage. In *Witthuhn v. M.N.R.* (1957), 17 Tax ABC 33, 57 D.T.C. 174, for example, the Board disallowed a medical expense deduction in respect of the cost of a full-time attendant for the taxpayer's bedridden wife, who could sit for a few hours a day in a special rocking chair, on the basis that she was not "necessarily confined by reason of illness, injury or affliction to a bed or *wheelchair*" (emphasis added) as required by then subparagraph 27(1)(c)(iv) of the 1952 Act.[133] According to W.S. Fisher (at Tax ABC 37):

> I am of the opinion that, on a strict interpretation of the statute as enacted, the appellant is not legally entitled to the deduction claimed, however much one may feel that, in equity, he should get the benefit thereof. As has been so often stated, however, there is, unfortunately, no equity in a taxation statute.

Do you agree with this interpretation? Why or why not? For other cases in which ambiguities in relieving provisions were resolved against the taxpayer, see *Lumbers v. M.N.R.*, [1943] C.T.C. 281, 2 D.T.C. 631 (Ex. Ct.), aff'd [1994] S.C.J. No. 15, [1944] S.C.R. 167 (S.C.C.) and *W.A. Sheaffer Pen Co. Ltd. v. M.N.R.*, [1953] C.T.C. 345, 53 D.T.C. 1223 (Ex. Ct.).

9.   Notwithstanding its dominance until *Stubart*, strict construction was never the only method used by English and Canadian courts to interpret tax statutes. In a number of early tax cases, Canadian courts referred to the purpose of the statute, the intentions of the legislature, the context in which the relevant statutory language was employed, and the consequences of alternative interpretations. These decisions are reviewed in Duff, "Interpreting the Income Tax Act — Part 1: Interpretive Doctrines".[134]

10.   The strict approach to the interpretation of tax statutes was formally rejected in *Stubart Investments Ltd. v. Canada*, [1984] S.C.J. No. 25, [1984] C.T.C. 294, 84 D.T.C. 6305 (S.C.C.). In a decision that dealt mainly with the issue of tax avoidance,[135] Estey J wrote (at para. 57) that:

> ...one must keep in mind the rules of statutory interpretation, for many years called a strict interpretation, whereby any ambiguities in the charging provisions of a tax statute were to be resolved in favour of the taxpayer; the taxing statute was classified as a penal statute. ...
>
> At one time, the House of Lords, as interpreted by Professor John Willis, had ruled that it was "not only legal but moral to dodge the Inland Revenue" (51 *Canadian Bar Review* 1 at 26), referring to *Inland Revenue Commissioners v. Levene*, [1928] AC 217, at 227. This was the high water mark reached in the application of Lord Cairns' pronouncement in *Partington v. Attorney-General* (1869), LR, 3 HL 100 at 122. ...

---

[133] This provision is the predecessor to para. 118.2(2)(c), which includes in the definition of medical expenses for which a credit may be claimed "remuneration for one full-time attendant upon the patient in a self-contained domestic establishment in which the patient lives" under certain circumstances. For a critical examination of the medical expenses tax credit, see David G. Duff, "Disability and the Income Tax" (2000) 45 McGill L. J. 797 at 809-23.

[134] (1999) Vol. 47 No. 3 Can. Tax J. 464 at 477-82.

[135] See Chapter 3, where this case is examined in considerable detail.

The converse was, of course, also true. Where the taxpayer sought to rely on a specific exemption or deduction provided in the statute, the strict rule required that the taxpayer's claim fall clearly within the exempting provision, and any doubt would there be resolved in favour of the Crown. ... Indeed, the introduction of exemptions and allowances was the beginning of the end of the reign of the strict rule.

Professor Willis, in his article, *supra*, accurately forecast the demise of the strict interpretation rule for the construction of taxing statutes. Gradually, the role of the tax statute in the community changed, as we have seen, and the application of strict construction to it receded. Courts today apply to this statute the plain meaning rule, but in a substantive sense so that if a taxpayer is within the spirit of the charge, he may be held liable. ...

While not directing his observations exclusively to taxing statutes, the learned author of *Construction of Statutes*, 2nd ed., (1983), at 87, E.A. Dreidger, put the modern rule succinctly:

Today there is only one principle or approach, namely, the words of an Act are to be read in their entire context and in their grammatical and ordinary sense harmoniously with the scheme of the Act, the object of the Act, and the intention of Parliament.

Two years later, in *Canada v. Golden*, [1986] S.C.J. No. 5, [1986] 1 C.T.C. 274, 86 D.T.C. 6138 (S.C.C.) a majority of the court held (at para. 10) that:

[i]n *Stubart Investments Ltd. v. Canada*, [1984] 1 S.C.R. 536, at 573-79; [1984] C.T.C. 294, at 313-17 the Court recognized that in the construction of taxation statutes the law is not confined to a literal and virtually meaningless interpretation of the Act where the words will support on a broader construction a conclusion which is workable and in harmony with the evident purposes of the Act in question. Strict construction in the historic sense no longer finds a place in the canons of interpretation applicable to taxation statutes. ...

Since *Golden*, the Supreme Court of Canada has reaffirmed this conclusion on several occasions. See, for example, *Bronfman Trust* ([1987] S.C.J. No. 1, [1987] 1 C.T.C. 117, 87 D.T.C. 5059 (S.C.C.) at para. 48); *McClurg* ([1990] S.C.J. No. 134, [1991] 1 C.T.C. 169, 91 D.T.C. 5001 (S.C.C.) at para. 44); *Corporation Notre-Dame de Bon-Secours v. Communauté Urbaine de Quebec*, [1994] S.C.J. No. 78, [1995] 1 C.T.C. 241, 95 D.T.C. 5017 (S.C.C.) (at paras. 29-30); and *Schwartz* ([1996] S.C.J. No. 15, [1996] 1 C.T.C. 303, 96 D.T.C. 6103 (S.C.C.) at para. 56).

11. In *Canada Trustco Mortgage Company v. Canada*, [2005] S.C.J. No. 56, [2005] 5 C.T.C. 215, 2005 D.T.C. 5523 (S.C.C.), the Supreme Court of Canada reaffirmed its rejection of the strict construction approach, declaring (at para. 11) that "[t]here is no doubt today that all statutes, including the [Income Tax] Act, must be interpreted in a textual, contextual and purposive way." At the same time, it suggested (at para. 10), "[w]hen the words of a provision are precise and unequivocal, the ordinary meaning of the words play [*sic*] a dominant role in the interpretive process." As a result, it emphasized (at para. 13), because the *Income Tax Act* is "dominated by explicit provisions with specific consequences", it necessarily "invite[s] a largely textual interpretation".

12.   Consistent with the court's rejection of strict construction in *Stubart*, the Supreme Court of Canada decision in *Corporation Notre-Dame de Bon-Secours* firmly rejected the presumption that ambiguities in relieving provisions should be resolved against the taxpayer. According to Gonthier J (at para. 34):

> it is no longer possible to apply automatically the rule that any tax exemption should be strictly construed. ... With respect, adhering to the principle that taxation is clearly the rule and exemption the exception no longer corresponds to the reality of present-day tax law. Such a way of looking at things was undoubtedly tenable at a time when the purpose of tax legislation was limited to raising funds to cover government expenses. In our time it has been recognized that such legislation serves other purposes and functions as a tool of economic and social policy. ... [T]here is nothing to prevent a general policy of raising funds from being subject to a secondary policy of exempting social works. Both are legitimate purposes which equally embody the legislative intent and it is thus hard to see why one should take precedence over the other.

13.   Notwithstanding the court's rejection of strict construction, subsequent Supreme Court of Canada decisions appear to have retained one feature of this doctrine in the form of a residual presumption in the taxpayer's favour. In *Canada v. Johns-Manville Corp.*, [1985] S.C.J. No. 44, [1985] 2 C.T.C. 111, 85 D.T.C. 5373 (S.C.C.), Estey J declared (at C.T.C. 126) that "where the taxing statute is not explicit, reasonable uncertainty or factual ambiguity resulting from lack of explicitness in the statute should be resolved in favour of the taxpayer". This presumption was invoked in *Fries v. Canada*, [1990] S.C.J. No. 109, [1990] 2 C.T.C. 439, 90 D.T.C. 6662 (S.C.C.) and *Symes v. Canada*, [1993] S.C.J. No. 131, [1994] 1 C.T.C. 40, 94 D.T.C. 6001 (S.C.C.), per L'Heureux-Dubé J (dissenting). In *Corporation Notre-Dame de Bon-Secours* (at C.T.C. 251), however, Gonthier J emphasized the exceptional and residual nature of this presumption, commenting that "recourse to the presumption in the taxpayer's favour is indicated when a court is compelled to choose between two valid interpretations" and that "this presumption is clearly *residual* and should play an exceptional part in the interpretation of tax legislation", and adopting the following passage from Pierre-André Côté, *The Interpretation of Legislation in Canada*, 2d ed. (Cowansville: Yvon Blais, 1990) at 412:

> If the taxpayer receives the benefit of the doubt, such a "doubt" must nevertheless be "reasonable". A taxation statute should be "reasonably clear". This criterion is not satisfied if the usual rules of interpretation have not already been applied in an attempt to clarify the problem. The meaning of the enactment must first be ascertained, and only where this proves impossible can that which is more favourable to the taxpayer be chosen.

B. Modern Rule

In *Stubart*, the Supreme Court of Canada rejected the strict construction rule for interpreting tax statutes, affirming instead Driedger's "modern rule" according to which "the words of an Act are to be read in their entire context and in their grammatical and ordinary sense harmoniously with the scheme of the Act, the object of the Act, and the intention of Parliament". Notwithstanding these words, subsequent Supreme Court of Canada judgments initially failed to settle on a preferred approach to the interpretation of tax legislation, favouring in some cases a "purposive" or "teleological" approach whereby courts should "first ... determine the purpose of the legislation" and read the words in light of this purpose, and on other occasions a "plain meaning rule" according to which the provisions of a tax statute "must be applied regardless of [their] object or purpose"[136] whenever they are "couched in specific language that admits of no doubt or ambiguity in [their] application to the facts".[137]

More recent Supreme Court of Canada decisions have returned to the modern rule, combining the textual emphasis of the plain meaning rule with the purposive consideration relied on in the teleological approach. A good example of this interpretive approach is the decision in *Will-Kare Paving & Contracting Ltd. v. Canada*, [2000] S.C.J. No. 35, [2000] 3 C.T.C. 463, 2000 D.T.C. 6467 (S.C.C.).

Will-Kare Paving & Contracting Ltd. v. Canada
[2000] S.C.J. No. 35, [2000] 3 C.T.C. 463, 2000 D.T.C. 6467 (SCC)

MAJOR J (L'Heureux-Dubé, Iacobucci, and Bastarache JJ concurring): This appeal concerns the appellant's ability to claim two manufacturing and processing tax incentives in respect of its 1988, 1989 and 1990 taxation years based upon the capital cost of an asphalt plant it constructed in 1988. The availability of both incentives, an accelerated capital cost allowance and an

---

[136] *Corporation Notre-Dame de Bon-Secours* ([1994] S.C.J. No. 78, [1995] 1 C.T.C. 241 at 250, 95 D.T.C. 5017 (S.C.C.)). For other decisions in which the Supreme Court of Canada has employed a purposive or teleological approach to the interpretation of the *Income Tax Act*, see *Bronfman Trust* ([1987] S.C.J. No. 1, [1987] 1 C.T.C. 117, 87 D.T.C. 5059 (S.C.C.)); *McClurg* ([1990] S.C.J. No. 134, [1991] 1 C.T.C. 169, 91 D.T.C. 5001 (S.C.C.)); and *Neuman* ([1998] S.C.J. No. 37, [1998] 3 C.T.C. 117, 98 D.T.C. 6297 (S.C.C.)). For a detailed discussion of purposive interpretation in the context of the *Income Tax Act*, see Duff, "Interpreting the Income Tax Act — Part I: Interpretive Doctrines" (1999) Vol. 47 No. 3 Can. Tax J. 464 at 485-504 and "... Part 2: Toward a Pragmatic Approach" (1999) Vol. 47 No. 4 Can. Tax J. 741 at 753-69.

[137] Peter W. Hogg and Joanne E. Magee, *Principles of Canadian Tax Law* (Scarborough: Carswell, 1995), at 454, cited with approval in *Friesen v. Canada*, [1995] S.C.J. No. 71, [1995] 2 C.T.C. 369, 95 D.T.C. 5551 (S.C.C.). For other Supreme Court of Canada decisions affirming a plain meaning rule, see *Canada v. Antosko* and *Duha Printers (Western) Ltd. v. Canada*, [1998] S.C.J. No. 41, [1998] 3 C.T.C. 303, 98 D.T.C. 6334 (S.C.C.). For a detailed discussion of Supreme Court of Canada decisions affirming a plain meaning rule of statutory interpretation, see Roger Taylor, "The Interpretation of Fiscal Statutes; The 'Plain Meaning' Approach in Recent Supreme Court of Canada Decisions", in *Report of Proceedings of the Forty-Eighth Tax Conference* (Toronto: Canadian Tax Foundation, 1997), 64:1-13; and Duff, "Interpreting the Income Tax Act — Part 1: Interpretive Doctrines" (1991) Vol. 47 No. 3 Can. Tax J. 464 at 504-17. For critical examinations of the plain meaning rule, see Brian Arnold, "Statutory Interpretation — Some Thoughts on Plain Meaning", in *Report of Proceedings of the Fiftieth Tax Conference* (Toronto: Canadian Tax Foundation, 1999), 6:1-36 and Duff, "Interpreting the Income Tax Act — Part 2: Toward a Pragmatic Approach" (1999) Vol. 47 No. 4 Can. Tax J. 741 at 769-79.

investment tax credit, turns upon whether using the plant to produce asphalt to be supplied in connection with paving services constitutes use primarily for the purpose of manufacturing or processing goods for sale.

I. Factual Background

The appellant, Will-Kare Paving & Contracting Limited ("Will-Kare"), paves driveways, parking lots and small public roadways for commercial and residential customers.

Until 1988, Will-Kare purchased all its asphalt from competitors, making it vulnerable in terms of price and availability. That year, Will-Kare constructed its own asphalt plant to remove its reliance upon third-party suppliers. As additional motivation, it anticipated that owning its own plant would allow it to bid on larger contracts. Finally, while Will-Kare's previous asphalt consumption did not justify construction of its own plant, it was confident that third-party sales of excess production would make the plant economically feasible.

After acquiring the plant, Will-Kare's sales and revenues from paving contracts increased as expected. For the taxation years in question, approximately 75 per cent of Will-Kare's asphalt output was utilized in its own paving business and approximately 25 per cent of its output was sold to third parties.

In the taxation years 1988, 1989 and 1990, Will-Kare included the plant and additions to it in Class 39 of Schedule II of the *Income Tax Regulations*, CRC 1978, c. 945 ("Regulations"), claiming that the plant was property used primarily in the manufacturing and processing of goods for sale. As such, Will-Kare claimed an accelerated capital cost allowance under s. 20(1)(a) of the *Income Tax Act*, S.C. 1970-71-72, c. 63 ("Act"). Will-Kare also claimed the s. 127(5) investment tax credit on the basis that the plant was "qualified property" within the meaning of s. 127(9) of the Act.

...

The Minister of National Revenue reassessed Will-Kare, reclassifying the plant as Class 8 property for capital cost allowance purposes and denying the investment tax credit, in both cases on the basis the plant was not being used primarily for the manufacturing or processing of goods for sale.

...

Will-Kare's appeals to both the Tax Court of Canada and the Federal Court of Appeal were dismissed.

II. Relevant Statutory Provisions

For ease of reference, the following statutory provisions are set out.
Income Tax Act, SC 1970-71-72, c. 63 (now R.S.C., 1985, c. 1 (5th Supp.))

20.(1) Notwithstanding paragraphs 18(1)(a), 18(1)(b) and 18(1)(h), in computing a taxpayer's income for a taxation year from a business or property, there may be deducted such of the following amounts as are wholly applicable to that source or such part of the following amounts as may reasonably be regarded as applicable thereto

(a) such part of the capital cost to the taxpayer of property, or such amount in respect of the capital cost to the taxpayer of property, if any, as is allowed by regulation;

127. ...

(5) There may be deducted from the tax otherwise payable by a taxpayer under this Part for a taxation year an amount not exceeding the lesser of

(a) his annual investment tax credit limit for the year,

(b) the aggregate of

(i) his investment tax credit at the end of the year in respect of property acquired, or an expenditure made, before the end of the year, and

(ii) ...

(9) In this section, ...

"investment tax credit" of a taxpayer at the end of a taxation year means the amount, if any, by which the total of

(a) the aggregate of all amounts each of which is the specified percentage of

(i) the capital cost to him of a qualified property ...

"qualified property" of a taxpayer means property ... that is ...

(b) prescribed machinery and equipment acquired by the taxpayer after June 23, 1975, that has not been used, or acquired for use or lease, for any purpose whatever before it was acquired by the taxpayer and that is

(c) to be used by him in Canada primarily for the purpose of

(i) manufacturing or processing goods for sale or lease, ...

"specified percentage" means

(a) in respect of a qualified property ...

(iii) acquired primarily for use in the Province of Nova Scotia, New Brunswick, Prince Edward Island, or Newfoundland or the Gaspé Peninsula,

(A) after November 16, 1978 and before 1989, 20%,

(B) after 1988 and before 1995, 15%,

Income Tax Regulations, C.R.C. 1978, c. 945

4600. ...

(2) Property is prescribed machinery and equipment for the purposes of the definition "qualified property" in subsection 127(9) of the Act if it is depreciable property of the taxpayer ... that is ...

(k) a property included in any of Classes 21, 24, 27, 29, 34, 39 and 40 in Schedule II; or

Schedule II ...

Class 8

(20 per cent)

Property not included in Class 1, 2, 7, 9, 11 or 30 that is

(a) a structure that is manufacturing or processing machinery or equipment;

...

Class 29

Property not included in Class 41 because of paragraph (c) or (d) of that class that would otherwise be included in another class in this schedule

(a) that is property manufactured by the taxpayer, the manufacture of which was completed by him after May 8, 1972, or other property acquired by the taxpayer after May 8, 1972,

          (i)   to be used directly or indirectly by him in Canada primarily in the manufacturing or processing of goods for sale or lease, ...

    (b) that is

          (i)   property that, but for this class, would be included in Class 8, ...

and

    (c) that is property acquired by the taxpayer

          (i)   before 1988, or

         (ii)   before 1990

                (A) pursuant to an obligation in writing entered into by the taxpayer before June 18, 1987,

                (B) that was under construction by or on behalf of the taxpayer on June 18, 1987, or

                (C) that is machinery or equipment that is a fixed and integral part of a building, structure, plant facility or other property that was under construction by or on behalf of the taxpayer on June 18, 1987.

Class 39

Property acquired after 1987 and before February 26, 1992 that is not included in Class 29, but that would otherwise be included in that class if that class were read without reference to subparagraphs (b)(iii) and (v) and paragraph (c) thereof.

III. Judicial History

A. Tax Court of Canada, 97 D.T.C. 506

Sarchuk TCCJ, in dismissing Will-Kare's appeal, viewed its entitlement to both the investment tax credit and the Class 39 accelerated capital cost allowance as depending upon whether the asphalt plant was acquired primarily for the purpose of manufacturing or processing goods for sale or lease. Adopting the reasoning in *Canada v. Hawboldt Hydraulics (Canada) Inc. (Trustee of)*, [1995] 1 F.C. 830 (C.A.), Sarchuk TCCJ concluded that use of the plant to produce asphalt for use in Will-Kare's own paving business did not constitute the manufacture of goods for sale, but rather for use in contracts for work and materials.

Sarchuk TCCJ also dismissed Will-Kare's argument that because potential third-party sales of asphalt were of equal importance in its decision to acquire the plant, the manufacturing of goods for sale was one of the plant's prospective primary uses. As third-party sales never represented more than 25 percent of total sales, Sarchuk TCCJ concluded that the plant's primary use could not be the manufacture of goods for sale.

B. Federal Court of Appeal, 98 D.T.C. 6203

Strayer JA dismissed the appeal and concluded that Sarchuk TCCJ correctly characterized the asphalt plant as not being acquired primarily for the manufacturing of goods for sale, but for the production of asphalt for use in Will-Kare's own paving business. Strayer JA also agreed that the phrase "goods for sale" be given the same meaning it would be given by the law of sale of goods to exclude contracts for work and materials. Therefore, Will-Kare had not acquired the plant primarily for the purpose of manufacturing or processing goods for sale.

IV. Issue

Does the capital cost of the Will-Kare's asphalt plant qualify for the investment tax credit provided for by s. 127(5) of the Act and the accelerated capital cost allowance provided for by Class 39 of Schedule II of the Regulations and s. 20(1)(a) of the Act?

V. Analysis

Will-Kare's ability to claim both the s. 127(5) investment tax credit and the Class 39 accelerated capital cost allowance depends on an interpretation of a statutory requirement common to both incentives.

It was not disputed that Will-Kare was entitled to depreciate its asphalt plant for tax purposes by claiming a capital cost allowance in accordance with s. 20(1)(a) of the Act. What is disputed, however, is into which of the asset pools enumerated in Schedule II of the Regulations Will-Kare's plant was to be placed.

Will-Kare clearly prefers that its plant be characterized as Class 39 property and, as such, be depreciated at an accelerated rate vis-à-vis the plant's alternate characterization as Class 8 property. Schedule II of the Regulations defines Class 39 property essentially as Class 29 property acquired after 1987. Therefore, for the plant to qualify as Class 39 property, Will-Kare must have acquired it "to be used directly or indirectly ... in Canada primarily in the manufacturing or processing of goods for sale or lease".

Will-Kare's ability to claim the s. 127(5) investment tax credit is contingent upon the plant being characterized as "qualified property" within the meaning of s. 127(9) of the Act, generally defined as prescribed machinery and equipment to be used by the taxpayer in Canada primarily for the purpose of manufacturing or processing goods for sale or lease. Pursuant to s. 4600(2)(k) of the Regulations, property is prescribed machinery and equipment if it is property included in, *inter alia*, Class 39 of Schedule II.

Therefore, for Will-Kare to receive the benefit of the above incentives, it must establish that it acquired the asphalt plant primarily for the purpose of manufacturing or processing goods for sale or lease.

...

Manufacturing or Processing Goods for Sale

Canadian jurisprudence to this point has adopted two divergent interpretations of the activities that constitute manufacturing and processing goods for sale. Without canvassing these authorities exhaustively, it may be helpful to outline briefly those cases which delineate these two distinct approaches.

One point of view is expressed in *Crown Tire Service Ltd. v. Canada*, [1984] 2 F.C. 219 (T.D.), where the court imports common law and provincial sale of goods law distinctions in defining the scope of the manufacturing and processing incentives' application. Only capital property used to manufacture or process goods to be furnished through contracts purely for the sale of such goods qualifies. Property used to manufacture or process goods to be supplied in connection with the provision of a service, namely through a contract for work and materials, is not viewed as being used directly or indirectly in Canada primarily in the manufacturing or processing of goods *for sale*, and as such, does not qualify for either the accelerated capital cost allowance or the investment tax credit.

The *Crown Tire* case related to whether the application of treads manufactured by the taxpayer to tires brought in by customers for repair constituted the manufacture or processing of goods for sale. Strayer J (later JA) disallowed the taxpayer's claim to the s. 125.1 manufacturing and processing profits deduction as the manufactured tread was supplied through a contract for work and materials, a characterization based upon the method through which property transferred to the buyer. See p. 223:

> In *Benjamin's Sale of Goods* (London, 1974), in considering the distinction between a contract of sale of goods and a contract for work and materials, it is stated:
>
> > Where work is to be done on the land of the employer or on a chattel belonging to him, which involves the use or affixing of materials belonging to the person employed, the contract will ordinarily be one for work and materials, the property in the latter passing to the employer by accession and not under a contract of sale. ...
>
> I believe that the situation here fits within the general principle as stated in *Benjamin*. With respect to the retreading of tires owned by customers, it appears to me that the customers retain ownership throughout the process.

A second line of authority departs from the point of view in *Crown Tire* and declines to apply statutory and common law sale of goods rules in delineating that capital property to which the manufacturing and processing incentives apply. Rather, these cases advocate a literal construction of "sale" such that the provision of a service incidental to the supply of a manufactured or processed good does not preclude receiving the benefit of the incentives. Any transfer of property for consideration would suffice. See *Halliburton Services Ltd. v. Canada*, 85 D.T.C. 5336 (F.C.T.D.), aff'd 90 D.T.C. 6320 (F.C.A.) and *Canada v. Nowsco Well Service Ltd.*, 90 D.T.C. 6312 (F.C.A.).

Halliburton and *Nowsco* considered the form of contract entered into between the taxpayer and customer to be irrelevant. In both cases the Federal Court of Appeal quoted with approval language from Reed J's decision in *Halliburton* at the Trial Division that appears to suggest an alternative test based upon the source of the taxpayer's profit. As stated by Reed J, at p. 5338:

> ... I do not find any requirement that the contract which gives rise to the taxpayer's profit must be of a particular nature, eg: one for the sale of goods and not one of a more extensive nature involving work and labour as well as the goods or material supplied. In my view it is the source of the profit, (arising out of processing) that is important ... not the nature of the taxpayer's contract with its customers.

Rolls-Royce (Canada) Ltd. v. Canada, 93 D.T.C. 5031 (F.C.A.), attempted to reconcile these diverging lines of authority by restricting *Crown Tire's* reasoning to circumstances that do not evidence the manufacture of a discrete and identifiable good prior or contemporaneous to the provision of a service. As stated by MacGuigan JA at p. 5034:

> The crucial distinction between *Crown Tire* and *Halliburton* seems to me to be ... that the processing in *Crown Tire* "did not involve the creation of a good antecedent to its use in the provision of a service".... The rubber strip in *Crown Tire* was not on the evidence manufactured or processed by the taxpayer, whereas the cement in *Halliburton* was made by the taxpayer, indeed was custom-made according to very exact specifications.

In *Hawboldt Hydraulics*, supra, the respondent taxpayer relied upon the *Rolls-Royce* interpretation of *Crown Tire* to claim a Class 29 accelerated capital cost allowance and s. 127(5) investment tax credit with respect to property used to manufacture parts for use in repair services. Rejecting the taxpayer's claim, the court reverted to the original *Crown Tire* approach. Isaac CJ wrote at p. 847:

> We are invited by the modern rule of statutory interpretation to give those words their ordinary meaning. But we are dealing with a commercial statute and in commerce the words have a meaning that is well understood. ... Strayer J was right, in my respectful view, to say in *Crown Tire* at page 225 that:
>
> > ... one must assume that Parliament in speaking of "goods for sale or lease" had reference to the general law of sale or lease to give greater precision to this phrase in particular cases.

In this appeal, Will-Kare admits that asphalt supplied in connection with its paving services is provided pursuant to a contract for work and materials. Nevertheless, Will-Kare requests that we adopt the *Halliburton* and *Nowsco* ordinary meaning interpretation such that the manufacturing of goods for sale includes all manufactured goods supplied to a customer for consideration, regardless of whether paving services are provided in connection with that supply. To the contrary, the respondent asserts that, as noted in *Crown Tire* and *Hawboldt Hydraulics*, use of the term sale in the manufacturing and processing incentives necessarily imports common law and statutory sale of goods concepts.

Both parties make extensive reference to *Hansard* as support for their respective interpretations of Parliament's intent in utilizing the words "goods for sale" in connection with the manufacturing and processing incentives. I do not propose to review this legislative material as I generally agree with the characterization ascribed to it by Isaac CJ in *Hawboldt Hydraulics*, supra, at pp. 846-47:

> ... it is clear from the total context of the legislation, including the passages from the House of Commons Debates to which I have referred, that Parliament's objective in enacting the legislation was encouragement of increased production of manufactured and processed goods to be placed on the domestic and international markets in competition with foreign manufacturers. That that is the activity which Parliament sought to encourage is, to my mind, plain from the Debates. It is equally plain that Parliament intended to benefit manufacturers and processors who engaged in those activities. In other words, the relevant statutory provisions were designed to give Canadian manufacturers and processors an advantage over their foreign competitors in the domestic and foreign markets. It is also clear that Parliament

> had in mind specific target groups and specific target activities. The legislation was not intended to benefit every manufacturing activity or every manufacturer. The language of the statute is clear that the activity to be benefitted was the manufacture of goods for sale or lease. ...

From the legislative material accompanying the manufacturing and processing incentives, it is clear that Parliament's objective was to encourage the manufacturing and processing sector's ability to address foreign competition in the domestic and international markets and foster increased employment in that sector of the Canadian economy. Furthermore, it is clear that Parliament did not wish to define exhaustively the scope of manufacturing or processing, words which do not have distinct legal meanings, but left it to the courts to interpret this language according to common commercial use. The language in *Hansard* is not helpful as to the meaning which Parliament intended to subscribe to the words "for sale or lease". It neither dictates, nor precludes, the application of common law sale of goods distinctions.

Notwithstanding this absence of direction, the concepts of a sale or a lease have settled legal definitions. As noted in *Crown Tire* and *Hawboldt Hydraulics*, Parliament was cognizant of these meanings and the implication of using such language. It follows that the availability of the manufacturing and processing incentives at issue must be restricted to property utilized in the supply of goods for sale and not extended to property primarily utilized in the supply of goods through contracts from work and materials.

It is perhaps true, as Will-Kare submitted and as noted in *Halliburton*, supra, at p. 5338, that the use of sale of goods law distinctions sometimes yields the anomalous result that the provision of services in connection with manufactured and processed goods will disqualify property that would, but for the services, qualify for the incentives. Nevertheless, it remains that in drafting the manufacturing processing incentives to include reference to sale or lease, Parliament has chosen to use language that imports relatively fine private law distinctions. Indeed, the Act is replete with such distinctions. Absent express direction that an interpretation other than that ascribed by settled commercial law be applied, it would be inappropriate to do so.

To apply a "plain meaning" interpretation of the concept of a sale in the case at bar would assume that the Act operates in a vacuum, oblivious to the legal characterization of the broader commercial relationships it affects. It is not a commercial code in addition to a taxation statute. Previous jurisprudence of this Court has assumed that reference must be given to the broader commercial law to give meaning to words that, outside of the Act, are well-defined. See *Continental Bank Leasing Corp. v. Canada*, [1998] 2 S.C.R. 298. See also P.W. Hogg, J.E. Magee and T. Cook, *Principles of Canadian Tax Law* (3rd ed. 1999), at p. 2, where the authors note:

> The *Income Tax Act* relies implicitly on the general law, especially the law of contract and property. ... Whether a person is an employee, independent contractor, partner, agent, beneficiary of a trust or shareholder of a corporation will usually have an effect on tax liability and will turn on concepts contained in the general law, usually provincial law.

Referring to the broader context of private commercial law in ascertaining the meaning to be ascribed to language used in the Act is also consistent with the modern purposive principle of statutory interpretation. As cited in E.A. Driedger, *Construction of Statutes* (2nd ed. 1983), at p. 87:

> Today there is only one principle or approach, namely, the words of an Act are to be read in their entire context and in their grammatical and ordinary sense harmoniously with the scheme of the Act, the object of the Act, and the intention of Parliament.

...

It would be open to Parliament to provide for a broadened definition of sale for the purpose of applying the incentives with clear language to that effect. Given, however, the provisions merely refer to sale, it cannot be concluded that a definition other than that which follows from common law and sale of goods legislation was envisioned.

For the taxation years in issue, approximately 75 per cent of the asphalt produced by the Will-Kare's plant was supplied in connection with Will-Kare's paving services. Thus the plant was used primarily in the manufacturing or processing of goods supplied through contracts for work and materials, not through sale. Property in the asphalt transferred to Will-Kare's customers as a fixture to real property.

The principles enunciated in *Crown Tire* and *Hawboldt Hydraulics*, to the extent they dictate reference to a common law and statutory definition of sale, offer a guide preferable to the broader interpretation of sale described in *Halliburton* and *Nowsco*.

Therefore I would dismiss the appeal with costs throughout.

BINNIE J (McLachlin CJC and Gonthier J, concurring in dissent): The fundamental issue in this case is the interpretation of everyday words used by Parliament in the context of a tax regime based on self-assessment. In 1997, the last year for which precise statistics are available, 20,453,540 tax returns were filed with Revenue Canada. Most taxpayers are not (and likely have no desire to be) learned in the law. When confronted as here with the phrase "primarily in the manufacturing or processing of goods for sale or lease" under s. 127(9) of the *Income Tax Act*, SC 1970-71-72, c. 63 ("Act"), he or she is entitled, in my opinion, to the benefit of the plain meaning of an everyday word like "sale". The taxpayer was denied that benefit by the Minister in this case. The millions of taxpayers who are not lawyers cannot be expected to reach for *Benjamin's Sale of Goods* to research the difference between a contract for the sale of goods and a contract for work and materials and to apply these distinctions in the assessment of their own income tax liability. I would therefore allow the appeal.

The taxpayer appellant, who was originally in the paving business, expanded his operation to include the manufacture of asphalt, and thereafter claimed an accelerated capital cost allowance under s. 20(1)(a) of the Act. (The appellant also seeks an investment tax credit pursuant to s. 127(5) of the Act.) Entitlement to the accelerated capital cost allowance ("fast tax write-off") turns on the taxpayer's ability to demonstrate that its investment in the asphalt plant was made to acquire property

> to be used directly or indirectly by him in Canada primarily in the manufacturing or processing of *goods for sale* or lease [Emphasis added.]

within the meaning of s. 20(1)(a) of the Act and Classes 39 and 29 in Schedule II of the *Income Tax Regulations*, C.R.C. 1978, c. 945. Entitlement to the investment tax credit turns on similar wording in s. 127(9)(c)(i).

The asphalt plant produced a manufactured product in a saleable condition. The asphalt came fully into existence prior to any paving services being rendered, obviously. The evidence is that about 25 per cent of the product was appropriated by the taxpayer and sold as is to customers. It disposed of the balance of the asphalt under various paving contracts for work and materials. None of the asphalt was retained by the taxpayer. The Minister denied the fast tax write-off because, while the asphalt plant produced a saleable product, the taxpayer chose to dispose of it primarily under contracts for work and materials rather than under contracts of sale within the meaning of the *Sale of Goods Act*, 1893 (UK), 56 & 57 Vic. c. 71, and various derivative provincial statutes.

It is common ground that if the taxpayer had sold to its paving customers the asphalt in one contract and the installation of it in another, it would be entitled to the deduction.

In this case, the Tax Court of Canada and the Federal Court of Appeal upheld the Minister's decision based on an interpretation developed by Strayer J in *Crown Tire Service Ltd. v. Canada*, [1984] 2 F.C. 219 (T.D.), where he said at p. 225:

> While the distinctions employed here may seem somewhat technical and remote from revenue law, one must assume that Parliament in speaking of "goods for sale or lease" had reference to the general law of sale or lease to give greater precision to this phrase in particular cases.

As applied to the facts of this case, however, the asphalt at the plant door was in fact "for sale". The Minister's interpretation requires that the statutory text be supplemented with additional words so that, as extended, it would read "goods to be disposed of under contracts for sale or lease". I agree in this respect with the approach of Reed J speaking of a comparable provision of the Act in *Halliburton Services Ltd. v. Canada*, 85 D.T.C. 5336 (F.C.T.D.), at p. 5338, aff'd 90 D.T.C. 6320 (F.C.A.):

> It seems to me to be quite clear that what was intended was a tax deduction with respect to profit arising out of the manufacturing and processing of goods, not a requirement that the goods had to be sold in a particular fashion.

Considerable argument was addressed to us and in the courts below about the percentage of asphalt that was disposed of under contracts of work and materials as opposed to contracts of sale. This debate was precipitated by the word "primarily" in the definition. In my view, the taxpayer's case, if it is to succeed, does not turn on these percentages, but on the proposition that all of the asphalt produced at the plant was for sale and asphalt disposed of under a contract for work and materials was a "sale" of the manufactured asphalt within the plain meaning of the Act.

Contracts for Work and Material

The appellant's standard form customer contract was "for furnishing all labour, materials and equipment required for the performance" of the work. In the sample contract provided in the appellant's Record, the handwritten notation undertook to "excavate unsuitable material, supply necessary gravel, grade, compact and pave with 2 ½" of asphalt". The global price for the job is then stipulated. The evidence was that about half of the contract price was for materials, of which about half was for asphalt. ...

I note at the outset that this case differs from the "repair cases" such as *Rolls-Royce Canada Ltd. v. Canada*, 93 D.T.C. 5031 (F.C.A.), application for leave to appeal to the Supreme Court of Canada refused, [1993] 2 S.C.R. x, where it was held that the overhauling of aircraft engines constituted "manufacturing or processing" but not "for sale" because the engines in issue were throughout owned by customers of the taxpayer. *Crown Tire*, supra, is to the same effect. No such issue arises here. In the beginning, the taxpayer owned the asphalt. At the end, the customer did. The only issue on this appeal is whether the asphalt as manufactured was for sale.

La Forest J pointed out in *H. W. Liebig & Co. v. Leading Investments Ltd.*, [1986] 1 S.C.R. 70, at p. 83, that "the primary meaning of sale is the transfer of property to another for a price". Referring to the definition in the *Oxford English Dictionary* of "sale" as "[t]he action or an act of selling or making over to another for a price; the exchange of a commodity for money or other valuable consideration", La Forest J said of the word "sale", in the admittedly different context of a real estate purchase agreement, "I do not think the technical meaning that lawyers may attach to a word for certain purposes should be substituted for the ordinary meaning of that word in everyday speech unless there is evidence that the parties intended to use it in that special or technical sense" (p. 84). In my view, ordinary words in the Act like "for sale" should also be interpreted in light of "the ordinary meaning of the word in everyday speech". Here, the supply of asphalt was specified, although the price was not allocated in the contract as between work and materials. The customer's objective was to obtain an asphalt driveway, and the services provided by the taxpayer were incidental to realization of that objective. The price was paid, and the customer became the owner of the asphalt in his driveway. The taxpayer and its customers were likely oblivious to the fact (relied on by the Minister) that, in the eye of the law, title to the steaming stretch of asphalt passed by accession.

This Court has frequently endorsed the "plain meaning" rule of interpretation in relation to the Act. ... This is not to say that the "plain meaning" is to be applied by a court oblivious to the context. In *Stubart Investments Ltd. v. Canada*, [1984] 1 S.C.R. 536, at p. 578, Estey J emphasized that "[c]ourts today apply to this statute [the *Income Tax Act*] the plain meaning rule, but in a substantive sense", which he elaborated by reference to the oft-quoted passage from E.A. Driedger, *Construction of Statutes* (2nd ed. 1983), at p. 87 (which Driedger styled "the modern rule"):

> Today there is only one principle or approach, namely, the words of an Act are to be read in their entire context and in their grammatical and ordinary sense harmoniously with the scheme of the Act, the object of the Act, and the intention of Parliament.

...

The strength of the "plain meaning" rule is its recognition that it is the words of the provision themselves that constitute the vehicle used by Parliament to convey its intent to the people who are trying to assess their rights and tax liabilities under the Act. As the Court said in *Antosko*, supra, at p. 326:

> While it is true that the courts must view discrete sections of the *Income Tax Act* in light of the other provisions of the Act and of the purpose of the legislation, and that they must analyze a given transaction in the context of economic and commercial reality, such techniques cannot alter the result where the words of the statute are clear and plain and where the legal and practical effect of the transaction is undisputed.

Even less attractive, I think, is the attempt in the present case to narrow the words "sale or lease" by reference to technical legal distinctions among various types of disposal contracts which are totally extraneous to the Act and are not easily accessible to the self-assessing taxpayer. Apart from everything else, such imported technical distinctions may frustrate not only the plain meaning, but the legislative purpose of the tax provision. Where (as here) Parliament has spoken in language that continues to speak plainly despite "successive circles of context", I think the taxpayer is entitled to the benefit voted by Parliament. It is the Minister (or the Minister's colleague, the Minister of Finance) who recommended the particular wording to Parliament, and it is the Minister or his colleague who may recommend amendments to the Act if it is thought desirable to narrow the tax benefit.

Commentary by the Tax Bar

The "plain meaning" approach as defined in *Stubart Investments*, supra, has been much discussed in the recent tax literature. ... More recently still, the "plain meaning" rule has been discussed in detail and criticized by Professor D.G. Duff in two articles titled "Interpreting the Income Tax Act" (1999), 47 *Can. Tax J* 471 and 741. At p. 770, Professor Duff says that by over-simplifying the interpretive task, the plain meaning rule in its pure form (i.e., before Estey J married the "plain meaning" rule to Driedger's "modern rule" in *Stubart Investments*, supra)

> ... obscures the process of statutory interpretation, artificially limits its scope, produces decisions contrary to legislative intentions and statutory purposes, permits substantial judicial discretion, and places an unreasonable burden on legislative drafters.

Whatever might have been said about the original "plain meaning" rule, I do not think that the modern plain meaning rule spelled out in *Stubart Investments* is fairly subject to these criticisms.

To take Professor Duff's points in reverse order, I do not think it unreasonable to require the legislative drafter to make it plain (if such be the intent) that the product must not only be manufactured for sale, but must be disposed of under a specific type of contract, e.g., excluding contracts for work and materials. It would be a simple matter to signal to the taxpayer in ordinary language that if he or she supplies services along with the manufactured product, the fast write-off and the investment tax credit will be forfeited.

Secondly, adoption of the plain meaning in this case reduces rather than enlarges judicial discretion. The Court respects the very words Parliament has used, and operates on the assumption that Parliament meant what it said ... . It does not complicate the Act with ideas borrowed from the *Sale of Goods Act, 1893*.

Thirdly, a review of the related text in the Act and the legislative history confirms the fact that the "plain meaning" accords with Parliament's intent expressed by the responsible Minister and senior officials, a type of evidence the Court has ruled admissible as part of the interpretive exercise. ... While the criticism may occasionally be made that "[j]udges have considerable freedom in formulating their descriptions of legislative purpose" (R. Sullivan, *Driedger on the Construction of Statutes* (3rd ed. 1994), at p. 60), the fact is that in this case there is a wealth of authoritative guidance on point.

On May 8, 1972, the Minister of Finance, the Honourable John Turner, introduced to the House of Commons a tax amendment to permit machinery and equipment required for manufacturing operations to be written off within two years ("the fast write-off") to provide "a substantial incentive for the establishment in Canada of new manufacturing enterprises and the expansion of existing enterprises by increasing the return that can ultimately be realized on capital investment" (*House of Commons Debates*, vol. III, 4th Sess., 28th Parl., at p. 2002). A major emphasis was on creating jobs. Asphalt plants create jobs irrespective of the form of the asphalt disposal contract.

The Minister of Finance returned to the theme of encouraging investment in manufacturing facilities in his budget address of February 19, 1973 (*House of Commons Debates*, vol. II, 1st Sess., 29th Parl., at p. 1428), and in the post-budget debate on June 13, 1973, when he pointed out that "increasing the after-tax rate of return on investment, these measures will help to achieve these national objectives by encouraging the establishment in many parts of the country of new manufacturing and processing industries and of supporting service industries" (*House of Commons Debates*, vol. V, 1st Sess., 29th Parl., at p. 4723). Whatever else may be said of the taxpayer's activities in this case, it acquired a new manufacturing plant and it worked the plant in conjunction with its paving service business.

On June 23, 1975, the Finance Minister returned to the same theme, explaining that "I am therefore proposing to introduce an investment tax credit as a temporary extra incentive for investment in a wide range of new productive facilities" (*House of Commons Debates*, vol. VII, 1st Sess., 30th Parl., at p. 7028).

In the same year, he explained to the Canadian Tax Foundation that:

We want the application of the policy to be clear as well. Grey areas in tax administration are no more popular with governments than with taxpayers.

To apply the reduced rate, a taxpayer must be able to answer two questions:

Am I carrying on a manufacturing or processing activity?

If I am, how much of my business income is subject to the reduced rate?

(Banquet Address, in Report of Proceedings of the Twenty-Fourth Tax Conference (1973), 278, at p. 281.)

In the following year, Mr. R. Weil, CA, of the Technical Interpretations Division of the Department of National Revenue, further explained the tax changes in an address to the Canadian Tax Foundation and gave an example which is apposite in the present appeal:

Where a company enters into a **supply and erect** contract, the **off-site** manufacturing of building products is not considered to be construction, whereas the activities of erecting and installing these products in place at the construction site are considered to be construction. Where a building product such as ready-mix concrete *or asphalt* is manufactured or processed off site *and then is installed* at the place of construction by the same company, *some concern may exist that there is no sale of the concrete or asphalt.* In these and similar circumstances, the product *is considered to be sold at the time the completed structure is sold and therefore such activities will qualify.* [bold in original; italics added.]

("Manufacturing and Processing Tax Incentives", in *Report of Proceedings of the Twenty-Fifth Tax Conference* (1974), 124, at p. 127.)

Administrative policy and interpretation are not determinative but are entitled to weight and can be an important factor in case of doubt about the meaning of legislation: per de Grandpré J, *Harel v. Deputy Minister of Revenue of Quebec*, [1978] 1 S.C.R. 851, at p. 859: *Nowegijick v. Canada*, [1983] 1 S.C.R. 29, per Dickson J, at p. 37. Bulletin No. IT-145 issued by the Department of National Revenue on February 5, 1974, incorporated Mr. Weil's interpretation as follows:

9. Where a building product such as ready-mix concrete or asphalt is manufactured or processed off site and then *is installed at the place of construction by the same corporation*, some concern may exist that there is no sale of the concrete or asphalt. In these and similar circumstances, *the product is considered to be sold* at the time the completed structure is sold and therefore such activities will qualify. [Emphasis added.]

These comments seem directed to construction projects which are a traditional heartland of work and materials contracts, and, I think, undermine the Minister's narrow interpretation urged here.

Moreover, this legislative history makes it clear that the distinction drawn from the niceties of contract law adopted by the Minister and the courts below to defeat the taxpayer's claim is unrelated to the purpose of the deductions. By basing the availability of the tax incentives on the distinction between a contract for the sale of goods and a contract for work and materials, the Minister applies doctrines developed in a non-tax context aimed at the totally different (and irrelevant) law governing the rights and obligations of buyers and sellers. There are, no doubt, provisions in the *Income Tax Act* which require for their proper understanding resort to commercial law or accounting practice, but the provisions at issue in the present appeal are not among them.

Notre-Dame de Bon-Secours, supra, recognized that, while at one time tax legislation was arguably limited to raising funds to cover government expenses, "[i]n our time it has been recognized that such legislation serves other purposes and functions as a tool of economic and social policy. ... Both are legitimate purposes which equally embody the legislative intent and it is thus hard to see why one should take precedence over the other". In my view, the legislative purpose here is to give positive encouragement to manufacturing and processing plants corroborates and reinforces the "plain meaning" of the Act. ...

Dismissed.

NOTES AND QUESTIONS

1. On what basis does the taxpayer in *Will-Kare Paving & Contracting* argue that it is entitled to the investment tax credit and accelerated capital cost allowance for property acquired "to be used directly or indirectly ... in Canada primarily in the manufacturing or processing of goods for sale or lease"? Why does Major J reject the taxpayer's argument? Why does Binnie J accept this argument?

2. What is the "ordinary meaning" of the words "manufacturing or processing of goods for sale"? What, if any, role should the "ordinary meaning" of these words play in the court's decision? Why does Binnie J prefer the "ordinary" or "plain" meaning of these words? Why does Major J reject this "plain" or "popular" meaning?

3. To what kinds of "external context" do the majority and dissenting judgments in *Will-Kare Paving & Contracting* refer? How do these contextual considerations affect their interpretations of the words "for sale" in the context of the incentive provisions at issue in the case?

4. To what extent do the opposing judgments in *Will-Kare Paving & Contracting* depend on different interpretations with regard to the purpose of the manufacturing and processing incentive provisions? How does Major J characterize this purpose? How does Binnie J define this purpose? How well does each judgment support its analysis of the purpose of the incentive provisions?

5. How do the opposing judgments in *Will-Kare Paving & Contracting* differ in their interpretations of Parliament's intent with respect to the application of the manufacturing and processing incentive provisions? Which of these interpretations do you find most persuasive? Why?

6. To what extent, if any, should courts rely on specific statements of legislative policy by Ministers and government officials? Does it make any

difference if these statements support the taxpayer's position? Does it make any difference if the taxpayer relied on or might reasonably have been expected to rely on these statements? How significant are these factors to your own view about the appropriate outcome of the case?

7.   According to Michael Livingstone, "Congress, the Courts and the Code: Legislative History and the Interpretation of Tax Statutes" (1991) 69 Tex. L. Rev. 819, at 831, the key issue in the interpretation of tax statutes "is not whether to rely on context, but rather *which* context is most persuasive on the given facts". In *Will-Kare Paving & Contracting*, which context is most persuasive to Major J? Which context is most persuasive to Binnie J? Which context do you find most persuasive? Why?

8.   Of what, if any, significance to your own view regarding the appropriate outcome in *Will-Kare Paving & Contracting* is the "anomalous result" noted by Major J that "the provision of services in connection with manufactured and processed goods will disqualify property that would, but for the services, qualify for the incentives"? Of what, if any, relevance is Binnie J's observation that the taxpayer would have been entitled to the deduction if it "had sold to its paying customers the asphalt in one contract and the installation of it in another"? What, if any, role should these consequential considerations play in the interpretation of tax legislation?

9.   In *Canada Trustco Mortgage Company v. Canada*, [2005] S.C.J. No. 56, [2005] 5 C.T.C. 215, 2005 D.T.C. 5547 (S.C.C.), the Supreme Court of Canada reaffirmed the "modern" approach to statutory interpretation adopted in the *Stubart* case [1984] S.C.J. No. 25, [1984] C.T.C. 294, 84 D.T.C. 6305 (S.C.C.) stating (at para. 11) that "[t]here is no doubt today that all statutes, including the [Income Tax] Act, must be interpreted in a textual, contextual and purposive way". At the same time, it declared (at para. 10), "[w]hen the words of a provision are precise and unequivocal, the ordinary meaning of the words play [sic] a dominant role in the interpretive process". As a result, it concluded (at para. 13), since the *Income Tax Act* is "dominated by explicit provisions dictating specific consequences", the Act necessarily "invite[s] a largely textual interpretation". This emphasis on the text of the *Income Tax Act* should not be confused with the plain meaning approach, however, since the court also emphasized (at para. 47) that "statutory context and purpose may reveal or resolve latent ambiguities" even where the meaning of a particular provision "may not appear to be ambiguous at first glance".

10.   In *Placer Dome Canada Ltd. v. Ontario (Minister of Finance)*, [2006] S.C.J. No. 20, 2006 S.C.C. 20 (S.C.C.), the Supreme Court of Canada summarized the "general principles" for interpreting tax statutes as follows (at paras. 21-24):

> In *Stubart Investments Ltd. v. The Queen*, [1984] 1 S.C.R. 536 (S.C.C.), this Court rejected the strict approach to the construction of taxation statutes and held that the modern approach applies to taxation statutes no less than it does to other statutes. That is, "the words of an Act

are to be read in their entire context and in their grammatical and ordinary sense harmoniously with the scheme of the Act, the object of the Act, and the intention of Parliament" (p. 578): see *65302 British Columbia Ltd. v. R.*, [1999] 3 S.C.R. 804 (S.C.C.), at para. 50. However, because of the degree of precision and detail characteristic of many tax provisions, a greater emphasis has often been placed on textual interpretation where taxation statutes are concerned: *Canada Trustco Mortgage Co. v. R.*, [2005] 2 S.C.R. 601, 2005 SCC 54 (S.C.C.), at para. 11. Taxpayers are entitled to rely on the clear meaning of taxation provisions in structuring their affairs. Where the words of a statute are precise and unequivocal, those words will play a dominant role in the interpretive process.

On the other hand, where the words of a statute give rise to more than one reasonable interpretation, the ordinary meaning of words will play a lesser role, and greater recourse to the context and purpose of the Act may be necessary: *Canada Trustco*, at para. 10. Moreover, as McLachlin C.J. noted at para. 47, "[e]ven where the meaning of particular provisions may not appear to be ambiguous at first glance, statutory context and purpose may reveal or resolve latent ambiguities". The Chief Justice went on to explain that in order to resolve explicit and latent ambiguities in taxation legislation, "the courts must undertake a unified textual, contextual and purposive approach to statutory interpretation".

The interpretive approach is thus informed by the level of precision and clarity with which a taxing provision is drafted. Where such a provision admits of no ambiguity in its meaning or in its application to the facts, it must simply be applied. Reference to the purpose of the provision "cannot be used to create an unexpressed exception to clear language": see P. W. Hogg, J. E. Magee and J. Li, *Principles of Canadian Income Tax Law* (5th ed. 2005), at p. 569; *Shell Canada Ltd. v. R.*, [1999] 3 S.C.R. 622 (S.C.C.). Where, as in this case, the provision admits of more than one reasonable interpretation, greater emphasis must be placed on the context, scheme and purpose of the Act. Thus, legislative purpose may not be used to supplant clear statutory language, but to arrive at the most plausible interpretation of an ambiguous statutory provision.

Although there is a residual presumption in favour of the taxpayer, it is residual only and applies in the exceptional case where application of the ordinary principles of interpretation does not resolve the issue: *Notre-Dame de Bon-Secours*, at p. 19. Any doubt about the meaning of a taxation statute must be reasonable, and no recourse to the presumption lies unless the usual rules of interpretation have been applied, to no avail, in an attempt to discern the meaning of the provision at issue.

IV. SOURCES OF INTERPRETATION

The various sources to which a court is likely to refer in order to interpret one or more provisions of the *Income Tax Act* clearly depend on the interpretive doctrine to which the court subscribes. To the extent that the court favours strict construction or an emphasis on the "plain meaning" of the statutory text, the primary emphasis is on the Act itself, as supplemented by authoritative judicial interpretations. Where the court adopts a more purposive or contextual approach, references to these primary sources are apt to be supplemented by references to extrinsic evidence of legislative intentions and statutory purposes. As well, courts frequently consider commentaries on the application of specific provisions or the scheme of the Act written by academics, practitioners, and the revenue department responsible for administering the *Income Tax Act*. This section reviews the various sources to which the courts refer as the foundation for Canadian income tax law.

A. Income Tax Act

The primary source of Canadian income tax law and the necessary starting point for any interpretation of the *Income Tax Act* is, of course, the statute itself. Originally enacted in 1948, when it replaced the preceding *Income War Tax Act*, the current *Income Tax Act* dates from 1972, when the previous legislation was repealed and replaced by a new statute containing a number of amendments following the *Report of the Royal Commission on Taxation* (Carter Commission).

Although the current statute dates from 1972, many rules are of more recent origin. Indeed the Act is amended so frequently that it is virtually impossible to rely on anything other than one of the consolidated versions published by Carswell or CCH:

- the *Practitioner's Income Tax Act*, published by Carswell each February and August;

- the *Stikeman Income Tax Act*, published annually by Carswell; and

- the *Canadian Income Tax Act with Regulations*, published each March and August by CCH.

Each edition contains the same basic primary material (the *Income Tax Act*, Income Tax Application Rules, Income Tax Regulations, the Canada-US and Canada-UK tax treaties, the federal *Interpretation Act* and a topical index) as well as historical or explanatory information, including references to related provisions and regulations, relevant cases, interpretation bulletins, and other extrastatutory references.[138] As a result, these commercial consolidations contain a wealth of valuable information in addition to the text of the *Income Tax Act* itself.

B. Income Tax Application Rules

A second source of Canadian income tax law is the Income Tax Application Rules or ITARs, which were introduced at the time of major tax reform in 1971, and provide transitional rules to accommodate adjustments from the pre-1972 rules to the current statutory scheme.[139] Although less and less relevant as time passes, the ITARs continue to play a role in the computation of capital gains and losses for property acquired before January 1, 1972. In order to exclude from

---

[138] For a detailed comparison of the three commercial consolidations, see David M. Sherman, *Canadian Tax Research: A Practical Guide*, 3d ed. (Scarborough: Carswell, 1997) at 41-46.

[139] The ITARs begin at s. 7 because they originally comprised the part of the statute that, in s. 1 to 6, repealed and replaced the pre-1972 Act and amended other statutes.

this computation most gains and losses that accrued before the introduction of capital gains tax in 1972, subsection 26(3) of the ITARs generally deems the cost of this property to be "the amount that is neither the greatest nor the least of": (a) the cost of the property to the taxpayer, (b) its fair market value on December 31, 1971, and (c) the taxpayer's proceeds of disposition of the property.

C. Income Tax Regulations

More important for our purposes than the ITARs are the Income Tax Regulations, which provide additional details for the computation and collection of tax beyond that of the statute itself. Authorized under section 221 of the Act, which permits the governor in council to make regulations "prescribing anything that, by this Act, is to be prescribed or is to be determined or regulated by regulation", regulations have the same force of law as the Act itself. As they are promulgated by the Governor General of Canada, acting on the advice of the federal Cabinet without the need for parliamentary debate or approval, they are useful to prescribe necessary information that is subject to frequent change and other details regarded as too technical or administrative for consideration by Parliament.

Within the Act itself, references to "prescribed" amounts or information indicate that one should refer to the regulations. For our purposes, the most important Regulations are found in Part XI and schedule II of the regulations, which set out rules for the deduction of "capital cost allowances" under paragraph 20(1)(a) of the Act. These rules are examined in detail in Chapter 5.

D. Tax Treaties

Tax treaties or conventions constitute yet another source of Canadian income tax law, and generally apply where Canadian residents obtain income from other jurisdictions and non-residents derive income from activities carried on in Canada. Canada has entered into tax treaties with more than 60 countries, including all of its major trading partners, but excluding so-called tax haven jurisdictions such as the Bahamas and the Cayman Islands. The purpose of these bilateral agreements is to prevent the double taxation of income that could otherwise occur, and to facilitate the administration and enforcement of income taxation by each contracting state.

While tax treaties themselves do not have the force of law in Canada, they acquire this status when they are made effective or ratified by enabling legislation. As a general rule, this legislation is quite brief, providing simply that the treaty is in force in Canada and prevails to the extent of any inconsistency between the treaty and any other law, and attaching the treaty itself as a schedule to the legislation. Although treaties are a central concern of a course on international tax law, they are not considered in this book.[140]

E. Tax Cases

Although subordinate to the Act, the ITARs, the Regulations, and tax treaties, judicial decisions constitute a further source of Canadian income tax law in addition to these primary legal sources. While Canadian courts occasionally refer to tax cases from other jurisdictions, these are merely persuasive, not authoritative legal sources. As in other areas of law, the weight given to a previous tax case depends on the level of court that arrived at the decision and the extent to which the reasoning applies to the facts of the subsequent case.

The court structure for tax appeals in Canada has changed several times since the *Income War Tax Act* was introduced in 1917. Until 1949, trials were held in the Exchequer Court, with appeals to the Supreme Court of Canada, and then to the Judicial Committee of the Privy Council. In 1949, the Income Tax Appeals Board (renamed the Tax Appeal Board in 1958) was established in order to provide a less formal procedure for the first level of tax appeals, decisions of which either party could appeal further by way of a new trial before the Exchequer Court. Also in 1949, appeals to the Privy Council for newly initiated cases were ended, though tax cases already under appeal continued to be heard by the Privy Council until 1955. From 1949 to 1971, therefore, appeals were heard first by the applicable board, then by the Exchequer Court by way of a new trial, and then by the Supreme Court of Canada.

In 1972, this structure was amended yet again, when the Tax Appeal Board was renamed the Tax Review Board, the Exchequer Court was replaced with the Federal Court Trial Division, and the Federal Court of Appeal was established in order to hear appeals from the Federal Court Trial Division. In 1983, the Tax Review Board became the Tax Court of Canada and board members became judges, though the procedure remained relatively informal compared with other court procedures. As appeals from the Tax Review Board and later the Tax Court of Canada to the Federal Court Trial Division were also by way of a new trial, this court structure provided for two levels of trial and two levels of appeal — an arrangement that continued to exist until 1991 when the Tax Court assumed the Federal Court Trial Division's jurisdiction over newly filed tax cases. Since 1991, therefore, tax cases are appealed first to the Tax Court of Canada, then to the Federal Court of Appeal, and then to the Supreme Court of Canada.[141]

Canadian tax cases are reported in two series of law reports: Canada Tax Cases (C.T.C.s), published by Carswell, and Dominion Tax Cases (D.T.C.s),

---

[140] For a brief introduction to tax treaties, see Sherman, *Canadian Tax Research: A Practical Guide*, 3d ed. (Scarborough: Carswell, 1997) at 57-61.

[141] For a more detailed discussion of the structure of Canadian tax appeals, see *ibid.*, at 31-35 and 84.

published by CCH. Federal Court of Canada and Supreme Court of Canada decisions are also published in conventional law reports, such as the Supreme Court Reports (S.C.R.), the Federal Court Reports (F.C.), or the National Reporter (NR). It is customary in tax writing to cite to the C.T.C.s and D.T.C.s. Tax cases are also available on CD-ROM products produced by Carswell (*TaxPartner*) and CCH (*TaxWorks*), each of which includes full texts of the *Income Tax Act*, ITARs, Regulations, and a wealth of other information in addition to all tax cases published by the respective company. Tax cases are also available online through various services.[142]

F. Other Statutes and Provincial Law

In order to interpret the *Income Tax Act*, courts are often required to consider other federal statutes as well as provincial law, both statutory and judicial. At the federal level, for example, the *Interpretation Act* contains several rules governing the interpretation of specific terms, as well as substantive rules of law regarding the effects of legislative amendments.[143] More generally, section 12 of this statute declares that "[e]very enactment is deemed remedial, and shall be given such fair, large and liberal construction and interpretation as best ensures the attainment of its objects". Surprisingly, however, this provision is rarely mentioned in tax cases.

In addition to the *Interpretation Act*, courts may refer to other federal statutes in order to interpret specific terms or provisions or to complete the statutory scheme of the Act, reading these statutes *in pari materia* as constituent elements of a single coherent system. For example, in *Yonge-Eglinton Building Ltd. v. M.N.R.*,[144] Gibson J suggested that the meaning of the word "interest" for the purposes of the deduction in then paragraph 11(1)(c) (now paragraph 20(1)(c)) of the *Income Tax Act* should be the same as the meaning given to this word for the purposes of the federal *Interest Act*, RSC 1970, c. I-18. Other tax cases have relied on caselaw addressing the federal *Interest Act* in order to determine the meaning of "interest" for the purposes of the *Income Tax Act*.[145] In *Symes v. Canada*,[146] L'Heureux-Dubé J (dissenting) relied on values of gender equality enshrined in the *Canadian Charter of Rights and Freedoms* to support the conclusion that child-care expenses could be deducted as an ordinary business expense and were not restricted to the more limited statutory deduction in section 63 of the Act. In *Markevich v. Canada*,[147] the Supreme Court of Canada

---

[142] For a more detailed discussion of available electronic sources, see *ibid.*, at 119-24.

[143] See the section on "Legislative Intent" earlier in this chapter in Section II. E.

[144] [1972] C.T.C. 542, 72 D.T.C. 6456 (F.C.T.D.), at para. 18 (aff'd [1974] F.C.J. No. 84, [1974] C.T.C. 209, 74 D.T.C. 6180 (F.C.A.)).

[145] See, for example, *Perini Estate v. M.N.R.*, [1982] F.C.J. No. 12, C.T.C. 74, 82 D.T.C. 6080 (F.C.A.). This case is excerpted in Chapter 5.

[146] [1993] S.C.J. No. 131, [1994] 1 C.T.C. 40, 94 D.T.C. 6001 at para. 248 (S.C.C.).

[147] [2003] S.C.J. No. 8, [2003] 2 C.T.C. 83, 2003 D.T.C. 5185 (S.C.C.).

relied on the six-year limitation period in section 32 of the *Crown Liability and Proceedings Act*, RSC 1985, c. C-50, to conclude that the revenue authorities could not in 1998 collect on a tax debt that was first asserted in a notice of assessment issued in 1986. Other cases have relied on section 87 of the *Indian Act*, RSC 1985, c. I-5, to conclude that the income of an "Indian" or "band" (within the meaning of the *Indian Act)* is exempt from tax where it is "situated" on a reserve.[148]

More generally, Canadian income tax law depends crucially on the private law that governs the legal rights and relationships to which the *Income Tax Act* applies absent specific statutory provisions to the contrary — private law that is ultimately determined by each province under its exclusive authority to make laws in relation to "Property and Civil Rights".[149] As Major J stated in *Will-Kare Paving & Contracting*,[150] "reference must be given to the broader commercial law to give meaning to words that, outside of the Act, are well-defined". For this reason, tax cases often refer to provincial private law, for example to determine the characterization of a taxpayer as an employee[151] or corporate director,[152] the existence of a partnership[153] or a gift,[154] or the ownership of property for the purpose of claiming capital cost allowance[155] or attributing income or losses.[156]

G. Legislative History

Legislative history comprises various extrastatutory materials, such as commission reports, white papers announcing a government's intention to amend legislation, budget statements announcing proposed amendments, explanatory information accompanying draft legislation, and legislative committee reports examining proposed legislation. As a general rule, federal tax policy is formulated by officials in the Department of Finance and introduced in

---

[148] See, for example, *R. v. Nowegijick*, [1983] S.C.J. No. 5, [1983] C.T.C. 20, 83 D.T.C. 5041 (S.C.C.) and *Williams v. M.N.R.*, [1992] S.C.J. No. 36, [1992] 1 C.T.C. 225, 92 D.T.C. 6320 (S.C.C.).

[149] *British North America Act*, 1867 U.K., 30-31 Vict., c. 3, s. 92(13) (since 1982, *Canada Act 1982* (U.K.), S.C. 1982, c. 11).

[150] [2000] S.C.J. No. 35, [2000] 3 C.T.C. 463, 2000 D.T.C. 6467 (S.C.C.) at para. 31.

[151] The leading case in this respect is *Wiebe Door Services Ltd. v. M.N.R.*, [1986] F.C.J. No. 1052, [1986] 2 C.T.C. 200, 87 D.T.C. 5025 (F.C.A.), which is excerpted in Chapter 4.

[152] See, for example, *Kalef v. Canada*, [1996] 2 C.T.C. 1, 96 D.T.C. 6132 (F.C.A.) and *Wheeliker v. Canada*, [1999] F.C.J. No. 401, [1999] 2 C.T.C. 395, 99 D.T.C. 5658 (F.C.A.).

[153] See, for example, *Continental Bank Leasing Corp. v. Canada*, [1998] S.C.J. No. 63, [1998] 4 C.T.C. 119, 98 D.T.C. 6505 (S.C.C.).

[154] See, for example, *Gagnon v. M.N.R.* (1960), 24 Tax ABC 309, 60 D.T.C. 347 (Tax A.B.C.) and *Aspinall v. M.N.R.*, [1970] Tax ABC 1073, 70 D.T.C. 1669 (Tax A.B.C.).

[155] See, for example, *M.N.R. v. Wardean Drilling Ltd.*, [1969] C.T.C. 265, 69 D.T.C. 5194 (Ex. Ct.) and *R v. Lagueux & Frères Inc.*, [1974] F.C.J. No. 118, [1974] C.T.C. 687, 74 D.T.C. 6569 (F.C.T.D.).

[156] See, for example, *Drescher v. Canada*, [1985] F.C.J. No. 23, [1985] 1 C.T.C. 229, 85 D.T.C. 5064 (F.C.T.D.) and *Côté v. Canada*, [1999] F.C.J. No. 1788, 2000 D.T.C. 6017 (F.C.A.).

Parliament by the Minister of Finance. While significant tax changes are generally introduced with annual budgets, other amendments are often introduced through so-called technical amendments bills, which have also tended to become an annual occurrence. Less frequently, tax reform is initiated by a commission or committee appointed by the Government in order to conduct a more comprehensive review of the tax system,[157] and/or by a white paper announcing the Government's intention to amend the *Income Tax Act* after discussion and consultation.

As a general rule, budgetary and other proposals to amend the income tax are introduced in the form of a notice of ways and means motion to amend the *Income Tax Act*. For the most part, these documents are relatively readable, expressing the Government's intentions in ordinary language. At the same time, or some months later if the proposed amendments are complex, the Department of Finance will release a draft of the proposed legislative changes, which have since 1983 been accompanied by explanatory notes or "technical notes" designed to explain the purpose of each amendment. Some time later, or concurrently if no lead time for public consultation is contemplated, a bill incorporating the proposed tax changes will be introduced in the House of Commons.

Assuming approval by a majority of the House, which is almost certain when the Government has a majority, the bill is subject to first and second reading in the House of Commons, after which it is studied by the House of Commons Standing Committee on Finance, which may recommend revisions before the bill is returned to the House for third reading. Having passed third reading in the House of Commons, a bill proceeds to the Senate for first and second reading, review by the Senate Standing Committee on Banking, Trade and Commerce, and third reading, before finally coming into force upon royal assent by the Governor General. Typically, tax legislation is made retroactive to the date when the proposed amendment was announced so that taxpayers have no opportunity to take measures to avoid the amendments before they come into effect.

Traditionally accepted by Canadian courts only as evidence of broad statutory purposes, extrastatutory materials comprising the legislative history of a statutory provision are increasingly accepted as evidence of Parliament's specific intentions, particularly where the legislation is ambiguous, the statement relied on is made by a person responsible for the legislation such as the minister of finance, and the statement itself is clear.[158] In *Symes v. Canada*,[159] for example, a majority of the Supreme Court of Canada relied on a federal

---

[157] An excellent example is the Royal Commission on Taxation (Carter Commission), which was discussed in Section II of Chapter 1. A more recent example is the Technical Committee on Business Taxation (Mintz Committee), which reported in 1998.

[158] See the sections on "Statutory Purposes" and "Legislative Intent", Sections II.D and II.E, respectively.

[159] [1993] S.C.J. No. 131, [1994] 1 C.T.C. 40, 94 D.T.C. 6001 (S.C.C.).

government white paper on tax reform to support its conclusion that the limited child-care expense deduction in section 63 of the Act constitutes a complete code, precluding the deduction of these expenses in computing a taxpayer's income from a business.[160] Likewise, in *Will-Kare Paving & Contracting v. Canada*,[161] Binnie J (dissenting) relied on statements in the House of Commons by then Minister of Finance John Turner to support the conclusion that the words "goods for sale" should be interpreted according to their plain or ordinary meaning rather than the technical or legal meaning established by commercial law. In other cases, the Federal Court of Appeal has relied on budget statements and Department of Finance technical notes to interpret applicable provisions.[162]

While the partisan nature of parliamentary debates and budget statements suggests that they should be treated with considerable caution as sources of statutory meaning,[163] these concerns are less significant for commission reports and white papers, and much less so for technical notes issued by the Department of Finance. Regardless, the Federal Court of Appeal has held that these considerations go to the weight that a court should accord to these extrinsic materials rather than their admissibility.[164]

H. Canada Revenue Agency Publications

In contrast to the Department of Finance, which is responsible for proposing and drafting changes to the *Income Tax Act*, the Canada Revenue Agency (CRA), formerly Revenue Canada, is responsible for administering the Act and collecting tax. While the Act itself provides for administration by "the Minister"[165] defined in subsection 248(1) of the Act as the Minister of National Revenue, subsection 220(1) authorizes the Commissioner of Customs and Revenue to exercise all the powers and perform the duties of the Minister under the Act, while subsection 220(2.01) permits the Minister to delegate these powers to officers employed for this purpose.

In order to administer the income tax, the CRA issues a number of forms and guides, as well more detailed information circulars (ICs), information bulletins (income tax or "IT" bulletins), and technical news releases, designed to provide information on tax matters to the general public and to convey the revenue

---

[160] Citing E.J. Benson, *Proposals for Tax Reform* (Ottawa: Department of Finance, 1969), paras 2.7 and 2.9 (proposing "on social as well as economic grounds to permit a tax deduction for child care expenses, under carefully controlled terms" to "assist many mothers who work or want to work to provide or supplement the family income, but are discouraged by the cost of having their children cared for"). This case is discussed in Chapter 7.

[161] [2000] S.C.J. No. 35, [2000] 3 C.T.C. 463, 2000 D.T.C. 6467 (S.C.C.).

[162] See *Lor-Wes Contracting* and *Maritime Telephone & Telegraph*, [1985] A.C.F. no. 178, [1985] 2 C.T.C. 79, 85 D.T.C. 5310 (F.C.A.).

[163] See, for example, *Heywood*, [1994] S.C.J. No. 101, 120 D.L.R. (4th) 348 (S.C.C.).

[164] *Fibreco Pulp v. Canada*, [1995] F.C.J. No. 934, [1995] 2 C.T.C. 172, 95 D.T.C. 5412 (F.C.A.).

[165] See, for example, subsection 150(1), which requires taxpayers to file an annual return with "the Minister".

agency's views on the applicable law.[166] CRA officials also make public statements that are widely reported and often cited as authoritative expressions of administrative practice.[167] Although these materials and public statements have no legal force, they represent useful and reliable summaries of applicable law, to which courts routinely refer as useful and persuasive aids to interpretation. In *R. v. Nowegijick*,[168] for example, the Supreme Court of Canada relied on an interpretation bulletin that supported the taxpayer's argument for tax-exempt status under the federal *Indian Act*, emphasizing that:

> [a]dministrative policy and interpretation are not determinative but are entitled to weight and can be an "important factor" in case of doubt about the meaning of legislation: per de Grandpré J, *Harel v. The Deputy Minister of Revenue of the Province of Quebec*, [1978] 1 SCR 851 at 859.

Likewise, in *Lowe v. Canada*,[169] (excerpted in Chapter 4), the Federal Court of Appeal relied on the revenue agency's own interpretation bulletin to support its conclusion that the taxpayer and his wife had not received a taxable employment benefit from a trip to New Orleans accompanying clients of the taxpayer's employer.

While it is the general policy of the revenue authority to assess taxpayers in accordance with its declared administrative practice, this is not always the rule, as the *Nowegijick* and *Lowe* cases illustrate.[170] Perhaps surprisingly, courts have consistently held that taxpayers may not rely on these administrative positions, and that the revenue authority is not estopped from assessing a taxpayer in a manner contrary to its declared view of the law.[171]

In addition to these materials the CRA also issues advance tax rulings (ATRs), explaining to taxpayers who pay a fee for the service, how the revenue agency will assess a transaction or series of transactions that the taxpayer is

---

[166] These materials are available at the CRA's Web site at <http://www.cra-arc.gc.ca/>.

[167] At the Canadian Tax Foundation's annual conference, for example, CRA officials respond to questions submitted in advance. The answers are reported in the Foundation's conference proceedings.

[168] [1983] S.C.J. No. 5 at para. 28, [1983] C.T.C. 20, 83 D.T.C. 5041 (S.C.C.).

[169] [1996] F.C.J. No. 319, [1996] 2 C.T.C. 33, 96 D.T.C. 6226 (F.C.A.).

[170] See also *Canada v. Fries*, [1989] F.C.J. No. 407, [1989] 1 C.T.C. 471, 89 D.T.C. 5240 (F.C.A.), rev'd [1990] S.C.J. No. 109, [1990] 2 C.T.C. 439, 90 D.T.C. 6662 (S.C.C.), which is excerpted in Chapter 4. For a thorough discussion of the principle of estoppel in Canadian income tax law, see Glen Loutzenhiser, "Holding Revenue Canada to its Word: Estoppel in Tax Law" (1999) 57 U. T. Fac. L. Rev. 127-64.

[171] The case that is most often cited for this position is *Stickel v. M.N.R.*, [1972] F.C.J. No. 53, [1972] C.T.C. 210, 72 D.T.C. 6178 (F.C.T.D.), rev'd on other grounds by the Federal Court of Appeal, [1973] F.C.J. No. 31, [1973] C.T.C. 202, 73 D.T.C. 5178 (F.C.A.), which decision was subsequently affirmed by the Supreme Court of Canada, [1974] S.C.J. No. 93, [1974] C.T.C. 416, 74 D.T.C. 6268. See also *M.N.R. v. Inland Industries*, [1971] S.C.J. No. 145, [1972] C.T.C. 27, 72 D.T.C. 6013 (S.C.C.); *Gibbon v. Canada*, [1977] A.C.F. no. 140, [1977] C.T.C. 334, 77 D.T.C. 5193 (F.C.T.D.); and *74712 Alberta v. M.N.R.*, [1994] F.C.J. No. 786, [1994] 2 C.T.C. 191, 94 D.T.C. 6392 (F.C.T.D.).

considering. Although case law suggests that the CRA is not estopped from assessing a taxpayer in a manner contrary to the position that it takes in an ATR,[172] the Department of Revenue declared at the inception of the formal ATR program in 1970 that an advance income tax ruling "will be regarded as binding on the Department", and there are no instances when the revenue authority has not adhered to a ruling. While ATRs are specifically limited to their own facts, they are released in "severed form" with names and other details omitted to protect the anonymity of the taxpayer, and may be considered as an indication of the revenue authority's "general attitude ... toward the appropriateness of the use of a particular provision in the Act for a particular purpose".[173]

I. Scholarly and Professional Publications

A final source to which Canadian courts refer to interpret the Income Tax Act consists of texts and other publications by legal academics and practitioners. Among legal tax texts and casebooks, the two most prominent in terms of legal citations are Peter W. Hogg, Joanne E. Magee, and Jinyan Li, *Principles of Canadian Income Tax Law*, 6th ed. (Toronto: Thomson Carswell, 2007) and Vern Krishna, *The Fundamentals of Canadian Income Tax Law*, 9th ed. (Toronto: Carswell, 2006), though others have also been considered.[174] In addition to these sources, courts frequently refer to books and articles published by the Canadian Tax Foundation, an independent tax research organization that publishes the Canadian Tax Journal four times a year, an annual conference report, and specialized monographs on assorted topics.[175] A final source of interpretive assistance is often found in services published by Carswell (Canada Tax Service) and CCH (Canadian Tax Reporter). Although published in looseleaf version, these services are also included in each publisher's CD-ROM product: TaxPartner for Carswell and TaxWorks for CCH.

---

[172] *Woon v. M.N.R.*, [1950] C.T.C. 263, 50 D.T.C. 871 (Ex. Ct.).

[173] Sherman, *Canadian Tax Research: A Practical Guide*, 3d ed. (Scarborough: Carswell, 1997) at 94.

[174] See, for example, B.G. Hansen, V. Krishna, and J.A. Rendall, eds., *Essays on Canadian Taxation* (Toronto: Butterworths, 1978); Edwin C. Harris, *Canadian Income Taxation*, 4th ed. (Toronto: Butterworths, 1986); Vern Krishna, *Tax Avoidance: The General Anti-Avoidance Rule* (Toronto: Carswell, 1990); Vern Krishna, *Income Tax Law* (Concord: Irwin Law, 1997); Tim Edgar, Jinyan Li, and Daniel Sandler, *Materials on Canadian Income Tax*, 12th ed. (Toronto: Carswell, 2000); and Norman C. Tobias, *Taxation of Corporations, Partnerships and Trusts*, 2d ed. (Toronto: Carswell, 2001).

[175] The Foundation is located in Toronto and has an excellent library that is open to the public. The full text of the Foundation's major publications is available on a CD-ROM product called TaxFind. The Foundation's Web site is <http://www.ctf.ca/>.

CHAPTER THREE

Introduction to Tax Avoidance

I. INTRODUCTION

Tax law depends not only on the interpretation of words, but also on the interpretation of facts. To the extent that tax consequences depend on the classification of amounts or transactions as being of one type rather than another, courts are confronted with the often difficult task of characterizing these amounts and transactions for the purposes of assessing tax. This task is rendered even more challenging by the fact that taxpayers, particularly those who are well advised regarding the tax consequences of alternative courses of action, may endeavour to arrange their affairs specifically in order to obtain a more favourable tax outcome. Indeed, these arrangements raise yet further interpretive issues about the character of the amounts or transactions to which the *Income Tax Act* ought to apply.

As opposed to tax "evasion", which involves an illegal breach of specific statutory duties such as failing to file a return or deliberately concealing or falsifying reported information,[1] these legal efforts to order one's affairs to minimize tax are labelled "tax avoidance". As the cases and statutory provisions examined in this chapter illustrate, the challenges posed by such tax avoidance have been a fertile source of judicial analysis and statutory reform. Section II reviews alternative approaches to tax avoidance adopted by the courts in Canada, the United Kingdom, and the United States. Section III considers specific anti-avoidance rules designed to prevent certain kinds of avoidance transactions considered sufficiently unacceptable to require a legislative response. Section IV examines the general anti-avoidance rule (GAAR) in section 245, which was enacted in 1988.

---

[1] See ss. 238 and 239 of the *Income Tax Act*, R.S.C. 1985, c. 1 (5th Supp.), as amended (herein referred to as "the Act"), which make tax evasion a criminal offence. See also ss. 162 and 163, which impose civil penalties for various acts and omissions. This book does not examine these provisions nor the investigatory powers that the revenue authorities may employ to determine the existence of tax evasion. For a brief summary of criminal prosecutions under the Act, see Peter W. Hogg, Joanne E. Magee & Ted Cook, *Principles of Canadian Income Tax Law*, 3d ed. (Toronto: Carswell, 1999) at 27-28.

II. JUDICIAL ANTI-AVOIDANCE DOCTRINES

The development of judicial doctrines in Canada, the United Kingdom, and the United States reflects widely different attitudes and approaches to taxpayer efforts to avoid or minimize their tax liabilities. Consistent with the doctrine of "liberal construction" applied by the US Supreme Court to the US *Internal Revenue Code*,[2] American courts were quick to adopt a critical approach to the phenomenon of tax avoidance.[3] In contrast, UK and Canadian courts, adhering to a doctrine of "strict construction," affirmed a distinctly laissez-faire attitude to tax avoidance, applying statutory provisions on the basis of legal relationships validly entered into by taxpayers regardless of the purpose — whether or not motivated by tax considerations — for which taxpayers entered into these relationships.[4]

While the attitude of UK and Canadian courts began to change by the mid-1970s and early 1980s,[5] the Supreme Court of Canada's decision in *Stubart Investments Ltd. v. Canada*,[6] signalled a reaffirmation of the traditional judicial approach to tax avoidance at the same time as it announced the demise of strict construction. Four years later, Parliament effectively overruled *Stubart* by enacting the GAAR.

As background to the specific anti-avoidance rules discussed in section III and the GAAR examined in section IV, this section reviews the various judicial anti-avoidance doctrines adopted by UK and Canadian courts. As an introduction, and by way of contrast, it considers the anti-avoidance doctrines adopted by the US courts.

A. US Approach

Among the earliest US cases adopting a critical approach to tax avoidance is *Gregory v. Helvering, Commissioner of Internal Revenue*, 293 U.S. 465 (1935), in which the taxpayer entered into a series of tax-motivated transactions to obtain the benefit of a statutory provision governing corporate reorganizations.

---

2 In *Commissioner v. Glenshaw Glass Co.*, 348 US 426 (1955).

3 *Gregory v. Helvering, Commissioner of Internal Revenue*, 293 US 465 (1935).

4 *Commissioners of Inland Revenue v. Duke of Westminster*, [1936] A.C. 1 (H.L.).

5 For Canadian cases, see *Dominion Bridge Company Ltd. v. Canada*, [1975] C.T.C. 263, 75 D.T.C. 5150 (F.C.T.D.), aff'd. [1977] C.T.C. 554, 77 D.T.C. 5367 (F.C.A.); and *M.N.R. v. Leon*, [1976] F.C.J. No. 134, [1976] C.T.C. 532, 76 D.T.C. 6299 (F.C.A.). For UK cases, see *W.T. Ramsay Ltd. v. IRC*, [1981] 1 All E.R. 865 (H.L.); *CIR v. Burmah Oil Co. Ltd.* (1981), 54 Tax Cas. 200, [1981] 42 T.R. 535 (H.L.); and *Furniss v. Dawson*, [1984] 1 All E.R. 530 (H.L.).

6 [1984] S.C.J. No. 25, [1984] C.T.C. 294, 84 D.T.C. 6305 (S.C.C.).

Gregory v. Helvering, Commissioner of Internal Revenue
293 U.S. 465 (1935)

SUTHERLAND J: Petitioner in 1928 was the owner of all the stock of United Mortgage Corporation. That corporation held among its assets 1,000 shares of the Monitor Securities Corporation. For the sole purpose of procuring a transfer of these shares to herself in order to sell them for her individual profit, and, at the same time, diminish the amount of income tax which would result from a direct transfer by way of dividend, she sought to bring about a "reorganization" under §112(g) of the *Revenue Act of 1928*, c. 852, 45 Stat. 791, 818, set forth later in this opinion. To that end, she caused the Averill Corporation to be organized under the laws of Delaware on September 18, 1928. Three days later, the United Mortgage Corporation transferred to the Averill Corporation the 1,000 shares of Monitor stock, for which all the shares of the Averill Corporation were issued to the petitioner. On September 24, the Averill Corporation was dissolved, and liquidated by distributing all its assets, namely, the Monitor shares, to the petitioner. No other business was ever transacted, or intended to be transacted, by that company. Petitioner immediately sold the Monitor shares for $133,333.33. She returned for taxation as capital net gain the sum of $76,007.88, based upon an apportioned cost of $57,325.45. Further details are unnecessary. It is not disputed that if the interposition of the so-called reorganization was ineffective, petitioner became liable for a much larger tax as a result of the transaction.

The Commissioner of Internal Revenue, being of the opinion that the reorganization attempted was without substance and must be disregarded, held that petitioner was liable for a tax as though the United Corporation had paid her a dividend consisting of the amount realized from the sale of the Monitor shares.

...

Section 112 of the *Revenue Act of 1928* deals with the subject of gain or loss resulting from the sale or exchange of property. Such gain or loss is to be recognized in computing the tax, except as provided in that section. The provisions of the section, so far as they are pertinent to the question here presented, follow:

Sec. 112. (g) *Distribution of stock on reorganization.*—If there is distributed, in pursuance of a plan of reorganization, to a shareholder in a corporation a party to the reorganization, stock or securities in such corporation or in another corporation a party to the reorganization, without the surrender by such shareholder of stock or securities in such a corporation, no gain to the distributee from the receipt of such stock or securities shall be recognized ...

(i) *Definition of reorganization.*—As used in this section ...

(1) The term "reorganization" means ... (B) a transfer by a corporation of all or a part of its assets to another corporation if immediately after the transfer the transferor or its stockholders or both are in control of the corporation to which the assets are transferred, ...

It is earnestly contended on behalf of the taxpayer that since every element required by the foregoing subdivision (B) is to be found in what was done, a statutory reorganization was effected; and that the motive of the taxpayer thereby to escape payment of a tax will not alter the result or make unlawful what the statute allows. It is quite true that if reorganization in reality was effected within the meaning of subdivision (B), the ulterior purpose mentioned will be disregarded. The legal right of a taxpayer to decrease the amount of what otherwise would be his taxes, or altogether avoid them, by means which the law permits, cannot be doubted. ... But the question for determination is whether what was done, apart from the tax motive, was the thing which the statute intended.

...

When subdivision (B) speaks of a transfer of assets by one corporation to another, it means a transfer made "in pursuance of a plan of reorganization" [§ 112(g)] of corporate business; and not a transfer of assets by one corporation to another in pursuance of a plan having no relation to the business of either, as plainly is the case here. Putting aside, then, the question of motive in respect of taxation altogether, and fixing the character of the proceeding by what actually occurred, what do we find? Simply an operation having no business or corporate purpose—a mere device which put on the form of a corporate reorganization as a disguise for concealing its real character, and the sole object and accomplishment of which was the consummation of a preconceived plan, not to reorganize a business or any part of a business, but to transfer a parcel of corporate shares to the petitioner. No doubt, a new and valid corporation was created. But that corporation was nothing more than a contrivance to the end last described. It was brought into existence for no other purpose; it performed, as it was intended from the beginning it should perform, no other function. When that limited function had been exercised, it immediately was put to death.

In these circumstances, the facts speak for themselves and are susceptible of but one interpretation. The whole undertaking, though conducted according to the terms of subdivision (B), was in fact an elaborate and devious form of conveyance masquerading as a corporate reorganization, and nothing else. The rule which excludes from consideration the motive of tax avoidance is not pertinent to the situation, because the transaction upon its face lies outside the plain intent of the statute. To hold otherwise would be to exalt artifice above reality and to deprive the statutory provision in question of all serious purpose.

Judgment affirmed.

NOTES AND QUESTIONS

1.   What was the Commissioner's argument in *Gregory*? What was the taxpayer's argument? How did the US Supreme Court frame the issue for determination?

2.   There are two ways to read the decision of the US Supreme Court in *Gregory*. On the one hand, it is arguable that the decision involved nothing more than the specific meaning of the expression "plan of reorganization", which,

when properly interpreted, excluded the sequence of transactions carried out by the taxpayer. Indeed, the court itself appears to have advanced this view, emphasizing the irrelevance of the taxpayer's motive and concluding that "the transaction upon its face lies outside the plain intent of the statute". On the other hand, given the explicit statutory definition of the term "reorganization", to which the transactions carried out by the taxpayer apparently conformed, the statutory intent that the court construed appears to be anything but "plain". On the contrary, despite the court's insistence that the taxpayer's motive was "not pertinent to the situation," the absence of a genuine business or non-tax purpose seems to have been essential to the court's conclusion that the taxpayer had not effected a "plan of reorganization" but merely "a preconceived plan, not to reorganize a business or any part of a business, but to transfer a parcel of corporate shares to the petitioner." From this perspective, the scope of the decision is much broader, pointing to a general interpretive principle that tax statutes are intended to apply to *bona fide* commercial transactions and ought not to produce the same results where transactions are entered into solely or primarily to obtain tax advantages not clearly intended by the statute.

3.   However tenuous its origins may have been in *Gregory*, a broad "business purpose test" emerged from the decision. US courts have since often employed this test to deny a tax benefit (for example, a deduction or the deferral of tax) in circumstances where the taxpayer had no business purpose entering into the transaction or series of transactions, which were carried out solely or primarily to obtain the tax benefit. See, for example, *Bazley v. CIR*, 331 US 737 (1947); and *Goldstein v. CIR*, 364 F2d 734 (2d Cir. 1966), cert. denied 385 US 1005 (1967).

4.   In the decision from which Mrs. Gregory appealed, 69 F2d 809, at 811 (2d Cir. 1934), Judge Learned Hand remarked of the transactions entered into by Mrs. Gregory that:

> [a]ll these steps were real, and their only defect was that they were not what the statute means by a "reorganization," because the transactions were no part of the conduct of the business of either or both companies, so viewed they were a sham.

The *Concise Oxford Dictionary*, 7th ed., defines the word "sham" as "imposture, pretence, humbug", Similarly, the US Supreme Court emphasized the simulated character of the transactions, denouncing the operation as "a mere device which put on the form of a corporate reorganization as a disguise for concealing its real character, ... an elaborate and devious form of conveyance masquerading as a corporate reorganization".

5.   In *Gregory*, the Commissioner of Internal Revenue claimed that "the reorganization attempted was without substance". On this basis, he argued, the transactions that were actually carried out "must be disregarded" and Mrs. Gregory should be "liable for a tax as though the United Corporation had paid her a dividend consisting of the amount realized from the sale of the Monitor shares". In other words, the Commissioner appears to have concluded that while

the transactions may have taken the *form* of a reorganization, in *substance* they amounted to a dividend and should be taxed as such.

Like the business purpose test, the doctrine that the economic or commercial substance of a transaction should prevail over its legal form has been employed in a number of US tax cases. See, for example, *CIR v. Court Holding*, 324 U.S. 331 (1945); and *Waterman Steamship Corp. v. CIR*, 430 F2d 1185 (5th Cir. 1970), cert. denied 401 U.S. 939 (1971). Nonetheless, the doctrine has been criticized on the grounds that it is either incoherent, given the availability of alternative ways of structuring transactions, or incomplete, given the absence of any specific explanation as to why one transaction or series of transactions should be assimilated to another:

> When the Revenue want to argue that the facts although coming under C should be taxed as if they fell under A because they are in substance A, the Revenue may be arguing one of two things. First, they may be asserting that *all* Cs are in substance As and therefore the A rule should apply. This is nonsense given the existence of the C rule since it will deny that the C rule will ever apply. Alternatively, they are arguing that these particular C facts are in substance A facts and therefore the A rule should apply rather than the C rule but it follows that they have to explain what is it about *these* C facts that makes them A facts.[7]

Indeed, Judge Learned Hand once described these concepts of "form" and "substance" as "anodynes for the pains of reasoning": *CIR v. Sansome*, 60 F2d 931, at 933 (2d Cir. 1932), cert. denied 287 U.S. 667 (1932).

In *Gregory*, the court seems to have treated the formal "reorganization" as a dividend "in substance" on the grounds that the payment of a dividend would have achieved Mrs. Gregory's main purpose in a straightforward manner whereas the organization of and transfer of shares to the Averill Corporation served no purpose other than the reduction of tax. Thus, the "business purpose test" appears to have provided the necessary reason to recharacterize the reorganization as a dividend.

In this light, the doctrine of economic or commercial "substance over form" appears to have functioned as a remedial adjunct to the "business purpose test". While the "business purpose test" provided the reason for recharacterization, the substance-over-form doctrine supplied the method of recharacterization. Although the substantive outcome may have been the same as the Commissioner sought, the process of reasoning was not.

B. Anglo-Canadian Approach

From the decision of the US Supreme Court in *Gregory v. Helvering*, one can trace at least three judicial anti-avoidance doctrines: substance over form, sham, and the business purpose test. The following cases and commentary consider the Anglo-Canadian approach to these doctrines and the development of a fourth

---

[7] John Tiley, "Judicial Anti-Avoidance Doctrines: The US Alternatives — Part II" [1987] 6 Brit. Tax Rev. 220 at 229-30.

judicial anti-avoidance doctrine directed at legally ineffective avoidance transactions.

1. Form and Substance

As *Gregory v. Helvering* is to the development of US tax law, so *Commissioners of Inland Revenue v. Duke of Westminster*, [1936] A.C. 1 (H.L.), is to the evolution of Anglo-Canadian tax law. With regard to a transaction apparently no less tax-motivated than that of Mrs. Gregory, the English House of Lords set a markedly different course from that of the US Supreme Court.

Commissioners of Inland Revenue v. Duke of Westminster
[1936] A.C. 1 (H.L.)

In August 1930, the respondent, the Duke of Westminster, drew up a deed in which he promised to pay Allman, a gardener in his employment, the annual sum of £98 16s. in weekly payments of £1 18s. for a period of seven years or during the joint lives of the parties. It was further agreed that these payments would be without prejudice to the remuneration to which Allman was entitled for services, if any, that he rendered after that time.

Before the deed was executed, the Duke's solicitors, on his instructions, wrote to Allman a letter. The material parts of the letter were as follows:

> On the 6th inst. we read over with you a deed of covenant which the Duke of Westminster has signed in your favour. We explained that there is nothing in the deed to prevent your being entitled to and claiming full remuneration for such further work as you may do, though it is expected that in practice you will be content with the provision which is being legally made for you for so long as the deed takes effect with the addition of such sum, if any, as may be necessary to bring the total periodical payment while you are still in the Duke's service up to the amount of the salary or wages which you have lately been receiving. You said that you accepted this arrangement, and you accordingly executed the deed. ... If you are still quite satisfied, we propose to insert the 6th inst. as the date of the deed, and we shall be obliged by your signing the acknowledgment at the foot of this letter and returning it to us.

Allman signed the acknowledgment. By doing so he accepted the provision made for him and agreed to the deed being dated and treated as delivered and binding on its parties. The acknowledgment was stamped with a sixpenny stamp.

The question was whether certain payments made by the Duke to various retainers and servants were annual payments within the meaning of section 27 of the *Income Tax Act, 1918*, and thus admissible as deductions in calculating the Duke's liability for surtax for the years 1929-1932.

The Duke appealed against the revenue authority's assessment of surtax for the three years. He claimed that in computing the amount of his total income liable to surtax, he was entitled to exclude the payments made under the deeds during the three years. The Commissioners of Inland Revenue decided that, except for payments to those covenantees who had already left their employment by the Duke, all payments under the deeds were in effect payments for services to be rendered to the Duke, and thus were not allowable as deductions from his income. At the Court of Appeal, the decision of the Commissioners was reversed. The Commissioners appealed to the House of Lords.]

LORD TOMLIN: ... [S]o far as I understand the argument the appellants, while admitting that Allman's annuity is payable under the deed, say that there is, having regard to the correspondence and in all the circumstances, another collateral contract between the Duke and the payee to the effect that the payee will serve the Duke in consideration of a salary or wage equal to the salary or wage he was receiving before the deed of covenant was executed, and that he will accept what he receives under the deed in part satisfaction of this salary or wage; and therefore that the annuity, so long as the payee remains in the Duke's service, is of a changed nature and is no longer a payment which the Duke is entitled to deduct from his income for the purposes of surtax.

...

[S]uch a contract if it could be inferred at all is in flat contradiction of the deed. Under the deed the payments are expressed to be without prejudice to such remuneration as the annuitant would become entitled to in respect of such services (if any) as the annuitant might thereafter render to the Duke. ...

In fact I do not think that upon the true construction of the relevant letter and written acknowledgment ... there was any such collateral contract as alleged. The letter of August 13, 1930, told the annuitant that there was nothing in the deed to prevent his being entitled to and claiming full remuneration for such future work as he might do, though it was expected that in practice he would be content in effect with the difference between the annuity and salary or wages which he had been lately receiving. I cannot think that a letter so framed can be construed as constituting a contract that the payee would serve the Duke upon terms in contradiction of the language of the letter—namely, that he should be entitled to less than the salary or wages which he had been then lately receiving. Further, the arrangement which the annuitant is stated in the letter to have accepted must, I think, on a proper reading of the letter refer to all that is set out in the letter as well as what is contained in the deed, and includes his right to full remuneration over and above what is received under the deed. Again, the acknowledgment signed by the annuitant at the foot of the letter is that he accepts the provision made for him by the deed, and that is a provision without prejudice to his right to full remuneration over and above what he receives under the deed. In short, it seems to me that there is no such contract as that which the appellants suggest can be inferred.

Apart, however, from the question of contract with which I have dealt, it is said that in revenue cases there is a doctrine that the Court may ignore the legal position and regard what is called "the substance of the matter," and that here the substance of the matter is that the annuitant was serving the Duke for something equal to his former salary or wages, and that therefore, while he is so serving, the annuity must be treated as salary or wages. This supposed doctrine (upon which the Commissioners apparently acted) seems to rest for its support upon a misunderstanding of language used in some earlier cases. The sooner this misunderstanding is dispelled, and the supposed doctrine given its *quietus*, the better it will be for all concerned, for the doctrine seems to involve substituting "the incertain and crooked cord of discretion" for "the golden and streight metwand of the law." Every man is entitled if he can to order his affairs so as that the tax attaching under the appropriate Acts is less than it otherwise would be. If he succeeds in ordering them so as to secure this result, then, however unappreciative the Commissioners of Inland Revenue or his fellow taxpayers may be of his ingenuity, he cannot be compelled to pay an increased tax. This so-called doctrine of "the substance" seems to me to be nothing more than an attempt to make a man pay notwithstanding that he has so ordered his affairs that the amount of tax sought from him is not legally claimable.

The principal passages relied upon are from opinions of Lord Herschell and Lord Halsbury in your Lordships' House. Lord Herschell LC in *Helby v. Matthews* observed: "It is said that the substance of the transaction evidenced by the agreement must be looked at, and not its mere words. I quite agree;" but he went on to explain that the substance must be ascertained by a consideration of the rights and obligations of the parties to be derived from a consideration of the whole of the agreement. In short Lord Herschell was saying that the substance of a transaction embodied in a written instrument is to be found by construing the document as a whole.

Support has also been sought by the appellants from the language of Lord Halsbury LC in *Secretary of State in Council of India v. Scoble*. There Lord Halsbury said: "Still, looking at the whole nature and substance of the transaction (and it is agreed on all sides that we must look at the nature of the transaction and not be bound by the mere use of the words), this is not the case of a purchase of an annuity." Here again Lord Halsbury is only giving utterance to the indisputable rule that the surrounding circumstances must be regarded in construing a document.

Neither of these passages in my opinion affords the appellants any support or has any application to the present case. The matter was put accurately by my noble and learned friend Lord Warrington of Clyffe when as Warrington LJ in *In re Hinckes, Dashwood v. Hinckes* he used these words: "It is said we must go behind the form and look at the substance ... but, in order to ascertain the substance, I must look at the legal effect of the bargain which the parties have entered into." So here the substance is that which results from the legal rights and obligations of the parties ascertained upon ordinary legal principles, and, having regard to what I have already said, the conclusion must be that each annuitant is entitled to an annuity which as between himself and the payer is liable to deduction of income tax by the payer and which the payer is entitled to treat as a deduction from his total income for surtax purposes.

There may, of course, be cases where documents are not *bona fide* nor intended to be acted upon, but are only used as a cloak to conceal a different transaction. No such case is made or even suggested here. The deeds of covenant are admittedly *bona fide* and have been given their proper legal operation. They cannot be ignored or treated as operating in some different way because as a result less duty is payable than would have been the case if some other arrangement (called for the purpose of the appellants' argument "the substance") had been made.

...

LORD RUSSELL OF KILLOWEN: My Lords, I would dismiss this appeal.

It is conceded that the deeds are genuine deeds, i.e., that they were intended to create and do create a legal liability on the Duke to pay in weekly payments the annual sum specified in each deed, whether or not any service is being rendered to the Duke by the covenantee. Further, it is conceded that the sums specified in the deeds were paid to the covenantees under the deeds.

...

My Lords, for myself I can find nothing in the letter and acknowledgment which constitutes or resembles a contract, notwithstanding the fact that the names of the solicitors were written across an adhesive stamp. There is an expression of a hope or anticipation or expectation that the covenantee will pursue a certain line of conduct, but he nowhere binds himself to do so, nor indeed is he even asked to do so. In my opinion the letter has no operation at all, and has no effect upon the legal rights and liabilities of the parties created by the deed.... The result is that payments, the liability for which arises only under the deed, are not and cannot be said to be payments of salary or wages. ... They cannot with any regard to the true legal position be said to arise from an employment.

...

The Commissioners ... took the opposite view on the ground that (as they said) looking at the substance of the thing the payments were payments of wages. This simply means that the true legal position is disregarded, and a different legal right and liability substituted in the place of the legal right and liability which the parties have created. I confess that I view with disfavour the doctrine that in taxation cases the subject is to be taxed if, in accordance with a Court's view of what it considers the substance of the transaction, the Court thinks that the case falls within the contemplation or spirit of the statute. The subject is not taxable by inference or by analogy, but only by the plain words of a statute applicable to the facts and circumstances of his case. As Lord Cairns said many years ago in *Partington v. Attorney-General:*

> As I understand the principle of all fiscal legislation it is this: If the person sought to be taxed comes within the letter of the law he must be taxed, however great the hardship may appear to the judicial mind to be. On the other hand, if the Crown, seeking to recover the tax, cannot bring the subject within the letter of the law, the subject is free, however apparently within the spirit of the law the case might otherwise appear to be.

If all that is meant by the doctrine is that having once ascertained the legal rights of the parties you may disregard mere nomenclature and decide the

156

question of taxability or non-taxability in accordance with the legal rights, well and good. ... If, on the other hand, the doctrine means that you may brush aside deeds, disregard the legal rights and liabilities arising under a contract between parties, and decide the question of taxability or non-taxability upon the footing of the rights and liabilities of the parties being different from what in law they are, then I entirely dissent from such a doctrine.

The substance of the transaction between Allman and the Duke is in my opinion to be found and to be found only by ascertaining their respective rights and liabilities under the deed, the legal effect of which is what I have already stated.

...

LORD ATKIN (dissenting): ... It was not, I think, denied — at any rate it is incontrovertible that the deeds were brought into existence as a device by which the respondent might avoid some of the burden of surtax. I do not use the word device in any sinister sense, for it has to be recognized that the subject, whether poor and humble or wealthy and noble, has the legal right so to dispose of his capital and income as to attract upon himself the least amount of tax. The only function of a Court of law is to determine the legal result of his dispositions so far as they affect tax.

...

It will be observed from the letter that on August 6, the solicitors had produced to the servant the deed already executed by the Duke but undated and had made the explanation set out in the letter; that the servant had accepted "this arrangement," and had executed the deed. Now what was the object of the letter and the signed acknowledgment which formed part of the document? The respondent gravely says merely to provide evidence that the servant was satisfied with the provision made for him by the deed and to protect the Duke against claims against him in the future for any increased pension. But the servant in no case had any legal claim to pension; in any case the deed was not to last for more than seven years; and finally, and as I suggest, conclusively, the servant had already signified his acceptance of the provision made in the deed by executing it "accordingly." Execution by the servant had been in law unnecessary.

In my opinion the facts and the terms of the letter indicate that the transaction was intended to have, and had, far more substantial results than the interchange of unnecessary assurances between master and servant. ... I am satisfied that a letter signed over a contract stamp and requiring the addressee to return it with the appended acknowledgment signed, addressed by the employer's solicitors to a workman at weekly wages would inevitably be understood by the recipient and would be intended by the writers to be understood as a representation that he was being asked to make a contract in the terms of the document.

...

I do not myself see any difficulty in the view taken by the Commissioners ... that the substance of the transaction was that what was being paid was remuneration. ... I agree that you must not go beyond the legal effect of the agreements and conveyances made, construed in accordance with ordinary rules in reference to all the surrounding circumstances. So construed the correct view of the legal effect of the documents appears to me to be the result I have mentioned.

...

[Lord Macmillan and Lord Wright also wrote judgments dismissing the appeal.]

NOTES AND QUESTIONS

1. In the *Duke of Westminster* case, the Commissioners had argued that "the substance of the transaction was that what was being paid was remuneration". Lords Tomlin and Russell rejected this argument and any doctrine suggesting that the courts "may ignore the legal position" (Lord Tomlin), "brush aside deeds, disregard the legal rights and liabilities arising under a contract between parties, and decide the question of taxability or non-taxability upon the footing of the rights and liabilities of the parties being different from what in law they are" (Lord Russell). For Lord Russell, this conclusion necessarily follows from a literal or plain meaning approach to statutory interpretation: "The subject is not taxable by inference or analogy, but only by the plain words of a statute applicable to the facts and circumstances of his case."

According to Lord Tomlin, the "supposed doctrine" that the courts may ignore "the legal position" and look to "the substance of the matter" stems from "a misunderstanding of language used in some earlier cases." Reviewing these cases, he concluded that "the substance is that which results from the legal rights and obligations of the parties ascertained upon ordinary legal principles". Likewise, Lord Russell said of the doctrine that the courts should look to the substance of a transaction rather than its form: "If all that is meant by the doctrine is that having once ascertained the legal rights of the parties you may disregard mere nomenclature and decide the question of taxability or non-taxability in accordance with the legal rights, well and good."

Thus, while Lords Tomlin and Russell rejected the doctrine of economic or commercial substance over form, they affirmed the statements in earlier cases that the courts may disregard the nomenclature used by the parties to a contract in favour of the "substance ... which results from the legal rights and obligations of the parties ascertained upon ordinary legal principles". This latter approach was neatly summarized by Viscount Simon in *CIR v. Wesleyan and General Assurance Society*, [1948] 1 All E.R. 555, 30 Tax Cas. 11 at 24-25 (H.L.) as follows:

> It may be well to repeat two propositions which are well established in the application of the law relating to income tax. First, the name given to a transaction by the parties concerned does not necessarily decide the nature of the transaction. To call a payment a loan if it is really an annuity does not assist the taxpayer, any more than to call an item a capital payment

> would prevent it from being regarded as an income payment if that is its true nature. The question always is what is the real character of the payment, not what the parties call it. Secondly, a transaction which, on its true construction, is of a kind that would escape tax is not taxable on the ground that the same result could be brought about by a transaction in another form which would attract tax.

This passage has been cited and followed in numerous Canadian tax cases. See, for example, *Front & Simcoe Ltd. v. M.N.R.*, [1960] C.T.C. 123, 60 D.T.C. 1081 (Ex. Ct.); *M.N.R. v. Ouellette*, [1971] C.T.C. 121, 71 D.T.C. 5094 (Ex. Ct.); *Perini Estate v. M.N.R.*, [1982] F.C.J. No. 12, [1982] C.T.C. 74, 82 D.T.C. 6080 (F.C.A.); *Regina News Limited v. M.N.R.*, [1993] T.C.J. No. 76, [1993] 2 C.T.C. 2136, 93 D.T.C. 358 (T.C.C.); and *Entre Computer Centers Inc. v. Canada*, [1996] T.C.J. No. 1311, [1997] 1 C.T.C. 2291, (1996) 97 D.T.C. 846 (T.C.C.).

2. In general, Canadian courts have accepted the doctrine that the *legal substance* of a contract or transaction is to prevail over the nomenclature employed by the parties, but not the more expansive doctrine of economic or commercial substance over form adopted in the United States. See, for example, *Donald MacDonald v. M.N.R.*, [1974] C.T.C. 2204, 74 D.T.C. 1161 (T.R.B.); and *Boardman v. Canada*, [1979] A.C.J. no 53, [1979] C.T.C. 159, 79 D.T.C. 5110 (F.C.T.D.).

Nonetheless, by failing to distinguish clearly between these two very different doctrines, Canadian courts have at times contributed to the same "misunderstanding of language" to which Lord Tomlin referred in *Duke of Westminster*. In *Dominion Taxicab Assn. v. M.N.R.*, [1954] S.C.J. No. 4, [1954] C.T.C. 34, 54 D.T.C. 1020 (S.C.C.), for example, the Supreme Court of Canada, though clearly referring to the narrow doctrine of *legal* substance over form, stated (at para. 10) that "[i]t is well settled that in considering whether a particular transaction brings a party within the terms of the *Income Tax Acts* its substance rather than form is to be regarded."

Canadian courts have also, on occasion, favoured a broader doctrine of economic or commercial substance over form. In *Bronfman Trust v. Canada*, [1987] S.C.J. No. 1, [1987] 1 C.T.C. 117 at 128, 87 D.T.C. 5059 (S.C.C.), for example, Dickson CJ noted (at para. 48) that:

> just as there has been a recent trend away from strict construction of taxation statutes ... so too has the recent trend in tax cases been towards attempting to ascertain the true commercial and practical nature of the taxpayer's transactions. There has been, in this country and elsewhere, a movement away from tests based on the form of transactions and towards tests based on ... "a common sense appreciation of all the guiding features" of the events in question.

Writing for a unanimous panel of six members of the court, Dickson CJ commented (at para. 49) that this trend was "laudable ... provided it is consistent with the text and purposes of the taxation statute", and proceeded to suggest that:

> [a]ssessment of taxpayers' transactions with an eye to commercial and economic realities, rather than juristic classification of form, may help to avoid the inequity of tax liability being

> dependent upon the taxpayer's sophistication at manipulating a sequence of events to achieve
> a patina of compliance with the apparent prerequisites for a tax deduction.

This passage was cited with approval in subsequent decisions of the Supreme Court of Canada in *McClurg v. Canada*, [1990] S.C.J. No. 134, [1991] 1 C.T.C. 169, [1990] 91 D.T.C. 5001 (S.C.C.), *Buanderie Centrale de Montreal Inc. v. Montreal (City)*, [1994] S.C.J. No. 80, [1995] 1 C.T.C. 223 (S.C.C.); and *Quebec (Communaute Urbaine) v. Corp Notre Dame de Bon Secours*, [1994] S.C.J. No. 78, [1995] 1 C.T.C. 241, (1994) 95 D.T.C. 5017 (S.C.C.).

In *Canada v. Antosko et al.,* [1994] S.C.J. No. 46, [1994] 2 C.T.C. 25, 94 D.T.C. 6314 (S.C.C.), however, Iacobucci J, writing for a unanimous panel of five members of the court, stated (at para. 29) that although the courts "must analyze a given transaction in the context of economic and commercial reality", this approach "cannot alter the result ... where the legal and practical effect of the transaction is undisputed".

3.   In light of the doctrine of form and substance developed in U.K. and Canadian jurisprudence, how do you interpret Lord Atkin's dissenting judgment in the *Duke of Westminster* case? Does he disagree with the approach to tax avoidance suggested by Lords Tomlin and Russell? Do you find his interpretation of the facts more or less persuasive?

2. Sham Doctrine

Toward the end of his judgment in the *Duke of Westminster* case, Lord Tomlin referred to "cases where documents are not *bona fide* nor intended to be acted upon, but are only used as a cloak to conceal a different transaction". Although the point is not made explicitly, the implication is clear that in these circumstances tax is to be assessed not on the basis of the documents that are "not intended to be acted upon", but according to the transaction that these documents are designed to conceal. Indeed, since tax consequences are to be based on "the legal rights and obligations of the parties ascertained upon ordinary legal principles", not on "mere nomenclature", this consequence follows as a matter of course.

Given a general rule that *legal* substance is to prevail over nomenclature, there is really no need for a separate judicial doctrine to address these cases. Nonetheless, the revenue authorities and the courts appear to have found it convenient to label these situations "shams" and to refer to a distinct "sham doctrine" to support the characterization of these transactions on the basis of the legal rights and obligations actually created by the parties rather than those that they have purported to create.

In Canada, the sham doctrine has been applied in a number of cases in which the courts have concluded that the legal relationships that the taxpayer has purported to create were not *bona fide*. See, for example, *M.N.R. v. Shields*, [1962] C.T.C. 548, 62 D.T.C. 1343 (Ex. Ct.); *Susan Hosiery Ltd. v. M.N.R.*, [1969] C.T.C. 533, 69 D.T.C. 5346 (Ex. Ct.); and *Dominion Bridge Co. v.*

Canada, [1975] C.T.C. 263, 75 D.T.C. 5150 (F.C.T.D.), aff'd [1977] C.T.C. 554, 77 D.T.C. 5367 (F.C.A.).

In *M.N.R. v. Cameron*, [1972] S.C.J. No. 137, [1972] C.T.C. 380, 72 D.T.C. 6325 (S.C.C.), the Supreme Court of Canada referred to the following definition of the word "sham" set out in *Snook v. London & West Riding Investments Ltd.*, [1967] 1 All E.R. 518 at 528 (C.A.) per Lord Diplock:

> acts done or documents executed by parties to the "sham" which are intended by them to give to third parties or to the court the appearance of creating between the parties legal rights and obligations different from the actual legal rights and obligations (if any) which the parties intend to create.

This definition was also cited in *Stubart Investments Ltd. v. Canada*, [1984] S.C.J. No. 25, [1984] C.T.C. 294, 84 D.T.C. 6305 (S.C.C.), where Estey J characterized a sham as a situation in which:

> [t]he transaction and the form in which it was cast by the parties and their legal and accounting advisers [can] be said to have been so constructed as to create a false impression in the eyes of a third party, specifically the taxing authority.

In two more recent decisions, however, the Supreme Court of Canada appears to have suggested a broader doctrine of "sham" more akin to the business purpose test or the expansive economic or commercial substance-over-form doctrine. See, for example, *Bronfman Trust v. Canada*, [1987] S.C.J. No. 1, [1987] 1 C.T.C. 117 at 128, 87 D.T.C. 5059 (S.C.C.); and *Friesen v. Canada*, [1995] S.C.J. No. 71, [1995] 2 C.T.C. 369 (S.C.C.). In *McClurg v. Canada*, [1990] S.C.J. No. 134, [1991] 1 C.T.C. 169, [1990] 91 D.T.C. 5001 (S.C.C.) and *Canada v. Antosko,* [1994] S.C.J. No. 46, [1994] 2 C.T.C. 25, 94 D.T.C. 6314 (S.C.C.), however, the Supreme Court of Canada reaffirmed the more narrow sham concept affirmed in *Stubart.*

3. Ineffective Transactions Doctrine

If tax consequences are to depend on the legal rights and obligations actually created by the taxpayer, it follows that the courts must scrutinize the conduct and documents by which these rights and obligations are established. As the Federal Court of Appeal explained in *Atinco Paper Products Ltd. v. M.N.R.*, [1978] F.C.J. No. 611, [1978] C.T.C. 566 at 577, 78 D.T.C. 6387 (F.C.A.):

> it is the duty of the Court to carefully scrutinize everything that a taxpayer has done to ensure that everything which appears to have been done, in fact, has been done in accordance with applicable law. It is not sufficient to employ devices to achieve a desired result without ensuring that those devices are not simply cosmetically correct, that is, correct in form, but, in fact, are in all respects legally correct, real transactions. If this Court, or any other court, were to fail to carry out its elementary duty to examine with care all aspects of the transactions in issue, it would not only be derelict in carrying out its judicial duties, but in its duty to the public at large.

In turn, where taxpayers have failed to follow the necessary formalities through which specific legal relationships are established, courts may conclude that the transactions that they have endeavoured to carry out are legally ineffective or incomplete. In these circumstances, tax will be assessed on the basis of the transactions actually entered into and the legal relationships actually created.

Like the sham doctrine, the doctrine of "legally ineffective or incomplete transactions" reflects the more general rule expressed in *Duke of Westminster* that tax consequences are to depend on the *legal* substance actually created by the parties rather than the form or nomenclature that they employ. Nonetheless, as with the sham doctrine, the revenue authorities and the courts have found it convenient to identify a distinct legal doctrine when faced with these situations.

As well, at least some decisions have suggested that the courts should more closely scrutinize transactions that are entered into deliberately in order to obtain tax advantages. In *Rose v. M.N.R.*, [1973] F.C.J. No. 12, [1973] C.T.C. 74 at 77, 73 D.T.C. 5083 (F.C.A.), for example, the court suggested that the tax-motivated aspects of an arrangement established to split income among the shareholders of various corporations warranted "a very careful appraisal of the evidence when considering whether what was projected with that end in view was actually carried out". On the other hand, in *Atinco Paper Products Ltd. v. M.N.R.*, [1978] F.C.J. No. 611, [1978] C.T.C. 566 at 577, 78 D.T.C. 6387 (F.C.A.), the court rejected "the suggestion, sometimes expressed, that there can be a strict or liberal view taken of a transaction, or series of transactions which it is hoped by the taxpayer will result in a minimization of tax".

In Canada, the doctrine of legally ineffective or incomplete transactions has generally been invoked to challenge tax-motivated transactions involving partnerships, trusts, and corporations. In *Atinco*, for example, an attempt to divide the income of a partnership among five separate taxpayers, two of which were trusts that were in turn designed to split income among various family members, was successfully challenged on the basis that two letters by which an aunt was alleged to have created the trusts did not in fact satisfy the legal formalities necessary to create a trust. See also *Kingsdale Securities v. M.N.R.*, [1974] F.C.J. No. 182, [1975] C.T.C. 10, 74 D.T.C. 6674 (F.C.A.).

Similarly, in *Lagacé v. M.N.R.*, [1968] C.T.C. 98, 68 D.T.C. 5143 (Ex. Ct.), the taxpayers' attempt to divert the profit from a real estate transaction to two corporations controlled by the taxpayers and their wives failed on the grounds that the actual transactions were negotiated by the taxpayers, who "subsequently arranged to the various intervening conveyances under which a large part of the profits arising from the dispositions were made to appear as having accrued to [the] companies" (at para. 5). Since the taxpayers could not establish that the conveyances were in fact "*bona fide* business transactions", the income was taxed in the hands of the taxpayers rather than the corporations. See also *Richardson Terminals Limited v. M.N.R.*, [1971] C.T.C. 42, 71 D.T.C. 5028 (Ex. Ct.), aff'd [1972] S.C.J. No. 36, [1972] C.T.C. 528, 72 D.T.C. 6431 (S.C.C.), where the taxpayer, which sought to transfer a profitable business to a related corporation with accumulated losses from prior years, failed to establish that the business, which the taxpayer purported to carry on after the alleged transfer as agent for the related company, had in fact been transferred. On the basis that the taxpayer carried on the business on its own behalf, not as agent for the related company, the income was taxable in the hands of the taxpayer rather than the related corporation.

4. Business Purpose Test

In Canada, where appeals to the Judicial Committee of the Privy Council continued until the 1950s, the judicial restraint of *Duke of Westminster* originally found greater favour than the judicial activism *of Gregory v. Helvering*.[8] By the mid-1970s, however, Canadian courts had begun to adopt a more activist approach to tax avoidance, akin more to *Gregory v. Helvering* than to *Duke of Westminster*.[9] Indeed, in the early 1980s, the English House of Lords itself began to qualify the *Duke of Westminster* principle, adopting a "step transactions" doctrine according to which tax-motivated transactions comprising part of a series of transactions could be disregarded, with tax based on the end result of the series.[10]

These judicial developments were reviewed in *Stubart Investments Ltd. v. Canada*, [1984] S.C.J. No. 25, [1984] C.T.C. 294, 84 D.T.C. 6305 (S.C.C.), where the Supreme Court of Canada considered the adoption of a judicial "business purpose test" like that adopted in the United States in *Gregory v. Helvering*. Although the *Stubart* decision was effectively overruled by the enactment of the GAAR in 1988, it remains the most authoritative statement of judicial anti-avoidance doctrines in Canadian tax law.

Stubart Investments Ltd. v. Canada
[1984] S.C.J. No. 25, [1984] C.T.C. 294, 84 D.T.C. 6305 (S.C.C.)

[Until 1951, corporations belonging to a related group could file a consolidated return in which the losses of one member of the group could be offset against the income of another profitable member of the group. In 1951, the Act was amended to prohibit the consolidation of separate corporate operations in a single return of income. While an individual proprietor may offset losses from one business against income from another, corporations carrying on business through more than one corporate vehicle may not combine the income and

---

[8] See, for example, *Pioneer Laundry and Dry Cleaners Ltd. v. M.N.R.*, [1939] S.C.R. 1, [1938-39] C.T.C. 401 (S.C.C.); *Malkin v. M.N.R.*, [1938] Ex. C.R. 225, [1938-39] C.T.C. 128 (Ex. Ct.); and *Foreign Power Securities Corp. v. M.N.R.*, [1966] C.T.C. 23, (1965) 66 D.T.C. 5012 (Ex. Ct.), aff'd [1967] S.C.J. No. 23, [1967] C.T.C. 116, 67 D.T.C. 5084 (S.C.C.).

[9] See, for example, *Dominion Bridge Co. Ltd. v. Canada*, [1975] C.T.C. 263, 75 D.T.C. 5150 (F.C.T.D.), aff'd. [1977] C.T.C. 554, 77 D.T.C. 5367 (F.C.A.); and *M.N.R. v. Leon*, [1976] F.C.J. No. 134, [1976] C.T.C. 532, 76 D.T.C. 6299 (F.C.A.).

[10] See *W.T. Ramsay Ltd. v. IRC*, [1981] 1 All E.R. 865 (H.L.); *CIR v. Burmah Oil Co. Ltd.* (1981), 54 Tax Cas. 200, [1981] 42 T.R. 535 (H.L.); and *Furniss v. Dawson*, [1984] 1 All E.R. 530 (H.L.).

losses of different corporations in order to pay income tax only on the net income of the group as a whole.

As a result, related corporations have engaged in a number of transactions in order to make use of the losses of unprofitable members of a corporate group to "shelter" the income of profitable members. One method, tried without success in *Richardson Terminals Limited v. M.N.R.*, [1971] C.T.C. 42, 71 D.T.C. 5028 (Ex. Ct.), was for a profitable corporation to sell its business to the unprofitable corporation under an agreement whereby the profitable corporation would continue to operate the business on behalf of the unprofitable corporation as its agent. In *Stubart*, the Minister challenged an arrangement such as this on the basis that it lacked a *bona fide* business purpose.]

ESTEY J (Ritchie, Beetz, and McIntyre JJ, concurring): The issue in this case is whether a corporate taxpayer, with the avowed purpose of reducing its taxes, can establish an arrangement whereby future profits are routed through a sister subsidiary in order to avail itself of the latter corporation's loss carry-forward.

The facts are, for a tax proceeding, quite straightforward. The holding company, Finlayson Enterprises Limited, referred to for convenience hereafter as the "parent company", incorporated the appellant in 1951. In 1962, the appellant purchased the assets of Stuart Brothers Company Limited which carried on the business of manufacturing and selling food flavourings and related products (sometimes for brevity referred to as "the business"). The appellant, at the time of this purchase, changed its original name to Stuart Brothers Limited in order to take advantage of the value of that name and the associated goodwill in the market. In 1969, the appellant again changed its name to the present name, Stubart Investments Limited.

The parent company, amongst its other subsidiaries, owned all of the shares of Grover Cast Stone Company Limited (hereinafter referred to as "Grover") which carried on the business of manufacturing and selling precast concrete products. By 1965, Grover had incurred substantial losses which were recognized as losses under the *Income Tax Act* SC 1970-71-72, c 63, as amended, for the purpose of the carry-forward provisions under the Act. In 1966, the tax advisers of the parent company established a plan whereby the assets of the appellant would be sold to Grover with effect January 1, 1966. Concurrent with the agreement of purchase and sale of these assets, Grover would appoint, by a separate agreement, the appellant as its agent to carry on the business for and to the account of Grover.

...

After this agreement of purchase and sale had been so performed and closed, the appellant proceeded to carry on the business on behalf of Grover, and at the end of each of the fiscal years 1966, 1967 and 1968, the appellant paid over to Grover the net income realized from the business. Grover, in turn, reported this income under the *Income Tax Act* in its corporate income tax returns for these three years. The Department of National Revenue subsequently reassessed the appellant, setting aside the entry transferring the net income to Grover, and charging such net income back to the taxable income of the appellant. It is from these assessments that this appeal was taken.

...

No section of the Act was isolated by the Attorney General of Canada as clearly authorizing the assessments which gave rise to these proceedings. Assuming for the moment there is no sham, the respondent asks the Court to find, without express statutory basis, that no transaction is valid in the income tax computation process that has not been entered into by the taxpayer for a valid business purpose. The respondent asserts that by definition, an independent business purpose does not include tax reduction for its own sake.

...

In the field of taxation ... the traditional position [appears] in *IRC v. Duke of Westminster*, [1936] AC 1 at 19 where it was stated:

> Every man is entitled if he can to order his affairs so as that the tax attaching under the appropriate Acts is less than it otherwise would be. If he succeeds in ordering them so as to secure this result, then, however unappreciative the Commissioners of Inland Revenue or his fellow taxpayers may be of his ingenuity, he cannot be compelled to pay an increased tax.

In the courts of the United States a different philosophy was developed in the oft-cited judgment in *Gregory v. Helvering, Commissioner of Internal Revenue* (1934), 293 US 465.

...

In the United Kingdom there is some evidence that the courts are moving from the principles enunciated in the older cases mentioned above to something approaching the United States *bona fide* business purpose rule.

...

The scene in Canada is less clear and has not, until this appeal, reached this Court. The first reference to "a business purpose" concept appears to be in the Exchequer Court in *Lagacé v. M.N.R.*, [1968] 2 Ex. CR 98; [1968] CTC 98; 68 DTC 5143 where President Jackett (as he then was) referred to a series of contrived conveyances as not representing a *"bona fide* business transaction." Later, at [101], he noted that the taxpayer had neglected to establish that each party was bound in "an actual *bona fide* contract that was in fact negotiated ... at the time of the negotiation of the business bargain." The court found that the profit resulted from the taxpayer's "own business transactions" and was taxable in respect of such transactions. The court [concluded that] ... the profits arose by reason of transactions made by the taxpayer, and the interposition of legal entities after the deal had been made did not separate the profits from the taxpayer. *Lagacé* was cited by the same court in *Richardson Terminals Ltd v. M.N.R.*, [1971] CTC 42; 71 DTC 5028, where, after a series of factual findings, the trial court found that the taxpayer had simply not followed a plan prescribed by its advisers for the transfer of a business to a loss company, and had simply attempted to transfer the net income from that business. The transferee company, the court found, neither in fact nor in law carried on the business in question in its own right. The appeal court, in oral reasons, reached the same conclusion ([1972] CTC 528; 72 DTC 6431). While *Lagacé* was also quoted in *Dominion Bridge Co Ltd v. The Queen*, [1975] CTC 263; 75 DTC 5150, Décary J, in the Federal Court Trial Division, found that the transactions between the parent company and its subsidiary, designed to transfer the profits of the parent to an off-shore subsidiary, were "a sham" (p. 271 [5155]) "to camouflage and hide" (p. 270 [5154]) the parent company's operations. The court then concluded that the operations in question "were those of the appellant taxpayer" (p. 270 [5154]) and the profits were properly assessed to the parent company. Again, in that case, the court found that the fixing of prices by the parent for purchases by it from the subsidiary was a device to transfer income from the taxpayer to its agent, the subsidiary, in a closed, inter-company sales transaction in which the agent subsidiary in fact performed no function. The business in question was that of the parent; the subsidiary was simply its purchasing department; and by this device the parent divested itself of its income arising from the transactions in question. ... The Federal Court of Appeal in [1977] CTC 554; 77 DTC 5367 held that there was no reason to interfere with the findings of fact made by the trial judge. The concept of "*bona fide* business purpose" played no part in the final outcome. Rather, this case falls into the "sham" category.

It was in *M.N.R. v. Leon*, [1976] CTC 532; 76 DTC 6299 that the Federal Court of Appeal may have incorporated the *bona fide* business purpose test into Canadian tax law. By a complex of management companies created by a group of brothers, each of whom owned all the shares of their respective management companies, the profits of a furniture business were routed through several corporate screens and eventually reached the original owners of the business after minimal taxation. In carrying out this plan, the brothers disregarded the advice of their accountants in which the true nature of the plan was discussed, and some of the documents were found to have been back-dated. The trial judge concluded that none of the companies had any employees (except the sole shareholder brother), no business facilities of any kind, and that the sole purpose of the interposition of the management companies was to reduce the brothers' taxes in the future. Heald J, in reviewing the evidence, stated, at 540 [6303]:

> Thus, the interposition of the management companies between the employer and the employee was a sham, pure and simple, the sole purpose of which was to avoid payment of tax.

In the course of reaching this conclusion, the Court of Appeal propounded the following rule (at 539 [6302]):

> It is the agreement or transaction in question to which the Court must look. If the agreement or transaction lacks a *bona fide* business purpose, it is a sham.

The Federal Court of Appeal in so phrasing the rule has mixed the older "sham" doctrine with the *bona fide* business purpose test, and has brought forth a hybrid rule. The judgment was met with immediate critical response from the taxation authors.

...

The statement of Heald J, supra, was not essential to the conclusion reached by the court. The interposition of the management company did not, in law, establish anything but a simple agency relationship between the taxpayer and the bare incorporation so established. The company itself had no business, and indeed no business facilities. The services were entirely personal and were at all times destined for delivery to the original, ongoing furniture business, owned in the first instance by the sole shareholders of the management companies. Nothing was changed by reason of the incorporation of the nest of wholly-owned management companies.

...

The Federal Court of Appeal shortly thereafter appears to have drawn back from the *Leon* proposition when Urie J wrote:

> I am not at all sure that I would have agreed with the broad principles relating to a finding of sham as enunciated in that case [*Leon*], and, I think, that the principle so stated should perhaps be confined to the facts of that case.

> *Massey-Ferguson Ltd v. The Queen*, [1977] CTC 6; 77 DTC 5013 at 16 [5020].

...

Returning then to the issue of interpretation now before this Court, there are certain broad characteristics of tax statute construction which can be discerned in the authorities here and in similar jurisdictions abroad. The most obvious is the fact that in some jurisdictions, such as Canada and Australia, the legislature has responded to the need for overall regulation to forestall blatant practices designed to defeat the Revenue. These anti-tax avoidance provisions may reflect the rising importance and cost of government in the community, the concomitant higher rates of taxation in modern times, and hence the greater stake in the avoidance contests between the taxpayer and the state. The arrival of these provisions in the statute may also have heralded the extension of the *Income Tax Act* from a mere tool for the carving of the cost of government out of the community, to an instrument of economic and fiscal policy for the regulation of commerce and industry of the country through fiscal intervention by government. Whatever the source or explanation, measures such as section 137 [former subsection 245(1)] are instructions from Parliament to the community on the individual member's liability for taxes, expressed in general terms.[11] This instruction is, like the balance of the Act, introduced as well for the guidance of the courts in applying the scheme of the Act throughout the country. The courts may, of course, develop, in their interpretation of section 137 [former subsection 235(1)], doctrines such as the *bona fide* business purpose test ...

In jurisdictions such as the United States and the United Kingdom, such doctrines have developed in the courts, usually in the guise of canons of

---

[11] For a discussion of former subs. 245(1), see paras. 1-3 in the "Notes and Questions" section following this case.

construction of the tax statutes ... Whether the development be by legislative measure or judicial action, the result is a process of balancing the taxpayer's freedom to carry on his commercial and social affairs however he may choose, and the state interest in revenue, equity in the raising of the revenue, and economic planning. In Canada the sham concept is at least a judicial measure for the control of tax abuse without specific legislative direction. The judicial classification of an ineffective transaction is another. In the United States, these doctrines have expanded to include the business purpose test. ... In sharp contrast is the approach of Noël J, as he then was, in *Foreign Power Securities Ltd v. M.N.R.*, [1966] CTC 23; 66 DTC 5012 at 52 [5027], where he stated:

> There is indeed no provision in the *Income Tax Act* which provides that, where it appears that the main purpose or one of the purposes for which any transaction or transactions was or were effected was the avoidance or reduction of liability to income tax, the Court may, if it thinks fit, direct that such adjustments shall be made as respects liability to income tax as it considers appropriate so as to counteract the avoidance or reduction of liability to income tax which would otherwise be effected by the transaction or transactions.

Perhaps the high water mark in the opposition to the introduction of a business purpose test is found in the reasoning of the learned authors, Ward and Cullity [supra], who stated, at 473-75, in answer to the question: can it be a legitimate business purpose of a transaction to minimize or postpone taxes?:

> If taxes are minimized or postponed, more capital will be available to run the business and more profit will result. Surely, in the penultimate decade of the twentieth century it would be naive to suggest that businessmen can, or should, conduct and manage their business affairs without regard to the incidence of taxation or that they are not, or should not, be attracted to transactions or investments or forms of doing business that provide reduced burdens of taxation.

I would therefore reject the proposition that a transaction may be disregarded for tax purposes solely on the basis that it was entered into by a taxpayer without an independent or *bona fide* business purpose. A strict business purpose test in certain circumstances would run counter to the apparent legislative intent which, in the modern taxing statutes, ... may have a dual aspect. Income tax legislation, such as the federal Act in our country, is no longer a simple device to raise revenue to meet the cost of governing the community. Income taxation is also employed by government to attain selected economic policy objectives. Thus, the statute is a mix of fiscal and economic policy. The economic policy element of the Act sometimes takes the form of an inducement to the taxpayer to undertake or redirect a specific activity. Without the inducement offered by the statute, the activity may not be undertaken by the taxpayer for whom the induced action would otherwise have no *bona fide* business purpose. Thus, by imposing a positive requirement that there be such a *bona fide* business purpose, a taxpayer might be barred from undertaking the very activity Parliament wishes to encourage. At minimum, a business purpose requirement might inhibit the taxpayer from undertaking the specified activity which Parliament has invited in order to attain economic and perhaps social policy goals.

...

Indeed, where Parliament is successful and a taxpayer is induced to act in a certain manner by virtue of incentives prescribed in the legislation, it is at least arguable that the taxpayer was attracted to these incentives for the valid business purpose of reducing his cash outlay for taxes to conserve his resources for other business activities. It seems more appropriate to turn to an interpretation test which would provide a means of applying the Act so as to affect only the conduct of a taxpayer which has the designed effect of defeating the expressed intention of Parliament. In short, the tax statute, by this interpretative technique, is extended to reach conduct of the taxpayer which clearly falls within "the object and spirit" of the taxing provisions. Such an approach would promote rather than interfere with the administration of the *Income Tax Act*, supra, in both its aspects without interference with the granting and withdrawal, according to the economic climate, of tax incentives. The desired objective is a simple rule which will provide uniformity of application of the Act across the community, and at the same time, reduce the attraction of elaborate and intricate tax avoidance plans, and reduce the rewards to those best able to afford the services of the tax technicians.

...

The question comes back to a determination of the proper role of the court in construing the *Income Tax Act* in circumstances such as these where the Crown relies on the general pattern of the Act and not upon any specific taxing provision.

...

[S]ome guidelines can be discerned for the guidance of a court faced with this interpretative issue.

1. Where the facts reveal no *bona fide* business purpose for the transaction, section 137 [former subsection 245(1)] may be found to be applicable depending upon all the circumstances of the case. It has no application here.

2. In those circumstances where section 137 [former subsection 245(1)] does not apply, the older rule of strict construction of a taxation statute, as modified by the courts in recent years, (*supra*), prevails but will not assist the taxpayer where:

    (a)   the transaction is legally ineffective or incomplete; or

    (b)   the transaction is a sham within the classical definition.

3. Moreover, the formal validity of the transaction may also be insufficient where:

    (a)   the setting in the Act of the allowance, deduction or benefit sought to be gained clearly indicates a legislative intent to restrict such benefits to rights accrued prior to the establishment of the arrangement adopted by a taxpayer purely for tax purposes;

(b)   the provisions of the Act necessarily relate to an identified business function. This idea has been expressed in articles on the subject in the United States:

> The business purpose doctrine is an appropriate tool for testing the tax effectiveness of a transaction, where the language, nature and purposes of the provision of the tax law under construction indicate a function, pattern and design characteristic solely of business transactions.

> Jerome R. Hellerstein, "Judicial Approaches to Tax Avoidance,"
> *1964 Conference Report*, p. 66.

(c)   "the object and spirit" of the allowance or benefit provision is defeated by the procedures blatantly adopted by the taxpayer to synthesize a loss, delay or other tax saving device, although these actions may not attain the heights of "artificiality" in section 137 [former subsection 245(1)]. This may be illustrated where the taxpayer, in order to qualify for an "allowance" or a "benefit," takes steps which the terms of the allowance provisions of the Act may, when taken in isolation and read narrowly, be stretched to support. However, when the allowance provision is read in the context of the whole statute, and with the "object and spirit" and purpose of the allowance provision in mind, the accounting result produced by the taxpayer's actions would not, by itself, avail him of the benefit of the allowance.

These interpretative guidelines, modest though they may be, and which fall well short of the *bona fide* business purpose test advanced by the respondent, are in my view appropriate to reduce the action and reaction endlessly produced by complex, specific tax measures aimed at sophisticated business practices, and the inevitable, professionally-guided and equally specialized taxpayer reaction. Otherwise, where the substance of the Act, when the clause in question is contextually construed, is clear and unambiguous and there is no prohibition in the Act which embraces the taxpayer, the taxpayer shall be free to avail himself of the beneficial provision in question.

In this appeal, the appellant taxpayer has done nothing to contrive the accumulated and recognized loss carry-forward of Grover. Neither has the parent nor the affiliated company Grover done so. The immediate payment in issue, the transfer of yearly profits from the business, was made by the appellant under a clear, binding legal obligation so to do. Grover's right to apply the tax loss to the income so received from the business is technically not here in issue. If it were in issue, it is difficult to see why Grover could not have acquired production assets from any source, including non-arm's length sources as here, so as to produce earnings *in futuro* in order to take advantage of its deficit accumulations before their expiry under the provisions of the *Income Tax Act*. Neither the loss carry-forward provisions, nor any other provision of the Act, have been shown to reveal a parliamentary intent to bar the appellant from entering into such a binding transaction and to make the payments here in question. Once the tax loss concept is included in the statute, the revenue collector is exposed to the chance, if not the inevitability, of the reduction of future tax collections to the extent that a credit [*sic*: should read deduction] is granted for past losses.

I would therefore allow the appeal, and direct that the notices of reassessment in question be vacated, with costs here and in the courts below to the appellant.

WILSON J (concurring): ... In my opinion, the Federal Court of Appeal in *Leon v. M.N.R.*, (*supra*), characterized a transaction which had no business purpose other than the tax purpose as a sham and was in error in so doing. I do not view that case as introducing the business purpose test as a test distinct from that of sham into our law and, indeed, if it is to be so viewed, I do not think it should be followed. I think Lord Tomlin's principle is far too deeply entrenched in our tax law for the courts to reject it in the absence of clear statutory authority. No such authority has been put to us in this case. For these reasons I concur in my colleague's disposition of the appeal.

NOTES AND QUESTIONS

1.   In the course of his judgment, Estey J referred to statutory anti-avoidance provisions "such as section 137", describing these measures as "instructions from Parliament to the community on the individual member's liability for taxes, expressed in general terms" and as "guidance" to the courts "in applying the scheme of the Act throughout the country." Although Estey J noted in the first of his three guidelines that this provision had "no application" in *Stubart*, it appears to have had a significant impact on his decision to reject the adoption of a judicial business purpose test in Canada.

According to subsection 137(1) of the 1952 Act:

> In computing income for the purposes of this Act, no deduction may be made in respect of a disbursement or expense made or incurred in respect of a transaction or operation that, if allowed, would unduly or artificially reduce the income.

This provision, derived from subsection 6(2) of the *Income War Tax Act*, was subsection 125(1) of the 1948 Act, and was renumbered subsection 245(1) in 1972. It was repealed in 1988 with the enactment of the GAAR In section 245 of the Act.

Although this rule was of general application to the *Income Tax Act* as a whole, it was limited in two ways. First, it applied only to a "deduction ... in respect of a disbursement or expense made or incurred in respect of a transaction or operation". Second, it applied only where this deduction, "if allowed, would unduly or artificially reduce ... income."

For present purposes, there is no need to examine the first branch of this test in any detail. Although the courts have differed in their interpretations of this requirement, higher courts have tended to adopt a broad view of the circumstances in which a deduction may be said to be "in respect of a disbursement or expense made or incurred".[12]

With respect to the second requirement, that the deduction "unduly or artificially reduce income", the courts have adopted two widely divergent approaches. On the one hand, several decisions have suggested that a deduction will produce an undue or artificial reduction of income where the transaction from which it arises is contrary to normal business practice. In *Shulman v. M.N.R.*, [1961] C.T.C. 385, 61 D.T.C. 1213 (Ex. Ct.), for example, the taxpayer incorporated a company to manage his legal practice, provided these management services himself as the company's agent, but received no salary from the company for the services that he performed. The court (at C.T.C. 400) disallowed the deduction of management fees paid to the management company by the taxpayer's legal practice on the basis that:

> [t]he non-payment of any direct remuneration to the [taxpayer] for the services performed as agent for [the management company] is opposed to the usual and natural relationship existing between a company and an agent who devotes from one-third to one-half of his time to the business of the company.

More generally, the court suggested (at C.T.C. 400) that:

> [a]ny artificiality arising in the course of a transaction may taint an expenditure relating to it and preclude the expenditure from being deductible in computing taxable income.

See also *Don Fell Ltd. v. Canada*, [1981] C.T.C. 363 at 375, 81 D.T.C. 5282 (F.C.T.D.), where "unduly" was defined as "excessively" or "unreasonably" and "artificially" as "not in accordance with normality".

In other cases, however, "artificial" has been defined as "simulated" or "fictitious". See, for example, *Spur Oil Ltd. v. Canada*, [1981] A.C.F. No. 193, [1981] C.T.C. 336 at 343, 81 D.T.C. 5168 (F.C.A.); *Canada v. Irving Oil*, [1991] F.C.J. No. 133, [1991] 1 C.T.C. 350 at 360, 91 D.T.C. 5106 (F.C.A.); and *Chambers v. Canada*, [1996] F.C.J. No. 71, [1996] 1 C.T.C. 265 (F.C.T.D). On this basis, as the court suggested in *Des Rosiers v. Canada*, [1975] F.C.J.

---

[12] See, for example, *Canada v. Alberta & Southern Gas Co*, [1977] A.C.F. no 161, [1977] C.T.C. 388 at 396, 77 D.T.C. 5244 (F.C.A.), aff'd. [1978] S.C.J. No. 70, [1978] C.T.C. 780, 78 D.T.C. 6566 (S.C.C.), where Jackett CJ stated of then subs. 245(1) that "considering it in its context in the scheme of the Act, [it] is applicable to every class of deductible expenses." See also *Harris v. M.N.R.*, [1966] S.C.J. No. 28, [1966] C.T.C. 226 at 241-42 (S.C.C.), where Cartwright J suggested in *obiter* that the words "a disbursement or expense made or incurred" in then subs. 137(1) "are, in my opinion, apt to include a claim for depreciation or for capital cost allowance"; and *Fording Coal Ltd. v. Canada*, [1995] F.C.J. No. 1535, [1996] 1 C.T.C. 230 (F.C.A.), where Strayer JA, emphasizing the broad scope of the words "in respect of," concluded that the deduction by a purchaser corporation of exploration and development expenses incurred by a vendor corporation was "in respect of a disbursement or expense made or incurred" by the vendor corporation. For more narrow interpretations of these words, see *Canada v. Esskay Farms Ltd*, [1976] C.T.C. 24, (1975) 76 D.T.C. 6010 (F.C.T.D.); and *McKee v. Canada*, [1977] C.T.C. 491, 77 D.T.C. 5345 (F.C.T.D.).

No. 31, [1975] C.T.C. 416, 75 D.T.C. 5298 (F.C.T.D.), the rule in former subsection 245(1) and its predecessors is no different from the sham doctrine.

2. In *Stubart*, the Crown did not attempt to rely on then subsection 137(1) of the Act, arguing instead that the transfer of the food-flavourings business to Grover should be disregarded on the basis that it served no business purpose. According to Estey J (at C.T.C. 299), however, it was "at least arguable that this section covers the 'disbursement' by the appellant of the profits earned for the account of Grover in the operation of the business":

> Clearly the cheque transferring the profit from the appellant to Grover at the end of the year is a disbursement, and it is a disbursement the deduction of which leaves no taxable income in the appellant from the business.

Commentary subsequent to the decision has questioned whether then subsection 137(1) might have applied to the transaction. According to T.E. McDonnell and R.B. Thomas, "The Supreme Court and Business Purpose: Is There Life After Stubart?" (1984) Vol. 32 No. 5 Can. Tax J. 853-69 at 859:

> The section is clearly directed at "deductions" in respect of outlays or disbursements otherwise claimed in computing income. We would have thought, then, that the subsection could have no application in a case in which there was no "deduction" of a disbursement in computing income. ... As we see it, if the arrangements between Stubart and Grover were, as the Court held, legally effective, then Stubart was the agent for Grover in carrying on the flavouring business. As such, the profits of the business never belonged to Stubart at all. The crediting of those profits to Grover could not, we suggest, be regarded as a "deduction" by Stubart in computing its income.

3. Although the Minister did not attempt to rely on then subsection 137(1) in *Stubart*, Estey J appears to have viewed its existence in the Act as one reason not to adopt a judicial business purpose test. After referring to the US Supreme Court decision in *Gregory v. Helvering*, for example, he explained (at C.T.C. 303) that the situation in Canada is different in part because "there are general provisions in the Act dealing with artificial transactions." Later, he observed (at C.T.C. 304) that:

> when examining the United States scene it is well to remember that the *Internal Revenue Code* and its predecessor statutes did not include an anti-tax avoidance provision in the nature of section 137 of the pre-1972 *Canadian Income Tax Act*.

Likewise, he suggested (at C.T.C. 306) that the evolution of the step transaction doctrine in the United Kingdom reflects "the role of the court in a regime where the legislature has enunciated taxing edicts in a detailed manner but has not superimposed thereon a general guideline for the elimination of mechanisms designed and established only to deflect the plain purpose of the taxing provision." He added (at C.T.C. 308) that:

> [i]t must be borne in mind that the United Kingdom tax statute, like the *Internal Revenue Code* of the United States under which the Helvering case, *supra*, was decided, contains no clause similar to our section 137.

However much Estey J may have regarded former subsection 245(1) and its predecessors as a "general guideline for the elimination of mechanisms designed and established only to deflect the plain purpose of the taxing provision", it was not perceived as such by Revenue Canada, the Department of Finance, or Parliament. Four years after the *Stubart* decision, Parliament amended the Act by replacing the rule against artificial transactions with the GAAR, now found in section 245 of the Act.

4.   Although the existence of then subsection 137(1) appears to have played a role in Estey J's decision to reject the adoption of a judicial business purpose test, the primary basis for his judgment appears to relate to the "dual purpose" of the income tax to "raise revenue to meet the cost of governing the community" and "to attain selected economic policy objectives". According to Estey J (at C.T.C. 315), since the statute may through various inducements deliberately encourage taxpayers to undertake specific activities that "would otherwise have no *bona fide* business purpose," a "strict business purpose test in [these] circumstances would run counter to the apparent legislative intent":

> by imposing a positive requirement that there be such a *bona fide* business purpose, a taxpayer might be barred from undertaking the very activity Parliament wishes to encourage. At minimum, a business purpose requirement might inhibit the taxpayer from undertaking the specified activity which Parliament has invited in order to attain economic and perhaps social policy goals.

Is this a valid concern if, as the decision in *Gregory v. Helvering* suggests, the business purpose test is based on an interpretive principle that tax statutes ought to apply differently to transactions entered into solely or primarily to obtain tax advantages *not clearly intended by the statute?* Consider the role of subsection 245(4) in responding to this concern in the context of the GAAR.

5.   Despite rejecting the business purpose test as a general interpretive principle, Estey J suggested in *Stubart* (at CTC 314), that the courts might develop a business purpose test in their interpretation of then subsection 137(1) of the Act. Likewise, in the first of his three guidelines, Estey J stated that:

> [w]here the facts reveal no *bona fide* business purpose for the transaction, section 137 may be found to be applicable depending upon all the circumstances of the case.

On the basis of these statements, one commentator described the decision as "a clear invitation to our courts to develop and apply the business purpose and step transaction doctrines to taxpayers' activities or planners' schemes in order to aid in a determination of whether such activities are proscribed by ... subsection 245(1)".[13] This occurred in *Fording Coal Ltd. v. Canada*, [1995] F.C.J. No. 1535, [1996] 1 C.T.C. 230 (F.C.A.), in which a majority of the Federal Court of Appeal disallowed resource expense deductions claimed by the

---

[13]   William J.A. Hobson, "New Guidelines from the Supreme Court of Canada and Other Canadian Courts: A Broad Interpretation of Subsection 245(1), the Interpretation Test, and Clearer Lines of Demarcation for Tax Avoidance and Tax Evasion," in *Report of Proceedings of the Thirty-Sixth Tax Conference*, 1984 Conference Report (Toronto: Canadian Tax Foundation, 1985), 148-55 at 149.

taxpayer corporation on the basis that they would unduly or artificially reduce the taxpayer's income because the transactions giving rise to the deductions had no independent purpose.

6.   The third of Estey J's guidelines in *Stubart* consists of three separate rules, each of which merits separate consideration.

According to the first rule, the formal validity of a transaction may be insufficient where "the setting in the Act of the allowance, deduction or benefit sought to be gained clearly indicates a legislative intent to restrict such benefits to rights accrued prior to the establishment of the arrangement adopted by a taxpayer purely for tax purposes." Though not entirely clear, it has been suggested that this rule should be read in light of Estey J's interpretation of the decisions in *Lagacé v. M.N.R.*, [1968] C.T.C. 98, 68 D.T.C. 5143 (Ex. Ct.), *Dominion Bridge Co. v. Canada*, [1975] C.T.C. 263, 75 D.T.C. 5150 (F.C.T.D.), and *M.N.R. v. Leon*, [1976] F.C.J. No. 134, [1976] C.T.C. 532, 76 D.T.C. 6299 (F.C.A.), each of which involved the interposition of a corporation or group of companies into a transaction that Estey J appears to have regarded as legally effective and complete "before the intermediate entity was created". As McDonnell and Thomas explain, at 864, this guideline "implies simply that any transaction entered into for tax purposes cannot have any retroactive effect and change the character for tax purposes of income that had accrued prior to the new arrangement". In this light, McDonnell and Thomas suggest that guideline 3(a) is "not unusual", "adds nothing to the law in this area", and "[i]n some respects ... is very close to the classical sham concept".

Pursuant to guideline 3(b), the formal validity of a transaction may also be insufficient where "the provisions of the Act necessarily relate to an identified business function". Although Estey J did not provide an example of such a provision, a good example might be paragraph 18(1)(a) of the Act, which permits the deduction of outlays and expenses in computing a taxpayer's income from a business or property only to the extent that they are made or incurred "for the purpose of gaining or producing income from the business or property". In *Moloney v. Canada*, [1992] F.C.J. No. 905, [1992] 2 C.T.C. 227, 92 D.T.C. 6570 (F.C.A.), for example, where the taxpayer sought to deduct expenses incurred to acquire an interest in a speed-reading course, which the trial judge determined to have had "no real business purpose" ([1989] F.C.J. No. 22, [1989] 1 C.T.C. 213, 89 D.T.C. 5099 (F.C.T.D.) (at para. 138)), the Federal Court of Appeal disallowed the deduction on the basis that the expense did not satisfy the business purpose test in paragraph 18(1)(a). According to Hugessen JA (MacGuigan and Linden JJA, concurring) (at para. 1):

> While it is trite law that a taxpayer may so arrange his business as to attract the least possible tax (see *Duke of Westminster's* case ...), it is equally clear in our view that the reduction of his own tax cannot by itself be a taxpayer's business for the purpose of the *Income Tax Act* ... .To put the matter another way, for an activity to qualify as a "business" the expenses of which are deductible under paragraph 18(1)(a) it must not only be one engaged in by the taxpayer with a reasonable expectation of profit, but that profit must be anticipated to flow from the activity itself rather than exclusively from the provisions of the taxing statute.

Similar conclusions have been reached in numerous other cases involving the same or similar tax avoidance schemes. See, for example, *Bendall v. Canada*, [1995] T.C.J. No. 1, [1995] 2 C.T.C. 2172, 96 D.T.C. 1626 (T.C.C.); *Watson v. Canada*, [1995] T.C.J. No. 230, [1995] 2 C.T.C. 2460 (T.C.C.); *Bennett v. The Queen*, [1996] 3 C.T.C. 2182 (T.C.C.); *La Liberté v. Canada*, [1996] T.C.J. No. 627, 96 D.T.C. 1483 (T.C.C.); *Lorenz v. Canada*, [1996] T.C.J. No. 1491, [1997] 1 C.T.C. 2484, 97 D.T.C. 756 (T.C.C.); *Carpini v. Canada*, [1997] T.C.J. No. 62, [1997] 2 C.T.C. 2434 (T.C.C.); *Tarves v. Canada*, [1997] T.C.J. No. 64, [1997] 2 C.T.C. 2439 (T.C.C.); and *Norton v. Canada*, [1997] T.C.J. No. 197, [1998] 1 C.T.C. 3197, 97 D.T.C. 1116 (T.C.C.).

Another example of a statutory business purpose test is subparagraph 20(1)(c)(i), which allows interest expenses to be deducted only where borrowed money is "used for the purpose of earning income from a business or property". In a number of notable cases considered in chapter 5, the courts appear to have relied on this statutory requirement to challenge transactions lacking any independent business purpose and to assess tax on the basis of their economic or commercial substance rather than their legal form. See, for example, *Bronfman Trust v. Canada*, [1987] S.C.J. No. 1, [1987] 1 C.T.C. 117 at 128, 87 D.T.C. 5059 (S.C.C.); *Mark Resources v. Canada*, [1993] T.C.J. No. 265, [1993] 2 C.T.C. 2259, 93 D.T.C. 1004 (T.C.C.); *Canwest Broadcasting Ltd. v. Canada*, [1995] T.C.J. No. 789, [1995] 2 C.T.C. 2780 (T.C.C.); *Singleton v. Canada*, [1996] T.C.J. No. 1101, [1996] 3 C.T.C. 2873, 96 D.T.C. 1850 (T.C.C.); and *Ludco v. Canada*, [1999] F.C.J. No. 402, [1999] 3 C.T.C. 601, 99 D.T.C. 5153 (F.C.A.). More recently, however, the Supreme Court of Canada appears to have rejected this approach in *Ludco Enterprises Ltd. v. Canada*, [2001] S.C.J. No. 58, [2002] 1 C.T.C. 95, 2001 D.T.C. 5505 (S.C.C.) and *Singleton v. Canada*, [2001] S.C.J. No. 59, [2002] 1 C.T.C. 121, 2001 D.T.C. 5533 (S.C.C.).

Finally, guideline 3(c) states that the formal validity of a transaction may be insufficient where the "object and spirit" of an "allowance" or "benefit provision" is "defeated" by "procedures blatantly adopted by the taxpayer to synthesize a loss, delay or other tax saving device, although these actions may not attain the heights of 'artificiality' in section 137". According to Estey J:

> [t]his may be illustrated where the taxpayer, in order to qualify for an "allowance" or a "benefit," takes steps which the terms of the allowance provisions of the Act may, when taken in isolation and read narrowly, be stretched to support. However, when the allowance provision is read in the context of the whole statute, and with the "object and spirit" and purpose of the allowance provision in mind, the accounting result produced by the taxpayer's actions would not, by itself, avail him of the benefit of the allowance.

Again, Estey J provided no example of when this rule might apply, though the decision in *Fording Coal*, supra, may be illustrative, since the Federal Court of Appeal concluded, among other things, that a transaction entered into between the corporate taxpayer and another corporation contravened the object and spirit of the relevant statutory provisions.

More challenging is to imagine a situation in which "procedures blatantly adopted by the taxpayer to synthesize a loss, delay or other tax saving device" contradict the "object and spirit" of the Act without attaining "the heights of 'artificiality' in section 137." In *Fording Coal*, for example, the Federal Court of Appeal concluded not only that the deductions were contrary to the object and spirit of the Act, but also that they would unduly and artificially reduce the taxpayer's income contrary to former subsection 245(1). Alternatively, where courts have held that transactions are not "artificial" within the meaning of former subsection 245(1), these transactions have also been considered to be within the object and spirit of the Act. See, for example, *Friedberg v. Canada*, [1989] F.C.J. No. 23, [1989] 1 C.T.C. 274, 89 D.T.C. 5115 (F.C.T.D.), aff'd [1991] F.C.J. No. 1255, [1992] 1 C.T.C. 1, 92 D.T.C. 6031 (F.C.A.), aff'd [1993] S.C.J. No. 123, [1991] 2 C.T.C. 306, 93 D.T.C. 5507 (S.C.C.); and *Mara Properties Ltd. v. Canada*, [1996] S.C.J. No. 56, [1996] 2 C.T.C. 54 (S.C.C.), aff'g McDonald JA's dissenting judgment ([1995] F.C.J. No. 278, [1995] 2 C.T.C. 86, 95 D.T.C. 5168 (F.C.A.)).

7.   In *Canada v. Antosko et al.*, [1994] S.C.J. No. 46, [1994] 2 C.T.C. 25, 94 D.T.C. 6314 (S.C.C.), the Supreme Court rejected the Minister's argument that a deduction apparently available to the taxpayer under subsection 20(14) of the Act should be disallowed on the basis that the series of transactions entered into by the taxpayer were contrary to the object and spirit of the provision to prevent double taxation. According to Iacobucci J (at para. 29):

> While it is true that the courts must view discrete sections of the Income Tax Act in light of the other provisions of the Act and of the purpose of the legislation, and that they must analyze a given transaction in the context of economic and commercial reality, such techniques cannot alter the result where the words of the statute are clear and plain and where the legal and practical effect of the transaction is undisputed.

Is this conclusion consistent with the object and spirit limit on deductibility suggested by Estey J's guideline 3(c)? Is it applicable to "avoidance transactions" as these are defined under the GAAR? See Section IV of this chapter, "General Anti-avoidance Rule".

III. SPECIFIC ANTI-AVOIDANCE RULES

The laissez-faire approach to tax avoidance adopted by the Canadian courts and the doctrine of strict construction from which it arose were, as Hogg et al. put it, "obviously highly sympathetic to tax avoidance."[14] In response, as Hogg et al. explain, Parliament was forced "to define the rules with great specificity, and to pass amendments adding more and more detail as avoidance techniques emerged and had to be blocked to protect the revenue."[15] The result is not only the detailed and ponderous drafting style apparent to anyone who attempts to read

---

[14] Peter W. Hogg, Joanne E. Magee & Ted Cook, *Principles of Canadian Income Tax Law*, 3d ed. (Toronto: Carswell, 1999) at 471.

[15] *Ibid.*

the Act, but a number of specific statutory provisions designed to prevent certain kinds of avoidance that have been considered sufficiently unacceptable to require a legislative response. Although commentators have devoted considerable attention to judicial anti-avoidance rules and the GAAR enacted in 1988,[16] these specific anti-avoidance rules have, as a group, been subject to much less analysis — perhaps not surprisingly, since these rules apply in a variety of different contexts and appear in numerous places throughout the *Income Tax Act.*[17]

This section does not attempt to provide a comprehensive list of the numerous specific anti-avoidance rules contained in the Act. As an introduction to the topic of tax avoidance, however, it identifies several specific anti-avoidance rules (most of which are examined more thoroughly in Part II of this book), and briefly describes the objectives that these rules are designed to advance. For the purposes of this overview, these rules may be categorized as: (1) rules mandating the inclusion of specific amounts in computing a taxpayer's income; (2) rules disallowing or limiting the deduction of specific amounts in computing a taxpayer's income; (3) rules governing the timing of inclusions or deductions in computing a taxpayer's income; and (4) "deeming provisions" that recharacterize specific amounts or their recipients for the purposes of computing tax under the Act.

A. Rules Mandating the Inclusion of Specific Amounts

In addition to general rules requiring taxpayers to include income from various sources, a number of statutory provisions mandate the inclusion of specific amounts as income from these sources.

In computing a taxpayer's income from an office or employment, for example, paragraph 6(1)(a) requires the taxpayer to include "the value of ... benefits ... received or enjoyed by the taxpayer in the year in respect of, in the course of, or by virtue of" the office or employment.[18] Other rules applicable to the computation of a taxpayer's income from an office or employment require taxpayers to include specific amounts in respect of allowances and particular categories of benefits.[19]

---

[16] See section IV of this chapter.

[17] For a notable exception to this pattern, see Thomas E. McDonnell, "Legislative Anti-Avoidance: The Interaction of the New General Rule and Representative Specific Rules," in *Report of Proceedings of the Fortieth Tax Conference*, 1988 Conference Report (Toronto: Canadian Tax Foundation, 1989), 6:1-34.

[18] This provision is examined in detail in Chapter 4.

[19] See, for example, para. 6(1)(b) (allowances), para. 6(1)(e), (k), and (l) and subs. 6(2) (automobile benefits), para. 6(1)(f) (insurance benefits), subs. 6(9), (15), and (15.1) (employee debt), subs. 6(19) to (23) (housing benefits), and s. 7 (stock options). These rules are examined in detail in Chapter 4.

In computing a taxpayer's income from a business or property, section 12 provides for the inclusion of various amounts that might not otherwise be included under the general rule in subsection 9(1).[20] Similarly, section 15 requires taxpayers to include as income various kinds of benefits that they or related persons may receive from corporations of which they are shareholders.[21]

Subdivision d, finally, requires taxpayers to include various other amounts otherwise excluded from the general concept of income from a source in paragraph 3(a). The inclusion of amounts received "as, on account or in lieu of payment of, or in satisfaction of ... a retiring allowance" in subparagraph 56(1)(a)(ii), for example, represents a legislative response to a series of cases in which amounts paid to a taxpayer on the termination of an office or employment were not included in the taxpayer's income from this source.[22]

While these provisions merely specify amounts that must be included in computing a taxpayer's income, they can be viewed as anti-avoidance provisions broadly defined to the extent that they foreclose what would otherwise be relatively simple methods of avoiding tax. If the value of benefits were not taxed as income from an office or employment, for example, employees could avoid income tax by arranging to receive their compensation in this form.

B. Rules Disallowing or Limiting Deductions

Alongside rules requiring taxpayers to include specific amounts in income, the *Income Tax Act* contains numerous rules disallowing or limiting the amount that taxpayers may deduct in computing their income from particular sources or their net income from all sources.

Several of these rules are designed to prevent the deduction of expenses that are primarily for personal or tax-motivated reasons, not for the purpose of earning income. In computing a taxpayer's income from a business or property, for example, paragraph 18(1)(a) prohibits the deduction of any outlay or expense "except to the extent that it was made or incurred by the taxpayer for the purpose of gaining or producing income from the business or property," while paragraph 18(1)(h) prohibits the deduction of "personal or living expenses."[23] Similarly, subparagraph 20(1)(c)(i) limits deductible interest expenses to

---

[20] See, for example, para. 12(1)(g) (payments based on the use of or production of property) and para. 12(1)(x) (inducements, reimbursements, contributions, allowances, or other assistance). These rules are examined in Chapter 5.

[21] The rules governing shareholder benefits in s. 15 are not examined in this book, and are properly considered in a course on the taxation of corporations and their shareholders.

[22] See, for example, *Canada v. Atkins*, [1976] F.C.J. No. 411, [1976] C.T.C. 497, 76 D.T.C. 6258 (F.C.A.). This case and others involving payments on the termination of an office or employment are discussed in Chapter 4 of this book. The inclusion of retiring allowances under subpara. 56(1)(a)(ii) is examined in Chapter 7.

[23] These provisions are examined in Chapter 5.

amounts in respect of a legal obligation to pay interest on borrowed money "used for the purpose of earning income from a business or property."[24] More specific rules reflect the assumption that certain kinds of expenses have a personal benefit by limiting the amount that taxpayers may deduct in respect of meals and entertainment,[25] home offices,[26] and luxury vehicles.[27] For similar reasons, section 31 limits the amount that certain taxpayers may claim as a loss from farming businesses in computing their net incomes.[28]

Other rules are designed to limit the availability of specific tax incentives to those taxpayers for whom the incentives are intended. Paragraph 18(1)(p), for example, prevents incorporated employees from claiming deductions to which unincorporated employees are not entitled.[29] Yet other rules, which are not considered in this book, are designed to protect Canadian income tax revenues by limiting amounts that taxpayers may deduct in respect of interest payments to non-residents.[30]

Section 67, finally, contains a general rule limiting the amount that may be deducted in respect of an otherwise deductible outlay or expense to the extent that the outlay or expense was reasonable in the circumstances.[31] Consistent with its anti-avoidance purpose, this provision has been employed to challenge income-splitting arrangements involving payments to non-arm's-length persons such as spouses and children,[32] and to limit the amount that a taxpayer may deduct in respect of expenses that have a marked personal character.[33] More recent decisions, however, may have limited the effectiveness of section 67 as an anti-avoidance rule.[34]

---

[24] This provision is examined in Chapter 5.

[25] See, for example, subs. 8(4), which applies in computing a taxpayer's income from an office or employment, and s. 67.1, which applies in computing a taxpayer's income from each source. Subsection 8(4) is examined in Chapter 4. s. 67.1 is examined in Chapter 8.

[26] See subs. 8(13), which applies in computing a taxpayer's income from an office or employment, and subs. 18(12), which applies in computing a taxpayer's income from a business. These provisions are examined in Chapters 4 and 5.

[27] See para. 13(7)(g), which applies in computing a taxpayer's income from a business or property, and ss. 67.2 to 67.4, which apply in computing a taxpayer's income from each source. Para. 13(7)(g) is discussed in Chapter 5. Sections 67.2 to 67.4 are discussed in Chapter 8.

[28] This provision is discussed in Chapter 5.

[29] Judicial and statutory responses to the incorporation of employees are examined in Chapter 4.

[30] See subs. 18(4) to (8), which are properly considered in a course on international tax.

[31] This provision is examined in Chapter 8.

[32] See, for example, *Maduke Foods Ltd. v. M.N.R.*, [1989] F.C.J. No. 841, [1989] 2 C.T.C. 284, 89 D.T.C. 5458 (F.C.T.D.). This case is discussed in Chapter 8.

[33] See, for example, *Mills v. M.N.R.*, [1981] C.T.C. 2995, 81 D.T.C. 909 (T.R.B.). This case is discussed in Chapter 8.

[34] See *Mohammad v. Canada*, [1997] F.C.J. No. 1020, [1997] 3 C.T.C. 321, 97 D.T.C. 5503 (F.C.A.); and *Shell Canada Ltd. v. Canada*, [1999] S.C.J. No. 30, [1999] 4 C.T.C. 313, 99 D.T.C. 5669 (S.C.C.). These cases are discussed in Chapters 5 and 8.

C. Rules Governing the Timing of Inclusions or Deductions

Anti-avoidance rules of another category prevent taxpayers from deferring taxes by delaying the accounting period in which amounts must be included in computing their incomes for the year or by accelerating the accounting period in which deductions may be claimed in computing their income for the year.

In computing a taxpayer's income from a business or property, for example, paragraphs 12(1)(a) and (b) require taxpayers to include certain receipts and amounts receivable in a taxation year that might not otherwise be required to be included in that taxation year under the general rules in subsection 9(1).[35] Other rules prevent the deferral of interest income by including in the taxpayer's income for a taxation year interest that has accrued during the taxation year, even if it was not received or receivable during the taxation year.[36] Similarly, although some rules permit taxpayers to defer income from an office or employment through employer contributions to certain deferred income plans,[37] other rules are designed to prevent the deferral of income from this source by taxing benefits in respect of a "salary deferral arrangement."[38]

Other rules prevent the deduction in a particular taxation year of expenditures that are likely to produce revenues in subsequent taxation years. Paragraph 18(1)(b), for example, prohibits any deduction in respect of "an outlay, loss or replacement of capital, a payment on account of capital or an allowance in respect of depreciation, obsolescence or depletion except as expressly permitted by this Part."[39] Together with specific allowances in paragraphs 20(1)(a) and (b),[40] this provision requires taxpayers to allocate deductions in respect of "capital expenses" over a period of time roughly corresponding to the economically useful life of the asset acquired by the initial expenditure. Likewise, other more specific rules require taxpayers to "capitalize" various categories of expenditures, thereby deferring their deduction to subsequent taxation years.[41]

Yet other provisions prevent taxpayers from deducting losses on the disposition of particular property where the taxpayer or an "affiliated" person

---

[35] These rules are examined in Chapter 5.

[36] See subs. 12(3), (4), (9), and (11). These rules are examined in Chapter 5.

[37] For example, employer contributions to registered pension plans and deferred profit-sharing plans are specifically excluded from inclusion as a taxable benefit under subpara. 6(1)(a)(i). Although payments under these plans are ultimately taxable to the beneficiary under subpara. 56(1)(a)(i) and para. 56(1)(i), the plans themselves are not taxable on the investment income, provided that they satisfy conditions set out in the Act. See para. 149(1)(o) and (s). These rules are discussed in Chapters 4 and 7.

[38] See subs. 6(11) to (14). These rules are examined in Chapter 4.

[39] The characterization of these "capital expenses" is examined in Chapter 5.

[40] These provisions are examined in Chapter 5.

[41] See, for example, subs. 18(2) and (3) (carrying charges on vacant land), subs. 18(3.1) to (3.6) (construction period "soft costs"), and subs. 18(9) (prepaid expenses). These provisions are examined in Chapter 5.

acquires the same property or an identical property within a stipulated period of time before or after the disposition.[42] By deferring the recognition of these "superficial losses, the Act prevents "wash sales" in which taxpayers trigger accrued but unrealized losses on property without ultimately disposing of an economic interest in the property.

D. Deeming Provisions

A final and more widely recognized group of anti-avoidance rules comprises deeming provisions that recharacterize specific amounts or their recipients for the purposes of computing tax under the Act. Although these provisions do not change the legal character of the payment or transaction at issue, they affect its tax consequences by changing its characterization for tax purposes. Beetz J explained in *R. v. Vermette*, [1978] S.C.J. No. 40, [1978] 2 S.C.R. 838 at 845 (S.C.C.):

> A deeming provision is a statutory fiction; as a rule it implicitly admits that a thing is not what it is deemed to be but decrees that for some particular purpose it shall be taken as if it were that thing although it is not or there is a doubt as to whether it is.

The purpose of a deeming provision, as Dickson J (as he then was) explained in *R. v. Sutherland*, [1980] S.C.J. No. 85, 2 S.C.R. 451 at 456 (S.C.C.), is "to impose a meaning, to cause something to be taken to be different from that which it might have been in the absence of the clause."

In the context of the *Income Tax Act*, deeming provisions are designed to prevent several kinds of tax avoidance. Subparagraph 40(2)(g)(iii), for example, prevents taxpayers from claiming losses on the disposition of property used primarily for personal use or enjoyment by deeming losses on all but certain types of "personal-use property" to be nil.[43] In this respect, the rule mirrors other provisions designed to prevent the deduction of expenses that are motivated primarily for personal reasons, not for the purpose of earning income.[44]

Other deeming rules require accrued but unrealized gains to be included in computing a taxpayer's income for a particular taxation year by deeming property to have been disposed of on the occurrence of various events, or by deeming the taxpayer to have received specific amounts on the disposition of property at death or by way of gift inter vivos. Subsection 104(4), for example, limits the ability to defer accrued capital gains on property held by a trust by

---

[42] See subs. 13(21.2) for depreciable property, subs. 14(12) for eligible capital property, subs. 18(13) to (16) for specific kinds of inventory, subpara. 40(2)(g)(i) and the definition of "superficial loss" in s. 54 for the disposition of non-depreciable capital property by an individual, and subs. 40(3.3) to (3.5) for the disposition of non-depreciable capital property disposed of by a corporation, trust or partnership. The concept of an "affiliated person" is defined in s. 251.1. These provisions are examined in Chapters 5 and 6.

[43] The term "personal-use property" is defined in s. 54. These provisions are examined in Chapter 6.

[44] See the discussion of these provisions earlier in this chapter in Section III. B. ("Rules Disallowing or Limiting Deductions").

deeming the trust to have disposed of all its capital property at intervals of 21 years.[45] Subsection 128.1(4) ensures that accrued gains are subject to Canadian tax by deeming taxpayers to have disposed of all their property immediately before ceasing to be residents of Canada.[46] Similarly, subparagraph 69(1)(b)(i) and subsection 70(5) require taxpayers who transfer property by gift or at death to pay tax on accrued but unrealized gains up to the time of the transfer by deeming the taxpayer to have received as proceeds for the transferred property an amount equal to the fair market value of the property at the time of the transfer.[47]

Yet another category of specific anti-avoidance rules affects the characterization of various payments for tax purposes by deeming them to be something other than they would be under the legal substance doctrine adopted in the *Duke of Westminster* case. Subsection 6(3), for example, is designed to prevent taxpayers from avoiding tax through the receipt of payments the economic or commercial substance of which is compensation for their services as an officer or employee by deeming amounts paid to a taxpayer while an officer or employee of the payer or in connection with an agreement "immediately prior to, during or immediately after a period that the payee was an officer of, or in the employment of, the payer" to be "remuneration for the payee's services" as an officer or employee:

> unless it is established that, irrespective of when the agreement, if any, under which the amount was received was made or the form or legal effect thereof, it cannot reasonably be regarded as having been received
>
> > (c)   as consideration or partial consideration for accepting the office or entering into the contract of employment,
> >
> > (d)   as remuneration or partial remuneration for services as an officer or under the contract of employment, or
> >
> > (e)   in consideration or partial consideration for a covenant with reference to what the officer or employee is, or is not, to do before or after the termination of the employment.[48]

Similarly, subsection 16(1) is designed to prevent taxpayers from avoiding tax through the receipt of payments under a contract or other arrangement the economic or commercial substance of which "can reasonably be regarded as being in part interest or other amount of an income nature and in part an amount of a capital nature" by deeming the part of the payments that can reasonably be so regarded, "irrespective of when the contract or arrangement was made or the form or legal effect thereof," to be interest or another amount of an income

---

[45]   This provision is not examined in this book, and is properly considered in a course on the taxation of trusts and estates.

[46]   This provision is not examined in this book, and is properly considered in a course on international taxation.

[47]   These provisions are examined in Chapter 6.

[48]   This provision is examined in detail in Chapter 4.

nature.[49] Likewise, section 68 prevents taxpayers from avoiding tax on the receipt of payments the economic or commercial substance of which "can reasonably be regarded as being in part the consideration for the disposition of a particular property of a taxpayer or as being in part consideration for the provision of particular services by a taxpayer" by deeming the parts that can reasonably be so regarded as being "proceeds of disposition of the particular property irrespective of the form or legal effect of the contract or agreement" or a payment for the services provided "irrespective of the form or legal effect of the contract or agreement."[50] Although judicial decisions have tended to interpret these provisions narrowly, with little regard to their anti-avoidance purposes,[51] the language of the provisions that apply where amounts can "reasonably be regarded" as something other than their legal substance "irrespective of the form or legal effect thereof" suggests a deliberate effort to overrule the legal substance doctrine in these specific circumstances.

A final category of deeming rules is designed to prevent income-splitting by attributing for tax purposes amounts received by one taxpayer to another, or by deeming the amount at which certain non-arm's-length transactions occur for tax purposes. Sections 74.1 to 74.5, for example, contain numerous rules deeming the income or loss from property transferred by an individual to a spouse or related minor to be the income or loss of the transferor and not that of the spouse or related minor.[52] Likewise, where taxpayers attempt to split income by directing or concurring in the payment or transfer of property to third parties either for their own benefit or for the benefit of the third party, by transferring rights to income to related persons, or by making interest-free or low-interest loans to related persons, other anti-avoidance rules attribute specific amounts back to the original taxpayer.[53] Finally, where a taxpayer acquires or disposes of anything to a person with whom the taxpayer does not deal at arm's length, subsection 69(1) prevents income splitting by deeming the taxpayer to have acquired or disposed of it for proceeds equal to its fair market value.[54]

IV. GENERAL ANTI-AVOIDANCE RULE

Three years after the Supreme Court of Canada rejected the business purpose test in *Stubart*, the federal government released a white paper on tax reform, proposing a number of amendments, among which was the repeal of former subsection 245(1) and the enactment of a new general anti-avoidance rule

---

[49] This provision is examined in detail in Chapter 5.

[50] This provision is examined in detail in Chapter 8.

[51] See the examination of these provisions in Chapters 4, 5, and 8.

[52] These rules are examined in detail in Chapter 8.

[53] See subs. 56(2), (4), and (4.1)-(4.3). Subsections 56(2) and (4) are examined briefly in Chapter 4. Subsections 56(4.1)-(4.3) are discussed in Chapter 8.

[54] This provision is examined in detail in Chapter 8.

designed "to prevent artificial tax avoidance arrangements."[55] According to the white paper: "This rule will introduce a "business purpose test" and a "step transaction" concept into the *Income Tax Act*." Thus, the white paper proposed to overrule *Stubart*.

The rationale for this amendment was explained as follows in a Department of Finance publication accompanying the white paper:

> The government believes that the existing provisions of the *Income Tax Act* are inadequate to deal with a number of blatant tax avoidance arrangements. The existing subsection 245(1), which disallows any deduction for a disbursement or expense that would reduce income artificially or unduly, is of limited application.
>
> The government is convinced that a change in direction is required to reduce what was succinctly described by the Supreme Court of Canada in the *Stubart* case ... as the "... action and reaction endlessly produced by complex, specific tax measures aimed at sophisticated business practices, and the inevitable, professionally guided and equally specialized taxpayer reaction."
>
> Therefore, the government proposes to repeal subsection 245(1) of the *Income Tax Act* and some other anti-avoidance rules aimed at specific types of avoidance and to introduce a new general anti-avoidance rule which is intended to prevent artificial tax avoidance arrangements. The new general anti-avoidance rule is intended to strike a balance between taxpayers' need for certainty in planning their affairs and the government's responsibility to protect the tax base and the fairness of the tax system. Not all tax avoidance transactions are artificial. The new rule will establish limits to acceptable tax avoidance.[56]

Although the Finance paper contained a draft version of the proposed rule, the current version was enacted more than a year later after considerable discussion and amendment.[57] In general, the current rule applies to transactions entered into on or after September 13, 1988.

The key substantive provisions of the GAAR are found in subsections 245(2), (3), and (4) of the Act. According to subsection 245(2):

> Where a transaction is an avoidance transaction, the tax consequences to a person shall be determined as is reasonable in the circumstances in order to deny a tax benefit that, but for

---

[55] Canada, Department of Finance, *The White Paper: Tax Reform 1987* (Ottawa: Department of Finance, June 18, 1987), reproduced in *White Paper on Tax Reform* (Don Mills, ON: CCH, 1987), 23 at 70.

[56] Canada, Department of Finance, *Tax Reform 1987: Economic and Fiscal Outlook* (Ottawa: Department of Finance, June 18, 1987), reproduced in *White Paper on Tax Reform, ibid.*, at 211.

[57] See, for example, David C. Nathanson, "The Proposed General Anti-Avoidance Rule," in *Report of Proceedings of the Thirty-Ninth Tax Conference*, 1987 Conference Report (Toronto: Canadian Tax Foundation, 1988), 9:1-27; Brian J. Arnold, "In Praise of the Business Purpose Test," in the 1987 Conference Report, 10:1-34; David A. Dodge, "A New and More Coherent Approach to Tax Avoidance" (1988) Vol. 36 No. 1 Can. Tax J. 1-22; and Howard J. Kellough, "A Review and Analysis of the Redrafted General Anti-Avoidance Rule" (1988), Vol. 36 No. 1 Can. Tax J. 23-78. See also Brian J. Arnold & James R. Wilson, "The General Anti-Avoidance Rule — Parts 1, 2, and 3" (1988) Vol. 36 Nos. 4-6 Can Tax J. 829-87, 1123-85, and 1369-1410; and Michael Hiltz, "Section 245 of the Income Tax Act" in *Report of Proceedings of the Fortieth Tax Conference*, 1988 Conference Report (Toronto: Canadian Tax Foundation, 1989) 7:1-9.

this section, would result, directly or indirectly, from that transaction or from a series of transactions that includes that transaction.

The term "avoidance transaction" is defined in subsection 245(3). Finally, subsection 245(4) stipulates that subsection (2) applies only if it may reasonably be considered that the transaction:

(a) would, if this Act were read without reference to [the GAAR], result directly or indirectly in a misuse of the provisions of any one or more of

(i) the Act,

(ii) the *Income Tax Regulations*,

(iii) the *Income Tax Application Rules*,

(iv) a tax treaty,

(v) or any other enactment that is relevant in computing tax or any other amount payable by or refundable to a person under [the] Act, or in determining any amount that is relevant for the purposes of that computation; or

(b) would result directly or indirectly in an abuse having regard to those provisions, other than [the GAAR], read as a whole.

For the purposes of this chapter, the GAAR is examined by considering in turn the test for an avoidance transaction in subsection 245(3), the additional requirement of a misuse or abuse in subsection 245(4), and the potential tax consequences if the GAAR applies.

A. Avoidance Transaction

According to subsection 245(2), the GAAR applies where a "transaction" is an "avoidance transaction." Subsection 245(1) defines the word "transaction" to include "an arrangement or event." Subsection 245(3) defines "avoidance transaction" as any transaction:

(a) that, but for this section, would result, directly or indirectly, in a tax benefit, unless the transaction may reasonably be considered to have been undertaken or arranged primarily for *bona fide* purposes other than to obtain the tax benefit; or

(b) that is part of a series of transactions, which series, but for this section, would result, directly or indirectly, in a tax benefit, unless the transaction may reasonably be considered to have been undertaken or arranged primarily for *bona fide* purposes other than to obtain the tax benefit.

To be characterized as an avoidance transaction, therefore, a transaction must satisfy two requirements. First, it must be a transaction or part of a series of transactions that, but for the GAAR itself, "would result, directly or indirectly, in a tax benefit." Second, it may not "reasonably be considered to have been undertaken or arranged primarily for *bona fide* purposes other than to obtain the tax benefit." The following discussion considers the concept of a "tax benefit," the role of the non-tax purpose test, and the application of the GAAR to transactions that are part of a series of transactions resulting in a tax benefit.

1. Tax Benefit

The term "tax benefit" is defined in subsection 245(1) as:

> a reduction, avoidance or deferral of tax or other amount payable under this Act or an increase in a refund of tax or other amount under this Act, and includes a reduction, avoidance or deferral of tax or other amount that would be payable under this Act but for a tax treaty or an increase in a refund of tax or other amount under this Act as a result of a tax treaty.

According to the Department of Finance technical notes accompanying the revised draft legislation, the language of the GAAR "is intended to encompass all types of abusive and artificial tax avoidance schemes including the types to which existing subsection 245(1) already applies." Unlike former subsection 245(1), however, which applied only to deductions in respect of disbursements or expenses, the scope of the GAAR is virtually unlimited, applying to any transaction (including an arrangement or event) resulting in any advantage under the *Income Tax Act* or a tax treaty, whether this involves the deduction of an amount; the reduction, avoidance, or deferral of tax by any other means; the reduction, avoidance, or deferral of other amounts payable under the Act, such as interest and penalties; or an increase in amounts refunded to the taxpayer on account of tax or other amounts such as interest and penalties. In *Canada Trustco Mortgage Co. v. Canada*, [2005] S.C.J. No. 56, [2005] 5 C.T.C. 215, 2005 D.T.C. 5523 (S.C.C.), the Supreme Court of Canada declared (at para. 19) that the existence of a tax benefit is "a factual determination, initially by the Minister and on review by the courts, usually the Tax Court." For this purpose, it held (at para. 63), the burden of proof is on the taxpayer to refute the "underlying assumptions of facts" on which the Minister's assessment is based.

In order to conclude that a transaction or series of transactions has resulted in a tax benefit, it might be thought that one must imagine a notional amount of tax or other amount payable or refundable absent the avoidance transaction or series of transactions of which the avoidance transaction is a part.[58] In some circumstances, this benefit might reasonably be assessed by comparing the tax consequences resulting from the transaction or series of transactions carried out by the taxpayer with the tax consequences resulting from an alternative or "benchmark" transaction or series of transactions that might reasonably have been carried out but for the existence of the tax benefit. In *Canada Trustco*, for example, the Supreme Court of Canada stated (at para. 20) that "[i]n some circumstances, it may be that the existence of a tax benefit can only be established by comparison with another arrangement." In cases where it is unreasonable to conclude that the taxpayer would have carried out any transaction or series of transactions but for the tax benefit, the tax benefit might

---

[58] See, *e.g.*, *McNichol v. Canada*, [1997] T.C.J. No. 5, [1997] 2 C.T.C. 2088, 97 D.T.C. 111 (T.C.C.), *per* Bonner TCJ at para. 20: "There is nothing mysterious about the subs. 245(1) concept of tax benefit. Clearly a reduction or avoidance of tax does require the identification in any given set of circumstances of a norm or standard against which reduction is to be measured."

reasonably be assessed by comparing the tax consequences resulting from the transaction or series of transactions with the tax consequences that would have resulted had the transaction or series of transactions not been carried out.[59] In either case, as Miller TCJ suggested in *Canada Trustco Mortgage Co. v. Canada*, [2003] T.C.J. No. 271, [2003] 4 C.T.C. 2009, 2003 D.T.C. 587 (T.C.C.) at para. 52, it seems reasonable to determine the existence of a tax benefit "in the context of the question of whether or not there is an avoidance transaction."

In *Canada Trustco*, however, the Supreme Cout of Canada also stated (at para. 20) that a deduction always results in a tax benefit "since a deduction results in the reduction of tax." This conclusion is unfortunate, since it lowers the threshold for a tax benefit in a manner that seems inconsistent with the structure and purpose of the GAAR to prevent artificial tax avoidance arrangements.

2. Non-Tax Purpose Test

The non-tax purpose test in subsection 245(3) has been aptly described as "an expanded version of the business purpose test."[60] In the draft legislation released with the 1987 white paper, the proposed rule stipulated that an avoidance transaction did not include a transaction reasonably considered to have been carried out "primarily for *bona fide* business purposes." Thus, as the white paper announced, the new rule contained an explicit business purpose test.

In response to this proposed rule, however, commentators observed that transactions may be carried out for legitimate purposes, such as personal reasons, that are not business-related.[61] As well, since the Act defines the word "business" in subsection 248(1), there was some concern that the rule might be interpreted in light of a statutory provision enacted for an entirely different purpose.[62] When revised draft legislation was released on December 16, 1987, the definition of an "avoidance transaction" was amended to refer to "*bona fide* purposes other than to obtain the tax benefit."

The technical notes explain that this amendment was made because the original business purpose test "might be found not to apply to transactions which are not carried out in the context of a business, narrowly construed." According

---

[59] Brian J. Arnold & James R. Wilson, "The General Anti-Avoidance Rule — Parts 1, 2, and 3" (1988) Vol. 36 Nos. 4-6 Can Tax J. 829-87, 1123-85, and 1369-1410, Part 2 at at 1154-55. In the case of a series of transactions that results in a tax benefit, however, it is unclear whether the appropriate tax benchmark is to be determined by disregarding the series as a whole or only tax-motivated steps inserted into the series.

[60] *Ibid.*, at 1159.

[61] Brian J. Arnold, "In Praise of the Business Purpose Test," in the 1987 Conference Report, *ibid.*, 10:31.

[62] Brian J. Arnold & James R. Wilson, "The General Anti-Avoidance Rule — Parts 1, 2, and 3" (1988) Vol. 36 Nos. 4-6 Can Tax J. 829-87, 1123-85, and 1369-1410, Part 2 at 1155.

to the technical notes, "[t]he vast majority of business, family or investment transactions will not be affected by proposed section 245 since they will have *bona fide* non-tax purposes."

Under the non-tax purpose test, a transaction will not be characterized as an avoidance transaction if it "may *reasonably* be considered to have been undertaken or arranged *primarily* for *bona fide* purposes other than to obtain the tax benefit." Although the technical notes do not address the use of the word "reasonably" in subsection 245(3), this statutory language suggests that the non-tax purpose test is intended to be objective rather than subjective — concerned "not [with] what was in the particular taxpayer's mind but [with] what a reasonable taxpayer [in the taxpayer's circumstances] would have considered to be the purpose of the transaction."[63] As the Supreme Court of Canada stated in *Canada Trustco* at para. 29:

> [t]he determination invokes reasonableness, suggesting that the possibility of different interpretations of events must be objectively considered.

As a result, for a transaction not to be characterized as an avoidance transaction, it is not sufficient that a transaction was in fact "undertaken or arranged primarily for *bona fide* purposes other than to obtain the tax benefit"; in addition, the *bona fide* non-tax purposes must provide a rational basis for the particular transaction under consideration. In *McNichol v. Canada*, [1997] T.C.J. No. 5, [1997] 2 C.T.C. 2088, 97 D.T.C. 111 (T.C.C.), for example, where the taxpayers argued that their primary purpose in selling the shares of a corporation was "to terminate their association with each other in the common ownership" of the company, Bonner TCJ noted (at para. 21) that this *bona fide* non-tax purpose could have been achieved either by "payment of a liquidating dividend"

---

[63] *Ibid.*, at 1157. Although Arnold and Wilson also argue that subs. 245(3) suggests an objective test by referring to the "purposes" of the transaction, not the taxpayer, this argument is difficult to accept both conceptually and textually. It is difficult to imagine a transaction having some kind of transcendent purpose independent of the purposes of the parties to the transaction. Moreover, the language of subs. 245(3) refers to transactions "undertaken or arranged ... *for*" bona fide purposes, not transactions *with* bona fide purposes, nor to the purposes of transactions. Textually, it seems more reasonable to conclude that the transactions to which the provision refers are transactions undertaken or arranged *by the parties to the transaction* for *their* purposes, not transactions undertaken or arranged on their own for their own purposes. Although the non-tax purpose test must be regarded as objective, given the insertion of the word "reasonably" in subs. 245(3), the issues considered in this note are not without consequence in the application of the GAAR. As suggested by the words "in the taxpayer's circumstances" inserted into the sentence quoted in the text, the objectivity of a rule that considers the purposes that a taxpayer may reasonably have undertaken or arranged a transaction is different from the objectivity of a rule that considers only the purposes of a transaction (assuming that these can be defined) independent of the purposes for which the taxpayer entered into the transaction. While neither approach recognizes purely subjective intentions of a taxpayer that cannot reasonably account for the transaction undertaken or arranged, only the former allows a taxpayer to argue that non-tax purposes that might not normally account for a particular transaction are in fact reasonable and bona fide in that taxpayer's circumstances.

or "sale of the shares." Since the payment of a liquidating dividend was regarded as the benchmark transaction, the taxpayers had the onus of proving that it was reasonable to conclude that the share sale was not undertaken primarily to obtain a tax benefit — an onus they failed to discharge.

The use of the word "primarily" in subsection 245(3) suggests that the characterization of a transaction as an avoidance transaction or otherwise depends on a comparative evaluation of the role that different purposes may reasonably have served to justify the particular transaction.[64] If any combination of non-tax purposes could reasonably have been the primary reason for which a transaction resulting in a tax benefit was undertaken or arranged, the transaction is not an avoidance transaction. Thus, as the technical notes explain, "a transaction will not be considered to be an avoidance transaction because, incidentally, it results in a tax benefit or because tax considerations were a significant, but not the primary, purpose for carrying out the transaction." Alternatively, if a transaction resulting in a tax benefit cannot reasonably be considered to have been undertaken or arranged primarily to fulfill one or more non-tax purposes, the transaction is an avoidance transaction. In this respect, the technical notes suggest that "transitory arrangements" such as "the establishment of an entity, such as a corporation or a partnership, followed within a short period by its elimination" ordinarily "would not be considered to have been carried out primarily for *bona fide* purposes other than the obtaining of a tax benefit."

As with the existence of a tax benefit, the Supreme Court of Canada has held that the determination that a transaction can reasonably be considered to have been primarily tax-motivated is a factual determination, in which the taxpayer bears the burden of disproving the "underlying assumptions of facts" on which the Minister's assessment is based: *Canada Trustco*, at para. 63. For this reason, the Court has also emphasized (at para. 77, subpara. 7) that appellate courts should accord considerable deference to the findings of the Tax Court judge, where these are "supported by the evidence."

3. Series of Transactions

By virtue of paragraph 245(3)(b), a transaction may be characterized as an avoidance transaction if it is part of a "series of transactions" that collectively results in a tax benefit, even though the individual transaction alone does not result in a tax benefit. In these circumstances, any step in the series of transactions will be an avoidance transaction even if it individually cannot reasonably be considered to have been undertaken or arranged primarily for *bona fide* non-tax purposes, provided that the series of transactions as a whole

---

[64] See, *e.g.*, *Canada Trustco Mortgage Co. v. Canada*, [2005] S.C.J. No. 56, [2005] 5 C.T.C. 215, 2005 D.T.C. 5523 (S.C.C.) at para. 28, concluding that subs. 245(3) mandates "an objective assessment of the relative importance of the driving forces of the transaction."

may reasonably be considered to have been undertaken or arranged primarily for *bona fide* non-tax purposes.

The technical notes state:

> New paragraph 245(3)(b) recognizes that one step in a series of transactions may not by itself result in a tax benefit. Thus, where a taxpayer, in carrying out a series of transactions, inserts a transaction that is not carried out primarily for *bona fide* non-tax purposes and the series results in a tax benefit, that tax benefit may be denied under subsection 245(2). This is accomplished by expressly defining an avoidance transaction in paragraph 245(3)(b) as including a step transaction (a step transaction being one that is part of a series of transactions) in a series that, but for new section 245, would result directly or indirectly in a tax benefit, unless that transaction has primary non-tax purposes. ... Thus, where a series of transactions would result in a tax benefit, that tax benefit will be denied unless the primary objective of each transaction in the series is to achieve some legitimate non-tax purposes. Therefore, in order not to fall within the definition of "avoidance transaction" in subsection 245(3), each step in such a series must be carried out primarily for *bona fide* non-tax purposes.

Thus, as announced in the 1987 white paper, the GAAR introduced into the Act a "step transaction" concept.

The Act does not define the term "series of transactions." Nonetheless, subsection 248(10) stipulates that for the purposes of the Act, a "series of transactions or events" is "deemed to include any related transactions or events completed in contemplation of the series." In *Canada Trustco* at para. 25, the Supreme Court of Canada concluded that the ordinary meaning of a "series of transactions" includes "a number of transactions that are 'pre-ordained in order to produce a given result' with 'no practical likelihood that the pre-planned events would not take place in the order ordained'".[65] With respect to the extended meaning in subsection 248(10), the court concluded (at para. 26) that the phrase could apply to events before or after the ordinary series of transactions and should be interpreted "not in the sense of actual knowledge but in the broader sense of 'because of' or 'in relation to' the series." Although it is not obvious that this interpretation is consistent with the text of subsection 248(10), which might more reasonably be interpreted to include only related transactions completed prior to an ordinary series of transactions but not related transactions completed after the series,[66] it is likely consistent with legislative intent and the purpose of subsection 248(10) to extend the ordinary meaning of a

---

[65] Citing *Craven v. White*, [1989] A.C. 398 (H.L.) at p. 514, *per* Lord Oliver; and *W.T. Ramsay Ltd. v. IRC*, [1981] 1 All E.R. 865 (H.L.).

[66] See David G. Duff, "Judicial Application of the General Anti-Avoidance Rule in Canada: *OSFC Holdings Ltd. v. The Queen*" (2003) 57 International Bulletin for Fiscal Documentation 278, at 286-87 (suggesting that subs. 248(10) should be amended "to include in addition to related transactions completed in contemplation of a series of transactions, related transactions in the contemplation of which a series of transactions is completed"). See also David G. Duff, "The Supreme Court of Canada and the General Anti-Avoidance Rule: Canada Trustco and Mathew" (2006) 60 Bulletin for International Taxation 54 at 64 (observing that the terms "because of" and "in relation to"do not correspond to dictionary definitions of the word "contemplation").

series of transactions to include related transactions that would not be included under the ordinary meaning of the term.[67]

B. Misuse or Abuse

According to subsection 245(4), the charging provision in subsection 245(2) applies to an avoidance transaction "only if it may reasonably be considered that the transaction":

> (a) would, if this Act were read without reference to [the GAAR], result directly or indirectly in a misuse of the provisions of any one or more of
>
> (i) the Act,
>
> (ii) the *Income Tax Regulations*,
>
> (iii) the *Income Tax Application Rules*,
>
> (iv) a tax treaty,
>
> (v) or any other enactment that is relevant in computing tax or any other amount payable by or refundable to a person under [the] Act, or in determining any amount that is relevant for the purposes of that computation; or
>
> (b) would result directly or indirectly in an abuse having regard to those provisions, other than [the GAAR], read as a whole.

Until 2005, this provision was drafted as an exception to the charging provision in subsection 245(2), stipulating that the GAAR did not apply where it could reasonably be considered that the avoidance transaction determined under subsection 245(3) "would not result directly or indirectly in a misuse of the provisions of [the] Act or an abuse having regard to the provisions of [the] Act, other than [section 245], read as a whole."

This provision did not appear in the original draft version of the proposed rule, which included a general interpretive provision indicating that the purpose of the section was "to counter artificial tax avoidance." In response to concerns that this interpretive provision was unclear and that the anti-avoidance rule might apply to tax-motivated transactions specifically encouraged by or consistent with provisions of the Act,[68] the interpretive provision was deleted and subsection 245(4) introduced in its place. While the 2005 amendment was

---

[67] See David G. Duff, "Judicial Application of the General Anti-Avoidance Rule in Canada *ibid.*, concluding that "[i]t is highly unlikely that Parliament could have intended to include in the statutory definition of 'series of transactions' related transactions completed in contemplation of a subsequent series of transactions, but not related transactions in the contemplation of which taxpayers completed a prior series of transactions", cited with approval in *Canada Trustco*, para. 26.

[68] See, for example, David C. Nathanson, "The Proposed General Anti-Avoidance Rule" in *Report of Proceedings of the Thirty-Ninth Tax Conference*, 1987 Conference Report (Toronto: Canadian Tax Foundation, 1988) 9:127 at 23-26.

made primarily to reverse two lower court decisions holding that the GAAR did not apply to the misuse or abuse of relevant enactments other than the *Income Tax Act*, such as Regulations or tax treaties,[69] the amended version also replaced the double negative language of the initial provision (stipulating that the GAAR does *not* apply if there is *not* a misuse or abuse) with an affirmative test stipulating that the GAAR applies "only if it may reasonably be considered that the transaction ... would ... result ... in a misuse ... or ... an abuse ...." Interestingly, the 2005 amendment was made retroactive to the initial introduction of the GAAR.[70]

Although the courts have not examined the amended version of subsection 245(4) in any detail, the former language was subject to extensive analysis in by the Federal Court of Appeal in *OSFC Holdings Ltd. v. Canada,* [2001] F.C.J. No. 1381, [2001] 4 C.T.C. 82, 2001 D.T.C. 5471 (F.C.A.) and by the Supreme Court of Canada in *Canada Trustco Mortgage Co. v. Canada*, [2003] T.C.J. No. 271, [2003] 4 C.T.C. 2009, 2003 D.T.C. 587 (T.C.C.). In *OSFC Holdings*, the court concluded (at para. 64) that the provision mandates "an object and spirit, or policy, analysis of the provisions in question or the provisions of the *Act* read as a whole" — with the misuse analysis directed at specific provisions at issue and abuse analysis based on the broader purpose, scheme or policy of the *Income Tax Act* as a whole. In addition, it continued (at para. 67):

> Determining whether there has been misuse or abuse is a two-stage analytical process. The first stage involves identifying the relevant policy of the provisions or the Act as a whole. The second is the assessment of the facts to determine whether the avoidance transaction constituted a misuse or abuse having regard to the identified policy.

Finally, the Court emphasized (at para. 69):

> to deny a tax benefit where there has been strict compliance with the Act, on the grounds that the avoidance transaction constitutes a misuse or abuse, requires that the relevant policy be clear and unambiguous.

In *Canada Trustco*, the Supreme Court of Canada endorsed the "two-stage analytical process" that the Federal Court of Appeal employed in *OSFC Holdings* (at para. 44) as well as the view that the GAAR should apply only when "the abusive nature of the transaction is clear" (at para. 50), but rejected any distinction between a misuse and abuse, concluding (at para. 43) that subsection 245(4) "requires a single, unified approach to the textual, contextual and purposive interpretation of the specific provisions of the *Income Tax Act* that are relied upon by the taxpayer in order to determine whether there was abusive tax avoidance". While the analytical separation of statutory interpretation from factual assessment seems eminently reasonable, the court's integration of the misuse and abuse tests into a "single, unified approach" is

---

[69] *Rousseau-Houle v. Canada*, [2001] T.C.J. No. 169, 2001 D.T.C. 250 (T.C.C.); and *Fredette v. Canada*, [2001] T.C.J. No. 170, [2001] 3 C.T.C. 2468, 2001 D.T.C. 621 (T.C.C.).

[70] S.C. 2005, c. 19, s. 52(2), applicable with respect to transactions entered into after September 12, 1988.

difficult to reconcile with the text of subsection 245(4), particularly in its amended form, which clearly contemplates separate inquiries into a misuse of specific "provisions" and an abuse "having regard to those provisions ... read as a whole."[71] One might also question the Court's conclusion in *Canada Trustco* that the GAAR should apply only where the existence of abusive tax avoidance is clear, on the basis that this standard is consistent with the double negative language of the former version of subsection 245(4) but not the affirmative language of the amended version.[72] Indeed, without commenting on the amended language in subsection 245(4), the more recent Supreme Court of Canada decision in *Lipson v. Canada*, [2009] F.C.J. No. 1, 2009 SCC 1, [2009] 1 C.T.C. 314 (S.C.C.), states (at para. 21) that "the burden is on the Minister to prove, *on the balance of probabilities*, that the avoidance transaction results in an abuse and misuse within the meaning of s. 245(4)" [emphasis added].

C. Tax Consequences

According to subsection 245(2), where a transaction is an avoidance transaction, "the tax consequences to a person shall be determined as is reasonable in the circumstances in order to deny [the] tax benefit" that would otherwise result from the transaction or series of which it is a part. Subsection 245(1) defines the term "tax consequences" broadly as "the amount of income, taxable income, or taxable income earned in Canada of, tax or other amount payable by or refundable to the person under this Act, or any other amount that is relevant for the purposes of computing that amount." Subsection 245(5) provides:

Without restricting the generality of subsection (2), and not withstanding any other enactment

(a)   any deduction, exemption or exclusion in computing income, taxable income, taxable income earned in Canada or tax payable or any part thereof may be allowed or disallowed in whole or in part,

(b)   any such deduction, exemption or exclusion, any income, loss or other amount or part thereof may be allocated to any person,

(c)   the nature of any payment or other amount may be recharacterized, and

---

[71]   For a critical evaluation of this conclusion, see Duff, "The Supreme Court of Canada and the General Anti-Avoidance Rule" (2006) 60 Bulletin for International Taxation 54 at 66 (arguing that the court's interpretation limits the effective operation of the GAAR by restricting its application to the abuse of "specific provisions" relied upon by the taxpayer to obtain the tax benefit).

[72]   See *ibid.*, at 67 (suggesting that a high burden of persuasion "flows logically from the double negative language of s. 245(4) as it formerly read, which stipulated that the GAAR did not apply to transactions that could reasonably be considered not to result in a misuse or abuse" but contradicts the amended language of subs. 245(4) according to which the GAAR applies if it may reasonably be considered that the transaction results in a misuse or abuse).

    (d)   the tax effects that would otherwise result from the application of other provisions of this Act may be ignored,

in determining the tax consequences to a person as is reasonable in the circumstances in order to deny a tax benefit that would, but for this section, result, directly or indirectly, from an avoidance transaction.

The procedural aspects of the rule are contained in subsections 245(6) to (8).

The scope of these remedial powers is extremely broad. Unlike former subsection 245(1), which applied only to deny the deduction of a disbursement or expense, subsections 245(2) and (5) authorize adjustments to any amount relevant to a taxpayer's current or future tax liability. Thus, for example, where an avoidance transaction is carried out in order to increase the cost of certain property for tax purposes, this cost may be adjusted in order to deny the tax benefit that might result from a subsequent sale of the property at a gain less than that which would have resulted in the absence of the avoidance transaction. As well, these remedial provisions apply to "any person," even one who was only indirectly or marginally involved in the avoidance transaction. As a result, where an avoidance transaction affects an amount that is relevant to the current or future tax liability of a marginal participant in the transaction, this amount may also be adjusted under the GAAR.

In order to deny the tax benefit, paragraph 245(5)(a) states that, "without restricting the generality" of subsection 245(2), "any deduction in computing income, taxable income, ... or tax payable or any part thereof may be allowed or disallowed in whole or in part." Consequently, the GAAR may be used to adjust not only deductions in computing a taxpayer's income from a source, but also deductions in computing a taxpayer's net income from all sources under section 3, deductions in computing the taxpayer's taxable income for the year under subsection 2(2), and tax credits available to reduce the amount of basic federal tax otherwise payable. Paragraph 245(5)(b) confirms that the GAAR may be used as an attribution rule to allocate any deduction, income, loss, or other amount or part thereof "to any person." Paragraph 245(5)(c) authorizes the CRA and the courts to recharacterize the nature of any payment or other amount, and paragraph 245(5)(d) provides that the tax effects that would otherwise result from the application of any other provisions of the Act may be ignored.

Under the basic remedial rule in subsection 245(2), the powers of the revenue authorities and the courts to determine the tax consequences of an avoidance transaction are limited in two ways: first, the tax consequences must be "reasonable in the circumstances"; and second, they must be determined "in order to deny the tax benefit." According to the technical notes, the reasonableness test in subsection 245(2) "recognizes that it is not possible to exhaustively prescribe the appropriate tax consequences for the range of avoidance transactions to which the rule might apply." The word "reasonable," as Arnold and Wilson observe, suggests "an objective standard that Revenue Canada and, ultimately, the courts must apply."[73]

The second of the limitations in subsection 245(2), that the tax consequences must be determined "in order to deny the tax benefit," clearly conditions the first. Arnold and Wilson explain:

> Revenue Canada and the courts are not authorized to do whatever they consider to be reasonable in the circumstances. Rather, the direction is more precise: to deny the tax benefit that would otherwise result from the avoidance transaction or series of transactions — the same tax benefit that must be identified as part of the determination that a particular transaction is an avoidance transaction.[74]

Thus, the tax consequences that are "reasonable in the circumstances" are those that are reasonable "in order to deny the tax benefit."

Because the tax consequences determined under the GAAR are those that are reasonable in order to deny the tax benefit, the considerations determining the remedial effects of the GAAR are necessarily related to those governing its application in the first place. In particular, just as the characterization of an avoidance transaction arguably depends on the identification of a "benchmark transaction" against which to measure the existence of a tax benefit, so also the determination of "reasonable tax consequences" requires a specification of the "benchmark transaction" in order to deny a tax benefit.

NOTES AND QUESTIONS

1. What is the relationship between the GAAR and the judicial anti-avoidance rules examined earlier in this chapter? Have these judicial anti-avoidance rules been rendered irrelevant by the introduction of the GAAR?

2. What is the relationship between subsection 245(4) and Estey J's guideline 3(c) in *Stubart Investments Ltd. v. Canada*, [1984] S.C.J. No. 25, [1984] C.T.C. 294, 84 D.T.C. 6305 (S.C.C.), according to which the formal validity of a transaction may be insufficient where the "object and spirit" of an "allowance" or "benefit provision" is "defeated" by "procedures blatantly adopted by the taxpayer to synthesize a loss, delay or other tax saving device"? If guideline 3(c) prohibits tax consequences that defeat the object and spirit of an allowance or benefit provision, and subsection 245(4) excludes from the operation of the GAAR transactions that do not contradict the "object and spirit" of the Act, is it arguable that the GAAR is meaningless?

Consider the following comments by Brian Arnold and James Wilson:

---

[73] Brian J. Arnold & James R. Wilson, "The General Anti-Avoidance Rule — Parts 1, 2, and 3" (1988) Vol. 36 Nos. 4-6 Can Tax J. 829-87, 1123-85, and 1369-1410, Part 2 at 1171. See also the discussion of the "reasonable in the circumstances" test in Howard J. Kellough, " A Review and Analysis of the General Anti-Avoidance Rule" (1988) Vol. 36 No. 1 Can. Tax J. 23-78 at 54-60.

[74] *Ibid.*, at 1172.

Section 245 applies as a provision of last resort; accordingly, a transaction must satisfy the other provisions of the Act before any question concerning the application of section 245 arises. According to the *Stubart* case and the modern rule of interpretation, the provisions of the Act must be interpreted and applied in accordance with their object and spirit; therefore, if a transaction is not in accordance with the object and spirit of the other provisions of the Act read in the context of the Act as a whole, those provisions should presumably be interpreted not to apply to the transaction. The general anti-avoidance rule is unnecessary in this situation. On the other hand, if a transaction is within the object and spirit of the other provisions of the Act, it must be determined whether the transaction is an avoidance transaction under subsection 245(3). Further, if the transaction is found to be an avoidance transaction, it must be determined whether subsection 245(4) applies, and if it does, subsection 245(2) will not be applied to deny the tax benefit of the transaction. But if the exception under subsection 245(4) is nothing more than an object and spirit test, it duplicates the test as originally applied in deciding whether the transaction was within the scope of the Act.

> In other words, if a transaction results in a misuse or abuse of the provisions of the Act, those provisions will not apply and the issue of the application of the general anti-avoidance rule will not apply. On the other hand, if a transaction is within other statutory provisions (that is. it is in accordance with the object and spirit of those provisions), inevitably the transaction is exempt from the general anti-avoidance rule by virtue of subsection 245(4).[75]

3.   What is the relationship between the GAAR and other, more specific anti-avoidance rules in the Act, such as those surveyed earlier in this chapter? If a transaction is not caught by a specific anti-avoidance rule, should it be excluded from the application of the GAAR?

For an analysis of these issues, see Thomas E. McDonnell, "Legislative Anti-Avoidance: The Interaction of the New General Rule and Representative Specific Rules," in *Report of Proceedings of the Fortieth Tax Conference*, 1988 Conference Report (Toronto: Canadian Tax Foundation, 1989), 6:1-34.

4.   Is the term "avoidance transaction" an appropriate term to characterize transactions that fall within the definition in subsection 245(3)? Should not a term like this be reserved for transactions that are caught by subsection 245(3) and not excluded by subsection 245(4)?

5.   According to technical notes accompanying the introduction of the GAAR:

> [s]ubsection 245(3) does not permit the "recharacterization" of a transaction for the purposes of determining whether or not it is an avoidance transaction. In other words, it does not permit a transaction to be considered to be an avoidance transaction because some alternative transaction that might have achieved an equivalent result would have resulted in higher taxes. It is recognized that tax planning — arranging one's affairs so as to attract the least amount of tax — is a legitimate and accepted part of Canadian tax law. If a taxpayer selects a transaction that minimizes his tax liability and this transaction is not carried out primarily to obtain a tax benefit, he should not be taxed as if he had engaged in other transactions that would have resulted in higher taxes.

Is this statement consistent with the decision in *McNichol v. Canada*, [1997] T.C.J. No. 5, [1997] 2 C.T.C. 2088, 97 D.T.C. 111 (T.C.C.)? Is it possible to

---

[75]   *Ibid.*, at 1172.

apply the GAAR without defining a benchmark transaction? How should such a benchmark transaction be determined?

6.   Although a taxpayer may incur accounting and legal fees to devise and implement an avoidance transaction, section 245 imposes no penalty on avoidance transactions other than nullifying the tax benefit that would otherwise result. Should taxpayers be further discouraged from engaging in avoidance transactions by the introduction of a specific penalty on these kinds of transactions?

Consider the following comments by Arnold and Wilson:

> Abusive tax avoidance imposes considerable costs on other taxpayers and on the tax system generally. In the absence of a penalty, some taxpayers may be willing to take the risk that a transaction may ultimately be determined to be subject to the general anti-avoidance rule, since the only costs would be the transaction costs and the interest on any unpaid taxes. ... A penalty would serve to reinforce the purpose of the general anti-avoidance rule and to increase its effectiveness, by discouraging taxpayers from engaging in abusive tax avoidance transactions.[76]

However, Arnold and Wilson also add that:

> [a] penalty is appropriate ... only if the general anti-avoidance rule is restricted to tax avoidance transactions that are clearly abusive. There is also some risk (depending on the severity of the penalty) that a penalty might discourage Revenue Canada and the courts from applying the rule and/or that it might discourage legitimate commercial transactions.[77]

7.   In order to ensure consistency in the application of the GAAR, the CRA has indicated that "proposed assessments involving the rule will be reviewed by ... Taxation Head Office".[78] In practice, decisions to apply the GAAR are made by a special GAAR committee of the CRA.

8.   In addition to the technical notes, there is an information circular outlining various circumstances in which the GAAR will or will not apply. See IC 88-2 and IC 88-2, Supplement 1, July 13, 1990.

9.   For discussions of the GAAR and judicial decisions in which it has been considered, see Harry Erlichmann, ed., *Tax Avoidance in Canada: The General Anti-Avoidance Rule* (Toronto: Irwin Law, 2002); Brian Arnold, "The Long, Slow, Steady Demise of the General Anti-Avoidance Rule" (2004) 52 Can. Tax J. 488-511; Brian J. Arnold, "Policy Forum: Confusion Worse Confounded — The Supreme Court's GAAR Decisions" (2006) 54 Can. Tax J. 167-209; and David G. Duff and Harry Erlichmann, *Tax Avoidance in Canada After Canada Trustco and Mathew* (Toronto: Irwin Law, 2007).

---

[76] *Ibid.*, at 1152.

[77] *Ibid.*

[78] *Information Circular* 88-2, "The General Anti-Avoidance Rule: Section 245 of the Act," October 21, 1998, para. 2.

PART TWO

Computation of Income or Loss

As the introduction to the basic structure of the income tax in Chapter 1 explained, the calculation of each taxpayer's tax payable in a taxation year begins with the computation of the taxpayer's aggregate income for the taxation year. According to section 3 of the *Income Tax Act*, R.S.C. 1985, c. 1 (5th Supp.), as amended, this aggregate income is computing by adding "all amounts each of which is the taxpayer's income for the year" from all "sources (paragraph 3(a)) and what can be described as the taxpayer's net taxable capital gains for the taxation year (paragraph 3(b)), and subtracting the total of all deductions permitted by subdivision e of Division B to the extent that they have not been taken into account in computing the taxpayer's income from specific sources under paragraph 3(a) (paragraph 3(c)) and the total of "all amounts each of which is the taxpayer's loss for the year from an office, employment, business or property or the taxpayer's allowable business investment loss for the taxation year" (paragraph 3 (d)). In computing a taxpayer's income or loss from each source and the taxpayer's capital gains and capital losses, moreover, the Act contains numerous rules specifying amounts that must be included, allowing deductions for costs that must be incurred in order to obtain this income, and providing for the exemption of specific amounts in particular circumstances. Other rules govern the timing of inclusions and deductions and the attribution of specific amounts to particular taxpayers. Together, these rules account for a large part of the Act, comprising subdivisions a to g of Division B of Part I of the Act, or sections 3 to 81.

The following chapters examine these provisions in detail, reviewing statutory rules and judicial decisions characterizing the source or kind of an income or loss, specifying amounts that must be included or may be deducted in computing a taxpayer's income or loss from specific sources, a taxpayer's capital gains and losses, and a taxpayer's aggregate income for the taxation year, and governing the timing of inclusions and deductions and the attribution of specific amounts to particular taxpayers. Chapter 4 considers the computation of a taxpayer's income or loss from an office or employment, examining the rules in subdivision a of Division B (sections 5 to 8). Chapter 5 examines the computation of a taxpayer's income from a business or property, reviewing key rules in subdivision b of Division B (sections 38 to 55). Chapter 7 considers other inclusions and deductions, examining notable inclusions in subdivision d of Division B (sections 56 to 59.1) and key deductions in subdivision e of

Division B (60 to 66.8). Chapter 8 reviews various rules relating to the computation of a taxpayer's income contained in subdivision f of Division B (sections 67 to 80). Section 81 of the Act (subdivision g of Division B) was examined in the discussion of exemptions in Chapter 1.

CHAPTER FOUR

Income or Loss from an Office or Employment

I. INTRODUCTION

According to paragraph 3(a) of the *Income Tax Act* a taxpayer's income for the year includes the taxpayer's income from each "office" and each "employment." In turn, paragraph 3(d) permits taxpayers to deduct their losses from each office and employment in computing their net income for the year.

The rules governing the computation of a taxpayer's income or loss from an office or employment are found in subdivision a of Division B of Part I of the Act, comprising sections 5 to 8. Subject to the rules in Part I of the Act, subsection 5(1) defines a taxpayer's income for a taxation year from an office or employment as "the salary, wages and other remuneration, including gratuities, received by the taxpayer in the year." Correspondingly, subsection 5(2) defines a taxpayer's loss for a taxation year from an office or employment as "the amount of the taxpayer's loss, if any, for the taxation year from that source computed by applying, with such modifications as the circumstances require, the provisions of the Act respecting the computation of income from that source." Sections 6 and 7 specify various amounts that must be included in computing a taxpayer's income from an office or employment, and section 8 sets out specific amounts that may be deducted in computing a taxpayer's income from an office or employment.

Because income from an office or employment is computed according to an identical set of rules, the distinction between these two sources is irrelevant for tax purposes. Therefore, unless otherwise stated, references in this book to income from "employment" should be read to include income from an office. In contrast, two significant tax consequences turn on the distinction between income from employment and income from a business. First, the deductions permitted under section 8 in computing a taxpayer's income from employment are much less generous than those available in computing a taxpayer's income from a business under subdivision b.[1] Second, employers are required to withhold and remit income and payroll taxes in respect of amounts paid to employees.[2] This imposes both an administrative and a financial obligation on employers, who must not only remit the employee's share of payroll taxes but also their own employer share of payroll taxes. As a result, both workers and the persons hiring them will usually prefer that the source of an amount be characterized as business rather than employment. For the revenue authorities, however, characterization as income from employment is typically more advantageous.

This chapter considers the characterization and computation of a taxpayer's income or loss from an office or employment. Section II surveys statutory and judicial rules governing the characterization of an occupation as an "office" or "employment." Section III examines statutory rules and judicial decisions regarding different amounts that are included in computing a taxpayer's income from these sources. Section IV reviews rules governing the deduction of specific amounts in computing a taxpayer's income from an office or employment. Section V considers the timing of inclusions and deductions.

II. CHARACTERIZATION

For the purposes of the *Income Tax Act*, the terms "office" and "employment" are defined in subsection 248(1) of the Act. An "office" is "the position of an individual entitling the individual to a fixed or ascertainable stipend or remuneration," including:

> a judicial office, the office of a minister of the Crown, the office of a member of the Senate or House of Commons of Canada, a member of a legislative assembly or a member of a legislative or executive council and any other office, the incumbent of which is elected by popular vote or is elected or appointed in a representative capacity and also includes the position of a corporation director.

"Employment" is defined as "the position of an individual in the service of some other person (including Her Majesty or a foreign state or sovereign)." Correspondingly, a person holding an employment position is referred to as a "servant" or "employee." The term "employee" is deemed to include "officers"

---

[1] On the deductions available in computing a taxpayer's income from an office or employment, see section IV of this chapter. Allowable deductions in computing a taxpayer's income from a business or property are considered in section IV of Chapter 5.

[2] See subs. 153(1) of the *Income Tax Act*, ss. 68 and 82 of the *Employment Insurance Act*, S.C. 1996, c. 23, s. 82, and ss. 9 and 21 of the *Canada Pension Plan*, R.S.C. 1985, c. C-8. In addition to these federal payroll taxes, a number of provinces levy payroll taxes in respect of amounts paid to employees. See, for example, *Employer Health Tax Act*, R.S.O. 1990, c. E.11, and the *Workplace Safety and Insurance Act*, S.O. 1997, c. 16. Under the *Canada Pension Plan* and some provincial payroll tax acts, self-employed individuals are required to make contributions equivalent to the sum of employer and employee contributions that would be payable if an employment relationship did exist.

(those persons holding an "office" as defined), and the term "employer" includes the person from whom an officer receives remuneration.

Whether because of the specificity of the statutory definition or the limited number of "offices" within the meaning of the statutory definition, few cases have considered the characterization of an "office" as a source of income or loss. Nonetheless, it has been suggested that an office typically "denotes a subsisting, permanent, substantive position which has an existence independent of the person who fills it, and which goes on and is filled in succession."[3] A mayor, an alderman, and a university professor in his official capacity were found to be officers in one trilogy of cases,[4] whereas an individual appointed to participate as a member of a royal commission was found not to have held an office due to the impermanent nature of the commissioner's appointment and the fact that a series of individuals were not appointed to complete the same duties.[5]

In contrast, the distinction between employment and business as sources of income or loss has been and continues to be a subject of considerable litigation, particularly in cases where an individual supplies services to another person. The following sections examine the various tests by which courts distinguish between employees and independent contractors, and judicial and statutory responses to taxpayer efforts to avoid characterization of a source as employment through incorporation.

A. Employees versus Independent Contractors

In private law, the existence of an employment relationship was traditionally based on the legal right of one party to control and direct the manner in which the employee performs contractual obligations.[6] According to *Black's Law Dictionary*, 8th ed., for example, an "employee" is defined as:

> who works in the service of another person (the employer) under an express or implied contract of hire, under which the employer has the right to control the details of work performance.

On this basis, courts have traditionally distinguished between a "contract of service" between an employee and an employer and a "contract for services" involving independent contractors.

Throughout the 20th century, however, the courts have developed several other tests to define the existence of an employment relationship. These tests, as well as the traditional control test, were considered in *Wiebe Door Services Ltd.*

---

[3] *MacKeen v. M.N.R.*, [1967] Tax ABC 374 at 380 (T.A.B.).

[4] See, respectively, *Badanai v. M.N.R.* (1951), 51 D.T.C. 378 (T.A.B.); *Mitchell v. M.N.R.* (1951), 51 D.T.C. 380 (T.A.B.); and *Blatz v. M.N.R.* (1951), 51 D.T.C. 382 (T.A.B.).

[5] See *MacKeen v. M.N.R.*, [1967] Tax ABC 374 (T.A.B.).

[6] See note 174 on the *Quebec Asbestos Corp. v. Couture* case in David Duff, "The Federal Income Tax Act and Private Law in Canada: Complementarity, Dissociation, and Canadian Bijurialism" (2003) Vol. 51 No. 4 Can. Tax J. 1.

v. M.N.R., [1986] F.C.J. No. 1052, [1986] 2 C.T.C. 200, 87 D.T.C. 5025 (F.C.A.), a leading Canadian case on the distinction between employment and business as sources of income.[7] In *Royal Winnipeg Ballet v. Canada (Minister of National Revenue – M.N.R.)*, [2006] F.C.J. No. 339 (F.C.A.) Sharlow JA said (at para. 34):

> *671122 Ontario Ltd. v. Sagaz Industries Canada Inc.*, [2001] 2 S.C.R. 983 (*Sagaz*) is the leading case from the Supreme Court of Canada on the determination of the status of a person as an employee or an independent contractor. However, before discussing *Sagaz*, it is useful to consider *Wiebe Door Services Ltd. v. M.N.R.*, [1986] 3 F.C. 553 (C.A.), because it forms an important part of the jurisprudential foundation for *Sagaz*.

Wiebe Door Services Ltd. v. M.N.R.
[1986] F.C.J. No. 1052, [1986] 2 C.T.C. 200, 87 D.T.C. 5025 (F.C.A.)

MacGUIGAN J (Pratte and Mahoney JJ concurring): This ... application is brought to set aside a decision by the Tax Court, which upheld an assessment against the applicant for the payment of Unemployment Insurance Premiums and Canada Pension Plan Contributions for the years 1979, 1980 and 1981. Counsel for the applicant admitted before this Court that the assessment for the 1979 year was correct, in that the only two persons then in question were admittedly employees in that year, but contended that the 12 persons in relation to whom the applicant was assessed in 1980 and 1981 were all independent contractors rather than employees.

The applicant is in the business of installing doors and repairing overhead doors in the Calgary area, with about 75 percent of its business being on the repair side. It carries on its business through the services of a considerable number of door installers and repairers, with each of whom it has a specific understanding that they would be running their own businesses and would therefore be responsible for their own taxes and any contributions for workers' compensation, unemployment insurance and Canada Pension Plan. Such an agreement is not of itself determinative of the relationship between the parties, and a court must carefully examine the facts in order to come to its own conclusion. ...

The essential part of the Tax Court's reasons for decision is as follows: ...

> Case law has established a series of tests to determine whether a contract is one of service or for the provision of services. While not exhaustive the following are four tests most commonly referred to:

---

[7] The case was directly concerned with determining whether the contractors who worked for Wiebe Door Services Ltd. were engaged in "insurable employment" for the purposes of the *Unemployment Insurance Act* and "pensionable employment" as defined by the *Canada Pension Plan*. Because this determination turns upon the distinction between individuals engaged as independent contractors engaged under contracts "for services" and employees engaged under contracts "of service," the tests and approaches described in *Wiebe Door* are equally applicable to cases concerning characterization arising under the *Income Tax Act*.

    (a)   The degree or absence of control, exercised by the alleged employer.

    (b)   Ownership of tools.

    (c)   Chance of profit and risks of loss.

    (d)   Integration of the alleged employees work into the alleged employers business.

Let us now subject the evidence to each of the above tests.

Firstly: The Control Test

The workers worked mostly on their own. They were free to accept or refuse a call. They were not required to work or attend at the Appellant's place of business, except to pick up a door or parts. The Appellant did exercise some measure of control over the workers. Firstly, the Appellant assigned the jobs to the installer. The job was guaranteed for one year. Within that time the Appellant would require the installer to correct any faulty or defective installation or repair. On the basis of the Control Test, the evidence is indecisive.

Secondly: Ownership of Tools

Each worker owned his own truck and tools. The Appellant provided only the special racks for transporting doors and the special cement drill, when required. On the basis of this test, the workers would seem to be independent contractors.

Thirdly: Chance of Profit or Risk of Loss

Each worker had a limited chance of profit. He got paid by the job. If he worked quickly and efficiently he could do more jobs per day if these were available. If on the other hand he was careless and did not properly complete the job, he would be required at his own expense as to gas, parts and services to redo or correct his work. On the basis of this test the workers would seem to be independent contractors.

Fourthly: The Integration Test

The Appellant was in the business of servicing and installing overhead electrically controlled doors. All the work performed by the installers formed an integral part of the Appellant's business. Without the installers, the Appellant would be out of business.

...

In the case before me, this test tips the scales in favour of a contract of service, and not a contract for services.

This appeal is therefore dismissed, and the determination of the Respondent is upheld.

The applicant argued before us that the Tax Court committed an error of law in its use of the so-called "integration" test, which it contended was rightly applied only in relation to workers possessed of a high degree of professional skill and therefore not applicable at all to the present facts.

...

The question of whether a contract is one *of service*, in which case it indicates a master-servant or employment relationship, or *for services*, in which case the relationship is between independent contractors, has arisen most often in the law of torts, as surveyed recently by Professor Joseph Eliot Magnet, "Vicarious Liability and the Professional Employee" (1978-79), 6 *CCLT* 208, or in labour law, as recently summarized by Professor Michael Bendel, "The Dependent Contractor: An Unnecessary and Flawed Development in Canadian Labour Law" (1982), 32 *UTLJ* 374.

The traditional common-law criterion of the employment relationship has been the control test, as set down by Baron Bramwell in *R v. Walker* (1858), 27 LJMC 207, 208:

> It seems to me that the difference between the relations of master and servant and of principal and agent is this: A principal has the right to direct what the agent has to do; but a master has not only that right, but also the right to say how it is to be done.

That this test is still fundamental is indicated by adoption by the Supreme Court of Canada in *Hôpital Notre-Dame de l'Espérance and Theoret v. Laurent et al.*, [1978] 1 SCR 605, at 613, of the following statement: "the essential criterion of employer-employee relations is the right to give orders and instructions to the employee regarding the manner in which to carry out his work."

Nevertheless, as Professor P.S. Atiyah, *Vicarious Liability in the Law of Torts*, London, Butterworths, 1967, p. 41, has put it, "the control test as formulated by Bramwell B ... wears an air of deceptive simplicity, which ... tends to wear thin on further examination." A principal inadequacy is its apparent dependence on the exact terms in which the task in question is contracted for: where the contract contains detailed specifications and conditions, which would be the normal expectation in a contract with an independent contractor, the control may even be greater than where it is to be exercised by direction on the job, as would be the normal expectation in a contract with a servant, but a literal application of the test might find the actual control to be less. In addition, the test has broken down completely in relation to highly skilled and professional workers, who possess skills far beyond the ability of their employers to direct.

Perhaps the earliest important attempt to deal with these problems was the development of the entrepreneur test by William O. (later Justice) Douglas, "Vicarious Liability and the Administration of Risk" (1928-29), 38 *Yale L.J.* 584, which posited four differentiating earmarks of the entrepreneur: control, ownership, losses, and profits. It was essentially this test which was applied by Lord Wright in *Montreal v. Montreal Locomotive Works Ltd. et al.*, [1947] 1 DLR 161 at 169-70; [1946] 3 WWR 748 at 756-58:

> In earlier cases a single test, such as the presence or absence of control, was often relied on to determine whether the case was one of master and servant, mostly in order to decide issues of tortious liability on the part of the master or superior. In the more complex conditions of modern industry, more complicated tests have often to be applied. It has been suggested that a fourfold test would in some cases be more appropriate, a complex involving (1) control; (2) ownership of the tools; (3) chance of profit; (4) risk of loss. Control in itself is not always conclusive. Thus the master of a chartered vessel is generally the employee of the shipowner though the charterer can direct the employment of the vessel. Again the law often limits the employer's right to interfere with the employee's conduct, as also do trade union regulations.

> *In many cases the question can only be settled by examining the whole of the various elements which constitute the relationship between the parties. In this way it is in some cases possible to decide the issue by raising as the crucial question whose business is it, or in other words by asking whether the party is carrying on the business, in the sense of carrying it on for himself or on his own behalf and not merely for a superior.* [Emphasis added.]

...

Taken thus in context, Lord Wright's fourfold test is a general, indeed an overarching test, which involves "examining the whole of the various elements which constitute the relationship between the parties." In his own use of the test to determine the character of the relationship in the *Montreal Locomotive Works* case itself, Lord Wright combines and integrates the four tests in order to seek out the meaning of the whole transaction.

A similar general test, usually called the "organization test" (though termed the "integration test" by the Tax Court here), was set forth by Denning LJ (as he then was) in *Stevenson, Jordan and Harrison, Ltd. v. MacDonald and Evans*, [1952] 1 TLR 101, 111:

> One feature which seems to run through all the instances is that, under a contract of service, a man is employed as part of the business, and his work is done as an integral part of the business; whereas under a contract for services, his work, although done for the business, is not integrated into it but is only accessory to it.

The organization test was approved by the Supreme Court of Canada in *Cooperators Insurance Association v. Kearney*, [1965] SCR 106 at 112; 48 DLR (2d) 1, at 22-33, where Spence J for the Court quoted with approval the following passage from Fleming, *The Law of Torts* (2nd ed. 1961) 328-29:

> Under the pressure of novel situations, the courts have become increasingly aware of the strain on the traditional formulation [i.e., the control test], and most recent cases display a discernible tendency to replace it by something like an "organization" test. Was the alleged servant part of his employer's organization? Was his work subject to co-ordinational control as to "where" and "when" rather than to "how"?

As Bendel points out, supra, at 381, the organization test is now "firmly established in Canada." He explains its attractiveness as follows, supra, at 382:

> The aspect of the organization test which makes it so attractive in the labour relations context is that integration into another person's business, the key feature of the test, is a very useful indicator of economic dependence.

...

The organization test has recently been described by MacKinnon ACJO for the Ontario Court of Appeal as an enlargement of, and presumably an advance upon, Lord Wright's test: *Mayer v. J. Conrad Lavigne Ltd.* (1979), 27 OR (2d) 129, at 132; 105 DLR (3d) 734, at 737. However, it has had less vogue in other common-law jurisdictions. In fact A.N. Khan, "Who is a Servant?" (1979), 53 *Austr. LJ* 832, 834, makes bold to say of the English and Australian cases:

> However, the "integration" or "organisation" test if applied in isolation can lead to as impractical and absurd results as the control test. The courts, therefore, came to the conclusion that a "multiple" test should be applied, in that all the factors should be taken into

account. Thus in *Morren v. Swinton & Pendlebury Borough Council* [[1965] 1 WLR 576], Lord Parker CJ stated that the control test was perhaps an over-simplification. His Lordship added that: "clearly superintendence and control cannot be the decisive test when one is dealing with a professional man, or a man of some particular skill and experience." Thus the courts started modifying and transforming the test into "common sense" test, [Somervell LJ in *Cassidy v. Minister of Health*, [1975] 2 KB 343] or "Multiple" test [Mocatta J in *Whittaker v. Minister of Pensions & National Insurance* [1967] 1 QB 156].

Professor Atiyah, supra, at 38-39, ends up with Lord Wright's test from the *Montreal Locomotive Works* case, as he finds it more general than Lord Denning's which he sees as decisive in only some cases.

I am inclined to the same view, for the same reason. I interpret Lord Wright's test not as the fourfold one it is often described as being but rather as a four-in-one test, with emphasis always retained on what Lord Wright, *supra*, calls "the combined force of the whole scheme of operations," even while the usefulness of the four subordinate criteria is acknowledged.

Lord Denning's test may be more difficult to apply, as witness the way in which it has been misused as a magic formula by the Tax Court here and in several other cases cited by the respondent, in all of which the effect has been to dictate the answer through the very form of the question, by showing that without the work of the "employees" the "employer" would be out of business ("Without the installers, the Appellant would be out of business"). As thus applied, this can never be a fair test, because in a factual relationship of mutual dependency it must always result in an affirmative answer. If the businesses of both parties are so structured as to operate through each other, they could not survive independently without being restructured. But that is a consequence of their surface arrangement and not necessarily expressive of their intrinsic relationship.

What must always remain of the essence is the search for the total relationship of the parties. Atiyah's counsel in this respect, *supra*, at 38, is, I believe, of great value:

> [I]t is exceedingly doubtful whether the search for a formula in the nature of a single test for identifying a contract of service any longer serves a useful purpose. ... The most that can profitably be done is to examine all the possible factors which have been referred to in these cases as bearing on the nature of the relationship between the parties concerned. Clearly not all of these factors will be relevant in all cases, or have the same weight in all cases. Equally clearly no magic formula can be propounded for determining which factors should, in any given case, be treated as the determining ones. The plain fact is that in a large number of cases the court can only perform a balancing operation, weighing up the factors which point in one direction and balancing them against those pointing in the opposite direction. In the nature of things it is not to be expected that this operation can be performed with scientific accuracy.
>
> This line of approach appears to be in keeping with what Lord Wright said in the little-known Privy Council decision in *Montreal Locomotive Works*. ...

Of course, the organization test of Lord Denning and others produce entirely acceptable results when properly applied, that is, when the question of organization or integration is approached from the persona of the "employee" and not from that of the "employer," because it is always too easy from the superior perspective of the larger enterprise to assume that every contributing cause is so arranged purely for the convenience of the larger entity. We must keep in mind that it was with respect to the business of the employee that Lord Wright addressed the question "Whose business is it?"

Perhaps the best synthesis found in the authorities is that of Cooke J in *Market Investigations, Ltd. v. Minister of Social Security*, [1968] 3 All ER 732, at 738-39:

> The observations of Lord Wright, of Denning LJ, and of the judges of the Supreme Court in the USA suggest that the fundamental test to be applied is this: "Is the person who has engaged himself to perform these services performing them as a person in business on his own account?" If the answer to that question is "yes," then the contract is a contract for services. If the answer is "no" then the contract is a contract of service. No exhaustive list has been compiled and perhaps no exhaustive list can be compiled of considerations which are relevant in determining that question, nor can strict rules be laid down as to the relative weight which the various considerations should carry in particular cases. The most that can be said is that control will no doubt always have to be considered, although it can no longer be regarded as the sole determining factor; and that factors, which may be of importance, are such matters as whether the man performing the services provides his own equipment, whether he hires his own helpers, what degree of financial risk be taken, what degree of responsibility for investment and management he has, and whether and how far he has an opportunity of profiting from sound management in the performance of his task. The application of the general test may be easier in a case where the person who engages himself to perform the services does so in the course of an already established business of his own; but this factor is not decisive, and a person who engages himself to perform services for another may well be an independent contractor even though he has not entered into the contract in the course of an existing business carried on by him.

There is no escape for the trial judge, when confronted with such a problem, from carefully weighing all of the relevant factors, as outlined by Cooke J.

It is patently obvious that the applicant's contention that Lord Denning's test should be applied only in the case of highly skilled workers is in no way supportable. It is, however, equally apparent that the Tax Court has erred in law in its use of that test.

...

What was the effect of the error of law in this case? If we excise the Tax Court's erroneous application of the organization or integration test from its decision, we are left with an inconclusive result, though on two tests out of three it found for the applicant. This Court cannot ... engage in an examination of the evidence as such, unless a particular result is so inevitable on the facts that any other conclusion would be perverse. I would therefore allow the application, set aside the decision of the Tax Court judge in respect of the 1980 and 1981 tax years, and refer the matter back to the Tax Court judge for a determination consistent with these reasons.

Application allowed.

NOTES AND QUESTIONS

1. Why did the Federal Court of Appeal reject the control test as the sole criterion for distinguishing between "contracts of service" (employment) and

"contracts for services" (independent contractor)? In light of the Court's reasoning in this regard, consider the following comments on the control test quoted in P.S. Atiyah, *Vicarious Liability in the Law of Torts* (London: Butterworths, 1967), 46:

> The control test was well-suited to govern relationships like those between a farmer and an agricultural labourer (prior to agricultural mechanization), a craftsman and a journeyman, a householder and a domestic servant, and even a factory owner and an unskilled "hand." It reflects the state of society in which the ownership of the means of production coincided with the possession of technical knowledge and skill and in which that knowledge and skill was largely acquired by being handed down from one generation to the next by oral tradition and not by being systematically imparted in institutions of learning from universities down to technical schools. The control test postulates a combination of managerial and technical functions in the person of the employer, i.e., what to modern eyes appears as an imperfect division of labour.

2.   In *Montreal v. Montreal Locomotive Works Ltd.*, [1947] 1 D.L.R. 161 (P.C.), Lord Wright suggested that in some cases it is appropriate to replace the traditional "control test" with a "fourfold test" to determine whether an employment relationship exists, looking at "(1) control; (2) ownership of the tools; (3) chance of profit; (4) risk of loss." Variously described as the "entrepreneur test," the "four-in-one test" (in *Wiebe Door Services Ltd. v. M.N.R.*, [1986] F.C.J. No. 1052, [1986] 2 C.T.C. 200, 87 D.T.C. 5025 (F.C.A.)) or the "economic reality test," this "fourfold test" is derived from economic arguments for vicarious liability in tort law, according to which the costs of accidents associated with a particular business activity should be borne directly by the business on the grounds that it can best control the factors contributing to the incidence of tortious damages and best distribute these costs among consumers. How did the Federal Court of Appeal in *Wiebe Door* interpret Lord Wright's test?

3.   A third test to determine the existence of an employment relationship that the court considered in *Wiebe Door* is the "organization" or "integration" test developed by Lord Denning in *Stevenson, Jordan and Harrison Ltd. v. MacDonald and Evans*, [1952] 1 T.L.R. 101 (C.A.) and approved by the Supreme Court of Canada in *Cooperators Insurance Association v. Kearney*, [1964] S.C.J. No. 55, [1965] S.C.R. 106 (S.C.C.).

Stevenson, Jordan and Harrison Ltd. involved a copyright dispute, in which the English Court of Appeal referred to this test to decide whether an accountant, who authored a textbook based on lectures written while he was engaged by an engineering firm, had written the work in the course of employment under a contract of service (in which case copyright became the property of the employer). In *Cooperators Insurance Association*, the Supreme Court of Canada relied on the test to conclude that an insurance agent, who had been injured in an automobile accident while accompanying an employee of the defendant to inspect a particular property, was eligible for worker's compensation on the basis (at 122) that he had been injured "by reason of the negligence of ... any person in the service of his employer acting within the scope of his employment". Finally, as Michael Bendel explains in "The Dependent Contractor: An Unnecessary and Flawed Development in Canadian Labour Law" (1982) 32 U.T.L.J. 374 at 382, the "organization" or "integration" test is also attractive in the labour relations context since "integration into another person's business ... is a very useful indicator of economic dependence."

4.   Why, according to the Federal Court of Appeal, did the trial court err "in its use of" the organization test? What role, if any, does the "organization" or "integration" test play in the passage excerpted from *Market Investigations Ltd. v. Minister of Social Security*, [1968] 3 All E.R. 732 (Q.B) which MacGuigan J approved as the "best synthesis" of tests for determining the existence of an employer-employee relationship? For divergent views on the test adopted in *Wiebe Door*, see Brian J. Wilson, "Employment Status Under the Income Tax Act," in *Income Tax and Goods and Services Tax Planning for Executive and Employee Compensation and Retirement*, 1991 Corporate Management Tax Conference (Toronto: Canadian Tax Foundation, 1991), 2:1-61 (arguing that the court approved the use of the integration test, provided that it is approached from the perspective of the employee); and Magee, "Whose Business Is It? Employees Versus Independent Contractors," *ibid.*, at 600 (noting that "although *Wiebe Door* redefined the integration test, it did not actually apply it or recommend its use").

5.   The approach adopted in *Wiebe Door* was approved in *671122 Ontario Ltd. v. Sagaz Industries Canada Inc.*, [2001] S.C.J. No. 61, 2001 S.C.C. 59 (S.C.C.). According to Major J (McLachlin CJC and Iacobucci, Bastarache, Binnie, Arbour, and LeBel JJ concurring) (at paras. 46-48):

> I agree with MacGuigan JA in *Wiebe Door* ... that what must always occur is a search for the total relationship of the parties ... .
>
> Although there is no universal test to determine whether a person is an employee or an independent contractor, I agree with MacGuigan JA that a persuasive approach to the issue is that taken by Cooke J in *Market Investigations, supra*. The central question is whether the person who has been engaged to perform the services is performing them as a person in business on his own account. In making this determination, the level of control the employer has over the worker's activities will always be a factor. However, other factors to consider include whether the worker provides his or her own equipment, whether the worker hires his or her own helpers, the degree of financial risk taken by the worker, the degree of responsibility for investment and management held by the worker, and the worker's opportunity for profit in the performance of his or her tasks.
>
> It bears repeating that the above factors constitute a non-exhaustive list, and there is no set formula as to their application. The relative weight of each will depend on the particular facts and circumstances of the case.

In *Royal Winnipeg Ballet v. M.N.R.*, [2006] F.C.J. No. 339, 2006 D.T.C. 6323 (F.C.A.), Sharlow JA (Desjardins J.A. concurring) described *Sagaz* as "the leading case from the Supreme Court of Canada on the determination of the status of a person as an employee or an independent contractor", and confirmed the ongoing relevance of *Wiebe Door* as "an important part of the jurisprudential foundation for *Sagaz*" (at para. 34).

6.   In applying the various tests from *Wiebe Door*, the Canada Revenue Agency and the courts may examine many specific details of the working relationship. In particular, they may consider whether the individual works for a single person over a particular length of time (suggesting employment), or for a number of people (suggesting the worker is carrying on an independent business). For example, in *Kilbride v. Canada*, [2007] T.C.J. No. 449, [2008] 4 C.T.C. 2172 (T.C.C.), aff'd 2008 FCA 335, 2009 D.T.C. 5502 (F.C.A.), the taxpayer was held to be an employee in part because all of his income was earned by providing accounting and management services to a company owned by himself and other family members, and he had not advertised his availability to work for anyone else.

The courts may also consider an individual's principal workplace in determining employment status. In *Martinez v. Canada*, [1995] T.C.J. No. 222, 96 D.T.C. 2017 (T.C.C.), for example, an engineer who entered into a long-term contract to design and build controls for heavy machinery was held to be self-employed in part because he worked primarily at home. See also *Tedco Apparel Management Services Inc. v. M.N.R.*, [1991] T.C.J. No. 423, [1991] 2 C.T.C. 2669, 91 D.T.C. 1391 (T.C.C.), where the court considered the fact that the taxpayer worked from his own home relevant in concluding that he could not reasonably be regarded as an employee of the company to which the services were provided.

In contrast, medical doctors with admitting privileges to hospitals are typically recognized as independent contractors despite the fact that they rely upon the facilities of a hospital to conduct their business. See, for example, *Cumming v. M.N.R.*, [1967] C.T.C. 462, 67 D.T.C. 5312 (Ex. Ct.) and *Henry v. M.N.R.*, [1969] C.T.C. 600, 69 D.T.C. 5395 (Ex. Ct.), in which hospital anaesthetists defeated the Minister's assertion that they were employees.

Courts have also considered the method of remuneration to be a relevant factor in distinguishing between a contract for services and a contract of service. In *Danggas v. M.N.R.* (1964), 35 Tax ABC 44 and *Di Francesco v. M.N.R.* (1964), 34 Tax ABC 380, 64 D.T.C. 106 (T.A.B.), insurance and real estate salesmen were held to be independent contractors since they were at liberty to determine their own working hours and find their own clients, and were paid solely on a commission basis. Similarly, in *Merrill v. M.N.R.* (1964), 35 Tax ABC 50 (T.A.B.), an electric organ salesman working solely on commission was found to be an independent contractor. In the latter case, the Tax Appeal Board referred to dictionaries that defined "employee" in terms of someone working for salary or wages.

In *Norgaard v. M.N.R.* (1964), 36 Tax ABC 449 (T.A.B.), on the other hand, a field manager for the Fuller Brush Company whose remuneration was calculated according to gross regional sales and who enjoyed a degree of independence in fulfilling his responsibilities controlling numerous commissioned salespersons was found to be an employee on the basis (at para. 11) that "he signed a contract with the said Company as an employee in the capacity of field manager... it was the [taxpayer's] only occupation and his activities were confined solely to the promotion and sale of his employer's products" and the selection and training of dealers. See also *Vango v. Canada*, [1995] T.C.J. No. 659, [1995] 2 C.T.C. 2757 (T.C.C.), where a stockbrocker whose income was calculated on a commission basis was held to be an employee on the grounds that he worked out of the employer's office; used the employer's telephones, promotional literature, and other facilities; relied upon the employer to mail reports to stockholders; and received one-third of all commissions charged by the employer to clients irrespective of whether they were paid to the employer.

Another factor to which Canadian courts sometimes refer is the "specific results" test suggested in *Alexander v. M.N.R.*, [1969] C.T.C. 715, 70 D.T.C. 6006 (Ex. Ct.). In this case, the director of radiology at the Trenton Memorial Hospital had agreed to provide "sufficient coverage" equivalent to 9,000 examinations per annum either by attending at the hospital himself or by hiring a substitute at his own cost. Concluding that the taxpayer was self-employed, the Court distinguished between a contract of service and a contract for services as follows:

> On the one hand, a contract of service is a contract under which one party, the servant or employee, agrees, for either a period of time or indefinitely, and either full time or part time, to work for the other party, the master or the employer. On the other hand, a contract for services is a contract under which the one party agrees that certain specified work will be done for the other. A contract of service does not normally envisage the accomplishment of a specified amount of work but does normally contemplate the servant putting his personal services at the disposal of the master during some period of time. A contract for services does normally envisage the accomplishment of a specified job or task and normally does not require that the contractor do anything personally.

The Canada Revenue Agency lists all of these specific factors and others as relevant to the determination of a worker's status in its guide titled *Employee or Self-Employed?* (RC4110(E) Revision 08).

7.   What weight should be given to the parties' express intentions in characterizing their legal relationship? Until recently the courts generally discounted such statements as less important than the objective features of the working relationship. Thus in *Wiebe Door*, though the taxpayer had a "specific understanding" with its workers that they would be self-employed, the Federal Court of Appeal stated that such an agreement "is not of itself determinative of the relationship between the parties, and a court must carefully examine the facts in order to come to its own conclusion". This approach was confirmed in *Standing v. M.N.R.*, [1992] F.C.J. No. 890, 147 N.R. 238 (F.C.A.), where the Federal Court of Appeal overturned a decision of the Tax Court that was based on the fact that the taxpayer and her alleged employer had agreed that she was an employee. In a frequently quoted passage, Stone JA asserted (at 239-40) that what the parties think their relationship is will not change the facts:

> There is no foundation in the case law for the proposition that such a relationship may exist merely because the parties choose to describe it to be so regardless of the surrounding circumstances when weighed in the light of the *Wiebe Door* test.

However, in several more recent decisions the Courts have placed more weight on the common intention of the parties as expressed in their agreement.

A key example is *Wolf v. Canada*, [2002] F.C.J. No. 375, [2002] 4 F.C. 396, 2002 D.T.C. 6853 (F.C.A.), involving an aerospace engineer who entered a contract with a placement agency ("Kirk-Meyer") to provide his services to an airplane manufacturer ("Canadair"). The contract described Mr. Wolf as "a consultant and an independent contractor" (at para. 6). It provided for hourly rates of pay and a bonus on completing the term of the contract. Wolf was not entitled to any pension or other benefits. He worked exclusively at Canadair's premises using its specialized equipment, reporting to a supervisor but working independently on the tasks assigned to him. The Federal Court of Appeal held unanimously that Wolf was an independent contractor, reversing the Tax Court of Canada. Desjardins JA followed the approach in *Wiebe Door*, holding that the parties' declared intentions were not determinative but that the actual relationship, especially the risk of loss assumed by Wolf, pointed to a contract for services (at para. 87):

> In consideration for a higher pay, the appellant, in the case at bar, took all the risks of the activities he was engaging in. He was not provided health insurance benefits nor a pension plan by Canadair. He had no job security, no union protection, no educational courses he could attend, no hope for promotion. The profit and the risk factors were his ...

While concurring in the result, the other two members of the court wrote separate reasons in which they emphasized the importance of the parties' intentions. DeCary JA wrote that the courts "have sometimes overlooked the very factor which is the essence of a contractual relationship, i.e., the intention of the parties" (at para. 117). He added (at para. 120):

> When a contract is genuinely entered into as a contract for services and is performed as such, the common intention of the parties is clear and that should be the end of the search. ... In our day and age, when a worker decides to keep his freedom to come in and out of a contract almost at will, when the hiring person wants to have no liability towards a worker other than the price of work and when the terms of the contract and its performance reflect those intentions, the contract should generally be characterised as a contract for services.

Noel JA held that (at para. 122):

> ... the manner in which parties choose to describe their relationship is not usually determinative particularly where the applicable legal tests point in the other direction. But in a close case such as the present one, where the relevant factors point in both directions with equal force, the parties' contractual intent, and in particular their mutual understanding of the relationship, cannot be disregarded.

In *Royal Winnipeg Ballet v. M.N.R.*, [2006] F.C.J. No. 339, [2006] F.C.A. 87, 2006 D.T.C. 6323 (F.C.A.), a majority of the Federal Court of Appeal confirmed the relevance of the parties' intentions, holding that dancers had been hired as independent contractors despite being subject to extensive control through the terms of a collective agreement. According to Sharlow JA (at para. 64):

> ... it seems to me wrong in principle to set aside, as worthy of no weight, the uncontradicted evidence of the parties as to their common understanding of their legal relationship, even if that evidence cannot be conclusive. The Judge should have considered the *Wiebe Door* factors in the light of this uncontradicted evidence and asked himself whether, on balance, the facts were consistent with the conclusion that the dancers were self-employed, as the parties understood to be the case, or were more consistent with the conclusion that the dancers were employees. Failing to take that approach led the Judge to an incorrect conclusion. ...

Dissenting, Evans JA asserted that "little if any weight" should be attached to the parties' own description of their relationship, including the concern that such statements may be self-serving, that the parties may not have equal bargaining power in setting the terms of the contract, and that honouring the parties' intentions may defeat the interests of third parties such as tort victims, tax authorities, or other workers who have a different understanding of the contract (at paras. 98-104).

In *Lang v. Canada*, [2007] T.C.J. No. 365, 2007 D.T.C. 1754 (T.C.C.), Bowman CJTC reviewed these and other recent decisions of the Federal Court of Appeal and concluded that (at para. 34),

> Intent is a test that cannot be ignored but its weight is as yet undetermined. It varies from case to case from being predominant to being a tie-breaker. It has not been considered by the Supreme Court of Canada. If it is considered by the Supreme Court of Canada the dissenting judgment of Evans J.A. in *Royal Winnipeg Ballet* will have to be taken into account.

The parties' intentions were also considered in *Kilbride v. Canada*, [2007] T.C.J. No. 449, [2008] 4 C.T.C. 2172 (T.C.C.), where the worker was nonetheless held to be an employee. After applying all of the tests referred to in *Wiebe Door*, including the integration test, Campbell J concluded that the parties' stated intention that Kilbride would be an independent contractor was not supported by "the reality of their relationship" (at para. 30), including the fact that he worked for only one firm, was not required to maintain a home office or purchase any other tools or equipment, and was paid at a set hourly rate. In affirming this decision the Federal Court of Appeal stated this was "not a close case where the *Wiebe Door* test is inconclusive, requiring the court to give greater weight to the intention of the parties" ([2008] F.C.J. No. 1524, 2008 FCA 335, (2009) D.T.C. 5502, at para. 11).

8. In determining the source of a taxpayer's income for tax purposes, courts have relied greatly on tests developed in the context of tort law and employment law. Nonetheless, according to Vern Krishna, *Fundamentals of Canadian Income Tax*, 5th ed. (Scarborough, Ont.: Carswell, 1995) at 192-93:

> Although not openly acknowledged, there is a difference in judicial attitudes in characterizing employment relationships in tax law and in other employment related areas. In employment law, there is a trend towards characterizing workers as employees to enable them to derive the benefits of legislation intended to protect the economically dependent and

vulnerable. In tax law, the advantage lies with the independent contractor and, hence, one may be inclined to view the relationship from a different perspective.

Given the different consequences associated with the characterization of an employment relationship under tax law, tort law, and employment law, is it reasonable to assume that the concept of employment should be controlled by a common set of tests in each of these areas?

Consider the decision in *Cormier v. Alberta (Human Rights Commission)*, [1984] A.J. No. 621, 33 Alta. L.R. (2d) 359 (Alta. Q.B.), where the Court of Queen's Bench affirmed that different tests for employment status may be appropriate depending on the particular mischief that the statute or common law in question is meant to address. Cormier was a truckdriver who had sought work with a company that supplied trucks and drivers to a mining company. Drivers owned and maintained their own trucks and were remunerated by the intermediary trucking company on an hourly wage basis with no deductions made except for union dues. The intermediary repeatedly refused to retain Cormier and Cormier laid a complaint under the Alberta *Individual's Rights Protection Act* to the effect that this action contravened the Act's prohibition of race-based discrimination in hiring employees. The Human Rights Commission declined jurisdiction on the basis that the trucking company did not enter into employer-employee relationships with its various trucker-contractors. In quashing this decision and ordering that the commission assume jurisdiction, the court quoted from a Labour Relations Board ruling, stating (at 370):

> We are inclined to believe that for purposes of *The Labour Relations Act* and the mischief at which it is aimed, together with the remedies it offers, the terms "employee" and "employer" are not, in all instances, necessarily applicable or confined to persons who may, for certain purposes, fall within the strict and traditional common law tests of the relationship of "master and servant." ... While common law criteria are not to be ignored and will apply in the absence of anything to the contrary, the precise meaning and scope of the terms "employee" and "employer" must, in the last analysis, of course, be derived from and tested within the statutory provisions and objects of *The Labour Relations Act.*

The court believed Cormier to be among that class of individuals the human rights legislation was intended to protect and consequently was prepared to expand the definition of "employment" accordingly. According to the court (at 377):

> words used in stating a legal rule in one context may not mean the same where the words may be used to express a legal rule in another context. This is so whether the rule is one of statute or of common law. The meaning of the same words may be found to be different if the two legal rules reflect different policy considerations and perform different social functions.

In contrast, consider Lord Denning's conclusion in *Stevenson, Jordan and Harrison Ltd. v. MacDonald and Evans*, [1952] 1 T.L.R. 101 (C.A.) (at 111), in proposing the "organization" or "integration" test, that:

> [o]ne perhaps cannot get much beyond this: "Was the contract a contract of service within the meaning which an ordinary person would give under the words?"

9.   In Quebec, article 2085 of the *Civil Code* stipulates:

> A contract of employment is a contract by which a person, the employee, undertakes for a limited period to do work for remuneration, according to the instructions and under the direction or control of another person, the employer.

Does this mean that the control test alone should be used to distinguish between employees and independent contractors in Quebec?

As a general rule, income tax cases arising in Quebec have applied the general test adopted in *Wiebe Door*, considering each of the subordinate tests considered by the Federal Court of Appeal in order to evaluate "the total relationship of the parties." For example, in *Tedco Apparel Management Services Inc. v. M.N.R.*, [1991] T.C.J. No. 423, [1991] 2 C.T.C. 2669, 91 D.T.C. 1391 (T.C.C.), the court rejected the taxpayer's argument that the control or subordination test should be given priority in Quebec on the basis (at 2695; 1431) that "in Quebec as in the other provinces in Canada further developments have deprived this test of its conclusive effect." See also *Beaulieu v. Canada*, [1993] T.C.J. No. 138, [1993] 2 C.T.C. 2323 (T.C.C.); and *Placements Marcel Lapointe Inc. v. M.N.R.*, [1992] T.C.J. No. 516, [1993] 1 C.T.C. 2506, 93 D.T.C. 809 (T.C.C.). Similarly, in *Wolf v. Canada*, [2002] F.C.J. No. 375, [2002] 3 C.T.C. 3, 2002 D.T.C. 6853 (F.C.A.), although citing provisions of the *Civil Code of Québec*, Desjardins JA relied on the various subordinate tests in *Wiebe Door*, on the basis (at para. 49) that "the distinction between a contract of employment and a contract for services under the *Civil Code of Québec* can be examined in light of the tests developed through the years both in the civil law and in the common law." In contrast, while recognizing (at para. 113) that both the civil and the common law look to "the terms of the relevant agreements and circumstances to find the true contractual reality of the parties," Décary JA's concurring judgment in *Wolf* emphasized (at para. 117) that for tax cases arising in Quebec "[t]he test ... is whether, looking at the total relationship of the parties, there is control on the one hand and subordination on the other." As a result, he observed (at para. 114) of Desjardins JA's judgment:

> I find it somehow puzzling that "control" is listed amongst the factors to be considered in an exercise the purpose of which is precisely under the *Civil Code of Quebec*, to determine whether or not there is control.

More recently, in *9041-6868 Québec Inc. v. M.N.R.*, [2005] F.C.J. No. 1720, [2005] F.C.A. 334 (F.C.A.), the Federal Court of Appeal concluded that in Quebec the characterization of an employment relationship for the purpose of the federal *Employment Insurance Act* should be based on the *Civil Code of Québec*. According to Décary JA (Létourneau and Pelletier JJA concurring) (at paras. 5-7):

> Section 8.1 of the *Interpretation Act* came into force on June 1, 2001. It codified the principle that the private law of a province and a federal statute are complementary, which had been recognized... but had not always been put into practice. When that section came into force, the immediate effect was to restore the role of the civil law in matters under the jurisdiction of this Court, to bring to light how the common law might have been borrowed

from, over the years, in cases where Quebec civil law applied or should have applied, and to caution us against any such borrowing in future.

It is possible, and in most cases even probable, that where contracts are similar they would be characterized similarly, whether the civil law or common law rules are applied. The exercise, however, is not a matter of comparative law, and the ultimate objective is not to achieve a uniform result. On the contrary, the exercise, as was in fact intended by the Parliament of Canada, is one of ensuring that the approach taken by the court is the approach that applies in the applicable system, and the ultimate objective is to preserve the integrity of each legal system. On that point, what was said by Mr. Justice Mignault in *Curley v. Latreille* (1920), 60 S.C.R. 131 (S.C.C.), at page 177 applies as well now as it did then:

> [TRANSLATION] It is sometimes dangerous to go outside a legal system in search of predecents in another system, based on the fact that the two systems contain similar rules, except, of course, where one system has borrowed a rule from the other that was previously foreign to it. Even when the rule is similar in the two systems, it may be that it has not been understood or interpreted in the same way in each of them, and because the legal interpretation — I am of course referring to interpretation that is binding on us — is in fact part of the law that it interprets, it may in fact happen that despite their apparent similarity, the two rules are not at all identical.
>
> I would therefore not base the conclusions that I think must be adopted in this case on any precedent taken from English Law ... (Emphasis added)

In other words, it is the *Civil Code of Québec* that determines what rules apply to a contract entered into in Quebec. Those rules are found in, inter alia, the provisions of the Code dealing with contracts in general (arts. 1377 C.C.Q. et seq.) and the provisions dealing with the "Contract of employment" (arts. 2085 to 2097 C.C.Q.) and the "contract of enterprise or for services" (arts. 2098 to 2129 C.C.Q.).

For similar conclusions, see also *Sauvé v. M.N.R.*, [1995] F.C.J. No. 1378, 132 D.L.R. (4th) 114 (F.C.A.); *Vaillancourt v. M.N.R.*, [2004] T.C.J. No. 685, [2005] CCI 328 (T.C.C.); and *Widrig v. Regroupement Mamit Innuat Inc.*, [2007] F.C.J. No. 1582, [2008] 4 C.T.C. 16 (F.C.).

For detailed considerations of this issue, see John W. Durnford, "Employee or Independent Contractor? The Interplay Between the Civil Code and the Income Tax Act," in *Mélanges Paul-André Crépeau*, (Cowansville, Quebec: Yvon Blais, 1997) at 273-310; David G. Duff, "The Federal Income Tax Act and Private Law in Canada: Complementarity, Dissociation, and Canadian Bijuralism" (2003) 51 Can. Tax J. 1-63; and Lara Friedlander, "What Has Tort Law Got to Do with It? Distinguishing Between Employees and Independent Contractors in the Federal Income Tax, Employment Insurance, and Canada Pension Plan Contexts" (2003) 51 Can. Tax J. 1467-1519.

10.   For an analysis of the tests used to distinguish employees and independent contractors in light of the increasing trend toward contract work, particularly in the information technology sector, see Magee, "Whose Business Is It? Employees Versus Independent Contractors" in *Income Tax and Goods and Services Tax Planning for Executive and Employee Compensation and Retirement*, 1991 Corporate Management Tax Conference (Toronto: Canadian Tax Foundation, 1991). For an extensive review of the legal tests to distinguish employees from independent contractors and of the tax implications of this

distinction, see Alain Gaucher, "A Worker's Status as Employee or Independent Contractor", in *Report of Proceedings of the Fifty-First Tax Conference*, 1999 Conference Report (Toronto: Canadian Tax Foundation, 2000), 33:1-98. For an analysis of Federal Court of Appeal jurisprudence since the decision in *Wolf v. Canada*, [2002] F.C.J. No. 375, 2002 DTC 6853, and the role of the common intention of the parties in characterizing their relationship, see Kurt G. Wintermute, "A Worker's Status as Employee or Independent Contractor: Recent Case Law, Trends, and Planning", in *Report of Proceedings of the Fifty-Ninth Tax Conference*, 2007 Conference Report (Toronto: Canadian Tax Foundation, 2008), 34:1-38

B. Incorporated Employees

Given the generally unfavourable tax consequences associated with the characterization of the source of a taxpayer's income as employment rather than business, it is not surprising that persons whose relationship might otherwise be characterized as one of employment might endeavour to structure their affairs in order to avoid this result. The most prominent of these avoidance strategies involves the interposition of a corporation between the individual performing the services and the person contracting for the performance of these services. In this circumstance, the individual performing the services can be described as an "incorporated employee."[8]

Since subsection 248(1) defines "office" and "employment" as positions "of an individual" and defines "individual" as "a person other than a corporation," payments to a corporation for services performed by an individual on its behalf must be characterized as income from a business rather than income from an office or employment. As a result, absent judicial or statutory anti-avoidance rules to the contrary, taxpayers who contract to perform services might be able to avoid any undesirable tax consequences associated with an employment relationship by arranging to perform the services through the inter-mediation of a private company. In addition, since the *Income Tax Act* provides for a low rate of tax for a portion of the "active business income" earned by qualifying corporations,[9] the interposition of such a corporation could also reduce the rate

---

[8] The term "incorporated employee" appears in the definition of a "personal services business" in subs. 125(7) of the Act. The rules governing personal services businesses are considered later in this section.

[9] This "small business deduction," which reduces the federal corporate tax rate from 28 per cent to 11 per cent for the first $400,000 of "active business income" received by a "Canadian-controlled private corporation," is found in subs. 125(1) of the Act (the dollar limit will rise to $500,000 as of January 1, 2009). The terms "income of the corporation for the year from an active business" and "Canadian-controlled private corporation" are defined in subs. 125(7). Although this chapter considers the anti-avoidance rule excluding "personal services businesses" from this low corporate tax rate, it does not examine the small business deduction in detail. The small business deduction is best examined in a course on corporate income taxation.

of tax payable by the taxpayer on the income received.[10] This advantage is even greater where the corporate income is split with non-arm's-length persons such as the taxpayer's spouse by the payment of salaries or dividends.

The following cases and commentaries consider alternative responses to this method of tax avoidance, considering the application of judicial anti-avoidance doctrines and specific anti-avoidance rules reviewed in Chapter 3. Although the cases and statutory provisions considered precede the introduction of the general anti-avoidance rule (GAAR) in 1988, it is useful to consider how the GAAR might have applied to the cases considered. In this light, one might evaluate the advantages or disadvantages of the GAAR as an alternative anti-avoidance measure.

1. Judicial Anti-Avoidance Doctrines

Chapter 3 reviewed the various anti-avoidance doctrines considered by the Canadian courts: the doctrine of substance and form, the sham doctrine, the doctrine of ineffective transactions, and the business purpose test. Each of these doctrines was considered in *Engel v. M.N.R.* (1982), 82 D.T.C. 1403 (T.R.B.).

Engel v. M.N.R.
(1982), 82 D.T.C. 1403 (T.R.B.)

M.J. BONNER: The appellant appeals from assessments of income tax for the 1975, 1976 and 1977 taxation years. The appellant was, before 1975 during most of that year, a television journalist employed by Global Communications Limited (hereinafter "Global"). Changes were then made. Late in 1975 the appellant incorporated a company, Reasoned Communications Limited (hereinafter "Reasoned"), he entered into an employment agreement with Reasoned and resigned from Global. Reasoned entered into a contract with Global whereby Reasoned undertook to "lend" the appellant's services to Global for a period of nine months, commencing December 1, 1975.

The Minister assessed tax on the basis that the appellant's income included the amounts paid to Reasoned by Global under the last-mentioned contract (and renewals thereof) and not just the amounts received by the appellant as salary from Reasoned under the contract between him and Reasoned. The appellant objected. The assessments were confirmed on the basis that the amounts added to declared income "... are (the appellant's) income from employment with

---

[10] Since payments by a corporation to an individual who actually performs the services are ultimately taxable in the individual's hands — whether in the form of salary, dividends, or other corporate distributions — the advantage of the low corporate rate is primarily one of tax *deferral* rather than outright tax *reduction*. To the extent that income received by the corporation is distributed to non-arm's-length persons whose income is subject to little or no tax, however, outright tax reduction may also be achieved.

Global Communications Limited ... in accordance with the provisions of section 3 and subsection 5(1) of the *Income Tax Act*."

The principal assumption of fact made on assessment was that:

... the interposition of Reasoned between the Appellant and Global and related assignment of the Appellant's services to Global were arrangements done for a fiscal purpose, lacked a *bona fide* business purpose, were shams, and a fiscal scheme whereby amounts which in fact and substance were salary, wages or other remuneration earned by the Appellant from Global were transferred or assigned to Reasoned.

The issue in these appeals is whether the Minister was correct in so assessing.

...

It was common ground that at the outset the appellant was employed by Global. The employment agreement was in writing and was to expire December 15, 1975. The appellant's duties were:

To act as business editor of Global News and to perform such other journalistic functions as may be required from time to time ... .

Clause 5 of the agreement required the appellant to:

... devote his full time efforts and ability to the performance of such services for Global in accordance with the requirements hereof.

Notwithstanding clause 5, the contract did appear to permit the appellant to perform services for others, provided he secured Global's consent in writing in advance.

Much was made of tax reduction as a purpose underlying the 1975 restructuring. The appellant, in evidence, said that his overall purpose was to make more money and he included tax reduction as a component of this comprehensive description of his purpose.

Another component of the appellant's purpose was the expansion of his activities as a free lance journalist. At the same time, he wanted to continue as business editor of Global. The appellant had joined the Global organization when it was first formed. As he and the rest of the Global staff gained experience and became more efficient, the appellant concluded that, but for one problem, he could find sufficient time both to discharge his duties to Global and to fulfil his wish to do more free lance work. The appellant experienced no difficulty securing Global's permission to do free lance work, although apparently no one bothered with the contractual requirement that such permission be in writing. Rather, the problem appeared to be that the appellant, as an employee, was expected to spend a reasonable amount of time each day at the Global premises. This requirement inhibited the appellant's efforts to promote and perform free lance work.

Another purpose given by the appellant for the creation of the new structure was his desire to charge his mother for financial and economic advice pertaining to her investments. The appellant had, in the past, given her such advice for nothing because he said he was not prepared to charge her for it so long as he had to pay tax at full personal rates on fees received.

It is quite plain that the appellant's desire to expand his free lance business led to the decision to change the relationship with Global from a contract of service to a contract for services. It is equally plain that the form of the remainder of the new structure was dictated by the appellant's desire to reduce his tax burden.

The first step in the 1975 restructuring was the incorporation, on October 20, 1975, of Reasoned. The Minister's counsel did not suggest that this corporation was not properly formed or that there was any failure to pass the necessary resolutions or otherwise observe the niceties of corporate behaviour.

The next step in the reorganization was the appellant's resignation from his position as an employee of Global. The employment agreement between the appellant and Global was for a term expiring December 15, 1975. It provided for early termination by notice in writing. The appellant resigned on November 30, 1975.

The appellant had entered into an agreement in writing with Reasoned dated October 27, 1975. By that agreement, Reasoned engaged the appellant to render his services as a broadcaster and writer solely and exclusively to it. The term of the employment was, according to that agreement, to commence October 27, 1975, and to run for a period of three years.

Reasoned entered into a contract with Global in writing dated November 19, 1975. By that contract Reasoned agreed to lend the services of the appellant to Global for a period of nine months to commence December 1, 1975. Under the agreement the appellant was to:

> ... act as the business editor of Global News and ... perform such other journalistic functions in connection therewith as may reasonably be required from time to time.

The latter agreement contained two further provisions which are of some relevance:

1. Reasoned agrees that Raoul Engel shall be subject to the absolute direction and control of Global at all times with respect to the manner and method of performance of the function of business editor as aforesaid: Reasoned hereby undertakes that Raoul Engel will abide by the policies, instructions, and directions of Global from time to time.

2. Reasoned further undertakes to make Raoul Engel available at such time or times as will enable him to devote his full time, effort and ability to the performance of the services herein contracted for.

The term of the agreement was extended from time to time so that it governed the relationship between Reasoned and Global throughout the period under consideration in these appeals.

It may be convenient to note at this point that the last quoted provision of the agreement between Reasoned and Global did have the effect of requiring the appellant, indirectly, to spend only so much time in working for Global as was necessary to do the work of the business editor and other connected journalistic functions. In short, the appellant was free to arrange his working hours as he wished, provided he produced the results required by Global.

It was contended by counsel for the respondent that the provisions as to direction and control effectively made the appellant the employee of Global. I cannot accept that contention. Employment is a relationship which is founded in contract. ... Following the appellant's resignation, privity of contract no longer existed between the appellant and Global.

It was further contended that the appellant did not resign from Global prior to December 15, 1975. The argument was based on the fact that no copy of a written resignation was produced in evidence. The appellant testified that his copy had been lost. I am satisfied that the appellant was correct in stating that he did resign effective November 30, 1975, both because of [his testimony to this effect], and because the appellant and Global conducted themselves in a manner consistent with the termination of the master-servant relationship at that time. Payment made by Global for work done by the appellant after November 30th was made to Reasoned.

It was argued that the new structure, and in particular the agreement between the appellant and Reasoned, was a sham. Counsel for the respondent pointed to the overlap period between October 27, 1975, when the exclusive services agreement between the appellant and Reasoned came into effect, and November 30, 1975, when the old employment contract between the appellant and Global was terminated. This overlap arose, according to the appellant's evidence, because Global's lawyers delayed in approving the new Reasoned-Global contract which was originally intended to come in force November 1st.

In my view, the failure of the appellant and Reasoned to amend their agreement is not, when considered in relation to the other evidence, indicative of sham, that is to say, a document not intended by the appellant and Reasoned to govern their relationship. The failure to amend the agreement between the appellant and Reasoned appears to indicate nothing more than a minor oversight in giving written expression to a common intention to defer the date of commencement of the agreement. Following November 30, 1975, all payments made by Global were not only made to Reasoned; all were deposited in the Reasoned bank account. All payments made by others for whom the appellant did free lance work during that subsequent period were similarly deposited in the Reasoned account. The appellant, who apparently had been well warned to exercise great care in giving effect to the legal relationships flowing from the new structure, made every possible effort to ensure that Global and all persons who sought his free lance services were informed from the very beginning that it was Reasoned which supplied such services. Further, all invoices sent were clearly prepared as invoices from Reasoned. In summary, the agreement between the appellant and Reasoned was intended to create a relationship between them of master and servant, whereby the appellant, as servant would perform the journalistic services sold by Reasoned, whether to Global or to others. I can see no basis for any suggestion that the relationship which the contract purported to create was not intended to be created or was not adhered to. There is no sham here.

Furthermore, the agreement between Global and Reasoned was not treated by either party as a sham. This is evident from:

(a)   Global's action in paying Reasoned after November 30, 1975;

(b)   Global's action in terminating employee benefits after November 30, 1975; and

(c)   the freedom accorded to the appellant to come and go as he pleased after November 30, 1975.

The Minister contended that the transaction between the appellant and Reasoned had no valid business purpose and should therefore be ignored. ... He pointed out that all money paid by Global for December 1975, for 1976 and for 1977, was paid for the services of the appellant. On the basis of the authorities mentioned, he submitted that I should ignore the non-arm's length transaction between the appellant and Reasoned and look at the end result. That end result was, he contended, the receipt by the appellant of the money which was paid by Global. I do not quite look at it that way. The end result that I see is that the money paid by Global was paid to, received by, and the property of Reasoned.

...

It might not be amiss to observe that the *Income Tax Act* imposes an obligation to pay tax on taxable income. It does not impose any obligation to earn income or to continue to earn income in the same way as in the past. Thus, the appellant was entirely at liberty to decide to work for his company, Reasoned, and to cease to work directly for Global. In *Atinco Paper Products Limited v. The Queen*, [1978] CTC 566; 78 DTC 6387, Urie J stated at 577 [6395]:

> It is trite law to say that every taxpayer is entitled to so arrange his affairs as to minimize his tax liability. No one has ever suggested that this is contrary to public policy. It is equally true that this Court is not the watch-dog of the Minister of National Revenue. Nonetheless, it is the duty of the Court to carefully scrutinize everything that a taxpayer has done to ensure that everything which appears to have been done, in fact, has been done in accordance with applicable law. It is not sufficient to employ devices to achieve a desired result without ensuring that those devices are not simply cosmetically correct, that is correct in form, but, in fact, are in all respects legally correct, real transactions. If this Court, or any other Court, were to fail to carry out its elementary duty to examine with care all aspects of the transactions in issue, it would not only be derelict in carrying out its judicial duties, but in its duty to the public at large.

I can only find that the scheme in question here stands up under the requisite scrutiny.

For the foregoing reasons the appeals will be allowed. The assessments in question will be referred back to the respondent for variation on the basis that the amounts paid by Global to Reasoned were the revenues of Reasoned and not the income of the appellant.

Appeal allowed.

NOTES AND QUESTIONS

1.   In *Engel*, what steps did the taxpayer and Global Communications take in order to restructure their relationship? What detail did the parties neglect in the course of this rearrangement? What role did this oversight play in the Minister's argument that amounts received by Reasoned should be included in computing the taxpayer's employment income? How did the board regard this oversight?

2.   What purposes did the taxpayer in *Engel* claim to have had in restructuring his relationship with Global Communications? What purpose did the board consider to have motivated the taxpayer? Of what importance, if any, were these purposes to the Minister's argument and the decision of the board?

3.   On what grounds did the Minister argue in *Engel* that the taxpayer remained an employee of Reasoned notwithstanding the steps taken by the parties to restructure their relationship? How did the board respond to each of these arguments?

4.   In *M.N.R. v. Leon*, [1976] F.C.J. No. 134, [1976] C.T.C. 532, 76 D.T.C. 6299 (F.C.A.), three brothers who managed a furniture business in which they held a controlling interest incorporated three management companies that contracted with the furniture business to supply the management services of each of the brothers, in consideration for which the furniture business paid bonuses to the management companies. Upholding the Minister's assessment, which included the bonuses in computing each of the brothers' employment income, the Federal Court of Appeal made the following comments on the business purpose test and the sham doctrine (at para. 20):

> it is one thing to concede a *bona fide* business purpose for *incorporation* and quite another thing to concede a *bona fide* business purpose for the interposition of the management companies in the *transaction* of providing management services. In my view, for the respondents to be successful in this appeal they must establish a *bona fide* business purpose in the *transaction*, which on the evidence in these cases, they have failed to do. It is the agreement or transaction in question to which the Court must look. If the agreement or transaction lacks a *bona fide* business purpose, it is a sham. It is, in my view, possible to have a company, the *incorporation* of which is not a sham, because of the existence of a *bona fide* business purpose for the incorporation, engaging in a *transaction* which is a sham, because of the absence of a *bona fide* business purpose for said transaction. [Emphasis in original.]

On this basis, the court concluded (at para. 25):

> In the case at bar, when the veil is pierced and the mask removed, it is clear that the three individual respondents who in fact "ran" the Ablan Leon Distributors furniture business, a very large business, also, in fact, earned the remuneration which was "diverted" to the management companies where the income attracted a lower rate of income tax. ... Thus, the interposition of the management companies between the employer and the employee was a sham pure and simple, the sole purpose of which was to avoid payment of tax. Accordingly, in my opinion, the transactions cannot be allowed to stand, the Minister's appeals should be allowed in all three cases and the assessments under review should be restored.

Leon was followed in *Fotheringham v. M.N.R.*, [1977] 77 D.T.C. 275 (T.R.B.) and *Kligman v. M.N.R.*, [1980] 80 D.T.C. 1088 (T.R.B.), in each of which the board disregarded interposed corporations on the basis that they had no *bona fide* business purpose. See also *Connor v. M.N.R.*, [1975] C.T.C. 2132, 75 D.T.C. 85 (T.R.B.), where the board dismissed the taxpayer's appeal on the basis (at para. 41) that it could not find "any sound business reason for the incorporation of this company in the light of the activities and actions of this appellant in the years subsequent to the incorporation".

5. The statements on the business purpose test and the sham doctrine in *M.N.R. v. Leon*, [1976] F.C.J. No. 134, [1976] C.T.C. 532, 76 D.T.C. 6299 (F.C.A.), were subsequently questioned in *Massey Ferguson Ind Ltd. v. Canada*, [1976] F.C.J. No. 196, [1977] C.T.C. 6, 77 D.T.C. 5013 (F.C.A.). Two years after the decision in *Engel*, the business purpose test was decisively rejected in *Stubart Investments Ltd. v. Canada*, [1984] S.C.J. No. 25, [1984] C.T.C. 294, 84 D.T.C. 6305 (S.C.C.).

In *Canada v. Parsons*, [1984] C.T.C. 354, 84 D.T.C. 6447 (F.C.A.), the Federal Court of Appeal relied on *Stubart* to uphold the taxpayers' appeals against assessments treating amounts received by personal management companies as employment income. Although the taxpayers acknowledged having had no business purpose apart from minimizing tax, the court held that the transactions by which the management companies were interposed between the taxpayers and their former employer ("Design") were "valid and complete ... in every respect". According to the court (at para. 20):

> The two management companies were not "bare incorporations" — they were fully clothed with all the legal relationships properly documented and acted upon. To ignore them would be to ignore the legal realities of corporate entities and the complete transactions created by the valid agreements which they entered into, particularly those between the management companies and Design. Neither Parsons nor Vivian was ever entitled to receive directly the amounts paid by Design to the management companies pursuant to those agreements nor could they, personally, have sued Design for the recovery of unpaid moneys. There is absolutely no evidence that the moneys received from Design were received as an agent, trustee or nominee of either Parsons or Vivian.

On a similar note, see *Société de Projets ETPA Inc. v. M.N.R.*, [1992] T.C.J. No. 705, [1993] 1 C.T.C. 2392, 93 D.T.C. 510 (T.C.C.).

6. In *Canada v. Daly*, [1981] F.C.J. No. 534, [1981] C.T.C. 270, 81 D.T.C. 5197 (F.C.A.), the taxpayer, who was general manager and chief operating officer of an Ottawa radio station (CKOY), incorporated a management company to which he assigned his employment contract with CKOY effective July 2, 1964. Although paycheques were subsequently made out to the management company, the assignment was not executed and approved by CKOY, the taxpayer did not formally resign as an employee of CKOY, and a renewal of the employment contract in 1967 was entered into not by CKOY and the management company but by CKOY and the taxpayer personally. Rejecting the taxpayer's argument that the legal relationships among the taxpayer, the management company, and CKOY were governed by an "oral arrangement" established in 1964, Heald DJ concluded (at para. 17):

> In a case of this kind, where it is acknowledged that what is sought by a certain course of action is a tax advantage, it is the duty of the Court to examine all of the evidence relating to the transaction in order to satisfy itself that what was done resulted in a valid, completed transaction. ... Applying that test and scrutinizing everything that the taxpayer has done in this case, it is my view that, at all material times, a valid contract of employment subsisted between the respondent and CKOY under which the respondent earned the fees paid for his services and thus they were properly included in his income by the income tax reassessments here in issue.

7.   For other cases in which the interposition of a corporation have been held to be legally ineffective, see *No. 594 v. M.N.R.* (1959), 59 D.T.C. 78 (T.A.B.) (corporation legally prohibited from practising medicine); *Kindree v. M.N.R.*, [1964] C.T.C. 386, 64 D.T.C. 5248 (Ex. Ct.) (corporation legally prohibited from practising medicine); *Petritz v. M.N.R.*, [1973] C.T.C. 299, 73 D.T.C. 5243 (F.C.T.D.) ("working agreement" between manufacturing company of which taxpayer was principal shareholder and management corporation incorporated by taxpayer not formally executed until after the taxation years at issue); *Galvin v. M.N.R.*, [1983] C.T.C. 2329, 83 D.T.C. 285 (T.R.B.) (documentation suggesting remuneration received by taxpayer personally not by management company); *Crichton v. M.N.R.*, [1985] 2 C.T.C. 2090, 85 D.T.C. 488 (T.C.C.) (absence of contract between interposed corporation and taxpayer's employer); and *Toushan v. M.N.R.*, [1989] T.C.J. No. 807, [1989] 2 C.T.C. 2324, 89 D.T.C. 568 (T.C.C.) ("interjection" of corporation between taxpayer and employer did not "effectively accomplish" its purpose).

8.   *Engel*, *Leon* and *Parsons* were decided before the introduction of the GAAR in 1988. How might the GAAR have applied to each of these cases?

2. Statutory Anti-Avoidance Rules

In addition to the judicial anti-avoidance doctrines just considered, the revenue authorities have relied on various statutory anti-avoidance rules to challenge the intermediation of a corporation between an employee and an employer. One set of rules involves the concept of "indirect receipt." Another set of rules was specifically enacted to eliminate various tax advantages otherwise available to "personal services businesses."

a. Indirect Receipt

The concept of indirect receipt underlies the anti-avoidance rules in subsections 56(2) and 56(4). According to subsection 56(2):

> A payment or transfer of property made pursuant to the direction of, or with the concurrence of, a taxpayer to some other person for the benefit of the taxpayer or as a benefit that the taxpayer desired to have conferred on the other person ... shall be included in computing the taxpayer's income to the extent that it would be if the payment or transfer had been made to the taxpayer.

According to subsection 56(4):

> Where a taxpayer has, at any time before the end of a taxation year, transferred or assigned to a person with whom the taxpayer was not dealing at arm's length the right to an amount ... that would, if the right had not been so transferred or assigned, be included in computing the taxpayer's income for the taxation year, the part of the amount that relates to the period in the year throughout which the taxpayer is resident in Canada shall be included in computing the taxpayer's income for the year unless the income is from property and the taxpayer has also transferred or assigned the property.

To the extent that a taxpayer directs an employer to make payments to an interposed corporation for the taxpayer's benefit, it is arguable that subsection 56(2) requires the payments to be included in computing the taxpayer's income. Alternatively, where the taxpayer transfers or assigns the right to what is in effect employment income to an interposed corporation with which the taxpayer does not deal at arm's length, it is arguable that subsection 56(4) mandates that this income be included in computing the taxpayer's income. In *Handa v. M.N.R.*, [1978] C.T.C. 2256, 78 D.T.C. 1191 (T.R.B.), the Minister relied on both of these provisions.

Handa v. M.N.R.
[1978] C.T.C. 2256, 78 D.T.C. 1191 (T.R.B.)

CHAIRMAN L.J. CARDIN, QC: ...

Facts

The appellant is a civil engineer who had studied in England, the Middle East and in South America. The appellant has his Master's degree and his doctorate in civil engineering and has been acting in the capacity of professor at the University of Waterloo for several years.

In 1971 the appellant incorporated Handa Systems Limited under a federal charter for the purpose of limiting his personal liability and keeping his consulting fees separate from his other income. The object of the company, of course, was to permit it to act as a consulting firm.

The evidence is that in 1971 and 1972 the company was inactive. In 1973 there were two or three transactions recorded in the company's books. It is alleged that the company was more active in 1974, but that it is presently not very active.

In 1973 the appellant received from his employment as professor at the University of Waterloo a salary of $23,992.42 which he properly included in income. In that year the appellant also received from the university an amount of $3,100 as consulting fees which the appellant did not include in his personal income, but which was included in Handa Systems Limited's returns for 1973.

There was no written contract between the university and Handa Systems Limited for the services rendered and for which an amount of $3,100 was paid. Nor was there any written agreement between the university and the appellant in that respect.

The remuneration for consulting services was by verbal agreement, based on a *per diem* basis.

The consulting services rendered by the appellant for which the amount of $3,100 was paid had to do with a proposal to the Canadian International Development Agency for a 5-year development grant for assistance and exchange of teaching staff between the University of Waterloo and the University of Paraiba, Brazil. ...

Submissions

Mr. Violi, an accountant who acted as agent for the appellant, admitted that the payment was made by the university to the appellant personally and not to Handa Systems Limited. However, he stated that although the appellant deposited the $3,100 in his personal account, the books of the company were credited with an income of $3,100 and that income was reflected in the company's return for 1973.

...

It was ... established that the reason why the $3,100 cheque was issued in the name of the appellant was because the university did not even know of the existence of Handa Systems Limited. Whatever oral contract or agreement that may have existed between the appellant and the university could not, under the circumstances, have been between the university and Handa Systems Limited. Any legal recourse the university may have had arising from the contract would have been against the appellant personally with whom the agreement had been made and not against the appellant's company.

...

In holding that Handa Systems Limited was merely a shell and a sham company, counsel for the respondent pointed out that no business purpose can be attributed to Handa Systems Limited. In my view, all of the appellant's activities in 1973 related exclusively to the appellant's professional competence. Since none of the services rendered in 1973 can be said to have been rendered by the corporation one might well ask for what purpose exactly was Handa Systems Limited incorporated.

Law

Counsel for the respondent indicated that the appellant's assessment was based on subsections 5(1), 56(2) and 56(4) of the *Income Tax Act*... .He concluded that since the $3,100 was paid directly to the appellant personally and a T4 slip to that effect was issued by the university, the relationship between the appellant and the university was one of employer and employee. The duties were executed at the request of and under the control of the Dean of the university. The report written by the appellant was referred back to and acted upon by the university.

In my view, the whole program of exchanging teaching staff has much to do with the university's general educational objectives and the appellant's employment as a professor at the university contributes to that general objective. The study and the report were made by the appellant in his capacity of professor of engineering.

...

The only logical reason for the incorporation of Handa Systems Limited in these circumstances is the possibility of transferring the appellant's personal income to that of the corporation for whatever tax advantage might be realized. This by itself, with no other business purpose, is not sufficient to justify the incorporation of the company and in that sense Handa Systems Limited is a sham company.

Subsections 56(2) and 56(4) taken together imply that any payment or transfer of property on the direction or concurrence of a taxpayer, particularly if the payment or the transfer of property is not at arm's length, the payment or the property will be included in the taxpayer's income.

There can be no question in my mind that the transfer of the appellant's personal income to the appellant and his wife, the only shareholders of Handa Systems Limited, is a non-arm's length transaction and the income must be included in computing the taxpayer's income. ...

Appeal dismissed.

NOTES AND QUESTIONS

1.   Why, according to the board, did the taxpayer in *Handa v. M.N.R.*, [1978] C.T.C. 2256, 78 D.T.C. 1191 (T.R.B.), incorporate Handa Systems Limited? Do you agree with this interpretation of the taxpayer's motives? Why or why not?

2.   On what basis did the board in *Handa* conclude that the consulting fees paid by the University of Waterloo were earned by the taxpayer personally and not by Handa Systems Limited? Does the decision turn on the absence of a business purpose for the incorporation of Handa Systems Limited? Was the arrangement a "sham" according to the definition from *Snook v. London & West Riding Investments Ltd.*, [1967] 1 All E.R. 518 (C.A.), which was accepted by the Supreme Court of Canada in *Stubart Investments Ltd. v. Canada*, [1984] S.C.J. No. 25, [1984] C.T.C. 294, 84 D.T.C. 6305 (S.C.C.)? What role, if any, did subsections 56(2) and (4) play in the board's decision?

3.   In *Adams v. M.N.R.* (1960), 60 D.T.C. 253, the taxpayer, who was the director of a stockbroking firm, incorporated two corporations to which the firm paid commissions to which he was entitled under the terms of his employment contract. Dismissing the taxpayer's appeal from an assessment which included the commissions in computing the taxpayer's employment income, R.S.W. Fordham, QC, concluded:

I regard what was done as nothing more or less than an assignment by the appellant, to the two companies, of income after it had been earned by him. I fail to comprehend how it could have been earned by the new companies. ... [T]he meagre evidence adduced in this particular regard does not satisfy me that either of them was actually carrying on a business of any kind. As I view the evidence brought before the Board, these corporate entities were merely the designated recipients of funds voluntarily transferred to or placed to their credit.

In the circumstances narrated, I do not think it matters much whether Section 16(1) [now subsection 56(2)] or Section 23 [now subsection 56(4)] is taken into account, although the latter section would seem to be the more applicable of the two. It appears to me that on the facts alone the appellant's appeal must fail. His alleged employment by either of the two new companies impresses me ... as notional rather than real; it was an idea conceived with a purpose. This was that by setting up an employer-and-employee relationship ... the appellant might be able to allocate his personal earnings in such a manner that appreciably less income tax would be attracted. It was legitimate, but ... ineffective for what was contemplated.

4.   For other cases in which payments to interposed corporations have been attributed to incorporated employees under subsection 56(2) or (4) or their predecessors, see *Goldblatt v. M.N.R.*, [1964] C.T.C. 185, 64 D.T.C. 5118 (Ex. Ct.); *Canada v. Burns*, [1973] C.T.C. 264, 73 D.T.C. 5219 (F.C.T.D.); *Barbeau v. Canada*, [1981] C.T.C. 496, 81 D.T.C. 5379 (F.C.T.D.); and *Dudley v. M.N.R.*, [1982] 82 D.T.C. 1153 (T.R.B.). In each of these cases, as in *Handa* and *Adams*, amounts were held to have been earned by the taxpayer directly and merely paid or assigned to the interposed corporation.

5.   In *Sazio v. M.N.R.*, [1968] C.T.C. 579, 69 D.T.C. 5001 (Ex. Ct.), the taxpayer, who was employed as the head coach of the Hamilton Tiger-Cats football team, incorporated a company (Ralph J. Sazio Limited) of which 499 of 1001 shares were issued to the taxpayer's wife. The taxpayer then resigned as head coach and entered into an employment contract with Ralph J. Sazio Limited, which itself contracted with the Hamilton Tiger-Cats to provide the taxpayer's coaching services for an amount identical to that formerly received by the taxpayer as an employee. Rejecting the Minister's argument that the payments to Ralph J. Sazio Limited were attributable to the taxpayer under the predecessors to subsections 56(2) and (4), the court concluded (at para. 37) that the company "was fully competent" to provide the football coaching services that it did and that "the agreements entered into between the appellant and the Company and the Club were *bona fide* commercial transactions all in furtherance of the Company's legitimate objects and that they govern and determine the relationship between the parties." According to the court (at paras. 38-40):

Here the appellant and his Company are two separate entities. In my view this is not a matter of form but rather a matter of substance and reality. Both the appellant and the Company could sue and be sued in its own right and indeed there is nothing to prevent the one from suing the other if need arose.

Ever since the *Salomon* case, [1897] AC 22, it has been a well settled principle, which has been jealously maintained, that a company is an entirely different entity from its shareholders. Its assets are not their assets, and its debts are not their debts. It is only upon evidence forbidding any other conclusion can it be held that acts done in the name of the company are not its acts or that profits shown in its accounts do not belong to it. The fact that a company may have been formed to serve the interests of a particular person is not sufficient to establish the relationship of principal and agent between that person and the company. In order to hold otherwise it must be found that the company is a "mere sham, simulacrum or cloak."

It is my view that the evidence in the present appeals is conclusive that such is not the case.

For similar results, relying on the decision in *Sazio*, see *O'Kane v. M.N.R.*, [1983] C.T.C. 2215; 83 D.T.C. 177 (T.R.B.) and *Shaw v. M.N.R.*, [1989] F.C.J. No. 260, [1989] 1 C.T.C. 386, 89 D.T.C. 5194 (F.C.T.D.).

6.   In *M.N.R. v. Cameron*, [1972] S.C.J. No. 137, [1972] C.T.C. 380, 72 D.T.C. 6325 (S.C.C.), the taxpayer and two other employees of a company ("Campbell Limited") that carried on business as a roofing and heating contractor incorporated a management company ("Independent Management Limited") that contracted to perform for Campbell Limited the same services formerly performed for it directly by the taxpayer and his two associates. Accepting the taxpayer's argument that the arrangement was designed to facilitate a *bona fide* business purpose to facilitate the acquisition of common shares of Campbell Limited, the Supreme Court of Canada rejected the Minister's argument that amounts received by the management company should be attributed to its three shareholder-employees under the predecessors to subsections 56(2) and (4). According to Martland J (at paras. 17-19):

> The appellant's submission really rests upon the contention that the agreement between Campbell Limited and Independent was nothing but a sham. ... I am not prepared to find that the agreement between Campbell Limited and Independent was a sham. The legal rights and obligations which it created were exactly those which the parties intended. The incorporation of Independent, the making of the agreement, the resignations of the respondent [and his associates] were all a part of an arrangement worked out between J.K. Campbell, who controlled Campbell Limited, and the three senior employees of that company. Mr. Campbell, who desired to deal with a company, and not with the three individuals, gave them the opportunity to provide management for his company, through a company, incorporated for that purpose, for a fee based, in part, on the net profits of Campbell Limited. This was done, and, as the learned trial judge says, "If a saving in income tax resulted to anyone that was incidental to the overall plan."

7.   Do the references to subsections 56(2) and (4) or their predecessors in these cases add anything to the judicial anti-avoidance doctrines examined earlier? If not, what, if any, purpose do these statutory provisions serve?

8.   Subsection 56(4) and its predecessors have also been considered in the context of income-splitting strategies involving interest-free or low-interest loans. See, for example, *Robinson v. M.N.R.*, [1985] 1 C.T.C. 2054, 85 D.T.C. 84 (T.C.C.) (considered in the section on the attribution rules in Chapter 8). More recently, subsection 56(4) has been applied to determine that "trailer fees" earned by an independent investment broker were properly included in his income from business though he had assigned the right to receive such fees to a family owned corporation: *Boutilier v. Canada*, [2007] T.C.J. No. 45, [2007] 3 C.T.C. 2007 (T.C.C.).

9.   For a useful discussion of the concept of "indirect receipt," see Brian Arnold, *Timing and Income Taxation: The Principles of Income Measurement for Tax Purposes*, Canadian Tax Paper No. 71 (Toronto: Canadian Tax Foundation, 1983) at 87-90.

b. Personal Services Business

By 1981, the federal government concluded that a specific statutory anti-avoidance rule was necessary to eliminate the tax advantages available to incorporated employees. In the federal budget of that year, the government announced that it would amend the *Income Tax Act* to exclude "personal service corporations" from the low corporate tax rate and to prevent such corporations from deducting expenses other than the payment of employment income to the incorporated employee. According to the budget:

> Executives and highly-paid employees of business firms can gain valuable tax advantages by incorporating themselves and continuing to provide services to their former employer through a personal corporation. A federal corporate tax rate of 23 ⅓%, rather than personal income tax rates, now applies to the corporation's earnings in such cases. There are other tax advantages in personal incorporations, including the possibility of income splitting among family members. This type of incorporation permits the conversion of employment income into business income of the personal corporation. The budget proposes to increase the federal corporate tax rate on such incorporated executives and employees to the general corporate tax rate of 36%. As a result, the combined federal and provincial corporate tax rate on such personal service corporations will be approximately 50%, equivalent to the maximum marginal tax rate that the budget proposes be applied to individuals.
>
> To further ensure that individuals who can channel their employment income through a private corporation do not receive undue advantages, the budget proposes that such corporations no longer be allowed tax deductions which are unavailable to ordinary employees. The deduction will generally be restricted to wages and salaries or other employment benefits paid to the person providing the services.

The statutory provisions effecting this anti-avoidance policy are found in the definitions of "active business carried on by a corporation" and "personal services business" in subsection 125(7) and the limitation on business expense deductions in paragraph 18(1)(p).

For the purposes of this chapter, the key statutory provision is the definition of a "personal services business," which is excluded from the low corporate tax rate under the definition of "active business carried on by a corporation" and restricted in the deductions that it may claim in computing its income by virtue of the limitation in paragraph 18(1)(p). According to this definition, a personal services business carried on by a corporation in a taxation year means:

a business of providing services where

(a)   an individual who performs services on behalf of the corporation (in this definition and paragraph 18(1)(p) referred to as an "incorporated employee"), or

(b)   any person related to the incorporated employee

is a specified shareholder of the corporation and the incorporated employee would reasonably be regarded as an officer or employee of the person or partnership to whom or to which the services were provided but for the existence of the corporation, unless

    (c)   the corporation employs in the business throughout the year more than five full-time employees, or

    (d)   the amount paid or payable to the corporation in the year for the services is received or receivable by it from a corporation with which it was associated in the year.

As defined in subsection 248(1), a "specified shareholder" of a corporation generally means a taxpayer who owns at least 10 per cent of the issued shares of any class of the corporation. As a result, where: (1) the taxpayer or a related person owns at least 10 per cent of the issued shares of a corporation on behalf of which the taxpayer performs services, and (2) the taxpayer performing the services would, but for the corporation, "reasonably be regarded as an employee" of the third party to whom services were provided, the corporation will be denied the low corporate tax rate and restricted in the deductions that it may claim in computing its income, *unless* it is excluded from the definition under paragraph (c) or (d).

Paragraph (c) is relatively straightforward and is designed to allow corporations with a sufficient number of full-time employees to deduct regular business expenses and to obtain the benefit of the low corporate tax rate.[11] Paragraph (d) is related to the structure of the small business deduction, which must be shared among "associated corporations" and need not concern us here. The key requirement that the taxpayer performing the services "would reasonably be regarded as an officer or employee of the person or partnership to whom or to which the services were provided but for the existence of the corporation" was considered in the following decision.

---

[11]   The Tax Court of Canada held this requirement was satisfied where a corporation had five full-time employees and two part-time employees. See *489599 B.C. Ltd. v. The Queen*, [2008] T.C.J. No. 251, 2008 T.C.C. 332, 2008 D.T.C. 4107 (T.C.C.), where Campbell J rejected as "incorrect" an earlier decision of the Federal Court Trial Division holding that "more than five full-time employees" means "at least six full-time employees," not five full-time employees and a part-time employee. See *Hughes & Co. Holdings v. M.N.R.*, [1994] F.C.J. No. 935, [1994] 2 C.T.C. 170, 94 D.T.C. 6511 (F.C.T.D.), considering the definition of "specified investment business" in subs. 125(7) of the Act. The CRA has indicated that it accepts the more recent decision in *489599 B.C. Ltd.* (see Technical Interpretation 2008-0299161I7, December 14, 2008).

Dynamic Industries Ltd. v. Canada
[2005] F.C.J. No. 997, [2005] 3 C.T.C. 225, 2005 D.T.C. 5293 (F.C.A.)

SHARLOW JA (Richard CJ and Malone JA concurring): ...

FACTS

Dynamic is a British Columbia corporation, incorporated on August 11, 1983. Its head office is in Cranbook, British Columbia. Since its incorporation, Dynamic has carried on the business of providing steel work services in Alberta and British Columbia. At all material times, the shares of Dynamic have been owned by Mr. Steven Martindale or his spouse, Ms. Shkwarok.

Mr. Martindale and Ms. Shkwarok have been employees of Dynamic from the outset. Mr. Martindale provided the services of an iron worker and a construction manager, as needed. Ms. Shkwarok provided administrative services.

Mr. Martindale is a certified ironworker, and a member of the Local 97 Ironworkers Union. In 1988, Mr. Martindale transferred his shares of Dynamic to Ms. Shkwarok to facilitate Dynamic becoming a "contractor signatory" to the Ironworkers, Local 97 Standard Collective Agreement. This was done because the constitution of the Ironworkers Union did not permit a member of the Union to be an owner of a contractor signatory. At approximately the same time, Mr. Martindale began working full time for Dynamic.

As a contractor signatory, Dynamic was able to provide steel work services to both union and non-union companies, as long as those employed by Dynamic were union members. As an employee of Dynamic, Mr. Martindale was therefore able to obtain work for himself in two ways, through Local 97 and through Dynamic as a contractor signatory company. ...

As construction manager for Dynamic, Mr. Martindale pursued and negotiated construction contracts for Dynamic on a per job basis. Mr. Martindale chose what work he wanted to do through Dynamic, where he wanted to do it and for what amount. Dynamic was able to charge hourly or daily rates, or accept cost-plus contracts or fixed-price contracts. These options would not have been available for any of the work offered through Local 97. ...

However, either kind of contract entailed a risk of non-payment. Unlike Mr. Martindale's work as a member of Local 97, work obtained through Dynamic was not covered by any surety. If a contractor to whom Dynamic was providing services became insolvent or otherwise unable to pay, Dynamic would have to turn to outside legal remedies to recover amounts owing to it.

As Mr. Martindale's experience in the industry progressed he worked less through Local 97 and more through Dynamic. Working with Dynamic was more lucrative for Mr. Martindale because of the flexibility in choosing work and the ability to negotiate. Also, Mr. Martindale could not have obtained, through the union hall, a position equivalent to construction manager.

Dynamic began by providing welding services, fabrication and erection services to various general contractors. As Mr. Martindale gained further experience, Dynamic undertook construction management projects and provided subcontracting services to a variety of companies between 1988 and 1995. ...

Dynamic later provided services to S.I.I.L. Maintenance Ltd. (SIIL). ... SIIL provided mostly maintenance work in coal mines. ... In 1994, Mr. Martindale took a position with Construction Management Ltd. of Calgary, acting as the representative of Fording Coal Ltd. He held that position for the duration of that year. Fording was the owner of three of the five mines in the Elk Valley, and was one of the largest employers in the industry at the time. In this position, Mr. Martindale was responsible for the management of Fording's operation of the project. The experience gave Mr. Martindale an opportunity to gain experience necessary to run and manage a large job and to gain the trust of Fording's management.

Beginning in 1995, SIIL was awarded its largest contracts to date with Fording. Dynamic provided SIIL with project management services in relation to those contracts. Dynamic, through Mr. Martindale, worked with SIIL to develop schedules, cost-estimates and time-lines for project proposals which were then used to bid on jobs with Fording. Mr. Martindale had no decision making authority with respect to what jobs SIIL chose to pursue. The management of SIIL would decide on its own if it wanted to bid for a particular job. If SIIL wanted to pursue a bid, Dynamic would put together the estimates of costs, time, equipment and people needed for a job and then SIIL would present the bid to Fording. If SIIL was awarded the contract, Dynamic had responsibilities which included coordinating the timing and sequence of sub-contracting work to be done as outlined in the proposals. Dynamic performed this construction management work at a pre-negotiated cost-plus contract price. If SIIL was not awarded the contract, Dynamic received no compensation for the time spent in preparing the estimates and proposals.

The contract between SIIL and Dynamic was not written. However, it is common ground that Dynamic was paid on a cost-plus basis for the work performed by Mr. Martindale at the rate of $45 per hour, with overtime rates of $63 per hour or $82 per hour, depending upon the circumstances, plus a living-out allowance, and GST. ...

If Dynamic had to fix an error it had made, the work was treated as "warranty work" by Dynamic. SIIL had no obligation to compensate Dynamic for the time or costs entailed in such warranty work. Overhead costs incurred to operate Dynamic were also not compensated by SIIL. ...

From 1995 to 1999, which includes the years under appeal, SIIL was the only source of income for Dynamic, except for a small amount of interest on invested money. Mr. Martindale testified that there was enough work, Dynamic made enough money and it wasn't slow enough at any one time that he needed to seek out other work for Dynamic, or for himself as a member of Local 97. ...

The contracts between Dynamic and SIIL did not require Mr. Martindale to keep regular hours of work, and he received no direction as to where he would work at any particular time. Mr. Martindale used his discretion as to when and where he was needed. There were no regular reporting sessions between Dynamic and SIIL. Mr. Martindale would keep SIIL informed on an ad hoc basis frequently, often daily, but there were no formal reporting requirements.

Dynamic invoiced SIIL for its project management work and the truck rental at various intervals. ...

Dynamic was given no form of security from SIIL to ensure payment of its invoices. However, Mr. Martindale believed that Fording would pay all of its contractors and eventually SIIL would have the money to pay Dynamic. The record indicates that at times payment from SIIL were delayed for as long as three months. SIIL was grateful for the flexibility and patience Dynamic gave to them in making their payments.

If a situation arose where Dynamic did not have enough money to pay its employees while it awaited payment from SIIL, Dynamic would borrow money from Mr. Martindale or Ms. Shkwarok, and repay it once it received payment from SIIL. ...

In late 1999 SIIL's share of the work in the Elk Valley began tapering off. As a result, the work of Dynamic began expanding outside the valley with other contractors beginning in 2000. As at the date of the hearing in the Tax Court in 2003, Mr. Martindale was actively negotiating and performing additional contracts with several companies other than SIIL.

In 2001, Dynamic was reassessed for 1997, 1998 and 1999 to disallow certain deductions on the basis of paragraph 18(1)(p) of the *Income Tax Act*. Dynamic appealed to the Tax Court, unsuccessfully, and now appeals to this Court.

...

In the most common situation involving paragraph 18(1)(p) of the *Income Tax Act*, no deduction is permitted for such ordinary business expenses as rent, telephone costs, administration and office costs, and remuneration to any employee other than the "incorporated employee". In this case, for example, most of the disallowed expenses over the three years under appeal represent remuneration paid to Ms. Shkwarok for administrative services. That expense was disallowed only because the Crown considered Dynamic to be carrying on a personal services business. There is no allegation that Ms. Shkwarok did not perform administrative services for Dynamic, or that her remuneration for those services was unreasonable.

Nothing in the *Income Tax Act* provides offsetting relief to the application of paragraph 18(1)(p). Thus, for example, Ms. Shkwarok would have been taxed on the remuneration she received from Dynamic, even though Dynamic was not permitted to deduct it.

APPLYING THE LAW TO THE FACTS

It is agreed that paragraph 18(1)(p) of the *Income Tax Act* applies in this case only if Dynamic carried on a "personal services business", as defined in subsection 125(7) of the *Income Tax Act*, during the years under appeal. Dynamic will have met that definition during any period in which Mr. Martindale (who the Crown say is the "incorporated employee" of Dynamic), would reasonably be regarded as an employee of SIIL, but for the existence of Dynamic. This hypothetical question arises from the words between paragraphs (b) and (c) of the definition of "personal services business", in what legislative drafters have been known to call the "mid-amble" (refer to the underlined portion of the definition, quoted above).

This case requires consideration of *Wiebe Door Services Ltd. v. Minister of National Revenue*, [1986] 3 F.C. 553, [1986] 2 C.T.C. 200, 87 D.T.C. 5025 (F.C.A.) and *671122 Ontario Ltd. v. Sagaz Industries Canada Inc.*, [2001] 2 S.C.R. 983, the leading cases in which the central question is whether an individual is providing services to another person as an employee, or as a person in business on his or her own account. I refer to this as the "Sagaz question" (*Sagaz*, paragraph 47). The factors to be taken into account in determining the Sagaz question will depend upon the particular case, but normally they will include the level of control the employer has over the worker's activities, whether the worker provides his or her own equipment, whether the worker hires his or her own helpers, the degree of financial risk taken by the worker, the degree of responsibility for investment and management undertaken by the worker, and the worker's opportunity for profit in the performance of his or her tasks. …

(d)   Ownership of tools

The Judge found that the "ownership of tools" factor favoured the position of the Crown because SIIL provided Mr. Martindale with office space, parking facilities, administrative facilities, and technical and maintenance services. The difficulty with this conclusion is that it is speculative. The record discloses no evidence to support this conclusion.

2.   Chance of profit and risk of loss

The Judge concluded that the evidence relating to the chance of profit and risk of loss also supported the Crown's position. In reaching this conclusion, the Judge appeared to focus on the fact that Mr. Martindale did not stand to share in the profits or losses of SIIL. With respect, that misses the point. The "chance of profit and risk of loss" factor is intended to reveal whether the activities of Mr. Martindale entail the kind of risks that are more typical of those borne by a business enterprise than an employee. The business enterprise is not that of SIIL, but that of Mr. Martindale himself. To quote *Sagaz* (at paragraph 47), it is "the worker's opportunity for profit in the performance of his or her tasks".

Mr. Martindale was remunerated for the services he provided to SIIL on a basis that in certain respects resembled that of an hourly employee. The remuneration was based on an hourly rate, with higher rates for overtime, and additional amounts to cover certain direct costs of the work. Also, at one point Mr. Martindale received a gratuitous bonus.

On the other hand, the manner in which the remuneration in this case was determined is also consistent with the kind of cost-plus contract that is commonly used by a subcontractor carrying on a business like that of Mr. Martindale. As well, there are three significant aspects of Mr. Martindale's remuneration that were not typical of an employment relationship. First, Mr. Martindale was not compensated for the time spent on working on estimates for SIIL if the estimate did not result in a contract. Second, Mr. Martindale was not remunerated on a regular or timely basis, with the result that he was compelled to provide his own financing to compensate for the delays. Third, the costs of "warranty work" (work required to correct Mr. Martindale's errors) were required to be borne by Mr. Martindale, rather than SIIL.

On balance, the manner in which Mr. Martindale was remunerated point away from the existence of an employment relationship. I conclude that the Judge erred in finding the contrary.

3.   Integration

The Judge found that Mr. Martindale's contribution to SIIL during the years under appeal made him an integral part of the operation of that corporation, and thus more like an employee rather than a person carrying on business on his own account. However, in reaching that conclusion, the Judge failed to consider the substantial body of evidence that the construction management business was carried on for a number of years before the years under appeal, and also afterward.

In the years under appeal, there was no change in the method in which the construction management business was conducted. In fact, the only thing that was unique about the years under appeal was that SIIL monopolized the services of Mr. Martindale because of the demands of their own contracts with Fording. In my view, the Judge was wrong to consider those years in isolation from the entire history of the business built up by Mr. Martindale, in which services were provided to numerous enterprises apart from SIIL.

From 1988 and into the early part of the 1990s, Mr. Martindale was seeking to avoid the limitations of being an ironworker employed solely through the union hall. He was developing the skills of an entrepreneur and a construction manager, which resulted in more and better opportunities for him than he could have achieved as an ironworker obtaining work through Local 97. This would suggest that if Dynamic did not exist, Mr. Martindale might have chosen, once he had learned the skills of project management in the early 1990s, to pursue various opportunities as a project manager through his own business, rather than as an employee of anyone. In that event, it would be reasonable to conclude that, during 1997, 1998 and 1999, the services he provided to SIIL would have been provided as an independent contractor, rather than an employee.

The fact that most favours the Crown's position is that during the years in question and in the two prior years, Mr. Martindale provided services only to SIIL. However, the monopolization of Mr. Martindale during that period did not arise because SIIL and Mr. Martindale were forging a relationship resembling that of employer and employee. Rather, it arose because SIIL was particularly successful during that period in obtaining work from Fording. There was no reason to believe that SIIL could reasonably expect that situation to continue, and in fact it did not continue after 1999.

4.   Control

The Judge did not mention the factor of control, that is, the degree to which SIIL controlled Mr. Martindale's activities as construction manager. In the context of this case, this was a significant factor, and it should have been addressed. The evidence on this point favours the position of Mr. Martindale. It establishes that Mr. Martindale was substantially independent, and that SIIL exercised no meaningful control over his activities.

CONCLUSION

Overall, the Judge failed to correctly apply all of the *Sagaz* factors to the facts in this case. It is my view, based on the considerations discussed above, that it would not be reasonable to conclude that, but for the existence of Dynamic, Mr. Martindale would have provided his services to SIIL as an employee in 1997, 1998 and 1999.

I would allow this appeal with costs in this Court and in the Tax Court. I would set aside the judgment of the Tax Court, and make an order referring this matter back to the Minister for reassessment on the basis that paragraph 18(1)(p) of the *Income Tax Act* does not apply to the appellant in 1997, 1998 or 1999.

NOTES AND QUESTIONS

1.   To what tests did the Court refer in *Dynamic Industries* to determine whether Mr. Martindale would reasonably be regarded as an employee of SIIL but for the existence of Dynamic Industries Ltd.? Of what relevance to the Court's decision was Mr. Martindale's previous experience of obtaining work individually through the ironworker's union? Of what relevance was the fact that Dynamic provided services only to SIIL during the years under appeal?

2.   In *533702 Ontario Ltd. v. M.N.R.*, [1991] T.C.J. No. 330, [1991] 2 C.T.C. 2102, 91 D.T.C. 982 (T.C.C.), Mrs. Joyce Brouwer was employed by the taxpayer which provided services managing the showroom of a plumbing and heating supply business owned by Brouwer Plumbing and Heating Ltd. ("BPH"), the shares of which were owned by Mrs. Brouwer's husband, Dick Brouwer. Concluding that the taxpayer provided services solely to BPH, that (at para. 12) "[t]he showroom had no commercial purpose apart from the plumbing

business of BPH" and that (at para. 18) "the showroom service carried on by the appellant had no commercial independence from the business of BPH," Mogan T.C.J. held that 533702 Ontario Ltd. carried on a personal services business.

Does the reasoning in this case suggest that a business purpose test may be relevant to determining whether an incorporated employee "would reasonably be regarded as an officer or employee of the person or partnership to whom or to which the services were provided but for the existence of the corporation" within the meaning of the definition of "personal services business" in subsection 125(7) of the Act?

3.   For other cases in which corporations have been held to have carried on a personal services business, see *Tedco Apparel Management Services Inc. v. M.N.R.*, [1991] T.C.J. No. 423, [1991] 2 C.T.C. 2669, 91 D.T.C. 1391 (T.C.C.); *Placements Marcel Lapointe Inc. v. M.N.R.*, [1992] T.C.J. No. 516, [1993] 1 C.T.C. 2506, 93 D.T.C. 809 (T.C.C.); *Camion Holdings Inc. v. M.N.R.*, [1999] T.C.J. No. 311 (T.C.C.), aff'd [2000] F.C.J. No. 863, [2000] 3 C.T.C. 208 (F.C.A.); and *W.B. Pletch Company Limited v. Canada*, [2005] T.C.J. No. 609, [2006] 1 C.T.C. 2582, 2006 D.T.C. 2065 (T.C.C.).

4.   For other cases in which corporations have been held not to have carried on a personal services business, see *David T. McDonald Co. v. M.N.R.*, [1992] T.C.J. No. 455, [1992] 2 C.T.C. 2607, 92 D.T.C. 1917 (T.C.C.); *Société de Projets ETPA Inc. v. M.N.R.*, [1992] T.C.J. No. 705, [1993] 1 C.T.C. 2392, 93 D.T.C. 510 (T.C.C.); *Crestglen Investments Ltd. v. M.N.R.*, [1993] T.C.J. No. 121, [1993] 2 C.T.C. 3210, 93 D.T.C. 462 (T.C.C.); *Healy Financial Corp. v. Canada*, [1994] T.C.J. No. 356, [1994] 2 C.T.C. 2168, 94 D.T.C. 1705 (T.C.C.); *Gitchee Gumee Consultants Ltd. v. Canada*, [1995] T.C.J. No. 353, [1995] 2 C.T.C. 2764 (T.C.C.); and *Galaxy Management Ltd. v. The Queen*, [2005] T.C.J. No. 504, [2006] 1 C.T.C. 2052, 2005 D.T.C. 1558 (T.C.C.).

5.   The CRA's views on the requirement in the definition of a "personal services business" that the taxpayer performing the services "would reasonably be regarded as an officer or employee of the person or partnership to whom or to which the services were provided but for the existence of the corporation" are found in *Interpretation Bulletin* IT-73R6, "The Small Business Deduction," March 25, 2002. According to paragraph 19, this requirement "is not met if, in the absence of the corporation, there would be no common law master-servant relationship and the individual who undertakes to perform the services would be viewed as a self-employed individual carrying on a business." According to the CRA:

> The determination of whether an incorporated employee would otherwise be regarded as self-employed or as an officer or employee of the entity to which the services were provided is a question of fact. The following lists of factors, although not exhaustive, are indications of employee status:
>
> (a)   the entity to which the services are provided has the right to control the amount, the nature and the direction of the work to be done and the manner of doing it;

(b)   the payment for work is by the hour, week or month;

(c)   payment by the entity of the worker's travelling and other expenses incidental to the payor's business;

(d)   a requirement that a worker must work specified hours;

(e)   the worker provides services for only one payor; and

(f)   the entity to which the services are provided furnishes the tools, materials and facilities to the worker.

6.   Where a corporation is held to have carried on a personal services business, the income from this business is subject to the limited deductions permitted by paragraph 18(1)(p) and excluded from the small business deduction provided under subsection 125(1). The income is not, however, attributed to the incorporated employee. As a result, since individuals must compute their income on a calendar-year basis, while corporations may select a fiscal period that does not coincide with a calendar year, incorporated employees may be able to defer tax even though the corporation is held to be carrying on a personal services business. In addition, to the extent that income received by the interposed corporation is distributed to non-arm's-length persons such as the spouse or children of the incorporated employee, income received by these non-arm's-length persons from the investment of corporate distributions may escape the attribution rules in sections 74.1 to 74.5.

Should the Act be amended to attribute the income of a personal services business to the incorporated employee? Might the GAAR be applied to prevent these tax benefits even though they are not caught by the specific anti-avoidance rules applicable to personal services businesses?

III. INCLUSIONS

Statutory provisions governing the inclusion of amounts as income from an office or employment are found in sections 5, 6, and 7 of the Act. According to subsection 5(1), a taxpayer's income for a taxation year from an office or employment is, subject to other rules in Part I of the Act, "the salary, wages and other remuneration, including gratuities, received by the taxpayer in the year." For the purposes of section 5, moreover, subsection 6(3) deems certain amounts to be "remuneration for the payee's services rendered as an officer or during the period of employment." In addition, paragraph 6(1)(c) requires taxpayers to include "director's or other fees received by the taxpayer in the year in respect of, in the course of, or by virtue of an office or employment."

To these amounts, paragraph 6(1)(a) adds, subject to various exceptions set out in subparagraphs (i) to (v), "the value of board, lodging and other benefits of any kind whatever received or enjoyed by the taxpayer in the year in respect of, in the course of, or by virtue of an office or employment," while paragraph 6(1)(b) requires taxpayers to include "all amounts received by the taxpayer in the year as an allowance for personal or living expenses or as an allowance for any other purpose," except various allowances specifically excluded from tax by virtue of subparagraphs (i) to (ix). Other provisions require taxpayers to include amounts allocated under an employee profit-sharing plan,[12] benefits in respect of an employer-provided automobile,[13] amounts received under various kinds of employment insurance benefit plans,[14] amounts received in respect of an employee benefit plan,[15] amounts allocated under an employee trust,[16] prescribed benefits under a group term life insurance policy,[17] benefits in respect of interest-free or low-interest loans,[18] amounts deemed to have been received under a salary deferral arrangement,[19] benefits related to the forgiveness of employee debt,[20] amounts paid in respect of an employee's housing loss,[21] employer-provided housing subsidies,[22] and stock options.[23] Yet other provisions exclude certain kinds of benefits or allowances from tax.[24]

Several of these statutory provisions concern the time when an amount must be included in computing an employee's income from employment and are examined in section V of this chapter. Others address highly specific kinds of benefits that do not merit detailed investigation for the purposes of this book. As a result, this section examines the most important statutory inclusions and exclusions, considering the characterization of a taxpayer's remuneration from an office or employment, the taxation of employment benefits under general and specific rules, the taxation of allowances under paragraph 6(1)(b), and statutory exclusions for employment at a special work site or remote work location and for various disability-related employment benefits.

---

[12] Paragraph 6(1)(d).

[13] See para. 6(1)(e) and subss. 6(2) and (2.1) (standby charges) and paras. 6(1)(k) and (l) (automobile operating expenses).

[14] Paragraph 6(1)(f).

[15] Paragraph 6(1)(g) and subs. 6(10). See also the definition of "employee benefit plan" in subs. 248(1).

[16] Paragraph 6(1)(h). See also the definition of "employee trust" in subs. 248(1).

[17] Subsection 6(4). See also the definition of "group term life insurance policy" in subs. 248(1), and sections 2700-2705 of the *Income Tax Regulations*.

[18] Subsection 6(9). See also the computational rule in subs. 80.4(1).

[19] Paragraph 6(1)(i) and subs. 6(11)-(14). See also the definition of "salary deferral arrangement" in subs. 248(1).

[20] Subsections 6(15) and (15.1). See also the definition of "forgiven amount" in subs. 80(1).

[21] Subsections 6(19)-(22). See also the definition of "eligible relocation" in subs. 248(1).

[22] Subsection 6(23).

[23] Section 7.

[24] See subs. 6(6) (employment at special work site or remote location) and (16) (disability-related employment benefits).

A. Remuneration

Together, paragraph 6(1)(c) and subsection 5(1) of the Act include in a taxpayer's income from an office or employment "fees," "salary," "wages," "gratuities," and "other remuneration." For the purposes of section 5, moreover, subsection 6(3) deems a payment "to be remuneration for... services rendered" as an officer or during a period of employment where it is "received by one person from another":

(a)   during a period while the payee was an officer of, or in the employment of, the payer, or

(b)   on account, in lieu of payment or in satisfaction of an obligation arising out of an agreement made by the payer with the payee immediately prior to, during or immediately after a period that the payee was an officer of, or in the employment of, the payer,

unless, "irrespective of when the agreement, if any, under which the amount was received was made or the form or legal effect thereof," the payment "cannot reasonably be regarded as having been received":

(c)   as consideration or partial consideration for accepting the office or entering into the contract of employment,

(d)   as remuneration or partial remuneration for services as an officer or under the contract of employment, or

(e)   in consideration or partial consideration for a covenant with reference to what the officer or employee is, or is not, to do before or after the termination of the employment.

As explained in Chapter 3, subsection 6(3) is a specific anti-avoidance rule designed to expand the scope of a taxpayer's income from an office or employment by including amounts that are connected to the employment relationship but not otherwise characterized as taxable remuneration.

Because none of the terms "fees," "salary," "wages," "gratuities," or "remuneration" is defined in the Act, the interpretation of these amounts must begin with ordinary dictionary definitions.[25] According to the *Concise Oxford Dictionary*, 7th ed., a "fee" is a "sum payable to a public officer for performing his function," while the words "salary" and "wage" are defined respectively as a "fixed payment made by employer at regular intervals, usu. monthly or quarterly, to person doing other than manual or mechanical work" and an "amount paid at regular intervals esp. by the day or week or month, for time

---

[25]   Although subs. 248(1) defines "salary or wages" as "the income of a taxpayer from an office or employment as computed under Subdivision A of Division B of Part I," this definition does not apply to s. 5 (indeed, cannot apply, since it would render the definition in subs. 248(1) circular).

during which the workman or servant is at employer's disposal." Similar definitions appear in *Black's Law Dictionary*:

Fee. A charge fixed by law for services of public officers .... A recompense for an official or professional service or a charge or emolument or compensation for a particular act or service. A fixed charge or perquisite charged as recompense for labor; reward, compensation, or wage given to a person for performance of services or something done or to be done.

Salary. A reward or recompense for services performed. In a more limited sense, a fixed periodical compensation paid for services rendered. A stated compensation paid periodically as by the year, month, or other fixed period, in contrast to wages which are normally based on an hourly rate.

Wages. A compensation given to a hired person for his or her services. Compensation of employees based on time worked or output of production.

In general, therefore, "fees" refers to fixed payments in respect of an office,[26] while "salaries" and "wages" describe regular payments to employees (which are distinguished from each other by reference to the type of work performed and/or the period to which the payments refer[27]).

The word "gratuity" is defined in the *Shorter Oxford English Dictionary*, 3d ed., as:

A gift or present (usu. of money), often in return for favours or services, the amount depending on the inclination of the giver; in a bad sense, a bribe. Now a "tip."

Likewise, *Black's Law Dictionary* defines a "gratuity" as:

Something acquired or otherwise received without bargain or inducement. ... Something given freely without recompense; a gift. Something voluntarily given in return for a favor or especially a service, hence, a bounty; a tip; a bribe.

In the context of subsection 5(1), therefore, gratuities may be understood as amounts paid to an officer or employee "on account of legally non-enforceable claims."[28]

Unlike "fees," "salary," "wages," and "gratuities," "remuneration" is a more general concept comprising these more specific kinds of payments. The *Shorter Oxford Dictionary*, for example, defines the verb "to remunerate" as "to pay (a person) for services rendered or work done," and the word "remuneration" as "payment, pay." Similarly, *Black's Law Dictionary* defines "remuneration" as:

---

[26] Typical offices in respect of which fees are included in a taxpayer's income under para. 6(1)(c) include the position of a corporate director, the administrator of an estate, and a juror. See *Interpretation Bulletin* IT-377R, "Director's, Executor's or Juror's Fees," January 27, 1989. For a case in which the predecessor to para. 6(1)(c) was applied to a payment to the executor of an estate, see *Buckley v. M.N.R.* (1961), 27 Tax ABC 222.

[27] See, for example, Peter W. Hogg, Joanne E. Magee, and Ted Cook, *Principles of Canadian Income Tax Law*, 3d ed. (Toronto: Carswell, 1999) at 173: "salary is usually computed by reference to a relatively long period, often a year, while wages are usually computed by reference to a relatively short period, often an hour or a week."

[28] *Fordham v. M.N.R.*, [1975] C.T.C. 2071, 75 D.T.C. 106 (T.R.B.).

Payment; reimbursement. Reward; recompense; salary; compensation.

In the context of subsection 5(1), moreover, the "limited class" principle of statutory interpretation (*ejusdem generis*) suggests that the general words "other remuneration" should take their meaning from the specific kinds of compensation with which they are grouped — namely, salaries, wages, and gratuities. For the purposes of subdivision a of Division B of Part I of the Act, therefore, "remuneration" is properly understood as a generic term that includes, among other unspecified payments, fees, salaries, wages, and gratuities.

Although a taxpayer's remuneration for an office or employment may take different forms, a common feature of these dictionary definitions is that the payment represents compensation "for services." Subsection 6(3), however, expands upon the scope of these provisions by including specified amounts that can "reasonably be regarded as having been received" from an employer or future employer not only as remuneration for services but also as consideration for accepting an office or entering into a contract of employment or as consideration for a covenant with respect to the employee's conduct before or after a termination of the employee's employment.

The following cases and text examine the scope of a taxpayer's remuneration from an office or employment, considering payments other than conventional fees, salaries, and wages that are received in the course of an office or employment. Since amounts that are not characterized as remuneration under the statutory provisions mentioned above may be included as income from an office or employment under other provisions or as income from another source under subdivision d or the general language in paragraph 3(a), these cases should be read in light of these other provisions.[29] Indeed, although most of the cases considered below refer to the statutory provisions governing taxable remuneration from an office or employment, others turn on other provisions including the general inclusion of income from all sources under paragraph 3(a).

1. Inducement Payments

Where a taxpayer is paid an amount as an inducement to accept an office or enter into a contract of employment, it is arguable that the payment is not remuneration for services rendered under the office or employment, and thus not taxable under subsection 5(1) of the Act. Although subsection 6(3) deems most such inducement payments to be taxable remuneration, this provision applies only where the inducement payment is "received by one person from another":

---

[29] See, for example, para. 6(1)(a), which includes the value of "benefits" that are received "in respect of, in the course of, or by virtue of an office or employment"; subpara. 56(1)(a)(ii), which includes "retiring allowances" as defined in subs. 248(1), and para. 56(1)(n), which includes, among other receipts, specific kinds of prizes. Paragraph 6(1)(a) is reviewed later in this chapter; subpara. 56(1)(a)(ii) and para. 56(1)(n) are examined in Chapter 7.

(a)   during a period while the payee was an officer of, or in the employment of, the payer, or

(b)   on account, in lieu or payment or in satisfaction of an obligation arising out of an agreement made by the payer with the payee immediately prior to ... a period that the payee was an officer of, or in the employment of, the payer.

As a result, on a strict reading, the provision does not apply where an inducement payment is made by someone other than the recipient's current or future employer.

In *Curran v. M.N.R.*, [1959] S.C.J. No. 66, [1959] C.T.C. 416, 59 D.T.C. 1247 (S.C.C.), the taxpayer received a payment before entering into a contract of employment not with the person making the payment but with a company controlled by the payer. At the Exchequer Court ([1957] C.T.C. 384, 57 D.T.C. 1270), Dumoulin J held that the payment was not caught by then section 24A (now subsection 6(3)), but fell within "the statutory meaning of income for the year from a source other than those particularized" in the Act. The taxpayer appealed to the Supreme Court of Canada.

Curran v. M.N.R.
[1959] S.C.J. No. 66, [1959] C.T.C. 416, 59 D.T.C. 1247 (S.C.C.)

KERWIN CJC (Locke and Judson JJ concurring): ... The appellant, a geologist and highly regarded in his field, was employed as manager of the producing department of Imperial Oil Limited. He had been connected with the latter for some years and in 1951 was earning $25,000 a year with the expectation that his salary would be increased, and had he continued until the retirement age of sixty-five he would have been entitled to a pension equal to approximately one-half the average of his salary for the five years immediately preceding his retirement. He had been offered a directorship in this company late in 1950 and early in 1951 but declined because he preferred to remain in the position he then occupied and to live in Calgary. The salary attached to the position of a director in Imperial Oil Limited is considerable.

In the spring of 1951 Robert A. Brown, Jr., approached the appellant with a view to inducing him to resign his position in Imperial Oil so that he might accept employment with Brown or one of the companies in which the latter was interested. Mr. Brown was a substantial shareholder of Federated Petroleums Limited and president and general manager of that company. The company itself held a large number of shares of Home Oil Company Limited. Calta Assets Limited was a small holding company, the shares of which were wholly owned by Mr. Brown and his brother and sister and it was a substantial shareholder in both Federated and Home Oil. Mr. Brown did not hold any office in Home Oil, of which Major Lowery was president and managing director and exercised both share and management control. Mr. Brown had become dissatisfied with the management of Home Oil and desired to secure the appellant's services as manager of Federated and Home Oil with the expectation that Major Lowery would then relinquish the active management of Home Oil. The negotiations between Brown and the appellant culminated in a written agreement, dated August 15, 1951, between Brown, called therein the grantor, and the appellant, referred to therein as the grantee. As the appellant emphasizes the terms of that agreement, it is set out in full:

WHEREAS the grantee is presently, at the age of 42 years, in charge of all Western Canadian Production for Imperial Oil Limited at a salary of $25,000 per year, having arrived at that position after eighteen years of service with the said Company or its affiliated companies (the said Company and its affiliates under the direction of the Standard Oil Company of New Jersey comprising together one of the largest groups of companies in the oil business with world wide production, refining and marketing facilities).

AND WHEREAS the grantee has acquired the right to a pension on retirement from Imperial Oil Limited or any of its affiliates which if his present salary scale remains the same until his retirement will yield to him the sum of $12,500 per year, and the probabilities are that if he remains with his present employers his salary will increase substantially over the years with corresponding increases in the pension payable to him.

AND WHEREAS his pension rights will cease entirely if he voluntarily severs his connection with the said Company and its affiliates.

AND WHEREAS the grantee has been mentioned as a prospective member of the Board of Directors of Imperial Oil Limited which if he were to be so appointed would mean an immediate substantial increase in salary and would in the ordinary course of events lead eventually to one of the senior positions in the oil organization of which Imperial Oil Limited forms a part.

AND WHEREAS it is not the policy of Imperial Oil Limited and its affiliates to reemploy in any part of such world wide organization anyone who has voluntarily left the service of any of the companies in or affiliated therewith.

AND WHEREAS FEDERATED PETROLEUMS LIMITED, a comparatively small oil company operating only in Canada and having no connection with Imperial Oil Limited or any of its affiliates, has recently intimated its willingness to offer the grantee a position as Manager at a salary equivalent to that which he draws from Imperial Oil Limited, which proposed offer the grantee has intimated that he would refuse solely by reason of the fact that he would be obliged to give up his chances of advancement with his present employers and their affiliates, would lose the opportunity for re-employment with them or any of them, thereby greatly limiting his field of possible future employment, and would lose all accumulated and future rights to pension.

AND WHEREAS the grantor holds a substantial interest in Federated Petroleums Limited, is of the opinion that the grantee's experience, capabilities and connections would be valuable to that Company, and is very desirous of persuading the grantee to resign from his present position in order that he may then be free to accept an offer of employment from Federated Petroleums Limited.

AND WHEREAS the grantor recognizes what the grantee is obliged to give up in the way of chances for advancement, pension rights, and opportunities for re-employment in the oil industry if he resigns from his present position in order to be free to accept the offered employment and has agreed to compensate him liberally therefor.

NOW THEREFORE THIS INDENTURE WITNESSETH

1. The grantor hereby agrees to pay to the grantee the sum of $250,000 in consideration of the loss of pension rights, chances for advancement, and opportunities for re employment in the oil industry, consequent upon the resignation of the grantee from his present position with Imperial Oil Limited, the said sum to be paid forthwith upon the grantee informing his

present employers that he is leaving their employ and whether or not employment has been offered to him by Federated Petroleums Limited or accepted by him, prior to that time.

2.   In consideration of the agreement of the grantor to pay the said sum, the grantee hereby agrees to resign his position with Imperial Oil Limited, such resignation to take effect not later than the 15th day of September, AD 1951.

Mr. Brown paid the $250,000 to the appellant, but Calta Assets Limited actually furnished the funds out of its own assets and from money borrowed from a bank. On the same day, August 15, 1951, the appellant entered into an agreement with Federated Petroleums to act as its general manager at a fixed salary of $25,000 per year and he was to serve as the directors of that company might determine from time to time as manager of any other company or companies in which Federated had a financial interest either in addition to or in lieu of serving as manager of Federated; but any salary from such other company or companies was to the extent thereof to be deemed satisfaction of the salary which under the terms of the agreement Federated was obligated to pay. The appellant was also given the option, within a limited time, to purchase twenty-five thousand shares of Home Oil Company at a given price.

The appellant resigned his position with Imperial Oil Limited shortly after August 15, 1951. He was never employed by Brown or Federated Petroleums or Calta Assets but became president and managing director of Home Oil at a salary of $25,000 per year with no superannuation benefits. Due to a disagreement with Brown the appellant resigned his position with Home Oil at the expiration of about one year.

...

As has been pointed out in the recent judgment of this Court in *Bannerman v. M.N.R.*, [1959] CTC 214, there is no extensive description of income such as appeared in the *Income War Tax Act*. The word must receive its ordinary meaning bearing in mind the distinction between capital and income and the ordinary concepts and usages of mankind. Under the authorities it is undoubted that clear words are necessary in order to tax the subject and that the taxpayer is entitled to arrange his affairs so as to minimize the tax. However, he does not succeed in the attempt if the transaction falls within the fair meaning of the words of the taxing enactment.

...

In the present case the substance of the matter was the engagement by the appellant to work for Mr. Brown or one of the companies in which the latter was interested and the agreement by the appellant with Federated Petroleums. It is true that in order to fulfil his obligations under the contracts the appellant was obliged to resign his position with Imperial Oil Limited and thereby gave up not only the annual salary, a like amount which he was to receive, but also his pension rights and further prospects. However, the payment of $250,000 was made for personal service only and that conclusion really disposes of the matter as it is impossible to divide the consideration. The mere fact that the first agreement of August 15, 1951, states that Brown agreed to pay the appellant $250,000 in consideration of the loss of pension rights, chances for advancement and opportunities for re-employment in the oil industry cannot change the true character of the payment. Its true nature must be found in the terms of the two agreements and the surrounding circumstances including the fact that the $250,000 did not come from Imperial Oil Limited. ... I should add that while, from the point of view of the respondent, I obtain no assistance from a consideration of Section 24A of the Act [now subsection 6(3)], I cannot agree with the submission on behalf of the appellant that it establishes non-taxability of the appellant.

The appeal should be dismissed with costs.

MARTLAND J (concurring): ... For the appellant it is contended that the payment represented a capital receipt and not income. The argument is based upon the proposition that the agreement made by him with Brown was to provide compensation for loss or relinquishment of a source of income, which source was of itself a capital asset of the appellant.

In support of this submission several English decisions and an Australian case were cited. ... All of these are cases in which the money payments to an employee have been held not to constitute taxable income because they were not made in respect of the performance of services by the employee, but rather in order to acquire from him rights which he had previously held against the employer.

...

In the present case it is clear that Mr. Brown was not seeking to acquire any rights which the appellant had under his existing employment contract with Imperial Oil Limited. The agreement made by Brown with the appellant and Brown's evidence make it clear that he was seeking to acquire the skilled services of the appellant as a manager. In order that those services might be available it was necessary that the appellant should resign from his position with Imperial Oil Limited and such resignation resulted in the foregoing by him of various advantages which his employment with Imperial Oil Limited carried and which are referred to in the agreement. However, the essence of the matter was the acquisition of services and the consideration was paid so that those services would be made available.

I, therefore, think that the payment made to the appellant by Brown, under the agreement of August 15, 1951, was income to the appellant within the meaning of Section 3 of the *Income Tax Act*. ...

...

Counsel for the respondent conceded that Section 24A [now subsection 6(3)] was not applicable to the circumstances of this case. Counsel for the appellant, however, urged that Section 24A was enacted in order to broaden the scope of Section 5 so as to tax certain kinds of income not otherwise taxable under Section 5. He pointed out that Section 24A might have applied to the payment in question here if it had been made to the appellant by Federated or by Home. Since it did not apply, because the payment was not made by the appellant's employer, he contended that the payment could not be regarded as income within Section 3, because so to hold would make Section 24A meaningless in its application.

It seems to me, however, that Section 24A was essentially a provision dealing with onus of proof and deemed certain payments as therein defined to be payments within Section 5, unless the recipient could establish affirmatively that a payment did not reasonably fall within the provisions of paragraphs (i), (ii) or (iii) of Section 24A [now paragraph 6(3)(c), (d), or (e)]. I do not think that it follows that payments which would fall within Section 24A, except for the fact that they were made by someone other than the employer, of necessity cannot be income within the provisions of Section 3.

In my opinion the appeal should be dismissed with costs.

[Taschereau J dissented, concluding that a portion of the $250,000 was paid for personal services and a portion as consideration for the loss of the taxpayer's prior benefits.]

Appeal dismissed.

NOTES AND QUESTIONS

1. On what basis did the majority in *Curran* agree with the Minister's assessment including the $250,000 payment in computing the taxpayer's income? What, according to the majority, was the source of the payment?

2. In *Curran*, Kerwin CJC (Locke and Judson JJ concurring) said of the payment to the taxpayer that "*the substance of the matter* was the engagement by the appellant to work for Mr. Brown or one of the companies in which the latter was interested and the agreement by the appellant with Federated Petroleums" (emphasis added). Similarly, Martland J stated that "*the essence of the matter* was the acquisition of services and the consideration was paid so that those services would be made available" (emphasis added). Is the decision an example of legal substance over nomenclature or economic substance over legal form?

3. Why did counsel for the Minister concede that then section 24A (now subsection 6(3)) did not apply? Might the Minister have argued that the court should disregard the separate existence of the payer (Mr. Brown), the party entering into the contract of employment (Federated Petroleums Limited), and the actual employer (Home Oil Company Limited) on the grounds that Brown controlled the two corporations? Does the language of the statutory provision, which operates "irrespective of when the agreement, if any, under which the amount was received was made or the form or legal effect thereof," suggest an appropriate approach to its application?

4.   For what purpose did counsel for the taxpayer refer to then section 24A (now subsection 6(3))? Do you agree with Martland J's response to this argument? Do you agree with his interpretation of then section 24A as "essentially a provision dealing with onus of proof"?

5.   In *MacInnis v. M.N.R.*, [1984] C.T.C. 2403, 84 D.T.C. 1370 (T.C.C.), the taxpayer, who negotiated the sale of all the shares of a company of which he was the president and a minority shareholder, received $58,775 from the purchaser pursuant to an agreement whereby the purchaser offered to continue the taxpayer's employment on specified terms should its offer be accepted. Rejecting the taxpayer's arguments that the payment was consideration for the disposition of his shares, the court characterized the amount (at para. 28) as remuneration "for services to be rendered" and "income within the meaning of section 3 of the *Income Tax Act*."

6.   In *Greiner v. M.N.R.*, [1984] F.C.J. No. 15, [1984] C.T.C. 92, 84 D.T.C. 6073 (F.C.A.), the taxpayer, whose employment as president of MEPC Canadian Properties Ltd. was terminated when MEPC amalgamated with a subsidiary of Morguard Properties Ltd., received $200,000 under an agreement with Morguard whereby he became employed as its president. Rejecting the taxpayer's argument that the money was received in consideration for the disposition of rights held under his previous employment contract, the court affirmed the decision of the trial judge, who concluded (at para. 18) that the payment was taxable under subsection 6(3) as "a payment arising out of an agreement made by Morguard with Greiner, immediately prior to the period that Greiner became an officer of or in the employment of Morguard."

7.   In *Volpé v. M.N.R.*, [1990] T.C.J. No. 337, [1990] 2 C.T.C. 2321, 90 D.T.C. 1703 (T.C.C.), the taxpayer, who accepted a new job that required him to move from Edmunston to Moncton, New Brunswick, received $27,000 pursuant to an agreement whereby his new employer promised to compensate him in the event that his former residence was sold for less than a stipulated amount. Rejecting the taxpayer's argument that the payment merely compensated him for a capital loss on the disposition of his former residence, Lamarre-Proulx TCJ concluded (at para. 9):

> I fail to see how I could say that such a payment was not received on account of an obligation resulting from an agreement between the payer and the payee immediately before a period in which this payee became an officer of the payer, and that this amount cannot reasonably be regarded as having been received as consideration or partial consideration for accepting the office, within the meaning of paragraphs 6(3)(b) and (c) of the Act.

For a similar decision, see *Pollesel v. Canada*, [1997] T.C.J. No. 839, 98 D.T.C. 1003 (T.C.C.).

2. Compensation for Breach or Waiver of Contractual Obligations

As with inducement payments received prior to the commencement of an office or employment, it is arguable that compensation received from an employer for the breach or waiver of a contractual obligation is not remuneration for services rendered under the office or employment, and thus is not taxable under subsection 5(1) of the Act. According to subsection 6(3), however, such compensation may be deemed to be remuneration where, "irrespective of when the agreement, if any, under which the amount was received was made or the form or legal effect thereof," it may reasonably be regarded as having been received:

(c)   as consideration or partial consideration for accepting the office or entering into the contract of employment,

(d)   as remuneration or partial remuneration for services as an officer or under the contract of employment, or

(e)   in consideration or partial consideration for a covenant with reference to what the officer or employee is, or is not, to do before or after the termination of the employee.

Among the many cases in which this provision had been applied to amounts received as compensation for the breach or waiver of a contractual obligation, one of the earliest is *Moss v. M.N.R.*, [1963] C.T.C. 535, 63 D.T.C. 1359 (Ex. Ct.).

Moss v. M.N.R.
[1963] C.T.C. 535, 63 D.T.C. 1359 (Ex. Ct.)

THORSON P: ... The appellant is a food broker and the president of F. Archibald Brokerage Ltd. and resides at Winnipeg. Prior to April 1, 1955, he had been with W.H. Escott Company Ltd. of Winnipeg for 15 years, first as an office boy, later as sales branch manager at Saskatoon and then as a salesman at Winnipeg. His salary with this company had never exceeded $5,000 per year.

On March 28, 1955, he entered into an agreement with Prairie Cereals Limited, a company that had its head office at Edmonton. ... There were other parties to the agreement referred to, namely, Albert Gaetz, who had a controlling interest in the Company, Edith Ryall, Selma Gaetz and Emma Gaetz, who were other shareholders in the Company, and The Toronto General Trusts Corporation as Trustee.

...

It was under the terms and conditions of this agreement that the appellant became employed by Prairie Cereals Limited, later Prairie Cereals Ltd., as its sales manager in Canada. Under the agreement he was entitled to ... specific payments [as well as an interest in a life insurance policy on the life of Albert Gaetz] and he also had the right... in the event of an intended sale of the assets or shares of the Company, to purchase the assets or shares at 90 per cent of the intended purchase price.

...

On April 1, 1955, the appellant commenced his employment by Prairie Cereals Limited as its sales manager in Canada under the terms and conditions set out in the agreement.

...

Late in 1955 or early in 1956, Albert Gaetz entered into negotiations for the sale of the assets of the Company to Martin & Robertson Ltd. The appellant was quite concerned about these negotiations for he had an option to purchase the assets, he was the beneficiary of a policy of insurance on the life of Albert Gaetz and he would have preferred to see the deal not made, for he knew that ultimately he was going to be the owner of the business. Being an interested party he was kept posted about the negotiations and was present when they were being discussed. Mr. Gaetz and Mr. T. Lacusta, his accountant, asked him to accompany them to Vancouver. While he was at Vancouver, he was handed a letter, dated March 24, 1956, signed by Prairie Cereals Limited and by Albert Gaetz, which read as follows:

> Dear Mr. Moss:
>
> In consideration for releasing Prairie Cereals Limited, and Albert Gaetz, and Edith Ryall, Selma Gaetz and Emma Gaetz from the provisions of the agreement between Prairie Cereals Limited, and Peter Moss, and Albert Gaetz and Edith Ryall, Selma Gaetz, and The Toronto General Trusts Corporation, dated March 28, 1955 Prairie Cereals Limited and Albert Gaetz hereby agree to pay to you the amount of Thirty Four Thousand Six Hundred Dollars ($34,600.00). This offer is made subject to the successful completion of the sale of the assets of Prairie Cereals Limited, to the Canada Rice Mills Ltd. or their agents of Vancouver, BC.

...

The appellant accepted the offer contained in the letter of March 24, 1956 and he and the Company, then Prairie Cereals Ltd., entered into an agreement, dated April 12, 1956. In view of its importance I set out its recitals as follows:

> WHEREAS by Agreement dated the 28th day of March, 1955, made between the Company of the First Part, Moss of the Second Part, Albert Gaetz of the Third Part, and others, it was agreed inter alia that the Company should not sell its undertaking and assets without first giving to Moss the prior and pre-emptive right for a period of Thirty (30) days to purchase the said assets at Ninety per cent (90%) of the proposed purchase price;
>
> AND WHEREAS by a Policy of Life Insurance No. 1320759, the Manufacturers Life Insurance Company has insured the life of Gaetz in the principal sum of One hundred thousand dollars ($100,000), Moss being the owner and named as beneficiary in the said Policy;
>
> AND WHEREAS the Company desires to sell its undertaking and assets to Martin & Robertson Ltd., and/or Prairie Maid Cereals Ltd., for the price and on the terms and conditions set forth in a proposed agreement to be dated May 1956 and to be made between the Company, the said Martin & Robertson Ltd., Gaetz, Moss and the said Prairie Maid Cereals Ltd.;
>
> AND WHEREAS the Company has requested Moss to consent to the said sale and to waive his pre-emptive right to purchase the said assets;

and paragraphs 1, 2 and 3 which contained the following provisions:

1. Moss waives any and all rights under the said Agreement dated the 28th day of March, 1955, or otherwise to purchase the assets of the Company and expressly consents to the sale of the said undertaking and assets by the Company to the said Martin & Robertson Ltd., and/or Prairie Maid Cereals Ltd.

2. Moss hereby transfers, sells and assigns to the Company all of the interest of Moss as owner or beneficiary of the said Policy of Life Insurance No. 1320759 issued by The Manufacturers Life Insurance Company on the life of the said Gaetz.

3. The Company shall pay to Moss on or before the First day of June, 1956, the sum of Thirty-four thousand, six hundred dollars ($34,600.00) or a sum equal to Ten per cent (10%) of the total purchase price paid or payable to the Company by Martin & Robertson Ltd., and/or Prairie Maid Cereals Ltd., for the undertaking and assets of the Company, whichever sum is the greater.

Following this agreement the appellant transferred his interest in the life insurance policy to the Company.

...

The Company concluded its arrangements for the sale of its assets to Martin & Robertson Ltd. and Prairie Maid Cereals Ltd. under the terms and conditions set out in an agreement, dated May 15, 1956. The appellant and Arthur Gaetz joined in it.

The sum of $34,600 referred to in the letter of March 24, 1956, and the agreement of April 12, 1956, was paid by Prairie Cereals Ltd. to the appellant and received by him at a date in respect of which the evidence is not clear. ... The appellant on his direct examination said that he received the amount by cheque at the end of May or early in June of 1956.

...

After Prairie Cereals Ltd. sold its assets to Martin & Robertson Ltd. and Prairie Maid Cereals Ltd. the appellant became the general manager of Prairie Maid Cereals Ltd. ... On August 3, 1956, he sent in his resignation as manager of Prairie Maid Cereals Ltd. but agreed to continue to act as manager until suitable arrangements could be made.

...

[T]he Minister in assessing the appellant for 1956 added $33,200 to the amount of income reported by him on his income tax return for the year, this being $1,400 less than the amount of $34,600 which he had received from Prairie Cereals Ltd., the said amount of $ 1,400 being the cash surrender value of [the insurance policy on the life of Albert Gaetz, the premiums for which were paid for by the company and included as a taxable benefit in computing the taxpayer's employment income for the 1955 taxation year].

The issue in the appeal is whether the said amount of $33,200 was properly included in the assessment under appeal. It was contended on behalf of the Minister that the amount was income within the meaning of Sections 3, 5 and 25 of the Act [now paragraph 3(a) and subsections 5(1) and 6(3)].

...

In my opinion, the agreement of March 28, 1955, was, so far as the appellant and Prairie Cereals Limited were concerned, a contract of employment of the appellant by Prairie Cereals Limited as its sales manager in Canada, on the terms and conditions set out in the agreement. Under this contract of employment the appellant was entitled to the remuneration for his services as an officer of and in the employment of Prairie Cereals Limited as set out in the agreement. Apart from the specific payments to which the appellant was entitled that were specified in paragraph 1 he also had the right specified in the proviso of paragraph 2, namely, that the Company should not sell its undertaking and entire assets without first giving him 30 days notice of its intention to effect such sale, the notice to specify the sale price and terms of payment and that thereupon he should have the first prior and pre-emptive right for the said 30 days to purchase the said assets at 90 per cent of the price mentioned in the notice on terms no less favourable than those set out in the said notice. This right was as much part of the consideration for accepting the office of sales manager and entering into the contract of employment and as much remuneration for his services as an officer or under the contract of employment as any of the payments specified in paragraph 1 of the agreement.

I now come to the contention advanced on behalf of the Minister that Section 25 [now subsection 6(3)] of the Act is applicable to the facts of the case and that the amount of $34,600 received by the appellant from Prairie Cereals Ltd. should be deemed for the purpose of Section 5 to be remuneration for the appellant's services rendered as an officer or during the period of employment.

The first enquiry is whether the amount was received during a period while the appellant was an officer of, or in the employment of Prairie Cereals Ltd. ... It could, in my opinion, be reasonably found on the evidence that the amount was received by the appellant from Prairie Cereals Ltd. during a period while he was an officer of and in its employment within the meaning of paragraph (a) of Section 25 [now paragraph 6(3)(a)]. Certainly, the appellant has failed to establish that the amount was received by him after he had ceased to be an officer of or in the employment of Prairie Cereals Ltd.

But, in any event, the facts bring the case within the ambit of paragraph (b) of Section 25 [now paragraph 6(3)(b)]. The amount of $34,600 was in satisfaction of the obligation arising out of the agreement made by Prairie Cereals Ltd. with the appellant, dated April 12, 1956, which implemented the offer made in the letter of March 1956, and its acceptance. The agreement was, therefore, made during the period that the appellant was an officer of and in the employment of Prairie Cereals Ltd. under the circumstances, the amount should be deemed, for the purpose of Section 5, to be remuneration for the appellant's services rendered as an officer or during the period of employment unless the conditions specified in subparagraphs (i), (ii) or (iii) are established [now paragraph 6(3)(c), (d), or (e)].

In my opinion, the specified conditions cannot be established. The amount paid in satisfaction of the obligation arising out of the agreement of April 12, 1956, relates back to the appellant's prior and preemptive right under the agreement of March 28, 1955, and was made in payment of it. It can, therefore, be reasonably regarded as having been received by the appellant as partial consideration for his acceptance of the office of sales manager of Prairie Cereals Limited and entering into the contract of employment of March 28, 1955, or as partial remuneration for his services as an officer of Prairie Cereals Limited or under his contract of employment.

Under the circumstances, I find that Section 25 is applicable in the present case and that the amount received by the appellant from Prairie Cereals Ltd. should be deemed, for the purpose of Section 5, to be remuneration for the appellant's services rendered as an officer of Prairie Cereals Ltd. or during his period of employment with it, and, therefore, taxable under the Act.

...

For the reasons given I am of the opinion that the Minister was right in assessing the appellant for 1956 as he did and I so find. It follows that the appeal herein must be dismissed with costs.

Judgment accordingly.

NOTES AND QUESTIONS

1. On what basis did Thorson P conclude in *Moss* that the $34,600 payment received by the taxpayer (less the $1,400 cash surrender value of the life insurance policy transferred to the company) was taxable as remuneration from his employment with Prairie Cereals Ltd.?

2. In *Blanchard v. Canada*, [1995] F.C.J. No. 1045, [1995] 2 C.T.C. 262, 95 D.T.C. 5479 (F.C.A.), the taxpayer, who worked at an oil-processing plant in Fort McMurray, Alberta, received $7,420 when the taxpayer's employer cancelled a housing program whereby a residence acquired from the employer's nominee Northward would be repurchased by Northward on the occurrence of specific events such as termination of the employee's employment. Referring to subsection 6(3) of the Act, the court concluded (at para. 23):

> Eugene Blanchard received a $7,240 payment while in the employ of the payor. This payment was made in satisfaction of an obligation arising out of an agreement entered into between Blanchard and be payor either at the time of or before the period of employment. This original agreement was clearly intended to induce and did induce Blanchard to accept the employment. It has not been established that this payment "cannot reasonably be regarded as having been received as consideration or a partial consideration for ... entering into the contract of employment." On the contrary, it is clear that the payment arising from the satisfaction of the obligation that arose under this agreement was received as "consideration or partial consideration" for entering into the contract of employment. It is, therefore, remuneration and is taxable.

3. In *Trottier v. M.N.R.*, [1981] C.T.C. 2581, 81 D.T.C. 572 (T.R.B.), the taxpayer, who worked for Quebec Hydro, received a lump-sum payment of

$6,500 when the employer discontinued a service providing free transportation to its employees' work sites. Rejecting the taxpayer's argument that the payment constituted non-taxable damages or a capital gain from the disposition of a property right, the board held that the payment was a gratuity within the meaning of subsection 5(1).

4.   In *Markin v. M.N.R.*, [1996] F.C.J. No. 992, 96 D.T.C. 6483 (F.C.T.D.), the taxpayer, who had acquired rights to a share of his employer's profits pursuant to an employee incentive program, received $389,760 in consideration for the cancellation of these rights on the termination of his employment. Rejecting the taxpayer's argument that the payment should be characterized as a capital gain from the disposition of his rights, Gibson J held that it was taxable under paragraph 6(1)(a) as a benefit from the taxpayer's employment or under subsection 6(3) as an amount "on account, in lieu of payment or in satisfaction of an obligation arising out of an agreement made by the payer with the payee ... during ... a period that the payee was ... in the employment of, the payer" that could reasonably be regarded as having been received "as ... partial remuneration for services ... under the contract of employment."

5.   In *Choquette v. Canada*, [1974] F.C.J. No. 78, [1974] C.T.C. 742, 74 D.T.C. 6563 (F.C.T.D.), the taxpayer received $25,000 in consideration for releasing his employer from an "irrevocable contract" extending his employment contract until the end of 1972. Citing *Curran* and *Moss*, Décary J held that the payment was taxable under section 3 as income "from a source which I regard as employment" or under then section 25 (now subsection 6(3)) on the grounds that it had been received during a period while the taxpayer was in the employment of the payer and could reasonably be regarded as having been received as remuneration for services under the contract of employment.

6.   In several cases, employees who have received compensation as arbitration awards or in settlement of a grievance against an employer under a collective agreement have argued that these payments are non-taxable damages excluded from the taxpayer's income from an office or employment. See *Gagnon v. M.N.R.* (1961), 26 Tax ABC 364, 61 D.T.C. 307 (T.A.B.); *Abramovici v. M.N.R.*, [1980] C.T.C. 2162, 80 D.T.C. 1151 (T.R.B.); *Norman v. M.N.R.*, [1987] T.C.J. No. 749, [1987] 2 C.T.C. 2261, 87 D.T.C. 556 (T.C.C.); *Vincent v. M.N.R.*, [1988] 2 C.T.C. 2075, 88 D.T.C. 1422 (T.C.C.); *Frank v. Canada*, [1998] T.C.J. No. 1110, [1999] 1 C.T.C. 2776 (T.C.C.); and *Kennedy v. Canada*, [1999] T.C.J. No. 401, [1999] 4 C.T.C. 2277 (T.C.C.). In each of these cases, payments were characterized as "salary, wages or other remuneration" under subsection 5(1) or as a benefit under paragraph 6(1)(a).

7.   Payments received by a taxpayer in consideration for the cancellation of stock options are subject to special rules in section 7 and are considered later in this chapter.

3. Payments On or After Termination of an Office or Employment

Also like inducement payments received prior to the commencement of an office or employment, amounts received by a taxpayer on or after the termination of an office or employment are not easily characterized as remuneration for services. As a result, the treatment of these amounts for tax purposes has been subject to considerable litigation and legislative action, culminating in the taxation of "retiring allowances" as income from an "other source" under subparagraph 56(1)(a)(ii) of the Act (see Chapter 7). In order to understand the cases and subsequent statutory amendments, it is useful to begin with the decision in *Quance v. Canada*, [1974] C.T.C. 225, 74 D.T.C 6210 (F.C.T.D.).

Quance v. Canada
[1974] C.T.C. 225, 74 D.T.C. 6210 (F.C.T.D)

CATTANACH J: ... The plaintiff is a professional engineer who in 1958 was engaged by McGraw-Edison of Canada Limited, which is a wholly-owned subsidiary of a parent company incorporated pursuant to the laws of one of the States of the United States of America under a corporate name somewhat similar to that of the subsidiary, in the capacity of president. At that time the subsidiary was in the business of manufacturing and dealing in small electrical appliances.

In time the operations of the subsidiary were expanded to include power systems. The plaintiff was designated the president of that division and more latterly became the managing director of that division.

The plaintiff was engaged under a verbal contract of hiring and accordingly there was no express term setting forth the duration of the contract. The plaintiff's salary was fixed on a yearly basis but he was paid the appropriate instalments semi-monthly. The plaintiff, during the period of his employment with the company beginning in 1958 and the termination of that employment on June 12, 1969, received four increases in salary. In 1969, his salary was $23,000 per annum. He was also permitted to participate in a stock option plan. Stock options were offered three times during the period of the plaintiff's employment. In addition he was the participant in a pension plan which appeared to have been tied in some way which was not explained in evidence to the profits of the company.

In the spring of 1969 the plant was struck by an employees' union. The plaintiff was negotiating settlement on behalf of his employer. Apparently the plaintiff's efforts were not satisfactory to the employer because he was replaced as negotiator by an employee of the parent company who held a title indicating that he was a specialist in labour relations. This employee settled the strike, which settlement, the plaintiff testified, was effected by a complete capitulation to the union demands.

On June 12, 1969, which was shortly after the settlement of the strike, the plaintiff was summoned into the presence of Mr. Gieseke who was the president of both the parent and subsidiary companies and Mr. G. Axson, the executive vice-president of the subsidiary, McGraw-Edison of Canada Limited and the plaintiff's superior.

At that meeting the plaintiff was invited to resign. He refused to do so. Thereupon the president terminated the plaintiff's employment as of 5 o'clock that day. The plaintiff was offered six and one-half months salary in lieu of notice. He refused this offer as inadequate and expressed the view that the offer should be at least one year's salary. He then left the interview. Later that day the president telephoned the plaintiff at his home and increased the offer in lieu of notice to nine and one-half months salary. This offer the plaintiff also rejected as being inadequate.

By letter dated June 17, 1969 the executive vice-president confirmed the termination of the plaintiff's employment and his rejection of the offer of salary in lieu of notice and withdrew that offer. However he expressed the willingness to discuss the matter further if the plaintiff wished to do so.

On receipt of that letter the plaintiff consulted his solicitors who wrote the plaintiff's former employer pointing out that in their view reasonable notice would have been one year. On behalf of the plaintiff they proposed settlement by payment of $33,256.68 to the plaintiff, that amount being made up of one year's salary at $23,000, $66 for hospitalization, $152.76 for group life insurance premiums, $37.92 for disability insurance premiums and an estimated loss of $4,000 for profit sharing pension plan and $6,000 for stock option benefits.

It was emphasized by the solicitors that the proposed amount was payment for damages for wrongful dismissal, not salary, wages, or other remuneration and should not be subject to withholding for income tax by the employer.

The company did not deign to reply to the solicitors' letter. Instead by letter dated July 24, 1969 the company forwarded to the plaintiff three cheques for the amount payable to him for the balance of June 1969 and for July 1969. The company announced its intention to pay the plaintiff his regular salary for nine and one-half months to cover his loss of employment based upon an income of $23,000 per year and that a cheque would be sent on the 15th and 30th of each month.

By letter dated August 8, 1969 the solicitors advised the company that the plaintiff was not prepared to accept the cheques as salary but would accept them as part-payment on account of damages and reiterated their request that the employer should not deduct income tax from the cheques. They also demanded payment of the amounts already deducted for that purpose.

Again the company ignored the solicitors' letter but continued to make semi-monthly payments to the plaintiff until the final payment forwarded by letter dated March 25, 1970. In that letter reference was made to the payment being "as per our arrangement re termination salary." The word "our" must be a use of the royal pronoun because the "arrangement" was unilateral. The plaintiff was not a consenting party thereto and denied the existence of any arrangement.

The total amount so paid to the plaintiff in his 1969 taxation year was $12,592.82 and in his 1970 taxation year the total amount was $5,748. It is upon these amounts that the Minister computed his assessments for the taxation years in question. The actual amounts received by the plaintiff in those respective years were $8,841.71 and $4,002.30, the differences of $3,751.65 and $1,745.70 represent the amounts of income tax deducted by the company and remitted to the Department of National Revenue.

On September 2, 1969 the plaintiff found other employment but at an annual salary of $ 17,500 which was $5,500 less per year than the salary he had been paid by his previous employer.

Upon receipt of the letter dated March 25, 1970 from McGraw-Edison of Canada Limited, enclosing the final payment of nine and one-half months salary in lieu of notice of dismissal, the plaintiff again consulted his solicitors. On their advice he did not sue for wrongful dismissal because as a result of the payment of the equivalent of nine and one-half months salary and the plaintiff's subsequent employment by another employer, although at a lesser salary, the quantum of damages would be reduced to an amount which would not warrant litigation.

The contract of employment between the plaintiff and McGraw-Edison of Canada Limited was an oral contract of general or indefinite hiring. In the absence of any express terms as to termination the general principle is that such a contract might be terminated on reasonable notice. It is an implied term of such a contract that reasonable notice shall be given. If such notice is not given the failure to do so constitutes a breach of the implicit term in the contract of employment and the dismissal will be actionable. The damages recoverable will be the salary which would have been earned during the period of notice. Accordingly it follows that payment of salary for a period coincident with the period of reasonable notice will prevent the dismissal from being wrongful and actionable for the payment of the salary is, in effect, the payment of liquidated damages in advance of the action.

What constitutes reasonable notice depends on the grade of employment. In essence the dispute between the plaintiff and his employer was the reasonableness of the period of notice and some other incidental benefits. That is not the dispute before me.

The issue before me is whether the amounts of $12,592.82 and $5,948 received by the plaintiff from his employer in the plaintiff's 1969 and 1970 taxation years under the circumstances outlined above are properly subject to income tax in his hands.

...

The plaintiff's employer was within its rights to dismiss the plaintiff upon giving him reasonable notice. However the employer dismissed him forthwith but it did continue the plaintiff's salary for a period of nine and one-half months presumably on the assumption that this was a period equivalent to a reasonable period of notice.

The amounts so received by the plaintiff from his employer were in satisfaction of an obligation arising out of the contract of employment between the plaintiff and his employer. That obligation was to give the plaintiff reasonable notice of the termination of his employment and upon failing to do so to pay him, in lieu thereof, the salary that would have been earned during the period of notice.

In my view those facts fall precisely within section 25 [now subsection 6(3)] of the *Income Tax Act* and accordingly the amounts paid are deemed thereby to be remuneration for the payee's services during his period of employment for the purposes of subsection 5(1) of the Act.

During his argument on behalf of the plaintiff counsel conceded that payments of salary made in lieu of notice of termination of an indefinite hiring are properly taxable as an obligation arising out of the agreement of employment but he contended that when the employee must sue to enforce that contract what is received are damages.

Mr. Justice Cameron considered the taxability of damages for loss of profits by infringement of a trade mark in *Donald Hart Ltd. v. Minister of National Revenue*, [1959] CTC 268, 59 DTC 1134, and said at page 270 [1135]:

> ... In income tax matters, the receipt of compensation by way of "damages" is neutral, without further evidence as to the nature and quality of the award. It is trite law to say that the receipt of an award of "damages" may or may not result in the receipt being taxable income.

He then went on to find that the damages awarded in that case were taxable and said at page 273 [1137]:

> Interpreting the judgment as best I can to ascertain the true nature and quality of the award for the purposes of income tax, I have reached the conclusion that it was made for the purpose of filling the hole in the appellant's profit which it could normally have expected to make, but which had been lost to it by reason of the tortious acts of the defendant therein. ...

As I have pointed out above the damages that the plaintiff would receive for dismissal without notice are to replace the income he was deprived of by not being given reasonable notice. That is the reason for awarding that item of damages for breach of a contract of employment. Accordingly such an award is imbued with the quality of income.

I fail to follow the logic of the contention that an obligation arising out of a contract of employment which is deemed to be income by the *Income Tax Act* is metamorphosed into a capital receipt because that obligation was the subject of a successful law suit resulting in a judgment for the amount of the obligation involved. In my view the nature and quality of the receipt remains unchanged but the simple and complete answer to this contention on behalf of the plaintiff is that the plaintiff did not sue. ...

Appeal dismissed.

NOTES AND QUESTIONS

1. On what words of what is now subsection 6(3) of the Act did Cattanach J rely to conclude that the facts in *Quance* "fall precisely within" the statutory provision? What was the obligation "on account, in lieu of payment or in satisfaction of" that the payments were deemed to remunerate under then section 25 (now subsection 6(3)) of the Act? How did Cattanach J respond to the taxpayer's argument that an amount paid as damages for breach of a contract of employment is not taxable?

2. *Quance* was followed in *Bye v. M.N.R.*, [1975] C.T.C. 2039, 75 D.T.C. 33 (T.R.B.), where the taxpayer, a teacher who was dismissed when her school was closed, received a lump-sum payment after a court held that her employment was properly terminated only two years after her dismissal. Finding (at para. 24) that "the School Board at no time effectively terminated this teacher's employment in 1970, and therefore from that date until the legal termination of her position in January of 1972 she never ceased to be an employee," the board concluded that "the sum received was income from employment." *Quance* was distinguished in *Pollard v. M.N.R.*, [1975] C.T.C. 2094, 75 D.T.C. 79 (T.R.B.), where the taxpayer received $6,500 in settlement of all claims arising from his dismissal in 1972. On the basis that the payment was for wrongful dismissal without cause, the board held (at para. 32) that the payment was a non-taxable "capital receipt."

3. In *Canada v. Atkins*, [1975] F.C.J. No. 509, [1975] C.T.C. 377, 75 D.T.C. 5263 (F.C.T.D.), the taxpayer received $18,000 in settlement of all claims related to the termination of his employment in October 1970. Distinguishing *Quance* on the grounds that the taxpayer in that case had received "continuing payments (at the same periods of time, for the same semi-monthly amounts... as before)" that were subsequently accepted without any exchange of releases or written agreement in respect of the monies received, the court characterized the severance payment as a non-taxable damage payment. According to Collier J (at para. 26):

> I agree with the ultimate result in the *Quance* case: that on the particular facts the moneys paid were salary, and became taxable as such. The facts before me are quite different. There is no evidence that the sum of $18,000 was intended by the employer or by the defendant to represent salary purely and simply, or that other factors deserving of compensation in damages were not included.

The court also rejected the Minister's further argument that the payment was subject to then section 25 (now subsection 6(3)), concluding that the payment was not "on account, in lieu of payment or in satisfaction of an obligation arising out of an agreement" but "in satisfaction of the breach of the employment contract and the right to damages that breach carried," and could not reasonably be regarded as having been received "in any of the qualities listed in subparagraphs (i), (ii), or (iii)" (now paragraph 6(3)(c), (d), or (e)).

On appeal ([1976] F.C.J. No. 411, [1976] C.T.C. 497, 76 D.T.C. 6258 (F.C.A.)), the Federal Court of Appeal affirmed the decision at the Trial Division. According to Jackett CJC (Pratte J and MacKay DJ concurring) (at paras. 3-4):

> Once it is conceded, as the appellant does, that the respondent was dismissed "without notice," moneys paid to him (pursuant to a subsequent agreement) "in lieu of notice of dismissal" cannot be regarded as "salary," "wages" or "remuneration" or as a benefit "received or enjoyed by him ... in respect of, in the course of, or by virtue of the office or employment." Moneys so paid (ie, "in lieu of notice of dismissal") are paid in respect of the "breach" of the contract of employment and are not paid as a benefit under the contract or in respect of the relationship that existed under the contract before that relationship was wrongfully terminated. The situation is not altered by the fact that such a payment is frequently referred to as so many months' "salary" in lieu of notice. Damages for breach of contract do not become "salary" because they are measured by reference to the salary that would have been payable if the relationship had not been terminated or because they are colloquially called "salary." The situation might well be different if an employee was dismissed by a proper notice and paid "salary" for the period of the notice even if the dismissed employee was not required to perform the normal duties of his position during that period. Having regard to what I have said, it is clear, in my view, that the learned trial judge was correct in holding that the payment in question did not fall within section 5 of the *Income Tax Act* as applicable to the taxation year in question.
>
> In so far as section 25 [now subsection 6(3)] is concerned, on the facts, it cannot be contended with any seriousness that the amount in question can reasonably be regarded as falling within paragraph (i), (ii) or (iii) of that section [now paragraph 6(3)(c), (d), or (e)].

With respect to the Minister's final argument that the payment should, as in *Curran*, [1959] S.C.J. No. 66, [1959] C.T.C. 416, 59 D.T.C. 1247 (S.C.C.), be taxable under section 3, the court stated (at para. 6):

> With reference to the further contention in this Court that the payment was income even if not income from an office or employment, this contention was based upon a line of cases which, in so far as relevant, held that remuneration for services is income. In my view, such authorities have no application to damages for wrongful dismissal.

Do you agree with the result in *Atkins*? Why or why not? For a critical comment on the decision, see Vern Krishna, "Characterization of Wrongful Dismissal Awards for Income Tax" (1977) 23 McGill L.J. 43.

4. *Atkins* was followed in a number of cases in which taxpayers were dismissed "without notice" and received payments "in lieu of notice" or in settlement of claims for wrongful dismissal. See, for example, *Burgess v. M.N.R.*, [1976] C.T.C. 2146, 76 D.T.C. 1119 (T.R.B.); *Grozelle v. M.N.R.*, [1977] C.T.C. 2432, 77 D.T.C. 310 (T.R.B.); *Krivy v. M.N.R.*, [1979] C.T.C. 2108, 79 D.T.C. 121 (T.R.B.); *Roy v. M.N.R.*, [1980] C.T.C. 2007, 80 D.T.C. 1005 (T.R.B.); *Beck v. M.N.R.*, [1980] C.T.C. 2851, 80 D.T.C. 1747 (T.R.B.); and *Brackstone v. M.N.R.*, [1980] C.T.C. 89, 80 D.T.C. 6060 (F.C.T.D.). In other cases, *Atkins* was distinguished on the basis that the taxpayer was not wrongfully dismissed but had been given adequate notice of termination — rendering the payments received salary within the meaning of subsection 5(1). See, for example, *Unaitis v. M.N.R.*, [1978] C.T.C. 2279 (T.R.B.); *Kok v.*

M.N.R., [1980] C.T.C. 2903, 80 D.T.C. 1762 (T.R.B.); and *Boychuk v. M.N.R.*, [1981] C.T.C. 2662, 81 D.T.C. 613 (T.R.B.).

5. In another series of cases, payments made on the termination of a taxpayer's employment were deemed to be remuneration under subsection 6(3) on the basis that they were received "on account, in lieu of payment or in satisfaction of an obligation arising out of an agreement made by the payer with the payee immediately ... after a period that the payee was ... in the employment of, the payer" and could reasonably be regarded as having been received "as remuneration or partial remuneration for services ... under the contract of employment." See *Love v. M.N.R.*, [1978] C.T.C. 2880, 78 D.T.C. 1630 (T.R.B.); *Gowling v. M.N.R.*, [1978] C.T.C. 2885, 78 D.T.C. 1624 (T.R.B.); and *Varin v. M.N.R.*, [1979] C.T.C. 2733, 79 D.T.C. 650 (T.R.B.).

Where a taxpayer agrees to a "covenant" about what the taxpayer "is, or is not, to do" on termination of an office or employment, payments received pursuant to this agreement are deemed to be remuneration under paragraphs 6(3)(b) and (e). See, for example, *Richstone v. Canada*, [1974] C.T.C. 155, 74 D.T.C. 6129 (F.C.A.) and *Mercier v. M.N.R.*, [1991] T.C.J. No. 908, [1992] 2 C.T.C. 2669, 92 D.T.C. 2306 (T.C.C.), where the "covenant" was a promise not to compete with the taxpayer's former employer. In *Galanov v. M.N.R.*, [1987] 2 C.T.C. 2353, 87 D.T.C. 647 (T.C.C.) the "covenant" was an agreement to repay a loan made by the employer to assist the taxpayer in purchasing a house.

6. In *Girouard v. Canada*, [1980] F.C.J. No. 137, [1980] C.T.C. 284, 80 D.T.C. 6205 (F.C.A.), the taxpayer entered into a five-year employment contract with a private hospital in Montreal (Villa Medica Inc.) that provided for liquidated damages of $30,000 in the event that he was dismissed without cause during the term of the contract. When his employment was terminated without cause, the hospital agreed to pay the $30,000 over a period of 24 months, provided that the taxpayer made no further claim against his former employer, undertook not to criticize the hospital or its staff, and further undertook not to work for another private hospital in Quebec for a period of two years. The taxpayer agreed to these terms on August 21, 1970.

Rejecting the Minister's argument that amounts received by the taxpayer pursuant to this agreement were remuneration under the deeming rule in then section 25 (now subsection 6(3)), the Federal Court of Appeal concluded that the payment could not reasonably be regarded as having been received as consideration for the taxpayer entering into the contract of employment, as remuneration under the contract of employment, or in consideration for a covenant with reference to what he was or was not to do after the termination of the employment. Referring to the taxpayer's covenants not to criticize the hospital or its staff and not to work for another private hospital in Quebec for a period of two years, Pratte J stated (at para. 8):

> it would seem that the circumstances contemplated by clause 25(iii) [now paragraph 6(3)(e)] have been fulfilled here. The matter is otherwise, however, if we look at all the evidence without giving undue importance to the "form" or "legal effect" of the agreement of August

21, 1970. It then appears, in my opinion, that the amount paid by Villa Medica Inc. cannot be reasonably regarded as having been received in consideration or partial consideration for appellant's undertaking not to work in a private hospital and not to criticize his former employer. Before the contract of August 21, 1970 was entered into Villa Medica Inc, which had just dismissed appellant, already owed him (and admitted owing him) the sum of $30,000 which it had undertaken to pay him as liquidated damages; and he was subsequently paid the $5,000 in question here in partial performance of this obligation. In other words, appellant in fact undertook not to criticize his former employer and not to work for another private hospital in Quebec, but in my opinion the evidence established that the sum of $30,000 promised by Villa Medica Inc did not constitute the consideration for this undertaking.

7.   In *obiter* comments in *Jack Cewe Ltd. v. Jorgenson*, [1980] S.C.J. No. 24, [1980] C.T.C. 314, 80 D.T.C. 6233 (S.C.C.), a case involving compensation for wrongful dismissal, the Supreme Court of Canada (at paras. 3-5) expressed "grave doubt" as to the validity of the reasoning in *Canada v. Atkins*, [1975] F.C.J. No. 509, [1975] C.T.C. 377, 75 D.T.C. 5263 (F.C.T.D.):

Damages payable in respect of the breach of a contract of employment are certainly due only by virtue of this contract. ... They clearly have no other source. ...

The basic principle governing the award of damages for breach of contract is that "the party complaining should, so far as it can be done by money, be placed in the same position as he would have been in if the contract had been performed." I fail to see any reason why this would not hold true towards the tax collector as well as towards the parties to the contract. ...

In my view, the present situation with respect to income tax on this award of "an identifiable sum for loss of earnings" must be considered legally insecure. This Court might well disagree with the conclusion reached by the Federal Court of Appeal in *Atkins*. In this respect, I will note that in that case consideration appears to have been given only to the question whether the damages for wrongful dismissal were income "from an office or employment" within the meaning of sections 5 and 25 of the *Income Tax Act* (RSC 1952) [now subsections 5(1), 6(1), and 6(3)]. No consideration appears to have been given to the broader question whether they might not be income from an unspecified source under the general provision of section 3.

After concluding that amounts received by the taxpayer constituted reasonable notice, the board in *Kok v. M.N.R.*, [1980] C.T.C. 2903, 80 D.T.C. 1762 (T.R.B.), cited the Supreme Court of Canada's *obiter* comments in *Jack Cewe Ltd.* as further grounds for including the payments in computing the taxpayer's income. According to the L.-J. L. Cardin, QC (at paras. 24-27):

The principles enunciated by the Supreme Court in the *Cewe (supra)* case, facilitate my decision in the instant appeal by inviting the courts to consider not only whether the damages for wrongful dismissal were income "from an office or employment" but to consider the broader question as to whether the income might not be from an unspecified source under general provisions of section 3 of the *Income Tax Act* ... .

Although there did exist at one time an employer/employee relationship between the appellant and the employer, whatever hesitation I may have had in concluding that the amount of $6,128.55 received by the appellant after he had been dismissed from office was income from employment, completely disappears when section 3 of the Act is considered in conjunction with subsection 6(3) of the *Income Tax Act* ... .

In my opinion, on the basis of the Supreme Court decision in the *Cewe* case, I would have to arrive at the same conclusion, whether I found that the amount received by the appellant was income from employment and had been paid in lieu of notice or received as damages for wrongful dismissal since in each instance the payments constitute income from an unspecified source but directly related to the taxpayer's employment.

8.   In *Canada v. Pollock*, [1984] C.T.C. 353, 84 D.T.C. 6370 (F.C.A.), the Minister argued that amounts received in settlement of a claim for wrongful dismissal should be included in computing the taxpayer's income pursuant to the Supreme Court of Canada's *obiter* comments in *Jack Cewe Ltd. v. Jorgenson*, [1980] S.C.J. No. 24, [1980] C.T.C. 314, 80 D.T.C. 6233 (S.C.C.). Rejecting this invitation to reconsider its prior decision in *Canada v. Atkins*, [1975] F.C.J. No. 509, [1975] C.T.C. 377, 75 D.T.C. 5263 (F.C.T.D.), the Federal Court of Appeal stated (at para. 2):

> While we do not doubt that this Court has the power to reconsider and refuse to follow one of its past decisions, we are of opinion that we should do so only when we are convinced that our previous decision was wrong. Here, ... we do not have that conviction.

9.   The Act was amended in 1978 to include "termination payments" as defined in subsection 248(1) in computing a taxpayer's income under subparagraph 56(1)(a)(viii). In 1981, these provisions were repealed and the Act was amended to add amounts received "in respect of the loss of an office or employment of a taxpayer" to the definition of a "retiring allowance" that must be included in computing a taxpayer's income under subparagraph 56(1)(a)(ii). These provisions are considered in Chapter 7.

10.   In several cases, taxpayers have entered into consulting agreements with former employers as part of an agreement that provides for their termination. Even though the taxpayer may provide no actual services and the parties may have intended that no services be provided, these payments are generally characterized as income from an office or employment. See, for example, *Bell v. M.N.R.*, [1962] C.T.C. 253, 62 D.T.C. 1155 (Ex. Ct.); *Smith v. M.N.R.* (1966), 41 Tax ABC 328; *M.N.R. v. Pannell*, [1973] C.T.C. 81, 73 D.T.C. 5038 (F.C.T.D.); and *Mountjoy v. M.N.R.*, [1979] C.T.C. 2232, 79 D.T.C. 250 (T.R.B.). Occasionally, however, amounts described as remuneration for continuing services are characterized as capital payments from the disposition of a business or shares on the basis that the written documents do not reflect the real agreement between the parties. See, for example, *M.N.R. v. Beaupré Estate*, [1973] C.T.C. 316, 73 D.T.C. 5255 (F.C.T.D.); *Gahrens v. Canada*, [1978] C.T.C. 651, 78 D.T.C. 6436 (F.C.T.D.); *Varga v. M.N.R.*, [1984] C.T.C. 2295, 84 D.T.C. 1278 (T.C.C.); and *Laperrière v. M.N.R.*, [1984] C.T.C. 2829, 84 D.T.C. 1650 (T.C.C.).

4. Tort Damages for Personal Injury or Death

Where a taxpayer receives tort damages for personal injury or death, this compensation typically includes special damages in respect of lost earnings. In *Cirella v. Canada*, [1978] C.T.C. 1, 77 D.T.C. 5442 (F.C.T.D.), the court addressed the taxation of these payments.

Cirella v. Canada
[1978] C.T.C. 1, 77 D.T.C. 5442 (F.C.T.D.)

THURLOW ACJ: The issue in this appeal is whether the plaintiff is liable for income tax in respect of an amount of $14,500, being part of a total amount of $34,400 awarded him by a judgment of the Supreme Court of Ontario in 1972 for damages for personal injuries sustained by him in a motor vehicle accident in 1968. The reasons for judgment indicate that the particular amount of $14,500 was awarded as special damages in respect of the plaintiff's loss of income for the period from the time of the injury to the end of 1971.

The plaintiff is a welder. At the time of the injury he was employed as such by a company known as "Indofab" and earning $108 per week. He went back to his employer after his recovery but, because of the permanent disability arising from his injuries, he was unable to do the heavy work involved in his job. Since then he has carried on a light welding business of his own. The precise date when the business was started is not clear; the evidence of the plaintiff being that it was in 1970 or 1971.

In reassessing the plaintiff for the 1972 taxation year, the Minister included the $14,500 in the plaintiff's income and his action in so doing was upheld by the Tax Review Board.

In support of the assessment, the defendant in the defence cited sections 3 and 9 of the *Income Tax Act*.... But as the evidence indicated that, prior to the injury, the plaintiff had been an employee of Indofab rather than engaged in carrying on his own business, counsel for the Crown also referred to and relied on subsection 5(1).

...

No case was cited, and I am not aware of any, in which the particular problem raised by this appeal, *viz*, the liability of a taxpayer for income tax in Canada in respect of special damages awarded for loss of income over a particular period of time resulting from the impairment of his earning capacity by personal injuries, has been decided. I was told by counsel for the plaintiff — without protest by counsel for the defendant — that such amounts have not heretofore been assessed. But whether that is so or not, the point was left open by the majority of the Supreme Court in *The Queen v. Jennings et al.*, [1966] SCR 532. There, Judson J. said at page 544:

> For what it is worth, my opinion is that an award of damages for impairment of earning capacity would not be taxable under the Canadian *Income Tax Act*. To the extent that an award includes an identifiable sum for loss of earnings up to the date of judgment the result might well be different. But I know of no decisions where these issues have been dealt with and until this has been done in proceedings in which the Minister of National Revenue is a party, any expression of opinion must be insecure....

The substance of the argument put forward by counsel for the defendant, as I understood it, was that the amount here in question was not damages for the loss of anything of a capital nature but was for loss of income for a particular period of time, that as such it replaced or compensated the plaintiff for income he would have earned and thus it should be brought into his income for tax purposes. He relied in particular on *London and Thames Haven Oil Wharves, Ltd. v. Attwooll*, [1967] 2 All ER 124, where an amount recovered for loss of use of a jetty for 380 days during repair following a collision by a ship with it was held to have been properly assessed as income, and *Raja's Commercial College v. Gian Singh & Co. Ltd.*, [1977] AC 312, where damages recovered for loss of the opportunity to earn a higher rent during a period in which tenants, who had been given notice to quit, overheld were considered to be assessable as income of the landlord.

I do not think the principle of these cases bears on the present situation. They were concerned with elements to be brought into account in computing the profits of businesses or properties where there had been a decrease or shortfall in the revenue, in the first case by damage done to an income-producing asset of the business and in the second by a tortious overholding of an income-producing property. In each case, the loss had been compensated for by the damages awarded. Here, there was no property in respect of which any loss arose and for any part of the period involved in the calculation of the damages here in question in which it might be concluded that the plaintiff was carrying on his newly-commenced business it cannot, in my view, be affirmed that there was any loss or shortfall of revenue of that business attributable to the tort for which he was compensated since the injuries had been incurred long before the business was commenced. I should add that I also doubt that the plaintiff could properly be regarded as an asset of his own business so as to treat damages recovered for personal injuries occasioned to him as filling a hole or shortfall of the revenue of the business resulting from his injury. In my view, therefore, the amount in question is not assessable in whole or in part as income of the plaintiff's business.

Nor do I think the amount can be regarded as income from employment. It was not salary or wages or a gratuity or other remuneration of employment, and it was not paid or received as such. [Compare *Canada v. Atkins*, [1976] F.C.J. No. 411, [1976] C.T.C. 497, 76 D.T.C. 6258 (F.C.A.).] It was not earned by working for or serving anyone. And it was not paid or received to induce the plaintiff to work for or serve anyone. [Compare *Curran v. M.N.R.*, [1959] S.C.R. 850, [1959] C.T.C. 416, 59 D.T.C. 1247 (S.C.C.).]

Moreover, in defining income from employment, the statute is very precise as to what is to be included, but nowhere does it specify that such an amount is to be included as such income.

There remains the question whether the amount is otherwise of an income nature so that it ought to be regarded as income from a source of income within the meaning of section 3. The wording of the judgment describes the amount in terms suggestive of income and calculates it in part on the basis of prospective income that, but for the injury, might have been earned. But the nature of the amount, as I see it, is determined not by that but by the nature of the award itself. What a court awards in personal injury cases is damages to compensate the injured person for the wrong done him. One of the elements frequently involved in such awards is the impairment of the earning capacity of the injured person resulting from his injuries and, in such cases, it is usual to assess the damages in respect thereof in two parts: one consisting of the loss up to the time of the judgment, which can generally be calculated with some approach to accuracy because the relevant events have already occurred; and the other, the loss for the future which can never be better than an informed and reasonable estimate. In both instances, however, they are for the same injury, the same impairment of earning power. There is but one tort and one impairment and, in my opinion, the damages therefor are all of the same nature.

The point is put thus in the 13th edition of *McGregor on Damages* at page 296:

> ...[I]t would seem that there is no "source" from which the amount given as damages can be said to come as income, for it represents not so much loss of earnings as the loss of future earning capacity, which is a capital value. Further... it would be fallacious to regard the special damages as taxable on the ground that they are loss of income and the general damages as not taxable on the ground that they are loss of a capital asset. For both are of the same nature, and it is only the accident of the time when the action is heard that will put a particular sum into the one category or the other. If the general damages for loss of future earning capacity are to be regarded as not taxable, then the same should be said in respect of the special damages, which in this case only represent a portion of the general damages for loss of earning capacity in a crystallised form. And indeed the plaintiff has not specifically earned, by working for them, the sums of damages awarded as special.

> ...

This view was followed by Gibbs, J in *Groves v. United Pacific Transport Pty Ltd. et al.*, [1965] Qd R 62 at 65:

> Although it is usual and convenient in an action for damages for personal injuries to say that an amount is awarded for loss of wages or other earnings, the damages are really awarded for the impairment of the plaintiff's earning capacity that has resulted from his injuries. This is so even if an amount is separately quantified and described as special damages for loss of earnings up to the time of trial. Damages for personal injuries are not rightly described as damages for loss of income.

Adopting, as I do, this view of the nature of the right of the plaintiff to the damages in question and having regard as well to the fact that they were in no sense earned or gained in the pursuit of any calling or trade or from property but arose from the injury done him, I am of the opinion that these damages are not of an income character and that the description of them in the judgment as damages for loss of income and the reasoning applicable thereto do not characterize the amount awarded as income but merely indicate the method by which a portion of the total award, which is of a capital rather than an income nature, was calculated. ...

Appeal allowed.

NOTES AND QUESTIONS

1.   On what grounds did the Minister argue that the special damages of $14,500 received by the taxpayer in *Cirella* should be included in computing his income? Why did the court in *Cirella* reject the Minister's arguments? On what basis did it distinguish the decisions in *London and Thames Haven Oil Wharves, Ltd. v. Attwooll*, [1967] 2 All E.R. 124, and *Raja's Commercial College v. Gian Singh & Co. Ltd.*, [1977] A.C. 312? Why did it conclude that the special damages were not income from the business carried on by the taxpayer after the injury? Why did it conclude that the special damages were not income from the employment in which the taxpayer was engaged prior to the injury? On what grounds did it conclude that the special damages were not income from a source within the meaning of paragraph 3(a)? Do you agree with the court's decision? Why or why not?

2.   If damages for the loss of income resulting from a personal injury are, as *McGregor on Damages* suggests, compensation for "loss of future earning capacity, which is a capital value," might these payments be characterized as "proceeds of disposition" within the meaning of the definition in section 54 of the Act? Can a person's earning capacity be characterized as "property" within the meaning of the definition in subsection 248(1)? If so, how should a gain or loss on the disposition or part disposition of this property be computed under subdivision c?

3.   *Cirella* was cited in *Kant v. Canada*, [2001] T.C.J. No. 257, [2001] 2 C.T.C. 2703 (T.C.C.), in which the taxpayer received a damage award of $490,000 after a motor vehicle accident left him permanently disabled and unable to work. Rejecting the Minister's argument that insurance benefits that were assigned to the defendant to prevent double recovery were taxable as benefits received under a "wage loss replacement plan" under paragraph 6(1)(f), the court concluded (at para. 25) that "[t]o include in taxable income an amount which goes to reduce the damages in effect is to tax damages which ... are not taxable."

4.   The CRA's views on the tax treatment of damages for personal injury or death are contained in *Interpretation Bulletin* IT-365R2, "Damages, Settlements and Similar Receipts," May 8, 1987. According to paragraph 2:

> Amounts in respect of damages for personal injury or death may be received by an injured taxpayer or by a dependant of a deceased taxpayer on account of:
>
> (a)   Special damages — examples are compensation for
>
>   (i)   out-of-pocket expenses such as medical and hospital expenses, and
>
>   (ii)   accrued or future loss of earnings and
>
> (b)   General damages — examples are compensation for
>
>   (i)   pain and suffering,

    (ii)   the loss of amenities of life,

    (iii) the loss of earning capacity,

    (iv) the shortened expectation of life and

    (v)   the loss of financial support caused by the death of the supporting individual.

> All amounts received by a taxpayer or the taxpayer's dependant, as the case may be, that qualify as special or general damages for personal injury or death will be excluded from income regardless of the fact that the amount of such damages may have been determined with reference to the loss of earnings of the taxpayer in respect of whom the damages were awarded. However, an amount which can reasonably be considered to be income from employment rather than an award of damages will not be excluded from income.

5.   Where a taxpayer suffers a personal injury or death while performing the duties of an office or employment, compensation is typically available under workers' compensation schemes, which generally bar any recovery in tort. Although such compensation is included in computing the recipient's net income under paragraph 56(1)(v) of the Act, an offsetting deduction is available under paragraph 110(1)(f) in computing the taxpayer's taxable income, effectively exempting these payments from tax. The tax treatment of workers' compensation payments is examined more fully in Chapter 7.

6.   Consider the policy implications of the non-taxation of workers' compensation payments and tort damages for personal injury or death. To the extent that the amount of these payments is determined on an after-tax basis, non-taxation does not increase the compensation paid to victims, but merely lessens the cost to employers, tortfeasors, and their insurers by enabling them to compensate victims on an after-tax basis. To the extent that employers and tortfeasors do not confront the full social costs of the accidents they may cause (which costs include lost tax revenues), economic theory suggests that negligent behaviour may be inadequately deterred. In this light, is the non-taxation of workers' compensation and tort damages for personal injury or death sound public policy? For a critical analysis of the policy rationales for non-taxation of personal injury damages see Tamara Larre, "Pity the Taxpayer: The Tax Exemption for Personal Injury Damages as Disability Policy" (2007) 33 Queen's L.J. 217-247.

5. Gratuitous Payments

In addition to "salary" and "wages," subsection 5(1) requires taxpayers to include "gratuities" in computing their income from an office or employment. Notwithstanding this language, taxpayers have often argued that gratuitous payments ought not to be included in computing their income from an office or employment on the basis that the payment was a gift or windfall, not remuneration for services provided within the scope of the taxpayer's office or employment. Although decided under the *Income War Tax Act*, *Goldman v.*

M.N.R., [1953] S.C.J. No. 7, [1953] C.T.C. 95, 53 D.T.C. 1096 (S.C.C.) remains the leading Canadian case on the characterization of gratuitous payments received in respect of a taxpayer's office or employment.

Goldman v. M.N.R.
[1953] S.C.J. No. 7, [1953] C.T.C. 95, 53 D.T.C. 1096 (S.C.C.)

KELLOCK J (Rinfret CJC and Locke and Fauteux JJ concurring): The facts found by the learned trial judge are essentially as follows: The appellant was active with two others in the formation of a committee of shareholders of a company then in receivership, and became its chairman. Shareholders of other classes, as well as bondholders, had also formed other committees. The reorganization of the company was, at this time, being attempted through the instrumentality of a negotiating committee appointed by the provincial government, and, ultimately, a scheme of arrangement was agreed upon.

The appellant had nominated a Mr. Black to be counsel for the shareholders' committee of which he was chairman, and the former was duly appointed and acted in that capacity throughout.

When the negotiation of a plan of reorganization was nearing its final stage, at a meeting of all the committees with the government committee, the appellant raised the question of remuneration for committee members. According to the evidence of Mr. Black, the chairman of the negotiating committee said that it had been understood throughout that there would be no remuneration for committee members "as such" but that counsel fees should be on a scale that the committees "could get something." After this meeting Mr. Black said to the appellant that while he did not like this arrangement, he was prepared to follow it out and see that, in that way, the appellant's committee did get something. Nothing was then said as to amount.

The scheme of arrangement provided that the company should pay the "costs and expenses" of the committees, but "not including any remuneration to the members of the said committees as such."

...

In a conversation between the solicitor for another shareholders' committee and Mr. Black, the subject of fees came up. The latter said he would be satisfied with $5,000 for himself, whereupon the other solicitor said that he would recommend that the bondholders' committee approve of $10,000, so as to provide $5,000 for the appellant's committee. According to Black, the appellant, on learning of this, was critical of Black for mentioning what the appellant regarded as a small amount, and Black was instructed to ask for $50,000.

The bondholders' committee refused to go beyond $8,000, which would have left $3,000 only for the appellant's committee and this was not acceptable to the appellant. At the appellant's insistence, Black then prepared a bill of costs for $75,000 for the purposes of taxation under the scheme. The appellant attended with Black on the taxation, on which occasion Black explained that the bill was not only for legal fees but also remuneration for the committee. In view of the terms of the scheme, however, the taxing officer could not and did not allow anything beyond legal fees. The bill was taxed at $20,000 plus some small disbursements. The appellant, pleased with the result, told Black he was going to tell his committee that Black's fee should be $6,000 instead of $5,000 and this was done.

Subsequently, it was arranged, with the approval of the department, that the amount taxed should be paid in three annual instalments, as the reorganization had occupied some three years. Upon the appellant stating to Black that he wanted his money assigned to him, Black assigned to the appellant the last two annual instalments amounting to $7,000 each. It is the first of these which is in question here. The appellant has taken the position that the amount was a gift to him and not taxable.

...

On the facts as found by the learned trial judge the inferences I think are plain. The appellant throughout his activity on the committee intended to be paid for his services if he could succeed in so doing. It has been already noted that the scheme of arrangement did not completely eliminate the possibility of the members of the committees being remunerated, but excludes direct payment to them for remuneration "as such." It was solely at the insistence of the appellant and for his benefit, that the taxation proceeded, and on this basis of the agreement between Black and the appellant that Black was to have no interest in any monies beyond the $6,000 which he had agreed to take.

The appellant having succeeded in obtaining the remuneration he set out to obtain, and which he has kept for himself, I do not consider that the form by which that result was brought about is important nor that if there be any illegality attaching to the agreement to divide the taxed costs, this can avail the appellant. What the appellant received, he received as remuneration as he intended. Mr. Stikeman admits that had the offer of the bondholders to approve payment of $8,000 been accepted, the $3,000 which would thereby have found its way to the appellant would have been taxable in the hands of the latter as remuneration. In my view the mere interposition of the certificate of taxation does not change the character of that which the appellant actually received.

"Income" is defined by Section 3(1) of the statute to mean, *inter alia*:

> ... the annual net profit or gain or gratuity, whether ascertained and capable of computation as being ... salary ...

Subsection (4) provides that:

> Any payment made to any person in connection with any duty, office or employment ... shall be salary of such person and taxable as income for the purposes of this Act.

In *Herbert v. McQuade*, [1902] 2 KB 631, the question for consideration arose under Schedule E, of the *Income Tax Act, 1842*, which imposed tax on "the persons respectively having, using or exercising the offices or employments of profit" in Schedule E for "all ... profits whatsoever accruing by reason of such offices, (or) employments..." Collins MR, at p. 649, referring to an earlier decision said that:

> a payment may be liable to income tax although it is voluntary on the part of the persons who made it, and that the test is whether, from the standpoint of the person who receives it, it accrues to him in virtue of his office; if it does, it does not matter whether it was voluntary or whether it was compulsory on the part of the persons who paid it.

In my view this reasoning is equally applicable to payments made to a person "in connection with" an office or employment. In the case at bar it is perfectly clear that the payment in question was made in connection with the appellant's office as chairman and as remuneration therefor.

In *Seymour v. Reed*, [1927] AC 554, Viscount Cave LC, at 599, stated the principle to be that the language of Schedule E rendered taxable:

> all payments made to the holder of an office or employment as such, that is to say, by way of remuneration for his services, even though such payments may be voluntary, but that they do not include a mere gift or a present (such as a testimonial) which is made to him on personal grounds and not by way of payment for his services.

In *Cowan v. Seymour*, [1920] 1 KB 500, it was held that a sum paid to the secretary of a company who had acted as liquidator in the voluntary winding-up without remuneration was not taxable income, the amount in question having been paid to him by the shareholders after the winding-up as a tribute or testimonial and not as payment for services.

In my opinion these authorities make it plain on which side of the line the amount received by the appellant in the case at bar falls. This was not received by him as a testimonial nor as anything but remuneration for the services which he had performed. That the services had been completed when payment was made or that there was no assurance from the beginning that the services would be remunerated do not prevent the amount in question being taxable income.

...

I would be, in any event, of the opinion that the payment here in question, being paid and received as remuneration, also falls within the words "the annual profit or gain from any other source" in Section 3, subsection (1), of the statute.

...

RAND J (concurring): ... That both parties intended the money to be paid and received as remuneration for services rendered by Goldman as committee chairman is not open to doubt. The solicitor became in fact a conduit between the company and Goldman. It was argued that the payment was voluntary. Apart from the question of a declared trust, it can be assumed that the solicitor was not legally bound to make the payment; but that he was bound by the common understanding, whatever it may be called or whatever its nature, is equally beyond doubt. He voluntarily undertook the obligation at least of his word given in an economic relation; but voluntariness of his consequent action is not to be confused with that present in gift. ...

Appeal dismissed.

NOTES AND QUESTIONS

1.   On what basis did the taxpayer in *Goldman* argue that the $7,000 payment at issue in the case was not taxable? Why did the court reject this argument?

2.   In *Mr. C v. M.N.R.* (1950), 2 Tax ABC 6 (T.A.B.), the taxpayer received $15,000 as an honorarium after serving on a provincial commission of inquiry. Rejecting the taxpayer's argument that the payment was a non-taxable gift, the board held that the payment was a "gratuity" within the meaning of then subsection 3(1) of the *Income War Tax Act* (now subsection 5(1) of the *Income Tax Act*).

3.   In *M.N.R. v. Gagnon*, [1965] C.T.C. 423, 65 D.T.C. 5268 (Ex. Ct.), the taxpayer, a principal clerk in the Dominion Bureau of Statistics, received an award of $170 under the Government of Canada Suggestion Award Plan Regulations after recommending "the use of IBM cards for the printing of the 'Street Index' for the Census Division of the DBS." Rejecting the taxpayer's argument that the payment was a non-taxable windfall, the Exchequer Court characterized the payment as remuneration for services within the meaning of subsection 5(1) (at para. 8):

> The short answer to the question as to the taxability of the award made to the respondent is to be found, in my view, in the determination of the character of all awards made under the Suggestion Award Plan Regulations. In my view, having regard to section 7 of the *Financial Administration Act*, all such awards must be "compensation or other rewards" for "suggestions or improvements." ... In my view, also, the creation, and formulation in usable form, of a suggestion for improvement in business or governmental operations, is a service of the kind that an employer may obtain either from officers or servants or from independent contractors (e.g. accountants, efficiency experts, etc.). It follows that, in my view, a payment for a suggestion is a payment for a service.

According to Jackett P (at para. 10):

> While there may be exceptions, I am of opinion that a payment for a service is ordinarily "income" from one of the recipient's "sources" within the meaning of those words in section 3 of the *Income Tax Act* whether the recipient receives the payment as an employee, as a person who operates a business of supplying services or as a person who has performed a service on an isolated occasion. ... Whether or not that view is too wide, there is no doubt in my mind that awards under the Suggestion Award Plan Regulations are income from an employment and fall within section 5 of the *Income Tax Act* because they are payable to employees of the Government of Canada for services performed for that Government. It is immaterial, in my view, that the particular services are not performed in the course of the execution of the normal duties of their positions. Parliament has expressly authorized awards as extra reward or compensation to be paid to public servants for services performed in addition to their normal duties. Such awards are, in my view, clearly within the words "other remuneration" in the introductory words of subsection (1) of section 5.

Gagnon was followed in *Dauphinée v. Canada*, [1980] C.T.C. 332, 80 D.T.C. 6267 (F.C.T.D.), where the taxpayer received $5,336.32 pursuant to regulations under the *Public Servants Inventions Act.* See also *Jarlan v. Canada*, [1984] C.T.C. 375, 84 D.T.C. 6452 (F.C.T.D.).

4.   Prizes and awards may also be included in computing a taxpayer's income from an office or employment as a benefit under paragraph 6(1)(a), which is considered later in this chapter. See, for example, *Offley v. M.N.R.*, [1974] C.T.C. 2139, 74 D.T.C. 1101 (T.R.B.) and *R. v. Savage*, [1983] S.C.J. No. 81, [1983] C.T.C. 393, 83 D.T.C. 5409 (S.C.C.). In addition, where a prize is not received in respect of an office or employment, the amount by which the prize exceeds $500 may be taxable under paragraph 56(1)(n), which is examined in Chapter 7.

5.   In *Kulka v. M.N.R.*, [1979] C.T.C. 2989, 79 D.T.C. 812 (T.R.B.), the taxpayer, a retired research chemist who continued to provide services to his former employer as a special consultant, received a $50,000 bonus in recognition of the "excellence and ingenuity" he demonstrated in carrying out his work. Rejecting the taxpayer's argument that the payment was a non-taxable prize or gift, the board held that the "voluntary payment" was taxable under the broad language of subsection 5(1).

6.   For other cases in which gratuitous payments on the termination of a taxpayer's office or employment have been characterized as remuneration from the office or employment, see *Buchanan v. M.N.R.*, [1966] C.T.C. 317, 66 D.T.C. 5257 (Ex. Ct.); *Fordham v. M.N.R.*, [1975] C.T.C. 2071, 75 D.T.C. 106 (T.R.B.); *Woodward v. M.N.R.*, [1978] C.T.C. 2385, 78 D.T.C. 1299 (T.R.B.); and *Denton v. M.N.R.*, [1981] C.T.C. 2358, 81 D.T.C. 313 (T.R.B.).

7.   As an alternative to taxation under section 5 or 6 of the Act, amounts that are received by a taxpayer (a) on or after retirement from an office or employment "in recognition of the taxpayer's long service" or (b) "in respect of a loss of an office or employment" may be taxable as a "retiring allowance" under subparagraph 56(1)(a)(ii). This provision is examined in Chapter 7.

8.   In *Heggie v. M.N.R.*, [1985] 1 C.T.C. 2417, 85 D.T.C. 357 (T.C.C.), the taxpayer received a gratuitous payment equivalent to his former salary for a period of five months after his employment as president and chief executive officer of a food-processing company was terminated when the shares of the company were sold to another company. On the basis that the payments were made by the purchaser, not the taxpayer's employer, the court rejected the Minister's argument that the payments were salary within the meaning of subsection 5(1). The court also rejected the Minister's alternative argument that the payment was a benefit within the meaning of paragraph 6(1)(a), reasoning (at para. 10) that "the appellant's anticipated unemployment rather than his prior employment" was "the real and proximate cause of the benefits he received."

Do you agree with this result? Might the payment now be taxable as a "retiring allowance" under subparagraph 56(1)(a)(ii)?

9.   In *Yaholnitsky-Smith v. M.N.R.*, [1991] T.C.J. No. 1125, [1992] 1 C.T.C. 2461 (T.C.C.), the taxpayer, a teacher in a Regina group home, received financial assistance from the charity that ran the group home (the Bosco Society)

in order to pursue an educational program at the Illinois School of Professional Psychology in Chicago. Although the taxpayer was not employed by the group home during the period of her studies, and was under no obligation to return to the group home after completing the program, the court (at para. 21) deemed the financial assistance to be remuneration under subsection 6(3) on the basis that:

> [t]he appellant has not established that the payments of money received by her in the taxation years under appeal cannot reasonably be regarded as having been received by her in consideration or partial consideration for her covenant to attend the institute in Illinois, such covenant, agreement and resulting obligation having been made before, during and immediately after the termination of her employment with Bosco.

Do you agree with this result? Why or why not?

10. In *Seary v. M.N.R.*, [1979] C.T.C. 2116, 79 D.T.C. 117 (T.R.B.), the taxpayer, who was denied tenure at the University of Toronto in 1973, received monthly payments of $1,000 (later $1,300) from the university after threatening legal action to reverse the decision in early 1975, and a lump-sum payment of $15,000 when tenure was ultimately granted in September 1975. Although the board held that the $15,000 payment was a taxable "gratuity" within the meaning of subsection 5(1), it concluded that the monthly payments were not taxable since the taxpayer held no office or employment at the time when they were paid. According to F.C. Dubrule, QC (at para. 9):

> The appellant was unemployed and had no contract with the University of Toronto when those monthly payments were received, as he had not had for some 20 months previously. ... If he had no employment or held no office for the year — How can be have income from the nonexistent office or employment?

Do you agree with this result? Might the monthly payments have been deemed to be remuneration under subsection 6(3)? Might they have been characterized as a taxable benefit received by the taxpayer "in respect of, in the course of or by virtue of an office or employment" within the meaning of paragraph 6(1)(a)? Might they have been characterized as income from an unspecified source under paragraph 3(a)?

6. Strike Pay

Unlike inducement payments, which are generally paid to employees as compensation for services to be rendered under the office or employment, strike pay provided by a union or affiliated organization is typically paid in respect of the *non-performance* of services by the employee. In *Canada v. Fries*, [1989] F.C.J. No. 407, [1989] 1 C.T.C. 471, 89 D.T.C. 5240 (F.C.A.), the Federal Court of Appeal referred to *Curran v. M.N.R.*, [1959] S.C.J. No. 66, [1959] C.T.C. 416, 59 D.T.C. 1247 (S.C.C.), to conclude that strike pay is taxable under paragraph 3(a) as income from an unspecified source. On appeal ([1990] S.C.J. No. 109, [1990] 2 C.T.C. 439 (S.C.C.)), the Supreme Court of Canada reversed the decision in a remarkably brief judgment, stating only:

> We are not satisfied that the payments by way of strike pay in this case come within the definition of "income ... from a source" within the meaning of section 3 of the *Income Tax Act.* In these circumstances the benefit of the doubt must go to the taxpayers.

The decision of the Federal Court of Appeal is reproduced below.

Canada v. Fries
[1989] F.C.J. No. 407, [1989] 1 C.T.C. 471, 89 D.T.C. 5240 (F.C.A.)

URIE JA (Hugessen and Desjardins JJA concurring): ... The appeal is from a judgment of Collier J in the Trial Division in which he allowed the appeal of the respondent from a decision of the Tax Review Board ("the Board") whereby the Board held that the assessment of the Minister of National Revenue ("the Minister"), taxing the payment of $880.80 to the appellant, by a union, as income received by him in the 1979 taxation year, was valid and properly levied.

It is not in dispute that the learned trial judge accurately summarized the facts as follows:

> The issue involves payment, by a union, of an amount of $880.80 to the defendant who was an employee of the Saskatchewan Liquor Board. He, and fellow employees, went out on a strike in support of other striking unionists. The $880.80 was equivalent to the defendant's normal net take home pay during the period he was on strike.
>
> In 1979, there existed, in Saskatchewan, a somewhat complicated organization in respect of employer-employee relationships with the provincial government, its various departments and other entities. The employees of forty-seven departments, boards, commissions or other agencies, controlled or operated by the Saskatchewan government, were divided into bargaining units. Among them was the Liquor Board. There were approximately 500 members in that bargaining unit. The largest bargaining unit of the Saskatchewan Government employees organization was the Public Service Bargaining Unit with roughly 12,000 members. Their employer was the Public Service Commission.
>
> All employees in the various bargaining units were members of the Saskatchewan Government Employees' Union (SGEU). That union had a Provincial Executive of twenty-eight members who came from twenty branches of the union. ...
>
> The collective agreement between the Public Service Commission and the Public Service Bargaining Unit had expired on October 1, 1979. On November 17, 1979, that unit went out on a legal strike.
>
> The collective agreement with the Liquor Board did not come up for renewal until March 1980.
>
> The evidence discloses that any contract, reached with the Public Service Bargaining Unit, usually became a flagship contract, setting the pattern for other agreements with other bargaining units, and other employers.
>
> The evidence indicates the negotiations, in what I will term the Public Service strike, were not proceeding satisfactorily from the union's point of view. It was decided to bring pressure on the employer to speed up negotiations and to try and obtain better offers. Meetings were held between representatives of the Provincial Executive of the SGEU and representatives of the bargaining unit of the Saskatchewan Liquor Board. The defendant, Fries, was chairman of the Liquor Board Branch of the union. The first meeting discussed "... the question of taking Liquor Board Branch members off the job to escalate the Public

279

Service/Government Employment strike." At a later meeting with the ... Advisory Committee of the Provincial Executive, Fries is said to have stated he was prepared:

> subject to a guarantee that members would be provided payloss for the days off the job and approval of the Executive of the Liquor Board Branch, to take a vote of the membership of the Liquor Board Branch on Saturday, November 24th regarding support for the Public Service/Government Employment Agreement group strike.

The above excerpts are taken from minutes attached to an Agreed Statement of Facts (Exhibit 2). At that stage, there was a recommendation by the Provincial Executive Advisory Committee that, if the Liquor Board union members went out in support, they be paid "pay loss for the duration of the time that they are out." The Provincial Executive adopted the minutes of the Advisory Committee.

The Liquor Board Branch employees voted in favour of a supporting strike. The members knew there would be a recommendation that they be reimbursed their full loss of pay. ...

From November 26, to December 17, 1979, a large number of Liquor Board employees, including the defendant, went on strike in support of the Public Service Bargaining Unit. ...

In the province of Saskatchewan, at that time, the strike by the Liquor Board employees was, in the circumstances, entirely legal, although their collective agreement with the Board did not expire until March 1980.

The defendant was paid the $880.80 out of the defence fund, or "strike fund," set up in the SGEU accounts. That fund, and other funds, came from union dues paid by the members, including the defendant.

The normal "strike stipend," the term used by the union, when any members were on strike, was usually $10 a week. ...

The evidence was that in other situations, the M.N.R. had never assessed any union members on the strike stipends received.

The learned trial judge, at trial, accepted the argument of counsel for Her Majesty that an enforceable contract existed between the SGEU and the individual members thereof employed by the Liquor Board.

...

It would appear that Collier J made his finding as to the existence of the contract largely because that was the way that the case was argued before him for the reason that will shortly appear. More importantly, he held that the payments were income in nature within the meaning of paragraph 3(a) of the *Income Tax Act* ("the Act").

...

Counsel for the appellant's primary contention was that the payment to the appellant was a strike benefit and strike benefits paid by a union to its members are not income for the purposes of the Act and, therefore, are not taxable. She conceded that nothing in the Act exempts them from being included in taxable income but pointed to Interpretation Bulletin IT-334R as indicating the Minister's administrative position with respect to strike benefits. Paragraph 3 of the Bulletin reads as follows:

Payments Received by Union Members

3.   Financial assistance paid by a union to its members during the course of a strike is not necessarily income of the member for the purposes of the Act. Such amounts, when received by a member, will be taxable if they are received as a consequence of the member being an employee of the union. Where union members receive funds that originated, or will originate, from the operation of a business by the union, the amounts will be treated as income subject to tax regardless of whether or not the receiving members participated in the business activity. Similarly, any amounts are taxable which are received by a taxpayer who is employed by or a consultant to a union, either permanently or as a member of a temporary committee, or who has withdrawn his services from his employer and has agreed to provide services, pursuant to an employment contract, to the union.

It was apparently to counter the effect of this Bulletin that counsel for the respondent endeavoured, successfully, to persuade the trial judge that the appellant and his union had entered into a contract whereby Mr. Fries would perform some sort of service on behalf of the union which would make the payment received for such service taxable in his hands. It was not necessary, in our view, to make such a finding for two reasons. First, as already noted, there is nothing in the Act which exempts strike pay, in its strictest sense, from taxability. Secondly, while administrative policy as set out in Interpretation Bulletins is "entitled to weight and can be 'an important factor' in case of doubt about the meaning of legislation" [*Nowegijick v. The Queen*, [1983] CTC 20, at 24 (SCC)], it cannot be determinative. Such doubt cannot exist in this case since there is no applicable legislation possibly giving rise to doubt. The Act does not provide specifically for the exclusion of strike benefits from taxation although administratively the Minister, apparently, does not usually assess tax thereon. That this is so does not mean that strike pay is not taxable. If, as here, he decides to assess, the person contesting such assessment must show that the benefits or pay he receives is not income in his hands within the meaning of that word in the Act. He cannot rely simply on past administrative practice as the foundation for his claim for exemption of such benefits from tax.

The nature of the word "income" as used in the Act was, as pointed out by Collier J, considered by the Supreme Court of Canada in *Curran v. M.N.R.*, [1959] SCR 850; [1959] CTC 416, where it was held by three of the members of the panel that [CTC 421]:

The word must receive its ordinary meaning bearing in mind the distinction between capital and income and the ordinary concepts and usages of mankind.

The trial judge on this basis made this finding [1986] 1 CTC at page 10:

In my view, where amounts, in this case money, are received by a person for his or her own benefit, those amounts, generally speaking, must be considered either as a receipt of a capital nature or as an income receipt. I know of no other categories; all tax cases appear to place such receipts in either one category or the other, unless, perhaps, the amounts are some kind of mere reimbursement. Gifts may, perhaps, be in a separate category — a kind of no-man's land.

In the circumstances of the present case, when applying the ordinary concept and usage of the word "income," I cannot conceive the monies received as being anything else but a receipt of income as opposed to a capital payment. They were neither a gift nor a windfall, nor payment for an asset or benefit of a permanent or semi-permanent nature. On the contrary, they were directly and solely related to the length of time over which the defendant payee acted (or refused to act) and the time during which the payor benefited from what the payee agreed to do.

The defendant, and his compatriots, received amounts similar to those normally received from their employer. The monetary calculation was based on their usual salaries. During the period in issue, the stipend amounts were paid from a new source, other than the employer. The Liquor Board employees exercised their then right to provide or withdraw their services to or from their employer, for tactical purposes, in union vs. management strategies.

While the test is not: if it is not capital, then it must inevitably be income, the amounts here received smack of income, rather than something else.

We agree that Mr. Justice Collier has accurately and succinctly demonstrated that the amounts paid to the appellant and others like him by his union are income in nature within the meaning of paragraph 3(a) of the Act, provided that the income is from a source inside or outside Canada. Among the possible sources is income from each office, employment, business and property but the source clearly is not confined to the specific enumerated sources.

The source of the payments in this case was from the "defence fund" or the strike fund set up by the union from the dues paid to it by its members. Those dues, which, according to the evidence, were deducted at source monthly from the members' wages, were paid at the rate of 1.2 per cent per month. The money received was then divided into three separate funds, namely (a) an operational account for the day to day operations of the union, (b) a defence fund which was accumulated by deducting from the monthly dues paid by each the sum of $1.50, and (c) a contingency fund. The annual dues paid by each member are deductible in the calculation of his or her taxable income [see subparagraph 8(1)(i)(iv), which is examined later in this chapter]. The gross income derived from such is not taxable in the hands of the union by virtue of paragraph 149(1)(k) of the Act.

The appellant submitted that the source of funds available for strike benefits is the members' income from their employment. There is, in counsel's submission, no new source. She analogized this situation to one in which each individual member might set up, by deductions from his income, his or her own personal strike fund. In such event, she said, withdrawals made by such person during a strike would not be taxable because they would be simply a return of that person's own money upon which he or she had already paid tax.

We do not agree that this is any way analogous to what was done here if only because personally compiled strike benefits would be paid only until the special fund was exhausted whereas, in the case of payments from a union's strike fund, they would be made for the duration of the strike or until the union executive decided to terminate the payments for whatever reason. However, the real difference, as the evidence clearly discloses, is that as soon as the dues are received by the union they go into a common fund which is divided in the manner earlier described, with no right of withdrawal by the paying members. The funds derived from such dues have completely lost their identity so far as each contributing member is concerned. The members have lost all control over them and their disposition is solely determined by the union, presumably through its executive. They, thus, provided the source of the income of the appellant's strike pay as the learned trial judge found. It is again, a conclusion with which we agree. Since, under the Act, such payments are income, they become subject to tax and assessment therefor. There is no basis, therefore, upon which the appellant can found his appeal.

Accordingly, the appeal will be dismissed with costs.

Appeal dismissed.

NOTES AND QUESTIONS

1.   On what grounds had the trial judge held that the taxpayer in *Fries* was taxable on the strike pay received in 1979? Why had the Minister argued that an enforceable contract had been entered into between the taxpayer and the Saskatchewan Government Employees' Union (SGEU)?

2.   On what basis did the Federal Court of Appeal conclude that the strike pay at issue in *Fries* should be included in computing the taxpayer's income? Why did the payment have the character of income? What, according to the court, was the source of the payment?

3.   How did the Federal Court of Appeal in *Fries* respond to the taxpayer's argument that taxation of strike pay was contrary to the revenue authority's stated administrative position that "[f]inancial assistance paid by a union to its members during the course of a strike is not necessarily income for the member for the purposes of the Act"? Do you agree with the court's response? Why or why not?

4.   In the trial decision in *Fries*, Collier J noted that the taxation of strike pay "was in fact raised, but never actually dealt with, when amendments to the *Income Tax Act* were enacted" in 1972. According to *Income Taxation in Canada*, Vol. II, looseleaf (Toronto: Prentice-Hall Canada) at para. 26,460:

> Strike pay is an anomaly. The amounts (union dues) from which strike pay is paid are fully deductible in the hands of employees, as are, for example, unemployment insurance premiums. By contrast, however, unemployment insurance benefits are taxed. On the assumption that strikes are voluntary and unemployment is involuntary, if there was to be an exception, one would have thought it might be unemployment benefits that were exempt. This anomaly, clearly, occurred at the cabinet table, as the first tax reform bill showed "strike pay" as a marginal note for amounts to be included in income, but without the corresponding legal language.

Does this legislative history suggest an intention to exclude strike pay from income? Is it relevant that the Act does not specifically exclude strike pay, or allow a deduction for these payments as it does for social assistance payments and workers' compensation under paragraph 110(1)(f)?

5.   On what basis did the Supreme Court of Canada reverse the decision of the Federal Court of Appeal in *Fries*? Is the court's approach consistent with the narrow limits subsequently placed on the residual presumption in favour of the

taxpayer in *Quebec (Communaute Urbaine) v. Corp Notre Dame De Bon Secours*, [1994] S.C.J. No. 78, [1995] 1 C.T.C. 241, 95 D.T.C. 5017 (S.C.C.) (as discussed in Chapter 2 in the section on Strict Construction)?

6.   Do you agree with the decision of the Supreme Court of Canada or the Federal Court of Appeal in *Fries*? Of what, if any, relevance is the fact that the taxpayer and other striking Saskatchewan Liquor Board employees "received amounts similar to those normally received from their employer"? Of what, if any, significance are the facts that labour organizations are exempt from tax under paragraph 149(1)(k) and union dues are deductible in computing a taxpayer's income from an office or employment under subparagraph 8(1)(i)(iv)? Might strike pay be characterized as a gift?

7.   In *Loeb v. Canada*, [1978] C.T.C. 56, 78 D.T.C. 6118 (F.C.T.D.), aff'd [1978] C.T.C. 460, 78 D.T.C. 6331 (F.C.A.), the taxpayer received $786.56 under a contract of employment with her teacher's federation, which was entered into in anticipation of a strike by Ottawa secondary school teachers and designed to enable teachers to continue making contributions to the teachers' pension fund as permitted under the *Teachers' Superannuation Act*, R.S.O. 1970, c. 455. Rejecting the taxpayer's argument that the arrangement was a sham without legal substance, the court held that the parties had created a *bona fide* legal relationship and that the payment was deemed to be employment income under subsection 6(3).

8.   In *Ferris v. M.N.R.*, [1977] C.T.C. 2034, 77 D.T.C. 17 (T.R.B.), the taxpayer was a member of a union that, together with other unions representing the employees of a Victoria publishing company, published a newspaper during the course of a labour dispute with the employer, distributing the profits from this enterprise as strike pay in accordance with a formula established by the union. Dismissing the taxpayer's appeal from an assessment including strike pay as taxable income, the board accepted the Minister's argument that the payments were income from a business venture. According to A.W. Prociuk, QC (at para. 15):

> I do not think that placing the taxable income from a commercial venture within the four walls of a union and then getting it back by way of a distribution pursuant to a certain formula, renders it tax-exempt. The form cannot change the substance.

For an opposing result, see *Canada v. O'Brien*, [1985] 1 C.T.C. 285, 85 D.T.C. 5202 (F.C.T.D.), where unions representing the employees of a Vancouver newspaper also published their own newspaper during the course of a labour dispute, distributing the profits as strike pay. Distinguishing *Ferris*, the court rejected the Minister's contention (at para. 24) that "the joint council which was operating the newspaper was merely an agent for all the individual union members who were joint venturers or independent contractors." According to Walsh J (at paras. 29-30):

> If this were simply a flow-through from profits of the newspaper to the individual members of the unions through the intermediary of the unions themselves, this conclusion could be

accepted, but as has been indicated, dealing with the facts is far more complex than that. Not only were not all of the profits distributed, but part of this distribution, although admittedly a small part, came from other sources (donations and contributions from other unions), and the individuals taxed had no right to claim them and were dependent on the unions themselves with respect to the amounts of such profits so distributed. As indicated I cannot accept the argument that the newspaper was being operated by the 1400-odd members of the union, most of whom did not even work on it but merely carried out union strike duties. It was operated by the unions themselves as appears from the masthead of the paper. They were certainly doing this for the benefit of their members but not as agents of them or under their direction.

Admittedly this conclusion hardly seems fair to the Department of National Revenue. By virtue of paragraph 149(1)(k) the unions who were actually operating the newspaper for the joint council are exempt from tax, and by virtue of the judgment herein, individual members of the union who received most of the profits from the operation are also exempt from tax, not being found to be individuals engaged in a business. As a result, the profits of a highly successful business remain tax exempt. The remedy may well lie in an amendment to the Act ... to deal with this problem, but as the law now stands I must maintain the appeals and refer the assessments of each of the plaintiffs herein back to the Minister for reassessment on the basis that supplemental strike benefits are not taxable.

Notwithstanding this statement, the *Income Tax Act* has not been amended to address the payment of strike pay in these or other circumstances.

9.   In the trial decision in *Canada v. Fries*, [1989] F.C.J. No. 407, [1989] 1 C.T.C. 471, 89 D.T.C. 5240 (F.C.A.), Collier J suggested that "Parliament should stipulate whether or not ordinary strike pay and any supplementary or extraordinary strike benefits should or should not be taxable." Do you agree? Why or why not? For a comparative analysis of the tax treatment of strike pay in several countries and recommendations for reform in Canada, see Benjamin Alarie and Matthew Sudak, "The Taxation of Strike Pay" (2006) 54 Can. Tax J. 426-449.

10.   For the CRA's current position on the tax treatment of strike pay, see *Interpretation Bulletin* IT-334R2, "Miscellaneous Receipts," February 21, 1992 at paragraph 12:

A member of a union who is on strike or locked out need not include in income payments of the type commonly referred to as "strike pay" that are received from his or her union, even if the member performs picketing duties as a requirement of membership. In the decision of the Supreme Court of Canada in *Wally Fries v. The Queen*, [1990] 2 CTC 439, 90 DTC 6662, payments by way of strike pay were held not to be "income from a source." On the other hand, payments made by a union to its members for services performed during the course of a strike are included in income if the member is employed by or is a consultant to the union whether permanently, as a member of a temporary committee or in some other capacity. Regular salary, wages and benefits received by employees of unions are subject to tax in the usual manner.

B. Benefits

In computing a taxpayer's income from an office or employment, paragraph 6(1)(a) includes, subject to various exceptions, "the value of board, lodging and other benefits of any kind whatever received or enjoyed by the taxpayer in the year in respect of, in the course of, or by virtue of an office or employment." Other provisions specify particular amounts that must be included in computing an individual's income from an office or employment in respect of specific kinds of benefits. The following cases and commentary examine the taxation of these benefits, looking first at the general rule in paragraph 6(1)(a) and then at specific rules applicable to particular kinds of benefits.

1. General Rule

Subject to a number of exceptions which need not be examined in detail,[30] paragraph 6(1)(a) applies where a "benefit" is received or enjoyed by a taxpayer "in respect of, in the course of, or by virtue of an office or employment" — in which case the "value" of the benefit must be included in computing the taxpayer's income from the office or employment. As a result, assuming that the benefit is not subject to one of the statutory exceptions, the application of paragraph 6(1)(a) involves three steps: (1) the characterization of a benefit, (2) the determination of a relationship between the benefit and the taxpayer's employment, and (3) the valuation of the benefit to be included in computing the taxpayer's income.

a. Characterization as Benefit

Although paragraph 6(1)(a) refers to "board" and "lodging" as specific kinds of benefits, the value of which may be included in computing a taxpayer's employment income, it also includes the value of "other benefits of any kind whatever," provided that they are received or enjoyed by the taxpayer in respect of, in the course of, or by virtue of an office or employment. In many cases, therefore, the first issue in applying paragraph 6(1)(a) involves the characterization of a benefit within the meaning of the statutory provision. A useful discussion of this characterization issue appears in *Lowe v. Canada*, [1996] F.C.J. No. 319, [1996] 2 C.T.C. 33, 96 D.T.C. 6226 (F.C.A.).

---

[30] Subparagraphs 6(1)(a)(i) to (v) create exceptions for three categories of benefits: (1) benefits involving various kinds of deferred income arrangements (registered pension plans, supplementary unemployment benefit plans, deferred profit-sharing plans, retirement compensation arrangements, employee benefit plans, employee trusts, and salary deferral arrangements) in respect of which amounts are included in computing a taxpayer's income elsewhere in s. 6 or under subs. 56(1); (2) other benefits, involving sickness or accident insurance, group term life insurance, or the use of an employer-provided vehicle, which are subject to special rules elsewhere in s. 6; and (3) benefits derived from an employer's contributions to a private health services plan or from specific categories of counselling services, which are exempt from tax.

Lowe v. Canada
[1996] F.C.J. No. 319, [1996] 2 C.T.C. 33, 96 D.T.C. 6226 (F.C.A.)

STONE JA (Strayer and Décary JJA concurring): This appeal from a judgment of the Tax Court of Canada arises out of an assessment of the appellant's income for the taxation year 1990, which included a portion of the cost of an expense-paid trip taken by the appellant and his wife to New Orleans on the basis that the appellant received in that year a taxable "benefit" under paragraph 6(1)(a) of the *Income Tax Act...* .

At all material times, the appellant was an account executive in the London, Ontario office of the Wellington Insurance Company and as such had responsibility for maintaining and developing relationships with independent insurance brokers and encouraging them to sell general insurance including home, auto and business policies. As Wellington had no sales force of its own, it relied on independent brokers who also sold the insurance of its competitors. According to the evidence at trial, all general insurers sell the same basic coverage. The appellant's job, therefore, was to promote his employer's insurance to the independent brokers and to create smooth relationships with them.

In 1989, Wellington brought out a broker incentive plan for its Ontario region, the purpose of which is described by the learned Tax Court Judge, at page 3 of his reasons:

> The program was a tool which account executives, such as Lowe, used to generate business for Wellington. Brokers who sold new business were awarded points and, upon achieving a certain quota, were eligible for a trip for two to New Orleans on the incentive program. In most, if not all, cases, the owner of the brokerage and his or her spouse would take the trip. During 1989, the brokers would have received brochures from Wellington detailing the trip and advertising the benefits awaiting the winners of the trip. Account executives, such as Lowe, would encourage the brokers during the year to purchase Wellington products.

The appellant and his wife attended at New Orleans with the successful brokers at the request of his employer and at the employer's expense. The expenses totalled $4,706 or $2,353 per person. In assessing the appellant, the Minister assumed, among other things, that the business portion of the cost of the trip "was no greater than 38% for the appellant, and no greater than 25% for his spouse," calculated as follows:

Hours

    total hours calculated as eight hours per day for 3 days = 24 hours
    4 hours were spent on formal business matters
    20 hours were unscheduled leisure activity

Appellant (employee)

    formal business hours: 4
    unscheduled activity (no more than 25% of 20 hours being business related): 5
    [total:] 9
    9/24 = 38%

Spouse

> formal business hours: 4
> unscheduled activity (no more than 10% of 20 hours being business related): 2
> [total:] 6
> 6/24 = 25%

The business portion of the cost for both spouses was allowed as not more than $1,482, i.e. 38% of $2,353 plus 25% of $2,353. In assessing, the Minister assumed that the appellant had received and enjoyed a benefit "in respect of, in the course of, or by virtue of his employment" which had a value of not less than $3,224 (arrived at by subtracting the business portion of the cost ($1,482) from the total cost to the employer ($4,706)) and that the primary purpose of the trip was "personal pleasure."

The appellant testified at trial as did two officers of Wellington Messrs. Evans and McConachie. The latter two witnesses had also attended in New Orleans. No witnesses were called by the respondent. The evidence of the witnesses is summarized by the Tax Court Judge at pages 4-7 of his reasons:

> ... Lowe attended the program in New Orleans as an employee of Wellington at the direction of his supervisor. The trip was not a holiday to Lowe and was not considered by Wellington to be a 'perk' to Lowe. He was to be present for four days to make sure the brokers for whom he was responsible had a good time. Wellington asked the account executives to go to New Orleans. They could not refuse; it was part of their job. Lowe testified it was his view he could not turn down the trip. His job in New Orleans, according to Evans and McConachie, was to maintain and promote the relationship with the brokers. At the same time, according to Evans and Lowe, Lowe's wife was to accompany him. The spouses of the brokers would be present and Wellington expected the spouses of its account executives to be present. Wellington paid for any babysitting expenses incurred by an account executive by virtue of his spouse attending at New Orleans. Evans said that unless there were compelling reasons, the spouse was expected to attend. Lowe considered his wife's presence in New Orleans as "part of my job." Her reason to be there, he said, was to be with brokers and build a rapport. "Anything she could do to improve relationships, she should do." Because he was "not given the choice for his wife not to attend," he felt he did not have the option of her not attending.

The initial brochure to the brokers offered:

> > ... a fabulous trip-for-two to New Orleans! Spend four sun-filled days and fun-filled nights at the breathtaking Royal Orleans Hotel in the French Quarter. Take a starlight Mississippi Riverboat cruise, ... And dine as you have never dined before!

> The group, consisting of approximately 50 brokers and their wives, including ten account executives and their spouses, as well as several of Wellington's senior management, arrived in New Orleans during the afternoon of March 28, 1990. At about 4:00 p.m., the account executives and their spouses, including Lowe and his wife, attended a two-hour meeting where they were given instructions on how to deal with the brokers, when to discuss business during the four days, where to sit during meals and also to arrange meetings with brokers and senior management of Wellington.

> The next morning, all the brokers and their spouses and the account executives and their spouses attended a business meeting for about two and a half hours. Various speakers made presentations. This culminated the formal business sessions. From then on, the attractions of New Orleans were available to the brokers. However, account executives had been instructed

to make sure that brokers signed up for the tours and other activities and to accompany them with their own spouse.

Lowe recalled discussing business with brokers to and from what was referred to as the "Honey Swamp Tour" while his wife had discussions with the spouses of the brokers. During the 45 minutes of the tour itself, no business was discussed.

Lowe also encouraged brokers to meet with senior management of Wellington and with the speakers who had given talks during the formal session. At meal time, account executives were strategically placed so that contact with brokers would be maintained. Each day, Evans would meet with account executives to make sure the brokers were happy.

Lowe testified that throughout the four days of the program, he and his wife had less than one hour to themselves (a bus trip through New Orleans); otherwise, he said, they were constantly occupied with the brokers and their wives. He admitted he enjoyed the trip, as he enjoyed his job. However, he said he was not free to do as he wished when in New Orleans. He was in New Orleans to serve his employer.

The Tax Court Judge concluded from the evidence that the Minister had erred in allowing only 38% as the business portion of the expenses incurred by the appellant. He was of the view that only 20% of this cost represented a taxable benefit. At the same time he left unchanged the Minister's assessment of the benefit enjoyed by the appellant's spouse.

The Minister's assumption that the primary purpose of the trip was personal pleasure was rejected by the Tax Court Judge who found, at pages 9-10:

The evidence suggests the primary purpose of the trip to New Orleans as far as Lowe is concerned was not personal pleasure. To the brokers and their spouses, it may have been so. As far as Lowe was concerned, he was present in New Orleans for the purposes of his employer's business and this function was the main purpose of his trip. ... Lowe's day was not the eight hours assumed by the Minister. The evidence states he was occupied from 7:30 in the morning to approximately 11:00 p.m. He did derive some enjoyment and pleasure from the trip, he admitted.

Evans revealed that not all Wellington account executives went to New Orleans. The account executives who went to New Orleans were those [who] had the most brokers travelling to New Orleans as well as the importance of the business relationship with the brokers. If an account executive convinced brokers to sell more Wellington policies, his chances of going to New Orleans increased. An account executive did not go to New Orleans if he had no brokers going there. To this extent, I believe, the trip to New Orleans was some type of reward to the account executive.

...

Paragraph 6(1)(a) of the *Income Tax Act* is of long standing and has been the subject of interpretation by the courts as well as by Revenue Canada. ... In his work *The Fundamentals of Canadian Income Tax*, 4th ed. (Toronto: Carswell, 1993), Professor V. Krishna discusses the purpose of paragraph 6(1)(a) as follows, at page 161:

The purpose of para. 6(1)(a) is simple: it is intended to equalize the tax payable by employees who receive their compensation in cash with the amount payable by those who receive compensation in cash and in kind. In the absence of this rule, the tax system would provide an incentive for employees to barter for non-cash benefits. The result would be a capricious and irrational tax system where tax burdens would be determined more by fortuitous circumstances of bargaining power than by principles of fairness.

He goes on immediately thereafter to suggest what should constitute a benefit for tax purposes:

> What, then, constitutes a benefit for tax purposes? There is no single test or determinative criterion which answers the question. Generally, the starting point is to determine whether the item under review provides the employee with an *economic advantage that is measurable in monetary terms*. If there is an advantage, one asks: does the primary advantage enure for the benefit of the employee or the employer? [Emphasis added.]

In *R v. Savage*, [1983] 2 SCR 428, [1983] CTC 393, 83 DTC 5409, ... Dickson J, as he then was, stated for the majority at page 441 (CTC 399; DTC 5414):

> I agree with what was said by Evans JA in *R v. Poynton*, [1972] 3 OR 727, at page 738, speaking of benefits received or enjoyed in respect of, in the course of, or by virtue of an office or employment:
>
> > I do not believe the language to be restricted to benefits that are related to the office or employment in the sense that they represent a form of remuneration for services rendered. If it is a *material acquisition which confers an economic benefit on the taxpayer* and does not constitute an exemption, e.g., loan or gift, then it is within the all-embracing definition of s. 3. [Emphasis added.] ...

I agree with counsel for the respondent that whether travelling expenses in a case such as this are to be viewed as a personal benefit turns heavily on the facts. In *Hale v. Minister of National Revenue*, [1968] CTC 477, 68 DTC 5326 (Ex. Ct.), the Court refused to treat an amount paid by a life insurance company for the expenses of the employee's wife in attending with him at a sales conference in Phoenix, Arizona as a taxable benefit under the predecessor of paragraphs 6(1)(a). It was clear that the taxpayer's wife, although having no formal connection to her husband's employer, was seen with her husband, as it was put by Cattanach J at page 479 (DTC 5327), "as the selling unit" in the employer's business.

...

In *Philp v. Minister of National Revenue*, [1970] CTC 330, 70 DTC 6237 (Ex. Ct.), the Court was called upon to determine to what extent, if any, a taxable benefit had been conferred by a grocery chain on employees and independent retail store managers in awarding them an expense-paid trip to Nassau in the Bahamas as a result of a competition in selling the chain's products. The appeal was allowed in part on the basis that "something of value in an economic sense" apart from the business purpose of the trip had been conferred on the recipients and should be taxed accordingly. At page 341 (DTC 6244), Thurlow J, as he then was, called attention, *inter alia*, to evidence which he regarded as supporting "something of value" to the taxpayer:

> ... apart from what was arranged for and carried out in the usual leisure or after hours of the day a considerable portion of the usual business or working hours of each day was made available for leisure with an organized programme of recreational activities arranged for those who wished to participate in them. These activities as well as transportation, hotel rooms, meals and receptions were all included in the project and were paid for by Oshawa. To my mind it is clear therefore that to persons interested in such an outing as a holiday, as

indeed many people are, the right to take such a trip represents *something of value in the material sense.* [Emphasis added.]

This "something of value" test was applied both by the Trial Division and by this Court in *Hart v. R*, [1981] CTC 91, 81 DTC 5070 (FCTD) and [1982] CTC 275, 82 DTC 6237 (FCA). That case involved a 23-day trip by the appellant and his wife, a farming couple, to Australia and New Zealand in 1977. Some of their activities involved visits to agricultural institutions and meeting with government agricultural officials, farmers or ranchers. The trial Judge, Mahoney J, as he then was, found, however, at page 92 (DTC 5071), that:

> A good deal of this activity related to matters of no immediate interest to Hartholm [the employer], notably sheep.

He went on to conclude, at page 93 (DTC 5071-72), that:

> ... the tour was of personal value to the Harts entirely apart from its business value. There may well be an incidental personal value inherent in many purely business trips but the personal benefit to the Harts in this case was not a mere incident of a business trip. A holiday oriented towards one's business or professional interests remains a holiday; it is not, per se, a business trip.

Viewing the cost of the trip as for a combination of business and pleasure, Mahoney J treated one-half of the husband's expenses as a personal benefit and upheld the Minister's assessment with respect to the expenses of the spouse. ... In dismissing the appeal from that decision, this Court saw no ground for interfering with what it regarded as "purely questions of fact and opinion," when "the view taken by the Trial Judge is not unreasonable or based on some erroneous principle" and the findings being "well supported by the evidence." Thurlow CJ described the tour to Australia and New Zealand, at page 276 (DTC 6239), in the following terms:

> The tour program, while predominantly concerned with activities that would be of interest to persons engaged in agricultural operations and which, for that reason, might be of little interest to persons of other callings was ... nevertheless a holiday. *It was a tour of such activities combined with visits to other points of interest to tourists generally and with activities and entertainment quite unrelated to agricultural pursuits. It is impossible, in my view, to conclude that such a tour was purely or even essentially a business trip* or that it had no value as a holiday and represented no economic benefit as a holiday trip received or enjoyed by the appellant. [Emphasis added.]

Although the *Philp* test is expressed in different words, it is not dissimilar from that of *Poynton* as approved in *Savage*, supra — "a material acquisition which confers an economic benefit on the taxpayer." It seems to me in light of existing jurisprudence that no part of the appellant's trip expenses should be regarded as a personal benefit unless that part represents a material acquisition for or something of value to him in an economic sense and that if the part which represents a material acquisition or something of value was a mere incident of what was primarily a business trip it should not be regarded as a taxable benefit within subparagraph 6(1)(a) of the Act. The Tax Court Judge found that the primary purpose of the appellant's trip to New Orleans was not for personal pleasure but for the purposes of the employer's business and allowed 80% of the appellant's costs as the business portion of the trip. His refusal to allow the whole as business expenses was based on the view that the trip to New Orleans was to an extent to "reward" him and because he derived some pleasure from the trip. When the time spent in New Orleans by the appellant on the employer's business is considered, it can be readily seen that the appellant had precious little time left over for personal pleasure. Nor is it clear that there was any element of "reward" for the appellant. It may well be, depending on the circumstances, that a true "reward" situation could support a conclusion that a trip was somehow earned by an employee so as to make the cost thereof, in whole or in part, taxable in the hands of the employee. The essential question in the present case, it seems to me, is whether on the facts the principal purpose of the trip was business or pleasure. Here it was found to be the former. Any pleasure derived by the appellant must, in my view, be seen as merely incidental to business purposes having regard to the fact that the overwhelming portion of the appellant's time in New Orleans was devoted to business activities.

I am similarly of the view, with respect, that the Tax Court Judge erred in treating the expenses of the appellant's spouse as a personal benefit under paragraph 6(1)(a). In concluding that the presence of the spouse in New Orleans was not necessary, the trial judge appears to have drawn heavily on his view that as a matter of law the spouse was under no obligation to be present and the employer could not require her presence in New Orleans. As he put it, at pages 10-11:

> In these days, as in 1989 and 1990, spouses, wives in particular, are under no obligation to follow the dictates of their spouses' employers, if this was ever the case. Times have changed. ... I am not satisfied that Lowe's wife's attendance in New Orleans was tantamount to being obligatory, as described by Cattanach J in *Hale* at page 5328.

In my view, while the existence of a legal obligation as in *Hale* is not present in the case at bar, the Tax Court ought nevertheless to have considered on the evidence, which was not contradicted, whether the spouse's presence with her husband in New Orleans at the request of the employer was primarily to serve the employer's business. The evidence seems clear that during the period of her stay in New Orleans the appellant's spouse attended the same meetings as did her spouse with the same objectives in mind and that she, like him, devoted the vast percentage of her time attending to the brokers and their wives. That evidence was not rejected or even commented upon unfavourably by the Tax Court Judge. No doubt she, like her husband, "enjoyed the trip," but enjoying a trip which is devoted primarily to the husband's role as an employee on behalf of his employer over the course of very lengthy work days should not, in my view, be seen in the circumstances of this case as giving rise to a personal benefit either to the spouse or to the employee. Any personal enjoyment of the trip by the spouse should, like that of the appellant, be viewed as merely incidental to what was primarily a business trip by both spouses for the purpose of advancing the employer's business interests.

Paragraph 6(1)(a) is cast in broad and somewhat vague language. I am, accordingly, satisfied that this is a proper case for having some regard to the

Department of National Revenue's own interpretations in construing paragraph 6(1)(a) even though they are non-binding.

...

Interpretation Bulletin IT-470R ... deals explicitly with the interpretation of various provisions of the Act including paragraph 6(1)(a) under the rubric of "employee's fringe benefits." Part A, dealing with "Amount to be Included in Income" includes under the subheading of "Holiday Trips, Other Prizes and Incentive Awards," ... the following:

> 11. In a situation where an employee's presence is required for business purposes and this function is the main purpose of the trip, no benefit will be associated with the employee's travelling expenses necessary to accomplish the business objectives of the trip if the expenditures are reasonable in relation to the business function. Where a business trip is extended to provide for a paid holiday or vacation, the employee is in receipt of a taxable benefit equal to the costs borne by the employer with respect to that extension.

> 12. There may be instances where an employee acts as a host or hostess for an incentive award trip arranged for employees, suppliers or customers of the employer. *Such a trip will be viewed as a business trip provided the employee is engaged directly in business activities during a substantial part of each day (e.g., as organizer of activities)* otherwise it will be viewed as a vacation and a taxable benefit, subject, of course, to a reduction for any actual business activity. [Emphasis added.]

Paragraph 15, under the subheading "Travelling Expenses of Employee's Spouse," reads:

> 15. Where a spouse accompanies an employee on a business trip the payment or reimbursement by the employer of the spouse's travelling expense is a taxable benefit to the employee *unless the spouse was, in fact, engaged primarily in business activities on behalf of the employer during the trip.* [Emphasis added.]

It can be seen on the particular record before us that the appellant's presence in New Orleans was required for his employer's business and that this was the main purpose of the trip. The record also shows that the spouse was engaged primarily in business activities on behalf of the appellant's employer during her stay in New Orleans.

I would allow the appeal with costs, set aside the Judgment of the Tax Court of Canada of February 27, 1995 except for the awarding of costs and would refer the matter back to the Minister for reconsideration and reassessment on a basis consistent with these reasons.

Appeal allowed.

NOTES AND QUESTIONS

1. How did the court in *Lowe* define the essential characteristics of a "benefit" for the purposes of paragraph 6(1)(a)? On what basis did the court conclude that the taxpayer in *Lowe* did not receive or enjoy a taxable benefit

from the trip to New Orleans? Do you agree with the court's conclusion that personal pleasure was "merely incidental" to the business purpose of the trip? Is it possible in a case like *Lowe* to separate business and pleasure? If not, should the characterization of a benefit within the meaning of paragraph 6(1)(a) depend on the "primary purpose" of the expense?

2. In *Lowe*, the court referred to earlier decisions in *Hart v. Canada*, [1981] C.T.C. 91, 81 D.T.C. 5070 (F.C.T.D.), aff'd [1982] C.T.C. 275, 82 D.T.C. 6237 (F.C.A.) and *Philp v. M.N.R.*, [1970] C.T.C. 330, 70 D.T.C. 6237 (Ex. Ct.), in each of which the taxpayer was held to have received a taxable benefit equal to half the cost of a trip involving business and pleasure. See also *Ferguson v. M.N.R.*, [1972] C.T.C. 2105, 72 D.T.C. 1097 (T.R.B.), where the board held that the taxpayer had received a taxable benefit equal to 10 per cent of the cost of a trip to Greece undertaken primarily for business reasons; *Dagenais v. Canada*, [1995] T.C.J. No. 20, [1995] 2 C.T.C. 2934 (T.C.C.), where the business component of the trip was held to be 15 per cent; *McMillan v. Canada*, [1995] T.C.J. No. 281, [1995] 2 C.T.C. 2766 (T.C.C.), where the taxpayer was required to include 40 per cent of the cost of two trips that he and his wife had taken at his employer's request in order to accompany other employees and distributors of the employer's products; and *Cales v. The Queen*, [1996] 1 C.T.C. 2110 (T.C.C.), in which the taxable share of the same trips as in *McMillan* was assessed at 85 per cent. Is this percentage approach to the assessment of a taxable benefit preferable to the "all-or-nothing" approach adopted in *Lowe*?

3. In *Romeril v. Canada*, [1998] T.C.J. No. 1044, [1999] 1 C.T.C. 2535, 99 D.T.C. 221 (T.C.C.), the court referred to Stone JA's reasons in *Lowe* in deciding that an employee did not receive a taxable benefit from his and his wife's attendance at a business convention in France.

Compare *Paton v. M.N.R.*, [1968] Tax ABC 200, where the taxpayer, who was the chief general manager of the Toronto-Dominion Bank, travelled to Winnipeg and Regina, where he and his wife, who accompanied him at the bank's request and expense, attended regional meetings of branch managers of the bank. Noting (at para. 14) that Mrs. Paton had not "spent any time in the head office of the bank to learn the details and intricacies of banking practice" and had no "special fitness or training to enable her to pass judgment on the abilities and qualities of the various people she would meet fleetingly at the social functions which were arranged or in which she engaged," the board upheld the Minister's assessment including Mrs. Paton's travel expenses as a taxable benefit to Mr. Paton.

For another case in which the travel costs of a wife's accompanying her husband on a business trip were held to be a taxable benefit, see *Shambrook v. M.N.R.* (1965), 40 Tax ABC 28 (T.A.B.).

4. The CRA's current views on taxable benefits associated with employer-provided trips are contained in *Interpretation Bulletin* IT-470R, "Employees' Fringe Benefits," October 8, 1999. According to this bulletin:

10. Where an employer pays for a vacation for an employee, the employee's family or both, the cost thereof to the employer constitutes a taxable benefit to the employee under paragraph 6(1)(a). Similarly, where a vacation property owned by an employer is used for vacation purposes by an employee, the employee's family or both, there is a taxable benefit conferred on the employee under paragraph 6(1)(a) the value of which is equivalent to the fair market value of the accommodation less any amount which the employee paid therefor to the employer. In any case, the taxable benefit may be reduced if there is conclusive evidence to show that the employee was involved in business activities for the employer during the vacation.

11. In a situation where an employee's presence is required for business purposes and this function is the main purpose of the trip, no benefit will be associated with the employee's travelling expenses necessary to accomplish the business objectives of the trip if the expenditures are reasonable in relation to the business function. Where a business trip is extended to provide for a paid holiday or vacation, the employee is in receipt of a taxable benefit equal to the costs borne by the employer with respect to that extension.

12. There may be instances where an employee acts as a host or hostess for an incentive award trip arranged for employees, suppliers or customers of the employer. Such a trip will be viewed as a business trip provided the employee is engaged directly in business activities during a substantial part of each day (e.g., as organizer of activities); otherwise it will be viewed as a vacation and a taxable benefit, subject, of course, to a reduction for any actual business activity.

For what purpose did the Court in *Lowe v. Canada*, [1996] F.C.J. No. 319, [1996] 2 C.T.C. 33, 96 D.T.C. 6226 (F.C.A.), refer to IT-470R? To what extent, if any, should the Courts refer to the revenue authority's interpretation bulletins? To what extent, if any, should the Crown be prejudiced by a published interpretation bulletin expressing a different interpretation from that argued in court?

5. In *Gernhart v. Canada*, [1996] T.C.J No. 821, [1996] 3 C.T.C. 2369 (T.C.C.), aff'd [1997] F.C.J. No. 1736, [1998] 2 C.T.C. 102, 98 D.T.C. 6026 (F.C.A.), the taxpayer, an American employee of General Motors who was posted in Canada from October 1988 to April 1991, received a "tax equalization payment" designed to provide an equivalent after-tax income to that which she had formerly received in the United States. Rejecting the taxpayer's argument that the equalization payment effected a reimbursement for a loss resulting from her employment in Canada, the Court held that the payment was taxable both as remuneration from the taxpayer's employment under subsection 5(1) and as a benefit under paragraph 6(1)(a). According to the Court (at paras. 12-14):

Remuneration is commonly adjusted to reflect advantages and disadvantages inherent in rendering services under an employment contract but does not for that reason cease to be remuneration for such services. ...

The tax equalization payment is an obvious benefit when the appellant's position is compared with that of any other resident of Canada in receipt of the same income but not in receipt of tax equalization. Inherent in the tax treatment sought by the appellant is a privilege offensive to the principle that individuals in similar financial circumstances should pay similar amounts of tax.

Do you agree with this decision? Why or why not?

6.   In *Guay v. Canada*, [1997] F.C.J. No. 470, [1997] 3 C.T.C. 276, 97 D.T.C. 5267 (F.C.A.), the taxpayer, who was employed as a foreign service officer with the Canadian Department of Foreign Affairs and International Trade, received $9,735 in 1991 as a reimbursement for tuition fees incurred in order to send his children to a private French-language school in Ottawa that was part of an international network of French-language institutions using the curriculum of the French Ministry of Education. On the grounds that the taxpayer's children were required to attend one of the network's institutions when the taxpayer was posted abroad, and that "it is difficult, and often impossible, to enrol a child in one of the network's institutions abroad if the child has not already begun or continued his or her education in Canada at an institution that is part of the network," the court held that the reimbursement was not a taxable benefit within the meaning of paragraph 6(1)(a). According to Décary JA (at para. 15):

> In the case at bar, the reimbursement by the Government of the cost of the applicant's children at the Lycée Claudel in Ottawa in no way increased the applicant's net worth; the reimbursement put him in the same position as if he had not been compelled by the nature of his employment to send his children there.

Were the educational expenses incurred by the taxpayer in *Guay* "compelled by the nature of his employment" or by the taxpayer's own choices both to have children and to educate them in the French language? Are the expenses associated with the care and education of children incurred primarily for the purpose of earning income or for personal reasons? See the discussion of child-care expenses in Chapter 7.

Note that the taxpayer in *Guay* would have been placed in the same economic position if his employer had increased his salary by an amount sufficient to provide an after-tax increase of $9,735 (for example, by $19,470 if the taxpayer's marginal tax rate had been 50 per cent). Should employers be able to reduce their employment expenses by paying tax-free compensation as in *Guay*?

7.   In *Huffman v. M.N.R.*, [1988] F.C.J. No. 1060, [1989] 1 C.T.C. 32, 89 D.T.C. 5006 (F.C.T.D.), aff'd [1990] F.C.J. No. 529, [1990] 2 C.T.C. 132, 90 D.T.C. 6405 (F.C.A.), the taxpayer, a plainclothes police officer with the Niagara Regional Police Force, received $500 pursuant to the terms of a collective agreement providing for the reimbursement of clothing expenses of plainclothes officers upon presentation of necessary receipts. On the grounds (at para. 9) that the taxpayer was required to purchase oversized clothing "to accommodate the on-duty equipment which he was required to carry (e.g. billy club, walkie-talkie, revolver, etc.)" and that the clothing became worn and stained from work in the field "examining fingerprints, footprints, blood stains, etc.," the court concluded (at paras. 14-15) that the payment "should not be considered as conferring a benefit under paragraph 6(1)(a) of the Act" but that the taxpayer "was simply being restored to the economic situation he was in before his employer ordered him to incur the expenses." See also *Shoveller v. M.N.R.*, [1984] C.T.C. 2207, 84 D.T.C. 1195 (T.C.C.), where Rip TCJ

concluded that the taxpayer had "not received any benefit, in the ordinary meaning of the word, as a result of being reimbursed for expenses."

According to paragraph 29 of IT-470R, the CRA does not consider an employee to have received a taxable benefit where the employee is required to wear a "distinctive uniform" while carrying out the duties of employment or provided with "special clothing (including footwear) designed for protection from the particular hazards of the employment." Nor, according to paragraph 30 of the same bulletin, does the department regard payments made by an employer "to a laundry or dry cleaning establishment for laundry or dry cleaning expenses of uniforms and special clothing, or directly to the employee in reimbursement of such expenses," to be a taxable benefit within the meaning of paragraph 6(1)(a).

8.   In *Cutmore v. M.N.R.*, [1986] 1 C.T.C. 2230, 86 D.T.C. 1146 (T.C.C.), the taxpayer's employer paid for senior employees to have their income tax returns prepared by professional accountants as part of a mandatory policy designed "to ensure that their [senior executives'] actions did not ... reflect on the credibility of the corporation" (at para. 6). Although concluding (at para. 10) that the employer's policy stemmed from "a *bona fide* business decision motivated by the desire to protect the Corporation's reputation for integrity," the court nonetheless held that the value of the accounting services was a taxable benefit within the meaning of paragraph 6(1)(a). According to Christie ACJTC (at para. 19):

> I do not regard the motivation behind the conferring of the benefits or the fact that the acceptance can be considered to have been a requirement of the appellant's employment to render paragraph 6(1)(a) inoperative in respect of them.

Is this conclusion consistent with the decision in *Lowe v. Canada*, [1996] F.C.J. No. 319, [1996] 2 C.T.C. 33, 96 D.T.C. 6226 (F.C.A.)? Should an employer be able to negate the characterization of a benefit to an employee by requiring the employee to accept the benefit as a condition of his or her employment? Might it matter whether the employee could reasonably be considered to have participated in the employer's decision requiring the employee to accept the benefit?

9.   In *Deitch v. M.N.R.*, [1989] 1 C.T.C. 2360, 89 D.T.C. 312 (T.C.C.), the taxpayer, a legal aid lawyer employed by the Law Society of Upper Canada, sought to exclude in computing his income for his 1984 taxation year $825 in professional liability insurance that his employer had paid on his behalf. Referring to the decision in *Cutmore v. M.N.R.*, [1986] 1 C.T.C. 2230, 86 D.T.C. 1146 (T.C.C.), the Court rejected the taxpayer's argument that the amount paid was "a mandatory term of his employment" from which he received no benefit. According to Sarchuk TCJ (at para. 11):

> Firstly, the payment of the fee by the employer was clearly an economic advantage of the appellant since the appellant would have been required to pay that amount himself, failing which he would not have been employable as a lawyer. Secondly, the provision of professional liability insurance by the employer protected the appellant from any personal

liability in respect of any acts of professional negligence. Frankly, that is a benefit which is of substantial economic benefit to the appellant. Thirdly, although more remote, I agree with counsel for the respondent that in certain circumstances the master or employer might be entitled to recover from his servant the amount of damages which it had been required to pay as a result of his negligence. The appellant, by virtue of this insurance is now protected, and that too is a benefit.

10. In *Dunlap v. Canada*, [1998] T.C.J. No. 757, [1998] 4 C.T.C. 2644, 98 D.T.C. 2053 (T.C.C.), the taxpayer was reassessed by including a benefit in respect of annual Christmas parties hosted by his employer in 1992 and 1993 at which employees ate, drank, and enjoyed the amenities of the Westin Hotel in Ottawa. Rejecting the taxpayer's argument that the parties did not constitute an economic benefit within the meaning of paragraph 6(1)(a), the court held that the benefits (the average cost of which were valued at $302 in 1992 and $278 in 1993) were "not ... trivial." In addition, Sarchuk TCJ stated (at para. 10):

> The fact that it was unilaterally conferred by the employer does not detract from its essential character, that of a benefit and a significant one, that was enjoyed by the Appellant. A benefit is a benefit even when unilaterally conferred.

According to paragraph 9 of IT-470R:

> An employer-provided party or other social event, which is generally available to all employees, will be accepted as a non-taxable privilege if the cost per employee is reasonable in the circumstances. As a guideline, those events costing up to $100 per person will be considered to be non-taxable. Ancillary costs, such as transportation home, would increase that amount. Parties costing more than that are generally considered to be beyond the privilege point and may result in a taxable benefit.

11. In *Faubert v. Canada*, [1998] T.C.J. No. 21, 98 D.T.C. 1380 (T.C.C.) and *Jex v. Canada*, [1998] T.C.J. No. 22, [1998] 2 C.T.C. 2688, 98 D.T.C. 1377 (T.C.C.), the taxpayers, each of whom worked for Revenue Canada, were reimbursed for tuition fees incurred by the taxpayers to enroll in accounting courses leading to their designation as certified management accountants and certified general accountants. Rejecting the taxpayers' argument that the courses were undertaken primarily for the benefit of the employer, which had a policy of encouraging employees to upgrade their skills by reimbursing tuition fees and required employees to meet specific academic qualifications in order to hold particular positions in the department, the court held that the payments were taxable benefits within the meaning of paragraph 6(1)(a). According to Sarchuk TCJ (at para. 14):

> The evidence does not support the suggestion that this Appellant was in some fashion legally obliged or was faced with job loss consequences if he failed to upgrade his skills. He was aware that specific qualifications existed for a position to which he aspired. The decision to seek educational upgrading for that purpose was purely personal in nature. ... The courses taken were primarily for the Appellant's benefit and in my view, the amount paid by his employer constitutes a taxable benefit in his hands under paragraph 6(1)(a) of the Act.

The CRA's views on the tax treatment of tuition reimbursements are found in IT-470R, paragraph 18:

When training is taken primarily for the benefit of the employer, there is no taxable benefit whether or not this training leads to a degree, diploma or certificate. A taxable benefit arises when the training is primarily for the benefit of the employee. ...

There are three broad categories of training:

Specific Employer-Related Training: Courses which are taken for maintenance or upgrading of employer-related skills, when it is reasonable to assume that the employee will resume his or her employment for a reasonable period of time after completion of the courses, will generally be considered to primarily benefit the employer and therefore be non-taxable. For example, fees and other associated costs such as meals, travel and accommodation which are paid for courses leading to a degree, diploma or certificate, in a field related to the employee's current or potential future responsibilities in the employer's business, will not result in a taxable benefit.

General Employment-Related Training: Other business-related courses, although not directly related to the employer's business, will generally be considered non-taxable. Examples of non-taxable training would include stress management, employment equity, first-aid and language skills. Normally, in-house training will not be considered a taxable benefit.

Personal Interest Training: Employer-paid courses for personal interest or technical skills that are not related to the employer's business are considered of primary benefit to the employee and thus taxable. For example, fees paid for a self-interest carpentry course would result in a taxable benefit.

Is this administrative position consistent with the decisions in *Faubert v. Canada*, [1998] T.C.J. No. 21, 98 D.T.C. 1380 (T.C.C.) and *Jex v. Canada*, [1998] T.C.J. No. 22, [1998] 2 C.T.C. 2688, 98 D.T.C. 1377 (T.C.C.)? Is it consistent with the Federal Court of Appeal decision in *Lowe v. Canada*, [1996] F.C.J. No. 319, [1996] 2 C.T.C. 33, 96 D.T.C. 6226 (F.C.A.)?

12.   In *Pellizzari v. M.N.R.*, [1987] T.C.J. No. 32, [1987] 1 C.T.C. 2106, 87 D.T.C. 56 (T.C.C.), the taxpayer, her husband, and a corporation of which she was an employee, sole director, and sole shareholder were charged with fraud. Although the charges were eventually dropped, the taxpayer was assessed on the basis that legal expenses of $7,500 incurred on her behalf by the corporation were a taxable benefit received by virtue of her employment. Rejecting the taxpayer's appeal, Couture CJTC stated (at para. 24):

In the present situation the appellant was defending herself against charges of alleged criminal acts committed by her while employed by the corporation. The fact that the charges were eventually withdrawn does not alter her involvement as the person directly affected by this whole affair and as the person who was seeking to vindicate herself from those accusations. The legal fees paid by Pamic were in my opinion her personal expenses and their payment by the corporation did constitute a benefit to her and therefore must be included in her income pursuant to paragraph 6(1)(a).

See also *Clemiss v. M.N.R.*, [1992] F.C.J. No. 851, [1992] 2 C.T.C. 232, 92 D.T.C. 6509 (F.C.T.D.), where a company incurred legal expenses of $146,533.37 to defend the taxpayer against criminal charges of conspiracy to defraud the company and theft of company property. Rejecting the taxpayer's argument that the legal expenses were incurred by reason of his employment, Reed J commented (at para. 59):

> In the present case the expenses were incurred by the plaintiff not in order to do the job but to answer criminal charges laid against him personally. The charges did not even involve charges against the company. The company was alleged to have been the victim. While the actions which gave rise to the criminal charges took place in the context of the plaintiff's employment with the company and his membership on the board of directors I could not find that there is the close nexus between their outlay and the plaintiff's position as an employee and director of the corporation, in order to conclude that they were incurred by reason of that employment or directorship.

On this basis, the court concluded, the legal expenses were properly included in computing the taxpayer's employment income under paragraph 6(1)(a).

13. In *R. v. Poynton*, [1972] O.J. No. 2014, [1972] C.T.C. 411, 72 D.T.C. 6329 (Ont. C.A.), the taxpayer, while an officer and employee of a corporation that carried on business as a building contractor in Toronto, fraudulently obtained over $21,000 from the employer by means of false invoices submitted by an accomplice. Rejecting the taxpayer's argument that the embezzled funds were not taxable income, the court characterized the money as a benefit under what are now paragraphs 3(a) and 6(1)(a) of the Act. According to Evans JA (Gale CJO and MacKay JA concurring) (at para. 24):

> I do not believe the language to be restricted to benefits that are related to the office or employment in the sense that they represent a form of remuneration for services rendered. If it is a material acquisition which confers an economic benefit on the taxpayer and does not constitute an exemption, e.g. loan or gift, then it is within the all-embracing definition of section 3.

14. For cases that have considered the characterization of board and lodging as taxable benefits, see *Williams v. M.N.R.*, [1955] C.T.C. 1 (Ex. Ct.), in which board and living accommodation on a BC ferry were held to be taxable under a predecessor to paragraph 6(1)(a); *Cockerill v. M.N.R.* (1965), 38 Tax ABC 446 (T.A.B.), in which a furnished apartment was characterized as a taxable benefit; *Lordly v. M.N.R.*, [1978] C.T.C. 2794, 78 D.T.C. 1569 (T.R.B.), where free accommodation at a motel operated by a company of which the taxpayer was the main shareholder was determined not to have been a taxable benefit since "the advantage was totally for the employer and not for the employee"; *Albrechtsen v. M.N.R.*, [1979] C.T.C. 2164, 79 D.T.C. 167 (T.R.B.), in which a furnished apartment used by the taxpayer on frequent business trips to Winnipeg was determined not to have produced an "economic benefit" within the meaning of paragraph 6(1)(a); *Hughes v. Canada*, [1993] T.C.J. No. 543, [1993] 2 C.T.C. 2894 (T.C.C.), where board and lodging at a bed-and-breakfast managed by the taxpayer was held to be a taxable benefit under paragraph 6(1)(a); and *Dhondge v. Canada*, [1996] T.C.J. No. 784 (T.C.C.), in which the court held that a live-in nanny was taxable on the value of board and lodging provided by her employer.

See also *McGoldrick v. Canada*, [2003] T.C.J. No. 502, [2004] 1 C.T.C. 2369, 2003 D.T.C. 1375 (T.C.C.), aff'd [2004] F.C.J. No. 849, [2004] 3 C.T.C. 264, 2004 D.T.C. 6407 (F.C.A.), where the taxpayer worked at "Casino Rama" near Orillia, Ontario, which provided one free meal per shift to all employees at an employee cafeteria called the Turtle Island Café. Notwithstanding that employees were not permitted to bring food onto the casino premises for sanitation reasons, that it was "impractical" to eat off-site due to the casino's location, and that the taxpayer "did not enjoy the experience" of eating at the Turtle Island Café, the Court upheld the Minister's assessment including a taxable benefit of $4.50 for each day that he worked more than five hours. Applying the test set out in *Lowe*, the Court concluded that the meals were provided primarily for a business purpose but that the personal benefit to the taxpayer was more than incidental. In a subsequent appeal the Tax Court of Canada reduced the quantum of the benefit by 50 per cent on the basis that the taxpayer accepted the free meal only half of the time. (*McGoldrick v. Canada*, [2005] T.C.J. No. 634, [2006] 1 C.T.C. 2454, 2006 D.T.C. 2045 (T.C.C.)).

The CRA's views on the taxation of board and lodging under paragraph 6(1)(a) are contained in IT-470R, paragraph 4:

> The *Income Tax Act* refers specifically to board and lodging as a benefit derived from employment. This includes board and lodging regularly furnished as a prerequisite of the employment, as is common for hotel employees and domestic and farm help. The value placed on this benefit should approximate its fair market value. Where subsidized board and lodging is provided to an employee the value of the benefit for "board" is determined on the basis described for subsidized meals (See ¶28 below); the "lodging" benefit will be valued at the fair market value of the accommodation less the amount charged to the employee.

According to paragraph 28:

> Subsidized meals provided to employees will not be considered to confer a taxable benefit provided the employee is required to pay a reasonable charge. A reasonable charge is generally defined as one that covers the cost of food, its preparation and service. Where less than a reasonable charge is paid, the value of the benefit is that cost less the amount paid by the employee.

15. As an administrative practice, the CRA excludes various "non-taxable privileges" from inclusion as taxable benefits under paragraph 6(1)(a) provided that the privilege does not constitute "a form of extra remuneration." According to IT-470R:

Discounts on Merchandise and Commissions on Sales

> 27. Where it is the practice of an employer to sell merchandise to employees at a discount, the benefits that an employee may derive from exercising such a privilege are not normally regarded as taxable benefits. However, this does not extend to an extraordinary arrangement with a particular employee or a select group of employees nor to an arrangement by which an employee is permitted to purchase merchandise (other than old or soiled merchandise) for less than the employer's cost. Furthermore, this treatment does not extend to a reciprocal arrangement between two or more employers whereby the employees of one can exercise such a privilege with another by whom the employees are not employed.
>
> ...

Transportation to the Job

> 32. Employers sometimes find it expedient to provide vehicles for transporting their employees from pick-up points to the location of the employment at which, for

security or other reasons, public and private vehicles are not welcome or not practical. In these circumstances the employees are not regarded as in receipt of a taxable benefit. ...

Recreational Facilities

33. Where employees generally are permitted to use their employer's recreational facilities (e.g., exercise rooms, swimming pools, gymnasiums, tennis, squash or racquetball courts, golf courses, shuffle boards) free of charge or upon payment of a nominal fee, the value of the benefit derived by an employee through such use is not normally taxable. ...

34. Similarly, where the employer pays the fees required for an employee to be a member of a social or athletic club the employee is not deemed to have received a taxable benefit where the membership was principally for the employer's advantage rather than the employee's. ...

Transportation Passes

42. Airline passes available to airline employees will become taxable only if the employee travels on a space-confirmed basis and is paying less than 50 per cent of the economy fare available on that carrier for that trip on the day of travel. The value of the benefit will be the difference between 50 per cent of the economy fare and any amount reimbursed to the carrier for that trip.

43. Employees of bus and rail companies will not be taxed on the use of passes.

44. Retired employees of transportation companies will not be taxed on pass benefits under any circumstances.

Where an employee is transported to a job as described in paragraph 32, the "benefit" may not involve a "material advantage." Other exceptions (for example, "discounts on merchandise and commissions on sales" discussed in paragraph 27 and the "transportation passes" described in paragraphs 42 and 43) may reflect a valuation of the benefit according to the marginal cost to the employer. The rationale for other exceptions (for example, "recreational facilities" described in paragraphs 33 and 34 and "transportation passes" for retired employees of transportation companies as described in paragraph 44) is less clear.

In *Rachfalowski v. The Queen*, [2008] T.C.J. No. 218, [2009] 1 C.T.C. 2073, 2008 D.T.C. 3626 (T.C.C.), Bowman CJ approved of paragraphs 33 and 34 of CRA's policy and held that an employer-paid golf club membership did not constitute a taxable benefit because it was "primarily for the benefit of the employer." The evidence established that the taxpayer was not a golfer, did not want the membership, and accepted it only to avoid the appearance of being a "rebel." Bowman CJ concluded that while the taxpayer did use the club occasionally to entertain clients and this "enhanced the company's image and prestige," the membership "was clearly not an advantage to him."

16. For a detailed discussion of the policy underlying the taxation of employment benefits and Canadian law on specific benefits, see Kim Brooks, "Delimiting the Concept of Income: The Taxation of In-Kind Benefits" (2004) 49 McGill L.J. 255-307. See also Antonio Di Domenico, "Employer Provided Benefits and the Environment: Transit Passes and Parking" (2006) 54 Can. Tax J. 115-141, in which the author makes a case for more consistent treatment of employer-provided parking and transit passes as taxable benefits.

b. Relationship to Office or Employment

For an amount to be included as a taxable benefit under paragraph 6(1)(a), the benefit must have been received or enjoyed by the taxpayer "in respect of, in the course of, or by virtue of an office or employment." The leading case on the relationship between a benefit and a taxpayer's office or employment is *R. v. Savage*, [1983] S.C.J. No. 81, [1983] C.T.C. 393, 83 D.T.C. 5409 (S.C.C.).

R. v. Savage
[1983] S.C.J. No. 81, [1983] C.T.C. 393, 83 D.T.C. 5409 (S.C.C.)

DICKSON J (Ritchie, McIntyre, Lamer, and Wilson JJ concurring): ... Mrs. Savage was employed by Excelsior as a research assistant. During 1976, she took three Life Office Management Association courses: Life Insurance Law, Economics and Investment, and Life Insurance Actuary Mathematics. The courses are designed to provide a broad understanding of modern life insurance and life insurance company operations, including management practices and personnel needs. The courses were voluntarily taken by Mrs. Savage to improve her knowledge in the life insurance field. She received from Excelsior $300 ($100 per course) as a result of passing the examinations. Such payment per course was available to all employees of Excelsior in accordance with company policy, designed to encourage self-upgrading of staff members. The courses, in both study time required and complexity of material, were comparable to university courses. Approximately 61 per cent of those taking the examinations in 1976 in the United States and Canada passed. One hundred or so Excelsior employees wrote the examinations in the spring and fall of 1976; the percentage passing slightly exceeded the overall United States and Canadian average results.

Excelsior reported the amount of $300 on a T4A Supplementary under "Other Income," indicating it was a "Prize for passing LOMA examinations," and claimed it as an expense of doing business. ... Mrs. Savage did not include the payment to her of $300 in the computation of her income for the 1976 taxation year. The Minister, by notice of reassessment, assessed the amount in the computation of her income on the basis that it constituted income of the taxpayer from an office or employment.

...

[T]he Federal Court of Appeal concluded the payments aggregating $300 were not within subsection 5(1) or paragraph 6(1)(a) because they were not payments "for services as an employee." LeDain J said:

> The sum of $100 paid to the appellant for successful completion of a course was not a payment for services rendered as an employee. It was not related in any way to her services as an employee. The courses were taken voluntarily, on her own time. There was no obligation as an employee to take them. The interest of the employer was that the courses would make her a more valuable employee. The payment was in the nature of a gift to encourage employees to take the courses and successfully complete them. The employment was certainly a condition of being able to receive the payment, but the payment was not received by reason of the employment but by reason of the successful completion of the course.

LeDain, J relied on *Estate of Phaneuf v. The Queen*, [1978] 2 FC 564 (TD) and *Ball (HM Inspector of Taxes) v. Johnson* (1971), 47 Tax. Cas. 155 (Ch. D).

The *Ball* case was much like the one at bar. The Midland Bank expected its staff, among whom was Mr. Johnson, to study and sit for examinations of the Institute of Banks, to qualify themselves better as bankers. The bank paid cash awards to those who passed, including Johnson. It was held the reason for the payments was Johnson's personal success in passing the examinations and they were not remuneration for his services with the bank. The case is of little relevance, however, because of the language of Rule 1 of Schedule E of the *Income Tax Act 1952* (Eng).

...

The provisions of section 156 of the *Income Tax Act 1952* of England are not unlike subsection 5(1) of the Canadian *Income Tax Act* but our Act goes further in paragraph 6(1)(a). In addition to the salary, wages and other remuneration referred to in subsection 5(1), paragraph 6(1)(a) includes in income the value of benefits "of any kind whatever... received or enjoyed ... in respect of, in the course of, or by virtue of an office or employment."

In *Phaneuf*, supra, the issue was whether Mr. Phaneuf was liable for income tax in respect of a benefit received by him on the purchase of shares. He acquired the shares in Charles Ogilvy Limited, his employer, pursuant to a bequest of the company's principal shareholder. The bequest gave the right to the Company's employees to acquire a number of shares at par value. The Company's Board of Directors revised the list of employees entitled to purchase shares and approved a formula for distribution based on service to some extent. Mr. Phaneuf bought shares of a par value of $2 although they had a market value at the time of $17.25. In the Federal Court, Mr. Justice Thurlow, then ACJ of the Trial Division, held that the benefit was conferred on Mr. Phaneuf as a person and not as an employee and as a personal gift rather than as remuneration, and hence not a taxable benefit.

...

I agree that the appropriate test in *Phaneuf* was whether the benefit had been conferred on Mr. Phaneuf as an employee or simply as a person. It would seem that Mr. Phaneuf received, as a person, the right to acquire the shares and therefore the case was correctly decided. With great respect, however, I do not agree ... that, to be received in the capacity of employee, the payment must partake of the character of remuneration for services. Such was the conclusion in the English cases but based on much narrower language. Our Act contains the stipulation, not found in the English statutes referred to, "benefits of any kind whatever ... in respect of, in the course of, or by virtue of an office or employment." The meaning of "benefit of whatever kind" is clearly quite broad; in the present case the cash payment of $300 easily falls within the category of "benefit." Further, our Act speaks of a benefit "in respect of an office or employment. In *Nowegijick v. The Queen*, [1983] CTC 20; 83 DTC 5041 this Court said, at 25 [5045], that:

> The words "in respect of" are, in my opinion, words of the widest possible scope. They import such meanings as "in relation to," "with reference to" or "in connection with." The phrase "in respect of" [is] probably the widest of any expression intended to convey some connection between two related subject matters.

...

It is difficult to conclude that the payments by Excelsior to Mrs Savage were not in relation to or in connection with her employment. ... [T]he employee took the course to improve his or her knowledge and efficiency in the company business and for better opportunity of promotion.

As Crown counsel submits, the sum of $300 received by Mrs. Savage from her employer was a benefit and was received or enjoyed by her in respect of, in the course of or by virtue of her employment within the meaning of paragraph 6(1)(a) of the *Income Tax Act*; it was paid by her employer in accordance with the company policy upon the successful completion of courses "designed to provide a broad understanding of modern life insurance and life insurance company operations" and "to encourage self-upgrading of staff members"; the interest of the employer "was that the courses would make her a more valuable employee"; Mrs. Savage took the courses to "improve [her] knowledge and efficiency in the company business and for better opportunity for promotion." Distinguishing this case from *Phaneuf*, there was no element of gift, personal bounty or of considerations extraneous to Mrs. Savage's employment.

I would hold that the payments received by Mrs. Savage were in respect of employment.

NOTES AND QUESTIONS

1.   On what basis did the Supreme Court of Canada in *Savage* distinguish the decision in *Phaneuf Estate v. Canada*, [1978] 2 F.C. 564, [1978] C.T.C. 21 (T.D.)? Must a benefit take the form of remuneration for services in order to be subject to tax under paragraph 6(1)(a)?

2.   Despite concluding that the $300 received by Mrs. Savage was a benefit "received ... in respect of... an office or employment," the Supreme Court of Canada proceeded to hold that the payment was exempt under a more specific

statutory provision governing prizes in paragraph 56(1)(n). This aspect of the decision, and its subsequent reversal by legislative amendment, are considered in Chapter 7.

3.   In *Mindszenthy v. Canada*, [1993] T.C.J. No. 338, [1993] 2 C.T.C. 2648 (T.C.C.), the taxpayer worked for a public relations company called the Beloff Group Inc., the president and controlling shareholder of which was Barry Beloff. After learning of a presentation that the taxpayer had made to the Department of External Affairs, for the purpose of which he had purchased as a prop an imitation Rolex watch for $40, Mr. Beloff gave the taxpayer a gold Rolex watch when the taxpayer was visiting Mr. Beloff at his home. Observing that the cost of the watch ($3,929) had been incurred and deducted by the Beloff Group Inc., the court rejected the taxpayer's argument that it was a personal gift and upheld the Minister's assessment as a taxable benefit. According to Bowman TCCJ (at para. 13):

> Where it is contended, as it is here, that a gift made to an employee by the president of a company is not given to him in his capacity of an employee but rather *qua* personal friend, it would require fairly cogent evidence to that effect. The intention of the donor would be an important factor and we have no evidence of that at all. ...
>
> As noted in *The Queen v. Savage*, ... paragraph 6(1)(a) is of extreme breadth. It speaks of benefits received or enjoyed by a taxpayer in the year "in respect of, in the course of, or by virtue of an office or employment." It would require much stronger evidence than we have here for a taxpayer to escape the wide net that paragraph 6(1)(a) casts. I might add that I have considerable sympathy for the appellant. He accepted the gift in good faith without being aware of the tax consequences. Had he known that it carried a tax burden, he might have refused to accept it. Instead of being a clear benefit, it gave rise to a liability and, as an economic matter, it forced him to pay in taxes a great deal more than he would have paid for a watch in the first place. He was, to some degree, the victim of an unasked for and perhaps unwanted generosity by Mr. Beloff, who was quite prepared at a later date to abandon him. This consideration, however, cannot affect my decision.

4.   Notwithstanding the decision in *Savage*, the CRA excludes certain gifts from the application of paragraph 6(1)(a) where they satisfy the administrative criteria set out in paragraph 9 of IT-470R:

> When the value of a gift commemorating a wedding, Christmas or similar occasion does not exceed $100 and when the employer does not claim its cost as an expense in computing taxable income, the gift is not required to be reported as income of an employee. This practice will only apply to one gift to an employee in a year, except in the year an employee marries in which case it will apply to two gifts.

More recently the CRA announced the following liberalization of its policy on gifts to employees (see Income Tax Technical News No. 22, January 11, 2002):

> ... Under our new position, employers will be able to give two non-cash gifts per year, on a tax-free basis, to employees for special occasions such as Christmas, Hanukkah, birthday, marriage or a similar event where the aggregate cost of the gifts to the employer is less than $500 per year.
>
> Similarly, employers will be able to give employees two non-cash awards per year, on a tax-free basis, in recognition of special achievements such as reaching a set number of years of

service, meeting or exceeding safety standards, or reaching similar milestones where the total cost of the awards to the employer is less than $500 per year. The employer will be able to deduct the cost of the gifts and awards.

...

This new position will be closely monitored and will be adjusted if abuse or undue revenue loss is identified.

...

The position would not apply to cash or near-cash gifts and awards. Accordingly, gift certificates, gold nuggets, or any other item that can easily be converted to cash would not fall within the new position, and the value of such awards and gifts will be considered a taxable employment benefit.

...

If the cost exceeds the $500 threshold, then the full fair market value of the gifts or awards will be included in the employee's employment income. The purpose of the new position is to allow employers to provide small non-monetary gifts and awards to employees without incurring the administrative burden of valuing these items for T4 reporting purposes. If the cost goes beyond the $500 limit, the assumption is that the gifts or awards form part of the employee's remuneration package.

5.   Notwithstanding the decision in *Savage*, in *McNeill v. Canada*, [1986] F.C.J. No. 532, [1986] 2 C.T.C. 352, 86 D.T.C. 6477 (F.C.T.D.) and *Segall v. Canada*, [1986] F.C.J. No. 904, [1986] 2 C.T.C. 364, 86 D.T.C. 6486 (F.C.T.D.), "accommodation differential allowances" paid to two anglophone air traffic controllers who were transferred from Montreal to Ottawa to diffuse tensions with francophone air traffic controllers were characterized as non-taxable benefits on the basis that they were not received "in respect of, in the course of, or by virtue of the taxpayers' employment as required by paragraph 6(1)(a). According to Rouleau J (at para. 39):

[T]he payments made to the transferring air traffic controllers did not arise by virtue of the contract of employment but rather pursuant to a separate agreement, which was entered into before the effective date of the transfers ... . But more importantly, the payment of the allowance with which I am concerned was primarily motivated by considerations extraneous to the employment, namely public and labour relations considerations.

Compare the reasoning in *Phillips v. M.N.R.*, [1994] F.C.J. No. 271, [1994] 1 C.T.C. 383, 94 D.T.C. 6177 (F.C.A.), where the taxpayer, an employee with the CNR who was transferred from Moncton to Winnipeg after the closing of the Moncton shops in 1987, received a relocation payment of $10,000 to compensate for higher housing costs in Winnipeg. Rejecting the taxpayer's argument that the payment was not received "in respect of, in the course of, or by virtue of" his employment, the court stated (at paras. 19-24):

[I]f an employee receives a payment on the condition that he or she continues to work for the employer, as is the case before us, then that payment can hardly be said to have stemmed from considerations extraneous to the employment relationship.

Collateral contracts, like all contracts, are only a means of providing objective evidence of subjective intent. By itself, a collateral contract cannot therefore be conclusive of whether a payment is received in the capacity of person or employee. To focus on the existence of a collateral contract to the exclusion of its context — the employment relationship — is to allow the form of the document to prevail over its substance. ...

> Applying the law as outlined in *Savage*, ... I am driven to the inescapable conclusion that the respondent received the $10,000 payment in his capacity as employee.

See also *Blanchard v. Canada*, [1995] F.C.J. No. 1045, [1995] 2 C.T.C. 262, 95 D.T.C. 5479 (F.C.A.), where the taxpayer argued that a payment of $7,420 pursuant to the cancellation of an employer housing arrangement "arose from factors 'extraneous' or 'collateral' to the respondent's employment." Rejecting this argument, Linden JA concluded (at para. 16):

> There is no doubt that the payment to the taxpayer came about as part of a real estate transaction. But this transaction was not a mere "house deal," totally divorced from the employment relationship of the taxpayer, which might take it out of the reach of paragraph 6(1)(a). That section, if I am to respect its unambiguous wording, requires only some connection between the receipt of a payment and the recipient's employment — nothing seems to turn on the source of the payment. It makes no difference whether a receipt arises from a land deal, a boat deal, a livestock deal, or any other type of deal, as long as the receipt is linked to the recipient's employment.

6.   In *Waffle v. M.N.R.*, [1968] C.T.C. 572, 69 D.T.C. 5007 (Ex. Ct.), the taxpayer was a co-owner and employee in a Ford dealership (Thorncrest) that, as a result of meeting its quota in a sales promotion campaign, was awarded a free Caribbean holiday for two. Rejecting the taxpayer's argument that the benefit was not received "in respect of, in the course of, or by virtue of his employment because the benefit was received directly from Ford, not his employer, Cattanach J concluded:

> I do not accede to the proposition that it follows from the fact that the person paying the cost is not the employer of the recipient, that such payment does not accrue to the recipient in respect of, in the course of, or by virtue of his office or employment.

For similar results, see *Robinson v. M.N.R.*, [1970] Tax ABC 1287 and *Dagenais v. Canada*, [1995] T.C.J. No. 20, [1995] 2 C.T.C. 2934 (T.C.C.).

7.   In *Giffen v. Canada*, [1995] T.C.J. No. 791, [1995] 2 C.T.C. 2767 (T.C.C.), the taxpayer, who was an employee of a company that required him to travel frequently by air in the course of his employment, was assessed on the value of "frequent flyer points" exchanged for free airline tickets valued at $15,369 in 1989 and $36,606 in 1990. Rejecting the taxpayer's argument that the points were not received or enjoyed "in respect of, in the course of, or by virtue of an office or employment" as required by paragraph 6(1)(a), the court held that the free travel was a taxable benefit "because it was available only to employees who travelled and who were members of a frequent flyer plan." According to the court (at para. 24):

> Where a benefit is received by reason of employment it is of no consequence that some other condition unconnected with employment must also be met. Free travel was not a benefit received in a personal capacity and wholly divorced from employment.

c. Valuation

Having determined that a "benefit" was received or enjoyed "in respect of, in the course of, or by virtue of an office or employment," it is necessary to place a value on the benefit in order to determine the amount to be included under paragraph 6(1)(a). In *Detchon v. Canada*, [1995] T.C.J. No. 1342, [1996] 1 C.T.C. 2475, 11 C.C.P.B. 291 (T.C.C.), the court considered different methods of valuing the benefit of free education provided to the taxpayer's children by a private educational institution at which the taxpayer was employed.

Detchon v. Canada
[1995] T.C.J. No. 1342, [1996] 1 C.T.C. 2475,
11 C.C.P.B. 291 (T.C.C.)

RIP JTCC: The appellants Eric Detchon and Clifford Goodwin appeal income tax assessments for the 1985 and 1986 taxation years on the basis neither of them received a benefit in respect of employment pursuant to paragraph 6(1)(a) of the *Income Tax Act*... as a result of their children attending their employer's school, and alternatively, if a benefit was conferred, the value of the benefit received by each of the appellants was less than determined by the Minister of National Revenue (the "Minister").

In assessing the appellants, the Minister considered that each of them received an employment benefit the value of which was equal to the tuition fees that the parents of other students were required to pay Bishop's College School ("BCS").

...

During the years in appeal the appellants were employed as teachers at BCS in Lennoxville, Quebec. BCS is a private educational institution incorporated as a non-profit corporation under the provisions of the *Quebec Companies Act*. It offers courses to males and females at the secondary level (grades 7 to 11) and grade 12. The school has both day students and boarding students.

Lawrence Sakamoto was Treasurer and Director of Finance at BCS in 1985 and 1986. At time of trial he was Treasurer. He stated BCS caters to people who in 1995 can afford to pay tuition and board aggregating $23,000 for their child's education. Students from Mexico, Japan, Venezuela, Spain, United States and Canada and other countries attend BCS.

For the years in appeal the teachers at BCS had no "formal" contract said Sakamoto. They simply received a letter setting out their salary for the year. Although it was not stated in writing, Sakamoto testified, the teachers at BCS had certain obligations due to the fact BCS was primarily a boarding school: the teachers had to live on campus, attend chapel every morning, be available 24 hours a day, seven days a week and send their school age children to BCS. The teachers were also expected to eat at the school cafeteria since a "family atmosphere" was encouraged. BCS employed "about 40 teachers" during the years in appeal.

309

On the other hand, Sakamoto explained, the teachers were aware of the school's policy of free tuition to children of staff. He described the free tuition as "part of the culture" of BCS. He stated staff "knew what is required of you by the nature of the place and what you are entitled to." Staff entitled to free tuition for their children included administrators, including Sakamoto who sent his child to BCS.

Sakamoto insisted that teachers' children were obliged to attend BCS. This was due to "the nature of the school." He explained members of staff live on campus with their families and would not be "good for our image if [teachers'] children of school age go to a public school."

"BCS" he said, "had no other choice." For a child to go to a public school would mean, Sakamoto declared, "the staff child [is] playing for the opposition."

Sakamoto said that if a teacher, for example, did not send his or her child to BCS "the teacher would have to think it over carefully." He stated BCS did not have a policy of dismissing a teacher if a child did not attend the school, but suggested the teacher would be reprimanded by the school's headmaster.

It was advantageous to BCS for the staff to send their children to the school, Sakamoto declared. Traditionally, he said, children of BCS staff do better academically than other students and so raise the average of the school. They also participate more actively in extra-curricular activities. These children are role models. He also stated that if the children attend BCS the staff is better able to devote their time to the school; their time is not disturbed with their child's daily travel to school in Lennoxville.

BCS has never achieved full capacity and its cost of having its staff's children attend is "virtually nothing," Sakamoto stated. These children, he said, "do not take places of other children." The children of BCS staff are fully integrated in the school's general population. They attend the same classes and follow the same programs as paying students.

Salaries are not dependent on whether their child is attending BCS, Sakamoto stated. There is no increase in a salary paid to a teacher, for example, once his or her child leaves the school. A staff parent cannot transfer his or her right to send a child to BCS to another person, for example, to a niece or nephew.

...

Sakamoto estimated that 14 or 15 children of BCS staff attended the school during 1985 and 1986. Approximately 300 students attended BCS during those years of which 240 were boarders and 60 were day students. Children of staff were day students. Fees for room and board were $11,000 for the 1984-1985 term and $11,950 for the 1985-1986 term. Fees for day students for the 1984-1985 term and 1985-1986 term were $6,900 and $7,470 respectively.

...

Based on a student population of 300, including staff children, the cost of instruction and related administration for each student was $5,013. Similar costs per student for 1986 and 1987 fiscal years were $5,504 and $5,023 respectively.

During 1985 and 1986 Detchon's salary from BCS was $25,582 and $30,621 respectively and Goodwin's salary was $28,675 and $26,619 respectively. Neither Detchon nor Goodwin paid any tuition for their children.

...

Submissions

... The essence of the argument of appellants' counsel was that if I find his clients received a benefit from their employer, the value of the benefit was less than the amount of the tuition charged by BCS. If what is assessed by paragraph 6(1)(a) of the Act is the fair market value of a benefit then one must refer to the standard definition of fair market value, that is, the value of a thing a person not obligated to buy would pay to a person not obligated to sell.

Parliament contemplated that in certain circumstances the word "value" in paragraph 6(1)(a) may mean something other than fair market, counsel declared. Revenue Canada has recognized, for example, "that subsidized meals provided to employees [are] not considered to confer a taxable benefit provided the employee is required to pay a reasonable charge," that is, the cost of the food, its preparation and service. Interpretation Bulletin IT-470, dated February 16, 1981. Counsel also referred to ... paragraphs 42 and 43 (airline employees who travel with airline passes on stand-by and bus and rail employees) of Bulletin IT-470R, dated April 3, 1988 (and December 11, 1989) where Revenue Canada recognizes value of a benefit to be something other than fair market value.

...

The appellants could have sent their children to public schools or a subsidized private school in Quebec at costs lower than those charged by BCS. ... Had the children gone to subsidized private schools, it was suggested the annual tuition in the years of appeal would have been in the neighbourhood of $500 to $600. If one examines the financial situation of the appellants, counsel stated, the tuition charged by BCS cannot be the criterion to determine value for purposes of paragraph 6(1)(a) since this would lead to an absurd situation; the appellants do not have the money to pay the tuition or the tax.

The word "value" in paragraph 6(1)(a) may have more than one meaning. It may mean "fair market value," or "cost" or something else. Counsel referred to the advice of Lord Hobhouse in *Simms v. Registrar of Probates*, [1990] AC 323 at 335, quoted in *Craies on Statute Law*, 7th edition, London: Sweet & Maxwell 1971 at page 87:

> Where there are two meanings, each adequately satisfying the meaning (of a statute), and great harshness is produced by one of them, that has a legitimate influence in inclining the mind to the other ... it is more probable that the legislature should have used the word ... in that interpretation which least offends our sense of justice.

...

M. Gauthier [counsel for the appellants] concluded that the policy of BCS to allow its staff to send their children to the school at no cost was for the advantage and benefit of BCS and not its employees. If there was any benefit to the employees, the value of the benefit was the incremental cost of having these children attend BCS, which was nil. Finally, he submitted that if I conclude the value of the benefit is not related to the incremental cost, the value of the benefit is the value of obtaining equivalent education elsewhere in Quebec.

M. Lefebvre, counsel for the respondent, argued that the appellants did receive a benefit from BCS in 1985 and 1986 and the value of the benefit was equal to the tuition charged by BCS. She added there was no other evidence of value other than the tuition at BCS.

...

Analysis

... I do not agree with appellants' counsel that the value of the benefit is the additional or incremental cost to BCS of having the appellants' children attend the school. ... I have been cited no Canadian authority permitting me to value the benefit to the appellants at BCS's incremental cost of having additional students and ignore both the average cost to BCS of teaching a student and the price paid to BCS.

I do not agree with M. Gauthier that the value of the benefit is the cost of obtaining education elsewhere in Quebec. ... The appellants educate their children at BCS and it is the value of the benefit at BCS which is to be considered.

...

There is no evidence before me that parents who are not employed by BCS, but who earn similar income to the appellants, may send their children to BCS for free or reduced tuition. If there was such evidence, I would be inclined to value the benefit to the appellants at the amount of fees, if any, paid by such parents.

There is no obligation for an employer to charge its employees for a good or service any more than its actual costs of the good or service. The employer need not add any profit element and indirect overhead costs to any good or service it provides to its employees: *ABC Steel Buildings Ltd. v. Minister of National Revenue*, [1974] CTC 2176, 74 DTC 1124 (TRB). ... [I]n the circumstances, valuing the benefit at the average cost per student is an appropriate method of valuation.

...

[I]t is obvious that the salaries of the appellants are insufficient to meet the tax assessed on the value of the benefit added to their incomes. However, it would not be just and reasonable to other Canadian taxpayers that employees, solely because of their occupations and low level salaries, obtain a tax free benefit from an employer who does not pay a higher wage. To permit such a tax advantage to one group of taxpayers is not within the object and spirit of the Act. The average cost to BCS of educating a student is a sensible method of valuing the benefit. ...

Appeals allowed.

NOTES AND QUESTIONS

1.   Assuming that the free education provided to the taxpayers' children in *Detchon* was a taxable benefit within the meaning of paragraph 6(1)(a), how, according to the taxpayers, ought the benefit to have been valued? Do you agree with the method chosen by the Court? Why or why not?

2.   In *Waffle v. M.N.R.*, [1968] C.T.C. 572, 69 D.T.C. 5007 (Ex. Ct.), the taxpayer argued that a free Caribbean vacation for two either should not be taxable since it was "not convertible into money" or should be taxable at its subjective value to the taxpayer. With respect to the first argument, Cattanach J observed (at paras. 40-41):

> The doctrine that no form of remuneration is taxable unless it is something which is money or money's worth and convertible into money stems from *Tennant v. Smith*, [1892] AC 150, decided in the House of Lords as long ago as 1892.
>
> I think that the language employed in Section 5 [now paragraph 6(1)(a)] to the effect that the "value of board, lodging and other benefits of any kind whatsoever," is to be included in taxable income, overcomes the principle laid down in *Tennant v. Smith* (supra). Obviously board which has been consumed and lodging which has been enjoyed cannot be converted into money by the taxpayer either subsequently or prior thereto and, in my view, the identical considerations apply to "other benefits of any kind whatsoever."

With respect to the alternative argument, he continued (at paras. 42-43):

> I fail to follow how the true measure of the value of the award can be other than the cost of the award to Ford. There is no other standard which is applicable. I can see no grounds for holding that the amount should be limited to an estimate of an amount which the appellant might have spent on the trip himself if Ford had not borne that cost. The appellant knew what was being offered to himself and his wife and he accepted the award, although he would not know the precise cost of the award to Ford.
>
> As I understand the intention of Section 5 it is simply to bring the benefits of any kind whatsoever from an office or employment into tax, that is to say, what has been spent to provide those benefits.

For a similar result, see *Philp v. M.N.R.*, [1970] C.T.C. 330, 70 D.T.C. 6237 (Ex. Ct.).

3.   In *Giffen v. Canada*, [1995] T.C.J. No. 791, [1995] 2 C.T.C. 2767 (T.C.C.), where the taxpayers were assessed on the basis that free air travel received in exchange for frequent flyer points acquired in the course of their employment was a taxable benefit within the meaning of paragraph 6(1)(a), the court discussed the value of the benefits as follows (at paras. 28-30):

> The decisions of the Exchequer Court in *Philp v. M.N.R.* ... and *Waffle v. M.N.R.* ... are not authority for the proposition that cost to the employer is a universally applicable measure of

the value of a benefit from employment. Here the benefits were not acquired by ordinary purchase in the open market.

> In my view the proper measure of the value of a benefit in the form of a reward ticket is the price which the employee would have been obliged to pay for a revenue ticket entitling him to travel on the same flight in the same class of service and subject to the same restrictions as are applicable to reward tickets. The sale price of a revenue ticket for travel in the same class on the same flight is only the starting point in the calculation. Care must be taken to adjust for the differences in value between revenue tickets and reward tickets attributable to restrictions on the latter. ...

> ... I conclude that an economy class reward ticket is unlikely to be worth more than the most heavily discounted economy ticket sold for the flight in question. Business class and first class revenue tickets are not discounted but, just as in the case of economy tickets, reward tickets for travel in those two classes cannot, because of restrictions, be regarded as equal in value to unrestricted revenue tickets. It seems likely that restrictions to which first class and business class reward tickets are subject reduce the value of them to the same extent that restrictions on economy class reward tickets reduce their value. Thus the value of a reward ticket in either business or first class is equal to that proportion of an unrestricted business or first class fare which the price of the most heavily discounted economy class fare on that flight is of the price of a full fare economy class ticket.

4.   In *Wisla v. Canada*, [1999] T.C.J. No. 821, [2000] 1 C.T.C. 2823 (T.C.C.), the Minister included in the taxpayer's income the amount of $562, representing the value of a gold ring given to all employees who had achieved 15 years of service with the employer. Although the court agreed with the Minister that the ring was a benefit received by the taxpayer in respect of his employment, it accepted the taxpayer's argument that because the ring was stamped with the corporate logo of the employer, its value was substantially reduced. The court concluded that the value of the ring in this case should be equal to its scrap value, which came to $73.

According to paragraph 9 of IT-470R:

> When an employee is rewarded by an employer with merchandise or other non-cash items, the fair market value of the award must be included in the employee's income. If an item is personalized with a corporate logo or engraved with the employee's name or a message, the fair market value of the item may be negatively affected. In such cases, the amount to be included in the employee's income may be reduced by a reasonable amount, having regard to all the circumstances. Depending on the value of a particular award, the existence of a logo may have little, if any, impact on the fair market value of the item. When the award given is a plaque, trophy or other memento of nominal value for which there is no market, it is not necessary to include any amount in an employee's income as a taxable benefit.

5.   In *Jelles v. Canada*, [1996] T.C.J. No. 1712, [1997] 2 C.T.C. 2122 (T.C.C.), the taxpayers, who were employed as resident caretakers of an apartment building, included $250 per month as a taxable benefit in respect of a suite that they occupied five nights a week, residing in a nearby home on weekends and statutory holidays. Accepting the taxpayers' evidence that they were required to be on call 24 hours per day and to stay in the suite as part of their caretaking duties, the court rejected the Minister's argument that the benefit should be valued at the suite's rental value of $965 per month.

6. In *Taylor v. Canada*, [1995] T.C.J. No. 294, [1995] 2 C.T.C. 2223 (T.C.C.), the taxpayer was held to have enjoyed a taxable benefit under paragraph 6(1)(a) from the exclusive personal use of a yacht worth $175,000. Rejecting the taxpayer's argument that the value of the benefit should be determined only for the summer months when the yacht was in use, the court accepted the Minister's method of valuation based on a presumed annual rate of return on the cost of the yacht.

7. In *Richmond v. Canada*, [1998] T.C.J. No. 258, [1998] 3 C.T.C. 2552, 98 D.T.C. 1804 (T.C.C.), a taxpayer was provided with a year-round reserved parking space by his employer in downtown Toronto. The taxpayer argued that because he usually walked to work and only used the space about once per week, the full market value of the annual parking spot (assessed at $1,800 by the Minister) should not be added to his income. Bell TCJ rejected this argument, explaining (at para. 7) that "[w]hether the appellant used the property is of little consequence. It was available to him and was accordingly a benefit to him."

2. Specific Rules

In addition to the general rule in paragraph 6(1)(a), sections 6 and 7 contain a number of specific rules pursuant to which particular kinds of benefits are also included in computing a taxpayer's income from an office or employment. The following cases and text examine the most important of these rules.

a. Automobile Benefits

Subparagraph 6(1)(a)(iii) specifically excludes from the general rule governing taxable benefits "any benefit ... that was a benefit in respect of the use of an automobile." In place of the general rule, automobile benefits are subject to specific rules in paragraphs 6(1)(e), (k), and (l) and subsections 6(1.1), (2), and (2.1). Paragraph 6(1)(e) and subsections 6(2) and (2.1) require employees to include a specific amount (described as a "reasonable standby charge") in respect of employer-provided automobiles. Paragraphs 6(1)(k) and (l) require an employee to include specific amounts where the employer pays for automobile operating expenses relating to the personal use of the automobile by the employee. For the purpose of these rules, subsection 248(1) defines an "automobile" as:

> a motor vehicle that is designed or adapted primarily to carry individuals on highways and streets and that has a seating capacity for not more than the driver and 8 passengers,

but does not include ambulances or emergency response vehicles and various other motor vehicles (taxis, buses, hearses, and certain kinds of vans and pickup trucks) used in the course of a business.

Finally, subsection 6(1.1) excludes from the exception in subparagraph 6(1)(a)(iii) "any amount or benefit related to the parking of the vehicle," making such benefits subject to the general rule in paragraph 6(1)(a). Although parking benefits were held to be taxable in *Monteith v. Canada*, [1997] T.C.J. No. 1282, [1998] 2 C.T.C. 2281, 98 D.T.C. 1306 (T.C.C.), the Court in *Chow v. Canada*, [2000] T.C.J. No. 902, [2001] 1 C.T.C. 2741, 2001 D.T.C. 164 (T.C.C.) concluded that free parking constituted an economic advantage to the taxpayer's employer rather than the taxpayer. See also *Adler v. Canada*, [2007] T.C.J. No. 166, [2007] 4 C.T.C. 2205, 2007 D.T.C. 783 (T.C.C.), an appeal by 16 taxpayers who were assessed in respect of free parking passes provided by their employer, Telus Communications Inc. Rowe J considered the circumstances of each taxpayer separately including the nature and extent of their use of the parking pass and the benefits to the employer of having them drive to work, including the costs saved on taxi fares and other alternative transport for those employees required to travel extensively in carrying out their job duties. On the basis of this review he concluded that 14 of the taxpayers had received a taxable benefit, while two had not.

i. STANDBY CHARGE

According to paragraph 6(1)(e), where a taxpayer's employer or a person related to the employer makes an automobile available to the taxpayer or a person related to the taxpayer, the taxpayer must include in computing his or her income from the office or employment:

the amount, if any, by which

    (i)   an amount that is a reasonable standby charge for the automobile for the total number of days in the year during which it was made so available

exceeds

    (ii)   the total of all amounts, each of which is an amount (other than an expense related to the operation of the automobile) paid in the year to the employer or the person related to the employer by the taxpayer or the person related to the taxpayer for the use of the automobile.

In general, therefore, where an employer makes an automobile available to an employee, the employee must include an amount equal to a "reasonable standby charge" less amounts paid in the taxation year to the employer for the use of the automobile.

For the purposes of paragraph 6(1)(e), subsection 6(2) defines the expression "reasonable standby charge" in terms of a formula the general effect of which is to include as a benefit, subject to the deduction in subparagraph 6(1)(e)(ii), an amount equal to 2 per cent of the cost of the automobile to the employer or two-thirds of the leasing cost (tax included[31]) for each month that the automobile is made available to the employee.[32]

Where the taxpayer is "required by the employer to use the automobile in connection with or in the course of the office or employment" and "the distance traveled by the automobile" while it is available to the taxpayer is "primarily in connection with or in the course of the office or employment," however, the standby charge may be reduced to the extent that the taxpayer's use of the automobile for personal purposes does not exceed 1,667 kilometres per month (about 20,000 kilometres per year).[33] As well, where the taxpayer was "employed principally in selling or leasing automobiles," the standby charge may be further reduced under subsection 6(2.1), the effect of which is to reduce the applicable percentage in subsection 6(2) from 2 per cent to 1½ per cent and to establish the cost of the automobile to the employer as the greater of the average cost of new automobiles acquired by the employer for sale or lease and the average cost of all such automobiles.

For our purposes, there is no need to examine the formula in subsection 6(2) in detail, nor the special rules in subsection 6(2.1).[34] However, since the application of these rules depends on the employer (or a person related to the employer) making an automobile "available" to the taxpayer or a person related to the taxpayer, it is useful to consider the meaning of this concept for the purposes of paragraph 6(1)(e). This was the issue in *Hewitt v. Canada*, [1995] T.C.J. No. 1339, [1996] 1 C.T.C. 2675 (T.C.C.).

Hewitt v. Canada
[1995] T.C.J. No. 1339, [1996] 1 C.T.C. 2675 (T.C.C.)

ROWE JTCC: The appellant appeals from assessments of income tax for his 1990 and 1991 taxation years. ... The sole remaining issue was whether the Minister was correct in including into income amounts calculated as a benefit

---

[31] See subs. 6(7), which requires tax payable in respect of the property or service to be included in the cost of any property, service, or lease payment required under section 6 to be included in computing a taxpayer's income for a taxation year.

[32] On this basis, where an automobile that costs an employer $20,000 (including tax) is made available to an employee throughout the year, the reasonable standby charge would be 0.02 × $20,000 × 12 = $4,800.

[33] See the description of A and B in subs. 6(2). According to the 2003 Federal Budget, the test to determine whether an automobile is used "primarily" in connection with or in the course of a taxpayer's office or employment is satisfied where "more than 50 percent" of the distance traveled by the automobile is for this purpose.

[34] For cases considering subs. 6(2.1), see *McKay v. M.N.R.*, [1990] 1 C.T.C. 2154, 90 D.T.C. 1064 (T.C.C.); *McCoy v. M.N.R.*, [1991] T.C.J. No. 334, [1991] 2 C.T.C. 2061, 91 D.T.C. 903 (T.C.C.); *Fillion v. M.N.R.*, [1994] T.C.J. No. 609, [1995] 2 C.T.C. 2741, 95 D.T.C. 79 (T.C.C.); and *Adams v. Canada*, [1998] F.C.J. No. 477, [1998] 2 C.T.C. 353, 98 D.T.C. 6266 (F.C.A.). See also IT-63R5, paras. 15 and 16.

flowing from a standby charge in the sum of $5,315 for 1990 and $5,315 in 1991, together with $359 attributable to the GST levy.

The appellant testified he resides in Quesnel, British Columbia, and is an electrician. He is the sole shareholder of Cariboo Industrial Electric Ltd. ("Cariboo"). He was employed by Cariboo during the years under appeal. Cariboo owned a 1990 Mazda Miata, which was purchased in November, 1989. The automobile was driven until October 31, 1990, at which time it had approximately 8,000 kilometres on the odometer. The appellant stated that 75 per cent of the total distance driven was for purposes of his employment with Cariboo. That percentage included a 1,000 kilometre return trip between Quesnel and Vancouver and another 4,000 kilometres incurred in travelling between Quesnel and Cranbrook, British Columbia to complete a contract for electrical installation. He did not maintain a log to record the purpose of the balance of the kilometres driven. After October 31, 1990, Cariboo had a contract in Quesnel which occupied the appellant for more than one year and he used a pick-up truck owned by Cariboo for purposes of carrying out his work. The Mazda Miata was stored in the appellant's garage at his home and was insured only for fire and theft. It did not have license plates or registration in 1991 which would have permitted the vehicle to have been operated lawfully on public highways. In June, 1992 the Miata was again insured and licensed for street use.

The appellant's position is that he should not be assessed a standby charge in respect of a motor vehicle that was not used by him and could not have been lawfully driven by him, owing to the lack of proper insurance and registration.

Counsel for the respondent submitted that the appellant, as sole shareholder of Cariboo, the corporation, had full control over potential use of the vehicle and it was stored in the garage at his personal residence.

The Minister's position is consistent with the content of paragraph 14 of Interpretation Bulletin IT-63R4 [now paragraph 18 of IT-63R5], which reads as follows: ...

> Where a shareholder is also an employee and an automobile is made available to the shareholder (or to a person related to the shareholder) in the capacity of an employee, the benefit is included in income under section 6 as income from employment, rather than under section 15 as a benefit conferred on a shareholder.

In IT-63R4, paragraph 15 [now paragraph 11 of IT-63R5], the subsection 6(2) formula — involving letters and numbers and fractions or percentages thereof — used to calculate the amount of the benefit, is set out. From its complexity, it may serve an extra purpose, perhaps to illustrate the exact proportion of constituents needed to produce rocket fuel. Then, the last sentence of paragraph 15 states:

> An automobile is available to the employee if it is used by the employee all day or for any part of the day or even if the automobile sits unused in the employee's garage or on the employee's driveway or parking spot.

...

There is no doubt that the appellant, as the sole shareholder of the corporation, Cariboo — also his employer — could have obtained proper insurance and registration for the Mazda vehicle any time he chose. However, between the end of October 1990 and the beginning of June, 1992 he, as the operating mind of Cariboo, decided the vehicle would not be required in the course of his employment. From the perspective of the appellant as an employee, it is difficult to understand what benefit was derived by him from the mere existence of the Miata, without proper insurance or license, sitting in his garage. I fail to see how the Minister is at any disadvantage in these situations as the same day a vehicle becomes insured and licensed for street use, then the basis of the standby charge would be valid and would continue to apply each day thereafter, even if the vehicle were never to be driven by the taxpayer. Otherwise, a damaged vehicle owned by a corporation, previously driven by an employee/shareholder, could be the subject of a standby charge assessment on the premise that the controlling shareholder could have, at his option, chosen to repair the car and render it usable. A vehicle, without lawful insurance or license, is not, in my view, "available" to someone for whom the automobile benefit provisions of the Act apply, any more than the proceeds of a corporation's bank account are "available" to the controlling shareholder, whether or not any funds are ever taken. The whole point of the legislation is that a benefit must be conferred on the taxpayer. Once it is found that a benefit has been conferred, then actual use or enjoyment by the taxpayer, in an active sense, is generally not required.

The Minister's assumption that the appellant did not reimburse Cariboo for the personal use of the Mazda was not challenged. During the 1990 taxation year, the appellant estimated that he used the Mazda less than 25 per cent of the time for personal use but it was available to him and he could have used it more until October 31, 1990, at which time the insurance — for street use — and the license expired. Accordingly, the standby charge for that period is appropriate.

The appeal is allowed, with costs, and the assessments are referred back to the Minister for reconsideration and reassessment on the following basis:

1.   1990 taxation year — the benefit with respect to automobile ... standby charge be calculated, on the basis of the facts found in these reasons, for the period January 1 to October 31, 1990.

2.   1991 taxation year — the amounts previously included relating to standby charge ... be deleted.

Appeal allowed.

NOTES AND QUESTIONS

1.   Do you agree with the Court's conclusion in *Hewitt* that the automobile was not "available" for the taxpayer's use from November 1, 1990 to June 1992? Why or why not?

2.   Before 1982, paragraph 6(1)(e) required the employer to have made an automobile available to an employee for the employee's "personal use (whether for his exclusive personal use or otherwise)." In *R v. Harman*, [1980] C.T.C. 83, 80 D.T.C. 6052 (F.C.A.), where an employer-provided automobile was made available to a travelling salesman whose personal use of the automobile accounted for 1,230 of 27,780 miles driven in 1972, the Federal Court of Appeal concluded that the automobile was not available for the employee's "personal use" within the meaning of the words in paragraph 6(1)(e) as it then read. See also *Bouchard v. Canada*, [1983] C.T.C. 173, 83 D.T.C. 5193 (F.C.T.D.), where Cattanach J held that a Rolls Royce owned by a company of which the taxpayer was the president and principal shareholder was not available for his personal use within the meaning of paragraph 6(1)(e) as it then read on the basis that the automobile was used to the extent of 90 per cent for business purposes.

In *Lavigueur v. M.N.R.*, [1991] 1 C.T.C. 2570, 91 D.T.C. 445 (T.C.C.), Dussault TCJ noted (at para. 13) that paragraph 6(1)(e) was amended "to neutralize the effect of the decision" in *Harman*, by requiring an employee to use the standby charge to compute an automobile benefit regardless of "whether the automobile was made available to the employee for personal use or not." Is this statutory history relevant to the decision in *Hewitt v. Canada*, [1995] T.C.J. No. 1339, [1996] 1 C.T.C. 2675 (T.C.C.)? Does it affect your conclusion as to the appropriate result?

3.   For other cases in which automobiles have been held not to have been available for a taxpayer's use within the meaning of paragraph 6(1)(e) as it currently reads, see *Franke v. Canada*, [1994] T.C.J. No. 263, [1994] 1 C.T.C. 2908, 94 D.T.C. 1524 (T.C.C.); *Rittinger v. Canada*, [1997] T.C.J. No. 67, [1997] 2 C.T.C. 2507 (T.C.C.); and *MacMillan v. The Queen*, [2005] T.C.J. No. 400, [2005] 4 C.T.C. 2463 (T.C.C.).

4.   In *Finochio v. Canada*, [1994] T.C.J. No. 840, 95 D.T.C. 197 (T.C.C.), the taxpayer objected to the inclusion of an automobile benefit under paragraph 6(1)(e) on the grounds that the automobile was available to other employees besides himself. Noting that neither paragraph 6(1)(e) nor subsection 6(2) requires the automobile to have been made available "exclusively" to the employee, the court dismissed the taxpayer's appeal. See also *Papa v. M.N.R.*, [1987] T.C.J. No. 745, [1987] 2 C.T.C. 2209, 87 D.T.C. 529 (T.C.C.), and *Adams v. Canada*, [1998] F.C.J. No. 477, [1998] 2 C.T.C. 353, 98 D.T.C. 6266 (F.C.A.).

5.   Because all or substantially all of the distance travelled by the automobile in *Hewitt v. Canada*, [1995] T.C.J. No. 1339, [1996] 1 C.T.C. 2675 (T.C.C.),

was not "in connection with or in the course of" the taxpayer's employment, the taxpayer was required to include as a standby charge an amount equal to 2 per cent of the automobile's cost for each month in which the automobile was available for his use. Since the automobile was available for the taxpayer's use for 10 months in 1990, the effect of the decision in *Hewitt* was to require the taxpayer to include as an automobile benefit for his 1990 taxation year an amount equal to 10/12 of the amount assessed by the Minister, or $4,429.17.

6.   Where a taxpayer is "required by the employer to use the automobile in connection with or in the course of the office or employment" and "all or substantially all of the distance travelled by the automobile" while it is available to the taxpayer is "in connection with or in the course of the office or employment," the standby charge may be reduced to the extent that the taxpayer's use of the automobile for personal purposes does not exceed 1,667 kilometres a month. For this purpose, paragraph 5 of *Interpretation Bulletin* IT-63R5, "Benefits, Including Standby Charge for an Automobile, from the Personal Use of a Motor Vehicle Supplied by an Employer — After 1992," August 21, 1995, states:

> In addition to what would obviously be considered use of a motor vehicle supplied by an employer that is not in connection with or in the course of the taxpayer's office or employment, i.e., personal use (e.g., vacation trips, personal shopping trips, etc.), such use includes travel between the employee's place of work and home, even though the employee may have to return to work after regular duty hours. An exception occurs, however, where (as required by the employer or with the employer's permission) the employee proceeds directly from home to a point of call other than the employer's place of business to which the employee reports regularly (e.g., to make repairs at customers' premises), or returns home from such a point. These particular trips are not considered to be of a personal nature. Also, where privately owned motor vehicles are prohibited from entering a restricted area where the employment duties are performed, and the distances to be travelled within the restricted area are such that a motor vehicle is necessary, the use and availability of the employer's motor vehicle within the restricted area is not considered to be for personal use. Employers and employees should keep records on the use of a motor vehicle so that the total kilometres driven in a calendar year by an employee or a person related to the employee may be properly apportioned between business use and personal use.

7.   In *Alston v. Canada,* [1997] T.C.J. No. 540, [1997] 3 C.T.C. 2283 (T.C.C.), the taxpayer, who was employed by the Municipality of Metropolitan Toronto as the director of operations for the Toronto Department of Ambulance Services, had use of a sport-utility vehicle equipped with emergency lights, a siren, and first aid equipment. Accepting the taxpayer's argument that the automobile was an "ambulance" to which the rules in paragraph 6(1)(e) and subsection 6(2) do not apply, the court nonetheless held that the taxpayer had received a benefit within the meaning of the general rule in paragraph 6(1)(a). Dismissing the taxpayer's appeal, the court implicitly accepted the Minister's valuation of the benefit under the rules in subsection 6(2).

ii. OPERATING EXPENSES

Paragraphs 6(1)(k) and (l) were enacted applicable to 1993 and subsequent taxation years in order to simplify the calculations and record-keeping requirements formerly involved in computing automobile operating expense benefits under the general rule in paragraph 6(1)(a).

Paragraph 6(1)(k) applies where an employee or person related to an employee is subject to paragraph 6(1)(e), the employer or a person related to the employer pays for automobile operating expenses relating to the personal use of the automobile by the employee or the person related to the employee, and the employee or related person does not reimburse the payer during the taxation year or within 45 days after the end of the taxation year. In these circumstances, the employee is generally required to include as an additional automobile benefit a fixed amount for each kilometre that the automobile is driven "otherwise than in connection with or in the course of the taxpayer's office or employment" less amounts reimbursed to the payer during the taxation year or within 45 days after the end of the taxation year.[35] For 2009, this fixed amount is 24 cents per kilometre or 21 cents per kilometre where the taxpayer is employed "principally in selling or leasing automobiles."[36]

Where the automobile is "used primarily in the performance of the duties of the taxpayer's office or employment" while it is available for the taxpayer's use, the taxpayer may use an alternative method of calculating the operating expense benefit, provided that the taxpayer notifies the employer in writing before the end of the taxation year of the taxpayer's intention to do so. In this case, the operating expense benefit is calculated as half the amount of the standby charge less amounts reimbursed to the payer during the taxation year or within 45 days after the end of the taxation year.[37]

Paragraph 6(1)(l) applies where an employer does not make an automobile available to an employee, but confers on an employee "a benefit in respect of the operation of an automobile" owned or leased by the employee himself or herself. In these circumstances, provided that the benefit is conferred on the employee "in respect of, in the course of or because of, the taxpayer's office or employment," the employee must include the "value" of the benefit in computing his or her income from the office or employment. According to paragraph 22 of IT-63R5:

> The value of the benefit is calculated by determining the ratio of the personal use kilometres to the total kilometres multiplied by the operating costs of the vehicle paid by the employer.

For this purpose, as explained in paragraph 6 of IT-63R5, "operating costs" include "running costs (e.g., gasoline, oil, maintenance charges and all repair expenses net of insurance proceeds) and some other costs (e.g., licenses and insurance)" but not the cost of acquiring or leasing the automobile.

---

[35] See subpara. 6(1)(k)(v) and the description of B in para. 6(1)(k).

[36] See re. 7305.1 and Department of Finance News Release, December 30, 2008.

[37] See subpara. 6(1)(k)(iv) and the description of B in para. 6(l)(k).

The 2008 Federal Budget announced that the CRA will attempt to reduce the record keeping burden on taxpayers in relation to automobile expenses and benefits. Instead of its current practice of requiring a detailed logbook to record all personal and business use of the automobile, CRA proposes to allow taxpayers to rely on a logbook for a sample period within each year that is representative of the vehicle's use. New guidelines had not yet been released when this edition went to press.

b. Insurance Benefits

Among other exceptions to the general rule in paragraph 6(1)(a), subparagraph 6(1)(a)(i) excludes benefits "derived from the contributions of the taxpayer's employer to or under a ... group sickness or accident insurance plan, private health services plan ... or group term life insurance policy." Subsection 248(1) defines a "group term life insurance policy" as:

> a group life insurance policy under which the only amounts payable by the insurer are
>
> (a)   amounts payable on the death or disability of individuals whose lives are insured in respect of, in the course of or because of, their office or employment or former office or employment, and
>
> (b)   policy dividends or experience rating refunds;

and a "private health services plan" as

> (a)   a contract of insurance in respect of hospital expenses, medical expenses or any combination of such expenses, or
>
> (b)   a medical care insurance plan or hospital care insurance plan or any combination of such plans,

except for specified provincial and federal health insurance plans. The Act does not define the term "group sickness or accident insurance plan."

Although excluded from the general rule in paragraph 6(1)(a), benefits derived from an employer's contributions under a group sickness or accident insurance plan are taxable under paragraph 6(1)(f), while those derived from an employer's contributions under a group life insurance policy are taxable under subsection 6(4). In contrast, benefits derived from an employer's contributions to or under a private health services plan are fully exempt from income tax.

For our purposes, there is no need to examine the exemption for private health service plan benefits in detail, except to note that it applies to dental as well as medical and hospital care plans,[38] and to pose the tax policy question

---

[38]   *Interpretation Bulletin* IT-339R2, "Meaning of 'Private Health Services Plan,'" August 8, 1989, para. 2. See also para. 8, which refers to medical and hospital insurance plans offered by Blue

whether it is fair and efficient to exempt these kinds of employer-provided benefits. Nor is it necessary to examine the taxation of employer-provided group term life insurance, which is subject to a complex set of rules in regulations 2700 to 2704.[39] The taxation of benefits received under a group sickness or accident insurance plan, however, has given rise to a number of interesting legal issues that merit more serious consideration.

In computing a taxpayer's income from an office or employment, paragraph 6(1)(f) requires the taxpayer to include:

> the total of all amounts received by the taxpayer in the year that were payable to the taxpayer on a periodic basis in respect of the loss of all or any part of the taxpayer's income from an office or employment, pursuant to

> (i) a sickness or accident insurance plan,

> (ii) a disability insurance plan, or

> (iii) an income maintenance insurance plan

> to or under which the taxpayer's employer has made a contribution,

subject to a limit that in effect permits a deduction for amounts that taxpayers themselves have contributed to the plan.

The Act does not define the terms "sickness or accident insurance plan," "disability insurance plan," or "income maintenance insurance plan," which are collectively described as "wage loss replacement plans" in *Interpretation Bulletin* IT-428, "Wage Loss Replacement Plans," April 30, 1979, paragraph 1. However, according to paragraph 5 of the bulletin:

> a plan to which paragraph 6(1)(f) applies is any arrangement, however it is styled, between an employer and employees, or between an employer and a group or association of employees, under which provision is made for indemnification of an employee, by means of benefits payable on a periodic basis, if an employee suffers a loss of employment income as a consequence of sickness, maternity or accident.

In the absence of a statutory definition, as explained in the *Interpretation Bulletin* IT-85R2, "Health and Welfare Trusts for Employees," July 31, 1986 at paragraph 2, "an employer's contribution to any of these three types of plans will be a contribution to a 'group sickness or accident insurance plan' as described in subparagraph 6(1)(a)(i), provided that the plan is a 'group' plan and an insured plan."

The characteristics of a "group" plan were considered in *Meyer v. M.N.R.*, [1977] C.T.C. 2581, 77 D.T.C. 413 (T.R.B.), where the taxpayer, the sole

---

Cross and various life insurers as examples of private health services plans within the meaning of the definition in subs. 248(1).

[39] See also CRA's *Employer's Guide: Taxable Benefits and Allowances* [T4130(E) Rev. 08], 15-16.

employee of a company of which the taxpayer and his wife were the sole shareholders, sought to exclude from his employment income premiums paid by the company to a life insurance company for a sickness and accident insurance policy on the basis that it was a group sickness and accident insurance plan within the meaning of subparagraph 6(1)(a)(i). Referring to another case in which the words "group insurance" were given their "ordinary and popular meaning" involving "a contact that provides for the insurance of a number of persons individually,"[40] the board dismissed the taxpayer's appeal from an assessment including the amount of the premiums in computing his income on the grounds (at para. 9) that the insurance that the company obtained "cannot be considered as a group insurance plan within the meaning of the exception of paragraph 6(1)(a) of the *Income Tax Act* when there is but one employee involved."

The characteristics of an "insured" plan are discussed in IT-428, in which the CRA explains that such a plan can include both formal arrangements "as evidenced by a contract negotiated between an employer and employees" and informal arrangements "arising from an understanding on the part of the employees, that wage loss benefits would be made available to them by the employer" (paragraph 5). Where the plan is not provided by an insurance company, however, the department emphasizes that "the plan must be one that is based on insurance principles, *i.e.*, funds must be accumulated, normally in the hands of trustees or in a trust account, that are calculated to be sufficient to meet anticipated claims" (paragraph 7).[41] On this basis, the department explains, paragraph 6(1)(f) does not apply to "uninsured employee benefits such as continuing wage or salary payments based on sick leave debits, which payments are included in income under paragraph 6(1)(a)" (paragraph 7).[42]

The combined result of these provisions is that employees are exempt from tax on the insurance coverage provided by a wage loss replacement plan to which their "employer has made a contribution," for example by paying all or any portion of insurance premiums. However, employees are taxed on periodic payments actually received under these plans. In contrast, under "employee-pay-all plans" (where the premiums are paid by employees themselves, whether by direct payments or by payroll deductions made by the employer on the employees' behalf), employees are taxable on the value of the premiums paid into the plan, but exempt from tax on payments received under the plan. (See IT-428, paragraphs 14 and 16.) Consequently, while characterization as a plan to which an employer has made a contribution is most advantageous *ex ante*,

---

[40] *Plumb v. M.N.R.*, [1964] C.T.C. 228, 64 D.T.C. 5145 (Ex. Ct.).

[41] Thus, the department adds: "If the arrangement merely consists of an unfunded contingency reserve on the part of the employer, it would not be an insurance plan."

[42] See, for example, *Heydom v. Canada*, [1997] T.C.J. No. 341, [1997] 2 C.T.C. 3088 (T.C.C.), in which $24,000 in accumulated sick leave credits received by the taxpayer were held to be a taxable benefit under para. 6(1)(a).

characterization as an employee-pay-all plan is most advantageous *ex post* for those who actually receive benefits under such a plan.

The question of when an employer has "made a contribution" to a wage loss replacement plan was considered in *Dagenais v. Canada*, [1995] F.C.J. No. 671, [1995] 2 C.T.C. 100, 95 D.T.C. 5318 (F.C.T.D.), where the taxpayers were employed under a collective agreement that provided for payment of a wage indemnity in the event of illness or injury. The Minister assessed the taxpayers on the basis that any payments received under this plan were included in income under section 6(1)(f). The taxpayers appealed, arguing that the union had negotiated the wage indemnity by accepting a lesser wage increase, so that in effect employees had paid the cost of the plan. In rejecting this argument the Court stated:

> In order to be exempt from taxation, the Court must be satisfied that it is in fact an employee-pay-all-plan, which means the entire premium must be paid by the employees. The onus of satisfying the Court that this is so rests with the plaintiff.

> ...

> I am satisfied that when the amendments to the relevant sections of the *Income Tax Act* were promulgated in the early 1970s, it was Parliament's intention that various benefits received by employees, including employment insurance benefits, are to be included in income unless they qualify as an exemption. There is no ambiguity created by the language used in section 6 of the Act. In particular, paragraph 6(1)(f) is clear and unambiguous that benefits, such as those in the present case, are to be included in computing a taxpayer's income.

> In order to succeed in their submission, that the benefits package in question was an employee-pay-all-plan, it was incumbent on the plaintiffs to establish that they paid for its entire cost. However, there is simply no evidence to substantiate a claim of that nature. Although there was some suggestion the employees accepted a lower hourly rate increase in order to gain improvements to their benefit package, no evidence was proffered with respect to any concise or exact amount which the employees allegedly paid for the benefits package. Neither was there any evidence as to the amounts which may have been contributed to the plan by the employee or the employer. In the absence of any indications to the contrary, I am unable to conclude that it was only the employees who contributed to the plan in question.

Dagenais was followed in *Leonard v. Canada*, [1996] F.C.J. No. 1171 (F.C.T.D.), where the Court rejected the taxpayer's argument that the sickness and accident insurance plan under which he received payments was an employee-pay-all plan funded by forgoing higher wages. According to Joyal J:

> In the case at bar, there is little substantive evidence leading me to conclude that the disability plan was a trade-off. Furthermore, I venture to suggest that any benefit plan under a collective agreement could easily be regarded as a trade-off, in which case paragraph 6(1)(f) would never apply to unionized employees enjoying disability or other benefits under their collective agreement.

For a similar result see *Pugh v. The Queen*, [2000] T.C.J. No. 585, [2000] 4 C.T.C. 2391, 2000 D.T.C. 3639 (T.C.C.).

The Courts have also had to decide whether a lump sum paid to settle an employee's rights under a wage loss replacement plan is taxable under section

6(1)(f). The Supreme Court of Canada considered this question in the following case.

Tsiaprailis v. The Queen
[2005] S.C.J. No. 9, [2005] 2 C.T.C. 1, 2005 D.T.C. 5119 (S.C.C.)

ABELLA J (Major and Lebel JJ concurring in dissent):

... As a result of the failure by an insurance company to pay disability benefits to her, Vasiliki Tsiaprailis sued for a declaration that she was entitled to those benefits. The parties settled and Ms. Tsiaprailis received a lump sum payment after signing a release in which the insurer denied all liability. The issue in this appeal by Ms. Tsiaprailis is whether a portion of the lump sum settlement is taxable.

I. Background

Ms. Tsiaprailis was employed by Tamco Limited. Under the terms of a collective agreement between Tamco and Ms. Tsiaprailis' union, she was entitled to long-term disability benefits through an insurance policy carried and paid for by her employer. The insurance company ultimately responsible for the policy was Manufacturers Life Insurance Company ("Manulife").

On November 10, 1984, Ms. Tsiaprailis was seriously injured in a car accident. From May 11, 1985 to May 10, 1993, she received long-term disability benefits in accordance with the insurance policy. In May 1993, however, Manulife terminated the benefits, claiming that Ms. Tsiaprailis was no longer totally disabled.

On March 30, 1994, Ms. Tsiaprailis sued Manulife for a declaration that she was entitled to a continuation of her disability benefits.

In the course of five letters exchanged between September 13, 1996 and October 11, 1996, a settlement was negotiated.

...

Manulife accepted [the taxpayer's final offer] ..., entering into a settlement agreement with Ms. Tsiaprailis on October 18, 1996 for a lump sum of $105,000, from which Ms. Tsiaprailis paid $18,068.97 in costs, plus GST and disbursements.

Ms. Tsiaprailis' release in favour of Manulife stated, in part:

IT IS UNDERSTOOD AND AGREED BY THE RELEASOR that this is a compromise settlement of a disputed claim and that the payment of consideration for this Release shall not be deemed nor construed as an admission of liability by the said Releasee in any manner whatsoever.

...

... On September 8, 1997, the Minister of National Revenue reassessed Ms. Tsiaprailis for the 1996 taxation year to include the full $105,000 as income. On

December 15, 1997, a further reassessment allowed her to deduct her legal expenses.

...

Ms. Tsiaprailis appealed the assessment to the Tax Court of Canada ([2001] T.C.J. No. 856, [2002] 1 C.T.C. 2858 (T.C.C. [General Procedure])). The issue before Bowman A.C.J. was whether the full settlement payment received by Ms. Tsiaprailis from Manulife was taxable pursuant either to s. 6(1)(*a*) or s. 6(1)(*f*) of the *Income Tax Act* ...

...

The trial judge held that only s. 6(1)(*f*) was potentially engaged by these facts. However, he concluded that the lump sum settlement was not taxable, holding that:

> The lump sum payment arrived at after a lawsuit was commenced and negotiated as a compromise cannot on any basis of statutory interpretation be described as an "amount ... payable to the taxpayer on a periodic basis". (para. 18)

The majority in the Federal Court of Appeal disagreed, and divided the total payment into a portion it attributed to arrears, and one attributed to future benefits ([2003] F.C.J. No. 431, [2003] 4 F.C. 112 (F.C.A.)). Pelletier JA, Strayer JA concurring, held that the portion of the lump sum payment attributable to arrears was taxable pursuant to s. 6(1)(*f*). Unlike the trial judge, they were of the view that Ms. Tsiaprailis had two kinds of claims against her insurance company: a claim for arrears and a claim for future benefits, claims that could and should be distinguished for tax purposes.

...

Even though they were in the form of a lump sum payment, the majority found the arrears to be "payable on a periodic basis" because, under the insurance policy, they were so payable. Because the settlement was "referable to" the insurance contract, it was, accordingly, paid "pursuant to" a disability insurance policy.

...

Evans JA, in dissent, disagreed with the majority's treatment of the arrears. In his view, the trial judge's interpretation of s. 6(1)(*f*) is the most obvious reading of that provision. He disagreed with both the majority's conclusion that the lump sum was "payable on a periodic basis", as well as its conclusion that it was paid "pursuant to a disability insurance plan". While he agreed that if a lump sum payment is made towards the arrears of periodic payments due under an insurance policy it can be considered "payable on a periodic basis", Evans J.A. found that this conclusion by itself provided no answer to whether the lump sum payment was made "pursuant to" a disability insurance contract. He concluded that the lump sum payment was made pursuant to a settlement agreement, not pursuant to the provisions of the insurance contract.

...

II. Analysis

... In its 1966 report, the Carter Commission recommended that all compensation for personal injuries, including disability insurance benefits, should be taxable as a form of income replacement: *Report of the Royal Commission on Taxation*, vol. 3 (1966), at p. 438. At the time, disability insurance benefits were not taxable. Parliament, however, chose not to follow this recommendation in the tax reform budget of 1971. Instead, Parliament rejected the wholesale taxation of compensation for personal injury, and chose to tax it only in certain defined circumstances as set out in what was then a new provision, s. 6(1)(*f*).

Section 6(1)(*f*) sets out two relevant requirements, both of which must be met if employment insurance plan benefits are to be taxed. First, the amount must be "payable to the taxpayer on a periodic basis". Second, the amount must be paid "pursuant to" a disability insurance plan. Unless the amount is payable "pursuant to" a disability insurance plan, it is irrelevant whether it is payable "on a periodic basis". In my view, the amount was not so payable, and it is therefore unnecessary to determine whether the lump sum payment was payable on a periodic basis.

The phrase "pursuant to" was applied by this Court in *Minister of National Revenue v. Armstrong*, [1956] S.C.R. 446 (S.C.C.). The taxpayer had been ordered to pay $100 per month to his former wife for child support. After payments had been made for two years, the taxpayer gave her a cash settlement of $4,000 in full satisfaction of her claim to further payments under the divorce decree. The issue before the Court was whether the lump sum payment was made "pursuant to" an order or judgment in a divorce or separation action, a condition precedent to taxation under the relevant section of the *Income Tax Act*. All three justices who wrote reasons agreed that the payment was not made "pursuant to" a decree, order or judgment. In the words of Locke J:

> It cannot ... be properly said that this lump sum was paid, in the words of the section, *pursuant* to the divorce decree. It was, it is true, paid *in consequence* of the liability imposed by the decree for the maintenance of the infant, but that does not fall within the terms of the section. [Emphasis in original.] (p. 449)

Kerwin CJ applied "pursuant to" similarly:

> The test is whether it was paid *in pursuance of* a decree, order or judgment and not whether it was paid *by reason of* a legal obligation imposed or undertaken. [Emphasis added.] (p. 447)

Kellock J reached the same conclusion:

> In my opinion, the payment here in question is not within the statute. It was not an amount payable "pursuant to" or "conformément à" ... the decree but rather an amount paid to obtain a release from the liability thereby imposed. (p. 448)

...

Even though *Armstrong* dealt with a settlement paid to extinguish a claim for future, not past benefits, that does not diminish its interpretive value. I share the view that "pursuant to" is different from and narrower than "as a result of".

Black's Law Dictionary (8th ed. 2004) also attributes a narrower definition to the phrase: "[i]n compliance with" or "in accordance with"; "[a]s authorized by"; and "[i]n carrying out". In this case, the lump sum settlement payment was not paid to Ms. Tsiaprailis "in compliance with" or "in accordance with" a disability insurance plan, it was paid "in compliance with" and "in accordance with" a settlement agreement.

Although the arrears component, assuming it was properly divisible from the rest of the settlement, was in consequence of a claim for arrears justified by the disability insurance plan, that does not, in my view, bring it within the scope of s. 6(1)(*f*). The payment to Ms. Tsiaprailis was not paid *pursuant to* the insurance contract, it was, as Kellock J said in *Armstrong*, "an amount paid to obtain a release" (p. 448) from the liability imposed, in this case, by the insurance policy.

. . .

Even if one applied the *surrogatum* principle, as the respondent urges, an application I question both on the facts of this case and the statutory provisions under consideration, I would not find the arrears to be taxable. Damage and settlement payments are inherently neutral for tax purposes and must therefore be classified to determine whether they are taxable. This is the *surrogatum* principle, as defined by Lord Diplock in *London & Thames Haven Oil Wharves Ltd. v. Attwooll (Inspector of Taxes)* (1966), [1967] 2 All E.R. 124 (Eng. C.A.) as follows:

> Where, pursuant to a legal right, a trader receives from another person compensation for the trader's failure to receive a sum of money which, if it had been received, would have been credited to the amount of profits . . . the compensation is to be treated for income tax purposes in the same way as that sum of money would have been treated if it had been received instead of the compensation.

When applying the *surrogatum* principle, the question is what the damage or settlement payment is intended to replace: *Canadian National Railway v. R.*, [1988] 2 C.T.C. 111 (Fed. T.D.), at p. 114. It is a factual inquiry: *Prince Rupert Hotel (1957) Ltd. v. R.*, [1995] 2 C.T.C. 212 (Fed. C.A.), at pp. 216-17.

. . .

In applying the *surrogatum* principle to this case, the general nature of the settlement payment was to release the insurance company from a claim that it was liable and, concurrently, to extinguish Ms. Tsiaprailis' claim for entitlement under the disability insurance policy. The lump sum settlement payment was negotiated based on three aspects of liability under the policy: an amount to extinguish Ms. Tsiaprailis' claim for accumulated arrears, an amount to extinguish her claim for future benefits, and an amount to extinguish her claim for costs.

. . .

As the release states, Manulife explicitly denied liability under the insurance contract. Moreover, throughout the settlement process, it disputed Ms. Tsiaprailis' claim that she was totally disabled and entitled to *any* payments under the policy. Although the parties' negotiations were undoubtedly related to what Ms. Tsiaprailis felt she was entitled to under the policy, those amounts were used more as a way to gauge the reasonableness of any compromise, rather than as a replacement mechanism.

III. Conclusion

The payment resulted from a court action seeking declaratory rights arising from and in consequence of disputed eligibility under a disability policy. The parties never came to an agreement about the value either of the arrears or the future benefits. They did not settle pursuant to liabilities flowing from the policy, but to avoid a judicial determination of what amounts, if any, were owed under it.

The lump sum payment is, in short, an amount paid to extinguish any liability for claims that might be asserted because of a disability policy. It is not, however, a payment made in accordance with or in compliance with that policy, and is not, therefore, a payment made pursuant to it.

...

Accordingly, I would allow the appeal, with costs.

CHARRON J (Bastarache, Binnie and Deschamps JJ concurring):

I have had the benefit of reading the reasons of my colleague Justice Abella. For the reasons that follow, I reach a different result and would dismiss the appeal.

Under the terms of a settlement of her claim against her group disability insurer, Vasiliki Tsiaprailis received a total of $105,000. This amount represented her entitlement to past benefits under the insurance plan, 75 percent of the present value of her future benefits, and an amount for costs, disbursements and GST. ... The details are set out in my colleague's judgment. The issue on this appeal is whether Ms. Tsiaprailis can be taxed on that portion of the settlement intended to compensate her for the past benefits.

The question turns on whether the amount allocated for past benefits was "payable on a periodic basis" and "pursuant to a disability insurance plan" within the meaning of s. 6(1)(f) of the *Income Tax Act.* ...

...

Ms. Tsiaprailis did not dispute before this Court that a lump sum paid in respect of an obligation to pay accumulated periodic payments would be taxable. She argued, however, that the payment was not made "pursuant to a disability insurance plan". Instead, she submitted that it was made pursuant to an agreement that settled a disputed obligation.

My colleague, Abella J, accepts Ms. Tsiaprailis' position and concludes that the settlement monies were not paid "pursuant to" the disability insurance plan because they were paid pursuant to a settlement agreement which extinguished any liability under the policy.

In my view, this conclusion runs counter to the principle that awards of damages and settlement payments are inherently neutral for tax purposes. My colleague takes no issue with this principle. As she explains, in assessing whether the monies will be taxable, we must look to the nature and purpose of the payment to determine what it is intended to replace. The inquiry is a factual one. The tax consequences of the damage or settlement payment is then determined according to this characterization. In other words, the tax treatment of the item will depend on what the amount is intended to replace. This approach is known as the *surrogatum* principle.

...

In determining the nature and purpose of the payment, Abella J concludes that the payment was not made "pursuant to" the insurance policy because it was paid to obtain a release from liability under the policy. My colleague relies on this Court's decision in *Minister of National Revenue v. Armstrong*, [1956] S.C.R. 446 (S.C.C.), in support of her analysis. In *Armstrong*, the Court concluded that a lump sum settlement paid in full satisfaction of a wife's claim to further payments under a divorce decree was not made "pursuant to" a decree, order or judgment. Rather, it was an amount paid "by reason of" or "in consequence of" a legal obligation imposed under the judgment. The distinction between a payment "pursuant to" a judgment and "by reason of" or "in consequence of" a judgment thus determined the outcome of the case in *Armstrong*.

Abella J correctly notes that, in *Armstrong*, the Court was not dealing with arrears but with future support payments payable under the judgment. However, she finds that this fact does not change the decision's interpretative value in relation to the meaning of the words "pursuant to". I do not quarrel with that observation but, in my view, the manner in which the case dealt with future obligations is highly relevant to the application of the *surrogatum* principle and explains the result reached in that case, a result that cannot follow here.

As noted by Kerwin CJ, Armstrong was under no obligation under the divorce judgment to pay a lump sum for future support payments. His obligation was to pay ongoing support at a rate of $100 per month. Hence it could not be said that the lump sum was paid "pursuant to" the judgment. To emphasize the fact that the settlement was not made pursuant to the underlying court order, Kellock J. pointed out that if Armstrong had agreed to purchase a house for his ex-wife in return for a release, he could not deduct the value of the house because "[s]uch an outlay made in commutation of the periodic sums payable under the decree is in the nature of a capital payment to which the statute does not extend" (p. 448). In Kellock J's view, the payment of a lump sum for future benefits would, like the house, be characterized as a capital payment.

When the reasoning in *Armstrong* is applied to the present case, it is clear that monies paid in settlement of any future liability under the disability insurance plan were not paid "pursuant to" the plan because there is no obligation to make such a lump sum payment under the terms of the plan. The part of the settlement for future benefits is in the nature of a capital payment and is not taxable under s. 6(1)(f) of the Act.

As we have seen, the decision in *Armstrong* relies on the application of the *surrogatum* principle, and concludes that Armstrong was not obligated by reason of the Court's judgment to pay a lump sum for future support payments. However, it does not suggest that past benefits like those at issue in this case are likewise not payable pursuant to or in consequence of a court's judgment or an insurance contract. Hence, I am of the view that the decision in *Minister of National Revenue v. Armstrong* does not lend support to the conclusion reached by my colleague.

My colleague further concludes that, even if one applied the *surrogatum* principle, the payment would not be taxable in this case because the liability under the policy was simply used as a way to gauge the reasonableness of the proposed settlement amount. I would not disagree that the fact that the parties may have used a taxable item as the reference point in calculating damages or negotiating a settlement does not conclusively determine whether the damages or settlement monies are taxable or non-taxable. Rather, the taxability will depend on the nature of the settled interest. However, with respect, I do not agree with the conclusion reached by my colleague in her application of the *surrogatum* principle on the facts of this case.

Abella J. appears to base her conclusion in large part on the fact that the insurer, by the terms of the release, explicitly denied liability under the insurance contract. In my view, this factor is of no moment to the inquiry. As aptly noted by the majority in the Federal Court of Appeal, it is the tax liability of the insured that is in issue and, on this point, I agree with the following observation:

> ... Ms. Tsiaprailis cannot assert the insurer's liability under the policy in her action, recover an amount from the insurer in that action, and then argue that the payment does not flow from the obligations of the insurer under the policy.

The determinative questions are: (1) what was the payment intended to replace? And, if the answer to that question is sufficiently clear, (2) would the replaced amount have been taxable in the recipient's hands? In this case, the evidence of what the amount was intended to replace is clear and cogent. As my colleague noted, the evidence established that the negotiated lump sum was "based on three aspects of liability under the policy: *an amount to extinguish Ms. Tsiaprailis' claim for accumulated arrears*, an amount to extinguish her claim for future benefits, and an amount to extinguish her claim for costs" ... (emphasis added) ... . Hence, it cannot be disputed on the evidence that part of the settlement monies was intended to replace past disability payments. It is also not disputed that such payments, had they been paid to Ms. Tsiaprailis, would have been taxable.

To conclude that the payment for past benefits was not made "pursuant to" the insurance disability plan in these circumstances is to render the *surrogatum* principle meaningless. Hence, I would conclude that the portion of the lump sum allocated to the accumulated arrears is taxable and I would dismiss the appeal, with no order as to costs.

Appeal dismissed.

NOTES AND QUESTIONS

1. On what basis did the majority in *Tsiaprailis* conclude that the portion of the settlement allocated to extinguish the claim for arrears of past disability insurance payments should be taxed differently than the portion allocated to extinguish her claim for future benefits? What reasons did Abella J. give in her dissenting reasons for rejecting this distinction? Which application of the *surrogatum* principle do you think is more persuasive? Of what relevance to the majority was the insurer's denial of liability under the policy? To the dissenting justices?

2. *Tsiaprailis* was followed in *Switzer v. Canada*, [2005] T.C.J. No. 124, [2005] 2 C.T.C. 2336, 2005 D.T.C. 431 (T.C.C.) and *Williams v. Canada*, [2008] T.C.J. No. 317, [2009] 1 C.T.C. 2487, 2008 D.T.C. 4432 (T.C.C.), in each of which the taxpayer was held to be taxable under section 6(1)(f) on a lump sum paid to settle a disputed claim for payments under a disability insurance plan. However, unlike *Tsiaprailis*, in neither case was any portion of the settlement found to be allocable to future benefits.

3. In *Ouimet v. M.N.R.*, [1979] C.T.C. 2172, 79 D.T.C. 16 (T.R.B.), the taxpayer, who received a single payment of $1,470.96 under a wage loss replacement plan, argued that the payment was not taxable under paragraph 6(1)(f) on the basis that it had not been paid "on a periodic basis" as required by the opening words of the provision. Dismissing the taxpayer's appeal, the Board concluded that:

> the fact that the payments came to the appellant through his employer and the fact that he did not receive them directly or immediately were not relevant. It is clearly stated in the contract that the payments were based on the appellant's monthly wages and that the benefits were payable periodically. The real issue is not when or how the benefits were *paid* but rather when and how they were *payable*. [Emphasis added.]

Ouimet was followed in *Marchand v. M.N.R.*, [1987] 2 C.T.C. 2309, 87 D.T.C. 629 (T.C.C.). See also *Ergen v. Canada*, [1995] 2 C.T.C. 2972 (T.C.C.) and *Leonard v. Canada*, [1996] F.C.J. No. 1171 (F.C.T.D.), where Joyal J held (at para. 13) that "so long as the contract or agreement calls for payments to be made on a periodic basis, the periodic character of the payments is not changed by the fact that they were not paid on time."

How did the Court in *Tsiaprailis* deal with the requirement under paragraph 6(1)(f) that insurance benefits be payable "on a periodic basis"?

4. According to paragraph 11 of IT-428, last updated in 1995, "If a lump sum payment is made in lieu of periodic payments, that amount will be considered to be income under paragraph 6(1)(f)." Following the Supreme Court of Canada's decision in *Tsiaprailis*, CRA has accepted that the portion of any such

settlement that is for extinguishment of a taxpayer's right to future benefits will not be taxable under section 6(1)(f). However, it has also taken the position in several private rulings that this portion may give rise to a taxable capital gain (see for example CRA documents 2005-0121521E5, April 21, 2005; and 2005-0159331E5, January 30, 2006). This position is based on the majority's conclusion that an amount allocable "for future benefits is in the nature of a capital payment and is not taxable under 6(1)(f)," and on the Federal Court of Appeal's earlier statement in the case that "in other circumstances, the disposition of a right to receive future amounts has been held to be a capital transaction" ([2003] F.C.J. No. 431, [2003] 3 C.T.C. 171, 2003 D.T.C. 5246 (F.C.A.), at para. 17). Where the payment can reasonably be considered to be proceeds from disposing of an interest in "an insurance policy" it will be exempt from capital gains tax under section 39(1)(a)(iii). However, CRA cautions that whether an employer provided disability plan constitutes an "insurance policy" is a question of fact to be determined on a case-by-case basis.

5.   In *Chapman v. Canada*, [1998] T.C.J. No. 78, [1998] 2 C.T.C. 2646, 98 D.T.C. 1443 (T.C.C.), the taxpayer, who was unable to work for two and a half years after she was injured in an automobile accident, received benefits under a wage-loss replacement plan insured by SunLife Assurance Company of Canada and an automobile insurance policy with Missisquoi Insurance Company, which paid 80 per cent of the insured's pre-accident gross weekly income, less any amounts received under the wage-loss replacement plan. When SunLife terminated benefits, the taxpayer assigned her rights to Missisquoi, which obtained $19,000 in the taxpayer's name. Concluding that Missisquoi acted as the taxpayer's agent and recovered disability benefits on her behalf, the court upheld the Minister's assessment including the $19,000 in computing the taxpayer's income under paragraph 6(1)(f) on the basis (at para. 19) that "any monies recovered from SunLife were constructively received by the Appellant even if such monies were paid directly or indirectly (*i.e.*, through a lawyer) to Missisquoi and retained by Missisquoi."

6.   In *Kant v. Canada*, [2001] T.C.J. No. 257, [2001] 2 C.T.C. 2703 (T.C.C.), insurance benefits of $19,000 payable to the taxpayer under a wage-loss replacement plan were assigned to the defendant in a tort action pursuant to section 267(1) of the *Insurance Act*, which operates to prevent double recovery. Rejecting the Minister's argument that the payments were taxable under paragraph 6(1)(f), the court distinguished *Chapman* on the basis (at para. 23) that the benefits were "assigned by operation of law and by Court order" and received by the defendant not as the taxpayer's agent. According to O'Connor TCJ (at para. 25):

> In the case at bar, the Appellant derived no benefits whatsoever from the amounts being assigned to the defendant ... . After the Ontario Court's judgment, not only could the Appellant not receive these amounts in his hands but he also did not derive any benefits or advantages from these amounts. The Appellant was entitled to the damage award notwithstanding the existence of the "wage loss replacement" benefits he was receiving. I conclude therefore that the Appellant did not, and could not "receive" the amounts as is

required by paragraph 6(1)(f) of the Act. In lieu of those amounts, the Appellant received the damage award which is non-taxable *Cirella v. R* (1977), 77 DTC 5442 (Fed. TD) ... . To include in taxable income an amount which goes to reduce the damages in effect is to tax damages, which ... are not taxable.

Do you agree with this result? Why or why not?

7. For a discussion of the potentially broad implications of the *Tsiaprailis* decision for the taxation of other types of replacement payments see Martha O'Brien, "Surrogatum, Source, and *Tsiaprailis*: Is There a Principled Basis for the Tax Treatment of Replacement Payments?" (2006) 54 Can. Tax J. 862-906.

c. Interest-free and Low-Interest Loans

In computing the income of a taxpayer from an office or employment, subsection 6(9) includes "an amount in respect of a loan or debt" that is "deemed by subsection 80.4(1) to be a benefit received in a taxation year by an individual." According to subsection 80.4(1), where a person "receives a loan or otherwise incurs a debt because of or as a consequence of a previous, the current or an intended office or employment of an individual," the individual is deemed to have received a benefit in a taxation year equal to the difference between:

1. the total of all interest on the loan or debt computed at a "prescribed rate" for the period it was outstanding (paragraph 80.4(1)(a)) and all interest paid or payable in respect of the loan or debt by the employer or a person (other than the debtor) related to the employer (paragraph 80.4(1)(b)), and

2. the total of interest paid on the loan or debt within 30 days after the end of the taxation year (paragraph 80.4(1)(c)) and any portion of any interest paid or payable by the employer or a person (other than the debtor) related to the employer that is reimbursed by the debtor in the year or within 30 days after the end of the taxation year (paragraph 80.4(1)(d)).

For the purpose of this provision, Regulation 4301(c) prescribes a rate of interest each quarter based on the yield on 90-day Government of Canada treasury bills. The effect of the rule is to require an individual to whom the provision applies to include as a benefit an amount equal to the difference between this prescribed rate and amounts paid by the debtor either as interest or by way of reimbursement of interest paid by the employer or a person related to the employer. Note that for purposes of computing this benefit the prescribed rate of interest may vary from quarter to quarter. For example, a $100,000 interest free loan to an employee that was advanced on January 1, 2006 and remained outstanding throughout the year would give rise to a benefit computed as follows for 2006:

¼ x 100,000 x 3% (prescribed rate in effect January-March 2006)
+ ½ x 100,000 x 4% (prescribed rate in effect April-September 2006)
+ ¼ x 100,000 x 5% (prescribed rate in effect October-December 2006)
= $4,000 benefit

According to subsection 80.4(3), subsection 80.4(1) does not apply where the rate of interest on the loan or debt is equal to or greater than commercial rates in effect at the time the loan was made or the debt was incurred, provided that the interest is paid by the debtor (paragraph 80.4(3)(a)), or where any part of the loan or debt was included in computing a taxpayer's income under Part I of the Act (paragraph 80.4(3)(b)). In *Archer v. M.N.R.*, [1989] T.C.J. No. 808, [1989] 2 C.T.C. 2300, 89 D.T.C. 571 (T.C.C.), Lamarre-Proulx TCJ suggested that the latter exception could apply to a loan or debt subsequently included in the recipient's income for the taxation year as a payment of salary. Likewise, this exception might apply where an amount is included in a taxpayer's income under subsection 6(15) on the forgiveness of the loan or debt.[43]

Special relief is provided for "home purchase loans" and "home relocation loans." In computing an employment benefit in respect of such loans, the prescribed interest rate cannot exceed the rate in effect when the loan was received or the debt was incurred for a period of five years, at which time the balance outstanding on the loan or debt is deemed to be a new home purchase loan for which the prescribed interest rate cannot exceed the rate in effect at that time for another five-year period, and so on.[44] As a result, the imputed interest benefit on such loans can decline during each 5-year period during which the loan is outstanding if the prescribed interest rate drops, but cannot rise. In addition, where section 80.4 deems a taxpayer to have received an interest benefit in respect of a home relocation loan, paragraph 110(1)(j) effectively

---

[43] See para. 11 of *Interpretation Bulletin* IT-421R2, "Benefits to Individuals, Corporations and Share holders from Loans or Debt." September 9, 1992, which notes, however, that "para. 80.4(3)(b) would not apply so as to reduce any benefit included in the employee's income pursuant to subsection 80.4(1) in a prior year in respect of such a loan."

[44] See subs. 80.4(4) and (6). Subsection 80.4(7) defines a "home purchase loan" as, among other things, "that portion of any loan received or debt otherwise incurred by an individual in the circumstances described in subs. (1) that is used to acquire, or to repay a loan or debt that was received or incurred to acquire, a dwelling ... for the habitation of ... the individual by virtue of whose office or employment the loan is received or the debt is incurred." The term "home relocation loan" is defined in subs. 248(1) as "a loan received by an individual or the individual's spouse or common-law partner in circumstances where the individual has commenced employment at a ... 'new work location' ... and by reason thereof has moved from the ... 'old residence' ... to a ... 'new residence' ... if (a) the distance between the old residence and the new work location is at least 40 kilometres greater than the distance between the new residence and the new work location, (b) the loan is used to acquire a dwelling ... for the habitation of the individual and is the individual's new residence, (c) the loan is received in the circumstances described in subs. 80.4(1), ... and (d) the loan is designated by the individual to be a home relocation loan."

exempts any benefit related to the first $25,000 of the loan by allowing the taxpayer to deduct any deemed interest on this amount in computing taxable income.

More importantly for the application of this provision is the requirement in the preamble to subsection 80.4(1) that the taxpayer must receive a loan or otherwise incur a debt "because of or as a consequence of a previous, the current or an intended office or employment of an individual, or because of the services performed or to be performed by a corporation carrying on a personal services business." This language, which is now subject to a specific interpretation rule in subsection 80.4(1.1), was considered in *Canada v. Hoefele (sub nom. Krull v. Canada)*, [1995] F.C.J. No. 1340, [1996] 1 C.T.C. 131, 95 D.T.C. 5602 (F.C.A.). Although the court's conclusion that the mortgage interest subsidy was not a benefit within the meaning of paragraph 6(1)(a) was subsequently reversed by the enactment of subsection 6(23), its analysis of subsection 80.4(1) continues to apply.

<h2 style="text-align:center">Canada v. Hoefele (sub nom. Krull v. Canada)</h2>

[1995] F.C.J. No. 1340, [1996] 1 C.T.C. 131, 95 D.T.C. 5602 (F.C.A.)

LINDEN JA (MacGuigan JA concurring): The sole issue raised in these five cases before this Court is whether a mortgage interest subsidy received by a taxpayer, after a relocation to a more expensive housing area, is taxable under either paragraph 6(1)(a) or section 80.4 of the *Income Tax Act*.

Facts

The relevant facts are not in dispute. The five taxpayers were each required in 1991 by their employer, Petro-Canada, to relocate from Calgary to the Toronto area as part of a company-wide reorganization. The relocation was mandatory, with affected employees given the option of moving or losing their jobs. The relocation was also purely geographical and involved no change in employee income.

To defray higher housing costs in the Toronto region and to encourage affected employees to accept relocation, Petro-Canada instituted a relocation incentive that worked as follows: A national real estate company was consulted to determine the market price differential between similar homes in Calgary and Toronto, which at the time of relocation came to 1.55. Petro-Canada then offered to pay any increase in interest charges on mortgages taken on costlier Toronto homes to a maximum set by the differential. Thus, a house that cost $100,000 in Calgary would be deemed to cost $155,000 in Toronto. The owner of such a house would be eligible for an interest subsidy paid by the employer to the extent of the interest payable on the increase in principal, that is, $55,000. The Relocation Program booklet distributed to the employees says the following about the interest subsidy:

> The Company will subsidize the interest on a portion of your mortgage financing. The maximum portion that the Company will subsidize will be the differential in housing prices as determined by the Company. ... The subsidy will be equal to the normal mortgage interest cost on a declining balance of your original differential in housing prices or the balance of your mortgage, whichever is the lessor [sic]. ...

As indicated, the mortgage interest subsidy was payable for ten years on a declining percentage basis, 100 per cent interest differential paid in the first year reducing gradually down to 50 per cent in the tenth. It would cease upon termination of employment. The subsidy was directed solely at defraying increased interest charges and it could not be applied to principal.

Also important to note is that the financing taken on the homes was to be arranged through normal methods by the relocated employees. The employer played no role assisting in this process, except that the mortgages were available only from Confederation Life, which billed Petro-Canada directly for the subsidy amount each year.

...

Is the Mortgage Interest Subsidy Taxable Under Subsections 80.4(1) and 6(9)?

The second issue in this appeal is whether the interest subsidy qualifies as a taxable benefit under subsection 80.4(1). ...

[F]or the 1992 and following taxation years, a receipt must be from a loan or debt incurred "because of or as a consequence of" employment. For taxation years prior to 1992, such loan or debt must have been incurred "by virtue of" employment. There is a slight difference in wording between the older and newly amended sections signifying little, if anything. Regardless, the focus of both versions is on the debt and not the receipt. It is not the benefit that must arise "because of," "as a consequence of," or "by virtue of" the employment; rather the loan or debt itself must be incurred "because of" or "as a consequence of" of "by virtue of" employment. In the present circumstances, the mortgage interest subsidy may well have been received "because of," "as a consequence of" or "by virtue of" the taxpayers' employment. But this is not the question before us. What must be determined is whether those portions of the mortgage loans taken out by the taxpayers in respect of the Toronto homes, and to which the interest subsidy was directed, came about "because of," "as a consequence of" or "by virtue of" employment.

In resolving this question, one must first note that subsection 80.4(1), whether in its older or newly amended form, requires a close connection between the loan or debt and employment, a connection much closer than that required by paragraph 6(1)(a) as between benefit and employment. In the latter, a benefit may arise if it is received merely "in respect of" employment. The phrase "in respect of" connotes only the slightest relation between two subjects and is intended to convey very wide scope.

...

On the other hand, the phrases used in the amended subsection 80.4(1), "because of," or "as a consequence of," as well as in the original version, "by virtue of," require a strong causal connection. I find little or no difference between the meanings of the phrases "because of," "as a consequence of" and "by virtue of." Each phrase implies a need for a strong causal relation between subject matters, not merely a slight linkage between them.

I do not see any strong causal relationship on the facts before us here. The employees who accepted the interest subsidy all owned houses prior to being relocated. To the extent that they incurred costs in trading a house in Calgary for a like house in the Toronto region they had to take mortgages out to cover those costs. Whether this meant simply increasing the principal on an already existing mortgage or taking out a new mortgage for the extra amount is of no consequence for subsection 80.4(1). Each taxpayer had simply to do what that taxpayer had to do. Each employee owned a house before relocating and traded like for like in the relocation. Each did what was needed to finance the trade and obtained such financing largely independently of employer involvement. They each had to qualify for the loans on their own merits. And each, in the end, was given an interest subsidy, on a declining ten-year basis, to defray part of the interest increases involved. I fail to see in this scenario a loan or debt incurred "because of," "as a consequence of" or "by virtue of" employment. No employee jumped from a rental to a mortgage situation, and none traded a principal residence for a non-principal residence. Such loans or debts that were incurred in each of these cases were incurred, then, in order to retain ownership of a house, not "because of," "as a consequence of" nor "by virtue of" employment.

...

ROBERTSON JA (dissenting): ... The taxpayers' argument is straight forward. It is submitted that they did not receive the mortgage loan from Confederation Life "because of or as a consequence of" their employment with Petro-Canada but, rather because they met the former's lending criteria. The existence of the subsidy had no bearing on the mortgage indemnity and approval requirements.

In my view, the taxpayers' argument can be disposed of readily. But for their employment with Petro-Canada, the taxpayers would not have received a monthly interest subsidy. But for that subsidy, and for the fact that Petro-Canada paid that subsidy directly to Confederation Life, the taxpayers would not have received a mortgage loan in which their monthly mortgage obligations were reduced by the amount of the subsidy paid by Petro-Canada. ... In effect, the taxpayers received their loans at a reduced interest rate, which is exactly what section 80.4 was designed to capture.

NOTES AND QUESTIONS

1. On what basis did a majority of the Federal Court of Appeal conclude in *Hoefele* that the mortgage interest subsidy received by the taxpayers was not deemed to have been a taxable benefit under subsections 80.4(1) and 6(9)? Why did Robertson JA disagree with this conclusion? How did the majority interpret

the words "because of or as a consequence of"? Do you agree with this interpretation? Why or why not?

2.   Of what, if any, relevance to the potential application of subsection 80.4(1) in *Hoefele* was the fact that Petro-Canada paid the mortgage interest subsidy directly to Confederation Life rather than the employees? Would a mortgage interest subsidy paid directly to an employee be subject to the deeming rule in subsection 80.4(1)?

3.   In *Funnell v. M.N.R.*, [1991] T.C.J. No. 129, [1991] 1 C.T.C. 2498, 91 D.T.C. 787 (T.C.C.), the taxpayer, whose position as president of a new employer required that he move from Toronto to Edmonton, received a $50,000 interest-free loan to "facilitate the relocation in Edmonton and to obtain a house comparable to the one owned in Toronto" (at para. 4). Noting that the benefit was conferred "as a term of acceptance of a contract of employment," the court applied subsections 6(9) and 80.4(1) to deem a taxable benefit in respect of the loan.

4.   In *Siwik v. Canada*, [1996] T.C.J. No. 280, [1996] 2 C.T.C. 2417 (T.C.C.), the taxpayer received an interest-free loan to assist in the acquisition of a new home when he was transferred from Montreal to Toronto. Allowing the taxpayer's appeal from an assessment deeming a taxable benefit under subsections 80.4(1) and 6(9), the court held that the payment was a non-taxable reimbursement under the authority of *Hoefele*. According to Taylor JTCC (at para. 7):

> It is not evident to me that there is a substantive difference between the employer ... foregoing the interest on the loan, and ... making a payment to the employee as reimbursement, or to a separate financial institution directly for the interest involved.

Do you agree with this conclusion? Why or why not?

5.   Effective for loans received and debts incurred after February 23, 1998, subsection 80.4(1.1) stipulates:

> A loan or debt is deemed to have been received or incurred because of an individual's office or employment, or because of services performed by a corporation that carries on a personal services business, as the case may be, if it is reasonable to conclude that, but for an individual's previous, current or intended office or employment, or the services performed or to be performed by the corporation,
>
> (a)   the terms of the loan or debt would have been different; or
>
> (b)   the loan would not have been received or the debt would not have been incurred.

According to supplementary information released with the 1998 Federal Budget in which this amendment was announced, this provision is intended to reverse the decision in *Siwik v. Canada*, [1996] T.C.J. No. 280, [1996] 2 C.T.C. 2417 (T.C.C.). Might this provision have affected the decision in *Canada v. Hoefele (sub nom. Krull v. Canada)*, [1995] F.C.J. No. 1340, [1996] 1 C.T.C. 131, 95 D.T.C. 5602 (F.C.A.)?

d. Forgiveness of Debt

For the purpose of paragraph 6(1)(a), paragraph 6(15)(a) deems a benefit to have been enjoyed by a taxpayer "at any time an obligation issued by any debtor (including the taxpayer) is settled or extinguished."[45] In these circumstances, paragraph 6(15)(b) deems the value of the benefit to be "the forgiven amount at that time in respect of the obligation." For this purpose, subsections 6(15.1) and 80(1) together stipulate that the "forgiven amount" is generally the lesser of the amount for which the obligation was issued (the loan proceeds) and the principal amount owing on the obligation (the unpaid balance of the loan) less any amount paid in satisfaction of the principal amount at the time that the obligation is settled or extinguished.

Although subsection 6(15) deems a benefit equal to the "forgiven amount" to have been enjoyed by a taxpayer when an obligation is settled or extinguished, it does not address the causal relationship between this benefit and the taxpayer's office or employment, which depends on the general rule in paragraph 6(1)(a). Among the many cases in which this causal connection has been considered, one of the most frequently cited is *McArdle v. M.N.R.*, [1984] C.T.C. 2277, 84 D.T.C. 1251 (T.C.C.). Although the case was decided before the enactment of subsection 6(15) in 1987, its analysis of the relationship between the forgiveness of a debt and a taxpayer's office or employment continues to be relevant to the application of this provision.

McArdle v. M.N.R.

[1984] C.T.C. 2277, 84 D.T.C. 1251 (T.C.C.)

CHRISTIE CJTC: This appeal relates to the appellant's 1978 taxation year. In that year he left his employment with Integrated Building Corporation Ltd. ("Integrated"). While employed he owed Integrated $14,774.72, the repayment of which was waived by it. By notice of reassessment mailed on June 9, 1981, the $14,774.72 was added to the appellant's total income for 1978. He objected to this in accordance with the statutory requirements and by notification dated April 1, 1982, the respondent confirmed his reassessment. Hence this appeal.

These facts are alleged in the notice of appeal and admitted by the respondent in paragraph 2 of the reply to the notice of appeal:

> (a) Prior to the commencement of my employment with Integrated ... Building Corp Ltd. I was employed by the Royal Bank of Canada. At the time of my resignation from the Bank, I was indebted to them in the amount of $17,158.76, being a preferential staff housing loan.

---

[45] For the purpose of this rule, reference should be made to subs. 248(26), which clarify the circumstances in which an obligation is considered to be issued by a debtor and subs. 248(27), which governs the partial settlement of obligations.

(b) As a condition of my employment, Integrated ... assumed the bank staff loan under the same terms and conditions as I had with my previous employer.

(c) I commenced employment with Integrated ... on July 1, 1976. Payments on the loan commenced September 1, 1976 and were made continuously through January 1, 1978 at $190.00 per month.

(d) I left employment with integrated (sic) on May 15, 1978 at which time there was $14,774.72 outstanding on my loan, which amount had been forgiven by Integrated ... .

In giving his evidence in chief the appellant stated that, while employed by Integrated, the relationship between him and his employer became strained and he saw no point in carrying on in what he described as a "disintegrating situation." He also testified that the forgiveness of the outstanding amount of the loan was not part of the arrangement under which employment with Integrated came to an end, but that Integrated, knowing the appellant was a person who could make collection very difficult, decided to write the loan off as a bad debt. In the course of cross-examination, however, counsel for the respondent confronted the appellant with a letter dated April 29, 1978 ... addressed to Mr. Peter R. Oluk of Integrated and signed by "J.E. McArdle." ... The document reads:

This letter will serve as my official Notice of Resignation to be effective February 15, 1978.

This is to certify that all expenses incurred by me on behalf of Integrated Building Corp Ltd. have been paid in full by the company.

Further, I would like to state that I am leaving the employ of Integrated on good terms and that Integrated has been most generous in paying me a resignation allowance and in the absolute forgiveness of my loan from the company (Copy of the note attached until the original is found) upon my resignation.

The appellant acknowledged his signature, although he added that he was not the author of the letter. He went on to testify unconvincingly that it did not reflect the reality of the situation. He alleged that the only reason he signed the letter was that, although he had taken other employment at Slave Lake, Alberta, in February 1978, he was to continue to receive payments from Integrated for a period up to May 15, 1978, and he did not wish to do anything which might jeopardize these payments.

I am satisfied that the forgiveness of the balance of the loan was an integral part of the arrangements under which the appellant's employment with Integrated was brought to an end by mutual agreement. This means there was a direct nexus between the course of action adopted by Integrated in respect of the loan and the appellant's employment. The thing which motivated the forgiveness of the loan was the existence of the contract of employment. This brings the $14,774.72 within those provisions of paragraph 6(1)(a) of the *Income Tax Act* ("the Act") which require that there shall be included in computing the income of a taxpayer for a taxation year as income from employment the value of a benefit of any kind whatever received by him in the year in respect of, in the course of, or by virtue of that employment. ...

Appeal dismissed.

NOTES AND QUESTIONS

1. On what basis did the taxpayer in *McArdle* argue that the amount of the debt that was forgiven by his former employer was not subject to paragraph 6(1)(a)? Why did the court reject this argument? Was the court's reasoning consistent with the Federal Court of Appeal decisions in *Canada v. Atkins*, [1975] F.C.J. No. 509, [1975] C.T.C. 377, 75 D.T.C. 5263 (F.C.T.D.) and *Canada v. Pollock*, [1984] C.T.C. 353, 84 D.T.C. 6370 (F.C.A.)? Would the taxpayer have been taxable if his former employer had paid him an additional $14,774.72 in lieu of notice and required him to repay the debt?

2. In *DeWaal v. M.N.R.*, [1975] C.T.C. 2160, 75 D.T.C. 127 (T.R.B.), the taxpayer was assessed on the basis that he had received a taxable benefit under paragraph 6(1)(a) when his former employer forgave a debt of $10,000 that was set off against severance pay payable on his termination. Rejecting the taxpayer's argument that the $10,000 was received as a non-taxable payment of damages for wrongful dismissal, the board concluded (at para. 17) that "DeWaal did in fact receive the benefit of the $10,000 by way of cancellation of debt, the same being offset as severance pay or bonus."

For similar results involving the forgiveness of debt on the termination of an employee's office or employment, see *Bolton v. Canada*, [1993] T.C.J. No. 696, [1993] 2 C.T.C. 3203, 95 D.T.C. 277 (T.C.C.); *Krampl v. Canada*, [1995] T.C.J. No. 767, [1995] 2 C.T.C. 2624 (T.C.C.); and *Klein v. Canada*, [1995] T.C.J. No. 147, [1995] 1 C.T.C. 2980 (T.C.C.), aff'd [1998] F.C.J. No. 327, [1998] 2 C.T.C. 326, 98 D.T.C. 6214 (F.C.A.).

3. In *Norris v. Canada*, [1994] T.C.J. No. 81, [1994] 1 C.T.C. 2495, 94 D.T.C. 1478 (T.C.C.), the taxpayer, who provided consulting services to Sunys International Inc. ("Sunys" and later "Romar") through a management company called Petroleum Marketing Corporation ("PMC"), received an interest-free loan of $135,000, which was subsequently forgiven. Citing *Waffle v. M.N.R.*, [1968] C.T.C. 572, 69 D.T.C. 5007 (Ex. Ct.), for the proposition that a taxable benefit within the meaning of paragraph 6(1)(a) need not be received from the taxpayer's employer directly, the court rejected the taxpayer's argument that any benefit attributable to the debt forgiveness was not received "in respect of, in the course of, or by virtue of an office or employment." According to Brulé JTCC (at para. 39):

> Pursuant to case law, the amount forgiven should be included in the appellant's income regardless of the source of the benefit. In addition, in light of the far-reaching definition given to the term "in respect of," it can be said that the appellant would not have benefitted from a loan granted by Sunys had he not been an employee of his own management company.

> The forgiveness of the loan must be seen at least as an indirect benefit of employment by virtue of section 6 of the Act and the jurisprudence arising out of the case law. It is not necessary that the appellant be found to be an employee of Sunys/Romar in order to have received a benefit from employment under the Act.

See also *Galon v. Canada*, [1995] T.C.J. No. 433, [1995] 2 C.T.C. 2521 (T.C.C.), in which a benefit from the forgiveness of a loan by a company to its president and principal shareholder was held to have been received "in respect of, in the course of, or by virtue of" his relationship as an employee, not as a shareholder.

4.   In *Cousins v. M.N.R.*, [1971] 72 D.T.C. 1055 (T.R.B.), the taxpayer, whose employer provided a second mortgage on his house pursuant to a company program that discharged the mortgage without payment if the employee remained with the employer for five years, was assessed as having received a taxable benefit in 1968 when his employer discharged the mortgage. Rejecting the taxpayer's argument that the discharge merely reimbursed him for a decline in value of his house, which he sold at a loss in 1970 after leaving his employment, the board held that the decrease in this loss resulting from the discharge was a taxable benefit within the meaning of then paragraph 5(1)(a) (now paragraph 6(1)(a)).

For a similar result, see *McIlhargey v. Canada*, [1991] F.C.J. No. 469, 91 D.T.C. 5381 (F.C.T.D.), in which the taxpayer, who had borrowed $305,000 from his employer in order to acquire 100,000 shares from its treasury, was assessed under paragraph 6(1)(a) when the employer forgave the balance of the loan when his employment was terminated in April 1984. Rejecting the taxpayer's argument that the debt forgiveness merely compensated him for a decrease in his net worth resulting from a decrease in the value of his shares, the court characterized the forgiven amount as a taxable benefit under paragraph 6(1)(a). According to Cullen J (at para. 13):

> The argument rejected in *Cousins v. M.N.R.*, [1971] 72 D.T.C. 1055 (T.R.B.), is precisely that which is advanced by the plaintiff in this case, i.e., that a forgiveness of a debt by an employer that has the effect only of reducing a loss suffered by the employee on the disposition of a capital asset is not a benefit. In the case at bar, the forgiveness of the outstanding balance of the loan had the very real benefit, admitted by the plaintiff, of avoiding a decrease in his net worth. I would therefore conclude that the forgiveness of the loan was a benefit within the meaning of paragraph 6(1)(a) of the Act.

For a contrasting result, see *Greisinger v. M.N.R.*, [1986] T.C.J. No. 919, [1986] 2 C.T.C. 2441, 86 D.T.C. 1802 (T.C.C.), where the taxpayer, who moved from Calgary to Edmonton to accept a new position with his employer, borrowed $140,000 from his employer to purchase a new home in Edmonton. When the real estate market collapsed and he was unable to sell his former residence in Calgary, he sold the Edmonton residence and moved back to Calgary, at which time his employer forgave $60,000 of the outstanding debt. Referring to the Exchequer Court decision in *Ransom v. M.N.R.*, [1967] C.T.C. 346, 67 D.T.C. 5235 (Ex. Ct), the court rejected the Minister's argument that this forgiveness of debt was a taxable benefit within the meaning of paragraph

6(1)(a) and characterized $46,040 of the forgiven amount as a non-taxable reimbursement for the taxpayer's loss on the disposition of the Edmonton residence.

5. By deeming a benefit to have been enjoyed "at any time an obligation issued by any debtor (including the taxpayer) is settled or extinguished," paragraph 6(15)(a) codifies the results in *Cousins v. M.N.R.*, [1971] 72 D.T.C. 1055 (T.R.B.) and *McIlhargey v. Canada*, [1991] F.C.J. No. 469, 91 D.T.C. 5381 (F.C.T.D.), and reverses the result in *Greisinger*.

6. In *Hendlisz v. The Queen*, [2000] T.C.J. No. 878, [2001] C.T.C. 2642 (T.C.C.), the taxpayer, who borrowed $100,000 from a new employer in order to finance the acquisition of a new residence when he was recruited in August 1991, repaid $75,000 of this amount after his employment was terminated in May 1992. Accepting the Minister's arguments (at para. 13) that the forgiveness was made "for the purpose of obtaining repayment of the mortgage loan and end a conflictual employment situation" and not "for the purpose of reimbursing losses," the court rejected the taxpayer's argument that the debt forgiveness compensated him for a decline in the value of his former residence in Montreal. According to Lamarre-Proulx TCJ (at para. 14):

> The courts must deal with what the taxpayer actually did and not what he would like it to be. In a matter of agreements, the courts have to determine the common purpose of the parties in reaching the agreement. There is no documentary evidence suggesting that the forgiveness of the amount of $25,000 was related to losses incurred by the Appellant on the disposition of his Montreal house. There had been no undertaking given by the Appellant's former employer to such a thing. No document executed by both the Appellant and his former employer made the slightest reference to these losses. The evidence has rather shown that the forgiveness of part of the loan was an integral part of a severance package relating to the Appellant's employment. ... Such a forgiven amount must be included in the calculation of the Appellant's income as a benefit conferred in respect of an employment, pursuant to paragraph 6(1)(a) and subsection 6(15) of the Act.

In light of this decision, how might you advise a taxpayer in Mr. Hendlisz's position?

e. Benefits in Respect of a Housing Loss

For the purpose of paragraph 6(1)(a), subsection 6(19) deems "an amount paid at any time in respect of a housing loss (other than an eligible housing loss) to or on behalf of a taxpayer or a person who does not deal at arm's length with the taxpayer in respect of, in the course of or because of, an office or employment" to be "a benefit received by the taxpayer at that time because of the office or employment." For this purpose, subsection 6(21) defines a "housing loss" at any time as the amount by which the greater of the cost of the residence and its highest fair market value during the previous six months exceeds its fair market value at the time if it is not disposed of or the lesser of its fair market value and the proceeds of its disposition if it is disposed of.

Subsection 6(20), in contrast, deems "an amount paid at any time in a taxation year in respect of an eligible housing loss to or on behalf of a taxpayer or a person who does not deal at arm's length with the taxpayer in respect of, in the course of or because of, an office or employment" to be "a benefit received by the taxpayer at that time because of the office or employment" only to the extent of:

the amount, if any, by which:

(a) one half of the amount, if any, by which the total of all amounts each of which is so paid in the year or in a preceding taxation year exceeds $15,000

exceeds

(b) the total of all amounts each of which is an amount included in computing the taxpayer's income because of this subsection for a preceding taxation year in respect of the loss.

For this purpose, subsection 6(22) defines an "eligible housing loss" in respect of a residence designated by a taxpayer as "a housing loss in respect of an eligible relocation of the taxpayer or a person who does not deal at arm's length with the taxpayer," and stipulates for this purpose that "no more than one residence may be so designated in respect of an eligible relocation." In turn, subsection 248(1) defines an "eligible relocation" as a relocation that enables a taxpayer to be employed at a new work location, provided that the taxpayer ordinarily resided at the old residence before the relocation and at the new residence after the relocation, and that the new residence is not less than 40 kilometres closer to the new work location than the old residence.

These provisions, which are generally applicable to relocations after February 23, 1998, limited the effect of the decision in *Ransom v. M.N.R.*, [1967] C.T.C. 346, 67 D.T.C. 5235 (Ex. Ct.). In *Ransom* the taxpayer received $3,617 from his employer as partial compensation for a loss on the sale of his old residence when he was transferred from Sarnia to Montreal, which the Minister assessed as a taxable benefit under then paragraph 5(1)(a) (now paragraph 6(1)(a)). Allowing the taxpayer's appeal, the court characterized the payment as a non-taxable reimbursement for a loss incurred in the course of the taxpayer's employment. According to Noël J (at paras. 50-53):

> In a case such as here, where the employee is subject to being moved from one place to another, any amount by which he is out of pocket by reason of such a move is in exactly the same category as ordinary travelling expenses. His financial position is adversely affected *by reason of* that particular facet of his employment relationship. When his employer reimburses him for any such loss, it cannot be regarded as remuneration, for if that were all that he received under his employment arrangement, he would not have received any amount for his services. Economically, all that he would have received would be the amount that he was out of pocket *by reason of* the employment. ...

> It appears to me quite clear that reimbursement of an employee by an employer for expenses or losses incurred by reason of the employment ... is neither remuneration as such [n]or a *benefit* "of any kind whatsoever."

For a critical analysis of this decision, see Brian J. Arnold and Jinyan Li, "The Appropriate Tax Treatment of the Reimbursement of Moving Expenses" (1996) 44: 1 Can. Tax J. 1-37.

The rationale for introducing subsections 6(19)-(22) was explained in supplementary information released with the 1998 Federal Budget as follows:

> To improve the fairness of the tax system, the budget ... proposes changes to the tax treatment of amounts paid by employers for a loss on a sale or diminishment in value of a former residence ... . The exclusion from income of these amounts provides a significant tax advantage to employees who are reimbursed by their employer for such expenses compared to those who must bear the costs themselves. The budget proposes that these employer-paid relocation expenses be included in the employee's income. However, to recognize that many employers require employees to relocate in circumstances where the employee would not have chosen to do so, the first $15,000 of amounts paid by the employer for a loss or diminishment in value of a former residence will not be taxed. One-half of such amounts in excess of $15,000 will be included in the employee's income.[46]

f. Relocation Assistance

In *Splane v. M.N.R.*, [1990] F.C.J. No. 622, [1990] 2 C.T.C. 199, 90 D.T.C. 6442 (F.C.T.D.), aff'd [1991] F.C.J. No. 60, [1991] 1 C.T.C. 406, 91 D.T.C. 5130 (F.C.A.), the taxpayer, who was transferred from Ottawa to Edmonton, was compensated by his employer for increased mortgage interest payments on a new residence attributable to higher interest rates prevailing at the time of the transfer. Rejecting the Minister's argument that the compensation was a taxable benefit under paragraph 6(1)(a), Cullen J concluded (at para. 18):

> No economic benefit of any significant value was conferred upon the plaintiff. The plaintiff moved at the request of his employer, incurred certain expenses on the move, and suffered a loss. The reimbursement of these expenses cannot be considered as conferring a benefit within the terms of the Act. The plaintiff was simply restored to the economic situation he was in before he undertook to assist his employer by relocating to the Edmonton office.

See also *Canada v. Hoefele (sub nom. Krull v. Canada)*, [1995] F.C.J. No. 1340, [1996] 1 C.T.C. 131, 95 D.T.C. 5602 (F.C.A.), in which the taxpayers, who were transferred from Calgary to Toronto, received a mortgage interest subsidy under a program established by their employer to compensate employees for increased interest charges on costlier Toronto homes. Observing that the subsidy did not increase the taxpayers' equity in their homes, a majority of the court rejected the Minister's argument that the subsidy was a taxable benefit under paragraph 6(1)(a). According to Linden JA (MacGuigan JA concurring) (at para. 24):

> No economic gain accrued to any of the taxpayers as a result of the subsidy. Their net worth was not increased. Thus, a fundamental requirement of paragraph 6(1)(a) was unfulfilled.

---

[46] Canada, Department of Finance, *Tax Measures: Supplementary Information* (Ottawa: Department of Finance, February 24, 1998).

Hoefele was followed in *Douglas v. Canada*, [1997] T.C.J. No. 841, [1998] 2 C.T.C. 2095, 98 D.T.C. 1001 (T.C.C.); *Fish v. The Queen*, [1996] 3 C.T.C. 2733 (T.C.C.); *D'Alessandro v. Canada*, [1997] T.C.J. No. 544, [1997] 3 C.T.C. 2756 (T.C.C.); and *Moore v. Canada*, [2000] T.C.J. No. 806, [2001] 1 C.T.C. 2395 (T.C.C.).

Compare the Court's approach in *Pezzelato v. Canada*, [1995] T.C.J. No. 884, [1995] 2 C.T.C. 2890 (T.C.C.), where the taxpayer, an employee of a pan-Canadian construction company who was transferred to Toronto, received $13,125 as a reimbursement of interest expenses on money that the taxpayer had to borrow in order to acquire a residence in Toronto while he was unable to sell his former residence in Ingersoll, Ontario. Rejecting the taxpayer's argument that this "bridge financing" merely compensated him for the loss otherwise incurred by his relocation at his employer's request, the Tax Court held that the payment was a taxable benefit within the meaning of paragraph 6(1)(a). According to Bowman JTCC (at para. 28):

> Here, the payment was to reimburse Mr. Pezzelato for the interest on a loan to buy a house in Toronto. ... I can see no difference in principle between paying an employee's mortgage interest and contributing to the principal amount of the purchase price of the house, or paying him a higher salary. If employers wish to ensure that their employees do not suffer a tax burden resulting from the conferral of benefits they should gross up the benefit by the tax cost, including the tax on the amount of the gross-up. After all, the employer can deduct it.

See also *Phillips v. M.N.R.*, [1994] F.C.J. No. 271, [1994] 1 C.T.C. 383, 94 D.T.C. 6177 (F.C.A.), where the taxpayer, a carman with the Canadian National Railway ("CNR"), received a $10,000 "relocation payment" after transferring from Moncton to Winnipeg when the CNR closed its Moncton shops in 1987. Allowing the Minister's appeal from the decision of the Federal Court Trial Division ([1993] F.C.J. No. 429, 2 C.T.C. 27 (F.C.T.D.)), which accepted the taxpayer's argument that the payment merely compensated him for increased housing costs associated with the move to Winnipeg without conferring an economic advantage, the Court concluded that the payment "enabled the respondent to acquire a more valuable asset" and increased his net worth. According to Robertson JA (at paras. 52-54):

> The respondent effectively argues that any payment received from an employer to compensate for higher housing costs in a new work location only serves to make the employee whole. As we have seen, this rationale is flawed. Moreover, nothing bars the extension of this same faulty reasoning to other purchases, such as new cars or appliances, in provinces with higher costs of living.

> I also observe that the problem of compensation directed at tax equalization is apparently of concern to tax lawyers familiar with the US multi-national practice of "grossing up" salaries of executives transferred to Canada ... . What of the employee who moves to a province with higher marginal rates of taxation? Why should he or she not be able to claim a tax-free benefit as well, assuming the employer is willing to provide such compensation? In my opinion, it is evident that the decision below creates a window of opportunity for those intent on structuring tax-free compensation packages for employees required to relocate to urban centres where costs of living are appreciably higher.

> When the above concerns are contemplated in light of the clear wording of paragraph 6(1)(a) of the Act ... and Parliamentary intent, it seems plain that the $10,000 payment is a taxable benefit.

For other cases in which compensation for increased housing costs at a new work location to which an employee has been transferred have been characterized as taxable benefits under paragraph 6(1)(a), see *Moore v. Canada*, [1996] T.C.J. No. 27, [1996] 1 C.T.C. 3004 (T.C.C.); *Robineau v. Canada*, [1997] T.C.J. No. 70, [1997] 3 C.T.C. 2865, 97 D.T.C. 234 (T.C.C.); *Lao v. M.N.R.*, [1997] F.C.J. No. 1409, [1998] 1 C.T.C. 118, 97 D.T.C. 5498 (F.C.A.); and *Des Rosiers v. Canada*, [1999] F.C.J. No. 98, [1999] 4 C.T.C. 47, 99 D.T.C. 5112 (F.C.A.).

For relocations after February 23, 1998, and for 2001 and subsequent taxation years for relocations before October 1998, subsection 6(23) stipulates:

> For greater certainty, an amount paid or the value of assistance provided by any person in respect of, in the course of or because of, an individual's office or employment in respect of the cost of, the financing of, the use of or the right to use, a residence is, for the purposes of [section 6], a benefit received by the individual because of the office or employment.

This provision effectively overrules the Federal Court of Appeal decisions in *Splane* and *Hoefele*, above, so that housing assistance on relocation of an employee is included in income regardless of the form in which such assistance is received.

The *Income Tax Act* recognizes some variations in living costs in section 110.7, which allows taxpayers residing in northern regions of the country to claim a specific deduction in computing taxable income, and in subsection 6(6), which provides an exemption for benefits or allowances in respect of board and lodging at and transportation to and from a remote location. Subsection 6(6) is considered later in this chapter.

Subsection 6(23) does not address the reimbursement of ordinary moving expenses by a taxpayer's employer. In *Pollesel v. Canada*, [1997] T.C.J. No. 839, [1997] 3 C.T.C. 3126, 98 D.T.C. 1003 (T.C.C.), the taxpayer's employer reimbursed him for moving expenses when he accepted a new job with the employer, which required that he move from Waterloo to Sudbury, Ontario. Allowing the taxpayer's appeal from an assessment that included the amount of this reimbursement as a taxable benefit under paragraph 6(1)(a), the Court held that the taxpayer had not received an economic benefit. See also *MacInnes v. Canada*, [2003] T.C.J. No. 119, [2003] 3 C.T.C. 2706 (T.C.C.), where the taxpayer received a lump-sum payment of $12,394 upon retirement from the Canadian military to cover the cost of moving from Trenton, Ontario, where he was based at retirement, to his original home in Sydney, Nova Scotia. Concluding (at para. 17) that "the military was simply moving the [taxpayer] back to where he came from when he joined the military" and that "he has received no economic gain, advantage or benefit." the Court allowed the taxpayer's appeal from an assessment which had included the payment as a taxable benefit under paragraph 6(1)(a). Do you agree with this result? Why or why not?

For the CRA's views on the reimbursement of moving expenses, see IT-470R, paragraphs 35 and 36:

35. Where an employer reimburses an employee for the expenses incurred by the latter in moving the employee and the employee's family and household effects either because the employee has been transferred from one establishment of the employer to another or because of having accepted employment at a place other than where the former home was located, this reimbursement is not considered as conferring a taxable benefit on the employee.

36. In addition, where the employer pays the expense of moving an employee and the employee's family and household effects out of a remote place at the termination of the employment there, no taxable benefit is imputed.

Where moving expenses are neither paid by the taxpayer's employer nor reimbursed in a non-taxable form, the taxpayer may deduct these expenses under section 62. This provision is examined in Chapter 7.

g. Options To Acquire Securities

The taxation of benefits arising from the issuance of securities by a corporation or mutual fund to an employee is governed by section 7, as well as paragraphs 110(1)(d), (d.01), and (d.1) and subsection 110(2.1). As a general rule, section 7 includes as an employment benefit the full amount of any gain resulting from the acquisition of securities or the disposition of an option to acquire securities, while paragraphs 110(1)(d) and (d.1) allow taxpayers to deduct half of this amount in computing their taxable incomes provided that the securities satisfy various conditions set out in these provisions and Regulation 6204.[47] Paragraph 110(d.01) and subsection 110(2.1) permit an additional deduction where the securities are donated to a qualifying charity.[48] Where applicable, the deductions

---

[47] In order to qualify for the deduction in para. 110(1)(d) the securities must be either non-convertible common shares or units of a widely-held class of units of a mutual fund trust, the exercise price must be no less than the fair market value of the security when the option is granted (less any amount paid by the employee to acquire the option), and at the time that the option is granted the employee must be dealing at arm's length with the grantor of the option, the employer, and any entity whose securities can be acquired under the option. The deduction under para. 110(1)(d.1) applies to benefits received after May 22, 1985, and is available where the taxpayer acquires a share of a "Canadian-controlled private corporation", does not dispose of or exchange the share within two years after the acquisition, and has not deducted an amount in respect of the benefit under para. 110(1)(d).

[48] Where an employee is entitled to a deduction under para. 110(1)(d), para. 110(1)(d.01) allows an additional deduction equal to ½ of the benefit included under section 7 where the employee donates the security to a qualifying charity during the year in which the employee acquires the security and no later than 30 days after its acquisition, effectively reducing the section 7 benefit to zero. Where an employee, in exercising an option to acquire a security, directs a broker or dealer approved or appointed by the grantor (or a qualifying person who does not deal at arm's length with the grantor) to sell the security immediately and donate all or part of the proceeds to a qualifying charity, subs. 110(2.1) allows the employee to claim a deduction under para.

reduce the benefit to an amount equivalent to the capital gains inclusion rate, though it is otherwise still treated as employment income.

In the absence of section 7, the general rule in paragraph 6(1)(a) would apply to the value of any benefit conferred on an employee through the granting or exercise of stock options (see *Robertson v. Canada*, [1990] F.C.J. No. 4, [1990] 1 C.T.C. 114, 90 D.T.C. 6070 (F.C.A.), discussed in the notes following the *Taylor* case, below). However, applying paragraph 6(1)(a) to stock options presents difficulties with respect to both the valuation and timing of when benefits should be recognized in income. Section 7 attempts to clarify the tax treatment of employee stock options by laying out a special regime that overrides the general rule in paragraph 6(1)(a). The treatment of employee stock options that fall outside of section 7 is discussed later in this section.

The Act does not use the colloquial term "employee stock option" but instead describes the circumstances in which section 7 will apply as follows, in subsection 7(3):

> If a particular qualifying person has agreed to sell or issue securities of the particular person, or of a qualifying person with which it does not deal at arm's length, to an employee of the particular person or of a qualifying person with which it does not deal at arm's length

> (a)   except as provided by this section, the employee is deemed to have neither received nor enjoyed any benefit under or because of the agreement.

For this purpose, subsection 7(7) defines a "qualifying person" as a corporation or a mutual fund trust and a "security" of such a person as a share of the capital stock of a corporation if the person is a corporation, and a unit of a trust if the person is a mutual fund trust. The effect of paragraph 7(3)(a) is to exclude the operation of section 6 to these arrangements. Instead, subsection 7(1) deems the employee (or certain others) to have received taxable benefits as defined in paragraphs 7(1)(a) to (e).[49] For this purpose, subsection 7(4) provides:

> where a person to whom any provision of subsection 7(1) would otherwise apply has ceased to be an employee before all things have happened that would make that provision applicable, subsection 7(1) shall continue to apply as though the person were still an employee and as though the employment were still in existence.

Subsection 7(5), however, stipulates that section 7 "does not apply if the benefit conferred by the agreement was not received in respect of, in the course of, or by virtue of, the employment." The following case considers the meaning of this threshold requirement.

110(d.01) equal to a portion of the deduction otherwise allowed under that provision based on the ratio of the amount paid to the charity to the proceeds of disposition of the security.

[49]   As discussed later in this section, this provision is subject to special rules in subss. 7(1.1) and (8), which affect the timing of inclusion for shares of a "Canadian-controlled private corporation" ("CCPC") and for "qualifying acquisitions" of non-CCPC shares.

Taylor v. M.N.R.
[1988] T.C.J. No. 732, [1988] 2 C.T.C. 2227, 88 D.T.C. 1571 (T.C.C.)

RIP TCJ: ... At all relevant times Mr. Taylor was a petroleum engineer who, through a corporation in which he was sole shareholder, provided consulting services to a number of resource companies, in particular in British Columbia. Two of these companies were Bianca Resources Limited ("Bianca") and Greenwood Explorations Limited ("Greenwood"). Mr. Taylor subsequently became a director of Bianca on April 27, 1979, and Greenwood on May 28, 1980, and received stock options in each of the two corporations.

Bianca granted him an option on April 27, 1979 to acquire 50,000 shares of the company at $2.70 per share on or before April 27, 1980. The appellant exercised his right to purchase 20,000 shares on March 3, 1980, and 30,000 shares on March 10, 1980, the values of each share on those dates were $5.40 and $4.40 respectively. Greenwood granted the appellant an option ... on June 30, 1980 ... to acquire 15,000 shares of the company at $3.75 per share on or before June 30, 1982. The appellant exercised this option on January 8, 1981, when the value of each share was $16.50.

In his capacity as a director of each corporation, the appellant attended directors' meetings, voted on resolutions of the Boards and generally performed the duties of his offices, albeit at a minimum level. As a director, Mr. Taylor had statutory responsibilities. Mr. Taylor testified — and there was no evidence or any suggestion to the contrary — that he was appointed to the Board of Directors of each of the two companies because each of Bianca and Greenwood desired to enhance its reputation by being associated with him.

...

The respondent submits that he has correctly included the stock option benefits from Bianca by virtue of Mr. Taylor's employment with Bianca and Greenwood respectively in accordance with paragraph 7(1)(a) of the Act. In the respondent's view, Mr. Taylor was director of Bianca and Greenwood and received stock option benefits by virtue of his employment as a director of the corporations.

...

The first requirement of subsection 7(1) is that the taxpayer must be an employee of either corporation or of a corporation with which it does not deal with at arm's length. Accordingly, Mr. Taylor's initial position is that because a corporation does not exercise any control over a director, a director can not be considered an employee and therefore he falls outside the ambit of the Act.

The words "office," "officer" and "employee" are defined in subsection 248(1) as:

> "office" means the position of an individual entitling him to a fixed or ascertainable stipend or remuneration and includes a judicial office, the office of a Minister of the Crown, the office of a member of the Senate or House of Commons of Canada, a member of a legislative assembly or a member of a legislative or executive council and any other office, the

incumbent of which is elected by popular vote or is elected or appointed in a representative capacity and also includes the position of a corporation director; and "officer" means a person holding such an office ... .

"employee" ... includes an officer.

Thus a directorship is an office: the holder of an office is an officer, and an officer is an employee. Therefore it would appear for the purposes of the *Income Tax Act* a director is an employee.

...

Mr. Taylor was granted the stock options subsequent to his appointments as a director. Accordingly, he received them while he was an employee of the corporations and the Minister's assessment would seem to meet the conditions set out in paragraph 7(1)(a).

The appellant, however, further submits that, even if he was an employee, he did not receive the options "by virtue of his employment," as required by subsection 7(5) of the Act. Subsection 7(5) provides that:

This section does not apply if the benefit conferred by the agreement was not received in respect of, in the course of, or by virtue of the employment.

There appear to be two elements to this argument. The first ... is that directors, although employees, do not have "employment." ... Presumably, the appellant seeks to restrict the scope of the word "employment" to that found in subsection 248(1), namely:

"employment" means the position of an individual in the service of some other person (including Her Majesty or a foreign state or sovereign). ...

Quite clearly, a directorship would not meet this test. But, the definitions provided by section 248 are not necessarily all inclusive, and the possibility still exists that the appellant may fall within some broader definition of the word employment.

"Employment" is defined as follows:

... A person's regular occupation or business; a trade or profession ....

(The Oxford English Dictionary, Vol. III)

Act of employing or state of being employed; that which engages or occupies; that which consumes time or attention ... .

(Black's Law Dictionary, 5th ed.)

These broader definitions are to be preferred to the more narrow statutory one for several reasons. Generally speaking, when an Act says that a word "means" something, it is understood that the legislature has intended to restrict the definition of that word to that set out in the Act: *vide*: *Yellow Cab v. Board of Industrial Relations*, [1980] 2 SCR 761, per Ritchie J, at page 768. But, this rule is only applicable where the particular statutory definition fits the context in which it is used. Where the context of a particular section clearly renders the statutory definition inapplicable, reference must be made to the ordinary meaning of the word. ...

To this end, implicit in the use of the phrase "by the employee by virtue of his employment" is the presumption that all employees are in employment. Indeed, it is only by accepting this relationship between the words "employee" and "employment" that the provisions of section 7 can have any logical meaning. ...

A statute must be expounded "according to the intent of them that make it" and should be interpreted to best ensure the attainment of its objects: *Fordyce v. Bridges* (1847), 1 HLC 4 ... . The purpose of subsection 7(5) is to exclude from income only the amount of any benefit received for consideration extraneous to a taxpayer's employment. ... The intent of the Act therefore would require that the word "employment" be given an inclusive, rather than exclusive, interpretation.

The second strand of the appellant's argument was that, even if he was an employee and was in "employment," he did not receive the stock options by virtue of such employment. ... Stripped to its essentials, the appellant argues that although he was a director and performed the duties inherent in this office, he, in common with all the other directors, received no remuneration as a consequence. Instead, the benefit which he did receive, namely the options, resulted from the companies' desire to enhance their reputations by virtue of their association with him.

...

To say that the appellant received the stock options because the companies wished to further their reputations begs the question. ... Here, the reputation of the companies was not advanced merely because the appellant's name appeared on a prospectus. Rather, it was because, having agreed to become a director, investors may have logically presumed that Mr. Taylor was performing the duties thereof, to the ultimate benefit of the companies. While the companies themselves may have been more interested in the prestige afforded by the appellant's name than by the manner or competence with which he performed his duties, the former flows directly from the latter.

As well, although it is necessary to relate the benefit received to the services performed, the connection need not be substantial. Subsection 7(5) only exempts those benefits which were not conferred "in respect of, in the course of, or by virtue of the employment," and as Dickson J, as he then was, indicated, in *Nowegijick v. The Queen*, [1983] 1 SCR 29 at 39; [1983] CTC 20 at 25:

> The words "in respect of" are, in my opinion, words of the widest possible scope. They import such meanings as "in relation to," "with reference to" or "'in connection with." The phrase "in respect of" is probably the widest of any expression intended to convey some connection between two related subject matters.

Ultimately, whatever the companies themselves hoped to gain through their association with the appellant, the bottom line is that he was "hired" as an employee in order, ostensibly at least, to perform as a director with all the statutory responsibilities of that office. Therefore, having structured their relationship in this manner the parties are bound by their choice.

Was Mr. Taylor remunerated by the companies? One may ask as well the question "why did Bianca and Greenwood grant the options to Mr. Taylor?" The evidence leads me to infer the options were granted in consideration of the services Mr. Taylor was to perform as a director and he received the options *qua* director, an employee of each of the corporations. The benefits he received by the exercise of his rights under the option agreements are taxable pursuant to subsection 7(1) since he received the benefits by virtue of his employment with the corporations.

NOTES AND QUESTIONS

1. On what grounds did the taxpayer in *Taylor* argue that his acquisition of shares in Bianca and Greenwood was not subject to the rule in paragraph 7(1)(a)? Why did the court reject these arguments? Do you agree with the court's reasoning? Why or why not?

2. Was it necessary for the court in *Taylor* to extend the meaning of the word "employment" beyond the statutory definition in subsection 248(1) in order to include the value of the stock options in computing the taxpayer's income from his offices with Bianca and Greenwood? If, as the taxpayer argued, section 7 did not apply because the benefit was not received in respect of, in the course of, or by virtue of the [taxpayer's] employment," might the benefit not have been taxable under the general rule in paragraph 6(1)(a)?

3. In *Busby v. Canada*, [1986] 1 C.T.C. 147, 86 D.T.C. 6018 (F.C.T.D.), the taxpayer, who had entered into a personal relationship with a German businessman named Wolfgang Rauball who persuaded her to serve as a nominal director of a resource company that required a Canadian-resident director, was granted a series of options to acquire shares in the company, which she exercised in 1978 and 1979. Allowing the taxpayer's appeal from an assessment that included benefits from the acquisition of these shares in computing the taxpayer's income from her office as a director, the court held (at para. 26) that "the benefits received by the plaintiff from the stock options were ... received by her as a person for considerations extraneous to such employment, namely ... her special relationship with Wolfgang Rauball." In addition, McNair J reasoned (at para. 18):

> it is noteworthy that subsection 7(5) specifically uses the words "the employment" without the usual coupling with the word "office" as in sections 3, 5 and 6 of the Act. In my view, it must be inferred that Parliament intended that the words "the employment" should stand alone on their own feet and without the support ... of the extended meaning accorded the words "Employed," "Employee," and "Office" by the dictionary of section 248.

In *Taylor*, Rip TCJ considered this argument, but dismissed it (at para. 17) as "*obiter* to the actual judgment."

4.   Which interpretation of parliamentary intent regarding subsection 7(5) do you find most persuasive: that in *Taylor* or that in *Busby*? Is it reasonable to presume that Parliament had a specific intent in using the words "the employment" in subsection 7(5) rather than the usual coupling with the word "office"? How should the courts approach these interpretive challenges?

5.   In *Scott v. Canada*, [1994] F.C.J. No. 3, [1994] 1 C.T.C. 330, 94 D.T.C. 6193 (F.C.A.), the taxpayer, who became a director of a company called Night Hawk Resources Ltd. ("Night Hawk") for which he performed services through a private company called Delso Realty Ltd. ("Delso") pursuant to a consulting contract between Night Hawk and another company ("D.Z.") for which Delso had agreed to provide a number of services, was granted options to acquire shares in Night Hawk, which he exercised in 1983 and 1984. Rejecting the taxpayer's argument that the stock options were not received "in respect of, in the course of, or by virtue of [any] employment" with Night Hawk, the Federal Court of Appeal affirmed the decision of the trial judge (at para. 16), who held that the taxpayer had become an employee of Night Hawk, "independently of his position as a director and an officer of the corporation" — "rendering practically full-time services" to it and its associated companies "without receiving any remuneration from it." In addition, the court observed (at para. 16), referring to the decision in *Taylor v. M.N.R.*, [1988] T.C.J. No. 732, [1988] 2 C.T.C. 2227, 88 D.T.C. 1571 (T.C.C.): "Pursuant to subsection 248(1) of the Act, an officer of a corporation is an employee of that corporation and necessarily has an employment relationship with the corporation."

6.   In *Grohne v. Canada*, [1989] F.C.J. No. 301, [1989] 1 C.T.C. 434, 89 D.T.C. 5220 (F.C.T.D.), the taxpayer, who was a director, shareholder, and president of a company called Ohio Resources Corporation ("Ohio"), received stock options as part of a shareholder rights offering. Referring to subsection 7(5), the court concluded that the options had been received by virtue of the taxpayer's relationship with the company as a shareholder, not as an officer or employee. For another case in which stock options were held to have been received by a taxpayer *qua* shareholder rather than *qua* employee, see *Bernstein v. M.N.R.*, [1977] C.T.C. 328, 77 D.T.C. 5187 (F.C.A.).

7.   In *Aylward v. Canada*, [1997] T.C.J. No. 194, [1997] 2 C.T.C. 2748, 97 D.T.C. 1097 (T.C.C.), the taxpayer, who had worked for his uncle's company, Aylward's Ltd., acquired shares of the company in December 1988, almost two years after he ceased to be an employee of the company. Referring to subsection 7(4) and concluding that the "agreement" to issue shares mentioned in the opening words of subsection 7(1) may involve an informal offer to issue shares, the Court held that the acquisition of the shares was subject to paragraph 7(1)(a).

8.   In *Robertson v. Canada*, [1990] F.C.J. No. 4, [1990] 1 C.T.C. 114, 90 D.T.C. 6070 (F.C.A.), the taxpayer was employed by another individual as a ranch manager and received an option right from his employer to purchase shares of a public corporation. Because the options were granted by a non-

corporate employer this arrangement clearly fell outside the parameters of section 7. The parties agreed that paragraph 6(1)(a) was broad enough to include the stock option but disagreed about when a benefit should be recognized under that provision. The taxpayer argued that the benefit was received in 1974 when the options were granted, citing the House of Lords decision to that effect in *Abbott v. Philbin*, [1960] 2 All E.R. 763 (H.L.). On this view the growth in the value of the shares between 1974 and 1980, when the options were exercised, would be taxed as a capital gain. The Federal Court of Appeal rejected this argument, holding that the taxpayer realized employment benefits on both the grant and the exercise of the options, but that only the latter could be quantified sufficiently to give rise to an income inclusion under paragraph 6(1)(a):

> ... while the second benefit can be measured by the discrepancy between the cost of exercising the option and the market value of the shares at the time of the acquisition, the first benefit, although a real one, eludes independent quantification.

Compare the more recent decision in *Henley v. Canada*, [2007] F.C.J. No. 1566, 2008 D.T.C. 6017 (F.C.A.), where the taxpayer received warrants to purchase shares of one of his employer's clients, as partial payment of fees owing in respect of the taxpayer's work for the client. The Court held that in this case paragraph 6(1)(a) applied to include an employment benefit in the taxpayer's income in the year the warrants were granted, and not in the year they were exercised to acquire shares. Writing for the Court, Ryer JA distinguished *Robertson* on the basis that the taxpayer there had only a conditional right to acquire shares under the option subject to continuing in the employer's service for some period of time, whereas Mr. Henley acquired an absolute right to exercise the warrants at any time (paragraphs 20-22). The Court did not address the appropriate method of valuing the warrants as the relevant year was not at issue in the appeal. However, it affirmed the decision of the Tax Court of Canada in which Sheridan TCJ made the following comments about valuation ([2006] T.C.J. No. 351, [2006] 5 C.T.C. 2459, 2006 D.T.C. 3431 (T.C.C.), at paragraphs 25-26):

> Though the concept of evaluating options is not new, since *Robertson* was decided, technology has increased dramatically the facility with which the data necessary for the calculation of their value may be obtained. In *Robertson*, it is not clear from the reasons what evidence was before the Court as to how such an evaluation could be made; at the hearing of this matter, however, the Appellant presented a sheaf of computer-generated documents containing the daily ranges of values of the UBS shares between May 1998 and September 2000. The Appellant also testified to the valuation methods he used as an investment banker. He explained that a share warrant has an "intrinsic value" when it is "in the money"; that is to say, when the share value on a particular day (assumed for the purpose, to be the day upon which an option is exercised) is higher than the exercise price of that warrant. In argument, counsel for the Appellant quoted from a publication outlining the ways in which that valuation may be made ... Indeed, the Canada Revenue Agency is no stranger to such methods. [Footnotes omitted]

Where section 7 applies to a stock option the statute resolves these difficult questions about the quantum and timing of the employment benefit. The operation of section 7 is discussed below.

I. QUANTUM OF BENEFIT INCLUDED UNDER SECTION 7

Where an employee acquires securities under a stock option agreement, paragraph 7(1)(a) stipulates that:

a benefit equal to the amount, if any, by which

    (i)   the value of the securities at the time the employee acquired them

exceeds the total of

    (ii)   the amount paid or to be paid to the particular qualifying person by the employee for the securities, and

    (iii)   the amount, if any, paid by the employee to acquire the right to acquire the securities

is deemed to have been received, in the taxation year in which the employee acquired the securities, by the employee because of the employee's employment.

Thus, where the value of the securities exceeds the sum of the exercise price and any amount paid by the employee to acquire the option right, the amount of this difference is included in computing the employee's income. For this purpose, the Federal Court of Appeal has held that the word "value" means "fair market value," which, in the case of publicly traded shares, is generally the market price at which the shares are traded.[50]

The operation of paragraph 7(1)(a) can be illustrated by a simple example.

Example

In year 1 an employee receives a right under a stock option agreement to purchase 1000 shares of the corporation which employs her, at a price of $40 per share. She is not required to pay any amount to the corporation to obtain the option right. The employee exercises the option in year 4, when the share value is $50.

The employment benefit under paragraph 7(1)(a) is computed as follows:

      $50,000 (value of shares at time option is exercised)
-    $40,000 (exercise price under the terms of the agreement)
= $10,000 benefit

Note that the employee has not yet realized the value of the shares in the form of cash. If in year 5 the employee sells the shares receiving proceeds of

---

[50] *Steen v. Canada*, [1988] F.C.J. No. 129, [1988] 1 C.T.C. 256, 88 D.T.C. 6171 (F.C.A.).

$57,000, the additional $7000 of appreciation will be subject to tax as a capital gain, not as a further employment benefit. The quantum of the employment benefit is fixed at the time the shares are acquired.

Where instead of exercising the option the employee "has transferred or otherwise disposed of" the option rights to an arm's length person, the employee is deemed by paragraph 7(1)(b) to have received a benefit equal to "the amount, if any, by which (i) the value of the consideration for the disposition exceeds (ii) the amount, if any, paid by the employee to acquire those rights." [51]

Example

Using the above hypothetical, if in year 3 the taxpayer had instead sold her option rights to another employee of the corporation with whom she deals at arm's length for total consideration of $3000, the benefit to the taxpayer would be computed as follows:

$$\begin{aligned} & \$3000 \\ - \quad & \underline{0} \\ = \quad & \$3000 \text{ benefit} \end{aligned}$$

For transactions or events occurring after December 23, 1998, subsection 248(1) defines a "disposition" of property to include, among other amounts,

(a) any transaction or event entitling a taxpayer to proceeds of disposition of the property, [and]

(b) any transaction or event by which, ...

(iv) where the property is an option to acquire or dispose of property, the option expires.

For transactions or events occurring up to this date, the Act did not define the words "transfer" or "dispose" for the purposes of paragraph 7(1)(b). According to the *Concise Oxford Dictionary*, 7th ed., however, the verb "transfer" is defined as "convey, remove, hand over," while the verb "dispose" is defined as "do what one will with, get rid of, sell, settle, finish, kill." In the context of other statutory provisions, moreover, the Supreme Court of Canada concluded in a 1979 decision that "the words 'disposed of should be given their broadest

---

[51] Where the employee transfers or otherwise disposes of these rights to a person with whom the employee does not deal at arm's length, the acquisition of shares or the subsequent transfer or disposition of the options by the transferee will give rise to a benefit in the hands of the employee under para. 7(1)(c) or (d).

possible meaning," including the destruction of property and the extinguishment of rights.[52]

Notwithstanding this judicial pronouncement and these dictionary definitions of the words "transfer" and "dispose," courts have concluded on several occasions that paragraph 7(1)(b) did not apply to amounts received as compensation for the cancellation of stock options generally resulting from the issuing company's amalgamation with another company.[53] In *Buccini v. Canada*, [2000] F.C.J. No. 1892, [2001] 1 C.T.C. 103, 2000 D.T.C. 6685 (F.C.A.), for example, the court concluded (at para. 16) that:

> [a] "disposition" in paragraph 7(1)(b) refers to a transaction in which the taxpayer voluntarily agrees to exchange property rights that have accrued under an employee stock option agreement for some other consideration.

Nor, according to the court, were these amounts taxable under paragraph 6(1)(a) or subsection 6(3), although earlier decisions had applied these provisions to include compensation received on the cancellation of stock options in computing the recipient's income from an office or employment.[54]

For amounts received on or after March 16, 2001, subsection 7(1.7) now stipulates for the purposes of paragraphs 7(1)(b) and 110(1)(d) that:

> where a taxpayer receives at a particular time one or more particular amounts in respect of rights of the taxpayer to acquire securities under an agreement referred to in subsection (1) ceasing to be exercisable in accordance with the terms of the agreement, and the cessation would not, if this Act were read without reference to this subsection, constitute a transfer or disposition of those rights by the taxpayer,
>
> (a) the taxpayer is deemed to have disposed of those rights at the particular time to a person with whom the taxpayer was dealing at arm's length and to have received the particular amounts as consideration for the disposition; and

---

[52] *Canada v. CIE Immobilière BCN,* [1979] S.C.J. No. 13, [1979] C.T.C. 71, 79 D.T.C. 5068 (S.C.C.), citing *Re Leven,* [1954] 3 All E.R. 81, where, according to the court, "it was said that the word 'disposition' taken by itself and used in its most extended meaning was 'wide enough to include the act of extinguishment.'"

[53] See, for example, *Reynolds v. M.N.R.,* [1975] F.C.J. No. 7, [1975] C.T.C. 85, 75 D.T.C. 5042 (F.C.T.D.), aff'd [1975] F.C.J. No. 905, [1975] C.T.C. 560, 75 D.T.C. 5393 (F.C.A.) aff'd [1976] C.T.C. 792, 77 D.T.C. 5044 (S.C.C.); *Bernier v. Canada,* [1999] F.C.J. No. 752, [2000] 1 C.T.C. 347, 2000 D.T.C. 6053 (F.C.A.); and *Buccini v. Canada,* [2000] F.C.J. No. 1892, [2001] 1 C.T.C. 103, 2000 D.T.C. 6685 (F.C.A.). For contrary results, in which amounts received in compensation for the cancellation of options were subject to para. 7(1)(b) on the basis that the taxpayer disposed of the options to the issuing corporation prior to its amalgamation with another company, see *Greiner v. M.N.R.,* [1984] F.C.J. No. 15, [1984] C.T.C. 92, 84 D.T.C. 6073 (F.C.A.); *Canada v. Harvey,* [1983] C.T.C. 63, 83 D.T.C. 5098 (F.C.T.D.); and *Dundas v. M.N.R.,* [1995] F.C.J. No. 106, [1995] 1 C.T.C. 184, 95 D.T.C. 5116 (F.C.A.).

[54] See *Kunten v. M.N.R.,* [1985] 2 C.T.C. 2251, 85 D.T.C. 575 (T.C.C.) (applying subs. 6(3)) and *McKay v. M.N.R.,* [1990] T.C.J. No. 901, [1990] 2 C.T.C. 2519, 90 D.T.C. 1926 (T.C.C.) (applying para. 6(1)(a)).

(b) for the purpose of determining the amount, if any, of the benefit that the taxpayer is deemed by paragraph (1)(b) to have received as a consequence of the disposition referred to in paragraph (a), the taxpayer is deemed to have paid an amount to acquire those rights equal to the amount, if any, by which

    (i) the amount paid by the taxpayer to acquire those rights (determined without reference to this subsection) exceeds

    (ii) the total of all amounts each of which is an amount received by the taxpayer before the particular time in respect of the cessation.

The effect of this provision is to reverse the result in *Buccini* and other cases in which paragraph 7(1)(b) was held not to apply to amounts received as compensation for the cancellation of options.

Note that the quantum of any benefit included in income under section 7 is determined by the provisions discussed above, regardless of the timing question of when that benefit must be included in income. We now turn to this second issue.

II. TIMING OF BENEFIT INCLUSION UNDER SECTION 7

The general rule under subsection 7(1) is that a stock option benefit "is deemed to have been received, in the taxation year in which the employee acquired the securities" (paragraph (a)) or in the taxation year in which the taxpayer "transferred or otherwise disposed of" the option rights to an arm's length party (paragraph (b)).

In applying paragraph 7(1)(a), then, it is necessary to determine whether a taxpayer acquired shares under the agreement, and if so when. In *Ball v. M.N.R.*, [1992] T.C.J. No. 539, [1992] 2 C.T.C. 2770, 92 D.T.C. 2123 (T.C.C.), the taxpayer was granted an option to purchase 25,000 shares of his employer, Calgroup Graphics Corporation Limited ("Calgroup"), which he purported to exercise on July 10, 1985, at which time he was issued a certificate for 25,000 shares, even though he had paid nothing for the shares. By September 23, 1985, when the Ontario Securities Commission issued a cease-trading order on Calgroup's shares, the taxpayer had sold 9,700 of the shares, for which he paid $19,885 pursuant to the terms of the stock option agreement. Rejecting the Minister's argument that the taxpayer had received a benefit under paragraph 7(1)(a) in respect of all 25,000 shares, the Court referred to the applicable corporations legislation prohibiting the issuance of shares until the consideration was fully paid, to conclude that the taxpayer had not "acquired" the remaining 15,300 shares as required by paragraph 7(1)(a).

See also *Mansfield v. Canada*, [1984] C.T.C. 547, 84 D.T.C. 6535 (F.C.A.), where the Court held that the conversion of a debenture to common shares pursuant to the terms of the debenture was an acquisition of shares within the meaning of paragraph 7(1)(a).

There are two exceptions to the general timing rule, both of which allow taxpayers to defer inclusion of their stock option benefit until the year they dispose of the securities. The first applies to Canadian-controlled private corporations ("CCPC's") which agree after March 31, 1977 to sell or issue their shares, or shares of a CCPC with which they do not deal at arm's length, to an employee. The employee must deal at arm's length with all the CCPC's which are party to the stock option arrangement. In these circumstances, subsection 7(1.1) stipulates that the reference in paragraph 7(1)(a) to "the taxation year in which the employee acquired the securities" shall be read as "the taxation year in which the employee disposed of or exchanged the securities." The deferral is mandatory if the conditions of subsection 7(1.1) are met. For our purposes, there is no need to consider the definition of a "Canadian-controlled private corporation" which appears in subsection 125(7) and is best examined in a course on the taxation of corporations.

A second exception was added following the 2000 federal budget. Subsection 7(8) applies where securities of a non-CCPC are acquired pursuant to a "qualifying acquisition" and the taxpayer elects in accordance with subsection 7(10) to have subsection 7(8) apply. For the purpose of this provision, subsection 7(9) defines a qualifying acquisition as:

- occurring after February 27, 2000;

- the benefit from which qualifies for the deduction under paragraph 110(1)(d);

- where the grantor is a corporation, the taxpayer was not a "specified shareholder" of the grantor, of a non-arm's length qualifying person that was the taxpayer's employer, or of a qualifying person whose securities the taxpayer had a right to acquire under the agreement;[55] and

- where the security is a share, it is of a class of shares that, at the time the acquisition occurs, is listed on a designated stock exchange as set out in the Regulations.

Subsection 7(10) requires the taxpayer to file an election in a prescribed form and manner before January 16 of the year following the year in which the acquisition occurs. In the absence of an election, the general rule will apply to include the stock option benefit in income in the year the taxpayer acquires securities under the agreement. Subsection 7(10) also requires the taxpayer to be resident in Canada at the time that the acquisition occurs, and limits the value of securities eligible for the deferral to an annual amount of $100,000 for each year in which the options are exercisable, determined at the time that the agreement

---

[55] For the purpose of this and other provisions of the Act, subs. 248(1) defines a specified shareholder as a taxpayer who owns directly or indirectly not less than 10 per cent of the issued shares of any class of the capital stock of the corporation or of any other corporation that is related to the corporation. For the purpose of this definition, the taxpayer is deemed to own shares owned by persons with whom the taxpayer does not deal at arm's length and shares owned by a trust or partnership in proportion to the taxpayer's beneficial interest in the trust or interest in the partnership, and persons who perform services on behalf of a personal services corporation are deemed to be specified shareholders if they or any person or partnership with which they do not deal at arm's length are or may become entitled directly or indirectly to not less than 10 per cent of the assets or shares of any class of the capital stock of the corporation or any related corporation.

was made. In these circumstances, subsection 7(8) stipulates that the reference in paragraph 7(1)(a) to "the taxation year in which the employee acquired the securities" shall be read as "the taxation year in which the employee disposed of or exchanged the securities."

The deferral in subsection 7(8) was announced in the federal budget on February 28, 2000. According to then Finance Minister Paul Martin, the provision was introduced in order "[t]o assist corporations in attracting and retaining high-calibre workers and make our tax treatment of employee stock options more competitive with the United States." For a critical evaluation of these rules and the Canadian tax treatment of stock options more generally, and a thorough comparison between Canadian and U.S. rules governing the taxation of stock options, see Daniel Sandler, "The Tax Treatment of Employee Stock Options: Generous to a Fault" (2001) 49 Can. Tax J. 259-319. For a more recent discussion of the policy issues involved in the tax treatment of stock options, see "Policy Forum: Comments on Tax and Financial Accounting for Employee Stock Options" (2003) 51 Can. Tax J. 1200-90.

The operation of these special timing rules can be illustrated by reference to the first example discussed above.

<u>Example</u>

Year 1: grant of option to acquire 1,000 shares at $40
Year 4: option exercised at a cost of $40,000, with shares valued at $50
Year 5: shares sold for proceeds of $57,000

If the taxpayer qualified for either of the deferred inclusions under subsections 7(1.1) or 7(8)/(9), the tax treatment would be as follows:

Year 1: no tax consequences
Year 4: no tax consequences
Year 5: taxpayer includes a benefit of $1,000 in employment income, computed in the same manner as above; taxpayer also realizes a $7000 capital gain.

C. Allowances

In addition to remuneration and benefits, in computing a taxpayer's income from an office or employment paragraph 6(1)(b) requires taxpayers to include, subject to specific exceptions listed in subparagraphs 6(1)(b)(i) to (ix), "all amounts received ... in the year as an allowance for personal or living expenses or as an allowance for any other purpose." Although the Act contains an extended definition of the expression "personal or living expenses,"[56] it does not define the word "allowance." The following cases and text consider the characterization of an "allowance" for the purposes of paragraph 6(1)(b) and some of the key exceptions in subparagraphs 6(1)(b)(i) to (ix).

1. Characterization

According to the *Concise Oxford Dictionary*, 7th ed., the word "allowance" means "money paid to cover special expenses." The leading case on the characteristics of an allowance for the purposes of paragraph 6(1)(b) is *MacDonald v. Canada (Attorney General)*, [1994] F.C.J. No. 378, [1994] 2 C.T.C. 48, 94 D.T.C. 6262 (F.C.A.).

MacDonald v. Canada (Attorney General)
[1994] F.C.J. No. 378, [1994] 2 C.T.C. 48, 94 D.T.C. 6262 (F.C.A.)

LINDEN JA (Mahoney and MacGuigan JJA concurring): ...

Facts

The respondent is a member of the Royal Canadian Mounted Police (RCMP) who was transferred from Regina to Toronto. After his transfer, the respondent was paid by the Department of Supply and Services $700 each month as a housing subsidy. The payment of this housing subsidy was authorized by Treasury Board and described in a Treasury Board Information Bulletin. It was payable to members of the RCMP "posted to Toronto ... who relocated ... on or after January 1, 1986, and who are subject to further rotational transfers."

The respondent did not include the housing subsidy in his income on his tax return, and he was reassessed by the Minister of National Revenue who determined that the money should be included in the respondent's income.

Relevant Legislation

It is necessary to begin by considering the relevant portions of the *Income Tax Act*. Section 5 of the Act provides that a taxpayer's income from an office or employment "is the salary, wages and other remuneration, including gratuities, received by him in the year." The phrase "salary, wages and other remuneration" is not broad enough to encompass all of those amounts flowing from an employer to an employee which are income from an office or employment, since remuneration is payment for services rendered or things done. Other advantages

---

[56] See the definition of "personal and living expenses" in subs. 248(1). This definition, which includes in "personal or living expenses" expenses of certain properties, insurance policies, and annuity contracts, need not concern us here.

may be received by employees which are not remuneration but which should be considered income.

The Act contains provisions for bringing amounts, other than remuneration, flowing from an employer to an employee within a taxpayer's income from an office or employment. Section 6 lists certain specific amounts that must be included in calculating a taxpayer's income from an office or employment. In this application, paragraph 6(1)(b) is the key provision. ... None of the exceptions to paragraph 6(1)(b) is applicable.

Paragraph 6(1)(b) has a companion paragraph, paragraph 6(1)(a), which requires a taxpayer to include in income benefits received in the course of employment. The purpose of paragraphs 6(1)(a) and 6(1)(b) is to include in a taxpayer's income from employment those gains or advantages arising from the taxpayer's employment that in effect increase the taxpayer's income from that employment. Paragraph 6(1)(a) is directed mainly towards benefits of a non-monetary nature, such as board or lodging, but can also include specific sums of money. Paragraph 6(1)(b), on the other hand, is designed mainly to capture money payments that meet the criteria of "allowances." As I already indicated, paragraph 6(1)(b) will be the focus of these reasons. In my view, the subsidy is a taxable allowance; it is not necessary, therefore, to discuss whether the subsidy is also a taxable benefit under paragraph 6(1)(a).

Analysis

The wording of paragraph 6(1)(b) provides little in the way of assistance in determining what constitutes an allowance. The paragraph simply requires taxpayers to include in their income from office or employment all amounts received in the year as an allowance for personal or living expenses or as an allowance for any other purpose. However, there are certain common sense aspects of the concept of an allowance which have surfaced in the jurisprudence.

The decision of the Exchequer Court in *Ransom v. M.N.R.*, [1967] C.T.C. 346, 67 D.T.C. 5235 (Ex. Ct), provides a good starting place in determining the qualities of an allowance. Noel J reasoned as follows at page 359 (DTC 5243):

> [A] reimbursement of an expense actually incurred in the course of the employment or of a loss actually incurred in the course of the employment is not an "allowance" within the meaning of the word in paragraph 5(1)(b) [now paragraph 6(1)(b)] as an allowance implies an amount paid in respect of some possible expense without any obligation to account.

He continued at page 361 (DTC 5244):

> An allowance is quite a different thing from reimbursement. It is, as already mentioned, an arbitrary amount usually paid in lieu of reimbursement. It is paid to the employee to use as he wishes without being required to account for its expenditure. For that reason it is possible to use it as a concealed increase in remuneration and that is why, I assume, "allowances" are taxed as though they were remuneration.

I agree with Noël J's definition of an allowance under paragraph 6(1)(b). An allowance is an arbitrary amount in that the allowance is not normally calculated to cover a specific expense. The amount may still be arbitrary even though it is roughly tailored to meet the employer's expectation of the magnitude of the expense or the proportion of the expense which the employer is prepared to bear. In other words, the amount of an allowance is predetermined without regard to the exact amount of a particular actual expense or cost, although the figure can be determined with reference to a projected or average expense or cost.

Another excellent definition of an allowance was ... expounded by E.C. Harris, in *Canadian Income Taxation* (4th ed. 1985) at page 108:

> An "allowance" is a round amount given to an employee to cover expenses that he will incur, such as travel or entertainment, on his employer's behalf. The employee is not required to account to the employer later for what he has actually spent. If the employee accounts to the employer for his actual expenses, neither an initial advance given him by his employer nor any subsequent payment by the employer to reimburse him for his expenses is an "allowance." The scope for abuse of allowances is greater: because the employee does not have to account for an allowance, large allowances might be given as a form of hidden remuneration. Hence the general rule that allowances form part of employment income.

Since an allowance does not have the character of reimbursement, it follows that the recipient of the allowance need not account for the manner in which the allowance is spent. The corollary of no accounting being required is that the recipient is free to disburse the money or not, as she or he pleases. This does not mean, however, that the allowance cannot be intended for a particular purpose. Indeed, the wording of paragraph 6(1)(b) captures allowances for personal or living expenses or "any other purpose." That an allowance is, in fact, used for its intended purpose or does not overcompensate its recipient does not lead to the conclusion, after the event, that there was an obligation to so use it.

...

[F]ollowing *Ransom*, ... the general principle defining an "allowance" for purposes of paragraph 6(1)(b) is composed of three elements. First, an allowance is an arbitrary amount in that it is a predetermined sum set without specific reference to any actual expense or cost. As I noted above, however, the amount of the allowance may be set through a process of projected or average expenses or costs. Second, paragraph 6(1)(b) encompasses allowances for personal or living expenses, or for any other purpose, so that an allowance will usually be for a specific purpose. Third, an allowance is in the discretion of the recipient in that the recipient need not account for the expenditure of the funds towards an actual expense or cost.

Applying these principles in this case, the housing subsidy has all the legal characteristics of a taxable allowance. This is not a case of reimbursement for a particular expense. First, the respondent received the $700 as a limited, predetermined, "round" amount, which might also be described as arbitrary, in that it was not calculated with respect to an actual cost or expense of the respondent's. Second, the money was for a particular purpose, namely to subsidize the respondent's accommodation costs. This is certainly a personal or living expense within the meaning of paragraph 6(1)(b) and paragraph 248(1)(a). Finally, the respondent received the money totally in his discretion; he was not required to account for buying a house in Toronto or paying a certain rent in order to receive the subsidy. No receipts had to be submitted. Instead, the respondent was not required to incur any accommodation expenses whatsoever in order to receive the monthly payment. We have here, therefore, a "hidden" or "concealed increase in remuneration," which, in all fairness, must be treated as income.

Application allowed.

NOTES AND QUESTIONS

1.   What, according to the Federal Court of Appeal in *MacDonald*, are the essential characteristics of an "allowance" for the purposes of paragraph 6(1)(b)?

2.   For other cases in which payments for increased living costs have been characterized as taxable allowances within the meaning of paragraph 6(1)(b), see *Bertrand v. Canada*, [1996] 1 C.T.C. 2992 (T.C.C.) (housing allowance following transfer from Ottawa to Montreal); *D'Alessandro v. Canada*, [1997] T.C.J. No. 544, [1997] 3 C.T.C. 2756 (T.C.C) (cost-of-living reimbursement following transfer from Thunder Bay to London, Ontario); *Middlestead v. Canada*, [1999] T.C.J. No. 134, [1999] 3 C.T.C. 2335 (T.C.C.) (non-accountable relocation allowance following transfer from Brandon, Manitoba to Calgary); and *Rio v. Canada*, [2003] F.C.J. No. 1610, [2004] 2 C.T.C. 221, 2004 D.T.C. 6079 (F.C.A.), aff'g [2002] T.C.J. No. 691, 2003 D.T.C. 1456 (T.C.C.) (housing, cost of living and official duties allowances paid during 7-year transfer from Montreal to Toronto).

3.   In *Lepine v. M.N.R.*, [1978] C.T.C. 2895, 78 D.T.C. 1637 (T.R.B.), the taxpayer, who worked for the Aluminum Company of Canada Ltd. ("Alcan"), received an "isolation bonus" of $700 per month when he was sent to the Republic of Guinea to "assist in setting up a bauxite dehydration plant." Referring to subsection 5(1) and paragraphs 6(1)(a) and (b), the board concluded (at para. 17):

> Regardless of whether these bonuses were received as salary, a gratuity or an allowance for personal or living expenses, they must be included in income because of the sections cited above, particularly paragraph 6(1)(b).

See also *Canada v. Demers*, [1980] F.C.J. No. 244, [1981] C.T.C. 282, 81 D.T.C. 5256 (F.C.T.D.), where a $4,280.92 "cost of living adjustment," paid to an employee of the Organization of the American States ("OAS") who was posted to Port-au-Prince, Haiti, was characterized as remuneration within the meaning of subsections 5(1) and 6(3), not as an "allowance" that might otherwise have been exempt under subsection 6(6).

4.   In *Oster v. Canada*, [1994] T.C.J. No. 758, [1995] 1 CTC 2224, 95 D.T.C. 104 (T.C.C.), the taxpayer, who was also a member of the RCMP, was paid a transfer allowance equal to a month's pay each time he was transferred from Nova Scotia to Prince Edward Island and back. Following *MacDonald v.*

Canada (Attorney General), [1994] F.C.J. No. 378, [1994] 2 C.T.C. 48, 94 D.T.C. 6262 (F.C.A.), the court concluded that the payment was taxable under paragraph 6(1)(b). For similar results in cases involving the payment of transfer allowances, see *McLay v. M.N.R.*, [1992] T.C.J. No. 610, [1992] C.T.C. 2649, 92 D.T.C. 2260 (T.C.C.); *McRae v. The Queen*, [1993] 3 C.T.C. 2482 (T.C.C.); *Berardo v. Canada*, [1995] 2 C.T.C. 2964D #2 (T.C.C.); *Morris v. Canada*, [1997] F.C.J. No. 1135, [1998] 1 C.T.C. 68 (F.C.A.); *McGuire v. Canada*, [1999] T.C.J. No. 194, [1999] 2 C.T.C. 2914 (T.C.C.); and *Shurtliff v. Canada*, [1999] T.C.J. No. 646, [1999] 4 C.T.C. 2864 (T.C.C.). For an opposing result, in which a payment of four weeks' salary to a taxpayer who was relocated from Quebec City to Montreal was characterized as a reimbursement of moving expenses, see *Côté v. M.N.R.*, [1990] T.C.J. No. 845, [1990] 2 C.T.C. 2617 (T.C.C.).

5.   In *Sheldon v. M.N.R.*, [1988] 2 C.T.C. 2039, 88 D.T.C. 1392 (T.C.C.), the taxpayer, who was employed by a mining company from 1970 to 1985 when his employment was terminated due to the closure of the mine, received $63,000 as a "housing subsidy" in compensation for the decrease in the resale value that his home would suffer as a result of the mine closure. Rejecting the taxpayer's argument that the payment was a non-taxable reimbursement for a loss suffered due to the mine closure, the court held that the taxpayer, who had not in fact sold his house, had received a taxable allowance within the meaning of paragraph 6(1)(b). See also *Vickery v. Canada*, [1993] T.C.J. No. 349, [1993] 2 C.T.C. 2678, 93 D.T.C. 993 (T.C.C.) and *Hodges v. Canada*, [1996] T.C.J. No. 478, [1996] 3 C.T.C. 2086 (T.C.C.), where lump-sum payments to railway employees on the relocation of railway operations were characterized as taxable allowances within the meaning of paragraph 6(1)(b).

6.   In *Huffman v. Canada*, [1990] F.C.J. No. 529, [1990] 2 C.T.C. 132, 90 D.T.C. 6405 (F.C.A.), the taxpayer, a plainclothes police officer with the Niagara Regional Police Force, received a $500 clothing allowance pursuant to a policy that required presentation of at least $400 in receipts. Referring to the trial decision ([1988] F.C.J. No. 1060, [1989] 1 C.T.C. 32, 89 D.T.C. 5006 (F.C.T.D.)), which found as a fact that the taxpayer had spent more than $500 on work-related clothing, the Federal Court of Appeal rejected the Minister's argument that the difference between the amount paid and the receipts actually submitted ($500 - $420.43 = $79.57) was a taxable allowance within the meaning of paragraph 6(1)(b). According to Heald JA (at para. 15):

> it is obvious that the $500 here in issue or any part of it cannot be said to be an allowance. Article 17.01 [of the collective agreement between the taxpayer's employer and the Niagara Police Association] provides for reimbursement only upon presentation of receipts. As noted by the trial judge ... a special exception was made in 1979 but only in respect of the $100 increase that year and in the interests of avoiding undue extra paperwork. This circumstance cannot operate so as to change the nature of the payment. It is still a reimbursement, not an allowance and the trial judge did not err in so finding.

For another case in which a clothing allowance was held to be a non-taxable reimbursement, see *McLay v. M.N.R.*, [1992] T.C.J. No. 610, [1992] 2 C.T.C. 2649, 92 D.T.C. 2260 (T.C.C.).

7.   In *North Waterloo Publishing Ltd. v. Canada* (appeal by *Verdun*), [1998] F.C.J. No. 165, [1998] 2 C.T.C. 327, 98 D.T.C. 6175 (F.C.A.), the taxpayer, who operated, edited, and published newspapers at two locations in southwestern Ontario, received a meal allowance of $1,440, which he excluded from his income on the grounds that it merely reimbursed him for evening meals consumed while working at one of the two locations. Dismissing the taxpayer's appeal from the trial decision ([1996] T.C.J. No. 1528, [1997] 1 C.T.C. 2557 (T.C.C.)), which held that the payment was a taxable benefit within the meaning of paragraph 6(1)(a), the court concluded that "this payment to the applicant is more properly described as an allowance." According to Linden JA (at para. 3):

> Even when these amounts are not used for any improper purpose, and even when they are reasonable estimations of the costs, our law treats them as additional renumeration, not as reimbursement of expenses, which require detailed receipts being submitted for reimbursement. This is felt to be necessary in order to ensure that allowable, reimbursed, personal expenses are accurately recorded and that the system is fair for all Canadians, even though extra accounting costs may be incurred.

Is the court's emphasis on receipts in this passage consistent with the decision in *Huffman v. Canada*, [1990] F.C.J. No. 529, [1990] 2 C.T.C. 132, 90 D.T.C. 6405 (F.C.A.)? Assuming that the taxpayer received no "material advantage" from the food consumed in Elmira (one of his two work locations), how might the taxpayer and his employer have arranged matters in order to avoid having to include the value of the food in computing the taxpayer's income from his employment? Is it consistent with the structure of section 6 of the Act that benefits should be taxable if received in cash but non-taxable if received in kind?

For another case in which meal allowances were held to be taxable under paragraph 6(1)(b), see *Lavoie v. M.N.R.*, [1978] C.T.C. 2452, 78 D.T.C. 1323 (T.R.B.).

8.   For the purpose of paragraph 6(1)(b), the CRA distinguishes among (a) an "allowance," which it defines as "any periodic or other payment that an employee receives from an employer, in addition to salary or wages, without having to account for its use"; (b) a "reimbursement," which it defines as "a payment by an employer to an employee to repay the employee for amounts spent by the employee on the employer's business"; and (c) an "accountable advance," which it defines as "an amount given by an employer to an employee for expenses to be incurred by the employee on the employer's business and to be accounted for by the production of vouchers and the return of any amount not so spent." Although an allowance is generally taxable, unless subject to a statutory exception, a reimbursement or accountable advance is generally not taxable, "unless it represents payment of the employee's personal expenses." See *Interpretation Bulletin* IT-522R, "Vehicle, Travel and Sales Expenses of Employees," March 29, 1996, paragraphs 40, 50, and 51.

2. Exceptions

The requirement in paragraph 6(1)(b) that a taxpayer must include all amounts received as "an allowance for personal or living expenses or ... for any other purpose" is subject to a number of exceptions in subparagraphs 6(1)(b)(i) to (ix), the most important of which for our purposes are found in subparagraphs 6(1)(b)(v), (vii), and (vii.1).[57] According to these provisions, a taxpayer is not required to include in computing the taxpayer's income from an office or employment:

(v)   reasonable allowances for travel expenses received by an employee from the employee's employer in respect of a period when the employee was employed in connection with the selling of property or negotiating of contracts for the employee's employer, ...

(vii)   reasonable allowances for travel expenses (other than allowances for the use of a motor vehicle) received by an employee (other than an employee employed in connection with the selling of property or the negotiating of contracts for the employer) from the employer for travelling away from

(A)   the municipality where the employer's establishment at which the employee ordinarily worked or to which the employee ordinarily reported was located, and

(B)   the metropolitan area, if there is one, where that establishment was located, in the performance of the duties of the employee's office or employment, [or]

(vii.1) reasonable allowances for the use of a motor vehicle received by an employee (other than an employee employed in connection with the selling of property or the negotiating of contracts for the employer) from the employer for travelling in the performance of the duties of the office or employment.

For the purpose of subparagraphs 6(1)(b)(v) and (vii.1), moreover, subparagraphs 6(1)(b)(x) and (xi) stipulate that an allowance for the use of a motor vehicle will be deemed not to be reasonable where the measurement of the use of the vehicle for the purpose of the allowance is not based solely on the number of kilometres for which the vehicle is used for employment purposes, or where the taxpayer receives both an allowance and a reimbursement in whole or in part in respect of the same use of the vehicle.

A common feature of these exceptions is that each involves allowances for "travel expenses" incurred by the employee on the employer's behalf and/or "travelling" by the employee in the performance of the duties of the employee's

---

[57] Subparagraphs 6(1)(b)(i) to (iv) apply to members of Parliament, members of the Canadian forces, and various categories of public servants. Subparagraph 6(1)(b)(vi) applies to members of the clergy. Subparagraph 6(1)(b)(v.1) was added in 2007 and exempts board and lodging allowances of up to $300 per month for amateur athletes. Subparagraph 6(1)(b)(viii), which has been repealed, applied to voluntary firefighters. Finally, subpara. 6(1)(b)(ix) applies to employees who, because of their work location, must send their children to an English- or French-language boarding school.

office or employment. Although the Act does not define these terms, their meaning was considered in *Blackman v. M.N.R.*, [1967] Tax ABC 480, 67 D.T.C. 347 (T.A.B.).

Blackman v. M.N.R.
[1967] Tax ABC 480, 67 D.T.C. 347 (T.A.B.)

MAURICE BOIVERT, QC: ... The appellants, in computing their income for each of the taxation years under review, failed to report in their income tax returns the amounts of the allowances they received from their employer, Furness, Withy & Company Limited, whose principal business was the transport of passengers and goods. The Minister revised the taxable income of each of the appellants and added for each taxation year during which an allowance was received the amount of such allowance.

...

[T]he appellants were employees of a firm engaged in the business of transporting passengers and goods. ... [T]he employer had to move the appellants from one place to another, at its convenience in the course of its operations. The employer was responsible for moving the appellants sometimes from Montreal to Halifax or to Saint John, NB, sometimes from the latter places to Montreal. The employer, in order to lessen the cost of living for the appellants because they were called to live outside the municipality where the employer had its regular and main establishment, used to pay to the appellants the allowances referred to above. ... The financial manager in Canada of Furness, Withy & Company Limited was Mr. Charles Naylor. He was called as witness and explained clearly the nature of the allowances paid to the appellants. In answer to questions by counsel he stated: ...

Q. Now, for what purpose is this allowance paid to the employees?

A. It covers out of pocket expenses and additional expenses whilst away from home.

Q. What do you mean by additional expenses whilst away from home?

A. Having experienced it myself about forty years ago. I know it cost me more to come to Montreal because every turn you take, such as laundry and transportation in a larger city and your meals would cost you more, you wouldn't be going home at noon and you had meals to buy and whilst you are away from home I know I found from my experience I wanted and I needed more entertainment because I couldn't sit and just look at the four walls. I had to go out at night and even walk the streets or go to the show. Being away from home, the minute you step out of the office you are among strangers so to speak. And at home you have all these things in front of you. You go home, pull off your shoes and that's it. ...

Q. According to the indication that we have with regard to the people who are under appeal and objection, the time away from home varies. In relation to this particular aspect, could you tell us generally what is the average time spent away from home office by an employee?

A. Well, these days it's three to four months.

...

From Mr. Naylor's evidence it is obvious that the sums of money paid to the appellants were not in the nature of travelling expenses but were personal and living expenses. The appellants were not travelling from one place to another but were living at different places in the performance of the duties of their employment. When they were away from their ordinary place of residence, the appellants received allowances which were reasonable but which were paid to them not because they were travelling but because they had to live away from their home for various periods of time.

...

Travelling is not defined in the Act. In common parlance it means to go on a journey, to move back and forth within a short period of time, which is quite different from sojourning somewhere which means to live temporarily in a place.

In the case at bar the employer's principal business was passenger and goods transport but the employee was not travelling on the ships used by the employer to transport goods or passengers. The appellants were not required by the duties of their employment to pay for their own meals and lodging while travelling.

The intention of the legislator in enacting the provisions of the Act with respect to deductibility of travelling expenses was to give the same treatment as to wages, salaries and remuneration to all employees of a designated trade or industry. For instance if an employee was required to travel in the performance of the duties of his employment and he could not deduct his travelling expenses under the provisions of the sections of the Act dealing with travelling expenses, then he would be underpaid vis-à-vis the other employees whose function is to accomplish stationary work. Similarly, if an employee, in the discharge of his duties, is called to sojourn or live for many months in places other than the municipality where his employer has his establishment and if he has the right to deduct the living expenses he is receiving to make up for personal expenditures he may incur on account of the fact that he was called to stay away from the locality where he habitually resides, then he will be overpaid vis-à-vis the other employees who, in order to carry out their duties, do not need to travel or sojourn away from their ordinary place of residence.

...

On the whole I have arrived at the conclusion that the appeals must be dismissed.

Appeals dismissed.

NOTES AND QUESTIONS

1.   On what basis did the taxpayers in *Blackman* argue that the allowances paid by their employer were not taxable as employment income? Why did the board reject this argument? How, for the purpose of then subparagraph 5(1)(b)(vii) (now subparagraph 6(1)(b)(vii)) did the board define "travelling expenses"?

2.   Although subparagraphs 6(1)(b)(v) and (vii) now speak of "travel expenses" rather than "travelling expenses" (the language used in former subparagraphs 5(1)(b)(v) and (vii)), there does not appear to be any significance to these amendments.

3.   Subsection 6(6), which was enacted in 1972, allows taxpayers in certain circumstances to exclude, among other things, reasonable allowances in respect of expenses incurred for board and lodging at a temporary work location. As a result, although per diems such as those in *Blackman* cannot be characterized as allowances for "travel expenses" within the meaning of subparagraph 6(1)(b)(vii), they might be excluded in computing a taxpayer's income from an office or employment under subsection 6(6). Subsection 6(6) is considered later in this chapter.

4.   In *Bouchard v. M.N.R.*, [1980] 80 D.T.C. 1785 (T.R.B.), the taxpayer, who lived in Quebec City where he was employed by the Quebec government for 32½ hours per week, received $1,500 as an allowance for travel and living expenses under a contract with the Université de Sherbrooke, where he was also employed as a part-time professor. Rejecting the taxpayer's argument that the payment was a non-taxable travel allowance within the meaning of subparagraph 6(1)(b)(vii), the board held (at para. 18) that the expenses in respect of which the payment was made were "personal expenses for travel from Quebec City to Sherbrooke voluntarily incurred by the appellant, just like the expenses he incurred in going from his residence in Quebec City to the Parliament Buildings, where he also worked."

5.   The outcome in *Bouchard* was legislatively reversed by the enactment of subsection 81(3.1), which exempts "an amount (not in excess of a reasonable amount) received by the individual from an employer with whom the individual was dealing at arm's length as an allowance for, or reimbursement of, travel expenses incurred by the individual in the year in respect of the individual's part-time employment in the year with the employer ... if ... throughout the period in which the expenses were incurred ... the individual had other employment or was carrying on a business," provided that "the duties of the individual's part-time employment were performed at a location not less than 80 kilometres from ... both the individual's ordinary place of residence and the place of the other employment or business." This provision was amended in 2001 to allow universities, colleges and other designated educational institutions to pay a tax exempt travel allowance to part-time teachers and professors

residing at least 80 kms away, without the requirement that they have other employment or operate a business.

6.   In *Campbell v. Canada*, [2003] T.C.J. No. 211, [2003] 3 C.T.C. 2790, 2003 D.T.C. 420 (T.C.C.), the taxpayers held offices with a regional school board, worked out of their homes, and received a per kilometre allowance for automobile travel between their homes and the school board's administrative building where they were required to attend meetings. Rejecting the Minister's argument that the allowance was taxable under paragraph 6(1)(b) of the Act, the court held that the allowance was exempt under subparagraph 6(1)(b)(vii.1) on the basis (at para. 13) that the taxpayers were "going from one place of business to another place of business" when they attended board meetings and (at para. 16) were therefore "travelling, in the performance of their duties."

7.   *Campbell* was distinguished in *Daniels v. Canada*, [2004] F.C.J. No. 573, [2004] 2 C.T.C. 377, 2004 D.T.C. 6276 (F.C.A.), in which the taxpayer, a municipal councillor in Alberta, received a per kilometre allowance for travel from his home to council meetings. Rejecting the taxpayer's argument that the allowance was exempt under subparagraph 6(1)(b)(vii.1) of the Act, the court concluded (at para. 11) that the travel was "essentially from his home and his home work base to his place of work ... not from one place or work to the other and ... not ... in the performance of the duties of his office."

8.   In *Canada v. Salter*, [1985] 2 C.T.C. 338, 85 D.T.C. 5525 (F.C.T.D.), the taxpayer, an engineer who was employed by the County of Wellington in Ontario, received a travel allowance of $70 per month as reimbursement for the use of his own automobile to acquire land for the county and to visit construction sites. Based on the taxpayer's testimony that he spent 2 per cent of his time in land acquisitions, the court held that $1.40 per month or $16.80 of the $840 received by the taxpayer in each of 1977 and 1978 was a non-taxable allowance within the meaning of subparagraph 6(1)(b)(v). With respect to the taxpayer's argument that the word "period" in subparagraph 6(1)(b)(v) "does not necessarily have to be one discrete time period" but "can import the whole taxation year, in a sense as yeast permeates dough, so long as any such selling or negotiating of contracts occurred at any time in the year," the court stated (at para. 9):

> The subparagraph might possibly bear such an interpretation if it provided, "... in respect of a taxation year during which he was employed for some period in connection with ... ." The subparagraph does not so provide. The subparagraph, in expressing "a period" means "any period" or "a discrete period" and they may be totalled for the year, but they cannot subsume the year unless the selling and negotiating referred to occupied the taxpayer all day, every day.

See also *Eggert v. M.N.R.*, [1985] 2 C.T.C. 343, 85 D.T.C. 5522 (F.C.T.D.).

9.   In *O'Connell v. Canada*, [1998] T.C.J. No. 624, [1998] 4 C.T.C. 2866, 98 D.T.C. 2155 (T.C.C.), the Court considered how to calculate a reasonable allowance for the use of a motor vehicle. The taxpayer in this case operated

retail clothing stores in St. Catharines and used a BMW, worth $66,000 in 1993, to travel to Montreal, Toronto, and New York in order to buy high fashion women's clothing. The Minister calculated a reasonable allowance for travel based on the aggregate of the actual costs of operating the vehicle in a year plus the annual capital cost allowance on the vehicle. The Minister also referred to paragraph 13(7)(g) of the Act and regulation 7307, which at that time limited the capital cost of vehicles to $24,000. The Court accepted the Minister's assessment, concluding (at para. 19) that "to determine what the word 'reasonable' contemplates in subsection 6(1), reference ought to be made to other provisions of the Act which are concerned with travel allowances and the capital cost of a passenger vehicle." Do you agree with this way of interpreting the meaning of the word "reasonable" in the context of subparagraph 6(1)(b)(vii.1)?

10. Subject to various restrictions, employees may deduct travel and motor vehicle travel expenses under paragraphs 8(1)(h) and (h.1). These provisions, which complement the exclusion of travel allowances in subparagraphs 6(1)(b)(v), (vii), and (vii.1) of the Act are considered in section IV of this chapter.

D. Statutory Exclusions

In addition to the numerous rules by which specific amounts are included in a taxpayer's income from an office or employment, the Act contains two rules specifically excluding certain benefits or allowances. Subsection 6(6) exempts certain benefits or allowances received by a taxpayer who is employed at a "special work site" or remote location. Subsection 6(16) exempts certain disability-related benefits or allowances. Each is considered in turn.

1. Employment at Special Work Site or Remote Location

Subsection 6(6) applies where an employee's duties at a special work site or remote location require the employee to be away from his or her principal place of residence or at the special work site or remote location for at least 36 hours. In these circumstances, paragraph 6(6)(a) exempts the value of, or a reasonable allowance in respect of, expenses that the taxpayer has incurred for board and lodging during the period that the taxpayer is at the special work site or remote location, while paragraph 6(6)(b) exempts benefits or allowances for transportation between a special work site and a taxpayer's principal place of residence or between a remote work location and any other location in Canada or in the country in which the taxpayer is employed. The following text and cases consider the characterization of a special work site and the characterization of a remote location for the purposes of subsection 6(6).

a. Special Work Site

Subparagraph 6(6)(a)(i) defines a "special work site" as:

> a location at which the duties performed by the taxpayer were of a temporary nature, if the taxpayer maintained at another location a self-contained domestic establishment as the taxpayer's principal place of residence
>
> (A) that was, throughout the period, available for the taxpayer's occupancy and not rented by the taxpayer to any other person, and
>
> (B) to which, by reason of distance, the taxpayer could not reasonably be expected to have returned daily from the special work site.

For this purpose, subsection 248(1) defines the term "self-contained domestic establishment" as "a dwelling-house, apartment or other similar place of residence in which place a person as a general rule sleeps and eats." The characterization of a location as a "special work site" was considered in *Guilbert v. M.N.R.*, [1991] T.C.J. No. 127, [1991] 1 C.T.C. 2705, 91 D.T.C. 737 (T.C.C.).

Guilbert v. M.N.R.
[1991] T.C.J. No. 127, [1991] 1 C.T.C. 2705, 91 D.T.C. 737 (T.C.C.)

DUSSAULT TCJ: ...

Summary of the Facts

In April 1984, the appellant, who until that time had been the president of the newspaper *La Voix de l'Est* in Granby, accepted the position of editor-in-chief of the newspaper *Le Soleil* in Quebec City, which was owned by the Groupe Unimedia. While this job is by its very nature a permanent position, the appellant says that he accepted it only temporarily on the basis of an undertaking that he would be appointed chairman of the newspaper *Le Droit* in Ottawa, which was also owned by the Groupe Unimedia, within a relatively short time. The health of the chairman of *Le Droit* was declining at that time, it seems, and the appellant could reasonably have expected to be appointed to replace him within a few months or more.

The facts show that the appellant continued to occupy his position in Quebec City with *Le Soleil* until March 1987, some months after learning that he would not be getting the position he desired with *Le Droit* in Ottawa, since another person who was already a member of that newspaper's organization had been appointed instead of him. The appellant thus states that his stay in Quebec City had initially been seen as of an essentially temporary nature, that the duties assigned to him related more to the day-to-day administrative management than to the editing of the newspaper on a permanent basis, and that accordingly, one of the agreed upon conditions of employment had been that the newspaper would provide him, free of charge, with an apartment in Quebec City during his stay. The appellant also stated that this arrangement seemed to him to be preferable to staying in a hotel.

The appellant occupied a six-room apartment, with three bedrooms, provided by *Le Soleil* and located in the Jardins Mérici in Quebec city, starting in April 1984 and throughout 1985 and 1986. However, he testified that during the years in question he always maintained his principal residence in Domaine Chéribourg, in Orford township, where he returned on the weekend, and where moreover, his wife lived, she having a permanent job in Sherbrooke, Quebec. The appellant's children, however, lived with him in the apartment in Quebec City during the school year, his daughter for one year and his son for two years during the period in question. Finally, the appellant stated that he had often been absent from Quebec City for business trips, conventions, conferences or other reasons during the years in question, so that he did not occupy the apartment made available to him for more than 50 per cent of the time during the period and, moreover, on occasion the apartment was used, at such times and even when he was there himself, as temporary housing for journalists or other members of the *Le Soleil* organization passing through Quebec City.

Analysis

The principle set out in paragraph 6(1)(a) of the Act is that there shall be included in computing the income of a taxpayer "the value of board, lodging and other benefits of any kind whatever received or enjoyed by him in the year in respect of, in the course of, or by virtue of an office or employment. ..."

On the other hand, subsection 6(6) of the Act provides an exception to this principle of including the value of benefits in income from an office or employment, in the case of employment at a special work site or at a remote location.

...

Essentially, the appellant argues that during the years in question his work in Quebec City was "of a temporary nature," his place of work at *Le Soleil* must be considered to be analogous to a "special work site" and he always maintained his principal place of residence in Domaine Cherbourg, in Orford township in the Eastern Townships.

Counsel for the respondent argued that the appellant's work for *Le Soleil* was of a permanent nature, the newspaper's premises were not a "special work site" and the appellant's principal place of residence was in the Jardins Mérici in Quebec City, in the apartment provided by *Le Soleil.*

...

Counsel for the respondent also submits that in the context of the tax reform that applied starting in 1972 the scope of the earlier provision, which applied only to construction workers working on remote sites, was considerably broadened, and on this point referred to the *Summary of 1971 Tax Reform Legislation* [at 10], and particularly to the following paragraphs:

Away from home expenses

Under existing law, construction workers at distant work sites may receive tax-free from their employers amounts covering expenses of transportation, board and lodging. The bill extends this to all employees.

The revision recognizes that many people besides construction workers must leave their normal residence and live and work temporarily at a place where they cannot reasonably be expected to establish homes for their wives and families.

The provision will apply, as it does now, only to an employee who leaves his ordinary residence. It will not apply to a single individual who does not maintain a permanent residence in which he supports a dependant. It is necessary that the employee be away from his ordinary residence for at least 36 hours and the work site must be far enough away that he could not reasonably be expected to return home daily.

Among those who will benefit are lumber and mining workers, oil well drillers, exploration crews, employees at isolated bases and those who work at remote construction sites but do not qualify as "construction workers."

The Act is indeed complex, and contains numerous definitions. However, we cannot assume, in the absence of a special statutory definition, that the usual words used by Parliament must have a meaning different from the generally recognized meaning set out in current dictionaries. A "work site" is a "work site" and this expression cannot refer to just any place of work. The newspaper's premises are not, in my humble opinion, a work site, or a "special work site," within the meaning intended by Parliament.

...

Thus, even if I could accept that the appellant's work was "of a temporary nature" and he maintained his principal place of residence in Domaine Chéribourg in the Eastern Townships, I believe that the exception set out in subsection 6(6) of the Act does not apply in this case. The examples set out in the *Summary of 1971 Tax Reform Legislation* are not the basis of my opinion, but would confirm it if this were necessary. ...

Appeal in the main dismissed.

NOTES AND QUESTIONS

1.   On what basis did the court in *Guilbert* conclude that the premises of *Le Soleil* in Quebec City were not a "special work site" within the meaning of subparagraph 6(6)(a)(i)? To what extent, if any, should the courts refer to documents like the *Summary of 1971 Tax Reform Legislation* in order to interpret provisions of the *Income Tax Act*? Was the court's interpretation consistent with the text of subparagraph 6(6)(a)(i)?

2.   In *Harle v. M.N.R.*, [1976] C.T.C. 2203, 76 D.T.C. 1151 (T.R.B.), the taxpayers sought to exclude "subsistence allowances" paid to members of the Legislative Assembly of Alberta who acquired a temporary residence in Edmonton for the purpose of attending the legislative session. Suggesting that "Parliament [could] not in its wildest dreams [have] consider[ed] a provincial legislative building such as the one in Edmonton to be a special work site," the

board held (at para. 9) that the taxpayers' duties were not "of a sufficiently temporary nature to qualify" within the meaning of the statutory exemption.

Compare the decision in *Jaffar v. R.*, [2002] T.C.J. No. 67, [2002] 2 C.T.C. 2204 (T.C.C.), where the taxpayer was employed as a systems analyst by Computec International. His employment contract provided that he would work at Computec's Malvern, Pennsylvania offices "or, if directed to do so, at the office of clients." After a few days in Malvern the taxpayer was assigned to work in Rochester, New York, at the offices of a client of Computec, an assignment which lasted one year and three months. During that time Computec paid for his apartment in Rochester and his expenses of traveling to Toronto on weekends to visit his family. The Court allowed his appeal, holding that these amounts did not have to be included in income under section 6(1)(b) as an allowance for personal or living expenses because they were exempt from tax under section 6(6)(a). The Court interpreted the phrase "special work site" as follows:

> Using *The Oxford English Dictionary*, 2nd Ed. definitions of the words "special work site": A "special" place is an unusual or exceptional place. To work is to perform or execute one's task. A site is a place. Thus the English version of the paragraph refers to an unusual place where an employee does his or her task. In this case the work site was established in evidence to be another firm's plant or factory in Rochester, New York, at which the Appellant performed temporary duties for a limited period of time. For that purpose his Employer paid for his board and lodging. The Appellant was initially hired to work at the Employer's place of business at Malvern, Pa. He went there to work and was assigned to another firm's premises in Rochester, New York. That in itself would be an unusual work place for an employee of a business. The fact that the Employer agreed to pay for his food, lodging and mileage in respect to this work establishes that the Employer considered it to be so.

> ...

> In this day, when carpenters, oilfield roughnecks, nurses, mechanics, engineers, computer technicians, civil servants, judges, lawyers and people in all sorts of callings do temporary work at sites remote from their homes or their places of business, a special work site is not the northern bush or a construction camp. A special work site may be any place in the world, including a large metropolitan city such as Toronto, New York or New Delhi; or it may be a place such as Afghanistan or Rochester, New York. Expertise in the modern world has become a contractual commodity for which the contract — like the Appellant's contract of employment — is not for a lifetime. Rather, it is often from job to job at work places other than the employer's place of business, that is, at "special work sites" such as where the Appellant worked in Rochester, New York.

See also *Rozumiak v. The Queen*, [2005] T.C.J. No. 629, [2006] 2 C.T.C. 2172, 2006 D.T.C. 2165 (T.C.C.), where the taxpayer was hired for a three year term by the Vancouver Ports Authority to open a Chicago office for the purpose of soliciting more shipping business to come through the Port of Vancouver. The Court held that the new office was a "special work site" and that amounts paid by the employer to cover the taxpayer's rent and other expenses while in Chicago were covered by s.6(6).

3.　　The CRA's views on the requirement in subparagraph 6(6)(a)(i) that the taxpayer's duties at the special work site be of a "temporary nature" are found in paragraphs 5 and 6 of *Interpretation Bulletin* IT-91R4, "Employment at Special Work Sites or Remote Work Locations," June 17, 1996:

5. The expression "duties performed by the taxpayer were of a temporary nature" as used in subparagraph 6(6)(a)(i) ... refers to the duration of the duties performed by the individual employee, not the expected duration of the project as a whole. For example, a project might take ten years to complete but the individual's duties at that project might take only a few months.

6. The term "temporary" is not defined in the *Income Tax Act*. However, as a general rule, duties will be considered to be of a temporary nature if it can reasonably be expected that they will not provide continuous employment beyond a period of two years. The determination of the expected duration of employment must be made on the basis of the facts known at its commencement. In this regard, particular consideration should be given to the following factors:

    •   the nature of the duties to be performed by the employee (certain types of work are, by their nature, short term engagements, such as repair work or trades which are involved only during a certain phase of a project);

    •   the overall time estimated for a project, or a particular phase of a project, on which the employee is engaged to perform duties; and

    •   the agreed period of time for which the employee was engaged according to the employment contract or other terms of the engagement.

Should these factors change after employment commences, it may be necessary to redetermine whether the duties undertaken by the employee are considered to be of a temporary nature for the purposes of the special work site exclusion.

4.   The CRA's views on the meaning of a taxpayer's "principal place of residence" for the purposes of subparagraph 6(6)(a)(i) are found in paragraphs 7 and 8 of IT-91R4:

7. An employee's "principal place of residence" is the place where the employee maintains a self-contained domestic establishment. The term "self-contained domestic establishment" is defined in subsection 248(1) as a dwelling-house, apartment or other similar place of residence where a person generally sleeps and eats. A residence is considered to be a self-contained domestic establishment if it is a living unit with restricted access that contains a kitchen, bathroom, and sleeping facilities. A room (or rooms) in a hotel, dormitory, boarding house or bunkhouse would not ordinarily be a self-contained domestic establishment. Where an employee maintains more than one self-contained domestic establishment (for example, the employee maintains a temporary place of residence at the work site while having a principal place of residence elsewhere), only the employee's principal place of residence has to meet the requirements set out in [subparagraph 6(6)(a)(i)].

8. A principal place of residence does not necessarily have to be in Canada. For example:

    •   a United States resident may be a construction worker sojourning in Canada, and may be subject to income tax in Canada because he or she is deemed by paragraph 250(1)(a) to be a resident of Canada by reason of being in Canada

183 days or more in the year. In these circumstances, for the purposes of subsection 6(6), the principal place of residence is the worker's home in the United States; or

- a non-resident, who stays in Canada for a short period of time, such as at a farm during harvesting, may maintain a self-contained domestic establishment outside Canada. In these circumstances, the non-resident's principal place of residence is in the country outside of Canada.

5.   In *Barrett v. Canada*, [1997] T.C.J. No. 1077, [1998] 1 C.T.C. 2138 (T.C.C.), the taxpayer's claim that a $40 per day board and lodging allowance was exempt under subparagraph 6(6)(a)(i) was dismissed on the basis (at para. 7) that the taxpayer, who had separated from his spouse while he worked at the Hibernia work site, had not established that he "maintained at another location a self-contained domestic establishment" as his "principal place of residence ... that was, throughout the period, available for [his] occupancy."

6.   The requirement in clause 6(6)(a)(i)(B) that the taxpayer maintain a principal place of residence "to which, by reason of distance, the taxpayer could not reasonably be expected to have returned daily from the special work site" has been considered in a number of cases.

In *Smith v. Canada*, [1998] T.C.J. No. 132, [1998] 2 C.T.C. 3218 (T.C.C.), where the taxpayer maintained a principal place of residence at Gooseberry, Newfoundland, 60 kilometres away from the location of his work on the Hibernia oil platform at Bull Arm, the court rejected his argument that an allowance for temporary accommodation near the work site was exempt under subparagraph 6(6)(a)(i), concluding (at para. 9) that "[i]t is not uncommon in Canada for people to commute 60 kilometres to work, spending an hour or more on a highway." See also *Leclair v. Canada*, [1997] T.C.J. No. 1071, 1 C.T.C. 2705 (T.C.C.), where the taxpayer maintained a principal place of residence 50 kilometres from his work site, and *Duperron v. M.N.R.*, [1984] C.T.C. 2463, 84 D.T.C. 1406 (T.C.C.), where the taxpayer lived 82 kilometres from his work site but returned home on a daily basis.

In *Charun v. M.N.R.*, [1983] C.T.C. 2681, 83 D.T.C. 623 (T.C.C.), on the other hand, where the taxpayer maintained a principal place of residence in Vancouver, roughly 60 kilometres from a temporary work site in Woodfibre, BC where he obtained temporary accommodation, the court held that an allowance for board and lodging was exempt under subparagraph 6(6)(a)(i) on the grounds that the taxpayer worked at the job for 12 hours a day, seven days a week, and that the trip from his home to the work site took an hour and a half, involving a winding, hilly, and at times treacherous section of the Whistler Road and a ferry from Squamish to Woodfibre across Howe Sound. According to Rip TCJ (at paras. 26-29):

In my view, it is not mere conjecture, but reasonable to interpret the phrase "by reason or distance" with the other words of subsection 6(6) of the *Income Tax Act* to mean more than only the space lying between Mr. Charun's ordinary place of residence and Woodfibre. This appeal is not to be decided simply by answering the question, "How far is far?" One must pay heed to the purpose of this exemption section which is to permit employees working away from their ordinary place of residence for a temporary period, who incurring certain expenses of room and board because of the difficulty of returning home on a daily basis, not to include in income allowances paid to them by their employer for expenses such employee would not have ordinarily been expected or required to incur.

In my view, any reasonable man faced with over one hour of travel over a route that is treacherous at more than several points, a work shift of 12 hours, the basic need to relax for just an hour a day, would have done what Mr. Charun did. Rather than commute daily to work and back, he would find board and lodging at the special worksite.

For purposes of determining the phrase "by reason of distance" in subparagraph 6(6)(a)(i) of the Act one must give weight not only to the length of the trip from a distance point of view, but also one must consider the hours of work the employee is required to perform in carrying out his duties, the type of roadway he must travel each day, the time of day he must travel and the general physical and mental health of the taxpayer.

A literal and strict interpretation of the phrase "by reason of distance" would not be consistent with the intent of subsection 6(6) of the Act and with the reality of certain employment situations.

For other cases in which courts have held that a taxpayer could not reasonably have been expected to have returned daily from a special work site to a principal place of residence, see *Canada v. Forestell*, [1979] C.T.C. 370, 79 D.T.C. 5289 (F.C.T.D.) and *King v. M.N.R.*, [1980] C.T.C. 2026, [1979] 80 D.T.C. 1037 (T.R.B.).

7.   The CRA's views on the requirement in subparagraph 6(6)(a)(i) that the taxpayer "by reason of distance ... could not reasonably be expected to have returned daily from the special work site" are found in paragraph 9 of IT-91R4:

This requirement will not be met if, in fact, the employee returns daily to his or her principal place of residence. As a general rule, an employee will not be expected to return to his or her principal place of residence if the work site is more than 80 kilometres (50 miles) from the employee's residence by the most direct route normally travelled in the circumstances. Cases not meeting this general rule are not necessarily disqualified from the exclusion under subsection 6(6) and factors such as the following will be considered:

- the number of hours of work which the employee is required to perform at the special work site each shift;

- the amount of time that would be required for travel and the time of day or night when travel would take place;

- the means of transportation available and the condition of the route that would be travelled (*e.g.*, quality of roadway, seasonal weather conditions, *etc.*);

- the length of rest period if the employee returned home daily; and

- the general physical and mental health of the employee.

b. Remote Work Location

Subparagraph 6(6)(a)(ii) refers to "a location at which, by virtue of its remoteness from any established community, the taxpayer could not reasonably be expected to establish and maintain a self-contained domestic establishment."

The language of this exemption was considered in *Dionne v. Canada* (1996), 97 D.T.C. 265 (T.C.C.), aff'd [1999] 2 C.T.C. 158, 99 D.T.C. 5282 (F.C.A.).

Dionne v. Canada
(1996), 97 D.T.C. 265 (T.C.C.)

ARCHAMBAULT JTCC: Luc Dionne is challenging an income tax assessment made by the Minister of National Revenue (Minister) under the *Income Tax Act* for the 1993 taxation year. The Minister added to Mr. Dionne's income an amount of $3,181.34 in respect of a benefit under paragraph 6(1)(a) of the Act or as an allowance under paragraph 6(1)(b) of the Act. This amount represents expenses incurred to transport food by air or mail paid or reimbursed by Mr. Dionne's employer (transportation allowance) for his benefit and that of his family.

Facts

In 1993, Mr. Dionne was living with his family in Akulivik, a village of approximately 400 inhabitants situated on Hudson's Bay, in Quebec, north of 60 degrees north latitude. There are only about 10 white residents in Akulivik, including two or three nurses. The suppliers and service providers generally found in the southern regions of Quebec are not established there. However, there is a cooperative-style store (Coop) where various products are sold, especially dry goods such as flour and, depending on incoming shipments, perishable foods as well such as fruit, vegetables and milk. However, quantities are limited and quality is mediocre.

Mr. Dionne worked in Akulivik as a teacher for the Commission Scolare Kativik (Kativik). Under the terms of the collective agreement between the Commission and its union association, Mr. Dionne enjoyed, in addition to a basic salary, a number of equalization adjustment measures to compensate for the quality of life and the high cost of living, including an isolation premium of $14,614 and living accommodations provided at below-market rent. Mr. Dionne was also entitled to three trips between Akulivik and his domiciliary origin. Kativik further paid a transportation allowance. The costs to transport perishable foods were generally billed directly to his employer's account. Mr. Dionne paid the postal charges to transport non-perishable foodstuffs, but was entitled to reimbursement of those charges by his employer. Clause 12-8.00 of the collective agreement provides:

[TRANSLATION]

12-8.01 Teachers who must provide for their own food supply in sectors I, II and III, shall receive payment, upon presentation of supporting documents, of transportation expenses for food up to the following weights:

(a)   727 kilograms per year per adult and per 12 years of age and over;

(b)   364 kilograms per year per child less than 12 years of age.

For the purposes of this clause, a maximum of 50 per cent of the allowed weight may be shipped by air freight, the difference to be shipped by parcel post.

While it is agreed that teachers may choose their own supply points, expenses reimbursed may not be greater than the cost of transportation between Montreal and the point of assignment.

His employer issued two T4 slips in respect of Mr. Dionne's remuneration totalling $54,974 and containing the following information:

Employment income: $43,492.16.

Allowance and taxable benefit (accommodation, board and lodging): $4,595.00.

Trips in a prescribed area: $6,705.49.

Other allowance and taxable benefit: $3,181.34 (transportation of food).

TOTAL: $57,973.99

Mr. Dionne is disputing only the inclusion of the transportation allowance of $3,181.34 in computing his income.

...

Subsection 6(6)

Counsel for Mr. Dionne contended ... that paragraph 6(6)(a) of the Act applied in the instant case and that his client was not required to include the transportation allowance in his income. ... [C]ounsel for Mr. Dionne rightly did not claim in his written submission or in his argument that the village of Akulivik constituted a special work site. He contended however that Mr. Dionne lived in a location at which, by virtue of its remoteness from any established community, the taxpayer could not reasonably be expected to establish and maintain a self-contained domestic establishment. This is the case provided for by subparagraph 6(6)(a)(ii) of the Act. It is quite clear that, if Akulivik constitutes an established community and Mr. Dionne maintained such an establishment which he had established there, he cannot meet the conditions of this subparagraph.

The first question that arises is thus whether Mr. Dionne had a self-contained domestic establishment at that location. The definition of this expression appears in subsection 248(1) of the Act:

"self-contained domestic establishment" means a dwelling-house, apartment or other similar place of residence in which place a person as a general rule sleeps and eats;

The evidence shows that Kativik made lodging available to Mr. Dionne where he lived with his family. In that house, he could take his meals and sleep.

Accordingly, Mr. Dionne's lodging represents a self-contained domestic establishment within the meaning of the Act.

Counsel for Mr. Dionne seems to be claiming that Akulivik did not constitute an established community ["agglomération" in the French text of subparagraph 6(6)(a)(ii) — Tr.] because it had few services. The *Nouveau Petit Robert* defines "agglomération" as follows:

> 3. (1861) Cluster of dwellings, a city, town or village. Rural, urban population centre [agglomération — Tr.]. To slow down on approaching a village or town [agglomération — Tr.]. "One of those enclosures, a minuscule collection [agglomération — Tr.] of four to six huts" (André Gide).

However, there are 400 inhabitants in Akulivik, where there are one Coop, nurses (presumably at a medical clinic) and a school. I believe the size of this village and the services found there are sufficient to conclude that it constitutes an established community ("agglomération") for the purposes of this paragraph.

There remains the question as to whether he had established and was maintaining a self-contained domestic establishment. Mr. Dionne contended that, in order to establish such an establishment, one had to have done so on a permanent basis. In his case, he could occupy his lodging only as long as he remained in Kativik's employ. Without this employment, he would not have been able to live in Akulivik.

...

The word "maintain" is used as the equivalent of the word "tenir" in the English version of subparagraph 6(6)(a)(ii) of the Act. In the *Nouveau Petit Robert*, the meaning most consistent with this English term is as follows:

> 3. To cause to remain in a certain state over a certain length of time. — to maintain.

The verb "établir" ["to establish" — Tr.] is defined as follows:

> [TRANSLATION]
>
> I.   Put or cause (something) to be kept in a place in a permanent manner. — to set, build, construct, erect, fix, found, install, 1. to place, put. "He began by building [établir — Tr.] a sort of road on the bank" (Flaubert). "In the middle of the drawing room, a footman ... had almost finished placing [établir — Tr.] a large table" (Stendhal). To erect [établir — Tr.] a factory, a printing plant in a city. — to create, found, introduce, put up. — Establish [établir — Tr.] one's domicile, residence in Paris. — to fix (cf. III, 1., below). — Put up [établir — Tr.] police roadblocks. — to set up.
>
> III. (1627) Fix one's residence (in a place). Go settle [s'établir — Tr.] in Paris. — to live, settle. She settled [s'est établie — Tr.] in the provinces.

The most striking feature in this definition is stability, not duration. In the example "Put up [établir — Tr.] police roadblocks," it may be seen that the time involved may be relatively short. Furthermore, by setting the word "maintain" ["tenir"] beside the word "establish" ["établir"], Parliament acknowledged that the notion of continuity was not included in the notion of "establishing."

Furthermore, nothing in the wording of this section requires the taxpayer to live permanently in that location: it does not contain expressions such as "definitively," "permanently," "for an indeterminate period" or "principal residence." On the contrary, the fact that this last expression appears in paragraph 6(6)(a)(i) of the Act and not in subparagraph 6(6)(a)(ii) clearly indicates that Parliament was not requiring this degree of permanence or importance.

There is no evidence in the instant case that Mr. Dionne had this other self-contained domestic establishment in the south. Even if that had been the case, I do not believe it would have prevented Mr. Dionne from establishing another elsewhere. Many Canadians have secondary residences which, in my view, may also constitute self-contained domestic establishments. If a person moves into a lodging where he eats and sleeps over many months, I believe that that is enough to "establish" and "maintain" a self-contained domestic establishment there for the purposes of this section.

Mr. Dionne lived in Akulivik for a number of years, including at least one with his entire family. If Mr. Dionne and his family had liked the location, they could have occupied the lodging for as long as he was engaged in teaching. He therefore could have remained in Akulivik for a lengthy period of time. In the circumstances, I believe that he "established" and "maintained" a self-contained domestic establishment there. The conditions of subparagraph 6(6)(a)(ii) were not met and the benefit provided for in paragraph 6(1)(a) may not be excluded from Mr. Dionne's income. For these reasons, Mr. Dionne's appeal is dismissed with costs.

Appeal dismissed.

NOTES AND QUESTIONS

1. On what grounds did the court in *Dionne* conclude that the allowance received by the taxpayer for the transportation of food was not exempt under subparagraph 6(6)(a)(ii)? How did the court define an "established community" for the purposes of the exemption? How did the court interpret the requirement in subparagraph 6(6)(a)(ii) that "the taxpayer could not reasonably be expected to establish and maintain a self-contained domestic establishment"? What interpretive method did the court employ? Do you agree with this method? Why or why not?

2. The CRA's views on the meaning of the words "established community" for the purposes of subparagraph 6(6)(a)(ii) are found in paragraph 15 of IT-91R4:

> The term "established community" is considered to mean a body of people who reside in the same locality and who are permanently settled in that location. A location will not be considered an established community if it lacks essential services or such services are not available within a reasonable commuting distance. In general, essential services would include:
>
> • a basic food store;
>
> • a basic clothing store with merchandise in stock (not a mail-order outlet);

- housing; and

- access to certain medical assistance and certain educational facilities.

3.   The CRA's views on the meaning of the word "remoteness" for the purposes of subparagraph 6(6)(a)(ii) are found in paragraph 14 of IT-91R4:

> When determining whether a work location is in fact remote from an established community, factors such as the following will be considered:
>
> - the availability of transportation;
>
> - the distance from an established community; and
>
> - the time required to travel that distance.

As a general rule, a work location will be considered to be remote if the nearest established community with a population of 1,000 or more is no closer than 80 kilometres (50 miles) by the most direct route normally travelled in the circumstances. Cases not meeting this general rule are not necessarily disqualified from the exclusion under subsection 6(6) and will be considered on their merits. If the work location is not remote from an established community, or if the work location itself can be considered an established community, the employee will, subject to 16 below, not qualify for the remote work location exclusion.

4.   The CRA's views on the requirement in subparagraph 6(6)(a)(ii) that the employee "could not reasonably be expected to establish and maintain a self-contained domestic establishment" at the work location are found in paragraphs 13, 16, and 17 of IT-91R4:

> 13.   Such a determination is made based on the facts of the particular case. If the employee has a reasonable expectation of establishing and maintaining a self-contained domestic establishment, the remote work location exclusion, of course, will not apply. A reasonable expectation is considered to exist in the following circumstances:
>
> - the employer provides a self-contained domestic establishment to the employee at the work location;
>
> - the employee is drawn from the local community itself where the employee's housing has already been established;
>
> - the employee opts to buy property and builds his or her own self-contained domestic establishment; or
>
> - the employee rents a self-contained domestic establishment at the work location. ...
>
> 16.   Where an established community is in an area which is not remote ... from a work location, the location will still [qualify for the exemption] if community services and (available) housing are limited to the extent that employees could not reasonably be expected to establish and maintain at that community a self-contained domestic establishment. Where there is more than one established community located in an area which is not remote from a work location, the sum total of the services and housing available in all established communities should be considered.
>
> 17.   Where the remote work location exclusion in subsection 6(6) applies for the reason that an employee could not reasonably be expected to establish and maintain a self-contained domestic establishment at a community that is not remote from a work

location, an improvement in service and an increase in the availability of housing at the community could result in a change in tax status. Conversely, an established community could become a remote work location if sudden growth renders the community's essential services insufficient. For example, an employer brings in a large number of employees to a small town and the town cannot accommodate the influx. As a result, ongoing reviews of the services and housing available in a community may be necessary in order to determine whether the exclusion in subsection 6(6) continues to apply.

5.   For other cases in which taxpayers have failed to bring themselves within the exemption in subparagraph 6(6)(a)(ii), see *Lepage v. M.N.R.*, [1982] C.T.C. 2538, 82 D.T.C. 1536 (T.R.B.); *Truemner v. M.N.R.*, [1989] F.C.J. No. 137, [1989] 1 C.T.C. 356, 89 D.T.C. 5149 (F.C.T.D.); *Dick v. Canada*, [1996] T.C.J. No. 519, [1996] 3 C.T.C. 2050 (T.C.C.); and *Theberge v. Canada*, [2008] 1 C.T.C. 2124, 2008 D.T.C. 3200 (T.C.C.).

2. Disability-Related Employment Benefits

In computing an individual's income from an office or employment, subsection 6(16) exempts benefits relating to or reasonable allowances in respect of expenses incurred by the individual for:

a.   the transportation of the individual between the individual's ordinary place of residence and the individual's work location (including parking near that location) if the individual is blind or is a person in respect of whom an amount is deductible, or would but for paragraph 118.3(1)(c) be deductible, because of the individual's mobility impairment, under section 118.3 in computing a taxpayer's tax payable under this Part for the year; or

b.   an attendant to assist the individual in the performance of the individual's duties if the individual is a person in respect of whom an amount is deductible, or would but for paragraph 118.3(1)(c) be deductible, under section 118.3 in computing a taxpayer's tax payable under this Part for the year.

Subsection 6(16) was enacted in 1991 in order to reduce barriers to workforce participation by disabled Canadians. According to supplementary information released with the 1991 Federal Budget:

Currently, where a disabled employee with a mobility or sight impairment receives employer-provided benefits such as subsidized parking, or allowances for taxis or specially designed public transportation (para-transport), these amounts are taxable in the hands of the employee. Furthermore, where the employer provides an allowance to a disabled employee for an attendant, this allowance is also considered a taxable benefit. These rules tend to discourage disabled Canadians from participating in the work force.

Allowances provided to employees for taxi fares, para-transport, and parking will no longer be considered as taxable benefits for those who are eligible for the disability tax credit by reason of a severe and prolonged mobility or sight impairment.

In addition, where an employer provides an allowance in respect of attendant care required to enable an employee who qualifies for the disability tax credit to perform employment duties (e.g., readers for the blind, signers for the deaf, coaches for the mentally handicapped), no taxable benefit will be imputed.

This provision has yet to be considered by the courts.

IV. DEDUCTIONS

Statutory provisions governing the deduction of amounts in computing a taxpayer's income from an office or employment are found in section 8 the Act. Indeed subsection 8(2) limits the amounts that may be deducted in computing a taxpayer's income from an office or employment to the amounts specifically listed in section 8. This contrasts with the rules for computing income from business or property which allow taxpayers to deduct a much broader range of expenses incurred to produce the income.[58] Historically, paragraph 8(1)(a) provided some recognition for unitemized employment expenses by allowing a general deduction equal to the lesser of $500 and 20 per cent of the taxpayer's income from all offices and employments. However, this was repealed as part of the 1988 tax reform. The 2006 Federal Budget announced a new non-refundable Canada Employment Credit, enacted as subsection 118(10). In 2009 the credit will effectively remove tax on $1,044 of employment income (this amount is indexed to inflation each year). In announcing this measure Minister of Finance James Flaherty stated that it "gives Canadians a break on what it costs to work, recognizing expenses for things such as home computers, uniforms and supplies." As this section demonstrates, such expenses are often non-deductible to employees under the rules in section 8.

According to subsection 8(1), taxpayers may in computing their income from an office or employment deduct specific amounts as indicated "as are wholly applicable to that source" or "as may reasonably be regarded as applicable thereto." The remainder of section 8 contains specific rules applicable to the deductions permitted in subsection 8(1).

For the purpose of these provisions, moreover, it may also be necessary to consider some of the general "rules relating to the computation of income" in subdivision f of Division B of Part I of the Act. Section 67.1, for example, limits the amount that may be deducted in respect of "the human consumption of food or beverages or the enjoyment of entertainment" to 50 per cent of the amount otherwise deductible, while sections 67.2 to 67.4 limit the amount that may be deducted in respect of a passenger vehicle. More generally, section 67 stipulates:

> In computing income, no deduction shall be made in respect of an outlay or expense in respect of which any amount is otherwise deductible under this Act, except to the extent that the outlay or expense was reasonable in the circumstances.

For the purposes of this chapter, there is no need to examine each of the deductions permitted by subsection 8(1), nor each of the rules governing these deductions in the remainder of section 8 or in subdivision f. (Section 67 and

---

[58] The deductions allowed in computing income from business or property are discussed in section IV of Chapter 5.

other rules in subdivision f are examined in Chapter 8.) Instead, this section considers the most important deductions that may be claimed in computing a taxpayer's income from an office or employment, considering deductions that are available to all employees and those available only to selected categories of employees.[59]

A. Travelling Expenses

Among the most common kinds of expenses that may be incurred by an employee in the course of an office or employment are travel expenses incurred in order to fulfill the duties of the office or employment. As a general rule, these expenses include costs of transportation, accommodation, and meals that are consumed during the period of travel. Where these expenses are reimbursed by an employer, the amount of the reimbursement is generally not regarded as a taxable benefit within the meaning of paragraph 6(1)(a) of the Act, nor an allowance within the meaning of paragraph 6(1)(b). Nor are reasonable travel allowances taxable, provided that they satisfy one of the criteria for exemption in paragraph 6(1)(b).

Where an employee incurs travel expenses that are not reimbursed or in respect of which the employer does not provide a reasonable travel allowance, these expenses are properly regarded as a cost of earning the taxpayer's income from the office or employment, which ought to be deductible in computing the taxpayer's income from this source. Not surprisingly, therefore, in computing a taxpayer's income from an office or employment, paragraph 8(1)(h) allows the taxpayer to deduct "amounts expended by the taxpayer in the year (other than motor vehicle expenses) for travelling in the course of the office or employment," provided that the taxpayer, in the year:

> (i)   was ordinarily required to carry on the duties of the office or employment away from the employer's place of business or in different places, and

> (ii)   was required under the contract of employment to pay the travel expenses incurred by the taxpayer in the performance of the duties of the office or employment,

except where the taxpayer

> (iii) received an allowance for travel expenses that was, because of subparagraph 6(1)(b)(v), (vi) or (vii), not included in computing the taxpayer's income for the year, or

> (iv)   claims a deduction for the year under paragraph (e), (f) or (g).

---

[59] For historical and policy purposes, it is also useful to mention former paras. 8(1)(k) and (l), which allowed taxpayers to deduct employment insurance premiums and Canada/Quebec Pension Plan (CPP/QPP) contributions. These provisions were repealed in 1987 and converted into a non-refundable tax credit in section 118.7.

Similarly, paragraph 8(1)(h.1) allows taxpayers to deduct amounts expended in respect of motor vehicle expenses incurred for travelling in the course of an office or employment, also provided that the taxpayer, in the year:

(i)   was ordinarily required to carry on the duties of the office or employment away from the employer's place of business or in different places, and

(ii) was required under the contract of employment to pay motor vehicle expenses incurred by the taxpayer in the performance of the duties of the office or employment,

and also except where the taxpayer

(iii) received an allowance for motor vehicle expenses that was, because of paragraph 6(1)(b), not included in computing the taxpayer's income for the year, or

(iv) claims a deduction for the year under paragraph (f).

Where a taxpayer may claim a deduction under paragraph 8(1)(h) or (h.1), moreover, paragraph 8(1)(j) allows the taxpayer to deduct interest payments and capital cost allowances related to the acquisition of a motor vehicle that is used to perform the duties of the taxpayer's office or employment or an aircraft that is required for the taxpayer's office or employment. (Deductions for interest expenses and capital cost allowances are examined in Chapter 5.) For 1988 and subsequent taxation years, however, subsection 8(10) stipulates that amounts otherwise deductible under paragraphs 8(1)(h) and (h.1) shall not be deductible "unless a prescribed form, signed by the taxpayer's employer certifying that the conditions set out in the applicable provision were met in the year in respect of the taxpayer, is filed with the taxpayer's return of income for the year."

As explained earlier in this chapter, paragraph 6(1)(b) requires taxpayers to include allowances in computing their income from an office or employment, but exempts various allowances including reasonable allowances for travel and motor vehicle expenses as indicated in subparagraphs 6(1)(b)(v), (vi), (vii), and (vii.1). Paragraph 8(1)(f), which is examined later in this section, allows the deduction of travel and other expenses incurred by taxpayers who are "employed in the year in connection with the selling of property or negotiating of contracts for the taxpayer's employer." Paragraphs 8(1)(e) and (g), which are not examined in this section, permit railway and transport employees to deduct amounts disbursed for meals and lodging where they are required to travel in the course of their duties.[60] The separate deduction for motor vehicle expenses in

---

[60] For cases on the application of para. 8(1)(e), see *English v. M.N.R.*, [1984] C.T.C. 2815, 84 D.T.C. 1714 (T.C.C.); *Ferguson v. M.N.R.*, [1985] 2 C.T.C. 2167, 85 D.T.C. 498 (T.C.C.); and *Edwards v. M.N.R.*, [1985] 2 C.T.C. 2171, 85 D.T.C. 496 (T.C.C.). For leading cases on the application of para. 8(1)(g), see *Canada v. Creamer*, [1976] C.T.C. 676, 76 D.T.C. 6422 (F.C.T.D.) (concluding that the principal business of the taxpayer's employer was not the transportation of passengers or goods); *Derrien v. M.N.R.*, [1980] C.T.C. 2848, 80 D.T.C. 1751 (T.R.B.) (defining the concept of "travel" for the purposes of para. 8(1)(f)); *Martin v. The Queen* (January 20, 1998), Doc. No. 97-1401 (IT)I; [1998] CarswellNat 25 (T.C.C.) (examining the

paragraph 8(1)(h.1), which was introduced for 1988 and subsequent taxation years, allows taxpayers to receive an exempt allowance in respect of these expenses without disqualifying the deduction of other travel expenses.

In order to qualify for the deductions in paragraphs 8(1)(h) and (h.1), therefore, an employee must generally satisfy three preliminary requirements:

1. the employee must have been "ordinarily required to carry on the duties of the office or employment away from the employer's place of business or in different places";

2. the employee must have been "required under the contract of employment to pay the travel expenses incurred ... in the performance of the duties of the office or employment"; and

3. the employee must not have received a travel allowance exempt from tax under paragraph 6(1)(b).

The following cases and commentary examine each of these requirements and the further stipulation that the amounts expended by the taxpayer must be for "travelling in the course of the office or employment."

1. Ordinarily Required To Carry On Duties Away from Employer's Place of Business or in Different Places

In order to deduct travel expenses under paragraph 8(1)(h) or (h.1), subparagraph (i) stipulates that the taxpayer must in the taxation year have been "ordinarily required to carry on the duties of the office or employment away from the employer's place of business or in different places." A useful discussion of this requirement appears in *Nelson v. M.N.R.*, [1981] C.T.C. 2181, 81 D.T.C. 190 (T.R.B.). At issue in this case is what is meant by "the employer's place of business" as well what is required of the employee to fulfill their duties.

Nelson v. M.N.R.
[1981] C.T.C. 2181, 81 D.T.C. 190 (T.R.B.)

L.-J. L. CARDIN, QC: ... The appellant, an architect and a lawyer since 1959, had over the years been employed with firms engaged in the management of large construction contracts and had acquired experience in contract management. ...

---

requirement that the duties of the taxpayer's employment require the taxpayer to "regularly" travel); *Canada v. Little*, [1974] C.T.C. 678, 74 D.T.C. 6534 (F.C.T.D.) (considering the location of the municipality where the taxpayer's establishment to which the taxpayer regularly reported for work); *Walls v. Canada*, [1976] F.C.J. No. 122, [1976] C.T.C. 501, 76 D.T.C. 6309 (F.C.T.D.) (examining the meaning of the words "municipality" and "metropolitan area" in the predecessor to subpara. 8(1)(f)(i)); and *McLean v. M.N.R.* (1956), 14 Tax ABC 369 (concluding that the word "vehicles" in subpara. 8(1)(f)(i) includes ships).

Early in February of 1976, the president of Konvey Construction Company Limited ... informed the appellant by phone that Konvey had a construction management contract with the Ministry of Government Services of Ontario (hereinafter referred to as MGS) for the construction of the Ontario Police College in Aylmer, Ontario, at a fixed management fee.

The company was experiencing difficulty with the project which was a little more than half finished and considerably behind schedule. The previous contract manager, Mr Anderson, having resigned, arrangements were made for the appellant to meet with Mr M.J. Watt, the project manager at the Aylmer construction site with a view to his employment in Konvey.

The appellant alleges that during his meeting with Mr. Watt, the responsibilities and the duties that would be given were very interesting. On February 23, 1976, the appellant accepted the position offered that of contract manager for a salary of $22,000 which employment was terminated on November 30, 1976.

...

[T]he difficulties in interpreting subparagraph 8(1)(h)(i) in this appeal centers on what is meant by:

(a)   the employer's place of business.

(b)   the duties of the taxpayer's employment.

(c)   ordinarily required to carry out the duties of employment away from the employer's place of business.

...

[I]n order to obtain the correct meaning of "the employer's place of business," subparagraph 8(1)(h)(i) of the Act should ... be read together with subsection 8(4) of the Act. [According to this provision, which is examined later in this chapter, no amount expended for meals may be deducted under paragraph 8(1)(h) unless "the meal was consumed during a period while the taxpayer was required by the taxpayer's duties to be away, for a period of not less than twelve hours, from the municipality where the employer's establishment to which the taxpayer ordinarily reported for work was located and away from the metropolitan area, if there is one, where it was located."] It appears to be logical ... to consider that the "employer's place of business" as used in subparagraph 8(1)(h)(i) of the Act, does not necessarily refer to the employer's head office or any one of its administrative offices but refer specifically to that establishment of the employer for which the taxpayer was hired, to which he was assigned and at which he ordinarily reports for work. In other words, the "employer's place of business" should in my opinion be interpreted in relation to the taxpayer.

...

The validity of considering the "employer's place of business" in relation to the employee's attendance in interpreting subparagraph 8(1)(h)(i) of the Act, can best be illustrated by the facts and the submissions made at the hearing.

The appellant alleges that he was hired as a senior management officer for the company's head office in Toronto. Other than the Ontario Police College project in Aylmer, Ontario, which took approximately four years to complete, it is the appellant's evidence that Konvey had at least two other places of business: one in Markham, Ontario, and one in the Toronto Dominion Centre in Toronto, both of which the appellant alleges to have attended on occasion in the course of his duties with the company.

...

The appellant further contends that the urgency of the Aylmer project and the amount of time he attended at Aylmer in the period of time he was employed by Konvey also seriously distorts the overall role he would have had to play in the company's general operations over a longer period of time and after the Aylmer project had been completed. The evidence is that the police college was completed two years after the appellant's employment with Konvey was terminated.

The point of the appellant's evidence of course is to establish that the appellant's employment contract with Konvey was not restricted to the Aylmer project, but was really a senior managerial position at the company's head office in Toronto and that therefore the company's place of business for the appellant was Toronto.

From this, the appellant concludes that, owing to his managerial position with the company while working on a full time basis in Aylmer, he was ordinarily required to carry on his duties of employment away from his "employer's place of business" in Toronto or in different places and therefore meets the requirements of subparagraph 8(1)(h)(i) of the Act.

The respondent's submission is that the "employer's place of business" was not Konvey's head office in Toronto but was the police college project in Aylmer and that in any event, the appellant was not by reasons of his employment ordinarily required to carry out his duties away from the employer's place of business.

Other than the appellant's rather vague statement that he believed he was being offered a senior managerial position at the company's head office in Toronto, there is no evidence which supports that allegation.

The written confirmation of the appellant's employment contract ... does not refer to either the Toronto head office or to Konvey's establishment in Markham as the "employer's place of business" for which the appellant was being hired and at which he would normally and regularly work. The facts, as disclosed by the appellant, which are in keeping with Konvey's letter of confirmation, leads one inevitably to conclude that the "employer's place of business" to which the appellant was assigned was the police college in Aylmer.

...

In the absence of any other evidence the "employer's place of business" for purposes of subparagraph 8(1)(h)(i) of the Act in this appeal can only be determined in relation to the appellant's attendance and work in a particular location. I can see no justification for concluding that because the appellant was hired by Konvey, whose head office is in Toronto, that the "employer's place of business" for the appellant must be Toronto.

Having concluded for purposes of this appeal that Aylmer and not Toronto is the "employer's place of business" within the meaning of subparagraph 8(1)(h)(i) of the Act, the duties of the appellant's employment must also be considered before determining whether the appellant was "ordinarily required to carry out the duties of his employment away from the 'employer's place of business' or in different places."

... [T]he appellant's duties in the instant appeal by their very nature were to be carried out at the "employer's place of business" in Aylmer. Indeed, in Konvey's confirmation letter in which the appellant's duties have been set out, travelling on company business away from the "employer's place of business" is considered as exceptional and must be cleared with the project manager located in Aylmer. The nature of the appellant's duties do not therefore ordinarily require that he carry out his duties away from the "employer's place of business."

...

Appeal dismissed.

NOTES AND QUESTIONS

1.   On what basis did the taxpayer in *Nelson* argue that the amounts that he expended travelling from Toronto to Aylmer and back were deductible under paragraph 8(1)(h) of the Act? Why did the board reject this argument? How did it interpret the words "employer's place of business" for the purpose of paragraph 8(1)(h)? Do you agree with the board's interpretation? Why or why not?

2.   In *Lowe v. M.N.R.* (1959), 21 Tax ABC 410 (T.A.B.), the taxpayer, an engineer in a fishing vessel, sought to deduct monthly payments paid by his employer but credited to his account payable for board on the vessel, on the basis that he was "ordinarily required to carry on the duties of [his] employment away from [his] employer's place of business" in Vancouver. Concluding (at para. 5) that the taxpayer "worked in a ship and not at any land establishment," the board disallowed the deduction on the grounds, within the meaning of then subsection 11(9) (now paragraph 8(1)(h)), the ship, not the employer's office on land, was the employer's place of business.

3.   In *Ronchka v. M.N.R.*, [1979] C.T.C. 3071, 79 D.T.C. 854 (T.R.B.), the taxpayer, who was hired by Ontario Hydro to work at its head office in Toronto, sought in computing his employment income for his 1977 taxation year to deduct accommodation and meal expenses incurred during a 4½ month period during which he was assigned to Ontario Hydro's training facilities in Rolphton,

Ontario, 300 miles from Toronto. Accepting that the taxpayer was required to carry on the duties of his employment away from the taxpayer's place of business in Toronto, the board nonetheless upheld the Minister's assessment, which disallowed the deduction on the basis that the taxpayer was not "ordinarily" required to carry on these duties in Rolphton. According to the board (at para. 12):

> "*Ordinarily required*" does not mean that during a certain period of time, i.e. *on a temporary assignment*, the employee was "required ... ordinarily to report for work" at a location other than his employer's place of business. "*Ordinarily required*" does mean that it was "normally," as opposed to "rarely," or "exceptionally" ... , "as a matter of regular occurrence" ... , that the taxpayer, during the year of his employment would be working away from his employer's place of business. There is no evidence in this appeal that Ronchka agreed that there would be such flexibility in his terms of employment, or that anything of such a nature was expected from him by Ontario Hydro. There is no indication that a situation in any way similar to the Rolphton assignment was anticipated or ever again arose. The contract of employment was not based upon any premise that in his state of employment, he was *ordinarily required* to work away from his employer's place of business.

Contrast *Ronchka* with the decision in *Tremblay v. Canada*, [1997] F.C.J. No. 1642, 98 D.T.C. 6008 (F.C.A.), where the taxpayer, a member of the RCMP who was required as a duty of his employment to attend an English-language course in Montreal from September 1991 to May 1992, sought to deduct $360 per month for room and board with a host family, which his employer deducted from his monthly salary. Rejecting the Minister's argument that the taxpayer was not "ordinarily" required to carry on the duties of his employment away from his employer's place of business, the court dismissed the interpretation in *Ronchka* as "incorrect," concluding (at para. 5) that:

> [e]ven a literal interpretation of subparagraph 8(1)(h)(i) leads to the conclusion that the [taxpayer] was ordinarily carrying on the duties of his employment away from his employer's place of business while he was assigned to Montreal during the 1991 and 1992 taxation years.

4.   In *Shangraw v. M.N.R.*, [1976] C.T.C. 2415, 76 D.T.C. 1309 (T.R.B.), the taxpayer, a floor-coverings salesman for the T. Eaton Co. Limited, sought to deduct among other amounts automobile expenses incurred to render in-home services to customers whose homes he was required to visit in the performance of his duties. Rejecting the Minister's argument that the taxpayer, whose duties were performed primarily at the Eaton's store in Oshawa, was not "ordinarily" required to carry on the duties of his employment away from his employer's place of business, the board stated (at para. 16):

> subparagraph 8(1)(h)(i) of the said Act can, of course, be interpreted as being essentially related to time, but the question as I see it is whether that is the only valid interpretation to be placed on the words "ordinarily required." In my opinion, interpreting those words as being related to the actual duties and responsibilities of the appellant's employment rather than to the time factor is also a legal and valid interpretation.

In *Krieger v. M.N.R.*, [1979] C.T.C. 2283, 79 D.T.C. 269 (T.R.B.), in contrast, the board disallowed the deduction of travelling expenses incurred by the taxpayer, an official receiver in bankruptcy who was required to be away from his office during the daytime about 24 to 30 days per year, on the grounds that the *Income Tax Act* "must be strictly interpreted" and that the taxpayer was not "ordinarily" required to carry on the duties of his employment away from his employer's place of business.

Which interpretation of the word "ordinarily" do you prefer, and why?

5.   In *Imray v. Canada*, [1998] F.C.J. No. 1409, [1998] 4 C.T.C. 221, 98 D.T.C. 6580 (F.C.T.D.), the taxpayers, teachers who were employed in Peace River, Alberta, sought to deduct travel expenses to attend a two-day teachers' convention in Grand-Prairie that they were required to attend as a duty of their employment. Rejecting the Minister's argument that attendance at an annual teachers' convention was not an ordinary requirement of their employment, the court accepted the taxpayers' argument (at para. 19) that "they were required to attend annual Teachers' Conventions, attended 'normally,' 'as a matter of regular occurrence,' 'commonly,' and 'usually,' and should, therefore, be allowed the deduction for their expenses." According to Campbell J (at paras. 21-24):

> On the authority of *Tremblay*, I do not agree with the assertion of a linear approach to the interpretation of "ordinarily" in s. 8(1)(h)(i). I do not think it is possible as a general rule, nor advisable, to say that a certain frequency of occurrence complies with the requirements of the provision, since an individual set of circumstances might be far more difficult to analyse fairly than this rather simple approach would allow. Accordingly, adoption of a linear approach would not generate a just result in each case, and rather than generate certainty as precedent, would generate confusion instead.
>
> Therefore, rather than viewing a particular set of facts as occupying a place on a frequency continuum, I find the mandated approach is to consider a particular set of facts as a function of the unique context in which they arise. This latter approach avoids the complication raised in argument by counsel for the Minister that, if I accede to the Imrays' argument, a dangerous precedent will be set, not only for cases of a like nature, but also for other cases in which the word "ordinarily" is used in different situations within the *Income Tax Act*. In addition, in response to this argument, I say that this decision is about the interpretation and application of "ordinarily" as used in s. 8(1)(h)(i), nothing more.
>
> The requirement of the Imrays' attendance at Teachers' Conventions is a function of legal, administrative and ethical expectations which apply to all teachers in Alberta. Within this context, the fact that Teachers' Conventions occur only once per year is a minor factor. As is the case for Mr. Imray, who has attended every year since being a teacher, save one, when because of a flood in his school he was unable to attend, the evidence establishes that most teachers in Alberta accept this responsibility.
>
> On this basis, I have no hesitation in finding that Teachers' Convention attendance is "normal," "a matter of regular occurrence," "commonly" and "usually" occurs, and is a requirement which takes teachers "from time to time away from the places which they usually work."

6.   In *Klue v. M.N.R.*, [1976] C.T.C. 2401, 76 D.T.C. 1303 (T.R.B.), the taxpayer, a detective sergeant with the Metropolitan Toronto Police Force, sought to deduct travel expenses incurred while off duty to attend Provincial Court for the purpose of giving evidence in cases in which he had been involved and filing permanent exhibits. Concluding (at para. 16) that "attendance at court

was an essential and important part of [the taxpayer's] duties as a police officer," the board allowed the taxpayer's appeal from an assessment disallowing the deduction on the basis, *inter alia*, that the taxpayer was ordinarily required to carry on duties of his employment away from the employer's place of business.

7.   In *Charlton v. M.N.R.*, [1984] C.T.C. 2616, 84 D.T.C. 1420 (T.C.C.), the taxpayer, a teacher who lived in Guelph, Ontario, sought to deduct automobile expenses incurred in 1980 when he was seconded by the Ontario Ministry of Education to teach at a school in Milton, Ontario, requiring road travel of 58 miles per day. Observing that the taxpayer had voluntarily chosen to teach in Milton, the court disallowed the deduction on the basis that the taxpayer was not "required" to carry on the duties of his employment away from his original employer's place of business in Guelph.

Do you agree with this conclusion? Why or why not? Might the court have concluded that the taxpayer was actually employed by the Ministry of Education during the period of his secondment and therefore did not carry on the duties of his employment away from this employer's place of business? Might the court also have concluded that the cost to commute from Guelph to Milton was not incurred in the course of the taxpayer's employment?

8.   In *M.N.R. v. Jeromel*, [1986] F.C.J. No. 410, [1986] 2 C.T.C. 207, 86 D.T.C. 6370 (F.C.T.D.), the taxpayer, a teacher who applied for and received a sabbatical leave in order to take courses leading to a master's degree in education, sought to deduct the cost of travelling from his home in Mabou, Nova Scotia, to classes held in Antigonish, New Glasgow, and Sydney. Noting that the taxpayer's contract permitted, but did not require, him to apply for a sabbatical leave, the court disallowed the deduction on the grounds that the taxpayer was not required to carry on the duties of his employment away from his employer's place of business.

See also *Mitchell v. Canada*, [1999] T.C.J. No. 302, [1999] 4 C.T.C. 2285, 99 D.T.C. 866 (T.C.C.), in which a university professor at the School of Business Administration at Acadia University, Wolfville, Nova Scotia, sought to deduct travel expenses incurred in order to carry on research in the West Indies during a sabbatical leave. Noting (at para. 23) that the sabbatical provided "choice as to what and where as well as the matter of costs to the person on leave," the court concluded that the taxpayer was not *required* to carry on the duties of his employment away from the university.

9.   For the CRA's views on paragraphs 8(1)(h) and (h.1), see IT-522R. According to paragraph 32 of this bulletin, for the purposes of subparagraphs 8(1)(h)(i) and (h.1)(i):

(a)   "ordinarily" means "customarily" or "habitually" rather than "continually," but there should be some degree of regularity in the travelling that the employee is required to do,

(b) "required" means that the travelling is necessary to the satisfactory performance of the employee's duties (it does not necessarily imply that the employer must order the employee to travel),

(c) "place of business" generally is considered to have reference to a permanent establishment of the employer such as an office, factory, warehouse, branch or store, or to a field office at a large construction job, and

(d) "in different places" generally refers to the situation where the employer does not have a single or fixed place of business. For example, a school inspector who has a number of schools to supervise and is required to travel from school to school meets this requirement. Similarly, an employee who is required to travel from building to building within the boundaries of the employer's property meets this requirement if the employer's property is very large and the distance between buildings is sufficient to justify the use of a "motor vehicle." On the other hand, where the employee is employed on a ship, the ship is the employer's place of business where the employee is ordinarily required to carry on the duties, and the fact that the ship may travel to different places is insufficient to meet this requirement.

10. Paragraph 8(1)(f) allows taxpayers who are employed "in connection with the selling of property or negotiating of contracts for [their] employer" to deduct amounts expended for the purpose of earning income from their employment, provided, *inter alia*, that they were "ordinarily required to carry on the duties of the employment away from the employer's place of business." This requirement, which is almost identical to that in subparagraphs 8(1)(h)(i) and (h.1)(i), is examined later in this chapter.

2. Required Under Contract of Employment To Pay Travel Expenses

In addition to the requirement in subparagraphs 8(1)(h)(i) and (h.1)(i) that the taxpayer must in the taxation year have been "ordinarily required to carry on the duties of the office or employment away from the employer's place of business or in different places," subparagraph (ii) of these provisions stipulates that the taxpayer must also have been "required under the contract of employment to pay the travel expenses incurred ... in the performance of the duties of the office or employment." Although distinguished in more recent cases, the leading case on the interpretation of this requirement is *Canada v. Cival*, [1983] C.T.C. 153, 83 D.T.C. 5168 (F.C.A.).

Canada v. Cival
[1983] C.T.C. 153, 83 D.T.C. 5168 (F.C.A.)

RYAN J (Kerr DJ and Heald J concurring): ... Mr. Cival is an employee of the Queen in right of Canada. During the 1977 taxation year, he was working in the Payroll Audit Section of the Department of National Revenue in Winnipeg. Mr. Cival used his own automobile in carrying out the duties of his employment under what, he said, was an arrangement with his Department, an arrangement in accordance with which the Department reimbursed him at a mileage rate. It is not questioned that he used his automobile at the request of his Department. During 1977, Mr. Cival's expenses for the use of his automobile in his work exceeded the mileage he received by $512.03. He claimed this sum as a deduction from his income. The Minister disallowed it.

The question in this appeal is whether Mr. Cival was entitled to this deduction under paragraph 8(1)(h). The answer depends on whether he was required by his contract of employment to pay the expenses incurred by him in using the automobile.

...

The trial judge clearly was of opinion that the arrangement respecting the use of Mr. Cival's car constituted a contract between Mr. Cival and his employer and that the contract was an employment contract. Under this contract, Mr. Cival, in his Lordship's view, was required by implication to pay the expenses incurred by him in using his car; at least to the extent they exceed his mileage reimbursement. I do not, with respect, agree that Mr. Cival was contractually bound under the arrangement to pay these expenses.

The terms of Mr. Cival's employment were contained in a collective agreement between Treasury Board and the Public Service Alliance which was in force during the 1977 taxation year. Mr. Cival was a member of the bargaining unit covered by the agreement. His terms of employment may also have included provisions of the Public Service Terms and Conditions of Employment Regulations; at least to the extent they were not inconsistent with the provisions of the collective agreement, and any statutory provisions concerning public employment applicable to him. It was not suggested that any term of employment contained in the collective agreement, in the Regulations or in any statutory provision required him to use his own car in performing his duties or to pay the expenses incurred in its use. To bring himself within subparagraph 8(1)(h)(ii), Mr. Cival would, therefore, have to establish that the arrangement about using his car was an employment contract under which he was required to pay the expenses incurred by him in using the car.

I am prepared to assume for purposes of this appeal that Mr. Cival could enter into an individual contract with his employer, covering an aspect of his employment, despite his being covered by the collective agreement, so long at least as the contract was not inconsistent with the terms of the agreement. In my view, the arrangement between Mr. Cival and his employer, if a contract at all, was at most what is sometimes called a unilateral contract. It was an arrangement under which his employer undertook to reimburse him on a mileage basis for expenses he incurred in using his car in the performance of his duties. I do not interpret the arrangement as involving a promise by Mr. Cival to use his car in performing his duties and to pay the expenses out of his own pocket in return for an undertaking by his employer to reimburse him. To put it another way: as I see the arrangement, Mr. Cival was not contractually bound to use his car in doing his job and to pay the expenses involved: if at any time during 1977 he had refused to use his car for this purpose, he would not have been suable by his employer for breach of contract. It follows that, to adopt the words used in subparagraph 8(1)(h)(ii), he was not required under his contract of employment to pay the expenses incurred by him in using his car in the performance of the duties of his employment. This is enough to dispose of the appeal. ...

Appeal allowed.

NOTES AND QUESTIONS

1. On what basis did the trial judge conclude in *Cival* that the taxpayer was required under the contract of his employment to pay the travel expenses that he incurred in the performance of the duties of his employment? Why did the Federal Court of Appeal disagree with this conclusion? Which interpretation do you find most persuasive? Why?

2. *Cival* was followed in *Denson v. M.N.R.*, [1985] 2 C.T.C. 2249, 85 D.T.C. 585 (T.C.C.), in which the taxpayer, a customer service adviser for Bell Canada whose duties required her to travel, sought to deduct the difference between automobile expenses that she incurred in the performance of her duties and a mileage allowance paid by her employer. Observing (at para. 7) that "there was no mandatory requirement for the [taxpayer] to use her vehicle in her work," the court disallowed the deduction. For a similar result, involving another Bell Canada employee, see *Mireault v. M.N.R.*, [1985] 1 C.T.C. 2167, 85 D.T.C. 170 (T.C.C.).

3. *Cival* was distinguished in *Rozen v. Canada*, [1985] F.C.J. No. 1002, [1986] 1 C.T.C. 50, 85 D.T.C. 5611 (F.C.T.D.), in which the taxpayer, who was employed by a firm of chartered accountants in Vancouver, incurred expenses travelling to clients' offices in the Vancouver area. Accepting (at para. 7) evidence that "it was the expectation of the employer that persons in the position of the [taxpayer] would use their own car for the purpose of going to work at clients' offices" and that "if an auditor did not have a car or was no longer able or willing to use it, the firm would probably dismiss him," the court concluded that the taxpayer was required under the contract of employment to pay the travel expenses incurred in the performance of his duties. According to Strayer J (as he then was) (at paras. 8-9):

> In the absence of any evidence to the contrary, I have concluded that the plaintiff was indeed required to use his automobile in order to do his job and that he was responsible for the costs of operating his automobile. This was basically an implied term of his contract and one which is apparently common with such auditors employed by accountancy firms. ... I believe this situation can be distinguished from that in *Cival*, ... where the Federal Court of Appeal held that the taxpayer was not obliged to use his own automobile in his work as a payroll auditor for the Department of National Revenue. The Court there held that nothing in the contract of employment obliged him to use his car even though provision was made for mileage allowance where he did use it. It was held that this was at most a "unilateral contract": that is, he did not have to use his car but if he did use it then he was entitled to be paid mileage. In the present case the employee did not have the option if he was to do his job properly.

> I believe also that subparagraph 8(1)(h)(ii) can be interpreted somewhat more broadly. Even if the plaintiff were not specifically required to use his car, he was required to pay his travelling expenses incurred by him in the performance of his duties and this would also bring him within the subparagraph. The evidence was clear that to do his job the plaintiff had to go to the offices of a variety of clients. No provision was made for reimbursement for transportation for getting to those offices except with respect to those outside of Vancouver where at least car mileage was allowed. If an employee is obliged to travel to do his work and his employer is not prepared to pay the exact and total cost of transportation, then he must come within the requirements of subparagraph 8(1)(h)(ii). This question was not under consideration before the Federal Court of Appeal in *Cival*.

For other cases in which courts have concluded that a contract implicitly required the taxpayer to pay travel expenses incurred in the performance of the taxpayer's duties of an office or employment, see *Peters v. M.N.R.*, [1986] 2 C.T.C. 2221, 86 D.T.C. 1662 (T.C.C.); *Canada v. Mina*, [1988] F.C.J. No. 260, [1988] 1 C.T.C. 380, 88 D.T.C. 6245 (F.C.T.D.); *Dallaire v. M.N.R.*, [1991] T.C.J. No. 1018, [1993] 2 C.T.C. 2773, 93 D.T.C. 193 (T.C.C.); and *Stokes v. M.N.R.*, [1993] C.T.C. 2066, (1992) 93 D.T.C. 201 (T.C.C.).

4.   In *Ain v. M.N.R.*, [1986] 2 C.T.C. 2024, 86 D.T.C. 1495 (T.C.C.), the taxpayer, a Crown attorney whose duties required him to travel from his office in Cornwall, Ontario to courts in nearby counties, sought to deduct travel expenses in excess of those reimbursed by the Ministry of the Attorney General. Distinguishing *Rozen v. Canada*, [1985] F.C.J. No. 1002, [1986] 1 C.T.C. 50, 85 D.T.C. 5611 (F.C.T.D.), the court disallowed the deduction on the grounds (at para. 17) that the taxpayer "was required to use his car but that there was no verifiable obligation that he was required to pay his expenses over and above the government allowance."

See also *Hudema v. Canada*, [1994] F.C.J. No. 443, [1994] 2 C.T.C. 42, 94 D.T.C. 6287 (F.C.T.D.), in which the taxpayer, a sales representative of the Canadian Broadcasting Corporation selling television advertising in Regina and the surrounding viewing area, sought to deduct automobile expenses incurred to travel within his sales area. Citing two clauses of the collective bargaining agreement (at para. 4) stipulating that "the use of employee's car in executing the business of the corporation is not compulsory, and he/she may at his/her discretion decline to use it" and that "[s]ales representatives authorized to use their cars on corporation business will be compensated" through a weekly car allowance and reimbursement of operating expenses, the court concluded (at para. 11) that the taxpayer "was not by his contract of employment required to use his car and thus pay the costs of operating the car." According to Strayer J (as he then was):

> The collective bargaining agreement specifically said that no employee was obliged to use his car but it contemplated that he could be authorized to use his car. It is not in dispute that the plaintiff was authorized to use his car for his sales work. I respectfully adopt the reasoning of the Federal Court of Appeal in *The Queen v. Cival*, ... where there was a rather similar set of facts. There was at best a kind of "unilateral contract" whereby if the plaintiff did use his car then he was entitled to the car allowance plus reimbursement for gas, oil, lubrication and parking. I distinguish this from my own decision in *Rozen v. The Queen*, ... because in that case there was clear evidence given by an officer of the employer to the effect

that there was an understanding between employer and employee that the employee would have to use his car. Further, he said the employer would probably dismiss an accountant employee if the latter was no longer able or willing to use his car in his work. In the present case there was no such evidence.

For a similar result, see also *Baxter v. Canada*, [1996] T.C.J. No. 1791, [1997] 1 C.T.C. 2384 (T.C.C.).

5.   According to paragraph 33 of IT-522R, the CRA considers the requirement in subparagraphs 8(1)(h)(ii) and (h.1)(ii) to be met where the following conditions are satisfied:

(a)   the employer must clearly indicate on the required form T2200 [as required by subsection 8(10)] that the employee is required to pay travel expenses incurred in the performance of duties; and

(b)   the employee's reasonable travel costs must not be fully reimbursed by the employer. In determining the reasonableness of the amount claimed by the employee for travel costs, consideration will be given to the mode of transportation used by the employee versus the mode of transportation that could be used to satisfy the requirement to travel.

6.   Among the other requirements to qualify for a deduction under paragraph 8(1)(f), a taxpayer who is employed "in connection with the selling of property or negotiating of contracts for the taxpayer's employer" must "under the contract of employment" have been "required to pay the taxpayer's own expenses." This requirement, which similar to that in subparagraphs 8(1)(h)(ii) and (h.1)(ii), is examined later in this chapter.

3. Receipt of Travel Allowance

In addition to the two requirements in subparagraphs (i) and (ii), subparagraphs 8(1)(h)(iii) and (h.1)(iii) impose a further requirement for the deductibility of amounts expended on travelling in the course of an office or employment that the employee must not have received a travel or motor vehicle allowance that is exempt from tax under paragraph 6(1)(b). An interesting examination of this requirement appears in *Yurkovich v. M.N.R.*, [1986] 2 C.T.C. 2300, 86 D.T.C. 1704 (T.C.C.).

Yurkovich v. M.N.R.
[1986] 2 C.T.C. 2300, 86 D.T.C. 1704 (T.C.C.)

TAYLOR TCJ: ... Mr. Yurkovich is, and was during 1981, an auditor with the Province of Alberta. ... In filing his income tax return the taxpayer had calculated that the total automobile expenses incurred amounted to $6,491.73 including depreciation; he had reported an amount of $2,152.01 received from his employer calculated at a rate per kilometre set under the terms of the collective union agreement governing his employment, as a deduction from this amount; he had concluded that his personal automobile had been used 56.2 per cent of the time on his employer's business; and finally he had calculated the disputed $2,438.72 as 56.2 per cent of the difference between his total automobile expenses of $6,491.73 (*supra*) minus his reimbursement of $2,152.01 ($6,491.73 - $2,152.01 × 56.2 per cent = $2,438.72). The Court notes that it is at least arguable that the automobile expenses which the appellant could claim against employment might be 56.2 per cent of the *total* automobile expense of $6,491.73 rather than 56.2 per cent of the net automobile expenses (after deduction of the receipt from his employer), but the mathematics of the taxpayer's claim did not arise as a specific point of dispute at the hearing.

...

The documentation and testimony satisfied the Court that the first two conditions under paragraph 8(1)(h) of the Act had been fulfilled. In other words, "... (he) was ordinarily required to carry on the duties of his employment away from his employer's place of business or in different places; and under the contract of employment was required to pay the travelling expenses incurred by him in the performance of the duties of his office or employment, ..." His difficulty ultimately rested on whether he qualified under subparagraph 8(1)(h)(iii) of the Act: "... (he) was not in receipt of an allowance for travelling expenses that was, by virtue of subparagraph 6(1)(b)(v), (vi) or (vii), not included in computing his income ... ." This then required an examination of subparagraph 6(1)(b)(vii) of the Act as it impinged on his claim.

Clearly that with which we are faced in the amount of $2.152.01 would normally be termed a "reimbursement" or "repayment." There was no evidence that the mileage rates were calculated and paid in advance, in anticipation of travel. Rather they were paid as a result of the claims made by the appellant subsequent to and dependent on such travel. That would appear to place this amount of $2,152.01 outside the "allowance" category, and if it is not an "allowance" at all, subparagraphs 6(1)(b)(vii) and 8(1)(h)(iii) have no application.

...

I can find no reason to deny Mr. Yurkovich the claim he has made, since he has met the first two conditions under paragraph 8(1)(h) of the Act, and the third condition is inapplicable. ...

Appeal allowed.

NOTES AND QUESTIONS

1.   On what basis did the court conclude that the taxpayer in *Yurkovich* satisfied the requirement in subparagraph 8(1)(h)(iii) that he did not receive an allowance for travel expenses that was exempt from tax under paragraph 6(1)(b)? Do you agree with this conclusion? Why or why not? Is the court's interpretation of an "allowance" for the purposes of paragraph 6(1)(b) consistent with the meaning adopted in *MacDonald v. Canada (Attorney General)*, [1994] F.C.J. No. 378, [1994] 2 C.T.C. 48, 94 D.T.C. 6262 (F.C.A.)?

2.   Do you agree with the manner in which the taxpayer computed the amount of the deduction under paragraph 8(1)(h)? Was the court not right to suggest that the 56.2 per cent figure should be applied to the total automobile expense of $6,491.73, rather than the net expense (after deducting the amount received from his employer) of $4,339.72 ($6,491.73 - $2,152.01)? Note that if the reimbursement is deducted from 56.2 per cent of the total automobile expense, the deductible amount decreases from the $2,438.72 claimed by the taxpayer (56.2 per cent of $4,339.72) to $1,496.34 (56.2 per cent × $6,491.73 - $2,152.01). Doesn't the taxpayer's approach permit a non-taxable reimbursement of personal expenses?

3.   For the CRA's views on the computation of allowable deductions under paragraph 8(1)(h) or (h.1), see IT-522R. According to paragraph 4 of this bulletin, the allowable deduction for motor vehicle expenses under paragraph 8(1)(h.1) should be computed by subtracting the amount of any reimbursement from the employment-related portion of the motor vehicle expenses.

4.   Notwithstanding the decision in *Yurkovich* and the *obiter* statement in *Cival*, the CRA appears to regard payments based on the distance travelled by employees in the performance of their duties as "allowances" within the meaning of paragraph 6(1)(b). According to paragraph 40 of IT-522R:

> In this bulletin, the word "allowance" means any periodic or other payment that an employee receives from an employer, in addition to salary or wages, without having to account for its use. It may be computed by reference to distance or time (for example a "motor vehicle" expense allowance based on the distance driven or a travel allowance based on the number of days away) or on some other basis.

Support for this position might be derived from the language of subparagraph 6(1)(b)(x), enacted subsequent to the decisions in *Yurkovich* and *Cival*, which stipulates that for the purposes of subparagraphs 6(1)(b)(v), (vi), and (vii.1):

> an allowance received in a taxation year by a taxpayer for the use of a motor vehicle in connection with or in the course of the taxpayer's office or employment shall be deemed not to be a reasonable allowance ... where the measurement of the use of the vehicle for the purpose of the allowance is not based solely on the number of kilometres for which the vehicle is used in connection with or in the course of the office or employment.

In this respect, see also paragraph 18(1)(r) and regulation 7306, which prohibit the deduction of "an amount paid or payable" by a taxpayer "as an allowance for the use by an individual of an automobile to the extent that the amount exceeds an amount determined in accordance with prescribed rules" based on the number of kilometres driven. See also *Lavigne v. Canada*, [1994] T.C.J. No. 58, [1995] 1 C.T.C. 2040, 94 D.T.C. 1571 (T.C.C.), which addresses the interpretation of similar language in paragraph 8(1)(f).

5.   In *Gauvin v. M.N.R.*, [1979] C.T.C. 2812, 79 D.T.C. 696 (T.R.B.), the taxpayer, who was employed as the director of research and development for a mining company and used his automobile to attend meetings and conferences, sought to deduct automobile expenses in excess of an allowance paid by his

employer on the grounds that the allowance was not a "reasonable allowance" within the meaning of subparagraph 6(1)(b)(vii) (now subparagraph 6(1)(b)(vii.1)). Concluding that the allowance was reasonable for the employer's purposes and that the additional expenses resulted from the taxpayer's personal decision to purchase a less economical vehicle than that contemplated by the allowance, the board disallowed the deduction. According to Mr. Taylor (at para. 9):

> to be "unreasonably low" would require, as I see it, a mileage allowance set *below the standard or reasonable amount for the functions it was intended to reimburse*, not merely lower than the total operating costs incurred. [Emphasis in original.]

For other cases in which travel expenses in excess of an allowance provided by the taxpayer's employer have been disallowed on the grounds that the taxpayer was unable to establish that the allowance was "unreasonably low," see *Hudema v. Canada*, [1994] F.C.J. No. 443, [1994] 2 C.T.C. 42, 94 D.T.C. 6287 (F.C.T.D.); *Dallaire v. M.N.R.*, [1991] T.C.J. No. 1018, [1993] 2 C.T.C. 2773, 93 D.T.C. 193 (T.C.C.); *Carter v. Canada*, [1993] T.C.J. No. 891, [1994] 1 C.T.C. 2330 (T.C.C.); *O'Neil v. Canada*, [2000] T.C.J. No. 534, [2001] 1 C.T.C. 2091, 2000 D.T.C. 2409 (T.C.C.); and *Henry v. Canada*, [2007] T.C.J. No. 290, [2008] 1 C.T.C. 2085, 2007 D.T.C. 1410 (T.C.C.).

6.   In *Canada v. Mina*, [1988] F.C.J. No. 260, [1988] 1 C.T.C. 380, 88 D.T.C. 6245 (F.C.T.D.), the taxpayers, psychological consultants for the North York Board of Education who were required to make daily trips between their offices and five different schools, for which they were paid a relatively small mileage allowance, sought to deduct automobile expenses in excess of this allowance under paragraph 8(1)(h) as it then read (now deductible under paragraph 8(1)(h.1)). Rejecting the Minister's argument that the allowance was "intended to pay all the relevant costs of the [taxpayers'] transportation," the court allowed the deduction on the grounds, *inter alia*, that the allowance was "woefully inadequate" (at para. 6).

See also *Faubert v. M.N.R.*, [1979] C.T.C. 2723, 79 D.T.C. 641 (T.R.B.), in which the board concluded that a motor vehicle allowance substantially less than travel expenses claimed by the taxpayer was not reasonable and did not preclude the deduction of excess expenses under paragraph 8(1)(h) as it then read.

7.   In *Evans v. Canada*, [1998] T.C.J. No. 1055, [1999] 1 C.T.C. 2609, 99 D.T.C. 168 (T.C.C.), the taxpayer, a school psychologist who was required to travel to various schools in order to carry out her duties, sought to deduct automobile expenses in excess of an allowance paid by her employer that covered the costs of travel between schools but not between her residence and the first and last schools that she visited each day. Rejecting the Minister's argument that the deduction should be disallowed under subparagraph 8(1)(h.1)(iii), the court concluded that the payment of a reasonable allowance for interschool travel did not preclude the deduction of expenses for travel

between the taxpayer's home and schools visited at the beginning and end of the day. According to Porter DJTC (at para. 22):

> It is clear that if a taxpayer travels 1,000 kilometres in the course of his or her employment and receives an allowance of say 25 cents per kilometre, which by reason of section 6(1)(b) is not included in income, he or she cannot then claim that allowance to be insufficient in respect of the same travel and that he or she should be entitled to claim, as a deduction, further expenses in relation to that travel, unless it falls into the "woefully inadequate" category referred to in the *Mina* case (above). The exception in paragraph 8(1)(h.1)(iii) is clearly a bar to this.

> However, the argument advanced by the Minister that such an allowance acts as a bar to a claim for expenses relating to different travel not covered by that allowance, could lead to absurd results, which clearly would not be within the contemplation of the legislation and is not supported by the case law on the issue. Say for example, the taxpayer was required as part of his or her employment to drive his own vehicle some 40,000 kilometres in a year and for whatever reason was only reimbursed by the employer for 100 of those 40,000 kilometres. Could it be said, that allowance should act as a bar to claiming as an expense against the employment income, the cost of travelling the remaining 39,900 kilometres. That would be an absurd result, which should be avoided. The allowance might be perfectly reasonable as it relates to the travel for which it was paid but it should have no bearing upon the travel for which it was not paid.

> The same principle was dealt with in the *Rozen* case (above), that if a taxpayer is required to use his vehicle for employment purposes, both within a city and outside the city, but is only reimbursed for travel outside the city by way of a non taxable allowance under subparagraph 6(1)(b)(vii.1), that taxpayer is still entitled to claim his or her expenses against employment income, for the travel within the city, as long as it meets all the other relevant criteria.

> In my view, the section makes complete and adequate sense if given the interpretation that if a taxpayer receives an allowance for motor vehicle expenses which, by reason of paragraph 6(1)(b), is not included in his or her taxable income, he or she can claim no further amounts in respect of motor vehicle expenses expended with respect to that same travel (unless "woefully inadequate" as per the *Mina* case above), even if the actual expenses exceeded the allowance for that travel. However, if he or she incurs expenses for travel, other than that covered by the allowance, done in the performance of duties under the contract of employment, express or implied, then the existence of that allowance is not a bar to a claim to set off those other expenses against employment income pursuant to subparagraphs 8(1)(h.1)(i) and (ii). In short, the exception under subparagraph 8(1)(h.1)(iii) relates only to the expenses of travel for which the allowance was paid and is not a bar to a claim for expenses relating to travel for which it was not paid.

Do you agree with this interpretation? Why or why not?

8.   With respect to the requirement in subparagraphs 8(1)(h)(iii) and (h.1)(iii) that a taxpayer must not have received a travel or motor vehicle allowance that is exempt from tax under paragraph 6(1)(b), paragraph 34 of IT-522R, states:

> (a)   where for one type of travel expense, an employee receives an allowance that is excluded from income by virtue of paragraph 6(1)(b), but the employee must pay a second type of travel expense for which no allowance or reimbursement is received, the second type of travel expense will not be disallowed provided it is otherwise deductible under paragraph 8(1)(h) or (h.1). For example, where an employee while on an out-of-town business trip receives a daily meal allowance that is excluded from income by virtue of subparagraph 6(1)(b)(vii) and the employee must bear the cost of

"motor vehicle" expenses, the employee will not be prevented from claiming the vehicle expenses if they are otherwise allowable under paragraph 8(1)(h) or (h.1), and

(b) where an employee receives an allowance for travel expenses that must be included in income, the employee may claim actual expenses under paragraph 8(1)(h) or (h.1) (and capital cost allowance and interest under paragraph 8(1)(j)) if the other requirements of paragraph 8(1)(h) or (h.1), and the requirement of subsection 8(10) ... are met.

9.   Among the other requirements to qualify for a deduction under paragraph 8(1)(f), subparagraph 8(1)(f)(iv) stipulates that the employee must not have been "in receipt of an allowance for travel expenses in respect of the taxation year that was, by virtue of subparagraph 6(1)(b)(v), not included in computing the taxpayer's income." This requirement, which is virtually identical to the requirements in subparagraphs 8(1)(h)(iii) and (h.1)(iii), is examined later in this chapter.

4. Travel in the Course of an Office or Employment

Where a taxpayer satisfies the various requirements in paragraphs 8(1)(h) and (h.1), these provisions authorize the deduction of "amounts expended by the taxpayer in the year ... for travelling in the course of the office or employment." One of the earliest cases to consider this language is *Luks v. M.N.R.*, [1958] C.T.C. 345, 58 D.T.C. 1194 (Ex. Ct.).

Luks v. M.N.R.
[1958] C.T.C. 345, 58 D.T.C. 1194 (Ex. Ct.)

THURLOW J: ... The appellant is an electrician and throughout the year in question he resided in the Township of North York. From January 1, 1954 to the end of June, 1954 he was employed by Eastern Electrical Construction Ltd. of Oshawa, for whom he worked on premises of General Motors at Oshawa in connection with the construction of a new building. ... Under the terms of a union contract governing the employment, the appellant was required to provide certain tools for use in his work. The list of tools so required was a lengthy one, and it is obvious that they would make a load that could not be conveniently carried without a vehicle of some sort. The appellant might have left them on the premises where he worked, but he would have done so at his own risk of loss, and no place to store them was provided. What he did was to carry them in his car which he used each day in travelling from his home to the place where he worked, a distance of 47 miles, and return. In June, 1954 he terminated this employment and secured employment on the same terms with Leslie Electric Co., an electrical contractor of Toronto. For this contractor the appellant worked on alterations to a building at Sunnyside, some 9½ miles from his home. This employment lasted until the end of August. From September 2 to December 8, 1954, the appellant was employed on the same terms by Standard Electric Co. of

Toronto, for whom he worked on the construction of a new building in Toronto, eight miles from his home. In each of these jobs, the appellant was paid at an hourly rate for the time during which he was engaged on the work, not including any of the time spent in travelling to or from his work.

...

In computing his income in his income tax return for 1954, the appellant deducted from the wages received in these employments $1,239.06 as travelling expenses incurred in travelling as above mentioned. The $1,239.06 was made up of $373.06 for gasoline, oil, repairs, and sundry automobile expenses, and $866 for capital cost allowance in respect of the automobile.

...

On his appeal to this Court, the appellant contended that because, under each of the contracts of employment, tools were "to be supplied" by the employee, the carrying of them to and from the place where he was employed was part of the duties of his employment and that he was entitled to deduct the travelling expenses and capital cost allowances so claimed under s-ss. (9) and (11) of s. 11 of the *Income Tax Act*, RSC 1952, c. 148 [now paragraphs 8(1)(h) and (h.1) and subparagraph 8(1)(j)(ii)].

...

It will be observed that under ss. (9), when the preliminary conditions for the application of the subsection are met what may be deducted is "amounts expended by the taxpayer in the year for travelling in the course of his employment." This raises the question whether any of the travelling expenses claimed by the appellant were "for travelling in the course of his employment."

In *Ricketts v. Colquhoun*, [1926] AC 1, the House of Lords considered the case of a London barrister who held the office of Recorder of Portsmouth and who had sought to deduct from the emoluments of that office his expenses of travelling several times each year from London to Portsmouth for the purpose of carrying out his duties as Recorder. He also sought to deduct the cost of transporting his robes of office as Recorder, which he required for the performance of the duties of that office. The section of the statute provided as follows:

> If the holder of an office or employment of profit is necessarily obliged to incur and defray out of the emoluments thereof the expenses of travelling in the performance of the duties of the office or employment, or of keeping and maintaining a horse to enable him to perform the same, or otherwise to expend money wholly, exclusively and necessarily in the performance of the said duties, there may be deducted from the emoluments to be assessed the expenses so necessarily incurred and defrayed.

With respect to the travelling expenses and the cost of conveying the robes, Viscount Cave said at p. 4:

> As regards the appellant's travelling expenses to and from Portsmouth ... , the material words of the rule are those which provide that, if the holder of an office is "necessarily obliged to incur ... the expenses of travelling in the performance of the duties of the office" the expenses so "necessarily incurred" may be deducted from the emoluments to be assessed.

The question is whether the travelling expenses in question fall within that description. Having given the best consideration that I can to the question, I agree with the Commissioners and with the Courts below in holding that they do not. In order that they may be deductible under this rule ... they must be expenses which the holder of an office is necessarily obliged to incur — that is to say, obliged by the very fact that he holds the office and has to perform its duties — and they must be incurred in — that is in the course of — the performance of those duties.

The expenses in question in this case do not appear to me to satisfy either test. They are incurred not because the appellant holds the office of Recorder of Portsmouth, but because, living and practising away from Portsmouth, he must travel to that place before he can begin to perform his duties as Recorder and, having concluded those duties, desires to return home. They are incurred, not in the course of performing his duties, but partly before he enters upon them, and partly after he has fulfilled them.

...

In the present case, travelling between the appellant's home and the several places where he was employed was not part of the duties of his employment, nor was it any part of the duties of his employment to take his tools from the place of employment to his home each day, nor to carry them each day from his home to the place of employment. This may well have been the practical thing for him to do in the circumstances, but the fact that it was a practical thing to do does not make it part of the duties of his employment. Both travelling from his home to the place of employment and carrying his tools from his home to the place of employment were things done before entering upon such duties, and both travelling home and carrying his tools home at the close of the day were things done after the duties of the employment for the day had been performed. The journeys were not made for the employer's benefit, nor were they made on the employer's behalf or at his direction, nor had the employer any control over the appellant when he was making them. The utmost that can be said of them is that they were made in consequence of the appellant's employment. That is not sufficient for the present purpose. In my opinion, neither the appellant's travelling nor the carrying of his tools was "travelling in the course of his employment" within the meaning of s. 11(9). It follows that the claim for the deduction of $1,239.06 for travelling expenses cannot be sustained and that it was properly disallowed. ...

Judgment accordingly.

NOTES AND QUESTIONS

1.   On what basis did the taxpayer in *Luks* contend that the cost of travelling to work sites in Oshawa, Sunnyside, and Toronto were deductible in computing his employment income? Why did the court reject this argument? Do you agree with the court's conclusion that the travelling expenses were incurred before and after the duties of the taxpayer's employment were performed, and not in the course of the taxpayer's employment? Why or why not?

2.   What, if any, reliance should the court in *Luks* have placed on the decision in *Ricketts v. Colquhoun*, [1926] A.C. 1 (H.L.)? Of what, if any, relevance to the

deductibility of these kinds of expenses is the preamble to subsection 8(1)? The preamble states:

> In computing a taxpayer's income for a taxation year from an office or employment, there may be deducted such of the following amounts as are wholly applicable to that source or such part of the following amounts as may reasonably be regarded as applicable thereto.

3.   In *Canada v. Diemert*, [1976] F.C.J. No. 77, [1976] C.T.C. 301, 76 D.T.C. 6187 (F.C.T.D.), the taxpayer, a locomotive engineer who lived in Regina, sought to deduct the cost of travelling to Assiniboia, where he reported to work and from where he made trips to other locations. Concluding that the taxpayer's employment duties commenced in Assiniboia, not Regina, the court dismissed the taxpayer's appeal from an assessment disallowing the deduction on the basis that the travel expenses were not incurred "in the course of [the taxpayer's] employment."

4.   For other cases in which courts have disallowed the deduction of expenses incurred by employees to travel between their home and their place of employment on the grounds that the expenses were not incurred "in the course of their employment," see *Martyn v. M.N.R.* (1962), 29 Tax ABC 305; *M.N.R. v. Pelletier*, [1963] C.T.C. 64, 63 D.T.C. 1059 (Ex. Ct.); *Madsen v. M.N.R.*, [1970] Tax ABC 713; and *Misfud v. M.N.R.*, [1978] C.T.C. 2537, 78 D.T.C. 1408 (T.R.B.); *Canada v. Wright*, [1981] C.T.C. 14, 81 D.T.C. 5004 (F.C.T.D.); and *Andrews v. M.N.R.*, [1987] 2 C.T.C. 2046, 87 D.T.C. 410 (T.C.C.).

5.   In *Chrapko v. Canada*, [1988] F.C.J. No. 908, [1988] 2 C.T.C. 342, 88 D.T.C. 6487 (F.C.A.), the taxpayer, who was employed as a parimutuel teller by the Ontario Jockey Club, sought to deduct the automobile expenses incurred in travelling from his home in Niagara Falls to each of three racetracks where he worked — Woodbine and Greenwood in Toronto and Fort Erie in Fort Erie, Ontario. Although disallowing the deduction of expenses incurred to travel to Toronto, where he worked 75 per cent of the time, the court allowed the deduction of expenses incurred to travel to Fort Erie on the grounds (at para. 6) that paragraph 8(1)(h) applies to expenses incurred "in travelling to a place of work away from the places at which [the taxpayer] usually worked, namely, Woodbine and Greenwood in Toronto."

Do you agree with this decision? Why or why not? Is the conclusion in *Chrapko* consistent with the decisions in *Luks v. M.N.R.*, [1958] C.T.C. 345, 58 D.T.C. 1194 (Ex. Ct.) and *Canada v. Diemert*, [1976] C.T.C. 301, 76 D.T.C. 6187 (F.C.T.D.)?

6.   In *M.N.R. v. Merten*, [1990] F.C.J. No. 924, [1990] 2 C.T.C. 444, 90 D.T.C. 6600 (F.C.T.D.), the taxpayer, who was employed as a project manager for an electrical contractor with a permanent office on 11th Avenue SW in Calgary, sought to deduct automobile expenses incurred to travel to different work sites in the Calgary area to which he frequently travelled directly from home before attending the employer's permanent office and from which he often returned directly home at the end of the day. Rejecting the Minister's argument

that the trips to and from home were not incurred "in the course of the [taxpayer's] employment," the court allowed the deduction of all travel expenses claimed by the taxpayer on the grounds (at para. 9) that the Federal Court of Appeal decision in *Chrapko* had "qualified" these words "by recognizing that a taxpayer can deduct expenses for travelling from his home to a place of work as long as that place of work is other than the place at which he 'usually' works." On this basis, Strayer J (as he then was) explained (at para. 9) "the *Luks* rationale can no longer be applied so as to preclude all deductibility where the travelling itself is not the performance of a service for the employer."

7.   *Chrapko* and *Merten* were applied in *Royer v. Canada*, [1999] T.C.J. No. 111, [2000] 1 C.T.C. 2688, 99 D.T.C. 683 (T.C.C.), to allow the deduction of automobile expenses incurred by the taxpayer, a heavy equipment operator, to travel from home to different railway yards at which he was required to carry on his duties.

8.   In *Evans v. Canada*, [1998] T.C.J. No. 1055, [1999] 1 C.T.C. 2609, 99 D.T.C. 168 (T.C.C.), the taxpayer, a school psychologist for the Calgary Board of Education who was required to travel to various schools in order to carry out her duties, sought to deduct automobile expenses incurred to travel in excess of an allowance paid by her employer that covered the costs of travel between schools but not between her residence and the first and last schools that she visited each day. Rejecting the Minister's argument that these amounts were personal expenses that were not incurred "for travelling in the course of [her] employment," the court concluded that the expenses related to duties that the taxpayer was required to carry on away from the employer's administrative office and in different places. According to Porter DJTC (at paras. 35-38):

> To the extent that the Appellant had to travel to or from schools which were further away than the administrative office at Parkdale, it would seem manifestly unfair that she should not be able to claim expenses for the additional distance either from the school board as a non taxable allowance under paragraph 6(1)(b)(vii.1) or as a claim against her employment income under paragraph 8(1)(h.1). These were clearly expenses incurred in the performance of her duties and simply because she did not attend at the administrative office first should not mean that she is not entitled to claim them.
>
> If the Appellant had simply to get herself between her residence and the various schools where she started and finished her days, it would seem to me that her travel expenses would properly be limited to the cost of such travel less the amount that she would have expended to travel on a daily basis to and from the administrative centre. In the normal course of events, her cost of travel between her residence and the administrative centre would be considered personal in nature. It is only the excess that she should be able to claim. Thus, if for example in a day she travelled 20 kilometres to the first school, 30 kilometres throughout the day up to the last school and 15 kilometres from the last school to home, and if the distance between her residence and the administrative centre was say 10 kilometres, she would in this scenario be entitled to claim the total of the 20 kilometres and the 15 kilometres, namely 35 kilometres (the total between the first and last schools and her residence) minus the 20 kilometres that she would normally have travelled going to work if she had gone first to the administrative centre. Thus, she would be able to claim the expenses for 15 kilometres for that day against her employment income and of course she would be

reimbursed by the employer for the 30 kilometers that she travelled between the various schools.

However, it seems to me that there is a further wrinkle in this particular case as it relates to the requirement to transport the voluminous amount of paper and materials around to her various work places requiring the exclusive use of the trunk of her car on a permanent basis throughout the school year. In my opinion, she had no alternative as part of her duties but to transport these back and forth between her residence and the first and last schools she visited on a daily basis. I have no hesitation in finding that it was an implied term of the contract not only that she had to have a car available to transport herself around, but also that she had to have all these materials on hand in order to carry out her duties. There was no other practical way in which she could do this but to take them back and forth to her residence. The situation seems to me to be no different in principle from that in the *Hoedel* case (above), involving the police officer who had to transport his police dog back and forth to his residence. As in that case, the Appellant was required to keep the materials in question with her at all times and to have them available at each of her appointments, including the first of the day. The evidence was clear that she could transport them in no other way, nor could she physically load and unload them on a daily basis.

I find therefore that the cost of transportation by automobile of the materials back and forth at the start and close of each day, was a necessary expense incurred in the performance of her duties.

Do you agree with this result? Why or why not? Is the court's conclusion consistent with the decision in *Luks*? Is it consistent with the decisions in *Chrapko*, *Merten*, and *Royer*?

9.   In *Hogg v. Canada*, [2002] F.C.J No. 704, [2002] 3 C.T.C. 177, 2002 D.T.C. 7037 (F.C.A.), the taxpayer, a judge in provincial court who was assigned to a base court and received a non-taxable vehicle allowance and was paid on a per kilometre basis for travel in excess of 15 kilometres when his duties required him to be away from his base court, sought to deduct motor vehicle expenses incurred in driving from his home to the base court and back home again at the end of the day on the basis that he was obliged to drive to the courthouse "by reason of security concerns". Concluding (at para. 13) that deductible motor vehicle expenses must have been incurred by the taxpayer "while performing the duties of his office", the Court disallowed the deduction on the basis (at para. 15) that the taxpayer's security concerns were "irrelevant with respect to whether or not [the taxpayer] is entitled to a deduction under paragraph 8(1)(h.1) of the Act." Do you agree with this conclusion? Why or why not?

10.   In *Toutov v. Canada*, [2006] T.C.J. No. 134, [2006] 3 C.T.C. 2275, 2006 D.T.C. 2928 (T.C.C.), the taxpayer was allowed to deduct expenses of traveling between his home office in Kingston and the offices of his employer's clients in Carleton Place, Ottawa, and other cities. Bowman CJTC held that while the costs of traveling from home to work are generally non-deductible personal expenses, an exception was warranted in the circumstances because (at para. 4),

The appellant's real base of operations is the office in his home, where he has equipment (including, at times, six computers). He travels to Carleton Place where he meets clients but he has no office there ... It is I think a fair conclusion on the evidence that his office in

Kingston is an extension of Oracle's place of business and Mr. Toutov's principal place of employment.

B. Meals

Although the *Income Tax Act* does not define the "travelling" expenses that may be deducted in paragraph 8(1)(h), it is generally accepted that these expenses include costs of transportation, accommodation, and meals that are consumed during the period of travel. Under subsection 8(4), however, taxpayers who seek to deduct the cost of meals as travelling expenses under paragraph 8(1)(h) or under the general deduction for salespersons in paragraph 8(1)(f) must satisfy a further requirement that:

> the meal was consumed during a period while the taxpayer was required by the taxpayer's duties to be away, for a period of not less than twelve hours, from the municipality where the employer's establishment to which the taxpayer ordinarily reported for work was located and away from the metropolitan area, if there is one, where it is located.

The leading case on the interpretation of subsection 8(4) is *Healy v. Canada*, [1979] C.T.C. 44, 79 D.T.C. 5060 (F.C.A.).

Healy v. Canada
[1979] C.T.C. 44, 79 D.T.C. 5060 (F.C.A.)

URIE J (MacKay DJ and Heald J concurring): ... The appellant at all material time resided in the Municipality of Metropolitan Toronto and was employed by the Ontario Jockey Club ... in the pari-mutuel operations of his employer. ...

The Ontario Jockey Club's head office ... is located in Rexdale, a part of the Municipality of Metropolitan Toronto. It operates six race tracks, including two in Metropolitan Toronto, namely, Woodbine and Greenwood and one at Fort Erie, Ontario, a municipality approximately 100 miles from Metropolitan Toronto. ... The appellant was assigned by the Club to work at different times in the year at each of the three tracks. In 1973, he worked at Fort Erie from April 15 to May 13 and from July 18 to September 1. While at Fort Erie he lived in a motel. He received no allowance or reimbursement from the Club for his travelling expenses to and from Fort Erie nor for the cost of accommodation and meal expenses incurred while he was in Fort Erie.

For the 1973 taxation year, the appellant deducted from his income the costs of transportation, accommodation and meals, incurred by him while he worked at Fort Erie. His claim for deduction of his transportation and accommodation expenses under paragraph 8(1)(h) of the *Income Tax Act* was allowed by the Minister of National Revenue, but his claim for the deduction of $504.00 for meal expenses was disallowed as not falling within the exception in subsection 8(4) of the Act. The quantum of the meal expense incurred was not disputed. The Tax Review Board sustained the appellant's appeal but the Trial Division reversed this decision and restored the assessment. It is from that judgment that this appeal is brought.

One of the other facts which should be mentioned is that while the Club has the right to determine where and when the employees ... will work from time to time, a list... is posted ... at each of the tracks to inform the employees of their work assignments. The evidence also discloses that the employees' salaries are paid from the Club's head office in Toronto and are delivered by courier to the employees at whichever track they may be working. Disciplinary matters are handled initially at the tracks but final disposition of such matters is the responsibility of a senior officer at head office.

...

The learned trial judge, after reviewing the evidence and ascertaining the dictionary meaning of "ordinarily" made the following finding:

> In the view I have of the facts, it was a matter of regular occurrence, normal and not exceptional for the defendant to carry out his duties during the racing season as required by his employer at at least two, if not three, different places, that is to say, at Toronto and at Fort Erie or at the Greenwood, Woodbine and Fort Erie racetracks. I conclude, therefore, that the defendant's situation fell within the meaning of paragraph 8(1)(h) and that he was entitled to a deduction in respect of his expenses of travelling in the course of his employment. Moreover such expenses would, I think, ordinarily include, but for the effect of subsection 8(4), the cost of his meals while at Fort Erie in the course of his duties.
>
> In subsection 8(4), the word "ordinarily" is part of the phrase "where the employer's establishment to which he ordinarily reported for work was located." In this context it modifies the expression "reported for work" and has the effect of narrowing what the phrase would include if the word were not there. The expression "reported for work" itself refers, I think, to the daily attendance by an employee for work. To give the word "ordinarily" its meaning, it appears to me to be necessary to conceive of and identify the establishment of the employer to which the employee "as a matter of regular occurrence," "usually" or "normally" reported for work.
>
> When this has been done, the wording of the subsection makes it necessary to go a step further and ascertain the municipality in which that establishment is located.
>
> In the present case there were, in my view, not one but three establishments of the Jockey Club to which the defendant in the course of the racing season usually, normally and as a matter of regular occurrence reported for work, that is to say, the Woodbine, Greenwood and Fort Erie racetracks, depending in each case, on the race meetings being held and the track to which the defendant was assigned. On the facts I am unable to see any valid basis for distinguishing, for present purposes, any one of the three tracks from the others and I am unable to reach the conclusion that any one of them alone was or that any two of them together were the establishment where the defendant ordinarily reported for work to the exclusion of the other or others.

I agree with the learned trial judge ... that the appellant falls squarely within the provisions of paragraph 8(1)(h) and was thus entitled to deduct his travelling expenses. However, with great deference, I disagree with his conclusion that subsection 8(4) precludes the appellant from deducting the cost of his meals while at Fort Erie in the course of his duties.

On the evidence, it is clear that:

(a)   the head office of the Club (the employer), in 1973 and at the time of trial, was in the Municipality of Metropolitan Toronto;

(b)   the employer from that head office assigned the employment schedules of its employees, disciplined them and paid them;

(c)   the appellant, who resided in the Municipality of Metropolitan Toronto, having been assigned his employment schedule by his employer, the Club, in 1973 worked approximately two-thirds of his working time in establishments operated by the Club in the Municipality of Metropolitan Toronto;

(d)   when the appellant worked at the Club's establishment in Fort Erie he was entitled to deduct his accommodation and travelling expenses pursuant to paragraph 8(1)(h) of the Act since he was ordinarily required to carry on the duties of his employment in different places.

From all of the above, it logically follows, in my view, that clearly the municipality in which the appellant usually worked was the Municipality of Metropolitan Toronto. In that municipality, the employer had two establishments to which the appellant usually reported for work, depending upon which of the two was operating at the relevant time. In 1973 that usual reporting was interrupted while he worked in another of the employer's establishments outside of Toronto, at Fort Erie, as part of his duties, for a period representing approximately one-third of his working time in that year. That, as I see it, was not "the municipality where the employer's establishment to which he ordinarily reported for work" was located. It was simply one of the "different places" at which he was required to work by virtue of the nature of his employment. On the facts of this case, it seems to me that, indisputably, the Municipality of Metropolitan Toronto was the municipality in which was located the establishments to which the appellant usually or commonly reported for work.

The question thus becomes — does that view of the appellant's employment situation in 1973 bring him within subsection 8(4) for the purpose of deduction of his meal expenses in the computation of his taxable income? I believe that it does. The Shorter Oxford English Dictionary defines "Ordinarily," *inter alia*, as

in most cases, usually, commonly.

Substituting, then, the word "ordinarily" for the expressions "commonly" and "usually" which are used in the analysis of the appellant's employment situation in the immediately preceding paragraphs, clearly leads to the conclusion that the appellant qualifies for the meal expense deduction unless the fact that there are two establishments in this base employment municipality affects the result. In my opinion, it ought not to. On any logical view of it, the purpose of the section is to first find the municipality where an employee usually reports for work and then to find whether or not he is entitled to meal expense deduction for having, in the course of his employment, to be away from that municipality for more than twelve hours. On that view of the section, it matters not whether there is only one or there are several establishments in the "base" municipality.

...

Where the learned trial judge erred, I respectfully suggest, was in finding that:

> In subsection 8(4), the word "ordinarily" is part of the phrase "where the employer's establishment to which he ordinarily reported for work was located." In this context it modifies the expression "reported for work" and has the effect of narrowing what the phrase would include if the word were not there. The expression "reported for work" itself refers, I think, to the daily attendance by an employee for work.

I think, on the contrary, that the expression "reported for work" when used with the word "ordinarily" applying the dictionary meaning of it, refers to the reporting in a larger sense, not a narrower one, namely, "in most cases" or as a general rule. To so interpret the words is consonant with what I think is necessary for the interpretation of subsection 8(4) which is to read it together with paragraph 8(1)(h).

The objective of paragraph 8(1)(h) is to enable employees who are required by their employment to work from time to time away from the places at which they usually work, to deduct their out-of-pocket expenses in so doing. Subsection 8(4) is designed to prevent abuses in the application of paragraph 8(1)(h) but not to prevent the legitimate deduction of expenses properly incurred while working at different places. As I see it, the rather restrictive interpretation adopted by the trial judge would unfairly detract from the overall objective of the sections. ...

Appeal allowed.

NOTES AND QUESTIONS

1.   On what basis did the trial judge conclude in *Healy* that the taxpayer could not deduct the meal expenses that he incurred during the periods while he was assigned to the race track in Fort Erie? Why did the Federal Court of Appeal allow the taxpayer's appeal?

2.   In *Healy*, how did the Federal Court of Appeal define the word "ordinarily" for the purpose of subsection 8(4)? Is this definition consistent with the court's subsequent interpretation in *Canada v. Tremblay*, [1997] F.C.J. No. 1642, 98 D.T.C. 6008 (F.C.A), of the word "ordinarily" in the context of subparagraphs 8(1)(h)(i) and (h.1)(i)? How, if at all, does the phrase "ordinarily reported for work" in subsection 8(4) differ from the expression "ordinarily required to carry on the duties of the office or employment" in subparagraphs 8(1)(h)(i) and (h.1)(i)?

3.   Of what, if any, relevance to the decision in *Healy* was the court's emphasis on the "overall objective" of paragraph 8(1)(h) and subsection 8(4)? Would the court have reached the same conclusion if it had applied a strict approach to the interpretation of these provisions?

4.   For the CRA's views on subsection 8(4), see paragraphs 55 to 57 of IT-522R. According to paragraph 56 of this bulletin:

The employer's establishment referred to in subsection 8(4) is the one to which the employee ordinarily reports for work. It includes an employer's place of business ... and may also include any place where the employer is carrying out a contract. Where the employer has more than one place of business to which an employee ordinarily reports on a continuing basis, the establishment referred to in subsection 8(4) is the one to which the employee reports most frequently. Where more than one of the employer's places of business is located within the same municipality or metropolitan area, all such places of business will be viewed as a single establishment for the purpose of subsection 8(4).

C. Legal Expenses

According to paragraph 8(1)(b), taxpayers may deduct "amounts paid by the taxpayer in the year as or on account of legal expenses incurred by the taxpayer to collect or establish a right to salary or wages owed to the taxpayer by the employer or former employer of the taxpayer." Until 1990, this deduction was limited to legal expenses incurred "in collecting" salary or wages owed by an employer or former employer, making it impossible for taxpayers to deduct legal expenses incurred in order to establish a right to the payment of salary or wages.[61] One of the first cases to examine the amended language in paragraph 8(1)(b) was *Werle v. The Queen*, [1995] 1 C.T.C. 2336 (T.C.C.).

Werle v. The Queen
[1995] 1 C.T.C. 2236 (T.C.C.)

BEAUBIER JTCC: ... The issue before the Court is whether the appellant is entitled to deduct legal fees he paid in 1992 on account of a law suit he brought against SaskEnergy for wrongful dismissal and for nine months' wages he claimed they contracted to pay to him in the event of dismissal. The dismissal occurred in March 1991. The appellant lost his law suit and paid legal fees of $30,928 in 1992. His claim to deduct this sum was not allowed. He appealed.

Paragraph 8(1)(b) of the *Income Tax Act* ... provides for the deduction claimed.

...

In particular respecting this matter, the words in (b) "... to establish aright to ..." were added by an amendment which was effective after 1989. It is these words which create the issue in this matter.

...

The amendment to the *Income Tax Act* in question appears to add two principles to the subsection in question. The first is that the legal fees in question may be for the purpose of establishing a right; in other words the litigation does

---

[61] See *Lyonde v. M.N.R.*, [1988] 2 C.T.C. 2032, 88 D.T.C. 1397 (T.C.C.) and *Côté v. M.N.R.*, [1989] 2 C.T.C. 2218, 89 D.T.C. 508 (T.C.C.), rev'd on other grounds [1998] F.C.J. No. 1824, [1999] 2 C.T.C. 270, 99 D.T.C. 5215 (F.C.T.D.).

not have to be successful. The second principle is that the "right" which may be litigated is a claim to an entitlement to salary or wages. Thus, whereas formerly the subsection merely allowed a taxpayer to deduct fees incurred to collect salary or wages, the amendment enables a taxpayer to deduct fees incurred to establish an entitlement to salary or wages which he or she can then collect.

Based upon the amendment to subsection 8(1), the Court finds that the appellant is entitled to deduct the legal fees incurred on account of his claim that he had a contract of employment which entitled him to nine months' wages in the event of dismissal. But the deduction is limited to the fees incurred in respect to this issue alone. It does not include the fees incurred in respect to a claim for wrongful dismissal and damages arising from that.

There is no evidence before the Court as to what portion of the legal fees related to each aspect of the unsuccessful law suit. The responsibility for this failure lies with both the appellant and the respondent, neither of whom brought these details out in evidence. The only evidence is that two issues were litigated. The result is that the Court finds that one-half of the legal fees incurred, namely $15,464, were incurred by the appellant in litigation, the purpose of which was to establish a right to the nine months' salary or wages owed to the taxpayer by his former employer.

This matter is referred to the Minister of National Revenue for reconsideration and reassessment on the foregoing basis. ...

Appeal allowed.

NOTES AND QUESTIONS

1.   On what basis did the court allow the taxpayer in *Werle* to deduct a portion of the legal expenses he paid in 1992? Do you agree with the court's interpretation that "the litigation does not have to be successful" in order for legal expenses to qualify for the deduction in paragraph 8(1)(b)? Why or why not? Should the deduction be available for legal expenses incurred in frivolous actions? Might the reasonableness limitation in section 67 be applied to limit the deduction of legal expenses in these circumstances?

CRA's position on this issue is set out in paragraph 23 of IT-99R5:

A deduction under paragraph 8(1)(b) is allowed only in respect of an amount "owed" by an employer or a former employer. If the taxpayer is not successful in court or otherwise fails to establish that some amount is owed, no deduction for expenses is allowed. However, failure to collect an amount established as owed to the taxpayer does not preclude a deduction under this paragraph.

2.   Why did the court in *Werle* disallow the deduction of a portion of the legal expenses incurred by the taxpayer? Do you agree with the court's approach to the allocation of the taxpayer's legal expenses?

3.   For other cases in which legal expenses incurred to secure damages or out-of-court settlements for wrongful dismissal have been held to be non-deductible under paragraph 8(1)(b), see *Maruscak v. M.N.R.*, [1985] 2 C.T.C. 2048, 85 D.T.C. 426 (T.C.C.) and *MacDonald v. M.N.R.*, [1990] 2 C.T.C. 2269, 90

D.T.C. 1751 (T.C.C.). For 1986 and subsequent taxation years, legal expenses incurred in order to collect or establish a right to damages following the termination of a taxpayer's office or employment are deductible under clause 60(o.1)(i)(B). This provision is examined in Chapter 7.

4.   In *Bongiovanni v. Canada*, [2000] T.C.J. No. 725, [2001] 1 C.T.C. 2186 (T.C.C.), the taxpayer incurred approximately $3,500 in legal expenses in order to obtain workers' compensation payments totalling $34,521. Accepting the Minister's argument that the expenses were not incurred to collect or establish a right to "salary or wages," the court disallowed the deduction.

For a similar result, involving legal expenses incurred to obtain compensation from the Quebec Commission de la santé et de la sécurité du travail ("CSST"), see *Marchand v. Canada*, [1995] 2 C.T.C. 2764 (T.C.C.).

5.   Where a taxpayer incurs legal expenses in order to obtain periodic benefits under a "wage loss replacement plan," these benefits are included in computing the taxpayer's income from an office or employment under paragraph 6(1)(f) and therefore constitute "salary or wages" according to the definition in subsection 248(1). According to the CRA, however, since these benefits are "generally received from an insurer" and not the "employer or former employer" referred to in paragraph 8(1)(b), these legal expenses cannot be deducted under this provision. See *Interpretation Bulletin* IT-99R5 "Legal and Accounting Fees," December 14, 2000, paragraph 24. Nor do these legal expenses appear to be deductible under paragraph 60(o) or (o.1), which permit the deduction of other legal expenses.

The Department of Finance has proposed to amend paragraph 8(1)(b) to permit the deduction of all "amounts paid by the taxpayer in the year as or on account of legal expenses incurred by the taxpayer to collect, or to establish a right to, an amount owed to the taxpayer that, if received by the taxpayer, would be required by this subdivision to be included in computing the taxpayer's income" (Former Bill C-10, *Income Tax Amendments Act, 2006*, Part 2, Technical Amendments, cl. 50(1)). The amendment aims to widen the scope of the current provision by allowing the deduction of legal expenses incurred in securing amounts owed to the taxpayer by parties other than the taxpayer's employer, that would otherwise be taxable as employment income. According to the Explanatory Notes accompanying the Bill:

> Concern has been expressed that where an amount is not owed to the employee directly by the employer, any legal expenses incurred by the taxpayer would not be deductible under paragraph 8(1)(b), even though the amount, when received, would be taxable as employment income. This would be the case, for example, with respect to legal fees incurred by a taxpayer to collect insurance benefits under a sickness or accident insurance policy provided through an employer.

Bill C-10 was passed by the House of Commons and received second reading in the Senate on December 4, 2007, but ceased to exist when the 2nd Session of the 39th Parliament was dissolved and an election was called for October 14, 2008. At the time of writing its provisions had not yet been reintroduced in a new Bill.

6.   In *L'Écuyer v. Canada*, [1994] T.C.J. No. 598, 95 D.T.C. 241 (T.C.C.), the taxpayer, who had been appointed to a provincial board the members of which were appointed for an indefinite period, incurred legal expenses in order to protect this right after he and other members of the board were informed that the appointment order had been amended to include a specified term. Emphasizing (at para. 16) that the deduction in paragraph 8(1)(b) is limited to legal expenses incurred by a taxpayer to collect or establish a right to salary or wages already "owed" to a taxpayer, "and not to establish future rights to salary or wages," the court disallowed the deduction. Do you agree with this interpretation? Why or why not?

In *Turner-Lienaux v. Canada*, [1996] T.C.J. No. 943, [1996] 3 C.T.C. 2810, 97 D.T.C. 261 (T.C.C.), aff'd [1997] F.C.J. No. 562, [1997] 2 C.T.C. 344, 97 D.T.C. 5294 (F.C.A.), the taxpayer, who was employed as a laboratory technologist at the Victoria General Hospital in Halifax, sought to deduct legal expenses incurred to challenge the results of a competition for a promotion that would have paid a higher salary than that which she received without the promotion. Citing *L'Écuyer* for the proposition (at para. 19) that "where a person sues for future wages or a right to future salary, those deductions are not available" under paragraph 8(1)(b), the court disallowed the deduction. According to Margeson JTCC (at paras. 36-37):

> This Court has some difficulty in concluding that a person is "owed" a salary or "wages" if he did not do the work or occupy the position that required the salary or wages to be paid. Further it has difficulty in concluding that a person could be found to have incurred legal expenses to establish a right to salary or wages when two Courts of competent jurisdiction actually found that the Appellant did not have the "right" that she was seeking to enforce by the legal action.

> There can be no doubt that the Appellant was not seeking to collect wages owed.

See also *Jazairi v. Canada*, [1999] T.C.J. No. 790, [2000] 1 C.T.C. 2300 (T.C.C.), aff'd [2001] F.C.J. No. 259, [2001] 2 C.T.C. 28, 2001 D.T.C. 5163 (F.C.A.) (denying a deduction for legal fees incurred by the taxpayer to pursue a human rights complaint after he was denied a promotion to full professor at York University were non-deductible); *Guenette v. Canada*, [2004] T.C.J. No. 81, [2004] 2 C.T.C. 2861, 2004 D.T.C. 2276 (T.C.C.) (denying a deduction for legal fees incurred by a federal civil servant who brought an action against his employer alleging harassment and abuse of authority); and *Cimolai v. Canada*, [2006] F.C.J. No. 1666, [2007] 1 C.T.C. 268, 2007 D.T.C. 5019 (F.C.A.) (denying a deduction for legal fees to pursue a defamation action against former colleagues after the taxpayer was suspended from his employment as a medical microbiologist with a hospital).

Do you agree with these results? Why or why not? Should the Act be amended to permit the deduction of legal expenses such as those incurred by these taxpayers?

7.   In *Loo v. Canada*, [2004] F.C.J. No. 1132, [2004] 3 C.T.C. 247, 2004 D.T.C. 6540 (F.C.A.), the taxpayer was one of several employees of the Federal

Department of Justice in British Columbia, who sued their employer, seeking the same salary as similarly classified employees in Toronto. Concluding that the taxpayer had incurred legal expenses in order to establish a right to the salary that he contended that he was owed as a legal right, the court allowed the deduction of these expenses. According to Sharlow JA (Létourneau and Malone JJA, concurring) at paras. 7-9:

> Paragraph 8(1)(b) has two branches. The first branch permits a deduction for legal expenses incurred in an action to collect salary or wages owed. It contemplates litigation resulting from the failure of an employer to pay the salary or wages due to an employee. In such a case, there may be no dispute as to the amount of salary or wages that the employee is entitled to be paid for the services the employee has performed, but there may be a factual dispute as to how much of the salary or wages remains unpaid.
>
> The second branch of paragraph 8(1)(b) contemplates a situation in which the matter in controversy is the legal entitlement to the salary claimed. The second branch applies if, for example, an individual incurs legal expenses in litigating a factual dispute as to whether he or she has actually performed the services required by the contract of employment, or a dispute as to the rate of salary payable for services performed. That would include, for example, a dispute as to the term and conditions of employment.
>
> It is common ground that in this case Mr. Loo has performed services for his employer, and that he has been paid some salary for those services. But he has been paid at the rate that his employer alleges is payable, not at the rate that Mr. Loo alleges is payable. The heart of the litigation is the dispute between Mr. Loo and his employer as to the terms and conditions of Mr. Loo's employment relating to the applicable salary. Mr. Loo's claim may or may not be well founded in law, and it may or may not succeed. But his claim, regardless of its merits, falls squarely within the words of paragraph 8(1)(b) because Mr. Loo is trying to establish by litigation that, for the services he has rendered to his employer, the law requires that he be paid more than he has been paid. It follows that Mr. Loo is entitled to deduct the legal fees he has claimed.
>
> The facts in this case are unlike the facts in *Jazairi* [*supra*]. In that case, legal fees were held not to be deductible if they were incurred to establish a right to a promotion which commanded a higher salary. The essence of the claim of the applicant in that case was that he should have been moved to a higher level in his professional hierarchy.

8. In *Blagdon v. Canada*, [2002] T.C.J No. 79, [2002] 2 C.T.C. 2332, 2003 D.T.C. 804 (T.C.C.), aff'd [2003] F.C.J. No. 945, [2003] 4 C.T.C. 107, 2003 D.T.C. 5491 (F.C.A.), the taxpayer sought to deduct $6,249 in legal fees for representation at a Transport Canada inquiry held to consider allegations of incompetence arising from an explosion on an oil tanker in 1997 of which he was the captain. Although expressing sympathy with the taxpayer, the Court disallowed the deduction on the basis that the legal expenses were not incurred in order to "collect or establish a right to salary or wages owed to the taxpayer" as required by paragraph 8(1)(b). Although disallowing the taxpayer's appeal, the Federal Court of Appeal nonetheless suggested (at para. 4) that "a broad entitlement to a deduction for legal expenses for persons in the situation of Captain Blagdon might be justified on policy grounds but that is a matter for Parliament not the courts."

9. In *Wilson v. Canada*, [1990] F.C.J. No. 230, [1990] 2 C.T.C. 169, 90 D.T.C. 6382 (F.C.T.D.), aff'd [1991] F.C.J. No. 528, [1991] 2 C.T.C. 69, 91

D.T.C. 5407 (F.C.A.), the taxpayer, a teacher who was charged with a criminal offence and dismissed from his position, sought to deduct legal expenses incurred to defend the criminal charge in computing his employment income for 1983. Emphasizing (at para. 5) that "[b]y no stretch of the imagination ... can legal expenditures made in defending a charge of rape and a charge of unlawful confinement be considered as expenses for the purpose of collecting salaries or wages owed to the [taxpayer] by the school board," the court disallowed the deduction.

For other cases in which taxpayers have unsuccessfully sought to deduct legal expenses incurred to defend against criminal proceedings under paragraph 8(1)(b), see *De Verteuil v. Canada*, [1993] 1 C.T.C. 2669 (T.C.C.) and *Young v. The Queen*, [1997] 1 C.T.C. 2634 (T.C.C.).

10.   Where a taxpayer receives an award or reimbursement in respect of legal expenses that are deductible under paragraph 8(1)(b), the amount of the award or reimbursement must be included in computing the taxpayer's income from an office or employment under paragraph 6(1)(j), except to the extent that it was otherwise so included or taken into account in computing the deduction claimed under paragraph 8(1)(b).

D. Professional Membership Dues

According to subparagraph 8(1)(i)(i), taxpayers may in computing their income from an office or employment deduct "annual professional membership dues the payment of which was necessary to maintain a professional status recognized by statute" to the extent that they have not been reimbursed and are not entitled to be reimbursed in respect thereof. One of the leading cases on the application of this provision is *M.N.R. v. Montgomery*, [1970] C.T.C. 115, 70 D.T.C. 6080 (Ex. Ct.).

M.N.R. v. Montgomery
[1970] C.T.C. 115, 70 D.T.C. 6080 (Ex. Ct.)

KERR J: This is an appeal from a decision of the Tax Appeal Board with respect to an assessment of income tax for the respondent's 1966 taxation year.

In computing his income the respondent claimed a deduction of $43.30 which he had paid as "wardroom dues" (sometimes called "mess dues") as an officer in the Royal Canadian Naval Reserve (RCNR) at HMCS Tecumseh, which is a unit or ship of the Royal Canadian Navy at Calgary. He claimed the deduction as "annual professional dues" under Section 11(10)(a) [now subparagraph 8(1)(i)(i)] of the *Income Tax Act* ... .

The appellant disallowed the deduction, and the respondent then appealed to the Tax Appeal Board, which allowed the appeal.

In this appeal the appellant says that the payment of the wardroom dues did not constitute the payment of annual professional membership dues within the meaning of Section 11(10)(a) of the Act, and that the payment was not necessary to maintain a professional status recognized by statute ... . The respondent says that in addition to being a barrister practising law in Calgary he was an officer of the Royal Canadian Naval Reserve (RCNR) at HMCS Tecumseh during his 1966 taxation year and had to pay the wardroom dues, as such officer, in order to remain in the naval reserve and maintain his professional status as an officer in that Reserve.

The issue is whether Section 11(10)(a) includes the said wardroom dues.

...

There is no doubt that the Wardroom Mess of HMCS Tecumseh and its Wardroom Mess Rules (Exhibit R-1) were duly established under authority which flowed from the *National Defence Act*, the Queen's Regulations and Orders (QR & O, Exhibit R-3) and Canadian Forces Administrative Order (CFAO) 27-1 (Exhibit R-4).

...

Evidence was given by the respondent and LCDR Gwillim, RCNR, who has served, like the respondent, as Executive Officer of HMCS Tecumseh. They said they had never known or heard of a refusal by an officer to pay wardroom dues, and they thought that if an officer refused to pay his dues the procedure would be for the Executive Officer to first discuss the matter with the officer and, if refusal persisted, it would be regarded as a breach of discipline and the matter would be referred to the Commanding Officer who would have several courses open to him, such as asking the officer to resign, declaring him *persona non grata* and refusing permission for him to be on the ship, making an administrative deduction of the dues from his pay, charging him with conduct to the prejudice of good order and discipline under Section 118 of the *National Defence Act*, and forwarding to Headquarters at Ottawa a recommendation for his release from the service.

They also regarded the wardroom mess as an integral part of the ship or unit in the tradition of the naval service, a place where the officers meet socially, eat their meals, hold mess functions, have entertainments, discuss matters of interest in their line of duty and service, a place that encourages and promotes a camaraderie essential to the service. Necessary funds for the mess are raised in various ways. The mess dues are used along with other money, including profits, if any, from the bar, in the operation of the mess, which includes such things as buying furniture, making grants to Sea Cadet Corps, providing wreaths at commemorative services, and making presentations to officers on their departure from the ship.

...

The meaning of the word "profession" is now much wider than it formerly was.

...

I am satisfied that in Section 11(10)(a) the word "professional" is not used in its widest sense, nor yet in its former restricted sense of the learned professions of the Church, Medicine and Law. Its meaning lies somewhere between those extremes.

The subsection was enacted in a framework of circumstances so as to deal, income tax-wise, with a known state of affairs, and we must try to reach the common sense meaning of the subsection, taken as a whole, in the light of the circumstances with reference to which it was enacted and the object, appearing from those circumstances and the words used, which Parliament had in mind and intended. Parliament had in mind, I feel sure, the present day concept of organized societies and associations of doctors, dentists, lawyers, engineers, chartered accountants and other professional persons, which have been given a special status by statute and have the power to make regulations governing the issue of certificates and licences to practise the profession, examinations of candidates for membership and the right to practise, discipline of members, and a variety of other matters, including the regulation of the practice and the professional conduct of its members.

Counsel for the appellant submitted that a lawyer, for example, who is carrying on a general practice, does not need Section 11(10)(a) in order to deduct his Barristers Society's dues, for such dues may be deducted as a business expense of carrying on his practice; but that the lawyer who is employed and receives a salary under a contract of employment requires Section 11(10)(a) in order to deduct such dues, which are dues that each of the lawyers must pay in order to maintain his membership in the Society and the right to practise which goes with such membership.

I am satisfied that as an officer in the RCNR the respondent is a person with a "profession," that the status of an officer in the RCNR is a professional status recognized by statute, i.e. the *National Defence Act*, that the wardroom mess of HMCS Tecumseh is composed of RCNR officers, and that it was necessary for the respondent to pay his wardroom dues.

But it does not follow that those wardroom dues fall within Section 11(10)(a). It is my opinion that the necessity that Parliament was contemplating in that subsection is directly related to the essential purpose to be served by the payment of the professional membership dues. Inherent in the subsection is a direct relationship between membership in a professional society and professional status. The status recognized by statute is a professional status that is dependent upon membership in the professional society. No membership, no status. Such dues are no doubt used for the needs of the society, but the primary purpose of their payment is retention of membership, with its rights and privileges. It is clear to me that wardroom dues are paid for a very different purpose, namely, to defray operational costs of the mess, which is a room or suite where the members meet, eat, converse, entertain, etc. ... The purpose of the payment of wardroom dues is not, in my opinion, to maintain a professional status. The status of a navy officer does not call for membership in a mess, unlike the practice of medicine, for example, which calls for membership in a medical society established by statute.

Officers receive their commissions from the Crown. No dues are paid to obtain or maintain their commissions and officer status. My attention was not drawn to any specific recognition of a wardroom mess in a statute, and I scarcely think that the status of membership in a wardroom mess is a professional status recognized by statute.

The consequence of failure on the part of an officer to pay his wardroom dues conceivably might be loss of his status as an officer, and in that negative and limited sense it may be said that payment is necessary to maintain his status, but, in my opinion, that possibility is remote from what Parliament was contemplating and endeavouring to provide in the *Income Tax Act* when enacting Section 11(10)(a). If it were intended to include dues payable for operation of messes in the armed forces, it would have been easy to have said so expressly.

In my opinion, therefore, the wardroom dues in question are not deductible under Section 11(10)(a). ...

Appeal allowed.

NOTES AND QUESTIONS

1.   On what basis did the taxpayer in *Montgomery* argue that the wardroom dues were deductible under then paragraph 11(10)(a) (now subparagraph 8(1)(i)(i)) of the Act? Why did the court reject this argument? Of what, if any, relevance to the court's decision was its interpretation of Parliament's intent in enacting then paragraph 11(10)(a)? Do you agree with the court's conclusion? Why or why not?

2.   *Montgomery* was followed in *Boyer v. Canada* (September 7, 1995), Doc. No. 95-698(IT)I; [1995] CarswellNat 1720 (T.C.C.), in which the taxpayer, an officer in the armed forces, sought to deduct officers' mess subscription fees, which he was required to pay under the Queen's Regulations and Orders for the Canadian Forces (QR & O). Emphasizing (at para. 44) that the fees entitled the taxpayer "to frequent premises but not to obtain his commission," the court disallowed the deduction on the grounds that the dues were not necessary to maintain the taxpayer's professional status.

3.   In *Canada v. Swingle*, [1977] C.T.C. 448, 77 D.T.C. 5301 (F.C.T.D.), the taxpayer, a chemical analyst employed by various departments of the government of Canada, sought to deduct under subparagraph 8(1)(i)(i) annual dues paid to the Forensic Society, the American Chemical Society, the Chemical Society of Britain, and the Canadian Institute of Chemistry, which the Minister disallowed on the grounds that the dues were not "necessary to maintain a professional status recognized by statute." Rejecting the Minister's basic argument that *Montgomery* stands for the proposition that "the only deductible dues are those which have the effect of maintaining one's professional status and, at the same time, are the source of the right to carry on the practice of the particular profession," Collier J replied (at para. 32):

I can visualize situations where a profession is recognized by statute, but where no annual dues are required to be paid in order to carry on that profession; yet at the same time it may be "necessary" to belong to organizations in order to remain qualified, in the practical and business sense; to be able effectively to perform, and earn income, in a particular profession.

For example, I think it indisputable that accountancy is a profession; that an accountant is a "professional." A particular person may be a highly qualified and skilled accountant. That profession is, in British Columbia for example, recognized by statute: see the *Chartered Accountants Act*, RSBC 1960, c 51, and the *Certified General Accountants Act*, RSBC 1960, c 47. But one is not bound to be a member of the Institute of Chartered Accountants or of the Association of Certified General Accountants in order to practise the general profession of an accountant. An outsider is merely prevented from using the designation chartered accountant or certified general accountant. I can foresee, however, that a highly qualified and skilled accountant (in the general sense) may well find it necessary to pay annual dues to an appropriate professional organization in order to maintain his high qualifications and skills, and so be able to continue selling his services to others, including an employer.

Nonetheless, he concluded, because the taxpayer's professional status as a chemical analyst was not recognized by any statute, the membership dues were not deductible.

4.   *Swingle* was followed in *Addie v. M.N.R.*, [1980] C.T.C. 2647, 80 D.T.C. 1556 (T.R.B.), in which the taxpayer, a geological engineer employed by an engineering firm specializing in geology, sought to deduct an annual fee of $35 paid for membership in the Canadian Institute of Mining and Metallurgy. Although disallowing the deduction on the grounds that the fees were not required to maintain the taxpayer's professional status as an engineer, the board expressed its opinion that the dues ought to have been deductible, but for the authority of *Swingle*. According to Mr. Goetz (at para. 12):

The appellant is a fully qualified geologist and specializing in the metallurgical and mining fields, which terms are used in the *Engineering Profession Act* and to be qualified as a professional engineer, he must have one of these qualifications or others relating to other branches of engineering to be registered and licensed under the provisions of the *Engineering Profession Act*. The membership in the Canadian Institute of Mining and Metallurgy is, in my view, an off-shoot of the definition of "practice of professional engineering" in a specialized field and in order to specialize in that field, the appellant maintains and derives great benefits from his membership in the Canadian Institute of Mining and Metallurgy. I take the position that the definition of "practice of professional engineering" as a mining specialist in mining and metallurgy is included in the words of subparagraph 8(1)(i)(i). Certainly this would seem logical in light of the constant attempts by various professional societies to upgrade the qualifications of their membership. Some lawyers, for instance, belong to the Canadian Tax Foundation and, specializing in the taxation field, find that this is vital to their practice. Most lawyers in Canada are members of the Canadian Bar Association which issues various publications and has annual conventions and sectional meetings for the on-going education of its members. The membership dues in the Canadian Bar Association are deducted by all practicing lawyers, whether they be partners or employees of a legal law firm.

I feel that the only logical and reasonable interpretation of subparagraph 8(1)(i)(i) is that it recognizes all branches of practice of professional engineering and would therefore permit the inclusion of fees and dues paid by a professional engineer specializing in a particular field of engineering to maintain and upgrade his qualifications in that specialized field. Perhaps Parliament, through the Department of National Revenue, should and could give this question some consideration.

In *Gagne v. M.N.R.*, [1983] C.T.C. 2502, 83 D.T.C. 474 (T.R.B.), the board questioned the statement in *Addie*, that membership dues in the Canadian Bar Association are deductible by "all practicing lawyers, whether they be partners or employees of a legal law firm." See also *Lucas v. M.N.R.*, [1987] F.C.J. No. 502, [1987] 2 C.T.C. 23, 87 D.T.C. 5277 (F.C.T.D.), where the court stated (at para. 14) that:

> [m]embership fees payable to an association are not deductible if the taxpayer can maintain his professional status without paying them, for example, membership fees paid by a lawyer to the Canadian Bar Association are not deductible.

5. In *Jolicoeur v. Canada*, [1997] T.C.J. No. 1359, [1998] 3 C.T.C. 2069 (T.C.C.), the taxpayer, a dental surgeon employed at the Hématite Health Center in Fermont, Quebec, sought to deduct annual dues paid to the Health Center's council of physicians, dentists, and pharmacists (CPDP), which the Minister disallowed on the basis that this membership, unlike his membership in the Quebec Association of Dental Surgeons, was not necessary to maintain his professional status as a dentist. Referring to provisions of the Act respecting health services and social services that mandated the establishment of such councils and provided for the collection of mandatory dues, the court allowed the taxpayer's appeal on the grounds that the fees were "necessary to maintain a professional status recognized by statute" as "a dentist in an institution." Rejecting the Minister's argument that the deduction in subparagraph 8(1)(i)(i) was limited to annual dues paid to maintain the taxpayer's professional status as a dentist, Tardif TCJ declared (at para. 14):

> I do not think that the Act authorizes such a strict, conservative interpretation. Moreover, such an interpretation goes against the present-day reality where professional associations are much more numerous. We are living in an era of ultra-specialization in which even the traditional professions are now segmented into several fields of practice.
>
> Such a development requires the professionals within each group or segment to get organized and establish a structure for themselves for a great many reasons and purposes, including the defence of their interests, the very existence of their status, the definition of their respective fields of activity and their working conditions. These many changes have so transformed the practice and fields of activity of professionals generally that they must now organize themselves to deal with the many new realities that are often restricting and always highly regulated.
>
> The professional status that the respondent believes is described or covered by the Act is outdated. The wording of the Act does not have the strict meaning attributed to it by the respondent. The words used by Parliament in no way preclude the deduction of several dues payments. Parliament did not express its intention as follows: "to maintain his or her professional status." The words used do not have an exclusive or limited meaning, but refer simply and clearly to the position of a member of a professional group. The only limit or restriction is the existence of a very specific condition: the dues must be "necessary to maintain a professional status recognized by statute."
>
> According to the usual meaning of the words used, the interpretation advanced by the respondent cannot stand.

Do you agree with this interpretation? Why or why not? Is it consistent with the decisions in *Montgomery* and *Swingle*?

6.   In *Stewart v. M.N.R.*, [1982] C.T.C. 2746, 82 D.T.C. 1767 (T.R.B.), the taxpayer, who was employed as chief appraiser with the Department of National Revenue (Taxation) in Ottawa, sought in computing his employment income for his 1980 taxation year to deduct an annual membership fee of $150 paid to the Appraisal Institute of Canada. Citing *Swingle*, the board disallowed the deduction on the grounds that the taxpayer's professional status as an appraiser was not recognized by statute in the province of his residence (Ontario) nor by the government of Canada.

For identical results, involving appraisers in Ontario and other jurisdictions, see *Petrin v. M.N.R.*, [1990] F.C.J. No. 1070, [1991] 1 C.T.C. 94, [1990] 91 D.T.C. 5266 (F.C.T.D.); *Canada v. Mousseau*, [1994] F.C.J. No. 1753, [1995] 2 C.T.C. 431, 95 D.T.C. 5089 (F.C.T.D.); and *Laithwaite v. M.N.R.*, [1995] T.C.J. No. 863, [1995] 2 C.T.C. 2738 (T.C.C.).

7.   In *Montgomery v. M.N.R.*, [1995] T.C.J. No. 1627, [1996] 1 C.T.C. 2796 (T.C.C.), the court allowed the deduction of annual memberships fees paid by the taxpayer to the Appraisal Institute of Canada on the grounds that provisions of the BC *Expropriation Act*, S.B.C. 1987, c. 23, requiring an "appraisal report" to be prepared by a persons "accredited" by institutes including the Appraisal Institute, amounted to statutory recognition of the taxpayer's professional status as an appraiser. According to Bowman JTCC (at para. 15):

> The view ... expressed by Kerr J in *Montgomery* is that the expression "recognized by statute" ("reconnu par la loi") is confined only to statutes setting up self-governing professional bodies. This interpretation does not appear to be consistent with the approach to statutory interpretation enunciated by the Supreme Court of Canada in *Québec (Communauté urbaine) c. Corp Notre-Dame de Bon secours*, [1994] 3 SCR 3, [1995] 1 CTC 241, 95 DTC 5017, which was decided over 20 years after the decision in *Montgomery*. There is no reason why a professional status that is given statutory recognition by a provincial statute should not be sufficient to confer upon a person the right to deduct under paragraph 8(1)(i) fees paid to an organization so recognized. The plain wording of the BC statute and the regulation compels this conclusion. To deny the deduction is to put a judicial gloss on an obvious legislative intent and to impose a restriction unwarranted by the statutory language.

On appeal ([1997] F.C.J. No. 1343, [1998] 1 C.T.C. 58 (F.C.T.D.)), McGillis J disallowed the deduction on the grounds (at para. 8) that "a statutory provision requiring the preparation of an appraisal by a member of the Appraisal Institute of Canada does not constitute a recognition by statute of the professional status of that group; it merely indicates that a member of that group must perform the appraisal required by the statutory provision." According to the court (at para. 8):

> A profession only possesses "... a professional status recognized by statute," within the meaning of subparagraph 8(1)(i)(i) of the *Income Tax Act*, following the enactment of legislation permitting it to regulate its affairs in accordance with express rights, duties and powers. In 1988, there was no legislation anywhere in Canada permitting the self-regulation of the Appraisal Institute of Canada or any of its affiliated groups as a profession. As a result, in 1988, a real estate appraiser did not have "... a professional status recognized by statute," within the meaning of subparagraph 8(1)(i)(i) of the *Income Tax Act*. I note in passing that, in 1994, New Brunswick enacted legislation permitting the New Brunswick Association of Real Estate Appraisers to regulate its affairs.

On appeal yet again ([1999] F.C.J. No. 444, [1999] 2 C.T.C. 196, 99 D.T.C. 5186 (F.C.A.)), the deduction was allowed on the grounds that the BC *Expropriation Act* and other statutes cited on appeal recognized the professional status of appraisers by requiring appraisals to be prepared by appraisers designated by the Appraisal Institute of Canada. According to Rothstein JA (Desjardins and Sexton JJA concurring) (at paras. 11-15):

> For purposes of subparagraph 8(1)(i)(i), the British Columbia and Alberta legislation suffer from the complication that the references to the Appraisal Institute of Canada, or the AACI designation, are found in regulations and not in the statutes themselves. However, the *Yukon Government Employees Housing Plan Act* provides that an appraiser is deemed to have satisfied the requirement that he be experienced in the making of appraisals of real property, if he is the holder of a certificate from the Appraisal Institute of Canada qualifying him to appraise the housing unit.

> The line of jurisprudence upon which the learned Trial Judge relied in adopting the view that "recognized" means that a statute must provide for the regulation of the professional organization, was based on cases commencing with *Minister of National Revenue v. Montgomery*, supra. However, we do not read the *ratio decidendi* in *Montgomery* to deal directly with the question of what "recognized" means in subparagraph 8(1)(i)(i), which is the question before us in this appeal. Indeed in *Montgomery*, Kerr J stated at page 120:

>> The purpose of the payment of wardroom dues is not, in my opinion, to maintain a professional status. The status of a navy officer does not call for membership in a mess, unlike the practice of medicine, for example, which calls for membership in a medical society established by statute. ...

>> My attention was not drawn to any specific recognition of a wardroom mess in a statute, and I scarcely think that the status of membership in a wardroom mess is a professional status recognized by statute.

> Subsequent cases appear to rely on the *obiter* comments of Kerr J at page 119:

>> I feel sure, the present day concept of organized societies and associations of doctors, dentists, lawyers, engineers, chartered accountants and other professional persons, which have been given a special status by statute and have the power to make regulations governing the issue of certificates and licences to practise the profession, examinations of candidates for membership and the right to practise, discipline of members, and a variety of other matters, including the regulation of the practice and the professional conduct of its members. (sic)

> We are of the respectful view that *Montgomery*, and the cases following it, read into the *Income Tax Act* words that are not there. ...

> The Respondent's approach requires us to supplement the word "recognized" in subparagraph 8(1)(i)(i) with words such as "incorporating" or "providing for the regulation of the profession or words of similar import. We have no doubt that many, and perhaps most, professional organizations will be established and regulated by statute. However, the *Income Tax Act* is not concerned with the incorporation or regulation of professional societies and there is no necessary implication that the word "recognized" in subparagraph 8(1)(i)(i) includes such requirements.

> Subparagraph 8(1)(i)(i) is concerned with allowing, as a deduction from income, professional dues paid in order to maintain a professional status recognized by statute. The purpose of the term "recognized by statute" is only to establish a standard against which the

validity of the professional status in question is measured. The dictionary definition of "recognized" is, in this context, "to acknowledge the existence, validity, character or claims of." See *Concise Oxford Dictionary*, 8th ed. Had Parliament intended to restrict the meaning of "recognized" to include the requirement of being "incorporated," "created" or "regulated" by statute, it was open to it to use words to that effect. It did not. ... There is statutory acknowledgement of the status of appraisers which status is associated with membership in the Appraisal Institute of Canada and which the parties agreed is a professional status. We are therefore satisfied in this case that there is statutory recognition of the professional status of appraisers for purposes of subparagraph 8(1)(i)(i).

Do you agree with this decision? Why or why not?

8.   The government has proposed to amend the opening words of paragraph 8(1)(i) to allow deduction of professional membership dues and other expenses listed in that paragraph if they are "... paid by the taxpayer in the year, or on behalf of the taxpayer in the year if the amount paid on behalf of the taxpayer is required to be included in the taxpayer's income for the year ..." (Former Bill C-10, *Income Tax Amendments Act, 2006*, Part 2, Technical Amendments, cl. 50(2)). Bill C-10 was passed by the House of Commons and received second reading in the Senate on December 4, 2007, but ceased to exist when the 2nd Session of the 39th Parliament was dissolved and an election was called for October 14, 2008. At the time of writing its provisions had not yet been reintroduced in a new Bill.

E. Union Dues

In computing their income from an office or employment, subparagraph 8(1)(i)(iv) allows taxpayers to deduct "annual dues" paid in the year in order to maintain membership in a qualifying trade union or association of public servants "the primary object of which is to promote the improvement of the members' conditions of employment or work." Similarly, subparagraph 8(1)(i)(v) permits a deduction for annual dues paid pursuant to the provisions of a collective agreement to a trade union or association of public servants of which the taxpayer was not a member, while subparagraphs 8(1)(i)(vi) and (vii) permit the deduction of dues paid to other bodies, "the payment of which was required under the laws of a province." Subparagraph 8(1)(i)(iv) was considered in *Lucas v. M.N.R.*, [1987] F.C.J. No. 502, [1987] 2 C.T.C. 23, 87 D.T.C. 5277 (F.C.T.D.).

Lucas v. M.N.R.
[1987] F.C.J. No. 502, [1987] 2 C.T.C. 23, 87 D.T.C. 5277 (F.C.T.D.)

CULLEN J: ...

Facts

At all material times (in his 1980 taxation year) the plaintiff was a resident of Edmonton and was a member in good standing of the Alberta Teachers'

Association (the Association). In 1980 every teacher employed by a school board in Alberta was required to be an active member of the Association. The plaintiff was employed by the Edmonton Public School Board as a school teacher. The Association was an association for the purposes of subparagraph 8(1)(i)(iv) of the *Income Tax Act.* ...

On May 27, 1980, teachers in Calgary went on strike. The Provincial Executive Council (of the Alberta Teachers' Association) made a discretionary decision to grant financial support to the striking Calgary teachers. In order to finance this decision the by-laws of the Association were amended so that the monthly dues of each member were increased by $50 per month for the months of September to December 1980 and $10 per month for the months of January through August 1981.

...

In his 1980 income tax return the plaintiff deducted all amounts paid to the Association in 1980, including the amount of $200 representing the extra $50 per month for the months of September to December 1980 which all members were required to pay.

...

The Crown's Position

The Crown maintains that the additional amount of $50 per month was a special levy rather than increased monthly dues. In assessing the plaintiff's tax liability for his 1980 taxation year, the Minister assumed that the $200 was not annual dues within the meaning of paragraph 8(1)(i) of the Act but rather it was a special levy on account of the cost of the strike action by the Calgary teachers.

The Plaintiff's Position

The plaintiff maintains that the extra $200 was annual dues. Pursuant to its by-laws the Association was entitled to levy either annual dues pursuant to by-law 8 or special dues pursuant to by-law 10. The dues in question were levied pursuant to by-law 8(2) and not by-law 10, and are therefore annual dues.

Tax Court of Canada's Decision

... The tax court relied on two cases, *Western Leaseholds v. M.N.R.*, [1961] CTC 490, 61 DTC 1309 and *Moss Empires Ltd. v. Inland Revenue Commissioner*, [1937] AC 785, [1937] 3 All ER 381, for the proposition that "annual" infers the quality of being recurrent or being capable of recurrence.

The Court then looked at the Minutes of the Association whereby fees were increased $50 per month for the last four months of 1980. The Tax Court found that what the Association was really attempting to do was to effect a special levy against all teachers in the Association to support the striking teachers. The resolution purporting to increase the "annual dues" was merely a device whereby the Association protected its substantial portfolio on account of dues, a special levy to support a strike of the Calgary teachers. The $200 sought to be deducted by the taxpayer was not of a recurrent nature nor did it fit within the generally accepted understanding of the word "annual" as it was not a yearly recurring expense. The amount in question did not come within the provisions of subparagraph 8(1)(i)(iv) of the Act.

Case Law

There are very few cases which deal with the meaning of the word "annual" as it is used in the *Income Tax Act* and specifically as it relates to the payment of union dues and professional membership dues described in subparagraphs 8(1)(i)(i) and (iv). One principle has clearly been established with regard to payments of trade union and other dues: such dues must be annual payments to maintain membership and any initial fee payable upon admittance to a union or association cannot be deducted (*Daley v. M.N.R.*, [1950] CTC 254, 4 DTC 877 and *Herbert Burke v. The Queen*, [1976] CTC 209, 76 DTC 6075).

...

In its decision the Tax Court of Canada relied on the decision of *Western Leaseholds Ltd. v. M.N.R.* (supra), which dealt with the meaning of "annual" as it related to annual payments. Thorson P held that the kind of annual payment contemplated by the section of the Act in question had the quality of being recurrent and did not include payments which were paid only once.

Of more relevance to this case is the decision in the *Burke* case (*supra*). In that case the taxpayer was seeking to deduct as union dues under subparagraph 8(1)(i)(iv) of the Act an amount of $383.87 paid by him in 1973 as regular monthly contributions. In disallowing the deduction one of the Crown's arguments was that the dues were not "annual" dues within the meaning of subparagraph 8(1)(i)(iv) because they were not paid on a recurring basis.

Thurlow ACJ (as he then was) rejected the Crown's argument. He was of the view that the language of the provision did not express such a limitation and there was no sound reason for applying one. He held that the use of the word "annual" in subparagraph 8(1)(i)(iv) was simply used to make it clear that only union dues of the recurring kind, as opposed to initiation or entrance dues paid once and for all on becoming a member, are to be deductible. At pages 217-18 (DTC 6081) Thurlow ACJ stated:

> Here the dues paid by the plaintiff were not initiation or entrance dues but dues of the recurring kind. They accrued in the taxation year and were the dues of the year, *the payment of which was required to maintain the plaintiff's membership for the year*. In my opinion, they are "annual" dues within the meaning of the provision and the fact that they were calculated monthly, that they varied in amount from month to month depending on the

member's earnings for the month and that they were paid monthly are all immaterial for this purpose. [Emphasis added.]

Accordingly, the Crown's argument and the finding of the Tax Court of Canada that the payments were not annual in this case must fail.

Second, the argument and the basis of the Tax Court's decision that the payments in fact represented a "special levy" do not seem to me to be supportable. I have read the minutes of the meeting of the Alberta Teachers' Association wherein it was agreed to increase monthly fees and I am unable to come to the same conclusion as that of the Tax Court, i.e. that the payments were in fact a special levy to support the striking Calgary teachers.

When any member of the Association took the trouble to read the amendment, it was quite clear to him that his annual dues had increased by $50 per month beginning September 1, 1980. The Association would probably have informed all members of the increase and the reason for it. There is no suggestion that the Association had no authority to replenish the special emergency fund and it did so by calling a special meeting and passing the necessary resolution.

It is true that the $200 did not recur but it was capable of recurring. Had the Calgary strike given any indication of lasting longer than the summer, or if Edmonton teachers went out, or if the whole membership of the Association had gone on strike, I daresay a further meeting would have been necessary.

I cannot find that subparagraph 8(1)(i)(iv) is sufficiently explicit to give the interpretation given to it by the defendant. Certainly the word "annual" is capable of two definitions, i.e. occurring from year to year or dues paid in that year. I have concluded that the section does not require a recurrence from year to year. In the final analysis, quoting Estey J in *Johns-Manville Canada Inc. v. The Queen*, [1985] 2 CTC 111 at 126, 85 DTC 5373 at 5384:

> Such a determination is, furthermore, consistent with another basic concept in tax law that where the taxing statute is not explicit, reasonable uncertainty or factual ambiguity resulting from lack of explicitness in the statute should be resolved in favour of the taxpayer. ...

Appeal allowed.

NOTES AND QUESTIONS

1. On what basis did the Minister argue in *Lucas* that the additional $200 paid by the taxpayer was not deductible under subparagraph 8(1)(i)(iv)? Why did the Federal Court — Trial Division reject this argument? How did the court define "annual dues" for the purpose of subparagraph 8(1)(i)(iv)?

2. *Lucas* was distinguished in *Hummel v. The Queen*, [1997] 2 C.T.C. 2791 (T.C.C.), in which the taxpayer, a school principal and member of a teachers' union who was required be at work and keep his school open regardless of a strike, sought to deduct $2,256 that was paid to the union pursuant to a resolution of the union requiring principals who remained at work to pay 0.1 per cent of their annual gross salary to the union for each day of the strike. Rejecting

the taxpayer's arguments that the dues were capable of recurring and that he was obligated to pay the levy in order to maintain his membership in the union, the court disallowed the deduction on the grounds (at para. 11) that any recurrence depended on the continuation of the strike, that the levy was imposed "only on principals and vice-principals in those schools where the teachers were on strike," and that it was imposed not "to maintain membership" in the union but to share in the financial hardship resulting from the strike.

Do you agree with this result? Why or why not? How, if at all, might the union have structured the levy to make it deductible to the taxpayer and other principals and vice-principals who were required to remain at work?

3.   In *Whitty v. M.N.R.*, [1989] T.C.J. No. 503, [1989] 2 C.T.C. 2091, 89 D.T.C. 348 (T.C.C.), the taxpayer, a medical doctor employed by the Ontario Workmen's Compensation Board, deducted $975 paid to the Ontario Medical Association (OMA), of which $675 represented annual dues and $300 was to support political action. Rejecting the taxpayer's argument (at para. 3) that the OMA functions as "a voluntary (trade) union and ... is given *de facto* recognition as a union by the Ontario Health Insurance Plan (OHIP) as a result of the legally binding negotiations between the OMA and OHIP," the court disallowed the deduction on the grounds that the $300 was a special assessment to support political action and that the OMA was not a trade union within the meaning of subparagraph 8(1)(i)(iv) of the Act. According to Mogan TCJ (at para. 4):

> In order to be deductible under that subparagraph, an amount must be "annual dues to maintain membership in a trade union" as defined in the *Canada Labour Code* or similar provincial legislation. "Trade union" is defined as follows in the *Canada Labour Code:*
>
> > "trade union" means any organization of employees, or any branch or local thereof, the purposes of which include the regulation of relations between employers and employees;
>
> > The OMA is a voluntary association which promotes and protects the interests of medical doctors in Ontario. The OMA could not, by any stretch of the imagination, be regarded as an organization of employees established to regulate the relations between employers and employees. The fact that the Ontario Government negotiates with the OMA to settle the fee schedule of OHIP does not cause the OMA to be a trade union because the medical doctors who practise in Ontario under OHIP are not employees of the Ontario Government — at least not yet.

Do you agree with this result? Why or why not? Might the fees have been deductible under subparagraph 8(1)(i)(i) as "annual professional membership dues the payment of which was necessary to maintain a professional status recognized by statute"?

4.   In *Crowe v. Canada*, [2003] F.C.J. No. 631, [2003] 3 C.T.C. 271, 2003 D.T.C. 5288 (F.C.A.), the taxpayers were provincial court judges in Alberta who sought to deduct $1,500 in annual dues paid to the Alberta Provincial Judges' Association under subparagraph 8(1)(i)(iv) of the Act. Concluding (at para. 39) that the term "association of public servants" was intended to include only "associations that, although not certified under federal or provincial labour law

as bargaining agents, did in fact negotiate collectively with the employer on behalf of their members for improvements to their working conditions," the court disallowed the deduction on the grounds (at para. 18) that the judges are not "public servants" within the ordinary meaning of the term and (at para. 45) are "constitutionally prohibited from bargaining with the government that pays them the terms and conditions under which they work."

5.   According to subsection 8(5):

> Notwithstanding subparagraphs (1)(i)(i), (iv), (vi) and (vii), dues are not deductible under those subparagraphs in computing a taxpayer's income from an office or employment to the extent that they are, in effect, levied
>
> (a)   or or under a superannuation fund or plan;
>
> (b)   or or under a fund or plan for annuities, insurance (other than professional or malpractice liability insurance that is necessary to maintain a professional status recognized by statute) or similar benefits; or
>
> (c)   or any other purpose not directly related to the ordinary operating expenses of the committee or similar body, association, board or trade union, as the case may be.

In *Burke v. Canada*, [1976] F.C.J. No. 104, [1976] C.T.C. 209, 76 D.T.C. 6075 (F.C.T.D.), the court relied on this provision to disallow the deduction of union dues paid by the taxpayer that were used to fund the union's mortuary benefit fund and old age benefit fund.

6.   For the CRA's views on subparagraphs 8(1)(i)(iv), (v), (vi), and (vii) and subsection 8(5), see *Interpretation Bulletin* IT-103R, "Dues Paid to a Union or to a Parity or Advisory Committee," November 4, 1988. According to paragraph 6 of this bulletin:

> Where a trade union incurs reasonable costs in prosecuting a legal strike (such as rental of strike headquarters, telephone expenses, publicity and advertising expenses and travelling expenses) and, during such strike provides relief payments to members in need but to which they are not entitled as a contractual right, such costs will be viewed as being related to the ordinary operating expenses of the trade union. For this reason, the part of the annual dues of a member that is levied for the purpose of providing for the current or anticipated costs of prosecuting legal strikes of the union is, if reasonable in the circumstances, deductible for tax purposes... . Levies made during a year on some or all members of a trade union to provide funds for the prosecution of a legal strike of the union will be considered to be annual dues provided that such levies are capable of recurring and have not been designated by the union as special assessments. On the other hand any such levies designated as special assessments are not annual dues and are, therefore, not deductible.

F. Cost of Supplies Consumed

According to subparagraph 8(1)(i)(iii), taxpayers may in computing their income from an office or employment deduct "the cost of supplies that were consumed directly in the performance of the duties of the office or employment and that the officer or employee was required by the contract of employment to supply and pay for." The words "required by the contract of employment" are largely indistinguishable from the words "required under the contract of employment" in subparagraphs 8(1)(h)(i) and (h.1)(i), which were considered earlier in this section. In *Martyn v. M.N.R.* (1964), 35 Tax ABC 428, 64 D.T.C. 461 (T.A.B.), the board considered the meaning of the words "supplies ... consumed directly in the performance of the duties" of an office or employment.

Martyn v. M.N.R.
(1964), 35 Tax ABC 428, 64 D.T.C. 461 (T.A.B.)

[In computing his income for his 1961 taxation year, the taxpayer, an airline pilot, sought to deduct the cost of clothing that he was required to wear while carrying out the duties of his employment. The Minister disallowed the deduction on the basis that expenditures for uniforms and accessories did not come within then paragraph 11(1)(c) of the Act (now subparagraph 8(1)(i)(iii)).]

J.O. WELDON, QC: ... The gist of the appellant's claim, which he substantiated by producing extracts from his employment contract with Trans-Canada Air Lines and from its Flight Operating Manual, was that he was required as a term of his employment to provide his own uniforms and accessories thereto, except as follows: TCA provided the hat, all insignia, paid 50% of the cost of the tunic and trousers, and made stocks of shirts and ties available to its pilots at what seemed to be special prices. With those exceptions the taxpayer herein had to pay for the various items of his uniform which also included — topcoat, raincoat, socks, shoes and so on, all of which were duly specified by the regulations in the Flight Operating Manual. His contention was that, since he had to dress while on duty precisely as directed by Trans-Canada Air Lines, he should be entitled to deduct in the relevant taxation year the actual cost of the annual replacements to his uniform from his taxable income.

...

To succeed in this appeal the appellant must bring his claim within ... Section 11(10)(c) [now paragraph 8(1)(i)(iii)] of the Act. His counsel submitted that several items of the appellant's TCA uniform — costing $98 as claimed — had to be replaced in his 1961 taxation year, and that those items were, in effect, supplies consumed directly in the performance of the taxpayer's employment as an airline pilot, and which he was required to supply and pay for, and for which he has not been and is not entitled to be reimbursed.

In the case of *Goodman v. M.N.R.*, 8 Tax ABC 320, R.S.W. Fordham, QC, now Assistant Chairman of the Board, held, first, that the Minister had been right in disallowing the cost of a RCAF pilot officer's uniform under the above-mentioned Section 11(10)(c) on the ground that the said outlay was a personal or living expense within the meaning of Section 12(1)(h) [now paragraph 18(1)(h)] of the Act, and secondly, that a uniform was also in the capital asset category. [These categories of expenditures are examined in Chapter 5.] Counsel for the appellant in the present appeal tried, but unsuccessfully in my view, to distinguish his client's TCA uniform from the uniform which was the subject matter of the *Goodman* case (supra), by seeking to establish that the TCA uniform did not wear nearly as long as other uniforms, such as those of the RCAF.

...

As I view this appeal the life of a TCA uniform is not the crux of the matter. The question is rather whether a TCA uniform can be regarded as coming under the heading of supplies that were consumed in the relevant taxation year directly in the performance of Mr. Martyn's duties as a TCA pilot. In my review of this matter since hearing the appellant's case I have decided to adopt my first impression and conclude that, while a uniform may be worn and worn until it is threadbare, it still cannot be said to be consumed in the ordinary meaning of that word, nor can it be regarded as coming under the heading of supplies in the ordinary meaning of that word. According to *The Shorter Oxford English Dictionary* the word "consume" means: make away with; destroy, as by fire etc.; to use up, and especially to eat up, drink up — the word "supply" as a noun means: a quantity or amount of something supplied or provided; a quantity of money or provisions supplied or to be supplied, and the word "supply" as a verb usually means: to furnish with regular supplies of a commodity. A "commodity" is defined in the above-mentioned dictionary as — a kind of thing produced for use or sale, and in its plural form as — goods, merchandise or produce. Therefore, from the above definitions it is obvious that the word "supplies" is not an appropriate term to use in connection with a uniform. The cloth out of which it was made was a commodity, but the combination of the material and tailoring skill that went into it produced a finished article of special personal value to its owner and capital in its nature.

...

Section 11(10)(c) of the Act does not, in my view, present any special problem of interpretation, at least so far as the present appeal is concerned. The word "supplies" is a common word and has a well understood meaning. Used in connection with the word "consumed," it denotes that which can be used up in the course of the taxpayer's employment and thereafter be unfit for further use in the performance of any similar employment ... . The term "supplies" as used in Section 11(10)(c) would seem to include such things as sandpaper, solder, litmus paper, bandages, stationery, gasoline for a blow torch, electric light bulbs and that type of thing, to give but a few examples. ...

Appeal dismissed.

NOTES AND QUESTIONS

1.   On what basis did the taxpayer in *Martyn* argue that he should be able to deduct the cost of purchasing his pilot's uniform? Why did the board reject this argument? How did the board interpret the words "supplies ... consumed directly in the performance of the duties" of an office or employment for the purpose of then paragraph 11(10)(c) (now subparagraph 8(1)(i)(iii))? Do you agree with the board's conclusion? Why or why not?

2.   Would the taxpayer in *Martyn* have been taxable on the value of a pilot's uniform if it had been provided to him by his employer? See paragraph 29 of IT-470R, in which the CRA expresses its view that an employee has not received a taxable benefit within the meaning of paragraph 6(1)(a) where the employee is required to wear a "distinctive uniform" while carrying out the duties of employment. Does it make sense to disallow the deduction of an expense the value of which would not have been included in an employee's income if provided by the employer? If you were advising an airline on the most tax-efficient method of employee compensation, how would you suggest that it should deal with employees' uniforms?

3.   For other cases in which the deduction of clothing expenses incurred by employees in the course of their duties has been disallowed on the grounds that clothes are not "supplies ... consumed directly in the performance of the [employee's] duties," see *Brownlee v. M.N.R.*, [1978] C.T.C. 2780, 78 D.T.C. 1571 (T.R.B.); *Thibault v. M.N.R.*, [1986] 2 C.T.C. 2062, 86 D.T.C. 1538 (T.C.C.); *Cuddie v. Canada*, [1998] T.C.J. No. 255, [1998] 3 C.T.C. 2232, 98 D.T.C. 1822 (T.C.C.); *Rouillard v. Canada*, [1999] T.C.J. No. 650, [2000] 4 C.T.C. 2065 (T.C.C.); and *Crawford v. Canada*, [2000] T.C.J. No. 110, [2003] 2 C.T.C. 2169 (T.C.C.).

4.   In *Luks v. M.N.R.*, [1958] C.T.C. 345, 58 D.T.C. 1194 (Ex. Ct.), the taxpayer, an electrician who worked at different sites in and around the city of Toronto, sought to deduct, in addition to travelling expenses, $44.34 to purchase a blow torch, screw drivers, pliers, and a chalk line, which he was required to provide at his own expense in order to carry out the duties of his employment. Rejecting the taxpayer's argument that the payment constituted "the cost of supplies ... consumed directly in the performance of [his] duties," the court disallowed the deduction on the grounds that the items purchased were not "supplies" but "tools falling within the general category of equipment," and that, even if they were regarded as supplies, there was no evidence that they were "consumed or worn out" in the performance of the taxpayer's duties as required by then paragraph 11(10)(c) (now subparagraph 8(1)(i)(iii)). According to Thurlow J (at para. 13):

> "Supplies" is a term the connotation of which may vary rather widely, according to the context in which it is used. In s. 11(10)(c) it is used in a context which is concerned with things which are consumed in the performance of the duties of employment. Many things may be consumed in the sense that they may be worn out or used up in the performance of duties of employment. The employer's plant or machinery may be worn out. The employee's clothing may be worn out. His tools may be worn out. And materials that go into the work, by whomsoever they may be provided, may be used up. "Supplies" is a word of narrower meaning than "things," and in this context does not embrace all things that may be consumed in performing the duties of employment, either in the sense of being worn out or used up. The line which separates what is included in it from what is not included may be difficult to define precisely but, in general, I think its natural meaning in this context is limited to materials that are used up in the performance of the duties of the employment. It obviously includes such items as gasoline for a blow torch but, in my opinion, it does not include the blow torch itself. The latter, as well as tools in general, falls within the category of equipment.

Do you agree with this conclusion? Why or why not?

5. *Luks* has been applied in several cases to disallow the deduction of various items acquired by taxpayers in order to carry out the duties of their employment on the grounds that these items were not "supplies" that are "consumed directly" but "equipment" that wears out over time. See, for example, *Payne v. M.N.R.*, [1976] C.T.C. 2302, 76 D.T.C. 1233 (T.R.B.) (records used by radio disc jockey); *Komarniski v. M.N.R.*, [1980] C.T.C. 2170, 80 D.T.C. 1134 (T.R.B.) (small tools used by aircraft mechanic); *Pyefinch v. Canada*, [1994] T.C.J. No. 575, [1995] 1 C.T.C. 2361 (T.C.C.) (tools used by auto mechanic); *Ellis v. Canada*, [1998] T.C.J. No. 638, [1998] 4 C.T.C. 2373, 98 D.T.C. 1885 (T.C.C.) (football equipment used by professional football player); and *Ouzilleau v. Canada*, [1998] T.C.J. No. 307, [1999] 1 C.T.C. 2701 (T.C.C.) (computers used by automobile salespersons).

6. In *Carson v. M.N.R.* (1966), 41 Tax ABC 249, the taxpayer, who was employed as a high school teacher, sought to deduct the cost of pencils, ballpoint pens, paperclips, and books used in the performance of his duties. Although disallowing the deduction of any expenses associated with the acquisition of books on the grounds that they are not "consumed" or "used up" in the performance of his duties, the board allowed the deduction of the other expenses under then paragraph 11(10)(c) (now subparagraph 8(1)(i)(iii)).

7. In *Fardeau v. Canada*, [2002] T.C.J. No. 264, [2002] 3 C.T.C. 2169 (T.C.C.), the taxpayer, an officer with the RCMP, sought to deduct the cost of a cellular phone, a pager and clothing in computing his employment income, which the Minister disallowed on the basis that these items were not "supplies ... consumed directly in the performance of the duties of the [taxpayer's] ... employment" under subparagraph 8(1)(i)(iii). Allowing the taxpayer's appeal, Bowman ACJTC reconsidered both the meaning of the word "supplies" as well as the concept of "consumption" for the purpose of this provision. With respect to the meaning of "supplies", he concluded (at para. 12):

> There is no unanimity in this court on the question whether such things as shirts, socks and other similar items are supplies. We are not talking about tools here. We are talking about shirts and socks that wear out. With respect I think it is time to reconsider the approach of Thurlow, J. in *Luks*. While it might be right for tools it may be unrealistically narrow for shirts, socks and boots in the context of modern employment practices. Such things as clothing are certainly supplies. In *Thibault* ..., Tremblay, J. after referring to the dictionary definitions held that clothing fell within the term "supplies". I agree. He was, however, of the view that clothing was not "consumed". I shall deal with this second point below.

With respect to the concept of consumption, he declared (at para.15):

> I think, adopting a teleological approach to the interpretation of this provision, it seems obvious that items of clothing that have to be worn by a police officer as part of his or her job are supplies that are consumed. If one steps back and asks what sort of employment expenses is subparagraph 8(1)(*i*)(iii) aimed at it seems the items of clothing that RCMP officers have to supply and pay for out of their own pockets are precisely what the subparagraph is intended to cover. No purpose is served by adopting a narrow and technical interpretation where ordinary common sense requires a different conclusion. Consumed is a word of some

elasticity. *The Oxford English Dictionary* ("*OED*") has three quarters of a page of definitions of consume. It is true that some of the definitions carry a connotation of destruction (as by fire) devouring (as by eating) or spending (as in the case of money). I do not however think there is any justification for requiring that there be instant annihilation. Consumption can be gradual. Perhaps one cannot consume a hammer but it does no violence to language to say that one consumes items of clothing by wearing them out. Indeed, one of the definitions of consume in the *OED* is:

> d. To wear out by use.

> 1878 HOOKER & BALL Marocco 156 The thin slippers universally used by the people are very soon consumed.

Finally, he held (at para. 17): "What of the monthly cost of the pager and cell phone? Certainly those services are "supplies". Just as obviously they are consumed."

See also *Glen v. Canada*, [2003] T.C.J. No. 667, [2004] 2 C.T.C. 2238, 2004 D.T.C. 2109 (T.C.C.), where the taxpayer, a real estate appraiser and part-time university professor, was permitted to deduct the cost of computer software as a "cost of supplies that were consumed directly" in the performance of his teaching duties.

8.   In *Drobot v. M.N.R.*, [1987] 2 C.T.C. 2098, 87 D.T.C. 371 (T.C.C.), the taxpayer, who was required by his employer to maintain an office in his house, sought to deduct various expenses associated with the maintenance of the office, including electricity, gas, repairs, and maintenance. Although allowing the deduction of these and other expenses under subparagraph 8(1)(i)(ii) of the Act as "office rent," the court rejected the characterization of these expenses as "the cost of supplies ... consumed directly in the performance of the [taxpayer's] duties." Concluding that these items were not "consumed" as the term is understood for the purposes of subparagraph 8(1)(i)(iii), the court also questioned whether any of the items could legitimately be classified as "supplies" within the meaning of the provision.

Notwithstanding this decision, the CRA regards expenses incurred by a taxpayer for the maintenance of a home office, "such as the cost of fuel, electricity, light bulbs, cleaning materials and minor repairs" as deductible "supplies" under subparagraph 8(1)(i)(iii). See *Interpretation Bulletin* IT-352R2, "Employee's Expenses, Including Work Space in Home Expenses," August 26, 1994, paragraph 5.

9.   The CRA's views on subparagraph 8(1)(i)(iii) appear in IT-352R2. According to paragraphs 9 and 10 of this bulletin:

> 9. The word "supplies" as used in subparagraph 8(1)(i)(iii) is limited to materials that are used up directly in the performance of the duties of the employment. In addition to certain expenses related to a work space in a home, ... supplies will usually include such items as

> > (a)   the cost of gasoline and oil used in the operation of power saws owned by employees in woods operations;

> > (b)   dynamite used by miners;

    (c)   bandages and medicines used by salaried doctors;

    (d)   telegrams, long-distance telephone calls and cellular telephone airtime that reasonably relate to the earning of employment income; and

    (e)   various stationery items (other than books) used by teachers, such as pens, pencils, paperclips and charts. ...

    10. Supplies, as used in subparagraph 8(1)(i)(iii), will not include:

    (a)   the monthly basic service charge for a telephone line;

    (b)   amounts paid to connect or licence a cellular telephone;

    (c)   special clothing customarily worn or required to be worn by employees in the performance of their duties; and

    (d)   any types of tools which generally fall into the category of equipment.

10. Employees generally are not permitted to deduct the cost of tools or equipment under subparagraph 8(1)(i)(iii), as interpreted by the courts in cases such as *Luks* and *Fardeau*. Further, unlike taxpayers earning income from business or property, employees generally are not entitled to deduct a percentage of such costs annually as capital cost allowance (discussed in Chapter 5, in the section on Timing Issues). Some specific provisions have been added to the Act to recognize tool and equipment expenses incurred by certain types of employees. Employees who are ordinarily required to carry on their duties away from their employer's place of business and who meet the other conditions for deducting expenses under paragraph 8(1)(f), (h) or (h.1) may also be entitled each year to deduct a percentage of the cost of purchasing a motor vehicle, or an aircraft required for use in performing the duties of employment, as capital cost allowance.[62] Similarly employed musicians may deduct capital cost allowance in respect of musical instruments they must provide as a term of their employment.[63] Since 2002, an individual who is employed as an "eligible apprentice mechanic" as defined in subsection 8(6) and who is required to provide certain tools for use in that employment can, upon meeting certain other conditions, deduct tool costs exceeding (for 2007 and subsequent years) $1,500 per annum (this threshold is subject to inflation indexing and rises by 5 per cent of income over $30,000).[64] As of 2006, "employed tradespeople" may deduct up to $500 of new tool costs each taxation year in excess of a $1,000 threshold, which will be indexed to inflation.[65] The definition of an "eligible tool" excludes most electronic communication devices and electronic data processing

---

[62] See para. 8(1)(j), Reg. 1100(1)(x), (x.1).

[63] See para. 8(1)(p), Reg. 1100 (1)(a)(viii).

[64] See para. 8(1)(r). Upon disposing of such tools the taxpayer may be required to include in income a portion of the proceeds of disposition to the extent of amounts previously deducted: see subs. 8(7), para. 56(1)(k).

[65] See para. 8(1)(s). This deduction is coordinated with the deduction for apprentice mechanic tools in para. 8(1)(r) to limit their combined value: see subsection 8(7).

equipment (cellular phones, handheld and other computers).[66] The term "tradesperson" is not defined in the Act.

G. Office Rent

According to subparagraph 8(1)(i)(ii), taxpayers may in computing their income from an office or employment deduct "amounts paid by the taxpayer in the year as ... office rent, ... the payment of which by the officer or employee was required by the contract of employment." This deduction was considered in *Prewer v. M.N.R.*, [1989] 1 C.T.C. 2337, 89 D.T.C. 171 (T.C.C.).

Prewer v. M.N.R.
[1989] 1 C.T.C. 2337, 89 D.T.C. 171 (T.C.C.)

SHERWOOD TCJ: This is an appeal from a confirmed reassessment whereby the respondent disallowed a deduction of $1,617.32 claimed as an expense for a "home office" by the appellant in her 1986 taxation year.

The appellant was employed by Inis International In-Store Sales Inc. (Inis) for 16 years to 1987. For most of that time her duties were those of administrative assistant. In 1986, Inis was experiencing difficulties and its few employees worked in a small office carrying extreme work loads. The appellant, in an effort to help Inis, agreed to add some sales activities to her heavy administrative duties. It was further agreed that she would do her sales work during normal business hours when Inis's clients' offices were open and would do most of her administrative and accounting work at home outside office hours in order to get it done on time. The appellant then converted the use of one bedroom of her residence to that of an office. The bedroom was one of three on the top level of four levels of a split-level townhouse which she owned with her husband. On the advice of her accountant she deducted ⅓ of the cost of maintaining the townhouse, not including mortgage interest, if any, or capital cost allowance. Her employer signed a tax form T2200 stating that she was required to maintain an office in her home and the form was included with her 1986 income tax return.

The appellant submits that she is entitled to the disallowed deduction and relies on the decision of Taylor TCJ in *Drobot v. M.N.R.*, [1987] 2 CTC 2098, 87 DTC 371.

The respondent's position is that the deduction was properly disallowed. He relies on the following facts and assumptions:

1. The appellant was not required by her contract of employment to maintain an office in her home.

---

[66] Subsection 8(6.1).

2. Her employer provided office space to her within a reasonable distance of her home.

3. She owned the premises where she maintained an office and therefore did not incur "office rent."

4. Alternatively, she was entitled to deduct only a reasonable portion of the expenses of maintaining the premises.

The appellant must bring herself within the provisions of paragraph 8(1)(i) of the *Income Tax Act* ... to be entitled to the deduction she claims. The Act permits no deductions from income except those it expressly provides.

I am satisfied that the appellant became required to maintain an office in her home at her own expense. She had no written contract of employment but such a requirement was implicit in her acceptance of sales responsibilities on top of her administrative duties in 1986. This finding disposes of the first of the facts relied on by the respondent. The second fact is irrelevant in light of the Court's finding on the first fact. In any event, there were compelling reasons for not using the Inis office. It was in an industrial area which was dark, semi-deserted and crime prone at night. It is also doubtful that the appellant, who is also a wife and homemaker, could have continued her employment if required to return to the Inis office for regular night and holiday work.

The appellant's response to the respondent's third fact is the case of *Drobot v. M.N.R.*, *supra*. The facts in this appeal are quite similar to those in *Drobot* wherein an appellant who was required to maintain a home office deducted 20 per cent of the expenses of his residence as an employment expense. The respondent did not (as he has done unsuccessfully in this appeal) dispute the requirement for a home office. He used subparagraph 8(1)(i)(iii) of the Act to disallow taxes, insurance and interest expenses claimed by *Drobot* while allowing 20 per cent of electricity, gas and repair expenses as being supplies consumed directly by the appellant in the performance of his duties.

Taylor TCJ rejected the contention that the expenses claimed were properly treatable as supplies. He found that the expenses claimed by *Drobot*, if deductible any place, would appear to fit into subparagraph 8(1)(i)(ii) as "rent." Addressing that issue, he reviewed some jurisprudence and concluded that he should interpret the subsection as "simply meaning that the contract of employment must require that the employee maintain an office and *himself be* responsible for any costs associated therewith, or, as in this case, any additional costs arising out of the provision of this space for purposes of gaining his income." Applying that conclusion, he allowed the appeal.

In the instant appeal the appellant could probably have issued cheques payable to her husband or to him and herself and characterized them as "rent" but that seems unnecessary. Why should the costlier expedient of renting a room from a neighbour qualify for a deduction but the cheaper and more convenient one of using part of her own home not qualify for deduction? I conclude that reasonable expenses of using space in one's own home to meet a requirement for office space away from an employer's establishment are deductible under subparagraph 8(1)(i)(ii).

This brings us to the final issue. Was the deduction claimed by the appellant a reasonable cost of her home office? The bedroom was one of three on the fourth level of a split-level townhouse. It is very difficult to accurately ascertain the expense of using part of a residence for business purposes. The appellant has claimed ⅓ of the total expenses of her residence. The residence includes common elements such as the dining room, kitchen, living room and family room. There is no evidence that any of the common elements were used as her office. Furthermore there is no justification for attributing any appreciable portion of the heat or hydro expenses to her home office. The office was only 1/12 of the space she had to heat. Major hydro users are such items as cooking stove, washer, dryer, water heater, etc., none of which have any significant relationship to her bedroom office. On the evidence presented not more than ten per cent of the residence expenses can be fairly attributed to the "home office" and I adopt that percentage.

The appeal is allowed in part and the matter is referred back to the respondent for reconsideration and reassessment on the basis that the appellant is entitled to a "home office" employment expense deduction of $485.10 in her 1986 taxation year. ...

Appeal allowed in part.

NOTES AND QUESTIONS

1.   On what grounds did the Minister disallow the deduction of the expenses claimed by the taxpayer in *Prewer*? On what basis did the court conclude that the expenses were deductible under subparagraph 8(1)(i)(ii) of the Act? How did the court respond to the Minister's argument that the taxpayer could not pay "office rent" because she owned the premises in which she maintained an office? Do you agree with the court's response? Why or why not?

2.   Why did the court in *Prewer* reduce the taxpayer's allowable deduction from $1,617.32 to $485.10? What, if any, statutory authority supports this reduction?

3.   In *Felton v. M.N.R.*, [1989] T.C.J. No. 205, [1989] 1 C.T.C. 2329, 89 D.T.C. 233 (T.C.C.), the taxpayer, who maintained an office in his home as required by his contract of employment, deducted one-sixth of his household expenses, including mortgage interest, property taxes, insurance, utilities, and maintenance, as "office rent" under subparagraph 8(1)(i)(ii). Concluding (at para. 4) that "'office rent' can only arise from a landlord and tenant relationship," the court refused to apply the reasoning in *Drobot v. M.N.R.*, [1987] 2 C.T.C. 2098, 87 D.T.C. 371 (T.C.C.), and disallowed the deduction. According to Rip TCJ (at para. 15):

When a lessor leases a property to a lessee for a rent, components of the rent usually include all those items claimed by Mr. Felton as a deduction. In fact, Mr. Felton was only deducting those expenses he actually incurred as a result of having the office in his home and the aggregate of those expenses may be less than or equal to any rent he may have paid to a lessor for an office in other premises. Unfortunately for Mr. Felton, however, Parliament legislated only those expenses specifically set out in section 8 as deductions from employment income, and office rent — not office expenses in general — is one of these expenses. Some office expenses may be deductible under subparagraph 8(1)(i)(iii). In many situations section 8 may be unfair, in particular since taxpayers earning income from a business, in computing their income, may deduct expenses, such as home office expenses, which employees are precluded from deducting in computing their income. In my view the Act does not permit Mr. Felton to deduct expenses incurred in his home as office rent because under this contract of employment he is required to have an office and be responsible for the costs associated with the office; such expenses were not payments of rent.

Do you agree with this conclusion? Why or why not?

4.   For other cases in which employees' home office expenses have been disallowed on the basis that the employee did not pay "office rent" as required by subparagraph 8(1)(i)(ii), see *Merleau v. M.N.R.*, [1986] T.C.J. No. 222, [1986] 1 C.T.C. 2381, 86 D.T.C. 1292 (T.C.C.); *Thompson v. M.N.R.*, [1989] F.C.J. No. 808, [1989] 2 C.T.C. 226, 89 D.T.C. 5439 (F.C.T.D.); and *Horbay v. Canada*, [2002] T.C.J. No. 684, [2003] 2 C.T.C. 2248 (T.C.C.). In *Thompson*, the court relied on "the plain meaning" of the words "office rent" in subparagraph 8(1)(i)(ii) to favour the approach in *Felton* over that in *Drobot* and *Prewer*.

5.   For 1991 and subsequent taxation years, paragraph 8(13)(a) stipulates that, not withstanding paragraphs 8(1)(f) (salesperson's expenses) and 8(1)(i):

no amount is deductible in computing an individual's income for a taxation year from an office or employment in respect of any part (in this subsection referred to as the "work space") of a self-contained domestic establishment in which the individual resides, except to the extent that the work space is either

    (i)   the place where the individual principally performs the duties of the office or employment, or

    (ii)   used exclusively during the period in respect of which the amount relates for the purpose of earning income from the office or employment and used on a regular and continuous basis for meeting customers or other persons in the ordinary course of performing the duties of the office or employment.

Where the conditions stipulated in subparagraphs 8(13)(a)(i) and (ii) apply, moreover, paragraphs 8(13)(b) and (c) prohibit the deduction of these "home office" expenses to the extent that they exceed the individual's income for the year from the office or employment otherwise determined, allowing the taxpayer to claim these disallowed losses as deductible expenses from the office or employment in subsequent taxation years.

This provision is almost identical in structure to subsection 18(12), which governs deductions for similar "home office" expenses in computing a taxpayer's income from a business or property. Subsection 18(12) is examined in Chapter 5.

6.   In *Haltrecht v. Canada*, [2000] T.C.J. No. 184, [2000] 2 C.T.C. 2749 (T.C.C.), the taxpayer, a part-time lecturer at York University who was not allocated an office at the university, deducted 14 per cent of the utilities and maintenance costs of his home, which the Minister disallowed. Approving the Minister's administrative practice to allow the deduction of utility expenses related to a home office as deductible "supplies ... consumed directly in the performance of the [taxpayer's] duties" under subparagraph 8(1)(i)(iii), and concluding that the taxpayer had, by taking 20 hours each week to prepare for two three-hour lectures, satisfied the further requirement in subparagraph 8(13)(a)(i) that the office is "the place where the individual principally performs the duties of the office or employment," the court allowed the taxpayer's appeal.

7.   The CRA's views on the deduction of "office rent" under subparagraph 8(1)(i)(ii) and the limitation in subsection 8(13) appear in IT-352R2. According to paragraph 5 of this bulletin:

> Regardless of whether the individual owns or rents the home, the work space expenses otherwise deductible as "supplies" under subparagraph 8(1)(i)(iii) consist of a reasonable proportion ... of expenses paid by the individual for the maintenance of the home, such as the cost of fuel, electricity, light bulbs, cleaning materials and minor repairs. If the work space is part of a home rented by the individual, a reasonable proportion of the rent is otherwise deductible under subparagraph 8(1)(i)(ii). However, no deduction can be made for the rental value of the work space area in a home owned by the individual.

H. Salary of Assistant or Substitute

In addition to the deduction of office rent, subparagraph 8(1)(i)(ii) also allows taxpayers to deduct "amounts paid by the taxpayer in the year as ... salary to an assistant or substitute, the payment of which by the officer or employee was required by the contract of employment." The expression "required by the contract of employment" is largely indistinguishable from the words "required under the contract of employment" in subparagraphs 8(1)(h)(i) and (h.1)(i), which were considered earlier in this section. In *Cruikshank v. M.N.R.*, [1985] 2 C.T.C. 2344, 85 D.T.C. 633 (T.C.C.), the court considered the meaning of the words "salary to an assistant or substitute."

Cruikshank v. M.N.R.
[1985] 2 C.T.C. 2344, 85 D.T.C. 633 (T.C.C.)

BRULÉ TCJ:

Issue

This is an appeal against an income tax assessment for the year 1981 in which the Minister of National Revenue disallowed an expense claimed by the taxpayer in filing his return in the amount of $447.88, under subparagraph 8(1)(i)(ii) of the *Income Tax Act* ... . The expense disallowed involved the payment of a telephone answering service which was necessary for the appellant's employment.

The appellant was employed by UniTrust Protection Services Ltd. and in his notice of appeal stated:

> The Declaration of Employment Conditions Form was signed by my employer as well as my employer's letter of March 11, 1982, which were both submitted to Revenue Canada Taxation and which both made clear that the Telephone and Answering Service were required and used for my work. As my substitute, the Telephone Answering Service wrote down messages and informed me when I was needed for work — particularly important in emergency situations which did occur and, thanks to the Telephone Answering Service taking calls and recording messages which they conveyed to me, I was able to report for work and prevent what would have been serious and expensive accidents at work.

Counsel for the Minister did not dispute any of the facts but rather took the approach that this expense did not come within the provisions of subparagraph 8(1)(i)(ii) of the Act and therefore must be disallowed. He did admit that if the appellant had hired telephone secretarial assistance, payment to such a person would have been a legitimate expense.

Analysis

Subparagraph 8(1)(i)(ii) allows a taxpayer, such as in this case, in computing his income for a taxation year a deduction from employment expenses for "office rent, or salary to an assistant or substitute" provided: (a) the taxpayer is required by his contract of employment to provide and pay for such expense; (b) the taxpayer has not been reimbursed and is not entitled to be reimbursed from his employer for such expense; and (c) the expense is incurred solely for the purpose of earning income from his employment.

While these conditions were met the respondent claimed the payment was not "salary to an assistant or substitute." He claimed that "substitute" meant a person taking the place of the claimant and that "salary" was as defined in the *Oxford Dictionary*, "a fixed payment made by an employer at regular intervals to a person doing other than manual or mechanical work."

The determination of the problem revolves around the interpretation and meaning of the words "salary" and "substitute."

The definition of "salary" as put forward by the respondent (supra) would seem to include a payment to a Telephone Answering Service as the latter would qualify as a "person" by [the] definition in subsection 248(1) of the Act. It must then be determined if the payment was to an "assistant or substitute." It was not to the former obviously and so to qualify the appellant's expense must have been made to a "substitute." While the respondent argued that the word "substitute" must be a person taking the place of the appellant I can find no jurisprudence to say that the word "substitute" must be a person.

Thorson P in the Exchequer Court of Canada decision of *W.A. Sheaffer Pen Company of Canada Limited v. M.N.R.*, [1953] CTC 345, 53 DTC 1223, said at 350 (DTC 1226):

It is thus a cardinal rule of interpretation that the context in which a word in the Act appears must always be considered in order to ascertain its true meaning.

The *Oxford English Dictionary*, Volume X, gives one definition of the word "substitute" as — "a thing put in place of another."

The *Random House Dictionary of the English Language*, 1981, published in Canada gives a definition for "substitute" as, "a person or thing acting or serving in place of another."

In this day of modern technology it must be recognized that substitutes are available, many of which are less expensive than former alternatives. In the present case a full or part-time telephone secretary would have been permitted at a much higher annual cost than $447.88. Here we do have people involved with the answering service who "wrote down messages and informed me when I was needed for work." This service acted as a "substitute" for the taxpayer when required and accordingly the expense of the appellant is one which qualifies under subparagraph 8(1)(i)(ii) of the Act.

This appeal is therefore allowed and the matter referred back to the Minister for reconsideration and reassessment on the basis that the amount of $447.88 was an allowable expense of the appellant in his 1981 taxation year.

Appeal allowed.

NOTES AND QUESTIONS

1. Why did the Minister disallow the deduction in *Cruikshank*? Why did the court allow the taxpayer's appeal? Do you agree with the court's decision? Why or why not? Even if the telephone-answering service was a "substitute" within the meaning of subparagraph 8(1)(i)(ii), was it appropriate to regard the amount paid for this service as a "salary"?

2. Where the payment of a salary to an assistant or substitute is deductible under subparagraph 8(1)(i)(ii) of the Act, paragraph 8(1)(1.1) allows the taxpayer to deduct employment insurance and pension plan payments that must be paid in respect of the employee. Might this provision aid in the interpretation of the meaning of the words "assistant or substitute" in subparagraph 8(1)(i)(ii)?

3. In *Watts v. M.N.R.* (1961), 27 Tax ABC 432, the taxpayer, who worked as a secretary at a Winnipeg law firm, sought to deduct payments to a housekeeper and babysitter that the taxpayer directed her employer to pay directly to the housekeeper/babysitter. Attributing the payments to the taxpayer under then subsection 16(1) (now subsection 56(2)), the board also disallowed the deduction of these payments under then paragraph 11(10)(b) (now subparagraph 8(1)(i)(ii)) on the grounds (at paragraph 7) that the housekeeper/ babysitter "was not hired at the request of the law firm" and "did not assist [the taxpayer] in the performance of her duties." According to Mr. Boisvert (at paragraph 8):

It is obvious that, when enacting Section 11(10)(b) [now subparagraph 8(1)(i)(ii)] which grants an employee the privilege of deducting from his income the salary paid by him to an assistant or substitute, the legislator had in mind that such an assistant could and would assist the employee *in the performance of his duties as an employee*. The "golden rule" of interpretation of statutes is that words ought to be given "their plain, fair, literal and natural meaning." It could hardly be said that a housekeeper and baby-sitter qualifies as an *assistant* to a secretary, within the meaning of Section 11(10)(b).

Do you agree with this result? Why or why not? Does subparagraph 8(1)(i)(ii) stipulate that the assistant or substitute must assist the taxpayer in the performance of his or her duties? Is it reasonable to read these words into this provision? Why or why not?

Although housekeeping expenses are generally not deductible in computing a taxpayer's income, child-care expenses are now deductible under a specific statutory provision enacted in 1972. This provision, section 63 of the Act, is examined in Chapter 7.

I. Expenses of Salespersons

Where a taxpayer is employed "in connection with the selling of property or negotiating of contracts for the taxpayer's employer," paragraph 8(1)(f) provides a more general rule for the deductibility of expenses, allowing the taxpayer to deduct all "amounts expended by the taxpayer in the year for the purpose of earning the income from the employment" other than the expenses listed in subparagraphs (v) to (vii),[67] provided that the taxpayer:

(i) under the contract of employment was required to pay the taxpayer's own expenses,

(ii) was ordinarily required to carry on the duties of the employment away from the employer's place of business,

(iii) was remunerated in whole or part by commissions or other similar amounts fixed by reference to the volume of the sales made or the contracts negotiated, and

(iv) was not in receipt of an allowance for travel expenses in respect of the taxation year that was, by virtue of subparagraph 6(1)(b)(v), not included in computing the taxpayer's income.

For the purpose of this provision, moreover, subsection 8(10) requires the taxpayer's employer to sign a prescribed form, "certifying that the conditions set out in the ... provision were met in the year in respect of the taxpayer," that must be filed with the taxpayer's return of income for the year. Where these expenses

---

[67] These provisions, which need not concern us here, disallow the deduction of capital expenses other than those permitted by para. 8(1)(j); deductions for the use of recreational facilities and club dues, which are prohibited under para. 18(1)(l); and payments in respect of automobile benefits that reduce the amount of a taxable employment benefit otherwise included in computing the taxpayer's income under para. 6(1)(e). For cases that deny the deduction of capital expenses to commissioned salespersons see *Gifford v. Canada*, [2004] S.C.J. No. 13, [2004] 1 S.C.R. 411, [2004] 2 C.T.C. 1, 2004 D.T.C. 6120 (S.C.C.) (cost of purchasing client list and interest on money borrowed for this purpose); and *Paes v. Canada*, [2007] T.C.J. No. 192, [2007] 5 C.T.C. 2110, 2007 D.T.C. 837 (T.C.C.) (cost of office furniture and equipment).

may be deducted, however, paragraph 8(1)(f) limits the aggregate amount that may be deducted to "the commissions or other similar amounts referred to in subparagraph (iii) and received by the taxpayer in the year," thereby disallowing the use of these deductions to produce a loss that might otherwise be deducted against other sources of income under paragraph 3(d) of the Act.[68]

In order to qualify under paragraph 8(1)(f), therefore, a taxpayer must satisfy five requirements:

1. the taxpayer must have been employed "in connection with the selling of property or negotiating of contracts for the taxpayer's employer";

2. the taxpayer must "under the contract of employment" have been "required to pay the taxpayer's own expenses";

3. the taxpayer must have been "ordinarily required to carry on the duties of the employment away from the employer's place of business";

4. the taxpayer must have been "remunerated in whole or part by commissions or other similar amounts fixed by reference to the volume of the sales made or the contracts negotiated"; and

5. the taxpayer must not have received a travel allowance exempt from tax under subparagraph 6(1)(b)(v).

Although the second, third, and fifth of these requirements are similar to the requirement for the deduction of travel and motor vehicle expenses under paragraphs 8(1)(h) and (h.1), paragraph 8(1)(f) has produced its own body of case law that merits separate examination. As a result, the following cases and commentary examine each of these five requirements.

1. Employed in Connection with Selling Property or Negotiating Contracts

The first requirement to qualify for the general deduction in paragraph 8(1)(f) is that the taxpayer must have been employed "in connection with the selling of property or negotiating of contracts for the taxpayer's employer." One of the

---

[68] For this reason, the court suggested in *Goldhar v. M.N.R.*, [1985] 1 C.T.C. 2187, 85 D.T.C. 202 (T.C.C.) (at para. 8), employees who satisfy the requirements of para. 8(1)(f) "*must* make any deductions claimed *under that section of the Act*" (emphasis in original) rather than other provisions under which specific amounts (for example, travelling expenses or office rent) might also be deductible. Whether this interpretation is consistent with the permissive "may be deducted" in the preamble to subs. 8(1) and the use of the words "claims a deduction" in subparas. 8(1)(h)(iv) and (h.1)(iv) is uncertain.

few cases in which this requirement has been considered explicitly is *Creighton v. M.N.R.* (1951), 4 Tax ABC 378 (T.A.B.).

Creighton v. M.N.R.
(1951), 4 Tax ABC 378 (T.A.B.)

R.S.W. FORDHAM (Chairman Fabio Money, KC concurring): The appellant is an assistant technician engaged by the Quinte District Cattle Breeders' Association and has entered an appeal from his income tax assessment for 1949.

During the year mentioned he claims to have incurred ... expenses in connection with an automobile owned by him and used in the performance of his duties. ...

These items ... amounted to $2,100 in all and this sum was deducted by the appellant from his total income for the year. The deduction was disallowed by the Minister of National Revenue....

The appellant stated that he resided and had an office at Napanee, Ontario, and that his duties involved the artificial inseminating of cows owned by members of the above-mentioned Association in the surrounding territory and that he drove his car about 30,000 miles in 1949 in order to do the work required of him, for which he claims seven cents per mile. His income tax return shows an additional 9,000 miles travelled in the same year for which he makes no claim. Seemingly the latter mileage related to pleasure or non-business driving.

The semen necessary for inseminating purposes was provided at Belleville and would either be sent from there to the appellant or he would drive from Napanee to Belleville for it, a distance of about 30 miles. He then had to drive to any farm where cows required attention. ... The area of his activities covered a radius of twenty miles from Napanee and he was responsible for the territory thus embraced.

On responding to a call received, the appellant would collect the farmer's membership fee, if it had not already been paid, and then charge the farmer $5.00 for each cow served. The appellant would remit all money so collected to the Association's office at Belleville and later would receive therefrom the sum of $3.00 for each cow treated.

...

I have no hesitation in finding that ... the arrangement between him and the Association constituted an employment and a permanent, full-time one with all the usual attributes of an employer and employee relationship attached thereto. ... Having so found, does section 11 [now section 8] authorize the deductions sought?

...

Just a cursory examination of section 11 is needed to make it clear that subsection 6 [now paragraph 8(1)(f)] thereof is the only provision that could possibly apply. It relates, however, to a person "employed in connection with the selling of property or negotiating of contracts for his employer." On the evidence the appellant did neither. He did not sell property of any kind. Instead he performed technical duties for farmers and others who had already made arrangements with the Association that entitled them to ask for the appellant's assistance at an agreed rate of remuneration payable to the Association. These arrangements were the subject of contracts made between the farmers and the Association, and there is no suggestion that the appellant negotiated them. ...

It may be that the agreement between the appellant and the Association is a burdensome one in that, under it, the former is left to pay his travelling expenses. In that case his remedy might be to negotiate, if he can, some arrangement therefor with the Association. In any event it seems clear that no relief such as that sought can be had under *The Income Tax Act*. ...

[W.S. Fisher dissented, observing that the deduction in what is now paragraph 8(1)(f) applies to persons "employed in connection with the selling of property," not persons "employed in selling property."]

Appeal dismissed.

NOTES AND QUESTIONS

1. On what basis did the majority of the board in *Creighton* conclude that the taxpayer was not eligible for the deduction in then subsection 11(6) (now paragraph 8(1)(f))? Why did W.S. Fisher dissent? Which view do you find more persuasive? Why?

2. In *Stromberg v. M.N.R.* (1954), 9 Tax ABC 393, 54 D.T.C. 28 (T.A.B.), the taxpayer, who managed the shoe department of a retail store, for which he was paid a fixed annual salary plus commission, sought to deduct travelling expenses incurred to visit shoe factories and the premises of competitors. Although disallowing the deduction on the basis that the taxpayer was not "ordinarily" required to carry on the duties of his employment away from his employer's place of business, the board rejected the Minister's argument that the expenses claimed related only to purchases, not sales, on the grounds that then subsection 11(6) (now paragraph 8(1)(f)) referred not only to the "selling of property" but also to the "negotiating of contracts."

2. Required Under Contract of Employment To Pay Own Expenses

The requirement in subparagraph 8(1)(f)(i), that the taxpayer "was under the contract of employment required to pay the taxpayer's own expenses," is similar to the requirement in subparagraphs 8(1)(h)(ii) and (h.1)(ii) that an employee must have been "required under the contract of employment to pay the travel expenses incurred ... in the performance of the duties of the office or employment." A useful discussion of this requirement appears in *Bowman v. M.N.R.*, [1985] 1 C.T.C. 2380, 85 D.T.C. 328 (T.C.C.).

Bowman v. M.N.R.
[1985] 1 C.T.C. 2380, 85 D.T.C. 328 (T.C.C.)

TAYLOR TCJ: This is an appeal heard in Toronto, Ontario, on February 20, 1985, against income tax assessments for the years 1977, 1978 and 1979 in which the Minister of National Revenue disallowed expenses claimed by the taxpayer in filing his returns, in the amounts of $2,933.66, $3,365 and $3,557 respectively, under paragraph 8(1)(f) of the *Income Tax Act* ... . A major portion of the expenses incurred by Mr. Bowman as a commission salesman for Pitney Bowes of Canada Ltd. was reimbursed to him by the employer, but he had expended the above amounts in excess of his reimbursements, in large measure for entertainment and promotion (although there were other types of expenses included). The rationale proposed by Mr. Bowman for this action is that he had a certain budget limit for such reimbursements, and that both he and the company expected that he would exceed this budget — at his own expense. Indeed, he felt, and certain documents he presented supported his opinion, that advancement in the company was governed to some degree by a salesman's (or a sales manager's) ability to contain costs to the company, while reaching or exceeding target sales limits. I quote from Exhibit R-2 submitted by the respondent as a letter from the vice-president of Pitney Bowes of Canada Ltd. to Mr. Bowman:

> A large portion of a Branch Manager's earnings are variable, based on sales attainment, (typically 30-35 per cent of total compensation would be comprised of bonuses and incentives.) Pitney Bowes expects Managers to achieve all quota assignments and they are judged accordingly. It is, therefore, understandable that a Branch Manager would be willing to invest some of his own money for specific promotions so as to maximize his earnings.

...

The appellant took the view that he really had no choice but to make the expenditures at issue, in order to earn his income. Counsel for the respondent contended that Mr. Bowman " — was not, under his contract of employment, required to pay his own expenses — ."

...

As I see it, while not part of the written contract of employment the accord between the parties — employer and employee — regarding reimbursement, was an integral part of that employment contract. But that accord, as per Mr. Bowman, was in the form of an understanding that such expenses would not exceed the budget allocation for them. ... So, accepting that we have a written "contract of employment" covering percentage commission, territories, etc, and an implied "contract of employment" covering expenses to be reimbursed by the company — where do we find a "contract of employment" covering the excess expenditures at issue in this appeal and mandating their dispersal? The closest comment to that possibility is to be found in Exhibit R-2 (supra), and I repeat the last sentence thereof:

> ... It is, therefore, understandable that a Branch Manager would be willing to invest some of his own money for specific promotions so as to maximize his earnings.

I would venture to say that an attempt to interpret that sentence as "under the contract of employment was required to pay his own expenses" (subparagraph 8(1)(f)(i)), as Mr. Bowman did, is a difficult task indeed. Quite the opposite, I view the sentence as the company specifically absolving itself of any possible involvement in excess expenditures which Mr. Bowman might incur, even though, at the same time the company made him aware, very forceably, of its desires and objectives with regard to such activity. The phrase "*with* some of *his* own money" (emphasis mine) says it all. It was simply expected that Mr. Bowman would be out of pocket by amounts in excess of the reimbursements he received to "maximize his earnings." The company did not say "pay some of his own expenses" nor did it say "advance some of his own funds," or a similar phrase. The message was clear and could be paraphrased as: "we expect it will cost you some of your own money, and that is your problem; at the same time we emphasize that you probably cannot reach your sales quotas without taking on such an obligation." That is an understandable position for an employer to take, but it is not a requirement that the employee pay his own expenses. ...

I have suggested recently in *Goldhar v. M.N.R.*, [1985] 1 CTC 2187, 85 DTC 202, that the term "his own expenses" 8(1)(f) may be different (I do not say is different) than the term "the (travelling) expenses," (brackets mine) 8(1)(h); and that possibly only the clear statement by an employer to an employee to that effect may suffice. In the instant appeal, if there were a statement such as: "you are required to pay your own expenses that exceed the reimbursement from this company" that distinction might arise in formulating this judgment. However, it is not an issue that requires a determination in this appeal. ...

Appeal dismissed.

NOTES AND QUESTIONS

1. On what basis did the court conclude in *Bowman* that the taxpayer was not required under the contract of employment with his employer to pay his own expenses? Do you agree with the decision? Why or why not? Is the decision in *Bowman* consistent with the decision of the Federal Court of Appeal in *Hoedel v. M.N.R.*, [1986] F.C.J. No. 669, [1986] 2 C.T.C. 419, 86 D.T.C. 6535 (F.C.A.)? Is it consistent with the decision of the Federal Court Trial Division in *Rozen v. Canada*, [1985] F.C.J. No. 1002, [1986] 1 C.T.C. 50, 85 D.T.C. 5611 (F.C.T.D.)?

2. Based on the decision in *Bowman*, how would you advise an employed commission salesperson who wishes to deduct amounts expended for the purpose of earning employment income?

3. For other cases in which courts have disallowed the deduction of expenses incurred by commissioned salespersons on the grounds that they were not required under a contract of employment to incur expenses in excess of those

reimbursed by their employer, see *Tozer v. M.N.R.*, [1982] C.T.C. 2835, 82 D.T.C. 1815 (T.R.B.); *Slawson v. M.N.R.*, [1985] 1 C.T.C. 2075, 85 D.T.C. 63 (T.C.C.); and *Canetti v. M.N.R.*, [1985] 1 C.T.C. 2426, 85 D.T.C. 401 (T.C.C.).

4.   For cases in which employees were determined to have been required under their contracts of employment to pay their own expenses, see *Goldhar v. M.N.R.*, [1985] 1 C.T.C. 2187, 85 D.T.C. 202 (T.C.C.) and *Baillargeon v. M.N.R.*, [1990] T.C.J. No. 712, [1990] 2 C.T.C. 2472, 90 D.T.C. 1943 (T.C.C.).

5.   In several cases, courts have disallowed the deduction of expenses under paragraph 8(1)(f) on the basis that the taxpayer failed to maintain adequate records in order to establish that expenses that they claimed to have made were in fact made. See, for example, *Vizien v. M.N.R.*, [1977] C.T.C. 2533, 77 D.T.C. 363 (T.R.B.); *Corrigan v. M.N.R.*, [1978] C.T.C. 2310, 78 D.T.C. 1256 (T.R.B.); *Litvinchuk v. M.N.R.*, [1979] C.T.C. 3141, 79 D.T.C. 899 (T.R.B.); *Coffey v. M.N.R.*, [1980] C.T.C. 2545, 80 D.T.C. 1478 (T.R.B.); and *Gadsby v. The Queen*, [1996] 2 C.T.C. 2145 (T.C.C.). In *Deutsch v. M.N.R.*, [1979] C.T.C. 217, 79 D.T.C. 5145 (F.C.T.D.), however, the court allowed the deduction of various expenses incurred by a commissioned salesperson, notwithstanding the absence of documentary substantiation.

3. Ordinarily Required To Carry On Duties Away from Employer's Place of Business

The third requirement in paragraph 8(1)(f), that the taxpayer be "ordinarily required to carry on the duties of the employment away from the employer's place of business," is virtually identical to the requirement in subparagraphs 8(1)(h)(i) and (h.1)(i), except that the latter provisions also permit these duties to be carried on "in different places." The leading case on this requirement in the context of paragraph 8(1)(f) is *Verrier v. M.N.R.*, [1990] F.C.J. No. 220, [1990] 1 C.T.C. 313, 90 D.T.C. 6202 (F.C.A.).

Verrier v. M.N.R.
[1990] F.C.J. No. 220, [1990] 1 C.T.C. 313, 90 D.T.C. 6202 (F.C.A.)

MAHONEY JA (Hugessen and MacGuigan JJA concurring): ... The appellant was a highly successful automobile salesman employed by a Winnipeg dealership. In 1980, sales of 269 vehicles at retail, 25 at wholesale and 175 fleet vehicles generated commissions of $65,977.32. He claimed $7,391.28 disputed expenses which the learned trial judge described as including:

> gas and oil for his demonstrator (provided free of charge by his employer) and for the two "courtesy" cars owned and provided by him to his customers for their own use when their cars were being serviced. The expenses claimed also include parking charges incurred while conducting business, advertising carried out by the plaintiff on his own to seek customers for himself, entertainment expenses (coffee and meals) incurred for the benefit of customers or prospective customers, and commissions or finders' fees paid by him to persons referring customers to him where the referral resulted in a sale.

...

There was no written contract of employment and, hence, no express condition readily at hand to demonstrate whether the appellant "was ordinarily required to carry on the duties of his employment away from his employer's place of business." The learned trial judge held that he was not. Some of the appellant's absences from the dealership, such as taking customers on test drives, taking sold vehicles elsewhere to get custom equipment installed and delivering their vehicles to purchasers, were characterized as "errands" which did not amount to "duties away from his employer's place of business." As to the rest, he held:

> However most of the activities relied on by the plaintiff involve means employed by him at his discretion to find customers, to encourage them to buy cars from him, and to encourage them to come back to him for future purchases through various follow-up services offered by him. Such activities include making contact with "bird-dogs" (persons encouraged by the plaintiff to refer customers to him), the demonstration of vehicles at the home or place of business of clients, picking up from customers cars already purchased to take them in for servicing and leaving with the customer a "courtesy car" owned by the plaintiff, entertaining customers with coffee or meals, etc. It is clear from the evidence that none of these activities of the plaintiff were specifically required by his employer. ... What the employer was interested in was results, i.e. sales. The plaintiff was a very successful salesman. No doubt the particular means which he employed were important to that success. But they were means chosen by him and to the extent that they took him away from the dealership that was his choice.

That entire finding is said to be founded on an error in law in that the learned trial judge is said to have misunderstood the clear intention of paragraph 8(1)(f). That misunderstanding is, it is said, manifest in his opinion that the provision is illogical, which he expressed more than once. At one point, he said:

> It is common ground that if [the requirements of subparagraphs (i) and (ii)] are met, the expenses deductible under paragraph 8(1)(f) are not limited to those attributable to the fact that the plaintiff was ordinarily required to carry on the duties of his employment away from his employer's place of business. In other words, once he can show that he meets the requirements of (subparagraphs (i) and (ii)) then any expenses however incurred for the purpose of earning income from his employment are deductible. The illogicality of this provision will be discussed later.

At another, he said:

> It is difficult to give a purposive interpretation of the words "ordinarily required" within the context of subparagraph 8(1)(f) because the expenses deductible under that paragraph bear no necessary relationship to the fact that a taxpayer is "ordinarily required to carry on the duties of his employment away from his employer's place of business." Once he establishes that he is so required, he can then deduct any expenses incurred for the purpose of earning income from the employment. The logic of this provision is far from apparent. For example, there are no doubt many commission salesmen (e.g. of clothing or furniture) who are never obliged to leave their employer's place of business for work purposes but who may well incur promotional expenses such as sending greeting cards to, or buying coffee for, customers or prospective customers. They are unable to claim under this paragraph. Similarly, salaried persons cannot claim under it, even though in many employment situations it is thought advantageous for those in supervisory roles to entertain members of their staff, at their own expense.

The learned trial judge seems to have felt that, somehow, the deductible expenses contemplated ought to relate to the necessity of the appellant's absence from the showroom but that sort of expense is dealt with by paragraph 8(1)(h) and subsection 8(4) makes clear, if that be necessary, that paragraphs 8(1)(f) and (h) deal with two different allowable deductions. The necessary interaction of subsection 8(4) and paragraph 8(1)(f) leads to the conclusion that an employee may be "ordinarily required" to carry on the duties of his employment away from the employer's establishment to which he "ordinarily reported" for work.

The criterion chosen by Parliament to differentiate between commission salesmen entitled to deduct their expenses and those not so entitled, namely that those entitled be "ordinarily required" to carry on their duties away from their employer's establishment, may be arbitrary but it is clear and the provision must be applied according to its plain meaning, whatever one's view of its logic. The legislative objective is apparent. A taxpayer entirely dependent on commissions directly related to sales volume and not entitled to claim his expenses from his employer is, in many respects relevant to the scheme of the *Income Tax Act*, more comparable to a self-employed person than to a conventional salaried employee. Such a taxpayer benefits from laying out the deductible expenses only because that results in increased income. Absent a 100 per cent tax rate, allowance of the deduction does not fully compensate the taxpayer for the outlay; that compensation is realized in increased sales, precisely what the learned trial judge found to be the interest of the appellant's employer, and concomitant increased commission income, the appellant's (and, one might have thought, the fisc's) interest.

I am of the opinion that the learned trial judge erred in law in his construction of paragraph 8(1)(f). It remains to consider whether that led him to the wrong result in the present case.

...

This Court had occasion, in *Hoedel v. The Queen*, [1986] 2 CTC 419, 86 DTC 6535, to consider the term "ordinarily required to carry on the duties of his employment away from his employer's place of business" as it is used in subparagraph 8(1)(h)(i), and held, per Heald JA at pages 422-3 (DTC 6538), that:

> if an employee's failure to carry out a task can result in an unfavourable assessment by his employer, it would seem to me that such a circumstance is compelling evidence that the task in issue is a duty of employment.

It would seem to me that if failure to sell enough cars would have resulted in the appellant's discharge and if both employer and salesman recognize that enough cars can only be sold if the salesman conducts some of his work away from the showroom, then the salesman is ordinarily required to carry on the duties of his employment away from his employer's place of business.

It follows that, in my opinion, the learned trial judge erred in concluding that the appellant was not entitled to claim the deduction of expenses under paragraph 8(1)(f) of the *Income Tax Act* in his 1979 and 1980 returns. ...

Appeal allowed.

NOTES AND QUESTIONS

1. On what basis did the Federal Court of Appeal conclude in *Verrier* that the taxpayer could deduct the various expenses he had claimed? On what basis did it conclude that the taxpayer was ordinarily required to carry on the duties of his employment away from his employer's place of business?

2. What rationale did the Federal Court of Appeal provide in *Verrier* for the more generous deductions available to commission salespersons? Do you agree with this rationale? Why or why not? How, if at all, does this rationale justify the requirement in subparagraph 8(1)(f)(ii) that the taxpayer must have been "ordinarily required to carry on the duties of the employment away from the employer's place of business"?

3. *Verrier* was followed in *McKee v. M.N.R.*, [1990] F.C.J. No. 207, [1990] 1 C.T.C. 317, 90 D.T.C. 6205 (F.C.A.), a similar case involving an automobile salesman who, the court concluded (at para. 2), was "ordinarily required to carry on the duties of his employment away from his employer's place of business ... if he was to sell enough vehicles to earn a living and keep his job."

4. For other cases in which *Verrier* has been applied to allow the deduction of expenses incurred by commissioned salespersons, see *M.N.R. v. Gilling*, [1990] F.C.J. No. 284, [1990] 1 C.T.C. 392, 90 D.T.C. 6274 (F.C.T.D.) and *Bober v. Canada*, [1997] T.C.J. No. 467, [1997] 3 C.T.C. 2396 (T.C.C.). In *Gilling*, the court cited *Verrier* for the proposition (at para. 37) that paragraph 8(1)(f) does not impose "technical considerations which would tend to defeat the intent and spirit of the legislation when the realities of any employer-employee contract are subject to scrutiny." According to Joyal J (at para. 38):

> The Court of Appeal ... has ... recognized that a specific requirement for an employee to pay his own expenses or to carry out duties outside of his normal place of business need not be patently expressed in a contract of employment. Courts, upon studying the experience of the relationship and all surrounding circumstances may well apply common sense and conclude that these are implied terms.

5. For earlier cases in which courts have considered the requirement in subparagraph 8(1)(f)(ii) or its predecessor that a taxpayer must have been "ordinarily required to carry on the duties of the employment away from the taxpayer's place of business," see *Stromberg v. M.N.R.* (1954), 9 Tax ABC 393, 54 D.T.C. 28 (T.A.B.) and *Neufeld v. M.N.R.*, [1981] C.T.C. 2010, 81 D.T.C. 18 (T.R.B.).

In *Stromberg*, the board disallowed the deduction of travelling expenses incurred by the manager of the shoe department of a retail store to visit shoe factories and the premises of competitors on the grounds, *inter alia*, that the taxpayer was "ordinarily in the retail store" and that "[h]is departures therefrom were only occasional and infrequent" (at para. 5). In *Neufeld*, the board disallowed the deduction of travel expenses incurred by a clothing store manager to make deliveries to customers, exchange stock between stores, make promotional public appearances, solicit new customers, and attend company sales meetings on the basis (at para. 10) that the taxpayer "was quite plainly 'ordinarily required' to be *in* his store and managing it." According to the board (at para. 13);

> The relevant jurisprudence leads me to the conclusion that the term "ordinarily required" from subparagraph 8(1)(f)(ii) of the Act should be applied to the main context of the "duties of employment" for which the taxpayer is responsible. In the instant case that is the position of manager in and of the clothing store. The fact that either through a general understanding with his employer or by his own choice Mr. Neufeld performed some of his duties away from the store does not serve to place him in the special category for expense deductions for those salesmen "ordinarily required" to do so "away from the employer's place of business" "in most cases, usually, or commonly."

Are these decisions consistent with the Federal Court of Appeal decision in *Verrier*? Are they consistent with judicial interpretations of the meaning of the word "ordinarily" in the context of subparagraphs 8(1)(h)(i) and (h.1)(i)?

4. Remuneration

In addition to the other criteria for the deductibility of employment expenses under paragraph 8(1)(f), subparagraph 8(1)(f)(iii) stipulates that the taxpayer must have been "remunerated in whole or part by commissions or other similar amounts fixed by reference to the volume of the sales made or the contracts negotiated." This requirement was considered in *Griesbach v. M.N.R.*, [1990] T.C.J. No. 910, [1990] 2 C.T.C. 2593, 91 D.T.C. 142 (T.C.C.).

Griesbach v. M.N.R.
[1990] T.C.J. No. 910, [1990] 2 C.T.C. 2593, 91 D.T.C. 142 (T.C.C.)

CHRISTIE ACJTC: ... In 1985 the appellant was one of a number of persons employed by Rideau Marine (Kingston) Ltd. of Kingston. His particular duties were those of assistant manager and salesman. His responsibilities as assistant manager were to manage the staff and the service aspect, i.e. providing dockage, fuel, etc., of the business in the absence of the general manager, Mr. Clayton Simonett, who was away a good deal of the time. His duties as salesman related to the sale of boats that ranged from 18 to 41 feet in length. Generally prices for these boats ranged from $25,000 to $125,000 although in 1985 a yacht was sold for $325,000.

In his return of income for 1985 he recorded that his employment income before deductions was $62,644.30 and this conforms with the T-4-1985 slip issued by Rideau Marine (Kingston) Ltd. At trial evidence was adduced that the $62,644.30 consisted of two components: $15,000 by way of salary and the balance of $47,644.30 was remuneration based on 20 per cent of the pre-tax gross profit of his employer in 1985.

Counsel for the respondent argues that remuneration arrived at under that formula is not "commissions or other similar amounts fixed by reference to the volume of the sales made or the contracts negotiated" within the meaning to be attributed to these words in subparagraph 8(1)(f)(iii) of the Act. I agree.

...

[I]n order for expenses to be deductible under ... paragraph [8(1)(f)] the remuneration pertaining thereto must be fixed by reference to the volume of the sales made or the contracts negotiated by the taxpayer claiming those deductions. Twenty per cent of the pre-tax gross profits of an employer with a number of employees is not synonymous with remuneration so fixed. ...

Appeal dismissed.

NOTES AND QUESTIONS

1. On what basis did the court conclude in *Griesbach* that the taxpayer could not claim any deductions under paragraph 8(1)(f)? How did the court interpret the meaning of the words "other similar amounts fixed by reference to the volume of the sales made or the contracts negotiated" for the purposes of subparagraph 8(1)(f)(iii)?

2. Do you agree with the court's decision in *Griesbach*? Why or why not? Should employees whose compensation is based on a percentage of their employer's profits be eligible for more generous deductions than other employees?

3. For other cases in which courts have disallowed the deduction of salespersons' expenses on the basis that taxpayers who received a percentage of net or gross profits were not "remunerated in whole or part by commissions or other similar amounts fixed by reference to the volume of the sales made or the contracts negotiated," see *No. 149 v. M.N.R.* (1954), 10 Tax ABC 147, 54 D.T.C. 142 (T.A.B.); *No. 150 v. M.N.R.* (1954), 10 Tax ABC 149, 54 D.T.C. 143 (T.A.B.); and *Claus v. M.N.R.* (1966), 40 Tax ABC 395, 66 D.T.C. 248 (T.A.B).

5. Receipt of Travel Allowance

The final requirement for the deductibility of expenses under paragraph 8(1)(f) is that the employee must not have received "an allowance for travel expenses in respect of the taxation year that was, by virtue of subparagraph 6(1)(b)(v), not included in computing the taxpayer's income." This requirement, which is similar to the requirements in subparagraphs 8(1)(h)(iii) and (h.1)(iii), was considered in *Barnard v. M.N.R.*, [1985] 1 C.T.C. 2178, 85 D.T.C. 210 (T.C.C.).

Barnard v. M.N.R.
[1985] 1 C.T.C. 2178, 85 D.T.C. 210 (T.C.C.)

CHRISTIE ACJTC: This appeal relates to the appellant's 1980 taxation year. The issue is whether she is entitled to deduct certain expenses claimed by her as a commission saleswoman. She was employed under a verbal contract by a corporation to sell knitting yarns in Hamilton and in an area of Ontario east of that city. In the year under review the appellant earned $15,019.13, which included commissions of $5,107.95. It is alleged by the respondent that the appellant received a reasonable allowance for travelling in the amount of $6,704. The appellant says she received $3,907.87. She also says that the amount expended by her in earning the $15,019.13 was $6,845.12.

...

In order for a person to make any deductions under subsection 8(1)(f) he must come within the ambit of each of subparagraphs 8(1)(f)(i), (ii) and (iv). This necessitates that he shall:

(a)   be required under his contract of employment to pay his own expenses,

(b)   be ordinarily required to carry on the duties of his employment away from his employer's place of business, and

(c)   not have been in receipt of a reasonable allowance for travelling expenses.

What is said in (c) reflects my understanding of the meaning of subparagraph 8(1)(f)(iv) because the kind of allowance described in the subparagraph is one that is to be excluded in computing the income of a taxpayer under subparagraph 6(1)(b)(v) and those allowances are "reasonable allowances for travelling expenses." As I see it, if a commission salesman receives an allowance for travelling expenses, whatever its adequacy may be in fact, and it is not included in computing his income, he fails to comply with subparagraph 8(1)(f)(iv) and is not entitled to make any deductions under paragraph 8(1)(f). That is to say if he receives a travelling allowance which he regards as unreasonable, but nevertheless does not include it in computing his income he has thereby, at the time of filing his return, chosen to act on it as a reasonable allowance and the respondent is entitled to assess or reassess on that basis. On the other hand, if he receives an allowance for travelling expenses and takes the position that it is not a reasonable allowance and includes it in his income, he is within subparagraph 8(1)(f)(iv) subject only to dispute which may arise regarding whether the allowance received was in fact reasonable. This could be important in some situations because, if a commission salesman is within paragraph 8(1)(f) he may, subject to any certain exceptions to which reference will be made, deduct all reasonable amounts expended by him for the purpose of earning income from his employment as a commission salesman, including any interest paid by him on borrowed money employed for the purpose of acquiring an automobile or aircraft used in the performance of his employment and such part of the capital cost to him of an automobile or aircraft used in the same manner as is allowed under Part XI of the *Income Tax Regulations*. Subparagraph 8(1)(f)(iv) relates only to travelling expenses so, if a commission salesman fails to include an allowance for travelling expenses in computing his income, even if he regards it as unreasonable, he is precluded from simultaneously deducting in calculating his income any other kind of expenses incurred by him for the purpose of earning income from his employment as commission salesman.

...

With respect to subparagraph 8(1)(f)(iv) it is important to bear in mind what constitutes an "allowance" within the meaning thereof.

...

I adopt as a correct statement of the law regarding the meaning of the word "allowance," in the context under consideration, this passage from *Canadian Income Taxation*, 3rd (1983) edition by Edwin C. Harris at page 102:

> An "allowance" is a round amount given to an employee to cover expenses that he will incur, such as travel or entertainment, on his employer's behalf. The employee is not required to account to the employer later for what he has actually spent. If the employee accounts to the employer for his actual expenses, neither an initial advance given him by his employer nor any subsequent payment by the employer to reimburse him for his expenses is an "allowance."

...

I have concluded that what the appellant received from her employer was not an "allowance for travelling expenses" within the meaning of paragraph 8(1)(f)(iv). These facts which I accept were in the appellant's testimony. Within her sales territory payment of her expenses was confined to specified geographical limitations. Precise amounts were prescribed for meals and lunch was not included. Monthly "expense reports" were sent by her to her employer. Furthermore, in his reply to the notice of appeal, the respondent alleges ... that the amount received by the appellant from her employer for travelling expenses for 1980 was $6,704. Counsel for the respondent reiterated this exact amount at the hearing. The $4 belies an allowance. Rather it suggests detailed accountability. Also in her 1980 return the appellant alleged that the amount received from her employer was $3,907.87. This figure also speaks for itself regarding accountability and it was submitted to Revenue Canada long before the eruption of the dispute which led to this appeal.

...

The appeal is allowed and the matter is referred back to the respondent for reconsideration and reassessment on the basis that the $3,907.87 received from her employer for expenses shall be included in computing her income as a commission saleswoman in her 1980 taxation year and there shall be deducted in computing that income $6,845.12 being the amount expended by her in 1980 for the purpose of earning it. ...

Appeal allowed.

NOTES AND QUESTIONS

1. In *Barnard*, how did the court define an "allowance" for the purpose of subparagraph 8(1)(f)(iv)? Is this definition consistent with the cases decided

under subparagraphs 8(1)(h)(iii) and (h.1)(iii)? Why did the court conclude that the taxpayer had not received an exempt travel allowance within the meaning of subparagraph 6(1)(b)(v)?

2.   In *Lavigne v. Canada*, [1994] T.C.J. No. 58, [1995] 1 C.T.C. 2040, 94 D.T.C. 1571 (T.C.C.), the taxpayer, a sales representative for a heavy truck dealer who was required to travel in the course of his employment, deducted automobile and other expenses (for accommodation, entertainment, supplies, and telephone), the former of which the Minister disallowed on the grounds that the taxpayer had received an automobile allowance computed at 25 cents per kilometre, which he had not included in computing his income in 1988 and 1989. Citing subparagraph 6(1)(b)(x) for the proposition (at para. 12) that "Parliament clearly considered a sum paid on the basis of the number of kilometres travelled as an allowance," and concluding (at para. 14) that the taxpayer and his employer "appear to have considered the allowance as reasonable since the allowances received in 1988 and 1989 were not included in ... his income pursuant to subparagraph 6(1)(b)(v) of the Act," the court affirmed the Minister's assessments.

Do you agree with this result? Why or why not? If the receipt of a reasonable travel allowance precludes the deduction of any employment expenses under paragraph 8(1)(f), on what, if any, statutory authority did the Minister allow the deduction of other expenses claimed by the taxpayer?

3.   For other cases in which salespersons' expenses have been disallowed on the basis that the taxpayer had received a reasonable allowance for travelling expenses the amount of which was not included in computing the taxpayer's income, see *Bourbonniere v. M.N.R.* (1957), 18 Tax ABC 134 and *Karp v. M.N.R.*, [1968] Tax ABC 1018 (T.A.B.).

J. Expenses of Musicians and Artists

Like taxpayers who are employed in connection with the selling of property or negotiating of contracts for their employers, musicians and artists are also eligible for a broader range of deductions than those available to other employees. According to paragraph 8(1)(p), "where the taxpayer was employed in the year as a musician and as a term of the employment was required to provide a musical instrument for a period in the year," the taxpayer may deduct:

an amount (not exceeding the taxpayer's income for the year from the employment, computed without reference to this paragraph) equal to the total of

(i)   amounts expended by the taxpayer before the end of the year for the maintenance, rental or insurance of the instrument for that period, except to the extent that the amounts are otherwise deducted in computing the taxpayer's income for any taxation year, and

(ii)   such part, if any, of the capital cost to the taxpayer of the instrument as is allowed by regulation.

According to paragraph 8(1)(q), where a taxpayer's income from an office or employment includes income from an "artistic activity":

(i) that was the creation by the taxpayer of, but did not include the reproduction of, paintings, prints, etchings, drawings, sculptures or similar works of art,

(ii) that was the composition by the taxpayer of a dramatic, musical or literary work,

(iii) that was the performance by the taxpayer of a dramatic or musical work as an actor, dancer, singer or musician, or

(iv) in respect of which the taxpayer was a member of a professional artists' association that is certified by the Minister of Canadian Heritage,

the taxpayer may deduct "amounts paid by the taxpayer before the end of the year in respect of expenses incurred for the purpose of earning income from those activities to the extent that they were not deductible in computing the taxpayer's income for a preceding taxation year," up to an amount "in respect of all such offices and employments of the taxpayer" equal to the amount, if any, by which:

(v) the lesser of $1,000 and 20% of the total of all amounts each of which is the taxpayer's income from an office or employment for the year, before deducting any amount under this section, that was income from an artistic activity described in any of subparagraphs [8(1)(q)(i)] to [8(1)(q)(iv)].

exceeds

(vi) the total of all amounts deducted by the taxpayer for the year under paragraph [8(1)(j)] or [8(1)(p)] in respect of costs or expenses incurred for the purpose of earning the income from such an activity for the year.

Paragraph 8(1)(p), which applies to 1988 and subsequent taxation years, allows taxpayers who are employed as musicians and required to provide a musical instrument "as a term of the employment" to deduct various expenses associated with the acquisition and maintenance of the instrument, including rental payments, insurance premiums, and capital cost allowances (which are computed at a rate of 20 per cent on a declining-balance basis).[69]

In *Belkin v. Canada*, [2005] T.C.J. No. 598, [2006] 1 C.T.C. 2399, 2006 D.T.C. 2016 (T.C.C.), the taxpayer was a professional musician and a music professor at the University of Montreal who sought to deduct capital cost allowance under paragraph 8(1)(p) in respect of a Macintosh computer which he

---

[69] For the purpose of the capital cost allowance rules, subs. 13(11) deems an amount deducted under subpara. 8(1)(p)(ii) to have been deducted under regulations made under para. 20(1)(a), which provides for the deduction of capital cost allowances in computing a taxpayer's income from a business or property. On this basis, musical instruments may be categorized as class 8 property under Schedule II of the *Income Tax Regulations*. Capital cost allowances are examined in Chapter 5.

used to conduct his teaching and research on computer-based composition and play back of music. In allowing the taxpayer's appeal Lamarre Proulx TCJ reasoned (at paragraphs 26-32):

> It appears rather evident that a computer cannot be considered a musical instrument if we begin the analysis by comparing traditional musical instruments such as a piano, violin or harp with a computer.
>
> However, a statute can apply to situations which did not exist when it was enacted, if justified by its aim and compatible with its wording.
>
> ...
>
> I believe that, for the purpose of giving effect to the legislative provision of paragraph 8(1)(p) of the Act, we have to look at the matter from a musician's perspective. What is the musician's tool to teach music, to create musical works, to reproduce musical sounds and even to produce sounds that a traditional music instrument cannot produce?
>
> ...
>
> In my view, the evidence has shown that times have evolved. This was revealed by the evolution of the type of courses taught at the Juilliard School as mentioned by the Appellant. In the field of music, a computer may now be used for artistic and creative purposes.
>
> My conclusion is that for the person who is employed as a musician and as a term of his employment is required to provide a computer for teaching musical subjects such as composition and orchestration, a computer is within the meaning of a musical instrument.

Paragraph 8(1)(q), which applies after 1990, allows taxpayers with income from an office or employment that "includes" income from a qualifying "artistic activity" to deduct amounts paid "in respect of expenses incurred for the purpose of earning income" from the qualifying artistic activity up to the amount by which the lesser of $1,000 and 20 per cent of the taxpayer's aggregate income from all offices and employments otherwise determined exceeds interest and capital cost allowances deducted under paragraph 8(1)(j) (motor vehicles and aircraft) and musical instrument costs deducted under paragraph 8(1)(p). The courts have yet to interpret paragraph 8(1)(q).[70]

V. TIMING ISSUES

In order to compute a taxpayer's income from an office or employment, it is necessary to determine not only the specific amounts that must be included or may be deducted, but also the taxation year in which these inclusions and deductions are taken into account or recognized for tax purposes. As a general rule, taxpayers will prefer to delay the recognition of inclusions and accelerate

---

[70] For the CRA's views on these provisions, see *Interpretation Bulletin* IT-504R2, "Visual Artists and Writers," December 2000, and *Interpretation Bulletin* IT-525R, "Performing Artists," August 17, 1995.

the recognition of deductions in order to reduce current tax liabilities and defer the payment of tax. However, where a taxpayer expects to face a higher tax liability in a subsequent taxation year — for example, because increased income is subject to tax at a higher rate — the taxpayer may prefer to accelerate the recognition of inclusions and/or delay the recognition of deductions. For the revenue authorities, of course, the incentives are generally reversed.

For the most part, income from an office or employment is computed on the basis of what is called the cash method of accounting. According to this approach, all items of income that are received in the accounting period are recognized for that period, and expenses paid in the period are recognized for that period. Although this accounting method can produce a distorted picture of a taxpayer's income in a taxation year in which a taxpayer receives or makes a payment in respect of amounts earned or expenses incurred in another taxation year, it is considerably simpler than other methods of accounting and relatively accurate for the computation of income from an office or employment, which is generally received in regular increments throughout the year and in respect of which deductions are relatively few and similarly recurring.

Notwithstanding these advantages, the cash method can create opportunities for tax avoidance where taxpayers deliberately delay the receipt of income in order to defer its recognition to subsequent taxation years. Although some provisions permit or even encourage this deferral subject to specific limits, other provisions are designed to prevent this deferral by including specific categories of income from an office or employment on an accrual basis, which requires that they be recognized for tax purposes when they have been earned, even if they have not been received.

This section considers timing issues in the computation of a taxpayer's income from an office or employment, examining statutory language and specific provisions governing the accounting period in which amounts must be included and may be deducted in computing a taxpayer's income from these sources.

A. Inclusions

According to subsection 5(1) of the Act, "a taxpayer's income for a taxation year from an office or employment is the salary, wages and other remuneration, including gratuities, *received* by the taxpayer *in the year*" (emphasis added). Similarly, paragraph 6(1)(a) requires taxpayers to include the value of benefits "*received or enjoyed* by the taxpayer *in the year*," while paragraph 6(1)(b) requires taxpayers to include "all amounts *received* by the taxpayer *in the year* as an allowance" and paragraph 6(1)(c) requires taxpayer to include "director's or other fees *received* by the taxpayer *in the year*" (emphasis added). For the purpose of paragraph 6(1)(a), moreover, subsections 6(19) and (20) define benefits in respect of housing losses in terms of amounts "paid" in respect of the loss. These words, as Canadian courts have held in other contexts,[71] denote a cash basis of accounting according to which income is recognized for tax purposes in the taxation year in which it is actually received, even though it may have been earned in a previous taxation year or may not yet have been earned.

In contrast to these general rules, however, other provisions allow taxpayers to defer the recognition of amounts that would otherwise be included in computing their income from an office or employment, while yet other rules prevent undue deferral by requiring taxpayers to include specific amounts notwithstanding the absence of actual receipts.[72] According to subparagraph 6(1)(a)(i), for example, in computing the value of any benefit received or enjoyed in the year in respect of, in the course of, or by virtue of an office or employment, taxpayers need not include the value of any benefits derived from an employer's contributions to or under a registered pension plan (RPP) or a deferred profit-sharing plan (DPSP), which are taxable under subparagraphs 56(1)(a)(i) and paragraph 56(1)(i), respectively, only when amounts are received in the form of pension benefits or payments under the DPSP. In contrast, where at the end of a taxation year a taxpayer has "a right under a salary deferral arrangement ... to receive a deferred amount," subsection 6(11) deems an amount equal to the deferred amount to have been received in the year, even if it was not actually received.

The following text and cases consider the concepts of "receipt" and "enjoyment" on which the timing of most inclusions is based in computing a taxpayer's income from an office or employment, as well as special rules governing the taxation of various kinds of deferred income from an office or employment. To the extent that the latter provisions are part of a more general statutory scheme including registered retirement savings plans ("RRSPs") and the taxation of amounts received from an RPP or a DPSP as income from an "other source" under subdivision d, the review of deferred income in this chapter should be read together with the discussion of related provisions in Chapter 7.

1. Receipt and Enjoyment

According to the *Canadian Oxford Dictionary*, the word "receive" is defined as "acquire or accept," "accept delivery of," or "be granted or have conferred upon one," while the word "enjoy" means "have the use or benefit of." Although the legal concept of a receipt is generally associated with the acquisition of a legal entitlement to the payment or item that is received,[73] the "enjoyment" associated with the "use or benefit" of an item does not necessitate legal entitlement or

---

[71] See, for example, *Trapp v. M.N.R.*, [1946] C.T.C. 30, 2 D.T.C. 784 (Ex. Ct.).

[72] One example of such special timing rules are the provisions governing employee stock option benefits, discussed above in Section III of this Chapter.

[73] See, for example, *Kenneth B.S. Robertson Ltd. v. M.N.R.*, [1944] C.T.C. 75, 2 D.T.C. 655 (Ex. Ct).

ownership. As a result, as Professor Krishna observes, the use of the word "enjoy" in paragraph 6(1)(a) "enlarges the benefit rule beyond actual receipt of the benefit."[74]

With respect to the timing of inclusions in computing a taxpayer's income from an office or employment, the use of the word "received" in subsection 5(1) and paragraphs 6(1)(b) and (c) and the words "received or enjoyed" in paragraph 6(1)(a) suggests that income from these sources will generally be recognized in the taxation year in which the recipient is legally entitled to the amounts in question (salary, wages, and other remuneration, including gratuities, allowances, and director's or other fees), except for benefits, the value of which may be included in a taxation year in which the taxpayer obtains the use of a good or service (for example, an automobile or free education) regardless of legal entitlement. A good discussion of the meaning of the word "received" in the context of computing a taxpayer's income from an office or employment appears in *Cliffe v. M.N.R.* (1957), 17 Tax ABC 207, 57 D.T.C. 305 (TA.B.).

Cliffe v. M.N.R.
(1957), 17 Tax ABC 207, 57 D.T.C. 305 (T.A.B.)

W.S. FISHER: The taxpayer appealed against his income tax assessment for the year 1954. When assessing him, the respondent added, to the income reported by the taxpayer in the return as filed, the sum of $3,333.91, which ... represented, in the respondent's view, "wages not withdrawn," and ... it was stated, further, that "when wages have been credited to your account by the Company and the funds are available they are considered to have been received by you."

In the notice of objection filed with the Minister, the taxpayer stated that his salary for 1954 was set by the company but that, "owing to commitments they had," it could not be paid to him; that he had reported as income the amount of salary he had received in 1954; and that he had paid tax on it. The taxpayer then gave as his reasons for objection to the assessment:

(a) That Section 5 of the Income Tax Act required him to report as income amounts received in the year;

(b) That the amount assessed additionally as taxable income was not received by him; and

(c) That when it was received he would report it as taxable income.

...

---

[74] Vern Krishna, *The Fundamentals of Canadian Income Tax*, 6th ed. (Toronto: Carswell, 2000) at 187.

With the exception of two shares, one held by his wife and one by his mother ... , all of the shares of Cliffe & Cliffe Logging Limited are held, in equal proportions, by the appellant and his father. The appellant is manager and president of the company, devoting all of his attention to the company's business. The company's fiscal year ends on July 31 in each year.

At some time in the fall of the year 1953, the appellant and his father discussed the question of salaries to be paid to them by the company, and it was agreed that the appellant should receive a salary of $7,500 for the company's fiscal year ending on July 31, 1954. During the company's 1953-54 fiscal year, its activities were entirely devoted to removing log poles for MacMillan and Bloedel Logging Company under a contract which Cliffe & Cliffe had with that company. Cliffe & Cliffe Logging was operating with a very limited amount of capital, and its expenses were being paid through advances received from MacMillan & Bloedel as and when log poles were delivered to that company. The total amount involved in the contract between Cliffe & Cliffe Logging Limited and MacMillan and Bloedel was in the neighbourhood of $60,000 to $65,000.

In February of 1954, the company received a statement from MacMillan & Bloedel which indicated that, instead of the latter company owing Cliffe & Cliffe Logging a considerable sum of money in respect of the contract, Cliffe & Cliffe Logging Ltd. owed MacMillan & Bloedel, for advances made in excess of the contract, the sum of $14,000 ... .

...

With this situation facing the company, and while discussions were taking place between Cliffe & Cliffe Logging Ltd. and MacMillan and Bloedel Ltd., it was felt that the company should not be called upon to pay out the full amount of the salaries which it had previously been agreed should be paid to the appellant and his father until the situation had improved. As shareholders of the company, the appellant and his father realized that there was a possibility of suffering a considerable loss on the MacMillan and Bloedel contract and, in any event, it would be necessary for the company to have funds on hand to engage in further operations under any other contracts which the company might receive in the spring or summer of 1954. The appellant stated that, for these reasons, he and his father merely drew from the company, in respect of the salaries owing to them, sufficient funds to enable them to finance their households from week to week. The balance of the appellant's salary and that of his father was not withdrawn or taken from the company in that calendar year.

The evidence indicated that, when Cliffe & Cliffe Logging Ltd. filed its income tax return for its fiscal period ended July 31, 1954, it claimed the full amount of the appellant's salary, as well as the full amount of the appellant's father's salary, as a deduction, as the company's auditors no doubt looked upon the balance of the salaries still unpaid as a debt owed by the company to the appellant and his father. It was contended on behalf of the respondent that, inasmuch as the appellant and his father had full control over the company through their ownership of the company's shares, the balance of their salaries undrawn should be looked upon as a loan by them to the company. I indicated at the hearing that I was unable to concur in this submission.

Respondent's counsel brought out, also, that as of July 31, 1954, Cliffe & Cliffe Logging Ltd. had sufficient moneys in its bank account to enable the company to pay the balance of the salaries due to the appellant and to his father had it so desired, and there would still have been some $1,000 in cash on hand at the bank. However, even in the light of this situation, it is my opinion that the company's officials were in the best position to determine whether it should pay out the moneys in question or whether, for the good of the company, it was necessary that a considerable amount of cash should be kept on hand to finance any possible operations which it might undertake under any future contracts which it might receive, as there was always the possibility that under a new contract the company might not be in a position to obtain advances against future deliveries of logs and would have to have money on hand to meet the expenses of carrying on business and to pay the wages of the loggers and other employees.

...

The evidence at the hearing did not disclose whether Cliffe & Cliffe Logging Ltd. had credited the balance owing to the appellant to an account in the appellant's name, or whether the balance owing in respect of the appellant's salary had merely been set up in the company's books as an account payable. It is quite possible, however, that it was the latter alternative which was adopted by the company, since the evidence indicated that neither the appellant nor his father intended to withdraw the balance of their salaries until such time as the company was in a sufficiently liquid position financially to enable the appellant and his father to be paid without harming the financial position of the company. The appellant's evidence was that, eventually, in the calendar year 1955, he did receive the full balance of the salary which was owing to him in respect of the company's 1954 fiscal period, although he did not receive, in the company's 1955 fiscal period, the full amount of the salary owing to him for that period.

...

In the circumstances of this case ... it is my opinion that the sum of $3,333.91 in dispute was not received by this taxpayer in the year 1954 and, accordingly, that it has been improperly included in computing his income for the purpose of the assessment appealed against.

In *Capital Trust Corporation et al. v. M.N.R.*, [1936] SCR 192; [1935-37] CTC 267, where the taxpayer during his lifetime had been an executor of his father's estate, under which he was entitled to be paid $500 a month "in addition to any sum which the courts or other proper authorities may allow him in common with the other executors," and nothing was paid to the testator's son for a number of years until finally a lump sum of $19,500 was paid to him to cover the period from December 5, 1923, to March 5, 1927, it was contended that the $500 per month which was payable in the years 1923, 1924, 1925, 1926 and

1927 for the months of the period indicated should be taxed in the appellant's hands in those years instead of the whole amount being taxed in the year of receipt, namely, 1927. In that case, there was no question but that the estate was quite capable of paying the $500 per month in each of the years in question and that the taxpayer had simply failed to request payment. The Supreme Court of Canada held that the sum of $19,500 was assessable for income tax in respect of the year 1927, the taxation year in which it was actually received, notwithstanding that $18,000 of that sum represented arrears that had fallen due during preceding years. In the judgment of the Court, delivered by Davis J, in which all references made are in connection with the old *Income War Tax Act*, it was stated, at p. 195:

> ... The statute here by section 3 defines income as "income received" and by section 9 imposes the tax upon "the income during the preceding year." Unfortunately in this case the taxpayer is bound to pay a larger amount than could have been levied and collected upon the same income had it been paid in instalments month by month as it became due and payable, but that cannot affect the liability plainly imposed by the statute.

This decision has been followed in a considerable number of cases since that time, and it is my opinion that it is equally applicable in the circumstances of the present case.

In *Vegso v. M.N.R.*, 14 Tax ABC 451, the appellant worked on her father's farm from 1943 to 1953 at a yearly wage of $800. $700 of the $800 earned each year was held in trust for her by her father until she married and, in 1954, the accumulated sum of $8,283 was paid to her. The Minister added the said sum to the appellant's declared income for 1954 and levied tax thereon as salary received in 1954, whereas the appellant contended that it should have been included in her income for the years 1943 to 1953, both inclusive. It was held that, although the appellant may have believed that her salary was held in trust, nevertheless it was taxable in the year in which it was received.

...

In his argument at the hearing of the present appeal, respondent's counsel referred to the decision of this Board in *Green v. M.N.R.*, 2 Tax ABC 218. In that case, however, the appellant, as a director of a finance company, had the privilege of depositing funds with the company and withdrawing such funds at any time, receiving 5% interest on the amounts deposited with the finance company. In the year 1946, his account was credited with $1,069.68 interest, which the Minister claimed was taxable in that year but which the appellant claimed he did not receive and that therefore he should not be taxed on that sum in that year. In the judgment ... it was pointed out that the appellant Green, as a director of the company, knew that the interest payable to him would be credited to his account; that he had agreed to this arrangement and had authorized the company to proceed thus; and that, by crediting the appellant's account each month with such interest as it had undertaken to pay to him, the company was discharging its obligation and the appellant was receiving, indirectly, the interest due on the money. The judgment continued, at p. 222 of the Tax Appeal Board Cases report:

> Since the appellant had agreed to the inclusion of the interest owed him by the company in the amount standing to his credit at the end of each month, I am of the opinion that, upon crediting the amount of interest to the appellant's account, the company fulfilled its obligation to pay the appellant the interest due, and the appellant received the amount of interest thus added to his balance. Indeed, it must be borne in mind that the appellant, having absolute control over the amount to his credit, including capital and interest, was at all times free to withdraw any funds from this account and even the whole amount. This could hardly have been done if he had not had the full ownership of this amount.

As already pointed out, there was no evidence before me in this case that the balance of this taxpayer's salary which owed to him had been credited to an account of his in the company's books. Notwithstanding the very able argument advanced on behalf of the respondent that the company had charged the balance of these salaries as expenses in determining its income for its 1954 fiscal period; that the appellant and his father were the controlling shareholders of the company and it was their decision which resulted in the non-payment of the balance of the salaries, so that they were not paid out in the year 1954; that the company had on hand sufficient cash at July 31, 1954, to enable it to pay the balance of the salaries in question; and that the amounts of salary allowed to remain in the hands of the company should be considered, in the circumstances, to have been a loan to the company by the two main shareholders, it is my opinion that the disputed amount of salary not actually received cannot be considered to come within the provisions of Section 5 of the Act, as it was not actually received in the year. ...

Appeal allowed.

NOTES AND QUESTIONS

1.   On what basis did the Minister in *Cliffe* add $3,333.91 in computing the taxpayer's employment income for his 1954 taxation year? Why did the board allow the taxpayer's appeal?

2.   Of what, if any, relevance to the board's decision in *Cliffe* was the absence of any evidence that the balance of the taxpayer's salary was not credited to an account of the taxpayer in the company's books? Would the $3,333.91 have been taxable in 1954 if the company had credited this amount to an account of the taxpayer during that year?

3.   In *M.N.R. v. Rousseau* (1958), 20 Tax ABC 333 (T.A.B.), aff'd [1960] C.T.C. 336, 60 D.T.C. 1236 (Ex. Ct.), the taxpayer was the controlling shareholder and manager of a company that agreed to pay him $22,000 in 1954 as salary and rent for premises occupied by the company, but actually paid only $15,263, crediting the remaining $6,737 to an account on the company's books from which the taxpayer could draw funds "at his discretion and according to his needs" (at para. 42). Rejecting the Minister's argument that the additional

amount was effectively received by the taxpayer in 1954, the board allowed the taxpayer's appeal. According to Mr. Boisvert (at paras. 50-53):

> It seems clear to me that the intention of the legislator was to tax the wage-earner on the wage or salary he receives, that is to say, on what he is paid in cash or otherwise, provided the funds come into his possession. If part of the wages remained in the possession of a third party — of a company as is the case here — it cannot be said that he received that part of his remuneration. ...
>
> The fact that an amount owing to the appellant had been credited to him cannot be considered payment within the meaning of the Act. Let us suppose for a moment that the limited company went bankrupt at the beginning of 1955, that the appellant was not paid his salary and in addition that it was obvious that the assets of the company were not sufficient to pay him, the effect would be that the taxpayer would be paying tax on salary he had not received and could not receive which, in my opinion, is not in accordance with the letter or spirit of the Act. If the legislator had intended that, he would not have used in Section 5 of the Act the words "that the taxpayer received."

For a similar result, relying on *Rousseau*, see *Phillips v. The Queen*, [1994] 2 C.T.C. 2416 (T.C.C.).

4.   Do you agree with the results in *Cliffe*, *Rousseau*, and *Phillips*? Of what, if any, relevance to your opinion is the fact that in each case the taxpayer's employer was a closely held company that was managed and controlled by the taxpayer? Of what, if any, relevance to your view is the fact that in each case the employer computed its income on an accrual basis and deducted the unpaid amount in the taxation year in which it was payable, even though it had not been paid? Should shareholder-managers of privately held companies be able to obtain this tax advantage by incurring obligations to pay salaries that are not actually paid during the taxation year?

5.   In response to transactions like those in *Cliffe* and *Rousseau*, the *Income Tax Act* was amended in the 1960s to disallow the deduction of amounts that remained unpaid beyond a stipulated period of time. According to subsection 78(1) of the Act:

> Where an amount in respect of a deductible outlay or expense that was owing by a taxpayer to a person with whom the taxpayer was not dealing at arm's length at the time the outlay or expense was incurred and at the end of the second taxation year following the taxation year in which the outlay or expense was incurred, is unpaid at the end of that second taxation year, either
>
> (a)   the amount so unpaid shall be included in computing the taxpayer's income for the third taxation year following the taxation year in which the outlay or expense was incurred, or
>
> (b)   where the taxpayer and that person have filed an agreement in prescribed form on or before the day on or before which the taxpayer is required by section 150 to file the taxpayer's return of income for the third succeeding taxation year, for the purposes of this Act the following rules apply:
>
>   (i)   the amount so unpaid shall be deemed to have been paid by the taxpayer and received by that person on the first day of that third taxation year ... , and

(ii) that person shall be deemed to have made a loan to the taxpayer on the first day of that third taxation year in an amount equal to the amount so unpaid minus the amount, if any, deducted or withheld therefrom by the taxpayer on account of that person's tax for that third taxation year.

According to subsection 78(2):

Where an amount in respect of a deductible outlay or expense that was owing by a taxpayer that is a corporation to a person with whom the taxpayer was not dealing at arm's length is unpaid at the time when the taxpayer is wound up, and the taxpayer is wound up before the end of the second taxation year following the taxation year in which the outlay or expense was incurred, the amount so unpaid shall be included in computing the taxpayer's income for the taxation year in which it was wound up.

More significantly for present purposes, subsection 78(4) stipulates:

Where an amount in respect of a taxpayer's expense that is a superannuation or pension benefit, a retiring allowance, salary, wages or other remuneration (other than reasonable vacation or holiday pay or a deferred amount under a salary deferral arrangement) in respect of an office or employment is unpaid on the day that is 180 days after the end of the taxation year in which the expense was incurred, for the purposes of this Act other than this subsection, the amount shall be deemed not to have been incurred as an expense in the year and shall be deemed to be incurred as an expense in the taxation year in which the amount is paid.

According to subsection 78(5), subsection 78(1) does not apply in any case where subsection 78(4) applies. As a result, where an employer incurs an obligation to pay wages, salary, or other remuneration to an employee, which amount remains unpaid 180 days after the end of the employer's taxation year, the unpaid amount must be added back in computing its income. In order to prevent this result, employers must actually pay the amount to the employee, triggering an income inclusion to the employee.

For cases in which these provisions have been considered in the context of closely held companies deducting unpaid salaries and bonuses to shareholder-managers, see *Canada v. V & R Enterprises Ltd.*, [1979] C.T.C. 465, 79 D.T.C. 5399 (F.C.T.D.); *Earlscourt Sheet Metal Mechanical Ltd. v. M.N.R.*, [1987] T.C.J. No. 1104, [1988] 1 C.T.C. 2045, 88 D.T.C. 1029 (T.C.C.); and *Berube v. Canada*, [1994] T.C.J. No. 133, [1994] 1 C.T.C. 2655 (T.C.C.). For the CRA's views on these provisions, see *Interpretation Bulletin* IT-109R2, "Unpaid Amounts," April 23, 1993.

6.   In *Park v. M.N.R.* (1950), 1 Tax ABC 391 (T.A.B.), the taxpayer, a substantial shareholder and vice-president of a company that had agreed to pay him an annual salary of $6,000 and a bonus of $3,000 for the year ending February 28, 1947, received $8,645.93 in 1946 and 1947, which he characterized as a non-taxable loan rather than remuneration. Observing (at paras. 53 and 56) that the taxpayer "signed no note or acknowledgement of debt in favour of the company," that "no mention was made regarding the rate of interest to be paid by him on these amounts," that "no term was set for the refund," and that if the taxpayer "had wanted to borrow from the company, he would have borrowed a substantial amount and would not ... have received

amounts of money several times per month," Mr. Monet concluded that "the relationship of borrower and lender never existed between the appellant and the company" and that the sum received was taxable remuneration.

For a contrasting result, see *Brum v. M.N.R.*, [1980] C.T.C. 2651, 80 D.T.C. 1607 (T.R.B.), in which the taxpayer, who was the president and controlling shareholder of a company (A & B Rail Contractors Ltd.) that built and repaired railway lines, withdrew funds on a regular basis every two weeks to pay his personal expenses, entering the amounts as indebtedness in the taxpayer's shareholder's loan account, which was credited a year later by the payment of "accrued salary payable." Even though "no promissory note was ever delivered nor were interest or conditions of repayment ever agreed on" (at para. 3), the board rejected the Minister's characterization of the payments as remuneration, not loans. According to Mr. Bonner (at para. 11):

> I do not regard [*Park*, supra] as setting down a rule of law that some or all of the list of indicia of a debtor-creditor relationship is or are necessary to establish the existence of that relationship. It is a question of fact to be decided on the evidence.
>
> Generally speaking bookkeeping entries do not create reality. They are useful only to the extent that they record or reflect reality. In this case, despite the use of the word "payable" in the phrase "accrued salary payable," I cannot find that the making of entries in that account reflected the creation of any enforceable obligation of the Company to pay to the appellant the amounts entered. The entries reflected only the creation of a contingent reserve. The approach taken by the [Minister] on assessment in effect anticipated, for the purpose of imposition of tax in each year, what did in fact regularly happen in the following year, that is to say, the finding of sufficient cash and the consequent crediting of the loan account of the accrued salary expense previously set upon in the books of A & B. The crediting was an event which need not necessarily have occurred as anticipated.

7.   In *Randall v. M.N.R.*, [1987] 2 C.T.C. 2265, 87 D.T.C. 553 (T.C.C.), the taxpayer, a lawyer with the Department of Justice, requested an advance on his salary in November 1985, which he received before the end of the year, covering a period in January 1986 when he planned to be on vacation and at a conference. Rejecting the taxpayer's argument that the advance was a non-taxable loan that he would have been required to repay had he ceased employment at the end of 1985, the court held that the sum was taxable in 1985. According to Taylor TCJ (at para. 3):

> In my view the proposition of the appellant that this should be considered a "loan" is not viable. Mr. Randall did not request a "loan" from his employer, he did request "pay in advance" and the evidence indicates that was what he received. ... Further, if he were sued for "non-performance," as he noted might happen, I am not persuaded even the recovery of the amount in a subsequent year by his employer, would have any direct bearing on its taxability in 1985. In the end analysis the amount is "pay" and therefore salary or wages, as indicated by subsection 5(1) of the Act.

For other cases in which advances of salary have been held to be taxable in the year they were received, see *Laberge v. M.N.R.* (1965), 38 Tax ABC 361 and *Ferszt v. M.N.R.*, [1978] C.T.C. 2860, 78 D.T.C. 1648 (T.R.B.).

8.   In *Meredith v. Canada*, [1994] T.C.J. No. 51, [1994] 1 C.T.C. 2538, 94 D.T.C. 1271 (T.C.C.), the taxpayer, who owned 50 per cent of the shares of a

real estate company of which he was a director and for which he worked as a commissioned salesperson, withdrew cash on a regular basis "as needed" during a period that the real estate business was in recession and the taxpayer was unable to earn sufficient commission income to meet his personal expenses. Rejecting the Minister's argument that the funds, which were described as "net advances receivable" in the company's financial statements, were taxable remuneration in the years in which they were received, the court relied on *Brum v. M.N.R.*, [1980] C.T.C. 2651, 80 D.T.C. 1607 (T.R.B.), to conclude that they were non-taxable loans. According to Kempo JTCC (at para. 41):

> Where there is no measurable degree of certainty concerning the earning and receipt of the future income, the advances made may ... be more accurately characterized as a loan. For the advances here to be considered income receipts, the Court must be able to find that under and by virtue of his contract of employment the appellant was entitled to commission based income and to advances on possible future earnings from time to time repayable solely out of that source which is to say that the future income if earned was to be the source and security for repayment with no liability to repay if it proved to be inadequate. If the latter represented the true situation then the recipient would enjoy receipt of these advances as a form of wages, salary or other remuneration within the meaning of subsection 5(1) of the Act.

Do you agree with this result? Why or why not? Is the decision consistent with *Randall v. M.N.R.*, [1987] 2 C.T.C. 2265, 87 D.T.C. 553 (T.C.C.)?

9.   Although the principal amount of a loan made to an officer or employee is not included in computing the recipient's income unless the loan is forgiven, a taxable benefit may be assessed under subsections 6(9) and 80.4(1) where the loan is low-interest or interest-free. See section III of this chapter. Where a corporation loans money to a shareholder, the principal amount of the loan is taxable under subsection 15(2). This provision, and others dealing with shareholder benefits, are best examined in a course on the taxation of corporations and shareholders.

10.   In *Markman v. M.N.R.*, [1989] 1 C.T.C. 2381, 89 D.T.C. 253 (T.C.C.), the taxpayer, a lawyer employed in the legislation-drafting section of the Department of Justice, was awarded a retroactive salary increase for the period April 1 to December 31, 1985, which was supposed to be received before the end of 1985 but was actually received on January 2, 1986 due to an administrative delay in the Compensation Services Branch. Rejecting the taxpayer's argument that the payment was intended to have been made in 1985 and therefore constructively received in that year, the court affirmed the Minister's assessment including the payment in computing the taxpayer's income for her 1986 taxation year.

11.   In *Blenkarn v. M.N.R.* (1963), 32 Tax ABC 321, 63 D.T.C. 581 (T.A.B.), the taxpayer was a paymaster in the Canadian Militia who delayed the receipt of salary owing in December 1960 by not making a requisition for the payment until the following year. Rejecting the taxpayer's argument that the payment was not taxable until it was received in 1961, the board concluded (at para. 5):

[T]here would seem to be little ground for finding that this was not income to the appellant which should be taxed in 1960. Being in a position to do so, he omitted to enter his name on the pay list which was a necessary step in the process of obtaining funds with which to make payment to his unit. Since that step and making requisition for funds was all that was required to enable the appellant to receive payment of salary due to the end of November, 1960, it seems that refusing, as it were, or neglecting to accept payment of an amount due does not make that amount anything but income when it is receivable.

Do you agree with this result? Why or why not? Is it consistent with the use of the word "received" in subsection 5(1)? According to Peter W. Hogg, Joanne E. Magee, and Ted Cook, *Principles of Canadian Income Tax Law*, 3d ed. (Toronto: Carswell, 1999) at 165, "[t]he payment was 'received' as soon as [the taxpayer] had an unconditional right to be paid, which was in 1960."

12. In *Morin v. Canada*, [1975] C.T.C. 106, 75 D.T.C. 5061 (F.C.T.D.), the taxpayer sought in computing his employment income to exclude amounts withheld for provincial income tax on the basis that he had not "received" these amounts within the meaning of subsection 5(1). Rejecting this argument, the court (at para. 29) cited an earlier Tax Review Board decision for the proposition that:

[t]he expression "touché" (received) does not necessarily mean that the full amount of the salary must be physically received by the payee or be deposited in full in his bank account.

According to the interpretation of section 5 it is sufficient to say that the amount of the salary was paid by the employer either to the employee himself or to his benefit, or that it was handed over to a third party under a federal or provincial statute.

For other applications of this "constructive receipt" doctrine in computing a taxpayer's income from an office or employment, see *Canada v. Kurisko*, [1988] F.C.J. No. 740, [1988] 2 C.T.C. 254, 88 D.T.C. 6434 (F.C.T.D.) and *M.N.R. v. Fairey*, [1991] F.C.J. No. 254, [1991] 1 C.T.C. 371, 91 D.T.C. 5230 (F.C.T.D.) (contributions to pension plans); *Dorval v. M.N.R.*, [1979] C.T.C. 2888, 79 D.T.C. 736 (T.R.B.) (payment of provincial health insurance premiums); and *Canada v. Hoffman*, [1985] 2 C.T.C. 347, 85 D.T.C. 5508 (F.C.T.D.) (payment of US social security contributions by US employer of US citizen employed and residing in Canada).

13. In *Hogg v. Canada*, [1987] F.C.J. No. 1019, [1987] 2 C.T.C. 257, 87 D.T.C. 5447 (F.C.T.D.), the taxpayer, an employee of a mining company that maintained an investment plan under which the custodian of the plan used funds contributed by the employer and employees to acquire shares of the mining company that could be withdrawn by employees after three years of participation in the plan, received 2,023 shares valued at $77,000 on his retirement in 1979. Accepting the taxpayer's argument that the taxable benefit had been "received" in prior years when the taxpayer's right to withdraw the shares had vested, the court allowed the taxpayer's appeal from an assessment including a taxable benefit in computing the taxpayer's employment income in 1979.

14. For the purposes of the Act, paragraph 248(7)(a) stipulates that "anything ... sent by first class mail or its equivalent shall be deemed to have been received by the person to whom it was sent on the day it was mailed." As a result, where a paycheque is mailed to an employee at the end of one taxation year but not actually received until the next taxation year, the payment must be included in computing the employee's income for the taxation year in which the cheque was mailed.

2. Deferred Income

As indicated earlier, the *Income Tax Act* both allows taxpayers to defer the recognition of amounts that would otherwise be included in computing their income from an office or employment and prevents undue deferral by requiring taxpayers to include specific amounts notwithstanding the absence of actual receipt. The following discussion reviews the most important of these rules, considering registered pension plans ("RPPs"), deferred profit savings plans ("DPSPs"), salary deferral arrangements ("SDAs"), and options to acquire securities.

a. Registered Pension Plans

Subsection 248(1) of the Act defines a "registered pension plan" as "a pension plan that has been registered by the Minister for the purposes of this Act, which registration has not been revoked." Subsection 147.1(2) provides that a "registered" plan must meet "prescribed" conditions set out in regulation 8501, while subsections 147.1(8) and (11) set out the circumstances under which the registration of a pension plan may be revoked. For our purposes, there is no need to examine these rules in detail.

In general, the *Income Tax Act* defines two kinds of pension plans: "money purchase" plans, the terms of which provide for a separate account for each member, the benefits from which depend on aggregate contributions to the plan, the return on these contributions over the years to the employee's retirement, and the value of the pension annuity that can be purchased with these accumulated investments at the time of the employee's retirement;[75] and "defined benefit" plans, the terms of which typically provide defined benefits according to a formula based on the number of years of service and a percentage of the employee's average annual earnings over a specified period (for example, the last three years of service).[76]

---

[75] See the definition of "money purchase provision" in subs. 147.1(1).

[76] See the definition of "defined benefit provision" in subs. 147.1(1). For example, where a pension plan provides a defined benefit calculated at 2 per cent of the average annual earnings during the last three years of service multiplied by the number of years of service, an employee who averaged $60,000 during the last three years and worked for 30 years would receive an annual pension of 0.02 × $60,000 × 30 = $36,000. In order to finance these benefits, annual

Under the scheme of the Act, contributions to a registered pension plan are deductible and not taxable as employment benefits,[77] and the investment income received by the plan is exempt from tax.[78] On retirement, pension benefits are subject to tax as income from an "other source" under subparagraph 56(1)(a)(i). The net effect is to defer tax on income contributed to an RPP and on the investment income produced by these savings until these funds are withdrawn from the plan in the form of pension benefits.

The favourable tax treatment available to these kinds of savings is subject to specific limits set out in the Act as well as the Regulations. For money purchase plans, the Act limits annual contributions to the lesser of 18 per cent of the employee's compensation from the employer for the year and a dollar limit that is set at $22,000 for 2009, after which it is to be indexed to annual increases in the average industrial wage.[79] For defined benefit plans, the annual contribution is limited to an amount that is actuarially determined to provide an accrued pension benefit of $1,722.22 or one-ninth of the dollar limit for money purchase plans, whichever is greater. This formula will generate an annual contribution limit of $2,444 in 2009 ($1/9$ x $22,000).[80]

These figures reflect an actuarial assumption that it requires an average contribution of $9 to finance a pension benefit of $1 commencing at age 65, a sociological assumption that individuals spend 35 years in the paid labour force, and a policy choice to limit the maximum tax-assisted retirement pension to the lesser of 2 per cent of an individual's compensation from each office or employment over a 35-year period and $85,556 (by 2009).[81] Alternatively, since it is assumed that a contribution of $9 is required to finance a pension of $1, an annual limit on tax-assisted retirement savings equivalent to 2 per cent of an individual's compensation from each office or employment implies an annual money purchase contribution limit equal to 18 per cent of this income.

b. Deferred Profit-Sharing Plans

Subsection 147(1) defines a "deferred profit sharing plan" as a "profit sharing plan" that is accepted by the Minister for registration on the basis that it

---

contributions must be determined by an actuary, taking into consideration factors such as actual and expected investment returns, employee turnover, and mortality rates.

[77] See para. 20(1)(q) and subs. 147.2(1) (deduction for employer contributions), para. 8(1)(m) and subs. 147.2(4) (deduction for employee contributions), and subpara. 6(1)(a)(i) (non-taxation as employment benefit).

[78] See paras. 149(1)(o), (o.1), and (o.2).

[79] See the "pension adjustment limits" in subs. 147.1(8) and the definitions of "compensation" of an individual from an employer and "money purchase limit" in subs. 147.1(1).

[80] See regulation 8500.

[81] For an excellent discussion of the policy choices leading to the current system of retirement savings, see Barbara Austin, "Preferences and Perversions in the Tax-Assisted Retirement Savings System" (1996), 41 McGill L.J. 571.

complies with the requirements of section 147. In turn, subsection 147(1) defines a "profit sharing plan" as:

> an arrangement under which payments computed by reference to an employer's profits from the employer's business, or by reference to those profits and the profits, if any, from the business of a corporation with which the employer does not deal at arm's length, are or have been made by the employer to a trustee in trust for the benefit of employees or former employees of that employer.

Where a profit-sharing plan qualifies as a DPSP, employer contributions are deductible under paragraph 20(1)(y) and subsection 147(8), benefits derived from these contributions are not taxable under paragraph 6(1)(a), and the investment income of the trust is exempt from tax under subsection 147(7) and paragraph 149(1)(s). Amounts received by a beneficiary under a DPSP, however, are taxable as income from an "other source" under paragraph 56(1)(i) and subsection 147(10). Like RPPs, therefore, DPSPs represent a statutorily sanctioned method whereby employees may defer the recognition of amounts that would otherwise be included in computing their income from an office or employment.

Like RPPs, moreover, the extent to which DPSPs can be used to provide tax-deferred compensation is specifically limited by the Act and the Regulations. According to paragraph 147(5.1)(a), for example, the maximum "pension credit" that may be provided under a DPSP in respect of each beneficiary is generally limited to the lesser of 18 per cent of the beneficiary's compensation from the employer for the year and one-half of the maximum dollar amount that may be contributed to a money purchase RPP ($11,000 in 2009, after which it is to be indexed to annual increases in the average industrial wage).[82] In addition, paragraph 147(5.1)(c) integrates the tax assistance available under RPPs and DPSPs by limiting the "pension adjustment" under these plans to the lesser of the maximum dollar amount that may be contributed to a money purchase RPP and 18 per cent of the beneficiary's compensation from the employer for the year.[83]

---

[82] For this purpose regulations 8301(2) and (3) generally define an individual's pension credit under a DPSP as the amount of any contribution in the year by the employer with respect to the individual and such portion of any forfeited amounts under the plan and earnings in respect thereof that are allocated to the individual.

[83] For the purpose of this provision, reg. 8301(1) generally defines the "pension adjustment" of an individual as the aggregate of the individual's pension credits under a DPSP or under the benefit provision of an RPP. In general, regulation 8301(4) defines the "pension credit" for a money purchase plan as the aggregate of contributions, forfeited amounts, and allocated surpluses, while reg. 8301(6) defines the "pension credit" for a defined benefit plan as nine times the individual's accrued benefit under the plan.

c. Salary Deferral Arrangements

Unlike RPPs and DPSPs, which allow taxpayers to defer the recognition of income from an office or employment subject to specific limits, the SDA rules are designed to prevent the deferral of income from these sources. Since income from an office or employment is generally computed on a cash basis, taxpayers might find it advantageous to defer the recognition of this income by delaying its actual receipt until a subsequent taxation year. In order to prevent this result, subsection 6(11) provides:

> Where at the end of a taxation year any person has a right under a salary deferral arrangement in respect of the taxpayer to receive a deferred amount, an amount equal to the deferred amount shall be deemed, for the purposes only of paragraph [6](1)(a), to have been received by the taxpayer as a benefit in the year, to the extent that the amount was not otherwise included in computing the taxpayer's income for the year or any preceding taxation year.

In addition, where the taxpayer is entitled to "any interest or other additional amount that accrued to, or for the benefit of, [the taxpayer] to the end of the year in respect of the deferred amount," subsection 6(12) deems this amount to be a deferred amount subject to the deeming rule in subsection 6(11). To the extent that these amounts are included under paragraph 6(1)(a), employers may claim a deduction under paragraph 20(1)(oo).

For the purpose of these provisions, subsection 248(1) defines a "salary deferral arrangement" in respect of a taxpayer as:

> a plan or arrangement, whether funded or not, under which any person has a right in a taxation year to receive an amount after the year where it is reasonable to consider that one of the main purposes for the creation or existence of the right is to postpone tax payable under this Act by the taxpayer in respect of an amount that is, or is on account or in lieu of, salary or wages of the taxpayer for services rendered by the taxpayer in the year or a preceding taxation year (including such a right that is subject to one or more conditions unless there is a substantial risk that any one of those conditions will not be satisfied),

other than various plans or arrangements indicated in paragraphs (a) to (l) of the definition. Subsection 248(1) defines a "deferred amount" at the end of a taxation year under a salary deferral arrangement in respect of a taxpayer as:

> (a) in the case of a trust governed by the arrangement, any amount that a person has a right under the arrangement at the end of the year to receive after the end of the year where the amount has been received, is receivable or may at any time become receivable by the trust as, on account or in lieu of salary or wages of the taxpayer for services rendered in the year or a preceding taxation year, and

> (b) in any other case, any amount that a person has a right under the arrangement at the end of the year to receive after the end of the year.

As a result, where a taxpayer is entitled under a plan or arrangement to receive an amount after the end of the taxation year (even if the right is subject to one or more conditions unless there is a substantial risk that a condition will not be satisfied), and one of the main purposes for the creation or existence of the right

483

is to postpone the payment of tax on compensation for services rendered by the taxpayer in the year or a preceding taxation year, the taxpayer must include the amount and any interest or other additional amount in respect of the deferred amount that accrued during the year as a taxable benefit for the year under paragraph 6(1)(a), unless the plan or arrangement is specifically excluded from the definition of a salary deferral arrangement under paragraphs (a) to (l) of the definition. Where amounts that were previously included in respect of an SDA are subsequently forfeited, however, paragraph 8(1)(o) permits a deduction in the subsequent taxation year to the extent of the forfeited amount.

Although the application of the SDA rules depend crucially on the conclusion that "it is reasonable to consider that one of the main purposes for the creation or existence of the right is to postpone tax payable," this criterion does not appear to have been subject to judicial or administrative interpretation. Professor Krishna, however, suggests that this requirement involves "[a]n intention to defer receipt for tax reasons."[84] Nonetheless, the words "reasonable to consider that'" suggest that the test is an objective one that does not turn on subjective intentions. In addition, although the word "main" can be interpreted as "chief or "principal,"[85] its use in the expression "one of the main purposes" suggests a somewhat broader meaning such as "major" or "substantial."

With respect to the inclusion of amounts in respect of rights that are "subject to one or more conditions unless there is a substantial risk that any one of those conditions will not be satisfied," paragraph 12 of *Interpretation Bulletin* IT-529, "Flexible Employee Benefit Programs," February 20, 1998, explains:

> the salary deferral arrangement rules cannot be avoided by making the employee's right to the funds subject to some condition which will likely be met anyway. For example, it is not relevant ... whether or not the receipt of the deferred amount is contingent on:
>
> - the employee remaining an employee for a minimum period of time;
>
> - the employee not being dismissed for the cause or commission of a crime;
>
> - the employee refraining from transferring or encumbering the employee's interest in the deferred amount; or
>
> - the employee abstaining from competition or being available for consultation after retirement or termination of employment.

According to the Department of Finance's technical notes that accompanied the introduction of the SDA rules in 1986:

---

[84] Vern Krishna, *The Fundamentals of Canadian Income Tax*, 6th ed. (Toronto: Carswell, 2000) at 207.

[85] *Ibid.*, at 208.

> As a general rule, a substantial risk of forfeiture would arise if the condition imposes a significant limitation or duty which requires meaningful effort on the part of the employee to fulfil and creates a definite and substantial risk that forfeiture may occur.

In these circumstances, it follows; the right to receive the amount is sufficiently contingent that it would be inappropriate to include it in computing the taxpayer's income until the condition is satisfied.

For our purposes, the most important feature of the SDA rules are the exceptions in paragraphs (a) to (l) of the definition in subsection 248(1), which exclude from definition of a salary deferral arrangement:

(a) a registered pension plan,

(b) a disability or income maintenance insurance plan under a policy with an insurance corporation,

(c) a deferred profit sharing plan,

(d) an employees profit sharing plan,

(e) an employee trust,

(f) a group sickness or accident insurance plan,

(g) a supplementary unemployment benefit plan,

(h) a vacation pay trust described in paragraph 149(1)(y),

(i) a plan or arrangement the sole purpose of which is to provide education or training for employees of an employer to improve their work or work-related skills and abilities,

(j) a plan or arrangement established for the purpose of deferring the salary or wages of a professional athlete for the services of the athlete as such with a team that participates in a league having regularly scheduled games,

(k) a plan or arrangement under which a taxpayer has a right to receive a bonus or similar payment in respect of services rendered by the taxpayer in a taxation year to be paid within 3 years following the end of the year, [and]

(l) a prescribed plan or arrangement.

Some of these exceptions (paragraphs (a) and (c)) involve deferred income plans, where the Act permits and encourages the deferral of tax on income that is saved in the form of an RPP or a DPSP. Others (paragraphs (b) and (f)) concern different kinds of wage loss replacement plans, benefits from which are taxable under paragraph 6(1)(f). Yet others (paragraphs (d), (e), and (g)) relate to various plans or trusts that are subject to separate rules and need not concern us here.[86] Similarly, paragraph (h), by reference to paragraph 149(1)(y),

---

[86] Benefits under employee profit-sharing plans, employee trusts, and supplementary employment benefit plans are subject to tax under paras. 6(1)(d) and (h) and para. 56(1)(g). The rules governing employee profit-sharing plans and supplementary employment benefit plans are found in ss. 144 and 145.

excludes from the SDA rules payments to trusts "established pursuant to the terms of a collective agreement between an employer or an association of employers and employees or their labour organization for the sole purpose of providing for the payment of vacation or holiday pay" to an employee or an heir or legal representative of the employee, which amounts are included in the employee's income in the taxation year when the contribution is made.[87] Paragraph (i) excludes amounts contributed to a plan or arrangement "the sole purpose of which is to provide education or training for employees of an employer," which amounts are not subject to tax.

Finally, paragraphs (j) to (l) permit limited forms of deferral for remuneration to professional athletes, bonuses or similar payments to be paid within three years, and various plans or arrangements prescribed by regulations 6801.[88]

B. Deductions

While most inclusions in computing a taxpayer's income from an office or employment are included in the taxation year in which they are received, most deductions that are allowed in computing a taxpayer's income from these sources are permitted in the taxation year in which deductible amounts are "paid,"[89] "expended,"[90] or "disbursed."[91] According to the *Canadian Oxford Dictionary*, the word "pay" means "give (a usu. specified amount)" or "hand over the amount," while "expend" is defined as "spend or use up," "disburse" is defined as "expend (money)," and "spend" means "pay out (money)." These

---

[87] *Interpretation Bulletin* IT-389R, "Vacation Pay Trusts Established under Collective Agreements," August 30, 1985, para. 7. Although this bulletin does not identify the statutory provision under which these amounts are included in computing the employee's income, vacation credits under such a trust are likely taxable as benefits under para. 6(1)(a). Where an employer does not set aside funds for the payment of vacation or holiday pay in the form of a trust, but merely continues to pay the employee's salary during the employee's vacation or holiday, the payments are taxable as remuneration in the taxation year in which they are received.

[88] Regulation 6801(a) pertains to leave of absence plans (for a leave of absence plan that satisfies the requirements of reg. 6801(a), see *Income Tax Ruling* ATR-39, "Self-Funded Leave of Absence," March 11, 1991); reg. 6801(b) pertains to leave of absence plans where salary deferral commenced before 1987; reg. 6801(c) pertains to SDAs for National Hockey League on-ice officials; and reg. 6801(d) pertains to "phantom" or "shadow" stock plans, under which amounts are received after the employee's death or retirement from or loss of the taxpayer's office or employment.

[89] See, for example, paras. 8(1)(b) (legal expenses), (i) (dues and other expenses of performing duties), and (q) (artists' employment expenses) and subpara. 8(1)(j)(i) (interest paid on borrowed money to acquire motor vehicle or aircraft).

[90] See, for example, paras. 8(1)(f) (salesperson's expenses), (h) (travelling expenses), and (h.1) (motor vehicle expenses); subpara. 8(1)(p)(i) (musical instrument costs); and subs. 8(4) (meals).

[91] See, for example, paras. 8(1)(e) (expenses of railway employees) and (g) (expenses of transport employees).

words, as Canadian courts have confirmed,[92] suggest a cash basis of accounting according to which amounts are neither included in computing a taxpayer's income until actually received nor deductible until actually paid out regardless of the taxation year in which amounts are earned and obligations are incurred.

As exceptions to these provisions, subparagraphs 8(1)(j)(ii) and 8(1)(p)(ii) limit deductions in respect of the "capital cost" of motor vehicles, aircraft, and musical instruments to "such part, if any," of that cost as is allowed by regulation. These "capital cost allowances" defer the deduction of amounts expended to acquire various categories of capital assets by allowing a deduction for a part of the capital cost of each asset in each year during which the asset is used to gain or produce income. Capital cost allowances are examined in detail in Chapter 5.

---

[92] See, for example, *Trapp v. M.N.R.*, [1946] C.T.C. 30, 2 D.T.C. 784 (Ex. Ct.).

CHAPTER FIVE

Income or Loss from a Business or Property

I. INTRODUCTION

Paragraph 3(a) of the *Income Tax Act*, R.S.C. 1985, c. 1 (5th Supp.), as amended, identifies each "business" and each "property," in addition to each office and employment, as sources of income from which taxpayers must include any income in computing their net income under section 3. Correspondingly, paragraph 3(d) permits taxpayers to deduct their losses from each business or property in computing their net income for the year.

The computation of a taxpayer's income or loss from a business or property is governed by subdivision b of Division B of Part I of the Act (sections 9 to 37). Subsection 9(1) defines the income of a taxpayer from a business or property as the "profit" from that business, a concept that implies the deduction of reasonable expenses incurred in order to obtain the income.[1] Subsection 9(2) defines a taxpayer's loss from a business or property as "the taxpayer's loss, if any, for the taxation year from that source computed by applying the provisions of this Act respecting computation of income from that source with such modifications as the circumstances require." Subsection 9(3) stipulates that the expressions "income from a property" and "loss from a property" do not include capital gains or losses from the disposition of that property.[2] Sections 10 and 11 contain special rules governing the timing of various inclusions and deductions. Sections 12 to 17 specify various amounts that must be included in computing a taxpayer's income from a business or property. Sections 18 to 21 contain numerous rules both limiting and permitting the deduction of specific amounts in computing a taxpayer's income from a business or property. Sections 22 to 25

---

[1] See, for example, *Symes v. Canada*, [1993] S.C.J. No. 131, [1994] 1 C.T.C. 40, (1993) 94 D.T.C. 6001 (S.C.C.), *per* Iacobucci J, citing *Daley v. M.N.R.*, [1950] C.T.C. 254, 50 D.T.C. 877 (Ex. Ct.).

[2] Draft legislation proposes to amend this provision to stipulate that "income or loss from a business or property does not include any capital gain or capital loss."

apply where a taxpayer ceases to carry on a business, while sections 26 to 37 apply to special cases as indicated.

Where the source of a profit or loss is characterized as a "business" or "property," income is fully taxable under subsection 9(1) and paragraph 3(a) of the Act and losses are fully deductible in computing the taxpayer's aggregate income for the year under paragraph 3(d). In contrast, where a gain or loss is of a capital nature, only one-half of the gain is taxable (section 38), whereas the loss is only one-half deductible (section 38) and deductible only against taxable capital gains for the year (paragraph 3(b)).[3] Alternatively, where an economic gain or loss is not contemplated by the Act, neither the gain nor the loss is recognized for tax purposes.

Where a taxpayer realizes a gain, therefore, it is generally to his or her advantage to argue either that the gain is not contemplated by the Act or (less advantageously) that the gain originated from the disposition of capital rather than a business or property. Where a taxpayer suffers an economic loss, however, it is generally more advantageous to characterize the loss as a loss from a business or property. For the revenue authorities, it follows, the incentives are typically reversed.

This chapter considers the characterization and computation of a taxpayer's income or loss from a business or property. Section II examines statutory and dictionary definitions of the words "business" and "property" and judicial decisions governing the characterization of an activity as a business or property for the purposes of the Act. Section III surveys various amounts that are included in computing a taxpayer's income from these sources. Section IV reviews statutory and judicial rules governing the deduction of specific amounts in computing a taxpayer's income from a business or property. Section V examines statutory and judicial rules governing the timing of inclusions and deductions.

II. CHARACTERIZATION

According to *The Concise Oxford Dictionary*, 7th ed., a "business" is defined as a "habitual occupation, profession, trade." Similarly, *Black's Law Dictionary*, 6th ed., defines a "business" as follows:

> Employment, occupation, profession, or commercial activity engaged in for gain or livelihood. Activity or enterprise for gain, benefit, advantage or livelihood. ... Enterprise in which person engaged shows willingness to invest time and capital on future outcome. ... That which habitually busies or occupies or engages the time, attention, labor, and effort of persons as a principal serious concern or interest or for livelihood or profit.

---

[3] Before 1972, capital gains and losses were not recognized for tax purposes. From 1972 to 1987, the inclusion rate was one-half. This rate was increased to two-thirds for 1988 and 1989 and three-quarters after 1990. The rate was subsequently reduced to two-thirds effective February 18, 2000 and one-half effective October 18, 2000.

Thus, as one Canadian commentator has written:

> "Business" is a term of broad meaning, embracing as it does a wide range of activities which
> have as their object the acquisition of gain through the utilization of labour and capital in
> varying combinations. Sometimes the labour factor is dominant — as in the professions —
> and in others, the capital factor is dominant — as in the business of renting land, buildings or
> chattels.[4]

The meaning of the word "property" is similarly broad in scope, defined in
The Shorter Oxford English Dictionary, 3d ed., as "the right (*esp.* the exclusive
right) to the possession, use, or disposal of anything," and in *Black's Law
Dictionary*, 6th ed., as "everything which is the subject of ownership, corporeal
or incorporeal, tangible or intangible, visible or invisible, real or personal."

For the purposes of the *Income Tax Act*, the words "business" and "property"
are given specific meanings in subsection 248(1). According to the definition of
"business" in subsection 248(1):

> "business" includes a profession, calling, trade, manufacture or undertaking of any kind
> whatever and ... an adventure or concern in the nature of trade but does not include an office
> or employment.

"Property" in turn is defined as "property of any kind whatever whether real or
personal or corporeal or incorporeal," including certain kinds of property which
need not concern us here. Thus, while the statutory definition of the word
"property" adds little to its ordinary dictionary definitions, the definition of
"business" both extends the ordinary dictionary meaning by including other
activities that might not otherwise be characterized as a business (for example,
an adventure or concern in the nature of trade), and restricts the ordinary
definition by specifically excluding an office or employment, which are subject
to a separate set of rules under subdivision a (discussed in Chapter 4 of this
text).

The distinction between income from a business and income from property
generally depends on the degree of activity involved in producing the income.[5]
As one commentator has written:

> Cast in terms of the economists' sources of wealth, income from business results from a
> combination of capital and labour in commercial enterprise, whereas income from property
> arises from capital alone, and is frequently described as investment income.[6]

---

[4]   Douglas J. Sherbaniuk, "The Concept of Income — The Receipts Side", Studies of the Royal
      Commission on Taxation No. 20 (Ottawa: Queen's Printer, February 1967) at 29-30.

[5]   See, generally, John Durnford, "The Distinction Between Income from a Business and Income
      from Property, and the Concept of Carrying On a Business" (1991) Vol. 39 No. 5 Can. Tax J.
      1131.

[6]   Douglas J. Sherbaniuk, "The Concept of Income — The Receipts Side", Studies of the Royal
      Commission on Taxation No. 20 (Ottawa: Queen's Printer, February 1967) at 103.

Likewise, Professors Hogg, Magee, and Cook explain:

> The distinction between the two types of income depends on whether the income is derived primarily from the ownership of property, in which case it is income from property, or whether the income is derived primarily from the activity of the owner or the owner's employees, in which case it is income from business.[7]

For present purposes, we need not concern ourselves with the distinction between income from a business and income from property, which is largely irrelevant to the computation of income under subdivision b.[8] Instead, this section considers the distinction between a business or property as sources of a taxpayer's income or loss and other sources that may or may not be recognized for tax purposes. For this purpose, the section begins by looking more closely at the statutory concept of a business both in the ordinary sense of the word and as it is modified by the extended definition in subsection 248(1). It then considers a judicially developed "reasonable expectation of profit" test according to which an economic loss may or may not be recognized for tax purposes.

A. Business

For the purposes of the Act, the concept of a business comprises both its ordinary meaning and the extended meaning set out in subsection 248(1). The following cases and text examine these ordinary and extended meanings.

1. Ordinary Meaning

In addition to the dictionary definitions outlined earlier, a number of cases have considered the question whether a given activity constitutes a business. In *Smith v. Anderson* (1880), 15 Ch. D 247 at 258 (C.A.), after citing various dictionary definitions of the word "business," Jessel MR said, "anything which occupies the time and attention and labour of a man for the purpose of profit is business."[9] This definition has been cited with approval in a number of Canadian cases,[10] including at least one case decided under the *Income War Tax Act*.[11] On the

---

[7] Peter W. Hogg, Joanne E. Magee, and Ted Cook, *Principles of Canadian Income Tax Law*, 3d ed. (Toronto: Carswell, 1999) 218.

[8] Although the distinction between business and property is irrelevant to the computation of a taxpayer's income or loss under subdivision b, it is crucial to the application of the attribution rules, which are considered in Chapter 8. It is also relevant to the application of a number of rules governing the taxation of corporate income.

[9] See also *Erichsen v. Last* (1881), 4 Tax Cas 422 at 427 (H.C.J. CA), where Cotton LJ stated that "when a person habitually does a thing which is capable of producing a profit for the purpose of producing a profit, he is carrying on a trade or business."

[10] See, for example, *Rideau Club v. City of Ottawa*, [1907] O.J. No. 32, 15 O.L.R. 118 at 122 (Ont. C.A.); and *Shaw v. McNay*, [1939] O.J. No. 480, [1939] O.R. 368 at 371 (Ont. H.C.J.), *per* Godfrey J.

[11] *Samson v. M.N.R.*, [1943] C.T.C. 47 (Ex. Ct.), *per* Thorson P.

basis of this definition, therefore, a business appears to involve an organized activity of any kind that is carried on for the purpose of making a profit. Each of these elements was considered in *M.N.R. v. Morden*, [1961] C.T.C. 484, 61 D.T.C. 1266 (Ex. Ct.).

M.N.R. v. Morden
[1961] C.T.C. 484, 61 D.T.C. 1266 (Ex. Ct.)

CAMERON J: The Minister of National Revenue appeals from a decision of the Income Tax Appeal Board dated October 26, 1956, 16 Tax ABC 81, which allowed the respondent's appeals from re-assessments made upon him for the taxation years 1949, 1951, 1952 and 1953. In the re-assessments, all dated September 13, 1954, the Minister added to the declared income of the respondent the following amounts:

1949	$1,500
1951 (reduced by the Minister's Notification from $10,250)	$10,000
1952	$860
1953	$1,500

The re-assessments indicated that the amounts so added were in relation to net gains from gambling activities. In Part B of the Minister's Notice of Appeal, it is alleged merely that these amounts were properly taken into account in computing the respondent's income for the years in question, that for the year 1953 being under the provisions of Sections 3 and 4 of the *Income Tax Act* [now sections 3 and 9] and the others being under the provisions of the same sections of the *Income Tax Act of 1948*. The Reply to the Notice of Appeal is merely a denial of these allegations.

...

In 1935, the respondent acquired the Morden Hotel in Sarnia, and operated it thereafter until 1957, when it was sold. ... His own evidence makes it abundantly clear that for a very considerable period of time the operation of the hotel was not his only, or possibly even his main, business interest. From about 1942 to 1948 he was the owner of a racing stable, having at times as many as twelve horses. A very substantial portion of his time was directed to training and racing these horses at many tracks in Canada and the United States and it is clear that throughout that period he was continuously placing bets on his own and other horses, paying a good deal of attention to racing information, attending the races, and gambling on horse races in a large way. For a long period of time he appears to have been an inveterate gambler, placing bets not only on horse races, but on a variety of card games and sporting events. He was a member of the Omega Club in Toronto where betting for heavy stakes was at least permitted and in which he participated. No records of his betting gains or losses was kept at any time. In 1948, he disposed of all his horses and, with the exception of one horse which he owned for a short time about 1952, has owned no race horses since that date.

His gambling activities up to the year 1948 were so extensively organized and occupied so much of his time and attention that, had they continued throughout the years in question, any net gain therefrom might possibly have been income from a business ... . It is submitted, however, that from 1949 to 1955, a period which includes all the taxation years in question, his gambling activities were only occasional and amounted to nothing more than indulging in a hobby or recreation, and that therefore his net income therefrom was not taxable.

...

Professional bookmakers accepting bets on race horses are taxable on the profits of what has been held to be their vocation (see *Partridge v. Mallandaine* (1886), 18 QBD 276). I think it would follow, also, that persons who make gains by organizing their efforts in the way that a bookmaker does are deriving income which is taxable.

In the well-known case of *Graham v. Green*, [1925] K.B. 37, 9 TC 209, Rowlatt J pointed out the distinction between the position of a bookmaker and the individual who bets with a bookmaker. In that case, the appellant for many years made substantial gains by betting on horses. ... It was proven that that was his main, if not his sole, means of livelihood. Rowlatt J, in holding that his winnings were not profits or gains assessable to tax, said that a winning bet was substantially in the same position as a gift or finding. At pages 313 *et seq.* he said:

> It has been settled that a bookmaker carries on a taxable vocation. What is a bookmaker's system? He knows that there are a great many people who are willing to back horses and that they will back horses with anybody who holds himself out to give reasonable odds as a bookmaker. By calculating the odds in the case of various horses over a long period of time and quoting them so that on the whole the aggregate odds, if I may use the expression, are in his favour, he makes a profit. That seems to me to be organising an effort in the same way that a person organises an effort if he sets out to buy himself things with a view to securing a profit by the difference in what I may call their capital value in individual cases.

> Now we come to the other side, the man who bets with the bookmaker, and that is this case. These are mere bets. Each time he puts on his money, ... I do not think he could be said to organise his effort in the same way as a bookmaker organises his. I do not think the subject matter from his point of view is susceptible of it. In effect all he is doing is just what a man does who is a skilful player at cards, who plays every day. He plays today and he plays tomorrow and he plays the next day and he is skilful on each of the three days, more skilful on the whole than the people with whom he plays, and he wins. But I do not think that you can find, in his case, ... that particular operations are marked in the conception of a trade. I think all you can say of that man, in the fair use of the English language, is that he is addicted to betting. ... There is no tax on a habit. I do not think "habitual" or even "systematic" fully describes what is essential in the phrase "trade, adventure, profession or vocation." All I can say is that in my judgment the income which this gentleman succeeded in making is not profits or gains, and that the appeal must be allowed, with costs.

...

To be taxable, gambling gain must be derived from carrying on a "business" as that term has been defined in Section 127(1)(e) [now subsection 248(1)]. Casual winnings from bets made in a friendly game of bridge or poker or from bets occasionally placed at the race track are, in my view, clearly not subject to tax. ... [E]ach case must depend on its own particular facts. A reasonable test in such matters seems to be that stated in *Lala Indra Sen* (1940), 8 ITR (Ind.) 187, where Braund J said at page 218:

> If there is one test which is, as I think, more valuable than another, it is to try to see what is the man's own dominant object — whether it was to conduct an enterprise of a commercial character or whether it was primarily to entertain himself.

In the present case, I find no evidence that the respondent during the years in question in relation to his betting activities conducted an enterprise of a commercial character or had so organised these activities as to make them a business, calling or vocation. After he sold his horses in 1948, he lost practically all interest in horse racing and placed only an occasional bet on such races on the few occasions when he attended the tracks at Detroit. True, he was an inveterate gambler and was prepared to place a bet on the outcome of baseball, hockey and football matches, and on card games, whether he was a player or merely placed side bets. His main winnings were on a few occasions when he attended the Grey Cup football play-offs in Toronto, where he placed bets on the game and also played cards for substantial stakes with friends or acquaintances at the Omega Club, at the hotel, or at the homes of his friends, or placed side bets on other card players. In Sarnia he was accustomed to playing card games for small stakes on Wednesday afternoons with friends who gathered in the basement of a nearby store. While his bets were high at times and his gains substantial, I can find no evidence that his operations amounted to a calling or the carrying on of a business. Gambling was in his blood and it provided him with the excitement which he craved. It was ... his hobby, but for the years in question it was not his vocation, calling or business. ...

Judgment accordingly

NOTES AND QUESTIONS

1. In *Graham v. Green (Inspector of Taxes)*, [1925] 2 K.B. 37, 9 TC 209 (U.K.), Rowlatt J distinguished between the organized effort involved in a bookmaker's "taxable vocation" and the "betting, pure and simple" of the gambler for whom betting is a habit or addiction. Is the distinction so clear-cut? Does the "skilful player of cards, who plays every day," not also organize his or her efforts?

2. What did Rowlatt J mean when he said that "the subject matter" of the gambler's activity is not susceptible to the organization of the bookmaker's vocation? Might this mean that a person who simply places bets can have no reasonable expectation of profit? If this is so, how could gambling be a

taxpayer's "main, if not ... sole, means of livelihood"? Are educated bets at the horse track any different than educated bets on the stock market? The concept of a reasonable expectation of profit is examined later in this chapter.

3.   In *Lala Indra Sen* (1940), 8 ITR (Ind.) 187, Braund J concluded that the main test to decide whether or not a gambling gain is income from a business is "to see what is the man's dominant object — whether it was to conduct an enterprise of a commercial character or whether it was primarily to entertain himself." Is this test the same or different from that employed by Rowlatt J in *Graham v. Green*? Is it consistent with the legal concept of a business set out in *Smith v. Anderson* (1880), 15 Ch. D 247 at 258 (C.A.)? What test does Cameron J employ in *M.N.R. v. Morden*?

4.   In *Morden*, Cameron J stated that a gambling gain, to be taxable, "must be derived from carrying on a 'business'" as that term is defined in the Act. Do you agree? Why or why not? Might a gambling gain be income from a business according to its extended definition in subsection 248(1)? Might it be characterized as income from an unspecified source under paragraph 3(a) of the Act?

5.   Most Canadian cases dealing with the taxation of gambling gains have held that the gains were not income from a business. See, for example, *No. 230 v. M.N.R.* (1955), 12 Tax ABC 136; *No. 364 v. M.N.R.* (1956), 16 Tax ABC 81 (T.A.B.); *Carey v. M.N.R.* (1957), 17 Tax ABC 97 (T.A.B.); *No. 469 v. M.N.R.* (1957), 18 Tax ABC 145; *M.N.R. v. Beaudin*, [1964] C.T.C. 70, 64 D.T.C. 5077 (Ex. Ct.); *Markowitz v. M.N.R.* (1964), 35 Tax ABC 348; *Chapman v. M.N.R.*, [1971] Tax ABC 81; *Hammond v. M.N.R.*, [1971] F.C.J. No. 27, [1971] C.T.C. 663, 71 D.T.C. 5389 (F.C.T.D.); *Chorney v. M.N.R.*, [1977] C.T.C. 2245, 77 D.T.C. 168 (T.R.B.); and *Canada v. Balanko*, [1988] F.C.J. No. 175, [1988] 1 C.T.C. 317, 88 D.T.C. 6228 (F.C.T.D.). Contrary decisions have been reached in *Badame v. M.N.R.* (1951), 3 Tax ABC 226 (T.A.B.); *Belawski v. M.N.R.* (1954), 11 Tax ABC 299 (T.A.B.); *Fraser v. M.N.R.* (1956), 16 Tax ABC 71; and *Hoare v. M.N.R.*, [1987] 2 C.T.C. 2040, 87 D.T.C. 408 (T.C.C.). Not one of these decisions considered the possibility that gambling gains might be taxable as an income from an unspecified source.

6.   In the United States, gambling winnings are fully taxable as income. Under paragraph 165(d) of the *Internal Revenue Code*, losses from "wagering transactions" are deductible but "only to the extent of the gains from such transactions."

7.   In 1994, the House of Commons Standing Committee on Finance recommended that lottery and casino winnings over $500 should be explicitly included in computing the income of a taxpayer for a taxation year, with losses

deductible against winnings.[12] Since lotteries and casinos have comprised an increasing share of provincial revenues over the last several years, implementation of this recommendation might be expected to result in a transfer of revenue from the provinces to the federal government. Do you agree or disagree with the committee's recommendation?

8.   In *MacEachern v. M.N.R.*, [1977] C.T.C. 2139, 77 D.T.C. 94 (T.R.B.), the taxpayer carried out the search for and recovery of treasure from a sunken ship. Income earned from the sale of gold and silver coins recovered from the wreck was found to be income from a business on the basis that at all times the taxpayer and his partners intended to sell for profit anything of value that was recovered. The board found that in the circumstances the search had the characteristics of a well-organized business endeavour. According to the board (at para. 8):

> In response to appellant's argument that the endeavour was a hobby, the Board points out that hobby though it may have been, it was clearly a hobby with a potential for profit, and under favourable circumstances, substantial profit. At the minimum this would tend to distinguish it from a hobby and endow it with characteristics somewhat akin to a business endeavour. ... The agreement between the parties ... gives ample evidence that they were prepared to invest time, money, and equipment in determining [the treasure's] location, physically acquiring, retaining and reselling it, all characteristics identifiable with the business treatment of stock-in-trade.

Is this decision consistent with the emphasis on the taxpayer's purpose in *Lala Indra Sen* (1940), 8 ITR (Ind.) 187? Might there be any reason to question the taxpayer's argument that "the endeavour was a hobby"?

9.   In *Tobias v. Canada*, [1978] C.T.C. 113, 78 D.T.C. 6028 (F.C.T.D.), the taxpayer was involved in an unsuccessful search for treasure rumoured to have been buried by pirates on Oak Island off the shore of Nova Scotia. Citing *MacEachern*, the court found that the operation was of a commercial nature, and allowed the costs of the search to be deducted as losses from a business. According to the court (at paras. 52-53):

> In the present appeals the plaintiff had assured himself to his satisfaction that there was a distinct possibility that treasure might be found, despite the failure of his predecessors, by the use of more modern methods and equipment. Regardless of the high degree of uncertainty as to the success of the project the prospect of the very substantial reward would compensate the plaintiff for the time, money and risk involved.
>
>   This is not unusual or peculiar to the plaintiff. Daily investors are persuaded to spend their money on projects where it is not known if there will be any future return but they are willing to do so in the belief that the substantial rewards in the event of success will compensate them for the uncertainty involved. I have in mind investors in penny mining stocks and prospectors and their grubstakers who spend a lifetime searching for the rich vein they may never find.

---

[12] Canada, House of Commons, *Confronting Canada's Deficit Crisis — Tenth Report of the Standing Committee on Finance* (Ottawa: Queen's Printer, 1994) 32.

Do you agree with this result? Why or why not?

10.   In *Cameron v. M.N.R.*, [1971] Tax ABC 645 (T.A.B.), the taxpayer, a self-employed fisher engaged principally in fishing for salmon and herring, joined with other fishers on two occasions to capture killer whales, which were sold to a number of aquariums. When the Minister added the taxpayer's share of the proceeds ($8,033.33) to the taxpayer's income for his 1968 taxation year, the taxpayer objected on the grounds (at para. 7) that he was not a whaler, that his boat was not equipped for whaling, and that, "due to the highly fortuitous and uncommon nature of the events, the money received was a windfall and not income." The Minister, on the other hand, contended (at para. 8) that because the taxpayer and the other fishermen "used their boats, fishing nets and knowledge of the sea in capturing the whales and intended to sell them at a profit ... , the share of the profit realized by the taxpayer was income in his hands."

Concluding (at para. 9) that the taxpayer was "a professional salmon fisherman and not a whaler," the board held that the two occasions were "fortuitous" and "not a business venture in the usual sense." Although speculating (at para. 10) that "[a] third catch, if it had taken place, might possibly have fallen into a different category," the board concluded that "both events should be considered as favourable to the taxpayer and that the gain realized is not taxable under the provisions of the *Income Tax Act*." Do you agree with this decision? Why or why not? Would the taxpayer have been taxable if he had caught tuna rather than salmon or herring?

2. Extended Meaning

To the ordinary meaning of the word "business," the extended definition in subsection 248(1) adds "a profession, calling, trade, manufacture or undertaking of any kind whatever and ... an adventure or concern in the nature of trade." According to *The Shorter Oxford English Dictionary*, 3d ed., a "profession" is defined as:

> a vocation in which a professed knowledge of some department of learning is used in its application to the affairs of others, or in the practice of an art founded upon it. Applied *spec.* to the three learned professions of divinity, law, and medicine.

Similarly, courts have defined professions according to the "special skill or ability or experience" possessed by persons carrying them on.[13]

While a "calling" is defined quite broadly as "a business; occupation; profession; trade; vocation,"[14] the word "trade" has both a general and a specific meaning, encompassing both "the practice of some occupation, business, or

---

[13]   See, for example, *Bower v. M.N.R.*, [1949] C.T.C. 77 (Ex. Ct.), *per* Thorson P, citing *Carr v. Inland Revenue Commissioners*, [1944] 2 All E.R. 163 (C.A.).

[14]   *The Dictionary of Canadian Law*, 2d ed. See also *The Shorter Oxford English Dictionary*, 3d ed., which defines a "calling" as an "ordinary occupation, business."

profession habitually carried on, esp. when practised as a means of livelihood or gain; a calling," and "the buying and selling or exchange of commodities for profit." In tax cases, it seems, the latter meaning is invoked more frequently than the former.[15]

The word "manufacture" is defined alternatively as the "making of articles by physical labour or machinery, esp. on large scale" or as "mechanical production" (in *The Shorter Oxford English Dictionary*, 3d ed.). For sales tax purposes, the word "manufacture" has been defined as "the production of articles for use from raw or prepared material by giving to these materials new forms, qualities and properties or combinations whether by hand or machinery."[16]

The word "undertaking" is defined as "an enterprise or activity, or a proposal, plan or program in respect of an enterprise or activity" (in *The Dictionary of Canadian Law*, 2d ed.). In one Canadian tax case, the court referred to the *Oxford English Dictionary* definition of the verb "undertaking" as "ready to undertake an enterprise, task, etc., esp. one involving some danger or risk" to conclude that an "undertaking" within the meaning of the *Income Tax Act* must involve an element of "danger" or "risk."[17]

As for an "adventure or concern in the nature of trade," the word "adventure" is defined in the *Concise Oxford Dictionary*, 7th ed., as a "daring enterprise" or "commercial speculation," while a "concern" is defined as a "matter that affects one," a "business" or a "firm." For an adventure or concern to be "in the nature of trade," moreover, the activity must presumably have at least some of the characteristics of a trading enterprise.

For the purposes of the *Income Tax Act*, little turns on the characterization of an activity as a "profession," "calling," "trade," or "manufacture," each of which appears to be encompassed by the ordinary meaning of the word "business."[18] Nor have Canadian courts made much of the words "undertaking of any kind whatever," despite its potentially broad application to various kinds of transactions resulting in economic gains.[19] In contrast, the category of an

---

[15] See, for example, *Grainger & Sons v. Gough*, [1896] A.C. 325, 3 Tax Cas 462 (H.L.), where Lord Davey said (at 345-46): "Trade in its largest sense is the business of selling, with a view to profit, goods which the trader has either manufactured or himself purchased."

[16] See, for example, *Canada v. York Marble Tile and Terrazzo Ltd.*, [1967] S.C.J. No. 85, [1968] S.C.R. 140, 68 D.T.C. 5001, 65 D.L.R. (2d) 449 (S.C.C.), *per* Spence J, citing *Canada v. Vandeweghe Limited*, [1934] S.C.J. No. 13, [1934] S.C.R. 244, [1928-34] C.T.C. 257 (S.C.C.).

[17] *Financial Collection Agencies (Quebec) Ltd. v. M.N.R.*, [1989] T.C.J. No. 1104, [1990] 1 C.T.C. 2178, 90 D.T.C. 1040 (T.C.C.).

[18] The characterization of a taxpayer as a "trader," however, is relevant to the application of subsection 39(4), by which a taxpayer can elect to characterize the source of gains and losses from the disposition of all "Canadian securities" as capital. This election is considered in Chapter 6.

[19] For a rare exception to this pattern, see *Drumheller v. M.N.R.*, [1959] C.T.C. 275, 59 D.T.C. 1177 (Ex. Ct.), where the taxpayer disposed of his rights and interest in a franchise to deliver natural gas to the town of Stettler, Alberta after having devoted time and energy to obtain the

"adventure or concern in the nature of trade" has been a source of considerable litigation, constituting the main boundary between characterization as income or loss from a business on the one hand and a capital gain or loss on the other. Although the characterization of an "adventure or concern in the nature of trade" remains one of the most litigated issues in Canadian income tax law, the leading case on the subject continues to be the first case to consider the expression after its enactment as part of the 1948 *Income Tax Act*: *M.N.R. v. Taylor*, [1956] C.T.C. 189, 56 D.T.C. 1125 (Ex. Ct.).

M.N.R. v. Taylor
[1956] C.T.C. 189, 56 D.T.C. 1125 (Ex. Ct.)

[The taxpayer was the president and general manager of the Canada Metal Company Limited, a wholly owned subsidiary of National Lead Company of New York, engaged throughout Canada in fabricating various products of non-ferrous metals, including lead.

The Canadian company was permitted by its parent to have on hand only a 30-day supply of raw metals and as a result experienced considerable difficulties from time to time due to shortages in supply. In 1949, when lead prices broke sharply and the metal became available abroad, the respondent requested permission from the parent company for his company to import foreign lead and to buy it for three months' future delivery. The parent company refused on the ground that it was against policy for the Canadian subsidiary to deal in futures. The taxpayer then asked the parent company whether he could purchase the lead himself and was granted this permission. The taxpayer believed that he could obtain the foreign lead and supplement the inadequate Canadian supply. Accordingly, he decided to buy the lead himself, sell it to the company, and assume personally whatever risk was involved in the transaction. The taxpayer then purchased 1,500 tons of lead, which was sold to the company through brokers. The taxpayer did not himself put up any money for the purchase of the lead. The taxpayer made a profit on the transaction of $83,712.24, which was assessed to him in 1949 and 1950. The Income Tax Appeal Board allowed the taxpayer's appeal. The Minister appealed to the Exchequer Court.

The main issue in the appeal was whether the respondent's purchase and sale of the lead was an adventure or concern in the nature of trade, in which case it was taxable as income from a business pursuant to then paragraph 127(1)(e) of the 1948 *Income Tax Act* (now the definition of "business" in subsection 248(1)).]

THORSON P: ... The expression "adventure or concern in the nature of trade" appeared for the first time in a Canadian income tax act in Section 127(1)(e) of

---

franchise on behalf of a producing corporation in expectation of becoming manager of the company and acquiring a 25 per cent interest in the franchise.

the 1948 Act. It was, no doubt, taken from the *Income Tax Act, 1918* of the United Kingdom. In that Act... tax was chargeable in respect of any trade ... and Section 237 defined trade as including "every trade, manufacture, adventure or concern in the nature of trade." Prior to its inclusion in the definition of trade by Section 237 of the *Income Tax Act, 1918*, the expression appeared in the *Income Tax Act* of 1849. In that Act provision was made ... for the charging of duties in respect of any "Trade, Manufacture, Adventure, or Concern in the nature of Trade," Indeed, the expression goes back to the Act of 1803.

It is, I think, plain from the wording of the Canadian Act, quite apart from any judicial decisions, that the terms "trade" and "adventure or concern in the nature of trade" are not synonymous expressions and it follows that the profit from a transaction may be income from a business within the meaning of Section 3 of the Act, by reason of the definition of business in Section 127(1)(e) [now subsection 248(1)], even although the transaction did not constitute a trade, provided that it was an adventure or concern in the nature of trade.

In view of the dearth of Canadian decisions on what constitutes an adventure or concern in the nature of trade resort may be had to Scottish and English decisions on the corresponding United Kingdom enactment.

...

The first definition of "trade" in the United Kingdom cases is that of Lord Davey in *Grainger and Son v. Gough* (1896), 3 RTC 462 at 474. There he said, in his speech in the House of Lords:

> Trade in its largest sense is the business of selling, with a view to profit, goods which the trader has either manufactured or himself purchased.

This definition is only partially helpful. It indicates that "trade" is included in "business" which latter term is of wider import than that of trade in that it embraces any gainful activity, but it does not define the term "trader."

An advance was made by the Lord Justice Clerk (Macdonald) of the Court of Exchequer (Scotland) in the famous case of *Californian Copper Syndicate Limited v. Harris* (1904), 5 TC 159. In that case the Company had been formed for the purpose, *inter alia*, of acquiring and reselling mining property and had acquired and worked several mining properties in California and then sold them to a second Company receiving payment in fully paid up shares of the latter Company. The Company was assessed in respect of the profit made on the transaction and appealed against the assessment so made but the Commissioners held ... that the Company had carried on an adventure or concern in the nature of trade ... and that the profits arising from the transaction whether received in cash or shares of another company were assessable to income tax. The Court of Session as the Court of Exchequer in Scotland agreed that the determination of the Commissioners was right. Its decision is of particular importance because of the objective test which the Lord Justice Clerk laid down for determining whether the gain from a transaction was a capital one or income subject to tax. At page 165, he said:

It is quite a well settled principle in dealing with questions of assessment of Income Tax, that where the owner of an ordinary investment chooses to realize it, and obtains a greater price for it than he originally acquired it at, the enhanced price is not profit ... assessable to Income Tax. But it is equally well established that enhanced values obtained from realisation or conversion of securities may be so assessable, where what is done is not merely a realisation or change of investment, but an act done in what is truly the carrying on, or carrying out, of a business. The simplest case is that of a person or association of persons buying and selling lands or securities speculatively, in order to make gain, dealing in such investments as a business, and therefore seeking to make profits. There are many companies which in their very inception are formed for such a purpose, and in these cases it is not doubtful that, where they make a gain by a realisation, the gain they make is liable to be assessed for Income Tax.

And then there follows the famous statement of the test to be applied:

What is the line which separates the two classes of cases may be difficult to define, and each case must be considered according to its facts; the question to be determined being — Is the sum of gain that has been made a mere enhancement of value by realising a security, or is it a gain made in an operation of business in carrying out a scheme for profitmaking?

The Lord Justice Clerk then proceeded to a review of the evidence and said, at page 166:

I feel compelled to hold that this Company was in its inception a Company endeavouring to make a profit by a trade or business, and that the profitable sale of its property was not truly a substitution of one form of investment for another. It is manifest that it never did intend to work this mineral field with the capital at its disposal. Such a thing was quite impossible. Its purpose was to exploit the field, and obtain gain inducing others to take it up on such terms as would bring substantial gain to themselves. This was that the turning of investment to account was not to be merely incidental but was, as the Lord President put it in the case of the Scottish Investment Company, the essential feature of the business, speculation being among the appointed means of the Company's gains.

...

The decision is subject to certain comments. In the first place, I think it is clear that when the Lord Justice Clerk used the expression "scheme of profit-making" he did not imply that the word "scheme" meant a multiplicity of transactions. There could be a scheme of profit-making even if there were only one transaction.

...

The case is also of importance for the stress which the Lord Justice Clerk put on the element of speculation as a determining factor in the decision that the transaction was not the realization of an investment and its transfer into another form but the gaining of profit by the sale of the property and thus a transaction that was characteristic of what a trader would do. This stress on the speculative element is of particular importance when it is coupled with the finding that the sale of a property, which by itself is productive of income and might be regarded as an investment, can be a trade in the property rather than a realization of an investment.

...

I now come to the decision in *CIR v. Livingston et al.* (1926), 11 TC 538, in which an attempt was made to define the expression "adventure in the nature of trade." There the facts were that three persons, a ship repairer, a blacksmith and a fish salesmen's employee purchased as a joint venture a cargo vessel with a view to converting it into a steam-drifter and selling it. They were not connected in business and had never previously bought a ship. Extensive repairs and alterations to the ship were carried out ... and on December 31, 1924, the owners sold the vessel at a profit. They were assessed to income tax on the profit so made and appealed to the Commissioners who allowed the appeal on the ground that the profit realized in the transaction in question was not made in the operation of business ordinarily carried on by the purchasers. Thereupon the Crown appealed to the Court of Session as the Court of Exchequer in Scotland and it unanimously reversed the decision of the Commissioners and held the owners of the ship assessable to income tax on the profit made by them. While all the judges agreed that the finding of the Commissioners should be reversed the case loses much of the value that it might otherwise have by reason of the divergence in the four reasons for judgment. In my opinion, the Lord President (Clyde) made the most useful contribution to the jurisprudence. At page 542, he said:

> I think the profits of an isolated venture, such as that in which the Respondents engaged, may be taxable ... provided the venture is "in the nature of trade." I say, "may be," because in my view regard must be had to the character and circumstances of the particular venture. If the venture was one consisting simply in an isolated purchase of some article against an expected rise in price and a subsequent sale of it might be impossible to say that the venture was "in the nature of trade"; because the only trade in the nature of which it could participate would be the trade of a dealer in such articles, and a single transaction falls as far short of constituting a dealer's trade, as the appearance of a single swallow does of making a summer. The trade of a dealer necessarily consists of a course of dealing, either actually engaged in or at any rate contemplated and intended to continue. But this principle is difficult to apply to ventures of a more complex character such as that with which the present case is concerned.

And then Lord Clyde put the test of whether a venture was in the nature of trade as follows:

> I think the test, which must be used to determine whether a venture such as we are now considering is, or is not, "in the nature of trade," is whether the operations involved in it are of the same kind, and carried on in the same way, as those which are characteristic of ordinary trading in the line of business in which the venture was made. If they are, I do not see why the venture should not be regarded as "in the nature of trade," merely because it was a single venture which took only three months to complete.

And he went on to say that the operations were the same as those which characterized the trade of converting and refitting secondhand articles for sale and that the transaction was "in the nature of trade."

...

A great step towards clarification of the meaning of the expression under review was taken by the Court of Session in *Rutledge v. CIR* (1929), 14 TC 490. There the appellant, who was a money lender and also interested in a cinema company and other businesses, being in Berlin on business connected with the cinema company, purchased very cheaply a large quantity of toilet paper from a bankrupt German firm and within a short time after his return to London sold the whole consignment to one person at a considerable profit. On being assessed on this profit he appealed to the Commissioners who found that the profit made was liable to assessment as being profit in the nature of trade and the Court unanimously dismissed the appeal from their finding. The judgment of the Lord President (Clyde) is illuminating. After ... expressing the opinion that the transaction was certainly an adventure [the Lord President] went on to say, at page 496:

> The question remains whether the adventure was one "in the nature of trade." The appellant's contention is that it could not be such, because it is essential to the idea of trade that there should be a continuous series of trading operations; and an observation made in the course of my opinion in *Inland Revenue v. Livingston*, 1927, SC 251, at p. 255, was founded on, according to which "a single transaction falls as far short of constituting a dealer's trade, as the appearance of a single swallow does of making a summer. The trade of a dealer necessarily consists of a course of dealing, either actually engaged in or at any rate contemplated and intended to continue." But the question here is not whether the appellant's isolated speculation in toilet paper was a trade, but whether it was an "adventure ... in the nature of trade"; and in the opinion referred to I said that, in my opinion, "the profits of an isolated venture ... may be taxable under Schedule D provided the venture is 'in the nature of trade.'" I see no reason to alter that opinion. It is no doubt true that the question whether a particular adventure is "in the nature of trade" or not must depend on its character and circumstances, but if — as in the present case — the purchase is made for no other purpose except that of re-sale at a profit, there seems little difficulty in arriving at the conclusion that the deal was 'in the nature of trade,' though it may be wholly insufficient to constitute by itself a trade.

Then the Lord President put his conclusion clearly, at page 497:

> It seems to me to be quite plain (1) that the Appellant, in buying the large stock of toilet paper, entered upon a commercial adventure or speculation; (2) that this adventure or speculation was carried through in exactly the same way as any regular trader or dealer would carry through any of the adventures or speculations in which it is his regular business to engage; and therefore (3) that the purchase and re-sale of the toilet paper was an "adventure ... in the nature of trade" within the meaning of the *Income Tax Act*, 1918.

Lord Sands agreed but put his opinion somewhat differently, stressing the nature and size of the subject matter. At page 497, he said:

> The nature and quantity of the subject dealt with exclude the suggestion that it could have been disposed of otherwise than as a trade transaction. Neither the purchaser nor any purchaser from him was likely to require such a quantity for his private use. Accordingly, it appears to me quite a reasonable view for the Commissioners to have taken that this transaction was in the nature of trade. From beginning to end the intention was simply to buy and to re-sell. ... I do not think that we can regard what was done here as other than an "adventure ... in the nature of trade" within the meaning of the Act.

...

The *Rutledge* case (supra) was followed in ... *CIR v. Fraser* (1949), 24 TC 498. There the respondent, a woodcutter, bought through an agent for resale a large quantity of whiskey which he sold at a large profit. The purchases and sales were made in three lots. This was his only dealing in whisky. He had no special knowledge of the whisky trade and did not take delivery of the whisky or have it blended or advertised. The purchase and the sales were made through an agent. On being assessed in respect of the profit on the transaction he appealed to the Commissioners who found that an adventure in the nature of trade had not been carried on, that merely an investment had been made and realized and that it was not assessable to income tax. Their finding was unanimously reversed by the Court of Session. The judgment of the Lord President (Normand) is clear cut. In the first place, he clearly realized the distinction between a trade and an adventure in the nature of trade. At page 502, he said:

> we must remind ourselves that we are not to decide whether the Respondent was carrying on a trade, but whether the transaction was an adventure in the nature of trade ... . It would be extremely difficult to hold that a single transaction amounted to a trade but it may be much less difficult to hold that a single transaction is an adventure in the nature of trade.

Lord President Normand then went on to discuss what criterion the Court should apply in determining whether a transaction was an adventure in the nature of trade and whether the transaction under review was an adventure in the nature of trade. I quote his opinion, at page 502:

> There was much discussion as to the criterion which the Court should apply. I doubt if it would be possible to formulate a single criterion. I said in a case which we decided only yesterday that one important factor may be the person who enters into the transaction ... . It is in general more easy to hold that a single transaction entered into by an individual in the line of his own trade (although not part and parcel of his ordinary business) is an adventure in the nature of trade than to hold that a transaction entered into by an individual outside the line of his own trade or occupation is an adventure in the nature of trade. But what is a good deal more important is the nature of the transaction with reference to the commodity dealt in. The individual who enters into a purchase of an article or commodity may have in view the resale of it at a profit, and yet it may be that that is not the only purpose for which he purchased the article or the commodity, nor the only purpose to which he might rum it if favourable opportunity of sale does not occur. In some cases the purchase of a picture has been given as an illustration. An amateur may purchase a picture with a view to its resale at a profit, and yet he may recognize at the time or afterwards that the possession of the picture will give him aesthetic enjoyment if he is unable ultimately, or at his chosen time, to realise it at a profit. A man may purchase stocks and shares with a view to selling them at an early date at a profit, but, if he does so, he is purchasing something which is itself an investment, a potential source of revenue to him while he holds it. A man may purchase land with a view to realising it at a profit, but it also may yield him an income while he continues to hold it. If he continues to hold it, there may be also a certain price of possession. But the purchaser of a large quantity of a commodity like whisky, greatly in excess of that could be used by himself, his family and friends, a commodity which yields no pride of possession, which cannot be turned to account except by a process of realisation, I can scarcely consider to be other than an adventurer in a transaction in the nature of a trade; and I can find no single fact among those stated by the Commissioners which in any way traverses that view. In my opinion the fact that the transaction was not in the way of the business (whatever it was) of the Respondent in no way alters the character which almost necessarily belongs to a transaction like this. Most important of all, the actual dealings of the Respondent with the whisky were exactly of the kind that take place in ordinary trade.

...

I next refer to certain expressions of opinion in *Commissioners of Inland Revenue v. Reinhold* (1953), 34 TC 389. There Lord Carmont said, at page 392:

Certain transactions show inherently that they are not investments but incursions into the realm of trade or adventures of that nature. In my opinion, it is because of the character of such transactions that it can be said with additional definiteness that certain profits are income from trade and not capital accretion of an investment, the purchase and sale of, for instance, whisky, as in *Fraser's* case, [1942] SC 493, was a trading venture and so too in regard to toilet paper: *Rutledge*, [1929] SC 379. This means that, although in certain cases it is important to know whether a venture is isolated or not, that information is superfluous in many cases where the commodity itself stamps the transaction as a trading venture, and the profits and gains are plainly income liable to tax.

...

The cases establish that the inclusion of the term "adventure or concern in the nature of trade" in the definition of "trade" in the United Kingdom Act substantially enlarged the ambit of the kind of transactions the profits from which were subject to income tax. In my opinion, the inclusion of the term in the definition of "business" in the Canadian Act, quite apart from any judicial decisions, has had a similar effect in Canada. I am also of the view that it is not possible to determine the limits of the ambit of the term or lay down any single criterion for deciding whether a particular transaction was an adventure of trade for the answer in each case must depend on the facts and surrounding circumstances of the case. But while that is so it is possible to state with certainty some propositions of a negative nature.

The first of these is that the singleness or isolation of a transaction cannot be a test of whether it was an adventure in the nature of trade. In *Atlantic Sugar Refineries Limited v. M.N.R.*, [1948] Ex. CR 622 at 631; [1948] CTC 326 at 333, I expressed the opinion that the fact that a transaction was an isolated one did not exclude it from the category of trading or business transactions of such a nature as to attract tax to the profit therefrom and cited several decisions in support of my statement. The decision in that case was affirmed by the Supreme Court of Canada, [1949] SCR 706; [1949] CTC 196, and has been followed in other cases: *vide*, for example, *Honeyman v. M.N.R.*, [1955] Ex. CR 200 at 208; [1955] CTC 151 at 158. This does not mean that the isolation or singleness of a transaction has no bearing on whether it was a business or trading transaction. On the contrary, it might be a very important factor.

But "trade" is not the same thing as "an adventure in the nature of trade" and a transaction might well be the latter without being the former or constituting its maker a "trader." And whatever merit the singleness or isolation of a transaction may have in determining whether it was a trading or business transaction it has no place at all in determining whether it was an adventure in the nature of trade. The very word "adventure" implies a single or isolated transaction and it is erroneous to set up its singleness or isolation as an indication that it was not an adventure in the nature of trade. ... In my opinion, it may now be taken as established that the fact that a person has entered into only one transaction of the kind under consideration has no bearing on the question whether it was an adventure in the nature of trade. It is the nature of the transaction, not its singleness or isolation, that is to be determined.

Nor is it essential to a transaction being an adventure in the nature of trade that an organization be set up to carry it into effect. ... [I]t is plain from ... *Rutledge* ... (supra) ... that a transaction can be an adventure in the nature of trade even although no organization has been set up to carry it into effect.

And [*Rutledge, supra,* is also] authority for saying that a transaction may be an adventure in the nature of trade even although nothing was done to the subject matter of the transaction to make it saleable, as in *CIR v. Livingston et al.* (supra).

Likewise, the fact that a transaction is totally different in nature from any of the other activities of the taxpayer and that he has never entered upon a transaction of that kind before or since does not, of itself, take it out of the category of being an adventure in the nature of trade. What has to be determined is the true nature of the transaction and if it is in the nature of trade, the profits from it are subject to tax even if it is wholly unconnected with any of the ordinary activities of the person who entered upon it and he has never entered upon such a transaction before or since.

And a transaction may be an adventure in the nature of trade although the person entering upon it did so without any intention to sell its subject matter at a profit. The intention to sell the purchased property at a profit is not of itself a test of whether the profit is subject to tax for the intention to make a profit may be just as much the purpose of an investment transaction as of a trading one. Such intention may well be an important factor in determining that a transaction was an adventure in the nature of trade but its presence is not an essential prerequisite to such a determination and its absence does not negative the idea of an adventure in the nature of trade. The considerations prompting the transaction may be of such a business nature as to invest it with the character of an adventure in the nature of trade even without any intention of making a profit on the sale of the purchased commodity. And the taxpayer's declaration that he entered upon the transaction without any intention of making a profit on the sale of the purchased property should be scrutinized with care. It is what he did that must be considered and his declaration that he did not intend to make a profit may be overborne by other considerations of a business or trading nature motivating the transaction.

Consequently, the respondent in the present case cannot escape liability merely by showing that his transaction was a single or isolated one, that it was not necessary to set up any organization or perform any operation on its subject matter to carry it into effect, that it was different from and unconnected with his ordinary activities and he had never entered into such a transaction before or since and that he purchased the lead without any intention of making a profit on its sale to the Company.

...

In addition to the negative propositions established by the cases they also lay down positive guides. There is, in the first place, the general rule that the question whether a particular transaction is an adventure in the nature of trade depends on its character and surrounding circumstances and no single criterion can be formulated.

But there are some specific guides. One of these is that if the transaction is of the same kind and carried on in the same way as a transaction of an ordinary trader or dealer in property of the same kind as the subject matter of the transaction it may fairly be called an adventure in the nature of trade. The decisions of the Lord President in the *Livingston* case (supra) and the *Rutledge* case (supra) support this view. Put more simply, it may be said that if a person deals with the commodity purchased by him in the same way as a dealer in it would ordinarily do, such a dealing is a trading adventure ... .

And there is the further established rule that the nature and quantity of the subject matter of the transaction may be such as to exclude the possibility that its sale was the realization of an investment or otherwise of a capital nature or that it could have been disposed of otherwise than as a trade transaction: *vide* the reasons for judgment of Lord Sands in the *Rutledge* case (supra). And there is the statement of Lord Carmont in the *Reinhold* case (supra) that there are cases "where the commodity itself stamps the transaction as a trading venture."

In my opinion, the principles laid down in the *Rutledge* case (supra) [and] the *Fraser* case (supra) are applicable to the present case and I have no hesitation in holding that the respondent's purchase and sale of 1,500 tons of lead was an adventure in the nature of trade. I do not see how it could possibly have been anything else. His transaction was certainly an adventure, a bold and imaginative one and highly successful, both for the Company and for himself, and the only question is whether it was in the nature of trade. If the alternatives are whether it was of a capital nature or in the nature of trade I am unable to see how there can be any doubt of which it was. The nature and quantity of its subject matter, namely, 1,500 tons of lead requiring 22 carloads to carry it, excluded any possibility that it was of an investment nature involving the realization of a security or resulted in a fortuitous accretion of capital or was otherwise of a capital nature. It is plain that the respondent had no considerations of a capital nature in mind. The nature and quantity of the subject matter of the transaction were such as to exclude the possibility that it was other than a transaction of a trading nature. The respondent could not do anything, with the lead except sell it and he bought it solely for the purpose of selling it to the Company. In my judgment, the words of Lord Carmont in the *Reinhold* case (supra) that "the commodity itself stamps the transaction as a trading transaction" apply with singular force to the respondent's transaction.

Moreover, he dealt with the lead in exactly the same manner as any dealer in imported lead would have done. He bought it from abroad and sold it to a user of lead in Canada, namely, the Company. If it had bought the lead it would have been subject to tax on the profit made by it on the sale of its products fabricated from the lead so bought. The respondent merely did what the Company would have done if his judgment in the matter had prevailed. But since the Company was not permitted by the parent company to deal in the lead the respondent dealt in it himself and did so exactly in the same manner as a trader or dealer in imported lead would have done. This brings his transaction within the decisions of the Lord President in the *Livingston* and *Fraser* cases (supra). It was a dealing in lead and, as such, it was ... essentially a trading adventure.

It is of no avail to the respondent that when he purchased the lead he did so without any intention of selling it to the Company at a profit. He did not pretend that his purchase was for an investment purpose. All his reasons were business reasons of a trading nature. His adventure was a speculative one. When lead prices broke others in the industry were unwilling to gamble but he did not hesitate. He saw advantages of a business nature in the transaction and these outweighed with him the risk of loss which he undertook. He calculated that the advantages outweighed the risk and he deliberately assumed it. He was justified in his speculative venture ... [and] succeeded in getting better supply terms from the Canadian supplier. As for himself his venture brought him the personal satisfaction of victory as well as an increase in salary and pension rights. These possible advantages were all contemplated by him. The evidence indicates that he entered into the transaction for a variety of purposes but they were all of a business nature and many of them were similar to those that would have motivated a trader. His transaction was a dealing in lead and nothing else. ...

Judgment accordingly.

NOTES AND QUESTIONS

1.   On what basis did Thorson P decide in *Taylor* that "the singleness or isolation of a transaction cannot be a test of whether it was an adventure in the nature of trade"? For what purposes, if any, might "the singleness or isolation of a transaction" be relevant?

2.   Among the "negative propositions" in *Taylor*, Thorson P stated that it is not essential to a transaction being an adventure in the nature of trade that "an organization be set up to carry it into effect," that something be "done to the subject matter of the transaction to make it saleable," that the taxpayer have "entered upon such a transaction before or since," or that the transaction be connected with "other activities of the taxpayer." For what, if any, purposes might these factors be relevant?

3.   In *Californian Copper Syndicate v. Harris* (1904), 5 Tax Cas 159 (Scot. Ct. of Ex.) the acquisition and development of mining properties was characterized as "the carrying on, or carrying out, of a business" and "an operation of business in carrying out a scheme for profitmaking." Was this an adventure or concern in the nature of trade? Is the organized activity and development of property involved in such a "scheme for profitmaking" necessary to the characterization of an adventure as being in the nature of trade?

4.   In *CIR v. Fraser* (1949), 24 Tax Cas 498, at 502 (Ct. of Sess.), Lord Normand suggested:

It is in general more easy to hold that a single transaction entered into by an individual in the line of his own trade (although not part and parcel of his ordinary business) is an adventure in the nature of trade than to hold that a transaction entered into by an individual outside the line of his own trade or occupation is an adventure in the nature of trade.

In *Taylor*, however, Thorson P rejected this criterion as a test for determining whether a transaction is an adventure in the nature of trade. How, if at all, might the relationship between an isolated transaction and a taxpayer's ordinary business be relevant to the characterization of a gain or loss from the transaction?

5.   On what grounds did Thorson P conclude in *Taylor* that "a transaction may be an adventure in the nature of trade although the person entering upon it did so without any intention to sell its subject matter at a profit"? Does the decision in *Taylor* suggest that the taxpayer's intention is irrelevant to the characterization of an adventure in the nature of trade? If not, how is this intention to be determined? What, if any, weight should be given to the taxpayer's argument that he "purchased the lead without any intention of making a profit on its sale to the Company"? Did the taxpayer intend to "profit" from the transaction in a broad sense of the word?

6.   In *Taylor*, Thorson P suggested that "the taxpayer's declaration that he entered upon the transaction without any intention of making a profit on the sale of the purchased property should be scrutinized with care." Do you agree with this proposition? Why or why not?

The doctrine that a taxpayer's statements regarding the purpose for which property was acquired should be carefully scrutinized has been affirmed on many occasions. See, for example, *M.N.R. v. Spencer*, [1961] C.T.C. 109, 61 D.T.C. 1079 (Ex. Ct.); *Scott (No. 2) v. M.N.R.*, [1961] C.T.C. 451, 61 D.T.C. 1285 (Ex. Ct.), aff'd [1963] S.C.J. No. 16, [1963] C.T.C. 176, 63 D.T.C. 1121 (S.C.C.); *Dignan Estate v. M.N.R.*, [1962] C.T.C. 297, 62 D.T.C. 1185 (Ex. Ct.); *M.N.R. v. Minden*, [1963] C.T.C. 364, 63 D.T.C. 1231 (Ex. Ct.); *Starko v. M.N.R.*, [1965] C.T.C. 246, 65 D.T.C. 5151 (Ex. Ct.); *Consolidated Building Corp. v. M.N.R.*, [1965] C.T.C. 360, 65 D.T.C. 5211 (Ex. Ct.); *Darius v. Canada*, [1974] C.T.C. 337, 74 D.T.C. 6260 (F.C.T.D.); *Reicher v. M.N.R.*, [1975] F.C.J. No. 1106, [1975] C.T.C. 659, 75 D.T.C. 6001 (F.C.A.); and *Walton v. The Queen*, [1982] C.T.C. 228, 82 D.T.C. 6220 (F.C.T.D.).

7.   Referring to *CIR v. Livingston et al.* (1926), 11 T.C. 538 (Ct. of Sess.) and *Rutledge v. CIR* (1929), 14 T.C. 490 (Ct. of Sess.), Thorson P affirmed as a "positive guideline" in *Taylor* the statement that "if the transaction is of the same kind and carried on in the same way as a transaction of an ordinary trader or dealer in property of the same kind as the subject matter of the transaction it may fairly be called an adventure in the nature of trade."

In *Livingston*, Lord Clyde suggested (at 542) that a single isolated transaction might not be an adventure "in the nature of trade," since "the only trade in the nature of which it could participate would be the trade of a dealer in such articles, and a single transaction falls as far short of constituting a dealer's trade, as the appearance of a single swallow does of making a summer." In *Rutledge*, however, he appeared to confine this statement, explaining (at 496):

> It is no doubt true that the question whether a particular adventure is "in the nature of trade" or not must depend on its character and circumstances, but if — as in the present case — the purchase is made for no other purpose except that of re-sale at a profit, there seems little difficulty in arriving at the conclusion that the deal was "in the nature of trade," though it may be wholly insufficient to constitute by itself a trade.

Do these cases suggest that a taxpayer's intention regarding the property that is the subject matter of a transaction is relevant in deciding whether the transaction is "of the same kind and carried on in the same way as a transaction of an ordinary trader or dealer"? What other factors might be relevant in determining whether a taxpayer deals with property in the same way as an ordinary trader or dealer? On what grounds did Thorson P conclude in *Taylor* that the taxpayer had "dealt with the lead in exactly the same manner as any dealer in imported lead would have done"?

8.   A second specific "positive guideline" mentioned by Thorson P in *Taylor* is the "established rule that the nature and quantity of the subject matter of the transaction may be such as to exclude the possibility that its sale was the realization of an investment or otherwise of a capital nature or that it could have been disposed of otherwise than as a trade transaction." Is this an independent test for determining whether a transaction is an adventure in the nature of trade, or a presumption with respect to the taxpayer's intention in entering into the transaction? On what basis did Thorson P conclude in *Taylor* that the "nature and quantity of the subject matter of the transaction" were such as to "exclude the possibility that it was other than a transaction of a trading nature"?

9.   In *Stringam Farms Ltd. v. M.N.R.*, [1977] C.T.C. 2438, 77 D.T.C. 317 (T.R.B.), the taxpayer, which operated a feed lot for cattle, owned land on which cattle were grazed, sold cattle for slaughter, and bought and sold futures contracts in cattle, rapeseed, soybeans, and barley, which it considered to be distinct and separate from its cattle-feeding operations and on account of capital. Dismissing the taxpayer's appeal, the Tax Review Board characterized the transactions in cattle futures as part of the taxpayer's principal business and the transactions in other futures contracts as adventures in the nature of trade. Referring to the taxpayer's intentions and the subject matter of the transactions, the board concluded (at para. 19):

> In the purchase of commodity futures which are by nature short-termed and highly speculative, it is inconceivable that the appellant's intention was to invest in long-term capital assets. ... [T]he appellant in the purchase of commodity futures in both cattle and grain was not making a long-term investment but was seeking to make a profit on a purchase and quick sale of the commodities. ... [T]his fact alone could preclude the appellant's transactions, in cattle and grain futures, from being considered as an investment which might give rise to eventual capital gains.

For similar results, see also *Tamas v. Canada*, [1981] C.T.C. 220, 81 D.T.C. 5150 (F.C.T.D.), where losses on the disposition of corn and silver futures acquired for speculative purposes were characterized as business losses from adventures in the nature of trade; and *Gavreau, Beaudry Ltée v. M.N.R.*, [1981] C.T.C. 2475, 81 D.T.C. 392 (T.R.B.), where gains from futures transactions involving the French franc were characterized as business income from adventures in the nature of trade.

10. Where a taxpayer acquires commodities or futures of a certain type and/or quantity, it is often reasonable to infer that the taxpayer's intention is to resell the commodities or futures at a profit. In contrast, where the nature and quantity of the property that is the subject matter of the transaction are such that it might reasonably be acquired as an income-producing asset or for personal use, these characteristics do not themselves stamp the transaction as an adventure or concern in the nature of trade. Indeed, as Lord President Normand suggested in *CIR v. Fraser* (1949), 24 Tax Cas 498 (at 502), a taxpayer may have more than one purpose in acquiring these kinds of property:

> An amateur may purchase a picture with a view to its resale at a profit, and yet he may recognize at the time or afterwards that the possession of the picture will give him aesthetic enjoyment if he is unable ultimately, or at his chosen time, to realise it at a profit. A man may purchase stocks and shares with a view to selling them at an early date at a profit, but, if he does so, he is purchasing something which is itself an investment, a potential source of revenue to him while he holds it. A man may purchase land with a view to realising it at a profit, but it also may yield him an income while he continues to hold it.

In *Regal Heights Ltd. v. M.N.R.*, [1960] S.C.J. No. 56, [1960] C.T.C. 384, 60 D.T.C. 1270 (S.C.C.), where the taxpayer acquired and then resold a parcel of vacant land in Calgary, the Supreme Court of Canada characterized the taxpayer's gain as business income from an adventure in the nature of trade on the basis that the taxpayer had a "secondary intention" to resell the property, notwithstanding that its primary purpose in acquiring the property was to develop a shopping centre. Subsequent decisions have emphasized that a transaction may be characterized as an adventure or concern in the nature of trade only where "the possibility of re-sale at a profit was one of the *motivating considerations* that entered into the decision to acquire the property in question" (emphasis added).[20] Although the courts have said little about the circumstances in which the possibility of resale at a profit will constitute a "motivating consideration" for entering into the decision to acquire the property in question, the language employed seems to suggest a "but for" test according to which a transaction may be characterized as an adventure or concern in the nature of trade where the taxpayer would not have acquired the property were it not for

---

[20] *Reicher v. M.N.R.*, [1975] F.C.J. No. 1106, [1975] C.T.C. 659, 76 D.T.C. 6001 (F.C.A.) (at para. 6). See also *Racine v. M.N.R.*, [1965] C.T.C. 150, 65 D.T.C. 5098 (Ex. Ct.); *Morev Investments Ltd. v. M.N.R.*, [1973] C.T.C. 429, 73 D.T.C. 5353 (F.C.A.); *De Salaberry Realties Limited v. M.N.R.*, [1976] F.C.J. No. 901, [1976] C.T.C. 656, 76 D.T.C. 6408 (F.C.A.); *Hawrish v. M.N.R.*, [1976] F.C.J. No. 912, [1976] C.T.C. 748, 76 D.T.C. 6455 (F.C.A.); *First Investors Corp. v. M.N.R.*, [1987] 1 C.T.C. 285, 87 D.T.C. 5176 (F.C.A.); and *Crystal Glass Canada Ltd. v. Canada*, [1989] F.C.J. No. 113, [1989] 1 C.T.C. 330, 89 D.T.C. 5143 (F.C.A.).

the possibility of resale at a profit. On this basis, a transaction might be characterized as an adventure in the nature of trade even though the primary reason for which the taxpayer acquired the property was for a purpose other than resale at a profit.

11. If the courts face a difficult challenge in determining an individual's motivations for acquiring and selling particular property, this task is often more difficult where the taxpayer engaging in the transaction is a legal entity such as a corporation or partnership. In *Anderson Logging Company v. British Columbia*, [1924] S.C.J. No. 52, [1917-27] C.T.C. 198, aff'd [1917-27] C.T.C. 210 (P.C.), the Supreme Court of Canada adopted a presumption that activities consistent with the stated objects of a corporation were necessarily carried out in the course of the corporation's business. In *Sutton Lumber and Trading Co. Ltd. v. M.N.R.*, [1953] S.C.J. No. 32, [1953] C.T.C. 237, 53 D.T.C. 1158 (S.C.C.), however, the court concluded (at para. 7) that: "[t]he question to be decided is not as to what business or trade the company might have carried on under its memorandum but rather what was in truth the business it did engage in."[21]

In *Regal Heights Ltd. v. M.N.R.*, [1960] S.C.J. No. 56, [1960] C.T.C. 384, 60 D.T.C. 1270 (S.C.C.), the court held that the "interest and intentions" of the taxpayer corporation, all the shares of which were held by three individuals, were "identical" with those of the controlling shareholders or directing minds of the company. See also *Vaughan Construction Co. Ltd. v. M.N.R.*, [1970] S.C.J. No. 62, [1970] C.T.C. 350, 70 D.T.C. 6268 (F.C.T.D.). In a more widely held company, the corporation's purposes are generally those of the natural persons by whom the company is managed and controlled, such as the directors. See, for example, *Metropolitan Motels Corp. v. M.N.R.*, [1966] C.T.C. 246, 66 D.T.C. 5208 (Ex. Ct.); and *Leonard Reeves Inc. v. M.N.R.*, [1985] 2 C.T.C. 2054, 85 D.T.C. 419 (T.C.C.). Where shareholders or directors disagree about the purpose for which property is acquired or held, however, the application of this "directing mind" test may be extremely difficult. See, for example, *Mohawk Horning Ltd. v. M.N.R.*, [1986] F.C.J. No. 327, [1986] 2 C.T.C. 89, 86 D.T.C. 6297 (F.C.A.).

Determining the purpose for which property is acquired and held by a partnership may be considerably more complicated. In some cases, the characterization of partnership property may be determined by a dominant partner. In other cases, the characterization of a gain or loss on property disposed of by a partnership may differ for different partners depending on their

---

21 Although new life may have been breathed into the presumption by the decision in *Canadian Marconi Company v. Canada*, [1986] S.C.J. No. 66, [1986] 2 C.T.C. 465, 86 D.T.C. 6526 (S.C.C.), the relevance of this doctrine may be fading since corporate statutes no longer require companies to list their corporate objects, but merely provide that corporations have the capacity, rights, powers, and privileges of a natural person. See, for example, the *Canada Business Corporations Act*, R.S.C. 1985, c. C-44, section 15; and the *Ontario Business Corporations Act*, R.S.O. 1990, c. B.16, section 15.

different purposes in the having the partnership acquire the property. See, for example, *Hyman et al. v. M.N.R.*, [1988] 1 C.T.C. 2516, 88 D.T.C. 1352 (T.C.C.).

12. The views of the CRA on the characterization of a transaction as an adventure or concern in the nature of trade are contained in *Interpretation Bulletin* IT-459, "Adventure or Concern in the Nature of Trade," September 8, 1980. According to paragraph 4:

> In determining whether a particular transaction is an adventure or concern in the nature of trade the Courts have emphasized that all the circumstances of the transaction must be considered and that no single criterion can be formulated. Generally, however, the principal tests that have been applied are as follows:
>
> (a) whether the taxpayer dealt with the property acquired by him in the same way as a dealer in such property ordinarily would deal with it;
>
> (b) whether the nature and quantity of the property excludes the possibility that its sale was the realization of an investment or was otherwise of a capital nature, or that it could have been disposed of other than in a transaction of a trading nature; and
>
> (c) whether the taxpayer's intention, as established or deduced, is consistent with other evidence pointing to a trading motivation.

Paragraphs 5 to 8 consider the manner in which the taxpayer deals with the property. According to the CRA:

> 5. The primary consideration is whether the taxpayer's actions in regard to the property in question were essentially what would be expected of a dealer in such a property. What is required, therefore, is to compare what dealers in the same kind of property ordinarily do with what the taxpayer did when he purchased the property, when he sold it and during the time when it was in his possession. ...
>
> 6. Evidence that efforts were soon made to find or attract purchasers or that a sale took place within a short period of time after the acquisition of the property by the taxpayer points to a trading intention.
>
> 7. During the time the taxpayer owned the property it is significant whether steps were taken with the intended result of improving its marketability. Where the property consisted of an operating business, such steps might involve various changes in the way the business was operated so as to improve the profit potential. The listing of the business for sale when the improved marketability was achieved would suggest that the business had not been acquired as an investment but had been acquired, improved and offered for sale in a manner similar to procedures followed by a dealer in businesses.
>
> 8. The fact that the taxpayer has a commercial background in similar areas or has had previous experience of a similar commercial nature has been held to be a pertinent consideration in some circumstances.

Paragraphs 9 to 11 address the nature of the property acquired:

9. Where property acquired by a taxpayer is of such a nature or of such a magnitude that it could not produce income or personal enjoyment to its owner by virtue of its ownership and the only purpose of the acquisition was a subsequent sale of the property, the presumption is that the purchase and sale was an adventure or concern in the nature of trade. This was a finding of the courts, for instance, where the property acquired was a large quantity of one kind of goods.

10. The property acquired may be capable of producing income but only if the taxpayer is in a position to operate or lease it, as for example, a cargo ship. If the taxpayer is not in a position to operate it and could make use of it only by selling it, the presumption again would be that the purchase and subsequent sale was an adventure or concern in the nature of trade.

11. Some kinds of property (e.g., a business, a security) are *prima facie* of an investment nature in that they are normally used to produce income through their operation or mere possession. Where property is of this kind and the taxpayer was in a position, if he so wished, to have operated or held it but he chose to sell it, then the manner in which he dealt with it and the intention when he acquired it must be the governing factors in deciding whether the transaction was an adventure or concern in the nature of trade.

According to paragraphs 12 and 13, which consider the taxpayer's intention:

12. A taxpayer's intention to sell at a profit is not sufficient, by itself, to establish that he was involved in an adventure or concern in the nature of trade. That intention is almost invariably present even when a true investment has been acquired, if circumstances should arise that would make it financially more beneficial to sell the investment than to continue to hold it. Where, however, one or other of the above tests clearly suggests an adventure or concern in the nature of trade, and, in addition, it can be established or inferred that the taxpayer's intention was to sell the property at the first suitable opportunity, intention will be viewed as corroborative evidence. On the other hand, inability to establish an intention to sell does not preclude a transaction from being regarded as an adventure or concern in the nature of trade if it can otherwise be so regarded pursuant to one of the above tests.

13. It must be recognized that a taxpayer may have more than one intention when a property is acquired. If the primary intention is said to be the holding of the property as an investment, regard must be had to whether, at the time of the acquisition, there was a secondary intention to sell the property if the primary intention could not be fulfilled. Secondary intention is particularly significant when the circumstances suggest that there was little likelihood of the property being retained by the taxpayer because of a lack of financial resources or for some other reason. Further, a taxpayer's intentions are not limited to the purposes for acquiring the property but extend to the time at which the disposition was made. A taxpayer's intention, if any, at the time of acquisition of the property may change at any time during ownership and up to disposition because the taxpayer may form an intention or otherwise change or abandon the primary, dominant or secondary intention with respect to the property.

The summary of the law in this interpretation bulletin was cited with approval by the Supreme Court of Canada in *Friesen v. Canada*, [1995] S.C.J. No. 71, [1995] 2 C.T.C. 369, 95 D.T.C. 5551 (S.C.C).

B. Reasonable Expectation of Profit

Where an activity such as gambling is not carried on for the purpose of making a profit, the courts have generally held that the activity is not a business within the meaning of the Act. In addition, as the court suggested in *Graham v. Green (Inspector of Taxes)*, [1925] K.B. 37, 9 TC 209 (U.K.), even if a taxpayer has a subjective intention to profit, an activity like gambling may not constitute a business if the activity is "not ... susceptible" of making a profit. On this basis, courts have generally concluded that gambling winnings are not included in computing a taxpayer's net income under section 3.

For the same reason, it follows; gambling losses are generally not deductible in computing a taxpayer's net income from all sources on the grounds that the source of the loss is not a business or property within the meaning of the Act. While these losses might reasonably be disallowed on the basis that the taxpayer's subjective purpose was not to make a profit but instead to enjoy a form of entertainment or personal consumption, consistency with the grounds for not taxing gambling winnings suggests that they might also be disallowed on the basis that the activity at issue is objectively not susceptible of making a profit. For this reason, Canadian courts have frequently supplemented the subjective profit-making purpose test for the existence of a business or property source with an objective "reasonable expectation of profit" (REOP) test to govern the deductibility of losses for a business or property. In *Stewart v. Canada*, [2002] S.C.J. No. 46, [2002] 3 C.T.C. 439, 2002 D.T.C. 6969 (S.C.C.), the Supreme Court of Canada reconsidered the scope of this test.

Stewart v. Canada
[2002] S.C.J. No. 46, [2002] 3 C.T.C. 439, 2002 D.T.C. 6969 (S.C.C.)

IACOBUCCI and BASTARACHE JJ:

I. Introduction

This appeal requires the Court to consider the appropriate use of what has come to be known as the "reasonable expectation of profit" test. The test originated with the following comments of Dickson J (as he then was) in the seminal case of *Moldowan v. The Queen*, [1978] 1 SCR 480, at p. 485:

> Although originally disputed, it is now accepted that in order to have a "source of income" the taxpayer must have a profit or a reasonable expectation of profit. Source of income, thus, is an equivalent term to business ...

Since then, decisions have varied in the application of this test. Although some cases have held that the reasonable expectation of profit test should only be used at the threshold stage of distinguishing between commercial and personal activities, others have used the test as a tool to assess the profitability of various *bona fide* commercial ventures in order to determine whether the taxpayer has a source of income, and is therefore entitled to deduct losses relating to that source.

The present appeal is just such a case. The appellant, Brian Stewart, purchased four condominium units from which he earned rental income. For the tax years in question, the appellant incurred losses, mainly as a result of significant interest expenses. These losses were disallowed by the Minister on the basis that the taxpayer had no reasonable expectation of profit, and therefore no source of income.

In our view, the reasonable expectation of profit analysis cannot be maintained as an independent source test. To do so would run contrary to the principle that courts should avoid judicial innovation and rule-making in tax law. Although the phrase "reasonable expectation of profit" is found in the *Income Tax Act*, SC 1970-71-72, c. 63 (the "Act"), its statutory use does not support the broad judicial application to which the phrase has been subjected. In addition, the reasonable expectation of profit test is imprecise, causing an unfortunate degree of uncertainty for taxpayers. As well, the nature of the test has encouraged a hindsight assessment of the business judgment of taxpayers in order to deny losses incurred in *bona fide*, albeit unsuccessful, commercial ventures.

It is undisputed that the concept of a "source of income" is fundamental to the Canadian tax system; however, any test which assesses the existence of a source must be firmly based on the words and scheme of the Act. As such, in order to determine whether a particular activity constitutes a source of income, the taxpayer must show that he or she intends to carry on that activity in pursuit of profit and support that intention with evidence. The purpose of this test is to distinguish between commercial and personal activities, and where there is no personal or hobby element to a venture undertaken with a view to a profit, the activity is commercial, and the taxpayer's pursuit of profit is established. However, where there is a suspicion that the taxpayer's activity is a hobby or personal endeavour rather than a business, the taxpayer's so-called reasonable expectation of profit is a factor, among others, which can be examined to ascertain whether the taxpayer has a commercial intent.

In the present appeal, the taxpayer purchased four rental properties which he rented to arm's length parties in order to obtain rental income. There was no personal element to the taxpayer's endeavour, and its commercial nature was never questioned. As a result, the appellant's rental activities constitute a source of income from which he is entitled to deduct his rental losses. We would therefore allow the appeal.

II. Facts

The appellant held senior positions with the Toronto Transit Commission in the years 1990 to 1992, the tax years relevant to this appeal. Between 1986, and 1992, his annual income ranged from $65,000 to over $90,000. The appellant was also an experienced real estate investor and had in the past acquired and disposed of several rental properties.

In 1986, the appellant acquired the four condominium rental units that are the subject of this appeal. The properties were part of a syndicated real estate development promoted by the Reemark Group, and were sold on the basis that the purchaser would be provided with a turnkey operation, that management would be provided, and that a rental pooling agreement would be entered into. The Reemark Group also arranged financing for the projects.

The first two units, the "White Oaks" units, located in London, Ontario, were purchased for $72,990 each. These units were financed by a first mortgage of $52,553, initially amortized over a 30-year period. Additional financing came in the form of two promissory notes totalling $19,437. The second two units, the "Park Woods" units, located in Surrey, British Columbia, were purchased for $74,990 and $58,990 and were similarly financed. All units were highly leveraged with the appellant paying only $1,000 cash for each unit. The appellant was provided with projections of rental income and expenses in respect of each of the properties. The projections contemplated payout of the promissory notes over a period of years terminating in 1994. They also projected negative cash flow and income tax deductions for a ten-year period in all cases. However, the actual rental experience of the four units ended up being worse than what had been set out in the projections provided by Reemark to the appellant, owing to worse than expected rental and vacancy rates.

The appellant tried to reduce the amount of financing on the units. In 1991, he increased the frequency of first mortgage payments on the units from monthly to weekly, thereby reducing the amortization period significantly. He sold one of the Park Woods units in 1991 and used the proceeds to pay down the debt on the other unit. By 1994, the appellant had paid off the promissory notes on all of the units. The appellant also exited the White Oaks rental pool arrangement in 1995 because of high vacancies and poor management and set up his own management company. In 1996, he changed management companies for the Park Woods unit.

For the taxation years 1990, 1991 and 1992, the appellant claimed losses of $27,814, $18,673 and $12,306, respectively. The losses resulted primarily from interest expenses on money borrowed to acquire the units. The Minister of National Revenue reassessed the appellant, disallowing his losses on the units for these taxation years solely on the basis that he had no reasonable expectation of profit for the years in question.

The appellant argued that the fact that the purchases were almost 100 percent financed was not determinative of whether he had a reasonable expectation of profit, and he argued that he should be able to deduct the carrying charges for monies borrowed to finance the rental losses. The respondent argued that the appellant had had no reasonable expectation of profit but had purchased the properties as a tax shelter, attracted by the promises of income tax deductions and capital gains projections promoted by the vendor Reemark. The appellant had followed the vendor's plan instead of following his usual investment practices, and chose not to pay down the debt owing at times when he clearly had money with which to do so.

The Tax Court of Canada found that the appellant's rental losses were not deductible in computing his income for income tax purposes because there was no reasonable expectation of profit. The Federal Court of Appeal dismissed the appeal.

...

V. Issues

A. Is the "reasonable expectation of profit" test set out by the Court in *Moldowan* the test for determining whether the taxpayer has a business or property source of income under the Act? If not, what is the test?

B. Did the courts below err in disallowing the appellant's interest expense deductions ... on the basis that there was no source of income?

VI. Analysis

A. The Test to Determine Whether the Taxpayer has a Business or Property Source of Income Under the Act

(1) A Brief Overview of the Cases Leading up to Moldowan

It is well accepted that the Canadian tax system adopted the concept of "source" from the English taxation statutes, and that the Act has always referred to income from various "sources": see V. Krishna, *The Fundamentals of Canadian Income Tax* (6th ed. 2000), at pp. 102-3. However, the term "source" is not defined in the Act, and it has been left to courts to determine the nature and scope of the various sources of income in the Act.

With respect to the phrase "reasonable expectation of profit," this wording first appeared in the *Income War Tax Act*, RSC 1927, c. 97 (previously SC 1917, c. 28) ("*IWTA*"), through a 1939 amendment which added a definition of "personal and living expenses" to the *IWTA*: SC 1939, c. 46, s. 2. That amendment defined "personal and living expenses" to include:

> ... the expenses of properties maintained by any person for the use or benefit of any taxpayer or any person connected with him by blood relationship, marriage or adoption, and not maintained in connection with a business carried on *bona fide* for a profit and not maintained with a reasonable expectation of a profit;

This definition was relevant to s. 6(f) of the *IWTA* which read, "[i]n computing the amount of the profits or gains to be assessed, a deduction shall not be allowed in respect of ... personal and living expenses." The phrase "reasonable expectation of profit" still appears in the virtually unaltered definition of "personal or living expenses" (now found in s. 248), which in turn relates to s. 18(1)(h). Section 18(1)(h) disallows the deduction of personal or living expenses from business or property income. It can be seen, therefore, that the statutory use of the phrase "reasonable expectation of profit" has changed little since its introduction into the *IWTA*.

Despite this fairly restrictive statutory use of the term "reasonable expectation of profit" (to disallow deductions for expenses of properties not maintained in connection with a business carried on with a reasonable expectation of profit), one author notes that several cases began to expand the use of the phrase in viewing "reasonable expectation of profit" as a general requirement of the "source of income" concept:

> The first suggestion to this effect actually appears in the 1964 decision of *J.S. Stewart v. M.N.R.*, a case concerning the raising of dogs for use in a display advertising business, in which the court stated (in obiter) that a business must be carried out in good faith with a reasonable expectation of profit." [[1964] CTC 45, at 51 (Ex. Ct.)]. Seven years later, in 1971, the Federal Court — Trial Division in *CBA Engineering Ltd. v. M.N.R.* [71 DTC 5282, at 5286], stated that farming could be either a hobby or an "operation with the expectation of profit," in which case it would be a source. *CBA Engineering Ltd.* was followed in 1972 by *O. Dorfman v. M.N.R.*, another farming case, in which the Federal Court — Trial Division stated, "In my view the words [source of income] are used in the sense of a business, employment, or property from which a net profit might reasonably be expected to come" [[1972] CTC 151, at 154],

> (C. Fien, "To Profit or Not to Profit: A Historical Review and Critical Analysis of the 'Reasonable Expectation of Profit' Test" (1995), 43 *Can. Tax J*, at p. 1298.)

From this, the author concludes at p. 1299 that "[i]t appears that *CBA Engineering Ltd.*, *Dorfman*, and [*D.A.*] *Holley* [*v. M.N.R.*, [1973] C.T.C. 539 (F.C.T.D.)] may well have been the springboard to Revenue Canada's adoption of a broadly based 'reasonable expectation of profit' test." In any event, these early cases were certainly germane to the decision in *Moldowan*.

In *Moldowan*, the taxpayer carried on a horse-racing activity. The Minister had conceded that this activity constituted a business; the issue before the Court was whether the taxpayer's farming was his *chief* source of income such that he could fully deduct his losses under s. 13 of the Act [now section 31].

[Where a taxpayer's "chief source of income for a taxation year is neither farming nor a combination of farming and some other source of income," subsection 31(1) generally limits the aggregate loss from all farming businesses carried on by the taxpayer to a maximum amount of $2,500 plus half of any net losses exceeding $2,500 up to $15,000. Subsection 31(1.1) defines any amount the deduction of which is prohibited by subsection 31(1) as "restricted farm loss," which can be carried over to other taxation years and deducted against net income from farming business under paragraph 111(1)(c) or added to the cost of the land under paragraph 53(1)(i) for the purpose of computing a gain or loss on its subsequent disposition. In *Moldowan*, the taxpayer, a Vancouver businessman who derived the bulk of his income from employment and investments, deducted the full amount of farm losses in computing his net income from all sources for the taxation years 1968 and 1969. Rejecting the taxpayer's argument that his chief source of income in these years was either farming or a combination of farming and another source of income, the Supreme Court of Canada held (at paras. 12 and 13) that a "chief source" of income turns on the taxpayer's "reasonable expectation of income from his various revenue sources and his ordinary mode and habit of work," while the "combination" of farming and another source specified in the provision "contemplates a man whose major preoccupation is farming" but who "may have other pecuniary interests as well, such as income from investments, or income from a sideline employment or business." As a result, Dickson J (as he then was) concluded (at para. 16), the *Income Tax Act* "envisages three classes of farmers": "(1) A taxpayer for whom farming may reasonably be expected to provide the bulk of income or the centre of work routine. Such a taxpayer, who looks to farming for his livelihood, is free of the limitation of subsection 13(1) [now subsection 31(1)] in those years in which he sustains a farming loss. (2) The taxpayer who does not look to farming, or to farming and some subordinate source of income, for his livelihood but carried on farming as a sideline business. Such a taxpayer is entitled to the deductions spelled out in subsection 13(1) in respect of farming losses. (3) The taxpayer who does not look to farming, or to farming and some subordinate source of income, for his livelihood and who carried on some farming activities as a hobby. The losses sustained by such a taxpayer on his non-business farming are not deductible in any amount."]

As such, the following comments of Dickson J at p. 485-86 relating to "reasonable expectation of profit" were *obiter*:

> Although originally disputed, it is now accepted that in order to have a "source of income" the taxpayer must have a profit or a reasonable expectation of profit. Source of income, thus, is an equivalent term to business: *Dorfman v. M.N.R.* [[1972] CTC 151]. See also s. 139(1)(ae) of the *Income Tax Act* which includes as "personal and living expenses" and therefore not deductible for tax purposes, the expenses of properties maintained by the taxpayer for his own use and benefit, and not maintained in connection with a business carried on for profit or with a reasonable expectation of profit. If the taxpayer in operating his farm is merely indulging in a hobby, with no reasonable expectation of profit, he is disentitled to claim any deduction at all in respect of expenses incurred.

> There is a vast case literature on what reasonable expectation of profit means and it is by no means entirely consistent. In my view, whether a taxpayer has a reasonable expectation of profit is an objective determination to be made from all of the facts. The following criteria should be considered: the profit and loss experience in past years, the taxpayer's training, the taxpayer's intended course of action, the capability of the venture as capitalized to show a profit after charging capital cost allowance. The list is not intended to be exhaustive. The factors will differ with the nature and extent of the undertaking: *The Queen v. Matthews* [(1974), 74 DTC 6193]. One would not expect a farmer who purchased a productive going operation to suffer the same start-up losses as the man who begins a tree farm on raw land.

Since this Court's decision in *Moldowan*, the "reasonable expectation of profit" or "REOP" test has been applied by the Minister and the courts in a variety of situations in order to determine whether a taxpayer has a source of income, whether business or property. However, as the above discussion indicates, equating the phrase "reasonable expectation of profit" with a "source" of income for the purposes of the Act is a case law expansion of the use of that phrase in the definition of "personal and living expenses" in the Act. As such, it is appropriate to examine the REOP test closely in order to determine whether it should be accepted as a stand-alone source test, or whether there is a better approach to assessing the existence of a source. Indeed, the wide range of approaches that courts have taken to the REOP test alone calls for clarification.

(2) Post-Moldowan REOP Cases

Since *Moldowan*, courts have differed in their acceptance of the REOP analysis as the appropriate test for the source of income determination, and a brief survey of some of these cases is a useful starting point for an evaluation of the *Moldowan* test.

Although cases where the Minister has disallowed deductions or losses on a "no reasonable expectation of profit" basis have taken a range of positions, they can generally be categorized into two groups: those which accept the use of the test where there is no personal element to the taxpayer's activities, and those which hold that the test has no application unless there is a personal or hobby aspect to the endeavour.

In *Landry v. Ministre du Revenu national* (1994), 173 NR 213 at paras. 1 and 3, the majority of the Federal Court of Appeal held that the taxpayer who had come out of retirement to practice law at the age of 71 did not satisfy the REOP test and thus had no source of income from which to deduct the losses that his practice had incurred. Writing for the majority, Décary JA quoted and accepted the Tax Court judge's application of the test:

> I see no reason why the reasonable expectation of profit test should not apply to any profession, liberal or otherwise, any occupation or activity which purports to be in the course of carrying on a business. As I see it, the *reasonable expectation of a profit* is a general rule applicable to any activity which may give rise to business income ... . [Emphasis added.]

Décary JA then concluded that:

> It is possible for someone, with the best will in the world, to practise an activity that takes all his or her time and that activity may still not be a business for the purposes of the *Income Tax Act*. ... For the purposes of determining whether there is a source of income, only an activity that is profitable or that is carried on with a *reasonable expectation of profit* is a business ... . [Emphasis added.]

This decision was followed in *Hugill v. The Queen*, 95 DTC 5311 (FCA), in which the taxpayer's deductions in respect of rental properties were disallowed. At p. 5311, the Federal Court of Appeal affirmed the Tax Court of Canada's determination that the taxpayer's business plan was unrealistic and therefore that there was no reasonable expectation of profit:

> In reaching this decision, the Tax Court judge had regard to: the constant losses suffered by the taxpayer since 1984; the lack of improvements required if the properties were to be rented during both the summer and winter seasons; and the fact that the venture "has been,

and continues to be, under capitalized." It is true that the applicant had a "plan" which if realized might reasonably have resulted in a profit but unfortunately it was a plan which changed from year to year as his personal financial circumstances changed. In the circumstances, the reasoning of Mr. Justice Décary in [*Landry v. Ministre du Revenu national* (1994), 173 NR 213 at paras. 1 and 3] is particularly apt: "There comes a time in the life of any business operating at a deficit when the Minister must be able to determine objectively ... that a reasonable expectation of profit has turned into an impossible dream."

A similar approach was taken in *Sirois v. M.N.R.*, 88 DTC 1114 (TCC), where the taxpayer ran a restaurant business that suffered losses from 1979 to 1984. The Minister disallowed the losses for the 1981 and 1982 taxation years. Couture CJTC reviewed the operations of the business, including seating capacity and opening hours in order to determine whether a reasonable expectation of profit existed so as to allow the taxpayer to deduct the losses. At p. 1115, he concluded that:

> ... for the 1981 taxation year, considering that the restaurant was operated with seating for only twenty (20), four days a week, and that since 1976 the operations had shown a loss, there was no realistic reasonable expectation of profit in these circumstances.
>
> For the 1982 taxation year, however, when the situation was entirely different, I am of the opinion that the respondent ... was not justified in presuming that there was no reasonable expectation of profit in such circumstances.

Although cases such as *Landry*, *Hugill*, and *Sirois* evidenced a willingness on the part of the Tax Court of Canada and the Federal Court of Appeal to reassess the business decisions of taxpayers, in *Tonn v. Canada*, [1996] 2 FC 73, the Federal Court of Appeal appeared to temper this approach somewhat. In that case, the taxpayers purchased a rental property which incurred losses. In allowing the taxpayers to deduct these losses, Linden JA, at paras. 26 and 28, made the following remarks with respect to the REOP test:

> But do the Act's purposes suggest that deductions of losses from *bona fide* businesses be disallowed solely because the taxpayer made a bad judgment call? I do not think so. The tax system has every interest in investigating the *bona fides* of a taxpayer's dealings in certain situations, but it should not discourage, or penalize, honest but erroneous business decisions. The tax system does not tax on the basis of a taxpayer's business acumen, with deductions extended to the wise and withheld from the foolish. ...
>
> ...
>
> The *Moldowan* test, therefore is a useful tool by which the tax-inappropriateness of an activity may be reasonably inferred when other, more direct forms of evidence are lacking. Consequently, when the circumstances do not admit of any suspicion that a business loss was made for a personal or non-business motive, the test should be applied sparingly and with a latitude favouring the taxpayer, whose business judgment may have been less than competent.

However, to this Linden JA added that it was open for courts to determine that "... though the taxpayer genuinely intended the pursuit of profit through a purely commercial activity, the intention was unrealistic, the expectation of profit unreasonable, and hence, the activity was not a business" (para. 36).

...

In contrast to the above cases, other decisions, particularly those of Bowman ACJ of the Tax Court of Canada, have taken a different view of the applicability REOP test. In *Allen v. The Queen*, 99 DTC 968 (TCC), aff'd 2000 DTC 6559 (FCA), Bowman JTCC (as he then was) held at paras. 18-25 that the REOP test had no application in a situation similar to the one at bar, where, with near 100 percent financing, the taxpayers formed a partnership which carried on a rental business and incurred losses:

> In my opinion, the respondent has misapplied the [REOP] doctrine. We are dealing here with two individuals who have invested, through a limited partnership, in a perfectly viable business that started making a profit in the second year. There was no personal element involved — neither appellant has any intention of residing in the apartments. ...
>
> ...
>
> How then does the fact that the acquisition of the limited partnership interests was financed substantially by the borrowing of money ... turn a viable and profitable business into one that had no reasonable expectation of profit and was, therefore, not a business and not a source of income? The investment was clearly long term and *bona fide*, with the expectation that in the fullness of time the debt would be paid down and ultimately paid off and the appellants would have a lasting investment. The Minister's position ... is that once the income from the partnership exceeded the interest charges, the non-business will become a business and the Minister will start to tax.
>
> ...
>
> Whatever else may be said about 99% financing of an investment, it certainly cannot be said that its result is that the vehicle in which the taxpayer has invested did not carry on a business. This is wrong as a matter of logic, law and common sense. The Minister is seeking to limit the deduction of the amount of interest ... by intoning the ritual incantation [REOP], where it is obvious and admitted that the partnership is carrying on a profitable business.
>
> ...
>
> The [REOP] principle may have some application where a person tries to write off losses from a hobby such as horseracing (*Rai v. The Queen*, February 8, 1999, file number 98-925(IT)I); or from collecting antique Coca-Cola bottles (*Kaye v. The Queen*, 98 DTC 1659); or renting a portion of the basement of that person's dwelling to a relative and trying to write off 2/3 of the costs of the house. *It operates at the liminal stage of questioning the existence of a business. Where there is no personal element and a genuine business exists the [REOP] doctrine has no application.* ... [Emphasis added.]

Bowman JTCC has expressed a similar view in a variety of cases: see, for example, *Nichol v. The Queen*, 93 DTC 1216 (TCC); *Bélec v. The Queen*, 95 DTC 121 (TCC); *Kaye v. The Queen*, 98 DTC 1659 (TCC).

It is evident from this brief review that the REOP test has not been interpreted and applied in a consistent manner. The cases dealing with this concept fall along a spectrum. At one end are the decisions which consider REOP to be the test by which the viability of the taxpayer's business plan is assessed, whatever the activity in question happens to be, and to determine whether this activity deserves to be considered a "source of income." At the other end of the spectrum are the cases which use the REOP analysis only where the activity in question contains a personal or hobby element, and then only as a factor in determining whether this activity is sufficiently commercial to be labelled a "source of income." The only coherent message that emerges from a survey of the cases which have followed *Moldowan* is that the proper role of "reasonable expectation of profit" is in need of clarification.

(3) Problems with the REOP Test

Since *Moldowan*, there has been a fair amount of judicial and academic criticism of the alleged misuse of the REOP test. These comments can be generally classified into two types. First, some critics allege that there is no statutory foundation for using "reasonable expectation of profit" as the test to determine whether a source of income exists. Second, it is argued that, even if *Moldowan* did set out a legitimate "source" test, the test is problematic and should be rejected.

In Dickson J's *obiter* comments with respect to reasonable expectation of profit, he cites *Dorfman v. M.N.R.*, [1972] CTC 151, as authority for the proposition that in order to have a source of income the taxpayer must have a reasonable expectation of profit. However, several commentators have pointed out that *Dorfman* stands for a slightly different proposition. In particular, in *Dorfman*, the Federal Court, Trial Division was dealing with an argument by the Minister that because the taxpayer had not realized net farming income for the year, that farming could not be a source of the taxpayer's income. In rejecting that argument, Collier J, at p. 154, stated that:

> I cannot accept the interpretation put by counsel for the Minister in this case on the words "source of income": that there must be net income before there can be a source. In my view the words are used in the sense of a business, employment, or property from which a net profit might reasonably be expected to come.

In other words, the court was addressing the contention that the phrase "source of income" required a net profit. In response to this particular argument, the court held that, where an activity had a reasonable *expectation* of net profit, this was enough to constitute a source of income. Put in other terms, the fact that an activity is being carried on with a reasonable expectation of profit is sufficient for the activity to constitute a source of income.

It has been pointed out that, as a matter of logic, the fact that an activity carried on with a reasonable expectation of profit is a *sufficient* requirement for a source of income (the proposition from *Dorfman*) does not entail that a reasonable expectation of profit is a *necessary* requirement for a source of income (the proposition from *Moldowan*): see B.S. Nichols, "Chants and Ritual Incantations: Rethinking the Reasonable Expectation of Profit Test," 1996 Conference Report, *Report of Proceedings of the Forty-Eighth Tax Conference*, Vol. 1, 28:1, at pp. 28:4-28:5; S. Silver, "Great Expectations: Are they Reasonable?," *Corporate Management Tax Conference 1995*, 6:1, at pp. 6:6-6:7. In other words, it is argued that by taking the comments from *Dorfman* out of their particular context and applying them generally, *Moldowan* mistakenly equated "source of income" with "reasonable expectation of profit."

Indeed, equating the term "business" with the phrase "reasonable expectation of profit" does not accord with the traditional common law definition of business, which is that "anything which occupies the time and attention and labour of a man for the purpose of profit is business" (*Smith v. Anderson* (1880), 15 Ch. D 247 (CA), at p. 258; *Terminal Dock and Warehouse Co. v. M.N.R.*, [1968] 2 Ex. CR 78, aff'd 68 DTC 5316 (SCC)). In addition, early cases dealing with the proper definition of a business rejected looking exclusively at one factor. For example, in *Erichsen v. Last* (1881), 4 TC 422, at p. 423, the English Court of Appeal stated:

> I do not think there is any principle of law which lays down what carrying on of trade is. There are a multitude of incidents which together make the carrying on [of] a trade, but I know of no one distinguishing incident which makes a practice a carrying on of trade, and another practice not a carrying on of trade. If I may use the expression, it is a compound fact made up of a variety of incidents.

Thus, to equate "source of income" with "reasonable expectation of profit," at least in the instance of a business source, is not in line with these earlier characterizations of "business."

The view has also been taken that Dickson J did not intend to set out a broadly applicable source test in *Moldowan*, but instead that he was simply distinguishing between mere hobbies and *bona fide* businesses: see J.R. Owen, "The Reasonable Expectation of Profit Test: Is There a Better Approach?" (1996), 44 *Can. Tax J* 979, at p. 1002. This view stems from the fact that in the same paragraph where Dickson J equates a business with a reasonable expectation of profit, he states "[i]f the taxpayer in operating his farm is merely indulging in a hobby, with no reasonable expectation of profit, he is disentitled to claim any deduction at all in respect of expenses incurred": *Moldowan, supra*, at p. 485. As well, various cases have held that the *Moldowan* test is only applicable where there is some personal element to the taxpayer's endeavour: *Hickman Motors Ltd. v. Canada*, [1997] 2 SCR 336, at paras. 69 and 72; *Allen, supra*; *Nichol, supra*; *Bélec, supra*.

In light of the definition of "business" developed in earlier cases, as well as the dubious scope of Dickson J's *obiter* reference to "reasonable expectation of profit" in *Moldowan*, which may also have been a mistaken application of that phrase as used in *Dorfman*, the REOP test should not be blindly accepted as the correct approach to the "source of income" determination. This conclusion is strengthened by the fact that subsequent cases have run the gamut with respect to the application of the REOP concept.

It has also been argued that the limited use of the phrase, "reasonable expectation of profit" in the Act, does not support its use as a stand-alone source test. As mentioned above, the phrase first appeared in the Act in the definition of "personal and living expenses." The current version of that definition, in s. 248 (RSC 1985, c. 1 (5th Supp.)), reads:

"personal or living expenses" includes

    (a)   the expenses of properties maintained by any person for the use or benefit of the taxpayer or any person connected with the taxpayer by blood relationship, marriage or common-law partnership or adoption, and not maintained in connection with a business carried on for profit or with a reasonable expectation of profit;

The phrase "personal or living expenses" relates to s. 18(1)(h) of the Act which now reads:

18. (1) In computing the income of a taxpayer from a business or property no deduction shall be made in respect of

             ...

    (h)   personal or living expenses of the taxpayer, other than travel expenses incurred by the taxpayer while away from home in the course of carrying on the taxpayer's business;

             ...

It can be seen, therefore, from an examination of the Act that the statutory provisions that employ a "reasonable expectation of profit" test are specific in nature and would not appear to support a broad application of this test by Revenue Canada and the courts.

Thus, the only way to accept "reasonable expectation of profit" as the test to determine whether a taxpayer has a source of income is to adopt an interpretive rule of law which is independent of the provisions of the Act. As this Court observed in *Ludco Enterprises Ltd. v. Canada*, [2001] 2 SCR 1082, 2001 SCC 62, at para. 53, "this Court has repeatedly stated that in matters of tax law, a court should always be reluctant to engage in judicial innovation and rule making." Although it is true that the term "source" is undefined in the Act, and courts must frequently determine whether a taxpayer has the requisite source of income, there is a distinction between judicial interpretation and judicial rule-making, and, in our respectful view, several cases have crossed the line between use of REOP as an interpretive aid to assess whether a source of income exists and use of REOP as a stand-alone "source" test. The fact that the REOP test has been applied to both business and property sources, activities with completely different natures, indicates that the test has transcended its use as a mere interpretive tool, and has taken on a life of its own. Indeed, in *Tonn, supra*, at para. 25, the *Moldowan* test was described as a "common law formulation respecting the purposes of the Act" which was "ideally suited to situations where a taxpayer is attempting to avoid tax liability by an inappropriate structuring of his or her affairs."

As stated by this Court in *Canderel Ltd. v. Canada*, [1998] 1 SCR 147, at para. 41, "[t]he law of income tax is sufficiently complicated without unhelpful judicial incursions into the realm of lawmaking." In our view, the range of uses and interpretations that courts have given to the phrase "reasonable expectation of profit," and the corresponding uncertainty this has created for the taxpayer, are illustrative of the dangers inherent in this type of judicial exercise. Moreover, even if one were to accept the use of the REOP test as a legitimate source of income standard, there are numerous practical difficulties which arise in its application that suggest to us that the test is ill-suited for this purpose.

It has been pointed out that it is unclear what exactly the REOP test refers to by the term "profit." For example, it is unclear whether the capacity for profit should be determined after taking into account depreciation and, if so, whether capital cost allowance or accounting depreciation should be used: see *Roopchan v. The Queen*, 96 DTC 1338, at p. 1341. Even if the basis for calculating profit was clear, it is still uncertain how much expected profit would be required, in what time frame, and whether the amount of expected profit should vary with the risk of the venture: see Fien, *supra*, at pp. 1304-6. For example, a high-risk venture may incur substantial losses which may be disallowed by virtue of a reasonable expectation of profit analysis; however, it is highly unlikely that, where such a venture does pay off, the Minister would abstain from an assessment on the ground that there was no reasonable expectation of profit and therefore no business.

The vagueness of the REOP test encourages a retrospective application which, as pointed out by Bowman JTCC in *Nichol, supra*, at p. 1219, causes uncertainty and unfairness:

> [The taxpayer] made what might, in retrospect, be seen as an error in judgment but it was a matter of business judgment and it was not one so patently unreasonable as to entitle this Court or the Minister of National Revenue to substitute its or his judgment for it, or penalize him for having made a judgment call that, with the benefit of 20-20 hindsight, that Monday morning quarterbacks always have, I or the Minister of National Revenue might not make today. ...

In addition, the way in which a particular venture is capitalized may have significant effects on its profitability. The extent of capitalization, rates of interest, and level at which a venture is capitalized (for example partner financing versus partnership financing, or corporate financing versus shareholder financing) may have significant effects on the bottom line, and it is difficult to see why the characterization of a commercial venture as a source should depend on the extent or method of financing: see Fien, *supra*, at pp. 1306-7.

To summarize, in recent years the *Moldowan* REOP test has become a broad-based tool used by both the Minister and courts in any manner of situation where the view is taken that the taxpayer does not have a reasonable expectation of profiting from the activity in question. From this it is inferred that the taxpayer has no source of income, and thus no basis from which to deduct losses and expenses relating to the activity. The REOP test has been applied independently of provisions of the Act to second-guess *bona fide* commercial decisions of the taxpayer and therefore runs afoul of the principle that courts should avoid judicial rule-making in tax law: see *Ludco, supra*; *Royal Bank of Canada v. Sparrow Electric Corp.*, [1997] 1 SCR 411; *Canderel, supra*; *Shell Canada Ltd. v. Canada*, [1999] 3 SCR 622. As well, the REOP test is problematic owing to its vagueness and uncertainty of application; this results in unfair and arbitrary treatment of taxpayers. As a result, "reasonable expectation of profit" should not be accepted as the test to determine whether a taxpayer's activities constitute a source of income.

(4) "Source of Income": The Recommended Approach

In our view, the determination of whether a taxpayer has a source of income, must be grounded in the words and scheme of the Act.

The Act divides a taxpayer's income into various sources. Under the basic rules for computing income in s. 3, the Act states:

> 3. The income of a taxpayer for a taxation year for the purposes of this Part is his income for the year determined by the following rules:
>
> (a) determine the aggregate of amounts each of which is the taxpayer's income for the year ... *from a source* inside or outside Canada, including, without restricting the generality of the foregoing, *his income for the year from each office, employment, business and property*; [Emphasis added.]

With respect to business and property sources, the basic computation rule is found in s. 9:

> 9. (1) Subject to this Part, a taxpayer's income for a taxation year from a business or property is his profit therefrom for the year.
>
> (2) Subject to section 31, a taxpayer's loss for a taxation year from a business or property is the amount of his loss, if any, for the taxation year from that source computed by applying the provisions of this Act respecting computation of income from that source *mutatis mutandis*.

It is clear that in order to apply s. 9, the taxpayer must first determine whether he or she has a source of either business or property income. As has been pointed out, a commercial activity which falls short of being a business, may nevertheless be a source of property income. As well, it is clear that some taxpayer endeavours are neither businesses, nor sources of property income, but are mere personal activities. As such, the following two-stage approach with respect to the source question can be employed:

(i)   Is the activity of the taxpayer undertaken in pursuit of profit, or is it a personal endeavour?

(ii)   If it is not a personal endeavour, is the source of the income a business or property?

The first stage of the test assesses the general question of whether or not a source of income exists; the second stage categorizes the source as either business or property.

Equating "source of income" with an activity undertaken "in pursuit of profit" accords with the traditional common law definition of "business," i.e., "anything which occupies the time and attention and labour of a man for the purpose of profit": *Smith, supra*, at p. 258; *Terminal Dock, supra*. As well, business income is generally distinguished from property income on the basis that a business requires an additional level of taxpayer activity: see Krishna, *supra*, at p. 240. As such, it is logical to conclude that an activity undertaken in pursuit of profit, regardless of the level of taxpayer activity, will be either a business or property source of income.

The purpose of this first stage of the test is simply to distinguish between commercial and personal activities, and, as discussed above, it has been pointed out that this may well have been the original intention of Dickson J's reference to "reasonable expectation of profit" in *Moldowan*. Viewed in this light, the criteria listed by Dickson J are an attempt to provide an objective list of factors for determining whether the activity in question is of a commercial or personal nature. These factors are what Bowman JTCC has referred to as "indicia of commerciality" or "badges of trade": *Nichol, supra*, at p. 1218. Thus, where the nature of a taxpayer's venture contains elements which suggest that it could be considered a hobby or other personal pursuit, but the venture is undertaken in a sufficiently commercial manner, the venture will be considered a source of income for the purposes of the Act.

We emphasize that this "pursuit of profit" source test will only require analysis in situations where there is some personal or hobby element to the activity in question. With respect, in our view, courts have erred in the past in applying the REOP test to activities such as law practices and restaurants where there exists no such personal element: see, for example, *Landry, supra*; *Sirois, supra*; *Engler v. The Queen*, 94 DTC 6280 (FC). Where the nature of an activity is clearly commercial, there is no need to analyze the taxpayer's business decisions. Such endeavours necessarily involve the pursuit of profit. As such, a source of income by definition exists, and there is no need to take the inquiry any further.

It should also be noted that the source of income assessment is not a purely subjective inquiry. Although in order for an activity to be classified as commercial in nature, the taxpayer must have the subjective intention to profit, in addition, as stated in *Moldowan*, this determination should be made by looking at a variety of objective factors. Thus, in expanded form, the first stage of the above test can be restated as follows: "Does the taxpayer intend to carry on an activity for profit and is there evidence to support that intention?" This requires the taxpayer to establish that his or her predominant intention is to make a profit from the activity and that the activity has been carried out in accordance with objective standards of businesslike behaviour.

The objective factors listed by Dickson J in *Moldowan* at p. 486 were: (1) the profit and loss experience in past years; (2) the taxpayer's training; (3) the taxpayer's intended course of action; and (4) the capability of the venture to show a profit. As we conclude below, it is not necessary for the purposes of this appeal to expand on this list of factors. As such, we decline to do so; however, we would reiterate Dickson J's caution that this list is not intended to be exhaustive, and that the factors will differ with the nature and extent of the undertaking. We would also emphasize that although the reasonable expectation of profit is a factor to be considered at this stage, it is not the only factor, nor is it conclusive. The overall assessment to be made is whether or not the taxpayer is carrying on the activity in a commercial manner. However, this assessment should not be used to second-guess the business judgment of the taxpayer. It is the commercial nature of the taxpayer's activity which must be evaluated, not his or her business acumen.

In addition to restricting the source test to activities which contain a personal element, the activity which the taxpayer claims constitutes a source of income must be distinguished from particular deductions that the taxpayer associates with that source. An attempt by the taxpayer to deduct what is essentially a personal expense does not influence the characterization of the source to which that deduction relates. This analytical separation is mandated by the structure of the Act. While, as discussed above, s. 9 is the provision of the Act where the basic distinction is drawn between personal and commercial activity, and then, within the commercial sphere, between business and property sources, the characterization of deductions occurs elsewhere. In particular, s. 18(1)(a) requires that deductions be attributed to a particular business or property source, and s. 18(1)(h) specifically disallows the deduction of personal or living expenses of the taxpayer ... .

It is clear from these provisions that the deductibility of expenses presupposes the existence of a source of income, and thus should not be confused with the preliminary source inquiry. If the deductibility of a particular expense is in question, then it is not the existence of a source of income which ought to be questioned, but the relationship between that expense and the source to which it is purported to relate. The fact that an expense is found to be a personal or living expense does not affect the characterization of the source of income to which the taxpayer attempts to allocate the expense, it simply means that the expense cannot be attributed to the source of income in question. As well, if, in the circumstances, the expense is unreasonable in relation to the source of income, then s. 67 of the Act provides a mechanism to reduce or eliminate the amount of the expense. Again, however, excessive or unreasonable expenses have no bearing on the characterization of a particular activity as a source of income.

In addition to the fact that the deductibility, or otherwise, of an expense is a separate question from the existence of the underlying source of income, it is also true that the profitability of the activity to which the expense relates does not affect the deductibility of the expense. In particular, there have been a number of cases where a taxpayer's large interest expenses have resulted in net losses, which in turn have caused the Minister to conclude that there is no reasonable expectation of profit, and therefore no source of income from which the interest expenses can be deducted. However, as stated above, reasonable expectation of profit is but one factor to consider in determining whether an activity has a sufficient degree of commerciality to be considered a source of income. Once that determination has been made, then the deductibility inquiry is undertaken according to whether the expense in question falls within the words of the relevant deduction provision(s) of the Act.

...

In summary, the issue of whether or not a taxpayer has a source of income is to be determined by looking at the commerciality of the activity in question. Where the activity contains no personal element and is clearly commercial, no further inquiry is necessary. Where the activity could be classified as a personal pursuit, then it must be determined whether or not the activity is being carried on in a sufficiently commercial manner to constitute a source of income. However, to deny the deduction of losses on the simple ground that the losses signify that no business (or property) source exists is contrary to the words and scheme of the Act. Whether or not a business exists is a separate question from the deductibility of expenses. As suggested by the appellant, to disallow deductions based on a reasonable expectation of profit analysis would amount to a case law stop-loss rule which would be contrary to established principles of interpretation, mentioned above, which are applicable to the Act. As well, unlike many statutory stop-loss rules, once deductions are disallowed under the REOP test, the taxpayer cannot carry forward such losses to apply to future income in the event the activity becomes profitable. As stated by Bowman JTCC in *Bélec, supra*, at p. 123: "It would be ... unacceptable to permit the Minister [to say] to the taxpayer ... 'The fact that you lost money ... proves that you did not have a reasonable expectation of profit, but as soon as you earn some money, it proves that you now have such an expectation.'"

B. Application of the Source Test to the Case at Bar

As stated above, whether or not a taxpayer has a source of income from a particular activity is determined by considering whether the taxpayer intends to carry on the activity for profit, and whether there is evidence to support that intention. As well, where an activity is clearly commercial and lacks any personal element, there is no need to search further. Such activities are sources of income.

In this case, the appellant was engaged in property rental activities. He owned four rental condominium units from which he earned rental income. The fact that there was no personal element to these properties was never questioned. The units were all rented to arm's length parties and there was no evidence that the appellant intended to make use of any of the properties for his personal benefit. In our view, a property rental activity which lacks any element of personal use or benefit to the taxpayer is clearly a commercial activity. For what purpose would the taxpayer have spent his time and money in this activity if not for profit? As a result, the appellant satisfies the test for source of income. Although this is sufficient to dispose of the appeal, in our view a few additional remarks are warranted.

Even if the appellant had made use of one or more of the properties for his personal benefit, the Minister would not be entitled to conclude that no business existed without further analysis. A taxpayer in such circumstances would have the opportunity to establish that his or her predominant intention was to make a profit from the activity and that the activity was carried out in accordance with objective standards of businesslike behaviour. Whether a reasonable expectation of profit existed may be a factor that is taken into consideration in that analysis.

The Minister and the courts below made much of the fact that the appellant anticipated a capital gain from the eventual sale of the properties. It was argued that it was this anticipated gain, and not rental profits, which motivated the taxpayer. As well, the Minister argued that an anticipated capital gain should not be included in assessing whether the taxpayer had a reasonable expectation of profit. As such, it was the Minister's submission that the appellant should not have been allowed to deduct his interest payments under s. 20(1)(c)(i) as amounts paid in respect of borrowed money used to produce income from a business or property. The application of the REOP test by the Minister was motivated by the policy concern that Canadian taxpayers should not have to subsidize mortgage payments made in respect of properties where the primary motivation is a long-term capital gain.

In response to this argument, it must be remembered that s. 20(1)(c)(i) is not a tax avoidance mechanism, and it has been established that, in light of the specific anti-avoidance provisions in the Act, courts should not be quick to embellish provisions of the Act in response to tax avoidance concerns: *Ludco*, *supra*, at para. 39; *Neuman v. M.N.R.*, [1998] 1 SCR 770, at para. 63. ... As such, the appellant's hope of realizing an eventual capital gain, and expectation of deducting interest expenses do not detract from the commercial nature of his rental operation or its characterization as a source of income. Moreover, in *Ludco*, *supra*, at para. 59, this Court specifically stated that s. 20(1)(c)(i) does not require the taxpayer to earn a net profit in order for interest to be deductible ....

Indeed, a clear analogy can be drawn between the facts in *Ludco*, and the facts in the case at bar. In *Ludco*, the taxpayer deducted approximately $6 million in interest charges on borrowed money used to purchase shares which yielded some $600,000 in dividends. On disposition of the shares the taxpayer realized a significant capital gain. The Minister disallowed the deduction of interest under s. 20(1)(c) on the basis that the borrowed money was not used for the purpose of earning income from property. This Court held at para. 54 that, in order to come within the scope of s. 20(1)(c)(i), the taxpayer had to show that "considering all the circumstances, the taxpayer had a reasonable expectation of income at the time the investment is made." The taxpayer satisfied this test, and the Court allowed the interest deduction.

Similarly, in this case, the taxpayer's interest payments exceeded his rental income for the years in question. Although the taxpayer only disposed of one of the properties during the relevant time period, the Reemark plan held out the prospect of an eventual capital gain on disposition. As in *Ludco*, the appellant used borrowed money to engage in a *bona fide* investment from which he had a reasonable expectation of income, and thus, he falls within the scope of s. 20(1)(c)(i).

With respect to whether or not an anticipated capital gain should be included in assessing whether the taxpayer has a reasonable expectation of profit, we reiterate that the expected profitability of a venture is but one factor to consider in assessing whether the taxpayer's activity evidences a sufficient level of commerciality to be considered either a business or a property source of income. Having said this, in our view, the motivation of capital gains accords with the ordinary business person's understanding of "pursuit of profit," and may be taken into account in determining whether the taxpayer's activity is commercial in nature. Of course the mere acquisition of property in anticipation of an eventual gain does not provide a source of income for the purposes of s. 9; however, an anticipated gain may be a factor in assessing the commerciality of the taxpayer's overall course of conduct.

VII. Conclusion

For these reasons, we conclude that the appellant's rental activities constituted a source of income. As a result, we would allow the appeal with costs throughout, set aside the judgment of the Federal Court of Appeal and refer the assessments for the taxation years in issue back to the Minister for reassessment on the basis that the taxpayer had a source of income from which he was entitled to deduct losses from the rental properties in question.

Appeal allowed with costs.

NOTES AND QUESTIONS

1.   On what grounds did the Minister disallow the deduction of the taxpayer's rental losses in *Stewart*? Of what relevance to the Minister's assessment was its view that the taxpayer was motivated primarily by an anticipated gain from the sale of the condominiums rather than net rental income? To the extent that the taxpayer was motivated mainly by the prospect of a gain on the sale of the condominiums, should such a subsequent gain be characterized as a capital gain or as income from a business?

2.   Why did the Supreme Court of Canada allow the taxpayer's appeal in *Stewart*? Why did it reject the reasonable expectation of profit ("REOP") test as an independent test to determine the existence of a business or property source within the meaning of the Act? Do you agree with the court's decision? Why or why not?

3.   Where taxpayers acquire property primarily for the purpose of subsequent resale at a profit, they may be willing to incur substantial annual losses while waiting for the property to increase in value. Indeed, so-called tax shelter investments are premised on the expectation of such losses, which may be used to reduce taxes payable on other sources of income. Indeed, the condominiums in *Stewart* had all the hallmarks of a tax shelter, because they were acquired primarily with borrowed money and were projected to generate tax losses for a 10-year period.

Is it appropriate to permit taxpayers to, in effect, finance the carrying cost of property acquired primarily for the purpose of resale by deducting annual losses against other sources of income? Might it be more appropriate for these losses to be added to the cost of the property in order to determine the profit on resale? In this respect, see subsection 18(2) of the Act, which prevents taxpayers from utilizing deductions for interest and property taxes to generate losses on land that is not used in the course of a business or held primarily for rental purposes, and paragraph 53(1)(h), which allows taxpayers to add the disallowed amount to the cost of the land for purposes of computing any gain or loss on resale. See also regulation 1100(11), which prevents taxpayers from using capital cost allowances on rental properties to generate losses from these properties. These provisions are considered later in this chapter.

4. In *Walls v. Canada*, [2002] S.C.J. No. 47, 2002 D.T.C. 6960 (S.C.C.), the taxpayers invested in a limited partnership that had been structured as a tax shelter designed to generate tax losses that investors could use to offset income from other sources. Although concluding (at para. 22) that the taxpayers "were clearly motivated by tax considerations when they purchased their interests in the Partnership," the court rejected the Minister's application of the REOP test to disallow the losses on the basis (at para. 21) that "the Partnership purchased and maintained an ongoing commercial operation."

5. In *Quebec (Deputy Minister of Revenue) v. Lipson*, [1979] S.C.J. No. 11, [1979] C.T.C. 247 (S.C.C.), the taxpayer was one of nine shareholders of a company incorporated in Ontario for the purpose of operating a 70-unit apartment building in Ottawa. When the building was ready for occupancy in November 1961, market conditions were poor and the company lost over $50,000 in six months. As a result, the shareholders formed a syndicate or joint venture that leased the building from the company under an arrangement that, in effect, shifted the losses from the company to the members of the syndicate. After incurring substantial losses for three years, the members of the syndicate exercised an option to renew the lease on identical terms for a further two years. In 1966, the syndicate lost $98,094.24. The taxpayer admitted that the sole purpose of these transactions was to enable the members of the syndicate to deduct the rental losses in computing their net income.

On appeal, the Supreme Court of Canada upheld the assessment under the Quebec *Income Tax Act*, R.S.Q. 1964, c. 69, which had disallowed the taxpayer's share of the syndicate's losses as a deduction in computing his income for purposes of provincial income tax. Although the losses were incurred in the context of a commercial transaction, the purpose of this transaction, according to the court, was not a genuine business purpose "to make a profit," but a purely tax-motivated purpose "to create a deductible loss by means of a disadvantageous contract":

> In the case at bar, there is no basis for finding that in renewing the lease for the last two years the members of the syndicate expected to make a profit. The only evidence submitted was as to the expectations they had on signing the lease, but these expectations were not realized,

and the factors which caused the losses in the first three years were still present when the lease was renewed. No one therefore could imagine that a loss would not be incurred. It is accordingly clear that the sole reason for the renewal was that stated by the respondent: to create a deductible loss by means of a disadvantageous contract, instead of advancing capital. The actual purpose of the operation was not to make a profit but to put money into the company by incurring a loss to its benefit.

Does this case suggest a category of commercial activities where it might be appropriate to employ a REOP test?

6.   Although the Supreme Court of Canada decision in *Stewart* rejected an independent REOP test to determine the existence of a business or property as a source of income, the concept remains relevant to the statutory definition of "personal or living expenses" in subsection 248(1) of the Act, the deduction of which is prohibited by paragraph 18(1)(h).

For cases in which losses from the rental of property to a related person have been disallowed under this provision, see *Maloney v. M.N.R.*, [1989] 1 C.T.C. 2402, 89 D.T.C. 314 (T.C.C.); *Volpé v. M.N.R.*, [1990] T.C.J. No. 337, [1990] 2 C.T.C. 2321, 90 D.T.C. 1703 (T.C.C.); *Huot v. M.N.R.*, [1989] T.C.J. No. 233, [1990] 2 C.T.C. 2364, 90 D.T.C. 1814 (T.C.C.); *Alves v. Canada*, [1994] T.C.J. No. 109, [1994] 1 C.T.C. 2500 (T.C.C.); *Martel v. M.N.R.*, [1996] 3 C.T.C. 2477 (T.C.C.); *Que v. The Queen*, [1996] 1 C.T.C. 2892 (T.C.C.); *Kirkaldy v. Canada*, [1997] T.C.J No. 15, [1997] 2 C.T.C. 2259 (T.C.C.); and *Yammine v. Canada*, [1997] T.C.J. No. 245, [1997] CarswellNat 370 (T.C.C.). For a case in which rental losses were allowed, even though the property was rented to a related person, see *Paiken v. M.N.R.*, [1987] 1 C.T.C. 2041, 87 D.T.C. 6 (T.C.C.).

For cases in which this statutory REOP test has been relied upon to disallow losses from the rental of part of a residence also inhabited by the taxpayer, see *Saleem v. M.N.R.*, [1984] C.T.C. 2660, 84 D.T.C. 1579 (T.C.C.); *Tollefson v. Canada*, [1994] T.C.J. No. 110, [1994] 1 C.T.C. 2507 (T.C.C.); *Russell v. The Queen*, [1996] 3 C.T.C. 2130 (T.C.C.); *Hall v. Canada*, [1997] F.C.J. No. 1674, [1997] 1 C.T.C. 2420 (T.C.C.), aff'd [1998] 1 C.T.C. 410, 98 D.T.C. 6027 (F.C.A.); *Sardinha v. Canada*, [1996] T.C.J. No. 1630, [1997] 2 C.T.C. 2049 (T.C.C.); *Goldstein v. Canada*, [1997] T.C.J. No. 275, [1997] 2 C.T.C. 2940 (T.C.C.); *Nardone v. Canada*, [1997] 2 C.T.C. 3021 (T.C.C.); and *Nguyen v. Canada*, [1997] T.C.J. No. 279, [1997] 2 C.T.C. 2997 (T.C.C.).

7.   In *Mason v. M.N.R.*, [1984] C.T.C. 2003, 84 D.T.C. 1001 (T.R.B.), the taxpayer, who accepted a teaching position at a school that required that he live on the school premises, incurred losses from renting out his house during the period that he was required to live at the school. Noting that the taxpayer "lived in the house except during the period while teaching at the school," the board concluded that the house had been maintained for the taxpayer's own benefit and disallowed the deduction of the rental losses on the basis that the rental operation was not carried on with a reasonable expectation of profit. For a similar result, see *Panford v. Canada*, [1996] T.C.J. No. 521, [1996] 3 C.T.C.

2123 (T.C.C.), where the taxpayer sought to deduct losses from the rental of a house in Brooks, Alberta during a one-year secondment in Edmonton.

In *Dallos v. M.N.R.*, [1985] 2 C.T.C. 2021, 85 D.T.C. 417 (T.C.C.), rental losses were disallowed on the basis that the taxpayer had built the property to use during his retirement, not for investment purposes. In *McNeill v. Canada*, [1989] F.C.J. No. 946, [1989] 2 C.T.C. 310, 89 D.T.C. 5516 (F.C.T.D.), on the other hand, losses from the rental of a condominium unit were allowed on the basis that the taxpayer had a "reasonable expectation of profit," even though the condominium was originally acquired for personal use.

8.   In *Moldowan v. Canada*, [1977] S.C.J. No. 55, [1978] 1 S.C.R. 480 (S.C.C.), the Supreme Court of Canada suggested (at para. 28) that the following criteria "should be considered" in determining whether a taxpayer has carried on an activity with a reasonable expectation of profit: "the profit and loss experience in past years, the taxpayer's training, the taxpayer's intended course of action, the capability of the venture as capitalized to show a profit after capital cost allowance." It also emphasized (at para. 28) that this list was "not intended to be exhaustive" and that the relevant considerations "will differ with the nature and extent of the undertaking."

In *Sipley v. Canada*, [1994] T.C.J. No. 1250, [1995] 2 C.T.C. 2073 (T.C.C.), the Court suggested (at para. 5) that this test includes "an examination of profit and loss experience over past years, also an examination of the operational plan and the background to the implementation of the operational plan including a planned course of action," as well as "an examination of the time spent in the activity as well as the background of the taxpayer and the education and experience of the taxpayer." In *Landry v. Canada*, [1994] F.C.J. No. 1314, [1995] 2 C.T.C. 3, 94 D.T.C. 6499 (F.C.A.), Décary JA stated (at para. 7):

> Apart from the tests set out by Mr. Justice Dickson, the tests that have been applied in the case law to date in order to determine whether there was a reasonable expectation of profit include the following: the time required to make an activity of this nature profitable, the presence of the necessary ingredients for profits ultimately to be earned, the profit and loss situation for the years subsequent to the years in issue, the number of consecutive years during which losses were incurred, the increase in expenses and decrease in expenses in the course of the relevant periods, the persistence of the factors causing the losses, the absence of planning, and the failure to adjust. Moreover, it is apparent from these decisions that the taxpayer's good faith and reputation, the quality of the results obtained and the time and energy devoted are not in themselves sufficient to turn the activity carried on into a business.

Although these tests were formulated in the context of the general REOP test that the Supreme Court of Canada rejected in *Stewart*, they may be relevant to the application of the statutory REOP test used to determine the existence of "personal or living expenses," the deduction of which is disallowed under paragraph 18(1)(h).

9.   The Federal Government responded to the Supreme Court of Canada decisions in *Stewart* and *Walls* in the budget delivered on February 18, 2003. According to the budget:

...these decisions could lead to inappropriate tax results where a taxpayer derives a tax loss by deducting interest expenses, even if under any objective standard there is no reasonable expectation that the taxpayer would earn any income (as opposed to capital gains), or where the presence or the prospect of revenue (as opposed to income net of expenses) is enough to conclude that an expenditure was incurred "for the purpose of earning income".

Explaining that "[n]either of these results is consistent with appropriate tax policy, nor would they have been generally expected under prior law and practice", the Budget announced that "legislative amendments to the Income Tax Act will be considered in order to provide continuity in this important area of law."

On October 31, 2003, the Department of Finance released draft legislation introducing a statutory reasonable expectation of profit text in proposed subsection 3.1 of the Act. According to proposed subsection 3.1(1):

A taxpayer has a loss for a taxation year from a source that is a business or property only if, in the year, it is reasonable to expect that the taxpayer will realize a cumulative profit from that business or property for the period in which the taxpayer has carried on, and can reasonably be expected to carry on, that business or has held, and can reasonably be expected to hold, that property.

For the purpose of this provision, proposed subsection 3.1(2) stipulates that "profit is determined without reference to capital gains or losses".

Explanatory notes released with the draft legislation emphasize that "[r]egard must be had to subsection 3.1(1) in each year in which the taxpayer seeks to report a loss from a business or property." From the perspective of that year, the explanatory notes state, it is necessary to assess cumulative expected profits and losses over the expected life of the business and property. In so doing, the explanatory notes provide no indication that expected profits or losses in future years should be discounted to their present value. The explanatory notes also stipulate that "it must be reasonable in the circumstances of *the particular taxpayer* to expect to profit from the property or business", but that the determination of a reasonable expectation of profit is to "be made on an objective, and not a subjective, basis." In other words, they add, "where a taxpayer has – or purports to have – expectations of profit that are objectively unreasonable, subjective beliefs will not suffice." Finally, the explanatory notes emphasize, section 3.1 distinguishes between a business and a source of income, adopting a more specific definition of a "business source" for the purposes of the *Income Tax Act* than the ordinary meaning of the word business:

Section 3.1 is intended to clarify that, in respect of businesses, it is only those losses from businesses that taxpayers carry on with a reasonable expectation of profit that are to be considered as losses from a source. This implies that a taxpayer may be conducting a business without the taxpayer having a reasonable expectation of profit from that business. This implication is deliberate, and is consistent with the description of "business" in subsection 248(1) of the Act and the general understanding that a business may exist whenever a taxpayer has the subjective intention to make a profit, whether or not there is objectively a reasonable expectation of profit.

With the release of the legislative proposals, the Department of Finance invited comments from the public and tax professionals. The proposed amendments generated a storm of criticism, most notably from tax, business and investment communities who argued that the changes go beyond restoring the pre-*Stewart* status quo and may have a severe effect on borrowing to invest in capital markets. At due time of writing, this draft legislation had yet to be enacted.

10. In *Morris v. Canada*, [2003] T.C.J. No. 288, [2003] 4 C.T.C. 2294 (T.C.C.), aff'd [2004] F.C.J. No. 595, 2004 D.T.C. 6295 (F.C.A.), Bowie TCJ applied the framework outlined in the Supreme Court of Canada's decision in *Stewart* to a taxpayer who had claimed substantial losses relating to fishing guide activities. The taxpayer had incurred expenses during the 1996-2001 tax years ranging from $7,090.00 in 1996 to $28,877.43 in 2001, with revenues over the same period ranging from $0 in 1996 to $1,250 in 2001. The taxpayer could name only two clients that he had guided over the six year period, did not engage in any type of advertising until 2001, and "kept no books, records or financial statements of any kind" relating to his guiding activities. Despite this, the taxpayer took the position that, "whenever he used the boat it was for business" and that even "[i]f he had no client along, which was almost all the time, it was nevertheless business use because he was investigating waters to which he would be able later to take clients." In denying the taxpayer's deduction of the losses, Bowie TCJ remarked that the taxpayer's activities had "a very substantial personal element" and that the taxpayer "was not engaged in an activity that could seriously be described as businesslike."

III. INCLUSIONS

According to subsection 9(1), a taxpayer's income from a business or property is the taxpayer's "profit" from that business or property. As numerous cases, such as *Symes v. Canada*, [1993] S.C.J. No. 131, [1994] 1 C.T.C. 40, 94 D.T.C. 6001 (S.C.C.); *65302 British Columbia Ltd. v. Canada*, [1999] S.C.J. No. 69, [2000] 1 C.T.C. 57, 99 D.T.C. 5799 (S.C.C.); and *Canderel Ltd. v. Canada*, [1998] S.C.J. No. 13, [1998] 2 C.T.C. 35, 98 D.T.C. 6100 (S.C.C.), have affirmed, profit is a net concept implying the deduction of reasonable expenses incurred for the purpose of gaining or producing the taxpayer's income from the business or property from the gross revenues obtained by the business or property. For this purpose, sections 12 to 17 specify various amounts that must be included in computing a taxpayer's income from a business or property, while sections 18 through 21 contain rules governing allowable deductions. Many of these provisions concern the accounting period in which amounts must be included or may be deducted in computing a taxpayer's income from a business or property. Others involve amounts received from or through corporations, partnerships, or trusts.[22]

---

[22] See, for example, paras. 12(1)(j), (k), (l), and (m) and s. 15, which require shareholders to include specific amounts in respect of various benefits conferred upon them by a corporation.

The deductions that a taxpayer may claim in computing the "profit" from a business or property and the timing of inclusions and deductions in computing this income are examined in sections IV and V of this chapter. Provisions involving amounts received from or through intermediary entities such as partnerships and corporations are best examined in courses examining the taxation of these entities. This section examines the scope of a business or property as sources of income, considering statutory and judicial rules governing the inclusion of specific amounts in computing a taxpayer's income from a business or property. While some inclusions are based on the concept of "profit" in subsection 9(1), others depend on specific statutory provisions in section 12.

A. Gains from Illegal Activities

Among the earliest issues considered under the *Income War Tax Act* is whether the income tax applied to gains from illegal activities. This early jurisprudence was examined in the Tax Appeal Board decision in *No. 275 v. M.N.R.* (1955), 13 Tax ABC 279 (T.A.B.).

No. 275 v. M.N.R.
(1955), 13 Tax ABC 279 (T.A.B.)

CHAIRMAN FABIO MONET QC: ... [T]he respondent determined the appellant's income in the sum of $2,495.56, of $4,366.02, of $7,916.05 and $8,825.67 for the taxation years 1949, 1950, 1951 and 1952 respectively. ...

The exactitude of these amounts is not disputed and the appellant's only grounds of appeal are: a) that her income for those years, being derived from her earnings as a prostitute, is not taxable, because it is not derived from a "business"; and b) that if it were held that it was derived from a business, it is nevertheless not taxable because derived from a business which is *malum in se* and not merely *malum prohibitum*. From the evidence adduced, there is no doubt that the appellant is a prostitute and that, except for a few dollars earned by her during the period under review from the illegal sale of liquor and some betting activities, all her earnings were derived from her sordid and contemptible way of living. The question in issue is whether the appellant's earnings, which are the fruits of prostitution, are taxable or not.

...

There is no doubt in my mind that the appellant's earnings are derived from a business within the meaning given to this word by Section 127(1)(e) [now the definition of "business" in subsection 248(1)] of the Act, and I do not agree with the appellant on her first ground of appeal.

The courts have been called upon many times to decide whether earnings from illegal operations or illicit businesses are subject to tax.

In *Smith v. The Attorney General of Canada*, [1924] Ex. CR 193; [1917-27] CTC 240, the facts are stated in the headnote as follows:

HELD,

1.   That profits arising within Ontario from an illicit traffic of liquor therein contrary to the *Ontario Temperance Act* are "income" within the meaning of Section 3, subsection 1 of the *Income War Tax Act, 1917*, and amendments and liable to be taxed under the provisions of the said Act.

2.   That the taxes imposed under the said Act are so imposed upon the person and not upon his trade, business or calling, and it is not necessary for the taxing power to inquire into the source of the income or revenue.

3.   That inasmuch as one is estopped from pleading his own illegality or wrongful act with a view of benefiting thereby, S could not claim that revenue from his illicit traffic was exempt from taxation, because it was illegally or improperly obtained.

and, in his judgment, Mr. Justice Audette, said, at page 194 (CTC at page 241):

This is not a case with a meritorious quality commending itself to a court of justice. The appellant invokes his own turpitude to claim immunity from paying taxes and to be placed in a better position than if he were an honest and legal trader, and asks the court to discriminate in his favour as against other honest traders. As against an innocent taxpayer no man shall set up his own iniquity to operate such discrimination in his favour. His claim rests upon and is tainted with illegality and no court will lend its aid to a person who rests his case on an illegal act.

The old rule, formulated as far back as 1584 in the *Heydon's* case, 2 Coke's R 18 at p. 20, is still in force and in harmony with the duty of the court in our days, where it says that

... the office of all judges is always to make such construction as shall suppress the mischief, and advance the remedy, and to suppress subtle inventions and evasions for continuance of the mischief, and *pro privato commodo*, and to add force and life to the cure and remedy, according to the true intent of the makers of the Act, *pro bono publico*.

To claim an immunity is to claim something that is in derogation of the proper incidence of taxation under the law. Any immunity of the individual shifts the burden that should have been borne by him on the shoulders of his fellow citizens.

...

The decision of Mr. Justice Audette was upheld by the Privy Council, [1927] AC 193; [1917-27] CTC 251. In his judgment, Viscount Haldane said, at page 197 (CTC at page 254):

Construing the Dominion Act literally, the profits in question, although by the law of the particular Province they are illicit, come within the words employed. Their Lordships can find no valid reasons for holding that the words used by the Dominion Parliament were intended to exclude these people, particularly as to do so would be to increase the burden on those throughout Canada whose businesses were lawful. Moreover, it is natural that the intention was to tax on the same principle throughout the whole of Canada, rather than to make the incidence of taxation depend on the varying and divergent laws of the particular Provinces. Nor does it seem to their Lordships a natural construction of the Act to read it as permitting persons who come within its terms to defeat taxation by setting up their own wrong. ...

...

It is clear from the above decisions that, when the question in issue is whether profits arising from illegal sources are liable to taxation or not, the courts are not concerned, either with the source of the taxpayer's income, or by the means taken by him to earn it, but merely with the question as to whether or not the said income is liable to tax under the provisions of the taxing statute. Once the courts are satisfied that the income is liable to tax, it is immaterial that it comes from a legal or an illegal business, or a business which is *malum in se* or *malum prohibitum*. ...

Appeal dismissed.

NOTES AND QUESTIONS

1.   In *Smith v. The Minister of Finance*, [1925] S.C.J. No. 18, [1917-27] C.T.C. 244 (S.C.C.), a unanimous panel of the Supreme Court of Canada allowed the taxpayer's appeal against Audette J's judgment in the Exchequer Court, [1924] Ex. C.R. 193, [1917-27] C.T.C. 240 (Ex. Ct.), which found the taxpayer taxable on profits from the "illicit traffic of liquor." According to Mignault J (at paras. 6-8):

> The real question however is whether we should place on the statute a construction which implies that Parliament intended to levy this income tax on the proceeds of crime or on the gain derived from a business which cannot be carried on without violating the law. Such a business should be strictly suppressed, and it would be strange indeed if under the general terms of the statute the Crown in right of the Dominion could levy a tax on the proceeds of a business which a provincial legislature, in the exercise of its constitutional powers, has prohibited within the province.

> Moreover what may be called the machinery clauses of the Act ... clearly show that it never was contemplated that an income tax would be levied on the gains derived from illicit businesses or from the commission of crime. ...

> ... It is difficult to conceive of the Minister requiring criminals to furnish information as to profits derived from the commission of crime, or demanding from them the keeping of books or records of their illicit and criminal operations. Furthermore if the gains derived from crime are within the contemplation of the statute, then the expenses incurred in making these gains, e.g. in the employment of criminal agents, would be chargeable as deductions against these gains, and, as to all information furnished by the wrongdoer, there would be a promise of secrecy for his protection. It is impossible to believe that anything like this was contemplated by Parliament.

This decision, however, was reversed by the Judicial Committee of the Privy Council, [1917-27] C.T.C. 251, which could find (at para. 6) "no valid reasons for holding that the words used by the Dominion Parliament were intended to exclude these people, particularly as to do so would be to increase the burden on those throughout Canada whose businesses were lawful."

2.   In the Exchequer Court decision in *Smith*, Audette J cited the rule in *Heydon's* case, (1584), 76 E.R. 637 at 638, according to which "the office of the

542

judge is always to make such construction as shall suppress the mischief, and advance the remedy, and to suppress subtle inventions and evasions for continuance of the mischief ... , and to add force and life to the cure and remedy, according to the true intent of the makers of the Act." Why might this rule of statutory construction have been applied to gains from illegal activities but not to other kinds of gains? Might the rationale for this broad interpretive approach also apply to avoidance transactions?

3.   In *Mann v. Nash* (1932), 16 Tax Cas 523, Rowlatt J considered the argument that by taxing gains from illegal activities, the government can be seen to be profiting from this illegality. Rejecting this view as "misconceived," he stated (at 530):

> The Revenue representing the State, is merely looking at an accomplished fact. It is not condoning it; it has not taken part in it; it merely finds profits made from what appears to be a trade, and the Revenue laws happen to say that the profits made from trades have to be taxed, and they say: "give us the tax." ... They are not partners; they are not principals in the illegality, or sharers in the illegality; they are merely taxing a man in respect of those resources. I think it is only rhetoric to say that they are sharing in his profits, and a piece of rhetoric which is perfectly useless for the solution of the question which I have to decide.

Do you agree or disagree? Why?

4.   For a recent decision concluding that embezzled funds were not income from a source, see *R. v. Fogazzi*, [1992] O.J. No. 1541, [1992] 2 C.T.C. 321, 92 D.T.C. 6421 (Ont. Ct. Gen. Div.). The decision was reversed by the Ontario Court of Appeal, [1993] O.J. No. 884, [1993] 2 C.T.C. 319, 93 D.T.C. 5183 (Ont. C.A.).

B. Damages and Other Compensation

Like gains from illegal activities, damages and other compensation are another category of amount the inclusion of which in computing a taxpayer's income from a business or property depends on judicial decisions rather than statutory rules. A leading Canadian case on the characterization of these amounts is *Canada v. Manley*, [1985] F.C.J. No. 140, [1985] 1 C.T.C. 186, 85 D.T.C. 5150 (F.C.A.).

Canada v. Manley
[1985] F.C.J. No. 140, [1985] 1 C.T.C. 186, 85 D.T.C. 5150 (F.C.A.)

[In exchange for a finder's fee, the taxpayer entered into an agreement with Benjamin Levy to find a purchaser for the controlling shares of a company owned by Mr. Levy and other members of the Levy family. When the taxpayer found a purchaser and the shareholders refused to pay the finder's fee, the taxpayer sued Mr. Levy and was awarded damages for breach of warranty of authority. The Minister included the damages in computing the taxpayer's income for his 1974 taxation year. On appeal, the Federal Court Trial Division vacated the assessment. The Crown appealed.]

MAHONEY J (Heald and Ryan JJ, concurring): ... The issue here is whether the damages for breach of warranty of authority were required, by sections 3, 9 and 248(1) of the *Income Tax Act*, to be included in the computation of the respondent's income for 1974.

...

The respondent relies on this Court's decision in *The Queen v. Atkins*, [1976] CTC 497; 76 DTC 6258, while recognizing that the payment in issue there related to wrongful dismissal. Some doubt may have been cast on the validity of that decision by the adverse *dicta* of the Supreme Court of Canada in *Jack Cewe Ltd. v. Jorgenson* (1980), 111 DLR (2d) 577, a case dealing with damages for wrongful dismissal as insurable earnings for purposes of the *Unemployment Insurance Act*, rather than, as had *Atkins*, the settlement of a claim for such damages as taxable income under the *Income Tax Act*. This Court has, however, very recently, in *The Queen v. Pollock*, [1984] CTC 353; 84 DTC 6370, found itself unconvinced that *Atkins* was wrongly decided.

That said, *Atkins* is to be understood in light of its facts. This Court, dismissing an appeal from the Trial Division, did so "for the reasons given by the learned trial Judge." It is necessary to look to the trial judgment, [1975] CTC 377; 75 DTC 5263, where, at 390 [5271], the trial judge made clear that the Minister's position was "that the payment in question represents salary (and nothing else) lost by the premature termination of the [employment] contract."

...

I take *Atkins* as authority, which I must respect, for the proposition that an amount paid in settlement of a claim for damages for wrongful dismissal is not salary, taxable as income from an office or employment under subsection 5(1) of the *Income Tax Act*. ... *Atkins* is not, and does not purport to be, authority for the proposition that damages, or an amount paid to settle a claim for damages, cannot be income for tax purposes.

The measure of damages for breach of warranty of authority is the amount that will put the party, to whom the representation of authority was made, in the position he would have been had the authority existed.

...

The respondent received, in damages, precisely what he would have realized, in profit, from his adventure in the nature of trade. As to whether the award of damages is properly to be regarded as profit from business for purposes of sections 3 and 9(1) of the *Income Tax Act*, I am of the view that the rule stated [the surrogatum principle] by Diplock, LJ, as he then was, in *London & Thames Haven Oil Wharves, Ltd. v. Attwooll*, [1967] 2 All ER 124 at 134 ff, is to be applied.

...

In that case, the taxpayer had received, in settlement of a claim in negligence, £21,404 for loss of use of an income earning asset during its period of repair. The issue before the Court was the assessment of that sum to tax. While the rule itself is stated in the second sentence of the second paragraph below, it is desirable to quote Diplock, LJ, at some length as its context is, in my opinion, compelling argument for its validity:

> ... The question whether a sum of money received by a trader ought to be taken into account in computing the profits or gain arising in any year from his trade is one which ought to be susceptible of solution by applying rational criteria; and so, I think, it is, I see nothing in experience as embalmed in the authorities to convince me that this question of law, even though it is fiscal law, cannot be solved by logic, and that, with some temerity, is what I propose to try to do.

> I start by formulating what I believe to be the relevant rule. Where, pursuant to a legal right, a trader receives from another person compensation for the trader's failure to receive a sum of money which, if it had been received, would have been credited to the amount of profits (if any) arising in any year from the trade carried on by him at the time when the compensation is so received, the compensation is to be treated for income tax purposes in the same way as that sum of money would have been treated if it had been received instead of the compensation. The rule is applicable whatever the source of the legal right of the trader to recover the compensation. It may arise from a primary obligation under a contract, such as a contract of insurance; from a secondary obligation arising out of non-performance of a contract, such as a right to damages, either liquidated, as under the demurrage clause in a charterparty, or unliquidated; from an obligation to pay damages for tort, as in the present case; from a statutory obligation; or in any other way in which legal obligations arise.

> ...

In the present case, the respondent was a trader; he had engaged in an adventure in the nature of trade. The damages for breach of warranty of authority, which he received from Benjamin Levy pursuant to a legal right, were compensation for his failure to receive the finder's fee from the Levy family shareholders. Had the respondent received that finder's fee it would have been profit from a business required by the *Income Tax Act*, to be included in his income in the year of its receipt. The damages for breach of warranty are to be treated the same way for income tax purposes. ...

Appeal allowed.

NOTES AND QUESTIONS

1. On what grounds did the taxpayer in *Manley* argue that the damage payment at issue in the case was not income from that business? Why did the court reject this argument? How did the court distinguish its earlier decisions in *Canada v. Atkins*, [1976] F.C.J. No. 411, [1976] C.T.C. 497, 76 D.T.C. 6258 (F.C.A.) and *The Queen v. Pollock*, [1984] C.T.C. 353, 84 D.T.C. 6370 (F.C.A.)?

2. In *Prince Rupert Hotel (1957) v. Canada*, [1995] F.C.J. No. 492, [1995] 2 C.T.C. 212, 95 D.T.C. 5227 (F.C.A.), the taxpayer received a lump sum in settlement of a legal action alleging negligence on the part of the taxpayer's

solicitors in drafting a partnership agreement governing the management of the Blackcomb Lodge in Whistler, British Columbia. Relying on its earlier decision in *Manley*, a majority of the court characterized the payment as business income on the basis that it replaced management fees to which the taxpayer would otherwise have been entitled. According to Strayer JA (at para. 9), the jurisprudence "requires that the trial judge determine as best as he can from the evidence for what the compensation was paid. If it was paid in lieu of money which the recipient would otherwise have received were it not for the loss of the business advantage, then it must be determined whether that money if received as originally contemplated would have been an income receipt or a capital receipt."

3.   In *Donald Hart Limited v. M.N.R.*, [1959] C.T.C. 268, 59 D.T.C. 1134 (Ex. Ct.), the taxpayer was awarded damages in a tort action for infringement of its trademark and passing off. Referring to the proceedings in which the damages were awarded, in which "the only evidence ... referred to as a basis for awarding damages was that relating to the appellant's loss of profits" (at para. 15), the court rejected the taxpayer's argument that the payment was a capital receipt in respect of a loss in the value of its trademark and its goodwill. According to Cameron J (at paras. 17-18):

> Interpreting the judgment as best I can to ascertain the true nature and quality of the award for the purposes of income tax, I have reached the conclusion that it was made for the purpose of filling the hole in the appellant's profit which it could normally have expected to make, but which had been lost to it by reason of the tortious acts of the defendant therein. Such acts constitute an injury to the appellant's trading. A case in point, although one arising out of a breach of contract, is *Burmah Steamship Co. Ltd. v. CIR*, 16 TC 67, a decision of the First Division of the Court of Sessions, in which the Lord President (Clyde) said at page 71:
>
>> Suppose some one who chartered one of the Appellant's vessels breached the charter and exposed himself to a claim of damages at the Appellant's instance, there could, I imagine, be no doubt that the damages recovered would properly enter the Appellant's profit and loss account for the year. The reason would be that the breach of the charter was an injury inflicted on the Appellant's trading, making (so to speak) a hole in the Appellant's profits, and the damages recovered could not therefore be reasonably or appropriately put by the Appellant — in accordance with the principles of sound commercial accounting — to any other purpose than to fill that hole. Suppose, on the other hand, that one of the Appellant's vessels was negligently run down and sunk by a vessel belonging to some other shipowner, and the Appellant recovered as damages the value of the sunken vessel, I imagine that there could be no doubt that the damages so recovered could not enter the Appellant's profit and loss account because the destruction of the vessel would be an injury inflicted, not on the Appellant's trading, but on the capital assets of the Appellant's trade, making (so to speak) a hole in them, and the damages could therefore — on the same principles as before — only be used to fill that hole.
>
>> My conclusion, therefore, is that the sum of $15,000 paid in the name of damages must be treated as a payment in place of loss of trading profits and not a payment for any loss in value of any capital assets.

4.   For other cases in which damage payments have been characterized as business income, see *M.N.R. v. Bonaventure Investment Co.*, [1962] C.T.C. 160, 62 D.T.C. 1083 (Ex. Ct.) (compensation to release payer from taxpayer's option to acquire land characterized as income from the taxpayer's business of building and selling houses); *Miller v. M.N.R.*, [1962] C.T.C. 488, 62 D.T.C. 1303 (Ex. Ct.) (compensation for optioner's failure to honour taxpayer's option to acquire land characterized as business income on the basis that the taxpayer's main source of income was trading in real estate); *McDonald v. Canada*, [1974] F.C.J. No. 1012, [1974] C.T.C. 836, 74 D.T.C. 6644 (F.C.A.) (compensation for expropriation of land held for purposes of resale characterized as income from an adventure in the nature of trade); *Zygocki v. Canada*, [1984] C.T.C. 280, 84 D.T.C. 6283 (F.C.T.D.) (compensation for purchaser's failure to complete sale of real property characterized as business income from an adventure in the nature of trade); *Violette Motors Ltd. v. M.N.R.*, [1987] T.C.J. No. 101, [1987] 1 C.T.C. 2205, 87 D.T.C. 136 (T.C.C.) (restitutionary damages for pickup and delivery charges imposed by Ford Motor Company in violation of a contractual agreement and paid by the taxpayer in order to avoid endangering its franchises characterized as business income on the basis that the taxpayer had deducted these charges in computing its income); and *Bellingham v. Canada*, [1995] F.C.J. No. 1602, [1996] 1 C.T.C. 187, 96 D.T.C. 6075 (F.C.A.) (compensation for expropriation of land characterized as business income from an adventure or concern in the nature of trade).

5.   For cases in which damage payments have been characterized as capital receipts, see *Canadian Automobile Equipment Limited v. M.N.R.* (1955), 13 Tax ABC 449 (T.A.B.) (compensation for expropriation of leasehold interest in premises where taxpayer carried on business characterized as being on account of capital, not income); *Farrell v. M.N.R.*, [1985] 2 C.T.C. 2429, 85 D.T.C. 706 (T.C.C.) (compensation for expropriation of farmland part of which was used for the business of gravel extraction on account of capital, not income, on the basis that the payment was for the land, not the gravel); *Anthes Equipment Ltd. v. M.N.R.*, [1987] 1 C.T.C. 2117, 87 D.T.C. 59 (T.C.C.) (replacement payments equal to twice the replacement cost of leased scaffolding and shoring equipment lost or damaged by lessee characterized as compensation for the loss of a capital asset and thus on account of capital); *Canadian Liquid Air Ltd. v. M.N.R.*, [1992] T.C.J. No. 372, [1992] 2 C.T.C. 2170, 92 D.T.C. 1822 (T.C.C.) (compensation by customers of taxpayer for loss of or damage to specialized cylinders used to deliver medical and industrial gas on account of capital on the basis that the cylinders were capital assets); and *Wighton v. Canada*, [1996] T.C.J. No. 76, [1996] 2 C.T.C. 2189 (T.C.C.) ($215,000 received in settlement of a legal action to enforce a right to first refusal to purchase commercial premises that the taxpayer had leased in order to carry on a restaurant business characterized as a capital receipt).

6.   In *M.V. Donna Rae Ltd. v. M.N.R.*, [1980] C.T.C. 2333, 80 D.T.C. 1284 (T.R.B.), the taxpayer received $60,000 from the government of the USSR in

settlement of a claim for destruction of fishing gear and loss of income after a Soviet fishing vessel motored through a string of the taxpayer's lobster traps while dragging its own nets. Concluding that the compensation was primarily for the lost lobster traps and secondarily for lost profits, the board considered 70 per cent of the payment to be on account of capital and the remaining 30 per cent on account of lost income.

7. In *The BC Fir and Cedar Company Ltd. v. M.N.R.* (1929), [1928-34] C.T.C. 35 (Ex. Ct.), the taxpayer, which carried on a business as a manufacturer and dealer in lumber products, received insurance proceeds of $43,000 for lost profits and $52,427.90 for fixed charges that it was required to incur for a period of 215 days after its plant was destroyed by a fire, which it sought to exclude in computing its income for its 1924 taxation year. On the grounds (at para. 7) that the insurance for lost profits substituted for "net profits that otherwise would presumably have been earned" and that the insurance for fixed charges compensated for payments that the taxpayer had deducted in computing its income, the court characterized both payments as income from the taxpayer's business.

8. For other cases in which insurance proceeds have been characterized as income from a taxpayer's business, see *No. 298 v. M.N.R.* (1955), 14 Tax ABC 106 (fire insurance for damaged cloth comprising stock in trade of the taxpayer's tailor business); *Custom Glass Ltd. v. M.N.R.*, [1967] C.T.C. 289, 67 D.T.C. 5207 (Ex. Ct.) (insurance received in respect of a warranty offered on the sale of windows); and *Seaforth Plastics Ltd. v. Canada*, [1979] C.T.C. 241, 79 D.T.C. 5174 (F.C.T.D.) (business interruption insurance received when the taxpayer's business premises were destroyed by fire). See also *Westar Mining Ltd. v. Canada*, [1992] F.C.J. No. 421, [1992] 2 C.T.C. 11, 92 D.T.C. 6358 (F.C.A.) (business interruption insurance characterized as income derived from the business of operating a mine).

9. In *H.A. Roberts Ltd. v. M.N.R.*, [1969] S.C.J. No. 41, [1969] C.T.C. 369, 69 D.T.C. 5249 (S.C.C.), the taxpayer, which carried on a real estate business in the course of which it managed mortgages for corporate clients, received $73,633.72 from one client and $10,000 from another when they discontinued long-term contracts with the taxpayer. Characterizing the taxpayer's mortgage department as a separate business that ceased to exist when the contracts were cancelled, and the contracts themselves as "capital assets of an enduring nature the value of which had been built up over the years" (at para. 12), the court accepted the taxpayer's argument that the payments were non-taxable capital receipts.

10. For other cases in which payments to cancel a long-term contract have been characterized as capital receipts on the basis that the cancellation effectively terminated a separate business of the taxpayer, see *Edgerton Fuels Ltd. v. M.N.R.*, [1970] C.T.C. 202, 70 D.T.C. 6158 (Ex. Ct.) (long-term contract to store and handle asphalt manufactured by the Shell Oil Company of Canada

characterized as distinct from taxpayer's primary business of storing and handling fuel oil); and *Pe Ben Industries Co. v. M.N.R.*, [1988] F.C.J. No. 558, [1988] 2 C.T.C. 120, 88 D.T.C. 6347 (F.C.T.D.) (long-term contract to transport supplies and equipment from Northern Alberta Railways yard at Fort McMurray to site of Syncrude heavy oil plant distinguished from taxpayer's ordinary business of transporting supplies and materials by truck to oil fields in northern Alberta).

11.   The CRA's views on the characterization of businesses as separate businesses for the purposes of the *Income Tax Act* are contained in *Interpretation Bulletin* IT-206R, "Separate Businesses," October 29, 1979. According to paragraphs 2 and 3 of this bulletin:

> 2. Whether the carrying on of two or more simultaneous business operations by a taxpayer is the same business is dependent upon the degree of interconnection, interlacing or interdependence and the extent of the unity embracing the business operations. The fact that the business operations of a taxpayer are of different natures, for example, manufacturing and selling, does not preclude them from being the same business if there is a sufficient interconnection, interlacing or interdependence between the operations.

> 3. When determining the degree of interconnection, interlacing or interdependence between simultaneous business operations, factors to be considered could include, but are not to be restricted to, the following:

> (a)   The extent to which the two operations have common factors that may be pertinent. For example, do the two operations have the same: processes, products, customers, services offered to customers, types of inventories, employees, machinery and equipment.

> (b)   Whether the operations are carried on in the same premises. For example, if a hardware store and a sporting goods store are operated in two distinct locations, it is possible that they should be looked upon as separate businesses, but if they are in one store, it is almost certain that they are one business.

> (c)   One operation may exist primarily to supply the other. An example of this might be the carrying on of market-garden operations chiefly for the purpose of supplying a hotel with fresh produce; in these circumstances, the two operations likely should be regarded as one business, even if a small amount of the market-garden produce is sold elsewhere.

> (d)   Whether the operations have differing fiscal year-ends.

> (e)   Whether the taxpayer's accounting system records the transactions of both operations as if they were those of one business, or whether separate complete sets of records are maintained throughout the year; if the latter, too much weight should not be given to the possible merging of the results into one statement at the year-end for tax and other reporting purposes.

12.   For other cases in which compensation received by a taxpayer on the cancellation of a business contract has been characterized as a capital receipt on

the basis that the contract was a capital asset of an enduring nature, see *Parsons-Steiner Limited v. M.N.R.*, [1962] C.T.C. 231, 62 D.T.C. 1148 (Ex. Ct.) (cancellation of exclusive agency agreement to distribute Doulton china in Canada); *M.N.R. v. Import Motors Ltd.*, [1973] C.T.C. 719, 73 D.T.C. 5530 (F.C.T.D.) (cancellation of Volkswagen distributorship franchise for the province of Newfoundland); *Courrier M.H. Inc. v. Canada*, [1976] C.T.C. 567, 76 D.T.C. 6331 (F.C.T.D.) (cancellation of two contracts to transport mail for Canada Post); *Akman Management Ltd. v. M.N.R.*, [1984] C.T.C. 3072, 85 D.T.C. 7 (T.C.C.) (termination of property management contract that represented the major part of the taxpayer's business); *Canada v. Goodwin Johnson (1960) Ltd.*, [1986] F.C.J. No. 174, [1986] 1 C.T.C. 448, 86 D.T.C. 6185 (F.C.A.) (termination of contract to manage logging operation); *Westfair Foods Limited v. M.N.R.*, [1990] F.C.J. No. 1154, [1991] 1 C.T.C. 146, 91 D.T.C. 5073 (F.C.T.D.), aff'd [1991] F.C.J. No. 1137, [1991] 2 C.T.C. 343, 91 D.T.C. 5625 (F.C.A.) (cancellation of long-term leases by landlord); and *T. Eaton Co. v. Canada*, [1999] F.C.J. No. 456, [1999] 2 C.T.C. 380, 99 D.T.C. 5178 (F.C.A.) (cancellation of participation clause in long-term lease for retail space in the Oshawa Shopping Centre which entitled taxpayer to 20 per cent of the landlord's net profits from the shopping centre). See also *Pepsi-Cola Canada Ltd. v. M.N.R.*, [1979] F.C.J. No. 921, [1979] C.T.C. 454, 79 D.T.C. 5387 (F.C.A.), where a payment of $100,000 on the termination of an agreement pursuant to which the taxpayer was the exclusive agent for bottling and selling Schweppes beverages in the greater Montreal area was characterized as proceeds for the disposition of goodwill established by the taxpayer.

13. For cases in which compensation for the cancellation of a business contract have been characterized as income from the taxpayer's business, see *The Great Lakes Paper Company, Ltd. v. M.N.R.* (1961), 27 Tax ABC 355 (T.A.B.) (payment on termination of contract to acquire a special type of paper pulp was received in respect of an ordinary commercial contract made in the course of carrying out the taxpayer's trade); *Bayker Construction Ltd. v. M.N.R.*, [1974] C.T.C. 2319, 74 D.T.C. 1236 (T.R.B.) (cancellation of contract with government department did not destroy or cripple taxpayer's earning structure); *Transcontinental Timber Co. v. Canada*, [1981] C.T.C. 152, 81 D.T.C. 5043 (F.C.A.) (compensation for cancellation of timber licences under which the licensee was required to pay a minimum amount regardless of quantity of timber cut received pursuant to contract made in the course of the taxpayer's licensing operations); *Packer Floor Coverings Ltd. v. Canada*, [1981] C.T.C. 506, 82 D.T.C. 6027 (F.C.T.D.) (termination of franchise to distribute Kraus line of carpets in Quebec did not materially cripple the taxpayer's profit-making apparatus, notwithstanding that the Kraus line had accounted for 50 per cent of taxpayer's sales, because the taxpayer proceeded to sell another brand of carpets made by the same manufacturer); *Brussels Steel Corp. v. Canada*, [1986] F.C.J. No. 21, [1986] 1 C.T.C. 180, 86 D.T.C. 6077 (F.C.T.D.) (compensation of $478,000 on cancellation of contract to acquire steel bars was received in

respect of ordinary commercial contracts made in the course of the taxpayer's business); *Canadian National Railway Company v. M.N.R.*, [1988] F.C.J. No. 524, [1988] 2 C.T.C. 111, 88 D.T.C. 6340 (F.C.T.D.) (compensation for cancellation of contract to transport supplies and materials to Syncrude oil field site in northern Alberta was to enable the taxpayer to "absorb the shock as one of the normal incidents to be looked for" and was "no more than a surrogatum for the future profits surrendered" — see IT-365R2, infra, note 14); *St-Romuald Construction Ltée v. Canada*, [1988] F.C.J. No. 638, [1989] 1 C.T.C. 205, 88 D.T.C. 6405 (F.C.T.D.) (failure to prove that compensation for cancellation of construction contract led to the sterilization of a major portion of the taxpayer's business); *Schofield Oil Ltd. v. M.N.R.*, [1989] F.C.J. No. 108, [1989] 1 C.T.C. 310, 89 D.T.C. 5128 (F.C.T.D.), aff'd [1991] F.C.J. No. 1082, [1992] 1 C.T.C. 8, 92 D.T.C. 6022 (F.C.A.) (cancellation of contract to sell waste oil to Imperial Oil Ltd. did not destroy the taxpayer's business, despite temporary setback); *Amaco Plumbing & Heating Co. v. M.N.R.*, [1990] T.C.J. No. 217, [1990] 1 C.T.C. 2482, 90 D.T.C. 1381 (T.C.C.) (compensation for cancellation of contract was for loss of profit, not "material dislocation" of taxpayer's business structure); and *Charles R. Bell Ltd. v. M.N.R.*, [1990] F.C.J. No. 722, [1990] 2 C.T.C. 333, 90 D.T.C. 6516 (F.C.T.D.), aff'd [1992] F.C.J. No. 823, [1992] 2 C.T.C. 260, 92 D.T.C. 6472 (F.C.A.) (compensation for cancellation of exclusive distributorship, which did not cripple or destroy the taxpayer's profit-making apparatus, was directly related to the loss of two years' profit).

14. The CRA's views on the characterization of payments received on the cancellation or non-performance of a business contract are set out in *Interpretation Bulletin* IT-365R2, "Damages, Settlements and Similar Receipts," May 8, 1987. According to paragraphs 8 and 9 of this bulletin:

> 8. An amount received by a taxpayer in lieu of the performance of the terms of a business contract by the other party to that contract may, depending on the facts, be either an income or capital receipt. If the receipt relates to the loss of an income-producing asset, it will be considered to be a capital receipt; on the other hand, if it is compensation for the loss of income, it will constitute business income. Again, while it is a question of fact as to whether a receipt is an income or capital amount, the following factors are important in making this distinction:
>
> > (a) if the compensation is received for the failure to receive a sum of money that would have been an income item if it had been received, the compensation will likely be an income receipt,
> >
> > (b) "where for example, the structure of the recipient's business is so fashioned as to absorb the shock as one of the normal incidents to be looked for and where it appears that the compensation received is no more than a surrogatum for the future profits surrendered, the compensation received is in use to be treated as a revenue receipt and not a capital receipt," and
> >
> > (c) "when the rights and advantages surrendered on cancellation are such as to destroy or materially to cripple the whole structure of the recipient's profit-making apparatus, involving the serious dislocation of the normal commercial

organization and resulting perhaps in the cutting down of the staff previously required, the recipient of the compensation may properly affirm that the compensation represents the price paid for the loss or sterilization of a capital asset and is therefore a capital and not a revenue receipt."

((b) and (c) above are quotations from the judgment in *Commissioner of Inland Revenue v. Fleming and Co. (Machinery) Ltd.*, 33 Tax Cas 57 (House of Lords).)

9. Where an amount received by a taxpayer as compensation for a breach of a business contract is a capital amount according to the comments in 8 above, that amount would relate either to a particular asset of the taxpayer or to the whole structure of the taxpayer's profit-making apparatus. If, on the basis of the facts of the case, such as the terms of a contract, settlement or judgment, the amount received relates to a particular asset (tangible or intangible) which is sold, destroyed or abandoned as a consequence of the breach of contract, it will be considered proceeds of disposition of that asset or a part thereof, as the case may be. Where the amount of compensation relates to a particular asset that was not disposed of, the amount will serve to reduce the cost of that asset to the taxpayer. On the other hand, where the amount of compensation is of a capital nature but it does not relate to a particular asset as indicated above, the amount will be considered as compensation for the destruction of, or as damages to, the whole profit-making apparatus of the taxpayer's business. Such compensation may result in an "eligible capital amount" for the purposes of subsection 14(1) and subparagraph 14(5)(a)(iv).

Subsection 14(1) is examined later in this chapter.

15. According to paragraph 7 of *Interpretation Bulletin* IT-359R2 "Premiums and Other Amounts with Respect to Leases," December 20, 1983, a payment from a landlord to a tenant on the cancellation of a lease is a capital receipt because "[t]he tenant is considered to have relinquished a right or rights in respect of a leasehold interest, and thus such an amount represents proceeds of disposition of part or all of the leasehold interest."

16. In *Bellingham v. Canada*, [1995] F.C.J. No. 1602, [1996] 1 C.T.C. 187, 96 D.T.C. 6075 (F.C.A.), the taxpayer received $114,272 pursuant to section 66(4) of Alberta's *Expropriation Act*, which requires the expropriating authority to pay additional compensation to persons whose land is expropriated when the compensation offered by the expropriating authority is less than 80 per cent of the compensation ultimately determined by the Land Compensation Board. Rejecting the Minister's arguments that the payment should be characterized as additional proceeds for the disposition of the taxpayer's land (and therefore business income from an adventure in the nature of trade) or as income from an unspecified source under paragraph 3(a), the Federal Court of Appeal held that the payment was a non-taxable windfall. Characterizing the payment as a "punitive damage award," Robertson JA (Stone and Décary JJ concurring) concluded (at para. 43):

An award ... under subsection 66(4) of the *Expropriation Act* is unrelated to the issue of fair compensation for expropriated lands. ... The taxpayer is the beneficiary ... of the legislature's desire to ensure that minimum standards of commercial behaviour are observed. The taxpayer's gain is the expropriating authority's loss. The payment in question does not flow from either an express or implied agreement between the parties. There is no element of bargain or exchange. There is no *quid pro quo*, on the part of the taxpayer. The payment is simply a windfall and, therefore, not income under paragraph 3(a) of the Act.

For a similar result, see *Cartwright and Sons Limited v. M.N.R.* (1961), 27 Tax ABC 272, 61 D.T.C. 499 (T.A.B.), where the taxpayer, which had published a reference of Canadian lawyers called *The Canadian Law List*, received $7,000 in settlement of a claim for infringement of copyright after The Carswell Company Limited, which printed *The Canadian Law List* on the taxpayer's behalf, published its own *Directory of Canadian Lawyers* using material supplied by the taxpayer. On the grounds that the taxpayer had not experienced any loss of income by Carswell's infringement of its copyright and that the payment constituted exemplary or punitive damages, the board rejected the Minister's argument that the payment was taxable under then sections 3 and 4 (now paragraph 3(a) and subsection 9(1)), concluding that "the sum paid to the appellant had no income feature."

Do you agree with these results? Why or why not? Are they consistent with the rule in *London & Thames Haven Oil Wharves, Ltd. v. Attwooll*, [1967] 2 All E.R. 124 (C.A.)?

C. Voluntary Payments

Unlike the amounts examined in the previous section, voluntary payments are made *ex gratia*, without any legal entitlement on the part of the recipient. In *Federal Farms Limited v. M.N.R.*, [1959] C.T.C. 98, 59 D.T.C. 1050 (Ex. Ct.), the Minister argued that the taxpayer should include as income from its farming business voluntary payments that it had received from a hurricane relief fund in order to compensate for lost crops and supplies.

Federal Farms Limited v. M.N.R.
[1959] C.T.C. 98, 59 D.T.C. 1050 (Ex. Ct.)

CAMERON J: ... The appellant carries on business on a large farm in the Holland Marsh near Bradford, Ontario, as a grower, packer and shipper of vegetables. On or about the 15th and 16th of October, 1954, during the flood resulting from the storm known as Hurricane Hazel, the appellant's farm was flooded to a very considerable depth. The appellant was then engaged in harvesting its vegetable crops, but due to the flood very substantial quantities of the vegetables in the ground were utterly destroyed and were of no value. In addition, the farm and the field and main ditches thereon were heavily damaged by erosion.

As is well known, Hurricane Hazel and the flooding which followed caused widespread damage, not only in Holland Marsh, but elsewhere. In order to alleviate the distress and to render assistance, four well-known and public-spirited gentlemen, including the Mayor of Metropolitan Toronto, secured letters patent from the province of Ontario by which the Ontario Hurricane Relief Fund was incorporated for the following objects:

(a) TO provide assistance and relief for persons in Ontario who suffered as a result of the storms and accompanying floods which occurred in Ontario on or about the fifteenth day of October, A.D. 1954, and the sixteenth day of October, A.D. 1954;

(b) TO accept donations from any person or persons in the Province of Ontario or elsewhere and to raise money by any other means; and

(c) TO invest and deal with the moneys of the Corporation not immediately required for the objects of the Corporation in such manner as may be determined by the board of directors.

...

As shown by the final report ... , the Relief Fund received in excess of $5,000,000 from donations, the estimated number of such donors being 250,000. Substantial amounts came from corporations, charitable foundations, churches, clubs, unions, employee groups and individuals. Its relief responsibilities to the community were defined as (1) To provide emergency assistance to hurricane flood victims; (2) To care for the dependents of some seventy-seven people who lost their lives; (3) To provide compensation for losses of household contents, clothing and other property not otherwise recoverable.

A special division was set up for the Holland Marsh area known as the Holland Marsh Division of the Ontario Hurricane Relief Fund. The flood affected some 7,000 acres in Holland Marsh and all farmers who applied for assistance from the Relief Fund received payments.

...

... [T]he appellant received $38,870 for crop losses ... and $1,274.08 ... [for] containers and supplies lost — a total of $40,144.08.

... [T]he money so received was spent in rehabilitating the farm, clearing up the debris, repairing equipment, in payment of accounts and for new supplies and seed purchased — and in general for getting the farm back into production for the following year. It is also established that for income tax purposes all of the expenses incurred in the seeding and cultivation of the crops destroyed were allowed as deductible operating expenses, as well as all the expenses occasioned by the flooding and in connection with which the amount in question was spent. The appellant carried no insurance for flood losses and received nothing from any other source in respect of the loss sustained.

The question to be decided is whether this sum was income within the provisions of Sections 3 and 4 of the *Income Tax Act*, RSC 1952, c. 148 [now paragraph 3(a) and subsection 9(1)]. ... The appellant's reasons are summarized in Part B of the Notice of Appeal as follows:

The Appellant claims that the said sum of $40,144.08 does not constitute income within the meaning of *The Income Tax Act*, that it was a receipt in the nature of a gift, casual gain or windfall, not derived from the operation of the Appellant's business, that it constituted compensation for damage to the Appellant's land and that the payments, having been made for a special purpose, in the public interest, that of assistance and relief to persons who suffered from the hurricane, were not of income nature.

Counsel for the Minister, on the other hand, submits that the amount received was income from the appellant's business. He takes the position that the amount received took the place of the growing crops which were the stock-in-trade of the appellant and that consequently it was a revenue receipt and one received in the course of the appellant's business.

A good many cases were cited to me by both parties. I think the position taken by the respondent may be stated by citing a passage of the judgment of the Master of the Rolls in *London Investment Co. v. CIR*, [1957] 1 All ER 277. After referring to the well-known cases of *J. Gliksten & Son, Ltd. v. Green*, [1929] AC 381, and *Newcastle Breweries Ltd. v. CIR*, 12 TC 927, Lord Evershed said at p. 282:

> It seems to me that these two cases support the view which has been fundamental to the Crown's argument, that, where a trader is dealing in any kind of commodity and where for any reason part of that commodity, his stock-in-trade, disappears or is compulsorily taken or is lost, and is replaced by a sum of cash by way of price or compensation, then *prima facie* that sum of cash must be taken into the account of profits or gains arising to the trader from his trade.

...

It is well settled that the whole of the amount received in respect of insurance policies on stock destroyed is a trade receipt and that compensation received for stock-in-trade which has been expropriated is also a trade receipt. Such cases now present no difficulty, the reported cases having decided that the compensation received was received in the course of or arising out of the trade, although the disposition of the stock was involuntary.

In the *London Investment Company* case (supra), it will be noted particularly that the taxpayer had made contributions under *The War Damage Act* and consequently, as a result of such contributions — which seem to have been something in the nature of insurance premiums — it was entitled to receive the value payments when loss of inventory was sustained by enemy action.

In the present case, I can find no analogy between the monies received from the Relief Fund and the monies received from insurance policies on stock-in-trade which has been destroyed by fire. Here the Relief Fund received nothing whatever from the appellant by way of contribution, insurance premiums, services, salvage or otherwise. The appellant had no legal right at any time to demand payment of any amount from the Relief Fund and clearly, at the time of its loss, had no expectation of getting anything. There was no contract of any sort between the donor and the donee, and the trustees of the Relief Fund, had they so desired, need not have paid the appellant anything. I can find nothing in the circumstances outlined which would indicate that the giving and receiving of the amount was in any sense a business operation or arose out of the taxpayer's business.

In truth, the monies received were in the nature of a voluntary personal gift and nothing more. Counsel for the respondent stressed the fact that the amount of the payment was related to and to some extent measured by the amount of the loss. That fact alone, however, cannot affect the nature or quality of the payment. In *Glenboig Union Fireclay Co. Ltd. v. CIR*, 12 TC 462 at 463 — a decision of the House of Lords — it was stated:

> ... there is no relation between the measure that is used for the purpose of calculating a particular result, and the quality of the figure that is arrived at by means of the application of that test.

There are, of course, many cases in which a voluntary payment has been found to be an income receipt (*Goldman v. M.N.R.*, [1953] CTC 95; *Ryall v. Hoare*, 8 TC 521; *Cowan v. Seymour*, [1920] 1 KB 500; *Australia (Commonwealth) Commissioner of Inland Revenue v. Souatting Investment Co. Ltd.*, [1954] 1 All ER 349 (PC)). In such cases, it was held that the payments, while voluntary, were for services rendered or arose out of or because of employment, or in respect of trading transactions. Nothing of that sort is to be found here, the payment having been an entirely gratuitous one.

The gift here in question, it seems to me, is of an entirely personal nature, wholly unrelated to the business activities of the appellant. The fact that the recipient is incorporated and that the gift was a large one does not affect the true nature of the payment, which, in my view, is precisely of the same kind as if the amount had been received by a neighbour of the appellant who had suffered flood damage but who was an individual and received less than did the appellant.

...

In this case, ... the payment was in no proper sense "compensation" or "income"; it was unlikely to ever occur again and did not result directly or indirectly from any business operation. It came about because of the losses suffered by the appellant in common with all others who had sustained flood losses and by reason of the sympathy engendered in the public mind for the difficulties in which such owners found themselves and which brought about a generous outpouring of funds for their relief. It could scarcely be contended that any of the tens of thousands of contributors to the fund had a thought that they, by their subscriptions, were entering into any business transaction with the flood sufferers or that any part of the sums so subscribed would be gathered in as "income" by the respondent. What they undoubtedly wanted to do — and all that they wanted — was to provide immediate relief to the needy and to assist the flood victims in getting back on their feet.

For these reasons, I have come to the conclusion that the amount in question was not "income" or a revenue receipt which must be brought into account. ...

Judgment accordingly.

NOTES AND QUESTIONS

1. On what basis did the court in *Federal Farms* distinguish the monies received by the taxpayer from the Ontario Hurricane Relief Fund from taxable payments received under a policy of insurance? In what way were the monies received from the taxpayer distinguishable from the payments referred to in *London Investment Co. v. C.I.R.*, [1957] 1 All E.R. 277 (C.A.)?

2. According to paragraphs 3 and 4 of *Interpretation Bulletin* IT-182, "Compensation for Loss or Business Income, or of Property Used in a Business," October 28, 1974:

> 3. Amounts paid to a taxpayer out of a relief fund established to provide aid to victims of some disaster (such as a flood, frost or explosion) are generally voluntary payments by the fund to which the taxpayer has no legal right. Such receipts by taxpayers (whether or not in business) are not income or proceeds of disposition of property.

> 4. However, where a taxpayer has a right to compensation for a property or income because of contract, statute law, order-in-council, etc., compensation paid for loss or destruction of capital property is considered to be proceeds received on the disposition of the property, and compensation for loss or destruction of inventory or for loss of profits is considered to be income from the carrying on of the taxpayer's business.

This interpretation bulletin was cancelled and replaced by *Interpretation Bulletin* IT-273R2, "Government Assistance — General Comments," September 13, 2000. According to paragraph 25 of this bulletin:

> When a natural disaster strikes, government assistance may be received in respect of the operation of a business, property held for the purpose of earning income, or a personal loss or expenditure. Generally, payments received by an individual from a government for personal losses and expenses incurred as a result of a disaster, including payments for temporary housing and meals during the disaster, are not included in income for tax purposes. As well, government compensation received for loss or damage to personal-use property does not ordinarily result in any tax consequences. However, assistance received in respect of capital property, whether business-related or personal, is ordinarily netted against the cost of the repairs made to that property or, if it relates to the replacement of that property, it normally reduces the cost or capital cost of the property so acquired. When government assistance is received for damaged inventory (e.g., spoiled milk, destroyed or damaged trees), the amount will be included in income under paragraph 12(1)(x) to the extent that the assistance does not reduce the amount of costs incurred related to that damage.

Paragraph 12(1)(x) is examined later in this chapter.

3. In *Federal Farms*, Cameron J characterized the amount received by the taxpayer as "a voluntary personal gift and nothing more." Do you agree or disagree? What are the characteristics of such a gift according to Cameron J? What factors do you think should be relevant to the characterization of a payment as a gift?

4. In *Federal Farms*, Cameron J noted that the monies received by the taxpayer from the Ontario Hurricane Relief Fund were "spent in rehabilitating the farm, clearing up the debris, repairing equipment, in payment of accounts

and for new supplies and seed purchased — and in general for getting the farm back into production for the following year." The court also noted:

> It is also established that for income tax purposes all of the expenses incurred in the seeding and cultivation of the crops destroyed were allowed as deductible operating expenses, as well as all the expenses occasioned by the flooding and in connection with which the amount in question was spent.

Should the taxpayer have been allowed to deduct amounts that it received from the Ontario Hurricane Relief Fund that were spent to rehabilitate the farm?

5.   In *German v. M.N.R.* (1959), 22 Tax ABC 302 (T.A.B.), the taxpayer received $20 in 1958 pursuant to *The Oil and Gas Royalties Divided Act*, S.A. 1957, c. 64, An Act To Enable Citizens of Alberta To Participate Directly in the Benefits Accruing from the Development of the Oil and Gas Resources of the Province, which the Minister added to the taxpayer's income for her 1958 taxation year, assessing an additional $6.60 in income tax. Notwithstanding that the provincial statute referred to the payment as a "dividend," the Tax Appeal Board concluded that the amount was non-taxable on the basis (at para. 7) that it was "entirely gratuitous" — "in the nature of a gift or windfall, albeit a small one, that was as surprising as it was unexpected."

6.   In *McMillan v. M.N.R.*, [1982] C.T.C. 2345, 82 D.T.C. 1287 (T.R.B.), the taxpayer, an insurance broker who operated his own agency through a corporation (Cox and McMillan Limited) in which he held 50 per cent of the shares, received $5,000 a year for three years from another insurance broker (Marsh & McLennan Limited) after a longstanding client (The Canada Life Assurance Company), which replaced Cox and McMillan with Marsh & McLennan, requested the latter to make the payments to Mr. McMillan. Rejecting the Minister's argument that the payment was a form of finder's fee to assist March & McLennan in obtaining the Canada Life account, the board held (at para. 38) that the payments were gratuitous payments "for which the appellant had no legal expectation" and a non-taxable "windfall." Do you agree with this result? Why or why not?

7.   In *Canada v. Cranswick*, [1982] C.T.C. 69, 82 D.T.C. 6073 (F.C.A.), the taxpayer, who held 640 shares of Westinghouse Canada Limited (WCL), received $2,144 from WCL's majority shareholder, Westinghouse Electric Corporation (WEC), after WEC offered to pay $3.35 per share to minority shareholders or purchase their shares for $26 per share "in the hope of avoiding controversy or potential litigation on behalf of minority shareholders of WCL" following a sale of WCL's household appliance division at an unfavourable price. Rejecting the Minister's argument that the payment should be characterized either as income from property under subsection 9(1) or income from an unspecified source under paragraph 3(a), the court held that the payment was a non taxable "windfall" to which the taxpayer "had no enforceable claim," for the receipt of which the taxpayer had engaged in "no organized effort," that was neither "sought after" nor "expected" by the

taxpayer, that had "no foreseeable element of recurrence," for which the payer (the majority shareholder) was "not a customary source," and for which the taxpayer had provided no consideration. According to LeDain J (Kelly and Urie JJ concurring) (at para. 15):

> I am of the opinion that the payment received by the respondent was not income earned by or arising from the respondent's shares, which are the only possible source of income in this case. In the absence of a special statutory definition extending the concept of income from a particular source, income from a source will be that which is typically earned by it or which typically flows from it as the expected return. The income which is typically earned by shares of capital stock consists of dividends paid by the company in which the shares are held. The payment in the present case was of an unusual and unexpected kind that one could not set out to earn as income from shares, and it was from a source to which the respondent had no reason to look for income from his shares.

Is this decision consistent with the rule in *London & Thames Haven Oil Wharves, Ltd. v. Attwooll*, [1967] 2 All E.R. 124 (C.A.)? Might the payment have been taxable as a capital receipt? What tax consequences might the taxpayer have expected to face if he had opted to sell his shares for $26 per share? Should the tax consequences have depended on which of the two options he selected?

8.   In *Mohawk Oil Co. v. M.N.R.*, [1992] F.C.J. No. 43, [1992] 1 C.T.C. 195, 92 D.T.C. 6135 (F.C.A.), the taxpayer received US$6 million from the Phillips Petroleum Company ("Phillips") in settlement of a claim for damages resulting from the negligent construction of a waste oil reprocessing plant installed in 1980 but taken out of service in 1981. Reversing the trial decision, [1990] F.C.J. No. 617, [1990] 2 C.T.C. 173, 90 D.T.C. 6434 (F.C.T.D.), which held that the payment was "akin to a windfall" and not income for tax purposes, the Federal Court of Appeal concluded that the payment had been received partly on account of income in recognition of lost profits, and partly on account of capital in recognition of the capital outlay involved in the construction of the plant. According to Stone JA (at paras. 18-19):

> The findings of the learned trial judge were that the settlement payment was agreed to by Phillips in order to "get rid" of Mohawk's claim and to preserve its reputation and that it was in excess of the amount provided for in the limitation of damages clause contained in the January 27, 1978 purchase agreement. The manner in which a settlement amount has been characterized by the payor in the course of negotiations would seem to be an unsafe test for determining its true nature. The payor's motives for settling a dispute may be many and varied in any given case, and it must be a difficult thing to know precisely what his true motivation may have been, especially where the settlement amount is represented by a lump sum which the documentation does not assign to any particular head of claim. I do not see how the settlement amount can be viewed as being "akin to a windfall" merely because the respondent says it was paid by Phillips to get rid of the claim.
>
> Nor am I persuaded that the settlement amount is to be viewed as "akin to a windfall" because it exceeded the amount provided for in the termination of damages clause of the purchase agreement. The evidence is clear that, while Phillips would not agree, the respondent sought from the outset and throughout the settlement negotiations to be made whole including compensation for lost profits and expenditures thrown away. The record

suggests that apart from lost profits, the respondent's other losses were for the cost of the plant itself and certain expenditures which were laid out either to acquire land and install auxiliary facilities or in attempting to make the plant operable. The evidence is also clear that the loss in respect of the land and auxiliary facilities did not materialize because those facilities were required for operating the new plant. As I see it, the settlement amount, of necessity, included compensation for lost profits and expenditures thrown away. Such compensation cannot, in my view, be regarded as "akin to a windfall."

Is this decision consistent with *Canada v. Cranswick*, [1982] C.T.C. 69, 82 D.T.C. 6073 (F.C.A.)?

9. In *Frank Beban Logging Ltd. v. Canada*, [1998] T.C.J. No. 44, [1998] 2 C.T.C. 2493, 98 D.T.C. 1393 (T.C.C.), the taxpayer, which carried on business as a logging contractor and logging-road contractor, received $800,000 from the province of British Columbia after its operations on the Queen Charlotte Islands came to an end when the federal and provincial governments agreed to create a national park on South Moresby Island. Emphasizing that the payment was not received pursuant to any legal or statutory right, and citing the decision in *Federal Farms Limited v. M.N.R.*, [1959] C.T.C. 98, 59 D.T.C. 1050 (Ex. Ct.), the court held that the payment was a non-taxable windfall. According to Rowe DJTC (at para. 29):

> In the event a government chooses to make a payment to an individual or corporation out of a sense of moral duty then it should have the right to perform an act of kindness in the absence of any legal obligation. Whether the payment was made purely as a political decision to remove a potential source of irritation that could emanate from a public discussion of the plight of [the taxpayer], a well-known British Columbia logging enterprise, during the waning days of a government about to call an election (which it lost convincingly) or whether it was done in the spirit of providing compensation, *ex gratia*, in order to "do the right thing" is not relevant. The key point is there is no question the nature of the payment was exactly as described under all of the circumstances and was not disguised in any way nor did it relate to any past, present or future dealings existing or contemplated between the payor and the recipient. Payments of this sort are not that uncommon if government decides to provide relief for a specific purpose under circumstances where there is not the remotest chance the government is ever going to be required to do so as a matter of law. Payments in the nature of flood relief or other damage or loss to individuals or entities from other weather related causes, or widespread economic deprivation due to a shutdown of a specific industry in a particular geographical location come to mind and I am not aware that it is ever intended, until otherwise specified in legislation or in the authorization permitting such payments to be made, that such amounts will be somehow taxable. If such payments were made as an expression of good will, then any warm feeling thus engendered would quickly evaporate around April 30th the following year.

Do you agree with this outcome? Why or why not?

10. In *Federal Farms Limited v. M.N.R.*, [1959] C.T.C. 98, 59 D.T.C. 1050 (Ex. Ct.), the court refers to "cases in which a voluntary payment has been found to be an income receipt" on the grounds that "the payments, while voluntary, were for services rendered or arose out of or because of employment, or in respect of trading transactions." One such case in which a gratuitous payment was characterized as income from a business is *Campbell v. M.N.R.* (1958), 21 Tax ABC 145, 59 D.T.C. 8 (T.A.B.). In this case, the taxpayer, who "enjoyed a wide reputation as a professional swimmer," entered into a contract with the

Toronto Star newspaper, under which she agreed to attempt to swim across Lake Ontario in 1956 in exchange for $600 and a further $5,000 upon completing the long-distance swim. Although the taxpayer attempted to complete the swim in summer of 1956, her coach pulled her from the water with only half a mile to go. Even though she had not completed the swim as agreed in the contract, the *Toronto Star* paid the taxpayer the $5,000 in recognition of her "magnificent effort to conquer Lake Ontario."

While the taxpayer treated this payment as a non-taxable gift, the Minister treated the payment as income and assessed the taxpayer for a further $945.34 in income tax. On appeal, the Tax Appeal Board expressed sympathy with the taxpayer, but concluded "with considerable reluctance" that the payment was taxable as income from a business within the meaning of the Act. According to the board:

> When officials of The Toronto Star Limited were successful in obtaining Shirley Campbell's consent to become a party to the contract they were, in effect, securing the services of Shirley Campbell as a professional swimmer. ...
>
> Although there may not have been any legal obligation on the part of The Toronto Star Limited to pay the sum of $5,000 to Miss Campbell when she failed by such a narrow margin to swim across the lake, nevertheless the prestige of the publication, under the circumstances, would have been sorely lessened in public opinion if there had been strict adherence to its technical legal position as a party to the contract. ...
>
> Under the circumstances can there be any conclusion other than that the Star felt obligated to pay Miss Campbell the sum of $5,000 for the services which she had rendered exclusively to that publication? It must be held that the true nature of this transaction was the performance of services for which payment was made. The money was paid in respect of services performed by Miss Campbell in a business context.

Do you agree with this decision? Why or why not?

11. For other cases in which voluntary payments have been characterized as business income, see *Galway v. M.N.R.*, [1972] C.T.C. 580, 72 D.T.C. 6493 (F.C.T.D.) (payment to taxpayer for arranging purchase and sale of a business characterized as "remuneration ... for services he performed in his capacity as a business broker" (at para. 66)); *Kenneth G. Mills v. M.N.R.*, [1978] C.T.C. 3166, 78 D.T.C. 1851 (T.R.B.) (voluntary payments to philosopher who held weekly meetings in Toronto area hotels characterized as income from a business); and *Winemaker v. Canada*, [1995] T.C.J. No. 110, [1995] 2 C.T.C. 2992, 96 D.T.C. 1156 (T.C.C.), aff'd [1995] F.C.J. No. 1737, 96 D.T.C. 6040 (F.C.A.) (payments of $50,011.70 and $17,859.34 received by the taxpayer in 1986 and 1987 characterized as remuneration for services of finding investors to purchase real estate in Florida, notwithstanding formal declaration describing payments as a "gift"). See also *Société d'ingénierie Cartier Ltée v. M.N.R.*, [1985] F.C.J. No. 1117, [1986] 1 C.T.C. 166, 86 D.T.C. 6025 (F.C.T.D.), where a payment received by taxpayer from its liability insurer, which negotiated the settlement of an action against the taxpayer by a client to recover costs for overruns and other

issues and an action by the taxpayer against the client for unpaid professional fees and out-of-pocket expenses, was characterized as business income on the basis that the payment, which was equal to half the unpaid professional fees owing, "would have been treated as professional fees and taxable income" if it had been received directly from the client.

D. Prizes and Awards

Like voluntary payments more generally, prizes and awards are often received without any legal entitlement on the part of the recipient. In some cases, however, the recipient may have provided valuable consideration in exchange for which the grantor confers either a prize or award itself, or the opportunity to receive a prize or award. In *Abraham v. M.N.R.* (1960), 24 Tax ABC 133 (T.A.B), the taxpayer, who operated a grocery store in Ottawa, won a sum of cash after entering a draw held by the distributor from whom he purchased his stock in trade.

Abraham v. M.N.R.
(1960), 24 Tax ABC 133 (T.A.B.)

JACQUES PANNETON: This is an appeal from a decision of the Minister against the ruling that an amount of money accepted in 1957 instead of a car in a draw, as a result of a contest award, is taxable.

The appellant operated an IGA Store at 565 Bronson Avenue in the City of Ottawa for several years and particularly in 1957. During such operations, stock in trade for resale was purchased from M. Loeb Ltd., exclusive distributor and administrator of IGA (Independent Grocers' Alliance) and tickets for the draw accompanied the deliveries of merchandise, at no extra cost and without specific request therefor.

The appellant signed his name to the tickets and returned them to M. Loeb Ltd. They were then deposited in a large container with all other tickets returned by other IGA merchants. On a fixed date, the draw was held, and the lucky ticket, drawn by pure chance, bore the appellant's name and he was declared the winner of an automobile. The appellant requested and received the sum of $2,275 instead of the car. ... He paid nothing for the tickets or the car. These tickets were in the form of vouchers attached to each order form filled out by an IGA merchant for merchandise required for delivery from M. Loeb Ltd., and there was no extra charge therefor. They were received absolutely free, and all the appellant did was sign them and return them for entry in the draw, as did other merchants who participated.

...

In his reply to the Notice of Appeal filed herein respecting the 1957 taxation year, and dated August 21, 1959, the respondent says that the sum of $2,275 was received by the appellant by virtue of his being in business as an IGA dealer; and that the said sum was therefore properly included in the calculation of the appellant's business income for the said year in accordance with Sections 3 and 4 of the *Income Tax Act* [now paragraph 3(a) and subsection 9(1)].

In giving evidence in support of his appeal, Mr. Michael Abraham stated that he was an independent grocer who owned his business and carried it on according to his own policy but subject to an agreement with the Independent Grocers' Alliance as to the actual merchandise he would sell in his store. However, he was under no obligation to stay with IGA for any length of time, and the latter had no share in the profits of his store. He just bought his goods from them as a wholesaler and not necessarily goods with the IGA label.

Mr. Abraham Bookman, who was then Executive Assistant to the President of M. Loeb Ltd., wholesale grocery and tobacco warehouse — (M. Loeb Ltd. and IGA are operated by the same people) — also gave evidence and said that a campaign or contest was initiated in the Ottawa-Hull district in 1957 for a period of about twelve weeks to highlight the fifth anniversary of the company. On May 20, 1957, a Dinner-Dance was held at the Chateau Laurier at which the draw took place, and Mr. Abraham won the car. The reason he gave for not accepting it was that he already had one, which seems to me to have been a very good reason.

I believe that, whether or not he took a cheque or cash instead of the car, what he received was still a prize, in one form or another. This car was won by pure chance and was not presented to the appellant as remuneration for services rendered. ...

Should the Board decide that a person in a case such as this is taxable on the value of a prize based upon chance or a lucky break, the Government would have to tax sweepstakes winners, bingo winners and gamblers who play poker or make casual bets.

...

[A]fter considering all the facts and the jurisprudence, I have come to the conclusion that the cheque for $2,275 which the appellant received was in the nature of a non-taxable prize.

Appeal allowed.

NOTES AND QUESTIONS

1.   In *Abraham*, the Tax Appeal Board noted that "the tickets for the draw accompanied the deliveries of merchandise" purchased for resale from M. Loeb Ltd., exclusive distributor and administrator of IGA. Consequently, although there was "no extra charge" for the tickets, was it right for the board to conclude that the tickets were received "absolutely free"? Does the fact that the prize was "not presented to the [taxpayer] as remuneration for services rendered" determine that it ought not to be included in computing the taxpayer's income from his grocery business?

2.   In *Abraham*, the board suggested that if the value of the prize was included in the taxpayer's income, "the Government would have to tax sweepstakes

winners, bingo winners and gamblers who play poker or make casual bets." Do you agree?

3. In *Poirier v. M.N.R.*, [1968] Tax ABC 319 (T.A.B.), the taxpayer was president of a Ford dealer that, having met a sales quota, participated in and won a lucky draw in which the prize was a holiday trip to the Caribbean, paid for by Ford. Having concluded that the benefit was not conferred on the taxpayer in his capacity as an employee nor as a shareholder, the board also rejected the Minister's alternative argument that the value of the trip should be included in computing the taxpayer's income from a business or property under then section 4 (now subsection 9(1)). According to the board (at para. 27):

> the advantage given to the appellant by Ford of Canada did not constitute an income because the origin of the advantage had none of the characteristics of a taxable income. The benefit to the appellant was neither rent, nor interest, nor dividend, nor profit, nor salary.

4. To what extent, if at all, do the decisions in *Abraham* and *Poirier* depend on the element of chance associated with the draw? What would the results have been if all IGA dealers who purchased a stipulated amount from Loeb were given a car and all Ford dealers meeting the sales quota were given a Caribbean holiday? What if the taxpayers' chances of winning the draw were 50 per cent, 80 per cent, or 99.9 per cent? Would it be appropriate to tax the recipient of a right to receive a prize on the expected value of this right?

5. In *Rother v. M.N.R.* (1955), 12 Tax ABC 379, 55 D.T.C. 227 (T.A.B.), the taxpayer, a professional architect, received $2,000 as one of six participants in a design competition for the National Gallery of Canada who, on the basis of designs submitted, were selected to participate in a final competition for the commission to design the gallery. On the grounds (at paras. 6-7) that the taxpayer was "not an officer of the National Gallery of Canada or of the Government of Canada" and "did not receive the two thousand dollars in question in payment for services rendered nor as a fee" nor as "the purchase price of the design submitted," the board concluded (at para. 8) that the payment was a non-taxable receipt "in the nature of a prize or gratuitous award received in the course of a competition."

6. In *M.N.R. v. Watts*, [1966] C.T.C. 260, 66 D.T.C. 5212 (Ex. Ct.), the taxpayer, who was also an architect, entered a design competition conducted by the Canadian Mortgage and Housing Corporation (CMHC), from which he received $4,000 as one of five entrants asked to submit further drawings and $15,000 as a prize for the best design. On appeal from a decision of the Tax Appeal Board (1965), 38 Tax ABC 64, which held that the amounts were not taxable on the authority of the decision in *Rother v. M.N.R.* (1955), 12 Tax ABC 379, 55 D.T.C. 227 (T.A.B.), Gibson J (at para. 16) characterized both payments as taxable income from a "contractual relationship" that had been created between the taxpayer and the CMHC by virtue of "the entering into this competition by the respondent and the filing of drawings pursuant to it."

7.   Where an employee receives a prize or award in respect of, by virtue of, or in the course of the employee's office or employment, the value of the prize or award is generally taxable as remuneration under subsection 5(1) or as a benefit under paragraph 6(1)(a) (see Chapter 4). Is there any reason why the tax treatment should differ where a prize is received in the course of a business?

8.   The Act was amended in 1972 to include in computing a taxpayer's income under paragraph 56(1)(n) "all amounts ... received by the taxpayer in the year ... as or on account of ... a prize for achievement in a field of endeavour ordinarily carried on by the taxpayer." Paragraph 56(1)(n) is considered in Chapter 7.

E. Interest

In computing a taxpayer's income from a business or property, paragraph 12(1)(c) specifically includes:

> any amount received or receivable by the taxpayer in the year (depending on the method regularly followed by the taxpayer in computing the taxpayer's income) as, on account of, in lieu of payment of or in satisfaction of, interest to the extent that the interest was not included in computing the taxpayer's income for a preceding taxation year.

The manner in which interest income is computed for income tax purposes is considered later in this chapter. For present purposes, we are concerned with the characterization of interest income as distinct from other amounts.

In many circumstances, this characterization issue is relatively straightforward. Where a debt obligation stipulates that "interest" is payable at a specific rate per annum, one can be reasonably confident that payments made pursuant to this obligation will be regarded as interest.[23] Nonetheless, it is also the case that payments specifically described as "interest" by the parties to an agreement may not be characterized as such for the purposes of the *Income Tax Act*. More generally, cases also occur in which payments that are functionally equivalent to interest are not described as such by the parties to a contract. In these circumstances as well, it is necessary to determine whether these amounts are in fact "interest" within the meaning of the Act.

The following cases and text consider the characterization of interest income in three contexts: (1) where the revenue department or the taxpayer seeks to characterize an amount "as, on account of, in lieu of payment of or in satisfaction of, interest" within the meaning of paragraph 12(1)(c) of the Act or its predecessor paragraph 6(1)(b) of the 1948 *Income Tax Act*; (2) where the taxpayer disposes of a capital property for an amount part of which is payable in one or more subsequent taxation years, and the revenue department seeks to characterize a portion of any deferred payment as interest; and (3) where the

---

[23]   See, for example, *West Coast Parts Co. v. M.N.R.*, [1964] C.T.C. 519 at 526, 64 D.T.C. 5316 at 5320 (Ex. Ct.), *per* Cattanach J.

taxpayer realizes a gain on a debt obligation acquired at a discount or disposed of at a premium, or on which a bonus is payable at maturity.

1. Characterization

Paragraph 12(1)(c) applies to payments "as, on account of, in lieu of payment of or in satisfaction of, interest." The Act, however, does not define the word "interest." Consequently, as Reed J explained in *Miller v. Canada*, [1985] 2 C.T.C. 139, 85 D.T.C. 5354 (F.C.T.D.) (at para. 7): "One must look to the general principles of interpretation, dictionary definitions and the jurisprudence." Among tax practitioners, these amounts are generally referred to as "legal interest."[24]

According to *The Concise Oxford Dictionary*, 7th ed., "interest" is defined as "money paid for the use of money lent or for not exacting repayment of debt." Similarly, *Black's Law Dictionary*, 6th ed., defines "interest" as "the compensation allowed by law or fixed by the parties for the use or forbearance of borrowed money" and as:

> Basic cost of borrowing money or buying on instalment contract. Payments a borrower pays a lender for the use of the money.

In contrast, the fourth edition of *Halsbury's Laws of England*, vol. 32, para. 32, contains a more precise definition of the word "interest":

> Interest is the return or compensation for the use or retention by one person of a sum of money belonging to or owed to another. Interest accrues from day to day even if payable only at intervals, and is therefore apportionable in respect of the time between persons entitled in succession to principal.

The leading case dealing with the meaning of the word "interest" for the purposes of the *Income Tax Act* is *Perini Estate v. M.N.R.*, [1982] F.C.J. No. 12, [1982] C.T.C. 74, 82 D.T.C. 6080 (F.C.A.).

Perini Estate v. M.N.R
[1982] F.C.J. No. 12, [1982] C.T.C. 74. 82 D.T.C. 6080 (F.C.A.)

[The taxpayer, who owned all the shares of All Records Supply of Canada Ltd. (ARS), sold these shares to Columbia Records of Canada (CRC) under an agreement providing for: (1) an initial payment of $660,000 on the closing date, November 27, 1968; (2) additional payments based on the post-tax net profits, if any, of ARS as determined by audited financial statements for the fiscal years ending on April 30 in 1969, 1970, and 1971, the total of which was not to exceed $400,000 by 1969, $800,000 by 1970, and $1,200,000 by 1971; and (3)

---

[24] See, for example, John M. Ulmer, "Taxation of Interest Income," in *Report of Proceedings of the Forty-Second Tax Conference*, 1990 Conference Report (Toronto: Canadian Tax Foundation, 1991) 8:1-30 at 8:2.

an amount described as "interest" on these additional payments, computed at an annual rate of 7 per cent from the closing date to the date of each additional payment. Under the terms of the agreement, the right to receive these payments was personal to the vendor, non-transferable, and terminable on the death of the vendor.

Pursuant to the agreement, the taxpayer received as "interest" $14,031.19 in 1969, $28,431.74 in 1970, and $119,262.60 in 1971, which the Minister characterized as interest income and included in computing the taxpayer's income for these years under then paragraph 6(1)(b) (now paragraph 12(1)(c)) of the Act. The taxpayer appealed.]

LeDain J (Heald J and Kelly DJ concurring): ... It is the appellant's contention that despite the name given to them in the agreement the payments were not interest but were part of the purchase price and were therefore not of an income nature. The contention is that while they are called interest, are calculated like interest, and serve the purpose of interest, they lack an essential characteristic of interest in that they did not accrue from day to day on an existing principal amount. The principal amount on which the sum referred to as "interest" was based did not come into existence until it had been determined by an audited financial statement following the close of the fiscal year. Until then there was no principal amount on which interest could accrue.

It is elementary, of course, that the name given by the parties to an amount... is not conclusive of its nature. See *Commissioners of Inland Revenue v. Wesleyan & General Assurance Society*, 30 TC 11 at 16 and 25. Counsel for the appellant cited several authorities as indicating the essential characteristics of interest. He relied particularly on what was said about the nature of interest in the Supreme Court of Canada in *Reference as to the Validity of Section 6 of the Farm Security Act, 1944, of the Province of Saskatchewan*, [1947] SCR 394, and in *The Attorney-General for Ontario v. Barfried Enterprises Ltd.*, [1963] SCR 570. In the *Saskatchewan Farm Security* case, Rand, J defined interest at 411 as "the return or consideration or compensation for the use or retention by one person of a sum of money, belonging to, in a colloquial sense, or owed, to another," and at 412 he said that "interest is referable to a principal in money or an obligation to pay money." At 417 in the same case Kellock, J said, "There can be no such thing as interest on principal which is non-existent." Counsel for the appellant attached particular importance to this statement as expressing the essence of his contention. In the *Barfried* case, Judson, J, after referring to the definition of interest by Rand, J in the *Saskatchewan Farm Security* case, said at 575: "The day-to-day accrual of interest seems to me to be an essential characteristic." In *Tomell Investments Limited v. East Marstock Lands Limited*, [1978] 1 SCR 974, Pigeon, J referred at 982 and 983 to "'interest' properly so-called" as "a charge for use of money accruing day by day." Thus it is appellant's contention that the amount paid ... could not be said to have accrued day by day from the date of closing because there was no principal sum in existence on which it could accrue during the period between that date and the time the additional sum payable was determined by an audited financial statement.

Counsel for the appellant also relied on the judgment of Thurlow, J, as he then was, in *R.G. Huston et al. v. M.N.R.*, [1962] Ex. C.R. 69; [1961] CTC 414; 61 DTC 1233, in which it was held that amounts paid as "interest" on awards from the War Claims Fund established after the Second World War were not interest within the meaning of paragraph 6[(1)](b) [now paragraph 12(1)(c)] of the *Income Tax Act*. The awards were made in 1958, and the applicable regulation provided that interest of 3% per annum should be paid on the awards from January 1, 1946. Thurlow, J concluded that, although the amounts were called interest, were calculated like interest, and served the purpose of interest, they were not interest because during the period from January 1, 1946 to the date of the awards the recipients were not legally entitled to a principal amount upon which interest could accrue. The essentials of the reasoning of Thurlow, J appear to me to be continued in the following passage from his reasons at 77-78 [422; 1238]:

> The facts are that the appellant's property had been partially destroyed in 1945, a misfortune for which, so far as has been made to appear, they had no right to legal redress against anyone, and, in any event, none against the Government of Canada. ... Despite what was going on in the meantime, that continued to be the legal position until October 10, 1958, when the Treasury Board approved the payments, which were made to them shortly afterwards. No principal sum was payable in the meantime, nor was interest accruing on any principal sum, nor were the appellants being kept out of any sum to which they were entitled. In truth, during the whole of the intervening period they had no right to compensation for their loss, and there was neither interest accruing to them nor loss of revenue being sustained in respect to which they would be entitled to interest by way of damages or compensation.

Thurlow, J added the following observations at 78 [423; 1238], which counsel for the appellant found particularly helpful to his contention:

> ... No case of which I am aware goes so far as to hold such an amount, call it interest or damages or compensation or any other name, to be interest or income when there was neither interest accruing in fact on the "principal" amount during the material period nor any right to the "principal" amount vested in the taxpayer during that period.

...

In the present case there was in existence on the closing date an obligation to pay a price to be determined according to the formula set out in ... the agreement, but the precise amounts of the additional payments, if any, to be made ... were not determined as of that date. The obligation to pay additional sums on account of the purchase price under these provisions was a conditional one or a contingent liability. It depended on two conditions which might or might not be fulfilled. There had to be post-tax net profits determined by audited financial statements, and the seller had to be living. Neither was a certainty. That was sufficient to make the liability for additional payments a contingent one. Unless and until these conditions were fulfilled there could not be an additional sum owing ... .

Reference was made in the course of argument to various cases indicating the nature of a contingent liability. ... What these cases do not touch on, and what appears to be the issue in the present case, is the effect, in so far as the essential characteristics of interest are concerned, that should be given to the fulfilment of the condition which makes the liability absolute. The learned trial judge concluded that the fulfilment of the condition had a retroactive effect. This conclusion is contained in the following passage from his reasons:

> Once it was ascertained that the profits had been made and could be calculated and the vendor was still alive his obligation for the payments in each of the years 1969, 1970 and 1971 became due, and the condition having been fulfilled it had a retroactive effect to the date of the contract. Interest ran from that day on the payments due in accordance with the terms of the contract.

He based this conclusion on the assumption that the common law as to the effect of the occurrence of a contingency did not differ in principle from the rule in article 1085 of the Quebec *Civil Code* that "The fulfillment of the condition has a retroactive effect from the day on which the obligation has been contracted."

...

[G]iven that such an effect is not clearly excluded by what we are able to ascertain from the cases of the common law concerning contingent liability, it is my opinion that it was open to the parties to the agreement of sale in this case to treat the occurrence of the contingency as having such effect, in so far as interest was concerned. Cf. *Trollope & Colls, Ltd. et al. v. Atomic Power Constructions, Ltd.*, [1962] 3 All ER 1035, in which it was held that parties to a contract could give their contract retrospective effect. There is no rule of law that prevented them from treating an additional sum payable on account of the purchase price ... as owing, for purposes of interest, from the closing date, as they appear to have done ... . There were sound business reasons for doing so since the sale had been concluded on that date and the over-all obligation to pay the purchase price contracted on that date. Because of the basis on which the balance of price, if any, was to be determined, the seller was obliged to wait for payment of the balance. Interest was the appropriate compensation for that delay. I think it is the existence on the closing date of a conditional obligation or contingent liability to pay the balance of price, which the parties were entitled to treat as having become absolute with retroactive effect, for purposes of interest, that distinguishes the present case from *Huston*. ...

Appeal dismissed.

NOTES AND QUESTIONS

1. In *Perini Estate*, the appellant cited three Supreme Court of Canada decisions "as indicating the essential characteristics of interest": *Reference as to the Validity of Section 6 of the Farm Security Act, 1944, of the Province of Saskatchewan*, [1947] S.C.J. No. 19, [1947] S.C.R. 394 (S.C.C.); *Attorney-General for Ontario v. Barfried Enterprises Ltd.*, [1963] S.C.J. No. 54, [1963] S.C.R. 570 (S.C.C.); and *Tomell Investments Limited v. East Marstock Lands Limited*, [1977] S.C.J. No. 91, [1978] 1 S.C.R. 974 (S.C.C.). The *Saskatchewan*

Farm Security Reference dealt with provincial legislation stipulating that, in the case of crop failure, the principal obligation of a mortgagor or purchaser of a farm should be reduced by 4 per cent in that year, but that interest should continue to be payable as if the principal had not been reduced. Emphasizing the relationship between interest and the principal sum to which it refers, the Supreme Court of Canada held that the legislation was *ultra vires* on the basis that it conflicted with federal jurisdiction over interest under section 91(19) of the *British North America Act*, 30 & 31 Vict., c. 3.

In *Barfried Enterprises*, the court considered the constitutionality of section 2 of the *Unconscionable Transactions Relief Act*, R.S.O. 1960, c. 410, under which a mortgage obligation with a face amount of $2,250 and interest payable at 7 per cent per annum, for which the borrower received only $1,500 less a commission of $67.50, was set aside and revised on the basis that the "cost of the loan" was "excessive" and the transaction was "harsh and unconscionable." Noting that the statute defined the expression "cost of the loan" to mean, among other things, "the whole cost to the debtor of money lent and includes interest, discount, subscription, premium, dues, bonus, commission, brokerage fees and charges," the lender and the attorney general of Canada argued that the legislation interfered with federal jurisdiction over interest under section 91(19) of the *British North America Act* and in particular with section 2 of the federal *Interest Act*, R.S.C. 1952, c. 156. According to the latter provision:

> Except as otherwise provided by this or by any other Act of the Parliament of Canada, any person may stipulate for, allow and exact, on any contract or agreement whatever, any rate of interest or discount that is agreed upon.

Emphasizing the distinction between the payment of a bonus and interest, particularly as these terms were understood for the purposes of the federal *Interest Act*, a majority of the court held (at 577) that the statute was "not legislation in relation to interest but legislation relating to annulment or reformation of contract," which was *intra vires* the provincial legislature under section 92(13) of the *British North America Act* as legislation in relation to property and civil rights.

Tomell Investments involved section 8(1) of the federal *Interest Act*, R.S.C. 1970, c. I-18, upon which the respondent relied to avoid payment of a bonus on the default of interest payments payable under a mortgage on real estate that it had acquired from the original mortgagor. According to this provision:

> No fine or penalty or rate of interest shall be stipulated for, taken, reserved or exacted on any arrears of principal or interest secured by mortgage of real estate, that has the effect of increasing the charge on any such arrears beyond the rate of interest payable on principal money not in arrears.

Rejecting the appellant's argument that section 8(1) was *ultra vires* the federal Parliament on the grounds that it applied to "charges" other than "interest," the Supreme Court of Canada held (at 987) that the provision was valid federal legislation in respect of its jurisdiction over interest under section 91(19) of the *British North America Act* because:

although it does not deal exclusively with interest in the strict sense of a charge accruing day by day, it is, insofar as it deals with other charges, a valid exercise of ancillary power designed to make effective the intention that the effective rate of interest over arrears of principal or interest should never be greater than the rate payable on principal money not in arrears.

To what extent should the characterization of "interest" for the purposes of the *Income Tax Act* be defined by cases concerned with the constitutional division of powers or the application of the federal *Interest Act*?

2. In *Perini Estate*, the Federal Court of Appeal held that the parties to a contract could give a contingent liability retroactive effect such that it could qualify as a principal sum to which interest could be referable. Similarly, in *Miller v. Canada*, [1985] 2 C.T.C. 139, 85 D.T.C. 5354 (F.C.T.D.), where the taxpayer received a retroactive salary increase with "interest" payable from the periods to which the salary related, the court held that these payments were referable to a principal sum, even though the amount of the principal to which the interest payments related was not determined prior to the commencement of the time period to which the interest related.

3. A number of cases have considered whether "interest" payments made pursuant to a statutory compensation scheme are properly characterized as "interest" within the meaning of paragraph 12(1)(c) of the *Income Tax Act*. In *Perini Estate*, for example, the court refers to *R.G. Huston v. M.N.R.*, [1962] Ex. CR 69, [1961] C.T.C. 414, 61 D.T.C. 1233 (Ex. Ct.), where the Exchequer Court held (at C.T.C. 419) that payments received from a war claims fund, though called interest and calculated as interest, were simply grants because the taxpayers "had no property or legal or equitable right of any kind in the amount on which the alleged 'interest' was computed." Likewise, in *Bellingham v. Canada*, [1995] F.C.J. No. 1602, [1996] 1 C.T.C. 187, 96 D.T.C. 6075 (F.C.A.), where the taxpayer received an amount pursuant to section 66(4) of the Alberta *Expropriation Act*, authorizing the payment of "additional interest" on compensation awarded by the Land Compensation Board where the compensation offered by the expropriating authority is less than 80 per cent of the amount ultimately awarded by the board, the Federal Court of Appeal characterized the payment as a punitive damage award rather than "interest."

In *Shaw v. Canada*, [1993] F.C.J. No. 160, [1993] 1 C.T.C. 221, 93 D.T.C. 5121 (F.C.A.), however, where the taxpayer received "interest" of $1,020,368 as part of the settlement of an action for additional compensation following the expropriation of a farm, the Federal Court of Appeal held that this payment was taxable as interest under paragraph 12(1)(c) of the Act, not as damages or compensation for the expropriation. Similarly, in *Bellingham*, the court held that "ordinary interest" referable to the amount of compensation for expropriated land and accruing from the date that the owner gives up possession to the time of payment was fully taxable under paragraph 12(1)(c).

4. In *Ahmad v. Canada*, [2002] T.C.J. No. 471, [2002] 4 C.T.C. 2429, 2002 D.T.C. 2065 (T.C.C.), the taxpayer received $388,212 as pre-judgment interest

after a successful legal action in which he sued Ontario Hydro for inducement of breach of contract. Rejecting the Minister's argument that the payment was taxable as interest income under paragraph 12(1)(c) of the Act, the court concluded (at para. 28) that there was no principal amount in reference to which interest could accrue until the judgment determined that he had been wronged, that he had suffered a loss from the wrong, and the amount of the loss.

For a contrasting result, see *Coughlan v. Canada*, [2001] T.C.J. No. 449, [2001] 4 C.T.C. 2004, 2001 D.T.C. 719 (T.C.C.), in which the taxpayer received damages and pre-judgment interest after the Nova Scotia Court of Appeal determined that the by-laws of a company of which he had been a director were required to indemnify him for the costs of defending himself against legal proceedings by the company alleging fraud, deceit, conspiracy and insider trading. Rejecting the taxpayer's argument that the pre-judgment interest should be characterized as an additional damage award, the court concluded (at para. 18) that the payment was "interest on liquidated amounts wrongfully withheld" and properly taxable under paragraph 12(1)(c) of the Act.

5.   In some cases, amounts have been taxable under paragraph 12(1)(c) or its predecessors on the basis that they were received "in lieu of interest." In *Hall v. M.N.R.*, [1970] C.T.C. 510 (Ex. Ct.), for example, where the taxpayer sold matured bearer coupons that he had clipped from a number of Canada bonds that he held, the Exchequer Court held that the amounts received for the bond coupons were taxable under then paragraph 6(1)(b), among other reasons, because the amounts received were "in lieu of payment of ... interest." This decision was affirmed by the Supreme Court of Canada, [1971] C.T.C. 401, 71 D.T.C. 5217 (S.C.C.).

In *The Queen v. Greenington Group Ltd.*, [1979] C.T.C. 31, 79 D.T.C. 5026 (F.C.T.D.), the taxpayer, through a nominee corporation, purchased a parcel of land from a company to which it had loaned money and from which it was owed $135,947 in arrears of interest. Regarding a corresponding reduction in the purchase price as an amount received "in lieu of payment of, or in satisfaction of, interest," the Minister assessed this amount as income under paragraph 12(1)(c). The assessment was upheld both by the Tax Review Board, [1977] C.T.C. 2494, 77 D.T.C. 343, and the Federal Court Trial Division.

6.   The characterization of an amount as interest has also been considered in the context of paragraph 20(1)(c) of the Act, which allows taxpayers to deduct interest expenses that satisfy specific statutory criteria examined later in this chapter. In *M.N.R. v. Yonge-Eglinton Building Ltd.*, [1974] F.C.J. No. 84, [1974] C.T.C. 209, 74 D.T.C. 6180 (F.C.A.), where the taxpayer borrowed money to finance the construction of an office building on terms whereby it agreed to pay quarterly interest computed at a yearly rate of 9 per cent and "additional interest" equal to 1 per cent of its annual gross rental income for 25 years, the court rejected the taxpayer's characterization of the additional payments as "interest" within the meaning of then paragraph 11(1)(c) [now paragraph 20(1)(c)].

In *Sherway Centre Ltd. v. Canada*, [1998] F.C.J. No. 149, [1998] 2 C.T.C. 343, 98 D.T.C. 6121 (F.C.A.), however, where the taxpayer financed the construction of a shopping centre in Toronto by issuing bonds paying fixed interest computed at an annual rate of 9.75 per cent and "participatory interest" equal to 15 per cent of the taxpayer's "operating surplus" in excess of $2.9 million and expected to yield a combined return of 10.25 per cent, the court stated (at para. 8) that "the jurisprudence interpreting the meaning of the definition of interest has not developed alongside of, or has not taken into account new and innovative financing schemes for new business ventures," and allowed the deduction under paragraph 20(1)(c). According to McDonald JA (Linden and Létourneau JJA, concurring) (at para. 9-16):

> The classic definition of interest is found in the 1947 Supreme Court of Canada case *Saskatchewan (Attorney General) v. Canada (Attorney General)* where Rand J defined interest broadly to include "the return or consideration or compensation for the use or retention by one person of a sum of money, belonging to, in a colloquial sense, or owed to another." This fairly broad definition has since been limited or more narrowly defined. For instance, in *Ontario (Attorney General) v. Barfried Enterprises Ltd.* Judson J, after considering the definition of interest provided by Rand J in *Saskatchewan (Attorney General) v. Canada (Attorney General)* and *Halsbury's Laws of England*, found that one of the essential characteristics of interest is that it accrues daily. ...
>
> Another limiting characteristic placed on Rand J's definition of interest in *Saskatchewan (Attorney General) v. Canada (Attorney General)* is found in *Balaji Apartments Ltd. v. Manufacturers Life Insurance Co.* (1979), 25 OR (2d) 275, 100 DLR (3d) 695 (Ont. HC), where the Ontario High Court of Justice held that in order to be interest, the payment must be a percentage of the principle [sic] sum. Based on these limiting characteristics to the broad definition of interest contemplated by Rand J in *Saskatchewan (Attorney General) v. Canada (Attorney General)*, the Tax Court Judge held that the payments were not interest because they did not accrue day-to-day and because they were not based on the principal outstanding at anytime but on the Operating Surplus of the shopping centre. I will deal with each of these findings in turn.
>
> On the issue of whether the payments accrue day-to-day, in my opinion, the appropriate interpretation to be given to daily accrual of interest is that each holder's entitlement to interest must be able to be ascertained on a daily basis. I therefore agree with the Respondent that the interpretation of the quotation from *Halsbury* should not be read as establishing a legal principle that "compensation for the use of money is not interest unless it is expressed on a daily basis." Indeed, I agree with the Respondent when he states that "an amount paid as compensation for the use of money for a stipulated period can be said to accrue day-to-day."
>
> While the participating interest in this case was only payable once a year, nonetheless, it was based on a percentage of the Operating Surplus for the year. It was, therefore, capable of being allocated on a day-to-day basis and therefore meets the test for day-to-day accrual.
>
> The more difficult issue is the requirement set out in *Balaji Apartments* that the interest must be a percentage of the principal sum. *Balaji Apartments* dealt with a mortgage which in addition to the mortgage payments also required the payment of a percentage of gross annual rentals after a bare figure was reached. The Court held that the payments related to the gross income were not interest because they were "not a percentage of, or in any way related to, the principal sum."

In my opinion, the *Balaji Apartments* case should not be read as limiting the deductibility of payments that while not directly related to the principal amount, nonetheless, are clearly related to that amount. Indeed, this case should be limited to facts similar to those on which it was decided — where it is clear that payment in question was in addition to the obligation to pay interest on the loan. ...

In the case at bar, the evidence reveals that the purpose of the participating interest was to compensate for having to issue the bonds at a lower interest rate (9.75% as opposed to 10.25%) because had the Respondent issued the bonds at the 10.25% rate, there was a very real possibility of the Respondent going bankrupt. The Participatory interest, therefore, was another means of ensuring that the end result was that those buying the bonds would receive payments corresponding to the 10.25% interest rate (the rate it would have used had it been able to do so in the absence of the risk of bankruptcy). Thus, the payments were not in addition to interest as in the *Balaji* case but, instead, were in pursuit of the objective of a 10.25% interest rate. Moreover, it is important to point out that Anderson J in *Balaji* contemplated that provided a payment was related to the principal sum it might be deductible as interest when he stated, "[t]he payment is not a percentage of, or in any way related to, the principal sum."

The question, therefore, is whether the participating interest paid to the bond holders in this case can be said to be a percentage of, or in any way related to, the principal sum. In my opinion it can because, as the Respondent points out, the participating interest was payable only so long as there was principal outstanding. The portion of the participatory interest received was directly proportional to the amount of principal owed and, because the only purpose the participating interest served was to provide a rate of return on the principal outstanding from time to time, over the term of the loan to approximate a normal rate of interest for the loan. To hold otherwise, that is, to construe this provision as narrowly as previous case-law has done and not allow the deduction would, in my opinion, be to ignore the new commercial realities that were not considered by the courts when their past decisions were rendered.

7.   The characterization of an amount as interest has also been considered in the context of other provisions of the *Income Tax Act* dealing with payments to non-residents. In *Lebern Jewellery Co. Ltd. v. M.N.R.*, [1976] C.T.C. 2422, 76 D.T.C. 1313 (T.R.B.), where the taxpayer agreed to pay a non-resident supplier of unassembled wristwatches "7.5% interest per annum on late payments," the Tax Review Board considered these late payment charges to be "part of the agreed selling price," not interest. See also *Taran Furs Inc. v. M.N.R.*, [1985] 1 C.T.C. 2255, 85 D.T.C. 188 (T.C.C.).

In *M.N.R. v. Thyssen Canada Ltd*, [1986] F.C.J. No. 818, [1987] C.T.C. 112, 87 D.T.C. 5038 (F.C.A.), on the other hand, the Federal Court of Appeal held (at C.T.C. 114) that late payment charges on steel purchased from the respondent's German parent "had all the characteristics of interest." Notwithstanding that the respondent had regarded these charges as part of its cost for the steel, Pratte J distinguished *Lebern Jewellery*, on the grounds that in *Thyssen* the late payment charges were not included in the price of the goods purchased:

The record shows clearly ... that, as between the respondent and its parent company, the late payment charges were not included in the price of the steel sold to the appellant. True, ... the respondent, in fixing the price at which it would sell to its customers, quite normally considered those late payment charges as part of its costs. However, this could not change the nature of the charges payable to the parent company; the nature of those charges was determined by the agreements entered into by the respondent and its parent company and could not be changed unilaterally by the respondent.

Thyssen has been followed in *Wenger's Ltd. v. M.N.R.*, [1992] T.C.J. No. 517, [1992] 2 C.T.C. 2479, 92 D.T.C. 2132 (T.C.C.); and *Taran Furs (Montreal) Inc. v. M.N.R.*, [1995] T.C.J. No. 1564, [1996] 1 C.T.C. 2819 (T.C.C.).

8.   The CRA's views on the characterization of interest income are set out in paragraphs 11 to 14 of *Interpretation Bulletin* IT-396R, "Interest Income," May 29, 1984. According to paragraph 12:

> 12. Interest, while not defined in the Act, has been described in general terms in the Courts as "the return or consideration or compensation for the use or retention by one person of a sum of money, belonging to, in a colloquial sense, or owed to, another." From this description, it follows that interest does not arise unless there is an amount due to, or belonging to, another person for the period for which the interest is calculated. Consequently, it is the Department's position that where, after 1983, an award for damages is made either by a court or by means of an out-of-court settlement which includes, or is augmented by, an amount stated, either by the court or in the terms of the settlement, to be in fact interest on all or a portion of the award, such amount will constitute interest income in the hands of the recipient thereof for all purposes of the Act. This position arises from the fact that a liability for damages is considered to originate on the date on which an injury occurred and there is therefore an amount owing to, or belonging to, the injured party from that date. It is immaterial that the amount owing was not determinable until a later date because once the right to receive damages has been established, that right exists from the time at which the injury giving rise to those damages occurred. Similarly, where an enforceable agreement for the sale of property is executed but the negotiated price is not paid until a subsequent date, any interest that is received by the vendor for the period from the date of the agreement to the date of payment is interest income in the vendor's hands. For example, an enforceable agreement for the purchase and sale of real property at a price of $100,000 is entered into with a closing date of January 1, 1981. However, payment of this amount is not made until May 1, 1982 and interest of $12,000 (calculated as 9% of $100,000 for 16 months), in addition to the $100,000, is paid by the purchaser to compensate the vendor for the delay. The $12,000 is interest income to the vendor. The foregoing remarks may apply with respect to interest on sums owing where property is expropriated. However, certain amounts described in some Expropriation Acts as "interest" are not necessarily interest income but are considered to be part of the disposal proceeds.

9.   For a useful analysis of the concept of interest from the perspectives of tax law and tax policy, see Tim Edgar, "The Concept of Interest Under the Income Tax Act" (1996) 44 Can. Tax J. 277.

2. Payments of Interest and Capital Combined

Paragraph 16(1)(a) applies where, "under a contract or other arrangement, an amount can reasonably be regarded as being in part interest ... and in part an amount of a capital nature." In these circumstances, the provision stipulates that "the part of the amount that can reasonably be regarded as interest shall, irrespective of when the contract or arrangement was made or the form or legal effect thereof, be deemed to be interest on a debt obligation held by the person to whom the amount is paid or payable."[25]

Paragraph 16(1)(a) is an anti-avoidance provision designed to enable the courts to characterize a reasonable part of a payment as interest where it is reasonable to regard the payment as being in part capital and in part interest. According to the provision, whether a part of an amount can reasonably be regarded as interest is to be determined "irrespective of when the contract or arrangement was made or the form or legal effect thereof." Thus, paragraph 16(1)(a) seems to permit the courts to characterize as interest not only payments that the parties themselves describe as something other than interest (which the courts can do as a matter of judicial interpretation irrespective of any statutory authority), but also payments that would not otherwise be characterized as interest on the basis of the legal relationships actually established. In so doing, paragraph 16(1)(a) appears to determine tax consequences on the basis of the economic or commercial substance of the contract or other arrangement rather than its legal form.

The leading case on the application of subsection 16(1) is *Groulx v. M.N.R.*, [1967] C.T.C. 422, 67 D.T.C. 5284 (S.C.C.).

Groulx v. M.N.R
[1967] C.T.C. 422, 67 D.T.C. 5284 (S.C.C.)

HALL, J (translation): The appellant is appealing from a judgment of the Exchequer Court of Canada ... allowing the appeal of the respondent, the Minister of National Revenue, from a decision of the Tax Appeal Board relating to assessments by the Minister for the appellant's 1958 and 1959 taxation years. The sole question in issue in this appeal is whether sums of $15,000 and $19,136.20, received by the appellant in 1958 and 1959 respectively, pursuant to the provisions of a contract of sale, may reasonably be considered as interest received by him within the meaning of s. 7(1) of the *Income Tax Act*, RSC 1952, c. 148 [now subsection 16(1)].

For some twenty years, the appellant had been the owner of a farm located in the parish of St-Laurent. He had occupied, and was at the time of the sale still occupying, a house situated on the farm, and for several years, right up to 1952, he had been operating the farm.

From 1950 to 1956 the appellant was approached by different persons asking him to sell his farm, but he refused all these offers because he did not like the conditions which would require him to leave the farm which he had operated for

---

[25] Paragraph 16(1)(b) applies where an amount can reasonably be regarded as being in part an amount "of an income nature" other than interest and in part an amount of a capital nature — for example, blended payments made under an agreement for the sale of a business under which the vendor agrees to provide consulting services to the purchaser for a specific period of time. This chapter considers only para. 16(1)(a).

such a long time. Around July 20, 1956, however, when property values were rising, he was approached by a company called Thorndale Investment Corporation with whom he had been negotiating to an extent, and was presented with an offer of purchase in the amount of $350,000. He still refused this offer, saying that he wanted $450,000 for the farm.

During the ensuing two days, intense negotiations took place between the appellant and Thorndale Investment Corp. ... After some discussion, the appellant dropped his price to $400,000, but this was still considered by the purchaser to be too high. The appellant then consented to a further reduction of $5,000 which was not considered sufficient by the purchaser corporation. Then, in order to consummate the sale, he decided to waive interest.

A notarized contract was accordingly signed on July 19, 1956, pursuant to which Mr. Groulx agreed to sell a large portion of his farm ... to Thorndale Investment Corp. for $395,000 ... , $85,000 on closing, with the balance of $310,000 payable before June 1, 1964, in annual instalments commencing in 1958. No interest was payable on the balance outstanding, unless the instalments fell into arrears, in which case the interest rate was to be 6%.

The main clauses of the contract of sale relevant to this appeal are the following [in English]:

(a) The present Sale is thus made for the price or sum of Three hundred and ninety-five thousand dollars ($395,000), on account whereof the Vendor acknowledges to have received from the Purchaser the sum of Eighty-five thousand dollars ($85,000) whereof quit for so much.

The balance of price, namely the sum of Three hundred and ten thousand dollars ($310,000) the Purchaser obliges itself to pay to the Vendor as follows: —

Fifteen thousand dollars ($15,000) on the first day of June, nineteen hundred and fifty-eight;

Twenty-five thousand dollars ($25,000) on the first day of June, nineteen hundred and fifty-nine;

Fifty thousand dollars ($50,000) on the first day of June, nineteen hundred and sixty;

Fifty thousand dollars ($50,000) on the first day of June, nineteen hundred and sixty-one;

Fifty thousand dollars ($50,000) on the first day of June, nineteen hundred and sixty-two;

Fifty thousand dollars ($50,000) on the first day of June, nineteen hundred and sixty-three; and

Seventy thousand dollars ($70,000) on the first day of June, nineteen hundred and sixty-four.

(b) The purchaser shall have the right to increase the amount of any payment or to make payments on account or pay the entire balance at any time.

(c) The said balance of price shall not bear any interest if the said instalments are paid on or before their due dates, but any instalment not paid on its due date shall bear interest at the rate of six per centum (6 %) per annum from such due date and compounded half-yearly but not in advance until paid.

(d) Should however, the Purchaser pay any instalment above set forth before its due date, it will be entitled to a discount calculated at the rate of five per cent (5%) per annum from the date upon which payment is made to the respective due date.

In his reasons for judgment, the learned Judge of the Exchequer Court, [1966] Ex. CR 447; [1966] CTC 115, held [at CTC 138-44 (translation)]:

... we have here to deal in particular with two questions of fact. First, was the Minister justified in arguing that, had the taxpayer in this case followed a well-recognized practice in the business world, the balance of $310,000 payable by instalments would have borne interest at the rate of 5% or 6% until fully paid?

This question must without doubt be answered affirmatively, since there was no argument on the point. In addition, I am of the opinion that the evidence produced by the appellant establishes that in cases such as this, it is almost the universal practice for the balance of the purchase price secured by hypothec to bear interest at the rate of 5%. ...

The second question for determination is whether the evidence enables us to conclude that the property was sold at a price in excess of its fair market value. ...

I am of the opinion that the appellant established, at least *prima facie* that the property was sold at a price in excess of its fair market value, and the respondent did not succeed, as it was incumbent upon him to do, in proving the contrary. ...

In my opinion the respondent was no ordinary farmer. As indicated in his income tax returns filed with this Court, his taxable income for the 1958 taxation year exceeded $12,500, and for 1959 it was some $15,000. Portions of these amounts were received by him as salary from a company of which he was the president, but the major part came from his investments. His testimony revealed that real estate transactions were not strange to him. As for his statement to the effect that he never thought of the tax being avoided by waiving interest, a child could calculate interest at 5% on a $310,000 outstanding balance of purchase price owing, and realize that this exceeds $15,000 per year.

A taxpayer as skilled in business as the respondent would instantly realize the pecuniary advantage in succeeding in not doubling his taxable income. ...

I feel that by sacrificing interest, the respondent demonstrated that his intention was to assure himself of a capital price of $395,000 — and his testimony failed to show anything other than that he was capitalizing interest.

I might add that certain other circumstances militate against the respondent's position, namely, the fact that the respondent himself proposed the non-payment of interest, the weakness of the reasons motivating this gesture, and the vague answers given by [the purchaser] when asked whether, if he had not been exonerated from paying interest, he would have paid $395,000. I must therefore hold that there was sufficient evidence to justify the assessments in question.

The evidence fully justifies the conclusions reached by Kearney, J, concerning the facts. The appeal is therefore dismissed, and the judgment of the Exchequer Court is affirmed with costs against the appellant.

Appeal dismissed.

NOTES AND QUESTIONS

1.   On what grounds did the Exchequer Court in *Groulx* conclude that the full amount of the instalment payment received by the taxpayer in 1958 and a portion of the instalment payment received in 1959 could reasonably be regarded as interest? Of what, if any, relevance to this determination is the fact that adherence to "well-recognized practice in the business world" would have resulted in interest payments on the unpaid principal of 5 or 6 per cent? Of what, if any, relevance is the relationship between the price paid for the land and its fair market value? Of what, if any, relevance are the purchaser's "vague answers ... when asked whether, if he had not been exonerated from paying interest, he would have paid $395,000"? Of what, if any, relevance is the contractual clause providing for a discount of 5 per cent per annum on the payment of any instalment before its due date? Of what, if any, relevance is the fact that the taxpayer himself "proposed the non payment of interest"?

2.   In *Vanwest Logging Co. Ltd. v. M.N.R.*, [1971] C.T.C. 199, 71 D.T.C. 5120 (Ex. Ct.), the taxpayer sold a tract of timber for $7.5 million, of which $1.5 million was payable on closing with the remainder due over the next five years in five equal annual instalments of $1.2 million each. The agreement did not provide for the payment of interest except in the case of overdue instalments, in which case interest was payable at a rate of 6 per cent per year. The Minister applied then subsection 7(1) (now subsection 16(1)) to characterize as interest a portion of the instalment payments. The taxpayer appealed.

According to the taxpayer (at para. 8):

unlike the *Groulx* case ... there is no evidence in these proceedings that interest was discussed or the payment of same waived at any stage during the negotiations, or that the price for which the sale was made was above the market value, or that there was any discount off the price for prepayment, or even that there was any clear indication that the practice in similar sales of timber limits is to charge interest on the unpaid balance. Neither is there any indication that the agreement reached was a sham and did not represent the true facts of what the parties had agreed upon, and that therefore the Minister has no right to find that it is reasonable to impute part of the payments to interest, unless he wishes to contend that there must always be an interest component whenever a sale calls for installment payments which do not carry interest, and this is not what Section 7 states.

In contrast, the Minister argued (at para. 10):

since, by virtue of Section 7(1), a breakdown of the payments into interest and capital elements can be made "irrespective of when the contract or arrangement was made or the form or legal effect thereof even an express statement in an agreement that no interest shall be charged on the unpaid balance does not prevent the inference being drawn, and that this is all the more true where the agreement contains no such express statement but merely makes no reference to interest (save with respect to the 6% interest to be paid on overdue instalments as mentioned above).

In addition, referring to a number of English cases in which instalment payments were broken down into interest and principal, the Minister also reasoned (at para. 10) that:

> if the British courts have, in the absence of a statutory provision like Section 7(1) seen fit in appropriate circumstances to isolate the interest element in installments payments, the courts in Canada have, partly because of the broader statutory powers under the *Income Tax Act* and partly because of a readiness to look beyond the form of a transaction to its substance (for example, *Dominion Taxicab Association v. M.N.R.*, [1954] SCR 82 at 85; [1954] CTC 34 at 38) been able to approach the problem on a broader basis, and that there is no justification for not looking at the commercial realities of the situation.

After considering these arguments and reviewing the judgment in *Groulx*, [1967] C.T.C. 422, 67 D.T.C. 5284 (S.C.C.), the court stated (at para. 11) that in order to determine whether part of each instalment payment could reasonably be regarded as in part a payment of interest, it was necessary to consider four criteria:

> [1] the terms of the agreement reached between the parties, ... [2] the course of the negotiations between them leading to it, ... [3] the relationship of the price paid to the apparent market value of the property at the time, and [4] the common practice with respect to payment of interest on the sale of timber limits.

Applying these criteria, the court allowed the taxpayer's appeal for the following reasons (at para. 48):

> [N]one of the factors on which the *Groulx* case concluded that it could reasonably be regarded that part of the payments represented interest and part were of a capital nature justifying the application of Section 7(1) by the Minister are present here, since there was no evidence that interest was considered by the vendor and affected the price it charged the purchaser, nor was there any evidence in this case that it is the invariable practice to charge interest on deferred payments in such sales of timber limits, nor was there evidence justifying a conclusion of fact that the price was excessive and could only be justified by not charging interest on the deferred instalments. The Minister is therefore left with nothing on which to base his "reasonable conclusion" save for the bare fact that it was obviously to the advantage of the vendor to sell for $7,500,000 without interest on the deferred payments rather than for $6,250,000 with interest. Since there is no indication, however, that in connection with the present sale the vendor ever considered selling for $6,250,000 with interest (nor for that matter that this offer had been made ...) this becomes a mere assumption on the part of the Minister, not based on any evidence and not a "reasonable" conclusion as required by Section 7(1). I do not consider that Section 7(1) can be applied by the Minister in all cases where no interest is claimed on deferred payments, but rather that it should only be used when something in the evidence indicates that it was the intention of the vendor to avoid taxation on interest by including it as part of a larger capital payment than would otherwise have been made.

Do you agree with this conclusion? Why or why not? Does subsection 16(1) suggest that evidence of the vendor's intention to avoid taxation is a prerequisite to the application of the rule? Should the courts adopt such a requirement notwithstanding the text of the provision?

3.   In *Rodmon Construction Inc. v. Canada*, [1975] C.T.C. 73, 75 D.T.C. 5038 (F.C.T.D.), the purchasers of a parcel of land assumed a non-interest-bearing mortgage payable by instalment to a non-resident. Allowing the taxpayer's appeal against an assessment that had imposed non-resident withholding tax on the purchasers on the basis that it was reasonable to regard the instalment payments as part interest and part principal, Décary J stated (at C.T.C. 75):

> It is well established that in similar cases the prime factor to be considered is whether or not the fair market value has been paid: if the price paid is in excess of fair market value, the excess is deemed interest; if the price reflects the fair market value then there is no element of interest in the payment.

Subsequent cases involving instalment sales have considered the four criteria referred to in *Vanwest Logging Co. Ltd. v. M.N.R.*, [1971] C.T.C. 199, 71 D.T.C. 5120 (Ex. Ct.), but have tended to regard the relationship between the price paid for property and its fair market value at the time of the purchase as the most important factor. See, for example, *Club de Courses Saguenay Ltée et al. v. M.N.R.*, [1979] C.T.C. 3022, 79 D.T.C. 579 (T.R.B.), where the board regarded the difference between the purchase price and the fair market value of assets sold as interest; and *J.E. Martin v. M.N.R.*, [1980] C.T.C. 2043, 80 D.T.C. 1052 (T.R.B.), where the board concluded (at C.T.C. 3034) that because a parcel of land was sold at its fair market value "it is unreasonable to presume that there was a part payment of interest."

A widely accepted definition of the term "fair market value" is "the highest price available in an open and unrestricted market between informed, prudent parties acting at arm's length and under no compulsion to act, expressed in terms of money or money's worth": *Connor v. Canada*, [1978] C.T.C. 669 at 677, 78 D.T.C. 6497 at 6503 (F.C.T.D.), aff'd [1979] C.T.C. 365, 79 D.T.C. 5256 (F.C.A.). See also *Mann Estate v. Minister of Finance*, [1972] 5 W.W.R. 23 (B.C.S.C.), aff'd [1973] C.T.C. 561 (B.C.C.A.), aff'd [1974] C.T.C. 222 (S.C.C.).

Does this definition suggest that an agreed-upon price will be equivalent to fair market value in most cases in which the parties to the transaction deal with each other at arm's length? If this is true, should the relationship between an agreed-upon price and the fair market value of property at the time of the sale be "the prime factor" in the application of subsection 16(1) of the Act?

4.   In *Peers v. M.N.R.* (1966), 40 Tax ABC 258 (T.A.B.), the Tax Appeal Board commented (at 263) that "Section 7(1) was clearly intended to cover the situation where the amount of interest was neither given in the contract under review, nor ... ascertainable from the facts contained therein." In *Vanwest Logging Co. Ltd. v. M.N.R.*, [1971] C.T.C. 199, 71 D.T.C. 5120 (Ex. Ct.), however, counsel for the Minister reasoned (at C.T.C. 204) that since these amounts could be subject to tax as interest under then paragraph 6(1)(b) (now paragraph 12(1)(c)) in any event, the purpose of then subsection 7(1) (now

subsection 16(1)) must be "to bring into income an amount that might not be taxed under Section 6(1)(b)." In this light, and emphasizing the words "irrespective of when the contract or arrangement was made or the form or legal effect thereof," he then argued that former subsection 7(1) could be applied notwithstanding "an express statement in an agreement that no interest shall be charged on the unpaid balance." Which interpretation do you find most persuasive? Why?

5.   The CRA's views on subsection 16(1) can be found in *Interpretation Bulletin* IT-265R3, "Payments of Income and Capital Combined," October 7, 1991 (archived by the CRA in 2004). According to paragraphs 8 and 9:

> 8. Where property of any kind is sold on a deferred or instalment payment basis, and no interest is specified in the contract other than for payments in arrears, it will be a question of fact whether or not each payment received by the vendor contains an income element (either interest or some other type of income). Even though the normal commercial practice is to charge interest in connection with the sale of property, a vendor and a purchaser could agree on a total selling price which will be payable over a period of time without interest charges.

> 9. Accordingly, subsection 16(1) does not apply unless there is sufficient evidence that the selling price of the property is greater than its fair market value. In these cases, the interest portion of the blended payment is not considered to be more than the lesser of:

> (a)   the excess of the selling price over the fair market value, and

> (b)   an amount computed with reference to the normal rate of interest prevailing at the time of the transaction.

6.   Subsection 16(4) provides that subsection 16(1) does not apply to any amount received by a taxpayer in a taxation year (a) as an annuity payment or (b) in satisfaction of the taxpayer's rights under an annuity contract. Although these amounts could otherwise fall within the ambit of subsection 16(1), they are governed by a specific set of rules and thus excluded from its application.

In general, annuity payments are fully taxable under paragraph 56(1)(d) of the Act, though a deduction is available under paragraph 60(a) for the capital element of the payment. Annuity contracts are also subject to special accrual rules under section 12.2. With respect to lump-sum payments in satisfaction of a taxpayer's rights under an annuity contract, gains are generally subject to tax under subsection 148(1), while losses are deductible under paragraph 20(20)(b).

7.   Subsection 16(5) states that subsection 16(1) does not apply in any case where subsection (2) or (3) applies. Subsections 16(2) and (3) apply to certain debt obligations issued at a discount by various non-taxable issuers, under terms whereby the effective annual yield from the discount exceeds $1\frac{1}{3}$ of the stipulated interest payable on the obligation. Under these circumstances, subsection 16(2), which applies only to debt obligations issued after December 20, 1960 and before June 19, 1971, requires the amount of the discount to be included in computing the income of the first owner of the obligation who is a resident of Canada and not exempt from tax for the taxation year in which he,

she, or it became the owner of the obligation. Subsection 16(3), which applies to debt obligations issued after June 18, 1971 other than "prescribed debt obligations" to which subsection 12(9) applies, requires the discount to be included in computing the income of the first owner of the obligation who is resident in Canada, is not exempt from tax, and holds the obligation as a capital property for the taxation year in which the owner acquired the obligation.

Subsection 16(3) is based on subsection 16(2), which was enacted in 1960 as then subsection 7(2) of the 1952 *Income Tax Act*. The origin and purpose of these provisions is explained in the following excerpt from Gibson J's decision in *J. Harold Wood v. M.N.R.*, [1967] C.T.C. 66 at 75-77, 67 D.T.C. 5045 (Ex. Ct.):

> In Canada about 1958 there developed a money market for so-called discount bonds. This became especially pronounced after a very substantial market break in the fall of 1959. ... The Government of Canada, for example, in March of 1959 sold a 2¼% issue due in thirteen months at $97.90 to yield 4.6%. This issue, in the main, as stated, was purchased by such corporate investors and such corporate investors treated the gain arising from this discount to maturity or the difference between the buying and selling price if sold prior to maturity as a capital gain or at least non-taxable income and paid corporate tax on the interest or coupon only. Provincial governments in Canada, also about this time, began to issue bonds at a discount. ... Between early 1958 and December, 1960 the Canadian Provinces and their authorities raised millions of dollars through the sale of discount bonds or notes with terms ranging from six months to two or three years. In the vast majority of cases a 2% coupon was used and the gross yield ranged from 2.40% to 5.65%.
>
> Then finally, in December, 1960 a three million dollar issue was done by a province. This issue was in two parts and each bore a 2% coupon. One part had a ten year term and was priced at $76.28 to yield 5.05%. The other was a fifteen year term and was priced at $66.95 to yield 5.20%.
>
> This led the Government of Canada to enact Section 7(2) of the *Income Tax Act*. This section then provided (and now provides) that for any new bonds issued where the coupon rate was less than 5% the gross or total yield on which the bond could be sold could not exceed the coupon by more than ⅓. If this gross yield exceeded the coupon by more than ⅓, then the whole of the discount would be deemed to be income in the hands of the first Canadian resident taxable holder of the instrument. This meant, for example, to avoid the income tax implication of Section 7(2) for a bond bearing a fixed or coupon rate of 2% the highest gross rate at which it could now be sold was 2.66%.
>
> The enactment of Section 7(2) of the Income Tax Act therefore brought an end to the issuance of these "deep discount" bonds.

Discounted debt obligations satisfying the description of a prescribed debt obligation in regulation 7000(1)(a) are also subject to special interest accrual rules under subsections 12(3), (4), and (9) and regulation 7000(2)(a). These rules are discussed later in this chapter.

3. Discounts and Premiums

Where a debt obligation is acquired at a price less than the principal amount payable on maturity, this "discount" constitutes an economic return in addition to any interest that may be payable on the debt. Likewise, debt obligations may provide an economic return in the form of a bonus in excess of the principal amount payable at maturity. To the extent that these kinds of economic returns can substitute for the payment of interest, one might expect that they should be included in computing the recipient's income from a business or property in the same way as ordinary interest. In order to characterize these amounts as "legal interest," however, judicial decisions have traditionally suggested that they must not only compensate for the use of borrowed money, but refer to the principal amount and accrue day by day. In *O'Neil v. M.N.R.*, [1991] T.C.J. No. 314, 91 D.T.C. 692 (T.C.C.), the court considered the characterization of discounts realized on the maturity of Government of Canada treasury bills.

O'Neil v. M.N.R.
[1992] T.C.J. No. 314, 91 D.T.C. 692 (T.C.C.)

LAMARRE-PROULX TCJ: ... On January 27, 1989, the Appellant acquired one Government of Canada treasury bill having a maturity value of $200,000 for a purchase price of $189,466.20. Its maturity date was July 26, 1989. It was redeemed on that date for a value of $200,000. On that same day, the Appellant purchased another treasury bill of a similar maturity value at a purchase cost of $189,108.90. The maturity date of this bill was January 1, 1990 and it was redeemed on that date. The treasury bills did not carry a stated interest, and it was mutually agreed that the rate of discount was slightly higher than the bank rates.

...

Appellant's position

... The appellant referred me to a publicity document ... issued by the investment dealer who sold the treasury bills to the Appellant. ... In [this] publicity document there was ... the following:

Tax Reminder — tax treatment of Treasury Bills

Government Treasury Bills carry no stated interest rate but instead are offered at a discount. It is the position of Revenue Canada (Interpretation Bulletin IT-114, paragraph 3) that the difference between the amount paid by the purchaser and the matured value of the Bill represents income in the nature of interest.

Agent for the Appellant brought this document to my attention in order to put forth the whole evidence but said that the Appellant was of the view that the Interpretation Bulletin was incorrect and he stated that it is not because an interpretation bulletin says something that this is how the law should be interpreted. This argument is valid but in this particular instance, I am of the view that, on this aspect, the Interpretation Bulletin is in accordance with the law and the case law.

Section 3 of the Interpretation Bulletin reads as follows:

3. A discount on the issue of a debt obligation which does not carry a stated interest rate normally, if not always, is interest. The Courts have held, however, that where a loan is made at or in excess of a reasonable commercial rate of interest as is applicable to a reasonably sound security there is no presumption that a discount at which the loan is made is in the nature of interest. The true nature of a discount therefore must be ascertained from all the circumstances of each particular case.

Here, it is a case where the debt obligation does not carry a stated interest rate and not a case where a loan is made at a reasonable commercial rate.

...

The Appellant referred me also to an article prepared by the Securities Department of the Bank of Canada entitled "Bank of Canada Review February 1991: The market for Government of Canada treasury bills" where it is said at pages 4, 11, 12 and 13:

Treasury bills are the shortest term debt instrument issued by the federal government. They serve a number of functions both for borrower and lender. For the Government, treasury bills are a key source of short-term financing in its overall borrowing program, and a flexible means of responding to the short-term ebb and flow of its cash balances. ...

The increased holdings by both the financial and non-financial general public can be attributed to the same characteristics that have made the treasury bill an attractive asset for banks: namely, its high quality, liquidity, and competitive yield. Treasury bills are particularly convenient from a cash management viewpoint because they are available in a variety of weekly maturities and there is an active "secondary" market in outstanding bills to accommodate sales prior to the maturity if needed. ...

Government of Canada treasury bills are issued through weekly auctions at the Bank of Canada in selected denominations ranging from $1,000 to $1 million. Bills are tendered in maturities of 91 days, 182 days and 364 days on a weekly basis, ...

Chartered banks, the Bank of Canada, and investment dealers eligible to act as primary distributors are authorized to submit competitive bids. Most of the purchases of bills by investment dealers and some of the chartered banks' purchases are subsequently made available to investors.

Respondent's position

Counsel for the Respondent ... relied on paragraph 12(1)(c) and section 9 of the Act. His argument is that the nature of the discount is interest and therefore should be included in the calculation of the taxpayer's income by virtue of subsection 12(1)(c). It could also be said that it is revenue from a property being income derived from a loan and subject to the provisions of section 9.

Jurisprudence

For this purpose, counsel for the Respondent referred the Court to three English cases which are:

Beck v. Lord Howard de Walden, [1940] TR 143;

CIR v. Thomas Nelson & Sons Ltd., (1938) 22 TC 175;

Lomax v. Peter Dixon & Sons Ltd., [1943] 1 KB 671.

In the first case, the facts as described in the headnotes were the following:

On the 11th December, 1933, the Appellant entered into agreements with four Canadian companies. It was common to all four agreements that the Appellant, in return for consideration moving from him to the company, was to receive from the company a series of 120 promissory notes payable without interest at the registered office of the company in Canada, the first to be payable on the 31st of March, 1934, and the remainder consecutively at intervals of three calendar months. These promissory notes were all issued and handed to the Appellant on the 11th December, 1933. The consideration moving from the Appellant was in one case purely a cash payment, and in the others a cash payment together with the release of the company concerned from its prior obligations to the Appellant.

On actuarial valuation, the consideration moving from the Appellant, whether cash or cash together with a release from prior obligations, was in each case less than the consideration moving from the company concerned, by a margin which represented in the one case exactly the present value of the promissory notes on a basis of 4 per cent interest and in the other cases closely approximated to that produced by interest at 4 per cent. ...

Held, that the promissory notes included an element of income.

...

With respect to the second case referred to me by counsel for the Respondent, the facts described in the headnotes are the following:

The Respondent Company lent a sum of money to an Indian company under an agreement which provided that interest was to be paid at 3% per annum and that on repayment of the principal sum or any part thereof there should also be paid a premium varying with the date of repayment. The full amount of the loan was ultimately repaid to the Respondent Company, together with the accrued interest and the premiums payable under the agreement.

On appeal against assessments ... the Respondent Company contended that the premiums were part of the principal sums repaid and were capital payments. ...

Held that the premiums were income ... .

The Lord President notes at pages 179, 180:

... Interest was to be paid at the remarkably low rate for an unsecured loan of this kind of 3 per cent. But the borrowers also agreed to repay the principal sums together with a premium varying with the date of payment, and they had an option to repay the principal in whole or in part, but not less than one-tenth of the amount at any one time, on the 1st September, 1924, or any subsequent first of September. The premiums prescribed by the agreement for each of the ten years of the currency of the loan are set out in the agreement; the first of them is at the rate of 2 per cent; the second is at 4 per cent; in each of the next five years there is an increase of 2½ per cent, in arithmetical progression, and for the last three years of the ten the rate of increase per annum is 3 per cent. Thus, if no repayment took place till the end of ten years, the whole principal would then fall to be repaid plus 25½ per cent.

On the question thus posed on the particular terms of the contract, I am of opinion that the premiums are in the nature of annual profits or gains ...

Let us consider now the third case referred to me by counsel for the Respondent. In that case, notes were issued by a company at a discount and redeemable at a premium but the notes were bearing interest at a reasonable commercial rate. It was held that the discount and the premiums were capital sums.

Lord Greene says the following at pages 262, 263:

It may be convenient to sum up my conclusions in a few propositions, (i) Where a loan is made at or above such a reasonable commercial rate of interest as is applicable to a reasonably sound security, there is no presumption that a "discount" at which the loan is made or a premium at which it is payable is in the nature of interest, (ii) The true nature of the "discount" or the premium, as the case may be, is to be ascertained from all the circumstances of the case and, apart from any matter of law which may bear upon the question (such as the interpretation of the contract), will fall to be determined as a matter of fact by Commissioners, (iii) In deciding the true nature of the "discount" or premium, in so far as it is not conclusively determined by the contract, the following matters together with any other relevant circumstances are important to be considered, viz., the term of the loan, the rate of interest expressly stipulated for, the nature of the capital risk, the extent to which, if at all, the parties expressly took or may reasonably be supposed to have taken the capital risk into account in fixing the terms of the contract.

In this summary I have purposely confined myself to a case such as the present where a reasonable commercial rate of interest is charged. Where no interest is payable as such, different considerations will, of course, apply. In such a case, a "discount" will normally, if not always, be ... [interest]. Similarly, a "premium" will normally, if not always, be interest. But it is neither necessary nor desirable to do more than to point out the distinction between such cases and the case of a contract similar to that which we are considering.

...

Analysis

Having regard to the nature of the Appellant's investment in treasury bills, which at the very beginning had a stated redemption value, it is reasonable to liken this investment to a loan to the Government of Canada and to find that the difference between the purchase price and the maturity value is interest pursuant to subsection 16(1) and therefore should be included in the calculation of the Appellant's income as income from a property, pursuant to section 9 or as interest received in a year pursuant to paragraph 12(1)(c). ... Having determined that the amount of the discount is in the nature of interest paid on money invested, it follows that paragraph 12(1)(c) applies. It was that paragraph that was referred to in the Respondent's assessment. ...

Appeal dismissed.

NOTES AND QUESTIONS

1. In *Lomax v. Peter Dixon & Sons*, [1943] 1 K.B. 671 (K.B.), on which Lamarre-Proulx TCJ relied in *O'Neil*, Lord Greene distinguished between debt obligations carrying a reasonable commercial rate of interest and debt obligations on which no interest is charged. In the case of the former, he

suggested, "there is no presumption that a 'discount' at which the loan is made or a premium at which it is payable is in the nature of interest." In the latter case, he concluded, a discount or premium will "normally, if not always, be interest."

This distinction has been referred to and followed in several Canadian cases. In *No. 593 v. M.N.R.* (1959), 21 Tax ABC 240 (T.A.B.), for example, where the taxpayer had loaned $100,000 to be repaid after six months with a bonus (or premium) of $13,000 with interest of 4 per cent per annum based on the amount of the principal and the bonus, the Tax Appeal Board, referring to the decision in *Lomax*, held (at para. 56) that the bonus was taxable under then paragraph 6(1)(b) (now paragraph 12(1)(c)) as "a receipt on account or in lieu or in satisfaction of the additional interest which the appellant might have received if he had not elected to accept the substantial lump sums."

Alternatively, in *West Coast Parts Co. Ltd. v. M.N.R.*, [1964] C.T.C. 519, 64 D.T.C. 5316 (Ex. Ct.), where the taxpayer loaned $125,000 to be repaid in less than two years with 10 per cent interest and a bonus (or premium) of $56,000, the amount of the bonus, though taxable as business income from an adventure in the nature of trade, was not regarded as interest within the meaning of then paragraph 6(1)(b). According to Cattanach J (at para. 36):

> When a person enters into a contract whereby he advances money to another person on terms that it is to be repaid at a fixed time together with an additional amount, if that additional amount is described as interest, there is no problem. Interest is income from property within Section 3 of the *Income Tax Act* and it is specifically required to be included in computing income by Section 6 [now paragraph 12(1)(c)]. When such a contract requires repayment with such an additional amount, but does not describe it as interest, it becomes a question of fact as to whether the additional payment is or is not in fact interest or, in any event, a profit from property in the sense of revenue derived from the money advanced. If the additional payment is the sole consideration for use of the money, there would appear to be a very strong probability that it is interest or a payment in lieu of interest. The problem is more complicated where, as here, the contract provides for repayment with interest as such plus an additional fixed amount. Usually the promise of such an amount is not regarded as being a payment for the use of the money, but as an inducement to the lender to incur the risk of not getting his money back in speculative circumstances. I cannot escape the conclusion that, in such event, the lump sum payment, not being payment merely for the use of the money, is, in the absence of very special circumstances, a profit from an adventure in the nature of trade.

2.   In *Puder v. M.N.R.*, [1963] C.T.C. 445, 63 D.T.C. 1282 (Ex. Ct.), the taxpayer, who had loaned a sum of money secured by a mortgage, agreed to a release of the mortgage in exchange for the payment of a bonus calculated as "the unearned interest for that portion of the three year period remaining" before the mortgagor was entitled under the mortgage agreement to repay the balance of the loan. Reversing a decision of the Tax Appeal Board (1962), 30 Tax ABC 219, Thurlow J held that this bonus was neither interest nor an amount "on account of, in lieu of payment of, or in satisfaction of, interest," nor income from property within the meaning of the predecessor to subsection 9(1) of the Act.

In response to the Minister's first argument that the payment was either interest or an amount "on account of, in lieu of payment of, or in satisfaction of, interest," the court stated (at para. 7):

In my opinion this contention cannot succeed. It disregards the fact that the appellant had other rights besides those to repayment of the principal and interest at the time when the release was requested and it overlooks as well the fact that the amount in question was never earned as interest. Interest, in my opinion, is essentially compensation for the use or retention of money for a period of time ... and here this element is lacking. The amount in question was not paid or received for or in respect of the use or retention of the principal sum for the period of 15 months or thereabouts during which the mortgage was in effect. Nor on the other hand was it paid or received for or in respect of the use of the principal sum for the remainder of the three-year period provided for in the mortgage for throughout that period the appellant had his principal sum and presumably the use of it as well and the mortgagor had neither. Though called interest the amount was accordingly not interest in fact and as it was not interest I do not think it can be regarded as having been "received as interest" within the meaning of Section 6(1)(b). ... Nor in my opinion can the amount properly be regarded as having been received 'on account of or in lieu of payment of, or in satisfaction of interest" within the meaning of Section 6(1)(b) since no part of the amount ever accrued as interest and no part of it was paid in lieu of or in satisfaction of any amount that ever accrued as interest.

With respect to the Minister's second argument that the bonus represented income from property, the court concluded (at para. 10):

In my opinion it is not correct either to regard the appellant's property, during the time when the mortgage was in effect, as consisting merely of his right to the principal sum which remained outstanding on the mortgage or to regard the gain (to use as neutral a word as I can find) represented by the amount here in question as a profit from his property. The transaction in which the mortgage was given appears to have been a mere investment of capital in which the appellant parted with or exchanged his $45,000 for the rights which the mortgage gave him. These rights were not however limited to a right of repayment of the principal sum or to that right plus the payment of interest to the date of repayment but included all the other enforceable legal rights given him by the mortgage including the right to insist on payment of the principal and interest at the times stated therein. It was the whole of these rights which the appellant surrendered when he gave a release of the mortgage and the amount he received at that time in my opinion represented his property itself rather than profit from his property ... . It appears to me to have been simply a sum received in respect of the relinquishment by the appellant of his right to insist on payment of the mortgage according to its tenor which in my opinion was not a right of an income nature even though retaining it would have resulted in income accruing to him.

For a similar result, see *Specht v. M.N.R.*, [1981] C.T.C. 2463, 81 D.T.C. 464 (T.R.B.).

3.   In *Gestion Guy Ménard Inc. v. Canada*, [1993] T.C.J. No. 425, [1993] 2 C.T.C. 2793, 93 D.T.C. 1058 (T.C.C.), the taxpayer, a private corporation engaged primarily in the business of obtaining medical supplies for Dr. Guy Ménard's medical practice, used surplus funds to acquire treasury bills. The bills were sold one day prior to maturity on the advice of Dr. Ménard's broker, who advised him that the company "could realize a capital gain instead of ordinary income" if the bills were sold in this manner. Emphasizing (at para. 17) that "the substance of the transactions [does] not change materially whether the bills are sold one day prior to maturity or held until maturity," P.R. Dussault TCCJ held that the gains were taxable under paragraph 12(1)(c) as amounts received "in lieu of payment of interest."

4.   In *O'Neil v. M.N.R.*, [1991] T.C.J. No. 314, 91 D.T.C. 692 (T.C.C.), Lamarre-Proulx TCJ stated that "it is reasonable to liken this investment to a loan to the Government of Canada," even though investors typically acquire treasury bills from and sell treasury bills to financial institutions or investment dealers, not the government of Canada. In *Ménard*, the taxpayer argued, among other things (at C.T.C. 2796), that because the treasury bills were neither purchased from nor sold to the government of Canada, "there was never a borrower/lender relationship between the government and the [taxpayer] during the period the bills were held so that interest could not be said to be payable or to accrue." Rejecting this argument, P.R. Dussault TCCJ concluded (at C.T.C. 2798):

> If one does not question that the government is in the position of a borrower when it issues a treasury bill, it seems difficult to sustain that a purchaser, even on the secondary market, is not in the position analogous to that of a creditor as a claim for payment can be made directly from the Bank of Canada at maturity if the bill is registered in the purchaser's name. Although at maturity an accredited institution or investment dealer would, in the normal course, pay the holder of a bill and then obtain payment from the government, it seems to me that the different transactions involve in substance if not in form an initial loan to the government by an accredited institution followed by a sale or assignment of the debt to persons such as the appellants. A second holder of a treasury bill can then certainly be considered a creditor of the amount payable by the government at maturity. In such a case, there is no doubt that the higher amount payable at maturity by the government represents ... in part the compensation for the use or retention by one person, for a certain period, of a sum of money owed to someone else.

5.   In *Gestion Guy Ménard Inc. v. Canada*, [1993] T.C.J. No. 425, [1993] 2 C.T.C. 2793, 93 D.T.C. 1058 (T.C.C.), the taxpayer also argued (at C.T.C. 2798-99) that "as the market price of treasury bills can vary due to the prevailing rates of interest on the market, the proceeds of disposition could not be said to represent a regular accrued yield on the purchase price. In other words, the discount obtained at the time of the purchase might not accrue day to day in those circumstances as interest would." In response, P.R. Dussault TCCJ stated (at C.T.C. 2799):

> It is true that the market value of a treasury bill can vary during the term according to prevailing returns on the monetary market but it is also true that it will never be worth more than the face value or the principal sum payable at maturity. Moreover, in my view, there is no longer any market influence one day before maturity so that the predetermined rate of return has accrued or been earned but for one day during the period.

The court also referred to the passage from *West Coast Parts Co. Ltd. v. M.N.R.*, [1964] C.T.C. 519, 64 D.T.C. 5316 (Ex. Ct.), and to the following broad definition of the word "interest" from *Re Unconscionable Transactions Relief Act*, [1962] O.R. 1103 at 1108 (C.A.):

> The word "interest" is not, then, a technical term and it is not restricted in any sense to compensation determinable by the application of a rate per centum to the principal amount of a loan. It may be for a fixed sum of money whether denominated a bonus, discount or premium, provided that it is referable to a principal money or obligation to pay money.

Ultimately, the court in *Ménard* held that the gains were taxable under paragraph 12(1)(c) as amounts received "in lieu of payment of interest."

See also *Gilmour v. Canada*, [1981] C.T.C. 401, 81 D.T.C. 5322 (F.C.T.D.), where in different circumstances Collier J held (at C.T.C. 405) that discounts were "from an acceptable accounting view and practice, and from an acceptable and realistic business viewpoint, a form of prepaid interest."

6.   As the taxpayer's second argument in *Gestion Guy Ménard Inc. v. Canada*, [1993] T.C.J. No. 425, [1993] 2 C.T.C. 2793, 93 D.T.C. 1058 (T.C.C.), suggests, "the market price of treasury bills can vary due to the prevailing rates of interest on the market." If market rates of interest increase, for example, the value of a treasury bill can be expected to decrease to the point where the return on the bill matches the new (higher) market rate of interest. Alternatively, if prevailing interest rates decrease, the value of the treasury bill can be expected to increase until the return on the bill is reduced to the new (lower) market rate of interest. As indicated by the following excerpt from *Ménard* (at C.T.C. 2796), where a treasury bill is disposed of prior to maturity, it is the CRA's administrative practice to distinguish between interest and capital elements of a gain or loss by computing the "effective yield" of the bill and subtracting from the proceeds both the cost of the bill and "interest" computed up to the date of the disposition on the basis of the effective yield:

> as a treasury bill does not carry a stated rate of interest, the difference between the purchase price and the face value is simply divided by the purchase price to obtain the effective yield. If a taxpayer disposes of the bill prior to maturity, the interest is computed for the period up until the date of disposition using that effective yield. A capital gain or loss is thereafter measured by subtracting from the proceeds of disposition both the adjusted cost base and any amount treated as interest.

In Ménard's case, where the treasury bill was sold one day prior to maturity, "the full amount of the discount was assessed as interest since the purported gain itself was negligible."

What, if any, statutory provision might be relied upon as authority for this administrative practice?

7.   In *O'Neil v. M.N.R.*, [1991] T.C.J. No. 314, 91 D.T.C. 692 (T.C.C.), Lamarre-Proulx TCJ held that the difference between the purchase price and the maturity value of the taxpayer's treasury bills "is interest pursuant to subsection 16(1) and therefore should be included in the calculation of the Appellant's income as income from a property, pursuant to section 9 or as interest received in a year pursuant to paragraph 12(1)(c)." Nonetheless, on the basis that "the amount of the discount is in the nature of interest paid on money invested," she then added that "it follows that paragraph 12(1)(c) applies." Similarly, in *Gestion Guy Ménard Inc. v. Canada*, [1993] T.C.J. No. 425, [1993] 2 C.T.C. 2793, 93 D.T.C. 1058 (T.C.C.), P.R. Dussault TCCJ relied on subsection 16(1) and paragraph 12(1)(c), but noted that if the gain is interest, "it should be treated as such under the more specific provisions of the Act applying to interest." In

Satinder v. Canada, [1995] F.C.J. No. 754, 95 D.T.C. 5340 (F.C.A.), Stone JA noted that "the holder of a treasury bill is paid a blend of principal and interest upon its redemption," but concluded that the discount was taxable under paragraph 12(1)(c).

Is subsection 16(1) necessary in these circumstances? Why or why not?

8.   The revenue authority's views on the tax treatment of discounts and premiums used to appear in *Interpretation Bulletin* IT-114, "Discounts, Premiums and Bonuses on Debt Obligations," August 3, 1973. This interpretation bulletin was cancelled by Special Release on June 10, 1994 "since it does not take into account the complex changes in financing transactions which have occurred in recent years." According to this release, the department "will continue to consider requests for opinions on specific provisions in the law relating to the taxation of discounts, premiums and bonuses on debt obligations, and will provide advance income tax rulings on specific proposed transactions."

F. Royalties

According to *Black's Law Dictionary*, 6th ed., "royalty" is defined as:

> Compensation for the use of property, usually copyrighted material or natural resources, expressed as a percentage of receipts from using the property or as an account per unit produced ... a share of product or profit reserved by owner for permitting another to use the property.

In the *Income Tax Act*, these payments are specifically included in a taxpayer's income from a business or property under paragraph 12(1)(g) which applies to "any amount received ... in the year" that was "dependent on the use of or production from property" (other than instalments of the sale price of agricultural land), "whether or not that amount was an installment of a sale price of the property." As a result, as Kerwin J observed in *M.N.R. v. Wain-Town Gas & Oil Co.*, [1952] S.C.J. No. 30, [1952] C.T.C. 147, 52 D.T.C. 1138 (S.C.C.), notwithstanding that an amount might otherwise be characterized as a capital receipt, it may nonetheless be taxable as income from a business or property under paragraph 12(1)(g).

Paragraph 12(1)(g) is derived from paragraph 3(1)(f) of the *Income War Tax Act*, which was enacted in 1934 shortly after the Privy Council decision in *M.N.R. v. Spooner*, [1933] A.C. 684, [1928-34] C.T.C. 184 (P.C.). In *Spooner*, the taxpayer had sold land to an oil company in exchange for $5,000 cash, $25,000 worth of shares, and 10 per cent of any oil produced from the land (a royalty that was actually paid in cash according to the market value of oil production). Although the Exchequer Court, [1928-34] C.T.C. 171, held that this royalty was income from property that the taxpayer had reserved in the sale agreement, the Supreme Court of Canada, [1928-34] C.T.C. 178, reversed on the grounds that the taxpayer had sold the property and received the royalty as a capital receipt from the sale. This decision was upheld by the Judicial Committee of the Privy Council.

According to paragraph 3(1)(f) of the *Income War Tax Act*, income was deemed to include:

> rents, royalties, annuities or other like periodical receipts which depend upon the production or use of any real or personal property, notwithstanding that the same are payable on account of the use or sale of any such property.

With the introduction of the *Income Tax Act* in 1948, this paragraph was renumbered 6(j) and amended to include in computing the income of a taxpayer for a taxation year:

> amounts received by the taxpayer in the year that were dependent upon the use of or production from property, whether or not they were instalments of the sale price of the property, but instalments of the sale price of agricultural land shall not be included by virtue of this paragraph.

Although paragraph 6(j) was later renumbered 6(1)(j) and became paragraph 12(1)(g) in 1972, the provision has remained essentially unchanged since 1948.

In applying paragraph 12(1)(g) and its predecessors, courts have grappled with two aspects of the statutory language: (1) the manner in which amounts received by the taxpayer must "depend on" the use of or production of property; and (2) the relationship between "amounts received in the year" and the use of or production from property. The following cases and commentaries examine each of these issues.

1. Dependence on the Use of or Production from Property

The leading case on the manner in which amounts received by the taxpayer must depend on the use or production from property within the meaning of paragraph 12(1)(g) is *M.N.R. v. Morrison*, [1966] C.T.C. 558, 66 D.T.C. 5368 (Ex. Ct.).

M.N.R. v. Morrison
[1966] C.T.C. 558, 66 D.T.C. 5368 (Ex. Ct.)

THURLOW J: ... The issue in the appeal is whether amounts of $2,500 and $14,500 received by the respondent in 1959 and 1960 respectively were taxable as income under Section 6(1)(j) of the *Income Tax Act*, RSC 1952, c. 148 [now paragraph 12(1)(g)].

...

The respondent is a bachelor who has earned his living by fishing, woodcutting, raising cattle, growing vegetables and working on the highways. He lives, as did his father and grandfather before him, on a 200-acre property at New Harris in Victoria County, Nova Scotia near an arm of the sea known as Big Bras d'Or.

...

In 1957 Provincial Government engineers, with [the respondent's] permission, made test drillings on his property for the purpose of ascertaining whether the rock under the surface was suitable for use in the construction of a causeway and bridge crossing of the Big Bras d'Or to be built near his property. The rock was found to be suitable and in the following year the respondent was approached by a representative of Municipal Spraying and Contracting Company Limited (hereinafter referred to as Municipal) with a proposal for the purchase of rock from his property for the purposes of its contract for the construction of the causeway. In an agreement in writing between the respondent and Municipal dated November 27, 1958, it is stated that the respondent, in consideration of one dollar and of the covenants and agreements thereinafter set forth:

> hereby sells to the purchaser all the rock required by the purchaser from the Vendor's land hereinafter described, for the purpose of the purchaser's contract for the construction of causeway in the Big Bras d'Or Lake, in the vicinity of Seal Island in the said lake.

After describing the respondent's property, the eastern side of which adjoined Sutherland property a portion of which had been or was later acquired by Municipal, the agreement went on to say:

> The Purchaser, its agents, servants and workmen, at all times within the period of two years from the date hereof shall have full and free liberty of entry through, over and upon the said land, for the purpose of digging, taking, removing, and carrying away the said rock, and with full right and liberty to bring, place, keep and maintain trucks, animals, carts and other vehicles, plant and equipment in and upon the said land, and to erect buildings necessary for the Purchaser's operations on the said land: and with full right and liberty to construct a road or roads from the said Sutherland land across the Vendor's said land, and if required, to construct a road or roads from the present highway to, through and over the said Vendor's land, for the operations of the purchaser.
>
> The price to be paid by the Purchaser to the Vendor for the said rock, and including the rights and privileges herein set forth, shall be Two and one-half cents (2½¢) per ton of 2,000 pounds, in accordance with Government scale, to be paid monthly within fifteen days after the end of each month; which the Purchaser hereby covenants and agrees to pay to the Vendor.
>
> The Purchaser agrees that it will remove all the rock required by the Purchaser, within two (2) years from the date hereof, and will also remove within the said period all the plant and equipment of the Purchaser, from the said land.
>
> The Purchaser shall take measures to protect, as far as possible, the Vendor's buildings on the said land from damage from the Purchaser's operations, and the Purchaser will repair any damage to such buildings so caused.

The construction of the causeway was begun in 1959 and was completed some 18 months later in 1960. In the process a large quantity of rock was removed from the respondent's property and from the adjoining Sutherland property, was weighed at a scale set up on government property nearby and was dumped into the water to form the causeway but no record of the portion thereof taken from the respondent's property was kept either by Municipal or by the respondent and none of the monthly payments required by the contract was made. Instead an advance of $2,500 was paid to the respondent in 1959, which is the amount in question in respect of the re-assessment for that year, and in 1960 when the work had been completed instead of calculating the quantity taken and paying for the same on the basis provided by the agreement the purchaser offered and the respondent accepted a further lump sum of $14,500 which is the amount in question in respect of the re-assessment for 1960.

Just what this sum of $14,500 was intended to cover is not clearly stated but I would infer that it, along with the $2,500 advanced earlier, was in settlement of whatever claims the respondent had against Municipal whether real or fancied and whether for rock or for damage to his house or both or for loss occasioned by the removal of the rock.

...

The Minister's case for including the amounts of $2,500 and $14,500 in computing the respondent's income is based entirely on Section 6(1)(j) of the Act. Two alternative grounds for supporting the assessment, that is to say, (1) that the amounts constituted income from a business and (2) that the amounts were received as rent for the use of land, were raised in the notice of appeal but these were abandoned in the course of the argument. The correct approach to the present problem, therefore, as I see it, is that the amounts in question may be subjected to tax if, but only if, they fall clearly within the provisions of Section 6(1)(j). If they do fall clearly within the scope of that provision they are of course taxable as income whether they are of an income nature or not. The provision itself makes it clear that such may be the result in some cases. But apart from the effect of Section 6(1)(j) and excepting the case of a sale in the course of a business there appears to me to be nothing about receipts from the sale of rock forming part of a taxpayer's property that would serve to characterize them as being of an income, as opposed to a capital, nature.

...

Section 6(1)(j) of the present statute is broader [than former paragraph 3(1)(f) of the *Income War Tax Act*] in some respects and possibly narrower in others. It applies to amounts of money and is not confined to such amounts when representing rents, royalties or annuities or periodical receipts of a like nature to rents, royalties or annuities. The only qualifications required of such an amount appear to be that it be one that (1) has been "received" by the taxpayer in the year and (2) was "dependent upon use of or production from property." While the words "rents, royalties, annuities or other like payments of a periodical nature," which by themselves suggest variability according to the extent of time or use or production, are not present in the section the qualification imposed by the words "dependent upon use of or production from property" in my opinion has the effect of limiting the "amounts" referred to amounts which vary with and are in that sense "dependent" in some way upon the extent of use of or production from property whether according to time or quantity or some other method of measurement.

Turning to the contract between the respondent and Municipal it seems doubtful to me that the payments contemplated by it, if made, would, as argued on behalf of the Minister, have fallen within the definition of Section 6(1)(j) as amounts that were dependent upon "use of the respondent's property, and particularly so if, as submitted, such payments were to be viewed as amounts received that were dependent upon "use of the land by the respondent himself. ... On the other hand if the payments had been made I should have had no difficulty in reaching the conclusion that the payments were amounts that were "dependent" upon the number of tons of rock removed from and thus, in my opinion, "upon production from" the respondent's property within the meaning of Section 6(1)(j).

The amounts contemplated by the contract were, however, never received. Instead what was received in 1959 consisted of an advance of $2,500, which was not related to the quantity of rock taken, and what was received in 1960 was a final payment of $14,500 making a total sum of $17,000, which was received by way of an accord and satisfaction of the respondent's rights to be paid both the sums payable for rock under the contract and the damage occasioned to his house. The sums so received were thus, as I view the case, not amounts that were "dependent upon use of or production from" the respondent's property but were amounts paid in settlement of unascertained claims which the respondent had against Municipal for rock removed and for damages to his house.

Even if, contrary to the view I take of the evidence, the amounts of $2,500 and $14,500 are regarded as having been paid and received entirely in respect of the rock taken it is in my opinion clear that they were not dependent upon the quantity taken, since this never was ascertained and as I have already indicated dependence upon the extent or quantity of production or use and the application thereto of some rate or standard appears to me to be an essential qualification of amounts which fall to be taxed under Section 6(1)(j). Moreover, while it might be possible to infer that from the point of view of the contractor the large, though unknown, quantity of rock obtained from the respondent's property was the prime consideration in reaching the figure of $17,000, from the point of view of the respondent I would infer that at that stage the chief elements in respect of which a satisfactory settlement was required were the losses of the accommodations which the property formerly afforded ... rather than the unknown quantity of rock in respect of which he was entitled to payment at the rate of 2½ cents per ton but had no way of knowing what that would amount to or whether it would be more or less than the losses which the removal of the rock entailed.

It might of course be said correctly of the amounts that they were received partly, if not entirely, "in lieu of payment of, or in satisfaction of" amounts that were dependent upon production from the respondent's property but while the expression "in lieu of payment of, or in satisfaction of appears in other clauses of Section 6(1), e.g., in 6(1)(a) and (b) [now paragraphs 56(1)(a) and 12(1)(c)], neither that nor any similar expression is found in Section 6(1)(j) and to read the clause as if such wording were present would in my opinion be unwarranted.

In my opinion therefore the amounts here in question did not fall clearly within the provisions of Section 6(1)(j) and as no other basis for taxing them has been advanced they cannot properly be included in the computation of the respondent's income. ...

Appeal dismissed.

NOTES AND QUESTIONS

1.   In what ways, according to the Exchequer Court in *Morrison*, must amounts received by a taxpayer depend on the use of or production from property in order to fall within the rule in then paragraph 6(1)(j) (now paragraph 12(1)(g))? On what basis did the Exchequer Court conclude that the payments received by the taxpayer did not depend on the use of or production from property? Would the payments have been caught by then paragraph 6(1)(j) if they had been based on the stated price of 2½ cents per ton?

2.   In *Morrison*, Thurlow J rejected the possibility that the payments might be taxable under then paragraph 6(1)(j) on the basis that they were received "in lieu of payment of, or in satisfaction of" amounts that were dependent on the use of or production from the taxpayer's property. See also *Randle v. M.N.R.* (1965), 39 Tax ABC 46 (T.A.B.), where then paragraph 6(1)(j) was held not to apply to amounts received by the taxpayer from the Department of Highways, which had negotiated for the removal of clay subsoil for road construction, on the basis (at para. 10) that the amount actually received bore no relation to the quantity of clay removed but was received as "compensation for the loss of a portion of a capital asset and for restoring it to its former state of productivity, nothing else." Are these conclusions consistent with the rule on the taxation of damage payments set out in the *London & Thames Haven Oil Wharves, Ltd. v. Attwooll*, [1967] 2 All E.R. 124 (C.A.), and adopted by the Federal Court of Appeal in *Canada v. Manley*, [1985] F.C.J. No. 140, [1985] 1 C.T.C. 186, 85 D.T.C. 5150 (F.C.A.)?

3.   In *M.N.R. v. Lamon*, [1963] C.T.C. 68, 63 D.T.C. 1039 (Ex. Ct.), then paragraph 6(1)(j) was held to apply where the taxpayer sold the rights to remove all the gravel from two parcels of land at prices based on the volume of gravel removed. Likewise, in *Chen v. M.N.R.*, [1984] C.T.C. 2451, 84 D.T.C. 1415 (T.C.C.), where the taxpayer contracted with a logging firm for the sale of timber at a price based on the number of cubic feet of timber logged, paragraph 12(1)(g) was applied to payments received pursuant to this contract.

In *Mouat v. M.N.R.* (1958), 20 Tax ABC 424 (T.A.B.), however, where the taxpayer sold all the merchantable timber on a parcel of land for an amount calculated according to the quantity of timber cut and payable in four instalments over two and a half months, the board refused to apply then paragraph 6(j) on the grounds (at para. 21) that:

> the legislator intended to tax, not *the fructus naturales* [the natural produce of the soil] but the *fructus industriales* [the fruits of industry] such as a crop, minerals, timber, which produce a periodical return as a result of yearly exploitation.

Similarly, in *Hoffman v. M.N.R.* (1965), 39 Tax ABC 220, 65 D.T.C. 617 (T.A.B.), where the taxpayer sold all the merchantable timber on his farm for an amount based on the type and quantity cut and payable in three instalments over two months, the board (at para. 11) rejected the application of then paragraph 6(1)(j) because "that statutory phrase, unquestionably, denotes a continuing activity — one that goes on from year to year." These interpretations have been reaffirmed more recently in cases involving the sale of all of the marketable timber on a taxpayer's property in order to clear the land for other uses. See *Mel-Bar Ranches Ltd. v. M.N.R.*, [1987] T.C.J. No. 651, [1987] 2 C.T.C. 2146, 87 D.T.C. 467 (T.C.C.), aff'd [1989] F.C.J. No. 219, [1989] 1 C.T.C. 360, 89 D.T.C. 5189 (F.C.T.D.); *Cromwell v. M.N.R.*, [1990] T.C.J. No. 201, [1990] 1 C.T.C. 2438, 90 D.T.C. 1335 (T.C.C.); and *Larsen v. Canada*, [1999] F.C.J. No. 1665, [2000] 1 C.T.C. 209, 99 D.T.C. 5757 (F.C.A.).

Do the words of paragraph 12(1)(g) require that the amounts received derive from "a continuing activity"? Should an activity that continues for a few months be distinguished from an activity that continues for a few years?

4.   In *Lackie v. Canada*, [1978] C.T.C. 157, 78 D.T.C. 6128 (F.C.T.D.), aff'd [1979] F.C.J. No. 700, [1979] C.T.C. 389 (F.C.A.), where the taxpayer received payments unrelated to the volume of gravel removed from his property, Dubé J applied paragraph 12(1)(g) and former paragraph 6(1)(j) on the basis that the amounts received depended on an exclusive right to remove gravel for a period of five years. See also *Mouat v. M.N.R.* (1963), 32 Tax ABC 269, 63 D.T.C. 548 (T.A.B.), where the Tax Appeal Board referred to the statutory definition of "property" as including "a right of any kind whatsoever" to conclude (at para. 20) that minimum annual payments received under an agreement granting an exclusive right to enter upon a taxpayer's property and remove shale for a period of 20 years depended on the use of "*property* ... as defined in section 139(1)(ag) [now subsection 248(1)] of the said Act." For other cases holding that the conferral of a right to enter upon land and remove gravel constitutes a "use of land" within the meaning of paragraph 12(1)(g) and its predecessors, see *Pallett v. M.N.R.* (1959), 22 Tax ABC 40, 59 D.T.C. 230 (T.A.B.); and *M.N.R. v. Lamon*, [1963] C.T.C. 68, 63 D.T.C. 1039 (Ex. Ct.).

5.   Several decisions have applied paragraph 12(1)(g) and its predecessors to payments for the use of intangible property rights such as franchises, licences, patents, and copyrights. See, for example, *M.N.R. v. Wain-Town Gas and Oil Co.*, [1952] S.C.J. No. 30, [1952] C.T.C. 147, 52 D.T.C. 1138 (S.C.C.); *Hould v. M.N.R.* (1965), 39 Tax ABC 233 (T.A.B.); *Gingras v. M.N.R.*, [1963] C.T.C. 194, 63 D.T.C. 1142 (Ex. Ct.); *Ladouceur v. M.N.R.*, [1968] Tax ABC 1057 (T.A.B.); and *Dunrobin Motors Ltd. v. M.N.R.*, [1979] C.T.C. 2717, 79 D.T.C. 619 (T.R.B.).

2. Amounts Received in the Year that Depend on Use or Production

Paragraph 12(1)(g) requires taxpayers to include in computing their income from a business or property not only "any amount ... that was dependent on the use of or production from property," but "any amount *received ... in the year* that was dependent on the use of or production from property" (emphasis added). This language dates from 1948, before which time paragraph 3(1)(f) of the *Income War Tax Act* applied to "rents, royalties, annuities or other like periodical receipts which depend upon the production or use of any real or personal property." The impact of the 1948 amendment on the kinds of receipts included under this provision was considered in *Huffman v. M.N.R.* (1954), 11 Tax ABC 167 (T.A.B.).

Huffman v. M.N.R.

(1954), 11 Tax ABC 167 (T.A.B.)

[In 1945 the taxpayer sold five placer mining leases for $25,000. The purchase price was payable in instalments of 25 percent of the value of the gold removed until the full price was paid, plus interest of 2½ percent per annum. The appellant received $2,000 in 1946, $2,000 in 1947, $2,500 in 1948, and $3,000 in 1949. The Minister, relying on paragraphs 3(1)(f) of the *Income War Tax Act* and paragraph 6(j) of the 1948 *Income Tax Act* (now paragraph 12(1)(g)), added these amounts in computing the appellant's income.]

W.S. FISHER: ... In considering the provisions of Section 3(1)(f)... , it must be noted that the amount received must first be in the nature of a rent, royalty, annuity, or other like periodical receipt before it is included in the definition of income and, in addition, any one of those four types of receipt must depend upon the production or use of any real or personal property. The clause then goes on to provide that, even although the amounts received are payable to the recipient on account of the sale of any such property, nevertheless, if they come within the description of any of the four types of receipt, they are to be treated as income.

After examining the agreement in question in this appeal and the receipts, it is my opinion that the amounts received in the years 1946, 1947 and 1948 cannot be brought within the provisions of Section 3(1)(f) as being rents, royalties, annuities, or other like periodical receipts, even if the payments in question here did depend upon the production or use of some real or personal property. In my view, the ... [taxpayer] ... here has sold his property for a sum which is to be paid in instalments, and when that is the case, the payments to him are not income. ...

In the instant case, the principal sum of $25,000 is to bear interest at 2½% and is to be paid by instalments. It is true that the instalments are not fixed as to a definite amount in respect of any particular calendar year subsequent to the date of the agreement, nor are the dates of payment of the instalments fixed by reference to a calendar date within the said respective calendar years. The dates of payment fixed by the agreement depend on the dates when the purchaser shall have gained certain gold from the placer mining claims, and the amounts of the payments are fixed, also, in relation to the amounts of gold gained by the purchaser at a particular time. In my opinion, however, this is merely a method of determining the amount of the instalment payment to be made in each year, including interest on the principal sum, and this method of calculation of the instalment payments, in the circumstances, does not bring the amounts within the provisions of Section 3(1)(f) of the *Income War Tax Act*.

...

With respect to the appeal against the 1949 assessment, the wording of Section 6(j) of the *Income War Tax Act* is quite different from that of Section 3(1)(f) of the *Income War Tax Act*, and reads as follows:

> 6. Without restricting the generality of section 3, there shall be included in computing the income of a taxpayer for a taxation year:
>
>> (j) amounts received by the taxpayer in the year that were dependent upon use of or production from property whether or not they were instalments of the sale price of the property, but instalments of the sale price of agricultural land shall not be included by virtue of this paragraph.

My interpretation of the wording of this section is that it is much wider than that of the former provision in Section 3(1)(f) of the *Income War Tax Act* in that it provides that any amount received in the year that was dependent upon the use of or production from property is to be included as income. Such amounts do not have to be rents, royalties, annuities, or other like periodical payments. This refinement or restriction in the *Income War Tax Act* has been completely wiped out by the use of the unqualified words "amounts received." In my opinion, Section 6(j) is wide enough to include as taxable income capital receipts such as those here in question where they are dependent upon the use of or production from property, and therefore wide enough to include the full amount of the payment received in the year 1949, even although a portion of it was received on account of the purchase price of $25,000.

In these circumstances, the appellant's appeal against his 1949 income tax assessment is dismissed.

Appeals allowed in part.

NOTES AND QUESTIONS

1.   Why did the board in *Huffman* conclude that the instalment payments were caught by then paragraph 6(j) of the 1948 *Income Tax Act*, but not by paragraph 3(1)(f) of the *Income War Tax Act*? Do you agree with the board's interpretation as to the effect of the 1948 amendment? Why or why not?

2.   In some cases, property is sold for a fixed price, with this amount payable by instalments based on the produce or profits of the property at various intervals. In *Huffman*, for example, the placer mining leases were sold for

$25,000, payable in instalments of 25 per cent of the value of the gold removed until the full price was paid, plus interest. Likewise, in *McDougall Estate v. M.N.R.*, [1950] C.T.C. 169, 50 D.T.C. 775 (Ex. Ct.), the taxpayer sold certain lands for $60,000, payable by instalments equal to 10 per cent of the value of oil and gas produced each month.

In these circumstances, provided that the fixed price is not unreasonably high, it is arguable that the *timing* of payments depends on the use of or production from property but that the aggregate *amount* does not. However, it is also arguable that paragraph 12(1)(g) should apply on the basis that the amount received by the taxpayer *in the year* depends on the use of or production from property. This appears to have been the conclusion in *Huffman*, based on the amended wording of the 1948 Act. The Exchequer Court arrived at the same result in *Ross v. M.N.R.*, [1950] C.T.C. 169, 50 D.T.C. 775 (Ex. Ct.), based on the earlier language of the *Income War Tax Act*.

3. In other cases, property may be sold for a specified percentage of output or revenue, subject to an agreement that payments will not fall below a minimum stipulated amount over a specific period of time. In *Porta-Test Systems Ltd. v. Canada*, [1980] C.T.C. 71, 80 D.T.C. 6046 (F.C.T.D.), for example, the taxpayer sold the exclusive rights to manufacture, use, and sell certain inventions within a specific area in exchange for a 15 per cent royalty with a minimum payment of $150,000 over the first three years. Similarly, in *Brosseau v. M.N.R.*, [1986] T.C.J. No. 355, [1986] 1 C.T.C. 2558, 86 D.T.C. 1412 (T.C.C.), the taxpayer, upon leaving an accounting firm of which he had been a partner, sold his former partners a list of his clients in exchange for 20 per cent of the revenue earned by the partners from these clients over five years, with a minimum payment of $100,000.

Where the royalty is equal to or less than the minimum payment over a given period of time, the aggregate amount of the payments will not depend on the use of or production from property. Nonetheless, while any "top-up payment" required to reach the minimum amount will not depend on the use of or production from property, amounts received as royalty payments in each previous year will depend on the use of or production of property. In *Porta-Test*, therefore, where the taxpayer was paid $75,040 in order to satisfy the minimum amount, the court held that this payment was a capital receipt that was not caught by paragraph 12(1)(g).

Where the royalty payments exceed the minimum stipulated amount over a specific period of time, both the total amount of all payments and the timing of each specific payment depend on the use of or production of property. Nonetheless, in *Brosseau*, where the taxpayer received royalty payments of roughly $125,000, the court held that the first $100,000 fell "outside the parameter of paragraph 12(1)(g)," which applied only to the payments in excess of the stipulated minimum.

The CRA's administrative position in these situations is set out in paragraph 5(d) of *Interpretation Bulletin* IT-462, "Payments Based on Production or Use," October 27, 1980:

> Where the agreement for sale provides for payments based on production or use but also stipulates that there is to be a minimum sale price (or minimum annual payments), the payments based on production or use are brought into income under paragraph 12(1)(g) regardless of whether they are less than, or in excess of, the minimum. However any other payments which must be made to meet the minimum requirements are treated as proceeds of disposition.

Is this position consistent with the decision in *Brosseau*? Is *Brosseau* consistent with the decisions in *Porta-Test* and *Huffman*?

4.   Property may also be sold for a fixed price, whether or not payable by instalment, with a proviso that this price will be adjusted downward if certain expectations regarding revenue or profitability are not met. In *Pacific Pine Co. Ltd. v. M.N.R.* (1961), 26 Tax ABC 41, 61 D.T.C. 95 (T.A.B.), for example, the taxpayer, which had acquired a timber licence in order to use the logs in its sawmill operations, sold the licence to a logging contractor for a fixed amount, payable in 16 quarterly instalments, subject to an agreement that the purchase price would be reduced if the quantity of timber was less than the taxpayer had represented.

Where the price of the property is reduced pursuant to such an agreement, it is arguable that the amount ultimately received depends on the use of or production from property. In *Pacific Pine*, however, the Tax Appeal Board held that the agreement to reduce the price if less than a specified amount of timber was logged from the property was not sufficient to bring the payments within the scope of then paragraph 6(1)(j). This conclusion is reflected in paragraph 9 of IT-462:

> Paragraph 12(1)(g) does not apply where the sale price of property is originally set at a maximum which is equivalent to the fair market value of the property at the time of the sale and which can be subsequently decreased if certain conditions related to production or use are not met in the future. In such a situation the proceeds will be on account of capital and if there is a reasonable expectation at the time of disposition of the property that the conditions will be met, then the disposition is treated in the ordinary manner, and the original maximum amount is considered to be the sale price of the property. If, subsequently, the conditions are not met then an appropriate adjustment will be made in the year in which the amount of the reduction in the sale price is known with certainty and will not vary in the future. Whether there is a reasonable expectation that conditions will be met is a question that is determined on the facts of the particular situation.

5.   Where shares of a corporation are sold under an "earnout agreement" whereby the sale price is determined wholly or partly by reference to future earnings generated by the corporation, the amount received by the vendor appears to depend on the use of or production from the property. Nonetheless, in *Interpretation Bulletin* IT-426R, "Shares Subject to an Earnout Agreement," September 28, 2004, the CRA indicates that it will not apply paragraph 12(1)(g) to these kinds of sales, provided that the following conditions are met:

(a) The vendor and purchaser are dealing with each other at arm's length.

(b) The gain or loss on the sale of shares of the capital stock of a corporation is clearly of a capital nature.

(c) It is reasonable to assume that the earnout feature relates to underlying goodwill the value of which cannot reasonably be expected to be agreed upon by the vendor and purchaser at the date of the sale.

(d) The earnout feature in the sale agreement must end no later than 5 years after the date of the end of the taxation year of the corporation (whose shares are sold) in which the shares are sold. For the purposes of this condition, the CRA considers that an earnout feature in a sale agreement ends at the time the last contingent amount may become payable pursuant to the sale agreement.

(e) The vendor submits, with his return of income for the year in which the shares were disposed of, a copy of the sale agreement. He also submits with that return a letter requesting the application of the cost recovery method to the sale, and an undertaking to follow the procedure of reporting the gain or loss on the sale under the cost recovery method as outlined below.

(f) The vendor is a person resident in Canada for the purpose of the Act.

Under these circumstances, the tax treatment of any gain or loss on the sale may be determined according to the "cost recovery method" according to which any gain is not taxable until the proceeds of the sale exceed the cost of the shares to the vendor, and no loss is recognized until the maximum amount receivable for the shares is irrevocably established to be less than the vendor's cost. Where the shares are sold at a gain, this treatment may be advantageous for the vendor, since taxation is deferred until the aggregate proceeds for the shares exceed their cost.

G. Rent

According to *Black's Law Dictionary*, 6th ed., "rent" is broadly defined as "the compensation or fee paid, usually periodically, for the use of any rental property, land, buildings, equipment, etc." So defined, rent appears to be a payment "dependent on the use of ... property" within the meaning of paragraph 12(1)(g).[26] However, Canadian courts and revenue authorities tend to refer not to this provision but to the more general language in subsection 9(1) and paragraph 3(a) to include rent in computing a taxpayer's income from a business or property. For this purpose, rent is characterized as income from a business or income from property depending on the extent to which the income is derived from the active participation of the taxpayer.[27]

---

[26] Indeed, the predecessor to para. 12(1)(g), para. 3(1)(f) of the *Income War Tax Act* explicitly referred to "rents ... or other like periodical receipts which depend upon the ... use of any real or personal property."

[27] See, for example, *Wertman v. M.N.R.*, [1964] C.T.C. 252, 64 D.T.C. 5158 (Ex. Ct.): *Walsh v. M.N.R.*, [1965] C.T.C. 478 (Ex. Ct); *Hollinger v. M.N.R.*, [1972] C.T.C. 592, 73 D.T.C. 5003 (F.C.T.D.), aff'd [1974] C.T.C. 693, 74 D.T.C. 6604 (F.C.A.); and *Canada v. Canadian-American Loan and Investment Corporation Ltd.*, [1974] F.C.J. No. 36, [1974] C.T.C. 101, 74 D.T.C. 6104 (F.C.T.D.). These cases are discussed in Chapter 8.

The distinction between rental income and payments on account of capital has arisen in a number of cases in which payments are made under a "lease option agreement" pursuant to which the lessee can apply some part or all of the payments to the purchase price of the property if the lessee chooses to purchase the property. One of the earliest of these cases is *Pitman v. M.N.R.* (1950), 2 Tax ABC 176 (T.A.B.).

Pitman v. M.N.R
(1950), 2 Tax ABC 176 (T.A.B.)

W.S. FISHER: Mr. Pitman appealed against income tax assessments for the years 1946 and 1947 in which were included as part of his income amounts of $148.75 in 1946 and $1,478.71 in 1947, which he considered and treated as repayments of principal under a lease option agreement between himself and one Peter Danyliw, and accordingly not subject to income tax.

The lease option agreement was dated 30th September, 1936, between the said Arthur Pitman as lessor and the said Peter Danyliw, of Lumsden, Sask., as lessee, and witnessed that, in consideration of the rents, covenants, promises, agreements and undertakings reserved and contained in the lease on the part of the lessee, the appellant as lessor demised and leased certain farm land therein described to the lessee for and during the term of five years, to be computed from the 31st day of October, 1936, the lessee yielding and paying therefor yearly during the said term a yearly rental of one-third share or portion of the whole crop of the different kinds and qualities of grain which shall be grown on the said land in each year of the said term without any deduction, defalcation, or abatement whatsoever; and yielding and paying therefor during the said term unto the lessor the sum of five dollars ($5) for each acre of the said land thereinafter agreed to be summerfallowed in that year that shall not be so summerfallowed. The lessee covenanted further that he would pay the said rental at the times specified in the agreement for payment thereof, and that he would at all times during the said term keep, and at the end thereof yield up, the said land in good and tenantable repair, accidents and damage to buildings from fire, storm and tempest, and reasonable wear and tear excepted.

After further covenants on the part of the lessee regarding the area to be summerfallowed each year, and other provisions which it is not necessary to cite for the purpose of this appeal, the parties agreed that an undivided one-third interest in all crops sown thereunder should vest in and become the property of the lessor forthwith upon the same being sown; and that as soon as the crop, or any portion thereof, had been severed from the land, the current year's rental should forthwith become due and payable.

The lease then provided for the option-to-purchase clause, as follows:

WHEN THE LESSOR'S SHARE of the crop as aforesaid, when converted into money, shall have amounted to the sum of $3,100.00, together with the taxes charged against the said lands and insurance premiums paid from and after January 1st, 1937, together with interest at 5 per cent on the sum of $6,100.00, and the amount of taxes and insurance premiums so paid, the lessor hereby grants unto the lessee the option to purchase the said land on the terms as set out in the attached agreement for sale and the lessor agrees to execute the said agreement if and when the lessee signifies his intention of taking advantage of the said option.

ALL THE COVENANTS of this lease on the part of the lessee having been done and performed, the lessor agrees should the amount of money in the immediately preceding paragraph not have been paid within the period of this lease, he will extend the term hereof for such further period or periods as may be sufficient for such purpose.

Until payment of the amount as required to entitle the lessee to take up the option to purchase the lessee shall have no interest in the said land other than as tenant.

The option to purchase the lease was not exercised within the five-year period ending on 31st October, 1941, and, according to the evidence given at the hearing, a renewal of the lease was given by the lessor, although a copy of this renewal was not filed with the Board. ...

In any event, according to the evidence and the exhibits filed, it is shown that, by 1st December, 1947, the lessee had paid to the appellant herein sums of money as rental and repayments of taxes on the farm property lease (which taxes had previously been paid by the appellant) sufficient to total $3,100 representing the value of the crop and, in addition, the taxes, and interest at 5% on the sum of $6,100 as referred to in the option clause of the lease, so that the lessee, if the option was still in existence, was entitled to exercise his option. In fact, a notice dated 7th January, 1948, signed by Peter Danyliw and addressed to the appellant, to the effect that the lessee Danyliw desired to exercise the option, was completed and forwarded as of that latter date ... .

It was the appellant's contention that, the option having been exercised, all payments made by the lessee to the lessor from the commencement of the lessee must be considered to have been payments on account of the capital purchase price of the lands in question and, accordingly, not taxable in his hands — excepting, of course, amounts which would represent the 5% interest on $6,100 as provided for in the computation specified in the option clause. The appellant contended, therefore, that in respect of the years 1946 and 1947 he should not be taxed on the amounts received by him from Mr. Danyliw in respect of the property with the exception of the 5% interest calculation on any balance of principal owing in those years. His appeal is based on the contention that, although the monies had been paid by the lessee under the terms of a lease in those years, their character changed immediately upon the option having been exercised, and that it would be most unjust that the appellant should have to pay tax on the $3,100 received by him in respect of the property over the years 1937 to 1947, both inclusive, even although those amounts, when received, were paid to him as rental and the purchaser under the lease option clause would be required to pay, subsequent to the exercise of the option, only some $3,000 on account of principal in respect of the land so purchased by reason of the exercise of the said option.

No cases were cited to the Board by counsel for the appellant in support of this contention that the exercise of the option had a retroactive effect insofar as the payments originally received as rental should now be considered to have been received as payments on account of capital.

...

Certain cases referred to in the 6th Edition of "Redman's Law of Landlord and Tenant" at p. 25 do seem, at first sight, to support the appellant's contention that, by the exercise of an option under an agreement for lease, the relationship of landlord and tenant might be changed — from the inception of the lease — to that of vendor and purchaser. It is there stated that:

> If the option be exercised after the landlord's death, it relates back to the date of the lease, operating as a conversion from that date, so as to make the purchase-money form part of the landlord's personal estate — *Lawes v. Bennett* (1785), 1 Cox 167; *Townley v. Bedwell* (1908), 14 Ves. 591; *Collingwood v. Row* (1857), 26 LJ. Ch. 649; — even though it is only exercisable after the landlord's death (*Re Isaacs*, [1894] 3 Ch. 506) — and revoking a specific devise in favour of the person to whom he may have left it by will (*Weeding v. Weeding* (1861), 1 J & H 424) or defeating the title of his heir-at-law when he has died intestate (*Re Isaacs*, supra).

A reading of the above cases indicates that the courts were more concerned in the circumstances therein with doing equity between the parties, and the decisions, in my opinion, are applicable only with respect to the conflicting interests of heirs-at-law of a deceased landlord, and are not applicable in so far as the relationship between the landlord and the tenant themselves is concerned. *Halsbury's Laws of England* in paragraph 72 of the article on "Landlord and Tenant" states that:

> The exercise of the option does not, so far as the lessor and lessee are concerned, date back to the commencement of the lease, so that, in the event of the premises being destroyed by fire, the lessee is not entitled to the insurance money in respect of the premises due under a policy taken out by the lessor. (*Edwards v. West* (1878), 7 Ch. D 858.)

In *S.S. Kresge Company Limited v. Granowitz*, [1948] 1 DLR 298 at p. 300; [1947] OWN 679 at 681; Barlow J, stated:

> The giving of a notice exercising the option to purchase terminated the tenancy, and the relationship of the parties was changed from that of landlord and tenant to that of vendor and purchaser: *Doe D. Gray v. Stanion* (1836), 1 M & W 695, 150 ER 614.

Accordingly I am of the opinion that the appellant cannot succeed in respect of his claim that the amounts received by him from Mr. Danyliw in 1946 and 1947 and which were paid to him as rental, should be treated as capital payments by reason of the exercise of the option by Mr. Danyliw in January, 1948. These payments were received by the appellant as rental and were income in his hands in those years and are taxable accordingly.

Appeal dismissed.

NOTES AND QUESTIONS

1.   On what basis did the taxpayer in *Pitman* argue that the amounts received in 1946 and 1947 were on account of capital rather than income? Why did the board reject this argument?

2. In *Katzman v. M.N.R.* (1963), 34 Tax ABC 213 (T.A.B.), the taxpayer, as lessor, entered into a five-year lease with an option pursuant to which the lessee could apply $150 of each monthly rental payment of $600 against the balance due on closing. Allowing the taxpayer's appeal against an assessment that included the full amount of the monthly payments in computing the taxpayer's income for his 1959 and 1960 taxation years, the board held (at para. 4) that the option operated as a "suspensive condition for the purpose of ascertaining whether the $150 a month is rent or a capital payment." On this basis, it concluded (at paras. 5 and 6), the "true substance of the monthly payments of $150" was "on account of the price of the property and not for its use."

3. In *J.F. Burns Sand & Gravel Ltd. v. M.N.R.*, [1968] Tax ABC 218, 68 D.T.C. 226 (T.A.B.), the taxpayer, which sold five acres of land under a lease option agreement whereby the lessee could apply 90 per cent of the annual payments of $1,600 against a purchase price of $16,000, sought in computing its income for its 1965 taxation year to deduct 90 per cent of the payments that it had included in computing its income for each of the previous three taxation years. Rejecting the taxpayer's argument (at para. 10), based on *Katzman*, that "an option to purchase in a lease 'can be regarded as a suspensive condition' in deciding whether a portion or the whole of a rental payment is rent or a capital payment," the board preferred the reasoning in *Pitman v. M.N.R.* (1950), 2 Tax ABC 176 (T.A.B.). According to J.O. Weldon (at para. 10):

> The *ratio decidendi* of that case appears to be that, since it has long been settled law that an option contained in a lease is collateral to, independent of and incidental to the relationship of landlord and tenant, the exercise of an option contained in a lease does not have a retroactive effect insofar as the payments originally received as rental payments are concerned so as to change the character of such rental payments to payments on account of capital. That impresses me as being sound law and should be regarded, at least in my view, as being the established rule in the ordinary lease-option arrangements.

For a similar result, see *Ages v. M.N.R.*, [1971] Tax ABC 86 (T.A.B.).

4. In *Foster v. M.N.R.* (1951), 4 Tax ABC 235 (T.A.B.), the taxpayer entered into an agreement titled "Lease and Option to Purchase" according to which the lessee was required to make certain monthly payments for four years, after which the taxpayer promised to transfer the property to the lessee without further payment. Allowing the taxpayer's appeal from an assessment that had included the monthly payments in the taxpayer's income, the Tax Appeal Board characterized the transaction as a sale on an instalment basis, not a true lease. According to the board (at para. 5):

> There is no doubt that many of the usual clauses found in a lease are to be found in the present instrument, but there is no doubt either that some of the provisions found in the instrument in question are entirely inconsistent with the true nature and character of a lease, but are definitely clauses found in a deed of sale. For instance, why would [the lessee], if he was to be only a lessee, have to pay all taxes and assessments levied against the land after the first day of July, 1944, which taxes are ordinarily paid by the landlord and not by the lessee; why would he have taken obligations to insure against damages by fire the buildings and the land and assigned the policy to the appellant as a security for the payment of sums payable

under that agreement; why would he have been given the privilege of paying at any time any sum in addition to the sums payable under the agreement; and why would he have the right to obtain from the appellant a transfer of the lands described in the agreement upon compliance with the terms of said agreement? These clauses of the agreement whereby [the lessee] was assuming obligations or was given certain rights ordinarily assumed by or given to a purchaser only indicate, to say the least, that the instrument in question is wrongly named when named a "lease and option to purchase."

Is this an example of commercial substance over form or legal substance over nomenclature? Which factors do you think were most important in characterizing the transaction as a sale rather than a lease? Which factors do you think should be regarded as most significant?

5.   Since rent is generally deductible in computing a lessee's income while payments on account of the purchase price of capital property are not, lessees will typically favour the characterization of lease option payments as rent. The characterization of lease option payments from the lessee's perspective is considered later in this chapter.

6.   For the CRA's prior views on the characterization of lease option payments, see *Interpretation Bulletin* IT-233R, "Lease-Option Agreements; Sale-Leaseback Agreements," February 11, 1983 (cancelled by Income Tax Technical News 21, June 14, 2001). According to paragraph 3 of this bulletin, a transaction is considered to be a sale rather than a lease where:

(a)   the lessee automatically acquires title to the property after payment of a specified amount in the form of rentals,

(b)   the lessee is required to buy the property from the lessor during or at the termination of the lease or is required to guarantee that the lessor will receive the full option price from the lessee or a third party (except where such guarantee is given only in respect of excessive wear and tear inflicted by the lessee),

(c)   the lessee has the right during or at the expiration of the lease to acquire the property at a price which at the inception of the lease is substantially less than the probable fair market value of the property at the time or times of permitted acquisition by the lessee. An option to purchase of this nature might arise where it is exercisable within a period which is materially less than the useful life of the property with the rental payments in that period amounting to a substantial portion of the fair market value of the property at the date of inception of the lease, or

(d)   the lessee has the right during or at the expiration of the lease to acquire the property at a price or under terms or conditions which at the inception of the lease is/are such that no reasonable person would fail to exercise the said option.

According to paragraph 4:

The option to purchase may be part of or separate from the lease agreement itself or may be a verbal agreement or undertaking. Where, although not specified in the agreement, it becomes apparent, for example, as a result of previous similar transactions undertaken by the parties involved, that it is the intention that the lessee be allowed to acquire the property at the termination of the lease for an amount that is less than its probable fair market value, the transaction is considered to be a sale.

7. A number of cases have considered the characterization of amounts paid to a lessor on the cancellation of a lease by a lessee. See, for example, *M.N.R. v. Farb Inv. Ltd.*, [1959] C.T.C. 113, 59 D.T.C. 1058 (Ex. Ct.); *Hill and Hill v. M.N.R.* (1960), 24 Tax ABC 382 (T.A.B.); *Grader v. M.N.R.*, [1962] C.T.C. 128 (Ex. Ct.); *MacDonald v. M.N.R.* (1963), 34 Tax ABC 317 (T.A.B.); *Industrial Leaseholds Ltd. v. M.N.R.* (1966), 40 Tax ABC 350, 66 D.T.C. 226 (T.A.B.); *Monart Corp. v. M.N.R.*, [1967] C.T.C. 263, 67 D.T.C. 5181 (Ex. Ct.); and *Berlin Motels Ltd. v. M.N.R.*, [1973] C.T.C. 2158, 73 D.T.C. 137 (T.R.B.). In each of these cases, lease cancellation payments were characterized as income from a business or property.

8. For the CRA's views on lease cancellation payments, see IT-359R2. According to paragraph 4: "Amounts a landlord receives from a tenant for cancelling a lease or sublease always constitute income to the landlord."

9. In *Front & Simcoe Ltd. v. M.N.R.*, [1960] C.T.C. 123, 60 D.T.C. 1081 (Ex. Ct.), the taxpayer, which, as landlord, had leased certain property in the city of Toronto for a five-year period under an agreement whereby the tenant could extend the term for two subsequent five-year periods, accepted $75,000 as consideration for releasing the tenant from its obligations under the original lease and entering into a new lease providing for a lower monthly payment. Rejecting the taxpayer's argument that the payment was on account of capital, Cameron J characterized the payment as prepaid rent.

10. For the CRA's views on the characterization of payments received by a landlord in exchange for granting or extending a lease or sublease, see IT-359R2:

    1. A premium or other amount received by a landlord or tenant, as the case may be, as consideration for granting or extending a lease or sublease, permitting a sublease, or cancelling a lease or sublease is business income to the recipient if renting property forms part or all of a business being carried on.

    2. Where a landlord, not in the business of renting property, receives a premium for granting or extending a lease and the rent charged is less than fair market value, the premium is included in income to the extent that it can reasonably be regarded as being in the nature of rent (e.g., "key money").

    3. Occasionally, a lease may provide for the payment of a "premium" but its terms indicate that what is called a premium is really a prepayment of rent. Such an amount is, in fact, additional rent and is income of the recipient.

H. Inducements, Reimbursements, and Refunds

Until May 22, 1985, the tax treatment of amounts received either as an inducement to undertake a particular course of action (for example, enter into a contract) or as a reimbursement for an expense already incurred by the recipient was governed by general principles according to which the character of the receipt depended on the character of the expense to which the payment related.

In *French Shoes Ltd. v. M.N.R.*, [1986] F.C.J. No. 380, [1986] 2 C.T.C. 132, 86 D.T.C. 6359 (F.C.T.D.), for example, a lease inducement payment that was "to be applied against inventory" was characterized as business income. Likewise, in *Ikea Ltd. v. Canada*, [1998] S.C.J. No. 15, [1998] 2 C.T.C. 61, 98 D.T.C. 6092 (S.C.C.), a lump-sum tenant inducement payment received by the taxpayer on entering into a long-term lease was characterized as business income on the grounds that the effect of the payment, which the taxpayer was free to spend as it saw fit, was to reimburse deductible lease payments.[28]

In *Woodward Stores Ltd. v. M.N.R.*, [1991] F.C.J. No. 30, [1991] 1 C.T.C. 233, 91 D.T.C. 5090 (F.C.T.D.), however, "fixturing allowances" received by the taxpayer upon agreeing to enter into long-term leases and open stores in two shopping centres were characterized as capital receipts on the grounds that they compensated for the capital cost of converting the retail spaces into premises suitable to the taxpayer's business.[29] Similarly, in *St. John Shipbuilding & Dry Dock Co. v. M.N.R.*, [1944] C.T.C. 106, 2 D.T.C. 663 (Ex. Ct.), a federal government subsidy to finance the construction of a dry dock was characterized as a capital receipt on the basis that it related to the acquisition of a capital asset, notwithstanding that the subsidy was payable for 35 years in annual amounts of $247,500.

Where a taxpayer receives a payment in respect of a capital asset, one might reasonably expect the amount of the payment to reduce the capital cost of the asset for the purpose of subsequent tax calculations (for example, computing capital cost allowances on depreciable property or computing a gain or loss on the disposition of the property). In a series of cases, however, Canadian courts held that reimbursements received by taxpayers on account of various capital expenses were neither taxable when received nor deductible in computing the cost to the recipient of property in respect of which the payment was provided.[30] In response to these decisions, the *Income Tax Act* was amended, effective for amounts received after May 22, 1985, by the enactment of paragraph 12(1)(x).

According to this provision, in computing their income from a business or property, taxpayers must include, subject to various exceptions:

> any particular amount (other than a prescribed amount) received by the taxpayer in the year, in the course of earning income from a business or property, from

---

[28] See also *Nesbitt Thomson Inc. v. M.N.R.*, [1991] T.C.J. No. 514, [1991] 2 C.T.C. 2352, 91 D.T.C. 1113 (T.C.C.); and *IBM Canada Ltd. v. M.N.R.*, [1993] T.C.J. No. 582, [1993] 2 C.T.C. 2860, 93 D.T.C. 1266 (T.C.C.).

[29] See also *Suzy Creamcheese (Canada) Ltd. v. M.N.R.*, [1992] F.C.J. No. 223, [1992] 1 C.T.C. 242, 92 D.T.C. 6291 (F.C.T.D.).

[30] See *Canada v. Canadian Pacific Limited*, [1977] C.T.C. 606, 77 D.T.C. 5383 (F.C.A.); *Canada v. Consumers' Gas Co.*, [1984] C.T.C. 83, 84 D.T.C. 6058 (F.C.A.); and *Canada v. Consumers' Gas Co.*, [1986] F.C.J. No. 838, [1987] 1 C.T.C. 79, 87 D.T.C. 5008 (F.C.A.).

(i)   a person or partnership (in this paragraph referred to as the "payer") who pays the particular amount

    (A)   in the course of earning income from a business or property,

    (B)   in order to achieve a benefit or advantage for the payer or for persons with whom the payer does not deal at arm's length, or

    (C)   in circumstances where it is reasonable to conclude that the payer would not have paid the amount but for the receipt by the payer of amounts from a payer, government, municipality or public authority described in this subparagraph or in subparagraph (ii), or

(ii)   a government, municipality or other public authority,

where the particular amount can reasonably be considered to have been received

(iii)   as an inducement, whether as a grant, subsidy, forgivable loan, deduction from tax, allowance or any other form of inducement, or

(iv)   as a refund, reimbursement, contribution or allowance or as assistance, whether as a grant, subsidy, forgivable loan, deduction from tax, allowance or any other form of assistance, in respect of

    (A)   an amount included in, or deducted as, the cost of property, or

    (B)   an outlay or expense.

Subparagraphs 12(1)(x)(v) and (vi) exclude from this rule amounts that are otherwise taken into account for tax purposes (typically by a reduction in the cost of property in respect of which the amount is received). Subparagraph 12(1)(x)(vii) allows taxpayers to exclude amounts otherwise included under paragraph 12(1)(x) where they make an election under subsection 12(2.2), 13(7.4), or 53(2.1) to account for the payment by reducing the amount of an outlay or expense, the capital cost of depreciable property, or the cost of non-depreciable capital property in respect of which the payment is obtained.[31] Subparagraph 12(1)(x)(viii) excludes any amount to the extent that it may "reasonably be considered to be a payment made in respect of the acquisition by the payer or the public authority of an interest in the taxpayer or the taxpayer's

---

[31]   Where the taxpayer elects to reduce the amount of an outlay or expense under subs. 12(2.2), the election will reduce the amount that the taxpayer might otherwise be able to deduct in respect of the outlay or expense. Where the taxpayer elects to reduce the capital cost of depreciable property under subs. 13(7.4), the election will reduce the amount that the taxpayer might otherwise be able to deduct in respect of capital cost allowance under para. 20(1)(a). Where the taxpayer elects to reduce the cost of non-depreciable capital property under subs. 53(2.1) and para. 53(2)(s), the election will increase any taxable capital gain or decrease any allowable capital loss on the subsequent disposition of the property.

business or property." For our purposes, there is no need to examine the meaning of a "prescribed amount," which is set out in regulation 7300.

Although the Act does not define the words "inducement," "refund," "reimbursement," "contribution," "allowance," or "assistance," subparagraph 12(1)(x)(iii) provides as examples of inducements and assistance grants, subsidies, forgivable loans, deductions from tax, and allowances. More generally, the word "inducement" may be defined as "what induces; attraction that leads one on," "assistance" as "aid," "contribution" as "help," "allowance" as "money paid to cover special expenses," and "refund" and "reimbursement" as "repayment" (per *The Concise Oxford Dictionary*, 7th ed.). Combined with the requirements of subparagraphs 12(1)(x)(i) and (ii) that the payment be received from a "government, municipality or other public authority" or from a person "who pays the particular amount... in the course of earning income from a business [or] property or in order to achieve a benefit or advantage," the provision applies primarily to various kinds of incentives including general or unrestricted payments to induce certain behaviour and more specific payments designed to defray or offset specific expenses incurred by the recipient. Nonetheless, the use of the word "refund" in subparagraph 12(1)(x)(iv), which was added in 1996 retroactive to amounts received after 1990,[32] suggests that the scope of the provision is somewhat wider, including also repayments of amounts such as sales taxes that may have been "included in, or deducted as, the cost of property" sold by the taxpayer in previous taxation years. The leading case on the interpretation of paragraph 12(1)(x) is *Iron Ore Co. of Canada Ltd. v. Canada*, [2001] F.C.J. No. 1092, [2001] 3 C.T.C. 281, 2001 D.T.C. 5411 (F.C.A.).

Iron Ore Co. of Canada Ltd. v. Canada
[2001] F.C.J. No. 1092, [2001] 3 C.T.C. 281, 2001 D.T.C. 5411 (F.C.A.)

LÉTOURNEAU JA (Richard CJ and Décary JA, concurring): This appeal raises the issue of whether Judge Lamarre-Proulx of the Tax Court of Canada erred in her interpretation of subparagraph 12(1)(x)(iv) of the *Income Tax Act* (Act) when she concluded that the refund received by the appellant for sales tax paid in error was a refund within the meaning of that subparagraph.

...

---

[32] This amendment reversed the decision in *Canada Safeway Ltd. v. Canada*, [1996] T.C.J. No. 1272, [1997] 1 C.T.C. 2194, 97 D.T.C. 187 (T.C.C.), aff'd [1997] F.C.J. No. 1632, [1998] 1 C.T.C. 120, (1997) 98 D.T.C. 6060 (F.C.A.), which held that the word "reimbursement" in subpara. 12(1)(x)(iv) as it then read did not include federal sales taxes erroneously paid and deducted in computing the taxpayer's income in the years 1985 to 1989 and refunded to the taxpayer in 1993.

Facts and Procedure

The case proceeded before the Tax Court of Canada upon an agreed statement of facts. It is fair to say that there was a bitter and long dispute between the appellant and Revenue Quebec which ended on October 19, 1993 by an out-of-court settlement, ratified on October 25, 1993 by the Quebec Court of Appeal. It is at this point that parts of the agreed facts become relevant for the present appeal. I am content to reproduce paragraphs 14 to 19 of the agreed statement of facts which read as follows:

> 14. Pursuant to the terms and conditions of the settlement, Appellant received during the 1994 calendar year five (5) monthly payments totalling $4,416,666.66 from Revenue Quebec.
>
> 15. This amount consisted of the following:
>
>   (a) refunded provincial sales tax paid in error by Appellant during the period extending from 1 April 1978 to 31 May 1985 in the amount of $950,000.00; and
>
>   (b) accrued interest in the amount of $3,466,666.66.
>
> 16. For its 31 December 1994 taxation year, Appellant included the accrued interest in the amount of $3,466,666.66 in computing its income.
>
> 17. By way of reassessment dated 20 August 1996, the Minister reassessed Appellant's 1994 taxation year by, *inter alia*, adding to Appellant's income the refunded provincial sales tax in the amount of $950,000.00. ...
>
> 19. The Minister relies on subparagraph 12(1)(x)(iv) of the *Income Tax Act* ... to include the refunded provincial sales tax in the computation of Appellant's income for its 1994 taxation year, while Appellant maintains that such amount should not come within the meaning of the said paragraph. ...

Basically, the argument of the appellant is that not every refund qualifies under subparagraph 12(1)(x)(iv) and, therefore, needs to be included in a taxpayer's income. The appellant avers that it has to be a refund which is in the nature or in the form of an assistance to the taxpayer. The appellant comes to this understanding of the scope and purpose of that subparagraph by way of a reading which calls into play the *noscitur a sociis* rule referred to in English as the "associated words rule." According to this rule, the word "refund," very much like the words "reimbursement," "contribution" and "allowance" in subparagraph 12(1)(x)(iv), would be qualified by a requirement of government assistance to the taxpayer because the appellant sees the notions of "assistance" and "any other form of assistance" appearing in the provision as a common feature applicable to all the terms appearing in the subparagraph. With respect, I think the appellant misreads subparagraph 12(1)(x)(iv) and that the *noscitur a sociis* rule has no application for the following reasons.

A proper reading of the impugned subparagraph, whether using the English or the French text, reveals that Parliament has identified three kinds of amounts under subparagraphs 12(1)(x)(iii) and (iv):

(a)   those that are received as an inducement;

(b)   those that are received as a refund, reimbursement, contribution or allowance, and

(c)   those that are received as assistance, whether as a grant, subsidy, forgivable loan, deduction from tax, allowance or any other form of assistance.

Both a textual and a contextual analysis leads to such a finding.

First, the use of the word "as" after the word "or" in the expression "or as assistance" found in ... subparagraph (iv) brings to an end the preceding enumeration of words and, therefore, the association of words. It introduces another category of amounts of a nature different from those which precede. In French, there is no ambiguity either. The subparagraph refers to amounts received "à titre de remboursement" or "à titre d'aide." Then, with respect to this second category, the text goes on to identify the form that this assistance or "aide" can take. The French words "sous forme de prime, de subvention, de prêt à remboursement conditionnel, de déduction de l'impôt ou d'indemnité ou sous toute autre forme" qualifies only a payment made "à titre d'aide".

Second, the words "allowance" and "indemnité" appear twice in the subparagraph, the first time as an amount akin to a refund, a reimbursement or a contribution and the second time as a form of assistance. The application of the *noscitur a sociis* rule would render meaningless and redundant the first use of the words "allowance" and "indemnité" in the subparagraph since, under the rule, an allowance or "indemnité" would have to be in the form of an assistance and, yet, assistance in the form of an allowance or "indemnité" would already be covered by the second use of the word.

Third, the words "any other form of assistance' found in the subparagraph clearly refer to an amount received "as assistance" and broaden the form of assistance enumerated in the subparagraph. In French, the words "sous toute autre forme" parallel the English text. They refer to an amount received "à titre d'aide, sous forme de prime, de subvention, etc." The French text is consistent with the English text and discards the application of the *noscitur a sociis* rule.

Fourth, this notion of assistance received from a government, whether as a grant, subsidy, forgivable loan, deduction from tax, allowance or any other form of assistance is a notion used in other provisions of the Act, independently of the concepts of refund or reimbursement. It is obviously a category of amounts existing on its own: see for example subsections 13(7.1), 13(7.2), paragraph 37(1)(d), subparagraphs 53(2)(k)(i), 66.1(6)(b)(ix), 66.2(5)(b)(xi), 66.4(5)(b)(viii) as well as the definition of "government assistance" in subsection 127(9) of the Act.

To sum up, the appellant's refund falls, in my view, into the second category of amounts which have to be included in a taxpayer's income in the taxation year in which it is received. Therefore, the learned Tax Court Judge made no error when she concluded that subparagraph 12(1)(x)(iv) applied in the circumstances of the present case. ...

Appeal dismissed.

NOTES AND QUESTIONS

1.   On what basis did the taxpayer in *Iron Ore of Canada Ltd.* argue that the refund of provincial sales taxes that it received in its 1994 taxation year was not subject to inclusion under paragraph 12(1)(x) in computing its income from its business? Why did the court reject this argument? Do you agree with the court's conclusion? Why or why not?

2.   For another decision holding that a refund of sales taxes must be included in computing the recipient's income under paragraph 12(1)(x), see *Bois Aisé de Roberval Inc. v. Canada*, [1998] T.C.J. No. 1089, [1999] 4 C.T.C. 2161, 99 D.T.C. 380 (T.C.C.). According to the court (at para. 33):

> Parliament added the word "refund" to put an end to [the] debate as to whether a refund of taxes paid in error constituted an "reimbursement" within the meaning of subparagraph 12(1)(x)(iv) of the Act. It is now clear that such amounts are covered by this provision.

3.   In *Westcoast Energy Inc. v. M.N.R.*, [1991] F.C.J. No. 333, [1991] 1 C.T.C. 471, 91 D.T.C. 5334 (F.C.T.D.), aff'd [1992] F.C.J. No. 225, [1992] 1 C.T.C. 261, 92 D.T.C. 6253 (F.C.A.), the Minister sought to apply paragraph 12(1)(x) to a payment received by the taxpayer in settlement of an action for negligence and breach of contract in the construction of a pipeline, on the basis that the payment was a "reimbursement" within the meaning of subparagraph 12(1)(x)(iv). Referring to dictionary definitions of the words "reimburse" and "reimbursement" and Parliament's intent in enacting paragraph 12(1)(x) to reverse a number of judicial decisions holding that certain payments need not be included in computing the recipient's income nor deducted from the cost to the recipient of property in respect of which the payment was made, the Court concluded that paragraph 12(1)(x) does not include damage awards. According to Denault J (at paras. 42-49):

> The word reimbursement in the ordinary sense, as defined in the Shorter Oxford English Dictionary, is as follows:
>
> Reimburse — to repay or make up to (a person) the sum expended: to repay, recompense (a person).
>
> Reimbursement — the act of reimbursing, repayment.
>
> *Black's Law Dictionary* also defines the word reimburse as: "to pay back, to make restoration, to repay that expended; to indemnify or make whole."

Examples of the word reimbursement in different legal relationships were cited. First, there is a compulsory payment. This is a situation where a person has been compelled by law to pay and pays money for which another is ultimately liable. The payer can make a claim for reimbursement from the latter individual. Second, there is the example of where a person makes repairs or improvements to property which he believes to be his own. He can claim a reimbursement against the owner of the property. Third, there is the situation where a person, such as a guarantor, discharges more than his proportionate part of a debt. He can take action for reimbursement against the co-guarantors. Finally, in the law of agency, a principal is liable to reimburse his agent for reasonable expenses incurred in an emergency, even if the agent exceeded his actual authority.

Based on the above analysis, I accept these examples as an accurate reflection of what the word means and the meaning that Parliament intended to capture by enacting paragraph 12(1)(x). ...

In this case, the damage award was a one time payment and it was not made at the behest of the party paying the sum. Rather, it was paid in order to release the defendant IPSCO from liability for its breach of contract.

In all of the examples of the word reimbursement, there exists a flow of benefits between the respective parties. The person who benefits is under a legal obligation to pay back the amount expended. In this case, the plaintiff expended a sum of money to replace a defective pipeline emanating from a breach of contract. There is no other reason why the plaintiff would have expended the money. Nor was there any legal obligation on the part of IPSCO to pay back the money expended. The legal obligation that IPSCO incurred arose when the action was settled out of court. I have found as a fact that the court settlement represented a damage award. There is no other reason why the defendant IPSCO would have given the plaintiff $20,250,000.

The strongest factor supporting the defendant's position is that the failed pipeline was replaced and the replacement factor weighed heavily in the plaintiff's lawsuit against IPSCO. The plaintiff paid over $6 million for the original pipeline, while it received more than $20 million in the settlement. Moreover, the plaintiff first built the new pipeline and then sought recovery for damages from IPSCO. These factors, in the defendant's submission constitute a reimbursement for the moneys expended. However, this course of action does not nullify the reason for which the plaintiff sought damages, which was for the negligence and breach of contract of IPSCO.

It is my conclusion that reimbursement does not include damage awards. It is not based on the evidence to say that the plaintiff received a reimbursement as defined in paragraph 12(1)(x). The ordinary and legal meaning of the word does not contemplate an award of damages. In this case, the plaintiff did not rebuild its pipeline at the request of IPSCO, to be reimbursed later by the cost as occurred in the *Consumers' Gas* case. Nor is it analogous to a landlord/tenant situation whereby the tenant will make a leasehold improvement which benefits him during his tenancy and which amounts to a leasehold improvement, thereby benefitting the landlord. In short, there was no flow of benefits between the parties.

I find that it was not Parliament's intention to include the jurisprudence on damage awards which I have outlined within paragraph 12(1)(x). ... The paragraph represented a legislative change and it was intended to remedy a particular gap in the law of taxation, which is exemplified in the *Consumers' Gas* case. There is no evidence that Parliament intended the paragraph to include the jurisprudence on damage awards under the word reimbursement.

Because the parties had narrowed the issues to the question whether the damage payment constituted a "reimbursement" within the meaning of subparagraph 12(1)(x)(iv), the court did not consider whether the damage payment should be otherwise included in computing the taxpayer's business income or deducted in calculating the cost of the pipeline.

4.   In *Tioxide Canada Inc. v. Canada*, [1993] T.C.J. No. 355, [1994] 1 C.T.C. 2569, 93 D.T.C. 1492 (T.C.C.), the taxpayer, which obtained tax credits from the Quebec government in connection with various research and development activities, objected to the inclusion of the value of these credits under paragraph 12(1)(x) on the grounds that it had not "received" an "amount" as required by the preamble to the provision, and that the credits, if received, were received not "from ... a government, municipality or public authority" as required by subparagraph 12(1)(x)(ii) but by virtue of the Quebec *Taxation Act.* With respect to the first argument, the court reasoned (at para. 19):

> The word "amount" is defined in subsection 248(1) of the *Income Tax Act* as meaning "money, rights or things expressed in terms of the amount of money or the value in terms of money of the right or thing." It follows that for each of the years in question the appellant benefited from a tax credit, and thus from a right conferred upon it by the aforementioned provincial legislation. As a consequence of this right, the appellant benefited from an "amount" within the meaning of subsection 248(1). If it can be said that the appellant benefited from an amount, it is also correct to say that the appellant "received" an amount in the years in question within the meaning of paragraph 12(1)(x), since during those years it benefited from the provincial tax credit in question which, in concrete terms, resulted in a reduction in the amount of income tax it had to pay to the Quebec Minister of Revenue. The appellant accordingly received a real monetary benefit during the years in question.

With respect to the taxpayer's second argument, the court referred to the definition of "government assistance" in subsection 127(9) (which applies for the purpose of the investment tax credits in subsections 127(5) and (6)), according to which:

> "government assistance" means assistance from a government, municipality or other public authority whether as a grant, subsidy, forgivable loan, deduction from tax, investment allowance or as any other form of assistance other than [the investment tax credits] under subsection 127(5) or 127(6),

and quoted the following passage from *Canada v. British Columbia Forest Products Ltd.*, [1986] 1 C.T.C. 1, 85 D.T.C. 5577 (F.C.A.), which involved the interpretation of similar language in subsection 13(7.1) (at para. 6):

> Parliament has expressly contemplated that a taxpayer may "receive" assistance from a government in the form of a "deduction from tax." Whatever violence that does to one's semantic scrupulosity, the Court is obliged to give effect to Parliament's clear and unambiguous intention if it can sensibly do so. The concept may be thought awkward, but it is clearly expressed. In Parliament's prescription, one can "receive" assistance when one takes advantage of an opportunity afforded to deduct from tax an amount that one would otherwise be required to pay.

5.   In *Everett's Truck Stop Ltd. v. Canada*, [1993] T.C.J. No. 343, [1993] 2 C.T.C. 2658, 93 D.T.C. 965 (T.C.C.), the taxpayer, which operated a service

station in Saskatchewan, entered into an agreement in 1987 to purchase petroleum products from Polar Oils Ltd. ("Polar") for five years at an enhanced price and to seek management assistance from Polar after Polar agreed to assume a debt that the taxpayer had incurred in order to expand its business. Rejecting the taxpayer's argument that the assumed debt was really a loan to the tax payer, the court characterized it as an "inducement" that must be included in computing the taxpayer's income for its 1987 taxation year under paragraph 12(1)(x) of the Act.

6. In *Supermarché Dubuc & Frère Inc. v. Canada*, [1993] T.C.J. No. 655, [1994] 1 C.T.C. 2215 (T.C.C.), the taxpayer, which operated a grocery business in Quebec, received $75,000 from Metro-Richelieu Inc. ("Metro") in 1988 in consideration for entering into a 20-year "purchasing loyalty agreement" whereby it agreed to acquire a minimum percentage of its supplies from Metro throughout this period, to grant Metro a right of first refusal on the sale of its business during this period, and to require any other purchaser of its business to undertake to observe the rights conferred on Metro for the remainder of the 20-year period. Characterizing the payment as an "inducement" within the meaning of subparagraph 12(1)(x)(iii) of the Act, the court nonetheless held that the amount was exempt under subparagraph 12(1)(x)(viii) as "a payment made in respect of the acquisition by the payer ... of an interest in the taxpayer or the taxpayer's business or property." According to Garon JTCC (at paras. 28, 32-35, and 37):

> I am inclined to believe that the acquisition of a right "in [its] property" mentioned in subparagraph 12(1)(x)(viii) implies the acquisition of real rights over the property of a taxpayer. First, the use of the preposition "in" seems to me unsuited to describing personal rights or the rights of a creditor in legal terminology. Second, in the context of a right pertaining to property the preposition "in" designates a close relationship to that property, a *jus in rea*. ...
>
> In the instant case it is clear that Métro did not acquire any real rights over the appellant's property. It only acquired a personal right or right to claim. A first refusal option in particular is clearly not a right.
>
> As to the part of subparagraph 12(1)(x)(viii) which mentions the acquisition "of an interest in the taxpayer," it seems to me that this part of the subparagraph cannot apply if the taxpayer is an individual. This kind of language can only be understood if it applies to a joint stock company. In civil law terminology, at least, there can be no question of a right "in" a natural person. In the case of an artificial person the subparagraph can be applied to a person owning shares in a joint stock company. If in the instant case Métro had by this agreement acquired the appellant's shares it could be said that Métro had acquired rights in the artificial person represented by the appellant. However, that is not the situation in the facts at issue here.
>
> It remains to consider the part of subparagraph 12(1)(x)(viii) which refers to the acquisition "of an interest in [the] business." The concept of a business involves the activities themselves, the operations associated with the management and functioning of an economic entity. Further, subsection 248(1) describes the word business in part as follows:

"business" includes a profession, calling, trade, manufacture or undertaking of any kind.

...

This word "business" does not include the property used in operating the business: see e.g., subsection 22(1) of the Act.

In view of the nature of the concept of a business, I think it is beyond question that Métro acquired rights relating to the activities of the appellant connected with the operation of its business. The appellant's hands were tied in several respects. In operating its business it was required, under the very wording of the agreement, to obtain suppliers from Métro and from suppliers designated by Métro to a very large degree. In other words, the appellant had to meet certain quotas or "fidelity ratios" in purchasing the classes of product covered by the agreement. This undertaking by the appellant is accompanied specifically by a penalty clause in Métro's favour. The appellant also could not cease doing business by selling its operation without first giving Métro the right to purchase the latter within the stated deadline. It was also provided that in the event Métro did not exercise its right to purchase the latter the appellant, as we have seen, had to make sure that the purchaser of the business signed a contract to be a member of Métro and observe the rights conferred on Métro by the aforesaid agreement for the unexpired portion of the term of that agreement. Métro thus held rights regarding how the appellant would cease operating its business in the circumstances I have just indicated. ...

I therefore consider that the amount of $75,000 received by the appellant can reasonably be considered a payment made for the acquisition by Métro of rights in the appellant's business within the meaning of subparagraph 12(1)(x)(viii) of the Act.

In *Supermarché Ste-Croix Inc. v. Canada*, [1994] T.C.J. No. 1157, [1996] 1 C.T.C. 2506, 95 D.T.C. 871 (T.C.C.), aff'd [1997] F.C.J. No. 268, 97 D.T.C. 5211 (F.C.A.), however, the court rejected the taxpayer's argument that a similar agreement between another company and Métro entailed an acquisition by Métro of "an interest in ... the taxpayer's business" such that an inducement payment received by the taxpayer in its 1988 taxation year was exempt under subparagraph 12(1)(x)(viii). According to Lamarre-Proulx JTCC (at paras. 42 and 44):

I am of the same view as our Court in *Supermarché Dubuc* as regards the meaning of the acquisition of an interest in the taxpayer and in his property. This means the acquisition of shares or of an interest in respect of shares or the acquisition of a share in a corporation and the acquisition of a real interest in respect of its property. Where my opinion differs is with respect to the meaning to be given to the words "acquisition of an interest in his business." ... I do not believe that the appellant's contractual obligations granted in consideration of the inducement payment can, in current legal language, be understood as interests acquired in a business. An interest in a business might possibly be a sharing in the business's profits or possibly a management interest. I will not attempt to give a descriptive and exhaustive definition of what an interest in a business would be, but I can say with certainty what it is not. It cannot be contractual obligations to which the recipient of the inducement payment has agreed. ...

An inducement payment is always granted in consideration of an obligation on the recipient's part. ... To interpret it otherwise would erase all effect of paragraph 12(1)(x) of the Act. This is what counsel for the respondent contended and I agree with that view.

Do you agree with this conclusion? Why or why not?

7.   In *CCLC Technologies Inc. v. The Queen*, [1996] F.C.J. No. 1226, [1996] 3 C.T.C. 246, 96 D.T.C. 6527 (F.C.A.), the taxpayer obtained financial and technological support from the government of Alberta for the development of a technological process allowing for the simultaneous upgrading of coal and heavy oil and liquefaction of coal. The support was obtained under a "Coal Research Agreement" pursuant to which the province obtained an equity interest in the project technology, which it was required to sell to the taxpayer if the project proved successful for an amount equal to the amount of its financial support plus interest costs. When the project did not prove to have commercial value, however, the province was left with its equity interest.

Rejecting the taxpayer's arguments that the support was not "assistance" within the meaning of subparagraph 12(1)(x)(iv), or, if it was assistance, that the support was exempt under subparagraph 12(1)(x)(viii), the Federal Court of Appeal held that the financial and technological support was subject to subparagraph 12(1)(x)(iv) on the basis that the agreement did not "establish an ordinary business arrangement between the parties" and could not "reasonably be considered to be a payment made in respect of the acquisition by the payer or the public authority of an interest in the taxpayer or the taxpayer's business or property." With respect to the taxpayer's first argument that the support was not "assistance" within the meaning of subparagraph 12(1)(x)(iv), the court concluded (at paras. 4-5):

> For its part the Government of Alberta undertook to provide technology and to pay money to the respondent. While in the short term the government obtained an equity interest, if the project were to prove commercially successful the Government would be obliged to sell its interest to the respondent, the price being simply the return of its money contribution plus its interest costs in having made that contribution. If the project did not prove to have commercial value, as in fact it did not during the period in question, the Government was entitled to nothing except an equity interest in a technology demonstrated not to have present commercial value. We find it impossible to characterize this as an ordinary business arrangement. Whatever public policy merits the agreement may have had from the standpoint of Alberta, it does not amount to an arrangement that a business would enter into to advance its business interests. A business which invested money in ventures on the basis that it could not receive any net profit if the venture succeeded, and would gain an equity interest only if the venture proved uncommercial, would not long survive.

> In the language of the *Income Tax Act*, subparagraph 12(1)(x)(iv), and the definition of "government assistance" in subsection 127(9), the government payments under the Coal Research Agreement became, in the circumstances of non-commercialization of the technology, a grant, subsidy, a forgivable loan, or similar form of assistance.

With respect to the taxpayer's second argument, the court noted that subparagraph 12(1)(x)(viii) "includes as income any payment which 'may not reasonably be considered to be made in respect of the acquisition' of the taxpayer's property." In light of the provisions of the agreement, it concluded (at para. 7):

> We are unable reasonably to consider the provisions of the Coal Research Agreement to be designed for the purpose of the Government of Alberta acquiring an interest in the respondent's property. As noted above, had the project been successful the Government of

Alberta would have acquired no lasting property rights in a going concern: in that circumstance it would instead have been obliged to sell its interest for merely a return of its money contributions plus interest. In the event of there being no commercial success, which was the case during the period in question, the Government was left with a half-share in a technology without demonstrated commercial value. In these circumstances its contribution if anything became of the nature of a grant, subsidy, or forgivable loan and cannot reasonably be considered a payment for the purpose of acquisition of property.

Do you agree with these conclusions? Why or why not?

8.   For the CRA's views on paragraph 12(1)(x), see IT-273R2.

IV. DEDUCTIONS

As the Supreme Court of Canada has affirmed on several occasions, the concept of profit in subsection 9(1) is a net concept that implicitly authorizes the deduction of legitimate expenses incurred in order to earn income from the business or property to which the expenses relate.[33]

In applying this provision, Canadian courts have long affirmed that the first test to determine the deductibility of a particular outlay or expense is "whether it was made or incurred by the taxpayer in accordance with ordinary principles of commercial trading or well accepted principles of business practice."[34]

In addition to this "business practices" test, the *Income Tax Act* contains a multitude of general and specific provisions governing the deductibility of different amounts in computing a taxpayer's income from a business or property. Among the more general provisions, for example, the income-producing purpose test in paragraph 18(1)(a) disallows the deduction of any outlay or expense "except to the extent that it was made or incurred by the taxpayer for the purpose of gaining or producing income from the business or property."[35] Paragraph 18(1)(h), however, prohibits the deduction of "personal or living expenses of the taxpayer, other than travel expenses incurred by the taxpayer while away from home in the course of carrying on the taxpayer's business." Section 67, moreover, which applies to the computation of income from all sources, limits the amount that may be deducted in respect of an

---

[33] See, *e.g.*, *Symes v. Canada*, [1993] S.C.J. No. 131, [1994] 1 C.T.C. 40, 94 D.T.C. 6001 (S.C.C.), *per* Iacobucci J. (at para. 40) (explaining that the concept of profit in subsection 9(1) is "inherently a net concept which presupposes business expense deductions); and *65302 British Columbia Ltd. v. Canada*, [1999] S.C.J. No. 69, [2000] 1 C.T.C. 57, 99 D.T.C. 5799 (S.C.C.), *per* Iacobucci J. (at para. 39) (affirming that "the concept of profit found in s. 9(1) authorizes the deduction of business expenses, as profit is inherently a net concept").

[34] *The Royal Trust Company v. M.N.R.*, [1957] Ex. C.J. No. 7, [1957] C.T.C. 32, 57 D.T.C. 1055 (Ex. Ct.) (at para. 27). The Supreme Court of Canada affirmed this test in *Symes v. Canada*, [1993] S.C.J. No. 131, [1994] 1 C.T.C. 40, 94 D.T.C. 6001 (S.C.C.).

[35] This provision is derived from para. 6(a) of the *Income War Tax Act*, which prohibited any deduction in respect of "disbursements or expenses not wholly, exclusively and necessarily laid out or expended for the purpose of earning the income."

otherwise deductible outlay or expense to an amount that is "reasonable in the circumstances."

In addition to these general provisions, other rules apply to the deduction of specific kinds of expenses, limiting or disallowing these expenses in some cases and authorizing their deduction in others. Subsection 18(12), for example, limits the amount that may be deducted in respect of a home office, while subparagraph 18(1)(l)(ii) prohibits the deduction of membership fees or dues in "any club the main purpose of which is to provide dining, recreational or sporting facilities for its members." Section 20, however, permits the deduction of numerous expenses, many of which are examined in section V of this chapter.

Although many tax cases involving the deductibility of a particular expense turn on the application of one or the other of these provisions, others consider a variety of statutory provisions, referring to the concept of profit in subsection 9(1), as well as the general rules in paragraphs 18(1)(a) and (h) and the general limitation in section 67. Yet others involve the reasonable expectation of profit ("REOP") test considered earlier in this chapter.

This section considers the deductibility of various amounts in computing a taxpayer's income from a business or property, examining general and specific statutory rules and significant tax cases in which these rules have been interpreted and applied. Since the deductibility question is often governed by several rules, the analysis is structured by reference to different categories of outlays and expenses, rather than by reference to the rules themselves. It is through their application in specific cases, moreover, that the meaning of these various statutory and judicial rules is best illustrated.

A. Illegal Payments

In computing a taxpayer's income from a business or property, it is well established that taxpayers must include gains from illegal activities: *Smith v. The Attorney General of Canada* (1924), [1917-27] C.T.C. 240 (Ex. Ct.), aff'd (1927), [1917-27] C.T.C. 251, 1 D.T.C. 92 (P.C.). In computing the income of an illegal business, moreover, Canadian courts have concluded that taxpayers may deduct ordinary expenses that are incurred for the purpose of gaining or producing this income. In *Angle v. M.N.R.*, [1969] Tax ABC 529 (T.A.B.), for example, the Tax Appeal Board stated (at para. 19):

> Any business legal or illegal is to be treated by the Crown in "its capacity of revenue-gatherer" on the same basis. The profit has to be established in the same manner as for any commercial or industrial enterprise.

In *Espie Printing Co. v. M.N.R.*, [1960] C.T.C. 145, 60 D.T.C. 1087 (Ex. Ct.), the court considered whether taxpayers could deduct payments that are themselves illegal.

Espie Printing Co. v. M.N.R.
[1960] C.T.C. 145, 60 D.T.C. 1087 (Ex. Ct.)

THURLOW J: These are appeals from re-assessments made on August 7, 1957, of income tax for the years 1944 to 1953 inclusive, in respect of the appellant's income. ... The Minister ...disputes the right of the appellant to deduct ... expenses ... incurred in carrying out illegal transactions.

...

There remains the question whether the sums which I have found were paid for overtime wages are deductible in computing income, in view of the fact that they, or some of them, were incurred in circumstances suggesting that there was something illegal about them. Just what the illegality was was not clearly brought out. In the earlier years, there were war-time regulations which probably were infringed and, for the years 1944 to 1948, there is evidence on which one may conclude that, in the case of some, if not all, of the employees in question, there was an illicit arrangement between the appellant and the employee to enable the employee to avoid payment of income tax. In these circumstances, the Minister submits that the taxpayer's expenses for wages paid were illegally incurred and that it would be contrary to public policy to permit the appellant to deduct them in computing its income for income tax purposes.

I do not think it can seriously be questioned that the profits of illicit businesses were subject to tax under the *Income War Tax Act*. ... The present problem is, however, not quite the same, since the appellant's business itself is not shown to have been an illegal one, and the taxpayer shows the illegality of what it has done not in the course of claiming that the statute does not apply but in the course of asserting a claim for a deduction in computing the income therefrom which is subject to the tax.

...

Among the commonest of the expenses which are ordinarily deductible for the purpose of ascertaining net profit or gain from a business and which are not prohibited by Section 6(a) [now paragraph 18(1)(a)] are the wages of employees engaged in carrying on the business and, apart from the point raised as to the illegality in the present case of the arrangements with the employees and of the payments to them, there could be no question but that these wages would be proper deductions for the purpose of ascertaining the profit or gain from the business in the ordinary sense and that their deduction was not prohibited by Section 6(a).

...

For my part, I do not see how the illegality of the arrangements with the employees or of the payments has any bearing on the question whether these wages were wholly, exclusively, and necessarily laid out or expended for the purpose of earning the income. ... I do not see how the net profit or gain can be properly computed without deducting such expenses whether they or some of

623

them bear the taint of illegality or not. I am accordingly of the opinion that the wages in question are deductible in computing the appellant's income for the years 1944 to 1948 inclusive. ...

Judgment accordingly.

NOTES AND QUESTIONS

1.   In *Espie Printing*, the court held that the illegality of payments made to the taxpayer's employees should have no bearing on the question of their deductibility. Should this conclusion be regarded as a general statement regarding the deductibility of illegal payments, or a more limited conclusion based on the specific facts of the case, in which the issue of illegality was both unclear and related to the manner in which payments that are ordinarily deductible in computing business income were made, not to the category of payments as a whole?

2.   In *Muller's Meats Ltd. v. M.N.R.*, [1969] Tax ABC 171, 69 D.T.C. 172 (T.A.B.), the taxpayer, a company engaged in the wholesale distribution of meat throughout the Niagara region, sought to deduct various "under the table" payments made to various chefs and purchasing agents of large hotels and restaurants in the region. Because of the nature of the payments, however, the taxpayer had no receipts evidencing that the payments had been made, and refused to disclose the names of any of the persons to whom the alleged payments had been made.

Though apparently accepting the taxpayer's argument that these payments were incurred for the purpose of gaining or producing income within the meaning of then paragraph 12(1)(a) (now paragraph 18(1)(a)), the board disallowed the deductibility of these amounts on the basis that the taxpayer had failed to discharge the onus of proving that the expenses had been incurred. According to the board (at para. 23):

> in the case of bribes or other improper payments, the burden of proof is, if anything, heavier than in the case of an ordinary and proper payment of a business expense, because the circumstances surrounding such payments are clouded with suspicion. If a taxpayer is willing to pay a bribe in order to do business, it throws open to question how much reliance can be placed upon his unsupported and uncorroborated evidence as to the actual amounts he paid to informants, or whether indeed he paid out any amounts at all in this fashion.

Furthermore, the board stated (at para. 24): "if a taxpayer fails to support with appropriate receipts his claims with regard to the deduction of specific items of expense, he has no one but himself to blame if the Minister of National Revenue declines to permit him to deduct such items from his income."

For a similar result, see *M.N.R. v. Eldridge*, [1964] C.T.C. 545, 64 D.T.C. 5338 (Ex. Ct.), where the taxpayer, who carried on a call-girl business in Vancouver, sought to deduct, among other things, various bribes allegedly paid to unnamed law enforcement officers and civic officials. Although Cattanach J appears to have accepted that these payments may have been incurred in order to gain or produce income from the taxpayer's business, the court disallowed any deduction on the basis that the taxpayer had not proven that these payments had actually been made. According to the court (at para. 36):

> I must assume that the law enforcement officers are conscientious in the exercise of their duties and are incorruptible and such assumption can only be rebutted by convincing evidence to the contrary. The evidence which I received was not of this nature and accordingly I have not been satisfied that payments for protection were made.

See also *Expofoods (Canada) Ltd. v. M.N.R.*, [1985] 1 C.T.C. 2026, 85 D.T.C. 42 (T.C.C.); and *Archambault v. Canada*, [2000] T.C.J. No. 17, 2000 D.T.C. 1809 (T.C.C.).

3. In *United Color and Chemicals Ltd. v. M.N.R.*, [1992] T.C.J. No. 100, [1992] 1 C.T.C. 2321, 92 D.T.C. 1259 (T.C.C.), the taxpayer corporation, which carried on the business of selling chemical and dye products to the paper and carpet industries, sought to deduct secret commissions or kickbacks paid in cash to customers' purchasing agents on the grounds that these arrangements were standard in the industry and necessary for the purpose of gaining or producing income. Despite the lack of detailed records, the court accepted the taxpayer's evidence that the amounts had been paid and were incurred for the purpose of gaining or producing income from the taxpayer's business. According to the court (at para. 24): "That the rebate arrangements were conducted secretly and carried an aura of impropriety are, apart from attracting a heavier burden of proof, not in themselves determinative."

4. Section 67.5, applicable to outlays made and expenses incurred after July 13, 1990, prohibits the deduction of certain payments made to government officials or employees in the public sector or the bribery of private sector agents or employees under circumstances where the making of the payment would constitute an offence under various provisions of the *Criminal Code*, R.S.C. 1985, c. C-46.

Section 119 of the *Criminal Code* applies to the bribery of judges, members of Parliament, and members of a provincial legislature. Section 120 refers to the bribery of officers involved in the administration of criminal law, such as police officers, justices, and officers of a juvenile court. Section 121 deals with payments to government employees or officials in order to obtain contracts or other benefits. Section 123 covers attempts to influence municipal officials through bribery, threats, deceit, etc. Section 124 refers to selling or paying for an appointment to an office. Section 125 deals with influencing or negotiating appointments and dealing in offices. Section 393 covers payments to a collector who fails to collect a fare or admission fee. Section 426 deals with secret commissions to an agent and deceiving the agent's principal. Section 465 sets out the offence of conspiracy to commit an act that is an offence under the *Criminal Code*. By including section 426 of the *Criminal Code* in the list of payments the deductibility of which is prohibited under section 67.5, this provision of the Act effectively overrules the decision in *United Color and Chemicals Ltd.*, [1992] T.C.J. No. 100, [1992] 1 C.T.C. 2321, 92 D.T.C. 1259 (T.C.C.).

5. In *Neeb v. Canada*, [1997] T.C.J. No. 13, 97 D.T.C. 895 (T.C.C.), the taxpayer, who pleaded guilty to charges of importing and trafficking in narcotics and income tax evasion, sought to deduct $6 million representing the alleged cost of marijuana and hashish seized by the US Drug Enforcement Agency. Acknowledging (at para. 29) that the cost of lost inventory "would normally be deductible in computing income ... as a part of the cost of goods sold," the court nonetheless disallowed the deduction on the grounds (at para. 19) that the amount had not been "established with any degree of particularity" and that to allow the deduction would contradict public policy. According to Bowman TCJ (at para. 30):

> I can see no reason why the Canadian public should be expected to subsidize a drug dealer's loss through forfeiture of illegal drugs, by allowing him to write-off the cost of drugs so forfeited, even if that cost had been established. If public policy has any role in fiscal matters it must deny such a claim.

See also *Burnett v. The Queen* (June 11, 1992), Doc. No. 92-41 (IT) (T.C.C.), where the loss of a van seized under the *Narcotic Control Act* was held to be a non-deductible expense on the basis, *inter alia*, of public policy.

Does public policy have a role to play in fiscal matters? To the extent that it does, should public policy considerations be determined by the courts, the legislature, or both? In *65302 British Columbia Ltd. v. Canada*, [1999] S.C.J. No. 69, [2000] 1 C.T.C. 57, [1999] 99 D.T.C. 5799 (S.C.C.), the Supreme Court of Canada rejected the judicial application of a public policy limitation to disallow the deduction of fines or penalties imposed under federal or provincial statutes. This decision is reproduced later in this chapter.

B. Damage Payments

Among the earliest cases to examine the statutory rules governing the deductibility of business expenses, one of the most notable is *Imperial Oil Limited v. M.N.R.*, [1947] Ex. C.J. No. 20, [1947] C.T.C. 353, 3 D.T.C. 1090 (Ex. Ct.), in which the taxpayer incurred a substantial damage payment resulting from the negligence of one of its employees. Although decided under the *Income War Tax Act*, the case remains the leading Canadian judgment on the deductibility of damage payments.

Imperial Oil Limited v. M.N.R.
[1947] Ex. C.J. No. 20, [1947] C.T.C. 353, 3 D.T.C. 1090 (Ex. Ct.)

THORSON P: The issue in this appeal ... is whether in computing the amount of its profits or gains to be assessed for the year 1930 a deduction of $526,995.35 should be allowed, this being the amount which the appellant was obliged to pay in settlement of damage claims arising out of a collision at sea between its motorship "Reginalite" and the steamship "Craster Hall" owned by the United States Steel Products Company.

...

The appellant's business is described on its return as the manufacturing and marketing of petroleum products. In addition to producing and refining petroleum it is engaged in the transportation of petroleum and petroleum products. It has a fleet of 20 oil tankers plying on the Great Lakes and in coastal and ocean going operations. These are handled under the supervision of its marine department. This was first established in 1912 when only Great Lakes vessels were operated, but in 1921 it was expanded and ocean going tankers were acquired. The greater part of the crude oil refined in Canada by the appellant comes from South America and is carried from there to Canadian ports in oil tankers. In 1927, it had 9 ocean going oil tankers in operation including the "Reginalite." For the most part they carried its own oil but also, on occasion, oil for others on voyage charters. Its marine operations were an important and profitable part of its business.

The facts relating to the collision and the payment of damages are not disputed. On June 19, 1927, the appellant's vessel, the motorship "Reginalite," had loaded a cargo of bunker fuel oil and commercial diesel oil for the International Petroleum Company Limited and was leaving the harbour of Talara in Peru bound for a port in Chile. The steamship "Craster Hall" was lying at anchor at the customary anchorage for vessels outside the harbour proper and was apparently swinging at her anchor slightly out into the channel. The "Reginalite" was headed out to sea and as she approached the "Craster Hall" the men on her bridge observed that she inclined to swing towards the "Craster Hall." An endeavour was made to correct this swing but it was not successful and she continued to swing. Then although the engines were reversed and the anchors dropped she collided with the "Craster Hall," which later sank and became a total loss. The "Reginalite" suffered practically no damage. The owners of the "Craster Hall" took proceedings in the United States against both the appellant and the "Reginalite." The damages originally claimed were estimated at $2,000,000. Negotiations for settlement continued from 1927 to 1930 when the claims were finally settled for $526,995.35, including fees. ... It is admitted that the collision was due to fault on the part of the "Reginalite" and that the amount paid was for damages resulting therefrom.

...

The issue turns upon whether the amount sought to be deducted is excluded from deduction by sec. 6(a) of the Act [now paragraph 18(1)(a)] which provides:

6. In computing the amount of the profits or gains to be assessed a deduction shall not be allowed in respect of:

(a) disbursements or expenses not wholly, exclusively and necessarily laid out or expended for the purpose of earning the income;

The profits or gains to be assessed are the net profits or gains described in sec. 3 [now subsection 9(1)] ... subject to sec. 6 [now section 18] with which sec. 3 must be read. The principles for the computation of such profits or gains are not defined in the Act but are stated in judicial decisions. In *Gresham Life Assurance Society v. Styles* (1892) AC 309 at 316 Lord Halsbury LC said:

> Profits and gains must be ascertained on ordinary principles of commercial trading.

The same view has often been expressed; for example, in *Usher's Wiltshire Brewery, Limited v. Bruce* (1915) AC 433 at 444 Earl Loreburn approved the statement that:

> profits and gains must be estimated on ordinary principles of commercial trading by setting against the income earned the cost of earning it,

and then pointed out that this was subject to the limitations prescribed by the Act, one of which was the rule in the English Act corresponding to sec. 6(a).

The section is couched in negative terms. It is not primarily concerned with what disbursements or expenses may be deducted and does not define them, so that their deductibility is determinable only by inference. But it is concerned with and does define the disbursements or expenses whose deduction is not allowed. ... The result is that the deductibility of disbursements or expenses is to be determined according to the ordinary principles of commercial trading or well accepted principles of business and accounting practice unless their deduction is prohibited by reason of their coming within the express terms of the excluding provisions of the section. ... The section ought not, in my opinion, to be read with a view to trying to bring a particular disbursement or expense within the scope of its excluding provisions. If it is not within the express terms of the exclusions its deduction ought to be allowed if such deduction would otherwise be in accordance with the ordinary principles of commercial trading or well accepted principles of business and accounting practice.

Counsel for the appellant argued that the transporting of petroleum and petroleum products was part of the appellant's business, that the income from its marine operations was part of the income earned by it, that the ordinary risks and hazards of that business must be accepted as part thereof including the possibilities of loss inherent in it, that the risk of collision at sea was an ordinary hazard of a shipping company and that negligence on the part of its seamen resulting in damages to another ship was a contingency that was to be expected, and that, while the amount of damage done in the present case was large, the accident was not extraordinary or unusual. His contention was that, under the circumstances, the amount which the appellant had to pay was a proper expense wholly and exclusively incurred in the course of and for the purpose of the marine operations portion of its business and the earning of income therefrom, and representing a liability inherent in such business which it was obliged to meet ... that it was properly deductible as a matter of accounting practice and that it was not excluded from deduction by sec. 6(a). I think that counsel's position was well taken, both on the facts and as a matter of law.

The case is of considerable importance in view of the fact that there are no Canadian decisions on the question whether the amount of damages paid by a taxpayer on account of the negligence of his servants, such as that sought to be deducted by the appellant, is a deductible item of expenditure under sec. 6(a). Counsel had, therefore, to rely upon decisions in other jurisdictions.

The leading English authority is *Strong & Co. Limited v. Woodifield* (1905) 2 KB 350; (1906) AC 448. There the appellants were a brewery company who owned an inn and conducted it through a manager. A customer sleeping in the inn was injured by the falling of a chimney upon him, and the appellants had to pay £1,490 in damages and costs because the fall of the chimney was due to the negligence of their servants, whose duty it was to see that the premises were in proper condition. The appellants sought to deduct this sum from the amount of their profits and gains assessable to income tax. The Commissioners thought that the deduction could not be allowed ... .

In the course of his speech in the House of Lords, Lord Loreburn LC, with whose view the majority of the other Lords concurred, summarized the English law on the subject, at page 452, as follows:

> In my opinion, however, it does not follow that if a loss is in any sense connected with the trade, it must always be allowed as a deduction; for it may be only remotely connected with the trade, or it may be connected with something else quite as much or even more than with the trade. I think only such losses can be deducted as are connected with in the sense that they are really incidental to the trade itself. They cannot be deducted if they are mainly incidental to some other vocation or fall on the trade in some character other than that of trader. The nature of the trade is to be considered. To give an illustration, losses sustained by a railway company in compensating passengers for accidents in travelling might be deducted. On the other hand, if a man kept a grocer's shop, for keeping which the house is necessary, and one of the window shutters fell upon and injured a man walking, in the street, the loss arising thereby to the grocer ought not to be deducted. Many cases might be put near the line, and no degree of ingenuity can frame a formula so precise and comprehensive as to solve at sight all the cases that may arise. In the present case I think that the loss sustained by the appellants was not really incidental to their trade as innkeepers, and fell upon them in their character not of traders, but of householders. Accordingly I think that this appeal must be dismissed.

The reason for disallowing the deduction was "that the loss sustained by the appellants was not really incidental to their trade as innkeepers, and fell upon them in their character not of the loss, but of householders." The decision turned on whether the loss was or was not really incidental to the business. If it had been it seems clear beyond doubt that the deduction would have been allowed. The case is, therefore, strong authority for the statement that if a trader has to pay damages for the negligence of his servants under such circumstances that the loss is really incidental to his trade then the amount so paid is deductible.

The same principle runs through the other cases cited. Two Australian cases were referred to. In *Todd v. Commissioners of Taxation* (1913) NSW Court of Review Decisions 6, a ferry company paid damages to passengers in respect of injuries received and claimed it as a loss incurred in the production of the company's income. ... The Commissioners having disallowed the deduction, an appeal was taken and Murray, DCJ allowed it. At page 7, he said:

> The question is whether this is a loss incurred by the taxpayer in the production of his income. ... The course of the production in this case is partly disembarking and embarking passengers. This was a loss that happened quite accidentally. There was misconduct on the

part of some employee; but so far as the company is concerned, it was purely accidental; and it did occur as a loss which might reasonably be contemplated to happen at some time or other in the course of events which were a necessary incident to the production of the income; because part of the carrying of passengers, for which they pay, is their embarkation and disembarkation.

The other Australian case was *Herald and Weekly Times Limited v. Federal Commissioner of Taxation* (1932) 48 CIR 113, a decision of the High Court of Australia. There the appellant, the proprietor and publisher of an evening newspaper, claimed to deduct from its assessable income moneys paid by way of compensation, either before or after judgment, to persons claiming damages in respect of libels published in that paper, and amounts representing the costs of contesting the claims or of obtaining advice in regard thereto. ... The Commissioner disallowed the deduction and the Supreme Court of Victoria dismissed an appeal from his ruling ... . The High Court of Australia reversed this judgment and allowed the deduction. At page 118, Gavan Duffy, CJ and Dixon, J said:

> None of the libels or supposed libels was published with any other object in view than the sale of the newspaper. The liability to damages was incurred, or the claim was encountered, because of the very act of publishing the newspaper. The thing which produced the assessable income was the thing which exposed the taxpayer to the liability or claim discharged by the expenditure. It is true that when the sums were paid the taxpayer was actuated in paying them, not by any desire to produce income, but, in the case of damages or compensation, by the necessity of satisfying a claim or liability to which it had become subject, and, in the case of law costs, by the desirability or urgency of defeating or diminishing such a claim. But this expenditure flows as a necessary or a natural consequence from the inclusion of the alleged defamatory matter in the newspaper and its publication.

Counsel also relied upon a number of South African decisions. ... The first case referred to was *Income Tax Case No. 8* (1923) 1 SA Tax Cases 57. There a tramway company in the course of its business found it necessary to pay compensation for injuries to persons and properties resulting from collisions, from accidents in connection with broken trolley wires and excavations made in the roadway, and from accidents due to passengers alighting while the trains were still in motion. The company also incurred expenditures in obtaining legal advice in respect of such claims. The Commissioner disallowed a claim to deduct these expenses but his decision was reversed. Ingrain, P held, on the facts, as follows:

> It appeared from the evidence that in the carrying on of an undertaking of this character expenditure, in compensation up to a certain amount is inevitable, and that this is so even where every precaution may be taken to guard against accident or the negligence of the servants of the company. It is a recurrent loss which has to be taken into consideration as a factor in the undertaking itself and having a direct bearing on the profit earning capacity. ... The occurrences they represent were not extraordinary or abnormal. They were incidental and pursuant to the course of the operations which produced the profits and formed a necessary risk undertaken to earn the profits. Such being the case they were losses incurred on income account. ... As regards the fees paid to attorneys in connection with claims arising out of such damages, such expenditure must be equally as inevitable as the actual damages and compensation to which it relates, and is also attributable to the ordinary operations of the company.

...

See also in *Income Tax Case No. 238* (1932) 6 SA Tax Cases 259. There the appellants carried on business in partnership as stevedores. In the course of such business they were unloading cargo from a vessel and while a portion of the cargo was being transferred in a net attached to a crane an article fell out of the net and killed a passer-by. The heirs of the person killed claimed damages from the appellants on the grounds that the accident was due to the negligence of their servants. On the advice of counsel they settled the claim and sought to deduct the amount paid. It was held on an appeal from the Commissioner that damage or loss of this kind must be regarded as incidental to a business such as stevedoring and therefore as a legitimate expense in connection with the earning of the appellants' income as stevedores.

...

If the present case were being determined under the law in force in any of the jurisdictions referred to I have no doubt that the deduction sought by the appellant would be allowed. The issue of fact is whether the payment made was in respect of a liability for a happening that was really incidental to the business. In my view, there is no doubt that it was. The undisputed evidence is that the transportation of petroleum and petroleum products by sea was part of the marine operations of the appellant and part of the business from which it earned its income, that the risk of collision between vessels is a normal and ordinary hazard of marine operations generally, and that, while the amount of the appellant's liability in the present case was unusually large, there was nothing abnormal or unusual about the nature of the collision itself. Negligence on the part of the appellant's servants in the operation of its vessels, with its consequential liability to pay damages for a collision resulting therefrom, was a normal and ordinary risk of the marine operations part of the appellant's business and really incidental to it.

That being so, the question is whether the law under sec. 6(a) of the *Income War Tax Act* is so fundamentally different from that of the other jurisdictions referred to as to exclude deductibility of the amount claimed. I have come to the conclusion that it is not.

...

It is obvious that the words "for the purpose of earning the income" in sec. 6(a), as applied to disbursements or expenses, cannot be construed literally for the laying out or expending of disbursement or expense cannot by itself ever accomplish the purpose of earning the income .... [I]ncome is earned not by the making of expenditures but by various operations and transactions in which the taxpayer has been engaged or the services he has rendered, in the course of which expenditures may have been made. These are the disbursements or expenses referred to in sec. 6(a), namely, those that are laid out or expended as part of the operations, transactions or services by which the taxpayer earned the income. They are properly, therefore, described as disbursements or expenses laid out or expended as part of the process of earning the income. This means that the deductibility of a particular item of expenditure is not to be determined by isolating it. It must be looked at in the light of its connection with the operation, transaction or service in respect of which it was made so that it may be decided whether it was made not only in the course of earning the income but as part of the process of doing so.

It is no answer to say that an item of expenditure is not deductible on the ground that it was not made primarily to earn the income but primarily to satisfy a legal liability. This was the kind of argument that was expressly rejected by the High Court of Australia in the *Herald & Weekly Times, Ltd.* case (*supra*), and it should be rejected here. In a sense, all disbursements are made primarily to satisfy legal liabilities. The fact that a legal liability was being satisfied has, by itself, no bearing on the matter. It is necessary to look behind the payment and enquire whether the liability which made it necessary — and it makes no difference whether such liability was contractual or delictual — was incurred as part of the operation by which the taxpayer earned his income. Where income is earned from certain operations, as it was by the appellant from its marine operations, all the expenses wholly, exclusively and necessarily incidental to such operations must be deducted as the total cost thereof in order that the amount of the profits or gains from such operations that are to be assessed may be computed. Such cost includes not only all the ordinary operations costs but also all moneys paid in discharge of the liabilities normally incurred in the operations. When the nature of the operations is such that the risk of negligence on the part of the taxpayer's servants in the course of their duties or employment is really incidental to such operations, as was the fact in the present case, with its consequential liability to pay damages and costs, then the amount of such damages and costs is properly included as one of the items of the total cost of such operations. It may, therefore, properly be described as a disbursement or expense that is wholly, exclusively and necessarily laid out as part of the process of earning the income from such operations. It cannot be said, under the circumstances, that the payment of such damages and costs is made out of profits. It is no such thing. Being an item of the total cost of the operations it must be deducted, along with the other items of cost, before the amount of the profits from the operations can be ascertained.

For the reasons given I have no hesitation in finding that the amount sought to be deducted by the appellant would properly be deductible according to the ordinary principles of commercial trading and well established principles of business and accounting practice as an item in the total cost of its marine operations, and that it falls outside the excluding provisions of sec. 6(a). The amount was, therefore, improperly added to the assessment and it should be amended accordingly. The appeal must therefore be allowed with costs.

Judgment accordingly.

NOTES AND QUESTIONS

1. On what grounds did the Exchequer Court decide in *Imperial Oil* that the damages resulting from the collision at sea were deductible in computing the taxpayer's income from its manufacturing and marketing of petroleum products? Of what significance to the court's decision is its statement that "the risk of collision between vessels is a normal and ordinary hazard of marine operations"? Of what relevance is the court's conclusion that "the transportation of petroleum and petroleum products by sea was part of the marine operations of the appellant and part of the business from which it earned its income"?

2. According to the Exchequer Court decision in *Imperial Oil*, "the deductibility of disbursements or expenses is to be determined according to the ordinary principles of commercial trading or well accepted principles of business and accounting practice" absent the application of a specific "excluding provision" to the contrary. What, if any, statutory authority underlies this "business practices" test? Is this statutory authority limited to the *Income War Tax Act*, or does it also apply to the current *Income Tax Act*?

3. In *Strong and Company of Romsey Limited v. Woodifield* (1905), 2 K.B. 350, [1906], A.C. 448 (K.B.), the test for deductibility under the English law was said to depend on the extent to which the expense is connected with the trade in the computation of the income of which the expense is sought to be deducted. According to Lord Loreburn LC, the only expenses that can be deducted are those "as are connected with in the sense that they are really incidental to the trade itself" (at A.C. 452). Similarly, in *Imperial Oil*, the court emphasized that:

> the deductibility of a particular item of expenditure is not to be determined by isolating it. It must be looked at in the light of its connection with the operation, transaction or service in respect of which it was made so that it may be decided whether it was made not only in the course of earning the income but as part of the process of doing so.

What, if any, statutory authority underlies this "remoteness" test? Is this statutory authority limited to the *Income War Tax Act*, or does it also apply to the current *Income Tax Act*?

4. In *Davis v. M.N.R.* (1964), 36 Tax ABC 36, 64 D.T.C. 485 (T.A.B.), the taxpayer, a pig farmer, sought to deduct damages and legal costs arising out of an automobile accident that occurred while he and his family were on their way to inspect two boars that had been purchased by his brother, who lived nearby. Concluding (at para. 10) that the accident "was in no way incidental to the business of farming or hog-raising," the board denied the deduction. According to the board (at paras. 10-11):

> If the business concerned had been that of a company engaged in the transportation of goods or passengers, such accidents might be found to be a hazard incidental to, or a part of, the *usual and ordinary conduct* of such a business, as was the situation in the *Imperial Oil Limited* case ... . Such, however, cannot be said to be the case where the business is farming or pig-raising. ... An item of expense such as damages resulting from the personal negligence

of the appellant cannot be said to be related to the operational expenses of the appellant's farm, nor does it fall within the exception contained in Section 12(1)(a) [now paragraph 18(1)(a)].

Do you agree with this conclusion? Why or why not? If not, can you imagine circumstances in which damages resulting from an automobile accident might be regarded as "incidental to the business of farming or hog-raising"?

5.   In *Fairrie v. Hall (Inspector of Taxes)* (1947), 28 Tax Cas 200 (K.B.), the taxpayer, a sugar broker who was angered at the government's buying policy, uttered a malicious libel against a government official who was also a sugar broker. Denying a deduction for damages payable as compensation for this libel, Macnaghten J concluded (at 206) that the libel was "only remotely connected" with the taxpayer's trade as a sugar broker.

   Contrast this conclusion with the decision in *Herald and Weekly Times Limited v. Federal Commissioner of Taxation* (1932), 48 C.L.R. 113 (H.C.), in which the High Court of Australia permitted the taxpayer, the proprietor and publisher of an evening newspaper, to deduct compensation paid in respect of libels published in the paper. Do you agree with this decision? Is the connection with the taxpayer's trade the only test that should be applied to determine whether an expense is deductible?

6.   In *Income Tax Case No. 8* (1923), 1 SA Tax Cases 57, the taxpayer, a tramway company, was allowed to deduct compensation for injuries on the basis that "in the carrying on of an undertaking of this character expenditure, in compensation up to a certain amount is inevitable." Likewise, in *Imperial Oil Limited v. M.N.R.*, [1947] Ex. C.J. No. 20, [1947] C.T.C. 353, 3 D.T.C. 1090 (Ex. Ct.), the court allowed the deduction of damages on the basis that they were paid "in discharge of the liabilities normally incurred in the operations." Do these statements suggest that deductibility might be disallowed for "abnormal" damages exceeding "a certain amount"?

7.   In *Poulin v. Canada*, [1996] F.C.J. No. 960, 96 D.T.C. 6477 (F.C.A.), the taxpayer, a real estate broker who was required to pay $385,802 in damages to a former client after the broker was determined to have made false and fraudulent representations resulting in the client's damages, sought to deduct the payment in computing the income from his brokerage business. Although accepting that "the risk of having to pay damages for wrongful professional activities, in the private law sense, is inherent in carrying on any trade and any profession," the court disallowed the deduction on the basis (at para. 11) that it did not "correspond to a risk that it was necessary for [the taxpayer] to assume in order to carry on his business as a real estate broker." According to Marceau JA (Hugessen and MacGuigan JJA concurring) (at para. 9):

> while it must be admitted that the commission of an involuntary fault in performing an act that is necessary for carrying on a trade or profession is inevitable, and accordingly that an obligation to pay compensation is a risk inherent in that activity, we cannot extend the idea to the commission of a delict in the civil law sense, to the commission of a reprehensible act committed deliberately with the aim of causing damage. The delictual act cannot in that case

> be considered as being necessary for carrying on the trade or profession. It was committed while carrying on the trade or profession, but it is completely foreign to it. There is therefore no ground for arguing that, in this case, the payment of an award of damages meets the requirement in paragraph 18(1)(a) of the Act.

Do you agree with this conclusion? Why or why not? Might the deduction have been disallowed under subsection 9(1) on the basis that the taxpayer's behaviour was contrary to "ordinary principles of commercial trading or well accepted principles of business and accounting practice"?

8.   In *McNeill v. Canada*, [2000] F.C.J. No. 348, [2000] 2 C.T.C. 304, 2000 D.T.C. 6211 (F.C.A.), the taxpayer, a chartered accountant who entered into an agreement to sell his practice, to provide consulting and accounting services to the purchaser for three years, and to refrain from competing with the purchaser within a specified geographical area for a further five years, was required to pay damages and costs of $465,908 after he was determined to have breached the provisions of the restrictive covenant. Citing the Supreme Court of Canada decision in *65302 British Columbia Ltd. v. Canada*, [1999] S.C.J. No. 69, [2000] 1 C.T.C. 57, 99 D.T.C. 5799 (S.C.C.), which held that fines and penalties are generally deductible in computing a taxpayer's income from a business or property, and observing (at para. 15) that the taxpayer's actions were "for the purpose of keeping his clients and his business," the court concluded (at para. 20) that the damage payment was "deductible as an expense under paragraph 18(1)(a)" of the Act. According to Rothstein JA (Richard CJ and Strayer JA concurring) (at para. 14):

> If a fine or penalty for breach of the law is deductible because nothing in paragraph 18(1)(a) precludes it, it follows that court ordered damages for breach of a contract should also be deductible. The analysis [in *65302 British Columbia Ltd.*, supra] ... is equally applicable to court awards of damages as to fines and penalties.

The Supreme Court of Canada decision in *65302 British Columbia Ltd.*, and the Department of Finance's response to the decisions are reproduced in the following section. Without yet reading this section, however, consider whether the court's conclusion in *McNeill* that the damages were deductible "under paragraph 18(1)(a)" is consistent with the scheme for the deductibility of expenses set out in *Imperial Oil Limited v. M.N.R.*, [1947] Ex. C.J. No. 20, [1947] C.T.C. 353, 3 D.T.C. 1090 (Ex. Ct.). Does paragraph 18(1)(a) authorize the deduction of expenses in computing a taxpayer's income from a business or property? Was the taxpayer's behaviour consistent with "ordinary principles of commercial trading or well accepted principles of business and accounting practice"?

9.   For the CRA's views on the deductibility of damage payments, see *Interpretation Bulletin* IT-467R2, "Damages, Settlements and Similar Payments," (November 13, 2002). According to paragraph 5:

> 5. In order to be deductible as a current expense in computing income from a business or property, damages must meet at least the following tests:

    (a)   the outlay must have been made for the purpose of gaining or producing income from the business or property (paragraph 18(1)(a)),

    (b)   the outlay must not be on account of capital (paragraph 18(1)(b)),

    (c)   the outlay must not be made for the purpose of gaining or producing exempt income (paragraph 18(1)(c)),

    (d)   the outlay must not be a personal expense (paragraph 18(1)(h)), and

    (e)   the outlay must be reasonable in the circumstances (section 67).

10. Consider the economics of allowing a deduction for tort damages. To the extent that damage payments are intended to internalize the costs of accidents in order to encourage potential injurers to take "cost-justified" precautions in order to prevent accidents, it might be argued that the deductibility of damage payments diminishes this "deterrent" role of the tort system, unless courts take into account the fact of deductibility in determining damages. However, to the extent that the costs of taking precautions to prevent accidents are deductible, it is arguable that damage payments should also be deductible in order to ensure that the tax system does not distort the incentives that the tort system creates to reduce the risk of accidents. Should the tax system be neutral with respect to the economics of accidents? Should it deliberately encourage accident prevention? Is the denial of a deduction for damages an efficient way to encourage accident prevention? What other tax incentives can you imagine to encourage accident prevention?

C. Fines and Penalties

Like damage payments, fines and penalties are another category of expense the deductibility of which the Canadian revenue authorities have often challenged. Traditionally, Canadian courts disallowed the deduction of fines and penalties on the grounds either that such payments were not incurred for the purpose of gaining or producing income as required by the *Income Tax Act* or that deductibility would contradict public policy. In *Horton Steel Works Ltd. v. M.N.R.*, [1972] C.T.C. 2147, 72 D.T.C. 1123 (T.R.B.), for example, the board disallowed the deduction of a penalty imposed under the federal *Excise Tax Act* on the basis (at para. 5) that "[a]s the business of the [taxpayer] could have been carried on without any infraction of the law, the penalty is not an outlay made for the *purpose* of producing income" (emphasis in original). As authority for this conclusion, the board cited *Commissioners of Inland Revenue v. Alexander von Glehn & Co.*, [1920] 2 K.B. 553 (C.A.), in which Lord Sterndale disallowed the deduction of a penalty resulting from the violation of wartime export restrictions on the grounds (at 565) that because "[t]he business could be perfectly well carried on without any infraction of the law," the penalty was neither "laid out or expended for the purpose of [its] trade" nor "connected with or arising out of such trade," but "was a fine imposed upon the company personally." Similarly, in *M.N.R. v. E.H. Pooler & Co. Ltd.*, [1962] C.T.C. 527, 62 D.T.C. 1321 (Ex. Ct.), the court disallowed the deduction of a fine imposed by the Toronto Stock Exchange on the grounds (at para. 11) that the actions taken by the taxpayer's vice-president, in respect of which the fine was imposed, were "at most a remote circumstance" and not "done in the course of or for the purposes of the [taxpayer's] business," as required by then paragraph 12(1)(a) (now paragraph 18(1)(a)) of the Act.

In *Luscoe Products Ltd. v. M.N.R.* (1956), 16 Tax ABC 239, 57 D.T.C. 32 (T.A.B.), in contrast, the board disallowed the deduction of fines arising from the sale of cough medicine containing insufficient medication and sufficient alcohol to qualify as liquor under the *Liquor Control Act* of Ontario on the public policy basis (at para. 13) that deductibility would allow the taxpayer "to share equally with the public revenue the loss to which it was condemned by its own unlawful act." Likewise, in *King Grain and Seed Company Ltd. v. M.N.R.* (1961), 26 Tax ABC 436 (T.A.B.), the board disallowed the deduction of a fine for operating an overloaded truck on the grounds (at para. 12) that "it would be contrary to accepted principles if the [taxpayer] ... was allowed to deduct the amount of this fine ... and thus be enabled to share with the public revenue the loss to which it was condemned by reason of its own negligence."

In *Day & Ross Inc. v. Canada*, [1976] F.C.J. No. 198, [1976] C.T.C. 707, 76 D.T.C. 6433 (F.C.T.D.), the court broke with this tradition by allowing the taxpayer to deduct provincial fines imposed for overweight trucking violations on the grounds (at paras. 49-50) that the penalties "resulted from the day-to-day operation of its transport business and were a necessary expense," and that the "ready availability of advance overweight permits" indicated that "weight restrictions can be easily overcome and that violations thereof are obviously not outrageous transgressions of public policy." Similarly, in *TNT Canada Inc. v. Canada*, [1988] F.C.J. No. 565, [1988] 2 C.T.C. 91, 88 D.T.C. 6334 (F.C.T.D.), the court allowed the deduction of fines imposed under the *Customs Act* and the *Excise Tax Act* on the grounds that the taxpayer's actions in failing to pay sales and excise tax on repairs to vehicles in the United States and having foreign-owned vehicles make more than one stop in Canada "were taken to earn income," and were too few to constitute a significant violation of public policy. Although departing from the traditional approach of Canadian courts to disallow the deduction of fines and penalties, each of these decisions adhered to the twofold test asking whether the expense was incurred for the purpose of gaining or producing income and whether its deduction would be contrary to public policy. In each of these cases, the court also commented that at least some of the penalties were "inevitable" or "unavoidable."[36]

---

[36] See also *Iogen Corp. v. Canada*, [1995] T.C.J. No. 667, [1995] 2 C.T.C. 2651, 95 D.T.C. 1993 (T.C.C.), *per* Lamarre-Proulx JTCC, emphasizing (at para. 14) that late remittances of source

In *Amway of Canada Ltd. v. Canada*, [1996] F.C.J. No. 211, [1996] 2 C.T.C. 162, 96 D.T.C. 6135 (F.C.A.), the Federal Court of Appeal reaffirmed the income-earning purpose and public policy tests for the deductibility of fines and penalties, and relied on the decisions in *Day & Ross Inc. v. Canada*, [1976] F.C.J. No. 198, [1976] C.T.C. 707, 76 D.T.C. 6433 (F.C.T.D.) and *TNT Canada Inc. v. Canada*, [1988] F.C.J. No. 565, [1988] 2 C.T.C. 91, 88 D.T.C. 6334 (F.C.T.D.), to affirm a further "avoidability" consideration in the application of the first of these tests.[37] According to Strayer JA (Stone and Décary JJA concurring) (at para. 35), "a fine or penalty cannot be considered to have been incurred for the purpose of producing income unless in all the circumstances the incurring of the fine or penalty must be seen as an unavoidable incident of carrying on the business." Since the taxpayer had engaged in "an intentional and cynical scheme" to avoid customs duties and excise taxes by falsifying the value of goods imported into Canada, the court held that the resulting penalties were avoidable and therefore not deductible. In addition, it explained, it would be "contrary to public policy" and "frustrate the purposes of the penalties imposed by Parliament" if a taxpayer incurring such a penalty were "then able to share the cost of that penalty ... with other taxpayers of Canada by treating it as a deductible expense and thus reducing his taxable income." According to the court (at para. 35): "it is contrary to public policy to allow the deduction of a fine or penalty as a business expense where that fine or penalty is imposed by law for the purpose of punishing or deterring those who through intention or lack of reasonable care violate the laws."

In two subsequent decisions, the Tax Court of Canada applied the avoidability test to allow the deduction of a fine or penalty in one circumstance and to disallow its deduction in another. In *Sunys Petroleum Inc. v. Canada*, [1996] T.C.J. No. 1147, [1996] 3 C.T.C. 2931, 96 D.T.C. 1759 (T.C.C.), Bell JTCC allowed the deduction of a penalty relating to the taxpayer's failure to remit sales and excise taxes on the grounds (at para. 37) that the taxpayer had reasonably relied upon its financial vice-president "to attend, among other things, to the very matters giving rise to the imposition of the penalty" and "could not reasonably have avoided the failure to make the required remittances." In *Port Colbourne Poultry Ltd. v. Canada*, [1997] T.C.J. No. 72, [1997] 2 C.T.C. 2480, 97 D.T.C. 237 (T.C.C.), however, Rowe DJTC

---

deductions, which resulted in penalties and interest expenses, were "intentional and in a field of activity where violations were avoidable."

[37] As further support for this avoidability criterion, the court cited *Commissioners of Inland Revenue v. Alexander von Glehn & Co.*, [1920] 2 K.B. 553 (C.A.), in which Lord Sterndale suggested that "[t]he business could perfectly well have been carried on without any infraction of the law," and *Imperial Oil Limited v. M.N.R.*, [1947] Ex. C.J. No. 20, [1947] C.T.C. 353, 3 D.T.C. 1090 (Ex. Ct.), in which the court emphasized that "the transportation of petroleum and petroleum products by sea was part of the marine operations of the appellant and part of the business from which it earned its income, that the risk of collision between vessels is a normal and ordinary hazard of marine operations generally."

disallowed the deduction of a fine for an environmental offence on the grounds that while a spill of poultry sludge on the taxpayer's property may have been inevitable, the decision to flush the material into a drainage ditch connected to a watercourse was "certainly avoidable."

In *65302 British Columbia Ltd. v. Canada*, [1999] S.C.J. No. 69, [2000] 1 C.T.C. 57, 99 D.T.C. 5799 (S.C.C.), the Supreme Court of Canada considered the deductibility of fines and penalties for the first time. Ultimately, the court held that the over-quota fines incurred by the taxpayer were deductible business expenses. In response to the case, the Department of Finance enacted section 67.6, applicable to fine and penalties imposed after March 22, 2004. According to this provision:

> In computing income, no deduction shall be made in respect of any amount that is a fine or penalty (other than a prescribed fine or penalty) imposed under a law of a country or of a political subdivision of a country (including a state, province or territory) by any person or public body that has authority to impose the fine or penalty.

Although the deduction of fines such as those incurred by the taxpayer in *65302 British Columbia* is now legislatively denied, the case provides a useful review of the development of the law in this area. The following summary of the facts is taken from David G. Duff, "Deductibility of Fines and Penalties Under the Income Tax Act: Public Policy, Statutory Interpretation and the Scheme of the Act in 65302 B.C. Ltd." (2001) 34 Can. Bus. L.J. 336 at 343-46:

> The taxpayer ... operated an integrated poultry operation in the Prince George area of British Columbia, deriving revenue both from meat production chickens ("broilers") and from egg-laying chickens ("layers"). In order to obtain the layers, the taxpayer acquired day-old chicks from hatcheries, which were classified as "pullets" until they became mature layers at 19 weeks. Under the *British Columbia Egg Marketing Scheme, 1967* (the "Scheme"), producers were allocated a maximum number of layers and required to pay a fixed levy for each of these chickens. During the years at issue in the case, the taxpayer's quota was 33,680 layers, for each of which it was required to pay $0.07 per week.
>
> In 1988, the BC Egg Marketing Board (the "Board") determined that the taxpayer had exceeded its quota by 7.61 per cent in 1984, 1.39 per cent in 1985, 6.96 per cent in 1986, 9.89 per cent in 1987, and 14.58 per cent in 1988. Although the taxpayer's owner-manager testified that "it was normal for such an operation to be 2 to 6 per cent over quota due to the differential survival rates of baby chicks and the problem of not being able to get rid of spent fowl through processing plants in time," evidence established that the taxpayer had made a deliberate decision to produce over-quota, pending the purchase of additional quota in order to supply a major customer which it feared it might otherwise lose. Evidence also established that the taxpayer had deliberately delayed the acquisition of additional quota, which was available in the Lower Mainland area during the years at issue but not in the Prince George area, making what it characterized as a "business decision" to wait for lower-priced quota in the Prince George area. Nor had the taxpayer voluntarily disclosed its over-quota production to the Board, which discovered the extra layers through an audit inspection after a change in Board policy required inspectors to check all barns on a producer's property, not only the egg-producing barns identified by the producers themselves. The taxpayer purchased additional quota in 1989 and was never found to be over quota thereafter.
>
> The Scheme and the Board were established under the *Natural Products Marketing (BC) Act* (the "BC Act"), the declared purpose of which is to provide for the promotion, control

and regulation of the production, transportation, packing, storage and marketing of natural products in the province. According to s. 20 of this statute:

> Every person who fails to comply with this Act or the regulations or an order, rule, regulation, determination or decision made by the Provincial board or a marketing board or commission ... is liable on conviction, to a fine of not less than $100 and not more than $500 or to imprisonment not exceeding 6 months or to both a fine and imprisonment.

In addition to this penalty provision, s. 13(1)(k) of the BC Act stipulates that marketing boards or commissions may be empowered to:

> fix and collect levies or charges from designated persons engaged in the production or marketing of the whole or part of a regulated product and for that purpose to classify these persons into groups and fix the levies or charges payable by the members of the different groups in different amounts, and to use those levies or charges and other money and licence fees received by the commission

> (i)   to carry out the purposes of the scheme;

> (ii)   to pay the expenses of the marketing board or commission;

> (iii)   to pay costs and losses incurred in marketing a regulated product;

> (iv)   to equalize or adjust returns received by producers of regulated products during the periods the marketing board or commission may determine; and

> (v)   to set aside reserves for the purpose referred to in this paragraph.

Pursuant to this provision and powers set out in the regulatory Scheme, the Board issued a Standing Order which included a number of levies, one of which imposed an over-quota levy of $0.08 per day "in respect of each layer kept or maintained by a registered producer ... at any time in excess of the number of layers which may be kept or maintained by that registered producer ... ." According to the controller of the Board in testimony accepted by the trial judge, ten to fifteen over-quota levies were issued every year in British Columbia, very few of which involved over-quota production in excess of one percent.

Having determined that the taxpayer exceeded its quota from 1984 to 1988, the Board assessed an over-quota levy of $269,629.69 and directed the taxpayer to dispose of the extra layers, which it did. After seeking legal advice, the taxpayer agreed to pay the levy over time with interest charged accordingly. In computing its business income for its 1988 taxation year, the appellant claimed the $269,629.69 over-quota levy as a deductible expense. The deduction of this amount produced a business loss of $61,876 for the year, which the taxpayer carried back pursuant to s. 111 of the ITA and deducted in computing its taxable income for its 1985 taxation year. In computing its business income for its 1989 taxation year, the taxpayer deducted interest expenses of $9,074.50 on the unpaid balance of the over-quota levy and $3,766 in legal expenses incurred in respect of the over-quota levy.

In 1991, the taxpayer was reassessed in respect of its 1985, 1988, and 1989 taxation years, and the deduction of the over-quota levy, loss carryback, interest and legal expenses [was] disallowed. Before the trial, both parties agreed that the issues of the loss carryback and the deductibility of the interest charges and legal expenses would turn on the deductibility of the over-quota levy.

65302 British Columbia Ltd. v. Canada
[1999] S.C.J. No. 69, [2000] 1 C.T.C. 57, 99 D.T.C. 5799 (S.C.C.)

IACOBUCCI J (Gonthier, McLachlin, Major, Binnie JJ concurring):

I. Introduction

At issue in the present appeal is whether levies, fines and penalties may be deducted as business expenses from a taxpayer's income. The resolution of this issue involves questions of statutory interpretation and the extent to which public policy considerations may enter into this interpretation. It is my opinion that as a general principle, it is Parliament, and not the courts, who should decide which expenses incurred for the purpose of earning business income should not be deductible. Parliament has made such decisions on many occasions; this is simply not one of them. As such, levies, fines and penalties which are incurred for the purpose of earning income are deductible business expenses.

...

VI. Analysis

A. Section 18(1)(a) of the Income Tax Act

(1) The Concept of Profit in s. 18(1)(a)

The central question in this appeal is whether an over-quota levy may be deducted as a business expense from a taxpayer's business income. ... Section 9(1) of the Act provides that a taxpayer's business income for the tax year is the profit from that business. It is well established that the concept of profit found in s. 9(1) authorizes the deduction of business expenses, as profit is inherently a net concept, and such deductions are allowed under s. 9(1) to the extent that they are consistent with "well accepted principles of business (or accounting) practice" or "well accepted principles of commercial trading": *Symes v. R*, [1993] 4 SCR 695 (SCC), at pp. 722-23. These expenses may nonetheless be prohibited by the limiting provisions found in s. 18(1), although many of these provisions are also consistent with well accepted principles of business practice. The present appeal concerns the language of s. 18(1)(a), which provides that, in computing taxable business income, no deduction may be made in respect of:

> an outlay or expense except to the extent that it was made or incurred by the taxpayer for the purpose of gaining or producing income from the business or property.

...

To rephrase this language in the context of the present appeal, the question to ask is: did the appellant incur the over-quota levy for the purpose of gaining or producing income from its business?

On its face, I would answer this question in the affirmative. ... [T]he levy was incurred as part of the appellant's day to day operations. The decision to produce over-quota was a business decision made in order to realize income. The appellant deliberately produced over-quota in order to maintain its major customer, who was then expanding in the area, until it could purchase additional quota at what it thought was an affordable price.

However, the respondent urges this Court to follow Lord Sterndale's distinction between "a loss connected with the business" and "a fine imposed upon the company personally": Commissioners of Inland Revenue v. Von Glehn, [1920] 2 KB 553 (Eng. CA). The argument is that the nature of the sanction is such that it is more properly viewed as attaching to the business entity itself rather than to the business of the entity. Alexander von Glehn has been followed in other common law jurisdictions: see Robinson v. Commissioner of Inland Revenue, [1965] NZLR 246 (New Zealand SC); Herald & Weekly Times v. Federal Commissioner of Taxation (1932), 2 ATD 169 (Australia HC); Mayne Nickless Ltd. v. Federal Commissioner of Taxation (1984), 71 FLR 168 (Australia Vic. Sup. Ct.).

I do not find these cases helpful to the present appeal given the differences in the applicable taxation statues. According to Lord Sterndale in *Alexander von Glehn, supra*, three rules of the *Income Tax Act, 1842*, governed the deductibility of the fine at issue in that case. The third rule that he cited provided (at p. 563):

> In estimating the balance of the profits or gains to be charged ... no sum shall be set against or deducted from ... such profits or gains, for any disbursements or expenses whatever, not being money *wholly and exclusively laid out or expended for the purposes of such trade*, manufacture, adventure, or concern, or of such profession, employment, or vocation.

> [Emphasis added.]

> ...

I note that the New Zealand and Australian cases cited by the respondent dealt with similarly worded taxation statutes to that at issue in *Alexander von Glehn*. Canada's *Income War Tax Act*, RSC 1927, c. 97, also prohibited the deduction of expenses not "wholly, exclusively and necessarily laid out or expended for the purpose of earning the income." However, in 1948 this section was replaced with the precursor to our current s. 18(1)(a) of the Act, dropping the language of "wholly, exclusively and necessarily laid out or expended." As this Court affirmed in *Symes* at p. 732:

> the current wording of s. 18(1)(a) is sufficient justification for the view that Parliament acted to amend its predecessor section in such a way as to broaden the scope for business expense deductibility.

In my view, following case law interpreting statutes that employed similarly restrictive language as our *Income War Tax Act* would be to ignore the clear intention exhibited by Parliament since 1948 to broaden the scope of deductible business expenses.

...

The respondent also asks this Court to follow the Federal Court of Appeal's decision in *Amway, supra*. The central issue in *Amway* was also the deductibility of fines and penalties pursuant to s. 18(1)(a) of the Act. Strayer JA held, for the court, that "one legitimate test of whether fines should be deductible as a business expense is that of avoidability of the offences" (p. 389). In support of this proposition, Strayer JA cited *Alexander von Glehn, supra, Imperial Oil, supra, Day & Ross, supra*, and *TNT, supra*.

I have already mentioned why I do not find *Alexander von Glehn*, helpful in the context of our current Act. For similar reasons, I would decline to follow *Imperial Oil*. In that case, Thorson P held that the damages and costs associated with a negligence action against the taxpayer were properly deducted as business expenses where "the nature of the operations is such that the risk of negligence on the part of the taxpayer's servants in the course of their duties or employment is really incidental to such operations" (p. 1100, emphasis added). However, *Imperial Oil* concerned the application of the *Income War Tax Act* which, as I have already outlined, required that an expense be "wholly, exclusively and necessarily" made for the purpose of earning income. ... In the absence of similar language in the current Act, I find it difficult to endorse the requirement that expenses need be incidental, in the sense that they were unavoidable, in order to be deductible under s. 18(1)(a).

Day & Ross, supra, is a more recent case, but at best I find it ambiguous on the issue. While Dubé J held that the fines at issue, levied for violations of provincial highway weight restriction laws, were in fact "necessary expenses" and "inevitable," it is not clear whether these considerations went to establish that the fines fell within the wording of s. 12(1)(a) (now s. 18(1)(a)) of the Act or that the fines were not "outrageous transgressions of public policy."

Indeed, in *TNT, supra*, Cullen J purports to follow *Day & Ross* and yet appears not to follow the avoidability test. At issue in *TNT* were two types of fines. The first type was held to fall clearly within the ratio of *Day & Ross*, as they were unavoidable. With respect to the second type of fine, levied because a "foreign carrier [was] used in Canada and made more than one stop which conduct is prohibited by law" (at p. 100), the Minister argued that the fines were avoidable and that the taxpayer was deliberately flouting the law. In response, Cullen J stated, at p. 100:

> Counsel also made this comment: "*it may have been good economics and more expeditious* but it was against public policy." That comment buttresses my own view that these actions were taken to earn income and therefore were a legitimate expense under paragraph 18(1)(a) of the Act. The taxpayer has certainly met the "purpose test" vis-à-vis this penalty.

> [Emphasis added by Cullen J.]

With respect, I differ from Strayer JA's interpretation of *TNT* in *Amway, supra*, as I do not read Cullen J's statement as a finding that the second type of fine was an unavoidable expense. Rather, I interpret his statement to mean that so long as the fines were incurred in order to earn income, they fell within the meaning of s. 18(1)(a) of the Act. Cullen J then held that the deduction of the fines should not be disallowed on the basis of public policy, since the amount of the second type of fine at issue was lumped together with the first type and could not easily be separated, and since the underlying offences were small in number (at p. 101).

Even if these cases clearly established a test of avoidability, I would decline to endorse it. As Strayer JA indicated in *Amway, supra*, this test would only apply to fines and penalties and not the deductibility of other types of expenses (at p. 390). With respect, I do not see how the language of s. 18(1)(a) can support a requirement of avoidability, let alone one that only attaches to fines and penalties.

(2) Statutory Interpretation and Public Policy

This Court has on many occasions endorsed Driedger's statement of the modern principle of statutory construction: "the words of an Act are to be read in their entire context and in their grammatical and ordinary sense harmoniously with the scheme of the Act, the object of the Act, and the intention of Parliament." See *Rizzo & Rizzo Shoes Ltd., Re*, [1998] 1 SCR 27 (SCC), at para. 21. This rule is no different for tax statutes: *Stubart Investments Ltd. v. R*, [1984] 1 SCR 536 (SCC), at p. 578.

However, this Court has also often been cautious in utilizing tools of statutory interpretation in order to stray from clear and unambiguous statutory language. In *Antosko v. Minister of National Revenue*, [1994] 2 SCR 312 (SCC), at p. 326-27, this Court held:

> While it is true that the courts must view discrete sections of the Income Tax Act in light of the other provisions of the Act and of the purpose of the legislation, and that they must analyze a given transaction in the context of economic and commercial reality, such techniques cannot alter the result where the words of the statute are clear and plain and where the legal and practical effect of the transaction is undisputed.

In discussing this case, P.W. Hogg and J.E. Magee, while correctly acknowledging that the context and purpose of a statutory provision must always be considered, comment that "[i]t would introduce intolerable uncertainty into the *Income Tax Act* if clear language in a detailed provision of the Act were to be qualified by unexpressed exceptions derived from a court's view of the object and purpose of the provision": *Principles of Canadian Income Tax Law* 2nd ed., 1997 at pp. 475-76. This is not an endorsement of a literalist approach to statutory interpretation, but a recognition that in applying the principles of interpretation to the Act, attention must be paid to the fact that the Act is one of the most detailed, complex, and comprehensive statutes in our legislative inventory and courts should be reluctant to embrace unexpressed notions of policy or principle in the guise of statutory interpretation.

The most compelling argument put to this Court in the present appeal is that Parliament could not have intended s. 18(1)(a) to permit the deduction of fines and penalties as such a result violates public policy. Therefore, even if fines and penalties are allowable expenses within the ordinary meaning of s. 18(1)(a), this meaning must be modified in order to conform to a broader appreciation of Parliament's intent, and thereby avoid a repugnant disharmony or absurdity. In *Amway, supra,* the Federal Court of Appeal also took this approach, holding, at para. 31, that even if the fine or penalty in question is unavoidable, its deduction should be disallowed where "that fine or penalty is imposed by law for the purpose of punishing or deterring those who through intention or a lack of reasonable care violate the laws." Similarly, Professor Neil Brooks argues that this consideration is legitimate for courts to invoke even in the absence of statutory language to that effect, because of "the broad interpretative principle that in discharging their function they [courts] should not construe one statute in such a way that the objectives of another statute are frustrated": "The Principles Underlying the Deduction of Business Expenses" in B. Hansen, V. Krishna and J. Rendall, eds., *Canadian Taxation* (1981), 189, at p. 242.

The United States Supreme Court took this position in *Tank Truck Rentals, Inc. v. CIR* (1958), 356 US 30 (US Sup. Ct.). At issue was whether fines imposed for the operation of trucks in violation of state maximum weight laws were "ordinary and necessary" business expenses under §23(a)(1)(A) of the *Internal Revenue Code* of 1939. The court held at pp. 33-35 that:

> A finding of "necessity" cannot be made ... if the allowance of the deduction would frustrate sharply defined national or state policies proscribing particular types of conduct, evidenced by some governmental declaration thereof. ...

> ... It is clear that assessment of the fines was punitive action and not a mere toll for use of the highways: the fines occurred only in the exceptional instance when the overweight run was detected by the police. Petitioner's failure to comply with the state laws obviously was based on a balancing of the cost of compliance against the chance of detection. Such a course cannot be sanctioned, for judicial deference to state action requires, whenever possible, that a State not be thwarted in its policy. We will not presume that the Congress, in allowing deductions for income tax purposes, intended to encourage a business enterprise to violate the declared policy of a State. To allow the deduction sought here would but encourage continued violations of state law by increasing the odds in favor of noncompliance. This could only tend to destroy the effectiveness of the State's maximum weight laws.

However, the court recognized that this presumption against congressional intent to encourage the violation of declared public policy had to be balanced against the congressional intent to tax only net income. The test for non-deductibility therefore turns on "the severity and immediacy of the frustration resulting from allowance of the deduction" (at p. 35). I note that in 1969 Congress amended §162 of the *Internal Revenue Code* to disallow, *inter alia,* the deduction of "any fine or similar penalty paid to a government for the violation of any law."

Invoking public policy concerns raises the question, as put by Richard Krever, of whose public policy should be furthered by courts in disallowing the deduction of fines and penalties ("The Deductibility of Fines: Considerations From Law and Policy Perspectives" (1984), 13 *Austl. Tax Rev.* 168, at p. 185). As he notes, "[a] taxpayer may incur a fine in one jurisdiction as a result of activities producing assessable income that are undertaken on a nation-wide basis and allowed in all other States" (p. 185). Further, Krever points out on the same page:

> A more difficult problem arises with fines incurred in foreign jurisdictions where the illegal activity was carried out to earn assessable income that is taxed in Australia. Does comity require our courts to give effect to the public policy of other jurisdictions? If so, would this policy extend to situations where the fine was levied for actions not considered illegal in Australia or considered to be contrary to our public policy?

> ...

In this connection, I note that in calculating income, it is well established that the deduction of expenses incurred to earn income generated from illegal acts is allowed. ... Allowing a taxpayer to deduct expenses for a crime would appear to frustrate the *Criminal Code*; however, tax authorities are not concerned with the legal nature of an activity. Thus, in my opinion, the same principles should apply to the deduction of fines incurred for the purpose of gaining income because prohibiting the deductibility of fines and penalties is inconsistent with the practice of allowing the deduction of expenses incurred to earn illegal income.

This brings us to the crux of the issue. While fully alive to the need in general to harmonize the interpretation of different statutes, the question here arises in the specific context of a tax collection system based on self-assessment. Parliament designed the system and it is open to Parliament, as part of that design, to choose for itself to resolve any apparent conflicts between policies underlying tax provisions and other enactments. Parliament has indicated its intention to perform this role, not only in the design of the self-assessment system, which requires individuals without legal training to work through a complex series of provisions to calculate net income, for which maximum explicit guidance is necessary, but more specifically in its identification in the Act itself of certain outlays which the taxpayer is not permitted to deduct, as discussed below. Having recognized the problem of potentially conflicting legislative policies, Parliament has provided the solution, which is that in the absence of Parliamentary direction in the *Income Tax Act* itself, outlays and expenses are deductible if made for the purpose of gaining or producing income.

The argument is also put to this Court that Parliament did not intend to dilute the deterrent effect of a fine or penalty. If this Court is to accept this argument, then it would have to determine whether any particular fine or penalty was in fact meant to be deterrent in nature. If a fine was instead meant to be compensatory then there is no public policy frustrated by allowing its deduction: see Brooks, *supra*, at p. 244-45. Furthermore, this argument requires a court to establish that the deduction of the fine or penalty would decrease its intended effect. As Professor Vern Krishna has noted, although concluding that certain fines and penalties should not be deductible, the dilution argument may be:

> turned around to ask whether the denial of a deduction may have the ultimate effect of increasing a civil or criminal penalty, which may or may not have been intended by the legislative policy behind the statute violated. Thus, it is conceivable that indiscriminate

judicial application of a public policy limitation to all situations may cause the legislative policy behind an enactment to be varied in an unintended manner.

("Public Policy Limitations on the Deductibility of Fines and Penalties: Judicial Inertia" (1978), 16 *Osgoode Hall LJ* 19, at pp. 32-33.)

These difficulties outlined above demonstrate that the public policy arguments ask courts to make difficult determinations with questionable authority. Moreover, they place a high burden on the taxpayer who is to engage in this analysis in filling out his or her income tax return and would appear to undermine the objective of self-assessment underlying our tax system: see Hogg and Magee, *supra*, at p. 243. In addition, it is my opinion that the fundamental principles and provisions of the Act in the final analysis dictate that the rule be deductibility.

Tax neutrality and equity are key objectives of our tax system. Tax neutrality is violated by tax concessions, since the purpose of such concessions is to influence people's behaviour through the tax system by providing incentives for engaging in certain types of behaviour. For example, a deduction for an RRSP or a charitable contribution is a tax concession. This is to be distinguished from deductions allowed for the purpose of gaining an accurate picture of a taxpayer's net income. One of the underlying premises of our tax system is that the state taxes only net, rather than gross, income because it is net income that measures a taxpayer's ability to pay. As has been pointed out, this results in business-related fines being deductible: see Hogg and Magee, *supra*, at p. 243. Moreover, Hogg and Magee, *supra*, note, at p. 40, "in a system that is generally related to ability to pay, the provisions that violate neutrality (tax concessions) tend also to violate equity by abandoning the criterion of ability to pay in favour of other policy objectives."

Business expenses allowed under s. 18(1)(a) are deductible because of the concern to tax only net income, not in order to provide tax concessions to businesses. Such deductions are therefore consistent with the principles of tax neutrality and equity. The argument to disallow fines and penalties is thus an argument that the court should violate these principles in the name of public policy.

While various policy objectives are pursued through our tax system, and do violate the principles of neutrality and equity, it is my view that such public policy determinations are better left to Parliament. Particularly apposite is this Court's statement in *Royal Bank v. Sparrow Electric Corp.*, [1997] 1 SCR 411 (SCC), at para. 112, that "a legislative mandate is apt to be clearer than a rule whose precise bounds will become fixed only as a result of expensive and lengthy litigation." This statement was approved of by the Court in *Canderel Ltd. v. R*, [1998] 1 SCR 147 (SCC), at para. 41, adding that "[t]he law of income tax is sufficiently complicated without unhelpful judicial incursions into the realm of lawmaking. As a matter of policy, and out of respect for the proper role of the legislature, it is trite to say that the promulgation of new rules of tax law must be left to Parliament."

This approach and conclusion are supported by the fact that Parliament has expressly disallowed the deduction of certain expenses on what appear to be public policy grounds. For example, s. 67.5, added by RS 1994, c. 7, Sch. II (1991, c. 40), s. 46, prohibits the deduction of any outlay or expense made

> for the purpose of doing anything that is an offence under any of sections 119 to 121, 123 to 125, 393 and 426 of the Criminal Code or an offence under section 465 of that Act as it relates to an offence described in any of those sections.

In the absence of s. 67.5, bribes to public officials would be deductible (and taxable in the hands of the "bribee"). This is a situation where Parliament specifically chose to prohibit a deduction which would otherwise have been allowed. In addition, taxpayers are prohibited from deducting payments of interest and penalties levied under the Act itself (s. 18(1)(t) added by RS 1990, c. 39, s. 8), statutory royalties (s. 18(1)(m)), and payments required under the *Petroleum and Gas Revenue Act* (s. 18(1)(1.1)).

These provisions in the Act also reduce the force of the argument that allowing the deduction of fines and penalties permits the taxpayer to profit from his or her own wrongdoing. This line of reasoning is often traced to the statement of Lord Atkin in *Beresford v. Royal Insurance Co.*, [1938] 2 All E.R. 602 (UK HL), at p. 607: "the absolute rule is that the Courts will not recognize a benefit accruing to a criminal from his crime." However, as several commentators note, *Beresford* involved a payment under an insurance policy where the insured had committed suicide, at a time when suicide was characterized as a heinous crime. See E. Krasa, "The Deductibility of Fines, Penalties, Damages, and Contract Termination Payments" (1990) 38 *Can. Tax J* 1399, at p. 1417 and Krishna, *supra*, at pp. 31-32. There is therefore little authority to extend Lord Atkin's statement more generally, especially when one considers the clear authority, as mentioned above, to the effect that expenses incurred in the pursuit of illegal activities are deductible expenses.

Moreover, given that Parliament has expressly turned its mind to the deduction of expenses associated with certain activities that are offences under the *Criminal Code*, outlined in s. 67.5 of the Act, I do not find a legitimate role for judicial amendment on the general question of deductibility of fines and penalties. Since the Act is not silent on the issue of restricting the deduction of some expenses incurred for the purpose of gaining income, this is a strong indication that Parliament did direct its attention to the question and that where it wished to limit the deduction of expenses or payments of fines and penalties, it did so expressly. I am also sceptical that the deduction of fines and penalties provides the taxpayer with a "benefit" or "profit" — indeed, their purpose is to calculate the taxpayer's profit, which is then taxed.

(3) Conclusion Regarding s. 18(1)(a)

I therefore cannot agree with the argument that the deduction of fines and penalties should be disallowed as being contrary to public policy. First and foremost, on its face, fines and penalties are capable of falling within the broad and clear language of s. 18(1)(a). For courts to intervene in the name of public policy would only introduce uncertainty, as it would be unclear what public policy was to be followed, whether a particular fine or penalty was to be characterized as deterrent in nature, and whether the body imposing the fine intended it to be deductible. Moreover, allowing the deduction of fines and penalties is consistent with the tax policy goals of neutrality and equity. Although it may be said that the deduction of such fines and penalties "dilutes" the impact of the sanction, I do not view this effect as introducing a sufficient degree of disharmony so as to lead this Court to disregard the ordinary meaning of s. 18(1)(a) when that ordinary meaning is harmonious with the scheme and object of the Act. When Parliament has chosen to prohibit the deduction of otherwise allowable expenses on the grounds of public policy, then it has done so explicitly.

Although there are many points in my colleague Bastarache J's reasons with which I agree, there are others on which I would like to comment.

My colleague proposes a test in which the distinction between deductible and non-deductible levies must be determined on a case-by-case basis. In my view, such an approach would be quite onerous for the taxpayer who would be forced to undertake the difficult task of determining the object or purpose of the statute under which the payment was demanded whenever he or she filled out a tax return. Indeed, he or she would have to ascertain whether the specific purpose of the section was meant to be deterrence, punishment or compensation. Moreover, difficulties and uncertainties would undoubtedly arise where the purpose of the statutory provision is mixed. While a taxpayer must inevitably make various determinations in filing a return in order to report all relevant income and expenses and estimate the amount of tax payable, the statutory interpretation inquiry into the purpose of a statute is one which even courts often find particularly challenging. Consequently, it is inevitable that disputes will often require courts to determine whether a particular levy can be deducted from his or her income. Undoubtedly, this would introduce a significant element of uncertainty into our self-reporting tax system. On the other hand, Parliament could expressly prohibit the deduction of fines and penalties in a way compatible with the objectives of self-assessment and ease of administration.

Finally, at para. 17, my colleague states that penal fines are not, in the legal sense, incurred for the purpose of gaining income. It is true that s. 18(1)(a) expressly authorizes the deduction of expenses incurred for the purpose of gaining or producing income from that business. But it is equally true that if the taxpayer cannot establish that the fine was in fact incurred for the purpose of gaining or producing income, then the fine or penalty cannot be deducted and the analysis stops here. It is conceivable that a breach could be so egregious or repulsive that the fine subsequently imposed could not be justified as being incurred for the purpose of producing income. However, such a situation would likely be rare and requires no further consideration in the context of this case, especially given that Parliament itself may choose to delineate such fines and penalties, as it has with fines imposed by the *Income Tax Act*. To repeat, Parliament may well be motivated to respond promptly and comprehensively to prohibit clearly and directly the deduction of all such fines and penalties, if Parliament so chooses.

...

BASTARACHE J (L'Heureux-Dubé J concurring):

I. Introduction

This appeal raises the narrow question of whether a levy imposed pursuant to a provincial egg marketing scheme can be deducted as a business expense for the purposes of the *Income Tax Act*. ... The broader question posed by my colleague Justice Iacobucci is whether fines or other types of payments may be deductible from a taxpayer's income. While I agree with his answer to the narrow question, as well as with his characterization of the payment as a current expense rather than a capital outlay, and adopt his statement of the facts and judgments of the lower courts, I respectfully cannot agree that all types of fines and penalties are deductible as a matter of course.

II. Analysis

1. The Concept of Profit and the Scheme of the Income Tax Act

The Act sets out the mechanism for deducting expenses for the purpose of determining taxable income in broad language. Section 9 provides that "a taxpayer's income for a taxation year from a business or property is the taxpayer's profit from that business or property for the year." The Act provides no definition of the term "profit." In *Symes v. R*, [1993] 4 SCR 695 (SCC), this Court examined the calculation of profit in detail and determined that the correct approach is to begin by asking whether a particular expense would be deductible according to well accepted principles of business practice. However, even if the deduction is otherwise consistent with the principles of commercial trading, it may still be disallowed through the express limitations in s. 18(1). In particular, s. 18(1)(a) prohibits deductions in respect of:

> ... an outlay or expense except to the extent that it was made or incurred by the taxpayer for the purpose of gaining or producing income from the business or property; ...

Symes, *supra*, explains that the calculation of profit is a question of law that does not necessarily coincide with generally accepted accounting principles. As Iacobucci J instructs, at p. 724, "the s. 9(1) test is a *legal* test rather than an accountancy test" (emphasis added). While the definition of profit for balance sheet purposes and for income tax purposes may coincide, they are not necessarily identical.

Accordingly, the question of statutory interpretation raised in the present case is whether levies, fines and other payments should, in the legal sense, be considered to be "made or incurred by the taxpayer for the purpose of gaining income from the business.

2. Legislative Intention and Statutory Interpretation

It is well established that the correct approach to statutory interpretation is the modern contextual approach, set out by E.A. Driedger in *Construction of Statutes* (2nd ed. 1983), at p. 87:

> ... the words of an Act are to be read in their entire context and in their grammatical and ordinary sense harmoniously with the scheme of the Act, the object of the Act, and the intention of Parliament.

The modern rule is again described in *Driedger on the Construction of Statutes* (3rd ed. 1994), by R. Sullivan, at p. 131:

> There is only one rule in modern interpretation, namely, courts are obliged to determine the meaning of legislation in its total context, having regard to the purpose of the legislation, the consequences of proposed interpretations, the presumptions and special rules of interpretation, as well as admissible external aids. In other words, the courts must consider and take into account all relevant and admissible indicators of legislative meaning.

See also P.-A. Côté, *Interprétation des lois* (3rd ed. 1999), at pp. 364-73.

...

When considering the operation of ss. 9 and 18 in their entire context, I am persuaded that it was not the intention of Parliament to allow all fines to be deductible. I principally reach this conclusion for the simple reason that to so allow would operate to frustrate the legislative purpose of other statutes.

The statute book as a whole forms part of the legal context in which an act of Parliament is passed. As Driedger notes in the second edition, at p. 159, "one statute may influence the meaning of the other, so as to produce harmony within the body of the law as a whole"; see also Côté, *supra*, at pp. 433-40. Sullivan in *Driedger on the Construction of Statutes* is even more explicit in this regard, at p. 288:

> The meaning of words in legislation depends not only on their immediate context but also on a larger context which includes the Act as a whole and the statute book as a whole. The presumptions of coherence and consistency apply not only to Acts dealing with the same subject but also, albeit with lesser force, to the entire body of statute law produced by a legislature. The legislature is presumed to know its own statute book and to draft each new provision with regard to the structures, conventions, and habits of expression as well as the substantive law embodied in existing legislation.
>
> ... It is presumed that the legislature does not intend to contradict itself or to create inconsistent schemes. Therefore, other things being equal, interpretations that minimize the possibility of conflict or incoherence among different enactments are preferred.

[Footnotes omitted.]

She explains, at footnote 14, that the Act as a whole combined with the statute book as a whole "constitutes the complete text of a legislative provision." Similarly, Côté, *supra*, explains, at p. 433, that:

[TRANSLATION] Different enactments of the same legislature are supposedly as consistent as the provisions of a single enactment. All legislation of one Parliament is deemed to make up a coherent system. Thus interpretations favouring harmony between statutes should prevail over discordant ones, because the former are presumed to better represent the thought of the legislator.

To allow all fines to be deductible as a matter of course would therefore be inconsistent with the modern contextual approach to statutory interpretation, which requires that weight be given to the total context of the Act, including its relationship to other statutes. As N. Brooks argues in "The Principles Underlying the Deduction of Business Expenses," in B. Hansen, V. Krishna and J. Rendall, eds., *Essays on Canadian Taxation* (1978), 249, at p. 297:

> If the legislative bodies and the courts are perceived as engaged in a cooperative venture of law-making, then the courts must assume the task of ensuring, as much as possible, that the matrix of statutory instruments do not operate at cross purposes.

This is similar to the approach adopted by the United States Supreme Court in *Tank Truck Rentals, Inc. v. CIR* (1958), 356 US 30 (US Sup. Ct.). At issue there was whether fines imposed for violations of state maximum weight laws were deductible. The court unanimously held they were not, explaining, at p. 35:

> We will not presume that the Congress, in allowing deductions for income tax purposes, intended to encourage a business enterprise to violate the declared policy of a state. To allow the deduction sought here would but encourage continued violations of state law by increasing the odds in favor of non-compliance. This could only tend to destroy the effectiveness of the State's maximum weight laws.

The court recognized, however, that this presumption against congressional intention to encourage violations of other laws had to be balanced against the intention to tax only the profits of a business.

I observe the same complexity in the Canadian context. Nevertheless, it would clearly frustrate the purposes of the penalizing statute if an offender was allowed to deduct fines imposed for violations of the *Criminal Code*, RSC, 1985, c. C-46, or related statutes as business expenses. The deduction of a fine imposed for a *Criminal Code* violation would suggest that the decision to commit a criminal offence may be a legitimate business decision. Moreover, such a deduction would have the unsavoury effect of reducing the penal and deterrent effect of the penalizing statute.

The Act has since been amended to prohibit the deduction of illegal bribery expenses (s. 67.5, added by 1994, c. 7, Sch. II (1991, c. 49), s. 46) and fines imposed pursuant to the Act itself (s. 18(1)(t), added by 1990, c. 30, s. 8). It is argued that this indicates that Parliament did not intend to prohibit the deduction of other fines and penalties. In my view, this observation does not address the general consistency issue or require that the principles sustaining the coherence of our statutory framework be set aside when deciding whether an expense is incurred for the purpose of producing income under s. 18(1)(a). Côté, *supra*, explains the frailties of the type of *a contrario* argument proposed by the appellant, at p. 426:

[TRANSLATION] *A contrario*, especially in the form *expressio unius est exclusio alterius*, is widely used. But of all the interpretative arguments, it is among those which must be used with the utmost caution. The courts have often declared it an unreliable tool, and, as we shall see, it is frequently rejected.

He concludes, at p. 429:

[TRANSLATION] Since it is only a guide to the legislature's intent, *a contrario* reasoning should certainly be set aside if other indications reveal that its consequences go against the statute's purpose, are manifestly absurd, or lead to incoherence and injustice that could not have been the desire of Parliament.

[Footnotes omitted.]

In this case, it is possible to interpret the Act in a manner that is consistent with the object of other legislative enactments. To adopt the position that fines are always or generally deductible, without reference to the Act under which the fine was imposed, ignores the obligation to consider the intention of Parliament and to determine whether the deduction would defeat or impair the effectiveness of other legislative enactments. Absent express provision to the contrary, the presumption that Parliament would not intend to encourage the violation of other laws must be considered.

In my view, it is important not to overlook the importance of the characterization of the expenditure. When considering other types of payments, such as fees levied under regulatory regimes with compensatory aims, it might be wholly consistent with the scheme to allow the charges to be deductible. Such charges, like user fees generally, are costs of engaging in a particular type of business and are levied to compensate for different types of regulated activities or to claw back profits earned in violation of the regulations. Allowing such charges to be deducted does not undermine their function, as the money still goes to the compensatory scheme. Thus, it would not undermine the charging statute for these levies to be deducted from a taxpayer's income.

...

The distinction between deductible and non-deductible payments must therefore be determined on a case-by-case basis. The main factor in such a determination is whether the primary purpose of the statutory provision under which the payment is demanded would be frustrated or undermined. Statutory provisions imposing payments either as punishment for past wrongdoing or as general or specific deterrence against future law-breaking would be undermined if the fine could then be deducted as a business expense.

In contrast, if the legislative purpose behind a provision is primarily compensatory, its operation would not generally be undermined by the deduction of the expense. Where the purpose is mixed and the charging provisions have both a penal and a compensatory aim, a court should look for the primary purpose of the payment. In approaching this task, the court should consider, in particular, the nature of the mischief that the provision was designed to address.

I agree with my colleague, Iacobucci J, that public policy determinations are best left to Parliament. However, I am not suggesting that the deduction of penal fines be disallowed for public policy reasons, but instead because their deduction, not specifically authorized by the Act, would frustrate the expressed intentions of Parliament in other statutes if they were held to come under s. 18(1)(a) of the Act. In my view, penal fines are not expenditures incurred for the purpose of gaining or producing income in the legal sense. This concern is not so much one of public policy, morality or legitimacy, but one consistent with a realistic understanding of the accretion of wealth concept and the court's duty to uphold the integrity of the legal system in interpreting the *Income Tax Act.* As explained by McLachlin J in *Hall v. Hebert*, [1993] 2 SCR 159 (SCC), at p. 169, in finding that a court could bar recovery in tort on the ground of the plaintiff's immoral or illegal conduct:

> The basis of this power, as I see it, lies in the duty of the courts to preserve the integrity of the legal system, and is exercisable only where this concern is in issue. This concern is in issue where a damage award in a civil suit would, in effect, allow a person to profit from illegal or wrongful conduct, *or would permit an evasion or rebate of a penalty prescribed by the criminal law.* The idea common to these instances is that the law refuses to give by its right hand what it takes away by its left hand.

[Emphasis added.]

3. Application to the Facts

The impugned levy in the case at bar was imposed under s. 6 of the *British Columbia Egg Marketing Board Standing Order* (Rev. Jan. 1989), which derives its authority from s. 13(1)(k) of the *Natural Products Marketing (BC) Act*, RSBC 1979, c. 296, (the "Marketing Act") permitting the Lieutenant Governor in Council to vest in a marketing board or commission the power to:

> ... fix and collect levies or charges from designated persons engaged in the production or marketing of the whole or part of a regulated product and for that purpose to classify those persons into groups and fix the levies or charges payable by the members of the different groups in different amounts, and to use those levies or charges and other money and licence fees received by the commission

> (i)   to carry out the purposes of the scheme;

> (ii)   to pay the expenses of the marketing board or commission;

> (iii)   to pay costs and losses incurred in marketing a regulated product;

> (iv)   to equalize or adjust returns received by producers of regulated products during the periods the marketing board or commission may determine; and

> (v)   to set aside reserves for the purposes referred to in this paragraph;

In contrast, penalties are authorized by s. 20 of the *Marketing Act* which contemplates both fines and imprisonment as punishment for failing to comply with the Act or subordinate legislation:

> (1) Every person who fails to comply with this Act or the regulations or an order, rule, regulation, determination or decision made by the Provincial board or a marketing board or commission or made by virtue of a power exercisable under the federal Act, is liable on conviction, to a fine of not less than $100 and not more than $500 or to imprisonment not exceeding 6 months or to both a fine and imprisonment.

The comparison of these two provisions confirms that the over-quota levy assessed by the board pursuant to s. 13 of the *Marketing Act* was primarily compensatory and not penal. I would thus accept the trial judge's determination that this type of levy was akin to a "fee for service" incurred for the purpose of producing income:

> ... I do not view the levy imposed by the Board under the authority of paragraph 6(e) of the Standing Order, as a penalty. Indeed, there is a specific section in the BC Act dealing with penalties (section 20), and I do not see that these levies are assessed as a punishment imposed by statute as a consequence of the commission of an offense, but rather as an additional cost to the producer in the carrying out of his business.

([1995] 2 CTC 2294, at p. 2304.)

The deduction of such a levy does not operate to frustrate or undermine the purposes of the *Marketing Act* or of the *British Columbia Egg Marketing Board Standing Order* because such levies are not primarily geared towards punishment or deterrence, but instead to the efficient operation of the regulatory scheme.

Thus, as the over-quota levy was a compensatory fee charged primarily to defray the costs of over-production and incurred for the purpose of gaining or producing income, I would allow its deduction for the purposes of the computation of profit. ...

Appeal allowed.

NOTES AND QUESTIONS

1. On what grounds did the majority decision in *65302 British Columbia Ltd.* allow the taxpayer to deduct the over-quota levy in computing its business income for its 1988 taxation year? In what ways does the minority judgment differ from that of the majority? Why did the minority nonetheless concur with the majority's disposition of the case?

2. What test or tests did the majority decision in *65302 British Columbia Ltd.* apply to determine the deductibility of the over-quota levy incurred by the taxpayer? What test or tests did the minority decision apply? Is the court's characterization of these tests consistent with the scheme of the *Income Tax Act* and the relationship between the concept of profit and the income-producing purpose test established in *Imperial Oil Limited v. M.N.R.*, [1947] Ex. C.J. No. 20, [1947] C.T.C. 353, 3 D.T.C. 1090 (Ex. Ct.), and other cases?

Consider the following argument in David G. Duff, "Deductibility of Fines and Penalties Under the Income Tax Act: Public Policy, Statutory Interpretation and the Scheme of the Act in 65302 B.C. Ltd." (2001) 34 Can. Bus. L.J. 336 at 375-78:

the scheme of the ITA for the deduction of business expenses comprises the concept of "profit" in s. 9(1) as well as statutory limitations on deductibility such as the income-earning purpose test in s. 18(1)(a). Under the former provision, Canadian courts have held, taxpayers may claim deductions that are consistent with "ordinary principles of commercial trading or well accepted principles of business practice." The latter provision, on the other hand, prohibits the deduction of an otherwise deductible amount "except to the extent that it was made or incurred by the taxpayer for the purpose of gaining or producing income from the business." As a result, courts have emphasized, it is the former provision, rather than the latter, that "authorizes the deduction of business expenses."

Despite this conceptual priority, Canadian courts have also noted the considerable overlap between the business practices test under s. 9(1) and the income-earning purpose test in s. 18(1)(a). In *Symes*, for example, Iacobucci J, writing for a majority of the Supreme Court of Canada, observed that "the well accepted principles of business practice encompassed by subsection 9(1) would generally operate to prohibit the deduction of expenses which lack an income earning purpose" in the same way as s. 18(1)(a). Likewise, he explained, in many cases "the real issue may be whether a deduction is prohibited by well accepted principles of business practice *for the reason* that it is not incurred for the purpose of earning income."

On the other hand, Canadian courts have suggested, s. 9(1) may also "operate in isolation" to prohibit deductions that are inconsistent with ordinary principles of commercial trading or well accepted principles of business practice, irrespective of the limitations in s. 18(1). Indeed, given the objective character of the business practices test under s. 9(1) and the subjective character of the income-earning purpose test in s. 18(1)(a), it is entirely possible that an expense the deduction of which would not be prohibited by the latter provision could be disallowed under the former. This might be the case, for example, where a taxpayer incurs a fine or penalty in respect of a course of action that is undertaken for the purpose of earning income but neither ordinary nor well-accepted in its trade or business.

Notwithstanding this statutory scheme, Canadian cases dealing with the deduction of fines and penalties have tended to ignore the business practices test in s. 9(1), conflating this test with the income-earning purpose test in s. 18(1)(a). As a result, instead of asking whether deductibility would be "in accordance with ordinary principles of commercial trading or well accepted principles of business practice," courts have tended to ask whether the fine or penalty was incurred for the purpose of gaining or producing income. ...

In *65302*, the Supreme Court of Canada reproduces the conceptual confusion of other cases involving the deductibility of fines and penalties by ignoring the business practices test under s. 9(1) and conflating this test with the income-earning purpose test in s. 18(1)(a). For the majority, therefore, the key question in the appeal is whether the taxpayer incurred the over-quota levy "for the purpose of gaining or producing income from its business." Concluding that the over-quota levy satisfies the ordinary meaning of this test, it then rejects any modification to the language of s. 18(1)(a) based on avoidability or public policy. Similarly, although emphasizing the specifically *legal* character of the ITA tests for business expense deductibility, the minority concurs that "the question ... in the present case is whether levies, fines and other payments should ... be considered to be 'made or incurred by the taxpayer for the purpose of gaining income from the business.'" Having accepted this formulation of the essential legal question, it must then adopt a strained interpretation of s. 18(1)(a) according to which "penal fines are not expenditures incurred for the purpose of gaining or producing income in the legal sense."

Returning to the statutory scheme and prior case law, there are two major problems with this approach. First, as the Supreme Court of Canada itself affirmed in *Symes*, it is incorrect to regard the income-earning purpose test as the authority, "even inferentially" for the deductibility of a business expense. By making this the only test for the deduction of fines and penalties, therefore, the Court ignores both the scheme of the ITA and its own jurisprudence. Second, by disregarding the business practices test under s. 9(1), the Court overlooks the possibility that avoidability and public policy considerations might be relevant to this more basic test of business expense deductibility.

3.   On what basis did the majority judgment in *65302 British Columbia Ltd.* reject the Minister's argument that the over-quota levy was not connected with the taxpayer's business but imposed on the taxpayer personally? Did the majority reject the application of any "remoteness" test to determine whether an expense was incurred for the purpose of gaining or producing income from a taxpayer's business?

Consider the following comments in David G. Duff, "Deductibility of Fines and Penalties under the Income Tax Act: Public Policy, Statutory Interpretation and the Scheme of the Act in 65302 B.C. Ltd." (2001) 34 Can. Bus. L. J. 336 at 378-80:

Canadian courts have often employed a remoteness test which asks whether the activity giving rise to the expense was sufficiently connected with the business to have been incurred for the purpose of gaining or producing income from that business. While this test was first affirmed under the more restrictive language of the Income War Tax Act, it has also been applied under the much broader language of the ITA. It was also employed by the English Court of Appeal in *Alexander von Glehn*, where Lord Sterndale disallowed the deduction of a penalty arising from a violation of wartime export restrictions on the grounds that because "[t]he business could be perfectly well carried on without any infraction of the law," the penalty was neither "laid out or expended for the purpose of [its] trade" nor "connected with or arising out of such trade" but "was a fine imposed upon the company personally ... ." Noting that *Alexander von Glehn* and other Commonwealth cases on which the Minister relied were decided under more restrictive statutory language like that of the Canadian Income War Tax Act, the majority judgment in *65302* rejects these cases as "not ... helpful to the present appeal given the differences in the applicable taxation statutes."

Although the majority is right to emphasize the differences in language between s. 18(1)(a) of the ITA and the statutory provisions under which *Alexander von Glehn* and other Commonwealth cases were decided, it does not follow that these cases are necessarily irrelevant to the interpretation of the ITA. In *Alexander von Glehn*, for example, a careful reading suggests that non-deductibility turned less on the requirement that the penalty was not "wholly and exclusively" expended for the purpose of the taxpayer's business, but on the more general conclusions that the amount was neither "laid out or expended for the purpose of [the taxpayer's] trade" nor "connected with or arising out of such trade." Likewise, in *Imperial Oil*, Thorson P's affirmation of a remoteness test related to the general requirement in s. 6(a) of the Income War Tax Act that a disbursement or expense be laid out or expended "for the purpose" of earning income, not the more restrictive language requiring a disbursement or expense to have been "wholly, exclusively and necessarily laid out or expended" for this purpose. In each case, therefore, the remoteness test would appear to carry over to the less restrictive language of the ITA.

657

In addition, Canadian courts have often employed this remoteness test under the ITA to decide whether an expense was truly incurred for the purpose of gaining or producing income from the taxpayer's business. In *M.N.R. v. E.H. Pooler*, moreover, the Court emphasized the differences in language between the ITA and the statutory provisions under which *Alexander von Glehn* and *Imperial Oil* had been decided, but nonetheless disallowed the deduction of a fine imposed by the Toronto Stock Exchange on the grounds that improper conduct by the taxpayer's vice-president which led to the fine was "at most a remote circumstance" and not "done in the course of or for the purposes of the [taxpayer's] business." That the majority decision in *65302* considers none of these cases is further reason to question its apparent rejection of a remoteness test in the application of s. 18(1)(a).

4.   On what grounds did the majority decision in *65302 British Columbia Ltd.* reject the "avoidability" test affirmed by the Federal Court of Appeal in *Amway of Canada Ltd. v. Canada*, [1996] F.C.J. No. 211, [1996] 2 C.T.C. 162, 96 D.T.C. 6135 (F.C.A.)? Do you agree with the court's analysis? Why or why not? Consider the following argument in David G. Duff, "Deductibility of Fines and Penalties Under the Income Tax Act: Public Policy, Statutory Interpretation and the Scheme of the Act in 65302 B.C. Ltd." (2001) 34 Can. Bus. L.J. 336 at 381-83:

> For an expense to be deductible under the ITA, it is not sufficient for it to have been incurred for the purpose of gaining or producing income. On the contrary, as the scheme of the Act and Canadian jurisprudence make clear, the first test to determine the deductibility of a particular expense is "whether it was made or incurred by the taxpayer in accordance with ordinary principles of commercial trading or well accepted principles of business practice." While Canadian courts have tended to conflate this business practices test with the income-earning purpose test under s. 18(1)(a) of the ITA, several decisions have also considered the inevitability or avoidability of the expense as a relevant factor in determining its deductibility.
>
> Although Canadian courts have generally considered this avoidability criterion together with the income-earning purpose test in s. 18(1)(a), this consideration seems more compatible with the business practices test under s. 9(1). Where an expense is inevitable or unavoidable, its deduction is likely to be "in accordance with ordinary principles of commercial trading or well accepted principles of business practice." Where the expense is avoidable and generally avoided, on the other hand, it is unlikely to be regarded as "ordinary" or "well-accepted" in the taxpayer's trade or business.
>
> Indeed, to the extent that the avoidability requirement is supported by the Exchequer Court decision in *Imperial Oil*, Thorson P's judgment suggests that this criterion originates in the business practices test for business expense deductibility, not the income-earning purpose test. While the Court's conclusion that the damage payment was "in respect of a liability for a happening that was really incidental to the business" addresses the requirement that an expense must be connected with the business in order to be incurred for the purpose of earning income, the conclusion that the risk of collision was "normal and ordinary" for a marine operation such as that of the taxpayer satisfies the initial requirement for business expense deductibility in computing a taxpayer's "profit" — that the expense be deductible according to "ordinary principles of commercial trading or well accepted principles of business practice." As a result, Thorson P concluded:
>
> > I have no hesitation in finding that the amount sought to be deducted by the appellant would properly be deductible according to the ordinary principles of commercial trading and well established principles of business and accounting

practice as an item in the total cost of its marine operations, and that it falls outside the excluding provisions of sec. 6(a).

From this perspective, the majority's rejection of the avoidability test in *65302* is as misguided as its understanding of the statutory scheme for the deductibility of business expenses more generally. Referring to *Imperial Oil*, for example, it ignores the passages cited by the Federal Court of Appeal in *Amway* in support of an avoidability test, conflates this test with the requirement that an expense be incidental to the business in order to be incurred for the purpose of earning income, and refuses to follow *Imperial Oil* on the basis that the language of s. 18(1)(a) of the ITA differs from that of the comparable provision of the Income War Tax Act. To the extent that the avoidability criterion relates to the business practices test, which applies to the ITA as much as it did to the Income War Tax Act, changes in the language of the income-earning purpose test are irrelevant to its continued application.

Nor is it damaging to the argument for an avoidability test that such a requirement seems incompatible with the language of s. 18(1)(a) of the ITA. On the contrary, if the avoidability concept originates in the business practices test for business expense deductibility, it is here where one should seek its compatibility with the language and scheme of the ITA, not s. 18(1)(a). Since the majority ignores the business practices test and conflates the concept of profit under s. 9(1) with the limitation on deductibility in s. 18(1)(a), however, it does not consider this possibility.

Nor does it affect the case for an avoidability test that *Day & Ross* and *TNT* were unclear on the issue, or that the Federal Court of Appeal suggested in *Amway* that such a requirement might apply only to fines and penalties and not other expenses. Since these decisions also ignored the business practices test, conflating this test with the income-earning purpose test, it is not surprising that they are not clear on the appropriate role and scope of any avoidability requirement. Indeed, to the extent that the avoidability criterion relates to the business practices test, it should apply to any category of expense, not only fines and penalties.

5.   On what grounds did the majority judgment in *65302 British Columbia Ltd.* reject the application of a judicially defined public policy limitation on the deductibility of fines and penalties? Why did the minority decision dissent on this point? Which approach do you find more persuasive? Consider the following argument for a public policy limitation in David G. Duff, "Deductibility of Fines and Penalties Under the Income Tax Act: Public Policy, Statutory Interpretation and the Scheme of the Act in 65302 B.C. Ltd." (2001) 34 Can. Bus. L.J. 336 at 383-88:

> Although various arguments have been advanced in favour of a public policy limitation on the deductibility of fines and penalties, the most persuasive is the interpretive argument that Parliament would not have intended the provisions of the ITA to contradict other statutes and regulatory schemes. Regardless of the moral severity of the offence or the deterrent effect of the sanction, deductibility of an expense associated with a violation of another statute might contradict the basic purpose of the other statute by suggesting that the violation is a legitimate business practice. To the extent that Parliament is presumed to legislate in a coherent manner, taking into account the statute book as a whole, interpretations that avoid these inconsistencies are preferable to those that do not. On the other hand, as the majority judgment in *65302* emphasizes, courts should be reluctant to depart from the ordinary meaning of statutory provisions "in order to conform to a broader appreciation of Parliament's intent, and thereby avoid a repugnant disharmony or absurdity."

[As with] the avoidability test ... , Canadian courts have been unclear on the statutory authority for a public policy limitation on the deductibility of fines and penalties. While some cases appear to regard it as an independent test, irrespective of any statutory basis in the ITA, others view it as a modification to the income-earning purpose test in s. 18(1)(a). In *65302*, the Supreme Court of Canada takes the latter view, with the minority arguing that "penal fines are not expenditures incurred for the purpose of gaining or producing income *in the legal sense*" and the majority rejecting the introduction of a public policy limitation through "judicial amendment" to the ordinary meaning of s. 18(1)(a) of the ITA.

Also like the avoidability test, however, a public policy limitation on the deductibility of fines and penalties may be more compatible with the business practice test under s. 9(1) of the ITA than the income-earning purpose test in s. 18(1)(a). Indeed, since the courts have characterized the former test as a specifically legal test, it is arguable that legal norms and public policies derived from other statutes and regulatory schemes might be legitimately incorporated into the "ordinary principles of commercial trading" and "well accepted principles of business practice" with which deductible business expenses must comply. Thus, for example, even if it were customary in a particular trade or business to hire contract killers to eliminate one's competitors, courts might reasonably disallow a deduction for their fees on the basis that such expenses are neither ordinary nor well-accepted within the legal system as a whole.

While this approach would avoid inconsistencies among different statutes and regulatory schemes without requiring any "judicial amendment" to the ordinary meaning of s. 18(1)(a), even this public policy test might be opposed on various grounds. In fact, critics have raised several objections to the introduction of any judicially established public policy limitation on the deductibility of fines and penalties, apparently irrespective of its particular form. ...

Beginning with the argument that it would be unfair to tax the profits of illegal activities while disallowing the deduction of fines and penalties, one can respond that these circumstances in no way correspond: that the taxation of illegal enterprises, unlike the deduction of fines and penalties, does not condone these activities, that the non-taxation of illegal enterprises, unlike the non-deductibility of fines and penalties, relieves the offender and shifts the tax burden to law-abiding citizens, and that Parliament could therefore reasonably have intended to tax illegal enterprises while disallowing deductions for fines and penalties. For similar reasons, one can challenge the assumed inconsistency of disallowing the deduction of fines and penalties while permitting the deduction of ordinary expenses incurred by illegal businesses. Although deductibility of fines and penalties can operate to condone the conduct in respect of which the fine or penalty is imposed, deductions for ordinary expenses incurred by illegal enterprises no more condone these activities than the taxation of these enterprises themselves. While non-deductibility of ordinary expenses incurred by illegal enterprises might help to deter these activities, the most persuasive public policy argument against the deductibility of fines and penalties does not depend on such deterrence arguments. ...

Turning to the argument that non-deductibility would contradict the basic scheme of the ITA, which taxes net income not gross income before deductions, one can respond that this important tax policy objective must be balanced against other public policies reflected in other statutes and regulatory schemes. To the extent that Parliament is assumed to legislate in a coherent manner, taking into account all statutes and regulatory schemes, it would be inappropriate to regard the ITA as a "self-contained code" operating independently of the broader legal context of which it is a part. Indeed, provisions like s. 67.5 can be viewed as a signal to the courts to interpret the ITA in light of this broader context more generally.

The remaining arguments against a judicially established public policy test emphasize conflicts among different jurisdictions, difficulties in discerning public policies, difficulties in the administration of any public policy limitation on the deductibility of otherwise deductible expenses, and the merits of clear legislative guidelines over uncertain judicial standards. Without examining each of these arguments in detail, their combined purport is to suggest that questions of public policy are better left to Parliament than the courts.

> Although the application of a specific public policy limitation to any otherwise deductible business expense is neither easy nor certain, it is not clear that legislatures are always better placed to make these decisions than the courts. On the contrary, since courts are called upon to evaluate particular expenses in the context of specific violations, they are often better able to identify and address unanticipated conflicts among different statutes and regulatory schemes. In contrast, it would be unreasonable to expect Parliament to survey each and every statute and regulatory scheme to identify and address potential conflicts in advance. In this respect, as I have argued elsewhere, "in the application of statutory provisions to concrete facts, comparative institutional competence rests with the courts, not the legislature."

6.   For other comments on the role of public policy considerations in the deductibility of fines and penalties, see Vern Krishna, "Public Policy Limitations on the Deductibility of Fines and Penalties: Judicial Inertia" (1978) 16 Osgoode Hall L.J. 19 at 31-33; Neil Brooks, "The Principles Underlying the Deduction of Business Expenses" in Brian G. Hansen, Vern Krishna, and James A. Rendall, *Canadian Taxation* (Toronto: De Boo, 1978) 249 at 297-302; Richard Krever, "The Deductibility of Fines: Considerations from Law and Policy Perspectives" (1984) 13 Australian Tax Review 168; Eva M. Krasa, "The Deductibility of Fines, Penalties, Damages, and Termination Payments" (1990) 38 Can. Tax J. 1399 at 1415-20; and Peter W. Hogg, Joanne E. Magee, and Ted Cook, *Principles of Canadian Income Tax Law*, 3d ed. (Toronto: Carswell, 1999) at 258-59.

7.   On what, if any, grounds might a court have disallowed the deduction of a fine or penalty after the Supreme Court of Canada decision in *65302 British Columbia Ltd. v. Canada*, [1999] S.C.J. No. 69, [2000] 1 C.T.C. 57, 99 D.T.C. 5799 (S.C.C.)? On what grounds would the government justify its decision to enact section 67.6?

8.   Until the decision in *65302 British Columbia Ltd.* and the enactment of section 67.6, the CRA's views on the deductibility of fines and penalties were contained in *Interpretation Bulletin* IT-104R2, "Deductibility of Fines or Penalties," May 23, 1993. According to paragraph 2, "judicial and statutory fines or penalties do not generally qualify as a deduction in computing income from a business or property under paragraph 18(1)(a)." According to paragraph 3, however:

> Where the expense satisfies all of the following tests and factors, fines or penalties for relatively minor matters, such as licensing infractions, may be deducted in computing income from a business or property:
>
> > (a)   the fine or penalty can be shown to have been laid out for the purpose of earning income;

      (b)   the nature and circumstances of the penalized conduct are such that allowing the deduction of the expense would not be contrary to public policy;

      (c)   incurring the particular type of fine or penalty is a normal risk of carrying on the business or earning the income and even though due care is exercised, the violation resulting in the imposition of the fine or penalty is inevitable and beyond the control of the taxpayer and the taxpayer's employees;

      (d)   the breach of the law giving rise to the fine or penalty does not result from negligence, ignorance or deliberate disobedience of the law and does not endanger public safety; and

      (e)   deduction of the expense is not otherwise prohibited under the Act ... .

According to paragraph 4:

For purposes of 3(c) above, where fines or penalties are a normal risk in carrying on business but the risk is accepted as an expedient way for realizing savings in expenses that would otherwise have been necessary in avoiding fines or penalties, these fines or penalties are not inevitable and not beyond the control of the taxpayer. In determining what is within the taxpayer's control, practical considerations will be taken into account based on the facts of each case. However, fines and penalties for most common violations, including pollution and speeding offenses, will not satisfy this condition of deductibility.

According to paragraph 5:

For the purposes of 3(b) and (d) above, a breach or infraction of the law which gives rise to a fine or penalty is not generally considered to endanger public safety nor is the deduction of the amount of the fine or penalty normally considered contrary to public policy provided that:

      (a)   the purpose of the fine is merely compensatory, as opposed to discouraging people from engaging in certain kinds of activities, and the amount of the fine bears a reasonable relation to the compensation required to remedy the harm caused; or

      (b)   legal means are available for avoiding the imposition of fines or penalties, such as in the case of overweight fines for trucks where advance overweight permits are readily available.

According to paragraph 7, penalties or fines imposed by governing bodies of specific businesses, professions, or trades, such as provincial law societies, that are empowered to levy fines and penalties against their members "will normally be imposed as a punishment or deterrent in connection with the infraction and will not be deductible from income." According to paragraph 8, however, penalties imposed by trade associations with respect to violations of voluntarily agreed upon standards of performance "will ordinarily be allowed as a deduction" where these penalties are "clearly related to the earning of income from business."

Interpretation Bulletin IT-104R2 was replaced by Interpretation Bulletin IT-104R3 on August 9, 2002. According to paragraph 3 of this Bulletin:

> 3. Paragraph 18(1)(a) of the Act provides that, in computing a taxpayer's income from a business or property, no deduction shall be made in respect of an outlay or expense except to the extent that it was made or incurred by the taxpayer for the purpose of gaining or producing income from the business or property. As stated by the Supreme Court of Canada in the *65302 British Columbia Ltd.* decision: "... if the taxpayer cannot establish that the fine was in fact incurred for the purpose of gaining or producing income, then the fine or penalty cannot be deducted ..."

> For purposes of establishing whether a fine or penalty has been incurred for the purpose of gaining or producing income:

> • the taxpayer need not have attempted to prevent the act or omission that resulted in the fine or penalty; and

> • the taxpayer need only establish that there was an income-earning purpose for the act or omission, regardless of whether that purpose was actually achieved.

> In the *65302 British Columbia Ltd.* decision, the Supreme Court of Canada also stated: "It is conceivable that a breach could be so egregious or repulsive that the fine subsequently imposed could not be justified as being incurred for the purpose of producing income." The Court did not, however, give any guidelines with respect to this statement other than to indicate that "... such a situation would likely be rare ...." It would have to be one in which the egregiousness or repulsiveness of the act or omission giving rise to the fine or penalty is sufficient to refute any allegation that the purpose of the act or omission was to gain or produce income.

9.   Paragraph 18(1)(t), applicable to the 1989 and subsequent taxation years, prohibits deductions in respect of any amount paid or payable under the *Income Tax Act*. According to the Department of Finance technical notes released with the amendment, the prohibition applies to taxes, interest, and penalties payable under the Act. In *Iogen Corp. v. Canada*, [1995] T.C.J. No. 667, [1995] 2 C.T.C. 2651 (T.C.C.), where the taxpayer sought to deduct penalties and interest that were payable under the *Income Tax Act* in taxation years prior to 1989, Lamarre-Proulx JTCC rejected the taxpayer's argument that the enactment of paragraph 18(1)(t) suggested that these penalties were deductible prior to 1989, commenting (at para. 16) that this provision was "enacted for greater certainty and did not change the law." See also *Godsell v. Canada*, [1995] T.C.J. No. 1757, [1996] 2 C.T.C. 2238 (T.C.C.), where Teskey JTCC suggested (at para. 19) that paragraph 18(1)(t) was enacted to confirm "long-standing jurisprudence to the effect that an amount paid pursuant to the *Income Tax Act* cannot be deducted in the calculation of income."

10.   According to section 162(f) of the US *Internal Revenue Code*, in deducting "ordinary and necessary expenses paid or incurred during the taxable year in carrying on any trade or business," taxpayers may not deduct "any fine or similar penalty paid to a government for the violation of any law."

For discussions of the US rule, see Andrew R. Shoemaker, "The Smuggler's Blues: Wood v. United States and the Resulting Horizontal Inequity Among Criminals in the Allowance of Federal Income Tax Deductions" (1992) 11 Va. Tax Rev. 659 at 666-67; and F. Philip Manns Jr., "Internal Revenue Code Section 162(f): When Does the Payment of Damages to a Government Punish the Payor?" (1993) 13 Va. Tax Rev. 271.

D. Theft

Like damages, fines, and penalties, losses attributable to theft may be either avoidable or remotely connected with the taxpayer's business. One of the earliest Canadian cases to consider the deductibility of stolen funds is *Thayer Lumber Company Limited v. M.N.R.*, (1957), 18 Tax ABC 284, 58 D.T.C. 48 (T.A.B.).

Thayer Lumber Company Limited v. M.N.R.
(1957), 18 Tax ABC 284, 58 D.T.C. 48 (T.A.B.)

CECIL L. SNYDER, QC: The appellant company was incorporated on January 27, 1954, continuing a business established in 1912 by the father of the appellant's president. The president, Cyril W. Thayer, has been associated with the business since 1946 in partnership with Claude Elliott. The company continued to carry on business in a manner similar to that followed by the founder of the business and with the staff previously employed. Mr. Thayer and Mr. Elliott are the principal shareholders of the appellant, a small number of shares being held by another. In April or May, 1955, when the company's accounts were balanced, it was discovered that there was a shortage of $8,122.15 in the appellant's receipts for 1954. The appellant deducted this sum in computing its taxable income for that year. This deduction was disallowed by the respondent in assessing the appellant's income and this appeal was taken from the assessment.

Mr. Thayer gave evidence that Mr. Elliott instructed an employee regarding her duties in accepting and recording cash receipts. Mr. Thayer said that he believed that each morning $50 in change was taken from the vault in the company's offices by this employee for use through the day and was returned to the vault at the end of the day together with the daily receipts. Mr. Thayer, Mr. Elliott, the above-mentioned employee and another employee accepted cash receipts. Mr. Elliott did most of the bookkeeping. The woman employed as cashier made deposits at the bank on behalf of the company. It appears that daily cash receipts were not checked against the daily sales record. The cash account was balanced only once a year.

Mr. Thayer said that when the loss was discovered in May, 1955, he at first thought that there was some explanation and it was only in December, 1955, that the loss was reported to the insurance company with which the appellant was bonded. In December, 1955, the local police were also informed of the loss. An investigation was conducted on behalf of the insurance company and the result was that the insurance company refused to reimburse the appellant for the loss or to accept any responsibility in the matter as there was no evidence that the vault had been broken into.

Mr. Thayer said that the method of handling cash was similar to the practice of his father in conducting the business for some forty years. The vault in which cash was retained was unlocked throughout the day in order that the two employees in the office might obtain cash when required. At the end of the day Mr. Thayer or Mr. Elliott locked the vault. During lunch hour a member of the staff was on duty but, as the vault was located on the opposite side of the hall from the general office, it would have been possible for someone to enter the hall and have access to the vault without her knowledge. Entrance to the hall could be gained from a door leading to the yard adjoining the company's mill. Mr. Thayer said that the same staff had been employed prior to incorporation of the company and no shortage had been found previously. He said, "you have to trust someone." However, since the loss was discovered a device has been attached to the vault door to indicate each time the vault is opened.

Evidence was given by the accountant engaged in October, 1955, by the appellant to make an investigation into the shortage which had been discovered. ... The accountant stated that the losses resulted from carelessness.

...

It was submitted on behalf of the appellant that the money was lost in the course of carrying on its business. The delay in reporting the loss was due to disbelief on the part of the appellant's officers that the shortage was due to theft. It was pointed out that the appellant's records could have been adjusted to show net income remaining after deduction of the sums lost. Instead the appellant chose to state the facts as they actually existed.

...

Counsel for the respondent contended that the sum under consideration did not come within the ambit of Section 12(1)(a) [now paragraph 18(1)(a)] and accordingly could not be deducted. An expense would be deductible if it was incurred in the ordinary course of doing business ... but it had not been shown that the deduction claimed herein was an amount lost as a result of an ordinary business risk.

...

[I]ncome tax legislation does not decree the manner in which a man must carry on his business. ... The present appellant's business was carried on in the same manner as it had been carried on for many years, in which time no loss was suffered. However, the appellant has learned that it is unwise and costly to place such responsibility upon employees and, indeed, to leave the door wide open to trespassing by others in premises where funds are retained. Where such a practice is permitted theft by employees or others is a risk inherent in the carrying on of the taxpayer's business.

...

The loss suffered by the present appellant occurred in business operations carried on in its usual manner. The appellant would surely be subject to criticism if, after the loss was discovered and verified, it had taken no steps to ensure that further losses would not occur. However, past experience had shown that the methods used until 1954 were quite satisfactory. ... [T]he loss was an extraordinary event but, nevertheless, it occurred in the usual routine of business activities.

...

In the present appeal there is no reason to believe that either of the principal shareholders misappropriated company funds. It appears that the loss occurred because of the long-standing practice of the founder, Mr. Thayer, Sr., adopted by his successor, the appellant company, in assuming that all people are honest.

Whether the monies were taken by an employee of the company or by others is unknown but the loss occurred in the usual course of the appellant's operations and is a deductible expense.

Appeal allowed.

NOTES AND QUESTIONS

1.   On what grounds did the Minister argue in *Thayer Lumber Company Limited* that the taxpayer should not be allowed to deduct the amount of the stolen funds in computing its business income? What, if any, statutory authority underlies the Minister's argument that the loss could be deducted only if it was incurred "in the ordinary course of doing business"? What, if any, statutory authority underlies the Minister's argument that the loss could be deducted only if the funds were stolen "as a result of an ordinary business risk"?

2.   On what grounds did the Tax Appeal Board allow the taxpayer's appeal in *Thayer Lumber Company Limited*? Of what, if any, relevance to the board's decision is its affirmation that "income tax legislation does not decree the manner in which a man must carry on his business"? Of what, if any, relevance is its observation that the taxpayer's business had been "carried on in the same manner ... for many years, in which time no loss was suffered"? Of what, if any, relevance is the board's conclusion that "theft by employees or others is a risk inherent in the carrying on of the taxpayer's business"? Of what relevance to the board's decision is its comment that "there is no reason to believe that either of the principal shareholders misappropriated company funds"?

3.   In *Thayer Lumber Company Limited*, the board observed that the taxpayer "would surely be subject to criticism if, after the loss was discovered and verified, it had taken no steps to ensure that further losses would not occur." Does this statement suggest that a subsequent loss would not be deductible if the taxpayer took no steps to ensure that further theft did not occur? Should

continued losses be deductible notwithstanding a taxpayer's carelessness in managing its cash?

4.   In *General Stampings of Canada Ltd. v. M.N.R.* (1957), 17 Tax ABC 1, 57 D.T.C. 163 (T.A.B.), the taxpayer sought to deduct $36,571.33, which was discovered to have been stolen by the taxpayer's general manager, who was also the registered holder of one share and a director of the taxpayer. Disallowing the deduction, the board stated (at para. 3):

> It appears that the General Manager conducted the Company's affairs to suit himself and was able to do just as he pleased with the funds on hand. The operation of the business was left entirely in his hands and none of the other directors interfered in any way. The monies involved had already been earned and were in the Company's coffers. The General Manager removed them by an improper exercise of the control that he possessed and this action on his part had nothing whatever to do with the conduct of the Company's income-earning activities. To quote from the judgment in [*Curtis v. J. & G. Oldfield, Ltd.* (1925), 9 TC 319, 41 T.L.R. 373], it was "dehors the trade altogether." This being the position, the loss suffered by the Company cannot be treated as deductible from income as though a loss incurred in the ordinary course of business.

For similar results involving the theft of a taxpayer's property by shareholders, directors, partners, or senior employees, see *Blue Bonnet Oil Co. v. M.N.R.* (1958), 20 Tax ABC 73, 58 D.T.C. 487 (T.A.B.); *Dessin General Drafting Inc. v. M.N.R.*, [1968] Tax ABC 327, 68 D.T.C. 239 (T.A.B.); *Miller v. M.N.R.* (1953), 8 Tax ABC 385, 53 D.T.C. 266 (T.A.B.); and *Cameron v. M.N.R.* (1959), 21 Tax ABC 193, 59 D.T.C. 64 (T.A.B.).

5.   For other cases in which losses attributable to theft by burglars or more subordinate employees have been allowed as deductible expenses, see *Weidman Brothers Limited v. M.N.R.* (1950), 2 Tax ABC 223, 50 D.T.C. 322 (T.A.B.); *Montreal Bronze Ltd. v. M.N.R.* (1962), 29 Tax ABC 345, 62 D.T.C. 371 (T.A.B.); and *Royal Holdings Ltd. v. M.N.R.*, [1969] Tax ABC 1169, 69 D.T.C. 775 (T.A.B.).

6.   In *Cassidy's Ltd. v. M.N.R.*, [1989] T.C.J. No. 930, [1990] 1 C.T.C. 2043, 89 D.T.C. 686 (T.C.C.), the taxpayer sought to deduct amounts that had been embezzled over a period of four years by a senior employee who held the positions of vice-president, general manager, and controller, the last of which gave him "complete discretion" over the financial operations of the taxpayer. Concluding that "[t]he case law distinguishes not so much as to the level of the employee in the employer's hierarchy but how and at what stage in the income earning process the money is stolen or embezzled," the court rejected the Minister's arguments that the losses were "non-deductible expenses resulting from the actions of a senior employee" and "did not constitute expenses incurred for the purpose of earning or producing income from a business within the meaning of paragraph 18(1)(a) of the Act," on the grounds (at para. 50) that the losses were incurred "in the normal course" of the taxpayer's business and were "deductible in computing profit in accordance with ordinary commercial principles and ... not prohibited by the Act." According to Rip TCJ (at para. 46):

> When a taxpayer carries on a business he is exposed to all of the risks of that business. The risks include damage to property used in the business, liability for the torts or delicts of its employees in the course of their employment as well as theft, embezzlement or defalcation by employees while working for the employer in the course of business. To protect themselves against such exposure businesses may insure their properties against damage and bond their employees. ... There is, in carrying on a business, an inherent risk that employees may steal. The use of employees in a business is necessary to carrying on that business. In hiring persons for employment an employer may hire dishonest people: that is a risk he takes in carrying on the business.

More importantly, he observed (at para. 49), the senior employee had drawn cheques on the taxpayer's account "in the same manner as when he drew cheques required in the normal course of carrying on the business." As a result, he concluded, citing *W.G. Evans & Co. Ltd. v. Commissioner of Inland Revenue*, [1976] 1 N.Z.L.R. 425 at 435, the senior employee had:

> misappropriated the money while dealing with it as part of the company's activities, and not by the exercise of overriding power or control outside those activities altogether. ... The risk of such defalcations was inherent in the operations of the company carried on by necessity in this way, and accordingly the resulting loss is fairly incidental to the production of the assessable income and is deductible.

7. In *Parkland Operations Ltd. v. M.N.R.*, [1990] F.C.J. No. 954, [1991] 1 C.T.C. 23, 90 D.T.C. 6676 (F.C.T.D.), the taxpayer corporation sought to deduct $563,396, which had been misappropriated by two shareholders and directors of the taxpayer who were authorized to sign cheques on the taxpayer's behalf. Allowing the deduction, the court accepted accounting evidence that deductibility was in accordance with generally accepted accounting principles, and held that the funds were misappropriated "in the course of the company's activities." According to Jerome ACJ (at para. 21), the directors "misappropriated the funds not in their capacity as shareholders, but rather as thieves, with neither the knowledge nor consent of the other shareholders."

When, if ever, might funds be misappropriated by shareholders or directors *qua* shareholders or directors, rather than shareholders or directors *qua* thieves? Is this a relevant criterion for determining deductibility?

8. The CRA's views on the deductibility of losses from theft, defalcation, or embezzlement appear in *Interpretation Bulletin* IT-185R, "Losses from Theft, Defalcation or Embezzlement," March 2001.

9. In some cases the taxpayer's entire venture may be characterized as a fraud, and losses denied on the fundamental basis that there was no business. See, for example, *Hammill v. Canada*, [2005] F.C.J. No. 1197, [2005] 4 C.T.C. 29, 257 D.L.R. (4th) 1, 338 N.R. 162 (F.C.A.), where the taxpayer's losses associated with the sale of his inventory of gems were denied because "the appellant was the subject of a scam from start to finish". The Federal Court of Appeal determined that "[t]his finding precludes the existence of a business" (at para. 47). In the alternative, the Federal Court of Appeal held that the expenses were unreasonable pursuant to section 67.

E. Legal Defence Costs

Where a taxpayer incurs legal expenses to defend against a civil or criminal proceeding, a separate question arises regarding the deductibility of these legal defence costs. One of the leading cases on this issue is *Rolland Paper Company Limited v. M.N.R.*, [1960] C.T.C. 158, 60 D.T.C. 1095 (Ex. Ct.).

Rolland Paper Company Limited v. M.N.R.
[1960] C.T.C. 158, 60 D.T.C. 1095 (Ex. Ct.)

[The taxpayer and other persons engaged in the business of manufacturing and selling fine paper were charged under section 498(1)(d) of the *Criminal Code* on the basis that they "did unlawfully conspire, combine, agree or arrange together and with one another ... to unduly prevent or lessen competition" during the years 1933 to 1952. On June 4, 1954, the accused parties were convicted by the Ontario High Court and sentenced to pay a $10,000 fine. Appeals to the Ontario Court of Appeal and the Supreme Court of Canada were dismissed. In order to pursue these appeals, the taxpayer incurred a legal expense of $5,948.27, which it deducted in computing its income for its 1955 taxation year. The Minister disallowed the deduction on the basis that the expense was not incurred for the purpose of gaining or producing income within the meaning of paragraph 12(1)(a) of the 1952 Act (now paragraph 18(1)(a)).]

FOURNIER J: ... The appellant submits that these legal expenses were made in accordance with the ordinary principles of commercial trading and well accepted principles of business practice. It urged that they were made in the course of its business and incurred for the purpose of defending its day-to-day trade practices which gave rise to income and were directly related to the earning of its income.

On the other hand, the respondent contends that the amount sought to be deducted was the amount of the legal costs incurred for the purpose of defending against an accusation made under the provisions of the *Criminal Code* and that in such cases these expenses, from the point of view of the law, are not to be deemed to have been made or incurred for the purpose of earning income. They relate to the cost of unsuccessfully defending a criminal action and from the point of view of strict business practices and within the framework of the law such expenses could not be admitted as deductions.

...

In the case of *M.N.R. v. L.D. Caulk Co. of Canada Ltd.*, [1952] Ex. CR 49; [1952] CTC 1, in 1947, the respondent, a manufacturer of dental supplies, at the invitation of the Commissioner under the *Combines Investigation Act* who was conducting an investigation into an alleged combine in the manufacture and sale of dental supplies in Canada, made representations before him, employing for the purpose solicitors to whom he paid a fee for their services. Later the respondent and others were charged under Section 498 of the *Criminal Code* that they did in fact constitute a combine in the manufacture and sale of dental supplies in Canada. At the trial the respondent was acquitted and an appeal taken by the Crown from such acquittal was dismissed. The respondent in 1948 paid legal fees to its solicitors and counsel who acted at the trial and appeal.

Although the facts dealt with in the dental trade as opposed to those dealt with in the fine paper trade were identical in terms of the indictment and charge, the results in the two instances were different. In the *Caulk* case *(supra)* the charge was dismissed and the company was not found guilty and was not fined. In the *Rolland Paper Co. Ltd.* case, the company was found guilty and fined. So the only difference material to this appeal between this case and the *Caulk* case is the difference between condemnation and acquittal.

Cameron J held [[1952] Ex. CR 49; [1952] CTC 12]:

> The payments [to its solicitors and counsel by respondent] were made in the usual course of business and were made with reference to a particular difficulty which arose in the course of the year, namely, the investigation by the Commissioner, the charge laid against the respondent and the unfavourable and damaging publicity which resulted therefrom, and which would have been greatly enhanced had the charge been sustained: the disbursements ... were made in an effort ... to establish that its trading practices were not illegal, and to enable it to carry on as it had in the past, unimperilled by charges that such practices were illegal.

The learned judge affirmed the decision of the Income Tax Appeal Board and held that certain legal expenses incurred by the respondent were deductible under the *Income War Tax Act* in ascertaining this taxable income.

On appeal from this decision to the Supreme Court of Canada, [1954] SCR 55; [1954] CTC 28, Rand, J, who delivered the judgment said at p. 56 [[1954] CTC 30]:

> ... The agreement or arrangement alleged to have been unlawful purported to regulate day to day practices in the conduct of the respondent's business ... and the payment to defend the usages under it was a beneficial outlay to preserve what helped to produce the income. These expenses included legal fees both for appearing before the Commissioner under the *Combines Investigation Act* and at the trial which resulted in acquittal.

After reading carefully the judgments of both Courts from which I have cited extracts, I have come to the conclusion that the facts therein stated are identical to those ... in the present case.

In each case, the parties' claim is for the deduction of legal expenses in the computation of their taxable income. Both claimants had been charged and prosecuted under the same section of the *Criminal Code* for having illegally conspired and combined to prevent or lessen competition in their respective trades of manufacturing, selling and distributing their commodities. The agreement or arrangements made or arrived at were to regulate their day to day practices in the conduct of their business activities. Their scheme was one to govern their operations from which they derived their income. The legal expenses were paid to defend their way of doing business and preserve the system under which they operated.

Certain remarks of Cameron J of the Exchequer Court in his notes and which were concurred in by Kellock J of the Supreme Court were discussed at length by counsel for both parties. The opinions expressed related to the fact that a conviction on the charge might have made a difference on the decision which was arrived at.

I quote the remarks of Cameron J [1952] Ex. CR 58 [[1952] CTC 10]:

> ... In view of the fact that the respondent was acquitted, I do not think that in this case the mere fact that the charge against the respondent was made under the *Criminal Code* has any bearing on the deductibility or otherwise of the expenses incurred in defence of that charge. The result might have been different had the respondent been found guilty of the charge, but as to that I need say nothing.

Kellock J made these observations, [1954] SCR 60 [[1954] CTC 33]:

> It must be assumed in the case at bar, by reason of the acquittal, that the trade practices involved were not illegal, and, as pointed out by Cameron, J, it is not necessary to consider the situation had the contrary been the case. The difference for the present purposes is substantial.

I do not believe that Cameron J meant to express the opinion that his decision would have been different had the respondent been found guilty. He might have had doubts, but he did not choose to give the reasons for any doubts he may have had because the fact was not an issue in the case submitted to his judgment. As to Kellock, J, there is no doubt that he thought the difference would have been substantial had the trade practices been illegal. He also refrained from expanding on this matter because the issue did not call for a decision on that point. I fail to see, in the remarks referred to, the expression of an opinion which could be binding in a case where the trade practices were illegal. In one instance, there was doubt; in the other, there was a statement which, in my view, was made to mean that illegal trade practices would have been considered in a different way than legal trade practices in the computation of the taxpayer's income under the *Income Tax Act*.

In the present case, I am not called upon to decide if the appellant's trade practices were legal or illegal. My duty is to determine whether the legal fees incurred and paid for by the appellant in defending itself on a charge alleging that its trade practices were illegal are deductible as having been incurred and made for the purpose of gaining or producing income from its business. Legal expenses in the course of a taxpayer's business have been considered by the Supreme Court as being deductible. It is the purpose of the legal expenses which is material in this issue.

...

In my view, there is no material difference between the facts relevant to the appellant in this case and those upon which the Supreme Court of Canada made its decision. The decision as set forth in the headnote of the judgment reads thus:

> The legal expenses incurred by the respondent companies in connection with an investigation into an alleged illegal combine and in successfully defending a charge under s. 498 of the *Criminal Code* regarding the operation of such alleged illegal combine, were deductible in ascertaining taxable income as they were "wholly, exclusively and necessarily laid out or expended for the purpose of earning the income" within the meaning of s. 6(1)(a) of the *Income War Tax Act*, RSC 1927, c. 97 (*Minister of National Revenue v. The Kellogg Company of Canada Ltd.*, [1943] SCR 58 followed).

...

The provision of the *Income Tax Act* to be considered in this instance is to the effect that deductions from revenue must have been made for the purpose of gaining or producing income from the business, whilst the provision of the *Income War Tax Act* considered in the *Caulk* case limits the disbursements or expenses as shown to have been laid out wholly, exclusively and necessarily for the purpose of earning the income. These terms seem to me to be more restrictive than the terms of Section 12(1)(a) which exclude deduction of outlays or expenses that are not made or incurred for the purpose of gaining or producing income from the business. Business purpose remains the test, but need not be exclusive.

...

In the *Caulk* case, where the facts were identical in terms of the indictment and charge to those of the present case, both the Exchequer Court and the Supreme Court found that the disbursements of legal expenses incurred to defend its right to use certain trade practices had been laid out for the purpose of its business and for the purpose of earning the income and were deductible in computing the taxpayer's taxable income.

Believing as I do that the appellant's trade practices in the operations of its business were used and followed for the purpose of earning income from the business, I find that lawful legal fees and costs incurred or made in defending such practices till a final decision on their legality or illegality was reached were made for the purposes of their trade and for the purpose of earning income and were deductible in ascertaining the appellant's taxable income within the meaning of Section 12(1)(a) of the *Income Tax Act*, RSC 1952. ...

Judgment accordingly.

NOTES AND QUESTIONS

1.   On what grounds did the Minister argue in *Rolland Paper Company Limited* that the taxpayer should not be allowed to deduct legal expenses incurred to defend against charges of illegal trade practices? Of what, if any, relevance to the Minister's argument is the fact that the taxpayer was determined to have been guilty of illegal trade practices? To what extent do the Exchequer Court and Supreme Court of Canada decisions in *M.N.R. v. L.D. Caulk Co. of Canada Ltd.*, [1952] Ex. C.R. 49, [1952] C.T.C. 1 (Ex. Ct.) support the Minister's arguments?

2.   Why did the Exchequer Court reject the Minister's arguments in *Rolland Paper Company Limited*? On what basis did it conclude that the legal expenses incurred by the taxpayer were deductible in computing its business income? Of what, if any, relevance to the judgment is the court's conclusion that illegal trade practices were "part of [the taxpayer's] trade" and "applied to the day to day operations of the [taxpayer's] business"? Of what, if any, significance is the court's statement that the legal expenses "were paid to defend [the taxpayer's] way of doing business and preserve the system under which [it] operated"?

3.   Do you agree with the result in *Rolland Paper Company Limited*? Should legal expenses to defend against criminal proceedings be deductible whenever they are paid to defend the taxpayer's "way of doing business and preserve the system under which [it] operated"? What if the taxpayer's "way of doing business" involved hiring professional contract killers to eliminate its competitors?

4.   In *No. 666 v. M.N.R.* (1959), 23 Tax ABC 208 (T.A.B.), the taxpayer incurred legal expenses appealing a decision of the Ontario Securities Commission, which had cancelled the taxpayer's registration as a broker-dealer on account of questionable sales practices. As a result of delays in proceeding with the appeal, the commission offered to substitute a six months' suspension for cancellation of the taxpayer's registration, which the taxpayer accepted. Upholding the Minister's assessment, which had disallowed a deduction for the legal expenses, the Tax Appeal Board commented (at para. 6) that "a business can perfectly well be carried on without any infraction of the law," and concluded that the legal expenses fell into "the category of disbursements not contemplated where a business is conducted in a legitimate way." Referring to the decision in *M.N.R. v. L.D. Caulk Co. of Canada Ltd.*, [1952] Ex. C.R. 49, [1952] C.T.C. 1 (Ex. Ct.), the board added (at para. 6):

> The theory that the success or failure of the proceedings in which legal expenses have been incurred should have an effect upon their deductibility has been criticized editorially in several publications, I notice, in connection with one or two earlier appeals, but it appears to me to find support in the trend of recently-reported cases on the subject. If a different rule obtained, a taxpayer in business could deduct legal expenses incurred through any flagrant disregard of provincial statutes and regulations that one in his particular calling would be expected to observe in the proper and ordinary course of his business.

5.   In *Neeb v. Canada*, [1997] T.C.J. No. 13, 97 D.T.C. 895 (T.C.C.), the taxpayer sought to deduct $155,000 paid to Toronto criminal lawyer Clayton Ruby related to his defence to criminal charges under the *Narcotic Control Act*. Disallowing the deduction, the court held that the legal expenses were not business expenses incurred for the purpose of gaining or producing income, but personal expenses incurred to reduce the length of his sentence. According to Bowman TCJ (at paras. 35-36):

> Mr. Neeb defended the narcotics charge not because he intended to carry on the illegal narcotics business, but because he wanted to stay out of jail, or at least avoid going to jail for any longer than he had to. He was not defending his business or his business practices.

> The situation may be contrasted with that in *Rolland Paper Co. Ltd. v. M.N.R.*, ... where a company was successful in deducting legal fees incurred in its unsuccessful defence against a charge under the *Criminal Code* of unlawful conspiracy to lessen competition. In that case, the court was dealing with a criminal activity relating to one aspect of the carrying on of an otherwise legitimate business. Here we are dealing with a charge of carrying on a business that by its very nature was criminal. I do not think that one can fairly describe the legal expenses incurred by Mr. Neeb as a legitimate deduction in computing income from his business, even though his carrying on of that business was the very thing that caused him to be charged. The distinction between Mr. Neeb's case and that of Rolland Paper is this: Rolland Paper was charged with an illegal business practice within the context of its business. Its defence against that charge was therefore directly related to the manner of

carrying on the business. The reason Mr. Neeb was charged was that he carried on a criminal business in the first place. In his defence he was not seeking to justify the manner in which he carried on his business ... . He was defending himself, not his business. The legal fees are, therefore, personal and are not in my view proper business expenses.

6.   In *Ben Matthews & Associates Ltd. v. M.N.R.*, [1988] T.C.J. No. 208, [1988] 1 C.T.C. 2372, 88 D.T.C. 1262 (T.C.C.), the taxpayer and its general manager were jointly charged with making false and deceptive statements in respect of inventory values in the corporation's tax returns for its 1966 to 1971 taxation years. In order to defend against these charges, which were tried and dismissed in 1979, the taxpayer paid legal fees of $30,000 in 1979, $15,000 in 1980, and $9,200 in 1981, which it sought to deduct in computing its income for each of these taxation years. Allowing these deductions, Rip TCJ concluded (at para. 36) that the legal expenses were incurred "to defend a prosecution against the [taxpayer] which arose directly from the practice of preparing financial statements in the normal course of business."

For a similar result, see *No. 166 v. M.N.R.* (1954), 10 Tax ABC 285 (T.A.B.), in which the taxpayer, a partner in a firm of chartered accountants, sought to deduct $1,250 for legal fees incurred in the successful appeal of a three-year suspension for misconduct issued by a committee of the Institute of Chartered Accountants. Referring to the decision in *M.N.R. v. L.D. Caulk Co. of Canada Ltd.*, [1952] Ex. C.R. 49, [1952] C.T.C. 1 (Ex. Ct.), the board allowed the deduction on the basis (at para. 5) that it was "imperative that the expense involved be incurred in order to enable the [taxpayer] to continue in his profession and to restore the firm to the position it had formerly enjoyed."

7.   In *Cormier v. M.N.R.*, [1989] 1 C.T.C. 2092, 89 D.T.C. 44 (T.C.C.), the taxpayer sought to deduct legal costs incurred in the unsuccessful appeal of a conviction for tax evasion for failing to report income received from the taxpayer's business operations for the taxation years 1976 to 1981. Referring to the decision in *Rolland Paper Company Limited v. M.N.R.*, [1960] C.T.C. 158, 60 D.T.C. 1095 (Ex. Ct.), Kempo TCCJ suggested (at para. 21) that the test for deductibility did not depend on the ultimate issue of legality or illegality but on the commercial necessity of the legal expenses "in that their purpose must have some measurable nexus to some kind of ... business-related expense." On this basis, the court rejected the taxpayer's claim that the legal expenses were incurred to defend his business practices, and held (at para. 25) that they were not deductible:

> In the case at bar, the appellant had been charged and convicted of wilfully failing to report substantial amounts of income which, in the context of this case, cannot be described as a normal business activity carried out in the course of business operations or which had been carried out for the purpose of gaining or producing income. The facts here simply do not support counsel for the appellant's submission that the legal expenses arose and occurred directly in defending the appellant's practice of paying assistants and employees in the course of his business and in computing the income from that business. Rather, ... the false statements wilfully made concerned non-reporting of over 50 per cent of the appellant's business income for each of the subject years. This activity, on these particular facts, lacks commerciality and simply does not fit within the jurisprudential phraseology of incurring

legal expenses to defend a way of doing business or to preserve a system under which a business operates.

8.   In *Sommers v. Canada*, [1993] T.C.J. No. 691, [1993] 2 C.T.C. 3122, 93 D.T.C. 1489 (T.C.C.), the taxpayer incurred legal fees in 1986 and 1987, successfully defending six charges of tax evasion for failing to report commission income deposited by his US employer in a US bank account, which he sought to deduct in computing his income for each of these taxation years. Referring to the decision in *Cormier v. M.N.R.*, [1989] 1 C.T.C. 2092, 89 D.T.C. 44 (T.C.C.), the court disallowed the deductions on the basis that the legal expenses had not been incurred "to defend a normal business activity carried out in the course of business operations or ... for the purpose of gaining or producing income." According to Teskey TCCJ (at para. 9):

> The money in the [US bank account] was the profit from the business. There is no dispute as to its calculation or as to the amount. The decision to declare or not to declare the income when earned is not a business decision, but a personal one.

> The appellant's argument that he was defending his way of doing business is not a valid argument. The charges against him arose because he did not report the United States income. The reporting or non-reporting of this income was not an integral part of his business. The legal expenses herein cannot be characterized as an outlay made for the purposes of gaining or producing income. The income had been gained or produced, it simply was not reported.

9.   In *Thiele Drywall Inc. v. Canada*, [1996] T.C.J. No. 623, [1993] 3 C.T.C. 2208 (T.C.C.), the taxpayer incurred legal expenses in an unsuccessful defence against tax-evasion charges arising from the taxpayer's participation in a scheme by which payments to various employees were falsely recorded as reimbursements for expenses in order to avoid income taxes and various payroll taxes. Referring to the test for the deductibility of fines and penalties adopted by the Federal Court of Appeal in *Amway of Canada Ltd. v. Canada*, [1996] F.C.J. No. 211, [1996] 2 C.T.C. 162, 96 D.T.C. 6135 (F.C.A.), the court suggested that the issue of deductibility depended on whether or not the taxpayer's evasion "was a normal or ordinary incident of carrying on its business." On the basis that the taxpayer's evasion was neither ordinary nor unavoidable, Rip TCCJ concluded that deduction of the legal expenses was neither sanctioned as an ordinary business expense under subsection 9(1) nor allowed as an expense incurred for the purpose of gaining or producing income under paragraph 18(1)(a).

10.   In *Border Chemical Co. Ltd. v. M.N.R.*, [1987] F.C.J. No. 837, [1987] 2 C.T.C. 183, 87 D.T.C. 5391 (F.C.T.D.), the taxpayer corporation incurred legal expenses defending its president against criminal charges of conspiracy and fraud for allegedly having offered secret commissions in a share promotion venture. On the basis that the criminal charges related to business activities of the accused that were unrelated to the business of the taxpayer, Muldoon J held that the connection between the criminal charges and the taxpayer's business activities was too remote to justify deductibility of the legal expenses as

expenses incurred for the purpose of gaining or producing the taxpayer's income.

For a similar result, see *William F. Koch Laboratories of Canada Ltd. v. M.N.R.* (1956), 16 Tax ABC (T.A.B.), where the board disallowed the deduction of amounts paid to indemnify the taxpayer's president for legal expenses incurred in a libel action against the publishers of an article that was critical of a method of cancer treatment developed by the president and employed by the taxpayer corporation.

11. In *Premium Iron Ores Limited v. M.N.R.*, [1966] S.C.J. No. 48, [1966] C.T.C. 391, 66 D.T.C. 5280 (S.C.C.), the taxpayer sought to deduct legal expenses that were incurred in order to pursue a successful objection to the imposition of US income and capital gains taxes. Rejecting the Minister's argument (at para. 78) that the legal expenses were incurred not "for the purpose of gaining or producing income" as required by then paragraph 12(1)(a) (now paragraph 18(1)(a)) but rather "for the purpose of preserving profits already earned by the [taxpayer] from a claim made by the United States tax authorities," a majority of the Supreme Court of Canada held that the expenses were deductible. According to Hall J (at paras. 28 and 45):

> A company such as the [taxpayer] exists to make a profit. All its operations are directed to that end. The operations must be viewed as one whole and not segregated into revenue producing as distinct from revenue retaining functions, otherwise a condition of chaos would obtain. ...

> In conclusion, as I see it, the expenditures here were ones which under sound accounting and commercial practice would be deducted in the Statement of Profit and Loss as expenditures for the year in determining the profit, if any, of the company for that year. ... [T]he expenditures in question had to be made to preserve the income and working capital from the unwarranted claim of a foreign taxing authority.

12. In 1964, the Act was amended by the introduction of paragraph 11(1)(w), permitting taxpayers, in computing their income for a taxation year, to deduct amounts paid in the year "in respect of fees or expenses incurred in preparing, instituting or prosecuting an objection to, or an appeal in relation to, an assessment of tax, interest or penalties" under the *Income Tax Act*. At the same time, paragraph 6(1)(q) was enacted, providing that amounts awarded as costs in respect of any expenses deductible under paragraph 11(1)(w) must be included in computing the taxpayer's income. These rules, which are now contained in paragraphs 60(o) and 56(1)(l), were subsequently amended to apply also to amounts paid in respect of fees or expenses incurred in objecting to or appealing assessments of tax, interest, or penalties imposed under a provincial income tax, under an income tax imposed by the government of another country, under the *Employment Insurance Act*, or under the *Canada Pension Plan* or comparable provincial pension plan.

F. Promotional Expenses

Unlike most of the expenses examined in this section thus far, promotional expenses are generally viewed as one of the most common categories of business expense, the deductibility of which might be assumed. In several cases, however, these expenses have been challenged on the basis that they were too remotely connected to the taxpayer's business to have been incurred for the purpose of gaining or producing income from that business. An excellent illustration of this principle is the decision in *Ace Salvage Alberta Ltd. v. M.N.R.*, [1985] 2 C.T.C. 2277, 85 D.T.C. 568 (T.C.C.).

Ace Salvage Alberta Ltd. v. M.N.R.
[1985] 2 C.T.C. 2277, 85 D.T.C. 568 (T.C.C.)

[In computing its income for the years 1979 to 1982 from carrying on a scrap-metal business, the taxpayer sought to deduct losses that it incurred from the training, maintenance, and racing of horses. Characterizing the horse-related activities as a separate "farming business" losses from which are restricted under subsection 31(1) of the Act, the Minister limited the deduction to $5,000 per year. The taxpayer appealed.]

TAYLOR, TCJ: ... Mr. Shulder, president of the appellant corporation, ... regarded the losses as advertising and business promotion for the salvage business, and consciously set out on that path. He claimed that a substantial portion of both his customers and suppliers were racetrack fans, and by these contacts his "salvage" business did receive the benefit from the expenses (losses) incurred. His evidence was that only very minimal other "advertising" was conducted by the company, but he believed his salvage business (Ace) was one of the most profitable, perhaps the most profitable in the area. He raced his horses under the name of "Ace Stables," and felt that his clients, even the general public made a direct connection between "Ace Stables" and "Ace Salvage Alberta Ltd."

In argument counsel for the appellant emphasized that there was no evidence or rationale for the Minister assessing the company on the basis that "Ace Stables" was a farming business separate and distinct from the salvage business.

...

[T]o view properly the issue before the Court, one can simply ask the question — what is the proper designation and treatment (for tax purposes) of the expenditures incurred for purchasing, training, boarding and racing the horses, under this set of circumstances? ... The appellant's position is that this was nothing different than *normally* expected (if somewhat unique) advertising and promotion expenses. In support of this proposition there are two main facts:

(1)   The appellant corporation alleges that in other forms of advertising, very little was spent; and

> (2)   The opinion of Mr. Shulder that salvage business resulted from the contacts he made at the race-track.

As opposed to these, there was no hard empirical evidence whatever that a connection existed between the horse-racing expenses and the salvage income; again, a situation which might not be completely fatal under certain circumstances, but is of serious proportions in this situation, because of the unusual nature of the proposition put forward by the appellant.

The bottom line, whether he realized it or not, is that Mr. Shulder was authorizing the expenditure of some part of the gross income earned from the salvage operations, for purposes for which the only support is *his* opinion — that it was to gain or produce income from the salvage operation. Certainly Mr. Shulder, as the president and major shareholder of Ace Salvage may authorize the use of funds of that company as he sees fit — but that of itself does not assure that such use of funds will be treated as a deduction from the salvage income of the company for income tax purposes. The expenditure of such funds may reduce the pool of funds available in the company, but that is not synonymous with acquiring the right to a deduction from income with respect to the earning of those funds. Otherwise, simply the authorization by the principal shareholder, president, board of directors, owner, or some other responsible body or person would be all that was needed to make an expenditure incurred a deductible expense.

...

[T]he *Income Tax Act* presupposes a tax on *all business income*, reduced only by the deductions scheduled and permitted. It must be *demonstrated* that the funds expended (and for simplicity of perspective we refer to 1982 estimated total of $124,916 in this instance) were so expended for the purpose of gaining or producing income for the salvage business. The Court recognizes that there is probably no more ethereal category than "advertising and promotion," and that indeed in general the interpretation of the tax laws by Revenue Canada has been flexible and generous in allowing the parameters around such a category to encompass a great range of tangential or obliquely related items. I do not doubt ... that some of the activity which surrounded the horse-racing provided contacts, information, leads and help which were of benefit to the salvage business. But it could also easily be argued that Mr. Shulder (a highly personable and congenial man) going for a cup of coffee, mowing his lawn, or attending a wedding could have (and probably has) done the same thing, perhaps even to the same degree. But it could *not* be argued (except under possibly the most extreme circumstances that are not easily evident to me) that going for a cup of coffee, mowing the lawn, or attending the wedding was for the "*purpose of gaining or producing income from the salvage business.*" (See paragraph 18(1)(a).) It might be argued that some small or modest part of the cost of doing so (coffee, lawn, wedding) which could be directly and clearly associated with the income-producing activities of the company might be the responsibility of the company — but no such limited and restricted effort was defined in this appeal.

...

Simply put, if the clear and primary purpose for an expenditure can be discerned, and that purpose, *prima facie* is markedly different than the normal business purpose of the payor entity, then the road to recognition that any subsidiary or ancillary benefit to the payor entity (from an income tax viewpoint) should be substituted for that reasonable, direct, and primary purpose for the expenditure is difficult indeed. Accordingly the purpose of the expenditures at issue in this matter was for purchasing, boarding, training and racing horses, *not* for purposes directly (perhaps not indirectly) associated with the salvage business purpose of the appellant. ...

Appeal dismissed.

NOTES AND QUESTIONS

1.   On what basis did the court in *Ace Salvage* conclude that the losses from the training, maintenance, and racing of horses were not deductible in computing the taxpayer's income from its salvage business? Do you agree or disagree with the decision? Why?

2.   Might the taxpayer in *Ace Salvage* have been more successful if it had argued that a portion of the expenses incurred in training, maintaining, and racing horses was deductible as a promotional expense in computing its income from the salvage business? Might the taxpayer have argued that expenses incurred by Mr. Shulder in going for a cup of coffee, mowing his lawn, or attending a wedding were deductible in computing the income of the salvage business?

3.   Why did the taxpayer in *Ace Salvage* seek to deduct losses from the training, maintenance, and racing of horses as promotional expenses for the purposes of computing its income from its salvage business, rather than as business losses deductible in computing a taxpayer's net income under paragraph 3(d) of the Act? Of what, if any, significance to the taxpayer's motives is the restricted farm loss provision in subsection 31(1) of the *Income Tax Act*?

4.   In *H.J. O'Connell Limited v. M.N.R.* (1966), 42 Tax ABC 174, 66 D.T.C. 714 (T.A.B.), the taxpayer, which carried on a construction business, sought to deduct as promotional expenses for this business amounts spent to operate a farm on which it raised prize cattle, show horses, and race horses either for exhibition at agricultural fairs or for races at various race tracks held in the province of Quebec. Observing (at para. 32) that the farm operated at a loss and that the taxpayer "wanted to deduct such losses from other sources of income," the board rejected the taxpayer's argument that the farm expenses were incurred for the purpose of gaining or producing income from its construction business

on the grounds that the farm was "autonomous by its very nature" and "too remotely connected" to the construction business. According to Roland St-Onge (at para. 33):

> The law, while not empowering the Minister to stipulate the forms of advertising to be used in a particular business, must draw a line between advertising costs directly with actual promotion and profit-making of business and other expenditures incurred in too remote a way for that purpose.

As a result, it followed, the taxpayer was subject to the restricted farm loss provision in then subsection 13(1) (now subsection 31(1)) of the Act.

In *Leffler v. M.N.R.*, [1971] Tax ABC 717 (T.A.B.), the taxpayer, who carried on business as an independent insurance agent, sought to deduct the cost of maintaining, training, and showing horses as "advertising and promotional expenses of his business." Upholding the Minister's reassessment, which disallowed the expenses on the basis that they were not incurred for the purpose of gaining or producing income, the board considered (at para. 4) the taxpayer's interest in horses to be a "hobby" the costs of which were "too remotely connected with the operation of his life insurance agency business" to be deductible.

See also *Blair Supply Co. v. M.N.R.*, [1984] C.T.C. 2560, 84 D.T.C. 1457 (T.C.C.), where the court rejected the taxpayer's appeal from a reassessment disallowing the cost of breeding and racing horses as a deduction in computing the taxpayer's income from a business of distributing building supplies. According to Taylor TCJ (at para. 11):

> The source of income to which the expenditures constituting the farming loss at issue in this appeal, while part of the overall business activity of the corporation, is not the same source of income as the main building supply business of this corporation. ... The loss from the one source is not deductible as an expense item from the profit from the other source.

As a result, the taxpayer was subject to the restricted farm loss provision in subsection 31(1) of the Act.

In *King v. Canada*, [2000] T.C.J. No. 580, [2000] 4 C.T.C. 2341, 2000 D.T.C. 2544 (T.C.C.), in contrast, the court allowed the taxpayers to deduct the cost of raising, maintaining, and showing horses and sponsoring horse shows in computing their income from an insurance business on the grounds that the business name was displayed prominently at the horse shows and that the horse-related activities were demonstrated to have produced customers for the business. According to Margeson TCJ (at paras. 119-120 and 128):

> The Court is satisfied that the raising, maintaining, showing, sponsorship and riding of show horses was not a hobby of the [taxpayers] but indeed was a way of doing business. All of these activities were an integral part of the business plan. ...
>
> The Court is satisfied that the facts in the case at bar can be distinguished from the facts in *Leffler, supra*, and it is satisfied that a significant connection has been established in the case at bar between the keeping of horses and the selling of life insurance not only through the evidence of the [taxpayers] but also through the evidence of other witnesses called on

behalf of the [taxpayers] who were significant business persons and testified to that very same effect. ...

In the end result the Court is satisfied that the expenses in question were incurred for the purpose of gaining or producing income from the [taxpayer's] insurance business, as required by paragraph 18(1)(a) of the *Act*; they were not "personal or living expenses," within the meaning of paragraph 18(1)(h) and subsection 248(1) of the *Act* and they were not unreasonable.

5.   In *No. 511 v. M.N.R.* (1958), 19 Tax ABC 248, 58 D.T.C. 307 (T.A.B.), the taxpayer, a company which carried on a business selling lumber in Canada and the United States, lost $22,500 after sponsoring a baseball team in order to obtain advertising for its business, which it sought to deduct in computing its income for its 1954 taxation year. Rejecting the Minister's argument that the amount was not incurred for the purpose of gaining or producing income from the taxpayer's lumber business as required by then paragraph 12(1)(a) (now paragraph 18(1)(a)) of the *Income Tax Act*, the board emphasized (at para. 32) that "we have to consider ... the purpose of one's action rather than the result" and noted in any event that the taxpayer's profits rose from $18,000 in 1953 to $100,000 in 1955. Applying the reasonableness limitation in then subsection 12(2) (now section 67), however, the court limited the amount that the taxpayer could deduct to $5,000. According to Maurice Boisvert, QC (at paras. 35-38):

Advertising today is a necessity of trade but it does not mean that one engaged in a business must spend on advertising all the profits produced from his business activity. It is legitimate to promote goodwill, the quality of goods, the efficiency of a service, even the name of a commercial firm, but, for the purpose of the *Income Tax Act*, the legitimacy of the thing does not always legitimate the expenditures. In determining the reasonableness of an advertising expense, it is well to take cognizance of the size of the business, the patronage to be expected in the future, the form of advertising, the locality where it is done, and the size of population reached by the advertising.

The circumstances revealed by the evidence do not give an opening to accept the full amount spent by the taxpayer as the result of its sponsorship as deductible from its income for the taxation year 1954. The size of the appellant company's business does not justify the Board to allow the full amount. If the Board did so, it would mean that the appellant company would deduct, for 1954, the sum of $22,500 out of a net income of $42,874, which is more than one-half of the said income. This would be unreasonable and in complete derogation of the letter and the spirit of Section 12 [now section 67] of said Act.

I see nothing in the evidence to permit me to arrive at such a conclusion. On the contrary, the evidence discloses that the advertising started in the month of July instead of in the month of May when it should have. Moreover, it must be accepted also, from the evidence, that the appellant company was a producer of lumber, and that the advertising was in relation to the name of the firm rather than to the marketable product which was sold through agencies. To be deductible, advertising expenditures must have some relation to the business in which one in engaged.

After having taken into consideration all the facts and the circumstances in this case, I arrive at a figure of $5,000 which would be about the expenditure of an advertising campaign during the summer in question in the daily newspaper and over the radio station of the City of which the appellant is a resident.

Do you agree with this result? Why or why not? Why did the taxpayer not deduct the $22,500 as a business loss in computing its net income from all sources?

6.   In *Varcoe v. Canada*, [2005] T.C.J. No. 444, [2005] 5 C.T.C. 2220, 2005 D.T.C. 1319 (T.C.C.), the taxpayer owned a truck repair business and sought to deduct the costs associated with his stock car racing activities. The taxpayer justified the deduction by arguing that the stock car racing helped to advertise his truck repair business and that through his racing activities he made business contacts. The court held that the expenses associated with the taxpayer's racing activities were not business expenses, but instead were merely expenses incurred for the taxpayer's personal amusement.

7.   In *Riedle Brewery Limited v. M.N.R.*, [1939] S.C.J. No. 9, [1938-39] CTC 312 (S.C.C.), the taxpayer, which carried on a business of brewing and selling beer in Manitoba, sought to deduct a sum of $4,206.40 computing its income for its 1933 taxation year, which it had spent "treating" customers at various establishments to beer, "practically all" of which was manufactured by the taxpayer. Accepting the taxpayer's arguments (at para. 24) that "the practice followed ... is one adopted by the other brewers in Manitoba, and followed by all as something considered by them, not merely as advisable, but as obligatory, to increase, or at least sustain, the volume of their sales," a majority of the court held that the taxpayer had expended the amount "wholly, exclusively and necessarily ... for the purpose of earning ... income" from its business, as required by then paragraph 6(a) of the *Income War Tax Act*.

8.   In *Olympia Floor & Wall Tile (Que.) Ltd. v. M.N.R.*, [1970] C.T.C. 99, 70 D.T.C. 6085 (Ex. Ct.), the taxpayer, in computing its business income for the taxation years 1962 and 1963, sought to deduct gifts to charitable organizations that were (at para. 2):

> headed up by men who, in their ordinary business lives, were in a position to cause purchases to be made of the appellant's goods, and who, as a consequence of the appellant's gifts to their charitable organizations, did, in the ordinary course of events as things were done in the particular part of the Montreal community that was involved, cause substantial purchases to be made of the appellant's goods that would not otherwise have been made.

Concluding (at para. 4) that the gifts "fall clearly within the authority of *Reidle Brewery Limited*," the court allowed the deduction, notwithstanding the Minister's argument that the deduction was implicitly disallowed by the statutory deduction for charitable contributions in then paragraph 27(1)(a) (now paragraph 110.1(1)(a)), which at the time limited deductible contributions to 10 per cent of the taxpayer's net income for the year. According to Jackett P (at paras. 17-19):

> In my view, when a taxpayer makes an outlay for the purpose of producing income — i.e. as part of his profit making process — even though that outlay takes the form of a "gift" to a charitable organization, it is not a "gift" within the meaning of that word in Section 27(1)(a) which, by reason of the place it holds in the process of computing taxable income, was

obviously intended to confer a benefit on persons who made contributions out of income and was not intended to provide deductions for outlays made in the course of the income earning process. ...

[T]he outlays made by the appellant for the purpose of maintaining or expanding sales, even though they took the form of contributions to charitable organizations, were not "gifts" within the meaning of that word in Section 27(1)(a) of the *Income Tax Act*.

For a similar result, see *Impenco Ltd. v. M.N.R.*, [1988] T.C.J. No. 121, [1988] 1 C.T.C. 2339, 88 D.T.C. 1242 (T.C.C.), where the taxpayer made a number of charitable donations in 1984, the total value of which exceeded the 20 per cent limit on deductible gifts under then paragraph 110(1)(a) of the Act (now paragraph 110.1(1)(a)). On the basis that the donations were made primarily to various Jewish charitable organizations for the purpose of gaining or producing income from a largely Jewish clientele, the court accepted the taxpayer's argument that the amounts were deductible in computing its business income and not excluded under paragraph 18(1)(a).

9.   Although advertising costs are generally deductible in computing a taxpayer's business income, subsection 19(1) prohibits any deduction "in respect of an otherwise deductible outlay or expense of a taxpayer for advertising space in an issue of a newspaper for an advertisement directed primarily to a market in Canada" unless:

(a)   the issue is a Canadian issue of a Canadian newspaper; or

(b)   the issue is an issue of a newspaper that would be a Canadian issue of a Canadian newspaper except that

(i)   its type has been wholly set in the United States or has been partly set in the United States with the remainder having been set in Canada, or

(ii)   it has been wholly printed in the United States or has been partly printed in the United States with the remainder having been printed in Canada.

The terms "Canadian issue" and "Canadian newspaper" are defined in subsection 19(5). Subsection 19(3) stipulates that the prohibition in subsection 19(1) does not apply "with respect to an advertisement in a special issue or edition of a newspaper that is edited in whole or in part and printed and published outside Canada if that special issue or edition is devoted to features or news related primarily to Canada and the publishers thereof publish such an issue or edition not more frequently than twice a year."

Section 19.01 limits the amount that may be deducted "in respect of an otherwise deductible outlay or expense for advertising space in an issue of a periodical for an advertisement directed at the Canadian market" to 50 per cent of the amount otherwise deductible, except for issues of periodicals containing at least 80 per cent "original editorial content" (for which advertising expenses are fully deductible). For the purpose of this provision, subsection 19.01(1) defines the expression "original editorial content" in respect of an issue of a periodical as "non-advertising content":

(a)   the author of which is a Canadian citizen or a permanent resident of Canada within the meaning assigned by the *Immigration Act* and, for this purpose, "author" includes a writer, a journalist, an illustrator and a photographer; or

(b)   that is created for the Canadian market and has not been published in any other edition of that issue of the periodical published outside Canada.

Subsection 19.1(1) prohibits any deduction "in respect of an otherwise deductible outlay or expense of a taxpayer made or incurred after September 21, 1976 for an advertisement directed primarily to a market in Canada and broadcast by a foreign broadcasting undertaking." The term "foreign broadcasting undertaking" is defined in subsection 19.1(4) as "a network operation or a broadcasting transmitting undertaking located outside Canada or on a ship or aircraft not registered in Canada." Subsection 19.1(2) sets out a transitional rule, allowing deductions otherwise prohibited by subsection 19.1(1) where they were made or incurred before September 22, 1977, pursuant to a written agreement entered into on or before January 23, 1975 or after January 23, 1975 and before September 22, 1976 "if the agreement is for a term of one year or less and by its express terms is not capable of being extended or renewed."

G. Recreation, Meal, and Entertainment Expenses

Among the most contentious categories of deductions in computing a taxpayer's income from a business or property are those related to amounts expended by the taxpayer for recreation, meals, or entertainment. Although these expenditures are often incurred for the purpose of business promotion, they also confer personal benefits both on the objects of the promotional activities and on the persons who conduct these activities on behalf of the business. One of the earliest Canadian decisions to consider this category of expenses was the Exchequer Court decision in *Royal Trust Co. v. M.N.R.*, [1957] Ex. C.J. No. 7, [1957] C.T.C. 32, 57 D.T.C. 1055 (Ex. Ct.). Although the specific decision in the case was reversed by the introduction of subparagraph 18(1)(l)(ii) in 1972, the court's analysis of the word "profit" and of the relationship between this concept and the general limitation in former paragraph 12(1)(a) (now paragraph 18(1)(a)) is of continuing relevance to this day.

The Royal Trust Company v. M.N.R.
[1957] Ex. C.J. No. 7, [1957] C.T.C. 32, 57 D.T.C. 1055 (Ex. Ct.)

THORSON, P: ... In its income tax return for [1952] the appellant claimed ... that it was entitled, in computing its taxable income to deduct as an expense the sum of $9,527.29 which it had paid to various social clubs in payment of the admission fees and annual membership dues of certain officers who were members of such clubs. ... In assessing the appellant the Minister ... added the sum of $9,597.29 to the amount of taxable income reported by it.

...

The appellant's business, as its name implies, covers a wide range of activity of a fiduciary and personal nature. It gives assistance in the planning and preparation of wills and trust deeds and supervises and manages estates and trusts; it acts as trustee of pension plans and under bond and debenture issue indentures; it acts as agent for corporations in the transfer and registration of shares; it manages corporate and personal investment portfolios; it acts as agent in the purchase and sale of real estate and manages properties; and it accepts deposits from its customers and clients. The most important part of its business is that of acting as executor and trustee of estates and trusts, which was described as the "bread and butter" part of its business, and its next most important activities are those of acting as trustee under bond and debenture issue indentures and as agent for corporations for the transfer and registration of their shares.

The appellant uses several means for getting business and gaining or producing income from it. While it is in somewhat the same position as lawyers and accountants it has one advantage over them in that it is free to advertise and it uses this means extensively. But its major effort to attract business is based on its belief, as the result of many years of experience, that personal contacts by its officers produce the best business results. The appellant, therefore, requires its senior executive officers and such other of its officers as are charged with the maintenance and promotion of its business, such as, for example, its branch managers and their assistants, to take every opportunity to develop personal contacts with those persons from whom it might reasonably expect trust company business. It is part of its policy to require such officers to take an active part in the community life of the locality in which they operate. Consequently, when one of its officers is appointed to a position which calls for the maintenance or promotion of its business he is required to join a social club in his community, take an active part in community organizations and campaigns such as Red Feather and other community welfare drives, join a service club and the local chamber of commerce or board of trade and generally make himself known in the community. He is to be regular in his attendance at club meetings and functions, take his part in club committee work and serve as a club officer if required to do so.

The details of the appellant's policy are carefully worked out. It decides which of its officers should join social clubs. They are those that would be likely to come into personal contact with clients or prospective clients, such as, for example, in addition to senior executive officers, branch managers and their assistants, trusts and estates officers, supervisors of pension funds, supervisors of investment folios, stock transfer officers and managers of real estate. The appellant also designates the clubs to which its officers should belong and takes the necessary steps for their introduction and admission.

...

685

The appellant has followed this policy for a great many years but it did not claim a deduction of the amounts paid by it in furtherance of it prior to the claim made in its income tax return for 1952. This was made on the advice of its financial adviser and tax consultant. ... It was in pursuance of this policy and in accordance with its long business practice that the appellant paid the social club admission fees and annual membership dues that are in question in this action.

...

The evidence is conclusive that the appellant's policy has resulted in business for it from which income was gained or produced. Mr. Pembroke belonged to three social clubs in Montreal and one in Ottawa. He used their facilities frequently and discussed business in them. He gave several specific instances of obtaining substantial business for the appellant by reason of being able to invite persons to lunch at one of the clubs and discuss business with them there. His officers frequently reported similar situations. He stated that the appellant's business was largely of a personal and confidential nature and that many persons could not find the time to go to the appellant's office but could go to one of the clubs. To that extent the club, in his opinion, was an extension of the appellant's office facilities. On many occasions a remark made at the club gave him a lead that he could follow up and a discussion there might end up with a will or a trust or a pension fund for the appellant. This did not mean that if he had not been a member of the club he would not have obtained the business. He might have done so but it was not as likely. Mr. Pembroke said that the appellant regarded its policy as an extension of its advertising but attached greater importance to it in that the use of the club facilities resulted in more direct dealing with persons from whom the appellant as a trust company might expect the bulk of its business.

Mr. Harrington's evidence was to the same effect. He was appointed manager of the appellant's Toronto branch and supervisor of its Ontario branches in 1952. Prior to that time he had been in the Montreal branch. He stated that he joined two clubs in Toronto and that the appellant paid his dues there. He found in his first year at Toronto that the fact that he was able to join social clubs there greatly facilitated his start in business. Before he went there steps had been taken to have his name proposed for membership and he was instructed to take an active part in the life of the clubs, meet the members and endeavour to get information that would result in business. He gave specific examples of having obtained profitable business for the appellant through joining the clubs. Soon after he arrived in Toronto he met at one of the clubs a person whose company had just successfully floated a bond issue and he was able to get a deposit from him of over a million dollars. One of his officers was able through his membership in a club to obtain about 25 will executor appointments. A luncheon discussion at the club with a lawyer resulted in the management of a $600,000 investment portfolio. And in his capacity as supervisor of the Ontario branches he had knowledge of business resulting to the appellant from membership in clubs.

There is no doubt that the appellant considered that its expenditures were in accordance with good business practice. Its experience over a long period was certainly to that effect. According to Mr. Pembroke, it was desirable that in the larger cities its officers should be members of several clubs in order to meet as many persons as possible but it was also vital in the smaller centres that its representative should belong to a club there. Indeed, as Mr. Pembroke put it, his failure to join might do him and the appellant active harm through creating the belief in the community that he was anti-social.

Moreover, the evidence shows that other trust companies, competitors of the appellant, followed the same policy as it does and considered it good business practice to do so. Mr. Pembroke's evidence was to that effect and it was confirmed by Mr. Harrington. As he put it, it was the general opinion of trust companies that it was important and essential and good business practice to have officers in social clubs and pay their club fees and dues. And finally, Mr. Arthur Gilmour, an experienced chartered accountant with the firm of Clarkson, Gordon and Company, expressed the opinion, as an accountant, that the amount paid to the clubs was a proper and necessary deduction in determining the amount of the appellant's profits and gains.

On these uncontradicted facts I proceed to consideration of the principles to be applied. The statutory provision primarily involved is Section 12(1)(a) of the *Income Tax Act*, to which I have already referred. For convenience, I repeat its terms:

12. (1) In computing income, no deduction shall be made in respect of

    (a)   an outlay or expense except to the extent that it was made or incurred by the taxpayer for the purpose of gaining or producing income from property or a business of the taxpayer,

This section replaced Section 6(a) of the *Income War Tax Act*, RSC 1927, c. 97, which provided:

6. In computing the amount of the profits or gains to be assessed a deduction shall not be allowed in respect of

    (a)   disbursements or expenses not wholly, exclusively and necessarily laid out or expended for the purpose of earning the income;

It is clear that the range of deductibility of an outlay or expense under the *Income Tax Act* is greater than that of disbursements or expenses under the *Income War Tax Act*. But there are certain tests of deductibility that are as applicable in the case of the later enactment as they were in the case of the earlier one.

This Court had occasion in several cases under the *Income War Tax Act* to consider what should be the primary approach to the question whether a disbursement or expense was deductible for income tax purposes. I dealt with this question at length in *Imperial Oil Limited v. M.N.R.*, [1947] Ex. CR 527;

[1947] CTC 353, and need not repeat what I said there beyond pointing out that it was held there that the deductibility of disbursements or expenses was to be determined according to the ordinary principles of commercial trading or well accepted principles of business and accounting practice unless their deduction was prohibited by reason of their coming within the express terms of the excluding provision of Section 6(a). I went on to say the section ought not to be read with a view to trying to bring a particular disbursement or expense within the scope of its excluding provisions, but that if it was not within the express terms of the exclusions its deduction ought to be allowed if such deduction would otherwise be in accordance with the ordinary principles of commercial trading or well accepted principles of business and accounting practice. It is manifest from the reasons for judgment in that case that the first approach to the question whether a particular disbursement or expense was deductible for income tax purposes was to, ascertain whether its deduction was consistent with ordinary principles of commercial trading or well accepted principles of business and accounting practice and that if it was the next enquiry should be whether the deduction was within or without the exclusions of Section 6(a). My only present observation is that I should have omitted the reference to accounting practice which I made in that case.

In the case of *Daley v. M.N.R.*, [1950] Ex. CR 516; [1950] CTC 254, I carried the analysis a step further and expressed the opinion that it was not correct to look at Section 6(a) as the authority, even inferentially, for permitting the deduction of a disbursement or expense. I put my view, at page 521, as follows:

> The correct view, in my opinion is that the deductibility of the disbursements or expenses that may properly be deducted "in computing the amount of the profits and gains to be assessed" is inherent in the concept of "annual net profit or gain" in the definition of taxable income contained in Section 3. The deductibility from the receipts of a taxation year of the appropriate disbursements or expenses stems, therefore, from Section 3 of the Act, if it stems from any section, and not at all, even inferentially from paragraph (a) of Section 6.

This led to the statement that in some cases it was not necessary to consider Section 6(a) at all, for if the deduction of a disbursement or expense was not permissible by the ordinary principles of commercial trading or accepted business and accounting practice, ... that was the end of the matter and it was not necessary to make any further enquiry, for if ordinary business practice could not sanction the deduction the expenditure could not possibly fall outside the exclusions of Section 6(a) but must automatically fall within its prohibition.

...

It follows from this line of reasoning, which is as applicable in the case of the *Income Tax Act* as it was in that of the *Income War Tax Act*, that instead of saying that the range of deductibility of an outlay or expense is greater under Section 12(1)(a) than that of a disbursement or expense under Section 6(a) of the *Income War Tax Act* it would be more accurate to say that the extent of the prohibition of the deduction of an outlay or expense is less under Section 12(1)(a) of the *Income Tax Act* than that of a disbursement or expense under the *Income War Tax Act*. Indeed, it was plainly intended that it should be so, with the result that the gap, if it may be so described, between the kind of an outlay or expense that is deductible according to ordinary principles of commercial trading and business practice and that which is deductible for income tax purposes is narrower now than it was under the former Act.

Consequently, if the correct approach to the question of whether a disbursement or expense was properly deductible in a case under the *Income War Tax Act* was the one which I have outlined, it follows, *a fortiori*, that it is the correct approach to the question of whether an outlay or expense is properly deductible in a case under the *Income Tax Act*. Thus, it may be stated categorically that in a case under the *Income Tax Act* the first matter to be determined in deciding whether an outlay or expense is outside the prohibition of Section 12(1)(a) of the Act is whether it was made or incurred by the taxpayer in accordance with the ordinary principles of commercial trading or well accepted principles of business practice. If it was not, that is the end of the matter. But if it was, then the outlay or expense is properly deductible unless it falls outside the expressed exception of Section 12(1)(a) and therefore, within its prohibition.

There is, in my opinion, no doubt that it was consistent with good business practice for a trust company like the appellant to make the payments in question. They were made as a matter of business policy that had been carefully considered, was well regulated and had been in effect for many years prior to the year in question. It was considered that the use of social club facilities by the appellant's officers was particularly suited to the kind of personal business done by a trust company and was a means for promoting business beyond that which advertising could produce. The experience over the years showed that the policy had worked out well and that its benefits to the appellant were real. Business contacts were made at the club and business was discussed there. Membership in the clubs had produced profitable business for the appellant. Moreover, the appellant's competitors followed policies similar to the appellant's and the evidence is that it was considered good business practice for a trust company to have its business getting officers become members of social clubs and pay their admission fees and annual membership dues. In addition to the business and commercial judgment of the appellant's officers that the payments made by them were properly deductible as business expenses there was the opinion of Mr. A. Gilmour as an accountant, for what it is worth that from an accounting point of view the deduction of the amount of the payments made by the appellant was a proper and necessary one for the ascertainment of its true profits and gains. Thus I find as a fact that the payments made by the appellant were made in accordance with principles of good business practice for trust companies.

I now come to the enquiry whether the deduction of the amount in question is prohibited by Section 12(1)(a) of the Act or falls within its expressed exception.

...

The essential limitation in the exception expressed in Section 12(1)(a) is that the outlay or expense should have been made by the taxpayer "for the purpose" of gaining or producing income "from the business." It is the purpose of the outlay or expense that is emphasized but the purpose must be that of gaining or producing income "from the business" in which the taxpayer is engaged. If these conditions are met the fact that there may be no resulting income does not prevent the deductibility of the amount of the outlay or expense. Thus, in a case under the *Income Tax Act* if an outlay or expense is made or incurred by a taxpayer in accordance with the principles of commercial trading or accepted business practice and it is made or incurred for the purpose of gaining or producing income from his business its amount is deductible for income tax purposes.

That is plainly the situation in the present case. I have already found that the payments by the appellant were made in accordance with principles of good business practice for a trust company. It is equally clear, in my opinion, that they were made by the appellant for the purpose of gaining or producing income from its business. The appellant's purpose was to increase its business through personal contacts of its officers with persons whom it would not otherwise readily reach. The clubs were to be used as extensions of its office facilities for persons who would rather go there than to its office. Its whole policy was for the purpose of furthering its business and so gaining or producing income from it. In my view, the payments in question were properly deductible and the Minister was in error in adding their amount to the taxable income reported by the appellant. ...

Judgment accordingly.

NOTES AND QUESTIONS

1.   How important to the decision in *Royal Trust* is the evidence that the taxpayer's policy of paying for club memberships actually produced income? Must an expenditure produce income in order to be deductible?

2.   How important to the decision in *Royal Trust* is the evidence that other trust companies, competitors of the taxpayer, followed a similar policy of paying for club memberships of employees?

3.   According to the expert evidence of a chartered accountant, "the amount paid to the clubs was a proper and necessary deduction in determining the amount of the appellant's profits and gains." Is this evidence relevant to the issue of deductibility? Is it determinative with respect to the issue of deductibility?

4.   In *Royal Trust* Thorson P referred to his earlier judgment in *Imperial Oil Limited v. M.N.R.*, [1947] Ex. C.J. No. 20, [1947] C.T.C. 353, 3 D.T.C. 1090 (Ex. Ct.), in which the deduction of an expense was held to depend on its consistency with "ordinary principles of commercial trading or well accepted principles of business and accounting practice." He then explained that "I should have omitted the reference to accounting practice which I made in that case."

Why did Thorson P delete the reference to accounting practice as governing the deductibility of expenses in computing a taxpayer's income from a business or property?

Consider the following excerpt from Iacobucci J's judgment in *Symes v. Canada*, [1993] S.C.J. No. 131, [1994] 1 C.T.C. 40, 94 D.T.C. 6001 (S.C.C.) (at para. 43):

> the determination of profit under subsection 9(1) is a question of law: *Neonex International Ltd. v. The Queen*, [1978] CTC 485, 78 DTC 6339 (FCA). Perhaps for this reason, and as *Neonex* itself impliedly suggests, courts have been reluctant to posit a subsection 9(1) test based upon "generally accepted accounting principles" (GAAP): see also "Business Income and Taxable Income" (1953 Conference Report: Canadian Tax Foundation) cited in B.J. Arnold and T.W. Edgar, eds.. *Materials on Canadian Income Tax* (9th ed. 1990), at page 336. Any reference to GAAP connotes a degree of control by professional accountants which is inconsistent with a legal test for "profit" under subsection 9(1). Further, whereas an accountant questioning the propriety of a deduction may be motivated by a desire to present an appropriately conservative picture of current profitability, the *Income Tax Act* is motivated by a different purpose: the raising of public revenues. For these reasons, it is more appropriate in considering the subsection 9(1) business test to speak of "well accepted principles of business (or accounting) practice" or "well accepted principles of commercial trading."

5.   What, according to Thorson P, is the relationship between the concept of "profit" in subsection 9(1) (then section 4) of the *Income Tax Act* and the general limitation on deductibility in paragraph 18(1)(a) (then paragraph 12(1)(a))? Which of these provisions constitutes statutory authority for the deduction of expenses incurred to produce income from a business or property?

6.   What, if any, differences are there between the general limitation on deductibility in paragraph 6(a) of the *Income War Tax Act* and the general limitation on deductibility found in current paragraph 18(1)(a)? Is the current limitation broader or narrower than the limitation in paragraph 6(a) of the *Income War Tax Act*?

7.   In order to satisfy the purpose test in paragraph 18(1)(a), must an expense be incurred "wholly," "primarily," or only "partially" for the purpose of gaining or producing income? Do the words "to the extent that" in paragraph 18(1)(a) provide any statutory direction with respect to the deduction of expenses incurred for mixed business and non-business (for example, personal) purposes? Does the decision in *Royal Trust Co. v. M.N.R.*, [1957] Ex. C.J. No. 7, [1957] C.T.C. 32, 57 D.T.C. 1055 (Ex. Ct), provide any guidance on these matters?

8.   The specific decision in *Royal Trust*, was effectively reversed by the enactment of subparagraph 18(1)(l)(ii) in 1972. According to this provision:

> In computing the income of a taxpayer from a business or property no deduction shall be made in respect of ... an outlay or expense made or incurred by the taxpayer after 1971 ... as membership fees or dues (whether initiation fees or otherwise) in any club the main purpose of which is to provide dining, recreational or sporting facilities for its members.

As a result, where a taxpayer pays "membership fees or dues" to "any club" the "main purpose" of which is the provision of "dining, recreational or sporting facilities for its members," the amount expended on these fees or dues is non-deductible. Although subsequent cases have not elaborated on the meaning of these words, the CRA suggests in *Interpretation Bulletin* IT-148R3, "Recreational Properties and Club Dues," July 21, 1997, paragraph 11, that:

> [w]hen determining the main purpose for which a club was organized, the instruments creating the club, such as the content of the club's by-laws to regulate its affairs, are to be considered. Also of importance in this determination is whether more than 50 percent of the club's assets are used in providing dining, recreational or sporting facilities.

According to paragraph 12:

> The payment or reimbursement of club dues or membership fees by an employer would generally be considered to be a taxable benefit to the employee. However, as indicated in the current version of IT-470, *Employees' Fringe Benefits*, if an employer pays the fees required for an employee to be a member of a social or athletic club, the employee is not considered to have received a taxable benefit when the membership is principally for the employer's advantage rather than the employee's. The use of an in-house recreational facility or a physical fitness facility that is owned by the employer for the use of the employees does not usually give rise to a taxable benefit to the employees. In addition, no taxable benefit will generally arise to the employees if the employer pays a related or unrelated organization to provide such facilities, as long as the facilities or membership is available equally to all employees. On the other hand, if the club membership is in the nature of a fringe benefit with little or no advantage to the employer's business, then the cost of membership is considered to be a taxable benefit to the employee and included in the employee's income, even though the dues or fees are not deductible by the employer because of paragraph 18(1)(l). The onus is on the employer and employee to establish that membership in the facility is primarily to the employer's advantage.

9.   Subparagraph 18(1)(l)(ii) was applied in *Damon Developments Ltd. v. M.N.R.*, [1988] T.C.J. No. 103, [1988] 1 C.T.C. 2266, 88 D.T.C. 1128 (T.C.C.), to disallow the deduction of membership fees paid by the taxpayer to the Saskatchewan Roughrider Football Club in order for its senior management personnel to obtain access to the club and host guests for promotional purposes. Would subparagraph 18(1)(l)(ii) have disallowed the deduction of football tickets acquired by the taxpayer in order that its senior management personnel to host guests for promotional purposes?

10.   In *No. 308 v. M.N.R.* (1955), 14 Tax ABC 237 (T.A.B.), the taxpayer, a manufacturer and distributor of wire coils, sought to deduct expenses incurred in operating and maintaining a lodge at which it entertained customers. Concluding (at para. 7) that there was "nothing in the Act, without straining its meaning, that can be said to embrace a financial outlay made purely for social entertainment of people who either are, or are expected to become, customers of the spender of the money involved," the board disallowed the deduction on the basis that the relationship between the entertainment expenses and the taxpayer's sales was "too remote."

11.   The decision in *No. 308* was codified and extended for 1972 and subsequent taxation years by the enactment of subparagraph 18(1)(l)(i). According to this provision:

> In computing the income of a taxpayer from a business or property no deduction shall be made in respect of ... an outlay or expense made or incurred by the taxpayer after 1971 ... for the use or maintenance of property that is a yacht, a camp, a lodge or a golf course or facility, unless the taxpayer made or incurred the outlay or expense in the ordinary course of the taxpayer's business of providing the property for hire or reward.

As a result, where a taxpayer expends an amount to "use" or "maintain" a "yacht," a "camp," a "lodge," or a "golf course or facility," the expenditure is non-deductible, unless it is made or incurred "in the ordinary course of the taxpayer's business of providing the property for hire or reward."

12. The leading case on the application of subparagraph 18(1)(l)(i) is *Sie-Mac Pipeline Contractors Ltd. v. M.N.R.*, [1992] 1 C.T.C. 341, 92 D.T.C. 6461 (F.C.A.), aff'd [1993] S.C.J. No. 33, [1993] 1 C.T.C. 226, 93 D.T.C. 5158 (S.C.C.), in which the taxpayer sought to deduct a sum of $12,800.65, which it spent to send seven customers, five employees, and two employees of a related company on a three-day trip to a fishing lodge ("the Hoeya Hilton") in a wilderness area of British Columbia, in order "to show its appreciation to its customers and inform them of new equipment and techniques" (at para. 2). Reversing the trial decision, [1990] F.C.J. No. 194, [1990] 2 C.T.C. 8, 90 D.T.C. 6344 (F.C.T.D.), which allowed the deduction on the grounds (at para. 19) that a "use of property" within the meaning of subparagraph 18(1)(l)(i) required "exclusive use such as is found in ownership or in renting from an owner," the Federal Court of Appeal held (at para. 5) that the amount was not deductible, "even though it may have been incurred for the purpose of producing income, because it falls within the language of subparagraph 18(1)(l)(i)." According to Linden JA (Heald and Stone JJA concurring) (at paras. 5-7):

> In 1971 Parliament decided to exclude as deductible expenses certain types of costs that had been allowed before that time. It was apparently felt that certain taxpayers may have been taking unfair advantage of the law, as it then stood, to provide recreational activities to its customers where the direct business purpose of the meeting may have been only marginal. Parliament, as a matter of policy, prepared a list of recreational sites that were prone to this type of perceived abuse and prohibited the deduction of the costs of their use and maintenance. Certainly, anyone who owned a yacht, camp, lodge or golf course could not deduct the cost of their maintenance as an expense, but, so too, a taxpayer who "used" any one of these facilities to entertain customers was precluded from deducting the cost. ...

> ...

> In this case there is no dispute that the "Hoeya Hilton" is a lodge within the meaning of subparagraph 18(1)(l)(i). The payments made on behalf of the customers were for the use of the lodge, in the sense of "utilisation" or "availing oneself of" or to "employ." (See *Black's Law Dictionary*, 6th Edition.) There is no need for the property to be "owned" or "rented" or "exclusively controlled" in order for it to be "used," as that word is employed here. If that were the meaning intended, Parliament could easily have shown that intention, which it did not.

As a result, as the CRA explains in IT-148R3, at paragraph 1:

> Subparagraph 18(1)(l)(i) is not restricted to a taxpayer who is the owner of a property described therein but also applies to a taxpayer who rents or uses such a property from the

owner and, in either case, the use of the property may be by the taxpayer or by the taxpayer's clients, suppliers, shareholders or employees.

13. In *Sie-Mac*, the court also rejected the taxpayer's alternative argument that, if subparagraph 18(1)(l)(i) applied, it should apply only to the cost of rooms in the "Hoeya Hilton" and not to other expenses (food, transportation, fishing and the canning of fish, licences, alcohol, and tobacco) that were included in the $12,800.65 that the taxpayer had attempted to deduct. According to Linden JA (Heald and Stone JJA concurring) (at para. 11):

> In my view, there is no merit to this contention. None of the costs incurred are deductible in this case. Had the customers been taken to dinner in Edmonton to discuss business the costs would have been deductible; if they had been flown to Vancouver, for a meeting at a hotel, these expenses too would have been allowable; however, the expense of flying up to a lodge for three days, even for a business purpose, is expressly non-deductible. This was the very kind of thing the subparagraph was meant to stop.

As a result, as Dussault TCJ suggested (at para. 15) in *Groupe Y. Bourassa & Associés Inc. v. Canada*, [1995] T.C.J. No. 1333, [1998] 1 C.T.C. 2511 (T.C.C.), the effect of subparagraph 18(1)(l)(i) is to prohibit "the deduction of both direct and indirect or incidental expenses relating to the use of a property referred to in that subparagraph." Do you agree with this interpretation? Why or why not?

14. Although subparagraph 18(1)(l)(i) disallows the deduction of amounts expended for the use or maintenance of the properties identified in the provision, it does not prohibit the deduction of capital cost allowances in respect of the capital cost of the property. For property acquired after December 31, 1974, however, regulation 1102(1)(f) prohibits the deduction of capital cost allowance in respect of any property for which the costs of use or maintenance are non-deductible by virtue of subparagraph 18(1)(l)(i).

15. For subparagraph 18(1)(l)(i) to apply, the property in respect of which the taxpayer has incurred expenses of use or maintenance must be a "yacht," a "camp," a "lodge," or a "golf course or facility." The meaning of these words is not defined in the *Income Tax Act*, but has been elaborated in judicial decisions and *Interpretation Bulletin* IT-148R3.

Yacht

In *John Barnard Photographers Ltd. v. M.N.R.*, [1979] C.T.C. 2678, 79 D.T.C. 592 (T.R.B.), the taxpayer sought to deduct the cost of maintaining a boat that it used for the purposes of research and photography in order to produce a fishing almanac which it hoped to sell to tourists. Emphasizing (at para. 10) that the provision "is aimed at recreational facilities including a yacht used for pleasure," and concluding (at para. 13) therefore that the meaning of the word "yacht" for the purpose of subparagraph 18(1)(l)(i) should be determined by considering "the use that is generally made" of the vessel, not simply whether it has "a bow, a stem, a hull, a cabin and a motor, regardless of the use it was put to," the board allowed the deduction. In *M.N.R. v. CIP Inc.*, [1988] 1 C.T.C. 32, 88 D.T.C.

6005 (F.C.T.D.), in contrast, the court allowed the taxpayer to deduct $28,963 and $52,222 in its 1979 and 1980 taxation years, which it paid to rent a converted tugboat for the purpose of business entertainment on the grounds (at paras. 9 and 10) that the vessel "could accurately be described only as a tugboat or perhaps as a converted tugboat" that was generally used as a personal residence by its owners and only "occasionally for recreational purposes (4 to 6 weeks in the summer ... and to some extent for day excursions and on weekends)."

According to paragraph 2 of *Interpretation Bulletin* IT-148R3:

> If a yacht is used primarily to entertain clients, suppliers, shareholders or employees, the deductibility of any interest expense on funds borrowed to purchase the yacht is generally denied by the application of subparagraph 18(1)(l)(i).
>
> Expenses incurred for food and beverages at a dining facility of a yacht will not be subject to subparagraph 18(1)(l)(i), if such dining facilities are used on their own and not in conjunction with the recreational nature of the property and there is a genuine business purpose to the use of the facilities.

For other cases in which subparagraph 18(1)(l)(i) has been applied to disallow the deduction of expenses to use or maintain a yacht, see *Voyageur Travel Insurance Ltd. v. M.N.R.*, [1984] C.T.C. 2590, 84 D.T.C. 1566 (T.C.C.) (cost of renting a boat to provide seminars to travel agents who sold the taxpayer's insurance policies non-deductible); and *Robitaille v. Canada*, [1997] 3 C.T.C. 2267, 97 D.T.C. 346 (T.C.C.) (cost to a criminal lawyer of maintaining a yacht to entertain clients non-deductible); and *West Hill Redevelopment Co. v. M.N.R.*, [1986] 2 C.T.C. 2235, 86 D.T.C. 1685 (T.C.C.) (deduction of expenses to operate a yacht allowed on the grounds that the taxpayer had incurred the expenses in the ordinary course of a distinct business of providing the yacht "for hire or reward," even though the taxpayer's ordinary business was the construction and sale of condominium units).

Camp or Lodge

The meaning of the words "camp" and "lodge" for the purpose of subparagraph 18(1)(l)(i) was considered briefly in *Fehrenbach v. M.N.R.*, [1994] T.C.J. No. 1191, [1995] 1 C.T.C. 2602, 95 D.T.C. 860 (T.C.C.), where the taxpayer sought to deduct expenses incurred to maintain a condominium in Collingwood, Ontario that the taxpayer, a partner in a law firm, used primarily for personal use but occasionally to entertain clients and prospective clients. Although observing (at para. 59) that "[t]he dictionary meaning of 'lodge' is so broad it could easily encompass not only the type of structure involved in the case at bar but every conceivable *abode* no matter how large or small it is, no matter whether its use is seasonal or permanent," the court refused (at para. 63) "to stretch the meaning of the word 'lodge' or 'camp' to include the condominium of the appellant" on the basis (at para. 59) that Parliament could not have intended "such a wide application" of subparagraph 18(1)(l)(i). Notwithstanding this conclusion, however, the court disallowed the deduction on the grounds that the expenses were neither "reasonable" within the meaning of section 67 nor incurred for the purpose of gaining or producing income within the meaning of paragraph 18(1)(a), but were "personal expenses" the deduction of which is prohibited by paragraph 18(1)(h).

According to paragraph 3 of *Interpretation Bulletin* IT-148R3:

The words "camp" and "lodge," as used in subparagraph 18(1)(l)(i), are not defined in the *Income Tax Act*. However, for this purpose, "lodge" is generally considered to mean an inn or resort hotel, particularly one that is a centre for recreational activities, as well as a dwelling occupied on a seasonal basis in connection with particular activities, such as hunting or fishing. It is a question of fact whether a hotel or inn is a "lodge." Some factors to consider in making this determination include the location of the hotel or inn, whether it is operated on a seasonal or year-round basis, the type of facilities offered, and whether the facilities offered are the primary or secondary focus, or are incidental to the hotel or inn.

The words "camp" and "lodge" are not considered to embrace a small cottage or other similar dwelling which is designed primarily for the restricted use of a single family. Whether or not a particular dwelling is a "lodge" or "camp" for this purpose will normally depend on the use to which it is put, rather than the physical characteristics or the nature of the design of the property. A reasonable proportion of the taxes, insurance and other like expenses incurred in the maintenance of a cottage may be claimed as a deduction in computing income if a self-employed individual is carrying on a business, or is an employed commission salesman who is required to supply his or her own office space, provided a portion of the cottage is used solely for such income-earning activities by the self-employed individual or employed commission salesman.

If a resort hotel or lodge is used for a genuine business purpose which does not include the entertainment or recreation of clients, suppliers, shareholders or employees, the related expenses are not considered to be subject to paragraph 18(1)(l). Notwithstanding the above, paragraph 18(1)(l) applies in situations where some business meetings may be involved but the main activity is recreation or entertainment.

For cases in addition to *Sie-Mac Pipeline Contractors Ltd. v. M.N.R.*, [1992] 1 C.T.C. 341, 92 D.T.C. 6461 (F.C.A.), in which subparagraph 18(1)(l)(i) has been applied to disallow the deduction of expenses incurred to use or maintain a "camp" or "lodge," see *Canada v. Jaddco Anderson Ltd.*, [1984] C.T.C. 137, 84 D.T.C. 6135 (F.C.A.) (cost of renting a fishing lodge to entertain clients disallowed); *Duramold Ltd. v. M.N.R.*, [1984] C.T.C. 2571, 84 D.T.C. 1498 (T.C.C.) (expenses related to meeting of the taxpayer's board of directors and principal employees at a fishing camp disallowed); and *Adams v. Canada*, [1995] T.C.J. No. 1566, [1996] 1 C.T.C. 2916, (1995) 96 D.T.C. 1145 (T.C.C.) (cost of annual meeting and fishing trip by partners in a medical practice disallowed on the grounds that they were paid "for the use" of the Miramichi Salmon Club, which was a "camp" or "lodge" within the meaning of subparagraph 18(1)(l)(i) of the Act).

Golf Course or Facility

In *Groupe Y. Bourassa & Associés Inc. v. Canada*, [1995] T.C.J. No. 1333, [1998] 1 C.T.C. 2511 (T.C.C.), the taxpayer, an insurance broker, sought to deduct, among other amounts, expenditures for golf tournaments conducted to promote the taxpayer's business among its clients. Disallowing the deductions, the court held that green fees were related to "the direct use of a golf course or facility," while the cost of meals and beverages consumed at the golf club and prizes purchased from the club's pro shop and were "incidental" expenses, the deduction of which was also prohibited by subparagraph 18(1)(l)(i).

According to paragraph 4 of *Interpretation Bulletin* IT-148R3:

> The word "facility'" as used in subparagraph 18(1)(l)(i), refers solely to a golf course and is intended to extend the words "golf course" to include any amenities provided by a golf club, such as a restaurant, dining room, lounge, banquet hall, conference room, health club, swimming pool, curling rink or tennis courts.
>
> Green fees or membership fees in a golf club are not deductible by virtue of paragraph 18(1)(l). In addition, expenses incurred for food and beverages at, and for the use of, a restaurant, dining room, lounge, banquet hall or conference room of a golf club in conjunction with a game of golf or other recreational activity at the golf club are not deductible by virtue of subparagraph 18(1)(l)(i). Expenses incurred for food and beverages at a restaurant, dining room, banquet hall or conference room of a golf club are not subject to paragraph 18(1)(l), provided there is a genuine business purpose to the use of the facilities and the expenses are not incurred in conjunction with a game of golf or other recreational activity at the golf club.

16.   In *Adaskin v. M.N.R.* (1953), 8 Tax ABC 356 (T.A.B.), the taxpayer, a producer of radio shows, sought to deduct $500 to host two parties for cast members held after the performance was finished and the actors had been paid. Rejecting the taxpayer's argument that the parties were essential "to show his appreciation of what the members of his cast had done and to cement his good relations therewith" (at para. 3), the board disallowed the deduction on the basis that the expenses had not been incurred for the purpose of gaining or producing income as required by then paragraph 12(1)(a) (now paragraph 18(1)(a)).

See also *Roebuck v. M.N.R.* (1961), 26 Tax ABC 11, 61 D.T.C. 72 (T.A.B.), where the taxpayer and his brother, who carried on a law practice in equal partnership, invited a number of clients and prospective clients to a bat mitzvah held for the taxpayer's daughter in order to recognize "a debt to their clients" and to establish goodwill with prospective clients. Disallowing the deduction of a percentage of the bat mitzvah expenses based on the ratio of business guests to all guests, the board concluded (at paras. 25 and 27) that the expenses were neither "in accordance with the principles of commercial trading or accepted business practice" nor "incurred for the purpose of gaining or producing income from the law business or practice which they conduct[ed] in the city of Toronto." According to the chair of the board (at para. 25):

> Nothing has been unearthed in the consideration of the present appeal which would make an outlay or expense deductible when such outlay or expense was made purely for social

entertainment following a religious ceremony and particularly when three-quarters of the guests consisted of customers, clients, business acquaintances, members of the judiciary and those engaged in the local administration of justice, and perhaps a number of fallen-away customers or clients.

Do you agree with these outcomes? Why or why not? Was the expense in *Roebuck* "purely for social entertainment"?

17. In *Fingold v. M.N.R.*, [1992] T.C.J. No. 485, [1992] 2 C.T.C. 2393, 92 D.T.C. 2011 (T.C.C.), the taxpayer, one of two primary shareholders of a private company called Fobasco, was assessed under subsection 15(1) on the basis that he had received a shareholder's benefit from the company, which had paid part of the cost of receptions held after the bar mitzvah of the taxpayer's son and after the wedding of the taxpayer's stepdaughter. Although the corporation paid only a proportionate share of the expenses based on the percentage of business guests invited, the court dismissed the taxpayer's appeal on the basis that there was no evidence that the business guests were aware that they were the guests of Fobasco rather than the taxpayer. According to Rip TCCJ (at para. 4):

> In my view when a taxpayer carrying on a business incurs expenses to promote the business ... the target of the expense, that is, the person who the taxpayer desires to think kindly of it, must be aware that the taxpayer, and no one else, has actually disbursed the funds for that purpose. Otherwise the whole exercise is in vain. ...
>
> There is no evidence that the invitations sent to the business guests were any different from those sent to personal guests. ... The business guests had no idea they were invited to these affairs as guests of Fobasco. When guests are invited to a Fobasco Christmas party they know Fobasco is the "host." I have no doubt the business guests knew they were invited because they had business dealings with the Fingolds but this is not sufficient for Fobasco to claim the guests as its own.

With respect to the deductibility of expenses in the course of personal functions such as weddings and bar mitzvahs, the court stated that:

> A very fine but definite line exists separating personal and business related expenses. It is common practice for principal shareholders of a corporation, sole proprietors of a business, professionals and others carrying on a business to invite customers and clients and others with whom business is carried on to family functions such as weddings and bar mitzvahs. The outlays or expenses made or incurred by a taxpayer or a person related to the taxpayer, for the purpose of an essentially personal function cannot be said at the same time to be made or incurred by that taxpayer for the purpose of gaining or producing income from a business. An expense is either a personal expense or a business related expense and where the expense is incurred essentially for personal purposes it cannot at the same time be incurred for the purpose of earning income from a business. There may be a slight difference in fact between the two but in law the difference is clear.

18. In *Grunbaum v. Canada*, [1994] T.C.J. No. 180, [1994] 1 C.T.C. 2687, 94 D.T.C. 1384 (T.C.C.), the taxpayer was the president and primary shareholder of a company that sought to deduct $12,477.79 expended on a wedding reception for the taxpayer's daughter. On the basis that these expenses were proportionate to the number of business guests invited to the reception, that the invitations were sent through the company and identified the trade name of the company on both the interior and exterior envelopes, and that all correspondence with the

business guests was handled exclusively by the company, the court held that the wedding expenses were a deductible expense to the company and not a taxable benefit to the taxpayer. According to Garon JTCC (at para. 69):

> It is true, as stressed by counsel for the respondent, that the event which triggered this reception is of a personal nature. However, a proper analysis of the situation shows that with respect to the invitations to the wedding reception two main decisions were made. One decision concerns the invitations to family and friends. This decision is unquestionably of a personal nature and the expenses made as a result of this decision are likewise of a personal nature and obviously not deductible. The other main decision relates to the act of inviting business guests to the wedding reception. This second decision is clearly, in my view, a business decision. This decision was made by the appellant Grunbaum and [the vice-president of the company] on behalf of the appellant company. The appellant Grunbaum could have decided that the wedding reception in honour of his daughter would be exclusively a family gathering and a private and personal affair. For reasons that concern the appellant Grunbaum and the appellant company, they took advantage of a personal event to make it in a large part a business promotion or a commercial endeavour. In this connection, I believe in particular the testimony of [the vice-president] when she in substance expressed the view that the invitations of the business guests to the wedding and the holding of the related reception procured in all likelihood tangible benefits to the appellant company's business. In fact, as a direct result of these promotional activities made through the vehicle of the wedding reception, the appellant company was awarded in respect of its products a sole distributorship for the United States because of a contact made at the wedding reception with one Bridget Downs from Hamilton Lamp. This distributorship was expected to generate over $100,000 a year in additional revenues.

Does the decision in *Grunbaum* reverse the holdings in *Adaskin v. M.N.R.* (1953), 8 Tax ABC 356 (T.A.B.) and *Roebuck v. M.N.R.* (1961), 26 Tax ABC 11, 61 DTC 72 (T.A.B.)?

19. For expenses incurred after June 17, 1987, subsection 67.1(1) limits the amount that a taxpayer may deduct "in respect of the human consumption of food or beverages or the enjoyment of entertainment" to a fixed percentage of the amount otherwise deductible — originally 80 per cent, but reduced to 50 per cent for amounts incurred after February 21, 1994. For the purpose of this provision, paragraph 67.1(4)(b) defines "entertainment" to include "amusement and recreation," while paragraph 67.1(4)(a) provides that "no amount paid or payable for travel on an airplane, train or bus shall be considered to be in respect of food, beverages or entertainment consumed or enjoyed while travelling thereon," thereby excluding items such as airplane meals and in-flight movies from the operation of the rule. Subsection 67.1(3) applies to amounts paid for conferences, conventions, seminars, or similar events at which food, beverages, or entertainment are provided. Subsection 67.1(2) sets out a number of exceptions to the limit in subsection 67.1(1). Section 67.1 is examined in Chapter 8.

20. In *Scott v. Canada*, [1998] F.C.J. No. 1037, [1998] 4 C.T.C. 103, 98 D.T.C. 6530 (F.C.A.), the taxpayer, a courier who delivered packages by foot and public transit, sought to deduct the cost of additional food and water that he consumed as part of his daily routine. Rejecting the Minister's argument that

these costs were "personal and living expenses" the deduction of which is prohibited by paragraph 18(1)(h), the court analogized the food and water to the gasoline used by couriers who deliver packages by automobile. According to McDonald JA (Strayer and Robertson JJA concurring) (at para. 10):

> Because the courier who drives the automobile is allowed to deduct his or her fuel, the foot and transit courier should be able to deduct the fuel his body needs. However, because we all require food and water to live, he can only deduct the extra food and water he must consume above and beyond the average person's intake in order to perform his job. This is similar to the automobile courier who is only entitled to deduct that portion of the fuel used for a business purpose. The extra fuel consumed for personal needs cannot be deducted. This result takes into account the different methods by which the same job is done and puts all couriers on an equal footing. Arguably, it also recognizes and encourages [rather than discourages, as a prohibition on this expense would] new environmentally responsible ways of producing income.

Do you agree with this result? Why or why not? Would the limitation in section 67.1 apply to any such deduction? Should it?

H. Clothing Expenses

Like recreation, meals, and entertainment, clothing that is acquired for business purposes may also provide a personal benefit. The deductibility of clothing expenses was considered in *No. 360 v. M.N.R.* (1956), 16 Tax ABC 28 (T.A.B.).

No. 360 v. M.N.R.
(1956), 16 Tax ABC 28 (T.A.B.)

CHAIRMAN FABIO MONET, QC: ... In her income tax return for the taxation year 1954, the appellant deducted from the income derived from her professional activities a sum of $950 for certain expenses which she described as follows: "The cost of making and altering her wardrobe, accessories for various dresses and the purchase of dresses for television purposes." The respondent did not allow that deduction and on August 10, 1955 assessed the appellant accordingly. On October 5 of the same year the appellant sent the respondent a notice of objection to the assessment and was advised on February 2, 1956 that:

> The Honourable the Minister of National Revenue having reconsidered the assessment and having considered the facts and reasons set forth in the Notice of Objection hereby confirms the said assessment as having been made in accordance with the provisions of the Act and in particular on the ground that expenses to the extent of $950.00 claimed as deductions from income were personal or living expenses within the meaning of paragraph (h) of subsection (1) of section 12 of the Act [now paragraph 18(1)(h)].

I must state that the respondent recognized the fact that the income of the appellant is derived from a "business" within the meaning given that word in Section 139(1)(e) of the *Income Tax Act* (RSC 1952, c. 148) [now subsection 248(1)] and admitted that she incurred the expense of $950. Therefore, it is solely a matter of deciding whether or not the appellant is entitled to the deduction she claims.

Actress, commentator and dramatic artist, the appellant is a star of the stage, radio and television — and occasionally of the screen — whose services are much sought after by directors and producers. It has been proved that her success is due both to her great talent as an actress and to her charm and grooming, and because of these qualities she has often been selected in preference to other as talented but less elegant artists. It is obvious that her concern about her dress leads her to spend large sums on her clothes. Besides, television makes many demands of its artists where dress is concerned. The appellant listed some of them; for example, black must be avoided; so must white and pale colours which may make the person wearing them appear stout; materials must be neither opaque nor too shiny; dresses must be simple in cut, without frills, bows, etc. During her testimony the appellant added that television made many other demands; for example, she declared that although she had been a natural brunette until the advent of television, she was required to become a blonde because blondes photograph more easily and "show up" better on television.

The evidence revealed that the CBC furnishes the costumes the artists wear in "period" plays but the artists must provide their own costumes for modern plays. In most of her television engagements the appellant is required to furnish her own dresses which have to be varied and always in the best taste, particularly for the programme in which she gives advice on beauty and elegance to an extremely exacting female audience. The appellant stated in her testimony that she even receives letters of protest from female viewers if she wears the same dress or the same jewelry on two or three occasions. For that reason, the appellant declared that she must buy a large number of dresses and accessories if she is to retain her television contracts. Furthermore, it was established that the intense lighting and the makeup required for television are hard on the artist's clothing.

The testimony of the appellant was corroborated by that of a well-known producer. The witness declared that he knew personally that on many occasions the appellant had been selected over other competitors of equal talent merely because she was the most elegant. Quoting a concrete example, the witness added that the appellant was chosen from among several candidates to star in a particular screen production. The reasons the jury gave for selecting her were (and I quote the words of the witness):

> ... because first of all, she was an artist — that was the prime condition. Secondly, because she was pretty. But thirdly, because she had style and was recognized for it. That was part of her stock-in-trade as an artist.

When cross-examined, the appellant admitted that she wears, or could wear, the dresses and accessories she purchases for her television engagements on other occasions.

Counsel for the appellant contended that she must maintain her reputation as a well-dressed woman both on and off the stage and that the expenses she incurred to do so are deductible because they are made for the purpose of earning or producing the income from her profession. On the other hand, counsel for the respondent submitted that different activities have different requisites; television, the radio and the theatre having their particular ones just like the professions, the trades, business and industry. Consequently, the clothing worn by the people belonging to these various groups is not the same. Some wear the same clothes at work as elsewhere; others choose to wear different clothing. The principle, however, remains the same; it is a personal expense.

The question here has arisen in a great number of cases heard by this Board. In all such cases it was decided that such expenses were personal expenses and a deduction was not allowed. I find nothing in the present case which would warrant a decision different from the one reached by my colleagues and myself in similar cases, to wit, that these are "personal or living expenses" within the meaning of Section 12(1)(h) of the Act and consequently are not deductible. ...

Appeal dismissed.

NOTES AND QUESTIONS

1. Do you agree with the decision in *No. 360*? Why or why not? Of what relevance is the taxpayer's admission that she wore, or could wear, the dresses and accessories she purchased for her television engagements on other occasions?

2. In *Giroux v. M.N.R.* (1957), 17 Tax ABC 116, 57 D.T.C. 238 (T.A.B.), the taxpayer, a stage and television artist, sought to deduct $236.78 incurred to purchase clothes and accessories that the taxpayer considered necessary for playing her roles, and a further amount for the cost of cleaning these items. Allowing the deduction, the board (at para. 12) distinguished between "an expenditure incurred by an artist for clothing he could not suitably wear except on stage or television but which he is required to provide or feels he should wear on account of the role he will play or the character he will portray, and an expenditure incurred by an artist for costumes or clothing he can wear either on stage, television or in private life" (at para. 15). Without analysis, however, the cleaning expenses were disallowed on the basis that they were "a purely personal expense whose deduction is not allowed by the Act."

3. For other cases in which the cost of clothes has been allowed as a deductible expense, see *No. 428 v. M.N.R.* (1957), 17 Tax ABC 236, 57 D.T.C. 310 (T.A.B.); and *Col. Sanders Kentucky Fried Chicken Ltd. v. M.N.R.*, [1970] Tax ABC 1013, 70 D.T.C. 1662 (T.A.B.).

4. Consider the following argument from Neil Brooks, "The Principles Underlying the Deduction of Business Expenses" in B.G. Hansen, V. Krishna, and J.A. Rendall, eds., *Essays on Canadian Taxation* (Toronto: Richard De Boo, 1978) 249 at 262-63:

Expenses for clothing must be incurred whether or not an individual is working. It is true that the clothes that one wears to work may not be identical to the clothes that one would wear if not working, however, even these clothes are at least in part a substitute for leisure clothes and can be worn for such a purpose. Also to the extent that work clothes are more expensive than the clothes one would wear for leisure, there is probably increased personal satisfaction derived from the clothes worn to work. While this increased personal satisfaction may not equal the cost of the clothes, the administrative difficulties of trying to determine how much of the expense is a consumption expense would be insurmountable. A rule disallowing all expenses for clothing worn to work is thus more likely to be just than a rule allowing the deduction of all such expenses, and is obviously more feasible than one which attempts to allocate the expense.

Some people wear special clothing or uniforms to work which are not suitable for off-the-job wear. Others, such as actors and actresses, have to spend a great deal of money for clothing, much of which is not suitable for off-the-job wear and much of which is worn once or twice. While these items of clothing take the place of clothing that would be worn in any event, because of their expense and because they cannot be worn off-the-job it is less clear that the personal satisfaction derived from them equals their cost. In the case law indeed there is some suggestion that expenses for clothing in these circumstances are deductible.

Do you agree or disagree with this argument? To what extent is the personal satisfaction derived from wearing certain kinds of clothing relevant to the issue of deductibility? Does the personal satisfaction derived from wearing certain kinds of clothes necessarily correspond to their cost? Is there any reason why the cost of clothing acquired for the purpose of gaining or producing income should be treated any differently for tax purposes from the cost of recreation, meals, or entertainment, from which taxpayers may also derive personal satisfaction?

I. Home Office Expenses

Also like payments for recreation, meals, and entertainment, amounts expended on a home office may provide personal benefits as well as business advantages. Perhaps not surprisingly, therefore, the deduction of home office expenses has given rise to considerable litigation and a detailed statutory rule in subsection 18(12). Before examining this specific provision, however, it is useful to consider the application of general principles to the deduction of home office expenses. An excellent example of the application of these general principles is the decision in *Locke v. M.N.R.* (1965), 38 Tax ABC 38, 65 D.T.C. 223 (T.A.B.).

Locke v. M.N.R.
(1965), 38 Tax ABC 38, 65 D.T.C. 223 (T.A.B.)

J.O. WELDON: The appellant is a barrister and solicitor practising his profession in partnership with David G. Humphrey under the firm name of Humphrey and Locke in the City of Toronto. During the year 1961 Mr. Locke resided in his own home in the Village of Thornhill which is situated on Yonge Street about 10 miles north of Toronto proper. Having fitted up one of the rooms in his Thornhill residence as a study or office, he proceeded to claim 1/6 of

2,217.16 being the total of his home expenses for 1961 or $369.53 as an expense incurred by him for the purpose of producing part of his income from the practice of his profession. The deduction so claimed was subsequently disallowed by the Minister and the resulting appeal herein in respect of the taxation year 1961 was heard in Toronto. The appellant acted for himself at the hearing.

In confirming the re-assessment made on April 30, 1963, the Minister stated: that the expenditures in respect of the taxpayer's residence amounting to $369.53 claimed as deductions from income were not outlays or expenses incurred by the taxpayer for the purpose of gaining or producing income within the meaning of paragraph (a) of subsection (1) of Section 12 of the *Income Tax Act*, RSC 1952, c. 148 [now paragraph 18(1)(a)], and that the said expenditures were personal or living expenses within the meaning of paragraph (h) of subsection (1) of Section 12 of the Act [now paragraph 18(1)(h)].

...

The facts of this matter were not in dispute and will now be given briefly. The appellant was married in 1953, and called to the bar in 1954. In the year 1961 he, his wife and their two young children were living in an 8-room house with two bathrooms in the Village of Thornhill, as already mentioned. The house was built for him in 1955, and an addition was added about 1958 consisting of three rooms, a bedroom, a bathroom and a study. Mr. Locke testified that the addition to the house was made for the purpose of providing him with an office in his home where he could take the numerous telephone calls which he received, and also return the 15 to 20 telephone calls which, apparently, accumulated during the day when he was out of his Toronto office, where he could see clients in the evening, and where he could read law and work at home, and that the study or office contained a desk, law library (as described by the taxpayer, this appeared to be quite a good working library for home use), chesterfield, chairs, a telephone extension (one of three in the house), dictaphone and possibly a television set.

The appellant also testified that his practice has grown in a general fashion, and has become one in which he does a substantial amount of matrimonial and criminal work as well as a reasonable amount of real estate and company work. He stressed the fact that his frequent attendances in court made it very difficult for him to see clients during the daytime, also a number of his clients were not free to see him during working hours. Apparently, he is able to deal with a great many details in connection with his work by telephone. During cross-examination by counsel for the Minister, Mr. Locke was unable to testify with definiteness as to the number of personal interviews he had had with clients in his home in the relevant taxation year in the course of a week. He said that it would be difficult to estimate that because in some weeks he would see clients every night, and in other weeks the whole seven days would pass without there being any appointments at all in his home. His conclusion was that he might have seen two clients a week in his home on the average, but that estimate, apparently, was a very rough approximation.

To summarize the taxpayer's evidence covering the relevant taxation year, he appeared to be a very active and industrious young lawyer who not only took home a brief-case full of work every night to work on for the next day, but who actually did do some work at home. He found it very convenient to have a room set aside for his use in his home, where he was able to look up points of law, receive and return numerous telephone calls, do preparatory work and see the occasional client. Thus, it is possible to see where Mr. Locke got the idea of charging a part of his home expenses against his professional income. It should be mentioned: that the appellant did not put up a brass plate or sign outside of his home bearing his name and profession; that the yellow pages of the Toronto Telephone Directory dated May 1961 listed the taxpayer under the lawyer classification as "Locke, Hugh R. 11 Adelaide St. W., Empire 3-7291" with no other address given, and that the Toronto Suburban North Directory dated June 16, 1961 showed the taxpayer listed as "Locke, Hugh R., 12 Riverside Blvd., Avenue 5-3192" with no mention of his occupation.

The case of *Heakes v. M.N.R.*, 32 Tax ABC 443, received considerable attention from both the appellant and counsel for the Minister at the hearing of this appeal. The facts of that case are very similar to the present appeal, the main similarities being: both appellants are lawyers practising in partnership with one other lawyer, Mr. Locke's firm having law offices in the city of Toronto, Mr. Heakes' firm having law offices in the Town of Weston which is part of the Municipality of Metropolitan Toronto — in other words, each taxpayer maintained and occupied business premises where he regularly practised his profession, kept his books of account, office files and law office paraphernalia and where his stenographic staff performed their duties; both appellants are married with two children — Mrs. Heakes has the advantage of being a well-trained legal secretary and has continued to do typing work for her husband; both appellants have provided themselves with homes wherein each has his own room which has been fitted up as an office-study; both appellants make themselves available to their clients in the evenings for a variety of reasons — in Mr. Heakes' case the stairs to his regular office are too steep for some of his elderly clients; both appellants appear to have seen on the average about one to two clients a week in their respective offices in their homes; neither appellant displayed a professional sign on his home premises, and both appellants claimed the same fraction of "1/6" of his total home expenses as a deduction from his professional income — Mr. Locke said that he simply adopted the fraction "1/6," used by Mr. Heakes, in his 1961 income tax return.

In dismissing the *Heakes* case, the Chairman of the Board said that the appellant's evidence fell far short of what was required to bring him within the exception contained in Section 12(1)(a) of the Act. He called attention to Section 12(1)(d) of the Act [now paragraph 18(1)(d)] which reads as follows:

12. (1) In computing income, no deduction shall be made in respect of

    (d)   the annual value of property except rent for property leased by the taxpayer for use in his business,

and quoted the following excerpt from the case of *English v. M.N.R.*, 15 Tax ABC 87:

> ... A private individual cannot be the owner of realty and his own tenant thereof at the same time; he cannot pay rent to himself. There was no payment or expense relating to the use of the study that would not have been made or incurred by the appellant in any event and regardless of whether or not a study was available.

Thus, on the basis of Section 12(1)(d) and the *English* case (*supra*), the present appellant was not entitled to treat a portion of his home expenses as rent. However, in a proper case, where a portion of the house has been definitely set aside for business purposes, and an appreciable amount of business has been transacted therein, not so found in the *Heakes* case, the taxpayer might be entitled to deduct a reasonable amount as an expense incurred in operating that business. That deduction might be characterized as arising from an apportionment of the taxpayer's home expenses between the taxpayer for personal living expenses, on the one hand, and the taxpayer for business expenses applicable to the business transacted in a portion of his home, on the other hand. It should be recognizable that the taxpayer has foregone the use of a definite part of his home for the sake of his business.

    ...

In his reasons for judgment in the *Heakes* case, the Chairman also mentioned: that no sign was affixed to the outside of Mr. Heakes' home to announce to the general public that a law office was being maintained therein; that the maintaining of an office in a home is a completely different situation to that of renting a second or branch office in business premises under a formal lease; that Mr. Heakes only saw one or two clients a week in his home office; that that office appeared to be mainly used for his convenience and was personal to him, and that, as a general comment, the fraction of 1/6 of the home expenses appeared too large under the circumstances. After comparing the facts of the present appeal with those in the *Heakes* case, I do not think that the cases can be distinguished from one another on any sound basis. Therefore, it should be concluded that the appellant herein has also fallen far short of bringing himself within the exception contained in Section 12(1)(a) of the Act.

Before claiming a deduction in respect of his business or professional income covering the use of a room in his home, a taxpayer would seem to be well advised to consider the following questions: was the room in question definitely separate from the living quarters of his family; was an appreciable amount of business transacted in the said room or was it just used for his convenience; was his house partially municipally assessed for business purposes; was his telephone ordered for business purposes; was there a sign on his house announcing to the general public that a law office was being maintained therein, and lastly, if he already has an office where he regularly practises his profession, was his home office, in fact, a second branch office. *Apropos* of an office in a home, some thought might be given for purposes of comparison to the example set by the medical profession. When a medical doctor practises in his home, there is no mistaking the fact. There is usually a brass name-plate, conspicuously in view, on his house, and a special entrance well-lighted for his patients. The office itself is usually completely separate from the doctor's living quarters, and is usually divided into a waiting-room, dispensary and consulting room. The patients never see the doctor's family, unless his wife happens to be acting as his receptionist.

While the Board has had nothing but admiration for the present appellant's industry and frankness, his appeal will have to be dismissed because his home office appeared to be used, in the relevant taxation year, principally for his own personal convenience. The great majority of lawyers, especially in the early days of their practice, do work at home, and are frequently called on the telephone by their clients. There is nothing unusual in that. I would say that there is a very heavy onus indeed on a lawyer who seeks to claim a deduction under Section 12(1)(a) of the Act, over and above the expenses applicable to his regular office, in connection with the use of a room in his home as an office-study.

For the reasons and observations set out above, this appeal should be dismissed and the relevant re-assessment confirmed.

Appeal dismissed.

NOTES AND QUESTIONS

1.   On what basis did the Tax Appeal Board in *Locke* disallow the deduction of the taxpayer's home office expenses? Do you agree with the board's decision? Why or why not?

2.   Under what circumstances did the board in *Locke* suggest that home office expenses might be deductible? Do you agree or disagree with these requirements? Why?

3.   In the course of his decision in *Locke*, J.O. Weldon referred to former paragraph 12(1)(d) (now paragraph 18(1)(d)), according to which no deduction is allowed in computing a taxpayer's income from a business or property for "the annual value of property except for rent for property leased by the taxpayer for use in the taxpayer's business."

Paragraph 18(1)(d) was formerly paragraph 12(1)(d), and is derived from paragraph 6(1)(c) of the *Income War Tax Act*. The expression "annual value of property" is derived from Schedule A of the UK *Tax Act*, which imposed tax on the imputed rental value of real property. The purpose of paragraph 18(1)(d) and its predecessors appears to be to deny a deduction for the imputed rental value of property owned by a taxpayer and used in the taxpayer's business. Paragraph 18(1)(d) contains an exception from the prohibition against (and thus permits) the deduction of "rent for property leased by the taxpayer for use in the taxpayer's business."

In *English v. M.N.R.* (1956), 15 Tax ABC 87 (T.A.B.), the Tax Appeal Board disallowed home office expenses (computed, as in *Locke*, as one-sixth of operating costs of the taxpayer's home) on the basis that they were personal and living expenses within the meaning of then paragraph 12(1)(h) and prohibited under then paragraph 12(1)(d). A similar conclusion was reached in *Heakes v. M.N.R.* (1963), 32 Tax ABC 443 (T.A.B.) and *Brooks v. Canada*, [1978] C.T.C. 761, 78 D.T.C. 6505 (F.C.T.D.), each of which involved a lawyer who sought to deduct one-sixth of the operating costs of his home as expenses incurred for the purpose of gaining or producing income from his legal practice.

Is it appropriate to characterize the costs of maintaining a home (for example, mortgage interest, property taxes, utilities, insurance, and depreciation) as "the annual value" of the property? Does this interpretation preclude the possibility of any deduction for home office expenses, even where they satisfy the conditions set out in *Locke*?

4.   In the course of his decision in *Locke v. M.N.R.* (1965), 38 Tax ABC 38, 65 D.T.C. 223 (T.A.B.), J.O. Weldon referred to "the example set by the medical profession" where "there is no mistaking the fact" when "a medical doctor practices in his home":

> There is usually a brass name-plate, conspicuously in view, on his house, and a special entrance well-lighted for his patients. The office itself is usually completely separate from the doctor's living quarters, and is usually divided into a waiting-room, dispensary and consulting room. The patients never see the doctor's family, unless his wife happens to be acting as his receptionist.

The deductibility of home office expenses of medical practitioners was considered in *Logan v. M.N.R.*, [1967] Tax ABC 276, 67 D.T.C. 189 (T.A.B.) and *Mallouh v. M.N.R.*, [1985] 1 C.T.C. 2297, 85 D.T.C. 250 (T.C.C.).

In *Logan*, the taxpayer, a heart surgeon who had a full-time business office at which he examined patients, sought to deduct expenses related to a home office where he consulted with and prepared written reports to submit to other doctors who referred patients to him. Accepting the taxpayer's evidence that his full-time office was unsuitable for night-time work, that he had deliberately acquired a home large enough to provide him with a study that he could use exclusively for his medical practice, and that "his income increased by $10,000 a year due to his having an office at home for the purpose of his medical practice," the Tax Appeal Board allowed the deduction of home office expenses based on the ratio of the area of the home office to the area of the house as a whole. According to the board (at para. 9):

> In this appeal, the appellant proved that (a) he purchased his house because he found out that a specific room was available in it where he could carry on his night work; (b) that room was separated from the rest of his house; (c) he had a telephone extension and a dictaphone; (d) five to eight doctors a week came to that room in his home to discuss the case of their respective clients, and (e) he used the office he was maintaining in his home for the purpose of report writing and consultation with doctors, which could not be done in the day-time as

he was then seeing patients in his downtown office and also visiting patients in hospitals. The fact that he had no sign on the door to indicate to casual clients that he had an office in his home is immaterial because he was known as a heart specialist by doctors and, in the evening, he was dealing only with doctors in his home office. It has also been put in evidence that the room he occupied in his home was not used by his family, or for entertaining guests or for anything else, but was used for the sole purpose of his medical practice. He had no radio, no television set in his home office. But he had the most complete medical library relating to heart diseases and so on.

Finally, the board suggested (at para. 8): "Who, if not the taxpayer himself, is in a better position to determine what is the best way to go about or the best method to follow in order to gain and produce a bigger income from his business?"

In *Mallouh*, however, where the taxpayer obstetrician and gynecologist maintained a home office in a portion of the basement served by a separate entrance, the Tax Court disallowed the deduction of related expenses on the grounds that the taxpayer did not treat or receive patients in the home office, had no business phone number for the office, nowhere indicated that he operated a medical office in his home, had not purchased his home with the primary purpose of establishing a medical office, and did not need a home office. According to the court (at para. 19), the expenses were "personal expenses whose sole purpose was for the [taxpayer's] convenience."

5.   For other cases in which deductions for home office expenses have been disallowed on the basis that they were personal or living expenses, see *Hill v. M.N.R.* (1963), 34 Tax ABC 169 (T.A.B.) and *Hagar v. M.N.R.*, [1969] Tax ABC 1180 (T.A.B.). For other cases in which deductions for home office expenses have been allowed, see *Kenton v. M.N.R.*, [1969] Tax ABC 981 (T.A.B); *Allen v. M.N.R.*, [1979] C.T.C. 3076, 79 D.T.C. 847 (T.R.B.); *Merchant v. M.N.R.*, [1982] C.T.C. 2742, 82 D.T.C. 1764 (T.R.B.); and *Roy v. M.N.R.*, [1985] 1 C.T.C. 2328, 85 D.T.C. 261 (T.C.C.).

6.   Effective for fiscal periods commencing after 1987, the deductibility of home office expenses is subject to specific statutory regulation under subsection 18(12), which applies notwithstanding any other provision of the Act. According to paragraph 18(12)(a), in computing an individual's income from a business for a taxation year:

> no amount shall be deducted in respect of an otherwise deductible amount for any part (in this subsection referred to as the "work space") of a self-contained domestic establishment in which the individual resides, except to the extent that the work space is either
>
> (i)   the individual's principal place of business, or
>
> (ii)   used exclusively for the purpose of earning income from business and used on a regular and continuous basis for meeting clients, customers or patients of the individual in respect of the business.

The term "self-contained domestic establishment" is defined in subsection 248(1) as "a dwelling-house, apartment or other similar place of residence in which place a person as a general rule sleeps and eats."

In general, therefore, where an amount in respect of a home office or "work space" would be "otherwise deductible" under general principles,[38] this amount will not be deductible except to the extent that the work space is the individual's "principal place of business" or is "used exclusively for the purpose of earning income from business and used on a regular and continuous basis for meeting clients, customers or patients of the individual in respect of the business."

Where the taxpayer satisfies one or both of these requirements, paragraph 18(12)(b) provides that the amount that may be deducted in respect of the home office may not exceed the taxpayer's income from the business to which the home office relates. In other words, home office expenses may not be used to generate losses that may be deducted against a taxpayer's income from other sources under paragraph 3(d). Finally, paragraph 18(12)(c) allows amounts the deduction of which is disallowed under paragraph 18(12)(b) to be carried forward indefinitely and deducted against future income from the business to which the home office relates.

The rationale for the enactment of subsection 18(12) was explained as follows in *Tax Reform 1987: Income Tax Reform*, a Department of Finance paper accompanying its *White Paper: Tax Reform 1987* (Ottawa: Department of Finance, June 18, 1987) at 87:

> Under present law, self-employed persons may deduct from business income all expenses related to a home office that is used for business purposes. ... The existing law thus allows a deduction for home office expenses in those circumstances where the use of the home office may not be required for the conduct of the business, but rather is incidental to the business activity.
>
> The new rules limit the deduction for expenses relating to a home office to those circumstances where maintaining a place of business in the home is necessary for the conduct of the business. The new rules seek to separate business costs from those costs that would have been incurred in any event in the normal course of maintaining a home.

In addition, the Department of Finance paper outlined various scenarios in which it suggested that subsection 18(12) will or will not apply (at 88):

- Lawyers, accountants, doctors and other professionals who have their principal offices outside of their homes will not be able to claim any expenses in respect of a home office unless they use the office exclusively for business purposes and regularly meet clients, customers or patients in the office.

- A university professor who has a consulting practice operated exclusively out of a home office devoted to the practice will be able to claim home office expenses. So will a life insurance salesperson who conducts business from a part of the home dedicated exclusively to the business. In both cases, the home

---

[38] See *Furlotte v. Canada*, [2000] T.C.J. No. 757, [2001] 1 C.T.C. 2044 (T.C.C.).

office expense deduction can be claimed to the extent of the income from the business.

- A person who lives in the building in which he or she operates a grocery store, a barber shop or a bed and breakfast business will be able to claim all currently allowable expenses to the extent of the income from that business.

7.   For the CRA's views on subsection 18(12), see *Interpretation Bulletin* IT-514, "Work Space in Home Expenses," February 3, 1989. Paragraph 2 discusses the requirement in subparagraph 18(12)(a)(i) that the work space must be the taxpayer's "principal place of business"; paragraph 3 discusses the two requirements in subparagraph 18(12)(a)(ii) that the work space must be used "exclusively for the purpose of earning income from business" and "on a regular and continuous basis for meeting clients, customers or patients of the individual in respect of the business"; and paragraph 4 discusses acceptable methods of apportioning home expenses between personal and business uses.

According to paragraph 2:

> The word "principal" is not defined in the Act but it is considered that the words "chief" and "main" are synonymous to it. Where, for example, a room in a contractor's residence is used to accomplish the functions relating to a contracting business, such as, receiving work orders, bookkeeping, purchasing and preparing payrolls while the remaining activities of the business, the performance of the contracts, are carried out at the customer's location, the room would be considered as the contractor's principal place of business. Similarly, the work space in a farmer's home utilized to operate the farming business would normally be the farmer's principal place of business. The room used by the contractor and the farmer's work space could also be used for personal purposes since they need not be used exclusively for the business in order to meet the 1(a) requirement.

According to paragraph 3:

> The first requirement [of subparagraph 18(12)(a)(ii)] that the work space must be used exclusively to earn business income ... is met if a segregated area, such as a room or rooms, is used in a business and for no other purpose. The second requirement is that the work space must be used for meeting clients, customers or patients on a regular and continuous basis. The regularity and frequency of meetings in a work space to meet the requirement of being on a regular and continuous basis will depend on the nature of the business activity and is determined on the facts of each situation. However, a work space in respect of a business which normally requires infrequent meetings or frequent meetings at irregular intervals would not meet the requirement. A home office used by a doctor to meet one or two patients a week is an example of a work space which would not be considered used on a regular and continuous basis for meeting patients. On the other hand, a work space used to meet an average of 5 patients a day for 5 days each week would clearly be used for that purpose on a regular and continuous basis.

According to paragraph 4:

> The expenses should be apportioned between business and non-business use on a reasonable basis, such as, square metres of floor space used. However, the reasonable basis should also take into consideration any personal use, if any, of a work space that is an individual's principal place of business [where the expenses are deductible under subparagraph 18(12)(a)(i)].

8.   In applying subsection 18(12), courts have considered both the meaning of the expression "any part ... of a self-contained domestic establishment" and the statutory requirement that the work space be either the taxpayer's "principal place of business" or "used exclusively for the purpose of earning income from business and used on a regular and continuous basis for meeting clients, customers or patients of the individual in respect of the business."

In *Ellis v. Canada*, [1994] T.C.J. No. 24, [1994] 1 C.T.C. 2349, 94 D.T.C. 1731 (T.C.C.), the taxpayer, who operated a business producing and selling pottery and stained glass out of a studio/store built over a flat-roofed garage at her residence and connected to the rest of the house through two interior passages, sought to deduct losses from this business in computing her net income from all sources. Rejecting the taxpayer's argument that the work space was not part of her "self-contained domestic establishment," the court applied paragraph 18(12)(b) to disallow the deduction of the losses. According to Rowe DJTCC (at para. 12):

> the studio/store area, falling within the definition of work space, is clearly a part of the residence of the appellant, which is indeed a self-contained domestic establishment. ... Although potential customers could enter the business premise from the outside, the studio was still physically connected to the house and was accessible therefrom without having to go outside and shared the electrical, water and heating facilities. It is probably safe to assume the legislators in enacting the subsection at issue had an eye on the typical home office in which a portion of the residence, although possessing a business identity, is still readily identifiable as forming a part of the domestic establishment. The appellant, for reasons of practicality and cost efficiency found it expedient to construct her business premises in the manner she did, and from the perspective of the public, was able to create a sense of a separate entity by design, provision of walkway, stairway and entrance, and by the appropriate use of signs. In such a way she was able to distinguish her business from what might ordinarily be expected from an "in-home" business establishment. However, such distinction by way of perception, does not detract from the fact the studio was an area which formed a part of the appellant's residence. In order to apply, the subsection does not require the smell of home-baked bread wafting into the work space. The Minister was correct in applying the limitation imposed by subsection 18(12) of the Act to the years under appeal.

See also *Dufour v. Canada*, [1998] T.C.J. No. 54, [1998] 3 C.T.C. 2741 (T.C.C.), in which a notary business carried on in an office constructed in the taxpayer's garage was determined to be part of the taxpayer's "self-contained domestic establishment" on the grounds that it was physically attached to, shared utility connections with, and was accessible from the interior of the taxpayer's home.

In *Maitland v. Canada*, [2000] T.C.J. No. 423, [2000] 3 C.T.C. 2840 (T.C.C.), the taxpayers operated a bed and breakfast business in a residence purchased for this purpose, residing on the top floor and part of the second floor and using the remainder of the second floor and the main floor in the business. Disallowing the deduction of losses from this business in computing the taxpayers' net income from all sources, the court held that the residence "was clearly their home" and fell within the statutory definition of a "self-contained domestic establishment." In *Sudbrack v. Canada*, [2000] T.C.J. No. 625, [2000] 4 C.T.C. 2688, 2000 D.T.C. 2521 (T.C.C.), however, the court allowed the taxpayer to deduct losses incurred in the operation of a country inn, even though the taxpayer and his family resided in the same building in which the business was carried on, on the grounds (at para. 19) that "the separate living quarters of the family, which are essentially a separate apartment within the inn, constitute the self-contained domestic establishment" without including the rest of the inn. In *Broderick v. Canada*, [2001] T.C.J. No. 286, [2001] 3 C.T.C. 2033 (T.C.C.), where the taxpayer lived in a basement apartment and operated a bed and breakfast in the rest of the "self-contained domestic establishment," *Sudbrack* was distinguished on the basis that the business was largely seasonal, making the residence fully available to the taxpayer and his family for seven months out of the year.

In *Lott v. Canada*, [1997] T.C.J. No. 1270, [1998] 1 C.T.C. 2869 (T.C.C.), the taxpayers sought to deduct losses from a day-care business operated out of their home. Rejecting the taxpayer's argument that subsection 18(12) applied only to a work space in "any part" of a self-contained domestic establishment, but not to a business carried out *throughout* the taxpayer's home, the court concluded (at para. 8) that "[t]he expression 'any part' clearly includes the whole." The court also rejected the taxpayers' alternative argument that paragraph 18(12)(b) should apply to disallow losses generated only by costs associated with the residence itself but not the land subjacent and adjacent to the residence.

In *Vanka v. Canada*, [2001] T.C.J. No. 663, [2001] 4 C.T.C. 2832 (T.C.C.), the taxpayer, a family physician who maintained an office in downtown Montreal, where he saw patients from 8:00 a.m. to 7:00 p.m. from Monday to Friday, sought to deduct expenses related to the operation of a home office where, on average, he saw one patient per week and received seven telephone calls each evening, accessing their medical files through a computer connection to his downtown office. Accepting the taxpayer's testimony that the office was used exclusively for the purpose of earning income from the business, the court allowed the deduction on the basis that the office was "used on a regular and continuous basis for meeting ... patients." According to Lamarre-Proulx TCJ (at para. 13):

> It is my view that if the seeing of a patient on an average of once a week at the home office could not suffice to make it a regular and continuous use of the home workspace, the receiving of an average of seven phone calls an evening by patients may be considered such a regular and continuous use of a home workspace ... . Although the words used in the provision are "meeting patients," I am not convinced that these words require the physical presence of the patients in the home workspace. It is my view that the physician met his patients by making himself available to answer his patients' queries by phone ... .

J. Travel Expenses

Travel expenses constitute yet another category of expenditure the benefits of which may be both personal and business-related. According to paragraph 18(1)(h), however, "travel expenses incurred by the taxpayer while away from home in the course of carrying on the taxpayer's business" are specifically excluded from other "personal and living expenses" the deduction of which is disallowed in computing a taxpayer's income from a business or property. Among the many cases that have considered the deduction of travel expenses, one of the most notable is *Cumming v. M.N.R.*, [1967] C.T.C. 462, 67 D.T.C. 5312 (Ex. Ct.).

Cumming v. M.N.R.
[1967] C.T.C. 462, 67 D.T.C. 5312 (Ex. Ct.)

[The taxpayer carried on a medical practice as an anaesthetist, and was appointed to the staff of the Ottawa Civic hospital, where he rendered all of his services to his patients. He also maintained an office in his home, located about half a mile from the hospital, where he reviewed medical journals, maintained business records, and prepared billings. Although the hospital contained a library and lounge that the taxpayer was free to use, there was no place at the hospital where he could carry out "the administrative functions of his practice." As a result, his typical routine was to go to the hospital each evening from 6:30 p.m. to 8:00 p.m. to visit patients and obtain the schedule of operations for the next day, to return the next morning in time for his first scheduled operation, and to return home at approximately 4:00 p.m. to work on his records. In addition to these duties, he was often on call for emergency work.

In computing his income for his 1962 and 1963 taxation years, the taxpayer claimed deductions of $1,454.01 and $1,002 for the use of a 1961 Chevrolet station wagon to travel "to and from the hospital ... or elsewhere in connection with his practice." The Minister disallowed all but $100 of the amounts claimed on the basis that "the expenses of ordinary travelling between these points at the beginning and end of the day's scheduled work at the hospital and of travelling between them in response to calls at a time when the appellant happens to be at his home (as opposed to travelling to the hospital on receipt of a call when actually engaged in working on his records at home) are not 'incurred for the purpose of gaining or producing income' from the appellant's business within the meaning of the exception to Section 12(1)(a) [now paragraph 18(1)(a)] of the *Income Tax Act* but are 'personal or living expenses' the deduction of which is prohibited by Section 12(1)(h) [now paragraph 18(1)(h)] of the Act." The taxpayer appealed.]

THURLOW J: ... The appellant considered it to be mandatory for him to have a car available for his use when required to go to the hospital in response to emergency calls and he also said that apart from this without a car the carrying on of his practice would be more complicated and his office work would pile up. There is evidence that the other anaesthetists practising in Ottawa also used automobiles to travel to and from the hospital and that the expenses of operating an automobile for that purpose were regarded as being properly deductible for the purpose of computing profit from the practice on commercial accounting principles.

...

The statutory provisions on which the present case is to be determined are ... Section 4 of the *Income Tax Act* [now subsection 9(1)], which defines income from a business for a taxation year as being subject to the other provisions of Part I of the Act, "the profit therefrom for the year" and paragraphs (a) and (h) of Section 12(1) of the Act [now subsection 18(1)].

...

It appears to have become established in England ... that where a professional man lives at a distance from the office or chambers where he carries on his practice the expenses of travelling between his home and his office or chambers are not to be regarded as having been incurred "wholly and exclusively" for the purposes of his practice but on the contrary are personal or living expenses, even though he may do at his home a considerable portion of the work by which his income is earned.

...

In the *Newsom v. Robertson* (1952), 33 TC 452, case the Court of Appeal in England had considered the case of a barrister who had chambers in London where he carried on his practice but resided in Whipsnade where he maintained a library and worked on professional matters during the evenings and weekends in term time and throughout the week days as well during the long vacation. He claimed deductions in respect of the expense of travelling between his residence and his chambers both in term time and during the vacation but the Court denied both.

Somervell LJ said at page 462:

> ... Whipsnade as a locality has nothing to do with Mr. Newsom's practice ... . Mr. Newsom's purpose in making the journeys was to get home in the evenings or at weekends. The fact that he intended to do professional work when he got there and did so does not make this even a subsidiary "purpose" of his profession.

...

Denning LJ said at page 463:

> In the days when Income Tax was introduced, nearly 150 years ago, most people lived and worked in the same place. The tradesman lived over the shop, the doctor over the surgery, and the barrister over his chambers, or, at any rate, close enough to walk to them or ride on his horse to them. There were no travelling expenses of getting to the place of work. Later, as means of transport quickened, those who could afford it began to live at a distance from their work and to travel each day by railway into and out of London. So long as people had a choice in the matter — whether to live over their work or not — those who chose to live out of London did so for the purposes of their home life because they preferred living in the country to living in London. The cost of travelling to and fro was then obviously not incurred for the purpose of their trade or profession.

Nowadays many people have only a very limited choice as to where they shall live. Business men and professional men cannot live over their work, even if they would like to do so. A few may do so, but once those few have occupied the limited accommodation available in Central London, there is no room for the thousands that are left. They must live outside, at distances varying from 3 miles to 50 miles from London. They have to live where they can find a house. Once they have found it, they must stay there and go to and from it to their work. They simply cannot go and live over their work. What is the position of people so placed? Are their travelling expenses incurred wholly and exclusively for the purposes of the trade, profession, or occupation? I think not. A distinction must be drawn between living expenses and business expenses. In order to decide into which category to put the cost of travelling, you must look to see what is the base from which the trade, profession, or occupation is carried on. In the case of a tradesman, the base of his trading operation is his shop. In the case of a barrister, it is his chambers. Once he gets to his chambers, the cost of travelling to the various courts is incurred wholly and exclusively for the purposes of his profession. But it is different with the cost of travelling from his home to his chambers and back. That is incurred because he lives at a distance from his base. It is incurred for the purposes of his living there and not for the purposes of his profession, or at any rate not wholly or exclusively; and this is so, whether he has a choice in the matter or not. It is a living expense as distinct from a business expense.

On this reasoning I have no doubt that the Commissioners were right in regard to Mr. Newsom's travelling expenses during term time. The only ground on which [the taxpayer's barrister] challenged their finding during term time was because Mr. Newsom has a study at his home at Whipsnade completely equipped with law books and does a lot of work there. The Commissioners did not regard this as sufficient to make his home during term time a base from which he carried on his profession, and I agree with them. His base was his chambers in Lincoln's Inn. His home was no more a base of operations than was the train by which he travelled to and fro. He worked at home just as he might work in the train, but it was not his base.

Romer LJ put the matter thus at page 465:

Now it is, of course, true that on days when Mr. Newsom has to appear in Court in the Chancery Division the expense of his journey to London from Whipsnade is incurred for the purpose of enabling him to do so in the sense that if he did not come to London he could not earn his brief fee. But if this view of the position were sufficient to justify the deduction of his fares to London for Income Tax purposes every taxpayer in England ... could claim as a permissible deduction his expenses of getting from his work of residence to his place of work. On the other hand, it could scarcely be argued that the cost of going home at the end of the day would be similarly eligible as a deduction and it would be a curious result ... that the morning journey should qualify for relief but that the evening journey should not ... . Moreover it cannot be said even of the morning journey to work that it is undertaken in order to enable the traveller to exercise his profession; it is undertaken for the purpose of neutralising the effect of his departure from his place of business, for private purposes, on the previous evening. In other words, the object of the journeys, both morning and evening, is not to enable a man to do his work but to live away from it.

Is the position altered, then, by the fact, as found by the Commissioners, that Mr. Newsom works in his house at Whipsnade as well as in his chambers in Lincoln's Inn? I am clearly of opinion that it is not. It seems to me impossible to say that this element assimilates the case to that of a man who possesses two separate places of business and, for the furtherance and in the course of his business activities, has to travel from one to another. The appellant could, if he liked, carry on the whole of his profession in London, though he certainly could not do so at Whipsnade if only for the reason that the Courts of the Chancery Division do not sit there. It seems to me accordingly that it is almost impossible to suggest that when the appellant travels to Whipsnade in the evenings, or at week-ends, he does so for the purpose of enabling him "to carry on and earn profits in his" profession — let alone that he does so exclusively for that purpose. That purpose, as I have said, could be fully achieved by his remaining the whole of the time in London. He goes to Whipsnade not because it is a place where he works but because it is the place where he lives and in which he and his family have their home. Even busy barristers occasionally have an evening free from legal labour, and I feel sure that if Mr. Newsom were lucky enough to have one he would not remain in London on the ground that there was no work to take him to Whipsnade.

Whether or not the reasoning of this decision is applicable in Canada, where the imposition of federal income tax has a history of but fifty years, and where the expression "not being money wholly and exclusively laid out or expended for the purposes of the trade, profession, etc." does not appear in Section 12(1)(a) [now paragraph 18(1)(a)] of the present *Income Tax Act*, is a matter on which I have some doubt. In the absence of such a decision it would not have occurred to me to think of expenses of operating an automobile for the purpose of getting to a place where the taxpayer's services are to be rendered and returning therefrom were in any ordinary sense "personal or living expenses." Nor would it have occurred to me to think that the expenses of the appellant in the circumstances described in this case in travelling between his home, where the administrative side of his practice was carried out, and the hospital, where his medical services were rendered, were not incurred by him for the purpose of gaining or producing income from his business. But, as I see it, the applicability or otherwise under the Canadian statute of the opinions expressed in *Newsom v. Robertson* as to the expenses there in question being personal or living expenses is a question which it is unnecessary to decide for in my view the decision rests on the particular facts of the case as well as on the applicable statutory provision and besides the differences in the statutory provisions the facts of the present case present a very different picture. It might well be observed of the barrister in the English case that his living at such a distance as to involve both car and train journeys to get from his home to his professional chambers was the result of a choice made for his personal, rather than his professional, reasons and that this coloured the expense of travelling between these points with a personal character. Here on the contrary, I would think that the appellant's choice of a location for his home about half a mile from the hospital was dictated either wholly or at least partially by the desirability for reasons relating to his practice of his living conveniently near to the place where his services were required as opposed to personal preference for that over any other location in Ottawa or elsewhere. ... I doubt therefore, as well, that the reasoning of this case has any clear application to facts such as I have described in the present case.

However, even assuming that the reasoning of the case may be applied for resolving the present problem, I am of the opinion that it does not support the Minister's position. The reasoning poses the question of the location of the base of the taxpayer's operation and proceeds to its conclusion after determining this point. On it the Minister's contention was that the base of the appellant's operation was the hospital, where the appellant rendered the services for which he was paid. It was, however, admitted in the course of argument that the appellant conducted part of his practice at his home, that the nature of the business was such that the bookkeeping and financial activities had to be carried on at a location different from that where the patients were treated and that there were no office facilities available to him at the hospital where he might have carried out this part of his business.

While I think it might be said in a particular sense that the appellant exercised his profession at the hospital, as I see it, he had no base of his practice there. His services were not performed in any one place in the hospital but in the numerous areas in which anaesthetics were administered, in the recovery rooms, in the areas where resuscitation procedures were carried out and in the various patients' rooms. The appellant had no space there but a locker that he could call his own. There was a cot in the office of the department of anaesthesia where he might go for a nap if he wished and time permitted between cases. There was also a library where he might study and a lounge where he could sit when not engaged with a patient. But these were not his nor were they for his use alone. They were for the use of all the anaesthetists. Nor had he an office or even a desk there to which he could repair to do the administrative work of his practice when he was not immediately engaged with a patient. The operations booking office was also a place to which he might go for some purposes such as to get a copy of the schedule of operations for the next day but I do not regard any of these places or the aggregation of them as having been any more in the nature of a base for his operation of practicing his profession than any other room which he may have visited for a purpose associated with the carrying out of his professional activity. And if the whole hospital were to be considered his base I fail to see why the area consisting of the whole hospital plus his house and the distance between them could not just as readily be said to be the base of his practice. As I view the matter the appellant had no more of a base for his professional business at the hospital than a barrister can be said to have at a court house where he attends frequently as required and in the course of a day may have occasion to be engaged in one or more court rooms on one or more cases and incidentally to spend some time in the barristers' robing room and possibly in the court registry office as well. In my view therefore there is no basis for holding that the base of the appellant's practice within the reasoning of *Newsom v. Robertson* was at the Ottawa Civic Hospital.

In my opinion the base of the appellant's practice if there was any one place that could be called its base, was his home. This was the place from which he was called when required and whence he set forth to serve patients, whether by scheduled appointment or in emergencies. It was the place where the records of his practice were kept, where he worked on them and where his studying for particular cases and for the purpose of keeping up with developments in his specialty was done. It was the place to which he returned during the day whenever the time available was long enough to enable him to make the trip and do some work of the kind which he did there. Indeed, though in fact he went nearly every day, he had no occasion to go to the hospital at all in connection with his practice except when there was some service to be rendered to a patient there. And when he had no work to do there he had no place of his own or base of his practice to repair to but his home where the administrative side of his practice was carried out.

It seems to me that if the appellant had not found it convenient to carry out at his home that part of the work of his practice in fact done there and had maintained an office for the purpose, whether near to or at some distance from the hospital, there could have been little doubt that such office was the base of his practice and that both the reasonable expense of maintaining it and the expense of travelling between it and the hospital would have been expense of his business. The result is, I think, the same where the office, such at it was, was at his home and the work was done there. In the present case it seems to me to be the only single place which could be regarded as the base from which his professional operation was carried on. The case is thus not like that of the barrister travelling from his home to his professional chambers — which, in *Newsom v. Robertson* was the base of his operation — but resembles more closely that of the same barrister's travelling between his chambers and the courts, the expense of which, had it involved expense, would, I apprehend, not have been regarded as personal or living expense and would, I also think, have been allowable as a deduction even under the stringent prohibition of the English statute. As I view the matter therefore *Newsom v. Robertson* affords no guide for the determination of the present case and it seems to me to be necessary to reach a conclusion by applying the words of Section 12(1)(a) and (h) of the Act without assistance from the jurisprudence of other countries.

In my view, since the appellant could not possibly live in or over the hospital so as to incur no expense whatever in getting to and from it when required and since he could not even carry out at the hospital all the activities of his practice necessary to gain or produce his income therefrom, it was necessary for the successful carrying on of the practice itself that he have a location of same sort somewhere off the hospital premises. This necessity of itself carried the implication that travel by him between the two points would be required. Where, as here, the location off the hospital premises was as close thereto as it might reasonably be expected to be from the point of view of his being available promptly when called as well as from the point of view of economizing on the expense of travelling between the two points it is, I think, unrealistic and a straining of the ordinary meaning of the words used in the statute to refer to any portion of the expense of travelling between these points in connection with his practice as "personal or living expenses" and this I think is so whether the taxpayer lives at or next door to his location off the hospital premises or not. There may no doubt be cases where a further element of personal preference for a more distant location has an appreciable effect on the amount of the expense involved in travelling between the two points but I do not think such an element is present here. In the appellant's situation there is, in my view, no distinction to be made either between journeys from his home to the hospital and returning therefrom in the course of his scheduled daily and evening routines and similar journeys made in response to emergency calls or between journeys of either of these types and those made either in response to a call when he was working on his records at home or from the hospital to his home for the purpose of working on his records and then returning to the hospital to attend another patient. In my view whenever he went to the hospital to serve his patients he was doing so for the purpose of gaining income from his practice and the expense both of going and of returning when the service had been completed were incurred for the same purpose. All such expenses, in my view, fall within the exception to Section 12(1)(a) and are properly deductible and none of them in my opinion can properly be classed as personal or living expenses within the prohibition of Section 12(1)(h). ...

Appeal allowed.

NOTES AND QUESTIONS

1.   On what basis did the court in *Cumming* conclude that the taxpayer's travelling expenses were deductible in computing his income from his medical practice? To what extent, if at all, did Thurlow J rely on the decision of the English Court of Appeal in *Newsom v. Robertson* (1952), 33 Tax Cas 452 (C.A.)? To what extent, if at all, do the reasons in *Newsom v. Robertson* apply for the purpose of determining the deductibility of travelling expenses under the Canadian *Income Tax Act*? Do you agree with the reasons in *Newsom v. Robertson*? Why or why not?

2.   The decision in *Cumming* was followed in *Prowse v. M.N.R.*, [1971] C.T.C. 736, 71 D.T.C. 5443 (F.C.T.D.), in which an anaesthetist attached to the PEI Hospital sought to deduct expenses incurred in travelling to and from his home, located one-third of a mile from the hospital. Noting that the taxpayer did not have an office set aside in the hospital for his personal use, Cameron DJ concluded that the "base" of the taxpayer's business was his home, such that the travelling expenses were incurred "in the course of carrying on his business" according to the language of then paragraph 12(1)(h).

In *Henry v. M.N.R.*, [1971] S.C.J. No. 143, [1972] C.T.C. 33, 72 D.T.C. 6005 (S.C.C.), however, the Supreme Court of Canada disallowed travelling expenses claimed by yet another anaesthetist, who sought to deduct expenses incurred in commuting between the Royal Jubilee Hospital in Victoria and his home, a mile and a half away. On the basis that the taxpayer also maintained a separate office, where records were kept and accounts were made up, Hall J distinguished *Cumming*, stating (at para. 4):

> even assuming that *Cumming* was properly decided which is not necessary to do in this appeal, I am of opinion that the appeal must fail. ... I am unable to discern any difference between the appellant and the self-employed owner of any business who maintains a home from which he leaves in the morning and returns in the late afternoon as a matter of course.

Although the Supreme Court did not specify the statutory basis on which these expenses were non-deductible, the decision of the Exchequer Court, [1969] Ex. C.J. No. 22, [1969] C.T.C. 600, 69 D.T.C. 5395, from which the taxpayer appealed, disallowed the deduction on the basis that the expense was a "personal and living expense" within the meaning of then paragraph 12(1)(h) of the Act and not incurred for the purpose of gaining or producing income from the taxpayer's business as required by then paragraph 12(1)(a).

3.   In *Canada v. Cork*, [1990] F.C.J. No. 429, [1990] 2 C.T.C. 116, 90 D.T.C. 6358 (F.C.A.), the taxpayer, a mechanical-design draftsperson who maintained an office in one room of his rented home, sought to deduct expenses incurred in travelling to construction sites at which he performed services on drafting tables supplied by those for whom his services were rendered with tools and materials of his own, which he brought with him to the sites. Allowing the deduction, Stone JA reasoned (at para. 15):

> In the present case, the learned trial judge found on the evidence that Mr. Cork used his home as a base of operations for his drafting business. There is, I think, much to be said for the correctness of that view. Mr. Cork had evidently set himself up at his home for the conduct of his business activities. ... Whether he arranged work directly or through a placement agency he did so from his home where he could be found. He used his home as a base or focal point for that purpose as well as for the performance of his work in the field. In my view, all of the findings have a basis in the evidence and ought not, therefore, to be disturbed. ...

> I am unable to agree with the appellant's submission that Mr. Cork's travel from home to work and back again was *qua* home rather than *qua* work. The trial judge drew the correct inference from the facts proven that the office in the home was used by Mr. Cork as a base of his business operations. It follows, of course, that the travel from the house and back again was *qua* work and not *qua* home. The answer to the question posed in argument by counsel for the appellant will, of course, depend upon the circumstances. I have no doubt that the travel by Mr. Cork was from and to his home *qua* place of work in the circumstances of this case. The travelling expenses were incurred by him while away from home in the course of carrying on his business.

4.   In *Forestell v. M.N.R.*, [1991] T.C.J. No. 600, [1991] 2 C.T.C. 2278, 91 D.T.C. 998 (T.C.C.), the taxpayer, an independent contractor engaged solely by the Royal Ontario Museum (ROM) from 1978 to 1990, resided in Campbellford, Ontario, commuting to Toronto on a weekly basis, where he rented a small apartment that he claimed to use as an office. In computing his income for his 1984 taxation year, he deducted $11,340 for travelling expenses, $13,880 for meals, and $2,600 for rent. In computing his income for his 1985 taxation year, he deducted $11,025 for travelling expenses, $7,800 for meals, and $2,808 for rent. Revenue Canada allowed the deductions for rent, but disallowed the deductions for travelling expenses and meals.

On appeal, the Tax Court (at para. 14) accepted the taxpayer's argument that his "base of operations" was in Campbellford, Ontario, although it doubted whether the activities performed at the taxpayer's home in Campbellford were "more than a very small part of the total business operation" and commented that "to a substantial degree, using Campbellford as the base of operations was a *choice* made by Mr. Forestell." Nonetheless, concluding (at para. 17) that "the Court must carry the known elements in these appeals to their logical conclusion," Taylor TCJ referred the matter back to Revenue Canada for reassessment on the basis that the expenses incurred for travelling to and from

Toronto and for meals while travelling were properly deductible. According to the court (at para. 15):

> once agreed that a taxpayer businessman has a "base of operations" in a given location, it is very difficult to limit that taxpayer's right to operate wherever and whenever his business requires away from his "base of operations" to the actual site of operations itself.

Do you agree or disagree with this result? Is the judgment in *Forestell* consistent with the decisions in *Cumming, Henry*, and *Cork*?

5.   For the taxation years relevant to the decision in *Forestell*, paragraph 18(1)(h) referred to "personal or living expenses of the taxpayer except travelling expenses (*including the entire amount expended for meals and lodging*) incurred by the taxpayer while away from home in the course of carrying on his business" (emphasis added). It is on this basis that the court in *Forestell* allowed the taxpayer to deduct the full amount expended on meals as well as the travelling expenses more narrowly defined.

Paragraph 18(1)(h) was amended for expenses incurred and amounts paid after 1987 by deleting the parenthetical reference to "the entire amount expended for meals and lodging." According to the Department of Finance technical notes, this amendment was made "as a consequence of the general restriction provided in section 67.1 on the deductibility of meal expenses to 80% [now 50 percent] of their cost."

6.   In *Brown v. Canada*, [1998] T.C.J. No. 92, [1998] 2 C.T.C. 2641 (T.C.C.), the taxpayer lived in Sault Ste. Marie and worked as an independent contractor in Toronto — staying at a variety of apartment hotels while in Toronto and returning to Sault Ste. Marie on weekends to visit his family. Referring to paragraph 4(1)(a) of the Act, Bowman TCJ (as he then was) disallowed the deduction of travel expenses on the basis that they were not reasonably attributable to the business that he carried on in Toronto.

7.   In *Friedland v. M.N.R.*, [1989] F.C.J. No. 506, [1989] 2 C.T.C. 79, 89 D.T.C. 5341 (F.C.T.D.), the taxpayer, an economics professor at York University who performed outside consulting work in business economics and finance, sought to deduct travelling expenses associated with the use of a Rolls Royce in 1973 and 1974 and a BMW in 1975, which, according to the court (at para. 44), were used "to get back and forth, three days a week, to York University," occasionally in the evenings for social events, to travel downtown to the office of a major client at least two days a week, and "to call on other clients as well." Notwithstanding this evidence, Collier J (at para. 44) accepted the taxpayer's testimony that "the cars were used 80 percent to 90 percent of the time" for business purposes, and allowed the deduction of automobile expenses totalling $4,860.00 in 1973, $3,960.00 in 1974, and $5,939.77 in 1975.

8.   Effective for fiscal periods commencing after June 17, 1987, the amount that a taxpayer may deduct in respect of a luxury automobile used in a business is limited under paragraphs 13(7)(g) and (h), subsection 20(16.1), and sections

67.2, 67.3, and 67.4. For the purpose of these provisions, reg. 7307 prescribes the amount that may be deducted. The effect of these provisions is discussed in *Interpretation Bulletin* IT-521R, "Motor Vehicle Expenses Claimed by Self-Employed Individuals" December 16, 1996.

9. In *Randall v. M.N.R.*, [1967] S.C.J. No. 37, [1967] C.T.C. 236, 67 D.T.C. 5151 (S.C.C.), the taxpayer, a resident of Vancouver engaged in the business of managing horse-racing activities at a number of race tracks in British Columbia, entered into an agreement with the Portland Turf Association to manage its business affairs and transactions arising from racetrack meetings in Portland, Oregon. In 1958, the taxpayer reported an income of $17,626.71 under this agreement from which he sought to deduct $5,241.53 as travelling expenses, including the entire amount expended for meals and lodging while in Portland.

On appeal to the Supreme Court of Canada, Judson J (dissenting) accepted the argument made by counsel for the Minister that the expenses were "personal and living expenses" incurred in order to be available to earn the income in Portland, not "travelling expenses" incurred "in the course of carrying on" the taxpayer's business in Portland. Accepting the taxpayer's argument that the Portland operation was only one base of a single business carried on in various geographic locations, however, a majority of the court allowed the deductions.

Randall was followed in *Waserman v. M.N.R.*, [1969] Tax ABC 599 (T.A.B.), where the taxpayer, who operated a furrier shop in Pembroke, Ontario, but resided 100 miles away in Ottawa, sought to deduct expenses incurred travelling between these two cities as well as expenses for meals and lodging while in Pembroke. According to the board (at para. 14):

> there is no doubt that the appellant was carrying on business in both cities as well as while travelling from one city to the other. He had offices, business telephones, bank accounts, fur storage service, and he advertised in both locations and personally looked after his Ottawa business while his employee looked after the Pembroke clientele when the appellant was not there. ... Besides, the appellant was looking for clientele everywhere in Ottawa, Pembroke and the general area between the two cities. ... This business must be considered as a whole just like that of any bank or other business that may have branches here and there. ... The appellant cannot be ubiquitous. He must incur expenses whether his headquarters is in Ottawa or in Pembroke and he found it far more profitable from a business standpoint to pay hotel bills in Pembroke rather than in Ottawa.

See also *Frank S. Ozvegy v. M.N.R.*, [1978] C.T.C. 3043, 78 D.T.C. 1772 (T.R.B.), where the taxpayer, a radiologist who rendered services at the Yarmouth General Hospital, sought to deduct the cost of meals and rent for a furnished apartment 158 miles away in Shelbourne, Nova Scotia, where he also rendered services 2½ days a week at the Roseway Hospital. Noting that the expenses were no more than would have been incurred if Dr. Ozvegy had stayed in a hotel, the expenses of which would have been deductible, the board allowed the taxpayer's appeal from an assessment that had disallowed the deductions.

10. As the decision in *Randall v. M.N.R.*, [1967] S.C.J. No. 37, [1967] C.T.C. 236, 67 D.T.C. 5151 (S.C.C.), indicates, the deductibility of travel expenses may depend on whether separate business operations are characterized as separate

operations of the same business or separate businesses altogether. For the CRA's views on this determination, see IT-206R.

11. In *A-1 Steel and Iron Foundry Ltd. v. M.N.R.* (1963), 31 Tax ABC 338, 63 D.T.C. 294 (T.A.B.), the taxpayer sought to deduct $3,426.80 in respect of the expenses of a trip to Europe taken by its president and controlling shareholder, who was accompanied by his wife. On the basis that only a small portion of the trip was devoted to visiting business contacts and inspecting techniques at other foundries, the board upheld the Minister's assessment, which had allowed only 35 per cent of half of the total expenses representing the taxpayer's share and disallowed the remainder on the basis that they were personal expenses.

In *Shaver v. Canada*, [2004] T.C.J. No. 3, [2004] 2 C.T.C. 2125, 2004 D.T.C. 2112 (T.C.C.) aff'd [2004] F.C.J. No. 1857, [2005] 1 C.T.C. 89, 2004 D.T.C. 6720, (F.C.A.), the taxpayer attempted to deduct travel expenses associated with attending monthly Amway business seminars throughout North America during 1996 and 1997. At the Tax Court of Canada, Lamarre TCJ held that these expenses were not deductible because they were not incurred "for the purpose of gaining or producing income" and thus did not satisfy paragraph 18(1)(a) of the Act. Moreover, the travel expenses were payments "on account of capital" since they contributed to training which would result in a lasting advantage to Shaver. As such, the deductions available to Shaver for these travelling expenses were limited by paragraph 18(1)(b) (denying deductions for payments "on account of capital" except as otherwise explicitly provided) and subsection 20(10) (limiting convention travel expenses to "not more than two conventions held during the year"). The Federal Court of Appeal, Stone J.A. (Sexton, and Malone, JJ.A., concurring) unanimously affirmed the decision.

For similar decisions in which expenses incurred on trips have been disallowed either in part or in whole, see *Kerr Farms Ltd. v. M.N.R.*, [1971] Tax ABC 804 (T.A.B.); and *Grunbaum v. Canada*, [1994] T.C.J. No. 180, [1994] 1 C.T.C. 2687, 94 D.T.C. 1384 (T.C.C.).

K. Interest Expense

Although most of the expenses that may be deducted in computing a taxpayer's income from a business or property are implicitly authorized by the concepts of "profit" and "loss" in subsections 9(1) and (2) of the Act, other expenses are explicitly deductible under specific statutory provisions. Among the most important of these provisions is subparagraph 20(1)(c)(i), which permits a deduction for:

> an amount paid in the year or payable in respect of the year (depending on the method regularly followed by the taxpayer in computing the taxpayer's income), pursuant to a legal obligation to pay interest on ... borrowed money used for the purpose of earning income from a business or property (other than borrowed money used to acquire property the income from

which would be exempt or to acquire a life insurance policy) ... or a reasonable amount in respect thereof, whichever is the lesser.[39]

As McLachlin J (as she then was) observed in *Shell Canada Limited v. Canada*, [1999] S.C.J. No. 30, [1999] 4 C.T.C. 313, 99 D.T.C. 5669 (S.C.C.), at para. 28, this provision has "four elements":

> (1) the amount must be paid in the year or be payable in the year in which it is sought to be deducted; (2) the amount must be paid pursuant to a legal obligation to pay interest on borrowed money; (3) the borrowed money must be used for the purpose of earning non-exempt income from a business or property; and (4) the amount must be reasonable, as assessed by reference to the first three requirements.

The first of these elements concerns the taxation year in which the amount may be deducted, and is addressed in section V of this chapter. The second element involves the characterization of "legal interest" and was examined earlier in this chapter. The fourth element, concerning the reasonableness of the amount, has received extremely little judicial attention, except for a brief discussion in *Shell Canada*.[40] In contrast, the third element, that the borrowed money must be used for the purpose of earning non-exempt income from a business or property, has been subject to considerable litigation. The leading case on the interpretation of this language is *Bronfman Trust v. Canada*, [1987] S.C.J. No. 1, [1987] 1 C.T.C. 117, 87 D.T.C. 5059 (S.C.C.).[41]

Bronfman Trust v. Canada
[1987] S.C.J. No. 1, [1987] 1 C.T.C. 117, 87 D.T.C. 5059 (S.C.C.)

DICKSON CJ (Beetz, McIntyre, Lamer, Wilson and La Forest, JJ concurring): In computing income for a taxation year, a taxpayer may deduct interest paid on borrowed money "used for the purpose of earning income from a business or property." In the present appeal, the trustees of a trust elected to make discretionary capital allocations to Phyllis Barbara Bronfman in 1969 and 1970. Instead of liquidating capital assets to make the allocations, the trustees

---

[39] Subparagraphs 20(1)(c)(ii) to (iv) extend the deduction to other amounts including interest on "an amount payable for property acquired for the purpose of gaining or producing income from the property or ... from a business." In addition, para. 20(1)(d) permits the deduction of compound interest that applies to basic interest that is deductible under para. 20(1)(c). For our purposes, there is no need to examine these provisions in detail.

[40] See discussion in Note 21 after *Bronfman Trust*.

[41] As a general rule, Canadian courts have characterized interest expenses on money borrowed to increase the financial capital of the borrower as payments "on account of capital" the deduction of which is prohibited by para. 18(1)(b) of the Act. In these circumstances, therefore, interest expenses may only be deducted where they comply with the statutory rule in para. 20(1)(c). Where loan proceeds constitute inventory of the borrower, however, as is the case with moneylenders, interest expenses are generally deductible as an ordinary business expense under subs. 9(1). See *Gifford v. Canada*, [2004] S.C.J. No. 13, [2004] 2 C.T.C. 1, 2004 D.T.C. 6120 (S.C.C.).

considered it advantageous to retain the trust investments temporarily and finance the allocations by borrowing funds from a bank. The issue is whether the interest paid to the bank by the trust on the borrowings is deductible for tax purposes; more particularly, is an interest deduction only available where the loan is used directly to produce income or is a deduction also available when, although its direct use may not produce income, the loan can be seen as preserving income-producing assets which might otherwise have been liquidated. A subordinate issue is whether the answer to this question depends upon the status of the taxpayer as a corporation, a trust, or a natural person.

...

Facts

By means of a deed of donation registered in Montreal on May 7, 1942 a trust was established by the late Samuel Bronfman in favour of his daughter, Phyllis Barbara Bronfman ("the beneficiary" or, under Quebec law, "the Institute") and her children. Under the terms of the deed, the beneficiary has the right to receive 50 per cent of the revenue from the trust property. In addition, the trustees "in their sole and unrestricted discretion" are empowered to make an allocation to the beneficiary from the capital of the trust if they consider it "desirable for any purpose of any nature whatsoever." The beneficiary has no children and in the event she dies without issue, the residue of the trust accrues for the benefit of her brothers and sisters.

The assets of the trust consist of a portfolio of securities having a cost base of more than $15 million. By the end of 1969 trust assets had a market value of about $70 million. Except for a Rodin sculpture, the holdings of the trust during the material period were in bonds and shares, assets which could be characterized generally as of an income-earning nature. I should add, however, that the investment portfolio of the trust produced a low yield: 1969, 1970 and 1971 earnings amounted to $324,469, $293,178 and $213,588 respectively, providing a return of less than one-half of one per cent on the portfolio's market value ... . Trust investment policies appear to have been focused more on capital gains than on income. Accordingly, the trust's very substantial asset base generated modest income-tax liabilities: the 1970 and 1971 income tax returns filed by the taxpayer show federal tax payable of $12,107.99 and $15,687.98 respectively and in 1972 (when some capital gains were realized and, for the first time, taxable) federal tax was listed as $31,878.

The low-yield investment portfolio of the trust undoubtedly had detrimental consequences for the beneficiary in respect of the amount of income available under her 50 per cent entitlement. Perhaps to mitigate those consequences, or perhaps for some other reason entirely, the trustees chose to make a capital allocation to the beneficiary of $500,000 (US) on December 29, 1969 and one of $2 million (Can.) on March 4, 1970. There is no suggestion by the trust that these allocations were in any way designed to enhance the income-earning potential of the trust. On the contrary, the inevitable result was to reduce the trust's net income-earning prospects both in the short-term and in the long run owing to the depletion of trust capital.

To make the capital allocations, the trust borrowed from the Bank of Montreal $300,000 (US) on December 29, 1969 and $1.9 million (Can.) on March 9, 1970. The amounts borrowed went into the account of the trust and were used to make the capital allocations to the beneficiary. The trust used uninvested earnings to finance the remaining approximately $300,000 of allocations to the beneficiary. There is no dispute concerning the immediate and direct use to which the borrowed funds were put. They were used to make the capital allocations to the beneficiary and not to buy income-earning properties.

The sole witness at trial was Mr. Arnold Ludwick, an accountant, executive vice-president of Cemp Investments and executive vice-president of Claridge Investments. Claridge Investments managed the business affairs of the taxpayer trust, subject of course to the ultimate authority of the trustees. Mr. Ludwick's evidence concerned the reasons for the borrowing. He testified that subject to various constraints on the marketability of some of the trust investments, "it certainly would have been possible to, in an orderly way, liquidate investments" to fund the capital allocation. The funds were borrowed because such a disposition of assets would have been commercially inadvisable. As testified by Mr. Ludwick:

> ... my reasoning that existed then [in 1969] still exists today, that precise timing of the sale of investments ought to be related to the nature of the investment, and not a possible immediate need for cash on any particular day, that the basic issue [is one] of managing the assets side separately from the liability and capital side.

In addition, most of the investments at the time were not readily realizable, in part because of securities law constraints and in part because the marketable securities that the trust did hold had dropped in value. Accordingly, the trustees considered it inappropriate to sell them at that point; it appeared to be more advantageous for the trust to keep the assets and borrow from the bank.

The evidence is unclear as to the precise amounts and dates of the loan repayments, but it is clear that the entire borrowings were repaid by 1972. In 1970 the trust realized $1,966,284 and in 1972, $1,026,198, from the sale of shares of Gulf Oil Canada Ltd. Some of the proceeds from these dispositions were used to repay the bank loans. Thus the loans postponed but did not obviate the need for an eventual reduction in the trust's capital assets. In the meantime, interest payments of $110,114 in 1970, $9,802 in 1971, and $1,432 in 1972 were incurred on the debts to the Bank of Montreal. It is the deduction of these interest payments from the trust's income which is contested in this appeal.

The trust argues that even if the loans were used to pay the allocations, they were also used for the purpose of earning income from property since they permitted the trust to retain income-producing investments until the time was ripe to dispose of them. The end result of the transactions, the trust submits, was the same as if the trustees had sold assets to pay the allocations and then borrowed money to replace them, in which case, it is argued, the interest would have been deductible. The Crown, on the other hand, takes the position that the borrowed funds were used to pay the allocations to the beneficiary, that the amounts of interest claimed as deductions are not interest on borrowed money used for the purpose of earning income from a business or property and as such are not deductible.

...

Judgments

(a) Tax Review Board

... Mr. Tremblay reviewed the jurisprudence, in particular the main case upon which the trust based its contention, *Trans-Prairie Pipelines Ltd. v. M.N.R.*, [1970] CTC 537; 70 DTC 6351, a decision of Jackett, P in the Exchequer Court. In that case the taxpayer corporation wanted to raise capital by way of bond issues for expansion of its business. It discovered, however, that it was impossible, practically speaking, to float a bond issue unless it first redeemed its preferred shares, because of the sinking fund requirements of its preferred share issue. Accordingly, the taxpayer borrowed $700,000, used $400,000 to redeem the preferred shares and the remaining $300,000 for expansion of its business. Jackett, P held the interest payments on the entire $700,000 loan deductible. He saw the borrowed funds as "fill[ing] the hole left by the redemption."

...

The main case on which the Crown relied to rebut the *Trans-Prairie* case was *Sternthal v. The Queen*, [1974] CTC 851; 74 DTC 6646 (FCTD). In *Sternthal*, a taxpayer with a large excess of assets over liabilities borrowed a sum of $246,800. On the same day he gave interest-free loans to his children totalling $280,000. The taxpayer argued that he was entitled to use his assets to make loans to his children and to borrow for the purpose of "filling the gap" left by the making of such loans. Therefore, he argued, as long as the assets which made the loan possible were used to produce income, interest on the borrowing was deductible. Mr. Justice Kerr did not agree. He held that the taxpayer used the borrowed money to make non-interest bearing loans to his children, not for the purpose of earning income. The taxpayer chose to find the money for the loans by borrowing and the fundamental purpose of the borrowing was to make the loans.

Mr. Tremblay, in the present case, was of the opinion that the facts before him were more similar to *Sternthal* than *Trans-Prairie*. ... Accordingly the appeal was dismissed.

(b) Federal Court, Trial Division

The trust took its suit to the Federal Court — Trial Division where it was heard *de novo* by Justice Marceau ([1980] 2 FC 453; [1979] CTC 524). The trust maintained its contention that even if the proceeds of the loans negotiated with the bank were actually used to pay the allocations made in favour of the beneficiary, they must still be deemed to have been "used for the purpose of earning income from property" within the meaning of the Act, since their use allowed the trust to retain securities which were income producing and which moreover increased in value before the loans were redeemed. Marceau, J said at 454 (CTC 525), "The defendant [i.e., the Crown] disagrees, and in my view rightly so." ... He, like Mr. Tremblay of the Tax Review Board, accepted the principle that it is the actual and real effect of a transaction or series of transactions that was relevant, rather than its "legal" or apparent aspect. If the transactions in the present case had merely changed the composition of the income-earning property of the trust by liquidating one debt and substituting another, then he would have accepted the proposition that the real purpose of the transactions was to earn income from the trust. He concluded, however, that the net effect of the trustees' actions was to reduce the income-earning property of the trust by some $2.5 million.

...

In the opinion of the trial judge the interest deduction was designed to encourage accretions to the total amount of tax-producing capital. Nothing was added to the capital base by the transactions of the trust. It followed that the Minister was right in disallowing the deductions.

...

(c) Federal Court of Appeal

In the Federal Court of Appeal ([1983] 2 FC 797, [1983] CTC 253), Thurlow CJ, Hyde DJ concurring, allowed the trust's appeal. Thurlow CJ held that the use of the borrowed money to pay the capital allocations was what enabled the trustees to keep the income-yielding trust investments and to exploit them by obtaining for the trust and the income they were earning. Chief Justice Thurlow said at 800-801 (CTC 255):

> Had the trustees sold income-yielding investments to pay the allocations, the income of the trust would have been reduced accordingly. Had they given the beneficiary income-yielding investments in lieu of cash, the income of the trust would have been reduced accordingly. By not doing either, by borrowing money and using it to pay the allocations, *the trustees preserved intact the income-yielding capacity of the trust's investments.* That, as it seems to me, is sufficient, in the circumstances of this case, to characterize the borrowed money as having been used in the taxation years in question for the purpose of earning income from the trust property.

[Emphasis added.]

With respect, I have some difficulty with this passage. In a narrow sense it might be said that the trustees preserved intact the income-yielding capacity of the trust's investments but the practical and business reality of the situation was that the net income-yielding capacity of the trust was reduced by the annual debt load from the bank borrowings which, as I have said, amounted to $110,114 in

1970. Thurlow CJ, however, characterized the borrowed money as having been used for the purpose of earning income from property and it made no difference, according to him, that the immediate use of the funds was to pay directly the capital allocations rather than to repurchase investments which might have been liquidated to pay the allocations. In his view, the focus of the statute was on the income-earning purpose of the trustees in continuing to hold the trust investments. Moreover, it did not matter that the trustees, in continuing to hold the investments, might also have had an eye to the possible appreciation of their capital value. The majority of the Court did, however, express one important reservation on the scope of its holding. The majority was careful to limit the ratio of its decision to trusts, as distinct from individuals:

> It should be noted that a trust such as that here in question has no purpose and the trustees have no purpose save to hold trust property, to earn income therefrom and to deal with such income and the capital of the trust in accordance with the provisions of the trust instrument. In that respect a trust differs from an individual person who may have many purposes, both business and personal. Compare *Sternthal v. Her Majesty The Queen* [(1974), 74 DTC 6646 (FCTD)] where the taxpayer, an individual, had no obligation to lend money to his children but invested his borrowings in interest-free loans to them.

Pratte J dissented. He agreed with Marceau, J that the borrowed funds were in fact used to pay capital allocations in favour of the beneficiary. The allocations could not, by any stretch of the imagination, be considered as having been used for the purpose of earning income. In his view, *Trans-Prairie* was not applicable. Unlike *Trans-Prairie*, where the money previously subscribed by preferred shareholders had been used by the company for the purpose of earning income from the business, in this case the money paid to the beneficiary had not already been used by the trust for the purpose of earning income. Justice Pratte said at 804 (CTC 257):

> Pursuant to the relevant provisions of the *Income Tax Act*, the interest here in question was not deductible unless the money borrowed from the Bank of Montreal had been "used for the purpose of earning income from a business or property." It was not so used but was, in fact, used to pay the capital allocations made by the Trustees in favour of Miss Bronfman. The appellant's argument, in my view, ignores the language of the Act.

With respect, I agree.

...

Eligible and Ineligible Uses of Borrowed Money

... I agree with Marceau J as to the purpose of the interest deduction provision. Parliament created subparagraph 20(1)(c)(i) ... in order to encourage the accumulation of capital which would produce taxable income. Not all borrowing expenses are deductible. Interest on borrowed money used to produce tax exempt income is not deductible. Interest on borrowed money used to buy life insurance policies is not deductible. Interest on borrowings used for non-income earning purposes, such as personal consumption or the making of capital gains is similarly not deductible. The statutory deduction thus requires a characterization of the use of borrowed money as between the eligible use of earning non-exempt income from a business or property and a variety of possible ineligible uses. The onus is on the taxpayer to trace the borrowed funds to an identifiable use which triggers the deduction. Therefore, if the taxpayer commingles funds used for a variety of purposes only some of which are eligible he or she may be unable to claim the deduction: see, for example, *Mills v. M.N.R.*, [1985] 2 CTC 2334; 85 DTC 632 (TCC), *No. 616 v. M.N.R.*, 22 Tax ABC 31; 59 DTC 247 (TAB).

The interest deduction provision requires not only a characterization of the use of borrowed funds, but also a characterization of "purpose." Eligibility for the deduction is contingent on the use of borrowed money for the purpose of earning income. It is well established in the jurisprudence, however, that it is not the purpose of the borrowing itself which is relevant. What is relevant, rather, is the taxpayer's purpose in using the borrowed money in a particular manner: *Auld v. M.N.R.*, 28 Tax ABC 236; 62 DTC 27 (TAB). Consequently, the focus of the inquiry must be centred on the use to which the taxpayer put the borrowed funds.

...

Original or Current Use of Borrowed Money

The cases are consistent with the proposition that it is the current use rather than the original use of borrowed funds by the taxpayer which is relevant in assessing deductibility of interest payments: see, for example, *Lakeview Gardens Corporation v. M.N.R.*, [1973] CTC 586; 73 DTC 5437 (FCTD), per Walsh J, for a correct application of this principle. A taxpayer cannot continue to deduct interest payments merely because the original use of borrowed money was to purchase income-bearing assets, after he or she has sold those assets and put the proceeds of sale to an ineligible use. To permit the taxpayer to do so would result in the borrowing of funds to finance the purchase of income-earning property which could be re-sold immediately without affecting the deductibility of interest payments for an indefinite period thereafter.

Conversely, a taxpayer who uses or intends to use borrowed money for an ineligible purpose, but later uses the funds to earn non-exempt income from a business or property, ought not to be deprived of the deduction for the current, eligible use: *Sinha v. M.N.R.*, [1981] CTC 2599; 81 DTC 465 (TRB); *Attaie v. M.N.R.*, [1985] 2 CTC 2331; 83 DTC 613 (TCC) (presently under appeal). For example, if a taxpayer borrows to buy personal property which he or she subsequently sells, the interest payments will become prospectively deductible if the proceeds of sale are used to purchase eligible income-earning property.

There is, however, an important natural limitation on this principle. The borrowed funds must still be in the hands of the taxpayer, as traced through the proceeds of disposition of the preceding ineligible use, if the taxpayer is to claim the deduction on the basis of a current eligible use. Where the taxpayer has expended the borrowings on an ineligible use, and has received no enduring benefit or saleable property in return, the borrowed money can obviously not be available to the taxpayer for a subsequent use, whether eligible or ineligible. A continuing obligation to make interest payments to the creditor therefore does not conclusively demonstrate that the borrowed money has a continuing use for the taxpayer.

In the present case the borrowed money was originally used to make capital allocations to the beneficiary for which the trust received no property or consideration of any kind. That use of the borrowings was indisputably not of an income-earning nature. Accordingly, unless the direct use of the money ought to be overlooked in favour of an alleged indirect income-earning use, the trust cannot be permitted to deduct the interest payments in issue in this appeal.

...

Direct and Indirect Uses of Borrowed Money

As I have indicated, the respondent trust submits that the borrowed funds permitted the trust to retain income-earning properties which it otherwise would have sold in order to make the capital allocations to the beneficiary. Such a use of borrowings, it argues, is sufficient in law to entitle it to the interest deduction. In short, the Court is asked to characterize the transaction on the basis of a purported indirect use of borrowed money to earn income rather than on the basis of a direct use of funds that was counter-productive to the trust's income-earning capacity.

In my view, neither the *Income Tax Act* nor the weight of judicial authority permits the courts to ignore the direct use to which a taxpayer puts borrowed money. One need only contemplate the consequences of the interpretation sought by the trust in order to reach the conclusion that it cannot have been intended by Parliament. In order for the trust to succeed, subparagraph 20(1)(c)(i) would have to be interpreted so that a deduction would be permitted for borrowings by any taxpayer who owned income-producing assets. Such a taxpayer could, on this view, apply the proceeds of a loan to purchase a life insurance policy, to take a vacation, to buy speculative properties, or to engage in any other non-income-earning or ineligible activity. Nevertheless, the interest would be deductible. A less wealthy taxpayer, with no income-earning assets, would not be able to deduct interest payments on loans used in the identical fashion. Such an interpretation would be unfair as between taxpayers and would make a mockery of the statutory requirement that, for interest payments to be deductible, borrowed money must be used for circumscribed income-earning purposes.

One finds in the Act not only the distinction within subparagraph 20(1)(c)(i) between eligible and ineligible uses of funds, but other provisions which also require the tracing of funds to particular uses in a manner inconsistent with the argument of the trust. Subsection 20(3) ... stipulates, for example, that interest on money borrowed [used] to repay an existing loan shall be deemed to have been used for the purpose for which the previous borrowings were used. This provision would, of course, be unnecessary if interest on borrowed money were deductible when the taxpayer had income-earning properties to preserve. On the contrary, however, for taxation years prior to the enactment of [the provision in 1953], it had been held that such interest was not deductible since the borrowings were used to repay a loan and not to earn income: *Interior Breweries Ltd. v. M.N.R.*, [1955] CTC 143 at 148; 55 DTC 1090 at 1093 (Exch. Ct.).

It is not surprising, therefore, that the cases interpreting subparagraph 20(1)(c)(i) and its predecessor provisions have not favoured the view that a direct ineligible use of borrowed money ought to be overlooked whenever an indirect eligible use of funds can be found. See *Sternthal* and also *Garneau Marine Co. v. M.N.R.*, [1982] CTC 2191; 82 DTC 1171 (TRB).

In a similar vein, it has been held repeatedly that an individual cannot deduct interest paid on the mortgage of a personal residence even though he or she claims that the borrowing avoided the need to sell income-producing investments. Some of the more recent cases include: *Toolsie v. The Queen*, [1986] 1 CTC 216; 86 DTC 6117 (FCTD), *Jordanov v. M.N.R.*, [1986] 1 CTC 2183; 86 DTC 1136 (TCC), *Day v. M.N.R.*, [1984] CTC 2200; 84 DTC 1184 (TCC), *Eelkema v. M.N.R.*, [1983] CTC 2311; 83 DTC 253 (TRB), *Zanyk v. M.N.R.*, [1981] CTC 2042; 81 DTC 48 (TRB), *Holmann v. M.N.R.*, [1979] CTC 2653; 79 DTC 594 (TRB), *Huber v. M.N.R.*, [1979] CTC 3161; 79 DTC 936 (TRB), *Dorman v. M.N.R.*, [1977] CTC 2355; 77 DTC 251 (TRB), and *Verhoeven v. M.N.R.*, [1975] CTC 2292; 75 DTC 230 (TRB). It has also been held in a number of cases that an estate cannot deduct interest paid on borrowings used to pay succession duties or taxes even though the estate claims to have borrowed in lieu of selling income-producing investments: *Shields v. M.N.R.*, [1968] Tax ABC 909; 68 DTC 668, *Auld v. M.N.R.*, *Cutten v. M.N.R.*, 16 Tax ABC 1; 56 DTC 454, *No. 228 v. M.N.R.*, 12 Tax ABC 83; 55 DTC 39, *No. 185 v. M.N.R.*, 11 Tax ABC 173; 54 DTC 395.

The leading case from this Court on the availability of the interest deduction, *Canada Safeway Ltd. v. M.N.R.* [[1957] CTC 335; 57 DTC 1239 (SCC)], also demonstrates a reluctance to overlook a clearly ineligible direct use of borrowed money in order to favour the taxpayer by characterizing the transaction on the basis of a less direct eligible use of borrowings. The taxpayer corporation in that case sought to deduct the interest on a series of debentures which the corporation used to finance the purchase of shares in another, related corporation. In the period in question, 1947-1949, dividends from shares of Canadian corporations were exempted from taxable income. To the extent to which the debentures were used to produce dividend income from shares, the taxpayer was accordingly ineligible for the interest deduction. The taxpayer corporation argued however that the share purchase not only provided dividend income, but also increased the taxpayer's income from its existing business operations by giving it control over a wholesale supplier. This conferred a considerable advantage on the taxpayer relative to its competitors and allowed it to increase significantly its net income. Nevertheless, the Court held that the interest payments were not deductible, Locke J dissenting. Justice Rand stated, at 726 (CTC 343):

No doubt there is in fact a causal connection between the purchase of the stock and the benefits ultimately received; but the statutory language cannot be extended to such a remote consequence; it could be carried to any length in a chain of subsidiaries; and to say that such a thing was envisaged by the ordinary expression used in the statute is to speculate and not interpret.

Referring to the interest expense deduction for borrowed money used for the purpose of earning income from business, Rand, J concluded at 727 (CTC 345):

What is aimed at by the section is an employment of the borrowed funds immediately within the company's business and not one that effects its purpose in such an indirect and remote manner.

Turning to borrowings used to generate income from property, he said:

There is nothing in this language to extend the application to an acquisition of "power" annexed to stock, and to the indirect and remote effects upon the company of action taken in the course of business of the subsidiary.

Although the *Canada Safeway* case did not relate specifically to an alleged indirect use of funds to preserve income-producing assets, the emphasis on directness of use of borrowed funds in the reasons of Justice Rand is antithetical to the submission of the taxpayer in the present appeal.

The respondent trust prefers the decision of Jackett P in *Trans-Prairie*. In that case, as I have already indicated, Jackett P relied on the proposition, perfectly correct in so far as it goes, that it is the current use and not the original use of borrowed money that determines eligibility for a deduction. As stated previously, however, the fact that the taxpayer continues to pay interest does not inevitably lead to the conclusion that the borrowed money is still being used by the taxpayer, let alone being used for an income-earning purpose. For example, an asset purchased with borrowed money may have been disposed of, while the debt incurred in its purchase remains unpaid.

With the exception of *Trans-Prairie*, then, the reasoning of which is, in my opinion, inadequate to support the conclusion sought to be reached by the respondent trust, the jurisprudence has generally been hostile to claims based on indirect, eligible uses when faced with direct but ineligible uses of borrowed money.

I acknowledge, however, that just as there has been a recent trend away from strict construction of taxation statutes (see *Stubart Investments Ltd. v. The Queen*, [1984] 1 SCR 536 at 573-79; [1984] CTC 294 at 313-316 and *The Queen v. Golden*, [1986] 1 SCR 209 at 214-15; [1986] 1 CTC 274 at 277), so too has the recent trend in tax cases been towards attempting to ascertain the true commercial and practical nature of the taxpayer's transactions. There has been, in this country and elsewhere, a movement away from tests based on the form of transactions and towards tests based on what Lord Pearce has referred to as a "common sense appreciation of all the guiding features" of the events in question: *B.P. Australia Ltd. v. Commissioner of Taxation of Australia*, [1966] AC 224 at 264; [1965] 3 All E.R. 209 at 218 (PC). ...

This is, I believe, a laudable trend provided it is consistent with the text and purposes of the taxation statute. Assessment of taxpayers' transactions with an eye to commercial and economic realities, rather than juristic classification of form, may help to avoid the inequity of tax liability being dependent upon the taxpayer's sophistication at manipulating a sequence of events to achieve a patina of compliance with the apparent prerequisites for a tax deduction.

This does not mean, however, that a deduction such as the interest deduction in subparagraph 20(1)(c)(i), which by its very text is made available to the taxpayer in limited circumstances, is suddenly to lose all its strictures. It is not lightly to be assumed that an actual and direct use of borrowed money is any less real than the abstract and remote indirect uses which have, on occasion, been advanced by taxpayers in an effort to achieve a favourable characterization. In particular, I believe that despite the fact that it can be characterized as indirectly preserving income, borrowing money for an ineligible direct purpose ought not entitle a taxpayer to deduct interest payments.

The taxpayer in such a situation has doubly reduced his or her long run income-earning capacity: first, by expending capital in a manner that does not produce taxable income; and second, by incurring debt financing charges. The taxpayer, of course, has a right to spend money in ways which cannot reasonably be expected to generate taxable income but if the taxpayer chooses to do so, he or she cannot expect any advantageous treatment by the tax assessor. In my view, the text of the Act requires tracing the use of borrowed funds to a specific eligible use, its obviously restricted purpose being the encouragement of taxpayers to augment their income-producing potential. This, in my view, precludes the allowance of a deduction for interest paid on borrowed funds which indirectly preserve income-earning property but which are not directly "used for the purpose of earning income from ... property."

Even if there are exceptional circumstances in which, on a real appreciation of a taxpayer's transactions, it might be appropriate to allow the taxpayer to deduct interest on funds borrowed for an ineligible use because of an indirect effect on the taxpayer's income-earning capacity, I am satisfied that those circumstances are not presented in the case before us. It seems to me that, at the very least, the taxpayer must satisfy the Court that his or her *bona fide* purpose in using the funds was to earn income. In contrast to what appears to be the case in *Trans-Prairie*, the facts in the present case fall far short of such a showing. Indeed, it is of more than passing interest that the assets which were preserved for a brief period of time yielded a return which grossly fell short of the interest costs on the borrowed money. In 1970, the interest costs on the $2.2 million of loans amounted to over $110,000 while the return from an average $2.2 million of trust assets (the amount of capital "preserved") was less than $10,000. The taxpayer cannot point to any reasonable expectation that the income yield from the trust's investment portfolio as a whole, or indeed from any single asset, would exceed the interest payable on a like amount of debt. The fact that the loan may have prevented capital losses cannot assist the taxpayer in obtaining a deduction from income which is limited to use of borrowed money for the purpose of earning income.

Before concluding, I wish to address one final argument raised by counsel for the trust. It was submitted — and the Crown generously conceded — that the trust would have obtained an interest deduction if it had sold assets to make the capital allocation and borrowed to replace them. Accordingly, it is argued, the trust ought not to be precluded from an interest deduction merely because it achieved the same effect without the formalities of a sale and repurchase of assets. It would be a sufficient answer to this submission to point to the principle that the courts must deal with what the taxpayer actually did, and not what he might have done: *Matheson v. The Queen*, [1974] CTC 186 at 189; 74 DTC 6176 at 6179 (FCTD) per Mahoney J. In any event, I admit to some doubt about the premise conceded by the Crown. If, for example, the trust had sold a particular income-producing asset, made the capital allocation to the beneficiary and repurchased the same asset, all within a brief interval of time, the courts might well consider the sale and repurchase to constitute a formality or a sham designed to conceal the essence of the transaction, namely that money was borrowed and used to fund a capital allocation to the beneficiary. In this regard, see *Zwaig v. M.N.R.*, [1974] CTC 2172; 74 DTC 1121 (TRB), in which the taxpayer sold securities and used the proceeds to buy a life insurance policy. He then borrowed on the policy to repurchase the securities. Under subparagraph 20(1)(c)(i) the use of borrowed money to purchase a life insurance policy is not a use entitling the taxpayer to an interest deduction. The Tax Review Board rightly disallowed the deduction sought for interest payments, notwithstanding that the form of the taxpayer's transactions created an aura of compliance with the requirements of the interest deduction provision. The characterization of taxpayers' transactions according to their true commercial and practical nature does not always favour the taxpayer. The taxpayer trust in this appeal asks the Court for the benefit of a characterization based on the alleged commercial and practical nature of its transactions. At the same time, however, it seeks to have the commercial and practical nature of its transactions determined by reference to a hypothetical characterization which reflects the epitome of formalism. I cannot accept that it should be allowed to succeed.

It follows that I would allow the appeal and restore the assessments of the Minister of National Revenue, with costs ...

Appeal allowed.

NOTES AND QUESTIONS

1.   On what basis did the Supreme Court of Canada conclude in *Bronfman Trust* that the interest expenses incurred by the taxpayer were not deductible? Did the court overrule the Exchequer Court decision in *Trans-Prairie Pipelines Ltd. v. M.N.R.*, [1970] C.T.C. 537, 70 D.T.C. 6351 (Ex. Ct.)? Must borrowed

money be used directly for the purpose of earning income from a business or property in order to be deductible under subparagraph (20)(1)(c)(i).

2.   Of what relevance to the Supreme Court's decision in *Bronfman Trust* is the presumed purpose of subparagraph 20(1)(c)(i)? Of what relevance are the consequences that would follow if taxpayers could deduct interest on borrowed money used to retain assets that might otherwise be sold to finance personal consumption? Of what relevance is the text of subparagraph 20(1)(c)(i) and the existence of subsection 20(3)? Of what relevance is the court's observation that "the assets which were preserved for a brief period of time yielded a return which grossly fell short of the interest costs on the borrowed money" and its conclusion that there was no "reasonable expectation that the income yield from the trust's investment portfolio as a whole, or indeed from any single asset, would exceed the interest payable on a like amount of debt"?

3.   On what basis did Dickson CJC conclude in *Bronfman Trust* that "Parliament created subparagraph 20(1)(c)(i) ... in order to encourage the accumulation of capital which would produce taxable income"? Do you agree with this interpretation of the purpose of subparagraph 20(1)(c)(i)? Why or why not?

4.   What concerns about tax fairness did Dickson CJC express in *Bronfman Trust* with respect to "the consequences of the interpretation sought by the trust"? Do you share these concerns? Why or why not? Of what significance, if any, should these tax policy considerations play in the interpretation of the *Income Tax Act* by the courts?

5.   In *Bronfman Trust*, the court suggested that "the focus of the inquiry" regarding the deductibility of interest expenses "must be centred on the use to which the taxpayer put the borrowed funds." Is this statement fully consistent with the text of subparagraph 20(1)(c)(i), which refers to the *purpose* for which borrowed money is used?

6.   In *Mark Resources Inc. v. Canada*, [1993] T.C.J. No. 265, [1993] 2 C.T.C. 2259, 93 D.T.C. 1004 (T.C.C.), the taxpayer, a profitable Canadian company with a wholly owned US subsidiary that had accumulated substantial business losses, borrowed US dollars, which it transferred to the American subsidiary as a contribution of capital, which invested the funds at a lower rate than that payable on the taxpayer's loan, using its prior years' losses to shelter taxes otherwise payable on the interest and paying the full amount of this income to the taxpayer as dividends that were deductible in computing the taxpayer's taxable income and subject only to a modest US withholding tax. Rejecting the taxpayer's argument that the borrowed funds were used by the taxpayer for the purpose of earning dividend income from its US subsidiary, the court held that the "overriding ultimate economic purpose for which the borrowed funds were used" was to enable the taxpayer to, in effect, import the losses of its US subsidiary. According to Bowman TCCJ (at para. 45):

The direct and immediate use [of the borrowed funds] was the injection of capital into a subsidiary with the necessary and intended consequence that the subsidiary should earn interest income from term deposits from which it could pay dividends. The earning of dividend income cannot, however, in my opinion, be said to be the real purpose of the use of the borrowed funds. Theoretically one might, in a connected series of events leading to a predetermined conclusion, postulate as [to] the purpose of each event in the sequence the achievement of the result that immediately follows but in determining the "purpose" of the use of borrowed funds within the meaning of paragraph 20(1)(c) the court is faced with practical considerations with which the pure theorist is not concerned. That purpose — and it is a practical and real one, and in no way remote, fanciful or indirect — is the importation of the losses from the US. This case is not the converse of *Bronfman*. The vague purpose of protecting assets that produced virtually no income was patently subservient to the direct and uneconomic purpose of distributing capital to a beneficiary of the trust. Here the immediate step of investing in a subsidiary that in accordance with the scheme must necessarily pay dividends was not the real purpose of the use of the funds. The earning of interest income by [the US subsidiary] and the payment by it of dividends to [the taxpayer] were integral but subservient and incidental steps to the real objective that lay behind the implementation of the plan. The amount of dividends, albeit deductible in computing taxable income, and based upon the interest from the term deposits, was less than the interest paid. ... It is true that the overall economic result, if all of the elements of the plan work, is a net gain to the appellant, but this type of gain is not from the production of income but from a reduction of taxes otherwise payable in Canada.

For a similar result, involving a much more complicated series of transactions designed to transfer accumulated tax losses among companies that were unrelated before the series of transactions commenced, see *Canwest Broadcasting Limited v. Canada*, [1995] T.C.J. No. 789, [1995] 2 C.T.C. 2780, 96 D.T.C. 1375 (T.C.C.). According to McArthur JTCC (at paras. 43-44):

> The situation the Supreme Court of Canada in *Bronfman* faced was very different from the one in the case at bar. In deciding that the "direct use of the funds" is the purpose which should be looked at, the Supreme Court chose a *"direct, ineligible"* use over an *"indirect, eligible"* use. Chief Justice Dickson restricted himself to situations in which the choice was between a direct ineligible use and an indirect, eligible use. There was no mention in the judgment as to which method should be applied in a situation, with which we are presented in this case. The Court noted with approval that there has been a recent trend in tax cases *towards attempting to ascertain the true commercial and practical nature of the taxpayer's transaction.*
>
> I find that the Court must look at the commercial, practical and economic reality of the taxpayer's transactions, and not permit form to override substance. The Court must ensure that the "purpose" which is used for a paragraph 20(1)(c) analysis is one that represents what the taxpayer's real intentions are, and not what he or she makes them appear to look. In *Bronfman*, the "real purpose" was the distribution of capital. In the present case, the "real purpose," as demonstrated by the evidence, was tax savings.

7. In *Bronfman Trust*, Dickson CJC suggested that "the recent trend in tax cases [has] been towards attempting to ascertain the true commercial and practical nature of the taxpayer's transactions." Is the "[a]ssessment of taxpayers' transactions with an eye to commercial and economic realities, rather than juristic classification of form," which Dickson CJC favoured, consistent with the traditional emphasis in Canadian tax law on the legal substance of transactions rather than their commercial or economic substance? Is an assessment of "the true commercial and practical nature of the taxpayer's

transactions" relevant to the statutory requirement in subparagraph 20(1)(c)(i) that borrowed money be used for the purpose of earning income from a business or property?

8. How did Dickson CJC respond to the taxpayer's argument in *Bronfman Trust* that "the trust would have obtained an interest deduction if it had sold assets to make the capital allocation and borrowed to replace them"? Is the court's reference to the sham doctrine consistent with the definition of a "sham" adopted by the Supreme Court of Canada in *M.N.R. v. Cameron*, [1972] S.C.J. No. 137, [1972] C.T.C. 380, 72 D.T.C. 6325 (S.C.C.) and *Stubart Investments Ltd. v. Canada*, [1984] S.C.J. No. 25, [1984] C.T.C. 294, 84 D.T.C. 6305 (S.C.C.)? Might the deduction of interest expenses be disallowed in this circumstance on the grounds that the "overriding ultimate economic purpose for which the borrowed funds were used" (*Mark Resources Inc. v. Canada*, [1993] T.C.J. No. 265, [1993] 2 C.T.C. 2259, 93 D.T.C. 1004 (T.C.C.)) was to make a capital allocation and not to acquire income-producing assets, notwithstanding the order in which the transactions were carried out?

9. In *Zwaig v. M.N.R.*, [1974] C.T.C. 2172, 74 D.T.C. 1121 (T.R.B.), the taxpayer sold securities to a brokerage firm on the understanding that he would repurchase them, used the proceeds to purchase a life insurance policy, and borrowed money in order to repurchase the securities. Disallowing the deduction of interest expenses on the borrowed funds, the board emphasized (at para. 17) that "[o]ne must look at the whole picture of the transaction to discover its substance and by the same token to find out if the borrowed money was used to earn income." On the facts of the case, it concluded, the borrowed money was "according to the form of the transaction ... used to repurchase the securities that had just been sold and, according to the substance of the transaction, to purchase a life insurance policy."

See also *Robitaille v. Canada*, [1997] T.C.J. No. 766, [1997] 3 C.T.C. 3031, 97 D.T.C. 1286 (T.C.C.), in which the taxpayer, a partner in a law firm, withdrew $100,000 from his partnership account on June 12, 1985 in order to purchase a home for $113,500 on June 13, 1985, and borrowed $100,000 on the security of the home later on June 13, 1985, which was used to make a capital contribution to his partnership account on June 14, 1985. Commenting (at para. 16) that "focus must be had not on the direct and immediate result of the use to which the funds were put but rather, in a real and practical manner, on the ultimate economic objectives sought by the transactions," the court disallowed the deduction of interest expenses incurred on the borrowed funds. According to Dussault TCJ (at para. 21):

> I consider that the analysis of the "true commercial and practical nature" of the transactions carried out by the appellant leads to the conclusion that their ultimate purpose was the purchase ... of his residence, not investment in the law firm in which he is one of the partners. Investment in the law firm already existed and the purpose of the loans was only to reimburse money withdrawn and used for personal purposes a few days earlier in 1985.

10. In *Singleton v. Canada*, [2001] S.C.J. No. 59, [2002] 1 C.T.C. 121, 2001 D.T.C. 5533 (S.C.C.), the taxpayer, a partner in a law firm in which he had invested capital of at least $300,000, engaged in a series of transactions on October 27, 1988 in which he borrowed $298,750 to contribute to his capital account in the partnership and withdrew $300,000 from this account in order to purchase a house. Relying on the "direct use" test from *Bronfman Trust v. Canada*, [1987] S.C.J. No. 1, [1987] 1 C.T.C. 117, 87 D.T.C. 5059 (S.C.C.), insisting that "the transactions must be viewed independently" (at para. 34), emphasizing that the court "must simply apply s. 20(1)(c)(i) rather than search for the economic realities of the situation" (at para. 31), and dismissing Dickson CJC's reference in *Bronfman Trust* to *Zwaig v. M.N.R.*, [1974] C.T.C. 2172, 74 D.T.C. 1121 (T.R.B.), as "more musing than jurisprudence" (at para. 42), Major J (Gonthier, Iacobucci, Binnie and Arbour JJ concurring) allowed the deduction on the basis that the taxpayer had "used the borrowed funds to refinance his capital account" (at para. 32). Dissenting, LeBel J (Bastarache J concurring) concluded that the statutory language of subparagraph 20(1)(c)(i) suggests an inquiry into the economic realities of the transactions (at para. 53), that Dickson CJC's comments in *Bronfman Trust*, were "precisely on point and should not be dismissed as mere *obiter dicta* on an hypothetical issue" (at para. 55), and that the borrowed funds were in fact used to finance the purchase of a private home (at para. 87). But see the decision in *Lipson v. Canada*, [2006] T.C.J. No. 174, 2006 CarswellNat 982, 2006 T.C.C. 148 (T.C.C.) where the Tax Court held that a taxpayer's attempt to convert non-deductible interest expenses into deductible expenses violated the general anti-avoidance rule in section 245.

11. In *Ludco Enterprises Ltd. v. Canada*, [2001] S.C.J. No. 58, [2002] 1 C.T.C. 95, 2001 D.T.C. 5505 (S.C.C.), the taxpayers incurred interest expenses of $6 million on borrowed money that was used to acquire shares in two companies located in an offshore tax haven, the declared goals of which were to pay little in the way of dividends in order to accumulate untaxed investment returns that would increase the value of investors' shares, resulting in capital gains on their subsequent disposition. Notwithstanding that the taxpayers received only $600,000 in dividends over an eight-year period during which they held the shares, and realized a capital gain of $9.24 million on the sale of the shares in 1985, the Supreme Court of Canada allowed the taxpayers to deduct the full $6 million of interest expense on the grounds that "the term 'income' in s. 20(1)(c)(i) does not refer to net income, but to income subject to tax" (at para. 61) and that "a taxpayer's ancillary purpose" to earn income so defined is "equally capable of providing the requisite purpose for interest deductibility in comparison with any more important or significant purpose" (at para. 51).

Is this decision consistent with the Supreme Court of Canada decision in *Bronfman Trust v. Canada*, [1987] S.C.J. No. 1, [1987] 1 C.T.C. 117, 87 D.T.C. 5059 (S.C.C.)? Is it consistent with the definition in subsection 9(1) of "a taxpayer's income ... from a business or property" as "the taxpayer's profit from that business or property"?

12.   In *722540 Ontario v. Canada*, [2003] F.C.J. No. 367, [2003] 3 C.T.C. 1, 2003 D.T.C. 5195 (F.C.A.), the taxpayer engaged in a complicated series of "pre-ordained" and "circular" transactions designed to obtain interest deductions by borrowing money and loaning it to a company with accumulated losses and no ongoing business. Although reversing the trial decision ((2001) CarswellNat 3015 (T.C.C.)), which relied on *Mark Resources Inc. v. Canada*, [1993] T.C.J. No. 265, [1993] 2 C.T.C. 2259, 93 D.T.C. 1004 (T.C.C.) and *Canwest Broadcasting Ltd. v. Canada*, [1995] T.C.J. No. 789, [1995] 2 C.T.C. 2780, 96 D.T.C. 1375 (T.C.C.) to disallow the deduction of interest expenses on the basis that the borrowed money was used to avoid tax, the court disallowed the deduction under former subsection 245(1) on the basis that the transactions would artificially reduce the taxpayer's income.

13.   In *M.N.R. v. Attaie*, [1990] F.C.J. No. 527, [1990] 2 C.T.C. 157, 90 D.T.C. 6413 (F.C.A.), the taxpayer, who left Iran at the time of the Islamic Revolution, purchased a home in Don Mills, Ontario in December 1978, for which he borrowed $54,000 under an open mortgage at 10¾ per cent, repayable at any time and maturing on November 30, 1983. According to the court:

> The respondent insisted on those terms, at the cost of paying further interest and against the advice of his real estate agent, in view of the fact that he had approximately $200,000 in funds in Iran. He expected to move such moneys out of that country within a matter of months and was anxious to repay the mortgage loan without notice or bonus.

When the taxpayer obtained access to these funds in the spring of 1979, however, interest rates had increased significantly, and the taxpayer decided to invest his funds in term deposits yielding a return of 14 to 16 per cent, rather than repaying the mortgage.

In a decision arrived at two years before the Supreme Court of Canada decision in *Bronfman Trust v. Canada*, [1987] S.C.J. No. 1, [1987] 1 C.T.C. 117, 87 D.T.C. 5059 (S.C.C.), the Tax Court, [1985] 2 C.T.C. 2331, 85 D.T.C. 613 (T.C.C.), allowed the taxpayer to deduct mortgage interest, notwithstanding that the taxpayer and his family occupied the home as a principal residence, on the basis (at para. 6) that the taxpayer was "in no different position than if the residential property title was clear and he would have been able to ... take out a mortgage on the residence and use the funds from that mortgage to earn income from term deposits." In *Bronfman Trust*, Dickson CJC appears to have interpreted this decision as an example of a situation in which "a taxpayer who uses ... borrowed money for an ineligible purpose, but later uses the funds to earn non-exempt income from a business or property, ought not to be deprived of the deduction for the current, eligible use."

Referring to the Supreme Court of Canada decision in *Bronfman Trust*, the Federal Court Trial Division, [1987] F.C.J. No. 862, [1987] 2 C.T.C. 212, 87

D.T.C. 5411, dismissed the Crown's appeal on the basis of a "common sense appreciation" of the facts, concluding (at para. 26):

> Here, the defendant's original purpose was to obtain funds to complete the purchase of the home. Once he received the funds from Iran that use of the borrowed funds, in a practical business sense, ceased. He made a carefully thought-out decision to maintain the borrowing in order to invest in attractive term deposits and earn income. This was done with an eye to the practical commercial and economic realities at the time.

On appeal, the Federal Court of Appeal disallowed the deduction of interest payments on the mortgage, concluding that the trial judge had committed "an error, both in fact and in law" in concluding that the ineligible use of the borrowed funds ceased when the taxpayer invested other funds in income-earning term deposits. According to the court (at paras. 11, 16, 17, and 21):

> Once the property became occupied as a personal residence, it could not be found that the direct and actual use of the borrowed moneys was for the purpose of earning moneys from a business or property. It should not, therefore, have been held that the interest on the mortgage was deductible under the provisions of subparagraph 20(1)(c)(i) of the Act. ...

> According to *Bronfman Trust*, the statutory provisions require that the inquiry to be made, be centred on the use to which the taxpayer put the borrowed funds. Their current use rather than their original use is relevant in assessing deductibility of interest payments. ...

> The fact that the respondent decided to maintain the borrowing and use the funds received from Iran to make a more profitable investment, does not render the interest paid on borrowing "interest on borrowed money used for the purpose of earning income from a business or property" as these words are found in subparagraph 20(1)(c)(i) of the Act. ...

> There is no tracing here of the borrowed funds to the income earned. The borrowed funds were put to a non-eligible use while the personal funds were used so as to produce income.

Do you agree with this decision? Why or why not? Might the result have been any different if the court had emphasized the purpose for which the borrowed funds were used rather than their direct use?

14. In *Grenier v. M.N.R.*, [1992] T.C.J. No. 21, [1992] 1 C.T.C. 2703, 92 D.T.C. 1678 (T.C.C.), aff'd [1998] 3 C.T.C. 243, 98 D.T.C. 6439 (F.C.T.D.), the taxpayer borrowed $66,000 on the security of his home, which was used to earn income from an automobile garage in Hull. When he subsequently moved to a new residence, he used the proceeds from the sale of the old residence to repay the original $66,000 loan, borrowed a further $151,700 to purchase the new residence, and sought to deduct the interest on the full amount of this new loan on the basis that it had replaced the original $66,000 loan. Allowing the taxpayer to deduct interest payable on $66,000 of the new loan, the court justified the decision on the grounds (at para. 10) that "the decision in *Bronfman Trust* does not seem to have overruled the reasoning in *Trans-Prairie Pipelines* ... with respect to circumstances where loans are replaced with subsequent loans." According to Lamarre-Proulx TCCJ (at paras. 12-15):

Is this a case where the principles set out in *Trans-Canada Pipelines* should be applied, that is, that the interest should be deductible in the years in which the borrowed money was used to earn income, and the deduction not be dependent upon the existence of the first loan contract when there is a subsequent loan contract under which the borrowed money may continue to be used in the business?

I am of the opinion that the answer should be in the affirmative with respect to the amount of $66,000, and the recent decision of Mr. Justice Strayer in *The Queen v. J. Shore* [1992] 1 CTC 34, 92 DTC 6059, dated January 2, 1992, confirms this conclusion. In circumstances which were analogous to those in the case at bar, the learned judge held that subsection 20(3) of the Act applied and decided in favour of the taxpayer.

This decision affirmed the decision of Judge Taylor of this Court, which is reported at [1986] 1 CTC 2360, 86 DTC 1253. I quote from the summary of that case which appears at page 2361 (DTC 1253):

> The taxpayer borrowed approximately $40,000 secured by a mortgage on his residence. He immediately loaned the money to a business corporation controlled by him with the repayment terms being the same as those in the mortgage. Since the interest received by the taxpayer from the company was taxable and the mortgage interest paid by the taxpayer was deductible, the net effect on the taxpayer's income was nil. In 1979 the taxpayer sold his residence with the purchaser assuming the mortgage. A short time later, the taxpayer purchased a new residence and assumed an existing mortgage which also had an outstanding balance of $40,000. The taxpayer continued to include the interest received by the company in his income and to deduct the mortgage interest.

I quote from Mr Justice Strayer, at page 35 (DTC 6060-61):

> Each case must turn on its own facts when a court is obliged to make such a characterization. In the present case when one looks at the commercial reality of the situation one sees that there was a series of transactions the net result of which was to enable the taxpayer to borrow money in order to earn income from his business, using his private homes as collateral for the loan. It is important to note that at the beginning of these transactions the taxpayer and his wife were owners of their Thamesford home. ...
>
> It is not disputed that the taxpayer and his wife gave a mortgage on their home to Guaranty Trust in order to raise approximately $42,000 to use in their new business, Joline Automobiles Ltd and that the net proceeds of that mortgage were loaned to the business. That amounted to a direct use of the money for purposes of the business. ...
>
> They found a house in Stratford which was encumbered by a mortgage of a similar amount to the mortgage on their previous house, and they were thus able to pay cash to mortgage to acquire the house in Stratford. In my view the reality of that transaction, in taking on a house encumbered by the mortgage in favour of Victoria and Grey Trust similar to the one on their previous residence, was in essence the replacement of one borrowing of money for the purpose of their business by another borrowing of money for the same purpose, thus bringing it within subsection 20(3) of the *Income Tax Act* so that such "borrowed" money could be deemed to be used for the same purpose as the original money borrowed from Guaranty Trust.

743

In the case at bar, the hypothec granted on the second house was not in the same amount as the hypothec on the Rosemere house. Perhaps it would have been preferable to grant two hypothecs, one of which would have been in the amount of $66,000. I cannot, however, find that this was essential.

I believe that we must consider the economic context of the transactions in question. When the taxpayer sold his first house, he received $110,000 cash less $66,000. Why did he not receive the full amount of $110,000? This was because part of the amount had been lent for the financial support of his business, which was an automobile garage. When the time came to purchase his other house, he did not have the full $110,000 in hand, again because the money was used in the business. The reason he mortgaged his second home by $66,000 and more is that he did not have the $66,000 he had lent to the business. In *Trans-Prairie Pipelines*, the replacement of borrowed money by other borrowed money concerned the corporation only. In the case at bar it involves an individual who borrowed money to earn income by lending this money to a corporation. He had to pay off the first loan secured by a hypothec on his house, because he sold the house. However, when he bought another house, he had to borrow money to make up for the decrease in his assets brought about by the loan to his business, or in other terms, to fill the hole left in his assets by the money he had lent to his business and that was still being used to earn income.

Do you agree or disagree with this decision? Is it consistent with the Supreme Court of Canada's emphasis on the "direct use of borrowed funds" in *Bronfman Trust v. Canada*, [1987] S.C.J. No. 1, [1987] 1 C.T.C. 117, 87 D.T.C. 5059 (S.C.C.)? Is it consistent with an emphasis on the real or true economic purpose for which the borrowed funds are used? Does subsection 20(3) apply to the facts in *Grenier*? Was it properly applied in *Shore v. M.N.R.*, [1992] F.C.J. No. 1, [1992] 1 C.T.C. 34, 92 D.T.C. 6059 (F.C.A.)?

15. In *Canadian Helicopters Ltd. v. Canada*, [2001] T.C.J. No. 219, [2001] 2 C.T.C. 2541, 2001 D.T.C. 339 (T.C.C.), aff'd [2002] F.C.J. No. 148, [2002] 2 C.T.C. 83, 2002 D.T.C. 6805 (F.C.A.), the taxpayer sought to deduct interest expenses on borrowed funds which were loaned to a parent company interest-free so that the parent company could purchase the shares of a competitor company. Accepting that the taxpayer's *bona fide* purpose in using the borrowed funds was to earn management fees from running the operations of the competitor and increasing business income through the amalgamation of operations, the court allowed the deduction of interest expenses on the basis that they were used for an eligible indirect use, notwithstanding that their direct use was not to earn income.

16. In *Tennant v. M.N.R.*, [1996] S.C.J. No. 16, [1996] 1 C.T.C. 290 (S.C.C.), the taxpayer borrowed $1 million in May 1981 with which he purchased a million common shares of an arm's-length corporation (Realwest Energy Corporation) at $1 per share. On July 25, 1985, the taxpayer disposed of the shares to an arm's-length holding company (TWL Holdings Ltd.) at a declared fair market value of $1,000, in exchange for 1,000 class B common shares of TWL. When the taxpayer continued to deduct interest on the full $1 million borrowed in May 1981, Revenue Canada reassessed, allowing the taxpayer a deduction for interest on the $1,000 value of the shares declared on July 25, 1985.

Concluding that the full amount of the borrowed funds could be traced to the taxpayer's interest in the 1,000 TWL shares, the Supreme Court of Canada allowed the taxpayer's appeal. According to Iacobucci J (La Forest, Sopinka, Gonthier, Cory, McLachlin, and Major JJ concurring):

> in order to deduct interest payments, the taxpayer must establish a link between the current eligible use property, the proceeds of disposition of the original eligible use property, and the money that was borrowed to acquire the original eligible use property. On the facts of this case, in order to deduct the interest payments, the appellant must establish a link between the TWL shares he now owns, the proceeds of disposition of the original shares, and the money that was borrowed to acquire the original shares. In my view, this has been done, as both the original shares and the TWL shares are directly traceable to the loan. The respondent has argued that it is only the amount of $1,000 that can be traced to an eligible use, and that the appellant, in disposing of his Realwest shares, did not merely alter the form of the investment, but "reduced his investment capital and therewith his income earning source to $1,000, which was the cost of the TWL shares."

> With respect, this view should be rejected. Money was borrowed and used by the taxpayer in order to produce investment income, and continued to be used for this purpose even though the investment vehicle for producing the income changed. The fact that the investment has changed is not of any consequence. ... The original Realwest shares, the first source of income, were exchanged for the TWL shares, a replacement source. In a sense, the first source continued in a new form, as both the Realwest and the TWL shares are directly and fully traceable to the loan, as all the proceeds of disposition were reinvested in the second source.

> ... [I]t is implicit in the principles outlined in *Bronfman Trust* that the ability to deduct interest is not lost simply because the taxpayer sells the income-producing property, as long as the taxpayer reinvests in an eligible use property. ... The appellant has replaced one eligible use property with another, and both are directly traceable to the same loan, as the appellant reinvested all the proceeds of disposition. ...

> In my opinion, the basis for an interest deduction pursuant to subparagraph 20(1)(c)(i) is not the value of the replacement property, in this case the TWL shares, but the amount of the original loan. The wording of subparagraph 20(1)(c)(i) itself supports this interpretation. The deduction is based on the amount of interest paid in the year, or payable in respect of the year, pursuant to a legal obligation to pay interest on that proportion of "borrowed money used for the purpose of earning income from a business or property" that is "wholly applicable to that source." As long as the replacement property can be traced to the entire amount of the loan, then the entire amount of the interest payment may be deducted. If the replacement property can be traced to only a portion of the loan, then only a proportionate amount of the interest may be deducted. Clearly, however, the amount of interest to be deducted relates to the amount of the loan, and not the value of the replacement property.

Is this interpretation consistent with the language and purpose of subparagraph 20(1)(c)(i)? Is it consistent with the tracing requirement outlined in *Bronfman Trust*?

17. In *Hills v. M.N.R.*, [1970] Tax ABC 639 (T.A.B.), the taxpayer sought to deduct interest payments on a bank loan obtained to acquire a home 25 per cent of the living space of which was used for rental purposes. Affirming the Minister's assessment, which had allowed the taxpayer to deduct only 25 per cent of the interest expense, the board (at para. 5) characterized the remaining 75

per cent of the interest expense as "a personal living expense ... not incurred for the purpose of producing income from a property or a business ... within the meaning of Sections 11(1)(c), 12(1)(a) and 12(1)(h) [now paragraphs 20(1)(c), 18(1)(a), and 18(1)(h)] of the *Income Tax Act*."

18. In *Emerson v. Canada*, [1985] 1 C.T.C. 324, 85 D.T.C. 5236 (F.C.T.D.), aff'd [1986] 1 C.T.C. 422, 86 D.T.C. 6184 (F.C.A.), the taxpayer borrowed $100,000 in 1980 to purchase shares of three small business corporations, which were sold at a loss of $35,000 in August 1981, at which time the taxpayer borrowed a further $63,750 to discharge the amount of the initial loan still outstanding. Rejecting the taxpayer's argument that interest on the second loan was deductible under subsection 20(3), the Federal Court Trial Division concluded that the taxpayer had failed to establish the existence of a source of income to which the interest expense continued to relate. In other words, because the borrowed funds could no longer be traced to an eligible use, the deductibility of interest expenses was disallowed.

While this result may have been reasonable on the facts of *Emerson*, the requirement that borrowed funds be traceable to a continuing source of income could result in hardship where a taxpayer borrowed money to invest in a source of income that ceased to have a reasonable expectation of profit or ceased to exist altogether. See, for example, Gordon D. Dixon and Brian J. Arnold, "Rubbing Salt into the Wound: The Denial of the Interest Deduction After the Loss of a Source of Income" (1991) 39 Can. Tax J. 1473. For 1993 and subsequent taxation years, this result is precluded by the enactment of section 20.1, which contains a complicated set of rules permitting the continuing deduction of certain interest expenses after the loss of a source of income.

19. In *Leslie v. Canada*, [1997] T.C.J. No. 1228, [1998] 1 C.T.C. 3296 (T.C.C.), the taxpayer, whose annual salary increased from between $20,000 and $30,000 to over $40,000 after she graduated with a bachelor of arts degree from the University of Toronto, sought to deduct interest on student loans under paragraph 20(1)(c) on the basis that the borrowed money was used for the purpose of earning income from the business of working as a salaried employee. Rejecting the taxpayer's argument, Bowie TCJ emphasized the distinction between employment and business in the context of the *Income Tax Act*, and concluded:

> absent an ongoing business with a reasonable expectation of profit against which the expenses might be set, ... the expenses of gaining an education, and interest paid upon money borrowed for the purpose of paying those expenses [are] personal or living expenses.

For 1998 and subsequent taxation years, a tax credit (computed at the lowest marginal tax rate) may be claimed under section 118.62 for interest paid on qualifying federal or provincial student loans during the taxation year or in any of the previous five taxation years after 1997.

20. In *Sinha v. M.N.R.*, [1981] C.T.C. 2599, 81 D.T.C. 465 (T.R.B.), the taxpayer, who had borrowed $4,530 in 1977 in the form of a Canada student

loan, did not use the funds for educational or living expenses, but invested the cash in interest-bearing securities. When the Canada student loan began to bear interest in 1978, the taxpayer deducted these payments, which were disallowed by Revenue Canada on the grounds that the interest payments "were not expended for the purpose of gaining or producing income from a business or property within the meaning of paragraph 20(1)(c) of the *Income Tax Act*, but were personal and living expenses of the appellant within the meaning of paragraph 18(1)(h) of the Act." Rejecting the Minister's argument that the deductions should be denied because "the money was not borrowed for the purpose of earning income," the Tax Review Board allowed the taxpayer's appeal in the basis that the taxpayer had used the funds to earn income, regardless of the original purpose for which they were borrowed. According to D.E. Taylor (at para. 5):

> It is the testimony of the appellant that during the year in question the money was not used for the reason it was loaned to him (to further his education) but instead was *used* to earn income. ... [I]n the absence of any evidence to the contrary, the appellant is entitled to have the Minister regard his *use* of the subject borrowed money during the year in question as for "earning income" rather than personal, irrespective of the purposes for which the loan was made. [Emphasis in original.]

21.   In *Shell Canada Limited v. Canada*, [1999] S.C.J. No. 30, [1999] 4 C.T.C. 313, 99 D.T.C. 5669 (S.C.C.), the taxpayer, which required approximately US$100 million for its general corporate purposes, entered into an elaborate series of transactions whereby it borrowed funds in a currency (New Zealand dollars) that was expected to depreciate against the US dollar, exchanged these funds for US dollars, and entered into a forward exchange agreement to purchase the New Zealand dollars as needed to make interest and principal payments on the loan. As a result of these transactions, the taxpayer incurred much higher interest expenses during the term of the loan than it would have incurred if it had borrowed US dollars (15.4 per cent versus 9.1 per cent), and corresponding foreign exchange gains on the payments of interest and principal. In computing its income for the taxation years at issue, the taxpayer deducted the Canadian equivalent of the New Zealand dollar interest expenses and reported the foreign exchange gains as capital gains. The Minister characterized the foreign exchange gains as business income and disallowed the deduction of interest expenses in excess of the US rate of 9.1 per cent.

At the Federal Court of Appeal, [1998] F.C.J. No. 194, [1998] 2 C.T.C. 207, 98 D.T.C. 6177 (F.C.A.), Linden JA (Strayer and Stone JJA concurring), concluded (at para. 55), *inter alia*, that "[t]he true or real purpose ... realized by borrowing NZ$ and paying the extra percentage was the reduction of taxation," and that the payment of interest at the higher New Zealand rate was not a "reasonable amount" as required by the postamble to paragraph 20(1)(c). Reversing this decision, the Supreme Court of Canada held that the borrowed funds were used by the taxpayer for the purpose of earning non-exempt income from its business, notwithstanding the purpose for which the New Zealand dollars were borrowed, and that the interest rate negotiated with the New

Zealand lender was a reasonable rate. According to McLachlin J (as she then was) (at paras. 32-34):

> Here, Shell borrowed NZ$150 million from the foreign lenders and immediately exchanged it for approximately US$100 million before applying it to its business. This exchange did not alter the basic character of the funds as "borrowed money." ... The US$100 million was simply the NZ$150 million transformed into a different currency which, although it changed its legal form and its relative value, did not change its substance. ... Viewed thus, it is apparent that all of the NZ$150 million that Shell borrowed from the foreign lenders was borrowed money currently and directly used for the purpose of producing income from Shell's business. The direct link between the borrowed money and the activity calculated to produce income can hardly be compared to the indirect use at issue in *Bronfman Trust, supra*. ...

> Therefore, the taxpayer is entitled to deduct the lesser of, (1) the actual amount paid or, (2) a reasonable amount in respect of "an amount paid ... pursuant to a legal obligation to pay interest on ... borrowed money used for the purpose of earning income from a business or property." Here, the borrowed money that was used for the purpose of earning income was the NZ$150 million. At trial, Christie ACJTC found that the market rate for a loan of NZ$ in 1988 for the five-year term specified in the Debenture Agreements was 15.4 percent per annum. That is the rate Shell paid. Where an interest rate is established in a market of lenders and borrowers acting at arm's length from each other, it is generally a reasonable rate: *Mohammad v. R* (1997), 97 DTC 5503 (Fed. CA) at p. 5509, per Robertson JA; *Irving Oil Ltd. v. R*, [1991] 1 CTC 350 (Fed. CA) at p. 359, per Mahoney JA.

In response to this decision, the federal government enacted section 20.3, applicable after February 27, 2000, which limits the deduction of interest expenses on "weak currency debt" to an amount that would have been payable if the taxpayer had incurred the debt directly in the final currency that is used for the purpose of gaining or producing income.

22. For an excellent survey of the law and policy regarding the deductibility of interest expenses, see Brian J. Arnold and Tim Edgar, "Deductibility of Interest Expense" (1995) 43 Can. Tax J. 1216. Arnold and Edgar argue, convincingly, that since interest is paid, like rent, for the use of capital over time, interest should almost always be considered to be a current expenditure. In their view, just as no one would dispute that rent paid for the use of a building occupied for business purposes should be deductible as a current expense, similarly it should not be disputed that interest paid to borrow funds that are used to earn income from business or property should be regarded as deductible. Although paragraph 18(1)(b) of the ITA precludes the current deduction of payments "on account of capital" except as explicitly provided in the ITA, paragraph 20(1)(c) explicitly provides for a deduction for interest paid on funds borrowed to earn income from business or property.

In *Gifford v. Canada*, [2004] S.C.J. No. 13, [2004] 2 C.T.C. 1, 2004 D.T.C. 6120 (S.C.C.), Major J. (McLachlin C.J., Bastarache, Binnie, Arbour, Deschamps, and Fish JJ. concurring) for the Supreme Court of Canada addressed the question of whether interest payments were payments "on account of capital" in the context of determining the deductibility of interest paid by an employee on $100,000 borrowed to acquire a client list from another employee.

Earlier decisions of the Supreme Court, such as *Canada Safeway Limited v. M.N.R.*, [1957] S.C.J. No. 50, [1957] C.T.C. 335, 57 D.T.C. 1239 (S.C.C.), had suggested that interest payments should almost always be considered payments "on account of capital." This term had been interpreted by many commentators, including Arnold and Edgar, to be consistent with a characterization of interest as a capital expenditure. However, in *Gifford* the court drew a clear distinction between describing interest as a payment "on account of capital" — a term that has become one of legislative art in the ITA — and a capital expenditure, as the term is commonly used and understood in finance and accounting. Instead, the court explained in *Gifford* that if funds are borrowed in order to add to the financial capital of a taxpayer, then interest payments thereon will be payments "on account of capital," regardless of whether the payments would otherwise be appropriately characterized as capital expenditures (which they would typically not). This judicial sleight of hand appears to reconcile the theoretical argument of Arnold and Edgar maintaining that interest is almost always appropriately regarded as a current expense, with the explicit wording of the ITA and the traditional treatment of interest by the courts considering interest payments to be payments "on account of capital."

23.   See also the discussion of *Lipson v. Canada* in Chapter 3, "Introduction to Tax Avoidance" at p. 194.

L. Other Financing Expenses

In addition to interest expense, other financing expenses that do not satisfy the legal definition of interest may be deducted under paragraphs 20(1)(e) to (g).[42] Paragraph 20(1)(f), for example, permits a deduction for discounts, which are one-half deductible in the case of so-called deep discounts (where the discount exceeds 3 per cent of the principal amount or the return on the discount exceeds 4/3 of the interest payable on the face value of the debt obligation) and fully deductible otherwise.[43] In addition, paragraph 20(1)(e.1) allows taxpayers to deduct certain guarantee fees and other transactions costs incurred to borrow money or reschedule a debt used for the purpose of earning taxable income from a business or property. Similarly, paragraph 20(1)(e.2) permits a deduction for premiums on life insurance policies that are required as collateral for a loan, provided that the interest on the loan is deductible in computing the taxpayer's income,[44] while paragraph 20(1)(g) allows corporate taxpayers to deduct fees to

---

[42]   See Brian Carr, "Interest Deductibility — Corporate Tax Planning" (2003) 51 Can. Tax J. 1422-1449.

[43]   Since most discounts are fully taxable to the recipient under para. 12(1)(c) or subs. 16(1), (2), or (3), critics have questioned the asymmetry of the limited deduction for deep discount debt obligations under para. 20(1)(f). See Peter W. Hogg, Joanne E. Magee, and Ted Cook, *Principles of Canadian Income Tax Law*, 3d ed. (Toronto: Carswell, 1999) at 237.

[44]   This provision, which applies to premiums payable after 1989, reverses the results in *Equitable Acceptance Corporation Ltd. v. M.N.R.*, [1964] C.T.C. 74, 64 D.T.C. 5045 (Ex. Ct.) and *Antoine*

list their shares on a stock exchange, amounts paid or payable to third parties to transfer the taxpayer's shares or remit dividends to shareholders, and expenses incurred in the year to print and issue a financial report to shareholders and other persons entitled by law to receive the report.

More generally, paragraph 20(1)(e) permits taxpayers to deduct amounts that are not otherwise deductible and are expenses incurred in the year or a preceding taxation year:

(i)   in the course of an issuance or sale of units of the taxpayer where the taxpayer is a unit trust, of interests in a partnership or syndicate by the partnership or syndicate, as the case may be, or of shares of the capital stock of the taxpayer,

(ii)   in the course of a borrowing of money used by the taxpayer for the purpose of earning income from a business or property (other than money used by the taxpayer for the purpose of acquiring property the income from which would be exempt),

(ii.1) in the course of incurring indebtedness that is an amount payable for property acquired for the purpose of gaining or producing income therefrom or for the purpose of gaining or producing income from a business (other than property the income from which would be exempt or property that is an interest in a life insurance policy), or

(ii.2) in the course of a rescheduling or restructuring of a debt obligation of the taxpayer or an assumption of a debt obligation by the taxpayer, where the debt obligation is

(A)   in respect of a borrowing described in subparagraph (ii), or

(B)   in respect of an amount payable described in subparagraph (ii.1),

and, in the case of a rescheduling or restructuring, the rescheduling or restructuring, as the case may be, provides for the modification of the terms or conditions of the debt obligation or conditions of the debt obligation or the conversion or substitution of the debt obligation to or with a share or another debt obligation.

For the purpose of this provision, moreover, deductible expenses specifically include "a commission, fee, or other amount paid or payable for or on account of services rendered by a person as a salesperson, agent or dealer in securities in the course of the issuance, sale or borrowing," and specifically exclude amounts paid or payable as or on account of interest or principal,[45] and amounts that are contingent or dependent on the use of, or production from, property, or

---

Guertin Ltée v. Canada, [1987] F.C.J. No. 1023, [1988] 1 C.T.C. 360, 88 D.T.C. 6126 (F.C.A.), in which such premiums were held to be non-deductible under para. 20(1)(e) and its predecessor para. 11(1)(cb) of the 1952 Act.

[45] For this purpose, subs. 248(1) defines a "principal amount" in relation to any obligation as "the amount that, under the terms of the obligation or any agreement relating thereto, is the maximum amount or maximum total amount, as the case may be, payable on account of the obligation by the issuer thereof, otherwise than as or on account of interest or as or on account of any premium payable by the issuer conditional on the exercise by the issuer of a right to redeem the obligation before the maturity thereof."

"computed by reference to revenue, profit, cash flow, commodity price or any other similar criterion or by reference to dividends paid or payable to shareholders of any class of shares of the capital stock of a corporation."[46] Since 1988, this deduction must be spread over a five-year period, with one-fifth of the amount deductible in each year.[47]

Paragraph 20(1)(e) was originally enacted in 1955 as paragraph 11(1)(cb) of the 1952 *Income Tax Act*. According to the Minister of Finance at the time, the provision was intended "to allow as a business expense the costs incidental to borrowing money and issuing shares" (House of Commons, *Debates*, April 5, 1955, at 2737). In 1978, the provision was broadened to include commissions, fees, or other amounts on account of "services rendered by a person as a salesperson, agent or dealer in securities in the course of the issuance, sale or borrowing," which previously had been expressly excluded from the deduction. The exclusion of amounts that are "contingent or dependent on the use of, or production from, property" and amounts "computed by reference to revenue, profit, cash flow, commodity price or any other similar criterion or by reference to dividends paid or payable to shareholders of any class of shares of the capital stock of a corporation" applies after November 1999.[48]

A key requirement in the application of paragraph 20(1)(e) is that the expense be incurred "in the course of" specific kinds of financing listed in subparagraphs 20(1)(e)(i) to (ii.2). The meaning of these words in the context of former paragraph 11(1)(cb) was considered in *M.N.R. v. Yonge-Eglinton Building Ltd.*, [1974] F.C.J. No. 84, [1974] C.T.C. 209, 74 D.T.C. 6180 (F.C.A.). Although the participating payments at issue in the case are now expressly excluded from the deduction in paragraph 20(1)(e), the case remains a leading statement on the kinds of expenses the deduction of which is permitted under paragraph 20(1)(e).

M.N.R. v. Yonge-Eglinton Building Ltd.
[1974] F.C.J. No. 84, [1974] C.T.C. 209, 74 D.T.C. 6180 (F.C.A.)

[To help finance the construction of an office building, the respondent obtained interim financing from Traders Realty Ltd. in 1962 in the amount of $6,500,000, undertaking (1) to pay interest at 9 per cent, (2) to pay 1 per cent of its gross

---

[46] Under the concept of interest adopted in *Sherway Centre Ltd. v. Canada*, [1998] F.C.J No. 149, [1998] 2 C.T.C. 343, 98 D.T.C. 6121 (F.C.A.), these amounts could be deducted under subpara. 20(1)(c)(i) as interest expenses.

[47] See subparas. 20(1)(e)(iii) and (iv). This five-year amortization period was introduced in 1988 in order to "achieve a better matching of expenses and revenues" (Canada, Department of Finance, *White Paper: Tax Reform 1987* (Ottawa: Department of Finance, June 18, 1987)).

[48] According to explanatory information accompanying the announcement of this amendment, the exclusion is intended to "clarify" that the provision does not apply to "profit participation and similar payments," which are either deductible as interest under para. 20(1)(c) or non-deductible payments of principal according to the definition of "principal amount" in subs. 248(1).

rental revenue for 25 years, and (3) to sell to Traders some of its capital stock at a nominal price. In fact, only $900,000 was borrowed from Traders and the line of credit was used as collateral to borrow the needed money from the bank. In issue was whether the respondent was permitted to deduct the payments made to Traders in 1965 to 1968 at the rate of 1 per cent of gross revenue. The Federal Court Trial Division held that the payments were deductible. The Minister appealed.]

THURLOW, J: ... I am ... of the opinion ... that the obligation to pay the amounts in question was ... of a capital nature the deduction of which is prohibited by paragraph 12(1)(b) [now paragraph 18(1)(b)].

It remains therefore to consider whether the amounts fall within and are deductible under paragraph 11(1)(cb) [now paragraph 20(1)(e)]. This paragraph, which was enacted in 1955, expands into another area the deductibility of expenses relating to capital used for the purpose of gaining or producing income which had formerly been provided under paragraphs 11(1)(c) and 11(1)(ca) [now paragraphs 20(1)(c) and (d)] only for interest and compound interest payable in respect of such capital.

...

The Minister's position, as I understand it, is not that the amounts were not expenses of borrowing money but that in order to qualify for deduction the expense must be one that is incurred at or around the time the borrowing takes place and that here the liability to pay the amounts was not incurred in the course of the borrowing but in years after the borrowing took place upon profits being earned from the operation of the building.

...

The respondent's position on the other hand is that the obligation to pay the amounts are expenses that arose in the course of borrowing the money to construct the building but that they could not be regarded as having been incurred until the years in which by reason of the respondent having a net profit from its operation the amount of such expense could be ascertained, that paragraph 1l(1)(cb) does not require that to be deductible the expense must be incurred in the year when the borrowing occurs and that the amounts in question accordingly fall within subparagraph (ii). ...

The general area of what is comprehended in subparagraph ... (ii) of paragraph 11(1)(cb) is I think indicated by the scope of what is expressly excluded ... for the fact that it was considered expedient to expressly exclude ... payments as or on account of principal or interest, to my mind, shows that what is referred to as "an expense incurred in the year" in the course of issuing or selling shares or borrowing money for the purpose referred to is capable of embracing a broad class of expenditures for such purposes. The easiest cases to think of are professional fees for necessary documentation and fees for registering documents but the wording is not confined to these or like expenses and to my mind it involves no stretch of the language used to treat it as including amounts of the kind here in question. I also think these amounts are to be regarded as expenses "incurred in the year" in which they became payable. The difficulty is with the wording "in the course of borrowing money" in the context of "an expense incurred in the year in the course of borrowing money" etc.

On this point I am of the opinion that the Minister's position is not sound. It does not seem to me to be a sensible or practical interpretation (and counsel for the Minister did not so contend) to hold that the deduction can only be made when the taxation year in which shares are issued or sold or money is borrowed is the same as that in which the expense is incurred because such a construction would arbitrarily exclude the deduction, for example, of professional fees incurred in connection with a share issue or a borrowing in a taxation year prior to the share issue or borrowing. It would also exclude the deduction, again for example, of expenses for formal documentation contemplated by the arrangements but incurred in a taxation year after that in which money has been borrowed on the strength of temporary or informal arrangements. There seems to be no good reason based on the language of the statute why the expenses referred to in either example should be excluded. But the Minister's suggestion that the incurring of the expense must be at or around the time of the issuing or selling or the borrowing if it is to be "in the course of the issuing or selling or borrowing appears to me to leave the deductibility of such expenses subject to a vague and uncertain test. It would be untenable if it meant that the expense must be incurred in the taxation year of the issuing or selling or borrowing and since it is impossible to know what is included in "around the time" it seems to me to be untenable on that basis as well. What appears to me to be the test is whether the expense, in whatever taxation year it occurs, arose from the issuing or selling or borrowing. It may not always be easy to decide whether an expense has so arisen but it seems to me that the words "in the course of in paragraph 11(1)(cb) are not a reference to the time when the expenses are incurred but are used in the sense of "in connection with" or "incidental to" or "arising from" and refer to the process of carrying out or the things which must be undertaken to carry out the issuing or selling or borrowing for or in connection with which the expenses are incurred. In my opinion therefore since the amounts here in question arose from and were incidental to the borrowing of money required to finance the construction of the respondent's building they fall within subparagraph 11(1)(cb)(ii) [now subparagraph 20(1)(e)(ii)] as expenses incurred in the year in the course of borrowing money etc.

...

LACROIX DJ (concurring): ... [I]n my view it is difficult not to say that this expense was incurred or that financial burden was assumed or accepted by the taxpayer, in the course of borrowing money for the purpose of earning income from a business or property, according ... to the terms of subparagraph (11)(1)(cb)(ii). ... The obligation arose with the agreement, but the expenses or part of the price or cost to be paid could naturally only be ascertained in the years when the rentals were being paid and consequently the expense or part of the price should be deducted in the year they were incurred.

...

SWEET DJ (dissenting): ... It occurs to me that the expenses dealt with in paragraph (cb) might merely be those incidental costs often incurred by a borrower, for example, professional fees, and not extended periodical payments here. However that was not a contention of the appellant and was not put in issue. In any event in the view which I take I need not decide it and I do not. I proceed to deal with the matter as though the amounts in question are "expenses" within the meaning of the paragraph.

...

The respondent's obligation to make the expenditures arose pursuant to the Traders agreement dated "as of the 3rd day of July 1962." As I see it, then, the Traders agreement would be said to have been entered into in the course of borrowing and the respondent's obligations under that agreement created in the course of borrowing. However the agreement to make an expenditure under certain circumstances in the future and the expenditure itself if and when those circumstances arise are not the same thing.

Since the last borrowing from Traders was on December 23, 1964 and the first year in which any such expense was incurred was 1965 those expenses, having been incurred after the last instalment had been lent, could not, in my opinion be said to have been incurred in the course of borrowing.

Had Parliament intended that all expenses incurred pursuant to an agreement made in the course of borrowing money be deductible it could, easily enough, have said just that. However that it did not say. By its wording paragraph (cb) refers only to expenses incurred in the course of borrowing.

I would allow this appeal with costs here and below.

Appeal dismissed.

NOTES AND QUESTIONS

1.   In *Yonge-Eglinton*, how did Thurlow J interpret the requirement in then paragraph 1l(1)(cb) (now paragraph 20(1)(e)) that the financing expense be incurred "in the course of borrowing money"? How did Sweet DJ (dissenting) interpret this requirement? With which interpretation, if either, do you agree? Why?

2.   *Yonge-Eglinton* was followed in *Sherway Centre Ltd. v. Canada*, [1996] T.C.J. No. 844, [1996] 3 C.T.C. 2687 (T.C.C.), aff'd [1998] F.C.J. No. 149, [1998] 2 C.T.C. 343, 98 D.T.C. 6121 (F.C.A.), in which "participating interest payments" like those in *Yonge-Eglinton* were held to be deductible under paragraph 20(1)(e). At the Federal Court of Appeal, however, the payments were also held to be deductible interest under subparagraph 20(1)(c)(i).

3.   In *Riviera Hotel Co. Ltd. v. M.N.R.*, [1972] F.C.J. No. 50, [1972] C.T.C. 157, 72 D.T.C. 6142 (F.C.T.D.), the taxpayer, which paid $13,108 to discharge a first mortgage prior to maturity in order to borrow additional capital to expand its hotel, sought to deduct the penalty under former subparagraph 11(1)(cb)(ii) (now subparagraph 20(1)(e)(ii)) as an expense incurred in the course of borrowing money used for the purpose of gaining or producing taxable income. Characterizing the payment as "an expense incurred in the course of repaying the money borrowed from the first lender" (at para. 28), not an expense incurred in the course of borrowing money, the court disallowed the deduction. See also *Neonex International Ltd. v. Canada*, [1978] F.C.J. No. 514, [1978] C.T.C. 485, 78 D.T.C. 6339 (F.C.A.), in which a similar payment was characterized as a non-deductible expense incurred by the taxpayer "to rid itself of the first lender," not "in the course of borrowing money from ... the second lender" (at para. 28). For payments made after 1984, subsection 18(9.1) reverses the results in *Riviera Hotel* and *Neonex International* by deeming as interest any amount paid in order to obtain a reduction in the rate of interest payable on a debt obligation or as a penalty or bonus on the repayment of a debt obligation before its maturity, to the extent that the payment relates to and does not exceed the amount of interest that would otherwise have been paid or payable on the debt obligation, provided that the payment cannot:

(a)   reasonably be considered to have been made in respect of the extension of the term of a debt obligation or in respect of the substitution or conversion of a debt obligation to another debt obligation or share,

and is not

(b)   contingent or dependent on the use of or production from property or ... computed by reference to revenue, profit, cash flow, commodity price or any other similar criterion or by reference to dividends paid or payable to shareholders of any class of shares of the capital stock of a corporation.

According to paragraph 7 of IT-104R3:

Subsection 18(9.1) applies in certain cases to a penalty or bonus payable by reason of the repayment before maturity of all or part of the principal of an outstanding debt obligation. It may also apply to a fee or penalty paid to reduce the rate of interest payable on such an obligation. These amounts are considered prepaid interest and, provided the other requirements of paragraph 20(1)(c) are satisfied, are deductible in computing a taxpayer's income from business or property over the period that the interest rate is to be reduced, or over the period that would have been (but for the prepayment) the remaining term of the debt obligation.

4.   In *Cara Operations Ltd. v. M.N.R.*, [1973] C.T.C. 2296, 73 D.T.C. 241 (T.R.B.) the taxpayer, which issued new shares when it converted from a private to a public company, sought to deduct as financing costs under then subparagraph 11(1)(cb)(i) (now subparagraph 20(1)(e)(i)) a transfer fee that it was required to pay to the Ontario Liquor Licence Board based on a percentage change in the ownership of the company's shares. Rejecting the taxpayer's argument that the expression "in the course of issuing shares" is "a flexible

expression" including "expenses which are a necessary incident to the issuance of shares" (at para. 22), the board disallowed the deduction on the grounds (at para. 23) that the provision applies only to "expenses which are inherent and essential to the actual issue of the shares and ... not ... expenses which are only consequential or resulting from the issue." Is this decision consistent with the broad approach to the interpretation of then subparagraph 11(1)(cb)(ii) in *M.N.R. v. Yonge-Eglinton Building Ltd.*, [1974] C.T.C. 209, 74 D.T.C. 6180 (F.C.A.)?

5. In *Burrard Dry Dock Company Ltd. v. M.N.R.*, [1975] C.T.C. 2011, 75 D.T.C. 22 (T.R.B.), the taxpayer incurred legal and accounting expenses in effecting a reorganization of its capital structure in order to allow it to issue new shares in the form of stock dividends paid to existing shareholders. Even though the reorganization did not increase the company's capital, but permitted it to distribute corporate surplus in the form of stock dividends, the court allowed the deduction of these expenses under then subparagraph 11(1)(cb)(i) (now subparagraph 20(1)(e)(i)) on the basis that the expenses were incurred "in the course of issuing shares."

6. In *MacMillan Bloedel Ltd. v. M.N.R.*, [1990] F.C.J. No. 200, [1990] C.T.C. 468, 90 D.T.C. 6219 (F.C.T.D.), the taxpayer, which borrowed US funds for the purpose of earning income in Canada, incurred a loss on foreign exchange contracts designed to hedge against fluctuations in the value of the Canadian dollar. Characterizing the loss as an expense of borrowing the US funds, the Court allowed the taxpayer to deduct the loss on the basis (at para. 44) that "it seems to fall clearly within subparagraph 20(1)(e)(ii)." Do you agree with this conclusion? Why or why not?

7. In *Canada v. MerBan Capital Corporation Ltd.*, [1989] F.C.J. No. 712, [1989] 2 C.T.C. 246, 89 D.T.C. 5404 (F.C.A.), the taxpayer was required to pay interest to the Toronto-Dominion Bank pursuant to an agreement whereby the bank loaned funds to a subsidiary of the taxpayer on the condition, *inter alia*, that the taxpayer would guarantee to pay interest up to $500,000 should the subsidiary be unable to make these payments. Rejecting the taxpayer's arguments that the payments were deductible as interest expenses or financing expenses, the court disallowed the deduction on the grounds that the payments were not legal interest on funds borrowed by the taxpayer as required by subparagraph 20(1)(c)(i) and that the borrowed funds were not used by the taxpayer for the purpose of earning income as required by subparagraph 20(1)(e)(ii). Do you agree with these conclusions? Why or why not?

8. For the CRA's views on paragraphs 20(1)(e), (e.1), (e.2), and (f), see *Interpretation Bulletin* IT-341R3, "Expenses of Issuing or Selling Shares, Units in a Trust, Interests in a Partnership or Syndicate and Expenses of Borrowing Money," November 29, 1995.

V. TIMING ISSUES

As with the computation of a taxpayer's income from an office or employment, the final task in computing a taxpayer's income from a business or property is to determine the taxation year in which specific amounts must be included and may be deducted. Unlike income from an office or employment, though, which is generally computed on a cash basis, with amounts included when actually received and deductible when paid, business income is typically computed on an accrual basis, according to which revenues are included in computing a taxpayer's income in the taxation year in which they are earned, even if they have not been received, and expenses are deducted in the taxation year in which they are incurred, even if they have not been paid.[49] While interest and rental income are also generally included on an accrual basis, however, other amounts are included in computing a taxpayer's income from a business or property only when they are received.[50] Other rules defer the taxation year in which specific kinds of expenditures may be deducted in computing a taxpayer's income from a business or property (see the discussions of inventory costs, capital expenses, and prepaid expenses in subsection B, infra), while yet others permit taxpayers to deduct specific amounts in respect of amounts that were previously included in computing their income from a business or property (see the discussions of reserves and bad debts in subsection B, infra).

This section considers timing issues in the computation of a taxpayer's income from a business or property, examining statutory and judicial rules governing the allocation of revenues and expenditures to specific taxation years.[51] Subsection A considers the taxation year in which amounts must be included in computing a taxpayer's income from a business or property. Subsection B reviews rules governing the taxation year in which allowable expenditures may be deducted in computing a taxpayer's income from a business or property.

---

[49] Notwithstanding this general approach, taxpayers may employ another method of computing income where it portrays a "truer picture" of the taxpayer's income for the year. See, for example, *Publishers Guild of Canada Ltd. v. M.N.R.*, [1956] Ex. C.J. No. 6, [1957] C.T.C. 1, (1956) 57 D.T.C. 1017 (Ex. Ct.); *Brown v. M.N.R.*, [1961] C.T.C. 432, 61 D.T.C. 1255 (Ex. Ct.); and *Boosey & Hawkes (Canada) Ltd. v. M.N.R.*, [1984] C.T.C. 2871, 84 D.T.C. 1728 (T.C.C.). In addition to this judicial principle, s. 28 of the Act explicitly allows taxpayers to compute income from a farming or fishing business on a cash basis.

[50] In addition to the exception for a farming and fishing business in s. 28 of the Act, see the statutory inclusions for royalties in para. 12(1)(g), for dividends in para.s 12(1)(j) and (k), and for inducements, refunds, reimbursements, and allowances in para. 12(1)(x).

[51] For a useful introduction to these timing issues, see Peter W. Hogg, Joanne E. Magee, and Ted Cook, *Principles of Canadian Income Tax Law*, 3d ed. (Toronto: Carswell, 1999) Chapter 11. For a more extensive, though now somewhat dated, analysis, see Brian J. Arnold, *Timing and Income Taxation: The Principles of Income Measurement for Tax Purposes*, Canadian Tax Paper No. 71 (Toronto: Canadian Tax Foundation, 1983) .

A. Inclusions

The statutory starting point for determining the taxation year in which amounts must be included in computing a taxpayer's income from a business or employment is section 9 of the Act, which defines a taxpayer's income for a taxation year from a business or property in subsection 9(1) as "the taxpayer's profit from that business or property for the year" and a taxpayer's loss for a taxation year from a business or property in subsection 9(2) as "the taxpayer's loss, if any, for the taxation year from that source computed by applying the provisions of this Act respecting computation of income from that source with such modifications as the circumstances require." In addition to these basic rules, however, section 12 contains a number of additional rules, the most important of which require taxpayers to include:

•   unearned amounts that are "received by the taxpayer in the year in the course of a business" (paragraph 12(1)(a));

•   amounts that are "receivable by the taxpayer in respect of property sold or services rendered in the course of a business in the year, notwithstanding that the amount or any part thereof is not due until a subsequent year, unless the method adopted by the taxpayer for computing income from the business and accepted for the purpose of [part I of the Act] does not require the taxpayer to include any amount receivable in computing the taxpayer's income for a taxation year unless it has been received in the year" (paragraph 12(1)(b));

•   amounts that are "received or receivable by the taxpayer in the year (depending on the method regularly followed by the taxpayer in computing the taxpayer's income) as, on account of, in lieu of payment of or in satisfaction of, interest to the extent that the interest was not included in computing the taxpayer's income for a preceding taxation year" (paragraph 12(1)(c));

•   amounts "received by the taxpayer in the year" that were "dependent on the use of or production from property" (paragraph 12(1)(g));

•   amounts "received by the taxpayer in the year as, on account or in lieu of payment of, or in satisfaction of," dividends of resident and non-resident corporations (paragraphs 12(1)(j) and (k) and sections 82 and 90);

•   amounts "received by the taxpayer in the year, in the course of earning income from a business or property" as an inducement, or as a refund, reimbursement, contribution, or allowance, or as assistance in respect of an outlay or expense or an amount included in, or deducted as, the cost of property (paragraph 12(1)(x)); and

•   interest income that has accrued during the year, regardless of whether it has been received or is receivable, to the extent that the interest was not included in computing the taxpayer's income for the year or a preceding taxation year (subsections 12(3), (4), (9), and (11), and regulation 7000).

Other rules allow taxpayers to claim deductions in respect of some of these inclusions, thereby deferring their effective inclusion until a subsequent taxation year.[52]

For our purposes, there is no need to examine each of these statutory rules in detail, several of which employ the same concept of an amount "received" in the year that appears in statutory provisions governing the inclusion of amounts in computing a taxpayer's income for a taxation year from an office or employment.[53] To the extent that the inclusion of other amounts in computing a taxpayer's income for a taxation year from a business or property depends on general principles governing the computation of a taxpayer's "profit" or "loss" for the taxation year or on the concept of an amount "receivable" in the year, however, these merit further examination. An excellent discussion of these concepts appears in *West Kootenay Power & Light Co. v. M.N.R.*, [1991] F.C.J. No. 1263, [1992] 1 C.T.C. 15, 92 D.T.C. 6023 (F.C.A.).

West Kootenay Power & Light Co. v. M.N.R.
[1991] F.C.J. No. 1263, [1992] 1 C.T.C. 15, 92 D.T.C. 6023 (F.C.A.)

MacGUIGAN, JA (Heald and Hugessen, JJA concurring): The issue in this case is one of tax timing: whether estimates of unbilled revenue at December 31, the end of the taxpayer appellant's taxation year, must be included in its income from business in that year.

I

The appellant is an investor-owned corporation engaged in the business of generating and distributing hydro-electric power in southeastern British Columbia and subject to regulation, including as to its rates, by the British Columbia Utilities Commission ("the BCUC"). Its residential customers were on a two-month billing cycle, and meter readings were made on a bi-monthly basis.

---

[52] See, for example, the deduction in respect of unearned amounts in para. 20(1)(m), the deduction for deferred payments in para. 20(1)(n), and the deductions for doubtful and bad debts in paras. 20(1)(l) and (p). These provisions are examined in subsection B, infra.

[53] See section V of Chapter 4. For a leading decision on the concept of an "amount received," see *Kenneth B.S. Robertson Ltd. v. M.N.R.*, [1944] Ex. C.J. No. 6, [1944] C.T.C. 75, 2 D.T.C. 655 (Ex. Ct.) (distinguishing between non-taxable advances and deposits, and taxable receipts to which the recipient's right is "absolute and under no restriction, contractual or otherwise, as to its disposition, use or enjoyment"). For other cases in which amounts "received" by a taxpayer in the course of a business have been held to be non-taxable deposits, see *Dominion Taxicab Assn. v. M.N.R.*, [1954] S.C.J. No. 4, [1954] C.T.C. 34, 54 D.T.C. 1020 (S.C.C.); *M.N.R. v. Atlantic Engine Rebuilders Ltd.*, [1967] S.C.J. No. 36, [1967] C.T.C. 230, 67 D.T.C. 5155 (S.C.C.); *Riverview Development (Ottawa) Ltd. v. M.N.R.*, [1967] Tax ABC 115 (T.A.B.); *Dartmouth Developments Ltd. v. M.N.R.*, [1968] Tax ABC 188 (T.A.B.); and *Canada v. Imperial General Properties*, [1985] 1 C.T.C. 40, 85 D.T.C. 5045 (F.C.A.).

At the relevant fiscal year-ends, 1983 and 1984, the appellant had delivered some electricity for which, as of those year-ends, the customers had not yet been billed. In fact, the BCUC-approved tariff did not permit the appellant to issue bills for electricity supplied to December 31 until the completion of the billing cycle ending after that date.

Until 1979, the accounting practice followed by the appellant did not take account of unbilled revenue, but in that year, on the advice of accountants, the appellant changed its practice and recorded income based on estimates of the revenue anticipated to be received, both for financial statements of its operation and for tax purposes. This accrual basis was continued through 1982.

In 1983, while maintaining the accrual basis for calculating income for its annual statements, the appellant changed from an accrual to a "billed" basis for its income tax return, eliminating from its income the estimate of revenue unbilled at year-end, and reported revenues only as billed.

The estimated sale price of the delivered but as yet unbilled electricity at year-end was $3,919,176 as of the end of 1983, and $3,874,834 as of the end of 1984 ("the unbilled revenue"). This unbilled revenue was added to the appellant's income by the Minister of National Revenue for the 1983 and 1984 taxation years by reassessments dated May 21, 1987.

The impact of generally accepted accounting principles ("GAAP") on this fact situation was partially covered by the partial agreed statement of facts, as follows ... :

> 3. Under generally accepted accounting principles as applied to the particular facts of this case, it would be acceptable to treat the unbilled revenues in either of the following ways:
>
> (a) either the plaintiff could include the unbilled revenues as of year-end in its computation of income for financial statement purposes (as the plaintiff in fact did in its Financial Statements for the years in issue); or
>
> (b) the plaintiff could exclude the unbilled revenue as of year-end from its computation of income for financial statement purposes. If the plaintiff chose this second option, the unbilled revenues would be included in the computation of its income for financial statement purposes in the following year when the amounts were billed and recorded as accounts receivable.
>
> 4. Under generally accepted accounting principles accounting policies followed by an enterprise should be consistent within each accounting period and from one period to the next. Changes in accounting policy should be made in a manner consistent with section 1506 of the Canadian Institute of Chartered Accountants Handbook, a copy of which is annexed hereto.
>
> ...

The relevant part of section 1506 of the *CICA Handbook*, section 1506.02, is as follows:

CHANGE IN AN ACCOUNTING POLICY

Accounting policies encompass the specific principles and the methods used in their application that are selected by an enterprise in preparing financial statements. There is a general presumption that the accounting policies followed by an enterprise are consistent within each accounting period and from one period to the next. A change in an accounting policy may be made, however, to conform to new Handbook Recommendations, Accounting Guidelines published by the Accounting Standards Steering Committee, Abstracts of Issues Discussed by the CICA Emerging Issues Committee or legislative requirements or if it is considered that the change would result in a more appropriate presentation of events or transactions in the financial statements of the enterprise.

The relevant provisions of the *Income Tax Act* ... are as follows:

9. (1) Subject to this Part, a taxpayer's income for a taxation year from a business or property is his profit therefrom for the year.

12. (1) There shall be included in computing the income of a taxpayer for a taxation year as income from a business or property such of the following amounts as are applicable: ...

    (b) any amount receivable by the taxpayer in respect of property sold or services rendered in the course of a business in the year, notwithstanding that the amount or any part thereof is not due until a subsequent year, unless the method adopted by the taxpayer for computing income from the business and accepted for the purpose of this Part does not require him to include any amount receivable in computing his income for a taxation year unless it has been received in the year, and for the purposes of this paragraph, an amount shall be deemed to have become receivable in respect of services rendered in the course of a business on the day that is the earlier of

        (i) the day upon which the account in respect of the services was rendered, and

        (ii) the day upon which the account in respect of those services would have been rendered had there been no undue delay in rendering the account in respect of the services; ...

    (2) Paragraphs (1)(a) and (b) are enacted for greater certainty and shall not be construed as implying that any amount not referred to therein is not to be included in computing income from a business for a taxation year whether it is received or receivable in the year or not.

The appellant used two methods in estimating for its financial statements the amount of unbilled revenue. The first was the "prorate method," in which by means of a computer program each customer's account was computed on the basis of consumption to date, previous rates of consumption and allowances for changing weather conditions or other factors. The second method, used primarily for checking purposes, was the "gross load method," in which an amount was determined based on production output to December 31, reduced by estimated line losses for energy lost in transmission.

MacKay, J at trial found as follows on the facts ... :

> ... While it would be possible in a theoretical sense to determine actual amounts owned to that date by "unbilled" customers, I accept that it was not possible in any reasonable, practical sense to do so. ... Thus, I accept that revenue attributable to unbilled accounts at year end could only be estimated on a reasonable basis without pretence that the estimate was accurate for any customer or for all customers.

This finding as to unbilled revenue does not, of course, determine the issue.

The trial judge went on to state the issue as he saw it... :

> In essence the issue presented by argument of the parties is whether a taxpayer who uses the accrual method of accounting for revenues, in accordance with GAAP, for purposes of its financial statements and general accounting, can utilize another method of accounting also consistent with GAAP, for purposes of its reporting for income tax purposes. Counsel for the Crown acknowledged that if in 1983 the company had reverted to its practice prior to 1979, accounting for revenues on the billed account basis for purposes of both its financial statements and its reporting for income tax purposes, the issue presented by the Minister's reassessments would not have been raised.

Since he analyzed the issue in terms of consistency between the financial statement and the tax return, the trial judge devoted a great deal of attention to the evidence of a chartered accountant, Dennis Culver, given on behalf of the respondent.

[Although MacGuigan JA uses the word "consistency" throughout the judgment when referring to this principle, most of the literature on this topic uses the word "conformity" to distinguish this principle from the principle of "consistency" expressed in section 1506.02 of the *CICA Handbook*, according to which the accounting practices followed by an enterprise should, subject to various exceptions stated in the rule, be consistent from one accounting period to the next. See, for example, Brian J. Arnold, "Conformity Between Financial Statements and Tax Accounting" (1981), vol. 29, no. 4 *Canadian Tax Journal* 476; Glen E. Cronkwright, "The Dilemma of Conformity: Tax and Financial Reporting — A Perspective from the Private Sector," in *Current Developments in Measuring Business Income for Tax Purposes*, 1981 Corporate Management Tax Conference (Toronto: Canadian Tax Foundation, 1981), 22; Barrie M. Philp, "Is It Time To Place More Reliance on GAAP?" in *Report of Proceedings of the Forty-Third Tax Conference*, 1991 Conference Report (Toronto: Canadian Tax Foundation, 1992), 25:1-55, at 25:12-15.]

Culver relied in particular on the *CICA Handbook*, section 1506.02, cited above. The trial judge summarizes Culver's evidence as follows ... :

> In the opinion of Mr. Culver the change in method of calculating revenue for income tax purposes only, while retaining the accrual method for financial statement purposes, was akin to trying to ride "two GAAP horses at one time." Having adopted the accrual method for accounting for financial statement purposes, Mr. Culver's opinion was that it would be inconsistent with GAAP to utilize another method, and that the method adopted for basic financial purposes is then applicable for all other financial reporting purposes for the same period.

In arriving at the applicable law, the trial judge followed the decision of Reed, J in *Maritime Telegraph and Telephone Co. v. Canada*, [1991] 1 CTC 28, 91 DTC 5038, where the corporate taxpayer, whose business was the provision of telephone and other telecommunication services, adopted for tax purposes the "billed" method of reporting income, although for general accounting purposes and for reporting to its regulator agency it continued to use the accrual method. Reed, J held that unbilled but earned revenues are not receivables under paragraph 12(1)(b) of the Act, but are caught rather under subsection 9(1), since this method gives a truer picture of income for the year then the alternative method.

MacKay, J therefore concluded ... :

> If the exclusion of unbilled revenue in accounting for profits for tax purposes is not required by the Act, is there a basis for support of the plaintiff's position that its exclusion, following a method consistent with one phase of generally accepted accounting principles, is permissible under the Act? The expert evidence of Mr. Culver, questioned but maintained in cross-examination, was clearly to the effect that adopting one method for financial statement accounts and another for reporting income for tax purposes is not supportable under GAAP, for that does not comply with the principle of consistency, particularly section 1506.02, applicable within each accounting period and from one period to the next. Further, the principles underlying the decisions of the Court of Appeal in *Neonex International Ltd. v. The Queen* [[1978] CTC 485; 78 CTC 6339 (FCA)], and *Canada v. Cyprus Anvil Mining Corporation* [[1990] 1 CTC 153; 90 CTC 6063 (FCA)], in my view, support the conclusion that the Act does not permit reporting revenues for tax purposes on a different basis than that adopted for purposes of accurately portraying the financial picture of a company for shareholders and creditors, aside from provisions of the Act which specifically require different treatment. In *Neonex*, in relation to claimed deductibility of expenses incurred in making unfinished signs under contract for payment upon completion, the Court relied on the principle of matching expenses and revenues to preclude a different treatment for tax purposes than that followed by the company in financial statements prepared for shareholders and general public purposes. In *Cyprus Anvil*, relying on the principle requiring consistency in accounting, the Court precluded calculation of profit on a basis different for tax purposes from that followed for the corporation's own financial accounting in a tax exempt period which affected the tax situation of the company in the succeeding period. While the facts of both cases are easily distinguished from the case before this Court, the general principle supports the conclusion set out that the Act does not permit reporting for tax purposes as the plaintiff here seeks to do. That conclusion is also supported by the interpretation of subsection 12(2) together with subsection 9(1) in the decision of Madame Justice Reed in *Maritime Telegraph*.

> I conclude that the *Income Tax Act* does not require or permit a taxpayer to account for revenues, and thus profits, on a billed basis for a taxation year when at the same time it accounts for financial statement purposes on an earned or accrued basis, including estimates of unbilled revenue in its account at year end. It may well be that the taxpayer could opt to calculate income on the billed basis, at least in the plaintiff's industry where either of the two treatments appears to be followed by individual companies, assuming appropriate reasons for so doing are supportable within GAAP, if it does so for purposes of both financial statements and for reporting for income tax purposes. That would simply put the plaintiff in this case in the same position that it followed prior to 1979.

II

In the submission of the appellant, the trial judge erred in two respects: (1) in deciding that the estimates of unbilled revenue were revenue for income tax purposes, ... and (2) in deciding that profit for tax purposes must be computed on the same basis used for computing profit for general financial purposes, even though there are two alternative generally accepted accounting principles. I shall deal with these errors in reverse order.

...

The trial judge cited *Neonex International Ltd. v. The Queen*, [1978] CTC 485, 78 DTC 6339 and *Canada v. Cyprus Anvil Mining Corporation*, [1990] 1 CTC 153, 90 DTC 6063, in support of the principle of consistency. *Neonex* had to do with the deductibility of expenses incurred in making unfinished signs, and the trial judge accurately stated that "the Court relied on the principle of matching expenses and revenues." But with respect, that is not the same as the asserted principle of consistency, which must amount to a rule of law rather than a factual determination. In *Neonex*, Urie, JA wrote for the Court (at pages 500-501 (CTC 6349)):

> In my opinion, the method used by the appellant in calculating its taxable income neither accorded with generally accepted accounting principles nor with the proper method of computing income for tax purposes. ... The expenses incurred in connection with the partially completed signs were laid out to bring in income in the next or some other taxation year, not in the year in which they were claimed. As a result, the income of the appellant would not be portrayed fairly nor accurately if it were permitted to adopt this method for tax purposes while for the purposes of its own creditors and shareholders it used the generally accepted accounting method presumably because that method fairly and accurately provides them with the profit or loss information to which they are entitled.

The decision made by this Court in *Neonex* was in the interests of the fair and accurate presentation of the company's income, and was based upon a factual determination that a different method from that used in its financial statement would not on the facts portray its position fairly and accurately.

In *Cyprus Anvil* this Court applied a principle of consistency, but that principle related to the taxpayer's own previous tax returns as well as to its financial statements, and was based on sound business or commercial principles ... . This is a different concept, it seems to me, than the principle of consistency as between financial and tax statements. It has to do, rather, with fairly and accurately portraying income on the basis of sound business or commercial principles.

Again, in *Maritime Telegraph* Reed, J relied on the method which accords a "truer picture" of the company's income (at page 30 (CTC 5039)):

> It is clear from the evidence that both methods of accounting are in accordance with generally accepted accounting principles (GAAP). At the same time, while there is some evidence that the billed method is used by some utility companies, there was no evidence that any large Canadian telephone company uses the billed method for its general financial statements. Also, it is fair to conclude that the earned method accords a "truer" picture of the company's income for the year in question than does the billed method. The plaintiff is

engaged in providing a continuing service which by its very nature results in revenues accruing daily.

Apart from the judicial authorities, I find myself in agreement with the following analysis by Professor Brian J. Arnold, "Conformity Between Financial Statements and Tax Accounting" (1981), 29 *Can. Tax J* 476 at page 487, as to the policy considerations involved:

> Any requirement of conformity between financial statements and income tax accounting is undesirable basically for two reasons. First, it will result in distinctions in the tax burdens on taxpayers on the basis of a criterion that is largely irrelevant to the tax system. The determination of business profit in accordance with ordinary accounting principles and practices entitles taxpayers occasionally to choose between alternative methods or practices. If this flexibility is unacceptable for income tax purposes (and it is very questionable that it is unacceptable), detailed provisions of the Act should be adopted to prescribe the rules that must be used for computing tax profit. But requiring conformity between a taxpayer's financial statements and his tax return simply shifts the flexibility from the tax return to the financial statements. Taxpayers in the same situation should be treated in the same way for income tax purposes whether or not they happen to use different accounting methods and practices for financial statement purposes. Second, any conformity requirement will operate unevenly with respect to different types of taxpayers. Corporations whose financial statements must be audited or are required by legislative enactment to follow prescribed accounting practices and methods will have less flexibility in reporting their income for income tax purposes than private corporations or individuals who will be more able to adopt alternative accounting practices in their financial statements.

> Many accountants have expressed the view from time to time that a requirement of conformity between the computation of profit for income tax purposes and the computation of profit for financial accounting purposes would have the undesirable effect of constraining the development of generally accepted accounting principles. The pressure of the development of financial accounting will be even greater if there is a requirement of conformity between financial statements and tax reporting. In order to reduce taxes, owners and managers are likely to attempt to persuade accountants to prepare the financial statements of the business on a basis that results in less tax being paid but that does not result in the disclosure of the best or most reliable information to other users of the financial statements.

In my view, it would be undesirable to establish an absolute requirement that there must always be conformity between financial statements and tax returns, and I am satisfied that the cases do not do so. The approved principle is that whichever method presents the "truer picture" of a taxpayer's revenue, which more fairly and accurately portrays income, and which "matches" revenue and expenditure, if one method does, is the one that must be followed.

The result often will not be different from what it would be using a consistency principle, but the "truer picture" or "matching approach" is not absolute in its effect, and requires a close look at the facts of a taxpayer's situation.

Because the practical results of the two principles are so closely related, it may be that the trial judge implicitly reached a conclusion as to the application of the truer picture approach, even though he did not do so clearly and unequivocally. For instance, he said of Culver's testimony, which he clearly found persuasive as a whole ... :

From the examination and cross-examination of Mr. Culver I conclude the following. It is his view that the accrual method of accounting better reflects the financial situation of a corporation because it is intended to match expenditures with revenues, and thus net income, for a given period, consistent with one of the basic tenets of GAAP.

Culver himself was very directly on point in his expert report ... :

Faced with a choice between the alternative of accruing or not accruing the unbilled income, I would opt for the former. In my opinion, the accruing of unbilled income more closely matches the revenues of the organization with its relevant costs ... and therefore produces a more accurate determination of net income for a particular period.

This conclusion of Culver's is less significant than two admissions by Stephen A. Ash, the Vice President of Finance of, and the only witness called by, the appellant. The more general admission was made in the context of the 1979 change of policy with respect to unbilled revenues ... :

Q. Would it be fair to say that by taking into account the unbilled revenues, you would more accurately reflect the profit picture for the company during the fiscal period?

A. We were trying to reflect what the revenue would be — ultimately what the revenue would be in the fiscal year.

Q. And would that be more accurate if you included unbilled revenues than if you excluded them?

A. That's why we did it, yes.

...

Finally, there is an acknowledgement by Ash as to the appellant's primary motive in its 1979 change of policy, which I believe is tantamount to an acceptance that the accrual method presents a truer picture of the company's income ... :

Q. Why was the company seeking to improve its income for financial statement to [sic] purposes at that time, for whose benefit?

A. It was for the benefit of the shareholders and we were in a serious position of potentially recording losses. We had a serious concern that we would be unable to raise capital if we got into a worse position. So we were seeking ways to improve our earnings at that time.

On the basis of this evidence I can conclude only to the fact that, even in the opinion of the appellant's directing mind, the accrual method of accounting adopted in 1979 for both financial and tax purposes presented a truer picture of the appellant's revenue because it more accurately and fairly matched revenue and expenditure — this, despite the fact that the estimate of revenue for the "stub-end" of the year could be only an approximation of the actual revenue.

Although, in my view, the learned trial judge was in error as to the legal principle to be applied, the approach which I propose to this problem leads to the same result, one which I believe he reached implicitly and in any event one to which he would inevitably have come if he had clearly directed his mind to the question.

III

The principal question remaining is as to whether the unbilled revenues in question come under the provisions of paragraph 12(1)(b) of the Act as an amount receivable, and, if so, whether they are exempted from that provision by the unless clause.

The word "receivable" is nowhere defined in the Act. The respondent's witness Culver acknowledged that, under GAAP, unbilled revenue at the end of a year is not considered an amount receivable for that year ... . That is, of course, relevant, but not decisive, as to the legal concept.

In *Maritime Telegraph* Reed, J held that the unbilled telephone charges there were not receivable under paragraph 12(1)(b), and that the case should be decided under subsections 9(1) and 12(2) (at pages 31-32 (CTC 5040-41)):

> I do not think the unbilled but earned revenues are "receivable" in the sense governed by paragraph 12(1)(b). It seems to me that that paragraph refers to amounts which have been billed as is the case with "accounts receivable." The paragraph is particularly applicable to businesses who deal in the sale of goods or the sale of services when those services are performed at a discrete time or times. The business in which the plaintiff engages is not of this nature. The service it provides to its customers is a continuous one and its profit therefrom is earned on a continuous basis. ...
>
> The earned but unbilled revenues of the taxpayer at year end are brought into income pursuant to subsection 9(1) of the Act and there is no need to rely upon paragraph 12(1)(b) for this purpose.
>
> ...
>
> Lastly, it is my view that subsection 12(2) is pertinent. That subsection makes it very clear that paragraph 12(1)(b) is not to be construed as implying that amounts not referred to therein are "not to be included in computing income." It seems to me the taxpayer's argument in the present case would require one to ignore that directive.

The trial judge in the case at bar seems to have been in agreement with Reed, J.

The *locus classicus* for the concept of "receivable" is *Minister of National Revenue v. John Colford Contracting Co.*, [1960] CTC 178, 60 DTC 1131, at pages 186-87 (CTC 1134-35), where Kearney, J said:

> As "amount receivable" or "receivable" is not defined in the Act, I think one should endeavour to find its ordinary meaning in the field in which it is employed. If recourse is had to a dictionary meaning, we find in the *Shorter Oxford*, Third Edition, the word "receivable" defined as something "capable of being received." This definition is so wide that it contributes little towards a solution. It envisages a receivable as anything that can be transmitted to anyone capable of receiving it. It might be said to apply to a legacy bestowed in the will of a living testator, but nobody would regard such a legacy as an amount receivable in the hands of a potential legatee. In the absence of a statutory definition to the contrary, I think it is not enough that the so-called recipient have a precarious right to receive the amount in question, but he must have a clearly legal, though not necessarily immediate, right to receive it. A second meaning as mentioned by Cameron, J, is "to be received," and Eric L. Kohler, in *A Dictionary for Accountants*, 1957 edition, page 408, defines it as "collectible, whether or not due." These two definitions, 1 think, connote entitlement.

The appellant argued that an amount which is not capable of quantification in any reasonable or practical sense and for which a claim of payment could not be made by virtue of the Tariff comprising the contractual basis upon which the appellant supplied, and the customers consumed, electricity, is not receivable within the meaning of that Act. The Act was said to be concerned with certainty rather than estimation, and the opinions that such estimates necessarily entail.

...

Applying the *Colford* rule to the facts at hand, at first blush the unbilled revenue would seem to qualify as receivable because based on appellants "clearly legal, though not necessarily immediate, right to receive it." Electricity produced, sold and consumed is a commodity or good: *Quebec Hydro-Electric Commission v.* [*Deputy Minister of National Revenue*], [1970] SCR 30, [1969] CTC 574, 69 DTC 5372 (SCC). It also falls under the definition of property in subsection 248(1) of the Act. Where property is sold, delivered and consumed, the rendering of an account is not a precondition to the right to payment: sections 31 and 32, *Sale of Goods Act*, RSBC 1979, c. 370.

The language of paragraph 12(1)(b) itself makes a distinction between "receivable" and "due" so that an amount may be receivable even though not due until a subsequent year. As this Court said in *The Queen v. Derbecker*, [1984] CTC 606, 84 DTC 6549 per Hugessen, JA "the words due to him look only to the taxpayer's entitlement to enforce payment and not to whether or not he has actually done so" (at page 607 (CTC 6549)).

The only contrary argument is that the unbilled revenue was not receivable because, for practical purposes, it could not be known exactly. Viscount Simon in *Commissioners of Inland Revenue v. Gardner Mountain & D'Anbrumenil Ltd.* (1947), 29 TC 69, at page 93 was willing to accept "an estimate of what the future remuneration will amount to" and even "a discounting of the amount to be paid in the future." In my opinion the amount here is sufficiently ascertainable to be included as an amount receivable.

I can have no doubt that the appellant was absolutely entitled to payment for any electricity delivered, and in an amount reasonably estimated. Suppose, for example, that a customer's residence was destroyed by fire at midnight on December 31. The appellant would surely have a legal right as of the due date to reimbursement for the electricity supplied since the previous billing, viz, through December 31, and a court would be prepared to fix the amount of entitlement, probably using something like the appellant's prorated method.

I must therefore conclude that the appellant had a clear legal right to payment: the amounts in question were sufficiently ascertainable to be receivables even though not yet billed or due, and therefore had to be included in income for the year then ending, provided only they are not exempted by the "unless" clause in paragraph 12(1)(b).

In my opinion, this clause does not provide an exemption because of the words "accepted for the purpose of this Part." As previously set forth, I believe the principle to be applied for purposes of this Part of the Act is the "truer picture" or "matching" principle, which, as applied here, has the effect of denying the appellant the right to use the billed account method.

In the light of this holding, it would be inappropriate to consider the applicability of subsection 9(1) taken apart from paragraph 12(1)(b) or of subsection 12(2).

...

Appeal dismissed.

NOTES AND QUESTIONS

1.   Why did the Federal Court of Appeal in *West Kootenay* reject the "consistency" principle adopted by the trial judge? What, if any, principle does the Federal Court of Appeal affirm in its place?

2.   Of considerable relevance to the relationship between generally accepted accounting principles ("GAAP") and the concept of "profit" in subsection 9(1) is the legislative history preceding the enactment of this language in 1948. Although draft legislation introduced in 1947 had stipulated that a taxpayer's income from a business or property should be "determined in accordance with generally accepted accounting principles," this language was rejected on the grounds that it was "too indefinite to be used in a statute, that it would require the development of a whole new case law and might require the taxation of certain forms of income not hitherto included" (Brian J. Arnold, Tim Edgar, Jinyan Li, and Daniel Sandier, *Materials on Canadian Income Tax*, 11th ed. (Scarborough, ON: Carswell, 1996) at 327). In response, the Minister of Finance withdrew the original proposal, accepting instead suggestions that a taxpayer's annual income from a business or property be defined in terms of its "profit" for the year — a more general term than "generally accepted accounting principles" that is more common in commercial parlance and allows a more flexible approach in computing the annual income or loss of a business or property to accommodate the diverse accounting practices employed by individual enterprises. For a useful summary of this history, see "Business Income and Taxable Income," in *Report of Proceedings of the Seventh Annual Tax Conference*, 1953 Conference Report (Toronto: Canadian Tax Foundation, 1954).

Notwithstanding this legislative history, some judicial decisions, like that of the trial judge in *West Kootenay Power & Light Co. v. M.N.R.*, [1991] F.C.J. No. 1263, [1992] 1 C.T.C. 15, 92 D.T.C. 6023 (F.C.A.), suggested that the computation of a taxpayer's profit or loss for a taxation year from a business or property should, absent any statutory rule to the contrary, follow GAAP. See, for example, *Bank of Nova Scotia v. Canada*, [1980] C.T.C. 57, 80 D.T.C. 6009 (F.C.T.D.), aff'd [1981] C.T.C. 162, 81 D.T.C. 5115 (F.C.A.); and *Canada v. Metropolitan Properties Co. Ltd.*, [1985] 1 C.T.C. 169, 85 D.T.C. 5128 (F.C.T.D.). On this basis, moreover, the Canadian revenue department announced in 1981 that:

(1) "the profit or loss from a business for the purposes of section 9 of the *Income Tax Act* should be determined in accordance with generally accepted accounting principles unless specific provisions of the Act require a departure therefrom" and

(2) "[w]hen more than one set of generally accepted accounting principles would be appropriate in determining the profit or loss for a particular business, ... the set utilized by the taxpayer for financial purposes should also be used for tax purposes."

See Robert C. Reed, "The Dilemma of Conformity: Tax and Financial Reporting — A Perspective from Revenue Canada" in *Current Developments in Measuring Business Income for Tax Purposes*, 1981 Corporate Management Tax Conference (Toronto: Canadian Tax Foundation, 1981), 1 at 20. Both of these principles were rejected in *West Kootenay Power & Light Co. v. M.N.R.*, [1991] F.C.J. No. 1263, [1992] 1 C.T.C. 15, 92 D.T.C. 6023 (F.C.A.).

3. The Supreme Court of Canada addressed the relationship between accounting practices and the computation of profit under subsection 9(1) of the Act in *Canderel Ltd. v. Canada*, [1998] S.C.J. No. 13, [1998] 2 C.T.C. 35, 98 D.T.C. 6100 (S.C.C.). According to Iacobucci J (Gonthier, Cory, Major, and Bastarache JJ concurring) (at paras. 32-38):

> The great difficulty which seems to have plagued the courts in the assessment of profit for income tax purposes bespeaks the need for as much clarity as possible in formulating a legal test therefor. The starting proposition, of course, must be that the determination of profit under s. 9(1) is a question of law, not of fact. Its legal determinants are two in number: first, any express provision of the *Income Tax Act* which dictates some specific treatment to be given to particular types of expenditures or receipts, including the general limitation expressed in s. 18(1)(a), and second, established rules of law resulting from judicial interpretation over the years of these various provisions.

> Beyond these parameters, any further tools of analysis which may provide assistance in reaching a determination of profit are just that: interpretive aids, and no more. Into this category fall the "well-accepted principles of business (or accounting) practice" which were mentioned in *Symes*, also referred to as "ordinary commercial principles" or "well-accepted principles of commercial trading," among other terms. A formal codification of these principles is to be found in the "generally accepted accounting principles" ("GAAP") developed by the accounting profession for use in the preparation of financial statements. These principles are accepted by the accounting profession as yielding accurate financial information about the subject of the statements, and become "generally accepted" either by actually being followed in a number of cases, by finding support in pronouncements of professional bodies, by finding support in the writings of academics and others, or by more than one of these methods: see Peter W. Hogg and Joanne E. Magee, *Principles of Canadian Income Tax Law* (2nd ed. 1997), at pp. 180-81. What must be remembered, however, is that these are non-legal tools and as such are external to the legal determination of profit, whereas the provisions of the Act and other established rules of law form its very foundation.

> That is not to minimize the key role played by such well-accepted business principles (as I shall hereafter refer to them) in the profit-computation process. ... In the absence of a statutory definition of profit, it would be unwise for the law to eschew the valuable guidance offered by well-established business principles. Indeed, these principles will, more often than not, constitute the very basis of the determination of profit. However, well-accepted business principles are not rules of law and thus a given principle may not be applicable to every case.

More importantly, these principles must necessarily take a subordinate position relative to the legal rules which govern.

The reason for this is simple: generally speaking, well-accepted business principles will have their roots in the methodology of financial accounting, which, as was expressed in *Symes*, is motivated by factors fundamentally different from taxation. Moreover, financial accounting is usually concerned with providing a comparative picture of profit from year to year, and therefore strives for methodological consistency for the benefit of the audience for whom the financial statements are prepared: shareholders, investors, lenders, regulators, etc. Tax computation, on the other hand, is solely concerned with achieving an accurate picture of income for each individual taxation year for the benefit of the taxpayer and the tax collector. Depending on the taxpayer's commercial activity during a particular year, the methodology used to calculate profit for tax purposes may be substantially different from that employed in the previous year, which in turn may be different from that which was employed the year before. Therefore, while financial accounting may, as a matter of fact, constitute an accurate determinant of profit for some purposes, its application to the legal question of profit is inherently limited. Caution must be exercised when applying accounting principles to legal questions.

I do not wish to be taken, however, as minimizing the role of GAAP in the determination of profit for income tax purposes. ... In fact, ... GAAP will generally form the very foundation of the "well-accepted business principles" applicable in computing profit. It is important, however, for the courts to avoid delegating the criteria for the legal test of profit to the accounting profession, and therefore a distinction must be maintained. That is, while GAAP may more often than not parallel the well-accepted business principles recognized by the law, there may be occasions on which they will differ, and on such occasions the latter must prevail. ...

Moreover, there will, of course, be situations in which GAAP will offer various acceptable options in the preparation of financial statements, and the taxpayer will be free, for financial accounting purposes, to adopt whichever option best suits his financial objectives at the given time. In such cases, GAAP will surely not be determinative as to the method by which an accurate picture of profit may be obtained for taxation purposes, though it may still be useful as a guide to the various acceptable methods of computation, one of which may yield the appropriate result for taxation.

4.   What is the relationship between the "matching approach" and the "truer picture" doctrine? On what basis did the Federal Court of Appeal conclude in *West Kootenay* that the inclusion of earned but unbilled revenues up to the end of the year presented a "truer picture" of the taxpayer's income? In *Canderel Ltd. v. Canada*, [1995] F.C.J. No. 221, [1995] 2 C.T.C. 22, 95 D.T.C. 5101 (F.C.A.), a majority of the court, referring to *West Kootenay*, stated (at para. 2) that "the matching principle of accounting has, at least in this Court, been elevated to the status of a legal principle." On appeal, however, the Supreme Court of Canada held that the matching principle was merely an "interpretive aid," not an established "rule of law." Referring to the statement in *West Kootenay* that "whichever method presents the 'truer picture' of a taxpayer's revenue, which more fairly and accurately portrays income, and which 'matches' revenue and expenditure, if one method does, is the one which must be followed," Iacobucci J (Gonthier, Cory, Major, Bastarache JJ concurring) stated (at paras. 44 and 50):

In the court below, Stone JA took this passage as grounding his conclusion that the matching principle of accounting has been elevated to a rule of law. ... I do not, with respect, subscribe to that point of view. To my mind, the significance of this statement is to confirm a much sounder proposition: that the goal of the legal test of "profit" should be to determine which method of accounting best depicts the reality of the financial situation of the particular taxpayer. If this is accomplished by applying the matching principle, then so be it. On the other hand, if some other method is appropriate, is permissible under well-accepted business principles, and is not prohibited either by the Act or by some specific rule of law, then there is no principled basis by which the Minister should be entitled to insist that the matching principle — or any other method, for that matter — be employed. MacGuigan JA in *West Kootenay* seemed to advert to this notion at p. 6028, in the passage immediately following the above-quoted portion:

> The result often will not be different from what it would be using a consistency principle, but the "truer picture" or "matching approach" *is not absolute in its effect, and requires a close look at the facts of a taxpayer's situation.* [Emphasis added.] ...

> It follows from all of this that in calculating his or her income for a taxation year, the taxpayer must adopt a method of computation which is not inconsistent with the Act or established rules of law, which is consistent with well-accepted business principles, and which will yield an accurate picture of his or her income for that year.

Based on this analysis the Court held that the taxpayer, Canderel Ltd., was entitled to deduct over $4 million of lump sum tenant inducement payments ("TIPs") in the year they were made. The Court rejected the Minister's argument that the deduction of TIPs should be spread or "amortized" over the term of the leases to which they related, concluding that GAAP permitted either of the accounting methods advocated by the parties and that "where no one method emerges as clearly superior or more properly applicable than another, the taxpayer should retain the option of ordering its affairs in accordance with any method which is in accordance with well-accepted business principles and which is acceptable in light of the reality of its business" (para. 64). For a similar result see *Toronto College Park Ltd. v. Canada*, [1998] S.C.J. No. 14, [1998] 2 C.T.C. 78, 98 D.T.C. 6088 (S.C.C.). For a critique of the *Canderel* framework and its potential to resolve timing issues in the computation of business and property income see Geoffrey Walker, "Timing and Recognition of Income", in *Report of Proceedings of Fifty-Third Tax Conference*, 2001 Tax Conference (Toronto: Canadian Tax Foundation, 2002) 29:1-42.

A third case heard together with *Canderel* and *College Park* considered when a lump sum TIP should be included in the tenant's income for tax purposes. In *Ikea Ltd. v. Canada*, [1998] S.C.J. No. 15, [1998] 2 C.T.C. 61, 98 D.T.C. 6092 (S.C.C.), the taxpayer, which received a $2,650,000 inducement payment during its 1986 taxation year in order to enter into a long-term lease agreement, sought to defer recognition of the payment by amortizing it over the term of the lease. Rejecting the taxpayer's argument that the income inclusion should be matched against subsequent rental expenses to which it could be said to relate, the Court held that the payment was fully taxable in the taxpayer's 1986 taxation year. According to Iacobucci J (at para. 39):

> The "matching principle" is not an overriding rule of law, and there is no reason to apply it as paramount to or in lieu of the "realization principle," which is of key importance in the present circumstances. Indeed, I cannot see how the amortization of the [tenant inducement payment] in this case could possibly yield a truer picture of income than its immediate deduction [sic]. Ikea received a large sum of money with no conditions attached as to its use. It was free to dispose of the money whenever it chose and in whatever manner it saw fit. In my view, it would constitute a serious distortion of Ikea's taxation picture to ignore the fact that this entire amount was freely available to it as of the 1986 taxation year.

All three of these Supreme Court of Canada decisions endorsed a cash method of accounting for TIPs as the most appropriate in the circumstances. The cash method has also been approved in certain other contexts.

In *Publishers Guild of Canada Ltd. v. M.N.R.*, [1956] Ex. C.J. No. 6, [1957] C.T.C. 1, (1956) 57 D.T.C. 1017 (Ex. Ct.), the taxpayer, which sold books and magazines through door to door canvassers, computed its annual income on an "instalment basis," according to which amounts receivable from door-to-door subscriptions were not brought into income until actually received, while expenses incurred in order to earn subscription income were not deducted until this income was received. Referring (at para. 31) to accounting evidence that the instalment basis of accounting was "more appropriate than the accrual basis ... in cases [such as that of the taxpayer] where the period of payment of the instalments is protracted, where the collection of the instalments is uncertain and the costs of collection high, where the accounts are of such doubtful value that they cannot be discounted or readily sold and where there are no valuable rights of repossession of the articles sold," Thorson P accepted the accounting method employed by the taxpayer on the basis (at para. 39) that "the instalment system of accounting as adopted by the taxpayer is an acceptable system, is appropriate to the taxpayer's business and more accurately reflects its income position than any other system of accounting would do." In the course of his judgment, Thorson P also made the following comments on the role of accounting principles in income tax cases (at paras. 37-38):

> The accountancy profession is not a static one and the system of accounting which accountants should apply to the accounts of the businesses in which they are called upon to act [is] not immutable. A system of accounting that would be appropriate to one kind of business is not necessarily appropriate to a different kind. Only an arbitrary minded person would contend that there is only one system of accounting of universal applicability. No reasonable person would do so. But while accountants devise changes in systems of accounting to meet the changing conditions in the business world and new ways of conducting business their guiding principle must always be the same. Accounting is really the recording in figures, instead of words, of the financial implications of the transactions of the business to which it is applied. The accountant is thus the narrator of the transactions, his narrative being in the form of figures instead of words. His narrative should be such as to disclose to persons understanding his language of figures the true position of his client's business at any given time or for any given period. The accountant cannot fulfill the duty thus required of him unless he has carefully considered the manner in which his client carries on his business and has applied to it the system of accounting that is appropriate to it and most nearly accurately reflects its financial position, including its income position, at the time or for the period required.

But the Court must not abdicate to accountants the function of determining the income tax liability of a taxpayer. That must be decided by the Court in conformity with the government income tax law. ... Thus the prime consideration, where there is a dispute about a system of accounting, is, in the first place, whether it is appropriate to the business to which it is applied and tells the truth about the taxpayer's income position and, if that condition is satisfied, whether there is any prohibition in the governing income tax law against its use. If the law does not prohibit the use of a particular system of accounting then the opinion of accountancy experts that it is an accepted system and is appropriate to the taxpayer's business and most nearly accurately reflects his income position should prevail with the Court if the reasons for the opinion commend themselves to it.

In *Boosey & Hawkes (Canada) Ltd. v. M.N.R.*, [1984] C.T.C. 2871, 84 D.T.C. 1728 (T.C.C.), the taxpayer, which was in the music publishing business, received royalties in its 1979 taxation year, which the Minister included in computing the taxpayer's income for its 1978 taxation year on the basis that these amounts were receivable at the end of that year. Although concluding that the royalties were receivable in 1978, the Court allowed the taxpayer's appeal on the grounds that the taxpayer had "consistently adopted" a cash method of reporting its income "since at least 1958" and that the Minister failed to establish that this method "did not accurately reflect the income of the appellant in the taxation year at issue." Curiously, neither the taxpayer nor the Court noted that royalties are taxed on a cash basis under paragraph 12(1)(g).

5.   In *Canadian General Electric Co. v. M.N.R.*, [1961] S.C.J. No. 57, [1961] C.T.C. 512, 61 D.T.C. 1300 (S.C.C.), the taxpayer, which had borrowed US funds from its American parent, included a foreign exchange gain on the value of the debt in terms of Canadian dollars (which appreciated in value during the term of the loan) as the gain accrued from 1950 to 1952, not when the debt was repaid in 1952. At the Exchequer Court, [1959] C.T.C. 350, 59 D.T.C. 1217, Cameron J rejected the taxpayer's argument that the accrual method of accounting, which required the taxpayer to revalue the debt at the end of each taxation year, presented a true picture of its income for each taxation year, concluding (at para. 10) that "the issue before me ... is one of law and not of accounting" and (at para. 51) that the foreign exchange gain was not made "until the time at which the several notes payable in US currency were actually paid. It was only then when the profits were ascertained and realized."

Referring to *Dominion Taxicab Assn. v. M.N.R.*, [1954] S.C.J. No. 4, [1954] C.T.C. 34, 54 D.T.C. 1020 (S.C.C.), in which Cartwright J held (at para. 10) that "profit must be determined on ordinary commercial principles unless the provisions of the *Income Tax Act* require a departure from such principles," the Supreme Court of Canada reversed the Exchequer Court decision. According to Martland J, because the funds were borrowed in US dollars and repaid in US dollars, the very existence of a foreign exchange gain could be said to arise only because the taxpayer estimated the amount of the debt when incurred in 1950 in terms of Canadian dollars. As a result, he concluded (at para. 26), "the valuation of the liability should continue to be revised in each year thereafter until the year of actual payment."

The Supreme Court of Canada decision in *Canadian General Electric* has been sharply criticized as an unjustified judicial exception to the so-called realization principle according to which accrued gains are generally not included in computing a taxpayer's income until they are determined by a sale or other disposition. See Douglas J. Sherbaniuk, "The Time Recognition of Foreign Exchange Gains and Losses on Revenue Account" (1969) 19 U.T.L.J. 522 at 558; and Brian J. Arnold, *Timing and Income Taxation: The Principles of Income Measurement for Tax Purposes*, Canadian Tax Paper No. 71 (Toronto: Canadian Tax Foundation, 1983) at 191-93. To what extent does the outcome in *Canadian General Electric* depend on the fact that the taxpayer, not the Minister, sought to include the foreign exchange gain as it accrued?

6.   How does the Federal Court of Appeal decision in *West Kootenay Power & Light Co. v. M.N.R.*, [1991] F.C.J. No. 1263, [1992] 1 C.T.C. 15, 92 D.T.C. 6023 (F.C.A.), define the concept of a "receivable" for the purpose of paragraph 12(1)(b) of the Act? On what basis does it conclude that the estimate of unbilled electricity delivered to the end of the year was a "receivable" according to this definition? Why does it conclude that the receivables were not exempted by the "unless" clause in paragraph 12(1)(b)? What does it mean for a method of accounting to be "accepted" for the purpose of Part I of the Act?

A number of cases have considered when an amount becomes receivable, and when amounts that are not yet receivable may nonetheless have to be included in income for tax purposes. In *M.N.R. v. John Colford Contracting Co.*, [1960] Ex. C.J. No. 8, [1960] C.T.C. 178, 60 D.T.C. 1131 (Ex. Ct.), aff'd [1962] C.T.C. 546, 62 D.T.C. 1338 (S.C.C.), the taxpayer carried on a business of furnishing and installing plumbing, heating, air conditioning, and ventilation equipment. In the course of its business, it entered into several contracts pursuant to which it received progress payments as work was carried out, of which a stipulated percentage was held back until the work was completed and certified by the supervising architect or engineer. Relying on Ontario law, according to which "the contractor has no legal right to the amount of the holdback until the issuance of the certificate, and no suit can be properly commenced ... before certification unless it is clear that the certificate has been improperly withheld," the court held that holdbacks on projects that had yet to be certified were not "receivables" under then paragraph 85B(1)(b) (now paragraph 12(1)(b)), while holdbacks on a project certified by the end of the taxpayer's taxation year were "receivables" in that year, even if the taxpayer had neither received the payment nor knew that the project had been certified before the end of the year.

In *Wilchar Construction Ltd. v. Canada*, [1981] C.T.C. 415, 81 D.T.C. 5318 (F.C.A.), the taxpayer, which had consistently included in its income holdbacks and progress claims for which architects' certificates had not been issued, responded to an assessment in respect of its 1968 taxation year by filing a notice of objection contending that the amount of the holdbacks should not have been included in its income for that year. Rejecting the taxpayer's argument that the holdbacks were not taxable by virtue of the decision in *M.N.R. v. John Colford*

Contracting Co., [1960] Ex. C.J. No. 8, [1960] C.T.C. 178, 60 D.T.C. 1131 (Ex. Ct.), Heald JA (LeDain and Kelly JJA concurring) stated (at para. 6):

> In my view, it is important to note that in *Colford* (*supra*) it was the Minister who was seeking to include in the 1953 income "amounts receivable" which, in the view of the Court, were not "amounts receivable." ... I agree with the learned trial judge that the *Colford* case (*supra*) is authority for the proposition that a taxpayer may exclude such amounts. But in the case at bar, the taxpayer did not exclude such amounts in any of its returns for the years 1962 to 1969 inclusive. I do not read the *Colford* case (*supra*) as deciding that in a factual situation like the present one where the taxpayer chose to include subject amounts in its 1968 taxation year, and the Minister agreed thereto, such a practice is prohibited by paragraph 85B(1)(b) of the Act. All that *Colford* (*supra*) is authority for, in, my opinion, where the facts are as in this case, is that the Minister could not require the taxpayer to take subject amounts into income. As stated earlier herein, the method chosen by the appellant and accepted by the Minister had the effect of anticipating rather than deferring tax liability. I can find nothing in the *Colford* (*supra*) judgment nor in the provisions of the Act which prohibit the adoption of this method of anticipating tax liability. Paragraph 85B(1)(b) does not, in my view, prohibit such a method. All that section provides is that where an amount is, at law receivable, the taxpayer is required to include that amount. The section is silent with respect to other amounts. The item here in issue is such an other amount since it was only contingently receivable in the taxation year 1968.

On the basis that GAAP required the taxpayer to maintain a consistent method of computing its income from one year to the next, the court held that the holdbacks were properly included in the taxpayer's income for its 1968 taxation year.

In *M.N.R. v. Benaby Realties Ltd.*, [1967] S.C.J. No. 73, [1967] C.T.C. 418, 67 D.T.C. 5275 (S.C.C.), the taxpayer, which was compensated on November 9, 1954 for two parcels of land that were expropriated on January 7, 1954, sought to include gains resulting from the expropriation in computing its income for its 1954 taxation year, the fiscal period of which ended on April 30, 1954. Rejecting the taxpayer's argument that "from the moment of expropriation, [it] no longer had its land but had instead the right to receive compensation" (at para. 4), Judson J (Fauteux, Abbott, Ritchie, and Spence JJ concurring) concluded (at paras. 7 and 11):

> It is true that at the moment of expropriation the taxpayer acquired a right to receive compensation in place of the land but in the absence of a binding agreement between the parties or of a judgment fixing the compensation, the owner had no more than a right to claim compensation and there is nothing which can be taken into account as an amount receivable due to the expropriation. ...
>
> My opinion is that the Canadian *Income Tax Act* requires that profits be taken into account or assessed in the year in which the amount is ascertained.

In *Commonwealth Construction Co. v. M.N.R.*, [1984] F.C.J. No. 416, [1984] C.T.C. 338, 84 D.T.C. 6420 (F.C.A.), the taxpayer, which received judgment on a mechanic's lien action in 1974 and an award of costs in 1975, argued that the amounts were not receivable until 1977 when the action was finally settled following an appeal. Referring to the Supreme Court of Canada decision in *Benaby Realties*, Urie JA (Pratte and Cowan JJA concurring) rejected the taxpayer's argument, stating (at para. 20):

I can see no difference in the principle to be applied in an expropriation case as enunciated by Judson, J and that applicable in a case in which the amount payable is determined by a judgment of a court of competent jurisdiction. The amounts payable for services performed in prior years were ascertained by a judgment in 1974 and 1975 so that they became receivable in the hands of the judgment debtor in those years and were in fact paid in the same years. Thus, they were taxable in the hands of the taxpayer having acquired "the quality of income" in those years. ... The possibility of a successful appeal does not ... derogate from the quality of income of the payments in issue at the time of receipt.

In *Stevenson & Hunt Insurance Brokers Ltd. v. Canada*, [1993] F.C.J. No. 176, [1993] 1 C.T.C. 383, 93 D.T.C. 5125 (F.C.T.D.), the taxpayer sold insurance policies in consideration for which insurance companies paid it regular sales commission plus additional commissions contingent on the profitability of the policies sold. At trial, the taxpayer argued that it depended on insurance companies to determine the amount of the contingent commissions and was not informed of the amount earned in the 1982 calendar year until after the end of its fiscal year on January 31, 1983. The Minister argued that the contingent commissions had been earned in 1982, that the amount of these commissions could have been estimated by the taxpayer, and that this estimate could have been adjusted when the commissions were subsequently determined and paid.

Rejecting the Minister's arguments, the Court concluded that the contingent commissions were not ascertainable and therefore not receivable until the taxpayer's 1984 taxation year. According to Rothstein J (at paras. 34, 38, and 39):

I am ... of the opinion that there was no practical way for Stevenson & Hunt to have reasonably estimated contingent profit commissions earned for the 1983 fiscal year by January 31, 1983. It was necessary for Stevenson & Hunt to rely on the actual information provided by insurance companies after the end of the fiscal year. ...

In the case at bar, the issue is not whether amounts can be "known exactly," it is whether indeed they could even be estimated. While estimates and, where necessary, discounting of amounts to be paid in the future appear to be acceptable practice, they must be predicated on an ability to approximate what is expected or knowledge of the amount to be discounted. Neither of these conditions is present in the case at bar.

I accept the principle that the accounting method chosen by the taxpayer for income tax purposes should most accurately reflect the profit of the company for the year in question. However, I do not think this contemplates mere guessing as to contingent profit commissions at the financial year end or keeping the books open passed [*sic*] the fiscal year end until contingent profit commissions are ascertained. The application of the principle has certain practical limitations and, in my opinion, those practical limitations preclude the use of the accrual method in the case at bar.

In *Outboard Marine Corp. of Canada v. M.N.R.*, [1990] T.C.J. No. 121, [1990] 1 C.T.C. 2444, 90 D.T.C. 1350 (T.C.C.), the taxpayer, which manufactured lawn mowers, outboard motors, engines, and related parts, was able to obtain rebates on customs duties paid on imported parts when the finished products into which they were incorporated were exported. Rejecting the Minister's argument that these rebates or "duty drawbacks" became receivable when the finished products were exported, the Tax Court accepted the taxpayer's argument that they were receivable only when the taxpayer submitted a claim for a rebate, which it did in batches rather than processing each claim individually. Emphasizing that "no legal right [to payment] arises before a claim is made," Brulé TCJ concluded (at para. 31):

> After the exportation of the goods involved the taxpayer has a right to make a claim but this is different to a right to receive the amount involved. To obtain such a right certain conditions must be met and until these are completed ... the taxpayer does not have an absolute right to be paid. He must be entitled at a particular time to the amount and the soonest this can arise is after a claim in proper form is made. Based on previous jurisprudence this is a condition precedent to obtaining the amount involved.
>
> In the present case while the appellant company may have made a claim after each article was exported such was not feasible. Each year there were thousands of items involved and the only practical way to deal with the claims was to group them together and verify the dates of shipment and the amounts involved. This took considerable time. It was a business judgment and a practical arrangement for the appellant. To make separate claims for each item exported would have inundated the Revenue Canada Office. The appellant suffered to some extent by not having his drawback as soon as the goods were shipped and from the evidence the delay in making a claim was not for any tax benefit but for expediency and good business management.

To what extent do you think that the court's decision depends on its conclusion that "the delay in making a claim was not for any tax benefit but for expediency and good business management"?

In *Maritime Telegraph and Telephone Co. v. Canada*, [1992] F.C.J. No. 131, [1992] 1 C.T.C. 264, 92 D.T.C. 6191 (F.C.A.), the taxpayer, which billed its customers on a monthly basis in nine separate billing groups billed three or four days apart, employed an earned method of accounting for tax purposes until 1984 (including estimated revenue earned up to its year-end, even though some customers had not been billed). In 1984, it adopted a billed method of accounting for tax purposes while retaining the earned method for its financial statements, which it defended on the basis of an amendment to paragraph 12(1)(b). That amendment added the following words:

> and for the purposes of this paragraph, an amount shall be deemed to have become receivable in respect of services rendered in the course of a business on the day that is the earlier of

> (i) the day on which the account in respect of the services was rendered, and

> (ii) the day on which the account in respect of those services would have been rendered had there been no undue delay in rendering the account in respect of the services.

Referring to the scheme of the Act and a Department of Finance technical note accompanying the amendment, the court held that the unbilled amounts were taxable in the taxation year in which they were earned. According to MacGuigan JA (Heald and Linden JJA concurring) (at paras. 18-23):

In my opinion, subsection 12(1) operates so as to expand subsection 9(1)'s ambit of inclusion ... . [T]he joint thrust of section 9 and subsection 12(1) is to include, not exclude, and subsection 12(2) has the effect of ensuring, at the very least, that nothing clearly included in section 9 is henceforth excluded.

This interpretation is, I believe, supported by the only extrinsic evidence available. The technical note accompanying the 1983 amendment reads as follows:

> 1982 TN — Paragraph 12(1)(b) of the Act requires any amount receivable in respect of property sold or services rendered in the course of a business in a year to be included in that year's income. This paragraph is amended to add a provision that treats an amount as having become receivable for services performed on the day the account would have been rendered had there been no undue delay in rendering the account for the services. This rule, which previously applied only to services rendered in the course of a professional business under section 34 of the Act, has been expanded to apply to all services.

Not only is there no suggestion in the note of such a major change in the law as would completely exempt all services from the application of the earned method of computation, but the emphasis of the note is entirely upon subparagraph 12(1)(b)(ii), relating to an imputed billing date where there is undue delay. This suggests to me that the principal intention of the amendment was to prevent undue extension of billing times in rendering accounts for services rather than to establish any exclusion from income.

From the time of the decision in *Ken Sleeves Sales Ltd. v. Minister of National Revenue*, [1955] CTC 47, 55 DTC 1044 (Ex. Ct.), it has been clear that receivables are included in income under section 9. ...

In this light the factual finding by the trial judge that the earned method gives a truer picture of the taxpayer's income therefore assumes capital importance, and leads immediately to her conclusion ... :

> The earned but unbilled revenues of the taxpayer at year end are brought into income pursuant to subsection 9(1) of the Act and there is no need to rely upon paragraph 12(1)(b) for this purpose. They were being accounted for by the taxpayer under subsection 9(1) prior to 1984 and they should equally be accounted for, pursuant to that subsection, after that date. ... The 198[3] amendment was not intended to allow or require taxpayers to change their method of accounting for profit from the earned to the billed method and thereby accomplish a significant deferral of taxes. It seems clear the amendment's purpose was entirely the opposite. It was intended to require taxpayers who report on a billed method, when there is undue delay in billing, to account for the income which has not yet been billed.

I am in full agreement with her conclusion. The purpose of paragraph 12(1)(b) is to ensure that income from a business is computed on the accrual basis, not a cash basis, with certain specified exceptions. It applies in cases where profit is not otherwise required to be computed on the accrual basis. In the present case, it has no application, because of the trial judge's factual finding that the earned method was the appropriate accounting method for this taxpayer. The appellant's earned revenues to the end of each taxation year were receivables in law, and therefore income for the ending year. ... The receivables already being recognized as profit under subsection 9(1), subsection 12(2) requires that that status be maintained.

7. Interest income is subject to several particular timing rules, starting with paragraph 12(1)(c) which requires taxpayers to include in income:

> ... any amount received or receivable by the taxpayer in the year (depending on the method regularly followed by the taxpayer in computing the taxpayer's income) as, on account of, in lieu of payment of or in satisfaction of, interest to the extent that the interest was not included in computing the taxpayer's income for a preceding taxation year.

While many interest payments are now subject to the accrual rules in subsections 12(3) and (4) (discussed below), it is worth examining first how the courts have interpreted paragraph 12(1)(c).

In *Freeway Properties Inc. v. Canada*, [1985] 1 C.T.C. 222, 85 D.T.C. 5183 (F.C.T.D.), the taxpayer, a corporation engaged in the business of land development, sold a parcel of land in 1979, for which it took back a $300,000 mortgage repayable in full on December 31, 1984, with interest owing during the term of the mortgage payable in three lump-sum instalments on September 30, 1979, December 31, 1979 and March 31, 1980. Rejecting the taxpayer's argument that $130,000 of prepaid interest received by the taxpayer in its 1980 taxation year should, in accordance with the accrual method of accounting employed by the taxpayer, be included over the term of the mortgage, the court concluded that this method of accounting, though consistent with GAAP, was precluded by paragraph 12(1)(c). According to Addy J (at C.T.C. 227):

> It appears clear from the ... text [of paragraph 12(1)(c)] that interest for taxation purposes can and must be taken into account as income in only two ways: when the taxpayer is entitled to account for income on a cash basis, interest is to be considered in computing income during the year of receipt; when the taxpayer, on the other hand, is accounting for income under the accrual method, interest must be taken into account when it is *receivable*. This section allows no other alternative. For instance, it does *not* say that if it is receivable in any one year it is not to be taken into account in that year where it is interest *in respect of* a period previous to or subsequent to the time when it is *receivable*.

In *Elm Ridge Country Club Inc. v. M.N.R.*, [1995] T.C.J. No. 729, [1995] 2 C.T.C. 2810, 95 D.T.C. 715 (T.C.C.), the taxpayer received an interest payment of $43,380 in August 1983, $41,565 of which it sought to include in computing its income for its 1982 taxation year on the grounds that this amount accrued during 1982 and it regularly reported its income on an accrual basis. Although acknowledging (at para. 64) that a taxpayer "can adopt different methods for reporting income from different properties, provided the taxpayer is consistent over the years in reporting his income from a particular source," the court affirmed the Minister's assessment accounting for the interest payment on a cash basis on the grounds that the taxpayer reported other interest income on a cash basis and had not reported the accrued interest in computing its income for its 1982 taxation year.

The CRA's views on the interpretation of paragraph 12(1)(c) are found in paragraphs 6 and 7 of *Interpretation Bulletin* IT-396R, "Interest Income," May 29, 1984. According to paragraph 6:

> The words in paragraph 12(1)(c) "depending upon the method regularly followed by the taxpayer in computing his profit" are interpreted to refer to the taxpayer's method of

accounting for net interest income from a particular source and not necessarily to the taxpayer's method of accounting for other types of income. For example, a taxpayer who might have consistently used the received (cash) method to report interest income from bonds without coupons and the receivable method to report interest income from bonds with coupons will have established a "method regularly followed." If that method is reasonable in the circumstances, paragraph 12(1)(c) requires the taxpayer to retain its use from year to year except where ... a change in method becomes obligatory or is made voluntarily. ... Although paragraph 12(1)(c) permits a taxpayer to report interest income from different sources using different methods, it is the Department's position that interest from the same source (i.e. same payer, on same type of interest-yielding property) must be reported, within the confines of that paragraph, using the same method.

According to paragraph 7, the department will permit taxpayers subject to paragraph 12(1)(c) to account for interest on a received basis, a receivable basis, or an accrual basis. In addition, while taxpayers may change from a received to a receivable or accrued basis, or from a receivable to an accrued basis, they may not change from an accrued or receivable basis to a cash basis.

For most debt obligations, interest income is now subject to tax on a pure accrual basis under subsection 12(3) or 12(4) of the Act. According to subsection 12(3):

in computing the income for a taxation year of a corporation, partnership, unit trust or any trust of which a corporation or a partnership is a beneficiary, there shall be included any interest on a debt obligation ... [other than certain excluded forms of debt] that accrues to it to the end of the year, or becomes receivable or is received by it before the end of the year, to the extent that the interest was not included in computing its income for a preceding taxation year.

Consequently, except for interest on certain excluded debt obligations that need not concern us here, subsection 12(3) requires the various business entities identified to include interest income in computing their income for the earliest of the taxation years in which it has accrued, becomes receivable or is received.

Subsection 12(4) applies to individual taxpayers and to trusts that are not subject to the accrual rule in subsection 12(3). According to this provision:

where in a taxation year a taxpayer (other than a taxpayer to whom subsection (3) applies) holds an interest in an investment contract on any anniversary day of the contract, there shall be included in computing the taxpayer's income for the year the interest that accrued to the taxpayer to the end of that day with respect to the investment contract, to the extent that the interest was not otherwise included in computing the taxpayer's income for taxation year or any preceding taxation year.

Subsection 12(11) defines an "investment contract" as "any debt obligation" other than various employment-related arrangements or plans governed by other statutory provisions (salary deferral arrangements, retirement compensation arrangements, employee benefit plans, foreign retirement arrangements, and prescribed contracts), the debt obligations excluded from subsection 12(3) (income bonds, income debentures, small business development bonds, net income stabilization accounts, and indexed debt obligations), and debt obligations in respect of which accrued interest is included in computing a taxpayer's income at periodic intervals of not more than one year irrespective of subsection 12(4). The term "anniversary day" is also defined in subsection 12(11) as:

(a)   the day that is one year after the day immediately preceding the date of issue of the contract,

(b)   the day that occurs at every successive one year interval from the day determined under paragraph (a), and

(c)   the day on which the contract was disposed of.

As a result, for debt obligations (other than excluded debt obligations) with a term of more than one year on which compound interest is payable at maturity ("compound debt obligations"), subsection 12(4) requires individual taxpayers and trusts to which subsection 12(3) does not apply to include in computing their income for a taxation year interest that has accrued on the debt obligation either over the course of a year ending in the taxpayer's taxation year, or up to the day when the debt obligation is disposed of during the taxation year. Thus, while subsection 12(4) requires taxpayers to include accrued interest on an annual basis, the amount of interest that must be included in a taxpayer's taxation year is the amount that has accrued up to the "anniversary day" occurring in that taxation year, rather than the amount that accrues during the taxpayer's taxation year.

According to Department of Finance technical notes accompanying amendments to these provisions, they were introduced in order to eliminate opportunities to defer the taxation of interest income by delaying the receipt or receivability of this income to a subsequent taxation year. In order to prevent the avoidance of these rules through such techniques as the issuance of discounted debt obligations paying little or no interest, moreover, yet other rules deem the return on these and other "prescribed debt obligations" to be interest for the purpose of the accrual rules. These anti-avoidance rules are found in subsection 12(9) and regulation 7000.

B. Deductions

As with inclusions, the taxation year in which amounts may be deducted in computing a taxpayer's income from a business or property is determined both by the general concepts of "profit" and "loss" in subsections 9(1) and (2) of the Act and by other rules that apply either generally to all expenditures or more narrowly to specific kinds of expenditures. Where taxpayers compute their income on an accrual basis, for example, expenses are generally deductible in the taxation year in which they are payable, even if they are not actually paid until a subsequent taxation year. Where taxpayers are permitted to compute their income from a business or property on a cash basis, on the other hand, expenditures are not deductible until the taxation year in which they are actually paid. Both methods of accounting are contemplated by paragraph 18(1)(a), which disallows any deduction in respect of an "outlay" (an actual payment) or

782

an "expense" (the assumption of an obligation to pay an amount), except to the extent that it was "made" (paid) or "incurred" (assumed) by the taxpayer, and by paragraph 20(1)(c), which permits a deduction for interest that is "paid in the year or payable in respect of the year (depending on the method regularly followed by the taxpayer in computing the taxpayer's income)." Other provisions allow taxpayers to deduct amounts that are "paid in the year,"[54] amounts that are "payable" in the year,[55] expenses that are "incurred in the year,"[56] and amounts that are "payable in respect of the year."[57] In addition to these provisions, moreover, other rules defer the taxation year in which taxpayers may deduct otherwise deductible outlays and expenses, while yet others permit a deduction in respect of amounts previously included in computing a taxpayer's income from a business or property, even if an amount is not paid or payable by the taxpayer in the taxation year.

This section examines statutory and judicial rules governing the taxation year in which amounts may be deducted in computing a taxpayer's income from a business or property, beginning with the general concept of an amount "payable" by a taxpayer in a taxation year, and then looking at special rules for the deduction of inventory costs, capital expenses, prepaid expenses, running expenses, reserves, bad debts, and transfers of debt obligations.

1. Amounts Payable

To the extent that income from a business or property is generally computed on an accrual basis, with amounts included in the taxation year in which they are "receivable," the "truer picture" principle by which Canadian courts have interpreted the concepts of "profit" and "loss" in subsections 9(1) and (2) of the Act suggests that deductions should be allowed in the taxation year in which expenses are "incurred" or "payable." A leading case on the concept of an "amount payable" is *J.L. Guay Ltée v. M.N.R.*, [1971] F.C.J. No. 21, [1971] C.T.C. 686, 71 D.T.C. 5423 (F.C.T.D.), aff'd [1972] F.C.J. No. 134, [1973] C.T.C. 506, (1972) 73 D.T.C. 5373 (F.C.A.), aff'd [1975] C.T.C. 97, 75 D.T.C. 5094 (S.C.C.).

J.L. Guay Ltée v. M.N.R.
[1971] F.C.J. No. 21, [1971] C.T.C. 686, 71 D.T.C. 5423 (F.C.T.D.)

NOËL ACJ: ... Appellant is a general building contractor which, in order to perform some of its building contracts, delegates performance of certain operations to other businesses, i.e. sub-contractors. In accordance with

---

[54] See, for example, the deduction for discounts in para. 20(1)(f).

[55] See, for example, the deduction for guarantee fees and other transactions costs in para. 20(1)(e.1).

[56] See, for example, the deduction for other financing costs in para. 20(1)(e).

[57] See, for example, the deduction for life insurance premiums in para. 20(1)(e.2).

established practice in the construction trade, appellant pays its sub-contractors on presentation by them of a monthly estimate showing what progress has been made. According to the terms of the contract with its sub-contractors, appellant withholds a percentage of the monthly estimates submitted and accepted, which it pays after the work is finally approved by the architect. Respondent in his assessment refused to admit as payable an amount of $277,428.48, representing the balances owing to the sub-contractors from appellant as a result of the amounts withheld each month during 1965. These balances, representing a percentage of the monthly estimates submitted by the sub-contractors and accepted by appellant, are, the latter submits, payable at a specific date. The fact is that appellant is under an obligation to pay on a certain date, i.e. the 35th day after final approval of the work by the architect, as provided in the contract between it and its sub-contractors. Appellant stated that the existence of this obligation is not subject to any suspensive or resolutory condition: the obligation does exist and only its performance is postponed till the end of the period. At any time after the period of 35 days following approval by the architect, the sub-contractor is entitled to demand payment of the balance owing. Thus, the appellant contends, these balances owing at a definite time constitute amounts payable within the meaning of the *Income Tax Act* and case law, and must, accordingly, be included in the contract expenses and deducted from appellant's profits for the year.

...

In support of his assessment respondent cites Sections 3, 4, 12(1)(a) and 12(1)(e) of the *Income Tax Act*, RSC 1952, c. 148 [now section 3, subsection 9(1), and paragraphs 18(1)(a) and 18(1)(e), according to which, in computing a taxpayer's income from a business or property, no deduction is permitted in respect of "an amount as, or on account of, a reserve, a contingent liability or amount or a sinking fund" except as expressly permitted by Part I of the Act]. He submits that the amounts thus withheld by appellant were not, during the taxation year 1965, amounts payable to its subcontractors. Payment of these amounts, he claims, was subject to the express condition that the work performed by the sub-contractors be approved by the architect in its final form on completion of the job. As the work for which the amounts were withheld was not so approved by the architect in appellant's 1965 taxation year, the said amounts could consequently not be used for a deduction in computing appellant's income.

...

Referring to the decision of this Court by Kearney J in *John Colford Contracting Co. Ltd. v. M.N.R.*, [1960] CTC 178, the learned member of the Tax Appeal Board stated that, although the facts in that case were the opposite of those established in the present case, he nevertheless felt obliged to apply the principles contained therein. In *Colford*, ... Kearney, J refused to include in a construction company's income amounts withheld during the current year and payable on the architect's approval. In Kearney, J's opinion, these amounts were not "receivables"; for them to be receivables they must, in the learned judge's view, be amounts which "the intended recipient has a clearly legal, though not necessarily immediate, right to receive."

According to Mr. Boisvert, applying that decision to the case which now concerns us, if the amount withheld could not constitute a debt due and payable to be included in a taxation year, because it represented a contingent debt, similarly an amount withheld which is due and payable in the future can only constitute an allowable deduction in the year in which it becomes certain and mandatory. Only then does it meet the condition set forth in Section 12(1)(a) [now paragraph 18(1)(a)], i.e. it becomes ... incurred by the taxpayer for the purpose of gaining income from a business ...

...

As stated by appellant, the contract does provide that, if the work is not found satisfactory by the architect, the sub-contractor will nevertheless have the right to be paid in full at the current market price for the work already done; this does not mean, however, that the contractor will always have to pay the amount so withheld in full. In fact, it must not be forgotten that the purpose of the provision which permits withholding of a certain percentage of the contract price is to ensure the payment of any damages the owner or the general contractor may incur from the sub-contractor's failure to perform the work or its faulty performance of it. If such damages correspond to, or exceed, the amounts so withheld, the owner or the general contractor may keep the entire amount; if, on the other hand, the damages are less, the subcontractor win be entitled to receive the difference.

It seems to me, therefore, that it is far from certain that the amounts so withheld will be paid in full to the sub-contractor. In fact, the payment of these amounts to the sub-contractor is perhaps to be regarded, if damages are incurred, as contingent. It is true that, once fixed, such damages may be offset by the amounts withheld, and that the general contractor will not benefit therefrom, but the damages have not yet been liquidated for 1965, and compensation cannot be paid until they are. Until then, and even after, until the architect has issued his certificate and 35 days have elapsed, the general contractor is under no obligation to pay this amount, and it is not claimable by the sub-contractor.

...

In most tax cases only amounts which can be exactly determined are accepted. This means that, ordinarily, provisional amounts or estimates are rejected, and it is not recommended that data which is conditional, contingent or uncertain be used in calculating taxable profits. If, indeed, provisional amounts or estimates are to be accepted, they must be certain.

...

[W]e are dealing with amounts withheld which are not only uncertain as to quantum if partial damages result from badly done work, but which will no longer even be due or payable if damages exceed the amounts withheld. How can it be claimed in such circumstances that a certain and current expense is involved, and that the amounts withheld, which appellant has full enjoyment of until it pays the amounts owing to the sub-contractor, or until compensation becomes due, may be deducted by appellant as it receives them from the owner.

...

Appeal dismissed.

NOTES AND QUESTIONS

1.   On what basis did the taxpayer in *J.L. Guay Ltée* argue that the amount of unpaid holdbacks were deductible in computing its income for its 1965 taxation year? Why did the court reject this argument? On the basis of the decision, how might one define a "contingent liability" for the purpose of paragraph 18(1)(e) of the Act? Must the obligation to make the payment be contingent?

2.   The decision in *J.L. Guay Ltée* was upheld by the Federal Court of Appeal, [1972] F.C.J. No. 134, [1973] C.T.C. 506, 73 D.T.C. 5373, and the Supreme Court of Canada, [1975] C.T.C. 97, 75 D.T.C. 5094. At the Federal Court of Appeal, the court stated (at para. 2) that "appellant's profit cannot be computed by taking, on the one hand, 90% of the value of all work done for the owner and, on the other hand, deducting the total sums paid by the appellant to the subcontractors for their work." The Supreme Court of Canada affirmed the decision without further reasons.

For other cases involving deductions in respect of holdbacks, see *Ellis Construction Ltd. v. M.N.R.*, [1982] C.T.C. 2604, 82 D.T.C. 1625 (T.C.C.); *Newfoundland Light & Power Co. Ltd. v. Canada*, [1990] F.C.J. No. 116, [1990] 1 C.T.C. 229, 90 D.T.C. 6166 (F.C.A.); *Wil Mechanical Ltd. v. M.N.R.*, [1990] F.C.J. No. 643, [1990] 2 C.T.C. 224, 90 D.T.C. 6475 (F.C.T.D.); *Imperial Financial Services Ltd. v. M.N.R.*, [1990] T.C.J. No. 949, [1991] 1 C.T.C. 2031, 91 D.T.C. 184 (T.C.C.); and *Wawang Forest Products Ltd. v. Canada*, [2001] F.C.J. No. 449, [2001] 2 C.T.C. 233, 2001 D.T.C. 5212 (F.C.A.).

In *Wil Mechanical*, the court distinguished *J.L. Guay Ltée* and *Newfoundland Light & Power* on the basis that the holdbacks at issue were not explicitly authorized by the contractual documents. Rejecting the Minister's argument that customary practice in the construction and contracting industries supported the existence of an implied term in each contract, McNair J held that the amounts withheld were "expenses or outlays made or incurred" within the meaning of paragraph 18(1)(a).

In *Imperial Financial Services*, the court allowed the taxpayer, a general contractor that was paid on the basis of the percentage of construction completed without any holdback but withheld 20 per cent of all progress payments made to subcontractors, to deduct uncertified holdbacks on the basis that these amounts were properly matched against revenues received in order to portray a true picture of the taxpayer's income. According to Teskey TCJ (at paras. 35 and 39):

The financial statements of the appellant as prepared using the percentage of completion method gave to the reader thereof the most accurate picture of the appellant's financial affairs and its true income position. If the appellant had reduced its expenses as the respondent has assessed, the income would have been distorted and misleading. ...

In this case, there is a matching of the expense to the income. This ... distinguishes the *Guay* decision. The *Guay* decision stands for the principle that a taxpayer contractor cannot compute profit by taking into income only 90 per cent of the value of all work done and deduct 100 per cent of the expenses (i.e., expense the holdbacks).

In *Wawang Forest Products Ltd.*, the taxpayer carried on a forestry business through independent contractors who were required to pay their own workers' compensation premiums under agreements that allowed the taxpayer to hold back a share of the contract price until it received a valid clearance certificate or other acknowledgement from the Workers' Compensation Board that premiums had been paid. Even though 1 to 5 per cent of the holdbacks were never paid, the court allowed their deduction in the year in which the work was completed on the grounds that they were payable at this time under the contract, only after which was the taxpayer entitled to withhold amounts as security against vicarious liability for the contractors' obligations under workers' compensation legislation. According to Sharlow JA (Rothstein and Malone JJA concurring) (at para. 30):

In my view, a legal obligation to pay an amount may exist even if there is some risk that the actual payment may be set off against potential counterclaims. Similarly, the fact that a liability remains unpaid does not mean that it never came into existence. For these reasons, I reject the argument of the Crown in this case that the taxpayers' contractual right of setoff for trespass penalties, or the fact that some of the holdbacks remained unpaid in 1994, proves that the holdbacks were contingent liabilities in the years under appeal.

3.   In *Time Motors Ltd. v. M.N.R.*, [1969] S.C.J. No. 15, [1969] C.T.C. 190, 69 D.T.C. 5149 (S.C.C.), the taxpayer, a used car dealer, deducted the value of "credit notes" for future automobile purchases that it issued in its 1961, 1962, and 1963 taxation years as partial payment for some of the used cars that it acquired. Rejecting the Minister's argument that any amount outstanding at the end of each taxation year in respect of the unredeemed credit notes was not a current liability, but a contingent reserve the deduction of which was prohibited under then paragraph 12(1)(e) (now paragraph 18(1)(e)), the Supreme Court of Canada held that the credit notes became actually existing obligations when issued.

Is this decision consistent with the concepts of an amount payable and a contingent liability in *J.L. Guay Ltée*? Consider the following comments on *Time Motors* in Brian J. Arnold, *Timing and Income Taxation: The Principles of Income Measurement for Tax Purposes*, Canadian Tax Paper No. 71 (Toronto: Canadian Tax Foundation, 1983) at 228-29:

It may be argued that the taxpayer's liability to redeem the credit notes in *Time Motors* was a contingent liability, because it was dependent upon the presentation of the note for redemption by the holder. In the absence of such presentation, the taxpayer would never be liable to honour the notes. This is a difficult point. Technically and legally, it seems clear that the taxpayer had no legal obligation to honour the notes unless they were presented for credit within the stipulated period. Given the nature of the notes, however, it also seems obvious that most, if not all, of the notes would in fact be presented for credit.

If this is an acceptable rationale, does it also extend to cases involving unredeemed trading stamps, tickets, or cash vouchers? In the absence of paragraph 20(1)(m), which authorizes the deduction of a reserve in respect of goods to be delivered or services to be rendered after the end of a taxation year, such amounts might not be deductible because of the possibility that the stamps, tickets, or vouchers would never be presented for redemption. These cases may be distinguished from *Time Motors* on the basis of an assessment of the likelihood that the liability will be ultimately incurred. This approach, however, is similar to the accounting treatment of contingencies and is not generally followed for income tax purposes.

Another difficulty with the result in the *Time Motors* case is distinguishing between the liability in that case to redeem the credit notes and the liability under a warranty or guarantee. The Supreme Court accepted the distinction proffered in evidence by the taxpayer's accountant: "... the credit note, while it is a liability, is also an existing obligation today. A warranty may be a liability in the future. It may be determinable in the future but isn't an existing obligation until the future. ..." A warranty obligation is not triggered until the property sold does not perform as warranted by the vendor; the vendor's liability is conditional upon this future occurrence. But the taxpayer's liability in *Time Motors* was also contingent in that the credit notes had to be presented for redemption by the purchasers. Consequently, either *Time Motors* is an aberration or the existing law requires an assessment of the likelihood of the occurrence of the future event. Where the future event is very likely to occur, as in *Time Motors*, the liability is deductible. Where it is not very likely, as with a warranty or trading stamps, the liability is a nondeductible contingent one. Unfortunately, subsequent cases have not clarified the scope or rationale of the *Time Motors* case.

Paragraph 20(1)(m), which permits a reserve for unearned amounts, and paragraph 20(7)(a), which deals with reserves in respect of "guarantees, indemnities or warranties," are considered later in this chapter.

4.   In *Canada v. Burnco Industries Ltd.*, [1984] F.C.J. No. 94, [1984] C.T.C. 337, 84 D.T.C. 6348 (F.C.A.), the taxpayer, which operated a gravel pit under a licence agreement with the city of Calgary requiring it to backfill areas excavated in the course of the year, sought to deduct $718,385 in computing its income for its 1974 taxation year as the estimated future cost of backfilling the gravel pit. Disallowing the deduction, the Federal Court of Appeal concluded (at para. 2) that:

> an expense, within the meaning of paragraph 18(1)(a) of the *Income Tax Act*, is an obligation to pay a sum of money. An expense cannot be said to be incurred by a taxpayer who is under no obligation to pay money to anyone. ... [A]n obligation to do something which may in the future entail the necessity of paying money is not an expense.

For a similar decision, disallowing deductions for estimated future reforestation costs, see *Northwood Pulp and Timber Limited v. Canada*, [1995] T.C.J. No. 1674, [1996] 2 C.T.C. 2123, 96 D.T.C. 1104 (T.C.C.), aff'd [1998] F.C.J. No. 1537, [1999] 1 C.T.C. 53, 98 D.T.C. 6640 (F.C.A.).

5.   In *Buck Consultants Ltd. v. Canada*, [1996] T.C.J. No. 584, [1996] 3 C.T.C. 2016 (T.C.C.), aff'd [1999] F.C.J. No. 1801, [2000] 1 C.T.C. 93, [2000]

D.T.C. 6015 (F.C.A.), the taxpayer, which had entered into a 15-year lease pursuant to which the first 14 months were rent-free, sought to deduct amounts during the rent-free period based on a notional payment schedule according to which rental payments were amortized over the duration of the lease. Rejecting the taxpayer's argument that the deduction conformed with GAAP and provided the truest picture of the taxpayer's income, the court disallowed the deduction on the basis that no outlay or expense had been made or incurred as required under paragraph 18(1)(a).

6.   In *North American Automobile Association Ltd. v. M.N.R.* (1963), 33 Tax ABC 395 (T.A.B.), the taxpayer, which sold memberships to motorists entitling them to various travel benefits, legal advice, and certain insurance benefits, sought to deduct at the end of its 1959 taxation year the estimated value of insurance premiums subsequently payable to an associated insurance company ("Pitts Insurance Company Limited") with which it had entered into an agreement to cover its obligations in respect of memberships sold. Noting that the premiums were not payable until June 1960, the board held that the deduction constituted a "reserve" within the meaning of then paragraph 12(1)(e). According to the board (at paras. 24-25):

> the taxpayer seeks to set aside in 1959 a part of premiums already received from insured members ... for the purpose of meeting a liability which might or might not arise in 1960. This method of calculating income would seem to have the effect of setting up a reserve as stated in Smails' *Accounting Principles and Practice* at 153:
>
>> (2) an estimate of the amount required to meet some liability which is known to exist but whose precise amount cannot be determined at the moment. ...
>
> [T]here is no doubt that the company acted in accordance with good accounting principles in setting aside the sum of $119,300 out of 1959 income to meet the possible requirements of the agreements with Pitts Insurance Company Limited. However, in the circumstances the deduction of the amount set aside is prohibited by the provisions of Section 12(1)(e) in computing the appellant's taxable income for 1959.

For a similar result, in which the court disallowed the difference between the maximum and the minimum premium payable on a reinsurance contract entered into by the taxpayer, see *Co-operators General Insurance Co. v. M.N.R.*, [1993] T.C.J. No. 22, [1993] 1 C.T.C. 2316, 93 D.T.C. 303 (T.C.C.).

For a contrary result, see *Day & Ross Ltd. v. Canada*, [1976] F.C.J. No. 198, [1976] C.T.C. 707, 76 D.T.C. 6433 (F.C.T.D.), in which the taxpayer sought to deduct during the taxation years 1969 to 1971 additional premiums relating to accident and cargo claims that occurred during each of these taxation years. Rejecting the Minister's argument that the deduction of these additional premiums was prohibited by then paragraph 12(1)(e), the court held (at para. 33) that "the amounts entered as expense were definitely owing and payable." According to Dubé J (at paras. 30-31):

> The terms "reserve" and "contingent account" of paragraph 12(1)(e) connote the setting aside of an amount to meet a contingency, an unascertainable and indefinite event which may or

may not occur; whereas the term "expense" in 12(1)(a) implies a liability present and certain, an amount definite and ascertainable. A standard yearly insurance premium would undoubtedly fit neatly under the generally accepted meaning of the term "expense," and no one would think of describing it as a "contingency" or a "reserve": the exact amount of the premium is known, ascertainable, admitted and payable.

The difficulty in the present case, of course, lies with the complex formula laid down by Lloyd's to establish plaintiff's yearly premiums. The amounts claimed by plaintiff as premiums payable were amounts entered in the books as liabilities in each year because they represent the cost of insurance coverage for the particular year. The amounts booked as accident and cargo claims were so entered for that year because the specific events leading to the claims had occurred in that year. The accountants did not set aside approximate amounts as "reserve" against contingencies, these amounts were booked as definitely payable because the premiums had been earned, the accidents had occurred, the claims had been filed, the investigations had taken place, the quantum of damage assessed, and the amounts entered.

7.   In *Transport Direct System Ltée v. M.N.R.*, [1984] C.T.C. 2845, 84 D.T.C. 1773 (T.C.C.), the taxpayer, in computing its income for its 1977 taxation year, sought to deduct its estimated liability for goods that were lost, damaged, or destroyed in the course of its transport business. Noting that this amount was based on damages incurred for which the taxpayer had not received a claim and claims received for which liability had not been determined, the court disallowed the deduction on the basis that the estimated amount was a contingent liability the deduction of which was prohibited under paragraph 18(1)(e). For a similar result on similar facts, see *TNT Canada Inc. v. Canada*, [1988] F.C.J. No. 565, [1988] 2 C.T.C. 91, 88 D.T.C. 6334 (F.C.T.D.).

8.   For other cases in which deductions have been disallowed under paragraph 18(1)(e) and its predecessors, see *Harlequin Enterprises Ltd. v. Canada*, [1977] C.T.C. 208, 77 D.T.C. 5164 (F.C.A.); *Mandel v. Canada*, [1978] C.T.C. 780, 78 D.T.C. 6518 (F.C.A.), aff'd [1980] S.C.J. No. 3, [1980] C.T.C. 130, 80 D.T.C. 6148 (S.C.C.); *Cummings v. Canada*, [1981] F.C.J. No. 524, [1981] C.T.C. 285, 81 D.T.C. 5207 (F.C.A.); *Northern & Central Gas Corp. v. Canada*, [1985] F.C.J. No. 111, [1985] 1 C.T.C. 192, 85 D.T.C. 5144 (F.C.T.D.); *Lakehead Newsprint Ltd. v. M.N.R.*, [1986] T.C.J. No. 345, [1986] 1 C.T.C. 2442, 86 D.T.C. 1353 (T.C.C.); *Samuel F. Investments Ltd. v. M.N.R.*, [1988] T.C.J. No. 3, [1988] 1 C.T.C. 2181, 88 D.T.C. 1106 (T.C.C.); *Dunblane Estates Ltd. v. M.N.R.*, [1989] T.C.J. No. 108, [1989] 1 C.T.C. 2248, 89 D.T.C. 137 (T.C.C.); *Foothills Pipe Lines (Yukon) Ltd. v. M.N.R.*, [1990] F.C.J. No. 925, [1990] 2 C.T.C. 448, 90 D.T.C. 6607 (F.C.A.); and *Canada v. Nomad Sand & Gravel Ltd.*, [1990] F.C.J. No. 1105, [1991] 1 C.T.C. 60, 91 D.T.C. 5032 (F.C.A.); *General Motors of Canada Ltd. v. Canada*, [2004] F.C.J. No. 1858, [2005] 1 C.T.C. 56; 2004 D.T.C. 6716 (F.C.A.), leave to appeal denied [2005] S.C.C.A. No. 3 (S.C.C.); and *General Motors of Canada Ltd. v. Canada*, [2008] F.C.J. No. 663, [2008] 4 C.T.C. 79; 2008 D.T.C. 6381 (F.C.A.).

In *Mandel*, the taxpayer, as a member of a limited partnership, purchased rights to a film for a total purchase price of $577,892, payable by a cash payment of $150,000 and the balance out of the earnings from the film.

Disallowing the taxpayer's claim for capital cost allowance based on the taxpayer's share of the $577,982 purchase price, the court concluded (at para. 15) that because the liability to pay more than $150,000 was "contingent on the happening of [an] uncertain event," capital cost allowance could be calculated only on the taxpayer's share of the $150,000 cash actually contributed.

In *Lakehead Newsprint*, the taxpayer, which operated a newsprint-processing factory, sought in computing its income for its 1980 taxation year to deduct the amount of a wage settlement payable for the period June 1 to December 31 but not ratified by the taxpayer and the employees until March 26, 1981. Rejecting the taxpayer's argument that the amount of the wage increase was accepted in principle by both parties by November 20, 1980, the court held (at para. 24) that the taxpayer "was under no legal obligation to pay money to anyone as at December 31, 1980." According to Sarchuk TCJ (at para. 24):

> while it is not disputed that generally accepted accounting principles should normally be applied for taxation purposes it is equally clear that these principles need not and indeed cannot be followed where the contrary is required by legislation. Such is the case here. I am satisfied that the amount in issue was not deductible as a result of the operation of paragraph 18(1)(e) of the *Income Tax Act*.

In *Samuel F. Investments*, the taxpayer, which resolved on December 27, 1978 to pay a management bonus of $147,000 to the corporation's president and sole shareholder at an undetermined future date, sought to deduct the amount of the unpaid bonus in computing its income for its 1978 taxation year, even though the bonus was not paid in 1978 or 1979 and was cancelled in 1980. Disallowing the deduction, Christie ACJTC concluded (at paras. 9 and 16) that:

> a liability to make a payment is contingent if the terms of its creation include uncertainty in respect of any of these three things: (1) whether the payment will be made; (2) the amount payable; or (3) the time by which payment shall be made. ...
>
> With respect to the appeal at hand, it appears to me that the director's resolution declaring a management bonus of $147,000 ... embodies uncertainties regarding the time or times of payment and whether payment would ever be made either in whole or in part with the result that the directors created a liability that is contingent in nature.

In *Dunblane Estates*, the taxpayer, which owned and operated a private nursing home, deducted accrued sick-leave credits, 50 per cent of which employees were entitled to claim upon ceasing to be employed by the taxpayer. Referring to the three aspects of contingency mentioned in *Samuel F. Investments*, the court disallowed the deduction under paragraph 18(1)(e).

In *Foothills Pipe Lines*, the taxpayer, which had been incorporated for the purpose of constructing together with other companies a pipeline through Canada to deliver Alaskan gas to the United States, excluded in computing its income for its 1982 and 1983 taxation years "Special Charges" on various producers shipping gas through segments of the uncompleted pipeline authorized by the National Energy Board. Rejecting the taxpayer's argument that the board had also required it to compensate these producers with interest "when the mainline commences operation," the Federal Court of Appeal held that the "Special Charges" were income to the taxpayer in its 1982 and 1983 taxation years and that any deduction in respect of these amounts was disallowed as a contingent liability. According to Urie JA (Marceau and Desjardins JJA concurring) (at paras. 35 and 38):

> If an amount received is, as here, in the nature of income, the fact that in the future the recipient may be under an obligation to repay it does not change the character of the receipt from income to a liability whether deferred or otherwise. ... As I see it, the possibility of any liability arising out of the Special Charges is uncertain and therefore is contingent. Furthermore, it is not possible to estimate with any degree of accuracy the quantum of liability or who the recipients of the repayments would be.

> A contingent liability, which refers to a contingency which may or may not occur, could, in my view, aptly describe the nature of the obligation imposed by the order of the Board in this case. It is not a present liability and nor is it a deferred one. By virtue of paragraph 18(1)(e) of the *Income Tax Act*, ... such a liability is not deductible in the computation of profits notwithstanding that such deductions may be, for financial reporting purposes, in accordance with generally accepted accounting principles.

In *Nomad Sand & Gravel*, the taxpayer, which operated a sand and gravel pit at Brighton, Ontario, sought to deduct payments made to the province of Ontario under the *Pits and Quarries Act*, calculated at $0.02 per ton of material extracted from the pit and payable as security toward the future cost of rehabilitating the area, which the taxpayer was obliged to carry out under the statute. Rejecting the taxpayer's argument that these amounts were deductible in the taxation years in which they were paid, the Federal Court of Appeal noted that regulations under the *Pits and Quarries Act* described these payments as "deposits" to be "held by the Treasurer of Ontario bearing simple interest at 6% per annum." On this basis, the court concluded, the payments were properly characterized as transfers to a reserve, the deduction of which was prohibited under paragraph 18(1)(e).

In the first *General Motors of Canada Ltd.* case the taxpayer ("GM") sought to deduct in its 1995 taxation year amounts it had accrued in a special contingency fund set up to finance a range of employee benefit programs, as required under a memorandum of understanding ("MOU") between GM and the union representing its employees (the "CAW"). The MOU prescribed the amounts to be accrued to the fund each year based on overtime hours worked by employees. The Federal Court of Appeal held that the 1995 accruals were not deductible in that year because they had not yet been used to pay for any benefits, and the taxpayer could satisfy its accrual obligations with nothing more than a bookkeeping entry. Malone JA reasoned that "since no funds were contributed to a qualified trustee or otherwise segregated or set aside from ordinary working capital, I can find no absolute liability or identifiable debt that was incurred by General Motors" (at para. 26). A deduction was prohibited by s. 18(1)(e) as payments from the fund were contingent on further decisions being made about the amount to be devoted to different benefit programs. The Supreme Court of Canada refused the taxpayer's application for leave to appeal.

Following the above decision GM and the CAW amended their MOU to state that "For greater certainty, the Company and the Union agree that the

Company's obligation to add to the Special Canadian Contingency Fund ... accrues and becomes absolute as the overtime hours described in the immediately preceding sentence are worked." Based on the amended MOU, GM deducted its 1996 accruals to the fund. The Minister reassessed once again on the basis that the MOU still created only a contingent liability. In the Tax Court of Canada, Miller J held in favour of the taxpayer on the grounds that while the amended MOU did not clearly create "an absolute liability to do anything more than calculate an amount," affidavit evidence of witnesses from GM and the CAW established "that the parties to the MOU intended to create, as overtime hours were worked, an absolute liability to expend the fund" ([2006] T.C.J. No. 563, [2007] 2 C.T.C. 2202, 2007 D.T.C. 272 (T.C.C.), at paras. 12 and 17). This decision was reversed in the Federal Court of Appeal, where Nadon JA held that the amended MOU was "not substantially different from its previous version" in that GM's accrual obligation could be satisfied by an accounting entry, and did not itself require any payments out of the fund ([2008] F.C.J. No. 663, [2008] 4 C.T.C. 79, 2008 D.T.C. 6381 (F.C.A.), at para. 43). Furthermore as the MOU was unambiguous about the nature of the obligation created, the Court held that Miller J was not entitled to consider the extrinsic affidavit evidence of the parties to the MOU (at para. 47). As such the 1996 accruals were a contingent liability the deduction of which was prohibited by s. 18(1)(e).

9. In *Meteor Homes Ltd. v. M.N.R.*, [1960] C.T.C. 419, 61 D.T.C. 1001 (Ex. Ct.), the taxpayer deducted sales taxes claimed by the province of Quebec, but unpaid pending the outcome of another case challenging the constitutionality of the tax. Rejecting the Minister's argument that the deduction of these amounts constituted a reserve for contingent liabilities prohibited under then paragraph 12(1)(e), Kearney J concluded (at para. 37):

> In the present case there was no condition precedent to prevent the provincial authorities from preferring a claim against the appellant; and whether the law under which the claim was instituted might later be declared *ultra vires* constituted a condition subsequent. In my opinion the validity of a statutory law must be presumed until the contrary is proved, and until then any monetary obligation which it imposes should be treated as an outstanding liability. In this case there is evidence that contractors in the province of Quebec generally set up the retail sales tax as a liability and paid it monthly. Whether some one contractor has attacked the Act on several counts including its constitutionality is not the criterion by which the instant case is to be judged.

For a similar result involving the deduction of unpaid licence fees that the taxpayer withheld to put pressure on the licensor to renegotiate the licence, see *Dibro Investments Ltd. v. M.N.R.*, [1987] T.C.J. No. 206, [1987] 1 C.T.C. 2281, 87 D.T.C. 210 (T.C.C.). See also *Fédération des caisses populaires Desjardins de Montréal & de L'Ouest-du-Québec v. Canada*, [2001] F.C.J. No. 266, [2001] D.T.C. 5173 (F.C.A.), in which a majority of the court allowed the taxpayer to deduct the cost of employer's contributions under provincial legislation regarding pensions, health and workers' compensation, and federal legislation for unemployment insurance in computing its income for its 1992 taxation year, even though the amounts were not paid until 1993, on the basis that the obligation to make the contributions arose when the taxpayer's employees performed the services in respect of which the contributions were payable, not when the contributions were actually required under federal and provincial legislation.

10.   In *Gluekler Metal Inc. v. Canada*, [2003] T.C.J. No. 236, [2003] 3 C.T.C. 2645; 2003 D.T.C. 431 (T.C.C.), the taxpayer corporation paid just over $500,000 to one of its major shareholders in 1994, on account of interest and administrative fees in respect of loans and services provided to it by the shareholder from 1989 to 1993. The Minister argued that claiming the entire deduction in 1994 instead of spreading it over the years to which it related did not present an accurate picture of the taxpayer's 1994 income. The Tax Court of Canada allowed the taxpayer's appeal. Relying on the Supreme Court of Canada's 1998 decision in *Canderel* (discussed above in the section on Inclusions), McArthur TCJ held that the taxpayer's entitlement to a deduction was a question of law rather than accounting principles. The Court found as a fact that the taxpayer had an arrangement with its shareholder in the past to provide financial and administrative services for inadequate compensation, but that they reached an agreement in 1994 at the urging of their bankers to make a one-time adjustment to compensate fully for these services. The decision to deduct the entire amount in 1994 was not inconsistent with s. 18(1)(a) as it was an expense incurred in that year to earn business income. Moreover, the full deduction of the expense gave the most accurate picture of the taxpayer's economic situation in 1994.

2. Inventory Costs

Where a taxpayer acquires or produces property for the purpose of sale in the course of a business, the property is generally characterized as inventory in the taxpayer's business. More specifically, though somewhat less descriptively, subsection 248(1) of the Act defines "inventory" as "a description of property the cost or value of which is relevant in computing a taxpayer's income from a business for a taxation year." Where a taxpayer's gains or losses from the disposition of property are characterized as business income, therefore, the cost or value of this property is relevant in computing the taxpayer's business income, making the property "inventory" within the meaning of subsection 248(1).[58]

Unlike ordinary business expenses, which are typically deductible in the taxation year in which they are incurred, costs to acquire or produce inventory

---

[58]   See, for example, *Friesen v. Canada*, [1995] S.C.J. No. 71, [1995] 2 C.T.C. 369, 95 D.T.C. 5551 (S.C.C.), distinguishing between inventory and capital properly according to "the type of income that the property will produce." The distinction between inventory and capital property is examined in detail in Chapter 6.

are generally deductible only in the year in which the inventory is sold or otherwise disposed of. By deferring the deduction of these costs until this subsequent taxation year, this approach "matches" revenues and expenses and provides a "truer picture" of the taxpayer's income from the business than would the deduction of inventory costs in the taxation year in which they are incurred.

Although subject to a number of statutory rules in section 10 of the Act, the characterization of a particular item of property as inventory and the allocation of specific costs to the acquisition or production of this inventory depends, as an initial matter, on general principles governing the computation of a taxpayer's income from a business. An excellent illustration of this dependence is the decision in *Neonex International Ltd. v. Canada*, [1978] F.C.J. No. 514, [1978] C.T.C. 485, 78 D.T.C. 6339 (F.C.A.).

Neonex International Ltd. v. Canada
[1978] F.C.J. No. 514, [1978] C.T.C. 485 78 D.T.C. 6339 (F.C.A.)

URIE J (Ryan and Le Dain JJA, concurring): ... [T]he appellant ... is engaged in the production and subsequent sale or rental of electrical signs. Each sign is custom built to meet the requirements and specifications of each customer. ... Most signs are sold under conditional sales contracts under which title does not pass until each sign is fully paid for. At year end, there is always a certain number of signs partially completed and in the course of construction. Until 1970 the appellant treated the uncompleted signs for both accounting and tax purposes as work in progress inventory. It continued to do so for accounting purposes thereafter but for the 1970, 1971 and 1972 taxation years the costs incurred to the end of the tax years in respect of partially completed signs were deducted, for the purpose of computing income for tax purposes, on the basis that they represented period expenses not required to be carried for income tax purposes as the cost of work in progress inventory. The amounts in issue in the respective years were $176,561, $111,724 and $24,963 which sums were disallowed as deductions by the Minister. The question simply put is was he right in so doing? The learned trial judge found that he was.

It is the Minister's contention that in reporting income for tax purposes the calculation thereof must be made in accordance with generally accepted accounting principles unless the *Income Tax Act* expressly imposes or permits some other method. Counsel for the respondent called as an expert witness a highly qualified chartered accountant who testified that generally accepted accounting practice does not permit the deduction of costs associated with incomplete signs until those costs can be matched with the revenue with which they are associated. Since there can be no revenue until the completed signs have been delivered to the customers, the proper accounting treatment for incomplete signs, according to him, is to carry them in the books of account as part of inventory until revenue is derived from their sales.

While agreeing that generally accepted accounting principles may favour the matching of costs with revenue, counsel for the appellant contended that that practice need not be followed for income tax purposes because paragraph 12(1)(a) of the Act, as it related to the 1970 and 1971 taxation years and paragraph 18(1)(a) of the Act as it applied to the 1972 taxation year, permit the deduction of expenses incurred for the purpose of gaining or producing income. In his submission, there need not be a causal connection between the expenditure of money and the realization of revenue in the year in which the expense was incurred, or at all, in order for the outlay to be deductible for income tax purposes. Because it carries no stock in trade, because it operates and produces signs only after a contract has been entered into and because it cannot earn the income it has a contractual right to receive without incurring the expense in issue, it has, in the course of producing the signs, incurred expenses for the purpose of gaining or producing income within the meaning of the *Income Tax Act* and the expenses are therefore deductible when incurred. Put another way, the principle of matching revenue and expenses, in the circumstances of the appellant's business, has no applicability for tax purposes.

The learned trial judge rejected the appellant's submissions and, in my opinion, rightly did so. He held that: —

> when a company, in submitting in a tax return a report of its expenditures and revenues during a taxation year with a view to establishing its profits or gains and tax base, purports to include as expenditures all the expenses incurred in realizing a manufactured article not yet finished but does not take into account the whole value of the article has for it at that time, it is not making an accurate report.

> ...

There is no doubt that the proper treatment of revenue and expenses in the calculation of profits for income tax purposes with a view to obtaining an accurate reflection of the taxable income of a taxpayer, is not necessarily based on generally accepted accounting principles. Whether it is so based or not is a question of law for determination by the Court having regard to those principles ... .

The uncontradicted evidence of the respondent's expert witness, John C. Bonnycastle, is succinctly summarized in the following excerpts from his statement: —

> The matching principle requires that at the end of an accounting period an effort be made to identify those costs which have been incurred during the period but which have not yet been expended in the revenue earning process so that they may be recorded as assets and carried forward to the accounting period in which the revenue they aid in producing is recorded. At that point in time the costs will be matched with the related revenues by including both revenues and costs in the statement of income.

> The objective that inventory accounting should give effect to the matching principle is implicit in the authoritative literature on the subject ... .

> ... when the amounts involved would have a material effect upon the income of an enterprise, generally accepted practice would require some costs to be allocated to inventories which are associated with revenues which, at the end of the accounting period

have not yet been included in income, even though there may be a number of acceptable alternatives for determining the amount of the costs to be so allocated.

...

This evidence I would accept, since it was not challenged, as establishing the accepted accounting treatment for partially completed signs being produced under contract by the appellant. The question then to be asked is whether the *Income Tax Act* requires or permits a different accounting treatment in the calculation of the appellant's income for income tax purposes than that which is applicable for the purposes of accurately portraying the financial picture of the company for shareholders and creditors.

...

In my opinion, the method used by the appellant in calculating its taxable income accorded neither with generally accepted accounting principles nor with the proper method of computing income for tax purposes ... . The expenses incurred in connection with the partially completed signs were laid out to bring in income in the next or some other taxation year, not in the year in which they were claimed. As a result, the income of the appellant would not be portrayed fairly nor accurately if it were permitted to adopt this method for tax purposes while for the purposes of its own creditors and shareholders it used the generally accepted accounting method presumably because that method fairly and accurately provides them with the profit or loss information to which they are entitled. For these reasons, I would dismiss the appeal on this issue.

Appeal dismissed.

NOTES AND QUESTIONS

1. On what basis did the Minister argue in *Neonex* that the taxpayer could not deduct the cost of uncompleted signs in computing its income for each of the taxation years at issue? On what grounds did the taxpayer argue that these expenses were properly deductible in the taxation years in which they were incurred? Why did the court reject the taxpayer's arguments?

2. According to paragraph 10(5)(a) of the Act: "property (other than capital property) of a taxpayer that is advertising or packaging material, parts or supplies or work in progress of a business that is a profession is, for greater certainty, inventory of the taxpayer." Notwithstanding this provision, however, paragraph 34(a) of the Act allows taxpayers to elect to exclude "work in progress" in computing any income for a taxation year from "a business that is the professional practice of an accountant, dentist, lawyer, medical doctor, veterinarian, or chiropractor." By excluding "work in progress" in computing the income from these professional practices, an election allows taxpayers to deduct the costs of partially completed work in the year in which they are incurred. Where such an election is filed, paragraph 34(b) requires the taxpayer to exclude work in progress inventory in computing his or her income in all

subsequent taxation years, "unless the taxpayer, with the concurrence of the Minister and on such terms and conditions as are specified by the Minister, revokes the election to have [paragraph 34(a)] apply."

3. Having characterized a particular item of property as inventory in a taxpayer's business, the next step in computing the taxpayer's income or loss from this business is to determine the specific expenses that must be allocated to the cost of this inventory. For inventory that is bought and sold without modification of any kind, the cost of unsold inventory generally comprises its acquisition cost and additional expenses (for example, taxes, transportation, and storage) that are incurred in order to "bring that particular item of inventory to its condition and location at the end of the taxation year." See *Interpretation Bulletin* IT-473R, "Inventory Valuation," December 21, 1998, paragraph 10. For inventory that is subject to some modification, such as land that is subdivided and/or developed, this cost generally includes these subdivision and development costs in addition to the purchase price of the land. See, for example, *Qualico Developments Ltd. v. Canada*, [1984] F.C.J. No. 101, [1984] C.T.C. 122, 84 D.T.C. 6119 (F.C.A.) (landscaping costs); *Canada v. Metropolitan Properties Co. Ltd.*, [1985] 1 C.T.C. 169, 85 D.T.C. 5128 (F.C.T.D.) (cost to construct municipal services, such as sewers and water mains); and *Interpretation Bulletin* IT-153R3, "Land Developers — Subdivision and Development Costs and Carrying Charges on Land," October 7, 1991, paragraphs 13 and 14. For a contrary result, however, see *Urbandale Realty Corp. v. M.N.R.*, [2000] F.C.J. No. 184, [2000] 2 C.T.C. 250, 2000 D.T.C. 6118 (F.C.A.), in which a majority of the court held that the taxpayer did not have to include a regional development charge in the inventory cost of land under development. For inventory that is produced or manufactured by the taxpayer, the cost of unsold work in progress or completed inventory necessarily includes direct labour and material costs and generally includes at least some overhead expenses. See IT-473R, "Inventory Valuation", December 21, 1998, paragraph 12.

4. Where particular items of inventory are unique or easily distinguished, as in *Neonex*, inventory accounting can be achieved directly by deferring the deduction of inventory costs until the taxation year in which the property is sold or otherwise disposed of. Where a taxpayer's inventory is numerous and relatively homogeneous, however, this result is generally achieved indirectly by deducting all expenses incurred in the year and *adding back* the cost of inventory that remains unsold at the end of the year. Indeed, since the "gross profit" (*GP*) from the sale of inventory is defined as the proceeds (*P*) resulting from the disposition of the property less the cost of the inventory disposed of (*C*), and the cost of inventory disposed of (*C*) may be defined as the cost of the taxpayer's inventory at the beginning of the year (C_0) plus the cost of inventory acquired or produced during the year (C_1) minus the cost of inventory remaining at the end of the year (C_2), it follows algebraically that gross profit can also be defined as the proceeds from sales minus the cost of unsold inventory at the

beginning of the year minus the cost of inventory acquired or produced during the year plus the cost of unsold inventory at the end of the year:

If $GP = P - C$ and $C = C_0 + C_1 - C_2$, then $GP = P - C_0 - C_1 + C_2$.

Where a taxpayer computes its income in this manner, the cost of inventory acquired or produced in the taxation year is relevant in computing the taxpayer's income from the business for that year, even if it has not been sold or otherwise disposed of during the year.

5.   Where inventory is numerous and homogeneous and acquired or produced at different costs, it is often impractical or impossible to track the cost of each individual item in order to determine the aggregate cost of inventory that remains at the end of each year. As a result, accounting practice has generally relied on different assumptions about the order in which inventory is disposed of. According to a "first in, first out" rule (FIFO), inventory is deemed to be disposed of in the order in which it was acquired or produced, such that the inventory that remains at the end of the year is deemed to comprise the most recently acquired or produced inventory. Under a "last in, first out" rule (LIFO), on the other hand, the most recently acquired or produced inventory is deemed to be that which is sold first, such that the inventory that remains at the end of the year is deemed to comprise inventory acquired or produced in the most distant previous years. According to an "average cost" rule, the cost of all inventory available for sale in a taxation year is averaged, so that the cost of inventory remaining at the end of the year is the same as the cost of inventory that is sold or otherwise disposed of in the taxation year. The effect of these different accounting conventions is best illustrated by a simple numerical example in which a business acquires two batches of inventory at different prices (for example, $10 and $20), and sells one of these batches before the end of the year, leaving one batch unsold at the end of the year. Assuming that the unsold inventory is the last batch acquired by the business (FIFO), the cost of this batch is $20 and the cost of the inventory sold during the year is $10. Assuming that the unsold inventory is the first batch acquired by the business (LIFO), the cost of this inventory is $10 and the cost of the inventory sold during the year is $20, resulting in a lower income for the year. Under the average cost approach, the cost of each batch is assumed to be $15, making the cost of the unsold batch $15 and the cost of the inventory sold during the year $15.

6.   In *M.N.R. v. Anaconda American Brass Ltd.*, [1955] J.C.J. No. 1, [1955] C.T.C. 311, 55 D.T.C. 1220 (P.C.), the taxpayer carried on a business of manufacturing metal sheets, rods, and tubes, in the course of which it purchased substantial quantities of copper. In 1947, at a time when metal prices were increasing after the removal of wartime price controls, the taxpayer adopted a LIFO method of accounting for the cost of its copper inventory, the effect of which was to increase the cost of products sold during the year and thereby reduce its income for the year. Although acknowledging (at para. 19) that "the

LIFO method is a generally acceptable, and in this case the most appropriate, method of accountancy," the Privy Council upheld the Minister's reassessment, which computed the cost of unsold copper on a FIFO basis, on the grounds (at para. 17) that this method more nearly than the LIFO method measured "the actual stock so far as it can be ascertained." According to Viscount Simmonds (at para. 19):

> It is in their Lordships' opinion the failure to observe, or, perhaps it should be said, the deliberate disregard of, facts which can be ascertained and must have their proper weight ascribed to them, which vitiates the application of the LIFO method to the present case.

The Privy Council decision in *Anaconda American Brass* was followed in *Handy & Harman of Canada Ltd. v. M.N.R.*, [1973] C.T.C. 507, 73 D.T.C. 5401 (F.C.T.D.), in which the taxpayer sought to compute the cost of unsold inventory on the basis of a modified LIFO method known as the "base stock method." See also *Wickett and Craig Ltd. v. M.N.R.*, [1978] C.T.C. 2516, 78 D.T.C. 1382 (T.R.B.).

7.   For the CRA's views on allowable methods of determining the cost of inventory, see IT-473R. According to paragraph 15:

> Where it is practical to identify costs by reference to specific items, the cost is determined by ascertaining the laid-down cost of the specific items. If it is not practical to determine cost by reference to specific items, it is necessary to use an arbitrary cost selection method which has the effect of making a presumption as to the order in which inventory is sold. Among the methods most commonly used in determining cost are:
>
> • specific item
>
> • average cost
>
> • first in, first out (fifo)
>
> The last in, first out method (LIFO) and the base stock method are not accepted for income tax purposes as methods of determining cost.
>
> The method used in determining cost for income tax purposes should normally be the same as the method used for financial statement purposes. However, if there is more than one acceptable method of determining cost according to generally accepted accounting principles, the method used for income tax purposes should be the one that gives the truer picture of the taxpayer's income. The method used must also be followed consistently from year to year and a change will only be accepted if the new method is more realistic in the circumstances and gives the truer picture of the taxpayer's income.

8.   As a general rule, the effect of inventory accounting is to defer the recognition of gains and losses from the disposition of particular items of inventory until the taxation year in which this property is sold or otherwise disposed of. Where inventory decreases in value in a taxation year prior to its disposition, however, inventory accounting has traditionally recognized these accrued losses by valuing this property at the lower of its cost and fair market value at the end of the year. See, for example, *Whimster & Co. v. Commissioners of Inland Revenue* (1925), 12 Tax Cas 813 (H.L.) and *BSC*

Footwear Ltd. v. Ridgway, [1971] 2 All E.R. 534 (H.L.). Although this "lower of cost and market" (LCM) rule constitutes an exception to the so-called realization principle according to which gains and losses are generally not taken into account for tax purposes until property is sold or otherwise disposed of, it is a well-established principle of business and accounting practice and is codified in subsection 10(1) of the *Income Tax Act*. Alternatively, regulation 1801 allows taxpayers to value "all the property described as inventories of the business at its fair market value," resulting in the recognition of accrued gains as well as accrued losses.

9.   In *Friedberg v. Canada*, [1993] S.C.J. No. 123, [1993] 2 C.T.C. 306, 93 D.T.C. 5507 (S.C.C.), the taxpayer traded in gold futures contracts, buying and selling contracts both to buy gold at future dates ("going long") and to sell gold at future dates ("going short"), in the course of which he realized substantial business losses ($512,126 in 1978, $934,387 in 1979, $1,276,172 in 1980, and $4,425,186 in 1981) by selling contracts that had decreased in value at the end of each taxation year and delaying the sale of contracts that had increased in value until the following taxation year. On the basis that the taxpayer's method of computing his income did not offer an "accurate reflection" of the taxpayer's "true financial position," the Minister employed a "marked to market" method of accounting that effectively netted the gains and losses against each other over the course of the year. Rejecting this argument, the Supreme Court of Canada held that the losses were properly deductible in each of the taxation years in which they were claimed on the grounds that they were actually incurred in these years while the gains were actually realized in the following taxation years. According to Iacobucci J (at para. 4):

> On the facts, the respondent reported his losses when they were actually incurred, and his gains when they were actually realized. In our view, the appellant has not demonstrated that there is any error in adopting this approach. While the "marked to market" accounting method proposed by the appellant may better describe the taxpayer's income position for some purposes, we are not satisfied that it can describe income for income tax purposes, nor are we satisfied that [it] is the appropriate measure of realized income for tax purposes.

Consider whether the general anti-avoidance rule ("GAAR") might be applied to tax-motivated transactions such as those considered in *Friedberg*. The Canadian revenue authorities have indicated that they intend to apply the GAAR to such transactions where they are entered into after the rule came into force on September 13, 1988.

10.   In the United States, comprehensive "mark-to-market" rules governing commodity straddles were enacted in 1981. See Richard R. Dailey, "Commodity Straddles in Retrospect: Federal Income Tax Considerations" (1981) 47 Brook. L. Rev. 313. In Canada, section 142.5 now requires "financial institutions" (as defined in subsection 142.2(1)) to adopt a "mark-to-market" method of reporting accrued gains or losses on various "mark-to-market properties" (as defined in subsection 142.2(1)) held at the end of a taxation year. Section 142.5 is applicable to taxation years ending after October 30, 1994.

11. In *Friesen v. Canada*, [1995] S.C.J. No. 71, [1995] 2 C.T.C. 369, 95 D.T.C. 5551 (S.C.C.), the taxpayer, who purchased a parcel of land ("the Styles property") for the purpose of reselling it at a profit, relied on the LCM rule to deduct as losses in computing his income for his 1983 and 1984 taxation years decreases in the value of the property during each of these years. Concluding that the Styles property was "inventory" within the meaning of the Act because it was relevant in computing the taxpayer's income for the taxation year in which it would be sold or otherwise disposed of, a majority of the court adopted a "plain reading" of subsection 10(1) as it then read to hold that the taxpayer could trigger accrued losses on the Styles property by valuing the property at its fair market value at the end of his 1983 and 1984 taxation years. Dissenting, Iacobucci J (Gonthier J concurring) would have limited the LCM rule to "stock-in-traders" for whom the cost or value of inventory remaining at the end of a taxation year is essential to the computation of gross profit during the year.

For a critical comment on the Supreme Court of Canada decision in *Friesen*, see David G. Duff, "Interpreting the Income Tax Act — Part 1: Interpretive Doctrines" (1999) Vol. 47 No. 3 Can. Tax J. 464, at 511-17 (arguing that although the Styles property was properly characterized as "inventory" in a "business" according to the definitions of these words in subsection 248(1) of the Act, the taxpayer should not have been able to use the LCM rule to trigger a loss before the property was sold or otherwise disposed of because this rule only applies "[f]or the purpose of computing income from a business," which, under general principles for the computation of profit, the taxpayer was neither required nor permitted to do until the loss was actually realized).

Four months after the Supreme Court of Canada decision in *Friesen* was released, the Department of Finance issued a press release announcing proposed amendments to the *Income Tax Act* to reverse the decision (Release No. 95-111, December 20, 1995). These amendments are reflected in the current language of subsection 10(1), which limits the LCM rule to taxpayers that carry on a business "that is not an adventure or concern in the nature of trade," and subsection 10(1.01), according to which inventory in an adventure or concern in the nature of trade "shall be valued at the cost at which the taxpayer acquired the property," thus precluding the recognition of any gain or loss until the property is actually sold or otherwise disposed of.

12. In *M.N.R. v. Cyprus Anvil Mining Corp.*, [1989] F.C.J. No. 1146, [1990] 1 C.T.C. 153, 90 D.T.C. 6063 (F.C.A.), the taxpayer, which opened a new mine that was exempt from income tax for a three-year period from February 1, 1970 to January 31, 1973, changed its method of accounting for inventory from the LCM method to the fair market value method during the years when it was tax-exempt, after which it returned to the LCM. Concluding that the changes distorted the taxpayer's income in its 1973 and 1974 taxation years, the court upheld the Minister's assessment computing the taxpayer's income on the LCM method. According to Urie JA (Pratte JA concurring) (at para. 23):

Admittedly, subsection 10(1), (a) neither contains a prohibition against changing the method of inventory valuation from time to time, nor (b) permits the method selected to be changed at will, nor (c) provides a departure from the generally accepted accounting practice of valuing inventory only at cost or the lower of cost or market. But, in my view, it must be construed within the context of the Act and be harmonious with its scheme and with the object and intention of Parliament. To permit the change in inventory valuations espoused by the respondent ... has the effect of distorting the respondent's profits in both the 1973 and 1974 tax years. In other words, by failing to adhere to the consistency principle in the computation of income, the respondent has not fairly and accurately portrayed its profit picture.

For a similar result, relying on the decision in *Cyprus Anvil*, see *Consoltex Inc. v. Canada*, [1995] T.C.J. No. 1567, [1996] 1 C.T.C. 2752, 96 D.T.C. 1812 (T.C.C.).

The decision in *Cyprus Anvil* was legislatively confirmed by the enactment of subsection 10(2.1), applicable to 1990 and subsequent taxation years. According to this provision:

Where property described in an inventory of a taxpayer's business that is not an adventure or concern in the nature of trade is valued at the end of a taxation year in accordance with a method permitted under this section, that method shall ... be used in the valuation of property described in the inventory at the end of the following taxation year for the purpose of computing the taxpayer's income from the business unless the taxpayer, with the concurrence of the Minister and on any terms and conditions that are specified by the Minister, adopts another method permitted under this section.

The principle of consistency affirmed in *Cyprus Anvil* is also reflected in subsection 10(2) of the Act, which stipulates:

Notwithstanding subsection 10(1), for the purpose of computing income for a taxation year from a business, the inventory at the commencement of the year shall be valued at the same amount as the amount at which it was valued at the end of the preceding taxation year for the purpose of computing income for that preceding taxation year.

For the purpose of this provision, subsection 10(3) authorizes the Minister to adjust the value of a taxpayer's inventory at the commencement of a taxation year to conform with the statutory scheme in subsection 10(1).

13. For the purpose of subsection 10(1), subsection 10(4) of the Act defines the fair market value of a professional's work-in-progress inventory to be "the amount that can reasonably be expected to become receivable in respect thereof after the end of the year," and the fair market value of advertising or packaging material, parts, supplies, or other property (other than work in progress of a profession) that is included in inventory to be "the replacement cost of the property." Where the inventory is "obsolete, damaged or defective" or "held for sale or lease or for the purpose of being processed, fabricated, manufactured, incorporated into, attached to, or otherwise converted into property for sale or lease," however, these valuation rules do not apply.

14. For the purpose of computing the income of an individual other than a trust from "a business that is the individual's artistic endeavour," moreover, subsection 10(6) of the Act allows the individual to make an election whereby

the value of any inventory of the business is deemed to be nil. For this purpose, subsection 10(8) defines the words "business that is an individual's artistic endeavour" as:

> the business of creating paintings, prints, etchings, drawings, sculptures or similar works of art, where such works of art are created by the individual, but does not include a business of reproducing works of art.

For income from this kind of business, subsection 10(6) permits individual taxpayers to adopt a type of cash basis accounting according to which the costs of creating qualifying artworks may be deducted in the year in which these costs are incurred, even if the artworks have yet to be sold. Where an individual files an election under subsection 10(6), subsection 10(7) requires the individual to continue to value inventory of the business as nil, "unless the taxpayer, with the concurrence of the Minister and on such terms and conditions as are specified by the Minister, revokes the election."

3. Capital Expenditures

In computing a taxpayer's income from a business or property, paragraph 18(1)(b) of the Act prohibits any deduction in respect of "an outlay, loss or replacement of capital, a payment on account of capital or an allowance in respect of depreciation, obsolescence or depletion except as expressly permitted by this Part." As a result, even if an outlay or expense has been made or incurred in a taxation year within the meaning of paragraph 18(1)(a), its deduction may be disallowed on the basis that it constitutes a capital loss or what is generally described as a "capital expenditure."[59] Except as expressly permitted under Part I of the Act, moreover, in computing a taxpayer's income from a business or property, no deduction may be made in respect of "an allowance in respect of depreciation, obsolescence or depletion."[60]

Where a taxpayer incurs a capital loss in a taxation year, the "allowable" portion of the loss (currently one-half) is generally deductible only against

---

[59] For this interpretation of the relationship between paras. 18(1)(a) and (b), see *British Columbia Electric Railway Co. v. M.N.R.*, [1958] S.C.J. No. 4, [1958] C.T.C. 21, 58 D.T.C. 1022 (S.C.C.), *per* Abbott J (Kerwin CJ and Fauteux J concurring).

[60] Depreciation refers to the decrease in the value of property over time, which typically occurs when tangible property is used to obtain income from a business or property; obsolescence denotes a decrease in the value of property due to innovation; and depletion means a decrease in the value of a resource property from exploitation of the resource. Although para. 18(1)(b) prohibits the deduction of allowances in respect of these items that a taxpayer may recognize for accounting purposes, Part I of the Act permits a deduction for "capital cost allowances" in para. 20(1)(a), a deduction in respect of a "terminal loss" in the value of depreciable property in subs. 20(16), and a deduction in respect of the depletion of resource properties in s. 65. Paragraph 20(1)(a) and subs. 20(16) are considered later in this chapter. This chapter does not consider the resource allowance in s. 65 of the Act.

taxable capital gains for the year,[61] and excluded from the rules governing the computation of a taxpayer's income or loss from a business or property.[62] Where a taxpayer makes or incurs a capital expenditure, the amount of this expenditure is added to the cost of the property in respect of which it is made or incurred, and (depending on the type of property) either subtracted from any proceeds of disposition in order to compute a capital gain or loss, or deductible over varying periods of time in computing the taxpayer's income from a business. As a result, capital expenditures, like inventory costs, are not fully deductible in the taxation year in which they are made or incurred, but must be deferred in whole or in part to subsequent taxation years in which gains or losses are realized or deductions are permitted by the Act. In this respect, like inventory accounting, the statutory scheme for capital expenditures ensures a "truer picture" of the taxpayer's income by matching the deduction of expenditures with the inclusion of revenues in subsequent taxation years.

The following text and cases consider the tax treatment of capital expenditures, examining statutory and judicial rules governing both the characterization of amounts as capital expenditures and the computation of deductible allowances in respect of "depreciable property" (capital cost allowances) and "eligible capital property" (eligible capital expenditures).

a. Characterization

Since the Act does not define the words "outlay of capital," "replacement of capital," or "payment on account of capital," the characterization of an amount as a capital expenditure depends on legal tests developed by the courts. A notable discussion of these judicial tests appears in *Canada v. Johns-Manville Corp.*, [1985] S.C.J. No. 44, [1985] 2 C.T.C. 111, 85 D.T.C. 5373 (S.C.C.).

Canada v. Johns-Manville Corp.
[1985] S.C.J. No. 44, [1985] 2 C.T.C. 111, 85 D.T.C. 5373 (S.C.C.)

[The taxpayer operated an open-pit asbestos mine in Quebec, in the course of which it was necessary to purchase land on a regular basis in order to extend the perimeter of the mine to maintain a gradual slope and prevent landslides. In computing its income for its 1969 and 1970 taxation years, the taxpayer deducted the cost of land acquired during the year as an ordinary business

---

[61] See para. 3(b) of the Act. Where the capital loss is characterized as a "business investment loss" within the meaning of para. 39(1)(c), the allowable loss (also one-half) is deductible against net income from all sources under para. 3(d). Where a taxpayer's allowable capital losses for a taxation year exceed taxable capital gains for the year, the excess is defined as a "net capital loss" under subs. 111(8), which may be deducted against net taxable capital gains in the previous three taxation years and any subsequent taxation year.

[62] See, for example, subs. 9(3), which stipulates that the words "loss from a property" do not include "any capital loss from the disposition of that property."

expense. The Minister disallowed the deductions on the basis that the cost of the land was a capital expenditure. The taxpayer appealed.]

ESTEY J (Dickson CJC, Beetz, McIntyre, Chouinard, Wilson JJ concurring): ... The learned trial judge concluded that these land expenditures were not in the nature of capital outlays but rather were expenses incurred in the mining operations and should be taken into account in the computation of net income in connection therewith. In the course of so determining, the learned justice stated: "The evidence also discloses that the acquisition of property at the periphery of its mining pit has been a constant part of the mining operations of Johns-Manville and purchases of land have occurred annually for almost 40 years. The acquisition cost of the purchases of such lands represent only ..." about three per cent of the average of the cost of sales of the appellant during the eight-year period from 1966 to 1973 inclusive. He continued:

> The subject expenditures did not add to or preserve the ore body. Instead, the lands purchased by these expenditures were in essence consumed for all practical purposes in the course of and as part of the mining operations of Johns-Manville and as a consequence were expenditures "incidental to the production and sale of the output of the mine" (cf *Denison Mines Limited v. M.N.R.*, [[1976] 1 SCR 245]) and were part of the cost in the determination of profits.

His Lordship concluded:

> Therefore, after considering the whole of the evidence, and as stated, looking at the character or quality of the expenditures based upon business or commercial practice rather than the character of the asset acquired by the expenditures, the conclusion is that the subject expenditures in the taxation years 1969 and 1970 were not on capital account within the meaning of section 12(1)(b) [now paragraph 18(1)(b)] of the *Income Tax Act*.

The Court of Appeal, Ryan J writing on behalf of the Court, reversed the trial court and concluded that these expenditures were of a capital nature and could not be charged as an expense in the computation of profit from the appellant's mining operations. In the course of his judgment, His Lordship acknowledged:

> It is no doubt true that the overburden, soil and rock removed in the course of blending the lots with the pit have little or no commercial value. It may also be true that, on completion of the mining of the ore, the site of the asbestos deposit and the pit may be a valueless wasteland — a real possibility.

Later in the judgment it was stated: "It may even be, as he [the trial judge] concluded, that the lots in question are in a way consumed." Indeed the Court of Appeal stated: "I accept the trial judge's basic findings of fact."

However, in reaching the conclusion that these expenditures were capital in nature, it was stated:

> As I see it, the lots were bought because they were adjacent to the pit and thus could be used to extend its slope, an extension that resulted in the lots becoming part of the pit. The lots, as part of the pit, serve as land on which the operation is in part carried on; for example, roads (the location of which may shift as the wall extends), spiralling up the side of the pit, are used to carry ore out of the pit.

And further, it was stated that the expenditures were:

> ... for purchases of lots of land which were incorporated in the operating structure of the enterprise ... [This] dominates the consideration that the lots are purchased annually in anticipation of the lowering of the level of the ore deposit. And it dominates that consideration that the lots may only remain as portions of a virtual wasteland when the mine ceases to operate.

...

The simple question which must here be decided, therefore, is this: can the taxpayer, when purchasing the additional surface area needed for the enlargement of the cone, charge the purchase price of the land as a production expense or must the taxpayer capitalize the land cost? The taxpayer's expense incurred in removing the overburden from these lands is not in issue. It should be noted that at one stage the Minister allowed a depletion allowance for part of the lands so acquired. This was acknowledged by both parties to be a conciliatory gesture rather than a supportable interpretation of the *Income Tax Act* depletion allowance provisions. These lands were not ore bearing and were not part of the surface overlaying the mineral deposit. The classification of these expenditures as capital would leave the taxpayer, of course, without any deductions from income in respect thereto. This of course is not decisive but may be of relevance in assessing the interaction of the "expense" and "capital" provisions in the overall pattern of the statute.

...

When one turns to the appropriate principles of law to apply to the determination of the classification of an expenditure as being either expense or capital, an unnerving starting place is the comment of the Master of the Rolls, Sir Wilfred Greene in *British Salmson Aero Engines Ltd v. CIR* (1938), 22 TC 29, at 43:

> ... there have been ... many cases where this matter of capital or income has been debated. There have been many cases which fall upon the borderline: indeed, in many cases it is almost true to say that the spin of a coin would decide the matter almost as satisfactorily as an attempt to find reasons. ...

This Court encountered paragraph 12(1)(b) in *M.N.R. v. Algoma Central*, [1968] SCR 447, [1968] CTC 161. Fauteux J, as he then was, at 449 (CTC 162), stated:

> Parliament did not define the expressions "outlay ... of capital" or "payment on account of capital." There being no statutory criterion, the application or non-application of these expressions to any particular expenditures must depend upon the facts of the particular case. We do not think that any single test applies in making that determination. ...

The Court thereupon expressed agreement with the decision of the Privy Council in *B.P. Australia Ltd. v. Commissioner of Taxation of the Commonwealth of Australia*, [1966] AC 224. The Privy Council there determined that a payment made by the taxpayer as an inducement to a service station operator to sign an exclusive agency contract was an income expenditure and not a capital outlay ... . After reviewing a number of different approaches to the problem of classifying in law and accounting the nature of the expenditure, Lord Pearce stated, at 264-65:

> *The solution to the problem is not to be found by any rigid test or description.* It has to be derived from many aspects of the whole set of circumstances some of which may point in one direction, some in the other. One consideration may point so clearly that it dominates other and vaguer indications in the contrary direction. *It is a commonsense appreciation of all the guiding features which must provide the ultimate answer.* Although the categories of capital and income expenditure are distinct and easily ascertainable in obvious cases that lie far from the boundary, the line of distinction is often hard to draw in border line cases; and conflicting considerations may produce a situation where the answer turns on questions of emphasis and degree. That answer:
>
> > "depends on what the expenditure is calculated to effect from a practical and business point of view rather than upon the juristic classification of the legal rights, if any, secured, employed or exhausted in the process"
>
> *per* Dixon J in *Hallstroms Pty. Ltd. v. Federal Commissioner of Taxation* (1946) 72 CLR 634, 648. [Emphasis added]

The Privy Council applied another test in the course of characterizing the expenditures in *BP Australia, supra*, at 271: "Finally, were these sums expended on the structure within which the profits were to be earned or were they part of the money-earning process?" This question is remarkably apt on the circumstances in the appeal now before this Court. The Privy Council's answer was that the expenditure was not to be taken as being on the structure but rather as part of the money-earning process. At 273, Lord Pearce, in considering the manner in which the benefit procured by the expenditure was to be used, stated that such benefit was to be used "in the continuous and recurrent struggle to get orders and sell petrol." In my view, the same result is reached on the circumstances existing in this appeal. The removal of the ore here was obviously the continuous and recurrent struggle in which the taxpayer was principally engaged, and the expenditure here was, as revealed by its uniform history over the years and by its role in the process of the recovery of ore, part of the essential profit-seeking operation of the taxpayer.

In the *Hallstroms* case, *supra*, Dixon J, as he then was, in discussing the difference between capital and income expenditures, stated, at 647, that the difference lay:

> between the acquisition of the means of production and the use of them; between establishing or extending a business organisation and carrying on the business; between the implements employed in work and the regular performance of the work ... ; between an enterprise itself and the sustained effort of those engaged in it.

Other tests have been adopted in other tax systems. Also in Australia, in the High Court decision in *Sun Newspapers Limited v. Federal Commissioner of Taxation* (1938), 61 CLR 337, the Court, speaking through Dixon J, enunciated three principles to be applied in determining the character of an expenditure by a taxpayer for the purposes of applying the taxation statute. He stated, at 363:

> There are, I think, three matters to be considered, (a) the character of the advantage sought, and in this its lasting qualities may play a part, (b) the manner in which it is to be used, relied upon or enjoyed, and in this and under the former head recurrence may play its part, and (c) the means adopted to obtain it; that is, by providing a periodical reward or outlay to cover its use or enjoyment for periods commensurate with the payment or by making a final provision or payment so as to secure future use or enjoyment.

On the preceding page, His Lordship, in explaining the test from another aspect, said:

> ... the expenditure is to be considered of a revenue nature if its purpose brings it within the very wide class of things which in the aggregate form the constant demand which must be answered out of the returns of a trade or its circulating capital and that actual recurrence of the specific thing need not take place or be expected as likely.

The Court on that occasion was concerned with the character to be ascribed to a payment made by one competitor to another to secure a discontinuance of a new and threatening adventure. The Court concluded the payment was capital in nature and should not be charged to revenue.

...

At one time, the test applied by the courts in discriminating as between revenue and capital was the "once and for all" test. This test was adopted by Viscount Cave LC in *British Insulated and Helsby Cables v. Atherton*, [1926] AC 205 at 213. Viscount Cave observed that the finding of revenue or capital was a question of fact, but then concerned himself with the answer to the question because of an imprecise finding below. The test he adopted at 213 was "... to say that capital expenditure is a thing that is going to be spent once and for all, and income expenditure is a thing that is going to recur every year," although he recognized that this test was not "to be a decisive one in every case." Later on the same page the Lord Chancellor elaborated:

> ... [W]hen an expenditure is made not only once and for all, but with a view to bringing into existence an asset or an advantage for the enduring benefit of a trade, I think that is a very good reason (in the absence of special circumstances leading to an opposite conclusion) for treating such an expenditure as properly attributable not to revenue but to capital.

...

After this review of the authorities it can be seen that the principles enunciated by the courts and the elucidation on the application of those principles is of very little guidance when it becomes necessary, as it is here, to apply those principles to a precise set of somewhat unusual facts.

...

[P]aragraph 11(1)(a) of the Act [now paragraph 20(1)(a)] ... authorizes the deduction of "such part of the capital cost to the taxpayer of property, or such amount in respect of the capital cost to the taxpayer of property, if any, as is allowed by regulation ... ." Regulation 1100(1) creates a series of capital cost allowances and Schedule B [now Schedule II] sets forth the classes of property to which these rates of allowances may be applied. The property here in question is not to be found in Schedule B and hence no capital cost allowance can be taken under section 11 with reference to the cost of these land acquisitions. Furthermore, subject to any concession made by the Minister, no depletion allowance is available on these lands as they are not used for mining purposes. Consequently, the taxpayer is in the position of either being permitted ... to deduct these expenditures as expenses "for the purpose of gaining or producing income," or being left with no tax relief of any kind with respect to these ongoing expenditures ... . On the other hand, if the property were to be treated as an undepreciable capital asset, then, on wind-up and disposition of all the properties and assets of the appellant, the question would arise as to whether the taxpayer had realized a capital gain or a capital loss depending upon the relationship between the proceeds on disposition and the cost of acquisition. A capital loss would, if the Act be as it is today, only be deductible by the appellant from realized capital gains. The capital gain would be taxable at half the rate applicable to the proceeds on disposition were they taken into income, again assuming the Act continues in its present form. This reasoning, of course does not conclusively lead to any result, either for or against either of the contending parties. On the other hand, if the interpretation of a taxation statute is unclear, and one reasonable interpretation leads to a deduction to the credit of a taxpayer and the other leaves the taxpayer with no relief from clearly *bona fide* expenditures in the course of his business activities, the general rules of interpretation of taxing statutes would direct the tribunal to the former interpretation. That is the situation here, in my view of these statutory provisions. These expenditures were clearly made for *bona fide* purposes. They clearly are not disqualified by paragraph 12(1)(a) nor by any other section of the *Income Tax Act* dealing with expenditures in the course of operating a business. The only possible basis in the statute for a denial of these *bona fide* expenditures closely associated with the conduct of the taxpayer's mining operations is the prohibition in paragraph 12(1)(b) relating to capital expenditures.

...

In this situation, ... it may be helpful to observe:

1.   The purpose of these expenditures, when viewed from the practical and business outlook, was the removal of a current obstacle in the operation of the taxpayer's mine and was not the acquisition of a capital asset;

2.   These expenditures were incurred year in and year out as an integral part of the day-to-day operations of the undertaking of the taxpayer;

3.   These expenditures form an easily discernible, more or less constant, element and part of the daily and annual cost of production;

4.   These lands were not acquired for any intrinsic value but merely by reason of location, and after the mining operation for the year in question had been completed, the land had acquired no intrinsic value, and indeed, as was found below, was "consumed" in the mining process;

5. These expenditures produced a transitional benefit and one which had no enduring value because similar expenditures were required in the future if the mining operation was to be continued at all;

6. The lands acquired in any given year do not produce a permanent wall or perimeter to the mining operation but are simply a transitional location of the wall representing the cone surrounding the mining undertaking; and to the extent that the wall of the cone is used for haulage of materials from the bottom of the pit on temporary roads, there may be some transitional asset created, but this asset disappears as the wall of the cone recedes in ensuing taxation years;

7. The nature of these expenditures is made clear when it is appreciated that they have been incurred annually for almost 40 years and there is no evidence whatever to indicate that mining operations can continue in the future without this annual expenditure;

8. The capitalization of these expenditures will not produce for the mining operator an asset which may be made subject to either capital cost or depletion allowances, the former because no asset recognized in the *Income Tax Act* is produced, and the latter because these lands contain no minerals which are being removed by the mining operations of the taxpayer;

9. These expenditures did not add to the ore body, nor did they increase the productive capacity of the mine, nor do they bear any relation to any asset engaged in the mining operation, but are simply expenditures for the removal of overburden which, if not removed, would bring the mining operation to a halt;

10. The expenditures relative to the cost of operating the mine are small and are directly related to the cost of operation averaging over a long period about three per cent per annum.

...

Here the taxpayer, at the end of the mining operations, is the owner of a large hole in the surface of the earth. The acquired lands represent segments down the wall of the hole, the older purchases being further down than the last purchases. There is no asset in the sense of a surface which can, by itself, be sold. The hole once filled in, at a likely considerable expense, would produce a surface which might have value in the market. Although the hole itself, and that part of the wall with which we are here concerned, might conceivably have some value, it can hardly be described as an asset which by itself has a real value. The evidence indicates that the life of this mine will end in the 1990s. Both courts below have concluded that at that time these lands will have disappeared for all practical purposes.

In applying the law to the above stated observations, one is thrown back to the pronouncement by Lord Wilberforce in *Tucker v. Granada Motorway Services*, [1979] 2 All ER 801, where he said at 804:

> It is common in cases which raise the question whether a payment is to be treated as a revenue or as a capital payment for indicia to point different ways. *In the end the courts can do little better than form an opinion which way the balance lies.* There are a number of tests which have been stated in reported cases which it is useful to apply, but we have been warned more than once not to seek automatically to apply to one case words or formulae which have been found useful in another. ... Nevertheless reported cases are the best tools that we have, even if they may sometimes be blunt instruments. [Emphasis added.]

We must also remember the previously cited words of Lord Pearce in *B.P. Australia, supra*, at 264: "It is a commonsense appreciation of all the guiding features which must provide the ultimate answer."

If we were to apply the three-step test adopted by the Australian court in *Sun Newspapers, supra*, these expenditures would qualify as expenses rather than being capital in nature. The character of the advantage sought is that of an advantage in the current operations of the taxpayer. The practice was recurring and the manner in which the object of the expenditures was applied was directly incorporated into the mining operations of the taxpayer. Finally, the means adopted by the taxpayer to gain this advantage was the periodic outlay of its funds ... which would formerly have been classified, in the vocabulary of that day, as circulating capital. In the words of Dixon J, as he then was, in *Sun Newspapers, supra*, at 362, we are here concerned with an expenditure of a revenue nature because:

> ... its purpose brings it within the very wide class of things which in the aggregate form the constant demand which must be answered out of the returns of a trade or its circulating capital and that actual recurrence of the specific thing need not take place or be expected as likely.

The same judge in *Hallstroms Pty. Ltd., supra*, at 648, reminds us that the classification of such expenditures "... depends on what the expenditure is calculated to effect from a practical and business point of view rather than upon the juristic classification of legal rights ... ," *supra*. The old rule of "once and for all" as well as the "common sense" test, *supra*, lead us to a result favourable to the taxpayer's contention.

The characterization in taxation law of an expenditure is, in the final analysis (unless the statute is explicit which this one is not), one of policy. ... The assessment of the evidence and the conclusions to be derived therefrom, and the application of the common sense approach to the business of the taxpayer in relation to the tax provisions, leads, in my respectful view, to the conclusion that ... the appropriate taxation treatment is to allocate these expenditures to the revenue account and not to capital. Such a determination is, furthermore, consistent with another basic concept in tax law that where the taxing statute is not explicit, reasonable uncertainty or factual ambiguity resulting from lack of explicitness in the statute should be resolved in favour of the taxpayer. This residual principle must be the more readily applicable in this appeal where otherwise, annually recurring expenditures completely connected to the daily business operation of the taxpayer, afford the taxpayer no credit against tax either by way of capital cost or depletion allowance with reference to a capital expenditure, or an expense deduction against revenue. ...

Appeal allowed.

NOTES AND QUESTIONS

1.   On what grounds did the trial judge in *Johns-Manville* conclude that the costs of land acquisitions that were incurred by the taxpayer in its 1969 and 1970 taxation years were deductible in the taxation years in which they were incurred? Why did the Federal Court of Appeal reject this conclusion? Why did the Supreme Court of Canada allow the taxpayer's appeal?

Of what relevance to the Supreme Court of Canada decision is the fact that the expenditures were incurred in order to remove "a current obstacle in the operation of the taxpayer's mine"? Of what relevance is the fact that the expenditures "were incurred year in and year out as an integral part of the day-to-day operations of the undertaking of the taxpayer"? Of what relevance is the fact that the expenditures comprised "an easily discernible, more or less constant, element and part of the daily and annual cost of production"? Of what relevance is the fact that "the lands were not acquired for any intrinsic value" and were "consumed" in the mining process? Of what relevance is the fact that the expenditures "produced a transitional benefit"? Of what relevance is the fact that the expenditures had been incurred annually for almost 40 years? Of what relevance is the fact that the costs, if capitalized, were not eligible for capital cost or depletion allowances? Of what relevance is the fact that the annual expenditures to acquire peripheral lands were only about 3 per cent of the taxpayer's annual cost to operate the mine? Of what relevance is the court's conclusion that the expenditures were incurred for *bona fide* business purposes?

2.   Why does the Supreme Court of Canada decision in *Johns-Manville* rely on an interpretive presumption in favour of the taxpayer? How does it define this presumption? Do you agree with this interpretive rule? Why or why not?

3.   On what legal tests does the Supreme Court of Canada rely in *Johns-Manville* to distinguish capital expenditures from ordinary business expenses? Do you agree with the court's statement that "[t]he characterization in taxation law of an expenditure is, in the final analysis ... one of policy"? If so, what is this policy?

4.   Among the various tests that courts have used to characterize capital expenditures, the most traditional is that in *British Insulated and Helsby Cables v. Atherton*, [1926] A.C. 205 at 213 (H.L.), according to which an expenditure is "on account of capital" where it is made "not only once and for all, but with a view to bringing into existence an asset or advantage for the enduring benefit of a trade." In this case, the taxpayer made a large lump-sum payment to establish a pension fund for its employees, which it deducted in computing its income for

the taxation year in which it was paid. Concluding (at 214) that "the object and effect of the payment" was "to enable the company to establish the pension fund and to offer to all its existing and future employees a sure provision for their old age, and so to obtain for the company the substantial and lasting advantage of being in a position throughout its business life to secure and retain the services of a contented and efficient staff," the House of Lords disallowed the deduction on the basis that it was a capital expenditure.

5.   For notable Canadian cases in which expenditures have been characterized as capital expenditures under the traditional test in *British Insulated and Helsby Cables v. Atherton*, see *Montreal Light, Heat & Power Consolidated v. M.N.R.* and *Montreal Coke & Manufacturing Co. v. M.N.R.*, [1942] S.C.J. No. 4, [1942] C.T.C. 1, 2 D.T.C. 535 (S.C.C.), aff'd on other grounds [1944] C.T.C. 94 (P.C.); *No. 237 v. M.N.R.* (1955), 12 Tax ABC 230 (T.A.B.); *British Columbia Electric Railway Co. v. M.N.R.*, [1958] S.C.J. No. 4, [1958] C.T.C. 21, 58 D.T.C. 1022 (S.C.C.); *Supertest Petroleum Corporation Ltd. v. M.N.R.* (1964), 35 Tax ABC 117 (T.A.B.); *M.N.R. v. Haddon Hall Realty Inc.*, [1961] S.C.J. No. 71, [1961] C.T.C. 509, 62 D.T.C. 1001 (S.C.C.); and *H.J. Levin v. M.N.R.*, [1971] C.T.C. 66, 71 D.T.C. 5047 (Ex. Ct.).

In *Montreal Light, Heat & Power Consolidated*, the taxpayer, which issued $15,000,000 in new bonds in order to discharge old bonds on which a higher rate of interest was payable, sought to deduct refinancing costs of $2,282,079.42 (comprising premium and foreign exchange paid on retiring the old bonds, discount on the sale of the new bonds, and certain incidental expenses), which it proposed to amortize over the life of the new bonds. Observing that the taxpayer's decision to amortize the expenses over a period of years suggested that they were not "ordinary annual expenditures," a majority of the court disallowed the deduction on the basis (at para. 6) that the refinancing costs were capital expenditures "made with a view to securing an enduring benefit, the reduction of the cost of borrowed capital over a period of at least fifteen years."

In *No. 237*, the taxpayer, which incurred legal expenses making representations to the federal government leading to a reduction in customs duties on imported materials used in the taxpayer's manufacturing business, sought to deduct these legal expenses as an expense incurred for the purpose of gaining or producing income. Rejecting the taxpayer's arguments that the reduction in customs duties was not a positive benefit and was of uncertain duration because the duties could subsequently be increased, the board characterized the legal expenses as capital expenditures on the grounds (at paras. 14-16) that: (1) the advantage paid for need not be "of a positive character" and may involve "getting rid of an item of fixed capital that is of an onerous character," and (2) "it is fundamental to the whole theory of our legal system that the state of the law today must be taken as a permanent and abiding thing." Ironically, given the board's comments about the assumed permanency of the law, the *Income Tax Act* was amended in 1965 to permit the deduction of such representation expenses under what is now paragraph 20(1)(cc). Pursuant to subsection 20(9), a taxpayer may elect to deduct expenses otherwise deductible under paragraph 20(1)(cc) in equal amounts during the taxation year in which the expenses are incurred and each of the subsequent 9 taxation years, thereby amortizing its cost over a 10-year period.

In *British Columbia Electric Railway*, the taxpayer, which operated a money-losing railway in the Lower Fraser Valley in British Columbia, paid a total of $220,000 to five municipalities in British Columbia in order to obtain their approval for a plan to replace rail service with bus service. Characterizing the termination of the unprofitable railway as "an advantage for the enduring benefit of the appellant's business" (at para. 39), Abbott J (Kerwin CJ and Fauteaux J concurring) held that the payment was "on account of capital." In a concurring opinion, Locke J (Cartwright J concurring) concluded that the benefit might not endure, but characterized the payments as capital expenditures in any event on the basis that they increased the value of the taxpayer's transportation franchises, which were capital assets.

British Columbia Electric Railway was followed in *Mandrel Industries Inc. v. M.N.R.*, [1965] C.T.C. 233, 65 D.T.C. 5142 (Ex. Ct.), in which the taxpayer, a subsidiary of which had in 1956 granted an exclusive right to distribute its products in Canada for a period of five years, paid US $150,000 in 1958 in order to terminate the distributorship. Concluding that the payment was made by the taxpayer to reacquire the right to sell its own products and to launch its own selling organization in Canada, the court held that the expenditure was a capital expense. According to Cattanach J (at para. 29):

> There is no question that the payment was made once and for all. I also think it is clear that what the payment brought into being was an advantage in that the appellant could operate its own selling operation in Canada without being in breach of its previously existing exclusive sales contract.

For similar results in which expenditures to terminate franchises have been characterized as capital expenses, see *Crystal Springs Beverage Co. v. M.N.R.*, [1964] C.T.C. 408, 64 D.T.C. 5253 (Ex. Ct.); and *Bomag (Canada) Ltd. v. M.N.R.*, [1984] F.C.J. No. 608, [1984] C.T.C. 378, 84 D.T.C. 6363 (F.C.A.).

In *Supertest Petroleum Corporation Ltd.*, the taxpayer incurred expenses to improve the premises of various dealers who, in consideration for these improvements, entered into "tying" agreements pursuant to which they agreed to sell only the taxpayer's products for periods averaging 10 years. Concluding (at para. 29) that the expenses were capital expenditures "made with a view to bringing into existence an asset or advantage for the enduring benefit of the trade," the board disallowed their deduction.

In *Haddon Hall Realty Inc*, the taxpayer, a company that owned and operated rental properties, sought in computing its income for its 1955 taxation year to deduct $11,675.95 that it spent during the year to replace stoves, refrigerators, and window blinds that had become worn out, obsolete, or otherwise unsatisfactory to its tenants. Emphasizing that "[e]xpenditures to replace capital assets which have become worn out or obsolete are something quite different from those ordinary annual expenditures for repairs which fall naturally into the category of income disbursements" (at para. 7), the court disallowed the deduction in the basis that the payments were "made once and for all with a view to bringing into existence an asset or advantage for the enduring benefit of the taxpayer's business."

In *Levin*, the taxpayer, a dentist practising in Toronto, sought to deduct tuition fees and travel expenses incurred to attend a course in prosthodontics at the College of Dentistry at New York University. Concluding (at para. 28) that the expenditures were "not of a recurrent nature" and "were made with a view to bringing into existence an advantage, i.e., a status as a prosthodontic specialist, for the enduring benefit of the appellant," the court disallowed the deduction of the tuition fees on the basis that they were on account of capital. For a similar result, see *Gridley v. M.N.R.* (1951), 4 Tax ABC 122 (T.A.B.), in which tuition fees paid by the taxpayer for a postgraduate course in cardiology and electrocardiology were characterized as a capital expenditure on the grounds (at para. 8) that "the payment was made once and for all; and that the knowledge gained by him is as much a capital asset as the knowledge gained by him when he took his original medical course which enabled him to obtain a licence to practice." See also *Daley v. M.N.R.* (1950), 1 Tax ABC 364 (T.A.B.), in which a $1,500 payment to be admitted to the Law Society of Upper Canada was characterized as a capital expenditure "which was made *once and for all* and which *created a lasting advantage for the appellant*" (at para. 16) (emphasis in original).

6.   For notable cases in which Canadian courts have refused to characterize an outlay or expense as a capital expenditure on the basis that the expenditure did not bring into existence an advantage of enduring benefit for the taxpayer's business, see *Johnston Testers Ltd. v. M.N.R.*, [1965] C.T.C. 116, 65 D.T.C. 5069 (Ex. Ct.); *Algoma Central Railway v. M.N.R.*, [1967] C.T.C. 130, 67 D.T.C. 5091 (Ex. Ct.), aff'd [1968] S.C.J. No. 24, [1968] C.T.C. 161, 68 D.T.C. 5096 (S.C.C.); *Canada Starch Co. Ltd. v. M.N.R.*, [1968] C.T.C. 466, 68 D.T.C. 5320 (Ex. Ct.); *Oxford Shopping Centres Ltd. v. Canada*, [1980] C.T.C. 7, 79 D.T.C. 5458 (F.C.T.D.), aff'd [1981] C.T.C. 128, 81 D.T.C. 5065 (F.C.A.); and *Central Amusement Co. v. M.N.R.*, [1992] F.C.J. No. 132, [1992] 1 C.T.C. 218, 92 D.T.C. 6225 (F.C.T.D.).

In *Johnston Testers Ltd.*, the taxpayer, which had entered into an agreement in 1956 to pay royalties until 1972 for the use of certain patents, paid $146,850 in 1958 to obtain a release from this obligation, which the taxpayer sought to deduct in computing its income for its 1958 taxation year. Distinguishing between cases in which such payments are made "in respect of a capital asset in order to *pro tanto* go out of business" and cases in which "such payment was made for the purpose of ... continuing [the] business" (at para. 43), the court allowed the deduction on the basis that the payment was made "to get rid of an annual charge against revenue in the future." According to Gibson J (at para. 53):

the true business purpose of this commutation payment ... was to get rid of an onerous annual expense in respect to a business that it proposed to and did carry on, and such payment was made in the course of such continuing business; and ... as a result no advantage or benefit ... accrued to the capital account of the appellant, but instead all the advantage and benefit obtained was of a revenue character and, therefore, the payment was not a capital outlay within the meaning of Section 12(1)(b) of the *Income Tax Act*.

For other cases in which lump-sum payments to obtain a release from a contractual obligation have been characterized as deductible current expenses, see *Dymo of Canada Ltd. v. M.N.R.*, [1973] F.C.J. No. 30, [1973] C.T.C. 205, 73 D.T.C. 5171 (F.C.T.D.); *Automatic Toll Systems (Canada) Ltd. v. M.N.R.*, [1974] F.C.J. No. 30, [1974] C.T.C. 30, 74 D.T.C. 6060 (F.C.T.D.); and *Angostura International Ltd. v. Canada*, [1985] 2 C.T.C. 170, 85 D.T.C. 5384 (F.C.T.D.).

In *Algoma Central Railway*, the taxpayer, which operated a railway through sparsely populated areas of northern Ontario, commissioned a five-year geological survey of the properties through which its railway ran, in the hope that this would lead to resource development and increased traffic on its lines. Concluding that the anticipated benefit of increased traffic was too remote and speculative to constitute an "advantage" of an enduring benefit within the meaning of the test in *British Insulated and Helsby Cables v. Atherton*, the court rejected the Minister's argument that payments for the survey of $43,603.40 in 1960, $85,189.06 in 1961 and $138,369.41 in 1962 were non-deductible capital expenditures. According to Jackett P (at para. 25):

In all ... cases ... to which reference was made during the argument, the "advantage" that was held to be of an enduring benefit to the taxpayer's business was the thing contracted for or otherwise anticipated by the taxpayer as the direct result of the expenditure. In all such cases it was the "advantage" so acquired that, it was contemplated, would endure to the benefit of the taxpayer's business. In my view, the information received by the appellant here, in consideration of the expenditures in dispute, is not such an "advantage" of an enduring benefit to the taxpayer's business.

Instead, he continued, these expenditures were not unlike advertising expenses, which, although "designed to benefit the business in an enduring way," are generally deductible as expenses in the year in which they are incurred.

In *Canada Starch Co. Ltd.*, the taxpayer, which produced and distributed cooking oils, industrial starches, and corn sweeteners, deducted an amount of $15,000 in computing its business income for its 1964 taxation year, which amount was paid to the owner of a registered trademark in consideration for which the latter withdrew its opposition to the taxpayer's registration of a similar trademark for a new cooking oil called "VIVA," which it introduced in that year. Rejecting the Minister's argument that the deduction should be disallowed on the basis that it was a capital expenditure, the court considered the nature of a trademark to conclude that the payment had not brought into existence an asset or advantage for the enduring benefit of the taxpayer's business. According to Jackett P (at para. 14):

in distinguishing between a capital payment and a payment on current account, in my view, regard must be had to the business and commercial realities of the matter. When the intricate

817

conditions of the *Trade Marks Act* are properly understood, they operate so that the statute only provides protection for a trade mark that is distinctive of the owner's wares or services. If it does not distinguish them, the registration is invalid (Section 18), and the protection afforded by Section 19 does not apply. The situation is, therefore, that if, as a result of the ordinary current operations of a business, a trade mark is distinctive, the action of passing off (and Section 7 of the *Trade Marks Act*) operates to give automatic protection; and additional protection can be obtained by registration. The trade mark, as an advantage for the enduring benefit of the business, is the product of the current operations of the business and is not the result of registration. Registration merely facilitates the businessman in enforcing the rights that accrued to him from his business operations. Either "VIVA" will be found, if it is ever tested, to have become distinctive of the appellant's wares by virtue of its trading operations, or its registration will be found to be invalid. Mere registration is an empty right if it is not based on a trade mark that has business or commercial reality as an incidental consequence of the current operations of the business. In my view, therefore, the trade mark in question as an "advantage for the enduring benefit of the ... business," if it is such an advantage, was not acquired by the payment of $15,000.

In *Oxford Shopping Centres Ltd.*, the taxpayer deducted $490,050 in computing its business income for its 1971 taxation year, which it paid in the year to the city of Calgary in consideration for which the latter agreed to construct a road interchange affecting access to the taxpayer's parking lot. Concluding (at para. 25) that the advantage obtained by the taxpayer was "no more permanent in nature than that expected to be realized from the geological survey which had been made in the *Algoma* case," the court rejected the Minister's argument that the payment was properly characterized as a capital expenditure. According to Thurlow ACJ (at paras. 26-28):

> if, as I think, the expenditure can and should be regarded as having been laid out as a means of maintaining, and perhaps enhancing, the popularity of the shopping centre with the tenants' customers as a place to shop and of enabling the shopping centre to meet the competition of other shopping centres, while at the same time avoiding the imposition of taxes for street improvements, the expenditure can, as it seems to me, be regarded as a revenue expense notwithstanding the once and for all nature of the payment on the more or less long term character of the advantage to be gained by making it. ...
>
> Moreover, while the undesirable effects of traffic congestion on the popularity of the shopping centre and on its prospects for competing with a rival shopping centre might conceivably have led to some other whole or partial solution involving an outlay of a capital nature, such as to restructure the shopping centre or its buildings or its means of access, and egress (and some such outlays may indeed have been made), this is not what the expenditure here in question was for. The money was not paid for changes in or additions to the appellant's premises or the buildings thereon or in connection with the structure of the appellant's business. Rather, it was paid to induce the city to make changes on city property that could be beneficial to the plaintiff in achieving its object of promoting its business by enhancing the popularity of its shopping centre.

For similar results, see *Cummings v. Canada*, [1981] F.C.J. No. 524, [1981] C.T.C. 285, 81 D.T.C. 5207 (F.C.A.) (expenses incurred pursuant to lease "pickup" obligations not capital expenditures) and *Baker Lovick Ltd. v. M.N.R.*, [1991] T.C.J. No. 428, [1991] 2 C.T.C. 2345, 91 D.T.C. 1041 (T.C.C.) (tenant inducement payments not capital expenses).

In *Central Amusement Co.*, the taxpayer deducted $175,026 in computing its business income for its 1983 taxation year, which it spent during the year to replace the circuit boards in 900 to 1,000 video and other arcade games (which cost roughly $4 million in total), thereby creating new games that satisfied the market for another few months. On the grounds that the expenditure was required "on a recurring and regular basis" and that the advantage obtained by the taxpayer by the purchase of new circuit boards "is temporary in nature," the court rejected the Minister's argument that the payments were on account of capital.

7. In *Damon Developments Ltd. v. M.N.R.*, [1988] T.C.J. No. 103, [1988] 1 C.T.C. 2266, 88 D.T.C. 1128 (T.C.C.), the taxpayer, which owned and operated a hotel in Regina, deducted in each of its taxation years from 1977 to 1983 the amount expended in each of these years to acquire various items (draperies, televisions, and washer and dryer machinery) to replace outmoded hotel equipment. Distinguishing *M.N.R. v. Haddon Hall Realty Inc.*, [1961] S.C.J. No. 71, [1961] C.T.C. 509, 62 D.T.C. 1001 (S.C.C.), on the basis that the items in question had a shorter useful life in the hotel business than when used by tenants in an apartment building, the court rejected the Minister's argument that the expenses were on account of capital on the grounds (at para. 10) that "expenditures for the hotel ... occur regularly at relatively short intervals and are therefore made to meet a continuous demand for expenditures."

8. In addition to the traditional test in *British Insulated and Helsby Cables v. Atherton*, [1926] A.C. 205 (H.L.), another test that courts have used to characterize capital expenditures is that adopted by the Privy Council in *B.P. Australia Ltd. v. Commissioner of Taxation of the Commonwealth of Australia*, [1966] A.C. 224 at 271 (P.C.), according to which expenditures are "on account of capital" where they are "expended on the structure within which the profits [are] earned" by the taxpayer, and "on revenue account" where they are expended as "part of the money-earning process." A similar test appears in *Sun Newspapers Limited v. Federal Commissioner of Taxation* (1938), 61 C.L.R. 337 at 359 (Aust. H.C.), where the High Court of Australia Court distinguished between "the business entity, structure, or organization set up or established for the earning of profit and the process by which such an organization operates to obtain regular returns by means of regular outlay," and in *Hallstrom's Pty. Ltd. v. Federal Commissioner of Taxation* (1946), 72 C.L.R. 634 at 647 (Aust. H.C.), another Australian decision in which the court distinguished "between the acquisition of the means of production and the use of them; between establishing or extending a business organisation and carrying on the business; between the implements employed in work and the regular performance of the work ... ; between an enterprise itself and the sustained effort of those engaged in it."

In *B.P. Australia*, the taxpayer made an inducement payment to a service station operator that entered into an exclusive agency agreement to distribute the taxpayer's products, which it deducted in computing its business income for the taxation year in which it was paid. Allowing the deduction, the Privy Council held (at 273) that the expenditure was made as part of the money-earning process "in the continuous and recurrent struggle to get orders and sell petrol."

In *Sun Newspapers*, the taxpayer made a lump-sum non-competition payment to a competitor, which it deducted in computing its business income for the taxation year in which it was paid. Concluding (at 354-55) that the expenditure was "a large non-recurrent unusual expenditure made for the purpose of obtaining an advantage for the enduring benefit of the appellants' trade ... namely, the exclusion of what might have been serious competition," the court characterized the payment as a non-deductible capital expenditure.

In *Hallstrom's*, the taxpayer incurred legal expenses to fight an application by a competitor to extend its patent on a refrigerator, which it deducted in computing its business income for the taxpayer year in which the expenses were incurred. Allowing the taxpayer's appeal from an assessment characterizing the expenses as a capital expenditure, a majority of the court held that the expenses were incurred in the process of gaining or producing income.

9. For Canadian cases in which expenditures have been characterized as capital expenditures under the tests adopted in *B.P. Australia*, *Sun Newspapers*, and *Hallstrom's*, see *Bennett & White Construction Ltd. v. M.N.R.*, [1948] S.C.J. No. 48, [1949] C.T.C. 1, 49 D.T.C. 514 (S.C.C.); *Cormack v. M.N.R.* (1965), 35 Tax ABC 437 (T.A.B.); *M.N.R. v. Canadian Glassine Co. Ltd.*, [1976] F.C.J. No. 61, [1976] C.T.C. 141, 76 D.T.C. 6083 (F.C.A.); *D.M. Firestone v. Canada*, [1987] F.C.J. No. 401, [1987] 2 C.T.C. 1, 87 D.T.C. 5237 (F.C.A.); and *Bancroft v. M.N.R.*, [1989] T.C.J. No. 104, [1989] 1 C.T.C. 2196, 89 D.T.C. 153 (T.C.C.).

In *Bennett & White Construction Ltd.*, the taxpayer company deducted commissions paid to three of its directors in consideration for their agreement to guarantee the company's indebtedness to a bank. Distinguishing between "expenditures made in providing capital for an enterprise and those for the carrying on of the trade from which its earnings are derived" (at para. 6), Locke J (Rinfret CJ concurring) disallowed the deduction on the grounds (at para. 6) that:

> the character of the payments in the present case does not differ in essence from those which were disallowed in the *Montreal Coke* case. They were, in my opinion, simply expenditures incurred in obtaining the capital to make the large deposits required, to purchase equipment and generally to finance the operations. A sum expended as interest for the use of capital is clearly to be distinguished from expenditures such as these, being the cost of obtaining guarantees without which the loans would not have been made by the bank, expenditures of the same character as the cost of floating issues of bonds or debentures or of selling shares for the purpose of obtaining capital.

Concurring in the decision, Rand J (at para. 14) regarded the payments as "preparatory to earning the income and ... no more part of the business carried on than would be the work involved in a bond issue." As a result, he concluded, they were incurred to "create part of the capital structure and are a capital payment."

In *Cormack*, the taxpayer, a medical practitioner who devoted much of his time to educational projects and subsequently opened a private school in Edmonton, sought to deduct the cost of a trip to Great Britain, the Netherlands, and Norway in 1961 to observe their schools, educational systems, and methods. Disallowing the deduction on the basis that it was a capital expense, the board commented (at para. 4):

> What the appellant did in so travelling abroad was not spend money in the earning of income, but for the purpose of increasing his knowledge of a special subject, or adding to what virtually was a capital asset. He may have been, and probably was, improving his means of earning income subsequently, but he earned nothing by proceeding to Europe in 1961 for the purpose mentioned and in no way augmented his income at that time.

In *Canadian Glassine*, the taxpayer, which manufactured lightweight specialty papers, entered into an agreement with Anglo-Canadian Pulp and Paper Mills Ltd. Anglo-Canadian undertook to construct at its own expense two underground pipelines to convey slush pulp and steam from its plant to that of the taxpayer and to supply slush pulp and steam to the taxpayer's plant for stipulated periods, in consideration for which the taxpayer issued to Anglo-Canadian shares and other securities valued at $268,623.48. Rejecting the taxpayer's argument that this sum should be deductible over the 25-year period stipulated in the contract to supply slush pulp, a majority of the Federal Court of Appeal disallowed the deduction on the basis that the cost was a capital expense incurred "for the establishment of the profit-making structure of the [taxpayer's] trade." Dissenting, LeDain J contended (at para. 38) that the expenditure was "simply part of the operating cost to the [taxpayer] of obtaining a supply of pulp and steam and did not obtain for it anything that can be regarded as an asset or advantage in the nature of fixed capital."

In *Firestone*, the taxpayer, the grandson of the founder of the Firestone Tire and Rubber Company, set out in 1968 to create his own "venture capital" business by acquiring financially distressed manufacturing businesses and making them profitable, and sought to deduct as current expenses a total of $77,590 incurred during the taxation years 1969 to 1972 to investigate potential businesses for acquisition. Disallowing the deduction, the court (at para. 15) characterized the expenditures as capital expenses incurred "in the course of putting together a new business structure." See also *Young v. M.N.R.*, [1989] F.C.J. No. 353, [1989] 1 C.T.C. 421, 89 D.T.C. 5234 (F.C.A.), where the cost of subscriptions in five investment publications was characterized as a capital expense on the basis (at para. 8) that the taxpayer was not a trader or dealer in securities and had used the information "for deciding on the purchase or sale of investments, managing such investments and generally in the administration of an expanding portfolio of capital assets."

In *Bancroft*, the taxpayer, a chartered accountant who acquired 700 acres of land near Gatineau Park with the expressed intention of opening a tourist resort, sought to deduct as business expenses roughly $132,000 incurred from 1982 to 1984 before he abandoned the project due to insufficient financing. Even though the taxpayer "never commenced his proposed business of a year-round country retreat," the court disallowed the deduction on the basis (at para. 30) that he "was in the process of creating a business structure." See also *Neonex International Ltd. v. Canada*, [1978] F.C.J. No. 514, [1978] C.T.C. 485, 78

D.T.C. 6339 (F.C.A.) (legal expenses of $260,000 incurred over the years 1970 to 1972 in connection with an unsuccessful takeover bid characterized as capital expenses); *Park Royal Shopping Centre Ltd. v. Canada*, [1995] T.C.J. No. 382, [1995] 2 C.T.C. 2117 (T.C.C.) (fees paid to a firm of architects to draw up plans for the proposed construction of a 14-storey office building to be erected adjacent to the taxpayer's shopping centre characterized as non-deductible capital expenses); and *Graham Construction and Engineering (1985) Ltd. v. Canada*, [1997] T.C.J. No. 343, 97 D.T.C. 342 (T.C.C.) (legal fees paid to an accounting firm and to two law firms for professional services relating to proposed acquisitions held to be capital expenses).

10.   For cases in which Canadian courts have refused to characterize an outlay or expense as a capital expenditure on the basis that the expenditure was incurred in the process of gaining or producing business income, see *Pantorama Industries Inc. v. Canada*, [2005] F.C.J. No. 635, [2005] 2 C.T.C. 336, 2005 D.T.C. 5230 (F.C.A.); *Bowater Power Co. Ltd. v. M.N.R.*, [1971] F.C.J. No. 36, [1971] C.T.C. 818, 71 D.T.C. 5469 (F.C.T.D.); *Wacky Wheatley's TV & Stereo Ltd. v. M.N.R.*, [1987] T.C.J. No. 811, [1987] 2 C.T.C. 2311, 87 D.T.C. 576 (T.C.C.); and *Inskip v. M.N.R.*, [1986] T.C.J. No. 1007, [1987] 1 C.T.C. 2009, (1986) 86 D.T.C. 1837 (T.C.C.).

In *Pantorama Industries*, Pantorama, the taxpayer corporation, sold casual clothing through over 200 leased premises located in shopping malls. Pantorama retained a firm called Snowcap Investments to find new locations for its stores and to negotiate new leases. Snowcap also regularly negotiated lease renewals, as required. Pantorama paid Snowcap a fixed periodic fee plus a variable fee based on the floor area and duration of the leases it entered into on behalf of Pantorama. In calculating its income, Pantorama did not capitalize any of the fees paid to Snowcap to match the duration of the leases, instead treating all fees as currently deductible. The Minister accepted that the fixed fees were a current expense, but argued that the variable fees were payments "on account of capital" and as such were not currently deductible. The Tax Court agreed with the Minister. The Federal Court of Appeal reversed the Tax Court, allowing Pantorama to treat the variable fees as current expenditures, stating that the Tax Court had erred in not considering the role the leases played in Pantorama's business, and ruling that the variable fees were not paid to Snowcap to secure an asset *per se*, but simply to allow it to continue to carry on business as it had done previously. At para. 22 of the judgment, in describing the large number of leases and continuity year-to-year with which they had to be entered into or renewed, Noël JA (Létourneau, Nadon JJA, concurring) observed that:

> In the present case, the nature of the payments is made clear when it is appreciated that they had to be made since 1979 and there is no suggestion that the appellant's business can continue without these payments being made every year ... What this shows, unequivocally in my view, is that the payments are required to insure the ongoing operation of the appellant's business.

In *Bowater Power*, the taxpayer, which generated and sold electrical power in Newfoundland, sought to deduct $18,195 in 1959 and $15,801 in 1960 for engineering studies undertaken to assess opportunities for increasing the generation of hydroelectrical power from its existing water sheds. Rejecting the Minister's argument that the cost of these studies should be characterized as capital expenditures, the court concluded (at para. 55) that they were "incurred ... while the business of the appellant was operating and [were] part of the cost of this business." According to Noël ACJ (at para. 57):

> I do not ... feel that merely because the expenditure was made for the purpose of determining whether to bring into existence a capital asset, it should always be considered as a capital expenditure and, therefore, not deductible. In distinguishing between a capital payment and a payment on current account, regard must always be had to the business and commercial realities of the matter. While the hydroelectric development, once it becomes a business or commercial realty is a capital asset of the business giving rise to it, whatever reasonable means were taken to find out whether it should be created or not may still result from the current operations of the business as part of the every day concern of its officers in conducting the operations of the company in a business-like way.

See also *Kruger Pulp & Paper Ltd. v. M.N.R.*, [1975] C.T.C. 2323, 75 D.T.C. 245 (T.R.B.), in which consulting services and legal fees incurred by the taxpayer with a view to acquiring timber-cutting rights and investigating a site for a plant were allowed as deductible expenses incurred in the operation of the business; and *M.N.R. v. M.P. Drilling Ltd.*, [1976] F.C.J. No. 12, [1976] C.T.C. 58, 76 D.T.C. 6028 (F.C.A.), in which expenses in the first three years after its incorporation that were incurred by the taxpayer in an unsuccessful attempt to get into the business of marketing propane and butane gas abroad were characterized as deductible expenses incurred in the course of the taxpayer's business, not startup costs incurred for the purpose of creating or acquiring a business structure.

In *Wacky Wheatley's*, travelling expenses incurred by various officers of the taxpayer (Michael Wheatley, Robert Wheatley, Douglas Wheatley, Murray Wheatley, and Bernard Caspick) in order to assess opportunities for business expansion in the Australian market were held to be deductible current expenses on the basis (at paras. 26 and 28) that the expenses "were anterior to any business decision to enter the Australian market" and "resulted from the current operations" of the taxpayer.

In *Inskip*, the taxpayer, a cattle rancher who held a licence enabling him to obtain water for irrigation purposes from a dammed lake on Crown land, sought in computing his income for his 1980 taxation year to deduct $37,529.65 that he was required to pay to the Crown for the purpose of reconstructing the dam. Concluding (at para. 15) that the expenditure was "made by the appellant in the course and for the purpose of his regular day-to-day business operations" and not "for the establishment of the profit-making structure of the respondent's trade," the court the rejected the Minister's argument that the payment was a capital expenditure.

11. Where a taxpayer incurs expenses in the course of its business in order to expand market share and develop goodwill, the decisions in *Canada Starch Co. Ltd. v. M.N.R.*, [1968] C.T.C. 466, 68 D.T.C. 5320 (Ex. Ct.), suggest that these expenses are properly deductible in computing the taxpayer's business income in the taxation year in which they are incurred. Where a taxpayer purchases existing goodwill in the form of a customer list or an ongoing business, however, this cost is generally characterized as a capital expenditure.

In *Southam Business Publications Ltd. v. M.N.R.*, [1966] C.T.C. 265, 66 D.T.C. 5215 (Ex. Ct.), for example, the taxpayer, which owned and operated a number of newspapers, sought in computing its income for its 1961 taxation year to deduct $50,000 that it paid in the year to acquire the circulation records and subscription lists of the *Financial Times*, pursuant to an agreement whereby it also acquired the exclusive right to publish the *Financial Times*, the right to the name, the vendor's advertising and other records, its furniture and fixtures, accounts receivable, inventory of newsprint, and goodwill, all for $25,000, and the vendor undertook to change its name and not compete. Rejecting the taxpayer's argument that the circulation records and subscription lists were analogous to the stock in trade of a business, the Exchequer Court characterized the payment as a capital expenditure to acquire the goodwill of a business purchased as a going concern. According to the court (at para. 15), "when all the circumstances of the present case are considered and all the authorities are looked at, it appears clearly that an asset such as that acquired by the taxpayer in the present case must be regarded as a non-tangible capital asset and, therefore, cannot be [deducted] as an operational expense."

More recently, in *Gifford v. Canada*, [2004] S.C.J. No. 13, [2004] 2 C.T.C. 1, 2004 D.T.C. 6120 (S.C.C.), the Supreme Court of Canada addressed the characterization of the purchase of a client list as a current or capital expenditure. The taxpayer, Thomas Gifford, was employed as a financial advisor at Midland Walwyn Capital Inc. in North Bay, Ontario. When another advisor at the same office decided to leave the firm, Gifford agreed to purchase the departing employee's client list for $100,000. The agreement required the departing employee to provide a written endorsement of Gifford to each client and to direct Midland Walwyn to transfer the clients to Gifford. The departing employee also agreed not to compete with Gifford for 30 months with respect to the clients on the list, and not to share any of the relevant client information with anyone. In characterizing the client list as a capital expenditure, Major J. for the Court (McLachlin C.J., Bastarache, Binnie, Arbour, Deschamps, and Fish JJ. concurring) held at para. 21 that the client list not only "significantly expanded Mr. Gifford's client network, the structure within which he earned his employment income," but "secured the discontinuance of competition," and that the payment was made "with the intention of securing an asset of enduring benefit that would provide Mr. Gifford with a lasting advantage." In addition, Major J. observed that "The purchase of someone else's accumulated goodwill is not the same as the recurring marketing expenses the appellant would have to incur to create his own goodwill." In so deciding, the court sharply disagreed with the characterization of the client list as a current expenditure by Bowman A.C.J. at the Tax Court of Canada, who had stated in support of his conclusion that "Clients are fleeting, volatile and evanescent." In response, Major J. reasoned at para. 22 that:

> The fact that, if not properly cared for, the asset may decrease in value cannot determine the question of what the asset was to the purchaser at the time of acquisition. A building purchased as a rental property does not lose its characterization as a capital asset if it burns down on the day after the sale closes.

See also *Metro Taxi Ltd. v. M.N.R.*, [1967] C.T.C. 88, 67 D.T.C. 5073 (Ex. Ct.), aff'd [1968] S.C.J. No. 30, [1968] C.T.C. 163, 68 D.T.C. 5098 (S.C.C.), in which the taxpayer spent $104,000 to acquire the business of another taxi company, which included 14 licences that were scheduled to expire a month later. Concluding that the taxpayer could reasonably expect to obtain a renewal of the licences, the court (at para. 37) characterized a portion of the payment as a capital expenditure for the acquisition of "an intangible, enduring advantage of a capital nature." For a similar result, in which the price of fishing licences was characterized as a capital expense on the grounds that the purchaser could reasonably expect a long series of renewals in future years, see *F.A.S. Seafood Producers Ltd. v. Canada*, [1998] T.C.J. No. 664, [1998] 4 C.T.C. 2794, 98 D.T.C. 2034 (T.C.C.).

For other cases in which the cost of purchasing all or part of a business as a going concern has been characterized as a capital expense, see *Riches v. M.N.R.* (1960), 24 Tax ABC 362, 60 D.T.C. 386 (T.A.B.); *M.N.R. v. Tomenson Inc.*, [1986] 1 C.T.C. 525, 86 D.T.C. 6267 (F.C.T.D.), aff'd [1988] 1 CTC 173, 88 D.T.C. 6095 (FCA); and *Robert Verrier & Fils Ltée v. M.N.R.*, [1989] T.C.J. No. 455, [1992] 2 C.T.C. 2464 (T.C.C.). See also *Aliments Ca-Mo Foods Inc. v. M.N.R.*, [1980] C.T.C. 75, 80 D.T.C. 6043 (F.C.T.D.), in which the taxpayer paid $60,000 to acquire a competitor's customer list as part of an agreement pursuant to which the competitor undertook not to operate the same time of business within a radius of 100 miles and gave the taxpayer an option on a building used in its business.

For contrasting outcomes, in which taxpayers have been allowed to deduct the cost of a customer list acquired without any agreement of non-competition by the vendor, see *Simon Voyer & Castelli Inc. v. M.N.R.*, [1979] C.T.C. 2503, 79 D.T.C. 41 (T.R.B.) and *Farquhar Bethune Insurance Ltd. v. Canada*, [1981] C.T.C. 35, 81 D.T.C. 5028 (F.C.T.D.).

12.   In *M.N.R. v. Dominion Natural Gas Co. Ltd.*, [1940] S.C.J. No. 46, [1940-41] C.T.C. 155, 1 D.T.C. 499-133 (S.C.C.), the taxpayer, which held a franchise to supply natural gas in the township of Barton, parts of which had been annexed to the city of Hamilton, incurred legal expenses to preserve its franchise in these annexed districts, which it deducted in computing its income for its 1934 taxation year. Concluding (at para. 16) that the expenditure was incurred "once and for all" and "for the purpose and with the effect of procuring for the company 'the advantage of an enduring benefit,'" Duff CJC (Davis J

concurring) characterized the expenses as non-deductible capital expenditures. In a concurring judgment, Kerwin J (Hudson J concurring) held (at para. 34) that the expenditure was "a 'payment on account of capital' as it was made ... 'with a view of preserving an asset or advantage for the enduring benefit of a trade.'"

Is this test the same as that set out in *British Insulated and Helsby Cables v. Atherton*, [1926] A.C. 205 at 213 (H.L.)? Is it consistent with the tests adopted in *B.P. Australia*, *Sun Newspapers*, and *Hallstrom's*?

13. For other cases in which expenses to protect or preserve intangible property have been characterized as capital expenditures, see *British Columbia Power Corp. v. M.N.R.*, [1967] S.C.J. No. 74, [1967] C.T.C. 406, 67 D.T.C. 5258 (S.C.C.); *Farmers Mutual Petroleum Ltd. v. M.N.R.*, [1967] S.C.J. No. 78, [1967] C.T.C. 396, 67 D.T.C. 5277 (S.C.C.); *McLaws v. M.N.R.*, [1970] C.T.C. 420, 70 D.T.C. 6289 (Ex. Ct.); *B.P. Pétroles Ltée v. Canada*, [1979] C.T.C. 174, 79 D.T.C. 5121 (F.C.T.D.), aff'd [1980] C.T.C. 408, 80 D.T.C. 6252 (F.C.A.); *Jager Homes Ltd. v. M.N.R.*, [1988] F.C.J. No. 40, [1988] 1 C.T.C. 215, 88 D.T.C. 6119 (F.C.A.); *Hoffman Estate v. M.N.R.*, [1992] T.C.J. No. 645, [1992] 2 C.T.C. 2645, 92 D.T.C. 2290 (T.C.C.); and *Upenieks v. Canada*, [1993] T.C.J. No. 335, [1993] 2 C.T.C. 2386 (T.C.C.), aff'd [1994] F.C.J. No. 1503, [1995] 1 C.T.C. 8, 94 D.T.C. 6656 (F.C.A.).

In *BC Power Corp.*, the taxpayer, the principal asset of which consisted of the common shares of a subsidiary company engaged in the business of distributing electricity in British Columbia, incurred legal expenses opposing the expropriation of this subsidiary by the British Columbia government, for the primary purpose of increasing the compensation paid for the taxpayer's shares. Referring to the decision in *M.N.R. v. Dominion Natural Gas Co. Ltd.*, [1940] S.C.J. No. 46, [1940-41] C.T.C. 155, 1 D.T.C. 499-133 (S.C.C.), the expenses were characterized as payments on account of capital.

In *Farmers Mutual Petroleum*, the taxpayer incurred legal expenses to defend its title to various resource properties. Rejecting the taxpayer's argument that the payments were deductible current expenses incurred in the course of the taxpayer's business operations, the Supreme Court of Canada characterized the expenses as a capital expenditure. According to Martland J (at paras. 19-21):

> It can certainly be said that the appellant, in resisting the lawsuits launched against it, was seeking to protect its income, because it was seeking to protect the assets from which its income was derived ... . The object and purpose of the lawsuits ... was to compel the restoration to the land owners of the mineral rights which the appellant had purchased. The learned trial judge has found, and the evidence establishes, that those rights were items of fixed capital, and were so regarded by the appellant. At the time the litigation occurred, the sum total of the mineral rights acquired by the appellant, all of which were of the kind involved in the litigation, represented all of the appellant's capital assets. The appellant did not trade in them, but intended to retain them perpetually.

> It was to protect those capital assets from attack that the legal costs of the litigation were incurred ... . The fact that the leases acquired by the appellant, along with the mineral rights, were more immediately connected with the production of income than was the franchise involved in the *Dominion* case does not affect the matter in principle. It is relevant in relation to the application of Section 12(1)(a), but in relation to Section 12(1)(b) we must ask the

question, was this outlay for the purpose of preserving a capital asset? In my opinion it clearly was and, if that is so, Section 12(1)(b) [now paragraph 18(1)(b)] prevents its deduction.

In *McLaws*, the taxpayer, a lawyer who owned all the shares of a corporation whose debts he had personally guaranteed, sought to deduct payments of $18,750 that he was required to make in each of the taxation years 1963 to 1965 when the bank called the company's loans and the taxpayer was required to make good on the guarantees. Disallowing the deduction, Kerr J concluded (at para. 24):

In my opinion the appellant's outlays were on account of capital ... and the claimed deductions are prohibited. In my view of the situation, the guarantee was given to protect and preserve the source of income, a business which was in immediate danger of bankruptcy and whose existence was imperilled. The character of the ensuing outlays in honouring the guarantee is quite different from expenditures which fall naturally into the category of income disbursements and business losses. In my opinion, the outlays are of the character of payments on account of capital. ...

On appeal, this statement was affirmed by the Supreme Court of Canada, [1972] S.C.J. No. 132, [1972] C.T.C. 165, 72 D.T.C. 6149 (S.C.C.).

In *B.P. Pétroles Ltée*, the taxpayer incurred legal expenses in an unsuccessful attempt to oppose an injunction sought by a neighbour to prohibit the operation of a service station. Citing *Dominion Natural Gas* and *Farmers Mutual Petroleum*, supra, the court disallowed a deduction for the expenses on the grounds that they were incurred in order to protect the very existence of the service station.

In *Jager Homes*, the taxpayer, which was controlled by another corporation ("Jager Holdings") 51 per cent of whose shares were owned by Mr. Jager and 49 per cent by Mrs. Jager, sought to deduct legal expenses incurred to defend against a winding-up action initiated by Mrs. Jager in conjunction with divorce proceedings. On the basis that "the legal fees were made in order to preserve the business entity, structure or organization, not as the kinds of expenditures which are made to earn profits from the operation of such business entities" (at para. 34), the Federal Court of Appeal characterized the legal expenses as a capital expenditure.

In *Hoffman Estate*, the taxpayer incurred legal expenses to defend its title to various capital assets ownership of which passed to the taxpayer on the death of Solomon Hoffman. Referring to the decisions in *Dominion Natural Gas* and *Farmers Mutual Petroleum*, the court characterized the legal expenses as capital expenses.

In *Upenieks*, the taxpayer sought to deduct $38,045 in legal expenses incurred in an unsuccessful libel action against the *Toronto Star* newspaper. Concluding that the taxpayer's professional reputation was a capital asset, the court disallowed the deduction under paragraph 18(1)(b) of the Act. For a similar result, relying on the decision in *Upenieks*, see *Hansen v. Canada*, [1998] T.C.J. No. 620, [1998] 4 C.T.C. 2412, 98 D.T.C. 2112 (T.C.C.).

14. Several important cases have considered whether transaction costs incurred on a takeover, merger or other corporate restructuring are on capital or income account. In *Boulangerie St-Augustin Inc. v. Canada*, [1994] T.C.J. No. 841, [1995] 2 C.T.C. 2149, 95 D.T.C. 56 (T.C.C.), aff'd (1996), 97 D.T.C. 5012 (F.C.A.), the taxpayer sought to deduct legal and accounting expenses of $62,122 to prepare information circulars in connection with three takeover bids that it was required to distribute to shareholders under the Quebec *Securities Act*. Rejecting the Minister's argument that these legal expenses were not incurred for the purpose of gaining or producing income within the meaning of paragraph 18(1)(a) of the Act, the court concluded that the costs of communicating with shareholders was a necessary business expense the deduction of which satisfied the tests in paragraphs 18(1)(a) and 18(1)(b). In the course of its judgement, however, it suggested (at para. 55) that expenses that the corporation might have incurred to fight the takeover bids, "in particular by hiring a business appraiser to show that those bids were not reasonable or other advisors to assist it in putting defence mechanisms into place" (for example, so-called poison pills) would have been characterized as payments on account of capital within the meaning of paragraph 18(1)(b).

In *Rona Inc. v. Canada*, [2003] T.C.J. No. 136, [2003] 4 C.T.C. 2974; 2003 D.T.C. 264 (T.C.C.), the Court held that professional fees paid to lawyers, accountants and stockbrokers to facilitate the expansion of the taxpayer's business through a series of acquisitions were capital expenditures within the meaning of s. 18(1)(b), because the "the advantage Rona sought through its growth strategy was the lasting expansion of its business structure, that is, its distribution network" (at para. 37).

Two other recent Tax Court of Canada decisions have permitted the deduction of merger or takeover transaction costs as current expenses. In *International Colin Energy Corp. v. Canada*, [2002] T.C.J. No. 585, [2003] 1 C.T.C. 2406, 2002 D.T.C. 2185 (T.C.C.), the taxpayer sought to deduct amounts paid to a financial advisor for help in arranging its merger with another corporation, following a period in which shareholders were unhappy with the taxpayer's poor financial results. Rejecting the Minister's argument that the expenses were incurred not for the purpose of earning income but rather for the purpose of maximizing the value of shareholder investments, or alternatively on capital account, Bowman ACJTC commented that (at paras. 46-48),

> If the shareholders' investment was improved by holding shares in a larger and commercially stronger entity, this was the result of an improvement in the income earning ability of the appellant within the larger combined entity. Obviously improved earnings enhance share prices and the value of the shareholders' investment. ... Patently here the services performed by ARC were intended to improve the appellant's income and the fees paid were laid out to earn income from the appellant's business ... no capital asset was acquired, nothing of an enduring benefit came into existence nor was any capital asset preserved.

B.J. Services Co. v. Canada, [2003] T.C.J. No. 706, [2004] 2 C.T.C. 2169, 2004 D.T.C. 2032 (T.C.C.) dealt with expenses incurred by a target company in responding to an unsolicited takeover bid, including professional fees paid to advisors, and a "hello" fee and break fee paid to another potential acquirer. Campbell TCJ rejected the Minister's argument against current deductibility of these expenses as "fundamentally inconsistent with the economic and business realities of the world of mergers and acquisitions. It is a basic common sense approach to view maximizing share price as inextricably interwoven with the business of any company" (at para. 36). Relying on the decision in *International Colin Energy Corp.*, Campbell TCJ held that the expenses were not capital outlays (at paras. 44-45):

> ... this case is an arguably stronger one, against characterization of the expenses as capital outlays, than in the International Colin case. In the case before Justice Bowman, the expenses were incurred voluntarily by the taxpayer and were motivated because of its financial problems and to preserve its business. Yet Justice Bowman rejected the argument on capital treatment. Here if it had not been for BJ's unsolicited takeover bid, Nowsco would never have sought to make changes to its capital structure. ... The entire process began and ended within an approximate 60-day window period, in the same financial period. I can see no justification for capitalizing these expenses and certainly no logic in applying them to some subsequent period where there is no causal link to the corporate activities ... No capital asset was acquired, no capital asset was preserved, and no enduring benefit was obtained in incurring these expenditures.

For detailed discussion of these and other recent decisions, and critical analysis of CRA's administrative policy regarding the deductibility of such expenses, see Stanley R. Ebel, "Transaction Costs", in *Report of Proceedings of Fifty-Seventh Tax Conference*, 2005 Tax Conference (Toronto: Canadian Tax Foundation, 2006), 35:1-27; and Nik Diksic and Christian Desjardins, "Tax Treatment of Transaction Costs", in *Report of Proceedings of Fifty-Eighth Tax Conference*, 2006 Tax Conference (Toronto: Canadian Tax Foundation, 2007), 38:1-37

15. In *M.N.R. v. Kellogg's Co. of Canada Ltd.*, [1943] S.C.J. No. 4, [1943] C.T.C. 1, 2 D.T.C. 601 (S.C.C.), the taxpayer, which manufactured cereal products in London, Ontario, incurred legal expenses defending its right to market a product known as "Shredded Wheat" in an action for trademark infringement initiated by the Canadian Shredded Wheat Company. Rejecting the Minister's argument that the legal expenses were non-deductible payments on account of capital, the Supreme Court of Canada distinguished its earlier decision in *M.N.R. v. Dominion Natural Gas Co. Ltd.*, [1940] S.C.J. No. 46, [1940-41] C.T.C. 155, 1 D.T.C. 499-133 (S.C.C.), on the basis (at para. 4) that the legal expenses incurred by the Kellogg Company were not incurred to defend "a right of property, or an exclusive right of any description, but the right (in common with all other members of the public) to describe their goods in the manner in which they were describing them."

16. In *Evans v. M.N.R.*, [1960] S.C.J. No. 15, [1960] C.T.C. 69, 60 D.T.C. 1047 (S.C.C.), the taxpayer, who by the combined effect of her first husband's and his father's will became entitled for the remainder of her life to the income of one-third of the father's estate, incurred legal expenses to successfully defend her right against members of her first husband's family. Rejecting the Minister's argument that these expenses were on account of capital, the Supreme Court of

Canada distinguished *Dominion Natural Gas*, on the basis that the life interest acquired by the taxpayer was "a bare right to be paid income" against which the that the legal expenses were properly deductible, not a capital asset for which any expense to preserve title would be on account of capital.

17. In *Canada v. Burgess*, [1981] C.T.C. 258, 81 D.T.C. 5192 (F.C.T.D.), the taxpayer, who was granted maintenance for herself and two children in an action for divorce, sought to deduct a portion of the legal expenses incurred in the divorce proceeding as an expense incurred for the purpose of gaining or producing income from property. Concluding that the taxpayer's right to maintenance came into existence only upon the order of the court in the divorce proceeding and not as a result of the marriage, the court distinguished the decision in *Evans*, supra, characterizing the legal expenses as a "capital expenditure" incurred to "bring the right into being" rather than a "revenue expenditure to enforce payment of income from a right in being" (at para. 55).

See also *Placements du Moulin Ltée v. Canada*, [1996] T.C.J. No. 850, [1997] 3 C.T.C. 2171, 97 D.T.C. 41 (T.C.C.), in which the taxpayer, which sold its shares to a second company, incurred legal expenses to collect the purchase price owing. Distinguishing between deductible legal expenses to collect the price of items sold "in the course of operating a business" and non-deductible legal expenses incurred to collect "the selling price of the business itself" (at paras. 25-26), the court disallowed the deduction of the legal expenses.

18. *Canada v. Burgess*, [1981] C.T.C. 258, 81 D.T.C. 5192 (F.C.T.D.) was questioned in *Gallien v. Canada*, [2000] T.C.J. No. 729, [2001] 2 C.T.C. 2676, 2000 D.T.C. 2514 (T.C.C.), in which the taxpayer sought to deduct legal fees incurred in order to obtain a support order as part of a divorce. Observing (at para. 21) that the right to support in divorce proceedings is created by legislation, not the courts, Lamarre Proulx TCJ concluded (at para. 22) that the legal fees were deductible expenses incurred "not to create a right but for the purpose of seeking and obtaining income to which [the taxpayer] was entitled." For similar conclusions, see *Donald v. Canada*, [1998] T.C.J. No. 866, [1999] 1 C.T.C. 2025 (T.C.C.); and *Nissim v. Canada*, [1998] T.C.J. No. 658, [1999] 1 C.T.C. 2119, [1998] 4 C.T.C. 2496 (T.C.C.).

Following the decision in *Gallien*, the Canada Revenue Agency reconsidered its position that legal expenses incurred to obtain the right to or an increase in spousal or child support are not deductible. According to Income Tax Technical News No. 24 (October 10, 2002):

> we now consider legal costs incurred to obtain spousal support under the *Divorce Act*, or under the applicable provincial legislation in a separation agreement, to have been incurred to enforce a pre-existing right to support. Consequently, these costs are deductible .... We also now accept that legal costs of seeking to obtain an increase in support ... are also deductible.

19. In *Canada Steamship Lines Limited v. M.N.R.*, [1966] C.T.C. 255, 66 D.T.C. 5205 (Ex. Ct.), the taxpayer, in computing its income for its 1956 and 1957 taxation years, deducted amounts paid in these years to repair several ships

by replacing both the floors and walls of cargo-carrying holds and the boilers by which the ships were powered. Distinguishing between the two classes of expenditure, the court characterized the former as deductible repair costs and the latter as non-deductible capital expenditures to replace distinct capital assets. According to Jackett P (at paras. 3-10):

> So far as the first class of expenditures is concerned, I do not, myself, have much difficulty in reaching the conclusion that these expenditures are deductible. In effect, the ship has a double bottom — an outside layer and an inside layer separated by appropriate structural members. If one or more plates constituting a part of the outside layer require to be replaced because they have been ... damaged, so long as the damage is not so extensive that the ship must be regarded as having been virtually destroyed and as having, in effect, ceased, from a businessman's point of view, to exist as a ship, their replacement is, I should have thought, the most typical kind of ship repair. Where the inside layer of the ship's bottom, which also serves as the floor for the ship's cargo-carrying holds, has to be replaced, in whole or in part, by reason of wear and tear and of damage caused by the cargo carried in the ship, it seems clear to me that the expense falls in the same class as the expenses of replacement of portions of the outside skin. So long as the ship survives as a ship and damaged plates are being replaced by sound plates, I have no doubt that the ship is being repaired and it is a deductible current expense. (I exclude, of course, a possible replacement by something so different in kind from the thing replaced that it constitutes a change in the character — an upgrading — of the thing upon which the money is expended instead of being a mere repair.)

> What I have said with reference to the replacement of all or part of the floors of the holds, which serve as the inner layer of the ship's bottom, applies in principle to the walls of the holds which are related to the sides of the ship in the same way as the floors of the hold are related to the ship's bottom.

> The Minister's argument against the conclusion that I have just expressed may, as I understand it, be summarized as follows: the expenditures are in respect of the replacement of a substantial part of the ship's holds, which are of "signal" importance in the operation of a cargo-carrying ship, and the cost of the replacement is substantial when compared with the value of the ship and the cost of repairs done to the ship in other years; such expenditures should, therefore, be regarded as being for capital repairs or renewals and not as being for current repairs. I have tried unsuccessfully to appreciate the full significance of the Minister's submission. I have not, however, been able to escape the conclusion that a replacement of a worn or damaged board or plate that is an integral part of an asset used in a business is a repair and that the costs of repairs are current expenses and not outlays of capital. I cannot accept the view that the cost of repairs ceases to be current expenses and becomes outlays of capital merely because the repairs required are very extensive or because their cost is substantial. There is, of course, in other types of case, a problem as to whether the thing replaced is, from the relevant point of view, an integral part of a larger asset or a distinct capital asset, that must be, from a businessman's point of view, treated separately. In deciding a problem of this kind, the amount of the expenditure for replacement in relation to the cost of the larger asset and in relation to past expenditures for repairs of the larger asset may well be significant. ...

> With reference to the expenditures in replacing the boilers in one of the appellant's ships, I have more difficulty. ...

> The problem arises here because, depending on one's conception of the facts, an expenditure made in replacing the boilers of a ship when they have worn out may be regarded as

(a)   being nothing more than an expenditure for the repair of the ship by replacing a worn out part, or

(b)   the acquisition of a new piece of plant or machinery to replace an old piece of plant or machinery which has an existence separate and distinct from the ship even though it is used in the ship and as part of the equipment by which the ship is propelled.

In the case of ... a ship, the function of which involves movement, I should have thought that it was a tenable or arguable view that the equipment or machinery required to effect such movement is, from a businessman's point of view, an integral part of the ship as a capital asset. If this were the right view, I should have thought that it would follow that the cost of the replacement of the whole of the propulsion machinery or of some unit thereof would be a current expense even though the thing replaced were an asset that, by itself, was an engine or machine that could be installed in a factory as a distinct and separate capital asset. I do not, however, feel free to consider whether I should adopt that approach in disposing of the present problem having regard to two previous decisions of this Court. I refer to *Thompson Construction (Chemong) Limited v. M.N.R.*, [1957] Ex. CR 96; [1957] CTC 155 and *M.N.R. v. Vancouver Tugboat Company, Limited*, [1957] Ex. CR 160; [1957] CTC 178. In each of these cases the result would have been different if the power plant, whereby the structure in which it was installed was moved from place to place, had been regarded as being merely an integral part of that structure.

20.   In *Thompson Construction v. M.N.R.*, [1957] C.T.C. 155, 57 D.T.C. 1114 (Ex. Ct.), the taxpayer, which carried on a general contracting business, sought to deduct an expense of $6,006.13 incurred in 1953 to install a new engine in a used power shovel purchased four years earlier at a cost of $27,075. Rejecting the taxpayer's arguments that the expense was "in the nature of a repair" and that the new engine was "a subsidiary part of the whole" (at para. 13), the court held that the payment was a capital expense. According to Cameron J (at paras. 17-19):

It may be conceded that as a general rule repairs necessitated by the wear and tear of equipment used in the business are allowed as deductions, although no specific reference is found in the *Income Tax Act* regarding "repairs." It may also be conceded that in normal circumstances the repairing of machinery frequently involves the necessity of replacing worn-out parts. But I think it is clear that if the outlay brings into existence a capital asset, such as a new piece of machinery, such outlay will not be allowed as a deduction.

In the instant case I have reached the conclusion that the outlay in question did bring into existence a new capital asset, namely, the new engine. The evidence is that the old engine was in use for at least five years and at the end of that period still had a substantial commercial value. It is probable that the new engine would have a useful life of at least the same number of years. The expenditure therefore brought into existence an advantage for the enduring benefit of the trade and which should be considered to be a capital asset (*Dominion Natural Gas Co. Ltd. v. M.N.R.*, [1941] SCR 19; [1940-41] CTC 155. In reaching the conclusion that the outlay was not one on revenue account, I am influenced in part ... by the magnitude of the outlay when related to the value of the power shovel as a whole. As pointed out above, the total cost of the new engine exceeded the written down value of the shovel as a whole after deducting all capital cost allowances made to the end of the appellant's taxation year 1953.

It seems to me, also, that to allow a deduction in full as an operating expense of an outlay such as this and which brought into existence a new capital asset, would be to frustrate the clear intent of the provisions of Section 11(1)(a) [now paragraph 20(1)(a)) and the regulations passed thereunder in regard to capital cost allowances. ... [C]laims for capital cost allowances were made in previous years in respect of the power shovel as a whole and were allowed. It was considered as a capital asset and having been purchased with the engine was treated as one asset. ... If, after a few years' use, it had been considered advisable to replace that engine with a new one, the appellant would have been required to bring into account the amount received on the sale so that depreciation already received might (in a proper case) be recovered, and also the cost of the new engine, so as to ascertain the amount to which the fixed rate of depreciation would be applied. I am unable to conclude that it should be otherwise merely on the ground, as in the instant case, that the engine was installed in the power shovel. The engine clearly was a marketable entity, readily detached from the power shovel by the removal of a few bolts, and capable of being used for other purposes. I am of the opinion that under the *Income Tax Act* and the special provisions relating to capital cost allowances, the sale of a capital asset — or of a substantial part thereof as in the instant case — and the replacement of the asset or part so sold by the acquisition of a new asset or such part, must be dealt with only as has been done in this case by the respondent in assessing the appellant.

21. In *M.N.R. v. Vancouver Tugboat Co.*, [1957] C.T.C. 178, 57 D.T.C. 1126 (Ex. Ct.), the taxpayer, which operated a tugboat service on the Pacific coast, sought in computing its income for its 1952 taxation year to deduct $42,086.71 incurred during the year to replace the engine in one of its tugboats. Concluding (at para. 18) that the expense was a capital expense "to cover the accumulations of past wear and tear and to prevent the necessity for so many repairs and so much loss of time in the future," the court indicated (at para. 19) that it was also "influenced by the size of the expenditure ... in relation to what were described as abnormally high repairs to the tug in the years 1949, 1950, and 1951, amounting to $15,833, $12,849, and $10,899.59 respectively." According to Thurlow J (at para. 19):

> These amounts were for repairs to the tug as a whole, not to its engine alone. In the light of this evidence and the evidence that a normal year's repairs should run to somewhat less than $10,000, I think it is apparent that the expenditure of a sum of $42,068.71 to replace a single part of the tug is one to replace a substantial portion of the capital asset rather than to renew some minor item in the course of carrying out the ordinary run of repairs.

22. In *Donohue Normick Inc. v. Canada*, [1995] F.C.J. No. 1476, [1995] 95 D.T.C. 5667 (F.C.A.), the taxpayer, which manufactured pulp and paper in a plant completed in 1982 at a cost of $210 million, of which $30 million was for a paper machine, sought to deduct $537,134 spent in 1985 and $519,843 spent in 1986 to acquire 17 spare parts for the paper machine, which were commercially necessary in order to allow the taxpayer to operate the paper machine on a continuous basis. Upholding the decision at trial, [1994] T.C.J. No. 502, 95 D.T.C. 731 (T.C.C.), which characterized the cost of the spare parts as capital expenses on the grounds that they cost more than $1 million altogether, were expected to last for ten years, and were not intended to be used for resale, the court also emphasized (at para. 14) that:

> (1) the parts in issue were durable: they were not to be thrown out after being used but were to be repaired or retooled;

(2) the parts were a significant asset for the respondent;

(3) the purchase cost of the parts in issue was not a regular, repeated expense;

(4) the parts had an intrinsic, permanent value;

(5) the parts were to alternate with identical parts already installed in the paper machine; they were in fact "alternative" rather than "spare" parts;

(6) the parts were made "to order" by the manufacturer specifically for the respondent; they were not easily available on a supplier's shelves.

23. In *Canaport Ltd. v. Canada*, [1993] T.C.J. No. 507, [1993] 2 C.T.C. 2830, 93 D.T.C. 1226 (T.C.C.), the taxpayer, a wholly owned subsidiary of Irving Oil Ltd. that operated an offshore crude oil tanker unloading and receiving facility at St. John, New Brunswick, sought in computing its income for its 1986 taxation year to deduct $4,047,470 spent to insert a fibreglass liner into a subsea crude oil pipeline to prevent leakage and extend the life expectancy of the pipeline. Comparing this expense to the cost of repairing the cargo-carrying holds in *Canada Steamship Lines Limited v. M.N.R.*, [1966] C.T.C. 255, 66 D.T.C. 5205 (Ex. Ct.), the court rejected the Minister's argument that the cost of the liner was a capital expense.

24. In *Canadian Reynolds Metals Co. v. Canada*, [1996] F.C.J. No. 593, [1996] 2 C.T.C. 261, 96 D.T.C. 6312 (F.C.A.), the taxpayer, in computing its income for its 1977, 1979, and 1980 taxation years, deducted expenditures made in these years to replace the carbon cathode lining in steel pots used to produce aluminium. Observing (at para. 5) that "the useful life of the linings increased from an initial 20 months at the plant's outset, to a period of 4 to 5 years during the taxation years in question and to a period of 7 to 9 years at the time of trial," the court characterized the cost of the new linings as capital expenditures to acquire "capital assets of an enduring nature." Is this decision consistent with the judgments in *Canada Steamship Lines Limited v. M.N.R.*, [1966] C.T.C. 255, 66 D.T.C. 5205 (Ex. Ct.), and *Canaport Ltd. v. Canada*, [1993] T.C.J. No. 507, [1993] 2 C.T.C. 2830, 93 D.T.C. 1226 (T.C.C.)?

25. In *Shabro Investments Ltd. v. M.N.R.*, [1979] F.C.J. No. 119, [1979] C.T.C. 125, 79 D.T.C. 5104 (F.C.A.), the taxpayer, which owned a two-storey building constructed on a garbage landfill site, sought to deduct as an operating expense in computing its income for its 1973 taxation year $95,198.10 incurred to (a) remove the bottom floor, which had become cracked and unusable, (b) install steel piles to support the new floor, (c) construct a new floor of concrete slab reinforced with steel to rest on the steel piles, and (d) repair and replace waterlines, drains, plumbing, and wiring that had become damaged as a result of subsidence. Characterizing these renovations as "improvements" rather than "repairs," the court disallowed the deduction of all but the costs incurred to repair and replace waterlines, etc., on the basis that the payment was on account of capital. According to Jackett CJ (at paras. 6-17):

Generally speaking, replacement of worn or damaged parts, even though substantial, are repairs and are to be contrasted with changes designed to create an enduring addition or improvement to the structure. In ordinary cases, the difference is evident. Unfortunately, this is not such an ordinary case.

In my view, on the uncontested facts, the learned Trial Judge reached the correct conclusion at least with reference to the installation of the steel piles for support of the floor.

When that part of the building in question was erected, there was a hidden defect in the structure thereof which adversely affected its intrinsic value but, being unrecognized, would not have affected its market value. When that defect became apparent, it seriously diminished, if it did not destroy, the market value of the part of the building involved. The installation of supporting piles for the basic floor was necessary to eliminate the defect, which had always existed but had just become apparent. Elimination of the defect was necessary to give the building the character of a long term usable asset that it had previously seemed to have but did not actually have. In my view, installation of the piles was a permanent addition to the structure of the building of a foundation that had not previously existed and was not a repair to the building as it had existed prior to their installation. An addition to the essential structure of a building for the period of life contemplated for it does not, in my view, become a "repair" merely because the necessity for it was overlooked when the building was built and it is added when the lack of it becomes apparent. In so far, therefore, as the expense of $95,198.10 can reasonably be regarded as attributable thereto, I am of opinion that it was properly disallowed as not being a current expense but as being an outlay on account of capital.

In so far as the outlay of $95,198.10 is reasonably attributable to the removal of the damaged floor and its replacement by a floor supported by the steel piles, I have more difficulty.

As indicated by the part of his Reasons that I have quoted, the learned Trial Judge seems to have taken the view that such expenditure cannot be regarded as a "repair" expenditure because

(a) the work was not done because of "any wear of the facilities" or "any aging of the materials previously in place," and

(b) the designing, engineering and construction of the new floor was quite different from that of the previous floor but was to meet conditions for which the previous floor did not qualify.

In my view, these are not reasons that necessarily disqualify money spent on remedying damage to the structure of a building from being treated as current expense on repairs. Damage caused by accident or vandalism, just as much as that caused by deterioration from wear and tear or aging, can call for "repairs" in the profit and loss sense; and, similarly, "repairs" do not become disqualified as "repairs" in that sense merely because they are carried out in the light of technology unknown when the original structure was built or because they take into account conditions (such as dampness) not taken into account when the original structure was built.

I am of the view that, if the replacement of the floor could otherwise be regarded as being the remedying of damage to the fabric of the building, it would have been properly deducted as a current expense on repairs notwithstanding

(a) that the damage arose from a hidden defect in the original structure and not from wear and tear, aging of materials or some accidental or malicious happening in the course of use, or

(b) that the damage was remedied in accordance with technology or knowledge as of the time thereof that incidentally effected an improvement in the structure over what it was when originally built.

The real problem, in my view, with regard to that part of the $95,198.10 that can reasonably be attributed to the replacement of the floor, is whether the replacement of the floor was merely the remedying of damage to the fabric of the building as it had theretofore existed or whether it was an integral component of a work designed to improve the building by replacing a substantial part thereof by something essentially different in kind.

My conclusion is that, prior to the change, the part of the building in question had a floor (consisting of concrete slabs resting on garbage fill) which made the lower floor of that part of the building unusable and that to remedy that situation and to improve the building by making the space in question usable it was necessary to replace that floor by a floor consisting of a concrete slab reinforced by steel resting on steel piles. With some hesitation, my view is that the improvement operation was the whole replacement work and not merely the sinking of the steel piles.

Again, I return to the fact that, while the difference between repairs and capital additions or improvements is obvious in certain cases, it becomes a matter of difficulty in others. Examples of cases that, I suggest, are evident, are

(a) if a building were built with a thatched roof, while filling in holes in the roof would be repairs, replacing the thatched roof, by reason of its unsuitability to modern living, with a modern roof, metal or wooden, would be a capital improvement in the structure of the building;

(b) if a building were built leaving one side without a wall but partially protected from the elements by a metal awning that was an essential part of the structure, remedying damage to the awning would be a "repair" but replacing it by a wall along the open side would be a capital improvement;

(c) if a building were built with the floor of the lowest storey consisting of dry fill spread on the ground, remedying losses of fill and smoothing it out would be a "repair" but replacing the dry fill with a concrete floor would be a capital improvement.

In each of such cases there has been, in the "replacing" operation, a substitution for some part of the building something that is essentially different in kind from what was there before and constitutes an improvement to the building rather than a mere repair thereto.

There is no doubt that, in this case, from the point of view of the persons making physical use of the building, once the floor was replaced, it was essentially the same as the old floor as it was before it subsided. So regarded, the replacement of the floor could be regarded as a repair of damage to the building. However, from the point of view of the owner or tenant of the building as such, a building the floor of which was "floating" on garbage fill has been changed into a substantially improved building, namely, a building the floor of which is supported by steel piles. Moreover, the removal of the old floor and construction of a floor consisting of a single concrete slab reinforced by steel so as to be suitable for being supported by piles was an essential part of that change. As already indicated, with some hesitation I have come to the conclusion that the problem must be so regarded and that the removal of the old floor, the sinking of the piles and the placing thereon of a concrete slab reinforced by steel was a single operation whereby an improvement was made to the building that was essentially different in kind from a repair to the building as it originally was.

In so far as the balance of the amount in question is concerned (viz, that part of the $95,198.10 that can reasonably be regarded as the cost of replacing or repairing of the waterlines, etc.), the learned Trial Judge was of the view that the cost attributable to them must be disallowed because what was done was not due to wear, aging or deterioration resulting from use or passage of time. I am of the view that that was not a reason for disallowing them. Whether or not this part of the amount in dispute or some part of it qualifies for deduction on current account, in my view, depends on whether, apart from what made the expenditures necessary, they are to be regarded as the cost of repairs or as an outlay on account of capital. In my view, it has been shown that this portion of the amount was disallowed on a wrong basis and that the matter should be referred back for reconsideration thereof on a proper basis.

I would allow the appeal, set aside the judgment of the Trial Division and the assessment in question and refer that assessment back for reassessment on the basis that any part of the $95,198.10 that is not reasonably attributable to the replacement of the old floor by a floor supported by steel piles and that would otherwise be deductible as a current expense should be allowed notwithstanding that its expenditure became necessary as a result of the subsidence or fracturing of the original floor.

26.   For other cases in which building construction costs have been characterized as capital expenses, see *Joseph Wilson Holdings Ltd. v. M.N.R.*, [1981] C.T.C. 2432, 81 D.T.C. 375 (T.R.B.) (cost of replacing a wooden retaining wall damaged during a severe storm with a steel wall); *Healey v. M.N.R.*, [1984] C.T.C. 2004, 84 D.T.C. 1017 (T.C.C.) (extensive renovations to a building that had been vacant for four years, most of which were characterized as capital expenses); *Coleman v. M.N.R.*, [1984] C.T.C. 2725, 84 D.T.C. 1637 (T.C.C.) (cost to restore roof, floors, and foundation of a rental building resulted not from normal wear and tear, but from the building's depreciation and deterioration over time); *Wager v. M.N.R.*, [1985] 1 C.T.C. 2208, 85 D.T.C. 222 (T.C.C.) (expenses to renovate a rental building shortly after acquisition by the taxpayer); *Méthé v. M.N.R.*, [1986] 1 C.T.C. 2493, 86 D.T.C. 1360 (T.C.C.) (expenses of $144,640.85 to renovate a six-unit apartment house purchased for $38,000 immediately before the renovation commenced, most of which were characterized as capital expenses); *Damon Developments Ltd. v. M.N.R.*, [1988] T.C.J. No. 103, [1988] 1 C.T.C. 2266, 88 D.T.C. 1128 (T.C.C.) (extensive renovation to a hotel's "beverage room"); *Dyer v. M.N.R.*, [1991] T.C.J. No. 130, [1991] 1 C.T.C. 2505, 91 D.T.C. 630 (T.C.C.) ($33,000 spent in 1982 to renovate a house purchased for $42,750 in 1981, most of which was characterized as a capital expense); *Earl v. Canada*, [1992] T.C.J. No. 740, [1993] 1 C.T.C. 2081, 93 D.T.C. 65 (TCC) ($32,000 — about 17 per cent of the value of the building — spent to replace a leaking roof that the taxpayer had repaired three years earlier at a cost of $4,200); *Fiore v. Canada*, [1993] F.C.J. No. 249, [1993] 2 C.T.C. 68, 93 D.T.C. 5215 (F.C.A.) (expenses of $326,648 to

renovate two rental properties purchased for $107,000, most of which were characterized as capital expenses); *Park Royal Shopping Centre Ltd. v. Canada*, [1995] T.C.J. No. 382, [1995] 2 C.T.C. 2117 (T.C.C.) (extensive renovations to a shopping centre on account of capital); and *Leclerc v. Canada*, [1997] T.C.J. No. 479, [1998] 2 C.T.C. 2578 (T.C.C.) (improvements to an unoccupied apartment to make the property rentable).

See also *Morel v. M.N.R.* (1951), 5 Tax ABC 213, 51 D.T.C. 431 (T.A.B.), in which the taxpayer, a hotel owner, had considerable work done to her premises, including moving the tap room and beverage room to different locations in the hotel, which required the installation of washrooms and heating equipment. Rejecting the taxpayer's argument that the expenses were deductible expenses that she "was compelled to make... to comply with the regulations of the Liquor Control Board of Ontario" (at para. 11), Chair Fabio Monet, KC concluded that "this fact would not in any way change the nature of the expenditure, for if an expenditure is *in se* a capital expenditure, I fail to see why the nature of the expenditure would be changed because a taxpayer has been compelled to incur it."

27. In *Gold Bar Developments Ltd. v. M.N.R.*, [1987] F.C.J. No. 219, [1987] 1 C.T.C. 262, 87 D.T.C. 5152 (F.C.T.D.), the taxpayer, which owned an apartment building worth about $8 million, sought to deduct in computing its income for its 1980 taxation year $241,665.76 spent to repair an exterior brick wall that an inspection revealed to have become unsound. Rejecting the Minister's argument that the repairs, which involved the replacement of the brick wall by a wall constructed of metal cladding, were on account of capital, the court characterized the expense as a deductible expense. According to Jerome J (at paras. 4-11):

> I do not think the solution to this problem can be found in the effect of the expenditure. It is expected that repairs to a capital asset should improve it. Where the source of income is a residential apartment building, that is always the case, especially where the repairs are substantial. Nor do I find the "once-in-a-lifetime" approach of much assistance. The more substantial the repair, the less likely it is to recur (certainly the fervent hope of the building owner) but it remains a repair expenditure nonetheless.

> I think it is more helpful to emphasize the purpose of the outlay by the taxpayer. What was in the mind of the taxpayer in formulating the decision to spend this money at this time? Was it to improve the capital asset, to make it different, to make it better? That kind of decision involves a very important elective component — a choice or option which is not present in the genuine repair crisis.

> It is not in dispute that the plaintiff discovered in 1979 that the bricks were coming loose and falling on the ground around the building used by tenants and passersby. Obviously, it was a risk that would be unacceptable to the public, but also one likely to meet a reaction from city officials, in the extreme even closure of the premises. In the circumstances, I cannot conclude that the plaintiff had any real choice. To ignore that condition would certainly have brought about a reduction in occupation, or in rental income.

It is also common ground that the cause of the premature break-down of the brick veneer was faulty work by the original subcontractor when the plaintiff had arranged to have the building constructed some ten years earlier. That is not directly relevant to the taxation issue, but certainly verifies the fact that the plaintiff had this decision forced upon him and did not initiate it. This was not a voluntary expenditure with a view to bringing into existence a new capital asset for the purpose of producing income, or for the purpose of creating an improved building so as to produce greater income. The plaintiff was faced with an unexpected deterioration in the walls of the building which put the viability of the property at risk. The decision to spend the money was a decision to repair to meet that crisis and despite the fact that I am sure the plaintiff's expectation was, and still is, that it will not recur in the lifetime of the building, it remains fundamentally a repair expenditure.

There remain two other considerations that arise from the jurisprudence. An expenditure which is in the nature of repair will not be allowed as a deduction from income if it becomes so substantial as to constitute a replacement of the asset. See *Canada Steamship Lines Limited v. M.N.R.* ... . Here, however, while the sum of money is certainly substantial, the undisputed evidence is that this building's value at the material time was in the range of $8 million so that the sum in issue represents less than three per cent of the value of the asset. There is no justification therefore to reclassify the expenditure on that basis.

Finally, there have been a number of decisions in which repairs, either alone or in combination with other work, have rendered the capital asset not simply restored to its original condition, but greatly improved because of its new-found resistance to those factors which caused the deterioration. See *Shabro Investments Ltd. v. The Queen* ... .

Counsel for the defendant invites me to reach that conclusion here because the walls to the plaintiff's building were not replaced with brick as before, but with a metal cladding that went beyond answering the defects, and made the building not only fully resistant to the problem of falling bricks, but also substantially improved in appearance. I cannot accept the suggestion, however, that once the decision to repair is forced upon the taxpayer, he must ignore advancements in building techniques and technology in carrying out the work. In remedying the situation, the plaintiff was given two or three options, including the replacement of the original brick. In pursuing the option of curtain-wall cladding, the plaintiff adopted an extremely popular modern construction technique. I am not satisfied that the appearance of the building was any better than it would have been had the original brick been replaced.

Nothing in this repair project attempted to change the structure of the building. What was done was neither more nor less than was required to replace the deteriorating and dangerous brick condition. The Minister was therefore in error in requiring the taxpayer to treat this as an expenditure on account of capital.

Do you agree with this decision? Why or why not? Is the court's approach consistent with the Federal Court of Appeal decision in *Shabro Investments Ltd. v. M.N.R.*, [1979] F.C.J. No. 119, [1979] C.T.C. 125, 79 D.T.C. 5104 (F.C.A.)? Is it consistent with Jackett P's comments on the characterization of "upgrades" in *Canada Steamship Lines Limited v. M.N.R.*, [1966] C.T.C. 255, 66 D.T.C. 5205 (Ex. Ct.)? Is it consistent with *Morel v. M.N.R.* (1951), 5 Tax ABC 213, 51 D.T.C. 431 (T.A.B.)?

28.   In *Marklib Investments II-A Ltd. v. Canada*, [1999] T.C.J. No. 716, [2000] 1 C.T.C. 2513, 2000 D.T.C. 1413 (T.C.C.), the taxpayer, which owned two apartment complexes from which it derived rental income, was required to

spend $3,457,385 in order to comply with work orders issued by the municipal authorities, which it deducted in computing its income for its 1991 taxation year, producing a net loss of $2,593,054. Rejecting the Minister's argument that the expenditure was a capital expense, the court allowed the taxpayer's appeal on the grounds that the repairs merely restored the building to its original condition and were undertaken to comply with municipal work orders. According to Brulé TCJ (at paras. 35 and 47):

> It is the purpose, rather than the result of an expenditure that determines whether it is characterized as a capital outlay or a current expense; and the focus of the test is on whether or not the expenditure brings into existence an asset of enduring value, rather than on the determination of the frequency or recurrence of the expenditure. The cases seem to promote the idea that as long as the repairs were done to preserve or conserve the asset and not to create a new asset then the repairs will be considered current expenses. ...

> The Court does not think the appellant should be penalized simply because it made a lot of large repairs in one year. As provided by Mr. Justice Jerome in *Gold Bar*, the appellant's intent and purpose must be kept in mind. Given the work orders and by-law changes there appears to be no intent of improving the asset or making substantial changes to the structure of the buildings. The purpose of most of the repairs was to comply with municipal requirements.

29. For other cases in which construction costs have been characterized as deductible current expenses for the purpose or repairing damaged property, see *Dubé v. M.N.R.*, [1979] C.T.C. 2241, 79 D.T.C. 10 (T.R.B.) (expenses of $24,605 to repair two buildings valued at $507,600); *Bergeron v. M.N.R.*, [1989] T.C.J. No. 923, [1990] 2 C.T.C. 2220, 90 D.T.C. 1505 (T.C.C.) (expense of $109,121 to renovate an apartment building purchased earlier in the year for $80,000, of which $82,652 was allowed as a deductible current expense incurred "for the purpose of returning the apartment building to its regular use"); *McLaughlin v. M.N.R.*, [1991] T.C.J. No. 1043, [1992] 1 C.T.C. 2001, 92 D.T.C. 1030 (T.C.C.) ($60,000 spent in 1987 to renovate a century-old house purchased for $113,000, of which the taxpayer capitalized $40,000 and claimed $20,000 as a deductible current expense); and *Chambers v. Canada*, [1997] T.C.J. No. 1244, [1998] 1 C.T.C. 3273 (T.C.C.) (expenses to repair a rundown rental building, other than amounts spent for refrigerators, stoves, and window blinds, considered deductible on the grounds that the cost was "not extraordinarily large in relation to [the cost of] the building").

30. In *Bowland v. Canada*, [1999] T.C.J. No. 588, [1999] 4 C.T.C. 2530, 99 D.T.C. 998 (T.C.C.), aff'd [2001] F.C.J. No. 839, [2001] 3 C.T.C. 109, 2001 D.T.C. 5395 (F.C.A.), the taxpayer, who owned a rental property that was damaged by fire, sought to deduct expenditures incurred to restore the building to a condition less than its original state. According to Hamlyn TCJ (at para. 18):

> These expenditures ... provided for permanent advantages as the taxpayer will not have to incur them every year. These repairs were a one-time occurrence. They gave rise to an enduring benefit. The effect of the expenditures brought the rental property back into existence. The house was virtually rebuilt and resulted in a new capital asset.

As a result, the court concluded, the expenditures were "capital in nature." See also *Speek v. Canada*, [1994] T.C.J. No. 677, [1994] 2 C.T.C. 2422 (T.C.C.), in which the taxpayer, who owned a bungalow from which she derived rental income, sought to deduct $29,343 that she spent in addition to insurance proceeds to construct a two-storey dwelling after the bungalow was destroyed by fire. Disallowing the deduction, the court commented that the original dwelling had been "destroyed and replaced by a new capital asset." Are these decisions consistent with the emphasis on the purpose of the expenditure in *Gold Bar Developments Ltd. v. M.N.R.*, [1987] F.C.J. No. 219, [1987] 1 C.T.C. 262, 87 D.T.C. 5152 (F.C.T.D.) and *Marklib Investments II-A Ltd. v. Canada*, [1999] T.C.J. No. 716, [2000] 1 C.T.C. 2513, 2000 D.T.C. 1413 (T.C.C.)?

31. For the CRA's views on the characterization of expenses related to the maintenance or improvement of depreciable property, see *Interpretation Bulletin* IT-128R, "Capital Cost Allowance — Depreciable Property," May 21, 1985. According to paragraph 4:

(a) Enduring Benefit — Decisions of the courts indicate that when an expenditure on a tangible depreciable property is made "with a view to bringing into existence an asset or advantage for the enduring benefit of a trade," then that expenditure normally is looked upon as being of a capital nature. Where, however, it is likely that there will be recurring expenditures for replacement or renewal of a specific item because its useful life will not exceed a relatively short time, this fact is one indication that the expenditures are of a current nature.

(b) Maintenance or Betterment — Where an expenditure made in respect of a property serves only to restore it to its original condition, that fact is one indication that the expenditure is of a current nature. This is often the case where a floor or a roof is replaced. Where, however, the result of the expenditure is to materially improve the property beyond its original condition, such as when a new floor or a new roof clearly is of better quality and greater durability than the replaced one, then the expenditure is regarded as capital in nature. Whether or not the market value of the property is increased as a result of the expenditure is not a major factor in reaching a decision. In the event that the expenditure includes both current and capital elements and these can be identified, an appropriate allocation of the expenditure is necessary. Where only a minor part of the expenditure is of a capital nature, the Department is prepared to treat the whole as being of a current nature.

(c) Integral Part or Separate Asset — Another point that may have to be considered is whether the expenditure is to repair a part of a property or whether it is to acquire a property that is itself a separate asset. In the former case the expenditure is likely to be a current expense and in the latter case it is likely to be a capital outlay. For example, the cost of replacing the rudder or propeller of a ship is regarded as a current expense because it is an integral part of the ship and there is no betterment: but the cost of replacing a lathe in a factory is regarded as a capital expenditure, because the lathe is not an integral part of the factory but is a separate marketable asset. Between such clear-cut cases there are others where a replaced item may be an essential part of a whole property yet not an integral part of it. Where this is so, other factors such as relative values must be taken into account.

(d) Relative Value — The amount of the expenditure in relation to the value of the whole property or in relation to previous average maintenance and repair costs often may have to be weighed. This is particularly so when the replacement itself could be regarded as a separate, marketable asset. While a spark plug in an engine may be such an asset, one would never regard the cost of replacing it as anything but an expense; but where the engine itself is replaced, the expenditure not only is for a separate marketable asset but also is apt to be very substantial in relation to the total value of the property of which the engine forms a part, and if so, the expenditure likely would be regarded as capital in nature. On the other hand, the relationship of the amount of the expenditure to the value of the whole property is not, in itself, necessarily decisive in other circumstances, particularly where a major repair job is done which is an accumulation of lesser jobs that would have been classified as current expense if each had been done at the time the need for it first arose; the fact that they were not done earlier does not change the nature of the work when it is done, regardless of its total cost.

(e) Acquisition of Used Property — Where used property is acquired by a taxpayer and at the time of acquisition it requires repairs or replacements to put it in suitable condition for use, the cost of such work is regarded as capital in nature even though, in other circumstances, it would be treated as current expense.

(f) Anticipation of Sale — Repairs made in anticipation of the sale of a property or as a condition of the sale are regarded as capital in nature. On the other hand, where the repairs would have been made in any event and the sale was negotiated during the course of the repairs, or after their completion, the cost should be classified as though no sale was contemplated.

32. In addition to judicial tests governing the characterization of capital expenditures, the *Income Tax Act* also contains specific rules that require taxpayers to "capitalize" stipulated amounts in specific circumstances. Subsection 18(2), for example, limits the extent to which taxpayers may deduct interest expenses and property taxes (generally referred to as "carrying charges") related to certain land. According to this provision:

Notwithstanding paragraph 20(1)(c), in computing the taxpayer's income for a particular taxation year from a business or property, no amount shall be deductible in respect of any expense incurred by the taxpayer in the year as, on account or in lieu of payment of, or in satisfaction of,

(a) interest on debt relating to the acquisition of land, or

(b) property taxes (not including income or profits taxes or taxes computed by reference to the transfer of property) paid or payable by the taxpayer in respect of land to a province or to a Canadian municipality,

unless, having regard to all the circumstances (including the cost to the taxpayer of the land in relation to the taxpayer's gross revenue, if any, from the land for the particular year or any preceding taxation year), the land can reasonably be considered to have been, in the year,

(c) used in the course of a business carried on in the particular year by the taxpayer, other than a business in the ordinary course of which land is held primarily for the purpose of resale or development, or

    (d)   held primarily for the purpose of gaining or producing income of the taxpayer from the land for the particular year,

except to the extent of the total of

    (e)   the amount, if any, by which the taxpayer's gross revenue, if any, from the land for the particular year exceeds the total of all amounts deducted in computing the taxpayer's income from the land for the year.[63]

Thus, where the land is not subject to one of the exceptions in paragraphs 18(2)(c) or (d),[64] the amount that a taxpayer may deduct in respect of the carrying charges referred to in paragraphs 18(2)(a) and (b) cannot exceed the net income from the land otherwise determined.[65] As a result, these carrying charges cannot be used to create or increase losses for tax purposes. Instead, the disallowed amount is added to the cost of the land under subsection 10(1.01) (where the land is inventory) or paragraph 53(1)(h) (where the land is capital property).

For the purpose of subsection 18(2), subsection 18(3) stipulates that the word "land" does not, "except to the extent that it is used for the provision of parking facilities for a fee or charge," include:

    (a)   any property that is a building or other structure affixed to land,

    (b)   the land subjacent to any property described in paragraph (a), or

    (c)   such land immediately contiguous to the land described in paragraph (b) that is a parking area, driveway, yard, garden or similar land as is necessary for the use of any property described in paragraph (a).

As a result, subsection 18(2) applies only to interest on a debt relating to the acquisition and property taxes paid or payable in respect of vacant land.

Among the few cases in which subsection 18(2) has been applied, one of the most interesting is *Ward v. M.N.R.*, [1988] F.C.J. No. 148, [1988] 1 C.T.C. 336, 88 D.T.C. 6212 (F.C.T.D.), in which the taxpayer, a doctor who invested in a golf course as a tax shelter, sought to deduct his share of annual losses, which

---

[63]   Paragraph 18(2)(f) and subs. 18(2.2)-(2.5) provide a more generous deduction for corporate taxpayers whose "principal business is the leasing, rental or sale, or the development for lease, rental or sale, or any combination thereof, of real property owned by it, to or for a person with whom the corporation is dealing at arm's length," generally equal to an amount that would be the interest on $1 million if computed at a rate prescribed by regulation 4301(c). For our purposes, there is no need to examine this additional deduction.

[64]   For the purpose of para. 18(2)(c), note that the definition of "business" in subs. 248(1) does not include an adventure or concern in the nature of trade.

[65]   For the purpose of para. 18(2)(a), note that subs. 18(3) specifies that the expression "interest on debt relating to the acquisition of land" includes, among other things, "interest paid or payable in a year in respect of borrowed money that cannot be identified with particular land but that may nonetheless reasonably be considered (having regard to all the circumstances) as interest on borrowed money used in respect of or for the acquisition of land." Paragraph (b) of the definition in subs. 18(3) refers to various non-arm's-length relationships that need not concern us here.

were generated by the deduction of interest expenses in excess of revenues derived from renting the property. Concluding that the property was held primarily for the purpose of resale and development, the court disallowed the deduction of these losses on the basis that the taxpayer was subject to the limitation in subsection 18(2).

For other cases in which subsection 18(2) has been applied, see *Wollenberg v. M.N.R.*, [1984] C.T.C. 2043, 84 D.T.C. 1055 (T.C.C.); *Shtabsky v. M.N.R.*, [1990] T.C.J. No. 503, [1990] 2 C.T.C. 2113, 90 D.T.C. 1621 (T.C.C.); *Volpé v. M.N.R.*, [1990] T.C.J. No. 337, [1990] 2 C.T.C. 2321, 90 D.T.C. 1707 (T.C.C.); *Anstel Holdings Ltd. v. M.N.R.*, [1991] T.C.J. No. 427, [1991] 2 C.T.C. 2515, 91 D.T.C. 1050 (T.C.C.); *Dupont v. M.N.R.*, [1993] 1 C.T.C. 2219, 93 D.T.C. 609 (T.C.C.); *Heinze v. Canada*, [1997] F.C.J. No. 420, 97 D.T.C. 5219 (F.C.T.D.); and *Magnowski v. Canada*, [2000] T.C.J. No. 330, 2000 D.T.C. 2244 (T.C.C.). For the CRA's views on subsection 18(2), see IT-153R3.

Like subsection 18(2), subsection 18(3.1) requires taxpayers to capitalize certain expenses that would otherwise be deductible in the taxation year in which they are made or incurred. Notwithstanding any other provision of the Act, in computing a taxpayer's income for a taxation year, paragraph 18(3.1)(a) provides that:

> no deduction shall be made in respect of any outlay or expense made or incurred by the taxpayer (other than an amount deductible under paragraph 20(1)(a), (aa) or (qq) or subsection 20(29)) that can reasonably be regarded as a cost attributable to the period of the construction, renovation or alteration of a building by or on behalf of the taxpayer ... and relating to the construction, renovation or alteration, or a cost attributable to that period and relating to the ownership during that period of land
>
> (i) that is subjacent to the building, or
>
> (ii) that
>
> (A) is immediately contiguous to the land subjacent to the building,
>
> (B) is used, or is intended to be used, for a parking area, driveway, yard, garden or any other similar use, and
>
> (C) is necessary for the use or intended use of the building.[66]

Instead, according to paragraph 18(3.1)(b), the amount of any such outlay or expense, the deduction of which is disallowed under paragraph 18(3.1)(a), is to be included in computing the cost or capital cost, as the case may be, of the building to the taxpayer.

While the direct costs of constructing, renovating, or altering a building are typically characterized as capital expenses under general principles, subsection

---

[66] Paragraph 18(3.1)(a) also applies to the same kinds of non-arm's-length relationships referred to in para. (b) of the definition of "interest on debt relating to the acquisition of land" in subs. 18(3). For our purposes, there is no need to examine the application of the rule to these situations.

18(3.1) mandates the capitalization of other costs that can "reasonably be regarded" as: (1) being "attributable to the period of the construction, renovation or alteration"; and (2) "relating to" either the construction, renovation, or alteration or the ownership of land subjacent or contiguous to the building as specified in subparagraph 18(3.1)(a)(ii). These costs, which include amounts such as interest and other financing costs, property taxes, mortgage insurance fees, legal and accounting expenses, site investigation fees,[67] and utility service connection costs,[68] are generally described as "soft costs" (as opposed to the "hard costs" associated with the construction, renovation, or alteration itself).

For the purpose of subsection 18(3.1), paragraph 18(3.2)(a) stipulates that "costs relating to the construction, renovation or alteration of a building or to the ownership of land" include:

> interest paid or payable by a taxpayer in respect of borrowed money that cannot be identified with a particular building or particular land, but that can reasonably be considered (having regard to all the circumstances) as interest on borrowed money used by the taxpayer in respect of the construction, renovation, or alteration of a building or the ownership of land.

Subsection 18(3.3) provides that for the purpose of subsection 18(3.1), "the construction, renovation or alteration of a building is completed at the earlier of the day on which the construction, renovation or alteration is actually completed and the day on which all or substantially all of the building is used for the purpose for which it was constructed, renovated or altered." As a general rule, the CRA interprets the expression "all or substantially all" to mean at least 90 per cent. Subsections 18(3.4) to (3.7) contain special and transitional rules that need not concern us here.

The exclusions to this provision include: paragraph 20(1)(a), which allows a deduction for capital cost allowance; paragraph 20(1)(aa), which permits a deduction for landscaping expenses;[69] paragraph 20(1)(qq), which allows a deduction for disability-related modifications to buildings; and subsection 20(29), which allows taxpayers to deduct construction-period "soft costs" to the extent that they do not exceed the taxpayer's income from the rental of the building for the year computed without reference to subsection 20(29) or subsection 20(28), which permits the deduction of certain capital cost allowances otherwise prohibited under subsection 13(26).[70] The combined effect

---

[67] Site investigation fees are otherwise deductible under para. 20(1)(dd).

[68] Utility service connection costs are otherwise deductible under para. 20(1)(ee).

[69] Notwithstanding para. 20(1)(aa) and the exclusion of landscaping expenses from subs. 18(3.1), taxpayers may be required to capitalize these expenses in the inventory cost of developed land. See *Qualico Developments Ltd. v. Canada*, [1984] F.C.J. No. 101, [1984] C.T.C. 122, 84 D.T.C. 6119 (F.C.A.).

[70] Subsection 13(26), which is discussed later in this chapter, prohibits the deduction of capital cost allowances on depreciable property that has been acquired by a taxpayer but is not "available for use" as defined in subs. 13(27) to (31). Where the depreciable property is a building, however, subs. 20(28) allows taxpayers to deduct an amount equal to the capital cost allowance that is

of subsections 18(3.1) and 20(29), therefore, is to permit the deduction of construction-period "soft costs" to the extent of any rental income from the building during the same taxation year, and to require the capitalization of all such costs exceeding any rental income for the year.

Among the few cases that have considered subsection 18(3.1), one of the most interesting is *Baggs v. M.N.R.*, [1990] T.C.J. No. 21, [1990] 1 C.T.C. 2391, 90 D.T.C. 1296 (T.C.C.), in which the taxpayer, who converted a garage in Burgeo, Newfoundland into two apartments, which were ready to be rented in 1983, spent over $20,000 to repair the building after its roof was blown away in a storm. Rejecting the Minister's argument that these costs were subject to the capitalization rule in subsection 18(3.1), the court held that the expenses at issue related to the building's repair, as opposed to its "construction, renovation or alteration." For other cases in which subsection 18(3.1) has been considered, see *Barat v. M.N.R.*, [1991] T.C.J. No. 604, [1991] 2 C.T.C. 2360, 91 D.T.C. 1097 (T.C.C.); *Clarke v. M.N.R.*, [1992] 2 C.T.C. 2741 (T.C.C.); *Kuhlmann v. Canada*, [1995] T.C.J. No. 229, [1995] 1 C.T.C. 2910, 95 D.T.C. 417 (T.C.C.); *Saskatchewan Wheat Pool v. Canada*, [1999] F.C.J. No. 494, [1999] 2 C.T.C. 369, 99 D.T.C. 5198 (F.C.A.); *Magnowski v. Canada*, [2000] T.C.J. No. 330, 2000 D.T.C. 2244 (T.C.C.); and *Trynchy v. Canada*, [2001] F.C.J. No. 1429, [2001] 4 C.T.C. 130, 2001 D.T.C. 5582 (T.C.C.).

33. In addition to subsections 18(2) and (3.1), which require taxpayers to capitalize otherwise deductible expenses, section 21 permits taxpayers to capitalize interest and other financing expenses that are incurred in order to acquire depreciable property. According to subsection 21(1):

> Where in a taxation year a taxpayer has acquired depreciable property, if the taxpayer elects under this subsection in the taxpayer's return of income under this Part for the year,
>
> (a) in computing the taxpayer's income for the year and for such of the 3 immediately preceding taxation years as the taxpayer had, paragraphs 20(1)(c), (d), (e) and (e.1) do not apply to the amount or to the part of the amount specified in the taxpayer's election that, but for an election under this subsection in respect thereof, would be deductible in computing the taxpayer's income (other than exempt income) for any such year in respect of borrowed money used to acquire the depreciable property or the amount payable for the depreciable property; and
>
> (b) the amount or the part of the amount, as the case may be, described in paragraph (a) shall be added to the capital cost to the taxpayer of the depreciable property so acquired by the taxpayer.

As a result, where a taxpayer who has acquired depreciable property files an election under this provision, otherwise deductible interest and financing

---

disallowed under subs. 13(26) up to the amount of any rental income from the building for the year.

expenses in respect of the acquisition of the property may be added to the capital cost of the property in the year of acquisition and each of the three preceding taxation years.

b. Allowances

Notwithstanding paragraph 18(1)(b), section 20 allows taxpayers to deduct a number of expenses that might otherwise be non-deductible capital expenditures. Paragraphs 20(1)(c) to (g), for example, which were examined in section IV of this chapter, *supra*, allow taxpayers to deduct interest and other financing expenses, even though these amounts are typically characterized as capital expenditures.[71] Other provisions also permit deductions for expenditures that are generally on account of capital.[72] Of the many statutory allowances in section 20, however, the most important are paragraphs 20(1)(a) and (b), which permit deductions for "capital cost allowances" and "eligible capital

---

[71] As a general rule, Canadian courts have characterized interest expenses on money borrowed to increase the financial capital of the borrower as payments "on account of capital" the deduction of which is prohibited by s. 18(1)(b), in which case they are deductible only if expressly allowed by s. 20(1)(c) or another provision of the Act. Where a taxpayer carries on a business of borrowing and lending money, however, interest and other financing expenses have generally been regarded as deductible current expenses. See *Gifford v. Canada*, [2004] S.C.J. No. 13, [2004] 2 C.T.C. 1, 2004 D.T.C. 6120 (S.C.C.). For useful discussions of the appropriate characterization of interest expenses see Brian J. Arnold, "Is Interest a Capital Expense?" (1992) 40:3 Can. Tax J. 533; and Joel Nitikman, "Is Interest a Current Expense?" Current Cases feature (2000) 48:1 Can. Tax J. 133.

[72] See, for example, paras. 20(1)(z) and (z.1), which permit a limited deduction for lease cancellation payments, subject to a limitation in para. 18(1)(q); para. 20(1)(bb), which allows taxpayers to deduct an amount, other than a commission, paid for advice or management of investments by a professional investment counsellor; para. 20(1)(dd), which permits taxpayers to deduct "an amount paid by the taxpayer in the year for investigating the suitability of a site for a building or other structure planned by the taxpayer for use in connection with a business carried on by the taxpayer"; para. 20(1)(ee), which allows a deduction for "an amount paid by the taxpayer in the year to a person (other than a person with whom the taxpayer was not dealing at arm's length) for the purpose of making a service connection to the taxpayer's place of business for the supply, by means of wires, pipes or conduits, of electricity, gas, telephone service, water or sewers supplied by that person, to the extent that the amount so paid was not paid (i) to acquire property of the taxpayer, or (ii) as consideration for the goods or services for the supply of which the service connection was undertaken or made"; and subs. 20(10), which allows a deduction in computing income from a business for "an amount paid by the taxpayer in the year as or on account of expenses incurred by the taxpayer in attending, in connection with the business, not more than two conventions held during the year by a business or professional organization at a location that may reasonably be regarded as consistent with the territorial scope of that organization." For cases in which subs. 20(10) has been considered, see *Graves v. M.N.R.*, [1990] F.C.J. No. 277, [1990] 1 C.T.C. 357, 90 D.T.C. 6300 (F.C.T.D.); *Friesen v. M.N.R.*, [1989] T.C.J. No. 926, [1990] 1 C.T.C. 2002, 89 D.T.C. 682 (T.C.C.); and *Wees v. Canada*, [1994] T.C.J. No. 1192, [1995] 1 C.T.C. 2711 (T.C.C.).

expenditures." The following text and cases examine the numerous statutory and judicial rules applicable to each of these deductions.

i. CAPITAL COST ALLOWANCES

For accounting purposes, the cost of tangible capital property with a limited useful life is generally depreciated over its expected life in order to match the expense of the asset with related revenues over the course of its useful life. Under the "straightline method" of depreciation, the cost of the property is deducted in equal annual increments over the course of its useful life until the unrecovered or undepreciated cost (or "book value") reaches zero. If an asset costing $1,000 is expected to last for 10 years, for example, straightline depreciation requires the owner to deduct $100 in each of the 10 years during which the asset is expected to produce income. Under the "declining-balance method," a percentage of the unrecovered or undepreciated cost is deducted each year, causing this book value to approach but never reach zero. Where an asset costing $1,000 is depreciated at a declining-balance rate of 40 per cent per year, for example, the schedule of deductions and undepreciated cost is as follows:

Year	Undepreciated cost	Depreciation
1	$ 1,000	$ 400
2	$ 600	$ 240
3	$ 360	$ 144
4	$ 216	$ 86.40
5	$ 129.60	$ 51.84
6	$ 77.76	$ 31.10
7	$ 46.66	$ 18.66
8	$ 28	$ 11.20
9	$ 16.80	$ 6.72
10	$ 10.08	$ 4.03

For tax purposes, deductions in respect of depreciation are explicitly prohibited under paragraph 18(1)(b). Notwithstanding this provision, however, paragraph 20(1)(a) allows a taxpayer to deduct "such part of the capital cost to the taxpayer of property, or such amount in respect of the capital cost to the taxpayer of property, if any, as is allowed by regulation." These "capital cost allowances" are the tax equivalent to depreciation for accounting purposes. Under the *Income Tax Act*, property acquired by a taxpayer for which capital cost allowance (CCA) may be claimed under paragraph 20(1)(a) is defined as "depreciable property."[73]

The regulatory and statutory rules governing CCAs are numerous and complex. At the outset, three basic features may be described. First, unlike accounting depreciation, which is generally calculated on a straightline basis, most CCAs are computed on a declining-balance basis.[74] For this purpose, part XI and schedule II of the Regulations set out a number of rates applicable to different classes of property.[75]

Second, unlike accounting depreciation, which is generally applied to individual assets, CCAs are generally computed by a "class method" according to which the rates specified in part XI and schedule II of the Regulations are applied not to the undepreciated cost of individual assets but to the undepreciated cost of similar kinds of property, the cost of each of which is aggregated to produce an undepreciated capital cost of the class as a whole.[76] This class method has important implications for the tax consequences associated with the disposition of depreciable property, which are examined later under the heading "Recapture and Terminal Loss."

Third, unlike accounting depreciation, which must be deducted in the relevant accounting period, the use of the words "there may be deducted" in the preamble to subsection 20(1) suggests that the deduction of CCAs under paragraph 20(1)(a) is optional. As a result, where taxpayers find it advantageous to do so, they may maintain the undepreciated capital cost of one or more classes of property by forgoing current deductions and deferring the tax value of these deductions to subsequent accounting periods.

The following text and cases consider the kinds of property that qualify as depreciable property, the tax consequences resulting from its acquisition and disposition, the deductions that may be claimed in respect of depreciable property, and rules governing the "recapture" of excessive CCA and the deduction of "terminal losses" remaining when depreciable property is disposed of for less than its undepreciated capital cost.

A. DEPRECIABLE PROPERTY

Subsection 13(21) of the Act defines "depreciable property" as "property acquired by the taxpayer in respect of which the taxpayer has been allowed, or would, if the taxpayer owned the property at the end of the year and this Act were read without reference to subsection (26), be entitled to, a deduction under

---

[73] See the definition of "depreciable property" in subs. 13(21), which applies to the Act as a whole by virtue of the definition of "depreciable properly" in subs. 248(1).

[74] A notable exception to this pattern involves patents, franchises, concessions, or licences for a limited period (class 14), the capital cost of which is deductible on a straightline basis during the period of the right.

[75] See also Schedules III to VI, which set out different methods of depreciation for specific categories of depreciable property.

[76] See the description of E in the definition of "undepreciated capital cost" in subs. 13(21).

paragraph 20(1)(a) in computing income for that year or a preceding taxation year."[77] By virtue of the definition of "depreciable property" in subsection 248(1) of the Act, this definition applies to the Act as a whole. In order to qualify as depreciable property, therefore, the property must be "acquired by the taxpayer" and must be property in respect of which a deduction has been allowed under paragraph 20(1)(a) or would be allowed if the taxpayer owned the property at the end of the year and the Act were read without reference to the "available for use" rule in subsection 13(26).

The requirement that a taxpayer have "acquired" the property for it to be characterized as depreciable property has been considered in numerous cases involving conditional sales agreements or financing leases under which legal title remains with the lessor, the lessee assumes the usual incidents of ownership such as possession, use, and risk, and the lessee is entitled to purchase the property during or at the end of the term of the lease. In common law provinces, courts have consistently held that these lease arrangements constitute an acquisition of property by the lessee, so that the lessee and not the lessor may deduct CCA. In *M.N.R. v. Wardean Drilling Ltd.*, [1969] C.T.C. 265, 69 D.T.C. 5194 (Ex. Ct.), for example, Cattanach J suggested (at para. 26) that:

> a purchaser has acquired assets of a class in Schedule B [now schedule II] ... when the purchaser has all the incidents of title, such as possession, use and risk, although legal title may remain in the vendor as security for the purchase price as is the commercial practice under conditional sales agreements.

In *Canada v. Henuset Brothers Ltd. (No. 2)*, [1977] C.T.C. 228, 77 D.T.C. 5169 (F.C.T.D.), the Court relied on this statement to allow the taxpayer, which had executed a conditional sales agreement to acquire 10 tractors, to deduct CCA on the tractors, even though legal title remained with the vendor. According to Bastin DJ (at para. 4):

> The clause in the conditional sales agreements obliging the buyer to insure the tractors against such risks as the vendor specified is evidence that the risk has passed to the buyer. ... On the completion of the sale the buyer had the right to use the tractors. ... It follows that all the incidents of ownership other than the legal title reserved in the vendor by the conditional sales agreements such as possession, risk and the right to use the tractors were acquired by the buyer. ... In my opinion the reservation of the legal title to the tractors in the vendor as security did not affect the issue any more than the taking of security on the tractors in the form of a chattel mortgage would have done.

Other cases involving lessors have generally adopted the same approach.[78]

---

[77] Subsection 13(26), which is examined later in this chapter, disallows the deduction of CCA on depreciable properly before the time the property is considered to have become available for use by the taxpayer.

[78] See, for example, *Chibougamau Lumber Ltd. v. M.N.R.*, [1973] C.T.C. 2174, 73 D.T.C. 134 (T.R.B.) and *Kamsel Leasing Inc. v. M.N.R.*, [1993] T.C.J. No. 12, [1993] 1 C.T.C. 2279, 93 D.T.C. 250 (T.C.C.). For a contrary result in which the lease was characterized as a "true" lease in which the usual incidents of ownership remained with the lessor, see *Tri-Star Leasing (London) Inc. v. M.N.R.*, [1992] T.C.J. No. 352, [1992] 2 C.T.C. 2099, 92 D.T.C. 1786 (T.C.C.).

In Quebec, however, where lease agreements are governed by the civil law, courts have reached differing conclusions as to whether conditional sales agreements and financing leases constitute an acquisition of property by the lessee. In *Canada v. Lagueux & Frères Inc.*, [1974] F.C.J. No. 118, [1974] C.T.C. 687, 74 D.T.C. 6569 (F.C.T.D.), in which the taxpayer leased machinery and equipment under contracts containing an option to purchase and requiring aggregate monthly payments equal to the cost of the machinery plus interest on the unpaid amount, the court held that the taxpayer had acquired the property — making rental payments non-deductible and limiting the taxpayer to the deduction of CCA and the interest component of the monthly payments (the remainder being payments on account of capital). In other cases, however, the Tax Court held that since the concept of ownership is absolute in civil law, lessors cannot be said to have acquired property within the meaning of the definition of depreciable property in subsection 13(21) of the Act so long as legal title remains with the lessor.[79] In *Canada v. Construction Bérou Inc.*, [1999] F.C.J. No. 1761, [2000] 2 C.T.C. 174, 99 D.T.C. 5868 (F.C.A.), a majority of the court favoured the former approach, concluding that the taxpayer, which had leased eight trucks for a term of 65 months with aggregate payments equal to the cost of the trucks plus interest and an option to purchase at a favourable price after 60 months, had acquired the property and could deduct CCA. Citing *M.N.R. v. Wardean Drilling Ltd.*, [1969] C.T.C. 265, 69 D.T.C. 5194 (Ex. Ct.), Létourneau JA concluded (at para. 14):

> I agree with this legal interpretation given for tax purposes to the word "acquired" contained in the definition of "depreciable property." For practical purposes this interpretation has the merit of recognizing, for tax legislation that applies throughout Canada, a business practice that has no boundaries and of avoiding the danger of becoming too embroiled in unnecessary, sectoral and above all sterile and inequitable legalism at a time when the trend in civil law is to approximate more closely the common law. In addition, it is significant that Parliament, which annually amends the Act *inter alia* to alter legislative provisions when they are so interpreted that they do not meet the objectives sought, has not thought it appropriate to overturn this thirty-year old interpretation. Further, this interpretation is consistent with the legislative intent stated in subsection 248(3) of the Act, which ... is intended to treat beneficial ownership of property in the same way as various forms of ownership recognized in the civil law of Quebec.

As well, he explained, this interpretation was consistent with the revenue department's longstanding administrative practice, according to which "a transaction is considered to be a sale rather than a lease" where, according to paragraph 3 of IT-233R:

> (a)   the lessee automatically acquires title to the property after payment of a specified amount in the form of rentals,

---

[79]   See, for example, *Fortin & Moreau Inc. v. M.N.R.*, [1990] 1 C.T.C. 2583, 90 D.T.C. 1436 (T.C.C.); *D. Dumais et Fits Inc. v. M.N.R.*, [1990] T.C.J. No. 1035, [1991] 1 C.T.C. 2650, 92 D.T.C. 1107 (T.C.C.); *Location Gaétan Lévesque Inc. v. M.N.R.*, [1991] T.C.J. No. 406, [1991] 2 C.T.C. 2795, 91 D.T.C. 1374, 91 D.T.C. 1380 (T.C.C.); and *Laurent Goulet & Fils Inc. v. M.N.R.*, [1991] T.C.J. No. 408, [1992] 1 C.T.C. 2419, 92 D.T.C. 1605 (T.C.C.).

(b) the lessee is required to buy the property from the lessor during or at the termination of the lease or is required to guarantee that the lessor will receive the full option price from the lessee or a third party (except where such guarantee is given only in respect of excessive wear and tear inflicted by the lessee),

(c) the lessee has the right during or at the expiration of the lease to acquire the property at a price which at the inception of the lease is substantially less than the probable fair market value of the property at the time or times of permitted acquisition by the lessee. An option to purchase of this nature might arise where it is exercisable within a period which is materially less than the useful life of the property with the rental payments in that period amounting to a substantial portion of the fair market value of the property at the date of inception of the lease, or

(d) the lessee has the right during or at the expiration of the lease to acquire the property at a price or under terms or conditions which at the inception of the lease is/are such that no reasonable person would fail to exercise the said option.

Concurring, Desjardins JA also referred to the revenue department's administrative practice and the policy underlying subsection 248(3) of the Act. Dissenting, Noël JA reasoned that the word "acquired" implies ownership "according to its ordinary meaning," that a lease transaction does not transfer ownership under civil law, and that the taxpayer therefore could not deduct capital cost allowance.

Given this diversity of judicial opinion on the appropriate characterization of conditional sales agreements and financing leases, it is perhaps not surprising that the legislature would take action to minimize uncertainty by amending the Act to specifically address transactions of this nature. For leases and subleases entered into after April 26, 1989, section 16.1 allows arm's-length parties to a leasing agreement for a term exceeding one year to elect to characterize the lease as a contract of purchase and sale financed by money borrowed from the lessor by the lessee.[80] Where the parties to a leasing transaction do not file such an election, the tax consequences of the transaction are determined according to the judicial principles set out in *M.N.R. v. Wardean Drilling Ltd.*, [1969] C.T.C. 265, 69 D.T.C. 5194 (Ex. Ct.) and *Canada v. Construction Bérou Inc.*, [1999] F.C.J. No. 1761, [2000] 2 C.T.C. 174, 99 D.T.C. 5868 (F.C.A.).

The kinds of property in respect of which a deduction has been allowed under paragraph 20(1)(a), or would be allowed if the taxpayer owned the property at the end of the year and the Act were read without reference to the "available for use" rule in subsection 13(26), are defined in part XI and schedule II of the Regulations. Some of the more prominent categories or "classes" of property include:

Class 1: Property not included in any other class that is ... (q) a building or other structure, or part thereof, including component parts such as electric wiring, plumbing, sprinkler systems, air-conditioning equipment, heating equipment, lighting fixtures, elevators and escalators. ...

---

[80] For our purposes, there is no need to examine this provision in detail.

Class 3: Property not included in any other class that is (a) a building or other structure or part thereof, including component parts ... , acquired by the taxpayer (i) before 1988, or (ii) before 1990 [under specific circumstances] ... .

Class 6: Property not included in any other class that is (a) a building of (i) frame, (ii) log, (iii) stucco on frame, (iv) galvanized iron, or (v) corrugated metal construction, including component parts ... , if the building (vi) is used by the taxpayer for the purpose of gaining or producing income from farming or fishing, [or] (vii) has no footings or any other base support below ground level ... .

Class 8: Property not included in [various other classes] that is ... (i) a tangible capital property that is not included in any other class in this Schedule [other than specific exceptions] ... .

Class 10: Property not included in any other class that is (a) automotive equipment ... [or] (f) general-purpose electronic data processing equipment and systems software therefor [with certain exceptions] ... .

Class 10.1: Property that would otherwise be included in Class 10 that is a passenger vehicle, the cost of which to the taxpayer exceeds $20,000 or such other amount as may be prescribed for the purposes of subsection 13(2) of the Act [now $30,000 before sales taxes]. ...

Class 12: Property not included in any other class that is ... (m) a motion picture film or video tape that is a television commercial message; (n) a certified feature film or certified production [as defined in subsection 1104(2) of the Regulations]; [or] (o) computer software ... .

Class 13: Property that is a leasehold interest [other than certain leasehold interests and the part of a leasehold interest representing buildings or other structures erected by a tenant or additions or alterations to leased buildings made by a tenant].

Class 14: Property that is a patent, franchise, concession or licence for a limited period in respect of property [other than certain kinds of excluded intangible property rights].

Class 43: Property acquired after February 25, 1992, that [is used by the taxpayer in Canada primarily in manufacturing or processing of goods for sale or lease] ...

Class 44: Property that is a patent, or a right to use patented information for a limited or unlimited period.

Schedule II includes most kinds of tangible property and some kinds of intangible property. Intangible property that is not described in schedule II of the Regulations (for example, purchased goodwill) is defined as eligible capital property, a percentage of which may be deducted on a declining-balance basis under paragraph 20(1)(b).[81]

The classes of depreciable property listed in schedule II are subject to specific exclusions in regulations 1102(1) and (2), which provide that the classes of property described in part XI and schedule II of the Regulations do not include property:

---

81   This provision is examined later in this chapter.

(a) the cost of which is deductible in computing the taxpayer's income if the Act were read without reference to sections 66 to 66.4 of the Act; ...

(b) that is described in the taxpayer's inventory;

(c) that was not acquired by the taxpayer for the purpose of gaining or producing income; ... [or]

(f) that is property referred to in paragraph 18(1)(l) of the Act [disallowing a deduction for the use of recreational facilities] acquired after December 31, 1974, an outlay or expense for the use or maintenance of which is not deductible by virtue of that paragraph;

nor "land upon which a property described therein was constructed or situated."

Regulation 1102(1)(a) prevents the deduction as CCA of amounts that are already deductible in computing a taxpayer's income.[82] Regulation 1102(1)(b) prohibits a deduction for CCA in respect of property acquired or manufactured by the taxpayer for the purpose of sale.[83] Regulation 1102(1)(c) is consistent with the policy underlying paragraph 18(1)(a), which prohibits any deduction in respect of an outlay or expense except to the extent that is was made or incurred for the purpose of gaining or producing income, and paragraph 18(1)(h), which prohibits the deduction of personal and living expenses.[84] Regulation 1102(1)(f) is consistent with the policy underlying subparagraph 18(1)(l)(i), which prohibits any deduction in respect of an outlay or expense for "the use or

---

[82] See, for example, *Denison Mines Ltd. v. M.N.R.*, [1972] F.C.J. No. 117, [1972] C.T.C. 521, 72 D.T.C. 6444 (F.C.A.), in which the taxpayer, which engaged in the business of mining uranium from a newly producing mine the income from which was exempt for three years, sought to deduct CCA in respect of "haulageways" (para. (f) of class 12) constructed to remove uranium ore from the mine. On the basis that the haulageways were constructed in the process of extracting uranium from ore bodies contained in the mine, the costs of which were properly deductible as current expenses under "ordinary business principles," the Federal Court of Appeal disallowed the deduction of CCA.

[83] For an application of this rule, see *Stein v. Canada*, [1996] T.C.J. No. 685, [1996] 3 C.T.C. 2279 (T.C.C.), in which the taxpayer, an experienced real estate developer who purchased a condominium with the intention of quickly reselling it at a profit, sought to deduct CCA in respect of the property during years in which it was held prior to sale. Referring to regulation 1102(1)(b) and to the matching principle, the court held that CCA and other carrying charges could not be deducted as running expenses in the year in which they were incurred. For a contrary result, see *Swire Enterprises Ltd. v. M.N.R.*, [1980] C.T.C. 2107, 80 D.T.C. 1109 (T.R.B.), in which the taxpayer, which acquired a parcel of land containing a service station and an old house, with the intention of selling the house and converting the service station into a Kentucky Fried Chicken outlet, demolished the house and constructed two stores for rental purposes after discovering that title to the entire parcel had become fused. Concluding (at para. 26) that "[t]he sale having been frustrated through no fault of the appellant, the property constituted a capital asset for the appellant," the court allowed the deduction of CCA on the house and a terminal loss on its demolition.

[84] The apparent contradiction between this provision and the preamble to subs. 20(1), which applies "[notwithstanding paras. 18(1)(a) ... and (h)," was noted in *Kier v. M.N.R.*, [1990] 1 C.T.C. 2055, 89 D.T.C. 710 (T.C.C.).

maintenance" of various recreational facilities.[85] Finally, subsection 1102(2) excludes all land from the categories of depreciable property in respect of which CCA may be claimed.[86] Of these exclusions, the most litigated is that in regulation 1102(1)(c). One of the first cases in which this provision was applied is *Ben's Limited v. M.N.R.*, [1955] C.T.C. 249, 55 D.T.C. 1152 (Ex. Ct.).

Ben's Limited v. M.N.R.
[1955] C.T.C. 249, 55 D.T.C. 1152 (Ex. Ct.).

CAMERON J: ... The appellant owns and operates a bakery on Pepperell Street in Halifax. In January, 1952, it purchased three adjoining residential properties, each consisting of land and a dwelling house. ... Early in June of the same year it sold the three buildings for $1,200 and shortly thereafter they were removed from the land. The business of the appellant company had increased and it became necessary to provide additional accommodation for its bakery and equipment. The three properties in question were acquired with the intention that the houses thereon would be removed and the land used as a site for the extension of the main building. At the time of the purchase, however, this scheme could not be carried out as all the properties were located in R2 Zone (Second Density Residential) under the existing by-laws of the city of Halifax and could not be changed from residential use to commercial or business purposes unless and until the property was re-zoned. Accordingly, on May 21, 1952, the appellant lodged a petition ... with the council of the city of Halifax and the Town Planning Board to re-zone the properties to C2 Zone (General Business Zone). In the result the proposed amendment to the zoning by-law was passed by the City Council on September 11, 1952, and approved by the Minister of Municipal Affairs on September 20, 1952. Shortly thereafter a contract was awarded for the construction of a concrete extension to the main factory and office building and the new extension was completed early in 1953.

In its ... income tax return for the year 1952, the appellant stated its costs of acquisition of the three properties ... to be $41,632.85, which it apportioned as follows: land — $3,000; buildings — $38,632.85. In respect of these buildings it deducted 10 per cent of that amount ($3,863.28) for capital cost allowance, but

---

[85] This provision was examined earlier in this chapter. For an application of this rule, see *Robitaille v. Canada*, [1996] T.C.J. No. 419, [1997] 3 C.T.C. 2267, 97 D.T.C. 346 (T.C.C.), in which the taxpayer, a criminal lawyer, sought to deduct the terminal loss on the sale of a yacht that he used to entertain clients.

[86] For an application of this rule, see *Sun Life Assurance Co. of Canada v. Canada*, [1997] T.C.J. No. 446, [1997] 3 C.T.C. 2593, 97 D.T.C. 422 (T.C.C.), in which the taxpayer, which acquired land on two corners in downtown Toronto with the intention of constructing two high-rise office buildings, sought to include in the capital cost of the buildings $4,124,803 that was spent to acquire increased density rights of a landowner across the street. Concluding that zoning determines what an owner can do with the land, the court disallowed the deduction of CCA on the payment on the basis that it was part of the cost of the land, not the buildings.

the full amount thereof (*inter alia*) was disallowed and added to the declared income in the re-assessment dated January 11, 1954. The appellant was advised that the disallowance was made on the ground that the entire amount had been expended for the purpose of acquiring the site on which the plant addition had been erected and that no portion of the payment was expended for the purpose of acquiring depreciable assets.

...

In its Notice of Appeal to this Court the appellant first submits that it is entitled, for capital cost allowance purposes, to amortize the net amount expended by it in acquiring the dwelling houses ($35,632.85) at the rate of 10 per cent, that being the maximum amount applicable to frame dwellings under Class 6 of Schedule B [now schedule II] of the Income Tax Regulations referable to capital cost allowances.

...

For the Minister it is contended that the property in question (namely, the frame houses) was not acquired by the appellant for the purpose of gaining or producing income, but was acquired merely as part of the land on which they stood; and that the entire outlay was incurred solely for the purpose of acquiring a site for the proposed extension of the main building.

If one were to approach the problem without paying strict attention to the precise wording of the Regulations, it might perhaps be said in general language that the whole of the *outlay* was "for the purpose of gaining or producing income." It was undoubtedly the intention of the appellant — as will be found later — to acquire a site for the purpose of extending its building and thereby increasing its business; in order to do so it had to purchase the land with the buildings. That, briefly, was the submission made on behalf of the appellant.

In my opinion, however, the Regulations require a somewhat different approach to the problem. All property which, *prima facie* at least, is entitled to the capital cost allowances, is broken up into "classes" as set out in Schedule B, and the rate of the applicable allowance for each such class is stated in Section 1100 of the Regulations. Then, by Section 1102(1)(c) of the Regulations (*supra*), these "classes of property" are deemed not to include property that was not acquired for the purpose of gaining or producing income. The only applicable item of property in Class 6 is "a building of frame."

In my view, therefore, the question is not whether the appellant's outlay as a whole as for the purpose of gaining or producing income, but rather this: "Was the property referred to in Class 6 as 'a building of frame' acquired by the appellant for the purpose of gaining or producing income?"

...

However difficult it may be in some cases to ascertain the intention or purpose of a transaction, no such problem here exists. It is abundantly clear from the evidence as a whole that the frame buildings located on the lands purchased were not acquired for the purpose of gaining or producing income and that the sole purpose in making the outlays was that of acquiring the land as a site for the extension of the factory.

...

An attempt was made, however, to establish that there was also a second purpose, namely, to use the buildings as they were as storage space for the business or as rent-producing property, if the petition to re-zone the property were denied. It was admitted, however, that the houses could not be put to any commercial use, such as warehousing, unless the by-law were changed. It is a fact that the appellant received rentals from one of the properties for a few months after it became the owner, but that was undoubtedly due to the fact that at the time the properties were acquired the tenants in possession held leases expiring May 1. The appellant secured vacant possession of the other properties at the time of purchase. No attempt was made to re-rent any of the properties at any time and it is patent that the appellant was not interested in renting any of them. What it desired was vacant possession so that the buildings could be removed at the earliest possible moment in order to secure the site for the proposed extension. It was not anticipated that there would be any serious difficulty in having the area re-zoned; in fact, the buildings were sold and entirely removed some months before the petition was finally granted. No opposition was filed to the petition.

On the evidence as a whole, I am satisfied that the sole purpose in making the purchase was to acquire a site for the extension of the factory. There never was any intention to acquire the frame houses for gaining or producing income; the sole intention in regard to the houses was to have them torn down and removed at the earliest possible moment, and that purpose was carried out. The mere fact that certain amounts of rental were obtained from one is attributable to the existing leases and does not affect in any way the real purpose of acquisition. Section 1102(1)(c) of the Regulations therefore bars the frame houses, under the circumstances, from being property which was subject to capital cost allowance. The appeal on this point is therefore disallowed.

...

Finally, the appellant submits that it is entitled to capital cost allowance on the net cost to it of the dwelling house at 149-151 Preston Street at the rate of 10 per cent applicable to frame buildings. This property was one of the three referred to above and it was from that property that a small amount of rent, totalling about $140, was received between the date of purchase and the time when the tenants went out of possession, namely, February 28 and April 30. It is submitted that as this property was purchased subject to the existing leases which expired May 1, the appellant acquired it "for the purpose of gaining or producing income." In view of the evidence which I have set out above as to the sole purpose of the appellant in purchasing all three properties, I am unable to conclude that the possibility of receiving rent for a few months from one of them formed any part of its purpose in making the purchases. There was only one purpose, namely, to secure a site for the extension. I regard the receipt of a few months rent as a merely fortuitous event. The appellant could not eject the tenants until the leases terminated. The receipt of rent was referable to the existing leases and not to any purpose of officials of the company had in mind as to the use to be made of the buildings.

For these reasons, the appeal from the decision of the Income Tax Appeal Board will be dismissed and the assessment affirmed. The respondent is entitled to costs after taxation.

Judgment accordingly.

NOTES AND QUESTIONS

1.   On what grounds did the taxpayer in *Ben's Limited* argue that it was entitled to claim CCA in respect of the three buildings that it acquired in January 1952? Why did the Exchequer Court reject these arguments?

2.   In acquiring the land and buildings adjoining its bakery, the taxpayer in *Ben's Limited* allocated $3,000 of the purchase price to the land and $38,632.85 to the buildings. Given that the buildings were sold for $1,200 and removed from the land shortly after their acquisition, was it reasonable for the taxpayer to allocate $38,632.85 of the purchase price to the buildings? See subsection 13(21.1), which is discussed later in this chapter, and section 68, which is considered in chapter 8.

3.   *Ben's Limited* was followed in *Glassman v. M.N.R.*, [1966] C.T.C. 374, 66 D.T.C. 5271 (Ex. Ct.), in which the taxpayer purchased several parcels of real estate in Vancouver, demolished the old houses situated on the property, and built high-rise apartments. Rejecting the taxpayer's argument that he acquired the old houses with a dual purpose of obtaining rental income and developing the property, the court disallowed deductions in respect of CCA on the old houses on the basis that the taxpayer's "basic or primary motive" was to acquire the property to build a high-rise apartment.

4.   In *Adanac Apparel Ltd. v. M.N.R.*, [1969] C.T.C. 484, 69 D.T.C. 5300 (Ex. Ct.), the taxpayer, which carried on a retail apparel business in Victoria, BC sought to deduct CCA in respect of a building situated on property adjacent to the taxpayer's shop, which the taxpayer acquired in 1963 with the intention of opening a "bargain barn" in the building. Although the taxpayer demolished the building and sold the property in 1965, the court allowed the CCA deduction on the basis that the taxpayer had acquired the building for the purpose of gaining or producing income from the expansion of its business.

See also *Moldaver v. M.N.R.*, [1992] T.C.J. No. 236, [1992] 2 C.T.C. 2055, 92 D.T.C. 1564 (T.C.C.), in which the taxpayer acquired a building zoned exclusively for use as dental offices in December 1985, sought unsuccessfully to obtain tenants, applied to rezone the property in February 1986, and subsequently demolished the building and constructed an apartment building for residential use. Concluding that the taxpayer had acquired the building for the purpose of gaining or producing rental income, the court allowed the taxpayer to deduct a terminal loss on the demolition.

5.   In *Gascho Farms Ltd. v. Canada*, [1996] T.C.J. No. 1368, [1997] 1 C.T.C. 2092 (T.C.C.), the taxpayer, which received a residential property as partial consideration for the sale of a family farm in 1990, claimed a terminal loss on the sale of the residence in December 1991 after a period during which it rented the residence at a loss. Concluding that the taxpayer acquired the property for the purpose of completing the sale of the farm and not for the purpose of gaining or producing income, the court disallowed the deduction.

6.   In *Bolus-Revelas-Bolus Ltd. v. M.N.R.*, [1971] C.T.C. 230, 71 D.T.C. 5153 (Ex. Ct.), the taxpayer, which owned land in Niagara Falls and 50 per cent of the shares of a company that had acquired land for an amusement area, acquired two amusement rides in 1965, which remained in storage throughout the year. Disallowing the deduction of CCA claimed by the taxpayer in computing its income for its 1965 taxation year, the court concluded (at para. 47) that although the taxpayer had acquired the rides "for the purpose of gaining or producing income generally from its business," it had not acquired the rides "for the purpose of gaining or producing income from the specific business of operating these two rides."

7.   In *Roywood Investment Ltd. v. M.N.R.*, [1981] F.C.J. No. 422, [1981] C.T.C. 206, 81 D.T.C. 5148 (F.C.A.), the taxpayer purchased land and buildings in 1965 for $589,132, of which it allocated $471,449.60 to the buildings and claimed CCA from 1965 to 1968. Noting that the property was subject to a head lease lasting almost a thousand years according to which the rent could be based on the value of the land alone without buildings or improvements, the court disallowed the deduction of CCA on the basis that the land alone, and not the buildings, was acquired for the purpose of gaining or producing income.

8.   For other cases in which the deduction of CCA or terminal loss has been disallowed on the basis that the taxpayer did not acquire property for the purpose of gaining or producing income, see *M.N.R. v. Gordon*, [1966] C.T.C. 722, 66 D.T.C. 5445 (Ex. Ct.), in which the court concluded that a furnished house acquired by the taxpayer was used for summertime occupancy by the taxpayer and his family, not for the purpose of gaining or producing income; *Campbellton Enterprises Ltd. v. M.N.R.*, [1990] T.C.J. No. 719, [1990] 2 C.T.C. 2413, 90 D.T.C. 1869 (T.C.C.), where the court concluded that a Florida condominium was acquired by the taxpayer for the purpose of providing accommodation for the taxpayer's shareholders and their spouses, not for the purpose of gaining or producing income; *Malatest v. Canada*, [1993] T.C.J. No. 904, [1994] 1 C.T.C. 2460, 94 D.T.C. 1779 (T.C.C.), aff'd [1996] F.C.J. No. 776, [1996] 2 C.T.C. 268, 96 D.T.C. 6377 (F.C.A.), in which the court disallowed the deduction of a terminal loss on the sale of a luxury condominium that the taxpayers sought to rent for a period of time during which they were unable to sell the property after moving into a new house; *Noonan v. Canada*,

[1997] T.C.J. No. 106, [1997] 2 C.T.C. 2593, 97 D.T.C. 1069 (T.C.C.), where the court concluded that the taxpayer, who acquired a luxury condominium in 1988 that remained vacant until he decided to move into the residence in 1991, had not intended to acquire the property "for the purpose of carrying on a profitable rental operation"; *Girouard v. Canada*, [1997] T.C.J. No. 114, [1998] 2 C.T.C. 2547, 97 D.T.C. 1038 (T.C.C.), where the court held that artwork acquired by the taxpayer was acquired for personal use, not for the purpose of gaining or producing income; and *Wallin v. Canada*, [2000] T.C.J. No. 70, [2000] 2 C.T.C. 2371 (T.C.C.), in which the court disallowed the deduction of a terminal loss on the sale of a condominium acquired by the taxpayer in order to carry on a business away from his principal residence.

9.   In *Hickman Motors Ltd. v. Canada*, [1997] S.C.J. No. 62, [1998] 1 C.T.C. 213, 97 D.T.C. 5363 (S.C.C.), the taxpayer, which carried on a car and truck dealership in St. John's, Newfoundland, sought to deduct CCA of $2,029,942 on leasing equipment with an undepreciated capital cost of $5,196,422, which it acquired on a tax-deferred windup of a subsidiary that had accumulated considerable losses (Hickman Equipment), and sold five days later to another subsidiary (Hickman Equipment (1985)). Even though the revenue produced by the leasing equipment during the period that it was held by the taxpayer was only $20,550, a majority of the court rejected the Minister's argument that the property was not acquired for the purpose of gaining or producing income on the grounds that the property produced rental income during the short period that it was held by the taxpayer and that regulation 1102(1)(c) does not require that depreciable property be held for any particular period of time. According to McLachlin J (LaForest and Major JJ concurring) (at paras. 7-8):

> The fact that the assets produced revenue ... establishes that they continued to be used for the purpose of producing income, avoiding ... the exclusion under Regulation 1102(1)(c). The fact that the revenue was small or earned over a short period of time does not take them out of this category. We need not decide whether a different result might flow if the evidence viewed as a whole showed that the assets possessed a non-revenue function: see *Clapham v. M.N.R.*, 70 DTC 1012; *Bolus-Revelas-Bolus Ltd. v. M.N.R.*, 71 DTC 5153 (Exch. Ct.). Nor is the case of assets held for such a short period of time that the revenue produced was too small to calculate ... before us. Here the assets served only one function, to produce income. That Hickman Motors may have intended to retransfer the assets to Hickman Equipment (1985) Ltd. is of no moment. The evidence admits of only one conclusion: that the assets were business assets associated with the production of income.

> The fact that the directors of the taxpayer may have intended to obtain a tax saving by acquiring the asset is irrelevant. It is a fundamental principle of tax law that "[e]very man is entitled if he can to order his affairs so as that the tax attaching under the appropriate Acts is less than it would otherwise be": *Inland Revenue Commissioners v. Duke of Westminster* (1935), [1936] AC 1 (UK HL), at p. 19, *per* Lord Tomlin. As Wilson J put it in *Stubart Investments Ltd. v. R*, [1984] 1 SCR 536 (SCC), at p. 540, "[a] transaction may be effectual and not in any sense a sham (as in this case) but may have no business purpose other than the tax purpose."

Do you agree with this result? Why or why not? If this transaction had been carried out after September 13, 1988, might the GAAR have applied?

B. ACQUISITION OF DEPRECIABLE PROPERTY

The CCAs permitted under paragraph 20(1)(a) and Regulation 1100(1) in respect of different classes of depreciable property are based on the "undepreciated capital cost" (UCC) to the taxpayer as of the end of the taxation year of property of that class. The term "undepreciated capital cost" is defined in subsection 13(21) by a lengthy formula, the essence of which is described by the terms A, B, E, and F, as follows:

$$UCC \text{ at any time} = [A + B] - [E + F]$$

The meaning of each part of this formula is discussed below but in basic terms:

A is the total cost of all properties acquired in the class before the time in question;

B is the amount of any "recapture" added to the taxpayer's income in previous years in respect of the class;

E is the "total depreciation" claimed for property of the class before the time in question (defined to include both CCA deductions and any "terminal losses"); and

F is the total amounts deducted from the UCC before the time in question as a result of dispositions of property of the class (for each disposition the lesser of the proceeds and cost of the asset is deducted from the UCC of the class) .

By virtue of the description of A in the definition of "undepreciated capital cost," "the capital cost to the taxpayer of a depreciable property of the class acquired before that time" is added to the UCC of the class for the purposes of computing CCA under regulation 1100(1). In determining the amount that may be added under item A in computing the UCC to a taxpayer of depreciable property of a prescribed class, two questions must be answered: what is the "capital cost" of the depreciable property, and when may this capital cost be added to the UCC of the class?

With respect to the first question, courts have held that there is no difference between the "capital cost" of a particular depreciable property and its cost as commonly understood.[87] In one frequently cited passage (*Cockshutt Farm Equipment of Canada Ltd. v. M.N.R.* (1966), 41 Tax ABC 386, 66 D.T.C. 544), the Tax Appeal Board concluded (at para. 28) that:

---

[87] *Ottawa Valley Paper Co. v. M.N.R.*, [1969] C.T.C. 642, 69 D.T.C. 5166 (Ex. Ct.).

the expression "capital cost to the taxpayer" as used in paragraph (a) of subsection (1) of section 11 of the *Income Tax Act* [now subsection 20(1)(a)] refers to the actual, factual or historical cost to the [taxpayer] of the depreciable property.

In accordance with the view that the meaning of the word cost should be interpreted in light of "ordinary business principles,"[88] a number of costs associated with the acquisition or construction of depreciable property have been held to be part of the "capital cost" of the depreciable property (for example, architect's fees,[89] the cost of preparing a site for the construction of a building,[90] and interest and other financing expenses incurred to finance the construction of a new mine[91]). Where a portion of the price to acquire a depreciable property represents a contingent liability, however, courts have concluded that this amount is not included in the capital cost of the property.[92]

On the basis of these cases, the CRA explains in paragraph 8 of *Interpretation Bulletin* IT-285R2, "Capital Cost Allowance — General Comments," March 31, 1994:

> The term "capital cost of property" generally means the full cost to the taxpayer of acquiring the property and includes:
>
> (a) legal, accounting, engineering or other fees incurred to acquire the property; and
>
> (b) in the case of a property a taxpayer manufactures for the taxpayer's own use, it includes material, labour and overhead costs reasonably attributable to the property, but nothing for any profit which might have been earned had the asset been sold.

The bulletin adds that construction "soft costs" that are capitalized under subsection 18(3.1) enter into the capital cost of any building that is constructed, renovated, or altered within the meaning of that provision.

In addition to these general principles and statutory rules, the capital cost of certain kinds of depreciable property is subject to specific rules in section 13 of the Act. Paragraphs 13(7)(g) and (h), for example, limit the capital cost of a

---

[88] See *Denison Mines Ltd. v. M.N.R.*, [1972] F.C.J. No. 117, [1972] C.T.C. 521, 72 D.T.C. 6444 (F.C.A.).

[89] *Oriole Park Fairways Ltd. v. M.N.R.* (1956), 16 Tax ABC 92, 56 D.T.C. 537 (T.A.B.).

[90] *George T. Davie & Sons Ltd. v. M.N.R.* (1961), 26 Tax ABC 70, 61 D.T.C. 109 (T.A.B.).

[91] *Sherritt Gordon Mines Ltd. v. M.N.R.*, [1968] C.T.C. 262, 68 D.T.C. 5180 (Ex. Ct.).

[92] See, for example, *Mandel v. Canada*, [1978] C.T.C. 780, 78 D.T.C. 6518 (F.C.A.), aff'd [1980] S.C.J. No. 3, [1980] C.T.C. 130, 80 D.T.C. 6148 (S.C.C.); *McKee v. Canada*, [1977] C.T.C. 491, 77 D.T.C. 5345 (F.C.T.D.); and *Lipper v. Canada*, [1979] C.T.C. 316, 79 D.T.C. 5246 (F.C.T.D.). Where a portion of the capital cost is offset by a guaranteed rate of return secured by a pledge of securities equal to the amount guaranteed, however, the capital cost is not reduced by the amount pledged, even if the taxpayer is not at risk for the full capital cost. See *Canada v. Gelber*, [1983] C.T.C. 381, 83 D.T.C. 5385 (F.C.A.). Where a taxpayer invests in a depreciable property through a limited partnership, the ability to deduct partnership losses that may be generated by the deduction of CCAs is now subject to specific "at-risk" rules in subs. 96(2.1) to (2.7). These provisions are best examined in a course on the taxation of partnerships.

passenger vehicle to $30,000 plus federal and provincial sales taxes.[93] Other provisions reduce the capital cost of depreciable property to the extent that the taxpayer has obtained various kinds of tax credits or any other form of public subsidy in respect of the acquisition of the property.[94] Yet other provisions define the capital cost of depreciable property acquired for a purpose other than gaining or producing income and subsequently used for this purpose; the capital cost of depreciable property used partly to gain or produce income and partly for another purpose; the capital cost of depreciable property acquired through non-arm's-length transactions; and the capital cost of rented property that is acquired for an amount less than its fair market value.[95]

With respect to the second question, concerning the time when the capital cost of depreciable property may be added to the undepreciated capital cost of the class, the description of A in the definition of "undepreciated capital cost" in subsection 13(21) suggests that the capital cost of a property may be added to the undepreciated capital cost of the class only when the property is "acquired" by the taxpayer. In *M.N.R. v. Wardean Drilling Ltd.*, [1969] C.T.C. 265, 69 D.T.C. 5194 (Ex. Ct.), the court stated (at para. 24) that "the proper test as to when property is acquired must relate to the title to the property in question or to the normal incidents of title, either actual or constructive, such as possession, use and risk." On this basis, the taxpayer, which did not obtain title to two pieces of drilling equipment until delivery, was unable to deduct CCA in respect of property that was purchased during the taxpayer's 1963 taxation year but not delivered until its 1964 taxation year. According to Cattanach J (at paras. 25-36):

> On the facts in the present appeal there is no question whatsoever that the contracts for the purchase and sale of the rig and substructure were completed prior to December 31, 1963. Accordingly, there is no question that as at the end of the respondent's 1963 taxation year it had rights under these contracts. Such rights are "property" within the meaning of Section 139(1)(a) [now the definition of "property" in subsection 248(1)] of the *Income Tax Act* but Schedule B [now Schedule II] to the Income Tax Regulations does not include a class of property which is subject to capital cost allowance such as properties which are contractual rights under the contracts here in question. In order to fall within any of the specified classes in Schedule B there must be a right in the property itself rather than rights in a contract relating to the property which is the subject matter of the contract.

> As I have indicated above, it is my opinion that a purchaser has acquired assets of a class in Schedule B when title has passed, assuming that the assets exist at that time, or when the purchaser has all the incidents of title, such as possession, use and risk, although legal title may remain in the vendor as security for the purchase price as is the commercial practice under conditional sales agreements. ...

---

[93] See regulation 7307(1), which prescribes an amount for the purposes of para. 13(7)(g) and subpara. 13(7)(h)(iii).

[94] See subs. 13(7.1) and (7.4). For our purposes, there is no need to examine these provisions in detail.

[95] See paras. 13(7)(b), (c), (d) and (e), and subs. 13(5.2). For our purposes, there is no need to examine these provisions in detail.

Property in the rig could have passed forthwith had the parties so intended. But the parties did not so intend. It was agreed ... that "Title to pass and notes issued as of date shipment." Delivery or shipment was not until February 18, 1964 and accordingly property in the rig did not pass to the respondent until that date.

The rule in *Wardean Drilling* has been adopted by the Canadian revenue authorities and applied in a number of subsequent cases involving deductions for CCA or terminal losses. According to paragraphs 17 to 20 of IT-285R2:

17. Generally, a taxpayer will be considered to have acquired a depreciable property at the earlier of:

(a)   the date on which title to it is obtained, and

(b)   the date on which the taxpayer has all the incidents of ownership such as possession, use, and risk, even though legal title remains in the vendor as security for the purchase price (as is commercial practice under a conditional sale agreement).

In order that the cost of an asset may fall within a specified class, the purchaser must have a current ownership right in the asset itself and not merely rights under a contract, of which the asset is the subject, to acquire it in the future.

18. In determining whether or not depreciable property is acquired by a taxpayer, the legal relationship between the vendor and the purchaser of the property should be reviewed. For example, where chattels are being acquired, the relevant sale of goods legislation would be applicable. Each of the provinces (other than Quebec) has a Sale of Goods Act pertaining to sales of chattels laying down substantially the same rules for the ownership rights to assets bought and sold. The basic rule is that property in respect of specific assets passes, and is therefore acquired by the purchaser, at the time when the parties to the contract intend it to pass as evidenced by the terms of the contract, the conduct of the parties and any other circumstances.

19. If, however, the intention of the parties is not evidenced as discussed above, the following rules apply to determine when property is to pass:

(a)   if there is an unconditional contract for the sale of a specific asset in a deliverable state, property will pass to the purchaser when the contract is made, and it is immaterial whether the time of payment or delivery or both are postponed;

(b)   if there is a contract for the sale of a specific asset and:

(i)   the seller is bound to do something to the asset to put it into a deliverable state, or

(ii)   the asset is in a deliverable state, but the seller must weigh, measure, test or do some other act or thing to ascertain the price,

then property does not pass until the seller has satisfied those conditions and the purchaser has notice thereof.

20. For the purpose of 18 and 19 above, property can pass and acquisition take place only if the asset is in existence and, even then, only if it is a "specific" asset, i.e., one that can be identified as the object of the contract. For example, this requirement is not met by a contract for the purchase of machinery which is described simply as being of a certain make and model, but it is met if the machinery is further identified by its serial number, since only one particular machine can be so described. It should be noted here that it is customary in some industries, for example, the automotive and other heavy equipment manufacturing industry, to issue contracts that describe the property being purchased as being of a certain make, model and even serial number at a time when the property does not exist but is scheduled for production. Under this type of contract, the purchaser acquires the property when the property has been produced and the purchaser has knowledge that it is in a deliverable state.

In *Kirsch Construction Ltd. v. M.N.R.*, [1988] F.C.J. No. 963, [1988] 2 C.T.C. 338, 88 D.T.C. 6503 (F.C.T.D.), in which the taxpayer claimed CCA for its 1977 taxation year on a piece of machinery ordered during the year but delivered in the subsequent taxation year, the Court relied on the written contract to conclude that the parties did not intend title to pass until the equipment was delivered. Similarly, in *Crown Cork & Steel Canada Inc. v. Canada*, [1990] F.C.J. No. 916, [1990] 2 C.T.C. 465, 90 D.T.C. 6586 (T.C.C.), where the taxpayer claimed CCA for its 1979 taxation year on custom machinery ordered by the taxpayer in 1978 but not manufactured until 1980, the court disallowed the deduction on the basis that the taxpayer could not have acquired the property until it was substantially completed. In *Gold Line Transport Ltd. v. M.N.R.*, [1992] T.C.J. No. 504, [1992] 2 C.T.C. 2561, 92 D.T.C. 2005 (T.C.C.), on the other hand, the Court allowed the taxpayer to deduct CCA for its 1988 taxation year on a truck that was neither delivered to nor registered in the name of the taxpayer until its 1989 taxation year, on the grounds that the truck was in a deliverable state and the parties intended title to pass before the end of the taxpayer's 1988 taxation year. Likewise, in *Rajotte v. M.N.R.*, [1990] T.C.J. No. 706, [1990] 2 C.T.C. 2333, 90 D.T.C. 1831 (T.C.C.), in which the taxpayer sought to deduct a terminal loss on a motor home purchased in November 1985 for $30,630 and sold in December 1985 for $22,000, the Court allowed the deduction on the basis that the parties to the original agreement intended title to pass at that time, even though the sale was conditional on financing that was not arranged until February 1986. In most of these cases, including *M.N.R. v. Wardean Drilling Ltd.*, [1969] C.T.C. 265, 69 D.T.C. 5194 (Ex. Ct.), courts have considered applicable sale of goods legislation to determine the time when the ownership of property is transferred.

In *Gartry v. Canada*, [1994] T.C.J. No. 240, [1994] 2 C.T.C. 2021, 94 D.T.C. 1947 (T.C.C.), where the taxpayer agreed to purchase a boat that sank in heavy seas before delivery had been made and before title had passed, the court relied on the broad definition of "acquisition" in *Wardean Drilling* to conclude that the cost of modifications to the boat, if not deductible as running expenses, could be deducted as a terminal loss. According to Bowman JTCC (at para. 33), the taxpayer's ability to arrange and supervise modifications to the boat demonstrated that he had "exercised sufficient dominion" over the boat to have "acquired a sufficient interest in the property and indicia of title thereto that it [became] depreciable property in his hands."

In addition to these general principles, the ability to claim CCA on newly acquired property is subject to specific limits in subsection 13(26) of the Act and regulation 1100(2). Subsection 13(26), which applies to property acquired after 1989, prohibits any addition to the undepreciated capital cost of a class of depreciable property of the capital cost to a taxpayer of "a property of that class ... before the time the property is considered to have become available for use by the taxpayer."[96] For this purpose, subsections 13(27) to (32) provide detailed rules on the time when particular kinds of depreciable property acquired by a taxpayer are considered to have become available for use by the taxpayer. Where a taxpayer acquires a building after 1989, however, subsection 20(28) allows the taxpayer to deduct an amount equal to the CCA that is disallowed under subsection 13(26) up to the amount of any rental income from the building for the year.

Regulation 1100(2) imposes a special limit known as the "half-year rule" on the CCA that may be claimed in respect of depreciable property acquired during a particular taxation year. In basic terms, where the amounts added to the UCC of a class in a taxation year as a result of acquisitions of property (under part A of the UCC definition) exceeds the aggregate amounts deducted from the UCC as a result of dispositions of depreciable property of the same class during the taxation year (under part F of the UCC definition), the CCA that a taxpayer may deduct in respect of property of that class is based on the UCC of the class otherwise determined less half of the net addition to the UCC during the year.[97] The effect of this "half-year rule" generally is to permit taxpayers who acquire depreciable property to claim only half the normal CCA in respect of that property during the taxation year in which the property is acquired.[98] The half-year rule was introduced in order to discourage the practice of acquiring new depreciable property near the end of a taxation year in order to increase CCA deductions and reduce the taxpayer's income for that taxation year.

C. DEDUCTIONS IN RESPECT OF DEPRECIABLE PROPERTY

For most classes of depreciable property, CCA is computed according to a specified rate of the UCC of property of the class at the end of the taxpayer's taxation year.[99] For these classes of depreciable property, CCA is determined on

---

[96] This rule does not apply to property that is a certified production according to the definition in regulation 1104(2).

[97] Regulations 1100(2)(a)(iii) and (iv) exclude from the application of this rule various types of property listed in classes 10 and 12 as well as all property included in any of classes 13, 14, 15, 23, 24, 27, 29, and 34.

[98] For a more detailed discussion of this rule, see Peter W. Hogg, Joanne E. Magee, and Ted Cook, *Principles of Canadian Income Tax Law*, 3d ed. (Toronto: Carswell, 1999) at 291-92.

[99] Exceptions to this pattern are found in regulations 1100(1)(b) and (c), referring to depreciable property belonging to classes 13 (leasehold interests), 14 (patents, franchises, concessions, or

a declining-balance basis determined according to the rate applicable to the class.

For this purpose, Regulation 1100(1)(a) sets out the various CCA rates applicable to specific classes of depreciable property. Regulation 1100(1)(a)(i), for example, defines the rate for class 1 (most buildings) as 4 per cent of the UCC of property of that class. Other rates include:

Class 3 (buildings acquired before 1988): 5 per cent

Class 6 (frame buildings without footing or other base support below ground level): 10 per cent

Class 8 (tangible capital property not included in any other class, e.g. furniture): 20 per cent

Class 10 (automotive equipment, computer hardware): 30 per cent

Class 10.1 (passenger vehicles costing more than $30,000): 30 per cent

Class 12 (certain films and computer software): 100 per cent

Class 43 (manufacturing or processing equipment): 30 per cent

Class 44 (patents or rights to use patented information): 25 per cent.

In theory, these rates are designed to approximate the rate of depreciation actually experienced by each kind of depreciable property. In practice, however, these rates tend to provide a more rapid recovery of the capital cost of depreciable property than the depreciation methods adopted for accounting purposes. In several cases, moreover, the CCA rates are especially generous in order to create incentives for taxpayers to invest in certain kinds of property (for example, certified firms).[100]

Notwithstanding these general provisions, other rules specifically limit the CCA that may be claimed in respect of certain kinds of depreciable property. Regulation 1100(11), for example, prevents taxpayers from using CCA deductions to create or increase rental losses in order to shelter income from other sources. According to this provision:

Notwithstanding [Regulation 1100(1)], in no case shall the aggregate of deductions, each of which is a deduction in respect of property of a prescribed class owned by a taxpayer that includes rental property owned by [the taxpayer], otherwise allowed to the taxpayer by virtue of [Regulation 1100(1)] in computing [the taxpayer's] income for a taxation year, exceed the amount, if any, by which

---

licences), the capital cost of which is deductible on a straightline basis. Further exceptions can be found in regulations 1100(1)(p), (q), (t), and (v). The capital cost of depreciable property used for the purpose of gaining or producing income from farming or fishing may also be deducted on a straightline basis. See regulations 1700 to 1704.

[100] See also regulation 1100(1), which sets out a number of "additional allowances" for certain kinds of depreciable property.

(a) the aggregate of amounts each of which is ... [the taxpayer's] income for the year from renting or leasing a rental property owned by [the taxpayer], computed without regard to paragraph 20(1)(a) of the Act ...

exceeds

(b) the aggregate of amounts each of which is ... [the taxpayer's] loss for the year from renting or leasing a rental property owned by [the taxpayer], computed without regard to paragraph 20(1)(a) of the Act ... .

For the purpose of this limitation, Regulation 1100(14) defines a "rental property" of a taxpayer as:

(a) a building owned by the taxpayer ... , whether owned jointly with another person or otherwise, or

(b) a leasehold interest in real property, if the leasehold interest is property of Class 1 [most new buildings], 3 [buildings acquired before 1988], 6 [frame buildings] or 13 [leasehold interests] in Schedule II and is owned by the taxpayer ... ,

provided that "in the taxation year in respect of which the expression is being applied, the property was used by the taxpayer ... principally for the purpose of gaining or producing gross revenue that is rent."[101]

Virtually identical provisions, preventing taxpayers from using CCA deductions to create or increase losses from the rental of a "leasing property," are contained in regulation 1100(15). For this purpose, Regulation 1100(17) defines a "leasing property" as depreciable property other than a rental property or a certified film feature or production that is owned by the taxpayer and "used by the taxpayer ... principally for the purpose of gaining or producing gross revenue that is rent, royalty or leasing revenue."[102]

Regulations 1100(1.1) to (1.3) prescribe a detailed set of rules to prohibit the deduction of CCA in respect of "specified leasing property" acquired by the taxpayer as part of a sale-leaseback transaction that is functionally equivalent to a loan of the purchase price to the vendor. For our purposes, it is not necessary to examine these rules in detail.[103]

---

[101] The provision also adds "for greater certainty" that the "rental property" of a taxpayer "does not include a property leased by the taxpayer ... to a lessee, in the ordinary course of the taxpayer's ... business of selling goods or rendering services, under an agreement by which the lessee undertakes to use the property to carry on the business of selling, or promoting the sale of, the taxpayer's ... goods or services."

[102] The provision also adds "for greater certainty" that the "leasing property" of a taxpayer "does not include a property leased by the taxpayer ... to a lessee, in the ordinary course of the taxpayer's ... business of selling goods or rendering services, under an agreement by which the lessee undertakes to use the property to carry on the business of selling, or promoting the sale of, the taxpayer's ... goods or services."

[103] For a brief discussion of the purpose and effect of these rules, see Peter W. Hogg, Joanne E. Magee, and Ted Cook, *Principles of Canadian Income Tax Law*, 3d ed. (Toronto: Carswell, 1999) at 283-85.

Where a taxpayer deducts an amount in respect of the capital cost of a particular class of depreciable property under paragraph 20(1)(a) of the Act, the UCC of property of that class is reduced by the CCA claimed, thereby reducing the amount of CCA that can be claimed in respect of the class in subsequent taxation years. This result is achieved by the description of E in the definition of "undepreciated capital cost" in subsection 13(21) of the Act, which, in computing the UCC to a taxpayer of depreciable property of a prescribed class at any time, subtracts "the total depreciation allowed to the taxpayer for property of the class before that time." The definition of "total depreciation" in subsection 13(21) includes "all amounts ... deducted by the taxpayer under paragraph 20(1)(a) in respect of property of that class."[104]

Finally, by virtue of the preamble to subsection 20(1), which says that amounts "may be deducted," taxpayers may defer the deduction of CCA in respect of one or more classes of depreciable property where it is to their advantage to do so.[105] Although the unclaimed CCA cannot be carried forward directly to subsequent taxation years, a failure to claim allowable CCA in respect of a specific class of depreciable property in a particular taxation year will preserve the balance of the taxpayer's UCC in respect of that class of depreciable property, permitting higher CCA deductions in subsequent taxation years than would otherwise be possible in respect of depreciable property of that class.

D. DISPOSITION OF DEPRECIABLE PROPERTY

In computing the UCC to a taxpayer of depreciable property of a prescribed class at any time, the description of F in the definition of "undepreciated capital cost" in subsection 13(21) of the Act requires taxpayers to subtract:

the total of all amounts each of which is an amount in respect of a disposition before that time of property ... of a taxpayer of the class, and is the lesser of

   (a)   the proceeds of disposition of the property minus any outlays and expenses to the extent that they were made or incurred by the taxpayer for the purpose of making the disposition, and

   (b)   the capital cost to the taxpayer of the property.

As a result, where a taxpayer disposes of a depreciable property of a particular class in a taxation year, the taxpayer must subtract the lesser of its proceeds of disposition and its capital cost in computing the UCC of the class. Where the

---

[104] The definition of "total depreciation" in subs. 13(21) also refers to "terminal losses" that may be deducted under subs. 20(16) or would be deductible but for subs. 20(16.1). Terminal losses are considered later in this chapter.

[105] This may be the case where a taxpayer has accumulated losses from prior years that may be deducted in computing taxable income, or where the taxpayer anticipates a higher level of income in subsequent taxation years, resulting in taxation at higher rates.

proceeds of disposition exceed the original capital cost of the property, the excess is subject to tax as a taxable capital gain.[106]

For the purposes of the CCA rules in section 13 of the Act, subsection 248(1) defines the words "disposition of property" to include "any transaction or event entitling a taxpayer to proceeds of disposition," and subsection 13(21) defines "proceeds of disposition" to include:

   (a)   the sale price of property that has been sold,

   (b)   compensation for property unlawfully taken,

   (c)   compensation for property destroyed and any amount payable under a policy of insurance in respect of loss or destruction of property,

   (d)   compensation for property taken under statutory authority or the sale price of property sold to a person by whom notice of an intention to take it under statutory authority was given,

   (e)   compensation for property injuriously affected, whether lawfully or unlawfully or under statutory authority or otherwise,

   (f)   compensation for property damaged and any amount payable under a policy of insurance in respect of damage to property, except to the extent that the compensation or amount, as the case may be, has within a reasonable time after the damage been expended on repairing the damage,

   (g)   an amount by which the liability of a taxpayer to a mortgagee or hypothecary creditor is reduced as a result of the sale of mortgaged or hypothecated property under a provision of the mortgage or hypothec, plus any amount received by the taxpayer out of proceeds of the sale, and

   (h)   any amount included because of section 79 [surrender of property of a debtor to a creditor] in computing a taxpayer's proceeds of disposition of the property.

Where a taxpayer receives compensation described in paragraph (b), (c), or (d) of this definition that is used to acquire a "replacement property" within a specified period of time, subsection 13(4) of the Act reduces the amount of the proceeds that must be subtracted in computing the UCC of the class by the lesser of the proceeds otherwise determined and the amount used to acquire the replacement property, thereby eliminating any tax consequences that would

---

[106] This is achieved by para. (a) of the definition of "capital properly" in s. 54 of the Act, which includes "any depreciable property of the taxpayer," and para. (a) of the definition of "adjusted cost base" in s. 54. which defines the adjusted cost base of depreciable property of a taxpayer as "the capital cost to the taxpayer of the property as of that time." These provisions are examined in Chapter 6.

otherwise result from such a disposition.[107] For this purpose, subsection 13(4.1) stipulates that a property is "a replacement for a former property," *inter alia*, where "(a) it is reasonable to conclude that the property was acquired by the taxpayer to replace the former property; [and] (a.1) it was acquired by the taxpayer and used by the taxpayer or a person related to the taxpayer for a use that is the same as or similar to the use to which the taxpayer or a person related to the taxpayer put the former property."

In addition to these statutory rules, other rules deem depreciable property to be disposed of for proceeds equal to fair market value where the taxpayer, "having acquired the property for the purpose of gaining or producing income, has begun at a later time to use it for some other purpose" (paragraph 13(7)(a)), and for proceeds equal to a proportion of the fair market value of the property where a taxpayer who has used depreciable property partly to gain or produce income and partly for another purpose decreases "the use regularly made of the property for the purpose of gaining or producing income" (subparagraph 13(7)(d)(ii)). Yet another statutory rule (subsection 13(21.1)) adjusts the proceeds of disposition of a building that is disposed of for proceeds less than its undepreciated cost in the same year as the land subjacent or immediately contiguous to the building is disposed of at a gain, reducing the amount of any loss on the building by the amount of any capital gain on the land by increasing the proceeds of disposition of the building and decreasing the proceeds of disposition of the land.[108]

In light of this statutory scheme, the Supreme Court of Canada has held, in *Canada v. Compagnie Immobilière BCN Ltée*, [1979] S.C.J. No. 13, [1979] C.T.C. 71, 79 D.T.C. 5068 (S.C.C.), that the words "disposition of property" should be given their broadest possible meaning, including the destruction of tangible property (for example, a building) or the extinction of an item of intangible property (for example, a patent or leasehold interest). Other judicial decisions have emphasized that a "disposition" by one party to a transaction corresponds to an "acquisition" by another party, and have relied on the rule in *M.N.R. v. Wardean Drilling Ltd.*, [1969] C.T.C. 265, 69 D.T.C. 5194 (Ex. Ct.), to conclude that taxpayers dispose of depreciable property when they divest themselves of "all of the duties, responsibilities and charges of ownership and also all of the profits, benefits and incidents of ownership" even though they retain legal title (*Olympia & York Developments Ltd. v. Canada*, [1980] C.T.C. 265, 80 D.T.C. 6184 (F.C.T.D.)). On this basis, the taxpayer in *Olympia & York*, which sold a building complex in August 1969 under an agreement providing that the purchaser would keep the property in repair and provide insurance until

---

[107] This "rollover" provision also applies where the taxpayer disposes of a "former business property" as defined in subs. 248(1) and uses the proceeds to acquire a replacement property. This rule is similar to s. 44 of the Act, which applies to dispositions of non-depreciable capital property and is examined in Chapter 6.

[108] This rule is designed to prevent the combination of a partly taxable capital gain on the disposition of the building and a fully deductible terminal loss on the sale of the building.

the consideration was paid in full, at which time title would pass, was determined to have disposed of the property in 1969, making it impossible to deduct CCA from 1970 to 1973. Similarly, in *Robert Bédard Auto Ltée v. M.N.R.*, [1985] 2 C.T.C. 2354, 85 D.T.C. 643 (T.C.C.), where the taxpayer, which carried on an automobile dealership, sold its business in 1976 under an agreement whereby land and buildings were leased for $2,000 per month with an option to purchase that was subsequently made mandatory, the court disallowed the deduction of CCA from 1976 to 1979 on the basis that the taxpayer had disposed of the buildings in 1976.[109]

In *M.N.R. v. Browning Harvey Ltd.*, [1990] F.C.J. No. 28, [1990] 1 C.T.C. 161, 90 D.T.C. 6105 (F.C.T.D.), however, where the taxpayer, a manufacturer and distributor of soft drinks, sought to deduct terminal losses on refrigerators costing $1,500 that were sold under supply agreements to shopkeepers for $2, half of which was payable at the time of the agreement and the other at the end of the seven-year agreement, the court held that the taxpayer did not dispose of the refrigerators at the time of the agreement. According to Martin J (at paras. 24-28):

> It is true that the shopkeepers had possession of the coolers but it was a limited possession. It was limited by the right of the defendant to retake possession in the event that the shopkeeper failed to comply with any of the several conditions set out in the agreement.
>
> The shopkeepers' use of the coolers was also limited. The shopkeepers could only use the coolers for the purpose of storing and displaying for sale soft drinks manufactured by the defendant and they could only use the coolers for that purpose at the shopkeepers' premises identified in the agreement unless the defendant consented to the shopkeepers using the coolers at some other location.
>
> Although the shopkeepers were required to keep the coolers insured against loss or damage by fire, wind, theft and accident it does not follow from that that [they were] bearing all the risks usually associated with the ownership of the coolers. The loss, for example, under the policy was required to be made payable to the [taxpayer] as its interest might appear which tends to show that the [taxpayer] retained an interest in the ownership of the coolers. Furthermore during the term of the agreement any repairs required were covered by the manufacturer's warranty given to the [taxpayer] for the first five years and during the last two years of the agreement the [taxpayer] itself paid for the cost of any necessary repairs. ...
>
> [I]n this matter, the shopkeepers had, under the terms of the agreement with the defendant, acquired some of the incidents of ownership but they did not acquire the right to use the coolers as they pleased for their personal use. They were not entitled to destroy the coolers, to dispose of them, or to use them as security for loans. In my view it is clear from the terms of the agreement that the defendant reserved to itself ownership in and title to the coolers for the full seven-year term of the agreement and by placing the limitations on the use of them which the defendant did in the agreement it refused to give to the shopkeepers

---

[109] See also *Larose v. M.N.R.*, [1991] T.C.J. No. 910, [1992] 2 C.T.C. 2339, 92 D.T.C. 2055 (T.C.C.), in which CCA was also disallowed; and *Kozan v. M.N.R.*, [1987] T.C.J. No. 136, [1987] 1 C.T.C. 2258, 87 D.T.C. 148 (T.C.C.), in which the taxpayer was held to have disposed property in 1979 rather than 1980.

sufficient of the essential incidents of ownership as would cause me to find that the parties to the agreement intended by its terms that property in the coolers would pass from the defendant to the shopkeepers at the time of the execution of the agreement. In my view a fair reading of the agreement shows an intention by the parties to it that the property in the cooler would not pass from the defendant to the shopkeeper until the expiration of the seven-year term set out in the agreement. Put another way, I find that at the time of the execution of the agreement there was not and the parties to the agreement did not intend there to be an acquisition of the property in the cooler by the shopkeeper or a disposition of the property in the cooler by the defendant and that the property in the cooler was not intended to pass from the defendant to the shopkeeper until the expiration of the seven-year term set out in the agreement upon payment by the shopkeeper of the balance of one dollar of the purchase price and on condition that the shopkeeper had, during the seven-year term, complied with all of its obligations under the terms of the agreement.

Similarly, in *Borstad Welding Supplies (1972) Ltd. v. Canada*, [1993] F.C.J. No. 892, [1993] 2 C.T.C. 266, 93 D.T.C. 5457 (F.C.T.D.), the court held that the taxpayer, which sold all of its working assets to another company (Union) on June 1, 1985 under an agreement providing that certain gas cylinders would be sold over the course of five years, with one-fifth purchased each year and the remainder leased for a monthly rent, did not dispose of this depreciable property until the dates stipulated in the agreement. According to Reed J (at paras. 26-28):

In the present case the parties expressly contracted that property was to remain in Borstad during the period of the lease and that Borstad could attach tags to specific cylinders to identify them if it wished. Union was obligated to indemnify Borstad for any claims arising out of the negligence of Union or the failure of Union to keep the cylinders in repair. Union was required to retain the cylinders in its sole possession and control. If Union defaulted on any term of the contract, for example, neglecting to pay rent, Borstad could immediately terminate the agreement respecting the cylinders. I do not think that the provisions of the agreement are consistent with a conclusion that Union acquired all the incidents of title to the cylinders except legal title. On June 1, 1985, Union acquired rights in a contract relating to property, it did not acquire the property itself.

Most important is the fact that while the parties intended a sale of the cylinders to occur they did not intend it to occur on June 1, 1985. They intended that there be five sales with one-fifth of the cylinders being purchased on each occasion. The purchase price for each one-fifth did not become payable until then. The plaintiff could not have sued for payment of any or all of the purchase price for the cylinders on June 1, 1985. The parties did not enter into a conditional sale or a chattel mortgage with respect to the cylinders. There was no question of the property in the goods being retained as security for the payment of the purchase price. The monthly rent which was paid for the cylinders prior to their sale approximated market price. ...

The parties thought they were entering into an agreement for the rental of the cylinders until such time as they were purchased, one-fifth of the total number of cylinders to be purchased in each of five consecutive years. I cannot characterize their agreement as other than what it purports to be. I cannot conclude that a disposition occurred on June 1, 1985.

The Federal Court of Appeal in *Hewlett Packard (Canada) Ltd. v. Canada*, [2004] F.C.J. No. 1084, [2004] 3 C.T.C. 230 (F.C.A.), carefully considered the point in time at which Hewlett Packard should be understood to have made a disposition of 750 vehicles which were purchased from, and resold to Ford each year. For the tax years at issue, Hewlett Packard provided new cars to its employees for work-related purposes. In order to maximize its CCA deductions, Hewlett Packard acquired the new Ford vehicles before its financial year-end and disposed of the previous year's cars to Ford shortly after its financial year-end. In its returns for 1995, 1996 and 1997, Hewlett Packard claimed entitlement to two years of CCA with respect to the vehicles, despite having had them for just over a year (but during three separate fiscal years). The Minister reassessed Hewlett Packard and refused the deduction for CCA for the previous year's cars on the basis that there had been a change of use of the vehicles before the end of the year such that they should be deemed to have been disposed of before the end of the fiscal year pursuant to subsection 13(7). The Minister's reassessments were confirmed by the Tax Court of Canada, although the court did not base its decision on a change of use of the vehicles, but rather on Hewlett Packard's having become entitled to the proceeds of disposition prior to the end of its fiscal year (although legal title had not yet passed). Upon appeal, Noel JA (Sexton and Evans JJA, concurring) reversed the Tax Court of Canada, holding at para. 51 that:

> Parliament ensured that the time of disposition of property corresponds with the time of its acquisition, a result that is not only desirable, but essential to the proper operation of the Act. I note in this regard that, according to the analysis of the Tax Court Judge, no one would own the old fleet for tax purposes on October 31, since HP would have disposed of it as of that date and Ford would not have acquired it until the next.

E. RECAPTURE AND TERMINAL LOSS

When a particular item of depreciable property is sold or otherwise disposed of, the proceeds from the disposition may be equal to, less than, or greater than the undepreciated cost in respect of the asset. Where these proceeds are exactly equal to this undepreciated cost, the rate at which the property was depreciated would appear to have been consistent with the actual depreciation in the value of the property. Where these proceeds are less than this undepreciated cost, however, it follows that the rate at which the asset was depreciated was insufficient to account for the actual depreciation in its value. As a result, the person disposing of the asset will suffer a loss (referred to as a "terminal loss") on the disposition. Alternatively, where the proceeds are greater than the undepreciated cost of the asset, the rate at which the asset was depreciated must have been excessive. In this situation, the person disposing of the property will realize a gain on the disposition, equivalent to the excessive depreciation recognized in previous accounting periods (referred to as "recaptured depreciation"). Where the proceeds exceed the original capital cost of the asset, moreover, the person disposing of the asset will realize a further gain representing this appreciation in the value of the asset above its original capital cost.

If each depreciable property acquired by a taxpayer comprised a separate class for the purpose of computing the taxpayer's CCA, the disposition of these assets would regularly give rise to terminal losses and recaptured depreciation, since it is unlikely that the CCA claimed by the taxpayer would correspond perfectly to the actual depreciation in the value of the asset. Because individual assets are generally aggregated into classes for the purpose of computing CCA, however, the disposition of most kinds of depreciable property does not necessarily result in a terminal loss or recaptured depreciation, even if the proceeds from the disposition are less than or greater than the undepreciated cost of the asset considered in isolation. On the contrary, since the description of F in the definition of "undepreciated capital cost" in subsection 13(21) of the Act requires the proceeds of disposition of a particular depreciable property (up to the capital cost of the property) to be subtracted in computing the UCC of the class, these terminal losses or recaptured gains are often not recognized during the year in which the taxpayer disposes of the depreciable property, but in subsequent years in the form of higher or lower permissible CCAs.[110] Where the proceeds of disposition of a particular depreciable property exceed its capital cost, however, the excess is subject to tax as a capital gain.

Although the *Income Tax Act* generally does not recognize recapture or terminal loss on the disposition of individual depreciable properties, it does so when the disposition of individual properties has certain consequences affecting the class as a whole.[111] In basic terms, any negative balance in the UCC of a class of property at the end of a taxation year must be included in income for that year as recapture. According to subsection 13(1) of the Act:

> Where, at the end of a taxation year, the total of the amounts determined for E to J in the definition "undepreciated capital cost" in subsection (21) in respect of a taxpayer's depreciable property of a particular prescribed class exceeds the total of the amounts determined for A to D in that definition in respect thereof, the excess shall be included in computing the taxpayer's income for the year.

As a result, where the aggregate of CCA claimed for a class of depreciable property and proceeds of disposition of depreciable property of the class (up to the capital cost) exceeds the capital cost of depreciable property acquired by the taxpayer (causing the UCC of the class to become negative) at the end of a taxation year, the excess amount is added to the taxpayer's income under subsection 13(1).[112] Under the description of B in the definition of "undepreciated capital cost" in subsection 13(21), this recaptured amount is

---

[110] Where a depreciable property is sold for less than its undepreciated cost, the amount subtracted in computing the UCC of the class will be less than it would otherwise be, resulting in higher permissible CCAs in subsequent years. Where a depreciable property is sold for more than its undepreciated cost, the amount subtracted in computing the UCC of the class will be more than it would otherwise be, resulting in lower permissible CCAs in subsequent years.

[111] As an exception to this rule, subs. 13(2) and 20(16.1) preclude the recognition of recapture or terminal loss on the disposition of passenger vehicles costing more than $30,000.

[112] Because this rule applies "at the end of a taxation year," taxpayers can avoid the inclusion of recaptured depreciation under subs. 13(1) by acquiring depreciable property with a capital cost equal or greater than the recaptured amount before the end of the taxation year.

added in computing the UCC of the class after that time, increasing the UCC account to nil.

Terminal losses are addressed in subsection 20(16) of the Act which provides:

Notwithstanding paragraphs 18(1)(a), (b) and (h), where at the end of a taxation year,

(a) the total of all amounts used to determine A to D in the definition "undepreciated capital cost" in subsection 13(21) in respect of a taxpayer's depreciable property of a particular class exceeds the total of all amounts used to determine E to J in that definition in respect of that property, and

(b) the taxpayer no longer owns any property of that class,

in computing the taxpayer's income for the year

(c) there shall be deducted the amount of the excess determined under paragraph (a), and

(d) no amount shall be deducted for the year under paragraph (1)(a) in respect of property of that class.

As a result, where a taxpayer disposes of all depreciable property of a class for proceeds less than the UCC of the class prior to the disposition, such that the taxpayer owns no property of a class that retains a positive balance in the UCC account at the end of a taxation year, subsection 20(16) prohibits the deduction of any CCA and requires the deduction of a terminal loss equal to the amount of the remaining UCC.[113] The amount of this terminal loss is included in the definition of "total depreciation" in subsection 13(21) of the Act and subtracted in computing the UCC to a taxpayer of depreciable property of a prescribed class by virtue of the description of E in the definition of "undepreciated capital cost" in subsection 13(21), thereby reducing the UCC account to nil.

Because the rules for recapture and terminal loss apply to classes of depreciable property rather than individual assets, the classification of depreciable properties into different classes has important implications for the tax consequences attributable to their disposition. Where an asset is one of many depreciable properties of the same class, for example, its disposition is unlikely to trigger recaptured depreciation (since the capital cost of other depreciable properties is likely to maintain a positive balance in the taxpayer's UCC account for the class) and cannot cause a terminal loss. Where a depreciable property is the only property of its class, however, its disposition will result in recaptured depreciation or a terminal loss whenever the proceeds differ from the property's UCC.

---

[113] Because this rule, like subs. 13(1), applies "at the end of a taxation year", no terminal loss may be claimed if the taxpayer acquires another depreciable property of the same class before the end of the taxation year.

In order to trigger these tax consequences in certain circumstances, the *Income Tax Act* requires or permits specific kinds of depreciable properties to be categorized as separate classes for the purpose of computing CCA, recapture, and terminal loss. According to regulation 1101 (1ac), for example, a separate class is generally prescribed for each rental property (as defined in regulation 1100(14)) with a capital cost of $50,000 or more, making it impossible to avoid the recognition of recaptured depreciation on a disposition for proceeds exceeding the UCC of the property.[114] Similarly, where a taxpayer acquires depreciable properties for the purpose of gaining or producing income from different businesses, regulation 1101(1) prescribes a separate class for properties acquired for the purpose of gaining or producing income from each business, making it impossible to rely on the UCC of depreciable property of one business to shelter recaptured depreciation on the disposition of depreciable property of another business.[115] In addition, regulations 1101(5p) and 1101(5q) allow taxpayers who have acquired rapidly depreciating electronic equipment as specified to elect to treat each such depreciable property as a separate class, making the taxpayer eligible for a terminal loss on its disposition. Where the property is held for five years, however, regulation 1103(2g) requires the property to be transferred back to the class in which it would have been included but for the election.

ii. ELIGIBLE CAPITAL EXPENDITURES

Before 1972, the *Income Tax Act* did not permit a deduction for the cost of intangible capital property such as purchased goodwill that was not included in the different classes of depreciable property listed in the Regulations. As a result, these expenses came to be known as "nothings." In order to address this perceived deficiency, the Act was amended by the introduction of a separate category of "eligible capital expenditures" three-quarters of which may be deducted on a declining-balance basis under a statutory scheme much like that for CCAs.[116]

---

[114] For the CRA's views on this provision, see *Interpretation Bulletin* IT-274R, "Rental Properties — Capital Cost of $50,000 or More," April 9, 1990.

[115] In *Dupont Canada Inc. v. Canada*, [2001] F.C.J. No. 557, [2001] 2 C.T.C. 315, 2001 D.T.C. 5269 (F.C.A.), the Minister relied on this rule to include recaptured depreciation of $24,066,437 from the disposition of the taxpayer's explosives manufacturing operation. Rejecting the Minister's argument that the explosives manufacturing operation was a distinct business separate from the taxpayer's other operations, the court allowed the taxpayer's appeal.

[116] Since the Act allows a deduction for only three-quarters of the cost of such property, it is best viewed as a hybrid between depreciable capital property, the cost of which is fully deductible as CCA, and non depreciable capital property, only part of the cost of which is recognized in the computation of a taxable capital gain or allowable capital loss. Until 2000, the deductible fraction for eligible capital expenditures matched the inclusion rate for taxable capital gains, increasing from one-half from 1972 to 1987 to two-thirds in 1988 and 1989 and three-quarters from 1990 to 2000. Although the capital gains inclusion rate was reduced to two-thirds in February 2000 and one-half in October 2000, the deductible fraction of eligible capital

Subsection 14(5) defines an "eligible capital expenditure" as "the portion of any outlay or expense made or incurred by the taxpayer, as a result of a transaction occurring after 1971, on account of capital for the purpose of gaining or producing income from the business," other than an outlay or expense:

(a) in respect of which any amount is or would be, but for any provision of this Act limiting the quantum of any deduction, deductible (otherwise than under paragraph 20(1)(b)) in computing the taxpayer's income from the business, or in respect of which any amount is, by virtue of any provision of this Act other than paragraph 18(1)(b), not deductible in computing that income,

(b) made or incurred for the purpose of gaining or producing income that is exempt income, or

(c) that is the cost of, or any part of the cost of,

    (i) tangible property of the taxpayer,

    (ii) intangible property that is depreciable property of the taxpayer,

    (iii) property in respect of which any deduction (otherwise than under paragraph 20(1)(b)) is permitted in computing the taxpayer's income from the business or would be so permitted if the taxpayer's income from the business were sufficient for the purpose, or

    (iv) an interest in, or right to acquire, any property described in subparagraphs (i) to (iii).

As a result, eligible capital expenditures are a residual of capital expenses that are incurred for the purpose of gaining or producing taxable income, that are not otherwise deductible, the deduction of which is not disallowed under any provision other than paragraph 18(1)(b) of the Act, and that are not incurred to acquire tangible property or intangible property that is depreciable property. Where a taxpayer incurs an eligible capital expenditure to purchase intangible property, this property is generally described as "eligible capital property."[117]

According to paragraph 20(1)(b) of the Act, taxpayers may deduct "such amount as the taxpayer claims in respect of a business, not exceeding 7% of the taxpayer's cumulative eligible capital in respect of the business at the end of the

---

expenditures remained unchanged. As explained below, however, the inclusion rate for recaptured eligible capital expenditures has decreased with reductions in the capital gains inclusion rate.

[117] See the definition of "eligible capital property" in s. 54, which, by virtue of the definition in subs. 248(1), applies to the Act as a whole. While this definition depends on the characterization of consideration for the disposition of the property as an "eligible capital amount" within the meaning of subs. 14(1), the definition of an "eligible capital amount" turns on the characterization of this consideration as an eligible capital expenditure if it had been made by the taxpayer.

year."[118] Subsection 14(5) defines a taxpayer's "cumulative eligible capital" (CEC) in respect of a business by means of a formula much like that for the UCC of depreciable property of a prescribed class, according to which three-quarters of the cost of eligible capital expenditures in respect of the business is added under A, amounts deducted under paragraph 20(1)(b) in respect of the business are subtracted under P and F, and three-quarters of the consideration for the disposition of eligible capital property of the business is subtracted under E.[119] Where the amount subtracted as consideration for the disposition of eligible capital property of the business causes the CEC account to become negative, subsection 14(1) of the Act generally requires two-thirds of this excess to be included in computing the taxpayer's income from the business for the year, effectively taxing half of any recaptured eligible capital expenditure and half of any gain exceeding the original cost of the eligible capital property.[120] In turn, three-halves of this recaptured amount is added in computing the taxpayer's CEC in respect of the business under the description of B in the definition of a taxpayer's "cumulative eligible capital" in subsection 14(5), increasing the CEC account to nil. Where a taxpayer has ceased to carry on a business and no longer owns any eligible capital property in respect of the business, however, subsection 24(1) prohibits the deduction of any cumulative eligible capital amount under paragraph 20(1)(b) and requires the deduction of a terminal loss equal to the amount of the remaining CEC.[121] Under paragraph 24(1)(c), finally, this terminal loss is deemed to be a deduction under paragraph 20(1)(b) for the purposes of the description of P in the definition of a taxpayer's "cumulative eligible capital" in subsection 14(5), thereby decreasing the CEC account to nil.

---

[118] Before 1988, the rate at which eligible capital expenditures could be written off for tax purposes was 10 per cent.

[119] The formula also includes several terms designed to deal with adjustments in the fraction of eligible capital expenditures and proceeds of disposition of eligible capital property that may be added and must be deducted in computing the taxpayer's cumulative eligible capital account. For our purposes, there is no need to examine these transitional provisions.

[120] Since the description of E in the definition of "cumulative eligible capital" in subs. 14(5) requires the taxpayer to deduct three-quarters of the proceeds of eligible capital property, the inclusion of two-thirds of any negative amount as income under subs. 14(1) implies an inclusion rate of $\frac{3}{4} \times \frac{2}{3} = \frac{1}{2}$ of the amount by which the proceeds exceed the taxpayer's CEC before to the disposition. Unlike the rules for depreciable property, which distinguish between fully taxable recaptured depreciation and partly taxable capital gains from the disposition of depreciable property for proceeds exceeding the original capital cost of the property, the rules for eligible capital property make no such distinction, since all amounts exceeding the taxpayer's CEC are effectively subject to a one-half inclusion rate.

[121] This rule is subject to subs. 24(2), which prohibits the deduction of a terminal loss where the taxpayer ceases to carry on a business and the taxpayer's spouse or a corporation controlled by the taxpayer carries on the business and acquires property that was eligible capital property in respect of the business, in which case the provision transfers from the taxpayer to the spouse or corporation, as the case may be, the various tax attributes of the eligible capital property to the taxpayer at the time of the disposition.

In applying these statutory provisions, courts have tended to consider two questions: whether an expense incurred by a taxpayer is properly characterized as an eligible capital expenditure or something else, and whether an amount received by a taxpayer constitutes consideration for the disposition of eligible capital property or something else. Each question is examined in turn.

A. CHARACTERIZATION

As explained earlier, an eligible capital expenditure is an expense that is incurred for the purpose of gaining or producing taxable income, that is not otherwise deductible, the deduction of which is not disallowed under any provision other than paragraph 18(1)(b) of the Act, and that is not incurred in order to acquire tangible property or intangible property that is depreciable property. The leading case on the characterization of these expenses is *Canada v. Royal Trust Corp. of Canada*, [1983] F.C.J. No. 303, [1983] C.T.C. 159, 83 D.T.C. 5172 (F.C.A.).

Canada v. Royal Trust Corp. of Canada
[1983] F.C.J. No. 303, [1983] C.T.C. 159, 83 D.T.C. 5172 (F.C.A.)

URIE J (Heald and LeDain JJ, concurring): It is common ground that the sole issue in this appeal from the Trial Division is whether the sum of $175,500 which the United Trust Company ("United Trust") paid to Pitfield, MacKay, Ross & Company Limited ("Pitfield") in 1972 was an "eligible capital expenditure" within the meaning of paragraph 14(5)(b) [now the definition of "cumulative eligible capital" in subsection 14(5)] of the *Income Tax Act*, RSC 1952, c. 148 as amended ("the Act") and, therefore, in part deductible pursuant to paragraph 20(1)(b) of the Act.

United Trust was a company incorporated under the provisions of The Loan and Trust Corporations Act of Ontario in 1964. Following a change of its name, the amalgamation, in 1976, of United Trust with the Royal Trust Corporation of Canada was effected, as a result of which the Respondent herein was formed. Prior thereto, in September 1972, after lengthy negotiations, United Trust had entered into an underwriting agreement with Pitfield, a well-known securities underwriter, the ultimate object of which, it is fair to say, was to cause the sale of 325,000 common shares of the capital stock of the company to the public. According to the prospectus filed by United Trust with the Ontario Securities Commission on September 7, 1972 for the purpose of carrying out the terms of the agreement and effecting the share distribution to the public and the listing of its shares on the Toronto and Montreal Stock Exchanges, the net proceeds of sale were to be "initially invested by the Company [to] enable it to continue the expansion of its operating facilities. The increase in shareholders' equity will enable the Company to increase the amount that may be accepted as deposits." It is clear that the prospectus constituted an offer by Pitfield to sell the shares of United Trust to members of the public at a price of $8.00 per share and disclosed that United Trust was to pay an underwriting commission of $0.54 per share to Pitfield.

The underwriting agreement was dated September 7, 1972. In it United Trust agreed to sell to Pitfield 325,000 of its shares at the price of $8 per share and to pay to Pitfield "a commission of $0.54 per share in consideration of our subscribing for the said 325,000 shares." 300,000 of the shares were to be delivered and were, in fact, delivered and paid for, in accordance with the terms of the agreement, on September 25, 1972. The balance of 25,000 shares were delivered and paid for, as required by the agreement, on October 10, 1972. On each of the respective closing dates the shares, which by those dates had been sold, were distributed to the purchasers thereof by Pitfield. On the same dates, and in compliance with the terms of the agreement, United Trust, by certified cheques, paid to Pitfield the respective sums of $162,000 and $13,500 as its commission.

...

For income tax purposes, United Trust treated the payment of $175,000 to Pitfield as an "eligible capital expenditure" within the meaning of paragraph 14(5)(b) of the Act. In accordance with subparagraph 14(5)(a)(i) of the Act, as it read at that time [now the description of A in the definition of "cumulative eligible capital" in subsection 14(5)], United Trust added one half of that amount, namely the sum of $87,750, to its "cumulative eligible capital" in each of its 1972, 1973, 1974 and 1975 taxation years in computing its taxable income for those years. The respective deductions were:

1971	$8,775
1972	$7,898
1974	$7,107
1975	$6,397

All of the deductions were disallowed by the Minister by notices of reassessment posted March 22, 1978 which disallowances were subsequently confirmed by him after consideration of the Respondent's notices of objection.

The Tax Review Board dismissed the Respondent's appeal from the reassessments. The Trial Division allowed the Respondent's appeal from that decision finding that the sum of $175,500 paid by the United Trust to Pitfield was an "eligible capital expenditure" one half of which became part of United Trust's "cumulative eligible capital" and deductible in accordance with subsection 20(1)(b) of the Act. It is from that judgment that this appeal is brought.

...

Counsel for the appellant attacked the impugned Judgment on three grounds:

(1) the 54¢ per share paid by United Trust to Pitfield was not an outlay or expense but was, rather, a discount or rebate from the purchase price paid for the

shares and, thus, was not an eligible capital expenditure ... deductible in the manner prescribed by paragraph 20(l)(b) of the Act[;]

(2) in the alternative, since subparagraph 14(5)(b)(i) [now paragraph (a) of the definition of "eligible capital expenditure" in subsection 14(5)] excludes generally any outlay or expense "... in respect of which any amount is, by virtue of any provision of this Act other than paragraph 18(1)(b), not deductible in computing such income" the specific prohibition against deduction provided by subparagraph 20(1)(e)(iii) must prevail with the result that the "commission" paid by United Trust to Pitfield is excluded from the purview of subparagraph 14(5)(b)(i) ... ;

[According to paragraph 20(1)(e) of the Act, as it then read, a taxpayer could deduct "an expense incurred in the year, (i) in the course of issuing or selling shares of the capital stock of the taxpayer, or (ii) in the course of borrowing money used by the taxpayer for the purpose of earning income from a business or property (other than money used by the taxpayer for the purpose of acquiring property the income from which would be exempt), but not including any amount in respect of (iii) a commission or bonus paid or payable to a person to whom the shares were issued or sold or from whom the money was borrowed or for or on account of services rendered by a person as a salesman, agent or dealer in securities in the course of issuing or selling the shares or borrowing the money, or (iv) an amount paid or payable as or on account of the principal amount of the indebtedness incurred in the course of borrowing the money, or as or on account of interest." This provision, which was amended in 1978 to make commissions on the sale of shares fully deductible, is examined later in this chapter.]

and

(3) in any event, even if otherwise it would have been an outlay or expense, it is not deductible in the circumstances of this case under paragraph 14(5)(b) [now the definition of "eligible capital expenditure" in subsection 14(5)] because it was not incurred for the purpose of gaining or producing income.

I will deal with each of the submissions in the order in which they were raised although, as will become apparent, each tends to blend in with the other.

1.   The ascertainment of whether or not a given outlay or expense is an "eligible capital expenditure" made "on account of capital for the purpose of gaining or producing income from the business," is one of fact. Whether or not such an outlay or expense is prohibited or permitted by any other provision in the Act is one of mixed law and fact. The first submission, therefore, would appear to relate essentially to findings of fact by the learned trial judge.

...

The trial judge reviewed the oral and documentary evidence in some detail and, *inter alia*, made the following findings:

The evidence discloses that in 1972, United Trust ... negotiated an agreement with Pitfield to underwrite an issue of 325,000 shares at a price of $8.00 each, with a commission of 54¢ per share. Both the share price and the commission were arrived at after extensive negotiations between the parties. The purpose of the transaction was, beyond any question, to achieve a distribution of the shares to the public and there is some evidence that the Plaintiff had requested, even insisted on as broad as possible a distribution, particularly to financial institutions with the intents of increasing its potential clientele. In response to this request, Pitfield wrote on September 8, 1972, to United Trust in the following terms.

> With respect to the public offering of 325,000 shares of United Trust Company, we hereby confirm to you that we shall endeavour to achieve a broad public distribution of the shares by asking our Banking Group members to limit sales to approximately 500 shares per purchaser on a best efforts basis. We also wish to confirm to you that it would be our intention to limit institutional placements to approximately 30% including the sale of 50,000 shares to Cemp Investments Limited. The foregoing, of course, will be subject to our judgment of market conditions as they develop during the course of the offering.

> This is one aspect of the services rendered in this transaction by the broker Pitfield but, in my opinion, there were many others. These included provision of expertise in the analysis of the price and the market possibilities, as well as the public commitment of Pitfield to the value of the shares at $8 each. There can be no doubt that for a junior company involved in its first public share offering, the quality of the broker involved in the underwriting commitment is a significant factor. The broker's service in bringing about actual sales to the public is also quite considerable and clearly upon the evidence includes the purely mechanical aspect of receiving the shares in one certificate from United Trust and accomplishing the actual distribution to the purchasers, as well as, obviously, the promotional aspect of locating the purchasers and finalizing the sales ... . It is my view that as a result of the rendering of all of these services by Pitfield, an agreement was entered into whereby United Trust shares were sold at $8.00 and that the intention of the parties for immediate re-sale by the broker was an element of the agreement from the beginning and in this case, was fully achieved since the issue was largely pre-sold.

There was, in my opinion, ample evidence to support the findings and the inferences drawn from the evidence by the Trial Judge. Appellant's counsel argued vigorously that the agreement of September 7, 1972 was simply an agreement to sell the shares in question to Pitfield and the agreement imposed no obligation on that firm to distribute them to the public. He further argued that the "commission" was not paid for services rendered but merely represented a discount from the purchase price. He premised this contention on the basis that no services were performed by Pitfield, according to his interpretation of the agreement, aside from taking the shares.

...

[A]s held by the learned trial judge, the evidence clearly discloses that the payments made were for the services to be performed by Pitfield in the distribution of shares. Some of those services were referred to in the judgment appealed from in the passage earlier cited herein. There was, thus, a basis for concluding that (a) the substance of the transaction was a distribution of United Trust shares to the public, (b) that the sale price for the shares was $8 per share, without any rebate or discount, (c) that the fee of 54¢ per share was negotiated by the parties as a fee for services to be rendered, and (d) those services were in fact rendered in the share distribution to the public.

All the documentary and oral evidence was considered by the learned trial judge and enabled him to conclude that:

> The 54¢ per share commission negotiated between the parties constituted compensation to Pitfield for all such services rendered and was therefore, a cost of the share issue, and as such, an expense to United Trust in 1972, in the amount of $175,500, clearly an eligible capital expenditure within the meaning of section 14(5)(b).

It is trite to say that an Appellate Court ought not to disturb the findings of fact of a trial judge unless it is satisfied that the judge had proceeded on a wrong principle or that he made some "palpable and overriding error which affected his assessment of the facts." [*Stein v. The Ship of "Kathy K"*, [1976] 2 SCR 802, at 808; see also 806 and 807.] Having reviewed the evidence I am satisfied that the learned trial judge in this case neither proceeded on a wrong principle nor did he ignore, misapprehend or otherwise make any palpable or overriding error affecting his assessment of the evidence. His finding that the payment here in issue was not a rebate or discount but was compensation for services rendered should not, therefore, be disturbed.

2.   For the sake of convenience I repeat the appellant's second ground of appeal as I understood it:

In the alternative, since subsection 14(5)(b)(i) excludes generally any outlay or expense "... in respect of which any amount is, by virtue of any provision of this Act other than paragraph 18(1)(b), not deductible in computing such income" the specific prohibition against deduction provided by subsection 20(1)(e)(iii) must prevail with the result that the "commission" paid by United Trust to Pitfield is excluded from the purview of subsection 14(5)(b)(i).

...

Paragraph (e) of subsection 20(1) refers to two kinds of expense deductions — those incurred in the course of issuing or selling capital stock of the taxpayer and those incurred in the course of borrowing money for the purpose of earning income. It is the former type of expense with which we are concerned here. Subparagraph (e)(iii) excludes the deduction in full of commissions paid for services of the kind performed by Pitfield in the case at bar. I can see nothing, however, which would preclude their inclusion in cumulative eligible capital within the meaning of paragraph 14(5)(a) of the Act, provided they meet all of the tests imposed by subsection 14(5)(b). In my opinion they do for the following reasons:

1.   The expenditures were made in respect of a business (that of United Trust),

2.   as a result of a transaction (the issuance of shares and the payment of a commission in connection therewith),

3.   which occurred after 1971,

4.   on account of capital (those moneys raised from the issuance of shares).

5. which, in turn, was for the purpose of producing income (as described in the prospectus earlier quoted herein) and

6. were outlays or expenses not otherwise deductible by virtue of any provision of the Act, other than subsection 18(1)(b), in computing income from the business. [This should read "not otherwise deductible in computing income from the business and not non-deductible by virtue of any provision of the Act, other than paragraph 18(1)(b)."]

The payment of $175,500 by United Trust to Pitfield meets all of the tests imposed by subsection 14(5)(b), in my opinion, and is, therefore, eligible for deduction in accordance with paragraphs 14(5)(a) and 20(1)(b).

In the recent unreported decision of the Supreme Court of Canada in *Nowegijick v. The Queen et al.* (pronounced January 25, 1983), Dickson, J reiterated the view first expressed by de Grandpré, J in *Harel v. The Deputy Minister of Revenue* for the Province of Quebec, [1978] 1 SCR 851; [1977] CTC 441, on reliance on administrative policy as an aid to statutory interpretation in the following way:

> Administrative policy and interpretation are not determinative but are entitled to weight and can be an "important factor" in case of doubt about the meaning of legislation. ...

It is, therefore, not without interest and significance in this case that Interpretation Bulletins IT-143R dated December 29, 1975 and IT-341R dated April 26, 1982 have each dealt with this question and interpreted it in the manner which I have concluded is the correct one. In paragraph 19 of IT-143R, for example, the following is stated:

> A provision such as paragraph 20(1)(e) that authorizes in qualified terms a deduction from income subject to certain exceptions is not always considered to have the effect of making the exceptions non-deductible for all purposes of the Act. Thus, such commission or bonus, not being non-deductible "by virtue of any provision of this Act other than paragraph 18(1)(b)" (see subparagraph 14(5)(b)(i)), is an eligible capital expenditure if the other requirements of paragraph 14(5)(b) are met.

It is my opinion that paragraph 20(1)(e) neither was intended to nor does it in fact limit the deduction of sums which are deductible under other provisions in the Act. It is not a specific provision overriding a general one as argued by the appellant. The two subsections relate to the same kinds of expenditures characterized and treated in different ways. Therefore, I am of the view that the appellant's second attack fails.

3. The appellant's third ground of attack must now be considered. It was appellant counsel's contention, it will be recalled, that, in any event, the expenditure of funds to Pitfield was not made for the purpose of gaining or earning income. I have already expressed the view that it was. I shall now endeavour to show why I have this view.

...

Counsel for the appellant submitted that the distinction between expenditures made in providing capital for a business and those for the carrying on of the business from which its earnings are derived is well recognized in the jurisprudence i.e., the expenditures incurred in providing capital as in this case are not, in counsel's submission, considered to be directly related to the earning of income. In support of this proposition counsel cited the decision of the Judicial Committee of the Privy Council in *Montreal Coke and Manufacturing Co. v. M.N.R.*, [1944] AC 126; [1944] CTC 94; 2 CTC 535 and of the Supreme Court of Canada in *Bennett & White Construction Co Ltd v. M.N.R.*, [1949] SCR 287; [1949] CTC 1; 4 CTC 514.

I do not believe that either of those cases assist the appellant's contention. Both cases arose under section 6 of the *Income War Tax Act*, the predecessor to *The Income Tax Act, 1948*. That section read as follows:

6(1) In computing the amount of the profits or gains to be assessed, a deduction shall not be allowed in respect of

(a) Expenses not laid out to earn income — disbursements or expenses *not wholly, exclusively and necessarily* laid out or expended for the purpose of earning the income;

(b) Capital outlays or losses, etc — any outlay loss or replacement of capital or any payment on account of capital or any depreciation, depletion or obsolescence, except as otherwise provided in this Act; (italics added)

Paragraphs 6(1)(a) and (b) were replaced in the *Income Tax Act, 1948* by paragraphs 12(1)(a) and (b) which read as follows:

12.(1) In computing income, no deduction shall be made in respect of

(a) an outlay or expense except to the extent that it was made or incurred by the taxpayer for the purpose of gaining or producing income from property or a business of the taxpayer,

(b) an outlay, loss or replacement of capital, a payment on account of capital or an allowance in respect of depreciation, obsolescence or depletion except as expressly permitted by this Part.

As will be seen those two subsections are identical to paragraphs 18(1)(a) and (b) of the present Act, *supra*. The subsections from the older Acts were the subject of comment by Abbott, J in *BC Electric Railway Company Limited v. M.N.R.*, [1958] SCR 133; [1958] CTC 21; 58 DTC 1022, as follows:

The less stringent provisions of the new section [the 1948 Act] should, I think, be borne in mind in considering judicial opinions based upon the former sections.

...

Mr Justice Abbott's warning is thus apt in considering the applicability of the reasoning in the *Montreal Coke* and the *Bennett & White* cases in the case at bar particularly because [subsection 14(5) and paragraph] 20(1)(b) relate to deductions for capital expenses. Deductions for such capital expenses were prohibited in the predecessor Acts. The concept of expenses arising from the raising of capital being deductible if all the statutory criteria are met, including whether or not they were incurred "for the purpose of gaining or earning income," could not have arisen under the old Acts. The issues facing the Courts under those Acts were, first, to determine whether the expense was one on account of income or of capital and, second, if it was found to be an income expense was it made for the purpose of gaining or producing income? Now, while it is true that both of those questions are still issues, the fact that the expenditure may have been on capital account does not, per se, prohibit the deduction. ... It is hard for me to conceive that expenditures incurred in the raising of capital to be used in the operations of the company, as described by the witnesses and in the prospectus, not being characterized as being "for the purpose of earning income." I am of the opinion, therefore, that none of the cases relied upon by the appellant are binding in the circumstances of this case and the expense of the underwriting in the sum of $175,500 was for the purpose of earning income. Accordingly, the appellant's third ground of attack must fail.

For all of the foregoing reasons, the appeal should be dismissed with costs.

Appeal dismissed.

NOTES AND QUESTIONS

1.   On what grounds did the Minister argue in *Royal Trust* that the underwriting commission paid by the taxpayer was not an "eligible capital expenditure" within the meaning of the definition in subsection 14(5) of the Act? Why did the court reject these arguments? Do you agree with the court's conclusions? Why or why not?

2.   In *Edmonton Plaza Hotel (1980) Ltd. v. M.N.R.*, [1987] F.C.J. No. 718, [1987] 2 C.T.C. 153, 87 D.T.C. 5371 (F.C.T.D), the taxpayer paid $216,000 to the city of Edmonton in order to obtain approval for a proposed extension that did not include additional parking. Characterizing the payment as a cost of the extension, the court rejected the Minister's argument that the payment was an eligible capital expenditure on the grounds that it was "part of the cost of tangible property," which is specifically excluded from characterization as an eligible capital expenditure by subparagraph (c)(i) of the definition.

3.   In *Cadillac Fairview Corp. Ltd. v. Canada*, [1996] T.C.J. No. 209, [1996] 2 C.T.C. 2197, 97 D.T.C. 405 (T.C.C.), the taxpayer, which paid $11,227,444 to the Holy Trinity Church in order to obtain increased density rights for the development of phase II of the Toronto Eaton Centre, sought to include this amount in its computing its cumulative eligible capital for the purpose of claiming deductions under paragraph 20(1)(b). Characterizing the cost of modifying rights relating to what one can do with land as "a cost attributable to the land," the court rejected the taxpayer's argument on the basis that it was "part of the cost of tangible property" within the meaning of subparagraph (c)(i) of the definition of an eligible capital expenditure in subsection 14(5).

4. In *Teck-Bullmoose Coal Inc. v. Canada*, [1996] T.C.J. No. 1403, [1997] 1 C.T.C. 2603, 97 D.T.C. 792 (T.C.C.), aff'd [1998] F.C.J. No. 700, [1998] 3 C.T.C. 195, 98 D.T.C. 6363 (F.C.A.), the taxpayer spent $2,930,643 to construct a public road on Crown land that was necessary to permit economically viable truck transportation from the taxpayer's mine to a rail transfer facility. Concluding that the payment was neither a deductible Canadian exploration expense nor a capital expense incurred to acquire depreciable property in the form of a leasehold interest, the court characterized the payment as an eligible capital expenditure.

5. For the CRA's views on the characterization of eligible capital expenditures, see *Interpretation Bulletin* IT-143R3, "Meaning of Eligible Capital Expenditure," August 29, 2002.

B. DISPOSITION OF ELIGIBLE CAPITAL PROPERTY

In computing a taxpayer's "cumulative eligible capital" in respect of a business, the description of E in the definition in subsection 14(5) of the Act requires the taxpayer to subtract ¾ of the amount, net of selling costs, that the taxpayer has or may become entitled to receive in exchange for consideration the payment for which would have been an eligible capital expenditure in respect of the business if it had been made by the taxpayer. In these circumstances, the net consideration received or receivable by the taxpayer is described as an "eligible capital amount," while the consideration given by the taxpayer is defined as "eligible capital property."[122] Where a disposition of eligible capital property causes a taxpayer's cumulative eligible capital in respect of a business to become negative, subsection 14(1) includes two-thirds of this negative amount in computing the taxpayer's income from the business, thereby taxing half of any recaptured eligible capital expenditure and half of any gain exceeding the original cost of the eligible capital property. The leading case in which these provisions has been considered is *Canada v. Goodwin Johnson (1960) Ltd.*, [1986] F.C.J. No. 174, [1986] 1 C.T.C. 448, 86 D.T.C. 6185 (F.C.A.).

R. v. Goodwin Johnson (1960) Ltd.
[1986] F.C.J. No. 174, [1986] 1 C.T.C. 448, 86 D.T.C. 6185 (F.C.A.)

URIE J (Heald J, concurring): ... The respondent, a company incorporated under the laws of the province of British Columbia, was engaged in the logging business. From 1967 to 1977, its primary business was the management and operation of Timber Sale License X-86695 at Naden Harbour, Queen Charlotte Islands, British Columbia. On March 6, 1970, it entered into an agreement with Kanematsu-Gosho (USA) Inc. ("Kanematsu") and Naden Harbour Timber Limited ("Naden") to record their respective obligations "for the orderly

---

[122] See subs. 14(1) and the definitions of eligible capital property in s. 54 and subs. 248(1).

development, exploitation and operation" of the Timber Sale Contract ("TSC") as defined in the agreement. That contract, which had been awarded in 1962 to Prince Rupert Sawmills Ltd., had been assigned to the respondent with the consent of the British Columbia Forest Service for the beneficial ownership of Kanematsu. Naden, a wholly-owned subsidiary of Kanematsu, was granted the exclusive authority to develop, exploit and conduct logging operations on the area covered by the TSC Naden, in turn, appointed the respondent as manager of Naden at the operational level "to administer, manage and operate the business of Naden as the same relates to the TSC" Kanematsu was to provide for the financial requirements for the operation.

Without recording here the full details of the compensation to be paid to the respondent for its efforts, suffice it to say that it covered pre-agreement activities in the sum of $300,000, post-agreement payments based on footage of timber cut from the TSC, a payment of $260,000 in the event of termination for any reason of the agreement and a non-interest bearing loan of $260,000 repayable in 10 equal annual instalments. An annual management fee of either one-half of the net profits of Naden before the payment of the management fees and taxes, or $75,000, whichever was the greater, was also specified in the agreement. There was also provision for payments in the event the annual cuts of timber permissible under the TSC were increased.

Lastly, paragraph 11 of the agreement provided for the termination of the agreement in the following terms:

> Either party in its sole and absolute discretion may by six (6) months notice terminate this agreement effective not earlier than the 31st day of May, 1972 subject to the rights of the respective parties hereto which shall have arisen prior to the effective date of such termination.

While, apparently, the operations proceeded reasonably well until the end of 1971, particularly to the satisfaction of the Forestry Service and its Minister, difficulties arose between the respondent and Kanematsu in respect of financing and construction of a mill. An action was instituted in the Supreme Court of British Columbia by Naden against the respondent in December 1974, arising as a result of the refusal of the respondent to deliver the TSC to Naden and to take any steps to effect the assignment thereof. It sought specific performance of the assignment provisions of the March 6, 1970, agreement, an injunction or, alternatively, rescission of the contract and a declaration, or damages. The respondent filed its defence and counterclaimed for damages for breach of contract and breach of fiduciary duty as well as other remedies.

On July 15, 1976, the respondent, Naden, Kanematsu and Goodwin Johnson and his wife Edna personally, entered into minutes of settlement of that action. The sum of $830,000 was paid by Naden to the respondent pursuant to paragraph 9 of those minutes:

> ... without admission of liability and accepted in full and final settlement of the claim of GJ [the Respondent] for compensation for the loss of the business related to the Agreement, that is to say, as damages for termination or cancellation of the Agreement. ...

...

The appellant ... said that the $830,000 received by the respondent was compensation for the destruction or loss of the whole profit-making structure of the respondent's business. It was, thus, an eligible capital amount which should have been included in its income as required by subsection 14(1) of the *Income Tax Act*, c. 63, SC 1970-71-72, as amended ("the Act").

...

Subsection 14(1) was described by counsel for the respondent as "the mirror image rule" because ... the test as to whether an amount received is an eligible capital amount is determined by the recipient being considered a notional payor of the amount which he, in fact, received, i.e., the inquiry necessarily is to ascertain whether or not the amount, if paid rather than received, would have been an eligible capital expenditure. By definition, to be such an expenditure it is required that:

(1)   the expenditure has been made in respect of a business,

(2)   as a result of a transaction,

(3)   which occurred after 1971,

(4)   was on account of capital,

(5)   was, in turn, for the purpose of producing income, and

(6)   was an outlay or expense not otherwise deductible by virtue of any provision, other than paragraph 18(1)(b), in computing income from the business.

[*R. v. Royal Trust Corp. of Canada*, [1983] CTC 159; 83 DTC 5172 (FCA). As indicated in an earlier note to the excerpt of this case, the last criterion should read "not otherwise deductible in computing income from the business and not non-deductible by virtue of any provision of the Act, other than paragraph 18(1)(b)."]

It is common ground that if the respondent had been the payor, the payment would have met all the tests of subsection 5 with the exception of number 4. The appellant says that, in so far as that test is concerned, the payment, not being deductible as a business expense, would have been a capital payment and, therefore, would have been an eligible capital expenditure since the other tests were met. It was the consideration paid to obtain the profit-making structure of the respondent which arose as a result of the operation of the agreement.

...

Counsel for the respondent, on the other hand, says that a payment in the settlement of a damage action is not a payment on account of capital although in the hands of the recipient it is a capital receipt. That is so because the payment would not be an outlay or expense made once and for all in order to secure or acquire an asset of a long term or enduring advantage. Rather, it would be an expense on revenue account and would be deductible as a business expense. It is, therefore, excluded by the definition, *supra* — test number 6.

With the respective positions of the parties in mind, it would be helpful in understanding the issue herein to adopt the terms used in subsection 14(1) to the facts of the case. An amount, $830,000, became payable to a taxpayer, the respondent in 1976, in respect of the logging business formerly carried on by it. The consideration given by the respondent for that amount was agreeing to settle the action for damages for breach of contract with Naden and, as a result, foregoing the benefits under the contract had it continued in existence. If the respondent had been the payor of that amount (a notional payor) in consideration of the contract cancellation, it would have been an eligible capital expenditure if it met the tests imposed by subsection 14(5) to be such an expenditure.

The issue raised by this appeal, therefore, is a very narrow one. The facts, the principles of law and the tests applicable, with the exception of one, have, as I have said, all been agreed upon. That issue is:

> Was the payment of $830,000 given by the Respondent as a notional payor, in return for the agreeing to the cancellation of the contract and the benefits flowing therefrom, an eligible capital expenditure or did it fail to be entitled to be so characterized because the consideration (the sum of $830,000) could not satisfy all of the tests of an eligible capital expenditure imposed by subparagraph 14(5)(b)(i) of the Act?

The payment deemed to have been made by the respondent as a notional payor was not, in my opinion, given for the transfer of the business or profit-making structure represented by the operations agreement as alleged by the appellant. I have this opinion for the following reasons:

(1) the action in the Supreme Court of British Columbia by Naden against the respondent was, as earlier observed, for specific performance and an injunction to restrain the respondent from disposing of the TSC or, alternatively, rescission of the contract. The respondent's counter-claim was for damages for breach of contract and breach of fiduciary duties, as well as other remedies, based on the existence of the contract. Neither did Naden seek, in this action, in any way to acquire the underlying business structure of the respondent, as alleged by the appellant, nor did the respondent seek to sell that structure, i.e., termination of the contract for the purpose of acquiring a capital asset was not sought. Those facts are crucial in the characterization of "the consideration given by the taxpayer. ..."

(2) While reference was made in paragraph 9 of the minutes of settlement, *supra*, to the "claim ... for the loss of the business related to the Agreement," that was amplified by the further words "that is to say, as damages for the termination ... of the Agreement." When that phrase is read in conjunction with the claims in both the statement of claim and counterclaim, as well as in conjunction with the overall terms of the settlement, there can be no question, in my view, that the $830,000 was paid as damages for breach of contract only.

(3) Cogent support for this view is derived from the termination provision of the contract, paragraph 11, *supra*. The underlying business structure could have been acquired by Naden having simply terminated the contract in accordance with the requirements of paragraph 11. It did not do so. For whatever reason, it elected not to terminate it but rather to seek its specific performance. The only reasonable inference to be drawn from these facts is that, when it could not obtain the remedies it sought, it agreed to pay to the respondent damages for breach of contract. It acquired nothing but peace in the litigation and rid itself of a bothersome partner. That was the purpose of the settlement.

...

In my opinion, it is clear that the expenditure was made "for the purpose of gaining or producing income" by getting rid of an operational contractual expense by paying damages for breach of that contract. The purpose could not remotely be described as being for the acquisition of a capital asset. That being so, subsection 14(1) does not come into play because if the respondent had been the payor, the payment made by it would not have been an eligible capital expenditure since it failed to meet one of the tests imposed by subparagraph 14(5)(b)(i) of the Act [now paragraph (a) of the definition of an "eligible capital expenditure" in subsection 14(5)], *viz.*, that the payment not be what, in general terms is described as, a deductible business expense.

...

Accordingly, I would dismiss the appeal with costs.

PRATTE J (dissenting): ... In order to know whether the sum of $830,000 was to be included in the income of the respondent under subsection 14(1), one must first specify ... what consideration was given by the respondent for that payment and, second, one must assume that the respondent made (rather than received) a payment for that consideration and determine whether that notional payment is an eligible capital expenditure. In this case, it is common ground that the notional payment that must be assumed to have been made by the respondent is an eligible capital expenditure if it is an expenditure made on account of capital. The narrow issue to be resolved, therefore, is simply whether that notional payment was on account of capital or not.

The amount of $830,000 was paid to the respondent pursuant to "Minutes of Settlement" which expressly provided that the sum in question was paid in settlement of the respondent's claim "for compensation for the loss of the business related to the Agreement, that is to say, as damages for termination or cancellation of the Agreement." The consideration given by the respondent, therefore, was its rights under the Agreement. That was what the respondent gave up in order to get the $830,000. That view of the matter is confirmed by the fact that the respondent has always treated that sum as being the proceeds of disposition of its rights under the Agreement.

Now, if the respondent, instead of having been paid to relinquish those rights, had paid to acquire them, that payment would have been a capital outlay since it would clearly have been made "once and for all ... with a view to bringing into existence an asset or an advantage for the enduring benefit" of the respondent's trade.

Counsel for the respondent challenged that conclusion on the ground that the payment received by the respondent had, in fact, been made by Naden Harbour to settle pending litigation. The settlement of the litigation, said he, was the consideration of that payment. If, therefore, the respondent had made, instead of received, a payment for that same consideration, it would have been in the same position as Naden Harbour was when it made the payment. And, according to counsel, it was clear that the payment made by Naden was not a capital outlay since it was not made to acquire a capital asset but merely made to obtain peace and get rid of a bothersome partner.

I am not persuaded by that argument. The terms of the "Minutes of Settlement" as well as the position taken by the respondent preclude it from advancing that the consideration for the payment of the $830,000 was something other than the relinquishment of the respondent's rights under the Agreement. Moreover, ... the question is not whether the payment made by Naden Harbour to the respondent was a capital outlay. It probably was not. The real and only question is whether the notional payment that must be assumed to have been made by the respondent was on account of capital. That question, as I have already said, must be answered in the affirmative.

I would allow the appeal with costs ... and refer the assessment back to the Minister for reassessment on the basis that the amount of $830,000 received by the respondent in its 1977 taxation year was a payment of the kind described in subsection 14(1) of the *Income Tax Act*, RSC 1952, c. 148, as amended by 1970-71-72, c. 63, s. 1.

Appeal dismissed.

NOTES AND QUESTIONS

1.   On what basis did the Minister argue in *Goodwin Johnson* that the payment received by the taxpayer was an eligible capital amount? Why did the majority of the Federal Court of Appeal reject this argument? Why did Pratte J dissent from this opinion? Which judgment do you find more persuasive? Why?

2.   Although concluding that the amount received by the taxpayer would have been deductible if made by the taxpayer, the majority in *Goodwin Johnson* also held that the payment was not income from the taxpayer's business but a capital receipt. On the basis of the trial judge's conclusion that the adjusted cost base of the agreement was equal to the amount received, moreover, the majority appears to have accepted the taxpayer's argument that the payment was not taxable but generated an allowable capital loss. The computation of taxable capital gains and allowable capital losses is examined in Chapter 6.

3.   *Goodwin Johnson* was followed in *Pe Ben Industries Company Limited v. M.N.R.*, [1988] F.C.J. No. 558, [1988] 2 C.T.C. 120, 88 D.T.C. 6347 (F.C.T.D.),

in which the taxpayer, which was in the business of transporting supplies and materials by truck to oil field sites in northern Alberta, received compensation of $1,152,354.60 on the cancellation of a contract with Northern Alberta Railways (NAR) to transport supplies and equipment from NAR's railway yard near Fort McMurray to the site of the Syncrude plant at Mildred Lake, 40 miles away. Concluding (at para. 14) that the payment by NAR was made to get "rid of any further obligations to pay what would normally be operating expenses under the contract," the court rejected the Minister's argument that the compensation was an eligible capital amount that must be included in computing the taxpayer's business income under subsection 14(1) of the Act. According to Strayer J (as he then was) (at para. 14):

> In other words the payment made by NAR to the [taxpayer] was for it in the nature of an operating expense which would be deductible as a business expense. By virtue of subparagraph 14(5)(b)(i) [now paragraph (a) of the definition of an "eligible capital expenditure" in subsection 14(5)] of the *Income Tax Act* it could therefore not be an "eligible capital expenditure" if it had been made by the plaintiff and therefore it cannot when received by the [taxpayer] be an "eligible capital amount." This was the rationale of the *Goodwin Johnson* decision and it is directly applicable here.

See also *Toronto Refiners & Smelters Ltd. v. Canada*, [2002] F.C.J. No. 1682, [2003] 1 C.T.C. 365, 2003 D.T.C. 5002 (F.C.A.), in which the taxpayer received $9 million from the City of Toronto as compensation for the loss of its business after its land was expropriated "due to concern regarding pollution and noxious use". Concluding (at para. 23) that a notional payment on account of a hypothetical expropriation by the taxpayer would not have been made for the purpose of gaining or producing income, the court rejected the Minister's argument that the payment was an eligible capital amount taxable under subsection 14(1). According to Sharlow JA (Linden and Sexton JJA, concurring) (at paras. 18-19):

> Counsel for the Crown wishes to hypothesize a commercial, profit motivated transaction where there is none. In this case, there was a termination of a business for a civic purpose, with statutory compensation being payable as a result. Those real circumstances must form the basis of the hypothetical questions asked by the mirror image rule.

> ... Counsel for the Crown may well be correct when he says that if his approach is not adopted, amounts may escape the section 14 net that are, in economic or functional terms, analogous to proceeds of disposition of goodwill. But that result flows from the words of section 14, as interpreted pursuant to the long standing authority of *Goodwin Johnson*. If section 14 is underinclusive because its drafters did not contemplate that the destruction of goodwill might be the subject of compensation by an expropriating authority, the remedy lies with Parliament.

Do you agree with this conclusion? Why or why not? Should Parliament amend the Act to ensure that payments like those in *Toronto Refiners & Smelters Ltd.* are subject to tax?

4.   In *Canadian Industries Ltd. v. M.N.R.*, [1980] C.T.C. 222; 80 D.T.C. 6163 (F.C.A.), the taxpayer, which manufactured trinitrotoluene (TNT) according to a process that it was licensed to use by a Swedish engineering firm that owned the

right to the process, entered into agreements with the US government to permit it to use the process for military purposes and to provide "knowhow" that it had developed, in exchange for which it received $378,000. Rejecting the taxpayer's arguments that it had disposed of a capital asset and lost its entire business of manufacturing TNT, the court characterized the payment as business income on the grounds that the agreement was "for a limited purpose ... and for a limited term" and not exclusive, and that the termination of the taxpayer's business of manufacturing TNT was not directly caused by the agreements with the US government.

5. *Canadian Industries Ltd.* was followed in *Canada v. Canadian General Electric Co.*, [1987] F.C.J. No. 38, [1987] 1 C.T.C. 180, 87 D.T.C. 5070 (F.C.A.), where the taxpayer, which operated a heavy water plant at Port Hawksbury, Nova Scotia under a long-term contract to supply heavy water to Atomic Energy of Canada Limited (AECL), received lump-sum payments of $750,000 in 1968 and $250,000 in 1971 in consideration for providing AECL with drawings, specifications, non-exclusive licences to certain patents, and "knowhow" to enable AECL to construct its own heavy water plant in Ontario. Reversing the decision of the trial judge, who held (at para. 17) that AECL's decision to build its own plant effectively eliminated the taxpayer's "opportunity to make further use, in Canada of the inventions and know-how generated in the design, construction and commissioning of the Port Hawksbury plant," a majority of the Federal Court of Appeal held that the payments were on account of income, not capital. Referring to the trial judge's emphasis on "the *de facto* consequence of AECL's decision to go it alone," MacGuigan J (Pratte J concurring) concluded (at para. 13):

> If the question were entirely open on the authorities, such a *de facto* approach might perhaps be the most fruitful pathway for the law. But it seems to me that the *C.I.L.* case stands for the proposition that the sale of knowhow will not normally be regarded as the sale of a capital asset, particularly when the sale is by a non-exclusive licence, and that any exception to this rule must be strictly established as a total loss of knowhow which is a direct and necessary result of the licence agreement. There is no more reason to make allowance in this case for *de facto* factors than there was in the *C.I.L.* case. If the *C.I.L.* case is strictly applied, as I believe it must be, the respondent cannot succeed.

In dissent, Urie J stated (at para. 36):

> My commonsense appreciation of all the guiding features as they relate to the facts of this case, leads me to the view that the trial judge correctly found the receipt in issue to be capital in nature. That characterization of the receipt was reached by an appreciation of all of the circumstances surrounding its acquisition

6. In *The Dixie Lee Company Limited v. M.N.R.*, [1971] Tax ABC 592 (T.A.B.), the taxpayer, which carried on business by "granting to restaurants in Ontario and elsewhere in Canada the right of using its franchise, name and formula [for preparing fried chicken] for a set period of time, upon specified conditions, and for an agreed consideration" (at para. 3), received a lump-sum payment of $23,000 when it "sold out its entire interest in the four Atlantic

provinces forever" (at para. 4). Allowing the taxpayer's appeal from an assessment that included the payment in computing the taxpayer's business income, the board concluded (at paras. 4 and 7):

> In so contracting, the appellant forewent its rights and all control, completely and irretrievably, as regards doing business in the Maritimes and thereby parted with what ... was an appreciable portion of a capital asset. ...

> The appellant relinquished something that it could not regain and ... by no process of reasoning could what was got in exchange be termed an income receipt. It was not in the business of selling franchises. There can be no doubt that it was engaged solely in the activity of licensing under its trademark rights. The sale of these rights was not in the normal or ordinary course of its business.

For other cases in which lump-sum payments to acquire franchises have been characterized as capital receipts, see *LaSalle Factories Ltd. v. M.N.R.*, [1979] C.T.C. 2098, 79 D.T.C. 91 (T.R.B.) and *Steinberg Inc. v. M.N.R.*, [1991] T.C.J. No. 425, [1992] 1 C.T.C. 2191, 92 D.T.C. 1478 (T.C.C.).

7.   In *Samoth Financial Ltd. v. Canada*, [1985] F.C.J. No. 954, [1985] 2 C.T.C. 275, 85 D.T.C. 5473 (F.C.T.D.), aff'd [1986] F.C.J. No. 347, [1986] 2 C.T.C. 107, 86 D.T.C. 6335 (F.C.A.), the taxpayer, which had purchased from a US company the exclusive right to sell Century 21 franchises to real estate brokers in Canada, received franchise fees on the sale of 10-year renewable franchises to various independent brokerage firms, which it regarded as eligible capital amounts only partly taxable under subsection 14(1) of the Act. Characterizing the taxpayer as a trader or dealer in real estate franchises, the court concluded that the franchises were not eligible capital property but stock in trade or inventory in the taxpayer's business.

For a similar result, see *Smitty's Pancake Houses Ltd. v. M.N.R.* (1965), 39 Tax ABC (T.A.B.), where the taxpayer, which held the franchise in perpetuity to operate Smitty's Pancake Houses in Canada, granted limited franchises for 10-year terms in various regions of Canada in consideration for lump-sum payments plus royalties. Concluding that the taxpayer was incorporated to deal in franchises and did so, the board characterized the lump-sum payments as business income from "a scheme for profit-making." See also *Red Barn System (Canada) Limited v. M.N.R.*, [1973] C.T.C. 2290, 73 D.T.C. 231 (T.R.B.), in which the taxpayer, which had entered into an agreement with Red Barn (US) to construct 60 restaurants with the exclusive right to handle the franchise in the whole of Canada, entered into "area agreements" with Red Barn Western and Red Barn Australia, whereby the taxpayer transferred its rights to the area under the agreement with Red Barn (US) in exchange for a lump sum for each new restaurant opened and a percentage of the gross receipts. Rejecting the taxpayer's argument that the lump-sum payments were on account of capital, the board concluded (at para. 16) that:

> the appellant has not disposed of any of its capital assets in an outright disposition. It has licensed "Western" and "Australia," subject to the same terms and conditions as were imposed upon the appellant itself by the original agreement ... with the appropriate changes

in wording. ... [A]ny sums recovered under those agreements must be income to the appellant in this case.

8.   In *Ananiadis v. M.N.R.*, [1985] 2 C.T.C. 2233, 85 D.T.C. 541 (T.C.C.), the taxpayer, who owned and operated a limousine service to and from Pearson International Airport, bought and sold licences to pick up and deliver passengers to the airport. Concluding that the licences were acquired not for the purpose of the taxpayer's limousine business but for the purpose of resale, the court concluded that the licences were inventory in a series of adventures in the nature of trade, not eligible capital property.

For a contrasting result, in which the taxpayer purchased a taxi owner's licence in 1979 for $1,500 and carried on a business of operating a taxi until 1987, when he sold the licence for $87,000, see *Mourtzis v. Canada*, [1993] T.C.J. No. 902, [1994] 1 C.T.C. 2801, 94 D.T.C. 1362 (T.C.C.). Concluding that the licence was an asset of enduring benefit that did not have a "limited period" as required by class 14 depreciable property, the court held that the proceeds were an eligible capital amount subject to taxation under subsection 14(1) of the Act.

9.   In *Consumers Software Inc. v. Canada*, [1993] T.C.J. No. 928, [1995] 2 C.T.C. 2851, 95 D.T.C. 518 (T.C.C.), the taxpayer, which had developed a computer program to audit spreadsheets, sold the program to a US software firm for US$750,000, which the Minister regarded as ordinary income from the taxpayer's business. Concluding that the program was the source of the majority of the taxpayer's business and that the taxpayer was "not a trader or dealer" in software, the court characterized the proceeds as an eligible capital amount subject to tax under subsection 14(1) of the Act.

10.   In *289018 Ontario Ltd. v. M.N.R.*, [1987] 1 C.T.C. 2095, 87 D.T.C. 38 (T.C.C.), the taxpayer, which had developed and operated a modular system applicable to instructional and educational environments, sold its business in 1980 in exchange for a fixed amount for certain assets transferred and a "royalty" determined as a percentage of future sales by the purchaser. Rejecting the taxpayer's argument that a royalty payment of $110,170.46 received in 1983 was an eligible capital amount only partly taxable under subsection 14(1), the court upheld the Minister's assessment, which included the full amount of the payment under paragraph 12(1)(g) of the Act as "an amount received in the year by the taxpayer that was dependent upon the use of or production from property."

For a contrasting result, see *Rouleau Estate v. M.N.R.*, [1989] T.C.J. No. 1030, [1991] 1 C.T.C. 2055, 91 D.T.C. 115 (T.C.C.), in which the taxpayer sold his accounting practice in 1976 for a price calculated as 20 per cent of the gross fees earned by the purchaser from the taxpayer's clientele for a period of five years. Rejecting the Minister's argument that the payments were fully taxable under paragraph 12(1)(g) of the Act, the court held that they were eligible capital amounts only partly taxable under subsection 14(1). According to Garon TCJ (at paras. 33-47):

[I]t seems clear to me that if paragraph 12(1)(g) of the *Income Tax Act* is applied to the amounts received leading [*sic*] to unexpected consequences that cannot logically be explained. ...

Let us take the case of a taxpayer who acquires the goodwill of a business for a certain price, as was the case here ... , and later disposes of it in return for compensation based entirely on a percentage of the fees to be received by the vendor over a period of time.

Given the provisions of the *Income Tax Act* in effect during the years with which we are concerned, the taxpayer in question would have to include under ... "cumulative eligible capital," half of his purchase price but could not, in disposing of this goodwill, include ... half of the proceeds of disposition of the said goodwill, because of the manner in which the compensation was payable. ...

This interpretation also leads to unexpected results that cannot be explained logically in cases where the compensation is partly in the form of a minimum lump-sum payment and partly in the form of future revenues from the disposition of the goodwill.

According to the interpretation supported by counsel for the respondent, in such a case paragraph 12(1)(g) would apply to the portion of the disposition consisting of a percentage of future gains, and the lump-sum payment, though representing only part of the compensation, would be included in the cumulative eligible capital.

This interpretation, whereby paragraph 12(1)(g) would apply to situations in which the amount of compensation depended in full or in part on future gains from the use of the eligible capital property, leads to absurdity and is unacceptable, at least where it is not evident that such is the clear, unambiguous intention of Parliament.

On the other hand, if section 14 is applicable in all cases, the form of compensation is unimportant; the result is a logical, easily explained tax treatment.

It could, in fact, then be said that in 1972 the Parliament of Canada established a "code" with respect to the tax treatment of expenditures and amounts payable upon acquisition or disposition of that category of property referred to as "nothings" under the former Act. ...

This interpretation, whereby section 14 applies in all circumstances, regardless of the form of compensation, has the particular advantage, in my view, of providing a similar tax treatment to related or analogous situations in economic terms.

According to this interpretation, the tax treatment of the amounts received in the present case by Mr. Rouleau, a total of close to $150,000 spread over a five-year period, would be identical to the tax treatment of similar amounts received by another taxpayer where compensation was expressed in the form of a lump-sum payment of the same order, payable, let us say, over an equal five-year period.

I accordingly conclude, on the basis of the rules of construction examined earlier, that paragraph 12(1)(g) does not apply to the amounts received by Mr. Rouleau over the years in question.

Notwithstanding the decision in *Rouleau Estate*, the revenue department adheres to the approach in *289018 Ontario Ltd. v. M.N.R.*, [1987] 1 C.T.C. 2095, 87 D.T.C. 38 (T.C.C.). According to paragraph 5 of *Interpretation Bulletin* IT-386R, "Eligible Capital Amounts," October 30, 1992:

Any portion of consideration received for EC [eligible capital] property that is dependent upon the use of or production from that property does not result in an EC amount but rather is taxable as income under paragraph 12(1)(g).

11. In *Fortino v. Canada*, [1996] T.C.J. No. 1457, [1997] 2 C.T.C. 2184, 97 D.T.C. 55 (T.C.C.), aff'd [1999] F.C.J. No. 1964, [2000] 1 C.T.C. 349, 2000 D.T.C. 6060 (F.C.A.), the taxpayers, who sold their shares of a company that operated a chain of food stores, received substantial payments for executing non-competition agreements (NCAs), which the Minister regarded as eligible capital amounts subject to tax under subsection 14(1) of the Act. Distinguishing between the shareholders who received the NCA payments and the corporation that carried on the retail business, the court dismissed the Minister's assessment on the grounds that the NCA payments were not received in respect of a business carried on or formerly carried on by the recipients as required by the description of E in the definition of a taxpayer's "cumulative eligible capital" in subsection 14(5) of the Act. According to Lamarre JTCC (at para. 71):

> In the present case, the evidence did not reveal that along the years the business was in reality carried on by the shareholders of Fortino's. Nothing put forward in evidence pointed to the fact that Fortino's acted as an agent for the appellants. Therefore, I cannot conclude that Fortino's was a mere conduit and for this reason I do not see how section 14, as it is actually drafted, could apply to shareholders who are not operating any business themselves.

12. For the CRA's views on the disposition of eligible capital property, see *Interpretation Bulletin* IT-123R6, "Transactions Involving Eligible Capital Property," June 1, 1997, and *Interpretation Bulletin* IT-386R, "Eligible Capital Amounts", October 30, 1992.

4. Prepaid Expenses

In addition to the statutory and judicial rules governing the deduction of inventory costs and capital expenditures, subsection 18(9) requires taxpayers to defer the deduction of various "prepaid expenses," prohibiting their deduction in the taxation year in which they are made or incurred, and allowing these amounts to be deducted instead in "the subsequent year to which [they] can reasonably be considered to relate." According to subsection 18(9), notwithstanding any other provision of the Act:

(a) in computing a taxpayer's income for a taxation year from a business or property (other than income from a business computed in accordance with the method authorized by subsection 28(1)), no deduction shall be made in respect of an outlay or expense to the extent that it can reasonably be regarded as having been made or incurred

(i) as consideration for services to be rendered after the end of the year,

(ii) as, on account of, in lieu of payment of or in satisfaction of, interest, taxes (other than taxes imposed on... insurance premiums ...), rent or royalties in respect of a period that is after the end of the year, or

    (iii) as consideration for insurance in respect of a period after the end of the year, other than

        (A) where the taxpayer is an insurer, consideration for reinsurance, and

        (B) consideration for insurance on the life of an individual under a group term life insurance policy where all or part of the consideration is for insurance that is (or would be if the individual survived) in respect of a period that ends more than 13 months after the consideration is paid; [and]

    (b) such portion of each outlay or expense (other than an outlay or expense of a corporation, partnership or trust as, on account of, in lieu of payment of or in satisfaction of, interest) made or incurred as would, but for paragraph (a), be deductible in computing a taxpayer's income for a taxation year shall be deductible in computing the taxpayer's income for the subsequent year to which it can reasonably be considered to relate.

For our purposes, there is no need to examine the remaining paragraphs of this provision.

The purpose of subsection 18(9), which applies to outlays or expenses made or incurred after December 11, 1979, was explained as follows in the 1979 budget statement:

> A change is proposed to deal with the timing of the deduction of certain advance payments made by taxpayers in calculating their business or property income. After December 11, 1979, expenditures made or incurred by a taxpayer for prepaid rent, interest, insurance and taxes, for services to be rendered in a subsequent taxation year ... will not be deductible until the year to which they relate. This change will more closely align the determination of business or property income for tax purposes with generally accepted financial reporting practice.

The purpose of this rule, therefore, as with rules governing the deduction of inventory costs and capital expenditures, is to provide a "truer picture" of the taxpayer's business income for each taxation year by matching expenses and revenues.

Although subsection 18(9) has been applied infrequently,[123] it has been considered in three notable cases. In *Urbandale Realty Corp. v. M.N.R.*, [2000] F.C.J. No. 184, [2000] 2 C.T.C. 250, 2000 D.T.C. 6118 (F.C.A.), a majority of the Federal Court of Appeal held that subsection 18(9) did not require the amortization of a regional development charge levied by the Regional Municipality of Ottawa-Carleton on the grounds that the one-time tax did not relate to a "period" as indicated in subparagraph 18(9)(a)(ii) and was not imposed in respect a period "after the end of the year." In *Toronto College Park Ltd. v. Canada*, [1996] F.C.J. No. 893, [1996] 3 C.T.C. 94, 96 D.T.C. 6407 (F.C.A.), rev'd [1998] S.C.J. No. 14, [1998] 2 C.T.C. 78, 98 D.T.C. 6088

---

[123] See, for example, *Langille v. Canada*, [2000] T.C.J. No. 852, [2001] 1 C.T.C. 2386 (T.C.C.), in which the Court applied subs. 18(9) to allocate the cost of three years of cell phone air time to each of the years to which the expense could reasonably be considered to relate.

(S.C.C.), the Federal Court of Appeal rejected the taxpayer's argument that the absence of tenant inducement payments from subsection 18(9) implicitly authorizes their immediate deduction on the basis that the kinds of expenses subject to subsection 18(9) are mostly expenditures that, unlike tenant inducement payments, cannot be easily matched to a specific source of income in subsequent taxation years. According to Robertson JA (Strayer JA and Chevalier DJ concurring) (at paras. 13-14):

> Subparagraph 18(9)(a)(ii) requires that prepaid rents be amortized over the period to which they relate. It is difficult to envisage a situation in which the payment of an overhead expense such as rent could *reasonably* or *directly* be attributed to the production of a specific revenue, that is matched with a corresponding item of revenue, as opposed to general expenditures paid to earn future and speculative income ... . [A]s a result, even though amortization is possible, it would not be required *but for* subsection 18(9) of the Act.
>
> Similarly, paragraph 18(9)(a)(i) relates to prepaid service contracts which would include, for example, a two year contract for the repair and maintenance of a building. This is a classic example of an overhead expense which cannot be related directly to a specific source of income: see *Naval Colliery Co. (The) v. Inland Revenue Commissioners (sub nom. Naval Colliery Co. v. Commissioners of Inland Revenue)* (1928), 12 Tax Cas. 1017 (KB) at page 1027.

In *Canderel Ltd. v. Canada*, [1998] S.C.J. No. 13, [1998] 2 C.T.C. 35, 98 D.T.C. 6100 (S.C.C.), however, the Supreme Court of Canada concluded that the taxpayer was not required to amortize amounts paid to induce tenants to enter into long-term leases on the grounds, *inter alia*, that subsection 18(9) does not include tenant inducement payments (TIPs) in the list of amounts that must be amortized. According to Iacobucci J (Gonthier, Cory, Major, and Bastarache JJ concurring) (at paras. 54-55):

> Section 18(9) of the Act does require the amortization of certain "prepaid expenses," but TIPs are not included in this provision.
>
> To my mind, this exclusion not only exempts TIPs from any statutory amortization requirement, but also provides a valuable hint as to Parliament's lack of intention to require such treatment of TIPs. I do not mean to suggest that the *expressio unius* maxim of statutory interpretation applies here, as s. 18(9) certainly does not purport to be an exhaustive compendium of amortizable expenses, and it is arguable that TIPs do not really fall into the same category as the prepaid expenses touched upon by the section, but the fact that Parliament has directed its mind to requiring the amortization of some expenses without requiring this of TIPs is nonetheless telling to some extent. Parliament would be free to institute this requirement, but has not done so.

For the CRA's views on subsection 18(9), see *Interpretation Bulletin* IT-417R2, "Prepaid Expenses and Deferred Charges," February 10, 1997.

5. Running Expenses

Notwithstanding judicial decisions suggesting that a matching of revenues and expenses produces a "truer picture" of a taxpayer's income for a taxation year from a business or property, English and Canadian courts have traditionally held that expenses that cannot be easily matched with specific revenues may be deducted in the year in which they are incurred, even if the amount of the deduction may be particularly large and distort the taxpayer's income for that particular year. An excellent discussion of this doctrine appears in *Oxford Shopping Centres Ltd. v. Canada*, [1980] C.T.C. 7, 79 D.T.C. 5458 (F.C.T.D.), which was subsequently affirmed without further analysis by the Federal Court of Appeal, [1981] C.T.C. 128, 81 D.T.C. 5065 (F.C.A.).

Oxford Shopping Centres Ltd. v. Canada
[1980] C.T.C. 7, 79 D.T.C. 5458 (F.C.T.D.), aff'd [1981] C.T.C. 128,
81 D.T.C. 5065 (F.C.A.)

[By an agreement made by the plaintiff, the owner of a shopping centre, with the city of Calgary, the plaintiff paid the city $490,050 in 1973 in respect of the construction by the city of a road interchange affecting the access and use of the plaintiff's parking area. The agreement stated that the payment was "in lieu of local improvement rates and taxes that might be payable" by reason of the works and improvements undertaken by the city. The plaintiff contended that the amount was an income expense and deductible in the year of payment. The Minister argued that the amount of the deduction should be amortized over a period of years.]

THURLOW ACJ: ... I turn now to the question whether in computing its income for tax purposes, the plaintiff was required to apportion the expenditure of the $490,050 over a period of years. That is what the appellant did in computing its profit for corporate purposes. In its balance sheet dated March 31, 1973, it showed as an asset an item described as "deferred charges" which included the $490,050. At that time though the amount had been paid to the city, the construction work had not yet been done. A note to the balance sheet states that the $490,050 will be amortized over fifteen years commencing in 1974. But for income tax purposes, the plaintiff deducted the whole $490,050 as an expense of the year 1973.

...

In the present case, the position taken on behalf of the Crown was that ... it was incumbent on the taxpayer to amortize it over a period of years and claim only a part of it as deductible each year. Counsel contended that, except where the *Income Tax Act* makes a specific provision, the recognized principles of commercial accounting apply for the purpose of determining the income from a business for the year and that to deduct the whole amount in the year 1973, rather than to amortize and deduct it over a period of years, distorts and unduly reduces the income for 1973. He made no attack on the accounting method adopted by the plaintiff in computing its profit for corporate purposes by amortizing the amount over a 15-year period.

In *Associated Investors of Canada v. M.N.R.*, [1967] 2 Ex. CR 96; [1967] CTC 138; 67 CTC 5096, Jackett, P (as he then was) in a footnote at 100 [142; 5098] said:

... In my view, while certain types of expense must be deducted in the year when made or incurred, or not at all, (e.g., repairs as in *Naval Colliery Co. Ltd. v. CIR* (1928), 12 TC 1017, or weeding as in *Vallambrosa Rubber Co. Ltd. v. Farmer* (1910), 5 TC 529), there are many types of expenditure that are deductible in computing profit for the year "in respect of" which they were paid or payable. ... Compare *IRC v. Gardner Mountain & D'Ambrumenil, Ltd.* (1947), 29 TC *per* Viscount Simon at 93: "In calculating the taxable profit of a business ... services completely rendered or goods supplied, which are not to be paid for till a subsequent year, cannot, generally speaking, be dealt with by treating the taxpayer's outlay as pure loss in the year in which it was incurred and bringing in the remuneration as pure profit in the subsequent year in which it is paid, or is due to be paid. In making an assessment ... the net result of the transaction, setting expenses on the one side and a figure for remuneration on the other side, ought to appear ... in the same year's profit and loss account, and that year will be the year when the service was rendered or the goods delivered." ... The situation is different in the case of "running expenses." See *Naval Colliery Co. Ltd. v. CIR, supra*, per Rowlatt, J at 1027: "... and expenditure incurred in repairs, the running expenses of a business and so on, cannot be allocated directly to corresponding items of receipts, and it cannot be restricted in its allowance in some way corresponding, or in an endeavour to make it correspond, to the actual receipts during the particular year. If running repairs are made, if lubricants are bought, of course no enquiry is instituted as to whether those repairs were partly owing to wear and tear that earned profits in the preceding year or whether they will not help to make profits in the following year and so on. The way it is looked at, and must be looked at, is this, that that sort of expenditure is expenditure incurred on the running of the business as a whole in each year, and the income is the income of the business as a whole for the year, without trying to trace items of expenditure as earning particular items of profit." See also *Riedle Brewery Ltd. v. M.N.R.*, [1939] SCR 253. ...

I think it follows from this that for income tax purposes, while the "matching principle" will apply to expenses related to particular items of income, and in particular with respect to the computation of profit from the acquisition and sale of inventory, it does not apply to the running expense of the business as a whole even though the deduction of a particularly heavy item of running expense in the year in which it is paid will distort the income for that particular year. Thus while there is in the present case some evidence that accepted principles of accounting recognize the method adopted by the plaintiff in amortizing the amount in question for corporate purposes and there is also evidence that to deduct the whole amount in 1973 would distort the profit for that year, it appears to me that as the nature of the amount is that of a running expense that is not referable or related to any particular item of revenue, the footnote to the *Associated Industries* [*sic*] case and the authorities referred to by Jackett P, and in particular the *Vallambrosa Rubber* case and the *Naval Colliery* case, indicate that the amount is deductible only in the year in which it was paid. ... [T]here is no specific provision in the Act which prohibits deduction of the full amount in the year it was paid. I do not think, therefore, that the Minister is entitled to insist on an amortization of the expenditure or on the plaintiff spreading the deduction in respect of it over a period of years.

There is another aspect of the matter. The 15-year period chosen has not much relation to the expected life of the street improvements. They may well last much longer. The period was probably selected for no better reason than that it is the period which the city would have used. On the other hand, it is not the expected life of the street improvements that should be considered. What, if anything, should be considered for such a purpose is the expected duration of the benefits to the popularity of the shopping centre that were expected to arise from the improvements and this, compounded as it is by the prospect of another shopping centre three miles away, and possibly other developments affecting the popularity of the plaintiff's shopping centre in a rapidly growing city, is imponderable. This confirms me in the view that the whole amount is deductible in the year of payment.

The appeal, therefore, succeeds and it will be allowed with costs and the re-assessment will be referred back to the Minister for re-assessment, accordingly.

Appeal allowed.

NOTES AND QUESTIONS

1.   On what grounds did the court in *Oxford Shopping Centres* permit the taxpayer to deduct the full amount of the $490,050 payment to the city of Calgary in computing its income for its 1973 taxation year? Do you agree or disagree with the decision? Why?

2.   What, according to the court in *Oxford Shopping Centres*, are the characteristics of a "running expense"? Why, according to the court, are these expenses not subject to the "matching principle"?

3.   In *Canderel Ltd. v. Canada*, [1998] S.C.J. No. 13, [1998] 2 C.T.C. 35, 98 D.T.C. 6100 (S.C.C.), Iacobucci J (Gonthier, Cory, Major, and Bastarache JJ concurring) made the following comment (at para. 46) on the decision in *Oxford Shopping Centres*:

> While on first glance, this decision might appear to fly in the face of the "accurate picture" principle, in my view, the facts of the case gave rise to a choice between two difficult positions: either to permit the distortion of the taxpayer's income for a single year by allowing the immediate deduction of a running expense, or to require the distortion of its income for a number of years by forcing the arbitrary amortization of an expense which was not clearly referable to any particular item of future revenue. Given this choice, it is apparent that Thurlow ACJ recognized that to apply the matching principle of accounting, as a well-accepted business principle, *not* a rule of law, would not have assisted in obtaining an accurate picture of the taxpayer's income. [Emphasis in original.]

4.   As the excerpt from *Oxford Shopping Centres* indicates, the key judicial sources for the doctrine that a "running expense" need not be matched against future revenue are the decisions in *Vallambrosa Rubber Co. Ltd. v. Farmer* (1910), 5 Tax Cas 529 (Ct. Sess.) and *Naval Colliery Co. Ltd. v. CIR* (1928), 12 Tax Cas 1017 (K.B.). In *Vallambrosa Rubber*, the taxpayer, which was in the first year of a new business involving the cultivation and sale of rubber, deducted the full costs of overseeing and maintaining its rubber plants, even though only one-seventh of the return from the plant was realized in the first year. Rejecting the Crown's argument that only one-seventh of the taxpayer's costs should be deducted in computing its income for this year, the court commented (at 534) that "nothing ever could be deducted as an expense unless

that expense was purely and solely referable to a profit which was reaped in the year." According to the court (at 535):

> I think the proposition only needs to be stated to be upset by its own absurdity. Because what does it come to? It would mean this, that if your business is connected with a fruit which is not always ready precisely within the year of assessment you would never be allowed to deduct the necessary expenses without which you could not raise that fruit. This very case, which deals with a class of thing that takes six years to mature before you pluck or tap it, is a very good illustration, but of course without any ingenuity one could multiply cases by the score. Supposing a man conducted a milk business, it really comes to the limits of absurdity to suppose that he would not be allowed to charge for the keep of one of his cows because at a particular time of year, towards the end of the year of assessment, that cow was not in milk, and therefore the profit which he was going to get from the cow would be outside the year of assessment. ... [W]hen you come to think of the expense in this particular case that is incurred for instance in the weeding which is necessary in order that a particular tree should bear rubber, how can it possibly be said that that is not a necessary expense for the rearing of the tree from which alone the profit eventually comes?

In the *Naval Colliery* case, the taxpayer incurred expenses to recondition its equipment after a national stoppage in the coal-mining industry, which the revenue authorities disallowed as a deduction in computing the taxpayer's excess profits duty for its 1921 taxation year on the basis that no expenditure was made until after this accounting period. In the course of his decision allowing the deduction, Rowlatt J stated (at 1027):

> Expenditure includes debts payable; and expenditure incurred in repairs, the running expenses of a business and so on, cannot be allocated directly to corresponding items of receipts, and it cannot be restricted in its allowance in some way corresponding, or in an endeavour to make it correspond, to the actual receipts during the particular year. If running repairs are made, if lubricants are bought, of course no enquiry is instituted as to whether those repairs were partly owing to wear and tear that earned profits in the following year and so on. The way it is looked at, and must be looked at, is this, that that sort of expenditure is expenditure incurred on the running of the business as a whole in each year, and the income is the income of the business as a whole for the year, without trying to trace items of expenditure as earning particular items of profit.

5. In *M.N.R. v. Tower Investment Inc.*, [1972] F.C.J. No. 30, [1972] C.T.C. 182, 72 D.T.C. 6161 (F.C.T.D.), the taxpayer, which constructed 24 apartment buildings in suburban Montreal, spent roughly $92,350 in 1963, $58,600 in 1964, and $2,350 in 1965 on an intensive advertising campaign in order to obtain tenants for the 660 apartments. For tax purposes, however, it deducted roughly $7,350 in 1963, $63,600 in 1964, and $82,350 in 1965. Rejecting the Minister's argument that the taxpayer was required to deduct the amounts actually expended in each of the taxation years in question, Collier J concluded (at para. 10) that "the method adopted by the taxpayer of deferring some of the advertising expense into future years was not only in accordance with generally accepted accounting principles but also more accurately reflected the truth about the taxpayer's income position."

In *Oxford Shopping Centres Ltd. v. Canada*, [1980] C.T.C. 7, 79 D.T.C. 5458 (F.C.T.D.), Thurlow ACJ said (at para. 40) of the decision in *Tower Investment*:

> All that appears ... to have been held in the ... case ... is that it was ... open to the taxpayer to spread the deduction there in question over a number of years. It was not decided that the whole expenditure might not be deducted in the year in which it was made, as the earlier authorities [*Vallambrosa Rubber*, supra, and *Naval Colliery*, supra] hold.

6.   The decision in *Oxford Shopping Centres* was followed in *Cummings v. Canada*, [1981] F.C.J. No. 524, [1981] C.T.C. 285, 81 D.T.C. 5207 (F.C.A.), where the taxpayer and his associates, who constructed a 15-storey office building in Montreal, incurred expenses (lease "pickups") to indemnify a key tenant for penalties and rental costs resulting from the decision to vacate other office space. Rejecting the Crown's argument that deductions for the lease pickups should be amortized over the term of the lease entered into by the tenant, the Federal Court of Appeal concluded (at para. 11) that the expenditure was:

> a "running expense" and in the same category as for example, an extensive advertising campaign to obtain tenants or an offer to a prospective tenant of a rent-free period as an inducement to enter into a long-term lease or a finder's fee for obtaining tenants and leases.

7.   In *Canderel Ltd. v. Canada*, [1998] S.C.J. No. 13, [1998] 2 C.T.C. 35, 98 D.T.C. 6100 (S.C.C.), the taxpayer, which carried on a business developing and managing commercial properties, spent over $1.2 million during its 1986 taxation year as inducements that were paid to tenants on the signing of leases, which ran from 3 and 10 years. Although these tenant inducement payments (TIPs) were, for accounting purposes, capitalized and amortized over the term of each lease, for tax purposes the taxpayer deducted the full amount of the payments in computing its income for its 1986 taxation year.

At trial, [1994] T.C.J. No. 7, [1994] 1 C.T.C. 2336, 94 D.T.C. 1133 (T.C.C.), Brulé J held that the TIPs were "running expenses" that could be fully deducted in the year in which they were incurred and need not be matched against future rental income from the resulting leases. On appeal, [1995] F.C.J. No. 221, [1995] 2 C.T.C. 22, 95 D.T.C. 5101 (F.C.A.), the Federal Court of Appeal concluded that the TIPs were not "running expenses" and were subject to the "matching principle." According to Desjardins JA (at paras. 60-62):

> What is at stake here is whether TIPs are expenses related to a particular item of income, or whether they are running expenses. If they are related to a particular item of income, the "matching principle" will apply. If they are running expenses, the taxpayer will have the option of deducting the amount in full or amortizing it.
>
> TIPs are clearly expenses related to particular items of income. They are not running expenses such as those disbursed for advertising the taxpayer's apartments over a period of years (*Tower Investment Inc.*) where the return is unknown or where, as in *Oxford Shopping Centres Ltd.*, the matching would have been inappropriate and, in any case, impossible. The essence of a running expense is that it is akin to an overhead item which cannot be traced to specific items of revenue. This, however, is a far cry from a TIP of the present kind where, as evident from the lease agreements themselves, there is a direct contractual relationship between the TIP and the stream of revenues gained over the period of the lease. The real and immediate effect of the TIPs is to pull a string of revenues. It is the revenues which, once they flow in, on account of the TIPs, have the remaining financial benefits described by the trial judge.

Matching of TIPs is compulsory.

According to Stone JA (Robertson JA concurring):

It is true, as the trial judge concluded, that in law as in accountancy, current expenses need not be matched with corresponding items of revenue for tax purposes if they are "running expenses," to be deducted in the year in which they are incurred. It is apparent, however, that the tenant inducement payments here in issue do not fit the classical description of "running expenses" in the oft-quoted passage from the judgment of Rowlatt J in *The Naval Colliery Co. v. CIR* (1928), 12 TC 1017 (KB) ... .

It can, however, be argued that the tenant inducement payments laid out by the respondent were in the nature of running expenses on the basis that they represented a cost of doing business in the 1986 taxation year and also that the respondent would likely have faced significant financial disadvantages if they had not been laid out and did achieve significant financial advantages by laying them out. It is a well-established principle that an expenditure becomes deductible in the year in which it was incurred even if the whole of the expenditure did not bear fruit in that year (*Vallambrosa Rubber Co. v. Farmer (Surveyor of Taxes)* (1910), 5 TC 529 (Ct. Sess.)). ...

In the present case, it is apparent that these expenditures were not incurred in earning income solely in the taxation year 1986 but in all of the years during which the respective leases were to run.

Nor am I able to equate these expenditures with the kind of outlay that was before the Court in *Oxford Shopping Centres Ltd. v. The Queen*. ... It is evident in that case that it was not possible to match the outlay with particular items of revenue. ...

In the present case, I share my colleague's view that the expenses in question could be matched with revenue from the particular leases in accordance with the matching principle discussed above. That they could be so matched is evident from the fact that they were matched for financial reporting purposes.

On further appeal, however, the Supreme Court of Canada concluded (at para. 65) that the TIPs were "running expenses to which the matching principle does not apply." According to Iacobucci J (Gonthier, Cory, Major, and Bastarache JJ concurring) (at paras. 60-66):

The accounting evidence adduced by the parties was somewhat inconclusive at best. It disclosed that at the time of the payments, GAAP allowed for three alternative and acceptable methods of accounting for TIPs. The payer was entitled to treat the payments either as operating expenses, fully chargeable to the results of operations in the year incurred, as capital expenditures to be added to the cost of the building and depreciated, or as deferred expenses to be amortized over the life of the relevant leases. The experts called by Canderel were of the opinion that the first option was to be preferred because the expenditures were incurred in the ordinary course of generating revenue from Canderel's business and that this method would thus give the most accurate picture of income. Those called by the Minister, as might be expected, testified that the preferred method was the third, as the payments were causally linked to rental revenue while any other benefits to which they gave rise were not revenue and could not be the subject of "matching." To my mind, this evidence is useful only to demonstrate that GAAP at the time endorsed the options contended for by both parties. However, I cannot draw from this alone any specific conclusion as to which method was preferable in terms of yielding the more accurate picture of Canderel's income.

But the findings of fact made by the trial judge are more instructive. Brulé J found that the payments yielded four primary benefits for Canderel: the prevention of a "hole in income" which otherwise would have been caused by maintaining a vacant building, the ability to satisfy the underlying requirements of its interim financing and to obtain permanent financing, the ability to meet its competition and to maintain its market position and reputation, and the generating of revenues through rentals and through management and development fees (which were to some extent contingent upon the rate of lease-up). From this, he concluded that the payments constituted "running expenses," as they could not be causally linked to any single or specific stream of revenue, and that the matching principle therefore did not apply in the circumstances, as contended for by the Minister.

It is immediately apparent that, while some of the benefits identified by Brulé J are of a type that would be realized over a period of years, others, such as the satisfaction of interim financing requirements and the maintenance of market position and reputation, are benefits that were immediately realized by Canderel in the year the payments were made. From this observation emerges one serious practical difficulty inherent in the Federal Court of Appeal's view of the law: even if it can properly be argued that the payments are "directly referable" to some future revenues, what is to be made of a situation where they are also referable to other, immediate benefits? It would be unduly arbitrary to allocate the expenses only to the specific revenues while ignoring the other, less tangible benefits. But there also exists no specific legal formula for the apportionment of the expenses among the various benefits. Perhaps some appropriate amortization formula could be devised to cover such an apportionment, but any such device would need to be a creature of statute; anything less would constitute judicial legislation of a very intrusive variety. It is similarly no answer to suggest that because the payments were amortized by Canderel for financial accounting purposes, they can be similarly amortized for taxation purposes. As I have already explained, the two portrayals of profit are substantially different in nature and purpose.

In its submissions before this Court, Canderel posited a variety of other questions which would arise out of the treatment of the matching principle as a compulsory rule of law. For example, if an induced tenant were to break its lease before the end of the term, how, and pursuant to what authority, would the balance of the TIP be deducted from income? What if the rate of rent varied over the term of the lease; would this affect the rate of amortization? Additionally, without any clear, principled distinction between this case and *Cummings, supra*, what other expenses incurred in the course of securing tenants for a building would be required to be amortized rather than currently deducted? Moreover, what would happen if the leased premises were disposed of before the TIPs were fully deducted? These are questions which simply cannot be answered by reference to the law as it presently exists, and for good reason: in a case such as this, there is simply no uniform solution by which the most accurate picture of the taxpayer's profit may be obtained. It is therefore an artificial and arbitrary solution to impose the matching principle, as a matter of law, upon circumstances where its application quite evidently creates serious difficulty.

. . .

In light of all of this, I find it difficult, particularly given the findings of the trial judge as to the various benefits generated by the TIPs, to conclude that the amortization of the payments over the terms of the leases, as contended for by the Minister, would provide a more accurate picture of Canderel's income than would their immediate deduction in the year expended. In such a case, where no one method emerges as clearly superior or more properly applicable than another, the taxpayer should retain the option of ordering its affairs in accordance with any method which is in accordance with well-accepted business principles and which is acceptable in light of the reality of its business. That is to say, just because a particular tactic is acceptable under well-accepted business principles will not necessarily justify its application in a given context if it is out of step with the actual manner in which the taxpayer conducts its affairs. However, once the taxpayer has established that the method adopted gives an accurate picture of its income, the onus is clearly on the Minister to prove that the method adopted by the taxpayer is inappropriate in the particular circumstances of each case. In the instant case, I believe that the findings of the trial judge make it impossible to conclude that the Minister has discharged this burden in the instant case.

Indeed, in my view, the fact that in the instant case, Brulé J found that the TIPs were properly attributable to a number of different expenses makes inevitable the conclusion that they constituted running expenses. As I have already noted, I do not see how, under these circumstances, it is possible with any accuracy to amortize the payments over the term of the lease, in the absence of an established formula acceptable for tax purposes, which was not advanced by the Minister. It follows, then, that the TIPs were not referable to any particular items of income, i.e., they cannot be correlated directly, or at least not principally, with the rents generated by the leases which they induced. They therefore qualify as running expenses to which the matching principle does not apply: see *Oxford Shopping Centres, supra*. The findings of fact made by Brulé J in this regard are entitled to considerable deference. There is no indication that these findings were unsupported by the evidence, and I can see no reason to reject them.

In light of the foregoing, I am compelled to the view that the Federal Court of Appeal erred in requiring that the TIPs be amortized over the terms of the leases which they induced, rather than being deducted entirely in the year incurred. As I have already made clear, there is no basis for treating the matching principle as a "rule of law," as the Federal Court of Appeal chose to do, and for my part, I am unable to conclude that to apply this particular principle of accounting to the present case would serve to achieve a more accurate picture, for tax purposes, of the taxpayer's financial position for the year in question than the immediate deduction of the expenses favoured by Canderel. While the matching principle will certainly be useful in some cases, its specific application in the present case is unnecessary, as the payments related at least partially to benefits realized entirely in the year incurred, and the taxpayer therefore should not be constrained to amortize. The method employed by Canderel was consistent both with the law and with well-accepted business principles, and gave at least as accurate a picture of the taxpayer's income as would the amortization method. Therefore, it ought not to be disturbed.

Do you agree with this result? Why or why not?

8.   The facts in *Oxford Shopping Centres Ltd. v. Canada*, [1980] C.T.C. 7, 79 D.T.C. 5458 (F.C.T.D.), preceded the enactment of subsection 18(9), which applies to outlays and expenses made or incurred after December 11, 1979. Would this provision have applied to require the taxpayer to deduct a portion of the expense in subsequent taxation years to which it could reasonably be considered to relate?

6. Reserves

Notwithstanding paragraphs 18(1)(a) and (e), which prohibit deductions in respect of unincurred expenses and contingent liabilities, subsection 20(1) allows taxpayers to deduct amounts in respect of reserves in respect of unearned amounts, deferred payments, and doubtful debts. This subsection considers each of these statutory reserves.

a. Unearned Amounts

Under paragraph 12(1)(a), a taxpayer must include amounts received but unearned in a taxation year and amounts received as deposits for "articles in or by means of which goods were delivered to a customer." Subject to subsection 20(6), however, where amounts described in paragraph 12(1)(a) have been included in computing a taxpayer's income from a business for a taxation year or a previous year, paragraph 20(1)(m) permits the taxpayer to deduct:

a reasonable amount as a reserve in respect of

(i) goods that it is reasonably anticipated will have to be delivered after the end of the year,

(ii) services that it is reasonably anticipated will have to be rendered after the end of the year,

(iii) periods for which rent or other amounts for the possession or use of land or chattels have been paid in advance, or

(iv) repayments under arrangements or understandings of the class described in subparagraph 12(1)(a)(ii) that it is reasonably anticipated will have to be made after the end of the year on the return or resale to the taxpayer of articles other than bottles.

Where an amount is deducted under paragraph 20(1)(m), the amount must be included in computing the taxpayer's income for the immediately following taxation year under subparagraph 12(1)(e)(i). Where the requirements of paragraph 20(1)(m) are satisfied in this subsequent taxation year, the taxpayer may deduct "a reasonable amount as a reserve" in this subsequent taxation year, in which case this amount must be included in the immediately following taxation year under subparagraph 12(1)(e)(i), and so on. The requirements that a taxpayer must satisfy to claim this reserve were considered in *Dominion Stores Limited v. M.N.R.*, [1966] C.T.C. 97, 66 D.T.C. 5111 (Ex. Ct.).

Dominion Stores Limited v. M.N.R.
[1966] C.T.C. 97, 66 D.T.C. 5111 (Ex. Ct.)

CATTANACH, J: ... The appellant company, the head office of which is in Toronto, Ontario, operates a chain of retail food stores throughout Canada, except in the Province of Newfoundland, the Yukon and Northwest Territories. Approximately 62 per cent of appellant's gross revenue is derived from its business conducted in the Province of Ontario and approximately 20 per cent is derived from its operations in the Province of Quebec.

As a matter of policy the appellant does not usually resort to the device of distributing trading stamps to attract and retain customers but, as an executive of the appellant company testified, the appellant was obliged to do so in the Province of Quebec and in those portions of Ontario bordering on Quebec in order to compete effectively with its business rivals.

...

The method of operating the trading stamp plans adopted by the appellant is this:

The appellant conducts its business on a cash basis exclusively. A customer on purchasing merchandise from the appellant is given trading stamps to the value of 1½ per cent of the price paid for the merchandise purchased. For example if the price of the merchandise was $10, the customer would be given 100 stamps having a redeemable value of 15 cents, or 3/20 of a cent each. The customer is also supplied with a small booklet in which the stamps are to be pasted. The booklet, when completely filled, has a redeemable value of $2.25. When a customer has filled booklets of these stamps he may then present them at the appellant's retail store where the merchandise was purchased where he is given a choice of articles illustrated in a catalogue which may have been given to him previously or is available for his inspection. The appellant then exchanges the article selected by the customer for a certain number of completed booklets, the number of booklets required being listed in the catalogue.

In all advertising media, and upon the catalogues and booklets the trading stamps and articles received by a customer in exchange therefor are described as being "free" — "gifts" and "free gifts."

I should have thought that the appellant would recoup itself for the cost of printing the trading stamps and the redeemable values thereof as well as sundry related administrative expenses, by appropriate increases in the prices of the merchandise sold to its customers. I should also have thought that the appellant would realize a profit by supplying articles in exchange for booklets of stamps. However, no satisfactory evidence was adduced upon either of the above points. An executive of the appellant company who was called as a witness could not say whether prices in those stores of the appellant in which a trading stamp plan was in vogue were increased to cover the cost of the stamp plan, nor did he know whether the premium articles given in exchange for stamps were purchased by the appellant at manufacturer's or wholesale cost and redeemed by it at the retail cost. The witness did say that prices varied from store to store in the appellant's chain in different areas and from store to store in the same areas, but that such variations in prices were attributable to so many factors that he was unable to attribute any part of the prices at which merchandise was sold to the introduction of a trading stamp plan. Neither could this witness state that a specific part of each sales dollar received by the appellant was allocated to an account for the redemption of trading stamps, or that a specific part of each sales dollar was allocated to the purchase price of the merchandise sold by the appellant. No such system of bookkeeping or segregation was set up although accounts were kept of the numbers and amounts of trading stamps issued.

It was positively established by evidence that when a customer made a purchase of merchandise in one of the appellant's stores where a trading stamp plan was in effect, he paid the asking price for the merchandise he received, he received or was entitled to receive trading stamps to the extent of 1½ per cent of the purchase price and he was entitled to present those trading stamps for redemption by the appellant. These were the conditions under which merchandise was sold by the appellant. If a customer did not wish to take the stamps he could not thereby obtain any reduction in the price of the merchandise that he wished to purchase. If the customer did not wish to take the stamps proffered to him, and did not take them, he would, in effect, be making a gift of them to the appellant.

It was a condition of acquiring trading stamps that a customer must purchase merchandise from the appellant. A person could not acquire stamps from the appellant except in connection with a purchase of merchandise in the manner I have described.

In addition to its trading stamp plan, the appellant also had in effect in some of its stores in some areas a variation thereof which was described as a "save-a-tape" plan. This plan worked in a manner identical to the trading stamp plan except that instead of trading stamps the customer was given cash register receipts in a specified colour which were also redeemable in the same manner and to the same values as trading stamps.

I should also add that a customer was given a further option by the appellant. A customer could exchange the trading stamps received by him (or the cash register receipts as the case might be) for the premiums listed in the catalogue or if the customer wished he might redeem the trading stamps for merchandise, that is groceries, sold by the appellant.

The appellant, in addition to distributing trading stamps in its own retail stores, also sold a much lesser quantity of trading stamps than it distributed itself to other retail merchants to disseminate or distribute among their customers. The customers of those other retail merchants were also entitled to present the trading stamps so received by them to the appellant to be exchanged for the premiums listed in the appellant's catalogue at the rates therein listed and the appellant also undertook to redeem those stamps.

The appellant also sold "gift certificates." These certificates were purchased from the appellant at a price equal to the face value printed thereon and were redeemable at any of the appellant's retail stores by the bearer for merchandise only, that is to say, the merchandise normally sold by the appellant but not for premiums listed in the gift catalogue. During the Christmas season the appellant also offered for sale turkey gift certificates which were for the same purpose as the gift certificates except that the merchandise to be received therefor was limited to turkeys.

Owing to the operation of trading stamp plans by the appellant in the conduct of its business, a problem arises in dealing with what are known as "unredeemed" stamps, that is to say, stamps that were distributed in the current accounting year or carried over from former years and that remain unredeemed at the end of the year. The problem is what account, if any, should be taken of such unredeemed stamps in computing the profits from the appellant's business for the year.

During the taxation years 1957 and 1958 the appellant operated its trading stamp plan under the name of the "Blue Chip Premium Stamp Plan." This plan was discontinued by the appellant in its 1958 taxation year and in its income tax return for that year the appellant deducted a reserve in respect of Blue Chip stamps then outstanding which the Minister disallowed as a deduction.

The appellant, in its 1959 and subsequent taxation years, continued to operate a premium trading stamp plan designated as the "Horizon Stamp Plan."

During its 1958 and subsequent taxation years the appellant also operated the "Save-a-Tape Plan" which has been described above.

In the appellant's 1959 and 1960 taxation years now under review, the Minister did allow claims for reserves with respect to trading stamps sold by the appellant to other retail merchants, and the issuance of gift certificates and Christmas turkey certificates, in amounts he considered to be reasonable, but he disallowed the claims for the reserves with respect to the "Blue Chip Plan," the "Horizon Stamp Plan" and the "Save-a-Tape Plan" made by the appellant for those taxation years by notification ... dated July 30, 1964, on the particular ground that:

> reserves for premium stamps and tapes supplied to customers claimed as deductions from income have been properly disallowed in accordance with the provisions of paragraph (e) of subsection (1) of Section 12 of the Act [now paragraph 18(1)(e)]; that no part of the taxpayer's receipts from customers represents an amount received in the year in the course of business that is on account of goods not delivered before the end of the year or that, for any other reason, may be regarded as not having been earned in the year or a previous year within the meaning of subparagraph (i) of paragraph (a) of subsection (1) of Section 85B of the Act [now subparagraph 12(1)(a)(i)] and accordingly the taxpayer is not entitled to a reserve under paragraph (c) of the said subsection (1) of Section 85B [now paragraph 20(1)(m)].

By such notification the Minister confirmed his prior assessments to which objections had been filed by the appellant. It is from these assessments that the appeals to this Court result.

...

The issue is whether the appellant is entitled to deduct an amount as a reserve in respect of the ... trading stamps and cash register receipts which it had distributed among its customers and which had not been redeemed during the respective taxation years in question.

...

The appellant's principal contention is, in effect, that the manner in which the appellant conducted its business, which has been described above, falls within the precise terms of Section 85 B [now subparagraph 12(1)(a)(i)] in that part of the purchase price received by the appellant in the course of each of its sales at a store where such a plan was in operation, was received on account of goods not delivered before the end of the year.

There is no question that the appellant is under a binding legal obligation to redeem trading stamps which it has issued under the plans that I have described when those stamps are presented to be exchanged for premiums in accordance with the terms of the respective plans under which they were issued. Counsel for the Minister readily concedes that such obligation is upon the appellant to redeem the trading stamps.

However, he submits that this obligation was voluntarily assumed by the appellant, that there was no evidence (as there was not) of an increase in price of the merchandise that the appellant sold in the normal course of its business to cover the cost of the premium plans when introduced and that there was no segregation or allocation of the revenue received to the merchandise sold, on the one hand, and to the trading stamps distributed on the other. He, therefore, suggests that the trading stamps were "free" as they were described in the appellant's advertising. On these grounds he submits that no amounts were received by the appellant in the years in question in respect of the trading stamps or the premiums to be given on their redemption. It would follow, therefore, that no amounts were included in computing the appellant's income and that a reasonable amount as a reserve was not permissible as a deduction under paragraph (c) of Section 85B [now paragraph 20(1)(m)]. In short, the contention on behalf of the Minister is, as I understand it, that the liability of the appellant to redeem the trading stamps issued by it cannot be related back to the period in which that liability arose, but rather any deductions should be brought into account when the trading stamps were actually redeemed and not before.

In my view the contention of the Minister cannot prevail.

The arrangement between the appellant and its customers is quite clear from the evidence. A customer paid the price demanded by the appellant when he purchased merchandise from the appellant. For this, he received the merchandise and in addition he received or was entitled to receive trading stamps which he was entitled to present to the appellant later for redemption either by way of premiums or the appellant's merchandise. The appellant was legally obligated to make this redemption. There was only one transaction and this was the only way in which the appellant would conduct its business at the particular stores. It does not follow that, because no specific amount is identifiable as being allocated to the cost of distributing and redeeming the stamps, the total amount is not attributable in part thereto. When two articles are sold together for one price without a price being put upon each separately, it does not follow that one article is free and that the price is attributable exclusively to the other article.

In my opinion, where the trading stamps and save-a-tape plans were in effect and trading stamps or premium tapes were issued to the appellant's customers, a portion of each amount received by the appellant from its customers was received on account of goods to be delivered on presentation of the trading stamps or tapes for redemption. All amounts received by the appellant in respect of such goods were included in the appellant's income in the year of receipt whether or not the trading stamps or tapes were redeemed in that year. Such amounts, with respect to trading stamps which remained outstanding at the end of each taxation year, were on account of goods not delivered before the end of the year. From this is follows that by virtue of Section 85B the appellant is entitled to deduct a reasonable amount for each of the two years in question as a reserve in respect of goods that it is reasonably anticipated will have to be delivered upon the redemption of trading stamps or premium tapes after the end of the year. ...

Appeal allowed.

NOTES AND QUESTIONS

1.   On what basis did the taxpayer in *Dominion Stores* argue that it could deduct a reserve in respect of unredeemed trading stamps under then paragraph 85B(c) (now paragraph 20(1)(m))? On what grounds did the Minister argue that the taxpayer could not deduct such a reserve? Why did the court reject the Minister's argument?

2.   In *Sussex Square Apartments Ltd. v. Canada*, [1998] T.C.J. No. 1109, [1999] 2 C.T.C. 2143, 99 D.T.C. 443 (T.C.C.), the taxpayer leased a number of apartment units in six buildings that it subsequently sublet to individuals under long-term leases in exchange for lump-sum payments. Characterizing these payments as prepaid rent, which must be included in computing the taxpayer's income under paragraph 12(1)(a) of the Act, the court allowed the taxpayer to deduct a reserve in respect of these amounts under subparagraph 20(1)(m)(iii).

3.   In *Argus Holdings Ltd. v. Canada*, [2000] F.C.J. No. 1887, [2001] 1 C.T.C. 115, 2000 D.T.C. 6681 (F.C.A.), the taxpayer operated a raquetball club, charging initiation fees a portion of which it promised to repay on a pro rata basis if the club failed within 10 years, and accounting for these fees on the basis that they should be included over a 10-year period with an equal amount included in the taxpayer's income each month. Even though the taxpayer had not explicitly included the initiation fees as income and claimed a reserve under paragraph 20(1)(m), the court affirmed the conclusion of the trial judge that, regardless of the manner in which the taxpayer described the amounts, it had in fact deducted a reserve under paragraph 20(1)(m).

4.   In *Burrard Yarrows Corp. v. M.N.R.*, [1986] F.C.J. No. 504, [1986] 2 C.T.C. 313, 86 D.T.C. 6459 (F.C.T.D.), var'd on other grounds [1988] 2 C.T.C. 90, 88 D.T.C. 6352 (F.C.A.), the taxpayer, a shipbuilder that entered into a contract with the Canadian government to build two icebreakers, sought to deduct a reserve under subparagraph 20(1)(m)(i) in respect of payments received as the work progressed. Noting that title to all materials, parts, and finished work paid for by each progress payment vested at that point in the purchaser, the court disallowed the deduction on the basis that paragraph 20(1)(m) did not apply. According to Joyal J (at paras. 23-25).

> the availability of a paragraph 20(1)(m) reserve depends entirely on whether an amount described in paragraph 12(1)(a) was included in computing the taxpayer's income. Therefore, to determine whether a paragraph 20(1)(m) reserve is available with respect to the progress payments in question, it must be determined whether they were brought into income pursuant to subparagraph 12(1)(a)(i), which in turn requires a determination of when they were "earned" or, in other words, when they took on the quality of income. ...

In the present case, the plaintiff, upon completing each of the various stages of construction, became absolutely entitled to receive the progress payments which had been agreed upon. Its right to those amounts was under "no restriction, contractual or otherwise, as to its disposition, use or enjoyment." The contract did not even contain a provision requiring refunding of the progress payments in the event of the plaintiff defaulting. As a result, I find that the progress payments had the quality of income when received and, hence, were earned amounts. It follows, therefore, that subparagraph 12(1)(a)(i) does not operate to bring the payments into income, and, further, that the Minister was correct in denying the plaintiff's claim for a paragraph 20(1)(m) reserve. The plaintiff must bring the progress payments into income in the year they are received.

5. Subsection 20(6) limits the deductible reserve in respect of articles of food, drink, or transportation to amounts included in computing the taxpayer's income from the business that were received or receivable in the year in respect of food, drink, or transportation not delivered or provided before the end of the year. By so doing, it prohibits the continued deduction of a reserve in respect of these items in subsequent taxation years, thereby limiting the duration of any reserve for these items to a single taxation year.

According to Brian J. Arnold, *Timing and Income Taxation: The Principles of Income Measurement for Tax Purposes*, Canadian Tax Paper No. 71 (Toronto: Canadian Tax Foundation, 1983) at 277, although the limitation in subsection 20(6) may result in a mismatching of certain items of revenue and the costs incurred in order to earn this revenue, it reflects a policy judgment that "food or drink coupons or transportation tickets that are outstanding for more than one year are unlikely ever to be redeemed; therefore, it is more appropriate to recognize the income in the year following the sale than to recognize it in the year in which it becomes unreasonable to expect the coupons or tickets to be redeemed."

6. Subsection 20(7) renders paragraph 20(1)(m) inapplicable for cash basis taxpayers, and prohibits the deduction under paragraph 20(1)(m) of a reserve in respect of "guarantees, indemnities or warranties" or a reserve in respect of insurance, subject to various exceptions with which we need not concern ourselves here. In *Mister Muffler Ltd. v. M.N.R.*, [1974] F.C.J. No. 172, [1974] C.T.C. 813, 74 D.T.C. 6615 (F.C.T.D.), the court adopted a broad definition of the words "guarantees, indemnities or warranties," disallowing the deduction of a reserve for the cost of replacing defective mufflers that the taxpayer guaranteed for as long as the purchaser continued to own the car. For similar results, see *Paul Burden Ltd. v. M.N.R.*, [1981] C.T.C. 2847, 81 D.T.C. 651 (T.R.B.); *Amesbury Distributors Ltd. v. Canada*, [1984] C.T.C. 667, 85 D.T.C. 5076 (F.C.T.D.); and *Sears Canada Inc. v. Canada*, [1986] F.C.J. No. 331, [1986] 2 C.T.C. 80, 86 D.T.C. 6304 (F.C.T.D.), aff'd [1988] F.C.J. No. 1119, [1989] 1 C.T.C. 127, 89 D.T.C. 5039 (F.C.A.). For a contrasting decision in which the court distinguished *Mr. Muffler*, see *Office Concepts Ltd. v. M.N.R.*, [1986] 2 C.T.C. 2178, 86 D.T.C. 1621 (T.C.C.).

7.   Effective for 1979 and subsequent taxation years, paragraph 20(1)(m.1) permits taxpayers who are required to include amounts under paragraph 12(1)(a) to deduct:

> a reasonable amount as a reserve in respect of goods or services that it is reasonably anticipated will have to be delivered or rendered after the end of the year pursuant to an agreement for an extended warranty

>> (i)   entered into by the taxpayer with a person with whom the taxpayer was dealing at arm's length, and

>> (ii)   under which the only obligation of the taxpayer is to provide those goods or services with respect to property manufactured by the taxpayer or by a corporation related to the taxpayer,

provided that the amount of the reserve is limited to "that portion of the amount paid or payable by the taxpayer to an insurer that carries on an insurance business in Canada to insure the taxpayer's liability under the agreement ... in respect of the period after the end of the year." As a result, unlike the reserve in paragraph 20(1)(m), a reserve under paragraph 20(1)(m.1) is available only where a taxpayer actually insures this liability and incurs premium expenses in respect of this insurance.

8.   Subsection 20(24) allows a taxpayer who pays a reasonable amount to another person as consideration for the assumption of the taxpayer's obligations in respect of an amount included in the taxpayer's income under paragraph 12(1)(a) to deduct the amount of the payment, in which case the taxpayer may not deduct a reserve under paragraph 20(1)(m). Under paragraph 20(24)(b), the amount of the payment to the person assuming the taxpayer's obligations is deemed to have been received under paragraph 12(1)(a), thereby permitting this person to claim a reserve in respect of this amount under paragraph 20(1)(m).

9.   The CRA's views on the meaning of the term "reasonable amount as a reserve" in paragraph 20(1)(m) can be found in *Interpretation Bulletin* IT-154R, "Special Reserves," February 19, 1988. According to paragraph 4:

> Where subsection 20(6) is not applicable, a reasonable amount for a reserve normally is the gross proceeds received by the taxpayer, in either the current or a preceding year, in respect of those goods and services which past experience or other factors indicate will have to be delivered or provided after the end of the year. There is no need to estimate the profit on such goods or services since the reserve is not restricted to the estimated costs of the goods to be delivered or the services to be rendered.

Do you agree with this interpretation? Consider the following comments in Brian J. Arnold, *Timing and Income Taxation: The Principles of Income Measurement for Tax Purposes*, Canadian Tax Paper No. 71 (Toronto: Canadian Tax Foundation, 1983) at 275-76:

> For accounting purposes, amounts received by a taxpayer that have not yet been earned are not considered to be income. The amount received is offset on the balance sheet by a corresponding liability in respect of the obligation to deliver goods or render services in a

917

future year. At first glance, it appears that the purpose of paragraphs 12(1)(a) and 20(1)(m) is to require taxpayers to include amounts in income at the earlier of the time at which they are received and the time at which they are earned. Where a taxpayer is required to include an amount in income that is received but not earned, the reserve under paragraph 20(1)(m) will allow the estimated future cost of earning such income to be matched against the amount received. It is, however, well established by administrative practice (though not by the jurisprudence) that this is not the case. Revenue Canada takes the position [spelled out in paragraph 4 of IT-154R]. ... Therefore, the reserve under paragraph 20(1)(m) operates as a complete offset to the inclusion of the amount received in income, and the profit from the transaction is subject to tax only in the year in which it is earned. The treatment for such pre-paid amounts, therefore, is the same for income tax purposes as it is for accounting purposes.

b. Deferred Payments

Where property is sold under an agreement according to which all or some of the proceeds are not due until a subsequent accounting period, amounts receivable may be included in computing the vendor's income for the taxation year in which the property is sold under section 9 or paragraph 12(1)(b). Consequently, where the property is sold at a gain, the vendor may be required to pay tax without having received sufficient proceeds to discharge this liability. As a concession to taxpayers in these circumstances, paragraph 20(1)(n) permits taxpayers to deduct a reasonable reserve in respect of any profit from the sale. More specifically, paragraph 20(1)(n) states that:

> where an amount included in computing the taxpayer's income from the business for the year or for a preceding taxation year in respect of property sold in the course of the business is payable to the taxpayer after the end of the year and, except where the property is real property, all or part of the amount was, at the time of the sale, not due until at least 2 years after that time, [there may be deducted] a reasonable amount as a reserve in respect of such part of the amount as can reasonably be regarded as a portion of the profit from the sale.

Where an amount is deducted under paragraph 20(1)(n), the amount must be included in computing the taxpayer's income for the immediately following taxation year under subparagraph 12(1)(e)(ii). Where the requirements of paragraph 20(1)(n) are satisfied in this subsequent taxation year, the taxpayer may deduct "a reasonable amount as a reserve" in this subsequent taxation year, in which case this amount must be included in the immediately following taxation year under subparagraph 12(1)(e)(ii), and so on.

In determining the reasonable amount that a taxpayer may deduct as a reserve under paragraph 20(1)(n), courts have noted that the reserve must relate to the profit from the sale rather than the gross amount that is receivable.[124] On this basis, the revenue department has adopted the administrative position (in paragraph 10 of IT-154R) that a reasonable reserve for the purposes of this provision is generally equal to a percentage of the profit from the sale based on the ratio of the amount due in a subsequent taxation year to the aggregate

---

[124] See, for example, *M.N.R. v. Burns*, [1958] C.T.C. 51, 58 D.T.C. 1028 (Ex. Ct.) and *Makis Construction Limited v. M.N.R.*, [1972] C.T.C. 2082, 72 D.T.C. 1101 (T.R.B.).

proceeds from the sale. Expressed as a formula, this amount is determined as follows:

$$\frac{\text{Amount Due after Year}}{\text{Gross Selling Price}} \times \text{Profit} = \text{Reserve}$$

Although the Federal Court of Appeal has questioned "the application of such a precise and inflexible formula" in all circumstances,[125] this approach has been accepted in several cases.[126]

In order to qualify for the reserve under paragraph 20(1)(n), three requirements must be met. First, an amount must have been included in computing the taxpayer's income from the business for the year or a preceding taxation year. Second, the amount included must be in respect of property sold in the course of the business. Third, except where the property is real property, all or part of the amount payable must, at the time of the sale, not be due until at least two years after the time of the sale. In addition, effective for property sold after November 12, 1982, paragraph 20(8)(b) prohibits a deduction under paragraph 20(1)(n) if "the sale occurred more than 36 months before the end of the year."[127] As a result, where an amount in respect of property sold in the course of a business qualifies for a reserve under paragraph 20(1)(n), the reserve may be claimed for a maximum of four years.[128]

The requirements to qualify for a reserve under paragraph 20(1)(n) were considered in *Odyssey Industries Inc. v. Canada*, [1996] T.C.J. No. 279, [1996] 2 C.T.C. 2401, 97 D.T.C. 498 (T.C.C.).

Odyssey Industries Inc. v. Canada
[1996] T.C.J. No. 279, [1996] 2 C.T.C. 2401, 97 D.T.C. 498 (T.C.C.)

[The taxpayer corporation disposed of certain assets during the 1985 taxation year. The disposition generated a capital gain as well as recaptured depreciation. In its tax return, the taxpayer reported the gain and the recaptured depreciation, and claimed a reserve for both under paragraph 20(1)(n) on the grounds that a portion of the sale proceeds were not due until a day that was more than two

---

[125] *Canada v. Ennisclare Corporation*, [1984] F.C.J. No. 129, [1984] C.T.C. 286, 84 D.T.C. 6262 (F.C.A.), where the court refused to apply this formula to the calculation of a reasonable reserve on the sale of real property subject to a mortgage assumed by the purchaser. For another case in which the Minister's formula was rejected, see *Dunn Holdings Ltd. v. M.N.R.*, [1985] 1 C.T.C. 2348, 85 D.T.C. 348 (T.C.C.).

[126] See, for example, *M.N.R. v. Burns*, [1958] C.T.C. 51, 58 D.T.C. 1028 (Ex. Ct.), and *Felgor Investments Ltd. v. M.N.R.* (1960), 24 Tax ABC 327 (T.A.B.).

[127] For our purposes, there is no need to examine the prohibition in para. 20(8)(a).

[128] The four-year period applies only where the property is sold on the last day of the taxpayer's taxation year. Otherwise, the manner in which para. 20(8)(b) is worded limits the maximum number of years that the reserve can be claimed to three years.

years after the date of sale and after the end of the 1985 taxation year. The Minister reassessed, allowing the reserve in respect of the capital gain but denying it with respect to the recaptured depreciation. The taxpayer appealed.]

SARCHUK, JTCC: ...

Appellant's Position

Paragraph 20(1)(n) of the Act permits a taxpayer to claim a deduction for a reserve in respect of amounts which are taxable as income but not due until a later year. Three preconditions must be met under paragraph 20(1)(n) in order for the Appellant to deduct a reserve under this paragraph. First, an amount must be included in computing the taxpayer's income from the business for the year. The Appellant contends that recaptured depreciation has the same character as income from which the capital cost allowance (CCA) was deducted and given that the CCA was deducted through the course of the Appellant's business, the amount of the recapture should also be income from the business. *Minister of National Revenue v. Bessemer Trust Co.*, [1973] CTC 12, 73 DTC 5045 at page 16 (CTC 5048) (FCA); *Arnos v. R*, [1981] CTC 176, 81 DTC 5126, at pages 177-79 (CTC 5127) (FCTD); IT-73R4, paragraph 6.

With respect to the second precondition, i.e. the amount which was included in income must be in respect of property sold in the course of the business. The relevant statutory words, i.e. "in the course of the business" must be examined "in their entire context and in their grammatical and ordinary sense harmoniously with the scheme of the Act, the object of the Act and the intention of Parliament." *Stubart Investments Ltd. v. R.* ... The Appellant contends that phrases such as "regular course of the business" and "in the ordinary course of business" have a narrower meaning than "in the course of the business" and that had Parliament meant to limit the availability of paragraph 20(1)(n) to such common and ordinary transactions, it could have done so by employing the phrase "in the ordinary course of the business," which refers to transactions which are "part of the undistinguished common flow of the company's business as carried on calling for no remark and arising out of no special situations." *BC Telephone Co. v. Minister of National Revenue*, [1986] 1 CTC 2410, 86 DTC 1286, at pages 2415-16 (CTC 1290) (TCC).

The Appellant contends that given the grammatical and ordinary meaning of the words "in the course of the business" and provided the business had not terminated prior to the sale of the assets or even if the sale was coincident with the cessation of the business, such sale must have been in the course of the business. *Andreychuk v. Minister of National Revenue*, [1983] CTC 2052, 83 DTC 20, at pages 2058-59 (CTC 25-26). Accordingly, the second precondition to paragraph 20(1)(n) has been satisfied.

The third precondition is that the amount included in income or some part of that amount must be due on a day that is more than two years after the day on which the property was sold and after the end of the taxation year. This precondition has also been met since a portion of the sale proceeds of the subject assets was not due until a day that was more than two years after the day on which they were sold and after the end of the 1985 taxation year.

The requirements of paragraph 20(1)(n) having been satisfied, the next step according to the Appellant, is to determine what portion of the amount included in income may reasonably be regarded as "a portion of the profit from the sale." Since profit is not defined in the Act, it must be determined using ordinary commercial principles. Under GAAP, profit is a synonym for income and is the excess of proceeds of sale of an asset over its book value. Under GAAP, on the disposition of a capital asset, the difference between the net proceeds on disposal and the net carrying amount is recognized in income in the period in which it is disposed of and for this purpose, the net carrying amount is equal to the original cost of the asset, less accumulated depreciation. In determining income for the purposes of the Act, the system of depreciation of capital assets which is used for financial statement purposes is replaced by the CCA system; both of these systems have as their purpose the deduction of the cost of capital assets computing income of the enterprise over a period of time (*Bessemer Trust Co., supra*). The income tax equivalent of the financial accounting concept of net carrying amount of a prescribed class of assets is the undepreciated capital cost of that class; undepreciated capital cost is the basis for the measurement of recaptured depreciation and it is submitted by the Appellant that undepreciated capital cost is the appropriate base from which to measure profit on the sale of depreciable property.

The Appellant's position is that it has established its entitlement to the reserve under paragraph 20(1)(n) of the Act. Since the recaptured depreciation is a component of the profit from the sale of the assets for this purpose, it is submitted that the amount of the reserve claimed may reasonably be regarded as a portion of the profit from the sale. Thus the method of calculation of the amount of the reserve claimed under paragraph 20(1)(n) of the Act was correctly done in accordance with the policies accepted and published by the Minister of National Revenue.

Respondent's Position

The Respondent's position is that the reserve provisions of paragraph 20(1)(n) do not apply to the recaptured depreciation when the sale has not been made "in the course of a business," as it is only in such case that a reserve is permitted by that paragraph. *Avril Holdings Ltd. v. Minister of National Revenue*, [1970] CTC 572, 70 DTC 6366 (SCC), at page 575-76 (CTC 6369). The assets in issue were not sold in the course of the Appellant's business.

The context of the *Income Tax Act* in which paragraph 20(1)(n) appears is important because the Act separates the taxation of income and the taxation of capital gains and in the present appeal, a reserve for the capital gains portion was in fact allowed. [In computing a taxpayer's gain from the disposition of capital property, clause 40(1)(a)(iii)(C) allows taxpayers to deduct "a reasonable amount as a reserve in respect of such of the proceeds of disposition of the property that are payable to the taxpayer after the end of the year as can reasonably be regarded as a portion of the [gain otherwise] determined." This provision is examined in chapter 6.] The Act defines the term "depreciable property" to mean assets for which a taxpayer is entitled to capital cost allowance. Depreciable property by definition is capital property. According to the *CICA Handbook*, the definition of a capital asset is that which is not sold in the course of business. The Respondent contends that the *Income Tax Act* recognizes the distinction between capital and non-capital property, the common example of the latter being inventory. Furthermore, the phrase "in the course of business" in paragraph 20(1)(n) of the Act is a reference to a sale which is a sale of inventory in a general sense and not the sale of a capital asset. The word "profit" is generally associated with non-capital property while the word "gain" is used with respect to capital property. The "property" contemplated by paragraph 20(1)(n) of the Act is not a reference to capital property.

The Respondent further contends that recaptured depreciation is not "profit from the sale," it is merely the calculated accumulation of an unwarranted charge made by the taxpayer. "Profit from the sale" would be the difference between the cost of the property sold and the amount for which it was sold, not the difference between the net depreciation value and the amount of the sale. The profit is the capital gain on the sale of the asset, unless it is established that the taxpayer in question was in the business of buying and selling such assets. The fact that the excess is brought into income by virtue of subsection 13(1) of the Act does not turn it into a "profit" for the purposes of paragraph 20(1)(n) of the Act (*Andreychuk, supra*, at pages 2059-60 (CTC 26)).

Last, it is the Respondent's position that GAAP has no application in the present case. If this were a question of quantum then such expert accounting evidence is relevant. It is however not relevant and of no assistance to the Court in determining the essential nature of the recapture and GAAP is not relevant in determining whether a receipt or expense is on revenue or capital account.

Conclusion

The Appellant, a corporation carrying on the business of providing freezer processing and warehousing facilities disposed of depreciable property of a prescribed class in its 1985 taxation year. The proceeds of disposition from the sale of the property exceeded both the adjusted cost basis (ACB) and the undepreciated capital cost (UCC) of the property. Accordingly, there was a capital gain from the dispositions which the Appellant reported after having deducted a reserve under subparagraph 40(1)(a)(iii) of the Act. The reserve claimed was allowed by the Minister. There was also a recapture of depreciation which the Appellant included in computing its income by virtue of subsection 13(1) of the Act and with respect to which it claimed a reserve pursuant to paragraph 20(1)(n) of the Act. The Minister disallowed the reserve on the recaptured depreciation.

The issue to be determined is whether the Appellant is entitled to claim the amount of $9,653,200 as a reserve pursuant to paragraph 20(1)(n) of the Act with respect to the recaptured depreciation taken into income under subsection 13(1) of the Act.

...

The Appellant's position is based on the proposition that recaptured depreciation is an element of profit for income tax purposes just as the gain on disposition of the same assets is an element of profit for financial statement purposes, even though the timing of recognition of the two amounts may differ due to differing methods of computation. It is in this context that the Appellant relied most heavily on the testimony of the expert witness, Casano.

I am not satisfied that the testimony of Casano is, or should be, determinative of the question which in this case is whether the excess recaptured depreciation brought into income by virtue of subsection 13(1) of the Act is profit for the purpose of paragraph 20(1)(n) of the Act. In my view, this question is ultimately one of law for the Court.

...

I am unable to accept the proposition advanced by the Appellant since the relevant language and in particular the word "excess" found in subsection 13(1) of the Act and the word "profit" in paragraph 20(1)(n) of the Act are not synonymous. They are terms that are used in the Act to achieve a specific legislative purpose. Subsection 13(1) of the Act was considered by D.E. Taylor, a Member of the Tax Review Board (as he then was), in *Andreychuk, supra*. He said at page 2060 (CTC 26):

> The critical word in subsection 13(1) (which brings the amount into income) is "excess," in the final phrase, "the excess shall be included in computing the income ..." The corresponding critical word in paragraph 20(1)(n) under which the taxpayer seeks relief is "profit," found in the last phrase "profit from the sale." In my analysis of the situation, the "recaptured depreciation" is not profit from the sale, it is not profit in any sense of the word — it is simply the calculated accumulation of an unwarranted charge made by the taxpayer, the quantity of which always existed but was determined only by virtue of the sale. But it is not "profit from the sale." In fact, it has nothing to do with the sale of the property, other than that the sale provides a number required in making the calculation for the excess depreciation charged. The "profit from the sale" would be the difference between the cost of the property sold and the amount for which it was sold, not the difference between the net depreciated value and the amount of the sale. Simply put, the profit is the capital gain on the sale of the asset, unless it is established that the taxpayer in question was in the business of buying and selling such assets. The fact that the "excess" is brought into income by virtue of subsection 13(1) of the Act does not turn it into a "profit" for purposes of paragraph 20(1)(n) of the Act. They are simply not interchangeable terms under these circumstances as would be necessary in order for the appellant to succeed. As I see it, therefore, the bar to the utilization of paragraph 20(1)(n) with respect to recaptured depreciation taken into income under subsection 13(1) of the Act may not arise out of the juxtaposition and comparative definitions of "going out of business" and "in the course of the business," nor out of the mere logic of such a disallowance, but rather out of the precise terminology used by the legislators in those two sections, particularly the words "excess" and "profit."

Notwithstanding the forceful submissions of counsel for the Appellant, I have not been convinced that the Judgment in *Andreychuk* was wrong. The reasons advanced therein constitute a clear and correct interpretation of the provisions of the Act in issue before me and I propose to adopt them. In my view, the recapture of the excess is merely a counterbalance to what are considered to have been excessive deductions of capital cost allowance on the asset in question that were made in computing the taxpayer's income for previous years. While there is substantial logic in the legislators' intent to require the inclusion of such amounts back into a taxpayer's income, it does not follow that these amounts constitute a "profit from the sale" for the purpose of paragraph 20(1)(n) of the Act.

For the foregoing reasons, the appeal is dismissed with costs to the Respondent.

Appeal dismissed.

NOTES AND QUESTIONS

1. On what basis did the taxpayer in *Odyssey Industries* argue that the reserve provided in paragraph 20(1)(n) should be available for recaptured depreciation under subsection 13(1)? How would the taxpayer have computed the reserve? Why did the court reject this argument? Do you agree with the court's interpretation? Why or why not?

2. In *Riverview Development (Ottawa) Ltd. v. M.N.R.*, [1967] Tax ABC 115 (T.A.B.), the taxpayer, which sold a 97-lot subdivision to an affiliated company, sought to deduct as a reserve under then paragraph 85B(1)(d) (now paragraph 20(1)(n)) an amount of $50,000 that it undertook in the sale agreement to "withhold from its profit" as "a fund against which the purchaser shall have recourse in the event that the cost of servicing ... should exceed $1,700 per lot" (at para. 14). Concluding that paragraph 85B(1)(d) was inapplicable where the payment had been received, the board characterized the amount as a contingent reserve the deduction of which was prohibited under then paragraph 12(1)(e) (now paragraph 18(1)(e)).

3. In *Earthquake Enterprises Inc. v. M.N.R.*, [1985] 1 C.T.C. 2387, 85 D.T.C. 352 (T.C.C.), the taxpayer, which was engaged in a business of land development and construction, sold real property on August 3, 1979 in exchange for a mortgage payable on demand, which by an amending mortgage dated September 2, 1980 became due and payable on September 2, 2000. Concluding that the debt, being payable on demand under the 1979 mortgage, was owing and payable and thus due in the 1980 taxation year, the court disallowed the deduction of a reserve under paragraph 20(1)(n) in computing the taxpayer's income for its 1980 taxation year.

4. In *Canada v. Esskay Farms Ltd.*, [1976] C.T.C. 24, 76 D.T.C. 6010 (F.C.T.D.), the taxpayer, which carried on a business of buying and selling real estate, received an offer from the city of Calgary to purchase 177 acres of land

for $247,000, of which the taxpayer requested $100,000 in 1976 and the balance in 1977. Since the city was precluded by statute from purchasing land over a period of years, the taxpayer agreed to sell the land to a trust company for the same price, payable in 1976 and 1977 with 7.5 per cent interest, which sold the land to the city for $247,000 cash. In computing its income for its 1976 taxation year, the taxpayer included the total amount receivable but deducted a reserve under paragraph 20(1)(n) in respect of a portion of the profit from the sale. Rejecting the Minister's argument, *inter alia*, that the trust company acted as the taxpayer's agent, the court held that the transaction was legally effective and not a sham and allowed the deduction.

5.   Where all or some of the proceeds from the sale of property are not due until a subsequent taxation year, it may be reasonable to regard a portion of these proceeds as interest within the meaning of subsection 16(1). See the analysis of this provision in section III.E.2 of this chapter.

c. Doubtful Debts

Subparagraph 20(1)(l)(i) allows taxpayers to claim as a reserve "a reasonable amount in respect of doubtful debts (other than a debt to which subparagraph (ii) applies) that have been included in computing the taxpayer's income for the year or a preceding taxation year." Subparagraph 20(1)(l)(ii) allows a reserve in respect of impaired loans or lending assets of a financial institution or moneylender "made or acquired by the taxpayer in the ordinary course of the taxpayer's business of insurance or the lending of money." For our purposes, there is no need to examine subparagraph 20(1)(l)(ii) in any detail.[129]

Where an amount is deducted under paragraph 20(1)(l), the amount must be included in computing the taxpayer's income for the immediately following taxation year under subparagraph 12(1)(d). Where the requirements of paragraph 20(1)(l) are satisfied in this subsequent taxation year, the taxpayer may deduct "a reasonable amount" as a reserve in respect of doubtful debts in this subsequent taxation year, in which case this amount must be included in computing the taxpayer's income in the immediately following taxation year under subparagraph 12(1)(d), and so on.

The availability of a reserve for doubtful debts was considered in *Coppley Noyes & Randall Ltd. v. M.N.R.*, [1991] F.C.J. No. 347, [1991] 1 C.T.C. 541, 91 D.T.C. 5291 (F.C.T.D.).

---

[129] For cases in which the availability of a reserve for doubtful debts has turned on whether loans were made "in the ordinary course of the taxpayer's business" of moneylending, see *Canada v. Pollock Sokoloff Holdings Corp.*, [1976] F.C.J. No. 52, [1976] C.T.C. 349, 76 D.T.C. 6181 (F.C.A.); *Highfield Corp. v. M.N.R.*, [1982] C.T.C. 2813, 82 D.T.C. 1835 (T.R.B.); *Muttart Industries Ltd. v. M.N.R.*, [1986] 1 C.T.C. 2373, 86 D.T.C. 1301 (T.C.C.); and *Akhtar v. Canada*, [1998] T.C.J. No. 416, [1998] 3 C.T.C. 2888 (T.C.C.).

Coppley Noyes & Randall Ltd. v. M.N.R.
[1991] F.C.J. No. 347, [1991] 1 C.T.C. 541, 91 D.T.C. 5291 (F.C.T.D.)

REED J: The issue in this case is whether the plaintiff's claim that a reserve of $3,084,000 for doubtful debts for its 1982 taxation year is reasonable, as required by paragraph 20(1)(l) of the *Income Tax Act*, RSC 1952, c. 148 (am. SC 1970-71-72, c. 63) (the "Act"). ...

Taxpayer's Assessment

... The plaintiff is in the business of manufacturing high quality men's clothing. It also does some importing of this type of clothing and in 1982 dealt in some items of ladies' wear as well. A substantial part of the plaintiff's business involves and involved, selling clothing to small independently owned retail shops specializing in the sale of quality men's wear. These were described as being typically "one-man shows" with the owner retailer being in the business because of his love of fine clothes. These businesses are often under capitalized, lack business experience and are very vulnerable to setbacks arising as a result of the individual characteristics of the owner retailer (e.g., lack of health) as well from negative economic conditions generally.

The plaintiff's year end is November 30. It prepares its financial statements and tax returns in the following March and April. For the purposes of both its financial statements and its tax returns for the 1982 year, Coppley Noyes reviewed its November 27, 1982 accounts receivable as of February 25, 1983. An estimate was made, as of that date, as to whether repayment of an account was doubtful and if so, the amount which should be recorded as a reserve for the fiscal year ending November 30, 1982. The February date was chosen not only because of its proximity to the date when financial statements and tax returns were prepared, but also because it approximates the end of a natural business cycle in the men's retail clothing industry. By that time of the year, fall and winter clothing (shipped and sold by the plaintiff to its retail customers in the summer and fall of the previous year) had usually been sold by the retailers; retailers who had unsold fall and winter inventory as of February of a given year would carry that inventory over to the following fall season.

The plaintiff assessed its accounts receivable by first looking at the age of its overdue accounts. It identified all those which had been owing as of November 27, 1982 and which were still owing as of February 25, 1983. In the plaintiff's experience there was a significant co-relation between a retail customer's inability to pay for fall-winter goods by the end of February and the likelihood that the customer was in financial difficulty. In 1983 this led to the identification of 145 accounts.

The plaintiff allowed its customers credit terms of 30 days from shipment for made to measure items (which comprised five per cent to ten per cent of the plaintiff's business) and 60 days from shipment for all other items. Thus, by February 25, 1983, the goods covered by the 145 overdue accounts would have been shipped, in the case of made to measure goods no later than 120 days earlier, and in the case of all other goods, no later than 150 days earlier.

After identifying the 145 accounts, the senior officers of the plaintiff (Mr. McWhinnie and Mr. Enkin) reviewed each individual account to determine whether, in their view, there was a real risk that the account would not be paid and if so, what amount should be included in the plaintiff's financial statements as a reserve therefor. In determining the degree of risk, the factors taken into account included the age of the overdue account, the customer's financial position including debts owed to the bank and others, the history if any, of NSF cheques on the account, whether the customer's sales were increasing or decreasing, the personal characteristics of the customer such as health, work ethic, ability to retain staff, the particular local conditions pertinent to the customer and whether amounts had been paid on the account since November 27, 1982. The plaintiff had credit files on each customer, in which it kept copies of the customer's financial statements, any credit reports that might exist (such as Dun and Bradstreet reports), reports on visits to the customer which had been made by Mr. Enkin, Mr. McWhinnie or others and information which might have been gleaned from the plaintiff's salesmen. In February of 1983, the assessment of the accounts receivable was done in the context of the recession which existed at that time. The recession started in 1980 and was particularly severe in the west where a number of the plaintiff's customers were located. Mr. McWhinnie's evidence was that in recessionary times men's clothing stores are particularly hard hit and that in 1981 in the west, sales in speciality shops dropped in some cases as much as 40 to 50 per cent. All 145 accounts which had been identified were determined to fall within the doubtful category.

In estimating the amount which should be allocated as a reserve for doubtful accounts, the plaintiff took into consideration the factors listed above as well as the amount the plaintiff might hope to realize (cents on the dollar) if the customer went bankrupt (referred to as the break-up value of the account). As has been noted, it took into account any amounts which had been paid by the customer between November 27, 1982 and February 25, 1983 ("since payments"). It also took into account whether additional amounts had become due from that particular customer between November 27, 1982 and February 25, 1983. The estimate of the reserve for each customer was a judgment call on the part of Mr. Enkin and Mr. McWhinnie. There was no precise formula applied.

Despite the fact that a customer was significantly in arrears the plaintiff, in general, continued to ship goods to that customer. This was true even in the case of next season's goods. The next season's goods had usually been specifically ordered by the customer some time previously and could not easily be placed elsewhere. More importantly however, since in many instances, the plaintiff was the customer's principal supplier, if further goods were not shipped the customer would with certainty be put out of business. Thus, continued shipments kept the possibility of repayment of the doubtful account alive. In addition, the business philosophy of Mr. Enkin, who had built the Coppley Noyes business since its purchase by the Enkin family in the early 1950s, was to extend extensive credit to fledgling or struggling retail stores. His business policy was to provide financial as well as business advice and assistance to these stores. It was Mr. Enkin's view that by sharing the business risk with these trade customers, he would encourage the development of retail businesses which would provide an increasing market for the plaintiff's products. This policy, while it would appear to have been a successful business policy, meant that the plaintiff extended credit to its customers far beyond what might normally be considered prudent.

In any event, the plaintiff's practice of assessing its November 1982 reserve for accounts receivable by reference not only to the payments received between November 27, 1982 and February 25, 1983 but also to amounts which had subsequently become overdue during that period meant that the amount of the reserve thus determined exceeded what it would have been, had only the former been taken into account.

...

The evidence establishes that the practice of estimating a reserve by reference not only to amounts paid after year end but also to amounts which become due after that date, is in accordance with generally accepted accounting principles.

...

I should note, as well, that the plaintiff's practice with respect to bad debt write-offs was to carry debts as receivables long after many businesses would have classified them as bad. The claimant was not quick to place accounts receivable in the bad debt category.

The plaintiff's procedure for assessing its reserve for doubtful debts for the 1982 taxation year was no different from that which it had followed in preceding years. The defendant had reassessed the plaintiff with respect to its 1976 and 1979 taxation years. The plaintiff appealed those reassessments and the dispute was settled in 1980 with the Minister agreeing that a reserve of $1,000,000 was appropriate for the 1976 year and $1,250,000 was appropriate for the 1979 taxation year. The taxpayer had claimed $1,533,800 and $2,003,000 respectively for those years; the latter amounts appear as reserves for doubtful accounts in the plaintiff's audited financial statements.

The amount agreed upon by the Minister and the plaintiff for the 1979 taxation year was $753,000 less than the amount which appeared in the taxpayer's audited financial statements for that year. The taxpayer reduced the reserves claimed for tax purposes each year subsequent to 1979, to an amount which was also $753,000 below the reserve appearing in its financial statements. Thus, for the 1982 taxation year, while the amount for doubtful debts which appeared in the plaintiff's audited financial statements and which is claimed in this litigation was $3,084,000, the amount which was included by the taxpayer in its 1982 tax return was $2,331,000.

Minister's Assessment

The defendant, through the instrumentality of the Minister of National Revenue, reassessed the plaintiff for its 1982 taxation year and allowed $1,400,000 for doubtful debts. As counsel for the Minister argues, the burden is on the taxpayer to disprove not only the Minister's assumptions (one of which, in this case, is that $1,400,000 is a reasonable allowance) but also to prove that the plaintiff's estimate is reasonable.

There seems little doubt that if GAAP apply to a determination of the amount of the reserve in question, then, the taxpayer has met both burdens. Mr. Luciani, the Department of National Revenue auditor started, first of all, with a comparison of the plaintiff's bad debt history: the amounts written off in a year as compared to the accounts receivable at the beginning of that year. It was his view that this type of comparison, over a period of years, would give a ratio which could be applied to the 1982 accounts receivable for the purpose of determining what would be a reasonable reserve for doubtful debts. This comparison was done for a six-year period; a ratio was obtained and applied to the 1982 accounts. This resulted in a figure of $285,000 being determined. The defendant's auditor regarded this as too low and abandoned that approach.

...

I would note that the reserve for doubtful debts claimed by the taxpayer had historically been much much larger than its bad debt write-off experience in the following tax year. For example, the reserve claimed in the 1981 taxation year was $2,235,000; the plaintiff's bad debt write-offs in 1982 were $510,840. The taxpayer's bad debt write-offs in 1983 were not quantitatively different than they had been in 1982. It was this difference between the plaintiff's bad debt history and the amounts included as a reserve for doubtful debts which prompted Mr. Luciani to review the plaintiff's 1982 reserve.

...

In any event, the defendant's auditor, having abandoned the idea of estimating a reasonable amount for doubtful debts on the basis of the ratio described above, turned to a review of the actual accounts the taxpayer had identified in February 1983 as being doubtful. Mr. Luciani's review was done in September 1983. He took into account any payments which had been made on the respective accounts after February 25, 1983 and up to September 30, 1983, as well as those made between November 27, 1982 and February 25, 1983. The former was, of course, information not available to the taxpayer when it prepared its financial statements and tax returns in the previous March and April.

Mr. Luciani was strongly influenced by the fact that the plaintiff had shipped new goods to the customers despite the fact that those accounts had been classified as doubtful by the plaintiff. Mr. Luciani considered this to be evidence that the plaintiff expected those accounts to be paid. In his view, when new goods had been shipped to customers, amounts with respect to those accounts should not have been included in computing the reserve for doubtful debts.

In preparing his estimate, Mr. Luciani looked primarily at whether there had been continued trading activity on the account and whether the customer had paid any further amounts to the plaintiff up to September 30, 1983. If the amount owing on fall goods as of November 27, 1982 had been paid off as of September 30, 1983, no reserve was allowed for that account regardless of whether additional amounts had become due on the account during the period. If an account was still active as of September 30, 1983 and the amount owing on fall goods as of November 27, 1982 had not been paid off, a reserve was allowed for the amount which was still owing. If, in Mr. Luciani's view, it was clear that the customer was unable to pay his account as of September 30, 1983, then, an amount somewhat higher than the unpaid portion of the November 1982 receivable was allowed.

Mr. Luciani's review of the plaintiff's accounts was admittedly subjective (as any such estimate must be). He determined that $1,368,000 was a reasonable reserve for tax purposes. This was subsequently rounded up to $1,400,000. Mr. Luciani admits that his assessment was not based on the same knowledge of the accounts that the plaintiff had and that he did not consider factors such as the break-up value of the account to the plaintiff. He did not talk to the officers of the taxpayer to ascertain why had they had included reserves with respect to certain accounts even though he admitted that the taxpayer's officers would be in the best position to evaluate the risk of non collection associated with an account. He had no knowledge of the particular business in which the plaintiff was engaged. He admitted that the amount outstanding on fall goods as of February 25, 1983 was of doubtful collectibility. Mr. Luciani's view is that the estimating of a reserve for tax purposes differs from the estimating of a reserve for financial statements purposes.

Legal Principles Applicable

The general principles applicable to the calculation of income for tax purposes, and to the interpretation of the *Income Tax Act*, are that they should be consonant with ordinary commercial and accounting principles and practices unless the *Income Tax Act* requires otherwise.

...

Thus, in determining a reserve for doubtful debts, the principles and factors that are used for the preparation of financial statements, as governed by the generally accepted accounting principles approved by the Canadian Institute of Chartered Accountants, are applicable, unless: (1) the *Income Tax Act* expressly requires otherwise or (2) the *Income Tax Act* implicitly requires otherwise. There is no definition of doubtful debts or other express provision in the *Income Tax Act* which requires a departure from GAAP in the circumstances of the present case. If a departure is required that result must arise because of a conflict of GAAP with other provisions or with the overall intent of the *Income Tax Act*.

Both counsel agree that the senior management of a corporate taxpayer is in the best position to determine, from its inspection of the company's accounts receivable, which accounts are likely to give rise to difficulty and might be of doubtful collection: *Atlas Steels Ltd. v. M.N.R.* (1961), 27 Tax ABC 331; 61 CTC 547 (TAB) at 334 (CTC 550) and *Kenora Miner and News Ltd. v. M.N.R.*, [1970] Tax ABC 337; 70 CTC 1228 (TAB). As counsel for the defendant stated, if this were not the case, the company would be in a sorry state indeed.

The jurisprudence which exists with respect to estimating reserves for doubtful debts, for tax purposes, indicates that delay in payment alone is not sufficient to justify including an amount in a reserve: *No. 409 v. M.N.R.* (1957), 16 Tax ABC 409; 57 CTC 136 (TAB). Among the factors which may be taken into consideration in estimating a reserve are the time element (the age of the overdue account), the history of the account, the financial position of the client, any increase or decrease in the client's total sales, the taxpayer's past bad debt experience, the general business condition in the country and the business condition in the particular locality: *No. 81 v. M.N.R.* (1953), 8 Tax ABC 82; 53 CTC 98 (TAB).

It is conceded that in order for an amount to be included as a reserve for doubtful debts there has to be more than just some doubt that the account might not be paid: *Picadilly Hotels Ltd. v. The Queen*, [1978] CTC 658; 78 CTC 6444 (FCTD). The decision in *No. 81 v. M.N.R.*, *supra*, rejected the assertion that every debt which is overdue is a doubtful one against which a reserve must be set up; see also *Brignall v. M.N.R.* (1961), 27 Tax ABC 233; 61 CTC 488 (TAB). There must be good and substantial reason to question the likelihood that the account will be paid. The Interpretation Bulletin issued by the Minister of National Revenue (No. IT-442, paragraph 22) describes the test as follows:

> For a debt to be classed as a bad debt there must be evidence that it has in fact become uncollectible. For a debt to be included in a reserve for doubtful debts it is sufficient that there be reasonable doubt about the collectibility of it. ...

In *Highfield Corporation Ltd. v. M.N.R.*, [1982] CTC 2812; 82 CTC 1835 (TAB) at 2828 (CTC 1847), it was said:

> A "Reserve for doubtful debts" established under section 20(1)(l) of the Act would seem to leave with the taxpayer a much greater degree of flexibility in using business judgment with regard to the inclusion of amounts in such a reserve than is permitted to a taxpayer in claiming a deduction under section 20(1)(p) of the Act for a "bad debt." The term "doubtful debt" in itself can mean only what it says   the debt is owing and possible of collection, but that possibility is not sufficiently certain in the mind of the taxpayer that he wishes to be placed in the disadvantageous position of having to pay income tax thereon before that possibility has become more of a certainty.

If there is a reasonable doubt that an account is not collectible, the degree of doubt is expressed as a proportion of the total debt taken as a reserve. In that sense the amount included in a reserve with respect to any given account is an estimate of the risk that the account will not ultimately be paid.

In *MacDonald Engineering Projects Ltd. v. M.N.R.*, [1987] 2 CTC 2237; 87 CTC 545 (TCC), the treatment of amounts paid on doubtful debts after year end but before a taxpayer filed his income tax return was in issue. The CTC headnote describes the decision:

> The Court found that the sum of approximately $35,600, which was actually paid before the taxpayer filed its tax return for the 1982 taxation year, could not reasonably be regarded as forming part of the reserve. However, in view of the general economic climate that existed at the time and in view of the history of the customer's accounts, the balance of the debt was properly regarded as doubtful.

This is consonant with normal accounting procedures which require that in preparing financial statements all current information be considered.

There is no jurisprudence dealing directly with the type of circumstances at issue in this case.

Defendant's Representation

The defendant's main contention is that what constitutes a reasonable reserve for doubtful debts for tax purposes differs from what is considered to be a reasonable amount for financial statement purposes. That is, while ... for financial statement purposes two factors should enter into the assessment, namely, the portion of the November 28, 1982 receivables that will not be collected and the eventual probable loss that will occur as a result of the policy of continued selling, it is argued that for tax purposes only the first is applicable.

...

Counsel for the Minister argues that GAAP expressly contemplates that a different regime will be used for tax purposes than is used in preparing financial statements. Paragraph 3020.14 of *CICA Handbook* states:

> The allowance [for doubtful debts] should be determined in accordance with generally accepted accounting principles regardless of how the allowance is determined for taxation purposes.

This admonition does not support the argument which it is sought to make. All that paragraph 3020.14 says is that the two reserves may differ but not that they must differ. This is entirely consistent with paragraph 24 of the Minister's Interpretation Bulletin IT-442 which provides that a taxpayer may claim an amount as a reserve that is less than the total amount which may be claimed and that that lesser amount will still be viewed as "reasonable." The Minister's Interpretation Bulletins, of course, are not authorities. Reference to them is made in these reasons only for the purpose of setting out the position which the Minister has taken in those publications. I do not consider them to be determinative of the issues which they address.

It is argued that GAAP are not applicable for tax purposes, when estimating a reserve, in a case such as the present, because under those principles a reserve can be claimed for a contingency. It is argued that GAAP allows a reserve to be claimed with respect to an anticipated loss that might occur two, three or five years later while for tax purposes only losses which are expected to occur in the immediate future can be considered. As I understand this argument, it is that for tax purposes the expectation of loss has to be more immediate and carry a higher degree of probability than is the case under GAAP. In addition, it is argued that the bad debt history of the taxpayer, while it might have limited relevance for financial statement purposes, has much greater significance for tax purposes. It is argued that, in this case, the fact that the taxpayer continued to ship goods to outstanding accounts after year end is very significant and indicates that the taxpayer expected the amounts outstanding on those accounts to be paid.

I have some difficulty with these conclusions. While counsel argues that under GAAP an allowance can be claimed for a contingency, the Interpretation Bulletin IT-442 indicates that this is equally the purpose of paragraph 20(1)(l):

> 21. Paragraph 20(1)(l), which authorizes a deduction in respect of doubtful debts of the kind described therein, is an exception to the general rule set out in paragraph 18(1)(e) that a deduction may not be claimed for losses that are contingent in nature. ...

In *Day & Ross v. The Queen*, [1976] CTC 707; 76 CTC 6433 (FCTD), it was held that a "reserve" in paragraph 12(1)(e) of the pre-1972 *Income Tax Act* (now paragraph 18(1)(e)) denotes the setting aside of an amount to meet a contingency, an unascertainable and indefinite event which may or may not occur. I have been referred to no authority or convincing argument which leads me to conclude that the test for estimating a reserve for doubtful debts has to be more restrictive and carry a higher probability of risk than is the case in applying GAAP. I am not convinced that an assessment of the taxpayer's real profit for a year is more accurately determined by assessing the reserve claimed without reference to ... the eventual probable loss that will occur because of the "continued sales to past due accounts" ... , than it is by reference to both factors which he considered should be taken into account in this taxpayer's case.

Also, I can not conclude from the evidence that the plaintiff's reserve was set up in anticipation of losses which it was thought would occur two, three, or five years down the road rather than during the 1983 year. The plaintiff simply did not know whether or when a doubtful debt would become a bad debt. In fact, given the recession which existed at that time (which was less severe in September 1983 when Mr. Luciani did his assessment than it was in February and March 1983) an earlier rather than a later date was more likely.

With respect to the conclusion the defendant seeks to draw from the post-year-end shipment of goods to customers, I have no doubt that the plaintiff hoped the accounts would be paid. Also, there is no doubt that the taxpayer shipped further goods to the customers for the purpose of avoiding immediate loss and to keep the possibility of repayment of those accounts alive. I do not conclude, however, that the accounts should not have been classified as doubtful. Indeed, at least part of the test which Mr. Luciani applied seems more akin to the identification of bad debts rather than doubtful debts.

Two other arguments made by the defendant must also be considered: the plaintiff identified doubtful accounts solely by reference to slowness of payment and the jurisprudence indicates that slow payment does not equate to doubtful debts; secondly, accountants proceed on the basis of a principle of conservatism, when calculating profits, and this is not appropriate in calculating income for tax purposes. With respect to the first, I could not conclude that the plaintiff's assessment was made solely on the basis of the age of the accounts in question. The evidence establishes that other considerations also entered into the plaintiff's identification of the doubtful accounts. With respect to the argument based on the "conservatism principle," this is too general a consideration to allow me to draw the kind of specific conclusion therefrom which the defendant would wish. In addition, ... that principle is always constrained by the requirement that financial statements fairly reflect the financial position of the company.

Amount of the Reserve

What then of the reasonableness of the plaintiff's estimate of the amount identified as a reserve for doubtful debts? Even if the correct principles have been chosen, the Minister argues that these were incorrectly applied. In addition, it is argued that it is not sufficient to demonstrate that Mr. Luciani applied wrong principles in assessing what would be an appropriate amount as a reserve for doubtful debts, but that the actual amount which was determined $1,400,000 must also be proven to be unreasonable.

Counsel for the defendant argues that I cannot refer this case back for a reassessment without identifying the exact figure which should be used as a reserve for the purposes of calculating the taxpayer's 1982 reserve for doubtful debts. He argues that to do otherwise would only encourage further litigation.

The Minister challenges the plaintiff's estimate of the reserve, $3,084,000, on the ground that it exceeds the amount outstanding on fall goods, in the 145 accounts, as of February 25, 1983. The total amount owing on the 145 accounts as of November 27, 1982 had been $4,537,900. The amount owing on these same accounts as of February 25, 1983 was $3,373,053. If the amount owing, as of February 25, 1983 is calculated so as to include all payments made on the accounts subsequent to November 27, 1982 but exclude all additional amounts which had become owing during that period then the February 25, 1983 balance would be $2,695,122 (amount outstanding on fall goods as of February 25, 1983).

The Minister argues that the estimated reserve must be adjusted downward from the amount it would have been at year end, as a result of amounts which have been paid by a customer between November 27, 1982 and February 25, 1983, but the reserve cannot be adjusted upward as a result of any additional amounts which became due during that same period. It is argued that this follows because the reserve allowed under paragraph 20(1)(l) is with respect to amounts which have already been included [a]s income. The plaintiff does not dispute the fact that "since" payments must result in a diminution of the amount of the reserve which would otherwise have been claimed. It claims, however, that it is equally entitled to take into account the fact that further debts have arisen on those same accounts.

As I understand it, the reserve for doubtful debts under paragraph 20(1)(l) must be adjusted downward as a result of amounts paid after November 27, 1982 because accounting principles require that all current information be taken into account when preparing financial statements subsequent to year end. Equally, it seems to me subsequent information concerning additional overdue amounts with respect to those same accounts should also be considered, as it is for financial statement purposes. In my view, it would be inconsistent to require a taxpayer to take into account after acquired information of one kind, but not of another. Conceptually, the reserve for doubtful debts relates to accounts receivable as of year end. The after acquired information, as I understand it, is used to assess the degree of risk attached to the collection of those accounts. The assessment of the accounts which is done subsequent to year end is not a recalculation of the amount which was owing at year end, as of a later period of time but an estimate of the degree of risk attached to the collection of the account. On that basis, I cannot conclude that because the reserve exceeds the amount outstanding on fall goods as of February 25, 1983, that the reserve is unreasonable. In addition, a finding that the amount of the reserve must never exceed the amount outstanding as of the date of the post-year-end review would mean that the "cap" thereby imposed would vary depending upon whether financial statements and tax returns were filed immediately on year end or one, two, three or six months later.

The plaintiff's estimate, as has been noted is $3,084,000. [One expert witness] gave evidence that the correct accounting principles and procedures had been used. He did not consider whether the estimate reached by the plaintiff was reasonable (for accounting purposes). [Another expert witness] gave evidence that the correct accounting principles and procedures had been used and that in his view a reasonable amount for a reserve would be within the range of 2.6 million to 3.0/3.1 million. His precise estimate had been $2,862,000.

...

I turn then to the Minister's estimate. As has already been indicated, I cannot conclude that it was based on proper principles. Too heavy a burden was placed on the taxpayer by concluding that, because goods were shipped after year end, the accounts to which those goods related could not be doubtful. The wrong principle was applied in refusing to consider all post-year-end information (the increased amounts owing after November 27, 1982 as well as amounts that had been paid on those accounts) when estimating the risk associated with collecting those accounts. Also, in my view, I have a serious doubt as to whether it is appropriate to take into account, when reassessing a taxpayer in circumstances such as the present, information not available to the taxpayer at the time that estimate was made. At the very least, such after acquired information must be used sparingly. In the present case, the economic outlook was brighter by September 1983 than it had been in February and March.

Although counsel may be right in saying that it is not enough to prove that the Minister's assessment proceeded on wrong principles or without taking into account all factors relevant to the method chosen, it is not open to a Court, in my view, to subjectively choose the Minister's assessment over that of the taxpayer's in the absence of an evidentiary basis establishing the appropriateness of the method the Minister used in reaching the assessment, or the appropriateness of some other method which would lead to approximately the same estimate. No direct evidence was called by the defendant in this case to support her position. Consequently, the Court is left with a situation in which, as between the taxpayer's and the Minister's estimates, the evidence leads to the conclusion that the taxpayer's estimate was appropriate.

...

Conclusion

I have not been persuaded in the circumstances of this case that the generally accepted accounting principles which are used for calculating doubtful accounts for financial statement purposes should not be followed for the purposes of paragraph 20(1)(l) of the *Income Tax Act*. There is no express requirement that a modification to those principles be adopted. There is no implied requirement. Indeed, in my view, the application of the principles is more consonant with the purposes of the Act than is a departure therefrom.

In the present case, generally accepted accounting principles were applied by the taxpayer to determine the amount of the reserve which was claimed. The evidence establishes that the actual numerical amount identified by the taxpayer falls within the range which is acceptable on the basis of the application of those principles. In my view, the amount is therefore reasonable for paragraph 20(1)(l) purposes subject to the minor corrections being made with respect to the reserves for those individual accounts mentioned-above which exceeded the amount overdue as of year end.

Appeal allowed.

NOTES AND QUESTIONS

1.   How did the taxpayer in *Coppley Noyes & Randall* determine the amount of the reserve for doubtful debts that it claimed in computing its income for its 1982 taxation year? On what basis did the Minister reassess the amount of the reserve allowed to the taxpayer under subparagraph 20(1)(l)(i)?

2.   How important to the Minister's assessment of a reasonable reserve in *Coppley Noyes & Randall* is the relationship between the doubtful debts claimed by the taxpayer and the bad debts claimed by the taxpayer in subsequent taxation years? How did the taxpayer explain this low ratio of bad debts to doubtful debts?

3.   In what ways did the taxpayer in *Coppley Noyes & Randall* take into account payments made and liabilities incurred in respect of doubtful accounts

after the end of its 1982 taxation year in determining the amount of a reasonable reserve for these accounts? Why did the Minister reject this approach?

4.   To what legal tests did the court in *Coppley Noyes & Randall* refer to determine whether the reserve for doubtful debts claimed by the taxpayer was reasonable? Of what significance to the assessment of a reasonable reserve under paragraph 20(1)(l) is the amount of the reserve allowed under GAAP?

5.   Why did the court in *Coppley Noyes & Randall* favour the amount of the reserve claimed by the taxpayer over that advanced by the Minister? Does the decision depend on a rule of conformity between financial accounting and tax accounting?

6.   In *92735 Canada Ltd. v. Canada*, [1999] T.C.J. No. 143, [1999] 2 C.T.C. 2661, 99 D.T.C. 771 (T.C.C.), the taxpayer loaned funds to a company engaged in the development of computer software, which had little revenue and paid no interest from 1987 to 1991. As a result, the taxpayer reported no income during these years. Although accepting the Minister's argument that accrued but unpaid interest must be included in computing the taxpayer's income during the years at issue under subsection 12(3) of the Act, the court concluded that the payment of interest was "doubtful from the outset" and "in [its] entirety." As a result, Bowman TCJ concluded (at para. 27):

> the interest that accrued each year became a doubtful debt in the year in which the interest accrued. The result is that the accruals for each year will be offset by the amount of the reserve [allowed under subparagraph 20(1)(l)(i)] so that effectively the [taxpayer's] income in each year is nil.

For a similar result, in which the taxpayer was required to include a receivable in computing his income for his 1985 taxation year, but was permitted to deduct the full amount of the inclusion as a doubtful debt under paragraph 20(1)(l), see *Remington v. Canada*, [1994] F.C.J. No. 1047, [1995] 1 C.T.C. 9, 94 D.T.C. 6549 (F.C.A.).

7.   In *Langdon v. Canada*, [2000] F.C.J. No. 371, [2000] 2 C.T.C. 375, [2000] D.T.C. 6203 (F.C.A.), the taxpayer, which carried on a business of buying and selling real properties, sought to deduct a doubtful debt on the sale of one property in computing his income for his 1991 taxation year, even though he had not reported the profit from the sale when the property was sold in 1989. Emphasizing the text of subparagraph 20(1)(l)(i), which permits a reserve for "doubtful debts *that have been included in computing the income of the taxpayer for that year or a preceding taxation year*," the court disallowed the deduction. According to Strayer JA (Richard CJ and Rothstein JA concurring) (at para. 9):

> paragraph 20(1)(l) allows for the deduction of doubtful debts "*that have been included* in computing the income of the taxpayer ..." (emphasis added). Such a condition would be almost meaningless if the words "included in computing" did not require the reporting of such income in a current or previous return. That is, the Minister must be able to track back

to a particular source of income if a deduction for doubtful debts is to be accepted in respect of that source.

Is this statement consistent with the decision in *92735 Canada Ltd. v. Canada*, [1999] T.C.J. No. 143, [1999] 2 C.T.C. 2661, 99 D.T.C. 771 (T.C.C.)?

8. For other cases in which courts have considered the deduction of a reserve for doubtful debts, see *Ferriss v. M.N.R.*, [1964] C.T.C. 491, 64 D.T.C. 5304 (Ex. Ct.); *Simpson v. Canada*, [1976] F.C.J. No. 162, [1976] C.T.C. 600, 76 D.T.C. 6350 (F.C.T.D.); *Gibraltar Mines Ltd. v. M.N.R.*, [1983] F.C.J. No. 526, [1983] C.T.C. 261, 83 D.T.C. 5294 (F.C.A.); *G.I. Norbraten Architect Ltd. v. M.N.R.*, [1983] C.T.C. 2145, 83 D.T.C. 121 (T.R.B.); and *Bell v. M.N.R.*, [1992] F.C.J. No. 5, [1992] 1 C.T.C. 35, 92 D.T.C. 6064 (F.C.T.D.).

9. For the CRA's views on the deduction of a reserve under paragraph 20(1)(l), see paragraphs 22 to 27 of *Interpretation Bulletin* IT-442R, "Bad Debts and Reserves for Doubtful Debts," September 6, 1991.

7. Bad Debts

Subparagraph 20(1)(p)(i) allows taxpayers to deduct the total of "all debts owing to the taxpayer that are established by the taxpayer to have become bad debts in the year and that have been included in computing the taxpayer's income for the year or a preceding taxation year." Subparagraph 20(1)(p)(ii) provides a comparable deduction for uncollectible loans made by insurers, moneylenders, or financial institutions. For our purposes, there is no need to examine this provision in any detail.[130]

Unlike the statutory reserves in paragraphs 20(1)(l), (m), and (n), there is no requirement that the deduction for a bad debt under paragraph 20(1)(p) must be included in computing the taxpayer's income in the immediately following or any subsequent taxation year. Nonetheless, if an amount on account of such a bad debt is subsequently received in any taxation year, it must be included in computing the taxpayer's income for that taxation year under paragraph 12(1)(i).

The criteria for determining whether and when a debt has become bad were considered in *Anjalie Enterprises Ltd. v. Canada*, [1994] T.C.J. No. 884, [1995] 1 C.T.C. 2802, 95 D.T.C. 216 (T.C.C.).

---

[130] For cases in which taxpayers have sought to deduct bad debts as business expenses on the basis that their "ordinary business included the lending of money," see *Orban v. M.N.R.* (1954), 10 Tax ABC 178, 54 D.T.C. 148; *Canada v. Lavigueur*, [1973] C.T.C. 773, 73 D.T.C. 5538 (F.C.T.D.); *Chaffey v. M.N.R.*, [1978] F.C.J. No. 116, [1978] C.T.C. 253, 78 D.T.C. 6176 (F.C.A.); *Global Communications Ltd. v. Canada*, [1998] F.C.J. No. 1511, [1999] 1 C.T.C. 23, 98 D.T.C. 6649 (F.C.T.D.); *Whitland Construction Co. v. Canada*, [1998] T.C.J. No. 899, [1999] 1 C.T.C. 2172, 99 D.T.C. 33 (T.C.C.); and *Loman Warehousing Ltd. v. Canada*, [2000] F.C.J. No. 1717, [2001] 1 C.T.C. 50, [2000] D.T.C. 6610 (F.C.A.).

Anjalie Enterprises Ltd. v. Canada
[1994] T.C.J. No. 884, [1995] 1 C.T.C. 2802, 95 D.T.C. 216 (T.C.C.)

LAMARRE JTCC: This is an appeal from an assessment issued against the appellant corporation for its 1989 taxation year, whereby the Minister of National Revenue, (hereinafter the Minister), disallowed the carryforward of a non-capital loss of $293,511 incurred by its predecessor corporation, Andrich Enterprises Ltd., (hereinafter Andrich), on the basis that the said non-capital loss originated in 1982 and was no longer available for carryforward in 1989.

Facts

Mr. Andrew Martin, principal shareholder in Andrich, was the only witness at trial. In March 1981, Andrich sold, to Forecastle Holdings Ltd. (hereinafter Forecastle), for $1,600,000, some real property it had acquired in late 1979 for $745,000. Forecastle granted a first mortgage to Ram Mortgage Corporation from which it borrowed an amount of $800,000 of which $600,000 was paid to Andrich.

In addition, the purchaser granted Andrich a second mortgage in the principal amount of $1,000,000. The second mortgage provided for a payment in reduction of principal of $75,000 on June 1, 1981, which Forecastle failed to make.

On July 30, 1981, Forecastle was legally advised by Andrich's lawyer of its failure and was asked to pay the full outstanding principal balance of $1,000,000 together with interest by September 8, 1981. Again, Forecastle did not execute the payment.

On November 6, 1981, Andrich instituted a petition for foreclosure seeking relief against Forecastle and the guarantors. On March 17, 1982, Andrich obtained an order from the Supreme Court of British Columbia granting it the conduct of sale of the property in the foreclosure action by Ram Mortgage Corporation.

On May 17, 1982, a modification of mortgage was signed between Andrich, Forecastle and guarantors whereby Andrich agreed to reduce the outstanding balance of principal and interest from $1,084,100 to $475,000 upon certain conditions. Again, Forecastle defaulted on the first payment, and on July 12, 1982, the Supreme Court of British Columbia granted an order nisi of foreclosure to Andrich. The redemption period was set at three months.

Andrich then listed the property for sale on September 1982 for $1,900,000 and in April 1983, for $1,750,000. No evidence was provided by the appellant to establish that these values were the result of a certified appraisal.

Andrich received no offer, and Forecastle never paid the outstanding debt. Mr. Martin was also advised on December 16, 1982 by his lawyer that an appraisal had been conducted on the property, and the market value was established at $700,000 on August 26, 1982, by a certified appraiser hired by Forecastle.

939

The first mortgage payable to Ram Mortgage Corporation attached to the property was in excess of $1,000,000 in September 1982. In addition, there were other creditors with additional claims that exceeded another $1,000,000 against the subject property that had to be paid before Andrich at that time. It was, therefore, not economically viable for Andrich as was said in a letter signed by Andrich's accountant to Revenue Canada in 1992, to repossess the subject property as it had been so severely encumbered by the purchase. According to the said letter, the purchaser filed for bankruptcy, and the asset values were insufficient to fully repay the first priority claim of Ram Mortgage. The date of bankruptcy is not indicated.

Andrich via its accountant filed its tax return for the year ended March 31, 1982 on December 31, 1982. By that time, it was apparent that there was no prospect of collecting the debt. ... As a result, Andrich claimed a deduction for a bad debt in computing its 1982 taxable income. Part of the loss, $132,177.64, was carried back in 1981. Andrich has not had any taxable income since.

On April 22, 1988, Andrich's accountant advised Revenue Canada in writing that Andrich erred in claiming a loss resulting from the above debt in its 1982 taxation year. The loss should have been claimed in the 1983 taxation year. On December 31, 1988, Anjalie Enterprises Ltd. and Andrich amalgamated to become the appellant company. Subsequent to that amalgamation, the appellant company deducted the loss in computing its income for the 1989 taxation year.

The Minister denied the deduction on the basis that the loss was incurred in Andrich's 1982 taxation year, and, therefore, could not be deducted in its 1989 taxation year as 1989 was past the five year carryforward period for 1982 losses.

Appellant's Position

Notwithstanding its treatment of its 1982 taxation year, it is the appellant's position that Andrich continued to seek recovery of the amount outstanding under the second mortgage from Forecastle and the guarantors until 1984 at least. As a result, Andrich erred in claiming the bad debt in its 1982 taxation year. Because it had prematurely treated the debt as bad, the appellant is arguing that the loss arising from the bad debt should be properly recognized in Andrich's 1983 taxation year.

Respondent's Position

The respondent's position is that the debt owing was established by Andrich to have become bad in the 1982 taxation year. Counsel for respondent relies on a decision of the Federal Court of Appeal in *Wilchar Construction v. The Queen*, [1981] CTC 415, 81 DTC 5318, to say that the taxpayer was estopped from changing the year in which it established the debt was bad.

...

Analysis

... In general the question of when a debt becomes bad is a question of fact to be determined according to the circumstances of each case. Primarily a debt is recognized to be bad when it has been proved uncollectible in the year. The question of when a debt is to be considered uncollectible is a matter of the taxpayer's own judgment as a prudent businessman. This has been stated by the Federal Court — Trial Division in *Picadilly Hotels Ltd. v. The Queen*, [1978] CTC 658, 78 DTC 6444.

In *Stikeman Canada Tax Service*, Volume 4, 1994 edition, page 20-1610, it is said that normally the debt should be written off as soon as but not before all normal collection procedures have been carried out without success. However, the taxpayer's own knowledge of the debtor's financial situation might dictate a deduction in an earlier or later year, depending on the circumstances.

The taxpayer should be in a position to satisfy the Minister not only that the debt was bad, but that it did not become bad in some earlier year. In *Bowyer-Boag Ltd. v. M.N.R.* (1950), 2 Tax ABC 202, 50 DTC 311, Mr. Fisher from the Tax Appeal Board stated ... :

> I am of the opinion that a taxpayer should not expect that he would be allowed to postpone the writing-off of what are in fact bad debts, for years after the date when in fact such debts became bad, and then to write them off in a year in which taxes happen to be imposed at high rate. All the surrounding circumstances, therefore, have to be taken into consideration in dealing with a claim such as has been put forward on behalf of this appellant.

Then, in trying to determine what constitutes a bad debt, Mr. Fisher stated in *Hogan v. M.N.R.* (1956), 15 Tax ABC 1, 56 DTC 183, that the issue of whether a debt becomes uncollectible in a given year must be based on the facts existing in that taxation year.

Moreover the determination of the bad debt cannot be revised in light of facts which only became apparent at a later date. Mr. Fisher stated ... and I quote:

> As already indicated, paragraph 11(1)(f) [now paragraph 20(1)(p)] states that the bad debts must be established to be bad in the year and not 18 months or two years afterwards. I am of the opinion, therefore, that the explicit provisions of the legislation in respect of this particular item preclude taking into consideration facts which have not become known until many months afterwards and which could not have been foreseen by the taxpayer at the time of his determination.

In addition, Mr. Fisher relied on *Anderton & Halstead Ltd. v. Birrell*, 16 TC 200, in which Rowlatt J stated at pages 208 and 209, and I quote:

> What the statute requires, therefore, is an estimate to what extent a debt is bad, and this is for the purpose of profit and loss account. Such an estimate is not a prophecy to be judged as to its truth by after events, but the valuation of an asset *de praesenti* upon an uncertain future to be judged as to its soundness as an estimate upon the then facts and probabilities.

In *Roy v. M.N.R.* (1958), 20 Tax ABC 385, 58 DTC 676, Mr. Boisvert for the Tax Appeal Board, adopted the views of Mr. Fisher in *Hogan*, *supra*, and added the following comment at page 391 (CTC 680), and I quote:

> As the Act does not define a bad debt, it is necessary to turn to recognized accounting principles of business practice. A debt is recognized to be bad when it has been proved uncollectable in the year.

In the more recent Tax Court of Canada case of *Berretti v. M.N.R.*, [1986] 2 CTC 2293, 86 DTC 1719 (TCC), Sarchuk J adopted the views of these previous cases at pages 2297-98 (CTC 1722-23). And I quote:

> Certain principles can be excerpted from these decisions. There is for example no necessity that a debt be absolutely irrecoverable ... and that possible recovery in the future is not per se a bar to a determination of uncollectability. ... These judgments also confirm the proposition that the determination of uncollectability is to be made by the appellant and not by an official of the respondent or some other person.

In the present case, as the case law demonstrates, the determination of when the second mortgage was uncollectible was to be made by the mortgagee, Andrich. The 1982 year-end financial statements reflected this bad debt. I assume the taxpayer and its auditors used generally accepted accounting principles in making this determination. Indeed, the appellant who relied on his accountant's judgment, did not call him as a witness, which testimony would have been helpful in dealing with the present case. It is therefore difficult for the appellant to argue that the realization of the mortgage loss in the 1982 taxation year was in error. The letter from the accountant on behalf of the appellant in 1992 to Revenue Canada confirmed that point, as he considered himself that the value of the property had declined to $700,000 by September 1982, and that there was an outstanding debt of $2,000,000 on the property on September 1982, before the appellant could be paid. In December 1982, at the time of filing the 1982 income tax return of Andrich, the decision was made by the appellant and its accountant to declare the bad debt in the year 1982.

If I follow the reasoning of Judge Collier in *Picadilly Hotels*, cited *supra*, I find that the appellant did not discharge his burden of proving that the debt was not uncollectible in the year 1982 on the balance of probabilities. On this point no evidence was adduced on the assets of the debtor company and on the date of its bankruptcy, and no evidence was adduced that the appellant did not consider in his business judgment the debt uncollectible in 1982.

In the *Picadilly* case, the plaintiff had the right to foreclose the property and could have forced the return of the asset, which he didn't. In the present case, Andrich obtained an order giving it the right to conduct the sale of the property and started the foreclosure procedure during the 1982 taxation year.

In the case of *Greensteel Industries v. M.N.R.*, [1975] CTC 2099, 75 DTC 63, Judge Cardin of the Tax Review Board said that the decision to treat the debt as bad or not rested entirely with the company. The Minister could not afterwards substitute his own judgment for that of the principal shareholder.

In the present case, the appellant used its business judgment at the end of 1982 and declared a loss on the bad debt in the 1982 taxation year. I do not believe that six years later it can change its business judgment in order to benefit from the changes in the Act.

[For 1983 and subsequent taxation years, the period for which non-capital losses could be carried forward to be deducted in computing a taxpayer's taxable income was increased from five years to seven years.]

The fact that Andrich continued to seek recovery of the amount outstanding under the mortgage until 1984, and that the Supreme Court of British Columbia did not grant the order nisi until after the 1982 taxation year had ended must have been considered at the time the tax return for 1983 was filed. In fact, the 1983 financial statements show that there were no more accounts receivable from Forecastle and no amendment was made at that time to change the year the debt should have been considered bad.

Furthermore, in the case of *Berretti* cited before, Sarchuk J concluded that there is no requirement that the debt be absolutely irrecoverable in the future for there to be a determination of irrecoverable in the present.

If I add to that the fact that the law was changed in 1983 so as to permit the carryback of non-capital losses for three years instead of one and a carryforward of seven years instead of five, which the appellant could not reasonably foresee in 1982, and the fact that by declaring the loss in 1982, it took the opportunity of carrying back the loss in 1981, I am more inclined to believe that the appellant's argument cannot prevail.

I therefore conclude that the Minister rightly denied the loss in the appellant's 1989 taxation year on the basis that the loss was incurred in Andrich's 1982 taxation year and, therefore, 1989 was past the five-year carryforward period for 1982 losses. ... For all these reasons, the appeal is dismissed with costs for the Minister.

Appeal dismissed.

NOTES AND QUESTIONS

1.   In *Anjalie Enterprises*, the taxpayer originally claimed a deduction for a bad debt in computing its income for its 1982 taxation year. Why did it subsequently want to claim that the debt became bad in its 1983 taxation year or later?

2.   On what basis did the court conclude that the debt owed to the taxpayer in *Anjalie Enterprises* had become bad in the taxpayer's 1982 taxation year?

3.   In *Flexi-Coil Ltd. v. Canada*, [1996] F.C.J. No. 811, [1996] 3 C.T.C. 57, 96 D.T.C. 6350 (F.C.A.), the taxpayer, a farm machine manufacturer that sold products to a 75 per cent owned UK subsidiary and a wholly owned Swiss subsidiary, deducted substantial amounts in 1987, 1988, and 1989 in respect of accounts receivable that it considered to have become bad debts within the meaning of paragraph 20(1)(p). Affirming the trial decision, which upheld the Minister's assessment disallowing the deduction in 1989 and reducing the allowable deduction in 1987 and 1988, the Federal Court of Appeal stated (at para. 8):

943

the courts should be vigilant in ensuring that a related creditor acted properly in determining that some debts had become uncollectible. After all, Flexi, the creditor in the non-arm's length relationship here, is not only omniscient about its subsidiaries' affairs, but also omnipotent. It is in a clear position to influence how their business is to be carried on, including determining whether the trade accounts are to be paid.

4.   For other cases in which deductions for bad debts have been considered, see *No. 415 v. M.N.R.* (1957), 17 Tax ABC 110 (T.A.B.); *Barzilay v. M.N.R.*, [1984] C.T.C. 2353, 84 D.T.C. 1290 (T.C.C.); *Honey Bunch Bakeries (Saskatoon 1975) Ltd. v. M.N.R.*, [1990] T.C.J. No. 402, [1990] 2 C.T.C. 2148, 90 D.T.C. 1549 (T.C.C.); *Williams Gold Refining Co. of Canada v. Canada*, [2000] T.C.J No. 25, [2000] 2 C.T.C. 2193, 2000 D.T.C. 1829 (T.C.C.); and *Burkes v. Canada*, [2000] T.C.J. No. 629, [2000] 4 C.T.C. 2511, 2000 D.T.C. 2576 (T.C.C.).

5.   For the CRA's views on the deduction of bad debts under paragraph 20(1)(p), see paragraphs 1 to 21 of *Interpretation Bulletin* IT-442R, "Bad Debts and Reserves for Doubtful Debts", September 6, 1991.

8. Transfers of Debt Obligations

Where a taxpayer sells a debt obligation on which interest has accrued without receipt, the price at which the obligation is sold is likely to include an amount equal to the value of the accrued but unpaid interest to which the purchaser will be entitled.[131] In this circumstance, subsections 12(3) and (4) provide that the accrued interest up to the time of the sale must be included in computing the vendor's income for the taxation year. Correspondingly, under subsection 52(1), accrued but unpaid interest that is included in computing the vendor's income under subsection 12(3) or (4) may be added to the cost of the debt obligation, thereby reducing the amount of any gain (or increasing the amount of any loss) on its disposition. In addition, where the debt obligation is disposed of for consideration equal to its fair market value at the time of the disposition, subsection 20(21) permits a deduction in the year of disposition in respect of accrued interest otherwise included in the vendor's income to the extent that it cannot reasonably be considered to have been received or to have become receivable.

For a taxpayer who acquires a debt obligation on which unpaid interest has accrued, the full amount of this interest must be included under paragraph 12(1)(c) in the year that it is received or receivable, even if the purchase price of the obligation is likely to have included an amount equal to the value of accrued but unpaid interest at the time of the transfer, which the vendor is required to

---

[131] Where interest rates have changed since the debt obligation was issued, the price of the obligation should also reflect a gain or loss on the principal amount of the debt. The value of the principal and interest elements of the debt may also decrease as a consequence of uncertainty regarding the financial stability of the debtor.

include as interest income pursuant to subsection 12(3) or (4). Absent any other rule, therefore, this accrued but unpaid interest would be taxable to both the vendor and the purchaser, with the only offsetting tax relief to the purchaser in the form of a higher cost base in the debt obligation, thereby affecting the amount of any gain or loss on the maturity or subsequent disposition of the obligation.

In order to prevent this anomaly, subsection 20(14), which predates the interest accrual rules in subsections 12(3) and (4), allows a deduction in computing the transferee's income for a taxation year of the amount of any accrued but unpaid interest at the time of the transfer to the extent that this amount is included under paragraph 12(1)(c) in computing the transferee's income for the year. Correspondingly, paragraph 53(2)(1) reduces the cost base of the debt obligation by any amount that is deductible under subsection 20(14). More specifically, subsection 20(14) stipulates:

> Where, by virtue of an assignment or other transfer of a debt obligation, other than an income bond, an income debenture, a small business development bond or a small business bond, the transferee has become entitled to an amount of interest that accrued on the debt obligation for a period commencing before the time of transfer and ending at that time that is not payable until after that time, that amount
>
> (a) shall be included as interest in computing the transferor's income for the transferor's taxation year in which the transfer occurred, except to the extent that it was otherwise included in computing the transferor's income for the year or a preceding taxation year; and
>
> (b) may be deducted in computing the transferee's income for a taxation year to the extent that the amount was included as interest in computing the transferee's income for the year.

Although subsection 20(14) was amended for transfers occurring after November 12, 1982, the provision remains essentially unchanged. The former language was considered in *Canada v. Antosko*, [1994] S.C.J. No. 46, [1994] 2 C.T.C. 25, 94 D.T.C. 6314 (S.C.C.).

Canada v. Antosko
[1994] S.C.J. No. 46, [1994] 2 C.T.C. 25, 94 D.T.C. 6314 (S.C.C.)

IACOBUCCI J (LaForest, L'Heureux-Dubé, Gonthier, and Major JJ concurring): These appeals concern the interpretation of subsection 20(14) of the *Income Tax Act*, RSC 1952, c. 148 (am. SC 1970-71-72, c. 63) (the "Act"). This section permits a transferee of a debt instrument to deduct from the calculation of his or her taxable income the interest accruing on the instrument prior to the date of transfer. The narrow issue in these appeals is whether, when the debt in question was transferred from a non-taxable government body to investors trying to rehabilitate a failing company, such a transaction came within the scope of subsection 20(14). As the three appeals are based on essentially identical facts, and indeed relate to the same transaction, I will refer to them collectively as "the appeal."

I. Facts

Atlantic Forest Products Ltd. (the "company") was the owner of a plant, located in Minto, New Brunswick, which manufactured charcoal briquettes. The New Brunswick Industrial Finance Board (the "board"), a provincially incorporated agency of the Province of New Brunswick, provided financing to the company. The board became the controlling shareholder of the company, holding 80 per cent of its issued and outstanding shares. In February and March 1971, the board guaranteed a $3 million loan from the Bank of Nova Scotia (the "bank") to the company. The company executed in favour of the board a fixed and floating charge debenture securing the board's guarantee of the loan. This debenture contained a covenant on the part of the company to repay all expenditures made by the board in protecting its security, together with interest, and to repay the bank loan according to a specified schedule. The parties agreed that, in the event of default by the company on the repayment, the board could pay to the bank the amounts in default and these payments would then constitute a further charge on the lands and premises of the company.

Between January 1972 and July 1973, the board made four direct loans to the company totalling $1.425 million. The board received four demand promissory notes for the principal amounts of these loans, with interest payable monthly at rates varying from five to 9.5 per cent. In September 1974, the company defaulted on the bank loan, and the board was compelled to make good on its guarantee. The board paid $3,375 million to the bank in full satisfaction of all outstanding principal and interest on the loan. By March 1975, the total indebtedness of the company to the board was approximately $5 million.

On March 1, 1975, the board entered into an agreement with the appellants, Antosko and Trzop, in which the appellants acquired all of the board's common shares in the company for a consideration of $1. The board also covenanted to ensure that the company was debt free, except for the indebtedness to the board in the amount of $5 million plus accrued interest, and to postpone the obligation to repay this indebtedness, and interest thereon, for a period of two years. In return, the appellants promised to operate the company during this two-year period in a good and business-like manner. The board agreed that, upon expiration of the two-year period and if all its conditions were met, it would then sell to the appellants the $5 million debt plus accrued interest for the sum of $ 10.

Following the execution of the above agreement, the appellants changed the name of the company to Resort Estates Ltd. In 1976, the obligations of the board passed to the Province of New Brunswick as represented by the Minister of Commerce and Development. The agreement, however, remained unchanged. The appellants satisfied their obligations under the agreement and thus, on July 6, 1977, the board sold to them the total indebtedness of the company. The Minister of Commerce and Development assigned to the appellants the debenture, promissory notes, realty mortgage and chattel mortgage that had been given as security for the outstanding indebtedness of the company to the board.

Interest on the debenture issued by the company as security for the $3.375 million paid by the board to the bank in fulfilment of its loan guarantee was treated as accruing daily at a rate of 11.5 per cent per annum from the date the bank was paid. Interest on the four promissory notes had also accrued daily. In the 1977 taxation year, the appellants each received $38,335 from the company in partial payment of interest which had accrued on the total debt prior to transfer. The appellants included this interest as income pursuant to paragraph 12(1)(c) of the *Income Tax Act*, and then claimed deductions of these amounts pursuant to paragraph 20(14)(b). In the 1980 taxation year, the appellant Trzop received $283,363 from the company as a similar partial payment of interest. This amount was also included as income and then claimed as a deduction.

The Minister of National Revenue disallowed the deductions. The appellants successfully appealed these disallowances to the Tax Court of Canada. ... An appeal by the respondent Minister to the Federal Court — Trial Division was allowed ([1990] 1 CTC 208, 90 DTC 6111), and a further appeal by the appellants to the Federal Court of Appeal was dismissed ([1992] 2 CTC 350, 92 DTC 6388), with the result that the deductions were disallowed. The appellants now appeal the decision of the Federal Court of Appeal to this Court.

...

V. Analysis

A. Does this transaction come within the ambit of subsection 20(14) of the Income Tax Act?

The Federal Court of Appeal ... held that the transaction in this appeal, within which the accrued interest was transferred, was not meant to give rise to a deduction pursuant to subsection 20(14).

For the purposes of analysis, I repeat the operative portion of subsection 20(14) [since amended]:

20(14) Where, by virtue of an assignment or other transfer of a bond, debenture or similar security ... the transferee has become entitled to interest in respect of a period commencing before the time of transfer and ending after that time that is not payable until after the time of the transfer, an amount equal to that proportion of the interest that the number of days in the portion of the period that preceded the day of transfer is of the number of days in the whole period:

    (a)   shall be included in computing the transferor's income for the taxation year in which the transfer was made, and

    (b)   may be deducted in computing the transferee's income for a taxation year in the computation of which there has been included

        (i)   the full amount of the interest under section 12, or

        (ii)   a portion of the interest under paragraph (a).

In order to come within the opening words of the subsection, two conditions must be satisfied. First, there must be an assignment or a transfer of a debt obligation. Second, the transferee must become entitled, as a result of the transfer, to interest accruing before the date of the transfer but not payable until after that date. All of the courts below agreed that these two conditions were met in fact.

...

While it is true that the courts must view discrete sections of the *Income Tax Act* in light of the other provisions of the Act and of the purpose of the legislation, and that they must analyze a given transaction in the context of economic and commercial reality, such techniques cannot alter the result where the words of the statute are clear and plain and where the legal and practical effect of the transaction is undisputed: *Mattabi Mines Ltd. v. Ontario (Minister of Revenue)*, [1988] 2 SCR 175, [1988] 2 CTC 294, at page 194 (CTC 304); see also *Symes v. Canada*, [1993] 4 SCR 695, [1994] 1 CTC 40, 94 DTC 6001.

It is quite true that, as the respondent points out, this transaction was not one where a debt obligation was purchased on the open market. It is equally true that the motivation of the parties was not specifically to buy and sell accrued interest. The parties were concerned with returning the company to a solvent and stable position so as to generate profit and preserve jobs in a small community. All this, however, is somewhat tangential to the application of subsection 20(14). The section requires the transfer of a debt obligation whose value includes interest accruing before the date of transfer, but payable after that date. The motives of the parties, and the setting in which the transfer took place, are simply not determinative of the application of the subsection.

...

In this appeal, despite conceding that these factual elements are present, the respondent is asking the Court to examine and evaluate the transaction in and of itself, and to conclude that the transaction is somehow outside the scope of the section in issue. In the absence of evidence that the transaction was a sham or an abuse of the provisions of the Act, it is not the role of the Court to determine whether the transaction in question is one which renders the taxpayer deserving of a deduction. If the terms of the section are met, the taxpayer may rely on it, and it is the option of Parliament specifically to preclude further reliance in such situations.

...

In this case, the substance of the transaction meets the requirements of subsection 20(14). The respondent argues that ... it is obvious from the nominal monetary consideration paid for the transfer of the debt obligation that its purchase price did not reflect the fact that interest had accrued. The Court of Appeal found, as did the other courts below, that a purchase of accrued interest by the appellants in the acquisition of debt obligations did occur. Once that is established, the adequacy of the consideration is not relevant, absent allegations of artificiality or of a sham. The issue in all commercial transactions, where there is no claim of unconscionability or of a similar vitiating factor, is the validity of the consideration. This principle is recognized in Interpretation Bulletin IT-410R, "Debt Obligations — Accrued Interest on Transfer," which states (in paragraph 3), "the amount, if any, of the interest determined for the purpose of subsection 20(14) is unaffected by either the prospects of its payment or non-payment or the nature or value of any consideration given by the transferee." Moreover, the consideration for the transfer at issue in this appeal included not only the nominal $10, but also the undertaking to operate the company in a good and business-like manner. It was only in fulfilment of this latter promise that the corresponding promise by the board to transfer the debt obligations became binding.

This transaction was obviously not a sham. The terms of the section were met in a manner that was not artificial. Where the words of the section are not ambiguous, it is not for this Court to find that the appellants should be disentitled to a deduction because they do not deserve a "windfall," as the respondent contends. In the absence of a situation of ambiguity, such that the Court must look to the results of a transaction to assist in ascertaining the intent of Parliament, a normative assessment of the consequences of the application of a given provision is within the ambit of the legislature, not the courts. Accordingly, I find that the transaction at issue comes within subsection 20(14).

B. Does subsection 20(14) permit the deductions?

The respondent argues in the alternative that, even if subsection 20(14) is *prima facie* applicable to the transaction in this case, the appellants are not entitled to claim a deduction pursuant to paragraph 20(14)(b), because the amount of interest accrued prior to the transfer was not included in the calculation of the income of the transferor, as required by paragraph 20(14)(a). It is not disputed in this case that the board, as transferor, is a non-taxable entity which did not file a tax return in the time period in question. The Trial Division found, and the Court of Appeal agreed, that these two paragraphs were to be interpreted conjunctively such that no deduction could be claimed under paragraph 20(14)(b) in the absence of evidence that the amount deducted had been included in the transferor's income under paragraph 20(14)(a). The respondent points to the word "and," which links the two subsections, and argues that an interpretation which precludes a deduction, unless the interest is included in the transferor's income, best accords with the object and spirit of the provision.

The respondent characterizes the purpose of subsection 20(14) as the avoidance of double taxation. I agree. Subsection 20(14) operates to apportion accrued interest between transferor and transferee so as to avoid the double taxation that would occur if both parties included all the interest accrued in their respective calculations of income. The interest that has accrued prior to the date of transfer is allocated to the transferor's calculation of income, based presumably on the reasoning that the transferor, as owner of the debt obligation, will be legally entitled to interest up to the date of transfer and that this fact will be reflected in the consideration to be paid by the transferee for the debt obligation. The accrued interest is therefore part of the income of the transferor, and not of the income of the transferee.

The respondent, however, goes on to argue that since amounts received or receivable as interest are included in the calculation of income under paragraph 12(1)(c), subsection 20(14) acts to ensure not only that double taxation is avoided, but also that the entire amount of interest is included in someone's taxable income. In my view, such an assertion transforms the proposition that the section is meant to avoid double taxation into one that the section is designed to ensure taxation of the entire amount of interest accrued during the taxation year. This is, however, not true, since if the board as non-taxable owner of the debt obligation did not transfer it, none of the accrued interest would be taxable. Parliament anticipates just such an outcome in creating a tax-exempt status for certain entities. Subsection 20(14) deals with the allocation of interest. Whether the government will ultimately recover tax on that interest is governed by other sections of the Act. In this regard I find helpful the comments of M.D. Templeton, in "Subsection 20(14) and the Allocation of Interest — Buyers Beware" (1990), 38 *Can. Tax J* 85, at pages 87-88, on the reasons of the Trial Division on this point:

> ... no words in subsection 20(14) or the Act as a whole make paragraph (b) of the subsection conditional on the application of paragraph (a). On the contrary, the grammatical construction of subsection 20(14) suggests that paragraphs (a) and (b) become applicable, independent of one another, once the conditions set out in the paragraph of subsection 20(14) that precedes paragraphs (a) and (b) are met.
>
> The grammatical structure of subsection 20(14) is similar to a number of other provisions in the Act in which Parliament lists the income tax consequences that arise when certain preconditions are met. Usually, the preconditions are set out in an introductory paragraph or paragraphs and the consequences in separate subparagraphs. We do not know of any canon of statutory interpretation that makes a tax consequence listed in the text of a provision subject to the taxpayer's compliance with all the other tax consequences listed before it.

To carry this observation further, where specific provisions of the *Income Tax Act* intend to make the tax consequences for one party conditional on the acts or position of another party, the sections are drafted so that this interdependence is clear: see, e.g., section 68 and subsections 69(5), 70(2), (3) and (5).

...

This conclusion is fortified by the consequences that would ensue were subsection 20(14) not read in this straightforward manner. Subsection 20(14) does not draw distinctions between the contexts in which debt instruments are transferred. The interpretation advanced by the Trial Division and endorsed by the Court of Appeal would be equally applicable in open-market bond transactions. It is simply unworkable to require market purchasers to discern whether the vendor of the bond is tax-exempt in order to be able to assess whether a paragraph 20(14)(b) deduction is permitted. Without this knowledge, the prospective purchaser would thus be unable to gauge the true value of the security.

Moreover, a debt instrument held by a non-taxable entity would be worth less than an identical instrument held by a body that was liable to tax. Any taxpayer who purchased a security previously held by either the federal or the provincial Crown, or by one of the persons enumerated in subsection 149(1) of the Act, would be disentitled from deducting. Given that many of the bonds sold on the open market are sold by the Bank of Canada, a body to whom paragraph 20(14)(a) does not apply, the interpretation of the section advanced by the respondent would mean that these bonds would have to be sold at a discount compared with identical bonds sold by other parties: Templeton, *supra*, at page 88; see also John M. Ulmer, "Taxation of Interest Income" (1990), 42 *Can. Tax Found.* 8:1, at page 8:20.

Therefore, I am of the view that, on the plain meaning of the section, the ability of a taxpayer to claim a deduction pursuant to paragraph 20(14)(b) is not dependent on the inclusion by the transferor pursuant to paragraph 20(14)(a) of the same amount in his or her calculation of income. The consequences of this straightforward grammatical reading do not persuade me that it is incorrect. In fact, the opposite is true.

Given that the inability of the transferor to include the amount of accrued interest transferred in its calculation of income is irrelevant to the ability of the appellants to claim a deduction of that interest, and in light of the earlier finding that there was in this case a transfer of a debt obligation which included interest accruing before the transfer but not payable until after the transfer, I am of the view that the appellants are entitled to rely on paragraph 20(14)(b) to claim a deduction of this interest.

C What is the amount of the deduction to which the appellants are entitled?

The respondent argued that, if the appellants were entitled to a paragraph 20(14)(b) deduction, the correct amount of the deduction was far less than the amounts claimed by the appellants. The appellants each claimed a deduction of $38,335 in the 1977 taxation year, and the appellant Trzop claimed a further $283,363 in 1980. As will be explained below, the respondent argues that the total deduction to which the appellants were entitled was $3,345.

... The respondent argued before the Tax Court judge that the accrued interest on the debt was far less than the approximately $1,000,000 calculated by the appellants, because the promissory notes stated that interest was not payable between 1975 and 1977, pursuant to the agreement between the board and the appellants to suspend repayment of the debt. The Tax Court judge rejected this argument, stating:

> It is obvious from the evidence adduced that what happened in the period between 1975 to 1977 was not a forgiveness of the accrued interest, but a suspension thereof. The appellants had the right to sue the company and obtain the accrued interest that they did receive in the years under appeal.

The reasons of the Tax Court judge do not indicate that he considered the alternate argument advanced by the respondent that most of the interest deducted by the appellants did not meet the requirement of subsection 20(14) that it must have accrued prior to the transfer but be payable after the transfer. The argument of the respondent, simply put, is that interest on the promissory notes accrued daily and was payable monthly, and that interest on the debenture accrued daily and was payable on demand. Therefore, nearly all of the interest accruing during the two-year period during which repayment of the debt was suspended became payable on demand at the time of the transfer of the debt to the appellants. The fact that the appellants chose not to collect on it immediately does not alter that fact.

Therefore, the respondent argues, since this interest was payable at the time of, rather than after, the transfer, it does not meet the terms of subsection 20(14). The only interest which satisfies the opening words of the subsection is the interest accruing on the four promissory notes between the June and July payment dates. The appellants are consequently entitled to deduct $3,325 as the amount which accrued prior to the transfer but was not payable until after the transfer.

This argument cannot succeed. The interest which accrued during the two-year period during which the debt was suspended was payable after the transfer and therefore meets the terms of subsection 20(14). This agreement to suspend repayment of accruing interest that would otherwise have been payable was legally enforceable by the appellants so long as they continued to fulfil their part of the agreement. Therefore, the accrued interest was not payable before the transfer.

Moreover, to say that the interest became payable at the very moment of the transfer, rather than after it, is somewhat artificial. It must be remembered that the board, as transferor, could not collect that accrued interest at all, so long as the appellants met the terms of the agreement. Therefore, the interest that accrued during that period became payable on demand immediately after the transfer of the debt to the appellants was completed. I find it difficult to understand how the appellants could have made a valid demand for payment of the interest until after the debt had been fully transferred to them. Therefore, this means that the interest accrued before the transfer but was payable after that time, and that it gave rise to a permissible deduction under paragraph 20(14)(b).

VI. Conclusion and Disposition

The appellants are entitled to a deduction of interest accruing prior to the transfer and payable thereafter. The transaction between the appellants and the board meets the requirements of subsection 20(14). The interest which accrued during the period that repayment of the debt was suspended did not become payable until after the transfer. However, the parties agree that this result may have other tax consequences for the appellants, such as a taxable capital gain pursuant to subsection 40(3). In this connection, these and any other possible consequences can be taken into account by the respondent in reassessment.

Therefore, the appeals are allowed, the judgment of the Federal Court of Appeal is set aside, and the matters referred back to the Minister for reassessment in accordance with these reasons. The appellants shall have their costs here and in the courts below.

Appeals allowed.

NOTES AND QUESTIONS

1.   On what grounds did the Supreme Court of Canada conclude in *Antosko* that the taxpayer may deduct under subsection 20(14) the interest he received in 1977 and 1980? Do you agree with the court's decision? Why or why not?

2.   What role, if any, did the Supreme Court of Canada's approach to statutory interpretation play in its decision in *Antosko*? How did the court define the proper approach to statutory interpretation? What method (or methods) of statutory interpretation did the court employ?

3.   Were the transactions carried out by the taxpayers within the "object and spirit" of subsection 20(14)? Might the deduction have been challenged under Estey J's guideline 3(c) as set out in *Stubart Investments Ltd. v. Canada,* [1984] S.C.J. No. 25, [1984] C.T.C. 294 (S.C.C.)? Might the deduction have been challenged under the rule against artificial transactions in former subsection 245(1)? If the same series of transactions occurred on or after September 13, 1988, might they be challenged under the GAAR?

4.   For a critical analysis of the decision in *Antosko*, see David G. Duff, "Interpreting the Income Tax Act — Part 1: Interpretive Doctrines" (1999) Vol. 47 No. 3 Can. Tax J. 464 at 509-11:

> Although the court's decision as to the proper reading of subsection 20(14) is unqualified and persuasive, its initial holding that the transaction fell within the scope of the provision is much less certain. First, as the court itself indicates, this conclusion depends on a prior judgment that the transaction was neither a "sham" nor "artificial." While the Minister conceded that the transaction was not a sham as it has been defined for the purposes of Canadian income tax law, the issue of artificiality does not appear to have been seriously argued. Nonetheless, on at least some interpretations of the word as contrary to normal business practice, the acquisition of $5 million of debt plus accrued interest for a cash payment of $10 might be construed as artificial. Moreover, as Estey J had suggested in *Stubart*, "the formal validity of [a] transaction may also be insufficient where ... 'the object and spirit' of [an] allowance or benefit provision is defeated by ... procedures blatantly adopted by the taxpayer to synthesize a loss, delay or other tax saving device, although these actions may not attain the height of 'artificiality.'" While the court in *Antosko* concluded that the transaction at issue was not "so blatantly synthetic as to be effectively artificial," this point also does not appear to have been seriously argued.

For these reasons alone, the court's conclusion that "clear and plain" words of a statutory provision must be applied regardless of "other provisions of the Act" and "the purpose of the legislation" must be read cautiously — contingent as it is on a prior conclusion that the transaction at issue is neither a "sham," nor "artificial," nor "blatantly synthetic." Moreover, since the enactment of the general anti-avoidance rule in 1988, this conclusion is further subject to an explicit "object and spirit" test in subsection 245(4) where the transaction may be characterized as an "avoidance transaction" within the meaning of subsection 245(3). In this context, therefore, any emphasis on the plain meaning of a statutory provision has been legislatively overruled.

5.   At the end of his decision in *Antosko*, Iacobucci J observes that the decision "may have other tax consequences for the appellants, such as a taxable capital gain pursuant to subsection 40(3)." As a general rule, subsection 40(3) deems a taxpayer to have realized a capital gain from the disposition of any property when the total of all amounts that must be deducted in computing the adjusted cost base of the property under subsection 53(2) exceeds the total of the cost of the property and any amount that must added to this cost in computing the adjusted cost base of the property under subsection 53(1) (that is, when the adjusted cost base of the property is negative).

Since amounts that may be deducted under subsection 20(14) must also be deducted in computing the adjusted cost base of the debt obligation under paragraph 53(2)(1), the deduction under subsection 20(14) of interest received by the taxpayers in 1977 and 1980 would have produced a negative adjusted cost base, resulting in a deemed capital gain under subsection 40(3). While the interest was fully deductible, however, only half of the deemed gain would have been taxable.

6.   In *Trzop v. R.*, [2000] T.C.J. No. 466, [2000] 4 C.T.C. 2093, [2000] D.T.C. 2364 (T.C.C.), one of the parties to the transactions in *Antosko* objected to the application of subsection 40(3) on the grounds that the Minister had adopted a new basis for assessing tax after the normal reassessment period had expired. Rejecting the taxpayer's argument that such a reassessment was impermissible without a showing of misrepresentation under subsection 152(4) of the Act, the court held that the reassessment was a legitimate exercise of the Minister's duties under subsection 164(4.1). According to Bowie TCJ (at para. 18):

The Minister did not reassess of her own volition under subsection 152(4) of the Act in this case, but under subsection 164(4.1), at the direction of the Supreme Court, to implement its judgment. Once the Appellant succeeded on the issue in dispute, it became the Minister's duty under subsection 164(4.1) of the Act to issue reassessments to give effect to the Supreme Court's judgment. That is done by making the assessments that the Minister would have made at the time of the original reassessments that were appealed from, if he had interpreted subsection 20(14) of the Act correctly at that time. The Minister has not now sought either to support the original reassessments, or to raise a new issue. She has simply computed the tax payable for the years in question, applying what the Supreme Court has now determined to be the correct interpretation of subsection 20(14) of the Act. The deeming of a disposition, and a gain on that disposition, are the logical and inevitable consequences of the Appellant being entitled to the deductions he sought.

The court also rejected the taxpayer's alternative argument that the adjusted cost base of the debt obligation should be increased by the value of the two years of unpaid labour that he put into the company. According to Bowie TCJ (at para. 24):

> The undertaking to operate the company in a good and business-like manner was part of the consideration, but that cannot be equated to an obligation on the part of the Appellant to work for two years without pay. He did that of his own volition, and the success of the enterprise was his reward for doing so. The computation of the ACB of a security is governed principally by section 53 of the Act, the operative words of which, so far as this case is concerned, are "... there shall be added to the cost to the taxpayer of the property ... ." Nothing that follows assists the Appellant's case, so for this argument to succeed he would have to bring the value of his labours within "... the cost to [him] of the property ... ." As there was no term in the agreement with the board that required him to work without pay, he cannot satisfy that requirement.

CHAPTER SIX

Taxable Capital Gains and Allowable Capital Losses

I. INTRODUCTION

In computing a taxpayer's net income for a taxation year, paragraph 3(b) includes what can be described as the taxpayer's "net taxable capital gain." This is determined by adding the taxpayer's "taxable capital gains" for the taxation year (other than gains from dispositions of "listed personal property") and the taxpayer's "taxable net gain for the year from dispositions of listed personal property" under subparagraph 3(b)(i), and deducting the taxpayer's "allowable capital losses" for the year (other than losses from the disposition of "listed personal property" and "allowable business investment losses") under subparagraph 3(b)(ii). Unlike business investment losses, which may be deducted in computing a taxpayer's net income from all sources under paragraph 3(d),[1] capital losses are generally deductible only against capital gains under paragraph 3(b). Similarly, losses from the disposition of listed personal property are deductible only against listed personal property gains,[2] with the net amount brought into income under clause 3(b)(i)(A) of the Act.

The rules governing the computation of these amounts are contained in subdivision c of Division B of Part I of the Act, comprising sections 38 to 55. In general, capital gains are determined by subtracting the cost of the property and the cost of selling the property from the proceeds received on its disposition, while capital losses occur where the sum of the cost and selling cost exceeds the

---

[1] The term "business investment loss" is defined in para. 39(1)(c) as a capital loss from the disposition of shares of or debt owing by a "small business corporation," which is defined in subs. 248(1) as "a Canadian-controlled private corporation all or substantially all of the fair market value of the assets of which" is generally "attributable to assets that are ... used principally in an active business carried on primarily in Canada by the particular corporation or a corporation related to it." The characterization of a capital loss as a business investment loss depends on a number of corporate tax provisions that are best examined in a course on corporate income taxation.

[2] See s. 41, which is discussed later in this chapter.

proceeds.[3] Section 38 of the Act defines the "taxable" portion of a capital gain and the "allowable" portion of a capital or business investment loss as one-half of the amount of the gain or loss otherwise determined under subdivision c.[4] Likewise, subsection 41(1) defines a taxpayer's "taxable" net gain from dispositions of listed personal property as one-half of the taxpayer's net gain from dispositions of listed personal property.[5]

As a result, although a taxpayer's income from each office, employment, business, or property is fully taxable under paragraph 3(a), only one-half of each capital gain is included in computing the taxpayer's net income under paragraph 3(b). However, while losses from each office, employment, business, or property are fully deductible in computing a taxpayer's net income from all sources under paragraph 3(d), capital losses are only one-half deductible in computing a taxpayer's net income and generally deductible only against taxable capital gains under subparagraph 3(b)(ii) or in computing a taxpayer's net gain from dispositions of listed personal property under subsection 41(2).[6] Where taxpayers dispose of property at a gain, therefore, it is generally to their advantage to characterize the source of the gain as capital not business or property. Alternatively, where property is disposed of at a loss, it is generally advantageous for taxpayers to characterize the source of the loss as business or property rather than capital. For the revenue authorities, on the other hand, the incentives are typically reversed. This is the practical context for most of the legal disputes involving the characterization of a gain or loss from the disposition of property.

This chapter considers the characterization and computation of a taxpayer's taxable capital gains, allowable capital losses, and taxable net gains from dispositions of listed personal property. Section II considers the characterization of gains and losses from the disposition of different kinds of property, reviewing statutory provisions and judicial decisions by which these gains and losses are identified as *capital* gains or losses. Section III examines statutory rules and judicial decisions governing the computation of these gains and losses, surveying general computational rules, recognition and non-recognition rules

---

[3] See subpara. 40(1)(a)(i) (defining a taxpayer's gain for a taxation year from the disposition of property) and para. 40(1)(b) (defining a taxpayer's loss for a taxation year from the disposition of property).

[4] This inclusion rate has varied since the Canadian income tax first recognized capital gains and losses in 1972, increasing from one-half during the taxation years 1972 to 1987 to two-thirds in 1988 and 1989 and three-quarters from 1990 to February 28, 2000, when the federal government reduced the inclusion rate to two-thirds. As of October 18, 2000, this fraction was further reduced to one-half. Paragraphs 38(a.1) and (a.2) reduce the inclusion rate to zero for charitable gifts consisting of publicly traded shares or ecologically sensitive land.

[5] The inclusion rate for these net gains has also varied since 1972, corresponding to the fraction applicable to capital gains and losses more generally.

[6] As explained earlier, "allowable business investment losses" may be deducted in computing a taxpayer's income from all sources under para. 3(d).

that apply to different categories of transactions or events, and special rules applicable to specific types of property.

II. CHARACTERIZATION

The *Income Tax Act* does not define the concept of "capital" for the purpose of determining the source of a taxpayer's gain or loss. According to paragraph 39(1)(a), however, "a taxpayer's capital gain for a taxation year from the disposition of any property" is defined as:

> the taxpayer's gain for the year determined under this subdivision (to the extent of the amount thereof that would not, if section 3 were read without reference to the expression "other than a taxable capital gain from the disposition of a property" in paragraph 3(a) and without reference to paragraph 3(b), be included in computing the taxpayer's income for the year or any other taxation year) from the disposition of any property of the taxpayer

other than specific kinds of property that need not concern us here.[7] Correspondingly, paragraph 39(1)(b) defines "a taxpayer's capital loss for a taxation year from the disposition of any property" as:

> the taxpayer's loss for the year determined under this subdivision (to the extent of the amount thereof that would not, if section 3 were read in the manner described in paragraph (a) of this subsection and without reference to the expression "or the taxpayer's allowable business investment loss for the year" in paragraph 3(d), be deductible in computing the taxpayer's income for the year or any other taxation year) from the disposition of any property of the taxpayer

other than various categories of property that we need not examine here.[8] According to subsection 248(1), these definitions apply for the purposes of the Act as a whole.

According to subsection 248(1) of the *Income Tax Act*, the word "property" means "property of any kind whatever whether real or personal or corporeal or incorporeal" including specific kinds of property that need not concern us here. Dictionary definitions are similarly broad, defining property as "the (exclusive)

---

[7] Of the various types of excluded property identified in subparas. 39(1)(a)(i) to (v), several are subject to special rules under which gains are otherwise included in computing a taxpayer's income — for example, "eligible capital property" proceeds from the disposition of which reduce the taxpayer's "eligible capital amount" under subs. 14(5). Subparagraph 39(1)(a)(i.1), on the other hand, exempts gains on the disposition of certain kinds of cultural property where the property is disposed of to a designated institution or public authority as defined in subs. 32(2) of the *Cultural Property Export and Import Act*.

[8] In addition to categories of property already identified in subparas. 39(1)(a)(i) to (v), subpara. 39(1)(b)(i) excludes from the definition of a capital loss any loss from the disposition of "depreciable property," which is subject to a special set of rules in s. 13. Where depreciable property of a particular class is disposed of at a loss, and the taxpayer no longer owns any property of the same class, the loss may give rise to a "terminal loss" under subs. 20(16). See the section on "Capital Cost Allowance" in Chapter 5.

right to the possession, use, or disposal of a thing,"[9] and "any external thing over which the rights of possession, use, and enjoyment are exercised."[10] In *Manrell v. Canada*, [2003] F.C.J. No. 408, [2003] 3 C.T.C. 50, 2003 D.T.C. 5225 (F.C.A.), however, the Federal Court of Appeal held that the concept of property in the Act requires "an exclusive and legally enforceable claim". The concept of a "disposition" of property was examined in context of capital cost allowances in Chapter 5, and is considered further in section III of this chapter.

Although other provisions deem specific kinds of gains and losses to be capital gains or losses,[11] paragraphs 39(1)(a) and (b) define capital gains and capital losses as a residual — that is, as gains or losses that would not otherwise be included or deductible in computing a taxpayer's income. Where a gain or loss from the disposition of property would, if the property were disposed of, be a capital gain or loss, the Act defines the property as "capital property."[12] Where the gain or loss would be characterized as income from a business, on the other hand, the property is described as inventory.[13] As a result, as the Supreme Court of Canada explained in *Friesen v. Canada*, [1995] S.C.J. No. 71, [1995] 2 C.T.C. 369, 95 D.T.C. 5551 (S.C.C.) (at para. 42):

> The Act defines two types of property ... Capital property ... creates a capital gain or loss upon disposition. Inventory is property the cost or value of which is relevant to the computation of business income. ... The characterization of an item of property as inventory or capital property is based primarily on the type of income that the property will produce.

As a general rule, a gain or loss from the disposition of property will be characterized as income or loss from a business where the property is disposed of in the course of a business according to its ordinary meaning or pursuant to an adventure or concern in the nature of trade.[14] Where the gain or loss is not so characterized, paragraphs 39(1)(a) and (b) define the amount as a capital gain or a capital loss. As a result, the characterization of gains and losses as *capital* gains and losses generally depends on the tests by which courts determine whether property is disposed of in the course of a business or as part of an adventure or concern in the nature of trade. The following cases and text examine the characterization of gains or losses from the disposition of different kinds of property.

---

[9] *The Shorter Oxford English Dictionary*, 5th ed.

[10] *Black's Law Dictionary*, 8th ed.

[11] See, for example, subs. 39(4) of the Act, which deems any gain or loss on the disposition of a "Canadian security" to be a capital gain or loss. This rule, and the definition of a "Canadian security" in subs. 39(6), are examined later in this chapter.

[12] See the definition of "capital property" in s. 54, which, according to subs. 248(1), applies to the Act as a whole. The definition of "capital property" in s. 54 also includes "depreciable property," which is defined in subs. 13(21) and was discussed in Chapter 5.

[13] See the definition of "inventory" in subs. 248(1) as "a description of property the cost or value of which is relevant in computing a taxpayer's income from a business for a taxation year." The computation of a taxpayer's profit or loss from the sale of inventory is discussed in Chapter 5.

[14] See part II of Chapter 5.

A. Real Property

Real property or real estate refers to "land and anything growing on, attached to, or erected on it, excluding anything that may be severed without injury to the land."[15] More generally, real property includes "any estate, interest or right" in land and fixtures, including a leasehold interest, but not including a mortgage secured by real property.[16]

The characterization of gains or losses from the disposition of real property is among the most litigated issues in Canadian income tax law. One of the most notable cases to consider this question is *Regal Heights Ltd. v. M.N.R.*, [1960] S.C.J. No. 56, [1960] C.T.C. 384, 60 D.T.C. 1270 (S.C.C.).

Regal Heights Ltd. v. M.N.R.
[1960] S.C.J. No. 56, [1960] C.T.C. 384, 60 D.T.C. 1270 (S.C.C.)

JUDSON J (Fauteux, Martland, and Ritchie JJ, concurring): ... The issue is whether the appellant was properly assessed on a profit of $135,704.73 arising from its dealings with certain real property in the City of Calgary. The appellant reported an income for the year 1955 of $970.94. The department re-assessed at $135,704.73. ... The question is whether the appellant's profit from the sale of this real estate in the 1955 taxation year was a profit derived from a venture or concern in the nature of trade and was therefore income from a business — within the meaning of Sections 3, 4 and 139(1)(e) of the *Income Tax Act*, RSC 1952, c. 148 [now sections 3 and 9 and subsection 248(1)].

In September 1952 one Benjamin Raber became interested in the purchase of 40 acres of land in the City of Calgary which was then being operated as the Regal Golf Course. Mr. Raber took in three other associates and the four, as partners, purchased the property for $70,000. They intended to attempt to establish a large shopping centre on the property.

In May 1953 the partners purchased for $14,700 a property on the other side of the road which would be useful in giving more ready access to a shopping centre. They also purchased in March 1954 an undivided one-third interest in a property some distance away which they proposed to use for the purpose of advertising the existence of the shopping centre. The total outlay of the partners for the acquisition of these properties was ... $88,700. In February 1954 they incorporated Regal Heights Limited and transferred all the property in question to the company in return for shares. The partners were the sole shareholders of the company. It became apparent in September 1954 that a shopping centre of the kind intended could not be established on the property. The reason was that a large department store, which the promoters hoped to interest in their centre,

---

[15] *Black's Law Dictionary*, 8th ed.
[16] *Pocket Dictionary of Canadian Law*, 4th ed.

announced publicly that it intended to locate in the neighbourhood but on another site 20 blocks away.

The company, in December 1954, disposed of 30 acres for $88,500. In May 1955 the shareholders passed a resolution to wind up the company. The company next sold the property on the other side of the road, which had been purchased for the purpose of access, for $20,000, and finally, in May 1955, it sold 6.3 acres of the remaining property for $143,200.

There is no doubt that the primary aim of the partners in the acquisition of these properties, and the learned trial judge so found, was the establishment of a shopping centre but he also found that their intention was to sell at a profit if they were unable to carry out their primary aim. It is the second finding which the appellant attacks as a basis for the taxation of the profit as income. The Minister, on the other hand, submits that this finding, is just as strong and valid as the first finding and that the promoters had this secondary intention from the beginning.

The appellant adduced much evidence concerning the efforts of the promoters to establish what was described as a "regional shopping centre." This means the largest of this type of enterprise and requires an area of from 30 to 60 acres. These promoters undoubtedly had the necessary land but a scheme of this kind involves an expenditure of anything from $2,000,000 to $5,000,000 and its financing and establishment depend upon the negotiation of leases with satisfactory tenants, and above all, upon the negotiation of a lease with a major department store as the centre of attraction.

It is necessary to set out the efforts made by the promoters to develop this property in this way. The acquisition of the two additional properties, the one for the purpose of easy access and the other for the purpose of advertising the centre, fits into the scheme. In February 1953 they secured a favourable opinion from the Calgary Planning Board that the property would be re-zoned from residential to commercial purposes although the Board withheld formal approval until there should be some indication that construction would begin. In addition, they had sketches made to show what the centre would look like. These sketches were no more than promotional literature. They made studies of other shopping centres; with professional help they compiled lists of prospective tenants; they entered into discussions with four department stores although the evidence shows that there was only one which might possibly be interested; they had discussions with one of the banks concerning the financing of the project; they had a special survey made at a fee of $3,000 for the purpose of influencing one particular department store and they incorporated this company.

These efforts were all of a promotional character. The establishment of a regional shopping centre was always dependent upon the negotiation of a lease with a major department store. There is no evidence that any such store did anything more than listen to the promoters' ideas. There is, understandably, no evidence of any intention on the part of these promoters to build regardless of the outcome of these negotiations. There is no evidence that these promoters had any assurance when they entered upon this venture that they could interest any such department store. Their venture was entirely speculative. If it failed, the property was a valuable property, as is proved from the proceeds of the sales that they made. There is ample evidence to support the finding of the learned trial judge that this was an undertaking or venture in the nature of trade, a speculation in vacant land. These promoters were hopeful of putting the land to one use but that hope was not realized. They then sold at a substantial profit and that profit, in my opinion, is income and subject to taxation.

...

What the promoters and the company did and intended to do is clear to me on the evidence, as it was to the learned trial judge. They failed to promote a shopping centre and they then disposed of their speculative property at a profit. This was a venture in the nature of trade and the profit from it is taxable within the meaning of Sections 3, 4 and 139(1)(e) of the *Income Tax Act*.

...

I would dismiss the appeal with costs.

CARTWRIGHT J (dissenting): ... In the case at bar the question whether the profit realized by the appellant is subject to tax is dependent upon whether in fact the true nature of the business in which it engaged was, (i) the purchase of lands with a view to reselling them at a profit or, (ii) the development of a shopping centre to be held and operated as an investment or, (iii) both of these.

As I read the reasons of the learned trial judge, he has accepted as truthful the evidence of the appellant's witnesses and has found that the "motivating intention" of the appellant and its promoters and directors was to purchase the lands as the first step in the erection and development of a shopping centre to be held and operated as a revenue-producing investment. He has however held the profit realized subject to tax on the ground that reasonable and experienced business men, such as the promoters were, must have envisaged the possibility of being unable to carry out the scheme of developing the shopping centre and have hoped in that event to dispose of the lands at a profit. Accepting this as a reasonable inference, it does not appear to me to justify the finding that the appellant was in fact engaged in the business of buying and selling lands. I do not think the evidence supports the view that the appellant or its promoters would have purchased, or did purchase, the lands in question as a speculation looking to re-sale.

... [I]t appears to me that the sales of the lands made by the appellant were a realization of its capital assets when the purpose for which they had been acquired was defeated by the decision of the department store mentioned in the evidence to build on a nearby site. To put the matter colloquially, the lands were acquired and disposed of not as the stock-in-trade or inventory of a dealer in land but as capital assets of a developer of a shopping centre which, owing to circumstances beyond the control of the appellant, it became impossible to develop. The result is not affected by the circumstance that these capital assets were held for a [relatively short] time. ...

I would allow the appeal with costs throughout and direct that the judgment of the Exchequer Court and the assessments should be set aside.

Appeal dismissed.

NOTES AND QUESTIONS

1. On what basis does a majority of the Supreme Court of Canada conclude in *Regal Heights*, that the gain was taxable business income rather than a capital gain (which was not subject to tax at the time)? Why does Cartwright J disagree? Is he right to suggest that the majority held that the taxpayer "was in fact engaged in the business of buying and selling lands"? Must the taxpayer carry on such a business for a gain from the disposition of land to be characterized as business income?

How, if at all, does the majority decision in *Regal Heights*, define the concept of a "secondary intention" to sell at a profit? If, as Cartwright J suggests in his dissenting opinion, reasonable and experienced developers generally envisage the possibility of being unable to carry out their plans and hope in that event to dispose of property at a profit, does the doctrine of "secondary intention" suggest that all such gains are business income from an adventure or concern in the nature of trade? Would this interpretation make sense of the statutory scheme for taxing gains from the disposition of property? How else might one understand the concept of a secondary intention?

2. In *Racine v. M.N.R.*, [1965] C.T.C. 150, 65 D.T.C. 5098 (Ex. Ct.), the taxpayers, each of whom had experience in the real estate business, borrowed money to purchase land and machinery of a bankrupt corporation, which they sold four to six weeks later at a profit of approximately $20,000 each. In view of the taxpayers' business experience, the method by which they financed the acquisition, and the brief period during which they owned the property, the Minister characterized the gain as business income from an adventure or concern in the nature of trade. Relying on the taxpayers uncontradicted testimony at trial that it had been their intention to carry on the business indefinitely as a long-term investment, the Exchequer Court rejected the Minister's further argument that they had a secondary intention to resell at a profit.

In subsequent cases involving the characterization of gains from the disposition of real property, courts have generally interpreted the "secondary intention" doctrine to require the possibility of resale at a profit as a "motivating" reason or consideration for the taxpayer's decision to acquire the property. See, for example, *Morev Investments Ltd. v. M.N.R.*, [1972] F.C.J. No. 801, [1972] C.T.C. 513, 72 D.T.C. 6421 (F.C.T.D.), aff'd [1973] F.C.J. No. 520, [1973] C.T.C. 429, 73 D.T.C. 5353 (F.C.A.); *Reicher v. M.N.R.*, [1975] F.C.J. No. 1106, [1975] C.T.C. 659, 75 D.T.C. 6001 (F.C.A.); *De Salaberry Realties Ltd. v. M.N.R.*, [1976] F.C.J. No. 901, [1976] C.T.C. 656, 76 D.T.C. 6408 (F.C.A.); *Hiwako Inv. Ltd. v. Canada*, [1978] F.C.J. No. 316, [1978] C.T.C. 378, 78 D.T.C. 6281 (F.C.A.); *Crystal Glass Canada Ltd. v. Canada*, [1989] F.C.J.

No. 113, [1989] 1 C.T.C. 330, 89 D.T.C. 5143 (F.C.A.); *Coady v. Canada*, [2006] T.C.J. No. 102, [2006] 3 C.T.C. 2089, 2006 D.T.C. 2717 (T.C.C.); and *Canada Safeway Ltd. v. Canada*, [2008] F.C.J. No. 82, [2008] 2 C.T.C. 149, 2008 D.T.C. 6074 (F.C.A.).

3.   Courts have grappled with the characterization of the gain on the purchase and sale of vacant land. For cases in which gains from the purchase and sale of vacant land have been characterized as business income, see *Watson & McLeod Ltd. v. M.N.R.*, [1966] C.T.C. 86, 66 D.T.C. 5101 (Ex. Ct.); and *Rivermede Dev. Ltd. v. M.N.R.*, [1993] F.C.J. No. 778, [1993] 2 C.T.C. 220, 93 D.T.C. 5365 (F.C.T.D.).

For cases in which gains on the sale of vacant land have been characterized as capital gains, see *M.N.R. v. Lawee*, [1972] C.T.C. 359, 72 D.T.C. 6342 (F.C.T.D.); *Riznek Construction Ltd. v. Canada*, [1979] F.C.J. No. 116, [1979] C.T.C. 197, 79 D.T.C. 5131 (F.C.T.D.); and *Montfort Lakes Estates Inc. v. Canada*, [1979] F.C.J. No. 1104, [1980] C.T.C. 27, 79 D.T.C. 5467 (F.C.T.D.).

4.   Of what, if any, relevance to the characterization of a gain or loss on the disposition of real property is the period of time during which the property was held by the taxpayer? Does a short holding period suggest that the property was acquired for the purpose of resale? Does a long holding period suggest that the property was acquired as a long-term investment?

For illustrative cases that consider the length of time that the real property has been held in characterizing the income on its disposition, see *McDonald v. Canada*, [1974] F.C.J. No. 1012, [1974] C.T.C. 836, 74 D.T.C. 6644 (F.C.A.); *H. Fine and Sons Ltd. v. Canada*, [1984] F.C.J. No. 816, [1984] C.T.C. 500, 84 D.T.C. 6520 (F.C.T.D.); *Gratl v. Canada*, [1993] T.C.J. No. 64, [1993] 2 C.T.C. 2035 (T.C.C.), aff'd [1994] F.C.J. No. 220, [1994] 2 C.T.C. 1, 94 D.T.C. 6255 (F.C.A.); and *Cayer v. Canada*, [2007] T.C.J. No. 75, [2007] 3 C.T.C. 2286, 2007 D.T.C. 557 (T.C.C.).

5.   Of what, if any, relevance to the characterization of a gain or loss on the disposition of real property is the circumstances responsible for its disposition? Might the fact that the taxpayer is compelled to sell the property under threat of expropriation or as a result of unexpected financial or personal circumstances, or induced to sell by an unexpected and unsolicited offer rebut an inference based on other factors (for example, a short holding period) that the property was acquired for the purpose of resale? Do efforts on the part of the owner to interest potential purchasers and/or bring the property to a more marketable condition suggest a trading intent? See *Barnett v. M.N.R.*, [1957] C.T.C. 355, 57 D.T.C. 1255 (Ex. Ct.); *Slater v. M.N.R.*, [1966] C.T.C. 53, (1965) 66 D.T.C. 5047 (Ex. Ct.); *Power v. M.N.R.*, [1975] F.C.J. No. 904, [1975] C.T.C. 580, 75 D.T.C. 5388 (F.C.T.D.); *Jarvie Holdings Ltd. v. M.N.R.*, [1980] F.C.J. No. 1102, [1980] C.T.C. 525, 80 D.T.C. 6395 (F.C.T.D.); *Carsons Camps Ltd. v. Canada*, [1983] F.C.J. No. 928, [1984] C.T.C. 46, 84 D.T.C. 6070 (F.C.T.D.); *N.L. Brousseau Realty Co. v. M.N.R.*, [1986] 1 C.T.C. 2277, 86 D.T.C. 1186 (T.C.C.);

Associated Investors of Canada Ltd. v. Canada, [1987] F.C.J. No. 256, [1987] 1 C.T.C. 285, 87 D.T.C. 5176 (F.C.A.); *Grouchy v. M.N.R.*, [1990] F.C.J. No. 287, [1990] 1 C.T.C. 375, 90 D.T.C. 6267 (F.C.T.D.); *Les Placements Richard Martineau Ltée v. M.N.R.*, [1991] T.C.J. No. 29, [1992] 1 C.T.C. 2170, (1991) 92 D.T.C. 1051 (T.C.C.); and *Iula v. Canada*, [1994] F.C.J. No. 1196, [1994] 2 C.T.C. 328, 94 D.T.C. 6614 (F.C.T.D.).

6.   Of what, if any, relevance to the characterization of a gain or loss on the disposition of real property is the manner in which the acquisition is financed and the ability of the property to produce a profit given a particular method of finance? Does the fact that property is acquired solely or primarily with borrowed funds suggest a trading intent? Might it be reasonable to draw such an inference where the property, as financed, does not generate a reasonable expectation of profit?

See *Jack Dichter Developments Ltd. v. M.N.R.*, [1979] C.T.C. 2706, 79 D.T.C. 608 (T.R.B.); *Walton v. Canada*, [1982] F.C.J. No. 410, [1982] C.T.C. 228, 82 D.T.C. 6220 (F.C.T.D.); *Zen v. Canada*, [1985] F.C.J. No. 935, [1985] 2 C.T.C. 313, 85 D.T.C. 5531 (F.C.T.D.); *Jordan v. M.N.R.*, [1985] 2 C.T.C. 2131, 85 D.T.C. 482 (T.C.C.); *Gratl v. Canada*, [1993] T.C.J. No. 64, [1993] C.T.C. 2035 (T.C.C.); *Belanger-Coady v. Canada*, [1993] T.C.J. No. 865, [1994] 1 C.T.C. 2097 (T.C.C.); *600166 Ontario Ltd. v. M.N.R.*, [1993] T.C.J. No. 225, [1993] 2 C.T.C. 2151, 93 D.T.C. 910 (T.C.C.); *L'Herault v. Canada*, [1993] T.C.J. No. 110, [1993] 2 C.T.C. 2612, 93 D.T.C. 1108 (T.C.C.); and *Saskatchewan Wheat Pool v. Canada*, [2008] T.C.J. No. 10, [2008] 3 C.T.C. 2329 (T.C.C.).

7.   Of what, if any, relevance to the characterization of a gain or loss on the disposition of real property is evidence of other activities carried on by the taxpayer or its principal shareholder(s)? Does the fact that the taxpayer or a principal shareholder bought and sold land on other occasions suggest that the property in question was also acquired for the purpose of resale? Does the fact that the taxpayer or a principal shareholder carries on a business as a developer or builder suggest that the property in question was acquired as part of this business? Alternatively, does the fact that the taxpayer or principal shareholder derives income from other real property suggest that the property was acquired as an investment?

See *Diamond Developments Ltd. v. M.N.R.*, [1984] C.T.C. 2992, 84 D.T.C. 1811 (T.C.C.) and *Rivermede Developments Ltd. v. M.N.R.*, [1993] F.C.J. No. 778, [1993] 2 C.T.C. 220, 93 D.T.C. 5365 (F.C.T.D.). See also *Muzyka v. M.N.R.* (1964), 34 Tax ABC 409, 64 D.T.C. 168 (T.A.B.); *Welton v. M.N.R.*, [1978] C.T.C. 3153, 78 D.T.C. 1848 (T.R.B.); *Schlamp v. Canada*, [1982] F.C.J. No. 520, [1982] C.T.C. 304, 82 D.T.C. 6274 (F.C.T.D.); *King Edward Hotel (Calgary) Ltd. v. M.N.R.*, [1990] F.C.J. No. 642, [1990] 2 C.T.C. 214, 90 D.T.C. 6468 (F.C.T.D.); *Grouchy v. M.N.R.*, [1990] F.C.J. No. 287, [1990] 1 C.T.C. 375, 90 D.T.C. 6267 (F.C.T.D.); *Gagnon v. M.N.R.*, [1990] T.C.J. No. 811,

[1991] 1 C.T.C. 2203, (1990) 91 D.T.C. 467 (T.C.C.); *Gratl v. Canada*, [1993] T.C.J. No. 64, [1993] 2 C.T.C. 2035 (T.C.C.); and *Belanger-Coady v. Canada*, [1993] T.C.J. No. 865, [1994] 1 C.T.C. 2097 (T.C.C.).

8.   Where property is held for personal use, a gain or loss on the disposition of the property is generally characterized as being on account of capital. In *Lemieux v. Canada*, [1973] C.T.C. 559, 73 D.T.C. 5428 (F.C.T.D.), for example, where the taxpayer made a profit of $17,230 on the sale of an old farmhouse near Mont Ste. Anne, which she had restored and used as a weekend retreat, the gain was characterized as a capital gain. The characterization and tax treatment of "personal-use property" as defined in section 54 is considered later in this chapter.

9.   For views of the CRA on the characterization of gains or losses from the sale of real property, see *Interpretation Bulletin* IT-218R, "Profit, Capital Gains and Losses from the Sale of Real Estate, Including Farmland, Inherited Land, and Conversion of Real Estate from Capital Property and *Vice Versa*," September 16, 1986. According to paragraphs 3 to 7 of this bulletin:

> 3. There is no provision in the *Income Tax Act* which describes the circumstances in which gains from the sale of real estate are to be determined as being either income or capital. However, in making such determinations, the courts have considered factors such as those listed below: (The list is not intended to be exclusive of any other factor.)
>
> (a)   the taxpayer's intention with respect to the real estate at the time of its purchase;
>
> (b)   feasibility of the taxpayer's intention;
>
> (c)   geographical location and zoned use of the real estate acquired;
>
> (d)   extent to which intention carried out by the taxpayer;
>
> (e)   evidence that the taxpayer's intention changed after purchase of the real estate;
>
> (f)   the nature of the business, profession, calling or trade of the taxpayer and associates;
>
> (g)   the extent to which borrowed money was used to finance the real estate acquisition and the terms of the financing, if any, arranged;
>
> (h)   the length of time throughout which the real estate was held by the taxpayer;
>
> (i)   the existence of persons other than the taxpayer who share interests in the real estate;
>
> (j)   the nature of the occupation of the other persons referred to in (i) above as well as their stated intentions and courses of conduct;
>
> (k)   factors which motivated the sale of the real estate;
>
> (l)   evidence that the taxpayer and/or associates had dealt extensively in real estate.
>
> 4. None of the factors listed in 3 above are conclusive in themselves for the purpose of determining that a gain arising on the sale of real estate constitutes income or a capital gain. The relevance of any factor to such a determination will vary with the facts of each case.

5. A taxpayer's intention at the time of purchase of real estate is relevant in determining whether a gain on its sale will be treated as business income or as a capital gain. It is possible for a taxpayer to have an alternate or secondary intention, at the time of acquiring real estate, of reselling it at a profit if the main or primary intention is thwarted. If this secondary intention is carried out any gain realized on the sale usually will be taxed as business income.

6. The more closely a taxpayer's business or occupation (e.g., a builder, a real estate agent) is related to real estate transactions, the more likely it is that any gain realized by the taxpayer from such a transaction will be considered to be business income rather than a capital gain (see 3(f) and (j) above).

7. The objects as stated in the charter of a corporation often offer little assistance in determining the intention of the corporation when real estate is acquired and later sold. Consequently, in any case where a corporation claims a capital gain in respect of real estate the corporate intention relative to the acquisition and sale thereof will be examined and determined by reference to factors such as those described in 3 above. In some cases (e.g., closely-held corporations) the corporate intention may be indistinguishable from that of its officers, directors and/or shareholders and in such cases their intentions, as based on their past and present conduct with respect to real estate, will accordingly be attributed to the corporation.

10. In many cases, real property that is originally acquired as an investment may be converted to inventory or vice versa. Although the Act contains specific rules deeming taxpayers to have disposed of and reacquired property at its fair market value when they acquire property for the purpose of gaining or producing income and commence to use the property for another purpose, or acquire property for another purpose and commence to use it for the purpose of gaining or producing income,[17] these rules do not apply where the purpose for which the property is used changes from one income-producing purpose to another.[18]

Where real property is converted from investment property to inventory, however, it is the CRA's view that "the ultimate sale of real estate that was so converted may give rise to a gain or loss on capital account, a gain or loss on income account or a gain or loss that is partly capital and partly income." According to paragraph 15 of *Interpretation Bulletin* IT-218R:

[w]here such real estate has been converted to inventory, capital gains or losses, if any, will be calculated on the basis that a notional disposition of such property occurred on the date of conversion. The amount of such a notionally determined capital gain or loss in respect of the real estate will be the difference between the adjusted cost base ... and its fair market value on the date of conversion. These notional capital gains or losses will be considered to give rise to taxable capital gains or allowable capital losses for the taxation year during which the actual sale of the real estate occurs and will be required to be reported in that same year. The amount of any income gain or loss arising on actual sale of the converted real estate will be determined in accordance with generally accepted accounting principles on the basis that its initial inventory value is its fair market value on the date of conversion.

---

[17] See paras. 13(7)(a) and (b) and para. 45(1)(c). These provisions are examined later in this chapter.

[18] See IT-218R, para. 11.

For this purpose, the CRA explains in paragraphs 12 to 14:

12. Vacant land that is capital property used by its owner for the purpose of gaining or producing income will be considered to have been converted to inventory at the earlier of

(a) the time when the owner commences or causes the commencement of improvements thereto with a view to selling it, and

(b) the time of making application to the relevant authority for approval of a plan to subdivide the land into lots for sale, provided that the taxpayer proceeds with the development of the subdivision. ...

13. The units in a multi-unit residential apartment, or an office, warehouse storage building or any similar structure that is held as capital property by the owner will be considered to have been converted to inventory at the time when application is made to the relevant authority for approval to change the title to any such building to strata title, provided that the owner proceeds with the sale of the units. ...

14. Where the relevant authority rejects an application referred to in 12 or 13 above, and the owner thereafter sells the property *en bloc*, the sale will ordinarily be treated as a sale of capital property if it would have been so treated had the property been sold before the application was made.

With respect to farmland and inherited land, however, which may be difficult to sell *en bloc*, the department accepts that "the filing of a subdivision plan and selling lots thereunder does not in itself affect the status of the gain notwithstanding that such subdivision may enhance the value of the land." According to paragraph 24 of *Interpretation Bulletin* IT-218R:

A gain on the sale of farming or inherited land will remain a capital gain if an examination of all other facts, both before and after subdivision, establishes this to be so. However, where the taxpayer goes beyond mere subdivision of the land into lots and installs improvements such as watermains, sewers or roads, or carries on an extensive advertising campaign to sell the lots, the taxpayer will be considered to have converted the land from a capital property into a trading property.

11. The CRA's views on the conversion of real property from inventory to investment property are found in paragraphs 20 to 22 of *Interpretation Bulletin* IT-218R. According to these paragraphs:

20. Where a taxpayer acquires real estate and allocates its cost to inventory in the taxpayer's accounting records, such accounting treatment will be considered to represent *prima facie* evidence that the real estate was initially acquired with the intention of reselling it at a profit at a propitious time. ... If such real estate is vacant land, it is the Department's position that any gain on its sale, as such, will be business income rather than a capital gain. See however, 21 below which discusses the conversion of improved land from inventory to capital.

21. A taxpayer who constructs buildings for sale and who originally intended to sell a particular building soon after it was completed may, however, permanently convert that building from inventory to capital property

(a) by establishing that the original intention to sell the building has been abandoned,

(b) by capitalizing the cost of the building and the cost of the lot (if owned by the taxpayer) upon which it sits, in the taxpayer's financial records, and

(c) by making use of the building as a capital asset for a period of time in a manner that is more indicative of investing than trading. Examples of such uses are as follows:

    (i) the rental of the building on a long term lease which does not provide the lessee with an option to purchase,

    (ii) the housing of the taxpayer's business, or

    (iii) the rental of part of the building on terms described in (i) and the occupation of the remainder thereof by the taxpayer for the purpose described in (ii).

The same considerations will apply with respect to real estate, other than vacant land, that was purchased for the purpose of resale.

    22. A taxpayer who constructs buildings for sale will not be considered to have converted inventory to capital property when part or all of any such building is temporarily rented for any reason.

12. A number of cases have considered the circumstances in which the purpose for which real property is used may be considered to have been changed from investment to resale at a profit or vice versa. Where real property is originally acquired as income-producing capital property, courts have held that concrete steps to rezone or subdivide the property must be taken to demonstrate a conversion in the use of the property to inventory: *Marshall v. M.N.R.*, [1983] C.T.C. 2664, 83 D.T.C. 592 (T.R.B.); *Hughes v. Canada*, [1983] F.C.J. No. 1124, [1984] C.T.C. 101, (1983) 84 D.T.C. 6110 (F.C.T.D.); *Turnbull v. M.N.R.*, [1984] C.T.C. 2800, 84 D.T.C. 1720 (T.C.C.); *Cantor v. M.N.R.*, [1985] 1 C.T.C. 2059, (1984) 85 D.T.C. 79 (T.C.C.); *Magilb Development Corp. Ltd. v. Canada*, [1986] F.C.J. No. 768, [1987] 1 C.T.C. 66, (1986) 87 D.T.C. 5012 (F.C.T.D.); *Roos v. Canada*, [1993] T.C.J. No. 867, [1994] 1 C.T.C. 2105, (1993) 94 D.T.C. 1094 (T.C.C.); and *Wierenga v. Canada*, [1996] T.C.J. No. 210, [1996] 2 C.T.C. 2371 (T.C.C.).

Where real property is originally acquired for the purpose of resale, the courts have held that there is a strong presumption that the land retains this character in the absence of clear and unequivocal acts implementing a change of intention: *Canada v. Fredericton Housing Ltd.*, [1975] F.C.J. No. 804, [1975] C.T.C. 537, 75 D.T.C. 5367 (F.C.A.); *Canada v. Randall Park Development Ltd.*, [1978] F.C.J. No. 1022, [1978] C.T.C. 826, 78 D.T.C. 6545 (F.C.T.D.); *Edmund Peachey Ltd. v. Canada*, [1979] F.C.J. No. 2, [1979] C.T.C. 51, 79 D.T.C. 5064 (F.C.A.); and *Mohawk Horning Ltd. v. M.N.R.*, [1986] F.C.J. No. 327, [1986] 2 C.T.C. 89, 86 D.T.C. 6297 (F.C.A.).

B. Tangible Personal Property

Personal property encompasses all kinds of property other than land and interests in land.[19] Corporeal or tangible property refers to all property with a physical or material existence.[20] As a result, tangible personal property constitutes "personal property that can be seen, weighed, measured, felt or touched or that is in any way perceptible to the senses."[21]

As with real property, the characterization of a gain or loss on the disposition of tangible personal property depends on the purpose for which the property is acquired and used by the taxpayer. Where tangible personal property is acquired and held by the taxpayer for the purpose of gaining or producing income from a business or property (for example, by leasing the property), the property is generally characterized as "depreciable property," gains from the disposition of which are characterized as capital gains to the extent that they exceed the capital cost of the property.[22] Where tangible personal property is acquired or manufactured to sell at a profit, on the other hand, the property is generally characterized as inventory in the taxpayer's business, gains and losses from the disposition of which are included or deducted in computing the taxpayer's income from the business. Where tangible personal property is acquired and used primarily for the personal use or enjoyment of the taxpayer or related persons, the property is characterized as "personal-use property" and subject to a special set of rules examined later in this chapter.

In *Canadian Kodak Sales Ltd. v. M.N.R.*, [1954] C.T.C. 375, 54 D.T.C. 1194 (Ex. Ct.), Thorson P considered the characterization of gains from the sale of tangible personal property that the taxpayer had originally acquired and held for the purpose of gaining or producing income by leasing the property to users on a monthly basis.

Canadian Kodak Sales Ltd. v. M.N.R.
[1954] C.T.C. 375, 54 D.T.C. 1194 (Ex. Ct.)

[The taxpayer ("Sales"), a wholly owned Canadian subsidiary of Eastman Kodak Company ("Eastman"), a US corporation, carried on a business of selling cameras and related photographic equipment and supplies manufactured by Canadian Kodak Company Limited ("Kodak"), another wholly owned Canadian subsidiary of Eastman. Until 1940, Eastman owned another Canadian subsidiary

---

[19] *The Canadian Oxford Dictionary*, 2d ed.

[20] *Pocket Dictionary of Canadian Law*, 4th ed.

[21] *Ibid.*

[22] See para. (a) of the definition of "capital property" in s. 54, which includes depreciable property as a form of capital property, and para. (a) of the definition of "adjusted cost base" in s. 54, which defines the adjusted cost base of depreciable property as "the capital cost to the taxpayer of the property as of that time." The characterization of property as "depreciable property" and the statutory rules governing this kind of capital property are examined in Chapter 5.

called Recordak Limited ("Recordak"), which leased and serviced specialized equipment known as recordaks, which were used to take reduced photographs and microfilms of documents. In 1940, the taxpayer took over Recordak's business and assets.

Until 1940, Recordak never sold any recordaks, but treated them as capital assets with respect to which it claimed capital cost allowance. When the taxpayer took over the business, it characterized it as a separate division for accounting purposes, and continued to treat the recordaks as capital assets, deducting capital cost allowance with respect to existing machines and new machines as they were acquired.

In 1951, the taxpayer changed its business policy with regard to recordaks, deciding to offer the machines for sale to existing users. According to the taxpayer's treasurer and assistant general manager, the change in policy reflected "a business decision made in the course of the [taxpayer's] business" and was designed to give the taxpayer "a wider distribution of the equipment and reduce the amount of capital invested in it." Despite the change in policy, the taxpayer hired no additional salespeople and continued to describe its business in its income tax returns as it had in previous years as "the sale of photographic supplies — wholesale." Pursuant to the new policy, the taxpayer sold approximately 40 per cent of its recordaks in 1951 and a further 5 per cent in 1952. Thereafter, the taxpayer continued to lease the recordaks that it did not sell, and continued to acquire new recordaks to lease or sell.

In computing its income for accounting purposes, the taxpayer reported a profit of $148,693.50 in 1951 and $20,518.00 in 1952 from the sale of recordaks, which it did not include in computing its income for tax purposes. The Minister added these amounts in computing the taxpayer's taxable income for each of these years. The taxpayer objected on the basis that "the machines were capital assets and any gain on their sale was a capital gain and that they were not sold in the ordinary course of its business and were not part of its profit-making activities.]

THORSON P: ... The issue in this case is whether the profit made by the appellant on the sale of the recordaks which it had previously leased was taxable income within the meaning of the *Income Tax Act*, SC 1948, c. 52.

...

It was contended for the appellant that the profit made by it was not a profit from its business. It was submitted that its recordaks had always been regarded by it as capital assets and accepted as such by taxing authority, that they had never acquired the characteristics of inventory or property held for sale but had always been held exclusively as revenue producing property from which income was received, that when they were sold the sale was not made with a view to making a profit but for the purpose of freeing capital and obtaining a wider distribution of machines, that they always retained their characteristics as capital assets and that when they were sold they were sold as capital assets with a resulting capital gain.

I cannot accept these submissions. On the contrary, I agree with the argument put forward by counsel for the respondent. He contended that the appellant was organized to be the selling instrument in Canada of the products of the Eastman Kodak Company, that its recordaks were not fundamentally different in principle from the wide range of cameras and photographic equipment and supplies sold by it, that the decision to sell the recordaks was a business decision made for business reasons to increase the appellant's sales and to increase its profits, that from the time of this decision the appellant was in the business of selling recordaks and that its profit therefrom was a profit from its business and taxable income within the meaning of the Act.

Moreover, I am unable to distinguish this case in principle from the case of *Gloucester Railway Carriage and Wagon Co. v. Inland Revenue Commissioners*, [1925] AC 467; 12 TC 720. In that case the company was formed to manufacture, buy, sell, hire and let on hire wagons and other rolling stock, and for many years it manufactured railway wagons, either selling them outright or on the hire-purchase system or letting them on simple hire. In the books of the company the wagons built to be let on hire were capitalized at a sum which included an amount added as profit on manufacture, and year by year an amount was written off the value of the wagons for depreciation. In 1920 the company decided to cease letting wagons on hire and to sell them. It then sold the entire stock of wagons used in that branch of its business for a sum in excess of the value of the wagons in the company's books. The surplus was included in an assessment to corporation profits tax on the company in respect of the profits of its business, and the company appealed contending that the surplus arose from the realization of capital assets used in its hiring business. The Special Commissioners disagreed with the contention of the company that the profit on the sales was an accretion of capital. They found as follows:

> We are unable to take this view. In our opinion we must have regard to the main object of the Company which is to make a profit in one way or another out of making wagons and rolling stock. We are unable to draw the very sharp line which we are asked to draw between wagons sold, wagons let on hire purchase and wagons let on simple hire, nor do we consider that this very sharp division in fact exists. We do not regard ourselves as precluded by the fact that as long as the wagons were let they were treated as "plant and machinery" subject to wear and tear, from deciding that they are stock in trade when they are sold, even though let under tenancy agreements, for they seem to us to have in fact the one or the other aspect according as they are regarded from the point of view of the users or the Company. In our view, shortly, it makes no difference that one way of making profit out of the wagons was given up, for the very giving up itself involved the making of a profit in another way out of the same wagons, and the purpose of the Company's trade is to make a profit out of wagons.

The decision of the Commissioners was affirmed by Rowlatt J of the King's Bench Division. An appeal from his decision to the Court of Appeal was dismissed, Pollock MR, dissenting. The judgment of the majority of the Court was clearly to the effect that the profit made by the company was profit arising from the business. On an appeal being taken to the House of Lords it was unanimously dismissed. I need quote only the last paragraph of Lord Dunedin's speech:

> The appellants argue that this is really a capital increment; and to say so they call these wagons plant of the hiring business. I am of the opinion that in calling them plant they really beg the whole question. The Commissioners have found — and I think it is the fact — that there was here one business. A wagon is none the less sold as an incident of the business of buying and selling because in the meantime before sold it has been utilized by being hired out. There is no similarity whatever between these wagons and plant in the proper sense, e.g., machinery, or between them and investments the sale of which plant or investments at a price greater than that at which had been acquired would be a capital increment and not an item of income. I think that the appeal fails.

The principles applied in the *Gloucester Railway Carriage and Wagon Company* case (*supra*) are applicable in this one. Counsel for the appellant sought to distinguish it from the present case on several grounds one of which was that in the case cited there was only one business whereas in the appellant's case there had always been a sharp separation between its recordak division and its other business so that the former was really a separate business, but the fact is that in each case there was only one business. The appellant's recordak division was not a separate business. The manner in which the appellant kept its accounts proves this beyond dispute. Moreover, just as in the case cited the Commissioners did not regard themselves as precluded by the fact that as long as the wagons were let they were treated as plant and machinery from deciding that they were stock in trade when they were sold, and Lord Dunedin considered that "a wagon is none the less sold as an incident of the business of buying and selling because in the meantime before sold it has been utilized by being hired out," so the fact that the appellant's recordaks were formerly leased and treated as capital assets ... does not prevent the profit from their sale being profit from the appellant's business once it had made the business decision to sell them and sold them in the course of its ordinary business of selling photographic equipment and supplies. It was in exactly the same position in which it would have been in if it had acquired the recordaks for resale. There was nothing of a capital nature in the sale of its recordaks and it is fanciful to say that they were realizations of investments. There was no difference in principle between its sales of recordaks and its sales of other photographic equipment. They were all sales in the course of the appellant's business.

I, therefore, find that the profit made by the appellant from the sales of its recordaks in each of the years under review was profit from its business and taxable income within the meaning of the Act. ...

Judgment accordingly.

NOTES AND QUESTIONS

1.   On what basis did the taxpayer in *Canadian Kodak Sales* argue that the gains on the sale of its recordaks in 1951 and 1952 were on account of capital, not income? Why did the court reject this argument?

2.   Among the taxpayer's arguments in *Canadian Kodak Sales*, is the argument that the recordak division was a "separate business" the sale of the property of which was, therefore, distinguishable from the *Gloucester Railway Carriage and Wagon Co. v. Inland Revenue Commissioners*, [1925] A.C. 469, 12 Tax Cas 720 (H.L.). Although Thorson P concluded that the recordak division was not a separate business, other decisions held that the sale of inventory as part of the sale of an entire business was a sale on account of capital, not income from the taxpayer's business.[23] These decisions were reversed by the enactment of section 85E [now section 23], effective with respect to sales made after April 5, 1955. According to subsection 23(1):

> Where, on or after disposing of or ceasing to carry on a business or a part of a business, a taxpayer has sold all or any part of the property that was included in the inventory of the business, the property so sold shall, for the purposes of this Part, be deemed to have been sold by the taxpayer in the course of carrying on the business.

For cases in which this deeming provision has been applied, see *M.N.R. v. Curlett*, [1967] S.C.J. No. 20, [1967] C.T.C. 62, 67 D.T.C. 5058 (S.C.C.); *Raby v. M.N.R.*, [1965] C.T.C. 138, 65 D.T.C. 5085 (Ex. Ct.); and *Lyon Development Corp. Ltd. v. M.N.R.* (1965), 40 Tax ABC 68 (T.A.B.). See also *Plewes v. M.N.R.*, [1984] C.T.C. 2585, 84 D.T.C. 1582 (T.C.C.), where the deeming provision was held not to apply to asparagus plants sold as part of the sale of a market garden business on the basis that the plants were not inventory, which is itself sold, but capital assets, which must remain in place in order to produce fruit.

3.   In *Anthes Equipment Ltd. v. M.N.R.*, [1987] 1 C.T.C. 2117, 87 D.T.C. 59 (T.C.C.), the taxpayer, who carried on a business of leasing and selling scaffolding and shoring equipment for use in construction, occasionally sold rental equipment to lessees, such sales being unsolicited and reluctantly made on the insistence of the lessee. Referring to *Canadian Kodak Sales Ltd. v. M.N.R.*, [1954] C.T.C. 375, 54 D.T.C. 1194 (Ex. Ct.), the Tax Court held that the proceeds from these sales were income from the taxpayer's business on the basis that the taxpayer had converted the property from capital property to inventory. Gains on sales of exhausted rental equipment for scrap, however, were held to be on account of capital.

4.   In *Sensibar Dredging Corp. Ltd. v. M.N.R.*, [1967] C.T.C. 298, 67 D.T.C. 5212 (Ex. Ct.), the taxpayer carried on a dredging business for the purpose of which dredges were occasionally designed by the taxpayer, built at the client's expense, and sold to the taxpayer after completion of the work. In the taxation year at issue, the taxpayer acquired and resold one such dredge from which it

---

[23] The leading Canadian case on this point is *Frankel Corp. Ltd. v. M.N.R.*, [1959] S.C.J. No. 52, [1959] C.T.C. 244, 59 D.T.C. 1161 (S.C.C.). See also *Empire Manufacturing Company Limited v. M.N.R.* (1951), 4 Tax ABC 203 (T.A.B.) and *M.N.R. v. McCord Street Sites Ltd.*, [1962] C.T.C. 387, 62 D.T.C. 1229 (Ex. Ct.).

realized a gain of $1,250,000. Notwithstanding that the arrangements to acquire the dredge were entered into before receiving an unsolicited offer from the subsequent purchaser, the court rejected the taxpayer's argument that the gain was a capital gain from the sale of a capital asset on the grounds (at para. 23) that the taxpayer was "influenced" by "trading considerations" and that "the negotiations leading up to the transaction" were "characteristic of trading rather than of mere realization of a capital asset."

For a contrary result, in which a gain from the purchase and sale of a tugboat was characterized as a capital gain, notwithstanding two other transactions in which the taxpayer bought and resold boats at a profit, on the basis that the taxpayer's sole intention in acquiring the boat had been to repair and refurbish it for living quarters and towing and air-sea rescue work, see *Bentzen v. Canada*, [1973] F.C.J. No. 902, [1973] C.T.C. 702, 73 D.T.C. 5517 (F.C.T.D.).

5. A number of cases have considered the characterization of gains on the sale of automobiles used by employees or as demonstration vehicles in the course of a sales business. See, for example, *M.N.R. v. British & American Motors Toronto Ltd.*, [1953] C.T.C. 177, 53 D.T.C. 1113 (Ex. Ct.); *M.N.R. v. J.T. Labadie Ltd.*, [1954] C.T.C. 90, 54 D.T.C. 1053 (Ex. Ct.); and *Maclin Motors Ltd. v. M.N.R.* (1954), 10 Tax ABC 377 (T.A.B.). For the most part, these gains have been characterized as income from the taxpayer's business on the basis that the vehicles were only temporarily removed from the taxpayer's inventory.

6. For the CRA's views on the conversion of property other than real property from capital property to inventory or vice versa, see *Interpretation Bulletin* IT-102R2, "Conversion of Property, Other than Real Property, to or from Inventory," July 22, 1985. According to paragraphs 3 to 7 of this bulletin:

> 3. Capital property, whether or not depreciable property of a prescribed class, that is used for the purpose of earning income from a business or property is not, as a general rule, converted to inventory simply because it is put on the market for sale. Accordingly, where capital property is sold, the sales proceeds will ordinarily be treated as proceeds of disposition of capital property for all purposes of the Act. It is, however, the Department's position that exceptions to this general rule will occur.
>
> 4. Where a taxpayer both sells and either rents or leases property of the same kind, it is the Department's position that all proceeds from the sale of property that has been rented or leased constitutes income of the taxpayer from the sale of inventory unless
>
> (a) the taxpayer operates a separate and clearly distinguishable leasing division, including the keeping of separate records,
>
> (b) specific property is set aside by the taxpayer for either renting or leasing and is factually so used, and
>
> (c) properties that are so rented or leased are normally sold for an amount that is less than their cost to the taxpayer.

Where the conditions in (a) to (c) above are complied with, the ultimate disposal of property used for renting or leasing will be treated as the disposal of capital property.

5. It is recognized that a taxpayer whose business consists only of the renting or leasing of property is, from time to time, required to renew such property by selling it after it has been rented or leased for a period of time, and purchasing new property. In these circumstances, where the proceeds from the disposal of each individual property normally exceed the taxpayer's cost thereof, the proceeds from the sale of all of the taxpayer's property that has been rented or leased will be considered to be received by the taxpayer on account of income rather than capital.

6. Notwithstanding 4 and 5 above, where, at any time, a particular property is leased

(a)   without option to purchase,

(b)   for a sufficiently long period of time so that the anticipated sales price of the particular property at the time of expiry of the lease will not ordinarily exceed its cost to the lessor, and

(c)   the particular property is not ordinarily replaced by other property during the currency of the lease,

the lessor may, from that time, treat the particular property as capital property rather than inventory for all purposes of the Act.

7. The facts of each case will determine whether or not a conversion of property ... has occurred. For example, a conversion is generally not considered to have taken place where

(a)   property that was purchased primarily for resale is temporarily withdrawn from inventory and used in a business to earn income, for example demonstrator or courtesy vehicles by a car dealer, salesmen's samples or the use of equipment by employees in carrying out their business responsibilities, or

(b)   the cost of property was incorrectly classified in the accounts of a business and has been reclassified to reflect the use made of the property, as capital property or inventory, as the case may be, since it was acquired.

According to paragraph 8:

Where capital property is converted to inventory, the action of conversion does not constitute a disposition within the meaning of paragraphs 13(21)(c) and 54(c). It is, however, recognized that the ultimate disposition of a property that was so converted may give rise to a gain or loss on capital account, a gain or loss on income account or a gain or loss that is partly capital and partly income. Accordingly, with respect to capital property that has been converted to inventory, taxpayers may calculate capital gains or losses, if any, on the basis that a notional disposition of such property occurred on the date of conversion. The amount of such a notionally determined capital gain or loss in respect of a property will be the difference between its adjusted cost base, as defined in paragraph 54(a), (subject to the ITAR rules for property held on December 31, 1971) and its fair market value on the date of conversion. These notionally determined capital gains or losses will be considered to give rise to taxable capital gains or allowable capital losses for the taxation year during which the actual disposition of the relevant property occurs and will be required to be so reported in that same year. The amount of any income gain or loss arising on actual disposition of the converted property will be determined in accordance with generally accepted accounting principles on the basis that its initial inventory value is its fair market value on the date of conversion.

Paragraphs 9 and 10 discuss the tax consequences associated with the conversion of inventory other than real property to capital property, but do not indicate whether a subsequent gain on the sale of property that is so converted results in a gain or loss on capital account alone or a gain or loss that is partly capital and partly income.

C. Corporate Shares

Corporate shares represent fractional interests in the ownership of the issuing corporation, conferring a proprietary interest in the corporation itself rather than the assets of the corporation. Like active income-producing real property, corporate shares can be acquired and held for the purpose of receiving a regular flow of income (typically in the form of dividends), for the purpose of resale at a profit, or for both purposes. The leading case on the characterization of gains from the disposition of this kind of property is *Irrigation Industries Ltd. v. M.N.R.*, [1962] S.C.J. No. 15, [1962] C.T.C. 215, 62 D.T.C. 1131 (S.C.C.).

Irrigation Industries Ltd. v. M.N.R.
[1962] S.C.J. No. 15, [1962] C.T.C. 215, 62 D.T.C. 1131 (S.C.C.)

CARTWRIGHT J (Judson J, concurring in dissent): This is an appeal from a judgment of Cameron J dismissing an appeal from a decision of the Tax Appeal Board whereby the re-assessment of the appellant for the taxation year ending December 31, 1953, was affirmed.

...

The appellant was incorporated on October 25, 1947, under *The Companies Act* of the Province of Alberta as a limited company. The original purpose of its promoters was to erect a mill for the dehydration of alfalfa, but this was abandoned by August, 1948. The appellant remained inactive until the autumn of 1952 when it purchased an office building in Calgary; it spent a substantial amount on alterations and, towards the end of 1955, sold the building for a sum equal to the total amount which it had spent on it.

Early in 1953 the directors of the appellant received a favourable report on the shares of the Brunswick Mining and Smelting Corporation Limited, hereinafter referred to as "Brunswick," and on or about February 23, 1953, the appellant purchased 4,000 treasury shares of that company at $10 per share, the total purchase price being $40,000. Between March 10 and March 13, 1953, the appellant sold 2,400 of these shares for a total of $38,513.50 and in June, 1953, it sold the remaining 1,600 shares for a sum in excess of $28,000. It is common ground that the appellant realized a total profit of $26,897.50 from the purchase and sale of these 4,000 shares.

With the exception of certain debentures purchased in 1955 after the sale of the building referred to above the appellant had no dealings in securities other than the purchase and sale of the 4,000 shares of Brunswick.

...

At the trial before Cameron J the only witness examined was Mr. Cheshire, the president of the appellant. The effect of his evidence was that the appellant purchased the Brunswick shares because it "felt that this was an excellent opportunity to invest money in a company which appeared to have an excellent chance for growth and development into a large mining operation," that the sales in March were prompted by the fact that the bank was pressing the appellant for repayment of a loan and those in June by the decision reached by the directors of the appellant at an informal meeting that the price of the shares had risen to such a point that, having regard to the aggregate value of Brunswick's known assets, it ceased to be in accordance with sound judgment to continue to hold them as an investment. There is, I think, an implication in the evidence of this witness that the shares were purchased as a long term investment rather than as a speculation looking to a quick turnover but there is no express statement to that effect.

Cameron J made the following finding of fact:

> On the facts in evidence and drawing what I consider to be the proper inferences therefrom, I have reached the conclusion that the purchase in question was not an investment, but a purely speculative purchase, and was entered into with the intention of disposing of the stock at a profit as soon as there was a reasonable opportunity of so doing.

The considerations which brought Cameron J to this conclusion were, (i) that the appellant at the time of purchasing the Brunswick shares had no funds of its own available for investment and used borrowed funds to pay for them, (ii) that the nature of the Brunswick undertaking was such that its shares were of speculative value, (iii) that even if Brunswick's operations proved successful its shares could not be expected to yield any dividends for a considerable time, and (iv) that the shares were held by the appellant only for the short time mentioned above.

After considering the whole record, in the light of the full and able argument of counsel, I find myself unable to say that the finding of fact made by Cameron J was not justified by the evidence, and in my opinion it should not be disturbed.

There are difficulties in ascertaining the intention of a corporation in entering into a transaction. In *CIR v. Fisher's Executor's*, [1926] AC 395, Lord Sumner said:

> In any case desires and intentions are things of which a company is incapable. These are the mental operations of its shareholders and officers. The only intention that the company has is such as is expressed in or necessarily follows from its proceedings. It is hardly a paradox to say that the form of a company's resolutions and instruments is their substance.

On the other hand in *Regal Heights Ltd. v. M.N.R.*, [1960] SCR 902; [1960] CTC 384, Judson J who gave the judgment of the majority of the Court held that the intentions of the appellant company were throughout its existence identical with those of its promoters who later became its directors.

In the case at bar there is no record of any resolution of the board of directors of the appellant or indeed of any formal proceeding to assist the Court in ascertaining its intention. The decisions in relation to the sale of the Brunswick shares appear to have been made at "informal meetings" of the directors. Mr. Cheshire's evidence regarding the appellant's intention was, as has been pointed out above, somewhat indefinite and it was proper for the learned trial judge to draw an inference as to what that intention was from the surrounding circumstances.

Having concluded that we should accept the finding of fact made by Cameron J and quoted above, the point which arises for decision may be briefly stated as follows. The appellant, which was not at any time engaged in the business of trading in securities, made an isolated speculative purchase of a block of shares, not with the intention of retaining them as an investment which would sooner or later yield an income by way of dividends but in the expectation and with the intention of disposing of the shares in the near future at an increased price; this expectation was realized as to part of the shares in less than a month and as to the balance within four months. The question is whether the resulting profit constitutes taxable income or a non-taxable capital gain.

...

Cameron J was of opinion that the purchase and sale of the Brunswick shares was an adventure or concern in the nature of trade. The respondent supports this view while the appellant contends that what occurred was simply the realization at an enhanced price of a capital asset or investment and did not constitute an adventure or concern in the nature of trade.

In the case at bar it appears to me that on the view which he took of the facts Cameron J was right in holding that the transaction in question was an adventure in the nature of trade and that consequently the profit arising from it was taxable.

Among the meanings of the word "adventure" given in the *Shorter Oxford Dictionary* are "a pecuniary venture" and "a speculation"; "venture" in turn is given the meaning, "a commercial enterprise in which there is considerable risk of loss as well as chance of gain." That the transaction was an adventure does not seem to me to admit of doubt.

Equally, I think, it was "in the nature of trade." In *Edwards v. Bairstow*, [1956] AC 14, Lord Radcliffe said, at page 38:

> Dealing is, I think, essentially a trading adventure, and the respondents' operations were nothing but a deal or deals in plant and machinery.

In the case at bar the appellant's transaction was a deal in mining shares.

There is nothing in the reasons of Cameron J or in what I have said above to throw the slightest doubt on the applicability to the *Income Tax Act* in this country of the principle stated by the Lord Justice Clerk, in *Californian Copper Syndicate Ltd. v. Harris* (1904), 5 TC 159 at page 165:

> It is quite a well settled principle in dealing with questions of assessment of Income Tax, that where the owner of an ordinary investment chooses to realize it, and obtains a greater price

for it than he originally acquired it at, the enhanced price is not profit in the sense of Schedule D of the *Income Tax Act* of 1842 assessable to Income Tax.

On the facts as found by Cameron J in the case at bar, the profit realized was not the enhancement in price of an ordinary investment but rather "a gain made in an operation of business in carrying out a scheme for profit-making." To hold otherwise would appear to me to be contrary to the reasoning of the majority in the *Regal Heights* case (*supra*).

I have arrived at this conclusion with some hesitation. It appears to me to involve the result that in cases of this nature the answer to the question whether a profit is or is not taxable depends on the purely subjective test as to the intention of the taxpayer when he acquired the shares which have subsequently been sold at a profit. If, for example, in the case at bar it had been found as a fact that the intention of the appellant when it acquired the shares was to hold them as an investment looking forward to the time when Brunswick would pay dividends the circumstance that a few weeks later it sold the shares at a profit would not have rendered that profit subject to tax. In *Bawlf Grain Co. v. Ross* (1917), 55 SCR 232 at page 255, Duff J as he then was, pointed out that the law does not as a rule "take note of subjective events in the stream of consciousness save in relation to or as manifested by some external word or deed." It seems strange that the question whether a certain profit is subject to tax should depend on the intention with which the taxpayer entered into the transaction from which it resulted, but the words of Bowen LJ in *Edgington v. Fitzmaurice* (1885), 99 Ch. D 459 at 483, have often been quoted with approval:

> ... the state of a man's mind is as much a fact as the state of his digestion. It is true that it is very difficult to prove what the state of a man's mind at a particular time is, but if it can be ascertained it is as much a fact as anything else.

The other cause of my hesitation is that while the expression "adventure or concern in the nature of trade" has been in the Acts in the United Kingdom for a century and a half and in the Act in this country for thirteen years counsel have not referred to any reported case in which the profit arising from one isolated purchase and sale of shares by a taxpayer not engaged in the business of trading in securities has been claimed to be taxable. However this is perhaps not the type of problem in the solution of which the maxim *omnis innovatio plus novitate perturbat quam utilitate prodest* is of assistance.

I would dismiss the appeal with costs.

MARTLAND J (Taschereau and Locke JJ, concurring): ... The facts are outlined in the judgment of my brother Cartwright and I will not repeat them here in full. There are, however, two matters which should be mentioned. The first is that the shares of Brunswick Mining and Smelting Company Limited (hereinafter referred to as "Brunswick") were purchased by the appellant directly from Brunswick being a part of an initial issue of shares by Brunswick to finance additional drilling and exploration work and for some underground development.

...

The other matter is that the purchase and sale of the Brunswick shares was not authorized by the Memorandum of Association of the appellant, or by the statutory powers conferred upon it by Section 19 of *The Companies Act*, RSA 1955, c. 53. There can, therefore, be no suggestion that in purchasing and selling the shares in question the appellant was engaged in a business which it had been created to carry on. The purchase and sale of the shares was outside the scope of its business activities and consequently nothing can turn on the fact that the appellant is a limited company as contrasted with an individual.

...

Cameron J held that there was an adventure in the nature of trade and the basis of his decision is stated as follows:

> On the facts in evidence and drawing what I consider to be the proper inferences therefrom, I have reached the conclusion that the purchase in question was not an investment, but a purely speculative purchase, and was entered into with the intention of disposing of the stock at a profit as soon as there was a reasonable opportunity of so doing. It was therefore an adventure or concern in the nature of trade.

The reasons leading to his conclusion that the purchase was not an investment are:

1. The fact that the appellant borrowed the funds necessary to effect the purchase of the shares;

2. The inference that the nature of Brunswick indicated that its shares were speculative in value and that dividends could not be expected for some years.

With respect, I would not think that the question of whether securities are purchased with the purchaser's own funds, or with money borrowed by him, is a significant factor in determining whether their purchase and subsequent sale is or is not an investment.

Similarly, the fact that there was no immediate likelihood of dividends being paid on the shares should not have much significance, for there are many corporate ventures, financed by the sale of shares to the public, in which immediate payment of dividends may not be anticipated, and yet the purchase of the treasury shares of a company embarking on a new enterprise is a well recognized method of making an investment.

However, assuming that the conclusion was correct that this purchase was speculative in that it was made, not with the intention of holding the securities indefinitely, with a view to dividends, but made with the intention of disposing of the shares at a profit as soon as reasonably possible, does this, in itself, lead to the conclusion that it was an adventure in the nature of trade?

It is difficult to conceive of any case, in which securities are purchased, in which the purchaser does not have at least some intention of disposing of them if their value appreciates to the point where their sale appears to be financially desirable. If this is so, then any purchase and sale of securities must constitute an adventure in the nature of trade, unless it is attempted to ascertain whether the primary intention at the time of purchase is to retain the security or to sell it. This, however, leads to the difficulty mentioned by my brother Cartwright that the question of taxability is to be determined by seeking to ascertain the primary subjective intention of the purchaser at the time of purchase.

I cannot agree that the question as to whether or not an isolated transaction in securities is to constitute an adventure in the nature of trade can be determined solely upon that basis. In my opinion, a person who puts money into a business enterprise by the purchase of the shares of a company on an isolated occasion, and not as a part of his regular business, cannot be said to have engaged in an adventure in the nature of trade merely because the purchase was speculative in that, at that time, he did not intend to hold the shares indefinitely, but intended, if possible, to sell them at a profit as soon as he reasonably could. I think that there must be clearer indications of "trade" than this before it can be said that there has been an adventure in the nature of trade.

...

The nature of the property in question here is shares issued from the treasury of a corporation and we have not been referred to any reported case in which profit from one isolated purchase and sale of shares, by a person not engaged in the business of trading in securities, has been claimed to be taxable.

...

Corporate shares ... constitute something the purchase of which is, in itself, an investment. They are not, in themselves, articles of commerce, but represent an interest in a corporation which is itself created for the purpose of doing business. Their acquisition is a well recognized method of investing capital in a business enterprise.

...

Furthermore, the quantity of shares purchased by the appellant in the present case would not, in my opinion, be indicative of an adventure in the nature of trade, as it constituted only 4,000 out of a total issue of 500,000 shares.

...

Were the operations involved in the present case of the same kind and carried on in the same way as those which are characteristic of ordinary trading in the line of business in which the venture was made?

The only operations of the appellant in the present case were the purchase of 4,000 treasury shares directly from Brunswick and their subsequent sale, presumably through brokers. This is not the sort of trading which would be carried on ordinarily by those engaged in the business of trading in securities. The appellant's purchase was not an underwriting, nor was it a participation in an underwriting syndicate with respect to an issue of securities for the purpose of effecting their sale to the public, and did not have the characteristics of that kind of a venture. What the appellant did was to acquire a capital interest in a new corporate business venture, in a manner which has the characteristics of the making of an investment, and subsequently to dispose, by sale, of that interest.

...

The only test which was applied in the present case was whether the appellant entered into the transaction with the intention of disposing of the shares at a profit so soon as there was a reasonable opportunity of so doing. Is that a sufficient test for determining whether or not this transaction constitutes an adventure in the nature of trade? I do not think that, standing alone, it is sufficient.

...

In my opinion, therefore, the appeal should be allowed. ...

Appeal allowed.

NOTES AND QUESTIONS

1. According to the majority decision in *Irrigation Industries*, corporate shares "constitute something the purchase of which is, in itself, an investment." Do you agree? Is it possible to determine the characterization of a gain or loss solely by reference to the subject matter of the property? Does the subject matter of certain kinds of property (for example, commodities or vacant land) completely determine the characterization of a gain or loss or simply raise an inference as to the taxpayer's purpose in acquiring the property? In *Irrigation Industries*, what inference was it reasonable to draw from the characteristics of the shares acquired by the taxpayer?

2. In *Irrigation Industries*, Martland J concluded that "there must be clearer indications of 'trade' than [speculative intent] before it can be said that there has been an adventure in the nature of trade." What indications does Martland J suggest should have been present in order to conclude that the acquisition of the shares was "in the nature of trade"? Do these indications exclude the possibility that an isolated transaction in shares can be characterized as an adventure in the nature of trade? If so, does Martland J's interpretation of the words "in the nature of trade" contradict Thorson P's conclusion in *Taylor v. M.N.R.*, [1990] T.C.J. No. 813, [1990] 2 C.T.C. 2466, 90 D.T.C. 1917 (T.C.C.), that a single trade may constitute an "adventure"?

3. In the course of his dissenting judgment in *Irrigation Industries*, Cartwright J expresses "some hesitation" in upholding the Exchequer Court decision, which "appears to involve the result that in cases of this nature" the characterization of a gain "depends on the purely subjective test as to the intention of the taxpayer when he acquired the shares which have subsequently been sold at a profit." Similarly, Martland J emphasizes "the difficulty mentioned by my brother Cartwright that the question of taxability is to be determined by seeking to ascertain the primary subjective intention of the purchaser at the time of the purchase." Is the inquiry into the taxpayer's purpose

in acquiring property a "purely subjective test"? Given the scheme of the *Income Tax Act*, is there any way to avoid this inquiry?

4. According to Cartwright J, the majority decision in *Irrigation Industries* "would appear ... to be contrary to the reasoning of the majority in the *Regal Heights* case [supra]." Do you agree? Why or why not?

5. In *Irrigation Industries*, the majority rejects the intention test for corporate shares, concluding that "the question as to whether or not an isolated transaction in securities is to constitute an adventure in the nature of trade" cannot be determined "solely upon that basis." Less than five years later, however, in *M.N.R. v. Foreign Power Securities Corp.*, [1967] S.C.J. No. 23, [1967] C.T.C. 116 at 117, 67 D.T.C. 5084 at 5085 (S.C.C.) Cartwright J (Taschereau CJC, Fauteux, Martland, Spence JJ, concurring) stated (at para. 4) that "[t]he question is essentially one of fact depending on the intention with which the respondent acquired the shares."

Despite the majority decision in *Irrigation Industries*, the intention test has been emphasized in subsequent decisions. See, for example, *Bossin v. Canada*, [1976] F.C.J. No. 402, [1976] C.T.C. 358, 76 D.T.C. 6196 (F.C.T.D.). Indeed, in a number of cases since *Irrigation Industries*, gains or losses from speculative sales of shares have been characterized as income or losses from adventures in the nature of trade. See, for example, *Interoceanic Investments Ltd. v. M.N.R.*, [1967] Tax ABC 1062 and *Tamas v. Canada*, [1981] F.C.J. No. 501, [1981] C.T.C. 220, 81 D.T.C. 5150 (F.C.T.D.).

6. In *Bossin*, Collier J distinguished *Irrigation Industries* on the basis that it concerned the acquisition of treasury shares obtained directly from the issuing corporation, rather than in the secondary market — for example, in a public stock exchange. To what extent does the majority decision depend on the fact that the shares were acquired directly from the issuing corporation?

7. In *Californian Copper Syndicate Ltd. v. Harris* (1904), 5 Tax Cas. 159 (Ex. Ct. (Scot.)), the taxpayer's gain from an isolated sale of shares was held to be business income on the basis that the taxpayer had entered into a scheme of profit making in order to increase the value of the shares for purposes of resale. On a similar basis, Canadian courts have often held that gains from isolated transactions in shares are income from a business within the ordinary meaning of the word. See, for example, *Robertson v. M.N.R.*, [1963] C.T.C. 550, 63 D.T.C. 1367 (Ex. Ct.); *Fraser v. M.N.R.*, [1964] S.C.J. No. 45, [1964] C.T.C. 372, 64 D.T.C. 5224 (S.C.C.); *Placements Bourg-Royal Inc. v. Canada*, [1974] F.C.J. No. 413, [1974] C.T.C. 362, 74 D.T.C. 6269 (F.C.T.D.); and *Western Wholesale Drug Ltd. v. Canada*, [1976] F.C.J. No. 1111, [1977] C.T.C. 1, (1976) 77 D.T.C. 5021 (F.C.T.D.). Likewise, losses on the disposition of corporate shares have been allowed on a similar basis. See, for example, *Factory Carpet Ltd. v. The Queen*, [1985] F.C.J. No. 823, [1985] 2 C.T.C. 267, 85

D.T.C. 5464 (F.C.T.D.) and *Leslie v. M.N.R.*, [1986] T.C.J. No. 21, [1986] 1 C.T.C. 2209, 86 D.T.C. 1152 (T.C.C.).

8.   In several cases, isolated share transactions have been characterized as adventures in the nature of trade on the basis that the share transaction was merely an alternative method of disposing of the underlying property owned by the corporation. See, for example, *William W. Siebens v. M.N.R.*, [1971] C.T.C. 557, 71 D.T.C. 5310 (F.C.T.D.), aff'd [1974] C.T.C. 889, 75 D.T.C. 5006 (F.C.A.); *Blok-Anderson v. M.N.R.*, [1972] C.T.C. 338, 72 D.T.C. 6309 (F.C.T.D.); *McKinley v. M.N.R.*, [1974] F.C.J. No. 10, [1974] C.T.C. 170, 74 D.T.C. 6138 (F.C.A.); *Cull v. M.N.R.*, [1987] F.C.J. No. 552, [1987] 2 C.T.C. 63, 87 D.T.C. 5322 (F.C.T.D.); and *Canada v. Dumas*, [1988] F.C.J. No. 910, [1989] 1 C.T.C. 52, (1988) 89 D.T.C. 5004 (F.C.A.). In contrast, where shares are sold in order to dispose of all or part of a business carried on by the taxpayer, a gain or loss on the sale is characterized as being on account of capital. See, for example, *M.N.R. v. Firestone Management Ltd.*, [1966] C.T.C. 771, 66 D.T.C. 5502 (Ex. Ct.).

9.   According to section 54.2:

> Where any person has disposed of property that consisted of all or substantially all of the assets used in an active business carried on by that person to a corporation for consideration that included shares of that corporation, the shares shall be deemed to be capital property of the person.

The term "active business" is defined in subsection 248(1) as any business carried on by a taxpayer except a "specified investment business" or a "personal services business" — which, in turn, are defined in subsection 125(7).

In essence, section 54.2 allows a taxpayer to incorporate an active business and obtain capital gains treatment on a subsequent sale of the shares. Note, however, that for the purposes of section 54.2, the extended definition of the term "business" in subsection 248(1) does not include an adventure or concern in the nature of trade. As a result, a taxpayer cannot convert business income from an adventure in the nature of trade into a capital gain by transferring the property that is the subject matter of the adventure to a corporation and disposing of the shares.

Section 54.2 was enacted by S.C. 1988, c. 55, section 32, applicable with respect to dispositions occurring after 1987. According to the Department of Finance technical notes released with the draft legislation:

> New section 54.2 provides that where a person disposes of all or substantially all the assets used in an active business to a corporation, the shares received in consideration shall be capital property of that person. The purpose of this new rule, which applies to dispositions occurring after 1987, is to ensure that the sale of a business through a sale of the shares of a corporation to which the business was recently transferred is not treated as a sale on income account. Thus, a parent corporation that would transfer a separate business to a subsidiary and subsequently sell the shares of that subsidiary would get capital gains treatment on the sale of the shares. A further example would be where an individual sells his business to a newly formed corporation in contemplation of a subsequent sale of all the shares of that corporation. In that case, the new rule will apply to ensure that the shares received as

consideration for the business will get capital gains treatment and will thus be eligible, provided other conditions are met, for the lifetime capital gains exemption for shares of a small business corporation.

A prerequisite to the application of the new rule is that the shares be issued as consideration for all or substantially all the assets used in an active business. Section 54.2 is not intended to apply where a taxpayer sells indirectly, through the sale of the shares of a corporation, non-business assets or only some of the assets used in a business.

An amendment to the definition of "business" in subsection 248(1) ensures that the disposition of the assets used in an adventure or concern in the nature of a trade will not qualify for the application of new section 54.2.

10.   In a number of cases, gains on the sale of shares have been characterized as income from a business on the basis that the taxpayer carried on a business of trading in securities. See, for example, *Gairdner Securities Ltd. v. M.N.R.*, [1954] C.T.C. 24, 54 D.T.C. 1015 (S.C.C.); *Osler Hammond & Nanton Ltd. v. M.N.R.*, [1963] S.C.J. No. 42, [1963] C.T.C. 164, 63 D.T.C. 1119 (S.C.C.); *Whittall v. M.N.R.*, [1967] S.C.J. No. 88, [1967] C.T.C. 377 (S.C.C.); *Georges Girard Inc. v. M.N.R.*, [1976] C.T.C. 2157, 76 D.T.C. 1128 (T.R.B.); *Karben Holding Ltd. v. Canada*, [1989] F.C.J. No. 624, [1989] 2 C.T.C. 145, 89 D.T.C. 5413 (F.C.T.D.); and *Forest Lane Holdings Ltd. v. M.N.R.*, [1990] F.C.J. No. 705, [1990] 2 C.T.C. 305, 90 D.T.C. 6495 (F.C.T.D.). Likewise, losses have been allowed on a similar basis. See, for example, *Admiral Investments Ltd. v. M.N.R.*, [1967] C.T.C. 165, 67 D.T.C. 5114 (Ex. Ct.); *Wellington Hotel Holdings Ltd. v. M.N.R.*, [1973] C.T.C. 473, 73 D.T.C. 5391 (F.C.T.D.); *Smith v. M.N.R.*, [1973] F.C.J. No. 905, [1973] C.T.C. 714, 73 D.T.C. 5526 (F.C.T.D.); *G.F. Mudge v. M.N.R.*, [1974] C.T.C. 2105, 74 D.T.C. 1084 (T.R.B.); and *Empire Paving Ltd. v. Canada*, [2008] T.C.J. No. 272, 2008 D.T.C. 4099 (T.C.C.).

11.   Alternatively where the taxpayer is considered to have acquired shares for investment purposes, gains or losses on the sale of shares prompted by market conditions or in order to take advantage of other investment opportunities have been characterized as being on account of capital. See, for example, *M.N.R. v. Foreign Power Securities Corp.*, [1967] S.C.J. No. 23, [1967] C.T.C. 116, 67 D.T.C. 5084 (S.C.C.); *Canada Permanent Mortgage Corp. v. M.N.R.*, [1971] C.T.C. 694, 71 D.T.C. 5409 (F.C.T.D.); *LeBel v. Canada*, [1987] F.C.J. No. 157, [1987] 1 C.T.C. 259, 87 D.T.C. 5154 (F.C.T.D.); *Imperial Stables (1981) Ltd. v. M.N.R.*, [1990] F.C.J. No. 38, [1990] 1 C.T.C. 213, 90 D.T.C. 6135 (F.C.T.D.), aff'd [1992] F.C.J. No. 140, [1992] 1 C.T.C. 263, 92 D.T.C. 6189 (F.C.A.); and *Pollock v. Canada*, [2008] T.C.J. No. 74, 2008 D.T.C. 2797 (T.C.C.).

12.   The CRA's views on the characterization of transactions involving corporate shares are found in *Interpretation Bulletin* IT-479R, "Transactions in Securities," February 29, 1984. According to this bulletin:

10. Where the whole course of conduct indicates that

(a) in security transactions the taxpayer is disposing of securities in a way capable of producing gains and with that object in view, and

(b) the transactions are of the same kind and carried on in the same way as those of a trader or dealer in securities,

the proceeds of sale will normally be considered to be income from a business and, therefore, on income account.

11. Some of the factors to be considered in ascertaining whether the taxpayer's course of conduct indicates the carrying on of a business are as follows:

(a) frequency of transactions — a history of extensive buying and selling of securities or of a quick turnover of properties,

(b) period of ownership — securities are usually owned only for a short period of time,

(c) knowledge of securities markets — the taxpayer has some knowledge of or experience in the securities markets,

(d) security transactions form a part of a taxpayer's ordinary business,

(e) time spent — a substantial part of the taxpayer's time is spent studying the securities markets and investigating potential purchases,

(f) financing — security purchases are financed primarily on margin or by some other form of debt,

(g) advertising — the taxpayer has advertised or otherwise made it known that he is willing to purchase securities, and

(h) in the case of shares, their nature — normally speculative in nature or of a non-dividend type.

12. Although none of the individual factors in 11 above may be sufficient to characterize the activities of a taxpayer as a business, the combination of a number of those factors may well be sufficient for that purpose. Further, subsection 248(1) defines the term "business" to include "an adventure or concern in the nature of trade" and the courts have held that "an adventure or concern in the nature of trade" can include an isolated transaction in shares where the "course of conduct" and "intention" clearly indicate it to be such.

13. A taxpayer's intention to sell at a gain is not sufficient, by itself, to establish that the taxpayer was involved in an adventure or concern in the nature of trade. That intention is almost invariably present even when a true investment has been acquired if circumstances should arise that would make it financially more beneficial to sell the investment than to continue to hold it. Where, however, one or other of the above tests clearly suggests an adventure or concern in the nature of trade and, in addition, it can be established or inferred that the taxpayer's intention was to sell the property at the first suitable opportunity, intention will be viewed as corroborative evidence. On the other hand, inability to establish an intention to sell does not preclude a transaction from being regarded as an adventure or concern in the nature of trade if it can otherwise be so regarded pursuant to one or more of the above tests. ...

15. All gains or losses of a taxpayer that relate to a participation in the promotion or underwriting of a particular issue of a security are on income account. Similarly, gains or losses made or incurred by an officer or employee of a firm or corporation that is engaged in the promotion or underwriting of securities are on income account if they result from the acquisition of securities promoted or underwritten by his employer. With regard to any other taxpayer who holds himself out to the public as a dealer in securities, there is a presumption that all gains or losses on security transactions are part of the normal operations of such a business and thus are on income account. Further, the gains and losses made by a corporation whose prime activity is trading in securities will be considered to be on income account, notwithstanding that the corporation does not hold itself out to the public as a trader or dealer in securities. ...

17. The presumption that gains and losses from security transactions are on income account will also be taken by the Department in any situation where it is apparent that the taxpayer has used special information not available to the public to realize a quick profit. ...

19. When the disposition of shares in a corporation is merely an alternative method of realizing income from the sale of a property held by the corporation (eg, real estate), the gains from the sale of those shares will be included in income as if the property itself had been sold.

D. Debt Obligations

A debt obligation is a generic term that comprises various kinds of financial instruments (for example, bonds, debentures, bills, notes, and mortgages) that represent indebtedness. Although debt obligations are often acquired for the purpose of receiving a regular flow of interest income, they may also be acquired for the purpose of resale at a premium or to obtain gains from holding discounted debt obligations to maturity. In some circumstances these gains may be characterized as interest income within the meaning of paragraph 12(1)(c) or deemed to be interest under paragraph 16(1)(a).[24] Where this is not the case, it remains to be determined whether the gain is a capital gain or income from a business within the meaning of the Act.

In a number of cases decided in the early 1960s, the Exchequer Court and the Supreme Court of Canada considered the characterization of gains realized by taxpayers who had acquired a number of debt obligations at a discount and held them to maturity. The decisions generally concluded that the gains were business income on the ground that the taxpayers had engaged in a "scheme of profit making" within the meaning of *Californian Copper Syndicate v. Harris*, (1904), 5 Tax Cas 159 (Ex. Ct. (Scot.)).[25] In *Wood v. M.N.R.*, [1969] S.C.J. No.

---

[24] See the section on "Interest Income" in Chapter 5.

[25] See *M.N.R. v. Spencer*, [1961] C.T.C. 109, 61 D.T.C. 1079 (Ex. Ct.); *M.N.R. v. Minden*, [1962] C.T.C. 79, 62 D.T.C. 1044 (Ex. Ct.); *M.N.R. v. Rosenberg*, [1962] C.T.C. 372, 62 D.T.C. 1216 (Ex. Ct.); *M.N.R. v. Wolfe*, [1962] C.T.C. 466, 62 D.T.C. 1281 (Ex. Ct.); *Associated Investors Ltd. v. M.N.R.*, [1962] C.T.C. 510, 62 D.T.C. 1315 (Ex. Ct.); *Scott v. M.N.R.*, [1963] S.C.J. No. 16, [1963] C.T.C. 176, 63 D.T.C. 1121 (S.C.C.); *M.N.R. v. MacInnes*, [1963] S.C.J. No. 27, [1963] C.T.C. 311, 63 D.T.C. 1203 (S.C.C.); *M.N.R. v. Minden*, [1963] C.T.C. 364, 63 D.T.C.

1, [1969] C.T.C. 57, 69 D.T.C. 5073 (S.C.C.), the Supreme Court of Canada considered the issue once again.

Wood v. M.N.R.
[1969] S.C.J. No. 1, [1969] C.T.C. 57, 69 D.T.C. 5073 (S.C.C.)

ABBOTT J: The appellant, a solicitor who has practised law in the City of Toronto since 1928, was at all material times a member of the firm Mackenzie, Wood & Goodchild. That firm had a general practice which included a "fairly substantial mortgage practice."

The firm, on behalf of clients, managed or supervised the collection of moneys lent on the security of mortgages and, between 1956 and 1963, the appellant had acquired personally an interest in thirteen mortgages. Eleven of these mortgages were acquired at a bonus or discount.

In July 1957, appellant, in association with a client, bought a first mortgage on which the amount then owing was $8,500 for principal, with interest at the rate of 6½ per cent per annum. The term of the mortgage was five years. Appellant and his client paid the sum of $7,100, each of them putting up one-half of the purchase price. The mortgage was paid off in full at maturity in July 1962.

Appellant was assessed for income tax in 1962 on $700 being his share of the discount on the said mortgage that he had collected in that year.

Before the Tax Appeal Board, the assessment was upheld on the finding, not that it was a profit from a business but that "it was a *quasi-bonus*" and therefore "interest *per se.*"

In the Exchequer Court, Gibson J did not wish to pass on the soundness of that conclusion and did not choose (those are his words) to make a finding that this was a profit from a business. He expressly founded his decision on the basis that this "was income from a 'source' within the meaning of the opening words of Section 3 [now paragraph 3(a)] of the *Income Tax Act*" adding:

> as far as I know there is no decision of this Court or of the Supreme Court of Canada in which a question of this kind has been resolved by deciding that such a discount was income from a "source" within the meaning of the opening words of Section 3 of the Act, without deciding whether it was income from any of the particular sources detailed in Section 3 or elsewhere in the Act.

...

At the hearing before this Court, counsel for the Crown abandoned the contention that the payment of $700 received by appellant in 1962 was interest and conceded that the issue of the appeal turns upon a finding as to whether or

---

1231 (Ex. Ct.); and *Lloyd Estate v. M.N.R.*, [1963] C.T.C. 518 (Ex. Ct.). For opposing results, see *Cohen v. M.N.R.*, [1957] C.T.C. 251, 57 D.T.C. 1183 (Ex. Ct.) and *M.N.R. v. MacInnes*, [1962] C.T.C. 350, 62 D.T.C. 1208 (Ex. Ct.), which was reversed on appeal, [1963] S.C.J. No. 27, [1963] C.T.C. 311, 63 D.T.C. 1203 (S.C.C.).

not the said sum was profit from a business or adventure in the nature of trade by virtue of paragraph (e) of subsection (1) of Section 139 [now the definition of "business" in subsection 248(1)] of the *Income Tax Act*.

Although certain specified receipts are declared to be income for the purposes of the Act, the *Income Tax Act* docs not purport to define income, it simply describes it. Section 3 [now paragraph 3(a)] mentions the three main sources of income, (1) business, (2) property, and (3) offices and employment, but without restricting the general meaning of income as being income from all sources.

The task of determining the meaning of income for income tax purposes has been left to the courts. The English courts, whose decisions on this point the Canadian courts tend to follow, have determined the meaning of income for tax purposes without reliance upon economic theory. Income is to be understood in its plain ordinary sense and given its natural meaning.

Since income tax is levied on an annual basis and capital gains are not included in income for tax purposes, it is necessary to determine whether a particular receipt, in a particular taxation year, is an income receipt or a capital receipt. In the case of a mortgage discount, such as the one in issue in this appeal, it is now well settled that the answer to that question depends upon whether the amount received should be classified as income from a business or as an accretion to capital.

· · ·

The appellant's investments, including investments in mortgages, were made entirely from savings not from borrowings, and his income from this source, including income from stocks and bonds, was a relatively modest part of his gross income. During the period from 1956 to 1963 inclusive, the appellant acquired eight first mortgages and five second mortgages all but two of them at a discount or bonus. This represents an average of one and one-half mortgages per year. The particulars of these mortgages are as follows:

1956	—	1 mortgage	—	$ 7,000
1957	—	1 mortgage	—	$ 7,100 (½ interest)
1958	—	No mortgages		
1959	—	1 mortgage	—	$ 2,500
1960	—	2 mortgages	—	$6,600
1961	—	4 mortgages	—	$22,412.20
1962	—	1 mortgage	—	$ 4,000.00 (no bonus or discount)
1963	—	3 mortgages	—	$17,000.00 (no bonus or discount)

As stated, appellant acquired his one-half interest in the mortgage in issue here in 1957, and it was the only acquisition in that year. Appellant's purchases were not speculative and, according to his evidence, they were made after he had inspected each property and reached a decision that each mortgage was a safe investment for him.

In my opinion, this pattern of appellant's activities was consistent with the making of personal investments out of his savings and not with the carrying on of a business. It follows that the amount of $700, received in 1962, represented a capital gain and not taxable income. ...

Appeal allowed.

NOTES AND QUESTIONS

1.   On what grounds does the Supreme Court of Canada conclude in *Wood* that the $700 discount realized by the taxpayer in 1962 was a capital gain and not taxable income? Of what relevance, if any, is the fact that the mortgages were acquired "entirely from savings not from borrowings"? Of what significance, if any, is the fact that the taxpayer's income from the mortgages "was a relatively modest part of his gross income"? How important is it that the taxpayer's half-interest in the mortgage at issue in the case was the taxpayer's only acquisition in 1957? Of what relevance, if any, is the fact that the taxpayer's law firm "had a general practice which included a 'fairly substantial mortgage practice'"? Does the court consider whether the discount might have been taxable as an adventure or concern in the nature of trade? Should it have considered this possibility?

For cases in which gains realized in the form of discounts and bonuses have been characterized as business income from an adventure in the nature of trade, see *No. 707 v. M.N.R.* (1960), 24 Tax ABC 246 (T.A.B.); *Bradford Investments Ltd. v. M.N.R.* (1961), 27 Tax ABC 205 (T.A.B.); *West Coast Parts Co. Ltd. v. M.N.R.*, [1964] C.T.C. 519, 64 D.T.C. 5316 (Ex. Ct.); *Feldstein v. M.N.R.*, [1969] C.T.C. 441, 69 D.T.C. 5298 (Ex. Ct.); *Ferguson v. M.N.R.*, [1970] Tax ABC 1199 (T.A.B.); *Aziz v. M.N.R.*, [1971] Tax ABC 203 (T.A.B.); and *Western Union Insurance Co. v. Canada*, [1983] F.C.J. No. 831, [1983] C.T.C. 363, 83 D.T.C. 5388 (F.C.T.D.).

For cases in which losses from the sale of bonds or other debt obligations acquired by taxpayers with the intention of selling the obligations at a profit have been characterized as business losses from an adventure in the nature of trade, see *Tamas v. Canada*, [1981] F.C.J. No. 501, [1981] C.T.C. 220, 81 D.T.C. 5150 (F.C.T.D.); and *Campbell v. Canada*, [1994] T.C.J. No. 1189, [1995] 1 C.T.C. 2597, (1994) 96 D.T.C. 1221 (T.C.C.). In each of these cases, speculative intent was inferred from the fact that the taxpayer had purchased the debt obligations with borrowed money, the interest payments attributable to which exceeded the interest received from the bonds.

2.   In *M.N.R. v. Sissons*, [1969] S.C.J. No. 16, [1969] C.T.C. 184, 69 D.T.C. 5152 (S.C.C.), the taxpayer, who carried on a successful stamp dealership through a private company, acquired for $15,000 shares and debentures (with a combined principal amount of $202,000) in two related companies ("Sonograph" and "Semco") each of which had accumulated losses and was on the verge of bankruptcy. In order to use these accumulated losses and generate

cash with which to redeem the debentures, the taxpayer caused his private company to sell its inventory of stamps to Sonograph. Sonograph then authorized the private company to retain physical possession of the inventory, to acquire additional stamps on its account, and to sell these stamps on its behalf. When Sonograph used the tax-sheltered profits from the sales of these stamps to repay an intercompany debt to Semco, and Semco used these payments to redeem for a combined amount of $102,000 two debentures held by the taxpayer, the Minister assessed the taxpayer on the difference between this amount and the $15,000 paid for the shares and debentures on the basis that this amount was profit from an adventure in the nature of trade.

Allowing the Minister's appeal from a decision of the Exchequer Court, [1968] C.T.C. 363, 68 D.T.C. 5236 (which held that the gain was on account of capital) the court held (at para. 14) that the series of transactions carried out by the taxpayer and the related companies had "none of the essential characteristics of an investment" but was a speculative "profit-making scheme" the purpose of which was "not to earn income from the securities but to make a profit on prompt realization."

The Supreme Court of Canada decision in *M.N.R. v. Sissons*, [1969] S.C.J. No. 16, [1969] C.T.C. 184, 69 D.T.C. 5152 (S.C.C.), has been followed in numerous cases involving the redemption of corporate debt obligations acquired as part of the reorganization of financially troubled companies. See, for example, *Dewar v. M.N.R.*, [1972] C.T.C. 2499, 72 D.T.C. 1421 (T.R.B.); *Bossin v. Canada*, [1976] F.C.J. No. 402, [1976] C.T.C. 358, 76 D.T.C. 6196 (F.C.T.D.); *Steeves v. Canada*, [1977] F.C.J. No. 507, [1977] C.T.C. 325, 77 D.T.C. 5230 (F.C.A.); *Canada v. Woods*, [1977] F.C.J. No. 1011, [1977] C.T.C. 597, 77 D.T.C. 5411 (F.C.T.D.); *Victor V. Spencer and Mary Spencer v. M.N.R.*, [1978] C.T.C. 2109, 78 D.T.C. 1129 (T.R.B.); *Modolo v. M.N.R.*, [1979] C.T.C. 3057, 79 D.T.C. 844 (T.R.B.); *Perkins v. Canada*, [1980] F.C.J. No. 131, [1980] C.T.C. 199, 80 D.T.C. 6154 (F.C.A.); *Canada v. Meronek*, [1982] F.C.J. No. 313, [1982] C.T.C. 248, 82 D.T.C. 6187 (F.C.T.D.); *Hall Estate v. M.N.R.*, [1986] F.C.J. No. 143, [1986] 1 C.T.C. 399, 86 D.T.C. 6208 (F.C.T.D.); and *Dally v. M.N.R.*, [1991] T.C.J. No. 112, [1991] 1 C.T.C. 2556, 91 D.T.C. 723 (T.C.C.).

3.   In *Eidinger v. Canada*, [1986] F.C.J. No. 748, [1987] 1 C.T.C. 36, (1986) 86 D.T.C. 6594 (F.C.A.), *Sissons* was distinguished on the basis (at para. 6) that the taxpayer's gain on the partial repayment of loans acquired for $1 was "part and parcel" of his "reacquisition of a business which he himself founded years earlier and which he wished to rescue from its financially perilous position." For this reason, the court concluded (at para. 6) that the loans were "unquestionably a capital investment." *Eidinger* was followed in *Blair v. Canada*, [1993] T.C.J. No. 868, [1994] 1 C.T.C. 2319, (1993) 94 D.T.C. 1126 (T.C.C.).

4.   In *M.N.R. v. Freud*, [1968] S.C.J. No. 81, [1968] C.T.C. 438, 68 D.T.C. 5279 (S.C.C.), the taxpayer incurred a loss after loaning money to a corporation that he had established in order to develop the prototype of a sports car, which

he hoped to sell to a manufacturer. Rejecting the Minister's argument that the loss was on account of capital, the court concluded (at para. 13) that:

> It is, of course, obvious that a loan made by a person who is not in the business of lending money is ordinarily to be considered as an investment. It is only under quite exceptional or unusual circumstances that such an operation should be considered as a speculation. However, the circumstances of the present case are quite unusual and exceptional. It is an undeniable fact that, at the outset, the operation embarked upon was an adventure in the nature of trade. It is equally clear that the character of the venture itself remained the same until it ended up in a total loss. Under those circumstances, the outlay made by respondent in the last year, when the speculative nature of the undertaking was even more marked than at the outset due to financial difficulties, cannot be considered as an investment.

A similar decision was reached in *Becker v. Canada*, [1983] C.T.C. 11, (1982) 83 D.T.C. 5032 (F.C.A.) (at para. 14), where the taxpayer had loaned money to a troubled company of which he had purchased 90 per cent of the shares "with the intention of transforming it in order to turn it into a profitable enterprise."

5.   In *United News (Wholesalers) Ltd. v. M.N.R.*, [1994] F.C.J. No. 942, [1994] 2 C.T.C. 180, 94 D.T.C. 6508 (F.C.T.D.), where the taxpayer, a distributor of books, magazines, and greeting cards, etc., lost $210,000, which it had advanced to a promoter to present "Toller Cranston and the Ice Show," the court concluded that "the advance amounted to the investment of a capital sum whose loss was a capital loss." Referring to the decision in *Freud*, the court explained (at para. 9) that:

> normally a person who lends money when he is not in the business of money lending makes an investment unless there are unusual circumstances. There were no unusual circumstances in the present case comparable to those in *Freud*...

See also *Stewart & Morrison Ltd. v. M.N.R.*, [1972] S.C.J. No. 125, [1972] C.T.C. 73, 72 D.T.C. 6049 (S.C.C.); *Chaffey v. M.N.R.*, [1978] F.C.J. No. 116, [1978] C.T.C. 253, 78 D.T.C. 6176 (F.C.A.); *Mandryk v. M.N.R.*, [1992] F.C.J. No. 329, [1992] 1 C.T.C. 317, 92 D.T.C. 6329 (F.C.A.); and *Easton v. Canada*, [1997] F.C.J. No. 1282, [1998] 3 C.T.C. 26, (1997) 97 D.T.C. 5464 (F.C.A.).

For a contrasting result, see *Berman & Co. v. M.N.R.*, [1961] C.T.C. 237, 61 D.T.C. 1150 (Ex. Ct.), in which the taxpayer made voluntary payments to the suppliers of a subsidiary that had defaulted on its obligations. Rejecting the Minister's argument that the payments were on account of capital, the court allowed the taxpayer to deduct the payments on the ground that it had been doing business with the suppliers and it wished to continue doing so in the future and make the payments to protect its own goodwill.

6.   In a number of cases, gains realized in the form of discounts and bonuses have been characterized as business income on the basis that the taxpayer was engaged in the business of money lending. See, for example, *No. 323 v. M.N.R.* (1956), 14 Tax ABC 384 (T.A.B.); *Stuyvesant-North Ltd. v. M.N.R.*, [1958] C.T.C. 154 (Ex. Ct.); *No. 667 v. M.N.R.* (1959), 23 Tax ABC 213 (T.A.B.); *Laplante v. M.N.R.* (1962), 28 Tax ABC 320 (T.A.B.); and *Canada v. RoyNat*

Ltd., [1981] C.T.C. 93, 81 D.T.C. 5072 (F.C.T.D.). In these circumstances, losses on the disposition of debt obligations acquired in the course of the business would be characterized as business losses rather than capital losses.

7.   Where a debt owing to a taxpayer is established to have become a bad debt, paragraph 20(1)(p) allows the taxpayer to deduct the amount of the debt if it was included in computing the taxpayer's income for a previous taxation year, if the taxpayer's "ordinary business included the lending of money," or if the taxpayer is an insurer or financial institution as defined in subsection 142.2(1). For cases in which taxpayers have sought to deduct bad debts under this provision on the basis that their "ordinary business included the lending of money," see *Orban v. M.N.R.* (1954), 10 Tax ABC 178, 54 D.T.C. 148 (T.A.B.); *Canada v. Lavigueur*, [1973] F.C.J. No. 1001, [1973] C.T.C. 773, 73 D.T.C. 5538 (F.C.T.D.); *Morflot Freightliners Ltd. v. M.N.R.*, [1989] F.C.J. No. 251, [1989] 1 C.T.C. 413, 89 D.T.C. 5182 (F.C.T.D.); *Beaudry v. Canada*, [1998] T.C.J. No. 353, [1998] 3 C.T.C. 2705, 98 D.T.C. 1898 (T.C.C.); *Global Communications Ltd. v. Canada*, [1998] F.C.J. No. 1511, [1999] 1 C.T.C. 23, (1998) 98 D.T.C. 6649 (F.C.T.D.); *Whitland Construction Co. v. Canada*, [1998] T.C.J. No. 899, [1999] 1 C.T.C. 2172, (1998) 99 D.T.C. 33 (T.C.C.); *Bird v. Canada*, [2000] T.C.J. No. 191, [2000] 2 C.T.C. 2699, 2000 D.T.C. 2067 (T.C.C.); *Singh v. Canada*, [2000] T.C.J. No. 176, [2000] 2 C.T.C. 2933, 2000 D.T.C. 2031 (T.C.C.); *Loman Warehousing Ltd. v. Canada*, [2000] F.C.J. No. 1717, [2001] 1 C.T.C. 50, 2000 D.T.C. 6610 (F.C.A.); and *Langhammer v. Canada*, [2000] T.C.J. No. 828, [2001] 1 C.T.C. 2372, 2001 D.T.C. 45 (T.C.C.).

8.   Where a debt that is capital property is established to have become a bad debt, and the taxpayer so elects, subsection 50(1) allows for the recognition of a capital loss on the debt by deeming the taxpayer to have disposed of the debt at the end of the year for proceeds equal to nil and to have reacquired it immediately after the end of the year at a cost equal to nil. Where an amount in respect of the debt is subsequently recovered, this amount will normally be taxable as a capital gain. For the CRA's views on subsection 50(1), see *Interpretation Bulletin* IT-159R3, "Capital Debts Established to be Bad Debts", May 1, 1989.

9.   In *Millford Development Ltd. v. M.N.R.*, [1993] F.C.J. No. 44, [1993] 1 C.T.C. 169, 93 D.T.C. 5052 (F.C.T.D.), the taxpayer, a real estate developer, incurred a loss on the sale of a mortgage that it assumed in order to sell land as part of its business operations. Notwithstanding that the taxpayer was not in the business of lending money, the court characterized the loss as a business loss on the ground (at para. 12) that "the taking back of the ... mortgage was solely for the purpose of effecting the sale of real property." According to the court, the resulting loss was held to be a business loss and not a capital loss. As Rothstein J reasoned:

> In this case the evidence is that the taking back of the ... mortgage was solely for the purpose of effecting the sale of real property. ... There is no evidence that the mortgage was acquired

for investment purposes. The total proceeds of the sale ... (including the proceeds represented by the mortgage back) were treated by [the taxpayer], for tax purposes, as revenue resulting in income and not capital gain. In my view, in this case the character of the discount resulting from the sale of the mortgage is influenced by the transaction giving rise to the mortgage. That transaction was a revenue transaction resulting in income. The effect is that, when the mortgage was sold at a discount, the discount had a character related to income and not to capital.

10. Several cases have considered the characterization of deemed gains resulting from the redemption of debt obligations acquired solely to obtain tax benefits in the form of scientific research tax credits (SRTCs). See, for example, *Smith v. M.N.R.*, [1989] T.C.J. No. 409, [1989] 2 C.T.C. 2069, 89 D.T.C. 331 (T.C.C.); *Financial Collection Agencies (Quebec) Ltd. v. M.N.R.*, [1989] T.C.J. No. 1104, [1990] 1 C.T.C. 2178, (1989) 90 D.T.C. 1040 (T.C.C.); *Stanley Drug Products Ltd. v. M.N.R.*, [1989] T.C.J. No. 632, [1990] 2 C.T.C. 2646, (1989) 90 D.T.C. 1664 (T.C.C.); *Morello v. M.N.R.*, [1993] T.C.J. No. 275, [1993] 2 C.T.C. 2357, 93 D.T.C. 1072 (T.C.C.); and *Loewen v. Canada*, [1994] F.C.J. No. 512, [1994] 2 C.T.C. 75, 94 D.T.C. 6265 (F.C.A.). Under this short-lived program, individual taxpayers acquiring a share or debt obligation of corporations satisfying certain statutory requirements with respect to scientific research and experimental development could obtain a federal tax credit under section 127.3 equal to 34 per cent of the amount up to the amount paid for the share or debt obligation "designated" by the corporation under subsection 194(4). In these circumstances, subsection 127.3(6) deemed the cost of the share or debt obligation to the taxpayer to be 50 per cent of its actual cost.

E. Canadian Securities

Subsection 39(4) allows taxpayers to make an election whereby every "Canadian security" owned by the taxpayer in that year or a subsequent year is deemed to be a capital property in those years and every disposition of such a security by the taxpayer is deemed to be a disposition of a capital property. The term "Canadian security" is defined in subsection 39(6) as "a security (other than a prescribed security) that is a share of the capital stock of a corporation resident in Canada, a unit of a mutual fund trust or a bond, debenture, bill, note, mortgage, hypothecary claim or similar obligation issued by a person resident in Canada." Subsection 39(5) provides that an election under subsection 39(4) does not apply to taxpayers who, at the time that the security is disposed of, are traders or dealers in securities, financial institutions as defined in subsection 142.2(1), corporations whose principal business is the lending of money or the purchasing of debt obligations or a combination thereof, non-residents, or any combination of these. Section 6200 of the regulations excludes from the definition of "Canadian security" shares whose value is primarily attributable to real property or resource property, debt of a corporation with which the taxpayer does not deal at arm's length, shares acquired from a non-arm's-length corporation or pursuant to a tax-deferred transfer of property to a corporation under subsection 85(1), exploration and development shares, and shares or debt substituted for any of the above.

In essence, these provisions allow taxpayers to characterize all gains on the disposition of all "Canadian securities" as capital gains — provided that all losses from the disposition of these securities are correspondingly characterized as capital losses. The purpose of these rules was outlined in the budget statement accompanying their introduction in 1977:

> where a taxpayer elects in his return of income for 1977 or any subsequent taxation year, all his gains and losses for the year and all subsequent years from the disposition of shares other than prescribed shares, bonds, debentures, notes, or similar obligations issued by a Canadian corporation, shall be deemed to be capital gains or losses of the taxpayer, except where the taxpayer is a dealer or a trader in securities, a bank, a trust company, credit union, life insurance corporation or similar institution.

The leading case dealing with these provisions is *Vancouver Art Metal Works Ltd. v. Canada*, [1993] F.C.J. No. 152, [1993] 1 C.T.C. 346, 93 D.T.C. 5116 (F.C.A.), which considered the meaning of the words "trader or dealer in securities" in paragraph 39(5)(a).[26]

Vancouver Art Metal Works Ltd. v. Canada
[1993] F.C.J. No. 152, [1993] 1 C.T.C. 346, 93 D.T.C. 5116 (F.C.A.)

LÉTOURNEAU JA (Marceau and Robertson JJA, concurring): Pursuant to Rule 474 of the *Federal Court Rules*, the parties had submitted the following question of law for a determination:

> Do the words "a trader or dealer in securities" in subsection 39(5) of the *Income Tax Act*, RSC 1952, c. 148 (am. SC 1970-71-72, c. 63) (the "Act") refer only to a person who is registered or licensed by regulatory authority to buy and sell securities, or to a person who in the ordinary course of business buys and sells securities on behalf of other persons; or are the words broad enough to include anyone other than a person engaged in an adventure or concern in the nature of trade?

Broadly stated, subsection 39(4) of the *Income Tax Act* authorizes a taxpayer, who disposes of Canadian securities in a given year, to elect in his return of income for that year or any subsequent taxation year to treat all his gains and losses resulting from these transactions as being capital in nature. However, subsection 39(5) denies this election to some taxpayers, including those who can be considered as traders or dealers in securities. Subsections 39(4) and (5) read as follows:

---

[26] Subsection 39(5) was amended in 1994 by repealing paras. 39(5)(c) to (e) and amending para. 39(5)(b) to refer to "a financial institution (as defined in subs. 142.2(1)." Pursuant to subs. 142.2(1) and the definition of a "restricted financial institution" in subs. 248(1), the financial institutions referred to in former paras. 39(5)(b) to (e) are now included within the general term "financial institution" in para. 39(5)(b). As a result, although the current language of subs. 39(5) differs from that examined in *Vancouver Art Metal Works*, its meaning should not.

39(4) *Election re: disposition of Canadian securities.* Except as provided in subsection (5), where a Canadian security has been disposed of by a taxpayer in a taxation year and the taxpayer so elects in prescribed form in his return of income under this Part for that year:

   (a)   every Canadian security owned by him in that year or any subsequent taxation year shall be deemed to have been a capital property owned by him in those years; and

   (b)   every disposition by the taxpayer of any such Canadian security shall be deemed to be a disposition by him of a capital property.

39(5) *Taxpayers to whom subsection (4) inapplicable.* An election under subsection (4) does not apply to a disposition of a Canadian security by a taxpayer who, at the time the security is disposed of, is

   (a)   a trader or a dealer in securities,

   (b)   a bank to which the *Bank Act* or the *Quebec Savings Banks Act* applies,

   (c)   a corporation licensed or otherwise authorized under the laws of Canada or a province to carry on in Canada the business of offering to the public its services as trustee,

   (d)   a credit union,

   (e)   an insurance corporation,

   (f)   a corporation whose principal business is the lending of money or the purchasing of debt obligations or a combination thereof, or

   (g)   a non-resident,

or any combination thereof.

In the Trial Division of this Court, the learned Associate Chief Justice ruled that such words were indeed limited to persons who are registered or licensed by regulatory authority to buy and sell securities and to those who in the ordinary course of business buy and sell securities on behalf of others. He proceeded to make a purposive interpretation of the statute by referring to the Parliamentary Debates in order to determine the context in which the provision was enacted.

Counsel for the appellant submits that the learned judge misinterpreted the provision and that "trader" or "dealer" refers to anyone who carries on a business of trading or dealing in securities, not only to brokers or professionals who are registered or licensed by a regulatory authority. In my respectful opinion, I believe her interpretation is the one intended by Parliament. Whether one makes a literal or a purposive interpretation of subsection 39(5) of the Act, one cannot come to the conclusion that the words "trader or dealer in securities" are as limited in scope as contended by the respondent.

Literally, one cannot read subsection 39(5) as if the words "registered or licensed by regulatory authority to buy and sell securities" appeared in the provision to qualify traders and dealers. There is no such qualification. In addition, as counsel for the appellant pointed out, paragraph 39(5)(c) does contain an express reference to a corporation "licensed or otherwise authorized".

Had Parliament intended such a restriction to apply to a "trader or dealer" under paragraph 39(5)(a), it would have said so.

...

Furthermore, my conclusion is also supported by a subsequent amendment made by Parliament to the *Income Tax Act*. As a matter of fact, section 47.1 was added to the Act in 1983-84, that is to say after the enactment of subsection 39(5), and the words "trader or dealer in securities" were introduced in relation to indexed security investment plans. The words were defined and limited to persons who are registered or licensed under the laws of a province to trade in securities. In adding that section to the Act, Parliament expressly restricted the application of that definition to section 47.1 and section 38 only. Had Parliament intended a similar restrictive definition of trader or dealer to apply as well to paragraph 39(5)(a) it would have done so.

By making reference to the budget speech delivered by the Minister of Finance on March 3, 1977, the learned Associate Chief Justice concluded that Parliament's intention in enacting subsection 39(5) was to exclude institutional investors or financial institutions from the right to elect under subsection 39(4). Hence his finding that the words "trader or dealer" in paragraph 39(5)(a) refer only to those who are brokers or who are licensed or registered by a regulatory authority. Counsel for the respondent submits that this finding can be justified by the rule of interpretation *noscitur a sociis*. According to that rule, "an expression's meaning may be revealed by its association with others" and where general and specific words are associated together and are capable of analogous meaning, the general words should be restricted to the specific meaning unless this would be contrary to the clear intention of Parliament.

However, for the rule to apply, there must be a distinct genus or category from which the general words can take their colour or meaning (see *Stouffville Assess. Comr. v. Mennonite Home Assn.*, [1973] SCR 189, 31 DLR (3d) 237). With respect, there is no such genus in subsection 39(5) which could justify the restrictive meaning, to wit institutional investor, given to the general words "trader or dealer in securities" found in paragraph 39(5)(a) of the Act. The paragraph refers to a non-resident, some corporations of different status (insurance company, lending company, corporation offering its services as trustee), a credit union and banks. ... It certainly cannot be said that the enumeration in paragraphs (b) to (g) of subsection 39(5) would be pointless if the general words "trader or dealer in securities" are given their ordinary meaning or are allowed to stand unrestricted. Indeed, because of its status, a lending corporation, for example, would be denied the right to elect even if its transactions fell short of making it a trader or dealer in securities. What, then, is the meaning of those words left undefined and unqualified?

In my view, the words "trader or dealer" should be given their ordinary meaning. They normally refer to a person who deals in merchandise, is engaged in buying and selling or whose business is trade or commerce. In *Black's Law Dictionary*, a "dealer" is defined as "any person engaged in the business of buying and selling securities for his own account, through a broker or otherwise, but does not include a bank, or any person insofar as he buys or sells securities for his own account, either individually or in some fiduciary capacity, *but not as a part of a regular business*" [emphasis added].

To a large extent, the two words "trader" and "dealer" overlap. So do the French equivalents "commerçant ou négociant," except that the word "négociant" (dealer) has, according to the *Dictionnaire encyclopédique Quillet*, a wider and less precise meaning than "commerçant" (trader). Both terms, however, import a notion of business or profession (*idem*).

I note in passing that the word "dealer" has been loosely translated in French by "courtier." A "courtier" is a "broker," that is to say a person employed as a middleman to transact business or negotiate bargains. The notion of "broker" necessarily involves the buying and selling on behalf of others. It is, therefore, narrower than either the term "trader" or "dealer." I hasten to add that it has no impact on the question submitted to us as the English version of paragraph 39(5)(a) contains no such ambiguity and the French word "commerçant" is, in any event, broad enough to include a broker.

I have no doubt that a taxpayer who makes it a profession or a business of buying and selling securities is a trader or a dealer in securities within the meaning of paragraph 39(5)(a) of the Act. As Cattanach, J stated in *Palmer v. M.N.R.*, [1973] CTC 323, 73 DTC 5248 (FCTD) at page 325 (DTC 5249), "it is a badge of trade that a person who habitually does acts capable of producing profits is engaged in a trade or business." It is, however, a question of fact to determine whether one's activities amount to carrying on a trade or business. Each case will stand on its own set of facts. Obviously, factors such as the frequency of the transactions, the duration of the holdings (whether, for instance, it is for a quick profit or a long term investment), the intention to acquire for resale at a profit, the nature and quantity of the securities held or made the subject matter of the transaction, the time spent on the activity, are all relevant and helpful factors in determining whether one has embarked upon a trading or dealing business.

In enacting subsections 39(4) and (5), Parliament had, in my view, no intention of allowing a taxpayer, who makes it a business or a profession of buying and selling securities, to convert his business income or losses into capital gains or losses as is the case for a simple investor engaged in an adventure in the nature of trade. Moreover, in my respectful opinion, to limit the scope of the exception to registered or licensed traders or dealers as found by the trial judge would lead to a strange result. A taxpayer who has a business of dealing in securities could make the election under subsection 39(4), convert his income into capital gains and avoid falling under the exception relating to dealers not because he is not a dealer, but simply because he has not registered or obtained a license as required by regulatory authorities.

Counsel for the respondent ably argued that Parliament's intention was to encourage investment in Canadian securities by providing certainty of tax treatment to taxpayers who make an irrevocable election to have all their gains and losses in Canadian securities taxed on capital account. Absolute certainty, in his view, can only be obtained if the words "trader or dealer in securities" are restricted, as the trial judge found, to those who are licensed or registered or buy and sell on behalf of others. Otherwise, there would have to be an *ad hoc* or case by case determination of a taxpayer's status with respect to the right to elect under subsection 39(4).

It is true that this kind of assessment will be necessary when a taxpayer's buying and selling amounts to carrying on a business of trading and dealing in securities. There is no doubt that Parliament could have achieved the absolute certainty sought by the respondent by either creating no exceptions at all or by creating a well-defined one with respect to traders and dealers in securities. Obviously, it chose neither course of action, hence the resultant uncertainty. It is clear that Parliament did not want the right to elect under subsection 39(4) to be a blanket provision applicable to every taxpayer irrespective of his status. It is also clear that it did not want the exception relating to traders and dealers to apply only to brokers and like professionals. By giving to the words "traders or dealer" their plain and ordinary meaning, this Court not only gives an interpretation which conforms to the text of the provision, but also one that does justice to Parliament's intent in enacting the election rule and its exceptions.

Conclusion

In conclusion, a taxpayer does not necessarily lose his election right under subsection 39(4) when he buys and sells securities for his own account. However, he loses such right to elect when he becomes a trader or a dealer, that is to say when his dealings amount to carrying on a business and can no longer be characterized as investor's transactions or mere adventures or concerns in the nature of trade.

In my opinion, the words "trader or dealer in securities" in paragraph 39(5)(a) of the *Income Tax Act* are broad enough to include anyone other than a person engaged in an adventure or concern in the nature of trade. ...

Minister's appeal allowed.

NOTES AND QUESTIONS

1.　On what grounds does the respondent in *Vancouver Art Metal Works* argue that the words "trader or dealer" refer only to persons registered or licensed by regulatory authority to buy and sell securities? What is the respondent's textual argument? What is the respondent's argument regarding parliamentary intent?

2.　Why does the Federal Court of Appeal reject the respondent's arguments in *Vancouver Art Metal Works*? To what textual considerations does the court refer? Why does the court reject the respondent's argument based on the "associated words rule" (*noscitur a sociis*)? How does the court interpret Parliament's intent? What role do the consequences of alternative conclusions play in the court's reasons? How does the court define the words "trader or dealer"? Which interpretation do you prefer and why?

3.   For other cases concerning the application of paragraph 39(5)(a), see *Robertson v. Canada*, [1996] T.C.J. No. 174, [1996] 2 C.T.C. 2269, 97 D.T.C. 449 (T.C.C.), aff'd [1998] F.C.J. No. 401, [1998] 3 C.T.C. 147, 98 D.T.C. 6227 (F.C.A.); *Woods v. Canada*, [1995] T.C.J. No. 264, [1995] 2 C.T.C. 2084 (T.C.C.); *Kane v. Canada*, [1994] F.C.J. No. 1512, [1995] 1 C.T.C. 1, (1994) 94 D.T.C. 6671 (F.C.T.D.); and *Howard v. Canada*, [2008] T.C.J. No. 75, [2008] 3 C.T.C. 2398 (T.C.C.). In *Robertson* Brulé JTCC distinguished (at para. 29) between the words "trader" and "dealer" as follows:

> It appears that "dealer" refers primarily to a professional trader, such as a broker or other licensed dealer, and that "trader" can be something less, including a person who is not a broker or other licensed dealer but who carries on a business activity that amounts to something more than an adventure in the nature of trade.

In *Woods*, the taxpayer acquired securities in a number of junior technology companies for which he arranged financing, many of which were sold at a gain when the shares were subsequently listed on a stock exchange. Rejecting the taxpayer's argument that he was not a "Bay Street" trader who "goes in and out of the market," buying and selling securities shares on a daily basis as their price fluctuates, the court concluded (at para. 17) that:

> What constitutes a trade on Bay Street and what constitutes a trade for purposes of the Act are not the same. The tests for tax purposes include whether a property is being purchased to hold as an investment or whether the property is being purchased in the course of a trade. An important test is the intention of the taxpayer and his course of conduct in dealing with the property. The subject matter being acquired, the length of ownership, the frequency or the number of similar transactions and the circumstances leading to the disposition of the eventual disposition of the property are also important factors to consider. However, in facts similar to those at bar, a key factor is the question of motive, that is, why did the taxpayer acquire the property in the first place? Woods did not beat around the bush in testifying. He was most candid in stating that he purchased the securities for the purposes of making a profit from them. Woods also stated that he looked for securities that did not yield a dividend since in his view securities that yield dividends are not susceptible of substantial growth. It is clear therefore that I do not need to canvas the intention of Woods when he first acquired these securities: it was for the purpose of selling at the opportune time. ...
>
> Woods participated in over 100 transactions in 1986 and 1987. The shares he acquired admittedly were not those which would yield dividends during his term of ownership. Woods did not even consider acquiring shares which would yield dividends. Woods stated that he acquired the shares for the purpose of selling them once it was profitable to do so. The time frame within which he held his shares was usually less than a year. Woods used borrowed funds to acquire the shares. Woods was an insider, he was director of several companies whose share he bought and sold. Notwithstanding Woods' unquestioned sincerity in investing in these companies in order to provide them with funds, he also wanted to sell the shares of these companies for a profit; this was his motive in the first place. He was trading in the securities of these corporations and the assessments issued to him in 1986 and 1987 were correct.

In *Kane*, Noël J distinguished (at paras. 21-23) between persons who engage in an adventure or series of adventures in the nature of trade (to whom the exclusion in paragraph 39(5)(a) does not apply) and "traders and dealers" by reference to "the legislative intent in enacting the limitation embodied in paragraph 39(5)(a) of the Act":

> It is recognized by all that paragraph 39(5)(a) was at least intended to prevent persons who are registered or licensed traders or dealers in securities from converting their income arising from that trade into capital gains. In the normal course, however, licensed dealers trade for the account of their clients and, in that context, paragraph 39(5)(a) is of no relevance to them. It is only of relevance to them when, from time to time, they choose to trade on their own account. In that context, it seems clear that the legislator did not intend individuals who, by their trade, have professional knowledge of the market in which they deal to benefit from the election.

> I believe that in determining the availability of the election to one who trades in securities without being licensed or registered, the focus should be the same, namely, does the author of the transactions in question possess a particular or special knowledge of the market in which he trades? To the extent that he does, he distinguishes himself from the common risk takers who "play the market" regularly or sporadically based on commonly available investment advice and information. That it seems is the guiding line which must delineate the scope of the election contemplated by section 39(4) of the Act and the limitation embodied in paragraph 39(5)(a).

On this basis he held that the taxpayer, who acquired and disposed of shares of a junior mining company of which he was a shareholder, director, and president, was a trader with respect to these shares and thus unable to elect capital gains treatment for these dispositions under subsection 39(4).

In *Howard*, the court relied on the reasoning in *Vancouver Art Metal Works* and *Kane* to hold a taxpayer who purchased and sold shares in the company where he was hired as a consultant was a "trader or dealer."

4.   For the CRA's views on the election in subsection 39(4), see paragraphs 2 to 8 of *Interpretation Bulletin* IT-479R, "Transactions in Securities," February 29, 1984. According to paragraph 5 of this bulletin:

> For the purposes of subsection 39(5) the Department interprets the term "trader or dealer in securities" to mean a taxpayer who participates in the promotion or underwriting of a particular issue of shares, bonds or other securities or a taxpayer who holds himself out to the public as a dealer in shares, bonds or other securities. The term is not considered to include an officer or employee of a firm or corporation that is engaged in the promotion or underwriting of issues of shares, bonds or other securities nor an officer or employee of a taxpayer who holds himself out to the public as a dealer in shares, bonds or other securities, unless that officer or employee transacts in securities as a result of the promoting or underwriting activities of this employer. Any person who, as a result of special knowledge of a particular corporation not available to the public, utilizes that knowledge to realize a quick gain is considered by the Department to be a "trader or dealer in securities" for those particular securities. Any corporation whose prime business activity is trading in shares or debt obligations is also considered to be a "trader or dealer" in securities, but this does not include a corporation whose prime business is the holding of securities and which sells such investments from time to time.

Is this interpretation consistent with the decisions in *Vancouver Art Metal Works*, *Robertson*, *Woods*, *Kane* and *Howard*?

5.   In *Satinder v. M.N.R.*, [1995] F.C.J. No. 754, 95 D.T.C. 5340 (F.C.A.), the taxpayer, who acquired a non-interest-bearing government of Canada treasury bill for $152,078 and redeemed it a year later at its face value of $170,000, argued that he was entitled to treat the discount giving rise to the gain as a capital gain on the basis that the treasury bill was a "Canadian security" subject to the election under subsection 39(4). According to the taxpayer (at para. 7), "the transaction [fell] squarely within the language of the subsection."

The Crown, however, argued that the taxpayer's argument was "based on a fundamental misunderstanding of the purpose underlying subsection 39(4) and on a failure to properly differentiate between the gain or return on an investment that is subject to the favourable tax treatment afforded by that subsection and the gain or return that is not to be so treated, but rather is to be treated as 'interest' taxable pursuant to paragraph 12(1)(c) of the Act." Emphasizing (at para. 9) that treasury bills are "capable of generating either a capital gain or capital loss, as well as interest income," the Crown argued that subsection 39(4) applied only to gains or losses in the principal value of the obligation arising from changes in market rates of interest, not to the interest element computed on the basis of the bill's effective yield.

Dismissing the taxpayer's appeal, the court concluded that the election under subsection 39(4) did not apply to discounts on treasury bills, which were properly characterized as interest income subject to taxation under paragraph 12(1)(c). Do you find this interpretation of subsection 39(4) persuasive? Why or why not?

6.   In a number of cases involving the redemption of debt obligations acquired to obtain scientific research tax credits, courts have interpreted the requirement in subsection 39(4) that taxpayers must file an election "in prescribed form" in their return of income "for that year" strictly, refusing to recognize late-filed elections that did not accompany the taxpayer's return when originally filed. See, for example, *Smith v. M.N.R.*, [1989] T.C.J. No. 409, [1989] 2 C.T.C. 2069, 89 D.T.C. 331 (T.C.C.); *Financial Collection Agencies (Quebec) Ltd. v. M.N.R.*, [1989] T.C.J. No. 1104, [1990] 1 C.T.C. 2178, (1989) 90 D.T.C. 1040 (T.C.C.); *Taylor v. M.N.R.*, [1990] T.C.J. No. 813, [1990] 2 C.T.C. 2466, 90 D.T.C. 1917 (T.C.C.); *Stanley Drug Products Ltd. v. M.N.R.*, [1989] T.C.J. No. 632, [1990] 2 C.T.C. 2646, (1989) 90 D.T.C. 1664 (T.C.C.); and *Loewen v. M.N.R.*, [1993] F.C.J. No. 128, [1993] 1 C.T.C. 212, 93 D.T.C. 5109 (F.C.T.D.), rev'd on other grounds [1994] F.C.J. No. 512, [1994] 2 C.T.C. 75, 94 D.T.C. 6265 (F.C.A.).

F. Foreign Exchange

For the purposes of computing Canadian income tax, amounts denominated in foreign currencies must be converted to Canadian dollars based on exchange rates prevailing at the relevant time. Where taxpayers dispose of assets or liabilities denominated in foreign currencies, this conversion may produce gains or losses due solely to fluctuations in the rates at which Canadian dollars can be exchanged for these foreign currencies. In these circumstances, an essential question concerns the characterization of these gains or losses for the purpose of computing Canadian income tax. The leading Canadian case on this issue is *Tip Top Tailors Ltd v. M.N.R.*, [1957] S.C.J. No. 49, [1957] C.T.C. 309, 57 D.T.C. 1232 (S.C.C.).

Tip Top Tailors Ltd. v. M.N.R.
[1957] S.C.J. No. 49, [1957] C.T.C. 309, 57 D.T.C. 1232 (S.C.C.)

RAND J: The appellant company deals in large scale manufacture of wearing apparel in the course of which quantities of cloth are purchased in lots from Great Britain. Its ordinary practice, prior to January 1948, was to pay for each lot according to the terms of the invoice by an individual purchase of sterling at the rate of exchange then prevailing. In that month the officers of the company, foreseeing the likelihood of a devaluation of sterling, made preparations to avail themselves of the benefit of that happening should it eventuate.

The company thereupon arranged with a Canadian bank having a branch office in London for a line of credit at that office to a maximum of £250,000 which could be called in by the bank at the end of each year. Although this credit may have been available for any purposes of the company, that it would be resorted to for some or all of its purchases of material for its business is quite evident, and no other purpose is suggested. The debit account accumulated until September 1949; interim payments during that period were from time to time made on the loan generally for the purpose of keeping it within what were considered to be desirable limits. In that month the pound was devalued and the amount then reached, approximately $588,000, was, in the course of weeks, liquidated by purchases of sterling at the lower rate.

During this period of approximately twenty months the purchases of goods were settled in the following manner: when the goods had been received in Canada, and within the terms of the invoice, a direction would be forwarded to the bank in London to make payment to the seller's at the same time the price would be entered in the books of the company in Canadian dollars at the then officially fixed rate of exchange; and when payment was made the purchase became a closed transaction. The total outstanding advances in September 1949, cleared at the lower rate, consisted solely of accumulated sums paid in this manner to sellers of cloth, i.e., goods bought by the company in the course of its trade. Up to devaluation the rate was $4.04 to the pound but the bank overdraft was paid on an exchange rate of $3.0875. The net profit was approximately $160,000 and the question is whether that profit is taxable as income.

The company's contention is that the profit was on a collateral borrowing of capital, a single and discrete transaction, not in the course of any business carried on by it, in effect, a temporary investment in foreign currency. As a profit on such an investment it is not within the scope of the taxing statute.

The Crown's answer is that this mode of financing was, as created, an inseparable part of and merged in the business in which the company was engaged; or if not, that it was a venture within Section 127(e) which defines "business" as including "an adventure or concern in the nature of a trade."

...

The proposition that the risk of a change in value of capital securities or investments is that of capital can be accepted. The capital machinery within and by means of which the business earning the income is carried on is distinct from that business itself; and the fluctuations in its value have no bearing on profits or losses from the business.

...

An analogous application was made in *McKinlay v. Jenkins*, 10 TC 372. A contractor, undertaking work which called for the use of Italian granite, purchased lira in advance of his requirements. The exchange value of the lira went up, the contractor sold at a profit and later repurchased when the value had fallen off. The gain was held to result from an isolated transaction in a capital dealing and was not income. In the language of Rowlatt J the profit was not "connected with the contract to construct"; it was an appreciation of a temporary investment, a dealing not merged in the business. So, too, in *Davies v. Shell Company of China Limited*, 32 TC 133. There the company sold petroleum products in China to agents who paid as the products were sold. To secure the seller's position the agents were required to deposit sums in Chinese dollars with the seller. The latter transferred the deposits to London and converted them into sterling. Three years later when the business in China was brought to a close the amounts due the agents in Chinese currency were repaid them. The value of that currency had declined and the company realized a substantial benefit in pound sterling, which was held not to be taxable income.

The dealings before us are not, in my opinion, within that differentiating conception. The loan produced working capital used in the course of the company's business; the loan was effected as each payment was made to a seller; but in substance the creation of debt in the bank was merely a substitution of creditor for the actual transactions: no advance was ever made or, so far as the case goes, was ever agreed to be made to the company itself. Mr. Phillips, in his plausible argument, stressed the arrangement as a temporary investment in foreign currency. But what, in the sense of *McKinlay*, is an investment? Surely it involves the putting at risk of an asset or interest of value by the investor from which an increment of additional return of value is ordinarily hoped for. Here there was simply an accumulation of debt as the transactions of the business proceeded. No asset was put at risk by the company; the obligation of the bank was to pay the sellers of the goods and them only. Even the elements here of a short sale of sterling do not, as a collateral investment, bring it within the meaning of *McKinlay*. What was intended and done was the creation of indebtedness to the bank arising directly out of the business and we cannot distort that into a purchase from the bank and a payment as a matter of choice, by the company to the supplier: actual sterling as a commodity never existed in the ownership of the company. The only difference between that course of dealing and the ordinary monthly arrangements with a bank lies in the possibly greater time allowed the outgoings to accumulate. It was a large scale process of overdraft through a substantial period of time which I am quite unable to view as an investment.

...

The dealings here are, I think, governed by a decision of the Court of Appeal of England, *Imperial Tobacco Company v. Kelly*, 25 TC 292. The Tobacco Company, an English incorporation, was a buyer of large quantities of tobacco leaf in the United States. During the first months of 1939 in preparation for that year's purchasing in the late summer and early autumn, the company bought $45,000,000 at rates of exchange varying between $4.63 and $4.68 and the moncy was remitted to the United States to be used to buy the ensuing year's stock. On September 3 the war with Germany broke out and on the 8th of that month the British Treasury requested the company to stop all further purchases. As a result of compliance, there remained of the American currency unusable approximately $25,755,000. On September 30 the British Treasury required the company to sell this surplus of dollars to it. Owing to the rise in the dollar exchange which had occurred, the price received by the company was much larger than that paid and the difference was included in the computation of taxable profits. It was held by Macnaghten J and by the Court of Appeal that the gain was attributable to the business carried on by the company. Lord Greene MR with whom MacKinnon LJ and du Parcq LJ concurred, took the view that the acquisition of the dollars was simply the first step in carrying out the purchases of the leaf and the payment of its price. Bought for that purpose, the currency took on revenue characteristic which was not lost when the surplus was sold. The argument against that seems to have been directed mainly to the circumstance that the disposal was not voluntary but dictated by the Treasury and a considerable part of the reasoning was to meet that consideration. *McKinlay's case* (*supra*) was examined and distinguished.

The principle there followed, however sound its application, and I do not imply a doubt of that, is, *a fortiori*, appropriate here. Every dollar of the accumulated debt represents the discharge of purchase price of goods bought. From the standpoint of investment, that case is much clearer; the sterling was bought generally and that allocated to the specific purchases was chargeable at the exchange existing at the moment of purchase. In both cases the foreign currency was used in the purchase of a commodity for the company's trade, but in that before us, the sterling representing the debt had no existence apart from that use.

Mr. Phillips urged the analogy of a loan by way of bonds or debentures repayable, say, in 1 or 2 years. If the money was raised for the purpose and used as here, that is, for and as working capital that was immediately employed in the course of the company's business, there would not seem to be any difference, and profit realized upon the redemption of the bonds or debentures might find itself gathered into income. It is difficult to distinguish a liability represented by bonds or debentures for a short period and mere indebtedness however represented when the character of the money and the purpose of its employment are the same. Bonds or other securities representing permanent or fixed features of the capital structure are entirely different in their nature and incidents.

Mr. Phillips also stressed the distinction between sterling as a commodity and as a medium of exchange, but, as already remarked, here no sterling was ever owned by the company as a commodity. A contractual right, assuming that the arrangement went so far, to have a bank pay bills on behalf of a purchaser as they are presented by sellers of goods, does not entail a purchase of a commodity for the company; and it is confusing the issue to speak of the arrangement as having produced a temporary investment: a debt is neither an asset nor an investment of the debtor, even though, as here, it may be exposed to the risk of variable value in terms of a foreign currency.

It follows that the appeal must be dismissed with costs.

LOCKE J (Kerwin CJC, concurring): The *Income Tax Act, 1948* does not contain any further definition of "income" which requires consideration in this case than that to be found in Sections 3 and 4 [now sections 3 and 9]. In this respect it differs from its predecessor, the *Income War Tax Act* (RSC 1927, c. 97) where the meaning to be assigned to the term in the Act was elaborately defined.

Section 3 of the 1948 Act says that the income of a taxpayer for a taxation year for the purposes of Part I of the Act is his income from all sources inside or outside Canada and without restricting the generality of the foregoing includes income from, *inter alia*, all businesses. Section 4 so far as it is relevant merely says that income for a taxation year from a business is the profit therefrom for the year. Accordingly the only question to be considered is whether the profit which was undoubtedly realized in the present matter is a profit from the business carried on by the appellant.

The relevant facts are detailed in the judgment of Cameron J delivered in the Exchequer Court. The purpose of the borrowing from the Canadian Bank of Commerce branch in London was stated during cross-examination of the witness Clayton, the secretary and controller of the appellant company, in these terms:

> It was felt that the pound sterling would be devalued, and after discussing the matter fully with the President and other top officials in the company we decided to deliberately pursue this policy of running a large overdraft in England in the hope of gaining the capital profit on devaluation.

And again:

> I contend that that profit is the result of a premeditated act on my part and other officials of the company to build up a liability in England when, in fact, we could have specifically paid out of funds that we had in Canada, and it had no relationship whatsoever with the merchandise, as you are saying it does, in that once we paid a supplier the transaction was completed with the supplier and we had no more recourse to him. In normal circumstances, for as long back as I can trace the records, the procedure was different, and it was only during this 18 months when we tried to go short of sterling and the procedure was different and resulted in a capital profit, and has no relationship, in my opinion, to the merchandise.

While the foregoing is rather more argument than a statement of facts it makes clear the purpose of the course that was followed. The question as to whether the gain made by the company is a capital profit is, of course, the point in the case.

It is, in my view, of importance to note that while, as Clayton's evidence indicated, the appellant intended to advance the claim that any profit realized as a result of devaluation of the pound was a capital gain resulting from what was to be a speculation in foreign exchange, the interest charges on the bank loan were charged in the years 1948 and 1949 as expenses of the operation of the business. In my opinion the present matter is concluded against the appellant by the decision of this Court in *Atlantic Sugar Refineries Limited v. M.N.R.*, [1949] SCR 706, [1949] CTC 196. I am unable to differentiate the position of the taxpayer in that case in respect to the profit made on the short sales of sugar from the position of the appellant in regard to the profit that was made due to the fall in value of the pound.

At the commencement of the year 1948 the appellant had a very small overdraft with the bank in London and from then until September 1949 used sterling borrowed from that bank to pay for the goods used in its manufacturing operations in Canada. The purpose of incurring the overdraft was made clear by Clayton. It was the hope that when it became necessary to pay the overdraft the value of the pound in relation to the Canadian dollar would have dropped, the practical result of which would be that the cost of the goods which had been used in the operations or purchased during that period would be reduced. In essence there appears to be no difference between the resulting profit, whether it be expressed as one realized by the reduction in the number of Canadian dollars needed to discharge a debt or as a reduction in the cost to the taxpayer of the merchandise which had been used and purchased during the period and that which would have resulted had the taxpayer sold sterling short to the requisite amount.

I agree with the learned trial judge that it was a scheme for profit-making in one necessary part of the appellant's trading operations, namely, the purchase of sterling funds and part of an integrated commercial operation being the purchase of the supplies and the payment for them in that currency. It was apparently treated as such in the preparation of the appellant's accounts for the years in question since if it was simply a speculation in sterling exchange divorced from the company's trading operations the interest payable on the bank loan would not have been deductible as an operating expense.

...

Everything that could be fairly urged on behalf of the appellant in the present matter has been said by the learned counsel who appealed on its behalf but, in my opinion, this appeal should fail for the above reasons.

CARTWRIGHT J (dissenting): The relevant facts out of which this appeal arises are undisputed.

The appellant has for many years carried on the business of manufacturing and selling clothes and in the course of that business makes large purchases of woolens in the United Kingdom the price of which is payable in sterling. For some years prior to January 1948 its practice was to purchase the necessary sterling funds to pay for each lot of goods bought but at about the date mentioned it arranged to borrow sterling from a bank in England. The funds borrowed were used to pay the vendors of the goods purchased and the cost of each lot of goods was charged in the appellant's books in dollars at the current rate of exchange which had for some time been pegged at $4.04 to the pound. Admittedly this arrangement was made in the expectation that the pound would be devalued and that a substantial saving to the appellant would result.

On September 20, 1949, the rate of exchange was altered to $3.0875. At this date the appellant owed the bank in round figures £178,000. In October 1949 the appellant paid off this indebtedness at the new rate of exchange. The amount in dollars required to make this payment was less by $169,614.96 than it would have been at the old rate. The respondent in assessing the appellant for the year 1949 added this sum to its declared income.

...

The gist of the decision of the Income Tax Appeal Board delivered by Mr. W.S. Fisher, QC, is contained in the following paragraph in his reasons:

> In the case of a debenture or bond issue floated by a company and subsequently liquidated or paid off for a smaller amount than that originally received, I am of the opinion that the difference would have been treated as a capital profit without question, and that this would be so even although the proceeds of the debenture or bond issue had been used in the business of the company for the purchase of raw materials utilized in the company's manufacturing and trading operations. In my opinion, the loan obtained from the British bank was borrowed capital, and when that loan was repaid by the appellant, the profit realized was a capital profit which was not subject to income tax under the Act. The profit in question did not arise out of the trading operations of the appellant company. The goods which it purchased in Great Britain were paid for promptly by it within a very short time after the goods were delivered, and the transaction was then closed. The fact that the payment was made out of monies borrowed from a bank does not, in my view, bring the bank loan into the category of ordinary day-to-day transactions carried on by the company. At all times, the position of the appellant in relation to the British bank was that of borrower to lender, and it was not part of the business of the appellant to deal in foreign exchange.

In the Exchequer Court, Cameron J after a careful review of a number of authorities reached the conclusion "that the profit made in the instant case was one made in the ordinary course of the respondent's business operations and while engaged therein on a scheme for profit making."

After considering all of the decisions referred to in the reasons of Cameron J and those discussed by counsel in the argument before us, it is my opinion that, in the case of a taxpayer carrying on a commercial undertaking such as that of the appellant whose business is not that of dealing in foreign exchange or borrowing and lending money, a gain or loss related to dealings between borrower and lender is *prima facie* one of capital and not of income. This appears to me to be a result of the decision in *Davies v. Shell*, 32 TC 133,

Montreal Coke and Manufacturing Co. v. M.N.R., [1944] AC 126, [1944] CTC 94; and *Bennett & White Construction Co. Ltd. v. M.N.R.*, [1949] SCR 287, [1949] CTC 1.

In the case at bar I can find nothing sufficient to displace this *prima facie* presumption that a saving made in discharging an obligation to a lender is properly treated as an item of capital and not of revenue. The circumstance that the payments of interest to the bank were charged as expenses of the operation of the appellant's business in the years 1948 and 1949 does not appear to me to assist the respondent. The money borrowed was used as part of the appellant's working capital and the interest was "an amount paid in the year ... pursuant to a legal obligation to pay interest on borrowed money used for the purpose of earning income from a business ..." and was properly deductible from taxable income under clause (c) of Section 11 of the *Income Tax Act*, Statutes of Canada, 1948, c. 52 [now paragraph 20(1)(c) of the Act].

...

For the reasons given by Mr. Fisher and for those set out above I would allow the appeal and restore the decision of the Income Tax Appeal Board with costs throughout.

Appeal dismissed.

NOTES AND QUESTIONS

1. On what basis did the taxpayer in *Tip Top Tailors* argue that the foreign exchange gain resulting from the anticipated devaluation in the British pound sterling was not taxable? On what grounds did the Crown contend that the foreign exchange gain in *Tip Top Tailors* should be taxable as business income?

2. Why does Rand J conclude that the foreign exchange gain was on account of income, not capital? On what basis does he distinguish the English decision in *McKinlay v. Jenkins* (1926), 10 Tax Cas 372?

3. Why does Locke J (Kerwin CJC, concurring) hold that the foreign exchange gain was taxable? Of what relevance is Locke J's observation that "there appears to be no difference between the resulting profit, whether it be expressed as one realized by the reduction in the number of Canadian dollars needed to discharge a debt or as a reduction in the cost to the taxpayer of the merchandise which had been used and purchased during the period"? Of what relevance is the fact that the taxpayer deducted the interest on the bank overdraft as a deductible expense?

4. Why does Cartwright J (dissenting) conclude in *Tip Top Tailors* that the foreign exchange gain was on account of capital, not income? Of what relevance is the fact that the taxpayer was not in the business of "dealing in foreign exchange or borrowing or lending money"?

5.   Which, if either, judgment do you find most persuasive in *Tip Top Tailors*? Why?

6.   *Tip Top Tailors* was followed in *Aluminum Union Ltd. v. M.N.R.*, [1960] C.T.C. 206, 60 D.T.C. 1138 (Ex. Ct.), in which the taxpayer, which sold aluminum and related products from 1934 to 1942 through a branch office in Osaka, Japan, realized a gain of $172,927 on the settlement in 1952 of a debt payable in yen that greatly depreciated in value immediately after the end of the Second World War. Observing (at para. 10) that the borrowed funds were used to pay duties on goods imported from Canada and elsewhere and "for business purposes, such as general administration, salaries, travelling expenses, and office furnishings," Fournier J held (at para. 22) that "[t]he borrowings were not made for investment purposes but to meet the expenditures incurred in the operation of its business activities." On this basis, he concluded (at para. 27), "the profit realized by [the taxpayer] on the settlement of its debt to the bank was includible in its revenue income and assessable for income tax purposes."

7.   For other cases addressing foreign exchange income see *Alberta Natural Gas Co. v. M.N.R.*, [1971] S.C.J. No. 126, [1971] C.T.C. 718, 71 D.T.C. 5400 (S.C.C.); *Alberta Gas Trunk Line Co. v. M.N.R.*, [1971] S.C.J. No. 127, [1971] C.T.C. 723, 71 D.T.C. 5403 (S.C.C.); *Columbia Records of Canada Ltd. v. M.N.R.*, [1971] C.T.C. 839, 71 D.T.C. 5486 (F.C.T.D.); *Salada Foods Ltd. v. Canada*, [1974] F.C.J. No. 106, [1974] C.T.C. 201, 74 D.T.C. 6171 (F.C.T.D.); *Neonex International Ltd. v. Canada*, [1978] F.C.J. No. 514, [1978] C.T.C. 485, 78 D.T.C. 6339 (F.C.A.); *The Weatherhead Company of Canada Ltd. v. M.N.R.*, [1982] C.T.C. 2839, 82 D.T.C. 1831 (T.R.B.); *Ethicon Sutures Ltd. v. Canada*, [1985] F.C.J. No. 436, [1985] 2 C.T.C. 6, 85 D.T.C. 5290 (F.C.T.D.); *I.S.E. Canadian Finance Ltd. v. M.N.R.*, [1986] T.C.J. No. 301, [1986] 1 C.T.C. 2473, 86 D.T.C. 1344 (T.C.C.); *MacMillan Bloedel Ltd. v. M.N.R.*, [1990] F.C.J. No. 200, [1990] 1 C.T.C. 468, 90 D.T.C. 6219 (F.C.T.D.); *Anstel Holdings Ltd. v. M.N.R.*, [1991] T.C.J. No. 427, [1991] 2 C.T.C. 2515, 91 D.T.C. 1050 (T.C.C.); *Netupsky v. M.N.R.*, [1992] T.C.J. No. 592, [1992] 2 C.T.C. 2531, 92 D.T.C. 2282 (T.C.C.); *CCLI (1994) Inc. v. Canada*, [2007] F.C.J. No. 684, [2007] 4 C.T.C. 19, 2007 D.T.C. 5372 (F.C.A.); and *Saskferco Products Inc. v. Canada*, [2007] T.C.J. No. 300, [2008] 1 C.T.C. 2566, 2007 D.T.C. 1183 (T.C.C.), aff'd [2008] F.C.J. No. 1363, 2008 FCA 297 (F.C.A.).

8.   Where a taxpayer has made a gain or sustained a loss "by virtue of any fluctuation after 1971 in the value of the currency or currencies of one or more countries other than Canada relative to Canadian currency," subsection 39(2) stipulates that:

(a)   the amount, if any, by which

(i)   the total of all such gains made by the taxpayer in the year (to the extent of the amounts thereof that would not, if section 3 were read in the manner described in paragraph (1)(a) of this section, be included in computing the taxpayer's income for the year or any other taxation year)

exceeds

(ii) the total of all such losses sustained by the amounts thereof that would not, if section 3 were read in the manner described in paragraph (1)(a) of this section, be deductible in computing the taxpayer's income for the year or any other taxation year) and

(iii) if the taxpayer is an individual, $200,

shall be deemed to be a capital gain of the taxpayer for the year from the disposition of currency of a country other than Canada, the amount of which capital gain is the amount determined under this paragraph; and

(b) the amount, if any, by which

(i) the total determined under subparagraph (a)(ii),

exceeds

(ii) the total determined under subparagraph (a)(i), and

(iii) if the taxpayer is an individual, $200

shall be deemed to be a capital loss of the taxpayer for the year from the disposition of currency of a country other than Canada, the amount of which capital loss is the amount determined under this paragraph.

As a result, the Act recognizes capital gains or losses of individuals from foreign currency exchanges only to the extent that these gains or losses exceed $200 Canadian.

9. Subsection 39(2) was considered in *MacMillan Bloedel Ltd. v. Canada*, [1999] F.C.J. No. 1058, [1999] 3 C.T.C. 652, 99 D.T.C. 5446 (F.C.A.); and *Imperial Oil Ltd. v. Canada*, [2006] S.C.J. No. 46, [2007] 1 C.T.C. 41, 2006 D.T.C. 6660, [2006] 2 S.C.R. 447 (S.C.C.).

10. In *Shell Canada Ltd. v. Canada*, [1999] S.C.J. No. 30, [1999] 4 C.T.C. 313, 99 D.T.C. 5682 (S.C.C.), the taxpayer corporation obtained capital for its US operations by borrowing funds in New Zealand and entering into a forward exchange contract to pay the interest and principal as they became due. As a result of the forward exchange contracts, the taxpayer locked in a foreign exchange gain of US $21 million, which it realized upon repayment of the principal in 1993. In determining that this gain was a capital receipt, the court followed the decision in *Tip Top Tailors Ltd. v. M.N.R.*, [1957] S.C.J. No. 49, [1957] C.T.C. 309, 57 D.T.C. 1232 (S.C.C.), and suggested (at para. 68) that "the characterization of a foreign exchange gain or loss generally follows the characterization of the underlying transaction." In finding that the purpose of the debenture agreements was to raise working capital, the court went on to find that

the foreign exchange gains made pursuant to these debentures were thus also on account of capital. The court also rejected the arguments raised by the Minister that the taxpayer was acting like a trader in acquiring the funds; and that the funds should be considered income because they did not arise fortuitously, but were guaranteed by the forward exchange contract.

11. On February 28, 2000, four months after the Supreme Court of Canada released its reasons in *Shell Canada*, the federal government announced that it would amend the *Income Tax Act*, effective from that date, to preclude any tax advantages from weak-currency borrowings. The amendment, in section 20.3, disallows the deduction of excess interest payments on a "weak currency debt", subtracting this disallowed interest in computing the foreign exchange gain or loss realized on repayment of the debt, and deeming any foreign exchange gain or loss on the repayment of the debt and on any associated hedge to be on income account.

12. For the CRA's views on the characterization of foreign exchange gains and losses, see *Interpretation Bulletin* IT-95R "Foreign Exchange Gains and Losses," December 16, 1980. According to paragraphs 2 to 6 of this bulletin:

> 2. Where it can be determined that a gain or loss on foreign exchange arose as a direct consequence of the purchase or sale of goods abroad, or the rendering of services abroad, and such goods or services are used in the business operations of the taxpayer, such gain or loss is brought into income account. If, on the other hand, it can be determined that a gain or loss on foreign exchange arose as a direct consequence of the purchase or sale of capital assets, this gain or loss is either a capital gain or capital loss, as the case may be. Generally, the nature of a foreign exchange gain or loss is not affected by the length of time between the date the property is acquired (or disposed of) and the date upon which payment (or receipt) is effected.

> 3. Generally, where borrowed funds are used in the ordinary course of a taxpayer's business operations, any foreign exchange gain realized on the repayment of the loan is considered to be an income gain and any foreign exchange loss incurred on repayment of the loan is considered to be an income loss. The fact that a company which borrowed in a foreign currency was not adequately capitalized does not automatically result in capital treatment of any foreign exchange gains or losses arising on repayment. Capital treatment will result where it can be shown that the borrowed funds form part of the permanent or fixed capital of the company, regardless of the use of the funds. In other cases of inadequate capitalization, the use made of the borrowed funds will determine whether such gains or losses should be on income account or on capital account.

> 4. Where current foreign funds, i.e., funds obtained as a result of transactions on income account, are used to make a capital payment, such as a payment to purchase a capital property or a payment on a capital debt obligation, the exchange gain or loss on those current funds is reflected on income account at the time of the capital payment as though the funds had been converted to Canadian dollars and the same amount of Canadian funds had been used to make the capita] payment. In such circumstances, there could subsequently be a capital gain or loss on the discharge of the capital debt obligation.

> 5. Sundry dispositions of foreign currency by individuals, such as a conversion of travellers cheques in foreign funds to Canadian dollars on return from a vacation, are

considered to be on account of capital. Foreign exchange losses sustained on the repayment of a debt which was given to acquire a personal-use property are also considered to be capital losses under subsection 39(2).

6. A taxpayer who has transactions in foreign currency or foreign currency futures that do not form part of business operations, or are merely the result of sundry dispositions of foreign currency by an individual, will be accorded by the Department the same treatment as that of a "speculator" in commodity futures — see 7 and 8 of IT-346R. However, if such a taxpayer has special "inside" information concerning foreign exchange, he will be required to report his gains and losses on income account.

III. COMPUTATION

In order to determine a taxpayer's taxable capital gain or allowable capital loss for a taxation year, it is necessary not only to characterize the gain or loss as a *capital* gain or loss, but also to compute the amount of the gain or loss. The remainder of this chapter examines key statutory and judicial rules governing the computation of taxable capital gains and allowable capital losses, considering general rules applicable to dispositions of all capital property, special rules applicable to specific types of capital property, and specific rules governing the recognition and non-recognition of capital gains and losses.

A. General Rules

As explained in the introduction to this chapter, the rules governing the computation of taxable capital gains and allowable capital losses are contained in subdivision c of division B of Part I of the Act, comprising sections 38 to 55. Paragraphs 38(a) and (b) define the "taxable" portion of a capital gain and the "allowable" portion of a capital loss as one-half of the amount otherwise determined under subdivision c (or one-quarter in the case of charitable gifts of publicly traded shares and ecologically sensitive land). In turn, paragraphs 39(1)(a) and (b) define the underlying concepts of capital gain and capital loss. Completing the definitional framework, the statutory rules dictating how to compute the amount of a taxpayer's gain or loss from the disposition of property are found in subsection 40(1).

According to subparagraph 40(1)(a)(i) of the Act, "a taxpayer's gain for a taxation year from the disposition of any property" in the year is defined as:

the amount, if any, by which the taxpayer's proceeds of disposition exceed the total of the adjusted cost base to the taxpayer of the property immediately before the disposition and any outlays and expenses to the extent that they were made or incurred by the taxpayer for the purpose of making the disposition.

Correspondingly, subparagraph 40(1)(b)(i) defines "a taxpayer's loss for a taxation year from the disposition of any property" in the year as:

the amount, if any, by which the total of the adjusted cost base to the taxpayer of the property immediately before the disposition and any outlays and expenses to the extent that they were made or incurred by the taxpayer for the purpose of making the disposition, exceeds the taxpayer's proceeds of disposition of the property.

Subparagraphs 40(1)(a)(ii) and (iii) permit taxpayers who dispose of property for proceeds some or all of which are payable after the end of the taxation year to defer the recognition of a portion of a gain through the deduction of a reserve,[27] while subparagraph 40(1)(b)(ii) requires taxpayers who realize a capital loss to recognize the full amount of the loss in the taxation year in which the property is disposed of by defining the amount of the capital loss in any other year as nil.

In order to determine the amount of a taxpayer's gain or loss for a taxation year from the disposition of capital property, therefore, it is necessary to determine the taxpayer's "proceeds of disposition of the property", the "adjusted cost base" to the taxpayer of the property immediately before the disposition, and the amount of any "outlays and expenses ... made or incurred by the taxpayer for making the disposition." The following text and cases examine each of these concepts, as well as the computation of a reserve where a taxpayer realizes a gain under paragraph 40(1)(a). As an initial matter, however, this section considers the basic statutory requirement for the recognition of a capital gain or loss that the taxpayer has disposed of capital property.

1. Disposition of Capital Property

For the purpose of the *Income Tax Act*, subsection 248(1) defines a "disposition" of property, except as expressly otherwise provided, to include "any transaction or event entitling a taxpayer to proceeds of disposition of property,"[28] other transactions or events involving the redemption, cancellation, settlement, conversion or expiry of shares, debt obligations, options and other kinds of intangible property,[29] and transfers of property to a trust or by a trust to a beneficiary of the trust.[30] Expressly excluded from the definition are the issuance of shares and debt obligations, transfers of property solely for the purpose of securing a debt or loan or for returning property used as security for a debt or loan, and various transfers of property resulting in a change of legal ownership without a change in beneficial ownership.[31] Section 54 defines "proceeds of disposition" to include "the sale price of property that has been sold,"[32] various kinds of compensation for property that is unlawfully taken,

---

[27] The computation of this reserve is discussed later in this chapter.

[28] See para. (a) of the definition of the word "disposition" in subs. 248(1).

[29] See para. (b) of the definition of the word "disposition" in subs. 248(1).

[30] See paras. (c) and (d) of the definition of the word "disposition" in subs. 248(1). For our purposes, there is no need to examine these provisions in detail.

[31] See paras. (e) to (m) of the definition of the word "disposition" in subs. 248(1). For our purposes, there is no need to examine these exclusions in detail.

[32] See para. (a) of the definition of "proceeds of disposition" in s. 54.

destroyed, expropriated, injuriously affected or damaged,[33] and specific amounts relating to the sale of a mortgaged property or the surrender of property in satisfaction of a debt.[34] Other rules specifically deem taxpayers to have disposed of property under specific circumstances.[35]

The most common type of disposition is undoubtedly a sale of property for valuable consideration. Nonetheless, the use of the word "includes" in the definition of a "disposition" in subsection 248(1) and the different categories of proceeds identified in the definition of "proceeds of disposition" in section 54 confirm that the statutory concept of a "disposition of property" encompasses much more than ordinary sales. In the context of a similar definition for depreciable property, for example, the Supreme Court of Canada held that the words "disposition of property" should be given their broadest possible meaning, including the destruction of tangible property (for example, a building) or the extinction of an item of intangible property (for example, a patent or leasehold interest).[36] In other cases, the Federal Court of Appeal has concluded that a taxpayer may dispose of property where the taxpayer conveys an economic interest in a corporation or partnership without explicitly transferring shares or an interest in the partnership.[37] Likewise, the CRA adopts the view that changes to the terms of securities, the redemption, cancellation, settlement, conversion, or expiry of which would be a "disposition" according to paragraph (b) of the statutory definition may also constitute a "disposition of property" where the change is sufficiently significant to affect the nature or economic value of the property.[38] According to paragraph 7 of Interpretation Bulletin IT-448, "Dispositions — Changes in Terms of Securities," June 6, 1980:

---

[33] See paras. (b) to (f) of the definition of "proceeds of disposition" in s. 54.

[34] See paras. (g) and (h) of the definition of "proceeds of disposition" in s. 54, and the rules governing the surrender of property to a creditor in s. 79. For our purposes, there is no need to examine this provision in detail.

[35] See for example, subs. 45(1), which deems taxpayers to have disposed of property where the purpose for which they use the property changes. This rule is examined later in this chapter.

[36] *Canada v. CIE Immobilière BCN Ltée*, [1979] S.C.J. No. 13, [1979] C.T.C. 71, 79 D.T.C. 5068 (S.C.C.) (at para. 35).

[37] See, for example, *M.N.R. v. Kieboom*, [1992] F.C.J. No. 605, [1992] 2 C.T.C. 59, 92 D.T.C. 6382 (F.C.A.) (transfer of value by taxpayer to spouse and children by causing corporation to issue shares to spouse and children for proceeds less than their fair market value); and *Stursburg v. Canada*, [1993] F.C.J. No. 594, [1993] 2 C.T.C. 76, 93 D.T.C. 5271 (F.C.A.) (series of transactions in which taxpayer's percentage interest in partnership was reduced on the withdrawal of funds while another partner's interest was increased on the contribution of funds characterized as disposition of partnership interest). For a critical examination of these and other cases, see Douglas S. Ewens and Michael J. Flatters, "Toward a More Coherent Theory of Dispositions" (1995) Vol. 43 No. 5 Can. Tax J. 1377. See also *Shepp v. Canada*, [1999] T.C.J. No. 53, [1999] 1 C.T.C. 2889, 99 D.T.C. 510 (T.C.C.), in which the court questioned whether the concept of a "disposition of property" includes the disposition of an economic interest.

[38] See Interpretation Bulletin IT-448, "Dispositions — Changes in Terms of Securities," June 6, 1980. For a critical evaluation of this interpretation bulletin, see Brian Arnold and David Ward, "Dispositions — A Critique of Revenue Canada's Interpretation" (1980) 28 Can. Tax J. 559.

The following changes in respect of the debt obligation itself (unless carried out pursuant to an authorizing provision in its original terms) are considered to be so fundamental to the holder's economic interest in the property that they almost invariably precipitate a disposition:

(a) a change from interest-bearing to interest-free or vice versa,

(b) a change in repayment schedule or maturity date,

(c) an increase or decrease in the principal amount,

(d) the addition, alteration or elimination of a premium payable upon retirement,

(e) a change in the debtor, and

(f) the conversion of a fixed interest bond to a bond in respect of which interest is payable only to the extent that the debtor has made a profit, or vice versa.

According to paragraph 14:

Following are examples of changes that are normally considered to be of sufficient substance to be regarded as dispositions:

(a) a change in voting rights attached to shares that effects a change in the voting control of the corporation;

(b) a change in a defined entitlement (e.g., a change in par value) to share in the assets of a corporation upon dissolution (preferred shares only);

(c) the giving up or the addition of a priority right to share in the distribution of assets of the corporation upon dissolution;

(d) the addition or deletion of a right attaching to a class of share that provides for participation in dividend entitlements beyond a fixed preferential rate or amount;

(e) a change from a cumulative to a non-cumulative right to dividends or vice versa.

Although these administrative positions have not been subject to judicial scrutiny, other cases have concluded that transactions or events are not dispositions of property where taxpayers transfer shares as security for a loan,[39] or receive a payment in exchange for extending the time limit for payment under a loan.[40] In contrast, where a shareholder transferred shares to the issuing

---

[39] See *106443 Canada Inc. v. Canada*, [1994] T.C.J. No. 6, [1995] 1 C.T.C. 2788, (1994) 94 D.T.C. 1663 (T.C.C.) (at para. 14) (transfer of shares for $1 with right to repurchase at prevailing value characterized as security for a loan made to a subsidiary of the taxpayer on the grounds that the shares were given to a trustee who could not sell them without the consent of the taxpayer, that the provisions of the share transfer agreement indicate "an intention to retain some measure of ownership and be able to recover ownership completely once certain conditions have been met," and that such a sale with a right of redemption is a common form of security contemplated by the Quebec Civil Code).

[40] *Quincaillerie Laberge Inc. v. Canada*, [1994] T.C.J. No. 842, [1995] 2 C.T.C. 2975, (1994) 95 D.T.C. 155 (T.C.C.) (at para. 32) (stating that a disposition requires "a fundamental transfer of

corporation to enable it to pay creditors, the court concluded that the transaction constituted a disposition of the shares on the grounds that the taxpayer did not transfer the shares as security for a loan but intended to and did give up ownership absolutely.[41]

With respect to the taxation year in which a disposition can be said to occur, courts have held in the context of a sale of property that "there is a disposal of property as soon as a taxpayer is entitled to the sale price of the property sold."[42] Where property is not sold outright, but is subject to a lease with an option to purchase, a disposition of property has been held to occur when the transferor divests itself of "all of the duties, responsibilities and charges of ownership and also all of the profits, benefits and incidents of ownership" even though they retain legal title.[43] In these and other cases, as commentators have suggested, the statutory concept of a "disposition" reflects a basic principle of income tax law that a gain generally must be realized by a taxpayer before the gain is subject to income tax.[44]

2. Proceeds of Disposition

As explained in the previous section, section 54 defines "proceeds of disposition" for the purpose of computing a capital gain or loss to include "the sale price of property that has been sold,"[45] various kinds of compensation for property that is unlawfully taken, destroyed, expropriated, injuriously affected or damaged,[46] and specific amounts relating to the sale of mortgaged property or

---

an interest in a property," concluding that the extension did not constitute a disposition of an interest under Quebec's civil law, and characterizing the payment as an inducement payment subject to tax under para. 12(1)(x) of the Act).

[41] *Fulljames v. Canada*, [1999] T.C.J. No. 736, [2000] 1 C.T.C. 2270, 2000 D.T.C. 1518 (T.C.C.). For a similar result, in which the court rejected the taxpayer's argument that an interest in real property had been transferred as a security interest for a loan, see *Hallbauer v. Canada*, [1998] F.C.J. No. 495, [1998] 3 C.T.C. 115, 98 D.T.C. 6275 (F.C.A.).

[42] *Victory Hotels Ltd. v. M.N.R.*, [1962] C.T.C. 614, 62 D.T.C. 1378 (Ex. Ct.). See also *Laurentide Rendering Inc. v. Canada*, [1982] F.C.J. No. 1018, [1982] C.T.C. 400, 83 D.T.C. 5066 (F.C.T.D.) and *Reilly Estate v. Canada*, [1983] F.C.J. No. 1114, [1984] C.T.C. 21, (1983) 84 D.T.C. 6001 (F.C.T.D.). For the CRA's views on when capital property is sold, see Interpretation Bulletin IT-170R, "Sale of Property — When Included in Income Computation," August 25, 1980.

[43] *Olympia & York Dev. Ltd. v. Canada*, [1980] C.T.C. 265, 80 D.T.C. 6184 (F.C.T.D.). See also *Kozan v. M.N.R.*, [1987] T.C.J. No. 136, [1987] 1 C.T.C. 2258, 87 D.T.C. 148 (T.C.C.), where the court concluded that the taxpayer had disposed of property of which the purchaser had taken possession in 1979, notwithstanding that transfer of title was not registered until 1980.

[44] See, for example, Brian Arnold and David Ward, "Dispositions — A Critique of Revenue Canada's Interpretation" (1980) 28 Can. Tax J. 559 at 576.

[45] See para. (a) of the definition of "proceeds of disposition" in s. 54.

[46] See para. (b) to (f) of the definition of "proceeds of disposition" in s. 54.

the surrender of property in satisfaction of a debt.[47] Specifically excluded from the definition are various types of deemed dividends that are best examined in a course on the taxation of corporations and shareholders.

Although the most common category of proceeds is the sale price of property that has been sold, the specific inclusion of other amounts in the statutory definition and the use of the word "includes" suggest that other amounts may also constitute proceeds of disposition. In *Robert v. M.N.R.*, [1990] 1 C.T.C. 2407, (1989) 90 D.T.C. 1277 (T.C.C.), the court considered the application of this statutory definition to a transaction in which the taxpayers settled a legal dispute by selling their interests in a real estate project for $1 plus the assumption of debt owing by the taxpayer.

Robert v. M.N.R.
[1990] 1 C.T.C. 2407, (1989) 90 D.T.C. 1277 (T.C.C.)

LAMARRE-PROULX TCJ: ... These are appeals relating to what is known by the abbreviation MURB in English and IRLM in French; a multiple unit residential building, that is, a building, in this case, which falls into class 32 of Schedule II of the *Income Tax Regulations*.

...

[T]he advantage of purchasing a MURB as opposed to another rental building is that the eligible capital cost allowance may be deducted from income other than rental income. [As a general rule, subsection 1100(11) of the regulations prohibits taxpayers from claiming capital cost allowance on rental properties in an amount exceeding the net income from all rental properties computed without accounting for CCA. During the years at issue in the case, subsection 1100(14) of the regulations excluded MURBs from the definition of rental properties.] On the other hand, in accordance with the provisions of the *Income Tax Act*, there is recapture of the capital cost allowance on resale as in the case of any disposition of depreciable property.

...

The Facts

In December 1979 the appellants purchased shares of 14 per cent, 7 per cent and 24 per cent respectively from Pierre Lavallée in the multiple unit residential property located in Longueuil known as "Les Jardins Chambly." The purchase price was $2,016,000, and was composed of the following amounts:

(1) $1,826,000, broken down as follows:

    (a) $36,000 — land

---

[47] See paras. (g) and (h) of the definition of "proceeds of disposition" in s. 54, and the rules governing the surrender of property to a creditor in s. 79.

    (b) $1,700,000 — buildings

    (c) $50,000 — equipment

    (d) $40,000 — parking

(2) $190,000, broken down as follows:

    (a) $20,000 — advertising attributable to rental of the buildings for a 5-year period, and

    (b) $ 170,000 — for management fees for the building and to guarantee cash flow.

Payment was made in the following manner:

    (1) $1,493,833.81 in mortgages, and

    (2) $522,166.19 from the purchasers.

With respect to the payment of the $522,166.19 to be made by the purchasers, it was in large part carried by the vendor in the form of promissory notes signed by the purchasers to the order of the vendor.

...

The purchase of this building had taken place specifically in response to a prospectus by the vendor, Pierre Lavallée. This prospectus indicated in the first point on the first page: [Translation] "Goal of the investment: to obtain the best legal means of reducing and deferring income tax by purchasing a building complex. In addition to tax savings, this investment will result in a cash flow surplus."

In the description of "10 benefits of having a tax shelter," benefit No. 7 reads as follows: [Translation] "Guarantee of operating funds. Our firm guarantees the project's operating funds, which means that if the project does not cover its expenses, our firm undertakes to make up the deficit."

...

The appellants quickly became dissatisfied with Pierre Lavallée's management for various reasons, but particularly because he had claimed operating deficits from them, contrary, in their opinion, to the promises made in the prospectus. Upon this demand being made to the appellants, to cover the operating deficit, they stopped their payments on the promissory notes and asked a firm of accountants in Montreal, Maheu, Noiseux, Roy et Associés, to prepare a report for them on the operation of the building. This report was produced on July 14, 1981.

To counteract the stopping of payments on the promissory notes and the refusal to cover the operating deficits, Pierre Lavallée brought two actions against the appellants on August 25, 1981: one, for payment on the promissory notes, and the other, for payment of the operating deficit, that is, the expenses that could not be covered by the income generated by the buildings.

...

After long and apparently tumultuous discussions, the appellants resold their respective shares to Mr. Lavallée on December 14, 1982 for the price of $1 plus assumption by the purchaser of the balance of the mortgages owing by the appellants. The effect of this sale at this price was to cause a terminal loss to the appellants.

The Law

The respondent contests part of this consideration, that is, the $1. He states that this consideration should be increased by the amount of the balance owing on the promissory notes and the operating losses that had been claimed and assumed by the manager despite himself. According to the respondent, for the years 1979 to 1981 the operating deficit before capital cost allowance was on the order of $115,448, which was absorbed by the purchaser at the time of the sale in 1981. The appellants' share would be about $77,000. This share should be included in calculating the proceeds of disposition of the buildings.

...

Counsel for the appellants ... argued that paragraph 54(h) [now the definition of "proceeds of disposition" in section 54] of the Act does not allow for inclusion of the remission of debts on the promissory notes as part of the proceeds of disposition because (a) this remission was not part of the sale price and (b) it is not included in the provisions of subparagraph 54(h)(vii) [now paragraph (g) of the definition of "proceeds of disposition" in section 54]. It may be, as submitted by counsel for the appellants, that this remission should not be included within the meaning of subparagraph 54(h)(vii), since this subparagraph seems to provide for cases of sale under a clause in a mortgage. This is not the case here. With respect to the argument that the remission of the debt in question cannot be covered by the provisions of any subparagraph of paragraph 54(h), I am of the opinion first that paragraph 54(h) is not drafted so as to be exhaustive, and second [that] the remission of this debt, which is one of the conditions for the transfer of ownership, must be calculated in the sale price. In order to determine the sale price, what we must look for is the true consideration for the transfer of ownership. In order to find what this consideration was, we must examine the sequence of events which led to the transfer of ownership.

...

With respect to the operating deficits of $77,000 which the manager, Pierre Lavallée, had claimed from the owners, which claim was settled by the sale of the building to the owner, the validity of including these deficits in the sale price of the building appears to me to be more uncertain. A purchase price is determined by mutual agreement. ... However, with respect to the value to be assigned to this mutual release, I am of the opinion that it is not possible to determine it in the circumstances of this case. If the parties had considered it advisable to put a value on this consideration ... , it was for them to do so. The evidence has shown that there was no agreement between the parties as to the amount and merits of these mutual claims.

Both sides have always argued that they did not owe anything and the legal actions in this respect are evidence that there was no agreement as to the validity of these claims. Moreover, the clause does not say that the purchaser releases claims that he has against the vendors, as in the case of the promissory notes; rather, we read that mutual releases are given: "The purchaser and the vendors shall each release the other from all claims that they have or may have between them."

Since the claim did not proceed in court and the resale of the building put an end to all such claims, I consider that it is not for me to put any value on these mutual releases, and in any event I could not do so. ...

Appeal allowed in part.

NOTES AND QUESTIONS

1.   What were the amounts that the Minister sought to add in computing the proceeds of disposition in *Robert*? On what grounds did the taxpayers argue that these amounts should not be included in computing their proceeds of disposition? What decision did the court reach? Why?

2.   In *Demers v. Canada*, [1985] F.C.J. No. 1145, [1986] 2 C.T.C. 321, (1985) 69 N.R. 120, 86 D.T.C. 6411 (F.C.A.), the taxpayers sold corporate stock for $7.8 million, pursuant to an agreement whereby they were also required to pay the purchaser the face value of $1.4 million for a debt obligation worth only $600,000. According to Pratte J (MacGuigan J concurring), the proceeds of disposition received by the taxpayer were only $7 million. Concurring in the outcome, Hugessen J characterized the $800,000 excess paid for the other asset as an expense of the disposition which was properly deductible in computing the taxpayer's capital gain.

3.   In *Sénécal v. M.N.R.*, [1993] T.C.J. No. 111, [1993] 2 C.T.C. 2218, 93 D.T.C. 1155 (T.C.C.), the taxpayer sold a parcel of real property for $90,000 cash plus a promissory note of $15,000 bearing no interest and payable only upon payment of all the purchaser's long-term debts. Although accepting the taxpayer's testimony that the promissory note had "no market value," the court held that the note was part of the sale price, which is statutorily included in the proceeds of disposition. Where the proceeds are not paid immediately, the court observed that the taxpayer may claim a reserve under subparagraph 40(1)(a)(iii). In addition, the court recognized that where a capital debt is determined to have become bad, subsection 50(1) permits the taxpayer to realize the loss by deeming the debt to have been disposed of and reacquired for a nil amount.

4.   Where the liability of a taxpayer to a mortgagee or hypothecary creditor is reduced as a result of mortgaged or hypothecated property under a provision of the mortgage or hypothec, the amount by which this liability is reduced plus any

amount received by the taxpayer out of the proceeds of sale are included in the statutory definition of "proceeds of disposition." Similarly, where a taxpayer surrenders property to a creditor after failing to pay interest or principal on a debt, these unpaid amounts are deemed to be the taxpayer's proceeds of disposition of the property under the statutory definition of "proceeds of disposition" and section 79 of the Act, which addresses the tax consequences of surrender of property by debtors.

In *Dunne v. Canada*, [1995] F.C.J. No. 375, [1995] 2 C.T.C. 108, 96 D.T.C. 6400 (F.C.T.D.), the taxpayers defaulted on the payment of a mortgage to the Canada Mortgage and Housing Corporation, which initiated mortgage sale proceedings at which time the taxpayers owed approximately $3.7 million, acquired the property when no bidder challenged its reserve bid, and subsequently sold the property to a third party for $1.7 million. Relying on the statutory definition of "proceeds of disposition," which includes "the amount by which the liability of a taxpayer to a mortgagee ... is reduced as a result of a sale of the mortgaged ... property," the court rejected the taxpayers' argument that the proceeds should be computed at $1.7 million, accepting instead the Minister's argument that they were $3.7 million.

See also *Corbett v. Canada*, [1996] F.C.J. No. 1419, [1997] 1 C.T.C. 2, (1996) 96 D.T.C. 6572 (F.C.A.), where the taxpayer owed $63,785 on a mortgage that had gone into default, resulting in a judicial sale to the mortgagee for $49,000. Rejecting the Minister's argument that the proceeds are deemed under section 79 and the statutory definition of "proceeds of disposition" to be the amount of the taxpayer's debt that was extinguished by the sale, the court held (at para. 10) that "a sale is a sale, whether it is done voluntarily or pursuant to a court order," and that the judicial sale resulted in a sale price of $49,000, which must be regarded as the proceeds of disposition. According to the court (at para. 12), section 79 is meant to apply only to "acquisitions by the lenders in a context where no fixed price is paid, and where it might take some time to ascertain the true value of what has been disposed of ... [such as] ... foreclosures and repossessions, where lenders may be forced to keep the property for some time before disposing of it and where different parties may calculate the value of the disposition differently."

5. Where property is taken under statutory authority, the statutory definition of "proceeds of disposition" includes "compensation" for such property. In *E.R. Fisher Ltd. v. M.N.R.*, [1986] F.C.J. No. 361, [1986] 2 C.T.C. 114, 86 D.T.C. 6364 (F.C.T.D.), this term was held to include all amounts received by the taxpayer as a result of an expropriation, whether or not the payments were specifically "compensatory" in character. More recent decisions have rejected this approach, distinguishing interest payments and other amounts from compensatory payments properly included in the taxpayer's proceeds of disposition. See *Shaw v. Canada*, [1993] F.C.J. No. 160, [1993] 1 C.T.C. 221, 93 D.T.C. 5121 (F.C.A.) and *Bellingham v. Canada*, [1995] F.C.J. No. 1602, [1996] 1 C.T.C. 187, (1995) 96 D.T.C. 6075 (F.C.A.).

6.   Where consideration is received or receivable by a taxpayer for "warranties, covenants or other conditional or contingent obligations given or incurred by the taxpayer in respect of [a] disposition" of capital property, section 42 requires the consideration to be included in computing the taxpayer's proceeds of disposition for the taxation year in which the taxpayer disposes of the property. Where the taxpayer is required in a subsequent taxation year to make or incur an outlay or expense "pursuant to or by reason of any such obligation," section 42 deems the amount of this outlay or expense to be a capital loss for that year.

7.   Notwithstanding the actual proceeds of disposition for a particular capital property, the *Income Tax Act* contains specific anti-avoidance rules that may apply to deem the taxpayer's proceeds of disposition to be another amount. According to section 68, for example, "[w]here an amount received or receivable from a person can reasonably be regarded as being in part the consideration for the disposition of a particular property of the taxpayer ... the part of the amount that can reasonably be regarded as being the consideration for the disposition shall be deemed to be proceeds of disposition of the particular property irrespective of the form or legal effect of the contract or agreement." Paragraph 69(1)(b), on the other hand, deems taxpayers who have disposed of anything by way of gift *inter vivos* or to persons with whom they do not deal at arm's length for no proceeds or for proceeds less than its fair market value at the time of the disposition, to have received proceeds of disposition equal to that fair market value. These provisions are examined in Chapter 8.

8.   In *Gaynor v. M.N.R.*, [1991] F.C.J. No. 348, [1991] 1 C.T.C. 470, 91 D.T.C. 5288 (F.C.A.), the taxpayer had acquired various securities with US funds, which were later sold for US proceeds, resulting in a gain that the taxpayer converted into Canadian currency for the purpose of computing her taxable capital gains. Referring to the language of paragraph 40(1)(a) of the Act, which defines a gain from the disposition of property as the "amount" by which the proceeds of disposition exceed the adjusted cost base, the court concluded that the proceeds and the cost must first be converted to Canadian currency before computing the amount of the gain. According to Pratte JA (at para. 4) (Heald and Desjardins JJA concurring):

> When that provision speaks of the "amount" of the capital gain, it obviously refers to an amount expressed in Canadian currency. As that amount is the result of a comparison between two other amounts, namely the amount representing the cost of the securities and the amount representing the value of the proceeds of disposition, it necessarily follows that both the cost of the securities and the value of the proceeds of disposition must be valued in Canadian currency which is the only monetary standard of value known to Canadian law. Once this is realized, it becomes clear that the cost of the securities to the appellant must be expressed in Canadian currency at the exchange rate prevailing at the time of their acquisition while the valuation of the proceeds of disposition of the same securities must be made in Canadian currency at the rate of exchange prevailing at the time of the disposition.

As a result, gains and losses on property acquired with and disposed of for another currency include both changes in the value of the property and changes in the value of the other currency relative to the Canadian dollar.

The Supreme Court of Canada recently addressed a perceived conflict between the provisions allowing for the full deduction of certain financing costs, including paragraph 20(1)(f) with the provisions providing for recognition of capital losses realized on foreign currency transactions in the case of *Imperial Oil Ltd. v. Canada*, [2006] 2 S.C.R. 447. The Court explicitly considered what the parties had referred to as the "*Gaynor* principle." Between 1989, when Imperial Oil issued $300,000,000 US worth of debentures, and 1999, when the debt was ultimately repaid, there was a significant appreciation of the US dollar against the Canadian dollar. This led to a large foreign currency loss for Imperial Oil. Imperial Oil argued it was entitled to a deduction under subparagraph 20(1)(f)(i) for the entire cost of redeeming the debt. Alternatively, Imperial Oil took the position that it was entitled to a deduction under subparagraph 20(1)(f)(ii) for 75 per cent of the loss and that the non-deductible 25 per cent was deductible as a capital loss under subsection 39(2). The Court was sharply divided, 4-3. LeBel J, for the majority of the Court, narrowed the holding of *Gaynor*, explaining that the decision in that case,

> does not support the proposition that all elements of a statutory formula must be converted into their Canadian dollar value at the relevant time. The implications of *Gaynor* are narrower than that. The decision was premised on the prior conclusion that the foreign exchange gains in issue were capital gains.

LeBel J instead held that the central question was one of statutory interpretation with respect to the role of paragraph 20(1)(f) in the scheme of the Act. In his view, the paragraph "was never intended to apply to foreign exchange losses" and that the "purpose of the provision is to address a specific class of financing costs arising out of the issuance of debt instruments at a discount." The majority of the Court therefore affirmed the Minister's treatment of the foreign currency losses, finding that the foreign currency losses were capital losses appropriately addressed solely under ss. 39(2) and 39(3) in subdivision c of division B of Part I of the Act, rather than under paragraph 20(1)(f).

Binnie J, in dissent, would have allowed the deduction under paragraph 20(1)(f), reasoning that, the majority's conclusion that "the language of s. 20(1)(f) should be read as limited to 'original issue discounts'" ignores the fact that "no such restriction is expressed in the section" and stating that he would "not imply it." Rather, in the view of the dissenting judges, Imperial Oil claimed deduction for the foreign currency loss "fits squarely with s. 20(1)(f)" and the appeal should have been dismissed.

3. Adjusted Cost Base

According to the definition in section 54 of the Act, the "adjusted cost base" to a taxpayer of a capital property is generally defined as:

(a) where the property is depreciable property of the taxpayer, the capital cost to the taxpayer of the property as of that time, and

(b) in any other case, the cost to the taxpayer of the property adjusted, as of that time, in accordance with section 53.

The "capital cost" of depreciable property is undefined in the Act and has been interpreted to mean "the actual, factual or historical cost to the [taxpayer] of the depreciable property,"[48] and was examined in Chapter 5. The "cost" of other capital property is similarly undefined and generally interpreted to include the purchase price of the property and "those costs intimately associated with its acquisition, such as delivery costs, legal fees, accounting fees, survey costs and the like."[49] Section 53 of the Act sets out a number of additions and deductions to the cost of capital property, most of which are highly technical and are not considered here.

It is important to note that as a transitional rule, for capital property acquired before 1972 subsection 26(3) of the *Income Tax Application Rules*, R.S.C. 1985, c. 2 (5th Supp.), as amended, generally deems the cost of the property to be "neither the greatest nor the least of" its actual cost to the taxpayer, its fair market value at the end of 1971, and the proceeds of disposition of the property. The effect of this rule is generally to disregard gains and losses that accrued prior to the statutory recognition of capital gains and losses in 1972.

In *Sterling v. Canada*, [1983] F.C.J. No. 320, [1983] C.T.C. 220, 83 D.T.C. 5252 (F.C.T.D.), rev'd. *Canada v. Stirling*, [1985] 1 C.T.C. 275, 85 D.T.C. 5199 (F.C.A.), the taxpayer sought to add to the acquisition cost of capital property amounts that were not explicitly included in the permitted statutory additions in computing the adjusted cost base to a taxpayer of capital property listed in subsection 53(1) of the Act. The following excerpts are drawn from the decision at trial and at the Federal Court of Appeal.

Sterling v. Canada
[1983] F.C.J. No. 320, [1983] C.T.C. 220, 83 D.T.C. 5252 (F.C.T.D.)

ROULEAU J: The plaintiff, during the years 1971 through 1975, acquired gold bullion and disposed of it in the years 1972 and 1975. The capital gain was declared, less carrying charges related to the financing of the acquisition as well as safekeeping charges. Both were disallowed by the Minister.

...

The question that arises in this appeal, is whether, in computing the capital gain from the disposition, there may be deducted only the price paid for the bullion; or, may he also deduct the interest paid on the money owed to the

---

[48] *Cockshutt Farm Equipment of Canada v. M.N.R.* (1966), 41 Tax ABC 386, 66 D.T.C. 386.

[49] D. Keith McNair, *The Meaning of Cost in Canadian Income Tax*, Canadian Tax Paper 69 (Toronto: Canadian Tax Foundation, 1982) at 71.

vendor, subsequent to the purchase, during the period the plaintiff held the gold; as well as safekeeping charges paid by him.

...

The plaintiff submits that when gold is purchased with borrowed money, held for a period of time under safekeeping arrangements, that costs before disposition, not only include the price paid for the gold, but also the interest on the borrowed money together with safekeeping charges.

The Minister argues that the latter cannot be added to make up the adjusted cost, because they are not provided for under the *Income Tax Act*. ... Counsel for the Minister submits that the acquisition and disposal of gold bullion is akin to a taxpayer acquiring and financing an automobile or a summer cottage. Upon the disposition of these items, one cannot deduct the carrying charges incurred. I find the analogy irrelevant, since the examples used are not of the same class and they are provided for specifically under paragraph 18(1)(h) of the *Income Tax Act*.

The plaintiff suggests that allowing the expense of the cost of the money and the safekeeping is a fair reading of the statutory provisions. Though the matter being litigated is not specifically dealt with under the *Income Tax Act*, he submits that by section 11 of the *Interpretation Act*, one is required, when reading an enactment that it: "shall be given such fair large and liberal construction and interpretation as best insures the attainment of its object" (section 11 of the *Interpretation Act*, RSC 1970, c I-23). Only such an interpretation could ensure the attainment of the object of the capital gain tax provisions, which were to bring all gains from disposition of property into the income base for taxation purposes.

He submits, that should I find that the Minister may exclude such costs from the computation of the gain, it would result in bringing something more than the actual gain into the computation of income; to that extent, the provision would fail in the attainment of its object, which is to impose a tax on "actual gain not otherwise, subject to tax."

Capital costs of property incorporated into a business or property acquired to produce income seems to be well-settled. There is no doubt that certain items may be added to the price paid for the property as costs to the vendor; and certain expenses after acquisition may be deducted upon disposition.

In *M.N.R. v. McCool Limited*, [1950] SCR 80, [1949] CTC 395, 4 DTC 700, Rand J states that when an asset is acquired as part of the capital structure of a business for a price, plus interest on the unpaid portion thereof, that interest was part of the "capital cost" to the taxpayer.

...

In *Sherritt Gordon Mines Limited v. M.N.R.*, [1968] CTC 262, 68 DTC 5180 at 287 [5195] states:

> In the absence of any definition in the statute of the expression "capital cost to the taxpayer of property" and in the absence of any authoritative interpretation of those words as used in section 11(1)(a) [now 20(1)(a)], insofar as they are being considered with reference to the

acquisition of capital assets, I am of opinion that they should be interpreted as including outlays of the taxpayer as a business man that were the direct result of the method he adopted to acquire the assets. In the case of the purchase of an asset, this would certainly include the price paid for the asset. It would probably include the legal costs directly related to its acquisition. It might well include, I do not express any opinion on the matter, the cost of moving the asset to the place where it is to be used in the business. When, instead of buying property to be used in the business, the taxpayer has done what is necessary to create it, the capital cost to him of the property clearly includes all monies paid out for the site and to architects, engineers and contractors. *It seems equally clear that it includes the cost to him during the construction period of borrowing the capital required for creating the property, whether the cost is called interest or commitment fee.*

and continuing at 288 [5196]:

The inclusion of interest during construction as part of the capital cost of property within the meaning and for the purposes of section 11(1)(a) [now 20(1)(a)], may present problems in some instances, but I do not think that an interpretation that includes such interest is inconsistent with the scheme of the Act or its capital cost allowance provisions. On the contrary, that treatment of interest during construction should, I think, help to accurately reflect the result of each taxation year's operations and the profit therefrom for that year for both business and income tax purposes, without unduly interfering with the smooth working of the Act.

Interpretation Bulletin No IT-174R seems to summarize it all and paragraph 1 states as follows:

The term "capital cost of property" generally means the full cost to the taxpayer of acquiring the property. It includes legal, accounting, engineering of other fees incurred to acquire the property.

It is important to note that when the capital gain provisions were added to the *Income Tax Act* in 1972, the purpose was to make other incomes subject to tax; one half of all gains from disposition of property, to the extent that such gains would not otherwise be included in the income that is subject to tax.

...

It is inconceivable to me that the spirit of the Act, its smooth working and its interpretation would not take into account the deductions from the gain that are being claimed by this taxpayer. If we carry the rationale to its extreme, I would like to present the following example, submitted by counsel, which would focus on an obvious inconsistency: A taxpayer acquires $100,000 worth of gold and owes the vendor the entire sum; if, after two years he has incurred $20,000 worth on interest charges and sold the gold for $110,000, there would be a net gain on the acquisition and disposition of the property, half of which, being $5,000, would have to be taken into additional income; his net loss would be $10,000. This seems totally contrary to the spirit and intent of the law. Had Parliament in 1972 foreseen the buying and selling of gold, which is more prevalent today, I am sure additional amendments would have been included in section 53. I agree with section 11 of the *Interpretation Act*, (*supra*) and give liberal construction and interpretation, as best ensures the attainment of the objectives of the *Income Tax Act* which I find is to tax actual gain.

I therefore find that when the plaintiff purchased gold with borrowed money, held during a period under safekeeping arrangements, then sold it, the cost incurred immediately prior to the disposition is not only the price paid for the gold, but the interest on the borrowed money for the period which it was held, together with the safekeeping charges for the same period. The interest and safekeeping charges are together and exclusively attributable to the gain derived for the acquisition and the disposition of the property. ...

Appeal allowed.

Canada v. Stirling
[1985] 1 C.T.C. 275, 85 D.T.C. 5199 (F.C.A.)

PRATTE J (Hugessen and MacGuigan JJ, concurring): The only issue on this appeal is whether the Trial Division was right in holding that, in computing his capital gain from the disposition of gold bullion, the respondent could deduct, as part of his cost, interest on the unpaid portion of the price of the bullion and safe keeping charges that he had incurred in respect of the period during which he had held the bullion.

In deciding that those interest and charges could be deducted, the learned trial judge did not rely on any provision of the *Income Tax Act* but rather on what, in his view, would have been the intention of Parliament had it given consideration to that question. We cannot agree with that approach.

In trying to support that judgment, counsel for the respondent argued in substance that capital gain should be computed according to the same rules as income from a business or property. That argument, while attractive, does not find any support in the *Income Tax Act*, which provides special rules for the computation of capital gain. Under those rules ... the interest and safe keeping charges here in question could be deductible only if they were part of the cost of the bullion. In our opinion, they were not. As we understand it, the word "cost" in those sections means the price that the taxpayer gave up in order to get the asset; it does not include any expense that he may have incurred in order to put himself in a position to pay that price or to keep the property afterwards.

The appeal will therefore be allowed with costs, the judgment of the Trial Division will be set aside, and the respondent's action will be dismissed with costs.

Appeal allowed.

NOTES AND QUESTIONS

1. On what basis did the Minister argue in *Stirling* that the interest and safekeeping expenses incurred by the taxpayer could not be added to the capital cost of the gold disposed of by the taxpayer? Why did the trial judge reject this argument? Why did the Federal Court of Appeal allow the Minister's appeal?

2.   On what basis did the Minister accept the taxpayer's characterization of the transactions in the gold bullion as yielding capital gains? Would the dispute have arisen if instead the taxpayer's transactions had been characterized by the Minister as being an "adventure or concern in the nature of trade," such as was the conclusion of the Exchequer Court in *M.N.R. v. Taylor*, [1956] C.T.C. 189, 56 D.T.C. 1125 (Ex. Ct.), where the taxpayer profited from buying and selling lead (analyzed in Chapter 5)?

3.   *Stirling* was followed in *Hastings v. M.N.R.*, [1988] T.C.J. No. 419, [1988] 2 C.T.C. 2001, 88 D.T.C. 1391 (T.C.C.), in which the taxpayer sought to deduct interest expenses on borrowed funds used to acquire commodities in computing the gain from the disposition of the commodities, which he characterized as capital gains. Rejecting the taxpayer's argument (at para. 4) that he should be entitled to deduct "whatever expenses relate to the acquisition of [his] commodities," the court stated that "the ordinary rules relating to expenses being deducted in the income earning process do not apply to the capital gains sections." Assuming that the commodities were in fact held as investment property, is this a persuasive reason to disregard interest expenses in computing the cost of the commodities to the taxpayer?

4.   In *Bodrug Estate v. Canada*, [1991] F.C.J. No. 1140, [1991] 2 C.T.C. 347, 91 D.T.C. 5621 (F.C.A.), the taxpayer had acquired shares that were deemed to have been disposed of for proceeds equal to their fair market value when he died on January 10, 1980. In computing the gain from these shares in January 1980, the taxpayer's estate sought to deduct as part of the adjusted cost base of the shares a substantial damage payment resulting from an insider trading action related to the taxpayer's initial acquisition of the shares. Citing *Stirling*, the court disallowed the deduction on the basis that the damage payments were not part of the cost of the shares. According to Stone JA (at para. 5) (Heald and Linden JJA concurring):

> The entire lawsuit having nothing to do with the deceased's title to the shares *per se*, it is my opinion that the damages for which the deceased was adjudged liable cannot be regarded as part of the price he had to give up in order to get the shares.

In contrast, where the taxpayer paid an amount to settle another action challenging his right to acquire the shares in the first place, the Minister and the court regarded the payment as a legitimate addition in computing the adjusted cost base of the shares.

5.   In *Jensen v. Canada*, [1986] T.C.J. No. 547, [1986] 2 C.T.C. 2047, 86 D.T.C. 1505 (T.C.C.), the taxpayer purchased a yacht in Florida in 1975, embarked on a year-long voyage ending in Vancouver, and sold the yacht in 1979. Objecting to the Minister's assessment of a capital gain on the disposition of the yacht, the taxpayer sought in computing the adjusted cost base of the yacht to include among other amounts expenses that he had incurred to repair and replace the yacht's transmission. Citing *Stirling* (at para. 7), for the

proposition that "a capital gain is to be computed in accordance with the special rules laid down in the *Income Tax Act* and not according to the rules which govern the computation of income from a business or property," the court disallowed the deduction. According to Bonner TCJ (at para. 7):

> The ordinary meaning of the words "... the capital cost to him of the property ..." to be found in the definition of the term "adjusted cost base" contained in [section 54] of the *Income Tax Act* does not encompass the cost of repairing or replacing or refurbishing parts of the property which have been worn or damaged or have deteriorated from use, misuse or the passage of time during the period of ownership. The amounts now in question, far from being part of the capital cost of the yacht, were quite simply part of the cost of using the yacht for a pleasure cruise.

Do you agree? Why or why not? Of what, if any, relevance to the court's decision is the fact that the yacht was used "for a pleasure cruise"?

For a similar result, see *Watkins v. M.N.R.*, [1990] F.C.J. No. 627, [1990] 2 C.T.C. 205, 90 D.T.C. 6432 (F.C.T.D.), in which the taxpayer acquired a horse for $1,000 in 1979 and sold it three years later for $24,700. Characterizing the horse as "personal-use property," the court rejected the taxpayer's argument that the adjusted cost base should include the cost of maintaining the horse for three years.

6.   In *MacDonald v. M.N.R.*, [1984] C.T.C. 2624, 84 D.T.C. 1602 (T.C.C.), the taxpayer objected to the assessment of a capital gain on a house that he purchased in 1975 and sold in 1978 on the basis that the real value of the house, after accounting for inflation, had actually declined during this period. Although sympathizing with "the logic" of the taxpayer's argument, the court dismissed his appeal on the grounds (at para. 7) that: "There is nothing in the *Income Tax Act* relating to capital gain or anything else whereby inflationary factors are taken into consideration when the Minister makes an assessment under this statute." For a similar result, see *Pappas Estate v. Canada*, [1981] F.C.J. No. 521, [1981] C.T.C. 266, 81 D.T.C. 5178 (F.C.T.D.). Do you agree with these decisions? Why or why not? Should the cost of capital property be indexed to prevent taxation of inflationary gains? If so, should interest deductions be limited to the so-called real interest rate, excluding amounts paid to the lender to compensate for expected decreases in the value of the principal amount of the loan?

7.   Where the total of all amounts that are deducted in computing the adjusted cost base of a particular property under subsection 53(2) of the Act exceeds the total of the cost of the property and all amounts that are added in computing its adjusted cost base under subsection 53(1), it appears that the adjusted cost base may be negative. According to paragraph (d) of the definition of "adjusted cost base" in section 54, however, "in no case shall the adjusted cost base to a taxpayer of any property at any time be less than nil." Instead, subsection 40(3) stipulates in these circumstances that the amount by which aggregate deductions in computing the adjusted cost base of the property exceed the cost of the property and additions in computing its adjusted cost base is generally deemed

to be "a gain of the taxpayer for the year from a disposition at that time of the property." In computing the adjusted cost base of the property thereafter, paragraph 53(1)(a) of the Act adds the amount of this deemed gain, thereby restoring its adjusted cost base to zero.

8. Where property is acquired partly for the purpose of gaining or producing income and partly for another purpose (for example, personal use or enjoyment), different tax consequences associated with these different uses makes it necessary to distinguish between the portion of the total cost of the property allocated to the income-producing purpose and the portion allocated to personal use. A similar allocation issue arises on the disposition of the property. For these reasons the Act contains specific rules allocating the cost and proceeds of disposition of property that is acquired and used for more than one purpose in proportion to these different uses. See paragraphs 13(7)(c) and 45(1)(b), which establish the result that the allocation of the costs of acquisition and the proceeds of disposition should be made proportionally to the parts of the property dedicated to these different uses.

9. Where a taxpayer disposes of part of a property while retaining another part, the adjusted cost base of each part is determined under subsection 43(1) and paragraph 53(2)(d). According to subsection 43(1):

> For the purpose of computing a taxpayer's gain or loss for a taxation year from the disposition of part of a property, the adjusted cost base to the taxpayer, immediately before the disposition, of that part is the portion of the adjusted cost base to the taxpayer at that time of the whole property that can reasonably be regarded as attributable to that part.

Correspondingly, paragraph 53(2)(d) stipulates that the amount determined under this provision must be deducted in computing the adjusted cost base of the part of the property that is retained by the taxpayer. Although the Act does not specify the manner in which a portion of the adjusted cost base of a property "may reasonably be regarded as attributable to" a part of the whole property, one plausible approach is to attribute to the part that is disposed of a portion of the adjusted cost base equal to the ratio of the proceeds from the disposition of the part to the fair market value of the whole property.[50]

Notwithstanding this approach, in certain circumstances, such as the granting of an easement that is less than 20% of the area of a property, or where compensation is received on account of damage done to an insubstantial part of a total property and the property is not repaired, so long as the amounts received are not excessive the CRA will accept as a reasonable portion of the adjusted cost base an amount equal to the proceeds from the disposition of part of a property: see Interpretation Bulletin IT-264R, "Part Dispositions," December 29, 1980. Because the portion of the adjusted cost base that is attributed to the

---

[50] See, for example, Vern Krishna, *The Fundamentals of Canadian Income Tax*, 6th ed. (Toronto: Carswell, 2000) at 405.

part of the property disposed of reduces the adjusted cost base of the property retained by the taxpayer, the effect of this approach is to defer the recognition of any gain resulting from the part disposition under these circumstances until the taxpayer disposes of all or part of the property that is retained.

10. Notwithstanding the ordinary rules for determining the cost of capital property, section 47 establishes an "average cost" rule for identical capital properties by deeming taxpayers who acquire one or more properties ("newly acquired properties") that are identical to one or more properties previously acquired by the taxpayer to have disposed of each such "previously-acquired property" immediately before the acquisition of the newly acquired property for proceeds equal to their adjusted cost base, and deeming the taxpayer to have acquired each identical property at that time at a cost equal to the average cost of all identical properties. Although the Act does not specifically define the term "identical properties," these are generally understood to refer to intangibles like shares or debt. According to subsection 248(12), moreover:

> For the purposes of the Act, one bond, debenture, bill, note or similar obligation issued by a debtor is identical to another such obligation issued by that debtor if both are identical in respect of all rights (in equity or otherwise, either immediately or in the future and either absolutely or contingently) attaching thereto, except as regards the principal amount thereof.

Where a taxpayer acquires identical debt obligations with different principal amounts, however, subsection 47(2) requires the average cost to be computed according to the ratio of the principal amount of each identical property to the principal amount of all such identical properties.[51]

4. Expenses of Disposition

In computing the gain or loss from the disposition of capital property, paragraphs 40(1)(a) and (b) allow taxpayers to deduct in addition to the adjusted cost base of the property "any outlays and expenses to the extent that they were made or incurred by the taxpayer for the purpose of making the disposition." The leading case on the interpretation of this language is *Avis Immobilien G.m.b.H. v. Canada*, [1996] F.C.J. No. 1551, 97 D.T.C. 5002 (F.C.A.).

---

[51] As a result, where a taxpayer acquires a debt obligation with a face amount of $1,000 for $100 and an identical debt obligation with a face amount of $4,000 at a cost of $900, the first debt obligation is deemed to be acquired for $100 + $900 / [($1,000 + $4,000) / $1,000] or $200, and the second debt obligation is deemed to be acquired for $100 + $900 / [($1,000 + $4,000) / $4,000] or $800, instead of averaging the cost of each debt obligation as ($100 + $900)/2 or $500.

Avis Immobilien G.m.b.H. v. Canada
[1996] F.C.J. No. 1551, 97 D.T.C. 5002 (F.C.A.)

HUGESSEN JA (Décary JJA and Chevalier DJA, concurring): The appellant, a corporation non-resident in Canada, purchased certain real properties in Montreal in 1982. The price was $16,500,000, of which $10,900,000 was paid in cash. To finance this purchase, the appellant borrowed 21,000,000 DM from its bank in Germany; at the time this was equivalent to the required amount in Canadian currency ($10,900,000). To secure repayment of its loan, the bank took out a hypothec on the properties in question. In addition to the formal clauses the loan instrument contained a clause prohibiting the appellant from disposing of the properties without the bank's permission and a clause prohibiting repayment of the debt before March 30, 1988.

In 1986, for commercial and economic reasons, the appellant decided to sell the properties to a party with which it had an arm's length relationship. The agreed price was $25,500,000. However, since the bank did not agree to deal directly with the purchaser, it became necessary for the appellant to repay the loan in advance and thus discharge the hypothec. The amount owing was at that time about 20,900,000 DM, which, owing to a decline in the value of the Canadian dollar in relation to the German mark, amounted to $14,300,000. Since the bank was not obliged to accept the advance payment, it required and obtained a penalty of $790,000 (1,149,225 DM).

The appellant therefore realized a capital gain on the disposition of its properties in Canada, which were [sic] taxable under ... the *Income Tax Act*. ... The gross amount of the gain was $9,000,000 ($25,500,000 — $16,500,000). The appellant claims it is entitled to deduct from this amount as outlays or expenses the following amounts:

— Losses resulting from the fluctuation in the exchange rate:

	$14,300,000-$10,900,00 =	$ 3,400,000
— Penalty:		$ 790,000
TOTAL:		$ 4,190,000

The net capital gain would then be $4,810,000 ($9,000,000 - $4,190,000).

The Minister, however, does not accept the deduction of the $3,400,000 representing the loss incurred in the currency conversions between the dollar and the mark in 1982 and 1986. Hence this litigation.

The appellant lost in the Tax Court of Canada. Here is the essential part of the reasons of the Tax Court judge:

The words "for the purpose of" are susceptible of different meanings depending on whether the purpose is immediate or ultimate, direct or indirect or initial or final. Subparagraph 40(1)(a)(i) provides a rule for determining what outlays and expenses may be deducted in calculating a taxpayer's capital gain. The words "for the purpose of in subparagraph 40(1)(a)(i) are directed to the action of making a particular disposition. The outlays and expenses in that provision are directed to a particular disposition and no other.

In the facts at bar Avis entered into two transactions prior to selling the properties; it repaid the loan and exchanged currencies. While the repayment of the loan may have been transacted in order to dispose of the properties, the exchange of currencies was transacted for the purpose of repaying the loan in German marks. In other words, it may be said that the transaction of converting the currency was made for the purpose of repaying the loan in a certain foreign currency and the repayment of the loan was made to dispose of the properties.

The words "for the purpose of" in subparagraph 40(1)(a)(i) mean "for the immediate or initial purpose of" and not the eventual or final goal which the taxpayer may have in mind. To give the words the latter meaning would permit the most indirect or most distantly related outlay or expense to reduce the amount of a gain. This could not have been Parliament's intent. We are not dealing in subparagraph 40(1)(a)(i) with the computation of income from a business, which is of an ongoing nature, but, rather, expenses or outlays made or incurred to dispose solely of capital properties. The statutory provision under consideration sets out a rule to determine a taxpayer's capital gain from the disposition of property and only expenses or outlays to be applied in reducing the gain are those incurred or made directly for the purposes of making the disposition. Subparagraph 40(1)(a)(i) does not contemplate expenses or outlays which may have merely facilitated the making of the disposition or which were entered into on the occasion of the disposition.

...

The appellant accuses the judge of "compartmentalizing" the transaction, not taking into account the overall economic reality of what was happening in 1986, and adding to the Act words that are not there.

None of these criticisms is warranted. They go to the form rather than the substance, the way in which the judge expressed himself rather than the correctness of his legal reasoning.

It is not compartmentalizing a transaction to ask oneself what a supposed outlay is for. In this case, the appellant reports three types of outlays it allegedly made: it paid the penalty of $790,000; it repaid the loan, the original dollar amount of which was $10,900,000; and it paid $3,400,000 representing the difference between this latter amount and the value of the loan in 1986, or $14,300,000.

The Minister did not dispute that in the case at bar the first of these amounts is deductible. The penalty would be the direct result of the repayment in advance of the loan, which conceivably was made "for the purpose of" the disposition of the properties.

The appellant, for its part, concedes that the repayment of the original amount of the loan in dollars is not deductible. The appellant simply paid off a pre-existing obligation. The disposition of the properties was the occasion but not the cause of the payment.

As to the disputed loss, the one suffered because of the dollar-mark conversions in 1982 and 1986, if it was indeed an "outlay" within the meaning of paragraph 40(1)(a), it seems obvious to us that it is linked to the repayment of the loan, which it was merely incidental to. Sooner or later, the appellant had to repay the loan in German currency. If it chose to do so in 1986 and to sell dollars at a loss for the purpose, this sale was not made "for the purpose of making the disposition" of the properties but rather for the purpose of making the payment of its debt. If a profit had been made on this dollar sale, it would not have been added to the appellant's taxable capital gain in Canada; the same applies to the loss, which is not deductible from the gain.

...

Finally, we do not think the judge actually added to the wording of the Act, something which would certainly not be permissible. In our opinion, the passage that begins "The words 'for the purpose of' ..." should be read in terms of the final sentence in that paragraph and thus be limited to the notion that outlays that simply facilitated the disposition or were incurred in the course of the disposition are not deductible. ...

Appeal dismissed.

NOTES AND QUESTIONS

1.   Why does the decision in *Avis Immobilien* distinguish between the penalty incurred by the taxpayer to repay the debt and the foreign exchange loss occasioned by the repayment? How does the court interpret the requirement in paragraphs 40(1)(a) and (b) of the Act that a deductible outlay or expense in computing a capital gain or loss must be made "for the purpose of making the disposition"?

2.   In Canada, foreign exchange losses are generally characterized as capital losses, the allowable portion of which may be deducted against taxable capital gains. Among other reasons why the court disallowed the deduction of the foreign exchange loss as an expense incurred for the purpose of making the disposition was the likely recognition of these losses in computing the taxpayer's income in Germany. According to the court (at para. 14):

> The economic substance of a transaction nowadays includes its tax consequences. In the circumstances of the case at bar, these consequences obviously include the tax impact of the transaction in Germany, the appellant's country of residence. Yet the appellant, who bore the onus, submitted no evidence concerning the tax treatment in Germany of a loss of the nature of the one at issue. We do not know, therefore, if it is allowable (or in the case of a gain, taxable) or, where applicable, if it is on account of income or on account of capital. Assuming that the German legislation is identical to ours, the appellant would be able to claim a capital loss in Germany which would be deductible in the computation of its taxable income in Germany.

3.   In *Campbellton Enterprises Ltd. v. M.N.R.*, [1990] T.C.J. No. 719, [1990] 2 C.T.C. 2413, 90 D.T.C. 1869 (T.C.C.), the taxpayer was required to pay a penalty or bonus on the prepayment of a mortgage on an apartment building that the taxpayer sold. Rejecting the taxpayer's argument that the penalty should be deductible as an interest expense under paragraph 20(1)(c) of the Act, the court suggested that the bonus should be deductible under subparagraph 40(1)(a)(i) as

"an outlay or expense made or incurred by the appellant for purposes of making the disposition of the apartment property." Effective for payments after 1984, subsection 18(9.1) generally deems penalties and bonuses that are payable on the repayment of debt obligations before maturity to be interest expenses that may be deducted under paragraph 20(1)(c).

4. In *Fraser v. M.N.R.*, [1985] 2 C.T.C. 2382, 85 D.T.C. 665 (T.C.C.), the taxpayer spent $1,229 in 1983 on promotion — long-distance telephone and parking charges relating to the entertainment of stockbrokers with whom the taxpayer dealt to acquire and sell securities. Although disallowing the deduction of these expenses as ordinary business expenses, the court referred the case back to the Minister for reassessment on the basis (at para. 3) that "the costs in issue are costs of acquisition or disposition of the capital assets that were stocks and bonds acquired and disposed of by the appellant during the year in question." Is this conclusion consistent with the Federal Court of Appeal's subsequent decision in *Avis Immobilien*?

5. In *Samson Estate v. M.N.R.*, [1989] T.C.J. No. 451, [1990] 1 C.T.C. 2223, (1989) 90 D.T.C. 1144 (T.C.C.), the taxpayer incurred professional fees to contest a municipal assessment and zoning bylaw that restricted the marketability of his property, which he sought to deduct as expenses of disposition in computing the gain from its subsequent disposition. Concluding (at para. 38) that there must be "some connection or relationship between the expenses and the disposition" to deduct an expense in computing the amount of a gain or a loss, the court allowed the deduction of fees spent to challenge the zoning bylaw, but disallowed the fees to contest the municipal assessment. According to Lamarre-Proulx TCJ (at paras. 39 and 40):

> The expense relating to the action to cancel the zoning by-law is not related to maintaining the property or financing the purchase price. In my view, it is an expense which, in certain circumstances, depending on the evidence, may be considered to be incurred for the disposition of a property. In this case, according to the evidence that I have heard, this was the purpose of the dispute. Since the public authorities were not buying, it was hoped to change the zoning so as to be able to dispose of it more easily to individuals. I am therefore of the opinion that the professional fees related to the zoning dispute fall within the terms of subparagraph 40(1)(a)(i).
>
> My conclusion is not the same with respect to the professional fees relating to the dispute of the municipal assessment. This was an expense related to the maintenance of the property which does not fall within the terms of subparagraph 40(1)(a)(i).

6. In *Akenhead v. M.N.R.*, [1983] C.T.C. 2111, 83 D.T.C. 105 (T.R.B.), the taxpayer's estate sought to deduct legal expenses to administer the estate in computing the gain from capital properties that were deemed under subsection 70(5) of the Act to have been disposed of by the taxpayer immediately before his death. Although accepting that legal expenses incurred to transfer property are generally deductible as amounts incurred "for the purpose of making the disposition," the board dismissed the taxpayer's appeal from an assessment

disallowing the deduction on the basis that no expenses were necessary to trigger the deemed disposition under subsection 70(5). According to the board (at para. 5):

> the deemed disposition which brings this matter to the foreground need involve no costs at all. In fact, no physical or actual disposition need ever occur. The "deemed disposition" determined by the provisions of the *Income Tax Act* is for the purpose of the calculation of income tax only and would be operative for that purpose and *only for that purpose* in any event. As I see it, the position taken by the appellants in this matter is tantamount to contending that unless an actual physical disposition takes place, the deemed disposition does not occur. Of course, that could not be the intention of the Act.

7.   In *Jensen v. Canada*, [1986] T.C.J. No. 547, [1986] 2 C.T.C. 2047, 86 D.T.C. 1505 (T.C.C.), the taxpayer, who purchased a yacht in Florida in 1975, embarked on a year-long voyage ending in Vancouver, and sold the yacht in 1979, sought in computing a capital gain on the disposition to deduct refinishing costs on the basis (at para. 8) that they were made "specifically for the purpose of making the disposition." Dismissing the taxpayer's appeal, the court concluded (at para. 8) that "[t]he evidence does not support a finding that the refinishing work was done for the purpose required by subparagraph 40(1)(a)(i)." Of what relevance to this conclusion is the fact that the yacht was used "for a pleasure cruise"?

5. Reserves

Where a taxpayer disposes of capital property for proceeds some or all of which are payable after the end of the taxation year in which the property is disposed of, subparagraph 40(1)(a)(iii) of the Act allows the taxpayer to deduct a reserve in computing the amount of the gain, the amount of which generally cannot exceed the lesser of:

> a reasonable amount as a reserve in respect of such of the proceeds of disposition of the property that are payable to the taxpayer after the end of the year as can reasonably be regarded as a portion of the amount determined under subparagraph (i) in respect of the property, and

> ... an amount equal to the product obtained when 1/5 of the amount determined under subparagraph (i) in respect of the property is multiplied by the amount, if any, by which 4 exceeds the number of preceding taxation years of the taxpayer ending after the disposition of the property.

Where a taxpayer deducts an amount under this provision in a particular taxation year, subparagraph 40(1)(a)(ii) includes this amount in computing a gain for the immediately following year. Where some or all of the proceeds remain payable after the end of this subsequent year, the taxpayer may again claim a reserve under subparagraph 40(1)(a)(iii), the amount of which is included in computing a gain for the subsequent year, and so on. The effect of these provisions is to allow taxpayers who dispose of capital property for proceeds some or all of which are payable after the end of the year to defer the recognition of a reasonable portion of the gain otherwise determined, provided that no less than one-fifth of this gain is recognized in the year in which the property is disposed of and in each of the following four taxation years.[52] Notwithstanding these rules, however, paragraph 40(2)(a) prohibits the deduction of a reserve by taxpayers who were either exempt from tax or not resident in Canada at the end of the year or at any time in the immediately following taxation year, and where the property is sold to a corporation with which the taxpayer is connected as set out in subparagraph 40(2)(a)(ii). Nor can a reserve be claimed in the year of a taxpayer's death,[53] except where the capital property at issue is disposed of to the taxpayer's spouse or a spousal trust.[54]

As a general rule, "a reasonable amount as a reserve" is the proportion of the gain otherwise determined based on the ratio of the amount payable after the end of the year to the aggregate proceeds of disposition. For example, where a taxpayer disposes of capital property for $10,000 only $1,000 of which is payable before the end of the year, realizing a gain otherwise determined of $4,000, a reasonable reserve would generally be computed as nine-tenths of the gain or $3,600, requiring the taxpayer to recognize one-tenth of the gain or $400 in the year in which the property is disposed of. Under clause 40(1)(a)(iii)(D), however, the maximum allowable reserve that may be claimed in the year in which the property is disposed of is limited to four-fifths of the gain otherwise determined or $3,200, requiring the taxpayer to recognize one-fifth of the gain or $800 in the year in which the property is disposed of.

In applying this provision, courts have generally addressed not the computation of the reserve, but the requirement under clause 40(1)(a)(iii)(C) as it read before February 22, 1994 that some or all of the proceeds must not be "due to the taxpayer until after the end of the year."[55] In a leading case on this issue, the Federal Court of Appeal held that a promissory note that is payable on demand is a current obligation and not due after the end of the year, making it impossible for the taxpayer to deduct a reserve under subparagraph 40(1)(a)(iii).[56] In another case, a corporate taxpayer, which disposed of a farm in exchange for non-transferable preferred shares of the purchaser corporation that were redeemable over a 10-year period was held to have received proceeds of

---

[52] Where the taxpayer disposes of land or depreciable property used in a farming business, shares of a family farm corporation, or shares of a small business corporation, subs. 40(1.1) extends the maximum deferral period to 10 years, requiring that at least one-tenth of the gain be recognized in the year of the disposition and each of the following 9 taxation years.

[53] Paragraph 72(1)(c).

[54] Paragraph 72(2)(b).

[55] In one other case worth mentioning, the Tax Review Board concluded that the reserve in subpara. 40(1)(a)(iii) does not apply to dispositions of eligible capital property, which are subject to a separate set of rules under s. 14 of the Act: *Andreychuk v. M.N.R.*, [1983] C.T.C. 2052, (1982) 83 D.T.C. 20 (T.R.B.).

[56] *Canada v. Derbecker*, [1984] C.T.C. 606, 84 D.T.C. 6549 (F.C.A.). For a similar result, see *Pineo v. M.N.R.*, [1986] F.C.J. No. 323, [1986] 2 C.T.C. 71, 86 D.T.C. 6322 (F.C.T.D.).

disposition in the form of the shares, making it ineligible for the reserve under subparagraph 40(1)(a)(iii), notwithstanding that the cash proceeds from the redemption of these shares was receivable over 10 years.[57] In another case, however, a taxpayer who disposed of a partnership interest for a piece of equipment and $50,000 to be paid when the cash flow from the business permitted was allowed to claim a reserve equal to the unpaid balance of the purchase price.[58] The continuing relevance of these cases appears to be unaffected by the 1994 amendments to clause 40(1)(a)(iii)(C), which replaced the words "are not due to the taxpayer until after the end of the year" with the words "are payable to the taxpayer after the end of the year."[59]

B. Special Rules

In addition to the general rules for the computation of a capital gain or loss and the recognition and non-recognition rules applicable to various kinds of transactions, the *Income Tax Act* contains a number of special rules governing the taxation of transactions involving specific kinds of property. For our purposes, the most important of these special rules are those for "personal-use property," "listed personal property," and the taxpayer's "principal residence."

1. Personal-Use Property

The term "personal-use property" is defined in section 54 of the *Income Tax Act* to include:

(a) property owned by the taxpayer that is used primarily for the personal use or enjoyment of the taxpayer or for the personal use or enjoyment of one or more individuals each of whom is

    (i) the taxpayer,

    (ii) a person related to the taxpayer, or

    (iii) where the taxpayer is a trust, a beneficiary under the trust or any person related to the beneficiary,

(b) any debt owing to the taxpayer in respect of the disposition of property that was the taxpayer's personal-use property, and

(c) any property of the taxpayer that is an option to acquire property that would, if the taxpayer acquired it, be personal-use property of the taxpayer.

---

[57] *Strager Securities Ltd. v. M.N.R.*, [1986] T.C.J. No. 550, [1986] 2 C.T.C. 2050, 86 D.T.C. 1507 (T.C.C.).

[58] *Andrews v. M.N.R.*, [1987] 1 C.T.C. 2165, 87 D.T.C. 118 (T.C.C.).

[59] The technical notes accompanying the proposed legislation provide that, "The purpose of this amendment is to avoid penalizing creditors who exercise 'acceleration' clauses pursuant to an agreement under which the creditor sold capital property and received as part of the consideration a note payable by the purchaser of the property. The acceleration clause would typically be exercised only if the purchaser defaulted on its obligations to a creditor."

Although this definition is not exhaustive, it is sufficiently broad to include most kinds of property the primary use of which is not for the purpose of gaining or producing income but for personal use or enjoyment.[60]

Where a taxpayer uses property primarily for personal use or enjoyment and subsequently disposes of the property for proceeds less than its original cost, the loss is generally attributable to the taxpayer's personal use of the property. Since the income tax generally disregards costs of personal consumption in computing a taxpayer's net income,[61] it is not surprising that it also disallows the deduction of capital losses from the disposition of personal-use property. According to subparagraph 40(2)(g)(iii) of the Act, notwithstanding the general rule for the computation of a capital gain or loss in subsection 40(1):

> a taxpayer's loss, if any, from the disposition of a property, to the extent that it is ... a loss from the disposition of any personal-use property of the taxpayer (other than listed personal property or a debt referred to in subsection 50(2)) ... is nil.

Similarly, where a decrease in the fair market value of personal-use property held by a corporation, partnership, or trust reduces the amount of a gain or increases the amount of a loss from the disposition of shares of the corporation or an interest in the partnership or trust, subsection 46(4) deems "the amount of the gain or loss, as the case may be, ... to be the amount that it would have been but for the decrease" in the fair market value of the personal-use property. As a result, although the Act recognizes capital gains from the disposition of personal-use property, it generally disregards capital losses from the disposition of this kind of property (except for listed personal property or personal-use property debts subject to the rule in subsection 50(2)).[62]

---

[60] Where property is owned by a partnership, the definition further adds that personal-use property includes "partnership property that is used primarily for the personal use or enjoyment of any member of the partnership or for the personal use of enjoyment of one or more individuals each of whom is a member of the partnership or a person related to such a member." In the case of property owned by a corporation, the combination of subpara. (a)(ii) of the definition of "personal-use property" in s. 54 and para. 251(2)(b) of the Act would include as personal-use property, corporate property that is used primarily for the personal use or enjoyment of an individual who controls the company, an individual who is a member of a related group that controls the company, or an individual who is related to a controlling individual or a member of a controlling related group.

[61] See, for example, paras. 18(1)(h) and (a) of the Act, which disallow the deduction of personal and living expenses and expenses that are not incurred for the purpose of gaining or producing income, and para. 1102(1)(c) of the *Income Tax Regulations*, which disallows the deduction of capital cost allowances on property that was not acquired for the purpose of gaining or producing income. Notwithstanding these provisions, however, it is arguable that the income tax acknowledges basic consumption expenses in the form of personal tax credits.

[62] Subsection 50(2) allows taxpayers who have realized a capital gain on the disposition of personal-use property to claim a capital loss on a debt arising from the disposition of the personal-use property that is established to have become a bad debt, up to the amount of the gain previously realized. Listed personal property is examined later in this chapter.

In addition to this loss non-recognition rule, the Act also contains a further rule applicable to personal-use property (other than "excluded property" in respect of the disposition of which the taxpayer may claim a charitable deduction or credit under section 110.1 or section 118.1), which deems both the adjusted cost base and the proceeds of disposition of personal-use property to be the greater of $1,000 and the amount otherwise determined to be the adjusted cost base or proceeds of disposition. This rule, which appears in subsection 46(1) of the Act, is designed to simplify tax administration and taxpayer compliance by exempting capital gains on most kinds of personal-use property worth less than $1,000 and eliminating the need for recordkeeping on the cost of personal-use property acquired for less than $1,000.

In order to prevent taxpayers from taking undue advantage of this rule by disposing of personal-use property through a series of partial dispositions, however, subsection 46(2) requires taxpayers to allocate the $1,000 minimum adjusted cost base and proceeds of disposition among each of the parts disposed of, based on the ratio of the adjusted cost base of the part disposed of as otherwise determined under section 43 of the Act to the adjusted cost base of the whole. Similarly, where a taxpayer disposes of a number of personal-use properties that would ordinarily be disposed of in a single disposition as a set to one person or to a group of persons who do not deal with each other at arm's length, and the fair market value of the set exceeds $1,000, subsection 46(3) deems the set to be a single personal-use property and each disposition to be a disposition of a part of that property.

Finally, where a taxpayer or a person with whom the taxpayer does not deal at arm's length acquires personal-use property "in circumstances in which it is reasonable to conclude that the acquisition of the property relates to an arrangement, plan or scheme that is promoted by another person or partnership and under which it is reasonable to conclude that the property will be the subject of a gift" that is eligible for a charitable deduction or credit under section 110.1 or section 118.1, subsection 46(5) defines the property as "excluded property" to which the $1,000 rule does not apply. The purpose of this exclusion is explained in the following passage from supplementary information released with the February 28, 2000 federal budget, when the amendment was first announced:

Certain charitable donation arrangements have been designed to exploit the $1,000 deemed adjusted cost base for personal-use property and to create a scheme under which taxpayers attempt to achieve an after-tax profit from such gifts. For example, arrangements have been designed under which a promoter acquires a number of objects for less than $50 each, invites taxpayers to purchase the objects for $250 each, and arranges for their appraisal at $1,000 each and their donation to a charity.

Based on the $1,000 appraised value, there would be a $750 capital gain per item to the donor but for the $1,000 deemed adjusted cost base for the gift. However, with the deemed adjusted cost base there is no gain for tax purposes. As a result, the cost to governments of the "$1,000 gift" is approximately $500 (i.e., the federal and provincial tax savings associated with a $1,000 charitable donation), which in many cases exceeds the amount that the charity can realize from the donated property. Such an arrangement intends that the "donor" achieve a tax-free profit of $250.

> The budget proposes to amend the *Income Tax Act* so that the $1,000 deemed adjusted cost base and deemed proceeds of disposition for personal-use property will not apply if the property is acquired after February 27, 2000, as part of an arrangement in which the property is donated as a charitable gift.

Like the rules in subsections 46(2) and (3), therefore, the exclusion in subsection 46(5) is designed to prevent abuse of the $1,000 rule.

In the years since the concept of personal-use property was first introduced in 1972, very few cases have considered the definition of the term or the loss non-recognition and $1,000 rules to which personal-use property is subject. The most litigated application of the concept, however, involves the characterization of losses from the sale of a residence the personal use of which could render the loss nil under subparagraph 40(2)(g)(iii) of the Act. An excellent example of this characterization issue appears in *Burnet v. Canada*, [1995] T.C.J. No. 479, [1995] 2 C.T.C. 2319, 96 D.T.C. 1686 (T.C.C.).

Burnet v. Canada
[1995] T.C.J. No. 479, [1995] 2 C.T.C. 2319, 96 D.T.C. 1686 (T.C.C.)

BOWMAN JTCC: These appeals are from assessments for the appellant's 1987 and 1989 taxation years. They have to do with the treatment of a loss sustained by the appellant in 1987 on the sale of property in West Vancouver. The 1989 appeal relates to the carryforward of a portion of that loss under section 111 of the *Income Tax Act*.

Introduction

The issue is apparent from a thumbnail sketch of the facts. In 1962 the appellant and his wife bought a house in West Vancouver on a one half acre lot, where they lived until about 1980. They moved to a house in North Vancouver that the appellant had inherited from his father. They demolished the house in West Vancouver and built a larger new home on the lot. In November 1981 the family moved back to the new house where they lived until 1985. In 1985 they leased the property to a tenant for one year and moved into rented premises. In 1986 they moved back to the new house where they lived until they sold it in 1987. A substantial loss was sustained on the sale and the appellant seeks to deduct that loss in the computation of his income, as a loss incurred in carrying out an adventure in the nature of trade. The respondent denies the deduction of the loss on the ground that the new house was the personal residence of the appellant and his wife and was personal use property that did not form part of a business undertaking.

The case involves a somewhat unusual role reversal. In a normal trading case the appellant realizes a profit which he or she seeks to characterize as a capital gain, and the Minister, in seeking to sustain the taxability of the profit as business income points to many of the same facts as those that the appellant here emphasizes in support of his claim to deduct the loss. The applicable principles are of course the same irrespective of whether a gain is realized or a loss sustained.

Facts

Many of the facts were agreed to and were supplemented by viva voce evidence. The appellant taught school until 1968 when he became a stockbroker, an occupation which he followed until 1988. In 1960, he married Mrs. Burnet, a lawyer with the British Columbia Attorney General's department. In 1962 they purchased, in joint tenancy, a house on a ½ acre lot at 2095-26th Street in West Vancouver for $12,000 (the "old house"). The Burnets and their family lived in the old house until 1980 when it was demolished and construction started on the new house on the West Vancouver property. Their family consisted of three children: Campbell, born in 1961, Samantha, born in 1965 and a foster child, Susan, born in 1964. In 1978 the appellant's father died and he inherited a house at 4118 Grace Crescent, North Vancouver (the "Grace Crescent house").

In 1979 and 1980 there was a boom in the real estate market in West Vancouver. The appellant decided to demolish the old house and erect on the lot in West Vancouver a much larger (4,183 square feet) new home (the "new house"). He testified that his intention was to construct a house for the upper end (i.e. affluent) market and sell it at a profit.

...

Demolition of the old house started in July 1980 and construction of the new house began in August 1980. It was originally scheduled to be completed in February 1981. It is agreed that in the spring of 1980 the appellant estimated the cost of constructing the new house would fall somewhere in the range of $127,000-$160,000.

[The builder] turned out to be unreliable. [He] missed the projected completion date, extended it to Easter 1981, which he also missed, and stopped turning up regularly in July.

Also, from January 1, 1981 to June 1982 real estate prices in West Vancouver declined by 50%. At the same time, it became apparent that the cost of constructing the new house was going to be significantly greater than anticipated, whether by reason of escalating prices or initial miscalculation. The CIBC mortgage was increased to $400,000 on June 23, 1981 based on a valuation made by the CIBC of $700,000, assuming the house was completed.

In the spring of 1981, [the builder] brought a real estate agent to the appellant. It is agreed that this person offered the appellant $715,000 for the house on an as is basis, but he rejected it on the advice of [the builder] who told him that if he waited he could get $1,000,000. As it turned out [the builder's] financial advice was as unreliable as his work. Finally the appellant took over the responsibility of general contractor.

After the demolition of the old house the Burnet family moved into the Grace Crescent house where they lived until about November 1981, at which time they moved back to the new house. A number of items were incomplete or defective, such as the plumbing, the landscaping, two stairwells, but by and large the house was liveable. In December of 1981 the Appellant sold the Grace Crescent house and netted $126,000 which he used to pay down the $400,000 CIBC mortgage which at that time bore interest at 20-24%.

By May of 1981 the cost of construction was $194,000. By November, S & J had billed $326,000, and this did not include the amounts spent by the appellant directly. Builders' liens were throughout the period being registered against the new house. In 1984 the new property was mortgaged for $18,000 to the appellant's account to complete landscaping and other aspects of the new house. In April 1984 the property was mortgaged for $325,815 to discharge the balance of the CIBC mortgage.

In September 1984 the appellant engaged an agent to find a tenant for the new house at $4,000 per month, but without success. In April 1985 another agent was engaged to rent or sell the house, which the appellant and his wife listed for $439,000. The house did not sell at that time but it was leased for a year, starting June 1, 1985 at $2,600 per month. During that period the appellant and his family lived in another house which they rented for $1,200 per month. On May 31, 1986 the Burnets moved back to the new house. During Expo '86 they rented out a portion of the house.

In November 1986 they listed the property with another agent for $456,000. Finally, they sold the property on March 31, 1987 for $385,000 and bought another property in North Vancouver where they continue to live.

...

In his 1987 return of income the appellant claimed a business loss of $520,920, the difference between the expenses claimed of $905,920 and the selling price. These figures are not disputed by the respondent.

...

Analysis

I come now to the most difficult part of this rather unusual case. That the entire project from beginning to end was a financial and emotional disaster for the Burnets cannot be gainsaid. It resulted from the combination of a variety of factors, some within their control and some not: a volatile real estate market in Vancouver, high interest rates, unreliable builders, unrealistic expectations by Mr. Burnet and flawed estimates of cost, to mention only a few. In the final analysis it boils down however to one question: was this an adventure in the nature of trade?

...

I can start from a reasonably firm footing: the credibility of the witnesses is not an issue. I have no reason to doubt their testimony. Whether the mere intention to develop and sell the family home is sufficient to turn the venture into a business is, of course, another matter. Most people expect to sell their principal residence at some time and, it is hoped, to realize a tax free capital gain. [The exemption for capital gains on the disposition of a taxpayer's principal residence is examined later in this chapter.] If this in itself were the test most sales of residential homes would result in taxable income. The converse of this proposition is that it is quite possible to speculate in one's principal residence, but it requires fairly cogent evidence to justify the conclusion that the house where one lives has become an object of trade: *Schlamp v. The Queen*, [1982] CTC 304, 82 DTC 6274 (FCTD). Here the case is complicated by the fact that the Burnets lived in the property for over five years and indeed rented it out for a year.

On balance I think that the evidence is more consistent with a trading intent. In reaching this conclusion I have endeavoured to balance a number of factors, some pointing in one direction and some in the other. On the one hand we have the incontrovertible fact that the West Vancouver property was, before the demolition of the old house, not only the principal residence of the appellant and his family but also a capital property in his hands. Moreover, when it was decided to demolish the old house and construct the new one the estimated costs were well within the appellant's means as a home in which the family could have lived. We have as well the fact that the family lived in the new house for several years, and rented it out. During the construction period the entire family participated in the design of the house — indeed the bedrooms were designated by the children's names — in a manner that is not inconsistent with an intention to live in it permanently. Counsel also emphasized that the contractor and architects were not told of the appellant's intention to sell the house. That the new house was the principal residence of the family during the period in which they occupied it is clear. That fact of course does not determine the matter. The exclusion from a taxpayer's income of the gain or loss on the disposition of a principal residence occurs only if the property, in addition to being a principal residence, is also capital property. A gain or loss realized or sustained on the disposition of a property in which the taxpayer ordinarily resides (i.e. a "principal residence" or a "personal use property" within the ordinary sense of those words and not because of the definitions in section 54 of the *Income Tax Act*) falls entirely outside the ambit of subdivision c of Division B [of Part I] of the Act if that property is not a capital property in the taxpayer's hands.

In support of the appellant's position we have his stated intention from the outset to sell the house and this intention was confirmed by his wife. Stated intentions in trading cases are of course not determinative. If they were, few taxpayers who appeal assessments in such cases would lose. The intention to realize a profit on the sale of a large house was, at the outset, although somewhat ill-conceived, at least understandable in the market that prevailed in 1979. Moreover, the house, if intended, as the respondent suggests, to be a permanent residence, was much too large and elaborate for the Burnet family. The sale of the Grace Crescent house and return to the property in West Vancouver was equally consistent with the financial exigencies that prevailed in 1981 — the escalating costs, the high interest rates and the collapse of the real estate market.

One could list many other factors on either side but the overall picture that emerges is that of a man with somewhat greater aspirations and optimism than business acumen who rather naively decided to capitalize on a housing boom and to embark on a venture in which he was, either in terms of experience or financial backing, ill-equipped to withstand the vicissitudes of a volatile real estate market. To this end he decided to use the family home which had a lot large enough to accommodate a luxury house. At the point at which he moved out of the old house and demolished it he converted what was clearly a capital property to inventory and notwithstanding the fact that he was forced for economic reasons to move back, when costs and interest rates escalated and the bottom fell out of the market, the West Vancouver property never ceased to be an asset that was held for sale in the course of an adventure in the nature of trade. The circumstances that impelled their moving back to the new house were more economic than familial.

Although the Minister had ample grounds on assessment for disallowing the loss — including the fact that the appellant and his family lived in the house, the fact that he assigned his children's names to the rooms, and the fact that the house was not listed for sale until 1985, nonetheless, I think that on balance the evidence discloses a consistent speculative intent that goes well beyond the normal hope that everyone has that he or she can sell his or her principal residence at a profit. I do not think it can fairly be inferred that the Burnets' intent, when they demolished the old house and started work on the new one, was to move back there. That move was dictated by the economic exigencies of the higher mortgage, the escalating costs and the high mortgage rates.

In the circumstances, I have concluded that on balance the appellant has made out his case. ...

Appeal allowed.

NOTES AND QUESTIONS

1. To which factors might one refer in *Burnet* to conclude that the new house constructed by the taxpayer in West Vancouver was personal-use property? What other factors convinced the court that the new house was not personal-use property? Do you agree with the court's decision? Why or why not?

2. Of what relevance to the characterization of property as personal-use property is its initial characterization as inventory or capital property? Why, according to the court in *Burnet*, does a gain or loss on the disposition of a property in which a taxpayer ordinarily resides escape the rules for personal-use property and principal residences in subdivision c of Division B of Part I of the Act "if the property is not capital property in the taxpayer's hands"?

3. In *Down v. M.N.R.*, [1993] T.C.J. No. 190, [1993] 2 C.T.C. 2027, 93 D.T.C. 591 (T.C.C.), the taxpayer, who had bought and sold between 80 and 100 properties in previous years, sought to deduct a loss of $112,818 incurred on the sale of a house on Granville Street in Vancouver, which he acquired in February

1982 and resided in until December 1982 while he carried out extensive renovations. Rejecting the Minister's argument that the property was personal-use property, a loss from the disposition of which is deemed to be nil, the court accepted the taxpayer's testimony that he had acquired the house for the purpose of renovating and reselling it as soon as possible. According to Bell TCCJ (at para. 13):

> On this basis I have no difficulty concluding that the Granville Street transaction was part of the appellant's business of dealing in real estate. Therefore, such property cannot, as was urged by respondent's counsel, be personal use property as defined in section 54 of the Act, that definition being expressed specifically to have application only for the purposes of [subdivision c] which deals with capital gains and capital losses.

For a similar result, see *Jason v. Canada*, [1995] T.C.J. No. 1062, [1996] 1 C.T.C. 2320 (T.C.C.), where the taxpayer sought to deduct a loss incurred on the sale of a residence acquired by the taxpayer and his wife on April 11, 1989 and sold on January 29, 1990. Although concluding that the taxpayer and his wife had lived in the residence for eight months and that the property had been acquired with the intention of using it as a principal residence, the court emphasized the fact that the purchase was 96.5 per cent debt-financed to conclude (at para. 20) that the taxpayer and his wife had "a secondary intention to sell for profit at the first opportunity." On this basis, the court held that the purchase and sale constituted an adventure or concern in the nature of trade, the loss from which was fully deductible in computing the taxpayer's net income.

For a contrasting result, see *McMillan v. M.N.R.*, [1987] T.C.J. No. 560, [1987] 2 C.T.C. 2038, 87 D.T.C. 358 (T.C.C.), in which the taxpayer, who resided in a newly constructed house from December 1981 until October 1982, sought to deduct a loss on the sale of the house on the grounds that the property was acquired as a speculative venture. Accepting (at para. 7) the Minister's argument that the taxpayer had purchased the property "with the sole intention that it be built as a principal residence for himself and that the possibility of reselling the property at a profit was not a motivating factor in the [taxpayer's] mind at the time of purchase," the court disallowed the deduction. According to Brulé TCJ (at paras. 9-11):

> The house was custom built as far as permissible to the specifications of the appellant. In my opinion, the evidence is clear that the appellant purchased this property and built the house for the sole purpose of establishing his principal residence there and for no other reason. On the basis of the evidence I must also conclude that the appellant's decision to sell the house ... was based upon his financial difficulties and was not part of a pre-determined plan to sell the property for a profit. ...

> In my view the property in question was clearly personal-use property. The lot was purchased for the sole purpose of building a custom home for the appellant and to establish a principal residence. As such he cannot get relief and comes within the provisions of subsection 40(2) of the *Income Tax Act*. The losses arising from such a transaction are clearly not deductible.

See also *Deacon v. Canada*, [1994] T.C.J. No. 1047, [1995] 1 C.T.C. 2476, 95 D.T.C. 793 (T.C.C.).

4.   In *Boudreau v. Canada*, [1999] T.C.J. No. 701, [2000] 1 C.T.C. 2242 (T.C.C.), the taxpayer purchased his parents' principal residence in February 1993 for $110,000, and rented the property to his parents at below market rates until December 1994, when he sold the property to his sister and her spouse for $103,000. Rejecting the taxpayer's argument that he had acquired the property as an investment for the purpose of gaining or producing rental income, the court disallowed the deduction of a terminal loss and the deduction of a capital loss on the basis that the property was personal-use property. According to Hamlyn TCJ (at paras. 17 and 18):

> The Property was not acquired for the purposes of gaining income from property. Not once did the Appellant rent the Property at fair market rental value. His parents enjoyed the Property on either a below market or minimal maintenance basis. The Property was used primarily for the enjoyment of the [taxpayer's] parents.
>
> The Property therefore being used for personal use, the loss was not a terminal loss. Moreover, the [taxpayer] is not entitled to claim a capital loss on the disposition of the Property because it relates to personal-use property as the loss on the disposition of the Property is deemed to be nil (subparagraph 40(2)(g)(iii)).

For a similar result, see *Paterson v. M.N.R.*, [1983] C.T.C. 2318, 83 D.T.C. 250 (TRB), where the taxpayer, whose estranged husband was transferred from Ontario to Winnipeg, purchased a house in Winnipeg, which she rented to her husband, who made the mortgage payments in lieu of rent. Disallowing the deduction of a capital loss on the sale of the property when the husband was transferred back to Ontario, the court concluded (at para. 23) that the property "must be considered personal-use property ... because it was for the use of the [taxpayer's] husband." The court did not consider whether the property provided the taxpayer with a reasonable expectation of profit.

5.   In *Sandoz v. M.N.R.*, [1981] C.T.C. 2116, 81 D.T.C. 181 (T.R.B.), the taxpayer, a retired civil servant who acquired a condominium for $42,500 in 1975 and sold it two years later for $40,000, claimed a capital loss on the grounds that he lived mostly at his cottage or with a friend, and had purchased the condominium while in the process of a marital separation in "an attempt to shelter his capital from legal attack by his wife's lawyer and also to provide a vehicle for financial improvement" in his retirement. Noting (at para. 21) that the taxpayer "stored his personal belongings" in the condominium, "had curtains and drapes put up," had put "the furniture ... in place," "lived in the condominium occasionally," "entertained a friend there on one occasion," and used the condominium address for his former employer's records, the board concluded (at para. 21) that "whether the [taxpayer] resided there or not, the condominium was purchased for his own personal use and advantage."

6.   For other cases in which capital losses have been disallowed on the basis that they resulted from the disposition of personal-use property, see *Carom v. M.N.R.*, [1977] C.T.C. 2085, 77 D.T.C. 67 (T.R.B.) (loss from the disposition of race horses acquired primarily for personal use or enjoyment and not as part of a business carried on with a reasonable expectation of profit); *Suojanen v. M.N.R.*, [1983] C.T.C. 2763, 83 D.T.C. 690 (T.C.C.) (loss from the theft of a watch and the disposition of a defective Franklin stove); *Gaudreault v. Canada,* [1998] T.C.J. No. 627, [1999] 1 CTC 2030 (T.C.C.) (loss from the disposition of a debt acquired on the sale of the taxpayer's principal residence to the taxpayer's son); and *Chartrand v. The Queen*, [2000] T.C.J. No. 201, [2001] 2 C.T.C. 2256 (T.C.C.) (loss of $8,115 resulting from the bankruptcy of a corporation in which the taxpayers had acquired a time share allowing them to use a vacation property for one week in August each year).

7.   For other cases in which taxpayers have successfully argued that losses did not result from the disposition of personal-use property, see *Mid-West Feed Ltd. v. M.N.R.*, [1987] T.C.J. No. 565, [1987] 2 C.T.C. 2101, 87 D.T.C. 394 (T.C.C.) (losses from the sale of a yacht and airplane acquired by the taxpayer corporation and used for business purposes) and *Woods Estate v. Canada*, [2000] T.C.J. No. 260, [2000] 3 C.T.C. 2179 (T.C.C.) (loss on the disposition of a principal residence acquired by the taxpayer estate in July 1993 and sold in January 1995).

8.   The CRA's views on the rules governing personal-use property formerly appeared in Interpretation Bulletin IT-332R, "Personal-use Property" November 28, 1984. This Interpretation Bulletin was archived in 2004.

2. Listed Personal Property

Listed personal property is defined in section 54 of the Act as personal-use property that is "all or any portion of, or any interest in or right to any (a) print, etching, drawing, painting, sculpture, or other similar work of art, (b) jewellery, (c) rare folio, rare manuscript, or rare book, (d) stamp, or (e) coin." Since capital losses from the disposition of these kinds of property generally reflect market fluctuations rather than personal use, the *Income Tax Act* excludes these losses from the general rule in subparagraph 40(2)(g)(iii), which deems capital losses from the disposition of personal-use property to be nil. As a compromise, however, capital losses from the disposition of listed personal property are deductible only against capital gains from the disposition of listed personal property. Like other kinds of personal-use property, however, listed personal property is also subject to the $1,000 rule in section 46 of the Act.

   The segregation of capital losses from the disposition of listed personal property is apparent in paragraph 3(b) of the Act as well as section 41. According to the former provision, taxable net gains from dispositions of listed personal property must be included under clause 3(b)(i)(B), while losses from dispositions of listed personal property are excluded from the general deduction for allowable capital losses under subparagraph 3(b)(ii). According to paragraph 41(2)(a) of the Act, a taxpayer's net gain for a taxation year from dispositions of listed personal property is generally defined as:

> the amount, if any, by which the total of the taxpayer's gains for the year from the disposition of listed personal property, other than property described in subparagraph 39(1)(a)(i.1) [exempting capital gains from the disposition of Canadian cultural property], exceeds the total of the taxpayer's losses for the year from dispositions of listed personal property,

while subsection 41(1) defines a taxpayer's taxable net gain for the year from dispositions of listed personal property as "½ of the amount determined ... to be the taxpayer's net gain for the year from dispositions of such property."

Where the total of the taxpayer's losses for the year from dispositions of listed personal property exceed the total of the taxpayer's gains for the year from dispositions of listed personal property (other than property described in subparagraph 39(1)(a)(i.1)), this amount is defined in subsection 41(3) as the taxpayer's "listed-personal-property loss" for the year. According to paragraph 41(2)(b) of the Act, in computing a taxpayer's net gain for the year from dispositions of listed personal property, taxpayers may deduct from the amount otherwise determined under paragraph 41(2)(a) "such portion as the taxpayer may claim of the taxpayer's listed-personal-property losses for the 7 taxation years immediately preceding and the 3 taxation years immediately following the taxation year."[63] This provision allows taxpayers to carry listed-personal-property losses in a particular taxation year back three years and forward seven years to offset net gains from dispositions of listed personal property in those years as otherwise determined under paragraph 41(2)(a) of the Act.

Given the highly specific statutory definition for listed personal property, it is perhaps not surprising that very few cases have considered the characterization of these kinds of personal-use property. In one case, however, the Tax Review Board held that Murray Schafer, a composer and musician who sold a number of documents to the National Library of Canada (including original manuscripts, a copy of his diary, sketches, and notes) for $25,000, had disposed of listed personal property rather than inventory in a business.[64]

---

[63] This provision is subject to a number of rules governing the manner in which listed personal property losses may be deducted in computing a taxpayer's net gains for a taxation year from dispositions of listed personal property. According to subpara. 41(2)(b)(i), listed personal property losses are deductible only to the extent that they have not been deducted in previous taxation years. Subparagraph 41(2)(b)(ii) requires taxpayers to deduct listed personal property losses from earlier years prior to the deduction of listed personal property losses from subsequent years. Finally, subpara. 41(2)(b)(iii) stipulates that listed personal property losses may be deducted only up to the amount of the taxpayer's net gains from dispositions of listed personal property otherwise determined under para. 41(2)(a).

[64] *Schafer v. M.N.R.*, [1981] C.T.C. 2261, 81 D.T.C. 226 (T.R.B.).

3. Principal Residence

Section 54 of the Act defines the "principal residence" of a taxpayer for a taxation year as:

> a particular property that is a housing unit, a leasehold interest in a housing unit or a share of the capital stock of a co-operative housing corporation acquired for the sole purpose of acquiring the right to inhabit a housing unit owned by the corporation and that is owned, whether jointly with another person or otherwise, in the year by the taxpayer, if
>
> > (a) where the taxpayer is an individual other than a personal trust, the housing unit was ordinarily inhabited in the year by the taxpayer, by the taxpayer's spouse or common-law partner or former spouse or common-law partner or by a child of the taxpayer,
> >
> > (a.1) where the taxpayer is a personal trust, the housing unit was ordinarily inhabited in the calendar year by a specified beneficiary of the trust for the year, by the spouse or common-law partner or former spouse or common-law partner of such a beneficiary or by a child of such a beneficiary, or
> >
> > (b) where the taxpayer is a personal trust or an individual other than a trust, the taxpayer
> >
> > > (i) elected under subsection 45(2) that relates to the change in use of the particular property in the year or a preceding taxation year, other than an election rescinded under subsection 45(2) in the taxpayer's return of income for the year or a preceding taxation year, or
> > >
> > > (ii) elected under subsection 45(3) that relates to a change in use of the particular property in a subsequent taxation year.

For the purpose of this definition, paragraph (e) provides that:

> the principal residence of a taxpayer for a taxation year shall be deemed to include, except where the particular property consists of a share of the capital stock of a co-operative housing corporation, the land subjacent to the housing unit and such portion of any immediately contiguous land as can reasonably be regarded as contributing to the use and enjoyment of the housing unit as a residence, except that where the total area of the subjacent land and of that portion exceeds ½ hectare, the excess shall be deemed not to have contributed to the use and enjoyment of the housing unit as a residence unless the taxpayer establishes that it was necessary to such use and enjoyment.

Paragraphs (c) and (c.1), on the other hand, stipulate that:

> subject to section 54.1, a particular property shall be considered not to be a taxpayer's principal residence for a taxation year
>
> > (c) where the taxpayer is an individual other than a personal trust, unless the particular property was designated by the taxpayer in prescribed form and manner to be the taxpayer's principal residence for the year and no other property has been designated for the purposes of this definition for the year
> >
> > > (i) where the year is before 1982, by the taxpayer, or
> > >
> > > (ii) where the year is after 1981,
> > >
> > > > (A) by the taxpayer,

(B)   by a person who was throughout the year the taxpayer's spouse or common-law partner (other than a spouse or common-law partner who was throughout the year living apart from, and was separated under a judicial separation or written separation agreement from, the taxpayer),

(C)   by a person who was the taxpayer's child (other than a child who was at any time in the year a married person, a person who is in a common-law partnership or 18 years of age or older), or

(D)   where the taxpayer was not at any time in the year a married person or 18 years of age or older, by a person who was the taxpayer's

(I)   mother or father, or

(II)   brother or sister, where that brother or sister was not at any time in the year a married person, a person who is in a common-law partnership or 18 years of age or older,

(c.1) where the taxpayer is a personal trust, unless

(i)   the particular property was designated by the trust in prescribed form and manner to be the taxpayer's principal residence for the year,

(ii)   the trust specifies in the designation each individual (in this definition referred to as a "specified beneficiary" of the trust for the year) who, in the calendar year ending in the year,

(A)   is beneficially interested in the trust, and

(B)   except where the trust is entitled to designate it for the year solely because of paragraph (b), ordinarily inhabited the housing unit or has a spouse or common-law partner, former spouse or common-law partner or child who ordinarily inhabited the housing unit,

(iii)   no corporation (other than a registered charity) or partnership is beneficially interested in the trust at any time in the year, and

(iv)   no other property has been designated for the purpose of this definition for the calendar year ending in the year by any specified beneficiary of the trust for the year, by a person who was throughout that calendar year such a beneficiary's spouse or common-law partner (other than a spouse or common-law partner who was throughout that calendar year living apart from, and was separated pursuant to a judicial separation or written separation agreement from, the beneficiary), by a person who was such a beneficiary's child (other than a child who was during that calendar year a married person or a person who is in a common-law partnership or a person 18 years or over) or, where such a beneficiary was not during that calendar year a married person or a person who is in a common-law partnership or a person 18 years or over, by a person who was such a beneficiary's

(A)   mother or father, or

(B)   brother or sister, where that brother or sister was not during that calendar year a married person or a person who is in a common-law partnership or a person 18 years or over, or

> (d)   because of paragraph (b), if solely because of that paragraph the property would, but for this paragraph, have been a principal residence of the taxpayer for 4 or more preceding taxation years,

while paragraph (f) of the definition deems "a particular property designated under paragraph (c.1) by a trust for a year ... to be property designated for the purposes of this definition by each specified beneficiary of the trust for the calendar year ending in the year."

According to paragraph 40(2)(b) of the Act, notwithstanding the general rule for the computation of a capital gain or loss in subsection 40(1):

> where the taxpayer is an individual, the taxpayer's gain for a taxation year from the disposition of a property that was the taxpayer's principal residence at any time after the date (in this section referred to as the "acquisition date") that is the later of December 31, 1971 and the day on which the taxpayer last acquired or reacquired it, as the case may be, is the amount determined by the formula

$$A - (A \times B / C) - D$$

> where

> A is the amount that would, if this Act were read without reference to this paragraph ... be the taxpayer's gain therefrom for the year,

> B is one plus the number of taxation years that end after the acquisition date for which the property was the taxpayer's principal residence and during which the taxpayer was resident in Canada, [and]

> C is the number of taxation years that end after the acquisition date during which the taxpayer owned the property whether jointly with another person or otherwise.

For our purposes, there is no need to consider the description of D, which applies only if the property was acquired before February 23, 1994 and an election to claim the lifetime capital gains exemption was made in respect of the property under subsection 110.6(19) of the Act.

The effect of the formula in paragraph 40(2)(b) is to exempt a portion of any capital gain on the disposition of a qualifying property based on the ratio of the number of years during which the property was the taxpayer's principal residence and the taxpayer was resident in Canada to the number of years during which the taxpayer owned the property. Where the property was the taxpayer's principal residence during each taxation year in which the taxpayer owned the property, any gain on the disposition of the property will be fully exempt. The words "one plus" in the description of B permit a taxpayer who disposes of one residence and reacquires another in the same taxation year to exempt the full amount of any capital gain on both properties.[65]

---

[65]   See Interpretation Bulletin IT-120R6, "Principal Residence," July 17, 2003, para. 10: "While only one property may be designated as a taxpayer's principal residence for a particular taxation year ... , the principal residence exemption rules recognize that the taxpayer can have two residences in the same year, i.e., where one residence is sold and another acquired in the same year. The effect of the 'one plus' in variable B (the numerator of the fraction) in the formula ... is

In order to examine this principal residence exemption, it is useful to consider each of its basic components: (1) the kinds of property that are eligible for the exemption; (2) the extent to which surrounding land qualifies for the exemption; and (3) the requirement that the property be designated as a principal residence. The following text and cases examine each of these features.

a. Eligible Property

According to the preamble to the definition in section 54, a principal residence must be "a housing unit, a leasehold interest in a housing unit or a share of the capital stock of a co-operative housing corporation acquired for the sole purpose of acquiring the right to inhabit a housing unit owned by the corporation ... that is owned, whether jointly with another person or otherwise, in the year by the taxpayer." According to paragraph (a), where the taxpayer is an individual other than a personal trust, the housing unit must be "ordinarily inhabited in the year by the taxpayer, by the taxpayer's spouse or common-law partner or former spouse or common-law partner or by a child of the taxpayer." Paragraph (a.1) contains a similar rule for a housing unit owned by a personal trust, requiring that it be "ordinarily inhabited in the calendar year ending in the year by a specified beneficiary of the trust for the year, by the spouse or common-law partner or former spouse or common-law partner of such a beneficiary or by a child of such a beneficiary." For this purpose, subparagraph (c.1)(ii) of the definition defines a "specified beneficiary" as an individual who is beneficially interested in the trust and specified by the trust in its designation of the property as a principal residence. As an alternative to the requirement that an eligible property be "ordinarily inhabited" by one of the persons identified in paragraphs (a) or (a.1), paragraph (b) extends the definition of a principal residence to include property subject to an election under subsection 45(2) or (3) on a change in use to or from the purpose of gaining or producing income. By virtue of paragraph (d) of the definition, however, qualification as a principal residence under paragraph (b) is generally limited to the four taxation years following an election under subsection 45(2) and the four taxation years preceding an election under subsection 45(3).[66]

---

to treat both properties as a principal residence in such a year, even though only one of them may be designated as such for that year."

[66] Section 54.1 creates an exception to this four-year limitation, where the taxpayer does not ordinarily inhabit the property "as a consequence of the relocation of the taxpayer's or the taxpayer's spouse's or common-law partner's place of employment while the taxpayer, spouse or common-law partner, as the case may be, is employed by an employer who is not a person to whom the taxpayer or the spouse is related," provided that the property was located at least 40 kilometres farther from this new place of employment than the taxpayer's subsequent place or places of residence, and "(a) the property subsequently becomes ordinarily inhabited by the taxpayer during the term of the taxpayer's or the taxpayer's spouse's or common-law partner's employment by that employer on or before the end of the taxation year immediately following the taxation year in which the taxpayer's or the spouse's or common-law partner's employment

The elections under subsections 45(2) and (3) of the Act are examined later in this chapter, along with other rules deeming taxpayers to have disposed of and reacquired property on a change in the use of the property. For now, therefore, the key requirements in the definition of "principal residence" in section 54 involve the meaning of the terms "housing unit" and "ordinarily inhabited," neither of which is defined in the Act. One of the more interesting discussions of these expressions occurs in *Flanagan v. M.N.R.*, [1989] T.C.J. No. 819, [1989] 2 C.T.C. 2395, 89 D.T.C. 615 (T.C.C.).

Flanagan v. M.N.R.
[1989] T.C.J. No. 819, [1989] 2 C.T.C. 2395, 89 D.T.C. 615 (T.C.C.)

RIP TCJ: The issue in these appeals from income tax assessments for 1982 and 1983 is whether a housing unit was ever located on two properties disposed of by the appellant, Patrick Gerald Flanagan ("Flanagan"), and, if so, whether the properties were part of his principal residence.

In January 1973 Flanagan purchased from his mother a vacant lot on which he hoped to build a home. The property was located in the Shuswap Regional District of British Columbia and fronted on Shuswap Lake, which was a source of fresh water supply. Mr. Flanagan was denied a building permit for his home by the municipal authorities. He was informed Shuswap Lake had a high water mark that would preclude construction and septic system approval; a permanent structure could not be built on the lot unless additional land was acquired for a septic system connected to the lakefront property in perpetuity. He also was informed by the municipal authorities that without a septic system no utility could be connected to the property.

Flanagan attempted to acquire an easement for the septic system from an owner of neighbouring land but the owner refused since she had "other plans" for her property. Eventually she sold the property to a developer. The developer also refused to grant Flanagan an easement but in 1975 entered into an agreement with Flanagan for the sale of a lot. In 1978 Flanagan acquired this second property. The second property was across a public road from the property he acquired from his mother ("first property"). Flanagan caused an easement in perpetuity to be placed on the second property in favour of the first property; a pipe ran beneath the road between the two properties.

In the meantime Flanagan wanted to put the property he acquired from his mother to the use intended. He purchased a 14-foot camper trailer in September 1973. The trailer contained a sink, stove, cupboards, bed and a portable toilet. He would drive the trailer to the property on weekends, when he had time off from work and when on vacation. He would live in the trailer during these times. At the end of a stay on the property he would drive the trailer to his parents'

---

by that employer terminates; or (b) the taxpayer dies during the term of the taxpayer's or the spouse's or common-law partner's employment by that employer."

home in Surrey where he would leave it when not in use and return to his rented apartment in Vancouver. The trailer was not left on the property for fear of vandalism. The trailer was used on the property during 1973 and 1974.

Also, in 1973 Flanagan purchased a van which also contained a trailer hitch. The van contained a bed, sink, cupboards, stove, toilet and lighting. Electrical power was available by means of an extension cord from a neighbour's property. A second van was acquired in 1978. The vans, like the trailer, were used by the appellant on the property as a place in which to sleep, eat and spend time, in short, to live. When he was away from the property Flanagan would leave the van parked near his apartment in Vancouver. The evidence indicates that in 1982 Flanagan made use of the second van on the first property.

Flanagan stated he never spent any spare time other than on the first property. All his vacations were spent on the property during the time he owned it; during this time, he explained, he continued attempts to obtain a building permit. He improved the property by raising it by three feet to prevent flooding. He also testified that he used the trailer, vans and tent only on the property. He did not, for example, make use of the trailer or vans when they were left parked in Surrey or Vancouver.

When he left his residence in Vancouver for the property he would take most of his clothing with him. He explained that during the time he owned the property his lifestyle did not require too much in the way of clothing and luxuries.

During the time he owned the property he would also occasionally put a tent on the property for shelter. On leaving the property he would take down the tent except if he intended to return within a week.

During 1976, Flanagan lived on the first property continuously from June to September; in any other year he estimates he spent at least 30 days a year on the property.

In 1982, a business Flanagan started was beginning to make demands on his time which affected his lifestyle. He decided to sell the properties. The first property was sold in 1982 and the second in 1983. In filing his income tax returns for those years he claimed the properties as principal residence and thus did not include any part of the capital gain in income.

The respondent denied the claims on the basis there was no housing unit that was ordinarily inhabited by the appellant on either of the two properties.

...

The original position taken by the respondent in disallowing the appellant's claim was that a "housing unit" does not include a trailer, van or tent. He relied on the English line of cases, the most recent of which is *Makins v. Elson (Inspector of Taxes)*, [1977] 1 All ER 572. In that appeal the taxpayer purchased land in 1970 for the purpose of building a "dwelling house"; he had received permission to build the home. A month after the purchase he moved to the property with a caravan and lived there with his family. He started to build a home but very little work was in fact done. While he lived on the property, water, telephone and electricity, which had been installed on the site, were connected to the caravan. The wheels had been taken off the caravan; it was jacked up and resting on bricks. In 1973 the taxpayer sold the caravan and property. The issue was whether the gains arising from the sale were exempt from capital gains tax on the ground the caravan was a chattel separate from the land and that the land did not constitute a dwelling-house or part of a dwelling-house within the meaning of paragraph 29(1)(a) of the *Finance Act, 1965* which was the taxpayer's only or main residence.

The Court, Chancery Division, took into account the installation of the telephone, electricity and water system, and the fact that the wheels of the caravan were not on the ground and found the caravan to be a "dwelling-house." [See also *Moore v. Thompson*, [1986] STC 170 (Ch. D), where it was held that a caravan sited in the courtyard of a farmhouse owned by the taxpayer and not connected to any services and that was used sporadically was not a dwelling house within the meaning of the UK *Capital Gains Tax Act*, 1979, section 101.]

...

The words "housing unit" are not defined in any dictionary available to me. The *Oxford English Dictionary*, Second Edition, (Oxford) defines "housing" as "... a shelter of a house, or such as that of a house; house accommodation; lodging. ... A house or building ..." *Le Grand Robert de la langue française*, deuxième édition (*Robert*) defines "logement" as "Local à usage d'habitation, et, plus spécial, Partie de maison, d'immeuble où l'on réside habituellement. ..."

...

A "housing unit" need not be a building. A house provides shelter to people who reside in it, and a building is not the sole means of shelter. A van and trailer, suitably equipped, are capable of providing the same type of shelter and comfort as a traditional house. Today one finds more than a few people residing in vans and trailers while some trailers, like the caravan in *Makins v. Elson*, *supra*, may rest on bricks and be supplied with services. Others may be mobile taking advantage of the very nature of the beast for travel. In either event the van or trailer easily may serve as a housing unit: it is a question of fact whether the van or trailer at any time is a housing unit. I do not find the lack of services to the appellant's van and trailer fatal to his appeal; there are, unfortunately, many buildings used as homes by Canadians which lack services normally available to the larger community and the lack of these services ought not to colour the very character of the building used as their housing unit. Similarly lack of services to a van or trailer, otherwise a housing unit, should not affect their character. A "housing unit" need not ... be a building or structure. The respondent has recognized that a trailer may be a housing unit for the purposes of [the definition of "principal residence" in section 54 of the Act] in its Interpretation Bulletin IT-120R3, published on February 16, 1984. Paragraph 5 of the bulletin states:

> The term "housing unit" includes a house, apartment in a duplex, or apartment building or condominium, cottage, mobile home, trailer or houseboat.

While administrative policy and interpretation are not determinative, they are entitled to weight and can be an "important factor" in case of doubt about the meaning of legislation: re de Grandpré J in *Harel v. Deputy Minister of Revenue of the Province of Quebec*, [1978] 1 SCR 851, [1977] CTC 441, 77 DTC 5438 at page 859, *Nowegijick v. The Queen et al.*, [1983] 1 SCR 29, [1983] CTC 20; 83 DTC 5041 at page 37 per Dickson J (as he then was).

Counsel for the respondent submitted that if a mobile home, van or trailer may be a "housing unit" and thus a principal residence for the purposes of [the definition in section 54 of the Act], it is only the mobile home or trailer itself that is the principal residence and not any land. The mobility of the mobile home, van or trailer suggests that many different lots, even roads in which they travel, may be subjacent to such a housing unit at any particular time.

This submission, in my view, ignores part of the statutory provision ... which provides that "principal residence ... shall be [deemed] to include ... the land subjacent to the housing unit and such portion of any immediately contiguous land as may be regarded as contributing to the taxpayer's use and enjoyment of the housing unit as a residence. ..."

"Subjacent" is defined by *Oxford* as "... situated underneath or below; underlying." "Sous-jacent" is defined by *Robert* as "... Qui s'étend, qui est situé au-dessous. ..." It is quite obvious that a van, trailer and tent must rest on something. Mr. Flanagan's van and trailer, as well as his tent, rested on the land he acquired from his mother; this land was situated underneath or below the van and trailer, as well as the tent, and in the normal sense of the word was subjacent to the housing unit used by Mr. Flanagan during his ownership of the first property.

In my view, the term "principal residence" in [section 54] includes land subjacent to a mobile home, van or trailer at the time the mobile home, van or trailer is in use as a housing unit. Hence where any of a mobile home, van or trailer is a housing unit ordinarily inhabited by the taxpayer, the land subjacent to such housing unit is part of the principal residence together with the housing unit itself.

The land contiguous to the land subjacent to the housing unit is to be included as part of Flanagan's principal residence in 1982 if it may reasonably be regarded as contributing to his use and enjoyment of the housing unit as a residence. With respect to the property he acquired from his mother, the land contributed to his use and enjoyment of the trailer, vans and tent. He did not spend all his time inside the van, the housing unit, in 1982. The purpose in acquiring the land was because of its lake frontage and surroundings. The first property was part of Flanagan's "principal residence" in 1982 within the meaning of [section 54] if it was "ordinarily inhabited" by him in 1982.

The courts have discussed on several occasions the meaning of the expression "ordinarily resident," as that expression was used in subsection 139(4) of the Act, as it read prior to 1972. In *Thomson v. M.N.R.*, [1946] SCR 209, [1946] CTC 51, 2 DTC 812 the Supreme Court of Canada found there was nothing of a casual or non-permanent character about the taxpayer's residence in

New Brunswick even though he lived there, during the years in appeal, from May to October, less than 183 days in each year. He resided the rest of year in the United States. Rand J on page 64 (DTC 815) stated that:

> The expression "ordinarily resident" carries a restricted signification, and although the first impression seems to be that of preponderance in time, the decisions on the English Act reject that view. It is held to mean residence in the course of the customary mode of life of the person concerned, and it is contrasted with special or occasional or casual residence. The general mode of life is, therefore, relevant to a question of its application.

Kellock J at pages 67 and 68 (DTC 819 and 820), stated as follows:

> "Ordinarily" is defined as "in conformity with rule or established custom or practice," "as a matter of regular practice or occurrence," "in the ordinary or usual course of events," "usually," "commonly," "as is normal or usual."
>
> ...

The word "ordinarily" does not, therefore, restrict a person to having residence in one country; a person may ordinarily inhabit more than one housing unit in a year if he does so in the course of the customary mode of his life: this too is a question of fact. The respondent agrees that a seasonal residence may be a taxpayer's principal residence. Paragraph 9 of the respondent's Interpretation Bulletin IT-120R3 reads as follows:

> The question of whether a residence was "ordinarily inhabited" during a taxation year by a taxpayer, the taxpayer's spouse or former spouse, or a child of the taxpayer must be resolved on the facts in each particular case. Where the residence has been occupied by such a person for only a short period of time during a taxation year (such as a seasonal residence occupied during a taxpayer's vacation or a house which was sold early or bought late in a taxation year), it is the Department's view that the taxpayer "ordinarily inhabited" that residence in the year, provided that the principal reason for owning the property was not for the purpose of gaining or producing income therefrom. In circumstances where a taxpayer receives incidental rental income from a seasonal residence, such property is not considered to be owned for the purpose of gaining or producing income therefrom.

Mr. Flanagan testified that in the normal course of living he spent all his free time at the first property. He did not visit the property only occasionally or use it for purposes other than ordinary habitation: see *Shlien v. M.N.R.*, [1988] 1 CTC 2244, 88 DTC 1152 at page 2247 (DTC 1154). The use of the vans, trailer and tent, as well as the lot he acquired from his mother was part of his lifestyle in 1982 prior to selling the property in that year. Cross-examination did not indicate that in 1982, up to the time of the sale of the property, Flanagan used the property any differently than in past years. In 1982, and prior years, the property was "ordinarily inhabited" by Mr. Flanagan.

Finally we arrive at the land Mr. Flanagan acquired in 1975, sometimes referred to as the second property, and sold in 1983. Prior to 1983 the land comprising this property was not contiguous to the land comprising the first property which was subjacent to the housing unit. The two properties were separated by a roadway and were not touching. Underground piping under the road connecting the two properties does not make the properties contiguous. Also in 1983 the first property was not part of Mr. Flanagan's principal residence since he no longer owned it. In any event at no time in 1983 was a housing unit owned by the appellant resting on the second property. The second property was not part of Flanagan's principal residence in 1983.

The appeal for 1982 will be allowed with costs, if any; the appeal for 1983 will be dismissed.

Appeals allowed in part.

NOTES AND QUESTIONS

1.   How does the court in *Flanagan* define the words "housing unit" for the purpose of the definition of "principal residence" in section 54 of the Act? Do you agree with the court's interpretation? Why or why not? Of the three types of shelter used by the taxpayer in *Flanagan*, which does the court characterize as a housing unit? Based on the court's interpretation, which of the following, if any, would qualify as a "housing unit": (i) a tent; (ii) a lean-to; (iii) a burrow or cave?

2.   Of what, if any relevance, to the court's interpretation of the words "housing unit" in *Flanagan*, is the revenue authority's administrative position expressed in paragraph 5 of Interpretation Bulletin IT-120R3, "Principal Residence," June 13, 1983? What, if any role, should these interpretation bulletins play in the interpretation of statutory provisions?

The CRA's current views on the kinds of property that are eligible for the principal residence exemption appear in Interpretation Bulletin IT-120R6, "Principal Residence," July 17, 2003. According to paragraph 3 of this bulletin:

> 3. The following are the types of property that can qualify as a "principal residence":
>
> - a housing unit, which includes:
>   - a house,
>   - an apartment or unit in a duplex, apartment building or condominium,
>   - a cottage,
>   - a mobile home,
>   - a trailer, or
>   - a houseboat;
> - a leasehold interest in a housing unit; or
> - a share of the capital stock of a co-operative housing corporation, if such share is acquired for the sole purpose of obtaining the right to inhabit a housing unit owned by that corporation. The term "co-operative housing corporation" means an association, incorporated subject to the terms and conditions of the legislation governing such incorporation, and formed and operated for the purpose of providing its members with the right to inhabit, by reason of ownership of shares therein, a housing unit owned by the corporation.
>
> Land on which a housing unit is situated can qualify as part of a principal residence, subject to certain restrictions.

3.   On what basis does the Minister argue in *Flanagan* that the taxpayer did not "ordinarily inhabit" the Shuswap property? Why does the court reject this argument? Of what, if any relevance, to the court's interpretation of the words

"ordinarily inhabited" is the revenue authority's administrative position expressed in paragraph 9 of IT-120R3? Do you agree with the court's interpretation? Why or why not?

The CRA's current views on the meaning of the words "ordinarily inhabited" for the purpose of the principal residence exemption appear in IT-120R6. According to paragraph 5:

> The question of whether a housing unit is ordinarily inhabited in the year by a person must be resolved on the basis of the facts in each particular case. Even if a person inhabits a housing unit only for a short period of time in the year, this is sufficient for the housing unit to be considered "ordinarily inhabited in the year" by that person. For example, even if a person disposes of his or her residence early in the year or acquires it late in the year, the housing unit can be considered to be ordinarily inhabited in the year by that person by virtue of his or her living in it in the year before such sale or after such acquisition, as the case may be. Or, for example, a seasonal residence can be considered to be ordinarily inhabited in the year by a person who occupies it only during his or her vacation, provided that the main reason for owning the property is not to gain or produce income. With regard to the latter stipulation, a person receiving only incidental rental income from a seasonal residence is not considered to own the property mainly for the purpose of gaining or producing income.

As a result, as paragraph 40 explains:

> A property that is located outside Canada can, depending on the facts of the case, qualify as a taxpayer's principal residence. ... A taxpayer that is resident in Canada and owns such a qualifying property outside Canada during a particular taxation year can designate the property as a principal residence for that year in order to use the principal residence exemption.

4.   In *Ennist v. M.N.R.*, [1985] 2 C.T.C. 2398, 85 D.T.C. 669 (T.C.C.), the taxpayers (husband and wife) entered into an agreement on September 17, 1980 to acquire a condominium in a building scheduled to be completed in May 1981, paying a deposit of $5,000. In December 1980, the taxpayer husband was offered a job in Ottawa, which he accepted and commenced in March 1981. When the condominium unit was finally ready for occupancy at the end of June 1981, the taxpayers took possession but sold the condominium two weeks later, deriving a capital gain of $33,363 against which they claimed the principal residence exemption. Rejecting the taxpayers' argument (at para. 16) that they had "ordinarily inhabited" the condominium by staying there for one night, the court concluded that the property was not a principal residence. According to Taylor TCJ (at para. 11):

> One of the cases cited by counsel for the respondent was that of *Ernest Neufeld v. M.N.R.*, [1981] CTC 2010, 81 DTC 18, in which the word "ordinarily" was examined. Therein the phrase "in most cases, usually, or commonly" seemed to suit as a definition in large measure. I have grave doubts that spending 24 hours in the condominium unit, in the circumstances of this appeal, would fulfill this condition and indeed the Minister's assessment could well be supported on that basis. Mr Ennist called upon the recent case of *Stubart Investments Ltd. v. The Queen*, [1984] CTC 294, 84 DTC 6305, as support for that which he readily admitted was an attempt in the "24-hour stay" to fulfill the "technical" wording of the Act, in that — (according to Mr. Ennist) — if the purpose of the 24-hour stay was only to escape tax (his interpretation of *Stubart* (supra)), that should not be used to deny him the deduction. I refrain from any comment on the accuracy or adequacy of Mr. Ennist's interpretation of the *Stubart* (supra) judgment. I do not feel required to examine *Stubart* (supra) to question the "ordinary"

part of "ordinarily inhabited," since I am not viewing that question based on a legal technicality, but I am examining it simply on a definition of the word. Further, if the lack of fulfillment of "ordinary" were not enough, these appellants face a greater challenge in the word "inhabit." I am not certain that one can view the word "inhabit" as totally synonymous with "visit" or even "occupy." In a definition of "inhabit" from the *Oxford English Dictionary* one finds — "to dwell in, *occupy* as an abode, to live permanently in ..." [emphasis mine]. And for the word occupy: — "to take possession of, take for one's own use, seize ..." I would be reluctant to reject the appellants' claim on this part of the appeal based solely on a very fine distinction one might see between the word "occupy" and "inhabit" — but I would suggest that whatever variation may exist, in terms of stability or continuity, the edge must go to "inhabit." However, when one combines the two critical words in the phrase "ordinarily inhabited," and puts forward as a definition the expression "in most cases, usually or commonly occupied as an abode" (a combination of the definitions provided above), I am quite prepared to say that the "24-hour stay" did not fill that requirement.

5.   In *Jukic v. Canada*, [1994] T.C.J. No. 173, [1994] 1 C.T.C. 2630 (T.C.C.), the taxpayer, who built and sold two houses and bought and sold a third between 1985 and 1989, claimed the principal residence exemption on gains from each sale on the grounds that in each case he and his wife had inhabited the residences while promoting and awaiting their sale. Accepting the Minister's argument that the properties were purchased or constructed primarily for the purpose of resale, the court dismissed the taxpayer's appeal. According to Taylor TCJ (at para. 3):

> the Court finally decided during the hearing that this pattern of conduct regarding the acquisition and disposition of properties had left him with business assets, not personal residences during this time. The Minister's contention that a major motivation was the possibility of turning a profit on the transaction was upheld. Despite the fact that he had "inhabited" the properties in question, the Court was not convinced that it could be said he had "ordinarily inhabited" them as would be required for the classification of "principal residence." His occupation of the properties appeared to be on an interim basis while promoting and awaiting a sale. The determination — that the properties in question were not "principal residences" eliminated any need to consider the gains as even on "capital account" — they were business assets as inventory for sale. The profit from the sales was on income account.

For similar results, in which taxpayers who have inhabited a residence have been denied the principal residence exemption on the grounds that they engaged in an adventure or concern in the nature of trade or carried a business of constructing or buying and selling houses, see *Hollo v. M.N.R.*, [1978] C.T.C. 2617, 78 D.T.C. 1450 (T.R.B.) where a gain from property acquired in May 15, 1974, occupied by the taxpayer during the summer of 1974, listed for sale in August 1974, and sold in October 1974, was characterized as business income from an adventure or concern in the nature of trade; *Gavrilovic v. Canada*, [1996] T.C.J. No. 1187, [1997] 1 C.T.C. 2096 (T.C.C.) in which gains from three residences bought and sold by a taxpayer between 1980 and 1994 characterized as income from the taxpayer's business of building and selling homes; and *Fournier v. Canada*, [1996] T.C.J. No. 1543, [1998] 2 C.T.C. 2001 (T.C.C.) where gains from the sale of the fourth of five homes built and sold by the taxpayers between 1983 and 1991, characterized as income from the taxpayers' residential construction company on the grounds that the residence, though more luxurious than the other homes built by the taxpayers, had no unique characteristics suggesting an intent to retain the property rather than sell it at a profit "as soon as the occasion arose."

For a contrary result, in which taxpayers bought and sold three residences on the same street between 1980 and 1988, see *Falk v. M.N.R.*, [1991] T.C.J. No. 918, [1991] 2 C.T.C. 2665, 91 D.T.C. 1445 (T.C.C.). Although acknowledging that "the house transactions, objectively, did portray a trading activity," the court allowed the taxpayer's appeal from an assessment disallowing the principal residence exemption on the grounds (at para. 6) that:

— neither [of the] appellants were [sic] sophisticated individuals with experience in the real estate industry, directly or indirectly;

— family needs and occupation was a primary operative motivation throughout;

— 261 Dadson Row was too small and full of their own construction errors which made it undesirable for the young family;

— 262 Dadson Row was a more desirable family home both as to situs and size; many personal custom features and colours were incorporated; an offer to buy during construction was refused; no record of costs were kept except those turned over to the Royal Bank for loan draw-downs; financing was not abnormal; sale effort was not aggressive or businesslike and was necessitated by external factors;

— 259 Dadson Row was smaller and cheaper, and was sold because of external factors [financial difficulties].

For these reasons, Kempo TCJ concluded (at para. 10) that "these series of transactions were principal residence use orientated, with acceptable explanations being given for all the sales" and that "no secondary motivations were at play."

6.   In *Johnstone v. M.N.R.*, [1987] F.C.J. No. 1106, [1988] 1 C.T.C. 48, (1987) 88 D.T.C. 6032 (F.C.T.D.), the taxpayer acquired a residential property in Vancouver in March 1979, sought approval to subdivide the property in May 1979, obtained approval to construct a duplex condominium in May 1980, sold one of the condominium units in March 1981, and moved into the other unit in May 1981. Rejecting the taxpayer's argument that a gain of almost $300,000 on the sale of the adjoining condominium unit was exempt under paragraph 40(2)(b) of the Act, the court observed that the taxpayer had never resided at the property when the unit was sold and concluded (at para. 10) that the taxpayer had acquired the property "with the intention of soon selling a half-interest in it in order to earn a monetary gain." As a result, the gain was fully taxable as business income from an adventure or concern in the nature of trade.

7.   In *Canada v. Mitosinka*, [1978] F.C.J. No. 809, [1978] C.T.C. 664, 78 D.T.C. 6432 (F.C.T.D.), the taxpayer owned a house with a common basement but divided in the middle to form a side-by-side duplex, living in one side with his family, while the other side was occupied by his parents until their death and afterward by tenants. Disallowing the principal residence exemption on the

whole of the building when the taxpayer sold it in 1973, the court concluded that the portion of the building inhabited by the taxpayer's parents and tenants was a separate "housing unit," which was not "ordinarily inhabited" by the taxpayer, his spouse, or his children.

For a contrasting result, see *Saccomanno v. M.N.R.*, [1986] 2 C.T.C. 2269, 86 D.T.C. 1699 (T.C.C.), where the taxpayer, who purchased a house in Toronto in 1979, divided it into three separate units, and resided in one of the units with his wife while renting out the other two, claimed the principal residence exemption on the entire property when it was sold in 1983. Observing (at para. 5) that the property "was originally built as a single family, self-contained dwelling, and prior to the acquisition by the taxpayer had been divided up, in a very informal way, to permit dwelling therein by three families," and concluding (at para. 5) that the prospect of "undoing the 'three-residence' accommodations which had been put together, and making the entire building into a single unit for himself and his wife" was "the main reason that he had purchased the property," the court allowed the taxpayer's appeal from an assessment limiting the exemption to one-third of the taxpayer's gain. According to Taylor TCJ (at para. 5):

> The problem in this appeal comes down to whether in the circumstances, the entire property could be and should be considered as the "principal residence" (the position now adopted by the taxpayer) or whether only that portion (approximately one-third) regularly and continuously occupied by the appellant's wife and ... the appellant. As I see it, either situation could be valid — depending on the circumstances and the perspective from which it is viewed. Clearly a taxpayer could acquire a property — primarily as a rental property — and use a portion thereof for a personal residence. That is the view taken by the Minister in this assessment. But I can think of no valid objection to a taxpayer doing exactly the opposite — buying a property for his own use, as a principal residence, and renting out a part of it. ...
>
> The essence of the Minister's assessment must be that he is considering the property as containing three separate "housing units."... That is as if this taxpayer had purchased a block of three "townhouses," which happened to have certain common physical elements, such as walls, but were nevertheless distinctly separate — and then rented two, and lived in one. I do not think that is a reasonable interpretation of the circumstances in this matter. In effect the Minister is saying that it would have been necessary for Mr. Saccomanno to physically and "ordinarily" inhabit each room in the building, in order that the entire building could qualify as his principal residence. That line of reasoning, if applicable, would mean that a taxpayer owning and inhabiting a single family home (a housing unit) who rented out one room, thereby gaining rental income, would risk having that part of the home declared as outside the principal residence category.
>
> As I perceive this situation, the entire house was a "housing unit," not three separate "housing units."... That a portion of it was rented has been explained satisfactorily to the Court, and does not appear to detract from its character as a "principal residence" under the circumstances of this appeal. I can find no basis in the legislation for the Minister's assessing the taxpayer in a divided interest manner — part principal residence and part not principal residence. The sections of the Act dealing with either "personal-use property" or "change in use" do not appear to me to adversely affect this taxpayer's claim.

Do you agree with this conclusion? Why or why not? Should the principal residence exemption apply to a portion of a residential property that is used for the purpose of gaining or producing income? Is the court's reasoning consistent with the allocation rule in paragraph 45(1)(b) of the Act?

8.   According to Interpretation Bulletin IT-120R6, paragraph 32, where a residential property is used partly as a principal residence and partly to earn income from a business or property, the CRA considers "the entire property" to be a principal residence "where all of the following conditions are met":

  (a)   the income-producing use is ancillary to the main use of the property as a residence,

  (b)   there is no structural change to the property, and

  (c)   no CCA is claimed on the property.

The Interpretation Bulletin further explains that:

> These conditions can be met, for example, where a taxpayer carries on a business of caring for children in his or her home, rents one or more rooms in the home, or has an office or other work space in the home which is used in connection with his or her business or employment. In these and similar cases, the taxpayer reports the income and may claim the expenses (other than CCA) pertaining to the portion of the property used for income-producing purposes.

9.   Among the other requirements that a taxpayer must satisfy in order to claim the principal residence exemption for a particular taxation year, is that the taxpayer must own the property in the year. For a detailed discussion of the circumstances in which a taxpayer will be considered to have owned a principal residence in a particular taxation year, see Interpretation Bulletin IT-437R, "Ownership of Property (Principal Residence)," February 21, 1994.

10.   On what basis did the Minister argue in *Flanagan* that the taxpayer's principal residence was limited to the van or trailer and did not include any land? Why does the court reject his argument? Do you agree with the court's interpretation? Why or why not? Why does the court distinguish between the "first property" acquired by the taxpayer from his mother in January 1973, and the "second property" acquired in 1978? Do you agree with the court's conclusion that the "second property" was not eligible for the principal residence exemption? Why or why not?

b. Surrounding Land

Where a property qualifies as a principal residence under the definition in section 54 of the Act, paragraph (e) of this definition stipulates that, except where the property is a share of the capital stock of a cooperative housing corporation, the principal residence is deemed to include:

> land subjacent to the housing unit and such portion of any immediately contiguous land as can reasonably be regarded as contributing to the use and enjoyment of the housing unit as a residence.

Where the total area of the subjacent land and the portion that can reasonably be regarded as contributing to the use and enjoyment of the housing unit as a residence exceeds ½ hectare (5,000 square metres or approximately 1.24 acres), however, paragraph (e) further states that:

the excess shall be deemed not to have contributed to the use and enjoyment of the housing unit as a residence unless the taxpayer establishes that it was necessary to such use and enjoyment.

For taxation years before 1982, the ½ hectare threshold was stipulated as being one acre.

Perhaps not surprisingly, the interpretation of this language has generated a substantial body of jurisprudence. Among the leading cases is the trial decision in *Canada v. Yates*, [1983] F.C.J. No. 211, [1983] C.T.C. 105, 83 D.T.C. 5158 (F.C.T.D.), which was affirmed without further comment by the Federal Court of Appeal, [1986] F.C.J. No. 927, [1986] 2 C.T.C. 46, 86 D.T.C. 6296.

Canada v. Yates
[1983] F.C.J. No. 211, [1983] C.T.C. 105, 83 D.T.C. 5158 (F.C.T.D.), aff'd
[1986] F.C.J. No. 927, [1986] 2 C.T.C. 46, 86 D.T.C. 6296 (F.C.A.)

MAHONEY J: ... The defendants acquired a ten acre parcel of vacant land near Guelph on which, in 1964, they built their home. Ten acres was the minimum residential parcel then permitted by the zoning. The zoning bylaw was subsequently amended to require a 25 acre minimum. The defendants continued to reside there as legal non-conforming users.

When they bought, the defendants did not want ten acres; they wanted only enough land for their residence but had to buy at least ten acres. They did not use more than an acre for residential purposes. The balance was rented to a neighbouring farmer who grew crops on it.

In 1978, the defendants sold 9.3 acres to the City of Guelph under threat of expropriation. The 9.3 acres did not include the residence. The defendants continued to reside on the remaining 0.7 acre plus an adjacent 0.225 acre transferred to them by the City as part of the consideration for the 9.3 acres.

The issue is whether the disposition of the 9.3 acres was a disposition of a principal residence. It was not argued that, by its very nature, a principal residence cannot be subject of a partial disposition. If the disposition of the 9.3 acres was a disposition of a principal residence, the capital gain thereon is exempted from tax by paragraph 40(2)(b) of the *Income Tax Act*.

...

In my opinion, the critical time is the moment before disposition. It is possible that a subjective test, involving the actual contribution of the immediately contiguous land to the taxpayer's use and enjoyment of the unit as a residence, may be admissible. ... However, whether or not a subjective test is properly to be applied, an objective test surely is and if, in its application, it is found that the taxpayer has discharged the onus on him, it is unnecessary to consider the subjective.

The defendants could not legally have occupied their housing unit as a residence on less than ten acres. It follows that the entire ten acres, subjacent and contiguous, not only "may reasonably" be regarded as contributing to their use and enjoyment of their housing unit as a residence; it must be so regarded. It also follows that the portion in excess of one acre was necessary to that use and enjoyment.

The disposition in issue was a disposition of a principal residence. ...

Appeal allowed.

NOTES AND QUESTIONS

1.   On what grounds did the Federal Court Trial Division conclude in *Yates* that the 9.3 acres that the taxpayers sold to the city of Guelph under threat of expropriation was "necessary" to their "use and enjoyment of the housing unit as a residence"? Do you agree with the court's conclusion? Of what, if any, significance to the question at issue in *Yates* is the fact that the taxpayers used no more than one acre of the property for residential purposes and rented out the remainder to a farmer who grew crops on the land? Might this suggest that the remainder was *not* necessary to the taxpayers' "use and enjoyment of the housing unit as a residence"? To what extent, if at all, should the statutory test depend on subjective factors that are personal to the taxpayer?

In *Rode v. M.N.R.*, [1985] 1 C.T.C. 2324, 85 D.T.C. 272 (T.C.C.), the taxpayers, who realized a gain on the sale of a 9.3 acre parcel of property in 1977, argued that the entire property was necessary to their use and enjoyment of their residence on the grounds that they preferred "seclusion and self-sufficiency in the production of their food to the extent feasible." Upholding the Minister's assessment, the court concluded that the taxpayers' "mode of existence" did not render the additional land necessary to the use and enjoyment of the taxpayers' housing unit as a residence. This seems to be a consistent finding, with courts in a number of other cases rejecting taxpayers' arguments that land exceeding the statutory threshold was necessary to the use or enjoyment of their residence on account of subjective factors. See, for example, *Madsen v. M.N.R.*, [1980] C.T.C. 3022, 81 D.T.C. 1 (T.R.B.); *Fraser v. M.N.R.*, [1983] C.T.C. 2522, 83 D.T.C. 448 (T.C.C.); *Cox v. M.N.R.*, [1985] 1 C.T.C. 2392, 85 D.T.C. 320 (T.C.C.); and *Todesco v. Canada*, [1999] T.C.J. No. 665, [2000] 1 C.T.C. 2144, (1999) 99 D.T.C. 1219 (T.C.C.).

2.   In your view, to what extent, if at all, should access to the principal residence exemption turn on what is possible or not possible according to various local zoning requirements? There is conflicting authority in the case law as to the relevance of zoning demands.

In *Watson v. M.N.R.*, [1985] 1 C.T.C. 2276, 85 D.T.C. 270 (T.C.C.), the taxpayers sought to apply the principal residence exemption to the whole of a 25 acre property when it was expropriated in 1978 for the purposes of a proposed airport. Notwithstanding the fact that it was impossible to sell the house and a strip of land required for the driveway without selling the entire parcel, the court upheld the Minister's assessment limiting the exemption to the gain on the residence and two acres of land on the basis that, "consideration as to what can lawfully and effectively be conveyed [is] irrelevant" because "the amount of land which contributes to the use and enjoyment of a housing unit is not" ... "made to depend on what can lawfully be bought and sold." For a similar result, see *Lewis Estate v. M.N.R.*, [1989] T.C.J. No. 410, [1989] 2 C.T.C. 2060, 89 D.T.C. 316 (T.C.C.), in which the court rejected the taxpayer's argument that 2.11 acres surrounding the taxpayer's residence were necessary to its use and enjoyment on the basis that the property could not be subdivided at any time prior to its sale in 1981.

For an opposing result, see *Michael v. M.N.R.*, [1985] 2 C.T.C. 2122, 85 D.T.C. 455 (T.C.C.), in which the court concluded that a 9.18 acre parcel of land was necessary to the use and enjoyment of the taxpayer's residence because a local zoning bylaw made it impossible to sever the property.

In *Augart v. M.N.R.*, [1993] F.C.J. No. 498, [1993] 2 C.T.C. 34, 93 D.T.C. 5205 (F.C.A.), the Federal Court of Appeal opined on the relevance of shifting zoning requirements. The taxpayer had acquired a home on 8.99 acres of land on the outskirts of Calgary in 1966, at a time when local bylaws required a minimum area of three acres for a residence and prohibited subdivisions of land parcels of less than 10 acres in size. On March 3, 1980, the minimum area for a residence was increased to 80 acres, with an exemption for existing properties that did not conform to the new bylaw. The taxpayer later sold the whole 8.99 acres to the city of Calgary, realizing a substantial capital gain in respect of which he claimed the principal residence exemption. In allowing the full gain on the sale of the property to qualify for the principal residence exemption, a majority of the Federal Court of Appeal held that the 1980 bylaw change made the old minimum area for residential occupation irrelevant at the time of the sale, and rejected the Minister's argument that subdivision restrictions are irrelevant to the characterization of surrounding land as part of a principal residence. See also, *Carlile v. Canada*, [1995] F.C.J. No. 1059, [1995] 2 C.T.C. 273, 95 D.T.C. 5483 (F.C.A.), and *Stuart Estate v. Canada*, [2004] F.C.J. No. 401, [2004] D.T.C. 6173 (F.C.A.), where the Federal Court of Appeal has reiterated that zoning requirements are relevant to a determination of how much land is necessary to the use and enjoyment of a housing unit as a principal residence.

3. Do you agree with the court's statement in *Yates* that "the critical time" to determine whether surrounding land is necessary to the use and enjoyment of a housing unit as a principal residence is "the moment before disposition"? Is this approach consistent with the structure of the principal residence exemption, which depends on the number of years during which the taxpayer owned the property that it qualified as a principal residence?

4. For the CRA's views on the extent to which surrounding land qualifies for the principal residence exemption, see Interpretation Bulletin IT-120R6, paragraphs 14-17:

Land Contributing to the Use and Enjoyment of the Housing Unit as a Residence

14. By virtue of paragraph (e) of the section 54 definition of "principal residence", a taxpayer's principal residence for a taxation year shall be deemed to include, except where the property consists of a share of the capital stock of a co-operative housing corporation, the land upon which the housing unit stands and any portion of the adjoining land that can reasonably be regarded as contributing to the use and enjoyment of the housing unit as a residence. Evidence is not usually required to establish that one-half hectare of land or less, including the area on which the housing unit stands, contributes to the use and enjoyment of the housing unit as a residence. However, where a portion of that land is used to earn income from business or property, such portion will not usually be considered to contribute to such use and enjoyment. Where the taxpayer claims a portion of the expenses related to the land (such as property taxes or mortgage interest) in computing income, the allocation of such expenses for this purpose is normally an indication of the extent to which he or she considers the land to be used to earn income.

Land in Excess of One-Half Hectare

15. Where the total area of the land upon which a housing unit is situated exceeds one-half hectare, the excess land is deemed by paragraph (e) of the section 54 definition of "principal residence" not to have contributed to the use and enjoyment of the housing unit as a residence and thus will not qualify as part of a principal residence, except to the extent that the taxpayer establishes that it was necessary for such use and enjoyment. The excess land must clearly be necessary for the housing unit to properly fulfill its function as a residence and not simply be desirable. Generally, the use of land in excess of one-half hectare in connection with a particular recreation or lifestyle (such as for keeping pets or for country living) does not mean that the excess land is necessary for the use and enjoyment of the housing unit as a residence. Land in excess of one-half hectare may be considered necessary where the size or character of a housing unit together with its location on the lot make such excess land essential to its use and enjoyment as a residence, or where the location of a housing unit requires such excess land in order to provide its occupants with access to and from public roads. Other factors may be relevant in determining whether land in excess of one-half hectare is necessary for the use and enjoyment of the housing unit as a residence, such as, for example, a minimum lot size or a severance or subdivision restriction (see ¶ 16). In all cases, however, it is a question of fact as to how much, if any, of the excess land is necessary for the use and enjoyment of the housing unit as a residence.

16. In order to acquire a property for use as a residence, a taxpayer may be required by a law or regulation of a municipality or province with respect to residential lots to acquire more than one-half hectare of the property. Such a law or regulation could, for example,

(a) require a minimum lot size for a residential lot in a particular area, or

(b) impose a severance or subdivision restriction with respect to residential lots in a particular area.

To the extent that a taxpayer, in order to acquire a property as a residence, is required because of such a law or regulation to acquire land that exceeds one-half hectare, the land that must be so acquired is generally considered to be necessary for the use and enjoyment of the housing unit as a residence throughout the period that the property is continuously owned by the taxpayer after the acquisition date. However, it should be noted that the mere existence of such a municipal law or regulation on the date the taxpayer acquired the property does not immediately qualify the excess land for purposes of the principal residence exemption. For example, if the taxpayer could have made an application for severance of the excess land and it is likely that such a request would have been approved, the taxpayer would generally not be considered to have been required to acquire the excess land. Furthermore, regardless of the above, where any portion of the land in excess of one-half hectare is not used for residential purposes but rather for income-producing purposes, such portion is usually not considered to be necessary for the use and enjoyment of the housing unit as a residence.

Disposition of Bare Land in Excess of One-Half Hectare

17. If the housing unit is situated on land in excess of one-half hectare and part or all of that excess land is severed from the property and sold, the land sold is generally considered not to be part of the principal residence unless the housing unit can no longer be used as a residence due to the land sale. If the housing unit can still be so used, such a sale indicates that the land sold was not necessary for the use and enjoyment of the housing unit as a residence. Circumstances or events beyond the taxpayer's control may cause a portion of the land to cease to be necessary for the use and enjoyment of the housing unit as a residence (e.g., a minimum lot size requirement or severance or subdivision restriction in effect at the date of acquisition is subsequently relaxed). If the taxpayer then subdivides the excess land, it will be considered to have been "necessary" until the time of its subdivision. After subdivision, each newly created lot is a separate property and only the property on which the housing unit is located may continue to be designated as the taxpayer's principal residence. Furthermore, it is possible for the vacant land which previously formed part of the principal residence to be considered to have been converted to inventory at the time of the subdivision.

c. Designation

In addition to the other requirements for a property to qualify as a taxpayer's principal residence, paragraphs (c) and (c.1) of the definition in section 54 require the taxpayer to designate the property "in prescribed form and manner" as the taxpayer's principal residence for the year, and disqualify the property as a principal residence where another property was designated as a principal residence for the year by the taxpayer, the taxpayer's spouse or common law partner, a child of the taxpayer who is under the age of 18 and neither married nor in a common law partnership, or (where the taxpayer was under the age of 18 and not married) by the taxpayer's mother or father or by brother or sister under the age of 18 who is neither married nor in a common law partnership.[67] As a result, as the CRA explains, for a property to be a taxpayer's principal residence for a particular taxation year, "no other property may have been designated as the principal residence of any member of the taxpayer's family unit for the year."[68]

According to section 2301 of the *Income Tax Regulations*, the designation that is required in order for a property to qualify as a principal residence need not be made every year in which the property is so designated, but "shall be made" with the taxpayer's tax return for any taxation year in which the taxpayer "has disposed of a property that is to be designated" as a principal residence, or "has granted an option to acquire such property." For this purpose, individuals may file form T2091, while trusts may file form T1079. As an administrative

---

[67] For taxation years before 1982, this disqualification applied only where the taxpayer designated another property as a principal residence, enabling each member of a family unit to designate a separate property as a principal residence any gain from which would be exempt from tax.

[68] Interpretation Bulletin IT-120R6, para. 6.

practice, however, the CRA does not require taxpayers to file a specific designation unless "a taxable capital gain on the disposition of the property remains after using the principal residence exemption formula."[69] In this circumstance, the CRA explains, the taxpayer "is still considered to have designated the property as his or her principal residence (that is, to have claimed the principal residence exemption for that property) for the years in question" — making it impossible to designate another property as the taxpayer's principal residence for those years.

The ability to designate different properties as a principal residence combined with the liberal interpretation of the "ordinarily inhabited" requirement creates an opportunity for taxpayers with more than one eligible property to choose the property designated as a principal residence in order to maximize the value of the exemption. As a general rule, this is accomplished by designating as the taxpayer's principal residence the property for which the average gain per year is greatest, subject to the use of the "one plus" aspect of the formula to maximize the number of years for which an exemption is available. The following example appears in Peter W. Hogg, Joanne E. Magee, and Jinyan Li, *Principles of Canadian Income Tax Law*, 5th ed. (Toronto: Carswell, 2005) at 323-24:

Example

A house was purchased by T in 1995 for $100,000, was ordinarily inhabited by T, and was sold in 1999 for $150,000.

A cottage was purchased by T in 1996 for $80,000, was ordinarily inhabited by T, and was sold in 1999 for $140,000.

A ski chalet was purchased by T in 1997 for $120,000, was ordinarily inhabited by T, and was sold in 1999 for $140,000.

In this example, T has sold three properties in 1999, and each of them is eligible for the principal residence designation. Only one can be designated each year. Which should be selected? Naturally, the principal residence designation should be used to minimize the capital gain that has to be reported by the taxpayer. This achieved by making a principal residence designation on the residence(s) with the biggest gain per year and by taking advantage of the "one plus" rule (which requires that you must designate a year to get the "one plus").

There is room for some variation in the actual calendar years designated for each property (although the property must be owned in the year of designation). One possible allocation would look like this:

	House	Cottage	Ski Chalet
Gain Otherwise Determined (1)	$50,000	$60,000	$20,000
Years Owned	5 (2001-2005)	4 (2002-2005)	3 (2003-2005)
Gain per Year	$10,000	$15,000	$6,667

---

[69] *Ibid.*

Years Designated	1 (2001)	3(2002-2005)	1 (2003)
Exemption (2)	$50,000 × (1 + 1)/5 = $20,000	$60,000 × (3 + 1)/4 = $60,000	$20,000 × (1 + 1)/3 = $13,333.33
Gain [(1)-(2)]	$30,000	$0	$6,666.67

Although taxpayers are generally unlikely to dispose of all residences in the same taxation year, subsection 70(5) deems taxpayers to have disposed of all capital property immediately before death, making the designation of a principal residence among different properties an important aspect of *ex post* tax planning for estates. In other cases where taxpayers own different properties that they or their family members "ordinarily inhabit," the designation of a property as a principal residence on the disposition of one property depends not only on the average gain per year of different properties and the potential use of the "one plus" aspect of the formula, but also on the time value of money and expectations regarding future changes in the value of any eligible property retained by the taxpayer. As Hogg et al. explain (at 324):

> If, for example, the ski chalet was not sold in 2005, and T had no intention of selling it in the near future, then the eventual gain on the property would be uncertain (it might even fall in value). Even if the property were likely to increase in value, the time value of money would diminish the value of any tax savings to be derived many years hence from the designation of the ski chalet, which has the lowest gain per year. On these facts, it might be better not to save a year of designation for the ski chalet, and to obtain the immediate tax saving that would be derived by designating the house for a second year.

C. Recognition and Non-Recognition Rules

The general and special rules governing the computation of a capital gain or loss depend on the existence of a "disposition," which triggers the recognition of accrued gains or losses for tax purposes. While a sale of property for valuable consideration is the most common kind of disposition, the statutory definition in subsection 248(1) of the Act includes various other kinds of transactions discussed earlier in this chapter. In addition to these rules, moreover, the Act contains other rules that either require taxpayers to recognize gains or losses in the absence of an actual disposition by deeming them to have disposed of capital property under specific circumstances, or defer the recognition of gains or losses from actual dispositions by deeming capital property to have been disposed of in other circumstances for proceeds equal to its adjusted cost base and "rolling over" this amount to the same property in the hand of another taxpayer and/or to other capital property in the hands of the first taxpayer by deeming this property to have been acquired at the same adjusted cost base. The following text and cases consider these recognition and non-recognition rules, examining key rules deeming taxpayers to have disposed of capital property under specific circumstances, important "rollover" rules permitting or requiring the deferral of gains or losses on actual dispositions of capital property, and "stop-loss" rules prohibiting the realization of losses under specific circumstances.

1. Deemed Dispositions

The *Income Tax Act* contains several rules deeming taxpayers to have disposed of various kinds of property in circumstances where no actual disposition has occurred. Where a taxpayer grants an option to acquire or dispose of a capital property, for example, subsection 49(1) of the Act generally deems the taxpayer to have disposed of "a property the adjusted cost base of which to the grantor immediately before the grant is nil" — the effect of which is to require the taxpayer to include any consideration received for the option as a capital gain for the year in which the option is issued.[70] Where a taxpayer holds capital property that is a bad debt or a share of a bankrupt company, subsection 50(1) allows the taxpayer to file an election pursuant to which the property is deemed to have been disposed of at the end of the year for proceeds equal to nil and to have been reacquired immediately thereafter at a cost equal to nil — thereby triggering a capital loss and requiring any amount that is subsequently recovered in respect of the property to be included as a capital gain in that taxation year. Where a taxpayer becomes resident or ceases to be resident in Canada, section 128.1 deems the taxpayer to have disposed of various kinds of property at that time for proceeds equal to their fair market value and to have reacquired this property at the same time at a cost equal to this fair market value — the effect of which is to exclude from Canadian tax gains and losses that have accrued before Canadian residency and to render a final account for gains and losses that have accrued while the taxpayer was a Canadian resident. Where a trust holds capital property, moreover, subsection 104(4) prevents the extended deferral of capital gains and losses by deeming the trust to have disposed of all of its capital property for proceeds of disposition equal to the fair market value of this property and to have immediately thereafter reacquired this property at a cost equal to these deemed proceeds every 21 years.[71]

For our purposes, there is no need to examine these rules in detail, as subsections 49(1) and 50(1) apply in highly specific circumstances, and section 128.1 and subsection 104(4) are best examined in courses on international taxation or the taxation of estates and trusts. In addition to these provisions,

---

[70] Where an option to acquire property (a "call option") is ultimately exercised by the party that has acquired the option, subs. 49(3) retroactively deems the granting of the option not to be a disposition of property, and adds the amount paid for the option to the vendor's proceeds of disposition and the purchaser's adjusted cost base. Where an option to dispose of property (a "put option") is exercised by a taxpayer who has paid valuable consideration for this option, subs. 49(3.1) also retroactively deems the granting of the option not to have been a disposition of property, and deducts the amount paid for the option in computing the vendor's proceeds of disposition and the vendor's cost of the property. For the purpose of these provisions, subs. 49(4) permits a retroactive adjustment of the grantor's tax return for the year in which the option was granted.

[71] This basic rule is subject to a number of exceptions which need not be considered here. For a brief explanation of these rules see Peter W. Hogg, Joanne E. Magee, and Jinyan Li, *Principles of Canadian Income Tax Law*, 5th ed. (Toronto: Carswell, 2005) at 469-70.

however, the Act contains two other recognition rules that merit closer attention: subsection 45(2), which deems taxpayers to have disposed of capital property where the purpose for which the property is used changes to or from an income-producing purpose, and subsection 70(5), which deems taxpayers to have disposed of each capital property immediately before their death.

a. Change in Use of Property

Where a taxpayer acquires property for the purpose of gaining or producing income and subsequently uses it for personal use or enjoyment, or vice versa, these changes in the use of the property can have significant tax implications. Although taxpayers can deduct the capital cost allowance (CCA) for depreciable property that is acquired for the purpose of gaining or producing income, for example, they cannot claim CCA for property that is acquired for personal use or enjoyment.[72] As well, while losses on the disposition of capital property acquired and used for the purpose of gaining or producing income are generally deductible in computing net taxable capital gains, losses on the disposition of personal-use property are generally not recognized for tax purposes.[73]

In order to distinguish the tax consequences associated with the use of property for one purpose from the tax consequences associated with its use for another purpose, the Act contains special rules deeming taxpayers to have disposed of property for proceeds of disposition equal to the property's fair market value and to have immediately reacquired the property at a cost equal to that fair market value whenever the purpose for which the property's use changes to or from the purpose of gaining or producing income. According to paragraph 45(1)(a), for example, for the purpose of subdivision c:

where a taxpayer,

> (i) having acquired property for some other purpose, has commenced at a later time to use it for the purpose of gaining or producing income, or

> (ii) having acquired property for the purpose of gaining or producing income, has commenced at a later time to use it for some other purpose,

the taxpayer shall be deemed to have

> (iii) disposed of it at that later time for proceeds equal to its fair market value at that later time, and

> (iv) immediately thereafter reacquired it at a cost equal to that fair market value.

Similar rules governing depreciable property appear in paragraphs 13(7)(a) and (b) of the Act.[74] Notwithstanding these deeming rules, subsections 45(2) and

---

[72] See the discussion of capital cost allowances in Chapter 5.

[73] See the discussion of personal-use property earlier in this chapter.

[74] See the discussion of these rules in Chapter 5. In addition to these rules, paras. 45(1)(c) and 13(7)(d) deem taxpayers to have disposed of and reacquired property at its fair market value

(3) allow taxpayers to preclude the application of these deemed dispositions by filing an election in respect of the property along with the taxpayer's tax return for the taxation year in which the property would otherwise be deemed to have been disposed and reacquired.

According to subsection 45(2), notwithstanding that a taxpayer has acquired property for some other purpose (for example, personal use or enjoyment) and commenced to use the property for the purpose of gaining or producing income, the taxpayer shall be "deemed not to have begun to use the property for the purpose of gaining or producing income" where the taxpayer "so elects in respect of the property in the taxpayer's return of income for the year." Although this rule overrides the deemed dispositions otherwise mandated under subparagraph 45(1)(a)(i) and paragraph 13(7)(b), the rule also prohibits the taxpayer from deducting CCA and other business expenses with respect to the property, which is deemed not to be used for the purpose of gaining or producing income. For this reason, also, any loss that accrues after the change in use is disallowed on the basis that the taxpayer is deemed not to have changed the use of the property from a non-income-producing (that is, personal) use. Under the definition of "principal residence" in section 54, however, a residence subject to an election under subsection 45(2) of the Act may be designated as a principal residence for each of the four years after the election notwithstanding that it is not ordinarily inhabited by the taxpayer or a related person.[75] Finally, where the taxpayer rescinds the election in a subsequent year in the return of income for that year, subsection 45(2) deems the taxpayer to have begun to use the property for the purpose of gaining or producing income on the first day of that subsequent year, and the residence can no longer qualify as a principal residence under paragraph (b) of the definition of "principal residence" in section 54.

Like subsection 45(2), subsection 45(3) permits taxpayers to prevent a deemed disposition under subsection 45(1) by filing an election, but permits this election only where property that was acquired by a taxpayer for the purpose of gaining or producing income ceases to be used for that purpose and becomes the taxpayer's principal residence.[76] If the taxpayer has deducted CCA in respect of the property for any taxation year after 1984, however, subsection 45(4) deems the election under subsection 45(3) not to have been made, thereby triggering

---

when "there has been a change in the relation between the use regularly made by the taxpayer of the property for gaining or producing income and the use regularly made of the property for other purposes." For our purposes, there is no need to examine these rules in detail.

[75] See the discussion of the principal residence exemption earlier in this chapter.

[76] This provision was introduced in 1985, applicable to property used by a taxpayer as a principal residence after 1981. Before the introduction of this amendment, taxpayers were required to compute capital gains and pay tax on deemed dispositions arising from the conversion of a property from rental properly to a principal residence. See, for example, *Leib v. M.N.R.*, [1984] C.T.C. 2324, 84 D.T.C. 1302 (T.C.C.) and *Derlago v. M.N.R.*, [1988] F.C.J. No. 447, [1988] 2 C.T.C. 21, 88 D.T.C. 6290 (F.C.T.D.).

tax consequences on the change of use. Finally, where a residence is subject to an election under subsection 45(3), the property may be designated as a principal residence for each of the four taxation years preceding the election.[77]

Perhaps surprisingly, given the frequency with which taxpayers might be expected to convert personal-use property to property used for the purpose of gaining or producing income and vice versa, the change-of-use rules in section 45 have been subject to relatively little judicial analysis. One of the more notable of these cases is *Duthie Estate v. Canada*, [1995] F.C.J. No. 770, [1995] 2 C.T.C. 157, 95 D.T.C. 5376 (F.C.T.D.).

Duthie Estate v. Canada
[1995] F.C.J. No. 770, [1995] 2 C.T.C. 157, 95 D.T.C. 5376 (F.C.T.D.)

ROTHSTEIN J: ... The issues are whether a land development business had been commenced by George Duthie in 1981 and whether, in 1981, there had been a change in use of Duthie's land pursuant to paragraph 45(1)(a) of the *Income Tax Act*, RSC 1952, c. 148 (am. SC 1970-71-72, c. 63) (the "Act"), which would have had the effect of converting the land from a capital asset to inventory.

The plaintiff's position is that a land development business had commenced in 1981 and that expenditures of the business incurred in 1982, 1983 and 1984 were deductible as expenses by George Duthie. Plaintiff also asserts there had been a change in use of the land from capital to inventory in 1981. In 1984 when George Duthie died, there had been a decline in value of the land in question since 1981. If the land was inventory, the decline in value may be treated as a business loss and deducted from income for tax purposes by the plaintiff in 1984 and by Duthie by way of loss carrybacks in 1981, 1982 and 1983.

...

Duthie and his wife moved to Invermere in the East Kootenay district of British Columbia in the 1950s. Duthie's wife acquired approximately 8.5 acres of land on which they constructed their principal residence. Duthie's wife died in 1979 and the land (with the exception of a portion which had already been conveyed to Duthie in 1957) was conveyed to Duthie in his own right.

In 1979 and 1980 the village of Invermere was growing and the economies in British Columbia and Alberta were also growing. In early 1981, Duthie made a decision to actively consider the development of his land. Duthie and his four sons attended formal meetings at which minutes were kept and at which various ways to proceed were considered. Reports were received, decisions taken and tasks assigned.

In March 1981, Duthie retained the services of an architect to prepare a "highest and best use study" for the land. In early May, it appears Duthie and his

---

[77] See the discussion of the principal residence exemption earlier in this chapter.

sons were still considering whether to sell the land or develop it themselves. At a meeting on May 3, 1981, they decided to obtain a market analysis on which to base a "go, no-go" decision. A few days later, Duthie and his sons met with a project manager. Matters began to move rapidly at this point. I turn to the agreed statement of facts:

16. In or about the second week in May 1981, Dr. Duthie engaged Thomas Consultants Inc. to prepare a condominium study (the "Thomas report") in respect of the development of the property. ... In the course of their family meetings during the remainder of May 1981, various aspects of the development were discussed. The minutes of meetings of May 3 and May 18, 1991 are included at Exhibit 1. ...

17. The Thomas report was issued on June 19, 1981. The Thomas report recommended, *inter alia*, that Dr. Duthie pursue the development of a 120-unit condominium development on the property (the "project"). The report further recommended that Phase I, consisting of 35 units, commence immediately.

18. Dr. Duthie attached considerable importance to the Thomas report.

19. Dr. Duthie and Mr. Ian Thomas formed a personal relationship which led Dr. Duthie to put a great deal of reliance in Mr. Thomas' opinions.

20. In late June, 1981, at a meeting among Dr. Duthie, Mrs. Thora Duthie, two of George Duthie's sons and representatives of LeBlond Koch Partnership, a decision was made to hire a project manager. A shortlist of project managers was prepared. ... By letter dated July 21, 1981, the firm of Pacer Developments Ltd. ("Pacer") submitted a proposal for project management services ... and by letter dated August 10, 1981, Pacer submitted a draft agreement for development management services. ...

21. In late June 1981, at a meeting in the village of Invermere, BC attended by Dr. Duthie, Mrs. Thora Duthie, two of Dr. Duthie's sons and representatives of the LeBlond partnership, it was decided that the Thomas report would be adopted and the LeBlond partnership was instructed to prepare a master plan for the property and a concept plan for the units to be constructed thereon. ...

22. In mid-July 1981, a meeting was held in Calgary to review the preliminary design drawings of the project dated July 16, 1981. A decision was taken at that time to develop the project to its full potential and that the project could be built as funds allow. The minutes of the meeting are included at Exhibit 1. ...

23. Pacer prepared a preliminary development concept for the Duthie Condominium Project Invermere, BC dated August, 1981 ... and prepared an estimate sheet dated August 5, 1981 for the project. ... By letter dated August 10, 1981 and addressed to John Duthie of Duthie Developments Ltd., Pacer submitted two copies of a draft agreement for the development management services for the project and the proposed Logic Network. ...

24. A meeting was held on August 20, 1981 to review the preliminary development concept and Logic Network prepared by Pacer. The minutes are included at Exhibit 1. ...

25. By letter dated August 20, 1981, George Duthie advised Vanhoutte Design Management Services Ltd. that Pacer was the successful bidder of the proposed 120-unit condominium — Invermere, BC. ...

The August 20, 1981 meeting signalled a turning point in Duthie's development activity. Up to this time, Duthie had been encouraged to get on with the development project. There was confidence in the economy. While Duthie had not secured financing for the project, the evidence was that this was not viewed as an impediment. However, shortly before the August 20, 1981 meeting, it began to become apparent to Ian Thomas, who had prepared the Thomas report and upon whom Duthie relied heavily, that resistance was building in the economy. Some projects that had been started were beginning to be put on hold. Thomas started to have concerns about the matter of financing.

Immediately after the August 20, 1981 meeting Thomas met with Duthie and some of his sons and expressed his concern. By letter dated August 25, 1981, he elaborated on the concern about the difficulty of obtaining financing. He recommended against Duthie entering into significant commitments with the architects and project manager until financing had been secured. He recommended various alternative forms of financing, including entering into a joint venture with another developer.

By September 3, 1981, the development project had been put on hold. For the next few months different avenues of financing were explored. However, there was no significant progress made on the project after September. By December, it was apparent that financing could not be arranged. The economy had gone into a severe recession, and the tax benefits afforded multiple unit residential buildings (MURBs), one method of financing, were to cease shortly.

Thereafter, Duthie kept the development project alive by ensuring that planning changes by the village of Invermere did not preclude development. However, there was no further progress on development. In October 1984, Duthie was killed in an airplane crash.

...

When Duthie filed his 1981 income tax return in April 1982, he claimed a 1981 business loss of $43,675.73. This was the total of the expenditures made by Duthie for architectural and project manager services, marketing consultants, property taxes, bank interest and other costs associated with the project. He did not, however, report any change in use of the land or any capital gain in respect of the land.

...

In his 1982 and 1983 returns, Duthie also deducted as business expenses, property taxes and bank interest and, in 1982 some accounting fees.

In the 1984 income tax return filed on behalf of the plaintiff on April 29, 1985, the estate deducted bank interest and property taxes as Duthie had in previous years. In addition, the estate claimed as a business loss, a decline in the value of the land from 1981 to 1984 ... [which the estate computed as $446,948].

The estate also requested that the resulting loss be carried back in respect of Duthie's 1981, 1982 and 1983 taxation years.

...

By notices of reassessment dated December 21, 1987 and September 21, 1989, the Minister reassessed Duthie's 1981, 1982 and 1983 taxation years and the 1984 taxation year of the Duthie estate. The Minister took the position that Duthie had not commenced carrying on a development business in respect of his property and that there had been no change in the use of the land so as to convert it from a personal capital asset into an inventory asset in 1981. Accordingly there was no business loss arising from the decline in value of the property from 1981 to 1984.

...

The issues are:

1.   Did Duthie carry on a land development business in 1981? If so, the expenditures he and the estate incurred after the business commenced and sought to deduct were business expenses and should be allowed.

2.   Was there a change in the use of Duthie's land in 1981 so as to convert the land from a personal capital asset into an inventory asset? If so, there would be a deemed disposition of the land in 1981 at its then fair market value. Except for the fact that the 1981 taxation year was statute-barred, Duthie would be liable for capital gains tax on that portion of the land not considered to be principal residence. To the extent the value of the land declined from 1981 to 1984, when Duthie died, the loss in value would be a business loss and the Duthie estate would be entitled to deduct the loss as a business expense in 1984 and carry the loss back for application to Duthie's 1981, 1982 and 1983 taxation years.

In my view, the two issues are inextricable. Duthie's land was the only reason for the development business. In the circumstances of this case, if it is determined that Duthie had commenced a development business in 1981, Duthie's personal capital asset became inventory of the business in that year. Indeed, Minister's counsel concedes that if it is determined Duthie commenced a business in 1981, a strong argument could be made that there had been a change in use of the land from capital to inventory in that year. However, he says that even if the plaintiff would otherwise be able to claim a change in use of the land, it is estopped from doing so. Counsel for the defendant says that by failing to report a deemed disposition of the land for capital gains purposes in 1981 in his income tax return, Duthie represented to the Minister there was no change in use of the land in that year. The Minister relied on that representation by taking no reassessment steps in respect of the capital gain on the land. In taking no steps, he acted to his detriment and later lost his right to reassess the plaintiff for capital gains tax in 1981 because reassessment of that year had become statute-barred. Accordingly, he says the plaintiff is now estopped from claiming a change in use of the land in 1981.

...

Facts to support the creation of a business and a change in use of land are:

1. There were frequent meetings held to progress the project.

2. Formal minutes were kept.

3. Consultants were engaged.

4. Business tasks were assigned to various family members and to consultants.

5. Duthie arranged to devote full time to the project for a number of months and took time off from his medical practice to do so.

6. One son, John Duthie quit his job in Edmonton to move to Invermere to work full-time on the project.

7. Over $43,000 was expended in 1981 on the land development project.

8. Accounting advice regarding the business organization and tax implications of land development had been obtained and a tax ruling sought.

9. Project managers were asked to and did submit proposals and a project manager was selected; the architect submitted a contract.

10. A logic network was prepared. Approval to proceed had been agreed to. The market study had been reviewed, and preliminary drawings prepared. The architect's proposal and schedule had been reviewed. Finalization of condominium unit sizes and amenities was in progress.

On the basis of ... these facts, I am also inclined to the view that there had been a change in the use of Duthie's land from capital to inventory in 1981. However, I think it is necessary to consider the arguments of the Minister to assess whether such a conclusion can properly be inferred from these facts. In essence, the Minister's position is that Duthie's activities were preliminary to a business. He says they were exploratory and that there had not been sufficient progress such that it could be said a business venture had been embarked upon. Nor had a change in the use of the land from capital to inventory occurred, in the Minister's view.

...

My interpretation of the documentary evidence is that up to approximately May 1981, the possibility of outright sale of the land was seriously being considered. However, as more information became available, it became apparent to Duthie that the most financially rewarding alternative would be to develop the land. This is confirmed by facts such as Duthie's call for proposals from project managers, the selection of project manager, the submission of a contract by the architect, that John Duthie quit his job in Edmonton to move to Invermere and consideration of condominium unit sizes. These activities are not consistent with an intention to sell outright. It is true that in correspondence from Duthie's accountant to Revenue Canada in June 1981, there is reference to outright sale. It is not clear how the accountants would have formed this opinion, but it is obvious from other documentation that outright sale was not, by that time, Duthie's intention.

I infer from the evidence cited thus far that the business had commenced likely by the month of June 1981, more specifically after the Thomas report was received. It was this report on which the "go, no-go" decision was to be based. In any event, according to the agreed statement of facts, a decision was taken in mid-July 1981, "to develop the project to its full potential and that the project could be built as funds allow." I have no doubt that the business had commenced by mid-July 1981, at the latest.

...

Duthie was on the verge of entering into such commitments. Proposals had been called for and submitted. The architects had submitted a draft contract. It seems clear that discussions and arrangements with consultants were those one would normally expect as a business was commencing. In this case, these arrangements were not linked to exploratory considerations, but to actual development activity.

...

[T]here had been approval to proceed which, in my view, was evidence of a critical step indicating that Duthie was proceeding with the development. There had also been other steps carried out. Drawings were reviewed and condominium unit sizes were being finalized. These are all activities consistent with the existence of a development business.

...

The Minister says that Duthie continued to live on the land and that there was no physical change to the land. While undoubtedly, had Duthie moved off the land and had there been a physical change, a change of use would have been clearer. However, I do not think moving off the land or physical change constitute conditions precedent to a change of use. *Peachey* [*Ltd. v. the Queen*, [1979] CTC 51; 79 DTC 5064 (FCA)] speaks of a clear and unequivocal positive act implementing a change of intention. Such words are not restricted to a physical change in the land. Here, I think that commencement of the business activity relative to the subject land constitutes such a clear and unequivocal positive act and is sufficient to evidence a change in use of the land in 1981 from capital to inventory.

...

Nonetheless, the Minister says the plaintiff is estopped from asserting a change in use of the land in 1981 because of Duthie's failure unequivocally to disclose that change of use in his 1981 tax return. The Minister concedes, however, that the 1984 tax return corrected the 1981 non-disclosure. When the Minister received the plaintiff's 1984 tax return which was filed on April 29,

1985, he was informed of the plaintiff's position that there had been a change in use of the land in 1981. The Minister still had until June 22, 1986, some 14 months, to reassess Duthie for 1981; see paragraph 152(4)(c).

Upon this view of the matter, estoppel does not arise. The Minister was informed shortly after April 29,1985, with the filing of the plaintiff's 1984 return, of the plaintiff's position with respect to change of use of the land in 1981. The Minister had some 14 months in which to consider the plaintiff's position and reassess for 1981 if he chose to do so. He chose not to do so. The Minister cannot now allege estoppel because he elected to act to his own detriment by not reassessing rather than by reassessing within the statutory time when he had the opportunity to do so.

...

In the circumstances, the expenses incurred in 1982, 1983 and 1984 must be considered to be expenses incurred for purposes of earning income. With respect to the land, there were clear and unequivocal positive acts which transformed the land from a capital asset to inventory in Duthie's name. These were not, as in *Peachey*, just expressed intentions. I do not think it is necessary that there be a physical change in the land or that some type of long-term commitment need be demonstrated. While undoubtedly, such evidence would more clearly support a change in use argument, it is not a condition. Here, there were sufficient acts of a positive nature as referred to in *Peachey* to demonstrate, on a balance of probabilities, the change of use. ...

Appeal allowed.

NOTES AND QUESTIONS

1.   On what grounds did the Minister disallow the deduction of a business loss on the deemed disposition of the Invermere property immediately before Dr. Duthie's death in 1984? Why did the court reject the Minister's arguments in *Duthie Estate*? Of what, if any, relevance to the issue of the deemed disposition in 1981 is the commencement by Dr. Duthie of a land development business during that year? Of what, if any, relevance are the facts that Dr. Duthie continued to live on the land after 1981 and that there was no physical change to the land? Of what, if any, relevance is the fact that Dr. Duthie did not report a change in the use of the property when he filed his tax return for his 1981 taxation year? What, if any, test does the court adopt to determine whether a change of use has occurred within the meaning of subsection 45(1) of the Act?

2.   In *Dawd v. M.N.R.*, [1981] C.T.C. 2999, 81 D.T.C. 888 (T.R.B.), the taxpayer, who had purchased six acres of land in 1967 with the intention of building a home for himself and his family, obtained an engineering study of the property for the purpose of developing the land in 1972, and approval of a draft plan of subdivision in 1973, and sold the land to a wholly owned corporation in 1977. Rejecting the taxpayer's argument that he had not commenced a land development business until September 1976, the court held (at para. 14) that the

taxpayer had "commenced a series of operations indistinguishable from those of a person carrying on the business of a land developer" no later than January 1, 1973.

For a similar conclusion, see *Jones v. M.N.R.*, [1990] T.C.J. No. 713, [1990] 2 C.T.C. 2406, 90 D.T.C. 1849 (T.C.C.), in which the court stated (at para. 9) that "actions and conduct by a taxpayer long in advance of actual registration of a subdivision plan may well be sufficient to establish a date or time at which a commitment to a change in use can be determined for a property."

3. In *Menzies v. M.N.R.*, [1990] T.C.J. No. 1101, [1991] 1 C.T.C. 2346, (1990) 91 D.T.C. 222 (T.C.C.), the taxpayers owned a house in Nanoose Bay on Vancouver Island, which they intended to sell when they moved to a new residence in Nanaimo in 1981, but decided to rent out when the real estate market declined. When the taxpayers returned to the home in Nanoose Bay in 1982, they sought to deduct an allowable capital loss of $10,000 on the land and a terminal loss of $16,484 on the building on the grounds that the property was subject to a deemed disposition under subparagraph 45(1)(a)(i) and paragraph 13(7)(b) when they rented the property out in 1981 and a deemed disposition under subparagraph 45(1)(a)(ii) and paragraph 13(7)(a) when they returned to the property a year later.

Concluding that the taxpayers had not commenced to use the property for the purpose of gaining or producing income when they decided to rent it out pending a change in the real estate market, the court disallowed the deductions. According to Christie AJTCC (at para. 17):

> In order for a taxpayer to successfully allege that real estate acquired by him as a principal residence has commenced later to be used for the purpose of gaining or producing income from a rental business, he must establish more than an agreement that, subject to contingencies regarding the anticipated sale of the property, may produce some income. The overriding intention must exist to use the property as an asset in a rental business and an arrangement that is essentially designed to defray costs pending the sale of the property and facilitate that sale will not suffice.

Do you agree with this result? Why or why not? How consistent is this conclusion with the decision in *Burnet v. Canada*, [1995] T.C.J. No. 479, [1995] 2 C.T.C. 2319, 96 D.T.C. 1686 (T.C.C.), discussed above in the context of the characterization of personal-use property?

4. In *Noonan v. Canada*, [1997] T.C.J. No. 106 (T.C.C.), the taxpayer, a Toronto lawyer who entered into an agreement on November 11, 1988 to acquire a luxury condominium for $450,000 on December 19, 1990, sought to deduct an allowable capital loss of $16,874 and a terminal loss of $174,264 after he moved into the condominium in the spring of 1991, on the basis that he had originally acquired the property as an investment for rental purposes and subsequently converted it to personal use, triggering a deemed disposition under subparagraph 45(1)(a)(ii) and paragraph 13(7)(a). Rejecting the taxpayer's claim that he had originally acquired the property for the purpose of gaining or

producing income, the court disallowed the deductions. According to Lamarre-Proulx JTCC (at para. 31):

> I find that the high cost of a one-bedroom apartment, the choice of the expensive material chosen to ornate it, without consideration as to whether it is capable of sustaining the wear and tear of tenants, the absolute failure of investigating the rental market and the total absence of search for tenants brings me to the inescapable conclusion that there is not one element of evidence adduced that is indicative of an intention of acquiring the property in question for the purpose of carrying a profitable rental operation. Therefore, when the Appellant took possession of the condominium unit, there was no deemed disposition of a property acquired for the purpose of gaining or producing income. The property might have been acquired for the purpose of an investment going to appreciate in value but the property cannot be found to have been acquired for the purpose of gaining or producing a profit from a rental operation.

Might the taxpayer have had a better chance of deducting the loss in value of the condominium if he had argued that it had acquired the property for the purpose of resale at a profit?

5.   For other cases in which courts have considered the change-of-use provisions in section 45 of the Act, see *Woods v. M.N.R.*, [1978] C.T.C. 2802, 78 D.T.C. 1576 (T.R.B.) (deemed disposition on return to former residence rented out for nine years) and *Taylor v. M.N.R.*, [1990] T.C.J. No. 423, [1990] 2 C.T.C. 2040, 90 D.T.C. 1574 (T.C.C.) (deemed disposition of books originally acquired by the taxpayer for personal use on commencement of a book-selling business).

6.   In *Browne v. M.N.R.*, [1979] C.T.C. 2376, 79 D.T.C. 342 (T.R.B.), the taxpayer and his wife sold their home in 1969 for $175,000, of which $125,000 took the form of a vendor take-back mortgage. When the purchaser defaulted in 1972, the taxpayer and his wife repossessed the property, which was rented for a period of time, and resold at a gain in 1973. Rejecting the taxpayer's argument that the property qualified as a principal residence in 1973, the board concluded that for the purposes of the relevant statutory provisions the property had been acquired in 1972, was not used as a principal residence, and was not subject to the deemed disposition in subsection 45(1) or the elective rule in subsection 45(2).

7.   For the CRA's views on changes in use from a principal residence to an income-producing property or vice versa, see Interpretation Bulletin IT-120R6. According to paragraph 25 of this bulletin:

Complete Change in Use of a Property from Principal Residence to Income-Producing

> 25. If a taxpayer has completely converted his or her principal residence to an income-producing use, he or she is deemed by paragraph 45(1)(a) to have disposed of the property (both land and building) at fair market value (FMV) and reacquired it immediately thereafter at the same amount. Any gain otherwise determined on this deemed disposition may be eliminated or reduced by the principal residence exemption. The taxpayer may instead, however, defer recognition of any gain to a later year by electing under subsection 45(2) to

be deemed not to have made the change in use of the property. This election is made by means of a letter to that effect signed by the taxpayer and filed with the income tax return for the year in which the change in use occurred. If the taxpayer rescinds the election in a subsequent taxation year, he or she is deemed to have disposed of and reacquired the property at FMV on the first day of that subsequent year (with the above-mentioned tax consequences). If capital cost allowance (CCA) is claimed on the property, the election is considered to be rescinded on the first day of the year in which that claim is made.

Subsection 220(3.2) of the Income Tax Act, in conjunction with section 600 of the Income Tax Regulations, provides the authority for [the CRA] to accept a late-filed subsection 45(2) election. Such a late-filed election may be accepted under certain circumstances, one of which is that no CCA has been claimed on the property since the change in use has occurred and during the period in which the election is to remain in force. For further particulars on the acceptance of late-filed elections, see the current version of *Information Circular* 92-1, Guidelines for Accepting Late, Amended or Revoked Elections.

According to paragraph 28:

Complete Change in Use of a Property from Income-Producing to Principal Residence

28. If a taxpayer has completely changed the use of a property (for which an election under subsection 45(2) is not in force) from income-producing to a principal residence, he or she is deemed by paragraph 45(1)(a) to have disposed of the property (both land and building), and immediately thereafter reacquired it, at FMV. This deemed disposition can result in a taxable capital gain. The taxpayer may instead defer recognition of the gain to a later year by electing under subsection 45(3) that the above-mentioned deemed disposition and reacquisition under paragraph 45(1)(a) does not apply. This election is made by means of a letter to that effect signed by the taxpayer and filed with the income tax return for the year in which the property is ultimately disposed of (or earlier if a formal "demand" for the election is issued by [the CRA]). Also, subsection 220(3.2) of the Income Tax Act, in conjunction with section 600 of the Income Tax Regulations, provides the authority for [the CRA] to accept a late-filed subsection 45(3) election. Such a late-filed election may be accepted under certain circumstances — for further particulars on the acceptance of late-filed elections, see the current version of Information Circular 92-1, Guidelines for Accepting Late, Amended or Revoked Elections.

Even if a subsection 45(3) election is filed in order to defer recognition of a gain from the change in use of a property from income-producing to principal residence, the net income from the property for the period before the change in use must still be reported. However, for purposes of reporting such net income, it should be noted that an election under subsection 45(3) is not possible if, for any taxation year ending after 1984 and on or before the change in use of the property from income-producing to a principal residence, CCA has been allowed in respect of the property to

- the taxpayer;
- the taxpayer's spouse; or
- a trust under which the taxpayer or his or her spouse is a beneficiary.

CCA so allowed would cause subsection 45(4) to nullify the subsection 45(3) election.

Paragraphs 30-32 deal with partial changes in the use of a property part of which is used as a principal residence:

Partial Changes in Use

30. If a taxpayer has partially converted a principal residence to an income-producing use, paragraph 45(1)(c) provides for a deemed disposition of the portion of the property so converted (such portion is usually calculated on the basis of the area involved) for proceeds equal to its proportionate share of the property's FMV. Paragraph 45(1)(c) also provides for a deemed reacquisition immediately thereafter of the same portion of the property at a cost equal to the very same amount. Any gain otherwise determined on the deemed disposition is usually eliminated or reduced by the principal residence exemption. If the portion of the property so changed is later converted back to use as part of the principal residence, there is a second deemed disposition (and reacquisition) thereof at FMV. A taxable capital gain attributable to the period of use of such portion of the property for income-producing purposes can arise from such a second deemed disposition or from an actual sale of the whole property subsequent to the original partial change in use. An election under subsection 45(2) or (3) cannot be made where there is a partial change in use of a property as described above.

31. The above-mentioned deemed disposition rule applies where the partial change in use of the property is substantial and of a more permanent nature, i.e., where there is a structural change. Examples where this occurs are the conversion of the front half of a house into a store, the conversion of a portion of a house into a self-contained domestic establishment for earning rental income (a duplex, triplex, etc.), and alterations to a house to accommodate separate business premises. In these and similar cases, the taxpayer reports the income and may claim the expenses pertaining to the altered portion of the property (i.e., a reasonable portion of the expenses relating to the whole property) as well as CCA on such altered portion of the property.

32. It is our practice not to apply the deemed disposition rule, but rather to consider that the entire property retains its nature as a principal residence, where all of the following conditions are met:

(a) the income-producing use is ancillary to the main use of the property as a residence,

(b) there is no structural change to the property, and

(c) no CCA is claimed on the property.

These conditions can be met, for example, where a taxpayer carries on a business of caring for children in his or her home, rents one or more rooms in the home, or has an office or other work space in the home which is used in connection with his or her business or employment. In these and similar cases, the taxpayer reports the income and may claim the expenses (other than CCA) pertaining to the portion of the property used for income-producing purposes. ... In the event that the taxpayer commences to claim CCA on the portion of the property used for producing income, the deemed disposition rule is applied as of the time at which the income-producing use commenced.

b. Death

Where the recognition of capital gains and/or recaptured depreciation on capital property depends on an actual disposition of the property, taxpayers have an incentive to hold on to this property in order to defer the tax liability that might otherwise be triggered by its disposition. This so-called "lock-in effect" can discourage the efficient allocation of resources among different uses and provide a considerable deferral advantage over other kinds of investments. For these reasons, paragraph 70(5)(a) of the Act limits the indefinite deferral of accrued gains and recaptured depreciation by deeming taxpayers who have died in a taxation year to have disposed of each capital property immediately before their death for proceeds equal to the fair market value of the property at that time. Where another person acquires any of this property as a consequence of a taxpayer's death, paragraph 70(5)(b) deems this person to have acquired the property at a cost equal to the fair market value of the property immediately before the taxpayer's death. Where the property that is deemed to have been disposed of before the taxpayer's death is depreciable property, moreover, and the original capital cost of the property exceeds its fair market value immediately before the taxpayer's death, paragraph 70(5)(c) deems the capital cost of the property to a person who acquires the property as a consequence of the taxpayer's death to be the original capital cost of the property to the taxpayer and the difference between this amount and the fair market value of the property immediately before the taxpayer's death to have been allowed to this person as capital cost allowance in previous taxation years. The effect of these rules is to trigger accrued capital gains and losses as well as recaptured depreciation and terminal losses in the year of the taxpayer's death, setting the cost of the property to persons who acquire the property as a result of the taxpayer's death at an amount equal to the fair market value of the property immediately before the taxpayer's death, and making this person liable for recaptured depreciation resulting from any subsequent increase in the value of depreciable property the original capital cost of which to the taxpayer exceeds its fair market value immediately before the taxpayer's death.

In applying subsection 70(5), courts have considered the effect of the stipulation that the taxpayer's capital property and the fair market value of this property are to be determined "immediately before the taxpayer's death." A useful illustration of the importance of these words is the decision in *Mastronardi Estate v. Canada*, [1976] C.T.C. 572, 76 D.T.C. 6306 (F.C.T.D.), aff'd [1977] C.T.C. 355, 77 D.T.C. 5217 (F.C.A.).

Mastronardi Estate v. Canada
[1976] C.T.C. 572, 76 D.T.C. 6306 (F.C.T.D.), aff'd [1977] C.T.C. 355, 77 D.T.C. 5217 (F.C.A.)

GIBSON J: What is the subject matter in this appeal from assessment is a deemed realization of a gain on capital property consisting of certain common shares in Mastronardi Produce Limited because of the death of the owner of these shares on February 20, 1973 while resident in Ontario. Such deemed realization of a gain is statutorily created by subsection 70(5) of the *Income Tax Act*.

By reason of subsection 70(5) of the Act, the deceased owner is "deemed to have disposed [of these shares, being capital property], immediately before his death ... and to have received proceeds of disposition therefor equal to the fair market value of the property at that time."

...

The parties have agreed to certain facts, among which are the following:

The Plaintiffs were confirmed as executors and trustees under the Last Will and Testament of the late Umberto Mastronardi, (hereinafter referred to as the deceased), by Grant of Probate dated July 5, 1973 issued by the Surrogate Court of the County of Essex in the Province of Ontario. ...

The deceased died suddenly and without warning of cardiac arrest on February 20, 1973 at which time he was a resident of the Province of Ontario.

...

(Since 1972, a five-year term insurance policy on the life of the deceased Umberto Mastronardi in the face amount of $500,000 reducing by $100,000 on each anniversary date was owned by Mastronardi Produce Limited.)

(It is common ground that prior to the death of the deceased, because of the special provisions of this term life insurance policy, an informed purchaser of the shares of Mastronardi Produce Limited would not pay any more for such shares of that company than he would have if that company did not own this term life insurance policy.)

...

In accordance with subsection 70(5) of the *Income Tax Act* as it applied during the 1973 taxation year, the deceased was deemed to have disposed, immediately before his death, of 311.4 common shares in Mastronardi Produce Limited and to have received proceeds of disposition therefor equal to the fair market value at that time.

Without having regard to any value attributable to the life insurance policy in question immediately before the death of the deceased each common share in question would have a fair market value equal to $323.58.

If the value of the corporation's assets were deemed to be increased by the face amount of the life insurance policy in question immediately before the death of the deceased it is common ground that each common share held by the deceased would have a fair market value equal to $778.59.

The Minister of National Revenue concluded that immediately before the death of the deceased the value of the policy was not less than $500,000.00 and that such amount would have to be taken into account in arriving at the net worth of the company and hence the value of the common shares immediately before the death of the deceased.

On reassessing the deceased's estate in respect of the deceased's 1973 taxation year, notice of which reassessment was dated July 21, 1975, the Minister of National Revenue added to taxable income a taxable capital gain of $70,845.05 in respect of the deemed disposition of 311.4 shares of Mastronardi Produce Limited at $778.59 per share less the valuation day value per share which was $323.58.

Among other things, the plaintiffs submitted that the capital property of the deceased represented by the common shares of Mastronardi Produce Limited owned by the deceased had a fair market value equal to $323.58 per share immediately before the death of the deceased and that no regard should be had to any value which might be added to the value of such shares attributable to the said term life insurance policy owned by Mastronardi Produce Limited in the amount of $500,000.

The respondent in the pleadings submitted that:

> ... immediately before the death of the deceased, the term insurance policy on his life, which was owned by Mastronardi Produce Ltd, had a value of $500,000.00, and that accordingly such value is to be considered in the determination of the fair market value of the shares in Mastronardi Produce Ltd which the deceased was deemed to have disposed of pursuant to subsection 70(5) of the *Income Tax Act.*

...

In the process of interpreting this statutory provision in relation to the facts of this case, it is apparent that there is a two-step fiction enacted by [subsection 70(5)] of the Act.

The first fiction is that the taxpayer after he dies is deemed to have disposed of the subject property "immediately before his death."

The second fiction is that he is deemed "to have received proceeds of disposition therefor equal to the fair market value of the property at that time."

...

The submission of the defendant in relation to the shares of Mastronardi Produce Limited is that they should not be valued anterior to the death of the deceased. Instead, the submission is that the words in [subsection 70(5)] of the Act "immediately before his death" are equivalent in meaning and intent to the instant of death. On that assumption then, it is submitted that the price that would be paid for each of the shares in a transaction between an informed vendor and an informed purchaser would be $778.59 because at the instant of death an informed purchaser would know that the company would receive the $500,000 proceeds from the said term life insurance policy.

On the other hand, the plaintiffs submit that the words in that subsection "immediately before his death" refer to a span of time before death which is relevant in determining the fair market value of these shares of the subject private company.

A number of English, Australian and Canadian authorities were submitted by the parties, but none of them are of substantial assistance in determining the legislative concept of [subsection 70(5)] of the *Income Tax Act.*

However, after careful consideration of these authorities, of the provisions of by [subsection 70(5)] of the *Income Tax Act* ... and of the facts of this case, I have come to the following conclusions:

The words "immediately before his death" in [subsection 70(5)] of the *Income Tax Act* should not be construed as meaning the equivalent of the instant of death; and also those words do not import a necessity of valuing capital property taking into account the imminence of death.

In the subject case, at the date of death of the deceased Umberto Mastronardi, [subsection 70(5)] of the Act, SC 1970-71-72, c 63, prescribed that the deemed realization took place "immediately before [the deceased's] ... death" and that at that time, as owner, he was deemed "to have received proceeds of disposition therefor equal to the fair market value of the property at that time."

...

In my view, therefore, in this case, both such valuations must be considered as having taken place at some other time rather than at the instant of death of the deceased and no premise of imminence of death of the deceased should form any part of such valuations.

It follows, therefore, as a result and I so find that the defence as pleaded is untenable, namely that "immediately before the death of the deceased, the term insurance policy on his life, which was owned by Mastronardi Produce Ltd, had a value of $500,000.00, and that accordingly such value is to be considered in the determination of the fair market value of the shares in Mastronardi Produce Ltd which the deceased was deemed to have disposed of pursuant to subsection 70(5) of the *Income Tax Act*." On the contrary, the finding is that no value of this term insurance policy is to be considered in the determination of the fair market value of these shares. ...

Appeal allowed.

NOTES AND QUESTIONS

1. On what basis did the Minister argue that the shares that were deemed to have been disposed of in *Mastronardi Estate* should be valued at $778.59 per share? Why does the court reject this approach? How does it interpret the words "immediately before [the taxpayer's] death" for the purpose of subsection 70(5) of the Act?

2. Do you agree with the result in *Mastronardi Estate*? Why or why not? Consider the following criticism in Wolfe D. Goodman, "Four Aspects of Valuation," in *Report of Proceedings of the Twenty-Eighth Tax Conference*, 1976 Conference Report (Toronto: Canadian Tax Foundation, 1977) 354 at 358:

> The key to Gibson J's decision in *Mastronardi Estate v. The Queen*, is his statement ... [that]:
>
> > The words "immediately before his death" in [subsection 70(5)] of the *Income Tax Act* should not be construed as meaning the equivalent of the instant of death; and also those words do not import a necessity of valuing capital property taking into account the imminence of death.
>
> It is easy to agree with the first part of Gibson J's statement but difficult to accept the last part. If one were to pick a point in time for valuation at which death was not regarded as imminent, one could always pick a point closer in time to the actual moment of death at

which it did become imminent. When then should valuation "immediately before death" not take into account the imminence of death?

> If "immediately before death" implies a time when death is known to be imminent, there can be little doubt that the value of the policy is equal to the proceeds payable on death. If we were dealing with two otherwise identical companies owned by the late Mr. Mastronardi, but one of these companies owned an insurance policy on his life, and if we imagined someone negotiating to purchase his shares immediately before his death and in the knowledge of his imminent death, why wouldn't the purchaser pay more for the company which owned the policy and why wouldn't the difference in price be based upon the increase in net worth which will result from maturity of the policy on Mr. Mastronardi's life?

3.   For deaths occurring after December 1, 1982, subsection 70(5.3) requires the fair market value of property that is deemed to be disposed of by a taxpayer under subsection 70(5) to be determined as though the fair market value at that time of any life insurance policy on the taxpayer's life were the cash surrender value of the policy immediately before the taxpayer's death. The purpose of this provision, as explained in a Department of Finance technical note accompanying amendments to the provision, is "to ensure that life insurance proceeds payable as a consequence of death are not reflected in share value and therefore do not give rise to a capital gain on death." In this respect, the provision codifies *Mastronardi Estate*.

This accommodates the outcome in a sensible way in light of the tax treatment of the proceeds of life insurance policies elsewhere in the Act. For example, for privately-held small business corporations, such as the one at issue in *Mastronardi Estate*, life insurance proceeds are typically considered to be received tax-free by the corporation. In addition, the proceeds are added to something called the "capital dividend account"[78] of the corporation, the balance of which can be distributed to shareholders as a tax-free capital dividend.[79] If the proceeds of life insurance policies of key shareholders such as Umberto Mastronardi are considered to augment the fair market value of the shares of the corporation, then these tax advantages, which are explicitly granted by another part of the Act, are effectively undermined when the deceased individual whose life is insured is also a shareholder.

Both the consistency of Gibson J's judgment with the scheme of the Act and the subsequent introduction of subsection 70(5.3) suggest that the court reached the right outcome in *Mastronardi Estate*.

4.   In *Nussey Estate v. Canada*, [2001] F.C.J. No. 519, [2001] 2 C.T.C. 222, 2001 D.T.C. 5240 (F.C.A.), the taxpayer died owning shares in a family-owned business that were subject to a shareholder's agreement providing that they would be deemed to be redeemed by the company the day preceding a shareholder's death. Rejecting the estate's argument that the shares were thereby redeemed and not subject to the deemed disposition in subsection 70(5) of the

---

[78] Subs. 89(1).
[79] Subs. 83(2).

Act, the court concluded that "the agreement could only operate once the taxpayer had died, by which time subsection 70(5) of the Act would have applied."

5.   Where a taxpayer disposes of capital property by way of gift inter vivos, paragraph 69(1)(b) deems the taxpayer to have received proceeds of disposition for the property equal to its fair market value at the time of the disposition. In turn, paragraph 69(1)(c) deems taxpayers who acquire property "by way of gift, bequest or inheritance" to acquire the property at its fair market value.

6.   The deemed disposition at death is subject to a number of "rollover" rules, which apply where property otherwise subject to subsection 70(5) is transferred to the deceased's spouse or spousal trust or where farm property is transferred to a child of the deceased. These provisions are examined later in this chapter.

2. Rollovers

In addition to the recognition rules examined in the previous section, the *Income Tax Act* contains numerous "rollover" provisions that permit actual dispositions to occur without triggering any tax consequences. Many of these rules apply where a disposition transforms the taxpayer's economic interest without effecting an ultimate disposition of the property, such as the transfer of property to a corporation or partnership in which the taxpayer holds an interest,[80] the conversion of debt into equity,[81] an exchange of one share for another,[82] and other corporate reorganizations.[83] By deferring the recognition of any accrued gains or recaptured depreciation that might otherwise arise on a disposition at fair market value, these rules remove tax impediments that might otherwise deter efficient reallocations of economic resources. A similar rationale underlies the rollover rules in subsections 13(4), 14(6), and 44(1), which permit taxpayers who dispose of specific kinds of property to defer any tax consequences from these transactions where they acquire a "replacement property" within a stipulated period of time.

In addition to these provisions, other rollover rules are designed to achieve other non-economic objectives. Where property is unlawfully taken, destroyed, taken under statutory authority, or sold to a person by whom, for example, notice of an intention to take it under statutory authority was given, subsections 13(4) and 44(1) also ensure that the taxpayer is not further burdened by the

---

[80]   See s. 85 (transfer of property to a corporation) and subs. 97(2) (transfer of property to a partnership).

[81]   Section 51.

[82]   See s. 85.1 (exchange of shares of target company for shares of purchasing company), s. 85 (transfer of property to a corporation), and subs. 97(2) (transfer of property to a partnership).

[83]   See s. 85 (transfer of property to a corporation) and subs. 97(2) (transfer of property to a partnership).

recognition of gains on these involuntary dispositions by allowing the taxpayer to defer any tax consequences that would otherwise apply by using the proceeds from the involuntary disposition to acquire a replacement property. Where a taxpayer transfers capital property at death or *inter vivos* to a spouse or common law partner, moreover, subsections 70(6) and 73(1) recognize the economic mutuality of these relationships by allowing the couple to defer the recognition of any gain or recaptured depreciation until the spouse or common law partner disposes of the property. A similar rollover rule applies for transfers of qualifying farm property to a taxpayer's child, facilitating the retention of a family farm from one generation to the next.[84]

For our purposes, there is no need to examine the various rollover rules that apply where a disposition transforms the taxpayer's economic interest without effecting an ultimate disposition of the property, since these rules are best examined in a course on the taxation of partnerships and corporations. The following text and cases consider each of the other rollover rules mentioned above: (a) where a taxpayer acquires a replacement property in exchange for property that was disposed of voluntarily or involuntarily; (b) where a taxpayer transfers capital property to a spouse or common law partner; and (c) where a taxpayer transfers qualifying farm property to a child.

a. Exchanges of Property

Notwithstanding the general rules governing the computation of a gain or loss in subsection 40(1) of the Act, subsection 44(1) allows taxpayers to defer the recognition of a gain on the disposition in a taxation year of a capital property (other than the share of the capital stock of a corporation) that is either:

> (a) property the proceeds of disposition of which are described in paragraph (b), (c) or (d) of the definition "proceeds of disposition" in subsection 13(21) or paragraph (b), (c) or (d) of the definition "proceeds of disposition" in section 54, or

> (b) a property that was, immediately before the disposition, a former business property of the taxpayer,

provided that the taxpayer has, within a specific period of time,[85] "acquired a capital property that is a replacement property for the taxpayer's former property." In these circumstances, where the taxpayer so elects, paragraph 44(1)(c) generally deems the taxpayer's gain from the disposition of the former property to be the lesser of the gain otherwise determined,[86] and the amount, if

---

[84] See subs. 70(9) to (11) (transfers of farm property as a consequence of the taxpayer's death), and subs. 73(3) and (4) (*inter vivos* transfers of farm property).

[85] Paragraphs 44(1)(c) and (d) specify these time periods as "before the end of the second taxation year" after the taxation year involving a disposition of property described in para. 44(1)(a), and "before the end of the first taxation year" following the taxation year of the disposition in any other case.

[86] Clause 44(1)(e)(i)(A).

any, by which the proceeds of disposition of the former property exceed the sum of the cost of the replacement property and any outlays and expenses made or incurred by the taxpayer for the purpose of making the disposition.[87] In turn, paragraph 44(1)(f) deems the cost to the taxpayer of the replacement property to be its actual cost minus the amount, if any, by which the gain otherwise determined on the disposition of the former property exceeds the difference between the proceeds of disposition of the former property and the sum of the actual cost of the replacement property and any outlays and expenses made or incurred by the taxpayer for the purpose of making the disposition. Where a taxpayer uses all the proceeds from a qualifying disposition to acquire a replacement property, the effect of this rule is to not recognize any gain on the disposition of the former property and to reduce the cost of the replacement property by the amount of this unrecognized gain, thereby "rolling over" the cost of the former property to the replacement property and deferring recognition of the gain until the taxpayer disposes of the replacement property. Where the proceeds from the disposition of the former property exceed the cost of the replacement property and the cost of the disposition, on the other hand, this excess is generally recognized as a gain in the taxation year in which the former property is disposed of.[88] The cost of the replacement property is reduced by the difference between the gain otherwise determined on the disposition of the former property and the amount by which the proceeds of disposition of this property exceed the sum of the actual cost of the replacement property and any outlays and expenses made or incurred by the taxpayer for the purpose of making the disposition — again causing the cost of the former property to "roll over" to the replacement property.

For the purpose of this and other provisions, the descriptions of "proceeds of disposition" in paragraphs (b), (c), and (d) of the definitions in subsection 13(21) and section 54 of the Act include various kinds of compensation for property that is unlawfully taken, destroyed, or expropriated. The term "former business property" is defined in subsection 248(1) as a capital property of the taxpayer that was real property or an interest in real property and was "used by the taxpayer or a person related to the taxpayer primarily for the purpose of gaining or producing income from a business," other than rental property, land subjacent to the rental property, contiguous land that is a parking area, driveway, yard, or garden that is otherwise necessary for the use of the rental property, or a

---

[87] Clause 44(1)(e)(i)(B). In computing the deemed gain for the taxation year in which the taxpayer disposes of the former property, subpara. 44(1)(e)(iii) permits the taxpayer to deduct a reserve in respect of proceeds of disposition that are payable after the end of the year. This reserve is identical to the reserve in subpara. 40(1)(a)(iii), which was examined earlier in this chapter.

[88] Where all or some part of the proceeds are payable in a subsequent taxation year, the taxpayer may reduce the amount of the gain that is recognized in the year by deducting a reserve under subpara. 44(1)(e)(iii). See the discussion above.

leasehold interest in any such property.[89] Finally, subsection 44(5) defines a "capital property" as a "replacement property for a former property" if:

(a) it is reasonable to conclude that the property was acquired by the taxpayer to replace the former property;

(a.1) it was acquired by the taxpayer and used by the taxpayer or a person related to the taxpayer for a use that is the same as or similar to the use to which the taxpayer or a person related to the taxpayer put the former property; [and]

(b) where the former property was used by the taxpayer or a person related to the taxpayer for the purpose of gaining or producing income from a business, the particular capital property was acquired for the purpose of gaining or producing income from that or a similar business or for use by a person related to the taxpayer for such a purpose.

A number of cases have considered the rollover rule in subsection 44(1), considering the definition of "former business property," the characterization of "replacement property," the requirement that the taxpayer acquire replacement property within a specified period of time, and the requirement that the taxpayer elect to have the rollover rule apply. The leading case on the application of this rollover provision is *Glaxo Wellcome Inc. v. Canada*, [1996] T.C.J. No. 6, [1996] 1 C.T.C. 2904, 96 D.T.C. 1159 (T.C.C.), aff'd [1998] F.C.J. No. 1476, [1999] 4 C.T.C. 371, 98 D.T.C. 6638 (F.C.A.).

Glaxo Wellcome Inc. v. Canada
[1996] T.C.J. No. 6, [1996] 1 C.T.C. 2904, 96 D.T.C. 1159 (T.C.C.), aff'd
[1998] F.C.J. No. 1476, [1999] 4 C.T.C. 371, 98 D.T.C. 6638 (F.C.A.)

BOWMAN JTCC: This appeal is from an assessment for the appellant's 1988 taxation year. The sole question is whether the appellant is entitled to treat property sold by it as a "former business property" within the meaning of section 44 of the *Income Tax Act* so as to defer the recognition by it of the capital gain realized on the sale.

...

In 1965, a predecessor of the appellant, Glaxo-Allenburys (Canada) Limited ("G-A") bought an 18.2 acre parcel of land on Eglinton Avenue East in Mississauga, Ontario. The Eglinton property was purchased with the specific intention of using it in an anticipated future expansion of G-A's pharmaceutical business. To this end consultants and architects were engaged with a view to constructing a facility on the Eglinton property.

---

[89] For the purpose of this definition, moreover, a "rental property'" of a taxpayer is generally defined as real property that is owned by the taxpayer, whether jointly or otherwise, and "used by the taxpayer ... principally for the purpose of gaining or producing gross revenue that is rent," excluding "a property leased by the taxpayer ... to a lessee, in the ordinary course of a business ... of selling goods or rendering services, under an agreement by which the lessee undertakes to use the property to carry on the business of selling or promoting the sale of the goods or services of the taxpayer or the related person."

In 1970 as the result of the acquisition in 1968 by G-A's parent of the parent of The British Drug Houses (Canada) Limited ("BDHC"), G-A and BDHC amalgamated to form Glaxo Canada Inc., the present appellant, (or, at all events, the predecessor to Glaxo Wellcome Inc.) ("Glaxo").

BDHC, prior to its amalgamation with G-A, operated a facility at 1025 The Queensway in Etobicoke, Ontario. That facility had enough room to accommodate the merged operations and accordingly Glaxo deferred its proposed construction on the Eglinton property.

It was, however, intended to expand and to this end the Eglinton property was retained. By 1987, Glaxo realized that its growth was of such a magnitude that a future expansion would require more space than the 18.2 acres comprising the Eglinton property. It therefore sold the Eglinton property for $9.5 million dollars in 1988 and bought a 61.58 acre site in Mississauga for $24,682,707 for its future expansion requirements.

From 1970 to a time subsequent to the acquisition of the Mississauga property in 1989 Glaxo operated primarily out of the Queensway property. The Eglinton property remained vacant throughout the entire period from its acquisition until its sale.

In its return of income for 1988 Glaxo filed elections under subsection 44(1) with a view to deferring the recognition of the capital gain realized on the sale of the property but this was denied on assessing. Hence this appeal.

In essence, section 44 permits a taxpayer to defer the recognition of a capital gain realized on the disposition of a "former business property" where before the end of the second taxation year following the year of disposition the taxpayer acquires a "replacement property." Both the former business property and the replacement property must be capital properties. There is no issue on the latter point, nor is there any issue that if the Eglinton property is a "former business property" the Mississauga property is a "replacement property."

Former business property is defined in section 248 in part as follows:

"former business property" of a taxpayer means a capital property that was used by him primarily for the purpose of gaining or producing income from a business, and that was real property or an interest therein of the taxpayer, but does not include. ...

In the French version of the *Income Tax Act* the expression is "ancien bien d'entreprise" which is defined in part as follows:

"ancien bien d'entreprise" S'entend d'un bien en immobilisation d'un contribuable utilisé par lui ou par une personne qui lui est liée principalement en vue de tirer un revenu d'une entreprise et qui était un bien immeuble du contribuable ou un droit y afferent. En sont exclus: ...

The entitlement of the appellant to the deferral contemplated by section 44 depends on the meaning to be ascribed to one word — used — (utilisé).

Why is this so difficult a question? The word "use" is one of the commonest and most frequently used in the English language, as is "utiliser" in French. Indeed, the definition of the verb "use" in the *New Shorter Oxford Dictionary of the English Language* is "make use of (a thing) esp. for a particular end or purpose; utilize, turn to account ...; work, till, occupy, (land, ground etc)." The noun "use" is defined as "act of using, fact of being used." After this exercise in circularity we are no wiser than before (or, for that matter, any better informed). Similarly, "utiliser" is defined in *Le Petit Robert 1 dictionnaire de la langue française* as "rendre utile, faire servir à une fin précise ... employer." I should not have thought that the resolution of this apparently (but deceptively) simple question would force me to bring to bear the vast array of principles of statutory interpretation that are regularly enunciated by our courts.

...

Obviously one starts with the plain words of the statute. If the words of the legislation are clear and unambiguous and admit of but one interpretation one need look no further. If they are not and are susceptible of more than one interpretation one must look to the scheme of the act and its object and spirit. It is only when recourse to all of the other tools of statutory interpretation fails to yield a clear answer that one is entitled to invoke the principle that in case of ambiguity the benefit of the doubt must go to the taxpayer.

...

Let us then start with the word "used." About as garden-variety a word as one is likely to find anywhere. A company uses a piece of land on which it locates its factory, and carries on its business. A farmer uses land on which he plants crops. Indeed, I would extend the word "use" to cover land that a farmer summer-fallows for a season. Unless some principle of interpretation compels me to ascribe a broader meaning to the word, "use" connotes actual utilization for some purpose, not holding for future use. "Used primarily for the purpose of gaining or producing income from a business" would, *prima facie*, imply that the land be put to some productive use in the business.

...

Counsel in this case referred to extrinsic materials in an attempt to draw some inference favourable to their interpretation. I did not find these materials added to or detracted from the strength of either position. The object is clear enough. Section 44 is a relieving provision that enables business-persons to dispose of property used in the business and acquire replacement property without incurring the immediate impact of taxation that such disposition would entail. One does not need to read *Hansard* to see that.

I do however obtain some assistance from the *Income Tax Act* itself. Cattanach J said in *AEL Microtel Ltd. v. R*, [1984] CTC 387, 84 DTC 6374 (FCTD) at 405 (DTC 6389):

> It is a rule of construction that, where in the same Act, and in relation to the same subject matter, different words are used such choice of different words must be considered intentional and indicative of a change in meaning or a different meaning.

...

Throughout the Act the expressions "used," "that was acquired for use" "that was intended to be used, "that was held" are found. It must be assumed that they are not interchangeable.

"Used or intended to be used" is found in clause 18(3.1)(a)(ii)(B) and paragraph 138(4.4)(d) of the *Income Tax Act*.

"Used or held" or "held" is used in the following provisions of the *Income Tax Act:* section 12.4 and paragraph 18(2)(d), subparagraph 18(3)(b)(ii), subsection 18(13), paragraph 85(1.l)(b), subparagraph 95(1)(a.1)(i), paragraph 129(4.1)(c), paragraph 129(4.2)(b), subsection 138(4.4), subparagraph 138(5)(b)(i), subparagraph 138(5)(b)(ii), subparagraph 138.l(1)(c)(ii) and subparagraph 138.1(1)(c)(iii).

"Acquired for use" appears in subsection 127(9). Indeed in the definition of certified property the two expressions "used" and "acquired for use" are juxtaposed.

It appears obvious that these expressions have a different meaning from "used" when that expression stands alone. As Mr. Justice Collier stated in *Evans v. R*, [1987] 1 CTC 316, 87 DTC 5226 (FCTD), in dealing with the words "was used" in subsection 1100(17) of the Income Tax Regulations at page 318 (DTC 5228):

> There was a difference of view, between the parties, as to whether Regulation 1100(17) applied in this case. Was the motorhome, in 1980, a leasing property? The regulation provides that leasing property is "depreciable property" owned by the taxpayer, if in the taxation year, the property
>
> ... was used by the taxpayer ... principally for the purpose of gaining or producing gross revenue that is rent, royalty or leasing revenue. ...
>
> The dispute centred on the words "was used." The plaintiff submitted the words must be given their ordinary meaning; on the evidence, the motorhome was not, in fact, used, in 1980, for the purpose of gaining or producing gross revenue.
>
> The defendant contends that, on the evidence, the plaintiff intended to rent out the motorhome to others; even though no rentals took place in 1980, it was used within the meaning of the regulation.
>
> I disagree. I concur with the plaintiff's submissions.
>
> The words "was used" must, in my opinion, be given their plain ordinary meaning. The leasing property must have, in fact, been used. Hoped for, or intended use, is not included.

Similarly, in *Stearns Catalytic Ltd. v. R (sub nom. Stearns Catalytic Ltd. v. Canada)*, [1990] 1 CTC 398, 90 DTC 6286 McNair J said at page 410 (DTC 6294):

> In my opinion, the words in subparagraph 127(10)(c)(i) "to be used" connote an actual physical or functional use of the prescribed machinery and equipment and spare parts stocked on shelves as an assurance against possible mechanical breakdown do not come within the concept of use, regardless of the soundness of the underlying business policy in stocking them.

In my opinion the Eglinton property was not "used" by Glaxo for the purpose of gaining or producing income from its business. It was intended to be used, it was waiting to be used, but in any meaningful sense of the term it was not being used. As Hugessen J said in *Qualico Developments Ltd. v. R (No. 1)*, [1984] CTC 122, 84 DTC 6119 at page 130 (DTC 6125-26):

> In my view, the "use" of a building in the context of paragraph 20(1)(aa) of the *Income Tax Act* requires something more than the passive holding of it, waiting for it to be sold.

Counsel for the appellant referred to a number of English authorities but I think they are distinguishable. In *British Motor Syndicate Ltd. v. Taylor & Son Ltd.*, [1900] 1 Ch. 577 it was held that the transport within the United Kingdom of patented articles was "making use" of them within the *Patent, Designs and Trade Marks Act*. At page 583 Stirling J said:

> The first meaning assigned to the word "use" in *Johnson's Dictionary* is "to employ to any purpose"; it is, therefore, a word of wide signification. It seems to me that the terms "use" and "make use of" are intended to have a wider application than "exercise" and "put in practice," and, without saying that no limit is to be placed on the two former expressions in the patent, I think, on the best consideration that I can give, that they are not confined to the use of a patented article for the purpose for which it is patented. In my opinion the transport within the United Kingdom of the articles made according to the plaintiffs' patent under the circumstances which occurred in this case was, indirectly at least, "making use of" those articles within the meaning of the patent, and consequently is an infringement.

Here we have the additional words "for the purpose of gaining or producing income from a business." The land was never put to any use in the business at all. It was held for future use.

In *Newcastle City Council v. Royal Newcastle Hospital*, [1959] AC 248, [1959] 1 All ER 734 (NSW PC) the question was whether vacant land adjoining a hospital was "used or occupied by a hospital for the uses thereof." Lord Denning said at pages 254-55 (All ER 735):

> The hospital acquired the land in a series of parcels from 1926 to 1946, namely, 92 acres in 1926, 4 acres in 1934, 10 acres in 1944, and 220 acres in 1946. There is no doubt that the hospital acquired all the land for the purposes of the hospital. Indeed, when the latest portion of it (220 acres) was compulsorily acquired in 1946, the Government Gazette expressly stated that it was "resumed for the purposes of the Newcastle Hospital." According to the evidence these purposes were to keep the atmosphere clear and unpolluted: to prevent building upon the land and so act as a barrier against the approach of factories and houses: to provide quiet and serene surroundings for the patients: and to give room to expand the activities of the hospital. The land was undoubtedly acquired and owned for those purposes. But was it used or occupied for those purposes? That is the question.
>
> Their Lordships are of opinion that it was used for those purposes. Mr. MacKenna submitted that an owner of land could not be said to use the land by leaving it unused: and that was all that had been done here. Their Lordships cannot accept this view. An owner can use land by keeping it in its virgin state for his own special purposes. An owner of a powder magazine or a rifle range uses the land he has acquired nearby for the purpose of ensuring safety even though he never sets foot on it. The owner of an island uses it for the purposes of a bird sanctuary even though he does nothing on it, except prevent people building there or disturbing the birds. In the same way this hospital gets, and purposely gets, fresh air, peace and quiet, which are no mean advantages to it and its patients. True it is that the hospital would get the same advantages if the land were owned by the Crown or by a trust which had determined to keep it in a natural state, or by an owner who was under a restrictive covenant not to build on the land. But the advantages then would be fortuitous or at any rate outside the control of the hospital. Here they are intended, and that makes all the difference.

I do not think the situation is the same here. The "use" of the vacant land by the hospital adjacent to the buildings was to assist in keeping the air clean and the atmosphere quiet. That is, in my view, quite a different matter from holding land that is not contiguous to the pharmaceutical company's premises with a view to future development and for no other purpose than the fulfilment of its future business plans.

In my opinion the Eglinton property was not used by Glaxo for the purpose of gaining or producing income from its business. Therefore it was not a former business property....

Appeal dismissed.

NOTES AND QUESTIONS

1.   On what basis did the taxpayer in *Glaxo Wellcome Inc.* argue that the parcel of land at issue in the case was "former business property" within the meaning of the definition in subsection 248(1) of the Act? Why does the court reject this argument? How does the court interpret the meaning of the words "was used ... for the purpose of gaining or producing income from a business" for the purposes of this definition?

2.   For other cases in which courts have disallowed a rollover under subsection 44(1) on the basis that the taxpayer had not established that the former property was used primarily by the taxpayer for the purpose of gaining or producing income from a business, see *Lefebvre v. M.N.R.*, [1990] T.C.J. No. 1130, [1991] 1 C.T.C. 2185, (1990) 91 D.T.C. 192 (T.C.C.) (land used in family farming, fishing, logging, and construction business acquired by taxpayers from their parents and sold five days later) and *Van Lathing & Holding Co. v. Canada*, [1996] T.C.J. No. 65, [1996] 2 C.T.C. 2008 (T.C.C.) (taxpayer's evidence that land was used in a farming business considered not believable).

3.   In *McKervey v. M.N.R.*, [1992] T.C.J. No. 269, [1992] 2 C.T.C. 2015, 92 D.T.C. 1570 (T.C.C.), the taxpayer carried on a number of businesses, including trucking, truck dismantling, and the sale of truck parts and building materials, for the purpose of which he had unsuccessfully attempted to rezone a parcel of land, which in the absence of such rezoning was used to store trucks and machinery. When the taxpayer sold this property and acquired another parcel of land, he elected to defer the gain under subsection 44(1), which the Minister considered inapplicable on the basis that the original property was not "used ... primarily for the purpose of gaining or producing income" from the taxpayer's business. Concluding (at para. 31) that a property need not be "used to full capacity all of the time" to qualify as "former business property" provided that "a reasonable amount of use is made of it and it is dedicated to and held in readiness for that use and provided further that it is not being put to any other significant use," the court allowed the taxpayer's appeal.

4.   In *Edwynn Holdings Ltd. v. M.N.R.*, [1990] 1 C.T.C. 2108, 89 D.T.C. 720 (T.C.C.), the taxpayer held 50 per cent of the shares of a numbered company that owned and operated a hotel, which it sold in 1980, after which it purchased a one-ninth interest in another hotel. Concluding that the shares of the numbered company were not real property and were not an interest in real property, the court affirmed the Minister's assessment disallowing the rollover in subsection 44(1).

5.   In *Buonincontri v. Canada*, [1985] F.C.J. No. 406, [1985] 1 C.T.C. 370, 85 D.T.C. 5277 (F.C.T.D.), the taxpayer, a tailor by trade who acquired nine different properties between 1967 and 1981 for the purpose of deriving rental income, sold an 11-suite apartment building in 1978, the proceeds of which he used to acquire a 10-suite apartment house in 1979. Concluding that the building sold in 1978 was a "rental property," which is specifically excluded from the definition of a "former business property" in subsection 248(1), the court held that the transactions did not qualify for the rollover under subsection 44(1).

For another case in which capital property was characterized as rental property, see *Colbert v. Canada*, [1994] F.C.J. No. 1171 (F.C.T.D.), where the taxpayers owned the land that was used in a farming business carried on by a wholly owned corporation. Concluding that the land was rented to the corporation, which used it for the purpose of gaining or producing income from a business carried on by it rather than the taxpayers, the court dismissed the taxpayer's appeal from an assessment disallowing the rollover in subsection 44(1).

6.   In *Macklin v. M.N.R.*, [1992] F.C.J. No. 1010, [1993] 1 C.T.C. 21, (1992) 92 D.T.C. 6595 (F.C.T.D.), the taxpayer sold a parcel of land for development purposes on April 11, 1980. The land had been used as farmland until the fall of 1979, when the crops were harvested and the topsoil removed in anticipation of the development. Rejecting the Minister's argument that the property was not, as required by paragraph 44(1)(b), "immediately before the disposition, a former business property" that was "used by the taxpayer ... primarily for the purpose of gaining or producing income from a business," the court adopted a broad interpretation of the word "immediately" consistent with commercial and economic reality and the purpose of the rollover. According to Rothstein J (at para. 42):

> In my view, the word "immediately" in the context of paragraph 44(1)(b) is not intended to specify a time in terms of a specific instance. I am of the opinion that it appears in paragraph 44(1)(b) to ensure that where taxpayers attempt to avail themselves of the relief provided by the replacement property provisions, that they do so for bona fide purposes consistent with the spirit and object of the provision. I cannot accept that the word "immediately" is included to catch taxpayers if the sequence of the property changing character and the disposition of the property is not in a particular order. Nothing in the paragraph indicates, and no rationale was put forward to suggest, that the word "immediately" is required to regulate the sequence of complicated steps that must be taken in such transitions. It seems to me to be unreasonable to expect taxpayers to ensure in all cases where they wish to avail themselves of the replacement property rules to defer recognition of capital gains, that disposition of property

in connection with its development must take place before or, in any event, not one instant after the property changes in character from its prior business purpose, in this case farming, to the development purpose. That would not take account of the practical nature of transactions and particularly the transaction in this case. It would not reflect commercial and economic reality.

7.   For the CRA's views on the characterization of capital property as "former business property," see Interpretation Bulletin IT-491, "Former Business Property," September 3, 1982. According to paragraphs 6 and 7 of this bulletin:

> 6. If a property that would otherwise qualify as a former business property is rented for a short period prior to its disposition, it is a question of fact as to whether or not the renting was simply an interim measure while *bona fide* attempts were being made to sell the property. If such is the case, the Department may accept that the status of the property as a former business property was maintained...

> 7. Likewise, if the property remained idle for a period of time while attempts were made to sell it, the Department would consider paragraph 44(1)(b) applicable provided the property otherwise qualifies as a former business property.

8.   For the CRA's views on the characterization of property as "replacement property" within the meaning of subsection 44(5), see Interpretation Bulletin IT-259R4, "Exchanges of Property," September 23, 2003. Where a taxpayer acquires a property to replace a former property that was not used for the purpose of gaining or producing income, paragraph 16 states that the replacement property will generally "bear the same physical description of the former property, for example, land replaced by land or a building by a building," but also notes that "there may be cases where a different type of property provides the same use or function as the former property." According to paragraph 17:

> Where the former property was used for the purpose of gaining or producing income from a business, another property will usually be considered to be a property acquired for the "same or a similar use" if it is acquired to gain or produce income from the same or a similar business and if it generally bears the same physical description as the former property. For example, a taxpayer may replace a warehouse with a manufacturing building used in the same or a similar business because both properties are buildings and the two uses are "similar" in that they are both part of the overall process of providing products from the same or a similar business to the consumer. It must be kept in mind, however, that the "same or a similar use" test ... is still a separate test from, and is not overridden by, the "same or a similar business" test.... Thus, for example, if a company owned a residential property used to house its employees, a building used to carry on the company's day-to-day operations would generally not be considered as having the "same or a similar use" even though both properties are real property and are used in the same business. Also, a property normally will not be a replacement property acquired for the same or a similar use when it is acquired to replace a former property and at the same time provide substantial other uses. An insignificant secondary use of a new replacement property is not a concern. A former business property cannot be replaced with a rental property.

According to paragraphs 18 to 21 of this bulletin:

> 18. The term "similar business" as used in the phrase "the same or a similar business" or "from that or a similar business" in paragraphs 13(4.1)(b), 14(7)(b) and 44(5)(b) ... are interpreted in a reasonably broad manner. In this respect, two businesses will be considered to be "similar" if they both fall within the same one of the following categories:

(a)   merchandising — retailing and wholesaling;

(b)   farming;

(c)   fishing;

(d)   forestry and forest products;

(e)   extractive industries, including refining;

(f)   financial services;

(g)   communications;

(h)   transportation;

(i)   construction, including subcontracting; and

(j)   manufacturing and processing.

19. With regard to the categories referred to in para. 18, where a business falls into more than one, a similar business will be one that falls into any one of these categories for which the business qualifies; for example, a plywood plant qualifies under category (d) - forestry and forest products, and under category (j) - manufacturing and processing. As a result, if the plywood plant is sold, any business that falls in category (d) or category (j) will be considered a "similar business."

20. A taxpayer who changes from one business category to another but continues to deal in the same product will normally be considered to be in a "similar business." For example, a taxpayer involved in the merchandising of a product may change to the manufacture and production of the same product and still be considered to be in a "similar" business. On the other hand, where a taxpayer carries on a number of separate businesses (see the current version of IT-206, *Separate Businesses*) and the same products are not involved, these businesses will not be considered to be similar businesses. For example, a taxpayer who operates a hotel business and a manufacturing business as separate businesses cannot be considered to have similar businesses.

21. Service industries, such as hotels, restaurants, repairs, professional services, barbershops, funeral parlours, laundries, real estate agencies, tourism, and entertainment, are not included in the categories referred to in para. 18, because most of these industries are too varied and different to permit categorization. Where there is a question of whether two businesses in a service industry or in any other industry not included in the categories in para. 18 are "similar businesses," the determination will have to be made on the facts of the case. For such cases, "similar business" will be interpreted in a reasonably broad manner.

9.   Since the rollover in subsection 44(1) requires the taxpayer to acquire a replacement property with specific periods of time after the year in which an amount becomes receivable by the taxpayer as proceeds of disposition of a capital property, the time when an amount becomes receivable as proceeds of disposition of a former business property and the time when the taxpayer acquires a replacement property may be crucial to the application of the provision. The time when a taxpayer acquires a replacement property depends on judicially developed principles governing the meaning of the word "acquisition" for the purposes of the Act. These principles were examined earlier in this chapter.

As a general rule, the time when an amount becomes receivable is also determined according to general principles — governing the characterization of amounts as receivables. Where a taxpayer obtains compensation for capital property that is unlawfully taken, destroyed, or expropriated, however, subsection 44(2) generally deems the time when the taxpayer has disposed of the property and an amount has become receivable by a taxpayer for the property to be the earliest of:

(a) the day the taxpayer has agreed to an amount as full compensation to the taxpayer for the property lose, destroyed, taken or sold,

(b) where a claim, suit, appeal or other proceeding has been taken before one or more tribunals or courts of competent jurisdiction, the day on which the taxpayer's compensation for the property is finally determined by those tribunals or courts, [and]

(c) where a claim, suit, appeal or other proceeding referred to in paragraph (b) has not been taken before a tribunal or court of competent jurisdiction within two years of the loss, destruction or taking of the property, the day that is two years following the day of the loss, destruction or taking,

and deems the taxpayer "to have owned the property continuously until the time so determined." For cases in which subsection 44(2) has been applied, see *Laurentide Rendering Inc. v. Canada*, [1988] F.C.J. No. 46, [1988] 2 C.T.C. 200, 88 D.T.C. 6133 (F.C.A.) and *Loukras v. M.N.R.*, [1990] T.C.J. No. 427, [1990] 2 C.T.C. 2044, 90 D.T.C. 1557 (T.C.C.).

10.   Where a taxpayer disposes of depreciable property of a prescribed class that is either "former business property" as defined in subsection 248(1) or property that is unlawfully taken, destroyed, or expropriated, subsection 13(4) provides a similar rollover to that in subsection 44(1), so long as the taxpayer acquires a replacement property within the same time periods and elects to have the rollover apply. For this purpose, subsection 13(4.1) contains a definition of "replacement property" that is virtually identical to the definition in subsection 44(5). A similar rollover rule for the disposition of eligible capital property appears in subsections 14(6) and (7).

b. Transfer of Property to Spouse or Common Law Partner

Where a taxpayer gives property to a person with whom the taxpayer does not deal at arm's length, paragraph 69(1)(b) of the Act generally deems the taxpayer to have disposed of the property for proceeds equal to fair market value, while paragraph 69(1)(c) deems a person who acquires property by way of gift to have acquired it at its fair market value. Similarly, where a taxpayer dies in a taxation year, paragraph 70(5)(a) deems the taxpayer to have disposed of all capital property immediately before death for proceeds equal to their fair market value, while paragraph 70(5)(b) deems the cost of capital property to a person who acquires this property as a consequence of a taxpayer's death to be the fair market value of the property immediately before the taxpayer's death.

Where the recipient of a gift *inter vivos* or transfer at death is the transferor's spouse or common law partner, however, subsections 73(1) and 70(6) provide for a rollover that applies by default unless the transferor, in the case of a gift, or the taxpayer's representative, in the case of a transfer at death, elects not to have these provisions apply.[90] According to subsection 73(1), where an individual transfers capital property to a spouse or common law partner, to a former spouse or common law partner in settlement of rights arising out of their common law relationship, or to a qualifying trust for the benefit of the spouse or common law partner, and the taxpayer does not elect not to have the rollover apply, the property is deemed:

(a) to have been disposed of at that time by the individual for proceeds equal to

    (i) where the particular property is depreciable property of a prescribed class, that proportion of the undepreciated capital cost to the taxpayer immediately before that time of all property of that class that the fair market value immediately before that time of the particular property is of the fair market value immediately before that time of all of that property of that class, and

    (ii) in any other case, the adjusted cost base to the taxpayer of the particular property immediately before that time; and

(b) to have been acquired at that time by the transferee for an amount equal to those proceeds.

For the purpose of this provision, subsection 73(1.1) ensures that the rollover applies to a court-ordered division and vesting of property by law on a marriage breakup by deeming an acquisition of capital property in this manner to be a transfer of property to a particular transferee. Where a transferee is deemed by this provision to have acquired depreciable property at a cost less than its capital cost to the transferor, moreover, subsection 73(2) deems the capital cost of the property to the transferee to be its original capital cost to the transferor, and the difference between this amount and the cost of the property to the transferee to have been allowed to the transferee as capital cost allowance in previous taxation years — making the transferee liable for recaptured depreciation on a subsequent disposition of this property.

Subsection 70(6) applies where capital property of a taxpayer that would otherwise be subject to a deemed disposition under subsection 70(5) is, as a consequence of the taxpayer's death, transferred or distributed to the taxpayer's spouse or common law partner, or to a qualifying trust for the benefit of the spouse or common law partner, and the property is demonstrated to have become "vested indefeasibly" in the spouse or common law partner or trust, as the case may be, within a period ending 36 months after the taxpayer's death or, where a written application has been made to the Minister within this period, such longer period as the Minister considers reasonable in the circumstances.[91] In these circumstances, paragraphs 70(6)(c) and (d) stipulate that:

---

[90] See the preamble to subs. 73(1) for gifts *inter vivos*, and subs. 70(6.2) for transfers at death.

[91] For the purposes of the Act, subs. 248(8) stipulates that a transfer, distribution, or acquisition of property shall be considered to have occurred as a consequence of a taxpayer's death where the transfer, distribution, or acquisition was made "(a) ... under or as a consequence of the terms of

(c)   paragraphs (5)(a) and (b) do not apply in respect of the property,

(d)   ... the taxpayer shall be deemed to have, immediately before the taxpayer's death, disposed of the property and received proceeds of disposition therefor equal to

(i)   where the property was depreciable property of a prescribed class, the lesser of the capital cost and the cost amount to the taxpayer of the property immediately before the death, and

(ii) in any other case, its adjusted cost base to the taxpayer immediately before the death, and the spouse or common-law partner or trust, as the case may be, shall be deemed to have acquired the property at the time of the death at a cost equal to those proceeds.

Where the property subject to this rollover was depreciable property, moreover, paragraph 70(5)(e) deems the capital cost of the property to the spouse, common law partner, or trust, as the case may be, to be the original capital cost of the property to the taxpayer and the difference between this amount and the cost of the property to the spouse, common law partner, or trust to have been allowed to this person as capital cost allowance in previous taxation years — making the spouse, common law partner, or trust liable for recaptured depreciation on a subsequent disposition of this property.

c. Transfer of Farming or Fishing Property to Child

Like the rollover rules in subsections 73(1) and 70(6), subsections 73(3) and 70(9) permit a rollover on the transfer of capital property to a taxpayer's child,

---

the will or other testamentary instrument of a taxpayer ... or as a consequence of the law governing the intestacy of a taxpayer ... [or] (b) ... as a consequence of a disclaimer, release or surrender by a person who was a beneficiary under the will or other testamentary instrument or on the intestacy of a taxpayer ... ." For a helpful discussion of the meaning of the words, "vested indefeasibly," see Interpretation Bulletin IT-449R, "Meaning of 'Vested Indefeasibly,'" September 25, 1987, which has been archived by the CRA. According to para. 1: "a property vests indefeasibly in [a person] ... when such a person obtains right to absolute ownership of that property in such a manner that such right cannot be defeated by any future event, even though that person may not be entitled to the immediate enjoyment of all the benefits arising from that right." According to para. 2: "Property is considered to vest indefeasibly in the person to whom it is bequeathed when that person has an enforceable right or claim to the ownership thereof. This will be so even though the formal legal conveyance and registration of ownership of property described in a specific bequest in a will will vest in the beneficiary immediately after the death of the testator. The ownership of property emanating out of a non-specific bequest will vest in the beneficiary when such property has been identified and the beneficiary has a binding right to receive it." For cases in which courts have considered whether property has vested indefeasibly within the period of time specified in subs. 70(6), see *Hillis Estate v. M.N.R.*, [1983] F.C.J. No. 817, [1983] C.T.C. 348, 83 D.T.C. 5365 (F.C.A.); *Hrycej Estate v. M.N.R.*, [1984] C.T.C. 2115, 84 D.T.C. 1089 (T.C.C.); *Parkes Estate v. M.N.R.*, [1986] 1 C.T.C. 2262, 86 D.T.C. 1214 (T.C.C.); *Van Son Estate v. M.N.R.*, [1990] F.C.J. No. 125, [1990] 1 C.T.C. 182, 90 D.T.C. 6183 (F.C.T.D.); and *Greenwood Estate v. M.N.R.*, [1990] F.C.J. No. 1007, [1991] 1 C.T.C. 47, (1990) 90 D.T.C. 6690 (F.C.T.D.), aff'd. [1993] F.C.J. No. 1340, [1994] 1 C.T.C. 310, (1993) 94 D.T.C. 6190 (F.C.A.).

but only for land or depreciable property that was, before the taxpayer's death "used principally in a fishing or farming business carried on in Canada in which the taxpayer, the taxpayer's spouse or common-law partner or any of the taxpayer's children was actively engaged on a regular and continuous basis." Similar rules in subsections 73(4) and 70(9.2) apply where the property transferred to a child consists of shares of the capital stock of a family farm or fishing corporation of an interest in a family farm or fishing partnership.[92] While these rollover rules operate like those for transfers of property to a spouse, common law partner, or qualifying trust for the benefit of a spouse or common law partner, the rules governing the transfer of farm or fishing property at death allow the taxpayer's legal representative to elect as the property's proceeds of disposition any amount between the property's cost and its fair market value.

For the CRA's views on the pre-2007 versions of these provisions, which were more limited in that they did not generally allow for the rollover of interests in family fishing businesses, see Interpretation Bulletin IT-268R4, "*Inter Vivos* Transfer of Farm Property to Child," April 15, 1996, and Interpretation Bulletin IT-349R3, "Intergenerational Transfers of Farm Property on Death," November 7, 1996. For cases in which these provisions have been considered, see *Lobsinger v. M.N.R.*, [1982] C.T.C. 2804, 82 D.T.C. 1810 (T.R.B.); *Penner Estate v. M.N.R.*, [1984] C.T.C. 2502, 84 D.T.C. 1444 (T.C.C.); *Gale Estate v. M.N.R.*, [1984] C.T.C. 3043, 85 D.T.C. 28 (T.C.C.); *Coleman Estate v. M.N.R.*, [1987] T.C.J. No. 1007, [1988] 1 C.T.C. 2010, (1987) 87 D.T.C. 664 (T.C.C.); *Lewis Estate v. M.N.R.*, [1989] T.C.J. No. 400, [1989] 2 C.T.C. 2011, 89 D.T.C. 291 (T.C.C.); *Boger Estate v. M.N.R.*, [1991] F.C.J. No. 805, [1991] 2 C.T.C. 168, 91 D.T.C. 5506 (F.C.T.D.).

3. Stop-Loss Rules

In addition to rollover rules that allow taxpayers to defer the recognition of a gain that would otherwise apply on the disposition of qualifying capital property, the Act contains other non-recognition rules that prevent the realization of a loss on the disposition of a particular property where the taxpayer or a person "affiliated" with the taxpayer acquires the particular property or a property identical to the particular property within a specified period of time before or after the disposition. The purpose of these "stop-loss rules" is to prevent the realization of accrued losses where the taxpayer's

---

[92] The terms "share of the capital stock of a family farm corporation," "share of the capital stock of a family fishing corporation," "interest in a family fishing partnership," and "interest in a family farm partnership" of a person are defined in subs. 70(10). According to these definitions, all or substantially all of the fair market value of the property of the corporation or partnership, as the case may be, must be attributable to property used by the corporation or partnership "principally in the course of carrying on the business of farming in Canada in which the person or a spouse, common-law partner, child or parent of the person was actively engaged on a regular and continuous basis."

economic interest in the property is not actually relinquished but continues through the acquisition of the property or an identical property by the taxpayer or an affiliated person shortly before or after the disposition. For the purpose of these provisions, subsection 251.1(1) defines as "affiliated persons" both "an individual and a spouse or common-law partner of the individual" as well as individuals, corporations, and partnerships that are connected with each other in specific ways listed in paragraphs 251(1)(b) to (f). For our purposes, there is no need to examine the latter categories of affiliation.

Although the Act contains several stop-loss rules,[93] the basic rules applicable to dispositions of capital property are found in subparagraph 40(2)(g)(i), the definition of a taxpayer's "superficial loss" in section 54, and paragraph 53(1)(f). According to the first of these provisions, a taxpayer's loss from the disposition of property is deemed to be nil to the extent that the loss is a "superficial loss." According to the definition of this term in section 54, a "superficial loss" means a loss from the disposition of a particular property where:

(a) during a period that begins 30 days before and ends 30 days after the disposition, the taxpayer or a person affiliated with the taxpayer acquires a property (in this definition referred to as the "substituted property") that is, or is identical to, the particular property, and

(b) at the end of that period, the taxpayer or a person affiliated with the taxpayer owns or had a right to acquire the substituted property,

except where the disposition was deemed by various provisions, including subsection 45(1) (change of use) and subsection 70(5) (death), or occurred in various other contexts that need not concern us here. In computing the adjusted cost base of any "substituted property," paragraph 53(1)(f) generally adds the amount of the superficial loss — thereby preserving the accrued loss for recognition when the substituted property is ultimately disposed of. While other stop-loss rules also prevent the recognition of losses on the disposition of a particular property where a taxpayer or an affiliated person acquires the property or an identical property within 30 days, this result is achieved not by adding the disallowed loss to the cost of the substituted property as in paragraph 53(1)(f), but by deferring recognition of the loss by the taxpayer until the taxpayer or affiliated person disposes of the property to an unaffiliated person. In this manner, these other stop-loss rules make it impossible to transfer accrued losses to an affiliated person, as was possible under earlier versions of these rules. Notwithstanding this possibility, however, the Supreme Court of Canada decision in *Mathew v. Canada*, [2005] S.C.J. No. 55, [2005] 5 C.T.C. 244, 2005 D.T.C. 5538 (S.C.C.) applied the general anti-avoidance rule to prohibit the use of subsection 18(13) (as it formerly read) to transfer accrued losses to partnership interests which were subsequently sold to arm's length parties who sought to deduct the losses when they were realized by the partnership.

---

[93] See also subs. 13(21.2), 14(12), 18(13) to (15), and 40(3.3) to (3.6).

CHAPTER SEVEN

Other Income and Deductions

I. INTRODUCTION

In addition to the economic gains and losses examined in Chapters 4 to 6, the *Income Tax Act*, R.S.C. 1985, c. 1 (5th Supp.), as amended, requires taxpayers to include income from the "other sources" specified in subdivision d of Division B of Part I (sections 56 to 59.1). These "other sources" of income are included in computing net income from all sources under paragraph 3(a). In addition to the amounts that may be deducted in computing a taxpayer's income from an office, employment, business, or property, paragraph 3(c) allows taxpayers to deduct amounts listed in subdivision e (sections 60 to 66.8), which, according to paragraph 3(c) may be deducted "except to the extent that those deductions, if any, have been taken into account" in computing the taxpayer's income from specific sources. This chapter reviews subdivisions d and e of Division B of Part I of the Act, examining key statutory rules and judicial decisions regarding these other sources of income and deductions.

Notably, subdivisions d and e of Division B of Part I of the Act contain rules addressing inclusions in and deductions from income relating to certain tax-advantaged plans, including registered retirement savings plans ("RRSPs"), registered retirement income funds ("RRIFs"), and registered education savings plans ("RESPs"). The majority of the provisions surrounding these plans appear in Division G of Part I of the Act, which is entitled, "Deferred and Other Special Income Arrangements," and are incorporated by reference in subdivisions d and e of Division B of Part I. These rules, and the rules surrounding the conceptually related but distinct tax-free savings accounts ("TFSAs"), introduced in January 2009, are addressed separately in section IV of the chapter. The inclusion and deduction provisions relating to these plans are discussed separately in this chapter not least because considering the inclusion and deduction elements jointly allows for a more systematic and transparent explanation of the structural features of each plan.

II. INCLUSIONS

Subdivision d of Division B of Part I of the Act contains a variety of income inclusions, several of which include amounts received under various deferred and special income arrangements;[1] thesee are discussed in section IV, below. Some of the other provisions in subdivision d are anti-avoidance rules designed to prevent income splitting.[2] For our purposes, there is no need to consider these rules in detail here. Other rules in subdivision d contribute significantly to the statutory scheme for taxing income from all sources and merit special examination. The following sections examine the most important of these inclusions.

A. Superannuation or Pension Benefits

Among the most important inclusions in subdivision d, subparagraph 56(1)(a)(i) requires taxpayers to include "any amount received by the taxpayer in the year as, on account or in lieu of payment of, or in satisfaction of ... a superannuation or pension benefit." For this purpose, subsection 248(1) defines a "superannuation or pension benefit" to include "any amount received out of or under a superannuation or pension fund or plan" or to the employer or former employer of the beneficiary under certain circumstances.[3] As well, in characterizing a payment as an amount "received out of or under a superannuation or pension fund or plan," clauses 56(1)(a)(i)(A) to (C.1) specifically include:

(A) the amount of any pension, supplement or spouse's or common-law partner's allowance under the *Old Age Security Act* and the amount of any similar payment under a law of a province,

(B) the amount of any benefit under the *Canada Pension Plan* or a provincial pension plan as defined in section 3 of that Act [that is, the *Quebec Pension Plan*],

(C) the amount of any payment out of or under a prescribed provincial pension plan, and

---

[1] See para. 56(1)(g) (supplementary unemployment benefit plan), (h) (registered retirement savings plan), (h.1) (home buyer's plan), (h.2) (lifelong learning plan), (i) (deferred profit-sharing plan), (j) (life insurance policy proceeds), (q) (education savings plan payments), (t) (registered retirement income fund), (w) (salary deferral arrangement), and (x), (y), and (z) (retirement compensation arrangement).

[2] See subs. 56(2) (indirect payments), 56(4) (transfer of rights to income), and 56(4.1) to (4.3) (interest-free or low-interest loans). According to subs. 56(5), these rules do not apply to amounts subject to a special "income-splitting tax" on passive income received by individuals under the age of 18—sometimes referred to as the "kiddie tax."

[3] The extended definition, which includes as a superannuation or pension benefit amounts paid to the employer or former employer of a beneficiary, was added to reverse the effect of *M.N.R. v. Eastern Abattoirs Ltd.*, [1963] C.T.C. 19, (1962) 63 D.T.C. 1023 (Ex. Ct.), in which a refund of previously deducted contributions to an employee's pension plan was determined to be not taxable.

(C.1) the amount of any payment out of or under a foreign retirement arrangement established under the laws of a country, except to the extent that the amount would not, if the taxpayer were resident in that country, be subject to income taxation in the country.

Clauses 56(1)(a)(i)(D) to (F) specifically exclude amounts otherwise taken into account in computing the recipient's income under paragraph 6(1)(g), dealing with employee benefit plans; amounts included under paragraph 56(1)(x) or (z), dealing with retirement compensation arrangements; and benefits received under section 71 of the *Canada Pension Plan* or a similar provision in a provincial pension plan as defined in section 3 of that Act (i.e. the *Quebec Pension Plan*).

For the purposes of this chapter, it is not necessary to examine the specific inclusions and exceptions in clauses 56(1)(a)(i)(A) to (F) in detail. However, since the general effect of the statutory provisions is to include all amounts "received out of or under a superannuation or pension fund or plan," it is useful to consider the meaning of these words for the purposes of the Act. Among the earliest cases to consider the meaning of these words is *Jackson v. M.N.R.*, [1951] C.T.C. 9, 51 D.T.C. 447 (Ex. Ct.), which involved similar language in the *Income War Tax Act*.

Jackson v. M.N.R.
[1951] C.T.C. 9, 51 D.T.C. 447 (Ex. Ct.)

CAMERON, J: ... On March 19, 1913, the appellant was appointed judge of the District Court of the District of Lethbridge, Alberta. ... He continued to be a judge of that court until August 3, 1935, when upon the reorganization of the District Courts of Alberta, he was appointed a judge of the District Court of the District of Southern Alberta. ... On June 1, 1945, he wrote to the Governor-General of Canada ... as follows:

> Pursuant to the provisions of section 26 and Amendments of Chapter 105, RSC 1927, I hereby resign my office of Judge of the District Court in the Province of Alberta as of July 1st, 1945, after more than thirty-two years of service in that office.

On October 2, 1945, by Letters Patent ... the appellant, under the provisions of section 26 and section 26A of the *Judges Act*, was granted a life annuity of $3,333.33, payable by monthly instalments out of the Consolidated Revenue Fund of Canada. In the taxation year 1945 the appellant received $824.35 from this annuity and, while he disclosed the receipt of that sum in a schedule attached to his income tax return, he considered it to be exempt from tax and therefore did not include it in his taxable income. The respondent, however, added that amount to his taxable income and assessed him accordingly. From that assessment an appeal is now taken.

The section of the *Judges Act* under which the appellant was entitled to resign and did resign, and under which the annuity was granted to him, was, in 1945, as follows:

26. (1) Every judge of a county court or of the district Court of Montreal who has attained the age of seventy-five years shall be compulsorily retired, and any judge of either of the said courts who has continued in office for a period of thirty years or upwards may resign his office; and to any judge who is retired, or who so resigns, His Majesty may grant an annuity equal to the salary of the office held by him at the time of his retirement or resignation.

(2) The annuity in either of the cases mentioned in this section shall commence immediately after the judge's retirement or resignation, and continue henceforth during his natural life.

Counsel for the appellant submits that the *Judges Act* (particularly section 26) makes a distinction between judges who have been retired upon reaching the age of seventy-five years and those who have resigned, like the appellant. He says that a judge who has been retired may still quite properly be referred to as a judge or a retired judge — and that even after his retirement such a judge retains certain powers and may be called upon again to perform the duties of a judge as provided for in section 35 of the Act...

He submits, however, that that is not the case with a judge who has resigned under section 26(1); that upon his resignation he ceased in every respect to be a judge, had no powers, duties, rights or responsibilities as a judge; and that not being a "retired judge" he could not be called upon to perform any duties of any sort under section 35, after his resignation. Then he says it must follow that the annuity provided for "judges" in section 26 and "the retiring allowances or annuities of the judges" which are payable out of the Consolidated Revenue Fund of Canada (section 29(1)) are limited to those judges who have retired; that the appellant having resigned on June 1, 1945, had no statutory right to the grant of an annuity and that the annuity granted to him by the Letters Patent of October 2, 1945, was granted to him in his personal capacity, the monies received by him thereunder being — as his counsel puts it:

they are a matter of largesse from a benevolent Monarch, completely independent of contract, completely independent of any obligation whatsoever, and completely independent of any right. They are granted pursuant to a permissive discretion and the annuity is granted to John Ainslie Jackson personally — to the person.

Such payments, he submits, are not taxable under any of the provisions of the *Income War Tax Act* as it was in 1945. He relies on the judgment of Maclean J in the case of *Fullerton v. Minister of National Revenue*, [1939] Ex. CR 13; [1938-39] CTC 207, to which reference will later be made.

I cannot agree with the interpretation which counsel for the appellant seeks to place upon section 26. In my view, that section is clear and unambiguous. It provides for the termination of office of the named judges in two ways: (a) by compulsory retirement upon reaching the age of seventy-five years; and (b) by voluntary resignation where service has continued for thirty years or more. Then provision is made for payment of an annuity which is the same [in] either case. The section does not in any way attempt to define the status of individuals concerned after they have been retired or have resigned, and there was no need to do so. The whole purport of the section was to require the withdrawal from office of such judges as had attained seventy-five years of age and to permit others who had been in service for thirty years or more (and were still under seventy-five years of age) to withdraw voluntarily from office should they desire to do so, and in either case to provide a pension or annuity. I have no doubt whatever that Parliament in enacting section 26 intended to confer the same right to an annuity on judges who had attained the age of seventy-five years and were retired compulsorily, as upon other judges who had given thirty years' service or over and who voluntarily resigned. The appellant herein at the time of his resignation was a judge of a district court and therefore, being "a judge ... who resigns," became entitled to the same annuity as "a judge who is so retired." The right to the annuity arises from his service in office as a judge in office and does not depend in any way upon the question as to whether or not he was entitled to the designation of "judge" after his resignation.

As I have stated above, appellant's counsel relies on the *Fullerton* case. There it was held that a lump sum payment made by the Canadian National Railways to the appellant after the termination of his office as Chairman of the Board of Trustees of the railways was not an annual net profit or gratuity directly or indirectly received from any office or employment but was a gratuity, personal to Mr. Fullerton, paid to him because he was no longer in office and because of the cessation of his office more than two years before the end of the period for which he was appointed, and was, therefore, not subject to income tax.

That case, in my opinion, is not of assistance to the appellant. There it was sought unsuccessfully to bring the monies paid to Mr. Fullerton — a lump sum payment — within "the annual net profit or gain or gratuity received from any office or employment." But that is not the case here.

...

In giving his decision on the appeal herein, the respondent affirmed the assessment:

> as having been made in accordance with the provisions of the Act and in particular on the ground that the taxpayer has been assessed in accordance with the provisions of subpara. (iv) of para. (d) of subsec. (1) of sec. 3 of the Act.

At the hearing, however, counsel for the respondent conceded that the payment made to the appellant would not properly come within "the salaries, indemnities or other remuneration of any judge ..." as provided by section 3(1)(d)(iv). He relied, however, on the general provisions of section 3(1) and particularly on subsection (c).

> 3. "Income." — 1. For the purpose of this Act "Income" means the annual net profit or gain or gratuity, whether ascertained and capable of computation as being wages, salary, or other fixed amount, or unascertained as being fees or emoluments, or as being profits from a trade or commercial or financial or other business or calling, directly or indirectly received by a person from any office or employment, or from any profession or calling, or from any trade, manufacture or business, as the case may be whether derived from sources within Canada or elsewhere; and shall include the interest, dividends or profits directly or indirectly received from money at interest upon any security or without security or from stocks, or from any

other investment, and, whether such gains or profits are divided or distributed or not, and also the annual net profit or gain from any other source including ...

> (c) any payment out of any superannuation or pension fund or plan: provided, however, that in the case of a lump sum payment out of any such fund or plan which is paid upon the death, withdrawal or retirement from employment of any employee or former employee in full satisfaction of all his rights in any such fund or plan, one-third only of such lump sum payment shall be deemed to be income.

The proviso to ss. (c) is here of no importance. I have no doubt whatever that the payments received by the appellant fall within the opening words of ss. (c) — "Any payment out of any superannuation [or pension] fund or plan" — and therefore constituted taxable income in his hands. In the sense in which the two words "superannuation" and "pension" are here used, I do not think it necessary in this case to draw any distinction between them. The *Shorter Oxford English Dictionary* (Third Edition) defines "to superannuate" as "to dismiss or discharge from office on account of age; esp. to cause to retire from service on a pension; to pension off"; and "pension" is defined as "an annuity or other periodical payment made, esp. by a government, a company, or an employer of labour, in consideration of past services or of the relinquishment of rights, claims, or emoluments."

An examination of the Letters Patent ... establishes beyond any question that the annuity therein granted to the appellant falls within the above definition of a pension. It provides for payments of an annual amount payable in monthly instalments. It recites the past services of the appellant in his office as District Judge for thirty years and upwards and refers to section 26 of the Judges Act as the authority for granting the annuity upon resignation. Had the services not been rendered there would have been no authorization for the payment of any annuity under section 26.

The payments also were made in accordance with a pension plan. "Plan" is merely a "scheme of action, project, design; the way in which it is proposed to carry out some proceeding" (*Shorter Oxford English Dictionary*, Third Edition). The *Judges Act* provided such a scheme or plan for all judges who retired or resigned, varying with the time of appointment, the length of service and the court in which the particular judge had held office, and other matters.

I find, therefore, that the payments in question fall within the provisions of section 3(1)(c) of the Act and constituted taxable income in the hands of the appellant. ...

Judgment accordingly.

NOTES AND QUESTIONS

1.   On what grounds did the taxpayer in *Jackson* argue that the annuity payment received in 1945 was not taxable under the *Income War Tax Act*? Why did the court reject these arguments? How did it distinguish *Fullerton*? How did it define the words "any payment out of any superannuation or pension fund or plan"?

2.   Since the taxpayer in *Jackson* had not contributed tax paid funds to the pension fund under the *Judges Act*, the full amount of each annuity payment was taxable as income. Similarly, to the extent that most superannuation or pension benefits are received from registered plans the contributions to which are either excluded in computing the beneficiary's income from an office or employment under subparagraph 6(1)(a)(i) (employer contributions) or deductible under paragraph 8(1)(m) (employee contributions), these payments also lack any capital element.

However, where an employer's contributions to a superannuation or pension plan or fund are taxable to the employee or the employee's contributions are not deductible, payments out of or under the fund or plan will usually include a capital element. Notwithstanding the resulting double taxation, several decisions have concluded that in these circumstances the full amount of the payment is taxable under subparagraph 56(1)(a)(i) and its predecessors. See, for example, *No. 157 v. M.N.R.* (1954), 10 Tax ABC 206 (T.A.B.); *Rea v. M.N.R.* (1961), 26 Tax ABC 33 (T.A.B.); *Stephan v. M.N.R.* (1963), 33 Tax ABC 330 (T.A.B); *Raven v. M.N.R.*, [1968] Tax ABC 1097 (T.A.B.); *Cooper v. M.N.R.*, [1981] C.T.C. 2031, 81 D.T.C. 40 (T.R.B.); and *Canada v. Herman*, [1978] C.T.C. 442, 78 D.T.C. 6311 (F.C.T.D.).

3.   For the views of the CRA on the taxation of superannuation or pension benefits, see Interpretation Bulletin IT-499R, "Superannuation or Pension Benefits," January 17, 1992. According to paragraph 4:

> Subject to the exceptions [in clauses 56(1)(a)(i)(D) and (E)], any amount received out of a superannuation or pension fund is income whether it is in the nature of a single payment or otherwise. This is so even if contributions to a particular fund or plan were not deductible for tax purposes. Furthermore, these payments are taxable despite the fact that the particular superannuation or pension fund or plan has not been registered by this Department.

According to paragraph 5:

> A pension payment which is taxable under subparagraph 56(1)(a)(i) of the Act cannot, either by will or otherwise, be changed into a capital receipt. The full amount received is always classed as a superannuation or pension benefit and not as an annuity payment. Consequently, a deduction is not allowed for what might otherwise be considered to be the capital element of an amount so received.

4.   In *Manuel v. Canada*, [1999] T.C.J. No. 427, [1999] 4 C.T.C. 2281 (T.C.C.), the taxpayer received a number of payments from her former husband, who, under a divorce settlement with the taxpayer, was required to share his pension with the taxpayer on an equal basis. Allowing the taxpayer's appeal from a reassessment characterizing the payment as pension income under subparagraph 56(1)(a)(i), the court concluded (at para. 10) that the payments "were not pension benefits but rather equalization payments in anticipation of a lump sum division of the pension." For a similar result, see *St.-Jacques v. Canada*, [1999] T.C.J. No. 929, [2001] 1 C.T.C. 2704 (T.C.C.).

5.   In *Mintzer v. Canada*, [1998] T.C.J. No. 325, [1998] 3 C.T.C. 2380 (T.C.C.), the taxpayer argued that Canada Pension Plan benefits that were

retained by the Minister pursuant to section 224.1 of the *Income Tax Act* to satisfy taxes owing in previous years were not taxable under subparagraph 56(1)(a)(i) on the basis that they had not been "received" by the taxpayer. Observing (at para. 6) that "an amount may be included in income even where it is only notionally or constructively received," the court upheld the Minister's assessment, which included the amount set off against taxes payable as a pension benefit that was received by the taxpayer within the meaning of subparagraph 56(1)(a)(i).

B. Death Benefits

According to subparagraph 56(1)(a)(iii), there shall be included in computing the income of a taxpayer for a taxation year any amount received by the taxpayer in the year as, on account or in lieu of payment of, or in satisfaction of, a death benefit. Pursuant to subsection 248(1), the term "death benefit" is defined as "the total of all amounts received by a taxpayer in a taxation year on or after the death of an employee in recognition of the employee's service in an office or employment minus"

(a) where the taxpayer is the only person who has received such an amount and who is a surviving spouse or common-law partner of the employee ... the lesser of
    (i) the total of all amounts so received by the taxpayer in the year, and
    (ii) the amount, if any, by which $10,000 exceeds the total of all amounts received by the taxpayer in preceding taxation years on or after the death of the employee in recognition of the employee's service in an office or employment, or
(b) where the taxpayer is not the surviving spouse or common-law partner of the employee, the lesser of
    (i) the total of all amounts so received by the taxpayer in the year, and
    (ii) that proportion of
        (A) the amount, if any, by which $10,000 exceeds the total of all amounts received by the surviving spouse or common-law partner of the employee at any time on or after the death of the employee in recognition of the employee's service in an office or employment

that

        (B) the amount described in subparagraph (i)

is of

        (C) the total of all amounts received by all taxpayers other than the surviving spouse or common-law partner of the employee at any time on or after the death of the employee in recognition of the employee's service in an office or employment.

As a result, where an amount is received "on or after the death of an employee in recognition of the employee's service in an office or employment," the amount must be included in computing the recipient's income only to the extent that the aggregate of all such amounts exceeds a $10,000 exemption, to which the surviving spouse or common law partner has first priority, after which the remaining exemption is distributed among recipients based on their respective ratios of the aggregate amounts paid. The meaning of "death benefit" was considered in *Canada v. Cumming*, [1976] C.T.C. 447, 76 D.T.C. 6265 (F.C.T.D.).

R. v. Cumming
[1976] C.T.C. 447, 76 D.T.C. 6265 (F.C.T.D.)

MAHONEY, J: ... Earl F. Cumming was a contributor to the *Canada Pension Plan* (hereinafter called "CPP"). He had worked for the same employer for over 25 years prior to his death in 1973. He left a will naming his wife, the defendant, sole executrix and heir if she survived him for 30 days. She survived; the will was not probated. She applied for the CPP death benefit on behalf of the estate and a cheque for $560 payable to "The Estate of Earl F. Cumming" was delivered to her in payment thereof. She endorsed the cheque personally, without reference in the endorsement to the estate or to her capacity as executrix, and deposited the proceeds in her own bank account. The $560 was not, of course, reported as income in the personal return filed for Earl F. Cumming for the portion of 1973 he lived. No return was ever filed for the estate as such.

In her own personal return for 1973 the defendant reported the $560 as income and claimed an offsetting [exemption].

...

The payment was to the estate not to the defendant. I do not, however, accept the plaintiff's argument that the *Income Tax Act* demands such a strict interpretation ... that a payment otherwise a death benefit for the purposes of the Act, destined in fact and in law to the [surviving spouse], would lose its character simply because it passed through the estate en route to her. The $560 paid by the CPP was "received" by the [surviving spouse] within the meaning of paragraph (a) [in the definition of "death benefit"] of subsection 248(1).

To be a death benefit under the *Income Tax Act* the payment must, *inter alia*, have been in recognition of the deceased's service in an office or employment. The ordinary meaning of the word "recognition" in the phrase "in recognition of" is:

> The acknowledgement or admission of a kindness, service, obligation or merit, or the expression of this in some way. [*The Oxford English Dictionary*]

> acknowledgement of something done or given esp. by making some return (a gift in — of a service) [*Webster's Third New International Dictionary*]

The defendant is correct in stating that the Act does not link the payer directly with the employment, but it does link the payment with a recognition of service in that employment. It is true that the deceased was a contributor to CPP because he was employed; it is equally true that the CPP death benefit became payable because he was a contributor but to say that it was paid "in recognition of his service in employment" is to do considerable violence to the idea plainly conveyed by those ordinary English words.

The death benefit payable under the *Canada Pension Plan Act* is not a "death benefit" within the meaning of subsection 248(1) of the Income Tax Act. It is, however, a benefit under the *Canada Pension Plan* and is specifically required to be included in its recipient's income by clause 56(1)(a)(i)(B). ...

Appeal allowed.

NOTES AND QUESTIONS

1.   Why did the court in *Cumming* conclude that the payment of a "death benefit" under the *Canada Pension Plan* was not a "death benefit" within the meaning of the *Income Tax Act*?

2.   In *Lamash Estate v. M.N.R.*, [1990] T.C.J. No. 929, [1990] 2 C.T.C. 2534, 91 D.T.C. 9 (T.C.C.), the taxpayer's estate received a "Guaranteed Five Year Minimum Benefit" under the *Public Service Superannuation Act*. Citing *Cumming*, the court held that the payment was a minimum benefit accruing under the deceased's superannuation plan, not a "death benefit" received in recognition of employment service within the meaning of the Act.

3.   In *Hiltemann v. M.N.R.*, [1986] T.C.J. No. 844, [1986] 2 C.T.C. 2279, 86 D.T.C. 1716 (T.C.C.), the taxpayer, who had lived for many years in a house that she and her husband rented from her husband's employer, purchased the house shortly after her husband's death for an amount substantially less than its fair market value. Concluding (at para. 14) that the taxpayer obtained "a price advantage that would never have been offered to a person dealing with [the vendor] as a stranger," the court characterized the discounted purchase price as a death benefit "received" by the taxpayer "in recognition of" his service as an employee.

4.   In *Walman v. M.N.R.*, [1979] C.T.C. 2286, 79 D.T.C. 272 (T.R.B.), the taxpayer received a payment, following her husband's death, from the insurance companies for which he worked. However, the evidence, including her husband's previously filed tax returns, showed that he was a self-employed, independent contractor and not an employee of the insurance companies. Since the husband was not an employee, the board determined that the payment could not be considered a "death benefit" as defined in subsection 248(1).

5.   For the CRA's views on death benefits and the calculation of death benefits in various situations see Interpretation Bulletin IT-508R, "Death Benefits — Calculation," February 12, 1996.

C. Retiring Allowances

Subparagraph 56(1)(a)(ii) requires taxpayers to include in computing their income for a taxation year "any amount received by the taxpayer in the year as, on account or in lieu of payment of, or in satisfaction of ... a retiring allowance" other than amounts received out of or under various deferred income plans, which are taxable as income from an office or employment. Subsection 248(1) defines the term "retiring allowance" as:

an amount (other than a superannuation or pension benefit, an amount received as a consequence of the death of an employee or a benefit described in subparagraph 6(1)(a)(iv)) received

    (a)   on or after retirement of a taxpayer from an office or employment in recognition of the taxpayer's long service, or

    (b)   in respect of a loss of an office or employment of a taxpayer, whether or not received as, on account or in lieu of payment of, damages or pursuant to an order or judgment of a competent tribunal,

by the taxpayer or, after the taxpayer's death, by a dependant or a relation of the taxpayer or by the legal representative of the taxpayer.

The essential elements of this definition were enacted with respect to amounts received in respect of the termination of an office or employment after November 12, 1981. Prior to this date, a "retiring allowance" was defined as:

an amount received upon or after retirement from an office or employment in recognition of long service or in respect of loss of office or employment (other than a superannuation or pension benefit), whether the recipient is the officer or employee or a dependant, relation or legal representative,

while "amounts received in respect of a termination of an office or employment" were included in the recipient's income as a "termination payment" under former subparagraph 56(1)(a)(viii), subject to a maximum inclusion equal to 50 per cent of the taxpayer's remuneration for the 12 months preceding the termination. This latter provision applied to amounts received in respect of a termination of an office or employment after November 16, 1978, and was enacted to reverse in part the decision in *Canada v. Atkins*, [1976] F.C.J. No. 411, [1976] C.T.C. 497, 76 D.T.C. 6258 (F.C.A.), in which the Federal Court of Appeal held that amounts received "in lieu of notice of dismissal" were not included in computing the recipient's income from the office or employment in respect of which the amounts were received. With the repeal of former subparagraph 56(1)(a)(viii) and the amendments to the definition of a "retiring allowance" in 1981, the legislative reversal of *Atkins* was made complete.

As it currently reads, the definition of a "retiring allowance" in subsection 248(1) includes two categories of payments: (1) amounts received "upon or after [the taxpayer's] retirement... from an office or employment in recognition of the taxpayer's long service"; and (2) amounts received "in respect of a loss of an office or employment of a taxpayer, whether or not received as, on account or in lieu of payment of, damages or pursuant to an order or judgment of a competent tribunal." The following cases and text examine each of these categories of payments.

1. Payments On or After Retirement in Recognition of Long Service

Paragraph (a) of the definition of a "retiring allowance" in subsection 248(1) requires that the amount be received "on or after [the taxpayer's] retirement ... from an office or employment" and "in recognition of the taxpayer's long service." Each of these requirements was considered in *Henderson v. M.N.R.*, [1991] T.C.J. No. 404, [1991] 2 C.T.C. 2048, 91 D.T.C. 1116 (T.C.C.), in which the taxpayer sought to characterize two payments as "retiring allowances" so that they would qualify for a deduction on transfers to a registered retirement savings plan under paragraph 60(j.1).

Henderson v. M.N.R.
[1991] T.C.J. No. 404, [1991] 2 C.T.C. 2048, 91 D.T.C. 1116 (T.C.C.)

BEAUBIER, TCJ: ... John Maxwell Henderson was born in 1932. Mr. Henderson graduated with his degrees and qualified as a pharmacist in 1959. He entered into employment with his father, E.M. Henderson, in his father's pharmacy in Campbellton, New Brunswick, after qualifying as a professional pharmacist and remained so employed until September 11, 1987, in Campbellton, New Brunswick. E.M. Henderson died in June 1987, and the appellant inherited his shares in E.M. Henderson Drugs Ltd. and became the sole shareholder of that corporation. The late E.M. Henderson had operated a drug store in Campbellton, New Brunswick, from approximately 1925 until 1971 when he incorporated E.M. Henderson Drugs Ltd. and transferred the drug store and its premises to the corporation at that time. Mr. E.M. Henderson became the majority shareholder of the new corporation and the appellant became a minority shareholder in the corporation. Due to the illness of the appellant and the age of the late E.M. Henderson, they commenced trying to sell the business in 1986. By an agreement of August 21, 1987, E.M. Henderson Drugs Ltd. sold the goodwill, customer lists, scheduled equipment and inventory of the drugstore to Koffler Stores (Eastern) Ltd. which is better known by its trade name Shoppers Drug Mart. The closing date was set at September 11, 1987, and the appellant entered into a personal covenant with the purchaser not to compete with the purchaser in the Campbellton area for three years from that date.

The employees of E.M. Henderson Drugs Ltd. went to work for the purchaser on September 11, 1987, and E.M. Henderson Drugs Ltd. ceased its operation as a drug store on that date. E.M. Henderson Drugs Ltd. also entered into a net lease of the entire premises of the drug store operation with the purchaser. The lessee thereupon not only had the drug store premises, but also took over the responsibility as landlord for leases by doctors and others in the building premises. The lease with the purchaser was for approximately ten years... The result was that after September 11, 1987, E.M. Henderson Drugs Ltd. merely paid its bills and collected its receivables on winding up its drug business and then received monthly rent cheques and reinvested moneys on hand quarterly in treasury bills. After September 11, 1987, the appellant worked part-time as a pharmacist for the franchisees of Shoppers Drug Mart in the same premises as his old drug store had been located. He also worked part-time as a pharmacist for another Shoppers Drug Mart franchise in the area, all within the confines of his personal covenant. After September 11, 1987, he did not work as a pharmacist from the end of May until October 1. All of the part-time work he did was performed at an hourly rate of $25 per hour, averaging substantially fewer hours per week than he had been accustomed to in his previous employment.

The only task the appellant did for E.M. Henderson Drugs Ltd. after September 11, 1987, was to attend to pay the bills and to collect the receivables of the drug store, to file corporate resolutions and financial statements, and to sign reinvestment authorities at the bank for treasury bills on a quarterly basis. He was not paid for this.

In 1987, the appellant was paid a salary of $26,790 by E.M. Henderson Drugs Ltd. to September 11, 1987. In February 1988, Mr. Henderson met with his accountant and the corporation declared a management bonus for the 1987 fiscal period of the corporation to September 11, 1987 (for the fiscal year ended December 31, 1987) which was paid in 1988 prior to June 30, 1988, in the amount of $38,611. The appellant was also paid a retiring allowance from E.M. Henderson Drugs Ltd. of $58,000 in 1987 and $43,500 in 1988. In each of 1987 and 1988 he filed his income tax return and claimed these payments as a transfer of eligible retiring allowance to a registered retirement savings plan. These claims were disallowed by the Minister of National Revenue and are the subject of this appeal. The appellant did not receive any other income after September 11, 1987, from E.M. Henderson Drugs Ltd. except by way of dividends.

As it applies to the appellant, retiring allowance is defined by subsection 248(1) of the *Income Tax Act*, RSC 1952, c. 148 (am. SC 1970-71-72, c. 63) (the "Act") to mean:

... an amount... received

    (a)   upon or after retirement of a taxpayer from an office or employment in recognition of his long service, or

    (b)   in respect of a loss of an office or employment of a taxpayer ... by the taxpayer ...

This is included in the taxpayer's income pursuant to subparagraph 56(1)(a)(ii) of the *Income Tax Act* and can be deducted pursuant to subsection 60(j.1) if the appellant retires.

In *Specht v. The Queen*, [1975] CTC 126; 75 DTC 5069, at 133 (DTC 5073), Collier, J dealt with the word "retirement" and subsection 31A(d) of the *Canada-United States of America Tax Convention Act, 1943*, which refers to the taxability of "a payment made by an employer to an employee or former employee upon or after retirement in respect of loss of office or employment." He said:

> The plaintiff did not retire or go into retirement from his occupation with MacMillan Bloedel within the ordinary meaning of "retire or retirement." That is, he did not *withdraw from his employment because he had reached a mutually stipulated age, or generally withdraw from his occupation or business activity.*

This was based in part upon the *Shorter Oxford English Dictionary*, 3rd ed. definition of retirement as "withdrawal from occupation or business activity." The *Oxford English Dictionary*, 2nd ed. currently defines "retire" as:

> To withdraw from office or an official position; to give up one's business or occupation in order to enjoy more leisure or freedom.

In *Lorenzen v. The Queen*, [1981] CTC 377; 81 DTC 5251, Grant DJ stated at page 379 (DTC 5253) that: "Retirement implies a complete cessation of one's profession or business." In that case, the taxpayer organized a second corporation and essentially carried on the same job in a new guise. He was found not to be retired.

...

Here the appellant did not withdraw from his employment because he had reached a mutually stipulated age. The corporation's main business changed from drug sales to merely being a collector of rents and interest.

...

Within the confines of the words describing a "retiring allowance" in subsection 248(1) the Minister of National Revenue disputes the following:

(1)   The appellant was not genuinely retired from his office or employment with the corporation.

(2)   The payments were not in recognition of the appellant's long service.

To dispose of (2) first, suffice it to say that the evidence is that the appellant served E.M. Henderson Drugs Ltd. for its entire life and its predecessor Mr. Henderson for a total of 28 years which is more than ½ of the average Canadian's working life. This is certainly by today's standards of job duration "long service." It was also all of the appellant's working life to September 11, 1987. Therefore the Court finds that the payments were quite properly made by the corporation in recognition of the appellant's long service. The problem then reverts to (1), that is: Was Mr. Henderson retired? He performed rudimentary corporate functions for E.M. Henderson Drugs Ltd. for which he was not paid and he worked part-time as a licensed pharmacist for third parties in the same premises after September 11, 1987.

The appellant did not hold an "office" in the corporation as that term is defined in subsection 248(1) of the *Income Tax Act*, since he was not entitled to a "fixed or ascertainable stipend." Whether he was employed after September 11, 1987, requires an examination of the definition "employment" in subsection 248(1) which reads:

"employment" means the position of an individual in the service of some other person (including Her Majesty or a foreign state or sovereign) and "servant" or "employee" means a person holding such a position.

To be "in the service of some other person" means that the employee has a duty to serve that other person who in turn has a right to those services pursuant to a contract of mutual rights and duties.

Here the only services the appellant performed for E.M. Henderson Drugs Ltd. after September 11, 1987, were gratuitous. He had no duty to that corporation and it had no contractual right to his services. Certainly the appellant ceased to have the corporation as a source of income for his labour since his employment had expired. Moreover, the retirement was genuine. After September 11, 1987, Mr. Henderson's duties in the drug store premises as a part-time pharmacist were directed by someone else who determined his hours of work, his daily tasks, and whether he was performing adequately. Thereafter he remained completely at leisure in June, July, August and September of each year.

This Court finds that Mr. Henderson was paid a retiring allowance of $58,000 in 1987 and $43,500 in 1988 by E.M. Henderson Drugs Ltd. after retirement from employment by reason of the elimination of his employment in the service of that corporation, or for his long service in the employ of that corporation...

Appeal allowed.

NOTES AND QUESTIONS

1.   On what basis did the court in *Henderson* conclude that the payments received by the taxpayer were received "on or after [the taxpayer's] retirement from an office or employment"? How did the court define the word "retirement" for the purposes of the definition of a "retiring allowance" in subsection 248(1)?

2.   On what basis did the court in *Henderson* conclude that the payments received by the taxpayer were "in recognition of the taxpayer's long service"? Is it sufficient for the taxpayer to have been in the service of the payer for a long time for the payment to be "in recognition" of that long service? Should the courts scrutinize payments to shareholder-managers of closely held companies such as those in *Henderson* to determine whether they are made "in recognition" of long service?

3.   For cases other than those cited in *Henderson* in which courts have considered the characterization of a payment as an amount received "on or after retirement of a taxpayer from an office or employment in recognition of the taxpayer's long service," see *Albino v. M.N.R.*, [1993] F.C.J. No. 1040, [1994] 1 C.T.C. 205, (1993) 94 D.T.C. 6071 (F.C.T.D.) and *Adler v. Canada*, [1994] T.C.J. No. 390, [1995] 1 C.T.C. 2590 (T.C.C.), aff'd [1994] F.C.J. No. 1326, [1995] 1 C.T.C. 181, (1994) 94 D.T.C. 6605 (F.C.A.).

4. The CRA's views on the characterization of amounts received "on or after retirement of a taxpayer from an office or employment in recognition of the taxpayer's long service" are contained in Interpretation Bulletin IT-337R4 (Consolidated), "Retiring Allowances," February 1, 2006. According to paragraphs 3 to 5:

> 3. To qualify as a retiring allowance, a payment must be in recognition of long service or in respect of loss of an office or employment. The term "long service" is usually considered to have reference to the total number of years in an employee's career with a particular employer or with affiliated employers. A payment for unused sick leave credits qualifies as a retiring allowance (see *J. Camille Harel v. The Deputy Minister of Revenue of the Province of Quebec* (77 DTC 5438, [1977] CTC 441)).

> 4. Whether an individual has retired is a question of fact. Continued participation in a former employer's health plan (for example, providing medical, dental and long term disability coverage) for a restricted period of time would not, in itself, indicate that employment has not terminated, particularly if the employer's plan specifically permits former employees to be covered under the plan. However, if pension benefits continue to accrue to the individual, the accrual indicates that there is an existing employment relationship, since such benefits only accrue to employees. The fact that the employer does not require an individual to report to work is not, by itself, determinative of whether the individual has retired. For example, an individual who has been given a leave of absence for educational purposes is still an employee.

> 5. A retiring allowance includes an amount received in respect of a loss of office or employment. In this context, the words "in respect of" have been held by the Courts to imply a connection between the loss of employment and the subsequent receipt, where the primary purpose of the receipt was compensation for the loss of employment. [...] Two questions set out by the Courts to determine whether a connection exists for purposes of a retiring allowance are as follows:

> 1- But for the loss of employment would the amount have been received? and,

> 2- Was the purpose of the payment to compensate a loss of employment?

> Only if the answer to the first question is "no" *and* the answer to the second question is "yes", will the amount received be considered a retiring allowance.

2. Payments in Respect of Loss of an Office or Employment

Paragraph (b) of the definition of a "retiring allowance" in subsection 248(1) requires that the amount be received "in respect of a loss of an office or employment of a taxpayer." In order to qualify as a "retiring allowance" under this paragraph, therefore, the payment must be "in respect of" the taxpayer's loss of an office or employment and the taxpayer must have suffered "a loss or an office or employment." Each of these two issues is considered in turn.

a. Relationship to Office or Employment

In the years since the definition of a "retiring allowance" was amended in 1981, a number of cases have considered whether a payment to a taxpayer is "in respect of" a taxpayer's loss of an office or employment within the meaning of these words in paragraph (b) of the definition of a "retiring allowance" in subsection 248(1). In *Mendes-Roux v. Canada*, [1997] T.C.J. No. 1287, [1998] 2 C.T.C. 2274 (T.C.C.), the Tax Court considered many of these cases.

Mendes-Roux v. Canada
[1997] T.C.J. No. 1287, [1998] 2 C.T.C. 2274 (T.C.C.)

LÉGER DJTC: The Appellant, who happens to be a lawyer, was employed with the Translation Bureau of New Brunswick for a period of seven years from 1987 to 1993. She acted as co-coordinator for Court interpreters. Her place of work was Bathurst, New Brunswick. The employment consisted of training, evaluating court interpreters and being a liaison officer between judges, lawyers, court interpreters and the Translation Bureau.

In April of 1993, the Appellant applied for and was granted maternity leave which was effective from June 7 to August 27, 1993. During her leave and without prior notice or discussion, she was informed that the Bathurst office of the Translation Bureau was to be closed and the court interpretation co-ordinating service was to continue to operate at the City of Fredericton effective September 1, 1993. She was also told she would be assigned to other duties but her salary and classification would remain the same. Finally in September 1993, the Appellant went to work at the Bathurst office and was told to report to the Fredericton office or her employment would be terminated under the heading of "Abandonment of Position."

The Appellant told us in effect that the Director of the province's Translation Bureau, her immediate superior, was a very cunning individual. She suspected he had reasons to be apprehensive of her and had a desire not to have her in his employ.

She was asked to elaborate on the above. She was very emotional during the time she gave evidence and counsel for the Respondent did not object to our hearing her contention. She told us that during the course of her employment she had uncovered and reported that a certain court interpreter was cheating the Translation Bureau. The discipline of the said employee had to be dealt with by ... the Director of the Translation Bureau. The said Director was not amused.

The Appellant alleged that it later appeared that the Director himself was involved in less than proper activities. These activities were in conflict with his duties and are described in a newspaper clipping attached to her written submission and marked K-2. Her submission is that her boss had an apprehension if she continued in her present position she might blow the whistle on his illicit activities. She submits the said Director organized a transfer of the Bathurst office to Fredericton while she was on leave. The allegations of the

1127

Appellant in regards to the motives of her boss to transfer the said office are just that, allegations and not proof. She also alleges the Director, being aware of her family commitments, knew she could not or would not accept a transfer to Fredericton.

The evidence discloses that the Appellant had three infant children of tender age and that her husband who is a lawyer was engaged in the practice of law in the City of Bathurst. The distance between Bathurst and Fredericton is far greater than acceptable to allow the Appellant to commute daily and still be able to attend to the needs of her husband and family.

After having heard the evidence it is obvious to this Court that the Appellant was wrongfully dismissed.

The Appellant after her dismissal claimed damages from her former employer for the wrong she suffered and the loss of benefits which she endured.

The evidence discloses that the husband of the Appellant, being a lawyer, negotiated a settlement with the province of New Brunswick which resulted in her receiving the sum of $25,376 according to a "Release" signed September 30, 1994.

The said Release which is set out in the 8th page from the end of the Appellant's submission reads as follows:

I, SYLVIA MENDES-ROUX, of the City of Bathurst, in the County of Gloucester and Province of New Brunswick in consideration of the payment to me of the sum of One Dollar ($1.00) and other valuable consideration, the receipt of which is hereby acknowledged, as payment of special damages incurred, general damages, legal costs and interest, by Her Majesty the Queen in right of the Province of New Brunswick as represented by the Minister of Supply and Services (thereinafter called the "Minister"), do hereby RELEASE, REMISE AND FOREVER DISCHARGE the Minister, his successors and assigns, from any and all claims of every nature and kind, including costs and interest thereon, which I may have against the Minister arising from the termination of my employment with the Translation Bureau of the Department of Supply and Services, in September, 1993.

I acknowledge that this payment is made without any admission of liability by the Minister, and I promise to keep confidential the details hereof.

...

The details of the settlement [were] not set out in any document. The Province obviously recognized the Appellant had a good course of action since it paid her the sum involved. For whatever reason the Province desired to keep the details of the settlement confidential.

The only document which throws any light on the subject is the Record of Employment ... attached to the submission of the Appellant. This is a form required by Revenue Canada which must be filled out by the employer. In answer to question number 15 the insurable earnings are set out as being $745 for one week. In answer to question number 17 "Payments or Benefits (other than regular pay)" it is indicated "Vacation pay $1,610.40 (8 ¼ days)"; and "Other monies (specify)" it is stated "see below number 22 — $25,376" which reads: "Comments ... was on child care leave prior to this record. She was dismissed. She made a claim for damages and the claim was settled."

Over and above this memo we have the sworn testimony of the Appellant. She said she does not know precisely how the amount of the settlement was calculated or arrived at. She told us she believed it was based on three months of salary, compensation for overtime earned, sick leave and earned vacation pay. The wages for three months would amount to about $8,900, the vacation pay $1,610.40; these amount to a total of $10,510.40. The other items were not proven. The Appellant claimed that most of the amounts accepted by her were for wrongful dismissal, loss of fringe benefits, legal fees, interest and pain and suffering. The Respondent has not refuted this claim.

The Respondent relies on the provisions of subparagraph 56(1)(a)(ii) and subsection 248(1) of the *Income Tax Act* and claims that the sum of $25,376 was received by the Appellant from the Province of New Brunswick as a retirement allowance as defined by the above sections of the Act.

...

[In] *Vachon v. R*, [1996] 3 CTC 2306 (TCC) ... the taxpayer was an employee of D Inc. and on April 12, 1993 his employment was terminated. He accepted a lump sum of $5,000 as a full and complete settlement of all claims arising from the termination of his employment. The issue was whether the $5,000 payment was a retiring allowance within the meaning of subsection 248(1). The taxpayer did not give evidence in this case. The release was introduced in evidence and relieved the employer from any action against it by reason of the cessation of the employment. The Court declared that the amount of $5,000 was a retirement allowance within the meaning of the Act.

[In] *Merrins v. Minister of National Revenue* [1995] 1 CTC 111 (FCTD) in May 1985 the taxpayer was laid off from his employment. He filed a grievance seeking reinstatement for breach of seniority provisions of the collective agreement. On April 7, 1988, the employer agreed to pay to the taxpayer the sum of $60,000 in order to conclude the arbitration proceedings The Minister considered the $60,000 payment a "retiring allowance" within the meaning of subsection 248(1) and included it in the taxpayer's income pursuant to subparagraph 56(1)(a)(ii). The taxpayer appealed and the Court held that on the facts of this case the amount received was in relation to his loss of his employment and therefore taxable.

[In] *Niles v. Minister of National Revenue*, [1991] 1 CTC 2540 (TCC)... an employee filed a complaint of discrimination under the Ontario Human Rights Code after being laid off. After negotiation, the parties settled the claim and the employee was awarded $5,000 in settlement of his claim for loss of employment. There was no finding of discrimination nor that the award might have altered the character of the payment. The Court held that the amount was taxable as a retirement allowance.

The case of *Young v. Minister of National Revenue* (1986), 86 DTC 1567 (TCC), was also cited. Here the facts are that the Appellant was awarded damages by court order in the following amounts: $10,000 for wrongful dismissal, $12,500 for exemplary damages, $12,500 for mental distress, [and] $5,000 for costs.

The Minister claimed all of the above amounts were taxable as being a retirement allowance. The Appellant did not testify. The above facts were agreed to by the parties. The Court dismissed the appeal and in so doing said the following in the second last paragraph of his decision:

> ... it would have taken some direct evidence or testimony to fulfill the appellant's total obligation thereunder, and the critical question of the origin of the amounts at issue was not addressed by the appellant.

Based on the above finding the Court declared the total amounts to be taxable.

The next case is *Bédard v. Minister of National Revenue* [1991] 1 CTC 2323 (TCC): in this case the Appellant was unjustly dismissed from his position with Relais Jeune Est of Matane. The reasons for his termination were broadcasted on radio and television where the Appellant lived. The Appellant denied the reasons and sought reinstatement and a public retraction. An arbitrator was brought in to settle the dispute and an agreement was reached whereby the Appellant was to receive six months' salary and "$32,000 (net) by way of compensation for the damage suffered." The Appellant claimed the $32,000 was meant to be non-taxable as he had received it as compensation for both economic loss and moral harm. The Respondent claimed that the amount was directly related to the Appellant's loss of employment and taxable as such.

The Court ruled that $16,000 should be included in the Appellant's income as compensation after he lost his job. The balance constituted damages for defamation that were not within the definition of retiring allowance and therefore not taxable as such. The appeal was allowed in part.

The appeal court judge reviewed the evidence in great detail and reviewed all the precedents cited to him. In the other cases, the decisions reached were that the amounts were taxable because there was a lack of evidence to establish the true nature of the payments. In this case, as well as in the case at bar, there was testimony upon which the Court could determine the amount which was paid for loss of employment and damages resulting from damages for loss of fringe benefits, mental distress, interest and costs.

I have thoroughly studied the cases cited. I have also given consideration to the evidence adduced before this Tribunal. After having given consideration to the proof advanced, this Court finds and decides that the Appellant has established that the settlement obtained by her included a sum for loss of wages of approximately three months compensation for earned overtime, earned vacation and earned sick leave. These items are taxable. The other factors such as damages for mental distress and costs are not taxable because they do not enter into the definition of retirement allowance as defined in subsection 248(1) of the *Income Tax Act*.

After having considered all of the evidence, the Court finds and declares that 50% of the sum of $25,376 was received by the Appellant as a "retirement allowance" and is therefore taxable. The balance was received by her as compensation for damages and is not taxable...

Appeal allowed.

NOTES AND QUESTIONS

1. On what grounds did the court in *Mendes-Roux* conclude that half of the $25,376 received by the taxpayer was non-taxable? Do you agree with the court's conclusion that "damages for mental distress and costs are not taxable because they do not enter into the definition of retirement allowance as defined in subsection 248(1)"?

2. In *Merrins v. M.N.R.*, [1994] F.C.J. No. 1582, [1995] 1 C.T.C. 111, 94 D.T.C. 6669 (F.C.T.D.), which Léger DJTC cited in *Mendes-Roux*, the taxpayer received $60,000 in settlement of a grievance in which he sought reinstatement pursuant to a collective agreement between his employer (Atomic Energy of Canada Limited) and the Society of Professional Engineers and Associates. Rejecting the taxpayer's argument that the payment was a capital gain from the disposition of his right to have his grievance arbitrated, the court held that the payment was a "retiring allowance" within the meaning of paragraph (b) of the definition in subsection 248(1). According to Pinard J (at paras. 5-7):

> Whether or not the validity of the arbitrator's award could have been successfully challenged before the courts is not relevant here. What is important is the fact that the award was not challenged and that the amount of $60,000 was received and the benefit accepted by the plaintiff. There is no doubt that the amount was received by the plaintiff in respect of the loss of his employment with AECL. Had there been no loss of employment, there would have been no grievance, no settlement, no award and, therefore, no payment of the sum to the plaintiff.

> The Supreme Court of Canada, in *The Queen v. Savage*, [1983] 2 SCR 428, [1983] CTC 393, 83 DTC 5409, concluded that the words "in respect of," in a provision of the *Income Tax Act*, ought to be given the widest possible scope. There, at page 440 (CTC 399; DTC 5414), Dickson J, as he then was, cited *Nowegijick v. The Queen*, [[1983] S.C.J. No. 5] [1983] 1 SCR 29, [1983] CTC 20, 83 DTC 5041, where the Court dealt with those words as follows:

>> The words "in respect of" are, in my opinion, words of the widest possible scope. They import such meanings as "in relation to," "with reference to" or "in connection with." The phrase "in respect of" is probably the widest of any expression intended to convey some connection between two related subject matters.

> Here, in my view, the use of those words within the definition of "retiring allowance" as found in subsection 248(1) of the Act surely conveys a connection between the plaintiff's loss of employment and his subsequent receipt of the amount of $60,000 as paid by his former employer, AECL. This amount, in the circumstances, is caught within the definition of "retiring allowance" and is therefore to be included when computing income under subsection 56(1).

See also *Niles v. M.N.R.*, [1991] T.C.J. No. 118, [1991] 1 C.T.C. 2540, 91 D.T.C. 806 (T.C.C.), where the court referred to the Supreme Court of Canada decisions in *Canada v. Savage*, [1983] S.C.J. No. 80, [1983] 2 S.C.R. 428, [1983] C.T.C. 393, 83 D.T.C. 5409 (S.C.C.) and *R. v. Nowegijick*, [1983] S.C.J. No. 5, [1983] 1 S.C.R. 29, [1983] C.T.C. 20, 83 D.T.C. 5041 (S.C.C.), in concluding that a payment received by the taxpayer in settlement of a human rights complaint following the termination of his employment was received "in respect of" the taxpayer's loss of an office or employment within the meaning of paragraph (b) of the definition of a "retiring allowance" in subsection 248(1).

3.   In *Stolte v. Canada*, [1996] T.C.J. No. 215, [1996] 2 C.T.C. 2421 (T.C.C.), the taxpayer received $9,368.50 from her former employer, of which $5,941 was paid "as compensation for pain, suffering and stress sustained as a consequence of the loss of Mrs. Stolte's employment" (at para. 15). Even though this amount was based on two month's salary, Bowman JTCC held (at paras. 20-21) that it was "not income within the meaning of the *Income Tax Act*," but "damages for the mental and physical injuries she sustained by reason of the insensitive, arrogant and wholly unacceptable treatment that she suffered at the hands of her employer prior to the termination of her employment."

For a similar result, see *Fournier v. Canada*, [1999] T.C.J. No. 495, [1999] 4 C.T.C. 2247 (T.C.C.), in which a lump-sum payment in settlement of a grievance and human rights complaint for physical and sexual harassment was characterized (at para. 14) as non-taxable damages arising from an injury "against the person of the taxpayer."

4.   In *Anderson v. Canada*, [1997] T.C.J. No. 1137, [1998] 1 C.T.C. 2522 (T.C.C.), the taxpayer received $93,809 in settlement of an action for wrongful dismissal, of which $42,345 was paid as a reimbursement for a real estate commission and legal fees on the sale of a house that the taxpayer acquired shortly after commencing his employment and sold shortly after the termination of his employment. Rejecting the taxpayer's argument that the $42,345 was not paid "in respect of a loss of an office or employment of the taxpayer" within the meaning of paragraph (b) of the definition of a "retiring allowance" in subsection 248(1), the court, referring to the Supreme Court of Canada decisions in *Canada v. Savage*, [1983] S.C.J. No. 80, [1983] 2 S.C.R. 428, [1983] C.T.C. 393, 83 D.T.C. 5409 (S.C.C.) and *R. v. Nowegijick*, [1983] S.C.J. No. 5, [1983] 1 S.C.R. 29, [1983] C.T.C. 20, 83 D.T.C. 5041 (S.C.C.), held (at para. 13) that there was "a sufficient connection between the receipt of the money by Mr. Anderson ... and his loss of employment." According to Rip TCJ (at para. 13):

> The damages received by Mr. Anderson arise from his loss of employment, and the incidental damages related to that loss of employment. This is not a case where damages were received extraneous to the loss of employment, such as where the taxpayer was defamed, as in *Bédard v. Minister of National Revenue* 91 DTC 573 (TCC), or for mental and physical injuries suffered during employment, as in *Stolte v. R*, [1996] 2 CTC 2421 (TCC). The $93,809 paid to Mr. Anderson by Genetech was on account of damages he suffered as a result of losing his job at Genetech and moving back to Scarborough. There is a causal link between the two. Accordingly, Mr. Anderson received an amount of money in

respect of a loss of employment with Genetech as damages, and such amount is properly regarded as a "retiring allowance" within the meaning of paragraph 248(1)(b) of the Act. By virtue of subparagraph 56(1)(a)(ii) these damages are to be included in his income for the 1990 taxation year.

5.   For other cases in which payments have been characterized as "retiring allowances" within the meaning of paragraph (b) of the definition in subsection 248(1), see *Blaker v. Canada*, [1993] T.C.J. No. 403, [1994] 1 C.T.C. 2242, (1993) 93 D.T.C. 1025 (T.C.C.); *Jasper v. Canada*, [1997] T.C.J. No. 1240, [1998] 1 C.T.C. 2690, 98 D.T.C. 1253 (T.C.C.); *Overin v. Canada*, [1997] T.C.J. No. 1264, 98 D.T.C. 1299 (T.C.C.); and *Saardi v. Canada*, [1999] T.C.J. No. 144, [1999] 4 C.T.C. 2488, 99 D.T.C. 767 (T.C.C.). In *Overin*, the court (at para. 9) rejected the taxpayer's argument that payments received from the province of British Columbia after his employer went into receivership were not a retiring allowance on the basis that it was immaterial that the payment originated from the province and not the employer:

> The definition of "retiring allowance" in subsection 248(1) is unequivocal, words should not be imported into the provision when Parliament has not seen fit to use them. The language of the provision is clear and does not impose the requirement that the payment originate with the employer.

See also *Graham v. Canada*, [2001] T.C.J. No. 461, [2001] 3 C.T.C. 2771 (T.C.C.), where the court held (at para. 15) that $22,000 to compensate the taxpayer for moving expenses and a loss on the sale of his home was "connected to the loss of the [taxpayer's] employment"; and *Jolivet v. Canada*, [2000] T.C.J. No. 48, [2000] 2 C.T.C. 2118 (T.C.C.), in which the court concluded (at para. 16) that there was "a sufficient nexus between the receipt and the loss of employment."

6.   In *Ahmad v. Canada*, [2002] T.C.J. No. 471, 2002 DTC 2065 (T.C.C.), the taxpayer received $488,525 as damages for inducement of breach of contract after Ontario Hydro induced his employer Atomic Energy of Canada Limited to terminate his employment. Dismissing the Minister's argument that the damages were taxable as a retiring allowance under subparagraph 56(1)(a)(ii) of the Act, Miller TCJ (at para. 14) distinguished between taxable damages for wrongful dismissal and non-taxable damages for the tort of inducing a breach of contract. According to Miller TCJ (at para. 15):

> Given its widest meaning, the expression "in respect of" as used in the context of damages "in respect of loss of employment" would cover any damage award if there were even some connection between the award and the loss of employment. This would then, for example, pick up damages of the employee physically injured in a car accident who could no longer work. If the judge in his calculation of damages considers the loss of future employment income, then the damages could be said to be "in respect of the loss of employment". This takes the expression well beyond what I believe the context of the definition of retiring allowance supports. To be "in respect of the loss of employment" suggests to me a primary purpose test. What is the first answer that leaps to mind when asked why did the injured employer receive damages? It is not, I would suggest, because he lost his job. It is because someone injured him in a car accident. Likewise, why did Dr. Ahmad receive damages from

Ontario Hydro? It is not because he lost his job. It is because Ontario Hydro wronged him in stripping him of the ability to ever conduct nuclear research.

7.   The CRA's views on the characterization of amounts received "in respect of a loss of an office or employment of a taxpayer" are contained in IT-337R4 (Consolidated). According to paragraphs 11-12:

11. The definition of a retiring allowance includes an amount received in respect of a loss of office or employment of a taxpayer, whether or not received as, on account or in lieu of payment of, damages or pursuant to an order or judgment of a competent tribunal. ... [T]he words "in respect of" denote a connection between the loss of employment and the subsequent receipt. Accordingly, where an individual receives compensation on account of damages as a result of a loss of employment, the amount received will be taxed as a retiring allowance. This applies to both special damages, as well as general damages received for loss of self-respect, humiliation, mental anguish, hurt feelings, etc.

12. Where personal injuries have been sustained before or after the loss of employment (for example, in situations of harassment during employment, or defamation after dismissal), the general damages received in respect of these injuries may be viewed as unrelated to the loss of employment and therefore non-taxable. In order to claim that damages received upon loss of employment are for personal injuries unrelated to the loss of employment, it must be clearly demonstrated that the damages relate to events or actions separate from the loss of employment. In making such a determination, the amount of severance that the employee would reasonably be entitled to will be taken into consideration.

Similarly, general damages relating to human rights violations can be considered unrelated to a loss of employment, despite the fact that the loss of employment is often a direct result of a human rights violations complaint. If a human rights tribunal awards a taxpayer an amount for general damages, the amount is normally not required to be included in income. When a loss of employment involves a human rights violation and is settled out of court, a reasonable amount in respect of general damages can be excluded from income. The determination of what is reasonable is influenced by the maximum amount that can be awarded under the applicable human rights legislation and the evidence presented in the case. Any excess will be taxed as a retiring allowance.

b. Loss of Office or Employment

In *Schwartz v. Canada*, [1996] S.C.J. No. 15, [1996] 1 C.T.C. 303, 96 D.T.C. 6103 (S.C.C.), the taxpayer received $360,000 in settlement of a claim for damages arising out of the cancellation of an employment contract prior to the date when the employment was to commence. At the Supreme Court of Canada, the Crown argued in the alternative that the payment was a "retiring allowance" under paragraph (b) of the definition in subsection 248(1) or income from an unspecified source within the meaning of paragraph 3(a).

Schwartz v. Canada
[1996] S.C.J. No. 15, [1996] 1 C.T.C. 303, 96 D.T.C. 6103 (S.C.C.)

LA FOREST J (L'Heureux-Dubé, Gonthier, and McLachlin JJ concurring): This appeal involves the issue whether compensation received by an "employee" from his "employer" pursuant to a settlement regarding liability for the employer's unilateral decision to cancel a contract of employment before the employee had become under obligation to provide services is taxable as income from an unenumerated source under the general provision of paragraph 3(a) of the *Income Tax Act* ... or, in the alternative, as a retiring allowance under subparagraph 56(1)(a)(ii) of the Act.

I. Background

In the spring of 1988, Mr. Schwartz, a lawyer, received a verbal offer of employment from the Dynacare Health Group Inc.'s Chairman, Albert J. Latner. The appellant accepted on the basis that the employment would begin on completion of an assignment by the appellant for the Government of Ontario, which was expected in November. Later, in May 1988 Mr. Schwartz wrote Mr. Latner a letter outlining the terms of their agreement. Mr. Latner accepted the proposed terms and signed the letter. They agreed that the appellant was to receive a salary of $250,000 annually as well as the option to acquire 1.25% of the existing non-voting shares of Dynacare, calculated at the date of the agreement, for the price of $0.01 per share. ... They also agreed that every effort would be made to minimize taxes payable by both parties. Within days, the appellant notified his partners of his intention to withdraw from the partnership at the end of his assignment.

The contract was never carried out. In late September, Dynacare informed the appellant that his services would not be required. Later, the appellant received a letter dated October 6, 1988 from Dynacare's solicitors confirming the cancellation of the employment, recognizing Dynacare's contractual obligation towards the appellant and offering him $75,000 in exchange for a full and final release. ... The appellant refused the offer. He continued to practise law until he withdrew from the partnership on January 31, 1989, as he had agreed with his partners. He commenced employment with an investment firm the next day at an annual salary of $175,000.

Negotiations for settlement were conducted by the parties' lawyers during the course of which two letters, later filed at trial, were exchanged. The first, dated June 13, 1989, was from Dynacare's solicitors and was addressed to the appellant's solicitors. It dealt specifically with the value of Mr. Schwartz's stock options and concluded that Dynacare considered them to be worth $267,000 for the purposes of the settlement. Dynacare's solicitors also stated that their client was "prepared to be flexible around the range of $267,000." The appellant's solicitors replied in a letter dated June 22, 1989, expressing disagreement with Dynacare's method of calculating the value of the stock options and stating that the appellant was owed $75,000 as lost salary. That letter contained an offer to settle the dispute for $400,000 plus costs.

A settlement was reached and a release was signed on August 21, 1989. Dynacare agreed to pay the appellant a lump sum of $360,000 as damages plus $40,000 on account of costs. At trial, Mr. Schwartz testified that in arriving at the amount of $360,000, losses on stock options, salary, embarrassment, anxiety and inconvenience resulting from the breach of the employment contract by

Dynacare were considered, but no specific allocation among such losses was made.

The respondent Crown assessed the damages as constituting a "retiring allowance" taxable under subparagraph 56(1)(a)(ii) of the Act. The appellant filed a notice of objection, but the respondent confirmed the assessment initially made. The appellant then appealed the assessment successfully to the Tax Court of Canada, [1993] 2 CTC 2125, 93 DTC 555, from whose decision the respondent appealed to the Federal Court of Appeal, which allowed the appeal: [1994] 2 CTC 99, 94 DTC 6249. This Court granted the appellant leave to appeal the latter decision on October 13, 1994, [1994] 3 SCR xi.

...

III. Judgments Below

Tax Court of Canada, [1993] 2 CTC 2125, 93 DTC 555

The Crown's principal contention before the Tax Court of Canada was that the settlement amount was taxable as a "retiring allowance." In considering this contention, Rip JTCC relied heavily on the ordinary meaning of the words of the Act dealing with retiring allowances. In his view, the ordinary meaning of the words "employment," "office," "employee," "officer," "position" and "holding" ought not be altered. The definition of "retiring allowance," he stated, does not refer to an "intended" or "prospective" employment, and one should not read into it words that are not present there. He confirmed that finding by considering English dictionary definitions of the word "position" and the French equivalent "poste" and found (at page 560) that an officer is "one who holds, has possession of or fills a position which grants him a right to stipend or remuneration" and that an employee is one who "occupies a position in the service of another."

The consideration of various factors led the trial judge to the conclusion that Mr. Schwartz was not an "employee" or in the "employment" of Dynacare when the cancellation of the employment agreement occurred. The appellant was still a partner in his law firm at the time. He was not performing any services for Dynacare, nor was he under any obligation to do so. He was not receiving any kind of remuneration and the directors of Dynacare had not yet appointed him. What the appellant lost when the contract was cancelled, Rip JTCC held, was not his employment or his position, but the legal right entitling him to employment in the future.

Rip JTCC rejected the respondent's submission that parliamentary documents and earlier cases supported its position by underlying the importance of the distinction to be made between termination of employment contracts occurring when employment had already commenced and those occurring before the employee had started providing any services to his employer. He therefore concluded that the damages were not a "retiring allowance" within the meaning of subsection 248(1) of the Act.

The judge also rejected the respondent's first alternative argument that if the damages were not a retiring allowance, they had been received by the appellant as a benefit by virtue of an office or employment and therefore fell within the purview of paragraph 6(1)(a) of the Act. He followed the Federal Court of Appeal's decisions in *R v. Atkins (sub nom. The Queen v. Atkins)*, [1976] CTC 497, 76 DTC 6258, and *Pollock v. R (sub nom. Pollock v. The Queen)*, [1984] CTC 353, 84 DTC 6370, and found that the damages received by the appellant could not be regarded as "salary," "wages" or "remuneration" or as a benefit "received or engaged [sic] by him ... in respect of, in the course of, or by virtue of the office or employment" within the meaning of section 5 and paragraph 6(1)(a) of the Act. He added that the fact that the appellant had not commenced employment at the time the breach occurred made the reasoning even more persuasive.

Finally, Rip JTCC dealt with the respondent's argument that the damages were taxable under section 3 as being "income from a source," the source being the employment contract. He found that the amount received by the appellant could not be considered "income," because the ordinary concept of income pertained to recurring receipts and did not extend to a lump sum received because a source of income had been taken away or destroyed. Consequently, in a case such as the one at bar, compensation for damages relating to future services was not to be considered "income." He noted that in the present situation, the damages received by the appellant did not relate in any way to past services.

In the course of his reasons, Rip JTCC stated (at page 557) that there was no evidence indicating any allocation of the settlement amount and made the following finding of fact, which was disturbed by the Federal Court of Appeal and which is at issue before our Court, at page 2135 (DTC 562):

> Schwartz suffered inconvenience and prejudice when he was informed his services would not be required. He had given notice of withdrawal to his law partnership. He had to begin to look for employment. Schwartz was never an employee or officer of the purported employer. *The damages he received was [sic] in a small part, if any, for loss of income for future services and to a larger part, according to the evidence, for embarrassment, anxiety and inconvenience.*

[Emphasis added.]

The respondent did not argue that the damages constituted a retiring allowance before the Federal Court of Appeal. Mahoney JA for the court nonetheless held that he was in substantial agreement with Rip JTCC's finding that the damages did not constitute a retiring allowance as contemplated by subparagraph 56(1)(a)(ii) and subsection 248(1) of the Act.

The critical issue before the Federal Court of Appeal was the Tax Court of Canada's finding of fact relating to apportionment. After stating the guidelines laid down by our Court in *Stein v. "Kathy K"*, [1976] 2 SCR 802, 62 DLR (3d) 1, Mahoney JA concluded that the Federal Court of Appeal was justified in overturning Rip JTCC's finding of fact because the latter had omitted to consider relevant documentary evidence. He found that the letters dated June 13, 1989 and June 22, 1989 from the parties' solicitors were contradictory to the oral evidence on the issue of allocation and he held that, on a balance of probabilities, $75,000 had been allocated for loss of salary and $267,000 for loss of the stock options, and that there was thus no reason not to conclude that $18,000 had been awarded for embarrassment, anxiety and inconvenience suffered by Mr. Schwartz. He preferred the documentary evidence over the appellant's testimony because ... the May 1988 agreement, which indicated concerns by both parties regarding taxes, and the self-serving nature Mr. Schwartz's testimony raised doubts as to his credibility.

The Federal Court of Appeal therefore held that the damages relating to lost salary and stock options ($342,000) were taxable under section 3 of the Act as income from employment. It followed the English decision *London & Thames Heaven Oil Wharves Ltd. v. Attwooll*, [1967] 2 All ER 124, 43 TC 491 (CA), which was approved by the Federal Court of Appeal in *R v. Manley (sub nom. Manley v. The Queen)*, [1985] 1 CTC 186, 85 DTC 5440 (leave to appeal to this Court refused: [1986] 1 SCR xi), and stated, at page 106 (DTC 6254):

> Where, pursuant to a legal right, a person receives from another compensation for the failure to receive a sum of money or benefit which, if it had been received, would have been income from an employment or office, the compensation is to be treated for income tax purposes in the same way as if the benefit or sum of money had been received instead of the compensation.

The Federal Court of Appeal held (at page 106 (DTC 6254)) that the source of the appellant's right was the contract of employment, "a source of income within the express contemplation of paragraph 3(a)," and that the $342,000 was therefore taxable as income from employment.

IV. Analysis

Before this Court, the Crown argued that the damages received by the appellant were taxable in two ways. Its main contention was that the money received by Mr. Schwartz relating to lost salary and stock options was taxable as income from an unenumerated source under the general provision of paragraph 3(a) of the Act — such unenumerated source being the employment contract terminated by Dynacare. The Crown also put forward an alternative argument, namely that the whole of the damages ($360,000) received by Mr. Schwartz were taxable under subparagraph 56(1)(a)(ii) of the Act as a retiring allowance.

For the reasons that follow, I am of the opinion that the appeal should be allowed. To deal with the substance of the Minister's main argument, it is necessary to address the correctness of the Federal Court of Appeal's decision to overturn Rip JTCC's finding of fact with respect to the allocation made by Dynacare and Mr. Schwartz of the compensation agreed upon. I conclude that the Federal Court of Appeal was wrong in doing so, a conclusion that is sufficient, technically, to dispose of the Crown's main argument in favour of the appellant. However, the substance of the Minister's main argument raises important questions that merit attention by this Court and it having been fully argued by the parties, I think it appropriate to deal with it on its merits. Regarding this issue, I have come to the conclusion that paragraph 3(a) of the

Act does contemplate taxability of income arising from sources other than those specifically provided for in paragraph 3(a) and in subdivision d of Division B of Part I of the Act. However, in the case at bar, an analysis of the way Parliament handled the taxability of payments such as the one received by Mr. Schwartz demonstrates that it is to the rules relating to retiring allowances that one should turn in assessing taxability. This brings us to a consideration of the Crown's alternative argument and, like the trial judge and the Federal Court of Appeal, I have come to the conclusion that the damages received by Mr. Schwartz do not constitute a retiring allowance.

Before dealing specifically with the issues raised in this appeal, however, I find it advisable to consider the manner in which Parliament has historically chosen to deal with the taxability of monies received by an employee from his ex-employer as a result of the latter's cancellation of the employment contract.

A. The Historical Background

The provisions on which the Crown relies in arguing that the amount received by Mr. Schwartz is taxable are all found in Part I of the Act, which is entitled "Income Tax." Section 3 states the basic rules to be applied in determining a taxpayer's income for a given year and identifies, in para. (a), the five principal sources from which income can be generated: office, employment, business, property and capital gains. Subdivisions a, b and c of Division B of Part I contain specific provisions relating to the characterization of income as being from either office, employment, business, property or as constituting capital gains. Section 56(1)(a)(ii) — which provides for the taxability of retiring allowances — is found in subdivision d of Division B of Part I, entitled "Other Sources of Income." As noted by Professor V. Krishna, *The Fundamentals of Canadian Income Tax* (4th ed. 1992), at page 525, these "other sources" relate to "certain types of income which cannot conveniently be identified as originating from, or relating to" the five sources enumerated in paragraph 3(a) of the Act.

Initially, damages received by an employee, from his ex-employer, as a result of the latter's cancellation of the employment contract, did not constitute income from office or employment taxable under subsection 5(1); nor did they constitute a retiring allowance taxable under subparagraph 56(1)(a)(ii).

On the first of these propositions, the Federal Court of Appeal, in *Atkins, supra*, stated that such payments did not constitute taxable income from an office or employment under subsection 5(1).

...

The principle laid down in *Atkins*, which was decided by the Federal Court of Appeal in May of 1976, was ... accepted as authoritative both by the courts and commentators (see *Krivy v. Minister of National Revenue*, [1979] CTC 2108, 79 DTC 121 (TRB); *Girouard v. R (sub nom. Girouard v. The Queen)*, [1980] CTC 284, 80 DTC 6205 (FCA); *Beck v. Minister of National Revenue*, [1980] CTC 2851, 80 DTC 1747 (TRB); *Grozelle v. Minister of National Revenue*, [1977] CTC 2432, 77 DTC 310 (TRB); E.C. Harris, *Canadian Income Taxation* (1979), at page 116; R.B. Goodwin, "Personal Damages" in Canadian Tax Foundation, *Report of the Proceedings of the Twenty-Eighth Tax Conference* (1977), 813, at pages 820-21; also W.A. MacDonald and G.E. Cronkwright, eds., *Income Taxation in Canada* (1977 (loose-leaf)), vol. 2, at T17,521; and L.M. Collins, "The Terminated Employee: Minimizing the Tax Bite," in *Report of the Proceedings of the Forty-Fifth Tax Conference* (1994), 31:1, at pages 31:18 and 31:19), although some questioned the correctness of the legal reasoning adopted by the Federal Court of Appeal at the time (see V. Krishna, "Characterization of Wrongful Dismissal Awards for Income Tax" (1977), 23 *McGill LJ* 43). P.W. Hogg and J.E. Magee, in their recent textbook *Principles of Canadian Income Tax Law* (1995), at pages 164-65, address this historical reality in these words:

> Before 1978, if the departing employee sued the employer for wrongful dismissal and recovered damages, then the damages would be received free of tax. This was because an award of damages for breach of contract (or for a tort or other cause of action) is not income for tax purposes. This was so, even though the amount of a damages award for wrongful dismissal would be computed by reference to exactly the same considerations (that is, the amount of salary that would have been paid during a required period of notice) as would be applied to the computation of a consensual severance payment. Since court-awarded damages were free of tax, it was also held that an out-of-court settlement of a wrongful dismissal action also escaped tax.

The position taken by the courts towards such payments was clearly accepted by the Minister of National Revenue. In Interpretation Bulletin IT-365, dated March 21, 1977, and entitled "Damages, Settlements, and Similar Receipts," it is stated:

> Receipts in Respect of Termination of Employment
>
> 2. An amount that a taxpayer receives on the termination of his employment may consist of many components such as amounts in respect of salaries, accumulated leave credits, retiring allowances, compensation for loss of job opportunity or for lack of adequate or reasonable notice, or other similar amounts. That part of the amount that represents salary or wages that the taxpayer would have received under the contract is taxable pursuant to the provisions of section 5 of the Act. The portion of the amount that is damages for breach of contract or loss of future job opportunity is not taxable. It is a question of fact whether all or some portion of the amount received is on account of salary, retiring allowance, or an obligation arising out of an agreement. For example a taxpayer may be dismissed with proper notice and be paid "salary" (which would be taxable) for the period of notice even if the dismissed employee was not required to perform the normal duties of his position during that period. *On the other hand, the fact that damages may be calculated by reference to salary that would have been payable if the relationship had not been terminated or because they are colloquially called "salary" does not alter the character of the payments to one of "salary."*

[Emphasis added.]

It was also settled that such payments did not constitute retiring allowances as contemplated by the Act. The definition of "retiring allowance" was different then and read:

> 248(1) ... "retiring allowance" means an amount received upon or after retirement from an office or employment in recognition of long service or in respect of loss of office or employment (other than a superannuation or pension benefit), whether the recipient is the officer or employee or a dependant, relation or legal representative;

At that time, retiring allowances related only to payments made by an employer following voluntary cessation of employment on the part of the ex-employee or again following cessation upon the arrival of a condition agreed upon by the parties, thus excluding from the scope of the definition payments made by the employer in pursuance of a judicial order or in settlement of pending or threatened litigation following unilateral dismissal of the ex-employee. The position adopted by the courts is best explained by reference to Collier J's reasons in *Specht v. R (sub nom. Specht v. The Queen)*, [1975] CTC 126, 75 DTC 5069 (FCTD), where the taxpayer had received from his ex-employer a payment in compensation for the consequences of the latter's unilateral decision to terminate employment. There Collier J had this to say, at page 133 (DTC 5073):

> In my view, the payment here was not made upon or after the plaintiff's retirement. The plaintiff did not retire or go into retirement from his occupation with MacMillan Bloedel within the ordinary meaning of "retire" or "retirement." That is, he did not withdraw from his employment because he had reached a mutually stipulated age, or generally withdraw from his occupation or business activity. I have obtained some assistance on this point, in endeavouring to ascertain the ordinary meaning of "retirement," from dictionary definitions:
>
> > *The Shorter Oxford English Dictionary* (3rd ed. rev): "withdrawal from occupation or business activity"
> >
> > *The Living Webster* (1st ed.): "retire" "to withdraw from business or active life."
>
> The *contract* of employment in this case (Exhibit 1) uses the words "retire" and "retirement" in clauses 1 and 2. Age 65 was stipulated, but extensions could be agreed upon. In my view, "retirement" was used by the parties in its ordinary meaning as set out above: a cessation of or withdrawal from work because of an age stipulation or because of some other condition agreed between employer and employee.

Although Collier J did not refer to any authority on the issue, his position was consistent with the jurisprudence applicable at that time; see *No. 45 v. Minister of National Revenue* (1952), 5 Tax ABC 417, 52 DTC 72 (TAB); *Larson v. Minister of National Revenue*, [1967] Tax ABC 112, 67 DTC 81 (TAB); *Jones v. Minister of National Revenue*, [1968] Tax ABC 1243, 69 DTC 4 (TAB); see also R.B. Goodwin, *supra*, at pages 829-32; B.G. Hansen, "The Taxation of Employees," in B.G. Hansen, V. Krishna and J.A. Rendall, eds., *Canadian Taxation* (1981), 117, at page 160; and A.R.A. Scace, *The Income Tax Law of Canada* (4th ed. 1979), at page 63. Collier J reiterated his position in *Atkins*, and applied the reasoning laid down in *Specht*. The Federal Court of Appeal did not deal with the issue in its reasons because, apparently, the Crown had abandoned the retiring allowance argument on appeal: Goodwin, *supra*, at page 830, and Krishna, "Characterization of Wrongful Dismissal Awards for Income Tax," *supra*, at page 53.

Here again, Interpretation Bulletins offer some helpful hindsight. The Minister wrote, in Interpretation Bulletin IT-337R, dated November 19, 1979, and entitled "Retiring Allowances":

1. Amounts received by a former employee arising out of or in consequence of the termination of employment are usually included as income from that employment under subsection 5(1) alone or together with paragraph 6(3)(b) (see IT-196R), or as a retiring allowance under subparagraph 56(1)(a)(ii). *One common exception is where the payment constitutes damages in respect of a breach of the contract of employment by the farmer employer.*

[Emphasis added.]

Clearly then, at the end of the 1970s, it had been settled and accepted by all, including the Minister of Revenue, that damages received by an employee, from his ex-employer, as a result of the latter's cancellation of the employment contract, did not constitute income from office or employment taxable under subsection 5(1) or a retiring allowance taxable under subparagraph 56(1)(a)(ii) of the Act.

This, without doubt, constitutes the mischief Parliament intended to remedy in 1979 when it amended the Act and introduced the concept of "termination payments." Termination payments were rendered taxable through subparagraph 56(1)(a)(viii) and were defined in subsection 248(1). ... In Interpretation Bulletin IT-365R, dated March 9, 1981, the Department of National Revenue stated its position on termination payments and emphasized that the portion of a payment exceeding the amount to be considered a "termination payment" under subsection 248(1) was considered to be a non-taxable benefit. This is consistent with the fact that before this amendment, amounts such as those received by Mr. Schwartz were not taxable under the Act.

Parliament again addressed the issue in 1983 by making termination payments of this kind taxable as retiring allowances. To that end, subparagraph 56(1)(a)(viii) and the definition of "termination payment" found in subsection 248(1) were repealed, and the definition of "retiring allowance" was amended in a form that is substantially the same as the definition applicable to this appeal. The purpose of this second series of amendments was to somehow broaden the scope of the Act with respect to such payments, which became fully taxable, as opposed to the partial taxability of termination payments.

As will become evident throughout these reasons, this historical perspective must be steadily kept in mind in considering the proper scope and the applicability to the case at bar of the provisions relied upon by the Minister in assessing the compensation received by Mr. Schwartz. I, therefore, turn to the specific grounds relied upon by the Crown before our Court.

B. The Taxability of the Compensation Received by Mr. Schwartz

As I noted at the outset, the Minister argued that the amount of compensation relating to lost salary and stock options ($342,000) constitutes income from a source taxable under the general provision of paragraph 3(a) of the Act, such source being the contract of employment. I pause here to mention that what the Crown argued before us differs somewhat from the approach adopted by the Federal Court of Appeal. Mahoney JA found that $342,000 of the $360,000 was income from employment since it had been received by Mr. Schwartz to compensate for loss of moneys that, if duly received, would have constituted income from employment taxable under subsection 5(1). Before us, the Crown did not argue that this amount constitutes income from employment. It first submitted that the application of the *surrogatum* principle, developed in the *London & Thames* case, *supra*, leads to the conclusion that $342,000 of the $360,000 received by Mr. Schwartz must be characterized as income from a source, since it compensates Mr. Schwartz for loss of moneys that, if received, would have constituted income from a source. The Minister then identifies that source as being the employment contract, a source other than the five enumerated in paragraph 3(a) and the "other sources" provided for in subdivision d of Division B of Part I of the Act. The difference lies in the Minister's argument relating to the specific source of the damages received by the appellant.

(1) Income from a Source: Taxability under Section 3(a) of the Act

In order to deal with the substance of the Crown's main argument, it is necessary to analyze the correctness of the premise on which it is based. This requires us to deal with the Federal Court of Appeal's decision to reconsider Rip JTCC's finding regarding the apportionment that was made by the parties of the compensation received by Mr. Schwartz.

(a) *The Finding of Fact*

... The essence of the Crown's argument, before the Federal Court of Appeal and this Court, is that Rip JTCC erred because in assessing the evidence on the question of apportionment, he failed to consider evidence which contradicted Mr. Schwartz's testimonial evidence. Rip JTCC found that the amount received by Mr. Schwartz in compensation was mostly for mental distress suffered as a result of the termination of the contract and that no specific allocation had been agreed upon by the parties. In the Federal Court of Appeal's opinion, that contradictory evidence consisted in the June letters, in which the parties' solicitors made offers to settle the litigation and calculated the proposed amounts by reference to lost salary and stock options.

To find that Rip JTCC erred in overlooking contradictory evidence on the allocation made by the parties of the settlement amount, one must obviously first be convinced that the June letters in fact do constitute evidence as to the allocation made by the parties of the settlement amount and that such evidence is in contradiction of Mr. Schwartz's testimonial evidence. I do not think that is the case.

The June letters certainly do constitute evidence that is relevant to this litigation. They establish that in arriving at the final settlement amount of $400,000, both Dynacare and Mr. Schwartz considered losses of salary and stock options, thereby supporting the appellant's testimony on this point. In that sense, the June letters are evidence of the fact that the amount of $360,000 is composed, at least in part, of amounts paid to Mr. Schwartz in compensation for losses of salary and stock options. But can they be considered evidence as to what portion of the $360,000 was allocated to such losses?

A global analysis of the evidence on the issue convinces me that this is not the case. There is no evidence that the $267,000 offered by Dynacare for the stock options was accepted by the appellant. Nor is there any evidence that the $75,000 claimed by the appellant for lost salary was agreed upon by Dynacare. The letters were written in June, while the final release was signed by the parties at the end of August.

...

It is difficult to see how the solicitors' letters could be seen as constituting evidence as to apportionment when Mr. Schwartz clearly testified to the contrary and Rip JTCC made no negative finding as to Mr. Schwartz's credibility. It is also noteworthy that the record at trial reveals that the Minister did not even argue that the letters constituted evidence as to apportionment contrary to Mr. Schwartz's testimony. Logically, the Minister should not have the burden of presenting, in every case where the apportionment of a general award is at issue, specific evidence amounting to an explicit expression of the concerned parties' intention with respect to that question. However, there must be *some* evidence, in whatever form, from which the trial judge will be able to infer, on a balance of probabilities, which part of that general award was intended to compensate for specific types of damages. I believe that the solicitors' letters, considered in the global evidentiary context of the case at bar, are insufficient to serve as a basis for such an inference.

The Federal Court of Appeal was, therefore, incorrect in inferring from the letters that the parties had agreed to allocate $342,000 of the $400,000 to losses of income relating to salary and stock options; consequently, it was wrong to conclude that the trial judge had failed to consider contradictory evidence. ... I, therefore, conclude that the Federal Court of Appeal erred in disturbing the trial judge's finding with respect to apportionment.

As mentioned earlier, the conclusion that the Federal Court of Appeal was wrong in interfering with the trial judge's finding of fact respecting apportionment disposes of the Minister's main argument. This is so because in order to find that some of the amount received by Mr. Schwartz was taxable under paragraph 3(a) as income from the employment contract, one must be able to identify what portion of the $360,000 was paid to Mr. Schwartz in compensation for amounts that he would have been entitled to receive *under the contract of employment*. Since the Federal Court of Appeal erred in its decision relating to the trial judge's assessment of the evidence, the factual situation is that there is evidence that the amounts received by Mr. Schwartz were, in part, received to compensate for the loss of amounts to which he would have been entitled under the employment contract entered into with Dynacare and, in part, to compensate for embarrassment, anxiety and inconvenience suffered by the appellant, and that there is *no* evidence tending to establish what portion of the

$360,000 was allocated to which head. Thus, absent a proper determination of that factual situation, the damages received by Mr. Schwartz cannot, in whole or in part, be found to be taxable under paragraph 3(a) of the Act as income from the employment contract.

As I mentioned at the beginning of my analysis, however, I propose to deal with the substance of the Minister's main contention since it raises important issues that merit attention and have been fully argued by the parties. I, therefore, turn to these submissions.

(b) *The Surrogatum Principle and Unenumerated Sources*

The Crown relies on the principle developed by Diplock LJ in *London & Thames*, *supra*, and argues that the portion of damages received by Mr. Schwartz relating to lost salary and stock options constitutes income from a source. In *London & Thames*, Diplock LJ had this to say, at page 134:

> Where, pursuant to a legal right, a trader receives from another person, compensation for the trader's failure to receive a sum of money which, if it had been received, would have been credited to the amount of profits (if any) arising in any year from the trade carried on by him at the time when the compensation is so received, the compensation is to be treated for income tax purposes in the same way as that sum of money would have been treated if it had been received instead of the compensation.

The Minister, quite correctly, noted that this principle was adopted and applied by the Federal Court of Appeal in *Manley*, *supra*.

...

In the present case, the Federal Court of Appeal applied this principle and found that, since part of the damages received by the appellant replaced lost salary and stock options which, if they had been paid to Mr. Schwartz, would have constituted income from employment taxable under subsection 5(1), such damages had to be treated in the same manner for tax purposes, i.e., as income from office or employment taxable under subsection 5(1) of the Act.

The solution arrived at by the Federal Court of Appeal is in contradiction with the findings in the *Atkins* case, *supra*, where the same court held that such damages could not be characterized as income from office or employment under subsection 5(1). The correctness of the conclusion arrived at in *Atkins* was reaffirmed in 1984 by the Federal Court of Appeal in *Pollock*, *supra*, despite the doubts expressed in an obiter dictum by Pigeon J in *Jorgenson v. Jack Cewe Ltd.*, [1980] 1 SCR 812, [1980] CTC 314, 80 DTC 6233, at pages 815-16 (CTC 315; DTC 6235).

However, the correctness of *Atkins* is not at issue before us since the Minister, as I have explained, is not arguing that the amounts are taxable as income from employment, but submits, rather, that they are income from an unenumerated source taxable under the general provision of paragraph 3(a) of the Act. Pigeon J, in *Jack Cewe*, had pointed out that the Federal Court of Appeal, in *Atkins*, had not considered whether such amounts were alternatively taxable under the general provision of paragraph 3(a):

This Court might well disagree with the conclusion reached by the Federal Court of Appeal in *Atkins*. In this respect, I will note that in that case consideration appears to have been given only to the question whether the damages for wrongful dismissal were income "from an office or employment" within the meaning of sections 5 and 25 of the *Income Tax Act* (RSC 1952) [now subsections 5(1) and 6(3)]. *No consideration appears to have been given to the broader question whether they might not be income from an unspecified source under the general provision of section 3.*

[Emphasis added.]

I pause here again to reaffirm what was implied by Pigeon J in *Jack Cewe*, that paragraph 3(a) does contemplate the possibility that income arising from sources other than those enumerated in paragraph 3(a) and subdivision d of Division B of Part I of the Act may nonetheless be taxable. Parliament has stated very clearly in that section that the five sources identified in paragraph 3(a) do not constitute an exhaustive enumeration. This is evident from the emphasized words in the paragraph, which I here reproduce:

3 ... (a) determine the aggregate of amounts each of which is the taxpayer's income for the year (other than a taxable capital gain from the disposition of a property) from a source inside or outside Canada, *including, without restricting the generality of the foregoing,* his income for the year from each office, employment, business and property;

Mr. Schwartz argues that the sources of income other than those contemplated in paragraph 3(a) are the "other sources" referred to in subdivision d of Division B of Part I of the Act and relies on this statement by E.C. Harris, *Canadian Income Taxation* (4th ed. 1986), at page 99:

While the Act recognizes that there may be other sources of income than [those specifically provided for in paragraph 3(a)], the case law under the former Act suggests that the only other sources of income and loss that are likely to be recognized are those that are specifically recognized in the Act.

However, this conclusion disregards the fact that Parliament, in the introductory part of subsection 56(1) of the Act, made clear that the enumeration that followed was not to be interpreted as restricting the generality of section 3:

56(1) *Without restricting the generality of section 3,* there shall be included in computing the income of a taxpayer for a taxation year. ...

Mr. Schwartz also submitted that, for policy reasons, an interpretation to the contrary would defeat the purpose and fundamental structure of the Act. However, as noted by Krishna, similarly valid policy concerns can be invoked to support an interpretation to the contrary. In his textbook *The Fundamentals of Canadian Income Tax, supra,* at pages 129-30, he writes:

The better view is that the named sources (office, employment, business, and property) are not exhaustive and income can arise from any other unnamed source. Hence, income from any source inside or outside Canada should be taxable under paragraph 3(a) of the Act. *This is justifiable both on the basis of the language of the statute and on policy grounds. To the extent that the income tax is based on the ability to pay, all accretions to wealth of an income nature are a measure of that ability and should be taxable regardless of source.*

[Emphasis added.]

In any event, policy concerns such as those raised by the appellant should not and cannot be relied on in disregard of Parliament's clearly expressed intention: *interpretatio cessat in claris*. In paragraph 3(a), when Parliament used the words "without restricting the generality of the foregoing," great care was taken to emphasize that the first step in calculating a taxpayer's "income for the year" was to determine the total of all amounts constituting income inside or outside Canada and that the enumeration that followed merely identified examples of such sources. The phrasing adopted by Parliament, in paragraph 3(a) and in the introductory part of subsection 56(1) is probably the strongest that could have been used to express the idea that income from *all* sources, enumerated or not, expressly provided for in subdivision d or not, was taxable under the Act.

This interpretation is also consistent with the approach adopted by this Court in the few other cases where this question was at issue. In *Curran v. Minister of National Revenue*, [1959] SCR 850, [1959] CTC 416, 59 DTC 1247, the taxpayer had received a $250,000 payment by a third party in return for which he was to resign from his employment and start working for another company. The payment did not constitute income from employment, since it had not been paid by the taxpayer's employer, but was assessed as constituting "income from a source" under the general provision of section 3 of the Act. This assessment was upheld by the Exchequer Court of Canada ([1957] CTC 384, 57 DTC 1270).

...

Dumoulin J, after concluding that the impugned payment was in the nature of income, held that it was taxable. He stated, at page 399 (DTC 1277):

For reasons somewhat differing from those propounded by respondent, I agree that the sum of $250,000 constitutes income.

Audette J in re *Morrison v. Minister of National Revenue*, (1917-27) CTC 343, 1 DTC 113, at page 350 (DTC 116), spoke thus:

Now the controlling and paramount enactment of section 3 defining the income is "the annual net profit or gain or gratuity." Having said so much the statute proceeding by way of illustration, but not by way of limiting the foregoing words, mentions seven different classes of subjects which cannot be taken as exhaustive since it provides, by what has been called the omnibus clause, a very material addition reading "and also the annual profit or gain from any other sources." The words "and also" and "other sources" make the above illustration absolutely refractory to any possibility of applying the doctrine of *ejusdem generis* set up at the hearing. The balance of the paragraph is added only *ex majori cautel* ... The net is thrown with all conceivable wideness to include all *bona fide* profits or gain made by the subject.

Despite a lapse of years, this interpretation of section 3 is still true of the amended text as it read in 1951.

In very wide terms, section 3 renders taxable "income for the year from *all sources* and without restricting the generality of the foregoing ..."

> Therefore, this controversial payment meets, I believe, the statutory meaning of income for the year from a source other than those particularized by subsections (a), (b) and (c) and was properly assessed as such.

[Emphasis in original.]

This decision was later confirmed by this Court. More recently, in *Fries v. Canada* ... [1989] 1 CTC 471, 89 DTC 5240, the Federal Court of Appeal expressly recognized that income from unenumerated sources was taxable under the general provision of paragraph 3(a) of the Act. In that case, the taxpayer was contesting the Minister's assessment, including in his yearly income strike pay he had received from his union. The court dismissed the taxpayer's claim and found that the amounts were taxable as constituting income from a source within the purview of paragraph 3(a) of the Act. Our Court, however, while implicitly holding that income from unenumerated sources was in fact taxable under the general provision of paragraph 3(a) of the Act, reversed this decision on the basis that the payments were not in the nature of "income ... from a source" within the meaning of paragraph 3(a); see *Fries*, [1990] 2 SCR 1322, [1990] 2 CTC 439, 90 DTC 6662.

In the case at bar, I do not think the Minister's argument should be accepted. In order to determine if a specific amount is taxable under the general provision of paragraph 3(a) of the Act, various considerations should be taken into account. Without providing a list of such considerations or attempting to suggest an approach to taxation under the general provision of paragraph 3(a) in an exhaustive way, I note that one must obviously go back to the concept of income and consider the whole scheme of the Act in order to properly analyze the issue in a given case. In the present case, accepting the argument made by the Crown would amount to giving precedence to a general provision over the detailed provisions enacted by Parliament to deal with payments such as that received by Mr. Schwartz pursuant to the settlement.

As indicated earlier, Parliament adopted a specific solution to a specific problem that resulted from a number of rulings by the courts respecting the taxability of payments similar to the one received by the appellant. Under these rulings, damages paid with respect to wrongful dismissal were not taxable as income from office or employment under subsection 5(1); nor were they taxable as constituting retiring allowances. The Crown had at that point many options. The Minister could have argued that such damages were taxable as income from a source under the general provision in paragraph 3(a) of the Act. It could also have sought an amendment to the Act making such payments expressly taxable as income from office or employment. But neither of these courses was taken. Instead, the Act was amended twice so that such amounts could be taxable under section 56 as income from "another" source. First, it was provided that termination payments were taxable. Then, the Act was amended to make such a payment taxable as constituting a retiring allowance. It is thus pursuant to these provisions that taxability should be assessed. To do otherwise would defeat

Parliament's intention by approving an analytical approach inconsistent with basic principles of interpretation.

...

To find that the damages received by Mr. Schwartz are taxable under the general provision of paragraph 3(a) of the Act would disregard the fact that Parliament has chosen to deal with the taxability of such payments in the provisions of the Act relating to retiring allowances. It is thus to those provisions that I will turn in assessing taxability.

(2) Retiring Allowance: Taxability under Subparagraph 56(1)(a)(ii)

Before this Court, the Crown argued, alternatively, that the damages received by Mr. Schwartz were taxable under subparagraph 56(1)(a)(ii) of the Act as constituting a retiring allowance. Both courts below refused to find these amounts could be so characterized, although the Crown abandoned this argument before the Federal Court of Appeal. At issue is whether the damages agreed to were received by Mr. Schwartz "in respect of a loss of an office or employment" within the meaning of para. (b) of the definition of "retiring allowance" found in subsection 248(1) of the Act. Section 248(1) also defines the words "employment" and "employee."

...

The essence of the Minister's argument is that "employment" as understood in subsection 248(1) of the Act commences the moment the contract of employment is entered into by the parties, regardless of whether or not the employee has the obligation to provide services from that point. Therefore Mr. Schwartz, by losing the benefit of the contract of employment entered into with Dynacare, lost "employment," and the damages received fall within the purview of subparagraph 56(1)(a)(ii) of the Act. I do not think the Minister's position is correct in law, in light of the definitions given by Parliament to the word "employment" and of the ordinary meaning of the words chosen by Parliament to define this term. The Minister's position is also inconsistent with the way Parliament has used the term "employment" in at least one other provision of the Act, while also being untenable when one considers the context in which the 1983 amendment was made.

The key element in the words chosen by Parliament to deal with this situation is the definition of "employment" which is the "position of an individual *in the service* of some other person." The statutory requirement that one must be "in the service" of another person to be characterized as an "employee" excludes, in my opinion, any notion of prospective employment when the phrase is given its ordinary meaning. An employee is "in the service" of his or her employer from the moment he or she becomes under obligation to provide services under the terms of the contract. At the basis of every situation of employment is a contract of employment; however, employment does not necessarily begin from the moment the contract is entered into. Before having any obligation to provide services, one cannot be considered to be "in the service" of his or her employer or, more accurately, his or her future employer. Consequently, there cannot be any *loss* of a position that has yet to be held, under the definition of "retiring allowance" found in subsection 248(1). I cannot see how, in the present case, Mr. Schwartz could be "in the service" of Dynacare from the moment the contract of employment was entered into in the spring of 1988 and how he could have "lost" employment when the contract was unilaterally cancelled by Dynacare. Both parties had agreed that Mr. Schwartz would start working upon completion of his assignment with the Government of Ontario. They both had agreed that the contract that had been entered into was a contract for future employment. Mr. Schwartz was not in any way — and had never been — obliged to provide any services to Dynacare at that moment; he was not "in the service" of Dynacare.

Therefore, when one considers the *ordinary meaning* to be given to the definition of "employment" in the Act, a distinction must be made between the start of the contractual relationship agreed upon by the employer and the employee and the moment, according to the terms of the contract, at which the employee is bound to start providing services to the employer. It is noteworthy that the Crown does not seriously contest the interpretation to be given under the ordinary meaning of the words Parliament chose to use. During oral argument, counsel admitted that an ordinary person would find that Mr. Schwartz was *not* an employee of Dynacare when the contract was cancelled.

The Minister's position is also inconsistent with Parliament's use of the word "employment" in subsection 80.4(1) of the Act. Section 80.4 is included in subdivision f of Division B of Part I of the Act, "Rules Relating to Computation of Income." It provides the method for determining how an amount in respect of interest-free or low-bearing-interest loans will be characterized as a benefit taxable as income from office or employment under subsection 6(9) of the Act, or again, in the case of corporations, as income from a business or property under paragraph 12(1)(w) of the Act. For the sake of convenience, I repeat the relevant provision, while [emphasizing] the crucial passages:

> 80.4 (1) Where a person or partnership received a loan or otherwise incurred a debt by virtue of the office or employment *or intended office or employment* of an individual, or by virtue of the services performed *or to be performed* by a corporation carrying on a personal services business (within the meaning assigned by paragraph 125(7)(d)), the individual or corporation, as the case may be, shall be deemed to have received a benefit ...

A parallel can be drawn between the concept of "intended employment" of an individual and services "to be performed" by a corporation carrying on a personal services business, in light of the fact that "employment" refers to the situation of an individual being "in the service" of a person. Clearly, in both cases, the intention of Parliament was to include within the scope of subsection 80.4(1) such loans made by virtue of a legal relationship involving the provision of services, by an individual or by a corporation, *regardless of whether or not the loans were made before the borrower became under obligation to provide any services.* The distinction made by Parliament is an implicit recognition that the term "employment" does not, in itself, have such a broad meaning.

It is a well-established principle of interpretation that words used by Parliament are deemed to have the same meaning throughout the same statute; see, for recent applications of the principle by this Court, *R v. Zeolkowski*, [1989] 1 SCR 1378, 61 DLR (4th) 725, 95 NR 149, and *Thomson v. Canada (Deputy Minister of Agriculture)*, [1992] 1 SCR 385, 89 DLR (4th) 218, 133 NR 345. This, as all principles of interpretation, is not a rule, but a presumption that must give way when circumstances demonstrate that such was not the intention pursued by Parliament. However, in the present circumstances, I see no reason to depart from that principle since, to the contrary, it confirms and is consistent with the ordinary meaning of the words "employment" and "retiring allowance" chosen by Parliament.

The Minister's position is also untenable when one considers the context in which the 1983 amendment was made. The amendment made by Parliament to subsection 80.4(1) of the Act was made through *An Act to amend the statute law relating to income tax (No. 2)*, SC 1980-81-82-83, c. 140, the same legislation by which the definition of "retiring allowance" was amended in 1983. If Parliament had wanted to include as retiring allowances payments made in respect of the cancellation of an employment contract occurring before the employee had become under obligation to provide services to the employer, it would, as counsel for the appellant argued, have specifically referred to the notion of prospective or intended employment as it did in subsection 80.4(1). This argument seems to me to be compelling and clearly establishes that the objective Parliament sought by amending the definition of "retiring allowance" was limited to termination of the employment relationship once the employee had come under the obligation to provide services to the employer.

The $360,000 received by Mr. Schwartz cannot, therefore, be considered a retiring allowance. As I have explained, "loss of employment" cannot occur before Mr. Schwartz became under obligation to provide services to Dynacare because he could not, before that moment, have been "in the service" of his future employer.

V. Disposition

For all these reasons, I would allow the appeal and restore the decision of the Tax Court of Canada with costs throughout.

MAJOR J (Sopinka and Iacobucci JJ concurring): I agree with the conclusion reached by La Forest J but, with respect, think his reasons go beyond those necessary to decide this appeal. I agree that on a plain meaning, subparagraph 56(1)(a)(ii) of the *Income Tax Act*, RSC 1952, c. 148 (now RSC, 1985, c. 1 (5th Supp.)), does not provide for the taxation of settlements for loss of intended employment. I agree as well that there was no factual foundation on which to argue that the settlement could be taxed under paragraph 3(a) of the *Income Tax Act* as income from the employment contract.

I do not agree with his conclusion on the taxation of income from unenumerated sources. Since the appeal was properly disposed of on other grounds, I do not think it was necessary to discuss this issue. Although La Forest J concluded that the settlement in this case could not be taxed under paragraph 3(a), his *obiter dicta* indicate that unenumerated sources are as a general matter taxable under paragraph 3(a). With respect, I disagree with my colleague on this point because I do not believe it is either necessary or desirable to decide the question. Given the conclusion reached in this case, it would seem preferable to avoid deciding whether, in theory, the Minister can tax on sources not specifically identified in the Act. I say this because a number of arguments can be and have been advanced on why this is not necessarily the case. I will briefly discuss these.

Section 3(a) ostensibly permits taxation of income from any source. The argument for the Minister, which is supported by the literal wording of the section, is that "office, employment, business and property" are only *examples* of sources which may be taxed. My colleague quotes with approval from *The Fundamentals of Canadian Income Tax* (4th ed. 1992), where Professor V. Krishna states that "all accretions to wealth of an income nature are a measure of [the] ability [to pay] and should be taxable regardless of source" (page 130).

However, a literal adoption of this position would arguably constitute a dramatic departure from established tax jurisprudence. It has long been recognized that not all "accretions to wealth" are included as income. Inheritances and gifts are "accretions to wealth" but are nevertheless not taxed because they are not income from employment, property, or business. Profits from hobbies are accretions to wealth, but they, too, are not taxed for the same reason.

If paragraph 3(a) were applied literally to provide for taxation of income from any source, then again it is arguable the existing jurisprudence would be placed in jeopardy. Despite the inclusive language of paragraph 3(a) and 56, many observers have pointed out that Canadian courts have always recognized that monies which do not fall within the specifically enumerated sources are not subject to tax. For example, E.C. Harris states in *Canadian Income Taxation* (4th ed. 1986), at page 99:

> While the Act recognizes that there may be other sources of income than [those specifically listed in paragraph 3(a)], the case law under the former Act suggests that the only other sources of income and loss that are likely to be recognized are those that are specifically recognized in the Act.

This view is reiterated in B.J. Arnold, T. Edgar and J. Li, eds., *Materials on Canadian Income Tax* (10th ed. 1993), at page 51. After noting that the literal wording of the statute does not require that income be from an enumerated source, the authors state:

> Nevertheless, Canadian courts have tended to adopt the approach of the English courts to the definition of income by restricting the scope of "source" to the traditional sources of income — employment, business, and property — rather than attempting innovatively to discover new sources of income.

To the same effect see J.A. Rendall, "Defining the Tax Base," in B.G. Hansen, V. Krishna and J.A. Rendall, eds., *Canadian Taxation* (1981), 59.

Contrary to the view of my colleague, accepting that unenumerated sources of income are taxable would seriously question a number of cases. For example, in the long line of decisions that distinguish a "business" from a "hobby," it has been consistently held that where the activity in question falls outside of the definition of "business," any profits recognized are not subject to tax under section 3. This is in accordance with the restrictive approach to paragraph 3(a).

In cases where a receipt of money has fallen outside of section 3 and subdivision d of Division B of Part I of the Act, the money has not been taxed. For example, in *Savage, supra*, the taxpayer received $300 as a prize for achievement. As a result, it fell outside of paragraph 56(1)(n), which provided for taxation of prizes over $500. The Minister claimed that the sum was still taxable as a "benefit" under paragraph 6(1)(a). Dickson J, as he then was, rejected this argument, because to do otherwise would have meant that paragraph 56(1)(n) had no meaning. As that sum was not specifically included in the Act it was not taxable. Thus one could state that that decision is inconsistent with a literal interpretation of paragraph 3(a). Moreover, it could be argued that the structure of the Act supports the conclusion that sources may be taxed only if specifically recognized in the Act. If paragraph 3(a) includes all income from any source, then there is no reason for subdivision d of Division B of Part I of the Act (sections 56 to 59.1; "Other Sources of Income"). Section 56 would be left with no purpose, since all sources it lists would already be covered by the general opening words of paragraph 3(a). However, I acknowledge in pointing this out that section 56 contains disclaiming words similar to those found in paragraph 3(a).

La Forest J finds support for his position in *Curran v. Minister of National Revenue, supra*, and *Canada v. Fries, supra.* With respect, my reading of those cases brings me to a different conclusion. I agree that the trial judge in *Curran* held that the payment in question was taxable under the general words of section 3. However, this Court did not approve or even mention the proposition that the payment could be taxed under the general provision of section 3. Instead, it was held that the payment amounted to income from employment, since it was made in exchange for personal service. Kerwin CJ found, "the payment of $250,000 was made for personal service only and that conclusion really disposes of the matter ... ." I do not agree that *Curran* is any authority for supporting taxation of unenumerated sources.

Likewise, I disagree that this Court in *Fries* implicitly held that unenumerated sources of income are taxable. This judgment allowed the appeal on the basis that strike pay did not come within the definition of "income ... from a source" within the meaning of section 3. If anything, this case leans *against* the proposition that unenumerated sources are taxable. This case follows the tradition of excluding any sources not specifically recognized in the Act.

If this Court intends to conclude that paragraph 3(a) should be applied literally, and permit taxation on income from any source whatsoever, it should only do so in circumstances which warrant such a decision because such a result is of fundamental importance. Moreover, as I have mentioned, so deciding can be viewed as a marked departure from previous tax jurisprudence. In 1966, the Carter Commission recommended the extension of taxation to all sources of income and all accretions to purchasing power, but its recommendations were not implemented by Parliament and it is hardly the role of the judiciary to do so.

Accordingly, it is my opinion that this Court in this case should not answer the question of whether paragraph 3(a) permits taxation of unenumerated sources. We should only do so when the question is properly and unavoidably before us.

I agree in all other respects with my colleague La Forest J and would dispose of the appeal in the manner he proposes.

Appeal allowed.

NOTES AND QUESTIONS

1. On what basis did the Supreme Court of Canada allow the taxpayer's appeal in *Schwartz*? Do you agree with the court's conclusion that "the Federal Court of Appeal erred in disturbing the trial judge's finding with respect to apportionment"? Given the exchange of letters between solicitors for Dynacare and the taxpayer, was it reasonable for the trial judge to conclude that the damages received by the taxpayer were "in a small part, if any, for the loss of income for future services and to a larger part... for embarrassment, anxiety and inconvenience"?

2. On what grounds did the Supreme Court of Canada conclude that the payment received by the taxpayer in *Schwartz* would not have been taxable as a "retiring allowance" even if it had been paid to compensate for the loss of amounts to which the taxpayer would have been entitled under the employment contract? Do you agree with the court's conclusion that a payment "in respect of a loss of an office or employment of the taxpayer" requires that the taxpayer have entered into the position of an employee? Why or why not? Do you agree with the court's conclusion that "the objective Parliament sought by amending the definition of 'retiring allowance' was limited to termination of the employment relationship once the employee had come under the obligation to provide services to the employer"? Why or why not?

3. On what grounds did the majority in *Schwartz* conclude that the payment received by the taxpayer would not have been taxable as income from a source under paragraph 3(a) even if it had been paid to compensate for the loss of amounts to which the taxpayer would have been entitled under the employment contract? Is the majority's conclusion that "Parliament has chosen to deal with the taxability of such payments in the provisions of the Act relating to retiring allowances" consistent with its subsequent conclusion that these specific provisions do not contemplate the receipt by the taxpayer of a payment in respect of the loss of an "intended employment"?

4.   Why did the minority in *Schwartz* reject the majority's *obiter dicta* on the scope of paragraph 3(a)? Which of the two interpretations do you prefer? Why?

5.   Might the Minister have argued in *Schwartz* that the payment received by the taxpayer was proceeds from the disposition of the taxpayer's rights under the employment contract? Consider the following passage from the decision of the trial judge, [1993] T.C.J. No. 8, [1993] 2 C.T.C. 2125, 93 D.T.C. 555 (T.C.C.) (at paras. 53-55):

> During the course of my preliminary review of the evidence I came to the view that there was an arguable case that the breach of contract by Dynacare resulted in a disposition of the employment agreement by Schwartz and the money he received from Dynacare constituted proceeds of disposition, or, perhaps as a result of the breach, Schwartz acquired a right of action which he disposed of for $400,000. I asked counsel for their comments on, amongst other things, whether Schwartz did dispose of the employment agreement as a capital asset.
>
>   In the Minister's view the employment agreement, because it is a source of income itself, cannot be a capital asset in the hands of the appellant. Counsel argued that an employment contract is not a capital asset that can be employed for the purpose of gaining income from business or property; it will generate income for the appellant and no one else. I cannot agree: the employment contract was a source of potential income to the appellant in the same way a rental building is to its owner. The employment agreement was an asset or advantage of enduring benefit to Schwartz and once it was acted on by the parties, would be the source of income and other advantages to him. ...
>
>   In my view the receipt of damages by Schwartz was not income "from a source inside or outside Canada" within the meaning of paragraph 3(a). The ordinary concept of income is that of recurring receipts and does not extend to a lump sum received because a source of income has been taken away or destroyed; Schwartz was deprived of an enduring right. He did not receive any income from, or as a result of, the employment agreement.

6.   For a critical analysis of the Supreme Court of Canada decision in *Schwartz*, see David Wentzell, "Taxation of Income from Unlisted Sources: An Analysis of Schwartz v. The Queen" in *Report of Proceedings of the Forty-Eighth Tax Conference*, 1996 Conference Report, Vol. 2 (Toronto: Canadian Tax Foundation, 1997), 67:1-15.

D. Employment Insurance and Adjustment Support

Subparagraphs 56(1)(a)(iv) to (vi) require taxpayers to include various amounts payable under the *Employment Insurance Act* and other federal statutes that provide income support for various kinds of labour market adjustment. Specifically excluded from the amounts otherwise required to be included under subparagraph 56(1)(a)(iv) are payments "relating to a course or program designed to facilitate the re-entry into the labour force of a claimant under that Act." Specifically included under Regulation 5502 as benefits prescribed for the purposes of subparagraph 56(1)(a)(vi) are:

(a)   benefits under the Labour Adjustment Benefits Act;

(b)   benefits under programs to provide income assistance payments, established pursuant to agreements under section 5 of the Department of Labour Act; and

(c) benefits under programs to provide income assistance payments, administered pursuant to agreements under section 5 of the Department of Fisheries and Oceans Act.

Regulation 5502 was added by PC 1995-1023, June 23, 1995, effective for benefits received after October 1991. In *Layton v. Canada*, [1995] T.C.J. No. 210, [1995] 2 C.T.C. 2408 (T.C.C.), the court considered the tax treatment of similar assistance received under a program that had not been prescribed for the purposes of subparagraph 56(1)(a)(vi).

Layton v. Canada
[1995] T.C.J. No. 210, [1995] 2 C.T.C. 2408 (T.C.C.)

BEAUBIER, JTCC: ... In 1993, Mr. Layton received $52,840.47 under the provisions of the Shipbuilders' Workers Adjustment Program ("SWAP"). This was assessed by the Minister of National Revenue as taxable income in 1993. This amount also caused the appellant to repay a portion of his Old Age Security Pension and disentitled him to the Goods and Services Tax Credit from July 1, 1994 to June 30, 1995 under section 122.5 of the *Income Tax Act*...

The Minister included the SWAP payment as "other income" under subparagraph 56(1)(a)(vi) of the *Income Tax Act*. ... Neither Crown counsel nor the Court was able to find any regulations under the *Income Tax Act*, or any other regulations, respecting the SWAP payments. Thus the payment or benefit was not "prescribed" and so does not fall within subparagraph 56(1)(a)(vi).

The payment is not income from an office, employment, business or property. According to the evidence, it is a grant from the government which was paid to the taxpayer after Versatile shipyards was closed. While it is alleged that government officials made a promise, the workers did not give any reciprocal promise or undertaking. They were simply laid off when Versatile shipyards closed. No agreement was made with them to pay them for that, nor did any regulations specify the nature of the payment in question.

The Court adopts the decision of the Supreme Court of Canada in *Fries v. The Queen*, [1990] 2 CTC 439, 90 DTC 6662, which states:

> We are not satisfied that the payments by way of strike pay in this case come within the definition of "income ... from a source" within the meaning of section 3 of the *Income Tax Act*. In these circumstances the benefit of the doubt must go to the taxpayers. The appeal is therefore allowed and the decision of the Tax Review Board is restored. The appellants are to have their costs throughout.

. . .

These matters are referred to the Minister of National Revenue for reconsideration and reassessment on the basis that the payment ... is not income.

Appeals allowed.

NOTES AND QUESTIONS

1.   Why did the court in *Layton* conclude that the payment to the taxpayer was not income? Do you agree with the outcome? Why or why not?

2.   *Layton* was followed in *Law v. The Queen*, [1996] 1 C.T.C. 2252 (T.C.C.), in which Beaubier JTCC held that a payment under the Program for Older Workers Adjustment, administered under the *Labour Adjustment Benefits Act*, was "not income." *Law* was decided before Regulation 5502 was added to the *Income Tax Regulations*.

E. Annuity Payments

Paragraph 56(1)(d) requires taxpayers to include "any amount received by the taxpayer in the year as an annuity payment," other than certain amounts that need not concern us here. Correspondingly, paragraph 60(a) allows the taxpayer to deduct the "capital element" of each annuity payment, which, in the case of an annuity paid under a contract, is prescribed by a detailed set of rules in Regulation 300. For our purposes, there is no need to examine these rules in any detail. The net effect of these rules is to require the recipient of an annuity payment to include the income element of each payment.

For the purposes of the *Income Tax Act*, an annuity is defined in subsection 248(1) to include "an amount payable on a periodic basis whether payable at intervals longer or shorter than a year and whether payable under a contract, will or trust or otherwise." This extended definition and the ordinary meaning of the words "annuity payment" were considered in *Short v. Canada*, [1999] T.C.J. No. 360, [1999] 4 C.T.C. 2085, 99 D.T.C. 1146 (T.C.C.).

Short v. Canada
[1999] T.C.J. No. 360, [1999] 4 C.T.C. 2085, 99 D.T.C. 1146 (T.C.C.)

MOGAN, TCJ:... The only issue is whether a certain amount received by each Appellant in August 1993 was income as an "annuity payment" within the meaning of paragraph 56(1)(d) of the *Income Tax Act* or capital as part of the proceeds of disposition of capital property.

In July 1988, Frederick W. Short Sr. (the father of both Appellants) applied to Great West Life Assurance Company ("GWL") for three different interest income annuities ... . The cost of each annuity was $50,000 and the specifications were for all practical purposes identical.

...

[The annuities were for a 20-year period, with a "guaranteed interest rate" of 11 percent, yielding $5,500 per year. Each annuity could be surrendered at any time in exchange for its "total cash value" — a defined amount that took into account the difference between the guaranteed interest rate on the surrendered annuity and the guaranteed interest rate offered by GWL at the time of surrender on other annuities with a term equal to the time remaining for the surrendered annuity.]

In May 1989, the father of the Appellants assigned two annuities ... to Frederick Short Jr. (one of the Appellants) and assigned the remaining annuity ... to John Short (the other Appellant). If I review the facts and decide the issue in the appeal of Frederick Short, the same result will follow in the appeal of John Short.

In August 1993, Frederick Short (the Appellant) elected to surrender both of his interest income annuities and receive the total cash value for each. He received $87,364.73 for each annuity making a total of $174,729.46. [At that time, the "accumulated value" of the annuity — the sum of the $50,000 principal amount and accrued interest that had not been paid — was $50,979.92, and the guaranteed interest rate offered by GWL on annuities with a term equal to the time remaining for the surrendered annuities was 6.375 percent per year.]

...

The market/surrender value of $87,364.73 is the amount which would have to be invested on August 17, 1993 at 6.375% per annum to produce annual interest of $5,500 for the remaining months in the interest guarantee period.... [A] so-called gain of $36,426.81 is the difference between the market/surrender value and the accumulated value. I would regard the true gain as the amount by which the market/surrender value exceeded the principal amount of $50,000.

At the end of 1993, GWL issued to Frederick Short a ... Statement of Investment Income showing accrued interest of $11,000 and other interest income of $74,729.46. The $11,000 was the annual interest amount at 11% paid to Frederick on June 13, 1993 with respect to his two annuities. The $74,729.46 was determined as follows:

Market/Surrender	$ 87,364.73
Value Less Principal Amount	50,000.00
Gain on one Annuity	$ 37,364.73
Gain on second Annuity	37,364.73
Total Gain	$ 74,729.46

When filing his income tax return for 1993, Frederick reported $11,000 as interest for the two annuities plus $74,729.46 as part of his income.... Upon being assessed for tax, Frederick filed a notice of objection claiming that the amount $74,729.46 was a capital gain from the disposition of the two annuities. That is the issue, income or capital, in these two appeals.

...

In defending the assessment against Frederick Short, the Respondent does not argue that the amount $37,364.73 with respect to the one annuity was interest. Instead, the Respondent argues that that amount was an "annuity payment" within the meaning of paragraph 56(1)(d) of the Act and as the word "annuity" is defined in subsection 248(1).

...

The complete answer to the Respondent's argument is that the amount of $37,364.73 was not "an amount payable on a periodic basis" by any standard or under any circumstances. In fact, it was the antithesis of an amount payable on a periodic basis because it was part of a lump sum payment made once and for all to terminate the annual interest payments of $5,500; to return the principal amount ($50,000) to the owner; and to pay the present value (as at August 17, 1993) of the stream of future interest payments over the remainder of the interest guarantee period.

Notwithstanding the definition of "annuity" in subsection 248(1), that same word is defined in the *Concise Oxford Dictionary*, Eighth Edition (1990) as follows:

1.   a yearly grant or allowance.

2.   an investment of money entitling the investor to a series of equal annual sums.

3.   a sum payable in respect of a particular year.

The root of the English word "annuity" is the Latin word "annus" meaning year. In the workaday world, an annuity is an amount payable yearly. The definition of "annuity" in subsection 248(1) as set out above confirms the ordinary meaning in the workaday world in the sense that it describes an amount payable on a periodic basis; and it expands that ordinary meaning to include intervals longer or shorter than a year. While the definition in subsection 248(1) is inclusive in the sense that it "includes an amount payable ..." that same definition does not state or suggest or even imply that an annuity, for income tax purposes, can be a large once-and-for-all payment like the amount of $87,364.73 ... derived from a consolidation of (i) a principal capital amount of $50,000; (ii) accrued interest of $937.92; and (iii) a balance of $36,426.81 which is dependent upon fluctuating day-to-day interest rates as determined on a particular valuation date.

Counsel for the Respondent argued that the word "annuity" as defined in subsection 248(1) cannot be confined to the words employed in the definition because of the word "includes." I accept that argument but I cannot conclude that Parliament intended that the word "annuity," for purposes of the *Income Tax Act*, have a meaning opposite to the ordinary dictionary meaning just because the definition in the Act commences with the word "includes." If the person drafting the Act had intended that the word "annuity" in the Act could mean a lump sum payment or a large once-and-for-all payment, that person would have used much more explicit language to demonstrate that the statutory meaning would include the antithesis of the ordinary dictionary meaning. ...

Appeals allowed.

NOTES AND QUESTIONS

1. On what basis did the Minister in *Short* argue that the gains realized by the taxpayers on the surrender of the annuities were fully taxable in computing their incomes for their 1993 taxation years? Why did the court reject this argument? How did the court interpret the words "annuity payment" for the purpose of paragraph 56(1)(d) of the Act? Do you agree with the court's decision? Why or why not?

2. Allowing the taxpayers' appeals in *Short*, the court concluded that "the amount of approximately $87,000 received from GWL represented proceeds of disposition of capital property having an adjusted cost base of $50,000." Do you agree with this conclusion? Shouldn't a portion of the gain representing accrued interest of $937.92 have been taxable as interest income?

3. In *Rumack v. M.N.R.*, [1992] F.C.J. No. 48, [1992] 1 C.T.C. 57, 92 D.T.C. 6142 (F.C.A.), the taxpayer won a "cash for life" lottery paying $1,000 a month for life, which was funded by an annuity purchased by and owned by the sponsor of the lottery (the Ontario Association for the Mentally Retarded) from the Sun Life Assurance Company for $135,337.55, but paid directly to the taxpayer by Sun Life. In her 1979 taxation year, the taxpayer received $12,000, of which the Minister assessed $8,155.20 as taxable income after deducting the capital element of these payments under paragraph 60(a). The taxpayer appealed, arguing that the full amount of each monthly payment was a non-taxable prize or windfall. In support of this argument, she also relied on paragraph 40(2)(f), which at the time deemed "a taxpayer's gain or loss from the disposition of (i) a chance to win a prize, or (ii) a right to receive an amount as a prize, in connection with a lottery scheme" to be "nil," and on subsection 52(4), which deems the cost of property acquired after 1971 "as a prize in connection with a lottery scheme" to be its fair market value at that time.

Rejecting the taxpayer's argument that the full amount of each monthly payment was a non-taxable prize or windfall, the court held that the income element was taxable by virtue of paragraphs 56(1)(d) and 60(a). According to Hugessen JA (Stone and Heald JJA, concurring) (at paras. 7-17):

> lottery prizes have traditionally been exempted from income tax in Canada. Originally, this was not as a result of any declared policy or legislative provision in the *Income Tax Act*. Instead, it was simply a consequence of the fact that income tax was only imposed upon income from a source. Lottery winnings did not have the character or quality of income and could not be traced to any source which might be identified as income producing. They were described as "windfalls"...
>
> With the introduction of capital gains tax in Canada in 1972, it became necessary to deal with the possibility that lottery winnings which were not income might nonetheless attract tax as capital gains. Clearly, a policy decision was reached that they should not be so taxed and the result was the enactment of paragraph 40(2)(f) and subsection 52(4) ... , both of which appear in subdivision c of Division B of Part I: "Taxable capital gains and allowable capital losses." ...

By its very nature a stream of payments of $1,000 monthly for life has the character and quality of income. Some of the features strongly indicative of that character in my view are the following: the payments are periodic, regular, certain, foreseeable, expected and enforceable; they are also to endure for the payee's lifetime and, subject only to that limitation, are inexhaustible. The fact that their present value is significantly less than their minimum face value over time shows that they contain a large component based upon interest or the productivity of money.

The source of the income constituted by the stream of payments is the contractual obligation undertaken by the Association at the time the respondent purchased the winning ticket. More immediately it is the annuity contract purchased by the Association from Sun Life for the respondent's benefit and in order to discharge its obligation to her. If it cost the Association $135,337.75 to meet its contractual obligation to her at the time she turned in her winning ticket in 1978, that is also surely the value of the prize which she won.

The respondent acquired through a lottery scheme a prize consisting of a stream of payments of $1,000 a month for life. That prize had a value of $135,337.75, and as such is clearly one which is intended to be covered, and is covered by the provisions of subsection 52(4). It is a "windfall" ... and is therefore not taxable as income. Since it is deemed to have been acquired by her at a cost equal to its fair market value, i.e., $135,337.75, it also does not attract capital gains tax.

The monthly payments received by the respondent are, however, an entirely different matter. It is true that each payment comes to her as a consequence of her having won a prize of a value of $135,337.75, but no payment or group of payments is itself the prize. The prize is the lifetime guaranteed stream of payments, each of which is composed, in large measure, of the income resulting from the tax exempt capital value of the prize. If she had won a lump sum and invested it there can be no doubt that the income from such investment would be taxable in her hands; only the capital would be free of tax by the operation of subsection 52(4). Here, the investment of the capital value of the prize was in effect compulsory, forced on her by the rules of the game itself, but that surely cannot change the result.

What the respondent has received in 1979 are 12 payments of $1,000 each. Those payments have been made under an annuity as that term is defined in subsection 248(1) .... As such they have the character of income and are required by paragraph 56(1)(d) to be included in computing the taxpayer's income. By the terms of paragraph 60(a) there may be deducted therefrom the amounts determined in prescribed manner to be a return of capital. Those amounts totalled $3,844.80 in 1979. The balance of $8,155.20 was taxable income and was properly assessed as such.

Do you agree with this result? Why or why not? Of what, if any, relevance is the fact that the sponsor of the lottery remained the owner of the annuity? Of what, if any, relevance is the fact that the taxpayer did not win a lump sum and decide to invest it, but was "in effect ... forced ... by the rules of the game" to invest the capital value of the prize?

F. Scholarships, Fellowships, Bursaries, and Research Grants

Paragraph 56(1)(n) requires taxpayers to include "the total of all amounts" received during the year "as or on account of a scholarship, fellowship or bursary" less a scholarship exemption, which is defined in subsection 56(3), and excluding amounts received "in the course of business," amounts received "in respect of, in the course of or by virtue of an office or employment," and payments under a registered education savings plan (RESP), which are taxable under paragraph 56(1)(q).[4]

Until 1999, the maximum exemption for scholarships, fellowships, and bursaries was $500. In 2007, subsection 56(3) was amended to provide a more generous exemption for scholarships, fellowships, and bursaries. More specifically, the scholarship exemption was increased to include the sum of three amounts—paragraphs 56(3)(a), (b), and (c). Paragraph 56(3)(a) provides that the scholarship exemption includes all scholarships, fellowships, and bursaries received in respect of "an elementary and secondary school educational program" or an "educational program in respect of which an amount may be deducted under subsection 118.6(2)" (section 118.6 is a provision in the Act that provides for an education tax credit based on the time of enrolment in an educational program at a "designated educational institution"). A "designated educational institution" is in turn defined in 118.6(1) and generally includes all Canadian universities, colleges, and other educational institutions recognized by various government operated student financial aid programs,[5] and universities located outside Canada.[6] Paragraph 56(3)(b) exempts the lesser of two amounts. The first of these is the amount included under 56(1)(n)(i) in respect of "a scholarship, fellowship, bursary, or prize that is to be used by the taxpayer in the production of a literary, dramatic, musical or artistic work." The second is "the total of all amounts each of which is an expense incurred by the taxpayer in the taxation year for the purpose of fulfilling the conditions" of the award. The joint effect of this provision is to exempt from inclusion under 56(1)(n) amounts that are received by the taxpayer as scholarships, fellowships, busaries, or prizes that is intended to be used for and are actually deployed to produce a literary, dramatic, musical or artistic work. Finally, the previous $500 exemption is retained in paragraph 56(3)(c).

It should be recognized that where the scholarship, fellowship, or bursary is received "in the course of business" or "in respect of, in the course of or by virtue of an office or employment," the payment is fully taxable as income from the applicable source and is ineligible for the exemption.

The consequence of the expanded scholarship exemption under subsection 56(3) is that most student financial aid received by Canadian students at the elementary, secondary, and post-secondary levels will be exempted from the inclusion in income provided for in paragraph 56(1)(n), because the amount otherwise included in the student's income under 56(1)(n)(i) will not exceed the scholarship exemption provided for in 56(3).

In contrast to paragraph 56(1)(n), paragraph 56(1)(o) requires taxpayers to include "the amount, if any, by which any grant received by the taxpayer in the

---

4   RESPs are discussed in section IV of this chapter.

5   Para. (a) of the definition of "designated educational institution" in subs. 118.6(1).

6   Para. (b) of the definition of "designated educational institution" in subs. 118.6(1).

year to enable the taxpayer to carry on research or any similar work exceeds the total of expenses incurred by the taxpayer in the year for the purpose of carrying on the work, other than":

(i)   personal or living expenses of the taxpayer except travel expenses (including the entire amount expended for meals and lodging) incurred by the taxpayer while away from home in the course of carrying on the work,

(ii) expenses in respect of which the taxpayer has been reimbursed, or

(iii) expenses that are otherwise deductible in computing the taxpayer's income for the year.

Unlike scholarships, fellowships, and bursaries, therefore, research grants are included in computing the recipient's income only to the extent that they exceed expenses incurred by the recipient for the purpose of carrying on the research. Also unlike scholarships, fellowships, and bursaries, however, research grants are not eligible for the scholarship exemption in subsection 56(3). As a result, characterization as a research grant is more advantageous to taxpayers with qualifying expenses exceeding the scholarship exemption as calculated under subsection 56(3), while characterization as a scholarship, fellowship, or bursary is preferable where qualifying expenses are less than this amount.

Because the *Income Tax Act* does not define the terms "scholarship," "fellowship," "bursary," or "grant ... to carry on research or ... similar work," this task has fallen to the courts. The leading judicial statement on the interpretation of these words is *Canada v. Amyot*, [1976] C.T.C. 352, 76 D.T.C. 6217 (F.C.T.D.).

Canada v. Amyot
[1976] C.T.C. 352, 76 D.T.C. 6217 (F.C.T.D.)

MAHONEY, J: The issue in this case is whether payments totalling $4,500 received by the defendant from the Canada Council in 1972 were on account of a scholarship, fellowship or bursary or on account of a research grant. Subject to any other deductions that may properly be taken, if the former, the entire amount thereof in excess of $500 must be included in his taxable income; if the latter, the expenses incurred in carrying out the research may be deducted. The amount of the expenses so incurred, $1,327.80, is not in dispute.

...

The evidence is that, in the North American academic community, the terms "bursary," "scholarship" and "fellowship" are mainly to be distinguished by the academic level of eligible recipients. Bursary pertains generally to the undergraduate level; scholarship to the master's level and fellowship to the doctoral level.

...

The receipts in issue were as a result of renewals, for twelve month periods, commencing April 1 in each of 1971 and 1972, of an award made sometime earlier. The evidence submitted to the Tax Review Board and adopted for purposes of this trial comprised the defendant's renewal applications and extracts from Canada Council brochures describing its 1971-72 and 1972-73 programs.

...

The authority of the Canada Council to make the payment in question is defined by section 8 of the *Canada Council Act*, RSC 1970, c C-2, the relevant portion of which follows:

> 8. (1) The objects of the Council are to foster and promote the study and enjoyment of, and the production of works in, the arts, humanities and social sciences, and, in particular, but without limiting the generality of the foregoing, the Council may, in furtherance of its objects, ...
>
> (b) provide, through appropriate organizations or otherwise, for grants, scholarships or loans to persons in Canada for study or research in the arts, humanities or social sciences in Canada or elsewhere or to persons in other countries for study or research in such fields in Canada; ...

The Canada Council clearly has the authority to award a research grant. Its nomenclature, "Doctoral Fellowship," is not, *per se*, evidence of the nature of the receipt for income tax purposes. That said, what was applied for and what was granted and renewed was, in its terminology, a Doctoral Fellowship.

The pertinent conditions as to eligibility in effect at the time of the original application, set forth in the memorandum of August 1968, were:

> *Eligibility*: Persons who, by the time of taking up the award can provide evidence that they
>
> 1) are registered in a programme of studies leading to a doctoral degree or the equivalent and
>
> 2) have no more than two years of course requirements to fulfill.

...

On December 4, 1968 the defendant applied for a Doctoral Fellowship of $3,500 tenable for twelve months from October 1, 1969. ... [T]he renewals were granted to permit him to pursue a program of research and study concerning the Italian Communist Party leading to a PhD from the University of Reading, England.

...

The Ordinances of the University of Reading provided that degree of PhD could be conferred upon the satisfactory completion of a thesis. No course work, examinations or, for that matter, bare attendance, at the University of Reading was necessarily required.

...

It appears that, in 1972 at least, the defendant ... did not set foot in England, much less Reading, at all. He lived in Rome and, except for August when he vacationed in Canada, spent the entire year in Italy. The expenses he claims were not his living expenses in Rome but rather the cost of meals and lodging elsewhere in Italy.

I have had recourse to a number of dictionaries, and have concluded that the appropriate definitions of "scholarship" and "fellowship" in *Webster's Third New International Dictionary* most closely [reflect] the ordinary meaning of those words in contemporary North American parlance. I think it reasonable, for this purpose, to ignore the rather particular significance attached to "scholarship" and "fellowship" in Great Britain. The payments in issue were made to a North American scholar by a North American institution and were made taxable by legislation adopted by the Parliament of Canada. Notwithstanding that the activity undertaken was done in Europe it must be concluded that the defendant in applying for the grant, the Canada Council in making it, and Parliament in seeking to tax it, have all acted in a North American frame of reference.

None of the dictionary definitions of "bursary" have any relevance to this action. The *Income Tax Act* does not, itself, define any of the terms. The following pertinent definitions are from *Webster's Third New International Dictionary*:

> *Fellowship*: a sum of money offered or granted by an educational institution, public or private agency, or organization, or foundation for advanced study or research or for creative writing.

> *Scholarship*: a sum of money or its equivalent offered (as by an educational institution, a public agency, or a private organization or foundation) to enable a student to pursue his studies at a school, college, or university.

Just as the Canada Council can make grants for either study or research, so the term "fellowship," in ordinary parlance, embraces grants for study or research, *inter alia*. A distinction must, however, be made for purposes of the *Income Tax Act*.

It is manifest that research is an essential element or ingredient or technique of study. Generally, the more eminent the station in the academic hierarchy of the student, the higher the quality and greater the quantity of research reasonably to be expected of him. I accept, without reservation, that what the defendant was doing, during 1972, in terms of activity, was research and nothing else.

The Act leaves one to search elsewhere for the meaning of the terms "bursary," "scholarship" and "fellowship" as used in paragraph 56(1)(n) but paragraph 56(1)(o) is explicit. It refers to "any grant received by the taxpayer ... to enable him to carry on research or any similar work." The phrase "or any similar work" may require interpretation on another occasion but it is not material here. As I have said, the defendant's 1972 activity was research and only research.

In order to bring the receipts within paragraph 56(1)(o), the purpose of the grant must have been to enable the defendant to carry on that research. The key question is the purpose of the payments he received from the Canada Council and not the means adopted, by necessity or choice, to achieve that purpose. If the purpose was the research itself, which is to say, in most cases, not research as an activity for its own sake but for the sake of the novel proposition, anticipated or otherwise, that might ensue upon it, then the grant was made for that purpose and fell within paragraph 56(1)(o). That would be so even if the defendant's advancement in the academic world was an active, but secondary, objective or an inevitable, but incidental, benefit. On the other hand, if the purpose of the grant was to assist the defendant to advance his academic career and the research undertaken was but a means, however essential, to carry out that purpose then the grant was a bursary, scholarship or fellowship and fell within paragraph 56(1)(n).

Notwithstanding the undisputed quality of the research in this case and the time devoted to it in 1972 to the exclusion of other activities, the object of the grant was not the defendant's contribution to the general body of knowledge on the Italian Communist Party; it was to assist the defendant toward his doctorate. Having regard to the defendant's level of academic attainment in 1972, the grant was a fellowship and the amounts received by him on its account fell within paragraph 56(1)(n) of the Act.

Appeal dismissed.

NOTES AND QUESTIONS

1. In *Amyot*, the court stated that the Canada Council's nomenclature "Doctoral Fellowship" "is not, *per se*, evidence of the nature of the receipt for income tax purposes." Do you agree? Why or why not? Is it reasonable to presume that the *Income Tax Act* and the *Canada Council Act* should be read *in pari materia*?

2. In determining the meaning of the terms "scholarship," "fellowship," and "research grant," Mahoney J relied on "the ordinary meaning of those words in contemporary North American parlance." Is this a "plain meaning" approach to statutory interpretation? Is it a "purposive" approach? Is it both? Do you agree with the court's interpretation? Why or why not?

3. In *Taylor v. M.N.R.*, [1979] C.T.C. 2356, 79 D.T.C. 331 (T.R.B.), the taxpayer, a university professor who spent his sabbatical leave doing research in Europe in the field of muscular physiology, obtained a "fellowship leave award" against which he deducted research expenses under paragraph 56(1)(o) of the Act. Allowing the taxpayer's appeal, the court held (at para. 14):

> In the instant appeal, the research done by the appellant, who already held a doctorate, was not to acquire a further academic degree but was aimed, among other things, at finding methods of isolating myosin from human biopsy samples. The research and resulting reports done by the appellant on this and other subjects with researchers in the Scandinavian countries were published in several publications and have added to the existing knowledge in the general field of muscular physiology. The grant awarded to the appellant and the research done by him in my view meet the requirements of the test set out by Mr. Justice Mahoney in the *Amyot* case. Paragraph 56(1)(o) is therefore applicable to the facts of this appeal and not paragraph 56(1)(n).

4.   In *Hoyt v. M.N.R.*, [1977] C.T.C. 2401, 77 D.T.C. 270 (T.R.B.), the taxpayer, a high school teacher who was granted a year's sabbatical leave at two-thirds of his regular salary, sought to deduct transportation expenses on the basis that the payments received during the year comprised a "research grant" within the meaning of paragraph 56(1)(o). Rejecting this argument, the board concluded (at para. 10) that the payments were "a special form of holiday pay from his employer and not within the ambit of said section 56(1)(o)."

For a similar result, see *Mitchell v. Canada*, [1999] T.C.J. No. 302, [1999] 4 C.T.C. 2285, 99 D.T.C. 866 (T.C.C.), in which the taxpayer, a tenured professor at the School of Business Administration at Acadia University in Wolfville, Nova Scotia, sought to deduct $15,551.68 in research expenses incurred to travel throughout North America and the Caribbean during his sabbatical year. Characterizing amounts paid to the taxpayer by the university during the year as salary rather than "a grant for the purpose of doing research on a specific project" (para. 12), the court rejected the taxpayer's argument that "because sabbatical leave is only granted by the University once the applicant's research program and expenses have been approved, any payment in lieu of salary during the leave is in essence a research grant within the meaning of paragraph 56(1)(o) of the *Act*, whether or not the University designates it as such." According to Sarchuk TCJ (at paras. 13-16):

> It is not disputed that the Appellant was an employee within the meaning of the [Collective] Agreement [with the University]. ... Article 21 of the Agreement provides for the remuneration of employees and sets out, *inter alia*, the salary grid for each of the taxation years in issue. Article 24.10 provides for a sabbatical leave which "is intended to provide an opportunity for employees to pursue scholarly interests related to their disciplines at other Universities or appropriate places" and also states: "sabbatical leave is the earned right of any employee who is granted leave by the Sabbatical Leave Committee." Article 24.11 provides that the salary for leave shall be according to the following scale: 12 month leaves ... six or more years of eligible service ... sabbatical salary 80%.
>
> I might add that the parties to this Agreement put their minds to the issue that expenses might be incurred by an employee in the course of conducting research at any time during his employment. For example, Article 25.00 — Fringe Benefits makes reference to a number of matters including the provision of "research monies" and funding for "professional development" and allocates the sum of $60,000 for the support of research in each academic year to be distributed amongst the various faculties. Requests for funds pursuant to this Article are made on an Application for Regular Research Grant form.
>
> In light of these provisions, it is not possible to consider that the amount received by him during the term of his sabbatical constituted anything other than the bargained-for portion of his salary. There is nothing in the relevant Articles of the Agreement to suggest that either the employer or the employee considered a sabbatical salary to be a grant or fellowship or any other form of remuneration.
>
> ... Paragraph 56(1)(o) can only apply where the receipt by a taxpayer is clearly and unequivocally a grant.

For another similar result, see *Ghali v. Canada*, [2001] T.C.J. No. 545, [2003] 3 C.T.C. 2513, 2001 D.T.C. 870 (T.C.C.), in which Tardif TCJ held (at para. 44) that amounts received by the taxpayer, a university professor, while on sabbatical were "not research grants at all, but one of the benefits related to the employment that the appellant held with Université Laval, the whole in accordance with the collective agreement."

5.   In *Subbarao v. M.N.R.*, [1986] T.C.J. No. 552, [1986] 2 C.T.C. 2089, 86 D.T.C. 1554 (T.C.C.), the taxpayer, an associate professor of administration at the University of Ottawa, received research grants totalling $18,180 during the 1980 taxation year, against which he deducted $16,244 to travel to India with his wife and two children. Rejecting the taxpayer's argument that the full amount of these expenses was deductible under subparagraph 56(1)(o)(i), the court affirmed the Minister's assessment, which disallowed any deduction for travelling expenses incurred by the taxpayer's wife and children, on the basis (at para. 12) that these amounts "cannot be construed as expenses incurred by the taxpayer for the purpose of carrying on his work as required by the provisions of paragraph [56(1)](o)." On the contrary, Couture CJTC emphasized (at para. 12), "[t]hey were not even remotely associated or related to such a purpose as the only and sole reason for the expense in question was to move his family with him to India where he was to carry on his research project."

6.   In *Scheinberg v. Canada*, [1996] T.C.J. No. 1, [1996] 2 C.T.C. 2089 (T.C.C.), the taxpayer, a tenured history professor at Concordia University in Montreal, received a $4,000 research grant to study the rise of the extreme right in Europe, against which he sought to deduct research expenses of $34,519.50, which included the cost of travelling to Europe and hiring his wife as a research assistant. Affirming the Minister's assessment, which disallowed the deduction of expenses exceeding the amount of the research grant, Bowman JTCC concluded (at paras. 7 and 10):

> Paragraph 56(1)(o) is not a provision that allows a deduction. It requires the inclusion in income of the amount of a research grant to the extent that it exceeds the expenses relating to the research. Where the expenses exceed the grant it does not authorize the deduction of the excess. If those expenses are to be deducted, the authority, if it exists at all, must be found elsewhere. ...
>
>   To the extent that the expenses were not personal or living expenses, they related not to any business that he carried on but to his employment with the university. Doing research and publishing are necessary concomitants of being a university professor and the cost of research and publishing ... relates to the employment as a professor.

7.   The CRA's views on the characterization of amounts as scholarships, fellowships, bursaries, and research grants appear in *Interpretation Bulletin* IT-75R4, "Scholarships, Fellowships, Bursaries, Prizes, and Research Grants," June 18, 2003. According to this bulletin:

Scholarships and Bursaries

    6. Scholarships and bursaries are amounts paid or benefits given to students to enable them to pursue their education. Scholarships and bursaries usually apply to education at a post-secondary level or beyond, such as at a university, college, technical institute or other educational institution. However, there are circumstances where scholarships or bursaries are awarded for education below the post-secondary school level. Scholarships and bursaries normally assist the student in proceeding towards a degree, diploma, or other certificate of graduation. Scholarships and bursaries may apply to any field of study, including an

academic discipline (such as the arts or sciences), a professional program (such as law or medicine) or a trade or skill (such as plumbing or carpentry). Normally, a student is not expected to do specific work for the payer in exchange for a scholarship or bursary. If a scholarship or bursary program provides allowances or reimbursements to pay for specific educational costs, such as those for lodging, personal travel, tools, books or equipment, those amounts are generally included under subparagraph 56(1)(n)(i). [...] Subparagraph 56(1)(n)(i) can also apply to the value of benefits in kind, such as free accommodation or equipment.

7. During or immediately after a period of employment, employees and employers sometimes make agreements under which the employer agrees to pay all or part of the employee's education costs on the condition that the employee returns to work for the employer when the education is completed. In such cases, the amounts so paid are employment income to the student under subsection 5(1) pursuant to subsection 6(3), and not scholarship or bursary income within the meaning of subparagraph 56(1)(n)(i).

...

Fellowships

11. Fellowships are similar to scholarships and bursaries in that they are amounts paid or benefits given to persons to enable them to advance their education. However, the recipient is generally a graduate student and the payer is generally a university, charity, or similar body. Fellowships are generally awarded for doctoral studies and post-doctoral work. An amount received on account of a fellowship is normally included as a fellowship under subparagraph 56(1)(n)(i), but it can sometimes be included as a research grant under paragraph 56(1)(o). The treatment depends upon the primary purpose for which the fellowship was granted as determined by reference to the terms and conditions attached to the award. If the primary purpose of the award is to further the education and training of the recipient in his or her individual capacity, such as studying for a doctoral degree, the award is included under subparagraph 56(1)(n)(i), even though research is undertaken as a means to achieve that purpose.

12. On the other hand, if the primary purpose of the award is to carry out research for its own sake (for example, to further knowledge in a particular field by discovering new facts, or by reinterpreting existing knowledge), the award is considered to be a research grant and is included under paragraph 56(1)(o). Where the recipient's education and training is also furthered by such research, such a benefit does not invalidate the primary purpose of the grant provided the benefit could be considered to be a secondary purpose of the grant or an inevitable but incidental benefit. ...

8. As a general rule, student loans, like other loans, are neither taxable when received nor deductible when repaid. According to paragraph 16 of IT-75R4:

> If a student receives a genuine loan to assist in financing the student's education, the loan is not considered to be an amount received as or on account of a scholarship, fellowship, or bursary for purposes of subparagraph 56(1)(n)(i). For a genuine loan to exist, provisions must generally be made for repayment within a reasonable time. In some cases, a forgivable loan may be included in income. If an amount included under subparagraph 56(1)(n)(i) or paragraph 56(1)(o) is later repaid, paragraph 60(q) may allow the taxpayer to deduct the repayment.

Although the benefit associated with an interest-free student loan might be characterized as a "scholarship, fellowship or bursary" within the meaning of paragraph 56(1)(n), the CRA does not appear to have addressed this issue.

9. For more detailed information about the CRA's treatment of forgivable loans, see *Interpretation Bulletin* IT-340R, "Scholarships, Fellowships,

Bursaries, and Research Grants — Forgivable Loans, Repayable Awards and Repayable Employment Income," September 26, 1984, paragraphs 2-4. Where a forgivable loan is in fact forgiven, one might assume that the forgiven amount constitutes a "scholarship, fellowship or bursary" within the meaning of paragraph 56(1)(n), which should be included in the recipient's income in that taxation year. This consequence, however, is not specified in the department's published administrative position, which refers only to the inclusion of forgiven amounts under paragraph 6(1)(a) where the forgiveness arises in the context of an employment relationship; see IT-340R, paragraphs 5 and 6.

10. The CRA defines a "repayable award," in contrast to a "forgivable loan," as "a scholarship, fellowship, bursary, or research grant which the recipient is committed to return if certain conditions are not met." See IT-340R, at paragraphs 2-3. Unlike forgivable loans, which are not included in computing the recipient's income in the taxation year in which they are received, repayable awards are regarded by the CRA as taxable income that must be "included in computing the recipient's income in the year received under paragraph 56(1)(n) or (o)." See IT-340R, at paragraph 8.

Where a taxpayer repays all or part of a repayable award that was previously included in computing the taxpayer's income under paragraph 56(1)(n) or (o), the amount repaid may be deducted under paragraph 60(q), provided that the payer and the recipient of the award deal with each other at arm's length; the amount was "paid to the taxpayer for the purpose of enabling the taxpayer to further the taxpayer's education"; and the taxpayer did not, during the period for which the award was paid, provide "other than occasional services to the payer as an officer or under a contract of employment." Moreover, where a repayable award is repaid, paragraph 56(1)(p) requires the original payer to include the amount in computing its income to the year in which the repayment is made.

G. Prizes

In addition to scholarships, fellowships, and bursaries, paragraph 56(1)(n) includes in the income of a taxpayer for a taxation year:

> the total of all amounts (other than ... amounts received in the course of business, and amounts received in respect of, in the course of or by virtue of an office or employment) received by the taxpayer in the year ... as or on account of ... a prize for achievement in a field of endeavour ordinarily carried on by the taxpayer, other than a prescribed prize,

less the $500 exemption provided for in paragraph 56(3)(c), discussed above. As a result, while a prize that is "received in the course of business" or "in the course of or by virtue of an office or employment" is fully taxable as business income or income from an office or employment, an amount received "as or on account of a prize for achievement in a field of endeavour ordinarily carried on by the taxpayer" is typically taxable only to the extent that it exceeds $500, unless it is a "prescribed prize," in which case it is explicitly exempt from tax.

The inclusion of prizes as income from a business or from an office or employment was considered in Chapters 4 and 5. The following cases and commentary consider the characterization of a "prize for achievement in a field of endeavour ordinarily carried on by the taxpayer" and the exemption for "prescribed prizes."

1. Prize for Achievement

The leading case on the meaning of a "prize for achievement in a field of endeavour ordinarily carried on by a taxpayer" is *Canada v. Savage*, [1983] S.C.J. No. 80, [1983] C.T.C. 393, 83 D.T.C. 5409 (S.C.C.), in which the taxpayer received $300 from her employer, a life insurance company, on successfully completing three courses in the areas of life insurance law, economics and investment, and life insurance actuary mathematics. Having concluded that the payment was a benefit received "in respect of, in the course of, or by virtue of an office or employment" within the meaning of paragraph 6(1)(a), Dickson J (as he then was) proceeded to consider whether the payment was non-taxable by virtue of the $500 exemption in paragraph 56(1)(n). At the time that the case was decided, paragraph 56(1)(n) did not contain the parenthetical words excluding "amounts received in the course of business, and amounts received in respect of, in the course of or by virtue of an office or employment."

Canada v. Savage
[1983] S.C.J. No. 80, [1983] C.T.C. 393, 83 D.T.C. 5409 (S.C.C.)

DICKSON, J: ... I turn then to the question of whether the sum received by Mrs Savage was a prize within the meaning of paragraph 56(1)(n) of the *Income Tax Act*. The Crown takes two points: (i) the word "prize" connotes a reward for superiority in a contest or competition with others, and (ii) in any event, paragraph 56(1)(n) is not an exemption provision and does not affect payments which fall within the other taxing provisions of the statute.

On the first point, the case of *The Queen v. McLaughlin*, [1979] 1 FC 470 is cited. The taxpayer had been given $10,000 as an award for his achievements as chairman of the Ontario Milk Marketing Board. Judge Marceau upheld the decision of the Tax Appeal Board which had held that the award did not come within the terms of paragraph 56(1)(n) of the Act, because it was not a prize for an endeavour ordinarily carried on by the taxpayer:

> In my opinion, the word "prize" connotes something striven for in a competition, in a contest, and I don't think there can be a competition or a contest in the real sense without the participants being aware that they are involved.

The word "prize," in ordinary parlance, is not limited to a reward for superiority in a contest with others. A "prize" for achievement is nothing more nor less than an award for something accomplished. There is no need to pluck the word "prize" out of context and subject it to minute philological examination, or to think of "prize" in the context of the medal or book one may have won at an earlier date on a field day or at school or in a music competition.

The word "prize" is surrounded in the *Income Tax Act* by other words which give it colour and meaning and content. I repeat them: "as or on account of a scholarship, fellowship, or bursary, or a prize for achievement in a field of endeavour ordinarily carried on by the taxpayer."

Three comments. First, paragraph 56(1)(n) is not concerned with the identity of the payer or the relationship, if any, between donor and donee. There is nothing in the section which renders the scholarship, fellowship, bursary or prize taxable on the ground that the donor or payer is the employer of the taxpayer. Second, the words "scholarship, fellowship or bursary," with which the word "prize" is associated, are normally employed in speaking of educational attainments, usually in the sphere of advanced studies, and "polite" learning. Third, the prize must be for "achievement," defined in the *Shorter Oxford Dictionary* (3rd Ed.) as "the action of achieving, anything achieved, a feat, a victory." "To achieve" is variously defined, including "to carry out successfully," "to attain." The "achievement" must be in a field of endeavour ordinarily carried on by the taxpayer. This rules out, for example, prizes won in games of chance or at a costume party or for athletic achievement. We are concerned with the field of endeavour ordinarily carried on by the taxpayer, in this instance, the life insurance business.

Funk and Wagnalls Standard College Dictionary (Canadian Edition) defines "prize" as:

1. That which is offered or won as an honor and reward for superiority or success, as in a contest; an award.

2. Anything to be striven for ...

Black's Law Dictionary (5th Ed.) gives, among others, this definition of a "prize": "An award or recompense for some act done; some valuable thing offered by a person for something done by others." This is broad language.

In my view, a "prize for achievement" does not necessarily connote an award for victory in a competition or contest with others. That places too narrow and inflexible a meaning on the words. In the case at bar the award was in recognition of bona fide accomplishment, successful completion of course studies, and examinations in a challenging and difficult field of endeavour, in which about 61 per cent of those writing were successful and about 39 per cent failed. Only the successful candidates were eligible to receive a prize.

It is important also to say that it is not suggested here that the system of awards was introduced as a colourable device intended to provide the employer with an opportunity of increasing the statutory exemption of employees by $500 per year. If and when such a case arises it can be considered on its facts.

. . .

For the foregoing reasons the Crown's contention, that the word "prize" in paragraph 56(1)(n) has application only in a contest or competition with others, in my opinion, fails.

The further submission on the part of the Crown is that, in any event, the $500 exclusion in paragraph 56(1)(n) is not an exemption, and does not affect payments which fall within other taxing provisions of the statute. In terms of this case, the Crown's position is that even if the $300 is a prize not taxable under paragraph 56(1)(n), the $300 is nonetheless taxable under sections 5 and 6 as income from employment.

It is true that the opening words of subsection 56(1) speak in terms of inclusion and not exclusion:

> 56. (1) Without restricting the generality of section 3, there shall be included in computing the income of a taxpayer for a taxation year...

Section 56 falls within Division B, subsection (d) headed "Other Sources of Income." The section enumerates examples of income that fall within s. 3, repeated below for ease of reference, as constituting "income ... from a source":

> 3. The income of a taxpayer for a taxation year for the purposes of this Part is his income for the year determined by the following rules:
>
> (a)   determine the aggregate of amounts each of which is the taxpayer's *income* for the year (other than a taxable capital gain from the disposition of a property) *from a source* inside or outside Canada, including, without restricting the generality of the foregoing, his income for the year from each office, employment, business and property;

I agree with counsel for Mrs Savage that the opening words "Without restricting the generality of section 3," in [subsection] 56(1) would seem to have been inserted to defeat an argument of *"expressio unius est exclusio alterius"* in order to relate income items contained in [subsection] 56(1) to the arithmetical calculation set out in section 3. Income can still be income from a source if it does not fall within section 56. Moreover, section 56 does not enlarge what is taxable under section 3, it simply specifies.

When section 56 is seen in this context, it is clear the Crown's submission cannot be sustained. The Crown's position, to repeat, is that a prize for achievement in a field of endeavour ordinarily carried on by the taxpayer, if less than $500, and if obtained in respect of, in the course of, or by reason of an office or employment, is taxable under sections 5 and 6, notwithstanding paragraph 56(1)(n). Paragraph 56(1)(n) makes it clear that a prize for achievement is income from a source under section 3 just as income from an office or employment is income from a source under section 3. If a prize under $500 would still be taxable under sections 5 and 6, it would have to follow on the Crown's argument that a prize under $500 would equally be taxable under section 3. That cannot be right. That would mean that a prize over $500 would be taxable under paragraph 56(1)(n) and a prize up to $500 would be taxable under section 3. The $500 exclusion in paragraph 56(1)(n) would never have any effect. It seems clear that the first $500 of income received during the year falling within the terms of paragraph 56(1)(n) is exempt from tax. Any amount in excess of $500 falls under paragraph 56(1)(n) and is taxable accordingly. If that is not the effect, what purpose is served by the subsection? ...

Appeal dismissed.

NOTES AND QUESTIONS

1.   What interpretive techniques did Dickson J (as he then was) employ in *Savage* to determine the meaning of the word "prize" in paragraph 56(1)(n)? Do you agree with his interpretation? Why or why not?

2.   On what basis did Dickson J (as he then was) conclude in *Savage* that the payment received by Mrs. Savage, though both an employment benefit under paragraph 6(1)(a) and a prize under paragraph 56(1)(n), was exempt under the latter provision? Do you agree with this interpretation? Why or why not?

3.   In the course of his decision, Dickson J (as he then was) stated that:

the opening words "Without restricting the generality of section 3," in [subsection] 56(1) would seem to have been inserted to defeat an argument of *"expressio unius est exclusio alterius,"* in order to relate income items contained in [subsection] 56(1) to the arithmetical calculation set out in section 3. Income can still be income from a source if it does not fall within section 56. Moreover, section 56 does not enlarge what is taxable under section 3, it simply specifies.

Is this statement *obiter* or part of the *ratio* of the decision? What significance might it have for the characterization of amounts as income under the Act?

4.   Effective for amounts received after May 23, 1985, paragraph 56(1)(n) was amended by excluding from the provision "amounts received in the course of business, and amounts received in respect of, in the course of or by virtue of an office or employment." As explained in the Department of Finance technical notes released with the draft legislation in November 1985, the purpose of this amendment was to reverse the result in *Savage*:

Paragraph 56(1)(n) includes in the income of a taxpayer for a year certain scholarships, bursaries and prizes for achievement to the extent that the total of such amounts exceeds $500. Some employers give awards, prizes or similar payments to their employees in the course of their employment. Generally, these payments represent taxable benefits to the employee and are intended to be fully included in income. However, a recent court decision indicated that certain of these awards might qualify for the $500 exemption. This amendment, which applies to amounts received after May 23, 1985, clarifies that work-related and business-related awards, prizes and similar payments do not qualify for the $500 exemption.

As a result of this amendment, courts are no longer confronted with the conflict between inclusion of a prize under paragraph 56(1)(n) and its inclusion as income from an office or employment or from a business.

Does this amendment affect the court's interpretation of the meaning of the words "prize for achievement in a field of endeavour ordinarily carried on by a taxpayer"? Does it affect its conclusions regarding the relationship between section 3 and subsection 56(1)?

5.   In *Turcotte v. Canada*, [1997] T.C.J. No. 828, [1997] 3 C.T.C. 2359 (T.C.C.), the taxpayer, a welfare recipient, who had worked as a cinema manager but had been unemployed for seven years, won $19,200 on a television game show ("Tous pour un") in which he answered questions on Quebec cinema, Charles de Gaulle, and Charlie Chaplin. Accepting the taxpayer's argument that the study of Quebec cinema, Charles de Gaulle, or Charlie Chaplin was not "a field of endeavour ordinarily carried on by the taxpayer," the court concluded that the payment was not taxable under paragraph 56(1)(n). According to Lamarre-Proulx TCJ (at para. 35):

> The ordinary field of endeavour was not at issue in [*Savage*]. In the instant case, can the phrase "field of endeavour ordinarily carried on" be given the broad meaning suggested by counsel for the respondent, namely the field of culture? In my opinion, it is difficult to regard the vast field of culture as an individual's ordinary field of endeavour within the meaning of the wording in s. 56(1)(n) of the *Act*. That surely is not the usual meaning of the wording. For most people, the phrase "field of endeavour ordinarily carried on" means a defined, specific field of endeavour continuously engaged in by that person.

Do you agree with this reasoning? Why or why not? Might the payment have been taxable under the more general language "income ... from a source" under paragraph 3(a)? Should the prize have been taxable?

2. Prescribed Prize

For the purposes of subparagraph 56(1)(n)(i), Regulation 7700 defines a "prescribed prize" as:

> any prize that is recognized by the general public and that is awarded for meritorious achievement in the arts, the sciences or service to the public but does not include any amount that can reasonably be regarded as having been received as compensation for services rendered or to be rendered.

The exemption for prescribed prizes was enacted in 1987, retroactive to 1983 and subsequent taxation years. The purpose of this amendment was explained as follows in the budget papers tabled in the House of Commons on February 18, 1987:

> The budget proposes a clarifying change for the 1983 and subsequent taxation years to the rules affecting the taxability of prizes for achievement. Amounts received by a taxpayer in a year, as or on account of a prize for achievement in a field of endeavour ordinarily carried on by the taxpayer, are technically required to be included in the taxpayer's income for the year. As a result of judicial decisions, the word "prize" has been interpreted more broadly than is appropriate. The budget therefore proposes to provide for regulation to prescribe the kind of prizes that will be excluded from a taxpayer's income. Such prizes would be limited to widely recognized prizes for meritorious endeavour.

On the basis of this language, the CRA has set out the following guidelines for "prescribed prizes" in paragraph 20 of IT-75R4:

> A prize meeting all of the criteria of a "prescribed prize" is not included in computing the income of the recipient, even if the prize relates to accomplishments in the recipient's ordinary field of endeavour. Section 7700 of the Regulations defines a prescribed prize as any prize that is recognized by the general public for meritorious achievement in the arts, the

sciences or service to the public. For example, a Nobel Prize given to a scientist or the Governor General's Literary Award given to a professional writer would qualify, as would many community service awards. Scholarships and bursaries awarded to students would not qualify. Furthermore, any amount that can reasonably be regarded as having been received as compensation for services rendered, or to be rendered, is not a prescribed prize.

The amended language of paragraph 56(1)(n) was considered in *Foulds v. Canada*, [1997] T.C.J. No. 87, [1997] 2 C.T.C. 2660 (T.C.C.), where the taxpayer, who operated a business known as "Real World Productions," the principal function of which was to manage a band called "Real World," received two music prizes referred to as the "Music Spirit East Award" and the "Ultimate Deal Award," the combined value of which was $31,600. On the basis that these awards fell within the definition of a "prescribed prize" in Regulation 7700 to the *Income Tax Act*, the taxpayer did not include this amount in computing her income for her 1992 taxation year. The Minister, however, assessed the taxpayer on the basis that these awards were received in the course of the taxpayer's business within the meaning of the 1985 amendment to paragraph 56(1)(n).

Having concluded that the prize was "for achievement in a field of endeavour ordinarily carried on by the taxpayer" and was not received "in the course of business" or "in respect of, in the course of or by virtue of an office or employment," Léger DJTC considered whether the awards fit within the definition of a "prescribed prize" in Regulation 7700. According to the court (at paras. 37-40):

> There is ample evidence before this Court that the prizes awarded were for "meritorious achievement in the arts." In order to succeed in the contest in question members of the band had to compose the music, compose the lyrics, prepare the arrangement for orchestration and finally give a rendition which was melodious and pleasing to the public and the judges. In exhibit A-3 we find the following provision in the rules and regulations for the contest:
>
> > Judging at the live venue for the winner will be based on the following criteria and weighted as indicated:
> >
> > | | |
> > |---|---|
> > | Musicianship | 20% |
> > | Commercial Appeal | 20% |
> > | Originality | 20% |
> > | Showmanship | 20% |
> > | Audience Response | 10% |
> > | X-Factor | 10% |
>
> Based upon the evidence heard during the appeal the Court finds as a fact that the prizes awarded were "for meritorious achievement in the arts" as provided for in Regulation 7700 of the *Income Tax Act*.
>
> The evidence also discloses that the contest was very well advertized in the press and on the radio over the various stations which were sponsors and this Court finds as a fact that the contest and the prizes were recognized by the general public as required by the Regulation 7700. I have perused Bulletin IT-75 R3 published by the Minister but found it to be of little assistance to me.

After having considered all of the evidence and the submissions of counsel, the Court finds and declares that the prizes received by the Appellant in the 1992 taxation year are not business income of the Appellant but fall within the taxing parameters of paragraph 56(1)(n) and further that such amounts are "prescribed prizes" within the meaning of Regulation 7700.

NOTES AND QUESTIONS

1. Do you agree with the court's conclusion that the prizes were "recognized by the general public" as required by regulation 7700? Is the decision in *Foulds* consistent with the purpose of the amendment as expressed in the Department of Finance technical notes? Is it consistent with the examples given in the Revenue Department's interpretation bulletin? To what extent, if at all, should the courts rely on these extrastatutory sources of interpretation?

2. In *Labelle v. The Queen*, [1994] T.C.J. No. 836, 96 D.T.C. 1115 (T.C.C.), the taxpayer, an accounting professor at the Université du Québec at Montréal, received a prize of US$5,000 for winning the second international Accounting Case Writing Competition organized by the Accounting Education Resource Centre of the University of Lethbridge in Alberta. Although the Crown conceded that the prize was not received "in the course of business" or "in respect of, in the course of or by virtue of an office or employment," it argued that prize was taxable under paragraph 56(1)(n) and not excluded as a "prescribed prize" on the basis that the prize was not "recognized by the general public." On the grounds (at paras. 10 and 13) that the Minister "did not explain why he was of the opinion that the prize was not recognized by the general public" and "had reassessed recipients of the same prize on the basis that the prize *was* recognized by the general public" ... Lamarre-Proulx JTCC allowed the taxpayer's appeal. According to the court (at para. 17):

> Determining whether a prize is recognized by the general public requires an element of evaluation or appreciation. The Minister cannot arrive at two opposing conclusions. He must make only one determination, and the criteria on which he based his evaluation or judgment must be given. It is not sufficient for the Minister to say that the prize is not recognized by the general public. The taxpayer must know why the prize is not, in the Minister's opinion, recognized by the general public. In other words, the Minister must adopt only one position with respect to a prize, which he must be capable of explaining.

Do you agree with this decision? Why or why not?

3. How "general" is the reference to the "recognizing public" in order for an award to fall within the definition of a "prescribed prize"? What constitutes "meritorious achievement in the arts, the sciences or service to the public"? On what basis should the courts give specific meaning to these words?

H. Art Production Grants

Where a taxpayer receives a scholarship, fellowship, bursary, or prize that is included under paragraph 56(1)(n) and that is "to be used by the taxpayer in the production of a literary, dramatic, musical or artistic work," paragraph 56(3)(c) of the Act increases the amount of the allowable exemption from thresholds otherwise applicable from paragraphs 56(3)(a) and (b) to the greater of these amounts and:

> the total of all amounts each of which is an expense incurred by the taxpayer in the year for the purpose of fulfilling the conditions under which the amount ... was received, other than:
>
> (A) personal or living expenses of the taxpayer (except expenses in respect of travel, meals and lodging incurred by the taxpayer in the course of fulfilling those conditions and while absent from the taxpayer's usual place of residence for the period to which the scholarship, fellowship, bursary or prize, as the case may be, relates),
>
> (B) expenses for which the taxpayer is entitled to be reimbursed, and
>
> (C) expenses that are otherwise deductible in computing the taxpayer's income.

For these "art production grants," therefore, this alternative exemption effectively allows taxpayers to deduct expenses incurred in order to fulfill the conditions of the grant. See IT-75R4, at paragraph 44, and *Interpretation Bulletin* IT-257R, "Canada Council Grants," March 31, 1995, paragraph 5. In administering these rules, the CRA has indicated that it will apply the same criteria as it applies to determining allowable deductions under similar language in paragraph 56(1)(o). There do not appear to be any reported cases on the characterization or computation of these art production grants.

I. Social Assistance

In Canada, social assistance is delivered at the federal level in the form of a guaranteed income supplement (GIS) and a spouse's allowance payable under the *Old Age Security Act* (OAS),[7] and at the provincial level under various welfare programs that provide benefits to individuals and families in need.[8] Although payments under the federal programs are specifically included in the recipient's income under clause 56(1)(a)(i)(A), payments under the provincial

---

[7] RSC 1985, c. O-9. The GIS is payable to recipients of an OAS pension who earn an income below a certain level as calculated in subs. 12(5). The spouse's allowance is payable to the spouse (or widow or widower) of the recipient of an OAS pension who is between the ages of 60 and 65, satisfies Canadian residency requirements, and together with his or her spouse earns an income below a certain level as calculated in subs. 22(3). OAS payments are subject to a "clawback" under Part I.2 of the *Income Tax Act*.

[8] See, for example s. 7(3) of the *Ontario Works Act*, S.O. 1997, c. 25, Sched. A, which provides that a person may be eligible for "income assistance" where "the budgetary requirements of the person and any dependants exceed their income and their assets do not exceed the prescribed limits, as provided for in the regulations." See also s. 12(1) of the Alberta *Social Development Act*, R.S.A. 1990, c. S-16, according to which, "[s]ubject to the regulations, when the Director considers that a person is in need of assistance he is responsible while the person is in Alberta for the provision of a social allowance to or in respect of that person in an amount that will be adequate to enable the person to obtain the basic necessities for himself and his dependents."

welfare programs are subject to tax under paragraph 56(1)(u), which includes social assistance payments "made on the basis of a means, needs or income test" in computing the income of the higher income-earning spouse or common law partner in the taxation year in which the payments are received. However, because social assistance payments based on "a means, needs or income test" and included under clause 56(1)(a)(i)(A) or paragraph 56(1)(u) may be deducted in computing the taxpayer's taxable income under paragraph 110(1)(f), these payments are effectively exempt from tax, although the inclusion in net income may affect the credits that may be claimed in computing tax payable. Social assistance payments received by individuals in respect of foster children within their care are fully exempt under paragraph 81(1)(h).[9]

Paragraph 56(1)(u) was enacted in 1981; previously, social assistance payments had been exempt under paragraph 81(1)(j). Since 1981, paragraph 56(1)(u) has been considered in at least two cases. In the first, a dentist sought to obtain the benefit of the deduction in paragraph 110(1)(f) by characterizing as payments of "social assistance" total amounts of $334,334.69 and $258,061.84 received in 1986 and 1987 directly from the governments of Canada and British Columbia in respect of treating certain patients on social assistance (*Hokhold v. Canada*, [1993] F.C.J. No. 672, [1993] 2 C.T.C. 99, 93 D.T.C. 5339 (F.C.T.D.)). In the second case, the taxpayer sought to obtain a marital tax credit under paragraph 118(1)(a) by characterizing a GIS received by his spouse as a social assistance payment that, under paragraph 56(1)(u), would have been included in computing his income rather than that of his spouse (*Brannen v. M.N.R.*, [1992] T.C.J. No. 22, [1992] 1 C.T.C. 2329, 92 D.T.C. 1147 (T.C.C.)).

In *Hokhold*, Rothstein J (as he then was) dismissed the taxpayer's appeal, stating (at para. 15):

> In my view, the taxpayer referred to in paragraph 56(1)(u) is the person to whom the means, needs or income test relates. I do not see how a provider of professional services such as a dentist could be said to be a taxpayer who received a social assistance payment made on the basis of a means, needs or income test.

Subsequent to this decision the Act was amended, retroactive to 1982, to exclude from the scope of paragraph 56(1)(u) payments that are "otherwise required to be included in computing the income for a taxation year of the taxpayer or the taxpayer's spouse or common-law partner."

In *Brannen*, Allan DTCCJ concluded (at paras. 8-11):

---

[9] See *Saulniers v. M.N.R.*, [1996] T.C.J. No. 1298, [1997] 2 C.T.C. 3033 (T.C.C.), where the court held (at para. 9) that the exemption in para. 81(1)(h) does not apply where the recipient "operates a business for profit." See also *Storey Group Homes Ltd. v. M.N.R.*, [1991] T.C.J. No. 787, [1992] 2 C.T.C. 2052 (T.C.C.), where para. 81(1)(h) was held not to apply on the basis that the recipient corporation, which operated foster and group homes for the care of adolescents, was not an "individual" as required by the Act.

Although "social assistance payment" might be thought to include a federal supplement under the *Old Age Security Act*, it cannot, in my view, have that meaning in section 56 of the *Income Tax Act*.

My reason for saying this is that paragraph 56(1)(a) specifically provides that "the amount of any pension, supplement, or spouse's allowance under the *Old Age Security Act*" shall be included in computing a taxpayer's income. And paragraph 56(1)(u) specifically requires a "social assistance payment" received by the taxpayer or the taxpayer's spouse also to be included in computing the taxpayer's income.

Logically, "supplement" must be assigned a meaning different from "social assistance payment" where, as here, they are specified separately in the same section as two kinds of income which are required to be included in a taxpayer's income.

The rules of statutory interpretation require words to be given meanings. Thus where two terms are used in the same statute, different meanings ordinarily ought to be ascribed to each in order to give each a meaning. *A fortiori*, where two terms or words or phrases are used in the same section of the statute, different meanings ought to be assigned to the different terms words or phrases.

On this basis, the GIS was included in computing the income of the taxpayer's spouse, thereby increasing her income such that the taxpayer could not claim the marital tax credit.

J. Workers' Compensation

Like social assistance payments, "compensation received under an employees' or workers' compensation law of Canada or a province in respect of an injury, a disability or death" must be included in computing the recipient's net income under paragraph 56(1)(v) but may be deducted in computing the recipient's taxable income under subparagraph 110(1)(f)(ii). The net result is that no tax is payable on workers' compensation benefits, though the inclusion in computing net income may affect the taxpayer's ability to claim tax credits in computing tax payable. In the case of compensation for injury, disability, or death received under section 5, 31, or 45 of the *Royal Canadian Mounted Police Pension Continuation Act* or under section 32 or 33 of the *Royal Canadian Mounted Police Superannuation Act*, payments are fully exempt under paragraph 81(1)(i).[10]

According to *Interpretation Bulletin* IT-202R2, "Employees' or Workers' Compensation," September 19, 1985, at paragraph 1(b), the "employees' or workers' compensation" referred to in paragraphs 56(1)(v) and 110(1)(f) means:

---

[10] See *Gingras v. Canada*, [1996] T.C.J. No. 794, [1998] 2 C.T.C. 2557 (T.C.C.) and *Dandurand v. Canada*, [1997] T.C.J. No. 7, [1998] 3 C.T.C. 2022 (T.C.C.), where the court held that a regular pension paid under the *Royal Canadian Mounted Police Superannuation Act* was taxable as a "superannuation or pension benefit" under subpara. 56(1)(a)(i) and not exempt under para. 81(1)(i).

the amount of an award, as adjudicated by a compensation board, which a worker or his or her dependants will receive as a result of the worker having suffered illness, injury or death in the performance of his or her duties of employment and includes any such compensation to which entitlement is provided under the *Government Employees Compensation Act* or any employees' or workers' compensation Act or Ordinance or a province or territory of Canada.

For this purpose, the bulletin explains at paragraph 1(a), a "compensation board" includes "any employees' or workers' compensation board or commission in any province or territory in Canada." In addition, the bulletin provides (at paragraph 4):

> For the purpose of paragraph 56(1)(v) the amount of compensation may be received either from a compensation board or from the employer or former employer of the person entitled thereto. An employee may, under the terms of an employment contract or collective agreement, or by reason of being granted injury leave with pay under the *Financial Administration Act*, be entitled to receive salary or wages during a period in which the employee is also entitled to compensation. Where, in these circumstances, the employee receives no payment from a compensation board, the amount received from his or her employer, to the extent that it does not exceed the compensation amount, will be included in the employee's income for the year, as compensation, under paragraph 56(1)(v). The excess, if any, will be included in the employee's income under subsection 5(1).

Although this administrative policy appears to be designed to make up for the fact that members of the Royal Canadian Mounted Police (RCMP) and the regular members of the Canadian Forces are excluded from the federal statute governing workers' compensation,[11] its legal basis was challenged in *Éthier v. Canada*, [1996] T.C.J. No. 130, [1997] 3 C.T.C. 3116 (T.C.C.), where payments received by an officer of the RCMP on sick leave were held to be taxable remuneration under subsection 5(1) and ineligible for the deduction under subparagraph 110(1)(f)(ii). See also *Goguen v. Canada*, [1996] T.C.J. No. 175, [1996] 2 C.T.C. 2343 (T.C.C.), and *Gingras v. Canada*, [1996] T.C.J. No. 794, [1998] 2 C.T.C. 2557 (T.C.C.), where disability payments were characterized as wage loss insurance benefits under paragraph 6(1)(f) rather than workers' compensation under paragraph 56(1)(v); and *Suchon v. Canada*, [2001] T.C.J. No. 695, [2002] 1 C.T.C. 2094 (T.C.C.), where employer-paid disability benefits were characterized as taxable employee benefits under paragraph 6(1)(a).

In *Whitney v. Canada*, [2001] T.C.J. No. 253, [2001] 2 C.T.C. 2714, 2001 D.T.C. 423 (T.C.C.), in contrast, the court characterized as workers' compensation eligible for the deduction in subparagraph 110(1)(f)(ii) amounts equal to the amount that would have been received under the provincial workers' compensation scheme that were paid by the taxpayer's employer (the province of New Brunswick), which operated as a "self-insured employer" for the purposes of the *Workers' Compensation Act*. According to Bowman ACJTC (at para. 20), there were four reasons for this conclusion:

> (a) ... Where the entitlement to workers' compensation is made by the WCB under the *WC Act* the receipt of that compensation constitutes a receipt under an employees'

---

[11] See s. 3 of the *Government Employees Compensation Act*, R.S.C. 1985, c. G-5.

or a workers' compensation law of a province. The Province of New Brunswick is an employer within the meaning of the *WC Act*. All of the procedures for claiming compensation by an injured employee conform to the *WC Act*, which determines the entitlement and duration of the compensation. The right to be paid compensation by the employer ... is entirely dependent upon the direction of the WCB.

(b)   The overall scheme of paragraphs 56(1)(v) and 110(1)(f) of the *Income Tax Act* is that payments of compensation to injured employees who cannot work are not taxable. The Crown's position would, in my view, run counter to this legislative scheme. ...

(c)   Moreover, the Crown's interpretation, if adopted, would lead to an absurdity in that it would mean that a member of CUPE who was employed by a self insured employer would have his or her compensation amount taxed simply because the right to compensation was determined under the *WC Act* but the compensation is paid by the employer under a collective agreement, whereas one who worked for a private employer and was paid 85% of his or her salary by the WCB and had that compensation "topped up" by the employer to an amount equal to his regular salary would not be taxed on the 85%. Where the two interpretations are possible and one leads to an absurdity and one does not, the latter must be chosen: *Victoria City v. Bishop of Vancouver Island*, [1921] 2 AC 384 at 388 (PC).

(d)   If there were any ambiguity or doubt in the application or interpretation of the legislation, that doubt must be resolved in favour of the subject. (*Fries v. The Queen*, 90 DTC 6662 (SCC))

On appeal, [2002] F.C.J. No. 948, [2002] 3 C.T.C. 476, 2002 D.T.C. 7145 (F.C.A.), the trial decision in *Whitney* was reversed on the grounds (at para. 10) that the compensation was "not paid under the Compensation Act," (at para. 9) but "under the collective agreement and pursuant to its terms", and (at para. 11) that the terms under which compensation was paid differed from those under the *Compensation Act*. The court also suggested that paragraph 4 of Interpretation Bulletin IT-202R2 was inconsistent with the relevant statutory provisions. Do you agree with this conclusion? Why or why not?

Another case in which a taxpayer sought to characterize as workers' compensation an amount otherwise taxable as income from an office or employment is *Vincent v. M.N.R.*, [1988] 2 C.T.C. 2075, 88 D.T.C. 1422 (T.C.C.), where the taxpayer received $6,507 in the form of a grievance arbitration award after his employer breached a flexible scheduling agreement contained in the collective agreement negotiated with the taxpayer's union. After rejecting the taxpayer's initial argument that the payment was a non-taxable windfall, the court addressed the taxpayer's alternative argument that the payment was "compensation received under an employees' or workers' compensation law of Canada or a province in respect of an injury, disability or death" within the meaning of paragraph 56(1)(v) and subparagraph 110(1)(f)(ii). According to Sarchuk TCJ (at paras. 51-53):

Counsel's characterization of the payment to Vincent as compensation received under an employee's or workmen's compensation law of the Province of British Columbia is not tenable. The reference in subsections 56(1) and 110(1) of the Act to "a workmen's compensation law of Canada or of a province" is a reference to specific enactments which are intended to provide compensation, medical assistance and services and pensions for employees injured in on-the-job accidents and which are funded for the most part by compulsory employer contributions. These statutes have been described as social legislation designed to achieve that purpose. (*Fleck v. Workmen's Compensation Board*, [1934] 2 DLR 145 (NBQB).)

Mignault, J dealing with the *Workmen's Compensation Act*, CSNB 1903, c. 79 in the case of *The Canadian Pacific Railway Company v. Cheeseman*, 57 SCR 439 said at page 450:

> The object of the ... Act was to give to the workman a remedy where none could be claimed under the common law, the risk of injury through the negligence of a fellow servant being a risk assumed by the workman at common law.

> The resolution of a contractual dispute between an employee and an employer and the awarding of compensation by an arbitrator pursuant to authority granted by the Code is not at all analogous to a payment of compensation by the Workmen's Compensation Board of the Province of British Columbia in respect of a death, personal injury, or for a disability from an injury (including by definition an industrial disease) arising out of and in the course of employment. The amounts paid to Vincent were not compensation received under an employee's compensation law within the meaning of paragraphs 56(1)(v) and 110(1)(f) of the Act.

As a result, the court held, the payment was remuneration from the taxpayer's employment within the meaning of subsection 5(1).

K. Non-Competition Payments

Where a former employee receives an amount as consideration for entering into an agreement not to compete with a former employer, this amount is generally deemed to be remuneration under subsection 6(3) of the Act and, therefore, taxable as income from an office or employment. In *Fortino v. Canada*, [1996] T.C.J. No. 1457, [1997] 2 CTC 2184, (1996) 97 D.T.C. 55 (T.C.C.), the court rejected the Minister's argument that non-competition payments not subject to the deeming rule in subsection 6(3) should be characterized as income from an unenumerated source under paragraph 3(a). In *Manrell v. Canada*, [2001] T.C.J. No. 792, [2002] 1 C.T.C. 2543, 2002 D.T.C. 1222 (T.C.C.), where the taxpayer also received amounts in exchange for an agreement not to compete with the purchaser of a business that he had carried on, McArthur TCJ held that the payments were proceeds from the disposition of a property right and therefore taxable as capital gains. On appeal, [2003] F.C.J. No. 408, [2003] 3 C.T.C. 50, 2003 D.T.C. 5225 (F.C.A.), however, the Federal Court of Appeal held that a right to compete is not "property" within the meaning of this word in the Act, as a consequence of which the payments were not taxable.

On October 7, 2003, the Minister of Finance announced that the results in *Fortino* and *Manrell* would be reversed by statutory amendments designed to tax such amounts as ordinary income. Where a non-competition agreement accompanies the sale of a business, however, the announcement explained that exceptions would allow taxpayers to characterize non-competition payments as capital receipts relating to the sale of the goodwill of the business or as proceeds from the sale of shares of a corporation or an interest in a partnership that carries on the business to the extent that the restrictive covenant increases the fair market value of the share or the partnership interest.

According to a pending amendment to the Act that has not yet taken force amd attempts to implement the accouncement of the Minister of Finance in October 2003, subsection 56.4(2) provides that:

> There is to be included in computing a taxpayer's income for a taxation year the total of all amounts each of which is an amount in respect of a restrictive covenant of the taxpayer that is received or receivable in the taxation year by the taxpayer or by a taxpayer with whom the taxpayer does not deal at arm's length (other than an amount that has been included in computing the taxpayer's income because of this subsection for a preceding taxation year or in the taxpayer's eligible corporation's income because of this subsection for the taxation year or a preceding taxation year).

For the purpose of this pending amendment, subsection 56.4(1) defines a "restrictive covenant" of a taxpayer as "an agreement entered into, an undertaking made, or a waiver of an advantage or right by the taxpayer … whether legally enforceable or not, that affects, or is intended to affect, in any way whatever, the acquisition or provision of property or services by the taxpayer or by another taxpayer that does not deal at arm's length with the taxpayer."

Subsection 56.4(3) of the pending amendment provides for several exceptions, stipulating that the inclusion in subsection 56.4(2) "does not apply to an amount received or receivable by a particular taxpayer in a taxation year in respect of a restrictive covenant granted by the particular taxpayer to another taxpayer (referred to in this subsection and subsection (4) as the "purchaser") with whom the particular taxpayer deals at arm's length … if"

(a) section 5 or 6 applied to include the amount in computing the particular taxpayer's income for the taxation year or would have so applied if the amount had been received in the taxation year;

(b) the amount would, if this Act were read without reference to this section, be required by the description of E in the definition "cumulative eligible capital" in subsection 14(5) to be included in computing the particular taxpayer's cumulative eligible capital in respect of the business to which the restrictive covenant relates, and the particular taxpayer elects (or if the amount is payable by the purchaser in respect of a business carried on in Canada by the purchaser, the particular taxpayer and the purchaser jointly elect) in prescribed form to apply this paragraph in respect of the amount; or

(c) subject to subsection (10), the amount directly relates to the particular taxpayer's disposition of property that is, at the time of the disposition, an eligible interest in the partnership or corporation that carries on the business to which the restrictive covenant relates, or that is at that time an eligible interest by virtue of paragraph (c) of the definition "eligible interest" where the other corporation referred to in that paragraph carries on the business to which the restrictive covenant relates, and

    (i) the disposition is to the purchaser (or to a person related to the purchaser),

    (ii) the amount is consideration for an undertaking by the particular taxpayer not to provide, directly or indirectly, property or services in competition with the property or services provided or to be provided by the purchaser (or by a person related to the purchaser),

(iii) the restrictive covenant may reasonably be considered to have been granted to maintain or preserve the value of the eligible interest disposed of to the purchaser;

(iv) if the restrictive covenant is granted on or after July 18, 2005, subsection 84(3) does not apply to the disposition,

(v) neither section 85 nor subsection 97(2) applies to the disposition of the eligible interest by the particular taxpayer,

(vi) the amount is added to the particular taxpayer's proceeds of disposition, as defined by section 54, for the purpose of applying this Act to the disposition of the particular taxpayer's eligible interest, and

(vii) the particular taxpayer and the purchaser elect in prescribed form to apply this paragraph in respect of the amount. the payment would be taxable as income from an office or employment under section 5 or 6.

Proposed subsection 56.4(4) defines the tax treatment of non-competition payments for the purchaser, providing that these are to be treated as wages if the payment is included in computing the recipient's income from an office or employment under section 5 or 6, as an outlay incurred by the purchaser on account of capital if the payment is taken into account in computing the recipient's cumulative eligible capital, and as a cost of the share or partnership interest if included in the recipient's proceeds of disposition of either kind of property. Subsections 56.4(5) to (14) provide for a series of detailed rules to provide greater certainty about the application of the forgoing provisions and to introduce two specific anti-avoidance rules. Finally, proposed subsection 56.4(15) stipulates that section 42 does not apply to an amount received or receivable for a restrictive covenant.

III. DEDUCTIONS

Subdivision e of Division B of Part I of the Act permits a variety of deductions that are generally not allowed in computing income or losses from specific sources or capital gains or losses.[12]

Like the inclusions in subdivision d of Division B of Part I of the Act, many of the deductions in subdivision e involve deferred and special income arrangements, permitting deductions for contributions to registered retirement

---

[12] See subs. 4(2) of the Act, which stipulates as a general rule that "no deductions permitted by ss. 60 to 64 apply either wholly or in part to a particular source or to sources in a particular place." Nonetheless, since para. 3(c) stipulates that the amounts specified in subdivision e may be deducted "except to the extent that those deductions, if any, have been taken into account" in computing the taxpayer's income from all sources under para. 3(a), the Act contemplates the possibility that amounts specified in subdivision e may also be deductible in computing income or loss from specific sources.

savings plans (RRSPs), registered retirement income funds (RRIFs), and qualifying pension plans.[13] Several of these provisions are examined in section IV of this chapter, below. Other rules provide allowances for the depletion of natural resources and special deductions for the exploration and development of natural resources.[14] For our purposes, there is no need to examine the rules associated with depletion of natural resources and exploration and development in detail.

In addition to these provisions, however, others permit deductions for specific kinds of payments that are not generally deductible in computing a taxpayer's income. Paragraph 60(b), for example, permits a deduction for certain support payments, which must be included in computing the recipient's income under paragraph 56(1)(b). Paragraphs 60(o) and (o.1) allow taxpayers to deduct qualifying legal expenses, and sections 62 to 64 permit deductions for qualifying moving expenses, child-care expenses, and attendant-care expenses. The following sections examine each of these deductions.

A. Support Payments

Until 1997, spousal and child support payments were generally deductible in computing the payer's income for the year and included in computing the income of the recipient spouse and custodial parent. Introduced in 1944, this "deduction-inclusion" system provided a form of statutory income splitting that, in theory, encouraged those with support obligations to make support payments and increased the after-tax resources available to separated families. More generally, a deduction-inclusion system reflects the logic of an individual income tax in which tax liabilities depend on the income to which each individual is legally entitled. To the extent that both parents are legally obliged to support a dependent child, however, a deduction-inclusion system arguably makes less sense than a basic exemption shared by the child's parents.

In 1995, the Supreme Court of Canada released its decision in *Thibaudeau v. Canada*, [1995] S.C.J. No. 42, [1995] 1 C.T.C. 382, 95 D.T.C. 5273 (S.C.C.), in which the taxpayer, a divorced mother of two children who was awarded custody of the children and $1,150 per month for their maintenance, challenged the inclusion of child support on the basis that it infringed her equality rights under section 15(1) of the *Canadian Charter of Rights and Freedoms*. Noting that the deduction-inclusion system produced aggregate tax savings to separated families of $240 million in 1988, a majority of the court dismissed the taxpayer's arguments on the basis that the tax system imposed no burden on

---

[13] See, for example, para. 60(i) (contribution to RRSP or RRIF), para. 60(j) (transfer of superannuation benefits to RRSP), para. 60(j.01) (transfer of registered pension plan surplus to RRSP), para. 60(j.02) (contributions to registered pension plans), para. 60(j.1) (transfer of retiring allowance to RRSP), para. 60(1) (RRSP rollover at death), and para. 60(v) (contribution to provincial pension plan).

[14] See ss. 65 to 66.8 of the Act.

single custodial parents. Dissenting, McLachlin J (as she then was) and L'Heureux-Dubé J noted that the deduction-inclusion system adversely affected almost 30 per cent of couples, and did not guarantee that tax savings would accrue to custodial parents, and concluded that the inclusion of child support payments in computing the custodial parent's income discriminated against custodial parents in a manner that could not be justified under section 1 of the Charter.

Notwithstanding this decision, or more likely because of the public attention that accompanied it, the federal government decided to eliminate the deduction-inclusion system for child support arrangements entered into after April 30, 1997, at which time the federal and provincial governments introduced a set of detailed guidelines for the calculation of child support.[15] As a result, while spousal support continues to be deductible to the payer and included in computing the recipient's income, child support is subject to this deduction-inclusion system only where the agreement or court order under which it is payable was entered into before May 1997.

The rules governing the deduction of support payments are found in paragraph 60(b) and section 60.1 of the Act. Corresponding rules for the inclusion of these payments by recipients appear in paragraphs 56(1)(b) and 56.1. According to paragraph 60(b), taxpayers may deduct:

the total of all amounts each of which is an amount determined by the formula

$$A - (B + C)$$

where

> A   is the total of all amounts each of which is a support amount paid after 1996 and before the end of the year by the taxpayer to a particular person, where the taxpayer and the particular person were living separate and apart at the time the amount was paid.

> B   is the total of all amounts each of which is a child support amount that became payable by the taxpayer to the particular person under an agreement or order on or after its commencement day and before the end of the year in respect of a period that began on or after its commencement day, and

> C   is the total of all amounts each of which is a support amount paid by the taxpayer to the particular person after 1996 and deductible in computing the taxpayer's income for a preceding taxation year.

The effect of this rule is to permit a deduction for "support amounts" paid in the year except to the extent that they represent "child support amounts" payable after the "commencement day" of the agreement or court order pursuant to which the support payments are made.

---

[15] For a useful discussion of the new rules and guidelines, see Glenn Feltham and Alan Macnaughton, "The New Child Support Rules and Existing Awards: Choosing the Best Tax and Family Law Regime" (1996) Vol. 44 No. 5 Can. Tax J. 1265.

For the purpose of this provision, subsection 60.1(4) incorporates the definitions in subsection 56.1(4), which defines a "support amount" as:

an amount payable or receivable as an allowance on a periodic basis for the maintenance of the recipient, children of the recipient or both the recipient and children of the recipient, if the recipient has discretion as to the use of the amount, and

(a) the recipient is the spouse or common-law partner or former spouse or common-law partner of the payer, the recipient and payer are living separate and apart because of the breakdown of their marriage or common-law partnership and the amount is receivable under an order of a competent tribunal or under a written agreement; or

(b) the payer is a natural parent of a child of the recipient and the amount is receivable under an order made by a competent tribunal in accordance with the laws of a province;

a "child support amount" as:

any support amount that is not identified in the agreement or order under which it is receivable as being solely for the support of a recipient who is a spouse or common-law partner or former spouse or common-law partner of the payer or who is a parent of a child of whom the payer is a natural parent;

and the "commencement day" of an agreement or court order as:

(a) where the agreement or order is made after April 1997, the day it is made; and

(b) where the agreement or order is made before May 1997, the day, if any, that is after April 1997 and is the earliest of

(i) the day specified as the commencement day of the agreement or order by the payer and recipient under the agreement or order in a joint election filed with the Minister in prescribed form and manner,

(ii) where the agreement or order is varied after April 1997 to change the child support amounts payable to the recipient, the day on which the first payment of the varied amount is required to be made,

(iii) where a subsequent agreement or order is made after April 1997, the effect of which is to change the total child support amounts payable to the recipient by the payer, the commencement day of the first such subsequent agreement or order, and

(iv) the day specified in the agreement or order, or any variation thereof, as the commencement day of the agreement or order for the purposes of this Act.

As a result of these definitions, support payments that are not specifically identified in the agreement or court order pursuant to which they are payable as being "solely for the support" of a spouse, common law partner, former spouse, former common law partner, or parent are characterized as child support amounts that are not subject to the deduction-inclusion system where they are payable pursuant to an agreement or court order that is made or varied after

April 1997 or where the payer and recipient jointly so elect.[16] In contrast, support payments that are not characterized as child support amounts may be deducted by the payer and must be included by the recipient where they are payable and receivable as "an allowance on a periodic basis for the maintenance of the recipient, children of the recipient or both the recipient and children of the recipient," provided that "the recipient has discretion as to the use of the amount" that was "receivable under an order of a competent tribunal or under a written agreement" (in the case of payments to a spouse or common law partner or former spouse or common law partner living separate and apart because of the breakdown of their marriage or common law partnership) or under an order made by a competent tribunal (in the case of a payment by a natural parent of the child).

In applying these provisions, it is necessary to determine whether the amount was payable as an "allowance"; whether amount was "payable ... on a periodic basis for the maintenance of the recipient, children of the recipient or both the recipient and children of the recipient"; whether the recipient has "discretion as to the use of the amount"; whether the payer and the recipient were living separate and apart because of the breakdown of their marriage or common law partnership; whether the amount was paid pursuant to a written agreement or court order;[17] when the agreement or order was made; and, for payments made after the "commencement day" of an agreement or order, whether the agreement or order specifies that amounts are payable solely for the support of the spouse, common law partner, former spouse, former common law partner, or parent. For our purposes, it will suffice to examine the two most litigated aspects of the rules: (1) the concept of an "allowance" and the condition of discretionary use; and (2) the stipulation that amounts must be payable on a periodic basis for the maintenance of the recipient and/or the recipient's children.

1. Allowance and Discretionary Use

The leading case on the concept of an "allowance" in the context of support payments context is *Gagnon v. Canada*, [1986] S.C.J. No. 17, [1986] 1 C.T.C. 410, 86 D.T.C. 6179 (S.C.C.), in which the taxpayer sought to deduct payments

---

[16] In recent years, several cases have considered whether child support payments have been made under an original agreement or court order made prior to May 1997, or pursuant to an agreement or court order made or varied after April 1997. See, *e.g.*, *Rosenberg v. Canada*, [2003] F.C.J. No. 1427, [2004] 1 C.T.C. 79, 2003 D.T.C. 5634 (F.C.A.); *Milliron v. Canada*, [2003] F.C.J. No. 1004, [2003] 4 C.T.C. 197, 2003 D.T.C. 5490 (F.C.A.); *Kennedy v. Canada*, [2004] F.C.J. No. 2122, [2005] 1 C.T.C. 206, 2005 D.T.C. 5039 (F.C.A.); and *Coombes v. Canada*, [2005] F.C.J. No. 874, [2005] 3 C.T.C. 75, 2005 D.T.C. 5263 (F.C.A.).

[17] Where an amount is not at the time paid pursuant to a written agreement or court order, subs. 60.1(3) and 56.1(3) deem the amount to have been paid and received "thereunder" where "a written agreement or order of a competent tribunal made at any time in a taxation year provides that an amount paid before that time and in the year or the preceding taxation year is to be considered to have been paid and received thereunder."

to his former wife to cover property taxes and the repayment of capital and interest on two hypothecs related to an immovable, which the Minister disallowed on the basis of an earlier Federal Court of Appeal decision, which defined an allowance as "a limited predetermined sum of money paid to enable the recipient to provide for certain kinds of expense ... determined in advance and, once paid, ... at the complete disposition of the recipient who is not required to account for it" (*Canada v. Pascoe*, [1975] C.T.C. 656, 75 D.T.C. 5427 (F.C.A.), at para. 7). Rejecting the Minister's argument that the third of these conditions, which derives from earlier jurisprudence on the concept of a "receipt" for tax purposes (*Kenneth B.S. Robertson Ltd. v. M.N.R.*, [1944] C.T.C. 75, 2 D.T.C. 655 (Ex. Ct.)), demands that the recipient be entitled to apply the amount "at her discretion and without being required to account for it," the Supreme Court allowed the deduction (at paras. 27-30) on the grounds that the third condition may be satisfied if "the recipient is able to dispose of the amount completely, and that, provided she benefits from it, it is not relevant that she has to account for it and that she cannot apply it to certain types of expense at her complete discretion."

In response to this decision, the federal government amended the *Income Tax Act* in 1988 by enacting new subsection 56(12), according to which an "allowance" for the purpose of the deduction-inclusion system was defined to exclude any amount with respect to which the recipient does not have "discretion as to the use of the amount." Subsection 56(12) was repealed in 1997, when the discretionary use requirement was included in the definition of a "support amount" in subsection 56.1(4). In addition, however, subsections 60.1(2) and 56.1(2) deem amounts payable under a court order or written agreement in respect of specific expenses to be payable and receivable as "an allowance on a periodic basis" and subject to discretionary use by the recipient, where "the order or written agreement, as the case may be, provides that [these subsections] shall apply to any amount paid or payable thereunder." In general, the amounts that may be so deemed under subsections 60.1(2) and 56.1(2) are expenditures "on account of a medical or education expense or in respect of the acquisition, improvement or maintenance of a self-contained domestic establishment" in which the recipient resides.[18]

The case cited most often on the requirement of discretionary use is *Armstrong v. Canada*, [1996] F.C.J. No. 599, [1996] 2 C.T.C. 266, 96 D.T.C. 6315 (F.C.A.), which also considered the language of subsections 60.1(1) and 56.1(1), which specify for the purposes of paragraphs 60(b) and 56(1)(b) that:

---

[18] See the description of A in subs. 60.1(2) and 56.1(2) of the Act. For expenditures in respect of "the acquisition or improvement of a self-contained domestic establishment ... , including any payment of principal or interest in respect of a loan made or indebtedness incurred to finance, in any manner whatever, such acquisition or improvement," the description of B in these provisions limits the amount that may be deducted to one-fifth of "the original principal amount of the loan or indebtedness" incurred to finance the acquisition or improvement.

where an order or agreement, or any variation thereof, provides for the payment of an amount by a taxpayer to a person or for the benefit of the person, children in the person's custody or both the person and those children, the amount or any part thereof

(a)   when payable, is deemed to be payable to and receivable by that person; and

(b)   when paid, is deemed to have been paid to and received by that person.

(The language of subsection 56.1(1) differs slightly from that of subsection 60.1(1), reproduced above, referring to "an amount to a taxpayer" instead of "an amount by a taxpayer to a person" and, more generally, to "the taxpayer" instead of "the/that person.")

Armstrong v. Canada
[1996] F.C.J. No. 599, [1996] 2 C.T.C. 266, 96 D.T.C. 6315 (F.C.A.)

STONE JA (Isaac CJ and Linden JA concurring): ... The issue raised is whether the payments made by the respondent to discharge a monthly mortgage obligation including municipal taxes and arrears with respect to the matrimonial home, may be deducted by the respondent in reporting his income subsequent to November 27, 1991, for the taxation years 1991 and 1992.

Following their marriage in 1981, the appellant and his former wife acquired a residential property in the City of Saskatoon, which became their matrimonial home. At the time of the acquisition, the couple assumed an existing mortgage which was transferred afterward to the Toronto-Dominion Bank. In March 1987, the couple separated and, after a short delay, the respondent moved out of the matrimonial home which remained in the exclusive possession of the spouse and her children. Divorce proceedings then ensued. On August 5, 1987, an order was made by the Court of Queen's Bench of Saskatchewan, which contains the following:

4. The petitioner, MURRAY ROBERT ARMSTRONG, shall pay the monthly mortgage obligation with respect to the matrimonial home and the Royal Bank loan payment as each falls due.

Payments under the Royal Bank loan are not in issue. The order made no provision for the payment of municipal property taxes on the matrimonial home. As these taxes were not paid in a timely fashion, in November 1990, the Toronto-Dominion Bank paid the arrears and added the additional debt to the balance owing under the mortgage with the result that each monthly mortgage payment was increased by $400.

On November 27, 1991, the Court of Queen's Bench made a further order upon the application of the respondent's former spouse, for the maintenance of the children. This order contains the following:

2. The Respondent [Murray Robert Armstrong] shall continue to pay the monthly mortgage obligation with respect to the matrimonial home. Such payment to include all municipal taxes and tax arrears.

When the respondent failed to meet the monthly mortgage obligation and taxes as required by this order, the spouse obtained garnishee orders under which the respondent was required to pay amounts equal to the obligation and taxes to the spouse's solicitor. The solicitors in turn remitted these funds to the spouse who applied them against the mortgage obligation and taxes.

When the Minister's assessments denied the deduction of the mortgage payments and taxes, the respondent appealed to the Tax Court of Canada. In its judgment of February 16, 1995, the Tax Court allowed the appeals with costs and referred the assessments back to the Minister for reconsideration and reassessment in accordance with his reasons for judgment in the matter.

It was the view of the learned Tax Court Judge that the case was governed by subsections 60.1(1) and (2) of the *Income Tax Act*. The word "allowance" as defined in subsection 56(12) of the Act, in his view, had no application. His reasons were twofold. First, to read that definition into subsection 60.1(1) would render that subsection "non-existent" because it could never be said that a payment made to a third party "for the benefit" of a former spouse could ever leave the former spouse with "a discretion as to the use" of the amounts paid to a third party on his or her behalf within the meaning of subsection 56(12). ... The Tax Court Judge was also of the view, in any event, that the payments in question were deductible from income under subsection 60.1(2) of the Act.

...

I shall deal with the Tax Court Judge's reasons for allowing the payments to be deducted in reverse order to that set forth above.

The view that subsection 60.1(2) applies can be dealt with shortly. In my view, the deeming provision employed by Parliament at the end of this subsection applies only "where the decree, order, judgment or written agreement ... provides that this subsection and subsection 56.1(2) shall apply to any payment made pursuant thereto." No such statutory language appears in either of the court orders. It follows, therefore, that subsection 60.1(2) can have no application in allowing the amounts to be deducted from the respondent's income.

...

I turn next to the remaining issue, which concerns the construction of subsection 60.1(1). After reviewing the cases of *R v. Pascoe*, [1976] 1 FC 372 (CA), [and] *Gagnon v. R*, [[1986] S.C.J. No. 17] [1986] 1 SCR 264, ... the Tax Court Judge stated, at page 8:

> ... The separated spouses have presumably agreed or in any event are bound by an Order directing that mortgage payments be made to the creditor. In such a case how can the supported spouse ever be said to have discretion? She may have had it prior to the Order and even may be considered to have exercised by it by agreement before the Order. After the Order however it is impossible for her to have a discretion. To insist that [the] third *Pascoe* condition must be met, even for third party payments, is to render section 60.1 non-existent in many cases such as the present.

...

Subsection 60.1(1) does not itself provide for the deduction of an amount paid and received. Instead, it enlarges the right of deduction made available under paragraph ... 60(b), ... by deeming "for the purposes of paragraph ... 60(b)," ... an amount "to have been paid and received by that person." In my view, the subsection 56(12) definition of "allowance" is to be read together with subsection 60.1(1) of the Act and the latter subsection construed accordingly. Accordingly, as the former spouse had no discretion as to the use of the moneys they cannot be deducted by the respondent from his income for the taxation years in question.

...

Tax relief is not altogether unavailable under the Act for a taxpayer in the position of the respondent who makes a payment to a third party on behalf of a former spouse or children or both. Provided its requirements are satisfied, subsection 60.1(2) deems "for the purposes of [section 60]" that an amount so paid is an amount paid by that taxpayer and received by a person on whose behalf it is paid to be "an allowance payable on a periodic basis" [and that the recipient "is deemed to have discretion as to the use of that amount"]. It was apparently the existence of this newly adopted subsection which [led] the Supreme Court of Canada to state in *Gagnon, supra*, at page 276:

> Before concluding, it should be noted that after this appeal was heard by this Court the *Income Tax Act* was amended by 1984 (Can.), c. 45, s. 20. As a result of these amendments, amounts like the ones at issue in the case at bar are, on certain conditions and up to certain maximum figures, deemed to be paid and received as allowances payable on a periodic basis. ...

Application allowed.

NOTES AND QUESTIONS

1. Why did the Tax Court in *Armstrong* allow the taxpayer to deduct amounts paid in 1991 and 1992 to discharge mortgage obligations and municipal taxes with respect to the matrimonial home? Why did the Federal Court of Appeal reverse the decision?

2. Do you agree with the court's conclusion in *Armstrong* that a court order or written agreement must specifically mention subsections 60.1(2) and 56.1(2) for these provisions to apply? Consider the following statement in *Mambo v. Canada*, [1995] T.C.J. No. 931, [1996] 1 C.T.C. 2388 (T.C.C.), at para. 12:

> The requirement that there be specific reference to these subsections in writing has two valid purposes. The first is to confirm that both parties know that there are tax consequences to such an order or agreement. The second is to comply with what provincial statutes across Canada now enact: that the parties participating in such a Court Order or signing such agreements each have independent legal advice due to their serious and permanent consequences.

In many other cases amounts that might otherwise have been deductible to the payer and included in computing the income of the recipient have been determined to be non-deductible to the payer or not included in computing the recipient's income on the basis that the court order or written agreement did not specifically mention subsections 60.1(2) and 56.1(2).

3.   In *Veilleux v. Canada*, [2002] F.C.J. No. 737, [2003] 1 C.T.C. 138 (F.C.A.), the taxpayer drafted a written agreement stipulating that support payments would be "net of tax." On the basis of this written agreement he deducted and his former spouse included these amounts in computing their incomes from 1990 to 1997. Allowing the taxpayer's appeal from an assessment which disallowed the deduction of these payments by the taxpayer on the basis that the written agreement had not specifically mentioned subsections 60.1(2) and 56.1(2), the court rejected a strict interpretation of the statutory provisions governing the deduction and inclusion of support payments. According to Létourneau JA (Desjardins and Pelletier JJA, concurring) (at paras. 23-24):

> Sections 56 and 60 allow a taxpayer to split his or her income for tax purposes. In this case, their purpose is to minimize the negative and in some cases devastating financial effects of a divorce for spouses and their children. They are intended to provide some assistance when the family unit breaks up. As a result of an unduly strict interpretation of subsection 56.1(2) and 60.1(2), a legislative measure enacted for the benefit of the family after the breakdown is becoming a measure enacted for the benefit of the government, one that is adverse to the interests of the distraught family that Parliament wanted to assist financially.
>
> I prefer the approach taken by Judge Archambault of the Tax Court of Canada in *Pelchat* ... and *Ferron* ..., which is more representative of Parliament's intention, consistent with the wording itself of the statutory provisions, and humane: an express reference to the numbers of subsections 56.1(2) and 60.1(2) is not required in the written agreement; it need only be apparent from the written agreement that the parties have understood the tax consequences of that agreement. A mere reference to the numbers of the subsections in the agreement is no better guarantee that the parties to the agreement understood their duties and their rights. On that point, stating and describing those duties and rights in the written agreement seems, in my view, to achieve Parliament's objective just as well as, if not better than, a mere magical reference to numbers of sections the substance of which is not stated in the agreement.

4.   In *Larsson v. Canada*, [1997] F.C.J. No. 1044, 97 D.T.C. 5425 (F.C.A.), the taxpayer made third-party mortgage payments during the years 1990 to 1992 pursuant to a series of court orders, which were followed by another court order in 1994 stipulating that the payments were payable under subsections 60.1(2) and 56.1(2). Concluding that the final order applied retroactively to the payments made from 1990 to 1992, the court held that the payments were deductible to the payer and included in computing the income of his former spouse.

5.   In *Arsenault v. Canada*, [1995] T.C.J. No. 241, [1995] 2 C.T.C. 2168, 96 D.T.C. 6131 (T.C.C.), the taxpayer entered into a separation agreement pursuant to which he was required to pay child and spousal support of $700 per month, which he discharged by providing his former spouse with rental cheques payable to her landlord. Allowing the taxpayer's appeal from an assessment that disallowed the deduction of these payments under paragraph 60(b) on the basis that the taxpayer's former spouse had no discretion as to the use of the funds, the court held that her consent to the arrangement, which was not legally binding,

constituted an exercise of discretion within the meaning of the Act. According to Brulé JTCC (at paras. 20-22):

> Here the Court is of the opinion that there was complete agreement between the appellant and the spouse. She received the cheques directed to the landlord ... and then paid them over. She could have insisted on payment to her but it was more convenient and beneficial to carry out the procedure adopted.
>
> The appellant's former spouse had constructive receipt of the amounts involved. She has acquiesced in the appellant's payment thereof to the landlord, thereby effectively constituting the landlord as her agent for the receipt and appropriate expenditure of the amounts involved. ...
>
> In this case the spouse had a legally enforceable right to demand payment to her, not to the landlord. This is where the discretion lies.

On appeal, [1996] F.C.J. No. 202, [1999] 4 C.T.C. 174, (1996) 96 D.T.C. 6131 (F.C.A.), Strayer JA (MacGuigan JA, concurring) affirmed the decision at trial, concluding in a two-paragraph decision (at para. 1) that "on the facts of this case the respondent's former spouse retained a discretion as to how the money was paid pursuant to the separation agreement and judgment and thus as to the use of that amount." Dissenting, Stone JA reasoned (at para. 3) that the taxpayer could not have had "discretion as to the use" of the payments "when it is clear that each of the cheques she received was payable to a third party and could be applied for no other purpose, even though it could be said that she had discretion to use each amount in that manner or return it to the appellant and demand of him that the cheques be made payable to her in accordance with the court order and separation agreement."

6.   In *Hak v. Canada*, [1998] T.C.J. No. 921, [1999] 1 C.T.C. 2633, (1998) 99 D.T.C. 36 (T.C.C.), the taxpayer and his wife entered into a separation agreement pursuant to which he was to pay $1,000 per month in the form of rent, utilities, and health-care premiums, the deduction of which the Minister disallowed on the grounds that the former spouse lacked discretionary use of the payments and that the agreement did not specifically refer to subsections 60.1(2) and 56.1(2) of the Act. Concluding (at para. 17) that the former spouse "had a discretion with respect to the entire $1,000, and she exercised that discretion by constituting her husband her agent to pay on her behalf certain expenses," the court allowed the taxpayer's appeal. According to Bowman TCJ (at para. 31):

> The payment of rent and utility expenses was simply an alternative means, agreed to by the spouses, of satisfying a portion of the appellant's obligation to pay his spouse the periodic allowance of $1,000 per month. The failure to mention [subsections 60.1(2) and 56.1(2)] in the agreement ... cannot be fatal to deductibility under paragraph 60(b).

7.   In *Serbey v. Canada*, [2001] T.C.J. No. 131, [2001] 2 C.T.C. 2420 (T.C.C.), the taxpayer's ex-husband was ordered to pay monthly maintenance, a portion of which was to be remitted directly to third parties on the taxpayer's behalf. Concluding that the taxpayer did not have discretion as to the use of the amounts remitted to third parties, the court allowed the taxpayer's appeal from an assessment that included this portion of the monthly maintenance payments

in computing her income under paragraph 56(1)(b) of the Act. According to Archambault TCJ (at paras. 12-13):

> In his argument, counsel for Ms. Serbey suggested that the *Hak* decision should be distinguished because there was in that case a written agreement between the parties and not a court order as is the case here. I do not believe that this is a valid distinction. I fail to see what difference it makes whether the loss of control of an ex-spouse over certain maintenance payments is agreed to by that ex-spouse or is ordered by a court. A distinction must be made between the time at which a maintenance agreement is concluded and the time at which the maintenance payments are made pursuant to such an agreement. For the purposes of the relevant time of subsection 56(12) of the Act, for determining whether a taxpayer has discretion as to the use of maintenance payments is the time these payments are made. Once an ex-spouse has agreed — whether voluntarily or not — to a loss of control over maintenance payments, that ex-spouse cannot thereafter exercise any discretion as to the use of such payments, unless both parties to the agreement consent to give the ex-spouse discretion or a court order is issued giving such discretion.
>
> With respect, I do not believe that Mrs. Hak had any more discretion than Ms. Serbey in this case. Once Mrs. Hak had agreed that her husband was to pay on her behalf certain expenses such as utility bills and rent, she could not have unilaterally given instructions to Mr. Hak to stop making these payments to third parties. This appears to me to be consistent with the intention of the parties. In paragraph 8 of the *Hak* decision, we find the following explanation for the agreement. Mr. Hak had testified that the payments to third parties had been agreed upon "because his wife was totally irresponsible about money and would simply take the cash and spend it on something else and not pay the rent or utility bills and would probably be evicted or have her utilities cut off." The very purpose of the agreement was apparently to remove any discretion in Mrs. Hak as to the use of the money. In short, she had discretion to agree or not to agree to this arrangement. However, once she had agreed to it, she could not thereafter unilaterally instruct her ex-husband to stop making the payments and, in my view, it cannot be said that she had retained any discretion as to the use of the funds.

8.   In *Hamer v. Canada*, [1997] T.C.J. No. 791, [1998] 3 C.T.C. 2030, (1997) 97 D.T.C. 1273 (T.C.C.), aff'd [1998] F.C.J. No. 829, [1999] 1 C.T.C. 45, (1998) 98 D.T.C. 6602 (F.C.A.), the taxpayer received child support payments that she sought to exclude in computing her income on the basis that she did not have discretion as to the use of these payments as required by then subsection 56(12) of the Act. Concluding that the taxpayer's interpretation would contradict the scheme of the Act by precluding any deduction for child support payments and excluding them from the custodial parent's income, the court rejected the taxpayer's argument.

9.   For the CRA's views on the deduction in paragraph 60(b) and the inclusion in paragraph 56(1)(b), see Interpretation Bulletin IT-530R, "Support Payments," July 17, 2003.

2. Periodic Maintenance Payments

In addition to the requirements that an amount be payable or receivable as an "allowance" with respect to which "the recipient has discretion as to the use of the amount," the definition of a "support amount" in subsection 56.1(4) of the Act also requires that the amount be payable or receivable "on a periodic basis for the maintenance of the recipient, children of the recipient or both the recipient and children of the recipient." The leading case on this further requirement is *McKimmon v. M.N.R.*, [1989] F.C.J. No. 1137, [1989] 1 C.T.C. 109, 90 D.T.C. 6088 (F.C.A.).

McKimmon v. M.N.R.
[1989] F.C.J. No. 1137, [1989] 1 C.T.C. 109, 90 D.T.C. 6088 (F.C.A.)

HUGESSEN JA (Pratt and Urie JJA concurring): ... The sole issue for determination is the deductibility, for tax purposes, of certain payments made by the taxpayer to his former wife in the years 1982 and 1983. Those payments were made pursuant to the provisions of a decree nisi of divorce pronounced by a local judge of the Supreme Court of British Columbia February 5, 1982. The relevant passages of the decree, given on consent, read as follows:

> AND THIS COURT FURTHER ORDERS, by consent, that the Respondent pay to the Petitioner the lump sum maintenance of ONE HUNDRED THIRTY THOUSAND ($130,000.00) DOLLARS and periodic maintenance in the sum of ONE HUNDRED FIFTEEN THOUSAND ($115,000.00) DOLLARS in satisfaction of all financial relief under the *Divorce Act* and *Family Relations Act*, payable in the manner following, that is to say:
>
> (a) Transfer to her of all that certain parcel or tract of land and premises situate at 33118 Whidden Avenue, Mission, British Columbia, more particularly known and described as:
>
> Lot 53, SW ¼, Section 28,
>
> Township 17, Plan 28357,
>
> New Westminster District
>
> free and clear of all encumbrances, subject to existing tenancies, at a deemed value for the purposes of this Action of ONE HUNDRED THIRTY THOUSAND ($130,000.00) DOLLARS; such transfer to be completed by the 1st day of April, 1982 with an adjustment date being the date of transfer;
>
> (b) Payment of the sum of ONE HUNDRED FIFTEEN THOUSAND ($115,000.00) DOLLARS in consecutive annual installments as follows:
>
> $25,000,00 on the first day of April, 1982
>
> $25,000.00 on the first day of January, 1983
>
> $25,000.00 on the first day of January, 1984
>
> $25,000.00 on the first day of January, 1985
>
> $15,000.00 on the first day of January, 1986
>
> together with and in addition to interest at the rate of TEN (10%) PERCENTUM per annum, on the balance of the said ONE HUNDRED FIFTEEN THOUSAND ($115,000.00) DOLLARS from time to time owing, such interest to commence accruing from and inclusive of the 1st day of April, 1982, and be computed half-yearly, not in advance, and become due and payable annually with the annual installments of principal as they become due and payable.

1197

AND THIS COURT FURTHER ORDERS, by consent, that the respondent cause Kapps Enterprises Ltd. to execute and deliver to the Petitioner a collateral mortgage of all its equity as Purchaser in and to all that certain parcel or tract of land and premises situate at 34054 Parr Avenue, Mission, British Columbia, more particularly known and described as:

> Lot 1, SE ¼, Section 27,
>
> Township 17, Plan 34254,
>
> New Westminster District

free and clear of all financial encumbrances (save and except the title interest of the unpaid Vendor) by the 1st day of April, 1982, such mortgage to be deemed collateral security for the payment of the said sum of ONE HUNDRED FIFTEEN THOUSAND ($115,000.00) DOLLARS and interest to the Petitioner as hereinbefore provided.

AND THIS COURT FURTHER ORDERS, by consent, that the Respondent shall have the privilege of prepaying the balance or any portion thereof owing under the aforesaid terms of payment, and collateral mortgage, without notice or bonus, subject nevertheless to the proviso that in the event of default of payment by the respondent of the principal or interest herein or any portion thereof, at the times and in the amounts provided, then and in every such case the principal sum and every portion thereof at the option of the Mortgagee shall forthwith become due and payable without notice; and further subject to the proviso that there shall be no acceleration of payment in the event of sale.

...

Prior to the pronouncement of the decree of divorce, the parties had lived separate and apart for approximately four years, during which time the taxpayer had paid to his wife the sum of $600 per month as interim alimony.

...

The problem of distinguishing between periodic payments made as an allowance for maintenance, which are deductible for income tax purposes, and periodic payments made as instalments of a lump or capital sum, which are not so deductible, is one which has given rise to considerable discussion and jurisprudence. It is not dissimilar, and is indeed related to the problem, common in income tax law, of determining if sums of money expended or received are of an income or of a capital nature. As with that problem there can be very few hard and fast rules. On the contrary, the Court is required to look at all the circumstances surrounding the payment and to determine what, in the light of those circumstances, is its proper characterisation. Because of the correlation between paragraphs 60(b) and 56(1)(b), a finding that a payment is deductible by the payer will normally result in its being taxable in the hands of the recipient. Conversely, a determination that a payment is not so deductible will result in the recipient having it free of tax.

The following are, as it seems to me, some of the considerations which may properly be taken, into account in making such a determination. The list is not, of course, intended to be exhaustive.

1. The length of the periods at which the payments are made. Amounts which are paid weekly or monthly are fairly easily characterised as allowances for maintenance. Where the payments are at longer intervals,

the matter becomes less clear. While it is not impossible, it would appear to me to be difficult to envisage payments made at intervals of greater than one year as being allowances for maintenance.

2. The amount of the payments in relation to the income and living standards of both payer and recipient. Where a payment represents a very substantial portion of a taxpayer's income or even exceeds it, it is difficult to view it as being an allowance for maintenance. On the other hand, where the payment is no greater than might be expected to be required to maintain the recipient's standard of living, it is more likely to qualify as such an allowance.

3. Whether the payments are to bear interest prior to their due date. It is more common to associate an obligation to pay interest with a lump sum payable by instalments than it is with a true allowance for maintenance.

4. Whether the amounts envisaged can be paid by anticipation at the option of the payer or can be accelerated as a penalty at the option of the recipient in the event of default. Prepayment and acceleration provisions are commonly associated with obligations to pay capital sums and would not normally be associated with an allowance for maintenance.

5. Whether the payments allow a significant degree of capital accumulation by the recipient. Clearly not every capital payment is excluded from an allowance for maintenance: common experience indicates that such things as life insurance premiums and blended monthly mortgage payments, while they allow an accumulation of capital over time, are a normal expense of living which are paid from income and can properly form part of an allowance for maintenance. On the other hand, an allowance for maintenance should not allow the accumulation, over a short period, of a significant pool of capital.

6. Whether the payments are stipulated to continue for an indefinite period or whether they are for a fixed term. An allowance for maintenance will more commonly provide for its continuance either for an indefinite period or to some event (such as the coming of age of a child) which will cause a material change in the needs of the recipient. Sums payable over a fixed term, on the other hand, may be more readily seen as being of a capital nature.

7. Whether the agreed payments can be assigned and whether the obligation to pay survives the lifetime of either the payer or the recipient. An allowance for maintenance is normally personal to the recipient and is therefore unassignable and terminates at death. A lump or capital sum, on the other hand, will normally form part of the estate of the recipient, is assignable and will survive him.

8. Whether the payments purport to release the payer from any future obligations to pay maintenance. Where there is such a release, it is easier to view the payments as being the commutation or purchase of the capital price of an allowance for maintenance.

Viewing the facts of the present case in the light of the foregoing criteria, it becomes quickly apparent that most of the indicators point strongly to the payments in issue being instalments of a lump sum settlement and that virtually none point the other way.

The payments are to be made only once a year. The amounts paid are not only greatly in excess of the prior alimony of $600 per month but also constitute a very large proportion of the taxpayer's declared income in the two years in question. Interest is, by the terms of the decree, payable on the balance of the total sum of $115,000 from time to time remaining due. The taxpayer is given a prepayment privilege at his option while, in the event of default, his former wife may require the accelerated payment of the whole of the balance. The total sum of $115,000 represents a significant capital amount when compared not only with the taxpayer's declared income but also with the deemed value of the real estate which was also transferred as part of the same consent decree. The payments are to be made over a fixed term and are not stated to be dependent upon the survival of either the payer or the recipient. Finally, the payments are stated to be "in satisfaction of all financial relief under the *Divorce Act* and *Family Relations Act*."

I conclude that the sums here in issue were not paid by the taxpayer as an allowance for the maintenance of his former wife. Accordingly they were not deductible from the taxpayer's income under paragraph 60(b) and are taxable in his hands rather than those of the recipient as would be required by paragraph 56(1)(b). ...

Appeal allowed.

NOTES AND QUESTIONS

1.   On what basis did the court in *McKimmon* conclude that the payments made by the taxpayer in 1982 and 1983 were not deductible under paragraph 60(b)? What criteria did the court suggest to determine whether an amount is payable "on a periodic basis for the maintenance of the recipient, children of the recipient or both the recipient and children of the recipient"?

2.   In *Urichuk v. Canada*, [1993] F.C.J. No. 161, [1993] 1 C.T.C. 226, 93 D.T.C. 5120 (F.C.A.), the taxpayer made one payment of $45,000 and three payments of $50,000 each to his former wife over a period of a little more than two years, which the parties characterized as "maintenance" in their separation agreement. Emphasizing (at para. 1) that the Minister "is entitled to rely on any available evidence to support his characterization of the payments in a manner different from that employed by the former spouses in the agreement itself," the

court disallowed the deduction claimed by the taxpayer on the basis that the payment was a capital payment to divide family property.

3.   In *Sills v. M.N.R.*, [1985] 1 C.T.C. 49, (1984) 85 D.T.C. 5096 (F.C.A.), the taxpayer was supposed to have received support payments of $300 per month in 1976 but instead received three payments of $1,000 in February, April, and December. Rejecting the taxpayer's argument that these were on account of arrears owing, not maintenance, and therefore need not be included in computing her income for the year under paragraph 56(1)(b), the court concluded (at para. 9) that because the payments were "payable" on a monthly basis, their late payment did not change their character as amounts payable on a periodic basis for the maintenance of the taxpayer and her children.

4.   In *Peterson v. Canada*, [2005] F.C.J. No. 1062, 2005 F.C.A. 223 (F.C.A.), the taxpayer received $36,000 from her former spouse in settlement of an action in which she sought enforcement of a separation agreement which had provided for increased child support under specific circumstances. Notwithstanding that the Minutes of Settlement characterized the payment as "retroactive additional periodic child support," the court held that the taxpayer was not taxable on the grounds (at para. 37) that the Minutes of Settlement recognized neither "a pre-existing child support obligation," nor "the existence of arrears of child support." According to Sharlow JA (Desjardins and Rothstein JJA, concurring) at para. 36:

> In my view, a written agreement or court order cannot be interpreted as obliging a person to pay arrears of child support unless, at the time the written agreement or court order is made, there is (1) an express or implied recognition of a pre-existing obligation to pay child support for a prior period, (2) an express or implied recognition of a complete or partial breach of that obligation, resulting in arrears of child support, and (3) an obligation set out in the written agreement or court order to pay the arrears in whole or in part.

See also *Kew v. Canada*, [2004] T.C.J. No. 346, [2004] 4 C.T.C. 2461, 2004 D.T.C. 2973 (T.C.C.), aff'd [2005] F.C.J. No. 167, [2005] 1 C.T.C. 371, 2005 D.T.C. 5106 (F.C.A.), in which the taxpayer sought to deduct $31,233 in unpaid child support after entering into an agreement with his former spouse to transfer his interest in the matrimonial home in exchange for $51,000 and a release from all claims. Concluding (at para. 7) that the transfer of the taxpayer's equity in the home was "to satisfy a variety of debts ... only a part of which may have been maintenance arrears," the court held that it could not be deducted as child support.

5.   In *Widmer v. Canada*, [1995] T.C.J. No. 1115, [1996] 1 C.T.C. 2647 (T.C.C.), the taxpayer accepted $15,000 in settlement of $50,590 of child support payments in arrears, at which time the parties also agreed to reduce monthly payments from $796 per month to $600 per month. Commenting (at para. 18) that "[w]hen the amount actually received ... is so different from and so much smaller than the amount owed ... , I cannot regard the amount received as having the same character as the amount owed," Mogan JTCC allowed the

taxpayer's appeal from an assessment that included the $15,000 in computing her income under paragraph 56(1)(b) on the basis that "the $15,000 amount was paid to obtain a release from existing obligations and a reduction in future obligations, and not for the maintenance of the three children."

6.   In *M.N.R. v. Armstrong*, [1956] S.C.J. No. 22, [1956] C.T.C. 93, 56 D.T.C. 1044 (S.C.C.), the taxpayer sought to deduct $4,000 paid "in full settlement" of all payments due or to become due under a court order obligating him to pay his former wife $100 per month as child support. Concurring in the majority decision, which disallowed the deduction on the basis that the payment was not made pursuant to a court order or separation agreement, Kellock J. held (at para. 7) that "an outlay made in commutation of the periodic sums payable under the decree is in the nature of a capital payment to which the statute does not extend."

B. Legal Expenses

In computing a taxpayer's income from an office or employment, paragraph 8(1)(b) permits a deduction for "amounts paid by the taxpayer in the year as or on account of legal expenses incurred by the taxpayer to collect or establish a right to salary or wages owed to the taxpayer by the employer or former employer of the taxpayer."[19] In computing a taxpayer's income from a business or property, legal expenses are similarly deductible to the extent that they are incurred for the purpose of gaining or producing income from the business or property and are reasonable in the circumstances.[20] In addition to these deductions, paragraphs 60(o) and 60(o.1) permit deductions for specific kinds of legal expenses that are not incurred in order to obtain income from these sources.

According to paragraph 60(o) of the Act, taxpayers may deduct "amounts paid by the taxpayer in the year in respect of fees or expenses incurred in preparing, instituting or prosecuting an objection to, or an appeal in relation to":

(i)   an assessment of tax, interest or penalties under this Act or an Act of a province that imposes a tax similar to the tax imposed under this Act,

(ii)   a decision of the Canada Employment and Immigration Commission, the Canada Employment and Insurance Commission, a board of referees or an umpire under the *Unemployment Insurance Act* or the *Employment Insurance Act*,

(iii) an assessment of any income tax deductible by the taxpayer under section 126 [foreign tax credits] or any interest or penalty with respect thereto, or

---

[19] The deduction of legal expenses in computing a taxpayer's income from an office or employment is examined in Chapter 4.

[20] See para. 18(1)(a) and s. 67 of the Act. The deduction of legal expenses in computing a taxpayer's income from a business or property is examined in Chapter 5.

(iv)   an assessment or a decision made under the *Canada Pension Plan* or a provincial pension plan as defined in section 3 of that Act.

Similarly, subject to certain limitations that we need not examine, paragraph 60(o.1) permits a deduction for "legal expenses (other than those relating to a division or settlement of property arising out of, or on a breakdown of, a marriage or common-law partnership) paid by the taxpayer in the year or in any of the 7 preceding taxation years to collect or establish a right to an amount of":

(A)   a benefit under a pension fund or plan (other than a benefit under the *Canada Pension Plan* or a provincial pension plan as defined in section 3 of that Act) in respect of the employment of the taxpayer or a deceased individual of whom the taxpayer was a dependant, relation or legal representative, or

(B)   a retiring allowance of the taxpayer or a deceased individual of whom the taxpayer was a dependant, relation or legal representative.

Although these provisions have been mentioned in a few cases, they have been subject to little in the way of judicial analysis. In *Cormier v. M.N.R.*, [1989] 1 C.T.C. 2092, (1988) 89 D.T.C. 44 (T.C.C.), however, where a taxpayer who was convicted of tax evasion sought to deduct legal expenses incurred in an unsuccessful effort to appeal the conviction, the court concluded that these expenses were not deductible under paragraph 60(o), which applies to objections and appeals to "an assessment of tax, interest and penalties" under Part I of the Act, not Part XV, which imposes criminal sanctions. Other cases have noted the limited scope of these deductions, which apply to legal expenses incurred to obtain employment insurance, pension income, and retiring allowances, but not to legal expenses incurred to obtain workers' compensation or support payments.[21] In more than one case, however, legal expenses incurred in order to collect support payments to which the recipient is legally entitled have been characterized as deductible expenses incurred for the purpose of gaining or producing income from property.[22] Other

---

[21]   See, for example, *Bergeron v. Canada*, [1999] T.C.J. No. 510, [2000] 1 C.T.C. 2001, (1999) 99 D.T.C. 1265 (T.C.C.) and *Bongiovanni v. Canada*, [2000] T.C.J. No. 725, [2001] 1 C.T.C. 2186 (T.C.C.).

[22]   See, for example, *Sembinelli v. M.N.R.*, [1993] 2 C.T.C. 2345 (T.C.C.), aff'd, [1994] F.C.J. No. 1352, [1994] 2 C.T.C. 378, 94 D.T.C. 6636 (F.C.A.), in which the Tax Court concluded (at para. 14) that the expenses were "incurred for the purpose of gaining income from an existing income producing right." See also *Haley v. Canada*, [2000] T.C.J. No. 233, [2000] 3 C.T.C. 2014 (T.C.C.); *St.-Laurent v. Canada*, [1998] T.C.J. No. 501, [1999] 1 C.T.C. 2478 (T.C.C.); *Donald v. Canada*, [1998] T.C.J. No. 866, [1999] 1 C.T.C. 2025 (T.C.C.); *Nissim v. Canada*, [1998] T.C.J. No. 658, [1999] 1 C.T.C. 2119, [1998] 4 C.T.C. 2496 (T.C.C.); *Gallien v. Canada*, [2000] T.C.J. No. 729, [2001] 2 C.T.C. 2676, 2000 D.T.C. 2514 (T.C.C.); *Nadeau v. Canada*, [2003] F.C.J. No. 1611, 2003 F.C.A. 400 (F.C.A.); and *Income Tax Technical News*, No. 24 (October 2002).

cases have questioned this conclusion on the basis that support payments are not income from a business or property.[23]

C. Moving Expenses

As with the costs of commuting to and from work, Canadian courts have traditionally regarded the cost of moving from one residence to another to be closer to a new or already existing place of business as non-deductible personal expenses incurred in order to be available to the taxpayer's employment or business but not "in the course of" carrying on the duties of the taxpayer's employment or the business. In *Stanley Karp v. M.N.R.*, [1968] Tax ABC 1018 (T.A.B.), for example, the Tax Appeal Board disallowed any deduction for expenses incurred to move the taxpayer's furniture from his former residence in Kansas to his new work location in Toronto, on the basis (at para. 3) that:

> [t]he whereabouts of a person's furniture at a given moment can have no bearing on that person's ability to earn income, albeit some inconvenience may be caused by the absence of such furniture.

On general principles, therefore, moving expenses have been held to be non-deductible personal expenses.

Effective January 1, 1972, however, the Act was amended to allow a limited deduction for moving expenses under section 62. According to subsection 62(1), taxpayers may in computing their income for a taxation year deduct "amounts paid by the taxpayer as or on account of moving expenses incurred in respect of an eligible relocation" subject to a number of limitations in paragraphs (a) to (d). The following cases and commentary examine the various elements of this deduction, considering the kinds of expenses that are eligible for the deduction, the concept of an "eligible relocation," and the limitations on deductibility in paragraphs 62(1)(a) to (d).

1. Eligible Expenses

For the purposes of the deduction in subsection 62(1), subsection 62(3) defines "moving expenses" to include "any expense incurred as or on account of":

(a) travel costs (including a reasonable amount expended for meals and lodging), in the course of moving the taxpayer and members of the taxpayer's household from the old residence to the new residence,

(b) the cost to the taxpayer of transporting or storing household effects in the course of moving from the old residence to the new residence,

(c) the cost to the taxpayer of meals and lodging near the old residence or the new residence for the taxpayer and members of the taxpayer's household for a period not exceeding 15 days,

---

[23] See, for example, *Mathieu v. Canada*, [2001] T.C.J. No. 542; [2001] CarswellNat 1813 (T.C.C.), and *Lemieux v. Canada*, [2001] T.C.J. No. 703, [2001] CarswellNat 2302 (T.C.C.).

(d)　the cost to the taxpayer of cancelling the lease by virtue of which the taxpayer was the lessee of the old residence,

(e)　the taxpayer's selling costs in respect of the sale of the old residence,

(f)　where the old residence is sold by the taxpayer or the taxpayer's spouse or common-law partner as a result of the move, the cost to the taxpayer of legal services in respect of the purchase of the new residence and of any tax, fee or duty (other than any goods and services tax or value-added tax) imposed on the transfer or registration of title to the new residence, and

(g)　interest, property taxes, insurance premiums and the cost of heating and utilities in respect of the old residence, to the extent of the lesser of $5,000 and the total of such expenses of the taxpayer for the period

　　(i)　throughout which the old residence is neither ordinarily occupied by the taxpayer or by any other person who ordinarily resided with the taxpayer at the old residence immediately before the move nor rented by the taxpayer to any other person, and

　　(ii)　in which reasonable efforts are made to sell the old residence, and

(h)　the cost of revising legal documents to reflect the address of the taxpayer's new residence, of replacing drivers' licenses and non-commercial vehicle permits (excluding any cost for vehicle insurance) and of connecting or disconnecting utilities.

In addition, "for greater certainty," the postamble to subsection 62(3) stipulates that the term "moving expenses" does not include costs, other than those referred to in paragraph (f), that are "incurred by the taxpayer in respect of the acquisition of the new residence."

The postamble to subsection 62(3) was added effective for costs incurred after May 25, 1976. Paragraph 62(3)(f) and the parenthetical exclusion of costs referred to in this paragraph from the general exclusion of acquisition costs in the postamble were added effective for costs incurred after December 31, 1976. The exclusion of goods and services and value-added taxes from the taxes, fees, and duties the deduction of which is otherwise allowed by paragraph 62(3)(f) was enacted in 1998, retroactive to the introduction of the goods and services tax (GST) in 1990.[24] Paragraphs 62(3)(g) and (h) were enacted effective for 1997

---

[24]　Prior to this amendment, courts has adopted conflicting positions on the deductibility of the GST on newly constructed homes, allowing the deduction in *Lachman v. Canada*, [1995] T.C.J. No. 63, [1995] 2 C.T.C. 2944 (T.C.C.) and *Mann v. Canada*, [1995] T.C.J. No. 64, [1995] 2 C.T.C. 2049 (T.C.C.), but disallowing the deduction in *Johnson v. Canada*, [1993] T.C.J. No. 931, [1995] 2 C.T.C. 2110 (T.C.C.) on the grounds (at para. 7) that the GST applies not, as the statute requires, to "the transfer or registration of title to the new residence" but instead to the transfer of the property itself. According to Department of Finance technical notes accompanying the amendment, the revised text "clarifies that the deduction in respect of taxes on the purchase of a new residence does not include any goods and services tax related to the purchase of that residence."

and subsequent taxation years, and reverse earlier cases in which the deduction of these expenses was disallowed.[25]

Among the first cases to consider the meaning of the term "moving expenses" was *Storrow v. Canada*, [1978] C.T.C. 792, 78 D.T.C. 6551 (F.C.T.D.), in which a tax lawyer sought to deduct various costs associated with moving from Ottawa to Vancouver in July 1975. Although paragraph 62(3)(f) and the postamble to subsection 62(3) had been enacted by the time the case came to trial, these amendments were not applicable in July 1975.

Storrow v. Canada
[1978] C.T.C. 792, 78 D.T.C. 6551 (F.C.T.D.)

[The plaintiff moved from Ottawa to Vancouver and claimed as part of his deductible moving expenses the following amounts, which the Minister disallowed: (1) $22,750, being the amount of the cost of his new residence in excess of the amount that he received on the sale of his former residence; (2) mortgage interest attributable to the amount of $22,750; (3) land registry fees paid on the purchase of the new residence; and (4) installation costs of a dishwasher and new door locks.]

COLLIER, J: ... The main issue, in this appeal, is whether the additional monies laid out by the taxpayer, when he moved, in acquiring a new residence reasonably comparable to his old residence, were:

---

[25] See *Webb v. M.N.R.*, [1983] C.T.C. 2305, 83 D.T.C. 245 (T.R.B.) (disallowing the cost of obtaining a new driving permit); *O'Gorman v. M.N.R.*, [1981] C.T.C. 2400, 81 D.T.C. 281 (T.R.B.) (disallowing the deduction of $832.12 in mortgage interest and property taxes paid on the taxpayer's old residence over a four-month period during which the taxpayer sought to sell the old residence on the grounds [at para. 14] that the costs were attributable to "*keeping*, not *selling* the former residence" and were incurred by the taxpayer "in his attempt to maximize his return from the sale of the old residence"); *Critchley v. M.N.R.*, [1983] C.T.C. 2365, 83 D.T.C. 278 (T.R.B.) (characterizing [at para. 17] interest expenses and property taxes in respect of the old residence as "expenses because the home is *not sold*" as opposed to "selling costs in respect of the sale"); *Stephen v. Canada*, [1995] T.C.J. No. 24, [1995] 2 C.T.C. 2963, 96 D.T.C. 3253 (T.C.C.) (disallowing [at para. 19] the deduction of "duplicate financing costs"); *Browning v. Canada*, [1996] T.C.J. No. 1776, [1997] 2 C.T.C. 3037 (headnote only) (T.C.C.) (disallowing the deduction of mortgage interest on an old residence sold five months after the taxpayer moved on the basis [at para. 25] that "the cost of carrying the older house are directly dependent upon one factor, the amount of money the vendor was willing to accept as the sale price of the older house"): and *Séguin v. Canada*, [1997] F.C.J. No. 1220, [1998] 2 C.T.C. 13, 97 D.T.C. 5457 (F.C.A.) (disallowing the deduction of mortgage interest on the old residence, which the taxpayer continued to pay until he was able to sell it). For contrasting decisions in which interest expenses and property taxes were allowed as deductible moving expenses, see *McLay v. M.N.R.*, [1992] T.C.J. No. 610, [1992] 2 C.T.C. 2649, 92 D.T.C. 2260 (T.C.C.); *Penner v. Canada*, [1996] T.C.J. No. 1387, [1997] 1 C.T.C. 2564 (T.C.C.); and *Graham v. Canada*, [1997] T.C.J. No. 176, 97 D.T.C. 1074 (T.C.C.).

amounts paid by him as or on account of moving expenses incurred in the course of moving from his old residence to his new residence.

I agree with certain initial propositions put forward by counsel for the plaintiff:

(a) Where a definition section uses the words "includes," as it does in ss 62(3), then the expression said to be defined includes not only those things declared to be included, but such other things "... as the word signifies according to its natural import." *The King v. BC Fir and Cedar Lumber Co Ltd.*, [1932] AC 441 at 448 (JCPC).

(b) The words "moving expenses" must be construed in their ordinary and natural sense in their context in the particular statute.

The plaintiff submits that a moving expense is an expense of moving from one dwelling to another; it includes all costs directly and solely related to the move from the time of the decision to leave to the time of resettlement. The additional monies laid out to acquire a comparable residence in Vancouver, the interest on that amount, and the costs of registration, of installing the dishwasher and new locks were all incurred, it is said, because of the move from one residence to another.

For the defendant, it is contended the amounts in issue are not really expenses at all; they are the extra costs incurred, in this case, in replacing an asset, the old residence. ... I agree generally with the defendant's contention. ... The disputed outlays were not, to my mind, moving expenses in the natural and ordinary meaning of that expression. The outlays or costs embraced by those words are, in my view, the ordinary out-of-pocket expenses incurred by a taxpayer in the course of physically changing his residence. The expression does not include (except as may be specifically delineated in subsection 62(3)) such things as the increase in cost of the new accommodation over the old (whether it be by virtue of sale, lcase, or otherwise), the cost of installing household items taken from the old residence to the new, or the cost of replacing or re-fitting household items from the old residence (such as drapes, carpeting, etc). Moving expenses, as permitted by subsection 62(3), do not, as I see it, mean outlays or costs incurred in connection with the acquisition of the new residence. Only outlays incurred to effect the physical transfer of the taxpayer, his household, and their belongings to the new residence are deductible. ...

Appeal dismissed.

NOTES AND QUESTIONS

1. Do you agree with Collier J's interpretation of the term "moving expenses" in *Storrow*? Why or why not? Considering the items specifically included as "moving expenses" in subsection 62(3), is it appropriate to limit the meaning of the words "moving expenses" to "ordinary out-of-pocket expenses incurred by a taxpayer in the course of physically changing his residence"?

2.   Do you agree with the disallowance of the particular expenses incurred by the taxpayer in *Storrow*? Why or why not? Note that the disallowance of land registry fees paid on the purchase of the new residence was legislatively overruled by the enactment of paragraph 62(3)(f), applicable to costs incurred after December 31, 1976. Although this paragraph originally referred only to "taxes imposed on the transfer or registration of title to the new residence," revisions enacted in 1998, applicable to 1990 and subsequent taxation years, confirm that a deduction is allowed for "any tax, fee or duty ... imposed on the transfer or registration of title to the new residence" other than "any goods and services tax or value-added tax."

3.   In *Ball v. Canada*, [1996] T.C.J. No. 542, [1996] 3 C.T.C. 2178 (T.C.C.), the taxpayer, an accountant residing in Newfoundland, spent $1,739 in 1993 to drive to Waterloo, Ontario with his wife to look for other business opportunities, a house, and a special school for their son, which he claimed as a moving expense when he and his family moved to Waterloo later in 1993. The Tax Court disallowed the expense on the basis (at para. 6) that section 62 "does not allow the deduction of expenses for house hunting and job hunting." Do you agree? Why or why not?

4.   In *Critchley v. M.N.R.*, [1983] C.T.C. 2365, 83 D.T.C. 278 (T.R.B.), the taxpayer sought to deduct as moving expenses, among other amounts, $19 veterinarian charges for tranquillizers and rabies shots incurred in moving the family dog. Allowing the deduction on the basis that the costs were "travel costs ... in the course of moving ... members of the taxpayer's household," the board concluded (at paras. 19-20):

> The Board thinks, contrary to the contention of counsel for the respondent, that the family dog is a member of the household. The *Income Tax Act* does not say "member of the family," but of the household. In the French version, it says "maisonnée" and not "famille." ...
>
> This question must be answered affirmatively because of paragraph 62(3)(a). ... [T]he words "... in the course of moving ..." are large enough to include the said expense. In the French version, one can read "frais de déplacement engagés pour le deménagement..."; the meaning of the word "engagés" is also very large.

5.   In *Yaeger v. M.N.R.*, [1986] 1 C.T.C. 2282, 86 D.T.C. 1217 (T.C.C.), the taxpayer sought to deduct as moving expenses $6,923.13 spent to move a horse and horse trailer, along with other related costs such as veterinarian and boarding fees. Rejecting the taxpayer's argument that these expenses were costs of "transporting or storing household effects," within the meaning of paragraph 62(3)(b), the court disallowed the deduction.

6.   In *Hasan v. Canada*, [2004] T.C.J. No. 377, [2004] 4 C.T.C. 2420, 2004 C.T.C. 3001 (T.C.C.), aff'd [2005] F.C.J. No. 556, [2005] 2 C.T.C. 181, 2005 D.T.C. 5220 (F.C.A.), the taxpayer was an architecture student at McGill University in Montreal who worked in Toronto during the summer of 2001, during which time she continued to pay rent on an apartment in Montreal where she stored some furniture, computer equipment and personal effects. Rejecting

the taxpayer's argument that the rental payments were deductible costs of storing household effects under paragraph 62(3)(b) of the Act, the court concluded (at para. 19) that "in order to qualify as a moving expense under paragraph 62(3)(b) of the Act, the amount paid must have been paid *when a taxpayer physically moves or changes her residence*" (emphasis in original).

7. In *Pollard v. M.N.R.*, [1988] 1 C.T.C. 2138, (1987) 88 D.T.C. 1110 (T.C.C.), the taxpayer, facing an interest penalty of $6,115 to discharge a five-year mortgage on his old residence, entered into an agreement with the mortgagee whereby he agreed to pay a higher rate of interest on a new mortgage on his new residence, resulting in an additional interest of $6,115 over the term of the new mortgage. Allowing the taxpayer's appeal, the Tax Court held (at para. 14) that the amount was a cost incurred in order to complete the sale, and "properly deductible" under section 62 as a "selling cost" within the meaning of paragraph 62(3)(e).

8. A few cases have considered whether a taxpayer has made "reasonable efforts" to sell an old residence within the meaning of subparagraph 62(3)(g)(ii) of the ITA. In *Lowe v. Canada*, [2007] T.C.J. No. 221, [2007] 5 C.T.C. 2406, 2007 D.T.C. 941 (T.C.C.), the taxpayer moved from Madoc, Ontario to Toronto in 2002 after he accepted a full time probationary position as a professor in the faculty of technology at George Brown College of Applied Arts and Technology, and moved back to Madoc in 2003 when he was offered a job at General Mills at a higher rate of pay. Concluding that the taxpayer had not made reasonable efforts to sell his residence in Madoc after moving to Toronto, the court disallowed the deduction of expenses that he incurred to maintain this residence. According to the court (at para. 8):

> Since the only effort that the [taxpayer] made in relation to selling the Madoc residence was to tell family and friends that the property would be for sale and, since the [taxpayer] indicated that he did not want to sell his property until the probationary period for his new job had expired (which would have been two years), the [taxpayer] was not making reasonable efforts to sell the Madoc residence during the period from January to June of 2003 (which is the period to which the expenses relate).

See also *Rosa v. Canada*, [2005] T.C.J. No. 206, [2005] 3 C.T.C. 2278, 2005 D.T.C. 805 (T.C.C.), in which the court disallowed the deduction of mortgage interest, utility payments and insurance in respect of the old residence on the grounds that because the taxpayer's son continued to reside in the old residence after he moved, reasonable efforts had not been made to sell the residence.

For a contrasting conclusion, see *Cusson c. Canada*, [2006] A.C.I. no 84, [2007] 2 C.T.C. 2331, 2006 D.T.C. 2472 (T.C.C.), where the taxpayer moved in April 2002, had two friends advertise that his old residence was for sale from April to October 2002, hired a real estate agent in October 2002, and sold the old residence in December 2002 with a closing date in January 2003. Rejecting the Minister's argument that the advertisements did not constitute "reasonable efforts" to sell the old residence, the court allowed the deduction of carrying costs in respect of the old residence from April 2002 to January 2003.

9.   In *Johnston v. Canada*, [2003] F.C.J. No. 589, [2003] 3 C.T.C. 298, 2003 D.T.C. 5295 (F.C.A.), the taxpayer borrowed funds to purchase a home at his new work location in Winnipeg, using his old residence in Toronto as security for the loans, and repaying the loans once he sold the Toronto home. Rejecting the taxpayer's argument that the interest expenses were "in respect of" his old residence, the court disallowed the deduction of these expenses under paragraph 62(3)(g). According to the court (at para. 6):

> The definition of "moving expenses", read in its entirety, indicates that interest on money borrowed to purchase a home in the new work location is not within the definition, even if the loan is secured by a mortgage on a home in the former work location.

10.   In *Cusson c. Canada*, [2006] A.C.I. no 84, [2007] 2 C.T.C. 2331, 2006 D.T.C. 2472 (T.C.C.), the taxpayer sought to deduct the cost of purchasing a Bell Express Vu antenna under paragraph 62(3)(h) as a cost of "connecting or disconnecting utilities" on the grounds that he had cable television at his old residence which was not available at the new residence. Apparently accepting that the cable television is a "utility" within the meaning of paragraph 62(3)(h), the court nonetheless disallowed the deduction (at para. 23) on the basis that the amount included "equipment and installation charges ... are not provided for in the paragraph since it refers to connection and disconnection costs."

2. Eligible Relocation

For the purpose of the moving expense deduction and other provisions of the Act, subsection 248(1) defines an "eligible relocation" as "a relocation of a taxpayer where":

(a)   the relocation occurs to enable the taxpayer

    (i)   to carry on a business or to be employed at a location in Canada (... referred to as "the new work location"), or

    (ii)   to be a student in full-time attendance enrolled in a program at a post-secondary level at a location of a university, college or other educational institution (... referred to as "the new work location"),

(b)   both the residence at which the taxpayer ordinarily resided before the relocation (... referred to as "the old residence") and the residence at which the taxpayer ordinarily resided after the relocation (... referred to as "the new residence") are in Canada, and

(c)   the distance between the old residence and the new work location is not less than 40 kilometres greater than the distance between the new residence and the new work location.

Where the taxpayer is "absent from but resident in Canada," the postamble to this definition drops the requirement in subparagraph (a)(i) that the new work location must be "in Canada" and the requirement in paragraph (b) that the old and new residences must be in Canada. Similarly, where the taxpayer relocates in order to be a student in full-time attendance at a post-secondary educational institution, subsection 62(2) drops the requirement that "both" the old and new residence must be in Canada, requiring only that "either" the old or new residence must be in Canada.

In applying this definition in the context of the moving expense deduction in subsection 62(1) of the Act, courts must consider three issues: (1) the purpose of the relocation; (2) the residences at which the taxpayer ordinarily resided before and after the relocation; and (3) the distance of the relocation. Each issue is considered in turn.

a. Purpose of Relocation

The first criterion for an "eligible location" is that the relocation must "occur to enable" the taxpayer to carry on a business, to be employed, or to be a full-time student at a post-secondary educational institution at the new work location. Applicable since 1999, this language replaces earlier versions of the moving expense deduction, which required the taxpayer to have "commenced" a business, employment, or full-time study at a new work location and "by reason thereof" to have moved from the old residence to the new residence.[26] Despite this amendment, judicial decisions addressing the "reason" for a move under the former language appear to be relevant to the current test. A useful example of this case law is *Beyette v. M.N.R.*, [1990] 1 C.T.C. 2001, (1989) 89 D.T.C. 701 (T.C.C.).

Beyette v. M.N.R.
[1990] 1 C.T.C. 2001, 89 D.T.C. 701 (T.C.C.)

TAYLOR TCJ: This is an appeal heard in Winnipeg, Manitoba, on October 5, 1989 against an income tax assessment for the year 1986 in which the Minister of National Revenue disallowed the deduction of moving expenses. The critical portion of the notice of appeal read:

> Mr. Beyette had a change in job location in December of 1981. It was his intention at that time and remained his intention from the date to the date of his residence move of October, 1986, to move to his new job site. He had engaged a realtor to locate a new home at the new job site, but by reasons of poor supply of homes, his lack of equity in his original house, high interest rates in 1981 and 1982, and intermittent health problems, the actual move had to be delayed.

> The reason for the move was the change in employment location and no other (see IT-178R2, May 26, 1978, paragraph 15).

In response thereto, the respondent stated:

> — In 1981, the Appellant resided and was employed in Winnipeg, Manitoba.

---

[26] See subs. 62(1) as it read before 1998. Before 1984, the provision required the taxpayer to have "ceased" a business, employment, or full-time study at an old location, "commenced" one of these activities at a new work location, and "by reason thereof to have moved from an old residence to a new residence."

— In December 1981, the Appellant commenced to be employed at a new work location in Beausejour, Manitoba.

— From December 1981 to September 1986, the appellant resided in Winnipeg and was employed in Beausejour. He commuted daily a distance of approximately 110 kilometres round-trip.

— In October 1986, the Appellant moved from his old residence in Winnipeg to his new residence in Beausejour.

— The move ... did not occur by reason of the commencement of employment at the new location....

The only issue raised in this appeal, is whether, all other conditions being met (and they were) the taxpayer is entitled to the deduction claimed for moving to his new employment site in 1986, from his old employment site after he had already been working at the new site (commuting daily) for the intervening five-year period. The respondent's assessment explanation read:

The general rule is that you may deduct moving expenses from your income if you move from the residence you ordinarily live in to commence employment at a new location. As the information submitted indicates that you commuted from Winnipeg to Beausejour for several years, you do not meet the above-mentioned criteria.

Counsel for the respondent argued that subsection 62(1) of the Act implied a certain time limit — between the change of work site and the move — and that five years was unreasonable. In addition the critical word in the legislation was "commenced," in his view and there was a requirement for a relationship between the "commencement of employment" and the "move."

I do not agree with either point raised by the respondent. In this matter, I was satisfied from the evidence and testimony that there were good reasons for which the taxpayer delayed his move from Winnipeg to Beausejour — illness, lack of housing in Beausejour, inactive real estate selling market in Winnipeg, etc. — but that is probably irrelevant. In my opinion, the taxpayer and he alone is left to determine the timing of the move, and the costs associated with the move, and no time limit is expressed by the wording of the Act. While clearly five years is an unusually long period of time between the change of work locale and the move, that cannot be put in issue — the respondent has no basis upon which to conclude (IT Bulletin 178R2) that there is some time frame that is "reasonable" and another that is unreasonable. As I read subsection 62(1) of the Act, it is a requirement that the taxpayer "... has ... commenced to be employed ..." previous to the move for which an expense claim is made. I do not see that one should read into the word "commenced" more than that. Mr. Beyette "commenced to be employed" in 1981 at the new work location, he "moved" in 1986 and is entitled to his costs of moving. ...

Appeal allowed.

NOTES AND QUESTIONS

1.   On what basis did the Minister disallow the deduction of the taxpayer's moving expenses in *Beyette*? Why did the court allow the taxpayer's appeal? Of what relevance to the decision is the old language of the moving expense deduction, which required the taxpayer to have "commenced" a qualifying activity at the new work location? Is it arguable that because the taxpayer was able to carry on the duties of his employment for five years by commuting from his old residence, the move was not motivated by the new employment but by personal considerations? Of what, if any, relevance to the court's decision was the taxpayer's explanation for the delay in moving?

2.   Would the moving expenses in *Beyette* have been deductible under the current definition of an "eligible relocation" in subsection 248(1) of the Act? Were the expenses incurred "to enable the taxpayer ... to be employed" at the new work location? If not, is the current language more restrictive than the former version?

Beyette was followed in *Beaudoin v. Canada*, [2005] T.C.J. No. 60, [2005] 1 C.T.C. 2821, 2005 D.T.C. 282 (T.C.C.), in which the taxpayer's job was relocated from Nanaimo to Courtenay, British Columbia, in 1996, but the taxpayer delayed moving to Courtenay until 2003. Without commenting on the amended language of the definition of an "eligible relocation" in subsection 248(1) of the ITA, the court rejected the Minister's argument (at para. 12) that this move did not enable the taxpayer to be employed in Courtenay and concurred (at para. 20) with the decision in *Beyette*.

3.   At the end of the decision in *Beyette*, the court referred to the requirement under subsection 62(1) as it then read that the taxpayer "has ... commenced to be employed" at the new work location "previous to the move for which an expense claim is made." On this basis, moving expenses incurred by a taxpayer seeking work at a new location were consistently disallowed, even though the taxpayer eventually found work at the new location. See, for example, *Pelchat v. M.N.R.*, [1984] C.T.C. 2964, 84 D.T.C. 1865 (T.C.C.); *Glaubitz v. Canada*, [1994] T.C.J. No. 753, [1994] 2 C.T.C. 2448 (T.C.C.); and *McLaren v. Canada*, [1999] T.C.J. No. 947, [2000] 2 C.T.C. 2633 (T.C.C.). Since the current language requires that the relocation occur "to enable the taxpayer" to carry on a business, be employed, or be a full-time student at a new work location, these decisions appear to have been legislatively reversed.

In *Abrahamsen v. Canada*, [2007] T.C.J. No. 39, [2007] 3 C.T.C. 2001, 2007 D.T.C. 412 (T.C.C.), the court confirmed that the amended language of the definition of an "eligible relocation" in subsection 248(1) allows for the deduction of expenses that were formerly disallowed on the basis that the taxpayer had not already obtained employment before moving. According to Mogan D.J. (at para. 9):

> In the definition of 'eligible relocation', I would not construe the words in paragraph (a) "to enable the taxpayer ... to be employed ..." as a requirement that the taxpayer have

employment at the new work location before making a move to the new location. In my view, the current legislation gives more latitude to the taxpayer than the pre-1988 legislation.

4.   In *Adamson v. Canada*, [2001] T.C.J. No. 609, [2001] 4 C.T.C. 2499 (T.C.C.), the taxpayer moved 67.8 kilometres from Toronto to Georgetown, Ontario, after he obtained a new position with his employer which required that he work from his home. Rejecting the Minister's argument (at para. 6) that the primary reason for the move was personal, the Court (at para. 7) accepted the taxpayer's testimony that the former residence was "too small to accommodate both his family and his office" and held that "the relocation occurred to enable the [taxpayer] to be employed at the new location selected by him for his home and office as required by paragraph (a) of the subsection 248(1) definition of 'eligible relocation.' Do you agree with this result? Why or why not?

5.   In *Howlett v. Canada*, [1998] T.C.J. No. 1035; [1998] CarswellNat 2257 (T.C.C.), the taxpayer was a sales representative who moved from Brantford to Waterdown, Ontario after he accepted a promotion that required him to spend more time at his employer's work location in Mississauga. On the basis that the taxpayer was not employed at a new work location, the court disallowed the deduction. Do you agree with this outcome? Why or why not? Should the Act be amended to allow a deduction for moving expenses in these circumstances?

Howlett was followed in *Broydell v. Canada*, [2005] T.C.J. No. 39, [2005] 1 C.T.C. 2826 (T.C.C.), in which the taxpayer moved from Innisfil to South Barrie, Ontario after his employer advised him to move closer to his work location when he experienced problems with the commuter train and missed work a number of times during the winter months. Emphasizing (at para. 6) that "Courts are bound by the statutory requirements and cannot extend them to capture a situation not envisaged by those statutory requirements," O'Connor T.C.J. disallowed the deduction of moving expenses on the basis that there was no new work location.

6.   In *Crampton v. M.N.R.*, [1980] C.T.C. 2269, 80 D.T.C. 1233 (T.R.B.), the taxpayer, who worked as an electrician at various job sites in the Vancouver area, sought to deduct expenses incurred in moving from one suburb of Vancouver to another. Concluding (at para. 7) that "there was no real difference in the nature of his employment or location of work sites before or after the move for which the appellant claims the deduction," the court affirmed the Minister's assessment disallowing the deduction.

7.   For cases in which moving expenses have been disallowed on the basis that the taxpayer never carried on a business, became employed, or attended a post-secondary educational institution at the new location, see *Letourneau v. Canada*, [1998] T.C.J. No. 209, [1998] 2 C.T.C. 3063 (T.C.C.) and *Sundararajan v. Canada*, [1999] T.C.J. No. 739, [2000] 1 C.T.C. 2367 (T.C.C.).

b. Residences Before and After Relocation

In order to determine whether a relocation is an "eligible relocation" within the meaning of the definition in subsection 248(1) of the Act, it is essential to determine not only the purpose of the move but where the taxpayer "ordinarily resided" before and after the relocation — defined in paragraph (b) of the definition of an "eligible relocation" as the "old residence" and the "new residence." According to paragraph (c) of this definition, moving expenses are deductible only where the new residence is at least 40 kilometres closer to the new work location than the old residence. As well, most of the eligible "moving expenses" in subsection 62(3) of the Act relate to costs of travelling and transporting household effects from the old residence to the new residence, as well as costs associated with the disposition of the old residence and the acquisition of the new residence. The case cited most often on the characterization of a taxpayer's residences for the purpose of the moving expense deduction is *Rennie v. M.N.R.*, [1989] T.C.J. No. 1105, [1990] 1 C.T.C. 2141, (1989) 90 D.T.C. 1050 (T.C.C.).

Rennie v. M.N.R.
[1989] T.C.J. No. 1105, [1990] 1 C.T.C. 2141, 90 D.T.C. 1050 (T.C.C.)

CHRISTIE, ACJTC: ... After some years of working for Domtar Ltd. and lecturing part-time in business administration at McGill University the appellant was employed by that university on a full-time basis. This employment was under two contracts for the academic year which runs from September to May. The second contract terminated in May 1981. This brought to an end his association with McGill. During the period just referred to the appellant, his wife and family resided in Montreal in a home he purchased in 1950. He was next employed by the University of Alberta at Edmonton. When he left Montreal he was uncertain regarding his length of employment in Edmonton so he only took with him a minimum of household effects such as a bedroom set, bedding and kitchen appliances and utensils. He turned his home over to a relative who only paid current expenses like heat, electricity and telephone. It was understood that the appellant could return and occupy this home at any time it suited him.

The appellant and his wife moved to Edmonton in August 1981. While there he had academic year contracts with the University of Alberta for employment in the position of Visiting Associate Professor in the faculty of Business Administration. They lived in a rented apartment. While in Edmonton they did not form an intention to reside there permanently. The appellant and his wife maintained ties with Montreal in the sense that they had relations and friends there with whom they kept in contact. When they visited Montreal they stayed at his home. He kept up his membership in the Montreal Athletic Association. After a year in Edmonton he learned that he could have a special non-resident membership so he applied for that change of status in the Athletic Association, which was granted.

The appellant enjoyed Edmonton and the university but he and his wife found the weather hard to take and, considering their age, they decided to explore Victoria as a place to settle. In June 1983 he opened negotiations with the University of Victoria and entered into a contract with that university for one academic year effective September 1, 1983. His employment there was that of Visiting Associate Professor in the Department of Economics. They moved to Victoria in August 1983 and took up residence in rented premises. When his contract was renewed by the University of Victoria at the end of his first year the appellant and his wife decided to make Victoria their permanent home. The Montreal home was thereupon sold and a home was purchased in Victoria.

...

In his 1981 tax return the appellant claimed and was allowed moving expenses from Montreal to Edmonton. He gave his "Former Residence" as 6531 Starnes, Montreal, and his "New Residence" as 11020-53rd Avenue, #1103, Edmonton. His "Former Employer" is stated to be McGill University and his "New Employer" the University of Alberta. This appears on the first page of the return. "Province or Territory of residence on December 31, 1981, was: Alberta." In his 1983 return the appellant claimed and was allowed moving expenses from Edmonton to Victoria. In his 1984 return of income the appellant makes this statement on page 1: "Your Province or Territory of residence on December 31, 1984, was: BC." Included in the claim for moving expenses he states that his "Former Residence" is 6531 Starnes, Montreal, and his "New Residence" is 317 Simcoe, Victoria. His "Former Employer" is said to be McGill University and his "New Employer" is the University of Victoria. July 20 to August 9, 1984, is given as the time of the move. The claimed deductions relate to the cost of transporting the balance of his household effects from Montreal to Victoria, the selling costs of his Montreal residence and legal fees and taxes in respect of his residence in Victoria. These are the deductions that gave rise to this litigation.

...

The argument made by counsel for the appellant, Mr. G. Jones, is founded on the proposition that a person can have two residences simultaneously. As I understand it from what was placed in evidence and said at trial, the argument evolves from that starting point in this way. The appellant had a residence in Victoria in 1984, but he had also continued to have one in Montreal from the time he went to Edmonton and therefore he was in a position to move from Montreal to Victoria within the meaning of section 62 in that year.

I do not believe that the concept of a person being capable of having more than one residence can be applied in the interpretation of the provisions of section 62 already cited in the manner propounded by the appellant. Those provisions relate to each other and constitute a framework that permits persons within it to deduct moving expenses. It is not the word "residence" that governs, but rather the phrase "ordinarily resided."

...

In *Thomson v. Minister of National Revenue*, [1946] SCR 209, [1946] CTC 51, 2 DTC 812 (SCC), the meaning of the words "ordinarily resident" in paragraph 9(a) of the *Income War Tax Act* was considered. Mr. Justice Estey said at page 70 (DTC 813):

> A reference to the dictionary and judicial comments upon the meaning of these terms indicates that one is "ordinarily resident" in the place where in the settled routine of his life he regularly, normally or customarily lives.

Mr. Justice Rand said at page 64 (DTC 815):

> The expression "ordinarily resident" carries a restricted signification, and although the first impression seems to be that of preponderance in time, the decisions on the English Act reject that view. It is held to mean residence in the course of the customary mode of life of the person concerned, and it is contrasted with special or occasional or casual residence. The general mode of life is, therefore, relevant to a question of its application.

In 1984 the place where, in the settled routine of the appellant's life, he normally lived was Victoria. That was his residence in the course of his customary mode of life at that time. He had moved from Montreal three years earlier and apart from a visit or visits there — the number or duration of which is not in evidence — his home was in Edmonton or Victoria. There is no evidence that the appellant was in Montreal at all in 1984. All of this clearly establishes that in that year the appellant was ordinarily resident in Victoria.

While there is judicial authority for the proposition that for some purposes a person may have more than one residence ..., I know of no authority that holds that a person can be ordinarily resident in two places at the same time. Nor is there anything in the wording of section 62 that suggests that possibility for the purpose of deducting moving expenses. Indeed what is essentially envisaged by the section is a taxpayer commencing to be employed and by reason thereof moving a prescribed minimum distance with the consequent termination of his then place of ordinary residence and the creation of a new and different place of ordinary residence. This is not what transpired regarding the appellant in 1984. ...

Appeal dismissed.

NOTES AND QUESTIONS

1. On what basis did the taxpayer in *Rennie* argue that the cost of transporting household effects from Montreal to Victoria, the selling costs of his Montreal residence, and legal fees and taxes in respect of his residence in Victoria were deductible moving expenses under subsection 62(1) of the Act? Why did the court reject this argument? How did the court determine where the taxpayer "ordinarily resided" in 1984?

2.   Do you agree with the decision in *Rennie*? Why or why not? Consider the following statement in *Jaggers v. Canada*, [1997] T.C.J. No. 477, [1997] 3 C.T.C. 2372, 97 D.T.C. 1317 (T.C.C.), at para. 28, in which Bowman TCJ allowed the taxpayer to deduct the costs of selling a former residence sold more than two years after the acquisition of a new residence:

> What section 62 is aimed at is the deduction of moving costs where a move is occasioned by a change of job. Its purpose would be defeated if an unduly narrow and technical approach were followed. We have here a taxpayer who moves to another city to take up new employment. He buys a home there but, sensibly, retains his old home until he is sure that the job will work out. He rents the old home as an interim measure. Because he does not evict the tenants as soon as he could — for reasons of commercial morality, it appears, rather than pure commerciality — he loses, in the view of the Department of National Revenue, the right to any deductions under section 62. I do not find this acceptable interpretation of section 62. These expenses are precisely the type contemplated by section 62.

3.   In *Neville v. M.N.R.*, [1979] C.T.C. 2288, 79 D.T.C. 344 (T.R.B.), the taxpayer, a university professor who accepted a government appointment in Winnipeg during a sabbatical leave in August 1973, sought to deduct moving expenses incurred in the spring of 1975 when he resigned his position at Trent University, sold his home in Peterborough, and transported various household effects from Peterborough to a new home that he purchased in Winnipeg. Objecting to the deduction of the expenses as moving expenses and noting that the taxpayer and his family had lived in Winnipeg since 1973 in rented accommodations, the Minister disallowed deductions relating to the sale of the Peterborough residence and the transportation of household effects on the basis that the Peterborough residence was no longer the taxpayer's "old residence" at the time of its sale. The Tax Review Board sided with the taxpayer, emphasizing (at para. 10) that "the appellant's domestic arrangements during the period prior to tendering his resignation were of a temporary nature." The Board allowed the taxpayer's appeal holding that "the appellant's 'old residence,' as the term is used in section 62, continued to be in Peterborough until the spring of 1975."

4.   In *Pitchford v. Canada*, [1997] T.C.J. No. 354, [1997] 3 C.T.C. 2645 (T.C.C.), the taxpayer, who moved from Victoria to Moose Jaw in 1993 and from Moose Jaw to Saskatoon in 1994, sought to deduct expenses incurred in transporting furniture, most of which remained in storage until the taxpayer and his family settled in Saskatoon. On the basis (at para. 13) that the taxpayer and his family "had no settled routine of life where they regularly, normally or customarily lived" until they settled in Saskatoon, the court allowed the deductions on the basis (at para. 14) that "the Appellant moved from his old residence in Victoria and did not take up a residence in which he ordinarily resided until he ... got all of [the family's] furniture out of storage and established his family in Saskatoon."

For a similar result, see *Simard v. Canada*, [1996] T.C.J. No. 626, [1998] 2 C.T.C. 2312, (1996) 97 D.T.C. 216 (T.C.C.), where the taxpayer occupied temporary lodgings near the new work location in Mont-Joli, Quebec for five years before selling his old residence and purchasing a new residence in Mont-

Joli in 1991. Concluding (at para. 17) that the taxpayer "did not 'ordinarily reside' in Mont-Joli prior to 1991," the court allowing the taxpayer to deduct moving expenses associated with the sale of the old residence and the transportation of household effects to the new residence.

See also *Dalisay v. Canada*, [2004] T.C.J. No. 67, [2004] 2 C.T.C. 2599 (T.C.C.), where the taxpayer moved from St. John's to Regina in July 2000 and from Regina to Edmonton seven weeks later. Allowing the taxpayer to deduct the cost of moving from St. John's to Regina against employment income earned after she moved to Edmonton, the court held that the taxpayer "was never 'ordinarily' resident in Regina" but had relocated from St. John's to Edmonton.

5.   In *Ringham v. Canada*, [2000] T.C.J. No. 224, [2000] 3 C.T.C. 2117, 2000 D.T.C. 2060 (T.C.C.), the taxpayer, a professional engineer who accepted an offer to work on a project in Budapest, Hungary, sold his home at Tiffany Place in Kanata, Ontario (near Ottawa), at the end of 1995, and rented a condominium at Robson Place in the same city, while travelling on a weekly basis to his employer's office in Thornhill, Ontario (near Toronto), where he stayed at the Holiday Inn. When delays in the commencement of the Budapest project became indefinite at the end of 1996, the taxpayer moved to Richmond Hill (near Thornhill) and started working full time at the employer's Thornhill office. The Minister disallowed the deduction of selling costs on the Kanata home on the basis that there were two moves: first, an ineligible relocation from the Kanata home to the condominium and, second, an eligible relocation from the condominium to Richmond Hill. Accepting the taxpayer's argument (at para. 12) that "there was realistically only one move" — from the Kanata home to Richmond Hill — the court allowed the taxpayer's appeal. According to Bowman ACJTC (at para. 13-15):

> The respondent's position does not take into account the unusual situation in which the appellant found himself as the result of the delays in, and ultimate abandonment of, the Budapest project. Robson Court was a temporary pied-à-terre, a way-station. It was never regarded by Mr. Ringham as his ordinary residence. He kept some of his furnishings in storage and he did not unpack many of the boxes which he stored at Robson Court. It is true he changed his mailing address to Robson Court but I do not regard this as determinative.

> It is not in my view realistic to say that he was "ordinarily resident" at Robson Court. He was expecting to move at any time to Budapest and kept himself in readiness for that move. It would make about as much sense to say that he was ordinarily resident in the Holiday Inn in Thornhill. He seems to have spent more time there than at Robson Court.

> After all, it took Odysseus ten years to get home to Ithaca from Troy, with numerous sojourns along the way. No one would ever suggest that notwithstanding his protracted stay with Circe on the island of Aeaea he was ever ordinarily resident there.

Do you agree with this decision? Why or why not? Where was Mr. Ringham "ordinarily resident" from the end of 1995 to the end of 1996? How long did it take for Mr. Ringham to move from Kanata to Richmond Hill?

The decision in *Ringham* was followed in *Jaschinski v. Canada*, [2002] T.C.J. No. 600, [2003] 1 C.T.C. 2571, 2002 D.T.C. 2183 (T.C.C.), where the taxpayer purchased a temporary home in Mississauga and subsequently moved to Campellville, Ontario, after he was transferred from Calgary to Toronto. Accepting the taxpayer's argument (at para. 4) that he had moved from Calgary to Campellville "with an interim stay in Mississauga to be considered as a hotel or stopover before finding a permanent home", the court allowed the taxpayer to deduct the cost of both moves.

Ringham was distinguished in *Calvano v. Canada*, [2003] T.C.J. No. 785, [2004] 2 C.T.C. 3004, 2004 D.T.C. 2471 (T.C.C.), in which the taxpayer moved from Brampton, Ontario to a rented house in Coquitlam, British Columbia in March 1995, but delayed selling his house in Brampton for 16 months after renting it to a tenant who insisted on a lease until June 1996 so that his children's school year would not be interrupted. The court rejected the taxpayer's argument that he resided in Coquitlam only temporarily until he sold the Brampton house, and disallowed the deduction of selling costs in respect of the Brampton house on the basis that the taxpayer ordinarily resided in Coquitlam in June 1996.

6. In *Turnbull v. Canada*, [1998] T.C.J. No. 173, [1999] 1 C.T.C. 2459 (T.C.C.), the taxpayer, who maintained a home in Newfoundland, worked in Edmonton in 1993, various locations in British Columbia in 1994, and Yellowknife in 1997. Noting that the taxpayer returned to Newfoundland each year, listed Newfoundland as his place of residence on his tax return, and rebuilt a house in Newfoundland on property that he had inherited from his father, the court disallowed the deduction of moving expenses to and from British Columbia in 1994 on the basis that the taxpayer was at all times ordinarily resident in Newfoundland.

For a similar result, see *MacDonald v. Canada*, [2007] T.C.J. No. 130, [2007] 4 C.T.C. 2166 (T.C.C.), where the taxpayer, who was unable to find work on Cape Breton Island, worked in Alberta for six weeks from October to December 2004. Disallowing the deduction of moving expenses to Alberta and back to Cape Breton, the court held (at para. 11) that the taxpayer was ordinarily resident in Cape Breton for the following reasons:

> He maintained a Nova Scotia driver's licence in 2004. He continued to be covered by the provincial health insurance plan of Nova Scotia. He did not take all of his belongings with him to Alberta (he only took what he could take in his truck). His common-law spouse remained in Nova Scotia. He had and maintained three houses in Nova Scotia. He did not purchase any property in Alberta. He did not relocate his bank accounts to Alberta. He did not change his mailing address to Alberta.

As a result, the court stated (at para. 12): "Unfortunately he simply incurred travel costs to find work in Alberta because work was not available in Nova Scotia."

In *Cavalier v. Canada*, [2001] T.C.J. No. 719, [2002] 1 C.T.C. 2001 (T.C.C.), in contrast, where the taxpayer accepted a teaching contract that required him to move from Delta, British Columbia, to Fort McMurray, Alberta, where he lived from January to April 1998, the court allowed the deduction of moving expenses to and from Fort McMurray, even though his wife remained at the Delta residence, his mail was addressed to that address, and he did not change his bank account.

The *Cavalier* decision was followed in *Persaud v. Canada*, [2007] T.C.J. No. 305, 2007 TCC 474 (T.C.C.), where the taxpayer, an electrician who was unemployed in 2005, traveled from Quispamsis, New Brunswick to Fort McMurray, Alberta in early May 2005 and back to Quispamsis in September 2005. Notwithstanding that the taxpayer did not obtain an Alberta driver's licence nor apply for Alberta health insurance and that his wife remained at their home in New Brunswick while he worked in Alberta, the court allowed the deduction of expenses incurred by the taxpayer to travel to and from Alberta on the grounds that he resided in Alberta for four months, that he opened a bank account in Alberta, and that his children were living in Alberta.

7. In *Klein v. Canada*, [1997] T.C.J. No. 590, [1997] 3 C.T.C. 2997 (T.C.C.), the taxpayer, who owned two homes in Montreal, one in Westmount and the other in Lachute, which had been purchased to accommodate his wife, who was confined to a wheelchair as a result of a stroke, sought to deduct the cost of selling both residences when he sold both homes and moved to Vancouver in 1993. Citing *Thomson v. M.N.R.*, [1946] C.T.C. 51, 2 D.T.C. 812 (S.C.C.) and *Rennie v. M.N.R.*, [1989] T.C.J. No. 1105, [1990] 1 C.T.C. 2141, (1989) 90 D.T.C. 1050 (T.C.C.), for the proposition that a person cannot have two ordinary residences, the court disallowed deductions for moving expenses related to the Lachute property. Do you agree with this conclusion? Why or why not?

8. In *Templeton v. Canada*, [1997] F.C.J. No. 396, [1998] 3 C.T.C. 207, (1997) 97 D.T.C. 5216 (F.C.T.D.), the taxpayer, an author, inventor, and former broadcaster who worked out of his own home, sought to deduct expenses incurred in moving from two residences — one that he owned in Penetanguishene, Ontario and the other that he rented in Toronto and occupied for about 105 days of the year — to a rented house in Don Mills, Ontario. Concluding that the taxpayer ordinarily resided in Penetanguishene, the court allowed the deductions on the basis that the taxpayer, who decided to devote more time to inventing, needed to be closer to business contacts in Toronto. Do you agree with this decision? Why or why not?

c. Distance of Relocation

According to paragraph (c) of the definition of an "eligible relocation" in paragraph 248(1) of the Act, "the distance between the old residence and the new work location" must be "not less than 40 kilometres greater than the distance between the new residence and the new work location." In other words, the new residence must be at least 40 kilometres closer to the new work location than the old residence.

For many years, the courts and revenue authorities measured this distance on a straightline basis "as the crow flies." The issue was reconsidered in

Giannakopoulos v. M.N.R., [1995] F.C.J. No. 1041, [1995] 2 C.T.C. 316, 95 D.T.C. 5477 (F.C.A.).

Giannakopoulos v. M.N.R
[1995] F.C.J. No. 1041, [1995] 2 C.T.C. 316, 95 D.T.C. 5477 (F.C.A.)

MARCEAU JA (Strayer and Linden JJA, concurring): ... The applicant was employed as a research interviewer with the University of Alberta when, in 1991, she accepted a new position as an administrative assistant with her employer, which required her to work at a different location. In order to be closer to her new workplace, she moved from Stony Plain to Edmonton, where the University administration offices are located.

...

Using the odometer in her car, the applicant calculated that her new residence was 44 kilometres closer to the University administration centre than her prior one. Considering herself to have met the conditions prescribed by the provisions of subsection 62(1) of the Act, the applicant claimed her moving expenses on her income tax returns for the 1991 and 1992 taxation years. The deduction, however, was disallowed and she was reassessed on the basis that, measured in a straight line, her new residence was only 36 kilometres closer to her workplace than the prior one. The applicant appealed to the Tax Court of Canada where the reassessment was confirmed, it being the jurisprudence of the Court ... that the "straight line method" was indeed the appropriate one.

...

Subsection 62(1) permits a taxpayer to deduct moving expenses when he moves closer to a new workplace. An employee must live within a reasonable distance of his work. When he accepts a new position, the employee may have to move in order to remain within a practical commuting distance of his job. Subsection 62(1) recognizes that relocation is a legitimate work-related expense. In order to prevent the provision from being invoked when a taxpayer simply desires a change in residence, the provision requires that the move bring the taxpayer at least forty kilometres closer to work. Usually, a taxpayer travels to work using ordinary routes of public travel, i.e. roads, highways, railways. In determining whether the taxpayer has really moved forty kilometres closer to work, it only makes sense to measure the distance he has moved using real routes of travel. A realistic measurement of travelling distance is necessary in order to give effect to the purpose of the provision. The straight line method bears no relation to how an employee travels to work. It is illogical to apply this technique to a provision which exists to recognize work-related relocation expenses. It leads to absurd results where the old residence and the new workplace are separated by a body of water. A taxpayer who moves across a river to be closer to his workplace may have only moved a few miles "as the crow flies" but may actually be several dozen miles closer to work. In fact, this is exactly what happened in *Cameron v. Minister of National Revenue* [supra] wherein the taxpayer moved across the Ottawa River from Aylmer, Quebec to Kars, Ontario. The Tax Court of Canada held that he could not deduct his moving expenses because the distance was less that 40 kilometres using a straight line measurement.

In one case before the Tax Court of Canada, *Bernier, J-C, Estate v. Minister of National Revenue* [supra], Lamarre-Proulx TCJ held herself to be bound by the prior decisions but only after expressing her own discordant personal view. She stated at page 2539 (DTC 1223):

> In my view, the remedy in subsection 62(1) should be interpreted in relation to the workers, and the distance in question should be measured by the worker's normal route or the route that he would normally take to go from home to his place of work.

While the use of the normal route notion is more realistic and more effectively furthers the purpose of the section, I would not go so far as Lamarre-Proulx TCJ would apparently have been prepared to go, i.e. to accept a measurement based merely on the worker's normal route or the route that he would normally take to go from home to his place of work. Such a subjective approach would introduce a source of uncertainty which might become "a trap for litigation," which was precisely the reason invoked by the judges to explain their adherence to the direct line approach. It is necessary to be more objective. The idea of the shortest route that one might travel to work should be coupled with the notion of the normal route to the travelling public. Thus, the shortest normal route would be a preferable test to the straight line method, for it is both realistic and precise. It also furthers the purpose of the provision. This test would prevent a taxpayer from being expected to use an extraordinary route such as a neglected or unpaved road. It would also leave room to consider travel not only on roads but on ferries and rail lines.

...

In my opinion, by applying the straight line rule to the calculation of the distance referred to in subsection 62(1) of the Act, the Tax Court of Canada has interpreted the word without regard to the context and, in so doing, has committed an error of law which must be reversed. ...

Application allowed.

NOTES AND QUESTIONS

1. Why did the trial judge disallow the deduction of the taxpayer's moving expenses in *Giannakopoulos*? Why did the Federal Court of Appeal reverse the decision at trial? Do you agree with the court's interpretation? Why or why not?

2. For an application of the approach suggested in *Giannakopoulos*, see *Higgins v. Canada*, [1995] T.C.J. No. 885, 96 D.T.C. 1291 (T.C.C.), where the court disallowed deductions for moving expenses incurred by the taxpayer on the basis (at para. 9) that the "shortest normal route" from the old residence to the new work location was by ferry, "a distance of approximately 15 to 20

kilometers, even though it may have been occasionally inconvenient for him because of freezing conditions on the Frazer [*sic*] River or the line-ups waiting for the ferry." Is this decision consistent with the spirit of *Giannakopoulos*?

3.   The approach in *Giannakopoulos* was also applied in *Nagy v. Canada*, [2007] T.C.J. No. 244, 2007 TCC 394 (T.C.C.), in which the revenue authorities disallowed the deduction of moving expenses claimed by the taxpayer on the basis that he had moved only 34.6 kilometres closer to his new work location. Rejecting the Minister's route for determining the distance between the old residence and the new residence, the court accepted the taxpayer's approach as more reasonable. According to Bowman, C.J.T.C. (at paras. 11-12):

> Counsel invites me to read the passage from *Giannakopoulos* as requiring that a mechanical measurement of all possible routes should be made and the shortest chosen, regardless of whether any reasonable person would follow such a route. The route suggested by the respondent as the shortest involves 18 left turns and 19 right turns and requires travelling on about 40 roads, some rural, as well as driving through the heavily congested City of Brampton.... The respondent's approach illustrates simply the triumph of mechanical irrationality over common sense. No rational person would follow such a route. Indeed, anyone trying to follow those instructions would get lost unless he or she had a navigator in the passenger seat giving directions. The approach advocated by the Crown represents an attempt to reverse the salutary effect of the Federal Court of Appeal's decision which endeavours to substitute a measure of common sense and rationality for the unthinking mechanical approach that prevailed prior to *Giannakopoulos*.
>
> The Federal Court of Appeal suggests no such robotic approach. In his reasons Marceau J.A. speaks of a *"realistic"* measurement of travelling distance". He also says that "the idea of the shortest route that one might travel to work should be coupled with the notion of the *normal* route to the travelling public" ... His use of "realistic" and "normal" implies that reason and common sense should play a part in the determination of distance. The 38 turn slalom suggested by the Crown is neither realistic, nor normal, nor reasonable, nor commonsensical. In some ways it is even more nonsensical than the straight line approach. The straight line approach would at least make sense to a crow. The 40 road zigzag approach makes sense to no one.

3. Limitations on Deductibility

In addition to permitting the deduction of moving expenses incurred in respect of an eligible relocation, subsection 62(1) limits the deduction of moving expenses in several ways. According to paragraph 62(1)(a), for example, moving expenses are not deductible to the extent that they were "paid on the taxpayer's behalf in respect of, in the course of or because of, the taxpayer's office or employment." Similarly, paragraph 62(1)(d) disallows the deduction of moving expenses to the extent that reimbursements or allowances received by the taxpayer in respect of the expenses are not included in computing the taxpayer's income. Most importantly, paragraph 62(1)(c) limits the amount that may be deducted in computing the taxpayer's income for a taxation year to the taxpayer's income for the year from carrying on a business or employment at the new work location where the relocation occurred to enable the taxpayer to carry on the business or be employed at the new work location, or to the aggregate of scholarships, fellowships, bursaries, prizes, and research grants where the relocation occurred to enable the taxpayer to attend a post-secondary educational institution. Finally, where the moving expenses that may be deducted in computing a taxpayer's income are limited by subsection 62(1), paragraph 62(1)(b) stipulates that non-deductible moving expenses for "the preceding taxation year" may be deducted in the subsequent taxation year. An interesting application of the limitation in what is now paragraph 62(1)(c) appears in *Hippola v. The Queen*, [2002] 1 C.T.C. 2156 (T.C.C.).

Hippola v. The Queen
[2002] 1 C.T.C. 2156 (T.C.C.)

HAMLYN TCJ: ... At all material times, the Appellant owned and maintained a residence located at 123 Saphir Avenue, Navan, Ontario. During the 1996 taxation year, the Appellant commenced employment with Dalsa Inc. in Waterloo, Ontario. While so employed, he resided in rental accommodation in Waterloo; his wife, son and daughter, however, continued to reside in Navan. In late 1998, the Appellant returned to the Ottawa area and started working for the Mitel Corporation.

...

The Appellant states that he moved to Waterloo in 1996 for employment purposes. Since his wife, son and daughter could not relocate with him, he continued to maintain the residence in Navan even though he was not living there, although he did try to sell the Navan residence between September 8, 1996 and June 30, 1997. Considering the increased expenses incurred as a consequence of maintaining these two residences and considering the desires of his family, the Appellant planned in 1998 to start a consulting business in his field of work in the Ottawa area. He stated that he moved back to the Ottawa area for the purpose of starting this business. However, while in the process of setting up the business in the Ottawa area, he was approached by Mitel Corporation and hired by Mitel after he moved back to Navan.

...

I conclude the Appellant ... ordinarily resided in Waterloo before he moved back to Navan in the latter part of 1998. In the present case, the Appellant's family stayed in the residence in Navan while he was living in Waterloo. However, in the settled routine of the Appellant's life he nevertheless regularly, normally or customarily lived in Waterloo during that period.

With this finding it is then necessary to determine whether the other conditions of subsection 62(1) of the Act are met. Pursuant to paragraph 62(1)(c), an amount may be deducted for expenses incurred in respect of an eligible relocation to the extent that it does not exceed the taxpayer's income for the year from his employment at the new work location or from carrying on a business at the new work location, as the case may be. In this appeal, the Appellant contends that he moved back to the Ottawa area for the purposes of starting to carry on a business. In fact he did not gain any income from the purported business since the Mitel Corporation offered him permanent employment, which he accepted instead of starting his business. Moreover, since the intention of working towards setting up his business, he has not gained any income from the business, nor indeed has the business got off the ground. Therefore, the Appellant is not entitled to the deduction of any amount since his income for the year from his business was nil.

My conclusion would be different if the evidence showed that Mitel hired the Appellant before he actually moved to Navan. If so, the Appellant could then submit that he moved back to Navan for the purposes of employment and accordingly could deduct his moving expenses to the extent that they did not exceed his income from this employment. However, it is only after the Appellant had moved back to Navan that Mitel approached him and offered him employment. The Appellant did not move to Navan to enable him to be employed by Mitel. ...

Appeal dismissed.

NOTES AND QUESTIONS

1.   On what basis did the court conclude in *Hippola* that the taxpayer could not deduct the cost of moving from Waterloo back to Navan? Does paragraph 62(1)(c) limit the deduction to income from the specific employment or business for which the relocation was made? Should it?

2.   For other cases in which moving expenses have been disallowed on the basis that the taxpayer did not earn employment or business income at the new work location, see *Avitan v. M.N.R.*, [1987] 1 C.T.C. 2434, 87 D.T.C. 336 (T.C.C.) and *Lopes v. Canada*, [1996] T.C.J. No. 1220, [1997] 1 C.T.C. 2169 (T.C.C.). Do you agree with these results as a matter of tax policy? Should taxpayers who relocate for the purpose of carrying on a business or obtaining employment at a new work location be prevented from deducting moving expenses if these plans are frustrated?

3.   In *James v. Canada*, [2001] T.C.J. No. 879, [2002] 2 C.T.C. 2376, 2002 D.T.C. 1723 (T.C.C.), aff'd [2003] F.C.J. No. 485, [2003] 3 C.T.C. 247, 2003 D.T.C. 5269 (F.C.A.), the taxpayer moved from Calgary to British Columbia in 1998, where he accepted an offer to provide information technology services to the provincial Liquor Distribution Branch under an agreement that required him to provide these services through a company that he was required to incorporate for this purpose. On the advice of his accountant, the taxpayer received no salary from his company, withdrawing funds solely in the form of dividends against which he sought to deduct moving expenses. Rejecting his appeal from an assessment that disallowed the deduction on the basis that the taxpayer did not receive business or employment income at the new work location, the court noted that the taxpayer could have deducted the expenses had he withdrawn

sufficient funds from his company in the form of a salary rather than dividends. According to the Federal Court of Appeal (at para. 3):

> In choosing to receive dividends on the advice of his accountant, the applicant derived certain advantages. But he thereby lost the possibility of deducting his moving expenses.

4.   Prior to 1998, subsection 62(1) stipulated that a taxpayer could only deduct moving expenses "in computing his income for the taxation year in which he moved from his old residence to his new residence or for the immediately following taxation year," permitting the deduction of moving expenses among other circumstances "to the extent that ... they were not deductible by virtue of this section in computing the taxpayer's income for the preceding taxation year." For 1998 and subsequent taxation years, the ITA does not explicitly limit the deduction of moving expenses to the year in which the taxpayer moved or "the immediately following taxation year" but continues to state in what is now paragraph 62(1)(b) that moving expenses may be deducted to the extent that they "were not deductible by virtue of this section in computing the taxpayer's income for the preceding taxation year."

Under the former language, two cases held that taxpayers who moved in one taxation year could deduct moving expenses only in that year or the immediately following taxation year. See *Duguay v. Canada*, [1996] T.C.J. No. 236, [1997] 3 C.T.C. 2212, (T.C.C.), where the taxpayer moved on March 4 1991, and sought to deduct moving expenses in computing his income for his 1992 and 1993 taxation years; and *Browning v. Canada*, [1996] T.C.J. No. 1776, [1997] 2 C.T.C. 3037 (T.C.C.), where the Court allowed the deduction of moving expenses in computing the taxpayer's income for his 1990 and 1991 taxation years, not his 1991 and 1992 taxation years, on the basis that he had moved on October 1, 1990, when they transported most of their furniture to their new residence (notwithstanding that they alternated between the old residence and the new residence until the old residence was sold in March 1991).

Under the amended language, three decisions have held that the carryforward for undeductible moving expenses is no longer limited to one year. In *Moodie v. Canada*, [2004] T.C.J. No. 337, [2004] 3 C.T.C. 2329 (T.C.C.), for example, Mogan T.C.J. declared (at para. 7) that:

> The words in the old provision which restricted the deduction of moving expenses to the taxation year "in which he moved" or the immediately following year do not appear in the new provision or in the new definition of "eligible relocation". I conclude that such restriction was intentionally omitted. In other words, Parliament intended that, for any taxation year after 1997, moving expenses may be deducted in the year of the move or any subsequent year to the extent that the taxpayer had employment or business income at a new work location against which the residual moving expenses could be applied.

Similarly, in *Edmond v. Canada*, [2004] T.C.J. No. 435, [2004] 5 C.T.C. 2423, 2004 D.T.C. 3244 (T.C.C.), Bowman A.C.J.T.C. (as he then was) observed (at para. 9) that:

> The words "to the extent that they were not deductible because of this section in computing the taxpayer's income for the preceding year..." do not, in my opinion, put a two-year limitation on the deductibility of moving expenses. Assume that an expense is incurred in

year one but the taxpayer's income for the new job is nil in that year and, say, is less than the moving expenses in year two. Clearly, the balance is deductible in year three when the income is sufficiently high. The amount deductible in year three is the amount that was not deductible in year two because of the limitation imposed by subsection 62(1). If Parliament wishes to put a limitation on the period in which expenses or losses can be carried forward or back it certainly knows how to say so, as it does with great specificity in section 111.

See also *Abrahamsen v. Canada*, [2007] T.C.J. No. 39, [2007] 3 C.T.C. 2001, 2007 D.T.C. 412 (T.C.C.) at para. 10, *per* Mogan T.C.J.:

> Under the pre-1998 legislation, moving expenses were deductible only in the taxation year when the taxpayer moved or "the immediately following taxation year". Under the current (post-1997) legislation, moving expenses are deductible to the extent that they were not deductible "because of this section ... for the preceding taxation year". Also, under paragraph 62(1)(*c*), moving expenses may be deducted only from the taxpayer's employment income at a new work location. In this appeal, if the Appellant did not have any employment income in Ontario in 2001 or in the last four months of 2000, then the 2002 taxation year would be the first taxation year in which his moving expenses would be deductible.

D. Child-Care Expenses

Like moving expenses, child-care expenses were also traditionally regarded as a non-deductible personal expense.[27] Effective January 1, 1972, however, the Act was amended to allow a limited deduction for child-care expenses under section 63. According to this provision, taxpayers may, subject to a number of limitations, deduct amounts paid "as or on account of child care expenses incurred for services rendered in the year in respect of an eligible child of the taxpayer." The following cases and commentary examine the various elements of this deduction, considering the definition of an "eligible child," the kinds of expenses that are eligible for the deduction, and statutory limitations on the deductibility of these expenses. A final section considers the decision in *Symes v. Canada*, [1993] S.C.J. No. 131, [1994] 1 C.T.C. 40, 94 D.T.C. 6001 (S.C.C.), which reconsidered the deductibility of child-care expenses as a business expense in light of the statutory deduction in section 63.

1. Eligible Child

The concept of an "eligible child" in relation to a taxpayer is defined in subsection 63(3) of the Act as:

(a)   a child of the taxpayer or of the taxpayer's spouse or common-law partner, or

---

[27]   See, for example, *No. 68 v. M.N.R.* (1952), 7 Tax ABC 110, 52 D.T.C. 333 (T.A.B.); *Nadon v. M.N.R.* (1965), 40 Tax ABC 33, 66 D.T.C. 1 (T.A.B.); *MacQuistan v. M.N.R.* (1965), 38 Tax ABC 23, 65 D.T.C. 236 (T.A.B.); *Pipe v. M.N.R.* (1966), 41 Tax ABC 132, 66 D.T.C. 388 (T.A.B.); *Lawlor v. M.N.R.*, [1970] Tax ABC 369, 70 D.T.C. 1248 (T.A.B.); and *King v. M.N.R.*, [1970] Tax ABC 1270, 71 D.T.C. 18 (T.A.B.).

(b)   a child dependent on the taxpayer or the taxpayer's spouse or common-law partner for support and whose income for the year does not exceed [the basic personal credit for the year, found in paragraph (c) of the description of B in subsection 118(1)]

provided that, "at any time during the year," the child

(c)   is under 16 years of age, or

(d)   is dependent on the taxpayer or on the taxpayer's spouse or common-law partner and has a mental or physical infirmity.

For the purpose of this provision, one should examine the extended definitions of "spouse" and "child" in section 252 and the definition of "common-law partner" in subsection 248(1).

Although the concepts of "dependence" and "support" have been addressed in the context of the personal tax credits in section 118 of the Act, judicial decisions do not appear to have considered these issues in the context of the child-care expense deduction. For the purposes of this chapter, there is no need to examine these concepts in any detail.

2. Eligible Expenses

For the purposes of the deduction in section 63, subsection 63(3) defines a "child care expense" as:

an expense incurred in a taxation year for the purpose of providing in Canada, for an eligible child of a taxpayer, child care services including baby sitting services, day nursery services or services provided at a boarding school or camp if the services were provided

(a)   to enable the taxpayer, or the supporting person of the child for the year, who resided with the child at the time the expense was incurred,

(i)   to perform the duties of an office or employment,

(ii)   to carry on a business either alone or as a partner actively engaged in the business, ...

(iv)   to carry on research or any similar work in respect of which the taxpayer or supporting person received a grant, or

(v)   to attend a designated educational institution or a secondary school, where the taxpayer is enrolled in a program of the institution or school of not less than three consecutive weeks duration that provides each student in the program spend not less than

(A)   10 hours per week on courses or work in the program, or

(B)   12 hours per month on courses in the program, and

(b)   by a resident of Canada other than a person

(i)   who is the father or mother of the child,

(ii)   who is a supporting person of the child or is under 18 years of age and related to the taxpayer, or

(iii) in respect of whom an amount is deducted under section 118 [personal tax credits] in computing the tax payable under this Part for the year by the taxpayer or by a supporting person of the child.

Paragraph (c) limits the amount that may be deducted in respect of camp and boarding school fees to a maximum dollar amount per week,[28] and paragraph (d) prohibits any deduction for amounts paid for "medical or hospital care, clothing, transportation or education or for board and lodging," except "as otherwise expressly provided" in the definition. In general, subsection 63(3) defines the term "supporting person" in relation to an eligible child of a taxpayer as "a person, other than the taxpayer, who is" the child's parent, the taxpayer's spouse or common law partner, or an individual who claimed the child as a dependant for the purpose of calculating tax credits under section 118, provided that this person "resided with the taxpayer at any time during the year and at any time within 60 days after the end of the year."

In order to satisfy this definition, an expense must satisfy three general requirements: (1) it must be for the purpose of providing "child care services, including baby sitting services, day nursery services or services provided at a boarding school or camp"; (2) the child-care services must be provided "to enable the taxpayer, or the supporting person of the child for the year, who resided with the child at the time the expense was incurred" to perform the duties of an office or employment, carry on a business or research in respect of which the taxpayer or supporting person received a grant, or attend a qualifying program at a secondary or post-secondary educational institution; and (3) the child-care services must be provided by a person other than the child's father or mother, a supporting person of the child, a person under the age of 18 who is related to the taxpayer, or a person in respect of whom a personal tax credit is deducted in computing the tax payable by the taxpayer or by a supporting person of the child. Each of these requirements is examined in turn.

a. Child-Care Services

Although the Act does not define the term "child care services," the definition of "child care expense" in subsection 63(3) of the Act states that these services include "baby sitting services, day nursery services or services provided at a boarding school or camp." In *Levine v. Canada*, [1995] T.C.J. No. 1487, [1995] 2 C.T.C. 2147 (T.C.C.), the court considered the scope of these services for the purposes of the child-care expense deduction.

---

[28] See the definitions of "periodic child care expense amount" and "annual child care expense amount" in subs. 63(3) of the Act. For 2000 and subsequent taxation years, the effect of these provisions is to cap deductible amounts for these expenses at $100 per week for children aged 7 or more at the end of the year, $175 per week for children under age 7 at the end of the year, and $250 per week for disabled children.

Levine v. Canada
[1995] T.C.J. No. 1487, 2 CTC 2147 (T.C.C.)

ARCHAMBAULT JTCC: ... In 1992, Mrs. Levine was a flight attendant working for Air Canada. Although she had been in Air Canada's employ for 15 years, she was still on call and had to accept flight assignments with very short notice. She went anywhere in the world and could be away as long as five days at a time. She usually worked 18 days per month and she was off 13 days. However, she could be asked to replace sick co-workers on her days off.

... Her husband, who testified on her behalf, estimated that she worked during weekends about half the time. Mr. Levine was a chartered accountant, an expert in forensic accounting, who worked long hours. His services could also be required on very short notice. He usually worked on Saturdays and sometimes on Sundays. In January 1992, the Levines had two children, aged seven and four. They had a live-in nanny to look after the children. The nanny worked no more than 50 hours a week and generally not on weekends. Mrs. Levine was able to make special arrangements with her to take into account her days off and trade weekend days for weekdays. The Levines also hired extra help from neighbours or got help from relatives for evenings and weekends.

As Mrs. Levine was expecting twins in the month of June, 1992, she stopped flying at the end of March and assumed ground duties until May 25 when the twins were born. Unfortunately for the Levines, the nanny decided to leave her employ soon after and they had a lot of difficulty finding a replacement. Many were hired but did not stay very long. They had to hire an agency to find a replacement. After two failures, the agency found a new nanny who is still working for them. They paid a finder's fee of $500 for this service. After the birth of the twins, Mrs. Levine took a 6-month maternity leave which was extended to March 1993.

In computing Mrs. Levine's income for 1992, the Minister refused the deduction of the following expenses:

Cost	Course
$169.00	Ballet Lessons
$77.00	Hampstead-Swimming
$155.79	Nautilus Plus Swimming
$135.00	Visual Arts Centre
$318.00	Mount Royal Ballet Lesson
$135.00	Ville Montréal Skating
$36.00	Hampstead-Swimming
$45.00	McGill University Tennis
$47.00	Pointe-Claire Swimming
$455.00	Hampstead Ski School
$170.00	Questo-Gymnastics
$50.00	Club Flexart-Gymnastics

$70.00	Côte St-Luc Skating
$35.00	Brownies
$500.00	Women's Domestic Service

The recreational activities described above represent lessons of a duration of one hour to one hour and a half once a week over a 12- to 13-week period, and in some instances over an 8-month period. The only exception is the ski school activity which was a whole day affair. They were either the activities of the seven year old or the four year old, but not both, except for the Nautilus swimming. They usually took place right after kindergarten or during the weekend.

...

Are the recreational expenses and the finder's fee deductible as child care expenses under section 63 of the *Income Tax Act* (Act)? The answer to this question depends on the application of the definition of child care expenses found in [subsection 63(3)] of the Act. ... It is useful to refer to the French version of the key words in [the definition of "child care expense" in subsection 63(3)]:

"frais de garde d'enfants" s'entend des frais engagés au cours d'une année d'imposition dans le but de faire assurer au Canada la garde de tout enfant admissible du contribuable, en le confiant à des services de garde d'enfants, y compris des services de gardienne d'enfants ou de garderie ou encore des services assurés dans un pensionnat ou dans une colonie de vacances, si les services étaient assurés. ...

What is the meaning and scope of "care" in English and "garde" in the French version? In the *Concise Oxford Dictionary*, "care" means, *inter alia*, "4 a. protection, charge, b. Brit. = child care." In *Le Petit Robert*, "garde" means:

Action de veiller sur un être vivant, soit pour le protéger (V. Défense, protection), soit pour l'empécher de nuire, (V. Surveillance). Confier un enfant à la garde de quelqu' un.

To better understand the scope of these words, it is useful to read them within the object and spirit of section 63 of the Act. This is in conformity with the teleological approach recently reiterated by the Supreme Court of Canada in *Québec (Communauté urbaine) v. Corporation Notre-Dame de Bon-Secours*, [1995] 1 CTC 241, 95 DTC 5017. ... We can find a review of the legislative intent of Parliament respecting section 63 in *Symes v. R*, [1994] 1 CTC 40, 94 DTC 6001, another decision of the Supreme Court of Canada. Iacobucci J there refers to the *Proposals for Tax Reform, 1969* where the following approach to child care expenses is described at page 15, para. 2.7:

We propose to permit deduction of the child care expenses that face many working parents today. The problem of adequately caring for children when both parents are working, or when there is only one parent in the family and she or he is working, is both a personal and a social one. We consider it desirable on social as well as economic grounds to permit a tax deduction for child care expenses, under carefully controlled terms, in addition to the general deduction for children.

In *McCluskie v. The Queen*, [1994] 1 CTC 2401, 94 DTC 1735 (TCC), Judge Rip of this Court made the following comments on the approach to be followed in interpreting section 63:

> Child care expenses were permitted by Parliament "under carefully controlled terms" and it is not for the courts to vary explicit terms. Where Parliament has drafted a provision of law in general terms, the Courts must use common sense in interpreting the provision.

Applying the above-mentioned principles, I conclude that the $500 finder's fee paid to Women's Domestic Service is a deductible expense because it was incurred for the purpose of providing child care services in Canada. The fee was paid to find a nanny to replace the previous one who had left. This expense was required to find the nanny who was to perform the child care services. In my view, it falls within the spirit of the section, which was to assist working parents in caring adequately for their children.

However, not all expenses incurred for the care of children are deductible. In particular, [paragraph (d) of the definition of "child care expense"] stipulates for greater certainty that education, medical and transportation costs are not child care expenses. I do not think that the recreational expenses disallowed by the Minister are child care expenses or "frais de garde d'enfants" within the meaning of [the definition of "child care expense" in subsection 63(3)] of the Act. These expenses were not incurred for the purpose of watching over the children to protect them, and therefore to enable the parents to earn income from employment. They were incurred to develop the physical, social and artistic abilities of the children. These expenses would have been incurred whether or not the parents had been working. The evidence has shown that these activities were carried out even if both parents were not working, that is, both during the period when Mrs. Levine was working and during her maternity leave. The fact that these activities were for a limited period of time, one hour to one hour and a half per week, sometimes just for a few weeks, also supports this conclusion. Attending a one-hour lesson can hardly be considered an effective way of watching over the children to protect them. It is, however, a very effective means of teaching children new physical and artistic abilities.

It was argued on behalf of the Appellant that these recreational activities had the benefit of providing care for the children.... It is true that the children, once they have been transported to the location of their lesson, are under the supervision of a responsible person. However, this person's primary role is not to watch over the children to protect them ["faire la garde" in French], but to teach ballet, swimming, skating, arts, etc. In my view, the children are being watched over is only an incidental benefit of the lessons. I do not believe that this type of expense was intended by the Canadian Parliament to be deductible. They are outside the scope of the "carefully controlled terms" of the Act. In conclusion, the recreational activities are not child care expenses within the meaning of [the definition of "child care expense" in subsection 63(3)] of the Act. ...

Appeal allowed in part.

NOTES AND QUESTIONS

1.   Why did the court in *Levine* allow the taxpayer to deduct the $500 finder's fee to find a replacement nanny? Why did it disallow the deduction of the other expenses claimed by the taxpayer? Do you agree with the court's conclusions? Why or why not?

2.   For other cases in which courts have disallowed the deduction of recreational expenses on the basis that the child-care services contemplated in subsection 63(3) are for the protection or guardianship of children, not the development of their physical, social, and artistic abilities, see *Keefer v. Canada*, [1999] T.C.J. No. 939, [2000] 2 C.T.C. 2622 (T.C.C.); *Bell v. Canada*, [2000] T.C.J. No. 844, [2001] 1 C.T.C. 2308 (T.C.C.); and *Burlton v. Canada*, [2001] T.C.J. No. 662, [2001] 4 C.T.C. 2710 (T.C.C.). In *Keefer*, for example, the court concluded (at para. 5) that:

> what is required and desired by Parliament is that the expenses be expenses, under carefully controlled terms, relating to the overwhelming component of guardianship, protection and child care. Had Parliament meant it to be broadened to include the type of expense claimed here by the Appellant, Parliament would have said so.

Similarly, in *Bell*, the court stated (at para. 16) that:

> to be deductible child care expenses must relate to the overwhelming component of guardianship, protection and child care. Recreational activities were never intended to be included as such an expense by Parliament, as these recreational activities do not have as their aim, providing care for the children. I believe that if one were to ask a volunteer hockey coach of young children if his primary duty was to be guardian or caregiver of these children, I do not believe his or her response would be in the affirmative. The protection and care giving are certainly a part of this activity but it is only secondary and incidental to the primary function that a hockey coach would view himself as having and that is to teach the basic skills of playing hockey.

3.   In *Acharya v. Canada*, [1996] T.C.J. No. 677, [1996] 3 C.T.C. 2173 (T.C.C.), the Minister disallowed the deduction of various expenses incurred in respect of the taxpayer's 13-year-old daughter on the grounds (at para. 4) that they were "tutorial in nature as opposed to child care" and that "a child of 13 does not really need much care or supervision." Allowing the taxpayer's appeal, the court stated (at para. 5) that "[e]ven if some education, musical or other, was involved, I would not find that sufficient in itself to hold that the amounts cannot qualify as child care." Although decided after *Levine v. Canada*, [1995] T.C.J. No. 1487, [1995] 2 C.T.C. 2147 (T.C.C.), the decision in *Acharya* did not refer to the decision in *Levine*.

4.   The CRA's views on the meaning of eligible child-care expenses are found in paragraphs 1 to 5 of *Interpretation Bulletin* IT-495R3, "Child Care Expenses," May 11, 2005. According to paragraph 3:

> 3. When an educational institution offers child care as well as an educational program, only the portion of the fees paid to the institution relating to child care (i.e., supervision before and after classes or during the lunch period) may qualify as child care expenses. However, when the payment made is for a child under the compulsory school age, the

services being provided are generally considered child care rather than education unless the facts indicate otherwise.

b. Purpose of Services

In order to qualify as deductible "child care expenses" under subsection 63(3) of the Act, not only must the expenses be incurred to provide "child care services," but these services must also be provided "to enable the taxpayer, or the supporting person of the child for the year, who resided with the child at the time the expense was incurred" to perform the duties of an office or employment, carry on a business or research in respect of which the taxpayer or supporting person received a grant, or attend a qualifying program at a secondary or post-secondary educational institution. A useful examination of this purpose requirement appears in *D'Amours v. M.N.R.*, [1990] T.C.J. No. 603, [1990] 2 C.T.C. 2355, 90 D.T.C. 1824 (T.C.C.).

D'Amours v. M.N.R.
[1990] T.C.J. No. 603, [1990] 2 C.T.C. 2355, 90 D.T.C. 1824 (T.C.C.)

LAMARRE-PROULX, TCJ: ... The appellant is a dental hygienist employed ... in Paspébiac. In late October 1984, when she was pregnant with her fourth child, she was allowed to leave her work as a preventive measure. The child was born on November 29, 1984. Under the collective agreement that applied to her the appellant continued to receive 95 per cent of her salary in accordance with the following formula: the employee received the benefits to which she was entitled under the unemployment insurance scheme and the employer made up the difference.

The appellant employed a babysitter in 1984 and kept this babysitter in her employ in the first four months of 1985. Between May and August the babysitter agreed temporarily to stop working for the appellant and began again in September, at which time the appellant returned to the duties of her employment. It is the expenses incurred for the services performed by this babysitter in the first four months of 1985 that are the subject of the dispute.

The respondent refused the deduction on the ground that the expenses were not incurred to enable the appellant to perform the duties of an office or employment, as required by [the definition of "child care expense" in subsection 63(3) of the Act]. The appellant's agent argued that the appellant was not unemployed or looking for work, that maternity leave was a benefit relating to employment and that the child care expenses were to be set off against earned income as defined in [subsection 63(3)] of the Act, which does not include benefits received under the *Unemployment Insurance Act, 1971* but includes such benefits as those described in paragraph 6(1)(f) of the Act that are paid pursuant to a sickness or accident insurance plan, a disability insurance plan or an income maintenance insurance plan.

...

1235

After mature reflection I feel that the appellant's argument is correct in law for the following reasons:

(1)   the babysitter was employed by the appellant prior to the maternity leave,

(2)   during the period in dispute the appellant kept her employment, and

(3)   the definition of earned income includes the sums received by the appellant from her employer during her maternity leave.

I shall consider each point in turn:

(1)   Since the babysitter was employed prior to the maternity leave, I accept the argument that she was employed for the purpose of enabling the appellant to perform her duties and not for strictly personal reasons. These were costs that the appellant had to continue to pay during her leave in order to ensure that the babysitter was still available when she returned to work. My decision would have been different if, for example, the services paid for were those of a casual employee who did not have to be kept in the appellant's employ during the maternity leave to ensure that she would be available when the appellant returned to work. In my judgment, these expenses would not then be covered by [subparagraph (a)(i) of the definition of "child care expense" in subsection 63(3)] but would be expenses incurred for strictly personal reasons.

(2)   The appellant kept her employment; it is a requirement of the provision in question that the taxpayer have an office or employment. The cost of child care must be incurred to enable the taxpayer to perform the duties of an office or employment.

(3)   If Parliament had wished to limit the application of this right to the period in which the person is physically at work, why would it have included in the definition of earned income certain sources of income other than earnings and gratuities such as, for example, the benefits described in paragraph 6(1)(f)? Parliament could have limited the definition of earned income to wages, salaries and other remuneration, including gratuities, received by the person in respect of, in the course of or by virtue of offices and employments. If the respondent's reasoning is taken to the limit, Parliament could even have excluded income earned during vacations from the definition of earned income. I am forced to conclude, therefore, that Parliament did not rule out situations where the person receives benefits in respect of, in the course of or by virtue of employment that he still holds, without being physically present at the work place, to the extent that the expenses claimed were incurred to perform the duties of the employment.

In a case such as this we must analyze the child care expenses claimed and determine whether they were related to the employment. I have concluded that the expenses claimed in this appeal were incurred to enable the appellant to perform the duties of her employment.

...

I believe that if I allow the deduction claimed by the appellant, I am taking into account the economic realities facing a parent who employs a babysitter, and I feel that my interpretation is consistent with both the wording and the object of the tax legislation.

The object of this legislation is, without any doubt, to enable parents who work to deduct child care expenses. It may happen that parents are unable to dismiss a babysitter or interrupt day care services not merely for personal reasons but because of economic reality. If a babysitter is dismissed, there may be little chance that she can be rehired at the end of the maternity leave. If a child is removed from day care, it may lose its priority on the waiting list and it may not be possible to have it readmitted to the day care at the desired time. This does not create the desirable permanence and quality of care for children that working parents need to enable them to perform their own jobs. In the circumstances, these expenses were not incurred for personal purposes but for purposes of employment. ...

Appeal allowed.

NOTES AND QUESTIONS

1.   Why did the Minister disallow the child-care expenses at issue in *D'Amours*? Why did the court allow the taxpayer's appeal? Of what relevance to the court's decision is the definition of "earned income" in subsection 63(3) of the Act? Would the expenses have been deductible if the taxpayer had not employed the nanny prior to her maternity leave? Would they have been deductible if she had quit her job before going on maternity leave? Do you agree with the decision? Why or why not?

2.   In *McCluskie v. Canada*, [1994] T.C.J. No. 13, [1994] 1 C.T.C. 2401, 94 D.T.C. 1735 (T.C.C.), the taxpayer applied in February 1990 to retain the services of a nanny who resided outside Canada, and hired the nanny when she arrived in Canada in July 1991, rather than waiting until the end of her maternity leave two months later. In computing her income for her 1991 taxation year, she sought to deduct payments made to the nanny during the months of July and August on the grounds (at para. 2) that:

> (1) she was required to hire a babysitter at the time the latter arrived in Canada or she would have risked losing the babysitter and then not be able to work, and (2) a training period for the babysitter and the three children of the appellant was necessary in that "a working parent cannot just leave their [*sic*] children with a stranger and hope everything is OK especially when the caretaker has just arrived from a foreign country."

Emphasizing the requirement in the definition of "child care expense" that the child-care services must be "provided ... to enable the taxpayer ... to perform the duties of an office or employment," the court disallowed the deduction of child-care expenses for the period before the taxpayer returned to work. According to Rip JTCC (at para. 33):

> The costs that a taxpayer incurs during leave while she or he is at home in order to ensure that the babysitter be available when the taxpayer eventually returns to work may be described as a "standby fee." The parent is at home presumably caring for the children and does not require a babysitter for that purpose. Nevertheless the parent realizes that if she or he wishes to retain that person's services when the parent returns to work, she or he must continue to pay that person. The babysitter, in these circumstances, is someone upon which the parent can rely and is paid a fee for the comfort of this reliance. The babysitter stands by the parent to render services in the future. This is a personal convenience to the parent. Such [a] fee is not a child care expense within the meaning of [the definition in subsection 63(3)].

Do you agree with this decision? Why or why not? Can *McCluskie* be reconciled with the decision in *D'Amours v. M.N.R.*, [1990] T.C.J. No. 603, [1990] 2 C.T.C. 2355, 90 D.T.C. 1824 (T.C.C.)?

3. In *McLelan v. Canada*, [1994] T.C.J. No. 951, [1995] 1 C.T.C. 2673 (T.C.C.), the taxpayer, who was on maternity leave from April 4, 1992 to October 10, 1992, sought to deduct payments made to a nanny who was hired immediately when she became available on August 2, 1992, "for fear of losing her and not being able later to find a good nanny." Referring to *D'Amours v. M.N.R.*, [1990] T.C.J. No. 603, [1990] 2 C.T.C. 2355, 90 D.T.C. 1824 (T.C.C.) and *McCluskie v. Canada*, [1994] T.C.J. No. 13, [1994] 1 C.T.C. 2401, 94 D.T.C. 1735 (T.C.C.), the Tax Court allowed the deduction, on the basis (at para. 12) that:

> although the appellant may not have required the nanny for the entire period, owing to market conditions relative to securing a good nanny, especially in her residential area, she felt that it was the most prudent thing to do to hire the nanny in question as soon as the nanny was available.

4. In *Sawicki v. Canada*, [1997] T.C.J. No. 1147, [1998] 1 C.T.C. 2448 (T.C.C.), the taxpayer, who suffered from depression but was able to work, sought to deduct as child-care expenses amounts allegedly paid to her nephew to care for her children on weekends and holidays. Notwithstanding the taxpayer's argument (at para. 5) that these services "uplift[ed] hers and her children's spirits" and "enabled her to continue working," Lamarre-Proulx TCJ concluded (at para. 9) that any such expense was "a personal expense that is not in the nature of a child care expense within the meaning of subsection 63(3) ... although it may in the end enable the taxpayer to work." According to the court (at para. 9):

> That subsection defines child care expenses. It is not an exhaustive definition but the services therein described indicate the scope of the meaning of child care services. *The meaning of a word depends on the context in which it is used (Dreidger on the Construction of Statutes*, 3rd ed. by Ruth Sullivan, Butterworths, p. 192). The child care services included in the definition are baby-sitting services, day nursery services or services provided at a boarding school or camp. It follows from the use of these associated words that the child care services

contemplated in s. 63 of the *Act* are services provided for the care of children when the parent cannot provide such care because of his employment or his business. It is in this sense that the child care services enable the parent to perform his employment duties or to carry on business.

Do you agree with this conclusion? Why or why not?

5.   Although the definition of child-care expenses in subsection 63(3) includes the cost of child-care services provided to enable the taxpayer to "perform the duties of an office or employment," it does not include the cost of child-care services to enable an unemployed taxpayer to search for an office or employment. Is this omission consistent with the purpose of the deduction outlined in IT-495R2, "to provide some relief for taxpayers who incur child care expenses in order to work, carry on a business or undertake certain training activities"? Is it consistent with the deductibility of expenses for child-care services to enable the taxpayer to attend a designated educational institution or secondary school?

According to Brian Arnold, "The Deduction for Child Care Expenses in the United States and Canada: A Comparative Analysis" (1973) 12 West. Ont. L. Rev. 1, at 11:

> In principle there is no difference between child care expenses while working and child care expenses while looking for work. However, a deduction for the latter expenses is subject to abuse because of the difficulty in determining when a taxpayer is "in active search for gainful employment."

6.   In *Lessard v. Canada*, [2003] T.C.J. No. 231, [2003] 4 C.T.C. 2097 (T.C.C.), the taxpayer deducted as child care expenses residence fees paid for her daughter while studying at the Royal Winnipeg Ballet School, which the Minister disallowed on the basis that the payments were not incurred in order to enable the taxpayer to perform the duties of an office or employment. Concluding (at para. 12) that the Act "does not require that the parent's choice of child care services be justified by the parent's work needs", the court allowed the taxpayer's appeal. According to Lamarre Proulx TCJ (at para. 12):

> The taxpayer is responsible for choosing the boarding school at which he or she wishes the child to study, or the child care services he or she wishes to use; the taxpayer makes this choice on the basis of the child 's needs, and this choice is an exercise of parental discretion. In the Court's opinion, the *Act* does not require that questions be asked about whether a particular form of child care is chosen on the basis of the parent's work needs or the child's needs.

Do you agree with this conclusion? Why or why not?

c. Child-Care Providers

According to paragraph (b) of the definition of the term "child care expense" in subsection 63(3), deductible expenses must be for child-care services provided by a person resident in Canada other than the mother or father of the child, a supporting person of the child, a person under the age of 18 years and related to the taxpayer, or a person whom the taxpayer or a supporting person of the child claimed as a dependant for the purpose of calculating tax credits under section 118. The categories of ineligible providers seem to be designed to prevent income splitting within the family unit, and appear to reflect the policy goal of the 1969 white paper to help address "[t]he problem of adequately caring for children when both parents are working, or when there is only one parent in the family and she or he is working." The exclusion of payments to specific providers in paragraph (b) of the definition of child-care expense in subsection 63(3) was considered in *Clogg v. Canada*, [1997] T.C.J. No. 292, [1997] CarswellNat 407 (T.C.C.).

Clogg v. Canada
[1997] T.C.J. No. 292, [1997] CarswellNat 407 (T.C.C.)

SOBIER, TCJ: The Appellant ... appeals ... from the assessment of the Minister for the 1993 and 1994 taxation years whereby the Minister disallowed the deduction of $10,000.00 in each of those years as child care expenses.

...

The day care centre into which the children of the Appellant were placed was operated by his wife, the children's mother, as a sole proprietorship.

Mr. Clogg maintains that by paying the money to a proprietorship operated by his wife under the name and style of "Wee People's Daycare," he is not paying it to his wife and therefore is not prohibited from claiming the child care expenses under [paragraph (b) of the definition of "child care expense" in subsection 63(3)] of the Act.

...

It is trite law that a sole proprietorship is carried on personally by the individual owning the proprietorship. It is not a separate and distinct entity such as a corporation. Therefore, the monies paid by Mr. Clogg were paid by him to his wife, the mother of the children for whom the day care was provided. Mrs. Clogg being the owner of the Wee People's Daycare provided the services and therefore the child care expense may not be claimed by Mr. Clogg.

Accordingly, the appeal with respect to the disallowance of the child care expenses is ... dismissed.

Appeal dismissed.

NOTES AND QUESTIONS

1.   Why did the court in *Clogg* disallow the deduction of child-care expenses claimed by the taxpayer? Might Mr. Clogg have been able to deduct the child-care payments if Mrs. Clogg had incorporated "Wee People's Daycare"? Might a tax-motivated incorporation of a day-care service to avoid the restrictions on the deduction of child-care expenses under section 63 be subject to the GAAR in section 245 of the Act?

2.   For another case in which child-care expenses have been disallowed on the basis that the services were provided by an ineligible person listed in paragraph (b) of the definition of "child care expense" in subsection 63(3), see *Babin v. Canada*, [2000] T.C.J. No. 581, [2000] WDFL 674, [2000] CarswellNat 1861 (T.C.C.), where child-care services were provided by the taxpayer's 17-year-old daughter.

3.   The statutory exclusion of payments to a spouse from the definition of the term "child care expense" in subsection 63(3) has been challenged, unsuccessfully, on the basis that it discriminates on the basis of family status, contrary to section 15(1) of the *Charter of Rights and Freedoms*. See *Ross v. Canada*, [1993] T.C.J. No. 237, [1993] 2 C.T.C. 2197 (T.C.C.) and *Boland v. M.N.R.*, [1993] T.C.J. No. 746, [1994] 1 C.T.C. 2001, (1993) 93 D.T.C. 1558 (T.C.C.). In *Boland*, Teskey JTCC stated (at para. 23):

> A reading of this history shows that the child care expense deduction was enacted to help working parents to adequately care for their children by enabling them to deduct part of the cost of hiring a third party to look after the children. The purpose of the deduction is to supplement the cost of child care where both parents or a single parent are working. It is not to subsidize in general the cost of raising children.

In *Ross*, Christie ACJTCC concluded (at para. 15):

> The basic social purpose of the legislation is certainly within the legislative competence of Parliament and I cannot appreciate how this Court could properly set the legislation aside in whole or in part because of the requirement that the child care services in respect of which the deduction for child care expense is sought be provided by someone other than the father or the mother of the eligible child. This condition precedent is perfectly reasonable and understandable in the light of the purpose of section 63 and it does not constitute discrimination of the kind alleged in this appeal.

Do you agree with these conclusions? Why or why not? Consider the following argument in David G. Duff, "Disability and the Income Tax" (2000) 45 McGill L. J. 797 at 857:

> [T]he requirement ... that child care expenses ... must be for services provided by a third party provider ... reflect a traditional view according to which child care is properly the responsibility of a stay-at-home parent and should be recognized for tax purposes only where this parent incurs expenses to engage in income-earning activities. To the extent that child care is viewed as a joint responsibility of both parents, however, which may be accomplished through payments to a third party or by a division of labour in which one parent works in the paid labour force while the other becomes the primary caregiver, it is arguable that the income tax should recognize alternative child care arrangements by ... allowing a parent participating in the paid labour force to deduct amounts paid to a caregiving parent up to the maximum amount permitted by the dollar ceilings. In addition to recognizing the economic partnership underlying this division of labour, this reform could enhance gender equality by encouraging transfers of income from higher income-earning breadwinners (who tend to be male) to lower income-earning caregivers (who tend to be female), and enable stay-at-home spouses who care for dependent children to accumulate independent Registered Retirement Savings Plan ("RRSP") contribution room and qualify more easily for CPP/QPP benefits and employment insurance.

Would such a reform risk reinforcing traditional female roles as homemakers and caregivers?

3. Limitations on Deductibility

Section 63 contains three general limitations on the deductibility of child-care expenses as these are defined in subsection 63(3). First, under subparagraph 63(1)(e)(ii) and the definition of "annual child care expense amount" in subsection 63(3), the amount that may be deducted cannot exceed $10,000 per year for each disabled child, $7,000 for each child who is under 7 years of age at the end of the year, and $4,000 for each other eligible child. Second, under subparagraph 63(1)(e)(i), the amount that may be deducted cannot exceed 2/3 of the taxpayer's "earned income for the year," as defined in subsection 63(3). According to this definition, "earned income" generally means the total of a taxpayer's incomes from all offices, employments, and businesses, as well as the taxable amount of scholarships, fellowships, bursaries and prizes, research grants, taxable earnings supplements, and amounts received "as, on account of, in lieu of payment of or in satisfaction of, a disability pension under the *Canada Pension Plan* or a provincial plan as defined in section 3 of that Act." Finally, by virtue of subsection 63(2), the deduction must generally be claimed by the parent or other supporting person with the lower income.[29] The impact of these limitations is exemplified in *Reinstein v. Canada*, [1995] T.C.J. No. 937, [1995] 2 C.T.C. 2924 (T.C.C.), in which the court also commented on the complexity of the statutory provisions by which they are defined.

---

[29] This result is achieved by para. 63(2)(b), which creates an exception to this general rule for "the number of weeks in the year during which child care expenses were incurred and throughout which the supporting person was" a qualifying student as defined in subpara. 63(2)(b)(iii), disabled according to subpara. 63(2)(b)(iv), confined to a prison or similar institution as set out in subpara. 63(2)(b)(v), or living separate and apart because of marriage breakdown at the end of the year and for a period of at least 90 days beginning in the year (subpara. 63(2)(b)(vi)). For a year in which a supporting person does not qualify under subpara. 63(2)(b)(iii)-(vi) at any time, the effect of subs. 63(2) is to disallow any deduction for child-care expenses incurred by a taxpayer whose income for the year exceeds the income of the supporting person. In these circumstances, the supporting person may, by virtue of para. 63(1)(b), deduct the child-care expenses under subs. 63(1) in computing his or her own income, subject to the limitations in subpara. 63(1)(e)(i) and (ii). Where the supporting person qualifies under one or more of subpara. 63(2)(b)(iii) to (vi) for one or more weeks in the taxation year in which the child-care expenses were incurred, the taxpayer may claim $150 per week for each eligible child who is under 7 years of age or disabled and $90 per week for each other eligible child, subject to the limitations in subpara.s 63(1)(e)(i) and (ii). Where the aggregate of these amounts is less than the maximum amounts in subpara. 63(1)(e)(ii), the supporting person may, by virtue of para. 63(1)(b), deduct an amount under subs. 63(1) in computing his or her own income, subject to the limitations in para. 63(1)(e) and (f). Finally, where the income of taxpayer is (without taxing into account any deduction for child-care expenses) equal to that of a supporting person in a taxation year, subs. 63(2.1) prohibits the deduction of any child-care expenses under s. 62 unless the taxpayer and the supporting person "jointly elect to treat the income of one of them as exceeding the income of the other for the year."

Reinstein v. Canada
[1995] T.C.J. No. 937, [1995] 2 C.T.C. 2924 (T.C.C.)

BELL JTCC: The appeals of Susan Maxwell and Arlen C. Reinstein were heard together. As these reasons apply to both Appellants, I shall refer to them individually by their surnames.

The Appellants are married and have three children, each of whom is an "eligible child" within the meaning of section 63 of the *Income Tax Act* ("Act"). The issue is whether Maxwell is entitled to a deduction of child care expenses [as] claimed by her in the 1992 taxation year and whether Reinstein is entitled to a deduction if Maxwell is not entitled. Generally, a taxpayer may deduct expenses incurred by him or her or by a "supporting person" of the child. Only payments made for child care services permitting either the taxpayer or the "supporting person" to earn income from an office, employment or business, to carry on research or to undertake occupational training may be deducted.

A taxpayer is entitled to a deduction only to the extent of "earned income," being income from business, an office or employment, training allowances, scholarships and research grants but not including investment income. Further, as between a taxpayer and a "supporting person," only the person with the lower income may claim the deduction unless that person is unavailable to take care of the children, for example, being a full time student or a prisoner.

In 1992, Maxwell paid $13,728 for child care services. Under the Act she could deduct only the lesser of two-thirds of her earned income and a formula determined amount based on the number of children under seven years of age. The amount determined under this formula is $12,000. Her earned income was $11,388.50 ... [She has a deduction of] two-thirds of that sum, namely $7,592.26.

Subsection 63(2) applies where the income of the taxpayer claiming a deduction is greater than that of the "supporting person." Reinstein was a "supporting person" of the children. However under that subsection, the amount that Maxwell could claim is the lesser of the amount actually claimed, namely $7,592.26 and another formula computed amount which in these circumstances is zero [because Reinstein had no earned income]. The result is that Maxwell, being entitled to a deduction of the lesser of those two amounts, is entitled to no deduction whatever for child care expenses.

Reinstein, by virtue of paragraph 63(1)(b) could [subject to the various limitations in section 63] deduct child care payments from his own income. His deduction is limited to the lesser of a fraction of his earned income (zero) and $4,000 per year for each eligible child, namely $12,000. Because Reinstein had no earned income in the taxation year, his income being from a registered retirement savings plan, unemployment insurance, investment, interest and dividends, he is entitled to no deduction during the year.

It is incredible that the legislation respecting child care expenses is so convoluted. Not only is the theory complex and arbitrary but the draftsmanship leaves one mired in legislative mud. It is bad enough for legislation to be as complex as it is in very technical areas such as the resource industry and foreign accrual property income. Where lawyers and judges struggle to comprehend provisions designed to help taxpayers in ordinary every day situations, how can those taxpayers be expected to make reasoned claims or to support claims made? Taxpayers should be able to file returns and claim deductions based upon the *Income Tax Act* and Regulations. That is virtually impossible for those seeking child care expense deductions.

Appeal dismissed.

NOTES AND QUESTIONS

1.   Aside from criticizing the manner in which section 63 is drafted, Bell JTCC in *Reinstein* describes the "theory" underlying the limitations on the deductibility of child-care expenses as "complex and arbitrary." Do you agree with this characterization? Why or why not?

2.   In a number of cases, deductions for child-care expenses have been limited or disallowed altogether on the basis that the amount claimed exceeded two-thirds of the taxpayer's earned income. For example, in *Lederhouse v. Canada*, [1993] T.C.J. No. 827, [1994] 1 C.T.C. 2094 (T.C.C.), the taxpayer, a professional geologist, sought to deduct child-care expenses during a year in which her income consisted mostly of employment insurance benefits and RRSP income, arguing (at para. 5) that:

> in order for me to remain employable, it was necessary for me to sustain my childcare situation. ... Most often, men seeking employment are available on short notice to fill a particular situation as they are not the principal caregivers for their children. In order to remain competitive, it was mandatory for me to be available on short notice as well.

On the basis that the taxpayer had no earned income for the year, the court disallowed the child-care expenses claimed by the taxpayer.

In *Matsi v. Canada*, [1994] T.C.J. No. 1178, [1995] 1 C.T.C. 2583 (T.C.C.), the taxpayer, who had started a new business from which he had yet to derive income, sought to deduct child-care expenses from an annual income of $17,138, comprised entirely of funds withdrawn from his RRSP. The court disallowed the deduction on the basis that the RRSP income was not "earned income" according to the definition in subsection 63(3).

In *McCoy v. Canada*, [1996] T.C.J. No. 680, [1996] 3 C.T.C. 2263 (T.C.C.), where the taxpayer participated in a job creation project for which she received unemployment insurance benefits in part of 1992 and 1993, deductions for child-care expenses in were limited to two-thirds of her employment income in each of these years. Responding to the taxpayer's argument that the limitation on deductibility was unfair given that the unemployment insurance benefits were taxable and participation in the job creation project required her to incur increased child-care expenses, Bowman JTCC concluded (at para. 10):

> I agree with Mrs. McCoy that the result seems unfair and anomalous. Unfortunately, the law is clear and there is nothing I can do for her. Her objection, which has merit, is essentially a political and not a legal one and this court is not the forum in which the situation can be rectified.

Is Mrs. McCoy's objection "essentially a political and not a legal one"? Might the definition of "earned income" in subsection 63(3) be subject to a legal challenge under the *Charter of Rights and Freedoms*? Should the definition of "earned income" be amended to include employment insurance benefits and income from an RRSP?

3.   What is the purpose of the limitation on deductible expenses to two-thirds of a taxpayer's "earned income"? Might this purpose be adequately achieved by the requirement that allowable child-care expenses must be incurred to enable the taxpayer to perform the duties of an office or employment, carry on a business or research in respect of which the taxpayer or supporting person received a grant, or attend a qualifying program at a secondary or post-secondary educational institution?

Consider the following criticism of this limitation in Brian Arnold, "The Deduction for Child Care Expenses in the United States and Canada: A Comparative Analysis" (1973) 12 West. Ont. L. Rev. 1 at 24:

> The effect of the limitation is to prevent taxpayers with small earned incomes from taking a full deduction. Therefore, the earned income limitation ... discriminates against taxpayers with small incomes. It might be argued that the limitation was designed to prevent a taxpayer from working for one day and taking a child care expense deduction for the whole year. But, the work requirement would seem to prevent this type of abuse in a much more equitable manner. By virtue of that requirement a taxpayer would be unable to deduct child care expenses for any period in which he was not employed or carrying on business. It is more likely that the earned income limitation reflects the judgment that a taxpayer, who incurs child care expenses in excess of two-thirds of his earned income, is working in order to be able to pay for child care services rather than incurring child care expenses in order to be able to work. Once again the work requirement would seem to be the more equitable way of dealing with this problem. If the taxpayer can satisfy the work requirement, the determination of an acceptable profit margin should be left to him. Since lower income taxpayers will be likely to find smaller profit margins acceptable, the earned income limitation discriminates against them without any justification. It should be deleted from the section.

Do you agree with this critique? Why or why not?

4.   In *Metcalf v. Canada*, [1995] T.C.J. No. 726, [1995] 2 C.T.C. 2740 (T.C.C.), the taxpayer reported employment income of $51,261.00 in 1993, while her husband, who was attempting to establish a woodworking business after losing his job, reported $10,859.00 in income derived from the redemption of an RRSP in order to invest in his business. Disallowing the deduction of child-care expenses by the taxpayer under subsection 63(2) on the grounds that the husband was a "supporting person" with a lower income, the Tax Court sympathized with the taxpayer's argument (at para. 14) that:

> [i]n the case of the small businessman who is working six, seven days a week but not bringing in a salary, I find that the law is inflexible, in that there is an assumption being made that my husband is at home and able to provide daycare or child care to his own child, and that assumption is incorrect. He is out working. He just doesn't have a salary to show for it. He's struggling to make a small business successful. ... I have a legitimate need to use an outside person other than somebody within my own family to provide that service to me. ... I

understand that there's a law in place. Maybe what needs to be done is the law needs to be changed.

According to Lamarre-Proulx JTCC (at paras. 14 and 17-18):

It is difficult not to agree with the Appellant's viewpoint. A review of the judgments of this Court on similar cases indicates to me that other judges of this Court thought in the same way: the legislative provision regarding the deduction of child care expenses, where the lower income of the supporting person comes from the carrying of a business, begs to be amended. ...

It seems clear that the object of section 63 of the Act is and was to ease the financial cost of providing for the care of children to working parents in the pursuit of earning income. However, the result of the legislation, as it stands now, is that parents employed in high-earning jobs will have, as a family unit, the benefit of a deduction for the care of their children ... [w]hereas, a family unit, in which one spouse earns income from employment and the other, having lost his well-paying job, tries his most to succeed in a business that does not yet yield income, does not have the benefit of any deduction for the care of the children although incurring the same expenses but with less assets.

It belongs to the Legislator to find a cure. The Tribunal can only bring the matter to the Legislator's attention and care. The relevant provisions of the Act being very clear, I have no option but to regretfully dismiss the appeal.

There are other cases in which child-care expenses have been disallowed on the basis that they must be claimed by a supporting person with a lower income. For example, in *Canada v. Copeland*, [1993] T.C.J. No. 584, [1993] 2 C.T.C. 3046 (T.C.C.), the taxpayer, whose wife was not employed and had no income, sought to deduct $1,448 in fees paid for his daughter to attend the Montessori Learning Centre in Ajax, Ontario. Rejecting the taxpayer's argument that the prohibition on deductibility in subsection 63(2) contravenes the equality rights provision of the *Charter of Rights and Freedoms*, Bowman TCCJ held (at paras. 8-9):

I cannot grant Mr. Copeland the relief he seeks without in effect rewriting section 63. This would necessitate tinkering with the other sections of the Act that are related within the overall legislative scheme. This is the prerogative of Parliament. It is not an endeavour upon which this court should embark merely because one group of Canadians is permitted a deduction and another is not. While I tend to agree with Mr. Copeland that section 63 can lead to anomalies and may well be unfair, it is not the function of the Charter or the business of the courts to remove those anomalies or to correct a perceived unfairness unless they can be attributed to the types of discrimination envisaged by section 15 of the Charter. Although I unequivocally reject the suggestion that the *Income Tax Act* is in some way immune to scrutiny under the Charter on the basis that to consider whether the provisions of Canada's most important piece of fiscal legislation are in accordance with the supreme law of Canada somehow "trivializes" the latter, nonetheless the purpose of the Charter must be kept in perspective. That purpose is, among others, to prevent discrimination against "discrete and insular minorities" based on the grounds set out in section 15, or grounds analogous thereto. Mr. Copeland's contention is that the "discrete and insular minority" to which he belongs is a group consisting of two parent families in which one parent has voluntarily chosen to stay at home and not earn income. Such a choice is a responsible and difficult one and it frequently, as Mr. Copeland points out, involves a financial sacrifice. To suggest that the work of a parent who stays at home for the sake of his or her children is any less onerous or important than that of one who chooses to join the workforce would be to belittle one of society's most sacred institutions.

> The choice, commendable as it may be, is, however, a voluntary one and it carries with it benefits and burdens — fiscal, financial and social. Persons, who make such a choice, as did Mr. and Mrs. Copeland, do not belong to the type of minority that it is the function of the Charter to protect. The treatment of such persons in a manner that differs from the treatment of persons who make a different choice is not discriminatory.

Do you agree with the decision in *Copeland*? Why or why not? Should deductions for child-care expenses generally be limited to the lower-income spouse? Do you think that the Montessori school fees in *Copeland* constituted a "child care expense" within the meaning of the definition in subsection 63(3) of the Act?

5.   In *Fiset v. M.N.R.*, [1988] T.C.J. No. 16, [1988] 1 C.T.C. 2335, 88 D.T.C. 1223 (T.C.C.), the taxpayer sought to deduct $4,000 in child-care expenses incurred in 1984 in respect of his two children, even though his new spouse, whom he married on December 21, 1984, was not employed and had no income. Accepting the taxpayer's argument that limitation in subsection 63(2) does not apply where the supporting person (the taxpayer's spouse) has *no* income, the Tax Court allowed the deduction. The same interpretation was subsequently accepted in *M.N.R. v. McLaren*, [1990] F.C.J. No. 827, [1990] 2 C.T.C. 429, 90 D.T.C. 6566 (F.C.T.D.), where the taxpayer, whose husband had no income in 1983, deducted $535 under section 63 in computing her income for the 1983 taxation year.

In response to these decisions, section 3 was amended, effective for 1990 and subsequent taxation years, to stipulate in paragraph 3(f) that where a taxpayer has no income, "the taxpayer shall be deemed to have income for the year in an amount equal to zero."

In *Fromstein v. Canada*, [1993] T.C.J. No. 155, [1993] 2 C.T.C. 2214, 93 D.T.C. 726 (T.C.C.), Sobier TCCJ registered his objection to the manner in which the Act was amended, stating (at paras. 1-2) that:

> in what was apparently a knee-jerk reaction to these cases, the *Income Tax Act* ... was amended badly, hastily, and without proper consideration of what it was doing. I think that by enacting paragraph 3(f) as it was enacted, without giving proper consideration to what was intended by section 63, was a quick patch-over and enacted in order to negate the effects of *McLaren* and *Fiset, supra.* They did so with a sledgehammer rather than with a scalpel. I believe that the problems could have been faced and dealt with in a more sophisticated fashion than they were, but they were not. They were using a very dull sword to cut out the heart of the decisions of *McLaren* and *Fiset*. However, cut out that heart they did. ... I would strongly urge the Ministry of Finance and the Ministry of National Revenue to rethink the blundering way in which they try to get around *McLaren* and *Fiset* and to take a look at what their real purpose was and that is to benefit a family of two working parents.

Is the enactment of paragraph 3(f) inconsistent with the policy underlying subsection 63(2)? Were the decisions in *Fiset* and *McLaren* consistent with the policy underlying subsection 63(2)? Is Sobier TCCJ's concern with the enactment of paragraph 3(f) or with the structure of section 63?

6.   As a further requirement for the deduction of child-care expenses, subsection 63(1) requires taxpayers to prove that amounts in respect of child-

care expenses have been paid "by filing with the Minister one or more receipts each of which was issued by the payee and contains, where the payee is an individual, that individual's Social Insurance Number."

In *Senger-Hammond v. Canada*, [1996] T.C.J. No. 1609, [1997] 1 C.T.C. 2728 (T.C.C.), where the taxpayer failed to submit appropriate receipts, the Tax Court considered whether this requirement was mandatory or merely directory. Allowing the deduction, Bowman JTCC concluded (at para. 28), "I think that the words in section 63 requiring the filing of receipts with the payee's social insurance numbers are directory rather than imperative, and that the failure to do so is not fatal to deductibility. This conclusion is consistent with the wording of the Act and its object." Do you agree or disagree with this interpretation? Why?

For an opposing view of the requirement that child-care expenses be proven by submitting appropriate receipts, see *Barclay v. Canada*, [1994] T.C.J. No. 576, [1995] 1 C.T.C. 2345 (T.C.C.). Other cases have distinguished *Senger-Hammond* on the grounds that the taxpayer failed to provide sufficient evidence to corroborate the actual payment of child-care expenses, failed to make reasonable efforts to comply with the requirements of section 63, or was grossly negligent in obtaining proper receipts: *Ritchie v. Canada*, [1997] T.C.J. No. 1176, [1998] 1 C.T.C. 2950 (T.C.C.); *Lachowski v. Canada*, [1997] T.C.J. No. 694, [1997] 3 C.T.C. 2924 (T.C.C.); *Bijai v. Canada*, [1998] T.C.J. No. 1051, [1998] CarswellNat 2369 (T.C.C.); and *Senechal v. R* (August 10, 2001), Doc. No. 97-3297(IT)I, [1998] CarswellNat 1680 (T.C.C.).

4. Business Expenses and the Statutory Deduction

Although child-care expenses were traditionally characterized as non-deductible "personal or living expenses," the cases in which these judgments were made were all trial level decisions rendered between 1952 and 1979.[30] In *Symes v. Canada*, [1993] S.C.J. No. 131, [1994] 1 C.T.C. 40, (1993) 94 D.T.C. 6001 (S.C.C.), the issue was reconsidered in light of changes in the social context for characterizing "personal or living expenses" as well as the introduction of section 63.

Symes v. Canada
[1993] S.C.J. No. 131, [1994] 1 C.T.C. 40, (1993) 94 D.T.C. 6001 (S.C.C.)

[The taxpayer, a practising lawyer and mother of one child from 1982 to 1984 and two children in 1985, employed a nanny at a salary of $10,075 in 1982, $11,200 in 1983, $13,173 in 1984, and $13,359 in 1985, which she sought to

---

[30] See, for example, *No. 68 v. M.N.R.* (1952), 7 Tax ABC 110, 52 D.T.C. 333 (T.A.B.); *Nadon v. M.N.R.* (1965), 40 Tax ABC 33, 66 D.T.C. 1 (T.A.B.); *MacQuistan v. M.N.R.* (1965), 38 Tax ABC 23, 65 D.T.C. 236; *Pipe v. M.N.R.* (1966), 41 Tax ABC 132, 66 D.T.C. 388 (T.A.B.); *Lawlor v. M.N.R.*, [1970] Tax ABC 369, 70 D.T.C. 1248 (T.A.B.); and *King v. M.N.R.*, [1970] Tax ABC 1270, 71 D.T.C. 18 (T.A.B.).

deduct in computing her professional income from her legal practice. Characterizing these payments as "personal or living expenses" the deduction of which is prohibited in computing a taxpayer's income from a business under paragraph 18(1)(h) of the Act, the revenue authorities disallowed the deduction of these amounts, substituting instead lesser amounts of $1,000 in 1982, $2,000 in each of 1983 and 1984, and $4,000 in 1985, as were then allowed under section 63 of the Act. The taxpayer appealed.]

IACOBUCCI J (Lamer CJ and LaForest, Sopinka, Gonthier, Cory and Major JJ concurring): ... My analysis of income tax law principles applicable to business deductions will proceed in the following way. Immediately below, I will describe the statutory framework which supports business expense deductibility. Then, I will examine deductibility issues *per se* under four headings. Under the first, I will discuss the interrelationship of subsection 9(1) and paragraphs 18(1)(a) and 18(1)(h) of the Act, in order to clarify the proper analytical approach in this case. Under the second, I will comment upon the historical classification of child care expenses as personal expenses, in order to define the relevance of paragraph 18(1)(h) of the Act. Under the third, I will examine paragraph 18(1)(a) of the Act in a search for indicia of business expenses which can be compared to the facts of this case. Finally, under the fourth, I will consider the relevance of the child care expense deduction in section 63 of the Act.

...

(i) Business income: The interrelationship of subsection 9(1), paragraphs 18(1)(a) and 18(1)(h)

Leaving aside for the moment the potential impact of section 63, three provisions of the Act which deal with business income determination are relevant in this case, and the language of each is worthy of note. First, by virtue of subsection 9(1), a taxpayer's income from business is stated to be the taxpayer's "profit therefrom for the year," "profit" being nowhere defined in the Act. Second, paragraph 18(1)(a) provides that in computing business income, no deduction shall be made for an expense "except to the extent that it was made or incurred by the taxpayer for the purpose of gaining or producing income." Finally, in paragraph 18(1)(h), a prohibition against deducting "personal or living expenses" is established. The proper approach to these three provisions is the initial point to be examined.

At one time, it was not clearly understood whether the authority for deducting business expenses was located within what is now subsection 9(1) or within what is now paragraph 18(1)(a). In a series of decisions culminating in *Royal Trust Co. v. Minister of National Revenue*, [1957] CTC 32, 57 DTC 1055 (Ex. Ct.), however, Thorson, P recognized that the deduction of business expenses is a necessary part of the subsection 9(1) "profit" calculation. In *Daley v. Minister of National Revenue*, [1950] CTC 254, 50 DTC 877 (Ex. Ct.),

Thorson, P commented upon section 3 (the forerunner to section 9) and subsection 6(a) (the forerunner to paragraph 18(1)(a)) of the *Income War Tax Act*, RSC 1927, c. 97, in the following terms (at page 261 (DTC 880)):

> The correct view, in my opinion, is that the deductibility of the disbursements and expenses that may properly be deducted "in computing the amount of the profits or gains to be assessed" is inherent in the concept of "annual net profit or gain" in the definition of taxable income contained in section 3. The deductibility from the receipts of a taxation year of the appropriate disbursements or expenses stems, therefore, from section 3 of the Act, if it stems from any section, and not at all, even inferentially, from paragraph (a) of section 6.

In other words, the "profit" concept in subsection 9(1) is inherently a net concept which presupposes business expense deductions. It is now generally accepted that it is subsection 9(1) which authorizes the deduction of business expenses; the provisions of subsection 18(1) are limiting provisions only.

...

Under subsection 9(1), deductibility is ordinarily considered as it was by Thorson, P in *Royal Trust, supra*, (at page 40 (DTC 1059)):

> ... the first approach to the question whether a particular disbursement or expense was deductible for income tax purposes was to ascertain whether its deduction was consistent with ordinary principles of commercial trading or *well accepted principles of business ... practice. ...*

...

Adopting this approach to deductibility, it becomes immediately apparent that the well accepted principles of business practice encompassed by subsection 9(1) would generally operate to prohibit the deduction of expenses which lack an income earning purpose, or which are personal expenses, just as much as paragraphs 18(1)(a) and (h) operate expressly to prohibit such deductions. For this reason, there is an artificiality apparent in the suggestion that one can first examine subsection 9(1) in order to determine whether a deduction is authorized, and can then turn to subsection 18(1) where another analysis can be undertaken: N. Brooks, "The Principles Underlying the Deduction of Business Expenses" in B.G. Hansen, V. Krishna and J.A. Rendall, eds., *Essays on Canadian Taxation* (1978), 249, at pages 253-54; V. Krishna, *The Fundamentals of Canadian Income Tax* (4th ed. 1992), at page 365, footnote 44, and page 367.

...

There is no doubt that, in some cases, subsection 9(1) will operate in isolation to scrutinize deductions according to well accepted principles of business practice. In this respect, I refer to cases, also noted by the trial judge, in which the real issue was whether a particular method of accounting could be used to escape tax liability: e.g. *Associated Investors of Canada Ltd. v. Minister of National Revenue*, [1967] CTC 138, 67 DTC 5096 (Ex. Ct.); *Canadian General Electric Co. v. Minister of National Revenue*, [1962] SCR 3, [1961] CTC 512, 61 DTC 1300. In other cases, including the present case, however, the real issue may be whether a deduction is prohibited by well accepted principles of business practice *for the reason* that it is not incurred for the purpose of earning income, or *for the reason* that it is a personal or living expense. In such cases, any treatment of the issue will necessarily blur subsection 9(1) with paragraphs 18(1)(a) and (h).

I proceed, therefore, to deal with closely related arguments respecting the specific language of paragraphs 18(1)(a) and 18(1)(h). In so doing, I mean to cast no doubt upon the proposition that subsection 9(1) contains the authority for deduction, nor do I wish to suggest that subsection 9(1) is not the first section against which a deduction is to be measured. Instead, I simply wish to acknowledge that, on the facts of this case, I cannot respond to the arguments of the parties without necessarily addressing the general language of subsection 9(1), and the specific language of paragraphs 18(1)(a) and 18(1)(h), at the same time.

(ii) Personal expenses and paragraph 18(1)(h)

I begin with paragraph 18(1)(h), since traditional tax analysis characterized child care expenses as personal expenses, such that in modern terms, paragraph 18(1)(h) would operate to specifically prohibit them .... [T]he line of reasoning supporting such a characterization is ultimately founded upon the English decision of *Bowers v. Harding* [(1891), 3 TC 22], and brief examination of that case can help to explain the historical classification of child care expenses as personal expenses.

In *Bowers, supra*, the Hardings (a married couple) were employed in the operation of a school, and they received a joint salary for this employment. Mr. Harding engaged a household servant, according to the admitted facts of the case, in order "to enable his wife to have time to perform her duties as schoolmistress" (page 23). Since the relevant tax legislation treated the couple's joint salary as Mr. Harding's alone, he sought to deduct the expense of the housekeeper upon the basis that it was incurred "wholly, exclusively, and necessarily in the performance of the duties of his ... employment": *Income Tax Act* (UK), 16 & 17 Vict., c. 34, section 51.

The attempted deduction was disallowed. In the eyes of the court, the Hardings were proposing a "but for" test for deductibility. In other words, they were arguing that "but for the housekeeper," the income could not have been earned. Baron Pollock rejected this test in the following terms (at page 564):

> When a man and a woman accept an office there are certain detriments as well as profits, but this is in no sense an expenditure which enables them to earn the income, in the sense of its being money expended upon goods, or in the payment of clerks, whereby a tradesman or a merchant is enabled to earn an income. ... If we were to go into these questions with great nicety, we should have to consider the district in which the person lives, the price of meat, and the character of the clothing that he would require, in many places indeed the character of the services and the wages paid to particular servants, and the style in which each person lives, before we could come to any conclusion.

I am aware that many people might question the applicability of the language and circumstances of *Bowers, supra*. Indeed, there are many ways that it might be distinguished. First, it deals with income from employment, rather than with income from business. Second, the expense in question related to "housekeeping," rather than to child care (or, at least, if child care was involved, the case report fails to disclose so). Third, the expense was compared against the very strict requirement that it be made "wholly, exclusively and necessarily" for the purpose of earning the income, and no identical requirement arises on the facts of this case. Finally, perhaps, like the trial judge below, one could merely focus upon the fact that the case came from "another age" and from "another system" (page 483 (DTC 5248)).

Even without distinguishing *Bowers, supra*, in this fashion, however, I believe that I should move beyond paragraph 18(1)(h) of the Act and the traditional classification of child care in the analysis of whether child care expenses are truly personal in nature. The relationship between expenses and income in *Bowers, supra*, was subsumed in that case, as it was in cases to follow, within an apparent dichotomy. As stated by Professor Arnold, "The Deduction for Child Care Expenses," supra, at page 27:

> The test established by the case for distinguishing between personal and living expenses involved a determination of the origin of the expenses. If the expenses arose out of personal circumstances rather than business circumstances the expense was a non-deductible personal expense.

There are obvious tautologies within this approach. "Personal expenses" are said to arise from "personal circumstances," and "business expenses" are said to arise from "business circumstances." But, how is one to locate a particular expense within the business/personal dichotomy?

This appeal presents a particular expense which has been traditionally characterized as personal in nature. If, in coming to a decision, this Court stated that since such expenses have always been personal, they must now be personal, the conclusion could be easily and deservedly attacked. For this reason, proper analysis of this question demands that the relationship between child care expenses and business income be examined more critically, in order to determine whether that relationship can be sufficient to justify the former's deductibility. This proposition, in my opinion, leads naturally to paragraph 18(1)(a), which sets out the relationship required by the *Income Tax Act*.

In turning to paragraph 18(1)(a), however, I must take pains not to eviscerate needlessly paragraph 18(1)(h) and its related jurisprudence. When faced with a particular expense, it may be both proper and expedient to refer to past decisions which have characterized the expense as "personal" within 18(1)(h), such that an extensive analytical approach involving the words of paragraph 18(1)(a) may not be required. On the facts of this case, paragraph 18(1)(a) may be of greater assistance than the simple prohibition against deducting "personal expenses" in paragraph 18(1)(h), as I re-examine whether child care expenses truly constitute personal expenses. However, not every expense which has been traditionally characterized as a personal expense will deserve a similar re-examination.

Why, in this case, is it appropriate to re-examine extensively whether child care expenses are appropriately characterized as personal expenses? Relying upon the evidence of the expert witness, Armstrong, the trial judge had this to say (at page 483 (DTC 5248)):

> ... There has been a significant social change in the late 1970s and into the 1980s, in terms of the influx of women of child-bearing age into business and into the workplace. This change post-dates the earlier cases dismissing nanny expenses as a legitimate business deduction and therefore it does not necessarily follow that the conditions which prevailed in society at the time of those earlier decisions will prevail now.

I consider the existence of the trend discussed in this paragraph to be relatively non-controversial, such that the point could have been accepted even without the assistance of an expert.

The decision to characterize child care expenses as personal expenses was made by judges. As part of our case law, it is susceptible to re-examination in an appropriate case. In *Salituro v. The Queen*, [1991] 3 SCR 654, 68 CCC (3d) 289, this Court had occasion to state the following (at page 670 (CCC 301)):

> Judges can and should adapt the common law to reflect the changing social, moral and economic fabric of the country. Judges should not be quick to perpetuate rules whose social foundation has long since disappeared. Nonetheless, there are significant constraints on the power of the judiciary to change the law. ... The judiciary should confine itself to those incremental changes which are necessary to keep the common law in step with the dynamic and evolving fabric of our society.

The increased participation of women in the Canadian workforce is undoubtedly a change in the "social foundation" within the meaning of *Salituro*. Accordingly, I do not feel that I must slavishly follow those cases which have characterized child care expenses as personal in nature. It now falls to be considered whether the alternative is appropriate. In other words, are child care expenses not prohibited by paragraph 18(1)(a) of the *Income Tax Act*?

(iii) Business expenses and paragraph 18(1)(a)

In order to be deductible as business expenses, the appellant's child care expenses must have been incurred "for the purpose of gaining or producing income from the business" within the meaning of paragraph 18(1)(a) of the Act.

...

As in other areas of law where purpose or intention behind actions is to be ascertained, it must not be supposed that in responding to this question, courts will be guided only by a taxpayer's statements, *ex post facto* or otherwise, as to the subjective purpose of a particular expenditure. Courts will, instead, look for objective manifestations of purpose, and purpose is ultimately a question of fact to be decided with due regard for all of the circumstances. For these reasons, it is not possible to set forth a fixed list of circumstances which will tend to prove objectively an income gaining or producing purpose. Professor Brooks has, however, in summarizing some reoccurring factual patterns, elucidated factors to be considered, and I find his discussion generally helpful: *supra*, at pages 256-59. In the following paragraphs, I will make reference to some of these factors.

It may be relevant in a particular case to consider whether a deduction is ordinarily allowed as a business expense by accountants. This is not to revert to the notion that accountancy will govern under subsection 9(1) of the Act, since accountants "have no special expertise in making" (Brooks, *supra*, at page 256) the business versus personal expense judgment. Instead, such evidence may simply indicate that a particular kind of expenditure is widely accepted as a business expense. Similarly, it may be relevant to consider whether the expense is one normally incurred by others involved in the taxpayer's business. If it is, there may be an increased likelihood that the expense is a business expense.

It may also be relevant to consider whether a particular expense would have been incurred if the taxpayer was not engaged in the pursuit of business income. Professor Brooks comments upon this consideration in the following terms (at page 258):

> If a person would have incurred a particular expense even if he or she had not been working, there is a strong inference that the expense has a personal purpose. For example, it is necessary in order to earn income from a business that a business person be fed, clothed and sheltered. However, since these are expenses that a person would incur even if not working, it can be assumed they are incurred for a personal purpose — to stay alive, covered, and out of the rain. These expenses do not increase significantly when one undertakes to earn income.

> ...

Here, the test suggests that "but for the gaining or producing of income, these expenses would still need to be incurred."

...

Taking up this last point, I note that in a tax system which is at least partly geared toward the preservation of vertical and horizontal equities ("[h]orizontal equity merely requires that 'equals' be treated equally, with the term 'equals' referring to equality of ability to pay" and "vertical equity merely requires that the incidence of the tax burden should be more heavily borne by the rich than the poor": V. Krishna, "Perspectives on Tax Policy" in *Essays on Canadian Taxation, supra*, at pages 5 and 6-7), one seeks to prevent deductions which represent personal consumption. To the extent that a taxpayer can make a lifestyle choice while maintaining the same capacity to gain or produce income, such choices tend to be seen as personal consumption decisions, and the resultant expenses as personal expenses. ... In some cases, it may be helpful to analyze expenses in these terms.

... [I]t may also be helpful to discuss the factors relevant to expense classification in need-based terms. In particular, it may be helpful to resort to a "but for" test applied not to the expense but to the need which the expense meets. Would the need exist apart from the business? If a need exists even in the absence of business activity, and irrespective of whether the need was or might have been satisfied by an expenditure to a third party or by the opportunity cost of personal labour, then an expense to meet the need would traditionally be viewed as a personal expense. Expenses which can be identified in this way are expenses which are incurred by a taxpayer in order to relieve the taxpayer from personal duties and to make the taxpayer available to the business. Traditionally, expenses that simply make the taxpayer available to the business are not considered business expenses since the taxpayer is expected to be available to the business as a quid pro quo for business income received. This translates into the fundamental distinction often drawn between the earning or source of income on the one hand, and the receipt or use of income on the other hand.

It remains to consider the appellant's child care expenses in light of this discussion. First, it is clear on the facts that the appellant would not have incurred child care expenses except for her business. It is relevant to note in this regard that her choice of child care was tailored to her business needs. As a lawyer, she could not personally care for her children during the day since to do so would interfere with client meetings and court appearances, nor could she make use of institutionalized daycare, in light of her working hours. These are points which were recognized by the trial judge.

Second, however, it is equally clear that the need which is met by child care expenses on the facts of this case, namely, the care of the appellant's children, exists regardless of the appellant's business activity. The expenses were incurred to make her available to practice her profession rather than for any other purpose associated with the business itself.

Third, I note that there is no evidence to suggest that child care expenses are considered business expenses by accountants. There is, however, considerable reason to believe that many parents, and particularly many women, confront child care expenses in order to work. There is, first of all, the evidence of the expert witness, already discussed above. In addition, the record before this Court includes a report by Status of Women Canada, entitled the *Report of the Task Force on Child Care* (1985), which demonstrates that a very large number of working parents require non-parental care for their children (see, e.g., Table 4.2). As well, the intervener Canadian Bar Association presented this Court with survey information which specifically addresses the experience of lawyers in Ontario. That information suggests that for lawyers with children, a significant proportion of child care responsibility is borne by paid child care workers, and the mean proportion is over 250 per cent greater for women (25.56 hours per week) than for men (9.53 hours per week): Law Society of Upper Canada, *Transitions in the Ontario Legal Profession* (1991). This demographic picture may increase the likelihood that child care expenses are a form of business expense.

Finally, as a fourth point of analysis, I am uncomfortable with the suggestion that the appellant's decision to have children should be viewed solely as a consumption choice. I frankly admit that there is an element of public policy which feeds my discomfort. In *Brooks v. Canada Safeway Ltd.*, [1989] 1 SCR 1219, 59 DLR (4th) 321, Dickson, CJ stated (at page 1243 (DLR 339)):

> That those who bear children and benefit society as a whole thereby should not be economically or socially disadvantaged seems to bespeak the obvious. It is only women who

bear children; no man can become pregnant ... it is unfair to impose all of the costs of pregnancy upon one half of the population.

The appellant and her husband freely chose to have children, and they further determined that the costs of child care would be paid by the appellant. However, it would be wrong to be misled by this factual pattern. Pregnancy and childbirth decisions are associated with a host of competing ethical, legal, religious, and socio-economic influences, and to conclude that the decision to have children should — in tax terms — be characterized as an entirely personal choice, is to ignore these influences altogether. While it might be factually correct to regard this particular appellant's decision to have children as a personal choice, I suggest it is more appropriate to disregard any element of personal consumption which might be associated with it.

...

The factors so far analyzed suggest that, considering only section 9 and paragraphs 18(1)(a) and 18(1)(h), arguments can be made for and against the classification of the appellant's child care expenses as business expenses. In another case, the arguments might be differently balanced, since the existence of a business purpose within the meaning of paragraph 18(1)(a) is a question of fact, and that the relative weight to be given to the factors analyzed will vary from case to case. However, in general terms, I am of the view that child care expenses are unique: expenditures for child care can represent a significant percentage of taxpayer income, such expenditures are generally linked to the taxpayer's ability to gain or produce income, yet such expenditures are also made in order to make a taxpayer available to the business, and the expenditures are incurred as part of the development of another human life. It can be difficult to weigh the personal and business elements at play.

...

I am aware that if I were compelled to reach a conclusion with respect to the proper classification of child care expenses with reference to only section 9 and paragraphs 18(1)(a) and 18(1)(h) of the *Income Tax Act*, such a conclusion would involve competing policy considerations. On the one hand, there is value in the traditional tax law test which seeks to identify those expenses which simply make a taxpayer available to the business, and which proceeds to classify such expenses as "personal" for the reason that a "personal need" is being fulfilled. On the other hand, however, it is inappropriate to disregard lightly the policy considerations which suggest that choice and consumption have no role to play in the classification of child care expenses.

In the Federal Court of Appeal, a needs-based analysis carried the day. The court concluded that "the concept of a business expense has been developed exclusively in relation to the commercial needs of the business, without any regard to the particular needs of those in charge" (page 9 (DTC 5403)). If other policy considerations are disregarded, an availability analysis virtually compels this conclusion. In this regard, however, I find interesting the comments of Professor Macklin which relate to the conclusion of the Federal Court of Appeal just quoted (A. Macklin, *"Symes v. Minister of National Revenue:* Where Sex Meets Class" (1992), 5 CJWL 498, at pages 507-8):

> This assertion failed to acknowledge that as long as business has been the exclusive domain of men, the commercial needs of business have been dictated by what men (think they) need to expend in order to produce income. The fact that these expenditures also have a "personal" element was never treated as a complete bar. It seems closer to the truth to suggest that these practices inhere in the way men, or some men, engage in business. Of course, since men have (until very recently) been the only people engaging in business, it is easy enough to conflate the needs of businessmen with the needs of business. Women's needs in doing business will necessarily be different, and one might reasonably demand a reconceptualization of "business expenses" that reflects the changing composition of the business class.

Although I wish to make no comment about expenses which have a "personal" element but which are nonetheless currently treated as business expenses, and although Professor Macklin fails to note the role of taxpayer availability in her discussion of "needs," it is difficult to argue that history has not conflated the "needs of businessmen with the needs of business" as Professor Macklin suggests. Therefore, to the extent that traditional income tax law would classify child care expenses as "personal" simply because such expenses are incurred in order to make the taxpayer "available" to the business — and in the absence of section 63 — it might be correct to assert that the changing composition of the business class and changing social structure demand a reconceptualization.

However, I find it unnecessary to determine whether reconceptualization is appropriate having regard to the presence of section 63 in the *Income Tax Act.* Section 63 cannot be lightly disregarded (E.A. Driedger, *Construction of Statutes* (2nd ed. 1983), at page 87):

> ... the words of an Act are to be read in their entire context and in their grammatical and ordinary sense harmoniously with the scheme of the Act, the object of the Act, and the intention of Parliament.

In fact, as I will now attempt to demonstrate, I do not believe that section 9 and paragraphs 18(1)(a) and 18(1)(h) can be interpreted to account for a child care business expense deduction, in light of the language used in section 63.

(iv) The effect of section 63

The appellant argues that the presence of section 63 in the *Income Tax Act* should not affect the deductibility of child care costs as business expenses. She suggests that the language of that provision does not operate to confine taxpayers in making deductions for child care expenses. Additionally, she relies upon the decision in *Olympia Floor & Wall Tile Co. (Quebec) v. Minister of National Revenue,* [1970] CTC 99, 70 DTC 6085 (Ex. Ct.) to suggest that when a taxpayer has expenses which exceed an amount made deductible by a specific provision of the Act, the taxpayer can have recourse to a more general provision in order to deduct the full amount. In my opinion, her arguments must fail.

Considering first the language of section 63, it is readily apparent that the Act's definition of "child care expenses" specifically comprehends the purpose for which the appellant incurred her nanny expenses. According to part of that definition, a child care expense is one incurred in order to provide child care services "to enable the taxpayer ... to carry on a business either alone or as a partner": [subparagraph (a)(ii) of the definition of "child care expense" in subsection 63(3)]. Furthermore, paragraph 63(1)(e) operates to cap the deduction with reference to "earned income," which is defined in [subsection 63(3)] to include "incomes from ... businesses carried on either alone or as a partner actively engaged in the business."

The fact that this language accurately describes the situation at hand — i.e., a law partner paying child care in order to work — is itself persuasive reason to suppose that section 9 and paragraphs 18(1)(a) and 18(1)(h) cannot be interpreted to permit a child care business expense deduction. Décary, JA, in the Federal Court of Appeal below, considered this language to be "clear and not open to question," and suggested that section 63 is "really a code in itself, complete and independent" (page 9 (DTC 5404)). In addition to the plain language of the quoted provisions, however, there are other reasons to believe that this is the correct interpretation.

One such reason is the structure of section 63 itself. Section 63 places a number of limitations upon the child care deduction. It varies the deduction according to the taxpayer's earned income, or, according to the product obtained when a fixed sum is multiplied by the number of children requiring care, subject to an annual ceiling. In addition, when two or more taxpayers have contributed during a year to the support of a child, the scheme established by section 63 ordinarily limits the deduction in a further way: it makes the deduction available only to the lower earning supporter (see subsection 63(2)).

To the extent that section 63 intends to limit child care expense deductions to lower earning supporters, the appellant's position could substantially undermine that intent. In this case, the appellant and her husband admittedly made a "family decision" to the effect that the appellant alone bears the financial burden of child care: see Federal Court of Appeal judgment, at page 3 (DTC 5399). By proffering evidence on this point, the appellant would seek to avoid the definition of "supporting person" in [subsection 63(3)] of the Act, which would statutorily define her husband as such a person, notwithstanding the "family decision." In the result, she would take a complete deduction of the child care expenses, free from the consideration of whether or not she is the lower earning supporter.

The appellant's approach is unworkable. For example, consider the case of two spouses living with an eligible child, one of whom is an employee earning a low income, and the other of whom is a businessperson earning a higher income. The approach of the appellant clearly invites this couple to make a "family decision" in order to establish that the cost of child care is the sole responsibility of the taxpayer with business income. Without casting aspersions upon the appellant, I fear that in many cases there would be more bookkeeping than reality about such a decision. The courts being poorly suited to assess the validity of "family decisions" of this sort, I am inclined to believe that the intent of section 63 is to prevent the need for such assessments. Further, by statutorily defining both parents to be responsible for child care expenses for tax purposes, [the definition of a "supporting person" in subsection 63(3)] is entirely congruent with a contemporary understanding of parental obligations in that regard.

Additionally, it is important to acknowledge the context of section 63 within the *Income Tax Act* as a whole. Section 63 exists within Division B, subdivision e of the Act. As set out in paragraph 3(c), the deductions permitted by this subdivision are made only after income from each of the various sources has been calculated. In this regard, it is relevant to consider section 4. Paragraph 4(1)(a) of the Act provides that each source of income is initially considered in isolation as one determines the taxpayer's overall income for the year. Then, subsection 4(2) provides that in applying subsection 4(1), "no deductions permitted by sections 60 to 63 are applicable either wholly or in part to a particular source."

Brief reference to subsection 4(2) is made in the respondent's factum. Aside from this reference, the section was not otherwise discussed by the parties in this case, and it has not been the subject of any significant commentary of which I have been made aware. For this reason, I do not wish to overstate the importance of subsection 4(2) to my analysis. Subsection 4(2) obviously means that the child care expense deduction in section 63 is not referable to a particular source of income. In other words, the section 63 calculation is not relevant to the computation of business income. Less obviously, however, it may also mean that the *type* of deduction provided for in section 63 (i.e., any deduction in respect of child care expenses) cannot occur within the source calculations. In other words, subsection 4(2) may be further evidence that section 63 is intended to be a complete legislative response to the child care expense issue.

At this point, it is appropriate to discuss *Olympia Floor & Tile, supra,* upon which the appellant relied in order to deny that the specific deduction allowed by section 63 must override the potential for a more general deduction elsewhere in the Act. In that case, unchallenged evidence was led to establish that between 25 and 30 per cent of a taxpayer's sales in each of two taxation years went toward charitable gifts. The taxpayer sought to deduct the full amount of such gifts, arguing that the sums were expended in order to increase future sales, and that for this reason, they constituted business expenses. The Minister took the position, however, that the deductibility of the gifts was governed by paragraph 27(1)(a) of the Act [now section 110.1] which established that a taxpayer could deduct charitable "gifts" not exceeding 10 per cent of the taxpayer's taxable income for the year.

Jackett P accepted the taxpayer's position. He was convinced that the taxpayer made the contributions largely, if not entirely, "for the purpose of increasing its sales and only subsidiarily, if at all, for charitable or benevolent reasons" (at page 101 (DTC 6086)). For this reason, he was satisfied that the expenses could constitute business expenses, and the important question became the effect of paragraph 27(1)(a). Jackett P recognized that paragraph 27(1)(a) calculated the allowable charitable deduction with reference to the taxpayer's income, and stated (at page 104 (DTC 6088)):

> ... it follows that what is being permitted by that provision is a deduction of an amount that has been given out of the corporation's income after it has been earned and not a deduction of an amount that has been laid out as part of the income earning process. ...

From this position, it was then a simple matter for Jackett P to conclude that the taxpayer's expense was not the sort of expense contemplated by the language of paragraph 27(1)(a). He did so in the following terms (at page 105-06 (DTC 6089):

> In my view, when a taxpayer makes an outlay for the purpose of producing income — i.e. as part of his profit making process — even though that outlay takes the form of a "gift" to a charitable organization, it is not a "gift" within the meaning of that word in paragraph 27(1)(a) which, by reason of the place it holds in the process of computing taxable income, was obviously intended to confer a benefit on persons who made contributions *out of income* and was not intended to provide deductions for outlays made in the course of the income earning process.

[Emphasis in original.]

In the result, therefore, the taxpayer could deduct the charitable donations as part of its business profit calculation, notwithstanding the specific provision relating to the deduction of charitable gifts.

...

I wish to express neither approval nor disapproval of the approach taken ... with respect to the charitable donation issue *per se*. Instead, it is sufficient to highlight the real basis for the decision in *Olympia Floor & Tile*. In my view, what that case says is that a particular expenditure, such as a charitable donation, may be made for more than one purpose. In such a case, it will be relevant to consider whether the actual purpose of the expenditure is addressed in the Act. If a specific provision exists which limits deductibility in respect of that purpose, then that should be the end of the matter. If, however, the purpose is not addressed in a specific provision, recourse may be had to more general rules governing deductibility.

In this case, the appellant willingly admits — indeed, she argues — that she has incurred child care expenses in order to gain or produce income. Only one purpose for the expenses has been advanced. On the facts of *Olympia Floor & Tile, supra*, a donation made with a truly charitable intent (out of a taxpayer's previously calculated "income") would undoubtedly have been limited by the specific language of paragraph 27(1)(a). Likewise, on the facts of this case, the purpose for which the appellant maintains she has incurred her child care expenses falls squarely within the language of section 63; they were, she argues, incurred in order to "enable" her to "carry on a business ... as a partner" within the meaning of [subparagraph (a)(ii) of the definition of "child care expense" in subsection 63(3)], and they were incurred for that reason alone. Since that purpose is specifically addressed in section 63 of the Act, she cannot claim a deduction employing that same purpose under section 9. Thus, I do not find persuasive support for the appellant's position from *Olympia Floor & Tile*, *supra*.

Although it is unnecessary to my conclusion, I wish to note, finally, that evidence of Parliamentary intent appears to support my view. At the outset of his reasons, Décary JA in the Federal Court of Appeal reviewed the fiscal history of child care expenses, as well as government policies on such expenses, and I consider his discussion helpful. I wish, however, to make particular note of the proposals which directly led to the 1972 introduction of section 63. In *Proposals for Tax Reform* (1969) (E.J. Benson, Minister of Finance), the following approach to child care expenses is advocated (at page 15):

> 2.7 We propose to permit deduction of the child care expenses that face many working parents today. The problem of adequately caring for children when both parents are working, or when there is only one parent in the family and she or he is working, is both a personal and a social one. We consider it desirable on social as well as economic grounds to permit a tax deduction for child care expenses, *under carefully controlled terms*, in addition to the general deduction for children. ...
>
> 2.9 This new deduction for child care costs would be a major reform. While it is not possible to make an accurate forecast of the number who would benefit from this new deduction, it seems likely to be several hundred thousand families. It would assist many mothers who *work or want to work* to provide or supplement the family income, but are discouraged by the cost of having their children cared for. ...

[Emphasis added]

These proposals suggest to me that section 63 was intended by Parliament to address comprehensively child care expenses. I cannot imagine that a system which allowed some parents to deduct expenses under general provisions respecting business income, but which confined others to a section 63 regime, would permit deductibility "under carefully controlled terms" within the meaning of the above quotation. Further, I am not impressed by the suggestion that Parliament intended section 63 to limit deductibility only for employees. The proposals do not specify the kind of "work" which is to be encouraged, and the language of section 63 clearly addresses income from business.

For these reasons, a straightforward approach to statutory interpretation has led me to conclude that the *Income Tax Act* intends to address child care expenses, and does so in fact, entirely within section 63. It is not necessary for me to decide whether, in the absence of sections 63 and 9, paragraphs 18(1)(a) and 18(1)(h) are capable of comprehending a business expense deduction for child care. Given section 63, however, it is clear that child care cannot be considered deductible under principles of income tax law applicable to business deductions.

L'HEUREUX-DUBÉ J (McLachlin J concurring in dissent): ... I do not agree with my colleague Iacobucci J's reasons with regard to section 63 of the Act...

and the eventual result he reaches. I do, however, substantially agree with the approach he has taken with regard to the definition of "business expense" through subsection 9(1), paragraphs 18(1)(a) and (h) of the Act and, as a result, I will not repeat a similarly detailed analysis in this regard, but will only review the essential points and provide my own insight into the two first questions at hand. In my view, the logical conclusion to my colleague's analysis, although he does not state it as such, is that section 9 and paragraphs 18(1)(a) and 18(1)(h) do not prevent the deduction of child care expenses as a business expense. My analysis, therefore, will focus primarily on the clear differences between our two positions, specifically with respect to section 63 of the Act.

...

As my colleague asserts, child care expenses have traditionally been viewed as expenses that were not incurred for the purpose of gaining or producing income, as they were considered personal in nature and, accordingly, could not be regarded as commercial. My colleague is of the view (at page 50) that:

> [T]here *is* value in the traditional tax law test which seeks to identify those expenses which simply make a taxpayer available to the business, and which proceeds to classify such expenses as "personal" for the reason that a "personal need" is being fulfilled.

[Emphasis in original]

In my view, such a test serves no purpose. The rationale of availability to the business is neither objective nor determinative. To be available for the business is the first requirement of doing business, otherwise, there can be no business. In this regard, it would be unthinkable for a business person's special needs, for example those associated with a disability, to be ineligible for deduction because they satisfy a "personal need." A woman's need for child care in order to do business is no different. One's personal needs can simply not be objectively determined, they are by their very definition subjective.

Courts in the past, and the Court of Appeal in this case, have also always assumed that commercial needs were an objectively neutral set of needs. As a consequence, they did not examine the close relationship between child care and women's business income.

...

When we look at the case law concerning the interpretation of "business expense," it is clear that this area of law is premised on the traditional view of business as a male enterprise and that the concept of a business expense has itself been constructed on the basis of the needs of businessmen. This is neither a surprising nor a sinister realization, as the evidence well illustrates that it has only been in fairly recent years that women have increasingly moved into the world of business as into other fields, such as law and medicine. The definition of "business expense" was shaped to reflect the experience of businessmen, and the ways in which they engaged in business. As Dorothy Smith points out in "A Peculiar Eclipsing: Women's Exclusion From Man's Culture" (1978), 1

Women's Studies Int. Quart. 281, when only one sex is involved in defining the ideas, rules and values in a particular domain, that one-sided standpoint comes to be seen as natural, obvious and general. As a consequence, the male standard now frames the backdrop of assumptions against which expenses are determined to be, or not to be, legitimate business expenses. Against this backdrop, it is hardly surprising that child care was seen as irrelevant to the end of gaining or producing income from business but rather as a personal non-deductible expense.

... [T]he world of yesterday is not the world of today. In 1993, the world of business is increasingly populated by both men and women and the meaning of "business expense" must account for the experiences of all participants in the field. This fact is enhanced by expert evidence which indicates that the practices and requirements of business women may, in fact, differ from those of businessmen. When we look at the current situation, it becomes clear that one of the critical differences in the needs of businessmen and business women is the importance of child care for business people with children, particularly women.

...

The reality of Ms. Symes' business life necessarily includes child care. The 1993 concept of business expense must include the reality of diverse business practices and needs of those who have not traditionally participated fully in the world of business.

...

In conclusion to the question of whether child care expenses are precluded from being deducted as a business expense under subsection 9(1) by the interplay of either paragraph 18(1)(a) or paragraph 18(1)(h) of the Act, I answer that child care may be held to be a business expense deductible pursuant to subsection 9(1) and paragraphs 18(1)(a) and (h) of the Act, all other criteria being respected. This result leads me to the most crucial consideration in this appeal, that is whether section 63 of the Act precludes the deduction of child care expenses as a business expense. Here, I part company with my colleague since, in my view, section 63 of the Act, properly interpreted, is no such bar.

...

The argument of the respondent rests on the proposition that the availability of deductions under section 63 is incompatible with the availability of child care deductions pursuant to subsection 9(1). In other words, the mere existence of section 63 prevents any deduction for child care under subsection 9(1) of the Act. My answer is twofold. First, there is nothing in the wording of section 63 that overrides the application of section 9. Second, such an interpretation is, in my view, in contradiction with the purpose and historical basis for the enactment of section 63, with traditional approaches to diverse deductions under the Act and, finally, with the Charter.

...

I suggest that... many of the same questions, that were examined with regard to the above analysis of subsection 9(1) and paragraphs 18(1)(a) and 18(1)(h), must take place in the context of section 63. Just as these sections of the Act have developed with regard solely to the needs of a traditionally male practice of business, so has the history of section 63 been tainted by a specific view of the world.

...

Section 63 was implemented in order to adapt to the needs of a society at that time. In 1972, when that section was enacted, societal ideals with regard to equality of the sexes and the equal participation of women in all aspects of society had not evolved to the point where they have today.

...

According to my colleague ... since the wording of section 63 of the Act clearly includes the appellant's nanny expenses, section 63 acts as a complete bar, rendering the appellant Symes ineligible to deduct her child care expenses as a business expense. I do not interpret section 63 of the Act in such a fashion. Section 63 and subsection 9(1), in my view, may co-exist. The fact that Parliament enacted a section to benefit all parents in the paid work force without distinction does not prevent a taxpayer who is in business from deducting an expense which can be legitimately claimed as a business expense. Section 63 provides general relief to parents, but nothing in its wording implies that deductions available under subsection 9(1) are abolished or restricted in this respect. Had Parliament intended to submit the deduction of child care expenses to the application of section 63 it would have expressed it in clear language. In providing that none of the deductions permitted by sections 60 to 63 are applicable to a particular source of income, subsection 4(2) of the Act clearly provides for some deductions which may legitimately fall under two sections of the Act. In addition, it is not insignificant that the text of section 63 is permissive as opposed to the negative wording of paragraphs 18(1)(b) and 18(1)(e), which are clearly intended to limit the allowable deductions to only those permitted under these paragraphs. Finally, it is important to note that the taxpayer in this case is not seeking to claim a section 63 deduction from a source, but is seeking a source deduction, independent of the section 63 deduction for child care, for a business expense.

The appellant argues that the availability of a deduction for child care expenses is consistent with principles of income tax as accepted in *Olympia Floor & Wall Tile, supra* ... . My colleague distinguishes *Olympia, supra*, in that the deduction there allowed is of a different order than that claimed in the case at hand. There, the taxpayer argued that the expense had been incurred for two distinct purposes, while, in the case at hand, only one purpose is argued. This, in my view, has absolutely no bearing on the interpretation of section 63, contrary to the view of my colleague. While it is true that the taxpayer in this case has claimed only that the child care expenses she has incurred are in order to gain or produce income from her business, the rationale in both cases is the same and the cases cannot be distinguished with any significance.

...

The fact that section 63 may be available to others or to the same taxpayer who would prefer to claim the deductions under that section does not in any way impede the application of section 9, which clearly applies to business expenses.

...

Regardless of whether the many factors I have set out above are determinative, certainly these many considerations lead one to the conclusion that, at the very least, section 63 is ambiguous in its effect on subsection 9(1). In such circumstances one must resort... to the general rules of statutory interpretation which make it clear that ambiguities are to be resolved in favour of the taxpayer.

...

Finally, in this regard, one must not lose track of the fact that section 63, which is general in nature, was drafted at a time when, as discussed by Iacobucci, J, child care expenses were considered an entirely personal expense. When Parliament enacted section 63, a new benefit, not then allowed under any other section of the Act, was conferred to taxpayers generally in order to better the position of working parents in society. From this perspective, it seems obvious that Parliament could not have intended to prohibit the deduction of child care as a business expense. To conclude that section 63 intends to limit the opportunity for a business woman to deduct child care expenses is antithetical to the whole purpose of the legislation, which was aimed at helping working women and their families bear the high cost of child care.

...

It is highly probable that the legislators did not even put their mind to the fact that women may some day enter into business and the professions in large numbers and that these women may approach the world of business differently than did their male predecessors. Most importantly, it was certainly not within the legislators' frame of mind that child care would be viewed as anything other than a personal expense.

Secondly, I wish to address the concern raised by many commentators, including my colleague Iacobucci, J, that to allow child care expenses to be deducted as a business expense would defeat and undermine the purpose of the provision of section 63, to allow a general deduction of child care expenses to all parents, whether employed or self-employed. Clearly, this analysis is very much tied to the purpose one attaches to the legislation. In a very thoughtful response to these concerns, Audrey Macklin, *supra*, notes that, even under the section 63 deduction, the more income a person has and, consequently, the higher tax bracket one falls into, the higher the deduction available ... . Further, the concern that employed persons and business people will not be treated in the same manner is a fact which stems from ... the Act itself: business deductions generally are restricted to those in business and are not available to an employed person. An employee cannot deduct an office at home, car expenses, meal and entertainment expenses, nor club dues or fees. In addition, employers who hire staff can deduct their salaries and employers who provide day care for their employees may deduct the expense (D. Goodison, "Nanny Means Business," *CGA Magazine*, September 1989, 15). Employees enjoy no such comparable deductions.

...

The basic premise upon which discussion with respect to the differential treatment between employees and business persons must be laid is the recognition that the Act can be viewed to operate in a discriminatory fashion.... However, in recognizing the distinction between the treatment of employees and business persons under the Act, in no way am I indicating that this may not constitute a real difficulty within our taxation system.

This said, this case is most fundamentally ... about ... the need to treat all business persons alike.

...

In conclusion, section 63 and subsection 9(1) of the Act may, in my view, co-exist. There is nothing in the wording of section 63 that excludes the application of section 9. In addition, any such interpretation is contrary to the purpose and historical basis for the enactment of section 63 and with traditional approaches to diverse deductions under the Act.... The definition of a business expense under the Act has evolved in a manner that has failed to recognize the reality of business women. It is thus imperative to recognize that any interpretation of section 63 which prevents the deduction of child care as a business expense may, in fact, be informed by this ... perspective. ...

Appeal dismissed.

NOTES AND QUESTIONS

1.   Why did the majority decision in *Symes* disallow the deduction of the taxpayer's child-care expenses as an ordinary business expense under subsection 9(1) of the Act? Did the majority accept the traditional view according to which child-care expenses were characterized as "personal or living expenses"? Did it conclude that the expenses were not incurred for the purpose of gaining or producing income? Of what relevance to the majority's decision is the structure and purpose of section 63 of the Act? Of what, if any, relevance is the language of subsection 4(2)? Of what, if any, relevance are the parenthetical words in paragraph 3(c), which allows subdivision e deductions "except to the extent that those deductions, if any, have been taken into account" in computing the taxpayer's income from specific sources under paragraph 3(a)?

2.   Why would the minority decision in *Symes* have allowed the taxpayer's appeal? How did the minority interpret the purpose of section 63? Of what relevance to the minority's judgment is its interpretation of this purpose?

3.   How did the majority decision in *Symes* distinguish the decision in *Olympia Floor & Wall Tile (Que.) Ltd. v. M.N.R.*, [1970] C.T.C. 99, 70 D.T.C. 6085 (Ex. Ct.), supra? Do you find Iacobucci J's reasoning persuasive? Why or why not?

4.   Which of the decisions in *Symes* do you find more persuasive? Of what, if any, relevance to your view is the inequity that would have occurred if taxpayers obtaining income from a business could deduct child-care expenses without any limit other than those applicable to other business expenses, while employees were limited to the deduction permitted by section 63? How did the minority decision address this concern?

Consider the following argument in David G. Duff, "Interpreting the Income Tax Act — Part 1: Interpretive Doctrines" (1999) Vol. 47 No. 3 Can. Tax J. 464 at 531-32:

> While the majority made a strong case that the deduction of child-care expenses as a business expense could "substantially undermine" the effect of section 63 to provide a limited deduction "under carefully controlled terms," it is difficult to dispute the minority's conclusion that this provision is itself shaped by the traditional assumption that child-care expenses are non-deductible personal expenses and should not, in an era in which "the world of business is increasingly populated by both men and women," be interpreted to preclude the possibility of a business expense deduction under the general rules governing the computation of business income. To the extent that the ... words of the Act are to be read in their "entire context," therefore, it is difficult to accept the majority's conclusion that section 63 unambiguously precludes the deduction of child-care expenses as a business expense. On the contrary, as the minority concludes, since the words of the Act do not explicitly preclude the business deductibility of child-care expenses, the resulting ambiguity might reasonably have been resolved in the taxpayer's favour.
>
> If the taxpayer had won, of course, Parliament would likely have responded by eliminating disparities in the resulting tax treatment of child care expenses incurred by business-persons (for whom child-care expenses would be fully deductible) and employees (for whom child-care expenses would be subject to the limits in section 63). Such a response, however, would have highlighted a more pervasive inequity in the Act arising from the general limitation on the deductibility of employment expenses under subsection 8(2), and necessitated a more contemporary explanation of the purpose and structure of the statutory deduction in section 63. In each respect, accepting the taxpayer's argument in *Symes* would have fostered democratic debate and placed the ultimate tax policy decision in the hands of the legislature, where it properly belongs.

5.   In the minority decision in *Symes*, L'Heureux-Dubé J noted that "even under the section 63 deduction, the more income a person has and, consequently, the higher tax bracket one falls into, the higher the deduction available." Does this suggest that any deduction for child-care expenses is inequitable? Does it suggest that all deductions are inequitable since they are worth more to taxpayers in higher tax brackets? For a critical examination of deductions for child-care expenses, see Claire F.L. Young, "Child Care A Taxing Issue?" (1994) 39 McGill L.J. 539.

6.   Having concluded that the taxpayer's child-care expenses were not deductible as business expenses, the majority decision in *Symes* also held that this result did not violate the taxpayer's equality rights under section 15(1) of the *Canadian Charter of Rights and Freedoms*. Accepting that "women disproportionately incur the *social costs* of child care" (emphasis in original), Iacobucci J reasoned that the taxpayer "must show that women disproportionately *pay child care expenses*" in order to demonstrate that section 63 has an adverse effect on women. On the basis that the taxpayer had failed to prove this point, Iacobucci J concluded that the taxpayer was "unable to demonstrate a violation of subsection 15(1) of the Charter with respect to section 63 of the Act." In response to these arguments, L'Heureux-Dubé J challenged the majority's "focus on section 63 of the Act rather than on business deductions as a whole" in considering the existence of a Charter violation, and questioned the majority's view that the taxpayer had to demonstrate that women disproportionately pay child-care expenses in order to establish that the tax restrictions on the deductibility of child-care expenses have an adverse impact on women.

E. Attendant-Care Expenses and the Disability Supports Deduction

Like moving expenses and child-care expenses, housekeeping expenses were traditionally regarded as non-deductible personal expenses, even for disabled taxpayers who obtained housekeeping services in order to generate income from a business.[31] In 1989, the Act was amended by the introduction of section 64, originally entitled "attendant care expenses," for taxpayers who were eligible for the disability tax credit in section 118.3. At the time of its introduction up to and including the 2003 taxation year, section 64 permitted a deduction for amounts "paid in the year ... as or on account of attendant care provided in Canada" less any reimbursement or assistance in respect of these amounts that is not included in computing the taxpayer's income. Like the deductions for moving expenses and child-care expenses, this deduction was available for amounts paid as or on account of attendant-care "to enable the taxpayer to" perform the duties of an office or employment, carry on a business, attend a secondary or post-secondary educational institution, or carry on research or similar work in respect of which the taxpayer received a grant. Also like the child-care expense deduction, the attendant-care expense deduction was limited to two-thirds of the taxpayer's earned income, and was available only where the recipient of the payment was "neither the taxpayer's spouse or common-law partner nor under 18 years of age." The deduction was unavailable where the taxpayer claimed attendant-care

---

[31]   See, for example, *Benton v. M.N.R.* (1952), 6 Tax ABC 230, 52 D.T.C. 196 (T.A.B.), in which the taxpayer (at para. 2), a "semi-invalid" who "had had a slight stroke and undergone an abdominal operation for cancer," sought to deduct payments to a housekeeper in computing his income from a farming business.

expenses as a medical expense under the medical expenses tax credit in section 118.2 of the Act.

From the 2004 taxation year onward, the attendant-care expenses deduction has been replaced with the "disability supports deduction." In keeping with the more general title, the disability supports deduction is broader and more generous than the attendant-care expenses deduction it replaced. The renamed version of section 64 allows full deductibility of eligible expenses up to the amount of income earned as a result, thereby doing away with the two-thirds limitation of the previous attendant-care expenses deduction, and recognizes a greater array of expenses.

In addition to the attendant-care expenses contemplated by the previous attendant-care expenses deduction, among the expenses eligible for deduction where prescribed by a medical practitioner are: (i) sign language interpretation services or real-time captioning services for taxpayers with speech or hearing impairments; (ii) teletypewriters or similar devices that enable deaf or mute individuals to make and receive telephone calls; (iii) equipment designed exclusively to be used by blind individuals in the operation of a computer; (iv) optical scanners or similar devices designed to be used by blind individuals to enable them to read print; and (v) electronic speech synthesizers that enable mute individuals to communicate by use of a portable keyboard.[32] Various other expenses are also deductible provided specified conditions are met.[33] These other expenses include: (i) voice-recognition software; (ii) tutoring services; and (iii) talking textbooks. Similar to the attendant-care expenses deduction, disability support expenses may not be claimed if they have been claimed as medical expenses tax credit pursuant to section 118.2 of the Act.[34]

IV. DEFERRED AND OTHER SPECIAL INCOME ARRANGEMENTS

In addition to the specific "other income" inclusions in subdivisions d and the various deductions from subdivision e of Division B of Part I of the Act, many of which have been covered in sections II and III of this chapter, there are a number of tax-advantaged plans, including registered pension plans ("RPPs"),[35] registered retirement savings plans ("RRSPs"),[36] registered retirement income funds ("RRIFs"),[37] deferred profit-sharing plans ("DPSPs"),[38] registered education savings plans ("RESPs"),[39] and registered disability savings plans

---

[32] See subpara. 64(a)(ii).

[33] For more detail on these conditions, see subparas. 64(a)(ii) and (iii).

[34] See subpara. 64(a)(iv).

[35] See subpara. 56(1)(a)(i); paras. 60(j.02), (j.03), and (j.04); and s. 147.1.

[36] See paras. 56(1)(h), (h.1), (h.2), and ss. 146, 146.01, and 146.02.

[37] See paras. 56(1)(h) and (t) and ss. 146 and 146.3.

[38] See para. 56(1)(i) and s. 147.

[39] See para. 56(1)(q) and s. 146.1

("RDSPs")[40] amounts from which may be included in a taxpayer's income as a result of inclusionary provisions in subdivision d and, in many cases, for which corresponding provision is made for the deduction of contributions through various rules in subdivision e. These inclusions and deductions in turn make reference to the rules established for these plans in Division G of Part I of the Act, entitled, "Deferred and Other Special Income Arrangements."

The plans that are provided for in Division G of Part I of the Act are used by taxpayers to secure tax advantages for certain types of economic gains, principally investment income and capital gains, under circumscribed conditions. It is no surprise that the plans each raise and address a number of detailed issues surrounding qualification for the various tax benefits. A complete discussion of each of the plans, which are frequently of considerable complexity, is beyond the scope of this chapter.[41] Nevertheless, for many Canadians, four of the Division G plans are likely to be quite important in practice and, therefore, it is useful to understand the basic structure and framework of each of these most frequently encountered plans.

The first and second of these most frequently encountered plans are RRSPs and RRIFs, amounts from which are included in income by virtue of paragraph 56(1)(h). RRSPs and RRIFs are tax post-paid plans, in the sense that no income tax liability is borne by contributions (which are deductible from other income when made) and investment income, including capital gains, accumulates tax-free within the plans (there is no recognition for capital or non-capital losses in these plans, however). Tax is deferred until amounts are withdrawn from the plans, at which point the full amount of the distribution is included in income by paragraph 56(1)(h).

The third and fourth most likely to be encountered plans are RESPs and tax-free savings accounts ("TFSAs").[42] TFSAs are a recent addition to the Act, available only from January 2009. RESPs and TFSAs are both considered to be tax pre-paid plans in the sense that contributions do not attract deductions (i.e. contributions to the plans are made with after-tax dollars) and so contributed amounts will have typically already borne some income tax liability. Like RRSPs and RRIFs, investment income (including capital gains) accumulates tax-free within the plans. Amounts received from RESPs bear little or no income tax liability in the hands of the beneficiaries of the plans (typically children of those who started the plan, who as post-secondary students include as income distributions from the plan, but can shield from tax most or all of the distribution

---

[40] See para. 56(1)(q.1) and s. 146.4.

[41] The CRA publishes a number of Guides and Infomration Circulars that assist taxpayers and tax advisors in navigating the detailed legislation pertaining to these plans. Among the Guides are: RC4092 "Registered Education Savings Plans (RESPs);" RC4112 "Lifelong Learning Plan (LLP);" and RC4135 "Home Buyers' Plan (HBP)." Relevant Information Circulars include IC72-22 "Registered Retirement Savings Plans;" IC78-18 "Registered Retirement Income Funds;" and IC93-3 "Registered Educational Savings Plan."

[42] See s. 146.2.

because of the basic personal amount and tuition tax credits). Amounts withdrawn from TFSAs are not considered to be income at all and are not subject to income tax. It is therefore appropriate to conceptualize RESPs and TFSAs as tax prepaid plans.[43]

The principal features of each of these tax-advantaged plans are addressed in this section.[44] It should be noted that the complexity of the rules applicable to these plans is easy to underestimate. What follows is only a basic description of the most important features of each of the four plans.[45]

A. Registered Retirement Savings Plans and Registered Retirement Income Funds

RRSPs and RRIFs are designed to provide a vehicle to promote and support retirement savings for Canadians. RRSPs allow taxpayers to contribute a fraction of their "earned income" to a special tax-deferred trust that is held for the benefit of the taxpayer by an approved institutional issuer.[46] Contributions may typically be made to a maximum limit of the lower of: (i) 18 per cent of a taxpayer's "earned income" in the foregoing taxation year; and (ii) the "money purchase limit" for the relevant taxation year ($22,000 for the 2009 taxation year).[47] The term "earned income" for the purposes of RRSPs is defined in subsection 146(1) as including income from one of the enumerated sources of income in paragraph 3(a) of the Act, subject to a number of limitations (particularly with respect to property income).[48] Amounts contributed to an RRSP may be deducted from a taxpayer's income for the year (or carried over to a future taxation year to be deducted then).[49] RRSPs can hold various types of

---

[43] This is the case even though there is no requirement that funds contributed to RESPs or TFSAs actually be from after-tax resources.

[44] Although they are not addressed in this section, it bears mentioning that the plans that are not discussed have features that are broadly similar to the plans that are discussed. For example, RPPs and DPSPs are tax post-paid plans that are similar (with some important differences) in their basic structure and operation to RRSPs and RRIFs. On the other hand, RDSPs are tax pre-paid plans, similar in many ways to RESPs and TFSAs, although not surprisingly with some important differences as well.

[45] Administrative guidance on these plans can be found in the following Interpretation Bulletins issued by the CRA: IT-124 "Contributions to Registered Retirement Savings Plans;" IT-167 "Registered Pension Funds or Plans — Employee's Contributions;" IT-307 "Spousal or Common-Law Partner Registered Retirement Savings Plan;" IT-320 "Qualified Investments — Trusts Governed by Registered Retirement Savings Plans, Registered Education Savings Plans and Registered Retirement Income Funds;" IT-412 "Foreign Property of Registered Plans;" IT-500 "Registered Retirement Savings Plans — Death of an Annuitant;" IT-528 "Transfers of Funds Between Registered Plans".

[46] See the definition of "retirement savings plan" in subs. 146(1), which outlines various financial institutions that may maintain RRSPs.

[47] See the definition of "money purchase limit" in subs. 147.1(1).

[48] See the definition of "earned income" in subs. 146(1).

[49] See the definition of "RRSP deduction limit" in subs. 146(1).

investments.[50] Since any income generated by the property owned within the RRSP will not be subject to tax until it is withdrawn, it frequently makes sense to the extent possible to hold investments that principally income-generating investments (such as bonds, which generate mostly interest income) inside an RRSP (or other tax deferred plan) and other investments, such as equities, which return a mix of dividend income and capital gains, outside a plan (but of course only to the extent that a taxpayer's savings exceed the contribution limits).

Provision is made for taxpayers to make contributions to a "spousal RRSP," which is a plan to which one spouse contributes to a plan the other spouse owns. A spousal RRSP is a useful planning tool that allows higher income-earning spouses to contribute to the savings of the lower-income earning spouses such that in retirement the lower income-earning spouse (and the couple regarded together) will pay less income tax on the withdrawals from the plan. Spousal RRSPs are of waning significance because of the introduction in 2007 of pension income-splitting.

RRSPs can be regarded as providing for three principal tax advantages that would not otherwise be available under the Act. Two of these advantages relate to the deferral of income tax liability. First, contributions may be deducted from a taxpayer's income at the time the contribution is made to the extent of the taxpayer's "RRSP deduction limit,"[51] which is calculated with reference, among other things, to the amount of RRSP contributions made in the current and previous taxation years. Second, once contributed funds are being held and invested within the RRSP there is tax-free realization of capital gains and investment income. A third, non-deferral, advantage relates to income-splitting. Amounts withdrawn from RRSPs may take advantage of certain income-splittting provisions that allow for the notional splitting of certain forms of retirement income between spouses.[52]

Generally, when amounts are withdrawn from an individual's RRSP, the amounts must be included in the taxpayer's income as a result of paragraph 56(1)(h), which provides for the inclusion of, "amounts required by section 146 in respect of a registered retirement savings plan or a registered retirement income fund to be included in computing the taxpayer's income for the year." This general rule is subject to some exceptions, such as under the "Home Buyer's Program"[53] or the "Lifelong Learning Program."[54] Another exception relates to the rollover of RRSP assets to a registered retirement income fund. Taxpayers who hold RRSPs in the year in which they reach the age of 71 will be considered to be holding "matured" RRSPs at the end of that calendar year and are required to collapse the plans. Because of this mandatory maturation of

---

[50] See the definitions of "qualified investment" and "non-qualified investment" in subs. 146(1).
[51] See the definition of "RRSP deduction limit" in subs. 146(1).
[52] See s. 60.03.
[53] See para. 56(1)(h.1).
[54] See para. 56(1)(h.2).

RRSPs, in the absence of a provision that allowed for a rollover into another type of tax-advantaged instrument, there would be a lump-sum inclusion in income in that year, much of which might be taxed at the highest applicable personal marginal tax rate. To escape the potentially large income inclusion and the correspondingly high tax burden, the Act provides for rollover treatment of RRSP assets to RRIFs.

RRIFs are plans that allow for the tax-deferred treatment of savings, and have many features — including eligible investments — in common with RRSPs. The key difference is that RRIFs have a schedule that requires withdrawals to be made from them at a minimum rate each year. Just as with RRSPs, these withdrawals are included fully in income by virtue of paragraph 56(1)(h). There are several sources of contributions to RRIFs, the most common of which are unmatured and matured RRSPs of a taxpayer. Less commonly, property from a deceased individual's RRIF or RRSP can be transferred into a taxpayer's RRIF where a taxpayer is a beneficiary of the plan of the deceased individual.

B. Registered Education Savings Plans

RESPs are tax-assisted savings plans under which contributors can accumulate funds in order to provide for a beneficiary's education at a post-secondary level. Although contributions to these plans, unlike those to registered retirement savings plans (RRSPs), are not deductible, an RESP is similar in that the income of a trust governed by an RESP is exempt from tax under subsection 146.1(5) and paragraph 149(1)(u) of the Act.

For the 2007 and subsequent taxation years, contributors may contribute up to the lifetime maximum at any time for each beneficiary of the plan. The lifetime limit as of 2009 is $50,000 for each beneficiary. In addition, regardless of family income for RESP contributions made in 2008, the federal government will make an additional contribution in the form of the basic Canada education savings grant (CESG). The basic CESG is equal to 20 percent of the annual amount contributed, up to a lifetime maximum of $7,200 per beneficiary over a period of 18 years. The annual maximum basic CESG is $500 in respect of each beneficiary (this is increased to $1,000 in CESG if there is unused grant room from a previous year). Depending on family income, it is also possible to receive an additional amount of CESG. This additional amount depends on family income. For 2008, if a child's family has income of $37,885 or less, then the additional CESG rate on the first $500 contributed to an RESP for a beneficiary under 18 years of age is 40 per cent (an extra 20 per cent on the first $500 contributed); if the child's family income for the year is more than $37,885 but is less than $74,769, then the rate of CESG is 30 per cent (an extra 10 per cent on the first $500 contributed).

Subsection 146.1(7) requires a taxpayer who is a beneficiary under an RESP to include in computing his or her income "all educational assistance payments paid out of registered education savings plans to or for the individual in the year." Subsection 146.1(1) defines an "educational assistance payment" as "any amount, other than a refund of payments, paid out of an education savings plan to or for an individual to assist the individual to further the individual's education at a post-secondary school level."

C. Tax-Free Savings Accounts

TFSAs allow individuals to contribute up to $5,000 per year on an after-tax basis (i.e., there is no deduction for contributions, unlike contributions to Registered Retirement Savings Plans, "RRSPs" or Registered Pension Plans, "RPPs").[55] Once a contribution to a TFSA is made, the account allows for tax-free compounding of investment income, tax-free capital gains, and tax-free withdrawals or, in the parlance of the legislation, "distributions."[56] Recontributions in the following calendar year are permitted to the extent of any amount distributed from a TFSA.[57] Under the TFSA regime the income attribution rules are suspended such that a higher-earning spouse can provide funds to the other to contribute to a TFSA without concerns regarding income attribution with respect to returns within the account.[58] In future taxation years the contribution limit of $5,000 for 2009 will be indexed for inflation (in $500 increments). Unused contribution room can be carried forward indefinitely.[59] It has been promised that distributions to taxpayers from a TFSA will not be considered to be income to the taxpayer and will therefore not affect eligibility for means-tested programs such as Old Age Security or the Guaranteed Income Supplement.[60]

---

[55] The term "TFSA dollar limit" is defined in subs. 207.01(1) to be $5,000 in the 2009 calendar year and "for each year after 2009, the amount (rounded to the nearest multiple of $500, or if that amount is equidistant from two such consecutive multiples, to the higher multiple) that is equal to $5,000 adjusted for each year after 2009 in the manner set out in section 117.1."

[56] Subsection 146.2(4) provides, subject to some qualifications, that a TFSA is not taxable unless it "carries on one or more businesses or holds one or more properties that are non-qualified investments."

[57] Subsection 207.01(1) provides that the "unused TFSA contribution room" for a taxation year is equal to a formula: A + B + C − D, where B "is the total of all amounts each of which was a distribution made in the preceding calendar year under a TFSA of which the individual was the holder at the time of the distribution" other than a "qualifying transfer" or a "prescribed distribution."

[58] Paragraph 74.5(12)(c) provides that the attribution rules in sections 74.1, 74.2, and 74.3 do not apply to an individual's spouse or common law partner while "the property, or property substituted for it, is held under a TFSA of which the spouse or common-law partner is the holder" and so long as the spouse or common-law partner does not is in an over-contribution situation under the TFSA. In addition, para. 75(3)(a) stipulates that subs. 75(2) does not apply to TFSAs.

[59] Subsection 207.01(1) provides that the "unused TFSA contribution room" for a taxation year is equal to a formula: A + B + C − D, where A "is the individual's unused TFSA contribution room at the end of the preceding calendar year."

[60] See Department of Finance Canada, *The Budget Plan 2008* (February 26, 2008) at p. 80.

TFSAs have a number of precedents in other developed countries. Similar plans have been in place in the U.K. since April 1999 (and there were related precursors as early as 1987) and in the US in the form of Roth IRAs since 1998. In many ways, therefore, the timing of the introduction of the TFSA scheme in Canada is auspicious for the prospects of getting the policy design right. There are limitations to the lessons that can be drawn from the U.K. and U.S. examples, however. For one thing, the tax systems in the U.K. and in the U.S. are different than the Canadian tax system in important respects. Another limitation is that the TFSA regime does not adopt the design features of either the ISA or the Roth IRA schemes wholesale. Instead, the TFSA regime has certain elements in common with ISAs and Roth IRAs. Nevertheless, it is related to both schemes in a way that suggests that the results here will be similar.

The ISA regime was introduced in the U.K. in April 1999. Many of the design features for ISAs in the U.K. are shared by the TFSA regime. For example, an ISA may be opened by any U.K. resident 18 years of age or older. There are no penalties for withdrawals from ISAs (unlike Roth IRAs), which suggests that the accounts are intended to be used for intermediate savings goals (and not necessarily for financing retirement). Contribution limits are fixed at an annual amount — for 2008, this amount is £7,200 — irrespective of earned income. A key difference from the TFSA regime is that once an ISA contribution is made that contribution room is exhausted once and for all. This loss of contribution room upon withdrawal is made up for in part by the relatively generous contribution limit (the 2008 ISA limit of £7,200 at current exchange rates is more than three times the $5,000 limit for TFSAs for 2009).

Roth IRAs were introduced in the U.S. in 1998. These accounts also have much in common with TFSAs. The contributions are made on an after-tax basis, accumulated gains are exempt from tax when withdrawn, and contributions are limited to an annual amount ($5,000) each year; however, this amount differs in three important respects from the TFSA contribution limit. One difference is that the limit is $5,000 or the lower of taxable "compensation" for the year. A second difference is that contributions to Roth IRAs are phased out with Adjusted Gross Income such that taxpayers filing jointly with income of greater than $169,000 in 2008 are not eligible to contribute to a Roth IRA. A final difference is that the limit is increased for older taxpayers ($6,000 for those 50 or older). Withdrawals from Roth IRAs are not as straightforward as they are from TFSAs, reflecting the Congressional intention that Roth IRAs are to be used to help finance retirement. For withdrawals to be made on a tax-free basis there is a minimum holding period of five years for Roth IRA contributions and the withdrawal must be made after the taxpayer reaches 59½ years of age. Early withdrawals of income earned in the Roth IRA are subject to a 10 per cent additional tax penalty (the original capital contributions can be withdrawn tax-free).

One leading 2004 study of the effects of ISAs in the U.K. suggests that savers tend to shift assets from conventional accounts to tax-preferred accounts, yielding little increase in aggregate savings. A subsequent 2005 study by the

U.K. Inland Revenue concluded that a mere 15% of ISA holders saved as a result of the availability of the tax-preferred accounts and would not have done so otherwise. In a 2007 study the OECD concluded that, "the introduction of ISAs might have caused a partial asset reshuffling of wealth from taxable to tax-preferred accounts, in particular for wealthier and older individuals. Nonetheless, there are some indications of creation of new savings, especially among moderate-income individuals."

American empirical studies on tax prepaid plans such as Roth IRAs is not yet well-developed. Studies of traditional tax-deferred accounts have found that participation rates and the value of contributions increases with earnings (up to the eligibility phase-out levels). New savings have been modest, and make up only about ¼ of the assets held in 401(k) accounts. Tax expenditures associated with tax postpaid accounts in the U.S. are such that the poorest ½ of the population receives about 10 per cent of the benefit, whereas the richest 10 per cent receives about 55 per cent of the tax benefits. The tentative lesson from these U.S. and U.K. studies (and those from other countries relied upon by the OECD meta-study) is that there is considerable reshuffling of taxable assets to capitalize on the tax-advantages associated with tax advantaged savings accounts, with modest new savings behaviour among those with low and middle incomes.

D. Tax Prepaid versus Tax Postpaid Plans: Assessing the Introduction of Tax-Free Savings Accounts

One might, not unreasonably, assume that TFSAs must be differentiated from RRSPs, RRIFs, and other tax postpaid plans in order for the introduction of this different policy instrument to be justified. This expectation is merited. Although with simplified assumptions about the nature of a tax system and the choices individuals make surrounding labour market participation, savings, investment, and consumption, tax prepaid and tax postpaid plans yield equivalent results, relaxing these assumptions somewhat shows that the approaches differ in at least three important respects. In addition, it should be noted that TFSAs are ostensibly intended to promote a different kind of savings behaviour than are RRSPs and RPPs, which are intended to be used by Canadians to finance retirement. TFSAs have been designed to facilitate the realization of intermediate savings goals, such as, for example, saving for a down-payment on the purchase of a home.

Aside from this apparent difference in the role to be played by TFSAs and RRSPs and RPPs, which is not necessarily associated with either tax prepaid or tax postpaid accounts, the central differences in these accounts from a theoretical perspective surround the present value of taxes paid in the presence of (a) lucky and unlucky investors; (b) differences in the pattern of income and the income tax rate structure over time; and (c) the timing of the payment and receipt of taxes. These differences are important because they affect how one assesses the introduction of TFSAs, assuming that the alternative would have been a modification of the currently offered tax postpaid options, such as RRSPs and RPPs.

First, lucky taxpayers are emphatically not in the same position as unlucky taxpayers and should not be taxed in the same way. Indeed, there is a relevant difference between taxpayers of the same annual income and savings, one of whom realizes tax prepaid account returns of 20 per cent compounded over a 30 year period and a taxpayer who realizes tax prepaid account returns of 3 per cent compounded over the same 30 year period. On what basis does it make sense to treat the two taxpayers the same with regard to lifetime income tax liability given their vast disparity in investment results? It really makes little difference to the unacceptability of this parity in treatment if one taxpayer experiences poorer investment returns than another out of sheer randomness. One could plausibly respond that the two taxpayers "decided to take their chances" at the time that they contributed to the tax prepaid account, but this is only partly responsive. The two taxpayers, while similarly situated *ex ante*, simply are not in the same position *ex post*. In general, income tax systems do not treat taxpayers with the same expected outcomes the same way. Instead, income tax liability is calibrated to how things turn. There is a strong argument in income taxation — indeed, it is a core principle of equity — that similarly situated taxpayers should not be taxed differently. To reiterate, a lucky investor is just not the same as an unlucky investor, even if at one point in the possibly distant past they were in the same position.

Second, in the abstract an individual who has an option to save in a tax prepaid and a tax postpaid account will take into account of two different considerations. First is a projection of future earnings and expenditures they expect to make in the future. Second is a projection of what they expect to happen to marginal tax rates and the tax system's rate structure as a whole. With respect to the future earnings and expenditures, holding the tax rate structure constant, if individuals expect that, as is ordinarily the case, they will tend to have lower incomes when they are in a position to draw down on their savings, they will tend to prefer to save in tax postpaid plans. The reason is that in the period of dissaving they will face a lower marginal tax rate than they do in the period during which they are saving. By using tax postpaid plans to smooth the realization of income, individuals can reduce the present value of the taxes they pay. If, on the other hand, individuals expect to have higher incomes later when they are dissaving, which would be unusual, then all else the same they would prefer to save in tax prepaid plans, since they will satisfy upfront the tax liability at a relatively low marginal tax rate.

Third and finally, tax prepaid and tax postpaid plans affect the timing of the imposition and receipt of tax revenue. In the absence of either type of plan, an income tax would impose tax liability from year to year as income is earned. Tax prepaid and tax postpaid schemes both depart from this matching of income with income tax liability. Tax prepaid plans accelerate the payment of tax whereas tax postpaid plans defer the payment of tax. Tax prepaid accounts will result in tax revenues being collected "upfront" from taxpayers with no later tax liability on investment returns or withdrawals.

Moving from the general to the specific, what about the particular design features of the RRSP and TFSA regimes? There are a number of important differences between the design of RRSPs on the one hand, and TFSAs on the other hand.

One of the major differences is that the ability to contribute to TFSAs does not turn on one's earned income. Contributions to RRSPs are limited by the lower of 18 per cent of one's earned income and a maximum contribution limit per year. TFSA contribution room grows by $5,000 (or a higher indexed amount for future taxation years) for each year a Canadian resident is the age of majority. This means that individuals who have no earned income can receive gifts from wealthier relatives, for example, and contribute those funds to a TFSA. This can yield dramatic intergenerational wealth transfers, entirely free of tax, particularly when *inter vivos* transfers are substituted for larger bequests that might otherwise be made at the death of a wealthy patriarch or matriarch. This feature suggests that some types of income that have not in fact borne tax will be transferred into TFSAs, such as bequests, inheritances, gifts, strike pay, illegal income, windfalls, gambling gains, etc. This is not something that is permitted with respect to RRSPs unless the individual also has available contribution room from past earned income. Although there is a limited ability to contribute to a spousal RRSP currently, the fact that pension and RRSP income can be split in retirement renders this a somewhat superfluous benefit.

One response to this concern is to point out that gifts from wealthy relatives of other assets can serve the same purposes as the modest ability to transfer wealth through TFSA contribution room. For example, if a wealthy relative gratuitously contributes the funds required to make a down-payment on a principal residence, the stream of consumption benefits, the mortgage interest savings, and any eventual capital gain on the principal residence will all escape inclusion in the Canadian income tax base. This is, of course, true. It is equally true, however, that it is difficult to achieve the same sorts of returns on investments in principal residences that are made possible by equity and debt investments in capital markets. In addition, because larger investments in principal residences are associated with higher carrying costs, such as utilities, property taxes, insurance, maintenance, and the like, there is a natural limit to the utility of older, wealthier, generations transferring assets through gifts for the purposes of transferring wealth inter-generationally.

Another possible response to the criticism of the flat $5,000 of contribution room is that TFSAs are intended to promote savings rather than to promote retirement savings. In addition, $5,000 of contribution room is more meaningful to a low or middle income Canadian than to a taxpayer with a higher income. This is true, insofar as it goes. To the extent this is the case, however, it is not obvious why a new account had to be introduced to secure the result. It would have been just as easy (if not easier) to have altered the formula for RRSP contributions to allow a fixed amount of contribution room each year regardless of earned income, and to allow withdrawals and recontributions of this amount. That is, a tax postpaid account with the same design features as TFSAs could just as easily have been used to promote savings as to promote retirement savings.

One argument made in support of TFSAs relative to RRSPs surrounds income-tested retirement income benefits such as OAS and GIS. The problem is that OAS and GIS benefits as they are currently structured result in high marginal effective tax rates in retirement for Canadians with low and middle incomes. The claim is that tax prepaid accounts can be setup so that distributions do not count as income and, therefore, that the clawbacks in these benefit programs will not have any effect on the eligibility of individuals for the benefits. That a distribution from a TFSA (or other tax prepaid plan) should not count as income for the purposes of OAS and GIS is a position that has been promoted repeatedly by Richard Shillington, who has been a tireless advocate for improving the savings environment for low and middle income Canadians. It is unclear, however, why the solution to the "high marginal tax rate due to clawbacks" problem should be the introduction of TFSAs, rather than addressing directly the sharp rate at which these income-support programs are phased out for seniors. For example, it might make more sense to universalize the provision of OAS and GIS for seniors or, if this were unacceptable, to consider only RRSP (or RRIF) distributions beyond a certain threshold to be income for the purposes of assessing benefit eligibility.

One way in which the design of TFSAs is quite good is in the way in which the regime addresses the concern that certain taxpayers will be capable of and inclined to disguise returns to entrepreneurial effort and skill as returns to savings. With regard to super-normal returns, TFSAs as they are currently structured prohibit certain types of investments, such as shares in closely-held corporations. Only qualified investments are permitted to be held within the accounts. These rules tend to piggyback on the rules that are used to demarcate permitted from unpermitted RRSP investments. To the extent that interests in closely-held corporations are not eligible investments, much of the scope to earn alpha or super-normal returns in TFSAs is attenuated. This is much to the better.

On the other hand, in choosing between TFSAs and RRSPs, there is greater revenue loss possible with tax prepaid options that with tax postpaid accounts, because at least with respect to RRSPs, there will be tax imposed on the super-normal returns eventually. With TFSAs, there is not the case. Moreover, with TFSAs there is the prospect of a much longer holding period (since there are no forced distributions associated with TFSAs, unlike RRSPs, which must be converted into RRIFs and which then must be liquidated at specified minimum rates). Cutting the other way, however, is the higher contribution room available with RRSPs for those with higher incomes; this greater contribution room may make it more attractive to invest efforts in generating alpha (and more possible, if it becomes easier to invest in certain kinds of investments, such as hedge fund units) within an RRSP as compared with a TFSA.

What happens if individual Canadian taxpayers regard with some suspicion the promise of future yield-exemption, and discount the probability that future governments will consider themselves to be bound fully by this promise? To the extent that each taxpayer has a choice between investing funds in RRSPs in which the promises of yield-exemption are not made, and the government "pays it forward" by offering an immediate deduction, one might well expect that they will take the sure thing and forgo the TFSA, at least for anything other than a minor float of savings that would otherwise go into a chequing or savings account for day-to-day use. There are taxpayers, however, who would, even if they though the yield-exemption promise was unlikely to be adhered to fully, be undeterred from investing in TFSAs heavily. These taxpayers are unlikely to be the ones that are the most attractive target for the accounts from the government's perspective, however, since they are the ones who have already topped-up their RRSP contributions and have additional savings available that are currently in non-registered accounts. They may also be taxpayers who receive *inter vivos* transfers from wealthier relatives in order to transfer wealth most tax-efficiently from one generation to the next. In neither case are the users of the accounts the most sympathetic from a distributional perspective. Nor are the savings in these circumstances apt to be "new savings."

In light of the foregoing, from a theoretical perspective, as an addition to the Canadian tax system TFSAs are not unambiguously desirable or undesirable. On the one hand, to the extent that TFSAs reduce the effective marginal tax rate on savings, the accounts can be expected to boost savings and investment by Canadians. To the extent that savings are currently overtaxed relative to consumption resulting in a bias towards current consumption (because leisure is not taxed but investment income on savings is), TFSAs can be expected to improve the neutrality of the Canadian tax system as regards the timing of consumption decisions and thereby improve efficiency. Moreover, to the extent that one sides with those who believe that a consumption tax is fairer than an income tax on the basis that those who consume later ought to bear the same present value of tax liability as those who consume currently, the TFSA regime can also, with some caveats, be regarded as improving the Canadian tax system.

On the other hand, there are a number of concerns that are raised by the introduction of TFSAs, most importantly whether the modest increase in new savings we can likely expect from low and middle income Canadian taxpayers will be worth the administrative and compliance costs associated with TFSAs and the income tax revenues forgone from taxable investments being shifted into TFSAs, mostly to the benefit of relatively affluent Canadians.

CHAPTER EIGHT

Rules Relating to the Computation of Income

I. INTRODUCTION

In addition to the specific rules in subdivisions a to e of Division B of Part I of the Act that govern the computation of different kinds of income and permit specific deductions in computing a taxpayer's net income for the year under section 3, subdivision f contains a number of computational rules that apply to all kinds of income and deductions. This chapter examines the most important of these rules, looking at provisions that limit amounts otherwise deductible in computing a taxpayer's income from a source, provisions that specify the amount at which certain transfers of property will be deemed to have occurred for tax purposes, and the attribution rules that deem certain amounts to have been received by someone other than the actual recipient.

II. LIMITATIONS ON DEDUCTIONS

In addition to specific limitations on allowable deductions in computing a taxpayer's income from various sources, subdivision f establishes further limitations on deductions irrespective of the kind of income to which the deduction applies. The most important of these limitations appears in section 67, which stipulates that "no deduction shall be made in respect of an outlay or expense in respect of which any amount is otherwise deductible under this Act, except to the extent that the outlay or expense was reasonable in the circumstances." In addition to this general rule, section 67.1 limits the amount that may be deducted in respect of meals and entertainment, and sections 67.2 to 67.4 limit the amount of interest and leasing expenses that may be deducted in respect of a passenger vehicle.

For our purposes, there is no need to examine sections 67.2 to 67.4 in any detail, because they contain little more than detailed formulas for computing the maximum interest or leasing expense that may be deducted over any period in which these amounts are paid by the taxpayer.[1] The following sections consider

---

[1] In general, s. 67.2 limits allowable interest expenses to $250 per month, and s. 67.3 limits allowable leasing expenses to $600 per month. Where two or more taxpayers own or lease a

the general limitation in section 67 and the specific limitation for meals and entertainment expenses in section 67.1.

A. Reasonableness

Section 67 is derived from subsection 6(2) of the *Income War Tax Act*, which, when originally enacted in 1933, allowed the Minister to "disallow as an expense the whole or any portion of any salary, bonus or commission or director's fee which in his opinion is in excess of what is reasonable for the services performed." In 1940, this provision was replaced with a more general rule, allowing the Minister to "disallow any expense which he in his discretion may determine to be in excess of what is reasonable or normal for the business carried on by the taxpayer, or which was incurred in respect of any transaction or operation which in his opinion has unduly or artificially reduced the income." In this form, it is possible to discern the predecessor not only to section 67 but also to the "artificial transactions" rule in former subsection 245(1). Like former subsection 245(1), therefore, section 67 should be regarded as an anti-avoidance rule.

When the *Income Tax Act* was adopted in 1948, the ministerial discretion in subsection 6(2) of the *Income War Tax Act* was abolished and the "reasonable" and "artificial" elements of the rule were separated, with the latter becoming subsection 125(1) of the 1948 Act, subsection 137(1) of the 1952 Act, and finally former subsection 245(1) of the 1972 Act. The "reasonableness" limitation became subsection 12(2), which provided:

> In computing income, no deduction shall be made in respect of an outlay or expense otherwise deductible except to the extent that the outlay or expense was reasonable in the circumstances.

Although relocated to section 67 in 1972, the rule has remained essentially unchanged since 1948.

The placement of the reasonableness limitation in the 1948 Act, immediately following the statutory limitations on deductibility in former subsection 12(1) (now subsection 18(1)), may be more suggestive of the rule's purpose than its current location in subdivision f ("Rules Relating to Computation of Income"). Indeed, section 67 and its predecessors have often been applied together with the limitations in paragraphs 18(1)(a) and (h), though generally to disallow only part but not all of an amount as a deductible expense. Thus, just as paragraphs 18(1)(a) and (h) may reinforce the "business practices" test for the deductibility of expenses under subsection 9(1), section 67 may provide a more flexible statutory instrument for achieving the policy goals underlying paragraphs 18(1)(a) and (h). For the same reason, the application of section 67 has been often considered in conjunction with the reasonable expectation of profit test. A

---

passenger vehicle jointly, s. 67.4 requires these limits to be allocated among these taxpayers based on their proportionate interest in the vehicle.

good example of a case in which section 67 has been applied is *Cipollone v. The Queen*, [1995] 1 C.T.C. 2598 (T.C.C.).

Cipollone v. Canada
[1994] T.C.J. No. 862, [1995] 1 C.T.C. 2598 (T.C.C.)

BOWMAN JTCC: ... These appeals are from reassessments for the appellant's 1987, 1988, and 1989 taxation years.

The appellant's real name is Nadine Cipollone , but she operates under the professional name of Dr. Phela Goodstein, having registered as a trade mark the words "Doctor of Humour". She owns and operates an organization known as the "Institute of Humour" at 6000 Yonge Street in North York, Ontario.

...

The appellant in 1986 registered under the Ontario *Partnerships Registration Act*, R.S.O. 1980, c. 371, a declaration of a sole proprietorship under the name of Dr. Phela Goodstein, the business activity of which was described as Humourologist.

Her business, if it can be so called, is variously described in her evidence and in the numerous newspaper articles and publicity releases that she submitted in evidence as clown, court jester, humour therapist, and humourologist. She has held humour therapy workshops and lectured on humour. She has appeared, for a fee, for such organizations as the Canadian Institute of Chartered Accountants, the Wellington-Dufferin-Guelph Health Unit, the Holistic Centre of Hamilton, the Corporation of the City of Burlington, the OSSTF (Ontario Secondary School Teachers Federation) in Thunder Bay, the Ontario Association of Registered Nursing Assistants, the Humber College Business and Industry Services, the North York General Hospital, the Disabled Women's Network, the York West Senior Citizens Centre, the Public Health Department of the City of York, the Bernard Betel Centre for Creative Living, the Ontario Gerontology Association.

She has been given unpaid publicity in such publications as *Toronto Life*, *The Sunday Sun*, *The Toronto Globe & Mail*, *The Financial Post* magazine, and the *Journal of the Canadian Psychology Association*, and as well, as recently as this morning, *The Toronto Star*.

She has contracts to appear before the employees of British Columbia Telephone Company in British Columbia and the Centennial College of Applied Arts and Technology.

Recognition of the appellant as a comedienne and humourist has been somewhat slow in coming and has occurred several years after the years under appeal. She is obviously a going concern. She is a person of enormous energy, enthusiasm, and dynamism, with apparently an unlimited optimism and virtually boundless belief in her own ability to succeed in the very competitive and difficult field of public comedy. She is undaunted by the fact that up to the present, since 1987, she has so far failed to realize a profit, at least given the very large deductions she has been claiming, her expenses for every year having exceeded her income.

The figures for the years since 1987 are rather revealing. In 1987, her revenues were $85.00 and expenses $14,588.00, for a loss of $14,503.00. In 1988, her revenues were $475.00 and her expenses were $7,693.00, for a loss of $7,218.00. For 1989, her revenues were $3,653.00 and expenses of $14,072.00, for a loss of $10,419.00. For 1990, her revenues were $1,327.00 and expenses were $11,370.00, for a loss of $10,043.00. For 1991, her revenues were $1,391.00 and her expenses were $12,998.00, for a loss of $11,607.00. The Department of National Revenue evidently did not have, or has at least not assessed, her 1992 return, but she had revenues of about $4,000.00 and expenses exceeding that amount. In 1993, she had revenues of $5,300.00 and $17,000.00 in expenses, giving rise to a loss of about $12,000.00.

It is hardly surprising that the Department of National Revenue, in reviewing her returns, concluded that with so great a discrepancy between her revenues and her expenses, her activities as a humour therapist had, to use the words of the Chief Justice of Canada in *Moldowan v. The Queen*, 1977 D.T.C. 5213, "no reasonable expectation of profit" and, therefore, no business, or that the expenses were not laid out for the purpose of gaining or producing income from a business. Mr. Cornfield, an auditor with the Department of National Revenue, testified, quite reasonably in my view, that on looking at the discrepancy between her receipts and her claimed expenditures, he concluded that she had no reasonable expectation of profit.

I quite agree that no business with the sort of revenues that she had and the amount of expenses that she was claiming could reasonably expect to earn a profit unless her revenues increased dramatically or her expenses decreased.

I do not, however, think that this approach is entirely consistent with the evidence I heard yesterday. The reason her losses were as great as they were was not because the business had no reasonable expectation of profit or because she was not expending money for the purpose of gaining or producing income from a business. I find as a fact that she was spending money in order to earn a profit and that her expectation of earning a profit was reasonable, if she had chosen to claim reasonable expenses. The problem lies not in the absence of a reasonable expectation of profit – businesses of this sort can be quite lucrative – but rather in the attempt to deduct unreasonable expenses.

Her claim for expenses was, in my opinion, unreasonable. The Crown pleaded that the Minister of National Revenue assumed that her expenses were not laid out for the purpose of gaining or producing income from a business within the meaning of paragraph 18(1)(a) of the *Income Tax Act* [R.S.C. 1985 (5th Supp.), c. 1 (the "Act")], and that since she had no reasonable expectation of profit that, therefore, they were personal and living expenses within the meaning of paragraph 18(1)(h) and section 248 of the *Income Tax Act*.

I think her activities constitute a business and that her evidence has demonstrated, on the balance of probabilities, that the assumption that she had none was wrong. I do not think it is appropriate that novel and possibly unusual types of businesses be discouraged if they are embarked on in good faith.

The portion of the Minister's case with which I do, however, agree is the assertion, not pleaded as an assumption but as a separate ground for upholding the assessment, that the expenses are unreasonable within the meaning of section 67. One needs only to compare the expenses with the revenues to see how disproportionate they are. Some of the expenses claimed are illustrative of what I am saying. For example, in 1987, she had automobile expenses of $2,968.95; clothes and accessories expenses of $3,706.00; entertainment, promotion, and travel, $2,334.56; office in the home, $2,681.00. In 1988, she had automobile expenses of $3,849.00; clothes and accessories of somewhat less at $994.00. In 1989, she had clothes expenses of $1,253.00; entertainment, $1,179.00. Comparing these expenses to the sort of revenues that she was generating, I think that they are unreasonable.

Since the Minister has pleaded as a separate head and not as an assumption that they are unreasonable, the onus is of course on him to establish the truth of the assertion. It is obvious that they are unreasonable, but within a range of indeterminate magnitude.

In disposing of this appeal I have three alternatives: (a) to allow the appeal and to permit the deductions claimed on the ground that the appellant has, on the balance of probabilities, shown that the pleaded assumptions were wrong; (b) to dismiss the appeal on the grounds that it was for the appellant to establish what would have been reasonable; or (c) to refer the matter back to the Minister of National Revenue on the basis that although the expenses were laid out to earn income and with a reasonable expectation of profit, they were unreasonable and that the Minister should consider what portion is reasonable on the basis that a reasonable portion of the expenses was properly deductible.

The first two dispositions are patently wrong, the first because it is unfair to the Minister of National Revenue to allow an excessive deduction and the second because it is unfair to the taxpayer because it allows her no reasonable costs of her business. Procedural fairness and common sense dictate the third alternative.

...

The appellant should be informed, however, that this may be something of a Pyrrhic victory because a good portion of her expenses may, on examination, turn out to be unreasonable. She may be able to persuade the departmental officials that it is reasonable, given her line of work, to deduct the cost of massages, for example; I remain somewhat skeptical. I think the clothes and automobile expenses are, in the context of this business, out of line.

...

Appeals allowed.

NOTES AND QUESTIONS

1.   On what grounds did the Minister reassess the taxpayer in *Cipolonne*? Why did the court reject these grounds? Why did apply section 67? Do you agree with the court's decision? Why or why not?

2.   The decision in *Cipolonne* was questioned in *Mohammad v. Canada*, [1997] F.C.J. No. 1020, [1997] 3 C.T.C. 321, 97 D.T.C. 5503 (F.C.A.), in which the Minister relied on section 67 to limit the deduction of interest expenses on borrowed funds that the taxpayer had used to purchase a residential property for rental purposes. Concluding that the reasonableness of an expense must be assessed on its own, not "collectively, when measured against revenues" (para. 22), and denouncing as arbitrary the notion that expenses cannot be disproportionate to revenues (para. 23), the court rejected the Minister's argument that it was unreasonable for the taxpayer to finance the purchase entirely with borrowed funds because expenses were bound to exceed revenues. More specifically, it declared (at para. 28):

> When evaluating the reasonableness of an expense, one is measuring its reasonableness in terms of its magnitude or quantum. Although such a determination may involve an element of subjective appreciation on the part of the trier of fact, there should always be a search for an objective component. When dealing with interest expenses, the task can be objectified readily. For example, it would have been open to the Minister to challenge the amount of interest being paid ... had the taxpayer agreed to pay interest in excess of market rates.

At the same time, the court acknowledged (at para. 29):

> ... there will be instances where the objective component will be difficult to isolate and, therefore, practical experience informed by commonsense will have to prevail. Such is true in respect of those expenses deemed to be unreasonable because they are believed to be excessive or extravagant: see *Cipollone*.

3.   In *Ammar v. Canada*, [2006] T.C.J. No. 100, [2006] 3 C.T.C. 2001, 2006 D.T.C. 2668 (T.C.C.), the taxpayer carried on an immigration and consulting business for students in Egypt and the Middle East wishing to study in Canada, for the purpose of which he rented an apartment in Cairo at an annual amount of $43,054 in 1997, $24,360 in 1998, $24,405 in 1999 and $43,219 in 2000. Concluding (at para. 8) that the Minister "provided sufficient objective evidence to demonstrate that the rental costs were excessive in 1997 and 2000" the court applied section 67 to limit the deductible amount to $25,000 for each of these years. According to Lamarre T.C.J. (at para. 8):

> Although it is not the CCRA's role to interfere with the appellant's business decision to rent an expensive apartment, and although the rentals for comparable apartments that were given by the respondent in court are for years subsequent to the taxation years at issue, it can be inferred from the evidence that a hotel room or comparable apartments could have cost less than half of what was claimed by the appellant. As a matter of fact, the appellant was able to negotiate half the rate for the apartment in 1998 and 1999. These considerations are in my view the kind of objective components referred to in the above-cited *Mohammad* case. I

would also add that the appellant did not provide the Court with rates for comparable apartments for the years at issue.

4.   In *Olympia Floor & Wall Tile (Que.) Ltd. v. M.N.R.*, [1970] C.T.C. 99, 70 D.T.C. 6085 (Ex. Ct.), where the taxpayer sought to deduct charitable donations as a business expense, the Minister argued, among other things, that the value of the gifts was unreasonable in the circumstances and thus contrary to then subsection 12(2) (now section 67). Referring to "unchallenged evidence that the contributions were necessary" to maintain 25 to 30 per cent of the taxpayer's sales, the court rejected this argument on the basis that a "necessary" expense must also be a "reasonable" expense. Finally, the court added (at para. 7):

> The fact that the business man makes a *bona fide* decision to make disbursements for business reasons raises a presumption in my mind that it was "reasonable" to make such disbursements unless facts are proved that establish that it was not "reasonable."

See also *Gabco Ltd. v. M.N.R.*, [1968] C.T.C. 313, 68 D.T.C. 5210 (Ex. Ct.), in which Cattanach J said (at para. 52) of then subsection 12(2):

> It is not a question of the Minister or this Court substituting its judgment for what is a reasonable amount to pay, but rather a case of the Minister or the Court coming to the conclusion that no reasonable business man would have contracted to pay such an amount having only [a] business consideration ... in mind.

Do these cases suggest that a business purpose test might be relevant to the application of section 67?

5.   Of what, if any, relevance to the reasonableness of an outlay or expense under section 67 is the likelihood that the taxpayer could derive a personal benefit from the expenditure? For cases in which section 67 has been applied to limit the deduction of expenses the benefits of which are likely to be both personal and business-related, see *No. 485 v. M.N.R.* (1957), 18 Tax ABC 358, 58 D.T.C. 69 (T.A.B.) (automobile and entertainment expenses incurred and gifts made by main shareholder of private corporation that owned two apartment buildings); *No. 589 v. M.N.R.* (1958), 21 Tax ABC 153, 59 D.T.C. 41 (T.A.B.) (expenses for travel, meals, and entertainment incurred by president of manufacturing company); *Niessen v. M.N.R.* (1960), 25 Tax ABC 62, 60 D.T.C. 489 (T.A.B.) (reduction in deductible capital cost allowance on automobile used by taxpayer in home renovation business); *Chabot v. M.N.R.* (1961), 26 Tax ABC 204 (T.A.B.) (entertainment expenses incurred by architect); *Meal v. M.N.R.* (1964), 36 Tax ABC 55 (T.A.B.) (entertainment and home office expenses incurred by salesperson); *Ivers v. M.N.R.* (1965), 39 Tax ABC 93 (T.A.B.) (capital cost allowance and expenses for automobile used in part for farming operation and in part personally); *Lewis v. M.N.R.* (1966), 41 Tax ABC 379 (T.A.B.) (capital cost allowance on automobile used in groceteria business); *W.J. Kent & Co. Ltd. v. M.N.R.*, [1971] Tax ABC 1158 (T.A.B.) (capital cost allowance on Rolls Royce used by the taxpayer's president to meet chief executive officers of large mining companies arriving at airports and once a week to drive to the president's cottage); *Upenieks v. M.N.R.*, [1973] C.T.C.

2284, 73 D.T.C. 218 (T.R.B.) (automobile and home office expenses incurred by physician); *Beauchemin v. M.N.R.*, [1977] C.T.C. 2029, 77 D.T.C. 26 (T.R.B.) (capital cost allowance on automobiles, including Porsche, claimed by plastic surgeon); *Mathieu v. M.N.R.*, [1978] C.T.C. 2646, 78 D.T.C. 1474 (T.R.B.) (capital cost allowance on automobile); *Duschesne v. M.N.R.*, [1978] CTC 2197, (1977) 78 D.T.C. 1156 (T.R.B.) (expenses for travel, meals, and entertainment incurred by real estate agent); *Mills v. M.N.R.*, [1981] C.T.C. 2995, 81 D.T.C. 909 (T.R.B.) (automobile, entertainment, and travel expenses incurred by real estate agent); *Graves v. Canada*, [1990] F.C.J. No. 277, [1990] 1 C.T.C. 357, 90 D.T.C. 6300 (F.C.T.D.) (automobile and home office expenses); *Qureshi v. M.N.R.*, [1991] T.C.J. No. 834, [1992] 1 C.T.C. 2370 (T.C.C.) (travel and home office expenses); *Bahl v. Canada*, [1993] F.C.J. No. 33, [1993] 1 C.T.C. 177, 93 D.T.C. 5074 (F.C.T.D.) (automobile expenses); and *Prefontaine v. Canada*, [2001] T.C.J. No. 94, [2001] 2 C.T.C. 2206 (T.C.C.), aff'd [2004] F.C.J. No. 202, [2004] 2 C.T.C. 278, 2004 D.T.C. 6087 (F.C.A.) (home office expenses). Note that many of these expenses would now be subject to specific limitations in sections 67.1 (meals and entertainment), sections 67.2 to 67.4 and paragraphs 13(7)(g) and (h) (passenger vehicles), and subsections 8(13) and 18(12) (home office expenses).

6. Of what, if any, relevance to the reasonableness of an outlay or expense under section 67 is the profitability of the taxpayer's enterprise? In *Bonin v. Canada*, [1999] T.C.J. No. 882, [2000] 2 C.T.C. 2011 (T.C.C.), the taxpayers carried on an Amway distributorship, which incurred net losses of $2,897 in 1984, $3,733 in 1985, $8,266 in 1986, $7,907 in 1987, $4,222 in 1988, $3,048 in 1989, $4,238 in 1990, $8,561 in 1991, $4,746 in 1992, $8,576 in 1993, $11,518 in 1994, $8,952 in 1995, $7,854 in 1996, and $5,822 in 1997. Noting (at paras. 24-25) that the losses in 1994 and 1995 were "the two largest losses in twelve years of business operation" and suggesting that the "continuance" of "losses of this order" beyond "the initial years" of the taxpayers' business "does not seem 'reasonable in the circumstances' of [their] operations," the court disallowed "the deduction of expenses" in excess of revenues in each of these years. Is this result consistent with the approach recommended in *Mohammad*?

7. Of what, if any, relevance to the reasonableness of an outlay or expense under section 67 is the fact that the payment was made to a non-arm's-length person? For cases in which section 67 or its predecessors have been employed to limit the amount that a taxpayer may deduct in respect of remuneration paid to a non-arm's-length party, see *No. 712 v. M.N.R.* (1960), 24 Tax ABC 282 (T.A.B.), which involved payments to the son of the taxpayer company's founder, president, and majority shareholder; *Mulder Bros. Sand & Gravel Ltd. v. M.N.R.*, [1967] Tax ABC 761, 67 D.T.C. 475 (T.A.B.), involving payments to the wife of one of the taxpayer's two shareholders; *Bartlett v. M.N.R.*, [1983] C.T.C. 2512, 83 D.T.C. 461 (T.R.B.), in which the taxpayer corporation sought to deduct amounts paid to the sons of the taxpayer's founder; *Doug Burns Excavation Contracting Ltd. v. M.N.R.*, [1983] C.T.C. 2566, 83 D.T.C. 528

(T.C.C.), where the taxpayer corporation sought to deduct payments to the wife of the corporation's majority shareholder; *Clarke v. M.N.R.*, [1984] C.T.C. 2944, 84 D.T.C. 1839 (T.C.C.), where the taxpayers sought to deduct payments to each of their children for farm labour; *Grant Babcock Ltd. v. M.N.R.*, [1985] 2 C.T.C. 2181, 85 D.T.C. 518 (T.C.C.), in which the taxpayer, a Canadian Tire dealership the shares of which were owned primarily by Mr. Babcock, sought to deduct salary and bonus payments made to Mrs. Babcock, which the court characterized as "not reasonable in accordance with good business considerations"; and *Maduke Foods Ltd. v. M.N.R.*, [1989] F.C.J. No. 841, [1989] 2 C.T.C. 284, 89 D.T.C. 5458 (F.C.T.D.), where the taxpayer paid substantial salaries to a shareholder's wife and children. For cases in which section 67 has been applied to limit deductions for rental payments to non-arm's-length parties, see *Cohen v. M.N.R.* (1963), 31 Tax ABC 216; *Geurts v. Canada*, [1994] T.C.J. No. 731, 95 D.T.C. 89 (T.C.C.); and *Produits pour Toitures Fransyl Ltée v. Canada*, [2005] A.C.I. no 156, 2005, 2008 D.T.C. 564 (T.C.C.), aff'd [2006] F.C.J. No. 405, [2007] 2 C.T.C. 71 (F.C.A.).

8. In *Humphrey v. Canada*, [2006] T.C.J. No. 107, [2006] 3 C.T.C. 2136, 2006 D.T.C. 2730 (T.C.C.), the taxpayer sought to deduct amounts that she paid back to her former employer from whom she had embezzled almost $100,000 during the years 1997 to 2000. Since the taxpayer had declared bankruptcy and consequently did not actually pay any tax on the embezzled funds, the court relied on section 67 to disallow the deduction on the basis that it would be "unreasonable for her to be able to deduct the repayments of amounts on which she has never paid tax" (para. 14).

B. Meals and Entertainment

For the purposes of the Act, other than the moving expense deduction in section 62, the child-care expense deduction in section 63, and the medical expenses tax credit in section 118.2, subsection 67.1(1) limits the amount that a taxpayer may deduct for amounts "paid or payable in respect of the human consumption of food or beverages or the enjoyment of entertainment" to 50 per cent of the lesser of "the amount actually paid or payable" and "an amount ... that would be reasonable in the circumstances." For this purpose, paragraph 67.1(4)(b) defines "entertainment" to include "amusement and recreation," and paragraph 67.1(4)(a) stipulates that "no amount paid or payable for travel on an airplane, train or bus shall be considered to be in respect of food, beverages or entertainment consumed or enjoyed while travelling thereon," thereby excluding items such as airplane meals and in-flight movies from the operation of the rule. In addition, where a taxpayer attends a "conference, convention, seminar or similar event," the fee for which "entitles the participant to food, beverages or entertainment (other than incidental beverages and refreshments made available during the course of meetings or receptions at the event)" and does not identify a reasonable portion as compensation for the food, beverages or entertainment, subsection 67.1(3) deems the amount payable in respect of food, beverages, or entertainment to be $50 per day.

Notwithstanding these rules, however, subsection 67.1(2) lists a number of exceptions to the percentage limitation in subsection 67.1(1), providing that this provision "does not apply to an amount paid or payable by a person in respect of the consumption of food or beverages or the enjoyment of entertainment where the amount":

(a) is paid or payable for food, beverages or entertainment provided for, or in expectation of, compensation in the ordinary course of a business carried on by that person of providing the food, beverages or entertainment for consumption;

(b) relates to a fund-raising event the primary purpose of which is to benefit a registered charity;

(c) is an amount for which the person is compensated and the amount of the compensation is reasonable and specifically identified in writing to the person paying the compensation;

(d) is required to be included in computing any taxpayer's income because of the application of section 6 in respect of food or beverages consumed or entertainment enjoyed by the taxpayer or a person with whom the taxpayer does not deal at arm's length, or would be so required but for subparagraph 6(6)(a)(ii) [exemption for board and lodging benefits at a remote work site];

(e) is an amount that

(i) is not paid or payable in respect of a conference, convention, seminar or similar event,

(ii) would, but for subparagraph 6(6)(a)(i) [exemption for board and lodging at a special work site], be required to be included in computing any taxpayer's income for a taxation year because of the application of section 6 in respect of food or beverages consumed or entertainment enjoyed by the taxpayer or a person with whom the taxpayer does not deal at arm's length, and

(iii) is paid or payable in respect of the taxpayer's duties performed at a work site in Canada that is

(A) outside any urban area, as defined by the last Census Directory published by Statistics Canada before the year, that has a population of at least 40,000 individuals as determined in the last census published by Statistics Canada before the year, and

(B) at least 30 kilometres from the nearest point on the boundary of the nearest such urban area;

(e.1) is an amount that

(i)   is not paid or payable in respect of entertainment or of a conference, convention, seminar or similar event,

(ii)   would, if this Act were read without reference to subparagraph 6(6)(a)(i), be required to be included in computing a taxpayer's income for a taxation year because of the application of section 6 in respect of food or beverages consumed by the taxpayer or by a person with whom the taxpayer does not deal at arm's length,

(iii)   is paid or payable in respect of the taxpayer's duties performed at a site in Canada at which the person carried on a construction activity or at a construction work camp referred to in subparagraph (iv) in respect of the site, and

(iv)   is paid or payable for food or beverages provided at a construction work camp, at which the taxpayer is lodged, that was constructed or installed at or near the site to province board and lodging to employees while they are engaged in construction services at the site; or

(f)   is in respect of one of six or fewer special events held in a calendar year at which the food, beverages or entertainment is generally available to all individuals employed by the person at a particular place of business of the person and consumed or enjoyed by those individuals.

Section 67.1 was enacted effective for amounts incurred after June 17, 1987, and originally limited the amount deductible in respect of food, beverages, and entertainment to 80 per cent of the lesser of the amount actually paid or payable and a reasonable amount. For expenses incurred after February 21, 1994 in respect of food and beverages consumed and entertainment enjoyed after February 1994, the percentage limitation on deductibility for these expenses was reduced from 80 per cent to 50 per cent.

Despite the relatively recent enactment of this provision, the idea of limiting the deductibility of business meals and entertainment has a long history in Canada. In the June 1961 budget speech, the Minister of Finance expressed concern about "abuse by some taxpayers of the provisions for the deduction of amounts expended for the purpose of gaining income from a business." According to the Minister:

> Since ours is a free enterprise economy, our income tax law assumes that the businessman is the best judge of the extent to which he should incur expenses of this nature, and naturally the government has been reluctant to recommend, and parliament to impose, rules that would restrict him unduly in this respect. However, the government has no intention of allowing so-called "expense account living" to thrive and I am consequently serving notice that in future the allowance of expenses of this nature will be subject to more intensive scrutiny. I am hopeful that more stringent legislation will not prove to be necessary.

The Minister of Finance returned to this theme in his June 1963 budget speech, expressing concern about "the way in which certain taxpayers seem to be able to eat, drink and entertain on a lavish scale on the basis of what is called a business expense but which is actually financed in large part at the expense of the public revenue." Instead of statutory reform, however, the government of the day announced that it would direct the revenue department "to tighten up its administration of the law and to pursue a policy of vigorous enforcement."

Twenty-four years later, in June 1987, the federal government announced in a document accompanying its 1987 *White Paper on Tax Reform* that it would limit the deductibility of expenses for business meals and entertainment to 80 per cent of the amount otherwise deductible, except for:

- the cost of meals or recreational events provided by an employer for the general benefit of employees (other than the direct operating cost to an employer of providing free or subsidized meals in a facility which is not accessible to employees generally);

- the cost to a restaurant, hotel or airline of providing meals to customers in the ordinary course of business;

- the cost of meals and entertainment to the extent that such costs are included as a taxable benefit to the employees or the employer is reimbursed for the costs; or

- meals or entertainment expenses relating to an event where the primary purpose is to benefit a registered charity.[2]

These exceptions are found in subsection 67.1(2).

The leading case on the purpose and application of section 67.1 is *Stapley v. Canada*, [2006] F.C.J. No. 130, 2006 D.T.C. 6075 (F.C.A.).

Stapley v. Canada
[2006] F.C.J. No. 130, 2006 D.T.C. 6075 (F.C.A.)

SEXTON JA (DECARY AND EVANS JJA concurring):

...During the 2000, 2001 and 2002 taxation years, the respondent was a self-employed real estate agent who marketed and sold residential properties. His business yielded commission income. In the 2000, 2001 and 2002 taxation years, he grossed amounts of $152,270.00, $113,440.00 and $165,610.00, respectively.

The respondent bought gift certificates for food and beverages and tickets to various concerts and sporting events for clients who had purchased or sold homes through his business. He gave these vouchers and tickets to his clients in the expectation that they would send him more business or refer more clients to him. In other words, the costs of the vouchers and tickets were marketing expenses. The respondent neither consumed the food or beverages obtained through the gift certificates, nor attended the sporting events or concerts to

---

[2] Canada, Department of Finance, *Tax Reform 1987: Income Tax Reform* (Ottawa: Department of Finance, 1987) at 86.

which the tickets provided admission. Indeed, the respondent had no control over how his client recipients used the vouchers and tickets.

The respondent deducted the costs of the vouchers and tickets – $20,125.00, $14,208.00 and $19,145.00 – for the 2000, 2001 and 2002 taxation years. In February 2004, the Minister reassessed the respondent and increased the respondent's net commission income by $10,062.00, $7,104.00 and $9,572.00 for the respective taxation years. In short, the Minister disallowed 50 percent of the deductions that the respondent had claimed for the gift certificates and tickets, pursuant to subsection 67.1(1) of the ITA.

...

IV The Findings of the Tax Court of Canada

The TCC held that the Minister was wrong to disallow 50 percent of the respondent's claimed deductions of $20,125.00, $14,208.00 and $19,145.00 pursuant to subsection 67.1(1).

For the TCC, the respondent's purchases were for the purpose of, or in respect of, earning income from his business and not consumption or entertainment. The amount the respondent paid for the vouchers and tickets constituted a reduction in, or a rebate of, his real estate commission. It was a form of discount for the purpose of gaining income. Since the respondent did not participate in the consumption or enjoyment, the purpose of the purchases was "in respect of earning a profit and nothing else."

V. Analysis

...

(2) Interpretation of Subsection 67.1(1)

a) The Grammatical and Ordinary Sense the Words

According to subsection 67.1(1):

> For the purposes of this Act, other than sections 62, 63 and 118.2, an amount paid or payable in respect of the human consumption of food or beverages or the enjoyment of entertainment shall be deemed to be 50% of the lesser of ...

The appellant contends that nothing in this wording limits the application of the provision to situations in which the taxpayer participated in the consumption of the food or beverages or in the enjoyment of the entertainment. Indeed, the provision certainly does not specify that a particular actor must consume or enjoy the goods in issue for the subsection to apply.

Moreover, the French version of subsection 67.1(1) indicates that if any person partakes in the purchased food, beverages or entertainment, then the provision is applicable:

Pour l'application de la présente loi, sauf des articles 62, 63 et 118.2, un montant payé ou payable pour des aliments, des boissons ou des divertissements pris par des personnes est réputé correspondre à 50% du moins élevé du montant réellement payé ou payable et du montant qui serait raisonnable dans les circonstances. [emphasis added]

The plain wording of the subsection thus suggests that there is no requirement of taxpayer use in subsection 67.1(1). Moreover, the words "in respect of" in subsection 67.1(1) are of "the widest possible scope." *Nowegijick v. The Queen et al.* (1983), [83 DTC 5041] 144 D.L.R. (3d) 193 (S.C.C.) ["*Nowegijick*"] at 200. According to *Nowegijick* at 200:

They import such meanings as "in relation to", "with reference to" or "in connection with". The phrase "in respect of" is probably the widest of any expression intended to convey some connection between two related subject-matters.

Accordingly, even though the respondent's expenditures were for a business purpose, it must also be acknowledged that they were "in respect of" the consumption of food and the enjoyment of entertainment. It seems, then, that the deductions in issue are caught by the plain wording of subsection 67.1(1), even though the respondent's clients consumed the purchased food and entertainment and the respondent did not. A contextual analysis sustains this conclusion.

b) The Scheme of the Act

Subsection 67.1(1) is a broadly drafted rule to which there are almost a dozen of what can be understood as "exceptions." Three of them are contained in subsection 67.1(1) itself. They address moving expenses (section 62), child care expenses (section 63) and the medical expense credit (section 118.2). Subsection 67.1(2) contains six more exceptions to the general deduction limitation in subsection 67.1(1). Subsection 67.1(3) arguably articulates an exception for fees relating to conferences, conventions, seminars and similar events. Finally, paragraph 67.1(4)(a) excludes amounts relating to airline, train and bus travel.

In my view, two conclusions can be drawn from this multitude of highly specific exceptions. First, had Parliament intended pure marketing expenditures, such as those in issue, to fall outside the scope of subsection 67.1(1), it clearly would not have been shy about adding a twelfth exception to that effect. However, the respondent's expenses are not covered by any of the exceptions to subsection 67.1(1). Second, at least two of the subsection 67.1(2) exceptions can be taken as suggesting that there is no requirement of taxpayer consumption or enjoyment in subsection 67.1(1). After all, were there such a requirement, these exceptions would be unnecessary.

For instance, according to paragraph 67.1(2)(a), subsection 67.1(1) does not apply to amounts:

paid or payable for food, beverages or entertainment provided for, or in expectation of, compensation in the ordinary course of a business carried on by that person of providing the food, beverages or entertainment for compensation;

This provision enables a taxpayer whose product is food, such as a restaurant, to deduct the full cost of its promotional samples. Arguably, this clarification would not be required were there a requirement of taxpayer consumption in subsection 67.1(1).

The same can be said of paragraph 67.1(2)(d), which excises from the deduction limitation in subsection 67.1(1) an amount that:

> is required to be included in computing any taxpayer's income because of the application of section 6 in respect of food or beverages consumed or entertainment enjoyed by the taxpayer or a person with whom the taxpayer does not deal at arm's length, or would be so required but for subparagraph 6(6)(a)(ii);

Because of paragraph 67.1(2)(d), the subsection 67.1(1) deduction limitation does not apply if the amount in issue would be included in an employee's income except for subparagraph 6(6)(a)(ii), which relates to employment at a remote location. In other words, an employer can fully deduct an amount paid for meals for employees at a location where, due to its remoteness from any established community, the employee could not reasonably be expected to establish and maintain a self-contained domestic establishment. Paragraph 67.1(2)(d) also exempts from the 50-percent limitation employer-provided allowances or reimbursements for meal or entertainment expenses that must be included in an employee's income. Evidently, this exception contemplates that subsection 67.1(1) speaks to consumption by individuals other than the taxpayer/employer.

In my opinion, if subsection 67.1(1) only covered cases in which the taxpayer participated in the consumption or enjoyment of the food or entertainment in issue, these two exceptions would be redundant. The legislative scheme thus suggests that subsection 67.1(1) does not contain a requirement of taxpayer use. If this is correct, the respondent would not be permitted to deduct 100 percent of the expenses in issue. This result, however, may not be entirely consistent with the purpose of section 67.1.

c) The Mischief Sought To Be Cured by the Provision

Subsection 67.1(1) is a rule that applies to the calculation of income. A taxpayer must include in income, income from a business. Income from a business is defined as the profit from a business [Section 9 of the Act]. In calculating the profit from a business, a taxpayer cannot deduct personal or living expenses [paragraph 18(1)(h) of the Act]. However, a taxpayer may deduct reasonable expenses made for the purpose of producing income from a business [paragraph 18(1)(a) of the Act]. Subsection 67.1(1) limits the quantum of paragraph 18(1)(a) deductions with respect to food, beverage and entertainment expenses.

Logic suggests that subsection 67.1(1) fulfills the following function in the legislative scheme. To reduce the amount of tax owing, a taxpayer will seek to minimize the value of income. One way to do so involves enlarging the size of paragraph 18(1)(a) deductions. Thus, the taxpayer may blend personal and business expenses and attempt to deduct them both as business expenses under paragraph 18(1)(a). For instance, a taxpayer might characterize the cost of a dinner eaten with a client as a wholly-deductible, paragraph 18(1)(a) business expense as opposed to a non-deductible, paragraph 18(1)(h) personal one. Recognizing this, subsection 67.1(1) arbitrarily apportions this kind of "dual-purpose" expense at fifty percent between income-earning and personal expenses.

Indeed, in *Racco Industrial Roofing Ltd. v. Canada*, [1997] T.C.J. No. 332 at paras. 4 and 5, Mogan T.C.J. commented:

> 4 ... I shall attempt to determine not the purpose of the Act [the ITA] as a whole but only the purpose of section 67.1. In my opinion, the purpose of section 67.1 can best be determined by looking at the law immediately before its enactment. This section was first enacted in 1988 applicable (generally speaking) to expenses incurred after 1987. Under paragraph 18(1)(a), any non-capital expense incurred for the purpose of gaining or producing income from business or property is deductible in computing income. Specifically, the cost of inviting a customer to lunch or dinner or to a theatrical or sporting event is deductible under paragraph 18(1)(a). By ordinary commercial standards, it is an accepted cost of promoting business akin to advertising. Treating a customer in this manner involves "the human consumption of food or beverages or the enjoyment of entertainment" in the words of subsection 67.1(1).

> 5 Before the enactment of section 67.1, any reasonable amount expended on the human consumption of food or beverages or the enjoyment of entertainment was deductible if it satisfied the "purpose" test in paragraph 18(1)(a). After the enactment of section 67.1, any such reasonable amount was deductible only to the extent of 80% [currently 50 percent] even if it did satisfy the "purpose" test in paragraph 18(1)(a), unless it fell within a specific exception in subsection 67.1(2). In *Lor-Wes Contracting Ltd. v. The Queen*, 85 D.T.C. 5310, the Federal Court of Appeal quoted a statement by the Minister of Finance in the House of Commons as a guide to the interpretation of a specific provision of the Income Tax Act. In this appeal, the origin of section 67.1 can be found in a document entitled "Income Tax Reform" issued by the Minister of Finance on June 18, 1987 in which he stated his intention to limit the deduction for "business meals and entertainment expenses". The document states at page 86:

>> As part of broadening the tax base to permit lower tax rates, the deduction for business meals (including food and beverages) and entertainment expenses (such as accommodation at a resort and tickets for the theatre, a concert, athletic event or other performance) will be limited to 80 percent of their cost.

>> ...

>> Business meals and entertainment involve an element of personal consumption and therefore some part of their cost can properly be characterized as a personal expense that should not be deductible. While it is difficult to ascertain what portion of the cost of meals and entertainment represents personal consumption, it is clear that a full deduction for such expenses simply because they are undertaken in the course of business allows the write-off of some part of expenses that are of a personal nature. Many countries have limited the deductibility of meals and entertainment expenses. For example, similar restrictions currently apply in the United Kingdom, Australia and the United States.

> Section 67.1 with its 80% limitation was enacted in 1988 as a direct consequence of the Minister's proposal for income tax reform announced on June 18, 1987.

[emphasis added]

Other extrinsic evidence affirms Mogan T.C.J.'s understanding of the purpose of section 67.1. For instance, according to December 1987 Tax Reform Supplementary Information:

> Currently, a taxpayer may deduct reasonable expenses for meals and entertainment incurred for business purposes. The present law effectively allows a deduction for some part of expenses that are personal in nature since business meals and entertainment necessarily involve an element of personal consumption.
>
> The White Paper proposed to limit the deduction for these expenses to 80% of their cost. The 80% limitation would apply to all business meals, including food and beverages, as well as to the cost of meals while travelling or attending a seminar, conference, convention or similar function. As well it would apply to tickets to an entertainment or sporting event, gratuities and cover charges, room rentals to provide entertainment, and the cost of private boxes at sports facilities. Where a taxpayer is reimbursed for the cost of a business meal or entertainment, the 80% limitation would apply to the person making the reimbursement.
>
> ...
>
> The restriction proposed received general support. It was also noted that similar, and in some cases more severe, restrictions apply in other countries. However, the Commons and Senate committees recommended that these expenses be deductible in full for persons in travel status.
>
> The government gave careful consideration to these suggestions but rejected the notion that out-of-town meals and entertainment should be excluded from the restriction, since they too involve an element of personal consumption. The government intends to proceed with the 80% limitation on business meals and entertainment expenses as proposed in the White Paper.

[emphasis added]

Budget Supplementary Information from 1994 is in a similar vein:

> The Canadian income tax system allows deductions for reasonable expenses incurred for the purpose of earning income from business, property or, in certain circumstances, employment. The deduction with respect to business meals and entertainment expenses is currently restricted to 80% of such expenses to reflect the fact that they contain an element of personal consumption.
>
> A similar restriction applies for the purposes of the Goods and Services Tax (GST) [section 236 of the Excise Tax Act-ed.] so that effectively only 80% of the GST paid on business meals and entertainment expenses may be recovered as an input tax credit. [This does not apply to registered charities-ed.]
>
> The government believes the tax system will be made fairer, and will better reflect the personal consumption element, by reducing the income tax deduction and the GST input tax credit for eligible business meals and entertainment expenses from 80% to 50%. This restriction will apply to expenses in respect of meals, beverages and entertainment consumed or enjoyed after February 1994.

[emphasis added]

The respondent did not consume the food or enjoy the entertainment in issue. Therefore, he was not attempting to deduct any personal or living expenses under the guise of business ones. In other words, his deductions are not an abuse targeted by subsection 67.1(1). A purposive approach, then, favours upholding the TCC's decision in this case.

d) Conclusions on the Question of Interpretation

While the first two interpretive aids — the plain meaning of the provision and the scheme of the legislation — suggest that the respondent's deductions are limited by subsection 67.1(1), the object of the provision leads to the opposite conclusion. In suggesting how to resolve these types of conflicts in *Canada Trustco* at para. 12, the Supreme Court of Canada quoted approvingly from *65302 British Columbia Ltd. v. Canada*, [1999] 3 SCR 804 at para. 51 (citing P. W. Hogg and J. E. Magee, Principles of Canadian Income Tax Law (2nd ed. 1997), at 475-76):

> It would introduce intolerable uncertainty into the Income Tax Act if clear language in a detailed provision of the Act were to be qualified by unexpressed exceptions derived from a court's view of the object and purpose of the provision.

Given that the respondent's expenditures do not fall under any of the express exceptions to subsection 67.1(1), I must find that he can only deduct 50 percent of them. The conclusion that his expenditures are caught by subsection 67.1(1) is confirmed by *Structures G.B. Ltée v. Canada*, [97 DTC 1146] [1996] T.C.J. No. 793 at paras. 11 and 12, wherein the TCC stated:

> 11 Secondly, counsel for the appellant argued that section 67.1 of the Act was intended to apply to entertainment expenses such as business meals and entertainment in which there was a personal component of enjoyment for the payer. He thus argued that the section does not apply in cases where the expenditure is made essentially for work purposes. This argument is not without weight, especially if one considers the title of section 67.1 of the Act: "Expenses for food, etc."

> 12 However, nothing in the wording of subsection 67.1(1) of the Act limits its application to amounts paid for food and beverages for entertainment purposes. Further, as counsel for the respondent noted, the list of exceptions described in subsection 67.1(2) of the Act, and especially in paragraph 67.1(2)(d), which excludes application of the 80 percent proportion in subsection 67.1(1) of the Act to food which must be included in calculating an employee's income, leads the Court to conclude that subsection 67.1(1) of the Act applies to any expense relating to food, beverages or entertainment. [internal citations omitted]

Nevertheless, I would like to note that, in my respectful opinion, it seems unfair to cut the respondent's deductions in half. The respondent could have purchased flowers or books for his clients and deducted 100 percent of their costs. Likewise, he could have fully "deducted" rebates on his real estate commission or gifts of cash to his clients. Thus, in its current form, section 67.1 interferes with taxpayers' business decisions and in particular, how they allocate their marketing budgets. It provides them with an incentive to forgo purchasing gifts of food and entertainment for the purpose of building and maintaining their client relationships. It is conceivable that the imposition of the arbitrary deduction limit of 50 percent can be justified for administrative reasons — that is, it could be too difficult in every case to determine what proportion of an expense was for personal consumption, if any. To achieve an equitable result, one might have thought that Parliament would have enabled the taxpayer to file evidence to rebut a presumption that the subsection 67.1(1) deduction limit applies.

In any event, the statute dictates the result in this case. While the respondent's expenses may have been in respect of producing income from a business, they were also "in respect of the human consumption of food or beverages or the enjoyment of entertainment." Therefore, they are caught by subsection 67.1(1) of the ITA.

The appeal should be allowed, the decision of the TCC should be set aside and the taxpayer's appeal from the assessments of tax should be dismissed.

Appeal allowed.

NOTES AND QUESTIONS

1.   On what basis did the Tax Court of Canada decision in *Stapley* conclude that subsection 67.1(1) did not apply to the expenses incurred by the taxpayer? Why did the Federal Court of Appeal reject this argument? Do you agree with the court's interpretation? Why or why not?

2.   For other cases in which section 67.1 has been considered, see *Kelowna Flightcraft Air Charter Ltd. v. Canada*, [2003] T.C.J. No. 302, [2003] 4 C.T.C. 2252, 2003 D.T.C. 611 (T.C.C.); *Vergos v. Canada*, [2001] T.C.J. No. 808, [2002] 1 C.T.C. 2613 (T.C.C.); *Ellis v. Canada*, [1998] T.C.J. No. 638, [1998] 4 C.T.C. 2373, 98 D.T.C. 1885 (T.C.C.); *Racco Industrial Roofing Ltd. v. Canada*, [1997] T.C.J. No. 332, [1997] 2 C.T.C. 3055, 97 D.T.C. 331 (T.C.C.); *Structures G.B. Ltée v. Canada*, [1996] T.C.J. No. 793, 96 D.T.C. 1590 (T.C.C.); *North Waterloo Publishing Ltd. v. Canada*, [1996] T.C.J. No. 1528, [1997] 1 C.T.C. 2557 (T.C.C.); and *Powrmatic du Canada Ltée v. Canada*, [1993] T.C.J. No. 589, [1994] 1 C.T.C. 2274, 94 D.T.C. 1196 (T.C.C.).

3.   The views of the CRA on section 67.1 are contained in *Interpretation Bulletin* IT-518R, "Food, Beverages and Entertainment Expenses," April 16, 1996. Unfortunately, the bulletin has not been revised to reflect the 1998 amendments that limited the exception in former paragraph 67.1(2)(e) (now paragraph 67.1(2)(f)) and introduced the new exception for expenses related to a special work site in paragraph 67.1(2)(e) as it currently reads. Nor does the bulletin address paragraph 67.1(2)(e.1), which allows full deductibility of expenses incurred after 2001 for meals provided to employees at work camps. In order to be fully deductible under paragraph 67.1(2)(e.1), the meal expenses must relate to meals provided to employees who are lodged at the site and who are engaged in providing construction services nearby. The bulletin is, nonetheless, relevant for other aspects of the statutory rule.

According to paragraph 17 of the bulletin, expenses for "food and beverages" include "any related expenses such as taxes and tips." In addition, the paragraph adds, "the cost of a restaurant gift certificate is considered to be an expense for food or beverages and is subject to this limitation."

Paragraph 18 elaborates on the statutory definition of "entertainment" in paragraph 67.1(4)(b), suggesting that entertainment expenses include:

(a)   the cost of tickets for a theatre, concert, athletic event or other performance:

(b)   the cost of private boxes at sports facilities;

(c)   the cost of room rentals to provide entertainment, such as a hospitality suite;

(d)   the cost of a cruise;

(e)   the cost of admission to a fashion show;

(f)   the cost of entertaining guests at night clubs, athletic, social and sporting clubs and on vacation and other similar trips.

Paragraph 19 emphasizes that an expense in respect of food, beverages, or entertainment must have been incurred for the purpose of earning income in order to be deductible even in part.

Paragraphs 5 to 13 of the bulletin address the exceptions in subsection 67.1(2) of the Act. According to paragraph 5 of the bulletin, the exception in paragraph 67.1(2)(a) is intended to exempt, "for example, restaurants, hotels and airlines from the 50 per cent limitation if the expenses are incurred to provide food, beverages, or entertainment to paying customers," as well as promotional samples where "a taxpayer's product or service is food, beverages or entertainment." According to paragraph 6 of the bulletin, the exception in paragraph 67.1(2)(b) applies only to events designed to raise funds for a registered charity, not to events carried on by a registered charity; as a result, it explains, "the cost of purchasing tickets for a client to attend a series of plays put on by an amateur theatre group that is a registered charity is not exempt from the 50% limitation."

Paragraph 7 of the bulletin explains the exception in paragraph 67.1(2)(c), according to which the 50 per cent limitation will not apply if the amount otherwise subject to the limitation is (1) an amount for which the person is compensated, (2) reasonable, and (3) specifically identified in writing to the person paying the compensation. For example, the bulletin explains, if "a self-employed individual expends a reasonable amount for meals while away from home" and furnishes clients with written bills identifying these amounts as expenses relating to meals, "[t]he self-employed individual would be entitled to fully deduct the meal expenses." In this circumstance, however, the bulletin adds, the client would then be subject to the 50 per cent limitation.

Paragraph 8 discusses the exceptions in paragraph 67.1(1)(d). Referring to subparagraph 6(6)(a)(ii), this paragraph explains that "amounts are not restricted if paid for food or beverages for employees at a location where, due to its remoteness from any established community, the employee could not reasonably be expected to establish and maintain a self-contained domestic establishment." The bulletin also notes that "an employer is not subject to the 50% limitation on allowances or reimbursements for meal or entertainment expenses that have to be included in an employee's income."

According to paragraph 9, the exception in former paragraph 67.1(2)(e) (now paragraph 67.1(2)(f)) "exempts costs incurred for a Christmas party or similar event to which all employees at a particular place of business have access." With respect to the expression "particular place of business," paragraph 10 of the bulletin suggests that:

> [f]or the purposes of paragraph 67.1(2)(e), a "particular place of business" could include a cluster of buildings, a building or a portion of a building, depending upon the circumstances. For example, an employer who occupies one storey of a building in the west of the city and a building in the east of the city would have two distinct places of business. On the other hand, an employer who occupies two or more buildings adjacent to each other might only have one particular place of business in respect of those buildings, depending on the surrounding circumstances. If access to the buildings is restricted for security, safety or other operational reasons, each of those buildings could be regarded as a separate place of business.

Paragraph 12 explains that, for the exception in former paragraph 67.1(2)(e) to apply, "it is not necessary for a party or other event to be held at the place of business; it may be held at a restaurant, rented hall or other location." It also notes that if the party or event is "only available to, or is primarily aimed at, selected employees or the owners, partners, managers or shareholders, the costs are not exempted from the 50% limitation." Nonetheless, it adds, "a party or event that is aimed only at employees of one or more specific divisions within a very large organization could qualify for the exemption, provided the event is open to all employees within that division." In addition, it states, the exception for special events also applies "to the costs of food, beverages and entertainment for the employees' spouses and children, provided these are offered to spouses and children of all employees."

4.   For a comparative examination of rules designed to limit the deductibility of entertainment expenses, see Claire F.L. Young, "Deductibility of Entertainment and Home Office Expenses: New Restrictions To Deal with Old Problems" (1989) 37(2) Can. Tax J. 227.

III. DEEMED PROCEEDS

Sections 68 and 69 are anti-avoidance rules that specify the amount at which certain transfers of property are deemed to have occurred for tax purposes. Section 68 applies "[w]here an amount received or receivable from a person can reasonably be regarded as being in part the consideration for the disposition of a particular property of a taxpayer or as being in part consideration for the provision of particular services by a taxpayer." Subsection 69 applies to various kinds of non-arm's-length transfers. The following cases and commentary examine section 68 and its predecessors and the basic rule applicable to non-arm's-length transfers in subsection 69(1).

A. Allocation on Disposition of Property or Provision of Services

Where a taxpayer enters into an agreement disposing of different kinds of property, or disposing of property and promising to provide services, in exchange for an aggregate amount, a question arises as to how these global proceeds should be allocated among the various kinds of property or services included in the sale. In addition to the global purchase price, the allocation of this price among different items is often a matter of considerable negotiation between the parties to the agreement.

As a general rule, vendors, who are likely to have claimed capital cost allowance (CCA) on depreciable property in previous taxation years, will prefer to allocate as much of the proceeds as possible to non-depreciable capital property (for example, land) and depreciable property on which little or no CCA has been claimed, in order to minimize any recapture on previously claimed CCA; maximize the amount of any capital gain, only half of which is taxable; and/or maximize any terminal losses that might be realized on the disposition of depreciable property. Purchasers, in contrast, will generally prefer to allocate as much of the proceeds as possible to inventory or services provided, since these are fully deductible in computing the purchaser's income, or to depreciable property, especially depreciable property with a high rate of CCA, in order to benefit from high CCAs and/or terminal losses on the subsequent disposition of this property. As a result, the interests of those selling and buying a business or property are generally opposed.

In some cases, however, vendors and purchasers may be able to agree on an allocation of the global proceeds from the disposition that minimizes their combined tax liability. For example, where a vendor has, because of accumulated losses from prior years, claimed little or no CCA in respect of depreciable property of one or more classes, it may be mutually beneficial to allocate a substantial portion of the proceeds of a sale to depreciable property, enabling the purchaser to claim substantial CCA with little or no recapture to the vendor. Alternatively, where the vendor has claimed substantial CCA on one or more classes of depreciable property and the purchaser has accumulated losses from prior taxation years, it may be mutually advantageous to allocate most of the proceeds to non-depreciable property, thereby avoiding recapture on the depreciable property and reducing the amount of CCA that the purchaser may subsequently claim. In these cases, the mutual tax benefit resulting from an agreed-upon allocation is likely to be shared between the parties through agreement on the global purchase price.

In order to limit opportunities for abuse in these circumstances, section 68 stipulates that "[w]here an amount received or receivable from a person can reasonably be regarded as being in part the consideration for the disposition of a particular property of a taxpayer or as being in part consideration for the provision of particular services by a taxpayer,":

> (a) the part of the amount that can reasonably be regarded as being the consideration for the disposition shall be deemed to be proceeds of disposition of the particular property irrespective of the form or legal effect of the contract or agreement, and the person to whom the property was disposed of shall be deemed to have acquired it for an amount equal to that part; and

> (b) the part of the amount that can reasonably be regarded as being the consideration for the provision of particular services shall be deemed to be an amount received or receivable by the taxpayer in respect of those services irrespective of the form or legal effect of the contract or agreement, and that part shall be deemed to be an amount paid or payable to the taxpayer by the person to whom the services were rendered in respect of those services.

Like subsections 6(3) and 16(1), this provision is an anti-avoidance rule that applies "irrespective of the form or legal effect" of a contract or agreement, where an amount can "reasonably be regarded" as something other than it would otherwise be according to the agreement entered into between the parties.

On February 27, 2004, draft legislation was introduced to amend the opening words of section 68. The proposed amendment would apply where "an amount received or receivable from a person can reasonably be regarded as being in part the consideration for the disposition of a particular property of a taxpayer, for the provision of particular services by a taxpayer, or for a restrictive covenant as defined by subsection 56.4(1) agreed to by a taxpayer." The proposed amendment is meant to apply in circumstances where consideration received or receivable by a taxpayer is in part for a restrictive covenant (as defined by new subsection 56.4(1)) agreed to by the taxpayer. The proposed amendment also includes a new subsection 68(c), which provides that in cases where an amount received or receivable is in consideration for a restrictive covenant:

> the part of the amount that can reasonably be regarded as being consideration for the restrictive covenant is deemed to be an amount received or receivable by the taxpayer in respect of the restrictive covenant irrespective of the form or legal effect of the contract or agreement, and that part is deemed to be an amount paid or payable to the taxpayer by the person to whom the restrictive covenant was granted.

It follows that in such a case, the part of the consideration that can reasonably be regarded as being for the restrictive covenant is considered to be an amount that is received or receivable by the taxpayer in respect of the restrictive covenant.

Section 68 is derived from paragraph 20(6)(g) of the 1952 *Income Tax Act*, which provided for a reallocation of proceeds "where an amount can reasonably be regarded as being in part the consideration for the disposition of depreciable property of a prescribed class and as being in part consideration for something else." Among the many cases in which this provision has been applied, one of the most illustrative is *Canadian Propane Gas & Oil Ltd. v. M.N.R.*, [1972] C.T.C. 566, 73 D.T.C. 5019 (F.C.T.D.).

Canadian Propane Gas & Oil Ltd. v. M.N.R.
[1972] C.T.C. 566, 73 D.T.C. 5019 (F.C.T.D.)

CATTANACH, J: ... The appellant is one of the largest retailers of propane gas in Canada. In addition to its own enterprise and marketing techniques the appellant achieved that pre-eminence in its trade by a systematic policy of purchasing smaller retailers in the same trade when those retailers are competitors in the same area or when the appellant wished to expand into a different geographic area.

...

The preference of the appellant was to purchase the assets whereas the vendor almost invariably wished to sell its shares.

The appellant usually began negotiations by an offer to purchase the assets. If the vendor was insistent upon selling its shares the appellant would comply but by a contract which was predicated upon conditions which would permit the appellant, after its examination of the vendor's records, to avoid the contract or alter it.

...

After having succeeded in getting access to the vendor's financial records the appellant would then prepare its own pro forma operating statement which was in reality a projection of potential earnings taking into account the assets involved, their location, the vendor's business in the area and the appellant's estimate of the better use it could make of these assets by the use of its superior marketing techniques and business experience. It also took into account any trade or marketing name in use by the vendor which the appellant could use as a "fighting" trade name.

The thinking which influenced the preparation of a projection of earnings is that the value of physical assets by themselves are best taken from "a value-in-use" viewpoint rather than the original cost or depreciated value to the vendor. The appellant directed its attention primarily to the likely future earning capacity of the assets to be acquired when in its hands.

The appellant, after having made its basic projection of earnings, taking into account all factors affecting that projection, would then estimate what amount it would be prepared to lay out to earn that estimated income over a predetermined period of years, normally five years, and that amount would be the amount that the appellant was willing to pay for the assets or shares of the vendor as the case might be.

The present assessments by the Minister which are under appeal resulted from three specific transactions of the general nature just described.

The appellant, on August 6, 1964, after prolonged bona fide arm's length negotiations made an offer to purchase all the assets of Zenith Propane Ltd. (hereinafter called Zenith). ... The offer ... was accepted ... and a formal bill of sale was entered into between them on September 15, 1964. ...

[A]n amount of $314,000 was paid for the fixed assets of Zenith. ... The sum of $39,660.88 was paid for inventory and the sum of $55,172.83 was paid for accounts receivable, making a total purchase price of $408,833.71.

This purchase price was deemed to cover all the assets of Zenith excluding cash but including goodwill which, for the purpose of the agreement, was valued at $1.

It was also a provision of the agreement that Zenith make available to the appellant the exclusive right to use the names "Zenith Propane" and "Zenigas" and assign to the appellant all trade names that Zenith owned.

Zenith also undertook, during the interval until final closing, to act as agent for the appellant for the purpose of retaining all of its customers for the benefit of the appellant. The purpose of the acquisition of Zenith, which operated in the area served by Calgary, Alberta, was that the area to the west, where the appellant had not previously conducted its business, would be served by the assets acquired from Zenith and in the area to the east where the appellant and Zenith were in competition, the expanded business of the appellant, because of its acquisition of Zenith, would be served both by its own assets and those acquired from Zenith.

...

If the appellant had purchased the shares of Zenith ... rather than purchasing the assets ... then the capital cost allowances would continue to have been based upon the [undepreciated capital cost of the assets] to Zenith because Zenith would continue to operate with those assets. However, upon the acquisition of the assets ... the appellant set up a much higher value therefor in its hands based upon the price of $314,000 agreed upon by the appellant and Zenith.

The second transaction, giving rise to the assessments of the appellant herein was the purchase by the appellant of the assets of Burro Gas & Electric Ltd. (hereinafter referred to as Burro) which operated in the area of Edmonton, Alberta. The same motives which prompted the appellant to acquire the assets of Zenith were present in the purchase of the assets of Burro.

The negotiations for this purchase were also protracted beginning in 1964 and were conducted at arm's length.

...

An offer of the appellant dated January 21, 1965 was accepted by Burro on January 22, 1965, the transfer to be effective as from November 30, 1964. The purchase price was $740,483.70 of which $539,335.66 was specified to be for certain described fixed assets and was specifically allocated to the fixed assets in the amounts set forth in a schedule to the offer.

...

By the agreement between the appellant and Burro an amount of $242,685 was allocated as the purchase price of the depreciable property acquired in Class 8 and $246,150 to the property within Class 10.

The original cost of such property to Burro was with respect to Class 8, $130,972.91 and Class 10, $12,584.89. This was known to the appellant.

...

Burro had not claimed any capital cost allowance on its depreciable property and accordingly it was not faced with any recovery thereof.

By paragraph 9 of ... the agreement between the appellant and Burro, the appellant was granted the right to the name "Burro" which it used as a fighting brand name. Burro undertook to and did change its corporate name and also undertook not to and did not compete with the appellant. Further, during the interval to closing, Burro undertook to retain its customers for the ultimate benefit of the appellant.

...

The third and last transaction was the purchase of the assets used by Grover's Propane Ltd. in the conduct of a propane retailing business by that company. This company operated in the area of Lethbridge, Alberta and it conducted a variety of diverse businesses under the corporate name of Grover's Propane Ltd. (hereafter called Grover's).

...

The negotiations for the purchase of this particular portion of Grover's business were ... prolonged because Grover's was undecided.

Eventually an agreement was entered into by the parent company and Grover's on December 16, 1966. The purchase price of the propane business to Grover's was $195,796 of which $187,061.76 was stated in the agreement to be for the described fixed assets and was specifically allocated in various amounts to various fixed assets.

It was estimated by the appellant that the original cost of Grover's assets acquired by the appellant was in the neighbourhood of $97,000.

Grover's was assessed to income tax on the basis of a 100% recapture of capital cost allowances. ... Grover's accepted the allocation of the price to the assets but insisted that it be compensated for the increased tax resulting from such recapture. This the appellant agreed to do and the purchase price was increased accordingly.

The appellant did not acquire the use of the Grover name because Grover's would continue its businesses other than propane retailing. However Grover's agreed to remove the word "propane" from its corporate name and did so.

Two separate agreements were entered into with the two principal shareholders in Grover's, both of whom bore the surname, Grover, that these two persons would not compete in the propanc business.

...

Mr. Dennis Anderson, the vice-president of the appellant ... testified that the appellant was not interested in buying the used physical assets as such, but only those assets in the locations in which they were gathered together and installed and he quite candidly testified that the appellant would not be interested in buying used physical assets so gathered and installed unless there was the prospect of retaining the customers of the vendors served by those assets.

The appellant foresaw that it could use those assets to continue to serve the customers of the vendors, either by themselves or in conjunction with the assets already owned by the appellant in the area.

In short what the appellant was buying was not only the physical assets as such but the whole business undertakings of the vendors. I should qualify this with respect to Grover's where what was acquired was the propane retailing business exclusive of the other businesses of Grover's. Mr. Anderson candidly admitted this to be so.

Mr. Anderson was equally frank in admitting that the appellant would not have purchased the assets of the vendors if that purchase was not accompanied by the definite prospect that the customers of the vendors would become the customers of the appellant.

...

The three transactions were in fact predicated upon that assumption. The appellant estimated the value-in-use to it of the assets acquired upon the earnings that those assets would generate in its hands. The assets in the appellant's hands could only gain income if there were customers to be served and it was a paramount consideration in estimating that income that the customers of the vendors would be served by the appellant after the purchase of the assets by it.

The provisions in the respective agreements with the vendors, that the vendors would not compete with the appellant, that the appellant was assigned the brand names of the vendors and that, in the interval before closing, the vendors would make every effort to preserve their customers for the appellant, to which provisions no value was assigned in the agreements, were all designed to ensure that the customers of the vendors would become the customers of the appellant. I would add that in all three agreements goodwill was included at the nominal value of $1.

The appellant, for the purpose of calculating its capital cost allowance allocated the consideration paid to each of the three vendors for the fixed assets acquired under the agreements with the vendors to land and depreciable assets as follows:

	Zenith	Burro	Grover's
Land		$ 19,500.00	
Class 6	$ 17,000.00	$ 21,000.00	
Class 8	$ 161,000.00	$ 242,685.00	$ 145,529.00
Class 10	$ 136,000.00	$ 246,150.00	$ 41,532.00
Class 13		$ 10,000.00	
Total	$ 314,000.00	$ 539,335.00	$ 187,061.00

The Minister accepted the appellant's figures with respect to the land acquired from Burro which had been appraised. There is no dispute with respect to Classes 6 and 13. The dispute centres on the consideration allocated by the appellant to Class 8 and Class 10 items as above indicated. There was no independent appraisal of the Class 8 and Class 10 property by the appellant. These were the prices paid to the vendors as allocated in the agreements with the vendors.

In assessing the appellant as he did the Minister invoked the provisions of paragraph 20(6)(g) [now section 68] of the *Income Tax Act* and accordingly reduced the capital cost of the Class 8 and Class 10 depreciable assets as follows:

	Class 8	Class 10	Total
Zenith			
Purchase Price	$ 161,000.00	$ 136,000.00	$ 297,000.00
Allowed by Minister	$ 55,685.00	$ 53,742.00	$ 109,427.00
Reduction	$ 105,315.00	$ 82,258.00	$ 187,573.00
Burro			
Purchase Price	$ 242,685.00	$ 246,150.00	$ 488,835.00
Allowed by Minister	$ 65,726.00	$ 78,337.00	$ 144,063.00
Reduction	$ 176,959.00	$ 167,813.00	$ 344,772.00
Grover's			
Purchase Price	$ 145,530.00	$ 41,532.00	$ 187,062.00
Allowed by Minister	$ 62,750.00	$ 30,532.00	$ 93,282.00
Reduction	$ 82,780.00	$ 11,000.00	$ 93,780.00

In determining the amounts that the Minister allowed as being reasonably regarded as being in part the consideration for the depreciable property within Classes 8 and 10, the Minister considered each item within those classes. ... These items consist mainly of trucks and automotive equipment within Class 10, some of which trucks had tanks installed, and storage tanks within Class 8. The amounts arrived at by the Minister ... were based on, in the case of Grover's, the value of similar new equipment determined by inquiry from suppliers and from suppliers' lists, with respect to items within Class 8, that is storage tanks and the like, added to which was the cost of fittings and installation. The value of such new equipment was selected because depreciation was negligible.

At this point I repeat that the original cost of this equipment to Grover's was, Class 8, $56,267.47 and Class 10, $37,626.53 for a total original cost of

$93,894. The amount allowed by the Minister was $93,282 being slightly less than the original cost to Grover's.

In the cases of Zenith and Burro the values were arrived at by the Minister for depreciable property within Class 8, i.e. storage tanks, from quotations received from suppliers for similar new equipment to which was added the cost of fittings and installation.

The values of depreciable property within Class 10, i.e. automotive equipment, in the cases of Zenith and Burro, were determined by the Minister by getting quotations from dealers for equipment in similar condition to that acquired by the appellant. For example a 1962 truck was valued as at the date of its acquisition by the appellant. However this practice was not uniformly followed by the Minister. In some instances the value of similar new equipment was taken.

Again, in the case of Zenith, the original capital cost was $14,983.05 for Class 8 property and $70,647.43 for Class 10 property, a total of $85,630.52. The Minister's allocation, in Schedule A, was for Class 8 property $55,685 and for Class 10 property $53,742 for a total of $109,427.

In the case of Burro the original capital cost of Class 8 property was $130,972.91 and $12,584.89 for Class 10 property for a total of $143,557.80. The allocation by the Minister was $65,726 for Class 8 property and $78,337 for Class 10 for a total of $144,063.

During the course of the trial the suggestion arose that in some instances the value given to some items by the Minister was too low. However no contradictory evidence was called and in the result the appellant accepted the figures arrived at by the Minister as accurate.

...

In applying [paragraph 20(1)(g) of the 1952 *Income Tax Act*] the matter for determination is not simply one of interpreting the contract or agreement or of giving effect to its provisions. The section states that the part of the amount that can reasonably be regarded as being the consideration for depreciable property shall be deemed to be the proceeds of disposition irrespective of the form or legal effect of the contract or agreement.

Rather, the first problem to be decided is whether the amount can be regarded as being in part the consideration for depreciable property and as being in part consideration for something else. In short is paragraph 20(6)(g) applicable?

If the first problem is answered in the affirmative the next problem that arises for determination is what amount of the total can reasonably be regarded as consideration for the depreciable property and what amount of the total can be reasonably regarded as consideration for something else. It seems to me that the determination of the foregoing respective amounts can best be determined by ascertaining the reasonable value of the property and the deduction of that amount from the total consideration results in the amount attributable to something else.

Reverting to the initial problem, that is whether the transactions here in question, fall within the ambit of paragraph 20(6)(g), the position in this respect taken by counsel for the appellant was, as I understood it, that since the parties to the agreements were dealing at arm's length and concluded the consideration for the physical assets in each of the three instances, which considerations were recited in the agreements as being for the assets, it cannot be concluded that the considerations allocated in the respective agreements are unreasonable for which reason paragraph 20(6)(g) is not applicable and the Minister cannot properly interfere.

On this subject Noel, J (now ACJ) pointed out in *Herb Payne Transport Limited v. M.N.R.*, [1964] Ex. CR 1 at 8; [1963] CTC 116 at 122; 63 DTC 1075 at 1078, that evidence is properly admissible that would otherwise be excluded if the contract or agreement alone governed the rights of the taxpayer and the Minister as parties to the proceeding.

In *Klondike Helicopters Limited v. M.N.R.*, [1966] Ex. CR 251 at 254; [1965] CTC 427 at 429-430; 65 DTC 5253 at 5254, Thurlow, J pointed out that the agreement is a circumstance to be taken into account in the overall enquiry and if the agreement purports to determine the amount paid for the depreciable property then, in the absence of other circumstances, the weight of the agreement "may well be decisive."

There is no question that in the present appeals what the appellant sought to acquire was the businesses of the vendors as going concerns. It was the policy of the appellant to do this by one or the other of two means, either to purchase the shares of a vendor company or to purchase its physical assets.

In the three transactions which give rise to the present appeals the appellant purchased the physical assets of the vendors. It was not interested in buying used equipment, but it bought that equipment as the means of acquiring the businesses of the vendors as going concerns and the price allocated to the assets was the price paid for the businesses. The price of the assets, determined upon a value-in-use to the appellant, was the yardstick by which the price of the businesses was measured. Value-in-use to the appellant presupposes the existence of something else. Value-in-use, which is the criterion used by the appellant, consists of the expectation of income from the property. A paramount consideration in the expectation of income from the acquisition of assets, which in the three transactions here involved is tantamount to the acquisition of the businesses as going concerns, is the expectation that the customers of the vendor will follow the business to the purchaser and become customers of the new owner.

It has been said that goodwill is something easy to describe but difficult to define. Some of the accepted elements of goodwill are the benefit and advantage of a good name, reputation and connection of a business. The expectation that the purchaser will have the customers of the vendor is certainly an element of goodwill.

In the present instance the agreements between the appellants and the vendor assigned only a nominal value to goodwill. Mr. Anderson on behalf of the appellant testified that the appellant considered that there was no value to the goodwill and accordingly so provided in the agreements.

The fact that no value is assigned to goodwill in the agreements is not conclusive of the matter.

The agreements did provide for the use by the appellant of brand names owned by the vendors, and the agreements also contained covenants that the vendors would not compete against the appellant and there were also provisions that the vendors would, until final closing, conduct its business in a manner to ensure that the appellant would succeed to the customers of the vendor.

...

It was frankly admitted on behalf of the appellant that if such expectation of succeeding to the vendors' customers was not present the appellant would not have purchased the three businesses.

It is not necessary for me to categorize such an expectation in the appellant as goodwill which is, of course, a non-depreciable asset. [For 1972 and subsequent taxation years, a fraction of purchased goodwill (currently one-half) may be deducted on a declining-balance basis under paragraph 20(1)(b) of the Act. This provision is examined in chapter 5.] It was a factor present in the mind of the appellant in making the purchases and that is sufficient to constitute "something else" within the meaning of paragraph 20(6)(g) to which an amount may be reasonably regarded as attributable. This being so it follows that paragraph 20(6)(g) is applicable to the transactions here in question.

Having concluded that paragraph 20(6)(g) is applicable, the next problem is what amount of the total price paid for the depreciable property can reasonably be regarded as consideration for that property and what amount of that total can be reasonably regarded as for something else.

In my view the crux of the issue between the parties is what was a reasonable consideration for the depreciable property.

On behalf of the appellant it was contended that since the purchases were negotiated on an arm's length basis for proper business motives and the prices at which the assets were sold were determined by *bona fide* bargaining between the parties to each sale, it follows the resultant written agreements ascribing prices to the assets must be conclusive.

...

In furtherance of its contention ... , it was pointed out that the assets were already assembled in particular locations. This to the appellant was an advantage for which it was prepared to pay a premium price. In effect what the appellant contends is that the assets had a value to it enhanced above the fair market value bearing in mind the motive of the appellant in acquiring the assets which was, of course, to expand its own business and thereby increase its income.

...

The Minister contends that, in the circumstances of this case, the fair market value of the assets which were determined by him upon enquiry of suppliers ...

is the acceptable standard. The Minister determined the replacement value or the fair market value and applied that standard in assessing the appellant as he did and it is his contention that this is the proper standard by which to determine the amount that can be reasonably regarded as the consideration attributable to the depreciable property.

...

Normally to an informed vendor and purchaser of a business there is a conflict of interest between them. It is to the purchaser's advantage to have a high price allocated to depreciable property in order to claim a high capital cost allowance. It is to the advantage of the vendor to have the price of depreciable property as low as possible to avoid recapture of capital cost allowance.

In my view there was no hard bargaining between the vendors and the appellant in the transactions as to the allocation of amounts of depreciable property.

...

The vendors' concern was exclusively that of getting as much as possible for their businesses. It was immaterial to them what the appellant assigned to each item of equipment so long as the aggregate thereof which the vendor received coincided with its estimate of what it could get for its business. In so stating I have not overlooked the fact that the vendors signed the agreements but it is my considered conclusion that the appellant was the dominant party in such allocation of prices to the depreciable property and that the vendors passively acquiesced thereto secure in the knowledge that the sum total met their prices for their businesses.

...

For the foregoing reasons I have concluded that the apportionment between depreciable property and something else was in effect unilaterally done by the appellant and that there was in reality no genuine negotiated apportionment as a result of bargaining between the parties to the agreement from which it follows that the allocations in the agreements are not decisive of what is reasonable.

The assumptions of the Minister in assessing the appellant as he did were that the amounts of $314,000, $539,335 and $187,061 can reasonably be regarded as being in part the consideration for the disposition of depreciable property of Zenith, Burro and Grover's respectively, and as being in part consideration for something else.

It was further assumed by the Minister that of the immediately foregoing amounts not in excess of $126,427, $175,063 and $93,282, respectively, can be reasonably regarded as the consideration for such disposition and, by virtue of paragraph 20(6)(g), are deemed to be the proceeds of the disposition of depreciable property and that the appellant is deemed to have acquired the property at a capital cost to it equal to the same parts of those amounts.

The figures of $126,427, $175,063 and $93,282 are the fair market value of the depreciable property within Classes 8 and 10 which was acquired by the appellant as determined by the Minister and which figures have been accepted by the appellant as accurate.

The onus of demolishing the Minister's assumptions falls on the appellant and, in my view, for the reasons expressed, the appellant has failed to discharge that onus. Accordingly it cannot be said that the assumptions of the Minister in assessing the appellant as he did were not warranted. ...

Appeals dismissed.

NOTES AND QUESTIONS

1.   On what basis did the taxpayer in *Canadian Propane Gas & Oil Ltd.* argue that the allocation of the proceeds in each of the three transactions was reasonable within the meaning of paragraph 20(6)(g) of the 1952 Act? On what basis did the Minister conclude that the taxpayer's allocation was not reasonable?

2.   Why did the court reject the allocation stipulated in the agreements of purchase and sale in each of the three transactions at issue in *Canadian Propane Gas & Oil Ltd.*? What allocation did the court consider reasonable and why?

3.   Should the allocation agreed upon by the parties to a transaction be conclusive as to its reasonableness within the meaning of former paragraph 20(6)(g) and current section 68? Does it matter whether the parties to the transaction engaged in "hard bargaining" over the allocation? Why or why not?

4.   In *Herb Payne Transport Ltd. v. M.N.R.*, [1963] C.T.C. 116, 63 D.T.C. 1075 (Ex. Ct.), the taxpayer sold its trucking business for $200,000, without any allocation among different kinds of property. Rejecting the Minister's argument that the full amount of the purchase price should be allocated to depreciable property, the court held that $50,000 of the proceeds could reasonably be allocated to goodwill. In the course of its decision, the court stated (at para. 20) that "ordinarily, the price of an asset arrived at by *bona fide* negotiations at arm's length in a commercial transaction should establish the value of that asset at that time and place." On this basis, Noël J concluded (at para. 25):

> There is ... no question that if the purchaser and vendor acting at arm's length, reach a mutual decision as to the apportionment of price against various assets which appear to be reasonable under the circumstances, they should be accepted by the taxation authority as accurate and they should be binding on both parties.

In *Leclerc, infra*, the court noted (at para. 6) that this conclusion "depends on whether the apportionment appears to be reasonable or not."

5.   In *Klondike Helicopters Ltd. v. M.N.R.*, [1965] C.T.C. 427, 65 D.T.C. 5253 (Ex. Ct.), Klondike's "fixed-wing flying operations" were sold to Connelly-Dawson Airways Ltd. for a global price of $100,000 of which the agreement allocated $50,000 to depreciable property and $50,000 to goodwill. For tax purposes, Klondike attributed $42,050 to class 16 property (aircraft and attached

furniture, fittings, and equipment), while Connelly-Dawson computed CCA on the fair market value of this property, which was conceded to be $71,300. Upholding the Minister's assessment, which had assessed both parties on the basis that $42,050 of the purchase price was attributable to class 16 property, Thurlow J commented (at para. 3) on then paragraph 20(6)(g):

> In applying this rule the matter for determination is not simply one of interpreting the contract or agreement or of giving effect to its provisions. Rather, when the rule applies, the problem is to decide, having regard to all the circumstances of the transaction, what part of an amount representing the consideration for disposition of depreciable assets of a prescribed class and for something else can reasonably be regarded as having been the consideration for the disposition of the assets of that prescribed class and for the purposes of the rule the amount so determined is to be regarded as the proceeds of disposition of such assets regardless of the form or legal effect of the contract or agreement. As pointed out by Noel J in *Herb Payne Transport Limited v. M.N.R.*, [1964] Ex. CR 1 at p. 8; [1963] CTC 116 at p. 122, in determining this question evidence will be admissible which would be excluded if the contract or agreement alone governed the rights of the taxpayer and the Minister as parties to the proceedings. The making of a contract or agreement in the form in which it exists is, however, one of the circumstances to be taken into account in the overall enquiry and if the contract purports to determine what amount is being paid for the depreciable property and is not a mere sham or subterfuge its weight may well be decisive.

For similar decisions involving similar facts, see *Coopérative Agricole de Granby v. M.N.R.*, [1970] Tax ABC 969, 70 D.T.C. 1620 (T.A.B.); *Bohun v. M.N.R.*, [1972] C.T.C. 2325, 72 D.T.C. 1268 (T.R.B.); and *Reynolds Construction Ltd. v. M.N.R.*, [1972] C.T.C. 2325 (T.R.B.).

6.   In *M.N.R. v. Clement's Drug Store (Brandon) Ltd.*, [1968] C.T.C. 53, 68 D.T.C. 5053 (Ex. Ct.), the taxpayer purchased for $110,000 an existing drug store business in leased premises, of which $45,000 was allocated to solid oak fixtures that had been custom-built and installed in 1913. When the oak fixtures were scrapped in the course of renovations two years later, the Minister reassessed the taxpayer on the basis that an allocation of $3,000 to these assets was reasonable within the meaning of then paragraph 20(6)(g). Commenting (at para. 37) that the oak fixtures were not "inefficient, obsolete or in need of replacement at the time of their purchase" and that the taxpayer "would have continued to use them for a long period of years" had it not been for unexpected renovations that became necessary to obtain a long-term lease, Cattanach J concluded (at para. 45):

> In my view the cost of the depreciable property here in question is $45,000 as determined by the contract among the parties to the sale thereof. That is the amount, under the terms of the contract, the respondent paid for the fixtures and equipment in question. The contract was the subject of arm's length negotiations over a protracted period and was not a mere sham or subterfuge but represents the bargain arrived at by the parties and in my opinion is decisive in the circumstances of this case.

See also *Kamsack Hotels Ltd. v. M.N.R.* (1965), 40 Tax ABC 1, in which the board rejected the Minister's argument that $25,650 of $245,250 spent by the taxpayer to purchase a hotel as a going concern should be allocated to goodwill, on the grounds that the purchasers in fact acquired little or no goodwill.

7. In *Canada v. Leclerc*, [1979] C.T.C. 527, 79 D.T.C. 5440 (F.C.T.D.), the vendors (Wise, Pollock, Sokoloff, and Burnstein) sold five apartment buildings in Montreal to the purchasers (Leclerc and Lemay) for $650,000, of which the deed of sale allocated $350,000 to depreciable property and $300,000 to the land. While the vendors computed recapture on the buildings according to the agreed-upon allocation of $350,000, the purchasers computed CCA on the basis that the capital cost of the buildings was $450,000. Rejecting the vendors' argument that the agreed-upon allocation should be accepted because it was arrived at by hard bargaining, the court commented (at paras. 7-8) that the decision in *Canadian Propane Gas & Oil Ltd. v. M.N.R.*, [1972] C.T.C. 566, 73 D.T.C. 5019 (F.C.T.D.):

> is not authority for the proposition ... that if there has been hard bargaining the result arrived at must be decisive. It is indeed only an element of proof to which considerable weight must be given but is in no way binding on the Minister in his determination of what is "reasonable." ...
>
> [T]he proper conclusion to be reached is that while the terms of the written agreement must be given considerable weight the Minister is certainly not bound to accept [such an] allocation as being reasonable and that appropriate weight must be given to other evidence in determining from an independent point of view what was in fact a reasonable allocation.

Thus, according to the court (at para. 12):

> When vendors and purchasers show a valuation for depreciable assets in a deed and then both use this figure in their tax return the Minister may or may not disallow it. While he would still have the right to do so it is unlikely that he would intervene to change such a negotiated figure unless it is clearly unreasonable. ... However when one or other of the parties uses a different figure for his tax returns it immediately puts the Minister on notice and he clearly cannot properly accept the use of one figure by the vendor and a different one by the purchaser for the same assets and must disallow one or both of them and issue reassessments accordingly. In the present case the vendors in good faith used the figure shown in the deed. The same cannot be said for Mr Lemay who ... increased the figure by $100,000. ... [H]aving agreed to a negotiated figure, upon which vendors had every right to rely in their own tax returns, purchasers by refusing to use it placed the Minister in a position where he had no choice but to have an independent assessment made, as a result of which not only the purchasers were assessed but also the vendors.

On the basis of the assessed value of the buildings for municipal tax purposes, the court upheld the Minister's conclusion that it was reasonable to regard $429,000 as consideration for the buildings.

8. For other cases in which the courts have referred to municipal assessments in deciding upon the reasonableness of consideration under former paragraph 20(6)(g), see *Monarch Marking Ltd. v. M.N.R.* (1965), 37 Tax ABC 348; *Blackstone Ltd. v. M.N.R.* (1966), 41 Tax ABC 224; *Mora Building Corp. v. M.N.R.*, [1967] Tax ABC 365, *Flanders Installations Ltd. v. M.N.R.*, [1967] Tax ABC 1018; and *Samuel-Jay Investments Ltd. v. M.N.R.*, [1968] Tax ABC 532.

9. For other cases in which former paragraph 20(6)(g) was applied to adjust an allocation of the purchase price agreed upon by the parties to the transaction, see *Nosa Holdings Ltd. v. M.N.R.*, [1970] Tax ABC 1153; *Canada v. Shok*, [1975] C.T.C. 162, 75 D.T.C. 5109 (F.C.T.D.); and *Erawan House Ltd. v. M.N.R.*, [1976] C.T.C. 2060, (1975) 76 D.T.C. 1049 (T.R.B.).

In *Nosa Holdings*, the taxpayer purchased a hotel as a going concern for $450,000, of which the agreement allocated $50,000 to the land, $230,000 to the building, $165,000 to furniture, linens, and equipment, and $5,000 to goodwill. Noting (at paras. 11 and 13) that the furniture, linens, and equipment were "very old" and insured for only $35,000, the board described the allocation in the agreement of purchase and sale as "far-fetched" and concluded that the amount allocated to goodwill was "much too low." On this basis, it upheld the Minister's assessment, which had allocated $53,000 to the furniture, linens, and equipment and $117,000 to the goodwill.

In *Shok*, the taxpayers purchased a hotel as a going concern for $405,000, of which the agreement allocated $15,000 to the land, $300,000 to the building, and $90,000 to contents and equipment. Referring to expert evidence that roughly $100,000 of the purchase price should have been allocated to goodwill, and noting (at para. 52) that "there was no real bargaining about the value of the depreciable assets," the court rejected the taxpayer's argument that this allocation was reasonable within the meaning of former paragraph 20(6)(g). Of the decision in *Klondike Helicopters Ltd. v. M.N.R.*, [1965] C.T.C. 427, 65 D.T.C. 5253 (Ex. Ct.), the court (at para. 42) concluded:

> Thurlow, J did not say the weight of what is said in the agreement, concerning depreciable property *must* be decisive, but only that it *may well* be decisive. He also stated that it was one of the circumstances to be considered.

In *Erawan House*, the taxpayer purchased two properties in the city of Ottawa: one (on Gladstone Avenue) for $395,000, of which $35,000 was allocated to the land and $360,000 to the buildings, and the other (on Elgin Street) for $400,000, of which $50,000 was allocated to the land and $350,000 to the building. Concluding (at para. 8) that "the specific allocation of values between the land and the buildings in the selling price" of each property was not "seriously negotiated between the parties through their agents," the board upheld the Minister's assessment, which had allocated $125,500 of the purchase price of the Gladstone property to the land and $269,500 to the buildings and $152,000 of the purchase price of the Elgin property to the land and $248,000 to the building.

10. In many cases, as in *Ben's Ltd. v. M.N.R.*, [1955] C.T.C. 249, 55 D.T.C. 1152 (Ex. Ct.) land and buildings are sold or expropriated and the buildings are subsequently demolished by a purchaser or expropriating authority intent on redeveloping the property. In these circumstances, the value to the purchaser is typically non-existent or negative since costs may have to be incurred in order to

tear down the building. From the vendor's perspective, a decision to allocate the proceeds entirely to the land may result in a terminal loss on the building.[3] Nonetheless, where the vendor used the building before the sale, it is arguable that its value to the vendor should not be based on its value to the purchaser.

In *M.N.R. v. Steen Realty Ltd.*, [1964] C.T.C. 133, 64 D.T.C. 5081 (Ex. Ct.), where the taxpayer sold land and buildings to a purchaser who immediately demolished the buildings in order to construct a 12-storey office building, the court concluded (at para. 16) that "it is not reasonable to regard any part of the $395,000 sale price as being the consideration for the disposition of the buildings." This decision was subsequently followed in *Stein v. M.N.R.* (1964), 35 Tax ABC 143; *Emco Ltd. v. M.N.R.*, [1968] C.T.C. 457, 68 D.T.C. 5310 (Ex. Ct.); *Baine, Johnston & Co. v. M.N.R.*, [1968] Tax ABC 1100; and *Moulds v. Canada*, [1977] C.T.C. 126, 77 D.T.C. 5094 (F.C.T.D.), aff'd [1978] C.T.C. 146, 78 D.T.C. 6068 (F.C.A.).

In many other cases, however, courts have accepted the Minister's view that the allocation of proceeds from the disposition of land and buildings in these circumstances should be based on the value of these assets to the vendor, not the purchaser. See, for example, *Chess v. M.N.R.* (1963), 32 Tax ABC 48; *Torrance v. M.N.R.* (1963), 35 Tax ABC 1; *Fielder v. M.N.R.* (1964), 36 Tax ABC 1; *Werle v. M.N.R.* (1966), 40 Tax ABC 337; *Gateway Lodge Ltd. v. M.N.R.*, [1967] C.T.C. 199, 67 D.T.C. 5138 (Ex. Ct.); *Stockport Investments Ltd. v. M.N.R.*, [1968] Tax ABC 921; *City Parking Properties & Development v. M.N.R.*, [1969] C.T.C. 508, 69 D.T.C. 5332 (Ex. Ct.); *Downsview Lumber & Supply Ltd. v. M.N.R.*, [1971] Tax ABC 662; and *Munday v. M.N.R.*, [1971] C.T.C. 585, 71 D.T.C. 5321 (F.C.T.D.).

11. In *Stanley v. M.N.R.*, [1972] C.T.C. 34, (1971) 72 D.T.C. 6004 (S.C.C.), the taxpayer owned land and a building that was expropriated for the Vancouver School Board for compensation of $90,200 determined by an appraiser, who allocated $20,500 to the land, $61,500 to the building, and $8,200 to other items. When the Minister assessed the taxpayer on recaptured depreciation of $31,066, the taxpayer argued that the building had been sold for $200, the price that the school board received in exchange for the removal of the building. Rejecting the taxpayer's argument, the Supreme Court of Canada held (at para. 1) that "of the sum of $90,200, received by the appellant ... at least the sum of $47,312.32 [the original capital cost of the building] could reasonably be regarded as the proceeds of disposition of his depreciable property."

---

[3] This would be the case where the vendor has no other depreciable buildings of the same class at the end of the year and the undepreciated capital cost (UCC) of the class is still positive. Where the vendor owns other buildings of the same class or acquires other buildings of the same class before the end of the taxation year, a disposition of the building for zero proceeds will not result in a terminal loss, but will preserve the balance of the UCC of buildings of the same class. As indicated earlier, regulation 1101(1ac) prescribes a separate class for each rental property the capital cost to the taxpayer of which was not less than $50,000.

12.   In *Canada v. Malloney's Studio Ltd.*, [1979] S.C.J. No. 52, [1979] C.T.C.
207, 79 D.T.C. 5124 (S.C.C.), the taxpayer, which owned and operated a
restaurant adjacent to a hospital that notified the taxpayer that it planned to
expropriate the taxpayer's property for expansion purposes, entered into an
agreement with the hospital pursuant to which it promised to deliver to the
hospital "vacant possession of the real property ... clear of all buildings" in
exchange for consideration of $280,000. Rejecting the Crown's argument that a
portion of the proceeds could reasonably be regarded as consideration for the
building within the meaning of paragraph 20(6)(g) of the 1952 Act, a majority of
the Supreme Court of Canada held that this provision did not apply to the facts
of the case. According to Estey J (Laskin CJ and Dickson J concurring) (at
paras. 8-9):

> There are two fatal obstacles to the application of this subsection of section 20 to the facts of
> this case. Firstly, it is argued by the appellant [the Crown] that demolition is equal to
> disposition and counsel for the respondent [the taxpayer] accepts this submission. However,
> that is not the end of the problem. In the opening portions of rule (g), provision is made for
> the allocation of so much of the consideration as can reasonably be regarded as being in part
> the consideration for the disposition of depreciable property and for the allocation otherwise
> of that part of the consideration which can be reasonably regarded as having been paid for
> "something else." The rule therefore applies to the situation where the taxpayer has disposed
> of two types of property, first depreciable property and secondly, something else. When this
> factual situation occurs, the rule then permits the allocation of that part of the consideration
> received in the total transaction to depreciable assets as "can reasonably be regarded as being
> in part the consideration for disposition of depreciable property of a taxpayer." The rule does
> not permit the Minister to characterize a transaction as one which could reasonably be
> regarded as being in part the sale of depreciable property and in part the sale of something
> else. The rule operates only as a second stage, the first stage being the agreement or valid
> determination that the sale involves both a sale of depreciable property and a sale of
> something else. Here the contract demonstrably relates only to the sale of vacant land. There
> is no contractual reference to depreciable property and no bill of sale or other transfer, deed,
> or assignment was delivered on closing relating to any depreciable asset. Only the deed
> conveying the land on which no buildings were then located, was delivered upon receipt of
> the consideration of $280,000.
>
> The second obstacle to the applicability of rule (g) when bare demolition occurs with
> nothing more arises from the portion of the rule appearing after the semicolon, which
> provides:
>
>> and the person to whom the depreciable property was disposed of shall be deemed
>> to have acquired the property ...
>
> Grammatically, the depreciable property there referred to is the same depreciable property as
> referred to in the opening of rule (g), and the past tense "was disposed of likewise refers back
> to the "disposition" mentioned in the second line of the opening part of rule (g). Thus it
> seems abundantly clear that for the purposes of the invocation of rule (g), the disposition in
> question must be bilateral and include both a disposer and "the person to whom the
> depreciable property was disposed of," whether or not such person may thereupon become
> entitled to any capital cost allowance under the Act. Here the demolition involved no
> recipient, at least as regards the hospital. It may conceivably be argued that the taxpayer
> disposed of the building by selling it to the demolition contractor and the proceeds of sale
> would at the most be the saving effected by the taxpayer in avoiding the cost of tearing the

building down himself. This is rather fanciful, and in any case, would not advance the position of the appellant. In both form and substance, the disposition here, in the bilateral sense, relates only to vacant land.

Dissenting, Pigeon J (Beetz J concurring) argued (at para. 20) that the taxpayer had disposed of the building, "whether ... by its agreement of sale of the land or by its demolition contract with a wrecker." In addition, referring to the words of former paragraph 20(6)(g) "irrespective of the form or legal effect of the contract or agreement," he concluded (at para. 27):

> I fail to see how it can be said that the value of the building was not part of the consideration of the agreement of sale, when it is established without contradiction that the sale price was arrived at on the basis of the value of the whole property to the owner; land, building, and improvements.

13. Effective for dispositions occurring after November 12, 1981, subsection 13(21.1) prevents taxpayers from claiming a terminal loss on the disposition of a building where subjacent or contiguous land is disposed of at a gain in the same year. Subsection 13(21.1) is discussed in Chapter 5.

14. In *Golden v. Canada*, [1983] C.T.C. 112, 83 D.T.C. 5138 (F.C.A.), aff'd [1986] S.C.J. No. 5, [1986] 1 C.T.C. 274, 86 D.T.C. 6138 (S.C.C.), the taxpayers, who owned an apartment complex on which they had claimed substantial CCA, sold the complex for $5.85 million, of which $5.1 million was allocated to the land and the remainder to the buildings and other depreciable property, after having received an unsolicited offer to sell the complex for $5.6 million, with $2.6 million allocated to the land, $2.4 million to the buildings, and $600,000 to other depreciable property. At trial, [1980] C.T.C. 488, 80 D.T.C. 6378 (F.C.T.D.), the court accepted that the land was worth $5.1 million to the purchaser, but held that the determination of reasonable consideration under section 68 must be approached from the view of the vendor, not the purchaser, and relied upon evidence of an expert valuator to allocate $2.32 million of the purchase price to the land and the remainder to the buildings and other depreciable property.

On appeal, the trial decision was reversed on the grounds that the determination of reasonable consideration should be approached from the perspective of the purchaser as well as the vendor, that the parties had engaged in arm's-length bargaining over the allocation of the purchase price, and that the trial judge himself had concluded that $5.1 million was not an unreasonable price for the purchaser to pay for the land alone. According to Heald J (Verchère DJ concurring) (at paras. 12-13):

> [T]he trial judge erred ... in deciding that the determination under section 68 is to be approached from the point of view of the vendor only. The trial judge was relying on the Exchequer Court decision of Dumoulin, J, in the case of *Munday v. M.N.R.*, [1971] CTC 585; 71 DTC 5321. That decision appears to me to be inconsistent with a number of other decisions of the Exchequer Court, the Trial Division of the Federal Court and the Federal Court of Appeal. In the case of *Herb Payne Transport Ltd. v. M.N.R.*, [1963] CTC 116; 63 DTC 1075, Noel, J (as he then was), in a determination under paragraph 20(6)(g), enunciated the following principles:

Because of the reciprocal effect on purchaser and vendor of any such finding here I am prepared to accept, as suggested by counsel for the respondent, that the matter should be considered from the viewpoint of the purchasers as well as from the viewpoint of the vendor.

There is also no question that if the purchaser and vendor acting at arm's length, reach a mutual decision as to apportionment of price against various assets which appear to be reasonable under the circumstances, they should be accepted by the taxation authority as accurate and they should be binding on both parties.

In another case before the Exchequer Court involving a determination under paragraph 20(6)(g), Ritchie, DJ, in making the determination, considered the situation from the point of view of both the vendor and the purchaser. In 1968, Mr. Justice Noël was called upon to again make a determination under paragraph 20(6)(g) in the case of *Emco Ltd. v. M.N.R.*, [1968] CTC 457; 68 DTC 5810. Here also, in making the necessary determination, the learned Justice considered the evidence as to the bargaining between the parties and the evidence as to the meeting of minds on both sides in the relevant transactions. Then, in 1977, in the Trial Division of the Federal Court, Marceau, J, in the case of *The Queen v. Godfrey G S Moulds*, [1977] CTC 126; 77 DTC 5094, in making a determination under paragraph 20(6)(g) followed the *Emco* decision of Mr Justice Noël and had regard to the bargaining between the parties and the meeting of minds on both sides in the transaction. The Federal Court of Appeal dismissed the appeal from the judgment of Marceau, J without specifically commenting upon the basis used by Marceau, J for making the determination under paragraph 20(6)(g).

A further decision of the Exchequer Court relevant to this issue is the decision of Thurlow, J (as he then was) in the case of *Klondike Helicopters Limited v. M.N.R.*, [1965] CTC 427; 65 DTC 5253. That was also a paragraph 20(6)(g) determination. At 5254 of the report, Thurlow, J said:

The making of a contract or agreement in the form in which it exists is, however, one of the circumstances to be taken into account in the overall enquiry and if the contract purports to determine what amount is being paid for the depreciable property and is not a mere sham or subterfuge its weight may well be decisive.

I find this series of cases to be persuasive when reaching a conclusion on the proper test to be utilized in making the determination required either under section 68 or its predecessor section, paragraph 20(6)(g). It is my opinion that the correct approach to a section 68 determination would be, as suggested by the above authorities, to consider the matter from the viewpoint of both the vendor and the purchaser and to consider all of the relevant circumstances surrounding the transaction. Where, as in this case, as found by the trial judge, the transaction is at arm's length and is not a mere sham or subterfuge, the apportionment made by the parties in the applicable agreement is certainly an important circumstance and one which is entitled to considerable weight. Furthermore, in this case, the trial judge made a specific finding of fact ... that the figure of $5,100,000 which the parties apportioned to land in the agreement was not an unreasonable price for the purchaser to pay for the land alone in March, 1973. Accordingly, based on that specific finding and on the other circumstances appearing from the evidence and addressing the question from the point of view of both the appellant and its purchaser, I am of the opinion that the amount that can reasonably be regarded as having been paid and received for the land apart from the buildings, etc., was $5,100,000 and for the buildings, equipment, roads, sidewalk, etc., was $750,000.

According to Thurlow CJ (at paras. 20-23):

The learned trial judge having, in my opinion, erred in approaching the determination to be made for the purposes of section 68 from the point of view of the vendor and not that of the purchaser it is, I think, open to the Court to reach its own determination of the amount that can reasonably be regarded as the proceeds of disposition of the depreciable property included in the subject matter of the sale. For this purpose the respective values of land alone and depreciable assets alone are no doubt relevant and may be taken into account in reaching a conclusion but it is to be remembered that the inquiry is not one as to reasonable value but as to proceeds of disposition. It is open to an owner to dispose of his property as he sees fit and for that purpose it is open to him, when he sees it to be to his advantage, to realize on the full potential of an asset of one kind even if as a result the greatest potential of a related asset cannot be realized in the transaction.

In the first offer an allocation of the price offered between land, building and equipment was proposed by the purchaser. The offer was rejected for several reasons including dissatisfaction with the proposed allocation. The vendors knew that the land was underdeveloped and believed that the purchaser's interest was in the land. They wanted to realize the full potential price for it. The learned trial judge found that $5,100,000 was not an unreasonable price for the purchaser to pay for the land alone. It was also, in my view, not an unreasonable amount for the vendors, for their own reasons, to insist on receiving for the land. It is also not unreasonable to think that the vendors would not have sold for $5,850,000 without the term providing for all the allocation of that amount between land and other assets included in the transaction. It must I think be assumed that they knew that there would be recapture of capital cost allowances which had been claimed on the buildings and that they would have to include the recaptured amount in the computation of their incomes and pay tax on it. Without an agreement allocating the purchase price or with an agreement allocating a higher amount to the depreciated assets the offer would not have been as attractive or as beneficial to them. From their point of view the consideration for the buildings and equipment and the amount they can reasonably be regarded as having received for them was the $750,000 provided by the agreement.

The allocation has a reciprocal effect. Its consequence from the point of view of the purchaser is that the cost of depreciable assets is less and the amount of capital cost allowance he can claim on the buildings and equipment is accordingly less whether he keeps or demolishes them. The amount he can reasonably be regarded as having paid for them is thus the $750,000 provided for in the agreement, a result which as I view it is confirmed by the learned trial judge's finding that the purchaser paid $5,100,000 for the land alone.

Given that the agreement was reached between parties who were dealing at arm's length and that it is not a sham or subterfuge, it appears to me that, notwithstanding the evidence of respective values on which the learned trial judge relied, the amount that can reasonably be regarded as the proceeds of disposition of the depreciable assets included in the transaction, irrespective of the form or legal effect of the contract, operating as it does only to govern the rights of the parties *inter se*, was the $750,000 for which the vendors agreed to sell and the purchaser agreed to purchase them.

Do you agree or disagree with these conclusions? Do they overrule the decisions in *Canadian Propane Gas & Oil Ltd. v. M.N.R.*, [1972] C.T.C. 566, 73 D.T.C. 5019 (F.C.T.D.) and *Canada v. Leclerc*, [1979] C.T.C. 527, 79 D.T.C. 5440 (F.C.T.D.)? Are they consistent with the purpose of section 68?

15. In *Petersen v. M.N.R.*, [1988] 1 C.T.C. 2071, (1987) 88 D.T.C. 1040 (T.C.C.), the taxpayer sold a day-care centre for $157,500, of which the agreement of purchase and sale allocated $45,000 to goodwill. Noting that the centre's licence had been cancelled, that the centre had suffered losses for five

consecutive years up to the time of the sale, and that two appraisal reports concluded that the centre's goodwill was non-existent, the Tax Court upheld the Minister's reallocation of the proceeds under section 68. Rejecting the taxpayer's argument that the agreed-upon allocation should be conclusive where the parties deal at arm's length and the allocation is not "a mere sham or subterfuge," Rip TCJ concluded (at paras. 46-51):

> While case law does provide some support for the appellant's position, it does not necessarily support its application in the present circumstances.
>
> In the case of *The Queen v. Golden*, [1986] 1 CTC 274; 86 DTC 6138, the Supreme Court of Canada considered the application of section 68. The majority of the Court held that the allocation established by the contract between the parties was reasonable for the reasons given by Mr. Justice Heald in the Federal Court of Appeal [1983] CTC 112 (83 DTC 5138) who stated at 116 (DTC 5142):
>
>> It is my opinion that the correct approach to a section 68 determination would be, as suggested by the above authorities, to consider the matter from the viewpoint of both the vendor and the purchaser and to consider all of the relevant circumstances surrounding the transaction. Where, as in this case, as found by the trial judge, the transaction is at arm's length and is not a mere sham or subterfuge, the apportionment made by the parties in the applicable agreement is certainly an important circumstance and one which is entitled to considerable weight. *Furthermore, in this case, the trial judge made a specific finding of fact ... that the figure of $5,100,000 which the parties apportioned to land in the agreement was not an unreasonable price for the purchaser to pay for the land alone in March, 1973. Accordingly, based on that specific finding* and on the other circumstances appearing from the evidence and addressing the question from the point of view of both the appellant and its purchaser, I am of the opinion that the amount that can reasonably be regarded as having been paid and received for the land apart from the buildings, etc., was $5,100,000 and for the buildings, equipment, roads, sidewalk, etc., was $750,000.
>
> [Emphasis added.]
>
> Notwithstanding that Mr. Justice Heald considered the finding by the trial judge that the agreement in the *Golden* case was not a sham or subterfuge his decision was based on the specific finding of fact that the amount apportioned by the parties was not an unreasonable amount. Where an agreement, although evidencing neither sham nor subterfuge, stipulates an amount which is clearly unreasonable in the circumstances, it is still very much open to the Court to conclude that section 68 should apply to reallocate the proceeds in a reasonable manner.
>
> In the case at bar there is no evidence, nor did the respondent even suggest, the agreement in issue was a sham or subterfuge. However the appellant's claim of $45,000 to goodwill is suspect. The business operated throughout its existence with losses and there was no indication of any change in the future. The evidence also indicated that problems existed with respect to the operation and licensing of the business.
>
> The courts have held that evidence of negotiations leading to an apportionment of value [is] an important factor in determining the weight to be given to the parties' allocation (see: *The Queen v. Shok et al.*, [1975] CTC 162; 75 DTC 5108 (FCTD)). The evidence in the case at bar indicates no bargaining between the parties as to allocation of purchase price.

The lack of any foundation for a value to goodwill in the business sold, let alone a value of $45,000, coupled with the absence of bargaining between the purchaser and vendor in allocating the purchase price would ordinarily lead me to conclude the allocation, in which approximately 30 per cent of the purchase price is said to be for goodwill is not reasonable.

16. In *H. Baur Investments v. M.N.R.*, [1987] T.C.J. No. 1112, [1988] 1 C.T.C. 2067, (1987) 88 D.T.C. 1024 (T.C.C.), aff'd [1990] F.C.J. No. 458, 2 C.T.C 122, 90 D.T.C. 6371 (F.C.T.D.), the taxpayer sold an apartment building for $2,990,000, of which $2,530,000 was allocated to the building by an amending agreement settled after the agreement of purchase and sale. On the basis of an appraiser's report, however, the taxpayer valued the building at $1,754,000 for the purpose of determining recaptured depreciation. Rejecting the taxpayer's argument, Taylor TCJ concluded (at paras. 10 and 12-13) that:

> Generally I agree with counsel's proposition that an "agreement" should not by itself be decisive — at least I have found nothing in the judgments of the higher courts ... which would clearly dictate the allocation for such an "agreement" to be paramount. ...
>
> But, as I see it, the thrust of the argument of counsel for the appellant in these appeals would urge the Court to ignore the viewpoint of the purchaser of the subject real estate and substitute therefor the sole viewpoint of the vendor. I reach that conclusion from the basis that since I am required to take into account the viewpoint of the purchaser (*Herb Payne* (*supra*)) then the sole indication I have of that perspective (of the purchaser) with regard to that party's allocation of costs is to be found in [the amending agreement to the agreement of purchase and sale]. ... It may well be that this clause represented some "trade-off," or last minute accord, or reflected particular circumstances, as now portrayed by the appellant in this matter. But that does not alter the basic fact that the Court must take into account the known view of the other party. The case law regarding section 68 does not dictate that an "agreement" on such allocation is the only or even the most important factor to be taken into account by the Court in usual circumstances. However, in this case, because it is the sole reflection of the purchaser's view, it cannot be overlooked and, in my opinion, must be the deciding factor for the Court. As I see the situation, it would be completely unreasonable for either the Minister, or this Court, to accept as an appropriate allocation any other breakdown of the selling price.

This passage was relied upon in *Damon Developments Ltd. v. M.N.R.*, [1988] T.C.J. No. 103, [1988] 1 C.T.C. 2266, 88 D.T.C. 1128 (T.C.C.), in which the court rejected the taxpayer's argument that depreciable property that it had sold should be valued for tax purposes on a different basis from that set out in the agreement of purchase and sale.

17. In *Léonard v. Canada*, [1990] T.C.J. No. 340, [1991] 1 C.T.C. 2353, (1990) 91 D.T.C. 545 (T.C.C.), the taxpayers, who purchased a farm in St-Valerian, Quebec after selling a farm in Earlton, Ontario, sought to deduct expenses pertaining to livestock and a milk quota based on their appraised values rather than the proceeds allocated to these assets in the deed of sale. Rejecting the Minister's argument that an agreed-upon allocation between parties dealing at arm's length must be accepted, the court stated (at paras. 39-43) that:

> In the instant cases the sellers and buyers have ... dealt with each other at arm's length, as in *Golden, supra*. In the instant cases, both parties similarly agreed on the prices to be allocated

to various items. It might even be added that both appellants had been farmers for about ten years, and that the forebears of at least the appellant Suzette Leonard were also farmers. ... Could the appellants have been unaware of the fiscal implications of such a transaction, after having just sold a farm in Ontario?

On the other hand, can we ignore the circumstances of the sale, which must be given due consideration according to Thurlow, CJ of the Court of Appeal, *supra*? Although the appellants should have been informed of the apportionment of the value of the assets several weeks prior to signing the contract, it was only provided to them at the last minute after a wait of more than two hours. It cannot be said in the instant cases that there were serious negotiations between the parties. Even if the appellants had been farmers in Ontario, that does not mean the prices were the same. Nonetheless, can it be said that the apportionment appears reasonable on the face of it?

The basis of the appraiser Beaudry's valuation appears reliable to me. Prices set by buyers in auction sales are good criteria for determining true market prices. I am [not] ignoring that true market value ... is not the applicable criterion for section 68, which is that of reasonableness; but true market value may be one factor in determining reasonableness.

With respect to the livestock, the difference between the market value and the price in the contract is $47,400 ($87,400 - $40,000), or 120 per cent. As for the milk quota, the difference is $58,000 ($88,000 - $30,000), or 193 per cent. Can such an apportionment be seen as reasonable?

I must respond in the negative. Accordingly, as agreed with counsel for the parties, these matters are referred back to the respondent for review so that a reasonable apportionment can be arrived at.

18. For other cases since the Supreme Court of Canada decision in *Golden v. Canada*, [1983] F.C.J. No. 68, [1983] C.T.C. 112, 83 D.T.C. 5138 (F.C.A.), in which section 68 has been considered, see *Schellenberg v. M.N.R.*, [1986] T.C.J. No. 452, [1986] 1 C.T.C. 2608, 86 D.T.C. 1463 (T.C.C.); *Humphreys Jones Realty Ltd. v. M.N.R.*, [1986] T.C.J. No. 928, [1986] 2 C.T.C. 2429, 86 D.T.C. 1807 (T.C.C.); *Zeiben v. M.N.R.*, [1991] T.C.J. No. 316, [1991] 2 C.T.C. 2008, 91 D.T.C. 886 (T.C.C.); *Staltari v. Canada*, [1994] T.C.J. No. 1114, [1995] 2 C.T.C. 2239 (T.C.C.); *Faucher v. Canada*, [1995] T.C.J. No. 87, [1996] 1 C.T.C. 2734 (T.C.C.); and *U.S.M. Canada Ltd. v. Canada*, [1996] T.C.J. No. 63, [1996] 2 C.T.C. 2289 (T.C.C.).

B. Non-Arm's-Length Transactions

Where one person disposes of something to another for proceeds greater than fair market value, the transaction creates an artificial gain or reduction in loss for the transferor that is matched by an artificially high cost to the transferee. Conversely, where a person disposes of something to another for proceeds less than fair market value, the transaction creates an artificial loss or reduction in gain for the transferor and an artificially low cost for the transferee. In either case, these transactions might be used to avoid tax by allocating gains to low-income taxpayers and losses to high-income taxpayers.

In order to prevent this kind of income splitting among non-arm's-length persons, paragraph 69(1)(a) deems taxpayers who have acquired anything from such persons for proceeds greater than fair market value to "have acquired it at that fair market value," while paragraph 69(1)(b) deems taxpayers who have disposed of anything to non-arm's-length persons for proceeds less than fair market value "to have received proceeds of disposition therefor equal to that fair market value." Although the Act does not define the word "anything," the meaning of this word is extremely broad and presumably includes both tangible and intangible property as well as services.[4] Because these rules do not adjust the seller's proceeds or the purchaser's cost, their effect is not only to prevent the income splitting that might otherwise result from transactions at amounts greater or less than fair market value, but also to penalize taxpayers who engage in these transactions by taxing the amount by which the proceeds stipulated by the parties differ from the fair market value both in the hands of the transferor and in the hands of the transferee.

For the purpose of these rules and other provisions of the Act, the concept of non-arm's-length relationships is defined in section 251. While paragraph 251(1)(c) makes the characterization of these relationships "a question of fact,"[5] paragraph 251(1)(a) provides greater certainty in specific situations by deeming "related persons" not to deal with each other at arm's length. For this purpose, paragraph 251(2)(a) defines related persons to include "individuals connected by blood relationship, marriage or common-law partnership or adoption"; paragraph 251(2)(b) specifies that a corporation is related to a person who controls the corporation, members of a related group that controls the corporation, and persons related to controlling persons and members of controlling related groups;[6] and paragraph 251(2)(c) lists the circumstances in which two corporations are related. For our purposes, there is no need to examine paragraph 251(2)(c) in detail. In turn, paragraph 251(6)(a) defines persons connected by "blood relationship" as lineal descendants and siblings, while paragraphs 256(6)(b) and (b.1) define persons connected by marriage or common law partnership as spouses and common law partners as well as persons connected by blood relationship to a spouse or common law partner, and paragraph 256(6)(c) defines persons connected by adoption as adopted children and their adoptive parents as well as adopted children and persons connected by blood relationship (other than siblings) with their adoptive parents.

Among the many cases to consider the rules in paragraphs 69(1)(a) and (b) and their predecessors, most involve transactions with corporations and other entities such as partnerships.[7] One of the clearest examples of these rules is

---

4   See *Interpretation Bulletin* IT-405, "Inadequate Considerations — Acquisitions and Dispositions," January 23, 1978 at para. 4, which states that the word "anything" has "a broad meaning and can include both tangible and intangible property."

5   In general, courts have adopted three tests to determine whether a *de facto* non-arm's-length relationship exists within the meaning of this provision: a "common mind" test, an "acting in concert" test, and a *de facto* control test. For our purposes, there is no need to examine the concept of *de facto* non-arm's-length relationships in detail.

6   For the purposes of the Act, subs. 251(4) defines a "related group" as "a group of persons each member of which is related to every other member of the group."

7   For a recent case dealing with a transaction between an individual and a partnership that was subject to the deeming rule in para. 69(1)(a) of the Act, see *Madsen v. Canada*, [2000] F.C.J. No. 2139, [2001] 1 C.T.C. 244, 2001 D.T.C. 5093 (F.C.A.).

Marcantonio v. M.N.R., [1991] T.C.J. No. 308, [1991] 1 C.T.C. 2702, 91 D.T.C. 917 (T.C.C.), in which paragraph 69(1)(a) was applied to prevent income splitting between the taxpayer and a company controlled by his wife.

Marcantonio v. M.N.R.
[1991] T.C.J. No. 308, [1991] 1 C.T.C. 2702, 91 D.T.C. 917 (T.C.C.)

MOGAN, TCJ: ... The appellant is an optometrist who practices his profession in the towns of Riverview and Sackville, New Brunswick. He examines the eyes of a patient for defects and faults of refraction and he is authorized to prescribe correctional lenses. A patient who is issued a prescription for glasses will go to an optician to have the prescription filled. ... [W]ithin the same office, the appellant provided the services of optometrist and optician.

On March 31, 1978, Andrea Enterprises Ltd. ("Andrea") was incorporated under the laws of the Province of New Brunswick. All of the issued shares of Andrea are beneficially owned by the appellant's wife. Originally, Andrea provided bookkeeping and office management services to the appellant. The appellant's wife had worked in a bank and, after their children were born, she wanted to go back to some form of business work. She commenced working at the bank on Monday and Friday of each week and she worked two or three of the other days for Andrea.

In 1983, a chain of optical stores invited the appellant to join them as an in-house optometrist. He declined the proposal but decided that Andrea should become his affiliated retailer for the dispensing of frames and lenses. In 1983, he arranged for Andrea to take over his former "optician business" and to commence selling frames and lenses to the public. From and after 1984, a patient would first come to the appellant for a consultation with him as an optometrist; and if he were to issue a prescription for eye glasses, the patient could then go to a separate counter within the same business premises operated by an employee of Andrea to have the prescription filled.

Prior to 1984, the appellant purchased all of his optometric supplies directly from the various suppliers. In 1983-84, Andrea started to purchase the optometric supplies but they were sold by the appellant in connection with his professional practice. In a typical transaction, the appellant would prepare an invoice and receipt with prescription attached ... making the following charges:

Examination Fee	$40
Lenses	$51
Frame	$86
	$177

...

He explained that he would retain the $40 as his professional fee plus 18 per cent of the remaining $137 ($51 plus $86) as a charge to Andrea for rent, heat, light and office supplies; he would then remit the balance to Andrea. The patients would see only the appellant's name within his office, on his outdoor sign, on his invoice and prescription. The name of Andrea was not displayed and, if a patient were buying eye glasses through the appellant's office, the patient would not know that he or she was buying the frames and lenses from Andrea. In 1984, Andrea sold only to and through the appellant's office.

In computing his income for 1984, the appellant ... deducted as an expense ... $155,457 ... paid to Andrea and about $21,000 was paid directly to the supplier of contact lenses which Andrea could not sell. By notice of reassessment dated June 6, 1986, the respondent added to the appellant's reported income for 1984 the amount of $42,130 determined as follows:

Purchases from Andrea			$ 155,457
Less: Andrea Costs		$ 101,051	
Salaries	$ 10,000		
Accounting	$ 625		
Bank Charges	$ 50		
	$ 10,675		
Plus 15%	$ 1,601	$ 12,276	$ 113,327
Total purchases disallowed			$ 42,130

When making the above reassessment, the respondent assumed that $155,457 exceeded the fair market value of the supplies purchased by the appellant from Andrea and that such amount was not a reasonable cost in the circumstances. The respondent relies on paragraph 69(1)(a) and section 67 of the *Income Tax Act* ... There is no doubt that the appellant and Andrea were not dealing at arm's length because Andrea was controlled by the appellant's wife. As I understand the above reassessment, the respondent has added to the appellant's reported income for 1984 almost all of the net profit which was reported by Andrea in its 1984 fiscal period. There was no evidence before me as to whether the respondent had issued a reassessment to Andrea to remove from Andrea's reported income for its 1984 taxation year that same amount of profit. I will return to this point later.

Counsel for the appellant argued that the respondent could not ignore Andrea and determine that the appellant was in the business of merchandising optometric supplies on his own account. That argument raises the question as to who was merchandising the optometric supplies (frames and lenses). The ultimate purchaser of the frames and lenses was the patient: the person who came first to the appellant as optometrist to determine if eye glasses were needed. If glasses were in fact needed, the appellant would fill out a form ... which is an all-inclusive invoice/receipt and prescription. The prescription is a detachable stub which may be taken to any person who sells frames and lenses. Both the invoice/receipt and the prescription stub display only the appellant's name. A patient who decided to purchase frames and lenses at the appellant's place of business would have no way of knowing that the person who filled the prescription for frames and lenses was an employee of Andrea or that Andrea was the purported vendor of the frames and lenses. The patient would issue a cheque to the appellant for the aggregate amount of the appellant's fee and the price of the frames and lenses. The appellant would cash the cheque and remit to Andrea only the specific amounts for frames and lenses less 18 per cent for rent and other overhead.

In my view, there was a contractual relationship between the appellant and patient with respect to his professional optometrist services and the sale of the frames and lenses but there was no contractual relationship between the patient and Andrea. How could it be said that Andrea was the vendor of the frames and lenses vis-à-vis the patient when the patient did not even know that Andrea existed? Andrea was the vendor of frames and lenses vis-à-vis the appellant but not the patient. With respect to the sale of frames and lenses, the commercial relationship between the appellant and his patient was retailer/customer whereas the commercial relationship between the appellant and Andrea was retailer/wholesaler. It appears, however, that the appellant was not buying from Andrea at wholesale prices. In fact, the appellant was buying from Andrea at retail prices out of which Andrea paid 18 per cent to the appellant for rent and other overhead. The respondent relies on paragraph 69(1)(a) of the *Income Tax Act.* ...

...

As stated above, the appellant and Andrea were not dealing at arm's length and were in a retailer/wholesaler relationship with respect to the sale of frames and lenses. That being the case, the "fair market value" of the frames and lenses in their particular relationship was the wholesale price and not the retail price. In other words, the appellant as retailer could not afford to buy the frames and lenses from Andrea at the same price at which he sold them to his patients. I find that the appellant did pay to Andrea for the frames and lenses an amount in excess of their fair market value (i.e., wholesale price) having regard to their retailer/wholesaler relationship. Accordingly, under paragraph 69(1)(a) of the *Income Tax Act*, the appellant is deemed to have purchased the frames and lenses at their wholesale price; and the respondent was justified in reducing the appellant's cost of frames and lenses.

...

I have decided for the above reasons that this appeal must be dismissed. There was no evidence before me on the question of whether the respondent had issued a reassessment to remove the amount of $42,130 from Andrea's reported income for 1984. I recognize, however, that the dismissal of this appeal would cause an undesirable result if any amount of income reported by Andrea were to be taxed in the hands of both the appellant and Andrea.

Appeal dismissed.

NOTES AND QUESTIONS

1. On what basis did the Minister in *Marcantonio* conclude that the taxpayer's purchases of frames and lenses from Andrea Enterprises Ltd. were at an amount in excess of fair market value? Of what relevance to the court's decision is the fact that purchasers of frames and lenses were not aware that they were dealing with Andrea?

2. In *Indalex Ltd. v. M.N.R.*, [1987] F.C.J. No. 1150, [1988] 1 C.T.C. 60, [1987] 88 D.T.C. 6053 (F.C.A.), the taxpayer, a wholly owned subsidiary of a Canadian public company 58 per cent of the shares of which were owned by a U.K. company, purchased aluminum from a Bermudan subsidiary of the U.K. company at a price that exceeded the discounted price at which the Bermudan company had purchased the aluminum from the original supplier. On the grounds that the aluminum was purchased at a price exceeding its fair market value and that the two companies did not deal with each other at arm's length, the court relied on paragraph 69(1)(a), as well as section 67 and the anti-avoidance rule in former subsection 245(1), to decrease the cost of the aluminum to the taxpayer.

For a contrary result in which the court concluded that oil purchased by the taxpayer through a Bermudan subsidiary had been acquired at a cost equal to its fair market value, see *Irving Oil Ltd. v. Canada*, [1988] F.C.J. No. 201, [1988] 1 C.T.C. 263, 88 D.T.C. 6138 (F.C.T.D.), aff'd [1991] F.C.J. No. 133, [1991] 1 C.T.C. 350, 91 D.T.C. 5106 (F.C.A.).

3. In *Caplan v. M.N.R.*, [1986] T.C.J. No. 448, [1986] 2 C.T.C. 2027, 86 D.T.C. 1489 (T.C.C.), the taxpayer owned one-third of the shares of a corporation ("Edgedale") that operated a home furnishings business out of adjoining premises, one owned by it and the other leased. In 1976, Edgedale sold its business to another corporation ("Marnec") but retained the premises, which were leased to Marnec. In February 1977, the taxpayer purchased the leased premises for $17,000. In July 1978, the taxpayer sold these premises for $17,000 to Edgedale, which sold it and the adjoining property to Marnec for $90,000, of which $45,000 was attributed to each parcel. Dismissing the taxpayer's argument that she had acquired the property as a trustee for Edgedale, the court affirmed the Minister's reassessment deeming the taxpayer to have disposed of the property to Edgedale for proceeds of $45,000, resulting in a taxable capital gain of $14,000.

For other cases in which paragraph 69(1)(b) or its predecessors have been applied to non-arm's-length dispositions for proceeds less than fair market value, see *No. 726 v. M.N.R.* (1960), 25 Tax ABC 257; *Ancaster Development*

Co. v. M.N.R., [1961] C.T.C. 91, 61 D.T.C. 1047 (Ex. Ct.); Rolka v. M.N.R., [1962] C.T.C. 637, 62 D.T.C. 1394 (Ex. Ct.); Thea Corporation v. M.N.R., [1967] Tax ABC 206; and Courier Trading & Enterprises Ltd. v. Canada, [1977] F.C.J. No. 510, [1977] C.T.C. 346, 77 D.T.C. 5220 (F.C.T.D.).

4. What is the "undesirable result" to which the court referred in the last paragraph of its decision in Marcantonio? Do you agree that the inclusion of the $42,130 that was disallowed as a deduction to the taxpayer should be subtracted from Andrea's reported income for 1984? Under what, if any, statutory authority might this adjustment be made?

5. In Allfine Bowlerama Ltd. v. M.N.R., [1972] C.T.C. 2603, 72 D.T.C. 1502 (T.R.B.), the taxpayer, which had accumulated operating losses of $107,000 over a period of years, purchased for $245,575 from a 50 per cent shareholder ("Amcan") a parcel of land worth $343,770, which it immediately sold to another company. After the Minister taxed the net gain of $83,014.83 in the hands of the shareholder under then subsection 17(2) (now paragraph 69(1)(b)), the taxpayer appealed on the basis that the same gain should not also be taxable in its hands. The board allowed the appeal (at paras. 6-7) on the following basis:

> There is a general presumption in law against taxing the same income dollars twice. Double taxation can only be considered to exist where it is equitable and/or the language of the taxing Act is clear and unequivocable [sic]. In this case we are dealing with a "deemed" transaction under subsection 17(2) of the Income Tax Act. The Minister of National Revenue "deemed" that the profit of $83,014.83 was income in the hands of Amcan and when Amcan did not contest this deemed allocation, that amount of income for tax purposes was proven to be income of Amcan and not that of the appellant and was no longer merely "deemed." Further, the substance of the transaction as opposed to the form leaves no doubt whatsoever in my mind that the dollars in question were the income dollars of Amcan and not those of the appellant. The Minister of National Revenue cannot in my opinion tax the $83,014.83 earned by Amcan as income dollars of the appellant.
>
> To permit the Minister to impose such a "tax" would be tantamount to allowing the masquerading of a penalty as a tax not permitted under the Income Tax Act. The Board has no alternative but to allow the appeal.

Do you agree with this conclusion? Why or why not? Does the rule in paragraph 69(1)(b) deem a gain in the hands of the transferor and not in the hands of the transferee? To what extent did the board's decision turn on its emphasis on the substance of the transaction over its form? Is this an example of economic or legal substance over form?

6. The CRA's views on paragraphs 69(1)(a) and (b) appear in Interpretation Bulletin IT-405, "Inadequate Considerations — Acquisitions and Dispositions," January 23, 1978. According to paragraphs 1 to 3 of this bulletin:

> 1. Except as expressly provided in the Act, where a taxpayer acquires anything from a person with whom he or she does not deal at arm's length at an amount in excess of its fair market value, the taxpayer is deemed by paragraph 69(1)(a) to have acquired it at its fair

market value. This provision has the effect of counteracting any attempt by the taxpayer to inflate the cost of a property in a non-arm's length transaction.

2. The vendor or transferor of the property is required to include the actual proceeds received in computing his or her income.

3. Except as expressly provided by the Act, where anything is disposed of by a taxpayer to a person with whom he or she does not deal at arm's length for no proceeds or for proceeds less than its fair market value, under paragraph 69(1)(b) the taxpayer is deemed to have received proceeds equal to its fair market value. Therefore, except in cases specially provided by the Act, a taxpayer is prevented from reporting artificially reduced amounts of proceeds in computing income.

7.   Where non-arm's-length persons are able to demonstrate that a transaction at an amount greater or less than fair market value occurred "by reason of an honest error and not by a deliberate attempt to evade or avoid tax," paragraph 5 of IT-405 states that the revenue authorities "may permit an adjustment in the amount of the proceeds of disposition or purchase price to reflect the amounts deemed by paragraph 69(1)(a) or 69(1)(b) to have been paid or received." According to this paragraph: "The onus will be on either or both taxpayers, as the case may be, to substantiate a claim that the incorrect valuation was caused by an honest error."

8.   In order to avoid the application of paragraph 69(1)(a) or (b), non-arm's-length parties may enter into an agreement to adjust the price in accordance with the revenue authorities' determination of fair market value. The CRA's views on these "price adjustment clauses" appear in *Interpretation Bulletin* IT-169, "Price Adjustment Clauses," August 6, 1974. According to paragraph 1 of this bulletin:

If the parties have agreed that, if the Department's value is different from theirs, they will use the Department's value in their transaction, that is their choice and the Department will recognize that agreement in computing the income of all parties, provided that all of the following conditions are met:

(a)   The agreement reflects a *bona fide* intention of the parties to transfer the property at fair market value and arrives at that value for the purposes of the agreement by a fair and reasonable method.

(b)   Each of the parties to the agreement notifies the Department by a letter attached to his return for the year in which the property was transferred

(i)   that he is prepared to have the price in the agreement reviewed by the Department pursuant to the price adjustment clause,

(ii)   that he will take the necessary steps to settle any resulting excess or shortfall in the price, and

(iii) that a copy of the agreement will be filed with the Department if and when demanded.

(c)   The excess or shortfall in price is actually refunded or paid, or a legal liability therefor is adjusted.

IV. ATTRIBUTION RULES

The attribution rules are designed to prevent income splitting by deeming certain amounts received by specific persons to whom an individual has transferred or lent property to have been received by the transferor and not the transferee. Originating in a single subsection of the *Income War Tax Act* in 1917,[8] these rules have grown considerably, as amendments have frequently been enacted in response to judicial decisions and to limit opportunities for tax avoidance.

The main attribution rules are found in sections 74.1 and 74.2.[9] According to subsection 74.1(1):

> Where an individual has transferred or lent property ... , either directly or indirectly, by means of a trust or by any other means whatever, to or for the benefit of a person who is the individual's spouse or common-law partner or who has since become the individual's spouse or common-law partner, any income or loss, as the case may be, of that person for a taxation year from the property or from property substituted therefor, that relates to the period in the year throughout which the individual is resident in Canada and that person is the individual's spouse or common-law partner, shall be deemed to be income or a loss, as the case may be, of the individual for the year and not of that person.

Similarly, subsection 74.1(2) deems any income or loss from property or from property substituted therefor that is transferred or lent by an individual to or for the benefit of a "related minor" (a person under 18 years of age who does not deal with the taxpayer at arm's length or who is the niece or nephew of the taxpayer) to be the income or loss or the individual and not that of the related minor, unless the related minor attains the age of 18 before the end of the taxation year.[10] Considering an earlier version of these rules, the Exchequer

---

[8]   According to subs. 4(4): "A person who, after the first day of August, 1917, has reduced his income by the transfer or assignment of any real or personal, movable or immovable property, to such person's wife or husvand, as the case may be, or to any member of the family of such person, shall nevertheless, be liable to be taxes as if such transfer or assignment has not been made, unless the Minister is satisfied that such transfer or assignment was not made for the purpose of evading the taxes imposed under this Act or any part thereof.

[9]   For the purpose of the attribution rules and the Act as a whole, para. 248(5)(a) states that: "where a person has disposed of or exchanged a particular property and acquired other property in substitution therefor and subsequently, by one or more further transactions, has effected one or more further substitutions, the property acquired by any such transaction shall be deemed to have been substituted for the particular property." This provision was originally enacted in 1950 as subs. 22(3) of the 1948 *Income Tax Act*, and reverses the result in *M.N.R. v. MacInnes*, [1954] C.T.C. 50; 54 D.T.C. 1031 (Ex. Ct.), in which the predecessor to subs. 74.1(1) was held not to apply to income from securities acquired by the taxpayer's wife with proceeds from the sale of other securities that she had substituted for cash and bonds given to her by the taxpayer. (This case is excerpted in Chapter 2.)

[10]   The *Income Tax Act* itself does not use the term "related minor," but merely refers to persons under 18 years of age who do not deal with the taxpayer at arm's length or are the taxpayer's

Court concluded that they apply only to income from property, not income from a business.[11] For this reason, the characterization of income as income from property can be essential to the application of the attribution rules.[12]

Section 74.2 extends the attribution rules to taxable capital gains and allowable capital losses from the disposition of property, or property substituted therefor, that an individual has lent or transferred to or for the benefit of the individual's spouse or common-law partner or a person who has since become the individual's spouse or common-law partner. In these circumstances, paragraph 74.2(1)(a) deems the excess of any taxable capital gains over allowable capital losses from dispositions of lent or transferred property or property substituted therefor (other than dispositions of listed personal property) to be a taxable capital gain of the individual from the disposition of property other than listed personal property, paragraph 74.2(1)(b) deems the exceess of any allowable capital losses over taxable capital gains from lent or transferred property or property substituted therefor (other than dispositions of listed personal property) to be an allowable capital loss of the individual from the disposition of property other than listed personal property, paragraph 74.2(1)(c) deems the excess of any gains over losses from dispositions of listed personal property that is lent or transferred property or property substituted therefor to be a gain of the individual from the disposition of listed personal property, paragraph 74.2(1)(d) deems the excess of any losses over gains from dispositions of listed personal property that is lent or transferred property or property substituted therefor to be a loss of the individual from the disposition of listed personal property, and paragraph 74.2(1)(e) deems any taxable capital gain or allowable capital loss or gain or loss that is taken into account in computing an amount under paragraphs 74.2(1)(a) to (d) not to be a taxable capital gain or allowable capital loss or a gain or loss, as the case may be, of the recipient.

As a general rule, the attribution rules do not apply to gains and losses from the disposition of property to a child or related minor, though section 75.1 attributes taxable capital gains and allowable capital losses from qualifying farming and fishing property that is transferred to a child on a rollover basis

---

nieces or nephews. The more convenient term "related minor" is used in *Interpretation Bulletin* IT-510, "Transfers and Loans of Property Made After May 22, 1985 to a Related Minor," December 30, 1987.

[11] *Robins v. M.N.R.*, [1963] C.T.C. 27, 63 D.T.C. 1012 (Ex. Ct.). This conclusion has been accepted by the Canada Revenue Agency. See *Interpretation Bulletin* IT-511R, "Interspousal and Certain Other Transfers and Loans of Property," February 21, 1994, para. 5; *Interpretation Bulletin* IT-510R, "Transfers and Loans of Property Made After May 22, 1985 to a Related Minor," December 30, 1987, para. 3; and *Interpretation Bulletin* IT-434R, "Rental of Real Property by an Individual," April 30, 1982, para. 11.

[12] See, *e.g.*, *Wertman v. M.N.R.*, [1964] C.T.C. 252, 64 D.T.C. 5158 (Ex. Ct.) (in which the taxpayer argued unsuccessfully that rental income from an apartment building was income from a business); and *Lackie v. M.N.R.*, [1979] F.C.J. No. 700, [1979] C.T.C. 389, 79 D.T.C. 5309 (F.C.A.) (in which the taxpayer argued unsuccessfully that royalty income from a gravel pit was income from business not property).

under subsection 73(3) or (4). Since these rollover rules deem the property to have been disposed of by the transferor and acquired by the transferee at its adjusted cost base, this attribution rule is necessary to prevent the transfer of accrued gains or losses for tax purposes.

In addition to these basic rules, the attribution rules contain numerous other provisions. Sections 74.3 and 74.4, for example, contain special rules defining the amounts attributed where property is transferred or lent to a trust or corporation in which a "designated person" (defined in subsection 74.5(5) as a spouse or common-law partner or a related minor) is a beneficiary or a shareholder. For our purposes, it is not necessary to examine these rules in any detail.

Section 74.5 contains further special rules, some of which exempt certain categories of transfers and loans from attribution, while others are designed to prevent opportunities for tax avoidance. Beginning with exemptions, subsections 74.5(1) and (2) provide that the attribution rules in subsections 74.1(1) and (2) and section 74.2 generally do not apply to any income or gain or loss from property, or property substituted therefor, that is transferred for fair market consideration or lent at an arm's length rate of interest.[13] Similarly, subsections 74.5(3) and (4) stipulate that these attribution rules do not apply to amounts received by a spouse or common law partner living separate and apart from the transferor because of a marriage breakdown, while subsection 74.5(12) exempts contributions to a spousal RRSPs and TFSAs as well as payments to a spouse or common law partner or related minor that are deductible in computing the individual's income and required to be included in computing the recipient's income. To the extent that individuals receive fair market consideration or a market rate of interest in exchange for property that it transferred or lent, income splitting is not achieved and it follows that the attribution rules generally should not apply. Likewise, attribution is generally inappropriate where an individual pays a deductible amount that is included in computing the recipient's income and where property is lent or transferred to a former spouse or common-law partner. Non-attribution of contributions to spousal RRSPs and TFSAs, on the other hand, represent deliberate policy decisions to permit income-splitting in these contexts.[14]

In addition to these rules, yet others are designed to foreclose possible strategies to avoid the attribution rules. Subsection 74.5(6), for example, ensures that the attribution rules apply where an individual transfers or loans property to another person on the condition that the other person transfers or loans property

---

[13] In order to prevent the transfer of accrued gains and losses to a spouse or common-law partner, a further requirement for the exemption in subs. 74.5(1) to apply to a transfer of property to or for the benefit of a spouse or common-law partner is that the transferor must have elected out of the rollover in subs. 73(1). See para. 74.5(1)(c).

[14] A similar policy objective underlies the parenthetical exclusion in subs. 74.1(1) of an assignment to a spouse or common law partner of a portion of a pension under the Canada or Quebec Pension Plans, and the similar exclusion in subs. 74.1(2) of amounts received in respect of related minors under the child tax benefit in s. 122.61 of the Act.

to or for the benefit of a spouse or common-law partner or related minor, subsection 74.5(7) extends the attribution rules to circumstances where an individual guarantees a loan made to a spouse or common-law partner or related minor, and subsection 74.5(9) deems a loans or transfers to a trust in which another taxpayer is beneficially interested to be a loan or transfer to or for the benefit of the other taxpayer. Finally, subsection 74.5(11) contains a specific anti-avoidance rule applicable to the attribution rules as a whole, declaring that:

> Notwithstanding any other provision in this Act, sections 74.1 to 74.4 do not apply to a transfer or loan of property where it may reasonably be concluded that one of the main reasons for the transfer or loan was to reduce the amount of tax that would, but for this subsection, be payable under this Part on the income and gains derived from the property or from propery substituted therefor.

This provision is designed to prevent so-called "reverse attribution" which might otherwise result from the transfer of property for fair market consideration to a spouse or common-law partner under circumstances where the transferor does not elect out of the rollover rule in subsection 73(1).[15]

The most notable judicial decision involving the attribution rules is the Supreme Court of Canada decision in *Lipson v. Canada*, [2009] 1 C.T.C. 314, 2009 D.T.C. 5528 (S.C.C.), in which the Court was asked to rule on the application of the GAAR in section 245 of the Act.

Lipson v. Canada
[2009] S.C.J. No. 1, [2009] 1 C.T.C. 314, 2009 D.T.C. 5015 (S.C.C.)

LEBEL J (Fish, Abella and Charon JJ concurring)

I. Introduction

These consolidated appeals raise the issue of what constitutes abusive tax avoidance for the purposes of the general anti-avoidance rule ("GAAR") provided for in the *Income Tax Act*, R.S.C. 1985, c. 1 (5th Supp.) ("*ITA*" or "*Act*"). More specifically at issue is whether a series of transactions beginning with a wife borrowing money to purchase shares in a family corporation and leading to the husband deducting the interest on the couple's home mortgage loan results in an abuse and misuse of one or more provisions of the Act, as contemplated in s. 245(4) of the *ITA*.

---

[15] Absent subs. 74.5(11), this result might be accomplished by the following series of transactions: (1) lower-income spouse borrows money from a bank to purchase income-producing property form a third party; (2) lower-income spouse transfers the property to higher-income spouse in exchange for fair market consideration, without electing out of the rollover in subs. 73(1); (3) lower-income spouse uses proceeds from transfer to repay loan. Since the lower-income spouse has not elected out of the rollover rule in subs. 73(1), subs. 74.5(1) does not apply, as a result of which the attribution rule in subs. 74.1(1) applies to attribute income from the property from the higher-income spouse to the lower-income spouse.

The framework for identifying abusive tax avoidance was set out in the cases of *Canada Trustco Mortgage Co. v. Canada*, 2005 SCC 54, [2005] 2 S.C.R. 601, and *Mathew v. Canada.*, 2005 SCC 55, [2005] 2 S.C.R. 643 (S.C.C.), (*"Kaulius"*). In those companion cases, the Court held that, for the purposes of s. 245(4), abusive tax avoidance occurs where the impugned transaction frustrates the object, spirit or purpose of one or more of the provisions relied on by the taxpayer.

For the reasons that follow, I agree with the courts below that the respondent has established abusive tax avoidance. The GAAR applies to one of the transactions within the series and can accordingly be used to deny one of the tax benefits sought by the appellants. As a result, the appeals should be dismissed.

II. Facts

These appeals were heard on the basis of a statement of agreed facts and conclusion, on which I will rely in reviewing the relevant facts. The appellant Earl Lipson ("Mr. Lipson ") conducted a series of transactions whose purpose, he concedes, was to minimize his income tax. He also concedes that his transactions were avoidance transactions within the meaning of s. 245(3) of the *ITA*. First, in April 1994, Mr. Lipson and his wife, Jordanna Lipson ("Mrs. Lipson"), entered into an agreement of purchase and sale for a family residence in Toronto. The purchase price was $750,000. On August 31, 1994, Mrs. Lipson borrowed $562,500 from the Bank of Montreal to finance the purchase at fair market value of 20 and 5/6 shares in Lipson Family Investments Limited, a family corporation. Mrs. Lipson did not earn enough income to pay the interest on this loan (the "share loan") and the bank would not have lent it to her on an unsecured basis but for the fact that Mr. Lipson had agreed to repay the loan in its entirety the following day. Mrs. Lipson paid the borrowed money directly to her husband, who transferred the shares to her.

...

Mr. and Mrs. Lipson obtained a mortgage from the Bank of Montreal for $562,500 (the "mortgage loan"), which was advanced on the closing date of September 1, 1994. They were joint chargers under the mortgage. That same day, they used the mortgage loan funds to repay the share loan in its entirety.

Mr. Lipson relied on four provisions of the *ITA* to claim a deduction of the mortgage loan interest on his 1994, 1995 and 1996 tax returns. The first was s. 73(1), pursuant to which a taxpayer may defer tax on interspousal transfers of property. Mr. Lipson did not elect out of this provision, as he was entitled to do. As a result, the transfer of shares from him to his wife was deemed to have occurred at his adjusted cost base rather than at fair market value, such that he neither sustained a loss nor realized a gain on the sale.

Second, s. 74.1 attributes any income or loss from property transferred from one spouse to another back to the transferring spouse for tax purposes. Thus, although Mrs. Lipson owned the shares acquired from her husband, the dividend income and losses were attributed to Mr. Lipson.

The third provision, although the shares were paid for with the proceeds of the share loan rather than the mortgage loan, was s. 20(3), which allows a deduction for interest on money borrowed to repay previously borrowed money if the interest on the original loan is deductible. As the Tax Court judge noted, the purpose of this provision is to facilitate refinancing (2006 TCC 148, [2006] 3 C.T.C. 2494 [General Procedure], para. 20). The mortgage loan was therefore treated as having funded the share purchase.

Finally, Mr. Lipson deducted the interest on the mortgage loan pursuant to s. 20(1)(c), which permits the deduction of interest on money borrowed "for the purpose of earning income from a business or property". It is not in dispute that the shares in Lipson Family Investments Limited were income-producing assets for Mrs. Lipson and that, were it not for the attribution rule of s. 74.1, she would be entitled, under s. 20(1)(c), to deduct the interest on the money borrowed to purchase the shares. As a result of that attribution rule, however, the dividend income and the interest expense were attributed to Mr. Lipson.

On his 1994, 1995 and 1996 tax returns, Mr. Lipson deducted the interest on the mortgage loan and reported the taxable dividends on the shares as income where applicable. The Minister of National Revenue ("Minister") disallowed the interest expenses of $12,948.19, $47,370.55 and $44,572.95, respectively, for those years and reassessed Mr. Lipson accordingly. The Minister originally disallowed the deductions on the basis that the true economic purpose for which the borrowed money was used was not to earn income and that the interest was therefore not deductible under s. 20(1)(c) of the *ITA*. However, by the time the case reached the Tax Court of Canada, this Court had rejected the "true economic purpose" approach in *Singleton v. Canada*, 2001 SCC 61, [2001] 2 S.C.R. 1046, aff'g [1999] 4 F.C. 484. The Minister therefore argued the case on the basis of the GAAR set out in s. 245 of the *ITA* and submitted that the series of transactions amounted to abusive tax avoidance.

III. Judicial History

The appellants appealed the Minister's reassessments to the Tax Court of Canada. The only issue at trial was whether the transactions, which the parties agreed were avoidance transactions resulting in a tax benefit, constituted abusive tax avoidance and were prohibited by the GAAR. Bowman C.J.T.C. relied on the approach to the GAAR set out by this Court in *Canada Trustco* and *Kaulius*. He held that "[t]he overall purpose as well as the use to which each individual provision was put was to make interest on money used to buy a personal residence deductible" (para. 23). He emphasized this overall purpose in relation to the purposes of each of the provisions in question and found that the series of transactions resulted in a misuse of ss. 20(1)(c), 20(3), 73(1) and 74.1 of the *ITA* (para. 23). He therefore dismissed the appeals.

On appeal to the Federal Court of Appeal, the appellants claimed that Bowman C.J.T.C. had erred by relying on the overall purpose of the series of transactions in concluding that the transactions resulted in a misuse of specific *ITA* provisions. They added that Bowman C.J.T.C. had relied on the economic purpose and substance of the transactions, which is not the test for interest deductibility under s. 20(1)(*c*). The proper approach, according to the appellants, would have been to assess each transaction, and the resulting legal relationships, separately, in which case the court could find no abuse and misuse of the provisions. They argued that this approach was consistent with the Supreme Court's rulings in *Canada Trustco* and *Kaulius*.

Noël J.A. agreed that, viewed separately and without regard to the overall purpose of the scheme, no single one of the transactions appeared abusive (2007 FCA 113, [2007] 4 F.C.R. 641, para. 33). However, he concluded that Bowman C.J.T.C. was entitled to consider the transactions as a series. Indeed, both s. 245(2) and s. 245(3)(*b*) contemplate the denial of a tax benefit resulting from a "series of transactions". Further, Noël J.A. quoted para. 46 of *Kaulius*, in which this Court spoke of assessing the "object, spirit or purpose" of the provision "in light of the series of transactions". He concluded that "the series cannot be ignored in conducting the abuse analysis" for the purposes of the GAAR (para. 45). He held that it had been open to Bowman C.J.T.C. to find, as he did, that the transactions resulted in a misuse of several provisions of the *ITA*. He dismissed the appeals.

IV. Analysis

A. Issues and Positions of the Parties

The appellants submit that the Minister has not established that abusive tax avoidance had occurred. They point out that it is not disputed that the share purchase transaction was a *bona fide*, legal transaction in which Mrs. Lipson acquired shares in Lipson Family Investments Limited. She earned income on those shares and, were it not for s. 74.1 of the *ITA*, would have been required to report that income for tax purposes but would, pursuant to s. 20(1)(*c*), have been entitled to deduct the interest paid on the money borrowed to purchase those shares. The purpose of s. 20(1)(*c*) is to encourage the accumulation of income-producing assets. The fact that the applicability of this provision depends on tracing (i.e., of the actual use of the borrowed funds) rather than on apportionment or ordering (based on assumptions about use) means that the provision is concerned with legal relationships rather than with the true economic purpose of the transaction or series of transactions .... This principle was confirmed in Singleton, where a taxpayer was effectively permitted to deduct his home mortgage interest under s. 20(1)(*c*) because the direct use of the funds in issue was to acquire an income-producing asset, not to purchase a house. Therefore, the transactions in that case did not frustrate the purpose of s. 20(1)(*c*).

Similarly, according to the appellants, the purposes of the other three provisions on which they rely are not frustrated. Section 20(3) contemplates the refinancing of a loan, and that was what the Lipsons did in using the mortgage loan to pay off the share loan. Section 73(1) applies automatically unless the taxpayer opts out, and s. 74.1 also applies automatically if the taxpayer does not elect out of s. 73(1). The provisions operated as intended. It would have been a misuse had they *not* applied.

The appellants argue that the courts below erred in their analysis of the GAAR by relying on the "overall purpose" of the transactions, since an "overall purpose" test is not part of the inquiry under s. 245(4). Further, to the extent that "overall purpose" is synonymous with "true economic purpose", this Court rejected the application of such a test under s. 20(1)(*c*) in Singleton and stated in *Canada Trustco* that "economic substance" is not determinative in the inquiry under s. 245(4) .... The effect of adopting an "overall purpose" test under s. 245(4) would be to cause uncertainty and inconsistency for taxpayers.

The respondent, on the other hand, submits that the appellants' approach effectively reads the GAAR out of the *ITA*. The very purpose of the GAAR is to negate arrangements that would result in a tax benefit "but for this section" (s. 245(2)). In other words, even if the provision being relied on allows a tax benefit, this does not preclude the transaction from being abusive under s. 245(4) of the Act.

A contextual and purposive approach to the GAAR, as is mandated by *Canada Trustco* and *Kaulius*, requires a court to consider the purpose of each provision relied on and whether that purpose was defeated by the transaction or series of transactions. According to the respondent, such an analysis leads inevitably to the conclusion that to allow the interest to be deducted in the case at bar would frustrate the purpose of the provisions being relied on. Specifically, the deduction of mortgage interest frustrates the purpose of s. 20(1)(*c*) because personal expenses such as home mortgage interest are not deductible under s. 20(1)(*c*), as is clear from ss. 18(1)(*a*) and 18(1)(h) of the *ITA*. Such a deduction also frustrates s. 74.1, because that provision is aimed at preventing income splitting. Section 74.1 is an anti-avoidance provision, but it was used here precisely to avoid tax. It cannot be consistent with the object, spirit or purpose of s. 20(1)(*c*), s. 73(1) or s. 74.1 to permit one spouse to deduct interest on money borrowed to fund a personal expense for the benefit of both spouses. The respondent therefore submits that the courts below were correct in finding that the transactions were prohibited by the GAAR.

B. Applicability of the Singleton Case to the Present Situation

As I mentioned above, the appellants consider this Court's decision in Singleton to weigh in their favour because of its focus on legal relationships. The Minister concedes that, were it not for the GAAR, Mr. Lipson could properly deduct the interest expense under s. 20(1)(*c*) .... If, as in Singleton, the issue in the instant case were whether the deduction was properly available under s. 20(1)(c), the Minister's concession would be fatal.

However, neither the GAAR nor s. 74.1 of the *ITA* was at issue in Singleton, so the present case is distinguishable. By treating Singleton as dispositive of the present appeals, the appellants in effect read the GAAR out of the *ITA*.

C. Interpretation of Tax Statutes and the Principle of Minimizing Tax Liability

It has long been a principle of tax law that taxpayers may order their affairs so as to minimize the amount of tax payable (*Inland Revenue Commissioners v. Duke of Westminster* (1935), [1936] A.C. 1 (U.K. H.L.)). This remains the case. However, the *Duke of Westminster* principle has never been absolute, and Parliament enacted s. 245 of the *ITA*, known as the GAAR, to limit the scope of allowable avoidance transactions while maintaining certainty for taxpayers (*Canada Trustco*, at para. 15). In brief, the GAAR denies a tax benefit where three criteria are met: the benefit arises from a transaction (ss. 245(1) and 245(2)); the transaction is an avoidance transaction as defined in s. 245(3); and the transaction results in an abuse and misuse within the meaning of s. 245(4). The taxpayer bears the burden of proving that the first two of these criteria are not met, while the burden is on the Minister to prove, on the balance of probabilities, that the avoidance transaction results in abuse and misuse within the meaning of s. 245(4).

...

Mr. Lipson concedes that all the transactions were avoidance transactions .... Therefore, the issue before us is whether any of the transactions result in a misuse and an abuse having regard to the provisions the taxpayers have relied on.

...

The approach to determining whether a transaction results in a misuse and an abuse for the purposes of s. 245(4) was set out in *Canada Trustco*, at paras. 44-62, the key portion of which reads as follows:

> The heart of the analysis under s. 245(4) lies in a contextual and purposive interpretation of the provisions of the Act that are relied on by the taxpayer, and the application of the properly interpreted provisions to the facts of a given case. The first task is to interpret the provisions giving rise to the tax benefit to determine their object, spirit and purpose. The next task is to determine whether the transaction falls within or frustrates that purpose. The overall inquiry thus involves a mixed question of fact and law. The textual, contextual and purposive interpretation of specific provisions of the *Income Tax Act* is essentially a question of law but the application of these provisions to the facts of a case is necessarily fact-intensive.

> This analysis will lead to a finding of abusive tax avoidance when a taxpayer relies on specific provisions of the *Income Tea Act* in order to achieve an outcome that those provisions seek to prevent. As well, abusive tax avoidance will occur when a transaction defeats the underlying rationale of the provisions that are relied upon. An abuse may also result from an arrangement that circumvents the application of certain provisions, such as specific anti-avoidance rules, in a manner that frustrates or defeats the object, spirit or

purpose of those provisions. By contrast, abuse is not established where it is reasonable to conclude that an avoidance transaction under s. 245(3) was within the object, spirit or purpose of the provisions that confer the tax benefit. [paras. 44-45]

...

Thus, the first analytical step is to interpret the four provisions at issue in the present case to determine their essential object, spirit and purpose.

...

At this step, it is important to identify which provisions are associated with each tax benefit. Here, it is clear that the tax benefit of deductibility of interest relates to ss. 20(1)(c) and 20(3). On the other hand, the tax benefit arising out of Mr. Lipson 's use of the attribution rules, namely the possibility of deducting the interest to reduce his income, is linked with ss. 73(1) and 74.1(1). By virtue of these provisions, Mr. Lipson retains, for tax purposes, the stream of income from the shares sold to his wife but is able to deduct the interest payments on the mortgage from his income.

Section 20(1)(c) allows taxpayers to deduct interest on borrowed money used for a commercial purpose. The purpose of this provision is to "create an incentive to accumulate capital with the potential to produce income" (*Entreprises Ludco ltée c. Canada*, 2001 SCC 62, [2001] 2 S.C.R. 1082, at para. 63), or to "encourage the accumulation of capital which would produce taxable income" (*Shell Canada Ltd. v. Canada*, [1999] 3 S.C.R. 622, at para. 57).

Section 20(3) was enacted "[f]or greater certainty" in order to make it clear that interest that is deductible under s. 20(1)(c) does not cease to be deductible because the original loan was refinanced. It serves "a practical function in the commercial world of facilitating refinancing" (Tax Court judgment, at para. 20).

The effect of s. 73(1) is to facilitate interspousal transfers of property without triggering immediate tax consequences (Tax Court judgment, at para. 21). This is an exception to the general rule that capital gains and losses are recognized when property is disposed of.

...

Finally, the attribution rules in ss. 74.1 to 74.5 are anti-avoidance provisions whose purpose is to prevent spouses (and other related persons) from reducing tax by taking advantage of their non-arm's length status when transferring property between themselves. The most common example of such a benefit is one derived from income splitting, but it is not the only example.... Thus, s. 74.1(1) is designed to prevent spouses from benefiting from their non-arm's length relationship by attributing, for tax purposes, any income or loss from property transferred to a spouse back to the transferring spouse.

The second step in the s. 245(4) analysis is to determine whether the avoidance transaction frustrates the object, spirit or purpose of the relevant provisions. The appellants submit that the courts below erred at this step of the analysis by relying on the "overall purpose" of the transactions in question, that is, by collapsing the series of legally effective transactions into a single

transaction and recharacterizing them by attributing an overall purpose to them
.... As I interpret the appellants' submissions, the objection to an "overall
purpose" approach is twofold: First, transactions under s. 20(1)(c) should be
assessed individually rather than as a series .... This is an objection to the
"overall" aspect of the "overall purpose" test. Second, this approach is legally
incorrect because the purpose of the transactions — whether in the sense of the
taxpayer's motivation, of the primary purpose or perhaps even of economic
substance — is not determinative in the s. 245(4) inquiry. This is an objection to
the "purpose" aspect of the "overall purpose" test.

It is true, as the appellants argue, that in assessing a series of transactions, the
misuse and abuse must be related to the specific transactions forming part of the
series. However, the entire series of transactions should be considered in order
to determine whether the individual transactions within the series abuse one or
more provisions of the *Act*. Individual transactions must be viewed in the
context of the series. Consideration of this context will enable a reviewing court
to assess and understand the nature of the individual parts of the series when
analysing whether abusive tax avoidance has occurred. At the same time, care
should be taken not to shift the focus of the analysis to the "overall purpose" of
the transactions. Such an approach might incorrectly imply that the taxpayer's
motivation or the purpose of the transaction is determinative. In such a context,
it may be preferable to refer to the "overall result", which more accurately
reflects the wording of s. 245(4) and this Court's judgment in *Canada Trustco*.

...

Turning to the Tax Court judge's reasons, it is not entirely clear what
Bowman CJTC meant by "overall purpose". He cited and applied the *Canada
Trustco* analysis (paras. 17-30), but also appeared, at times, to rely on the
taxpayers' motivation and on the economic substance of the transactions. For
example, in para. 31, he mentioned that the primary objective of the transactions
was to make the interest on the purchase of the house tax deductible. However,
as I mentioned above, Bowman C.J.T.C. seems to have focussed on the result of
the series of transactions. I will now turn to a review of the specific transactions
within the series at issue.

D. Abuse and Misuse

According to the framework set out in *Canada Trustco*, a transaction can
result in an abuse and misuse of the Act in one of three ways: where the result of
the avoidance transaction (a) is an outcome that the provisions relied on seek to
prevent; (b) defeats the underlying rationale of the provisions relied on; or (c)
circumvents certain provisions in a manner that frustrates the object, spirit or
purpose of those provisions (*Canada Trustco*, at para. 45). One or more of these
possibilities may apply in a given case. I should reiterate that in a case like the
one at bar, the individual tax benefits must be analysed separately, but always in
the context of the entire series of transactions and bearing in mind that each step

may have an impact on the others, in order to determine whether any of the provisions relied upon for each tax benefit was misused and abused.

First of all, in accordance with the analytical approach described above, we must consider the tax benefit conferred on Mrs. Lipson by ss. 20(1)(c) and 20(3), namely the entitlement to deduct the interest. In my opinion, the respondent has not established that in view of their purpose, these provisions have been misused and abused. Mr. Lipson sold his shares to his wife and bought the residence with the proceeds of that sale .... In the result, Mrs. Lipson financed the purchase of income-producing property with debt, whereas Mr. Lipson financed the purchase of the residence with equity. To this point, the transactions were unimpeachable. They became problematic when the parties took further steps in their series of transactions. The problem arose when Mr. Lipson and his wife turned to ss. 73(1) and 74.1(1) in order to obtain the result contemplated in the design of the series of transactions, namely to have Mr. Lipson apply his wife's interest deduction to his own income. This was contrary to the purpose of s. 74.1(1).

As I mentioned above ..., the purpose of s. 74.1(1) is to prevent spouses from reducing tax by taking advantage of their non-arm's length relationship when transferring property between themselves. In this case, the attribution to Mr. Lipson of the net income or loss derived from the shares would enable him to reduce the dividend income attributed to him by the amount of the interest on the loan that financed his wife's purchase of those shares. However, before the transfer, when the dividend income was in Mr. Lipson's hands, no interest expense could have been deducted from it. It seems strange that the operation of s. 74.1(1) can result in the reduction of the total amount of tax payable by Mr. Lipson on the income from the transferred property. The only way the Lipsons could have produced the result in this case was by taking advantage of their non-arm's length relationship. Therefore, the attribution by operation of s. 74.1(1) that allowed Mr. Lipson to deduct the interest in order to reduce the tax payable on the dividend income from the shares and other income, which he would not have been able to do were Mrs. Lipson dealing with him at arm's length, qualifies as abusive tax avoidance. It does not matter that s. 74.1(1) was triggered automatically when Mr. Lipson did not elect to opt out of s. 73(1). His motivation or purpose is irrelevant. But to allow s. 74.1(1) to be used to reduce Mr. Lipson 's income tax from what it would have been without the transfer to his spouse would frustrate the purpose of the attribution rules. Indeed, a specific anti-avoidance rule is being used to facilitate abusive tax avoidance.

...

In summary, the tax benefit of the interest deduction resulting from the refinancing of the shares of the family corporation by Mrs. Lipson is not abusive viewed in isolation, but the ensuing tax benefit of the attribution of Mrs. Lipson's interest deduction to Mr. Lipson is. It follows that this latter tax benefit can be denied under s. 245(2), which is triggered because the transactions in the series include the attribution of the interest deduction under s. 74.1(1) and this attribution frustrates the object, spirit and purpose of that provision. I must now briefly consider the tax consequences of the denial of the tax benefit and the application of the GAAR.

E. Determination of the Tax Consequences of the Application of Section 245(2)

The Minister seeks to deny the deductibility of the interest expense in the hands of Mr. Lipson, while still attributing the dividend income back to him .... The appellants respond that such an outcome is impossible, since s. 74.1(1) only attributes the income or loss back to the transferor .... Thus, the tax consequences of the application of s. 245(2) are in issue here.

Section 245(5), without restricting the generality of s. 245(2), sets forth a scheme for determining the tax consequences of the application of that provision.

...

When considering the application of s. 245(5), a court must be satisfied that there is an avoidance transaction that satisfies the requirements of s. 245(4), that s. 245(5) provides for the tax consequences and that the tax benefits that would flow from the abusive transactions should accordingly be denied. The court must then determine whether these tax consequences are reasonable in the circumstances. In the present case, disallowing the interest deduction in computing the income or loss attributed to Mr. Lipson and attributing that deduction back to Mrs. Lipson is a reasonable outcome.

...

BINNIE J (Deschamps J concurring in dissent): How healthy is the *Duke of Westminster*? There is cause for concern. Although this Court in *Canada Trustco Mortgage Co. v. Canada*, 2005 SCC 54, [2005] 2 S.C.R. 601, affirmed, at para. 11, the continuing viability of the principle that taxpayers are entitled to arrange their affairs to minimize the amount of tax payable (a principle enshrined in *Commissioners of Inland Revenue v. Duke of Westminster*, [1936] A.C. 1 (H.L.)), the traditional approach is now tempered by the application of the general anti-avoidance rule ("GAAR"). The question in these appeals, as it was in *Canada Trustco*, is where the appropriate balance is to be struck.

The GAAR is a weapon that, unless contained by the jurisprudence, could have a widespread, serious and unpredictable effect on legitimate tax planning. At the same time, of course, the GAAR must be given a meaningful role. That role is circumscribed by the requirement in s. 245(4) of the *Income Tax Act*, R.S.C. 1985, c. 1 (5th Supp.), that the transaction[s] not only be shown to be "avoidance transaction[s]", i.e. transactions structured primarily to obtain a tax benefit, but *in addition* that the Minister demonstrate that the tax benefit results from a misuse/abuse of the provisions of the Act relied upon to produce it.

The tax plan at issue in this case is "*Singleton* with a spousal dimension" – or *Singleton* with a twist – see *Singleton v. Canada*, 2001 SCC 61, [2001] 2 S.C.R. 1046. In that case, the taxpayer used $300,000 of existing equity in his law firm to purchase a house. He refinanced his law firm equity with borrowed money. He deducted the interest on the loan claiming that the borrowed money now represented his investment in the law firm. Despite the Minister's objection, our Court held that he was entitled to do so.

Singleton was not a GAAR case, and it did not involve the spousal attribution rules. Its outcome turned on the Court's view of s. 20(1)(c) interest deductibility. Nevertheless, it is important to emphasize at the outset that the Minister is not asking the Court to revisit Singleton. He does not claim that the GAAR would have applied on the facts of that case.

In the Statement of Agreed Facts and Conclusion, the Minister acknowledged that it is common ground that the interest was deductible (para. 15). Applying Singleton, the only question is whether the deduction becomes "abusive" when income or losses are attributed back to the transferor (appellant) by the spousal attribution rules in ss. 73(1) and 74.1(1).

In my opinion, the spousal "twist" added to Singleton should not cause the entire series of transactions to be characterized as abusive. After all, there is nothing in the Act to discourage the transfer of property at fair market value between spouses. Indeed, by allowing a spouse to transfer property to the other spouse at the transferor's adjusted cost base, Parliament intended to make such transfers attractive.

...

Counsel for the Minister argues that the appellant "wanted to take advantage of the tax-free rollover. He wanted to sell the shares to his wife in order to trigger the income-earning use, but he didn't want the consequences that a sale of shares would normally carry with it" .... But this is precisely the outcome contemplated by Parliament when it enacted the spousal attribution rules. The outcome was not so much an abuse "of the specific provisions" as it was a fulfilment of them....

In my opinion the Minister has failed to identify a specific policy shown to be frustrated by the appellant's plan.

...

Since the appellant did not opt out of s. 73(1), any income or loss from the shares in the hands of Jordanna are deemed to be that of the appellant pursuant to s. 74.1(1) of the *Income Tax Act*. This is understandable. If for tax purposes there is no realization of the property, then for tax purpose Parliament has decided that the income or losses should stay with the transferor....

...

In other words, ...the tax consequence my colleague condemns is presicely the consequence called for by s. 74.1(1) unless the taxpayer opts out.

...

In my view, Parliament must have contemplated that by giving taxpayers a choice under s. 73(1), they would exercise it in a tax-minimizing manner.... [F]ar from offending the "object, spirit or purpose" of the spousal attribution rules,, the appellant's tax plan fulfilled them, or at a minimum did not abuse them.

...

ROTHSTEIN J (dissenting)

Introduction

I have had the benefit of reading the reasons of my colleagues Binnie J. and LeBel J. I am in agreement with their analyses insofar as ss. 20(1)(c) and 20(3) of the *Income Tax Act*, R.S.C. 1985, c. 1 (5th Supp.) (the "Act"), are concerned. There is no reason why taxpayers may not arrange their affairs so as to finance personal assets out of equity and income earning assets out of debt.

However, I am unable to agree with either of my colleagues' approaches to the attribution rules.

With respect to the views of my colleague, LeBel J., I do not believe it was appropriate for the Minister to rely on the general anti-avoidance rule ("GAAR") in this case. In my opinion, the GAAR does not apply here because there is a specific anti-avoidance rule that pre-empted its application. Had the Minister reassessed Mr. Earl Lipson using the relevant specific anti-avoidance provision, s. 74.5(11), the tax benefit that resulted from Mr. Lipson's use of the attribution rules would have been precluded.

...

Analysis

The Relationship Between the GAAR and Section 74.5(11)

In my opinion, the Minister could not reassess Mr. Lipson's use of the attribution rules on the basis of the GAAR. The Minister can only resort to the GAAR when he has no other recourse. In *Canada Trustco Mortgage Co. v. Canada*, 2005 SCC 54, [2005] 2 S.C.R. 601, McLachlin C.J. and Major J. stated at para. 21:

> The GAAR was enacted as a provision of last resort in order to address abusive tax avoidance, it was not intended to introduce uncertainty in tax planning.

In my respectful view, the Minister did have other recourse in this case. Section 74.5(11) provides:

> Notwithstanding any other provision of this Act, sections 74.1 to 74.4 do not apply to a transfer or loan of property where it may reasonably be concluded that one of the main reasons for the transfer or loan was to reduce the amount of tax that would, but for this subsection, be payable under this Part on the income and gains derived from the property or from property substituted therefor.

Section 74.5(11) is a specific anti-avoidance rule that precludes the use of the attribution rules where one of the main reasons for the transfer of property was to reduce the amount of tax that would be payable on the income derived from the property. As I will explain, that is what occurred here.

The fact that the GAAR is a provision of last resort is indicated by the words of s. 245 itself. Section 245(2) provides:

> Where a transaction is an avoidance transaction, the tax consequences to a person shall be determined as is reasonable in the circumstances in order to deny a tax benefit that, but for this section, would result, directly or indirectly from that transaction or from a series of transactions that includes that transaction.

For the Minister to invoke the GAAR, a tax benefit must result unless the GAAR were applied to prevent it.

The wording of s. 245(4) is to the same effect:

> Subsection (2) applies to a transaction only if it may reasonably be considered that the transaction
>
> (a) would, if this Act were read without reference to this section, result directly or indirectly in a misuse of the provisions of any one or more of
>
> (i) this Act
>
> ...
>
> (b) would result directly or indirectly in an abuse having regard to those provisions, other than this section, read as a whole.

Again, it is apparent that in order for there to be a finding of misuse and abuse in respect of a transaction, the Act must be read without reference to the GAAR. In other words, s. 245(4) requires that all other relevant provisions of the Act be read before the Minister may have recourse to the GAAR. This would include not only the enabling provision that is alleged to be misused and abused, but also provisions that themselves would prevent the use of the enabling provision for the purpose objected to by the Minister. If there is a specific anti-avoidance rule that precludes the use of an enabling rule to avoid or reduce tax, then the GAAR will not apply.

The Application of Section 74.5(11)

The issue here is whether s. 74.5(11) applies to preclude the attribution back to Mr. Lipson of the net income or loss with respect to the shares transferred to Mrs. Lipson. As I read s. 74.5(11), it provides that there can be no attribution under s. 74.1(1) when one of the main reasons for the transfer of property (the transfer of the shares from Mr. Lipson to Mrs. Lipson) was to reduce the amount of tax that would, but for s. 74.5(11), be payable on the income (dividends less interest) derived from the property (the shares).

It is uncontroversial that one of the main reasons for the transfer of shares to Mrs. Lipson was to use mortgage interest on a loan to reduce or eliminate the income from the dividends on the shares. There were other reasons, but certainly it is reasonable to conclude that this was one of the main reasons.

In 1995, the dividend income exceeded the interest expense and so there was net income. But that net income was less than what it would have been had the transfer not taken place. Without the transfer, the dividends in Mr. Lipson's hands would not have been reduced by any interest expense. In 1994 and 1996, the interest expense exceeded the gross dividend income and no tax was payable on the dividends. There was a net loss. Again, there would have been tax payable by Mr. Lipson on the dividends had the transfer not taken place, whereas with the transfer, no tax was payable on the dividend income.

By using s. 74.1(1), Mr. Lipson was presumably able to apply the net loss on the dividends in 1994 and 1996 to offset his other income in those years. While reducing tax on income earned from sources other than the transferred property would not be caught directly by s. 74.5(11), offsetting other income cannot take place without the income on the dividends first having been reduced to zero. That is because under s. 74.1(1) the amount attributed back to the transferor, Mr. Lipson, would be the net income or loss from the property transferred. Therefore, the transfer had to have as one of its main purposes the reduction of tax on the income from the transferred property, namely the dividends on the shares transferred to Mrs. Lipson.

In the circumstances, s. 74.5(11) precluded the application of s. 74.1(1). As a result, if it had been invoked by the Minister as the basis for reassessing in respect of the use of s. 74.1(1) by Mr. Lipson, the tax benefit in his hands would have been precluded. By the same reasoning, there could be no misuse and abuse of s. 74.1(1) for purposes of the GAAR because its use would have been pre-empted by s. 74.5(11).

The Minister was obliged to resort to s. 74.5(11) in order to reassess Mr. Lipson in respect of his use of s. 74.1(1). Section 245 did not apply and could not be relied upon by the Minister. The Minister's failure to invoke s. 74.5(11) is fatal to his reassessment in respect of s. 74.1(1).

...

Conclusion

I accept that the tax benefit that the Minister sought to prevent was obtained by the series of transactions involving ss. 20(1)(c) and 20(3) as well as s. 74.1(1). If the Minister wished to reassess in respect of the transactions, relying on the use of all three sections, then his recourse was to reassess in respect of the alleged misuse and abuse of ss. 20(1)(c) and 20(3) by invoking the GAAR and s. 74.1(1) by invoking s. 74.5(11).

Had the Minister reassessed on the basis of s. 74.5(11), his remedy would simply have been to disallow Mr. Lipson's use of the attribution rules and leave the dividend income and interest deduction in the hands of Mrs. Lipson. The rollover of the shares from Mr. to Mrs. Lipson at their adjusted cost base would not have been affected.

It may seem anomalous that the rollover would be allowed to stand while the attribution rules would not apply. However, that is the way in which s. 74.5(11) must be interpreted. It does not prevent the operation of s. 73(1) which enables a taxpayer to elect either to rollover the shares to his or her spouse or sell them to him or her at fair market value and pay whatever tax may be applicable on any capital gains on the shares. Section 74.5(11) is the Minister's remedy when the attribution rules are being used to reduce tax on income from transferred property and it applies "[n]otwithstanding any other provision of this Act", including the GAAR. It is the remedy that Parliament provided in the circumstances. If it does not go far enough in some cases, it is up to the Minister to ask Parliament to change it.

Because there was no abuse of ss. 20(1)(*c*) and 20(3) of the Act and because the Minister could not invoke the GAAR to reassess in respect of Mr. Lipson's use of s. 74.1, I am of the opinion that the appeals should be allowed with one set of costs in this Court and the courts below.

Appeal dismissed.

NOTES AND QUESTIONS

1.   On what grounds does LeBel J's decision in *Lipson* conclude that the transactions are subject to the GAAR? Which provisions does LeBel J consider to have been misused or abused? Do you agree with the majority's conclusions in this respect? Why or why not?

2.   Why does Binnie J conclude that the GAAR should not have applied to the transactions in *Lipson*? Do you agree with his reasons? Why or why not?

3.   In response to Binnie J.'s judgment, LeBel J states (at para. 52) that "my colleague Binnie J essentially guts the GAAR and reads it out of the *ITA* under the guise of an exercise in legal interpretation." Do you agree? Why or why not?

4.   Why does Rothstein J conclude that the GAAR should not have applied to the transactions in *Lipson*? Do you agree? Why or why not?

5.   In response to Rothstein J, LeBel J states (at paras. 44-46):

> Although I agree with Rothstein J. that this Court is not bound to adopt, on a question of law, an interpretation on which the parties agree, it is quite another matter to settle their dispute on a basis of a construction and an application of the statute expressly disavowed by all parties throughout the proceedings. Our decision must turn on the issues as framed in the proceedings and litigated in the courts below and on appeal to this Court. The issue in these appeals was whether the GAAR applies to the impugned transactions.

> In my view, for the reasons set out above, the GAAR applies to these transactions. It is true that courts should avoid extending the GAAR beyond its statutory purpose. But, bearing this purpose in mind, where the language of and principles flowing from the GAAR apply to a transaction, the court should not refuse to apply it on the ground that a more specific provision -- one that both the Minister and the taxpayers considered to be inapplicable throughout the proceedings -- might also apply to the transaction.

In this context, I need not decide whether the taxpayers could have succeeded under s. 74.5(11) ITA. I seriously doubt that that provision would have properly addressed the complex series of transactions before this Court in the present appeals. It may have been mentioned in factums and in questions at the hearing, but its interpretation and application were not the issues litigated by the parties in this case. The GAAR was and remains the focus of the present appeals. I would leave the issue of the interpretation of s. 74.5(11) ITA for another day.

See also Binnie J's response (at para. 61):

> My colleague Rothstein J. finds in s. 74.5(11) a sort of *deus ex machina* to dispose of the appeals on a basis not advanced by any of the parties. When asked at the hearing of the appeal by Rothstein J. about the possible application of s. 74.5(11), counsel for the Minister stated that in the Minister's view s. 74.5(11) "did not address the particular problem[s] of this case" because "the transfer of the shares by the appellant to the wife was not merely to reduce the tax payable on any future dividends. It was really to get the interest expense up to the appellant" (tr. p. 41). The Minister was not prepared even to argue as a matter of *fact* "that one of the main reasons in the transfer or loan was to reduce the amount of tax that would, but for this subsection, be payable" within the meaning of s. 74.5(11). The appellant taxpayer was not called on to meet a case under s. 74.5(11) and I do not believe we should assume a factual basis for the application of s. 74.5(11) ("one of the *main* reasons") which none of the parties was prepared to support. The Minister defends the disputed reassessment squarely on the basis of the GAAR. The appellant responds that the GAAR, in its own terms, has no application. The proper limits of the GAAR raise questions of considerable interest to both taxpayers and tax collectors. I believe we should respond to these questions and leave the more narrowly circumscribed role of s. 74.5(11) to another day when one or other of the parties sees fit to allege a factual basis for its application.

Do you agree with these arguments? Why or why not?

6.   Among the many statutory requirements for the attribution rules to apply, one of the most litigated is whether an individual has "transferred property" to or for the benefit of a spouse, common-law partner or related minor. In *Fasken Estate v. M.N.R.*, [1948] C.T.C. 265 (Ex. Ct.), Thorson P concluded (at paras. 33 and 36) that:

> The word "transfer" is [a] term of wide meaning.
>
> ...
>
> The word "transfer" is not a term of art and has not a technical meaning. It is not necessary to a transfer of property from a husband to his wife that it should be made in any particular form or that it should be made directly. All that is required is that the husband should so deal with the property as to divest himself of it and vest it in his wife, that is to say, pass the property from himself to her. The means by which he accomplishes this result, whether direct or circuitous, may properly be called a transfer.

On this basis, he held that the taxpayer had "transferred" property to his wife when he conveyed a debt to a trust of which she was the beneficiary. For similar results, see *Murphy v. Canada*, [1980] F.C.J. No. 706, [1980] C.T.C. 386 (F.C.T.D.) (addition of spouse as beneficiary of estate); *Heller v. M.N.R.*, [1987] T.C.J. No. 1120, [1987] 1 C.T.C. 2135 (T.C.C.) (transfer of property to trust); and *Naiberg v. M.N.R.* (1969), Tax ABC 492 (T.A.B.) ("skilfully-conceived scheme" in which three taxpayers transferred shares in various companies to each other's wives).

7.   In *Kieboom v. M.N.R.*, [1992] F.C.J. No. 605, [1992] 2 C.T.C. 59, 92 D.T.C. 6382 (F.C.A.), the Court addresseed a more difficult question when the Minister applied the attribution rules to income and capital gains from shares that a private corporation controlled by the taxpayer had issued to the taxpayer's spouse for nominal consideration which was much less than their fair market value. On the basis that the words "transfer of property" in the attribution rules are used in "broad sense" (para. 22), the Court concluded that the income and capital gains were subject to the attribution rules in what are now subsections 74.1(1) and 74.2(1). According to Linden JA (Heald and Décary JJA, concurring) at paras. 22-27:

> Both of the nouns in the phrase are general and non-technical. As for the word transfer, Lord Justice James in *Gathercole v. Smith* (1880-81), 17 Ch. D. 1 stated at page 7 that the noun transfer was "one of the widest terms which can be used.".
>
> ...
>
> As for the word "property," it too has been widely interpreted. The *Income Tax Act*, subsection 248(1) defines property as "... property of any kind whatever whether real or personal or corporeal or incorporeal and, without restricting the generality of the foregoing includes (a) a right of any kind whatever, a share or a chose in action. ..." Lord Langdale once stated that the word property is the "most comprehensive of all the terms which can be used inasmuch as it is indicative and descriptive of every possible interest which the party can have." (See *Jones v. Skinner* (1836), 5 L.J. (N.S.) Ch. 87, at p. 90; see also *Re Liness* (1919) 46 O.L.R. 320, at p. 322; *Estate of Fasken, supra,* at p. 496 [DTC 496]; and *Vaillancourt v. M.N.R.*, [1991] 3 F.C. 66).
>
> In this case, therefore, the taxpayer transferred property to his wife, that is, he gave a portion of his ownership of the equity in his company to his wife. The 40% capital interest in his company which he gave to his wife was clearly property. His beneficial interest in his company was reduced by 40% and hers was increased by 40%. The fact that this transfer of property was accomplished through causing his company to issue shares makes no difference. Subsection 74(1) [now subsection 74.1(1)] covers transfers that are made "directly or indirectly" and "by any other means whatever." The transfer, which in this case was indirect, in that the taxpayer arranged for his company to issue shares to his wife, is nevertheless a transfer from the husband to the wife. There is no need for shares to be transferred in order to trigger this provision of the Act, as was erroneously concluded by the Tax Court judge. By this transfer of property to his wife, he divested himself of certain rights to receive dividends should they be declared. Hence, when the dividends were paid to the wife in 1982, that was income from the transferred property and was rightly attributable to the taxpayer.
>
> In addition, the property transferred to Mrs. Kieboom in 1980 was a portion of his ownership equity. As a result of the transfer, the taxpayer's entitlement of 40% was transferred to Mrs. Kieboom.... Mrs. Kieboom disposed of part of that interest when she transferred a part of that equity to the children. On the same reasoning as above, the ... capital gain on that disposition must also be attributed to the taxpayer under subsection 74(2) [now subsection 74.2(1)].

Do you agree with this conclusion? Why or why not?

8.   *Kieboom* was followed in *Romkey v. Canada*, [1999] F.C.J. No. 1922, [2000] 1 C.T.C. 390, 2000 D.T.C. 6047 (F.C.A.), in which a corporation that was controlled by two brothers issued shares for no consideration to two trusts

in favour of their children, on which dividends of $167,000 were paid between November 21, 1988 and May 2, 1990. Citing *Kieboom* (at para. 18) for the proposition that "property" can be "transferred" either in the form of a portion of the taxpayer's equity in a company or by the divestiture of certain rights to receive dividends should they be declared, the Court attributed the dividends to each of the brothers under subsection 74.1(2) of the Act on the basis (at para. 21) that:

> by causing the … shares to be issued to the trusts the [brothers] effectively forwent the right to receive an increased measure of any future dividends declared and paid by the Company.

9.   Notwithstanding the broad interpretation of the word "transfer" in *Fasken Estate*, the Exchequer Court held in two decisions that the attribution rules, which at the time referred only to property "transferred" but not "lent," did not apply to loans (*Dunkelman v. M.N.R.*, [1959] C.T.C. 375, 59 D.T.C. 1242 (Ex. Ct.)), even interest-free loans the primary purpose of which could reasonably be regarded as being avoidance of the attribution rules (*Oelbaum v. M.N.R.*, [1968] C.T.C. 244, 68 D.T.C. 5176 (Ex. Ct.)). On the basis of these cases, the revenue authorities affirmed in paragraphs 8 and 9 of *Interpretation Bulletin* IT-258R2, "Transfers of Property to a Spouse," May 11, 1982:

> A transfer does not include a genuine loan made by a person to his spouse. No all-inclusive statement can be made as to when a loan can be considered to be "genuine," but a written and signed acknowledgement of the loan by the borrower and an agreement to repay it within a reasonable time ordinarily is acceptable evidence that it was so. If, in addition, there is evidence that the borrower has given security for the loan, that interest on the loan has been paid, or that actual repayments have been made, it is accepted that the loan was genuine. The fact that no interest is required to be paid does not mean, in itself, that a genuine loan has not been made.

> Where there is a genuine loan and there is no evidence that the terms of that loan are not being honoured, the Department considers that such a loan made directly to a spouse is not a transfer of property for the purpose of subsection 74(1).

Virtually identical language appeared in paragraphs 3 and 4 *of Interpretation Bulletin* IT-260R, "Transfer of Property to a Minor," November 12, 1979.[16]

---

[16] The "genuineness" of a loan for these purposes was addressed by the Tax Court of Canada in *Harvey v. Canada*, [1994] T.C.J. No. 391, [1995] 1 C.T.C. 2507 (T.C.C.), where the taxpayer transferred a large sum of money to his spouse for her to hold on behalf of their three infant children. The spouse signed promissory notes on the children's behalf promising that they would repay the amounts on demand with 20 per cent interest in the event of default. Concluding that the transfer of funds was not a genuine loan, Bowman TCCJ commented (at para. 12):

> I do not think that we can push the principle in *Dunkelman* too far. A *bona fide* loan to a properly constituted trust may well meet the criteria in *Dunkelman* to avoid the provisions of subsection 75(1). A somewhat loose arrangement between husband and wife where the wife, without any form of documentation, calls herself a guardian of the infant children does not. It must be recognized that subsection 75(1) is designed to prevent income splitting and if one wishes to avoid the section on the basis of *Dunkelman* the formalities

Not surprisingly, therefore, interest-free demand loans became widely used as a method to avoid the application of the attribution rules. Despite this practice, Parliament took no action to prohibit this avoidance technique until 1985, 26 years after the 1959 decision concluding that a loan was not a transfer within the meaning of the attribution rules, and 17 years after the decision holding that the attribution rules did not apply to interest-free demand loans. As the current statutory language in subsections 74.1(1) and (2) and subsection 74.2(1) indicates, the attribution rules now apply to transfers *and loans*.

The 1985 budget speech commented on the introduction of these new rules as follows:

> The *Income Tax Act* currently provides rules intended to prevent a taxpayer from splitting his or her income among family members to reduce the total amount of tax payable. For example, where an income-earning security is transferred by a taxpayer to a spouse or minor child, the income thereon will be attributed to the taxpayer so that the taxpayer, rather than the family member to whom the security was transferred, pays tax on the income. However, in interpreting the term "transfer" in the context of the income attribuiton rules, the courts have concluded that a loan is not a transfer. Consequently, taxpayers could avoid the application of these rules by making a low-interest or interest-free loan to a spouse or child. This could result in a significant tax reduction depending on the tax bracket of the spouse or child.
>
> The budget proposes to extend the income attribution rules to the income from property acquired from the proceeds of a loan outstanding on May 22, 1985 or after that date.

In commenting on the new rules in the House of Commons, a member of the governing Progressive Conservative party (Mr. Redway) explained that:

> the courts have held that while one cannot get around the income tax attribution rules by giving away money and investments one can get around them by loaning the money either interest free or with a low interest rate. This Bill plugs that loophole as well. There is another loophole which members of the Opposition wished that they had plugged. They had 20 years to do it and they did not.[17]

Although the amended language applies to loans outstanding on or after May 22, 1985, the amending legislation included transitional relief for loans outstanding on May 22, 1985, providing that attribution would not apply until 1988.

10. Also notwithstanding the broad interpretation of the word "transfer" in *Fasken Estate*, English caselaw suggested that the concept of an "indirect transfer" might not encompass transfers made "to" third parties (for example, trusts, corporations, or creditors) "for the benefit of" a transferor's spouse or minor children. In *Potts Executors v. C.I.R.*, [1951] 1 All E.R. 76 (H.L.), the House of Lords considered section 40(1) of the United Kingdom *Finance Act, 1938*, which provided that any capital sum paid "directly" or "indirectly" by trustees of a settlement "to the settlor" was to be treated as income to the settlor

---

of a real trust must be set up. While a real trust could presumably borrow funds, an infant cannot do [so] directly. Such a contract is void.

[17] Canada, House of Commons, *Debates*, November 27, 1985, 8897.

to the extent of the available income arising under the settlement. Despite the statutory reference to "indirect" payments, the court concluded that amounts paid by the trustees to third parties on behalf of the settlor, for charitable subscriptions, taxes, and the like were not subject to tax in the hands of the settlor. According to Lord Norman (at 82):

> It was said, however, that a payment made by the settlor's request to an agent of other person accountable to him is in law a payment made directly to the settlor and, therefore, that the word "indirectly" must have a wider significance than I have assigned to it. That is, with respect, to beg the question. In a taxing Act designed to prevent tax evasion by affecting with liability to tax sums paid to a settlor otherwise than as income, it was obviously necessary to provide for the case where persons accountable to the settlor or interposed between the payer and the settlor for the purpose of disguising the transaction. That is a satisfactory explanation of the words "directly or indirectly." There is, therefore, no reason for extending the meaning of "indirectly" so as to include payments to third parties which the settlor has an interest to make whether in discharge of his legal liabilities or furtherance of charities favoured by him. If that had been the intention, other words would have been added.

Among the many amendments to the attribution rules in 1985, the language of the provisions was amended to ensure that they would apply where property is transferred or loaned "to or for the benefit of" the transferor's spouse or a related minor. The technical notes accompanying the draft legislation explained:

> The new attribution rules apply when property is transferred by an individual *to or for the benefit of* his spouse or a person under 18 years of age. This language is utilized to clarify and confirm the interpretation given to the existing attribution rules in respect of certain indirect transactions. For example, the new rules clarify that attribution will occur when an individual transfers property to a trust in which his spouse or a person under 18 years of age is beneficially interested. The income that is subject to that attribution rules in such a case is the income of the trust that would otherwise be taxed in the hands of the spouse or the person under 18 years of age. Income that accumulates and is taxed in the trust is not subject to the attribution rules.

Index

Q